SCHOOL
DICTIONARY 1

The circus images on the cover of this book celebrate the magic of language—a magic that transforms letters into the words we use to name all the wonders of our world.

MACMILLAN

Macmillan Publishing Company
New York

Collier Macmillan Publishers
London

Macmillan Publishing Company
866 Third Avenue
New York, New York 10022
Collier Macmillan Canada, Inc.

Printed in the United States of America
ISBN 0-02-195003-2/3-5
9 8 7 6 5 4 3

Editorial Staff

Editor in Chief	Judith S. Levey
Managing Editor	Helen Adele Chumbley
Senior Editors	Deirdre Dempsey, Michael E. Agnes
Editors	Ronald J. Bogus, Carol G. Braham, Kathleen Derzipilski, John P. Elliott, Lona Greenhouse (mathematics), William C. Hale (etymologies), Bonny Hart (life sciences), Walter M. Havighurst, Archie Hobson, Susan J. Lacerte (botany), Paul G. Lagassé, Edward J. Moran (physical sciences), Carolyn Quinn, Peggy Seeger, Gloria Mihályi Solomon (pronunciation)
Production Manager	Karen L. Tates
Editorial Production	Milica Govich, Mary Ann Maderer, John Mariano, Susan R. Norton, Nick Scelsi, Patricia Clements Shuldiner
Proofreaders/Keyboarders	Jerilyn Famighetti, Robert B. Gampert, Phyllis Ger, Mibo Shim Lee, Ezra Maurer, Dana M. Schwartz, John F. Scorza, Stephanie Sweeney
Production Assistants	Margot A. Bonelli, Joseph D. Henry
Lexicographic Consultant	Sidney I. Landau

Art Staff

Design Director	Zelda Haber
Associate Design Director	Joan Gampert
Senior Designer	Marvin Friedman
Designers	Norman Dane, Emil Chendea, Anna Sabin
Photo Research	Omni-Photo Communications, Inc.
Artists	Howard Berelson, Howard Friedman, Mordecai Gerstein, James Gordon Irving, Dan Todd, Ruth Adam, Dorothea and Sy Barlowe, Kenneth Barr, Ann Brewster, George Buctel, Eva Cellini, Alex Ebel, Alan Eitzen, Fred Irvin, René Martin, Erica Merkling, Harry McNaught, Sam Sirdotsky
Cover Design	Barnett-Brandt Design
Cover Art	Fred Winkowski
Frontmatter/Backmatter Design	MKR Design

Illustrations: Frontmatter: Fred Winkowski; Backmatter: Time Line, R29–R32, Joel Snyder; Birds, flowers, flags, R33–R45, Alex Bloch; Maps, R52–R56, R. R. Donnelly Cartographic Services; Math art, R56–R59, Simon Galkin; Math technical art, R60, Tom Cardamone Associates; Solar System, R61, Deborah Morse; Inside the Earth, R64, Deborah Morse

Acknowledgments

The publisher gratefully acknowledges permission to reproduce the following copyrighted materials:

For photograph of the cover of the 1989 WORLD ALMANAC: THE WORLD ALMANAC & BOOK OF FACTS, 1989 edition, copyright © Newspaper Enterprise Association, Inc. 1988, New York, NY 10166. Used by permission.

For photograph of the cover of the 1989 INFORMATION PLEASE ALMANAC and photograph of page 696 from above volume: From INFORMATION PLEASE ALMANAC 1989. Copyright © 1988 by Houghton Mifflin Company. Reprinted by permission of Houghton Mifflin Company.

Photograph of covers/spines of *Collier's Encyclopedia* and photograph of pages 90–91 in Volume 10 of above: Reprinted with permission from *Collier's Encyclopedia* © 1984 Macmillan Educational Company.

Photograph of page 53 in *Rand McNally Road Atlas*: From ROAD ATLAS © Copyright 1989 Rand McNally & Company, R.L. 89-S-S.

Photo Credits (A-Z Section): **abreast:** Michal Heron/Woodfin Camp; **abstract:** ''Creole Dance'' by Henri Matisse-Three Lions/Superstock; **accompany:** Menschenfreund/Taurus; **accordion:** Eric Kroll/Taurus; **acrobat:** Paolo Koch/Photo Researchers; **adjacent:** S. Zeiberg/Taurus; **aerial:** John Reis Photography/Stock Market; **affection:** Barbara Kirk/Stock Market; **aide:** Michal Heron/Woodfin Camp; **airport:** George Hall/Woodfin Camp; **album:** Michal Heron/Woodfin Camp; **alpaca:** Ted Levin/Animals Animals; **anemone:** Jeanne White/Photo Researchers; **antique:** Lee Boltin; **aqueduct:** Adam Woolfitt/Woodfin Camp; **archery:** Bill Backman/Photo Researchers; **assembly line:** Joseph Nettis/Photo Researchers; **astride:** Lenore Weber/Taurus; **atop:** DiMaggio & Kalish/Stock Market; **attract:** Kenneth Karp/Omni-Photo Communications, Inc.; **autumn:** Richard Steedman/Stock Market; **awning:** Claudia Parks/Stock Market; **bagpipe:** Harvey Lloyd/Stock Market; **ballerina:** Sisse Brimberg/Woodfin Camp; **banister:** Toby Rankin/Image Bank; **basket:** Lisl/Image Bank; **bear:** Jose L.G. Gruade/Photo Researchers; **bicycle:** G. Cloyd/ Taurus; **birthday:** David Barnes/Stock Market; **blast-off:** Spinelli/Woodfin Camp; **blindfold:** Albert Moldvay/Woodfin Camp; **blowtorch:** Alec Duncan/Taurus; **bolt:** Joseph Nettis/Photo Researchers; **boot:** Dean Krakel II/Photo Researchers; **bottle:** Charles Krebs/Stock Market; **bow:** David Hundley/Stock Market; **brace:** Michael Manheim/Stock Market; **brass:** Cynthia Matthews/ Stock Market; **buffalo:** James R. Simon/Photo Researchers; **bugle:** Catherine Ursillo/Photo Researchers; **burlap:** Catherine Ursillo/Photo Researchers; **butte:** Craig Aurness/Woodfin Camp; **campfire:** Stephanie Stokes/Stock Market; **canyon:** Oxford Scientific Films/Earth Scenes; **caravan:** M&E Bernheim/Woodfin Camp; **carve:** Lowell Georgia/Photo Researchers; **castle:** Steve Elmore/Stock Market; **cello:** Brownie Harris/Stock Market; **chaps:** Guy Gillette/Photo Researchers; **checkers:** Richard Hutchings/ Photo Researchers; **chopsticks:** Lawrence Migdale/Photo Researchers; **circus:** Blair Seitz/Photo Researchers; **clarinet:** Farrell Grehan/Photo Researchers; **cleaver:** William Hubbell/Woodfin Camp; **clown:** Richard Hutchings/Photo Researchers; **coconut:** J.H. Robinson/Photo Researchers; **community:** Omni-Photo Communications, Inc.; **complete:** John Lei/Omni-Photo Communications, Inc.; **computer graphics:** Joe Sohm-Chromosome/Stock Market; **congratulate:** Gabe Palmer/Stock Market; **construction:** William R. Wright/Taurus; **contrast:** Leonare Lee Rue III/National Audubon Society/Photo Researchers; **costume:** Suzanne Szasz/Photo Researchers; **countryside:** Robert Frerck/Woodfin Camp; **crab:** Tom McHugh/Photo Researchers; **crane:** George H. Cardozo/Photo Researchers; **create:** Richard Hutchings/Photo Researchers; **crossing:** Mark Mittelman/Taurus; **cultivate:** Bill Ross/Woodfin Camp; **cymbal:** Kenneth Karp/Omni-Photo Communications, Inc.; **dam:** Breck P. Kent/Earth Scenes; **dashboard:** Cadillac Motor Car Div.; **deck:** Franke Keating/Photo Researchers; **decoy:** M. Warren Williams/Photo Researchers; **demonstration:** Lowell Georgia/Photo Researchers; **dependent:** Ira Block/Woodfin Camp; **desert¹:** Arthur Gloor/ Earth Scenes; **detector:** Philip Jon Bailey/Taurus; **dimple:** Pam Hasegawa/Taurus; **disc jockey:** Gabe Palmer/Stock Market; **diskette:** John Lei/Omni Photo Communications, Inc.; **distort:** Ted Horowitz/Stock Market; **dragon:** Laurence Rosenberg/ Taurus; **drawbridge:** Charles Mayer/Photo Researchers; **drum:** Ehnenn/Taurus; **easel:** Susan McCartney/Photo Researchers; **electric:** Steve Benbow/Woodfin Camp; **embroider:** Julie Habel/Woodfin Camp; **enclosure:** G.R. Roberts/Omni-Photo Communications, Inc.; **enormous:** Brownie Harris/Stock Market; **enthrall:** Will McIntyre/Photo Researchers; **escalator:** Tom McHugh/Photo Researchers; **everyone:** Randy Duchaine/Stock Market; **exercise:** Blaine Harrington III/Stock Market; **expressway:** P. Saloutos/Stock Market; **eyeglasses:** Timothy Eagan/Woodfin Camp; **farm:** Dick Durrance II/Woodfin Camp; **feather:** Joel Greenstein/Omni-Photo Communcations, Inc.; **feel:** Tom McCarthy/Stock Market; **figurehead:** David Hamilton/ Image Bank; **fireworks:** Jerry Cooke/Photo Researchers; **flatcar:** George E. Jones III/Photo Researchers; **float:** Lawrence Migdale/Photo Researchers; **flute:** Lawrence Migdale/Photo Researchers; **folk dance:** L. Villota/Stock Market; **football:** Jerry Wachter/Photo Researchers; **foreground:** Dean Brown/Omni-Photo Communications, Inc.; **forge:** Black Mamba/Omni-Photo Communications, Inc.; **fountain:** Anne Heimann/Stock Market; **framework:** Dick Durrance II/Woodfin Camp; **French horn:** Pam Hasegawa/Taurus; **gallop:** Guido Alberto Rossi/Image Bank; **garden:** Craig Aurness/Woodfin Camp; **geyser:** Art Twomey/ Photo Researchers; **glitter:** Geoffrey Gove/Image Bank; **gondola:** E. Wheather/Image Bank; **gourd:** Zig Leszcynski/Earth Scenes; **graze:** H. Wendler/Image Bank; **group:** John Lei/Omni-Photo Communications, Inc.; **guard:** Bruce Stromberg/Stock Market; **guitar:** Katrina Thomas/Photo Researchers; **habit:** Stephanie Stokes/Stock Market; **hammock:** Wasyl Szkodzinsky/Photo Researchers; **hang glider:** Alexander Hubrich/G&J Images/Image Bank; **harvest:** Catherine Ursillo/Photo Researchers; **hatch:** Charles Krebs/Stock Market; **haystack:** Earth Scenes; **helicopter:** Michele Burgess/Stock Market; **helmet:** Craig Aurness/ Woodfin Camp; **home plate:** Melchior DiGiacomo/Image Bank; **hopscotch:** Benn Mitchell/Image Bank; **hose:** George Hall/ Woodfin Camp; **hurdle:** Janeart Ltd./Image Bank; **icicle:** Edmund Appel/Photo Researchers; **impression:** Brownie Harris/Stock Market; **incline:** Gabe Palmer/Stock Market; **industrious:** Richard Hutchings/Photo Researchers; **ingot:** Guido A. Rossi/Image Bank; **inscribe:** Jim Brown/Stock Market; **instructor:** Brownie Harris/Stock Market; **intercept:** Bill Weems/Woodfin Camp; **interview:** D. Hayes/Omni-Photo Communications, Inc.; **intricate:** Bruce Brander/Photo Researchers; **irrigation:** Jack Parsons/ Omni-Photo Communications, Inc.; **ivory:** Marc & Evelyne Bernheim/Raho Guillumette/Woodfin Camp; **jewelry:** C. Krishna/ Taurus; **jump rope:** Mike Yamashita/Woodfin Camp; **Jupiter:** NASA/Omni-Photo Communications, Inc.; **kayak:** Annie Griffiths/Woodfin Camp; **kimono:** Steve Elmore/Stock Market; **kite:** R. Steedman/Stock Market; **koala:** Tom McHugh/Photo Researchers; **ladder:** Craig Aurness/Woodfin Camp; **lasso:** Janeart Ltd./Image Bank; **leash:** Catherine Ursillo/Photo Researchers; **lei:** Al Satterwhite/Image Bank; **life preserver:** Roy Morsch/Stock Market; **lighthouse:** Murray & Associates, Inc./Stock Market; **litter:** Portraiture by Allan/Image Bank; **lock¹:** Harvey Lloyd/Stock Market; **loom¹:** Bruce Roberts/Rapho-Photo Researchers; **lot:** George Hall/Woodfin Camp; **lumber¹:** Arthur D'Arazien/Image Bank; **magician:** Blair Seitz/Photo Researchers; **magnifying glass:** Gabe Palmer/Stock Market; **makeup:** Ann Hagen Griffiths/Omni-Photo Communications, Inc.; **map:** Blair Seitz/Photo Researchers; **marionette:** DPI; **Mars:** NASA/Omni-Photo Communications, Inc.; **mass production:** Arthur D'Arazien/Image Bank; **medal:** Bill Strode/Woodfin Camp; **memorial:** Wally McNamee/Woodfin Camp; **merry-go-round:** Jack Jones/Photo Researchers; **microchip:** J.M. Barrs/DPI; **miniature:** Adam Woolfitt/Woodfin Camp; **monorail:** Paolo Koch/Photo Researchers; **mountain:** Saul Mayer/Stock Market; **muffler:** J.T. Miller/Stock Market; **mural:** G & J Images/Image Bank; **navigator:** Luis

Villota/Stock Market; **neon:** Timothy Eagan/Woodfin Camp; **net:** Joe DiStefano/Photo Researchers; **noodle:** Kenneth Karp/ Omni-Photo Communications, Inc.; **northern lights:** Jack Finch/SPL/Photo Researchers; **nozzle:** Robert Frerck/Woodfin Camp; **oasis:** DPI; **observatory:** Robin Scagell/Photo Researchers; **office:** Peter Vadnai/Stock Market; **oil well:** Paul Chauncey/Stock Market; **ornate:** Adam Woolfitt/Daily Telegraph Magazine/Woodfin Camp; **outrigger:** Paul Slaughter/Image Bank; **oval:** Patti McConville/Image Bank; **overgrow:** Hans Wolf/Image Bank; **pagoda:** Claudia Parks/Stock Market; **parade:** Lawrence Migdale/ Photo Researchers; **partition:** Dick Luria/Photo Researchers; **pastel:** Eric Kroll/Taurus; **peacock:** Pete Saloutos/Stock Market; **pedestal:** Steve Elmore/Stock Market; **pendulum:** Co Rentmeester/Image Bank; **perpendicular:** Ben Simmons/Stock Market; **perspective:** Larry Mulvehill/Photo Researchers; **piano:** Randa Bishop/DPI; **piggyback:** Ben Simmons/Stock Market; **pinto:** Chris Bjornberg/Photo Researchers; **plaid:** Bruce Roberts/Photo Researchers; **plan:** Michal Heron/Woodfin Camp; **plastic:** Sepp Seitz/Woodfin Camp; **playground:** Liama Druskis/Taurus; **pollen:** Peter Ward/Bruce Coleman; **pose:** Stan Goldblatt/Photo Researchers; **poster:** Granger Collection; **prehistoric:** Chris Rogers/Stock Market; **press:** Arthur D'Arazien/Image Bank; **prize[1]:** Jay Dorin/Omni-Photo Communications, Inc.; **profile:** William Hubbel/Woodfin Camp; **prohibit:** Art Attack/Photo Researchers; **prospector:** Christina Thomson/Woodfin Camp; **protect:** Ken Karp/Omni-Photo Communications, Inc.; **pueblo:** Adam Woolfitt/ Woodfin Camp; **puppet:** Nancy J. Pierce/Photo Researchers; **quetzal:** John S. Dunning/Photo Researchers; **quilt:** Linda Barlett/ Photo Researchers; **rainbow:** Annie Griffiths/Woodfin Camp; **ranger:** Michal Heron/Woodfin Camp; **rear[2]:** J. Bichet/Image Bank; **receive:** Richard Hackett/Omni-Photo Communications, Inc.; **rectangle:** Omni-Photo Communications, Inc.; **redwood:** Dick Durrance/Woodfin Camp; **reflection:** Charlie Ott/DPI; **relay race:** Focus on Sports; **repair:** Jay Freis/Image Bank; **resemble:** Shelley Rotner/Omni-Photo Communications, Inc.; **restore:** David Hiser/Image Bank; **revolve:** Luis Casteneda/Image Bank; **rigging:** George Haling/Photo Researchers; **rink:** Randa Bishop/DPI; **robot:** Tom McHugh/Photo Researchers; **rolling pin:** Richard Hutchings/Photo Researchers; **rowboat:** Al Satterwhite/Image Bank; **ruin:** Jake Rajs/Image Bank; **rung[2]:** J.C. Lozouet/ Image Bank; **salesperson:** Gabe Palmer/Stock Market; **sari:** Luis Villota/Stock Market; **Saturn:** NASA/Omni-Photo Communications, Inc.; **scale[1]:** David R. Frazier/Photo Researchers; **scatter:** Susan McCartney/Photo Researchers; **sculpture:** Dean Brown/Omni-Photo Communications, Inc.; **seat belt:** Charles E. Schmidt/Taurus; **seismograph:** Tom McHugh/Photo Researchers; **sentry:** Chuck O'Rear/Woodfin Camp; **sewing machine:** L.L.T. Rhodes/Taurus; **shaggy:** DPI; **shopping center:** Disario/Stock Market; **sign language:** L.L.T. Rhodes/Taurus; **silo:** G. Cloyd/Taurus; **sit-up:** Mario Taglienti/Image Bank; **skyscraper:** Joel Greenstein/Omni-Photo Communications, Inc.; **slide:** Eric Kroll/Taurus; **sluice:** Mark E. Gibson/Stock Market; **smokestack:** Eric Kroll/Taurus; **snowy:** Omni-Photo Communications, Inc.; **soccer:** Ann Hagen Griffiths/Omni-Photo Communications, Inc.; **soloist:** Omni-Photo Communications, Inc.; **spacewalk:** NASA/Omni-Photo Communications, Inc.; **spectrum:** Garfield/Stock Market; **spiral:** James H. Carmichael, Jr./Image Bank; **spool:** C.B. Jones/Taurus; **staircase:** Nicholas Foster/Image Bank; **stamp:** Garry Gay/Image Bank; **start:** Richard Hutchings/Photo Researchers; **steamboat:** John Lewis Stage/ Image Bank; **stilt:** Richard W. Brown/Stock Market; **stoplight:** Peter B. Kaplan/Photo Researchers; **strength:** Ken Karp/ Omni-Photo Communications, Inc.; **studio:** Steve Dunwell/Image Bank; **submerge:** Armando Jenik/Image Bank; **subway:** George Dodge/ DPI; **sunset:** Bill Bridge/DPI; **surf:** Pete Saloutos/Stock Market; **symmetry:** Stephen Frink/Stock Market; **table tennis:** Dilip Mehta/Contact Press Images-Woodfin Camp; **takeoff:** David Lawrence/Stock Market; **tap:** Dan Budnik/Woodfin Camp; **telescope:** John Bova/Photo Researchers; **tent:** Gary Cralle/Image Bank; **test tube:** Peter Beck/Stock Market; **thermometer:** DPI; **thread:** Michal Heron/Woodfin Camp; **tiara:** Wally McNamee/Woodfin Camp; **timberline:** Joan Teasdale/Stock Market; **toadstool:** Michael E. Agnes; **torch:** Gary Faber/Image Bank; **toss:** Will-Deni McIntyre/Photo Researchers; **tractor:** Richard Hutchings/Photo Researchers; **trampoline:** Suzanne Szasz/Photo Researchers; **triangle:** P.W. Grace/Photo Researchers; **tribal:** Jack Parsons/Omni-Photo Communications, Inc.; **triumphant:** Janeart Ltd./Image Bank; **trumpet:** Luis Villota/Stock Market; **tugboat:** Michael Tamborrino/Stock Market; **turquoise:** Adam Woolfit/Woodfin Camp; **umbrella:** Al Satterwhite/Image Bank; **unearth:** Cara Moore/Image Bank; **unicycle:** Peter Frey/Image Bank; **uproot:** G.R. Roberts/Omni-Photo Communications, Inc.; **Uranus:** NASA; **vase:** Murray Alcosser/Image Bank; **veterinarian:** Michal Heron/Woodfin Camp; **violin:** Stan Goldblatt/Photo Researchers; **volcano:** F. Salmoiraghi/Stock Market; **wagon:** John Lei/Omni-Photo Communications, Inc.; **wax:** Richard B. Peacock/Photo Researchers; **weigh:** Ken Karp/Omni-Photo Communications, Inc.; **wheelchair:** Michal Heron/Woodfin Camp; **whittle:** Bill Weems/Woodfin Camp; **wisteria:** A.W. Ambler/Photo Researchers; **workshop:** Babette & Marshall Druck/Photo Researchers; **zinnia:** Luis Villota/Stock Market

Photo Credits (Backmatter):

R25-R28, Reader's Resources, Richard Haynes; Time Line R30: George Washington, Smithsonian Institution/painting by Rembrandt Peale 1853; Samuel Morse, from the Macmillan Photo Library; Lee/Grant, photo: Russ Finley/painting: Louis Mathieu Didier Guillaume; R31: Thomas Edison, from the Macmillan Photo Library; Sputnik, Sipa-Press/Tass; Explorer XV-46, NASA; R32: Kennedy, Black Star/Art Rickerby; King, Bettmann Newsphotos; Begin/Carter/ Sadat, Gamma/Dick Halstead; O'Connor, Black Star/Dennis Brack; Reagan/Gorbachev, Sipa-Press/Trippett; R46-R51: White House Historical Association: Photographs by National Geographic Society; R51: Bush, Uniphoto/Gary Kieffer; R62-R63: Mercury, Photo Researchers, Inc./NASA/Science Source; Venus, NASA; Earth, Photo Researchers, Inc./John Giannicchi/Science Source; Mars, Uniphoto; Jupiter, Photo Researchers, Inc./NASA/Science Source; Saturn, Photo Researchers, Inc./NASA/Science Source; Uranus, Photo Researchers, Inc./NASA/Science Source; Neptune, NASA/83-HC-218; Pluto, Photo Researchers, Inc./ NASA/Science Source

Contents

Introduction

TO STUDENTS

The *Macmillan School Dictionary I* is a special book written for you. It will answer many of your questions about words. It will tell you what words mean. It will tell you how to say them and how to spell them. It will also tell you stories about where certain words come from.

The *Macmillan School Dictionary* is a list of words with their meanings and information about how to use them. The words in this book are the words you are most likely to see when you read. All of the words are listed in alphabetical order so you can find them easily.

When you look up a word, you are looking for an entry. The entry gives you a lot of information. First, it tells you the meaning, or meanings, of the word you are looking for. Then, it gives example sentences. These sentences help make the meaning of the word clear. They also show you how to use the word correctly in your own writing. The example sentences are written clearly. They are complete sentences, just like those you would find in a book or newspaper.

The first part of this book is a guide to the dictionary. It tells you about the information in the dictionary. It also tells you how to use the dictionary. Your teacher will help you through these pages.

The last part of this book has other information you can use. It has a thesaurus to help you choose among words that have different shades of meaning. It has answers to questions about how to use other books, like an atlas or encyclopedia. Maps of the world and the United States are included. You will also find information about the Presidents and the states of the United States, tables of weights and measures, and a chart about the planets.

The world of words is an exciting place. You can learn all kinds of new things in this world. The *Macmillan School Dictionary* is a great place to start your adventure.

TO PARENTS AND TEACHERS

The *Macmillan School Dictionary I* is a special book designed to help students learn about the English language and to use it more effectively. It contains a number of features intended to help words come alive and help students enjoy learning about them and using them.

The *Macmillan School Dictionary* has special features designed not only to provide information for students but also to excite their interest in learning more about language. In the front section of this book, the features of the dictionary are explained in clear, concise language, and a series of "Your Turn" exercises are included to help students practice their dictionary skills.

The back section of this dictionary provides reference materials and resources related to Language Arts and Reading, Social Studies, and Mathematics and Science, to help make this book even more valuable to students in all content areas.

The *Macmillan School Dictionary* provides clear, understandable information about words and how to use them. It provides example sentences to show how words are used, and drawings and photographs to illustrate and clarify word meanings. As this dictionary becomes familiar to students, it will help open up to them a whole new world of language.

Dictionary Preview

MAIN ENTRY

caboose   A railroad car that is at the end of a freight train. The train crew live, rest, or work in the caboose.
ca·boose (kə büs′) *noun, plural* **cabooses.**

DEFINITION

candle   A stick of wax or tallow with a string called a wick inside it. When the wick is lit, the candle slowly burns and gives off light.
can·dle (kan′dəl) *noun, plural* **candles.**

EXAMPLE SENTENCE

cane   A stick used to help someone walk. Canes are made of wood, metal, or other material. I needed to use a *cane* after I sprained my ankle.
cane (kān) *noun, plural* **canes.**

SYLLABLE DIVISION

canyon   A deep valley with very high, steep sides. A canyon often has a stream.
can·yon (kan′yən) *noun, plural* **canyons.**

PRONUNCIATION

carp   A fish that lives in fresh water and is sometimes used as food.
carp (kärp) *noun, plural* **carp** or **carps.**

IDIOM

cat   A small furry animal that has short ears and a long tail. Cats are kept as pets.
• **to let the cat out of the bag.**   To reveal a secret. The children were so excited about the surprise birthday party that they *let the cat out of the bag.*

PART OF SPEECH

cat (kat) *noun, plural* **cats.**

VERB FORMS

cater   To provide food, supplies, and other services. A restaurant *catered* the wedding dinner.
ca·ter (kā′tər) *verb,* **catered, catering.**

checkers   A game for two people played on a checkerboard with twelve pieces for each player.
check·ers (chek′ərz) *plural noun.*

ILLUSTRATION

checkers

HOMOPHONES

Chile   A country in southern South America.
▲ Other words that sound like this are **chili** and **chilly.**
Chil·e (chil′ē) *noun.*

GUIDE WORDS

COMPOUND WORD

civil war   1. A war between groups of citizens of the same country.   2. **Civil War.** The war between the northern and southern states of the United States that occurred between 1861 and 1865.

clever   1. Having a quick mind; bright and alert. The *clever* child soon learned to use the new toy.

ADJECTIVE FORMS

clev·er (klev′ər) *adjective*, **cleverer, cleverest.**

constellation   A group of stars. A constellation forms a pattern in the sky that looks like a picture.

PLURAL

con·stel·la·tion (kon′stə lā′shən) *noun*, *plural* **constellations.**

Word History

The word **constellation** comes from the old French name for a group of stars. This French word came from two Latin words meaning "together" and "stars."

WORD HISTORY

contraction   A shortened form. "Wouldn't" is the contraction of "would not."

con·trac·tion (kən trak′shən) *noun*, *plural* **contractions.**

Language Note

Contractions are used very commonly in spoken English. Here are some that you are likely to hear and use often: I'm (I am), you're (you are), aren't (are not), who'll (who will).

LANGUAGE NOTE

HOMOGRAPHS

cricket¹   A black or brown insect that hops.
crick·et (krik′it) *noun*, *plural* **crickets.**
cricket²   An English game like baseball.
crick·et (krik′it) *noun*.

at; āpe; fär; câre; end; mē; it; īce; pîerce; hot; ōld; sông; fôrk; oil; out; up; ūse; rüle; pull; tûrn; chin; sing; shop; thin; this; hw in white; zh in treasure. The symbol ə stands for the unstressed vowel sound in about, taken, pencil, lemon, and circus.

PRONUNCIATION KEY

A11

*F*inding Words in the Dictionary

MAIN ENTRIES: Words Listed in the Dictionary

A dictionary is a long list of words with their meanings and other information. Each word in the list is called a **main entry**. The word *entry* means "a place through which one enters; an entrance." One kind of entry you know is a doorway. When you go through a doorway, you go into a place. Think of main entries as the doorways to the dictionary. When you look up a main entry, you go into the dictionary.

Main entries are easy to find. They are printed in heavy black type—**like this**. You will find them at the left-hand side of each column on the dictionary page.

Main entries are only part of an entry. An entry tells many things about a word. Read the entry for *arch*.

> **arch 1.** A curved structure over an open space. An arch is usually built to support the weight of the material above it. Four *arches* supported the bridge across the river. **2.** A monument that contains an arch or arches. **3.** Anything like an arch in shape or use. The curved part of the foot between the toes and the heel is called the arch. *Noun.*
> —To form in an arch; curve. The cat *arched* its back in anger. *Verb.*
> **arch** (ärch) *noun, plural* **arches;** verb, **arched, arching.**

ALPHABETICAL ORDER: How Words Are Listed

The *Macmillan School Dictionary* has thousands of entry words. All of these words are listed in a special order. This order is called **alphabetical order**. It is sometimes called "ABC order." All the words that begin with the same letter are grouped together. Then the groups are arranged in order of the letters of the alphabet.

Many different words begin with each letter of the alphabet. For example, you can find fifty-two pages just for words beginning with the letter **a**. The dictionary must list all these **a** words in alphabetical order so we can find them.

Because so many words begin with the same letter, you must also look at the second letter in the word to find its correct alphabetical order.

1. able
acrobat
adapt

2. ape
aquarium
arbor

In many words, both the first and the second letters are the same. Sometimes the third or fourth letters are the same, too. Then you have to look at the next letter in the word to find the word's right place in alphabetical order.

1. about
absent
abyss

2. affect
affirm
afford

3. astray
astride
astronaut

Entry words beginning with **b, c,** and all the other letters are put in alphabetical order in the same way.

YOUR TURN 1

On your own paper, write the words in each list below in alphabetical order.

1. oboe
vase
relay

2. bobwhite
borrow
boat

3. sluice
slouch
slogan

4. family
marble
honey

5. vanish
various
valiant

6. crow's-
nest
crowbar
crown

Now put *all* these words in one longer list in alphabetical order.

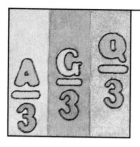

DICTIONARY SECTIONS: Three Thirds

Words beginning with **a** or **z** are easy to find quickly. But the farther you get from the ends of the alphabet, the harder it is to decide just where to open the dictionary. Searching through the book wastes a lot of time, so it helps to have a plan. You need to have a good idea of where to find words beginning with each letter.

The middle of the alphabet comes between **m** and **n.** So you might think that the middle of the dictionary should come between **m** words and **n** words.

abcdefghijklm / nopqrstuvwxyz

However, if you were to turn to the exact middle page of the dictionary, you will find that you are not in the exact middle of the alphabet. You will be in the first half, among the **l** words such as *laser.* The middle of the book is not the middle of the alphabet because some letters of the alphabet include more words than others. A lot more words begin with **b** or **c,** for example, than with **q** or **x.**

Here is a way to help you open the dictionary to the section you want. Think of this dictionary as being divided into three parts: the first third, the middle third, and the last third. About one third of the pages are in each part. This is how the letters of the alphabet are grouped within the book:

First Third	Middle Third	Last Third
A–F	G–P	Q–Z

You can use these thirds as guides to help direct you to the part of the dictionary you want. Try to find the word *hand-spring*, for example, by thinking about it this way: "**H** is in the second third. It comes just after **g**, a little more than one third of the way through the dictionary.'' Try it. See if you can open up the book to the **h** words.

The *Macmillan School Dictionary* has a special feature designed to make finding words even easier when you use the thirds of the dictionary. If you look at the side of the book, you will notice three color bars: blue, red, and green. There is a different color for each third of the dictionary. If you want to find a word in the first third, you would look in the section with the blue bar. The middle third has a red bar, and the last third has a green bar.

Using the three thirds is a good plan for finding words quickly. It is the first step in a strategy for finding information in the dictionary.

YOUR TURN

Read the words below. In which third of the dictionary would you find each word?

1. **kernel**	2. **lariat**	3. **yonder**
4. **universe**	5. **cocoon**	6. **forestry**
7. **oval**	8. **fuse**	9. **heroic**
10. **aphid**	11. **plume**	12. **computer**

Now see if you can open this dictionary to the section in which each word appears.

GUIDE WORDS:
The First and Last Entry Words on a Page

Suppose you want to find the word *newt* in the dictionary. There are many pages with **n** words. But you do not have to hunt through every **n** page to find *newt*.

There are pairs of words at the top outside corners of dictionary pages that can help you find the page with the word you are looking for. They are called **guide words.** *Guide* means "to show the way." Guide words show you the way to the word you are looking for. The first guide word tells you the first entry word on the page. The second guide word tells you the last entry word on the page. If the word you want comes in alphabetical order between the two guide words, it can be found on that page.

Look at the first pair of guide words below. They are *nearly* and *needless. Newt* cannot be on the same page with these guide words. *Newt* comes after *needless* in alphabetical order. You must look further on. Look at the last pair of guide words, *North Pole* and *note.* You will see that you have gone too far. *North Pole* comes after *newt* in alphabetical order. So *newt* cannot be on this page. You will find *newt* on the page with the guide words *newspaper* and *night. Newt* comes between these words in alphabetical order.

nearly/needless   newspaper/night   North Pole/note

Look up each of the following entry words in this dictionary. On your own paper, write each word. Next to it write the guide words that are on the page with that word.

1. auk	2. cashew	3. mercury
4. flute	5. impala	6. insignia
7. kimono	8. jerkin	9. obstacle

Checking Your Spelling

In the first part of this section of the dictionary, called "Finding Words in the Dictionary," you learned how to find words by the way they are spelled. But suppose you hear a new word that you cannot spell. If this new word does not look the way it sounds, how would you be able to find it in the dictionary? The Table of English Spellings can help you match the sound of a word with the way the word is spelled. You will find the Table of English Spellings on pages A46–A47. Turn to these pages and look at the sound represented by the letter **n**. This sound can be spelled five ways.

You can use the Table of English Spellings to help you spell a word. The story that follows shows you how.

One day Judy heard her mother talking on the telephone. She heard her say, "Oh, that Judy has a *knack* for cooking." Judy was not happy. She didn't think she had ever used a knack when she cooked. She looked among the pots and pans, but she didn't see any knacks. So she decided to find out what a *knack* really was.

Judy started to look in the dictionary. Then she realized she didn't know how to spell the word. It sounded like "nak," but she could not find a word spelled "nak." So she looked at the Table of English Spellings. She thought about the word. The first part of the word sounded like **n**. So she looked under *Sound* and found the **n**. This is what she saw.

Sound	Spelling	Example
n	**n,nn,kn,gn,pn**	**n**ice, fu**nn**y, **kn**ee, **gn**ome, **pn**eumonia

She wrote down the letters that spell the **n** sound. Then she thought about the other sounds that make up the word *nak*. She looked up each and found a list of ways to spell it. She wrote them all down like this.

n		a		k		
n	gn	a		c	cc	cq
nn	pn	au		k	qu	cu
kn		ai		ck	q	que
				ch		

Then she put the spellings together in different ways. Here are some of the ways she spelled the word: *nack, nach, knaik, knack, gnak, gnack.* She looked up each spelling in the dictionary until she found the right one.

> **knack** A special ability or skill for doing something easily. My classmate has a *knack* for repairing things.
> **knack** (nak) *noun.*

"Well, I guess I don't mind having a *knack* for cooking," Judy decided. She walked right into the kitchen and asked her mother if she could make lunch.

When you need to look up a word but you're not sure how to spell it, you can use the Table of English Spellings as Judy did. Think about how each part of the word sounds. Then look up each sound in the table.

YOUR TURN Use this dictionary to check the spelling of each word below. If a word is an entry word in the dictionary, that means it is spelled correctly. If it is *not* an entry word, it is not spelled correctly. Use the Table of English Spellings to help you find the correct spelling. Write each word on your own paper.

1. **skwat**
2. **byootee**
3. **flox**
4. **posse**
5. **goast**
6. **koff**
7. **nayshun**
8. **vakseen**

Discovering Word Meanings

I'M A MARIONETTE

THE DEFINITION: What a Word Means

From the dictionary you can learn many things about a word. But most of the time you will only want to know one thing. You will only want to know what a word means. The meaning of a word is also called its **definition.** The definition helps you understand a word clearly.

In this dictionary, the definition of a word is easy to find. It comes right after the entry word. You do not have to read other information before you read the definition.

The example below shows the entry for *marionette.* The first part of the definition is short and easy to read. Just a few words tell you what a marionette is—"a doll or puppet."

> **marionette** A doll or puppet moved by strings or wires that are held from above. It is usually made of wood.
> **mar·i·o·nette** (mâr′ē ə net′)
> *noun, plural* **marionettes.**

After the short definition, you may find more information about the entry word. Look below at the example from this dictionary. The sentences for **flax** answer three questions. What is flax? Where does it come from? What can flax be used for?

> **flax** **1.** A fiber that comes from the stem of a certain plant. This fiber is spun into thread, and the thread is used to make linen. Flax can also be used to make rope and rugs. **2.** The plant that produces this fiber. A kind of oil comes from the seeds of flax plants.
> **flax** (flaks) *noun.*

ILLUSTRATIONS:
How to Learn About a Word From a Picture

"A picture is worth a thousand words" is an old saying. In a book of words like a dictionary, a picture can be very helpful. Why does a book about words need pictures? Sometimes a picture can help you understand something more clearly than the definition alone can. Read the definition below.

> **geyser** A hot, underground spring from which steam and hot water shoot into the air.
> **gey·ser** (gī′zər) *noun, plural* **geysers.**

What does a geyser look like when it shoots into the air? Look at the picture below. The picture gives you a better idea of how to answer the question.

SYNONYMS: Words Having Almost the Same Meaning

Often in a definition you will see a single word by itself. This word is a **synonym.** A synonym is a word that has nearly the same meaning as another word. *Funny* and *humorous* are synonyms.

Synonyms you know can help you understand definitions. Synonyms can also help you write. They can help you say things in a different way.

Fghij

> **jovial** Full of fun; merry; jolly. I'm always in a *jovial* mood on my birthday.
> **jo·vi·al** (jō′vē əl) *adjective.*

The word *jovial* has two synonyms, *merry* and *jolly*. So you could say "Timothy is *jovial*" instead of "Timothy is *merry*." Both sentences mean nearly the same thing.

Write each word below on your own paper. Then write a synonym for each. Use this dictionary to check your work.

1. firm
2. brag
3. crisp
4. act
5. notion
6. devour

MULTIPLE MEANINGS:
Words With More Than One Meaning

Sometimes one word can mean many different things. Some words in this dictionary have five different meanings. Others have as many as twenty different meanings. When a word has more than one meaning, the different definitions are numbered.

> **field** **1.** A piece of open or cleared land. We could see the farmer in the wheat *field*. **2.** Land that contains or gives a natural resource. There are about ten oil wells in the oil *field*. **3.** An area of land on which a game is played. The players have just come out onto the football *field*. **4.** An area of interest or activity. The two friends both hope to work in the *field* of medicine when they get out of college. *Noun.*
> —To catch, stop, or pick up a ball that has been hit in baseball. The shortstop *fielded* the ball and threw it to first base. *Verb.*
> **field** (fēld) *noun, plural* **fields;** *verb,* **fielded, fielding.**

The first meaning listed for a word is the one that is used most often. It has the number **1** in front of it. The second most common meaning comes next, and so on.

Read this sentence:

We went down to the baseball *field* to watch the game.

Which meaning of *field* is used in this sentence? If you said meaning **3**, you are correct. From the words in the rest of the sentence, you know that this *field* is "an area of land on which a game is played."

YOUR TURN 6

Read each sentence below. Look at the underlined word. Use this dictionary to find the meaning of each underlined word. On your own paper, write the meaning of the word as it is used in the sentence.

1. Jimmy saw the figure 7 appear on his computer screen.
2. Kate will twist her ankle walking on that log.
3. Our strawberry plants have new runners.
4. Mr. Best used a pattern to make a new coat.
5. We watched June dribble the ball past the whole team.

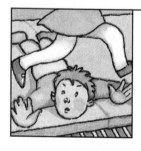

IDIOMS:
Phrases Made of Words That Do Not Mean What They Say

Suppose someone tells you that she "ran across an old friend today." You know she does not really mean that she knocked her friend down and ran over him. Rather, "to run across" someone means to meet that person by chance.

> **run** **1.** To go or cause to go quickly; move at a faster pace than a walk. The child had to *run* to catch the bus. I *ran* for help when I saw the fire break out. The rider *ran* the horse until it was exhausted.
> - **in the long run.** In the last part of a course of events; at the end; finally. The project started well, but *in the long run*, we abandoned it because we didn't have enough money.
> - **to run across.** To meet or find by chance. If you *run across* any bargains at the book sale, buy something for me.

The phrase "to run across" means something quite different from what each of the words usually means. Phrases like this are called **idioms.** The word *idiom* comes from a word that means "something strange in language." The meaning of an idiom certainly seems strange when you compare it to the usual meanings of the words in the idiom.

Idioms are listed in this dictionary. To find the definition of an idiom, look up the entry for the most important word in the idiom. There you will find a definition of the idiom. And you will find an example of how to use the idiom in a sentence.

YOUR TURN 7

Look up each of the entry words below. Read all the idioms listed under each word. Choose one idiom for each entry word and use it in a sentence. Write the sentence on your own paper.

1. turn   **2. take**   **3. get**   **4. put**

L earning About How Words Are Used

So far you have learned how to find words in the dictionary and how to discover the meaning of a word. This section will help you to learn about how words are used.

Look at the two pictures above. The picture on the left shows a paddle. But if you do not know what a paddle is, this picture does not help you much. The picture on the right shows two people using paddles. This picture tells you quite a bit more about a paddle. It shows how the paddle is used.

It is the same way with words. You can learn more about a word when you see how it is used. The definition tells you what the word means. Example sentences show how the word is used. In the *Macmillan School Dictionary,* almost every definition has at least one example sentence.

Do you know what the word *rustle* means? Read the example sentence from this dictionary. "The leaves *rustled* in the wind." You can probably figure out that *rustle* means "to make soft, fluttering sounds," like the sound leaves on a tree make when the wind blows.

Now read this example sentence. "There is a *plaza* with benches and a large fountain at the center of town." You might not know what *plaza* means. But you would know from the sentence that it is a place or area in a town. A *plaza* is "a public square or open space in a city or town."

You can learn many new words without ever using the dictionary. You hear people around you use new words. Most

of the time they use the words in sentences. These sentences give you clues to what words mean. Example sentences in the dictionary teach you about new words in the same way.

Many words have more than one meaning. Many words can also be used in more than one way, as different parts of speech. The example sentences can help you learn the different meanings of a word and how the word is used. For example, read these words and their definitions.

humble . . . **2.** Not big or important; lowly.

plane¹ . . . **1.** A level or grade.

riddle² . . . To make many holes in.

Are you sure of what the words mean? If you are not, read them again in the definitions below. Example sentences have been put in where they belong. The example sentences help make the meaning of the entry words clearer.

> **humble** . . . **2.** Not big or important; lowly. They lived in a *humble* cottage on a farm.
> **plane** . . . **1.** A level or grade. The book was on such a high *plane* that I couldn't understand it.
> **riddle²** . . . To make many holes in. The soldier *riddled* the target with bullets.

All of the examples in the *Macmillan School Dictionary* are in complete sentences. The examples serve as models to help you use words correctly and write clear sentences.

PARTS OF SPEECH: How Words Are Used

Many words can be used in different ways and in different forms. The dictionary tells you how each word can be used.

Words are divided into groups. These groups are called **parts of speech.** A word's part of speech is its job in the sentence. There are eight parts of speech in the *Macmillan School Dictionary*. They are: **noun, verb, adjective, adverb, pronoun, preposition, conjunction,** and **interjection.** In this dictionary, each entry tells you the word's part of speech. The part of speech comes right after the pronunciation.

> **par·a·sol** (par′ ə sôl′) *noun.*
> **cal·cu·late** (kal′kyə lāt′) *verb.*
> **rain·y** (rā′ nē) *adjective.*
> **quite** (kwīt) *adverb.*
> **up·on** (ə pon′) *preposition.*
> **and** (and) *conjunction.*
> **wow** (wou) *interjection.*

Often a word can be used as more than one part of speech. If a word is used as more than one part of speech, definitions for the different parts of speech are given in separate groups. You will find the part of speech at the end of each group of definitions. The part of speech that is used most often comes first. Then comes the second most common part of speech, and so on.

> **bristle** A short, stiff hair. Hogs have bristles. My toothbrush is made of *bristles. Noun.*
>   —**1.** To have the hairs on the neck or body rise. The dog *bristled* when it saw the fox. **2.** To stand up stiffly. The porcupine's quills *bristled. Verb.*
>   **bris·tle** (bris′əl) *noun, plural* **bristles;** *verb,* **bristled, bristling.**
> **diagonal** Having a slant. The dress had a pattern of *diagonal* stripes. *Adjective.*
>   —A straight line that connects the opposite corners of a rectangle. *Noun.*
>   **di·ag·o·nal** (dī ag′ə nəl) *adjective; noun, plural* **diagonals.**

YOUR TURN 8

Find each word below in this dictionary. On your own paper, write a sentence using the word as the part of speech shown in parentheses.

1. human (noun)   **2. report** (noun)
3. pleat (verb)   **4. direct** (adverb)

PLURALS: Words Meaning "More than One"

A **noun** is a word that names a person, place, or thing. For example, *boy, sea,* and *clam* are nouns. *Plural* means "having to do with the form of a word that refers to more than one." The dictionary shows you how to form the plurals of nouns.

Most plurals are formed by adding **-s.**

boy + s = boys   sea + s = seas   clam + s = clams

Sometimes the spelling changes when you form a plural. For example, the plural for *woman* is *women*. The plural for *wolf* is *wolves*. The plural for *diary* is *diaries*. Once in a while, the noun and its plural are exactly the same, as in **sheep**, *plural* **sheep**.

ox/oxen	party/parties	mouse/mice
goose/geese	child/children	couch/couches

YOUR TURN 9

Find each word below in this dictionary. On your own paper, write the plural of each.

1. elf
2. man
3. deer
4. dove[1]
5. fox
6. life
7. fly[1]
8. berry
9. bush
10. cabin
11. tree
12. loss

VERB FORMS:
Changes to Show When Something Happens

A **verb** is a word that is used to express an action or condition. Verbs can also be changed. A verb is changed to show the time when something happens, happened, or will happen.

jump	walk	fold
jumped	walked	folded
jumping	walking	folding

You usually change verbs by adding **-ed** or **-ing**. Most of the time, the ending **-ed** shows the past. The ending **-ing** can be used to show the present.

I <u>look</u> at the picture now.
I am <u>looking</u> at the picture now.
I <u>looked</u> at the picture yesterday.

Some verbs have very different forms to show when something happened. They do not use the **-ed** or **-ing** ending. They show when something happened in different ways.

run	**grow**	**go**
ran	**grew**	**went**
running	**grown**	**gone**
	growing	**going**

The dictionary tells you how each verb changes. After the word *verb*, the entry for each word shows the past and present participle forms of the verb. These forms of the verb are shown in heavy black type.

stop (stop) *verb*, **stopped, stopping.**
know (nō) *verb*, **knew, known, knowing.**
say (sā) *verb*, **said, saying.**

YOUR TURN 10

Copy the following sentences on your own paper. Then complete each sentence by using the correct form of each verb. Check your work in this dictionary.

clean	**visit**	**mop**
see	**find**	**explore**

1. Yesterday I _____ the new house.
2. I have _____ the house every day this week.
3. Now I am _____ the house again.

ADJECTIVES:
Words That Describe or Modify Nouns and Pronouns

An **adjective** is a word that describes or modifies a noun or pronoun. It tells how many, what kind, or which one. For example, "We saw <u>three</u> robins. They flew into a <u>tall</u> tree. I think it was <u>that</u> tree."

Adjectives can change to show the idea of *more* or *most*. For adjectives that have one syllable, you usually add the letters **-er** to show the meaning of "more." "My feet are *longer* (more long) than your feet." You usually add **-est** to show the meaning of "most." "His feet are the *longest* (most long) of all."

Sometimes when you add **-er** or **-est**, the spelling of the word changes.

happy + er = happier   sad + est = saddest

When an adjective has more than one syllable, you often do not add **-er** or **-est**. Instead, you leave the word as it is. Then use *more* or *most* in front of it. You should say "more peaceful" and "most wonderful," for example.

high	foolish	beautiful
higher	more foolish	more beautiful
highest	most foolish	most beautiful

In this dictionary, many entries for adjectives show the ways that the word can change.

> **fun·ny** (fun' ē) *adjective*, **funnier, funniest.**
> **glad** (glad) *adjective*, **gladder, gladdest.**

If there are no changes after the word *adjective*, that means you would use *more* or *most* with the word instead of adding **-er** or **-est**.

On your own paper, write the *more* or *most* forms of each adjective below. Then check your work in this dictionary.

1. old
2. red
3. friendly
4. afraid
5. cute
6. good
7. fortunate
8. many
9. luxurious

ADVERBS:
Words That Describe or Modify Verbs, Adjectives, and Adverbs

An **adverb** is a word that describes or modifies a verb, an adjective, or another adverb. The adverb tells how, when, or where. For example, "He walked *slowly*. I saw him *yesterday*. He went *inside*."

Like adjectives, adverbs can change to show the idea of *more* or *most*. When an adverb has only one syllable, you usually add the letters **-er** to mean "more." "She runs *faster* (more fast) than I do." You usually add **-est** to mean "most." "Pete runs *fastest* (most fast) of all."

Many adverbs end in **-ly**. For example, "He works *quickly*. They played *happily*. She slept *quietly*." When an adverb has more than one syllable, you do not usually add **-er** or **-est**. Instead, you leave the word as it is. Then use *more* or *most* in front of it. You would say "more quickly" and "most quietly," for example.

ABBREVIATIONS: Short Forms of Words

Sometimes you will see a short form of a word or words, usually followed by a period. This is called an **abbreviation**. The abbreviation stands for a whole word or for more than one word. For example, **Mr.** stands for *Mister,* and **Nov.** stands for *November.*

If you do not know the meaning of an abbreviation, you can look it up in the dictionary. Abbreviations are alphabetized in the dictionary just as whole words are.

YOUR TURN 12

Look up each abbreviation below in this dictionary. Then on your own paper, write the word or words that it stands for.

1. St.   2. lb.   3. Apr.   4. Rd.
5. co.   6. Feb.   7. Ave.   8. Mt.

CAPITAL LETTERS: Capitalizing Words

Most entry words in the *Macmillan School Dictionary* start with a small letter. For example, *new, island, ocean.* But some words begin with **capital letters**. Words that name certain places, people, and things begin with capital letters. These words are called **proper nouns**.

Proper adjectives are adjectives that refer to certain places, people, or things. Proper adjectives begin with capital letters.

French horn   Irish Setter   Arabic numerals

If you are not sure when a word should have a capital letter, check the word in the dictionary.

YOUR TURN 13

Look up each word or phrase below in this dictionary to see if it needs a capital letter or letters. Then write the word or phrase correctly on your own paper.

1. july   2. area code
3. hockey   4. sunday
5. house of   6. democratic party
   representatives   8. arctic ocean
7. egyptian

Pronouncing Words

If you see a word you do not know, you may not know how to say the word correctly. The *Macmillan School Dictionary* can make it easy to find out how to pronounce new words.

SYLLABLES: Parts of Words

After the definitions of each word in this dictionary, the main word is printed again in smaller black letters. This time, it is divided into smaller parts by black dots.

leg·end·ar·y   sal·a·man·der

These parts of a word are called **syllables**. When you want to spell a word, it can help to think of it as being divided in this way.

Knowing how to divide a word into syllables can help you when you write, too. Sometimes a whole word will not fit at the end of a line. Suppose you are writing the word *salamander*. You do not have room for the whole word on one line. You must decide where to break the word. You can break it wherever there is a black dot. Put a **hyphen** (-) where you break the word. The hyphen shows that there is more of the word to come on the next line.

We saw an orange **sala-**
mander near the brook.

YOUR TURN 14

Look up each word below in this dictionary. On your own paper, rewrite each word to show the syllable divisions marked with black dots.

1. pentagon   2. watermelon   3. gelatin
4. voluntary   5. anthracite   6. conspicuous
7. demonstrate   8. tourniquet   9. evening

PRONUNCIATION RESPELLINGS:
A Special Alphabet

The dictionary can tell you how to say a new word. The way a word is spoken is called its **pronunciation**. In the *Macmillan School Dictionary,* the pronunciation comes right after the syllable division. The pronunciation is not written in the same way as words you see in books, magazines, or newspapers. For example:

gorge (gôrj)   plea·sure (plezh′ər)

The pronunciation has its own special alphabet. As you can see, some of the letters in this alphabet look just like ordinary letters. Other letters have special marks above them. We use the twenty-six letters in the regular alphabet when we write. But we use more than forty different sounds when we speak. Think about the letter **e**. It is said one way in *me,* another way in *end,* and still another way in *taken.* In the dictionary, the special alphabet is used to show all the different sounds.

THE PRONUNCIATION KEY: Unlocking the Code

The pronunciation in a dictionary may seem a little like a strange language or a secret code. You can unlock this code. But to do it, you must use a special key. This key is called the **Pronunciation Key**. It is on page A48.

You will find all the different sounds of the English language in this Pronunciation Key. You will also find the different ways these sounds can be written. But you do not have to turn back to this Pronunciation Key whenever you use this dictionary. Instead, you can look at the bottom of most right-hand pages in this book.

The Pronunciation Key looks like this:

at; āpe; fär; câre; end; mē; it; īce; pîerce; hot; ōld; sông; fôrk; oil; out; up; ūse; rūle; pull; tûrn; chin; sing; shop; thin; this; hw in white; zh in treasure. The symbol ə stands for the unstressed vowel sound in about, taken, pencil, lemon, and circus.

Look at the key. All the letters in it are regular alphabet letters. Some have special signs above them. (There is one special symbol you will read about below.) The letters in this key are used to show you how to pronounce each word in the dictionary.

Let's look at these two words.

bone (bōn)   **copy (kop′ ē)**

By using the key, you can see that *bone* is pronounced with the **b** sound, then **o** as in *old,* then the **n** sound. If you put these sounds together, you will know how to pronounce *bone. Copy* is pronounced with a **k** sound, then **o** as in *hot,* the **p** sound, and **e** as in *me.* Put the sounds together to pronounce *copy.*

YOUR TURN 15

Look up each word below in this dictionary. Use the pronunciation key to find out how to pronounce it. Then on your own paper, write a word you know that rhymes with each one.

1. loot	2. taut	3. bead	4. though
5. soul	6. veil	7. could	8. heir

ACCENTS: Stressing Syllables

There is one symbol used for pronunciation. It looks like an upside down **e**. It is called a *schwa* (schwä). The schwa vowel sound can be in any word that has the letters **a, e, i, o,** or **u**. Say the following words.

about   taken   pencil   lemon   circus

Think about how you said the **a** in *about,* the **e** in *taken,* the **i** in *pencil,* the **o** in *lemon,* and the **u** in *circus.* The sounds are all the same. This sound is the schwa vowel sound.

When you say a long word, you say parts of it with more force than you do others. You say the first part of the word *breakfast* with more force than the second part. You say the second part of *tonight* with more force than the first part. This kind of force is called **stress.**

The dictionary shows you which part of a word is spoken with more stress. Black marks called **accent marks** show which part to say with more force. An accent mark comes after the part that is spoken with the most stress.

con·test (kon′test)   be·gin·ning (bi gin′ing)

Some long words have more than one part that is spoken with stress. A lighter mark shows the other part or parts of the word you speak with stress. But do not say it with as much stress as the part with a heavy black mark.

pic·tur·esque (pik′chə resk′)

YOUR TURN 16

Say the words below softly to yourself. Then on your own paper, write each word with the correct accent marks. Check your work in this dictionary.

1. **fi·es·ta**
   (fē es tə)
2. **hel·i·cop·ter**
   (hel i kop tər)
3. **la·dy·bug**
   (lā dē bug)
4. **suc·cess·ful**
   (sək ses fəl)

*E*xploring the World of Words

You have learned to find words and their meanings in the dictionary. You have also learned how to find the pronunciation of words. By now you can see that the dictionary has a lot of information. But there is so much more.

Words can be fascinating. Think of your dictionary as a huge house with hundreds of rooms. Every room you go into has new treasures for you to find. This section is about exploring words. It tells you about many of the kinds of words you will find in the dictionary.

COMPOUND WORDS:
Two or More Words Put Together

One kind of word is a **compound word**. A compound word is a word made up of two or more words. *Campfire, houseboat,* and *candlestick,* for example, are compound words.

In some cases, a compound word is written as one word with no space between. But others are written with hyphens, and many are written as two words.

lumberjack　　　　　　**good-by**　　　　　　**number line**

Compound words have their own entries in the dictionary because they have special meanings. Even if you know every word in the compound, you may not know what the compound means. An *Adam's apple,* for example, is not an apple. (It does not belong to Adam either.) You cannot live in a *cottage cheese.*

Compound words are listed in alphabetical order in the dictionary. They are all listed as if each were written as one word with no space between.

Find the compound in each list below.

contrast	girder	lattice
control tower	girl	laugh
convene	Girl Scouts	launching pad

YOUR TURN 17

Read each question below. Use this dictionary to find the meaning of each underlined compound. Then on your own paper, write the answer to the question. Give a reason for each answer by telling what the compound means.

1. Does a bird live in a <u>crow's-nest</u>?
2. How many fingers are there on the <u>upper hand</u>?
3. If you travel <u>first-class</u> are you in first grade?
4. Are <u>field glasses</u> used to drink water on a baseball field?
5. Is a <u>Great Dane</u> a famous person from Denmark?

NO. I DON'T KNOW.

HOMOPHONES: Words That Sound Alike

Some words sound the same, but they are spelled differently. These words are called **homophones**. The name comes from two Greek words. *Homo* means "same," and *phone* means "sound." (Think of the word *telephone*. When you answer it, you hear sounds.) Words such as *no* and *know, ate* and *eight,* or *sun* and *son* are examples of homophones. Can you see how homophones can make our language tricky?

Suppose a friend describes a trip to the zoo. She tells you about an animal you have never heard of. Its name sounds like this: "nu." You are curious about this strange animal. So you look up the word that seems to go best with this sound, *new.* But you certainly do not learn anything about a kind of animal. Then you might look up another common word with the same sound, *knew.* The same thing will happen.

But this dictionary has a way to get you to the right place. At the end of the definitions for *new* you will read: "Other words that sound like this are **knew** and **gnu**." The *gnu* is what you're hunting for!

gnu A large animal that lives in Africa. A gnu is a kind of antelope but has a large head and a stocky build like an ox. ▲ Other words that sound like this are **knew** and **new**.
   gnu (nü *or* nū) *noun, plural,* **gnus** or **gnu**.

Watch for a blue triangle like this (▲) at the end of an entry. It may tell you that there are other words that sound just like the word you have looked up.

pier 1. A structure built out over the water. It is used as a landing place for boats or ships. **2.** A pillar or other kind of support that is used to hold up a bridge. Modern bridges have steel piers to support them. ▲ Another word that sounds like this is **peer**.
   pier (pîr) *noun, plural* **piers**.

YOUR TURN 18

Read each sentence below. The underlined word in each sentence is incorrect. Look up the word in this dictionary. Find the homophone that fits the sentence. Then on your own paper, write the sentence with the correct word.

1. Water began to <u>floe</u> out of the bathtub.
2. Susan climbed all the way up to the mountain <u>peek</u>.
3. Just as the game started, the <u>reign</u> fell.
4. Blood goes back to the heart through each <u>vane</u>.
5. The actor took a <u>bough</u> while everyone applauded.

HOMOGRAPHS: Words That Are Spelled Alike

You know that two or three different words can sound alike. But two or three different words can also be spelled the same way. Suppose you read this sentence: "The captain sailed the junk into the bay." You probably know about the

kind of junk that is old pieces of metal, wood, rags, or other things that are thrown away. But the idea of a captain sailing junk into a bay might sound strange.

The dictionary can solve this problem. It has two different entries for **junk**.

> **junk¹** Old pieces of metal, wood, rags, or other things that are thrown away; trash.
> **junk** (jungk) *noun.*
> **junk²** A sailing ship usually found in China and southeastern Asia.
> **junk** (jungk) *noun. plural* **junks.**

The second entry for *junk* fits the sentence.

Words like these are called **homographs**. The word *homograph* comes from two Greek words. *Homo* means ''same'' and *graph* means ''writing.'' (*Autograph* and *paragraph* are two other words made with *graph*.) Entry words that are homographs have a small number after them. There are two or more entries in such groups of homographs.

It would be quite confusing to list all the different meanings for the two words under just one spelling. So this dictionary lists each homograph separately.

All homographs look the same, and many are pronounced in the same way.

> **bowl¹** **1.** A rounded dish that holds things. I put lettuce in the salad *bowl*. Pour some milk into a *bowl* for the cat. **2.** Something shaped like a bowl. The round end of a spoon is called a bowl. A football stadium is sometimes called a bowl. ▲ Another word that sounds like this is **boll.**
> **bowl** (bōl) *noun, plural* **bowls.**
> **bowl²** A wooden ball used in a game. *Noun.*
> —**1.** To play the game of bowling. My classmates like to *bowl* on Saturday night. **2.** To roll a ball in bowling. It is your turn to *bowl. Verb* ▲ Another word that sounds like this is **boll.**
> **bowl** (bōl) *noun, plural* **bowls;** *verb,* **bowled, bowling.**

Some homographs are spelled the same but pronounced differently. *Tear* is an example.

---

tear¹ **1.** To pull or become pulled apart by force. I *tore* the letter up and started over. *Tear* off a sheet from the pad of paper. This thin cloth *tears* easily. **2.** To make a hole or cut into by force; rip. I *tore* my shirt when I caught it on a nail. **3.** To remove or divide by force. We couldn't *tear* ourselves away from the interesting program. The country was *torn* by civil war. **4.** To move very quickly; rush. When the door was opened, the dog *tore* out of the house. *Verb.*
—A torn part or place. The tailor sewed the *tear* in my coat. *Noun.*
 tear (târ) *verb*, **tore, torn, tearing;** *noun, plural* **tears.**
tear² **1.** A drop of clear, salty liquid that comes from the eye. Tears help keep the surface of the eye clean. Extra tears form when you cry, or when you get something in your eye. **2. tears.** The act of crying. The baby fell and burst into *tears*. ▲ Another word that sounds like this is **tier.**
 tear (tîr) *noun, plural* **tears.**

YOUR TURN 19

Read each sentence below. The underlined word in each sentence is a homograph. Look up the underlined word in this dictionary. Then on your own paper, write the definition of the word as it is used in the sentence.

1. Mrs. Gray put some ice cubes in the punch.
2. Mom asked me to wind up the garden hose and put it away.
3. We swept up a pile of refuse from the parking lot.
4. The heavy load causes the boat to list.
5. Kenney rubbed his temple with his fingers.

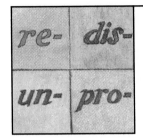

PREFIXES: Word Parts Added to the Beginning of Words

A number of entries in this dictionary are not words at all. Some are prefixes. A **prefix** is a word part that is added to the beginning of a word. You find prefixes in the dictionary because they help to form words.

The word to which a prefix is added is called the **base word**. For example, look at the word *unhappy*. **Un-** is a prefix that means "not." *Happy* is the base word.

You may sometimes see a word that is formed with a prefix and not be able to find that word in the dictionary. You can find the meaning of such a word by looking up the meaning of the prefix. Then look up the meaning of the base word.

For example, you might read that two teams are going to "*replay* a game." You might wonder what the word *replay* means. This word is not listed in the dictionary. So you must look up its parts, **re-** and **play**. They appear in the dictionary.

> **re-** *prefix* **1.** Again. . .
> **play** . . . **2.** To be in or have a game. Let's *play* tag. . .

From these two entries, you can figure out that *replay* means "to be in a game again." The two teams will play the game again.

YOUR TURN 20

Read each sentence below. Find the meaning of the underlined word in each sentence. If necessary look up the meaning of the base word and the meaning of the prefix. Then on your own paper, write a definition for each word.

1. We had to <u>repaint</u> the doghouse.
2. Mr. Green put <u>antifreeze</u> in his car.
3. Megan <u>dislikes</u> cold weather.
4. Dick has always felt <u>unlucky</u>.
5. Ms. Hunter <u>misunderstood</u> the directions.

-ly -ful
ment -er

SUFFIXES: Word Parts Added to the End of Words

You have learned that a prefix is added to the beginning of a word. Another kind of word part is a suffix. A **suffix** is added to the end of a word. You will find suffixes in the dictionary, too. They can also be used to form new words.

The word to which a suffix is added is called the **base word**. For example, look at the word *painter*. **Paint** is the base word. The ending **-er** is the suffix. It means "a person or thing that does something." A *painter* is a person who paints.

You may sometimes see a word that is formed with a suffix and not be able to find that word in the dictionary. You can find the meaning of such a word by looking up the meaning of the suffix. Then look up the meaning of the base word.

For example, you might read this sentence: "He spoke *softly* to the dog." You might wonder what the word *softly* means. This word is not listed in the dictionary. So you must look up its parts, **soft** and **-ly**. These parts do appear in the dictionary.

> **soft** ...**3.** Gentle or light; not harsh or sharp. The police officer's *soft* voice calmed the lost child.
>   **soft** (sôft) *adjective*, **softer, softest.**
> **-ly**[1] *suffix* **1.** In a certain way or manner. *Perfectly* means in a perfect way...

From these two entries, you can figure out that *softly* means "in a gentle or light way," or "in a soft manner." He spoke to the dog in a gentle way.

YOUR TURN 21

Read each sentence below. Find the meaning of the underlined word in each sentence. If necessary look up the meaning of the base word and the meaning of the suffix. Then on your own paper, write a definition for each word.

1. Ms. James held a <u>professorship</u> for ten years.
2. Tony has a list of jobs she has to do <u>monthly</u>.
3. Mr. Murphy has been <u>jobless</u> for six weeks.
4. Cathy was filled with <u>happiness</u> when she heard the news.
5. Julie finds such <u>enjoyment</u> in making her own clothes.

Sometimes you will see a word that has both a prefix and a suffix. You can find the meaning of such a word in the same way. Look up the meaning of the prefix. Then look up the meaning of the base word. Then look up the meaning of the suffix.

For example, you might see the word *unkindly.* To find out what it means, you can look up the prefix **un-**. Then look up the base word, **kind**. Then look up the suffix **-ly**. By putting the meanings of the word parts together, you can figure out that *unkindly* means "not in a kind way."

Remember that *suffix* comes from a word meaning "to fasten at the back." *Prefix* comes from a word that means "to fasten at the front."

Special Information About Words

This dictionary contains special articles with information on words and language. You will find these articles throughout the dictionary printed in boxes beneath colored banners.

WORD HISTORIES: Where Words Come From

Many words have an interesting story to tell us. They may have been borrowed from a foreign language, or they may have changed their meaning greatly since they were first used. This dictionary offers these stories in the form of Word Histories, which are printed in a red box.

For example, did you know that the word *circus* comes from a Latin word meaning "a ring" or "a circle"? Find the entry for the word *circus* and read the information under the red banner with the words "Word History." Now look up the entry *comet* and read the Word History. Where did this word come from?

In this dictionary, there is a Word History for every state in the United States. Look up the entry for the state that you live in. What does the Word History tell you about the name of your state? Does it come from a Spanish word? Was it based on an American Indian name?

Modern English has adopted words from many different languages. From the Spanish language come these words:

corral   **ranch**   **canyon**   **patio**

The German language has given us these words:

pretzel   **nickel**   **kindergarten**

We still use words the American Indians used, including:

moccasin   **hickory**   **raccoon**

Reading the Word History features will tell you the story behind many words you use everyday.

LANGUAGE NOTES: How Words Are Used

Language Notes are short articles that will help you use a word correctly. They are given after the entry and are printed in a blue box. When you are reading an entry, be sure to read the Language Note if there is one.

For example, do you know when to use the word *among* and when to use the word *between*? Look up the entry for *among* and read the Language Note. Now do you know? How is the word *good* used differently from the word *well*? There is a Language Note at the entry for *good* that will explain the differences.

 **YOUR TURN 22**

Find the answer to each question below by reading the Language Note or Word History sections for the words in heavy black type. On your own paper, use complete sentences to write your answer.

1. Where did **America** get its name?
2. Why was the first **sandwich** made?
3. Who was the month of **July** named after?
4. Why is there a "lion" in **dandelion**?
5. What did Roman soldiers use their **salary** for?
6. Where does the word **Wednesday** come from?
7. What did the Latin word **alibi** mean?
8. What can a **bilingual** person do?
9. From what language did we get our word **constellation**?
10. What Greek term explains the meaning of **etymology**?

Table of English Spellings

SOUND	SPELLING	EXAMPLE
a	a, au, ai	hand, laugh, plaid
ä	a, e, ea, ua	father, sergeant, heart, guard
ā	a, a-consonant-e, ai, ay, eigh, et, ea, ei, ey, au	paper, rate, rain, pay, eight, ballet, steak, veil, obey, gauge
âr	are, air, ayer, ere, ear, eir	care, fair, prayer, there, bear, heir
b	b, bb	bit, rabbit
ch	ch, t, tch, ti, c	chin, nature, batch, mention, cello
d	d, dd, ed	dive, ladder, failed
e	e, ea, a, ai, ie, eo, u, ae, ay, ei, ue	met, weather, many, said, friend, jeopardy, bury, aesthetic, says, heifer, guess
ē	e, y, ee, ea, e-consonant-e, i-consonant-e, ie, ei, ey, ae, ay, oe, eo	he, city, bee, beach, cede, machine, field, deceive, key, Caesar, quay, amoeba, people
f	f, ph, ff, gh	fine, physical, off, laugh
g	g, gg, gue, gh	go, stagger, catalogue, ghost
h	h, wh	how, whole
hw	wh	wheel
i	i, i-consonant-e, a-consonant-e, y, ie, ui, ei, ia, e, ee, u, o	sit, give, damage, myth, sieve, build, counterfeit, carriage, pretty, been, busy, women
ī	i-consonant-e, i, y, igh, ie, ei, eigh, uy, ai, ey, ye, eye	fine, tiger, try, high, tie, stein, height, buy, aisle, geyser, dye, eye
îr	ear, eer, ere, er, ier, ir, yr	near, deer, here, imperial, fierce, delirious, Syria
j	g, j, dg, d, gg, di	magic, jump, ledger, graduate, exaggerate, soldier
k	c, k, ck, ch, cc, qu, q, cq, cu, que	cat, key, tack, chord, account, liquor, Iraq, acquaint, biscuit, bisque
l	l, ll	line, hall
m	m, mm, mb, mn	mine, hammer, climb, hymn
n	n, nn, kn, gn, pn	nice, funny, knee, gnome, pneumonia
ng	ng, n, ngue	sing, link, tongue
o	o, a	lock, watch

SOUND	SPELLING	EXAMPLE
ō	o, o-consonant-e, oa, ow, ou, ough, oe, au, eau, oo, ew, oh	so, bone, boat, know, soul, though, foe, mauve, beau, brooch, sew, oh
ô	o, a, au, aw, ough, augh, oa	toss, fall, author, jaw, bought, caught, broad
ôr	or, ore, orr, oar, aur, our	order, more, horrible, soar, aural, four
oi	oi, oy, uoy	foil, toy, buoy
ou	ou, ow, ough	out, now, bough
p	p, pp	pill, happy
r	r, rr, wr, rh	ray, parrot, wrong, rhyme
s	s, ss, c, sc, ps, st, sch	song, mess, city, scene, psychology, listen, schism
sh	ti, sh, ci, ssi, si, ss, ch, s, sci, ce, sch	nation, shin, special, mission, expansion, tissue, machine, sugar, conscience, ocean, schist
t	t, tt, ed, pt, th	ten, bitter, topped, ptomaine, thyme
th	th	thin
th	th	them, bathe
u	u, o, ou, o-consonant-e, oo, oe	sun, son, touch, come, flood, does
u̇	u, oo, ou, o	full, look, should, wolf
ü	oo, u, o, u-consonant-e, ou, ew, ue, o-consonant-e, ui, eu, oe	tool, luminous, who, flute, soup, jewel, true, lose, fruit, maneuver, canoe
ū	u, u-consonant-e, ew, eu, ue, iew, eau, ieu, ueue	music, use, new, feud, cue, view, beautiful, adieu, queue
ûr	er, or, ur, ir, yr, our, ear, err, eur, yrrh	fern, worst, turn, thirst, myrtle, courage, earth, err, amateur, myrrh
v	v, f	vine, of
w	w, u, o	we, queen, choir
y	i, y, j	onion, yes, hallelujah
z	s, z, x, zz, ss	has, zoo, xylophone, fuzz, scissors
zh	si, s, g, z, zi	division, treasure, mirage, azure, brazier
ə	o, a, i, e, ou, u, y, ai	lemon, about, pencil, taken, furious, circus, analysis, bargain

Pronunciation Key

a	at, bad	d	dear, soda, bad
ā	ape, pain, day, break	f	five, defend, leaf, off, cough, elephant
ä	father, car, heart	g	game, ago, fog, egg
âr	care, pair, bear, their, where	h	hat, ahead
e	end, pet, said, heaven, friend	hw	white, whether, which
ē	equal, me, feet, team, piece, key	j	joke, enjoy, gem, page, edge
i	it, big, English, hymn	k	kite, bakery, seek, tack, cat
ī	ice, fine, lie, my	l	lid, sailor, feel, ball, allow
îr	ear, deer, here, pierce	m	man, family, dream
o	odd, hot, watch	n	not, final, pan, knife
ō	old, oat, toe, low	ng	long, singer, pink
ô	coffee, all, taught, law, fought	p	pail, repair, soap, happy
ôr	order, fork, horse, story, pour	r	ride, parent, wear, more, marry
oi	oil, toy	s	sit, aside, pets, cent, pass
ou	out, now	sh	shoe, washer, fish, mission, nation
u	up, mud, love, double	t	tag, pretend, fat, button, dressed
ū	use, mule, cue, feud, few	th	thin, panther, both
ü	rule, true, food	<u>th</u>	this, mother, smooth
u̇	put, wood, should	v	very, favor, wave
ûr	burn, hurry, term, bird, word, courage	w	wet, weather, reward
ə	about, taken, pencil, lemon, circus	y	yes, onion
b	bat, above, job	z	zoo, lazy, jazz, rose, dogs, houses
ch	chin, such, match	zh	vision, treasure, seizure

A a

1. The oldest form of the letter **A** was used about 4,000 years ago by tribes in the Middle East.

2. In the early Hebrew alphabet, this letter looked something like an **A** turned on its side.

3. The Greeks then borrowed a form of this letter about 3,000 years ago.

4. Later, the Greeks changed the letter to look more like our modern capital **A**.

5. The Romans borrowed the letter from the Greeks nearly 2,700 years ago.

6. Our English letter **A** looks like the late Greek and Roman letters.

a, A The first letter of the alphabet.
  a, A (ā) *noun, plural* **a's, A's.**

a **1.** Any. *A* dog would love that bone. **2.** One. My cousin has *a* new bicycle. **3.** One kind of. The orange is *a* fruit. **4.** In each; in every. We wash our car once *a* week. **5.** For each; for every. The piece of meat was two dollars *a* pound.
  a (ə *or* ā) *indefinite article.*

aardvark An animal that has a pointed snout, a long, sticky tongue, and sharp claws. The aardvark lives mainly in Africa, where it digs into the nests of ants and termites and uses its tongue to catch the insects.
  aard·vark (ärd′värk′) *noun, plural* **aardvarks.**

AB Postal abbreviation for *Alberta.*

abacus A frame with beads that slide on wires or in grooves. An abacus is used to add, subtract, multiply, or divide.
  ab·a·cus (ab′ə kəs) *noun, plural* **abacuses.**

abalone A large sea snail that has a flat shell. The lining of the shell is colorful and shiny like a pearl and is used to make buttons and ornaments. The meat of the abalone is used for food.
  ab·a·lo·ne (ab′ə lō′nē) *noun, plural* **abalones.**

abandon **1.** To leave without intending to return; desert. The sailors *abandoned* the sinking ship. **2.** To give up completely. Because of heavy rain, the climbers *abandoned* their efforts to reach the top of the mountain that day.
  a·ban·don (ə ban′dən) *verb,* **abandoned, abandoning.**

abandoned Left behind; no longer used or lived in. The porch of the *abandoned* house is overgrown with vines.
  a·ban·doned (ə ban′dənd) *adjective.*

abate To make or become less in amount or intensity. The storm finally passed, and the wind and rain *abated.*
  a·bate (ə bāt′) *verb,* **abated, abating.**

abbey A building or buildings where monks or nuns live a religious life.
  ab·bey (ab′ē) *noun, plural* **abbeys.**

abbreviate To make shorter. We *abbreviate* the words "United States of America" as "U.S.A."
  ab·bre·vi·ate (ə brē′vē āt′) *verb,* **abbreviated, abbreviating.**

abbreviation A letter or group of letters that stand for a longer word or phrase. "N.Y." is an abbreviation for "New York," "c" is an abbreviation for "centimeter," "Jan." is an abbreviation for "January," and "Fri." is an abbreviation for "Friday."

ab·bre·vi·a·tion (ə brē′vē ā′shən) *noun,* *plural* **abbreviations.**

Language Note

People use abbreviations in writing when they do not want to write out the full word that the abbreviation stands for. Many abbreviations have a period at the end. For example, "gal." is the abbreviation for the word "gallon." Other abbreviations may use more than one period, or they may use no period at all. Some abbreviations begin with a capital letter, and some have all capital letters.

---

abdicate To give up power. When the king *abdicated,* his oldest son became king.
ab·di·cate (ab′di kāt′) *verb,* **abdicated, abdicating.**

abdomen **1.** The hollow part of the body that lies between the chest and the hips. The abdomen contains the stomach, intestines, kidneys, and liver. **2.** The rear part of the body of an insect.
ab·do·men (ab′də mən *or* ab dō′mən) *noun,* *plural* **abdomens.**

Abdomen
abdomen of an insect

abduct To carry off by force; kidnap. In the movie, creatures from one planet *abducted* those from another planet and took them aboard their spacecraft.
ab·duct (ab dukt′) *verb,* **abducted, abducting.**

abide **1.** To continue to live or dwell. The family *abided* on a farm for many years. **2.** To put up with; bear; endure. My parents cannot *abide* a messy room.
• **to abide by.** **1.** To accept and obey. A good citizen *abides by* the law. **2.** To be faithful to; carry out. I was sure you would *abide by* your promise.
a·bide (ə bīd′) *verb,* **abided, abiding.**

ability **1.** The power to do something; capability. People are the only mammals that have the *ability* to speak. **2.** Talent or skill. That singer also has great *ability* as a painter.
a·bil·i·ty (ə bil′i tē) *noun,* *plural* **abilities.**

able **1.** Having the power to do something. A deer is *able* to run very fast. **2.** Having more than usual ability or talent. You are an *able* pianist.
a·ble (ā′bəl) *adjective,* **abler, ablest.**

–able A *suffix* that means: **1.** Able to be; capable of being. *Movable* means able to be moved. **2.** Likely to; tending to. *Agreeable* means likely to agree. **3.** Worthy of being. *Likable* means worthy of being liked.

abnormal Not normal, average, or usual. It is *abnormal* for it to be so cold in July.
ab·nor·mal (ab nôr′məl) *adjective.*

aboard In, on, or into a ship, train, airplane, or other vehicle. The ship left the dock just after we got *aboard.*
a·board (ə bôrd′) *adverb; preposition.*

abolish To end; stop. The purpose of that law is to *abolish* the dumping of toxic materials into the ocean.
a·bol·ish (ə bol′ish) *verb,* **abolished, abolishing.**

abolition The act of abolishing. The *abolition* of slavery in the United States occurred in 1865.
ab·o·li·tion (ab′ə lish′ən) *noun.*

abolitionist A person who was in favor of abolishing slavery in the United States before the Civil War.
a·bo·li·tion·ist (ab′ə lish′ə nist) *noun,* *plural* **abolitionists.**

abominable **1.** Causing hatred or disgust. The bombing of the school was an *abominable* act. **2.** Very unpleasant; offensive. You have *abominable* table manners.
a·bom·i·na·ble (ə bom′ə nə bəl) *adjective.*

aborigine One of the first people to live in a place. The Eskimo are among the *aborigines* of North America.
ab·o·rig·i·ne (ab′ə rij′ə nē) *noun, plural* **aborigines.**

abound To be present in great amounts; be plentiful. Buffalo used to *abound* on the western plains of North America.
a·bound (ə bound′) *verb,* **abounded, abounding.**

about **1.** Having to do with; concerning. We are reading a book *about* the exploration of outer space. **2.** On every side of; around. Look *about* you and you'll see birds everywhere. *Preposition.*
—**1.** Very close to; approximately. There were *about* twenty people waiting to buy tickets. **2.** Nearly; almost. Are you *about* ready to go? **3.** In several directions; all around. I looked *about* to find my dog. *Adverb.*
• **about to.** Very near the time when something will happen or begin; ready to. It is *about to* rain. We are *about to* leave.
a·bout (ə bout′) *preposition; adverb.*

above In or to a higher place; overhead. Stars glittered *above. Adverb.*

—**1.** Over or higher than. The kite flew *above* the trees. **2.** Higher in rank. A captain is *above* a lieutenant in the army. **3.** More than; over. Don't pay *above* ten dollars for the ticket. *Preposition.*
a·bove (ə buv′) *adverb; preposition.*

aboveboard Honest. The traders were open and *aboveboard* in their business.
a·bove·board (ə buv′bôrd′) *adjective.*

abreast Next to each other; side by side. The students walked two *abreast.*
a·breast (ə brest′) *adverb; adjective.*

children standing **abreast**

abridge To make shorter by using fewer words. The book I am reading was *abridged* from a much longer book.
a·bridge (ə brij′) *verb,* **abridged, abridging.**

abroad Outside of one's country. We went *abroad* to visit relatives in France.
a·broad (ə brôd′) *adverb.*

abrupt **1.** Without warning; sudden. The bus made an *abrupt* stop at the traffic light. **2.** Not polite or gentle; blunt. The impatient clerk gave us an *abrupt* answer.
a·brupt (ə brupt′) *adjective.*

abscess A collection of pus in some part of the body. It usually is caused by an infection.
ab·scess (ab′ses) *noun, plural* **abscesses.**

absence **1.** The condition of being away. In the teacher's *absence,* a substitute teacher taught our class. **2.** A period of being away. After an *absence* of a year, my cousin came home from college. **3.** The condition of being without; lack. The *absence* of rain caused the plants to wilt.
ab·sence (ab′səns) *noun, plural* **absences.**

absent **1.** Not present; away. My friend was *absent* from school because of a cold. **2.** Not existing; missing. Leaves are *absent* on trees in winter.
ab·sent (ab′sənt) *adjective.*

absentee A person who is absent from school, a job, or some other place where he or she is supposed to be. The teacher listed three *absentees* on the attendance record.
ab·sen·tee (ab′sən tē′) *noun, plural* **absentees.**

absent-minded **1.** Not paying attention to what is going on. The child stared out the window in an *absent-minded* way. **2.** Forgetful. *Absent-minded* people often misplace things.
ab·sent-mind·ed (ab′sənt mīn′did) *adjective.*

absolute **1.** Complete; entire; whole. The witness told the *absolute* truth. **2.** Not limited or restricted. Some rulers have *absolute* power. **3.** Without any doubt; positive. The family had *absolute* proof that the land belonged to them.
ab·so·lute (ab′sə lüt′) *adjective.*

absolutely **1.** Completely. He is *absolutely* right about that. **2.** Without any doubt; positively. I was *absolutely* sure that I wanted to buy that shirt.
ab·so·lute·ly (ab′sə lüt′lē *or* ab′sə lüt′lē) *adverb.*

absorb **1.** To soak up or take in. A towel *absorbed* the spilled water. **2.** To hold the interest of. The book about animals *absorbed* me. **3.** To take in and hold without reflecting back. Thick draperies *absorb* sound.
ab·sorb (ab sôrb′ *or* ab zôrb′) *verb,* **absorbed, absorbing.**

absorbent Able to soak up water or moisture. These towels are very *absorbent.*
ab·sorb·ent (ab sôr′bənt *or* ab zôr′bənt) *adjective.*

absorption The act or process of absorbing. A sponge picks up water by *absorption.*
ab·sorp·tion (ab sôrp′shən *or* ab zôrp′shən) *noun.*

abstain To keep oneself from doing something. I *abstained* from eating candy.
ab·stain (ab stān′) *verb,* **abstained, abstaining.**

---

at; āpe; fär; câre; end; mē; it; ice; pîerce; hot; ōld; sông, fôrk; oil; out; up; ūse; rüle; pùll; tûrn; chin; sing; shop; thin; <u>th</u>is; hw in white; zh in treasure. The symbol ə stands for the unstressed vowel sound in about, taken, pencil, lemon, and circus.

abstract **1.** Expressing a quality thought of apart from the person or thing that has the quality. "Sourness" is an abstract word. "Lemon" is not an abstract word. **2.** Hard to understand. This book on physics is too *abstract* for me. **3.** Having to do with a style of art that does not show real objects, but uses lines, shapes, and colors.
ab·stract (ab′strakt *or* ab strakt′) *adjective.*

an **abstract** painting

absurd Silly, foolish, or untrue. It is *absurd* to believe that the moon is made of green cheese.
ab·surd (ab surd′ *or* ab zurd′) *adjective.*

abundance A very large amount; a quantity that is more than enough. The farmer had an *abundance* of food.
a·bun·dance (ə bun′dəns) *noun.*

abundant More than enough; plentiful. Rockets need an *abundant* amount of fuel when they are launched.
a·bun·dant (ə bun′dənt) *adjective.*

abuse **1.** To use in a way that is bad or wrong; misuse. We must not *abuse* our natural resources. **2.** To treat roughly or cruelly; harm. In the story, the villain was punished for *abusing* the servants. **3.** To attack with harsh or insulting words. *Verb.*
—**1.** Bad or wrong use; misuse. The ruler's *abuse* of power caused the people to revolt. **2.** Rough or cruel treatment. During the trip on the old, bumpy road our car took a lot of *abuse.* **3.** Harsh or insulting words. *Noun.*
a·buse (ə būz′ *for verb;* ə būs′ *for noun*) *verb,* **abused, abusing;** *noun, plural* **abuses.**

abyss A hole so deep that it seems impossible to measure.
a·byss (ə bis′) *noun, plural* **abysses.**

acacia A small tree with featherlike leaves and yellow or white flowers that look like fuzzy balls. This tree is found in warm areas.
a·ca·cia (ə kā′shə) *noun, plural* **acacias.**

academy **1.** A private high school. **2.** A school that trains people in a special field or subject. I take violin lessons at the music *academy.*
a·cad·e·my (ə kad′ə mē) *noun, plural* **academies.**

accelerate To move or cause to move faster. The bicycle *accelerated* as it went down the hill.
ac·cel·er·ate (ak sel′ə rāt′) *verb,* **accelerated, accelerating.**

acceleration An increase in speed; moving faster. The sudden *acceleration* of the car frightened the passengers.
ac·cel·er·a·tion (ak sel′ə rā′shən) *noun, plural* **accelerations.**

accent **1.** The stress or stronger tone of voice given to a word or part of a word. In the word "happy," the *accent* is on the first syllable. In "forget," the *accent* is on the second syllable. **2.** A mark used on a word to show which syllable is spoken with an accent. In this dictionary, the mark ′ is used to show the syllable in the word spoken with the most stress. The mark ′ is used to show a syllable with a weaker accent. In the word "abbreviation," we place the accents like this: ə brē′vē ā′shən. **3.** A particular way in which people in one part of a country pronounce words. My cousins from Georgia have a Southern *accent.* **4.** A particular way in which people pronounce words in a language that is not their first language. My grandparents from Holland speak English with a Dutch *accent. Noun.*
—To pronounce or mark a word or syllable with a stronger tone of voice. You *accent* the first syllable of the word "apple." *Verb.*
ac·cent (ak′sent *for noun;* ak′sent *or* ak sent′ *for verb*) *noun, plural* **accents;** *verb,* **accented, accenting.**

accept **1.** To take something that is given. I *accepted* the birthday gift from my cousin. **2.** To receive or admit, often with favor or approval. Our class *accepted* the new teacher immediately. **3.** To agree to; answer "yes" to. The author *accepted* the invitation to give a speech to our book club. **4.** To think of as true, satisfactory, or correct. My parents *accepted* my reason for being late.

ac·cept (ak sept′) *verb*, **accepted, accepting.**

acceptable Good enough to be accepted; satisfactory. Our plan for the bazaar was *acceptable* to everyone in the club.

ac·cept·a·ble (ak sep′tə bəl) *adjective.*

acceptance **1.** The act of taking something given or offered. Your *acceptance* of my invitation pleased me. **2.** A favorable reception; approval. The new television series won immediate *acceptance.*

ac·cept·ance (ak sep′təns) *noun, plural* **acceptances.**

access **1.** The act of approaching or entering. *Access* into the abandoned house was easy. **2.** The right to approach, enter, or use. Only military personnel had *access* to the missile base. **3.** A way or means of approaching or entering. The only *access* to the lake is through the woods.

ac·cess (ak′ses) *noun, plural* **accesses.**

accessory **1.** Something that is added to a more important thing. A radio is an *accessory* for a car. **2.** A person who helps another person commit a crime. Two suspects have been arrested as *accessories* to the theft. *Noun.*
—Useful but not necessary; additional. The listing of street addresses is an *accessory* feature of a telephone book. *Adjective.*

ac·ces·so·ry (ak ses′ə rē) *noun, plural* **accessories;** *adjective.*

accident **1.** Something that happens for no apparent reason and is unexpected. The discovery of oil on the farm was a happy *accident.* **2.** An unfortunate event that is not expected. During the snowstorm there were many *accidents* on the highways. **3.** Chance; fortune. I found the missing watch by *accident* while looking for my comb.

ac·ci·dent (ak′si dənt) *noun, plural* **accidents.**

accidental Not planned or expected; happening by chance. We did not know we would see each other; our meeting was *accidental.*

ac·ci·den·tal (ak′si den′təl) *adjective.*

acclaim To welcome with strong approval; praise. The crowd *acclaimed* the astronauts. *Verb.*
—Enthusiastic praise or welcome. The tennis champion was greeted with *acclaim. Noun.*

ac·claim (ə klām′) *verb*, **acclaimed, acclaiming;** *noun, plural* **acclaims.**

accommodate **1.** To have room for; hold. That movie theater *accommodates* 600 people. **2.** To supply with a place to stay or sleep. That motel *accommodates* about forty guests each night. **3.** To do a favor for; help out. The police officer *accommodated* us when we asked for directions.

ac·com·mo·date (ə kom′ə dāt′) *verb*, **accommodated, accommodating.**

accommodation **1.** A convenience or favor. Giving me a ride to school on your way to work was a big *accommodation.* **2. accommodations.** A place to stay or sleep, often one where food is served. When we were traveling, we found good *accommodations.*

ac·com·mo·da·tion (ə kom′ə dā′shən) *noun, plural* **accommodations.**

accompaniment **1.** Something that acts or is used together with something else. Cranberry sauce is a delicious *accompaniment* to turkey. **2.** A musical part that is played as background for a main part. The soloist performed with a piano *accompaniment.*

ac·com·pa·ni·ment (ə kum′pə ni mənt) *noun, plural* **accompaniments.**

accompany

accompany **1.** To go together with. One of my parents always *accompanies* me to the movies. **2.** To happen at the same time as. Wind often *accompanies* rain. **3.** To play a musical accompaniment. While I played the flute, my cousin *accompanied* me on the piano.

ac·com·pa·ny (ə kum′pə nē) *verb*, **accompanied, accompanying.**

at; āpe; fär; câre; end; mē; it; īce; pîerce; hot; ōld; sông, fôrk; oil; out; up; ūse; rüle; pull; tûrn; chin; sing; shop; thin; <u>th</u>is; hw in white; zh in treasure. The symbol ə stands for the unstressed vowel sound in about, taken, pencil, lemon, and circus.

5

accomplice A person who helps another person do something that is illegal or wrong.
ac·com·plice (ə kom′plis) *noun, plural* **accomplices.**

accomplish To carry out or complete; perform. We *accomplished* more work than we had planned.
ac·com·plish (ə kom′plish) *verb,* **accomplished, accomplishing.**

accomplishment **1.** The act of accomplishing; completion. The *accomplishment* of our goal will be very difficult. **2.** Something accomplished; achievement. The first landing on the moon was a great *accomplishment.* **3.** A special skill or ability that is usually gained by training. Practice has certainly increased your *accomplishment* as a pianist.
ac·com·plish·ment (ə kom′plish mənt) *noun, plural* **accomplishments.**

accord **1.** Agreement; harmony. A higher wage is in *accord* with the demands of the workers. **2.** An agreement made, such as a treaty between nations. *Noun.*
—To agree or be in harmony. Her opinions on politics *accord* with his. *Verb.*
ac·cord (ə kôrd′) *noun, plural* **accords;** *verb,* **accorded, according.**

accordance Agreement. Thank you for acting in *accordance* with my request.
ac·cord·ance (ə kôr′dəns) *noun.*

according According to. **1.** In agreement with. Everything went *according to* our plan. **2.** In proportion to. People were paid *according to* the amount of work they did. **3.** On the authority of. *According to* the weather report, it will probably rain tomorrow.
ac·cord·ing (ə kôr′ding).

accordion A musical instrument with keys, metal reeds, and a bellows. The bellows forces air past the reeds to produce musical tones.
ac·cor·di·on (ə kôr′dē ən) *noun, plural* **accordions.**

account **1.** A spoken or written statement; report. There was an *account* of the baseball game in the newspaper. **2.** A record of money spent or received. Who takes care of the household *accounts* for your family? **3.** A sum of money that a person allows a bank to hold until it is needed. How much do you have in your savings *account?* **4.** Importance or worth. This old watch is of little *account. Noun.*
—To consider to be. I *account* them a happy couple. *Verb.*

• **to account for.** **1.** To explain. How do you *account for* your lateness? **2.** To be the reason for. The heavy snow *accounts for* the closing of school today. **3.** To explain what happened to or what was done with. The police have *accounted for* everyone who was on the boat when it capsized.
ac·count (ə kount′) *noun, plural* **accounts;** *verb,* **accounted, accounting.**

accountant A person who is trained to take care of the financial records of a person or business.
ac·count·ant (ə koun′tənt) *noun, plural* **accountants.**

accumulate To gather or pile up; collect. My cousin *accumulated* a number of books at college. The mail *accumulated* while we were on vacation.
ac·cu·mu·late (ə kū′myə lāt′) *verb,* **accumulated, accumulating.**

accumulation **1.** The act of accumulating; piling up. The *accumulation* of snow during the blizzard created traffic problems. **2.** An amount accumulated; collection; heap; mass. There was an *accumulation* of dust under the bed.
ac·cu·mu·la·tion (ə kū′myə lā′shən) *noun, plural* **accumulations.**

accuracy Freedom from errors or mistakes; correctness; exactness; precision. Check the *accuracy* of your arithmetic answers. You can trust the *accuracy* of the scale in the doctor's office.
ac·cu·ra·cy (ak′yər ə sē) *noun.*

accordion

accurate   **1.** Being correct, exact, or precise. The newspaper stories about the accident were not *accurate*.   **2.** Making few or no errors or mistakes; exact. We need an *accurate* typist for this job.
ac·cu·rate (ak′yər it) *adjective.*

accusation   A statement that a person has done something wrong or illegal; charge. What is the *accusation* against the prisoner?
ac·cu·sa·tion (ak′yə zā′shən) *noun, plural* **accusations.**

accuse   To state that a person has done something wrong or illegal. The store manager *accused* the clerk of stealing.
ac·cuse (ə kūz′) *verb,* **accused, accusing.**

accustom   To make familiar through experience or use. You have to *accustom* yourself to a new school when your family moves.
ac·cus·tom (ə kus′təm) *verb,* **accustomed, accustoming.**

accustomed   Usual. The dog lay in its *accustomed* place by the fire.
• **accustomed to.**   Familiar with; used to. The police officer was *accustomed to* the noisy traffic.
ac·cus·tomed (ə kus′təmd) *adjective.*

ace   **1.** A playing card having one mark in the center.   **2.** A person who is an expert at something. You're an *ace* at bowling. *Noun.*
—Of the highest quality; expert. It takes years to become an *ace* pitcher. *Adjective.*
ace (ās) *noun, plural* **aces;** *adjective.*

ace
of hearts

ache   **1.** To hurt with a dull or constant pain. My whole body *ached* after I did those new exercises.   **2.** To want very much; be eager. After being away for a month, we *ached* to get back home. *Verb.*
—A dull or constant pain. I had an *ache* in my side from running so far. *Noun.*
ache (āk) *verb,* **ached, aching;** *noun, plural* **aches.**

achieve   **1.** To do or carry out; accomplish. Did you *achieve* all that you had set out to do?   **2.** To gain or to reach by one's own effort. Marie and Pierre Curie *achieved* fame as scientists.
a·chieve (ə chēv′) *verb,* **achieved, achieving.**

achievement   **1.** Something accomplished or achieved. The invention of the telephone was a great *achievement*.   **2.** The act of achieving.
a·chieve·ment (ə chēv′mənt) *noun, plural* **achievements.**

acid   **1.** Sour, sharp, or biting to the taste. A lemon has an *acid* taste.   **2.** Sharp or biting in actions or speech. The *acid* remark hurt my feelings. *Adjective.*
—A chemical compound that can unite with a base to form a salt. Acids have a sour taste when dissolved in water. An acid will cause blue litmus paper to turn red. *Noun.*
ac·id (as′id) *adjective; noun, plural* **acids.**

acid rain   Rain that contains chemical pollution and that can harm plants and other parts of the environment.

acknowledge   **1.** To admit the existence or truth of; concede. The scientists *acknowledged* the mistakes of their research.   **2.** To recognize the ability or authority of. The teacher *acknowledged* you as the best speller in the class.   **3.** To make known that one has received something. I *acknowledged* the invitation with a phone call.
ac·knowl·edge (ak nol′ij) *verb,* **acknowledged, acknowledging.**

acknowledgment   **1.** The act of acknowledging. My *acknowledgment* that I was wrong made me feel better.   **2.** A response made to show that one has received something. Have you sent an *acknowledgment* of your gift?
ac·knowl·edg·ment (ak nol′ij mənt) *noun, plural* **acknowledgments.**

acne   A skin disease in which a person has pimples, especially on the face. Acne is caused by inflammation of the oil glands under the skin. People often get acne in their teens when these glands are very active.
ac·ne (ak′nē) *noun.*

acorn   The nut of the oak tree.
a·corn (ā′kôrn *or* ā′kərn) *noun, plural* **acorns.**

acquaint   To make familiar. All swimmers must *acquaint* themselves with the rules of the swimming pool.
ac·quaint (ə kwānt′) *verb,* **acquainted, acquainting.**

acquaintance   **1.** A person one knows, but who is not a close friend.   **2.** Knowledge of something gained from experience. I have an *acquaintance* with the game of chess.
ac·quaint·ance (ə kwān′təns) *noun, plural* **acquaintances.**

at; āpe; fär; câre; end; mē; it; īce; pîerce; hot; ōld; sông, fôrk; oil; out; up; ūse; rüle; pùll; tûrn; chin; sing; shop; thin; this; hw in white; zh in treasure. The symbol ə stands for the unstressed vowel sound in about, taken, pencil, lemon, and circus.

acquire To get or gain as one's own. I *acquired* the ability to speak Spanish while I lived in Mexico.
ac·quire (ə kwīr′) *verb,* **acquired, acquiring.**

acquit To free from a charge of a crime; declare not guilty. The jury *acquitted* the person accused of the crime.
ac·quit (ə kwit′) *verb,* **acquitted, acquitting.**

acre A measure of land equal to 43,560 square feet. An acre is slightly smaller in size than a football field.
a·cre (ā′kər) *noun, plural* **acres.**

acreage An area of land measured in acres; number of acres. How much *acreage* does the farmer own?
a·cre·age (ā′kər ij) *noun.*

acrobat A person who is skilled at performing stunts such as walking on a tightrope or swinging on a trapeze.
ac·ro·bat (ak′rə bat′) *noun, plural* **acrobats.**

across From one side to the other. We came *across* in a rowboat. *Adverb.*
—**1.** From one side of to the other; over. We drove *across* the bridge. **2.** On the other side of; beyond. They live *across* the street from me. **3.** In a direction that crosses. The cat walked *across* our path. *Preposition.*
a·cross (ə krôs′) *adverb; preposition.*

act **1.** Something that is done; a deed. Saving the child's life was an *act* of bravery. **2.** The process of doing something. The thief was caught in the *act* of opening the safe. **3.** A law. The United States can declare war only by an *act* of Congress. **4.** One of the main parts of a play, opera, or ballet. Our school play this year has five *acts.* **5.** A short performance that is usually one of several on a program. The magician's *act* follows the intermission. *Noun.*
—**1.** To do something. After the accident, the doctor *acted* quickly to help the victims. **2.** To be an actor; play a part. Did you ever *act* in a play? **3.** To conduct oneself; behave. They *acted* as though they had no manners. **4.** To have or produce an effect. The medicine *acted* slowly. *Verb.*
 • **to act on** or **to act upon.** **1.** To behave according to; follow. We will *act on* your orders. **2.** To have an effect upon; influence. This acid *acts on* metal.
 • **to act up.** **1.** To behave in a mischievous or playful way. The children are *acting up* again. **2.** To cause trouble. My stomach *acted up* after dinner.
act (akt) *noun, plural* **acts;** *verb,* **acted, acting.**

acrobats

action **1.** The process of doing something. Throwing a ball, jumping over a fence, and running down a hill are all *actions.* **2.** Something that is done; an act. Helping a blind person across a street is a kind *action.* **3. actions.** Behavior; conduct. We couldn't understand their strange *actions* at the party. **4.** A way of working or moving. This washing machine has a very gentle *action.* **5.** Fighting in battles; combat. Many soldiers were wounded in *action* during the war.
ac·tion (ak′shən) *noun, plural* **actions.**

action verb A verb that shows action. *Take, write, cut, send, vote, run,* and *practice* are some examples of action verbs.

activate To cause to work or operate. Pushing the button *activates* the machine.
ac·ti·vate (ak′tə vāt′) *verb,* **activated, activating.**

active **1.** Moving around or doing something much of the time; lively; busy. My grandparents are still very *active.* Are you very *active* in your club? **2.** Doing something or capable of doing something; functioning; working. Steam rose from the *active* volcano.
ac·tive (ak′tiv) *adjective.*

activity **1.** The condition of doing something or moving around; action; movement.

There was a lot of *activity* during recess. **2.** A thing to do or to be done. I take part in many school *activities*.

ac·tiv·i·ty (ak tiv′i tē) *noun, plural* **activities.**

actor A person who plays a part in a play, movie, television program, or radio program.

ac·tor (ak′tər) *noun, plural* **actors.**

actress A girl or woman who plays a part in a play, movie, television program, or radio program.

ac·tress (ak′tris) *noun, plural* **actresses.**

actual Real; existing. That book is about *actual* people, not imaginary ones.

ac·tu·al (ak′chü əl) *adjective.*

actually In fact; really. Were you *actually* sick on the day you missed class?

ac·tu·al·ly (ak′chü ə lē) *adverb.*

acupuncture The practice of relieving pain or treating a disease by putting needles into the skin at certain points on the body. Acupuncture has been practiced in China for thousands of years.

ac·u·punc·ture (ak′yü pungk′chər) *noun.*

acute **1.** Very keen or quick. My vision became *acute* when I started wearing glasses. **2.** Sharp and severe. I got an *acute* pain in my side from running too far. **3.** Very important; urgent; critical. The lack of rain this year has led to an *acute* water shortage.

a·cute (ə kūt′) *adjective.*

acute angle An angle that is less than 90 degrees.

ad A short form of the word **advertisement.** Look up **advertisement** for more information. ▲ Another word that sounds like this is **add.**

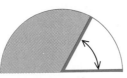

acute angle

ad (ad) *noun, plural* **ads.**

A.D. The abbreviation for the Latin words *Anno Domini,* meaning "in the year of the Lord." It is used in giving dates since the birth of Jesus. A.D. 1000 means 1,000 years after the birth of Jesus.

adage An old and familiar saying that is believed to be true; proverb. "The early bird catches the worm" is an adage.

ad·age (ad′ij) *noun, plural* **adages.**

adapt **1.** To change in order to make suitable. The authors *adapted* their play for television. **2.** To make or become used to. When the family moved to Florida, they had to *adapt* to the warm weather.

a·dapt (ə dapt′) *verb,* **adapted, adapting.**

add **1.** To find the sum of two or more numbers. If you *add* 2 and 7, you get 9 because 2 + 7 = 9. **2.** To put in or on as something extra. I like to *add* fruit to my yogurt. We plan to *add* a porch to our house. **3.** To put more onto something written or said. I thanked them for the gift and *added* that it was just what I wanted. ▲ Another word that sounds like this is **ad.**

add (ad) *verb,* **added, adding.**

addend Any number to be added to another number. In the problem 5 + 3 = 8, the *addends* are 5 and 3.

ad·dend (ad′end *or* ə dend′) *noun, plural* **addends.**

adder A kind of snake. The type of adder found in Europe is poisonous, while the type found in North America is not poisonous.

ad·der (ad′ər) *noun, plural* **adders.**

adder

addict **1.** A person who has a strong need for something, especially a drug. **2.** A person who is a very enthusiastic fan. My cousin is a science fiction *addict. Noun.*
—To make a person have a strong need for something, especially a drug. *Verb.*

ad·dict (ad′ikt *for noun;* ə dikt′ *for verb*) *noun, plural* **addicts;** *verb,* **addicted, addicting.**

addiction The condition of not being able to control the need for something, especially a drug.

ad·dic·tion (ə dik′shən) *noun, plural* **addictions.**

addition **1.** The adding of two or more numbers. 9 + 2 + 5 = 16 is an example of

at; āpe; fär; câre; end; mē; it; īce; pîerce; hot; ōld; sông, fôrk; oil; out; up; ūse; rüle; pùll; tûrn; chin; sing; shop; thin; this; hw in white; zh in treasure. The symbol ə stands for the unstressed vowel sound in about, taken, pencil, lemon, and circus.

A

addition.   **2.** The act of adding. The *addition* of herbs helped give flavor to the soup. **3.** Something that is added. Our neighbors built an *addition* to their house.
  • **in addition** or **in addition to.**   Besides. I don't want to go to the movies, and, *in addition,* I have no money. *In addition to* checkers, we also play chess.
  ad·di·tion (ə dish′ən) *noun, plural* **additions.**

additional   More; extra. You can get *additional* information for your report from the library.
  ad·di·tion·al (ə dish′ə nəl) *adjective.*

additive   A small amount of a substance added to another substance to change or improve it. Some packaged foods have *additives* that keep the food from spoiling.
  ad·di·tive (ad′i tiv) *noun, plural* **additives.**

address   **1.** The place at which a person lives or an organization is located. My cousin's *address* is 90 Pine Lane. That store's *address* is 595 Main Street.   **2.** The writing printed on a piece of mail that tells where it is to be delivered. I can't read the *address* on this letter.   **3.** A formal speech. The president's *address* to the nation will be on television. *Noun.*
  —**1.** To speak or give a formal speech to. The mayor *addressed* the audience in the town hall.   **2.** To put directions for delivery on. Please *address* these envelopes. *Verb.*
  ad·dress (ə dres′ *or* ad′res *for noun;* ə dres′ *for verb*) *noun, plural* **addresses;** *verb,* **addressed, addressing.**

adenoids   Small masses of tissue that grow at the top of the throat in back of the nose. Adenoids can become swollen and make it hard to breathe and speak.
  ad·e·noids (ad′ə noidz′) *plural noun.*

adept   Skillful; expert. It takes practice to be an *adept* skater.
  a·dept (ə dept′) *adjective.*

adequate   **1.** As much as is needed; enough. Those plants will not grow without *adequate* rain.   **2.** Satisfactory but not outstanding. The actor's performance was no more than *adequate.*
  ad·e·quate (ad′i kwit) *adjective.*

adhere   **1.** To stick tightly; become attached. The chewing gum *adhered* to my shoe.   **2.** To follow closely; be faithful. They *adhered* to their principles even though it meant they would lose their jobs.
  ad·here (ad hîr′) *verb,* **adhered, adhering.**

adhesive   A substance that makes things stick together. Glue and paste are *adhesives. Noun.*

—Having a sticky surface that will hold tight to other things. An *adhesive* bandage will stick to your skin. *Adjective.*
  ad·he·sive (ad hē′siv) *noun, plural* **adhesives;** *adjective.*

adios   The Spanish word that means "goodbye."
  a·di·os (ä′dē ōs′) *interjection.*

adjacent   Next to or near. The garage is *adjacent* to the house.
  ad·ja·cent (ə jā′sənt) *adjective.*

adjacent houses

adjective   A word that describes or modifies a noun or pronoun. In the sentence "The large suitcase is green," the words "large" and "green" are adjectives.
  ad·jec·tive (aj′ik tiv) *noun, plural* **adjectives.**

adjoin   To be very close or next to. The tennis courts *adjoin* the golf course.
  ad·join (ə join′) *verb,* **adjoined, adjoining.**

adjourn   **1.** To bring to an end for a while. The class president *adjourned* the meeting until next week.   **2.** To stop work. The senate will *adjourn* for the summer.
  ad·journ (ə jûrn′) *verb,* **adjourned, adjourning.**

adjust   **1.** To change or regulate so as to correct or improve. The mechanic had to *adjust* the brakes on the car.   **2.** To be used to; adapt. We found it hard to *adjust* to our new schedule.
  ad·just (ə just′) *verb,* **adjusted, adjusting.**

adjustment   **1.** The act of making a change to correct or improve something. *Adjustment* of the thermostat took no time at all. **2.** The act of becoming used to or comfortable in a situation. *Adjustment* to their new home was difficult at first.
  ad·just·ment (ə just′mənt) *noun, plural* **adjustments.**

ad-lib To do or say something that has not been planned or practiced. I forgot part of my speech, so I *ad-libbed*.
ad-lib (ad'lib') *verb*, **ad-libbed, ad-libbing.**

administer **1.** To control the operation of; manage; direct. Who *administers* the company's sales department? **2.** To provide or dispense. The Red Cross *administered* first aid to the victims of the earthquake. A judge's duty is to *administer* justice.
ad·min·is·ter (ad min'ə stər) *verb*, **administered, administering.**

administration **1.** The control of the operations of a business or other organization. Since you once ran a business with several employees, you have some experience in *administration*. **2.** A group of people in charge of the operation of something. The principal is the head of the school *administration*. **3. the Administration.** The president of the United States, together with the cabinet and the other officials who make up the executive branch of the government. **4.** The period of time during which a government holds office. American astronauts first traveled in space during the *administration* of President John F. Kennedy.
ad·min·is·tra·tion (ad min'ə strā'shən) *noun, plural* **administrations.**

admirable Worthy of approval or respect. The senator has an *admirable* record.
ad·mi·ra·ble (ad'mər ə bəl) *adjective*.

admiral A naval officer of the highest rank. The four ranks of admiral in the United States Navy are **rear admiral, vice admiral, admiral,** and **fleet admiral.** The highest rank of admiral is fleet admiral.
ad·mi·ral (ad'mər əl) *noun, plural* **admirals.**

admiration A feeling of approval or respect. The astronauts have earned the *admiration* of the whole country.
ad·mi·ra·tion (ad'mə rā'shən) *noun*.

admire **1.** To approve of or respect. I *admire* a person who is always honest. **2.** To look at or speak of with appreciation and pleasure. I *admired* my friend's new coat.
ad·mire (ad mīr') *verb*, **admired, admiring.**

admission **1.** The act of allowing to enter. Who is in charge of the *admission* of patients to that hospital? **2.** The privilege or right to enter. **3.** The price a person must pay to enter. The *admission* to the park was one dollar. **4.** The act of making known that something is true; confession. I couldn't make the *admission* that I had lost my friend's ring.
ad·mis·sion (ad mish'ən) *noun, plural* **admissions.**

admit **1.** To allow to enter; let in. We were *admitted* to the club last week. **2.** To make known that something is true; confess. They *admitted* that they had broken the lamp.
ad·mit (ad mit') *verb*, **admitted, admitting.**

admittance The right or permission to enter. This ticket gives you *admittance* to the movie theater.
ad·mit·tance (ad mit'əns) *noun*.

adobe **1.** A sandy kind of clay used to make bricks. Bits of straw are sometimes mixed with the clay, and the bricks are dried in the sun. Many buildings in Mexico and the southwestern United States are made of adobe. **2.** A building made with adobe bricks.
a·do·be (ə dō'bē) *noun, plural* **adobes.**

adobe
a building made of **adobe**

adolescent A person who is growing out of childhood but is not yet an adult.
ad·o·les·cent (ad'ə les'ənt) *noun, plural* **adolescents.**

adopt **1.** To take into one's family according to the law and raise as one's own child. The couple *adopted* the baby from an orphanage. **2.** To take and use as one's own. The English language has *adopted* many words from other languages. **3.** To accept or approve. The people of the town voted to *adopt* the plan for a new library.
a·dopt (ə dopt') *verb*, **adopted, adopting.**

adoption The act of adopting. The *adoption* of the baby took two months.
a·dop·tion (ə dop'shən) *noun, plural* **adoptions.**

at; āpe; fär; câre; end; mē; it; īce; pîerce; hot; ōld; sông, fôrk; oil; out; up; ūse; rüle; pull; tûrn; chin; sing; shop; thin; this; hw in white; zh in treasure. The symbol ə stands for the unstressed vowel sound in about, taken, pencil, lemon, and circus.

adorable Delightful; lovable; charming. The fluffy kittens are really *adorable*.
a·dor·a·ble (ə dôr′ə bəl) *adjective*.

adore **1.** To love and admire very much. We *adore* our parents. **2.** To honor for being divine; worship. Religious people *adore* God. **3.** To like very much. I *adore* folk music.
a·dore (ə dôr′) *verb*, **adored, adoring**.

adorn To add something beautiful to; decorate. We *adorned* the room with flowers.
a·dorn (ə dôrn′) *verb*, **adorned, adorning**.

adrift Moving freely with the current or wind; drifting.
a·drift (ə drift′) *adverb; adjective*.

adult **1.** A person who is fully grown; grown-up. **2.** A plant or animal that is fully grown. *Noun*.
—Having grown to full size; mature. An *adult* elephant is a huge animal. *Adjective*.
a·dult (ə dult′ *or* ad′ult) *noun, plural* **adults**; *adjective*.

adulthood The period of a person's life when he or she is an adult.
a·dult·hood (ə dult′hůd) *noun, plural* **adulthoods**.

advance **1.** To move forward. I *advanced* the hands of the clock to the correct time. **2.** To help the progress or growth of; further. The scientists hoped that their experiments would *advance* the exploration of outer space. **3.** To offer; propose. The club's president *advanced* a new plan for a camping trip. **4.** To move up in position. The private *advanced* to the rank of colonel. **5.** To give before it is due. My parents *advanced* me my allowance for the next week. *Verb*.
—**1.** A move forward. The army made a steady *advance* toward the city. **2.** Progress; improvement. The development of the airplane was an *advance* in long-distance travel. **3.** A payment given before it is due. Did you receive an *advance* on your salary? *Noun*.
• **in advance.** Before the time when something is due to happen; ahead of time. If you want tickets for the concert, order them *in advance*.
ad·vance (ad vans′) *verb*, **advanced, advancing**; *noun, plural* **advances**.

advanced **1.** Beyond the level of others in development or progress. The *advanced* civilization of ancient Egypt is known for the Pyramids and other achievements in architecture. **2.** Beyond the beginning level; not elementary. I'm taking a class in *advanced* algebra. **3.** Very old. My grandparents lived to an *advanced* age.
ad·vanced (ad vanst′) *adjective*.

advancement **1.** Progress; improvement. The *advancement* of technology has made space travel possible. **2.** A move up in position; promotion. That job offers good opportunities for *advancement*.
ad·vance·ment (ad vans′mənt) *noun, plural* **advancements**.

advantage Something that is helpful or useful; benefit. Being tall is an *advantage* for a basketball player.
• **to take advantage of.** **1.** To use in a helpful or beneficial way; benefit by. We *took advantage of* the opportunity to learn French. **2.** To use or treat in an unfair or selfish way. Don't *take advantage of* your friend's willingness to be helpful.
ad·van·tage (ad van′tij) *noun, plural* **advantages**.

advantageous Giving an advantage; favorable; beneficial. Capturing my opponent's queen put me in an *advantageous* position in the chess game.
ad·van·ta·geous (ad′vən tā′jəs) *adjective*.

adventure **1.** Something a person does that is difficult and dangerous. The astronauts' landing on the moon was a great *adventure*. **2.** An exciting or unusual experience. Their first trip by airplane was an *adventure* for the whole family.
ad·ven·ture (ad ven′chər) *noun, plural* **adventures**.

adventurous **1.** Willing to risk danger in order to have exciting or unusual experiences; bold. The *adventurous* campers hiked into the wilderness. **2.** Full of danger or risks. The first voyages to the New World were *adventurous* journeys.
ad·ven·tur·ous (ad ven′chər əs) *adjective*.

adverb A word that describes or modifies a verb, an adjective, or another adverb. In the sentence "Two very large vans drove quite slowly down the street," the words "very," "quite," and "slowly" are adverbs.
ad·verb (ad′vûrb′) *noun, plural* **adverbs**.

adversary A person or group that opposes another person or group in a contest or fight; opponent or enemy. The American colonists and Great Britain were *adversaries* in the American Revolution.
ad·ver·sar·y (ad′vər ser′ē) *noun, plural* **adversaries**.

adverse **1.** Not helpful to what is wanted; not favorable. The football game was played under *adverse* conditions because of the heavy rain. **2.** Unfriendly or hostile. Your *adverse* remarks about the party hurt my feelings. **3.** Acting in an opposite direction; opposing. The ship met *adverse* winds.
ad·verse (ad vûrs′ *or* ad′vûrs) *adjective*.

A

adversity Misfortune, suffering, or difficulty. The shipwrecked sailor showed courage in the face of *adversity*.
ad·ver·si·ty (ad vûr′si tē) *noun, plural* **adversities.**

advertise **1.** To make known to the public the good qualities of. That company *advertises* its toothpaste on television. **2.** To make known to the public. The school *advertised* the play by putting up posters. **3.** To place an advertisement. Our parents *advertised* for a babysitter in the town newspaper. That department store *advertises* frequently.
ad·ver·tise (ad′vər tīz′) *verb,* **advertised, advertising.**

advertisement A notice or announcement that makes something known to the public. Some advertisements describe the good qualities of a product or a service. Other advertisements tell about a future event, such as a sale or performance.
ad·ver·tise·ment (ad′vər tīz′mənt *or* ad vûr′tis mənt) *noun, plural* **advertisements.**

advice An idea that is offered to a person about how to solve a problem or how to act in a certain situation; suggestion; recommendation. Our friends gave us *advice* about how to take care of our new puppy.
ad·vice (ad vīs′) *noun.*

advisable Showing good sense; sensible; wise; recommended. It is *advisable* to drive at a slower speed on wet roads.
ad·vis·a·ble (ad vī′zə bəl) *adjective.*

advise **1.** To give advice to. The doctor *advised* us to exercise regularly. **2.** To give information to; notify. The letter *advised* me that I had won first prize in the contest.
ad·vise (ad vīz′) *verb,* **advised, advising.**

adviser A person who gives advice. High schools have *advisers* who help students decide what to study. This word is also spelled **advisor.**
ad·vis·er (ad vī′zər) *noun, plural* **advisers.**

advocate To speak in favor of; urge; recommend. The senator *advocated* strict penalties against businesses that pollute the air and water. *Verb.*
—A person who speaks in favor of someone or something. *Noun.*
ad·vo·cate (ad′və kāt′ *for verb;* ad′və kit *for noun) verb,* **advocated, advocating;** *noun, plural* **advocates.**

adz A tool that looks like an ax. It has a curved blade and is used to shape logs and other large pieces of wood. This word is also spelled **adze.**
adz (adz) *noun, plural* **adzes.**

aerial Of or in the air. Trapeze artists do *aerial* acrobatics. *Adjective.*
—A radio or television antenna. *Noun.*
aer·i·al (âr′ē əl) *adjective; noun, plural* **aerials.**

aerial view of a neighborhood

aerobics Exercises that help the body to take in and use more oxygen. If aerobics are done regularly, they can strengthen the heart and lungs. Running, biking, and swimming are three kinds of aerobics.
aer·o·bics (â rō′biks) *plural noun.*

aeronautics The science that deals with flight. Aeronautics is concerned with designing, building, and flying aircraft. ▲ The word *aeronautics* is used with a singular verb.
aer·o·nau·tics (âr′ə nô′tiks) *noun.*

aerosol A mass of very fine particles of a solid or a liquid that are suspended in a gas. Smoke and fog are aerosols that occur in nature. There are also aerosols of paint and other materials that are sealed in cans and released in the form of a spray.
aer·o·sol (âr′ə sôl′) *noun, plural* **aerosols.**

aerospace **1.** The earth's atmosphere and outer space. The region in which aircraft and spacecraft operate is called *aerospace.* **2.** The science that deals with aerospace.
aer·o·space (âr′ō spās′) *noun.*

aesthetic Of or having to do with art and beauty or with things that are beautiful. The architect judged the building on both its *aesthetic* and practical merits.
aes·thet·ic (es thet′ik) *adjective.*

at; āpe; fär; câre; end; mē; it; īce; pîerce; hot; ōld; sông, fôrk; oil; out; up; ūse; rüle; pùll; tûrn; chin; sing; shop; thin; this; hw in white; zh in treasure. The symbol ə stands for the unstressed vowel sound in about, taken, pencil, lemon, and circus.

afar To a great distance away or at a distance; far away. The explorers traveled *afar* to discover new lands.
a·far (ə fär') *adverb.*

affable Pleasant to be with and talk to; friendly. The country doctor was an *affable* person.
af·fa·ble (af'ə bəl) *adjective.*

affair 1. A thing that is done or has to be done. Moving to the new home was a confusing *affair*. 2. Something that happens; event; occasion. The dance is going to be a formal *affair*. 3. **affairs.** Business matters. An accountant takes care of the company's *affairs* when the owner is on vacation.
af·fair (ə fâr') *noun, plural* **affairs.**

affect[1] 1. To make something happen to; have an effect on. The lack of rain may *affect* the crops. 2. To influence the feelings of; touch; move. The photographs of the hungry children *affected* us. ⏺ Another word that sounds very similar to this is **effect.**
af·fect (ə fekt') *verb,* **affected, affecting.**

affect[2] To pretend to have or feel. They *affected* bravery, but they were really afraid. ⏺ Another word that sounds very similar to this is **effect.**
af·fect (ə fekt') *verb,* **affected, affecting.**

affection A feeling of tenderness, fondness, or love. I have deep *affection* for my sister and brother.
af·fec·tion (ə fek'shən) *noun, plural* **affections.**

affection

affectionate Full of or showing affection; tender, fond, or loving. The *affectionate* boy gave his baby sister a hug.
af·fec·tion·ate (ə fek'shə nit) *adjective.*

affiliate To join or unite. Our local television station is *affiliated* with a national network.
af·fil·i·ate (ə fil'ē āt') *verb,* **affiliated, affiliating.**

affirm To state in a positive way; assert; declare. The patriots *affirmed* their belief in freedom.
af·firm (ə fûrm') *verb,* **affirmed, affirming.**

affirmative Saying that something is true; saying "yes." They gave an *affirmative* answer to my question by nodding their heads.
af·firm·a·tive (ə fûr'mə tiv) *adjective.*

affix To attach or fasten. I *affixed* labels to the packages. *Verb.*
—A syllable or group of syllables added to a word to change its meaning; a prefix or suffix. In the word *unbreakable, un-* and *-able* are affixes. *Noun.*
af·fix (ə fiks' *for verb;* af'iks *for noun*) *verb,* **affixed, affixing;** *noun, plural* **affixes.**

afflict To cause pain or trouble; make miserable. The campers were *afflicted* by a rash caused by poison ivy.
af·flict (ə flikt') *verb,* **afflicted, afflicting.**

affliction 1. The condition of being afflicted; pain or trouble. The *affliction* of poverty affects many people. 2. A cause of pain or trouble. Influenza can be a severe *affliction.*
af·flic·tion (ə flik'shən) *noun, plural* **afflictions.**

affluent Having a large amount of money; rich; wealthy. The jewelry store had many *affluent* customers.
af·flu·ent (af'lü ənt) *adjective.*

afford 1. To have enough money to pay for. Can you *afford* a new car? 2. To be able to spare or give. They couldn't *afford* the time to help us. 3. To be able to do without causing harm. I can't *afford* to skip breakfast. 4. To give or provide. A vacation *affords* us time to rest.
af·ford (ə fôrd') *verb,* **afforded, affording.**

affront A deliberate, open insult. Your rude comment about my home was an *affront* to me. *Noun.*
—To insult deliberately and openly. The audience *affronted* the speaker by booing. *Verb.*
af·front (ə frunt') *noun, plural* **affronts;** *verb* **affronted, affronting.**

Afghanistan A country in south-central Asia.
Af·ghan·i·stan (af gan'ə stan') *noun.*

afire On fire; burning. The old wooden ship was *afire*. It was hard to set the damp log *afire.*
a·fire (ə fīr') *adjective; adverb.*

afloat Floating on water or in the air. The lifeboat was made to stay *afloat*. The dandelion seeds are *afloat* in the wind.
a·float (ə flōt') *adjective; adverb.*

A

afoot **1.** By walking; on foot. I left my bicycle and continued *afoot.* **2.** Going on; in progress. Plans for the attack were *afoot.*
a·foot (ə fŭt′) *adverb; adjective.*

afraid **1.** Feeling fear; frightened. Are you *afraid* of snakes? **2.** Feeling unhappy or sorry. I'm *afraid* I can't play now.
a·fraid (ə frād′) *adjective.*

Africa A continent south of Europe and between the Atlantic and Indian Oceans.
Af·ri·ca (af′ri kə) *noun.*

African Of or having to do with Africa or its people. *Adjective.*
—**1.** A person who was born or is living in Africa. **2.** A person who is a citizen of an African country. *Noun.*
Af·ri·can (af′ri kən) *adjective; noun, plural* **Africans.**

African-American A black American. *Noun.*
—Of or having to do with African-Americans. This museum has *African-American* art. *Adjective.*
African-American (af′ri kən ə mer′i kən) *noun, plural* **African-Americans;** *adjective.*

African violet A small plant with fuzzy leaves and pink, purple, or white flowers.

Afro-American Another word for **African-American.** Look up **African-American** for more information.
Af·ro-A·mer·i·can (af′rō ə mer′i kən) *noun, plural* **Afro-Americans;** *adjective.*

aft At or toward the rear of a boat or aircraft. The sailor walked *aft.*
aft (aft) *adverb.*

after **1.** Following in place or order; behind. My dog walked *after* me. **2.** With the purpose of following, finding, or catching. The police went *after* the thieves. **3.** Following in time; later than. I arrived *after* dark. *Preposition.*
—**1.** Following in place; behind. Our parents walked ahead, and we walked *after.* **2.** Following in time; later. They left on Sunday, and I left three days *after. Adverb.*
—Following the time that. It happened *after* you left. *Conjunction.*
af·ter (af′tər) *preposition; adverb; conjunction.*

afternoon The part of the day between noon and evening.
af·ter·noon (af′tər nün′) *noun, plural* **afternoons.**

afterward or **afterwards** At a later time. We swam and *afterward* we rested.
af·ter·ward or **af·ter·wards** (af′tər wərd *or* af′tər wərdz) *adverb.*

again Once more; another time. I failed that test once, but I took it *again* and passed.
a·gain (ə gen′) *adverb.*

against **1.** In opposition to. The senator voted *against* the bill. **2.** In the opposite direction to. The salmon swam *against* the current. **3.** In contact with. We leaned our bicycles *against* the building. **4.** So as to strike or come into contact with. I threw the ball *against* the wall. **5.** As a protection or defense from. We covered the windows with plywood *against* the hurricane.
a·gainst (ə genst′) *preposition.*

agate **1.** A kind of quartz that has layers or masses of different colors. **2.** A marble used in games that is made of agate or a material that looks like agate.
ag·ate (ag′it) *noun, plural* **agates.**

a cross section of **agate**

age **1.** The amount of time that a person, animal, or thing has lived or existed. My *age* is eleven. **2.** A particular time of life. My grandparents are enjoying their old *age.* **3.** The latter part of life; old age. The judge has the wisdom and experience of *age.* **4.** A particular period of history. The second part of the twentieth century might be known as the *age* of the computer. *Noun.*
—**1.** To make or become old. Having a hard life can *age* a person. **2.** To become ready to be used. Some cheese tastes better after it *ages. Verb.*
age (āj) *noun, plural* **ages;** *verb,* **aged, aging** or **ageing.**

aged **1.** Old; elderly. The children take care of their *aged* grandparents. **2.** Having the age of. She had a brother *aged* three.
a·ged (ā′jid *for definition 1;* ājd *for definition 2) adjective.*

agency **1.** A company or a person that does business for other companies or people. That advertising *agency* prepares the advertisements for several large companies. **2.** A special department of the government. A federal *agency* set the safety rules followed in the factory.
a·gen·cy (ā′jən sē) *noun, plural* **agencies.**

at; āpe; fär; câre; end; mē; it; īce; pîerce; hot; ōld; sông, fôrk; oil; out; up; ūse; rüle; pùll; tûrn; chin; sing; shop; thin; this; hw in white; zh in treasure. The symbol ə stands for the unstressed vowel sound in about, taken, pencil, lemon, and circus.

agent   **1.** A person who acts for some other person or company. The real estate *agent* sold the couple a new house.   **2.** Something that produces a certain effect. Soap is a cleaning *agent*.
a·gent (ā′jənt) *noun, plural* **agents.**

aggravate   **1.** To make worse. Being out in the rain *aggravated* my cold.   **2.** To irritate; bother; annoy. Their constant complaining *aggravated* us.
ag·gra·vate (ag′rə vāt′) *verb,* **aggravated, aggravating.**

aggression   An attack or warlike action, especially one that is not provoked. A country that sends an army to take over the land of another country has committed an act of *aggression*.
ag·gres·sion (ə gresh′ən) *noun, plural* **aggressions.**

aggressive   **1.** Ready and eager to attack or start a fight. The neighborhood bullies get into trouble because they are so *aggressive*.   **2.** Very forceful and bold. An *aggressive* salesperson does not easily accept "no" for an answer.
ag·gres·sive (ə gres′iv) *adjective.*

aghast   Feeling amazement, shock, or horror. We were *aghast* at the number of houses that were ruined by the tornado.
a·ghast (ə gast′) *adjective.*

agile   **1.** Able to move and react quickly and easily. A cat is an *agile* animal.   **2.** Able to think quickly. Astronauts need *agile* minds.
ag·ile (aj′əl) *adjective.*

agility   The ability to move or think quickly and easily. An acrobat must have *agility*.
a·gil·i·ty (ə jil′i tē) *noun.*

aging   Growing old. Losing the sense of hearing may be a sign of *aging*.
ag·ing (ā′jing) *noun.*

agitate   **1.** To move or shake in a rough, irregular way. The wind *agitated* the water and made waves.   **2.** To disturb the feelings of; excite. The report that a hurricane was approaching *agitated* the people in the area.   **3.** To try to stir interest in the public. A group of employees from the factory *agitated* for safer working conditions.
ag·i·tate (aj′i tāt′) *verb,* **agitated, agitating.**

aglow   Bright with light or warmth; glowing. During the festival the park was *aglow* with colored lights.
a·glow (ə glō′) *adjective; adverb.*

ago   Before now. They left ten minutes *ago*. Dinosaurs lived long *ago*.
a·go (ə gō′) *adjective; adverb.*

agony   Great pain or suffering of the mind or body. I was in *agony* from the toothache. We suffered *agony* at the death of our dog.
ag·o·ny (ag′ə nē) *noun, plural* **agonies.**

agree   **1.** To have the same opinion or feeling. My friends all *agreed* that it was a good movie.   **2.** To say that one is willing; give permission. Will you *agree* to lend me your bicycle?   **3.** To come to an understanding. The car dealer and the customer *agreed* on a price.   **4.** To be alike; correspond. Their stories about the car accident don't *agree*.
• **to agree with.**   To be healthful or suitable for. Humid weather does not *agree with* me.
a·gree (ə grē′) *verb,* **agreed, agreeing.**

agreeable   **1.** Nice; pleasant. Our new neighbors are very *agreeable*.   **2.** Willing to give permission. I will come to the party if my parents are *agreeable*.
a·gree·a·ble (ə grē′ə bəl) *adjective.*

agreement   **1.** An understanding between people or groups. The two nations signed a peace *agreement*.   **2.** The condition of agreeing; harmony. My parents are in *agreement* about what color to paint the house.
a·gree·ment (ə grē′mənt) *noun, plural* **agreements.**

agricultural   Having to do with farming or farms. Because of their interest in farming, my cousins went to an *agricultural* college.
ag·ri·cul·tur·al (ag′ri kul′chər əl) *adjective.*

agriculture   The science and business of raising crops and farm animals; farming.
ag·ri·cul·ture (ag′ri kul′chər) *noun.*

ah   A word used to show concern, hurt, joy, admiration, surprise, or other strong feelings. *Ah*, now I understand.
ah (ä) *interjection.*

aha   A word used to show triumph, satisfaction, discovery, or other feelings. *Aha!* I caught you sneaking up on me!
a·ha (ä hä′) *interjection.*

ahead   **1.** In front. At the end of the race I moved *ahead* of the other runners.   **2.** In advance. We planned *ahead* for your visit.
a·head (ə hed′) *adverb.*

ahoy   An expression used by sailors as a greeting or to attract attention. When the sailors saw the other ship, they yelled "Ship *ahoy!*"
a·hoy (ə hoi′) *interjection.*

aid   To give help or support. We *aided* the farmers in their search for the lost cattle. *Verb.*
—**1.** Help or support; assistance. My friends came to my *aid* when I climbed too high in

the tree. **2.** A person or thing that is helpful. A dictionary is an *aid* in learning new words. *Noun.* ◢ Another word that sounds like this is **aide.**

 aid (ād) *verb,* **aided, aiding;** *noun, plural* **aids.**

aide A person who helps or supports; assistant. During the summer, I worked as a nurse's *aide.* ◢ Another word that sounds like this is **aid.**

 aide (ād) *noun, plural* **aides.**

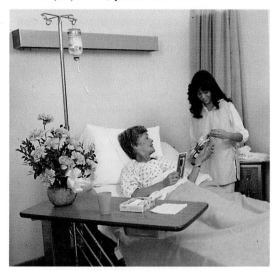

an **aide** in a hospital

ail **1.** To cause illness or trouble for. What *ails* the twins? **2.** To be ill; feel sick. They have been *ailing* for a month. ◢ Another word that sounds like this is **ale.**

 ail (āl) *verb,* **ailed, ailing.**

ailment An illness; sickness. My *ailment* was cured by a long rest.

 ail·ment (āl′mənt) *noun, plural* **ailments.**

aim **1.** To direct or point a weapon or a blow. Take careful *aim,* then release the arrow. **2.** To intend for; direct toward. I *aimed* my speech at the classmates who might vote for me in the election. *Verb.*
—**1.** The act of pointing or directing a weapon or blow. The child's *aim* was not good enough to hit the target. **2.** Goal; purpose. My *aim* is to become the best doctor in town. *Noun.*

 aim (ām) *verb,* **aimed, aiming;** *noun, plural* **aims.**

aimless Without purpose or aim. They took an *aimless* walk through the fields.

 aim·less (ām′lis) *adjective.*

ain't **1.** Am not. **2.** Is not; are not. **3.** Has not; have not.

 ain't (ānt).

air **1.** The mixture of gases that surrounds Earth and forms its atmosphere. Air is made up mainly of nitrogen and oxygen, with small amounts of other gases. The *air* is fragrant with roses. **2.** The open space above Earth; sky. I threw the ball into the *air.* **3.** Fresh air. Please open the window and let in some *air.* **4.** A look or manner. The principal has a very serious *air.* **5. airs.** Showy manners used to impress others. Don't put on *airs* at the restaurant. **6.** A melody or tune. I whistled a cheerful *air* while I worked. *Noun.*
—**1.** To let air through; freshen. Please open the windows and *air* the room. **2.** To expose to air so as to dry or make fresh. We *aired* our summer clothes after taking them out of the trunk. **3.** To make known; express. The workers *aired* their complaints about having to work such long hours. *Verb.* ◢ Other words that sound like this are **ere** and **heir.**

 • **off the air.** Not broadcasting or being broadcast. That program has been *off the air* for two years.
 • **on the air.** Broadcasting or being broadcast. That program will be *on the air* at 6:30.

 air (âr) *noun, plural* **airs;** *verb,* **aired, airing.**

air conditioner A machine that cools air and removes dust and humidity from it. An air conditioner is used to move air around in an enclosed space, such as a room or automobile.

 air con·di·tion·er (kən dish′ə nər).

aircraft Any machine made to fly in the air. Airplanes, helicopters, gliders, and balloons are all aircraft.

 air·craft (âr′kraft′) *noun, plural* **aircraft.**

airfield An area of land where aircraft can take off and land; landing field.

 air·field (âr′fēld′) *noun, plural* **airfields.**

air force The branch of a country's armed forces trained to fight using aircraft. ▲ The words *air force* are often capitalized when they mean the air force of a particular country.

airline An organization or business that carries passengers and freight from one place to another by airplane.
air·line (âr′līn′) *noun, plural* **airlines.**

airliner A large airplane that carries passengers.
air·lin·er (âr′lī′nər) *noun, plural* **airliners.**

airmail **1.** A system of transportation that carries mail by airplane. **2.** Mail carried by airplane. *Noun.*
—To send by airmail. I am going to *airmail* this letter to our senator. *Verb.*
—Having to do with or sent by means of airmail. Our cousin in Canada sent us an *airmail* letter. *Adjective.*
—By means of airmail. Please send this package *airmail* so it will arrive quickly. *Adverb.*
air·mail (âr′māl′) *noun; verb,* **airmailed, airmailing;** *adjective; adverb.*

airman An enlisted person in the United States Air Force who ranks below a sergeant.
air·man (âr′mən) *noun, plural* **airmen** (âr′mən).

airplane A machine with wings that flies. An airplane is heavier than air, and is driven by propellers or jet engines.
air·plane (âr′plān′) *noun, plural* **airplanes.**

airport

airport A place where airplanes can take off and land. An airport has buildings for sheltering and repairing airplanes and for receiving passengers and freight.
air·port (âr′pôrt′) *noun, plural* **airports.**

air pressure The force that air puts on things. Air pressure in the atmosphere is caused by the weight of the air high above the earth pressing down on the air that is below.

airship An aircraft that is filled with gas and is lighter than air. It is driven by a motor and can be steered.
air·ship (âr′ship′) *noun, plural* **airships.**

airsick Having nausea or feeling dizzy when riding in an aircraft.
air·sick (âr′sik′) *adjective.*

airstrip A paved or cleared area where aircraft can take off and land.
air·strip (âr′strip′) *noun, plural* **airstrips.**

airtight **1.** So tight that no air or gases can get in or out. The jelly was packed in an *airtight* jar so that it would stay fresh. **2.** Having no weak points that could be easily attacked. The police had an *airtight* case against the car thieves.
air·tight (âr′tīt′) *adjective.*

airy **1.** Light as air; delicate. The costume was made of an *airy* material. **2.** Open to the movement of air. I love to sit on our *airy,* cool porch.
air·y (âr′ē) *adjective,* **airier, airiest.**

aisle The space between two rows or sections of something. There are several *aisles* in the supermarket. I like to sit on the *aisle* when I fly. ▲ Other words that sound like this are **I'll** and **isle.**

ajar Partly open. The front door was *ajar.*
a·jar (ə jär′) *adjective; adverb.*

AK Postal abbreviation for *Alaska.*

akimbo With the hands on the hips and the elbows turned outward.
a·kim·bo (ə kim′bō) *adjective.*

akin **1.** Belonging to the same family; related. My cousin and I are *akin.* **2.** Like each other; similar. Love and friendship are *akin.*
a·kin (ə kin′) *adjective.*

AL Postal abbreviation for *Alabama.*

Ala. An abbreviation for *Alabama.*

Alabama A state in the southeastern United States. Its capital is Montgomery.
Al·a·bam·a (al′ə bam′ə) *noun.*

Word History

The name **Alabama** comes from two Indian words that mean "people who gather plants" or "people who clear land." The words were used first as the name of an Indian tribe that lived near the Alabama River. The tribe's name was used for the river, and the state of Alabama was later named for the river.

alabaster   A smooth, white stone. It is used to make sculptures.
　a·la·bas·ter (al′ə bas′tər) *noun.*

alarm   **1.** A bell, buzzer, or other device used to wake people up or to warn them of danger. Set the *alarm* for seven o'clock. The bank has an *alarm* that alerts the police in case of a robbery.   **2.** A sudden fear of danger. The loud thunder filled the child with *alarm.*   **3.** A warning of danger. The radio broadcast spread the *alarm* that a hurricane was approaching. *Noun.*
　—To make afraid; frighten. The news that the river was rising *alarmed* us. *Verb.*
　a·larm (ə lärm′) *noun, plural* **alarms;** *verb,* **alarmed, alarming.**

alarm clock   A clock that can be set to ring, buzz, or make some other sound at a particular time. People use alarm clocks to wake them up in the morning.

alas   An expression used to show sorrow, regret, or disappointment. *Alas!* All of our plans have failed.
　a·las (ə las′) *interjection.*

Alas.   An abbreviation for *Alaska.*

Alaska   The largest state of the United States. It is located in the northwestern part of North America. The capital of Alaska is Juneau.
　A·las·ka (ə las′kə) *noun.*

Word History

The name **Alaska** comes from an Eskimo word meaning "mainland." The Eskimo who named Alaska lived on islands off of its coast.

Albania   A country in southeastern Europe.
　Al·ba·ni·a (al bā′nē ə) *noun.*

albatross   A large, black and white bird that has a long, hooked beak and webbed feet. The albatross has very large wings and is able to fly great distances. It is usually found in the southern oceans of the world.
　al·ba·tross (al′bə trôs′) *noun, plural* **albatrosses.**

Alberta   A province in western Canada. Its capital is Edmonton.
　Al·ber·ta (al bûr′tə) *noun.*

albino   A person, animal, or plant that lacks normal coloring. An albino rabbit has white fur and pink eyes.
　al·bi·no (al bī′nō) *noun, plural* **albinos.**

album   **1.** A book with blank pages. People use albums to hold things like photographs and stamps.   **2.** A phonograph record or set of records in one container. You have more jazz *albums* than anyone else I know.
　al·bum (al′bəm) *noun, plural* **albums.**

an **album** of photographs

alcohol   A clear liquid that has no smell. Alcohol burns easily and evaporates quickly. It comes from certain grains and fruits, or it can be made in a laboratory. One kind of alcohol is found in drinks like whiskey, wine, and beer. Alcohol is also used in making medicines and chemicals.
　al·co·hol (al′kə hôl′) *noun, plural* **alcohols.**

alcoholic   **1.** Containing or caused by alcohol. At the party the host served *alcoholic* drinks as well as soft drinks.   **2.** Suffering from alcoholism. *Adjective.*
　—A person who suffers from alcoholism. *Noun.*
　al·co·hol·ic (al′kə hô′lik) *adjective; noun, plural* **alcoholics.**

alcoholism   A disease in which a person has a very strong desire to drink alcoholic beverages and finds it hard to control the desire.
　al·co·hol·ism (al′kə hô liz′əm) *noun.*

alcove   A small area of a room that opens out from a main area. I study in an *alcove* off our living room.
　al·cove (al′kōv) *noun, plural* **alcoves.**

alder   A tree or shrub that has rough bark and oval leaves with jagged edges. The alder

at; āpe; fär; câre; end; mē; it; īce; pîerce; hot; ōld; sông, fôrk; oil; out; up; ūse; rüle; pùll; tûrn; chin; sing; shop; thin; <u>th</u>is; hw in white; zh in treasure. The symbol ə stands for the unstressed vowel sound in about, taken, pencil, lemon, and circus.

is related to the birch tree. Alders grow in cool, moist places.

al·der (ôl′dər) *noun, plural* **alders.**

Leaf

alder

ale   An alcoholic drink, similar to beer, that is made from malt and hops. ▲ Another word that sounds like this is **ail.**

ale (āl) *noun, plural* **ales.**

alert   **1.** Watching carefully; attentive. The rabbit was *alert* to the slightest movement. **2.** Quick to act or learn. The goalie was *alert* and didn't let anyone score. *Adjective.*
—A signal that warns of possible danger; alarm. A siren sounded the *alert. Noun.*
—To make aware of; warn. The Coast Guard *alerted* the town to the coming hurricane. *Verb.*

a·lert (ə lûrt′) *adjective; noun, plural* **alerts;** *verb,* **alerted, alerting.**

Aleut   A member of a people living on the Aleutian Islands, a chain of islands that are part of Alaska.

Al·eut (ə lüt′) *noun, plural* **Aleut** or **Aleuts.**

alfalfa   A plant that has bluish purple flowers and groups of three leaflets like clover leaves. Alfalfa is grown as a food for cattle and other livestock.

al·fal·fa (al fal′fə) *noun.*

algae   Simple living things that are composed of one or more cells. Most algae are plants that do not have roots or flowers. Some kinds of algae are neither plants nor animals. Seaweed and some other ocean plants are algae.

alfalfa

al·gae (al′jē) *plural noun.*

algebra   The branch of mathematics that deals with the relations between known and unknown numbers. In an algebra problem, letters are used to stand for unknown numbers. In the algebra problem X + Y = 7, if X = 3, then Y = 4.

al·ge·bra (al′jə brə) *noun.*

Algeria   A country in northern Africa.

Al·ge·ri·a (al jîr′ē ə) *noun.*

alias   A name used to hide one's real name. The criminal had three *aliases. Noun.*
—Otherwise called; also known as. Lee Hunter, *alias* Kim Tracey, was wanted by the police for questioning. *Adverb.*

a·li·as (ā′lē əs) *noun, plural* **aliases;** *adverb.*

alibi   **1.** A claim or proof that one was somewhere else when a crime was committed. The suspects in the robbery had good *alibis.* **2.** An excuse. Do you have an *alibi* for being late?

al·i·bi (al′ə bī′) *noun, plural* **alibis.**

Word History

The word **alibi** comes from a Latin word that means "somewhere else." Persons accused of a crime would try to prove that they were in another place at the time of the crime. The claim or proof that a person was somewhere else became known as an *alibi.*

alien   **1.** A person who is not a citizen of the country in which he or she lives; foreigner. **2.** A being from some place outside of the earth or its atmosphere. The movie was about *aliens* that tried to take over the earth. *Noun.*
—**1.** Of or from another country. This city has a large *alien* population.   **2.** Not familiar; different. The customs of those people are *alien* to me. *Adjective.*

al·ien (āl′yən *or* ā′lē ən) *noun, plural* **aliens;** *adjective.*

alight[1]   **1.** To get down or get off. The door of the plane opened, and the passengers *alighted.*   **2.** To come down from the air; land. The bee *alighted* on the flower.

a·light (ə līt′) *verb,* **alighted** or **alit** (ə lit′), **alighting.**

alight[2]   **1.** Lit up; glowing. The child's face was *alight* with joy.   **2.** On fire; burning. Is the charcoal *alight* yet?

a·light (ə līt′) *adjective.*

align   To put in a straight line. The captain *aligned* the troops for the parade.

a·lign (ə līn′) *verb,* **aligned, aligning.**

alike In the same way; similarly. The twins often dress *alike*. *Adverb.*
—Like one another; similar. No two people have fingerprints that are exactly *alike*. *Adjective.*
a·like (ə līk′) *adverb; adjective.*

alimentary canal A long tube that carries food through the body. It includes the esophagus, stomach, small intestine, and large intestine. It is a part of the digestive system.
al·i·men·ta·ry canal (al′ə men′tə rē *or* al′ə men′trē).

alive 1. Having life; living. These plants must be given water if you want them to stay *alive*. 2. In existence or operation; active. The results of the poll kept the candidate's hopes *alive* during the campaign.
a·live (ə līv′) *adjective.*

all 1. The whole of. We ate *all* the ice cream. 2. Every one. Students from *all* the schools in town were in the swimming meet. *Adjective.*
—1. The whole amount or number. *All* of us are going to the party. *All* of the sugar is gone. 2. Everything or everyone. *All* were saved from the fire. *Pronoun.*
—Completely. The work is *all* finished. *Adverb.*
—Everything that one has. The team gave its *all* during the game and won. *Noun.* ▲ Another word that sounds like this is **awl**.
all (ôl) *adjective; pronoun; adverb; noun.*

Allah God, in the Muslim religion.
Al·lah (al′ə) *noun.*

all-around 1. Having talent, skill, or knowledge in many areas. Some events in the Olympic games require *all-around* athletes, and others involve a particular skill. 2. Wide in range; not limited; broad. That school will give you an *all-around* education.
all-a·round (ôl′ə round′) *adjective.*

allege To say or declare positively but without final proof. The villagers *alleged* that the sawmill caused the water pollution.
al·lege (ə lej′) *verb,* **alleged, alleging.**

allegiance Faithful feelings and behavior; loyalty and devotion to a country, person, group, or cause. Americans owe *allegiance* to the United States.
al·le·giance (ə lē′jəns) *noun.*

allergic 1. Having an allergy. Are you sniffling because you're *allergic* to pollen? 2. Of or caused by an allergy. A rash is sometimes an *allergic* reaction.
al·ler·gic (ə lûr′jik) *adjective.*

allergy A condition that causes a person to have an unpleasant reaction to certain things that are harmless to most people. A person can have an allergy to pollen, dust, certain foods, and other substances. Rashes and sneezing are some of the reactions that allergies can cause.
al·ler·gy (al′ər jē) *noun, plural* **allergies.**

alley 1. A narrow street or passageway between or behind buildings. There is an *alley* behind those apartments where people can park their cars. 2. A long, narrow lane down which bowling balls are rolled. The pins to be knocked down by the ball are at the far end of the alley.
al·ley (al′ē) *noun, plural* **alleys.**

alliance An agreement between two or more countries, groups, or people to work together in doing something. The two nations had an *alliance* by which each promised to defend the other.
al·li·ance (ə lī′əns) *noun, plural* **alliances.**

allied 1. Joined together by an alliance. The *allied* countries fought on the same side during the war. 2. Related or similar. Drawing and painting are *allied* arts.
al·lied (ə līd′ *or* al′īd) *adjective.*

alligator An animal with a long head and tail and a thick, tough skin. Alligators live in rivers and swamps in the southeastern United States and China. Alligators are reptiles. They are closely related to crocodiles but have shorter, wider heads.
al·li·ga·tor (al′i gā′tər) *noun, plural* **alligators.**

Alligator

Crocodile

alliteration The repetition of the same sound at the beginning of several words in a phrase or sentence. "The bees buzzed in the

at; āpe; fär; câre; end; mē; it; īce; pîerce; hot; ōld; sông, fôrk; oil; out; up; ūse; rüle; půll; tûrn; chin; sing; shop; thin; <u>th</u>is; hw in white; zh in treasure. The symbol ə stands for the unstressed vowel sound in about, taken, pencil, lemon, and circus.

birches in back of the barn" is an example of alliteration.

al·lit·er·a·tion (ə lit′ə rā′shən) *noun, plural* **alliterations.**

allot **1.** To give out as a share. The money raised at the bazaar was *allotted* to three charities. The chairperson *allotted* ten minutes to each speaker. **2.** To reserve for some use. The city council *allotted* funds for a new library.

al·lot (ə lot′) *verb,* **allotted, allotting.**

allow **1.** To give permission to or for; permit. Will you *allow* me to use your bicycle? The manager does not *allow* smoking in the restaurant. **2.** To make provision for; assign. We *allowed* an extra hour to make the trip in case of heavy traffic.

• **to allow for.** To provide for some future need or possibility. We *allowed for* medical expenses in preparing the household budget.

al·low (ə lou′) *verb,* **allowed, allowing.**

allowance **1.** A sum of money or quantity of something given at regular times or set aside for a particular purpose. How much is your weekly *allowance?* **2.** A reduction in price made for a special reason; discount. We got an *allowance* of $600 when we traded in our old car for a new one.

al·low·ance (ə lou′əns) *noun, plural* **allowances.**

alloy A substance made by melting and mixing two or more metals or a metal and another substance. Brass is an *alloy* of copper and zinc.

al·loy (al′oi *or* ə loi′) *noun, plural* **alloys.**

all right **1.** Acceptable; good enough. The book was not as good as I had hoped, but it was *all right.* **2.** Not hurt or ill; safe; well. Our friend asked if we were *all right* after the accident. **3.** Yes. *All right,* I'll do it.

allude To mention briefly or refer to indirectly. The reporter *alluded* to the errors made by the shortstop.

al·lude (ə lüd′) *verb,* **alluded, alluding.**

ally To unite in order to do something. Great Britain and the United States *allied* themselves during World War II. *Verb.*
—A person, group, or nation united with another in order to do something. France was an *ally* of the American colonies during the Revolutionary War. *Noun.*

al·ly (ə lī′ *for verb;* al′ī *or* ə lī′ *for noun*) *verb,* **allied, allying;** *noun, plural* **allies.**

almanac **1.** A book that contains facts and figures on many different subjects. Almanacs are published every year. **2.** A book that

gives facts about the weather, the tides, and the rising and setting of the sun for each day of the year.

al·ma·nac (ôl′mə nak′) *noun, plural* **almanacs.**

almond An oval nut. It grows on a tree that is also called an almond.

al·mond (ä′mənd *or* am′ənd) *noun, plural* **almonds.**

Fruit

Nut   Kernel

almond

almost Very close to; nearly. I am *almost* finished with the work.

al·most (ôl′mōst) *adverb.*

aloft **1.** Far above the ground; high up. There were many kites *aloft* at the beach last weekend. **2.** High up on the mast or rigging of a ship. The sailors climbed *aloft* on ladders made of rope.

a·loft (ə lôft′) *adverb; adjective.*

aloha The Hawaiian word that means both "hello" and "good-bye."

a·lo·ha (ə lō′ə *or* ä lō′hä) *noun, plural* **alohas;** *interjection.*

alone **1.** Apart from anyone or anything else. We were *alone* all day on the beach. **2.** With no other person, group, or thing; only. The Supreme Court *alone* can declare a law unconstitutional. *Adjective.*
—**1.** Without anyone or anything else. My cousin lives *alone.* **2.** Without help or support. Can you finish the job *alone? Adverb.*

• **to leave alone** or **to let alone.** To not bother, interrupt, or interfere with. Please *leave* me *alone* for an hour so I can finish reading this book.

a·lone (ə lōn′) *adjective; adverb.*

along **1.** Over or following the length of. Flowers grew *along* the path. We walked *along* the highway. **2.** At some place on. Can we stop *along* the way for lunch? *Preposition.*
—**1.** Toward what is ahead; farther on; onward; forward. After we got through the traffic jam, we were able to drive *along* quickly. **2.** With oneself. Don't forget to bring *along* your umbrella. *Adverb.*

• **to get along.** **1.** To manage successfully. How are you *getting along* with your new business? **2.** To be in harmony; agree. The children *get along* well.

a·long (ə lông′) *preposition; adverb.*

A

alongside   At, close to, or by the side. Another car pulled up *alongside* and then passed us. *Adverb.*
—By or at the side of; beside. The truck was parked *alongside* the curb. *Preposition.*
a·long·side (ə lông′sīd′) *adverb; preposition.*

aloof   **1.** Having or showing little or no concern or friendliness. The queen and king had an *aloof* manner toward their subjects. **2.** Not involved; apart. When my friends argue, I always try to remain *aloof.*
a·loof (ə lüf′) *adjective.*

aloud   Using the voice so as to be heard; out loud. Students will read their reports *aloud* to the class.
a·loud (ə loud′) *adverb.*

alpaca   An animal that lives in the mountains of South America and has long, silky wool. The alpaca is related to the camel and the llama.
al·pac·a (al pak′ə) *noun, plural* **alpacas.**

alpacas

alphabet   The letters or characters that are used to write a language, arranged in their proper order.
al·pha·bet (al′fə bet′) *noun, plural* **alphabets.**

Word History

The word **alphabet** comes from *alpha* and *beta,* the names of the first two letters in the Greek alphabet.

alphabetical   Arranged in the order of the letters of the alphabet. The words in a dictionary are listed in *alphabetical* order.
al·pha·bet·i·cal (al′fə bet′i kəl) *adjective.*

alphabetize   To put in alphabetical order. The teacher asked me to *alphabetize* the names of all the students in my class.
al·pha·bet·ize (al′fə bə tīz′) *verb,* **alphabetized, alphabetizing.**

already   By a certain time. When we got to the bus station the bus had *already* left.
al·read·y (ôl red′ē) *adverb.*

also   In addition; as well; too. My cousin swims well and is *also* a good tennis player.
al·so (ôl′sō) *adverb.*

Alta.   An abbreviation for *Alberta.*

altar   A table or a raised place that is used for religious services. ▴ Another word that sounds like this is **alter.**
al·tar (ôl′tər) *noun, plural* **altars.**

alter   To make or become different; change. The tailor *altered* the coat to fit me. The new student's attitude has *altered* greatly since the beginning of the year. ▴ Another word that sounds like this is **altar.**
al·ter (ôl′tər) *verb,* **altered, altering.**

alternate   **1.** To take turns. My brother and sister *alternate* washing the car each week. **2.** To happen or appear with one thing following another. Red stripes *alternate* with white stripes on the American flag. **3.** To pass or change back and forth. The act *alternated* between singing and dancing. *Verb.*
—**1.** Happening or appearing one after another. The dessert had *alternate* layers of cake and icing. **2.** First one, then the other; every other. I have piano lessons on *alternate* Mondays. **3.** Taking the place of another; substitute. Please think of an *alternate* plan in case the first plan doesn't work. *Adjective.*
—A person or thing that takes the place of another; substitute. In case you cannot attend the meeting, can you send an *alternate? Noun.*
al·ter·nate (ôl′tər nāt′ *for verb;* ôl′tər nit *for adjective and noun) verb,* **alternated, alternating;** *adjective; noun, plural* **alternates.**

alternating current   An electric current that flows first in one direction and then in the opposite direction. These changes in direction occur several times a second.

alternative   **1.** A choice between two or more things. We had the *alternative* of going to the beach with our friends or going on a picnic with our family. **2.** One of two or more things that may be chosen. We chose the first *alternative,* and went to the beach. *Noun.*

at; āpe; fär; câre; end; mē; it; īce; pîerce; hot; ōld; sông, fôrk; oil; out; up; ūse; rüle; pùll; tûrn; chin; sing; shop; thin; <u>th</u>is; hw in white; zh in treasure. The symbol ə stands for the unstressed vowel sound in about, taken, pencil, lemon, and circus.

—Being or giving a choice between two or more things. We were offered the *alternative* plans of leaving that day or the next. *Adjective.*

al·ter·na·tive (ôl tûr′nə tiv) *noun, plural* **alternatives;** *adjective.*

although In spite of the fact that; though. *Although* I ate a big dinner, I was hungry again in an hour.

al·though (ôl t͟hō′) *conjunction.*

altimeter An instrument that shows how high something is above the ground or above sea level. An altimeter is used in an airplane to show the pilot how high the airplane is above the ground.

al·tim·e·ter (al tim′i tər *or* al′tə mē′tər) *noun, plural* **altimeters.**

altitude The height that something is above the ground or above sea level. The pilot flew at an *altitude* of 8,000 feet. As we drove up the mountain we passed a sign that said the *altitude* was 4,000 feet above sea level.

al·ti·tude (al′ti tüd′ *or* al′ti tūd′) *noun, plural* **altitudes.**

alto 1. The lowest female singing voice or the highest male singing voice. 2. A singer who has such a voice. 3. A musical instrument that has the range of an alto voice.

al·to (al′tō) *noun, plural* **altos.**

altogether 1. Completely; entirely; wholly. The arrow missed the target *altogether*. 2. With everyone or everything counted; in all. There were twelve of us *altogether* at the party. 3. With everything considered; on the whole. *Altogether,* I think the project was successful.

al·to·geth·er (ôl′tə get͟h′ər) *adverb.*

aluminum A light, soft, silver-white metal. Aluminum is the most abundant metal in the earth's crust. It conducts heat and electricity well and does not tarnish easily. It is used in making pots and pans, trucks, airplanes, and machines. It is also used as a building material. Aluminum is a chemical element.

a·lu·mi·num (ə lü′mə nəm) *noun.*

always 1. All the time; continuously. There is *always* snow and ice at the North Pole. 2. Every time; at all times. No matter when I schedule our meetings, you are *always* late. 3. For all time; forever. I'll remember their kindness *always*.

al·ways (ôl′wāz *or* ôl′wēz) *adverb.*

am A form of the present tense of **be** that is used with *I*. I *am* happy that you can come to my party. I *am* going to the circus tomorrow. Look up **be** for more information.

am (am *or* əm) *verb.*

a.m. or **A.M.** An abbreviation used when referring to the time of day between midnight and noon.

Word History

A.M. comes from the first letters of the Latin words *ante meridiem. Ante meridiem* means "before noon."

---

amateur 1. A person who does something for the pleasure of doing it, not for pay. Only *amateurs* in sports are allowed to take part in the Olympic games. 2. A person who does something without much experience or skill. The star of the play was a professional, but the rest of the performers were *amateurs. Noun.*

—Done by or made up of amateurs. I will run the mile in the *amateur* track meet. *Adjective.*

am·a·teur (am′ə chər *or* am′ə tər) *noun, plural* **amateurs;** *adjective.*

amaze To surprise greatly; astonish. The child's speed at solving mathematical problems *amazed* us.

a·maze (ə māz′) *verb,* **amazed, amazing.**

amazement Great surprise or wonder; astonishment. The people watching the whales swim by were filled with *amazement.*

a·maze·ment (ə māz′mənt) *noun.*

ambassador 1. An official of a government who is sent to represent his or her country in another country. 2. Any person who acts as a representative or messenger. A group of high school athletes were sent as *ambassadors* of good will to European countries.

am·bas·sa·dor (am bas′ə dər) *noun, plural* **ambassadors.**

amber 1. A hard, yellowish to brownish material that is used to make jewelry. Amber is a fossil that is formed from the resin of pine trees that grew millions of years ago. 2. A yellowish to brownish color.

am·ber (am′bər) *noun.*

ambiguous Having more than one possible meaning; not clear. The sentence "The Johnsons told the Browns that their dog had won the prize" is ambiguous. We cannot be sure to which family the dog belongs.

am·big·u·ous (am big′ū əs) *adjective.*

ambition A strong desire to do or succeed at something. My cousin's *ambition* is to become a sculptor.

am·bi·tion (am bish′ən) *noun, plural* **ambitions.**

ambitious **1.** Having a strong desire to succeed at something; having ambition. The *ambitious* clerk hoped to be president of the company someday. **2.** Requiring great ability or effort. The governor proposed an *ambitious* plan to end water pollution in the state.
am·bi·tious (am bish′əs) *adjective.*

Word History

The word **ambitious** goes back to a Latin word meaning "going around trying to get votes." In ancient Rome, men who wanted to be chosen for a government job would walk around the city in white robes to seek support for their election.

---

amble To walk or move at a slow pace. We *ambled* through the town, looking for a restaurant.
am·ble (am′bəl) *verb,* **ambled, ambling.**

ambulance A special vehicle that is used to carry sick or injured people to a hospital.
am·bu·lance (am′byə ləns) *noun, plural* **ambulances.**

ambush **1.** A surprise attack made by people who are in a hidden place. In the jungle the troops were always afraid of an *ambush* by the enemy. **2.** A hidden place from which people can make a surprise attack. The bandits waited in *ambush* to hold up the stagecoach. *Noun.*
—To make a surprise attack from a hidden place. The soldiers *ambushed* the enemy near the river. *Verb.*
am·bush (am′bush) *noun, plural* **ambushes;** *verb,* **ambushed, ambushing.**

ameba A tiny living cell. An ameba is so small that it can be seen only through a microscope. It is always moving and changing shape. An ameba eats by wrapping itself around its food. This word is also spelled **amoeba.**
a·me·ba (ə mē′bə) *noun, plural* **amebas.**

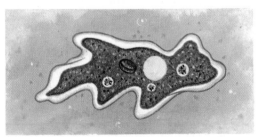

ameba

amen **1.** A word said at the end of a prayer to mean "may it come true" or "may it be so." **2.** A word used after a statement to show agreement or approval.
a·men (ā′men′ *or* ä′men′) *interjection.*

amend To change formally, according to an official procedure. It is a complicated procedure to *amend* the Constitution of the United States.
a·mend (ə mend′) *verb,* **amended, amending.**

amendment A formal change made according to official procedures. In 1920, women were given the right to vote by an *amendment* to the Constitution.
a·mend·ment (ə mend′mənt) *noun, plural* **amendments.**

amends To make amends. To make up for a wrong. I tried *to make amends* for my rude behavior by apologizing to the teacher after class.
a·mends (ə mendz′) *plural noun.*

Amer. An abbreviation for *America* or *American.*

America **1.** Another name for the **United States.** **2.** Another name for **North America** or **South America.** **3.** Another name for the **Western Hemisphere.** Look up **Western Hemisphere** for more information.
A·mer·i·ca (ə mer′i kə) *noun.*

Word History

The name **America** comes from *Amerigo* Vespucci, an Italian explorer. Some people gave him credit for discovering the New World and put his name on early maps of those lands.

American **1.** Of or having to do with the United States. July 4, 1776 is an important date in *American* history. **2.** Of or having to do with North America, Central America, or South America. The coyote is an *American* animal. *Adjective.*
—**1.** A person who was born in or is a citizen of the United States. **2.** A person who was born in or is a citizen of a country in North

---

at; āpe; fär; câre; end; mē; it; īce; pîerce; hot; ōld; sông, fôrk; oil; out; up; ūse; rüle; pùll; tûrn; chin; sing; shop; thin; this; hw in white; zh in treasure. The symbol ə stands for the unstressed vowel sound in about, taken, pencil, lemon, and circus.

America, Central America, or South America. *Noun.*

A·mer·i·can (ə mer′i kən) *adjective; noun, plural* **Americans.**

American English The variety of English that is used by most people who live in the United States.

American Revolution The war between Great Britain and the thirteen American colonies that was fought from 1775 to 1783. It resulted in the Americans setting up a free and independent country. This war is also called the **Revolutionary War.**

amethyst Quartz that has a purple or bluish purple color. Amethyst is used as a gem.

am·e·thyst (am′ə thist) *noun, plural* **amethysts.**

amiable Friendly and kind; good-natured. The owners of the shop are an *amiable* couple who don't mind people coming in just to browse.

a·mi·a·ble (ā′mē ə bəl) *adjective.*

amid or **amidst** In the middle of. The house stood *amid* a grove of pine trees.

a·mid or **a·midst** (ə mid′ *or* ə midst′) *preposition.*

amigo A Spanish word that has the same meaning as "friend."

a·mi·go (ə mē′gō) *noun, plural* **amigos.**

amiss Not right or proper; wrong. I knew something was *amiss* when they said they didn't want to go to the baseball game.

a·miss (ə mis′) *adjective; adverb.*

ammonia **1.** A gas that is a mixture of nitrogen and hydrogen. It has no color but has a very sharp smell. **2.** A mixture of ammonia in water that is used as a cleanser.

am·mo·nia (ə mōn′yə) *noun.*

ammunition Bullets, shells, grenades, bombs, and other things that can be fired from guns or exploded in some other way.

am·mu·ni·tion (am′yə nish′ən) *noun.*

amnesia A partial or total loss of memory. Amnesia is caused by injury to a person's brain or by sickness or shock.

am·ne·sia (am nē′zhə) *noun.*

amoeba A spelling sometimes used for the word **ameba.** Look up **ameba** for more information.

a·moe·ba (ə mē′bə) *noun.*

among **1.** In the middle of; surrounded by. The campers pitched their tents *among* the trees. **2.** In the company of; in association with; with. We spent last summer *among* friends in Canada. **3.** In the number, class, or group of; part of. Elephants and whales are *among* the largest animals in the world.

4. With a portion or share for each of. The dessert was divided *among* the six children. **5.** To or through every part of; throughout. The excitement quickly spread *among* the crowd outside the auditorium.

a·mong (ə mung′) *preposition.*

Language Note

Among is only used when you write about more than two people or things. The house stands *among* a group of tall trees. The preposition **between** is usually used when you write about just two people or things. Please sit here *between* my friend and me.

amount **1.** The sum of two or more numbers or quantities. What is the *amount* of money you spent this week? **2.** Quantity. No *amount* of hard work will keep me from going to college. *Noun.*
—**1.** To be equal in number or quantity; add up. The bill *amounts* to ten dollars. **2.** To be equal; be the same. Their story *amounts* to a big lie. *Verb.*

a·mount (ə mount′) *noun, plural* **amounts;** *verb,* **amounted, amounting.**

amphibian **1.** Any of a group of cold-blooded animals with backbones. Amphibians have moist skin without scales. They usually live in or near water. Frogs and toads are amphibians. **2.** An airplane that can take off from and land on both land and water. **3.** A tank or other vehicle that can travel both on land and in water.

am·phib·i·an (am fib′ē ən) *noun, plural* **amphibians.**

amphibious **1.** Able to live both on land and in water. Not all amphibious animals are amphibians. The seal and the frog are amphibious animals. **2.** Able to travel or operate both on land or in water. The soldier drove an *amphibious* tank.

am·phib·i·ous (am fib′ē əs) *adjective.*

amphitheater A circular or oval building that is used as a stadium or theater. An amphitheater has seats rising in rows around a central open space.

am·phi·the·a·ter (am′fə thē′ə tər) *noun, plural* **amphitheaters.**

ample **1.** More than enough; abundant. We bought *ample* food for our camping trip. **2.** Large in size or capacity; roomy. The car has an *ample* trunk.

am·ple (am′pəl) *adjective,* **ampler, amplest.**

amplify **1.** To add to; expand. The teacher asked me to *amplify* my report by giving more details. **2.** To make louder or stronger. The microphone will *amplify* the speaker's voice so that everyone can hear.
am·pli·fy (am′plə fī′) *verb*, **amplified, amplifying.**

amputate To cut off. The doctor had to *amputate* the soldier's wounded leg.
am·pu·tate (am′pyə tāt′) *verb*, **amputated, amputating.**

amt. An abbreviation for *amount.*

amuse **1.** To cause to laugh or smile. The silly clowns *amused* the children. **2.** To keep interested or busy in a way that gives pleasure; entertain. I *amused* myself by reading an exciting book.
a·muse (ə mūz′) *verb*, **amused, amusing.**

amusement **1.** The condition of being amused and entertained. The magician did tricks for our *amusement* . **2.** Something that amuses or entertains. Playing baseball is my favorite outdoor *amusement.*
a·muse·ment (ə mūz′mənt) *noun, plural* **amusements.**

amusement park A park where there are rides, games, and other kinds of entertainment.

an Another word for *a.* It is used before words that begin with the letters *a, e, i, o,* or *u,* and before words that begin with an *h* that is not pronounced. I ate *an* ear of corn. The nurse checks patients once *an* hour.
an (an *or unstressed* ən) *indefinite article.*

anaconda A very large snake found in South America. The anaconda can kill another animal by wrapping itself around the animal so tightly that it cannot breathe.
an·a·con·da (an′ə kon′də) *noun, plural* **anacondas.**

anaconda

analysis **1.** The separation of something into the parts that make it up. In chemistry class we made *analyses* of several compounds. **2.** A careful examination and study of something. An *analysis* of the play will show you why it remains popular.
a·nal·y·sis (ə nal′ə sis) *noun, plural* **analyses** (ə nal′ə sēz′).

analyze **1.** To find out what something is made of by separating it into parts. If we *analyze* air we find that it is made up mostly of nitrogen and oxygen. **2.** To study something carefully. The detective *analyzed* the evidence in the crime.
an·a·lyze (an′ə līz′) *verb*, **analyzed, analyzing.**

anarchy The complete absence of government. After the revolution, the country was in a state of *anarchy.*
an·ar·chy (an′ər kē) *noun.*

anatomy **1.** A science that deals with the structure of animals or plants. **2.** The structure of an animal or plant or one of its parts. We are studying the *anatomy* of the frog in science class.
a·nat·o·my (ə nat′ə mē) *noun, plural* **anatomies.**

ancestor A person from whom one is descended. Your grandparents and great-grandparents are among your *ancestors.*
an·ces·tor (an′ses tər) *noun, plural* **ancestors.**

anchor **1.** A heavy metal device that is attached to a ship by a chain or cable. When an anchor is dropped overboard, it digs into the ground below the water and keeps the ship from drifting. **2.** Any device that holds something in place. *Noun.*
—1. To hold something in place with an anchor. We will *anchor* the boat while we fish. **2.** To fasten firmly. *Anchor* the shelf to the wall. *Verb.*
an·chor (ang′kər) *noun, plural* **anchors;** *verb,* **anchored, anchoring.**

anchovy A small, silver fish that lives in salt water and is used for food. Anchovies are related to sardines.
an·cho·vy (an′chō vē *or* an chō′vē) *noun, plural* **anchovies.**

ancient **1.** Of or having to do with times very long ago. The archaeologist found the ruins of an *ancient* city buried under the ashes. **2.** Very old. Marriage is an *ancient* custom.
an·cient (ān′shənt) *adjective.*

and **1.** As well as; in addition to; also. The twins are tall *and* strong for their age. **2.** Added to; plus. Two *and* two make four.

at; āpe; fär; câre; end; mē; it; īce; pîerce; hot; ōld; sông, fôrk; oil; out; up; ūse; rüle; pu̇ll; tûrn; chin; sing; shop; thin; this; hw in white; zh in treasure. The symbol ə stands for the unstressed vowel sound in about, taken, pencil, lemon, and circus.

3. Then as a result. Treat us fairly, *and* we'll be fair with you. **4.** To. Try *and* finish the work today.
> **and** (and *or* ənd *or* ən) *conjunction.*

andiron Either of two metal supports that are used for holding wood in a fireplace.
> **and·i·ron** (and′ī′ərn) *noun, plural* **andirons.**

android A creature in science fiction stories that is not human but has the form or appearance of a human being.
> **an·droid** (an′droid) *noun, plural* **androids.**

anecdote A short story about an interesting or funny event or incident. The newscast on the election featured *anecdotes* about the candidates.
> **an·ec·dote** (an′ik dōt′) *noun, plural* **anecdotes.**

anemia A condition in which the blood does not have enough red cells or when a person has lost blood. A person with anemia often feels tired and weak.
> **a·ne·mi·a** (ə nē′mē ə) *noun.*

anemometer An instrument used to measure the speed of the wind.
> **an·e·mom·e·ter** (an′ə mom′i tər) *noun, plural* **anemometers.**

anemone A plant that has delicate white, red, pink, or purple flowers.
> **a·nem·o·ne** (ə nem′ə nē) *noun, plural* **anemones.**

anemones

anesthesia The loss of all feeling, especially pain. This loss of feeling may be in all or part of the body. Doctors give patients drugs that produce *anesthesia* before surgery.
> **an·es·the·sia** (an′əs thē′zhə) *noun.*

anesthetic A drug or other substance that causes a loss of feeling or consciousness. The doctor gave me an *anesthetic* before setting my broken arm.
> **an·es·thet·ic** (an′əs thet′ik) *noun, plural* **anesthetics.**

anew Once more; again. I accidentally crumpled my sketch in art class, so I began *anew*.
> **a·new** (ə nü′ *or* ə nū′) *adverb.*

angel **1.** In the Bible and other writings, a heavenly being who serves God as a helper and messenger. **2.** A person who is admired for his or her goodness or beauty.
> **an·gel** (ān′jəl) *noun, plural* **angels.**

anger A strong feeling caused by a person or thing that opposes, displeases, or hurts one. I had a fit of *anger* when the heavy traffic made me late for my appointment. *Noun.*
—To make or become angry. The students' rudeness *angered* their teacher. My cousin *angers* easily. *Verb.*
> **an·ger** (ang′gər) *noun; verb,* **angered, angering.**

angle **1.** The figure formed by two lines or flat surfaces that extend from one point or line. **2.** The space between these lines or flat surfaces. **3.** A corner. The sculpture has many *angles* and curves. **4.** A way of thinking or feeling about something; point of view. I was having trouble solving the problem, so I tried to look at it from another *angle. Noun.*
—To move or turn so as to form an angle. The road *angles* to the right as it goes up the mountain. *Verb.*
> **an·gle** (ang′gəl) *noun, plural* **angles;** *verb,* **angled, angling.**

Angola A country in southwestern Africa.
> **An·go·la** (ang gō′lə) *noun.*

angora Yarn or cloth made from the long, silky hair of a kind of rabbit or goat. Angora feels soft and fluffy and is used to make sweaters and other clothing.
> **an·gor·a** (ang gôr′ə) *noun.*

angry **1.** Feeling or showing anger. I was *angry* with my friends for breaking my model airplane. I gave them an *angry* look. **2.** Giving a sign of something bad, dangerous, or harmful; threatening. We were afraid to sail in the *angry* sea. **3.** Inflamed and painful. I had an *angry* sore on my knee.
> **an·gry** (ang′grē) *adjective,* **angrier, angriest.**

anguish Great suffering of the body or mind; agony. The children were in *anguish* over the death of their dog.
> **an·guish** (ang′gwish) *noun.*

animal **1.** A living thing that takes in food and moves about and that is made up of many cells. Unlike plants, animals do not have to stay in one place, and they cannot make their own food. Jellyfish, worms, clams, insects, birds, fish, mammals, and hu-

man beings are all animals.   **2.** Animals other than humans. My aunt and uncle raise *animals* on their farm.
an·i·mal (an′ə məl) *noun, plural* **animals.**

animosity   Deep hatred; hostility. The *animosity* between the two countries led to war.
an·i·mos·i·ty (an′ə mos′i tē) *noun, plural* **animosities.**

ankle   The joint that connects the foot and the leg.
an·kle (ang′kəl) *noun, plural* **ankles.**

anklet   A short sock that reaches just above the ankle.
an·klet (ang′klit) *noun, plural* **anklets.**

annex   To add or attach to something larger. The United States *annexed* the independent republic of Texas and made it a state in 1845. *Verb.*
—A wing added to a building or a separate building used as an addition to a main building. The school needs an *annex* with extra classrooms. *Noun.*
an·nex (ə neks′ *for verb;* an′eks *for noun*) *verb,* **annexed, annexing;** *noun, plural* **annexes.**

annihilate   To destroy completely; wipe out. The earthquake *annihilated* the town.
an·ni·hi·late (ə nī′ə lāt′) *verb,* **annihilated, annihilating.**

anniversary   The occurrence each year of the date on which an event happened in the past. On February 15 the couple will celebrate the tenth *anniversary* of their wedding.
an·ni·ver·sa·ry (an′ə vûr′sə rē) *noun, plural* **anniversaries.**

announce   To make something known in an official or formal way. The principal *announced* that the school would be closed because of the blizzard.
an·nounce (ə nouns′) *verb,* **announced, announcing.**

announcement   **1.** The act of making known officially or formally. *Announcement* of the election results brought cheers from the audience.   **2.** A public statement that makes something known. The president will make an important *announcement* on television tonight.
an·nounce·ment (ə nouns′mənt) *noun, plural* **announcements.**

announcer   A person on radio or television who does such things as introduce programs, present advertisements, and read the news.
an·nounc·er (ə noun′sər) *noun, plural* **announcers.**

annoy   To bother or disturb. The sound of that loud radio *annoys* me.
an·noy (ə noi′) *verb,* **annoyed, annoying.**

annoyance   **1.** A person or thing that annoys. Their constant complaining was an *annoyance* to me.   **2.** The condition of being annoyed. Your *annoyance* at being teased was easy to understand.
an·noy·ance (ə noi′əns) *noun, plural* **annoyances.**

annual   **1.** Measured by the year. The average *annual* rainfall in my state is 15 inches.   **2.** Happening or returning once a year. Thanksgiving is an *annual* holiday that we celebrate in November.   **3.** Living its full life in one year or one growing season. Corn is an *annual* plant. *Adjective.*
—A plant that lives only one year or growing season. We plant *annuals* in our garden every spring. *Noun.*
an·nu·al (an′ū əl) *adjective; noun, plural* **annuals.**

annual ring   One of the rings of wood on the inside of the trunk of a tree. Annual rings are visible on the cut edge of the stump of a tree. Each new ring represents one year of growth.

anoint   To put oil on during a ceremony. The archbishop *anointed* the king.
a·noint (ə noint′) *verb,* **anointed, anointing.**

anonymous   **1.** From or by someone whose name is not known or given. The police got an *anonymous* phone call telling them where to find the robbers.   **2.** With a name not known or given. The person who donated the money wanted to remain *anonymous.*
a·non·y·mous (ə non′ə məs) *adjective.*

another   **1.** One more; an additional. Do you want *another* apple?   **2.** A different; some other. I saw *another* coat that I liked better than the first one. *Adjective.*
—**1.** One more; an additional one. When you have read that book, I have *another* I think you'll like.   **2.** A different person or thing. That plan didn't work, so we'll use *another. Pronoun.*
an·oth·er (ə nuth′ər) *adjective; pronoun.*

answer   **1.** Something said or written in reply. I could not get an *answer* to my question. Did you get an *answer* to your letter?   **2.** Something, such as an action or movement, done as a response. The employer's

at; āpe; fär; câre; end; mē; it; īce; pîerce; hot; ōld;
sông, fôrk; oil; out; up; ūse; rūle; pùll; tûrn; chin;
sing; shop; thin; <u>th</u>is; hw in white; zh in treasure.
The symbol ə stands for the unstressed vowel
sound in about, taken, pencil, lemon, and circus.

answer to the workers' complaints was to raise their pay.   **3.** The solution to a problem. To find the right *answer,* multiply by 12. *Noun.*
—**1.** To speak or write as a reply. I *answered* my friend's long letter.   **2.** To do in response to. I ran to *answer* the doorbell.   **3.** To agree with; match. The suspect *answers* to the description of the person seen by witnesses. *Verb.*
> **an·swer** (an′sər) *noun, plural* **answers;** *verb,* **answered, answering.**

ant   A small insect related to bees and wasps. Ants live together in large groups called colonies. ▲ Another word that sounds like this is **aunt.**
> **ant** (ant) *noun, plural* **ants.**

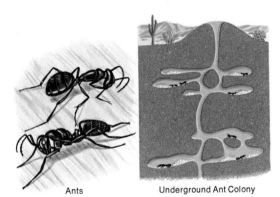

Ants   Underground Ant Colony

antagonism   A strong feeling against a person or thing. After their quarrel, the children felt *antagonism* toward each other.
> **an·tag·o·nism** (an tag′ə niz′əm) *noun, plural* **antagonisms.**

antagonize   To cause dislike in; irritate. The clerk's rude manner *antagonized* many customers.
> **an·tag·o·nize** (an tag′ə nīz′) *verb,* **antagonized, antagonizing.**

antarctic   Of or having to do with the South Pole or the region around the South Pole. The expeditions made by *antarctic* explorers have always been difficult and dangerous. *Adjective.*
—the **Antarctic.** Another name for **Antarctica.** The explorers set sail for *the Antarctic.* Look up **Antarctica** for more information. *Noun.*
> **ant·arc·tic** (ant ärk′tik *or* ant är′tik) *adjective; noun.*

Antarctica   The continent at the South Pole. Antarctica is almost completely covered with ice all year long.
> **Ant·arc·ti·ca** (ant ärk′ti kə *or* ant är′ti kə) *noun.*

Antarctic Ocean   The water around Antarctica that includes the most southern parts of the Atlantic, Pacific, and Indian oceans.
> **Ant·arc·tic** (ant ärk′tik *or* ant är′tik).

anteater

anteater   An animal with a long head, sticky tongue, and strong claws. Anteaters claw into ant nests and use their tongues to capture ants, termites, and other insects. Anteaters live in Central America and South America.
> **ant·eat·er** (ant′ē′tər) *noun, plural* **anteaters.**

antecedent   The word or group of words in a sentence that a pronoun in the same sentence refers to. In the sentence "The secretary typed the letter and then mailed it," the antecedent of "it" is "the letter."
> **an·te·ced·ent** (an′tə sē′dənt) *noun, plural* **antecedents.**

antelope   A slender, swift animal that has long horns without branches. Antelopes look like deer, but they are closely related to goats. Antelopes are found in Africa and Asia.
> **an·te·lope** (ant′ə lōp′) *noun, plural* **antelopes.**

antenna   **1.** A metallic device, such as a rod or wire, used to send out or receive radio or television signals.   **2.** One of a pair of long, thin body parts, such as that on the head of an insect or a lobster; feelers. Antennae are used to sense touch and smells.
> **an·ten·na** (an ten′ə) *noun, plural* **antennas** *for definition 1* or **antennae** (an ten′ē) *for definition 2.*

anthem   **1.** A song of gladness, praise, or patriotism. The national *anthem* of the United States is "The Star-Spangled Banner."   **2.** A religious song, usually with words from the Bible.
> **an·them** (an′thəm) *noun, plural* **anthems.**

anther   The upper part of the stamen of a flower. The anther contains the flower's pollen.
> **an·ther** (an′thər) *noun, plural* **anthers.**

anthill   A mound of earth made by ants around the entrance to their underground nest.
> **ant·hill** (ant′hil′) *noun, plural* **anthills.**

anthology A book or other collection of writings, such as poems, stories, or articles.
an·thol·o·gy (an thol′ə jē) *noun, plural* **anthologies.**

anthracite A very hard, shiny black coal that burns with a low flame and gives off little smoke. This kind of coal is sometimes called **hard coal.**
an·thra·cite (an′thrə sīt′) *noun.*

anthropology The study of the physical, cultural, and social characteristics of human beings. Anthropology deals with the development of these characteristics from prehistoric times to the present.
an·thro·pol·o·gy (an′thrə pol′ə jē) *noun.*

anti– A *prefix* that means opposed to or against. *Antifreeze* means something that works against freezing. *Antiwar* means against a war.

antibiotic A drug that is used in medicine to kill or slow the growth of germs that cause disease.
an·ti·bi·ot·ic (an′tē bī ot′ik) *noun, plural* **antibiotics.**

antibody A substance produced by the body's white blood cells to destroy or weaken germs.
an·ti·bod·y (an′ti bod′ē) *noun, plural* **antibodies.**

anticipate **1.** To look forward to; expect. I *anticipate* their arrival at noon. **2.** To think of and do something about in advance. We *anticipated* your objection to our plan and thought of another one that you might like.
an·tic·i·pate (an tis′ə pāt′) *verb,* **anticipated, anticipating.**

anticipation The act of anticipating; expectation. In *anticipation* of a hot summer, we bought an air conditioner.
an·tic·i·pa·tion (an tis′ə pā′shən) *noun, plural* **anticipations.**

antidote A medicine that works against the effects of a poison. The doctor prescribed an *antidote* for the child who accidentally swallowed poison.
an·ti·dote (an′ti dōt′) *noun, plural* **antidotes.**

antifreeze A substance that is added to a liquid to help keep the liquid from freezing. Antifreeze is added to the cooling liquid used in the radiators of cars and trucks.
an·ti·freeze (an′ti frēz′) *noun.*

antique Of times long ago; very old. We went to an exhibit of *antique* carriages. *Adjective.*
—Something made very long ago. The museum has *antiques* from the time of colonial America. *Noun.*

an·tique (an tēk′) *adjective; noun, plural* **antiques.**

an **antique** rocking horse

antiseptic A substance that kills germs or stops their growth. Alcohol and iodine are antiseptics.
an·ti·sep·tic (an′ti sep′tik) *noun, plural* **antiseptics.**

antitoxin A substance produced by the body that protects a person from a poison produced by a living thing. For example, the body makes antitoxins when stung by a bee.
an·ti·tox·in (an′ti tok′sin) *noun, plural* **antitoxins.**

antler One of the two bony growths on the head of a deer and certain other animals. Antlers usually have branches. Animals with antlers shed them each year and grow new ones.
ant·ler (ant′lər) *noun, plural* **antlers.**

antonym A word that has the opposite meaning of another word. "High" is the antonym of "low," and "hot" is the antonym of "cold."
an·to·nym (an′tə nim′) *noun, plural* **antonyms.**

Language Note

Not every word has an **antonym,** but many do. You can improve your vocabulary by thinking of pairs of words that are opposite in meaning. Some subjects *fascinate* me, and others *bore* me. Elephants are *gigantic,* but ants are *tiny.* Can you think of others?

---

at; āpe; fär; câre; end; mē; it; ice; pîerce; hot; ōld; sông, fôrk; oil; out; up; ūse; rüle; púll; tûrn; chin; sing; shop; thin; this; hw in white; zh in treasure. The symbol ə stands for the unstressed vowel sound in about, taken, pencil, lemon, and circus.

anvil   An iron or steel block on which metals are hammered into shape. Metals are usually softened by heating before they are placed on an anvil.
an·vil (an′vəl) *noun, plural* **anvils.**

anvil

anxiety   A feeling of fearful worry or uneasiness about what may happen. We were filled with *anxiety* about our boat capsizing in the stormy sea.
anx·i·e·ty (ang zī′i tē) *noun, plural* **anxieties.**

anxious   **1.** Nervous, worried, or fearful about what may happen. My cousin was *anxious* about driving on the slippery mountain roads.   **2.** Wanting very much; eager. I was *anxious* to make friends at my new school.
anx·ious (angk′shəs) *adjective.*

any   **1.** One or some. Sit in *any* chair. Did they eat *any* lunch?   **2.** Every. *Any* child can do this problem. *Adjective.*
—**1.** Any one or ones. *Any* of these books is sure to interest you. *Any* of you who are ready can leave now.   **2.** Any quantity or part. Did you finish *any* of your work? *Pronoun.*
—To any extent or degree. Are you feeling *any* better? *Adverb.*
an·y (en′ē) *adjective; pronoun; adverb.*

anybody   Any person whatever; anyone. Has *anybody* seen the teacher?
an·y·bod·y (en′ē bod′ē) *pronoun.*

anyhow   **1.** No matter what happens; in any case. Maybe it won't rain, but we should be prepared *anyhow.*   **2.** Without being stopped or prevented by that; in spite of that. Our best player was hurt, but we won the game *anyhow.*
an·y·how (en′ē hou′) *adverb.*

anymore   Now; nowadays. Now that I can ride a bicycle I don't use my tricycle *anymore.*
an·y·more (en′ē môr′) *adverb.*

anyone   Any person whatever; anybody. *Anyone* who lives in this town can go swimming in the town pool.
an·y·one (en′ē wun′) *pronoun.*

anyplace   In, at, or to any place; anywhere. Take the car and drive *anyplace* you want.
an·y·place (en′ē plās′) *adverb.*

anything   Any thing whatever. I'll do *anything* you ask. *Pronoun.*
—In any way; at all. You aren't *anything* like your twin. *Adverb.*
an·y·thing (en′ē thing′) *pronoun; adverb.*

anytime   At any time. You may leave *anytime* you want.
an·y·time (en′ē tīm′) *adverb.*

anyway   No matter what happens; in any case. The water is cold, but I want to go swimming *anyway.*
an·y·way (en′ē wā′) *adverb.*

anywhere   In, at, or to any place. Just put the books down *anywhere.*
an·y·where (en′ē hwâr′ *or* en′ē wâr′) *adverb.*

aorta   The main artery of the body. The aorta carries blood from the left side of the heart to all parts of the body except the lungs.
a·or·ta (ā ôr′tə) *noun, plural* **aortas.**

Apache   A member of an American Indian tribe of the southwestern United States.
A·pach·e (ə pach′ē) *noun, plural* **Apache** or **Apaches.**

apart   **1.** Away from each other in space or time. The houses are 2 miles *apart.* The trains left three hours *apart.*   **2.** In or into two or more parts or pieces. In sewing class, we tore a coat *apart* at the seams and then sewed it back together.
• **to take apart.**   To separate into two or more parts or pieces. The mechanic *took* the engine *apart* to find out what was wrong with it.
a·part (ə pärt′) *adverb.*

apartheid   The government policy of racial segregation that is followed in South Africa.
a·part·heid (ə pär′tīd *or* ə pärt′hāt) *noun.*

Word History

Apartheid is a word borrowed from Afrikaans, the form of Dutch that is spoken in South Africa. It means "being apart."

---

apartment   A room or group of rooms usually used to live in. There are twenty *apartments* in that building.
a·part·ment (ə pärt′mənt) *noun, plural* **apartments.**

apathy   A lack of feeling, interest, or concern; indifference. *Apathy* kept some people from voting in the election.
ap·a·thy (ap′ə thē) *noun.*

A

ape A large animal with no tail that is able to stand and walk in an almost upright position. Chimpanzees, gorillas, gibbons, and orangutans are all types of apes. *Noun.*
—To imitate; mimic. My cousin likes to *ape* famous politicians. *Verb.*
   ape (āp) *noun, plural* **apes;** *verb,* **aped, aping.**

aphid A small insect that lives by sucking juices from plants.
   a·phid (ā′fid *or* af′id) *noun, plural* **aphids.**

aphid

apiece For or to each one; each. These red pencils are fifteen cents *apiece.* The store manager gave us five dollars *apiece* for our work.
   a·piece (ə pēs′) *adverb.*

apologize To say one is sorry or embarrassed; make an apology. I *apologized* to my parents for being rude.
   a·pol·o·gize (ə pol′ə jīz′) *verb,* **apologized, apologizing.**

apology A statement that one is sorry or embarrassed about something, such as an offense or a mistake. Please accept my *apology* for being late.
   a·pol·o·gy (ə pol′ə jē) *noun, plural* **apologies.**

Apostle One of the early Christian leaders, especially one of the twelve disciples chosen by Jesus.
   A·pos·tle (ə pos′əl) *noun, plural* **Apostles.**

apostrophe A punctuation mark (') that is used in the following ways: **1.** To show that one or more letters or numbers have been left out. For example, "you're" means "you are," and '91 can mean *1991.* **2.** To form a possessive noun or possessive pronoun that shows that something belongs to a person or thing. In the sentence "My cousin's bike is red" the word "cousin's" means that the bike belongs to my cousin. **3.** To form the plural of letters and numbers, for example, "I got three B's on my report card."
   a·pos·tro·phe (ə pos′trə fē) *noun, plural* **apostrophes.**

apothecary A person who prepares and sells drugs and medicine; druggist.
   a·poth·e·car·y (ə poth′ə ker′ē) *noun, plural* **apothecaries.**

appall To fill with horror or terror; shock or terrify. We were *appalled* by the news of the airplane crash.
   ap·pall (ə pôl′) *verb,* **appalled, appalling.**

apparatus Anything that is used for a particular purpose. Gymnasium equipment, chemistry sets, tools, and machinery are all different kinds of apparatus.
   ap·pa·rat·us (ap′ə rat′əs *or* ap′ə rā′təs) *noun, plural* **apparatus** or **apparatuses.**

apparel Clothing; clothes. That store sells children's *apparel.*
   ap·par·el (ə par′əl) *noun.*

apparent **1.** Easily seen or understood. It's *apparent* that you did not comb your hair. It was *apparent* they were enjoying themselves. **2.** Seeming real or true even though it may not be. The *apparent* size of a star is much smaller than its real size.
   ap·par·ent (ə par′ənt) *adjective.*

apparently As far as one can judge by the way things appear. *Apparently,* it is going to rain.
   ap·par·ent·ly (ə par′ənt lē) *adverb.*

appeal **1.** An earnest request for something needed or wanted. Each year that church makes an *appeal* for money to aid poor people. **2.** The power to interest or attract. Sports have a great *appeal* to people of every age. **3.** A request to have a legal case heard again by a higher court. If they lose their case, the lawyer will certainly *appeal. Noun.*
—**1.** To make an earnest request. The people of the town *appealed* to the governor for help after the flood. **2.** To be attractive or interesting. Camping out in the woods does not *appeal* to me. **3.** To request to have a case heard again before a higher court of law. *Verb.*
   ap·peal (ə pēl′) *noun, plural* **appeals;** *verb,* **appealed, appealing.**

appear **1.** To come into sight; be seen. The snowy mountain peaks *appeared* in the distance. **2.** To give the impression of being; seem; look. They *appeared* interested in the game, but they were really bored. **3.** To come before the public. That actor has often *appeared* on television. **4.** To come before a court of law. They were ordered to *appear* in the county court.
   ap·pear (ə pir′) *verb,* **appeared, appearing.**

appearance **1.** The act of appearing or coming into sight. The sun made a sudden

at; āpe; fär; câre; end; mē; it; īce; pîerce; hot; ōld; sông; fôrk; oil; out; up; ūse; rüle; pu̇ll; tûrn; chin; sing; shop; thin; this; hw in white; zh in treasure. The symbol ə stands for the unstressed vowel sound in about, taken, pencil, lemon, and circus.

appearance through the clouds. **2.** The way a person or thing looks; outward look. I could tell from your *appearance* that you were disappointed. **3.** The act of coming before the public. That was the actor's first *appearance* in the movies.
ap·pear·ance (ə pîr′əns) *noun, plural* **appearances.**

appease 1. To make content or calm. The owner of the business *appeased* the striking workers by giving them more pay. **2.** To supply with what is needed or wanted; satisfy. The sandwich *appeased* my appetite.
ap·pease (ə pēz′) *verb,* **appeased, appeasing.**

appendicitis An inflammation of the appendix. It causes sharp pain on the lower right side of the abdomen.
ap·pen·di·ci·tis (ə pen′də sī′tis) *noun.*

appendix 1. A short, hollow pouch that is attached to the large intestine. **2.** A section at the end of a book or other piece of writing. An appendix gives more information about the subject of the book.
ap·pen·dix (ə pen′diks) *noun, plural* **appendixes** or **appendices.** (ə pen′də sēz′).

appetite 1. A desire for food. When I was sick I had no *appetite.* **2.** Any strong desire. Some people have no *appetite* for adventure and excitement.
ap·pe·tite (ap′i tīt′) *noun, plural* **appetites.**

appetizing Pleasing or stimulating the appetite; tasty. We made some *appetizing* sandwiches for our picnic.
ap·pe·tiz·ing (ap′i tī′zing) *adjective.*

applaud 1. To show approval or enjoyment of something by clapping the hands. The children *applauded* the clown's funny tricks. **2.** To approve or praise. The public *applauded* the mayor's plan for lower taxes.
ap·plaud (ə plôd′) *verb,* **applauded, applauding.**

applause 1. Approval or enjoyment shown by clapping the hands. Everyone joined in the *applause* at the end of the act. **2.** Approval or praise. The author's first novel received the *applause* of the critics.
ap·plause (ə plôz′) *noun.*

apple A round fruit with red, yellow, or green skin. Apples have firm white flesh surrounding a core with small seeds. Apples grow on a tree that is also called an apple.
ap·ple (ap′əl) *noun, plural* **apples.**

applesauce A food made from pieces of apple that have been sweetened with sugar and cooked in water until soft.
ap·ple·sauce (ap′əl sôs′) *noun.*

appliance A device or small machine that has a particular use. Refrigerators, washing machines, toasters, and irons are household appliances.
ap·pli·ance (ə plī′əns) *noun, plural* **appliances.**

applicant A person who makes a request for something, such as a job. There were several *applicants* for the position of school custodian.
ap·pli·cant (ap′li kənt) *noun, plural* **applicants.**

application 1. The act of putting something to use. The *application* of scientific knowledge has made space exploration possible. **2.** The act of putting something on. The *application* of paint made the old house look like new. **3.** Something that is put on, such as an ointment. This *application* will soothe your bruise. **4.** A way of being used. Many scientific discoveries have practical *applications.* **5.** A request. I made an *application* for the job of gardener's assistant.
ap·pli·ca·tion (ap′li kā′shən) *noun, plural* **applications.**

apply 1. To use. You have to *apply* force to open the locked door. **2.** To put on. They *applied* two coats of paint to the wall. **3.** To ask; make a request. I *applied* for a summer job at the grocery store. **4.** To devote oneself with effort. We *applied* ourselves to the task of cleaning the basement. **5.** To be suitable or have to do with. The law against speeding *applies* to all drivers.
ap·ply (ə plī′) *verb,* **applied, applying.**

appoint 1. To name or select for a position, office, or duty. The president *appointed* Judge Smith to the Supreme Court. **2.** To decide on; set; fix. The judge *appointed* the date of the trial.
ap·point (ə point′) *verb,* **appointed, appointing.**

appointment 1. The act of naming or selecting for a position, office, or duty. The *appointment* of the new judge was announced

Blossom

Fruit

apple

in the newspaper.   **2.** A position or office to which one is appointed. The doctor was offered an *appointment* on the staff of a major hospital.   **3.** An agreement to meet or see someone at a certain time and place. I have an *appointment* with the dentist at ten o'clock.
  ap·point·ment (ə point′mənt) *noun, plural* **appointments.**

appraise   **1.** To estimate the value of; set a price for. A real estate agent *appraised* our house.   **2.** To judge the quality, importance, or worth of. The critic *appraised* the concert in a newspaper review.
  ap·praise (ə prāz′) *verb,* **appraised, appraising.**

appreciate   **1.** To understand the value of. Everyone *appreciates* loyal friends.   **2.** To be grateful for something. I *appreciate* your running these errands for me.   **3.** To be fully aware of; realize. Do you *appreciate* the difficulties involved in that experiment? **4.** To rise in value. Real estate has *appreciated* in that town.
  ap·pre·ci·ate (ə prē′shē āt′) *verb,* **appreciated, appreciating.**

appreciation   **1.** An understanding of the value of something. After studying carpentry, I had a better *appreciation* of fine woodworking.   **2.** A feeling of being thankful; gratitude. I want to show my *appreciation* for your help.   **3.** An increase in value. The *appreciation* of our property has been very great.
  ap·pre·ci·a·tion (ə prē′shē ā′shən) *noun.*

apprehend   **1.** To capture and arrest. The police *apprehended* the suspects.   **2.** To understand. Did you fully *apprehend* the meaning of the speech?
  ap·pre·hend (ap′ri hend′) *verb,* **apprehended, apprehending.**

apprehension   **1.** A fear of what may happen. The thought of going to the dentist filled me with *apprehension*.   **2.** Arrest or capture. The chase ended with the *apprehension* of the suspects.   **3.** Understanding. I have no *apprehension* of the way a computer works.
  ap·pre·hen·sion (ap′ri hen′shən) *noun, plural* **apprehensions.**

apprentice   A person who works for a skilled worker in order to learn a trade or art. The students worked as *apprentices* in a woodworking shop. *Noun.*
  —To take on or place as an apprentice. When I was *apprenticed* to the tailor, I learned to sew and run the business. *Verb.*
  ap·pren·tice (ə pren′tis) *noun, plural* **apprentices;** *verb,* **apprenticed, apprenticing.**

approach   **1.** To come near. The plane *approached* the airport. The car *approached* at a high speed.   **2.** To go to with a plan or request. I *approached* my parents with the hope of getting a higher allowance.   **3.** To begin to work on. How should we *approach* the problem? *Verb.*
  —**1.** The act of coming near. I always look forward to the *approach* of summer.   **2.** A method of doing something. My *approach* to training the dog was to be very patient.   **3.** A way of reaching a place or person. The only *approach* to the town was blocked by snow. *Noun.*
  ap·proach (ə prōch′) *verb,* **approached, approaching;** *noun, plural* **approaches.**

appropriate   Suitable;   proper;   correct. Warm clothes are *appropriate* for a cold day. I began my letter to the ambassador with an *appropriate* greeting. *Adjective.*
  —To reserve for a particular use. Congress *appropriated* money to add land to the park system and to maintain campgrounds. *Verb.*
  ap·pro·pri·ate (ə prō′prē it *for adjective;* ə prō′prē āt′ *for verb) adjective; verb,* **appropriated, appropriating.**

approval   **1.** Favorable   opinion;   acceptance. The mayor's plan to attract businesses to the city had the *approval* of most of the people.   **2.** Permission or consent. I got my parents' *approval* to give a Halloween party.
  ap·prov·al (ə prü′vəl) *noun, plural* **approvals.**

approve   **1.** To have or give a favorable opinion. My parents don't *approve* of my staying up very late.   **2.** To consent or agree to officially; authorize. The town recently *approved* the construction of a public swimming pool.
  ap·prove (ə prüv′) *verb,* **approved, approving.**

approximate   Nearly correct or exact. My *approximate* weight is 100 pounds. *Adjective.*
  —To be nearly the same as; come close to. Your estimate *approximates* the actual cost of the repairs. *Verb.*
  ap·prox·i·mate (ə prok′sə mit *for adjective;* ə prok′sə māt′ *for verb) adjective; verb,* **approximated, approximating.**

---

at; āpe; fär; câre; end; mē; it; īce; pîerce; hot; ōld; sông, fôrk; oil; out; up; ūse; rüle; pùll; tûrn; chin; sing; shop; thin; this; hw in white; zh in treasure. The symbol ə stands for the unstressed vowel sound in about, taken, pencil, lemon, and circus.

approximately   Nearly; about. We had *approximately* 4 inches of snow yesterday.
ap·prox·i·mate·ly (ə prok′sə mit lē) *adverb.*

Apr.   An abbreviation for *April.*

apricot   A round, yellowish orange fruit that looks like a small peach. Apricots grow in warm climates on a tree that is also called an apricot.
a·pri·cot (ā′pri kot′ *or* ap′ri kot′) *noun, plural* **apricots.**

April   The fourth month of the year. April has thirty days.
A·pril (ā′prəl) *noun.*

apricots

Word History

April goes back to the Latin name for this month. In Latin the month may have been named after *Aphrodite,* the Greek goddess of love.

---

apron   A garment worn over the front of the body to protect one's clothing. The cook's *apron* was made of white cloth.
a·pron (ā′prən) *noun, plural* **aprons.**

apt   **1.** Likely; inclined. You're *apt* to hurt yourself if you're not more careful.   **2.** Appropriate; suitable. My friend gave me some *apt* suggestions for my science project.   **3.** Quick to learn. You are an *apt* student in mathematics.
apt (apt) *adjective.*

aptitude   **1.** A natural ability or talent. The twins seem to have an *aptitude* for drawing.   **2.** Quickness in learning. There were many students with great *aptitude* in my class.
ap·ti·tude (ap′ti tüd′ *or* ap′ti tūd′) *noun, plural* **aptitudes.**

aqualung   A device used by a person to breathe underwater. The trademark for this device is **Aqua-lung.**
aq·ua·lung (ak′wə lung′) *noun, plural* **aqualungs.**

aquarium   **1.** A tank, bowl, or similar container in which fish, other water animals, and water plants are kept. An aquarium is usually made of glass or some other material that one can see through.   **2.** A building used to display collections of fish, other wa-ter animals, and water plants. People visit aquariums for pleasure or to study the animals and plants kept there.
a·quar·i·um (ə kwar′ē əm) *noun, plural* **aquariums.**

aqueduct   **1.** A large pipe or other channel that carries water over a long distance.   **2.** A structure like a bridge used to support such a pipe or channel.
aq·ue·duct (ak′wi dukt′) *noun, plural* **aqueducts.**

aqueduct

AR   Postal abbreviation for *Arkansas.*

Arab   **1.** A member of one of the Arabic-speaking peoples who live in southwestern Asia and northern Africa.   **2.** A person who was born in or is a citizen of an Arabian country. *Noun.*
—Of or having to do with the Arabs or Arabia. *Adjective.*
Ar·ab (ar′əb) *noun, plural* **Arabs;** *adjective.*

Arabia   A peninsula in southwestern Asia.
A·ra·bi·a (ə rā′bē ə) *noun.*

Arabian   Of or having to do with Arabia or the people of Arabia. *Adjective.*
—A person who was born in or is a citizen of an Arabian country. *Noun.*
A·ra·bi·an (ə rā′bē ən) *adjective; noun, plural* **Arabians.**

Arabic   Of or having to do with the Arabs or their language. *Adjective.*
—The language of the Arabs. *Noun.*
Ar·a·bic (ar′ə bik) *adjective; noun.*

Arabic numerals   The number symbols 1, 2, 3, 4, 5, 6, 7, 8, 9, and 0.

arable   Suitable for farming. Irrigation can turn a desert into *arable* land.
ar·a·ble (ar′ə bəl) *adjective.*

arbitrary   Based on personal opinions, feelings, or wishes rather than on reason or on a rule or law. Judges may not make *arbitrary* decisions when they decide legal cases.
ar·bi·trar·y (är′bə trer′ē) *adjective.*

arbitrate **1.** To settle a dispute or disagreement. The umpires *arbitrated* between the two teams. **2.** To settle by or submit to arbitration. The union and the company agreed to *arbitrate* their dispute.
　　ar·bi·trate (är′bi trāt′) *verb,* **arbitrated, arbitrating.**

arbitration A way of settling a dispute or disagreement by agreeing to accept the decision of a person or group that is not involved. The strike was finally ended by *arbitration.*
　　ar·bi·tra·tion (är′bi trā′shən) *noun.*

arbor A place that is covered and shaded by trees or shrubs or by vines growing on a frame.
　　ar·bor (är′bər) *noun, plural* **arbors.**

arc **1.** A curved line between two points on a circle. **2.** Any line curving in this way. The rainbow formed an *arc* in the sky. ▲ Another word that sounds like this is **ark.**
　　arc (ärk) *noun, plural* **arcs.**

arcade **1.** A passageway that is covered by a curved roof. Arcades often have a row of shops along each side. **2.** A place with a selection of video games, for which a person pays to play.
　　ar·cade (är kād′) *noun, plural* **arcades.**

arch **1.** A curved structure over an open space. An arch is usually built to support the weight of the material above it. Four *arches* supported the bridge across the river. **2.** A monument that contains an arch or arches. **3.** Anything like an arch in shape or use. The curved part of the foot between the toes and the heel is called the arch. *Noun.*
　　—To form into an arch; curve. The cat *arched* its back in anger. *Verb.*
　　arch (ärch) *noun, plural* **arches;** *verb,* **arched, arching.**

arch

archaeology The study of the way humans lived a long time ago. Archaeologists dig up the remains of ancient cities and towns and then study the tools, weapons, pottery, and other things they find. This word is also spelled **archeology.**
　　ar·chae·ol·o·gy (är′kē ol′ə jē) *noun.*

archbishop A bishop of the highest rank.
　　arch·bish·op (ärch′bish′əp) *noun, plural* **archbishops.**

archeology Another spelling for **archaeology.** Look up **archaeology** for more information.
　　ar·che·ol·o·gy (är′kē ol′ə je) *noun.*

archer A person who shoots with a bow and arrow.
　　arch·er (är′chər) *noun, plural* **archers.**

archery The skill or sport of shooting with a bow and arrow.
　　arch·er·y (är′chə rē) *noun.*

archery

archipelago **1.** A large group of islands. **2.** A large body of water having many islands in it.
　　ar·chi·pel·a·go (är′kə pel′i gō′) *noun, plural* **archipelagoes** or **archipelagos.**

architect A person who designs buildings and supervises their construction.
　　ar·chi·tect (är′ki tekt′) *noun, plural* **architects.**

architecture **1.** The science, art, or profession of designing buildings. **2.** A particular style or method of building. We studied Greek *architecture* in art class.
　　ar·chi·tec·ture (är′ki tek′chər) *noun.*

arctic **1.** Of or having to do with the North Pole or the region around the North Pole.

---

at; āpe; fär; câre; end; mē; it; īce; pîerce; hot; ōld; sông, fôrk; oil; out; up; ūse; rüle; pùll; tûrn; chin; sing; shop; thin; <u>th</u>is; hw in white; zh in treasure. The symbol ə stands for the unstressed vowel sound in about, taken, pencil, lemon, and circus.

Reindeer live in the *arctic* wilderness. **2.** Very cold; frigid. The *arctic* weather lasted long into the spring.
　arc·tic (ärk′tik *or* är′tik) *adjective.*

Arctic Ocean　The ocean surrounding the North Pole.

are　A form of the present tense of **be** that is used with *you, we, they,* or the plural form of a noun. You *are* late. We *are* glad you could come. How *are* your friends? Look up **be** for more information.
　are (är) *verb.*

area　**1.** The amount of surface within a given boundary. The *area* of our yard is 400 square feet. **2.** A particular space, region, or section. We moved from the city to a rural *area.* **3.** A field of interest, study, or activity. What *area* will you specialize in at college?
　ar·e·a (âr′ē ə) *noun, plural* **areas.**

area code　A set of three numbers assigned to each area into which the United States and Canada are divided for telephone service. You dial these three numbers before the local number when you call from one area to another.

arena　**1.** A space that is used for contests or entertainment. In the arenas of ancient Rome, gladiators fought each other. Today, circuses and sports events take place in arenas. **2.** A building with an arena. **3.** An area or scene of activity or conflict. My cousin is interested in getting into the political *arena.*
　a·re·na (ə rē′nə) *noun, plural* **arenas.**

aren't　Shortened form of "are not." Why *aren't* you going with us?
　aren't (ärnt *or* är′ənt) *contraction.*

Argentina　A country in southern South America.
　Ar·gen·ti·na (är′jən tē′nə) *noun.*

argue　**1.** To have a difference of opinion; disagree. My parents always *argue* about politics. **2.** To give reasons for or against something. I *argued* against going to the beach because it looked like it might rain.
　ar·gue (är′gū) *verb,* **argued, arguing.**

argument　**1.** A discussion of something by people who do not agree. They had an *argument* about who was the better musician. **2.** An angry disagreement; quarrel. I was unhappy after the *argument* with my best friend. **3.** A reason or reasons given for or against something. The children's *argument* for getting new bicycles was that they needed them to deliver newspapers.
　ar·gu·ment (är′gyə mənt) *noun, plural* **arguments.**

arid　Getting very little rain; dry. A desert is an *arid* region.
　ar·id (ar′id) *adjective.*

arise　**1.** To rise from a sitting, kneeling, or lying position; get up. The audience *arose* and applauded at the end of the play. **2.** To move upward; rise. A mist slowly *arose* from the lake. **3.** To come into being; appear. Questions often *arise* in our minds as we read about new things.
　a·rise (ə rīz′) *verb,* **arose, arisen, arising.**

aristocracy　**1.** A class of people who are born into a high social position; nobility. Members of an aristocracy usually have more wealth and enjoy more privileges than the rest of society. **2.** Any group of people who are thought to be outstanding because of wealth, intelligence, or ability.
　ar·is·toc·ra·cy (ar′ə stok′rə sē) *noun, plural* **aristocracies.**

aristocrat　**1.** A person who belongs to an aristocracy. **2.** A person who has the tastes, manners, and attitudes of an aristocracy.
　a·ris·to·crat (ə ris′tə krat′) *noun, plural* **aristocrats.**

arithmetic　**1.** The science and technique of figuring with numbers. Arithmetic deals with addition, subtraction, multiplication, and division. **2.** The act of adding, subtracting, multiplying, or dividing. You are good at *arithmetic.*
　a·rith·me·tic (ə rith′mə tik′) *noun.*

Ariz.　An abbreviation for *Arizona.*

Arizona　A state in the southwestern United States. Its capital is Phoenix.
　Ar·i·zo·na (ar′ə zō′nə) *noun.*

Word History

　Arizona comes from an Indian word that means "a place where there is a little spring." This was the name of a part of the state where explorers found silver. The name became famous, and people began to use it for the whole area that became the state of Arizona.

---

ark　**1.** In the Bible, the ship that Noah built to save himself, his family, and two of every kind of animal from the flood God sent to punish humanity. **2.** A chest carried by the ancient Hebrews. It contained the two stone tablets on which the Ten Commandments were written. ▲ Another word that sounds like this is **arc.**
　ark (ärk) *noun.*

Ark.　An abbreviation for *Arkansas.*

Arkansas A state in the south-central United States. Its capital is Little Rock.
Ar·kan·sas (är′kən sô′) *noun.*

Word History

Arkansas was an Indian name for a tribe that lived near the Arkansas River. French explorers later used the word as the name of the river, and later still it was used as the name of the state.

arm¹ **1.** The part of the body between the shoulder and the wrist. **2.** Anything shaped or used like an arm. The *arms* of the green chair are loose.
arm (ärm) *noun, plural* **arms.**

arm² Any weapon. Guns and bombs are arms. *Noun.*
—**1.** To supply with weapons. The sheriff *armed* the deputies before they searched for the bandits. **2.** To supply with anything that protects or strengthens. A porcupine is *armed* with quills. *Verb.*
arm (ärm) *noun, plural* **arms;** *verb,* **armed, arming.**

armada A large group of warships.
ar·ma·da (är mä′də) *noun, plural* **armadas.**

armadillo A small animal that has a hard bony shell, a long snout, sharp claws, and a long tail. It digs into the ground looking for insects to eat. The armadillo is a mammal. It is found in South America and parts of the southern United States.
ar·ma·dil·lo (är′mə dil′ō) *noun, plural* **armadillos.**

armadillo

armaments The military forces, weapons, equipment, and supplies of a country.
ar·ma·ments (är′mə mənts) *plural noun.*

armchair A chair with parts on both sides that support a person's arms or elbows.
arm·chair (ärm′châr′) *noun, plural* **armchairs.**

armed forces All of a nation's military branches. The Army, Navy, Marine Corps, Air Force, and Coast Guard are the armed forces of the United States.

armistice A temporary stop in fighting agreed on by those who are fighting; truce.
ar·mi·stice (är′mə stis) *noun, plural* **armistices.**

armor **1.** A covering for the body, usually made from metal. In former times it was worn for protection during battle. **2.** Any protective covering. The metal plates on a tank or warship are armor. The hard shell of a turtle is armor.
ar·mor (är′mər) *noun.*

armor

armored Protected or equipped with armor. The pope rode in an *armored* car.
ar·mored (är′mərd) *adjective.*

armory **1.** A place where weapons are kept. **2.** A building in which a military unit is trained.
ar·mor·y (är′mə rē) *noun, plural* **armories.**

armpit The hollow part under the arm at the shoulder.
arm·pit (ärm′pit′) *noun, plural* **armpits.**

at; āpe; fär; câre; end; mē; it; īce; pîerce; hot; ōld; sông, fôrk; oil; out; up; ūse; rüle; pùll; tûrn; chin; sing; shop; thin; this; hw in white; zh in treasure. The symbol ə stands for the unstressed vowel sound in about, taken, pencil, lemon, and circus.

A

army 1. A large, organized group of soldiers who are armed and trained to fight on land. ▴ The word *army* is often capitalized when it means the branch of a country's armed forces that is trained to fight on land. In some nations, the Army also includes the Air Force. A United States *Army* recruiting poster was on the wall. 2. Any large group of people or things. An *army* of teenagers came to the concert to hear the famous singing group.
ar·my (är′mē) *noun, plural* **armies.**

aroma A pleasant or agreeable smell; fragrance. The bread we were baking gave off a delicious *aroma.*
a·ro·ma (ə rō′mə) *noun, plural* **aromas.**

arose Past tense of **arise.** I *arose* at seven o'clock this morning. Look up **arise** for more information.
a·rose (ə rōz′) *verb.*

around 1. In a circle or path that surrounds. I wore a belt *around* my waist. We walked *around* the block. 2. On all sides of. Flowers were planted *around* the house. 3. Here and there in. Tourists wandered *around* the city. 4. Somewhat near in place, time, or amount. Please stay *around* the house. I'll meet you *around* noon. That watch is worth *around* ten dollars. 5. On or to the other side of. Their house is *around* the corner. *Preposition.*
—1. In a circle. The wheel spun *around.* 2. In circumference. The column measures 3 feet *around.* 3. On all sides; in various directions; here and there. We looked *around* but couldn't see anyone. 4. Somewhere near. Why not stay *around* for a few minutes? 5. In or to the opposite direction. I turned *around* quickly. *Adverb.*
a·round (ə round′) *preposition; adverb.*

arouse 1. To cause an action or strong feeling; excite; stir. Your rudeness *aroused* everyone's anger. 2. To awaken. The alarm clock *aroused* me in time for school.
a·rouse (ə rouz′) *verb,* **aroused, arousing.**

arrange 1. To put in some kind of order or position. The teacher *arranged* the names of the children in alphabetical order. 2. To prepare for; plan. Who *arranged* this meeting? 3. To adapt a piece of music for instruments, voices, or a style of performance for which it was not originally written.
ar·range (ə rānj′) *verb,* **arranged, arranging.**

arrangement 1. The act of putting in order or position. *Arrangement* of the books took two hours. 2. Something arranged. They made a flower *arrangement* for the party. 3. **arrangements.** Plans or preparations. We made *arrangements* for our class party. 4. A piece of music that has been arranged. The band played a new *arrangement* of an old folk song.
ar·range·ment (ə rānj′mənt) *noun, plural* **arrangements.**

array 1. An orderly grouping or arrangement. The books in the shop window were in an attractive *array.* 2. A large or impressive group or display. There was quite an *array* of food at the banquet. 3. Beautiful or splendid clothing. The monarch appeared in royal *array. Noun.*
—1. To put in order or position. We *arrayed* the family photographs on the shelf. 2. To dress beautifully or splendidly. The couple were *arrayed* like a queen and king. *Verb.*
ar·ray (ə rā′) *noun, plural* **arrays;** *verb,* **arrayed, arraying.**

arrest 1. To seize and hold by authority of the law. The police officer *arrested* the suspect. 2. To stop or hold. We hope to *arrest* pollution in our country. 3. To catch and hold; attract and keep. The commotion *arrested* our attention. *Verb.*
—The act of seizing by authority of the law. The *arrest* of the suspects was reported on the morning newscast. *Noun.*
ar·rest (ə rest′) *verb,* **arrested, arresting;** *noun, plural* **arrests.**

arrival 1. The act of arriving. The reporters were waiting for the *arrival* of the president. 2. A person or thing that arrives or has arrived. New *arrivals* waited in line for their baggage at the airport.
ar·riv·al (ə rī′vəl) *noun, plural* **arrivals.**

arrive 1. To come to a place. We will *arrive* in Florida at midnight. 2. To come. The week of my cousin's visit has *arrived.*
• **to arrive at.** To come to or reach. Has the jury *arrived at* a decision yet?
ar·rive (ə rīv′) *verb,* **arrived, arriving.**

arrogant Having or showing too much pride or feelings of superiority. The *arrogant* visitors were surprised and upset when they lost the game to our school's team.
ar·ro·gant (ar′ə gənt) *adjective.*

arrow 1. A straight, slender stick that has a sharp point at one end and feathers at the other. An arrow is made to be shot from a bow. 2. Something that is like an arrow in shape. The road sign had an *arrow* to show which way traffic should go.
ar·row (ar′ō) *noun, plural* **arrows.**

arrowhead The pointed tip or head of an arrow.
ar·row·head (ar′ō hed′) *noun, plural* **arrowheads.**

arroyo A ditch with steep sides that has been cut in the ground by the force of running water; gully. Arroyos are dry most of the year.
ar·roy·o (ə roi′ō) *noun, plural* **arroyos.**

arsenal A place for making or storing weapons and ammunition.
ar·se·nal (är′sə nəl) *noun, plural* **arsenals.**

arsenic A gray, very poisonous substance that has no taste. Arsenic is used in rat, insect, and weed poisons. Arsenic is a chemical element.
ar·se·nic (är′sə nik) *noun.*

arson The crime of deliberately setting fire to a building or other property.
ar·son (är′sən) *noun.*

art 1. An activity by which one creates a work that has beauty or special meaning. Painting, sculpture, composing, and writing are forms of art. 2. The works created by this kind of activity. Murals, ballets, and poems are examples of such works. 3. A skill, craft, or occupation that requires study, practice, or experience. You have an *art* for making people feel at ease. The *art* of cooking came easily to me.
art (ärt) *noun, plural* **arts.**

artery 1. One of the blood vessels that carry blood away from the heart. 2. A main road or channel. This highway is the major *artery* between the two cities.
ar·ter·y (är′tə rē) *noun, plural* **arteries.**

arthritis A painful inflammation of a joint or joints of the body. People who suffer from arthritis often find certain activities very painful.
ar·thri·tis (är thrī′tis) *noun.*

artichoke A plant like a thistle, with large, coarse leaves and purple flowers. The immature greenish yellow flower head is cooked and eaten as a vegetable.
ar·ti·choke (är′ti chōk′) *noun, plural* **artichokes.**

artichoke

article 1. A composition written for a newspaper, magazine, or book. The scientist wrote an *article* on space travel for the encyclopedia. 2. A particular thing or object; item. Several *articles* were stolen from the house. 3. A separate section of a formal document. There are articles in treaties, constitutions, and contracts. 4. Any one of the words *a, an,* or *the* used to modify a noun. *A* and *an* are indefinite articles. *The* is a definite article.
ar·ti·cle (är′ti kəl) *noun, plural* **articles.**

articulate Able to speak or express oneself clearly. The professor was *articulate* on the subject of mathematics. *Adjective.*
—To speak or express oneself clearly. I was so upset that I could not *articulate* my feelings. *Verb.*
ar·tic·u·late (är tik′yə lit *for adjective;* är tik′yə lāt′ *for verb) adjective; verb,* **articulated, articulating.**

artificial 1. Made by people, not by nature; not natural. The *artificial* flowers were made of plastic. 2. Not sincere or true. The actor's smile seemed cold and *artificial.*
ar·ti·fi·cial (är′tə fish′əl) *adjective.*

artificial respiration The forcing of air into and out of the lungs of a person who has stopped breathing. This helps the person to start breathing normally again.

artillery 1. Large firearms that are too heavy to carry. They are fixed on stationary bases, supported by wheels, or mounted on vehicles with wheels or tracks. 2. The part of the army that uses such firearms.
ar·til·ler·y (är til′ə rē) *noun.*

artisan A person who is skilled in a particular craft. Carpenters, plumbers, and electricians are artisans.
ar·ti·san (är′tə zən) *noun, plural* **artisans.**

artist 1. A person who is skilled in painting, music, literature, or any other form of art. 2. A person whose work shows talent or skill. This restaurant's chef is an *artist.*
art·ist (är′tist) *noun, plural* **artists.**

artistic 1. Of or having to do with art or artists. My teacher has *artistic* interests. 2. Having or showing talent or skill. The dancer gave an *artistic* performance.
ar·tis·tic (är tis′tik) *adjective.*

---

at; āpe; fär; câre; end; mē; it; ice; pîerce; hot; ōld; sông, fôrk; oil; out; up; ūse; rüle; pùll; tûrn; chin; sing; shop; thin; this; hw in white; zh in treasure. The symbol ə stands for the unstressed vowel sound in about, taken, pencil, lemon, and circus.

as To the same amount or degree. The first movie was exciting, but the second was not *as* good. *Adverb.*
—**1.** To the same degree or extent that. They were proud *as* they could be. **2.** In the same way or manner that. Pronounce the word *as* I am pronouncing it. **3.** At the same time that; while or when. My parents arrived *as* we were leaving. **4.** For the reason that; because; since. *As* you are not ready, we will wait for you. *Conjunction.*
—In the manner, role, or function of. I'm speaking to you *as* a friend. *Preposition.*
• **as if** or **as though.** In the way it would be if. The children behaved *as if* they had no manners.
• **as of.** By or up to a certain time. *As of* Wednesday, we had read four books for our English class.
• **as yet.** Up to now; yet. Our new television set hasn't arrived *as yet.*
as (az) *adverb; conjunction; preposition.*

asbestos A grayish mineral. Its fibers can be woven or pressed into material that does not burn or conduct electricity. Fibers of asbestos can be dangerous if they enter the lungs.
as·bes·tos (as bes′təs *or* az bes′təs) *noun.*

ascend To move or go up; rise or climb. The elevator *ascended* to the twentieth floor. The hikers *ascended* the hill.
as·cend (ə send′) *verb,* **ascended, ascending.**

ascent **1.** The act of moving or going up. A heavy snowstorm made an *ascent* of the mountain impossible. **2.** A place or way where one ascends; upward slope. Ahead of us there was a steep *ascent.*
as·cent (ə sent′) *noun, plural* **ascents.**

ascertain To find out definitely; determine. The police quickly *ascertained* the whereabouts of the gang.
as·cer·tain (as′ər tān′) *verb,* **ascertained, ascertaining.**

ash¹ A small amount of grayish white powder left after something has burned. A pile of *ashes* was all that remained of the burned leaves.
ash (ash) *noun, plural* **ashes.**

ash² A tree that has a strong wood. Ash is used in construction and in making baseball bats.
ash (ash) *noun, plural* **ashes.**

ashamed **1.** Feeling shame; upset or guilty because one has done something wrong or silly. The student was *ashamed* for having failed the arithmetic test. **2.** Not wanting to do something because of fear or shame. I was *ashamed* to admit that I had broken my friend's bicycle.
a·shamed (ə shāmd′) *adjective.*

ashore On or to the shore or land. The children paddled the canoe *ashore.* Most of the ship's passengers are already *ashore.*
a·shore (ə shôr′) *adverb; adjective.*

Asia The largest continent. Asia lies between the Pacific Ocean and Europe and Africa.
A·sia (ā′zhə) *noun.*

Asian Of or having to do with Asia or the people of Asia. I am studying *Asian* history. *Adjective.*
—A person who was born or is living in Asia. *Noun.*
A·sian (ā′zhən) *adjective; noun, plural* **Asians.**

aside **1.** On or to one side. I turned my bike *aside* so the riders behind me could pass. **2.** Out of one's thoughts or consideration. Put your worries *aside* and have a good time! **3.** So as to be available at some future time. The librarian is keeping the book *aside* for me.
a·side (ə sīd′) *adverb.*

ask **1.** To put a question about something; inquire. We *asked* how to get to town. **2.** To put a question to. I *asked* a police officer where the nearest post office was. **3.** To call for an answer to. Don't *ask* that question again. **4.** To make a request. May I *ask* for your help? **5.** To invite. We *asked* our friends to the party.
ask (ask) *verb,* **asked, asking.**

askew At or to one side; turned the wrong way. The picture hung *askew.*
a·skew (ə skū′) *adverb; adjective.*

Leaf

ash²

asleep **1.** Not awake; sleeping. Be quiet because the baby is *asleep.* **2.** Without feeling; numb. My foot is *asleep. Adjective.*

—Into a condition of sleep. The children fell *asleep* while they were watching television. *Adverb.*

a·sleep (ə slēp′) *adjective; adverb.*

asparagus The young, green shoots of a garden plant. They are shaped like spears and have large, scaly leaves at the tip. Asparagus is cooked and eaten as a vegetable.

as·par·a·gus (ə spar′ə gəs) *noun.*

asparagus

aspect 1. A particular way in which something can be looked at and thought about. The mayor's committee considered every *aspect* of the traffic problem. 2. Look; appearance. The deserted house had a gloomy *aspect.*

as·pect (as′pekt) *noun, plural* **aspects.**

aspen A tree whose leaves shake in the slightest breeze. Its wood is used to make pulp for paper. An aspen is a kind of poplar.

as·pen (as′pən) *noun, plural* **aspens.**

asphalt A brown or black substance found in the ground or obtained when petroleum is refined. It is mixed with sand or gravel and is used to pave roads.

as·phalt (as′fôlt) *noun.*

aspire To want or try very strongly to achieve some goal; seek ambitiously. My cousin *aspires* to a career in medicine.

as·pire (ə spīr′) *verb,* **aspired, aspiring.**

aspirin A kind of drug used to ease pain and reduce fevers. Some people take aspirin when they have a cold or a headache.

as·pi·rin (as′pər in) *noun, plural* **aspirins.**

ass 1. An animal that is closely related to the horse but is smaller and has longer ears; donkey. 2. A stupid or silly person.

ass (as) *noun, plural* **asses.**

assassin A murderer. Assassins are often paid or chosen to kill their victims. The victims are usually important or famous people.

as·sas·sin (ə sas′in) *noun, plural* **assassins.**

assassinate To murder an important or famous person. The plot to *assassinate* the ambassador was foiled by the police.

as·sas·si·nate (ə sas′ə nāt′) *verb,* **assassinated, assassinating.**

assault 1. A sudden, violent attack. The troops retreated under the *assault* of the enemy. 2. An unlawful attempt or threat to do physical harm to someone. The suspect was charged with *assault. Noun.*
—To make an assault on; attack. The soldiers *assaulted* the fort. *Verb.*

as·sault (ə sôlt′) *noun, plural* **assaults;** *verb,* **assaulted, assaulting.**

assemble 1. To come or bring together. A crowd began to *assemble* for the rally. I have *assembled* a large shell collection. 2. To put or fit together. We had to *assemble* the parts of the bicycle.

as·sem·ble (ə sem′bəl) *verb,* **assembled, assembling.**

assembly 1. A group of people gathered together for some purpose. An *assembly* of school principals met to discuss new topics in education. 2. A group of people who make laws. In some states of the United States, one of the houses of the legislature is called the **Assembly.** 3. The act of putting or fitting together. Robots were used for the hazardous jobs in the *assembly* of the automobiles. 4. A group of parts that fit or work together. The plane was grounded when a crack in the wing *assembly* was discovered.

as·sem·bly (ə sem′blē) *noun, plural* **assemblies.**

assembly line A line of workers and machines used for putting together a product step by step in a factory. As the product is moved along an assembly line, a part is added or some other work is done until the product is finished.

assembly line

at; āpe; fär; câre; end; mē; it; īce; pîerce; hot; ōld; sông, fôrk; oil; out; up; ūse; rüle; pull; tûrn; chin; sing; shop; thin; <u>th</u>is; hw in white; zh in treasure. The symbol ə stands for the unstressed vowel sound in about, taken, pencil, lemon, and circus.

assent To express approval; agree; consent. The town council *assented* to changes in the budget. *Verb.*
—Approval, agreement, or consent. The community gave its *assent,* and the new traffic light was added at the intersection. *Noun.*
as·sent (ə sent′) *verb,* **assented, assenting.** *noun.*

assert 1. To state in a positive way. The scientists *asserted* that their theory was correct. 2. To insist on; claim. As children mature, they feel a need to *assert* their independence.
as·sert (ə sûrt′) *verb,* **asserted, asserting.**

assess 1. To set the value of property for taxation. That farm is *assessed* at $100,000. 2. To set the amount of a fine or tax. The judge *assessed* a fine of fifty dollars. 3. To charge or tax. The library *assesses* a person five cents for each day a book is overdue.
as·sess (ə ses′) *verb,* **assessed, assessing.**

asset 1. Something valuable or useful; advantage. Being tall is a great *asset* for a basketball player. 2. **assets.** Property and other things of value that belong to a person or organization. Their *assets* include a house, a car, and a boat.
as·set (as′et) *noun, plural* **assets.**

assign 1. To give out as a task. Our teacher will *assign* a different science project to each student. 2. To appoint. The mayor *assigned* three people to the committee on education. 3. To fix definitely; name. The coach *assigned* the date for the championship game.
as·sign (ə sīn′) *verb,* **assigned, assigning.**

assignment 1. Something that is assigned. My arithmetic *assignment* is to do ten multiplication problems. 2. The act of assigning. The company's president is responsible for the *assignment* of tasks to employees.
as·sign·ment (ə sīn′mənt) *noun, plural* **assignments.**

assist To help; aid. All the people in the town got together to *assist* the family whose house had burned down.
as·sist (ə sist′) *verb,* **assisted, assisting.**

assistance The act of assisting; help; aid. We will need some *assistance* in carrying the packages upstairs.
as·sist·ance (ə sis′təns) *noun.*

assistant A person who assists; helper; aide. The manager's *assistant* helps to run the store. *Noun.*
—Acting to assist another person. The head football coach has four *assistant* coaches. *Adjective.*
as·sist·ant (ə sis′tənt) *noun, plural* **assistants;** *adjective.*

associate 1. To connect in one's mind. I always *associate* summer with picnics at the beach. 2. To join as a friend, companion, or partner. At first the new student was too shy to *associate* with the rest of us. *Verb.*
—A friend, companion, or partner. One of the *associates* in the business left to work for another company. *Noun.*
—1. Closely connected with another or others in work, responsibility, or status. The two *associate* judges went to the same law school. 2. Having or giving some, but not all, rights, and privileges. My parents have an *associate* membership in the club. *Adjective.*
as·so·ci·ate (ə sō′shē āt′ *or* ə sō′sē āt′ *for verb;* ə sō′shē it *or* ə sō′sē it *for noun; adjective*) *verb,* **associated, associating;** *noun, plural* **associates;** *adjective.*

association 1. A group of people joined together for a common purpose. My friends and I belong to an *association* that helps preserve forests. 2. The act of associating or the condition of being associated. My friends and I are proud of our long *association.* 3. A thought or feeling one has in connection with a person, place, or thing. This house has many happy *associations* for me. *Noun.*
as·so·ci·a·tion (ə sō′sē ā′shən *or* ə sō′shē ā′shən) *noun, plural* **associations.**

associative property A characteristic of addition and multiplication that allows you to add or multiply three or more numbers in any order and still get the same answer. For example, $(6 + 5) + 2$ gives the same answer as $5 + (6 + 2)$, and $(2 \times 3) \times 4$ gives the same answer as $3 \times (4 \times 2)$.
as·so·ci·a·tive property (ə sō′shē ā′tiv *or* ə sō′sē ā′tiv).

assortment A collection of different kinds. That store carries a large *assortment* of sports equipment.
as·sort·ment (ə sôrt′mənt) *noun, plural* **assortments.**

assume 1. To take for granted; suppose. I *assume* we will arrive on time. 2. To take upon oneself; undertake. You will have to *assume* the responsibility of feeding the dog. 3. To take for oneself; seize. The military leaders *assumed* control of the country. 4. To give a false impression of; pretend. I *assumed* a lack of interest in the party because I had not been invited.
as·sume (ə süm′) *verb,* **assumed, assuming.**

assumption 1. The act of taking for granted. A member of a jury must make the *assumption* that a person is innocent until proven guilty. 2. Something that is taken for granted. Your *assumption* turned out to be wrong.
as·sump·tion (ə sump′shən) *noun, plural* **assumptions.**

assurance 1. A statement that is supposed to make a person certain or sure. We had their *assurance* that they would help with our project. 2. Freedom from doubt; certainty. 3. Confidence in one's own ability. The speaker had the *assurance* that comes from knowledge and experience.
as·sur·ance (ə shùr′əns) *noun, plural* **assurances.**

assure 1. To state positively. I *assure* you that I won't be late. 2. To make certain or sure. Their hard work *assured* the success of the project. 3. To give confidence to. We *assured* the child that the dog was friendly.
as·sure (ə shùr′) *verb,* **assured, assuring.**

aster A flower like a daisy that has white, pink, purple, or yellow petals around a yellow center. Asters bloom in the fall.
as·ter (as′tər) *noun, plural* **asters.**

asters

asterisk A mark (*) shaped like a star that is used in printing or writing to tell the reader to look somewhere else on the page for more information.
as·ter·isk (as′tə risk′) *noun, plural* **asterisks.**

astern 1. At or toward the rear of a ship. The ship's crew gathered *astern* to watch the sunset. 2. Behind a ship. A sailboat followed *astern.* 3. Backward. The ship pulled *astern* into the dock.
a·stern (ə stûrn′) *adverb.*

asteroid Any of the thousands of small planets that revolve around the sun. Most of them are between the orbits of Mars and Jupiter. Some asteroids are less than 1 mile wide. Others are as big as 500 miles wide.
as·ter·oid (as′tə roid′) *noun, plural* **asteroids.**

asthma A disease that makes it difficult to breathe and causes wheezing and coughing. Sometimes asthma is caused by an allergy.
asth·ma (az′mə) *noun.*

astir In motion; active. Very few people were *astir* at dawn.
a·stir (ə stûr′) *adjective.*

astonish To surprise very much; amaze. The news that I had won the contest *astonished* me.
as·ton·ish (ə ston′ish) *verb,* **astonished, astonishing.**

astonishment Great surprise; amazement. The child was filled with *astonishment* when the magician pulled a rabbit out of a hat.
as·ton·ish·ment (ə ston′ish mənt) *noun.*

astound To surprise very much; amaze; astonish. The first flight in outer space *astounded* the whole world.
as·tound (ə stound′) *verb,* **astounded, astounding.**

astray Off the right way or path. The family was sad because their dog had gone *astray* and gotten lost.
a·stray (ə strā′) *adverb.*

astride With one leg on each side of.
a·stride (ə strīd′) *preposition.*

sitting **astride** a rocking horse

astrology The study of the influence that the stars and planets are supposed to have on people and events.
as·trol·o·gy (ə strol′ə jē) *noun.*

at; āpe; fär; câre; end; mē; it; īce; pîerce; hot; ōld; sông, fôrk; oil; out; up; ūse; rüle; pùll; tûrn; chin; sing; shop; thin; this; hw in white; zh in treasure. The symbol ə stands for the unstressed vowel sound in about, taken, pencil, lemon, and circus.

astronaut   A person trained to fly in a spacecraft. The *astronauts* landed safely on the moon.
as·tro·naut (as′trə nôt′) *noun, plural* **astronauts.**

Word History

The word **astronaut** is made up of two Greek words that mean "star" and "sailor." An astronaut is thought of as sailing among the stars.

---

astronomer   A person who works or specializes in astronomy.
as·tron·o·mer (ə stron′ə mər) *noun, plural* **astronomers.**

astronomical   **1.** Of or having to do with astronomy. The spacecraft radioed *astronomical* information to earth.   **2.** Very great or large. The cost of the yacht was *astronomical.*
as·tro·nom·i·cal (as′trə nom′i kəl) *adjective.*

astronomy   The science that deals with the sun, moon, stars, planets, and other heavenly bodies.
as·tron·o·my (ə stron′ə mē) *noun.*

asylum   **1.** A place where people who cannot care for themselves receive care. People who are mentally ill may live in an asylum.   **2.** A place of refuge or protection. A church may be an asylum where criminals are safe from arrest.   **3.** Protection given to a refugee. Some people leave their own country to seek *asylum* in another country.
a·sy·lum (ə sī′ləm) *noun, plural* **asylums.**

at   **1.** In, on, or by. I stood *at* my parents' side. The race started *at* the top of the hill.   **2.** To or toward. Look *at* this picture.   **3.** In a place or condition of. The children are *at* home. The nations were *at* war.   **4.** On or near the time or age of. We rise *at* dawn. Some people retire *at* sixty-five.   **5.** In the amount of; for. The car was sold *at* a low price.
at (at) *preposition.*

ate   Past tense of **eat.** We *ate* all the pie. Look up **eat** for more information. ▲ Another word that sounds like this is **eight.**
ate (āt) *verb.*

atheist   A person who does not believe that God exists.
a·the·ist (ā′thē ist) *noun, plural* **atheists.**

athlete   A person who is trained in sports or other exercises that take strength, skill, and speed. Baseball players, hockey players, swimmers, skiers, and runners are athletes.
ath·lete (ath′lēt) *noun, plural* **athletes.**

athlete's foot   An infection of the foot caused by a fungus. Athlete's foot causes blisters that itch.

athletic   **1.** Of or having to do with an athlete or athletics. Our school has just bought new *athletic* equipment.   **2.** Active and strong. My grandparents are very *athletic;* they love to swim and ice-skate.
ath·let·ic (ath let′ik) *adjective.*

athletics   Athletic games, sports, or activities. *Athletics* are often an important part of a student's education.
ath·let·ics (ath let′iks) *plural noun.*

Atlantic   The ocean that separates Europe and Africa from North America and South America. This is also called the **Atlantic Ocean** *Noun.*
—Of, on, near, or having to do with the Atlantic Ocean. We sailed down the *Atlantic* coast of Florida. *Adjective.*
At·lan·tic (at lan′tik) *noun; adjective.*

atlas   A book of maps. We took a road *atlas* along when we drove to Canada.
at·las (at′ləs) *noun, plural* **atlases.**

Word History

In Greek mythology, *Atlas* was a giant who was made to hold the sky on his shoulders. In the front of early books of maps, there was often a picture of Atlas holding up the sky. So people began to call a book of this kind an **atlas.**

---

atmosphere   **1.** The layer of gases that surrounds the Earth. The atmosphere is made up of oxygen, nitrogen, carbon dioxide, and other gases. Outer space lies beyond the Earth's atmosphere.   **2.** The layer of gases that surrounds any heavenly body. Scientists do not think people could live in the *atmosphere* of Mars.   **3.** The air in a particular place. This attic has a hot, stuffy *atmosphere.*   **4.** Character or mood. Our house has a happy *atmosphere* at holiday time.   **5.** Environment; surroundings. We moved to the country because we wanted to live in a quiet *atmosphere.*
at·mos·phere (at′məs fîr′) *noun, plural* **atmospheres.**

atmospheric   Of, in, or having to do with the atmosphere. Severe *atmospheric* disturbances were reported by the weather bureau.
at·mos·pher·ic (at′məs fer′ik) *adjective.*

atoll A coral island or string of coral islands that surrounds a lagoon.
at·oll (at′ôl *or* ə tôl′) *noun, plural* **atolls.**

atom **1.** The smallest particle of a chemical element that has all the properties of that element. An atom has a central nucleus of protons and neutrons that is surrounded by electrons. All matter in the universe is made up of atoms. **2.** Any very small particle; tiny bit. There was not an *atom* of sense in their solution to the problem.
at·om (at′əm) *noun, plural* **atoms.**

atomic **1.** Of or having to do with an atom or atoms. Those scientists are performing *atomic* research. **2.** Using atomic energy. An *atomic* submarine can stay underwater for long periods of time.
a·tom·ic (ə tom′ik) *adjective.*

atomic bomb A very powerful bomb. Its great force and the radiation it produces come from the energy released by the splitting of atoms. This bomb is also called an **atom bomb.**

atomic energy A term that is sometimes used for **nuclear energy.** Look up **nuclear energy** for more information.

atone To make up for a wrong; make amends. I *atoned* for my rude behavior by apologizing to them.
a·tone (ə tōn′) *verb,* **atoned, atoning.**

a bird **atop** a hat

atop On top of. There were ten candles *atop* my birthday cake.
a·top (ə top′) *preposition.*

atrocious **1.** Very bad or unpleasant. Their manners are *atrocious.* What *atrocious* weather we've been having! **2.** Cruel, brutal, or wicked.
a·tro·cious (ə trō′shəs) *adjective.*

attach **1.** To fasten. You can *attach* the sign to the wall with nails. **2.** To add or include at the end. They *attached* their signatures to the document. **3.** To bind by a strong feeling. I am very *attached* to my family. **4.** To think of as belonging; assign. We *attach* great importance to our parents' advice.
at·tach (ə tach′) *verb,* **attached, attaching.**

attachment **1.** The act of attaching. The *attachment* of the wrecked car to the tow truck was difficult. **2.** A strong feeling of affection or devotion. The children had a great *attachment* to their dog. **3.** A part or device that is connected to a thing. The camera has an *attachment* for winding the film automatically.
at·tach·ment (ə tach′mənt) *noun, plural* **attachments.**

attack **1.** To begin to fight against with violence; assault. The enemy troops *attacked* the town at dawn. **2.** To write or speak against. The newspaper editorial *attacked* the mayor's speech. **3.** To begin to work on with energy. We *attacked* the job of setting up the tent. **4.** To act harmfully on. A plant disease *attacked* many of the trees in our yard. *Verb.*
—**1.** The act of attacking. The *attack* on the fort came without warning. **2.** A sudden occurrence of sickness or disease. A doctor was called when my cousin had an *attack* of asthma. *Noun.*
at·tack (ə tak′) *verb,* **attacked, attacking;** *noun, plural* **attacks.**

attain **1.** To get by hard work; achieve. I *attained* my ambition to work on the school newspaper. **2.** To arrive at; reach. My grandparents have *attained* the ages of ninety and ninety-one.
at·tain (ə tān′) *verb,* **attained, attaining.**

attempt To make an effort; try. The kitten *attempted* to follow the squirrel up the tree. *Verb.*
—**1.** A try; effort. We made an *attempt* to learn how to ski. **2.** An attack. The traitor

at; āpe; fär; câre; end; mē; it; īce; pîerce; hot; ōld; sông, fôrk; oil; out; up; ūse; rüle; půll; tûrn; chin; sing; shop; thin; <u>th</u>is; hw in white; zh in treasure. The symbol ə stands for the unstressed vowel sound in about, taken, pencil, lemon, and circus.

made an *attempt* on the monarch's life. *Noun.*
> **at·tempt** (ə tempt′) *verb,* **attempted, attempting;** *noun, plural* **attempts.**

attend 1. To be present at. I have to *attend* a club meeting this afternoon. 2. To be with as a helper or companion. Three aides *attended* the ambassador. 3. To take care of. Doctors and nurses *attended* the victims of the accident. 4. To listen carefully. *Attend* to what the doctor tells you. 5. To devote oneself. *Attend* to your work.
> **at·tend** (ə tend′) *verb,* **attended, attending.**

attendance 1. The act of being present. Your *attendance* at band practice was poor last year. 2. The number of people present. The *attendance* at the baseball game was over 500.
> **at·ten·dance** (ə ten′dəns) *noun.*

attendant A person who takes care of someone or provides service to other people. The *attendant* at the park showed us where we could rent a canoe.
> **at·ten·dant** (ə ten′dənt) *noun, plural* **attendants.**

attention 1. The act or power of watching, listening, or concentrating. The magician had the children's *attention.* The noise called our *attention* to the airplane flying above us. 2. Careful thought with the intention to act; consideration. Pollution of our rivers and lakes requires immediate *attention.* 3. Care, kindness, and affection. The children gave their grandparents much *attention.* 4. attentions. Kind, polite, or affectionate acts. The host's many *attentions* made every guest at the party feel welcome. 5. A military position in which a person stands very straight, with arms at the sides, heels together, and eyes looking ahead. The troops stood at *attention* while waiting for the parade to start.
> **at·ten·tion** (ə ten′shən) *noun, plural* **attentions.**

attentive 1. Paying attention. The audience was *attentive* throughout the concert. 2. Considerate; thoughtful; courteous. When you have a party, you try to be *attentive* to your guests.
> **at·ten·tive** (ə ten′tiv) *adjective.*

attest To be the proof of; show clearly. Your high grades *attest* your good study habits.
> **at·test** (ə test′) *verb,* **attested, attesting.**

attic The space just below the roof of a house. We use our *attic* to store trunks of old clothes.
> **at·tic** (at′ik) *noun, plural* **attics.**

attire Apparel; clothing. The queen and king were clothed in royal *attire. Noun.*
> —To dress; clothe. The children were *attired* in their best clothes. *Verb.*
> **at·tire** (ə tīr′) *noun; verb,* **attired, attiring.**

attitude 1. A way of thinking, acting, or feeling. Your *attitude* toward school is more enthusiastic than mine. 2. A position of the body. The body's attitude often shows the feelings or thoughts of a person.
> **at·ti·tude** (at′i tüd′ *or* at′i tūd′) *noun, plural* **attitudes.**

attorney A lawyer. An *attorney* presented the case to the judge and jury.
> **at·tor·ney** (ə tûr′nē) *noun, plural* **attorneys.**

attract 1. To cause to come near; draw by physical force. A magnet will *attract* an iron bar. 2. To draw by gaining the attention or admiration of. The beautiful scenery in these mountains *attracts* many tourists.
> **at·tract** (ə trakt′) *verb,* **attracted, attracting.**

the magnet **attracts** metal

attraction 1. The act or power of attracting. The *attraction* of the magnet drew the nails across the table. 2. A person or thing that attracts. The clowns were the main *attraction* at the circus.
> **at·trac·tion** (ə trak′shən) *noun, plural* **attractions.**

attractive Having a quality that attracts people; appealing; pleasing. Friendly people are naturally *attractive.*
> **at·trac·tive** (ə trak′tiv) *adjective.*

attribute To think of as belonging to or being caused by. We *attribute* stubbornness to mules. The coach *attributed* the team's victory to training and practice. *Verb.*
> —A quality that is thought of as belonging to a person or thing; characteristic. One of your

greatest *attributes* is your kindness. *Noun.*
at·trib·ute (ə trib′ūt *for verb;* at′rə būt′ *for noun*) *verb,* **attributed, attributing;** *noun, plural* **attributes.**

auction A public sale at which things are sold to the person who offers the most money. My cousin bid five dollars for a rocking chair at the village *auction. Noun.*
—To sell at an auction. Before we moved to our new house, my parents *auctioned* off some of our old furniture. *Verb.*
auc·tion (ôk′shən) *noun, plural* **auctions;** *verb,* **auctioned, auctioning.**

audible Loud enough to be heard. The music became *audible* after you turned up the volume of the radio.
au·di·ble (ô′də bəl) *adjective.*

audience 1. A group of people gathered to hear or see something. The *audience* applauded at the end of the play. 2. All the people who give attention to something. That television program has a large *audience.* 3. A formal meeting with a person of very high rank. The diplomat was granted an *audience* with the king and queen.
au·di·ence (ô′dē əns) *noun, plural* **audiences.**

audio Of or having to do with sound or how sound is recorded, sent, or received. I bought new *audio* equipment because my old stereo no longer worked.
au·di·o (ô′dē ō′) *adjective.*

audition A short performance that demonstrates the ability of an actor, singer, or other performer. If I give a successful *audition,* I might be asked to play in the band. *Noun.*
—To perform or test in an audition. The young actor *auditioned* for a small role in the play. The conductor *auditioned* three pianists this afternoon. *Verb.*
au·di·tion (ô dish′ən) *noun, plural* **auditions;** *verb,* **auditioned, auditioning.**

auditorium A large room or building where a group of people can gather. The concert will be in the school *auditorium.*
au·di·to·ri·um (ô′di tôr′ē əm) *noun, plural* **auditoriums.**

auditory Having to do with hearing or the organs of hearing.
au·di·to·ry (ô′di tôr′ē) *adjective.*

Aug. An abbreviation for *August.*

auger A tool for boring holes in wood.
au·ger (ô′gər) *noun, plural* **augers.**

augment To make greater; increase. Some people *augment* their incomes by working at two jobs.
aug·ment (ôg ment′) *verb,* **augmented, augmenting.**

August The eighth month of the year. August has thirty-one days.
Au·gust (ô′gəst) *noun.*

Word History

The Romans named the month of **August** in honor of *Augustus* Caesar, the first emperor of Rome.

auk Any of various diving birds that live along northern sea coasts. Auks have webbed feet, short wings that are used as paddles in swimming, and black and white feathers.
auk (ôk) *noun, plural* **auks.**

aunt 1. The sister of one's mother or father. 2. The wife of one's uncle. ▲ Another word that sounds like this is **ant.**
aunt (ant *or* änt) *noun, plural* **aunts.**

auricle Either of the two upper chambers of the heart. The auricles receive blood from the veins and send it to the ventricles.
au·ri·cle (ôr′i kəl) *noun, plural* **auricles.**

aurora borealis Shining bands of lights sometimes seen in the sky at night, especially in areas near the North Pole. The lights are caused by particles from the sun that strike the Earth's atmosphere. Another name for this is **northern lights.**
au·ro·ra bo·re·al·is (ə rôr′ə bôr′ē al′is)

Word History

Aurora borealis is a Latin phrase meaning "dawn of the north." The colored lights in the sky reminded people of the light of early dawn.

Australia 1. A continent southeast of Asia, between the Indian Ocean and the Pacific Ocean. It is the smallest continent. 2. A country made up of this continent and the island of Tasmania.
Aus·tra·lia (ô strāl′yə) *noun.*

Australian A person who was born in or is a citizen of Australia. *Noun.*
—Of or having to do with Australia or its people. *Adjective.*

at; āpe; fär; câre; end; mē; it; ice; pîerce; hot; ōld; sông, fôrk; oil; out; up; ūse; rüle; pùll; tûrn; chin; sing; shop; thin; this; hw in white; zh in treasure. The symbol ə stands for the unstressed vowel sound in about, taken, pencil, lemon, and circus.

Aus·tra·lian (ô strāl′yən) *noun, plural* **Australians;** *adjective.*

Austria A country in central Europe.
Aus·tri·a (ôs′trē ə) *noun.*

authentic **1.** Worthy of belief; reliable; true; correct. This book gives an *authentic* account of the Civil War. **2.** Being what it appears or claims to be; real; genuine. These are *authentic* signatures of famous people.
au·then·tic (ô then′tik) *adjective.*

author A person who has written a book, story, play, article, or other work of literature.
au·thor (ô′thər) *noun, plural* **authors.**

authoritative **1.** Worthy of belief; reliable. No one believed the rumor because it did not come from an *authoritative* source. **2.** Showing authority. The principal has an *authoritative* manner.
au·thor·i·ta·tive (ə thôr′i tā′tiv) *adjective.*

authority **1.** The power or right to make decisions, command, act, or control. The captain has *authority* over the sailors on a ship. **2.** A person or group having this power or right. We reported the car accident to the *authorities.* **3.** A good source of information or facts. That professor is an *authority* on the life of Abraham Lincoln.
au·thor·i·ty (ə thôr′i tē) *noun, plural* **authorities.**

authorize **1.** To give authority to. My parents *authorized* the real estate agent to sell our house. **2.** To approve officially. The governor *authorized* the building of the new highway.
au·thor·ize (ô′thə rīz′) *verb,* **authorized, authorizing.**

auto A short form of the word **automobile.** Look up **automobile** for more information.
au·to (ô′tō) *noun, plural* **autos.**

autobiography The story of a person's own life written by that person.
au·to·bi·og·ra·phy (ô′tə bī og′rə fē) *noun, plural* **autobiographies.**

autograph A person's signature written in that person's own handwriting. *Noun.*
—To write one's name in one's own handwriting. Will you *autograph* a copy of your book for me? *Verb.*
au·to·graph (ô′tə graf′) *noun, plural* **autographs;** *verb,* **autographed, autographing.**

automatic **1.** Operating by itself. We have an *automatic* dishwasher. **2.** Done without a person's control. Digestion is an *automatic* action of the body.
au·to·mat·ic (ô′tə mat′ik) *adjective.*

automation The development and use of machines to do jobs that used to be done by people. Automobiles are now built by *automation.*
au·to·ma·tion (ô′tə mā′shən) *noun.*

automobile A vehicle that usually has four wheels and is powered by an engine that uses gasoline; car. An automobile is used mainly to carry passengers.
au·to·mo·bile (ô′tə mə bēl′) *noun, plural* **automobiles.**

autopsy A medical examination of a dead body to find the cause of death.
au·top·sy (ô′top sē) *noun, plural* **autopsies.**

autumn The season of the year coming between summer and winter; fall. In *autumn* the leaves fell from the trees.
au·tumn (ô′təm) *noun, plural* **autumns.**

autumn in the Northeast

auxiliary **1.** Giving aid or support. This sailboat has an *auxiliary* engine in case there is no wind. **2.** Additional; extra. The mayor put *auxiliary* police on duty during the president's visit. *Adjective.*
—A person, group, or thing giving aid or support. Our town has a firefighters' *auxiliary.* Noun.
aux·il·ia·ry (ôg zil′yə rē) *adjective; noun, plural* **auxiliaries.**

auxiliary verb A verb that helps a main verb to express an action or condition. *Be, have, do, can, must,* and *may* can be used as auxiliary verbs. In the sentence "They must have returned by now," the verbs "must" and "have" are used as auxiliary verbs. An auxiliary verb is also called a **helping verb.**

available **1.** Possible to get. There are still a few seats *available* for the game. Strawberries become available in early summer. **2.** Ready for use or service. The telephone is now *available.*
a·vail·a·ble (ə vā′lə bəl) *adjective.*

avalanche The swift, sudden fall of a mass of snow, ice, earth, or rocks down a mountain slope. The *avalanche* completely covered the village with mud.
   av·a·lanche (av'ə lanch') *noun, plural* **avalanches.**

Ave. An abbreviation for *Avenue* used in a written address.

avenue A street. Avenues are often wider than other streets.
   av·e·nue (av'ə nū' *or* av'ə nü') *noun, plural* **avenues.**

average **1.** A number found by adding two or more quantities together, and then dividing the sum by the number of quantities; mean. The *average* of 2, 4, 6, and 8 is 5. **2.** The usual amount or kind. This year's rainfall came close to the *average. Noun.*
   —**1.** Found by figuring an average. The *average* grade on the test was 81. **2.** Usual; typical; ordinary. You are of *average* height and weight. *Adjective.*
   —**1.** To find the average of. I *averaged* my three bowling scores and got 126. **2.** To have as an average. That basketball player *averages* twenty points a game. *Verb.*
   av·er·age (av'ər ij *or* av'rij) *noun, plural* **averages;** *adjective; verb,* **averaged, averaging.**

avert **1.** To turn away or aside. *Avert* your eyes from the glare of the sun. **2.** To prevent; avoid. The driver *averted* a crash by steering carefully to the side of the road.
   a·vert (ə vûrt') *verb,* **averted, averting.**

aviation The science or techniques of flying aircraft.
   a·vi·a·tion (ā'vē ā'shən) *noun.*

aviator A person who flies an airplane or other aircraft; pilot.
   a·vi·a·tor (ā'vē ā'tər) *noun, plural* **aviators.**

avid **1.** Very eager or enthusiastic. I am an *avid* fan of mystery novels. **2.** Having a great desire; greedy. Some people are so *avid* for wealth that they commit crimes to get it.
   av·id (av'id) *adjective.*

avocado A tropical fruit that is shaped like a pear. It has a dark green skin, a large seed, and yellowish green pulp. Avocados grow on trees.

avocado

av·o·ca·do (av'ə kä'dō) *noun, plural* **avocados.**

avoid To keep away from. We took a back road to *avoid* the heavy highway traffic.
   a·void (ə void') *verb,* **avoided, avoiding.**

await **1.** To wait for. The parents had long *awaited* the day of their children's graduation from college. **2.** To be ready for; be in store for. Many changes *await* you in your new school.
   a·wait (ə wāt') *verb,* **awaited, awaiting.**

awake To wake up. The barking of the dog *awoke* everyone in the house. *Verb.*
   —**1.** Not asleep. We were *awake* most of the night because of the noise outside. **2.** Alert; aware. Are you *awake* to the risks in the plan? *Adjective.*
   a·wake (ə wāk') *verb,* **awoke** or **awaked, awaking;** *adjective.*

awaken To wake up. I *awakened* at dawn.
   a·wak·en (ə wā'kən) *verb,* **awakened, awakening.**

award **1.** To give after careful thought. The judges *awarded* my dog first prize at the dog show. **2.** To give because of a legal decision. The jury *awarded* money to the people who had been injured in the accident. *Verb.*
   —Something that is given after careful thought. My cousin received the *award* for writing the best essay. *Noun.*
   a·ward (ə wôrd') *verb,* **awarded, awarding;** *noun, plural* **awards.**

aware Knowing or realizing; conscious. We were not *aware* that you were planning a party for us.
   a·ware (ə wâr') *adjective.*

away **1.** From this or that place. The frightened rabbit hopped *away*. **2.** At a distance. They stood far *away* from us. **3.** In another direction; aside. I turned *away* to hide my tears. **4.** From or out of one's possession or use. Throw *away* that old coat. **5.** At or to an end; out of existence. The sound of footsteps faded *away*. **6.** Without interruption; continuously. I worked *away* at my typewriter for two hours. *Adverb.*
   —**1.** Distant. The town is 3 miles *away*. **2.** Absent; gone. My cousin has been *away* for three weeks. *Adjective.*
   a·way (ə wā') *adverb; adjective.*

at; āpe; fär; câre; end; mē; it; īce; pîerce; hot; ōld; sông, fôrk; oil; out; up; ūse; rüle; pǔll; tûrn; chin; sing; shop; thin; this; hw in white; zh in treasure. The symbol ə stands for the unstressed vowel sound in about, taken, pencil, lemon, and circus.

awe Great wonder, fear, and respect. They read with *awe* the news of the astronauts' landing on the moon. *Noun.*
—To fill with awe. We were *awed* by the violence of the thunderstorm. *Verb.*
awe (ô) *noun; verb,* **awed, awing.**

awesome Causing wonder or fear. The huge whale was an *awesome* sight.
awe·some (ô′səm) *adjective.*

awful **1.** Causing fear, dread, or awe; terrible. The earthquake was an *awful* disaster. **2.** Very bad. I thought that movie was *awful.* **3.** Very large; great. A million dollars is an *awful* lot of money.
aw·ful (ô′fəl) *adjective.*

awfully **1.** Very much; badly; terribly. My knee hurt *awfully* where I had scraped it. **2.** Very. I am *awfully* glad you won the prize.
aw·ful·ly (ô′fə lē *or* ô′flē) *adverb.*

awhile For a short time. They rested *awhile* before playing another game of tennis.
a·while (ə hwīl′ *or* ə wīl′) *adverb.*

awkward **1.** Lacking grace or poise in movement or behavior; clumsy or uncomfortable. The colt was *awkward* and had trouble standing up. **2.** Difficult or embarrassing. It was an *awkward* moment when the teacher found out that I hadn't done my homework. **3.** Difficult to use or handle. The piano was an *awkward* piece of furniture to move.
awk·ward (ôk′wərd) *adjective.*

awl A pointed tool used for making small holes in leather or wood. ▲ Another word that sounds like this is **all.**
awl (ôl) *noun, plural* **awls.**

awning A cover of canvas, metal, or other material that serves as a small roof over a door or window. An awning is used as a shelter from the sun or rain.
aw·ning (ô′ning) *noun, plural* **awnings.**

awnings

awoke Past tense of **awake.** I *awoke* at seven o'clock this morning. Look up **awake** for more information.
a·woke (ə wōk′) *verb.*

ax A tool that has a metal blade attached to a handle. An ax is used for cutting down trees and chopping wood. This word is sometimes spelled **axe.**
ax (aks) *noun, plural* **axes** (ak′siz).

axis A real or imaginary straight line through the center of an object, around which the object turns. The earth rotates on its *axis* once every twenty-four hours.
ax·is (ak′sis) *noun, plural* **axes** (ak′sēz).

axle A bar or shaft on which a wheel or pair of wheels turns. The front *axle* of our car is broken.
ax·le (ak′səl) *noun, plural* **axles.**

axis

aye Yes. All in favor of the plan say "*aye.*" *Adverb.*
—A vote of yes or a person who votes yes. *Noun.* ▲ Other words that sound like this are **eye** and **I.**
aye (ī) *adverb; noun, plural* **ayes.**

AZ Postal abbreviation for *Arizona.*

azalea A shrub with dark green leaves and clusters of pink, orange, or white flowers.
a·za·lea (ə zāl′yə) *noun, plural* **azaleas.**

Word History

The **azalea** takes its name from a Greek word meaning "dry." It was once thought that azaleas grow best in dry soil.

Aztec A member of an American Indian people of central Mexico. The Aztec developed an advanced civilization and controlled an empire in the thirteenth and fourteenth centuries.
Az·tec (az′tek) *noun, plural* **Aztec** or **Aztecs.**

azure A clear blue color; the color of a clear blue sky. *Noun.*
—Having a clear blue color. *Adjective.*
az·ure (azh′ər) *noun, plural* **azures;** *adjective.*

B b

1. This is the oldest form of the letter **B**, written by tribes in the Middle East.

2. The Greeks borrowed this letter 3,000 years ago, writing it like a backwards capital **B**.

3. Later, the Greeks turned the letter around, making it similar to our **B** today.

4. The Romans then borrowed the letter **B** from the Greeks 2,700 years ago.

5. Our **B** in Modern English looks very similar to the **B** written by the Greeks and Romans.

b, B   The second letter of the alphabet.
   b, B (bē) *noun, plural* **b's, B's.**

baa   The sound that a sheep makes. *Noun.*
—To make such a sound. *Verb.*
   baa (bä) *noun, plural* **baas;** *verb,* **baaed, baaing.**

babble   **1.** To make sounds that have no meaning. Babies *babble* before they learn to talk.   **2.** To talk in a foolish way; chatter. The children *babbled* during the long car ride.   **3.** To make a low, murmuring sound. The brook *babbled* as it flowed. *Verb.*
—**1.** Sounds that are confused or not clear or have no meaning.   **2.** A low, murmuring sound.
   bab·ble (bab'əl) *verb,* **babbled, babbling;** *noun, plural* **babbles.**

babe   A baby.
   babe (bāb) *noun, plural* **babes.**

baboon   A large monkey that has a face like a dog's. Baboons live in open country in parts of Africa. They live together in large groups, and they travel great distances in search of food.
   ba·boon (ba bün') *noun, plural* **baboons.**

baboon

baby   **1.** A very young child; infant. The *baby* is learning how to walk.   **2.** The youngest person in a family or group. I am the *baby* of the family.   **3.** A person who acts in a childish way. Don't be such a *baby* when you can't have what you want. *Noun.*
—**1.** Of or for a baby. We put the infant in the *baby* carriage.   **2.** Very young. *Baby* bears are called cubs. *Adjective.*
—To treat like a baby. My parents *babied* me when I was sick. *Verb.*
   ba·by (bā'bē) *noun, plural* **babies;** *adjective; verb,* **babied, babying.**

baby-sit   To take care of children while their parents are away. I *baby-sit* for the neighbors on Friday nights.
   ba·by-sit (bā'bē sit') *verb,* **baby-sat** (bā'bē sat'), **baby-sitting.**

baby-sitter A person who takes care of children while their parents are not at home. **ba·by-sit·ter** (bā′bē sit′ər) *noun, plural* **baby-sitters.**

baby tooth One of the first teeth of infants and baby mammals. Baby teeth fall out and are replaced by permanent teeth.

bachelor A man who has not married. **bach·e·lor** (bach′ə lər) *noun, plural* **bachelors.**

back **1.** The part of the human body behind the chest. My *back* itches just below the shoulder. **2.** The upper part of the body of an animal. The puppy likes to be petted on its *back*. **3.** The part of anything that is opposite the front part. The bank teller asked me to sign my name on the *back* of the check. The visitors sat in the *back* of the classroom. *Noun.*
—**1.** To move backward. *Back* the car out of the garage. The frightened child *backed* away from the growling dog. **2.** To help or support. If you run for class president, I'll *back* you. *Verb.*
—**1.** Behind the front part. We went around the house to the *back* door. **2.** Past; old. We threw away *back* copies of magazines. *Adjective.*
—**1.** Toward the back; backward. We moved *back* to let other people get into the bus. **2.** In the place where something used to be. Put the keys *back* in your purse. **3.** In or to a time or place in the past. That happened a few years *back*. **4.** In reply or in return. I'll give you *back* your pen in a moment. *Adverb.*
  • **back and forth.** First in one direction and then in the other. When we read, our eyes move *back and forth* across the page.
  • **behind one's back.** Without someone's knowledge or approval. We wanted the party to be a surprise, so we planned it *behind your back*.
  • **in back of.** At the rear of; behind. There is a porch *in back of* the house.
  • **to back out** or **to back out of.** To not keep a promise or agreement. You said you would help, so please don't *back out* now.
  • **to back up.** **1.** To move backward in an automobile. **2.** To give support to; back. Try to *back up* your opinions with facts.
back (bak) *noun, plural* **backs;** *verb,* **backed, backing;** *adjective; adverb.*

backboard The board to which the basket is attached in basketball. **back·board** (bak′bôrd′) *noun, plural* **backboards.**

backbone The column of bones running down the center of the back; spine. People, dogs, birds, fish, frogs, and snakes all have backbones. The backbone supports the body. **back·bone** (bak′bōn′) *noun, plural* **backbones.**

backfire A small explosion inside a gasoline engine that causes a loud noise. **back·fire** (bak′fīr′) *noun, plural* **backfires.**

backgammon A game for two people that is played on a special board. The players throw dice to see how they may move their pieces. **back·gam·mon** (bak′gam′ən) *noun.*

background **1.** The part of a picture or scene that seems to be in the distance. **2.** In a design, the empty space around figures or objects. The bedspread has yellow flowers printed on a green *background*. **3.** A person's past experience or learning. The former tennis player has a good *background* for coaching our tennis team. **back·ground** (bak′ground′) *noun, plural* **backgrounds.**

backhand A kind of stroke in tennis and other games. It is made with the back of the hand turned forward. **back·hand** (bak′hand′) *noun, plural* **backhands.**

backpack A bag that is used to carry things on the back. It has straps for the shoulders and sometimes has a metal frame. *Noun.*
—To go hiking or camping while carrying a backpack. We *backpacked* through the mountains for a week. *Verb.* **back·pack** (bak′pak′) *noun, plural* **backpacks;** *verb,* **backpacked, backpacking.**

backward **1.** Toward the back. I heard a sudden noise behind me and looked *backward*. **2.** With the back first. The clown was walking *backward* and fell. Baseball catchers usually wear their caps *backward. Adverb.*
—Toward the back. The winning runner never gave a *backward* glance during the whole race. *Adjective.* **back·ward** (bak′wərd) *adverb; adjective.*

backwards Another spelling of the adverb **backward.** **back·wards** (bak′wərdz) *adverb.*

backyard A yard behind a house or other building. **back·yard** (bak′yärd′) *noun, plural* **backyards.**

bacon Meat from the back and sides of a hog. Bacon is flavored with salt and treated with smoke to preserve it. **ba·con** (bā′kən) *noun.*

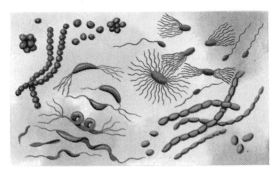

These are different types of **bacteria** as seen under a microscope.

bacteria Tiny living cells. Bacteria are so small that they can only be seen through a microscope. Some bacteria cause diseases. Others do useful things, like making soil richer.
bac·te·ri·a (bak tîr′ē ə) *plural noun, singular* **bacterium**.

bacterium The singular of **bacteria**. Look up **bacteria** for more information.
bac·te·ri·um (bak tîr′ē əm) *noun, plural* **bacteria**.

bad **1.** Having little quality or worth. How can anyone watch such a *bad* television program? **2.** Not good or moral; wrong; evil. Stealing the toy was a *bad* thing to do. **3.** Having a harmful effect; damaging. Eating candy is *bad* for your teeth. **4.** Severe or violent. Butterflies hide under leaves during *bad* storms. **5.** Having errors; incorrect. Try to improve your *bad* spelling. **6.** Not well or happy, especially because of regret or sadness; sorry. I felt *bad* when my dog was run over. **7.** Unpleasant; disagreeable. The *bad* news upset all of us. **8.** Rotten or spoiled. Milk turns *bad* if it is not kept cool.
• **not bad** or **not half bad** or **not so bad.** Fairly good; acceptable. This soup you made is *not bad*.
bad (bad) *adjective,* **worse, worst.**

badge Something worn to show that a person belongs to a certain group or has received an honor. Police officers wear *badges* on their uniforms. We were awarded a merit *badge* for our exhibit at the science fair.
badge (baj) *noun, plural* **badges.**

badger A furry animal with short legs and long claws. Badgers live in holes in the ground, which they dig with their claws. They hunt for food at night. *Noun.*
—To bother with questions or requests; pester. I'll keep *badgering* you until you give me an answer. *Verb.*
badg·er (baj′ər) *noun, plural* **badgers;** *verb,* **badgered, badgering.**

badly **1.** In a bad way. The team played *badly* and lost the game. **2.** Very much. You *badly* need new shoes.
bad·ly (bad′lē) *adverb.*

badminton A game for two or four players. In badminton, the players use rackets to hit a small object, called a shuttlecock, back and forth over a high net.
bad·min·ton (bad′min tən) *noun.*

Word History

The game of **badminton** was named after an English duke's estate where the game was first played.

baffle To be too confusing for someone to solve or understand. The message "EM TI-SIV EMOC" *baffled* me until I read it from right to left.
baf·fle (baf′əl) *verb,* **baffled, baffling.**

bag **1.** Something used to hold things. Bags are made of paper, cloth, plastic, or other soft material. The cashier put the groceries in a large *bag*. We bought a *bag* of grass seed. **2.** A handbag; purse. **3.** A suitcase. Have you packed your *bags* for the trip?
bag (bag) *noun, plural* **bags.**

bagel A round roll with a hard, shiny crust and a hole in the center. Bagels are cooked in water before they are baked.
ba·gel (bā′gəl) *noun, plural* **bagels.**

baggage The suitcases, trunks, or bags that a person takes when going on a trip.
bag·gage (bag′ij) *noun.*

badger

at; āpe; fär; câre; end; mē; it; īce; pîerce; hot; ōld; sông, fôrk; oil; out; up; ūse; rüle; pùll; tûrn; chin; sing; shop; thin; this; hw in white; zh in treasure. The symbol ə stands for the unstressed vowel sound in about, taken, pencil, lemon, and circus.

B

baggy Hanging loosely; sagging. *Baggy* trousers make a person look sloppy.
bag·gy (bag′ē) *adjective*, **baggier**, **baggiest**.

bagpipe A musical instrument made of a leather bag and pipes. A person makes music by blowing air into the bag and then pressing the bag so that the air is forced out through the pipes. The bagpipe is often played in Scotland and Ireland.
bag·pipe (bag′pīp′) *noun, plural* **bagpipes**.

bagpipe

bail¹ Money given to a court of law to allow an arrested person to remain out of jail until the time of his or her trial. The money is returned when the person appears for trial. *Noun.* ▲ Another word that sounds like this is **bale**.
- **to bail out.** **1.** To arrange for the temporary release of a person who has been arrested. Who *bailed* them *out* of jail? **2.** To help or assist, as by giving money. When my friends' business was failing, their families *bailed* them *out*.
bail (bāl) *noun, plural* **bails**; *verb*, **bailed**, **bailing**.

bail² To take water out of a boat with a pail or other container. The campers will have to *bail* water out of their rowboat or it will sink. ▲ Another word that sounds like this is **bale**.
- **to bail out.** To jump out of an airplane with a parachute. The pilot *bailed out* when the plane stalled.
bail (bāl) *verb*, **bailed**, **bailing**.

bait **1.** Food put on a hook or in a trap to attract and catch fish or other animals. When we fish, we use worms as *bait*. **2.** Something that tempts or attracts. Using the costumes and masks as *bait*, we soon got the children at the window to come out and play. *Noun.*
—**1.** To put bait on. We *baited* the trap with cheese to catch the mouse. **2.** To tease again and again in a mean way. The bully *baited* the smaller children by calling them names. *Verb.*
bait (bāt) *noun, plural* **baits**; *verb*, **baited**, **baiting**.

bake **1.** To cook by dry heat in an oven. We *bake* bread on Saturdays. The potatoes *baked* slowly. **2.** To harden or dry by heating. People *bake* clay bowls and dishes in ovens called kilns. The sun *baked* the earth until it cracked.
bake (bāk) *verb*, **baked**, **baking**.

baker A person who bakes and sells bread, cakes, cookies, and pastries.
bak·er (bā′kər) *noun, plural* **bakers**.

bakery A place where bread, cakes, cookies, and pastries are baked or sold.
bak·er·y (bā′kə rē) *noun, plural* **bakeries**.

baking powder A powder used in baking and frying to make dough or batter rise.

baking soda A white powder that is used in cooking and as a medicine to soothe an upset stomach.

balance **1.** The condition in which opposite sides or parts of something are the same in weight, amount, or force. The two children kept the seesaw in *balance*. **2.** A steady, secure position. I lost my *balance* and fell on the ice. **3.** A scale that looks like a small seesaw and is used for weighing things. The things to be weighed are placed in two flat pans hanging from an upright post. The chemist weighed the powder on the *balance*. **4.** The part that is left over; remainder. We'll do most of the gardening in the morning, and the *balance* after lunch. *Noun.*
—**1.** To make equal in weight, amount, or force. Try to *balance* the two sides of the scale. **2.** To put or keep in a steady position. I can *balance* a book on my head. *Verb.*
bal·ance (bal′əns) *noun, plural* **balances**; *verb*, **balanced**, **balancing**.

balanced diet A diet that includes all the different kinds of food that the body needs to stay healthy and to grow. A balanced diet is made up of the proper amounts of these foods.

balcony **1.** A platform that juts out from the outside wall of a building. A balcony has a low wall or railing on three sides. **2.** An upper floor that juts out into a large room or auditorium. Churches and theaters often have balconies with seats.

bal·co·ny (bal′kə nē) *noun, plural* **balconies.**

bald **1.** Having little or no hair on the head. When I was first born, I was *bald*. **2.** Without a natural covering. The *bald* hilltop had no trees or shrubs.

bald (bôld) *adjective,* **balder, baldest.**

bald eagle A large eagle of North America. A fully grown bald eagle is brown with a white head, neck, and tail. The bald eagle is the national symbol of the United States.

bale A large bundle of things tied together tightly for shipping or storing. The farmer stored the *bales* of hay in the barn for the winter. ⏴ Another word that sounds like this is **bail.**

bale (bāl) *noun, plural* **bales.**

balk **1.** To stop short and refuse to go on. The mule *balked* and would not move. **2.** To keep from going on; hinder. The guards *balked* the prisoners' plans to escape from jail.

balk (bôk) *verb,* **balked, balking.**

ball¹ **1.** A round object. I wound the kite string into a *ball*. **2.** A roundish object used in various games. Baseball, football, and jacks are all played with different *balls*. **3.** A game played with a ball. Let's play *ball* after school today. **4.** A pitch in baseball that the batter does not swing at and that does not pass over home plate in the area between the batter's knees and shoulders. ⏴ Another word that sounds like this is **bawl.**

ball (bôl) *noun, plural* **balls.**

ball² A large, formal party for dancing. In the story, the two main characters met at a costume *ball*. ⏴ Another word that sounds like this is **bawl.**

ball (bôl) *noun, plural* **balls.**

ballad A simple poem or song that tells a story. The singer sang *ballads* about the old West.

bal·lad (bal′əd) *noun, plural* **ballads.**

ballast Something heavy carried in the bottom of a ship to keep it steady and balanced in the water. Sand or rocks are used as ballast.

bal·last (bal′əst) *noun, plural* **ballasts.**

ball bearing A bearing made up of a number of small metal balls in a groove. A moving part can slide easily on a ball bearing. The wheels of my roller skates turn on *ball bearings.*

ballerina A woman or girl who dances ballet.

bal·le·ri·na (bal′ə rē′nə) *noun, plural* **ballerinas.**

ballerinas in a ballet class

ballet **1.** A form of dance in which dancers use certain formal steps and movements. I have studied *ballet* for three years. **2.** A presentation by a dancer or dancers using ballet steps. A ballet usually tells a story. In the *ballet* that we saw, a mechanical doll turned into a real person.

bal·let (ba lā′ *or* bal′ā) *noun, plural* **ballets.**

ball game A game that is played with a ball. Baseball is a ball game.

balloon A rubber or plastic bag filled with air or other gas. Small balloons are used as children's toys or for decoration. Large balloons are filled with hot air or some other very light gas so that they rise and float. These balloons have cabins or baskets for carrying passengers or scientific instruments. *Noun.*
—To swell out or grow larger like a balloon. The parachute *ballooned* when it opened. *Verb.*

bal·loon (bə lün′) *noun, plural* **balloons;** *verb,* **ballooned, ballooning.**

ballot **1.** A printed form or other object used in voting. A voter checks or writes down a choice on a paper ballot or on a ballot

at; āpe; fär; câre; end; mē; it; īce; pîerce; hot; ōld; sông, fôrk; oil; out; up; ūse; rüle; pùll; tûrn; chin; sing; shop; thin; <u>th</u>is; hw in white; zh in treasure. The symbol ə stands for the unstressed vowel sound in about, taken, pencil, lemon, and circus.

57

that appears on the face of a machine. Later the ballots are counted to see who has won the election.   **2.** The act or the right of voting. Student council decisions are made by *ballot*. The United States granted women the *ballot* in 1920. *Noun.*
—To use a ballot for voting. The students *balloted* to choose a class president. *Verb.*
   bal·lot (bal'ət) *noun, plural* **ballots;** *verb,* **balloted, balloting.**

Word History

The word **ballot** comes from an Italian word meaning "little ball." People would cast their votes by putting little balls into a voting box. A white ball meant a vote for the candidate, but a black ball meant a vote against.

---

ballpoint pen   A pen whose point is a small metal ball that rolls the ink from a container inside the pen onto the paper.
   ball·point pen (bôl'point').

ballroom   A large room where dances and other parties are given.
   ball·room (bôl'rüm' *or* bôl'rùm') *noun, plural* **ballrooms.**

balsa   A strong and very light wood from a tropical American tree. Balsa is easy to cut and carve. It is used to make airplane and boat models.
   bal·sa (bôl'sə) *noun.*

balsam fir   A fragrant evergreen tree that grows in North America. Wood from the balsam fir is used as lumber and to make boxes, crates, and pulp.
   bal·sam (bôl'səm).

bamboo   A tall plant that is related to grass. The bamboo has woody stems that are often hollow and are used to make fishing poles, canes, and furniture.
   bam·boo (bam bü') *noun, plural* **bamboos.**

ban   To forbid by law; prohibit. The government *banned* the hunting of animals in that national park. *Verb.*
—An official order that forbids something. There is a *ban* on bringing pets into that building. *Noun.*
   ban (ban) *verb,* **banned, banning;** *noun, plural* **bans.**

banana   A slightly curved fruit that has a thick yellow or red skin. Bananas grow in bunches on a tree-like plant that has very large leaves. They grow in tropical regions of the world.
   ba·nan·a (bə nan'ə) *noun, plural* **bananas.**

band¹   **1.** A group of people or animals. We saw a *band* of stray dogs in the park.   **2.** A group of musicians playing together. The school *band* played at the football game. *Noun.*
—To gather together in a group. The neighbors *banded* together to clean up litter in the vacant lot. *Verb.*
   band (band) *noun, plural* **bands;** *verb,* **banded, banding.**

band²   **1.** A strip of cloth or other material. I tied a red *band* around my head. There were metal *bands* around the barrel.   **2.** A stripe of color. The beach umbrella had wide *bands* of red and white on it.   **3.** A range of frequencies in radio broadcasting. *Noun.*
—To put a band on. Scientists *banded* the leg of the pigeon so that they could later identify it. *Verb.*
   band (band) *noun, plural* **bands;** *verb,* **banded, banding.**

bandage   A strip of cloth or other material used to cover a wound or protect an injured part. Be sure to put a *bandage* on that cut finger. *Noun.*
—To cover or protect with a bandage. The nurse *bandaged* the bicyclist's scraped knee. *Verb.*
   band·age (ban'dij) *noun, plural* **bandages;** *verb,* **bandaged, bandaging.**

bandanna   A large handkerchief with a bright pattern on it. The workers wore red *bandannas* around their necks. This word is sometimes spelled **bandana.**
   ban·dan·na (ban dan'ə) *noun, plural* **bandannas.**

bandit   A robber or outlaw. *Bandits* stopped the stagecoach and demanded money.
   ban·dit (ban'dit) *noun, plural* **bandits.**

bang   A loud, sudden noise or blow. The door swung shut with a *bang. Noun.*
—**1.** To make a loud, sudden noise. The

Fruit

Flower

banana

door *banged* shut. **2.** To strike or hit noisily. The judge *banged* the table with a gavel. *Verb.*
  bang (bang) *noun, plural* **bangs;** *verb,* **banged, banging.**

Bangladesh A country in south-central Asia.
  Ban·gla·desh (bang′glə desh′) *noun.*

bangs Hair cut short and worn over the forehead. I wear my hair in *bangs.*
  bangs (bangz) *plural noun.*

banish **1.** To punish someone by making him or her leave a country. The ruler *banished* the person who had been a spy for the enemy. **2.** To send or drive away. The children *banished* their friend from the game for cheating.
  ban·ish (ban′ish) *verb,* **banished, banishing.**

banister A railing along a staircase, and the posts that support this railing.
  ban·is·ter (ban′ə stər) *noun, plural* **banisters.**

banister

banjo A musical instrument that has a round body, a long neck, and five strings. A banjo is played by plucking the strings with the fingers or with a pick.
  ban·jo (ban′jō) *noun, plural* **banjos** or **banjoes.**

bank¹ **1.** A long mound or heap. A *bank* of earth protected the town from flood waters.

2. The rising ground along a river or lake. We go fishing along the river's *bank. Noun.*
—To form into a bank; pile; heap. The plow *banked* the snow along the side of the road. *Verb.*
  bank (bangk) *noun, plural* **banks;** *verb,* **banked, banking.**

bank² **1.** A small, strong container for storing coins and other money. **2.** A place of business where people store, borrow, and exchange money. I went to the *bank* to deposit cash in my savings account. **3.** A place for storing a reserve supply of something. Hospitals keep *banks* of blood for people who need transfusions. *Noun.*
—To do business with a bank. We *bank* at the savings bank around the corner. *Verb.*
  bank (bangk) *noun, plural* **banks;** *verb,* **banked, banking.**

banker A person who helps run a bank.
  bank·er (bang′kər) *noun, plural* **bankers.**

bankrupt Not able to pay what one owes. When the business failed, its owners went *bankrupt. Adjective.*
—To make bankrupt. The fire in the store *bankrupted* the owner. *Verb.*
  bank·rupt (bangk′rupt) *adjective; verb,* **bankrupted, bankrupting.**

Word History

The word **bankrupt** comes from two Italian words that mean "broken bench." In the Middle Ages in Italy, bankers kept their money in benches. When a banker could not pay people what they were owed, the bench was broken.

---

banner A flag or other piece of cloth that has a design and sometimes writing on it. The fans at the baseball game hung *banners* from the grandstand. *Noun.*
—Important; outstanding. With the hedges and roadsides full of raspberries, it was a *banner* season for raspberry pickers. *Adjective.*
  ban·ner (ban′ər) *noun, plural* **banners;** *adjective.*

at; āpe; fär; câre; end; mē; it; īce; pîerce; hot; ōld; sông, fôrk; oil; out; up; ūse; rüle; pùll; tûrn; chin; sing; shop; thin; <u>th</u>is; hw in white; zh in treasure. The symbol ə stands for the unstressed vowel sound in about, taken, pencil, lemon, and circus.

banquet A large formal dinner prepared for many people. A banquet is given for a special occasion. The school gave a *banquet* for the students who won scholarship awards.
ban·quet (bang′kwit) *noun, plural* **banquets.**

banter Playful teasing or joking. The interview was full of *banter* between the mayor and the reporters. *Noun.*
—To tease or make jokes in a playful way. After the game we *bantered* about the mistakes that both teams had made. *Verb.*
ban·ter (ban′tər) *noun; verb,* **bantered, bantering.**

baptism A religious ceremony for admitting a person into a Christian church. In this ceremony a person is dipped in water or sprinkled with water.
bap·tism (bap′tiz əm) *noun, plural* **baptisms.**

baptize To make a person a member of a Christian church by dipping in water or sprinkling with water. The minister *baptized* the baby.
bap·tize (bap tīz′ *or* bap′tīz) *verb,* **baptized, baptizing.**

bar **1.** A piece of metal, wood, soap, or other solid material that is longer than it is wide. There is a *bar* of soap in the shower. The windows of the jail have *bars* on them. **2.** Something that blocks the way. The child's small body was a *bar* to becoming a football player. **3.** A stripe or band of color. My favorite shirt has *bars* of blue and yellow on it. **4.** In music, an upright line placed on a staff to mark the division between two equal measures of time. **5.** A unit of music between two bars; measure. **6.** The profession of a lawyer. The young law student passed the examination and was admitted to the *bar.* **7.** A place with a counter where foods or drinks are served. *Noun.*
—**1.** To use a bar to fasten something. We *barred* the cabin door with a heavy piece of wood. **2.** To keep out. Visitors are *barred* from the hospital in the morning. *Verb.*
bar (bär) *noun, plural* **bars;** *verb,* **barred, barring.**

barb A sharp point that sticks out backward or at an angle from something else. The *barb* of the fishhook caught in the fish's mouth.
barb (bärb) *noun, plural* **barbs.**

barbarian A person who belongs to a tribe or a people that is savage or uncivilized. *Barbarians* conquered that country about 1,500 years ago.
bar·bar·i·an (bär bâr′ē ən) *noun, plural* **barbarians.**

barbecue **1.** A meal cooked outdoors over an open fire. **2.** A grill or small fireplace that uses gas or charcoal for fuel. It is used for cooking food outdoors. *Noun.*
—To cook a meal outdoors over an open fire. We *barbecued* the chicken. *Verb.*
bar·be·cue (bär′bi kū′) *noun, plural* **barbecues;** *verb,* **barbecued, barbecuing.**

barbed wire Wire with barbs attached. It is used in fences.
barbed wire (bärbd).

barber A person whose work is cutting hair and trimming or shaving beards.
bar·ber (bär′bər) *noun, plural* **barbers.**

barbed wire fence

bare **1.** Without covering or clothing; naked. We walked on the beach with *bare* feet. In winter the trees are *bare.* **2.** Empty. After we took all the books out, the shelves were *bare.* **3.** Just enough; mere. The campers brought only the *bare* necessities on their trip. *Adjective.*
—To uncover. The doctor asked me to *bare* my chest by opening my shirt. The cat *bared* its claws. *Verb.* ▲ Another word that sounds like this is **bear.**
bare (bâr) *adjective,* **barer, barest;** *verb,* **bared, baring.**

bareback On the back of a horse without a saddle. My cousin is a *bareback* rider in the circus. *Adjective.*
—Without a saddle. The cowhand rode the horse *bareback. Adverb.*
bare·back (bâr′bak′) *adjective; adverb.*

barefoot Having the feet bare. The *barefoot* children waded across the creek. *Adjective.*
—With the feet bare. Let's walk *barefoot* on the grass. *Adverb.*
bare·foot (bâr′fut′) *adjective; adverb.*

barely Only just; scarcely. There was *barely* enough food to go around.
bare·ly (bâr′lē) *adverb.*

bargain **1.** Something offered for sale or bought at a low price. At only ten cents, this ballpoint pen is a *bargain.* **2.** An agreement. We made a *bargain* that I would wash the dishes if you would dry them. *Noun.*

—To talk over the price of a sale or the terms of an agreement. I *bargained* with the salesperson to get a good price on the used bicycle. *Verb.*
> **bar·gain** (bär′gin) *noun, plural* **bargains;** *verb,* **bargained, bargaining.**

barge A boat with a flat bottom. Barges are used to carry freight on canals and rivers.
> **barge** (bärj) *noun, plural* **barges.**

baritone **1.** A man's singing voice that is lower than tenor and higher than bass. **2.** A singer who has such a voice.
> **bar·i·tone** (bar′i tōn′) *noun, plural* **baritones.**

Word History

The word **baritone** comes from the Italian name for this singing voice. The Italian word comes from two Greek words meaning "deep" and "tone."

barium A soft, silver-colored metal. Barium is a chemical element. Some compounds of barium are used as white pigments for paints and ceramics. One compound of barium absorbs X rays. Doctors give this compound to patients whose digestive systems will be examined by X rays.
> **bar·i·um** (bar′ē əm) *noun.*

bark¹ The outer covering of the trunk, branches, and roots of a tree. Bark is usually rough and dark in color. *Noun.*
—To scrape or rub the skin off. If you climb that tree in shorts, you might *bark* your legs. *Verb.*
> **bark** (bärk) *noun, plural* **barks;** *verb,* **barked, barking.**

bark² The short, loud sound that a dog makes. *Noun.*
—**1.** To make the short, loud sound that a dog makes. The watchdog *barked* at the stranger. Seals *bark* too. **2.** To speak loudly and sharply. The sheriff *barked* "Hands up!" at the outlaw. *Verb.*
> **bark** (bärk) *noun, plural* **barks;** *verb,* **barked, barking.**

barley The grain of a plant that is like grass. Barley is used as animal feed, in cooking, and to make malt.
> **bar·ley** (bär′lē) *noun.*

barn A building on a farm that is used to store hay and grain, and to house cows and horses.
> **barn** (bärn) *noun, plural* **barns.**

barnacle Any of a group of small, saltwater shellfish. Barnacles attach themselves to animals, rocks, ship bottoms, and other objects in the water. Some barnacles can be eaten.
> **bar·na·cle** (bär′nə kəl) *noun, plural* **barnacles.**

barnyard An area around a barn that is surrounded by a fence. The cows grazed in the *barnyard* while waiting to be milked.
> **barn·yard** (bärn′yärd′) *noun, plural* **barnyards.**

barometer An instrument for measuring the pressure of the atmosphere. A barometer is used to forecast changes in the weather.
> **ba·rom·e·ter** (bə rom′i tər) *noun, plural* **barometers.**

baron A nobleman of the lowest rank. ◣ Another word that sounds like this is **barren.**
> **bar·on** (bar′ən) *noun, plural* **barons.**

baroness A noblewoman of the lowest rank.
> **bar·on·ess** (bar′ə nis) *noun, plural* **baronesses.**

barracks A building or group of buildings where soldiers or workers live. Barracks are usually found on military bases. This *barracks* needs to be cleaned by noon today. The *barracks* are inspected every week. ◣ The word barracks may be used with a singular or plural verb.
> **bar·racks** (bar′əks) *plural noun.*

barracuda A fierce fish that lives in warm seas. The barracuda has a long, narrow body and a large mouth with sharp teeth.
> **bar·ra·cu·da** (bar′ə kü′də) *noun, plural* **barracuda** or **barracudas.**

barracuda

barrage A heavy amount of cannon, rocket, or gun fire aimed at an area. The *barrage* kept the enemy from attacking the town.
> **bar·rage** (bə räzh′) *noun, plural* **barrages.**

at; āpe; fär; câre; end; mē; it; ice; pîerce; hot; ōld; sông, fôrk; oil; out; up; ūse; rüle; půll; tûrn; chin; sing; shop; thin; <u>th</u>is; hw in white; zh in treasure. The symbol ə stands for the unstressed vowel sound in about, taken, pencil, lemon, and circus.

barrel   1. A large, round, wooden container with curved sides. The farmer packed the apples in *barrels*. 2. A metal tube that forms part of a gun. Bullets are fired through the barrel.
    bar·rel (bar′əl) *noun, plural* **barrels.**

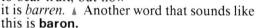

barrel

barren   Not able to produce anything. No plants could grow in the sandy, *barren* soil. This apple tree used to bear fruit, but now it is *barren*. ▲ Another word that sounds like this is **baron.**
    bar·ren (bar′ən) *adjective.*

barrette   A small clasp or clip used to hold hair in place.
    bar·rette (bə ret′) *noun, plural* **barrettes.**

barricade   A structure put up quickly to block the way or for protection. The police set up wooden *barricades* on each side of the street before the parade. *Noun.*
—To block the way with a barricade. The settlers piled up logs to *barricade* the entrance to the fort. *Verb.*
    bar·ri·cade (bar′i kād′) *noun, plural* **barricades;** *verb,* **barricaded, barricading.**

barrier   Something that blocks the way. The fallen tree was a *barrier* to traffic on the road.
    bar·ri·er (bar′ē ər) *noun, plural* **barriers.**

barrio   In a city of the United States, a district where Spanish is the main language that is spoken.
    bar·ri·o (bär′ē ō *or* bar′ē ō) *noun, plural* **barrios.**

barter   To trade things for other things without using money. The pioneers *bartered* grain for blankets with the natives. *Verb.*
—The trading of goods or services without the use of money. Among early settlers in this country much business was carried on by *barter. Noun.*
    bar·ter (bär′tər) *verb,* **bartered, bartering;** *noun.*

base¹   1. The part that something rests or stands on; the lowest part. That lamp has a wooden *base*. The hikers camped at the *base* of the mountain. 2. The main part of something. Many kinds of soup have a chicken *base*. 3. A starting place. The airplanes got back to the *base* safely. 4. One of the four corners of a baseball diamond. The batter reached first *base* when I dropped the ball. 5. A chemical that joins with an acid to form a salt. Bases have a bitter taste when dissolved in water. A base will cause red litmus paper to turn blue. *Noun.*
—To put on a base or foundation. The builders *based* the house on concrete. Writers often *base* stories on their own experiences. *Verb.* ▲ Another word that sounds like this is **bass.**
    base (bās) *noun, plural* **bases** (bā′siz); *verb,* **based, basing.**

base²   1. Not brave or honorable; cowardly or bad. Telling lies about what happened was a *base* thing to do. 2. Low in value when compared with something else. Iron is a *base* metal; gold is a precious metal. ▲ Another word that sounds like this is **bass.**
    base (bās) *adjective,* **baser, basest.**

baseball   1. A game played with a ball and bat by two teams of nine players each. Baseball is played on a field with four bases that form a diamond. To score a run, a player on one team must reach home base by touching first, second, and third bases before that team is put out. Each team is allowed three outs in an inning, and a game is made up of nine innings. 2. The ball used in this game.
    base·ball (bās′bôl′) *noun, plural* **baseballs.**

basement   The lowest floor of a building, below or partly below the ground.
    base·ment (bās′mənt) *noun, plural* **basements.**

bashful   Embarrassed and shy around people. The *bashful* child hid behind the chair when the babysitter arrived.
    bash·ful (bash′fəl) *adjective.*

basic   Forming the most important part; fundamental. Food is a *basic* human need. The *basic* parts of a bicycle are the wheels, handlebars, and frame. A *basic* difference between the two friends is that one likes to play baseball and the other likes to read.
    ba·sic (bā′sik) *adjective.*

BASIC   A computer language that is simple enough for beginners to use to write programs.
    BASIC (bā′sik) *noun.*

basin   1. A round or oval bowl for holding liquids. Fill the *basin* with water. 2. An enclosed or sheltered area containing water. The harbor has a boat *basin*. 3. All the land that is drained by a river and by all the streams flowing into the river. Iowa, Missouri, and Montana are all in the *basin* of the Mississippi River.
    ba·sin (bā′sin) *noun, plural* **basins.**

basis The part that something rests or depends on; foundation. The idea that toads give you warts has no *basis* in fact.
ba·sis (bā′sis) *noun, plural* **bases** (bā′sēz).

bask To lie in and enjoy a pleasant warmth. The cat *basked* in the sun.
bask (bask) *verb,* **basked, basking.**

basket **1.** A container woven from twigs, straw, strips of wood, or other material. They bought two *baskets* of strawberries from the farmer. **2.** A metal hoop with a net hanging from it, used in basketball. The ball is thrown through the basket to score a goal.
bas·ket (bas′kit) *noun, plural* **baskets.**

basket

basketball **1.** A game played with a large, round ball on a court by two teams of five players each. To score, a player must throw the ball through a raised basket at the opponent's end of the court. **2.** The ball used in this game.
bas·ket·ball (bas′kit bôl′) *noun, plural* **basketballs.**

bass[1] **1.** The lowest man's singing voice. **2.** A singer who has such a voice. **3.** A musical instrument that has a similar range.
▲ Another word that sounds like this is **base.**
bass (bās) *noun, plural* **basses.**

bass[2] Any of a number of North American fish found in streams and lakes, and in the sea. Bass are used for food.
bass (bas) *noun, plural* **bass** or **basses.**

bass drum A very large drum that gives a deep, booming sound when it is struck.
bass drum (bās).

bassoon A musical instrument that makes a low sound when it is played. The bassoon has a long, straight, wooden body attached to a smaller, curved, metal tube. It is played by blowing into the metal tube and pressing holes and keys on the body.
bas·soon (bə sün′) *noun, plural* **bassoons.**

bass viol The largest musical instrument that has strings. It gives a very low sound when it is played. The bass viol is shaped like a violin, but it is played standing upright on the floor. The musician plays a bass viol with a bow or by plucking with the fingers.
bass vi·ol (bās vī′əl).

baste[1] To put melted butter, fat, gravy, or other liquid on food to keep it moist while it is roasting. You can use a large spoon or a brush to *baste* the chicken.
baste (bāst) *verb,* **basted, basting.**

baste[2] To sew with long, loose stitches. You should *baste* the seam of the dress in place before sewing it on the sewing machine.
baste (bāst) *verb,* **basted, basting.**

bat[1] A strong wooden stick or club. A bat is used to hit the ball in baseball and softball. *Noun.*
—To hit the ball with a bat. I *batted* the ball out of the park. It is your turn to *bat. Verb.*
• **at bat.** Having a turn to hit the ball in a baseball or softball game. The visiting team is *at bat* first.
bat (bat) *noun, plural* **bats;** *verb,* **batted, batting.**

bat[2] A small, furry animal that flies. It has a body like a mouse and wings of thin skin.
bat (bat) *noun, plural* **bats.**

bat[2]

batch A group of things prepared together or gathered loosely together. We baked a *batch* of muffins.
batch (bach) *noun, plural* **batches.**

bath **1.** A washing of something in water. Let's give the dog a *bath.* **2.** The water used for bathing. The *bath* was too hot. **3.** A place or room for bathing; bathroom. The house has two bedrooms and one *bath.*
bath (bath) *noun, plural* **baths** (ba<u>th</u>z or baths).

at; āpe; fär; câre; end; mē; it; īce; pîerce; hot; ōld; sông, fôrk; oil; out; up; ūse; rüle; pull; tûrn; chin; sing; shop; thin; <u>this</u>; hw in white; zh in treasure. The symbol ə stands for the unstressed vowel sound in about, taken, pencil, lemon, and circus.

bathe   **1.** To wash something in water. The nurse *bathed* the cut finger before bandaging it. I *bathe* every night.   **2.** To go swimming. The children liked to *bathe* in the lake in the summer.   **3.** To seem to cover as if with a liquid. Sunlight *bathes* our bedroom in the morning.
   bathe (bāth) *verb*, **bathed, bathing.**

bathing suit   A piece of clothing worn while swimming.

bathrobe   A loose piece of clothing similar to a coat. It is usually worn before and after bathing or when relaxing.
   bath·robe (bath′rōb′) *noun, plural* **bathrobes.**

bathroom   A room that has a sink and a toilet, and often a bathtub or shower.
   bath·room (bath′rüm′ or bath′rüm′) *noun, plural* **bathrooms.**

bathtub   A large tub to bathe in.
   bath·tub (bath′tub′) *noun, plural* **bathtubs.**

baton   A stick or rod. The conductor used a *baton* to direct the orchestra.
   ba·ton (bə ton′) *noun, plural* **batons.**

battalion   A large section of an army, made up of companies. A battalion forms part of a regiment.
   bat·tal·ion (bə tal′yən) *noun, plural* **battalions.**

batter[1]   To hit over and over again with heavy blows. The sailor was afraid the high waves would *batter* the small boat to pieces.
   bat·ter (bat′ər) *verb*, **battered, battering.**

batter[2]   A mixture of flour, milk or water, and other things. Batter is fried or baked to make pancakes, biscuits, or cakes.
   bat·ter (bat′ər) *noun, plural* **batters.**

batter[3]   A person whose turn it is to bat in a game of baseball or softball.
   bat·ter (bat′ər) *noun, plural* **batters.**

battering ram   A heavy beam once used in war to batter down walls or gates.

battering ram

battery   **1.** A device that produces an electric current by chemical changes in the materials inside it. Flashlights must have *batteries* to work.   **2.** A group of things that are alike or that work together. A *battery* of microphones stood in front of the mayor as the speech began.
   bat·ter·y (bat′ə rē) *noun, plural* **batteries.**

battle   **1.** A fight between two armed persons or groups. Battles happen during wars. The two armies fought a *battle*.   **2.** A long, hard effort or contest; struggle. Life in the Arctic is a constant *battle* against the cold. *Noun.*
   —To fight or struggle. The armies *battled* for control of the city. *Verb.*
   bat·tle (bat′əl) *noun, plural* **battles;** *verb*, **battled, battling.**

battlefield   A place where a battle was fought or is being fought. Gettysburg is a famous *battlefield* of the Civil War.
   bat·tle·field (bat′əl fēld′) *noun, plural* **battlefields.**

battleground   A battlefield.
   bat·tle·ground (bat′əl ground′) *noun, plural* **battlegrounds.**

battlement   A low wall built along the top of a fort or tower. A battlement has a series of openings for soldiers to shoot through.
   bat·tle·ment (bat′əl mənt) *noun, plural* **battlements.**

battleship   A large warship with very powerful guns and thick, heavy armor.
   bat·tle·ship (bat′əl ship′) *noun, plural* **battleships.**

bawl   To cry or shout loudly. The child fell on the sidewalk and started to *bawl*. *Verb.*
   —A loud cry or shout. *Noun.* ▲ Another word that sounds like this is **ball.**
   • **to bawl out.** To scold loudly. Our neighbor *bawled* us *out* for making so much noise.
   bawl (bôl) *verb*, **bawled, bawling;** *noun.*

bay[1]   A part of an ocean or lake that is partly enclosed by the coastline.
   bay (bā) *noun, plural* **bays.**

bay[2]   The deep, long barking or howling of a dog. The hunter heard the *bay* of the hounds chasing a rabbit. *Noun.*
   —To bark or howl with deep, long sounds. The dog *bayed* at the moon. *Verb.*
   bay (bā) *noun, plural* **bays;** *verb*, **bayed, baying.**

bayonet   A large knife that fits on the end of a rifle. A bayonet is used to stab an opponent in close fighting.
   bay·o·net (bā′ə nit or bā′ə net′) *noun, plural* **bayonets.**

bayou A stream that flows slowly through a swamp or marsh. Bayous are found in the southern United States.
bay·ou (bī′ü *or* bī′ō) *noun, plural* **bayous.**

bazaar **1.** A market made up of rows of small shops or stalls. **2.** A sale of different things for some special purpose. We baked a carrot cake for the church *bazaar.*
ba·zaar (bə zär′) *noun, plural* **bazaars.**

BC Postal abbreviation for *British Columbia.*

B.C. An abbreviation for *before Christ.* It is used in giving dates before the birth of Jesus Christ. 100 *B.C.* means 100 years before the birth of Jesus.

be **1.** To have reality; exist. There *is* one apple left. Once there *was* a little child. **2.** To take place; happen. My birthday *was* last week. **3.** To occupy a place or situation; lie. A caterpillar *was* in the jar. That person *is* in trouble. **4.** To come or go. Have you ever *been* to California? **5.** To stay or continue. I have *been* in the house all day. **6.** A linking verb that is used to join the subject of a sentence and a word or words that tell something about the subject. The grapes *are* purple. That house *is* the largest one in town. Let X *be* 10. **7.** An auxiliary verb that is used to form special verb tenses. When *be* is used as an auxiliary verb, the main verb is a present participle or a past participle. We *are* studying for a test. They will *be* going soon. The child *was* lifted high in the air. ⌁ Another word that sounds like this is **bee.**
be (bē) *verb.*

beach The land along the edge of an ocean or other body of water. A beach is covered with sand or pebbles. *Noun.*
—To run a boat onto a beach. They *beached* the sailboat so they could paint it. *Verb.* ⌁ Another word that sounds like this is **beech.**
beach (bēch) *noun, plural* **beaches;** *verb,* **beached, beaching.**

beacon A light or other signal that warns or guides ships or aircraft. The *beacon* from the lighthouse guided the ship through the fog.
bea·con (bē′kən) *noun, plural* **beacons.**

bead **1.** A small, round piece of glass, wood, plastic, or other material that has a hole through it. Beads are often strung together on a wire or string. The dancer wore a necklace of red *beads.* **2.** Any small, round thing. *Beads* of sweat rolled down my face. *Noun.*
—To decorate with beads. *Verb.*
bead (bēd) *noun, plural* **beads;** *verb,* **beaded, beading.**

beagle A small dog with short legs, a smooth coat, and drooping ears. Beagles are kept as pets and also are used to hunt squirrels, rabbits, and other small animals.
bea·gle (bē′gəl) *noun, plural* **beagles.**

beagle

beak The hard, projecting mouth part of a bird or a turtle. Hawks and eagles have sharp, hooked beaks. Finches have small beaks for eating seeds.
beak (bēk) *noun, plural* **beaks.**

beaker A glass cup or container with a lip shaped to make pouring easier. Beakers are used in laboratories to hold liquids or chemicals.
beak·er (bē′kər) *noun, plural* **beakers.**

beam **1.** A long, strong piece of wood or metal. Beams are used in building to support floors or ceilings. **2.** A narrow ray of light. *Beams* of sunlight came through the window. The campers could see the path by the *beams* of their flashlights. *Noun.*
—**1.** To shine brightly. The sun *beamed* down on the field. **2.** To smile happily. The parents *beamed* with pride as their child sang on the stage. *Verb.*
beam (bēm) *noun, plural* **beams;** *verb,* **beamed, beaming.**

bean **1.** A pod or seed that is eaten as a vegetable. There are many kinds of beans, including the lima bean, string bean, and kidney bean. **2.** Any seed that looks like a bean. The grocer ground the coffee *beans.*
bean (bēn) *noun, plural* **beans.**

bear¹ **1.** To hold up; support or carry. Beams *bear* the weight of the roof of our house. Don't climb that tree because its branches won't *bear* your weight. **2.** To produce offspring. The peach tree *bears* fruit. Our dog will *bear* puppies soon. **3.** To put up with patiently; stand. My friend cannot *bear* being teased. The child was able to *bear* the pain of a broken arm bravely. **4.** To

at; āpe; fär; câre; end; mē; it; īce; pîerce; hot; ōld; sông, fôrk; oil; out; up; ūse; rüle; pùll; tûrn; chin; sing; shop; thin; <u>th</u>is; hw in white; zh in treasure. The symbol ə stands for the unstressed vowel sound in about, taken, pencil, lemon, and circus.

have as a visible mark or feature; show. You *bear* a resemblance to your father. ▲ Another word that sounds like this is **bare**.
  • **to bear down.** To press or weigh down.
  • **to bear with.** To be patient toward; tolerate. Please *bear with* me today if I seem in a bad mood.
  bear (bâr) *verb,* **bore, borne** or **born, bearing.**

bear² A large, heavy animal with thick, shaggy fur. A bear has sharp claws and a very short tail. There are many kinds of bears, including the black bear, brown bear, grizzly bear, and the polar bear. ▲ Another word that sounds like this is **bare**.
  bear (bâr) *noun, plural* **bears.**

bear²

beard **1.** The hair that grows on a man's face. **2.** A growth of hair that is like a beard. That goat has a *beard* on its chin.
  beard (bîrd) *noun, plural* **beards.**

bearing **1.** The way that a person walks, stands, or acts. That slim, strong person has the *bearing* of an athlete. **2.** Connection in thought. That silly remark has no *bearing* on our conversation. **3. bearings.** Knowledge of one's position or direction. The campers lost their *bearings* and wandered for a long time before they found the right path again. **4.** A part of a machine that holds a moving part and allows it to move with less friction. The mechanic replaced a worn *bearing* in the automobile engine.
  bear·ing (bâr′ing) *noun, plural* **bearings.**

beast **1.** Any animal that has four feet. At the zoo we saw tigers, elephants, and other *beasts* of the jungle. **2.** A person who is coarse or cruel.
  beast (bēst) *noun, plural* **beasts.**

beat **1.** To hit again and again; pound. The leader of the parade *beat* a drum. The cruel animal trainer *beat* the lion. The ocean waves *beat* against the pier. **2.** To do better than; defeat. Our spelling team *beat* their team. My friend *beat* me at checkers. **3.** To thump or throb. You could feel the kitten's heart *beat*. **4.** To move up and down; flap. The eagle *beat* its wings. **5.** To stir or mix with force. I *beat* three eggs for the omelet. *Verb.*
—**1.** A blow made over and over again. We could hear the *beat* of the drum before we could see the parade. **2.** A pounding sound, rhythm, or sensation. The dance music had a loud *beat*. If you put your hand to your chest, you can feel the *beat* of your heart. **3.** A regular route or round. We saw a police officer patrolling the *beat*. **4.** The basic unit of time in music. There are three *beats* to a measure in this waltz. *Noun.* ▲ Another word that sounds like this is **beet**.
  beat (bēt) *verb,* **beat, beaten** or **beat, beating;** *noun, plural* **beats.**

beaten Past participle of **beat.** When the eggs are well *beaten,* set them aside. Have we ever *beaten* that team? Look up **beat** for more information. *Verb.*
—**1.** Worn by use. The hikers followed a *beaten* path through the woods. **2.** Defeated. The *beaten* football team hoped to do better in the next game. *Adjective.*
  beat·en (bē′tən) *verb; adjective.*

beautiful Pleasing to look at, hear, or think about. There are *beautiful* paintings at the museum. The band played some *beautiful* music. We had *beautiful* weather for our picnic.
  beau·ti·ful (bū′tə fəl) *adjective.*

beautify To make beautiful. We *beautified* the yard around our house by planting flowers and shrubs.
  beau·ti·fy (bū′tə fī′) *verb,* **beautified, beautifying.**

beauty **1.** A quality that makes a person or thing pleasing to look at, hear, or think about. The garden is a place of *beauty* when all the flowers are in bloom. **2.** A person or thing that is beautiful. That new bicycle is a *beauty.*
  beau·ty (bū′tē) *noun, plural* **beauties.**

beaver A furry, brown animal that has a broad, flat tail and webbed hind feet to help it swim. The beaver lives in or near the water in a house built of branches, stones, and mud. It can build dams from these same materials to keep the water around its house. Most beavers live in North America.
  bea·ver (bē′vər) *noun, plural* **beavers.**

became Past tense of **become**. The train *became* hot when the air conditioning broke. Look up **become** for more information.
be·came (bi kām′) *verb.*

because For the reason that. You're cold *because* you did not wear your sweater. I drank two glasses of water *because* I was thirsty.
• **because of.** On account of. They were late for the wedding *because of* a flat tire.
be·cause (bi kôz′) *conjunction.*

beckon To make a sign or signal by moving the hand or head. I *beckoned* to my friends to come closer so they could hear me.
beck·on (bek′ən) *verb,* **beckoned, beckoning.**

become **1.** To grow to be; come to be. Tadpoles *become* frogs. I *became* tired after running six laps. **2.** To look good on; flatter; suit. That blue shirt *becomes* you.
• **to become of.** To happen to. What has *become of* my pencil?
be·come (bi kum′) *verb,* **became, become, becoming.**

becoming Looking good on; flattering. The color green is *becoming* to you.
be·com·ing (bi kum′ing) *adjective.*

bed **1.** Something used to sleep or rest on. This *bed* needs a new mattress. The deer slept on a *bed* of leaves. **2.** A piece of ground used to grow plants in. We planted roses in the flower *bed.* **3.** The ground at the bottom of a river, lake, or other body of water. The stream had a *bed* of sand and pebbles. **4.** A foundation or support. The road was built on a *bed* of gravel. *Noun.*
—To give a place to sleep to. The farmer decided to *bed* the dogs in the barn. *Verb.*
bed (bed) *noun, plural* **beds;** *verb,* **bedded, bedding.**

bedding Sheets, blankets, and other coverings used on a bed. Extra *bedding* is kept in the hall closet.
bed·ding (bed′ing) *noun.*

bedpan A pan used as a toilet by a person who cannot get out of bed.
bed·pan (bed′pan′) *noun, plural* **bedpans.**

bedraggled Wet, limp, and dirty. We found a *bedraggled* kitten under the porch during the thunderstorm.
be·drag·gled (bi drag′əld) *adjective.*

bedrock Solid, unbroken rock beneath the soil or looser rock.
bed·rock (bed′rok′) *noun.*

bedroom A room for sleeping. Our dog likes to sleep in my *bedroom.*
bed·room (bed′rüm′ or bed′rùm′) *noun, plural* **bedrooms.**

bedside The space beside a bed. The nurse hurried to the patient's *bedside.*
bed·side (bed′sīd′) *noun, plural* **bedsides.**

bedspread A top cover for a bed.
bed·spread (bed′spred′) *noun, plural* **bedspreads.**

bedtime The time at which a person goes to bed. My *bedtime* is nine o'clock during the week.
bed·time (bed′tīm′) *noun, plural* **bedtimes.**

bee **1.** An insect that has a thick, hairy body, four wings, and, sometimes, a stinger. A bee feeds on nectar and pollen. Some bees live in colonies and make honey and beeswax. **2.** A gathering of people to work on something together or to have a contest. The fifth graders won the spelling *bee.* The club members gathered for a sewing *bee.* ⟁ Another word that sounds like this is **be.**
bee (bē) *noun, plural* **bees.**

beech A tree that has smooth, light gray bark and small, sweet nuts. ⟁ Another word that sounds like this is **beach.**
beech (bēch) *noun, plural* **beeches.**

Leaf in Autumn

beech

beef The meat of a steer, cow, or bull.
beef (bēf) *noun.*

beefsteak A slice of beef to be broiled or fried.
beef·steak (bēf′stāk′) *noun, plural* **beefsteaks.**

at; āpe; fär; câre; end; mē; it; īce; pîerce; hot; ōld; sông, fôrk; oil; out; up; ūse; rüle; pùll; tûrn; chin; sing; shop; thin; this; hw in white; zh in treasure. The symbol ə stands for the unstressed vowel sound in about, taken, pencil, lemon, and circus.

beehive   A nest or house that bees live in.
bee·hive (bē′hīv′) *noun, plural* **beehives.**

Commercial Beehive

beehive

been   Past participle of **be.** I have *been* visiting my grandparents for a week. ▲ Another word that sounds like this is **bin.**
been (bin) *verb.*

beer   An alcoholic drink made from specially treated grains, called malt, and the fruit of a certain plant, called hops.
beer (bîr) *noun, plural* **beers.**

beeswax   The yellow wax given out by honeybees and used by them to make their honeycombs.
bees·wax (bēz′waks′) *noun.*

beet   A plant with a thick, round, fleshy root. The leaves grow on long stalks from the top of the root. The leaves and roots are cooked and eaten as vegetables. ▲ Another word that sounds like this is **beat.**
beet (bēt) *noun, plural* **beets.**

beetle   An insect with hard front wings that cover the thin hind wings when they are folded. Beetles have chewing mouth parts.
bee·tle (bē′təl) *noun, plural* **beetles.**

befall   To happen to or happen. We were sad that misfortune had *befallen* our friends.
be·fall (bi fôl′) *verb,* **befell** (bi fel′), **befallen, befalling.**

before   1. In front of; ahead of. There were four people *before* me in line. We arrived at the airport *before* three o'clock.   2. In the presence of. The criminals stood *before* the judge for sentencing. *Preposition.*
—1. At an earlier time; previously. I've seen them *before.*   2. In front; in advance. Some soldiers went on *before* to scout. *Adverb.*
—1. Earlier than the time when. It grew dark *before* the children finished the game.

2. Rather than; sooner than. I would beg *before* I would steal. *Conjunction.*
be·fore (bi fôr′) *preposition; adverb; conjunction.*

beforehand   Ahead of time. Let's find out *beforehand* what we're having for dinner.
be·fore·hand (bi fôr′hand′) *adverb.*

befriend   To become a friend to. My family *befriended* our new next-door neighbors.
be·friend (bi frend′) *verb,* **befriended, befriending.**

beg   1. To ask in a humble way. The late guest *begged* to be excused. I *beg* your pardon.   2. To ask in an eager or insisting way; plead. The child *begged* to go to the rodeo.   3. To ask for money or food as charity.
beg (beg) *verb,* **begged, begging.**

began   Past tense of **begin.** The train *began* to move. Look up **begin** for more information.
be·gan (bi gan′) *verb.*

beggar   A person who asks others for money, food, or clothes in order to live.
beg·gar (beg′ər) *noun, plural* **beggars.**

begin   1. To do the first part of something; make a start. The workers will *begin* to build the house next month. *Begin* your homework now.   2. To come into being; start. Spring *begins* in March.
be·gin (bi gin′) *verb,* **began, begun, beginning.**

beginner   A person who is starting to do something for the first time. This swimming class is for *beginners.*
be·gin·ner (bi gin′ər) *noun, plural* **beginners.**

beginning   1. The first part. The *beginning* of the story was exciting.   2. The time when something begins; start. Yesterday was the *beginning* of summer vacation.
be·gin·ning (bi gin′ing) *noun, plural* **beginnings.**

begonia   A tropical plant with flowers that are white, yellow, red, purple, or pink.
be·gon·ia (bi gōn′yə) *noun, plural* **begonias.**

begun   Past participle of **begin.** The game has already *begun.* Look up **begin** for more information.
be·gun (bi gun′) *verb.*

begonia

B

behalf **1. In behalf of.** For the benefit or good of; for. The school held a fair *in behalf of* the town hospital. **2. On behalf of.** As a representative of. The class president spoke *on behalf of* the whole class at the student assembly.
be·half (bi haf′) *noun.*

behave **1.** To do things in a certain way; act. You *behaved* bravely after you hurt your knee. **2.** To act in a good way. The children promised to *behave* themselves at the party if they were allowed to stay longer.
be·have (bi hāv′) *verb,* **behaved, behaving.**

behavior A way of behaving or acting. The children's *behavior* was good. The science class studied the *behavior* of grasshoppers.
be·hav·ior (bi hāv′yər) *noun.*

behead To cut off someone's head. Criminals were once executed by being *beheaded.*
be·head (bi hed′) *verb,* **beheaded, beheading.**

behind **1.** At the back of. I sit *behind* my best friend in school. The spy hid *behind* a tree. **2.** Later than; after. The second bus came ten minutes *behind* the first bus. **3.** Less advanced than; not as far or as high as. I've been sick, so I'm *behind* the rest of the class in my studies. Our team is three points *behind* the other team. **4.** In support of; backing. The whole town got *behind* the minister's plan. *Preposition.*
—**1.** At the back. I sneaked up on my friend from *behind.* **2.** In a place just left. When the picnic was over, I stayed *behind* to clean up. **3.** Less advanced than most others; below a goal or standard. They fell *behind* in their work. *Adverb.*
be·hind (bi hīnd′) *preposition; adverb.*

behold To look at; see. The campers stayed up late to *behold* the beauty of the stars.
be·hold (bi hōld′) *verb,* **beheld** (bi held′), **beholding.**

beige A pale brown color. *Noun.*
—Having the color beige. *Adjective.*
beige (bāzh) *noun, plural* **beiges;** *adjective.*

being Present participle of **be.** The baby is *being* washed. Look up **be** for more information. *Verb.*
—**1.** The state of existing; existence. Many of our customs came into *being* years ago. **2.** A person or animal. Platypuses are strange *beings. Noun.*
be·ing (bē′ing) *verb; noun, plural* **beings.**

belated Late. I received a *belated* birthday present a week after my birthday.
be·la·ted (bi lā′tid) *adjective.*

belch **1.** To let out gas from the stomach through the mouth; burp. **2.** To throw out or be thrown out violently or suddenly. The chimney *belched* smoke and sparks. Flames *belched* from the windows of the burning building. *Verb.*
—The act of belching. The baby gave a quiet *belch* after drinking from the bottle. *Noun.*
belch (belch) *verb,* **belched, belching;** *noun, plural* **belches.**

belfry A tower or a room in a tower where bells are hung. Some churches have a belfry.
bel·fry (bel′frē) *noun, plural* **belfries.**

Belgium A country in northwestern Europe.
Bel·gium (bel′jəm) *noun.*

belief **1.** A feeling that something is true, real, or worthwhile. My *belief* in God is strong. *Belief* in ghosts is not common. **2.** Something that is believed to be true; conviction. Our country was founded on the *belief* that all people are created equal.
be·lief (bi lēf′) *noun, plural* **beliefs.**

belfry

believe **1.** To feel sure that something is true, real, or worthwhile. The police didn't *believe* the story they were hearing. I *believe* in getting regular exercise. **2.** To feel sure that someone is telling the truth. They say they ran five miles, and I *believe* them. **3.** To think; suppose. I *believe* peanuts grow underground, but I'm not sure.
be·lieve (bi lēv′) *verb,* **believed, believing.**

bell **1.** A hollow metal object that is shaped like a cup. A bell makes a ringing sound when struck. **2.** Something that makes a ringing sound like a bell. The *bell* at our front door is an electric buzzer.
bell (bel) *noun, plural* **bells.**

belligerent **1.** Wanting to fight. That *belligerent* child always picks on other students.

at; āpe; fär; câre; end; mē; it; īce; pîerce; hot; ōld; sông, fôrk; oil; out; up; ūse; rüle; pull; tûrn; chin; sing; shop; thin; <u>th</u>is; hw in white; zh in treasure. The symbol ə stands for the unstressed vowel sound in about, taken, pencil, lemon, and circus.

2. Busy fighting; at war. The two *belligerent* countries fought a long battle.
bel·lig·er·ent (bə lij'ər ənt) *adjective.*

bellow To make a loud, deep sound; roar. The bull *bellowed* in the pasture. The angry giant *bellowed* at the children. *Verb.*
—A loud, deep sound; roar. *Noun.*
bel·low (bel'ō) *verb,* **bellowed, bellowing;** *noun, plural* **bellows.**

bellows A bag between two handles that has an opening. It makes a strong current of air when it is pumped open and closed. ▲ The word **bellows** may be used with a singular or plural verb. A *bellows* is used to make fires burn faster. *Bellows* are also used to produce sound in accordions and some other musical instruments.
bel·lows (bel'ōz) *plural noun.*

belly **1.** The front part of the body below the chest and above the legs; abdomen. **2.** The stomach. **3.** The underside of the body of an animal. A snake crawls on its *belly.* **4.** The under surface of something. The airplane made an emergency landing on its *belly.* *Noun.*
bel·ly (bel'ē) *noun, plural* **bellies.**

bellybutton The round scar on the belly of humans and most other mammals; navel.
bel·ly·but·ton (bel'ē but'ən) *noun, plural* **bellybuttons.**

belong **1.** To have a special or right place. The coat *belongs* in the closet, not on the floor. **2.** To be owned by someone. That book *belongs* to me. **3.** To be a member. Some stamp collectors *belong* to clubs.
be·long (bi lông') *verb,* **belonged, belonging.**

belongings Things owned by a person; possessions. I packed my *belongings* in a large box when we moved.
be·long·ings (bi lông'ingz) *plural noun.*

beloved Loved very much. The friendly dog was *beloved* by the whole neighborhood.
be·lov·ed (bi luv'id *or* bi luvd') *adjective.*

below In or to a lower place. From the roof we could see the street *below.* *Adverb.*
—**1.** In a lower place than; beneath. Our grandparents' apartment is just *below* ours. **2.** Less than. It was 5 degrees *below* 0 this morning. *Preposition.*
be·low (bi lō') *adverb; preposition.*

belt **1.** A strip or band of cloth, leather, or other material. People wear belts around the waist to hold up clothing. **2.** A region or area. We drove through the farm *belt* and saw many cows. **3.** A band that forms a loop and is wound around two wheels or pulleys. A belt transfers power or motion from one wheel or pulley to another. **4.** An endless band in a factory that carries objects that are being worked on by a row of people.
belt (belt) *noun, plural* **belts.**

bench **1.** A long seat. The friends sat on the park *bench* and talked. **2.** A long table for doing work on. The carpenter repaired the broken chair on a *bench.* **3.** The position or job of a judge in a court of law. The lawyer was appointed to the *bench.* *Noun.*
—To keep a player from playing. The coach *benched* the exhausted football player. *Verb.*
bench (bench) *noun, plural* **benches;** *verb,* **benched, benching.**

bend **1.** To change the shape of something by making it curved or crooked. We *bent* pieces of wire to make hooks. The stream *bends* to the left just beyond those trees. **2.** To move the top part of the body forward and down; stoop; bow. Can you *bend* over and touch your toes? *Verb.*
—Something bent. The campers' tent is just beyond the *bend* in the trail. *Noun.*
bend (bend) *verb,* **bent, bending;** *noun, plural* **bends.**

a **bend** in a river

beneath **1.** Lower than; below; under. We stood *beneath* the stars. The cellar is *beneath* the house. **2.** Unworthy of. Telling a lie is *beneath* you. *Preposition.*
—In a lower place; below. The house has an attic above and a basement *beneath.* *Adverb.*
be·neath (bi nēth') *preposition; adverb.*

beneficial Having a good effect; tending to help. Some insects are *beneficial* to plants.
ben·e·fi·cial (ben'ə fish'əl) *adjective.*

benefit Something that helps a person or thing; advantage. Plenty of sunshine is one of the *benefits* of living in Arizona. *Noun.*
—To be helpful to; be helped by. Rain will *benefit* the farmer's crops. *Verb.*
ben·e·fit (ben'ə fit) *noun, plural* **benefits;** *verb,* **benefited, benefiting.**

bent Past tense and past participle of **bend.** The bicycle fender was *bent* from the accident. Look up **bend** for more information. *Verb.*

70

—**1.** Curved or crooked. After the accident, the car had a *bent* fender. **2.** Determined; set. We were *bent* on going to the mountains for our vacation. *Adjective.*
bent (bent) *verb; adjective.*

beret A soft, round, flat cap.
be·ret (bə rā') *noun, plural* **berets.**

berry A small, juicy, fleshy fruit that has one or more seeds. Blueberries and grapes are berries that can be eaten. ⟁ Another word that sounds like this is **bury.**
ber·ry (ber'ē) *noun, plural* **berries.**

berth **1.** A bed or bunk on a train or ship. I had the upper *berth* on our train trip. **2.** A place for a ship to dock. The freighter was in its *berth* in the harbor. ⟁ Another word that sounds like this is **birth.**
berth (bûrth) *noun, plural* **berths.**

beseech To ask someone in a pleading way; beg. I *beseech* you to help me.
be·seech (bi sēch') *verb,* **besought** (bi sôt') or **beseeched, beseeching.**

beset To surround and attack. The hunter and the dogs *beset* the bear.
be·set (bi set') *verb,* **beset, besetting.**

beside **1.** At the side of; next to. Sit down *beside* me. You can put that book *beside* the lamp on the table. **2.** Compared with. This bicycle looks tiny *beside* that motorcycle. **3.** Not connected with. What you just said is *beside* the point.
be·side (bi sīd') *preposition.*

besides In addition; also. I don't want to go; *besides,* I have work to do. We have two dogs and a cat *besides. Adverb.*
—In addition to. *Besides* you, no one else is coming to lunch. *Preposition.*
be·side (bi sīdz') *adverb; preposition.*

besiege **1.** To surround in order to capture. The soldiers *besieged* the fort. **2.** To crowd around. The fans *besieged* the famous singer.
be·siege (bi sēj') *verb,* **besieged, besieging.**

best **1.** Of the highest quality; better than all others. My friend is the *best* pitcher on our baseball team. **2.** Most preferred; most suitable. What is the *best* way home from here? **3.** Largest. The canoe trip took the *best* part of a day. *Adjective.*
—**1.** With the most success or effectiveness. I work *best* when I work by myself. **2.** Most. I like all fruits, but I like peaches *best. Adverb.*
—Something or someone of the highest quality. I studied all week so that I would do my *best* on the test. They're all good swimmers, but Sandy is the *best. Noun.*

—To do better than; defeat. Our chess team *bested* the other team in a close match. *Verb.*
best (best) *adjective; adverb; noun; verb,* **bested, besting.**

bestow To give. The school *bestowed* a medal on the outstanding athlete.
be·stow (bi stō') *verb,* **bestowed, bestowing.**

bet An agreement to pay money to another person if that person is right about something and you are wrong. I made a *bet* with my friend that our team would win. The other team won, so I lost the *bet. Noun.*
—**1.** To agree to pay money to another person if that person is right about something and you are wrong; make a bet. I *bet* my friend that I could do twenty push-ups, and I won. **2.** To say with confidence; be certain. I *bet* it won't rain tomorrow. I *bet* we arrive by nightfall. *Verb.*
bet (bet) *noun, plural* **bets;** *verb,* **bet** or **betted, betting.**

betray **1.** To give help to the enemy of. They *betrayed* their country by giving secret information to the invaders. **2.** To be unfaithful to. You should not *betray* your friends by telling their secrets to others.
be·tray (bi trā') *verb,* **betrayed, betraying.**

better **1.** Of higher quality. These are *better* pants than those torn ones. **2.** More preferred; more suitable. A firm mattress is *better* for your back. **3.** Improved in health. I was sick with the flu, but I'm much *better* now. **4.** Larger; greater. We spent the *better* part of Saturday cleaning the attic. *Adjective.*
—**1.** With more success or effectiveness. Cactuses grow *better* in dry soil. **2.** To a higher degree; more. I like painting *better* than gardening. *Adverb.*
—Something or someone of higher quality. Which is the *better* of these two books? *Noun.*
—**1.** To make better; improve. You can *better* your piano playing if you practice more. **2.** To do better than; outdo. The runner *bettered* the school record for the 100-yard dash. *Verb.*
- **better off.** In a better situation or condition. We'll be *better off* staying here until the rain stops.

---

at; āpe; fär; câre; end; mē; it; īce; pîerce; hot; ōld; sông; fôrk; oil; out; up; ūse; rüle; pùll; tûrn; chin; sing; shop; thin; <u>th</u>is; hw in white; zh in treasure. The symbol ə stands for the unstressed vowel sound in about, taken, pencil, lemon, and circus.

• **had better.** Ought to. You *had better* start studying if you want to do well on the science test.
bet·ter (bet'ər) *adjective; adverb; noun, plural* **betters;** *verb,* **bettered, bettering.**

between **1.** In the space or time separating. The table is *between* the chairs. There is a rest period *between* classes. **2.** Joining; connecting. There is a bridge *between* the island and the mainland. **3.** Involving; among. A quarrel broke out *between* two students. **4.** By the combined action of. *Between* us, we can clean our room in an hour. **5.** By comparing. You can choose *between* pancakes and oatmeal for breakfast. *Preposition.* ▲ Look up **among** for a Language Note about this word.
—In the space or time separating two things. A sandwich is two pieces of bread with a filling *between. Adverb.*
be·tween (bi twēn') *preposition; adverb.*

beverage A liquid for drinking. Orange juice, milk, and cocoa are beverages.
bev·er·age (bev'ər ij) *noun, plural* **beverages.**

beware To be on one's guard; be careful. *Beware* of the traffic when you cross the street. *Beware* of that dog.
be·ware (bi wâr') *verb.*

bewilder To confuse or puzzle; mix up. The hard arithmetic problem *bewildered* the student.
be·wil·der (bi wil'dər) *verb,* **bewildered, bewildering.**

bewitch **1.** To cast a spell over someone using magic. In the story, the wicked fairy *bewitched* the prince and turned him into a frog. **2.** To charm. The child's beautiful smile *bewitched* everyone.
be·witch (bi wich') *verb,* **bewitched, bewitching.**

beyond **1.** On the far side of. Our camp is just *beyond* those trees. **2.** Later than. The children stayed awake well *beyond* their bedtime. **3.** Outside the reach or limits of; too advanced for. What the scientist told us about computers was *beyond* me. The veterinarian told us that our old dog was *beyond* help. *Preposition.*
—Farther on. Look *beyond,* and you'll see the mountains in the distance. *Adverb.*
be·yond (bē ond') *preposition; adverb.*

bi- A *prefix* that means "having or involving two." *Bilevel* means "having two levels."

bias A strong feeling for or against a person or thing that keeps someone from being fair. A good judge never shows *bias* during a trial. *Noun.*

—To cause to have or show bias. Don't be *biased* against the movie just because I didn't like it. *Verb.*
bi·as (bī'əs) *noun, plural* **biases;** *verb,* **biased, biasing.**

Bible **1.** The sacred writings of the Christian religion, contained in the Old Testament and the New Testament. **2.** The Old Testament alone, which is part of the sacred writings of the Jewish religion.
Bi·ble (bī'bəl) *noun.*

biblical Found in the Bible; relating to the Bible. The story of Noah's ark is a *biblical* story. Joshua is a *biblical* name.
bib·li·cal (bib'li kəl) *adjective.*

bibliography A list of books about a subject. This book on dinosaurs has a *bibliography* in the back.
bib·li·og·ra·phy (bib'lē og'rə fē) *noun, plural* **bibliographies.**

biceps The large muscle that runs down the front of the arm from the shoulder to the elbow. When it is contracted, the arm bends.
bi·ceps (bī'seps) *noun, plural* **biceps** or **bicepses.**

bicker To quarrel in a noisy way about something that is not very important. The two brothers *bickered* over whose turn it was to mow the lawn.
bick·er (bik'ər) *verb,* **bickered, bickering.**

bicuspid A tooth with two points. A grown person has eight bicuspids.
bi·cus·pid (bī kus'pid) *noun, plural* **bicuspids.**

bicycle A light vehicle with two wheels, one behind the other. It has a seat, handlebars to steer with, and two foot pedals to turn the wheels and make it go forward. *Noun.*
—To ride a bicycle. Sometimes I *bicycle* to school. *Verb.*
bi·cy·cle (bī'si kəl) *noun, plural* **bicycles;** *verb,* **bicycled, bicycling.**

bicycles

bid   **1.** To give an order to; command. The general *bid* the soldiers to march.   **2.** To say when meeting or leaving someone. The children *bid* their friend good-bye.   **3.** To offer to pay. We *bid* thirty-five dollars for the old desk at the auction. *Verb.*
—An offer to pay money. The rug was sold to the person who made the highest *bid. Noun.*
   bid (bid) *verb* **bid** or **bidden, bidding;** *noun, plural* **bids.**

bide   **To bide one's time.** To wait for the right moment or chance. I'm going to *bide my time* until I find a bicycle that I really want to buy.
   bide (bīd) *verb,* **bided, biding.**

big   **1.** Great in size or amount; large. Chicago is a *big* city. A redwood is a *big* tree.   **2.** Very important. That was a *big* moment in my life.   **3.** Proud and boasting. Some people are *big* talkers, but get little done.
   big (big) *adjective,* **bigger, biggest.**

Big Dipper   A group of seven bright stars that looks like a ladle in outline. It is found in the northern part of the sky.

bighorn   A wild sheep that lives in the Rocky Mountains of North America. Bighorn have large, curled horns.
   big·horn (big′hôrn′) *noun, plural* **bighorn** or **bighorns.**

bike   A bicycle. *Noun.*
—To ride a bicycle. Let's *bike* down to the park and back. *Verb.*
   bike (bīk) *noun, plural* **bikes** *verb,* **biked, biking.**

bile   A bitter yellow or green liquid made in the liver. Bile helps the body to digest food.
   bile (bīl) *noun.*

bilingual   **1.** Speaking or writing two languages. My Canadian friends are *bilingual;* they speak both French and English very well.   **2.** Spoken or written in two languages. There are several *bilingual* dictionaries in our library.
   bi·lin·gual (bī ling′gwəl) *adjective.*

Word History

Bilingual comes from a Latin word meaning "two tongues." The Latin word for "tongue" can also mean "language" or "speech." A bilingual person does not have two tongues but does speak two languages.

bill¹   **1.** A notice of money owed for something bought or for work done. Mom pays the telephone *bill* every month. Why is the *bill* for repairs on my bike so high?   **2.** A piece of paper money. The shopper paid for the book with a five-dollar *bill.*   **3.** A poster or sign with an advertisement. A *bill* on the wall advertised a sale at the store.   **4.** A suggested law. The new tax *bill* was passed by Congress. *Noun.*
—To send a written notice of money owed to someone. The store will *bill* us for the things we are buying today. *Verb.*
   bill (bil) *noun, plural* **bills;** *verb,* **billed, billing.**

bill²   The hard, projecting mouth part of a bird or a turtle; beak. The woodpecker has a heavy, pointed bill. The duck has a broad, flat bill.
   bill (bil) *noun, plural* **bills.**

bill²

billboard   A large board placed outdoors for displaying signs or advertisements. Billboards are often seen along highways.
   bill·board (bil′bôrd′) *noun, plural* **billboards.**

billfold   A folding case for paper money. Many billfolds also have places for a driver's license, cards, and other things.
   bill·fold (bil′fōld′) *noun, plural* **billfolds.**

billiards   A game played with hard balls that are hit with a long stick called a cue. Billiards is played on a large, felt-covered table with a raised edge.
   bil·liards (bil′yərdz) *noun.*

billion   One thousand times one million; 1,000,000,000.
   bil·lion (bil′yən) *noun, plural* **billions;** *adjective.*

billow   A great swelling wave of something. *Billows* of smoke poured out of the burning house. *Noun.*
—To rise or swell in billows. Smoke *billowed* from the chimney of the factory. The sail of the boat *billowed* in the wind. *Verb.*
   bil·low (bil′ō) *noun, plural* **billows;** *verb,* **billowed, billowing.**

at; āpe; fär; câre; end; mē; it; īce; pîerce; hot; ōld; sông, fôrk; oil; out; up; ūse; rüle; pull; tûrn; chin; sing; shop; thin; this; hw in white; zh in treasure. The symbol ə stands for the unstressed vowel sound in about, taken, pencil, lemon, and circus.

bin A closed place or box for holding or storing something. Coal for the furnace is stored in a *bin*. ▲ Another word that sounds like this is **been**.
bin (bin) *noun, plural* **bins**.

binary system A system of numbers that uses only 0 and 1. In the binary system, any number can be expressed by 0, 1, or a combination of these. The ordinary decimal number 2 is the same as the binary number 10. Many electronic computers use the *binary system* of numbering.
bi·na·ry system (bī′nə rē).

bind 1. To tie together; fasten. The clerk *bound* the packages with string. 2. To tie a bandage around. The nurse will *bind* your sprained ankle. 3. To fasten together between covers. This machine *binds* the pages into a book. 4. To force by a promise or an obligation; oblige. The agreement *binds* me to work for the company for three years.
bind (bīnd) *verb,* **bound, binding**.

bingo A game in which each player covers numbers on a card as they are called out. The winner is the first player to cover a row of numbers or the whole card.
bin·go (bing′gō) *noun.*

binoculars A device that makes distant objects look larger and closer. Binoculars are made up of two small telescopes joined together, so that a person can look at distant objects with both eyes.
bi·noc·u·lars (bə nok′yə lərz) *plural noun.*

biodegradable Able to decay and to be absorbed by the environment. Food and paper are biodegradable. When they decay, they become part of the earth's natural resources.
bi·o·de·grad·a·ble (bī′ō di grā′də bəl) *adjective.*

biography A true story of someone's life written by another person.
bi·og·ra·phy (bī og′rə fē) *noun, plural* **biographies**.

biologist A person who works or specializes in biology.
bi·ol·o·gist (bī ol′ə jist) *noun, plural* **biologists**.

biology The study of living things. Biology deals with the way in which plants and animals and other living things live and grow, and where they are found.
bi·ol·o·gy (bī ol′ə jē) *noun.*

bionic Having to do with mechanical or electronic devices that work like the things in nature from which they are copied. A bionic arm and a real arm are both worked by signals from the brain.
bi·on·ic (bī on′ik) *adjective.*

birch Any of a large group of trees that have hard wood. One kind of birch has white bark.
birch (bûrch) *noun, plural* **birches**.

bird An animal that has wings, two legs, and a body covered with feathers. Birds have a backbone, are warm-blooded, and lay eggs. Most birds can fly. Eagles, robins, and penguins are birds.
bird (bûrd) *noun, plural* **birds**.

birth 1. The time when a person or animal first comes from its mother. The *birth* of the puppies was a happy occasion. 2. The start of something; beginning. The *birth* of the United States took place in 1776. ▲ Another word that sounds like this is **berth**.
• **to give birth to.** 1. To produce offspring. Our beagle *gave birth to* four puppies. 2. To produce or be the cause of something. The artist's work *gave birth to* a new style of painting.
birth (bûrth) *noun, plural* **births**.

birthday 1. The day on which a person is born. My best friend's *birthday* was December 12, 1980. 2. The return each year of this day.
birth·day (bûrth′dā′) *noun, plural* **birthdays**.

a **birthday** celebration

birthmark A mark on the skin that was there at birth.
birth·mark (bûrth′märk′) *noun, plural* **birthmarks**.

birthplace The place where a person was born. My *birthplace* was New Orleans. My grandparents' *birthplace* was Ireland.
birth·place (bûrth′plās′) *noun, plural* **birthplaces**.

birthright   A right or possession that a person is entitled to because of having been born into a certain family or at a certain time or place. The right to vote is a *birthright* of anyone born in the United States.
  birth·right (bûrth′rīt′) *noun, plural* **birthrights.**

biscuit   **1.** A small cake of baked dough. **2.** A cracker.
  bis·cuit (bis′kit) *noun, plural* **biscuits.**

Word History

Biscuit comes from an old French word meaning "baked twice." When dough was put in the oven twice, it became crisp and dry.

bisect   To divide into two equal parts. An angle is bisected when a straight line is drawn through the middle of it.
  bi·sect (bī sekt′ *or* bī′sekt) *verb.*

bishop   **1.** A Christian church official who has a high rank.   **2.** A piece in the game of chess.
  bish·op (bish′əp) *noun, plural* **bishops.**

Word History

Centuries ago, English borrowed the word **bishop** from a Greek word meaning "a person who watches over." The bishop was the person who watched over the religious life of the people.

bison   A large animal that has a big, shaggy head with short horns and a hump on its back; buffalo. Bison are found in North America.
  bi·son (bī′sən *or* bī′zən) *noun, plural* **bison.**

bison

bit¹   **1.** The metal piece of a bridle that goes into the horse's mouth. **2.** The part of a drilling tool that makes holes in wood or other material. A bit fits into the part of a tool called the brace.
  bit (bit) *noun, plural* **bits.**

bit¹

bit²   **1.** A small piece or part. They threw a *bit* of meat to the dog. The glass fell and broke into *bits*. **2.** A short while. Wait a *bit*.
  • **a bit.**   A little; slightly. Let's rest a while; I am *a bit* tired.
  bit (bit) *noun, plural* **bits.**

bit³   Past tense and a past participle of **bite.** The child *bit* into the sandwich. The cat was *bit* in the ear. Look up **bite** for more information.
  bit (bit) *verb.*

bit⁴   The smallest unit of memory in a computer. A bit may be either 0 or 1.
  bit (bit) *noun, plural* **bits.**

bite   **1.** To seize, cut into, or pierce with the teeth. The child *bit* off a piece of carrot. **2.** To wound with teeth, fangs, or a stinger. I smacked the mosquito before it could *bite* me.   **3.** To make something sting. The icy wind will *bite* our cheeks.   **4.** To take or swallow bait. The fish are not *biting* today. *Verb.*
  —**1.** A seizing or cutting into something with the teeth. The dog's *bite* caused a bad sore.   **2.** A wound made by biting. The cat scratched at the flea *bite*.   **3.** A piece bitten off. Do you want a *bite* of my apple?   **4.** A sharp sensation; sting. When I went out I felt the *bite* of the cold air. *Noun.*
  bite (bīt) *verb,* **bit, bitten** *or* **bit, biting;** *noun, plural* **bites.**

bitten   A past participle of **bite.** I had already *bitten* into the peach before I realized it wasn't ripe. Look up **bite** for more information.
  bit·ten (bit′ən) *verb.*

at; āpe; fär; câre; end; mē; it; īce; pîerce; hot; ōld; sông, fôrk; oil; out; up; ūse; rüle; pùll; tûrn; chin; sing; shop; thin; this; hw in white; zh in treasure. The symbol ə stands for the unstressed vowel sound in about, taken, pencil, lemon, and circus.

bitter **1.** Having a biting, harsh, bad taste. The strong coffee tasted *bitter*. I did not like the *bitter* cough medicine. **2.** Causing or showing sorrow or pain. The children shivered in the *bitter* cold. **3.** Showing anger, resentment, or hatred. The two rivals were *bitter* enemies.
bit·ter (bit′ər) *adjective.*

black **1.** The darkest of all colors; the opposite of white. **2.** A member of one of the major divisions of the human race; Negro. Blacks often have dark skin. *Noun.*
—**1.** Having the darkest of all colors. Coal is *black*. My favorite sneakers are *black*. **2.** Having no light; dark. When the lights went out, the room became *black*. **3.** Of or being a member of one of the major divisions of the human race; Negro. Both white and *black* families live in this neighborhood. **4.** Unhappy or gloomy. When they lost all their money, their future looked *black*. *Adjective.*
black (blak) *noun, plural* **blacks;** *adjective,* **blacker, blackest.**

blackberry A sweet, juicy black fruit. Blackberries grow on a prickly bush.
black·ber·ry (blak′ber′ē) *noun, plural* **blackberries.**

blackbird Any of various birds that are mostly black. Grackles, crows, and meadowlarks are blackbirds.
black·bird (blak′bûrd′) *noun, plural* **blackbirds.**

blackberries

blackboard A hard, smooth board made of slate or other material. Blackboards are used for writing or drawing on with chalk. Some blackboards are black, while others are green.
black·board (blak′bôrd′) *noun, plural* **blackboards.**

blacken **1.** To make or become black. Smoke from the fireplace *blackened* the walls of the room. The white curtains may *blacken* from the smoke. **2.** To do harm to. Don't *blacken* your reputation by lying.
black·en (blak′ən) *verb,* **blackened, blackening.**

black eye A bruise on the skin around the eye. A black eye is usually caused by a blow to the eye.

black hole An invisible object in space that has a pull of gravity so strong that nothing can escape from it, not even light.

blackmail The attempt to get money from a person by threatening to tell things that would harm the person's reputation. *Noun.*
—To try to get money from someone by threatening to tell bad things about that person. *Verb.*
black·mail (blak′māl′) *noun; verb,* **blackmailed, blackmailing.**

blackout A sudden loss of electrical power in a large area. Were you in an elevator when the *blackout* began?
black·out (blak′out′) *noun, plural* **blackouts.**

blacksmith A person who makes and repairs iron objects. A blacksmith heats the iron in a forge and then hammers it into shape on an anvil. A blacksmith can make horseshoes.
black·smith (blak′smith′) *noun, plural* **blacksmiths.**

blacktop A black material that is used for paving roads, playgrounds, and other surfaces. *Noun.*
—To pave a surface with this material. *Verb.*
black·top (blak′top′) *noun; verb,* **blacktopped, blacktopping.**

black widow A black spider. The female black widow is poisonous and has a red mark on her body. The female black widow is larger than the male, and often eats the male after mating.

bladder A small balloon-like part in the body. The bladder stores urine from the kidneys.
blad·der (blad′ər) *noun, plural* **bladders.**

blade **1.** The sharp part of anything that cuts. That knife has a sharp *blade*. **2.** A leaf of grass. **3.** The wide, flat part of something. I dipped the *blade* of the oar into the water. The *blades* of the fan spun around and crated a breeze. **4.** The runner of an ice skate.
blade (blād) *noun, plural* **blades.**

blame **1.** To find fault with. I don't *blame* you for getting angry at me when I took your bike without asking. **2.** To hold responsible for something wrong or bad. The neighbor *blamed* us for breaking the window. *Verb.*
—Responsibility for something wrong or bad. The other driver took the *blame* for the accident. *Noun.*
blame (blām) *verb,* **blamed, blaming;** *noun.*

blank **1.** Without writing or printing; unmarked. The teacher asked the class to turn

B

to a *blank* page in their notebooks. **2.** With empty spaces to be filled in. Please fill in the *blank* order form. **3.** Without thought; vacant. The sleepy child gave me a *blank* stare. *Adjective.*
—**1.** An empty space to be filled in. Fill in the *blank* with your name and address. **2.** A paper with spaces to be filled in. Everyone must fill in an application *blank* to open a bank account. **3.** A cartridge with gunpowder but no bullet. *Noun.*
blank (blangk) *adjective,* **blanker, blankest;** *noun, plural* **blanks.**

blanket **1.** A covering made of wool, nylon, or other material. Blankets are used on beds to keep people warm while they sleep. **2.** Anything that covers like a blanket. A *blanket* of fog lay over the town. *Noun.*
—To cover with a blanket. A foot of snow *blanketed* the city. *Verb.*
blan·ket (blang′kit) *noun, plural* **blankets;** *verb,* **blanketed, blanketing.**

blare **1.** To make a loud, harsh sound. The car horns *blared* in the traffic jam. **2.** To send or be sent out with loud, harsh sounds. The radio *blared* the news. Music *blared* from the loudspeakers at the baseball game. *Verb.*
—A loud, harsh sound. The *blare* of the horn awakened the baby. *Noun.*
blare (blâr) *verb,* **blared, blaring;** *noun, plural* **blares.**

blast **1.** A strong rush of wind or air. A *blast* of cold air blew into the room. **2.** A loud noise made by a horn. We heard the *blast* of trumpets in the marching band. **3.** An explosion. When the old building was blown up, the *blast* made the windows of our house rattle. *Noun.*
—**1.** To blow up with explosives. The workers *blasted* a hole in the rock with dynamite. **2.** To ruin. The rain *blasted* our hopes to have a picnic. *Verb.*
• **to blast off.** To take off into flight propelled by rockets. The spacecraft will *blast off* in an hour.
blast (blast) *noun, plural* **blasts;** *verb,* **blasted, blasting.**

blast-off The launching of a rocket or space vehicle. *Blast-off* is scheduled for noon tomorrow.
blast-off (blast′ôf′) *noun, plural* **blast-offs.**

blaze¹ **1.** A bright flame; a glowing fire. We could see the *blaze* of the burning building. **2.** A bright light. We shielded our eyes from the *blaze* of the sun. **3.** A bright display. The circus parade was a *blaze* of color. *Noun.*
—**1.** To burn brightly. The campfire *blazed*

all night. **2.** To shine brightly. The tree will *blaze* with lights on Christmas. *Verb.*
blaze (blāz) *noun, plural* **blazes;** *verb,* **blazed, blazing.**

blaze² A mark made on a tree or rock to show a trail or boundary. A blaze is made with paint or by chipping off a piece of bark. *Noun.*
—To show a trail or boundary by putting marks on trees or rocks. The hikers will *blaze* a trail through the woods. *Verb.*
blaze (blāz) *noun, plural* **blazes;** *verb,* **blazed, blazing.**

bleach To make something white. The sun *bleached* the sheets. We will *bleach* these shirts when we wash them. *Verb.*
—A substance used for bleaching. I used *bleach* to remove the stains in the sink. *Noun.*
bleach (blēch) *verb,* **bleached, bleaching;** *noun, plural* **bleaches.**

bleachers A group of seats or benches in rows placed one above and behind another. People sit in bleachers to watch an event, such as a baseball game or a parade.
bleach·ers (blē′chərz) *plural noun.*

blast-off

bleak   **1.** Open and not protected from the wind; bare. There were no trees growing on the *bleak* mountain top.   **2.** Cold and gloomy. It was a *bleak* December day. Everyone thought that the *bleak* old house was haunted.
bleak (blēk) *adjective*, **bleaker, bleakest.**

bled   Past tense and past participle of **bleed.** The cut finger *bled.* My bruised knee had *bled* only a little. Look up **bleed** for more information.
bled (bled) *verb.*

bleed   **1.** To lose blood. If you cut yourself, you will *bleed.*   **2.** To lose sap or other liquid. The tree will *bleed* if you cut into its trunk.
bleed (blēd) *verb*, **bled, bleeding.**

blemish   Something that spoils beauty or perfection; flaw. The scar is a *blemish* on his face. One day's absence was the only *blemish* on her attendance record. *Noun.*
—To spoil the beauty or perfection of something. Worm holes *blemish* an apple. *Verb.*
blem·ish (blem′ish) *noun, plural* **blemishes;** *verb*, **blemished, blemishing.**

blend   **1.** To   mix   together   completely. *Blend* the flour, milk, and eggs in a bowl. The voices in the choir *blend* well.   **2.** To shade into each other. The sea and sky seemed to *blend* on the horizon. *Verb.*
—A mixture. This drink is a *blend* of fruit juices. *Noun.*
blend (blend) *verb*, **blended, blending;** *noun, plural* **blends.**

bless   **1.** To make holy by a religious ceremony. The minister will *bless* the new chapel.   **2.** To ask God's help for. The minister *blessed* everyone in the church.   **3.** To make happy or fortunate. Members of our family have been *blessed* with good health.
bless (bles) *verb*, **blessed** or **blest, blessing.**

blessing   **1.** A prayer asking for God's favor, or giving thanks. The priest gave a *blessing* at the end of the church service.   **2.** A person or thing that brings happiness. The helpful child was a *blessing* to the disabled people in the building.   **3.** A wish for happiness or success; good wishes. Our old friends sent their *blessings* for a happy new year.
bless·ing (bles′ing) *noun, plural* **blessings.**

blew   Past tense of **blow.** I *blew* on the hot soup to cool it. Look up **blow** for more information. ⏃ Another word that sounds like this is **blue.**
blew (blü) *verb.*

blight   **1.** A disease of plants. Blight makes a plant wither and die.   **2.** Something that spoils the looks or health of something else. Those abandoned buildings are a *blight* on our city.
blight (blīt) *noun, plural* **blights.**

blimp   An airship that does not have a rigid framework to form its shape.
blimp (blimp) *noun, plural* **blimps.**

blind   **1.** Without sight; unable to see. The *blind* person asked the waiter what was on the menu.   **2.** Not easily seen; hidden. The sign warned of a *blind* driveway on the road ahead.   **3.** Done with instruments only and not with the eyes. The pilot of the airplane had to make a *blind* landing because of the storm.   **4.** Closed at one end. The thief ran into a *blind* alley and could not escape the police.   **5.** Without thinking or using one's judgment. If you don't know the answer to the question, make a *blind* guess. *Adjective.*
—**1.** To make unable to see. The sun will *blind* you if you look at it too long.   **2.** To take away thought or good judgment. Fear *blinded* the people in the theater when the fire broke out. *Verb.*
—Something that blocks a person's sight or keeps the light out. The teacher lowered the *blinds* of the window. *Noun.*
blind (blīnd) *adjective; verb*, **blinded, blinding;** *noun, plural* **blinds.**

blindfold   To cover someone's eyes with a strip of cloth or a bandage. We took turns *blindfolding* each other for the game. *Verb.*

blindfold

—A strip of cloth or other cover for the eyes. *Noun.*

blind·fold (blīnd′fōld′) *verb,* **blindfolded, blindfolding;** *noun, plural* **blindfolds.**

blink **1.** To close and open the eyes quickly. Everyone *blinked* as they walked out of the dark theater into the light of day. **2.** To flash on and off; twinkle. Stars *blinked* in the sky.

blink (blingk) *verb,* **blinked, blinking.**

bliss Great happiness. We were filled with *bliss* at the thought of our vacation.

bliss (blis) *noun.*

blister **1.** A sore place on the skin that looks like a small bubble. A blister is filled with a liquid. It is usually caused by rubbing or by a burn. There is a *blister* on my heel where my shoe rubbed it. **2.** Any small bubble or swelling. *Blisters* formed on the new coat of paint. *Noun.*
—To form a blister on; have blisters. Touching the hot iron made my finger *blister. Verb.*

blis·ter (blis′tər) *noun, plural* **blisters;** *verb,* **blistered, blistering.**

blizzard A heavy snowstorm with very strong winds.

bliz·zard (bliz′ərd) *noun, plural* **blizzards.**

bloat To make or become too full with a lot of liquid or gas; swell. Eating too much *bloated* our stomachs.

bloat (blōt) *verb,* **bloated, bloating.**

blob A drop or small lump of something soft. I got a *blob* of paint on my overalls.

blob (blob) *noun, plural* **blobs.**

block **1.** A piece of something hard and solid, with flat surfaces. The workers built a wall with *blocks* of stone. **2.** An area in a town or city with four streets around it. We walk our dog around the *block* every morning. **3.** The length of one side of a block in a town or city. I live three *blocks* from school. **4.** A number of things that are alike. The teacher bought a *block* of theater tickets so our class could sit together. **5.** Something that stops or obstructs something else; obstacle. The fallen tree was a *block* to traffic. **6.** A pulley in a frame. *Noun.*
—To get in the way of; obstruct. A tall building *blocks* the view from my window. The football player *blocked* the pass. *Verb.*

block (blok) *noun, plural* **blocks;** *verb,* **blocked, blocking.**

blockade A shutting off of an area to keep people and supplies from going in or out. During a war, a country may use ships to set up a blockade around an enemy country. *Noun.*

—To shut off with a blockade. A line of ships *blockaded* the enemy's harbor for one month. *Verb.*

block·ade (blo kād′) *noun, plural* **blockades;** *verb,* **blockaded, blockading.**

blockhouse **1.** A strong building made of wooden timbers or logs. It has holes in the walls to shoot weapons from. Blockhouses were formerly used as forts. **2.** A strong building near the launch pad of a rocket. A blockhouse is used to protect people who are watching rockets launch.

block·house (blok′hous′) *noun, plural* **blockhouses** (blok′hou′ziz).

blockhouse

blond **1.** Light yellow. He has *blond* hair like his mother. The bookcase is made of *blond* wood. **2.** Having light yellow hair and usually light-colored eyes and skin. Most of the members of that family are *blond. Adjective.*
—A person with light yellow hair and usually light-colored eyes and skin. *Noun.*
▲ This word is also spelled **blonde** when the person is a girl or woman.

blond (blond) *adjective,* **blonder, blondest;** *noun, plural* **blonds.**

blood **1.** The bright red liquid that is pumped by the heart. Blood circulates in the arteries and veins through all parts of the body. It carries oxygen and food to the body and takes away waste materials. **2.** Family relationship. The cousins are related by

at; āpe; fär; câre; end; mē; it; īce; pîerce; hot; ōld; sông, fôrk; oil; out; up; ūse; rüle; pùll; tûrn; chin; sing; shop; thin; <u>th</u>is; hw in white; zh in treasure. The symbol ə stands for the unstressed vowel sound in about, taken, pencil, lemon, and circus.

blood because their mothers are sisters. **3.** National origin; descent. *The scout was of Indian* blood.
blood (blud) *noun.*

blood bank A place where blood is collected and stored until it is needed to replace the blood someone has lost in an operation or an injury.

bloodhound A large dog with long, drooping ears and a wrinkled face. Bloodhounds have a good sense of smell. They are often used to track escaped criminals or find people who are lost.
blood·hound (blud′hound′) *noun, plural* **bloodhounds.**

bloodhound

bloodshed The loss of blood or life. *The king's soldiers won the battle without much* bloodshed.
blood·shed (blud′shed′) *noun.*

bloodshot Irritated and marked with reddish veins. When the eyes are tired, sometimes they become bloodshot.
blood·shot (blud′shot′) *adjective.*

bloodstream The blood flowing through the body.
blood·stream (blud′strēm′) *noun, plural* **bloodstreams.**

bloodthirsty Eager to cause bloodshed; cruel. *Bloodthirsty pirates sometimes attacked trading ships.*
blood·thirst·y (blud′thûr′stē) *adjective.*

blood vessel Any of the tubes in the body through which the blood flows. Arteries and veins are blood vessels.

bloody **1.** Covered or stained with blood. *The bandage on my cut knee was* bloody. **2.** Causing much bloodshed. *Many soldiers were killed in the* bloody *battle.*
blood·y (blud′ē) *adjective,* **bloodier, bloodiest.**

bloom **1.** The flower of a plant. *The forsythia branches were covered with yellow* blooms. **2.** The time of flowering. *The roses are in* bloom. *Noun.*
—To have flowers; blossom. *Cherry trees* bloom *in the spring. Verb.*
bloom (blüm) *noun, plural* **blooms;** *verb,* **bloomed, blooming.**

blossom **1.** The flower of a plant or tree, especially one that produces fruit. *We gathered* blossoms *from the apple trees.* **2.** The time of flowering. *The lilacs are in* blossom. *Noun.*
—**1.** To have flowers or blossoms; bloom. *The peach trees* blossom *in the spring.* **2.** To grow; develop. *The awkward child* blossomed *into a graceful adult. As the artist worked, the sketch* blossomed *into a detailed portrait. Verb.*
blos·som (blos′əm) *noun, plural* **blossoms;** *verb,* **blossomed, blossoming.**

blot **1.** A spot or stain. *The letter was neat, except for a* blot *at the end.* **2.** Something that spoils or mars. *Those billboards along the highway are a* blot *on the beautiful countryside. Noun.*
—**1.** To spot or stain. *Spilled ink* blotted *my letter.* **2.** To soak up or dry with a blotter. *Blot your signature so the ink won't smear. Verb.*
blot (blot) *noun, plural* **blots;** *verb,* **blotted, blotting.**

blotch A large spot or stain. *The spilled jelly left a* blotch *on the tablecloth. The rash covered my arms with red* blotches. *Noun.*
blotch (bloch) *noun, plural* **blotches.**

blotter A piece of soft, thick paper used to soak up or dry wet ink. *The lawyer used a* blotter *on the contract to dry the fresh ink.*
blot·ter (blot′ər) *noun, plural* **blotters.**

blouse A loose piece of clothing for the upper part of the body. A blouse may be worn with a skirt or pants.
blouse (blous *or* blouz) *noun, plural* **blouses.**

blow¹ **1.** A hard hit or stroke. A blow may be made with the fist, a tool, or some other object. *A heavy* blow *with a hammer drove the nail into the board.* **2.** A sudden event that causes great shock or unhappiness. *The death of their dog was a* blow *to the family.*
blow (blō) *noun, plural* **blows.**

blow² **1.** To move with speed or force. *An autumn breeze* blew *the leaves across the yard.* **2.** To send out a strong current of air. *Blow on your hands to warm them.* **3.** To move by a current of air. *My hat* blew *off as I ran to catch the bus.* **4.** To form or shape by a current of air. *Children love to* blow *soap bubbles.* **5.** To sound by a blast of air.

When the whistle *blows* the race will start.
6. To clear by forcing air through. I *blew* my nose.   **7.** To break or destroy by an explosion. The soldiers *blew* the enemy's bridge to pieces.   **8.** To burst because of being worn out, filled too much, or used too much.

- **to blow out.   1.** To stop burning or stop from burning. The lantern *blew out* during the storm. Make a wish and *blow out* the candles on the cake.   **2.** To burst. We drove to the side of the road when one of our tires *blew out.*
- **to blow up.   1.** To explode. The gasoline truck crashed and *blew up.*   **2.** To fill with air or gas. They *blew up* balloons for the party.   **3.** To lose one's temper. I'll *blow up* if they are this late again.   **4.** To start; arise. A storm *blew up* during the night.

blow (blō) *verb,* **blew, blown, blowing.**

blown   Past participle of **blow.** The telephone pole was *blown* down during the storm. Look up **blow** for more information.
blown (blōn) *verb.*

blowtorch   A small torch that shoots out a very hot flame. Blowtorches are used to melt metal and to burn off old paint.
blow·torch (blō'tôrch') *noun, plural* **blowtorches.**

blowtorch

blubber   A layer of fat under the skin of whales, seals, and some other sea animals. The oil made from whale blubber used to be burned in lamps. *Noun.*
—To cry and sob noisily. *Verb.*
blub·ber (blub'ər) *noun, plural* **blubbers;** *verb,* **blubbered, blubbering.**

blue   The color of the clear sky in the daytime. The colors of the American flag are red, white, and *blue. Noun.*
—**1.** Having the color blue.   **2.** Unhappy; discouraged. Before I made new friends, I felt *blue* during the first week away at camp. *Ad-*

jective. ▲ Another word that sounds like this is **blew.**

- **out of the blue.**   Suddenly and unexpectedly. The reason we were so shocked by the news was that it came *out of the blue.*

blue (blü) *noun, plural* **blues;** *adjective,* **bluer, bluest.**

blueberry   A small, dark blue, sweet berry with tiny seeds. Blueberries grow on a shrub.
blue·ber·ry (blü'ber'ē) *noun, plural* **blueberries.**

bluebird

bluebird   A small songbird of North America that has blue feathers on its back.
blue·bird (blü'bûrd') *noun, plural* **bluebirds.**

bluefish   A blue or green saltwater fish that lives in coastal waters in various parts of the world. It is caught for sport or food.
blue·fish (blü'fish') *noun, plural* **bluefish** or **bluefishes.**

bluegrass   A grass that has bluish green stems. Bluegrass is raised as food for cattle and horses and is used for lawns.
blue·grass (blü'gras') *noun, plural* **bluegrasses.**

blue jay   A bird of North America that has a crest on its head and blue feathers with black-and-white marks. A blue jay is a kind of jay.

blue jeans   Pants or overalls made of blue denim.

blueprint   **1.** A paper printed with white lines on a blue background. It is used to show the plan for building something. The construction workers looked at the *blueprints* as they built the house.   **2.** A detailed plan for

at; āpe; fär; câre; end; mē; it; īce; pîerce; hot; ōld; sông, fôrk; oil; out; up; ūse; rüle; půll; tûrn; chin; sing; shop; thin; <u>th</u>is; hw in white; zh in treasure. The symbol ə stands for the unstressed vowel sound in about, taken, pencil, lemon, and circus.

how to do or make something. The U.S. Constitution is a *blueprint* for democracy.
blue·print (blü′print′) *noun, plural* **blueprints.**

blues **1.** Sadness; low spirits. I've had the *blues* ever since my best friend moved away. **2.** Music that sounds sad and has a jazz rhythm.
blues (blüz) *plural noun.*

blue whale A blue-gray whale. The blue whale is the largest mammal that has ever lived.

bluff¹ A high, steep bank or cliff. As the ship came within sight of the shore they saw the *bluffs* jutting up from the sea.
bluff (bluf) *noun, plural* **bluffs.**

bluff² To try to fool people with a false show of courage, confidence, or knowledge. "Of course I know how to play," I said, but I was only *bluffing. Verb.*
—A false show of courage, confidence, or knowledge that is put on to fool other people. All your boasting about being able to speak Spanish and French turned out to be a big *bluff. Noun.*
bluff (bluf) *verb,* **bluffed, bluffing;** *noun, plural* **bluffs.**

blunder A careless or stupid mistake. Forgetting my friend's birthday was a *blunder. Noun.*
—**1.** To make a careless or stupid mistake. You really *blundered* when you said that Abraham Lincoln was the first president of the United States. **2.** To move in a clumsy way. The lost campers *blundered* through the woods looking for the path. *Verb.*
blun·der (blun′dər) *noun, plural* **blunders;** *verb,* **blundered, blundering.**

blunt **1.** Having a dull edge or point; not sharp. This pencil is *blunt* and needs to be sharpened. **2.** Very outspoken and frank about what one thinks. My friend's *blunt* criticism of my essay hurt my feelings. *Adjective.*
—To make less sharp; make dull. Don't *blunt* the scissors by using them to cut wire. *Verb.*
blunt (blunt) *adjective,* **blunter, bluntest;** *verb,* **blunted, blunting.**

blur To make dim or hard to see; make less clear. Fog began to *blur* the outline of the boat. Old age had *blurred* the artist's eyesight. *Verb.*
—Something that is dim or hard to see. The faces of the crowd were only a *blur* to the driver of the racing car. *Noun.*
blur (blûr) *verb,* **blurred, blurring;** *noun, plural* **blurs.**

blurt To say suddenly or without thinking. I was sorry after I *blurted* out the secret.
blurt (blûrt) *verb,* **blurted, blurting.**

blush To become red in the face. A person blushes when feeling ashamed, embarrassed, or confused. The shy student *blushed* when praised by the teacher. *Verb.*
—A becoming red in the face because of shame, embarrassment, or confusion. I listened with a *blush* as my parents corrected me. *Noun.*
blush (blush) *verb,* **blushed, blushing;** *noun, plural* **blushes.**

bluster **1.** To blow in a noisy or violent way. The wind *blustered* through the trees. **2.** To talk in a loud or threatening way. The store manager told the angry customer to stop *blustering* and calm down. *Verb.*
—**1.** A noisy, violent blowing. The *bluster* of the storm kept us awake all night. **2.** Loud, threatening talk. That bully is full of *bluster* but doesn't fight. *Noun.*
blus·ter (blus′tər) *verb,* **blustered, blustering;** *noun.*

Blvd. An abbreviation for *Boulevard* used in a written address.

boa constrictor

boa constrictor A large snake that is found in Mexico and in Central and South America. A boa constrictor is not poisonous. It kills its prey by coiling around it and squeezing it to death.
bo·a constrictor (bō′ə).

boar A wild pig that has bristles and a long snout. Boars live in forests in Europe and Asia. ◢ Another word that sounds like this is **bore.**
boar (bôr) *noun, plural* **boars.**

board **1.** A long, flat piece of sawed wood. Boards are used in building houses and other things. **2.** A flat piece of wood or other material used for some special purpose. Get the *board* and we'll play a game of checkers. **3.** A group of people who are chosen to manage or direct something. The school *board* helps to run the school. **4.** Meals served daily to guests for pay. The student found a

good room with *board* near campus. *Noun.*
—**1.** To cover with boards. The owner *boarded* up the broken window of the store. **2.** To get a room to sleep in and meals for pay. I *boarded* with a family in France last summer. **3.** To get on a ship, plane, or train. We will *board* the plane ten minutes before it leaves. *Verb.*

• **on board.** On, onto, or in a ship, plane, or train; aboard. When the plane took off, there were seventy-five people *on board.*

board (bôrd) *noun, plural* **boards;** *verb,* **boarded, boarding.**

boarding school A school that provides meals and a place to live for its students when the school is in session.

boast 1. To talk too much or with too much pride about oneself; brag. Those two are always *boasting* of their good grades. **2.** To be proud of having. Our town *boasts* a big new sports arena. *Verb.*
—A statement in which one brags. I try not to listen to the bullies' *boasts* about their strength. *Noun.*

boast (bōst) *verb,* **boasted, boasting;** *noun, plural* **boasts.**

boat 1. A small vessel that is used for traveling on water. A boat is moved by using oars, paddles, sails, or a motor. Passengers in a boat usually sit in the open air. **2.** A ship. An ocean liner is a boat. *Noun.*
—To go in a boat. We want to spend the vacation *boating* and fishing. *Verb.*

boat (bōt) *noun, plural* **boats;** *verb,* **boated, boating.**

boathouse A building for sheltering or storing boats. They keep the sailboat in a *boathouse* during the winter.

boat·house (bōt′hous′) *noun, plural* **boathouses** (bōt′hou′ziz).

bob¹ To move up and down or back and forth with a jerky motion. The ball *bobbed* on the waves. The hen *bobbed* its head as it pecked its food. *Verb.*
—A jerky motion. The bus driver answered my question with a *bob* of the head. *Noun.*

bob (bob) *verb,* **bobbed, bobbing;** *noun, plural* **bobs.**

bob² 1. A short haircut for a woman or child. **2.** A float or cork of a fishing line. *Noun.*
—To cut hair short. *Verb.*

bob (bob) *noun, plural* **bobs;** *verb,* **bobbed, bobbing.**

bobbin A spool around which yarn or thread is wound. A bobbin is used in weaving and in sewing on a sewing machine.

bob·bin (bob′in) *noun, plural* **bobbins.**

bobcat

bobcat A small wildcat of North America. A bobcat has reddish brown fur with dark stripes or spots and a short tail.

bob·cat (bob′kat′) *noun, plural* **bobcats.**

bobolink A songbird of North and South America that lives in fields.

bob·o·link (bob′ə lingk′) *noun, plural* **bobolinks.**

bobsled A long sled for racing. A bobsled has two sets of runners, a steering wheel, and brakes.

bob·sled (bob′sled′) *noun, plural* **bobsleds.**

bobsled

at; āpe; fär; câre; end; mē; it; īce; pîerce; hot; ōld; sông, fôrk; oil; out; up; ūse; rüle; pull; tûrn; chin; sing; shop; thin; this; hw in white; zh in treasure. The symbol ə stands for the unstressed vowel sound in about, taken, pencil, lemon, and circus.

bobwhite A North American bird that has a reddish brown body with white, black, and tan markings. Its call sounds a little like its name. A bobwhite is a kind of quail.
 bob·white (bob′hwīt′ *or* bob′wīt′) *noun, plural* **bobwhites.**

bode To be a sign of. Those dark clouds *bode* a storm.
 bode (bōd) *verb,* **boded, boding.**

bodily Of the body. The people in the automobile accident were frightened but they suffered no *bodily* harm.
 bod·i·ly (bod′ə lē) *adjective.*

body **1.** The whole physical structure that makes up a person, animal, or plant. An athlete must have a strong *body.* **2.** The main part of a human being or animal, without the head, arms, and legs. This bathing suit covers the *body* but leaves the limbs bare. **3.** The main part of something. The *body* of the new jet airplane is very large. **4.** A group of persons or things. The student *body* at the high school is headed by a president. **5.** A separate mass. The Atlantic Ocean is a huge *body* of water. The sun, the moon, and the stars are heavenly *bodies.*
 bod·y (bod′ē) *noun, plural* **bodies.**

bodyguard A person or persons who protect someone from danger or attack. That senator will not travel without a *bodyguard.*
 bod·y·guard (bod′ē gärd′) *noun, plural* **bodyguards.**

bog Wet, spongy ground; marsh; swamp. Cranberries grow in *bogs. Noun.*
 —To become stuck. The car will *bog* down if you drive in the mud. I got *bogged* down on the last arithmetic problem. *Verb.*
 bog (bog) *noun, plural* **bogs;** *verb,* **bogged, bogging.**

boil¹ **1.** To heat or be heated so that bubbles form and steam is given off. Let's *boil* water for tea. Water *boils* at 212 degrees Fahrenheit. **2.** To cook by boiling. We *boiled* the potatoes for dinner. *Verb.*
 —The condition of boiling. Bring the water to a *boil* and then add the noodles. *Noun.*
 boil (boil) *verb,* **boiled, boiling;** *noun.*

boil² A red swelling beneath the skin that hurts. A boil is caused by infection and is full of pus.
 boil (boil) *noun, plural* **boils.**

boiler **1.** A large tank in which water is heated and turned into steam. The steam made in a boiler is used to heat buildings and to run engines. **2.** A pan or pot in which something is heated or boiled. We cooked the ears of corn in a large *boiler.*
 boil·er (boi′lər) *noun, plural* **boilers.**

boiling point The temperature at which a liquid begins to boil. The boiling point of water at sea level is 212 degrees on a Fahrenheit thermometer, or 100 degrees on a Centigrade thermometer.

bold **1.** Not afraid; brave. A person who is bold is willing to do dangerous things. The *bold* explorer pushed on into the jungle. The firefighter made a *bold* rescue of the child from the burning roof. **2.** Not polite; rude; fresh. The *bold* child talked back to the teacher. **3.** Very easy to see; standing out clearly. The jagged mountains make a *bold* outline against the sky.
 bold (bōld) *adjective,* **bolder, boldest.**

Bolivia A country in west-central South America.
 Bo·liv·i·a (bə liv′ē ə) *noun.*

boll The seed pod of a cotton or flax plant. ▲ Another word that sounds like this is **bowl.**
 boll (bōl) *noun, plural* **bolls.**

boll weevil A beetle that lays eggs in the seed pods of the cotton plant. Boll weevils cause a great deal of damage to cotton plants.
 boll wee·vil (wē′vəl).

bolster A long pillow or cushion. *Noun.*
 —To give support or strength to. The beams *bolstered* the roof of the cabin. The sight of land *bolstered* the sailors' low spirits. *Verb.*
 bol·ster (bōl′stər) *noun, plural* **bolsters;** *verb,* **bolstered, bolstering.**

bolt **1.** A rod used to hold things together. A bolt usually has a head at one end and screw threads for a nut at the other. **2.** A sliding bar for fastening a door. I closed the door and slid the *bolt* shut. **3.** The part of a lock that is moved by a key. **4.** A sudden spring or start. The frightened deer made a *bolt* for the woods. **5.** A flash of lightning. **6.** A roll of cloth or paper. *Noun.*

bolts of cloth

—1. To fasten with a bolt. *Bolt* the door for the night after you let the dog in. **2.** To spring or move suddenly. The child *bolted* out the door. The horse *bolted* and its rider fell off. **3.** To swallow quickly or without chewing; gulp down. My parents are always telling us not to *bolt* our breakfast. *Verb.*
bolt (bōlt) *noun, plural* **bolts;** *verb,* **bolted, bolting.**

bomb A hollow case filled with something that can explode. It is used as a weapon. A bomb explodes when it strikes something or when it is set off by a fuse or a timing device. *Noun.*
—To throw or drop a bomb on. The planes *bombed* the bridge so the soldiers could not attack the city. *Verb.*
bomb (bom) *noun, plural* **bombs;** *verb,* **bombed, bombing.**

bombard **1.** To attack with bombs or heavy fire from big guns. The attacking army used cannons to *bombard* the fort. **2.** To aim many questions or criticisms at. The reporters *bombarded* the candidates with questions.
bom·bard (bom bärd′) *verb,* **bombarded, bombarding.**

bomber An airplane used to drop bombs.
bomb·er (bom′ər) *noun, plural* **bombers.**

bond **1.** Something that fastens or holds together. The prisoner's *bonds* were made of rope. **2.** A feeling or understanding that holds people together; tie. There is a *bond* of friendship between the two teenagers. **3.** A certificate given by a government or a business for a loan of money. A bond is a promise to pay back the money borrowed on a certain date with interest.
bond (bond) *noun, plural* **bonds.**

bondage Slavery; lack of freedom. Abraham Lincoln freed the slaves from *bondage* in 1863.
bond·age (bon′dij) *noun.*

bone One of the parts of the skeleton of an animal with a backbone. Bones are hard and firm. Our star football player broke an ankle *bone* during the game. *Noun.*
—To take out the bones of. We *boned* the fish before cooking it. *Verb.*
bone (bōn) *noun, plural* **bones;** *verb,* **boned, boning.**

bonfire A large fire built outdoors. We sat around the *bonfire* at camp and sang songs.
bon·fire (bon′fīr′) *noun, plural* **bonfires.**

bongo drums A pair of small drums played with the hands while being held between the knees.
bon·go drums (bong′gō).

bonnet **1.** A covering for the head. A bonnet is usually tied under the chin by ribbons or strings. **2.** A covering for the head made of feathers. It is worn during ceremonies by North American Indians.
bon·net (bon′it) *noun, plural* **bonnets.**

bonus Something extra given or paid in addition to what is due or expected. At the end of the year, the workers received a *bonus* in addition to their wages.
bo·nus (bō′nəs) *noun, plural* **bonuses.**

bony **1.** Made of bone. The skeleton is a *bony* structure. **2.** Full of bones. The fish we caught was so *bony* that it was hard to eat. **3.** Very thin. A *bony* old dog came to our back door begging for food.
bon·y (bō′nē) *adjective,* **bonier, boniest.**

boo A sound made to frighten or to show dislike. My cousin leaped out of the closet and yelled *"Boo!" Interjection.*
—To show that one does not like something by shouting "boo." The crowd *booed* the baseball player who made an error. *Verb.*
boo (bü) *interjection; verb,* **booed, booing.**

book **1.** Sheets of paper fastened together between two covers. The pages of a book usually have writing or printing on them. I just read a *book* about whales. I like the pictures in this *book.* **2.** A section of a long printed work. There are sixty-three *books* in my Bible. *Noun.*
—To arrange for ahead of time. My parents *booked* rooms at the motel before we left on our trip. *Verb.*
book (bùk) *noun, plural* **books;** *verb,* **booked, booking.**

bookcase A set of shelves for holding books.
book·case (bùk′kās′) *noun, plural* **bookcases.**

bookkeeper A person who keeps the records of a business. The *bookkeeper* at the grocery store keeps a record of the store's sales.
book·keep·er (bùk′kē′pər) *noun, plural* **bookkeepers.**

booklet A small, thin book. Booklets usually have paper covers. A *booklet* of recipes came with the mixer.
book·let (bùk′lit) *noun, plural* **booklets.**

---

at; āpe; fär; câre; end; mē; it; īce; pîerce; hot; ōld; sông, fôrk; oil; out; up; ūse; rüle; pùll; tûrn; chin; sing; shop; thin; <u>th</u>is; hw in white; zh in treasure. The symbol ə stands for the unstressed vowel sound in about, taken, pencil, lemon, and circus.

B

bookmark   A piece of paper, a ribbon, or something similar that is placed in a book to show the page the reader wishes to return to.
book·mark (bùk′märk′) *noun, plural* **bookmarks.**

bookmobile   A truck or other vehicle that travels around with a collection of books that can be borrowed. Our librarian drives a *bookmobile* to nearby small towns and rural areas where there are no libraries.
book·mo·bile (bùk′mə bēl′) *noun, plural* **bookmobiles.**

boom¹   **1.** A deep, hollow sound. We heard the *boom* of thunder and knew that a storm was coming.   **2.** A time of fast growth. There was a *boom* in the sale of overshoes at the store after the heavy snowstorm. *Noun.*
—**1.** To make a deep, hollow sound. Our voices *boomed* in the empty house.   **2.** To grow suddenly and rapidly. The number of people at baseball games *booms* as summer comes closer. *Verb.*
boom (büm) *noun, plural* **booms;** *verb,* **boomed, booming.**

boom²   **1.** A long pole or beam used to stretch the bottom of a sail.   **2.** The long movable arm of a crane or derrick. The load being lifted hangs from the end of the boom.
boom (büm) *noun, plural* **booms.**

boomerang   A flat curved piece of wood. A boomerang can be thrown so that it returns to the thrower. A boomerang is used as a weapon by the native people of Australia.
boom·er·ang (bü′mə rang′) *noun, plural* **boomerangs.**

boon   A help; benefit. The rain was a big *boon* to my vegetable garden after so much dry weather.
boon (bün) *noun, plural* **boons.**

boost   **1.** A push or shove up. Give me a *boost* to help me climb up the tree.   **2.** Something that gives support or encouragement. The teacher's praise of my drawing gave me a *boost. Noun.*
—**1.** To push or shove up. I *boosted* my little brother over the fence.   **2.** To give support to; encourage. During the long hike, we found that singing *boosted* our spirits.   **3.** To make greater; increase. The factory *boosted* its production of cars. *Verb.*
boost (büst) *noun, plural* **boosts;** *verb,* **boosted, boosting.**

booster shot   An extra injection of a vaccine. A booster shot is given to continue the protection given by an earlier injection.
boost·er shot (bü′stər).

boot   A covering for the foot and lower part of the leg. Boots are usually made of leather or rubber. Put on your *boots* if you are going out to play in the snow. *Noun.*
—To kick. The player *booted* the football. *Verb.*
boot (büt) *noun, plural* **boots;** *verb,* **booted, booting.**

boots

bootee   A soft shoe for a baby. We bought a pair of *bootees* for our neighbor's baby that were knitted from wool. ▲ Another word that sounds like this is **booty.**
boot·ee (bü′tē) *noun, plural* **bootees.**

booth   **1.** A stall where things are sold or shown. People crowded around the refreshment *booth* at the fair.   **2.** A small closed place. I made a telephone call from a telephone *booth.* There was a long line of people at the ticket *booth* for the movie theater.
booth (büth) *noun, plural* **booths** (bü<u>th</u>z *or* büths).

booty   Things taken from people by force; plunder, loot. The *booty* that the pirates had gained by attacking ships included jewelry, coins, and silk. ▲ Another word that sounds like this is **bootee.**
boot·y (bü′tē) *noun, plural* **booties.**

border   **1.** A line where one country or other area ends and another begins; boundary. That fence marks the *border* between our yard and theirs.   **2.** A strip along the edge of something. This skirt has a pretty red *border. Noun.*
—**1.** To lie on the edge of. California *borders* Oregon.   **2.** To put an edging on. The handkerchief was *bordered* with lace. *Verb.*
bor·der (bôr′dər) *noun, plural* **borders;** *verb,* **bordered, bordering.**

bore¹   **1.** To make by digging or drilling. The road builders *bored* a tunnel through the mountain.   **2.** To make a hole in. The carpenter *bored* the wood with a drill. ⏴ Another word that sounds like this is **boar**.

bore (bôr) *verb,* **bored, boring.**

bore² To make very tired or restless by being uninteresting and dull. You can *bore* people by telling them the same jokes over and over again. *Verb.*

—A person or thing that is uninteresting and dull. That television program is a *bore.* *Noun.* ⏴ Another word that sounds like this is **boar**.

bore (bôr) *verb,* **bored, boring;** *noun, plural* **bores.**

bore³ Past tense of **bear.** We both *bore* our defeat in the spelling contest very well and congratulated the winner. Look up **bear** for more information. ⏴ Another word that sounds like this is **boar**.

bore (bôr) *verb.*

boredom The condition of being bored. *Boredom* with my job caused me to quit.

bore·dom (bôr′dəm) *noun.*

born **1.** Brought into life or being. The cat has newly *born* kittens. **2.** By birth; natural. That runner is a *born* athlete who plays almost every sport very well. *Adjective.*

—A past participle of **bear.** I was *born* and raised on a farm. Look up **bear** for more information. *Verb.* ⏴ Another word that sounds like this is **borne**.

born (bôrn) *adjective; verb.*

borne A past participle of **bear.** My friend has *borne* the pain of a sprained ankle without crying. Look up **bear** for more information. ⏴ Another word that sounds like this is **born**.

borne (bôrn) *verb.*

borough **1.** In some states of the United States, a town or village that governs itself. **2.** One of the five divisions of New York City. ⏴ Other words that sound like this are **burro** and **burrow**.

bor·ough (bûr′ō) *noun, plural* **boroughs.**

borrow **1.** To take something from another person with the understanding that it must be given back. I have no bicycle, but I can *borrow* my neighbor's. We *borrow* books from the library. **2.** To take something and use it as one's own. The word "chipmunk" was *borrowed* from the American Indians.

bor·row (bôr′ō *or* bor′ō) *verb,* **borrowed, borrowing.**

bosom The upper, front part of the chest. I hugged the kitten to my *bosom. Noun.*

—Close and dear. The visiting student and I soon became *bosom* buddies. *Adjective.*

bos·om (bùz′əm) *noun, plural* **bosoms;** *adjective.*

boss A person who watches over and plans the work of others. The *boss* hired three new people to help get the job done. *Noun.*

—To act like the boss of. The older campers tried to *boss* us around. *Verb.*

boss (bôs) *noun, plural* **bosses;** *verb,* **bossed, bossing.**

botany The study of plants. People who study botany learn about many kinds of plants and how they grow and where they grow.

bot·a·ny (bot′ə nē) *noun.*

both One and also the other; the two. *Both* players are left-handed. *Adjective.*

—The one and also the other. You may need a pencil and paper, so bring *both. Pronoun.*

—Equally; as well. That bowl you made is *both* beautiful and useful. *Conjunction.*

both (bōth) *adjective; pronoun; conjunction.*

bother **1.** To give trouble to; annoy. Noise *bothers* me when I study. **2.** To make concerned or worried. It *bothers* me that my parents aren't home yet. **3.** To take the trouble. Don't *bother* to make lunch for me. *Verb.*

—A person or thing that troubles or annoys. I think making my bed is a *bother. Noun.*

both·er (bo<u>th</u>′ər) *verb,* **bothered, bothering;** *noun, plural* **bothers.**

Botswana A country in south-central Africa.

Bot·swa·na (bot swä′nə) *noun.*

bottle A container to hold liquids. A bottle has a narrow neck that can be closed with a

bottles

at; āpe; fär; câre; end; mē; it; īce; pîerce; hot; ōld; sông, fôrk; oil; out; up; ūse; rüle; pùll; tûrn; chin; sing; shop; thin; <u>th</u>is; hw in white; zh in treasure. The symbol ə stands for the unstressed vowel sound in about, taken, pencil, lemon, and circus.

cap or stopper. Bottles are usually made of glass or plastic. *Noun.*
—To put in bottles. That company *bottles* soft drinks. *Verb.*
- **to bottle up.** To hide or control; hold in. I tried to *bottle up* my anger at their rude behavior.

bot·tle (bot′əl) *noun, plural* **bottles;** *verb,* **bottled, bottling.**

bottom 1. The lowest part. The ball rolled to the *bottom* of the hill. 2. The under or lower part. The *bottom* of the rowboat needs painting. 3. The ground under a body of water. The *bottom* of the pond is sandy. 4. The most important part; basis. The detective tried to get to the *bottom* of the mystery by asking questions. *Noun.*
—Lowest or last. I hid my money in the *bottom* drawer of my bureau. *Adjective.*

bot·tom (bot′əm) *noun, plural* **bottoms;** *adjective.*

bough A large branch of a tree. We fastened the swing to a *bough* of the tree. ▲ Other words that sound like this are **bow¹** and **bow³**

bough (bou) *noun, plural* **boughs.**

bought Past tense and past participle of **buy.** We *bought* groceries at the store. They have already *bought* tickets to the play. Look up **buy** for more information.

bought (bôt) *verb.*

boulder A large, usually rounded rock. The *boulder* fell off the cliff and blocked the road below.

boul·der (bōl′dər) *noun, plural* **boulders.**

boulevard A wide city street. A boulevard often has trees growing along its sides.

boul·e·vard (bùl′ə värd′) *noun, plural* **boulevards.**

bounce 1. To spring back or up after hitting something. The rubber ball *bounced* off the wall and back to me. 2. To cause to spring back or up. I *bounced* the basketball against the sidewalk. *Verb.*
—A spring; bound. With one *bounce* the ball disappeared over the fence. *Noun.*

bounce (bouns) *verb,* **bounced, bouncing;** *noun, plural* **bounces.**

bound¹ 1. Fastened; tied. The bank robbers left the guard *bound* and gagged. 2. Certain; sure. The team is *bound* to lose the game if the players don't practice. 3. Have an obligation; obliged. I am *bound* by my promise to keep the secret. *Adjective.*
—Past tense and past participle of **bind.** We *bound* the carton of books with rope. I *bound* up my hurt knee with a bandage. Look up **bind** for more information. *Verb.*

bound (bound) *adjective; verb.*

bound² 1. To leap; spring; jump. The rabbit *bounded* away into the woods. 2. To spring back after hitting something. The ball *bounded* off the wall. *Verb.*
—A long or high leap. With one *bound* the deer was across the stream. *Noun.*

bound (bound) *verb,* **bounded, bounding;** *noun, plural* **bounds.**

bound³ A line that marks the farthest edge; boundary. We marked the *bounds* of the volleyball court with string. *Noun.*
—To form the boundary of. A road *bounds* the farmer's land on the north. *Verb.*
- **out of bounds.** 1. Beyond the limits of a playing field or court. The soccer ball rolled *out of bounds.* 2. Not allowed; prohibited. The swimming pool is *out of bounds* to students after six o'clock.

bound (bound) *noun, plural* **bounds;** *verb,* **bounded, bounding.**

bound⁴ Going or intending to go; headed. The train is *bound* for New York.

bound (bound) *adjective.*

boundary A line that marks the edge of a country, state, or other area; border. The Rio Grande forms the *boundary* between Mexico and the United States.

bound·a·ry (bound′ə rē *or* boun′drē) *noun, plural* **boundaries.**

bountiful More than enough; abundant. The farmer had a *bountiful* harvest.

boun·ti·ful (boun′tə fəl) *adjective.*

bounty 1. A reward for killing a dangerous or destructive animal. 2. Generosity; goodness. Many poor people were helped by the rich family's *bounty.*

boun·ty (boun′tē) *noun, plural* **bounties.**

bouquet A bunch of flowers. I brought a *bouquet* of tulips to my sick friend.

bou·quet (bō kā′ *or* bü kā′) *noun, plural* **bouquets.**

bout 1. A trial of skill; contest. The two boxers will fight in the second *bout.* 2. An attack or outburst; fit; spell. The sick child had a *bout* of coughing.

bout (bout) *noun, plural* **bouts.**

bouquet

bow¹ 1. To bend forward. People bow to show respect, to greet someone, or to accept the applause of an audience. 2. To give in;

bow¹

submit. I *bowed* to my parents' wishes. *Verb.*
—A bending forward of the head or body.
Noun. ⓐ Another word that sounds like this
is **bough.**
> **bow** (bou) *verb,* **bowed, bowing;** *noun,*
> *plural* **bows.**

bow² **1.** A weapon for shooting arrows. A
bow is made of a strip of wood that is bent
by a string fastened to each end. **2.** A knot
with two or more loops. I'll tie a green *bow*
on the package. **3.** A long piece of wood
with horsehairs stretched from one end to
the other. This bow is used to play the violin
and other instruments that have strings.
> **bow** (bō) *noun, plural* **bows.**

bow³ The front end of a boat. ⓐ Another
word that sounds like this is **bough.**
> **bow** (bou) *noun, plural bows.*

bowels **1.** A long tube that forms the part
of the digestive system below the stomach;
intestines. **2.** The deepest part of something. The coal mine was in the *bowels* of the
earth.
> **bow·els** (bou'əlz) *plural noun.*

bowl¹ **1.** A rounded dish that holds things.
Will you please pour some milk into a *bowl*
for the cat? **2.** Something shaped like a
bowl. The round end of a spoon is called a
bowl. A football stadium is sometimes called
a bowl. ⓐ Another word that sounds like this
is **boll.**
> **bowl** (bōl) *noun, plural* **bowls.**

bowl² A wooden ball used in a game. *Noun.*
—**1.** To play the game of bowling. My classmates like to *bowl* on Saturday night. **2.** To
roll a ball in bowling. *Verb.* ⓐ Another word
that sounds like this is **boll.**
> **bowl** (bōl) *noun, plural* **bowls;** *verb,*
> **bowled, bowling.**

bowlegged Having legs that curve outward at the knee when the ankles are together.
> **bow·leg·ged** (bō'leg'id) *adjective.*

bowling A game that you play by rolling a
heavy ball so as to knock down wooden pins.
The balls are rolled on a wooden alley or a
smooth lawn.
> **bowl·ing** (bō'ling) *noun.*

box¹ **1.** A stiff container, usually having
four sides, a bottom, and a cover. A box is
made of cardboard, wood, or other material.
The clerk put the books in a large *box.* A ring
is missing from the jewelry *box.* **2.** A
closed-in area or place. We sat in a *box* at the
theater. *Noun.*
—To put in a box. I asked the farmer to *box*
the vegetables that I bought. *Verb.*
> **box** (boks) *noun, plural* **boxes;** *verb,*
> **boxed, boxing.**

box² A blow made with the open hand or
the fist. In the old movie, the mad scientist
woke the sleeping assistant with a *box* on the
ear. *Noun.*
—**1.** To hit with the open hand or the fist.
2. To fight someone with the fists as a sport.
The two fighters will *box* each other for the
championship. *Verb.*
> **box** (boks) *noun, plural* **boxes;** *verb,*
> **boxed, boxing.**

boxcar A car of a railroad train used to
carry freight. A boxcar is enclosed on all
sides and is loaded through a sliding door on
the side.
> **box·car** (boks'kär') *noun, plural* **boxcars.**

boxer **1.** A person who fights with the fists
as a sport. The *boxer* knocked out an opponent in the third round. **2.** A dog that has a
wide face and short hair. The boxer has a
tan or reddish-brown coat, sometimes with
white markings. Boxers are related to bulldogs.
> **box·er** (bok'sər) *noun, plural* **boxers.**

boxing The sport of fighting with the fists.
> **box·ing** (bok'sing) *noun.*

Boxing Day A holiday observed the first
weekday after Christmas in England, Canada, and some other countries.

boy A male child from birth to the time he
is a young man.
> **boy** (boi) *noun, plural* **boys.**

boycott To join with others in refusing to
buy from or deal with a person, nation, or
business. We *boycotted* the store to show
support for the strike by its employees. *Verb.*

---

at; āpe; fär; câre; end; mē; it; īce; pîerce; hot; ōld;
sông, fôrk; oil; out; up; ūse; rüle; pull; tûrn; chin;
sing; shop; thin; <u>th</u>is; hw in white; zh in treasure.
The symbol ə stands for the unstressed vowel
sound in about, taken, pencil, lemon, and circus.

—A planned joining with others in refusing to buy from or deal with a person, nation, or business. The people in our neighborhood led a *boycott* against the toy company because its toys were not safe. *Noun.*
boy·cott (boi'kot) *verb*, **boycotted, boycotting;** *noun, plural* **boycotts.**

Word History

About one hundred years ago a man named Captain Charles **Boycott** collected rent from farmers in Ireland. The owner of the land was English, and the farmers thought they should own the land themselves, instead of someone from another country. So they refused to pay their rent to Captain Boycott. None of the people would talk to him. Captain Boycott finally had to give up his job and go back to England. Since then, the word **boycott** has been used in talking about actions of this kind.

boyhood The time of being a boy. He spent his *boyhood* on a farm.
boy·hood (boi'hùd') *noun, plural* **boyhoods.**

boyish Of a boy; like a boy.
boy·ish (boi'ish) *adjective.*

boy scout A member of the Boy Scouts.

Boy Scouts An organization for boys. The Boy Scouts teaches boys outdoor skills, physical fitness, and good citizenship.

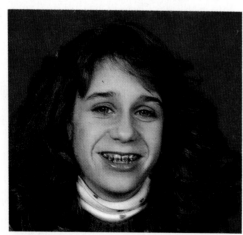
braces

brace 1. Something that holds parts together or holds a thing steady. The roof of the old shed needs a *brace* to hold it up. 2. **braces.** Metal wires used to help teeth to grow straight. 3. A tool that is like a handle. It is used to hold a drill or bit. 4. A pair. The pirate held a *brace* of pistols. We saw a *brace* of geese. *Noun.*
—1. To hold steady; support. The gardener *braced* the tree with wires so that the wind wouldn't blow it over. 2. To prepare for a shock. *Brace* yourself for some bad news. 3. To give energy to. The cold winter air *braced* us. *Verb.*
brace (brās) *noun, plural* **braces;** *verb,* **braced, bracing.**

bracelet A band or chain worn around the wrist as an ornament.
brace·let (brās'lit) *noun, plural* **bracelets.**

bracket 1. A piece of wood, metal, or stone fastened to a wall to support something. The shelf was held up by *brackets.* 2. One of two marks, [ ], used to enclose words or numbers. 3. Group. These books are for children in the 8-to-11 age *bracket. Noun.*
—1. To put words or numbers in brackets. 2. To group together. The teacher will *bracket* the students according to their reading speeds. *Verb.*
brack·et (brak'it) *noun, plural* **brackets;** *verb,* **bracketed, bracketing.**

brad A thin nail with a small head.
brad (brad) *noun, plural* **brads.**

brag To speak with too much praise about what one does or owns; boast. Stop *bragging* about how smart you are. The children *bragged* to their friends about their new swimming pool.
brag (brag) *verb,* **bragged, bragging.**

braid A strip made by weaving together three or more long pieces of hair, straw, or cloth. I wear my hair in *braids.* Our band uniform is decorated with gold *braid. Noun.*
—To weave together long pieces of hair, straw, or cloth. I *braided* a belt from strips of leather. *Verb.*
braid (brād) *noun, plural* **braids;** *verb,* **braided, braiding.**

braille A system of printing for blind people. The letters of the alphabet in braille are formed by raised dots. Blind people read braille by touching the dots with their fingers.
braille (brāl) *noun.*

Word History

The word **braille** comes from the name of the blind Frenchman, Louis *Braille,* who invented this way to read and write.

B

brain   **1.** The large mass of nerve tissue that is inside the skull of persons and animals. The brain is the main part of the nervous system. The brain controls the actions of the body. It is also the center of thought, memory, learning, and the emotions. **2. brains.** Intelligence. It takes *brains* to figure out this puzzle. *Noun.*
—To hit on the head. *Verb.*
  brain (brān) *noun, plural* **brains;** *verb,* **brained, braining.**

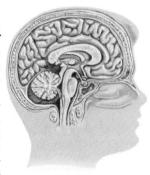

brain

brainstorm   A sudden, bright idea; inspiration. I tried for hours to find an answer to our problem, and then I had a *brainstorm.*
  brain·storm (brān′stôrm′) *noun, plural* **brainstorms.**

brake¹   A device used to stop or slow the movement of a vehicle. Many brakes work by pressing a pad against the moving wheel. *Noun.*
—To cause something to stop or slow down by using a brake. The rider *braked* the bicycle by pressing the pedals backward. The truck driver had to *brake* suddenly when a dog ran into the street. *Verb.* ▲ Another word that sounds like this is **break.**
  brake (brāk) *noun, plural* **brakes;** *verb,* **braked, braking.**

brake²   An area of ground covered with shrubs and bushes. ▲ Another word that sounds like this is **break.**
  brake (brāk) *noun, plural* **brakes.**

brakeman   A person who helps the conductor of a railroad train. In the past, the brakeman's job was to operate the train's brakes.
  brake·man (brāk′mən) *noun, plural* **brakemen** (brāk′mən).

bramble   A bush with thorny stems. The blackberry plant is a kind of bramble.
  bram·ble (bram′bəl) *noun, plural* **brambles.**

bran   The outer covering of wheat or other grains. The bran is separated from the flour by sifting. Bran is used in breakfast cereals and other foods.
  bran (bran) *noun.*

branch   **1.** A part of a tree or bush that grows out from the trunk. **2.** Something that goes out of or into a main part, like the branch of a tree. The main railroad line has many *branches.* The Missouri and Ohio rivers are *branches* of the Mississippi River. **3.** A division, office, or part of a large thing. I borrow books at my neighborhood *branch* of the city library. Arithmetic is a *branch* of mathematics. *Noun.*
—To divide into branches. Our cat got stuck in a place where the tree *branched.* Turn left at the place where the path *branches. Verb.*
  branch (branch) *noun, plural* **branches;** *verb,* **branched, branching.**

brand   **1.** A kind or make of something. We like that *brand* of orange juice. I tried a new *brand* of soap. **2.** A mark made on the skin of cattle or other animals. A brand is often made with a hot iron. It shows who owns an animal. **3.** A mark of disgrace. In former times a brand was burned on the skin of criminals. *Noun.*
—**1.** To mark with a brand. The cowhands will *brand* the cattle. **2.** To call by a bad or shameful name. I didn't want to be *branded* as a coward. *Verb.*
  brand (brand) *noun, plural* **brands;** *verb,* **branded, branding.**

brand-new   Completely new. The *brand-new* car didn't have any scratches or dirt on it.
  brand-new (brand′nü′ *or* brand′nū′) *adjective.*

brandy   An alcoholic drink that is made from fermented fruit juice or wine.
  bran·dy (bran′dē) *noun, plural* **brandies.**

brass trays

brass   **1.** A yellow metal that is a mixture of copper and zinc melted together.

---

at; āpe; fär; câre; end; mē; it; īce; pîerce; hot; ōld; sông, fôrk; oil; out; up; ūse; rüle; pull; tûrn; chin; sing; shop; thin; **this;** hw in white; zh in treasure. The symbol ə stands for the unstressed vowel sound in about, taken, pencil, lemon, and circus.

2. brasses. Wind instruments made of brass or other metal, such as trumpets and trombones.
    brass (bras) *noun.*

brat A child who misbehaves or has bad manners.
    brat (brat) *noun, plural* **brats.**

brave Having courage. A person who is brave can face danger or pain without being overcome by fear. The *brave* lifeguard jumped into the water to save the drowning child. *Adjective.*
—To face danger or pain without being overcome by fear. The firefighter *braved* the burning house to rescue the family. *Verb.*
    brave (brāv) *adjective,* **braver, bravest;** *verb,* **braved, braving.**

bravery The ability to face danger or pain without being overcome by fear; courage.
    brav·er·y (brā′və rē) *noun.*

Brazil A country in eastern South America.
    Bra·zil (brə zil′) *noun.*

breach A break made in something. Water poured through the *breach* in the dam. *Noun.*
—To make a break in; break through. The soldiers *breached* the enemy's lines. *Verb.*
    breach (brēch) *noun, plural* **breaches;** *verb,* **breached, breaching.**

bread **1.** A food made by mixing flour or meal with water or milk, and then baking it in an oven. **2.** The food and other things needed for a person to live. We earn our daily *bread* by working. ▲ Another word that sounds like this is **bred.**
    bread (bred) *noun, plural* **breads.**

breadth The wideness of something measured from one side to the other side; width.
    breadth (bredth) *noun.*

break **1.** To come apart or make something come apart by force; separate into pieces. The child dropped the glass and *broke* it. The mirror fell and *broke.* **2.** To crack a bone. Our best player *broke* a wrist during volleyball practice. **3.** To open the surface of. The scrape barely *broke* my skin. It's time to *break* ground for planting. **4.** To make or become useless because of damage; ruin. If you play roughly with that calculator, you might *break* it. **5.** To stop; end. It's hard to *break* a habit like biting your nails. **6.** To fail to obey or fulfill. Don't *break* the law. I never *break* a promise. **7.** To go beyond; surpass. This heat could *break* a record. **8.** To fill with sorrow. The disappointment *broke* my heart. **9.** To tell; reveal. I'll try to *break* the bad news gently. *Verb.*
—**1.** A broken place; something broken. We slipped through a *break* in the fence. The

break in my leg took a long time to heal. **2.** A sudden rush; dash. The children made a *break* for the door. **3.** A sudden change. Let's hope for a *break* in this rainy weather. **4.** A short rest period. I painted for an hour and then took a *break. Noun.* ▲ Another word that sounds like this is **brake.**

- **to break down.** **1.** To stop or stop working. Our car *broke down* on the road. **2.** To become ill physically or mentally. My cousin *broke down* from the strain of overwork. **3.** To lose one's self-control; act in an emotional way. I *broke down* and cried when my best friend moved away. **4.** To separate into smaller or simpler parts. The chemist *broke down* the substance into its elements.
- **to break in.** **1.** To make ready for use or wear. I'm *breaking in* a new pair of sneakers. **2.** To enter by force. A thief *broke in* through the back door. **3.** To interrupt. The student *broke in* with a question while the teacher was talking.
- **to break off.** To stop suddenly. The speaker *broke off* to take a drink of water.
- **to break out.** **1.** To start suddenly. A fire *broke out* in the basement. **2.** To become covered with a rash or pimples. The poison ivy made my skin *break out.* **3.** To escape. Three prisoners *broke out* last night.
- **to break up.** **1.** To separate, scatter, or disperse. The ice on the pond is *breaking up.* **2.** To come or bring to an end. The meeting *broke up* very late. The teacher *broke up* the fight.

    break (brāk) *verb,* **broke, broken, breaking;** *noun, plural* **breaks.**

breakdown **1.** A failing to work. Because of the *breakdown* of the car, we had to walk. **2.** A sudden loss of good health; collapse. When people work too hard, they sometimes suffer a *breakdown.*
    break·down (brāk′doun′) *noun, plural* **breakdowns.**

breaker A large wave that foams as it breaks on rocks or the shore.
    break·er (brā′kər) *noun, plural* **breakers.**

breakers

breakfast The first meal of the day. The children had *breakfast* before going to school. *Noun.*
—To eat breakfast. *Verb.*
break·fast (brek′fəst) *noun, plural* **breakfasts;** *verb,* **breakfasted, breakfasting.**

Word History

The word *fast* means "a time of eating little or no food." The morning meal **breakfast** was given its name because it is the meal that "breaks" the "fast" that lasts from after supper until waking up the next morning.

breast **1.** The front part of the body, between the stomach and the neck; chest. I pressed the baby to my *breast.* **2.** Either of the two milk glands of women.
breast (brest) *noun, plural* **breasts.**

breastbone The flat narrow bone in the center of the breast. The ribs are joined to the breastbone.
breast·bone (brest′bōn′) *noun, plural* **breastbones.**

breath **1.** Air drawn into and forced out of the lungs when you breathe. I can smell onions on your *breath.* **2.** The act of breathing; respiration. The doctor asked me to take deep *breaths* during the examination. **3.** The ability to breathe easily. It took only a few minutes for me to get my *breath* back after the race. **4.** A slight flow of air. There was not a *breath* of fresh air in the room.
• **to catch one's breath.** To rest or relax long enough to regain one's normal rhythm of breathing. I had to sit down to *catch my breath* after the long climb.
breath (breth) *noun, plural* **breaths.**

breathe **1.** To draw air into the lungs and then release it. The dog was *breathing* evenly as it slept. **2.** To whisper. Promise not to *breathe* a word of the secret.
breathe (brēth) *verb,* **breathed, breathing.**

breathless **1.** Out of breath. The messenger was *breathless* after running all the way. **2.** Holding the breath because of excitement or fear. The children were *breathless* as they watched the acrobats at the circus.
breath·less (breth′lis) *adjective.*

bred Past tense and past participle of **breed.** My friend *bred* puppies to sell. Look up **breed** for more information. ▲ Another word that sounds like this is **bread.**
bred (bred) *verb.*

breeches Pants that reach to or just below the knees. Men and boys wore breeches in the past.
breech·es (brich′iz) *plural noun.*

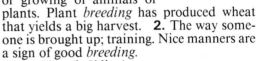
breeches

breed **1.** To raise plants or animals. They *breed* orchids in their greenhouse. Some farmers *breed* chickens to sell at the market. **2.** To bring forth young. **3.** To give rise to; produce. War and famine *breed* human misery. *Verb.*
—A particular kind of plant or animal. Dachshunds and collies are breeds of dogs. *Noun.*
breed (brēd) *verb,* **bred, breeding;** *noun, plural* **breeds.**

breeding **1.** The raising or growing of animals or plants. Plant *breeding* has produced wheat that yields a big harvest. **2.** The way someone is brought up; training. Nice manners are a sign of good *breeding.*
breed·ing (brē′ding) *noun.*

breeze A mild, gentle wind. The *breeze* made the flag flutter. *Noun.*
—To move in an easy or quick way. The older students *breezed* into the room. You will all *breeze* through this simple homework. *Verb.*
breeze (brēz) *noun, plural* **breezes;** *verb,* **breezed, breezing.**

brew **1.** To make beer or ale. Beer and ale are brewed by soaking, boiling, and fermenting malt and hops. **2.** To make by soaking in hot or boiling water. We *brewed* fresh coffee for the visitors. **3.** To bring about; cause. Those two children always seem to be *brewing* mischief. **4.** To form; gather. A storm is *brewing. Verb.*
—A drink made by brewing. *Noun.*
brew (brü) *verb,* **brewed, brewing;** *noun, plural* **brews.**

briar A thorny shrub. This word is usually spelled **brier.** Look up **brier** for more information.
bri·ar (brī′ər) *noun, plural,* **briars.**

at; āpe; fär; câre; end; mē; it; īce; pîerce; hot; ōld; sông, fôrk; oil; out; up; ūse; rüle; pùll; tûrn; chin; sing; shop; thin; <u>th</u>is; hw in white; zh in treasure. The symbol ə stands for the unstressed vowel sound in about, taken, pencil, lemon, and circus.

B

bribe   Money or gifts given to try to make a person do something wrong or something the person does not want to do. The crooks offered the police officer a *bribe* to let them go. *Noun.*
—To give a bribe to. I tried to *bribe* the child to stop crying by offering a toy. *Verb.*
> **bribe** (brīb) *noun, plural* **bribes;** *verb,* **bribed, bribing.**

brick   A block of clay baked in a kiln or in the sun. Bricks are used in building. The walls of my house are made of *bricks*.
> **brick** (brik) *noun, plural* **bricks.**

bride   A woman who has just married or is about to be married.
> **bride** (brīd) *noun, plural* **brides.**

bridegroom   A man who has just married or is about to be married.
> **bride·groom** (brīd′grüm′ *or* brīd′grüm′) *noun, plural* **bridegrooms.**

bridge   **1.** A structure built across a river, road, or railroad track so that people can get from one side to the other.   **2.** The top, bony part of a person's nose.   **3.** A raised structure on the deck of a ship. The captain or another officer guides or runs the ship from the bridge. *Noun.*
—To build a bridge across. The pioneers *bridged* the river with logs. *Verb.*
> **bridge** (brij) *noun, plural* **bridges;** *verb,* **bridged, bridging.**

bridle   The part of a horse's harness that fits over the animal's head. The bridle is used to guide or control the horse. *Noun.*
—**1.** To put a bridle on. The groom saddled and *bridled* a horse for me to ride.   **2.** To hold back; control. You should learn to *bridle* your bad temper. *Verb.*

bridle

> **bri·dle** (brī′dəl) *noun, plural* **bridles;** *verb,* **bridled, bridling.**

brief   **1.** Short in time. My cousins are in town for a *brief* visit.   **2.** Using few words. The business letter was very *brief. Adjective.*
—To give important details or facts to. The commander *briefed* the pilots just before their mission. *Verb.*
> **brief** (brēf) *adjective,* **briefer, briefest;** *verb,* **briefed, briefing.**

brier   A bushy plant with thorns. The raspberry plant and the blackberry plant are sometimes called briers. The thorns on these plants are also called briers. This word is also spelled **briar.**
> **bri·er** (brī′ər) *noun, plural* **briers.**

brig   **1.** A sailing ship with square sails on two masts.   **2.** A prison on a ship.
> **brig** (brig) *noun, plural* **brigs.**

brig

brigade   **1.** A large part of an army, made up of two or more battalions.   **2.** A group of people organized for a special purpose. My cousin belongs to a volunteer fire *brigade.*
> **bri·gade** (bri gād′) *noun, plural* **brigades.**

bright   **1.** Giving much light; filled with light. The *bright* light of the sun hurt the swimmer's eyes. The waxed floor has a *bright* shine.   **2.** Clear; strong. Let's paint the chair a *bright* red.   **3.** Smart; clever. *Bright* children often make up their own games. Poking that hornet's nest with a stick wasn't a very *bright* thing to do.
> **bright** (brīt) *adjective,* **brighter, brightest.**

brilliant   **1.** Very bright; sparkling. The diamond shone with a *brilliant* light.   **2.** Very fine; splendid. The fielder made a *brilliant* catch.   **3.** Very intelligent. The *brilliant* scientist won many awards.
> **bril·liant** (bril′yənt) *adjective.*

brim   An edge or rim. My glass is filled to the *brim*. That beach hat has a wide *brim. Noun.*
—To be full to the brim. The bathtub was *brimming* with water. *Verb.*
> **brim** (brim) *noun, plural* **brims;** *verb,* **brimmed, brimming.**

brine   Water that is full of salt. Brine is used for pickling foods.
> **brine** (brīn) *noun.*

bring   **1.** To cause something or someone to come with you. Remember to *bring* your books home. Come to the party, and *bring* your friend.   **2.** To cause something to come or happen. The heavy rains will *bring* floods.

3. To cause to reach a certain condition. The neighbors *brought* the fire under control. *Bring* the water to a boil. **4.** To be sold for. The silver necklace *brought* a high price.
- **to bring on.** To lead to; cause. That chilly wind *brought on* my stiff neck.
- **to bring out. 1.** To make clear; show. That shirt *brings out* the color of your eyes. **2.** To offer to the public; present. The producer is *bringing out* a new movie.
- **to bring up. 1.** To take care of during childhood; raise. After their parents died, their grandparents *brought* them *up*. **2.** To offer as a subject for discussion or consideration; mention. I *brought up* what happened at the game.

bring (bring) *verb,* **brought, bringing.**

brink 1. The edge at the top of a steep place. The old chief stood on the *brink* of the cliff to look down at the valley below. **2.** The point just before something happens. The baby is on the *brink* of tears. The two countries were on the *brink* of war.

brink (bringk) *noun, plural* **brinks.**

brisk 1. Quick and lively. The hike leader walked at a *brisk* pace. **2.** Refreshing; keen; bracing. We went out into the *brisk* winter air.

brisk (brisk) *adjective,* **brisker, briskest.**

bristle A short, stiff hair. Hogs have bristles. My toothbrush is made of *bristles.* *Noun.*
—**1.** To have the hairs on the neck or body rise. The dog *bristled* when it saw the fox. **2.** To stand up stiffly. The porcupine's quills *bristled. Verb.*

bris·tle (bris′əl) *noun, plural* **bristles;** *verb,* **bristled, bristling.**

Brit. An abbreviation for *Britain* or *British.*

Britain The countries of England, Scotland, and Wales; Great Britain.
Brit·ain (brit′ən) *noun.*

British Of Great Britain or the people of Great Britain. Drinking tea in the late afternoon is a *British* custom. *Adjective.*
—**the British.** The people of Great Britain. *Noun.*

Brit·ish (brit′ish) *adjective; noun.*

British Columbia A province in southwestern Canada. Its capital is Victoria.
Co·lum·bi·a (kə lum′bē ə).

brittle Very easily broken. The *brittle* icicles snapped in two when I touched them.
brit·tle (brit′əl) *adjective.*

broad 1. Large from one side to the other side; wide. There is a *broad* driveway in front of the school. **2.** Wide in range; not limited.

That collector has a *broad* knowledge of foreign stamps and coins. **3.** Clear and open. The thief robbed the bank in *broad* daylight.
broad (brôd) *adjective,* **broader, broadest.**

broadcast 1. To send out music, news, or other kinds of programs by radio or television. That radio station *broadcasts* twenty-four hours a day. The networks *broadcast* the president's speech. **2.** To make widely known. You shouldn't *broadcast* that secret to the whole school. *Verb.*
—Something that is broadcast; a radio or television program. My parents listen to the news *broadcast* every evening. *Noun.*
broad·cast (brôd′kast′) *verb,* **broadcast** or **broadcasted, broadcasting;** *noun, plural* **broadcasts.**

broaden To make or become broad or broader. The workers *broadened* the road. The path *broadens* just ahead.
broad·en (brô′dən) *verb,* **broadened, broadening.**

brocade A heavy cloth with patterns woven into it. The queen wore a robe of gold *brocade.*
bro·cade (brō kād′) *noun, plural* **brocades.**

broccoli A plant whose thick green stems and flower buds are eaten as a vegetable.
broc·co·li (brok′ə lē) *noun, plural* **broccoli.**

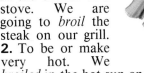
broccoli

broil 1. To cook over an open fire or under the flame in the broiler of a stove. We are going to *broil* the steak on our grill. **2.** To be or make very hot. We *broiled* in the hot sun on the beach. The hot sun *broiled* us.
broil (broil) *verb,* **broiled, broiling.**

broiler A pan, grill, or part of a stove that is used to broil food.
broil·er (broi′lər) *noun, plural* **broilers.**

broke Past tense of **break.** The cat knocked over the lamp and *broke* it. Look up **break** for more information. *Verb.*
—Having no money. I could not buy a new ball because I was *broke. Adjective.*
 broke (brōk) *verb; adjective.*

broken Past participle of **break.** You must have *broken* your watch when you dropped it. Look up **break** for more information. *Verb.*
—**1.** In pieces. You can throw away that *broken* dish. **2.** Not kept. You ought to say you're sorry for your *broken* promise. **3.** Not working; damaged. Our old television set is *broken.* **4.** Not spoken perfectly. The European tourists spoke *broken* English. *Adjective.*
 bro·ken (brō'kən) *verb; adjective.*

bronchial tubes The branches of the windpipe. Air flows to and from the lungs through the bronchial tubes.
 bron·chi·al tubes (brong'kē əl).

bronchitis A sickness from an inflammation of the bronchial tubes. When you have bronchitis you have a bad cough.
 bron·chi·tis (brong kī'tis) *noun.*

bronco A small, partly wild horse of the western United States. Broncos are descendants of the horses first brought to the New World by the Spanish.
 bron·co (brong'kō) *noun, plural* **broncos.**

brontosaur A huge dinosaur with a long neck and tail and a small head. It ate plants. This dinosaur is also called **brontosaurus.**
 bron·to·saur (bron'tə sôr') *noun, plural* **brontosaurs.**

bronze **1.** A reddish brown metal made by melting together copper and tin. Bronze is made into dishes, jewelry, and statues. **2.** A reddish brown color. *Noun.*
—Reddish brown. *Adjective.*
—To make reddish brown. The sun had *bronzed* the lifeguard's back. *Verb.*
 bronze (bronz) *noun, plural* **bronzes;** *adjective; verb,* **bronzed, bronzing.**

brooch A pin worn as an ornament. A brooch is fastened with a clasp.
 brooch (brōch *or* brüch) *noun, plural* **brooches.**

brood The young birds that are hatched from eggs at the same time. *Noun.*
—**1.** To sit on eggs in order to hatch them. Hens, robins, and other birds brood until the baby birds hatch from their eggs. **2.** To think or worry about for a long time. After I lost my new jacket, I *brooded* over it. *Verb.*
 brood (brüd) *noun, plural* **broods;** *verb,* **brooded, brooding.**

brook A small stream.
 brook (brŭk) *noun, plural* **brooks.**

broom **1.** A brush with a long handle, used for sweeping. **2.** A bush that has long, thin branches, small leaves, and usually yellow flowers.
 broom (brüm *or* brŭm) *noun, plural* **brooms.**

broth A thin soup. Broth is made by boiling meat, fish, or vegetables in water.
 broth (brôth) *noun, plural* **broths.**

brother A boy or man having the same parents as another person.
 broth·er (bruth'ər) *noun, plural* **brothers.**

brotherhood **1.** The close feeling between brothers or among a group of males. **2.** A group of people united by interest or aims. Labor unions are sometimes called brotherhoods.
 broth·er·hood (bruth'ər hŭd') *noun, plural* **brotherhoods.**

brother-in-law **1.** The brother of one's husband or wife. **2.** The husband of one's sister.
 broth·er·in·law (bruth'ər in lô') *noun, plural* **brothers-in-law.**

brought Past tense and past participle of **bring.** My friend *brought* me a birthday present. Have you *brought* your glasses? Look up **bring** for more information.
 brought (brôt) *verb.*

brow **1.** The part of the face above the eyes; forehead. The puppy wrinkled its *brow* when it heard the cat meow. **2.** The curved line of hair above the eye; eyebrow. **3.** The edge of a steep place. From the *brow* of the hill we could see for miles around.
 brow (brou) *noun, plural* **brows.**

brown A dark color like that of chocolate or cocoa. *Noun.*
—Having the color brown. *Adjective.*
—To make or become brown. The cook *browned* the onions in a frying pan. *Verb.*
 brown (broun) *noun, plural* **browns;** *adjective,* **browner, brownest;** *verb,* **browned, browning.**

brownie **1.** An elf or goblin. Brownies are supposed to do good things for people. **2.** A small, flat chocolate cake with nuts in it. **3. Brownie.** A girl who belongs to the junior division of the Girl Scouts.
 brown·ie (brou'nē) *noun, plural* **brownies.**

brownout A lessening of the electric power supplied to an area. Our lights dimmed during the *brownout.*
 brown·out (broun'out') *noun, plural* **brownouts.**

browse **1.** To look through something in a casual way. I *browsed* through the library books before choosing one. My cousin likes to *browse* in antique shops. **2.** To feed or nibble on the leaves or twigs of a tree or shrub. The giraffe *browsed* on the tree.
 browse (brouz) *verb*, **browsed, browsing.**

Word History

 Browse comes from a French word meaning "to feed on young shoots or sprouts." *Browse* was first used to describe the way some animals feed on the leaves of bushes and other plants. Later *browse* was used to describe the way people look around in a library or bookstore.

bruise **1.** An injury that does not break the skin but makes a bluish or blackish mark on it. A bruise is caused by a fall, blow, or bump. **2.** A mark on a fruit, vegetable, or plant caused by a blow or bump. *Noun.*
 —To cause a bruise on the skin of. I *bruised* my arm when I fell off my bicycle. *Verb.*
 bruise (brüz) *noun, plural* **bruises;** *verb,* **bruised, bruising.**

brunette **1.** Dark brown. The dancer had long, *brunette* hair. **2.** Having dark brown hair and dark-colored eyes. Your parents are both *brunette. Adjective.*
 —A person with dark-brown hair and dark-colored eyes. My relatives are all *brunettes. Noun.*
 bru·nette (brü net′) *adjective; noun, plural* **brunettes.**

brush¹ **1.** A tool that is used for scrubbing, smoothing, sweeping, or painting. A brush is made of bristles or hairs attached to a stiff back or to a handle. I used a clothes *brush* to get the cat hairs off my coat. **2.** The act of using a brush. Give your hair a good *brush.* **3.** A light touch in passing. I felt a *brush* on my arm as the bee flew by. *Noun.*
 —**1.** To scrub, smooth, sweep, or paint with a brush. *Brush* your teeth every day. **2.** To remove with a brush or with quick movements of the hand. I *brushed* the crumbs from my lap. **3.** To touch lightly in passing. Leaves and branches *brushed* our faces as we walked through the woods. *Verb.*
 • **to brush up.** To go over something again so as to refresh one's memory. We started the class by *brushing up* on our fractions.
 brush (brush) *noun, plural* **brushes;** *verb,* **brushed, brushing.**

brush² **1.** Shrubs, small trees, and bushes growing together. The frightened rabbit disappeared into the *brush.* **2.** Twigs or branches cut or broken off from trees. We cleared the *brush* from the yard.
 brush (brush) *noun.*

Brussels sprouts A leafy plant with a thick stem that has small buds that look like cabbages growing from it. The buds are eaten as a vegetable. These buds are also called Brussels sprouts.
 Brus·sels sprouts (brus′əlz).

Brussels sprouts

brutal Causing or allowing pain without caring; cruel. It's *brutal* to make children work in coal mines.
 bru·tal (brü′təl) *adjective.*

brute **1.** An animal. A brute cannot reason or feel the way a human being does. **2.** A cruel person. I saw that *brute* kicking an old dog.
 brute (brüt) *noun, plural* **brutes.**

bu. An abbreviation for *bushel.*

bubble A small round body of air or other gas, usually in or on the surface of a liquid. There are *bubbles* in soda water. The children blew soap *bubbles* with a pipe. *Noun.*
 —To form bubbles. Water *bubbles* when it is boiling. *Verb.*
 bub·ble (bub′əl) *noun, plural* **bubbles;** *verb,* **bubbled, bubbling.**

buck A male deer, antelope, rabbit, or goat. *Noun.*
 —**1.** To jump into the air with the back arched and the head down. The horse *bucked* and threw off the rider. **2.** To work or push against. We had to *buck* heavy traffic on the highway. *Verb.*
 buck (buk) *noun, plural* **bucks;** *verb,* **bucked, bucking.**

at; āpe; fär; câre; end; mē; it; īce; pîerce; hot; ōld; sông, fôrk; oil; out; up; ūse; rüle; pull; tûrn; chin; sing; shop; thin; this; hw in white; zh in treasure. The symbol ə stands for the unstressed vowel sound in about, taken, pencil, lemon, and circus.

bucket A sturdy container with a round, open top and a flat bottom; pail. Buckets are used for carrying water, sand, or other things.
buck·et (buk′it) *noun, plural* **buckets.**

buckle **1.** A fastener used to hold together the two ends of a belt or strap. My belt has a silver *buckle.* **2.** A bend or bulge in a flat surface. The heat caused a *buckle* in the surface of the road. *Noun.*
—**1.** To fasten with a buckle. The pilot told us to *buckle* our seat belts. **2.** To bend or bulge. The shelf began to *buckle* because I put too many books on it. *Verb.*
• **to buckle down.** To devote oneself with energy and determination. I *buckled down* and finished all my tasks.
buck·le (buk′əl) *noun, plural* **buckles;** *verb,* **buckled, buckling.**

buckskin A yellowish tan leather made from the skins of deer or sheep. Buckskin is strong and soft.
buck·skin (buk′skin′) *noun, plural* **buckskins.**

bucktooth An upper front tooth that sticks out. Braces are sometimes used to straighten buckteeth.
buck·tooth (buk′tüth′) *noun, plural* **buckteeth** (buk′tēth′).

buckwheat A plant whose seeds are used as feed for animals or are ground into flour.
buck·wheat (buk′hwēt′ *or* buk′wēt′) *noun, plural* **buckwheats.**

bud A small swelling on the stem or branch of a plant. A bud will later grow into a flower, leaf, or branch. *Noun.*
—To form buds. The trees are beginning to *bud. Verb.*
bud (bud) *noun, plural* **buds;** *verb,* **budded, budding.**

Buddha An Indian religious leader who was born about 563 B.C. and died about 483 B.C.
Bud·dha (bůd′ə *or* bü′də) *noun.*

Buddhism A religion based on the teachings of Buddha.
Bud·dhism (bůd′iz əm *or* bü′diz əm) *noun.*

buddy A close friend; pal. My *buddy* and I enjoy camping together.
bud·dy (bud′ē) *noun, plural* **buddies.**

budge To move just a little. The refrigerator wouldn't *budge* when I pushed it. We couldn't *budge* the heavy box.
budge (buj) *verb,* **budged, budging.**

budget A plan for using money. A budget shows how much money a person will have and the ways it will be spent. Mother and Father made a *budget* for household expenses for the month. The cost of building highways is a part of the *budget* of a state. *Noun.*

—To make a plan for the spending of money. If you *budget* your allowance carefully, you'll have enough left over for a treat at the end of the week. *Verb.*
budg·et (buj′it) *noun, plural* **budgets;** *verb,* **budgeted, budgeting.**

Word History

Budget comes from a word meaning the "leather bag" or "leather pouch" in which people put their money for safekeeping. Their coins represented all of the money they owned or could spend. Today *budget* still shows how much money is available for spending.

buff **1.** A soft, strong yellowish brown leather. Buff was formerly made from the skin of buffalo and is now made from the skin of oxen. **2.** A yellowish brown color. **3.** A wheel or stick with a soft covering, used for polishing things. *Noun.*
—Having the color of buff; yellowish brown. *Adjective.*
—To polish; shine. The soldier *buffed* the shoes to make them shiny. *Verb.*
buff (buf) *noun, plural* **buffs;** *adjective; verb,* **buffed, buffing.**

buffalo **1.** A large North American animal that has a big shaggy head with short horns and a hump on its back; bison. **2.** Any of various oxen of Europe, Asia, and Africa.
buf·fa·lo (buf′ə lō′) *noun, plural* **buffaloes** or **buffalos** or **buffalo.**

buffalo

buffet **1.** A piece of furniture. A buffet has a flat top to serve food from and drawers or shelves for storing dishes, silver, and table linen. **2.** A meal laid out on a buffet or a table so that guests may serve themselves.
buf·fet (bə fā′ *or* bü fā′) *noun, plural* **buffets.**

B

bug **1.** Any of a group of insects with front wings that fold across the back. Bugs have mouth parts that are like a beak and are for sucking. **2.** Any insect or crawling animal. Ants, spiders, and cockroaches are bugs. **3.** A germ that causes a disease. A lot of pupils missed school because of the flu *bug*. **4.** A fault in the working of a machine or a plan. There is some *bug* in the car engine that makes it stall. **5.** A hidden microphone used to overhear conversations. *Noun.*
—To hide a small microphone in. The spy *bugged* the room in order to overhear the secret conversation. *Verb.*
   bug (bug) *noun, plural* **bugs;** *verb,* **bugged, bugging.**

buggy A light carriage with four wheels. A buggy is pulled by one horse.
   bug·gy (bug′ē) *noun, plural* **buggies.**

bugles

bugle A brass musical instrument shaped like a trumpet. Bugles are used in the army and navy to sound signals.
   bu·gle (bū′gəl) *noun, plural* **bugles.**

bugler A person who plays a bugle.
   bu·gler (bū′glər) *noun, plural* **buglers.**

build **1.** To make by putting parts or materials together. I *built* a bookcase with boards and nails. The state will soon *build* a new highway near our farm. Beavers *build* dams. **2.** To form little by little; develop. That store owner is trying to *build* a successful business. You can *build* up your muscles by exercising. *Verb.*
—The way in which someone is put together. That football player has a strong *build. Noun.*
   build (bild) *verb,* **built, building;** *noun, plural* **builds.**

building **1.** Something built, especially a permanent structure for people to live or do things in. Houses, hotels, schools, stores, and garages are buildings. **2.** The act of making houses, stores, bridges, and similar things.
   build·ing (bil′ding) *noun, plural* **buildings.**

built Past tense and past participle of **build.** The children *built* a tree hut. The White House was *built* in the 1790s. Look up **build** for more information.
   built (bilt) *verb.*

built-in Built as a permanent part of something. Our den has *built-in* shelves and cabinets.
   built-in (bilt′in′) *adjective.*

bulb **1.** A round, underground part of some plants from which the plants grow. These plants live in the form of a bulb until the growing season comes and they put forth leaves and flowers. Onions, lilies, and tulips grow from bulbs. **2.** Any object with a rounded part. Put a new electric light *bulb* in the lamp. Mercury is contained in a *bulb* at the bottom of a thermometer.
   bulb (bulb) *noun, plural* **bulbs.**

Bulgaria A country in southeastern Europe.
   Bul·gar·i·a (bul gâr′ē ə *or* bùl gâr′ē ə) *noun.*

bulge A rounded part that swells out. The big rag made a *bulge* in the mechanic's back pocket. *Noun.*
—To swell out. The bag *bulged* with groceries. *Verb.*
   bulge (bulj) *noun, plural* **bulges;** *verb,* **bulged, bulging.**

bulk **1.** Large size. The *bulk* of the elephant made it hard for it to move around in its cage. **2.** The largest or main part. The farming family grew corn on the *bulk* of their land.
   bulk (bulk) *noun.*

bull **1.** The fully grown male of cattle. **2.** The fully grown male of some other animals, such as the elephant, moose, or seal.
   bull (bùl) *noun, plural* **bulls.**

bulldog A small, muscular dog. A bulldog has a large head, square jaws, short legs, and a smooth coat. The bulldog is known for the strong, stubborn grip of its jaws.
   bull·dog (bùl′dôg′) *noun, plural* **bulldogs.**

bulldozer A tractor with a powerful motor and a heavy metal blade in front. Bulldozers are used for clearing land by moving earth and rocks.
   bull·doz·er (bùl′dō′zər) *noun, plural* **bulldozers.**

---

at; āpe; fär; câre; end; mē; it; īce; pîerce; hot; ōld; sông, fôrk; oil; out; up; ūse; rùle; pùll; tûrn; chin; sing; shop; thin; <u>th</u>is; hw in white; zh in treasure. The symbol ə stands for the unstressed vowel sound in about, taken, pencil, lemon, and circus.

bullet   A small piece of rounded or pointed metal. A bullet is made to be shot from a small firearm, such as a gun or rifle.
bul·let (bùl′it) *noun, plural* **bullets.**

bulletin   **1.** A short announcement of the latest news. We heard a *bulletin* on the radio about the coming hurricane.   **2.** A small newspaper or magazine published regularly. Our club *bulletin* lists the dates of meetings.
bul·le·tin (bùl′i tin) *noun, plural* **bulletins.**

bullfight   A public show in which performers face and try to kill bulls in an arena. The performers do this in ways that display their skill and courage. Bullfights are popular in Spain, Mexico, and South America.
bull·fight (bùl′fīt′) *noun, plural* **bullfights.**

bullfrog   A large green or reddish brown frog. The male bullfrog has a loud, bellowing croak. The bullfrog is the largest frog in the United States.
bull·frog (bùl′frôg′ *or* bùl′frog′) *noun, plural* **bullfrogs.**

bull's-eye   **1.** The center circle of a target. The archer's arrow hit the *bull's-eye*.   **2.** A shot that hits this circle.
bull's-eye (bùlz′ ī′) *noun, plural* **bull's-eyes.**

bully   A person who likes to frighten or threaten others. Bullies usually pick on smaller or weaker people. *Noun.*
—To frighten or threaten into doing something. Those two tough students tried to *bully* us into carrying their books. *Verb.*
bul·ly (bùl′ē) *noun, plural* **bullies;** *verb,* **bullied, bullying.**

bumblebee   A large bee with a thick, hairy body. Most bumblebees have yellow and black stripes.
bum·ble·bee (bum′bəl bē′) *noun, plural* **bumblebees.**

bump   **1.** To strike or knock suddenly. The two cars *bumped* each other. Did you *bump* your knee on the chair?   **2.** To move with jerks and jolts. The wagon *bumped* along the dirt road. *Verb.*
—**1.** A heavy knock or blow. The *bump* on my head made me dizzy. **2.** A swelling or lump. There is a *bump* on my leg where the baseball hit it. The wasp's sting left a little *bump. Noun.*
bump (bump) *verb,* **bumped, bumping;** *noun, plural* **bumps.**

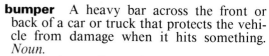
bumblebee

bumper   A heavy bar across the front or back of a car or truck that protects the vehicle from damage when it hits something. *Noun.*
—Very large. Our neighbor had a *bumper* crop of tomatoes this year. *Adjective.*
bump·er (bum′pər) *noun, plural* **bumpers;** *adjective.*

bun   A baked piece of bread dough or cake batter; roll. I would like my hamburger on a toasted *bun.*
bun (bun) *noun, plural* **buns.**

bunch   **1.** A number of things fastened or growing together. We bought a *bunch* of grapes at the fruit store.   **2.** A group of people. A *bunch* of us went to the movies. *Noun.*
—To gather together. The kittens *bunched* together to keep warm. *Verb.*
bunch (bunch) *noun, plural* **bunches;** *verb,* **bunched, bunching.**

bundle   A number of things tied or wrapped together. Put that *bundle* of newspapers in the trash can. *Noun.*
—To tie or wrap together. Help me *bundle* these dirty clothes for the laundry. *Verb.*
bun·dle (bun′dəl) *noun, plural* **bundles;** *verb,* **bundled, bundling.**

bungalow   A small house. A bungalow usually has only one story. We spent the weekend in a *bungalow* by the beach.
bun·ga·low (bung′gə lō′) *noun, plural* **bungalows.**

Word History

The word **bungalow** comes from the country of India, where it meant "a house built in the style of Burma." Burma is a country near India.

bunk   A narrow bed, especially one that is built against a wall like a shelf. *Noun.*
bunk (bungk) *noun, plural* **bunks.**

bunny   A small animal with long ears, a short tail, and soft fur; rabbit.
bun·ny (bun′ē) *noun, plural* **bunnies.**

Bunsen burner   An instrument that uses a mixture of air and gas to make a very hot, blue flame. Bunsen burners are often used in science laboratories.
Bun·sen burner (bun′sən).

bunt   To tap a baseball pitch so that the ball goes only a short distance. The batter *bunted* the ball. *Verb.*
—**1.** The act of bunting.   **2.** A baseball that has been bunted. *Noun.*
bunt (bunt) *verb,* **bunted, bunting;** *noun, plural* **bunts.**

100

buoy   1. A floating object that is anchored. Buoys are used to warn ships of dangerous rocks or to show the safe way through a channel.   2. A device used by a person to keep afloat in water; life preserver.
bu·oy (bü′ē *or* boi) *noun, plural* **buoys.**

bur   Another spelling for **burr.** Look up **burr** for more information.
bur (bûr) *noun, plural* **burs.**

burden   1. Something that is carried; load. The mule carried its *burden* of logs easily.   2. Something very hard to bear. Having an unusual name can be a *burden* to a child. *Noun.*
—To put too heavy a load on. Snow *burdened* the branches of the small tree. *Verb.*
bur·den (bûr′dən) *noun, plural* **burdens;** *verb,* **burdened, burdening.**

bureau   1. A chest of drawers. I keep my sweaters, shirts, and socks in my *bureau.*   2. A department of a government. I listen to the reports from the weather *bureau* on the radio every morning.   3. An office or agency. We bought our airplane tickets at the travel *bureau.*
bu·reau (byùr′ō) *noun, plural* **bureaus.**

burglar   A person who breaks into a house, store, or other place to steal something. *Burglars* broke into the hotel room and stole some valuable jewels.
bur·glar (bûr′glər) *noun, plural* **burglars.**

burial   The act of putting a dead body in the earth, a tomb, or the sea. Many people were present at the *burial* of the famous general.
bur·i·al (ber′ē əl) *noun, plural* **burials.**

burlap   A coarse cloth. Burlap is used for making bags, curtains, and wall coverings.
bur·lap (bûr′lap) *noun, plural* **burlaps.**

burly   Big, strong, and sturdy. A *burly* police officer was able to break through the locked door.
bur·ly (bûr′lē) *adjective,* **burlier, burliest.**

Burma   A country in southeastern Asia.
Bur·ma (bûr′mə) *noun.*

burn   1. To set on fire; be on fire. We helped *burn* the pile of leaves. The wood *burned* slowly.   2. To injure by fire, heat, or certain rays, like those of the sun. Be careful

buoy

not to *burn* your hand on the hot stove.   3. To make by fire or heat. A spark from the campfire *burned* a hole in the scout's jacket.   4. To feel or cause to feel very hot. The child *burned* with fever. The pepper *burned* my tongue.   5. To use as fuel to make light or heat. Our furnace *burns* oil. *Verb.*
—An injury caused by fire or heat. I got a *burn* on my hand from the hot iron. *Noun.*
• **to burn down** or **to burn up.** To destroy or be destroyed by fire. Three buildings *burned down* before the fire could be put out. The windmill completely *burned up* in one hour.
burn (bûrn) *verb,* **burned** or **burnt, burning;** *noun, plural* **burns.**

burner   The part of a stove or furnace from which the flame comes. Put the pot on the back *burner* of the stove.
burn·er (bûr′nər) *noun, plural* **burners.**

burnt   A past tense and a past participle of **burn.** The spark *burnt* a hole in the rug. The forest fire had *burnt* down many trees. Look up **burn** for more information.
burnt (bûrnt) *verb.*

burp   1. To let out gas from the stomach through the mouth; belch.   2. To cause to burp. He *burped* the baby by patting her lightly on the back.
burp (bûrp) *verb,* **burped, burping.**

burlap bags

at; āpe; fär; câre; end; mē; it; īce; pîerce; hot; ōld; sông, fôrk; oil; out; up; ūse; rüle; pùll; tûrn; chin; sing; shop; thin; **th**is; hw in white; zh in treasure. The symbol ə stands for the unstressed vowel sound in about, taken, pencil, lemon, and circus.

B

burr   **1.** A prickly covering of the fruit of some plants. Burrs stick to cloth and fur. **2.** Any plant that has burrs. This word is also spelled **bur.**
   burr (bûr) *noun, plural* **burrs.**

burro   A small donkey. Burros are used for riding and for carrying loads. ⋏ Other words that sound like this are **borough** and **burrow.**
   bur·ro (bûr′ō) *noun, plural* **burros.**

burrow   A hole dug in the ground by an animal. Rabbits, gophers, woodchucks, and other animals use burrows. *Noun.*
   —**1.** To dig a hole in the ground. Moles *burrow* in search of worms to eat.   **2.** To search. I *burrowed* in my pocket for the key to our house. *Verb.* ⋏ Other words that sound like this are **borough** and **burro.**
   bur·row (bûr′ō) *noun, plural* **burrows;** *verb,* **burrowed, burrowing.**

burst   **1.** To break open suddenly. The balloon *burst* when I stuck it with a pin. The buds on the roses were ready to *burst* into bloom.   **2.** To be very full. My closet is *bursting* with clothes.   **3.** To come or go suddenly. Please don't *burst* into my room. **4.** To show strong emotion suddenly. The baby *burst* into tears. We all *burst* out laughing. *Verb.*
   —**1.** The act of bursting; outbreak. There was a *burst* of laughter after I told the joke. **2.** A sudden effort. With a *burst* of speed, the runner won the race. *Noun.*
   burst (bûrst) *verb,* **burst, bursting;** *noun, plural* **bursts.**

bury   **1.** To put in the earth, a tomb, or the sea. When their dog died, they *buried* it beneath a tree on their farm.   **2.** To cover up; hide. The letter was *buried* in a pile of papers. ⋏ Another word that sounds like this is **berry.**
   bur·y (ber′ē) *verb,* **buried, burying.**

bus   A large motor vehicle with rows of seats for carrying many passengers. Buses usually go along a regular route. Many children go to school by *bus. Noun.*
   —To carry or go in a bus. Our town *buses* pupils to school. *Verb.*
   bus (bus) *noun, plural* **buses** or **busses;** *verb,* **bused** or **bussed, busing** or **bussing.**

bush   A low shrub. A bush is smaller than a tree and has many branches near the ground. Berries and roses grow on bushes.
   • **to beat around the bush.**   To speak in an indirect way and avoid getting to the point. Tell me what's worrying you and stop *beating around the bush.*
   bush (bush) *noun, plural* **bushes.**

bushel   A measure for grain, fruit, vegetables, and other dry things. A bushel is equal to 4 pecks, or 32 quarts. We bought a *bushel* of corn to roast for our picnic.
   bush·el (bush′əl) *noun, plural* **bushels.**

bushy   Thick and spreading like a bush. A squirrel has a *bushy* tail.
   bush·y (bush′ē) *adjective,* **bushier, bushiest.**

business   **1.** The work that a person does to earn a living. My *business* is farming. **2.** An activity that is carried on to make money, along with the place and equipment used. Stores and factories are businesses. The motel owner sold the *business.*   **3.** The buying and selling of things; trade. The kite shop does a big *business* in summer.   **4.** Matters or affairs. Don't meddle in other people's *business.*
   busi·ness (biz′nis) *noun, plural* **businesses.**

businessman   A man who owns or works in a business. The store manager and the farmer are *businessmen.*
   busi·ness·man (biz′nis man′) *noun, plural* **businessmen** (biz′nis men′).

businesswoman   A woman who owns or works in a business. The factory owner and the banker are *businesswomen.*
   busi·ness·wom·an (biz′nis wum′ən) *noun, plural* **businesswomen** (biz′nis wim′ən).

bust   A statue of a person's head and shoulders. There is a *bust* of that poet on a stand in our library.
   bust (bust) *noun, plural* **busts.**

bustle   To move or hurry in an excited or noisy way. Mother and Father *bustled* around getting everything ready for the birthday party. *Verb.*
   —Noisy, excited activity. There was much *bustle* as the family packed to go away on vacation. *Noun.*
   bus·tle (bus′əl) *verb,* **bustled, bustling;** *noun.*

busy   **1.** Doing something; active. I am *busy* tonight, so I can't baby-sit for the neighbors.   **2.** Full of activity. The airport is a *busy* place.   **3.** In use. When I telephoned, your line was *busy. Adjective.*
   —To make busy; keep busy. While they waited, they *busied* themselves with cleaning the room. *Verb.*
   bus·y (biz′ē) *adjective,* **busier, busiest;** *verb,* **busied, busying.**

busybody   A person who prys into or meddles in the affairs of other people.
   bus·y·bod·y (biz′ē bod′ē) *noun, plural* **busybodies.**

but **1.** On the other hand; in contrast. I am tall, *but* my best friend is short. **2.** In spite of this; nevertheless. My bruised knee hurt, *but* I did not cry. **3.** Other than; except. There is no direct route *but* through the center of town. *Conjunction.*
—Other than; except. Everyone has signed the card *but* you. *Preposition.*
—Only; just. I saw them *but* a few minutes ago. *Adverb.* ▲ Another word that sounds like this is **butt.**
but (but) *conjunction; preposition; adverb.*

butcher A person who cuts up or sells meat. I bought a roast from the *butcher.*
butch·er (bŭch′ər) *noun, plural* **butchers.**

Word History

The related words **buck** and **butcher** both come from words having to do with male goats. At one time, the word *buck* meant only "a male goat." *Butcher* comes from a French word meaning "a person who sells goat meat."

---

butler A male servant. A butler is the head servant in a household.
but·ler (but′lər) *noun, plural* **butlers.**

butt¹ **1.** The thicker or larger end of something. The hunter held the *butt* of the rifle against his shoulder. **2.** An end that is left over. Please throw out those cigarette *butts.* ▲ Another word that sounds like this is **but.**
butt (but) *noun, plural* **butts.**

butt² A person or thing that people make fun of. The mascot of the rival team was the *butt* of the children's teasing. ▲ Another word that sounds like this is **but.**
butt (but) *noun, plural* **butts.**

butt³ To strike hard with the head or the horns. The goat *butted* the gate. *Verb.*
—A push or blow with the head or the horns. The calf gave me a playful *butt. Noun.* ▲ Another word that sounds like this is **but.**
butt (but) *verb,* **butted, butting;** *noun, plural* **butts.**

butte A mountain or hill that stands alone. A butte has steep sides and, usually, a flat top.
butte (būt) *noun, plural* **buttes.**

butter **1.** A solid, yellowish fat. Butter is separated from cream or milk by churning. Butter is used as a spread for bread and in cooking. **2.** A spread that is like butter. Butter can be made from apples or from peanuts. *Noun.*
—To spread with butter. Please *butter* the bread for the sandwiches. *Verb.*
but·ter (but′ər) *noun, plural* **butters;** *verb,* **buttered, buttering.**

buttercup A plant that grows close to the ground and has yellow flowers shaped like cups.
but·ter·cup (but′ər kup′) *noun, plural* **buttercups.**

butterfat The yellow fat in milk. Butter is made from butterfat.
but·ter·fat (but′ər fat′) *noun.*

butterfly An insect with a thin body and four large, often brightly colored wings. Butterflies fly in the daytime.
but·ter·fly (but′ər flī′) *noun, plural* **butterflies.**

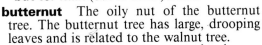

butterfly

buttermilk The sour liquid that is left after milk or cream has been churned to make butter.
but·ter·milk (but′ər milk′) *noun.*

butternut The oily nut of the butternut tree. The butternut tree has large, drooping leaves and is related to the walnut tree.
but·ter·nut (but′ər nut′) *noun, plural* **butternuts.**

butte

at; āpe; fär; câre; end; mē; it; īce; pîerce; hot; ōld; sông, fôrk; oil; out; up; ūse; rüle; pull; tûrn; chin; sing; shop; thin; <u>th</u>is; hw in white; zh in treasure. The symbol ə stands for the unstressed vowel sound in about, taken, pencil, lemon, and circus.

butterscotch A candy made from brown sugar and butter.
but·ter·scotch (but'ər skoch') *noun.*

button 1. A small, round, flat thing that is used to fasten clothing or to ornament it. The coat was fastened in front with a row of *buttons.* 2. A knob or disk that is turned or pushed to make something work. Press the elevator *button* if you want to stop at this floor. *Noun.*
—To fasten with buttons. Be sure to *button* your overcoat, because it is cold outside. *Verb.*
but·ton (but'ən) *noun, plural* **buttons;** *verb,* **buttoned, buttoning.**

buttonhole A hole or slit that a button is put through in order to fasten a piece of clothing. *Noun.*
—To stop someone and make that person listen to you. My parents *buttonholed* the neighbor next door and talked a long time about problems on our street. *Verb.*
but·ton·hole (but'ən hōl') *noun, plural* **buttonholes;** *verb,* **buttonholed, buttonholing.**

buttress A strong, heavy structure built against a wall to hold it up or make it stronger. *Noun.*
—To make stronger with a buttress. The walls of the cathedral were *buttressed. Verb.*
but·tress (but'ris) *noun, plural* **buttresses;** *verb,* **buttressed, buttressing.**

buy To get something by paying money for it; purchase. In this shop you can *buy* an apple for twenty-five cents. Our family *bought* a new car last year. *Verb.*
—Something offered for sale at a low price; bargain. That used car is a good *buy. Noun.*
▲ Another word that sounds like this is **by.**
buy (bī) *verb,* **bought, buying;** *noun, plural* **buys.**

buyer A person who buys. My set of weights is for sale, but there have been no *buyers.*
buy·er (bī'ər) *noun, plural* **buyers.**

buzz A low humming sound. A bee makes a buzz. The *buzz* of talking stopped when the teacher came into the room. *Noun.*
—1. To make the low, humming sound that a bee makes. The fly *buzzed* in my ear. 2. To fly an airplane low over something. The pilot *buzzed* the bridge. *Verb.*
buzz (buz) *noun, plural* **buzzes;** *verb,* **buzzed, buzzing.**

buzzard A very large bird that has a sharp, hooked beak and long, sharp claws.
buz·zard (buz'ərd) *noun, plural* **buzzards.**

buzzer An electrical device that makes a buzzing sound as a signal. I pressed the *buzzer,* and my friend opened the door.
buzz·er (buz'ər) *noun, plural* **buzzers.**

by 1. Close to; beside. There is a small table *by* my bed. 2. Up to and beyond; past. The express train went *by* our train. 3. Through the means of. I went to the city *by* bus. 4. Through the action of. This book was written *by* a famous author. 5. In units of. We buy milk *by* the gallon. 6. According to. Let's play the game *by* the rules. 7. Not later than. Please be here *by* eight o'clock. 8. To the extent of. I am older than my cousin *by* five years. 9. During; at. Some animals sleep *by* day. 10. And in the other dimension. The room measures three yards *by* four. *Preposition.*
—1. Near. I just stood *by* and watched. 2. Past. Years went *by. Adverb.* ▲ Another word that sounds like this is **buy.**
• **by and by.** In a little while; shortly; soon. I phoned to say we'd get to their place *by and by.*
by (bī) *preposition; adverb.*

bygone Gone by; past; former. The old couple thought of their *bygone* school years. *Adjective.*
—**bygones.** Something gone by or past. Let's end our quarrel and let *bygones* be *bygones. Noun.*
by·gone (bī'gôn' or bī'gon') *adjective; plural noun.*

bypass A road that allows someone to avoid a town or other place by passing it or going around it. We took the *bypass* to avoid all the traffic in the center of town. *Noun.*
—To go around by a bypass. The highway was built to *bypass* the town. *Verb.*
by·pass (bī'pas') *noun, plural* **bypasses;** *verb,* **bypassed, bypassing.**

by-product Something useful that comes from the making of something else. Buttermilk is a *by-product* of the making of butter.
by·prod·uct (bī'prod'əkt) *noun, plural* **by-products.**

bystander A person who is at a place while something is happening but does not take part in it. Several *bystanders* watched as the workers poured the concrete.
by·stand·er (bī'stan'dər) *noun, plural* **bystanders.**

C c

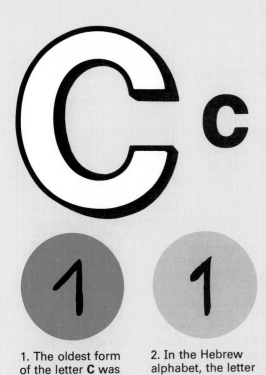

1. The oldest form of the letter **C** was the third letter in the alphabet used by ancient tribes in the Middle East.

2. In the Hebrew alphabet, the letter **C** stood for the hard *g* sound, as the *g* in game.

3. The ancient Greeks borrowed this letter from the Hebrew alphabet 3,000 years ago.

4. An ancient tribe north of Rome used **C** to stand for the hard *g* sound and the *k* sound.

5. The Romans, about 2,300 years ago, used the **C** to stand for the *k* sound and created a new letter, **G**, to stand for the hard *g* sound.

6. Since Roman times, the letter **C** has stood for the *k* sound. It now also stands for the *ch* sound in *cheese* and for the *s* sound in *face*.

c, C 1. The third letter of the alphabet. 2. The Roman numeral for 100.
c, C (sē) *noun, plural* **c's, C's.**

C or **C.** An abbreviation for *Celsius* or *centigrade.*

CA Postal abbreviation for *California.*

cab 1. An automobile that carries people for a charge; taxicab. We took a *cab* to the airport. 2. A small carriage that carries people for a charge. It has a driver and is pulled by one horse. 3. The enclosed part of a truck, steam shovel, or other big machine. The driver or operator of the machine sits in the cab.
cab (kab) *noun, plural* **cabs.**

cabbage A plant that has thick green or reddish purple leaves that form a round head. The leaves of the cabbage are eaten as a vegetable.
cab·bage (kab′ij) *noun, plural* **cabbages.**

cabin 1. A small, simple house. Cabins are often built of rough boards or logs. Our family lived in a *cabin* on a lake last summer. 2. A private room on a ship. The passengers stayed in their *cabins* during the storm. 3. A place in an aircraft for passengers, crew members, or cargo. The workers loaded the baggage into the *cabin.*
cab·in (kab′in) *noun, plural* **cabins.**

cabin

cabinet 1. A piece of furniture that has shelves or drawers. Many cabinets have doors. The kitchen *cabinet* is full of dishes, cups, and glasses. 2. A group of people who give advice to the leader of a nation. A cabinet is made up of the heads of the different departments of the government.
cab·i·net (kab′ə nit) *noun, plural* **cabinets.**

cable 1. A strong, thick rope. Most cables are made up of wires that are twisted together. That suspension bridge hangs from huge steel *cables.* 2. A bundle of wires that has a covering around it for protection. This kind of cable is used to carry an electric current. Telegraph messages are sent across the ocean by underwater cable. 3. A message

C

that is sent under the ocean by cable. The *ca-ble* from my parents in Puerto Rico said, "Come home." *Noun.*
—To send a message by cable. I *cabled* the news that I had arrived safely at my grand-parents' house. *Verb.*
ca·ble (kā′bəl) *noun, plural* **cables;** *verb,* **cabled, cabling.**

cable car **1.** A small car that hangs from a cable. A *cable car* takes skiers up the steep mountain. **2.** A vehicle like a trolley that moves on tracks and is pulled by a cable. We took a *cable car* to the top of the hill.

cable television A system that sends tele-vision programs by wire instead of through the air. People who want to receive the pro-grams must pay a fee.

caboose A railroad car that is at the end of a freight train. The train crew live, rest, or work in the caboose.
ca·boose (kə büs′) *noun, plural* **cabooses.**

cacao An evergreen tree found in warm tropical climates. Its seeds are used in mak-ing cocoa and chocolate.
ca·ca·o (kə ka′ō *or* kə kā′ō) *noun, plural* **cacaos.**

cackle To make a shrill, broken cry, like the sound a hen makes. The children *cackled* with delight when the jack-in-the-box sprang open. *Verb.*
—A shrill, broken sound like the one a hen makes. *Noun.*
cack·le (kak′əl) *verb,* **cackled, cackling;** *noun, plural* **cackles.**

cactus A plant that has a thick stem cov-ered with spines instead of leaves. Cacti are found in desert areas of North and South America. Most cacti produce bright flowers and edible fruit.
cac·tus (kak′təs) *noun, plural* **cacti** (kak′tī), **cactuses,** or **cactus.**

cacti

cadet A young man or woman who is a stu-dent in a military academy. Cadets train to be officers in the armed forces.
ca·det (kə det′) *noun, plural* **cadets.**

cafe A small restaurant. They sat at the out-door *cafe* to have something to drink.
ca·fe (ka fā′) *noun, plural* **cafes.**

cafeteria A restaurant where customers buy food at a counter and carry it to tables themselves. We ate lunch at the school *cafe-teria.*
caf·e·te·ri·a (kaf′i tîr′ē ə) *noun, plural* **cafeterias.**

caffeine A bitter substance found in coffee and tea and added to many soft drinks. Caf-feine stimulates the body and can keep a per-son from feeling sleepy. The *caffeine* in my soft drink kept me from falling asleep. This word is also spelled **caffein.**
caf·feine (ka fēn′) *noun.*

cage **1.** A box that has sides made of bars or wires with open spaces between them. Cages are used to house animals. The bird *cage* held a large green parrot. Lions are kept in *cages* at the zoo. **2.** A small room with one or more walls made of of bars, wires, or glass. The cashier at the amusement park sat in a *cage. Noun.*
—To put or keep in a cage. The scientist will *cage* the mice during the experiment. *Verb.*
cage (kāj) *noun, plural* **cages;** *verb,* **caged, caging.**

cake **1.** A baked mixture of flour, eggs, sugar, and flavoring. We baked a vanilla *cake* with chocolate frosting for the party. **2.** A flat, thin mass of food that is baked or fried. A pancake is a kind of cake. **3.** A flat-tened or shaped mass of something. Please give me a *cake* of soap. *Noun.*
—To become a hard, solid mass. The mud on my boots *caked* as it dried. *Verb.*
cake (kāk) *noun, plural* **cakes;** *verb,* **caked, caking.**

Cal. An abbreviation for *California.*

C

calcium A soft, silver-white metal. Bones, teeth, and blood need calcium. Calcium is a chemical element. It combines with other elements to make chalk and limestone.
cal·ci·um (kal′sē əm) *noun.*

Word History

Calcium comes from a Latin word meaning "limestone." Limestone is mostly made up of calcium.

calculate 1. To find out by using addition, subtraction, multiplication, or division. Let's *calculate* how much each person owes for the trip. 2. To estimate by examining numbers or quantities. The campers *calculated* that they had packed enough food for five days. 3. To plan; intend. The route was *calculated* to get us home quickly.
cal·cu·late (kal′kyə lāt′) *verb,* **calculated, calculating.**

calculation The act or result of calculating. By the *calculation* of scientists, the sun is about 93,000,000 miles away from the earth.
cal·cu·la·tion (kal′kyə lā′shən) *noun, plural* **calculations.**

calculator A small computer that can solve mathematical problems. Many calculators run on batteries and can be held in one hand.
cal·cu·la·tor (kal′kyə lā′tər) *noun, plural* **calculators.**

calendar 1. A chart showing the days, weeks, and months of a year. The *calendar* shows that my birthday falls on a Wednesday this year. 2. A schedule of events that will take place. In a court of law, cases to be tried are listed on a *calendar.*
cal·en·dar (kal′ən dər) *noun, plural* **calendars.**

Word History

The word **calendar** comes from a Latin word meaning "the first day of the month." In ancient Rome, that was the day when people paid their bills, so it was important to have a calendar to know when the first day of the month would come.

calf¹ 1. The young of cattle and related animals. A young cow or bull is a calf. 2. A young seal, elephant, or whale. 3. Leather that is made from the skin or hide of a calf.
calf (kaf) *noun, plural* **calves.**

calf² The fleshy part of the back of the leg, between the knee and the ankle.
calf (kaf) *noun, plural* **calves.**

calico A cotton material that has small, brightly colored designs printed on it. I have a bedspread made of *calico. Noun.* —1. Made of calico. That *calico* dress is on sale. 2. Having large spots or blotches of different colors. Our neighbors have a *calico* cat. *Adjective.*
cal·i·co (kal′i kō′) *noun, plural* **calicoes** or **calicos;** *adjective.*

calico cat

Calif. An abbreviation for *California.*

California A state in the western United States, on the Pacific Ocean. Its capital is Sacramento.
Cal·i·for·nia (kal′ə forn′yə *or* kal′ə fôr′nē ə) *noun.*

Word History

California was the name of a make-believe island in a very old Spanish story. When the Spanish explorers landed on the southern end of California, they thought they were on an island. So they named it after the island in the story. Other Spanish explorers went farther north and also called that area California. The name was finally used for all the land that became the state of California.

call 1. To speak or say in a loud voice. Please raise your hand when I *call* your name. 2. To ask or order to come. The cat will come if you *call.* We had to *call* the fire department to put out the fire. 3. To make a request; ask. One of the workers got tired

at; āpe; fär; câre; end; mē; it; ice; pîerce; hot; ōld; sông, fôrk; oil; out; up; ūse; rüle; pùll; tûrn; chin; sing; shop; thin; this; hw in white; zh in treasure. The symbol ə stands for the unstressed vowel sound in about, taken, pencil, lemon, and circus.

and *called* for a break. **4.** To give a name to; name. We are going to *call* our new puppy "Daisy." **5.** To telephone. They will *call* us from the airport when they arrive. **6.** To make a short visit or stop. We will *call* at your house tomorrow afternoon. *Verb.*
—**1.** The act of speaking or saying in a loud voice; shout; cry. There was a *call* for help from someone trapped in the burning building. **2.** A particular sound or cry made by a bird or animal. Some people can recognize many different bird *calls.* **3.** The act of telephoning someone. I will expect your *call* at about four o'clock. **4.** A short visit or stop. Some old friends made a *call* to visit. *Noun.*
- **on call.** Able to be telephoned or summoned when needed; available. Even when the repair shop is closed, there is always someone *on call* for emergencies.
- **to call for. 1.** To require because it is necessary or appropriate. This job *calls for* patience. Our victory *calls for* a celebration. **2.** To come and get in order to accompany. I'll *call for* you at 6 o'clock.
- **to call up. 1.** To telephone. I'll *call* you *up* after the game. **2.** To summon for military duty. My cousins were *called up* just after they finished college. **3.** To cause to remember. The music *called up* the first dance I went to.

call (kôl) *verb,* **called, calling;** *noun, plural* **calls.**

call number A group of numbers or numbers and letters that are assigned to a book. The call number is used to help locate the book in a library.

callus A hardened and thickened area of skin. Calluses are caused by repeated pressing or rubbing.
cal·lus (kal′əs) *noun, plural* **calluses.**

calm 1. Not moving; still. The sea was *calm* after the storm. **2.** Not excited or nervous; quiet. The people in the building stayed *calm* during the fire and got out safely. *Adjective.*
—A time of quiet or stillness. A barking dog broke the *calm* of the afternoon. *Noun.*
—To make or become calm. I tried to *calm* the frightened child by speaking softly. *Verb.*
calm (käm) *adjective,* **calmer, calmest;** *noun, plural* **calms;** *verb,* **calmed, calming.**

calorie 1. A unit that is used to measure the amount of heat in something. **2.** A unit that is used to measure the amount of energy produced by food. Some foods have more *calories* in an ounce than others.
cal·o·rie (kal′ə rē) *noun, plural* **calories.**

calves Plural of **calf.** Look up **calf** for more information.
calves (kavz) *plural noun.*

Cambodia A country in southeastern Asia. Its official name is **Kampuchea.**
Cam·bo·di·a (kam bō′dē ə) *noun.*

camcorder A portable device that includes a television camera and a videocassette recorder in one unit. The reporter used a *camcorder* to record the holiday parade.
cam·cord·er (kam′kôr′dər) *noun, plural* **camcorders.**

came Past tense of **come.** My friend *came* to dinner last night. Look up **come** for more information.
came (kām) *verb.*

camel A large animal that has a hump on its back, long legs, and a long neck. Camels live in deserts. They are very strong and can live for many days without water. They are used for riding and carrying loads. The camel of northern Africa and the Middle East has one hump, and the camel of central Asia has two humps.
cam·el (kam′əl) *noun, plural* **camels.**

camel

camera A device for taking photographs or motion pictures. A camera consists of a box with a small hole. When the hole is uncovered, light enters the camera and makes an image on the film inside. Most cameras have a lens to focus the image on the film.
cam·er·a (kam′ər ə *or* kam′rə) *noun, plural* **cameras.**

Cameroon A country in west-central Africa.
Cam·er·oon (kam′ə rün′) *noun.*

camouflage A disguise or false appearance that is used to hide something by making it look like its surroundings. The tan coat of a lion is a natural camouflage because it matches the color of the dry grasses where the lion lives. *Noun.*

—To change the appearance of something in order to hide or trick. The soldiers *camouflaged* the tank by covering it with bushes and branches. *Verb.*
> **cam·ou·flage** (kam′ə fläzh′) *noun, plural* **camouflages;** *verb,* **camouflaged, camouflaging.**

camp **1.** An outdoor place with tents or cabins where people live or sleep for a time. The soldiers set up *camp* near the river. My friend and I are going to a *camp* in the mountains this summer. **2.** The people staying at a camp. The whole *camp* woke up at dawn. *Noun.*
—To establish, equip, and live in a camp. Last summer we were *camping* in western Canada. *Verb.*
> **camp** (kamp) *noun, plural* **camps;** *verb,* **camped, camping.**

campaign A series of actions that are planned and carried out to bring about a particular result. The general's *campaign* was aimed at getting control of the enemy's territory. The candidate's whole family worked on the *campaign* for election as mayor. *Noun.*
—To carry on or take part in a campaign. Are you going to *campaign* for anyone for class president? *Verb.*
> **cam·paign** (kam pān′) *noun, plural* **campaigns;** *verb,* **campaigned, campaigning.**

camper **1.** A person who stays at or lives in an outdoor place with tents or cabins. The *campers* gathered firewood. **2.** A car or trailer that is built or used for camping. Our family slept in the *camper* during our trip this summer.
> **cam·per** (kam′pər) *noun, plural* **campers.**

campfire An outdoor fire that is used for cooking or keeping warm in a camp.
> **camp·fire** (kamp′fīr′) *noun, plural* **campfires.**

campfire

campground A place for camping, such as a park. For our fishing trip we stayed at a *campground* on the lake.
> **camp·ground** (kamp′ground′) *noun, plural* **campgrounds.**

camphor A white substance that has a strong odor. Camphor is used in products that repel moths, some medicines, and in making plastics.
> **cam·phor** (kam′fər) *noun.*

campus The grounds and buildings of a school, college, or university.
> **cam·pus** (kam′pəs) *noun, plural* **campuses.**

can¹ An auxiliary verb that is used to express the following meanings: **1.** To have the ability, skill, or knowledge to; be able to. My neighbor *can* speak French and Spanish. Elephants *can* move with surprising speed. *Can* you fix this broken radio? **2.** To have the right to; be entitled to. You *can* vote when you are eighteen. **3.** To have permission to; may. My parents said I *can* stay up late tonight.
> **can** (kan) *verb, past tense* **could.**

Language Note

At one time people were careful to use the word **can** to mean only "to be able to" and to use the word **may** to mean "to have permission to." Many people still prefer to use these words carefully with different meanings, especially in writing.

can² A container made of metal and usually shaped like a cylinder. Most cans have airtight tops or covers that fit tightly. Please put the old rags in the garbage *can*. Many fruits and vegetables are sold in *cans*. *Noun.*
—To put into or preserve in a can. We are going to *can* peaches this year. *Verb.*
> **can** (kan) *noun, plural* **cans;** *verb,* **canned, canning.**

Can. An abbreviation for *Canada.*

Canada A country in North America that is north of the United States.
> **Can·a·da** (kan′ə də) *noun.*

at; āpe; fär; câre; end; mē; it; īce; pîerce; hot; ōld; sông; fôrk; oil; out; up; ūse; rüle; pu̇ll; tûrn; chin; sing; shop; thin; this; hw in white; zh in treasure. The symbol ə stands for the unstressed vowel sound in about, taken, pencil, lemon, and circus.

Canada Day A holiday in Canada that falls on July 1. It celebrates the day when the first four provinces of Canada joined together. In the past, this holiday was called **Dominion Day**.

Canadian A person who was born in or is a citizen of Canada. *Noun.*
—Of Canada. Ice hockey is a *Canadian* sport. *Adjective.*
Can·a·di·an (kə nā′dē ən) *noun, plural* **Canadians;** *adjective.*

canal A waterway dug across land. A canal is used for boats and ships to travel through, and for carrying water from lakes or rivers to places that need it.
ca·nal (kə nal′) *noun, plural* **canals.**

canary **1.** A small yellow songbird. Canaries are often kept as pets. **2.** A light, bright yellow color. *Noun.*
—Having the color canary; light, bright yellow. *Adjective.*
ca·nar·y (kə nâr′ē) *noun, plural* **canaries;** *adjective.*

cancel **1.** To decide not to do, have, or go; call off. Why did you *cancel* your dental appointment? The baseball game was *canceled* because of rain. **2.** To cross out or mark with a line or lines to show that it cannot be used again. The post office *cancels* stamps on letters.
can·cel (kan′səl) *verb,* **canceled, canceling.**

cancer A disease in which cells in or on the body begin to divide and grow more rapidly than is normal. The growing cancer cells can crowd out healthy tissues and organs and use the food meant for them.
can·cer (kan′sər) *noun.*

candidate A person who seeks or is put forward by others for an office or honor. The senator will be a *candidate* for president.
can·di·date (kan′di dāt′) *noun, plural* **candidates.**

canary

Word History

Candidate comes from a Latin word meaning "clothed in white." In ancient Rome, a man who was a *candidate* for office would wear a white toga.

candle A stick of wax or tallow with a string called a wick inside it. When the wick is lit, the candle slowly burns and gives off a light.
can·dle (kan′dəl) *noun, plural* **candles.**

candlestick A holder for a candle.
can·dle·stick (kan′dəl stik′) *noun, plural* **candlesticks.**

candy A sweet food made of sugar or syrup with flavorings, nuts, or fruit. *Noun.*
—To cover or cook with sugar. At home, we *candy* apples and pears for special holidays. *Verb.*
can·dy (kan′dē) *noun, plural* **candies;** *verb,* **candied, candying.**

cane **1.** A stick used to help someone walk. Canes are made of wood, metal, or other material. I needed to use a *cane* after I sprained my ankle. **2.** The long, woody, jointed stem of bamboo, reed, and other tall grass plants. **3.** A plant that has a long, woody, flexible stem. Bamboo is a cane.
cane (kān) *noun, plural* **canes.**

canine **1.** Any member of the dog family, including dogs, foxes, wolves, and coyotes. **2.** One of the pointed teeth that people, dogs, and other animals use to tear off pieces of food. There is a canine on each side of the top and bottom front teeth. *Noun.*
—Having to do with a dog or any member of the dog family. *Adjective.*
ca·nine (kā′nīn) *noun, plural* **canines;** *adjective.*

cannibal **1.** A person who eats human flesh. **2.** An animal that eats other animals of its own kind.
can·ni·bal (kan′ə bəl) *noun, plural* **cannibals.**

cannon A large, heavy gun that is mounted on wheels or some other base.
can·non (kan′ən) *noun, plural* **cannons** or **cannon.**

cannot Can not; be unable to. I *cannot* understand this arithmetic problem.
can·not (kan′ot *or* ka not′) *verb.*

canoe A light, narrow boat. A person moves and steers a canoe with a paddle. Most canoes are pointed at both ends. *Noun.*
—To paddle or ride in a canoe. We will *canoe* across the lake after lunch. *Verb.*
ca·noe (kə nü′) *noun, plural* **canoes;** *verb,* **canoed, canoeing.**

canopy A covering that is made of cloth or other material. A canopy is hung over a bed, throne, or entrance to a building.
can·o·py (kan′ə pē) *noun, plural* **canopies.**

can't Shortened form of "can not." I *can't* lift this heavy box, can you?
can't (kant) *contraction.*

C

cantaloupe A kind of melon that has a rough, pale green or yellow skin and sweet, yellowish orange flesh.
can·ta·loupe (kan′tə lōp′) *noun, plural* **cantaloupes.**

canteen **1.** A small metal container for carrying water or other liquids to drink. **2.** A store in a school or factory that sells food and drinks.
can·teen (kan tēn′) *noun, plural* **canteens.**

canvas A strong, heavy cloth made of cotton, flax, or hemp. It is used to make things that must be strong and last for a long time. Tents, sails, coats, and boat covers are made of canvas. Oil paintings are painted on pieces of canvas.
can·vas (kan′vəs) *noun, plural* **canvases.**

canyon A deep valley with very high, steep sides. A canyon often has a stream running through it.
can·yon (kan′yən) *noun, plural* **canyons.**

canyon

cap **1.** A close-fitting covering for the head. Most caps have a short brim or no brim. Nurses and police officers wear caps. **2.** Something that is used or shaped like a cap; a cover or top. I took the *cap* off the bottle of maple syrup. **3.** A paper wrapping or covering that contains a small amount of explosive. Caps are used in toy guns. *Noun.*
—**1.** To put a cap on; cover with a cap. Please *cap* the toothpaste when you're finished. **2.** To follow with something equal or better; match. The speaker *capped* that joke with a funnier one. *Verb.*
cap (kap) *noun, plural* **caps;** *verb,* **capped, capping.**

capability The quality of being capable; ability. I admire you for your *capabilities* as a student and athlete.
ca·pa·bil·i·ty (kā′pə bil′i tē) *noun, plural* **capabilities.**

capable Having skill or power; able. A *capable* mechanic can fix many things.
• **capable of.** Having the ability needed for. I'm *capable of* running 2 miles.
ca·pa·ble (kā′pə bəl) *adjective.*

capacity **1.** The amount that can be held in a space. The car's gas tank has a *capacity* of 20 gallons. **2.** Ability or power. Everyone has the *capacity* to learn. **3.** A job or position with duties. In my *capacity* as club president, I ran the club's meetings.
ca·pac·i·ty (kə pas′i tē) *noun, plural* **capacities.**

cape¹ A piece of clothing without sleeves. A cape is worn loosely over the shoulders.
cape (kāp) *noun, plural* **capes.**

cape² A piece of land that sticks out from the coastline into the sea or a lake.
cape (kāp) *noun, plural* **capes.**

caper A playful act or trick; prank.
ca·per (kā′pər) *noun, plural* **capers.**

capillary One of the tubes that connect the arteries and veins. Capillaries are the smallest of the blood vessels.
cap·il·lar·y (kap′ə ler′ē) *noun, plural* **capillaries.**

capital¹ **1.** A city or town where the government of a country or state is located. Austin is the *capital* of Texas. Washington, D.C., is the *capital* of the United States. **2.** A large form of a letter of the alphabet. *A* and *B* are capitals; *b* and *c* are not. **3.** The total amount of money or property that is owned by a company or person. That corporation has a large amount of *capital.* **4.** Money accumulated to start a business or to invest in other businesses. My family has enough *capital* to start its own business. *Noun.*
—**1.** Being where the government is located. Madrid is Spain's *capital* city. **2.** Being the large form of a letter. *T* and *L* are *capital* letters. **3.** Very good or satisfying; excellent. This is a *capital* plum pudding! **4.** Being or punished by death. Murder is a *capital* crime in some places. *Adjective.* ▲ Another word that sounds like this is **Capitol.** Look up **Capitol** for a Language Note about this word.
cap·i·tal (kap′i təl) *noun, plural* **capitals;** *adjective.*

at; āpe; fär; câre; end; mē; it; ice; pîerce; hot; ōld; sông, fôrk; oil; out; up; ūse; rüle; pùll; tûrn; chin; sing; shop; thin; <u>th</u>is; hw in white; zh in treasure. The symbol ə stands for the unstressed vowel sound in about, taken, pencil, lemon, and circus.

capital²   The top part of a column or pillar. The columns of the building had carved *capitals*. ▲ Another word that sounds like this is **Capitol.**
cap·i·tal (kap′i təl) *noun, plural* **capitals.**

capitalism   An economic system in which land, factories, and other means of producing goods are owned and controlled by individual people instead of by the government. The economic system of the United States is based on capitalism.
cap·i·tal·ism (kap′i tə liz′əm) *noun.*

capital²

capitalize   To write or print with a capital letter or letters, or begin with a capital letter. You should always *capitalize* proper names.
cap·i·tal·ize (kap′i tə līz′) *verb,* **capitalized, capitalizing.**

Capitol   **1.** The building in which the U.S. Congress meets in Washington, D.C. **2. capitol.** The building in which a state legislature meets. ▲ Another word that sounds like this is **capital.**
Cap·i·tol (kap′i təl) *noun.*

Language Note

Even though the words **Capitol** and **capital** sound the same, they have different meanings. It's important to spell them correctly. A capital is a city, but the Capitol is a building. When we visited Washington, D.C., our country's *capital,* we stood on the steps of the *Capitol* to have our picture taken.

---

capsize   To turn upside down. The strong wind *capsized* the small sailboat. The sailors held on to the sides of the boat after it *capsized.*
cap·size (kap′sīz *or* kap sīz′) *verb,* **capsized, capsizing.**

capsule   **1.** A small, thin case that encloses something tightly. Some plant seeds grow in capsules. Another kind of capsule holds a small amount of medicine and dissolves in the stomach after it is swallowed. **2.** A compartment of a spacecraft that carries astronauts or instruments. The space capsule usually separates from the main rocket after the spacecraft is launched.
cap·sule (kap′səl) *noun, plural* **capsules.**

captain   **1.** A person who is the leader of a group. Who is *captain* of the volleyball team? **2.** A person who is in charge of a ship. The *captain* of the fishing boat wore a blue and gold cap. **3.** An officer in the armed forces. In the United States Army, Marine Corps, or Air Force, a captain ranks just below a major. In the United States Navy, a captain ranks just below an admiral. *Noun.*
—To be the captain of; lead. Who will *captain* the basketball team next year? *Verb.*
cap·tain (kap′tən) *noun, plural* **captains;** *verb,* **captained, captaining.**

caption   The word or words under a picture that tell who or what appears in the picture. There is a *caption* under most pictures in this dictionary.
cap·tion (kap′shən) *noun, plural* **captions.**

captive   A person or animal that is captured and held by force; prisoner. The soldiers kept the *captive* in a jail inside the fort. *Noun.*
—Held prisoner. The *captive* lion was kept in a cage. *Adjective.*
cap·tive (kap′tiv) *noun, plural* **captives;** *adjective.*

capture   **1.** To catch and hold a person, animal, or thing. The explorers *captured* the tiger in a large net. **2.** To attract and hold. The film's strange title *captured* my interest. **3.** To succeed in showing or expressing something. The story *captures* what it is like to be an only child. *Verb.*
—The act of catching and holding a person, animal, or thing. The *capture* of the bank robber took place the day after the robbery. *Noun.*
cap·ture (kap′chər) *verb,* **captured, capturing;** *noun, plural* **captures.**

car   **1.** An automobile. A car is a vehicle with four wheels and an engine. **2.** Any kind of vehicle that moves on wheels and is used to carry people or things from one place to another. A railroad train is made up of different cars that are joined together. **3.** The compartment of an elevator in which people and things are carried.
car (kär) *noun, plural* **cars.**

caramel   **1.** Sugar that is browned and melted by being heated slowly. Caramel is used in cooking to color and flavor gravy, cookies, and other foods. **2.** A light-brown, soft candy flavored with caramel.
car·a·mel (kar′ə məl *or* kär′məl) *noun, plural* **caramels.**

carat   A unit of weight for diamonds and other precious stones. A carat is the same weight as $\frac{1}{5}$ of a gram. ▲ Another word that sounds like this is **carrot.**
car·at (kar′ət) *noun, plural* **carats.**

caravan   A group of people who travel together. Arab merchants and their camels travel in caravans across the desert. A *caravan* of army trucks and soldiers moved slowly along the highway.
   car·a·van (kar'ə van') *noun, plural* **caravans.**

caravan

carbohydrate   A compound made up of carbon, hydrogen, and oxygen. Carbohydrates are made by green plants. Starches and sugars are carbohydrates.
   car·bo·hy·drate (kär'bō hī'drāt) *noun, plural* **carbohydrates.**

carbon   A chemical element that is found in all livings things and in coal and charcoal. Diamonds and graphite are carbon in the form of crystals.
   car·bon (kär'bən) *noun.*

carbon dioxide   A gas that is made up of carbon and oxygen. Carbon dioxide has no color or odor. It is part of the air we breathe and is used in soft drinks and fire extinguishers.
   carbon di·ox·ide (dī ok'sīd).

carbon monoxide   A poisonous gas that has no color or odor. Carbon monoxide is formed when carbon burns with too little air. It is found among the exhaust gases of automobiles.
   carbon mon·ox·ide (mə nok'sīd).

carburetor   The part of an engine in which gasoline is mixed with air to make a mixture that the engine burns when it runs.
   car·bu·re·tor (kär'bə rā'tər) *noun, plural* **carburetors.**

carcass   The body of a dead animal.
   car·cass (kär'kəs) *noun, plural* **carcasses.**

card   A flat piece of stiff paper that has words or numbers or some kind of design on it. People have membership cards for libraries and for clubs they belong to. We play many games with decks of playing cards.
   card (kärd) *noun, plural* **cards.**

cardboard   A heavy, stiff paper. Cardboard is used to make boxes and posters.
   card·board (kärd'bôrd') *noun.*

cardinal   **1.** One of the group of important officials who rank just below the pope in the Roman Catholic Church. The cardinals help the pope govern the church, and when he dies, they meet and elect the new pope. Cardinals wear bright red robes and hats. **2.** A songbird that has a crest of feathers on its head. The male cardinal has bright red feathers with a black patch around its bill. *Noun.*
—Of the greatest importance; chief. One of the *cardinal* issues in the town election was the vote on the new park and playground. *Adjective.*
   car·di·nal (kär'də nəl) *noun, plural* **cardinals;** *adjective.*

cardinal

cardinal number   A number that tells how many. Numbers such as one, two, three, and four are cardinal numbers.

care   **1.** Close and serious attention. Be sure to dry the dishes with *care*. **2.** A feeling of worry or unhappiness. I have so many *cares* that it is hard to fall asleep. We didn't have a *care* in the world as we ran down the beach splashing in the waves. **3.** Keeping or custody; protection. When they were on vacation, they left their cats in the *care* of a neighbor. The sick child was under a doctor's *care*. *Noun.*
—**1.** To have an interest, liking, or concern about a person or thing. My parents *care* about me and how I do in school. I don't *care* for sweets. **2.** To have a feeling against; mind. Do you *care* if I borrow your bicycle? **3.** To want or wish. Would you *care* to go to the movies with me? **4.** To protect or provide care. When our neighbors go away, I *care* for their plants. *Verb.*

at; āpe; fär; câre; end; mē; it; īce; pîerce; hot; ōld; sông, fôrk; oil; out; up; ūse; rüle; pùll; tûrn; chin; sing; shop; thin; this; hw in white; zh in treasure. The symbol ə stands for the unstressed vowel sound in about, taken, pencil, lemon, and circus.

- **in care of.** At the address of. The letter was sent to us *in care of* the hotel where we were staying.
- **to take care of.** **1.** To provide whatever care is necessary for the protection, well-being, or upkeep of. A nurse *took care of* me when I was home with pneumonia. Two gardeners were hired to *take care of* the flowers in the park. **2.** To devote one's attention and effort to. Please *take care of* the most important tasks first.
  care (kâr) *noun, plural* **cares;** *verb,* **cared, caring.**

career The work that a person does through life. My cousin chose a *career* as a doctor.
ca·reer (kə rîr′) *noun, plural* **careers.**

carefree Happy with nothing to worry about. We all felt absolutely *carefree* as we started off on our picnic.
care·free (kâr′frē′) *adjective.*

careful **1.** Paying close attention to what one is doing or saying; watchful. Be *careful* and look both ways before you cross the street. **2.** Done with care. A *careful* check of the paragraph showed two mistakes.
care·ful (kâr′fəl) *adjective.*

careless **1.** Not paying close enough attention to what one is doing or saying. I was *careless* when I ran down the stairs, and I tripped and fell. **2.** Done without close attention or care. You will not get a good grade on your report if you make *careless* spelling mistakes.
care·less (kâr′lis) *adjective.*

caress To touch or stroke gently and with love; pet. The child *caressed* the kitten fondly. *Verb.*
—A gentle, loving touch or stroke. The *caress* made the kitten purr. *Noun.*
ca·ress (kə res′) *verb,* **caressed, caressing;** *noun, plural* **caresses.**

caretaker **1.** A person who takes care of a building or property; custodian. The park's *caretaker* mows the grass every week in summer. **2.** Someone who takes care of other people. Nurses, foster parents, and baby-sitters are caretakers.
care·tak·er (kâr′tā′kər) *noun, plural* **caretakers.**

carfare The money a person must pay for a ride, as in a bus, subway, or taxi.
car·fare (kär′fâr′) *noun.*

cargo The goods carried by a ship, airplane, truck, or other vehicle. The workers unloaded a *cargo* of rice from the ship.
car·go (kär′gō) *noun, plural* **cargoes** or **cargos.**

Caribbean A sea between North America and South America. It is next to the Atlantic Ocean.
Car·ib·be·an (kar′ə bē′ən *or* kə rib′ē ən) *noun.*

caribou A large animal in the deer family that lives in northern regions. In Europe and Asia caribou are called reindeer. The female caribou is the only female deer that has antlers.
car·i·bou (kar′ə bü′) *noun, plural* **caribou** or **caribous.**

caries Decay of the teeth or bone. Brushing the teeth after every meal helps prevent dental *caries.* ▲ The word **caries** is used with a singular verb.
car·ies (kâr′ēz) *noun.*

carnation A flower that has a spicy, fragrant smell and comes in many colors. The carnation grows on a plant that has narrow, pointed leaves.
car·na·tion (kär nā′shən) *noun, plural* **carnations.**

carnival A fair or festival that has games, rides, and other amusements. A special roller coaster was built just for our city's spring *carnival.*
car·ni·val (kär′nə vəl) *noun, plural* **carnivals.**

carnations

carnivore An animal that eats the flesh of other animals. Lions and dogs are carnivores.
car·ni·vore (kär′nə vôr′) *noun, plural* **carnivores.**

carnivorous Eating the flesh of animals. Wolves, lions, dogs, and cats are carnivorous animals.
car·niv·o·rous (kär niv′ər əs) *adjective.*

carol A joyful song or hymn. The choir practiced singing *carols. Noun.*
—To sing joyously. The children went from house to house *caroling. Verb.*
car·ol (kar′əl) *noun, plural* **carols;** *verb,* **caroled, caroling.**

carp A fish that lives in fresh water and is sometimes used as food.
carp (kärp) *noun, plural* **carp** or **carps.**

carpenter A person who builds and repairs houses and other things made of wood.
car·pen·ter (kär′pən tər) *noun, plural* **carpenters.**

carpet **1.** A covering for a floor, usually made of heavy woven fabric. **2.** Anything like a carpet. The lawn was covered with a *carpet* of snow. *Noun.*
—To cover with a carpet. We are going to *carpet* the stairs in our house. *Verb.*
car·pet (kär′pit) *noun, plural* **carpets;** *verb,* **carpeted, carpeting.**

car pool An arrangement made by a group of people who ride to work together or whose children ride to school together in a car. Each person in the group takes a turn at driving.

carriage **1.** A vehicle that moves on wheels. Some carriages are pulled by horses and carry people. Others, such as baby carriages, are small and light and are pushed by people. **2.** A movable part of a machine that carries or holds up some other part. A carriage on a typewriter is the part that holds the paper and moves back and forth.
car·riage (kar′ij) *noun, plural* **carriages.**

carrier A person, machine, or organization that carries something. Railroads are carriers.
car·ri·er (kar′ē ər) *noun, plural* **carriers.**

carrot **1.** The long, orange-colored root of a plant. Carrots are eaten as a vegetable. **2.** The plant that produces this root. ▲ Another word that sounds like this is **carat.**
car·rot (kar′ət) *noun, plural* **carrots.**

carrot

carry **1.** To hold or contain something while moving it or while it is being moved. Will you *carry* my suitcase if it is too heavy for me? The pipes in our house *carry* water. **2.** To have something. If a store carries rubber boots, it has them there for you to buy. **3.** To keep doing something; continue. If you *carry* your teasing too far, the puppy will become angry. **4.** To move a number from one column or place and add it to another. When I added 23 and 39, I got 52 instead of 62 because I forgot to *carry* the 1 from the right-hand column.
 • **to carry on.** **1.** To go on; continue. The visitors to the classroom told the students to *carry on* with their work. **2.** To behave in a wild, foolish, or silly way. The student who *carried on* when the teacher left the room was punished.

 • **to carry out.** **1.** To obey; follow. The soldier *carried out* the order promptly. **2.** To do; accomplish; complete. We don't have the money to *carry out* our plans for the party.
car·ry (kar′ē) *verb,* **carried, carrying.**

carsick Having nausea or feeling dizzy when riding in a car, train, or bus. The motion of the vehicle can make a person feel carsick.
car·sick (kär′sik′) *adjective.*

cart **1.** A strong wagon with two wheels that is used to carry a load. Carts are usually pulled by horses, mules, or oxen. **2.** A light vehicle that is pushed by a person. We use carts in supermarkets to hold the groceries we take from the shelves. *Noun.*
—To move something in a cart. In many countries, farmers *cart* the vegetables they grow to the nearest town to sell them. *Verb.*
cart (kärt) *noun, plural* **carts;** *verb,* **carted, carting.**

cartilage A strong, flexible material that forms parts of the body of humans and other animals that have a backbone. Cartilage is not as stiff or as hard as bone. Much of a person's nose is formed of cartilage.
car·ti·lage (kär′tə lij) *noun.*

carton A box or container that is made of cardboard, paper, or other materials and that comes in many shapes. Egg cartons hold each egg separately. Milk and juice sometimes are sold in cartons. Our new television set was delivered in a strong *carton.*
car·ton (kär′tən) *noun, plural* **cartons.**

cartoon A drawing, often with words or a caption, that shows people or things in a way that makes you laugh. Some cartoons are made as motion pictures. Comic strips are groups of cartoons that appear in magazines and newspapers.
car·toon (kär tün′) *noun, plural* **cartoons.**

cartridge **1.** A small case that holds gunpowder and a bullet. Cartridges are made to load into a gun. **2.** Any small case that holds something. Some pens are loaded with cartridges full of ink. Some cameras have special cartridges that hold the film. The needle of a record player is held in a cartridge.
car·tridge (kär′trij) *noun, plural* **cartridges.**

at; āpe; fär; câre; end; mē; it; īce; pîerce; hot; ōld; sông, fôrk; oil; out; up; ūse; rüle; pùll; tûrn; chin; sing; shop; thin; this; hw in white; zh in treasure. The symbol ə stands for the unstressed vowel sound in about, taken, pencil, lemon, and circus.

cartwheel **1.** The wheel of a cart. **2.** A kind of jump from one's feet to one's hands and back again. If you keep your arms and legs straight when doing a cartwheel, they look like the spokes of a wheel as it turns. Acrobats often do cartwheels.

cart·wheel (kärt′hwēl′ *or* kärt′wēl′) *noun, plural* **cartwheels.**

carving wood

carve **1.** To cut something into a shape. Artists *carve* statues out of wood and stone. Some furniture is *carved* with designs of flowers and animals. **2.** To cut meat into slices or pieces. You will need a sharp knife to *carve* the turkey.

carve (kärv) *verb,* **carved, carving.**

cascade Water falling over a steep slope or series of slopes. *Noun.*
—To flow down like a waterfall. Water from the overflowing sink *cascaded* onto the floor. *Verb.*

cas·cade (kas kād′) *noun, plural* **cascades;** *verb,* **cascaded, cascading.**

case¹ **1.** An example of something. The forest fire was an obvious *case* of carelessness. **2.** The facts; state of affairs. They say the key is lost, and if that is the *case,* we are all locked out. **3.** An instance of sickness or injury. Local doctors reported ten *cases* of measles to the health department.
4. A matter to be investigated or decided by law. The police had no suspects in the *case.* The judge will make a decision on the trespassing *case* tomorrow.

cascade

- **in case.** If. *In case* anything happens, call me right away.
- **in case of.** If there is. *In case of* rain, we will go to the movies rather than play tennis.

case (kās) *noun, plural* **cases.**

case² A box or other container made to hold or protect something. The new camera came in a leather *case.* We ordered a *case* of soft drinks for the picnic.

case (kās) *noun, plural* **cases.**

cash Money in the form of coins and paper bills. Instead of paying for the coat with a check, I paid for it with *cash. Noun.*
—To get or give cash for. We have to stop at the bank and *cash* a check before we can buy groceries. *Verb.*

- **to cash in on.** To take advantage of; put to good use. I *cashed in on* my knowledge of plants and got a job as a gardener.

cash (kash) *noun; verb,* **cashed, cashing.**

cashew An edible nut that is shaped like a bean. It grows on an evergreen tree that is found in tropical countries.

cash·ew (kash′ü) *noun, plural* **cashews.**

cashier A person whose job it is to receive or pay out money. In a store or restaurant the cashier takes money from customers who are paying for something.

cashew

cash·ier (ka shîr′) *noun, plural* **cashiers.**

cash machine A machine that works by means of a computer and allows bank customers to take out and put in money.

cashmere A very soft woolen fabric that is woven from the hair of Asian goats. Sweaters made of *cashmere* are very comfortable.

cash·mere (kazh′mîr *or* kash′mîr) *noun, plural* **cashmeres.**

cask A wooden barrel that is used to hold wine or other liquids.

cask (kask) *noun, plural* **casks.**

casket **1.** A box made of wood or metal, in which the body of a dead person is put to be buried; coffin. **2.** A case or box for keeping jewels and other valuables.

cas·ket (kas′kit) *noun, plural* **caskets.**

casserole **1.** A deep dish in which food can be cooked and served. **2.** Food prepared in such a dish. The shrimp *casserole* was baked in the oven.

> **cas·se·role.** (kas′ə rōl′) *noun, plural* **casseroles.**

cassette A small case holding recording tape to place in a tape recorder or player. We played one of our music *cassettes* and everyone danced.

> **cas·sette** (kə set′) *noun, plural* **cassettes.**

cast **1.** To throw through the air. We *cast* our fishing lines into the stream. **2.** To send or put. Each student *cast* a vote in the election for class president. The tree *cast* a long shadow on the ground. **3.** To pick the actors who will take different roles in a play. They *cast* me as the wicked magician in the class play. **4.** To shape by pouring a soft material into a mold to harden. The artist *cast* a statue of a horse. *Verb.*
—**1.** The act of throwing something. Try to make a long *cast* with your fishing line. **2.** Something that is given shape in a mold. The student made a plaster *cast* of a deer. **3.** The actors in a play or other show. The whole *cast* came on stage to bow together. **4.** A wet bandage, made of plaster and cloth, that is shaped around a broken bone and allowed to dry. When the cast is dry and hard it protects the broken bone and keeps it from moving. The doctor put a *cast* on my broken arm. *Noun.*

> • **to cast off.** **1.** Discard or shed. Birds *cast off* old feathers when they molt. **2.** To release. We *cast off* the boat from the dock.
>
> **cast** (kast) *verb,* **cast, casting;** *noun, plural* **casts.**

castanet One of a pair of small, wooden pieces that look like the two shells of a clam. They are clicked together in a person's hand in time to the rhythm of a dance.

> **cas·ta·net** (kas′tə net′) *noun, plural* **castanets.**

cast iron A mixture of iron and other materials that are heated together until they melt into a liquid and are then poured into a mold. Cast iron is usually hard and brittle.

castle **1.** A large building or group of buildings having high, thick walls with towers. Many castles had moats around them for defense against attack. **2.** One of the pieces in a chess game; rook.

> **cas·tle** (kas′əl) *noun, plural* **castles.**

casual **1.** Done or happening without serious thought or planning. Our neighbors sometimes make a *casual* visit to our house without calling beforehand. **2.** Informal. You may wear *casual* clothes to dinner.

> **cas·u·al** (kazh′ü əl) *adjective.*

casualty A person who is injured or killed in an accident or a war. Soldiers who are captured by the enemy are also called casualties. The police reported 25 *casualties* in the fire.

> **cas·u·al·ty** (kazh′ü əl tē) *noun, plural* **casualties.**

cat **1.** A small furry animal that has short ears and a long tail. Cats are kept as pets and for catching mice and rats. **2.** Any animal of the family that includes lions, tigers, leopards, and the cats that are kept as pets.

> • **to let the cat out of the bag.** To reveal a secret. The children were so excited about the surprise birthday party that they *let the cat out of the bag.*
>
> **cat** (kat) *noun, plural* **cats.**

catalog A list. Libraries have catalogs of the titles, authors, and subject matter of all their books. Stores publish catalogs with pictures and prices of the things they have for sale. *Noun.*
—To make a list of; put in a list. I *cataloged* the stamps in my collection. *Verb.* This word is also spelled **catalogue.**

> **cat·a·log** (kat′ə lôg′ *or* kat′ə log′) *noun, plural* **catalogs;** *verb,* **cataloged, cataloging.**

cataract **1.** A large, steep waterfall. **2.** A cloudiness in the lens of a person's or animal's eye, causing partial or total blindness. Cataracts can usually be corrected by surgery.

> **cat·a·ract** (kat′ə rakt′) *noun, plural* **cataracts.**

castle

at; āpe; fär; câre; end; mē; it; īce; pîerce; hot; ōld; sông, fôrk; oil; out; up; ūse; rüle; pùll; tûrn; chin; sing; shop; thin; this; hw in white; zh in treasure. The symbol ə stands for the unstressed vowel sound in about, taken, pencil, lemon, and circus.

catastrophe   A great, often sudden disaster. The plane crash was the worst *catastrophe* of the year.
   ca·tas·tro·phe (kə tas′trə fē′) *noun, plural* **catastrophes.**

catbird   A gray songbird with a long, slender beak. The bird got its name because its call sounds like a cat meowing.
   cat·bird (kat′bûrd′) *noun, plural* **catbirds.**

catch   **1.** To take or get hold of something or someone that is moving. I can *catch* a ball with one hand. Use a pail to *catch* the water leaking from the roof.   **2.** To be in time for. We will have to hurry to *catch* the school bus.   **3.** To become hooked or fastened. My sweater *caught* on a branch.   **4.** To come upon suddenly; surprise; apprehend. The police hoped to *catch* the thieves before they got on the airplane.   **5.** To get; receive. Dress warmly or you will *catch* a cold. *Verb.*
   —1. The act of catching something or someone. The shortstop made a great *catch*.   **2.** Something that holds or fastens. The *catch* on the door was broken.   **3.** Something that is caught. Our *catch* for the day was three fish.   **4.** A game in which a ball is thrown back and forth between the players.   **5.** A hidden reason or condition; trick. This arithmetic problem seems so easy that there must be a *catch* to it. *Noun.*
   • **to catch on.   1.** To understand. A friend had to explain the joke to me three times before I *caught on*.   **2.** To become fashionable or popular. That style of dressing *caught on* very quickly.
   • **to catch up.**   To move fast enough to come from behind into an even position. I *caught up* with the leading runner near the end of the race.
   catch (kach) *verb*, **caught, catching;** *noun, plural* **catches.**

catcher   A person or thing that catches. In a baseball game the catcher is the player who crouches behind home plate to catch balls that are thrown by the pitcher.
   catch·er (kach′ər) *noun, plural* **catchers.**

catching   **1.** Spread from one person to another by infection; contagious. Measles is very *catching*.   **2.** Easily passed on to another. The excitement of the people watching the parade was *catching*.
   catch·ing (kach′ing) *adjective.*

category   A group or class of things. The books on that shelf are divided into two *categories*, history and geography.
   cat·e·go·ry (kat′i gôr′ē) *noun, plural* **categories.**

cater   To provide food, supplies, and other services. A restaurant *catered* the wedding dinner. This laundry service *caters* to large families.
   ca·ter (kā′tər) *verb*, **catered, catering.**

caterpillar   The larva of a butterfly or moth. A caterpillar looks like a short worm and is sometimes hairy. Look up the word **larva** for more information.
   cat·er·pil·lar (kat′ər pil′ər) *noun, plural* **caterpillars.**

caterpillar

catfish   A type of fish that has long feelers around its mouth that look like whiskers. Catfish are often used as food.
   cat·fish (kat′fish′) *noun, plural* **catfish** or **catfishes.**

cathedral   **1.** The official church of a bishop.   **2.** A large and important church.
   ca·the·dral (kə thē′drəl) *noun, plural* **cathedrals.**

Word History

   The word **cathedral** comes from the Greek word for "chair." A bishop's official seat, which indicates his or her position of authority, is in a *cathedral.*

Catholic   Having to do with the Christian church that is headed by the pope; Roman Catholic. *Adjective.*
   —A person who is a member of the Catholic Church; Roman Catholic. *Noun.*
   Cath·o·lic (kath′ə lik) *adjective; noun, plural* **Catholics.**

catsup   A spicy red tomato sauce. This word is usually spelled **ketchup.** Look up **ketchup** for more information.
   cat·sup (kat′səp *or* kech′əp) *noun, plural* **catsups.**

cattail   A tall plant with long flat leaves that grows in marshes. Cattails have long, furry brown flower spikes.
   cat·tail (kat′tāl′) *noun, plural* **cattails.**

cattle   Cows, bulls, and steers that are raised for meat, milk products, and their hides.
   cat·tle (kat′əl) *plural noun.*

cattleman   A person who owns or helps take care of cattle on a ranch.
   cat·tle·man (kat′əl mən) *noun, plural* **cattlemen** (kat′əl mən).

caught Past tense and past participle of **catch**. I *caught* the butterfly in a net. Look up **catch** for more information.
caught (kôt) *verb.*

cauliflower A plant that has a round, usually white head with green leaves around it. The head of a cauliflower is eaten as a vegetable.
cau·li·flow·er (kô′lə flou′ər) *noun.*

cauliflower

caulk To fill with tar or another substance to prevent leaking; make watertight or airtight. We *caulked* the seams of the new rowboat before putting it in the water.
caulk (kôk) *verb,* **caulked, caulking.**

cause 1. A person or thing that makes something happen. The hurricane was the *cause* of great damage to the town. 2. Something a person or group believes in. Stopping the pollution of our air and water is a *cause* many people work for. *Noun.*
—To make something happen; result in. A fire *caused* the barn to collapse. *Verb.*
cause (kôz) *noun, plural* **causes;** *verb,* **caused, causing.**

causeway A raised road or path. Causeways are often built across swamps, shallow water, or low ground.
cause·way (kôz′wā′) *noun, plural* **causeways.**

caution 1. Close care; watchfulness. Use *caution* when you leave a campfire, and be sure it is completely out. 2. A warning about something. There was a sign giving drivers a *caution* about falling rocks. *Noun.*
—To tell to do something with great care; warn. The cook *cautioned* us not to touch the pot because it was hot. *Verb.*
cau·tion (kô′shən) *noun, plural* **cautions;** *verb,* **cautioned, cautioning.**

cautious Using caution. Always be *cautious* when you ride your bicycle.
cau·tious (kô′shəs) *adjective.*

cavalry A group of soldiers fighting on horseback or from tanks and other armored vehicles.
cav·al·ry (kav′əl rē) *noun, plural* **cavalries.**

cave A natural hollow or hole in the ground or in the side of a mountain. *Noun.*

• **to cave in.** To fall in or down. The walls of the old mine are about *to cave in. Verb.*
cave (kāv) *noun, plural* **caves;** *verb,* **caved, caving.**

cave dweller A human being of the Stone Age who lived in a cave.
cave dwell·er (dwel′ər).

cave-in A collapse, as of a mine or tunnel. The *cave-in* closed the tunnel to traffic.
cave-in (kāv′in′) *noun, plural* **cave-ins.**

cave man A term sometimes used for **cave dweller.**

cavern A large cave.
cav·ern (kav′ərn) *noun, plural* **caverns.**

cavity 1. A hollow place; hole. The explosion left a large *cavity* in the ground. 2. A softened place on a tooth caused by decay. The dentist cleaned out and filled two *cavities* in my teeth.
cav·i·ty (kāv′i tē) *noun, plural* **cavities.**

CD An abbreviation for *compact disc.*

cease To come or bring to an end; stop. The rain *ceased* in the afternoon. The soldiers *ceased* firing.
cease (sēs) *verb,* **ceased, ceasing.**

cedar An evergreen tree that has needle-shaped leaves. The reddish wood of the cedar is very fragrant and strong and is used for making chests and cabinets and for lining closets.
ce·dar (sē′dər) *noun, plural* **cedars.**

Needles and Cone
cedar

ceiling 1. The inside overhead surface of a room. The tall guest reached up and almost touched the *ceiling.* 2. The distance from

at; āpe; fär; câre; end; mē; it; īce; pîerce; hot; ōld; sông, fôrk; oil; out; up; ūse; rüle; pu̇ll; tûrn; chin; sing; shop; thin; <u>th</u>is; hw in white; zh in treasure. The symbol ə stands for the unstressed vowel sound in about, taken, pencil, lemon, and circus.

the earth to the bottom of the lowest clouds. The airport canceled all flights because there was a low *ceiling*. **3.** An upper limit. The class treasurer put a *ceiling* of ten dollars on how much we could spend on the party.
ceil·ing (sē′ling) *noun, plural* **ceilings.**

celebrate **1.** To observe or honor a special day or event with ceremonies and other activities. The Chinese *celebrate* each new year with parades, fireworks, and feasts. **2.** To perform with the proper ceremonies. Members of the clergy *celebrate* religious rituals.
cel·e·brate (sel′ə brāt′) *verb,* **celebrated, celebrating.**

celebration **1.** The ceremonies and other activities that are carried on to observe or honor a special day or event. All the members of the winning team were at the victory *celebration*. **2.** The act of celebrating. We were there for the *celebration* of my cousin's graduation from high school.
cel·e·bra·tion (sel′ə brā′shən) *noun, plural* **celebrations.**

celebrity A person who is well-known or often in the news. The stars and other *celebrities* attended the opening of the new movie.
ce·leb·ri·ty (sə leb′ri tē) *noun, plural* **celebrities.**

celery The crisp, green or cream-colored stalks of a plant that is also called celery. The stalks are eaten raw or cooked.
cel·er·y (sel′ə rē) *noun.*

cell **1.** A small, plain room in a prison, convent, or monastery. **2.** The very small, basic unit of living matter. All living things are made of cells. Cells consist of a mass of cytoplasm surrounded by a membrane. **3.** A small hole or space. Honeycombs contain many cells.

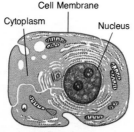

Cell Membrane
Cytoplasm
Nucleus
animal **cell**

4. A device that changes chemical or solar energy into electrical energy. A battery is made up of one or more cells. ▲ Another word that sounds like this is **sell.**
cell (sel) *noun, plural* **cells.**

cellar A room or group of rooms built underground. Most cellars are under buildings and are used for storage.
cel·lar (sel′ər) *noun, plural* **cellars.**

cello A musical instrument that is like a violin but is larger and lower in tone. A cello is held between the knees when it is played.
cel·lo (chel′ō) *noun, plural* **cellos.**

cellophane A thin, clear material made from cellulose. Cellophane is used to wrap food and to make clear tape.
cel·lo·phane (sel′ə fān′) *noun.*

celluloid A strong, clear plastic that burns easily. It is made from alcohol, camphor, and a mixture of cellulose and certain acids.
cel·lu·loid (sel′yə loid′) *noun.*

cellulose The tough material that forms the walls of plant cells. Cellulose makes up the woody part of trees and plants.
cel·lu·lose (sel′yə lōs′) *noun.*

Celsius On or of a temperature scale on which the freezing point of water is at 0 degrees and the boiling point of water is at 100 degrees. The Celsius scale is also called the **centigrade** scale.
Cel·si·us (sel′sē əs *or* sel′shəs) *adjective.*

cement **1.** A powder that is made by burning a mixture of limestone and clay. Cement is mixed with water, sand, and rock to form concrete, a mixture that becomes hard when it dries. **2.** Any soft, sticky substance that hardens to make things hold together. Some types of glue are called cement. *Noun.*
—1. To cover with cement or concrete. The workers *cemented* the cracks in the sidewalk. **2.** To fasten with cement. The instructions said to *cement* the wing to the model airplane. **3.** To make firm or secure; bind. The secret that we shared *cemented* our friendship. *Verb.*
ce·ment (sə ment′) *noun, plural* **cements;** *verb,* **cemented, cementing.**

cello

cemetery A place where the dead are buried.
> **cem·e·ter·y** (sem′ə ter′ē) *noun, plural* **cemeteries.**

census An official count of the people living in a country or district. A census is taken to find out how many people there are, and their age, sex, and kind of work.
> **cen·sus** (sen′səs) *noun, plural* **censuses.**

cent A coin of the United States and Canada. One hundred cents is equal to one dollar. ▲ Other words that sound like this are **scent** and **sent.**
> **cent** (sent) *noun, plural* **cents.**

centennial The hundredth-year anniversary of an event or the celebration of that anniversary. Three parades and a fair are planned to celebrate the *centennial* of the founding of our city. *Noun.*
—Of or relating to a hundredth anniversary. The *centennial* celebration ended with fireworks. *Adjective.*
> **cen·ten·ni·al** (sen ten′ē əl) *noun, plural* **centennials;** *adjective.*

center **1.** The middle point of a circle or sphere. It is the same distance from any point on the circumference of the circle or any point on the surface of the sphere. **2.** The middle point, part, or place of something. We put the flowers in the *center* of the table. **3.** A main person, place, or thing. The new baby was the *center* of attention. That city is a leading *center* of trade. **4.** A player on a team who has a position in the middle of the playing line or area. I am the *center* on our soccer team. *Noun.*
—**1.** To put in or at the center. We *centered* the picture on the wall. **2.** To come together or gather around a point or points; concentrate. Crowds at beaches often *center* around the lifeguards. *Verb.*
> **cen·ter** (sen′tər) *noun, plural* **centers;** *verb,* **centered, centering.**

centi– A *prefix* that means: **1.** One hundred. *Centigrade* means divided into one hundred grades, or degrees. **2.** One hundredth ($\frac{1}{100}$) of. *Centimeter* means $\frac{1}{100}$ of a meter.

centigrade On or of the Celsius temperature scale. Look up **Celsius** for more information.
> **cen·ti·grade** (sen′ti grād′) *adjective.*

centimeter A unit of length in the metric system. A centimeter is equal to $\frac{1}{100}$ of a meter. One inch equals about two and a half centimeters.
> **cen·ti·me·ter** (sen′tə mē′tər) *noun, plural* **centimeters.**

centipede A small animal that has a long body divided into many segments. Each segment has two legs.
> **cen·ti·pede** (sen′tə pēd′) *noun, plural* **centipedes.**

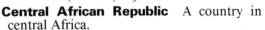
centipede

central **1.** In, at, or near the center or middle. The railroad station is in the *central* part of town. **2.** Very important; main; chief. They both work in the *central* office of the bank.
> **cen·tral** (sen′trəl) *adjective.*

Central African Republic A country in central Africa.

Central America The long, narrow strip of land that connects North America and South America.

century A period of one hundred years. From 1651 to 1750 is one century.
> **cen·tu·ry** (sen′chə rē) *noun, plural* **centuries.**

ceramic Made of baked clay. These *ceramic* tiles were made in Mexico. *Adjective.*
—An object made of baked clay. My cousin collects English *ceramics. Noun.*
> **ce·ram·ic** (sə ram′ik) *adjective; noun, plural* **ceramics.**

ceramics The art of making bowls, dishes, vases, and other things out of baked clay.
> **ce·ram·ics** (sə ram′iks) *noun.*

cereal **1.** Any grass whose grains are used for food. Wheat, oats, rye, barley, and rice are cereals. **2.** A food that is made from this grain. Oatmeal is a cereal. ▲ Another word that sounds like this is **serial.**
> **ce·re·al** (sîr′ē əl) *noun, plural* **cereals.**

Word History

The word **cereal** goes back to a Latin word meaning "having to do with growing crops of grain." The Latin word comes from the name *Ceres,* goddess of farming and crops in Roman mythology.

at; āpe; fär; câre; end; mē; it; īce; pîerce; hot; ōld; sông, fôrk; oil; out; up; ūse; rüle; pùll; tûrn; chin; sing; shop; thin; <u>this</u>; hw in white; zh in treasure. The symbol ə stands for the unstressed vowel sound in about, taken, pencil, lemon, and circus.

ceremony **1.** A formal act or set of acts done on a special or important occasion. At the graduation *ceremony,* each student received a diploma from the principal. **2.** Very polite or formal behavior. The usher showed us to our seats with great *ceremony,* bowing twice.
cer·e·mo·ny (ser′ə mō′nē) *noun, plural* **ceremonies.**

certain **1.** Sure; positive. I am *certain* that my answer is correct because I checked it. **2.** Known but not named; some; particular. *Certain* animals hunt for food at night. *Certain* people already know who won the contest.
cer·tain (sûr′tən) *adjective.*

certainly Without a doubt; surely. Those dark clouds *certainly* mean it will rain.
cer·tain·ly (sûr′tən lē) *adverb.*

certainty The state or quality of being sure or certain. I watched them leave, so I can say with *certainty* that they are not here.
cer·tain·ty (sûr′tən tē) *noun, plural* **certainties.**

certificate A written statement that is accepted as proof of certain facts. Your birth *certificate* tells where and when you were born.
cer·tif·i·cate (sər tif′i kit) *noun, plural* **certificates.**

Chad A country in central Africa.
Chad (chad) *noun.*

chain **1.** A row of rings or links that are connected to each other. Most chains are made of metal and are used to fasten, hold, or pull something. I fastened my bicycle to the fence with a *chain.* **2.** A series of things that are connected or related to each other. The *chain* of mountains runs across the state. That family owns a *chain* of grocery stores. **3. chains.** Rows of rings or other objects that are used to fasten together the wrists or ankles of a prisoner. The escaped prisoner was brought back in *chains. Noun.*
—To fasten or hold with a chain. *Chain* the goat to the post so it can't get into the garden. *Verb.*
chain (chān) *noun, plural* **chains;** *verb,* **chained, chaining.**

chain

chair **1.** A piece of furniture for one person to sit on. A chair has a seat, legs, and a back. Some chairs have arms. **2.** A chairperson.
chair (châr) *noun, plural* **chairs.**

chairman A person, especially a man, who is in charge of a meeting or committee.
chair·man (châr′mən) *noun, plural* **chairmen** (châr′mən).

chairperson A person who is in charge of a meeting or committee.
chair·per·son (châr′pûr′sən) *noun, plural* **chairpersons.**

chairwoman A woman who is in charge of a meeting or committee.
chair·wom·an (châr′wùm′ən) *noun, plural* **chairwomen** (châr′wim′ən).

chalk **1.** A type of soft white or gray limestone that is made up mostly of the tiny fossils of seashells. Chalk is used to make lime and cement and as a fertilizer. **2.** A piece of this substance, used for writing and drawing on a blackboard. *Noun.*
—To mark, write, or draw with chalk. I *chalked* a circle on the sidewalk for a game of marbles. *Verb.*
• **to chalk up.** **1.** To score or record. The hockey team *chalked up* three more goals. **2.** To think or say that something is caused by something else. You can *chalk up* my mistake to ignorance.
chalk (chôk) *noun, plural* **chalks;** *verb,* **chalked, chalking.**

chalkboard A hard, smooth board that is made to be written or drawn on with chalk; blackboard. Look up **blackboard** for more information.
chalk·board (chôk′bôrd′) *noun, plural* **chalkboards.**

challenge **1.** To ask to take part in a contest or fight. They *challenged* us to a race around the block. **2.** To stop someone and demand identification. The guard *challenged* us at the door of the building. **3.** To question the truth or correctness of; doubt or dispute. They *challenged* my claim that bats are mammals. **4.** To make someone think, work, or try hard; make demands on. The puzzle *challenged* us all. *Verb.*
—**1.** A call to take part in a contest or fight. Our football team has accepted their team's *challenge.* **2.** A call to stop and give an explanation. The soldier answered the guard's *challenge* with the password. **3.** A questioning of the truth or correctness of something; objection. There was a legal *challenge* to the election, because some votes were not counted. **4.** Something that calls for work, effort, and the use of one's talents. I find chemistry to be a real *challenge. Noun.*
chal·lenge (chal′ənj) *verb,* **challenged, challenging;** *noun, plural* **challenges.**

chamber **1.** A room in a house or other building. While exploring the castle, we discovered a secret *chamber* in the tower. **2.** The office of a judge, usually in a courthouse. **3.** A hall where a lawmaking body meets. In Philadelphia, you can see the *chamber* where the Declaration of Independence was signed. **4.** A legislature or other group of lawmakers. The Senate and the House of Representatives are the two *chambers* of Congress. **5.** An enclosed space in the body of an animal or plant. The human heart has four *chambers*. **6.** The part of the barrel of a gun into which the shell is put.
cham·ber (chām′bər) *noun, plural* **chambers.**

chameleon A small lizard that can change its color to look like its surroundings.
cha·me·leon (kə mēl′yən) *noun, plural* **chameleons.**

champion **1.** A person or thing that is the winner of first place in a contest or game. Our school is the *champion* in basketball. **2.** A person who fights or speaks for another person or a cause. That senator is a *champion* of the rights of the poor.
cham·pi·on (cham′pē ən) *noun, plural* **champions.**

championship **1.** A contest held to decide who is the champion. We have tickets to the basketball *championship* tomorrow night. **2.** The title or position held by a champion. Their team is so good that they've held the *championship* for the last three years.
cham·pi·on·ship (cham′pē ən ship′) *noun, plural* **championships.**

chance **1.** A good or favorable opportunity. I'm so glad I had this *chance* to meet you. **2.** The possibility of something happening. There's a *chance* that it may rain tomorrow. **3.** A risk. Never take *chances* by swimming alone. *Noun.*
—**1.** To risk. The prisoners decided to *chance* an escape. **2.** To happen accidentally. I *chanced* to meet them in the park. *Verb.*
—Not expected or planned; accidental. We learned about the surprise party through a *chance* remark. *Adjective.*
• **by chance.** Accidentally. It was only *by chance* that I noticed the mistake.
chance (chans) *noun, plural* **chances;** *verb,* **chanced, chancing;** *adjective.*

chancellor A very high official. In certain European countries the head of the government is called the chancellor.
chan·cel·lor (chan′sə lər) *noun, plural* **chancellors.**

chandelier A kind of light that hangs from the ceiling. Most chandeliers have several lights arranged on branches.
chan·de·lier (shan′də lîr′) *noun, plural* **chandeliers.**

Word History

The word **chandelier** comes from a French word meaning "candlestick." This French word goes back to a Latin word meaning "candle."

change **1.** To make or become different; alter. I *changed* the way I signed my name. I *changed* my mind about going to the movies. The weather *changed* as we drove farther south. **2.** To replace with another or others; exchange. We went home and *changed* our wet clothes. Can you *change* a quarter for five nickels? Let's *change* our seats. **3.** To put on other clothes. I *changed* and went for a swim. *Verb.*
—**1.** The act or result of making something different. We made a *change* in our plans. **2.** Something that can be put in place of another. Bring a *change* of clothing on the camping trip. **3.** The money that is given back when the amount paid is more than the amount owed. I gave the clerk a dollar bill and got forty cents in *change*. **4.** Coins. I have lots of *change* in my pocket. *Noun.*
change (chānj) *verb,* **changed, changing;** *noun, plural* **changes.**

channel **1.** The deepest part of a river, harbor, or other waterway. **2.** A body of water that connects two larger bodies of water. The Strait of Gibraltar is a narrow *channel* between the Atlantic Ocean and the Mediterranean Sea. **3.** A band of frequencies that a radio or television station uses to send out electronic signals. This old television set can pick up only one *channel*. *Noun.*
—To form a channel in. The flood *channeled* the bed of the stream. *Verb.*
chan·nel (chan′əl) *noun, plural* **channels;** *verb,* **channeled, channeling.**

chant A singing or shouting of words over and over. Chants usually have a strong

at; āpe; fär; câre; end; mē; it; īce; pîerce; hot; ōld; sông, fôrk; oil; out; up; ūse; rüle; pull; tûrn; chin; sing; shop; thin; <u>th</u>is; hw in white; zh in treasure. The symbol ə stands for the unstressed vowel sound in about, taken, pencil, lemon, and circus.

rhythm. The crowd yelled a *chant* before the basketball game began. *Noun.*
—To sing or shout a chant. The worshipers *chanted* a prayer. *Verb.*
> **chant** (chant) *noun, plural* **chants**; *verb,* **chanted, chanting.**

Chanukah Another spelling for **Hanukkah.** Look up **Hanukkah** for more information.
> **Cha·nu·kah** (hä′nə kə) *noun, plural* **Chanukahs.**

chaos Complete confusion; great disorder. The village was in *chaos* after the earthquake struck.
> **cha·os** (kā′os) *noun.*

chap¹ To make or become dry, cracked, and rough. In the winter, the cold, dry air *chaps* my face and hands.
> **chap** (chap) *verb,* **chapped, chapping.**

chap² A man or boy; fellow. Our camp counselor is a nice *chap.*
> **chap** (chap) *noun, plural* **chaps.**

chapel A room, small building, or other place for worship.
> **chap·el** (chap′əl) *noun, plural* **chapels.**

chaplain A member of the clergy who leads services and does counseling for a military unit, school, prison, or other group.
> **chap·lain** (chap′lin) *noun, plural* **chaplains.**

chaps Strong leather coverings worn over trousers. Chaps are sometimes worn by cowhands to protect their legs while riding horses.
> **chaps** (chaps *or* shaps) *plural noun.*

chaps

chapter 1. A main part of a book. My history book has fifteen *chapters.* 2. A local branch or division of a club or other organization. The fan club has a *chapter* in every large city.
> **chap·ter** (chap′tər) *noun, plural* **chapters.**

character 1. All the qualities that make a person or thing different from others. That writer's stories all have a frightening *character.* The countryside has a different *character* as you travel west. 2. What a person really is; inner nature. You can judge a person's character by the way that person feels, thinks, and acts. 3. Strength of mind, courage, and honesty taken together. Political leaders should be persons of great *character.* 4. A person in a book, play, story, or motion picture. Who is your favorite *character* in that movie? 5. A person who is different, funny, or strange. Everyone thought the storekeeper who wore funny ties was a *character.* 6. A mark or sign used in writing or printing. The letters of the alphabet are characters.
> **char·ac·ter** (kar′ik tər) *noun, plural* **characters.**

characteristic A quality or feature that belongs to and helps to identify a person or thing. Kindness and honesty are two good *characteristics* of my neighbor. The ability to fly is a *characteristic* of most birds. *Noun.*
—Belonging to and helping to identify a person or thing; typical. The *characteristic* taste of a lemon is sour. *Adjective.*
> **char·ac·ter·is·tic** (kar′ik tə ris′tik) *noun, plural* **characteristics**; *adjective.*

characterize 1. To be an important quality or characteristic of; distinguish. The ability to hop great distances *characterizes* the kangaroo. 2. To describe the character or qualities of. The author of the book *characterizes* the town as a quiet place by the ocean.
> **char·ac·ter·ize** (kar′ik tə rīz′) *verb,* **characterized, characterizing.**

charcoal A soft, black substance that is a form of carbon. It is made by partially burning wood or other plant or animal matter. Charcoal is used as a fuel and in pencils for drawing.
> **char·coal** (chär′kōl′) *noun.*

charge 1. To ask as a price. The shop *charged* ten dollars to repair the radio. 2. To ask to pay for something. The neighbor *charged* the children for the window that they broke. 3. To put off paying for something until later. We *charged* the clothes at the store and paid for them at the end of the month. 4. To blame; accuse. The police *charged* them with robbery. 5. To rush at; attack. The angry bull *charged* the farmer. The troops *charged* toward the fort. 6. To fill or load. The soldier *charged* the cannon with shot. The mechanic *charged* the car's battery with electricity. 7. To give a task or responsibility to; trust with a duty. The life-

guard was *charged* with the care of the swimmers. *Verb.*
—**1.** The price asked for something. The *charge* for the repair of the car was sixty dollars. **2.** Care or responsibility. I had *charge* of my brother and sister while our parents were away. **3.** A statement that someone has committed a crime; accusation. They were arrested on a *charge* of robbery. **4.** A rushing at an opponent; attack. The enemy's *charge* was turned back by the king's soldiers. *Noun.*
- **in charge.** Having the power or right to act, order, or make decisions. One worker in the crew was *in charge.*
- **in charge of.** Assigned the duty of; responsible for. You must cook dinner, and I'm *in charge of* washing the dishes.

charge (chärj) *verb,* **charged, charging;** *noun, plural* **charges.**

chariot A vehicle with two wheels that is drawn by horses. Chariots were used in ancient times in warfare, races, and processions.
char·i·ot (char′ē ət) *noun, plural* **chariots.**

chariot

charity **1.** The giving of money or help to those who need it. The family had to depend on *charity* for a month after their house burned down. **2.** A fund or organization for giving help to those who need it. We give money to a *charity* for orphans. **3.** Kindness or forgiveness toward other people. I try to show *charity* even to people who are unkind to me.
char·i·ty (char′i tē) *noun, plural* **charities.**

charm **1.** The power to attract or delight greatly. That fairy tale holds much *charm* for people of all ages. **2.** A small ornament worn on a bracelet or necklace. **3.** An act, saying, or thing that is supposed to have magic power. Do you carry a rabbit's foot as a *charm* for good luck? *Noun.*
—To attract or delight greatly. The magician's clever tricks *charmed* the children. *Verb.*
charm (chärm) *noun, plural* **charms;** *verb,* **charmed, charming.**

charming Full of charm; attractive or delightful. The baby had a *charming* smile. We rested under the *charming* arbor.
charm·ing (chär′ming) *adjective.*

chart **1.** A sheet that shows information in the form of a list, diagram, table, or graph. We made a *chart* of the temperatures for each day of the last month. **2.** A map. Sailors use *charts* that show where rocks, harbors, and channels are. *Noun.*
—To make a map or chart of. The explorers *charted* the coastline. *Verb.*
chart (chärt) *noun, plural* **charts;** *verb,* **charted, charting.**

charter **1.** A written document giving and explaining certain rights and obligations. A charter is given by a government or ruler to a person, group of people, or company. The insurance company was granted a *charter* by the state. **2.** A renting or hiring of a bus, aircraft, or automobile. Those planes are available for *charter. Noun.*
—**1.** To rent or hire by charter. The school band *chartered* a bus for the trip. **2.** To give a charter to. The state *chartered* a new bank. *Verb.*
char·ter (chär′tər) *noun, plural* **charters;** *verb,* **chartered, chartering.**

chase **1.** To run after and try to catch. The cat *chased* the mouse across the room. The police *chased* after the thief. **2.** To cause to go away quickly; drive away. We *chased* the birds out of our vegetable garden. *Verb.*
—The act of running and trying to catch. The children caught the puppy after a long *chase. Noun.*
chase (chās) *verb,* **chased, chasing;** *noun, plural* **chases.**

chasm A deep crack or opening in the earth's surface.
chasm (kaz′əm) *noun, plural* **chasms.**

chasm

C

chassis The main framework that supports the body of an automobile or airplane, or the parts of a radio or television set.
chas·sis (chas′ē *or* shas′ē) *noun, plural* **chassis** (chas′ēz *or* shas′ēz).

chat To talk in a light, friendly, or relaxed way. The two friends *chatted* as they ate their lunch. *Verb.*
—A light, friendly, or informal talk. *Noun.*
chat (chat) *verb,* **chatted, chatting;** *noun, plural* **chats.**

chatter 1. To talk quickly and without serious thought or purpose. The students *chattered* on and on about the coming vacation. 2. To knock or click together quickly. My teeth *chattered* from the cold. *Verb.*
—1. Quick talk without serious thought or purpose. We couldn't be heard above the *chatter* of the others. 2. Quick, short sounds. We could hear the *chatter* of monkeys in the next cage. *Noun.*
chat·ter (chat′ər) *verb,* **chattered, chattering;** *noun, plural* **chatters.**

chauffeur A person whose work is driving someone else's automobile.
chauf·feur (shō′fər *or* shō fûr′) *noun, plural* **chauffeurs.**

cheap 1. Low in price; not costing much. Milk is *cheap* in that store. 2. Charging low prices. Let's find a *cheap* restaurant. 3. Having little value; not of good quality. Clothing made of *cheap* material does not last long.
cheap (chēp) *adjective,* **cheaper, cheapest.**

cheat 1. To act in a dishonest or unfair way. Do not *cheat* when playing games. 2. To take something away from dishonestly; swindle. The crook *cheated* them out of their share of the money. *Verb.*
—A person who cheats; dishonest person. *Noun.*
cheat (chēt) *verb,* **cheated, cheating;** *noun, plural* **cheats.**

check 1. A test or other way of finding out if something is correct or as it should be. The teacher made a *check* of the classroom to see if everyone was present. 2. A mark (✓) used to show that something has been approved or is correct. The club secretary put a *check* by the name of each person who was present at the meeting. 3. A written order directing a bank to pay a certain amount of money. The money comes from the account of the person who signs the check and goes to the person named on the check. I'll give the store a *check* to pay for the new lamp. 4. A slip of paper showing what is owed for food or drink in a restaurant. The total on the *check* for our lunch was ten dollars. 5. A ticket, tag, or token given to a person who has left or stored something so that the article can be claimed later. 6. A pattern of squares. The skirt has black and white *checks.* 7. A sudden stop. A lack of time put a *check* on our plans to clean the yard. 8. A person or thing that stops, controls, or limits. The leash was a *check* on the dog. *Noun.*
—1. To test or compare to find out if something is correct or as it should be. The mechanic *checked* the car's engine. I will *check* my answers with those in the back of the book. 2. To mark with a check. Please *check* the right answer to each question. 3. To leave something for a time. We *checked* our coats at the door. 4. To bring to a sudden stop. The army *checked* the attack of the enemy soldiers. 5. To hold in control; curb. I had to *check* the urge to laugh at the mistake my friend made during the speech. *Verb.*
• **to check in.** To register as a guest in a hotel or motel. We *checked in* at a hotel on the beach.
• **to check out.** 1. To pay one's bill and depart from a hotel or motel. We didn't like the hotel so we *checked out* a day early. 2. To add up prices and accept payment for. I have a job on weekends *checking out* groceries in a supermarket.
check (chek) *noun, plural* **checks;** *verb,* **checked, checking.**

checkerboard A square board marked off into sixty-four squares of two alternating colors. It is used in playing checkers and chess.
check·er·board (chek′ər bôrd′) *noun, plural* **checkerboards.**

checkers A game for two people played on a checkerboard with twelve pieces for each player.
check·ers (chek′ərz) *plural noun.*

playing **checkers**

checkup 1. A complete examination of the body to find out if a person is healthy. The

C

doctor gave the children *checkups* before they started school. **2.** Any complete inspection. People sometimes give their cars a *checkup* before taking a long trip.

    check·up (chek′up′) *noun, plural* **checkups.**

cheek   **1.** Either side of the face below the eye. **2.** Boldness or rudeness; disrespect. I was shocked that the new student had the *cheek* to talk back to the teacher.

    cheek (chēk) *noun, plural* **cheeks.**

cheer   **1.** A shout of happiness, encouragement, or praise. We greeted our team with *cheers* when it appeared on the field. **2.** Good spirits; happiness. Summer vacation brings many students feelings of *cheer*. *Noun.*

  —1. To give a shout of happiness, encouragement, or praise. The crowd *cheered* the batter for the home run. **2.** To make or become happy. My friend's funny joke *cheered* me up. *Verb.*

    cheer (chîr) *noun, plural* **cheers;** *verb,* **cheered, cheering.**

cheerful   **1.** Showing or feeling happiness or good spirits. The *cheerful* carpenter whistled while building the shed. **2.** Bringing a feeling of happiness and good spirits. Our kitchen is a *cheerful* room.

    cheer·ful (chîr′fəl) *adjective.*

cheese   A food made by pressing the less watery parts of curdled milk into a solid piece. Most cheeses are seasoned and aged.

    cheese (chēz) *noun, plural* **cheeses.**

cheetah   A wild cat that has solid black spots on its coat. Cheetahs live in Africa and southern Asia. They can run very fast.

    chee·tah (chē′tə) *noun, plural* **cheetahs.**

chef   The head cook of a restaurant or hotel.

    chef (shef) *noun, plural* **chefs.**

chemical   Having to do with or made by chemistry. Rusting is a *chemical* process in which metal combines with oxygen. *Adjective.*

  —A substance made by or used in chemistry. Ammonia is a *chemical* used in household cleansers. *Noun.*

    chem·i·cal (kem′i kəl) *adjective; noun, plural* **chemicals.**

chemist   A person who works or specializes in chemistry.

    chem·ist (kem′ist) *noun, plural* **chemists.**

chemistry   The science that deals with substances, what they are made of, what characteristics they have, and what kinds of changes happen when they combine with other substances.

    chem·is·try (kem′ə strē) *noun.*

chemotherapy   The use of chemical substances to treat diseases.

    chem·o·ther·a·py (kē′mō ther′ə pē *or* kem′ō ther′ə pē) *noun, plural* **chemotherapies.**

cherish   To love and treat tenderly; hold dear. The whole class *cherished* the pet guinea pig.

    cher·ish (cher′ish) *verb,* **cherished, cherishing.**

Cherokee   A member of an American Indian tribe of the southeastern United States. The Cherokee now live mostly in Oklahoma.

    Cher·o·kee (cher′ə kē′) *noun, plural* **Cherokee** or **Cherokees.**

cherries

cherry   **1.** A small, round red fruit with a smooth skin and a pit in the center. Cherries grow on a tree that has many clusters of white or pink flowers in the spring. **2.** A bright red color.

    cher·ry (cher′ē) *noun, plural* **cherries.**

cheetah

at; āpe; fär; câre; end; mē; it; īce; pîerce; hot; ōld; sông, fôrk; oil; out; up; ūse; rüle; pull; tûrn; chin; sing; shop; thin; <u>th</u>is; hw in white; zh in treasure. The symbol ə stands for the unstressed vowel sound in about, taken, pencil, lemon, and circus.

chess A game played by two people on a board, with sixteen pieces for each player.
  chess (ches) *noun.*

chest **1.** The upper, front part of the body of a person or other animal. The chest is enclosed by the ribs. The lungs and the heart are in the chest. **2.** A large, strong box used for holding things.
  chest (chest) *noun, plural* **chests.**

chestnut **1.** A sweet-tasting nut that grows inside a large, prickly bur. It grows on a tree that is also called a chestnut. **2.** A reddish brown color.
  chest·nut (ches'nut') *noun, plural* **chestnuts.**

chew **1.** To crush and grind something with the teeth. It's important to *chew* food thoroughly. **2.** To make by chewing. The puppy *chewed* a hole in the slipper.
  chew (chü) *verb,* **chewed, chewing.**

chewing gum A sweet gum for chewing. It usually comes in sticks or small squares.

Cheyenne A member of a tribe of American Indians that used to live on the plains of North America. The Cheyenne now live mostly in Montana and Oklahoma.
  Chey·enne (shī en' *or* shī an') *noun, plural* **Cheyenne** or **Cheyennes.**

Chicano An American of Mexican birth or descent.
  Chi·ca·no (chi kä'nō) *noun, plural* **Chicanos.**

chick A young chicken or other young bird.
  chick (chik) *noun, plural* **chicks.**

chickadee A small bird that has a gray back and wings and a black head and throat. Chickadees live in North America. They have a call that sounds like their name.
  chick·a·dee (chik'ə dē') *noun, plural* **chickadees.**

chickadee

chicken **1.** A bird that is raised on farms for its meat and eggs. Chickens may be of many different colors. They usually stay on the ground and fly only for short distances. **2.** The meat of a chicken used for food. We had fried *chicken* on our picnic.
  chick·en (chik'ən) *noun, plural* **chickens.**

chicken pox A mild disease caused by a virus that is easily passed from one person to another. Chicken pox causes a fever and rash.
  chicken pox (poks).

chief A person who is highest in rank or power; leader of a group. The *chief* of police will lead the parade. The *chief* of the Indian tribe was the oldest and wisest member. *Noun.*
  —**1.** Highest in rank; in charge of a group. My cousin is *chief* counselor at that camp. **2.** Most important; main. Corn and soybeans are the *chief* farm crops of Iowa. *Adjective.*
  chief (chēf) *noun, plural* **chiefs;** *adjective.*

chiefly **1.** Mainly; mostly. The house was made *chiefly* of wood. **2.** More than anything; especially. I am *chiefly* interested in becoming a doctor.
  chief·ly (chēf'lē) *adverb.*

chieftain A leader of a tribe or clan. The *chieftain* of the clan was respected by all the clan's members.
  chief·tain (chēf'tən) *noun, plural* **chieftains.**

chigger A mite that gets under the skin of people and animals and causes a rash and itching.
  chig·ger (chig'ər) *noun, plural* **chiggers.**

chihuahua A tiny dog that has big, pointed ears and usually a short tan coat. It is the smallest breed of dog.
  chi·hua·hua (chi wä'wə) *noun, plural* **chihuahuas.**

child **1.** A son or daughter. The parents were very proud of their only *child.* **2.** A young boy or girl. That is a good book for a *child* of ten. **3.** A baby; infant.
  child (chīld) *noun, plural* **children.**

childbirth The act of giving birth to a child or children.
  child·birth (chīld'bûrth') *noun, plural* **childbirths.**

childhood The period of a person's life when he or she is a child. The children liked to hear their grandparents' stories about their *childhood.*
  child·hood (chīld'hùd') *noun, plural* **childhoods.**

childish Of, like, or suitable only for a child. Refusing to try new kinds of food is *childish* behavior.
  child·ish (chīl'dish) *adjective.*

children Plural of **child.** Three *children* stood at the bus stop. Look up **child** for more information.
  chil·dren (chil'drən) *plural noun.*

Chile A country in southern South America. Other words that sound like this are **chili** and **chilly.**
  Chil·e (chil'ē) *noun.*

C

chili 1. The dried pod of a kind of pepper plant, used to make a hot spice. Most chilies are either red or green. 2. A spicy food made of chilies, chopped meat, and usually beans and tomatoes. ▲ Other words that sound like this are **Chile** and **chilly**.
chil·i (chil′ē) *noun, plural* **chilies.**

chill 1. A mild but unpleasant coldness. There was a *chill* in the air this morning. 2. A feeling of coldness in the body that makes a person shiver. He got a *chill* from sleeping without blankets. As she listened to the ghost story she felt a *chill* go through her. *Noun.*
—To make or become cold. We should *chill* the sodas before we drink them. Without mittens, your hands will soon *chill* in the cold winter air. *Verb.*
—Unpleasantly cold; chilly. There was a *chill* wind blowing across the lake. *Adjective.*
chill (chil) *noun, plural* **chills;** *verb,* **chilled, chilling;** *adjective.*

chilly 1. Causing or feeling coldness; unpleasantly cold. It was a *chilly* morning so I put on an extra sweater. 2. Not warm and friendly. I was disappointed at the *chilly* welcome I got at the new school. ▲ Other words that sound like this are **Chile** and **chili**.
chill·y (chil′ē) *adjective,* **chillier, chilliest.**

chime 1. One of a set of bells or pipes that are tuned to make musical sounds at different pitches. Chimes are usually played by being hit with small hammers. 2. The sound made by these bells or pipes or a similar sound. I didn't hear the *chime* of the doorbell. *Noun.*
—To make a musical sound by ringing. The bells *chimed* in the steeple. *Verb.*
chime (chīm) *noun, plural* **chimes;** *verb,* **chimed, chiming.**

chimney An upright, hollow structure that is connected to a fireplace or furnace. It carries away the smoke from the fire.
chim·ney (chim′nē) *noun, plural* **chimneys.**

chimpanzee A small ape with a dark coat that lives in groups in the forests of central and eastern Africa. Chimpanzees sleep in nests that they build in trees. They are very intelligent.

chimney

chim·pan·zee (chim′pan zē′ *or* chim pan′zē) *noun, plural* **chimpanzees.**

chimpanzee

chin The part of the face below the mouth and above the neck. The chin forms the front of the lower jaw. *Noun.*
—To lift oneself up to an overhead bar by pulling with the arms until the chin is level with or above the bar. How many times can you *chin* yourself? *Verb.*
chin (chin) *noun, plural* **chins;** *verb,* **chinned, chinning.**

china 1. A fine, hard pottery. It is usually white and can have colored designs baked on it. 2. Dishes and other things made of china. We set the table with our best *china* for dinner.
chi·na (chī′nə) *noun.*

China A large country in eastern Asia. More people live in China than in any other country in the world.
Chi·na (chī′nə) *noun.*

chinchilla A small South American animal that looks like a squirrel. A chinchilla is a rodent that has a thick, soft, silver-gray fur.
chin·chil·la (chin chil′ə) *noun, plural* **chinchillas.**

Chinese 1. A person who was born in or is a citizen of China. 2. The language spoken in China. *Noun.*
—Having to do with China. *Adjective.*
Chi·nese (chī nēz′ *or* chī nēs′) *noun, plural* **Chinese;** *adjective.*

at; āpe; fär; câre; end; mē; it; īce; pîerce; hot; ōld; sông, fôrk; oil; out; up; ūse; rüle; pùll; tûrn; chin; sing; shop; thin; <u>th</u>is; hw in white; zh in treasure. The symbol ə stands for the unstressed vowel sound in about, taken, pencil, lemon, and circus.

chink A small, narrow opening; crack. Light came through *chinks* in the walls of the log cabin.
   chink (chingk) *noun, plural* **chinks.**

chip **1.** A very small piece that has been broken off or cut off something. *Chips* of wood flew as I chopped the logs. **2.** A place on an object where a small piece has been broken or cut off. The glass had a *chip* on the rim. **3.** A short form of the word **microchip.** Look up **microchip** for more information. *Noun.*
—To break off in a small piece or pieces. We had to *chip* the old paint off the woodwork before repainting it. The cup *chipped* when I knocked it against the sink. *Verb.*
   • **to chip in.** To join with others in giving money or help; contribute. I *chipped in* to buy flowers for our teacher.
   chip (chip) *noun, plural* **chips;** *verb,* **chipped, chipping.**

chipmunk A small animal that has brown fur with dark stripes on its back and tail. Chipmunks are rodents and are related to squirrels.
   chip·munk (chip'mungk) *noun, plural* **chipmunks.**

chipmunk

chirp A short sound with a high pitch made by birds, insects, and other small animals. I heard the *chirp* of a cricket. The *chirp* of a sparrow woke me up. *Noun.*
—To make a chirp. Our canary *chirps* when it is happy. *Verb.*
   chirp (chûrp) *noun, plural* **chirps;** *verb,* **chirped, chirping.**

chisel A metal tool that has a sharp edge at the end of a blade. A chisel is used to cut or shape wood, stone, or metal. *Noun.*
—To cut or shape with a chisel. The sculptor carefully *chiseled* the stone. *Verb.*
   chis·el (chiz'əl) *noun, plural* **chisels;** *verb,* **chiseled, chiseling.**

chivalry The qualities that a good knight was supposed to have. Chivalry included politeness, bravery, honor, and the protecting of people who needed help.
   chiv·al·ry (shiv'əl rē) *noun.*

Word History

The word **chivalry** comes from an old French word meaning "a knight." This French word goes back to a common Latin word for "horse," because a knight was a mounted warrior on horseback.

---

chlorine A greenish yellow poisonous gas that has a strong, unpleasant odor. Chlorine is used to kill germs and to bleach things. Chlorine is a chemical element.
   chlo·rine (klôr'ēn) *noun.*

chlorophyll The green substance in plants that absorbs energy from sunlight. Plants use chlorophyll to change carbon dioxide and water into food and oxygen.
   chlo·ro·phyll (klôr'ə fil') *noun.*

chocolate **1.** A food substance made from cacao beans that have been roasted and ground. Chocolate is used to make drinks and candy. **2.** A drink made by dissolving chocolate in milk or water. We had some hot *chocolate* after we went ice skating. **3.** A candy made of or coated with chocolate. **4.** A dark brown color. *Noun.*
—**1.** Made with chocolate. That restaurant serves *chocolate* cake for dessert. **2.** Having a dark brown color. *Adjective.*
   choc·o·late (chô'kə lit *or* chôk'lit) *noun, plural* **chocolates;** *adjective.*

choice **1.** The act or result of choosing. It took me a long time to make a *choice* between the two sweaters I liked. I think my *choice* was the right one. **2.** The chance to choose. We were given a *choice* between going to the movies and visiting the zoo. **3.** A person or thing that is chosen. Fresh fruit salad was my *choice* for dessert. **4.** A variety or number of things from which to choose. By reading the catalog, I learned that the school offers a large *choice* of courses. *Noun.*
—Of very good quality; excellent. We searched through the woods for a *choice* spot to have a picnic. *Adjective.*
   choice (chois) *noun, plural* **choices;** *adjective,* **choicer, choicest.**

choir A group of singers who sing together, especially in a church.
   choir (kwīr) *noun, plural* **choirs.**

C

choke **1.** To stop or hold back the breathing of by squeezing or blocking the wind pipe. That tight collar could *choke* the dog. **2.** To make or become unable to breathe easily. The smoke from the fire *choked* us. I *choked* on a bone. **3.** To block or clog; fill up. Grease *choked* the kitchen drain. **4.** To keep from growing or progressing normally. Weeds *choked* the flowers in the garden.

• **to choke back.** To keep from showing; hold in; restrain. I *choked back* my anger.
choke (chōk) *verb,* **choked, choking.**

choose **1.** To decide to take one or more from all that are available; pick. If you could have either a bicycle or a pair of ice skates, which one would you *choose?* **2.** To decide or prefer to do something. You can come to the game with us if you *choose.*
choose (chüz) *verb,* **chose, chosen, choosing.**

chop **1.** To cut by a quick blow or blows with something sharp. The firefighter had to *chop* the door down with an ax. **2.** To cut into small pieces. They *chopped* onions to put in the stew. *Verb.*
—**1.** A quick blow with something sharp. It took many *chops* with the ax to cut down the tree. **2.** A small piece of meat that has a rib in it. We are having lamb *chops* for dinner. *Noun.*
chop (chop) *verb,* **chopped, chopping;** *noun, plural* **chops.**

chopsticks A pair of long, thin sticks that are used to eat with. Chopsticks are held between the thumb and fingers of one hand.
chop·sticks (chop′stiks′) *plural noun.*

using **chopsticks**

chord¹ A combination of three or more notes of music that are sounded at the same time to produce a harmony. ▲ Another word that sounds like this is **cord.**
chord (kôrd) *noun, plural* **chords.**

chord² A straight line that connects any two points on the circumference of a circle. ▲ Another word that sounds like this is **cord.**
chord (kôrd) *noun, plural* **chords.**

chore **1.** A small job or task. Feeding the chickens every morning was one of my *chores* on the farm. **2.** A hard or unpleasant task. At first, shoveling snow was fun, but soon it became a *chore.*
chore (chôr) *noun, plural* **chores.**

chorus **1.** A group of people who sing or dance together. We three are going to sing in the *chorus* at school. The *chorus* danced in a line behind the soloist. **2.** A part of a song that is sung after each stanza. It was hard to remember all the words of the song, but everyone knew the *chorus. Noun.*
—To sing or say at the same time. All the children *chorused* "good morning" to the guest. *Verb.*
cho·rus (kôr′əs) *noun, plural* **choruses;** *verb,* **chorused, chorusing.**

chose Past tense of **choose.** I *chose* a book on tennis to read over the weekend. Look up **choose** for more information.
chose (chōz) *verb.*

chosen Past participle of **choose.** The basketball team has *chosen* its new captain. Look up **choose** for more information.
cho·sen (chō′zən) *verb.*

chowder A thick soup made with fish or clams and vegetables. I made a *chowder* of clams, potatoes, and corn for supper.
chow·der (chou′dər) *noun, plural* **chowders.**

Christ Jesus, the founder of the Christian religion.
Christ (krīst) *noun.*

christen **1.** To give a name to a person during baptism. The minister *christened* the twins Sarah and Thomas. **2.** To receive into a Christian church by means of baptism.
chris·ten (kris′ən) *verb,* **christened, christening.**

Christian A person who believes in Jesus and follows his teachings. *Noun.*
—**1.** Having to do with Jesus or the religion based on his teachings. The cross is a *Christian* symbol. **2.** Believing in Jesus and fol-

at; āpe; fär; câre; end; mē; it; īce; pîerce; hot; ōld; sông, fôrk; oil; out; up; ūse; rüle; pŭll; tûrn; chin; sing; shop; thin; this; hw in white; zh in treasure. The symbol ə stands for the unstressed vowel sound in about, taken, pencil, lemon, and circus.

lowing his teachings. Easter is a holiday that is celebrated by *Christian* people. *Adjective.*
Chris·tian (kris′chən) *noun, plural* **Christians;** *adjective.*

Christianity The religion based on the teachings of Jesus.
Chris·ti·an·i·ty (kris′chē an′i tē) *noun.*

Christmas A Christian holiday on December 25 celebrating the anniversary of the day Jesus was born.
Christ·mas (kris′məs) *noun, plural* **Christmases.**

Christmas tree A tree that is decorated with lights and ornaments at Christmas.

chromium A hard silver-white metal that does not easily rust or become dull. Chromium is a chemical element. Chromium is used to coat the bumpers and metal trim on automobiles so that they will stay shiny.
chro·mi·um (krō′mē əm) *noun.*

chronic 1. Lasting a long time or happening again and again. Arthritis is a *chronic* illness. 2. Done by habit; habitual; constant. Their *chronic* complaining irritated us.
chron·ic (kron′ik) *adjective.*

chrysanthemum A round flower with many small petals. Chrysanthemums may be yellow, white, or some other color.
chry·san·the·mum (krə san′thə məm) *noun, plural* **chrysanthemums.**

chubby Round and plump. The baby had *chubby* legs.
chub·by (chub′ē) *adjective,* **chubbier, chubbiest.**

chrysanthemum

chuckle To laugh in a quiet way. When we chuckle we are often laughing to ourselves. I *chuckled* when I read the letter from my friend. *Verb.*
—A quiet laugh. *Noun.*
chuck·le (chuk′əl) *verb,* **chuckled, chuckling;** *noun, plural* **chuckles.**

chum A close friend; pal. After they became *chums,* they went everywhere together.
chum (chum) *noun, plural* **chums.**

chunk A thick piece or lump. I cut the bread into big *chunks.*
chunk (chungk) *noun, plural* **chunks.**

chunky 1. Full of chunks. I don't like *chunky* peanut butter, but I do like soups

that are *chunky.* 2. Short and solid in build or form; stocky. I have a *chunky* build, so I thought I should try out for the football team.
chunk·y (chung′kē) *adjective,* **chunkier, chunkiest.**

church 1. A building where people gather together for Christian worship. Many families go to *church* on Sundays. 2. A group of Christians having the same beliefs; denomination. The Roman Catholic and Episcopalian *churches* share many beliefs and rituals.
church (chûrch) *noun, plural* **churches.**

churn A container in which cream or milk is shaken or beaten to make butter. *Noun.*
—1. To shake or beat cream or milk in a special container to make butter. 2. To stir or move with a forceful motion. The water *churned* around the rocks at the bottom of the waterfall. A plow *churns* up the soil. *Verb.*
churn (chûrn) *noun, plural* **churns;** *verb,* **churned, churning.**

chute A steep passage or slide through which things can pass. The clothes that we put in the laundry *chute* slide down to the laundry room. ⚠ Another word that sounds like this is **shoot.**
chute (shüt) *noun, plural* **chutes.**

cider The juice that is pressed from apples. Cider is used as a drink and in making vinegar.
ci·der (sī′dər) *noun, plural* **ciders.**

cigar A finger-shaped roll of tobacco leaves that is used for smoking.
ci·gar (si gär′) *noun, plural* **cigars.**

cigarette A small roll of finely cut tobacco leaves wrapped in thin white paper and used for smoking.
cig·a·rette (sig′ə ret′ *or* sig′ə ret′) *noun, plural* **cigarettes.**

cinder A piece of coal, wood or other material that has been burned up or that is still burning but no longer flaming.
cin·der (sin′dər) *noun, plural* **cinders.**

cinnamon 1. A reddish brown spice. Cinnamon is made from the dried bark of a tropical tree. 2. A light, reddish brown color. *Noun.*
—Having a light, reddish brown color. *Adjective.*
cin·na·mon (sin′ə mən) *noun; adjective.*

circle 1. A closed, curved line made up

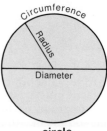
circle

of points that are all the same distance from a point inside called the center. **2.** Anything that has a shape like a circle. We sat in a *circle* around the campfire. **3.** A group of people who have interests that they share and enjoy together. Most of my *circle* of friends are interested in baseball. *Noun.*
—**1.** To make a circle around. We were told to *circle* the right answer on the page. **2.** To move around in a circle. The airplane *circled* the airport. The flock of birds *circled* overhead. *Verb.*
 cir·cle (sûr′kəl) *noun, plural* **circles;** *verb,* **circled, circling.**

circuit **1.** A movement around. The earth takes one year to make its *circuit* around the sun. **2.** A course or route that someone travels regularly; round. The mail carriers start their *circuits* in my town early each morning. **3.** The path of an electric current. Electricity in a house moves in a circuit that takes it from wires outside the house to the different wall sockets, switches, and appliances in the house.
 cir·cuit (sûr′kit) *noun, plural* **circuits.**

circuit breaker A safety switch that automatically prevents current from flowing through an electric circuit. When the current becomes dangerous because it is too strong for the circuit, the circuit breaker interrupts the circuit and stops the flow.

circular Having or making the shape of a circle; round. The skaters moved in a *circular* path around the ice rink. *Adjective.*
—A letter or an advertisement that is sent to many people. The store sent out *circulars* to announce the big sale. *Noun.*
 cir·cu·lar (sûr′kyə lər) *adjective; noun, plural* **circulars.**

circulate **1.** To move around freely or widely among different places. The fan in the window *circulates* air around the room. The blood in our bodies *circulates* from the heart through the arteries and then back through the veins to the heart. **2.** To pass from person to person. Bills and coins *circulate*. Don't *circulate* gossip.
 cir·cu·late (sûr′kyə lāt′) *verb,* **circulated, circulating.**

circulation **1.** Movement around many different places or from person to person. Keep your windows open to increase the *circulation* of air. The government is putting some new coins into *circulation*. **2.** The average number of copies of each issue of a newspaper or magazine that are sold. The *circulation* of that newspaper is over 100,000.
 cir·cu·la·tion (sûr′kyə lā′shən) *noun.*

circulatory system The system in the body made up of the heart, the blood vessels, the blood, and the lymph system.
 cir·cu·la·to·ry system (sûr′kyə lə tôr′ē).

circumference **1.** A curved line that forms the outside edge of a circle. Look up **circle** for a picture of this. **2.** The distance around something. The *circumference* of our round kitchen table is 9 feet. That tree trunk is 15 feet in *circumference*.
 cir·cum·fer·ence (sər kum′fər əns) *noun, plural* **circumferences.**

circumstance A condition, act, or event that exists or happens along with other things and that may have an effect on them. Weather is a *circumstance* beyond our control.
 cir·cum·stance (sûr′kəm stans′) *noun, plural* **circumstances.**

circus

circus A show with trained animals and acrobats, clowns, and other people who entertain. A circus is often given in a huge tent and moves from town to town.
 cir·cus (sûr′kəs) *noun, plural* **circuses.**

Word History

The word **circus** comes from a Latin word meaning "ring" or "circle." The ancient Romans held chariot races and other public events in a large oval theater which they called "the Circus."

---

at; āpe; fär; câre; end; mē; it; īce; pîerce; hot; ōld; sông, fôrk; oil; out; up; ūse; rüle; ṗùll; tûrn; chin; sing; shop; thin; <u>this</u>; hw in white; zh in treasure. The symbol ə stands for the unstressed vowel sound in about, taken, pencil, lemon, and circus.

cite **1.** To repeat the words of another person exactly; quote. I *cited* a paragraph in the encyclopedia that supported my theory. **2.** To mention as proof or support. The firefighters *cited* the fire in the garage as an example of the danger of collecting oily rags. **3.** To single out for praise or honor. The mayor *cited* our school for our community activities. ▴ Other words that sound like this are **sight** and **site**.
cite (sīt) *verb*, **cited, citing.**

citizen **1.** A person who was born in a country or who chooses to live in and become a member of a country. When you are a citizen of the United States, you have the right to vote for people who hold government office. You also have responsibilities, such as serving in the military. **2.** Any person who lives in a town or city. The *citizens* of our city voted against the increase in bus fares.
cit·i·zen (sit′ə zən) *noun, plural* **citizens.**

citizenship The position of being a citizen of a country with all the rights, duties, and privileges that come with it. We had to pass a test in order to gain *citizenship* in our new country.
cit·i·zen·ship (sit′ə zən ship′) *noun.*

citrus Of or having to do with a group of trees whose fruits are juicy and often have a thick rind. Oranges, grapefruits, lemons, and limes are citrus fruits.
cit·rus (sit′rəs) *adjective.*

city A large area where many people live and work. A city is larger than a town.
cit·y (sit′ē) *noun, plural* **cities.**

civic **1.** Having to do with a city. Keeping our streets and parks clean is a matter of *civic* pride. **2.** Having to do with the responsibilities or privileges of a citizen or citizenship. It is a person's *civic* duty to vote.
civ·ic (siv′ik) *adjective.*

civics The study of the duties, rights, and privileges of citizens in relation to their government. ▴ The word "civics" is used with a singular verb.
civ·ics (siv′iks) *noun.*

civil **1.** Having to do with a citizen or citizens. I am studying the *civil* life of ancient Rome. **2.** Not connected with military or church affairs. The couple was married in a *civil* ceremony. **3.** Polite but not friendly; courteous. I was very angry but still managed to give a *civil* answer.
civ·il (siv′əl) *adjective.*

civilian A person who is not in the armed forces. Soldiers were sent to aid *civilians* during the disaster. *Noun.*
—Relating to civilians. It must feel funny to be wearing *civilian* clothes again after being in the Navy. *Adjective.*
ci·vil·ian (si vil′yən) *noun, plural* **civilians;** *adjective.*

civilization A condition of human society in which agriculture, trade, government, art, and science are highly developed. Civilization is often characterized by the use of writing and the growth of cities. In school we study the *civilization* of ancient Egypt.
civ·i·li·za·tion (siv′ə lə zā′shən) *noun, plural* **civilizations.**

civilize To bring out of a primitive or ignorant condition; educate in the arts, science, government, and agriculture.
civ·i·lize (siv′ə līz′) *verb,* **civilized, civilizing.**

civil rights The rights of every citizen of a country. In the United States, a citizen's civil rights include the right to vote, the right to live anywhere, and the right to equal protection under the law.

civil service The branch of government service that is not part of the armed forces, the court system, or the legislature. Postal employees belong to the civil service.

civil war **1.** A war between groups of citizens of the same country. **2. Civil War.** The war between the northern and southern states of the United States that occurred between 1861 and 1865.

clad A past tense and past participle of **clothe.** We *clad* the baby in a warm sweater. The actor was *clad* in a blue leotard. Look up **clothe** for more information.
clad (klad) *verb.*

claim **1.** To declare or take as one's own. The settlers *claimed* the land along the river. **2.** To say that something is true. The witnesses *claimed* that the robber wore glasses. **3.** To take up; require; occupy. My hobbies *claim* most of my free time. *Verb.*
—**1.** A demand for something as one's right. After the fire, we filed a *claim* with the insurance company. **2.** A statement that something is true. Their *claim* was that their team was the best. **3.** Something that is claimed. The miner's *claim* is a piece of land in the hills. *Noun.*
claim (klām) *verb,* **claimed, claiming;** *noun, plural* **claims.**

clam An animal that has a soft body and a hinged shell in two

clam

parts. Clams are found in the ocean and in fresh water. Many kinds of clams are used for food. *Noun.*
—To dig in the sand or mud for clams. *Verb.*
clam (klam) *noun, plural* **clams;** *verb,* **clammed, clamming.**

clambake An outdoor party or meal at which clams and other foods are served. The food at a clambake is usually steamed or baked over heated stones placed in a hole in the ground or sand at a beach.
clam·bake (klam′bāk′) *noun, plural* **clambakes.**

clamber To climb by using both the hands and the feet. We *clambered* slowly up the dunes behind the beach.
clam·ber (klam′bər) *verb,* **clambered, clambering.**

clamor 1. A loud continuous noise; uproar. The *clamor* of automobile horns filled the air on the crowded highway. 2. A loud protest or demand. The people made a *clamor* against pollution in the town. *Noun.*
—To make a clamor. The crowd *clamored* for the umpire to change the decision. *Verb.*
clam·or (klam′ər) *noun, plural* **clamors;** *verb,* **clamored, clamoring.**

clamp A device used to hold things together tightly. Use a *clamp* to hold the pieces of wood together until the glue dries. *Noun.*
—To fasten together with a clamp. I *clamped* the horn onto my bicycle. *Verb.*
clamp (klamp) *noun, plural* **clamps;** *verb,* **clamped, clamping.**

clan A group of families united by the belief that they are all descended from the same ancestor.
clan (klan) *noun, plural* **clans.**

clap 1. A sharp, sudden sound like two flat pieces of wood striking each other. There was a *clap* of thunder, and then it began to rain. 2. A friendly slap. My pal gave me a *clap* on the shoulder. *Noun.*
—1. To strike together. I *clapped* my hands twice to signal the start of the ceremony. 2. To strike one's hands together again and again, especially so as to show approval or enjoyment. The children all *clapped* when the magician's show was over. 3. To strike in a friendly way. They all *clapped* me on the back and congratulated me for winning the prize. *Verb.*
clap (klap) *noun, plural* **claps;** *verb,* **clapped, clapping.**

clarify To make something easier to understand; explain clearly. Please *clarify* the instructions for me.
clar·i·fy (klar′ə fī′) *verb,* **clarified, clarifying.**

clarinet A musical instrument shaped like a tube. A clarinet is played by blowing into the mouthpiece and pressing keys or covering holes with the fingers to change the pitch.
clar·i·net (klar′ə net′) *noun, plural* **clarinets.**

clarinets

clarity Clearness. The directions for playing the game are written with great *clarity.*
clar·i·ty (klar′i tē) *noun.*

clash 1. A loud, harsh sound like pieces of metal striking against each other. The band ended the parade music with a *clash* of cymbals. 2. A strong disagreement. There was a *clash* between the members of my family about where we should go for our vacation. *Noun.*
—1. To come together with a clash. The pots and pans *clashed* when they fell on the kitchen floor. 2. To disagree strongly. The two groups *clashed* over what to do with the vacant lot. 3. To be in sharp conflict; not match. That suit jacket *clashes* with your sneakers. *Verb.*
clash (klash) *noun, plural* **clashes;** *verb,* **clashed, clashing.**

at; āpe; fär; câre; end; mē; it; ice; pîerce; hot; ōld; sông, fôrk; oil; out; up; ūse; rüle; půll; tûrn; chin; sing; shop; thin; this; hw in white; zh in treasure. The symbol ə stands for the unstressed vowel sound in about, taken, pencil, lemon, and circus.

135

clasp **1.** A device used to hold two parts or objects together. A hook or a buckle is a clasp. The *clasp* of my watch is broken. **2.** A close or tight grasp. They said good-bye with a *clasp* of hands. *Noun.*
—**1.** To fasten with a clasp. Don't forget to *clasp* every buckle on the boot. **2.** To hold or grasp close or tight. The young child *clasped* the glass with both hands. *Verb.*
  clasp (klasp) *noun, plural* **clasps;** *verb,* **clasped, clasping.**

class **1.** A group of persons or things alike in some way. Pencils, pens, and crayons all belong to the *class* of writing tools. The mammals form one *class* of animals. **2.** A group of people who share a similar way of life and have the same rank or status in society. Members of the upper *class* looked to the king and queen as models in manners and dress. **3.** A group of students studying or meeting together. There are thirty students in my *class.* **4.** A period of time during which a group of students meets. A bell rings when the *class* is over. **5.** A grade or quality. That farmer grows a very high *class* of vegetables. *Noun.*
—To group in a class; classify. I have *classed* the stamps in my collection by the country from which they come. *Verb.*
  class (klas) *noun, plural* **classes;** *verb,* **classed, classing.**

classic Excellent in the opinion of many people, past and present; of high, lasting quality. *Robinson Crusoe* is a *classic* adventure story. That building is a *classic* example of modern architecture. *Adjective.*
—**1.** A very fine book or other work of art. That play by William Shakespeare is a *classic.* **2. the classics.** The writings of ancient Greece and Rome. *Noun.*
  clas·sic (klas′ik) *adjective; noun, plural* **classics.**

classical **1.** Relating to the literature, art, and way of life of ancient Greece or Rome. That museum has a collection of *classical* statues. **2.** Traditional; not experimental or new. It was a *classical* sort of play, in three acts. **3.** Of or having to do with music that follows forms and styles developed over a long period by educated musicians. Classical music is different from popular or folk music. Symphonies, quartets, and operas are *classical* music.
  clas·si·cal (klas′i kəl) *adjective.*

classification Arrangement in classes. The *classification* of the stamps in the album is according to the countries they come from.
  clas·si·fi·ca·tion (klas′ə fi kā′shən) *noun, plural* **classifications.**

classify **1.** To arrange in groups. The librarian *classified* the books according to the authors who wrote them. **2.** To assign to a class. Would you *classify* this stone as a pebble, a rock, or a boulder?
  clas·si·fy (klas′ə fī′) *verb,* **classified, classifying.**

classmate A member of the same class in school. I invited all my *classmates* to my birthday party.
  class·mate (klas′māt′) *noun, plural* **classmates.**

classroom A room in which classes are held.
  class·room (klas′rüm′ or klas′rùm′) *noun, plural* **classrooms.**

clatter A loud, rattling noise. The *clatter* of dishes from the kitchen was a sign that dinner was almost ready. *Noun.*
—To make a loud, rattling noise. The pots and pans *clattered* as we put them away. *Verb.*
  clat·ter (klat′ər) *noun, plural* **clatters;** *verb,* **clattered, clattering.**

clause **1.** A group of words that contains a subject and a predicate. In the sentence "I watched television before I went to bed," "I watched television" is the main clause because it can stand alone as a sentence. "Before I went to bed" is another clause. Its meaning depends on the main clause of the sentence. **2.** A separate part of a law, treaty, or other formal agreement. There is a *clause* in our lease that says we can't keep pets in our apartment.
  clause (klôz) *noun, plural* **clauses.**

claw **1.** A sharp, curved nail on the foot of a bird or animal. A cat has very sharp *claws.* An eagle uses its *claws* to seize and kill its prey. **2.** One of the grasping parts of a lobster or crab. **3.** Anything like a claw. The forked end of the head of a hammer that is used to pull out nails is called a claw. *Noun.*
—To scratch or tear with claws or hands. The puppy *clawed* the door because it wanted to come inside. *Verb.*
  claw (klô) *noun, plural* **claws;** *verb,* **clawed, clawing.**

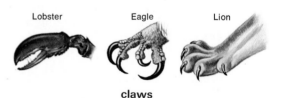

Lobster   Eagle   Lion

claws

clay A kind of fine earth. Clay can be easily shaped when wet, but it becomes hard when it is dried or baked. Clay is used to make pottery and bricks.

clay (klā) *noun, plural* **clays.**

clean **1.** Free from dirt. After playing football, we changed into *clean* clothes. The air is not very *clean* in some big cities. **2.** Honorable or fair. The coach wants our team always to play *clean* football. **3.** Complete; thorough. The dog seized the hamburger and made a *clean* escape. *Adjective.*
—Completely. The arrow went *clean* through the target. *Adverb.*
—To make clean. I have to *clean* my room today. *Verb.*

clean (klēn) *adjective,* **cleaner, cleanest;** *adverb; verb,* **cleaned, cleaning.**

cleaner **1.** A person whose work or business is cleaning. The window *cleaner* washed the windows of the apartment house. **2.** Something that removes dirt. I used a liquid *cleaner* to get the coffee stain off the rug.

clean·er (klē′nər) *noun, plural* **cleaners.**

cleanliness The condition of being clean; the habit of always keeping clean. Cats are known for their *cleanliness.*

clean·li·ness (klen′lē nis) *noun.*

cleanly[1] Always clean or kept clean. The guest's room was a *cleanly* and tidy place.

clean·ly (klen′lē) *adjective,* **cleanlier, cleanliest.**

cleanly[2] In a clean way. The ax cut *cleanly* through the log.

clean·ly (klēn′lē) *adverb.*

cleanse To make clean. The nurse *cleansed* the cut on my knee with soap.

cleanse (klenz) *verb,* **cleansed, cleansing.**

cleanser Something that is used for cleaning. You can scrub away the stains in the sink with a *cleanser.*

cleans·er (klen′zər) *noun, plural* **cleansers.**

clear **1.** Free from anything that darkens; bright. The summer day was warm and *clear.* **2.** Easily seen through. The water of the pond was so *clear* that you could see the bottom. **3.** Easily seen, heard, or understood; plain; distinct. The shout for help was loud and *clear.* The directions we got weren't very *clear.* **4.** Without guilt or some other burden. I did the right thing and have a *clear* conscience. *Adjective.*
—Completely; without obstruction. From the cliff we could see *clear* across the valley. *Adverb.*
—**1.** To make or become free from anything that darkens or clouds. The storm *cleared* the sky of smog. After the rain stopped, the sky

cleared. **2.** To remove or remove things from. We *cleared* the dishes. Please finish *clearing* the table. **3.** To go by, under, or over without touching. The runner *cleared* the fence with a leap. **4.** To approve or get approved. The council *cleared* the proposal. First I *cleared* my idea with the teacher. **5.** To remove suspicion or guilt from; declare innocent. The suspect was innocent and was *cleared* of all charges. Everyone knows I didn't take the wallet, so I should be able to *clear* my name. *Verb.*

• **to clear up.** **1.** To explain; clarify. The detective *cleared up* the mystery of who stole the jewels. **2.** To become clear. The sky *cleared up* after the storm.

clear (klîr) *adjective,* **clearer, clearest;** *adverb; verb,* **cleared, clearing.**

clearance **1.** The act of clearing. City officials ordered the *clearance* of three streets for the parade. **2.** The space in between two things that allows one or both things to move without touching each other. There was enough *clearance* for the truck to go under the bridge.

clear·ance (klîr′əns) *noun, plural* **clearances.**

clearing A piece of land that is free of trees or brush. We made our camp in a *clearing* in the woods.

clear·ing (klîr′ing) *noun, plural* **clearings.**

cleaver A tool that has a short handle and a broad blade. A cleaver is used by butchers for cutting up meat.

cleav·er (klē′vər) *noun, plural* **cleavers.**

cleaver

at; āpe; fär; câre; end; mē; it; īce; pîerce; hot; ōld; sông, fôrk; oil; out; up; ūse; rūle; půll; tûrn; chin; sing; shop; thin; this; hw in white; zh in treasure. The symbol ə stands for the unstressed vowel sound in about, taken, pencil, lemon, and circus.

clef A sign placed on a staff in music. A clef shows the pitch of the notes on the various lines and spaces.
   clef (klef) *noun, plural* **clefs.**

cleft A space or opening made by splitting; crack. You can climb the cliff by holding on to the *clefts* in the rocks. *Noun.*
   —Divided by a crack or split. Two of my cousins have *cleft* chins. *Adjective.*
   cleft (kleft) *noun, plural* **clefts;** *adjective.*

clench **1.** To close together tightly. People often *clench* their fists when they are angry. **2.** To grasp or grip tightly. I *clenched* the arm of the chair when I heard the scream.
   clench (klench) *verb,* **clenched, clenching.**

clergy Ministers, priests, and rabbis. The clergy consists of all the people who are appointed to carry on religious work.
   cler·gy (klûr′jē) *noun, plural* **clergies.**

clergyman A member of the clergy; minister, priest, or rabbi.
   cler·gy·man (klûr′jē mən) *noun, plural* **clergymen** (klûr′jē mən).

clerk **1.** A person who keeps records and files in an office. **2.** A person who sells goods to customers in a store. *Noun.*
   —To work as a clerk. I *clerk* in the department store on Saturdays. *Verb.*
   clerk (klûrk) *noun, plural* **clerks;** *verb,* **clerked, clerking.**

Word History

The word **clerk** comes from a Latin word used by the church meaning "clergyman." In the Middle Ages, priests and monks were nearly the only people who could read and write. So *clerk* came to mean "someone who writes and keeps records."

---

clever **1.** Having a quick mind; bright and alert. The *clever* child soon learned to use the new toy. **2.** Showing skill or intelligence. The cook had a *clever* way of cracking two eggs with one hand.
   clev·er (klev′ər) *adjective,* **cleverer, cleverest.**

click A light, sharp sound. We heard the *click* of a key in the lock. *Noun.*
   —To make a click. *Verb.*
   click (klik) *noun, plural* **clicks;** *verb,* **clicked, clicking.**

client A person or organization that uses the services of another person or organization. Our family's lawyer advises many *clients* besides us. That advertising agency has some large corporations as *clients.*
   cli·ent (klī′ənt) *noun, plural* **clients.**

cliff A high, steep face of rock or earth. From the edge of the *cliff*, we could see the beach far below.
   cliff (klif) *noun, plural* **cliffs.**

climate The average weather conditions of a place or region throughout the year. Climate includes average temperature, rainfall, humidity, and wind conditions. The *climate* in those mountains is cool and dry in the summer.
   cli·mate (klī′mit) *noun, plural* **climates.**

climax The highest or most exciting moment or event. The *climax* of our trip came when we canoed down the river.
   cli·max (klī′maks) *noun, plural* **climaxes.**

climb **1.** To move upward or in some other direction over, across, or through something, using the hands and feet. The prisoner *climbed* over the wall. *Climb* down the ladder carefully. **2.** To grow upward or upward on. The ivy *climbed* the side of the house. **3.** To go steadily upward; rise. Prices could *climb* a little higher next month. *Verb.*
   —**1.** The act of climbing. Their *climb* of the hill took an hour. **2.** A place to be climbed. That mountain is a difficult and dangerous *climb. Noun.*
   climb (klīm) *verb,* **climbed, climbing;** *noun, plural* **climbs.**

clinch **1.** To make definite; settle. The deal was *clinched* when they agreed to our terms. **2.** To make certain of winning. By winning today's game, we *clinched* the race for first place.
   clinch (klinch) *verb,* **clinched, clinching.**

cling To stick closely. Mud *clings* to your shoes. Little children sometimes *cling* to their parents when they are frightened. We all *clung* to the hope of victory.
   cling (kling) *verb,* **clung, clinging.**

clinic A place where medical care is given to people who do not need to stay in a hospital. I went to the dental *clinic* to have my teeth examined.
   clin·ic (klin′ik) *noun, plural* **clinics.**

clip¹ To cut; cut short. A good tailor *clips* the loose ends of thread with scissors after finishing sewing. I tried to *clip* the hedge evenly. *Clip* the article about the game out of the newspaper. *Verb.*
   —A rate of speed or pace. The bus moved along at a fast *clip. Noun.*
   clip (klip) *verb,* **clipped, clipping;** *noun, plural* **clips.**

clip² A device used to hold things together. A *clip* for papers is made of bent wire. You can hold a tie in place with a *clip. Noun.*
—To fasten with a clip. Please *clip* these papers together. *Verb.*
clip (klip) *noun, plural* **clips;** *verb,* **clipped, clipping.**

clipper 1. A tool used for cutting. The *clipper* for the hedges is not sharp enough. The veterinarian used a *clipper* to trim the cat's claws. 2. A fast sailing ship. American *clippers* were once used as cargo ships and sailed all over the world.
clip·per (klip′ər) *noun, plural* **clippers.**

clipping A piece that is cut out or off, especially one that is cut out of a magazine or newspaper. My friend keeps an album of *clippings* about favorite baseball players. Sweep the grass *clippings* from the sidewalk and add them to the compost.
clip·ping (klip′ing) *noun, plural* **clippings.**

cloak 1. A loose outer piece of clothing, with or without sleeves. 2. Something that covers or hides something else. A *cloak* of haze concealed the valley. *Noun.*
—To cover or hide with a cloak. Fog *cloaked* the city. *Verb.*
cloak (klōk) *noun, plural* **cloaks;** *verb,* **cloaked, cloaking.**

clock A device used for measuring and showing the time. A clock may have hands that pass over a dial marked to show hours and minutes, or it may have numerals that change to show the hour and minute. *Noun.*
—To find out the speed of something by using a device like a clock. While the runners were practicing, we *clocked* them with a stopwatch. *Verb.*
clock (klok) *noun, plural* **clocks;** *verb,* **clocked, clocking.**

clockwise In the direction in which the hands of a clock move. Move the dial *clockwise* to turn on the radio.
clock·wise (klok′wīz′) *adverb; adjective.*

clog To block; fill up. Grease could *clog* the drain. Heavy traffic *clogged* the roads. *Verb.*
—A shoe with a thick wooden sole. *Noun.*
clog (klog) *verb,* **clogged, clogging;** *noun, plural* **clogs.**

cloister 1. A covered walk along the wall of a building. A cloister is often built around the courtyard of a monastery, church, or college building. 2. A convent or a monastery.
clois·ter (kloi′stər) *noun, plural* **cloisters.**

close 1. To shut. Please *close* the door. The grocery store *closed* for the night. 2. To bring or come together. The dog's teeth *closed* on the bone. 3. To bring or come to an end. I *closed* the letter with a promise to write again soon. *Verb.*
—1. With little space or time between; near. Our house is *close* to the school. Spring vacation is *close.* 2. Having affection for each other; intimate. My neighbor and I are *close* friends. 3. Without fresh air; stuffy. It is *close* in this room with the window shut. 4. Nearly even; almost equal. It was a *close* race. 5. Careful; thorough. Pay *close* attention. *Adjective.*
—In a close position or way. Your car is not parked *close* enough to the curb. *Adverb.*
—End; finish. At the *close* of the day, we all went home. *Noun.*
close (klōz *for verb and noun;* klōs *for adjective and adverb) verb,* **closed, closing;** *adjective,* **closer, closest;** *adverb; noun.*

closet A small room for storing things. Get the mop and pail from the *closet.* Hang your coat in the clothes *closet.*
clos·et (kloz′it) *noun, plural* **closets.**

clot A soft lump formed when substances in a liquid thicken or stick together. A *clot* of blood formed over the cut. *Noun.*
—To form clots. The bleeding stopped when the blood *clotted. Verb.*
clot (klot) *noun, plural* **clots;** *verb,* **clotted, clotting.**

cloister

at; āpe; fär; câre; end; mē; it; īce; pîerce; hot; ōld; sông, fôrk; oil; out; up; ūse; rüle; pùll; tûrn; chin; sing; shop; thin; this; hw in white; zh in treasure. The symbol ə stands for the unstressed vowel sound in about, taken, pencil, lemon, and circus.

cloth **1.** Material made by weaving or knitting fibers. Cloth is made from cotton, wool, silk, linen, or other fibers. **2.** A piece of cloth used for a particular purpose. Use this *cloth* to dust the living room.
  cloth (klôth) *noun, plural* **cloths.**

clothe To put clothes on someone; dress; provide with clothes. I *clothed* the baby warmly because it was cold outdoors.
  clothe (klōth) *verb,* **clothed** or **clad, clothing.**

clothes Things worn to cover the body. I hung my coat, shirts, and other *clothes* neatly in the closet.
  clothes (klōz *or* klōthz) *plural noun.*

clothespin A clamp or forked piece of wood or plastic used to fasten clothes to a line.
  clothes·pin (klōz′pin′ *or* klōthz′pin′) *noun, plural* **clothespins.**

clothing Things worn to cover the body; clothes. The explorers wore very warm *clothing* when they went to the North Pole.
  cloth·ing (klō′thing) *noun.*

cloud **1.** A gray or white mass of tiny drops of water or bits of ice floating high in the sky. Rain falls from clouds. **2.** Something like a cloud. The cowhands rode off in a *cloud* of dust. A *cloud* of birds filled the sky. *Noun.*
  —**1.** To cover with a cloud or clouds. Smoke from the burning house *clouded* the whole street. **2.** To become cloudy. The sky suddenly *clouded* and it started to rain. *Verb.*
  cloud (kloud) *noun, plural* **clouds;** *verb,* **clouded, clouding.**

cloudburst A sudden, heavy rainfall. We were caught in the *cloudburst* and got very wet.
  cloud·burst (kloud′bûrst′) *noun, plural* **cloudbursts.**

cloudy **1.** Covered with clouds. The sky was *cloudy* and dark. **2.** Not clear. The stream was so *cloudy* that you couldn't see below the surface.
  cloud·y (klou′dē) *adjective,* **cloudier, cloudiest.**

clove¹ The dried flower bud of a tree that grows in the tropics. Cloves are used as a spice.
  clove (klōv) *noun, plural* **cloves.**

clove² One of the sections of a garlic bulb.
  clove (klōv) *noun, plural* **cloves.**

clover A small plant having leaves made up of three leaflets and rounded, fragrant flower heads of white, red, or purple flowers. Clover is used as food for cows.
  clo·ver (klō′vər) *noun, plural* **clovers.**

clown A person who makes people laugh by playing tricks or doing stunts. A clown in a circus often wears funny clothing and makeup. *Noun.*
  —To act like a clown. Don't *clown* around when you are supposed to be doing your homework. *Verb.*
  clown (kloun) *noun, plural* **clowns;** *verb,* **clowned, clowning.**

clowns

club **1.** A heavy stick that is often thicker at one end. A club is used as a weapon. **2.** A stick or bat used to hit a ball in various games. Clubs are used in the game of golf. **3.** A group of people who meet together for fun or some special purpose. My chess *club* meets Tuesday afternoons. **4.** The place where a club meets. I'll see you at the swimming *club.* **5.** A playing card marked with one or more figures shaped like this: ♣. **6. clubs.** The suit of cards marked with this figure. *Noun.*
  —To beat or strike with a club. *Verb.*
  club (klub) *noun, plural* **clubs;** *verb,* **clubbed, clubbing.**

clue A hint that helps solve a problem or mystery. A fingerprint was the *clue* that solved the robbery. If you can't solve the riddle, I'll give you a *clue.*
  clue (klü) *noun, plural* **clues.**

clump **1.** A group or cluster. The rabbit hopped out of a *clump* of bushes. **2.** A thick mass or lump. A *clump* of dirt clung to my shoe. **3.** A heavy, thumping sound. The dead branch fell off the tree and landed with a *clump. Noun.*

—To walk with heavy and noisy steps. The tired hikers *clumped* home across the wooden bridge. *Verb.*

clump (klump) *noun, plural* **clumps;** *verb,* **clumped, clumping.**

clumsy **1.** Awkward; not graceful. My *clumsy* puppy always knocks over its food bowl. **2.** Poorly made or done. The *clumsy* gate kept scraping the ground.

clum·sy (klum′zē) *adjective,* **clumsier, clumsiest.**

clung Past tense and past participle of **cling.** The monkey *clung* to its trainer's arm. Look up **cling** for more information.

clung (klung) *verb.*

cluster A number of things of the same kind that grow or are grouped together. Grapes grow in *clusters.* There was a *cluster* of houses in the distance. *Noun.*

—To grow or group in a cluster. We all *clustered* around the campfire and sang songs. *Verb.*

clus·ter (klus′tər) *noun, plural* **clusters;** *verb,* **clustered, clustering.**

clutch **1.** To grasp tightly. I *clutched* the money in my hand on the way to the grocery store. **2.** To try to grasp or seize. I *clutched* at the railing when I slipped on the stairs. *Verb.*

—**1.** A tight grasp. The girl kept a *clutch* on her little brother's hand so he wouldn't get lost in the crowd. **2.** A device in a machine that connects or disconnects the motor. *Noun.*

clutch (kluch) *verb,* **clutched, clutching;** *noun, plural* **clutches.**

clutter A messy collection of things; litter. We all helped pick up the *clutter* of cans and bottles after the picnic. *Noun.*

—To litter or fill with a messy collection of things. Dust and old books *cluttered* the attic floor. *Verb.*

clut·ter (klut′ər) *noun, plural* **clutters;** *verb,* **cluttered, cluttering.**

cm An abbreviation for *centimeter.*

co- A *prefix* that means: **1.** With. *Co-worker* means a person who works with others. **2.** Together. *Cosign* means to sign together.

co. An abbreviation for *company* or *county.*

CO Postal abbreviation for *Colorado.*

coach **1.** A large, closed carriage pulled by horses. A coach has seats inside for passengers and a raised seat outside for the driver. **2.** A railroad car for passengers. **3.** A section of low-priced seats on a bus, airplane, or train. **4.** A teacher or trainer of athletes or performers. The basketball *coach* made the team practice extra hours this week. *Noun.*

—To teach or train. My friend *coached* me when I was learning my part in the play. *Verb.*

coach (kōch) *noun, plural* **coaches;** *verb,* **coached, coaching.**

coal **1.** A black mineral that is burned as a fuel to heat buildings or make electricity. Coal is mostly carbon and is formed from decaying plants buried deep in the earth under great pressure. **2.** A piece of glowing or burned wood. We roasted hot dogs over the hot *coals* of the campfire.

coal (kōl) *noun, plural* **coals.**

coarse **1.** Made up of rather large parts; not fine. Some of the grains of *coarse* sand were almost as big as small pebbles. **2.** Thick and rough. The *coarse* wool of the sweater made my skin itch. **3.** Crude; vulgar. The parents scolded the child for *coarse* table manners. ▴ Another word that sounds like this is **course.**

coarse (kôrs) *adjective,* **coarser, coarsest.**

coast The land next to the sea; seashore. We saw a fleet of fishing boats just off the *coast. Noun.*

—To ride or slide along without effort or power. We *coasted* down the hill on our sleds. *Verb.*

coast (kōst) *noun, plural* **coasts;** *verb,* **coasted, coasting.**

coastal Near or along or at a coast. High waves washed away part of the *coastal* highway.

coast·al (kōs′təl) *adjective.*

Coast Guard A branch of the United States armed forces that patrols and defends the nation's coasts. In wartime, it becomes part of the United States Navy. The *Coast Guard* cutter prevented the smugglers from landing.

coastline The outline or shape of a coast. You can see on the map that the state of Maine has an irregular *coastline.*

coast·line (kōst′līn′) *noun, plural* **coastlines.**

coat **1.** A piece of outer clothing with sleeves. I have a new winter *coat.* **2.** The outer covering of an animal. Our dog has a shaggy brown *coat.* **3.** A layer. The painters put a new *coat* of paint on our house. *Noun.*

C

at; āpe; fär; câre; end; mē; it; īce; pîerce; hot; ōld; sông, fôrk; oil; out; up; ūse; rüle; pûll; tûrn; chin; sing; shop; thin; this; hw in white; zh in treasure. The symbol ə stands for the unstressed vowel sound in about, taken, pencil, lemon, and circus.

141

—To cover with a layer. Dust *coated* the furniture in the old house. Sand the floor and *coat* it with wax. *Verb.*

coat (kōt) *noun, plural* **coats**; *verb,* **coated, coating.**

coating A layer covering a surface. A thin *coating* of ice on the roads made driving dangerous.

coat·ing (kō′ting) *noun, plural* **coatings.**

coat of arms A design on and around a shield or on a drawing of a shield. A coat of arms can serve as the emblem of a person, family, country, or organization.

coat of arms

coax To persuade or influence by mild urging or pleasing actions. I tried to *coax* my parents into letting me go to camp next summer by promising to work hard in school.

coax (kōks) *verb,* **coaxed, coaxing.**

cob The hard center part of an ear of corn. The kernels grow on the cob in rows.

cob (kob) *noun, plural* **cobs.**

cobalt A silver-white metal. Cobalt is used in making alloys and paints. Cobalt is a chemical element.

co·balt (kō′bôlt) *noun.*

cobbler 1. A person whose work is mending or making shoes. The *cobbler* put new heels on my shoes. 2. A fruit pie baked in a deep dish. For dessert we had a delicious apple *cobbler.*

cob·bler (kob′lər) *noun, plural* **cobblers.**

cobblestone A round stone. Cobblestones were formerly used to pave streets.

cob·ble·stone (kob′əl stōn′) *noun, plural* **cobblestones.**

cobra A large, poisonous snake found in Africa and Asia. When a cobra becomes excited it spreads the skin about its neck so that the skin looks like a hood.

co·bra (kō′brə) *noun, plural* **cobras.**

cobra

cobweb A web that is made by a spider.

cob·web (kob′web′) *noun, plural* **cobwebs.**

cock¹ 1. A male chicken; rooster. 2. The male of the turkey and other birds. 3. A faucet or something like it used to turn the flow of a gas or a liquid on and off. *Noun.*
—To pull back the hammer of a gun so that it is ready for firing. The hunter *cocked* the rifle before taking aim. *Verb.*

cock (kok) *noun, plural* **cocks**; *verb,* **cocked, cocking.**

cock² To turn up; tip upward. The dog *cocked* its ears when it heard a meow. *Verb.*
—An upward turn. With a *cock* of the arm, the pitcher threw the ball. *Noun.*

cock (kok) *verb,* **cocked, cocking**; *noun, plural* **cocks.**

cockatoo A parrot that has a large crest. Cockatoos live in Australia and Asia.

cock·a·too (kok′ə tü′) *noun, plural* **cockatoos.**

cocker spaniel A dog with long, silky hair and short legs. Like other spaniels, the cocker spaniel was a hunting dog. It is now kept as a pet.

cock·er spaniel (kok′ər).

cockle A sea clam with a shell that looks like a heart. Cockles are used for food.

cock·le (kok′əl) *noun, plural* **cockles.**

cockatoo

cockpit The space in an airplane or a small boat where the pilot sits.

cock·pit (kok′pit′) *noun, plural* **cockpits.**

cockroach A brown or black insect that has a long, flat body and long feelers. Cockroaches are common household pests.

cock·roach (kok′rōch′) *noun, plural* **cockroaches.**

cocky Too sure of oneself. That bully is rude and *cocky.*

cock·y (kok′ē) *adjective,* **cockier, cockiest.**

cocoa 1. A brown powder that tastes like chocolate. Cocoa is made by grinding the dried seeds of the cacao tree and removing the fat. 2. A drink made by mixing cocoa powder, sugar, and milk or water. That restaurant serves hot *cocoa* in the winter.

co·coa (kō′kō) *noun.*

coconut The large, round, brown fruit of a palm tree. A coconut has a hard shell that is lined with a sweet, white meat. It is filled with a white liquid called coconut milk.
co·co·nut (kō′kə nut′) *noun, plural* **coconuts.**

coconuts on a **coconut** palm tree

cocoon The silky case that a caterpillar or other insect larva spins around itself. The larvae live in their cocoons while they are becoming moths or butterflies or other adult insects. Look up **silkworm** for a picture of a cocoon.
co·coon (kə kün′) *noun, plural* **cocoons.**

cod A large fish that lives in cold, northern ocean waters. Cod are used for food.
cod (kod) *noun, plural* **cod** or **cods.**

C.O.D. An abbreviation for *cash on delivery* or *collect on delivery.*

code **1.** Any set of signals, words, or symbols used to send messages. The *code* used in sending messages by telegraph uses long and short sounds that stand for letters. **2.** Any set of laws or rules that people live by. The building *code* in our town requires all apartment buildings to have smoke alarms and fire escapes. *Noun.*
—To put into a code. Spies *code* secret information so the enemy will not understand it. *Verb.*
code (kōd) *noun, plural* **codes;** *verb,* **coded, coding.**

coeducation The education of both boys and girls in the same school.
co·ed·u·ca·tion (kō ej′ə kā′shən) *noun.*

coffee **1.** A dark brown drink. Coffee is made from the roasted and ground seeds of a small tropical tree. Coffee seeds look like beans and are often called beans. **2.** The whole or ground seeds of the coffee tree.
cof·fee (kô′fē) *noun, plural* **coffees.**

coffin A box in which the body of a person who has died is buried.
cof·fin (kô′fin) *noun, plural* **coffins.**

cog One of the teeth on the outer edge of a wheel. Cogs are made to fit between the cogs of another wheel so that one wheel can cause the other to turn. Wheels with cogs are used to run machinery.
cog (kog) *noun, plural* **cogs.**

coil **1.** Anything wound into rings. Wind the hose into a *coil* when you finish watering the flowers. **2.** A wire wound into a spiral for carrying electricity. *Noun.*
—To wind round and round. I keep my kite string *coiled* around a stick. The snake *coiled,* ready to strike. *Verb.*
coil (koil) *noun, plural* **coils;** *verb,* **coiled, coiling.**

coin A piece of metal used as money. A coin is stamped with official government markings to show how much it is worth. Pennies, nickels, dimes, and quarters are coins. *Noun.*
—**1.** To make money by stamping metal. The government *coins* money at a mint. **2.** To invent. If you *coined* a new word, do you think other people would begin to use it? *Verb.*
coin (koin) *noun, plural* **coins;** *verb,* **coined, coining.**

coincide **1.** To happen at the same time. I don't know what to do, because my piano lesson *coincides* with my appointment with the dentist. **2.** To occupy the same place. The two roads *coincide* outside of town. **3.** To be exactly alike; to be identical. That photograph of you *coincides* with the way you look.
co·in·cide (kō′in sīd′) *verb,* **coincided, coinciding.**

coincidence The happening of two events at the same time or place. A coincidence seems remarkable because although it looks planned, it really is not. It was just a *coincidence* that the two couples went to the same movie.
co·in·ci·dence (kō in′si dəns) *noun, plural* **coincidences.**

coke A grayish black substance used as fuel for making metals in special furnaces. Coke is made when coal is heated in an oven that has very little air in it.
coke (kōk) *noun.*

at; āpe; fär; câre; end; mē; it; īce; pîerce; hot; ōld; sông, fôrk; oil; out; up; ūse; rüle; pull; tûrn; chin; sing; shop; thin; **this;** hw in white; zh in treasure. The symbol ə stands for the unstressed vowel sound in about, taken, pencil, lemon, and circus.

C

Col. An abbreviation for *Colorado*.

cold **1.** Having a low temperature; not warm. In some places *cold* weather brings the promise of ice skating. My dinner was *cold* because I was late. **2.** Feeling a lack of warmth; chilly. The children were *cold* after playing outside in the snow. **3.** Not friendly or kind. My angry friend greeted me with a *cold* smile. *Adjective.*
—**1.** A lack of warmth or heat. The *cold* made my teeth chatter. **2.** A common sickness that causes sneezing, coughing, and a running or stuffy nose. *Noun.*
• **to catch cold.** To become ill with a cold. I *caught cold* last week in the rain.
cold (kōld) *adjective*, **colder, coldest;** *noun, plural* **colds.**

cold-blooded **1.** Having a body temperature that changes with the temperature of the surrounding air or water. Snakes, fish, and turtles are cold-blooded animals. Cats and dogs are warm-blooded. **2.** Without any feeling or emotion; cruel.
cold-blood·ed (kōld′blud′id) *adjective.*

coleslaw A salad made from shredded cabbage and a dressing.
cole·slaw (kōl′slô′) *noun.*

coliseum A large building or stadium used for sports or other entertainments. We went to an ice skating show at the *coliseum*.
col·i·se·um (kol′ə sē′əm) *noun, plural* **coliseums.**

collage A picture made by pasting paper, cloth, metal, and other things in an arrangement on a surface.
col·lage (kə läzh′) *noun, plural* **collages.**

collapse **1.** To fall in; break down or fail. The force of the explosion caused the walls of the house to *collapse*. **2.** To fold together. This cot *collapses* so that it can be stored easily. **3.** To lose strength or health. The heat caused some of the marchers in the parade to *collapse*. *Verb.*
—The act of falling in, breaking down, or failing. Many miners were injured in the *collapse* of the mine shaft. The *collapse* of the talks between the two countries threatened world peace. *Noun.*
col·lapse (kə laps′) *verb*, **collapsed, collapsing;** *noun, plural* **collapses.**

collar A band or strap that is worn around the neck. Our dog has a red leather *collar* with its name on it. The *collar* of this dress is made of lace. *Noun.*
—**1.** To put a collar on. *Collar* the dog before you take it outdoors. **2.** To seize; capture. *Verb.*
col·lar (kol′ər) *noun, plural* **collars;** *verb*, **collared, collaring.**

collarbone The bone connecting the breastbone and the shoulder blade.
col·lar·bone (kol′ər bōn′) *noun, plural* **collarbones.**

collard **1.** A green, leafy vegetable. Collards are related to cabbages. **2. collards.** The green leaves of a collard, used as food.
col·lard (kol′ərd) *noun, plural* **collards.**

colleague A fellow worker. Our principal asked a *colleague* to speak at the assembly.
col·league (kol′ēg) *noun, plural* **colleagues.**

collect **1.** To gather together. The campers *collected* wood for the fire. Dust often *collects* under beds. **2.** To get payment for. The state *collects* tolls on this highway.
col·lect (kə lekt′) *verb*, **collected, collecting.**

collection **1.** A gathering together. The *collection* of garbage is the job of the city sanitation department. **2.** A group of things gathered together. The museum has a large *collection* of dinosaur bones. **3.** Money that is collected. We took up a *collection* to buy our teacher a present.
col·lec·tion (kə lek′shən) *noun, plural* **collections.**

college A school that offers more advanced education than high school. A college gives degrees to show that a person has completed certain studies.
col·lege (kol′ij) *noun, plural* **colleges.**

collide **1.** To crash against each other. The car and the truck *collided* at the corner. **2.** To disagree very strongly; clash. The mayor *collided* with the governor over plans for a new highway.
col·lide (kə līd′) *verb*, **collided, colliding.**

collie A large dog that has a long, narrow head. Some collies have long, coarse hair. Others have short, thick hair. Collies were originally raised to herd sheep.
col·lie (kol′ē) *noun, plural* **collies.**

collie

collision The act of colliding; a crash. The two bicycle riders had a *collision,* but neither one was hurt.
    col·li·sion (kə lizh′ən) *noun, plural* **collisions.**

Colo. An abbreviation for *Colorado.*

Colombia A country in northwestern South America.
    Co·lom·bi·a (kə lum′bē ə) *noun.*

colon¹ A punctuation mark (:) that is used mainly after a word to direct attention to something that follows, such as a list, a quotation, or an explanation.
    co·lon (kō′lən) *noun, plural* **colons.**

colon² The main part of the large intestine.
    co·lon (kō′lən) *noun, plural* **colons.**

colonel An officer in the armed forces. In the United States Army, Marine Corps, or Air Force, a colonel ranks below a general but above a major. The two ranks of colonel are **lieutenant colonel** and **colonel.** ▲ Another word that sounds like this is **kernel.**
    colo·nel (kûr′nəl) *noun, plural* **colonels.**

colonial 1. Relating to a colony. Great Britain was once a *colonial* power, ruling Canada, India, South Africa, and many other lands. 2. Relating to the thirteen British colonies that became the United States of America. People marching in the parade were dressed in *colonial* costumes.
    co·lo·ni·al (kə lō′nē əl) *adjective.*

colonist A person who helps found or lives in a colony; a settler. The early *colonists* of Canada were from France and England.
    col·o·nist (kol′ə nist) *noun, plural* **colonists.**

colonize To found a colony or colonies in. Spain *colonized* much of South America.
    col·o·nize (kol′ə nīz′) *verb,* **colonized, colonizing.**

colonnade A row of columns. A colonnade is often used to support the roof of a building.
    col·on·nade (kol′ə nād′) *noun, plural* **colonnades.**

colony 1. A group of people who leave their own country and settle in another land. A *colony* of English Puritans settled in Massachusetts. 2. A territory that is ruled by another country. Colonies are often far away from the country that governs them. Alaska was a Russian *colony* until the United States purchased it in 1867. 3. **the Colonies.** The thirteen British colonies that became the first states of the United States. 4. A group of animals or plants of the same kind that live together. Ants live in *colonies.*
    col·o·ny (kol′ə nē) *noun, plural* **colonies.**

color 1. A quality of light as we see it with our eyes. Red, blue, yellow, and green are colors. The color of something depends on how it reflects light. The *color* of grass is green. 2. The coloring of the skin. I see you have healthy *color* now that you are well again. The company hires workers without regard to race, religion, or *color. Noun.*
—To give color to. Young children usually enjoy drawing and *coloring* pictures with crayons. *Verb.*
    col·or (kul′ər) *noun, plural* **colors;** *verb,* **colored, coloring.**

Colorado 1. A state in the western part of the United States. Its capital is Denver. 2. A river in the western United States. It flows southwest from Colorado into Mexico.
    Col·o·rad·o (kol′ə rad′ō *or* kol′ə rä′dō) *noun.*

Word History

The name **Colorado** comes from a Spanish word meaning "reddish colored." Spanish explorers gave this name to a small river. Later the name was given to the Colorado River. The state of Colorado takes its name from the river.

---

color-blind Not able to see the difference between certain colors. Most people who are color-blind confuse red and green.
    col·or-blind (kul′ər blīnd′) *adjective.*

colorful 1. Full of color. Everyone admired the *colorful* photographs of birds. 2. Inter-

colonnade

at; āpe; fär; câre; end; mē; it; īce; pîerce; hot; ōld; sông, fôrk; oil; out; up; ūse; rüle; pŭll; tûrn; chin; sing; shop; thin; <u>th</u>is; hw in white; zh in treasure. The symbol ə stands for the unstressed vowel sound in about, taken, pencil, lemon, and circus.

esting or vivid. My grandparents tell many *colorful* stories of how they lived as children.

col·or·ful (kul′ər fəl) *adjective.*

coloring **1.** The way in which anything is colored. We drove into the country to see the brilliant *coloring* of the autumn leaves. **2.** Something used to give color. We used food *coloring* to make the icing on the cake pink.

col·or·ing (kul′ər ing) *noun, plural* **colorings.**

colt A young horse or similar animal, such as a donkey or zebra. A colt is usually a male.

colt (kōlt) *noun, plural* **colts.**

columbine A graceful plant related to the buttercup. The flowers of the columbine have five long petals.

col·um·bine (kol′əm bīn′) *noun, plural* **columbines.**

column **1.** An upright structure shaped like a post; pillar. A column is used as a support or ornament for part of a building. The roof of the porch on our house is held up by *columns.* **2.** Anything shaped like a column. A *column* of black smoke rose from the chimney. **3.** A narrow, vertical section of printed words on a page. This page has two *columns.* **4.** A part of a newspaper written regularly by one person. I like to read that writer's sports *column* in the evening paper. **5.** A long row or line. The band marched down the road in three *columns.*

col·umn (kol′əm) *noun, plural* **columns.**

column

comb **1.** A piece of plastic, metal, or other material that has a row of teeth. A comb is used to smooth, arrange, or fasten the hair. Another kind of comb is used to straighten out fibers of wool or cotton before spinning. **2.** A thick, fleshy red crest on the head of chickens and other birds. *Noun.*
—**1.** To smooth or arrange with a comb. I *comb* my dog's fur ev-

comb of a rooster

ery week to get the tangles out. **2.** To look everywhere in; search thoroughly. The police *combed* the woods for the lost child. *Verb.*

comb (kōm) *noun, plural* **combs;** *verb,* **combed, combing.**

combat Fighting; battle. The soldier was wounded in *combat. Noun.*
—To fight against. Scientists have developed vaccines to *combat* the spread of certain diseases. *Verb.*

com·bat (kom′bat *for noun;* kəm bat′ *or* kom′bat *for verb*) *noun, plural* **combats;** *verb,* **combated, combating.**

combination **1.** Something that is formed by putting several things together. The sandwich was a *combination* of ham and cheese. **2.** A series of numbers or letters used to open certain locks. Only the owner and the manager of the store knew the *combination* to the safe.

com·bi·na·tion (kom′bə nā′shən) *noun, plural* **combinations.**

combine To join together; unite. We *combined* eggs, flour, and milk to make the batter for the pancakes. The thirteen colonies *combined* to form the United States. *Verb.*
—A farm machine that harvests and threshes grain. *Noun.*

com·bine (kəm bīn′ *for verb;* kom′bīn *for noun*) *verb,* **combined, combining;** *noun, plural* **combines.**

combustible Capable of catching fire and burning. Paper and dry leaves are *combustible.*

com·bus·ti·ble (kəm bus′tə bəl) *adjective.*

combustion The act or process of burning. The car's engine runs by the *combustion* of gasoline.

com·bus·tion (kəm bus′chən) *noun.*

come **1.** To move toward. Does your dog *come* to you when you call it? Please *come* here a minute. **2.** To reach a place; arrive. All my friends say they will *come* to my party. The problem has *come* to my attention. The water *came* to a boil. Snow *came* early in October last year. **3.** To originate or take life from. The senator *comes* from a well-known family. Apples *come* from trees. **4.** To turn out to be; become. Our fear that it might rain during our picnic *came* true.

• **to come across.** To find or meet by chance. I *came across* these old clothes in the attic.

• **to come down.** To become sick. Our neighbor *came down* with the flu.

• **to come out.** **1.** To become known or be revealed. The truth about the crime has finally *come out.* **2.** To speak out in public. The candidate *came out* for lower taxes. **3.** To be presented to the public. That movie *came out* last year. **4.** To end; result; turn out. Everything will *come out* all right.

• **to come to. 1.** To become conscious again. When did the patient *come to?* **2.** To be equal to; add up to. The bill for dinner *comes to* eight dollars. **3.** To concern; have to do with. I'm a pretty good student when it *comes to* spelling.

come (kum) *verb,* **came, come, coming.**

comedian A person who makes people laugh by telling jokes or acting out funny stories.

co·me·di·an (kə mē′dē ən) *noun, plural* **comedians.**

comedy A play, motion picture, or television show that is funny or that has a happy ending.

com·e·dy (kom′i dē) *noun, plural* **comedies.**

comet A bright object in space that looks like a star with a long tail of light. A comet is made up of ice, frozen gases, and dust particles. A comet travels along an oval path around the sun.

com·et (kom′it) *noun, plural* **comets.**

Word History

The word **comet** comes from a Greek word that means "having long hair." The Greeks called a comet a "long-haired star" because the comet's tail looked like long hair flying behind it.

---

comfort **1.** A pleasant condition with freedom from worry, pain, or want. Although my family doesn't have a lot of money, we live in *comfort.* **2.** A person or thing that gives relief. When I was in the hospital, the card that you sent was a *comfort. Noun.*
—To ease the sorrow or pain of someone. We tried to *comfort* the lost child by giving him something to eat. *Verb.*

com·fort (kum′fərt) *noun, plural* **comforts;** *verb,* **comforted, comforting.**

comfortable **1.** Giving ease or comfort. My own bed was so *comfortable* after all those nights I had spent in a sleeping bag on our camping trip. **2.** At ease. After a few weeks, the family began to feel very *comfortable* in their new home.

com·fort·a·ble (kum′fər tə bəl *or* kumf′tə bəl) *adjective.*

comic Funny; amusing. The tiny kitten chasing the big, frightened dog was a *comic* sight. *Adjective.*
—**1.** A person who makes people laugh; comedian. That *comic* has a weekly show on television. **2. comics.** A group of comic strips. Our Sunday newspaper has *comics* printed in color. *Noun.*

com·ic (kom′ik) *adjective; noun, plural* **comics.**

comical Funny; amusing. We all laughed at the clown's *comical* tricks.

com·i·cal (kom′i kəl) *adjective.*

comic book A magazine or booklet of comic strips.

comic strip A group of drawings that tell a story or part of a story. Comic strips tell stories that are funny or full of adventure.

comma A punctuation mark (,) that is used to separate words, phrases, or clauses in a sentence.

com·ma (kom′ə) *noun, plural* **commas.**

command **1.** To give an order to; direct. The trainer *commanded* the dog to sit still. **2.** To have power over; rule. The general *commands* the army. **3.** To deserve and get. The teacher *commanded* our respect. *Verb.*
—**1.** An order; direction. The soldiers obeyed the sergeant's *command.* **2.** The power to command. The sheriff had *command* of the search party. **3.** The ability to use or control. My friends from France had a good *command* of the English language after a year here. *Noun.*

com·mand (kə mand′) *verb,* **commanded, commanding;** *noun, plural* **commands.**

commander **1.** A person who is in command; leader. **2.** A naval officer. In the United States Navy or Coast Guard, a commander is below a captain but above a lieutenant. The two ranks of commander are **lieutenant commander** and **commander.**

com·mand·er (kə man′dər) *noun, plural* **commanders.**

commandment A law or command.

com·mand·ment (kə mand′mənt) *noun, plural* **commandments.**

commemorate To honor or maintain the memory of. American postage stamps *commemorate* many of our country's presidents.

com·mem·o·rate (kə mem′ə rāt′) *verb,* **commemorated, commemorating.**

---

at; āpe; fär; câre; end; mē; it; īce; pîerce; hot; ōld; sông, fôrk; oil; out; up; ūse; rüle; pull; tûrn; chin; sing; shop; thin; this; hw in white; zh in treasure. The symbol ə stands for the unstressed vowel sound in about, taken, pencil, lemon, and circus.

commence To begin; start. The opening ceremonies for the new gymnasium *commenced* with everyone singing the national anthem.
    com·mence (kə mens′) *verb,*
    commenced, commencing.

commencement **1.** A beginning; a start. January 1 marks the *commencement* of a new year. **2.** The day or ceremony of graduation. At commencement, a school or college gives diplomas or degrees to students who have completed a course of study.
    com·mence·ment (kə mens′mənt) *noun,*
    plural **commencements.**

commend To speak of with approval; praise. I heard the teacher *commend* you for your fine book report.
    com·mend (kə mend′) *verb,* **commended, commending.**

comment A remark or note. A comment explains something or gives an opinion. After the game, the coach made a few *comments* in praise of the team's playing. *Noun.*
—To make a comment; remark. The principal would not *comment* on the rumor that the school was going to be closed. *Verb.*
    com·ment (kom′ent) *noun, plural* **comments;** *verb,* **commented, commenting.**

commentator A person who comments on something. Radio and television stations, newspapers, and magazines hire commentators to explain or give opinions about the news. The *commentator* felt that the new highway would increase business downtown.
    com·men·ta·tor (kom′ən tā′tər) *noun,*
    plural **commentators.**

commerce The buying and selling of goods; trade; business. There is much *commerce* between states of the United States.
    com·merce (kom′ərs) *noun.*

commercial **1.** Relating to business or trade. I plan to take accounting and other *commercial* subjects in high school. **2.** Having to do with making a profit. So many people paid to see the exhibit that it became a *commercial* success within a few weeks. *Adjective.*
—An advertising message on radio or television. The television show was interrupted every few minutes by a *commercial. Noun.*
    com·mer·cial (kə mûr′shəl) *adjective;*
    noun, plural **commercials.**

commission **1.** A group of persons who are chosen to do certain work. The mayor named a *commission* to find out the causes of pollution in the city. **2.** Money for work done. I receive a *commission* for every new customer I sign up on my paper route.

3. The act of committing. There has been a rise in the *commission* of crimes in the city. **4.** A position of military rank. The soldiers received their *commissions* as lieutenants after completing a training course. **5.** A thing that a person or persons is asked and trusted to do. The ambassador was given a *commission* to arrange a new agreement on trade. **6.** Working order. A dead battery has put our car out of *commission. Noun.*
—**1.** To give a person the right or power to do something. The school *commissioned* the architect to design a new gymnasium. **2.** To put something into active service. The ship will be *commissioned* after its crew is chosen. *Verb.*
    com·mis·sion (kə mish′ən) *noun, plural* **commissions;** *verb,* **commissioned, commissioning.**

commissioner **1.** A person on a commission. The *commissioners* decided that automobiles were the main cause of pollution in the city. **2.** A person who is in charge of a department of a government. The park *commissioner* has just announced plans to build a skating rink in the park.
    com·mis·sion·er (kə mish′ə nər) *noun,*
    plural **commissioners.**

commit **1.** To do or perform. The baseball player *committed* two errors in the first inning. **2.** To put into the care or under the charge of a person or institution, such as a prison. **3.** To devote; pledge. The town *committed* itself to raising money for the new hospital.
    com·mit (kə mit′) *verb,* **committed, committing.**

committee A group of persons who are chosen to do certain work. The decorations *committee* decorated the gym for the school dance.
    com·mit·tee (kə mit′ē) *noun, plural* **committees.**

commodity Something that can be bought and sold. Wheat, corn, and rice are agricultural *commodities.*
    com·mod·i·ty (kə mod′i tē) *noun, plural* **commodities.**

common **1.** Happening often; familiar; usual. Where I live, snow is *common* in the winter. **2.** Belonging equally to all; shared by all alike. It is *common* knowledge that the earth is round. **3.** Ordinary; average. The dandelion is a *common* weed.
• **in common.** Enjoyed, owned, or used together; shared. The two friends had many interests *in common.*
    com·mon (kom′ən) *adjective,* **commoner, commonest.**

common cold A sickness that can cause sneezing, coughing, or a sore throat. The common cold is caused by a virus.

common denominator A denominator that is the same in two or more fractions. The fractions ⅜ and ⅞ have the common denominator 8.

common noun A noun that names any one of a group of persons, places, or things. A common noun is not capitalized. In the sentence "My cousin took me to the movie," "cousin" and "movie" are common nouns.

commonplace Ordinary; not interesting, new, or remarkable. Snow is *commonplace* in Alaska but not in Florida.
com·mon·place (kom′ən plās′) *adjective.*

common sense Ordinary good judgment. A person learns common sense from experience and logical thinking, not from school or study. It is *common sense* to take an umbrella with you if there is a chance of rain.

commonwealth A nation or state that is governed by the people. The United States is a commonwealth. Certain states call themselves commonwealths.
com·mon·wealth (kom′ən welth′) *noun, plural* **commonwealths.**

commotion A noisy confusion; disorder. There was a *commotion* at the stadium as the crowd booed the referee's decision.
com·mo·tion (kə mō′shən) *noun, plural* **commotions.**

communicable Able to be carried or passed from one person to another. The common cold is a *communicable* disease.
com·mu·ni·ca·ble (kə mū′ni kə bəl) *adjective.*

communicate To exchange or pass along feelings, thoughts, or information. People communicate with each other by speaking or writing. When I was at camp, I *communicated* with my family by writing letters.
com·mu·ni·cate (kə mū′ni kāt′) *verb,* **communicated, communicating.**

communication **1.** An exchanging or sharing of feelings, thoughts, or information. The telephone makes *communication* over great distances possible. Some American Indian tribes used smoke signals as a means of *communication.* **2.** A message or news that is exchanged or shared. The *communication* from Dad said Mom's flight was late. **3. communications.** A system for sending messages by telephone, telegraph, computers, radio, or television. *Communications* in the flooded town are still not working.
com·mu·ni·ca·tion (kə mū′ni kā′shən) *noun, plural* **communications.**

communion **1.** A sharing of feelings or thoughts. There was a close *communion* between the parents and their children. **2. Communion.** A religious service commemorating the last meal of Jesus and his apostles.
com·mun·ion (kə mūn′yən) *noun, plural* **communions.**

communism A social and economic system in which property and goods are owned by the government and are to be shared equally by all the people. The governments of the Soviet Union, China, and other countries are based on this system.
com·mu·nism (kom′yə niz′əm) *noun.*

communist A person who believes in communism as a way of life or who belongs to a communist party.
com·mu·nist (kom′yə nist) *noun, plural* **communists.**

communist party A political party that is in favor of communism.

community **1.** A group of people who live together in the same place. Our *community* voted to build a new library. My grandparents live in a rural *community.* **2.** A group of people who share a common interest. The scientific *community* was excited by the landing on the moon. **3.** A group of different plants and animals that live together in the same area and depend on each other for their survival.
com·mu·ni·ty (kə mū′ni tē) *noun, plural* **communities.**

The **community** is having a plant sale.

at; āpe; fär; câre; end; mē; it; īce; pîerce; hot; ōld; sông, fôrk; oil; out; up; ūse; rüle; pùll; tûrn; chin; sing; shop; thin; this; hw in white; zh in treasure. The symbol ə stands for the unstressed vowel sound in about, taken, pencil, lemon, and circus.

commutative property A characteristic of addition and multiplication that allows you to add or multiply two numbers in any order and still get the same answer. For example, $4 + 6$ gives you the same answer as $6 + 4$, and 7×5 gives you the same answer as 5×7.
com·mu·ta·tive property (kom′yə tā′tiv *or* kə mū′tə tiv).

commute To travel regularly to and from work or school over quite a long distance. Many of our neighbors *commute* to the city every day by train.
com·mute (kə mūt′) *verb,* **commuted, commuting.**

commuter A person who travels a long distance to and from work or school. Every weekday evening the roads are filled with the cars of *commuters* driving home.
com·mut·er (kə mū′tər) *noun, plural* **commuters.**

compact¹ **1.** Tightly packed together; dense. We pressed the snow into *compact* snowballs. **2.** Taking up a small amount of space. We have very *compact* cooking equipment for camping trips. *Adjective.*
—**1.** A small case that holds face powder. **2.** An automobile that is smaller than a standard model. *Noun.*
—To pack tightly together. The school has a machine that *compacts* trash. *Verb.*
com·pact (kəm pakt′ *or* kom′pakt *for adjective;* kom′pakt *for noun;* kəm pakt′ *for verb*) *adjective; noun, plural* **compacts;** *verb,* **compacted, compacting.**

compact² An agreement. The Mayflower *Compact* was an agreement among the Pilgrims concerning how their new colony would be governed.
com·pact (kom′pakt) *noun, plural* **compacts.**

compact disc A flat, round piece of plastic that holds stored music. The music is reproduced by putting the compact disc in a special machine that uses a laser to read the stored music. The trademark is **Compact Disc.**
com·pact disc (kom′pakt).

companion **1.** A person who often goes along with another; friend; comrade. We three students were constant *companions* at camp last summer. **2.** Something that matches something else; one of a pair. I lost the *companion* to this glove at the theater.
com·pan·ion (kəm pan′yən) *noun, plural* **companions.**

companionship The relation between good companions; friendship. I missed the *companionship* of my friends when I moved to a new town.
com·pan·ion·ship (kəm pan′yən ship′) *noun.*

company **1.** A guest or guests. We are having *company* for dinner. **2.** A business firm or organization. My parents both work for small *companies.* **3.** Companionship. When the rest of the family is away, I am grateful for my dog's *company.* **4.** A friend or friends; companions. You can often judge people by the *company* they keep. **5.** A group of people gathered together. The guide led the *company* of tourists through the museum. **6.** A group of performers. A *company* of musicians will present a concert at the town hall tonight. **7.** A group of soldiers. A captain commands a company.
com·pa·ny (kum′pə nē) *noun, plural* **companies.**

comparative **1.** Having to do with or showing a comparison of one thing with another. We made a *comparative* study of a frog and a worm in science class. **2.** Measured or judged by comparing with something else. I've met your uncle many times, but your aunt is a *comparative* stranger to me, because we've only met once. *Adjective.*
—The form of an adjective or adverb that shows a greater degree or more of whatever is expressed by the basic form. For example, *taller* is the comparative of *tall. Noun.*
com·par·a·tive (kəm par′ə tiv) *adjective; noun, plural* **comparatives.**

compare **1.** To study in order to find out how persons or things are alike or different. We *compared* our watches and saw that your watch was five minutes ahead of mine. **2.** To say or think that something is like something else. The writer *compared* the boom of big guns to the sound of thunder. **3.** To be thought alike; be worthy of being compared. Seeing photographs of the Grand Canyon cannot *compare* with visiting it.
com·pare (kəm pâr′) *verb,* **compared, comparing.**

comparison **1.** The finding out of the likenesses and the differences between persons or things. A *comparison* of the two teams seems to show that Saturday's game will be close. **2.** A likeness; similarity. There is no *comparison* between those two cars when it comes to speed. **3.** A change in the form of an adjective or adverb that shows a difference in degree of what is expressed.
com·par·i·son (kəm par′ə sən) *noun, plural* **comparisons.**

compartment A separate division or section. My desk drawer has *compartments* for pencils, erasers, rubber bands, and paper clips.

com·part·ment (kəm pärt′mənt) *noun*, *plural* **compartments.**

compass **1.** An instrument for showing directions. A compass has a magnetic needle that points to the north. Airplane pilots, ship captains, and many other people use compasses. **2.** An instrument for drawing circles or measuring distances. A compass is made up of two arms joined together at the top. One arm ends in a point and the other one holds a pencil.

compass

com·pass (kum′pəs) *noun*, *plural* **compasses.**

compassion Sympathy for someone else's suffering or misfortune, together with the desire to help. They had *compassion* for the poor and helped deliver food to them.

com·pas·sion (kəm pash′ən) *noun*.

compel To force. The police *compelled* the owner to leave the burning building.

com·pel (kəm pel′) *verb*, **compelled, compelling.**

compensate **1.** To make up for something. The new player's speed *compensated* for lack of experience. **2.** To pay. The government *compensated* the farmers for the land it took to build the highway.

com·pen·sate (kom′pən sāt′) *verb*, **compensated, compensating.**

compensation **1.** Something that makes up for something else. Going to the zoo was our *compensation* for missing the parade last week. **2.** Wages; pay. When people do the same work, their *compensation* should be the same.

com·pen·sa·tion (kom′pən sā′shən) *noun*, *plural* **compensations.**

compete To try to win or gain something from another or others. The two students *competed* against each other for first prize in the spelling contest.

com·pete (kəm pēt′) *verb*, **competed, competing.**

competent Able to perform basic skills; capable. Only *competent* swimmers should use the deep end of the pool.

com·pe·tent (kom′pi tənt) *adjective*.

competition **1.** The act of trying to win or gain something from another or others. Our team was in *competition* with three others for the championship. **2.** A contest. I think I'll enter the swimming *competition*.

com·pe·ti·tion (kom′pi tish′ən) *noun*, *plural* **competitions.**

competitive **1.** Involving or decided by competition. I won top honors in a *competitive* examination. **2.** Enjoying or successful in competition. The *competitive* spirit of our team captain helps us all to do our best.

com·pet·i·tive (kəm pet′i tiv) *adjective*.

competitor A person or thing that tries to win or gain something from another or others. My main *competitor* in the election for school president was my best friend. That gas station has two *competitors* nearby.

com·pet·i·tor (kəm pet′i tər) *noun*, *plural* **competitors.**

compile To collect or put together in a list or report. The newspaper reporter *compiled* all the facts and then wrote the story.

com·pile (kəm pīl′) *verb*, **compiled, compiling.**

complacent Satisfied with oneself. We should not become *complacent* about our success, but continue to work for excellence.

com·pla·cent (kəm plā′sənt) *adjective*.

complain **1.** To say that something is wrong; find fault. The passengers *complained* that the train was never on time. **2.** To make an accusation or charge. We *complained* to the police about our noisy neighbors.

com·plain (kəm plān′) *verb*, **complained, complaining.**

complaint **1.** A statement that something is wrong. We took our *complaint* about the rude clerk to the store manager. **2.** A cause for complaining. I have no *complaints* about this restaurant. **3.** An accusation or charge. The storekeeper made a *complaint* against the person who had robbed the store.

com·plaint (kəm plānt′) *noun*, *plural* **complaints.**

complement Something that completes or makes a thing whole or perfect. Going to see a movie would be the perfect *complement* to this weekend. *Noun.*

at; āpe; fär; câre; end; mē; it; īce; pîerce; hot; ōld; sông, fôrk; oil; out; up; ūse; rüle; pùll; tûrn; chin; sing; shop; thin; this; hw in white; zh in treasure. The symbol ə stands for the unstressed vowel sound in about, taken, pencil, lemon, and circus.

C

151

—To make complete. The background music nicely *complements* the acting in the movie. *Verb.* ▲ Another word that sounds like this is **compliment.**
   com·ple·ment (kom′plə mənt *for noun;* kom′plə ment′ *for verb*) *noun, plural* **complements;** *verb,* **complemented, complementing.**

complete   **1.** Having all its parts; whole; entire. Our school library has the *complete* writings of William Shakespeare.   **2.** Ended; finished. I cannot go out to play until my homework is *complete.*   **3.** Thorough; perfect. The laughter of the audience showed that the comedian was a *complete* success. *Adjective.*
—**1.** To make whole or perfect. Do you mean you've finally *completed* your collection of baseball cards?   **2.** To bring to an end; finish. After you *complete* the test, you may go to lunch. *Verb.*
   com·plete (kəm plēt′) *adjective; verb,* **completed, completing.**

The girl is about to **complete** the puzzle.

completion   **1.** The act of completing or finishing. With the *completion* of the flight, the pilot was able to relax.   **2.** The condition of being completed. I hoped to bring this science project to *completion* before spring vacation.
   com·ple·tion (kəm plē′shən) *noun.*

complex   **1.** Hard to understand or do. I don't know how to solve this *complex* arithmetic problem.   **2.** Made up of many connected parts. The sweater had a *complex* pattern of shapes and colors in its design.
   com·plex (kəm pleks′ *or* kom′pleks) *adjective.*

complexion   **1.** The color and look of a person's skin, especially of the face. You have a clear and smooth *complexion.*   **2.** The general look or character of anything. The substitution of two new players on our team changed the whole *complexion* of the game, and we won.
   com·plex·ion (kəm plek′shən) *noun, plural* **complexions.**

complexity   The quality of being complex. The *complexity* of the arithmetic problem puzzled the class.
   com·plex·i·ty (kəm plek′si tē) *noun, plural* **complexities.**

complicate   To make hard to understand or do. My friend's attempts to help only *complicated* the job of washing the car.
   com·pli·cate (kom′pli kāt′) *verb,* **complicated, complicating.**

complicated   Hard to understand or do. The directions for putting together the bicycle were too *complicated* for me to follow.
   com·pli·cat·ed (kom′pli kā′tid) *adjective.*

complication   A confused or difficult condition. The snowstorm that closed down the airport caused a *complication* in our travel plans.
   com·pli·ca·tion (kom′pli kā′shən) *noun, plural* **complications.**

compliment   **1.** Something good that is said out of praise or admiration. You must receive many *compliments* on your piano playing.   **2. compliments.** Friendly greetings. Your friends asked me to send you their *compliments. Noun.*
—To express praise or admiration. I heard the teacher *complimented* you on your well-written composition. *Verb.* ▲ Another word that sounds like this is **complement.**
   com·pli·ment (kom′plə mənt *for noun;* kom′plə ment′ *for verb*) *noun, plural* **compliments;** *verb,* **complimented, complimenting.**

complimentary   **1.** Containing or expressing praise or admiration. The teacher made a *complimentary* remark about the student's hard work.   **2.** Without charge; free. The store attracted customers by giving away *complimentary* concert tickets.
   com·pli·men·ta·ry (kom′plə men′tə rē *or* kom′plə men′trē) *adjective.*

comply   To act in agreement with a request or rule. I *complied* with the doctor's orders and stayed home until my cold was better.
   com·ply (kəm plī′) *verb,* **complied, complying.**

compose   **1.** To form the basis of; make up. The material in this dress is *composed* of

cotton and rayon. Twelve people *compose* a jury. **2.** To put together; create. We *composed* a new school cheer. The musician *composed* an opera. **3.** To make quiet or calm. At first I cried when I heard the sad news, but soon I *composed* myself.
▸ **com·pose** (kəm pōz′) *verb*, **composed, composing.**

composer A person who writes something, especially a musical work.
▸ **com·pos·er** (kəm pō′zər) *noun, plural* **composers.**

composite Made up of various parts. The artist made a *composite* drawing by combining different sections from several pictures.
▸ **com·pos·ite** (kəm poz′it) *adjective.*

composition **1.** The act of putting together to form a whole. *Composition* of the opera took two years. **2.** The parts that together form something. The scientist studied the moon rock to find out its *composition.* **3.** Something that is put together or created, especially something written or a piece of music. I wrote a *composition* for English class about life in colonial America. A symphony is a kind of musical *composition.*
▸ **com·po·si·tion** (kom′pə zish′ən) *noun, plural* **compositions.**

compost A mixture of decaying leaves, vegetables, manure, or other organic matter, used to make the soil better for gardening.
▸ **com·post** (kom′pōst) *noun.*

composure Self-control; calmness. The family's *composure* during the fire helped them all escape injury.
▸ **com·po·sure** (kəm pō′zhər) *noun.*

compound Made up of two or more parts. Look up **leaf** for a picture of a compound leaf. *Adjective.*
—To mix or combine. The chemist *compounded* a new formula out of simple ingredients. *Verb.*
—**1.** A mixture or combination. **2.** A substance that is formed by the chemical combination of two or more elements. Water is a *compound* that is made of hydrogen and oxygen. **3.** A word that is made up of two or more words. *Comic strip, merry-go-round,* and *nighttime* are compounds. *Noun.*
▸ **com·pound** (kom′pound *for adjective and noun;* kəm pound′ *for verb) adjective; verb,* **compounded, compounding;** *noun, plural* **compounds.**

compound sentence A sentence that contains two or more simple sentences that are joined by the conjunctions *and, or,* or *but.* "I like movies, but my friend prefers books" is a compound sentence.

comprehend To understand. The teacher felt that the students still did not *comprehend* how to add and subtract fractions.
▸ **com·pre·hend** (kom′pri hend′) *verb,* **comprehended, comprehending.**

Word History

The word **comprehend** comes from a Latin word that originally meant "to grasp" or "to take hold of." The Latin word later came to mean "to take hold of with the mind" or "to understand."

comprehension Understanding or the ability to understand. Your clear and accurate report on the book shows your *comprehension* of it.
▸ **com·pre·hen·sion** (kom′pri hen′shən) *noun, plural* **comprehensions.**

comprehensive Covering or including everything or almost everything. The *comprehensive* map of the town shows even the smallest streets.
▸ **com·pre·hen·sive** (kom′pri hen′siv) *adjective.*

compress To press or squeeze together into less space. The city has trucks that *compress* garbage so it will not take up so much room at the dump. *Verb.*
—A pad or cloth used to put pressure, heat, or cold on some part of the body. The nurse put a cold *compress* on the head of the child who had a fever. *Noun.*
▸ **com·press** (kəm pres′ *for verb;* kom′pres′ *for noun) verb,* **compressed, compressing;** *noun, plural* **compresses.**

comprise To include or consist of; be composed of. The state of Hawaii *comprises* eight main islands and many smaller ones.
▸ **com·prise** (kəm prīz′) *verb,* **comprised, comprising.**

compromise The settlement of an argument or dispute by agreeing that each side will give up part of its demands. The fight over washing the dishes ended with a *compromise* in which they decided to share the chore. *Noun.*

at; āpe; fär; câre; end; mē; it; īce; pîerce; hot; ōld; sông, fôrk; oil; out; up; ūse; rüle; pùll; tûrn; chin; sing; shop; thin; this; hw in white; zh in treasure. The symbol ə stands for the unstressed vowel sound in about, taken, pencil, lemon, and circus.

—To reach a settlement by agreeing that each side will give up some part of its demands. When the two children wanted to watch different television programs, they *compromised* and watched parts of both. *Verb.*
com·pro·mise (kom′prə mīz′) *noun, plural* **compromises;** *verb,* **compromised, compromising.**

compulsory Required by law or rules. Gym class is *compulsory* in this school unless a student has an excuse from a doctor.
com·pul·so·ry (kəm pul′sə rē) *adjective.*

compute To find out or calculate by using mathematics; reckon. The builder *computed* the cost of a new garage. Scientists have *computed* how far away other planets are from the earth.
com·pute (kəm pūt′) *verb,* **computed, computing.**

computer An electronic device that can store and work with large quantities of information. Computers can do difficult mathematical calculations rapidly, can retrieve information quickly, and can help a person work with words and pictures.
com·put·er (kəm pū′tər) *noun, plural* **computers.**

computer graphics Pictures and drawings that a computer can display on its screen or print on paper.
computer graph·ics (graf′iks).

computer graphics

computer language A set of words and symbols that are used to give instructions to a computer and to write programs. LOGO and BASIC are computer languages.

computer literacy The understanding of how computers work and how they can be used to perform tasks.
computer lit·er·a·cy (lit′ər ə sē).

computer science The study of computers and the equipment and programs that are used with computers.

comrade A friend who shares the same work or interests with another; companion.
com·rade (kom′rad) *noun, plural* **comrades.**

concave Curved inward. The inside of a spoon is *concave.* The arch of your foot is *concave.*
con·cave (kon kāv′ or kon′kāv) *adjective.*

conceal To put or keep out of sight; hide. Don't forget to *conceal* the house keys under the porch. I *concealed* my anger by smiling.

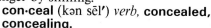

concave and convex

con·ceal (kən sēl′) *verb,* **concealed, concealing.**

concede **1.** To admit as true. After I tried it myself, I *conceded* that the lamp no longer worked. **2.** To yield to someone else or admit defeat. The candidate for mayor would not *concede* the election until all the votes were counted.
con·cede (kən sēd′) *verb,* **conceded, conceding.**

conceited Having too high an opinion of oneself or of one's ability to do things. People may think you are *conceited* if you talk about yourself too much.
con·ceit·ed (kən sē′tid) *adjective.*

conceive To form an idea of or imagine; think up. Scientists *conceived* the plan for the first spacecraft. It is hard to *conceive* of what life was like thousands of years ago.
con·ceive (kən sēv′) *verb,* **conceived, conceiving.**

concentrate **1.** To bring together into one place. The population of our country is *concentrated* in the cities. The team *concentrated* their efforts on winning the game. **2.** To make stronger or thicker. We can *concentrate* the liquid by boiling off some water. **3.** To pay close attention. We could not *concentrate* on our homework because the room was too noisy.
con·cen·trate (kon′sən trāt′) *verb,* **concentrated, concentrating.**

concentration **1.** The act of concentrating or the state of being concentrated. There was a great *concentration* of people in the small and crowded room. **2.** Close attention. My *concentration* on the television program was so deep that I didn't hear you ring the doorbell.
con·cen·tra·tion (kon′sən trā′shən) *noun, plural* **concentrations.**

C

concept A general idea; thought. Our country honors the *concept* of individual freedom.
con·cept (kon′sept) *noun, plural* **concepts.**

conception An idea; concept. Learning about travel in space gives you some *conception* of how enormous the universe must be.
con·cep·tion (kən sep′shən) *noun, plural* **conceptions.**

concern **1.** To be important to. What my parents said about saving money *concerns* our whole family. **2.** To have to do with; be about. This chapter of our book *concerns* the American Revolution. **3.** To worry; trouble. Your bad cough *concerned* us all. *Verb.*
—**1.** Something that is important to a person. Taking care of the puppy is my *concern.* **2.** Serious interest or worry. We were full of *concern* for our future after the flood destroyed our home. **3.** A business. I was hired to work for a clothing *concern. Noun.*
con·cern (kən sûrn′) *verb,* **concerned, concerning;** *noun, plural* **concerns.**

concerning About; having to do with; regarding. My friend wrote me a long letter *concerning* our vacation plans.
con·cern·ing (kən sûr′ning) *preposition.*

concert A performance, usually a musical performance by a number of musicians. We went to a band *concert* in the park.
con·cert (kon′sərt) *noun, plural* **concerts.**

concerto A piece of music for one or more musical instruments and an orchestra.
con·cer·to (kən cher′tō) *noun, plural* **concertos.**

concession **1.** The act of conceding or yielding. My parents made a *concession* and let me stay up late to watch the football game. **2.** Something that is conceded. Your admission that you were wrong was a *concession.* **3.** The permission to do something granted by a government or other authority. The town gave our neighbor the *concession* to sell hot dogs in the park.
con·ces·sion (kən sesh′ən) *noun, plural* **concessions.**

conch **1.** A kind of shellfish with a large, coiled shell. **2.** The shell of this animal.
conch (kongk *or* konch) *noun, plural* **conchs** or **conches.**

concise Expressed in few words. The coach's instructions to the team were clear and *concise.*
con·cise (kən sīs′) *adjective.*

conch

conclude **1.** To bring to an end; finish. When the band *concluded* the playing of the national anthem, the baseball game began. **2.** To decide after thinking. After studying all the facts, the judge *concluded* that no crime had been committed.
con·clude (kən klüd′) *verb,* **concluded, concluding.**

conclusion **1.** The end of something. The *conclusion* of the movie was very exciting. **2.** Arrangement; settlement. The *conclusion* of the treaty between the two countries took many months. **3.** Something decided after thinking. I have come to the *conclusion* that I want to be a doctor when I grow older.
con·clu·sion (kən klü′zhən) *noun, plural* **conclusions.**

concoct **1.** To prepare by combining several different things. We *concocted* a meal from leftovers. **2.** To devise; make up. They *concocted* a wonderful surprise party for their parents.
con·coct (kon kokt′) *verb,* **concocted, concocting.**

concord Peaceful agreement; harmony. The *concord* between the two nations prevented war.
con·cord (kon′kôrd *or* kong′kôrd) *noun, plural* **concords.**

concrete Able to be seen and touched. A chair is a *concrete* object. *Adjective.*
—A mixture of cement, pebbles or sand, and water. Concrete becomes very hard when it dries. It is used in buildings, bridges, and other structures, and in paving roads and sidewalks. *Noun.*
con·crete (kon′krēt *or* kon krēt′) *adjective; noun, plural* **concretes.**

concur To agree; have the same opinion. The judges *concurred* in awarding first prize to that science project.
con·cur (kən kûr′) *verb,* **concurred, concurring.**

concussion **1.** A sudden, violent shaking. The house shook from the *concussion* of the explosion. **2.** An injury to the brain or spine caused by a fall or blow. Diving into the shallow pool caused my *concussion.*
con·cus·sion (kən kush′ən) *noun, plural* **concussions.**

at; āpe; fär; câre; end; mē; it; īce; pîerce; hot; ōld; sông, fôrk; oil; out; up; ūse; rüle; pùll; tûrn; chin; sing; shop; thin; this; hw in white; zh in treasure. The symbol ə stands for the unstressed vowel sound in about, taken, pencil, lemon, and circus.

condemn **1.** To express strong opposition to; disapprove of. Many doctors *condemn* smoking. **2.** To order as a punishment. The judge *condemned* the thief to ten years in jail. **3.** To declare to be no longer safe or fit for use. The city government *condemned* the old building.
con·demn (kən dem′) *verb*, **condemned, condemning.**

condensation **1.** The act of condensing something. The *condensation* of steam causes it to change into water. **2.** Something condensed. I decided I would read a *condensation* of the long novel.
con·den·sa·tion (kon′den sā′shən) *noun*, *plural* **condensations.**

condense **1.** To make or become less in size or volume. Milk *condenses* when the water in it is boiled away. The writer *condensed* the long story to a short story. **2.** To change from a gas to a liquid form. Steam *condenses* to water when cooled.
con·dense (kən dens′) *verb*, **condensed, condensing.**

condition **1.** The way that a person or thing is; the state something is in. That athlete keeps in good *condition* by doing exercises. **2.** Something needed for another event or thing to occur; something required. Being a good skater is one of the *conditions* for getting on the hockey team. **3.** An illness or an unhealthy state of the body or a part of the body. **4. conditions.** State of affairs; circumstances. Poor working *conditions* caused the employees to complain. *Noun.*
—**1.** To put in a healthy state or good shape. I exercise to *condition* my body. **2.** To make used to something; accustom. Living at the North Pole soon *conditioned* the explorers to cold weather. *Verb.*
con·di·tion (kən dish′ən) *noun*, *plural* **conditions;** *verb*, **conditioned, conditioning.**

condominium **1.** An apartment building in which each apartment is owned by the person or persons living in it. **2.** A single apartment that is owned by the person or persons living in it.
con·do·min·i·um (kon′də min′ē əm) *noun*, *plural* **condominiums.**

condor A large bird with a hooked bill and a head and neck without feathers. A condor is a kind of vulture. It is found in the mountains of South America.
con·dor (kon′dər) *noun*, *plural* **condors.**

conduct The way someone behaves. Our teacher stresses the importance of good *conduct. Noun.*
—**1.** To behave. I know you were disappointed, but you *conducted* yourself very well. **2.** To direct or lead. Our music teacher will *conduct* the school orchestra. **3.** To take charge of; control; manage. It is a challenge to *conduct* a successful business. **4.** To carry or transmit. Cast iron *conducts* heat evenly. *Verb.*
con·duct (kon′dukt *for noun;* kən dukt′ *for verb*) *noun;* *verb*, **conducted, conducting.**

conductor **1.** A person who conducts. Our music teacher is also the *conductor* of the school orchestra. **2.** A person on a train or bus who collects fares and assists passengers. The *conductor* walked down the aisle and called out the name of the next stop. **3.** Something that transmits heat, electricity, or sound. Iron and copper are excellent *conductors* of heat.
con·duc·tor (kən duk′tər) *noun*, *plural* **conductors.**

cone **1.** A solid object that has a flat, round base with straight sides that come together at a point. **2.** Something shaped like a cone. I like to eat ice cream in a *cone.* **3.** A cone-shaped object with overlapping scales that grows on many evergreen trees. The cone bears the seeds.
cone (kōn) *noun*, *plural* **cones.**

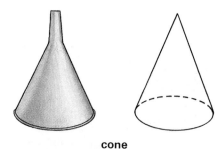

cone

confederacy **1.** A group of countries, states, or people joined together for a common purpose. The five Indian tribes joined to form a *confederacy.* **2. the Confederacy.** The eleven southern states that declared

condor

themselves separate from the United States in 1860 and 1861.
> **con·fed·er·a·cy** (kən fed′ər ə sē) *noun, plural* **confederacies.**

confederate **1.** A person or group that joins with another for a common purpose. The bank robbers and their *confederates* were arrested by the police. **2. Confederate.** A person who fought for or supported the Confederacy. *Noun.*
—**1.** United in an alliance. The two presidents signed a treaty that declared their countries *confederate* states. **2. Confederate.** Of the Confederacy. *Adjective.*
> **con·fed·er·ate** (kən fed′ər it) *noun, plural* **confederates;** *adjective.*

confederation **1.** The act of joining together to form a confederacy. The two neighboring countries began plans for *confederation.* **2.** A group of countries or states joined together for a common purpose; a league or alliance. From 1781 to 1789 the American states formed a *confederation.*
> **con·fed·er·a·tion** (kən fed′ə rā′shən) *noun, plural* **confederations.**

confer **1.** To meet and talk together. The three referees *conferred* to decide how to rule on the play. **2.** To give or bestow upon. The general will *confer* a medal on the brave soldier.
> **con·fer** (kən fûr′) *verb,* **conferred, conferring.**

conference A meeting to talk over important matters. A *conference* of doctors from all over the state was held to discuss new ways to treat disease.
> **con·fer·ence** (kon′fər əns) *noun, plural* **conferences.**

confess **1.** To admit. I *confess* that I don't enjoy that new television program. **2.** To tell a priest sins to be forgiven.
> **con·fess** (kən fes′) *verb,* **confessed, confessing.**

confession The admitting of something, especially guilt. The criminal made a full *confession* to the crime.
> **con·fes·sion** (kən fesh′ən) *noun, plural* **confessions.**

confetti Very small pieces of colored paper. Confetti is thrown into the air to celebrate a festive occasion. The baseball champions were showered with *confetti* as they rode in the parade.
> **con·fet·ti** (kən fet′ē) *noun.*

confide To tell a secret to someone who is trusted. I often *confide* in my best friends. I *confided* my worries to the school counselor.
> **con·fide** (kən fīd′) *verb,* **confided, confiding.**

confidence **1.** Trust or faith. I have *confidence* in your honesty. **2.** Faith in oneself. If you studied the lesson well, you can give your answer with *confidence.* **3.** Trust that a person will not tell a secret. I would never reveal something told to me in *confidence.* **4.** Something told as a secret to be kept.
> **con·fi·dence** (kon′fi dəns) *noun, plural* **confidences.**

confident **1.** Having trust or faith; sure. I am *confident* that our team will win the game. **2.** Having faith in oneself or one's own abilities.
> **con·fi·dent** (kon′fi dənt) *adjective.*

confidential Secret. The president received a *confidential* letter from the ambassador.
> **con·fi·den·tial** (kon′fi den′shəl) *adjective.*

confine To hold or keep in; limit. The sheriff *confined* the outlaw in a jail cell. My bad cold *confined* me to my bed. *Verb.*
—**confines.** Limits; boundaries. The dog was not allowed to go outside the *confines* of the yard. *Noun.*
> **con·fine** (kən fīn′) *verb,* **confined, confining; con·fines** (kon′fīnz) *plural noun.*

confirm **1.** To show to be true or correct. The newspaper *confirmed* reports of a flood. **2.** To consent to; approve. The Senate *confirmed* the trade agreement. **3.** To make definite. I called my friend to *confirm* our date for Saturday. **4.** To admit a person to full membership in a religious congregation.
> **con·firm** (kən fûrm′) *verb,* **confirmed, confirming.**

confirmation **1.** The act of confirming something. Please call the hotel to get *confirmation* of our reservation. **2.** Something that confirms or proves. **3.** The ceremony of admitting a person to full membership in a church or synagogue.
> **con·fir·ma·tion** (kon′fər mā′shən) *noun, plural* **confirmations.**

confiscate To take something by authority. The government *confiscated* the property when no one would pay the taxes on it.
> **con·fis·cate** (kon′fis kāt′) *verb,* **confiscated, confiscating.**

conflict **1.** A long fight; war. The War of 1812 was a *conflict* between America and

---

at; āpe; fär; câre; end; mē; it; īce; pîerce; hot; ōld; sông, fôrk; oil; out; up; ūse; rüle; pùll; tûrn; chin; sing; shop; thin; <u>this</u>; hw in white; zh in treasure. The symbol ə stands for the unstressed vowel sound in about, taken, pencil, lemon, and circus.

England.   **2.** A strong disagreement. The two newspaper stories about the cause of the fire are in *conflict. Noun.*
—To disagree strongly. The two accounts of the accident *conflict. Verb.*
con·flict (kon′flikt *for noun;* kən flikt′ *for verb*) *noun, plural* **conflicts;** *verb,* **conflicted, conflicting.**

conform   **1.** To act or think in a way that agrees with a rule or a standard. New students were told that they must *conform* to the rules of the school.   **2.** To be or make the same; be like. The house *conformed* to the architect's plans.
con·form (kən fôrm′) *verb,* **conformed, conforming.**

confront   To meet or face. The soldiers *confronted* the enemy soldiers. A difficult problem *confronted* us.
con·front (kən frunt′) *verb,* **confronted, confronting.**

confuse   **1.** To mix up; bewilder. That street sign *confuses* drivers and causes them to take a wrong turn.   **2.** To mistake for another; not see the difference between. People are always *confusing* the twins. Be careful not to *confuse* the word "principle" with the word "principal."
con·fuse (kən fūz′) *verb,* **confused, confusing.**

confusion   **1.** The condition of being confused; disorder. In my *confusion,* I gave the wrong answer. Everything in my desk drawer was in *confusion.*   **2.** A mistaking of one person or thing for another.
con·fu·sion (kən fū′zhən) *noun, plural* **confusions.**

congeal   To become thick, stiff, or hard through exposure to cold or to air. The pudding I spilled on the rug *congealed* into a clump.
con·geal (kən jēl′) *verb,* **congealed, congealing.**

congestion   **1.** Too much mucus or blood in a part of the body. I had *congestion* in my nose when I had a cold.   **2.** A very crowded condition. There is always *congestion* on the highway after work.
con·ges·tion (kən jes′chən) *noun.*

Congo   A country in west-central Africa.
Con·go (kong′gō) *noun.*

congratulate   To give good wishes or praise for someone's success or for something nice that has happened. We *congratulated* them on doing such a good job on their science project.
con·grat·u·late (kən grach′ə lāt′) *verb,* **congratulated, congratulating.**

congratulation   **1.** The act of congratulating.   **2. congratulations.** Good wishes or praise given for a person's success or for something nice that has happened. We offered *congratulations* to the winning team.
con·grat·u·la·tion (kən grach′ə lā′shən) *noun, plural* **congratulations.**

congregate   To come together in a crowd. People *congregated* around the famous movie star to get an autograph.
con·gre·gate (kong′grə gāt′) *verb,* **congregated, congregating.**

congregation   **1.** A gathering or crowd of people or things. There was a large *congregation* of tourists at the fair.   **2.** The people present at a religious service.
con·gre·ga·tion (kong′grə gā′shən) *noun, plural* **congregations.**

congress   **1.** An assembly of people who make laws. Many nations that are republics have a congress.   **2. Congress.** A branch of the government of the United States that makes laws. Congress is made up of the Senate and the House of Representatives.
con·gress (kong′gris) *noun, plural* **congresses.**

congressman   A member of Congress. When people say congressman, they usually mean a member of the House of Representatives.
con·gress·man (kong′gris mən) *noun, plural* **congressmen** (kong′gris mən).

congresswoman   A woman who is a member of Congress. When people say congresswoman, they usually mean a member of the House of Representatives.
con·gress·wom·an (kong′gris wùm′ən) *noun, plural* **congresswomen** (kong′gris wim′ən).

a graduate being **congratulated**

C

congruent Exactly equal in shape and size. Two triangles are congruent if the sides and angles of one are the same as the sides and angles of the other.
con·gru·ent (kong′grü ənt *or* kən grü′ənt) *adjective.*

conjunction A word that joins other words or groups of words. In the sentence "My friends and I were late because we missed the bus," the words "and" and "because" are conjunctions.
con·junc·tion (kən jungk′shən) *noun, plural* **conjunctions.**

Conn. An abbreviation for *Connecticut.*

connect 1. To fasten or join together. We had no trouble *connecting* the trailer to the car. 2. To consider as related; associate. We *connect* robins with spring. 3. To join together in an electrical circuit. They will *connect* our telephone tomorrow.
con·nect (kə nekt′) *verb,* **connected, connecting.**

Connecticut A state in the northeastern United States. Its capital is Hartford.
Con·nect·i·cut (kə net′i kət) *noun.*

Word History

The name **Connecticut** comes from an Indian word that means "a place beside the long river." Settlers then gave the name to the river, too. Soon they used it for villages near the Connecticut River. Later they used it for the state in which this river is located.

---

connection 1. The act of fastening or joining things. The *connection* of the pipes under the sink was hard work. 2. Relationship; association. The city council is studying the *connection* between heavy traffic and air pollution. 3. Something that connects. The electrician looked for the bad *connection* in the radio.
con·nec·tion (kə nek′shən) *noun, plural* **connections.**

conquer To overcome; defeat. The army *conquered* the small country. I *conquered* my feelings of being homesick after my second day at summer camp.
con·quer (kong′kər) *verb,* **conquered, conquering.**

conqueror A person who conquers. In ancient times, Alexander the Great was a powerful *conqueror.*
con·quer·or (kong′kər ər) *noun, plural* **conquerors.**

conquest 1. The act of conquering something. *Conquest* of the country took the invading army many months. 2. Something conquered. Mexico was once a *conquest* of Spain.
con·quest (kon′kwest *or* kong′kwest) *noun, plural* **conquests.**

conscience A feeling about what is right and what is wrong. Your conscience tells you to do right and warns when you are doing something wrong. If you tell a lie, it will trouble your *conscience.*
con·science (kon′shəns) *noun, plural* **consciences.**

conscientious Showing honesty, thought, and care. Your *conscientious* work at school has improved your grades.
con·sci·en·tious (kon′shē en′shəs) *adjective.*

conscious 1. Knowing or realizing; aware. I was *conscious* of someone tapping my shoulder. 2. Able to see and feel things; awake. I was still *conscious* after being hit by the car. 3. Done on purpose. I made a *conscious* effort to stop laughing.
con·scious (kon′shəs) *adjective.*

consecutive Following one after another without a break. The numbers 1, 2, 3, and 4 are *consecutive* numbers.
con·sec·u·tive (kən sek′yə tiv) *adjective.*

consent To give permission; agree. My parents would not *consent* to my going camping by myself. *Verb.*
—Permission. My parents had to give their *consent* before I could go on the field trip with my class. *Noun.*
con·sent (kən sent′) *verb,* **consented, consenting;** *noun, plural* **consents.**

consequence 1. The result of an action. One *consequence* of going to sleep late at night is waking up tired. 2. Significance; importance. The president of this company is someone of *consequence.*
con·se·quence (kon′si kwəns) *noun, plural* **consequences.**

consequently As a result; therefore. I forgot to wear my boots when it rained, and *consequently* I got my shoes wet.
con·se·quent·ly (kon′si kwent′lē) *adverb.*

---

at; āpe; fär; câre; end; mē; it; īce; pîerce; hot; ōld; sông, fôrk; oil; out; up; ūse; rüle; pull; tûrn; chin; sing; shop; thin; this; hw in white; zh in treasure. The symbol ə stands for the unstressed vowel sound in about, taken, pencil, lemon, and circus.

conservation **1.** The act of conserving. **2.** The protection and wise use of the forests, rivers, minerals, and other natural resources of a country.
con·ser·va·tion (kon'sər vā'shən) *noun.*

conservative **1.** Wanting things to be as they used to be or to stay as they are; not usually favoring change or new ideas. **2.** Wanting to avoid risks; using caution. The doctor talked about the *conservative* use of medicines. *Adjective.*
—A person who is conservative. *Noun.*
con·serv·a·tive (kən sûr'və tiv) *adjective; noun, plural* **conservatives.**

conserve To keep and protect from harm, loss, or change. We tried to *conserve* our energy for the hike.
con·serve (kən sûrv') *verb,* **conserved, conserving.**

consider **1.** To think carefully about before deciding. I'm *considering* whether or not to go to college. **2.** To think of as; believe to be. I *consider* that movie the best I've ever seen. I hope you *consider* me your friend. **3.** To show concern and care for; respect. Always try to *consider* other people's feelings. **4.** To keep in mind. My grandparents are very healthy if you *consider* their age.
con·sid·er (kən sid'ər) *verb,* **considered, considering.**

considerable Great in amount or extent. We had *considerable* trouble driving up the icy hill.
con·sid·er·a·ble (kən sid'ər ə bəl) *adjective.*

considerate Thoughtful of other people and their feelings. It's *considerate* to leave some peanuts for the rest of the family.
con·sid·er·ate (kən sid'ər it) *adjective.*

consideration **1.** Thoughtfulness for other people and their feelings. Please show *consideration* for the neighbors by not playing your radio too loud. **2.** Careful thought before deciding about something. After much *consideration,* my cousin decided to study to be a lawyer. **3.** Something thought about before deciding. One *consideration* when moving to a new city is the quality of the schools.
con·sid·er·a·tion (kən sid'ə rā'shən) *noun, plural* **considerations.**

consist To contain; be made up. Bricks *consist* mostly of clay. A year *consists* of twelve months.
con·sist (kən sist') *verb,* **consisted, consisting.**

consistency **1.** Thickness or stiffness of a liquid. This paint has the *consistency* of glue. **2.** A keeping to one way of thinking or acting. Since you change your mind so often, there is no *consistency* to what you say or believe.
con·sist·en·cy (kən sis'tən sē) *noun, plural* **consistencies.**

consistent **1.** Keeping to one way of thinking or acting. My parents are *consistent* in applying rules, so you usually know what they will allow and what they won't. **2.** In agreement. What they said about the accident is not *consistent* with what really happened.
con·sist·ent (kən sis'tənt) *adjective.*

console¹ To comfort or cheer. You try to console a person who is sad or disappointed about something. Both parents tried to *console* the weeping child for the loss of the gerbil.
con·sole (kən sōl') *verb,* **consoled, consoling.**

console² The cabinet of a radio, television set, or phonograph that rests on the floor.
con·sole (kon'sōl) *noun, plural* **consoles.**

consolidate To join together; combine. The two stores *consolidated* to form one large store.
con·sol·i·date (kən sol'i dāt') *verb,* **consolidated, consolidating.**

consonant A letter of the alphabet that is not a vowel. Consonants include the letters *b, d, f, g, m, p, t,* and others.
con·so·nant (kon'sə nənt) *noun, plural* **consonants.**

conspicuous Easily seen; attracting attention. The blue ink left a *conspicuous* stain on the white tablecloth.
con·spic·u·ous (kən spik'ū əs) *adjective.*

conspiracy Secret planning together with others to do something wrong. Several members of a gang were arrested for *conspiracy* to rob a bank.
con·spir·a·cy (kən spir'ə sē) *noun, plural* **conspiracies.**

conspire To plan secretly with others to do something bad or illegal. The outlaws *conspired* to rob the stagecoach.
con·spire (kən spīr') *verb,* **conspired, conspiring.**

constable **1.** A member of the police force in England; policeman or policewoman. **2.** A law officer in a town who is in charge of keeping order.
con·sta·ble (kon'stə bəl *or* kun'stə bəl) *noun, plural* **constables.**

constant **1.** Not changing; continuing. Your *constant* talking will make the teacher angry. **2.** Faithful; loyal. I am lucky to have such *constant* friends.
con·stant (kon'stənt) *adjective.*

constellation A group of stars. A constellation forms a pattern in the sky that looks like a picture. The Big Dipper and the Little Dipper are parts of constellations.
con·stel·la·tion (kon′stə lā′shən) *noun, plural* **constellations.**

Word History

The word **constellation** comes from the old French name for a group of stars. This French word came from two Latin words meaning "together" and "stars."

---

constituent Forming a needed part. Hydrogen and oxygen are the *constituent* parts of water. *Adjective.*
—**1.** A needed part. Wood pulp is an important *constituent* of paper. **2.** A voter in a particular district. The senators were expected to vote for the laws that their *constituents* wanted. *Noun.*
con·stit·u·ent (kən stich′ü ənt) *adjective; noun, plural* **constituents.**

constitute **1.** To make up; form; equal. Four quarts *constitute* a gallon. **2.** To set up; establish. Congress *constitutes* our laws. **3.** To appoint or elect. The club plans to *constitute* you as its president.
con·sti·tute (kon′sti tüt′ *or* kon′sti tūt′) *verb,* **constituted, constituting.**

constitution **1.** The basic principles used to govern a state, country, or organization. The people voted for numerous changes in their state *constitution.* **2. Constitution.** The document containing the law and plan of government of the United States. **3.** The way in which a person or thing is made. The healthy child has a strong *constitution.*
con·sti·tu·tion (kon′sti tü′shən *or* kon′sti tū′shən) *noun, plural* **constitutions.**

constitutional Having to do with a constitution. The United States has a *constitutional* form of government. *Adjective.*
—A walk taken to stay healthy. *Noun.*
con·sti·tu·tion·al (kon′sti tü′shə nəl *or* kon′sti tū′shə nəl) *adjective; noun, plural* **constitutions.**

constrict To make smaller or narrower by pressing together; to squeeze. The dog's tight collar *constricted* its neck.
con·strict (kən strikt′) *verb,* **constricted, constricting.**

constrictor A large snake that can kill small animals by squeezing them in its coils

constrictor

so that they cannot breathe. The python, anaconda, and boa constrictor are different kinds of constrictors.
con·stric·tor (kən strik′tər) *noun, plural* **constrictors.**

construct To make by putting parts together; build. We *constructed* a bike shed in the backyard. The state will *construct* a new highway to the town.
con·struct (kən strukt′) *verb,* **constructed, constructing.**

construction The act of constructing something; building. *Construction* of the new gym began last summer and will be finished next spring.
con·struc·tion (kən struk′shən) *noun, plural* **constructions.**

construction

---

at; āpe; fär; câre; end; mē; it; īce; pîerce; hot; ōld; sông, fôrk; oil; out; up; ūse; rüle; pull; tûrn; chin; sing; shop; thin; this; hw in white; zh in treasure. The symbol ə stands for the unstressed vowel sound in about, taken, pencil, lemon, and circus.

C

161

constructive Serving to make better; helpful. The coach always gives *constructive* criticism so that the players can improve their performance.
con·struc·tive (kən struk′tiv) *adjective.*

consul A person appointed by a government to live in a foreign city. A consul protects his or her country's citizens and business there.
con·sul (kon′səl) *noun, plural* **consuls.**

consult 1. To go to for advice or information. When you are ill, you *consult* a doctor. We *consulted* a map to find out where the town was located. 2. To talk together. My teacher *consulted* with my parents about my grades.
con·sult (kən sult′) *verb,* **consulted, consulting.**

consume 1. To use up or destroy. A car *consumes* gasoline. The fire *consumed* the garage and part of the house. 2. To eat or drink up. I *consumed* two sandwiches at lunch.
con·sume (kən süm′) *verb,* **consumed, consuming.**

consumer A person who buys and uses up things. A person who shops for food in a grocery store is a consumer. People who buy radios, books, cars, and many other things are consumers.
con·sum·er (kən sü′mər) *noun, plural* **consumers.**

consumption The using up of something. The *consumption* of gasoline is usually greater in a big car than in a small car.
con·sump·tion (kən sump′shən) *noun, plural* **consumptions.**

contact A touching or meeting of persons or things. The plastic bowl began to melt when it came in *contact* with the hot stove. I don't want to lose *contact* with my friends when I move away. *Noun.*
—To get in touch with; communicate with; reach. Why don't you try to *contact* your friend by telephone? *Verb.*
con·tact (kon′takt) *noun, plural* **contacts;** *verb,* **contacted, contacting.**

contact lens A thin plastic lens worn on the eyeball to improve vision.

contagious Able to be spread from person to person. Nearly everyone in the class caught chicken pox because it is so *contagious.*
con·ta·gious (kən tā′jəs) *adjective.*

contain 1. To hold. The jar *contains* candy. The shelf *contains* books. 2. To include as a part of; be made up of. This candy *contains* sugar. 3. To keep or hold back. I tried to *contain* my laughter when your chair tipped over backwards.
con·tain (kən tān′) *verb,* **contained, containing.**

container A box, can, or jar that holds something. I bought a *container* of milk at the grocery store.
con·tain·er (kən tā′nər) *noun, plural* **containers.**

contaminate To make dirty; pollute. Garbage thrown in the river will *contaminate* the water.
con·tam·i·nate (kən tam′ə nāt′) *verb,* **contaminated, contaminating.**

contemplate To think about or look at carefully for a long time. The young student sat and *contemplated* the future. We quietly *contemplated* the lovely scenery.
con·tem·plate (kon′təm plāt′) *verb,* **contemplated, contemplating.**

contemporary 1. Belonging to the same time. Julius Caesar and Cleopatra were *contemporary* figures in ancient history. 2. Modern; up-to-date. The furniture in our house is *contemporary. Adjective.*
—A person who belongs to the same time as another person. *Noun.*
con·tem·po·rar·y (kən tem′pə rer′ē) *adjective; noun, plural* **contemporaries.**

contempt 1. A feeling that a person or act is bad, mean, or worth nothing; scorn. I have nothing but *contempt* for people who are cruel to animals. 2. The condition of being scorned. The noisy students were held in *contempt* by their classmates who were trying to study.
con·tempt (kən tempt′) *noun.*

contend 1. To compete. Only three students *contended* for the swimming championship. 2. To argue. I *contended* that we ought to go to the beach instead of seeing a movie. 3. To struggle. The explorers had to *contend* with very cold weather at the North Pole.
con·tend (kən tend′) *verb,* **contended, contending.**

content Happy and satisfied. We are seldom *content* to stay home and play games on rainy days. *Adjective.*
—To make happy; satisfy. A pat on the head and a kind word *contents* my dog. *Verb.*
—A feeling of being happy or satisfied. After eating, the baby went to sleep in complete *content. Noun.*
con·tent (kən tent′) *adjective; verb,* **contented, contenting;** *noun.*

contented Happy and satisfied. A contented person is happy with what he or she is

or has. The *contented* kitten purred and rubbed against my leg.
con·tent·ed (kən ten′tid) *adjective.*

contents **1.** What something holds. When the bag broke, its *contents* fell all over the floor. **2.** What is written or spoken about. The *contents* of the letter upset me.
con·tents (kon′tents) *plural noun.*

contest **1.** A game or race that people try to win; competition. Our team won the swimming *contest*. The school held a *contest* for the best essay on safety. **2.** A struggle; fight. The *contest* between the two armies for the town lasted into the night. *Noun.*
—**1.** To struggle or fight for. The enemy troops *contested* the fort. **2.** To argue against. The loser of the race *contested* the judge's decision. *Verb.*
con·test (kon′test *for noun;* kən test′ *for verb*) *noun, plural* **contests;** *verb,* **contested, contesting.**

contestant A person who takes part in a contest. Were you a *contestant* in the swimming meet? The *contestant* on the television quiz show won a trip to Hawaii.
con·test·ant (kən tes′tənt) *noun, plural* **contestants.**

context The words that come before and after a word or phrase. The context influences the meaning of a word or phrase. It was clear from the *context* that they were only joking when they said that.
con·text (kon′tekst) *noun, plural* **contexts.**

continent One of the seven large land areas on the earth. The continents are Asia, Africa, North America, South America, Europe, Antarctica, and Australia.
con·ti·nent (kont′ə nənt) *noun, plural* **continents.**

continual Happening again and again. I had to make *continual* visits to the doctor until my leg healed.
con·tin·u·al (kən tin′ū əl) *adjective.*

continue **1.** To keep on happening, being, or doing; go on without stopping. The rain *continued* for two days. *Continue* reading until you reach the end of the page. **2.** To go on or do after stopping. We will *continue* the meeting after lunch.
con·tin·ue (kən tin′ū) *verb,* **continued, continuing.**

continuous Going on without stopping; unbroken. The river has a *continuous* flow of water.
con·tin·u·ous (kən tin′ū əs) *adjective.*

contour The outline or shape of something. The astronauts could see the curved *contour* of the earth.
con·tour (kon′tùr) *noun, plural* **contours.**

contract **1.** To make or become shorter or smaller. A turtle can *contract* its neck to draw its head into its shell. The words "you had" *contract* to form "you'd." **2.** To get or acquire. I *contracted* the flu. **3.** To make an agreement. The worker *contracted* to paint the house for $600. *Verb.*
—An agreement. The singer signed a *contract* to make records for the record company. *Noun.*
con·tract (kən trakt′ *for verb, definitions 1 and 2;* kən trakt′ *or* kon′trakt *for verb, definition 3;* kon′trakt *for noun*) *verb,* **contracted, contracting;** *noun, plural* **contracts.**

contraction **1.** The act of contracting or the state of being contracted. The *contraction* of the heart forces blood into the arteries. **2.** A shortened form. "Wouldn't" is the contraction of "would not."
con·trac·tion (kən trak′shən) *noun, plural* **contractions.**

Language Note

Contractions are used very commonly in spoken English. Here are some that you are likely to hear and use often: I'm (I am), you're (you are), she's (she is *or* she has), he'll (he will), they'd (they would *or* they had), aren't (are not), don't (do not), who'll (who will).

---

contradict To say the opposite of; disagree with. The newspaper *contradicted* what had been said on the radio about the accident.
con·tra·dict (kon′trə dikt′) *verb,* **contradicted, contradicting.**

contradictory **1.** Contradicting; opposing; inconsistent. There are two *contradictory* versions of what happened. **2.** Likely to contradict or to have a different opinion. My *contradictory* cousin often disagrees with me.
con·tra·dic·to·ry (kon′trə dik′tə rē) *adjective.*

---

at; āpe; fär; câre; end; mē; it; īce; pîerce; hot; ōld; sông, fôrk; oil; out; up; ūse; rüle; pùll; tûrn; chin; sing; shop; thin; <u>th</u>is; hw in white; zh in treasure. The symbol ə stands for the unstressed vowel sound in about, taken, pencil, lemon, and circus.

contralto   **1.** The lowest female singing voice.   **2.** A singer who has such a voice.
con·tral·to (kən tral′tō) *noun, plural* **contraltos.**

contrary   **1.** Entirely different; opposite. My cousin's ideas about sports and music are *contrary* to my own.   **2.** Liking to argue and oppose. That *contrary* child never agrees with what other people say. *Adjective.*
—Something completely different; the opposite. We thought it would rain, but the *contrary* happened; it was sunny. *Noun.*
• **on the contrary.**   Just the opposite of what has been said. You are not a clumsy dancer; *on the contrary,* you are very graceful.
con·trar·y (kon′trer ē *for adjective, definition 1 and noun;* kon′trer ē *or* kən trâr′ē *for adjective, definition 2*) *adjective; noun.*

contrast   To show differences that are based on comparing. The teacher *contrasted* life in a big city and life on a farm. Red and white *contrast* with each other. *Verb.*
—**1.** A difference. There is a great *contrast* between the weather at the North Pole and the weather in the tropics.   **2.** A person or thing that is compared to another and shows differences. Our new car is quite a *contrast* to our old car. *Noun.*
con·trast (kən trast′ *for verb;* kon′trast *for noun*) *verb,* **contrasted, contrasting;** *noun, plural* **contrasts.**

contrast in size

contribute   **1.** To give. The citizens of the town *contributed* food and clothing to the family whose house had burned down. Do you *contribute* to a charity?   **2.** To write for a newspaper or magazine. My aunt and uncle *contribute* articles to their town's newspaper.
• **to contribute to.**   To help bring about.

A lack of rain *contributed to* the poor harvest of potatoes.
con·trib·ute (kən trib′ūt) *verb,* **contributed, contributing.**

contribution   **1.** The act of contributing; giving something. The wealthy family's *contribution* of money will help build a new hospital.   **2.** Something contributed. We gave *contributions* to help hungry children in other countries.
con·tri·bu·tion (kon′trə bū′shən) *noun, plural* **contributions.**

contrive   To plan or design cleverly. They are *contriving* a surprise party. The inventor *contrived* a car that would run on sunlight.
con·trive (kən trīv′) *verb,* **contrived, contriving.**

control   **1.** Power, authority, or regulation. The dictator had complete *control* over the country. The car went out of *control.*   **2.** The power or ability to hold back or hold in. The police lost *control* of the mob. People do not always keep their anger under *control.*   **3.** Something that is used to operate, regulate, or guide a machine or other device. Where is the volume *control* on this television set? The pilot operates the *controls* of an airplane. *Noun.*
—**1.** To command or regulate by using power or authority. Our dog does exactly what it wants; I can't *control* it. The federal government *controls* the handling and delivery of mail.   **2.** To adjust or regulate. This knob *controls* the loudness on my radio.   **3.** To hold back or hold in. The dam could not *control* the flooded river. I always try to *control* my temper. *Verb.*
con·trol (kən trōl′) *noun, plural* **controls;** *verb,* **controlled, controlling.**

control tower   A tower at an airport. The movement of airplanes landing and taking off is directed from the control tower.

controversial   Causing an argument. Politics is often a *controversial* subject.
con·tro·ver·sial (kon′trə vûr′shəl) *adjective.*

controversy   A disagreement; dispute. The new tax caused much *controversy.*
con·tro·ver·sy (kon′trə vûr′sē) *noun, plural* **controversies.**

convalescent   **1.** Recovering from illness. *Convalescent* patients often sleep a lot.   **2.** For or relating to the process of recovering from illness. In the *convalescent* room, patients can sit in the sun. *Adjective.*
—A person who is recovering from illness. *Noun.*
con·va·les·cent (kon′və les′ənt) *adjective; noun, plural* **convalescents.**

convection The transfer of heat through a gas or a liquid by currents. Fireplaces heat a room by convection through the air.
con·vec·tion (kən vek′shən) *noun.*

Word History

Convection comes from a Latin word meaning "to carry along with." A convection oven carries its heat along with the circulating air inside.

convene To come or bring together for a meeting; assemble. Congress will *convene* again after the election.
con·vene (kən vēn′) *verb,* **convened, convening.**

convenience 1. Ease and comfort. I like the *convenience* of canned foods. 2. Something that gives ease or comfort. A washing machine is a modern *convenience.*
con·ven·ience (kən vēn′yəns) *noun, plural* **conveniences.**

convenient Giving ease and comfort; useful; handy. A dishwasher is very *convenient* if you have many dishes to wash.
con·ven·ient (kən vēn′yənt) *adjective.*

convent 1. A group of nuns living together. 2. A building where a group of nuns live.
con·vent (kon′vent) *noun, plural* **convents.**

convention 1. A formal meeting for some special purpose. Every four years the political parties hold *conventions* to choose candidates for president. 2. An accepted way of acting or doing something; custom. Shaking hands when you are introduced to someone is a *convention.*
con·ven·tion (kən ven′shən) *noun, plural* **conventions.**

Word History

Convention comes from two Latin words meaning "to come" and "together."

conventional Following customs. Saying "hello" is a *conventional* greeting.
con·ven·tion·al (kən ven′shə nəl) *adjective.*

conversation Talk between two or more persons. I had a long *conversation* with my parents about my plans for the summer.
con·ver·sa·tion (kon′vər sā′shən) *noun, plural* **conversations.**

converse To talk together. My friend and I often *conversed* by telephone.
con·verse (kən vûrs′) *verb,* **conversed, conversing.**

conversion 1. The changing of something. The *conversion* of our garage into a den took six months. 2. The changing of a person's belief, especially religious belief.
con·ver·sion (kən vûr′zhən) *noun, plural* **conversions.**

convert 1. To change something into something different. The new owner *converted* the large house into an inn. 2. To cause a person to change a belief. The political party tried to *convert* the voters to its beliefs. *Verb.*
—A person who has changed his or her beliefs. *Noun.*
con·vert (kən vûrt′ *for verb;* kon′vûrt *for noun) verb,* **converted, converting;** *noun, plural* **converts.**

convertible Able to be changed. The *convertible* sofa can be made into a bed. *Adjective.*
—An automobile with a roof that can be folded back or removed. It was sunny, so we drove the *convertible* with the top down. *Noun.*
con·vert·i·ble (kən vûr′tə bəl) *adjective; noun, plural* **convertibles.**

convex Curving outward. The outside of a bowl is convex. Look up **concave** for a picture of something that is convex.
con·vex (kon veks′ *or* kon′veks) *adjective.*

convey 1. To take from one place to another; carry. These pipes *convey* water from the well to the house. 2. To make known; express. Our parents *conveyed* the excitement of their trip in letters they wrote to us.
con·vey (kən vā′) *verb,* **conveyed, conveying.**

conveyor belt A long, moving belt that is used to carry objects from one place to another. Conveyor belts are often used in factories.
con·vey·or belt (kən vā′ər).

convict To declare or prove that a person is guilty of a crime. The jury *convicted* the gang members of robbery. *Verb.*
—A person who is serving a prison sentence.

at; āpe; fär; câre; end; mē; it; īce; pîerce; hot; ōld; sông, fôrk; oil; out; up; ūse; rüle; pull; tûrn; chin; sing; shop; thin; this; hw in white; zh in treasure. The symbol ə stands for the unstressed vowel sound in about, taken, pencil, lemon, and circus.

165

The police were looking for two *convicts* who had escaped from a nearby prison. *Noun.*
con·vict (kən vikt′ *for verb;* kon′vikt *for noun*) *verb,* **convicted, convicting;** *noun, plural* **convicts.**

conviction **1.** The act of declaring or proving that a person is guilty of a crime. The new evidence led to the *conviction* of the thief. **2.** The state of being found guilty of a crime. The criminals' *conviction* for robbery meant that they would probably be sent to prison. **3.** A strong belief. My teacher has the *conviction* that most people are good at heart.
con·vic·tion (kən vik′shən) *noun, plural* **convictions.**

convince To cause a person to believe or do something; persuade. I *convinced* my parents to let me see the scary movie.
con·vince (kən vins′) *verb,* **convinced, convincing.**

Word History

The word **convince** comes from a Latin word meaning "to conquer" or "to overcome." When you convince someone of something, you overcome the person's doubts or objections.

convulse To shake or disturb violently. The explosion *convulsed* the building. The audience was *convulsed* with laughter by the comedian's jokes.
con·vulse (kən vuls′) *verb,* **convulsed, convulsing.**

convulsion **1.** A violent, involuntary contraction of the muscles; spasm. The crash victim's injuries were so severe that they caused *convulsions.* **2.** A fit of laughter. The joke caused a *convulsion* in the audience.
con·vul·sion (kən vul′shən) *noun, plural* **convulsions.**

cook **1.** To make food ready for eating by using heat. You can cook food by broiling, roasting, baking, boiling, or frying it. **2.** To be cooked. The peas will *cook* quickly. *Verb.*
—A person who cooks. *Noun.*
cook (kůk) *verb,* **cooked, cooking;** *noun, plural* **cooks.**

cookbook A book of recipes and other information about food. I looked in a *cookbook* to find out how to roast a turkey.
cook·book (kůk′bůk′) *noun, plural* **cookbooks.**

cookie A small, flat, sweet cake.
cook·ie (kůk′ē) *noun, plural* **cookies.**

cookout An outdoor gathering at which food is cooked and eaten. We offered to have the *cookout* in our yard because we have a large grill.
cook·out (kůk′out′) *noun, plural* **cookouts.**

cool **1.** Somewhat cold. A *cool* breeze feels good on a hot summer day. **2.** Protecting or giving relief from heat. The *cool* shirt is made of thin cloth. **3.** Not excited; calm. Everyone kept *cool* and got out of the burning building safely. **4.** Not warm or friendly. I'm not surprised that they were very *cool* to you after you insulted them. *Adjective.*
—Something cool. We took a walk in the *cool* of the early morning. *Noun.*
—To make or become cool. You can *cool* your soup by blowing on it. *Verb.*
cool (kůl) *adjective,* **cooler, coolest;** *noun; verb,* **cooled, cooling.**

coop A cage or pen for chickens, rabbits, or other small animals. Our neighbor keeps rabbits in a *coop* behind the house. *Noun.*
• **to coop up.** To put or keep in a coop or other small space. We *cooped* the dog *up* in the kitchen until the guests left. I feel *cooped up* having to study in this small room.
coop (küp) *noun, plural* **coops;** *verb,* **cooped, cooping.**

cooperate To work together. The three classes *cooperated* in planning a picnic at the end of the school year.
co·op·er·ate (kō op′ə rāt′) *verb,* **cooperated, cooperating.**

cooperation The act of working together. Keeping the streets of our town clean takes the *cooperation* of all the people who live here.
co·op·er·a·tion (kō op′ə rā′shən) *noun.*

coordinate To work or cause to work well together; bring or put into proper working order. A good athlete's muscles *coordinate* well. In this dance, it is important to *coordinate* the movements of the feet to the beat of the music.
co·or·di·nate (kō ôr′də nāt′) *verb,* **coordinated, coordinating.**

coordination **1.** The act of coordinating. Who is responsible for *coordination* of the class picnic? **2.** The ability of parts of the body to work together well. Athletes need good *coordination* to perform their best.
co·or·di·na·tion (kō ôr′də nā′shən) *noun.*

cope To handle with success. Some students had trouble *coping* with the extra homework.
cope (kōp) *verb,* **coped, coping.**

copper **1.** A reddish metal. Copper is soft and easy to shape. It is also an excellent conductor of heat and electricity. Copper is a chemical element. **2.** A reddish brown color. *Noun.*
—**1.** Made of copper. This frying pan has a *copper* bottom. **2.** Having the color copper; reddish brown. Our dog has a *copper* coat. *Adjective.*
cop·per (kop′ər) *noun; adjective.*

Word History

The word **copper** comes from a Latin word meaning "from Cyprus." Cyprus is an island where many ancient peoples mined copper ore.

copperhead A poisonous snake found in the eastern part of the United States. It has a copper-colored head and a light brown body with dark brown markings.
cop·per·head (kop′ər hed′) *noun, plural* **copperheads.**

copperhead

copy **1.** Something that looks exactly like something else; imitation; duplicate. **2.** One of a number of books, magazines, or newspapers printed at the same time. The store has only one *copy* of the new book on football. *Noun.*
—**1.** To make a copy of. *Copy* your book report neatly. **2.** To make or do something that is exactly like something else. The students in the ballet class *copied* the teacher's steps. *Verb.*
cop·y (kop′ē) *noun, plural* **copies;** *verb,* **copied, copying.**

coral **1.** A hard substance that is like stone found in tropical seas. Coral is made up of the skeletons of tiny sea animals. **2.** The tiny sea animal that makes coral. **3.** A pinkish red color. *Noun.*
—**1.** Made of coral. A *coral* reef surrounds the island. **2.** Having the color coral; pink-ish red. I wore a *coral* sweater. *Adjective.*
cor·al (kôr′əl) *noun, plural* **corals;** *adjective.*

coral snake A poisonous American snake that has a narrow head and red, black, and yellow bands on its body.

cord **1.** A string or thin rope. Cord is made of several strands twisted or woven together. Tie the books together with *cord.* **2.** A covered wire that is used to connect a toaster, lamp, or other appliance to an electrical outlet. **3.** A structure in the body that is like a cord. The spinal *cord* extends from the brain down through the backbone. **4.** An amount of cut wood equaling 128 cubic feet. A cord is a pile of wood 4 feet wide, 4 feet high, and 8 feet long. ⏃ Another word that sounds like this is **chord.**
cord (kôrd) *noun, plural* **cords.**

cordial Warm and friendly; hearty. The mayor gave us a *cordial* greeting when we arrived.
cor·dial (kôr′jəl) *adjective.*

corduroy **1.** A cloth with rows of ribs. It is usually made of cotton. **2. corduroys.** Trousers made from corduroy.
cor·du·roy (kôr′də roi′) *noun, plural* **corduroys.**

core **1.** The hard part in the middle of apples, pears, and certain other fruits. The seeds are in the core. **2.** The central part of the earth. **3.** The central, most important, or deepest part of anything. The *core* of the teacher's talk was that the class needed to study more. *Noun.*
—To remove the core of. We *cored* the apples before baking them. *Verb.* ⏃ Another word that sounds like this is **corps.**
core (kôr) *noun, plural* **cores;** *verb,* **cored, coring.**

cork **1.** The light, thick outer bark of a kind of oak tree. Cork is used for such things as bottle stoppers, insulation, and floats for rafts. **2.** A stopper for a bottle or other container. Corks can be made of cork, rubber, plastic, or glass. *Noun.*
—To stop with a cork. *Cork* the bottle and put it in the cupboard. *Verb.*
cork (kôrk) *noun, plural* **corks;** *verb,* **corked, corking.**

at; āpe; fär; câre; end; mē; it; īce; pîerce; hot; ōld; sông, fôrk; oil; out; up; ūse; rüle; půll; tûrn; chin; sing; shop; thin; ᵗʰis; hw in white; zh in treasure. The symbol ə stands for the unstressed vowel sound in about, taken, pencil, lemon, and circus.

corkscrew A device for taking corks out of bottles. Corkscrews usually have a pointed, metal spiral mounted in a handle. *Noun.*
—Shaped like a corkscrew; spiral. *Adjective.*
cork·screw (kôrk′skrü′) *noun, plural* **corkscrews;** *adjective.*

corn **1.** A grain that grows in rows on the ears of a tall plant. Corn is used for food and grows on a plant that is also called corn. Corn is also called **Indian corn.**
corn (kôrn) *noun.*

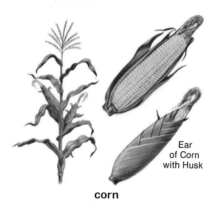

Ear of Corn with Husk

corn

corncob The long, woody core of an ear of corn. The corn kernels grow in rows on the corncob.
corn·cob (kôrn′kob′) *noun, plural* **corncobs.**

cornea The clear outer covering of the front of the eyeball. The cornea covers the iris and the pupil.
cor·ne·a (kôr′nē ə) *noun, plural* **corneas.**

corner **1.** The place or point where two lines or surfaces come together. I hit my leg on the sharp *corner* of the table. The television set is in the *corner* of the room. **2.** The place where two streets come together. There is a mailbox on the *corner.* **3.** A region or place, usually a distant one. The company has offices in many *corners* of the world. **4.** A place or position that is dangerous or difficult. The sudden thunderstorm put the hikers in a *corner. Noun.*
—At or near a corner. My friend works at the *corner* drugstore after school. *Adjective.*
—To force or drive into a dangerous or difficult place or position. The dog *cornered* the cat under the bed. *Verb.*
cor·ner (kôr′nər) *noun, plural* **corners;** *adjective; verb,* **cornered, cornering.**

cornet A brass musical instrument that is like a trumpet.
cor·net (kôr net′) *noun, plural* **cornets.**

cornmeal Corn that is coarsely ground.
corn·meal (kôrn′mēl′) *noun.*

coronation The ceremony of crowning a king or queen.
cor·o·na·tion (kôr′ə nā′shən) *noun, plural* **coronations.**

corporal **1.** A rank in the army, air force, and marines. It is below the rank of sergeant. **2.** Someone who holds this rank.
cor·po·ral (kôr′pər əl *or* kôr′prəl) *noun, plural* **corporals.**

corporation An organization made up of a number of people who are allowed by law to act as a single person. A corporation has the right to buy and sell property, borrow and lend money, and to enter into contracts.
cor·po·ra·tion (kôr′pə rā′shən) *noun, plural* **corporations.**

corps **1.** A group of soldiers trained for special service. The lieutenant was a member of the medical *corps.* **2.** A group of persons who act or work together. That restaurant has a large *corps* of waiters and waitresses.
▲ Another word that sounds like this is **core.**
corps (kôr) *noun, plural* **corps.**

corpse A dead human body.
corpse (kôrps) *noun, plural* **corpses.**

corpuscle A small cell that is part of the blood. Red and white blood cells are *corpuscles.*
cor·pus·cle (kôr′pus′əl) *noun, plural* **corpuscles.**

corral An area with a fence around it. A corral is used to keep cattle, horses, and other animals from straying. *Noun.*
—**1.** To drive or put into a corral. The cowhands *corralled* the herd of horses. **2.** To get control or hold of by surrounding or gathering. We *corralled* all the chicks in the corner of the barn and put them back in their pen. *Verb.*
cor·ral (kə ral′) *noun, plural* **corrals;** *verb,* **corralled, corralling.**

corral

C

correct **1.** Not having any mistakes; accurate. This is the *correct* answer to the arithmetic problem. **2.** In agreement with an accepted or approved way or example; proper. It is *correct* to thank people for gifts that they give you. *Adjective.*
—**1.** To mark the mistakes in; change to make right. The teacher *corrected* our spelling tests. **2.** To make agree with some standard. The doctor *corrected* my poor eyesight with glasses. **3.** To punish or scold in order to improve. The parents *corrected* their child for behaving badly. *Verb.*
cor·rect (kə rekt′) *adjective; verb,*
corrected, correcting.

correction **1.** The act of correcting. *Correction* of the trouble in the car's engine took the mechanic several hours. **2.** A change that is made to correct an error. I kept a list of the *corrections* I made in the report. **3.** The act of punishing in order to improve. Criminals are sent to prison for *correction.*
cor·rec·tion (kə rek′shən) *noun, plural*
corrections.

correspond **1.** To agree; match. Your answer to the question does not *correspond* with mine. **2.** To be similar. The gills of a fish *correspond* to the lungs of a human being. **3.** To write letters to one another. My friends *corresponded* with me when I was away at summer camp.
cor·re·spond (kôr′ə spond′) *verb,*
corresponded, corresponding.

correspondence **1.** Agreement or similarity. The police found a close *correspondence* between the stories of the two witnesses. **2.** The writing of letters to one another. We kept up a *correspondence* for many years after they moved. **3.** Letters sent or received. I enjoy reading the *correspondence* from my Canadian friends.
cor·re·spon·dence (kôr′ə spon′dəns)
noun.

correspondent **1.** A person who writes letters to someone and receives letters in return. **2.** A person who reports news. The newspaper *correspondent* in France has been writing stories about the elections there.
cor·re·spon·dent (kôr′ə spon′dənt) *noun,*
plural **correspondents.**

corridor A long hallway or passageway in a building. A corridor often has rooms opening onto it.
cor·ri·dor (kôr′i dər) *noun, plural*
corridors.

corrode To eat or wear away, little by little. Rust *corroded* the iron gate.
cor·rode (kə rōd′) *verb,* **corroded,**
corroding.

corrosion **1.** The act or condition of being eaten away or worn away. A leaking battery caused the *corrosion* of my flashlight. **2.** Something produced by corrosion.
cor·ro·sion (kə rō′zhən) *noun.*

corrugated Shaped into parallel ridges or folds; wrinkled. *Corrugated* cardboard is used to make boxes and to pack furniture.
cor·ru·gat·ed (kôr′i gā′tid) *adjective.*

corrupt **1.** Able to be bribed; crooked; dishonest. The *corrupt* mayor was not reelected. **2.** Wicked. *Adjective.*
—**1.** To cause to be dishonest. That judge cannot be *corrupted.* **2.** To make wicked. Bad friends may *corrupt* a good person. *Verb.*
cor·rupt (kə rupt′) *adjective; verb,*
corrupted, corrupting.

corsage A flower or small bunch of flowers worn by a woman at the shoulder or waist, or on the wrist.
cor·sage (kôr säzh′) *noun, plural*
corsages.

cosmetic A preparation used on the face, hair, or another part of the body. Lipstick and powder are cosmetics.
cos·met·ic (koz met′ik) *noun, plural*
cosmetics.

cosmic Of or relating to the whole universe.
cos·mic (koz′mik) *adjective.*

cosmonaut An astronaut from the Soviet Union. Soviet *cosmonauts* have worked together with American astronauts on space missions.
cos·mo·naut (koz′mə nôt′) *noun, plural*
cosmonauts.

Word History

The word **cosmonaut** comes from the Russian word meaning "astronaut." The Russian word comes from two Greek words meaning "universe" and "sailor." A *cosmonaut* is thought of as sailing through the universe.

cosmos The universe considered as an ordered and harmonious system.
cos·mos (koz′məs) *noun, plural* **cosmos**
or **cosmoses.**

at; āpe; fär; câre; end; mē; it; īce; pîerce; hot; ōld;
sông, fôrk; oil; out; up; ūse; rüle; pùll; tûrn; chin;
sing; shop; thin; this; hw in white; zh in treasure.
The symbol ə stands for the unstressed vowel
sound in about, taken, pencil, lemon, and circus.

cost **1.** An amount of money paid or charged for something; price. The *cost* of that book is five dollars. **2.** Something lost or sacrificed. The war was won at the *cost* of many lives. *Noun.*
—**1.** To be gotten or bought at the price of. The bicycle *cost* too much, so my parents didn't buy it. **2.** To cause the loss of. The accident almost *cost* the dog its life. *Verb.*
cost (kôst) *noun, plural* **costs;** *verb,* **cost, costing.**

Costa Rica A country in Central America.
Cos·ta Ri·ca (kos′tə rē′kə).

costly Costing much. Collecting rare stamps can be a *costly* hobby. The loss of many lives made the battle a *costly* one.
cost·ly (kôst′lē) *adjective,* **costlier, costliest.**

costume **1.** Clothes worn in order to look like someone or something else. I wore a ghost *costume* to the Halloween party. **2.** Clothes worn at a particular time or place or by particular people. My cousins collect dolls dressed in the national *costumes* of different countries.
cos·tume (kos′tüm *or* kos′tūm) *noun, plural* **costumes.**

costumes

cot A narrow bed. Cots usually have a frame that can be folded and put away.
cot (kot) *noun, plural* **cots.**

cottage A small house. We have a summer *cottage* at the beach.
cot·tage (kot′ij) *noun, plural* **cottages.**

cottage cheese A soft, white cheese made from sour skim milk.

cotton **1.** A fluffy mass of soft white or gray fibers that grow in the large seed pod of a plant. Cotton is used to make thread or cloth. **2.** Thread or cloth made from fibers of cotton. *Noun.*
—Made of cotton. Some people prefer *cotton* shirts. *Adjective.*
cot·ton (kot′ən) *noun; adjective.*

cotton plant

cottonmouth A poisonous snake that lives in swamps in the southeastern part of the United States; water moccasin.
cot·ton·mouth (kot′ən mouth′) *noun, plural* **cottonmouths.**

cottontail An American rabbit that has brown or grayish fur and a short, fluffy, white tail.
cot·ton·tail (kot′ən tāl′) *noun, plural* **cottontails.**

couch A piece of furniture that two or more people can sit on at the same time. Couches often have soft cushions.
couch (kouch) *noun, plural* **couches.**

cougar A member of the cat family that has a small head, long legs, and a slender, strong body. Cougars live in the mountains of North and South America. A cougar is also called a **puma** and a **mountain lion.**
cou·gar (kü′gər) *noun, plural* **cougars.**

cough **1.** To force air from the lungs with a sudden, sharp sound. I stayed home today because I had a cold and *coughed* all the time. **2.** To force out of the body by coughing. The baby *coughed* up a piece of cookie. **3.** To make a noise like coughing. The car *coughed* when the driver started it. *Verb.*
—**1.** The sharp sound that is made when air is suddenly forced from the lungs. **2.** A sickness that causes a person to cough. *Noun.*
cough (kôf) *verb,* **coughed, coughing;** *noun, plural* **coughs.**

could An auxiliary verb that is used in the following ways: **1.** To express the past tense of **can**[1]. I asked my parents if I *could* leave the table. **2.** To say that something is possible. It *could* rain today, but we're not sure. **3.** To express ability. Many countries *could* do more to reduce pollution. **4.** To make polite requests. *Could* you help us move this desk, please? **5.** To ask permission. *Could* I borrow your spelling book? **6.** To offer a suggestion. You *could* start over and do it a different way.
could (kùd) *verb.*

couldn't Shortened form of "could not." The little child *couldn't* reach the high shelf.
could·n't (kŭd'ənt) *contraction.*

council A group of people called together to discuss a problem or other matter. A council can give advice or make a decision. A group of people elected to make laws for or help run a city or town is called a city council or a town council. ▲ Another word that sounds like this is **counsel.**
coun·cil (koun'səl) *noun, plural* **councils.**

counsel 1. Ideas or suggestions about what to do; advice. A wise friend can often give good *counsel.* 2. A lawyer or lawyers who give legal advice. The *counsel* for the family advised them to buy more insurance. *Noun.*
—To give ideas or suggestions to; advise. My folks *counseled* me to work harder. *Verb.*
▲ Another word that sounds like this is **council.**
coun·sel (koun'səl) *noun, plural* **counsels;** *verb,* **counseled, counseling.**

counselor 1. A person who helps or gives advice. Our *counselor* at camp taught us how to paddle a canoe. 2. A lawyer.
coun·se·lor (koun'sə lər) *noun, plural* **counselors.**

count¹ 1. To find out how many of something there are; add up. *Count* the number of books on the shelf. 2. To say or write down numbers in order. Can you *count* up to 100 really fast? 3. To include or be included when things are added up. There were forty people in the bus, *counting* the driver. 4. To have importance; be worth something. Try to make every day of vacation *count.* 5. To believe to be; think of as. Our teachers *count* us as one of their best classes. 6. To depend; rely. Can I *count* on you if I need help? *Verb.*
—1. The act of counting. We made a *count* of the cows in the barn. 2. The number of things there are when you add them up; total. *Noun.*
count (kount) *verb,* **counted, counting;** *noun, plural* **counts.**

count² A European nobleman.
count (kount) *noun, plural* **counts.**

countdown The counting of time backward from a certain time to zero. This tells how much time is left before the start of something, such as the launch of a spacecraft.
count·down (kount'doun') *noun, plural* **countdowns.**

counter¹ 1. A long table. Stores have counters at which things are sold. Some restaurants have counters on which meals are served. 2. Something used for counting. Some games have round, colored disks called counters to help keep score.
count·er (koun'tər) *noun, plural* **counters.**

counter² Opposite. The student acted *counter* to instructions and wrote in pencil instead of ink. *Adverb.*
—Opposite. Your idea is *counter* to my idea. *Adjective.*
—To go against; oppose. My friends *countered* my idea for a picnic and said they wanted to go to the movies instead. *Verb.*
coun·ter (koun'tər) *adverb; adjective; verb,* **countered, countering.**

counter– A *prefix* that means: 1. Against; opposing; opposite. *Counterclockwise* means in a direction opposite to the direction in which the hands of a clock move. 2. Similar; matching. *Counterpart* means something that matches another thing.

counterclockwise In the direction opposite to the direction in which the hands of a clock move. Turn a screw *counterclockwise* to take it out.
coun·ter·clock·wise (koun'tər klok'wīz') *adverb; adjective.*

counterfeit To make a copy or imitation of something in order to cheat or fool people. It is a serious crime to *counterfeit* money. *Verb.*
—A copy or imitation made in order to cheat or fool someone. The twenty-dollar bill I found was a *counterfeit. Noun.*
—Not genuine. It is a crime to make *counterfeit* money. The angry driver's smile seemed *counterfeit. Adjective.*
coun·ter·feit (koun'tər fit') *verb,* **counterfeited, counterfeiting;** *noun, plural* **counterfeits;** *adjective.*

counterpart A person or thing that is very much like or equal to another. The United States Congress is the *counterpart* of the Canadian Parliament.
coun·ter·part (koun'tər pärt') *noun, plural* **counterparts.**

at; āpe; fär; câre; end; mē; it; īce; pîerce; hot; ōld; sông, fôrk; oil; out; up; ūse; rüle; pŭll; tûrn; chin; sing; shop; thin; this; hw in white; zh in treasure. The symbol ə stands for the unstressed vowel sound in about, taken, pencil, lemon, and circus.

C

countess A European noblewoman, usually the wife of a count.
count·ess (koun'tis) *noun, plural* **countesses.**

countless Too many to be counted. There are *countless* grains of sand in the desert.
count·less (kount'lis) *adjective.*

country **1.** Any area of land; region. We have a summer cabin in mountain *country.* **2.** An area of land that has boundaries and has a government that is shared by all the people; nation. The United States and Canada are *countries.* **3.** The land that a person was born in or is a citizen of. France was their *country* until the war forced them to leave. **4.** The people of a nation. The whole *country* feared the cruel ruler. **5.** The land outside of cities and towns. We decided to go for a drive in the *country. Noun.*
—Having to do with land outside of cities or towns; rural. We drove along narrow *country* roads. *Adjective.*
coun·try (kun'trē) *noun, plural* **countries;** *adjective.*

countryman **1.** A person who was born in or is a citizen of one's own country. **2.** A person who lives in the country.
coun·try·man (kun'trē mən) *noun, plural* **countrymen** (kun'trē mən).

countryside The land outside cities and towns.
coun·try·side (kun'trē sīd') *noun.*

countryside

countrywoman **1.** A woman who was born in or is a citizen of one's own country. **2.** A woman who lives in the country.
coun·try·wo·man (kun'trē wùm'ən) *noun, plural* **countrywomen** (kun'trē wim'ən).

county **1.** One of the sections into which a state or country is divided. Counties have their own local government. **2.** The people living in a county.
coun·ty (koun'tē) *noun, plural* **counties.**

couple **1.** Two things that are the same or go together in some way; pair. **2.** A man and woman who are together. My father and mother are a happy *couple. Noun.*
—To join together. They *coupled* the trailer to the car. *Verb.*
cou·ple (kup'əl) *noun, plural* **couples;** *verb,* **coupled, coupling.**

coupon A ticket or part of a ticket. A coupon can be exchanged for a gift or for a discount on the price of something. The *coupon* in the box of cereal was worth ten cents toward the price of the next box.
cou·pon (kü'pon *or* kū'pon) *noun, plural* **coupons.**

courage The strength to overcome fear and face danger; bravery. The teenager showed great *courage* in swimming out to save the drowning child.
cour·age (kûr'ij) *noun.*

courageous Having the strength to overcome fear and face something that is dangerous, very hard, or painful. The *courageous* firefighter went into the burning building to lead the people out.
cou·ra·geous (kə rā'jəs) *adjective.*

course **1.** A moving onward from one point to the next; progress. The bush grew four inches in the *course* of a year. **2.** A way; route; track. The airplane flew off its *course.* The river had a winding *course.* **3.** A way of acting. The most sensible *course* would be to go home now before it starts to rain. **4.** An area used for certain sports or games. The race will be held on the *course* in our town. **5.** A series of classes or lessons. I am taking a *course* in cooking. **6.** A part of a meal that is served at one time. Our first *course* was soup and the second *course* was salad. *Noun.*
—To move very quickly; run; flow. The stream *coursed* down the steep hill. *Verb.*
▲ Another word that sounds like this is **coarse.**
• **of course. 1.** Certainly; surely. *Of course* I'll help you with your work. **2.** As is or was expected; naturally. The rain began to fall, and, *of course,* we went inside to keep dry.
course (kôrs) *noun, plural* **courses;** *verb,* **coursed, coursing.**

court **1.** An open space that is surrounded by walls or buildings; courtyard. **2.** A short street. **3.** A space or area that is marked off for certain games. The gym has a basketball *court.* **4.** The place where a king or queen and his or her attendants live. **5.** The family, friends, and advisers of a king or queen. The entire *court* attended the royal ball.

C

6. An official gathering headed by a judge or judges. A court hears legal cases and decides them. The *court* heard the witness describe the accident. **7.** A room or building where trials are held or where other matters are decided by law. *Noun.*
—**1.** To try to win the favor or love of a person. In the fairy tale, the young woman was *courted* by a prince. The politician *courted* the voters throughout the state. **2.** To act in a way that invites; tempt. Driving a car too fast *courts* disaster. *Verb.*
> **court** (kôrt) *noun, plural* **courts;** *verb,* **courted, courting.**

courteous Having good manners; polite. A courteous person is always thoughtful of the feelings of others.
> **cour·te·ous** (kûr′tē əs) *adjective.*

courtesy **1.** A way of behaving that shows good manners and thoughtfulness toward other people; politeness. Everyone likes the grocery clerks here because of their *courtesy* to all the customers. **2.** A polite and thoughtful act; favor. This store offers its customers a free cup of coffee as a *courtesy.*
> **cour·te·sy** (kûr′tə sē) *noun, plural* **courtesies.**

courthouse **1.** A building in which courts of law are held. **2.** A building in which the offices of a county government are located.
> **court·house** (kôrt′hous′) *noun, plural* **courthouses** (kôrt′hou′ziz).

courtyard An open area that is surrounded by walls or buildings. The rooms of the palace looked out onto the *courtyard.*
> **court·yard** (kôrt′yärd′) *noun, plural* **courtyards.**

cousin The son or daughter of an aunt or uncle. First cousins have the same grandparents; second cousins have the same great-grandparents.
> **cou·sin** (kuz′in) *noun, plural* **cousins.**

cove A small, sheltered bay or inlet.
> **cove** (kōv) *noun, plural* **coves.**

cove

cover **1.** To put something over or on. *Cover* the baby with a blanket. Snow *covered* the ground during the night. **2.** To hide. The new grass *covered* the old path. **3.** To travel over. I *covered* the distance from my house to yours in five minutes. **4.** To deal with; include. That magazine *covers* sports. *Verb.*
—**1.** Something that is put on or over something else. Put a *cover* on the pot. **2.** Something that hides or protects. Most owls prefer to hunt under the *cover* of darkness. The hikers took *cover* in a barn when the storm broke. *Noun.*
> **cov·er** (kuv′ər) *verb,* **covered, covering;** *noun, plural* **covers.**

covered wagon A large wagon with a canvas top that is spread over hoops. American pioneers traveled in covered wagons when they settled the West.

covered wagon

covering Anything that covers. A rug is a covering for a floor.
> **cov·er·ing** (kuv′ər ing) *noun, plural* **coverings.**

covet To want something very much or with a feeling of envy. The losing runner *coveted* the winner's prize.
> **cov·et** (kuv′it) *verb,* **coveted, coveting.**

cow **1.** The fully grown female of cattle. Cows are raised for their milk, meat, and hide. **2.** The female of some other large mammals. A female moose, elephant, or whale is called a cow.
> **cow** (kou) *noun, plural* **cows.**

---

at; āpe; fär; câre; end; mē; it; īce; pîerce; hot; ōld; sông, fôrk; oil; out; up; ūse; rüle; pull; tûrn; chin; sing; shop; thin; this; hw in white; zh in treasure. The symbol ə stands for the unstressed vowel sound in about, taken, pencil, lemon, and circus.

coward   A person who lacks courage or is afraid of anything that is dangerous or hard to do.
   cow·ard (kou′ərd) *noun, plural* **cowards.**

cowardly   Afraid of anything that is dangerous or hard to do; lacking courage.
   cow·ard·ly (kou′ərd lē) *adjective.*

cowboy   A man who herds and takes care of cattle on a ranch.
   cow·boy (kou′boi′) *noun, plural* **cowboys.**

cowgirl   A woman who herds and takes care of cattle on a ranch.
   cow·girl (kou′gûrl′) *noun, plural* **cowgirls.**

cowhand   A person who works on a cattle ranch; cowboy or cowgirl.
   cow·hand (kou′hand′) *noun, plural* **cowhands.**

cowhide   **1.** The hide of a cow.   **2.** Leather made from the hide of a cow. The suitcase was made of *cowhide.*
   cow·hide (kou′hīd′) *noun, plural* **cowhides.**

coworker   A person who works with others at the same place or on the same project; colleague; fellow worker.
   co·work·er (kō′wûr′kər) *noun, plural* **coworkers.**

coyote

coyote   A North American animal that looks like a small, thin wolf. Coyotes are closely related to wolves, foxes, and dogs.
   coy·o·te (kī ō′tē *or* kī′ōt) *noun, plural* **coyotes** *or* **coyote.**

cozy   Warm and comfortable; snug. The kitten slept in a *cozy* spot by the fire.
   co·zy (kō′zē) *adjective,* **cozier, coziest.**

crab   An animal that lives in the water and is covered by a hard shell. Crabs have a wide, flat body, four pairs of legs, and a pair of claws. Many kinds of crabs are used for food.
   crab (krab) *noun, plural* **crabs.**

crab apple   A small, hard, sour apple that can be used to make jelly. Crab apples grow on trees that have many clusters of flowers in the spring.

crack   **1.** A break or narrow opening between the parts of something. A crack does not make a thing fall into parts. The window has a *crack* in it where the ball hit it. There are *cracks* between the floor boards in my room.   **2.** A sudden, sharp noise like that made by something breaking. When a bat hits a baseball you hear a crack.   **3.** A sharp, hard blow. The swinging door gave me a painful *crack* on the head. *Noun.*
   —**1.** To break without coming completely apart; split. The cup *cracked* when it fell into the sink. The squirrel *cracked* the acorn with its teeth.   **2.** To break with a noise that is sharp and sudden. The chair *cracked* loudly under the elephant's foot.   **3.** To make a sudden, sharp noise. The cowhand showed us how to *crack* the whip.   **4.** To hit with a sharp, hard blow. I *cracked* my head on the door. *Verb.*
   • **to crack down.**   To become strict or harsh in enforcing laws or regulations. The mayor promised to *crack down* on people who littered.
   crack (krak) *noun, plural* **cracks;** *verb,* **cracked, cracking.**

cracker   A thin, crisp biscuit.
   crack·er (krak′ər) *noun, plural* **crackers.**

crackle   To make slight, sharp snapping sounds. Dry leaves *crackle* when you walk on them. Some breakfast cereals *crackle* when you pour on milk. *Verb.*
   —A slight, sharp, snapping sound. The *crackle* of the burning logs was a pleasant sound. *Noun.*
   crack·le (krak′əl) *verb,* **crackled, crackling;** *noun, plural* **crackles.**

cradle   **1.** A small bed for a baby. Many cradles are set on rockers so the baby can be rocked to sleep.   **2.** The place where something starts or begins to grow. Philadelphia, Pennsylvania is the *cradle* of American independence.   **3.** Anything like a cradle in

crab

shape or use. A box on rockers used to wash gold from earth is a cradle. The part of a phone that holds the receiver is called a cradle. *Noun.*
—To put or hold in a cradle or as if in a cradle. The students *cradled* their books in their arms. *Verb.*
  cra·dle (krā′dəl) *noun, plural* **cradles;** *verb,* **cradled, cradling.**

craft **1.** A special skill that a person has. The chair was carved with great *craft.* **2.** A trade or work that needs special skill. Woodworking is a *craft* that takes years to master. **3.** Skill in deceiving people; cunning. The magician showed great *craft* in making things disappear. **4.** A boat or airplane. The harbor is filled with small sailing *craft* on sunny afternoons.
  craft (kraft) *noun, plural* **crafts** *(for definition 2)* or **craft** *(for definition 4).*

craftsman A person who has a special skill in making or doing something; artisan.
  crafts·man (krafts′mən) *noun, plural* **craftsmen** (krafts′mən).

crafty Skillful in deceiving; sly; cunning. The *crafty* photographer took my picture when I didn't expect it.
  craft·y (kraf′tē) *adjective,* **craftier, craftiest.**

crag A steep, rugged rock or cliff.
  crag (krag) *noun, plural* **crags.**

cram **1.** To force or crowd into a tight or crowded space. I tried to *cram* another book into the carton, but it was full. **2.** To fill completely or with more than is normally or easily held. The ship was *crammed* with survivors rescued from the disaster. **3.** To study hastily and intensely. We *crammed* all night for the test.
  cram (kram) *verb,* **crammed, cramming.**

cramp¹ **1.** A sharp pain in a muscle that suddenly gets tight. A *cramp* in the leg forced the runner to leave the race. **2. cramps.** Sharp pains in the abdomen. *Noun.*
—To cause a sharp pain in a muscle. Holding the pencil tightly for so long *cramped* my hand. *Verb.*
  cramp (kramp) *noun, plural* **cramps;** *verb,* **cramped, cramping.**

cramp² To limit; confine. Space on the boat was *cramped.*
  cramp (kramp) *verb,* **cramped, cramping.**

cranberry A sour, red berry that grows on low bushes in bogs and swamps. Cranberries are used to make sauce, juice, and jelly.
  cran·ber·ry (kran′ber′ē) *noun, plural* **cranberries.**

crane **1.** A large bird that has thin, very long legs and a long neck and bill. Cranes live near water and wade along the shore looking for food. **2.** A large machine with a long arm that can be moved up and down and in a circle. Cables at the end of the crane's arm are used to lift and move heavy objects. *Noun.*
—To stretch out the neck in order to see better. The people in back of the crowd *craned* their necks to see the parade. *Verb.*
  crane (krān) *noun, plural* **cranes;** *verb,* **craned, craning.**

The **crane** is lifting a heavy cement divider.

crank **1.** A part of a machine that has a handle attached to a rod. When the handle is turned, the rod turns with it and makes the machine work. The storekeeper turned the *crank* of the store's awning to lower it. **2.** A person who has strange ideas. An inventor with a new idea may seem to be a *crank.*

at; āpe; fär; câre; end; mē; it; īce; pîerce; hot; ōld; sông, fôrk; oil; out; up; ūse; rüle; pull; tûrn; chin; sing; shop; thin; this; hw in white; zh in treasure. The symbol ə stands for the unstressed vowel sound in about, taken, pencil, lemon, and circus.

C

3. A person who is always grouchy or cross. It's hard to be friendly with someone who is a *crank*. *Noun.*
—To turn a crank so that something will work. Years ago people had to *crank* the engine of a car to start it. *Verb.*
  crank (krangk) *noun, plural* **cranks;** *verb,* **cranked, cranking.**

cranky   Cross or in a bad temper; irritable; grouchy.
  crank·y (krang′kē) *adjective,* **crankier, crankiest.**

crash   **1.** A sudden, loud noise like something breaking or smashing. There was a *crash* when the ball broke the window.   **2.** A violent collision. We read about the terrible plane *crash*.   **3.** A sudden ruin or failure in business. Much money was lost in the *crash* of the stock market. *Noun.*
—**1.** To make a sudden, loud noise. The lamp *crashed* to the floor.   **2.** To collide or cause to collide violently. The car *crashed* into a wall.   **3.** To move or push forward with noise and strong force. The cows *crashed* through the fence.   **4.** To enter without being asked or having a ticket. Some people I didn't know tried to *crash* my party. *Verb.*
  crash (krash) *noun, plural* **crashes;** *verb,* **crashed, crashing.**

crate   A box made of slats of wood. Crates are used to hold and protect things that are being stored or moved. My grandparents sent us a *crate* of oranges. *Noun.*
—To pack in a crate or crates. The farmer *crated* the lettuce before shipping it to the market. *Verb.*
  crate (krāt) *noun, plural* **crates;** *verb,* **crated, crating.**

crate

crater   A hollow area that looks like the inside of a bowl. There are many *craters* on the surface of the moon. The explosion made a *crater* in the ground.
  cra·ter (krā′tər) *noun, plural* **craters.**

crave   To long or yearn for; desire eagerly. I *crave* a sunny day after all this rain.
  crave (krāv) *verb,* **craved, craving.**

crawl   **1.** To move very slowly. Babies *crawl* by moving on their hands and knees. Worms *crawl* by pulling their bodies along the ground. Traffic *crawled* along the highway.   **2.** To be covered or feel as if covered with crawling things. The picnic table was *crawling* with ants. The ghost story made my skin *crawl*. *Verb.*
—**1.** A very slow movement. Traffic slowed to a *crawl* in the fog.   **2.** A fast swimming stroke. When you do the crawl, your face is down, and you lift your arms over your head one after the other while you kick your feet. *Noun.*
  crawl (krôl) *verb,* **crawled, crawling;** *noun, plural* **crawls.**

crayfish   An animal that looks like a small lobster and lives in fresh water. Crayfish are a kind of shellfish and are used as food.
  cray·fish (krā′fish′) *noun, plural* **crayfish** or **crayfishes.**

crayon   A colored stick made of a wax material used for drawing or writing. Crayons come in different colors. *Noun.*
—To use crayons to draw or color. We *crayoned* pictures of our houses. *Verb.*
  cray·on (krā′on *or* krā′ən) *noun, plural* **crayons;** *verb,* **crayoned, crayoning.**

crazy   **1.** Having a mind that is sick; insane; mentally ill.   **2.** Foolish. Putting three dogs and two cats in the same room was a *crazy* thing to do.   **3.** Very enthusiastic. I'm *crazy* about fishing.
  cra·zy (krā′zē) *adjective,* **crazier, craziest.**

creak   To make a sharp, squeaking sound. The old stairs *creak* when you step on them. *Verb.*
—A sharp, squeaking sound. The rusty gate opened with a loud *creak*. *Noun.* ▲ Another word that sounds like this is **creek.**
  creak (krēk) *verb,* **creaked, creaking;** *noun, plural* **creaks.**

cream   **1.** The yellowish white part of milk. Cream has fat in it and is thicker than milk. Butter is made from cream.   **2.** A food like or made from cream. *Cream* of mushroom soup has a rich taste.   **3.** A soft, thick lotion or foam that is put on the skin. Hand cream and shaving cream are kinds of cream.   **4.** The best part of something. The *cream* of society came to the party. *Noun.*
—To stir or mix until smooth like cream. I *creamed* two sticks of butter before adding the other ingredients in the recipe. *Verb.*
  cream (krēm) *noun, plural* **creams;** *verb,* **creamed, creaming.**

creamy **1.** Containing cream. This soup is thick and *creamy*. **2.** Having the texture or color of cream. The *creamy* gravy had no lumps.
cream·y (krē′mē) *adjective,* **creamier, creamiest.**

crease A line or mark made by folding or wrinkling something. The rain ruined the *crease* in your slacks. *Noun.*
—To make or get a line or mark in by folding or wrinkling. I *creased* my shirt badly when I packed it. *Verb.*
crease (krēs) *noun, plural* **creases;** *verb,* **creased, creasing.**

create To cause something to exist or happen. The lack of rain during the summer *created* a shortage of wheat the next winter. An author *creates* characters in a novel.
cre·ate (krē āt′) *verb,* **created, creating.**

creating designs with paper

creation **1.** The act of causing something to exist or happen. *Creation* of the motion picture took many months. **2.** Anything that has been made. A sculpture, a painting, or a book is a creation. **3.** The world and all the things in it.
cre·a·tion (krē ā′shən) *noun, plural* **creations.**

creative Having or showing ability to make or do something in a new way. A *creative* person did this unusual painting.
cre·a·tive (krē ā′tiv) *adjective.*

creator **1.** A person who makes something. That author is the *creator* of many novels. **2. the Creator.** God.
cre·a·tor (krē ā′tər) *noun, plural* **creators.**

creature A living person or animal. Deer, bears, and wolves are *creatures* of the forest.
crea·ture (krē′chər) *noun, plural* **creatures.**

credit **1.** Belief in the truth of something; faith. Nobody gave full *credit* to the strange story. **2.** Reputation. The retired mayor is a citizen of great *credit* in our town. **3.** Praise or honor. The person who did most of the cooking deserves *credit* for the dinner. **4.** Trust in a person to pay a debt later. Several stores have given me *credit*. **5.** Something that is owed to a person. I have a twenty-five-dollar *credit* at that department store. *Noun.*
—**1.** To believe; trust. I *credit* the story of a person who is always honest. **2.** To put an amount of money that is owed to someone into an account for that person. The store *credited* our account with ten dollars when we returned the shirt. *Verb.*
cred·it (kred′it) *noun, plural* **credits;** *verb,* **credited, crediting.**

credit card A card from a bank or a store that gives a customer the right to buy things and pay for them later. I will have to use my *credit card* to buy the coat because I do not have enough money with me.

creditor A person or institution to whom a debt is owed. The business promptly paid the bills it received from *creditors*.
cred·i·tor (kred′i tər) *noun, plural* **creditors.**

creed A statement of what a person or group of people believe in. "Always be honest" is part of my *creed*.
creed (krēd) *noun, plural* **creeds.**

creek A small stream. A creek is usually bigger than a brook but smaller than a river. ▲ Another word that sounds like this is **creak.**
creek (krēk *or* krik) *noun, plural* **creeks.**

creep **1.** To move slowly and quietly; crawl. A baby *creeps* on hands and knees. The last days before vacation seemed to *creep* by. **2.** To grow along the ground or over a surface. The ivy *creeps* over the fence in our yard. **3.** To feel as if things were crawling over one's skin. The howling of the dog made my flesh *creep*. *Verb.*

at; āpe; fär; câre; end; mē; it; īce; pîerce; hot; ōld; sông, fôrk; oil; out; up; ūse; rüle; pùll; tûrn; chin; sing; shop; thin; this; hw in white; zh in treasure. The symbol ə stands for the unstressed vowel sound in about, taken, pencil, lemon, and circus.

C

—1. The act or condition of moving slowly. Traffic slowed to a *creep*. **2. the creeps.** A feeling as if things were crawling over the skin. The ugly mask gave me the *creeps*. *Noun*.
 creep (krēp) *verb*, **crept, creeping;** *noun*, *plural* **creeps.**

crepe **1.** A cloth that has a crinkled surface. Crepe is used to make clothes. **2.** A thin, light pancake. A crepe is usually served with a filling.
 crepe (krāp) *noun*, *plural* **crepes.**

crepe paper A thin paper with a crinkled surface used for decorating rooms for parties. Streamers can be made with crepe paper.

crept Past tense and past participle of **creep.** The crabs *crept* along the sand. Look up **creep** for more information.
 crept (krept) *verb*.

crescent **1.** The shape the moon has when you can only see a thin, curved part of it. **2.** Something shaped like the moon when you can only see a thin, curved part of it. The slice of cantaloupe formed a *crescent*. *Noun*.
 —Shaped like the moon when it is thin and curved. *Adjective*.
 cres·cent (kres′ənt) *noun*, *plural* **crescents;** *adjective*.

crest **1.** A tuft of longer feathers on the head of a bird. A bluejay has a *crest* on its head. **2.** A plume or other decoration on the top of a helmet. **3.** The highest part of something. We have a long climb before we reach the *crest* of the hill. The *crest* of the wave was white with foam. **4.** A decoration above a coat of arms.
 crest (krest) *noun*, *plural* **crests.**

crest on a bird

crew A group of people who work together. The people who work on and run a ship, airplane, or train are called the crew.
 crew (krü) *noun*, *plural* **crews.**

crib **1.** A small bed for a baby. Cribs have high sides that can be moved up and down. **2.** A box or trough that holds food for cattle and horses to eat from. **3.** A small farm building or bin in which grain or corn is stored.
 crib (krib) *noun*, *plural* **cribs.**

cricket¹ A black or brown insect that hops and looks like a short grasshopper. The male makes a chirping noise by rubbing its front wings together.
 crick·et (krik′it) *noun*, *plural* **crickets.**

cricket² An English game like baseball that is played with a ball and bats on a grass field. Each team has eleven players and instead of home base, there is a goal, called a wicket, at each end of the field.
 crick·et (krik′it) *noun*.

cried Past tense and past participle of **cry.** The baby *cried* because the bottle was empty. Look up **cry** for more information.
 cried (krīd) *verb*.

crime **1.** Anything that is against the law. Robbery is a crime, and a person who robs someone else can be sent to jail. **2.** Anything that seems wrong or foolish. It's a *crime* to waste food when other people are starving.
 crime (krīm) *noun*, *plural* **crimes.**

criminal A person who does something that is a crime. The robber was a *criminal* and was sent to prison. *Noun*.
 —Having to do with crime or the laws about crime. That person is studying to be a *criminal* lawyer. *Adjective*.
 crim·i·nal (krim′ə nəl) *noun*, *plural* **criminals;** *adjective*.

crimson A deep red color. *Noun*.
 —Having the color crimson. The setting sun turned *crimson*. *Adjective*.
 crim·son (krim′zən) *noun*, *plural* **crimsons;** *adjective*.

crinkle **1.** To form or cause to form wrinkles or ripples; wrinkle; crumple. The paper *crinkled* in the fire and then burst into flame. **2.** To make or cause to make a rustling or crackling sound. I *crinkled* the paper to catch the kitten's attention.
 crin·kle (kring′kəl) *verb*, **crinkled, crinkling.**

cripple A person or animal that cannot move some part of the body in the usual way because of an injury or a disease. The fox was a *cripple* after its leg was crushed in the trap. *Noun*.
 —**1.** To badly injure a person or animal. A car accident *crippled* a neighbor of ours. **2.** To damage something or affect it so that it cannot work properly. The heavy snowstorm *crippled* the airport for several days. *Verb*.
 crip·ple (krip′əl) *noun*, *plural* **cripples;** *verb*, **crippled, crippling.**

crisis **1.** A very important turning point that helps decide if things will get better or worse. Having to decide whether or not to go to college was the first real *crisis* in my life.

2. A difficult or dangerous situation. The sudden death of the prime minister caused a *crisis* in that country.

cri·sis (krī′sis) *noun, plural* **crises** (krī′sēz).

crisp **1.** Hard or firm but breaking easily into pieces. Fresh lettuce, celery, and radishes should be *crisp*. **2.** Clear and cool; brisk. It's nice to go walking on *crisp* autumn days. **3.** Short and to the point. The coach gave *crisp* instructions to the team. *Adjective.*

crisp (krisp) *adjective,* **crisper, crispest.**

crisscross Marked with lines that cross one another. *Adjective.*

—A design made by crossing lines. A plaid is a *crisscross* of lines and colors. *Noun.*

—**1.** To mark with or make lines that cross one another. I could see where the footprints *crisscrossed* in the snow. **2.** To go across back and forth. We *crisscrossed* the neighborhood to find our dog. *Verb.*

criss·cross (kris′krôs′) *adjective; noun, plural* **crisscrosses;** *verb,* **crisscrossed, crisscrossing.**

critic **1.** A person whose job is to say or write an opinion about what is good or bad about books, motion pictures, music, art, or plays. The *critic* wrote about the new movie for the newspaper. **2.** A person who finds something wrong. Don't be a *critic;* say something nice about the house.

cri·tic (krit′ik) *noun, plural* **critics.**

critical **1.** Finding something wrong with things. You were *critical* of every plan that we suggested. **2.** Having to do with a person whose job is to be a critic. There is a *critical* review of the new book in the newspaper. **3.** Having to do with a crisis; dangerous; serious. There is a *critical* shortage of water in the town.

crit·i·cal (krit′i kəl) *adjective.*

criticism **1.** The act of saying what is good or bad about something. I read the newspaper's *criticism* of the artist's work. **2.** The act of finding something wrong; disapproval. My parents' *criticism* of my manners made me change them.

crit·i·cism (krit′ə siz′əm) *noun, plural* **criticisms.**

criticize **1.** To say what is good or bad about something. The newspaper hired someone to *criticize* new movies. **2.** To find fault with something. Why do you always *criticize* the way I sing?

crit·i·cize (krit′ə sīz′) *verb,* **criticized, criticizing.**

croak A deep, hoarse sound like one made by a frog. *Noun.*

—To make a deep, hoarse sound. The frogs *croaked* in the pond. *Verb.*

croak (krōk) *noun, plural* **croaks;** *verb,* **croaked, croaking.**

crochet To make something by looping thread or yarn into connected stitches with a needle that has a hook at one end. I *crocheted* a blanket for the baby.

cro·chet (krō shā′) *verb,* **crocheted, crocheting.**

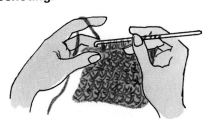

crochet

crocodile A long animal with short legs, thick, scaly skin, and a long, strong tail. Crocodiles live in and near water in America, Asia, and Africa. They are reptiles and are closely related to alligators. Look up **alligator** for a picture of a crocodile.

croc·o·dile (krok′ə dīl′) *noun, plural* **crocodiles.**

crocus A small flower that grows from an underground bulb. Crocuses can be purple, white, or yellow and have thin leaves like blades of grass. They bloom early in the spring.

cro·cus (krō′kəs) *noun, plural* **crocuses.**

crook **1.** A bent part; curve. I carry my umbrella in the *crook* of my arm. **2.** A shepherd's staff with a hook at the top. **3.** A person who is not honest. *Noun.*

crocus

—To bend; curve; hook. The clerk *crooked* a finger at us to tell us to come over. *Verb.*

crook (krùk) *noun, plural* **crooks;** *verb,* **crooked, crooking.**

crooked **1.** Not straight; bent or curving. The path that we followed through the woods was very *crooked.* **2.** Not honest. Only a *crooked* person would cheat at card games.

crook·ed (krùk′id) *adjective.*

crop **1.** Plants that are grown to be used as food or to be sold for profit. Cotton is an important *crop* in the South. **2.** The total amount of a plant grown as a crop that is gathered; harvest. We had a huge *crop* of tomatoes this year. **3.** A group of persons or things that come at the same time. There was a large *crop* of new students at school this fall. **4.** A pouch near the bottom of the throat of a bird. Food is held in the crop and is prepared for digestion. **5.** A short whip that has a loop at the end instead of a lash. Some horseback riders use crops. *Noun.*

—To cut or bite off the top part of something. The deer *cropped* the bushes behind our house. *Verb.*

• **to crop up.** To arise or appear. Unexpected problems always *crop up* in a project like this.

crop (krop) *noun, plural* **crops;** *verb,* **cropped, cropping.**

croquet An outdoor game played with sticks called mallets that are used to hit wooden balls along the ground and through wire hoops called wickets.

cro·quet (krō kā′) *noun.*

cross **1.** A post or stake that has a bar across it. The cross is the symbol of Christianity because Jesus died on a cross. **2.** Anything shaped like a cross. On some tests you make a *cross* next to the right answer to a question. **3.** Any difficulty or suffering. The patient bore the *cross* of the illness without complaining. **4.** A mixing of animals or plants of different kinds. A mule is a *cross* between a horse and a donkey. *Noun.*

—**1.** To move or go from one side of something to the other. The ship *crossed* the ocean in seven days. **2.** To go across and divide; lie across. There's a traffic light where Main Street *crosses* Maple Street. **3.** To draw a line across or through. You *cross* a "t" in writing. **4.** To put or lay one thing across another. I *crossed* my legs when I sat down. **5.** To pass while going in different directions. Your letter must have *crossed* mine in the mail. **6.** To go against; oppose. It angers my cousin to be *crossed.* **7.** To mix plants or animals of different kinds in order to get

a new kind. A horse *crossed* with a donkey will give birth to a mule. *Verb.*

—In a bad temper; grouchy. People sometimes get *cross* when you point out their mistakes. *Adjective.*

cross (krôs) *noun, plural* **crosses;** *verb,* **crossed, crossing;** *adjective,* **crosser, crossest.**

crossbow A weapon that was used in the Middle Ages that had a bow mounted across a wooden stock.

cross·bow (krôs′bō′) *noun, plural* **crossbows.**

cross-eyed Having one or both eyes turned inward toward the nose.

cross-eyed (krôs′īd′) *adjective.*

crossing **1.** A place where two lines or other things cross each other. We stopped at the railroad *crossing* to let the train go through. **2.** A place where a street or river may be crossed. There is a shallow *crossing* just down the stream.

cross·ing (krô′sing) *noun, plural* **crossings.**

children **crossing** the street

cross-reference A reference from one part of a book or index to another part, pointing out where more information can be found. Under the entry **crocodile** there is a cross-reference to the picture under **alligator.**

cross-ref·er·ence (krôs′ref′ər əns) *noun, plural* **cross-references.**

crossroad **1.** A road that crosses another road or a road that leads from one main road to another. **2. crossroads.** The place where two or more roads cross each other. There were four stop signs at the *crossroads.*

cross·road (krôs′rōd′) *noun, plural* **crossroads.**

C

cross section **1.** A slice or piece made by cutting straight across something. When you cut an orange through the middle you make cross sections. **2.** A sample of people or things that is thought to show what the whole group of people or things is like. A poll of a *cross section* of the state's voters showed that the candidate for senator would probably be elected.

crosswalk A path marked off for use by pedestrians in crossing a street. Cars are supposed to stop before they get to the crosswalk.
cross·walk (krôs′wôk′) *noun, plural* **crosswalks.**

crossword puzzle A puzzle that has a pattern of squares that a person fills with words or phrases, putting one letter in each square.
cross·word puzzle (krôs′wûrd′).

crotch The place where the body divides into two legs, or where a branch of a tree grows out at an angle from the trunk or from another branch.
crotch (kroch) *noun, plural* **crotches.**

crouch To stoop or bend low with the knees bent. The cat *crouched* in the bushes, ready to spring if a bird came close. *Verb.*
—The act or position of crouching. The child got into a *crouch* to hide. *Noun.*
crouch (krouch) *verb,* **crouched, crouching;** *noun, plural* **crouches.**

croup A children's disease of the throat and windpipe that causes difficulty in breathing and a barking cough.
croup (krüp) *noun.*

crow¹ **1.** To make the loud, sharp cry of a rooster. The farmer's rooster *crows* every morning when the sun rises. **2.** To make a happy yell or cry. The fans *crowed* with delight when the home team scored the first goal. *Verb.*
—**1.** The loud, shrill cry of the rooster. The rooster's *crow* at sunrise could be heard a mile away. **2.** A delighted, happy cry. The winner's *crow* echoed in the stadium. *Noun.*
crow (krō) *verb,* **crowed, crowing;** *noun, plural* **crows.**

crow² A large bird with shiny black feathers and a harsh cry.
crow (krō) *noun, plural* **crows.**

crow²

crowbar A heavy steel or iron bar that has one flattened end. A crowbar is used to lift things up or pry things apart.
crow·bar (krō′bär′) *noun, plural* **crowbars.**

crowbar

crowd A large number of people gathered together. There was a *crowd* of people waiting to get into the theater. *Noun.*
—**1.** To put or force too many people or things into too small a space; fill too full. My cousin *crowded* the shelf with books. **2.** To gather closely or in large numbers. We *crowded* around the table to get our food. **3.** To move by pushing or shoving. We asked the people behind us in line not to *crowd* us. *Verb.*
crowd (kroud) *noun, plural* **crowds;** *verb,* **crowded, crowding.**

crown **1.** A covering for the head worn by kings and queens. A crown is often made of gold and silver set with jewels. **2.** A king or queen; government headed by a king or queen. The *crown* was overthrown by a revolution. **3.** A wreath or band worn on the head. The winner of the race was given a *crown* of laurel leaves. **4.** The highest or top part of anything. I squashed the *crown* of your hat when I accidentally sat on it. **5.** The part of a tooth that can be seen above the gums or a substitute for this part. *Noun.*
—**1.** To make a person a king or queen at a special ceremony during which a crown is put on his or her head. **2.** To declare officially to be. The boxer was *crowned* champion. **3.** To be on the top of. The state flag *crowned* the office building. *Verb.*
crown (kroun) *noun, plural* **crowns;** *verb,* **crowned, crowning.**

at; āpe; fär; cãre; end; mē; it; īce; pîerce; hot; ōld; sông, fôrk; oil; out; up; ūse; rüle; pùll; tûrn; chin; sing; shop; thin; this; hw in white; zh in treasure. The symbol ə stands for the unstressed vowel sound in about, taken, pencil, lemon, and circus.

crow's-nest A small platform near the top of a ship's mast. Sailors use it as a lookout tower.
crow's-nest (krōz'nest') *noun, plural* crow's-nests.

crucial Very important; decisive. When a thing is crucial it means that it will decide whether something else succeeds or fails. The last inning of the baseball game was *crucial* to our team.
cru·cial (krü'shəl) *adjective.*

crude 1. In a natural or raw state. *Crude* oil is oil as it is pumped from the ground. 2. Done or made without skill; rough. The children built a *crude* shack in the woods out of wood they had found. 3. Lacking good manners or taste; not refined; rude. It was *crude* of them to laugh at the child who fell off the chair.
crude (krüd) *adjective,* cruder, crudest.

cruel 1. Willing to cause pain or suffering to others. It would be *cruel* to beat an animal. 2. Causing pain or suffering. A *cruel,* cold wind swept across the plains, destroying crops and damaging homes.
cru·el (krü'əl) *adjective,* crueler, cruelest.

cruelty 1. The causing of pain or suffering to others. I dislike people who show *cruelty* to animals. 2. A cruel act. The soldiers suffered many *cruelties* in the enemy prison camp.
cru·el·ty (krü'əl tē) *noun, plural* cruelties.

cruet A small glass bottle that vinegar, oil, or other dressings are served in.
cru·et (krü'it) *noun, plural* cruets.

cruise 1. To sail from place to place. The sailboat *cruised* along the coast. 2. To move or ride from place to place. A police car *cruises* through our neighborhood each night. *Verb.*
—A trip in a boat taken for pleasure. I would love to take a *cruise* to Hawaii. *Noun.*
cruise (krüz) *verb,* cruised, cruising; *noun, plural* cruises.

cruets

cruiser 1. A warship that is faster than a battleship and carries fewer guns. 2. A motorboat with a cabin that has space for cooking and sleeping. 3. A police car that patrols the streets.
cruis·er (krü'zər) *noun, plural* cruisers.

crumb A tiny piece of bread, cake, cracker, or cookie. We put out *crumbs* for the birds.
crumb (krum) *noun, plural* crumbs.

crumble 1. To break into small pieces. The muffin *crumbled* when I tried to butter it. 2. To fall apart or be destroyed. The old house is slowly *crumbling.* The team's hopes for winning the game *crumbled* when the best player got sick.
crum·ble (krum'bəl) *verb,* crumbled, crumbling.

crumple 1. To press or crush into wrinkles or folds. We *crumpled* sheets of newspaper to start the fire. 2. To fall down or collapse. The old shack *crumpled* when the bulldozer rammed it.
crum·ple (krum'pəl) *verb,* crumpled, crumpling.

crunch To chew or crush with a noisy, crackling sound. The rabbit *crunched* on a carrot. The thin ice *crunched* under my shoes. *Verb.*
—A crushing, crackling sound. We heard the *crunch* of the hiker's boots in the snow. *Noun.*
crunch (krunch) *verb,* crunched, crunching; *noun, plural* crunches.

crusade 1. Any of the military expeditions undertaken by the Christian people of Europe between the years 1095 and 1291 to take Palestine away from the Muslims. 2. A strong fight against something evil or for something good. We started a *crusade* to clean up the town parks. *Noun.*
—To fight in a crusade. Our senator is *crusading* against the pollution of our nation's lakes and rivers. *Verb.*
cru·sade (krü sād') *noun, plural* crusades; *verb,* crusaded, crusading.

crusader A person who fights in a crusade.
cru·sad·er (krü sā'dər) *noun, plural* crusaders.

crush 1. To squeeze very hard. When you crush something, it is broken, put out of shape, or hurt in some way. This machine *crushes* ice into small bits. The garbage can was *crushed* when the truck ran over it. 2. To press into wrinkles; crumple. The dress was *crushed* because it was poorly packed. 3. To put down; subdue. Our hopes of going to the circus were *crushed* when we couldn't get tickets. *Verb.*
—1. A very strong pressure or squeezing. The *crush* of the crowd pushed the student against the door of the gym. 2. A sudden,

strong liking for a person. I used to have a *crush* on that movie star. *Noun.*

crush (krush) *verb,* **crushed, crushing;** *noun, plural* **crushes.**

crust **1.** The hard, crisp outside part of bread, rolls, or other food. A pie has a *crust* of dough. We fed the birds *crusts* of bread. **2.** Any hard outside part or coating. The pond was covered with a *crust* of ice. The *crust* of the earth is a layer of rock 20 miles deep. *Noun.*
—To cover or become covered with a crust. Ice *crusted* the pond. *Verb.*

crust (krust) *noun, plural* **crusts;** *verb,* **crusted, crusting.**

crustacean An animal that has a hard shell and lives mostly in water. Lobsters, crabs, shrimp, and barnacles are crustaceans.

crus·ta·cean (kru stā′shən) *noun, plural* **crustaceans.**

crustacean

crutch A support that helps a lame person in walking. A crutch is a pole that usually has a padded part at the top that fits under the arm so a person can lean on it.

crutch (kruch) *noun, plural* **crutches.**

cry **1.** To shed tears; weep. The hungry baby *cried.* Many in the audience *cried* during the sad movie. **2.** To call loudly; shout. The people in the burning building *cried* for help. **3.** To utter a special sound, as a bird or other animal does. The gulls *cried* to each other as they flew by. *Verb.*
—**1.** A loud call or shout. My cousin gave a *cry* of surprise when we tapped on the window. The family heard a *cry* for help from the lake. **2.** A fit of weeping. I had a long *cry* when I learned that we had to move. **3.** The special sound that an animal makes. Late at night we listened to the *cries* of the owls. *Noun.*

cry (krī) *verb,* **cried, crying;** *noun, plural* **cries.**

crystal **1.** A clear kind of rock. Quartz is a kind of crystal. **2.** A body that is formed by certain substances when they change into a solid. Crystals have flat surfaces and a regu-

lar shape. Salt forms in crystals. Snowflakes are crystals. **3.** A very fine, clear glass used to make drinking glasses, bowls, plates, and vases. Crystal sparkles in the light. **4.** The transparent covering that protects the face of a watch. *Noun.*
—**1.** Made of crystal. The *crystal* bowl had a crack in it. **2.** Like crystal; clear. You can see the bottom of the lake through the *crystal* water. *Adjective.*

crys·tal (kris′təl) *noun, plural* **crystals;** *adjective.*

crystallize To form into crystals. Cold winds *crystallized* the vapor in the air into snowflakes.

crys·tal·lize (kris′tə līz′) *verb,* **crystallized, crystallizing.**

CT Postal abbreviation for *Connecticut.*

cu. An abbreviation for *cubic.*

cub A very young bear, wolf, lion, or tiger.
cub (kub) *noun, plural* **cubs.**

Cuba An island country in the Caribbean Sea.
Cu·ba (kū′bə) *noun.*

Cuban A person who was born in or is a citizen of Cuba. *Noun.*
—Of or having to do with Cuba or its people. *Adjective.*
Cu·ban (kū′bən) *noun, plural* **Cubans;** *adjective.*

cube **1.** A solid figure with six equal, square sides. **2.** Something shaped like a cube. Put more ice *cubes* in my iced tea, please. **3.** The product of a number that is multiplied by itself twice. The *cube* of 2 is 8 because 2 x 2 x 2 = 8. *Noun.*
—**1.** To cut or make into cubes. We *cubed* potatoes to make potato salad. **2.** To multiply a number by itself twice. *Verb.*

cube (kūb) *noun, plural* **cubes;** *verb,* **cubed, cubing.**

The building block is a **cube.**

cubic **1.** Shaped like a cube. These building blocks are *cubic.* **2.** Describing or measur-

at; āpe; fär; câre; end; mē; it; īce; pîerce; hot; ōld; sông, fôrk; oil; out; up; ūse; rüle; pùll; tûrn; chin; sing; shop; thin; <u>th</u>is; hw in white; zh in treasure. The symbol ə stands for the unstressed vowel sound in about, taken, pencil, lemon, and circus.

C

ing length, breadth, and thickness. The volume of an object is given in cubic measures, such as cubic inches or cubic feet.
cu·bic (kū′bik) *adjective.*

cub scout A boy who is a junior member of the Boy Scouts.

cuckoo

cuckoo A bird that has a long tail and a call that sounds like its name. Most cuckoos have brown or gray feathers.
cuck·oo (kü′kü *or* kŭk′ü) *noun, plural* **cuckoos.**

cucumber A long, green vegetable with white flesh and many seeds inside. The cucumber grows on a vine. Cucumbers are eaten raw in salads or made into pickles.
cu·cum·ber (kū′kum bər) *noun, plural* **cucumbers.**

cud Food that comes back into the mouth from the first stomach of cows, sheep, and some other animals so that they can chew it again.
cud (kud) *noun, plural* **cuds.**

cuddle **1.** To hold close in one's arms; hold tenderly. I *cuddled* the cat, and it fell asleep. **2.** To lie close and snug. They *cuddled* together for warmth.
cud·dle (kud′əl) *verb,* **cuddled, cuddling.**

cue¹ A signal that tells someone when to do something. The ring of the telephone was the actor's *cue* to walk on stage. Take a *cue* from me and leave the room when I do. *Noun.*
—To give a signal to someone to tell them when to do something. Your job is to stand in the wings and *cue* the actors. *Verb.*
cue (kū) *noun, plural* **cues;** *verb,* **cued, cuing.**

cue² A long, thin stick that is used to strike the ball in playing pool or billiards.
cue (kū) *noun, plural* **cues.**

cuff¹ **1.** A band of material at the bottom of a sleeve. **2.** A fold of material that is

turned up at the bottom of the leg of a pair of trousers.
cuff (kuf) *noun, plural* **cuffs.**

cuff² To hit with the hand. The grocer *cuffed* the child on the head for stealing an apple. *Verb.*
—A hit with the hand; slap. Give the dog a *cuff* if its snaps at you. *Noun.*
cuff (kuf) *verb,* **cuffed, cuffing;** *noun, plural* **cuffs.**

culprit A person who is guilty of doing something that is wrong. My sister and brother are the *culprits* who put salt in the sugar bowl.
cul·prit (kul′prit) *noun, plural* **culprits.**

cultivate **1.** To prepare and use land for growing vegetables, flowers, or other crops. To cultivate land, you dig it, fertilize it, and remove weeds from it before you plant seeds. **2.** To plant and help grow. That farmer *cultivates* corn. **3.** To work hard to improve or develop. Try to *cultivate* good study habits.
cul·ti·vate (kul′tə vāt′) *verb,* **cultivated, cultivating.**

cultivating a garden

cultivator A tool or machine used to loosen the soil and pull up weeds around growing plants.
cul·ti·va·tor (kul′tə vā′tər) *noun, plural* **cultivators.**

cultural Having to do with culture. This book is about the *cultural* history of England.
cul·tur·al (kul′chər əl) *adjective.*

culture **1.** The arts, beliefs, and customs that make up a way of life for a group of people at a certain time. We are studying the *culture* of the Eskimo. **2.** An appreciation of the arts, knowledge, and good taste and manners that are the result of education. A per-

C

son of great *culture* gave these paintings to the museum.   **3.** The growing and improvement of plants or animals. Animal culture has resulted in the development of many new breeds.   **4.** The growing of living cells or microorganisms, such as bacteria or viruses, for medical or scientific study.
>**cul·ture** (kul′chər) *noun, plural* **cultures.**

cumbersome   Not easy to manage or carry; unwieldy. I struggled up the stairs with the *cumbersome* box.
>**cum·ber·some** (kum′bər səm) *adjective.*

cunning   Very clever at fooling or deceiving others; sly. *Adjective.*
—Cleverness at fooling or deceiving others. Foxes are said to show much *cunning* in escaping from hunters. *Noun.*
>**cun·ning** (kun′ing) *adjective; noun.*

cup   **1.** A small bowl with a handle that is used to drink from.   **2.** The amount that a cup holds. I would like a *cup* of water.   **3.** A unit of measure equal to eight ounces. There are four cups in a quart.   **4.** Anything that has the shape of a cup. A silver *cup* was the prize for the winner of the sailing race. *Noun.*
—To shape like a cup. *Cup* your hands when you catch the ball. *Verb.*
>**cup** (kup) *noun, plural* **cups;** *verb,* **cupped, cupping.**

cupboard   A cabinet or closet with shelves to store dishes or food.
>**cup·board** (kub′ərd) *noun, plural* **cupboards.**

cupcake   A small cake. Cupcakes are baked in metal pans with several hollows shaped like cups.
>**cup·cake** (kup′kāk′) *noun, plural* **cupcakes.**

cupful   **1.** The amount that a cup holds. The size of this kind of cupful depends on the size of the cup.   **2.** The amount held by a standard cup in liquid or dry measurement. A *cupful* of water is eight ounces of water, or half a pint.
>**cup·ful** (kup′fül′) *noun, plural* **cupfuls.**

curb   **1.** A border of concrete or stone along the side of a road or sidewalk. We found a place to park along the *curb* in front of the restaurant.   **2.** Anything that holds back or controls an action. Our family keeps a *curb* on spending by following a strict budget.   **3.** A chain or strap that is fastened to a horse's bit. It is used to control the horse when the reins are pulled. *Noun.*
—To hold back or control. I tried to *curb* my anger by counting silently to ten before I spoke. *Verb.*
>**curb** (kûrb) *noun, plural* **curbs;** *verb,* **curbed, curbing.**

curd   The thick part of milk that separates from the watery part when the milk sours. Curds are used in making cheese.
>**curd** (kûrd) *noun, plural* **curds.**

curdle   To form or cause to form into a curd. This milk has *curdled* overnight. Heat *curdles* milk.
>**cur·dle** (kûr′dəl) *verb,* **curdled, curdling.**

cure   **1.** To make a person or animal healthy again. The veterinarian *cured* our dog.   **2.** To get rid of. To *cure* a cold you should stay in bed and rest.   **3.** To preserve or prepare meat and fish for use by drying, smoking, or salting. Farmers *cure* the meat of pigs to make ham. *Verb.*
—**1.** Something that makes a person or animal healthy again. Aspirin is the best *cure* for my headache.   **2.** A return to good health. The patient's *cure* required a week in the hospital. *Noun.*
>**cure** (kyür) *verb,* **cured, curing;** *noun, plural* **cures.**

curfew   A fixed time at night when a person has to be indoors or at home. At camp we had a ten o'clock *curfew* for being in bed.
>**cur·few** (kûr′fū) *noun, plural* **curfews.**

Word History

The word **curfew** comes from two old French words meaning "cover" and "fire." In the Middle Ages, a bell was rung to tell people when it was time to put out or cover their fires for the night. This signal became known as the *curfew*.

---

curiosity   **1.** A strong wish to learn about things that are new, strange, or interesting. The locked closet aroused our *curiosity*.   **2.** Something that is interesting because it is strange, rare, or unusual. A horse and buggy is a *curiosity* today.
>**cu·ri·os·i·ty** (kyür′ē os′i tē) *noun, plural* **curiosities.**

curious   **1.** Eager to learn about things that are new, strange, or interesting. I was really *curious* about the new student.   **2.** Strange or unusual. That is a *curious* old coin.
>**cu·ri·ous** (kyür′ē əs) *adjective.*

---

at; āpe; fär; câre; end; mē; it; īce; pîerce; hot; ōld; sông, fôrk; oil; out; up; ūse; rüle; pùll; tûrn; chin; sing; shop; thin; *th*is; hw in white; zh in treasure. The symbol ə stands for the unstressed vowel sound in about, taken, pencil, lemon, and circus.

curl To twist in curved rings or coils. I *curled* my hair for the party. The smoke *curled* from the chimney. The cat *curled* up for a nap. *Verb.*
—**1.** A curved lock of hair. The child's *curls* were hidden by a hat. **2.** Something shaped like a ring or coil. A *curl* of smoke rose upward out of the chimney. *Noun.*
  curl (kûrl) *verb,* **curled, curling;** *noun, plural* **curls.**

curly Forming or having curls. You have *curly* hair.
  curl·y (kûr′lē) *adjective,* **curlier, curliest.**

currant **1.** A small, sour berry that grows in bunches on a bush. Currants are used to make jelly. **2.** A small seedless raisin used in cakes, pies, and buns. ▲ Another word that sounds like this is **current.**
  cur·rant (kûr′ənt) *noun, plural* **currants.**

currency **1.** The money that is used in a country. Dollars, quarters, and dimes are part of the currency used in the United States and Canada. Pesos are part of the currency of Mexico. **2.** General use or acceptance. As more people use a new word, they begin to give it *currency.*
  cur·ren·cy (kûr′ən sē) *noun, plural* **currencies.**

current **1.** Belonging to the present time. My *current* address is on the envelope. **2.** Commonly used or accepted. At one time the belief was *current* that people lived on the planet Mars. *Adjective.*
—**1.** A part of the air or of a body of water that is moving along in a path. The rubber raft was caught in the *current* and carried out to sea. A cold *current* of air flowed into the room through the door. **2.** A flow of electricity. A plug lets a household appliance use the *current* in the wires of houses. **3.** The way events or thoughts seem to move along a path; trend. The *current* of public opinion today seems to be that the mayor should resign. *Noun.* ▲ Another word that sounds like this is **currant.**
  cur·rent (kûr′ənt) *adjective; noun, plural* **currents.**

curse **1.** A wish that something evil or harmful will happen to a person or thing. A curse is often made by calling on God or gods. **2.** A word or words used when swearing. A curse is usually said in anger. **3.** Something that brings or causes evil, harm, or suffering. War has been a *curse* throughout human history. *Noun.*
—**1.** To wish that something evil or harmful will happen to a person or thing. The soldier *cursed* the enemy. **2.** To say a word or words that show hate or anger; swear. **3.** To cause evil, harm, or suffering to. Our neighbor has been *cursed* with a weak back for years. *Verb.*
  curse (kûrs) *noun, plural* **curses;** *verb,* **cursed, cursing.**

cursor A special symbol on a computer monitor that shows where the next letter or number will appear. Some cursors flash on and off.
  cur·sor (kûr′sər) *noun, plural* **cursors.**

curt Rudely brief; abrupt. I asked directions politely, but all I got was a *curt* reply.
  curt (kûrt) *adjective,* **curter, curtest.**

curtain **1.** A piece of cloth hung across an open space. Curtains are hung at windows, in doorways, and across the front part of a stage. **2.** Anything that screens or covers like a curtain. A *curtain* of fog hid the tops of the tall buildings. *Noun.*
—To put a curtain over; screen. We *curtained* off a part of the basement as a workshop. *Verb.*
  cur·tain (kûr′tin) *noun, plural* **curtains;** *verb,* **curtained, curtaining.**

curtsy A bow showing respect made by bending the knees and lowering the body slightly. Women and girls make a *curtsy,* and men and boys make a bow. *Noun.*
—To make a curtsy. The women *curtsied* and the men bowed when the monarch greeted them. *Verb.*
  curt·sy (kûrt′sē) *noun, plural* **curtsies;** *verb,* **curtsied, curtsying.**

curve **1.** A line that keeps bending in one direction. A curve has no straight parts or angles. **2.** Something that has the shape of a curve. The baby looked snug in the *curve* of the nurse's arm. *Noun.*
—To bend or move in a curved line. The road *curves* on the other side of the bridge. *Verb.*
  curve (kûrv) *noun, plural* **curves;** *verb,* **curved, curving.**

curve in a road

cushion **1.** A pillow or soft pad used to sit, lie, or rest on. Our couch has three *cushions* on the seat. **2.** Something like a cushion in shape or use. I sat on a *cushion* of grass. **3.** Anything that softens a blow or protects against harm. Shoes are a *cushion* against shock for a runner's feet. *Noun.*
—**1.** To make a pillow or soft pad for. If you *cushion* the rocking chair it will be more comfortable. **2.** To soften a blow or shock. The pile of leaves *cushioned* my fall from the tree. *Verb.*
　cush·ion (kush'ən) *noun, plural* **cushions;** *verb,* **cushioned, cushioning.**

custard A sweet dessert made of eggs, milk, and sugar. Custard may be cooked or frozen.
　cus·tard (kus'tərd) *noun, plural* **custards.**

custodian A person who is responsible for the care of a person or thing. The school *custodian* made sure the buildings were kept clean and in good repair.
　cus·to·di·an (kə stō'dē ən) *noun, plural* **custodians.**

custody The care and keeping of a person or thing. I was in my grandparents' *custody* while my parents were in France for a month. The suspected thief was in the *custody* of the police until bail was arranged.
　cus·to·dy (kus'tə dē) *noun, plural* **custodies.**

custom **1.** A way of acting that has become accepted by many people. Customs are learned and passed down from one generation to another. Fireworks displays on the Fourth of July are an American *custom.* **2.** The usual way that something is done; habit. It is my *custom* to walk to school every morning. **3. customs.** Taxes that a government collects on products that are brought in from a foreign country. We had to pay *customs* on the sweaters we had bought in Scotland. *Noun.*
—Made the way the buyer wants or needs. The *custom* color of the paint on our house was mixed for us at the store. *Adjective.*
　cus·tom (kus'təm) *noun, plural* **customs;** *adjective.*

customary Usual. It is *customary* in our family to have Thanksgiving dinner at our grandparents' house.
　cus·tom·ar·y (kus'tə mer'ē) *adjective.*

customer A person who buys something at a store or uses the services of a business establishment. Most of the bakery's regular *customers* shop there at least once a week.
　cus·tom·er (kus'tə mər) *noun, plural* **customers.**

cut **1.** To divide, pierce, open, or take away a part with something sharp. We could not untie the knot so we had to *cut* the string. *Cut* the pie into six slices. I *cut* my foot on the sharp rock. We have to *cut* the grass today. The cold wind *cut* through the light jacket. **2.** To make by using a sharp tool. We *cut* a hole in the door so the cat could come in and go out. **3.** To do the work of a sharp tool. This saw *cuts* well. **4.** To be capable of being cut. This steak *cuts* easily. **5.** To make shorter or smaller; lessen. I *cut* my speech because it was too long. The store will *cut* all its prices for the big sale. **6.** To have a tooth or teeth grow through the gum. The baby *cut* a new tooth yesterday. **7.** To put an end to or interrupt. That last bolt of lightning *cut* the electricity for a minute. **8.** To cross or pass. The river *cuts* through the valley. Let's *cut* through the park instead of walking around it. **9.** To be absent from, usually without permission. The two students failed because they *cut* classes. *Verb.*
—**1.** An opening or slit made with something sharp. The *cut* on my hand is from the broken glass. **2.** A piece or part that has been cut or cut off. We had a nice *cut* of beef for dinner. **3.** A decrease. The store announced a *cut* in its prices. **4.** The way or shape in which a thing is cut; style. The *cut* of that dress is old-fashioned. *Noun.*
　cut (kut) *verb,* **cut, cutting;** *noun, plural* **cuts.**

cute Delightful or pretty; charming. This is the *cutest* puppy I've ever seen.
　cute (kūt) *adjective,* **cuter, cutest.**

cuticle A tough layer of dead skin. We have cuticles around the edges of our fingernails.
　cu·ti·cle (kū'ti kəl) *noun, plural* **cuticles.**

cutlass A sword with a wide, flat, curved blade.
　cut·lass (kut'ləs) *noun, plural* **cutlasses.**

cutter **1.** A person whose job it is to cut out things. A diamond *cutter* cuts away bits of the stone to give a diamond a special shape. A dress *cutter* cuts out dresses from fabric. **2.** A tool or machine that is used to cut out things. It is fun to use cookie *cutters* to make different shapes. **3.** A small, fast ship. The coast guard uses *cutters* to rescue people who are having trouble at sea.
　cut·ter (kut'ər) *noun, plural* **cutters.**

at; āpe; fär; câre; end; mē; it; īce; pîerce; hot; ōld; sông, fôrk; oil; out; up; ūse; rüle; pull; tûrn; chin; sing; shop; thin; <u>th</u>is; hw in white; zh in treasure. The symbol ə stands for the unstressed vowel sound in about, taken, pencil, lemon, and circus.

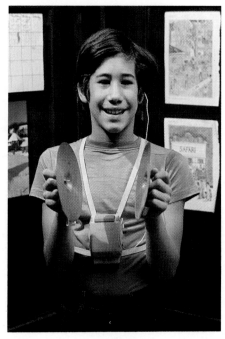

cymbals

cutting **1.** Able to make a slit or other opening in; sharp. The *cutting* edge of a knife is thinner than the other edge. **2.** Hurting a person's feelings. Think before you make a *cutting* remark to a friend, or you might be sorry. *Adjective.*
—**1.** A small part cut from a plant that is used to grow a new plant. If you take a *cutting* from ivy and put it in water, it will grow roots. **2.** An article or picture cut out of a newspaper or magazine; clipping. *Noun.*
    cut·ting (kut'ing) *adjective; noun, plural* **cuttings.**

cycle **1.** A series of events that happen one after another in the same order, over and over again. Spring, summer, autumn, and winter are the *cycle* of the four seasons of the year. **2.** A bicycle, tricycle, or motorcycle. *Noun.*
—To ride a bicycle, tricycle, or motorcycle. We plan to *cycle* in the park. *Verb.*
    cy·cle (sī'kəl) *noun, plural* **cycles;** *verb,* **cycled, cycling.**

cyclone A storm that is characterized by very powerful winds. The winds in a cyclone move around and around and can cause much damage.
    cy·clone (sī'klōn) *noun, plural* **cyclones.**

cylinder A solid or hollow object that is shaped like a drum or a soup can.
    cyl·in·der (sil'ən dər) *noun, plural* **cylinders.**

cylindrical Having the shape of a cylinder.
    cy·lin·dri·cal (sə lin'dri kəl) *adjective.*

cymbal A metal musical instrument that is shaped like a plate. A cymbal is hit against another cymbal or with a drumstick to make a clashing sound. ▲ Another word that sounds like this is **symbol.**
    cym·bal (sim'bəl) *noun, plural* **cymbals.**

cypress Any of various evergreen trees that have small leaves like scales. The wood of cypress trees is very hard and is used for building.
    cy·press (sī'pris) *noun, plural* **cypresses.**

Cyprus An island country in the eastern Mediterranean Sea.
    Cy·prus (sī'prəs) *noun.*

cyst An abnormal sac on the inside or the outside of the body. Cysts contain liquid and often are removed by surgery.
    cyst (sist) *noun, plural* **cysts.**

cytoplasm A substance that is like jelly and that holds all the parts inside a cell.
    cy·to·plasm (sī'tə plaz'əm) *noun.*

czar One of the male rulers of Russia before the revolution of 1917.
    czar (zär) *noun, plural* **czars.**

Word History

Czar is the Russian word for "Caesar." Julius Caesar was the first Roman emperor, and the name *Caesar* became the standard title for later Roman emperors, as well as for the Russian *czars.*

---

czarina The wife of a czar or a woman who ruled Russia before the revolution of 1917.
    cza·ri·na (zä rē'nə) *noun, plural* **czarinas.**

1. The earliest shape of the letter **D** was a triangle, used by ancient tribes in the Middle East.

2. Later, the ancient Greeks borrowed this letter and changed its name, calling it *delta*.

3. An ancient tribe near Rome used the letter *delta* about 2,800 years ago. They changed it by rounding two sides of the triangle.

4. The Romans then borrowed this letter about 2,400 years ago. They wrote the letter **D** much as we write it today.

5. Our modern English **D** looks much like the one written 2,800 years ago by the ancient tribe near Rome.

d, D **1.** The fourth letter of the alphabet. **2.** The Roman numeral for 500.
d, D (dē) *noun, plural* **d's, D's.**

dab **1.** To touch lightly and gently; pat. The school nurse *dabbed* my cut knee with cotton. **2.** To put on lightly and gently. You should *dab* lotion on those sunburned arms. *Verb.*
—**1.** A small, moist mass of something. I took a *dab* of clay and molded it with my fingers. **2.** A little bit. Would you like a *dab* of butter on your mashed potatoes? *Noun.*
dab (dab) *verb,* **dabbed, dabbing;** *noun, plural* **dabs.**

dabble **1.** To work at or do something a little, but not in a serious way. Some pupils *dabble* at playing the piano and don't practice enough. **2.** To splash in and out of the water. The children sat on the dock to *dabble* their feet in the water.
dab·ble (dab'əl) *verb,* **dabbled, dabbling.**

dachshund A small dog with a long body, very short legs, and drooping ears.
dachs·hund (däks'hunt' *or* däks'hund') *noun, plural* **dachshunds.**

dad Father. I call my father *Dad.*
dad (dad) *noun, plural* **dads.**

daddy Father. Young children often call their father *Daddy.*
dad·dy (dad'ē) *noun, plural* **daddies.**

daddy–longlegs An animal that looks like a spider. It has a small round body and eight very long, thin legs.
dad·dy–long·legs (dad'ē lông'legz') *noun, plural* **daddy-longlegs.**

daffodil A plant that has long, narrow leaves and yellow or white flowers shaped like trumpets. Daffodils grow from underground bulbs.
daf·fo·dil (daf'ə dil') *noun, plural* **daffodils.**

daffodil

dagger A small weapon that looks like a knife. A dagger has a pointed blade that is used for stabbing.
dag·ger (dag'ər) *noun, plural* **daggers.**

daily Appearing, done, or happening every day. Many people read the *daily* newspaper on the way to work. *Adjective.*
—Every day. That train runs *daily. Adverb.*
—A newspaper published every day or every weekday. *Noun.*
dai·ly (dā'lē) *adjective; adverb; noun, plural* **dailies.**

dainty   **1.** Delicate and pretty. The fine handkerchief was decorated with a *dainty* design.   **2.** Hard to please. The *dainty* eater wouldn't accept leftovers.
　dain·ty (dān′tē) *adjective*, **daintier, daintiest.**

dairy   **1.** A place where milk and cream are stored or made into butter and cheese.   **2.** A store or business that sells milk, cream, yogurt, and other milk products.   **3.** A farm where cows are raised for their milk and milk products are sometimes produced.
　dair·y (dâr′ē) *noun*, *plural* **dairies.**

dais   A slightly raised platform for a throne, a speaker's desk, or seats for guests of honor.
　da·is (dā′is) *noun*, *plural* **daises.**

daisy   A plant with a flower of pink, white, or yellow petals around a yellow center.
　dai·sy (dā′zē) *noun*, *plural* **daisies.**

Word History

　Daisy comes from the earlier phrase "the day's eye," a poetic name for this flower. The daisy was thought to resemble the sun.

dale   A valley.
　dale (dāl) *noun*, *plural* **dales.**

Dalmatian   A large dog that has a short white coat with small black or brown spots.
　Dal·ma·tian (dal mā′shən) *noun*, *plural* **Dalmatians.**

dam

dam   A wall built across a stream or river to hold back the water and form a lake or pond. Dams can be used to prevent floods or generate electricity. *Noun.*
—To hold back with a dam. Beavers *dam* streams with mud and sticks. *Verb.*
　dam (dam) *noun*, *plural* **dams;** *verb,* **dammed, damming.**

damage   Harm or injury that makes something less valuable or useful. The flood caused great *damage* to the farms in the area. *Noun.*
—To harm or injure. Rain came through the open window and *damaged* the books on the window sill. *Verb.*
　dam·age (dam′ij) *noun*, *plural* **damages;** *verb,* **damaged, damaging.**

dame   **1.** A woman who has a high social position or a position of honor.   **2.** An elderly woman.
　dame (dām) *noun*, *plural* **dames.**

damp   A little wet; moist. Spilled milk can be wiped up with a *damp* sponge. It was a *damp* and chilly day. *Adjective.*
—Slight wetness; moisture. The *damp* in the cellar made the paint on the walls peel. *Noun.*
　damp (damp) *adjective*, **damper, dampest;** *noun.*

dampen   **1.** To make a little wet or moist. *Dampen* the rag before you wipe the table.   **2.** To lessen the force or strength of. Losing the game *dampened* the team's spirits.
　damp·en (dam′pən) *verb,* **dampened, dampening.**

dance   **1.** To move the body or feet in time to music. We put on a record and *danced.* The ballerina *danced* across the stage.   **2.** To move or jump about quickly or lightly. Sunlight *danced* on the lake. *Verb.*
—**1.** A particular set of steps or movements done in time to music. The waltz, the polka, and the reel are *dances.*   **2.** A party where people dance. There will be a *dance* Friday night at the high school. *Noun.*
　dance (dans) *verb,* **danced, dancing;** *noun*, *plural* **dances.**

dancer   A person who dances. The band stopped playing, and the *dancers* sat down.
　danc·er (dan′sər) *noun*, *plural* **dancers.**

dandelion   A plant with a bright yellow flower and jagged leaves. Dandelion leaves are sometimes eaten in salads or cooked as a vegetable.
　dan·de·li·on (dan′də lī′ən) *noun*, *plural* **dandelions.**

Word History

　The word **dandelion** comes from the old French name for this flower, which meant "lion's teeth." The plant probably got its name because its leaves are pointed like teeth.

dandruff   Small white pieces of dead skin that fall from the scalp.
dan·druff (dan′drəf) *noun.*

dandy   A man who is very proud of his clothes and the way he looks. *Noun.*
—Very good; excellent. You can make *dandy* curtains out of those sheets. *Adjective.*
dan·dy (dan′dē) *noun, plural* **dandies;** *adjective,* **dandier, dandiest.**

Dane   A person who was born in or is a citizen of Denmark.
Dane (dān) *noun, plural* **Danes.**

danger   **1.** The chance that something bad or harmful will happen. There is great *danger* in skating on thin ice.   **2.** Something that may cause harm or injury. Icy roads are a *danger* to drivers.
dan·ger (dān′jər) *noun, plural* **dangers.**

dangerous   Likely to cause something bad or harmful to happen. Driving too fast is *dangerous.* Wild animals can be *dangerous.*
dan·ger·ous (dān′jər əs) *adjective.*

dangle   To hang or swing loosely. Some old kite string *dangled* from a branch of the tree.
dan·gle (dang′gəl) *verb,* **dangled, dangling.**

Danish   The language of Denmark. *Noun.*
—Of or having to do with Denmark, its people, or its language. *Adjective.*
Dan·ish (dā′nish) *noun; adjective.*

dare   **1.** To ask someone to do something as a test of courage or ability; challenge. I *dared* my friend to jump off the diving board.   **2.** To be bold enough to try; have the courage for. No one *dared* to go into the dark cave. *Verb.*
—A challenge. I accepted my friend's *dare* and jumped across the stream. *Noun.*
dare (dâr) *verb,* **dared, daring;** *noun, plural* **dares.**

daredevil   A person who performs bold or dangerous stunts; a person who is reckless. We were almost hit by the *daredevil* who skied too fast down the hill. *Noun.*
—Bold; reckless. *Daredevil* driving is foolish and unsafe. *Adjective.*
dare·dev·il (dâr′dev′il) *noun, plural* **daredevils;** *adjective.*

daring   Courage or boldness; bravery. The first pilots to fly airplanes were famous for their *daring. Noun.*
—Courageous and bold; brave; fearless. The police officer was given a medal for the *daring* rescue of a drowning child. *Adjective.*
dar·ing (dâr′ing) *noun; adjective.*

dark   **1.** Having little or no light. The night was *dark* because the clouds were covering the moon.   **2.** Black or brown rather than light in color. Some people's skin becomes *dark* when they spend time in the sun. *Adjective.*
—**1.** A lack of light. I keep a light on in my room at night because I am afraid of the *dark.*   **2.** Night or nightfall; the end of daylight. My grandparents asked us to be home before *dark. Noun.*
• **in the dark.**   Without knowledge; not aware. The teacher kept us *in the dark* about the surprise party.
dark (därk) *adjective,* **darker, darkest;** *noun.*

darken   To make or become dark or darker. The baseball players watched the rain clouds *darken* the sky. The white paint had *darkened* with age.
dark·en (där′kən) *verb,* **darkened, darkening.**

darling   A person who is loved very much. The proud couple called their new baby *darling. Noun.*
—**1.** Very much loved; dear. My grandparents wrote a letter to me at camp that began with the words "Our *darling* grandchild."   **2.** Cute and adorable. Everyone thought the kittens were *darling. Adjective.*
dar·ling (där′ling) *noun, plural* **darlings;** *adjective.*

darn   To mend by making stitches back and forth across a hole or tear. You can use woolen yarn to *darn* that hole in your sock.
darn (därn) *verb,* **darned, darning.**

dart   **1.** A thin, pointed object that looks like a small arrow.   **2. darts.** A game in which darts are thrown at a target. *Noun.*
—**1.** To jump or move suddenly and quickly. We watched the rabbit *dart* into the bushes.   **2.** To throw or send suddenly and quickly. The frog *darted* out its tongue to catch the fly. Why did you *dart* that angry look at me? *Verb.*
dart (därt) *noun, plural* **darts;** *verb,* **darted, darting.**

dash   **1.** To move fast; rush. We tried to teach our dog not to *dash* after cars.   **2.** To hit or throw with force; smash. High waves *dashed* against the ship during the storm.   **3.** To destroy or ruin. Spraining my ankle *dashed* my hopes of running in the race.

at; āpe; fär; câre; end; mē; it; īce; pîerce; hot; ōld; sông, fôrk; oil; out; up; ūse; rüle; pull; tûrn; chin; sing; shop; thin; this; hw in white; zh in treasure. The symbol ə stands for the unstressed vowel sound in about, taken, pencil, lemon, and circus.

4. To make, write or finish quickly. I *dashed* off a short letter to a friend. *Verb.*
—**1.** A fast movement or sudden rush. The hikers made a *dash* for cover when the rain started. **2.** A small amount that is added or mixed in. Add a *dash* of pepper to the beef stew. **3.** A short race. Both schools had runners in the 50-yard *dash.* **4.** A punctuation mark (–) that is used to show a pause or a break in the thought that a sentence expresses. A dash is also used to show that something has been left out of a sentence. *Noun.*
  dash (dash) *verb,* **dashed, dashing;** *noun, plural* **dashes.**

dashboard

dashboard A panel under the windshield in an automobile. It has dials and instruments to help the driver operate the car.
  dash·board (dash′bôrd′) *noun, plural* **dashboards.**

data **1.** Individual facts, figures, and other items of information. These *data* from the computer don't seem to be accurate. ▲ The singular of **data** in this sense is **datum.** **2.** Information as a whole. Adequate *data* on that subject is sometimes difficult to find.
  da·ta (dā′tə *or* dat′ə) *plural noun, noun.*

database A collection of information that can be examined and changed with a computer. This word is also spelled **data base.**
  da·ta·base (dā′tə bās′ *or* dat′ə bās′) *noun, plural* **databases.**

date¹ **1.** The day, month, year, or time when something happened or happens. The *date* of my birthday is June 3. The *date* that the thirteen colonies declared their independence from Great Britain was July 4, 1776. What is today's *date?* **2.** Writing or numerals that say when something was made or written. The *date* on the coin was 1883. **3.** An agreement to meet or be with someone at a certain time and place. The two friends made a *date* to meet for lunch on Thursday.

4. A person with whom one has such an agreement. My cousin doesn't have a *date* for the dance yet. *Noun.*
—**1.** To mark with a time or date. Be sure to *date* your test paper. **2.** To find out or fix the time of. The scientists at the museum were able to *date* the dinosaur bones. **3.** To belong to or come from a certain time. The old chair in the living room *dates* from the late 1800s. **4.** To meet socially with a person for companionship. They have been *dating* for six months. I *dated* one of my classmates during the summer. *Verb.*
  • **out of date.** No longer fashionable; old-fashioned. I gave away some clothes that were *out of date.*
  date (dāt) *noun, plural* **dates;** *verb,* **dated, dating.**

date palm tree

date² A sweet fruit that grows on a kind of palm tree. The tree that this fruit grows on is also called a date. It grows in warm areas.
  date (dāt) *noun, plural* **dates.**

datum One piece of information. Look up **data** for more information.
  da·tum (dā′təm *or* dat′əm) *noun, plural* **data.**

daughter A female child. A girl or woman is the daughter of her mother and father.
  daugh·ter (dô′tər) *noun, plural* **daughters.**

daughter-in-law The wife of a son.
  daugh·ter-in-law (dô′tər in lô′) *noun, plural* **daughters-in-law.**

dawn **1.** The first light that appears in the morning; daybreak. **2.** The beginning or first sign. The *dawn* of civilization took place thousands of years ago. *Noun.*
—**1.** To begin to get light in the morning; become day. We sat on the beach and watched the day *dawn.* **2.** To begin to be clear or un-

192

derstood. It *dawned* on us that we were being teased. *Verb.*

> **dawn** (dôn) *noun, plural* **dawns;** *verb,* **dawned, dawning.**

day **1.** The period of light between the rising and setting of the sun. The farmer worked all *day* long. **2.** The twenty-four hours of one day and night. We have a vacation of ten *days* in the spring. **3.** The part of a day spent working. My school *day* ends at three o'clock in the afternoon. **4.** A time or period. In the present *day,* more Americans live in cities than on farms.

> **day** (dā) *noun, plural* **days.**

daybreak The time each morning when light first appears; dawn.

> **day·break** (dā′brāk′) *noun, plural* **daybreaks.**

day–care center A place where adults take care of and teach small children during the day. It is often used by children whose parents are not home during the day because they go to work.

> **day-care center** (dā′kâr′).

daydream Pleasant thinking or wishing about things one would like to do or have happen. I had a *daydream* of being a famous writer someday. *Noun.*
—To think about pleasant things as if dreaming. The boss told the employees to get to work and not to *daydream* all day. *Verb.*

> **day·dream** (dā′drēm′) *noun, plural* **daydreams;** *verb,* **daydreamed, daydreaming.**

daylight **1.** The light of day; daytime. **2.** The dawn; daybreak. The farmer was up doing chores before *daylight.*

> **day·light** (dā′līt′) *noun.*

daytime The time when it is day; daylight.

> **day·time** (dā′tīm′) *noun.*

daze To confuse or stun; bewilder. The fall from the tree *dazed* me. *Verb.*
—A confused or stunned condition. The car accident left the driver in a *daze. Noun.*

> **daze** (dāz) *verb,* **dazed, dazing;** *noun, plural* **dazes.**

dazzle **1.** To make almost blind by too much light. The bright sun on the beach *dazzled* our eyes. **2.** To impress with something very showy or brilliant. The acrobat's spectacular tricks *dazzled* the audience.

> **daz·zle** (daz′əl) *verb,* **dazzled, dazzling.**

DC or **D.C.** **1.** An abbreviation for *District of Columbia.* **2.** An abbreviation for *direct current.*

de- A *prefix* that means: **1.** To do the opposite of; undo. *Desegregate* means to do the opposite of segregate. **2.** To remove. *De-*frost means to remove frost. **3.** Down; lower. *Depression* means a place that is lower than the area around it.

DE Postal abbreviation for *Delaware.*

deacon **1.** A church officer who helps a minister. **2.** A member of the clergy who ranks just below a priest.

> **dea·con** (dē′kən) *noun, plural* **deacons.**

dead **1.** No longer living or having life. The plant was *dead* because it had not gotten enough water and sun. **2.** Not having life. Rocks are *dead* matter. **3.** Without power, activity, or interest. I can't make a phone call because the telephone is *dead.* Winter is a *dead* time for the stores at the beach. **4.** Complete; total. When the curtain rose in the theater, there was *dead* silence. **5.** Sure or certain; exact. Try to hit the target at *dead* center. *Adjective.*
—**1.** Completely. The hikers were *dead* tired. **2.** Directly; straight. The exit from the highway is *dead* ahead. *Adverb.*
—**1.** People who are no longer living. The minister led us in a prayer for the *dead.* **2.** The time of greatest darkness or coldness. A noise woke me up in the *dead* of night. *Noun.*

> **dead** (ded) *adjective,* **deader, deadest;** *adverb; noun.*

deaden To dull or weaken. The dentist gave me an injection to *deaden* the pain in my sore tooth.

> **dead·en** (ded′ən) *verb,* **deadened, deadening.**

dead end A street or passage that is closed at one end.

deadline A set time by which something must be finished; time limit. The *deadline* for handing in our book reports is Friday.

> **dead·line** (ded′līn′) *noun, plural* **deadlines.**

deadly **1.** Causing or likely to cause death. A knife can be a *deadly* weapon. **2.** Meaning to kill or destroy. The two countries became *deadly* enemies when they went to war.

> **dead·ly** (ded′lē) *adjective,* **deadlier, deadliest.**

deaf **1.** Not able to hear, or not able to hear well. The *deaf* children were using sign lan-

---

at; āpe; fär; câre; end; mē; it; īce; pîerce; hot; ōld; sông, fôrk; oil; out; up; ūse; rüle; pùll; tûrn; chin; sing; shop; thin; <u>th</u>is; hw in white; zh in treasure. The symbol ə stands for the unstressed vowel sound in about, taken, pencil, lemon, and circus.

guage to speak to one another. **2.** Not willing to hear or listen. Most people were *deaf* to the beggar's calls for help.

deaf (def) *adjective,* **deafer, deafest.**

deafen To make unable to hear. The noise of the machines *deafened* us for a moment.

deaf·en (def'ən) *verb,* **deafened, deafening.**

deal **1.** To have to do; be about. I'm looking for a book that *deals* with dogs. **2.** To act or behave. The principal *dealt* harshly with the fighting students. **3.** To conduct business; trade. That store *deals* in newspapers and magazines. **4.** To give or deliver. Whose turn is it to *deal* the cards? *Verb.*
—A bargain or agreement. According to our *deal,* I make breakfast and you wash the dishes. *Noun.*
• **a great deal** or **a good deal.** A large amount or quantity. My cousin spends *a great deal* of time making furniture. I don't paint, but I draw *a good deal.*

deal (dēl) *verb,* **dealt, dealing;** *noun, plural* **deals.**

dealer **1.** A person who buys or sells something for a living. We bought our new car from a car *dealer.* **2.** A person who gives out cards in a card game.

deal·er (dē'lər) *noun, plural* **dealers.**

dealt Past tense and past participle of **deal.** I read a book that *dealt* with the discovery of North America. Look up **deal** for more information.

dealt (delt) *verb.*

dear **1.** Much or greatly loved. This is my *dearest* friend. That doll was *dear* to me. **2.** High in price; expensive. Strawberries are *dear* in the winter. **3.** Respected; esteemed. We start a letter by writing *"Dear"* and following it with the name of the person we are writing to. *Adjective.*
—A much loved person. You are such a *dear* to come over and help. *Noun.*
—An exclamation of surprise, disappointment, or trouble. Oh *dear!* I've missed the bus. *Interjection.* ▲ Another word that sounds like this is **deer.**

dear (dîr) *adjective,* **dearer, dearest;** *noun, plural* **dears;** *interjection.*

dearly Very much; a great deal. We *dearly* love our grandparents.

dear·ly (dîr'lē) *adverb.*

death **1.** The end of life in people, plants, or animals. Highway accidents cause many *deaths.* **2.** The end of something; destruction. The *death* of silent movies came in about 1930.

death (deth) *noun, plural* **deaths.**

debate A discussion between two persons or groups who disagree; argument. There was much *debate* about where we should go on our vacation. The candidates for mayor had a *debate* on budget cuts. *Noun.*
—**1.** To argue about or discuss at a public meeting. The state representatives *debated* whether or not to change the highway speed limit. **2.** To think about; consider. Sometimes on a cloudy day I *debate* whether to take an umbrella with me. *Verb.*

de·bate (di bāt') *noun, plural* **debates;** *verb,* **debated, debating.**

debris The scattered remains of something that has been broken or destroyed. *Debris* from the plane crash littered a large area of the town.

de·bris (də brē') *noun.*

debt **1.** Something that is owed to another. I was able to pay my *debts* when I got my allowance. **2.** The condition of owing. My parents are in *debt* to the bank because they borrowed money to buy our house.

debt (det) *noun, plural* **debts.**

debtor A person who owes something to someone else. I never borrow money, because I think it is unwise to be a *debtor.*

debt·or (det'ər) *noun.*

Dec. An abbreviation for *December.*

decade A period of ten years.

dec·ade (dek'ād) *noun, plural* **decades.**

decal A design or picture on specially treated paper. The decal can be transferred to a hard flat surface, such as wood or glass. We used a knife to scrape the old *decal* off the car window.

de·cal (dē'kal *or* di kal') *noun, plural* **decals.**

decanter A glass bottle with a stopper. Decanters are usually used to hold wine or liquor.

de·cant·er (di kan'tər) *noun, plural* **decanters.**

decanter

decay **1.** A slow, natural breaking down of plant or animal matter; rot. The dentist told me to brush my teeth at least twice a day to prevent tooth *decay.* The wooden beams of the old house showed *decay.* **2.** A slow lowering of quality or strength; decline. The subway system showed signs of *decay* because repairs had not been made for so long. *Noun.*

—**1.** To rot slowly. The oranges turned moldy and began to *decay*. **2.** To decline slowly in quality or strength. *Verb.*
de·cay (di kā′) *noun, plural* **decays;** *verb,* **decayed, decaying.**

deceased Dead. Our school is named after a *deceased* president. *Adjective.*
—**the deceased.** A dead person or persons. *Noun.*
de·ceased (di sēst′) *adjective; noun.*

deceit **1.** The act of lying or cheating. The salespersons were guilty of *deceit* when they told the customer that the used bicycle was new. **2.** The quality that makes someone lie or cheat. The thieves were full of *deceit* as they pretended to know nothing about the missing money.
de·ceit (di sēt′) *noun, plural* **deceits.**

deceive To make someone believe something that is not true; mislead. I *deceived* my parents by telling them I had no homework.
de·ceive (di sēv′) *verb,* **deceived, deceiving.**

December The twelfth and last month of the year. December has thirty-one days.
De·cem·ber (di sem′bər) *noun.*

Word History

December comes from the Latin word for "ten." The early Roman calendar began with March, making December the tenth month.

decent **1.** Proper and respectable. It is not *decent* to listen to other people's private conversations. **2.** Kind or generous. It was *decent* of them to help you with your chores. **3.** Fairly good; satisfactory. I'll never be an A student, but I get *decent* grades.
de·cent (dē′sənt) *adjective.*

decide **1.** To make up one's mind. I want to be a doctor or a teacher, but I haven't *decided* which. **2.** To settle or judge a question or argument. The judge *decided* in favor of the prisoner. **3.** To settle the outcome of. The last touchdown *decided* the game.
de·cide (di sīd′) *verb,* **decided, deciding.**

decimal Based on the number 10. In the United States money is based on the *decimal* system. *Adjective.*
—A fraction with a denominator of 10, or a multiple of 10 such as 100 or 1,000. The decimal .5 is another way of writing ⁵⁄₁₀. This is also called a **decimal fraction.** *Noun.*
dec·i·mal (des′ə məl) *adjective; noun, plural* **decimals.**

decimal point A period put before a decimal fraction. The periods in .5, .30, and .052 are decimal points.

decipher **1.** To figure out the meaning of something difficult to read or understand. No one could *decipher* the scribbled handwriting. **2.** To change secret writing into ordinary writing. The enemy *deciphered* our general's message and discovered our plans for a surprise attack.
de·ci·pher (di sī′fər) *verb,* **deciphered, deciphering.**

decision The act or result of making up one's mind. Think carefully about a problem before you make a *decision*.
de·ci·sion (di sizh′ən) *noun, plural* **decisions.**

decisive **1.** Deciding something finally and completely. The army suffered a *decisive* defeat and was forced to surrender to the enemy. **2.** Showing firmness and determination. The *decisive* customer quickly picked out a suit to buy.
de·ci·sive (di sī′siv) *adjective.*

deck of a ship

deck **1.** The floor on a ship or boat. A deck may have a roof or covering over it or be completely open. **2.** A platform that is like the deck of a ship or boat. We built a *deck*

D

at; āpe; fär; câre; end; mē; it; īce; pîerce; hot; ōld; sông, fôrk; oil; out; up; ūse; rüle; pull; tûrn; chin; sing; shop; thin; this; hw in white; zh in treasure. The symbol ə stands for the unstressed vowel sound in about, taken, pencil, lemon, and circus.

onto the back of the house so we could sit out in the sun.   **3.** A set of playing cards. It's your turn to shuffle the *deck* and deal the cards. *Noun.*
—To dress or decorate. We all *decked* ourselves out in funny costumes for Halloween. *Verb.*

> **deck** (dek) *noun, plural* **decks;** *verb,* **decked, decking.**

declaration   **1.** The act of announcing or of making something known. The *declaration* of war is a power given to the Congress by the Constitution of the United States.   **2.** A statement that makes something known. The two friends exchanged *declarations* of loyalty.

> **dec·la·ra·tion** (dek′lə rā′shən) *noun, plural* **declarations.**

Declaration of Independence   A statement made on July 4, 1776, that the thirteen American colonies were independent of Great Britain.

declarative sentence   A sentence that makes a statement. An example of a declarative sentence is "The game ended in a tie."

> **de·clar·a·tive sentence** (di klar′ə tiv).

declare   **1.** To announce or make something known. The two countries *declared* war.   **2.** To say strongly and firmly. They *declared* that they were right and nothing would change their minds.

> **de·clare** (di klâr′) *verb,* **declared, declaring.**

decline   **1.** To refuse politely. I wrote a note to *decline* the invitation to the birthday party.   **2.** To grow less or weaker; decrease. The membership *declined* in the club. *Verb.*
—A lessening or weakening of power, health, value, or amount. The empire suffered many wars during its *decline*. My grandparents' health went into a *decline* that winter. *Noun.*

> **de·cline** (di klīn′) *verb,* **declined, declining;** *noun, plural* **declines.**

decode   To change secret writing into ordinary language. The spy *decoded* the secret message.

> **de·code** (dē kōd′) *verb,* **decoded, decoding.**

decompose   To rot or decay. Dead leaves slowly *decompose* and become part of the soil.

> **de·com·pose** (dē′kəm pōz′) *verb,* **decomposed, decomposing.**

decorate   **1.** To make more beautiful; ornament. The children *decorated* the Christmas tree with lights. The family *decorated* the living room by hanging pictures on the walls.   **2.** To give a badge or medal to. The army *decorated* the soldier for bravery.

> **dec·o·rate** (dek′ə rāt′) *verb,* **decorated, decorating.**

decoration   **1.** The act of making more beautiful; decorating. The *decoration* of the gym for the dance took all day.   **2.** Something that is used to decorate; ornament. We took down the balloons, crepe paper, and other *decorations* after the party.   **3.** A badge or medal. All the children in the scout troops wore their *decorations* for the Fourth of July parade.

> **dec·o·ra·tion** (dek′ə rā′shən) *noun, plural* **decorations.**

decoys

decoy   **1.** A model of a bird used to attract real birds into a trap or to within shooting distance of a hunter. The hunter floated a wooden *decoy* on the lake.   **2.** A person who leads another person into danger or into a trap. The police *decoys* dressed as old people and arrested a criminal who tried to rob them. *Noun.*
—To attract or lead into danger or into a trap. They tried to *decoy* the rabbit into the trap by leaving a trail of pieces of lettuce. *Verb.*

> **de·coy** (dē′koi *or* di koi′ *for noun;* di koi′ *for verb) noun, plural* **decoys;** *verb,* **decoyed, decoying.**

decrease   To make or become less. The driver *decreased* the speed of the car as we came to our exit on the highway. The population of the town *decreased* when the coal mine closed. *Verb.*
—**1.** The act of becoming less. I noticed a *decrease* in people on the beach as it got colder.   **2.** The amount by which something becomes less. There was a *decrease* of 10 degrees in the temperature during the night. *Noun.*

> **de·crease** (di krēs′ *for verb;* dē′krēs *or* di krēs′ *for noun) verb,* **decreased, decreasing;** *noun, plural* **decreases.**

decree An official order or decision. The king and queen sent out a *decree* that all taxes would be raised. *Noun.*
—To order or decide officially. The dictator *decreed* the arrest of all people who were against the government. *Verb.*
de·cree (di krē′) *noun, plural* **decrees;** *verb,* **decreed, decreeing.**

dedicate To set apart for or devote to a special purpose or use. Many scientists have *dedicated* themselves to finding a cure for cancer.
ded·i·cate (ded′i kāt′) *verb,* **dedicated, dedicating.**

dedication 1. A setting apart for or devotion to a special purpose or use. At the *dedication* of the new school, people gave speeches and the building was officially named. 2. Great concentration on a purpose or goal. The guitar player practiced the piece with *dedication.*
ded·i·ca·tion (ded′i kā′shən) *noun, plural* **dedications.**

deduct To take away or subtract from a total. The teacher will *deduct* five points for each wrong answer on the test.
de·duct (di dukt′) *verb,* **deducted, deducting.**

deduction 1. The method or process of reaching a conclusion based on some condition that is known. That detective was a master of *deduction.* 2. A conclusion that has been reached based on some condition that is known. 3. The taking away from a total; subtraction. The store made a *deduction* of ten dollars from the price of the radio.
de·duc·tion (di duk′shən) *noun, plural* **deductions.**

deed 1. Something done; act; action. You did a good *deed* by helping the blind person across the street. 2. A written, legal agreement. When we bought our house, we received a *deed* to show that we owned it.
deed (dēd) *noun, plural* **deeds.**

deep 1. Far down from the surface. I don't swim in the *deep* end of the swimming pool because the water is over my head. 2. Great in degree; intense; extreme. The weary child fell into a *deep* sleep. 3. Difficult to understand. My cousin's chemistry book is too *deep* for me. 4. Completely occupied with something; absorbed. You didn't hear the doorbell ring because you were *deep* in thought. 5. Low in pitch. The bass singer had a *deep* voice. *Adjective.*
—In, at, or to a great depth. The explorers went *deep* into the jungle. *Adverb.*
deep (dēp) *adjective,* **deeper, deepest;** *adverb.*

deer An animal that has hooves, chews its cud, and runs very fast. A male deer has antlers that are shed every year and grow back the next year. Deer are closely related to elk, moose, and caribou. ▲ Another word that sounds like this is **dear.**
deer (dîr) *noun, plural* **deer.**

deer

deface To damage the surface or appearance of. The children *defaced* the statue by writing on it.
de·face (di fās′) *verb,* **defaced, defacing.**

defeat To win a victory over; overcome in a contest. Our basketball team easily *defeated* the visiting team. The troops in the fort *defeated* the attacking enemy. *Verb.*
—The condition or fact of being defeated in a contest. Our team's *defeat* ended our hopes of winning the championship. *Noun.*
de·feat (di fēt′) *verb,* **defeated, defeating;** *noun, plural* **defeats.**

defect A flaw or weakness. That glass bowl has a chip, a crack, and other *defects.*
de·fect (dē′fekt *or* di fekt′) *noun, plural* **defects.**

defective Having a flaw or weakness; not perfect. *Defective* electrical wiring is a cause of fires in homes.
de·fec·tive (di fek′tiv) *adjective.*

defend 1. To guard against attack or danger; protect. A goalie's job is to *defend* the goal against the opposing team. 2. To speak or act in support of. The lawyer agreed to de-

at; āpe; fär; câre; end; mē; it; īce; pîerce; hot; ōld; sông, fôrk; oil; out; up; ūse; rūle; pull; tûrn; chin; sing; shop; thin; this; hw in white; zh in treasure. The symbol ə stands for the unstressed vowel sound in about, taken, pencil, lemon, and circus.

fend the person accused of the robbery. Express your opinion, and *defend* it with facts and arguments.

de·fend (di fend') *verb,* **defended, defending.**

defense **1.** The act of guarding against attack or danger. The country prepared for the *defense* of its borders by setting up barriers. **2.** A person or thing that protects. The dam was the city's only *defense* against floods. **3.** Support. When the movie was unfairly criticized, I spoke up in its *defense.* **4.** The defending team or players in a game. Our hockey team has such a good *defense* that the other team never scored a goal.

de·fense (di fens') *noun, plural* **defenses.**

defensive Guarding or protecting against attack. Knights used to put on *defensive* armor before going into battle.

de·fen·sive (di fen'siv) *adjective.*

defer¹ To put off to a future time; delay. The judge asked the jury to *defer* their judgment in the case until they had heard all the evidence.

de·fer (di fûr') *verb,* **deferred, deferring.**

defer² To stop opposing the opinion or wishes of someone else; yield respectfully. When we disagree, I usually *defer* to my older friend's judgment.

de·fer (di fûr') *verb,* **deferred, deferring.**

defiance Bold refusal to obey or respect authority. The hoodlums showed their *defiance* of the law by breaking a window of the police station.

de·fi·ance (di fī'əns) *noun.*

deficiency **1.** A lack of something needed or necessary. Some people take vitamin pills every morning to help keep healthy and prevent a vitamin *deficiency.* **2.** The amount by which something is lacking. The banker counted the money in the safe after the robbery and found a *deficiency* of $10,000.

de·fi·cien·cy (di fish'ən sē) *noun, plural* **deficiencies.**

define **1.** To give the meaning or meanings of. A dictionary *defines* words. **2.** To describe or fix exactly. The deed for this piece of property *defines* its boundaries.

de·fine (di fīn') *verb,* **defined, defining.**

definite Certain; clear. Let's set a *definite* time to meet again. My answer was a *definite* no.

def·i·nite (def'ə nit) *adjective.*

definite article The article *the.* The definite article is used to refer to a particular person or thing. In the sentence "Give me the magazine you were reading," the definite article refers to a particular magazine.

definition An explanation of the meaning of a word or group of words. A definition for the word "house" is "a building in which people live."

def·i·ni·tion (def'ə nish'ən) *noun, plural* **definitions.**

deform To spoil the form or shape of. Constant winds had *deformed* and bent the tree.

de·form (di fôrm') *verb,* **deformed, deforming.**

defrost To make free of ice or frost; thaw. I *defrosted* the refrigerator this morning.

de·frost (di frôst') *verb,* **defrosted, defrosting.**

deft Skillful and clever; nimble. The musician's *deft* fingers raced over the piano keys.

deft (deft) *adjective.*

defy **1.** To show disrespect for by refusing to obey. Some drivers *defy* the law by going faster than the speed limit. **2.** To challenge someone to do something that seems impossible. I *defy* you to name all the presidents of the United States. **3.** To resist stubbornly; withstand. The stain *defied* all my attempts to bleach it.

de·fy (di fī') *verb,* **defied, defying.**

degrade To lower in character, quality, or rank. The boss's cruel treatment *degraded* the employees.

de·grade (di grād') *verb,* **degraded, degrading.**

degree **1.** A stage or step in a process or series. A young child learns to walk by *degrees.* **2.** Amount or extent. A high *degree* of skill is needed to weave a rug. **3.** A title given by a school or college to a student who has finished a course of study. **4.** A unit for measuring temperature. A person's normal body temperature is 98.6 *degrees* Fahrenheit. **5.** A unit for measuring angles or arcs. Two perpendicular lines form a 90-*degree* angle.

de·gree (di grē') *noun, plural* **degrees.**

The **degrees** are marked on the thermometer.

deity A god or goddess. Mars was the Roman *deity* of war.

de·i·ty (dē'i tē) *noun, plural* **deities.**

dejected Sad or depressed. The basketball team felt *dejected* after losing the game.

de·ject·ed (di jek'tid) *adjective.*

Del. An abbreviation for *Delaware*.

Delaware A state in the eastern United States. Its capital is Dover.

Del·a·ware (del′ə wâr′) *noun.*

The name **Delaware** comes from the name of the first governor of Virginia, Lord "De la Warr." An English captain named the Delaware Bay after this governor. Later, the name was given to the land west of the bay, which became the state.

delay **1.** To put off to a later time; postpone. The leader had to *delay* the start of the hike because of rain. **2.** To make late. We would have come sooner, but we were *delayed* by a flat tire. **3.** To slow down; linger. I will miss my bus if I *delay. Verb.*
—The act of delaying or the condition of being delayed. I answered the letter without *delay.* There will be a *delay* of fifteen minutes before the train arrives. *Noun.*

de·lay (di lā′) *verb,* **delayed, delaying;** *noun, plural* **delays.**

delegate A person who is chosen to act for others; representative. Each country that belongs to the United Nations is represented by a *delegate. Noun.*
—To choose or to be responsible for doing a task; assign. The club *delegated* me to make arrangements for a holiday party. *Verb.*

del·e·gate (del′i gāt′ *or* del′i git *for noun;* del′i gāt′ *for verb*) *noun, plural* **delegates;** *verb,* **delegated, delegating.**

delegation A group of delegates or representatives. A *delegation* from the fire department marched in the Fourth of July parade.

del·e·ga·tion (del′i gā′shən) *noun, plural* **delegations.**

deliberate **1.** Done or said on purpose. The bully played a *deliberate* trick to insult the new student. **2.** Careful and slow; not hasty or rash. The person with the cane walked with *deliberate* steps. *Adjective.*
—To think over or discuss carefully. The jury *deliberated* for hours before giving a decision. *Verb.*

de·lib·er·ate (di lib′ər it *for adjective;* di lib′ə rāt′ *for verb*) *adjective; verb,* **deliberated, deliberating.**

delicate **1.** Fine or dainty. The threads of a spider's web are *delicate.* **2.** Pleasing in smell, taste, or color; mild or soft. There was a *delicate* scent of roses in the air. **3.** Easily

damaged; fragile. Don't put those *delicate* glasses in the dishwasher because they break easily. **4.** Very sensitive. *Delicate* instruments detected an earthquake thousands of miles away. **5.** Requiring careful skill. The doctors repaired the nerves of the injured hand in a *delicate* operation.

del·i·cate (del′i kit) *adjective.*

delicatessen A store that sells food that is ready to eat. Cold meats, cheeses, and salads are sold in a delicatessen.

del·i·ca·tes·sen (del′i kə tes′ən) *noun, plural* **delicatessens.**

delicious Pleasing or delightful to the taste or smell. The stew cooking for dinner smelled *delicious.*

de·li·cious (di lish′əs) *adjective.*

delight Great pleasure; joy. The children beamed with *delight* as they watched the circus. *Noun.*
—**1.** To give great pleasure or joy to; please very much. The puppet show *delighted* the children. **2.** To have or take great pleasure. My grandparents *delight* in telling us stories about their childhood. *Verb.*

de·light (di līt′) *noun, plural* **delights;** *verb,* **delighted, delighting.**

delightful Very pleasing. We had a *delightful* time playing games at the party.

de·light·ful (di līt′fəl) *adjective.*

deliver **1.** To carry or take to the proper place or person. The department store *delivered* our new television set on Friday. **2.** To say; utter. The mayor *delivered* a long speech at the meeting. **3.** To strike or throw. The pitcher *delivered* a curve ball to the batter. **4.** To save from danger; rescue. The slaves were finally *delivered* from bondage.

de·liv·er (di liv′ər) *verb,* **delivered, delivering.**

delivery **1.** The act of carrying or taking something to the proper place or person. The mail carrier makes a mail *delivery* every day except Sundays and holidays. **2.** A way of speaking or singing. The singer's *delivery* was loud and energetic.

de·liv·er·y (di liv′ə rē) *noun, plural* **deliveries.**

delta An area of land at the mouth of a river. A delta is formed by deposits of mud,

at; āpe; fär; câre; end; mē; it; īce; pîerce; hot; ōld; sông, fôrk; oil; out; up; ūse; rüle; pùll; tûrn; chin; sing; shop; thin; this; hw in white; zh in treasure. The symbol ə stands for the unstressed vowel sound in about, taken, pencil, lemon, and circus.

sand, and pebbles. It is often shaped like a triangle.

del·ta (del′tə) *noun, plural* **deltas.**

demand **1.** To ask for urgently or forcefully; claim as a right. The customers *demanded* their money back for the defective radio. The judge *demanded* silence in the court. **2.** To call for; need. Portrait painting *demands* skill and close observation. *Verb.* —**1.** The act of demanding. The child's *demand* for more spinach surprised everyone. The teacher will provide extra paper on *demand.* **2.** Something that is demanded. Higher pay and safer conditions were among the *demands* of the factory workers. **3.** The willingness to buy or use something offered; desire for a product or service. The supermarket manager says that the *demand* for turkeys is very high at Thanksgiving time. *Noun.*

de·mand (di mand′) *verb,* **demanded, demanding;** *noun, plural* **demands.**

demerit Something on a person's record that shows he or she broke a rule. The two apprentices had received so many *demerits* for lateness that they were fired.

de·mer·it (dē mer′it) *noun, plural* **demerits.**

democracy **1.** A government that is run by the people who live under it. In a democracy, the people may run the government indirectly by electing representatives who govern for them. Or they may run it directly by having meetings to which everyone may come. **2.** A country in which the government is a democracy. The United States is a *democracy.*

de·moc·ra·cy (di mok′rə sē) *noun, plural* **democracies.**

democrat **1.** A person who believes that a government should be run by the people who live under it. **2. Democrat.** A person who belongs to the Democratic Party. **3.** A person who believes that all people are equal or should have equal rights.

dem·o·crat (dem′ə krat′) *noun, plural* **democrats.**

democratic **1.** Of or supporting a democracy. The United States is a *democratic* country. **2.** Believing that all people should be treated as equals.

dem·o·crat·ic (dem′ə krat′ik) *adjective.*

Democratic Party One of the two major political parties in the United States.

demolish To tear down or destroy. The workers *demolished* the old factory to make way for a new office building.

de·mol·ish (di mol′ish) *verb,* **demolished, demolishing.**

demon **1.** An evil spirit; devil. **2.** A person who does something with great enthusiasm or energy. We worked like *demons* to finish the boat in time for the race.

de·mon (dē′mən) *noun, plural* **demons.**

demonstrate **1.** To explain, prove, or show clearly. A salesperson *demonstrated* the new food processor at the department store. **2.** To take part in a public meeting or parade to show feelings about a matter. A group of citizens *demonstrated* against the pollution of the river by wastes from the factory.

dem·on·strate (dem′ən strāt′) *verb,* **demonstrated, demonstrating.**

a **demonstration** of carving

demonstration **1.** Something that explains, proves, or shows clearly. The firefighters' rescue of the family from the burning house was a *demonstration* of their

bravery. **2.** A public meeting or parade to show feelings about a matter. A group of people held a *demonstration* in the park to protest the war.
dem·on·stra·tion (dem′ən strā′shən) *noun, plural* **demonstrations.**

den **1.** A place where wild animals rest or sleep. The bear uses a cave as a *den* during its long winter sleeps. **2.** A small, cozy room for reading or studying. **3.** A group of about eight Cub Scouts.
den (den) *noun, plural* **dens.**

denial The act of saying "no" or "not true" to something. The judge listened to the prisoner's *denial* of the charges against him.
de·ni·al (di nī′əl) *noun, plural* **denials.**

denim **1.** A heavy cotton cloth used for work or sports clothes. **2. denims.** Pants or overalls made of this cloth.
den·im (den′im) *noun, plural* **denims.**

Denmark A country in north-central Europe.
Den·mark (den′märk) *noun.*

denomination **1.** A religious group or sect. **2.** One kind of unit in a system. A dime and a nickel are coins of different *denominations.*
de·nom·i·na·tion (di nom′ə nā′shən) *noun, plural* **denominations.**

denominator The number below the line in a fraction. The denominator shows the number of equal parts into which the whole is divided. In the fraction ½, 2 is the denominator.
de·nom·i·na·tor (di nom′ə nā′tər) *noun, plural* **denominators.**

denote **1.** To be a sign of; show. A dark sky and high winds usually *denote* the coming of a storm. **2.** To be a name for; mean. The word "dentist" *denotes* a doctor who takes care of people's teeth.
de·note (di nōt′) *verb,* **denoted, denoting.**

denounce **1.** To speak out against; object to. The letter in the newspaper *denounced* bicyclists who ignore traffic lights. **2.** To give information against; accuse.
de·nounce (di nouns′) *verb,* **denounced, denouncing.**

dense Packed closely together; thick. The campers wandered away from the trail and got lost in the *dense* woods.
dense (dens) *adjective,* **denser, densest.**

density Closeness; thickness. Pea soup has a greater *density* than water. The *density* of population is greater in a big city than it is in the country.
den·si·ty (den′si tē) *noun, plural* **densities.**

dent A small hollow made in the surface of something by a blow or pressure. The accident put a *dent* in the front fender of my bike. *Noun.*
—To make a dent or hollow in. I *dented* the soft clay with my thumb. *Verb.*
dent (dent) *noun, plural* **dents;** *verb,* **dented, denting.**

dental **1.** Having to do with the teeth. Good *dental* care helps prevent tooth decay. **2.** Having to do with a dentist's work.
den·tal (den′təl) *adjective.*

dental floss A specially treated thread used to clean between the teeth.

dentin or **dentine** The hard, bony material that forms the main part of the tooth. It is covered by the enamel. Dentin is very sensitive to heat, cold, and touch.
den·tin or **den·tine** (den′tin *or* den tēn′) *noun.*

dentist A doctor who specializes in the care of the teeth and mouth.
den·tist (den′tist) *noun, plural* **dentists.**

deny **1.** To say that something is not true. The prisoners *denied* that they had robbed the bank. **2.** To refuse to give or grant. The company *denied* the workers' request for longer vacations.
de·ny (di nī′) *verb,* **denied, denying.**

depart **1.** To go away; leave. The train is due to *depart* from the station at ten o'clock. **2.** To change or differ. We *departed* from our usual routine and held the class outdoors.
de·part (di pärt′) *verb,* **departed, departing.**

department A separate part of a large organization; division. The English *department* at school has three new teachers this fall. In the United States, the *Department* of the Treasury is in charge of printing paper money and making coins.
de·part·ment (di pärt′mənt) *noun, plural* **departments.**

department store A large store that sells many different kinds of goods in different departments.

departure The act of departing. The plane's *departure* was delayed two hours.
de·par·ture (di pär′chər) *noun, plural* **departures.**

at; āpe; fär; câre; end; mē; it; īce; pîerce; hot; ōld; sông, fôrk; oil; out; up; ūse; rüle; pùll; tûrn; chin; sing; shop; thin; <u>th</u>is; hw in white; zh in treasure. The symbol ə stands for the unstressed vowel sound in about, taken, pencil, lemon, and circus.

depend **1.** To rely or trust. You can always *depend* on my friend to be on time. **2.** To get help or support. Children *depend* on their parents. **3.** To be determined by how something else turns out. Whether we go on the hike *depends* on the weather.
de·pend (di pend′) *verb,* **depended, depending.**

dependable Reliable or trustworthy. A person who is dependable can be trusted to do a job without being watched or checked.
de·pen·da·ble (di pen′də bəl) *adjective.*

dependence The state of being dependent. A baby animal's *dependence* on its mother diminishes as it gets older.
de·pen·dence (di pen′dəns) *noun.*

dependent **1.** Relying on someone else for what is needed or wanted. Baby birds are *dependent* on their parents to feed them. **2.** Determined by how something else turns out. Our plans for the picnic are *dependent* on the weather. *Adjective.*
—A person whose home, food, and other basic needs are provided by someone else. My parents support five *dependents*: their own two children, a foster child, and my grandparents. *Noun.*
de·pen·dent (di pen′dənt) *adjective; noun, plural* **dependents.**

The baby animal is **dependent** on its mother.

depict **1.** To show by drawing or painting. The artist tried to *depict* the movement of the ocean's waves. **2.** To represent in words; describe. The story *depicts* a typical Chinese family.
de·pict (di pikt′) *verb,* **depicted, depicting.**

deposit **1.** To put money or valuable things in a bank or other safe place. I *deposited twenty dollars in my savings account.* **2.** To put or set down; place. The shopper *deposited* the groceries on the kitchen table. The river *deposits* silt at its mouth. *Verb.*
—**1.** Something put in a bank or other safe place. We made a *deposit* of fifty dollars. **2.** Something given as a partial payment, with the rest to be paid later. I made a *deposit* of twenty dollars on the new bicycle. **3.** Something that has settled and is left as a layer. There was a *deposit* of dust on the window sill. **4.** A large amount of mineral in rock or in the ground. Texas has large *deposits* of oil underground. *Noun.*
de·pos·it (di poz′it) *verb,* **deposited, depositing;** *noun, plural* **deposits.**

depot A railroad or bus terminal.
de·pot (dē′pō) *noun, plural* **depots.**

depress To make sad or gloomy. The death of their dog *depressed* the whole family.
de·press (di pres′) *verb,* **depressed, depressing.**

depression **1.** Sadness; gloom. My troubles at home and at school contributed to my *depression.* **2.** A low place or hollow. The car bumped over a *depression* in the road. **3.** A time when business is slow and people are out of work. Many people lost their jobs during the *depression* of the 1930s.
de·pres·sion (di presh′ən) *noun, plural* **depressions.**

deprive To keep from having or doing. The selfish child *deprived* others of a chance to play with the toy. The dictator *deprived* the people of freedom of speech.
de·prive (di prīv′) *verb,* **deprived, depriving.**

depth **1.** The distance from top to bottom or from front to back. The *depth* of the pool was 5 feet. The *depth* of our backyard is 50 feet. **2.** The quality of being deep; deepness. The parents' *depth* of understanding helped their children deal with their problems.
depth (depth) *noun, plural* **depths.**

deputy A person appointed to act for, or with the same powers as, someone else. The sheriff appointed a *deputy* to help keep order in the town.
dep·u·ty (dep′yə tē) *noun, plural* **deputies.**

D

derby A man's stiff round hat with a narrow rolled brim.

der·by (dûr′bē) *noun, plural* **derbies.**

derive To get from a source; obtain. The word "dandelion" is *derived* from a French word. I *derive* pleasure from reading.

de·rive (di rīv′) *verb,* **derived, deriving.**

derrick **1.** A machine for lifting and moving heavy objects. It has a long arm attached to the base of an upright post. **2.** The framework over an oil well or other drill hole that supports the drilling machinery.

der·rick (der′ik) *noun, plural* **derricks.**

descend **1.** To move or come from a higher place to a lower one. They rode up the hill in a cable car but *descended* on skis. **2.** To come down from an earlier source or ancestor. My family *descends* from French settlers in Canada.

de·scend (di send′) *verb,* **descended, descending.**

descendant A person who comes from a particular ancestor or group of ancestors. Our neighbor is a *descendant* of the early Dutch settlers in New York.

de·scen·dant (di sen′dənt) *noun, plural* **descendants.**

descent **1.** A coming from a higher place to a lower one. The quick *descent* of the elevator made my stomach feel funny. **2.** A downward slope. The slide had a steep *descent.* **3.** Ancestors or birth. We are of Polish *descent.* ▴ Another word that sounds like this is **dissent.**

de·scent (di sent′) *noun, plural* **descents.**

describe To give a picture of something in words; tell or write about. The boy *described* his adventures at camp.

de·scribe (di skrīb′) *verb,* **described, describing.**

Word History

The word **describe** comes from a Latin word meaning "to write down" or "to represent." This word later came to mean "to represent in words," whether the words were written down or spoken.

description **1.** An account that gives a picture in words; a statement that describes. The *description* of the lost dog said that it was a small collie with a bushy tail. **2.** Kind; sort; variety. There were automobiles of every *description* in the show.

de·scrip·tion (di skrip′shən) *noun, plural* **descriptions.**

descriptive Giving a picture in words. The tourists were given *descriptive* pamphlets about places to visit and things to do in the city.

de·scrip·tive (di skrip′tiv) *adjective.*

desegregate To do away with the system of having separate schools and other facilities for people of different races. The government ordered the town to *desegregate* its public schools.

de·seg·re·gate (dē seg′ri gāt′) *verb,* **desegregated, desegregating.**

desert¹ A hot, dry, sandy area of land with few or no plants growing on it. *Noun.*
—Not lived in or on; desolate. The sailor was shipwrecked on a *desert* island. *Adjective.*

des·ert (dez′ərt) *noun, plural* **deserts;** *adjective.*

desert¹

desert² To go away and leave a person or thing that should not be left; abandon. That family *deserted* their dog when they moved away. The soldiers *deserted* their company. ▴ Another word that sounds like this is **dessert.**

de·sert (di zûrt′) *verb,* **deserted, deserting.**

deserve To have a right to; be worthy of. The dancers *deserve* praise for their beautiful performance.

de·serve (di zûrv′) *verb,* **deserved, deserving.**

at; āpe; fär; câre; end; mē; it; īce; pîerce; hot; ōld; sông, fôrk; oil; out; up; ūse; rüle; pủll; tûrn; chin; sing; shop; thin; this; hw in white; zh in treasure. The symbol ə stands for the unstressed vowel sound in about, taken, pencil, lemon, and circus.

design   **1.** A drawing or outline made to serve as a guide or pattern. Everyone liked the architect's *design* for the new school. **2.** An arrangement of shapes, parts, or colors; pattern.

The moccasins are decorated with **designs**.

The carpet in the living room has a blue and green *design*. **3.** A plan, especially a secret or evil one; a plot or scheme. The burglar's *design* was to climb through a basement window. *Noun.*
—To make a plan, drawing, or outline of; make a pattern for. They *designed* costumes for the play. *Verb.*
de·sign (di zīn′) *noun, plural* **designs;** *verb,* **designed, designing.**

designate   **1.** To mark or point out; show. A blue line is used to *designate* rivers on many maps. **2.** To call by a particular name or title. The head of the executive branch of the United States is *designated* "president." **3.** To give a job or office to; appoint. I was *designated* to lead the hike across the canyon.
des·ig·nate (dez′ig nāt′) *verb,* **designated, designating.**

desirable   Worth having or wishing for; pleasing. That corner lot is a *desirable* place for a baseball field.
de·sir·a·ble (di zīr′ə bəl) *adjective.*

desire   To wish for; long for. The waiter asked us if there was anything else we *desired. Verb.*
—A longing; wish. The cold, hungry traveler had a great *desire* for a hot meal. *Noun.*
de·sire (di zīr′) *verb,* **desired, desiring;** *noun, plural* **desires.**

desk   A piece of furniture with a flat or sloping top. A desk is used for reading or writing. It usually has drawers.
desk (desk) *noun, plural* **desks.**

desolate   **1.** Without people; deserted. In the winter, that beach is *desolate.* **2.** Destroyed; ruined. The fire left the forest *desolate.* **3.** Miserable; cheerless. The lost child was *desolate.*
des·o·late (des′ə lit) *adjective.*

despair   A complete loss of hope. The family was filled with *despair* when the fire destroyed their house. *Noun.*
—To give up or lose hope; be without hope. I *despaired* of ever finding my lost watch in the pond. *Verb.*
de·spair (di spâr′) *noun; verb,* **despaired, despairing.**

desperate   **1.** Reckless because of having no hope. A desperate person is ready or willing to try anything. The *desperate* player hurled the basketball at the net just as the game was ending. **2.** Very bad or hopeless. The workers trapped in the mine were in a *desperate* situation.
des·per·ate (des′pər it) *adjective.*

desperation   A reckless or sinking feeling coming from loss of hope. They gripped the log in *desperation* as they floated toward the waterfall.
des·per·a·tion (des′pə rā′shən) *noun.*

despise   To look down on as very bad; scorn. I always tell the truth and *despise* lying of any kind.
de·spise (di spīz′) *verb,* **despised, despising.**

despite   In spite of; regardless of. I went to school *despite* my bad cold.
de·spite (di spīt′) *preposition.*

dessert   A food served at the end of a meal. Fruit, pie, cheese, and ice cream are desserts. ▴ Another word that sounds like this is **desert.**
des·sert (di zûrt′) *noun, plural* **desserts.**

destination   A place to which a person is going or a thing is being sent. I told the train conductor that my *destination* was New York.
des·ti·na·tion (des′tə nā′shən) *noun, plural* **destinations.**

destine   To set apart for a particular purpose or use; intend. That land is *destined* for a new hospital.
des·tine (des′tin) *verb,* **destined, destining.**

destiny   What happens to a person or thing, especially when it seems to be determined in advance; fortune. I felt that it was my *destiny* to run the family business someday.
des·ti·ny (des′tə nē) *noun, plural* **destinies.**

destroy   To ruin completely; wreck. The earthquake *destroyed* the city.
de·stroy (di stroi′) *verb,* **destroyed, destroying.**

destroyer   A small, fast warship.
de·stroy·er (di stroi′ər) *noun, plural* **destroyers.**

destruction   **1.** The act of destroying. We watched the *destruction* of an old building and the construction of a new one in its place. **2.** Great damage or ruin. The earthquake caused widespread *destruction.*
de·struc·tion (di struk′shən) *noun, plural* **destructions.**

destructive Causing destruction. Moths can be *destructive* to clothes made of wool.
 de·struc·tive (di struk′tiv) *adjective.*

detach To unfasten and separate; take off. The salesperson *detached* the price tag from the gift before wrapping it.
 de·tach (di tach′) *verb,* **detached, detaching.**

detail 1. A small part of a whole; item. First I drew a rough sketch of the face, then I added *details* like the nostrils, eyelids, wrinkles, and shadows. 2. A dealing with matters one by one. They told us they had a plan, but they didn't go into *detail. Noun.*
 —To tell or describe item by item. The speakers *detailed* their experiences as travelers in India and China. *Verb.*
 de·tail (di tāl′ *or* dē′tāl) *noun, plural* **details;** *verb,* **detailed, detailing.**

detain 1. To keep from going; hold back; delay. Band practice *detained* me at school this afternoon, so I was late getting home. 2. To keep in custody. The police *detained* the person who was suspected of robbery.
 de·tain (di tān′) *verb,* **detained, detaining.**

detect To find out; discover. I called the fire department after I *detected* smoke coming from the garage.
 de·tect (di tekt′) *verb,* **detected, detecting.**

detective A police officer or other person whose work is finding information about crimes and trying to solve them. *Noun.*
 —Having to do with detectives and their work. Do you like to read *detective* stories? *Adjective.*
 de·tec·tive (di tek′tiv) *noun, plural* **detectives;** *adjective.*

detector A device that detects something such as smoke, metal, or radioactivity.
 de·tect·or (di tek′tər) *noun, plural* **detectors.**

deter To discourage from doing something because of fear or doubt. The huge waves *deterred* us from going swimming.
 de·ter (di tûr′) *verb,* **deterred, deterring.**

detergent A chemical substance that is used for washing things. It may be a liquid or powder.
 de·ter·gent (di tûr′jənt) *noun, plural* **detergents.**

deteriorate To make or become steadily worse. Our car *deteriorated* as it got older.
 de·te·ri·o·rate (di tîr′ē ə rāt′) *verb,* **deteriorated, deteriorating.**

determination 1. A definite and firm purpose. Their *determination* to become doctors made the medical students study very hard. 2. The act of deciding or settling ahead of time. The campers' *determination* of what to take on their trip took a long time. 3. The act of finding out something by watching or checking. For the proper *determination* of your height, you should take off your shoes and stand up straight.
 de·ter·mi·na·tion (di tûr′mə nā′shən) *noun, plural* **determinations.**

determine 1. To decide or settle definitely or ahead of time. The members of the club *determined* the date for their next meeting. 2. To find out by watching or checking. We *determined* the name of the flower by looking for its picture in a book about plants. 3. To be the cause of. Sunlight, rainfall, and soil *determine* how well a plant grows.
 de·ter·mine (di tûr′min) *verb,* **determined, determining.**

determined Firm in sticking to a purpose; showing determination. The *determined* students kept phoning the senator's office until somebody answered.
 de·ter·mined (di tûr′mind) *adjective.*

detest To dislike very much; hate. Drivers *detest* icy roads.
 de·test (di test′) *verb,* **detested, detesting.**

detector

at; āpe; fär; câre; end; mē; it; īce; pîerce; hot; ōld; sông, fôrk; oil; out; up; ūse; rüle; půll; tûrn; chin; sing; shop; thin; <u>th</u>is; hw in white; zh in treasure. The symbol ə stands for the unstressed vowel sound in about, taken, pencil, lemon, and circus.

detour A roundabout or indirect way. We had to take a *detour* because the main highway was being repaired. *Noun.*
—To cause to make a detour. The police *detoured* the traffic because of the accident. *Verb.*
  de·tour (dē′tùr) *noun, plural* **detours;** *verb,* **detoured, detouring.**

detract To take away from the value or beauty of something. The noisy people *detracted* from our enjoyment of the movie.
  de·tract (di trakt′) *verb,* **detracted, detracting.**

devastate To destroy; ruin. The hurricane *devastated* the small towns along the coast.
  dev·as·tate (dev′ə stāt′) *verb,* **devastated, devastating.**

develop **1.** To bring or come gradually into being. I *developed* an interest in computers while in the third grade. A rash *developed* on the baby's skin. **2.** To grow or cause to grow; expand. Skill in juggling *develops* with practice. You can *develop* your muscles by exercising. **3.** To change gradually. The little trading post *developed* into a great city. **4.** To put to use; make available. That country has not *developed* its natural resources. **5.** To treat photographic film with a chemical so that an image appears.
  de·vel·op (di vel′əp) *verb,* **developed, developing.**

development **1.** The act or process of developing. The *development* of a spacecraft that could reach the moon took many years. **2.** An event or happening. New *developments* in the story were broadcast every hour. **3.** A group of houses or other buildings on a large area of land. The houses often look alike and are built by one builder.
  de·vel·op·ment (di vel′əp mənt) *noun, plural* **developments.**

device **1.** Something made or invented for a particular purpose. A can opener, a toothbrush, and a clock are devices. **2.** A plan or scheme; trick. Clearing the throat is sometimes just a *device* for getting attention.
  de·vice (di vīs′) *noun, plural* **devices.**

devil **1. the Devil.** The chief spirit of evil. **2.** A wicked, mischievous, or very energetic person.
  dev·il (dev′əl) *noun, plural* **devils.**

devise To think out; invent; plan. We *devised* a secret code that no one could decipher.
  de·vise (di vīz′) *verb,* **devised, devising.**

devote To give effort, attention, or time to some purpose; dedicate. I want to *devote* all my energy to studying dancing. The scientists *devoted* themselves to discovering the secrets of the atom.
  de·vote (di vōt′) *verb,* **devoted, devoting.**

devoted Loyal; faithful. My *devoted* friend would do anything for me.
  de·vot·ed (di vō′tid) *adjective.*

devotion A strong affection; loyalty; faithfulness. They felt great *devotion* to their grandparents.
  de·vo·tion (di vō′shən) *noun, plural* **devotions.**

devour **1.** To eat; consume. The lion *devoured* the deer. The hungry child *devoured* the sandwich. **2.** To destroy. Fire *devoured* the house.
  de·vour (di vour′) *verb,* **devoured, devouring.**

devout **1.** Very religious. *Devout* Muslims pray five times a day. **2.** Sincere; earnest. You have my *devout* wishes for your success in the school play.
  de·vout (di vout′) *adjective.*

dew Moisture from the air that forms drops on cool surfaces. Dew gathers on grass, plants, and trees during the night. ⊿ Other words that sound like this are **do** and **due.**
  dew (dü *or* dū) *noun, plural* **dews.**

dewlap The loose hanging skin under the throat of cattle and certain other animals.
  dew·lap (dü′lap′ *or* dū′lap′) *noun, plural* **dewlaps.**

dexterity Skill in using the hands or body. Both magicians and gymnasts need great *dexterity.*
  dex·ter·i·ty (dek ster′i tē) *noun.*

Word History

The word **dexterity** goes back to a Latin word meaning "right" or "right hand." Since most people are right-handed, the right side used to be associated with strength, skill, and ability.

---

diabetes A disease in which there is too much sugar in the blood. A person with diabetes either cannot make or cannot use enough insulin, the substance the body needs to use sugar properly. ⊿ The word **diabetes** is used with a singular verb.
  di·a·be·tes (dī′ə bē′tis *or* dī′ə bē′tēz) *noun.*

diabetic Having or having to do with diabetes. *Adjective.*
—A person who has diabetes. *Noun.*
  di·a·bet·ic (dī′ə bet′ik) *adjective; noun, plural* **diabetics.**

diagnosis The act of finding out what is wrong with a person or animal by examination and the study of symptoms. The doctor's *diagnosis* was that the sick child had chicken pox.
di·ag·no·sis (dī′əg nō′sis) *noun, plural* diagnoses (dī′əg nō′sēz).

diagonal Having a slant. The dress had a pattern of *diagonal* stripes. *Adjective.*
—A straight line that connects the opposite corners of a rectangle. *Noun.*
di·ag·o·nal (dī ag′ə nəl) *adjective; noun, plural* diagonals.

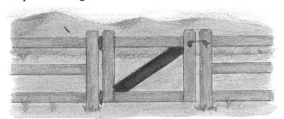
diagonal

diagram A plan or sketch that shows the parts of a thing or how the parts are put together. We'll use this *diagram* of the model airplane when we build it. *Noun.*
—To show by a diagram; make a diagram of. It's easier to *diagram* my house than to explain where all the rooms are. *Verb.*
di·a·gram (dī′ə gram′) *noun, plural* diagrams; *verb,* diagramed, diagraming.

dial 1. The face of an instrument. A dial is marked with numbers, letters, or other signs. A pointer moves over these markings and shows time, quantity, or some other value. A clock, a compass, and a meter usually have dials. 2. The disk on a radio or television set that is turned to tune in a station or channel. 3. The disk on some telephones that is turned by the finger when the caller is selecting the number being called. *Noun.*
—1. To tune in by using a radio or television dial. *Dial* another channel and find a better program. 2. To select numbers when making a telephone call. The caller *dialed* a wrong number. *Verb.*
di·al (dī′əl *or* dīl) *noun, plural* dials; *verb,* dialed, dialing.

dialect A form of a language that is spoken in a particular area or by a particular group of people.
di·a·lect (dī′ə lekt′) *noun, plural* dialects.

dialogue Conversation, especially in a play, movie, or story. That play is full of funny *dialogue.*
di·a·logue (dī′ə lôg′ *or* dī′ə log′) *noun, plural* dialogues.

diameter 1. A straight line passing through the center of a circle or sphere, from one side to the other. Look up **circle** for a picture of this. 2. The length of such a line; the width or thickness of something round. The *diameter* of the earth is about 8,000 miles.
di·am·e·ter (dī am′i tər) *noun, plural* diameters.

diamond 1. A mineral that consists of pure carbon in the form of a clear or pale crystal. It is the hardest natural material known. Diamonds are used in industry for cutting and grinding. Cut and polished diamonds are used as jewels. 2. A figure having four sides and four angles that is shaped like this: ♦. 3. A playing card marked with one or more red diamonds. 4. diamonds. The suit of cards marked with this figure. 5. The space on a baseball field that is inside the lines that connect the bases.
di·a·mond (dī′mənd *or* dī′ə mənd) *noun, plural* diamonds.

The sign has a **diamond** shape.

diaper A baby's underwear made of soft, folded cloth or other material.
di·a·per (dī′pər *or* dī′ə pər) *noun, plural* diapers.

diaphragm 1. A thin layer of muscles that divides the chest from the abdomen. The diaphragm helps control breathing. It is part of the respiratory system. 2. A flexible disk used to change sound into electrical signals, or to change electrical signals into sound. It is used inside telephones and microphones.
di·a·phragm (dī′ə fram′) *noun, plural* diaphragms.

diarrhea A condition in which a person or animal has frequent and watery bowel movements.
di·ar·rhe·a (dī′ə rē′ə) *noun.*

at; āpe; fär; câre; end; mē; it; īce; pîerce; hot; ōld; sông, fôrk; oil; out; up; ūse; rüle; pùll; tûrn; chin; sing; shop; thin; this; hw in white; zh in treasure. The symbol ə stands for the unstressed vowel sound in about, taken, pencil, lemon, and circus.

diary A written record of the things that one has done or thought each day. I wrote down the day's events in my *diary*.

   di·a·ry (dī′ə rē) *noun, plural* **diaries.**

dice Small cubes of wood, plastic, or other material marked on each side with from one to six dots. Dice are used in some games. *Noun.*

—To cut into small cubes. Please *dice* the potatoes for the stew. *Verb.*

   dice (dīs) *plural noun, singular* **die;** *verb,* **diced, dicing.**

a pair of **dice**

dictate 1. To say or read something aloud to be written down by someone else. The banker *dictated* a letter to a secretary, who wrote it down and typed it later. 2. To order by authority. The nation that won the war *dictated* the terms of the peace treaty. *Verb.*

—A rule or command that tells what to do. They believe in following the *dictates* of the law. *Noun.*

   dic·tate (dik′tāt *or* dik tāt′ *for verb;* dik′tāt *for noun*) *verb,* **dictated, dictating;** *noun, plural* **dictates.**

dictator A person who rules a country without sharing power or consulting anyone else. The *dictator* took away the people's right to vote.

   dic·ta·tor (dik′tā tər *or* dik tā′tər) *noun, plural* **dictators.**

dictionary A book that has words of a language arranged in alphabetical order, together with information about them. This dictionary tells what words mean, how they are spelled, how they are used, how they are pronounced, and where they come from.

   dic·tion·ar·y (dik′shə ner′ē) *noun, plural* **dictionaries.**

did Past tense of **do.** *Did* you know that person? Look up **do** for more information.

   did (did) *verb.*

didn't Shortened form of "did not." I *didn't* do my homework.

   did·n't (did′ənt) *contraction.*

die¹ 1. To stop living; become dead. Many soldiers *died* in the war. The flowers *died* during the cold spell. 2. To lose force or strength; come to an end. The wind suddenly *died* as the sailboat neared the shore. The music *died* away in the distance. 3. To feel a great need or desire. The hikers were *dying* for a cold drink of water. ◢ Another word that sounds like this is **dye.**

   die (dī) *verb,* **died, dying.**

die² 1. A small cube used in games. Look up **dice** for more information. 2. A metal block or plate used to stamp designs or letters on coins. ◢ Another word that sounds like this is **dye.**

   die (dī) *noun, plural* **dice** *(for definition 1)* or **dies** *(for definition 2).*

diesel engine An engine that burns fuel oil. The oil is set on fire by heat produced by the compression of air in the engine.

   die·sel engine (dē′zəl).

diet 1. The food and drink usually eaten by a person or animal. My *diet* is made up of meat, vegetables, and fruit. A giraffe's *diet* is mostly leaves. 2. A special selection of food and drink chosen by a person for health reasons or for losing or gaining weight. *Noun.*

—To eat a special selection of foods in order to be healthy or to lose or gain weight. My overweight classmate *dieted* for many weeks and lost 12 pounds. *Verb.*

   di·et (dī′it) *noun, plural* **diets;** *verb,* **dieted, dieting.**

dietitian A person who is trained to plan balanced meals for both healthy and sick people. A dietitian usually works at a hospital or school.

   di·e·ti·tian (dī′i tish′ən) *noun, plural* **dietitians.**

differ 1. To be unlike; not be the same. The two children *differ* greatly in looks, even though they are twins. 2. To have a different opinion; disagree. My cousin *differs* with the rest of our family about where to go on our vacation.

   dif·fer (dif′ər) *verb,* **differed, differing.**

difference 1. The state or quality of being unlike or different. Do you notice a *difference* in how people talk? 2. A way of being unlike or different. One of the *differences* between alligators and crocodiles is that crocodiles have longer heads. 3. The amount left after one quantity is subtracted from another; remainder. The *difference* between 16 and 12 is 4. 4. A disagreement about something. They were able to settle their *differences* without a fight.

• **to make a difference.** To have an effect on or change something; matter. Getting enough sleep *makes a difference* in how I feel.

   dif·fer·ence (dif′ər əns *or* dif′rəns) *noun, plural* **differences.**

different 1. Not alike or similar. The two opposing teams wore *different* uniforms. The moon is *different* from the sun. 2. Not the same; separate. It rained two *different* times this afternoon.

   dif·fer·ent (dif′ər ənt *or* dif′rənt) *adjective.*

difficult **1.** Needing much effort; hard to do; not easy. This is a *difficult* arithmetic problem. **2.** Hard to get along with or please. Some people become *difficult* when they can't have their way.
dif·fi·cult (dif′i kult′) *adjective.*

difficulty **1.** The fact of being difficult. The *difficulty* of learning how to ride a bicycle discouraged me at first. **2.** Something that is hard to do, understand, or deal with. We had *difficulty* fitting everything into one suitcase.
dif·fi·cul·ty (dif′i kul′tē) *noun, plural* **difficulties.**

dig **1.** To break up or turn over the earth with a shovel, the hands, or claws. Our dog likes to *dig* in the yard for bones. I *dig* in the vegetable garden with a spade. **2.** To make or get by digging. The settlers had to *dig* a well for water. We *dig* clams at the seashore when the tide is low. **3.** To try to find or discover by searching or by study. The reporter had to *dig* to find the facts about the robbery. **4.** To push or thrust. The cat loved to *dig* its claws into the tree.
dig (dig) *verb,* **dug, digging.**

digest To break down food in the mouth, stomach, and intestines. When we digest food, we change it into a form that can be absorbed and used by the body. *Verb.*
—A summary of a longer book or document. I read a *digest* of a long novel. *Noun.*
di·gest (di jest′ *or* dī jest′ *for verb;* dī′jest *for noun*) *verb,* **digested, digesting;** *noun, plural* **digests.**

digestion The process of breaking down food into a form that can be absorbed and used by the body. Digestion starts in the mouth and is completed in the intestines.
di·ges·tion (di jes′chən *or* dī jes′chən) *noun, plural* **digestions.**

digestive Relating to or helping digestion. Saliva is the first of the *digestive* juices that break down food.
di·ges·tive (di jes′tiv *or* dī jes′tiv) *adjective.*

digestive system The system that breaks food down so that it can be used by the body. In humans, the digestive system includes the mouth, the esophagus, the stomach, and the intestines. It also includes certain chemicals that help to break down the food.

digit **1.** One of the numerals 0, 1, 2, 3, 4, 5, 6, 7, 8, or 9. Sometimes 0 is not considered to be a digit. **2.** A finger, toe, or claw.
dig·it (dij′it) *noun, plural* **digits.**

digital Using or showing information in the form of numerical digits. My *digital* watch displays the time and the date.
di·gi·tal (dij′i təl) *adjective.*

dignified Having or showing self-respect and self-control; proud and calm. All the guests at the wedding exhibited *dignified* behavior during the ceremony.
dig·ni·fied (dig′nə fīd′) *adjective.*

dignity The condition of being aware of one's honor and worthiness, as shown in a proud, calm appearance or manner. Despite great hardship and poverty, my grandparents kept their *dignity.*
dig·ni·ty (dig′ni tē) *noun, plural* **dignities.**

dike A dam or high wall of earth built to hold back the waters of a sea or river.
dike (dīk) *noun, plural* **dikes.**

dilapidated Fallen into ruin or decay; broken down. I am going to build a new tool shed to replace the *dilapidated* one.
di·lap·i·dat·ed (di lap′i dā′tid) *adjective.*

diligent Working hard and steadily; applying much effort and care. The more *diligent* students checked all their answers.
dil·i·gent (dil′i jənt) *adjective.*

dilute To make thin or weaker by adding a liquid. If the paste is too thick, *dilute* it by adding water.
di·lute (di lüt′ *or* dī lüt′) *verb,* **diluted, diluting.**

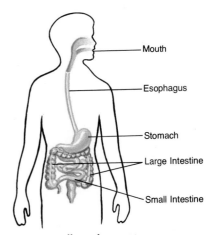

Mouth
Esophagus
Stomach
Large Intestine
Small Intestine

digestive system

at; āpe; fär; câre; end; mē; it; īce; pîerce; hot; ōld; sông, fôrk; oil; out; up; ūse; rüle; půll; tûrn; chin; sing; shop; thin; <u>th</u>is; hw in white; zh in treasure. The symbol ə stands for the unstressed vowel sound in about, taken, pencil, lemon, and circus.

dim **1.** Having or giving little light; not bright. There was only a *dim* light in the hallway. **2.** Not clear; not distinct. I could see a *dim* outline of the building through the fog. **3.** Not seeing, hearing, or understanding clearly. The old dog's eyes were growing *dim*. *Adjective.*
—To make or become dim. A good driver always *dims* the car headlights at night when passing cars going in the other direction. *Verb.*
> **dim** (dim) *adjective,* **dimmer, dimmest;** *verb,* **dimmed, dimming.**

dime A coin in the United States and Canada that is worth ten cents.
> **dime** (dīm) *noun, plural* **dimes.**

dimension **1.** The measurement of length, width, or height. The *dimensions* of the room are 15 feet long, 12 feet wide, and 8 feet high. **2.** Size or importance. Few people seem to realize the true *dimensions* of this social problem.
> **di·men·sion** (di men'shən) *noun, plural* **dimensions.**

diminish To make or become smaller. The campers' supply of food *diminished* as the days wore on.
> **di·min·ish** (di min'ish) *verb,* **diminished, diminishing.**

diminutive Very small; tiny. A baby has *diminutive* hands and feet.
> **di·min·u·tive** (di min'yə tiv) *adjective.*

dimmer A device that regulates the brightness of an electric light or automobile headlight. *Dimmers* gradually turned out the lights in the theater as the movie began.
> **dim·mer** (dim'ər) *noun, plural* **dimmers.**

dimple A small hollow on or in something. There are many children and adults who have *dimples* in their cheeks whenever they smile. *Noun.*
—To mark with or form dimples. The pebbles we threw *dimpled* the surface of the water. *Verb.*
> **dim·ple** (dim'pəl) *noun, plural* **dimples;** *verb,* **dimpled, dimpling.**

din A loud noise that goes on for some time. The *din* of the car horns kept us awake. *Noun.*
—To say over and over. The coach *dinned* into our ears that we must run faster and faster. *Verb.*
> **din** (din) *noun, plural* **dins;** *verb,* **dinned, dinning.**

dine To eat dinner. My parents *dined* at a restaurant on their anniversary.
> **dine** (dīn) *verb,* **dined, dining.**

diner **1.** A person who is eating dinner. **2.** A small restaurant that is usually inexpensive. That *diner* is a favorite stop for truck drivers on their way through town.
> **din·er** (dī'nər) *noun, plural* **diners.**

dinette A small dining room.
> **di·nette** (dī net') *noun, plural* **dinettes.**

dinghy A small rowboat. The sailors rowed a *dinghy* from the ship to shore.
> **din·ghy** (ding'ē) *noun, plural* **dinghies.**

dingy Having a dirty and dull appearance; not bright. The *dingy* curtains needed to be washed.
> **din·gy** (din'jē) *adjective,* **dingier, dingiest.**

dining room A room where meals are served and eaten. We eat breakfast in the kitchen and dinner in the *dining room.*

dinner **1.** The main meal of the day. On Sunday we eat *dinner* at four o'clock in the afternoon. **2.** A formal meal in honor of some person or event. The school gave the members of the soccer team a *dinner* to celebrate their winning season.
> **din·ner** (din'ər) *noun, plural* **dinners.**

dinosaur One of a large group of extinct reptiles that lived millions of years ago. Some dinosaurs were the largest land animals that have ever lived, and others were as small as cats.
> **din·o·saur** (dī'nə sôr') *noun, plural* **dinosaurs.**

This boy has **dimples** in his cheeks.

Word History

The word **dinosaur** comes from two Greek words meaning "terrible lizard." Scientists named these animals this because of their great size.

diocese A church district that is under the authority of a bishop.
  di·o·cese (dī′ə sis *or* dī′ə sēz′) *noun, plural* **dioceses** (dī′ə sēz′ *or* dī′ə sis′iz).

dip **1.** To put into a liquid or a container for a moment. I *dipped* my hand into the pond. Carefully *dip* the brush into the paint can. **2.** To go in water and come out quickly. We *dipped* in the swimming pool to cool off. **3.** To lift out by using a scoop or ladle. I *dipped* some oats from the bag. **4.** To lower and raise again. The soldier *dipped* the flag in salute as the president of the United States rode by. **5.** To sink or go down. The sun *dipped* below the horizon as evening came. *Verb.*
  —**1.** The act of dipping. Let's take one last *dip* in the ocean before we go home. **2.** A liquid into which something is dipped for cleaning or coloring. We put the eggs in a *dip* to color them for Easter. **3.** An amount taken out in a scoop or ladle. Would you like a *dip* of ice cream? **4.** A sinking or drop. The car ahead of us suddenly disappeared because of a *dip* in the road. **5.** A thick liquid food that is scooped up on crackers or vegetables. *Noun.*
  dip (dip) *verb,* **dipped, dipping;** *noun, plural* **dips.**

diploma A printed piece of paper given by a school or college to a graduating student that says he or she has finished a course of study.
  di·plo·ma (di plō′mə) *noun, plural* **diplomas.**

diplomat **1.** A person whose job is to handle relations between his or her own country and other countries. **2.** A person who is good at dealing with people without making enemies or hurting anyone's feelings.
  dip·lo·mat (dip′lə mat′) *noun, plural* **diplomats.**

dinosaur

diplomatic **1.** Of or having to do with diplomats. I hope some day to join the *diplomatic* service. **2.** Good at dealing with people without hurting feelings; showing tact. It's *diplomatic* to thank someone for a gift even if you don't like it.
  dip·lo·mat·ic (dip′lə mat′ik) *adjective.*

dipper A cup with a long handle that is used to lift water or other liquids.
  dip·per (dip′ər) *noun, plural* **dippers.**

direct **1.** To manage or control; guide. A police officer *directs* traffic at the busy intersection. **2.** To supervise and guide the performers in the making of a play, movie, or other performance. The music teacher *directed* our class play. **3.** To order; command. The general *directed* the troops to attack. **4.** To tell or show someone the way. Can you *direct* me to the nearest bus stop? **5.** To turn or send in a particular direction or to a particular place. I *directed* the hose at the flowers. *Verb.*
  —**1.** Going in a straight line without stopping or turning. Main Street is a *direct* route between my house and yours. **2.** Plain and straightforward. "Yes" and "no" are *direct* answers to a question. "If you say so" and "maybe" are not *direct* answers. *Adjective.*
  —In a straight line without stopping or turning. This plane goes *direct* to New York from Los Angeles. *Adverb.*
  di·rect (di rekt′ *or* dī rekt′) *verb,* **directed, directing;** *adjective; adverb.*

direct current An electric current that flows only in one direction. Batteries generate direct current.

direction **1.** Management or control; guidance. The young doctor performed the operation under the *direction* of an older, more experienced doctor. **2.** The line or course along which something moves, faces, or lies. We decided to walk in the *direction* of the lake. **3.** An order or instruction on how to do something or how to act. Follow the doctor's *directions* and take two pills four times a day. The *directions* on the package say to cook the vegetables in boiling water for seven minutes.
  di·rec·tion (di rek′shən *or* dī rek′shən) *noun, plural* **directions.**

at; āpe; fär; câre; end; mē; it; īce; pîerce; hot; ōld; sông, fôrk; oil; out; up; ūse; rüle; půll; tûrn; chin; sing; shop; thin; <u>th</u>is; hw in white; zh in treasure. The symbol ə stands for the unstressed vowel sound in about, taken, pencil, lemon, and circus.

directly **1.** In a direct line or manner; straight. The fielder threw the ball *directly* to a teammate covering first base. **2.** At once; without delay. Please come home *directly* after the concert.
di·rect·ly (di rekt′lē *or* dī rekt′lē) *adverb.*

direct object A word or group of words in a sentence that tells who or what directly receives the action expressed by the verb. In the sentence "I like oatmeal," the noun "oatmeal" is the direct object because it directly receives the action of the verb "like."

director A person who supervises and guides the performers in a play, movie, or other performance.
di·rec·tor (di rek′tər *or* dī rek′tər) *noun,* plural **directors.**

directory A list of names and addresses. A telephone directory lists the telephone numbers of people living in a particular area.
di·rec·to·ry (di rek′tə rē *or* dī rek′tə rē) *noun, plural* **directories.**

dirigible A large aircraft that has areas filled with gas to make it float. A dirigible is driven by a motor and can be steered.
dir·i·gi·ble (dir′i jə bəl *or* də rij′ə bəl) *noun,* plural **dirigibles.**

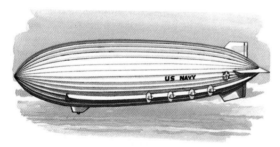
dirigible

dirt **1.** Mud, dust, or other material that makes something unclean. The children washed the *dirt* off their hands before coming to dinner. **2.** Loose earth or soil. The gardener filled the pots with *dirt* before planting the bulbs in them.
dirt (dûrt) *noun.*

dirty **1.** Soiled; not clean. The children put all their *dirty* clothes in a pile for the laundry. Cleaning out the garage was a hard and *dirty* job. **2.** Not honest or decent; unfair or low. That's a *dirty* lie. **3.** Full of spite; angry or resentful. The bully gave us a *dirty* look.
dirt·y (dûr′tē) *adjective,* **dirtier, dirtiest.**

dis– A *prefix* that means: **1.** Not or opposite. *Disapprove* means not to approve. *Disinfect* means to do the opposite of infect. **2.** Lack of. *Disrespect* means lack of respect.

disable To take away ability; cripple. A broken leg can *disable* a person for months.
dis·a·ble (dis ā′bəl) *verb,* **disabled, disabling.**

disadvantage **1.** Something that makes it harder to succeed. Being short is a *disadvantage* to a basketball player. **2.** A loss or injury; harm. It will be to your *disadvantage* if you don't have a car.
dis·ad·van·tage (dis′ad van′tij) *noun,* plural **disadvantages.**

disagree **1.** To differ in opinion. I think living in a city is fun, but my cousin *disagrees.* **2.** To quarrel; argue. They *disagreed* violently and then made up. **3.** To be different or unlike. The stories of the two witnesses *disagreed* so much that the police didn't know which one to believe. **4.** To cause indigestion or discomfort. Hot, spicy foods *disagree* with me.
dis·a·gree (dis′ə grē′) *verb,* **disagreed, disagreeing.**

disagreeable **1.** Not pleasant or likable; unpleasant. The strange food had a *disagreeable* taste. **2.** Likely to go against other people's wishes or opinions. Since my friend seemed to be in a *disagreeable* mood, I decided not to ask for the favor then.
dis·a·gree·a·ble (dis′ə grē′ə bəl) *adjective.*

disagreement **1.** A difference of opinion. There is much *disagreement* about how to solve the problems of pollution. **2.** A quarrel; argument. They settled their *disagreement* and shook hands.
dis·a·gree·ment (dis′ə grē′mənt) *noun,* plural **disagreements.**

disappear **1.** To go out of sight. We watched the sun *disappear* behind a cloud. **2.** To stop existing; become extinct. Dinosaurs *disappeared* from the earth about 65 million years ago.
dis·ap·pear (dis′ə pîr′) *verb,* **disappeared, disappearing.**

disappearance The act or fact of disappearing. The *disappearance* of the two mountain climbers worried us all.
dis·ap·pear·ance (dis′ə pîr′əns) *noun,* plural **disappearances.**

disappoint To fail to live up to the hopes of. You will *disappoint* the children if you do not keep your promise to them.
dis·ap·point (dis′ə point′) *verb,* **disappointed, disappointing.**

disappointment **1.** A feeling of being disappointed. The class couldn't hide its *disappointment* when it rained and the picnic was called off. **2.** A person or thing that disappoints. My new boots were supposed to be

very warm, but they are a *disappointment.*
dis·ap·point·ment (dis′ə point′mənt)
noun, plural **disappointments.**

disapprove To have a strong feeling against. My parents *disapprove* of smoking.
dis·ap·prove (dis′ə prüv′) *verb,*
disapproved, disapproving.

disaster An event that causes much suffering or loss. The flood was a *disaster.*
dis·as·ter (di zas′tər) *noun, plural*
disasters.

disbelief Lack of belief; refusal to believe. Thanks to my *disbelief* in ghosts, I wasn't afraid of the empty old house.
dis·be·lief (dis′bi lēf′) *noun, plural*
disbeliefs.

disc **1.** A phonograph record. **2.** Another spelling for **disk.** Look up **disk** for more information.
disc (disk) *noun, plural* **discs.**

discard To throw aside or give up as useless, worthless, or not wanted. I *discarded* all my worn-out clothes.
dis·card (dis kärd′) *verb,* **discarded, discarding.**

discharge **1.** To let go or release; dismiss. When the company went out of business it had to *discharge* all its workers. **2.** To unload or remove. The ship *discharged* its cargo at the dock. **3.** To fire or shoot. It is illegal to *discharge* a firearm within the city limits. **4.** To send off or let out. The factory should not be allowed to *discharge* its wastes into the river. *Verb.*
—1. The act of letting go or unloading. The *discharge* of the airplane's passengers will be at gate ten. **2.** Dismissal from service or a job. Many soldiers received their *discharges* from the army in 1946. **3.** A firing of a weapon. The *discharge* of the cannon made the ship shudder. *Noun.*
dis·charge (dis chärj′ *for verb;* dis′chärj *for noun*) *verb,* **discharged, discharging;** *noun, plural* **discharges.**

disciple **1.** A person who believes in a leader or a leader's teachings. The young doctor was a devoted *disciple* of the famous surgeon. **2.** One of the twelve original followers of Jesus; Apostle.
dis·ci·ple (di sī′pəl) *noun, plural* **disciples.**

discipline **1.** Training that develops skill, good character, or orderly behavior. Those wild children have had no *discipline* from their parents. **2.** Punishment given to train or correct someone. If you break a rule here, you will receive severe *discipline.* **3.** A field of study. Mathematics and science are related *disciplines. Noun.*

—1. To train to be obedient. An officer in the army must be able to *discipline* troops. **2.** To punish. We *disciplined* our dog for barking too much. *Verb.*
dis·ci·pline (dis′ə plin) *noun, plural* **disciplines;** *verb,* **disciplined, disciplining.**

disc jockey **1.** An announcer on a radio program that broadcasts recorded music. **2.** A person who selects, announces, and plays recordings of music at clubs or parties.

disc jockey

disclose To make known. I promise not to *disclose* this secret to anyone.
dis·close (dis klōz′) *verb,* **disclosed, disclosing.**

discomfort The condition or fact of being uncomfortable or uneasy. The cold wind caused us some *discomfort.*
dis·com·fort (dis kum′fərt) *noun, plural* **discomforts.**

disconnect To separate from another part or from a source of electricity; break the connection of. You must *disconnect* the television set before fixing it.
dis·con·nect (dis′kə nekt′) *verb,* **disconnected, disconnecting.**

discontented Unhappy and restless. The worker was *discontented* with the dull job.
dis·con·tent·ed (dis′kən ten′tid) *adjective.*

discontinue To put an end to; stop. We asked the telephone company to *discontinue* our service when we moved.
dis·con·tin·ue (dis′kən tin′ū) *verb,* **discontinued, discontinuing.**

---

at; āpe; fär; câre; end; mē; it; īce; pîerce; hot; ōld; sông, fôrk; oil; out; up; ūse; rüle; pull; tûrn; chin; sing; shop; thin; <u>th</u>is; hw in white; zh in treasure. The symbol ə stands for the unstressed vowel sound in about, taken, pencil, lemon, and circus.

discord   A lack of agreement or harmony; disagreement. There was much *discord* among the members of the committee.
dis·cord (dis′kôrd) *noun.*

discount   An amount subtracted from the regular price. I bought a suit on sale at a 25 percent *discount.*
dis·count (dis′kount′) *noun, plural* **discounts.**

discourage   **1.** To cause to lose courage, hope, or confidence. Failing to have your first story published should not *discourage* you from becoming a writer.   **2.** To try to keep a person from doing something. They *discouraged* us from starting our trip because of the heavy snowstorm.
dis·cour·age (dis kûr′ij) *verb,* **discouraged, discouraging.**

discourteous   Impolite; rude. It is *discourteous* to interrupt people.
dis·cour·te·ous (dis kûr′tē əs) *adjective.*

discover   **1.** To see or find out for the first time. Marie and Pierre Curie *discovered* radium.   **2.** To notice; come upon. I *discovered* a spelling error in my essay.
dis·cov·er (dis kuv′ər) *verb,* **discovered, discovering.**

discovery   **1.** The act of seeing or finding out something for the first time. The *discovery* of America by Christopher Columbus happened in 1492.   **2.** Something that is seen or found out for the first time. Electricity was an important *discovery.*
dis·cov·er·y (dis kuv′ə rē) *noun, plural* **discoveries.**

discriminate   **1.** To treat some people differently from others for unfair reasons. It is against the law for an employer to *discriminate* against people because of their race, religion, sex, or age.   **2.** To tell the difference between things. Can you *discriminate* between a dolphin and a porpoise?
dis·crim·i·nate (di skrim′ə nāt′) *verb,* **discriminated, discriminating.**

discrimination   **1.** An unfair difference in treatment. That company hires people without *discrimination* as to race or sex.   **2.** The act or ability of seeing differences.
dis·crim·i·na·tion (di skrim′ə nā′shən) *noun.*

discuss   To talk over; speak about. After dinner my friends and I *discussed* our hopes and plans for the future. The council *discussed* plans for building a new city hall.
dis·cuss (di skus′) *verb,* **discussed, discussing.**

discussion   The act of talking something over; a serious exchange of opinions. My question about when a person becomes a grown-up started an interesting *discussion.*
dis·cus·sion (di skush′ən) *noun, plural* **discussions.**

disease   **1.** A condition in which something, other than an injury, keeps the body or part of the body from working in a normal way; sickness; illness. Chicken pox is a *disease* that people usually get when they are children.   **2.** A similar condition of a plant.
dis·ease (di zēz′) *noun, plural* **diseases.**

disfavor   Lack of favor or approval; dislike. The students looked with *disfavor* on the plan to shorten spring vacation.
dis·fa·vor (dis fā′vər) *noun.*

disgrace   **1.** The loss of honor or respect; shame. The president of the company resigned in *disgrace* when the police learned about the stolen money.   **2.** A person or thing that causes a loss of honor or respect. Dirty streets and littered sidewalks are a *disgrace* to our city. *Noun.*
—To bring shame to. *Verb.*
dis·grace (dis grās′) *noun, plural* **disgraces;** *verb,* **disgraced, disgracing.**

disguise   **1.** To change the way one looks in order to hide one's real identity or look like someone else. The children *disguised* themselves as ghosts, pirates, and monsters on Halloween.   **2.** To hide. We *disguised* our hiding place with branches and leaves. *Verb.*
—Something that changes or hides the way one looks. A mustache was part of the thief's *disguise. Noun.*
dis·guise (dis gīz′) *verb,* **disguised, disguising;** *noun, plural* **disguises.**

disgust   A sick feeling caused by strong dislike. I felt *disgust* when I smelled the rotting garbage. *Noun.*
—To cause a sick feeling of strong dislike in. *Verb.*
dis·gust (dis gust′) *noun; verb,* **disgusted, disgusting.**

dish   **1.** A plate or shallow bowl used for holding food. We set the table with our good china *dishes.* I ate a *dish* of yogurt.   **2.** Food made in a particular way. Spaghetti with tomato sauce is my favorite *dish. Noun.*
—To put or serve in a dish. We *dished* up dinner as soon as everyone sat down. *Verb.*
dish (dish) *noun, plural* **dishes;** *verb,* **dished, dishing.**

dishonest   Not fair or honest. A student who cheats on a test is *dishonest.*
dis·hon·est (dis on′ist) *adjective.*

dishonor   Loss of honor or reputation; disgrace; shame. It is no *dishonor* to admit you are wrong if you have made a mistake. *Noun.*

—To cause disgrace or shame. *Verb.*
dis·hon·or (dis on'ər) *noun, plural*
dishonors; *verb,* **dishonored,**
dishonoring.

dishwasher   A machine that washes dishes,
glasses, and pots.
dish·wash·er (dish'wô'shər *or*
dish'wosh'ər) *noun, plural* **dishwashers.**

disinfect   To destroy germs that cause disease. The nurse *disinfected* the thermometer
before I used it.
dis·in·fect (dis'in fekt') *verb,* **disinfected,**
disinfecting.

disinfectant   A substance used to destroy
germs that can cause diseases or infections.
dis·in·fect·ant (dis'in fek'tənt) *noun,*
plural **disinfectants.**

disintegrate   To break into many small
pieces. A blow with the heavy hammer
caused the stone to *disintegrate*.
dis·in·te·grate (dis in'ti grāt') *verb,*
disintegrated, disintegrating.

disinterested   Free from selfish interest;
impartial. A referee should remain *disinterested*.
dis·in·ter·est·ed (dis in'trə stid *or*
dis in'tə res'tid) *adjective.*

disk   **1.** A flat, thin, round object.   **2.** A device that stores information in a computer.
This word is also spelled **disc.**
disk (disk) *noun, plural* **disks.**

disk drive   The device inside or attached to
a computer that allows the computer to store
and retrieve information on a disk.

putting a **diskette** into a computer

diskette   A small piece of plastic in a square
cover that is used to store information for a
computer. Some diskettes are floppy disks.
disk·ette (di sket') *noun, plural* **diskettes.**

dislike   A feeling of not liking or of being
against something. I have a *dislike* of base-

ball so I did not try out for the team. *Noun.*
—To have a feeling of not liking or of being
against. Our messy neighbor *dislikes* doing
housework. *Verb.*
dis·like (dis līk') *noun, plural* **dislikes;**
verb, **disliked, disliking.**

dislocate   To put out of a proper or normal
position. I *dislocated* my hip when I slipped
and fell on the ice.
dis·lo·cate (dis'lō kāt' *or* dis lō'kāt) *verb,*
dislocated, dislocating.

dislodge   To move or force out of a place or
position. The flood *dislodged* two of the supports that held up the bridge.
dis·lodge (dis loj') *verb,* **dislodged,**
dislodging.

dismal   Causing gloom or sadness; dreary;
miserable. The weather has been rainy and
dismal lately.
dis·mal (diz'məl) *adjective.*

dismay   To make afraid or discouraged because of danger or trouble. The rising flood
dismayed the people of the town. *Verb.*
—A feeling of fear or being discouraged in
the face of danger or trouble. The family was
filled with *dismay* when they learned that the
fire was approaching their house. *Noun.*
dis·may (dis mā') *verb,* **dismayed,**
dismaying; *noun.*

dismiss   **1.** To send away or allow to leave.
The teacher decided to *dismiss* the class
early.   **2.** To take away the job of; fire. The
supervisor *dismissed* the employee for being
late too often.
dis·miss (dis mis') *verb,* **dismissed,**
dismissing.

dismount   To get off or down from. The
soldiers *dismounted* from their horses.
dis·mount (dis mount') *verb,* **dismounted,**
dismounting.

disobedient   Refusing or failing to obey.
The *disobedient* child crossed the road without the babysitter's permission.
dis·o·be·di·ent (dis'ə bē'dē ənt) *adjective.*

disobey   To refuse or fail to obey. The
driver *disobeyed* the traffic laws by not stopping at a red light.
dis·o·bey (dis'ə bā') *verb,* **disobeyed,**
disobeying.

at; āpe; fär; câre; end; mē; it; īce; pîerce; hot; ōld;
sông, fôrk; oil; out; up; ūse; rüle; pùll; tûrn; chin;
sing; shop; thin; <u>th</u>is; hw in white; zh in treasure.
The symbol ə stands for the unstressed vowel
sound in about, taken, pencil, lemon, and circus.

215

disorder 1. A lack of order; confusion. The room was in complete *disorder* after the birthday party. 2. A sickness; ailment. Doctors are investigating ways to treat lung *disorders. Noun.*
—To disturb the order of; throw into confusion. The sudden downpour of rain *disordered* the parade. *Verb.*
  dis·or·der (dis ôr′dər) *noun, plural*
  disorders; *verb,* **disordered, disordering.**

disorderly 1. Messy; untidy. The old newspapers lay in a *disorderly* pile. 2. Behaving without proper self-control in public; unruly. The *disorderly* crowd had to be held back by the police.
  dis·or·der·ly (dis ôr′dər lē) *adjective.*

dispatch To send off quickly. The travelers *dispatched* a telegram to announce their time of arrival. *Verb.*
—A written message or report. The newspaper received a *dispatch* from its reporter in England. *Noun.*
  dis·patch (di spach′) *verb,* **dispatched, dispatching;** *noun, plural* **dispatches.**

dispel To drive away or cause to disappear. The babysitter's kind words helped to *dispel* the child's fear of the dark.
  dis·pel (di spel′) *verb,* **dispelled, dispelling.**

dispense To give out. The town *dispensed* food and clothing to the homeless people. There is a machine in the movie theater that *dispenses* popcorn.
  dis·pense (di spens′) *verb,* **dispensed, dispensing.**

disperse To break up and scatter in different directions. The police *dispersed* the angry crowd before anyone got hurt.
  dis·perse (di spûrs′) *verb,* **dispersed, dispersing.**

displace 1. To take the place of. The airplane *displaced* the train as the fastest way to travel. 2. To move from the usual or proper place. You can use my desk, but please don't *displace* the things on it.
  dis·place (dis plās′) *verb,* **displaced, displacing.**

display To show or exhibit. The art museum was planning to *display* some paintings. This song *displays* the singer's talent well. *Verb.*
—A show or exhibit. Have you seen the *display* of new toys in that store? A hug is a *display* of affection. *Noun.*
  dis·play (di splā′) *verb,* **displayed, displaying;** *noun, plural* **displays.**

displease To make dissatisfied or annoyed; disappoint. You *displeased* the teacher when you didn't do your homework.
  dis·please (dis plēz′) *verb,* **displeased, displeasing.**

disposable Made to be thrown away after being used. We used *disposable* paper plates at the picnic.
  dis·pos·a·ble (di spō′zə bəl) *adjective.*

disposal The act of disposing of something. The city is responsible for the *disposal* of garbage.
  dis·pos·al (di spō′zəl) *noun, plural* **disposals.**

dispose To dispose of 1. To get rid of. I *disposed of* the wrappers by putting them in a garbage can. 2. To finish up with; settle. We quickly *disposed of* our morning chores so we could go to the zoo in the afternoon.
  dis·pose (di spōz′) *verb,* **disposed, disposing.**

disposition 1. A person's usual way of acting, thinking, or feeling; nature. You always have a cheerful *disposition,* even when you're tired. 2. A natural tendency. I have a *disposition* to agree with others too readily.
  dis·po·si·tion (dis′pə zish′ən) *noun, plural* **dispositions.**

dispute 1. To argue against; disagree with. They *disputed* your statement that you were a faster swimmer. 2. To argue or fight over. The two countries are *disputing* the boundary between them. *Verb.*
—An argument or quarrel. A judge had to settle the *dispute* between the farmers. *Noun.*
  dis·pute (dis pūt′) *verb,* **disputed, disputing;** *noun, plural* **disputes.**

disqualify To make or declare not fit or able to do something. Your age *disqualifies* you from voting. The judges *disqualified* the runner from the race for starting too soon.
  dis·qual·i·fy (dis kwol′ə fī′) *verb,* **disqualified, disqualifying.**

disregard To pay no attention to; ignore. I tried to *disregard* the noise on the bus and read my book. *Verb.*
—Lack of attention or consideration; neglect. Playing the radio loudly shows a *disregard* for your neighbors. *Noun.*
  dis·re·gard (dis′ri gärd′) *verb,* **disregarded, disregarding;** *noun.*

disrespect Lack of respect. Some spectators showed their *disrespect* for the judge by talking loudly during the trial.
  dis·re·spect (dis′ri spekt′) *noun.*

disrupt To break up or apart. By talking together, the two pupils were *disrupting* the whole class.
  dis·rupt (dis rupt′) *verb,* **disrupted, disrupting.**

dissatisfaction A feeling of being displeased or disappointed; discontent. My *dissatisfaction* with my running shoes grew until I finally bought a new pair.
dis·sat·is·fac·tion (dis'sat is fak'shən) *noun.*

dissatisfied Not content; displeased. The salesperson said that if we were *dissatisfied* with the encyclopedia, we could return it.
dis·sat·is·fied (dis sat'is fīd') *adjective.*

dissent To differ in opinion; disagree. Six judges of the Supreme Court agreed on the decision, but three judges *dissented. Verb.*
—A difference of opinion; disagreement. The dictator did not allow *dissent* against the actions of the government. *Noun.* ▲ Another word that sounds like this is **descent.**
dis·sent (di sent') *verb,* **dissented, dissenting;** *noun.*

dissolve 1. To mix thoroughly and evenly with a liquid. *Dissolve* the powder in milk to make the instant pudding. 2. To bring to an end. The club members voted to *dissolve* the dance committee after the dance.
dis·solve (di zolv') *verb,* **dissolved, dissolving.**

distance 1. The amount of space between two things or points. The *distance* from my house to the school is two blocks. 2. A point or place that is far away. The driver saw a large truck in the *distance.*
dis·tance (dis'təns) *noun, plural* **distances.**

distant 1. Far away in space or time; not near. The novel told of a family that had traveled to America from a *distant* country. Dinosaurs lived in the *distant* past. 2. Away. The farm was 10 miles *distant* from the nearest town. 3. Not friendly. The two roommates have been *distant* since their quarrel.
dis·tant (dis'tənt) *adjective.*

distasteful Unpleasant; offensive.
dis·taste·ful (dis tāst'fəl) *adjective.*

distemper A very contagious disease that dogs and other animals can catch. Distemper is caused by a virus.
dis·tem·per (dis tem'pər) *noun.*

distill To purify a liquid by heating it until it becomes a vapor and then cooling the vapor until it becomes a liquid again. Gasoline is *distilled* from petroleum.
dis·till (di stil') *verb,* **distilled, distilling.**

distinct 1. Not the same; separate; different. The envelopes were sorted into three *distinct* piles. 2. Easy to see, hear, or understand; clear. The words on the street sign became *distinct* when we walked closer. The

coach noticed a *distinct* improvement in the team's playing.
dis·tinct (di stingkt') *adjective.*

distinction 1. The act of making or noticing a difference between things. It is not always easy to make a *distinction* between poison ivy and some other plants. 2. Something that makes a thing different or exceptional. The cheetah has the *distinction* of being the fastest animal on land. 3. Excellence; worth. The senator was a person of *distinction.*
dis·tinc·tion (di stingk'shən) *noun, plural* **distinctions.**

distinctive Making something or someone easy to recognize; characteristic. I recognized the *distinctive* smell of roast turkey. I spotted you from a distance, because you have a *distinctive* walk.
dis·tinc·tive (di stingk'tiv) *adjective.*

distinguish 1. To know or show that there is a difference between certain things. The jeweler *distinguished* the real diamond from the fake one. 2. To make something special or different; set apart. The male cardinal's bright red feathers *distinguish* it from other birds. 3. To see or hear clearly. We could not *distinguish* your faces in the dark. 4. To make famous or deserving of special honor or attention; make well known. The doctors *distinguished* themselves by their work in cancer research.
dis·tin·guish (di sting'gwish) *verb,* **distinguished, distinguishing.**

The images in the reflection are **distorted.**

distort 1. To twist or bend out of shape. The curved mirror *distorted* my image.

at; āpe; fär; câre; end; mė; it; īce; pîerce; hot; ōld; sông, fôrk; oil; out; up; ūse; rüle; pùll; tûrn; chin; sing; shop; thin; this; hw in white; zh in treasure. The symbol ə stands for the unstressed vowel sound in about, taken, pencil, lemon, and circus.

2. To change so as to be misleading. Don't *distort* the facts when you tell what happened.
> **dis·tort** (di stôrt') *verb,* **distorted, distorting.**

distract To draw one's attention away from what one is doing or thinking. The noise *distracted* me from my homework.
> **dis·tract** (di strakt') *verb,* **distracted, distracting.**

distress **1.** Great pain or sorrow; misery. My grandfather's illness was a great *distress* to me. **2.** Danger, trouble, or great need. The ship sent a message that it was in *distress. Noun.*
—To cause pain, sorrow, or misery. The bad news *distressed* us. *Verb.*
> **dis·tress** (di stres') *noun; verb,* **distressed, distressing.**

distribute **1.** To give out in shares. The teacher *distributed* new books to the class. **2.** To spread something out over a large area; scatter. The farm machines *distributed* seed over the plowed field. **3.** To arrange or sort into groups. The post office *distributed* the letters into boxes according to which town they were going to.
> **dis·trib·ute** (di strib'ūt) *verb,* **distributed, distributing.**

distribution The act of distributing. The fire department supervised the *distribution* of food and clothing to the flood victims.
> **dis·tri·bu·tion** (dis'trə bū'shən) *noun, plural* **distributions.**

distributive property A law of mathematics that allows you to multiply a group of numbers and get the same answer that you would by multiplying each member of the group separately. For example, $5 \times (2 + 3 + 4) = (5 \times 2) + (5 \times 3) + (5 \times 4) = 45$.
> **dis·trib·u·tive property** (di strib'yə tiv).

district An area that is a special part of a larger area. That store is in the business *district* of the city.
> **dis·trict** (dis'trikt) *noun, plural* **districts.**

District of Columbia An area in the eastern United States between Maryland and Virginia. It is completely occupied by the city of Washington, the national capital.
> **District of Co·lum·bi·a** (kə lum'bē ə).

Word History

The **District of Columbia** was named after Christopher Columbus, the Italian explorer who sailed across the Atlantic and landed in America in 1492.

disturb **1.** To make uneasy or nervous; upset. Loud music *disturbs* my grandmother. The news of the terrible accident *disturbed* us all. **2.** To break in on; interrupt. The telephone call *disturbed* everyone's sleep. **3.** To upset or change the order or arrangement of things. The children *disturbed* the books on the shelf.
> **dis·turb** (di stûrb') *verb,* **disturbed, disturbing.**

disturbance **1.** An interruption. After the phone call, I went back to work without further *disturbance.* **2.** Something that disturbs. The laughter was a *disturbance* to the students who were reading. When people complained of a barking dog, the police went to investigate the *disturbance.*
> **dis·turb·ance** (di stûr'bəns) *noun, plural* **disturbances.**

ditch A long, narrow hole dug in the ground. Ditches are used to drain off water.
> **ditch** (dich) *noun, plural* **ditches.**

dive **1.** To plunge headfirst into water. At first, I was afraid to *dive* from the high board into the pool. **2.** To plunge downward quickly and at a steep angle. We watched the eagle *dive* from the sky. **3.** To go, move, or drop suddenly and quickly. The sound of thunder made the frightened puppy *dive* under the bed. *Verb.*
—**1.** A headfirst plunge into water. It's not safe to do a *dive* from the rocks into the lake. **2.** A quick, steep plunge. The plane went into a *dive* when it was hit by enemy fire. *Noun.*
> **dive** (dīv) *verb,* **dived** or **dove, dived, diving;** *noun, plural* **dives.**

diver **1.** A person who dives. **2.** A person who works or explores underwater. Divers usually carry tanks of air on their backs so that they can breathe underwater.
> **div·er** (dī'vər) *noun, plural* **divers.**

diverse Not all the same; varied. The students in the class come from *diverse* backgrounds.
> **di·verse** (di vûrs' *or* dī vûrs') *adjective.*

diversion **1.** A changing of the direction in which something is going. The *diversion* of the train to a different track was necessary because the regular tracks were being repaired. **2.** Something that turns the attention in a different direction. You create a *diversion,* and we'll sneak up from behind to surprise them. **3.** Entertainment; amusement; pastime. My favorite *diversions* are drawing and listening to music.
> **di·ver·sion** (di vûr'zhən *or* dī vûr'zhən) *noun, plural* **diversions.**

D

diversity Great difference; variety. The exhibition of paintings included a *diversity* of styles.
di·ver·si·ty (di vûr′si tē *or* dī vûr′si tē) *noun, plural* **diversities.**

divert **1.** To change the direction in which something is going. The police *diverted* traffic from the street where the accident happened. **2.** To turn the attention in a different direction. I tried to *divert* the crying baby by singing a song. **3.** To entertain; amuse. The television show *diverted* me while I waited for dinner.
di·vert (di vûrt′ *or* dī vûrt′) *verb,* **diverted, diverting.**

divide **1.** To separate into parts, pieces, or groups. The cook *divided* the pie into ten slices. The class *divided* into two teams for the spelling contest. **2.** To separate into parts or pieces and give some to each; share. The three children who found the lost dog *divided* the reward money. **3.** To show how many times one number contains another number. When you *divide* 6 by 2 you get 3, because the number 6 contains the number 2 three times. **4.** To split into opposing sides because of different feelings or opinions. The class *divided* on the choice of a site for the picnic. *Verb.*
—A ridge of land that separates two areas that are drained by different rivers. *Noun.*
di·vide (di vīd′) *verb,* **divided, dividing;** *noun, plural* **divides.**

dividend **1.** A number that is to be divided by another number. When you divide 6 by 3, the *dividend* is 6. **2.** Money that is earned by a business; profit.
div·i·dend (div′i dend′) *noun, plural* **dividends.**

divine **1.** Of or from God or a god. The workers trapped in the mine prayed for *divine* mercy. **2.** Religious; sacred. The church bell called the people to *divine* worship.
di·vine (di vīn′) *adjective.*

diving board A board that swimmers use for jumping or diving into water. One end of the board is attached to the ground or a support, and the other end sticks out over the water.

divisible Capable of being divided. The number 8 is evenly *divisible* by the numbers 8, 4, 2, and 1.
di·vis·i·ble (di viz′ə bəl) *adjective.*

division **1.** The act of dividing or the condition of being divided. The *division* of the house into apartments provided homes for five families. **2.** One of the parts into which something is divided. A month is a *division* of a year. Asian history is one of the *divisions* of our social studies course. **3.** Something that divides or separates. The wooden fence formed a *division* between the farms. **4.** A large unit of an army that is made up of different regiments.
di·vi·sion (di vizh′ən) *noun, plural* **divisions.**

divisor A number by which another number is to be divided. When you divide 6 by 3, the divisor is 3.
di·vi·sor (di vī′zər) *noun, plural* **divisors.**

divorce The legal ending of a marriage. *Noun.*
—To legally end a marriage. The couple *divorced* after ten years of marriage. She *divorced* her husband. *Verb.*
di·vorce (di vôrs′) *noun, plural* **divorces;** *verb,* **divorced, divorcing.**

dizzy Having the feeling of spinning and being about to fall. The children ran in circles until they were *dizzy.*
diz·zy (diz′ē) *adjective,* **dizzier, dizziest.**

do **1.** To carry out an action; perform. Let's *do* something this afternoon. Please *do* me a favor. **2.** To produce or create; make. First the artist *did* a sketch. **3.** To bring to an end; finish. I've already *done* my homework. **4.** To take care of. Let's *do* the dishes. **5.** To work out; solve. I can't *do* this mathematics problem. **6.** To cause; result in . It *does* little good to complain. **7.** To act in a certain way; behave. The naughty children never *did* as they were told. **8.** To get along; manage. How are you *doing* with that homework assignment? I'm *doing* well. **9.** To be suitable. That light jacket won't *do* for cold weather. **10.** Used in place of a verb or a verb phrase that has just been used. You can ice-skate as well as I *do.* **11.** An auxiliary verb that is used in asking questions, in making negative statements, and in making another verb seem stronger. *Do* horses run faster than dogs? I *do* not want to go. Now I *do* understand. ▲ Other words that sound like this are **dew** and **due.**
• **to do away with. 1.** To put an end to; get rid of. The Thirteenth Amendment to the Constitution *did away with* slavery in

at; āpe; fär; câre; end; mē; it; īce; pîerce; hot; ōld; sông, fôrk; oil; out; up; ūse; rüle; pull; tûrn; chin; sing; shop; thin; this; hw in white; zh in treasure. The symbol ə stands for the unstressed vowel sound in about, taken, pencil, lemon, and circus.

219

the United States. **2.** To kill. The poison *did away with* the rats in our basement.
- **to make do.** To manage; get along. They can *make do* without new clothes for spring.

do (dü) *verb*, **did, done, doing.**

Doberman pinscher A dog that has a long head, slender legs, and a shiny black or brown coat. Doberman pinschers are often kept as watchdogs.

Do·ber·man pin·scher (dō′bər mən pin′shər).

Doberman pinscher

docile Easy to teach, train, or handle. A child can pet and ride that *docile* pony.

doc·ile (dos′əl) *adjective.*

dock **1.** A platform where boats or ships are tied up. A dock is built along the shore or out into the water. Docks are used for loading and unloading a ship's cargo and passengers. **2.** An area of water between two piers where boats and ships tie up. The tugboat towed the ocean liner into the *dock. Noun.*
—**1.** To bring or come to a dock. The pilot *docked* the ship. The tanker *docked* and unloaded its cargo. **2.** To bring two spacecraft together in space. *Verb.*

dock (dok) *noun, plural* **docks;** *verb,* **docked, docking.**

doctor **1.** A person who has been trained and licensed to treat the sick and injured. A physician, a dentist, and a veterinarian are all doctors. **2.** A person who has the highest degree from a university.

doc·tor (dok′tər) *noun, plural* **doctors.**

doctrine Something that is believed by a group of people. The beliefs of a religion and the ideals of a political party are doctrines.

doc·trine (dok′trin) *noun, plural* **doctrines.**

document A written or printed statement that gives official proof and information about something. A birth certificate, a deed to a house, and a diploma are documents.

doc·u·ment (dok′yə mənt) *noun, plural* **documents.**

dodge **1.** To keep away from something by moving aside quickly. I *dodged* the snowball that someone threw at me. **2.** To get away from something in a tricky way. The witness *dodged* the lawyer's question by pretending not to remember. *Verb.*
—**1.** A quick move to the side. The boxer avoided being hit by making a *dodge* to the left. **2.** A trick that is used to fool or cheat someone. I tried every *dodge* I could think of to avoid taking the history test. *Noun.*

dodge (doj) *verb,* **dodged, dodging;** *noun, plural* **dodges.**

dodo A large bird that no longer exists. Its wings were so small that it was not able to fly.

do·do (dō′dō) *noun, plural* **dodos** or **dodoes.**

doe **1.** A female deer. **2.** The female of several other animals, such as the antelope or hare. ▲ Another word that sounds like this is **dough.**

doe (dō) *noun, plural* **does.**

does A form of the present tense of **do** that is used with *she, he, it* or the name of a person, place, or thing. The artist *does* beautiful paintings. Look up **do** for more information.

does (duz) *verb.*

doesn't Shortened form of "does not." That cup *doesn't* hold much milk.

does·n't (duz′ənt) *contraction.*

dog An animal that has four legs and makes a barking noise. Dogs have claws and sharp teeth for eating meat. Dogs are related to coyotes, wolves, and foxes. *Noun.*
—To follow closely in the way a hunting dog would. I *dogged* the babysitter through the park so that I wouldn't get lost. *Verb.*

dog (dôg) *noun, plural* **dogs;** *verb,* **dogged, dogging.**

dogwood A tree or shrub that has small flowers with a greenish yellow center and pink or white leaves that look like petals.

dog·wood (dôg′wu̇d′) *noun, plural* **dogwoods.**

Blossom

dogwood in spring

D

doily A small piece of linen, lace, paper, or some other material. Doilies are usually placed under something, such as a vase or plate, as a decoration or to protect furniture.
doi·ly (doi′lē) *noun, plural* **doilies.**

doings Activities, deeds, or events. The *doings* of the club were reported on the news.
do·ings (dü′ingz) *plural noun.*

doll A toy that looks like a baby, a child, or a grown-up.
doll (dol) *noun, plural* **dolls.**

dollar A unit of money in the United States and in Canada. A dollar is worth one hundred cents.
dol·lar (dol′ər) *noun, plural* **dollars.**

dolphin A sea animal that has two flippers and a snout that is like a beak. Although a dolphin looks like a fish, it is a mammal. Dolphins are closely related to porpoises and whales. They are very intelligent animals.
dol·phin (dol′fin) *noun, plural* **dolphins.**

dolphin

domain 1. All the land that is controlled by a ruler or government. The news spread throughout the king's *domain*. 2. A field of knowledge or interest. Volcanoes and earthquakes fall within the *domain* of geology.
do·main (dō mān′) *noun, plural* **domains.**

dome A round roof that looks like an upside down cup. Domes are built on a base that is circular or has many sides. Some state capitol buildings have domes.
dome (dōm) *noun, plural* **domes.**

domestic 1. Having to do with the home and family. We all take turns doing the cleaning, cooking, and other *domestic* chores in our house. 2. Not wild; tame. Dogs, cows, and chickens are *domestic* animals. 3. Having to do with one's own country; not foreign. The president of the United States handles both foreign and *domestic* affairs.
do·mes·tic (də mes′tik) *adjective.*

domesticate To train or change a wild animal so that it can live with or be used by people; tame. People first *domesticated* wild horses to pull loads and help in farming.
do·mes·ti·cate (də mes′ti kāt′) *verb,* **domesticated, domesticating.**

dominant Most powerful or important. Blue is the *dominant* color in our kitchen. Rome was the *dominant* power in Europe 2,000 years ago.
dom·i·nant (dom′ə nənt) *adjective.*

dominate To rule or control because of power, strength, or importance. The United States and the Soviet Union dominate large parts of the world today.
dom·i·nate (dom′ə nāt′) *verb,* **dominated, dominating.**

Dominican Republic A country that occupies part of an island in the Caribbean Sea.
Do·min·i·can Republic (də min′i kən).

dominion 1. A land or territory that is controlled by a ruler or government. In 1770, Virginia was still among the *dominions* of Great Britain. 2. The power to rule; authority. An able ruler held *dominion* over the land for forty years.
do·min·ion (də min′yən) *noun, plural* **dominions.**

Dominion Day The former name of **Canada Day.** Look up **Canada Day** for more information.

domino 1. One of a set of small black tiles marked with dots. Dominoes are used in playing a game. 2. **dominoes.** The game that is played with these tiles.
dom·i·no (dom′ə nō′) *noun, plural* **dominoes.**

donate To give; contribute. The family *donated* their old clothes to people who needed them.
do·nate (dō′nāt) *verb,* **donated, donating.**

donation A gift; contribution. The hospital fund received *donations* of more than $1,000 from the citizens in our town.
do·na·tion (dō nā′shən) *noun, plural* **donations.**

done Past participle of **do.** The carpenters have *done* a very good job on our new kitchen. Look up **do** for more information. *Verb.*
—Cooked. When the meat is *done*, we can start our dinner. *Adjective.*
done (dun) *verb; adjective.*

donkey A tame ass. Donkeys are related to horses but have longer ears and a shorter

at; āpe; fär; câre; end; mē; it; īce; pîerce; hot; ōld; sông, fôrk; oil; out; up; ūse; rüle; pùll; tûrn; chin; sing; shop; thin; <u>th</u>is; hw in white; zh in treasure. The symbol ə stands for the unstressed vowel sound in about, taken, pencil, lemon, and circus.

mane than horses do. They are often used to pull or carry loads.

don·key (dong′kē *or* dung′kē) *noun, plural* **donkeys.**

donor A person who gives or contributes something. The name of the *donor* who had given the book to the library was printed inside the cover.

do·nor (dō′nər) *noun, plural* **donors.**

don't Shortened form of "do not." Please *don't* tell anyone else the secret.

don't (dōnt) *contraction.*

doom A sad end or death; a terrible fate. The mountain climbers met their *doom* when their rope snapped. *Noun.*
—To make sure that a bad end will come; destine to fail or die. When our boat began to sink, I was afraid we were *doomed. Verb.*

doom (düm) *noun, plural* **dooms;** *verb,* **doomed, dooming.**

door A movable object that is used to open or close an entrance in something. Doors are usually made of wood, metal, or glass.

door (dôr) *noun, plural* **doors.**

doorbell A bell or buzzer that is rung by someone who is outside a door and who wants to come in.

door·bell (dôr′bel′) *noun, plural* **doorbells.**

doorknob A rounded handle used to open and close a door. We were locked in the room because the *doorknob* was jammed.

door·knob (dôr′nob′) *noun, plural* **doorknobs.**

doorstep A step or flight of steps leading from the outside door of a building to the ground or sidewalk.

door·step (dôr′step′) *noun, plural* **doorsteps.**

doorway An opening in a wall that leads in and out of a room or building and can be closed by a door.

door·way (dôr′wā′) *noun, plural* **doorways.**

dope **1.** A very stupid person. **2.** A harmful drug that causes addiction. **3.** A varnish or similar liquid. Dope is used in building models of airplanes.

dope (dōp) *noun, plural* **dopes.**

dormant Not active. A volcano that had been *dormant* for years suddenly erupted.

dor·mant (dôr′mənt) *adjective.*

dormitory A building in which there are many bedrooms. Many colleges have dormitories where students live.

dor·mi·to·ry (dôr′mi tôr′ē) *noun, plural* **dormitories.**

dormouse An animal that looks like a small squirrel with black or gray fur. Dormice are rodents and are found in Europe and northern Africa. They hibernate in the winter.

dor·mouse (dôr′mous′) *noun, plural* **dormice** (dôr′mīs′).

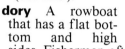
dormouse

dory A rowboat that has a flat bottom and high sides. Fishermen often use dories.

do·ry (dôr′ē) *noun, plural* **dories.**

dose An amount of medicine that a person is given at one time. The doctor prescribed a small *dose* of aspirin for the sick child.

dose (dōs) *noun, plural* **doses.**

dot A small, round mark; small spot or speck. The *dot* on the map showed the location of the town. *Noun.*
—**1.** To mark with a dot or dots. Don't forget to *dot* your i's. The child's face is *dotted* with freckles. **2.** To be scattered here and there. Small houses *dotted* the seashore. *Verb.*

dot (dot) *noun, plural* **dots;** *verb,* **dotted, dotting.**

dote To give too much affection. The grandparents *doted* on their two grandchildren and spoiled them.

dote (dōt) *verb,* **doted, doting.**

double **1.** Twice as many or as much. A grown-up who is 6 feet tall is *double* the height of a child who is 3 feet tall. The worker got *double* pay for the extra hours of work. **2.** Having or made up of two parts. People stood in a *double* line in front of the theater. That author led a *double* life during the war as a German citizen and a spy for the British. *Adjective.*
—Two instead of one; in pairs. The ride on the merry-go-round made me feel dizzy and see everything *double. Adverb.*
—**1.** Something that is twice as much. Ten is the *double* of five. **2.** A person or thing that is very much or just like another. I saw your *double* on the street today. **3.** A hit in baseball that lets the batter reach second base. *Noun.*
—**1.** To make or become twice as many or as much. I asked my parents to *double* my weekly allowance. **2.** To bend, fold, or turn over or back. The funny story made the lis-

222

teners *double* over with laughter. **3.** To be a substitute. Another actor *doubled* for the star when we saw the play. **4.** To serve a second purpose. This sofa *doubles* as a bed. **5.** To hit a double in baseball. *Verb.*
  dou·ble (dub′əl) *adjective; adverb; noun, plural* **doubles;** *verb,* **doubled, doubling.**

double-cross To cheat or betray someone by not doing what one has promised. The robber *double-crossed* a partner by running off with the money that they were supposed to share.
  dou·ble-cross (dub′əl krôs′) *verb,* **double-crossed, double-crossing.**

double-header Two games that are played one right after the other on the same day.
  dou·ble-head·er (dub′əl hed′ər) *noun, plural* **double-headers.**

doubt **1.** To be uncertain about; not believe or trust fully. The judge *doubted* that the prisoner was telling the truth. **2.** To think of as unlikely. I brought my umbrella, even though I *doubt* that it will rain. *Verb.* —**1.** A feeling of not believing or trusting. I had *doubts* about the honesty of the salesperson who was trying to sell me the car. **2.** A state of being undecided or unsure. The result of the race was in *doubt* until the horses reached the finish line. *Noun.*
  doubt (dout) *verb,* **doubted, doubting;** *noun, plural* **doubts.**

doubtful Feeling, showing, or causing doubt; not sure or certain. The outcome of the game was *doubtful* until the last minute.
  doubt·ful (dout′fəl) *adjective.*

doubtless Without doubt; certainly. A person who draws as well as you will *doubtless* become an artist someday.
  doubt·less (dout′lis) *adverb.*

dough A thick mixture of flour, liquid, and other ingredients that is usually baked. Dough is used to make bread, cookies, pie crusts, and other food. ▲ Another word that sounds like this is **doe.**
  dough (dō) *noun, plural* **doughs.**

doughnut A small, round cake that has a hole in the middle. A doughnut is cooked in fat.
  dough·nut (dō′nut′) *noun, plural* **doughnuts.**

---

dove¹ Any member of a group of plump birds with small heads; pigeon. A white dove is sometimes used as a symbol of peace.
  dove (duv) *noun, plural* **doves.**

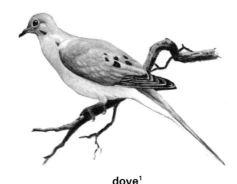

dove¹

dove² A past tense of **dive.** The swimmer *dove* from the rocks into the lake. Look up **dive** for more information.
  dove (dōv) *verb.*

down¹ **1.** From a higher to a lower place. The painter climbed *down* from the ladder. **2.** To or in a lower position, level, or condition. The price of milk has gone *down.* The train slowed *down.* **3.** To or on the ground or floor. I fell *down.* The wind almost knocked them *down.* **4.** To a calmer condition. The noisy crowd quieted *down.* *Adverb.* —From a higher to a lower place; along, through, or into. We rolled *down* the hillside. The water flows *down* that pipe. *Preposition.* —**1.** To bring or put down. The cowhand lassoed the calf and *downed* it. **2.** To swallow quickly. It's best to *down* the bitter medicine in one gulp. *Verb.* —One of four chances that a football team gets to move the ball 10 yards. If it does not move the ball that far, the other team gets possession of the ball. *Noun.*
  down (doun) *adverb; preposition; verb,* **downed, downing;** *noun, plural* **downs.**

down² Fine, soft feathers. Baby birds have *down* until their regular feathers grow in.
  down (doun) *noun.*

downpour A very heavy rain.
  down·pour (doun′pôr′) *noun, plural* **downpours.**

Word History

The word **doughnut** developed from an earlier form of the word *dough-nought,* a "dough circle." *Nought* is an old-fashioned word for "zero."

---

at; āpe; fär; câre; end; mē; it; īce; pîerce; hot; ōld; sông, fôrk; oil; out; up; ūse; rüle; pùll; tûrn; chin; sing; shop; thin; <u>th</u>is; hw in white; zh in treasure. The symbol ə stands for the unstressed vowel sound in about, taken, pencil, lemon, and circus.

downright Thorough; complete. The rumor about me is a *downright* lie. *Adjective.*
—Thoroughly; completely. First I was annoyed by the delay, then I became *downright* angry. *Adverb.*
down·right (doun′rīt′) *adjective; adverb.*

downstairs **1.** Down the stairs. The child tripped and fell *downstairs.* **2.** On or to a lower floor. From our room, we could hear our parents talking *downstairs. Adverb.*
—On a lower or main floor. We have an upstairs bathroom and a *downstairs* bathroom. *Adjective.*
down·stairs (doun′stârz′) *adverb; adjective.*

downstream Moving in the same direction as the current of a stream. *Downstream* river traffic is faster than upstream traffic. *Adjective.*
—**1.** Down a stream. The raft drifted *downstream.* **2.** At a point farther down the stream. The water becomes rough *downstream. Adverb.*
down·stream (doun′strēm′) *adjective; adverb.*

downtown To or in the main part or business district of a town. We went *downtown* to see a movie. *Adverb.*
—Going to or located in the main part or business district of a town. The *downtown* stores are larger than the stores in our neighborhood. *Adjective.*
down·town (doun′toun′) *adverb; adjective.*

downward From a higher to a lower place. The road is level and then goes *downward* into the valley. *Adverb.*
—Moving from a higher place to a lower place. The hikers followed the *downward* course of the stream from the mountain top. *Adjective.*
down·ward (doun′wərd) *adverb; adjective.*

downwards Another spelling of the adverb **downward.**
down·wards (doun′wərdz) *adverb.*

dowry The money or property that a woman brings to her marriage.
dow·ry (dou′rē) *noun, plural* **dowries.**

doz. An abbreviation for *dozen.*

doze To sleep lightly or for a short time; take a nap. I *dozed* on the couch for an hour before supper. *Verb.*
—A short, light sleep. *Noun.*
doze (dōz) *verb,* **dozed, dozing;** *noun, plural* **dozes.**

dozen A group of twelve. We bought three *dozen* doughnuts.
doz·en (duz′ən) *noun, plural* **dozens** or **dozen.**

Dr. An abbreviation for *doctor.*

drab Not cheerful or bright; dull. The dark, *drab* room was much nicer after we put up new curtains.
drab (drab) *adjective,* **drabber, drabbest.**

draft **1.** A current of air in an enclosed space. I could feel a cold *draft* from the open window. **2.** A device that controls the flow of air in something. Furnaces, fireplaces, and some stoves have drafts. **3.** A sketch, plan, or rough copy of something written. The author wrote three *drafts* of the novel. **4.** The selecting of persons for military service or some other special duty. During World War II, most young men in the United States were subject to the *draft. Noun.*
—**1.** To make a sketch, plan, or rough copy of something. I *drafted* the letter in pencil and then typed it. **2.** To select a person or persons for some special duty. Many people were *drafted* to serve in that war. *Verb.*
—Used for pulling loads. Elephants are used as *draft* animals in some countries. *Adjective.*
draft (draft) *noun, plural* **drafts;** *verb,* **drafted, drafting;** *adjective.*

drag **1.** To pull or move along slowly or heavily. The mover *dragged* the heavy trunk across the room. Time *dragged* on while we waited for the train that was late. **2.** To trail along the ground. The dog's leash *dragged* behind it. **3.** To search the bottom of a body of water with a hook or net. The sailors *dragged* the bottom of the lake for the sunken rowboat.
drag (drag) *verb,* **dragged, dragging.**

dragon

dragon An imaginary beast that is supposed to look like a giant lizard with claws and wings.
drag·on (drag′ən) *noun, plural* **dragons.**

D

dragonfly An insect that has a long, thin body and two pairs of wings. Dragonflies eat mosquitoes and other insects. They live near fresh water.

drag·on·fly (drag′ən flī′) *noun, plural* **dragonflies.**

dragonfly

drain **1.** To empty water or other liquid from something. The workers *drained* the water from the swimming pool. The thirsty players *drained* a pitcher of lemonade. **2.** To tire or use up; exhaust. The long hike *drained* our energy. *Verb.*
—**1.** An opening, pipe, or other device that draws off water or another liquid. The *drain* in the sink is clogged. **2.** Something that uses up or exhausts. Having to buy lunch every day is a *drain* on my allowance. *Noun.*

drain (drān) *verb,* **drained, draining;** *noun, plural* **drains.**

drainage A drawing off or emptying of water or other liquid. The *drainage* of the swamp made it possible for the farmer to plant crops there.

drain·age (drā′nij) *noun, plural* **drainages.**

drainpipe A pipe used for carrying water or sewage away.

drain·pipe (drān′pīp′) *noun, plural* **drainpipes.**

drake A male duck.

drake (drāk) *noun, plural* **drakes.**

drama **1.** A story that is written for actors to perform on the stage; play. **2.** A happening that is as exciting or interesting as a play. The newspaper reported the *drama* of the rescue of the family from the burning building. **3.** The quality of excitement and suspense that good plays and stories have. We enjoyed the movie, because it was full of *drama.*

dra·ma (drä′mə *or* dram′ə) *noun, plural* **dramas.**

dramatic **1.** Of or having to do with plays or acting. My cousin is studying *dramatic* literature. **2.** As exciting and interesting as a good play or story. Our team won a *dramatic* victory by scoring the winning point in the last minutes of the game.

dra·mat·ic (drə mat′ik) *adjective.*

dramatist A person who writes plays.

dram·a·tist (dram′ə tist *or* drä′mə tist) *noun, plural* **dramatists.**

dramatize **1.** To write or perform something as a play. The class *dramatized* several stories from the books they had read. **2.** To make something seem very exciting. I *dramatized* what happened so that it sounded like a great adventure.

dram·a·tize (dram′ə tīz′ *or* drä′mə tīz′) *verb,* **dramatized, dramatizing.**

drank Past tense of **drink.** I *drank* three glasses of water. Look up **drink** for more information.

drank (drangk) *verb.*

drape **1.** To cover or decorate with cloth that hangs loosely. I *draped* a shawl over my shoulders. **2.** To arrange or spread loosely. You *draped* your feet over the chair. *Verb.*
—Cloth that is hung at a window; drapery. I opened the *drapes* to let sunlight into the room. *Noun.*

drape (drāp) *verb,* **draped, draping;** *noun, plural* **drapes.**

drapery Cloth that is hung in loose folds. Draperies are usually used as window curtains.

dra·per·y (drā′pə rē) *noun, plural* **draperies.**

drastic Very strong or harsh; extreme. Fasting is a *drastic* way to lose weight.

dras·tic (dras′tik) *adjective.*

draw **1.** To move by pulling; haul. Four horses *drew* the hay wagon. **2.** To move; shift. The train *drew* near the station. **3.** To take out; bring out. The nurse carefully *drew* the splinter from my foot. **4.** To make a mark or picture with lines, using a pencil, crayon, or other writing tool. I *drew* a cat with chalk on the blackboard. Would you like to learn how to *draw?* **5.** To cause to come; attract. That band always *draws* a large audience. **6.** To bring forth; result in. The mayor's mistakes *drew* a lot of criticism. **7.** To close; shut. Please *draw* the curtains. **8.** To take in by inhaling. *Draw* a deep breath. *Verb.*
—**1.** The act of drawing. The hero in the movie was quick on the *draw* and fired first. **2.** A game or contest that ends with an even score or no winner; tie. The chess game ended in a *draw. Noun.*

• **to draw up.** To come or bring to a stop.

at; āpe; fär; câre; end; mē; it; īce; pîerce; hot; ōld; sông, fôrk; oil; out; up; ūse; rüle; pùll; tûrn; chin; sing; shop; thin; this; hw in white; zh in treasure. The symbol ə stands for the unstressed vowel sound in about, taken, pencil, lemon, and circus.

The taxi *drew up* in front of our house.
draw (drô) *verb*, **drew, drawn, drawing;**
noun, plural **draws.**

drawback　A thing that makes something more difficult or unpleasant; disadvantage. One *drawback* of our new house is that it is so far away from my school.
draw·back (drô′bak′) *noun, plural* **drawbacks.**

drawbridge　A kind of bridge that can be raised or moved so that ships can pass under it.
draw·bridge (drô′brij′) *noun, plural* **drawbridges.**

a raised **drawbridge**

drawer　A box that fits into a piece of furniture and can be pulled out and pushed in. Bureaus, desks, and cabinets have drawers.
drawer (drôr) *noun, plural* **drawers.**

drawing　**1.** A picture or design made using a pencil, pen, chalk, or other writing tool; sketch.　**2.** The choosing of a winning chance or ticket in a raffle or other contest. The *drawing* for the winning number will be next Saturday night.
draw·ing (drô′ing) *noun, plural* **drawings.**

drawl　To speak slowly, drawing out the vowel sounds. The sleepy child *drawled* an answer to the question. *Verb.*
—A slow way of speaking, with the vowel sounds drawn out. Many people from the South speak with a *drawl. Noun.*
drawl (drôl) *verb*, **drawled, drawling;**
noun, plural **drawls.**

drawn　Past participle of **draw.** The artist has *drawn* many sketches of the church. Look up **draw** for more information.
drawn (drôn) *verb.*

drawstring　A string or cord that is used to close an opening or to make something tighter. My pajamas have a *drawstring* around the waist.
draw·string (drô′string′) *noun, plural* **drawstrings.**

dread　To look forward to with fear; be very afraid or anxious about. I *dreaded* going to the dentist. *Verb.*
—A feeling of great fear. I think of mountain climbing with *dread* because I am afraid of heights. *Noun.*
—Causing fear; dreadful. Smallpox is one of the *dread* diseases that has been almost completely wiped out. *Adjective.*
dread (dred) *verb*, **dreaded, dreading;**
noun; adjective.

dreadful　**1.** Very frightening; terrible. The *dreadful* storm damaged many trees.
2. Very bad; awful. The movie was so *dreadful* that we left before it was over.
dread·ful (dred′fəl) *adjective.*

dream　**1.** A series of thoughts, feelings, and apparent sights that a person has while asleep. I had a *dream* last night that I was flying through the air.　**2.** A hope or ambition to do or succeed at something. My great *dream* is to become an actor. *Noun.*
—**1.** To see, feel, or think about in a dream. I dozed off and *dreamed* about riding a white horse.　**2.** To imagine. I didn't take an umbrella because I never *dreamed* it would rain. *Verb.*
dream (drēm) *noun, plural* **dreams;** *verb,* **dreamed** or **dreamt, dreaming.**

dreamt　A past tense and a past participle of **dream.** I *dreamt* I was living in a castle. Look up **dream** for more information.
dreamt (dremt) *verb.*

dreary　Sad or dull; gloomy. Painting the dark room bright yellow made it less *dreary.*
drear·y (drir′ē) *adjective*, **drearier, dreariest.**

dredge　A large machine that scoops up mud, sand, and other material from the bottom of a body of water. The engineers used a *dredge* to make the canal deeper. *Noun.*
—To clean out or deepen with a dredge. The machine *dredged* mud from the river. *Verb.*
dredge (drej) *noun, plural* **dredges;** *verb,* **dredged, dredging.**

dregs　Small pieces that settle at the bottom of a liquid. There were *dregs* at the bottom of the coffee cup.
dregs (dregz) *plural noun.*

drench　To make something completely wet; soak. The big wave *drenched* the children on the raft.
drench (drench) *verb*, **drenched, drenching.**

dress　**1.** An outer garment for a woman or girl. A dress is usually one piece and extends from the neck to just above or below the knees.　**2.** Clothing or a particular style of

clothing. The guests at the ball were all wearing formal *dress*. *Noun.*
—**1.** To put clothes on. I *dressed* quickly because I was late for school. **2.** To select and wear clothes. Salespersons often *dress* in the latest styles. **3.** To decorate; trim. Thank you for helping us *dress* the store windows for the holidays. **4.** To comb and arrange the hair. I went to the barber to have my hair *dressed*. **5.** To clean and prepare for use or sale. The butcher *dressed* the turkey for us. **6.** To clean and treat with medicine. The nurse *dressed* my wound and bandaged it. *Verb.*
   • **to dress up.** To put on clothing more elaborate or fancy than what is usually worn. It's fun to *dress up* for parties.
   dress (dres) *noun, plural* **dresses;** *verb,* **dressed, dressing.**

dresser A piece of furniture that has drawers for storing clothes and other things. A dresser often has a large mirror attached to it.
   dress·er (dres′ər) *noun, plural* **dressers.**

dressing **1.** A sauce that is put on salads and some other foods. **2.** A mixture of bread crumbs and seasonings that is used to stuff turkey, chicken, or other fowl. **3.** A medicine or bandage that is put on a wound or sore.
   dress·ing (dres′ing) *noun, plural* **dressings.**

drew Past tense of **draw.** I *drew* a map of the town. The visitors *drew* their chairs closer to the table. Look up **draw** for more information.
   drew (drü) *verb.*

dribble **1.** To flow or let flow in small drops; trickle. Rain *dribbled* through the cracks in the roof. **2.** To move a ball along by bouncing or kicking it. Players *dribble* the ball in basketball and soccer. *Verb.*
   —A dripping; trickle. A *dribble* of juice from the plum ran down the child's chin. *Noun.*
   drib·ble (drib′əl) *verb,* **dribbled, dribbling;** *noun, plural* **dribbles.**

dried Past tense and past participle of **dry.** I washed my hair and then *dried* it. Look up **dry** for more information.
   dried (drīd) *verb.*

drier Comparative of **dry.** The clothes were *drier* after they hung on the line for an hour. Look up **dry** for more information. *Adjective.*
   —A spelling sometimes used for the word **dryer.** Look up **dryer** for more information. *Noun.*
   dri·er (drī′ər) *adjective; noun, plural* **driers.**

drift **1.** To move because of a current of air or water. We stopped rowing and let our boat *drift* downstream. **2.** To pile up in masses from the action of the wind. The snow drifted to 6 feet outside our cabin. **3.** To move from place to place without a goal or purpose. The tramp *drifted* from town to town. *Verb.*
   —**1.** Movement caused by a current of air or water. Scientists measured the *drift* of the glacier over the past one hundred years. **2.** Something that has been moved along or piled up by air or water currents. The storm caused *drifts* of snow more than 10 feet deep. *Noun.*
   drift (drift) *verb,* **drifted, drifting;** *noun, plural* **drifts.**

driftwood Wood that floats on water or is brought to the shore by water.
   drift·wood (drift′wu̇d′) *noun.*

drill **1.** A tool that is used to cut holes in wood, plastic, and other hard material. A drill usually has a long, pointed end that is turned with a crank or by an electric motor. **2.** Training or teaching by making someone do something again and again; practice. For our social studies *drill*, the teacher asked us to name the capital of each state. *Noun.*
   —**1.** To make a hole in something with a drill; use a drill. The carpenter *drilled* a hole in the wood. The company *drilled* for oil. **2.** To train or teach by having someone do something again and again. The school band *drilled* by marching back and forth. I will *drill* you for your spelling test. *Verb.*
   drill (dril) *noun, plural* **drills;** *verb,* **drilled, drilling.**

drink **1.** To swallow a liquid. I *drink* a glass of milk with every meal. **2.** To soak up. The plants *drank* in the rain. **3.** To drink alcoholic beverages. *Verb.*
   —**1.** A liquid for drinking. Lemonade is my favorite *drink* in the summer. **2.** A portion of liquid to be swallowed. The tennis players stopped to have a *drink* of orange juice. **3.** An alcoholic beverage. *Noun.*
   drink (dringk) *verb,* **drank, drunk, drinking;** *noun, plural* **drinks.**

drip To fall or let fall in drops. Please don't *drip* paint from the brush onto the floor. *Verb.*

at; āpe; fär; câre; end; mē; it; īce; pîerce; hot; ōld; sông, fôrk; oil; out; up; ūse; rüle; pu̇ll; tûrn; chin; sing; shop; thin; this; hw in white; zh in treasure. The symbol ə stands for the unstressed vowel sound in about, taken, pencil, lemon, and circus.

—A falling of liquid in drops. There was a *drip* of water from the faucet. *Noun.*

drip (drip) *verb*, **dripped, dripping**; *noun, plural* **drips.**

drive **1.** To operate and steer a car or other vehicle. My parents will teach me to *drive* when I am sixteen years old. The farmer *drove* a truck to the market. **2.** To go or carry in a car or other vehicle. We plan to *drive* to the city on Saturday. I'll *drive* you to school. **3.** To move with a strong force. The waves *drove* the ship toward the rocks. **4.** To strike or send with a powerful blow. The carpenter *drove* nails into the plank. The baseball player tried to *drive* the ball over the fence. **5.** To force into some act or condition. The noises were *driving* us crazy. **6.** To supply the power for; set and keep going. Electricity *drives* this motor. *Verb.*
—**1.** A trip in a car or other vehicle. The *drive* to the city was unpleasant because there was so much traffic. **2.** A road or driveway. The visitor parked the car in the *drive* and walked to the front door. **3.** A strong hit. In the golf tournament, the winner hit a *drive* more than 250 yards. **4.** A special group effort to do something; campaign. The town started a *drive* to raise money for a new hospital. *Noun.*

drive (drīv) *verb*, **drove, driven, driving**; *noun, plural* **drives.**

drive-in A restaurant, movie theater, or bank that can take care of customers in their cars.

drive-in (drīv'in') *noun, plural* **drive-ins.**

driver A person who drives an automobile, truck, or other vehicle.

driv·er (drī'vər) *noun, plural* **drivers.**

driveway A private road that leads from a street to a house, garage, or other building.

drive·way (drīv'wā') *noun, plural* **driveways.**

drizzle To rain steadily in fine, misty drops. *Verb.*
—A fine, misty rain. *Noun.*

driz·zle (driz'əl) *verb*, **drizzled, drizzling**; *noun, plural* **drizzles.**

dromedary A kind of camel that has one hump. Dromedaries live in Arabia and northern Africa.

drom·e·dar·y (drom'ə der'ē) *noun, plural* **dromedaries.**

drone¹ A male bee.

drone (drōn) *noun, plural* **drones.**

drone² **1.** To make a low, steady, humming sound. The small airplane *droned* as it climbed higher. **2.** To talk in a dull, boring way. The speaker *droned* on and on. *Verb.*

—A low, steady humming sound. The *drone* of the car's engine could be heard down the road. *Noun.*

drone (drōn) *verb*, **droned, droning**; *noun, plural* **drones.**

drool To let saliva drip from the mouth. Babies often *drool* when they are teething.

drool (drül) *verb*, **drooled, drooling.**

droop To hang or sink down; sag. After a few days the flowers in the vase began to *droop*.

droop (drüp) *verb*, **drooped, drooping.**

drop **1.** To fall or cause to fall to a lower position; move or fall down. The wet dish *dropped* from my hand. You tripped and *dropped* the book you were carrying. The temperature *dropped* to below freezing last night. **2.** To go into a less active condition. After a while I must have *dropped* off to sleep. **3.** To stop talking about or pursuing. No one seemed interested, so I decided to *drop* the subject. **4.** To pay a casual, unplanned visit. Our neighbor *dropped* by to say hello. **5.** To let out of a vehicle. The bus *drops* the children in front of the school. **6.** To leave out; omit. I accidentally *dropped* a stitch as I knitted. *Verb.*
—**1.** A very small amount of liquid. A drop is usually shaped like a tiny ball. There was a *drop* of blood on my hand where the cat had scratched me. **2.** The act of dropping or falling. The weather reporter said there would be a *drop* in temperature tonight. **3.** The distance between one thing and another thing that is below it. From the top of the cliff to the beach was a *drop* of 100 feet. *Noun.*

- **to drop in.** To pay a visit that is informal or not planned. We were passing your house and decided to *drop in*.
- **to drop off.** To deliver. Please *drop off* this order at the grocery on your way to school.

dromedary

drop (drop) *verb*, **dropped** or **dropt**, **dropping**; *noun, plural* **drops**.

drought   A long period of time when there is very little rain or no rain at all.
drought (drout) *noun, plural* **droughts**.

drove[1]   Past tense of **drive**. We *drove* downtown in the car. Look up **drive** for more information.
drove (drōv) *verb*.

drove[2]   **1.** A group of animals that move or are driven along together. The cowhands brought a *drove* of cattle to the ranch.   **2.** A large number of people; crowd. People went to the beach in *droves* on the hot summer day.
drove (drōv) *noun, plural* **droves**.

drown   **1.** To die by suffocating in water or another liquid. The swimmer went out too far and almost *drowned*.   **2.** To kill by keeping under water or another liquid and not getting air to breathe. Two people were *drowned* in the flood.   **3.** To cover up the sound of something by a louder sound. We tried to say good-bye, but our words were *drowned* by the roar of the airplane engines.
drown (droun) *verb*, **drowned**, **drowning**.

drowsy   Half asleep; sleepy. I felt *drowsy* after dinner and decided to take a nap.
drow·sy (drou′zē) *adjective*, **drowsier**, **drowsiest**.

drudgery   Hard, unpleasant, and uninteresting labor. Compared to the *drudgery* of scrubbing the floor, dusting the shelves was enjoyable.
drudg·er·y (druj′ə rē) *noun*.

drug   **1.** A chemical substance taken to treat a disease or make a person feel better.   **2.** A harmful substance that can make a person who takes it become addicted. *Noun*.
—To give a drug to. The nurse *drugged* the patient so that falling asleep would be easier. *Verb*.
drug (drug) *noun, plural* **drugs**; *verb*, **drugged**, **drugging**.

druggist   **1.** A person who has a license to make and sell medicine; pharmacist.   **2.** A person who owns or runs a drugstore.
drug·gist (drug′ist) *noun, plural* **druggists**.

drugstore   A store where medicines and drugs are sold. Drugstores often also sell cosmetics, candy, magazines, and other things.
drug·store (drug′stôr′) *noun, plural* **drugstores**.

drum   **1.** A musical instrument that is hollow and covered at the top and at the bottom with material that is stretched tight. A drum is beaten to make sounds.   **2.** A container that is shaped like a drum. The oil was stored in large metal *drums*. *Noun*.
—**1.** To beat or play on a drum.   **2.** To make a sound like a drum. The woodpecker *drummed* on the tree trunk with its bill.   **3.** To force into a person's head by repeating. I finally *drummed* the idea into your head that I don't like to be called by my nickname. *Verb*.
drum (drum) *noun, plural* **drums**; *verb*, **drummed**, **drumming**.

drums

drum major   A person who leads a marching band.

drum majorette   A girl who twirls a baton while marching with a band in a parade.
drum ma·jor·ette (mā′jə ret′).

drummer   A person who plays drums.
drum·mer (drum′ər) *noun, plural* **drummers**.

drumstick   **1.** A stick used to beat a drum.   **2.** The lower part of the leg of a cooked chicken, turkey, or other fowl.
drum·stick (drum′stik′) *noun, plural* **drumsticks**.

drunk   Past participle of **drink**. Have you *drunk* your milk yet? Look up **drink** for more information. *Verb*.

at; āpe; fär; câre; end; mē; it; īce; pîerce; hot; ōld; sông, fôrk; oil; out; up; ūse; rüle; půll; tûrn; chin; sing; shop; thin; this; hw in white; zh in treasure. The symbol ə stands for the unstressed vowel sound in about, taken, pencil, lemon, and circus.

D

—Having had too much to drink of an alcoholic beverage. A person who is *drunk* should not drive a car. *Adjective.*

—A person who has had or often has too much to drink of an alcoholic beverage. *Noun.*

> **drunk** (drungk) *verb; adjective,* **drunker, drunkest;** *noun, plural* **drunks.**

dry **1.** Not wet or damp; with very little or no water or other liquid. Cactuses grow well in a *dry* climate. The farmer had to bring water from the stream because the well was *dry.* **2.** Not in or under water. After the long voyage, the sailors were happy to be back on *dry* land again. **3.** Thirsty. I was so *dry* after playing tennis that I drank three glasses of water. **4.** Not interesting; dull. The long, *dry* speech put some of the listeners to sleep. *Adjective.*

—To make or become dry. If you wash the dishes, I'll *dry* them. Your bathing suit will *dry* fast if you hang it outside in the sun. *Verb.*

> **dry** (drī) *adjective,* **drier, driest;** *verb,* **dried, drying.**

dry cell An electric cell or battery in which the substance that conducts the electrical current is made of a paste so that it will not spill.

dry-clean To clean clothes by using chemicals instead of water. I *dry-cleaned* my wool suit.

> **dry-clean** (drī′klēn′) *verb,* **dry-cleaned, dry-cleaning.**

dryer A machine or device for drying something. I put the wet laundry in the clothes *dryer.* This word is also spelled **drier.**

> **dry·er** (drī′ər) *noun, plural* **dryers.**

dual Made up of or having two parts. The driving instructor and the student used a car that had *dual* controls. ▲ Another word that sounds like this is **duel.**

> **du·al** (dü′əl *or* dū′əl) *adjective.*

duchess The wife or widow of a duke.

> **duch·ess** (duch′is) *noun, plural* **duchesses.**

duck¹ **1.** A water bird that has a broad, flat bill and webbed feet that help it to swim. There are both wild and tame ducks. Tame ducks

duck¹

are often raised for food. **2.** A female duck. The male is often called a drake.

> **duck** (duk) *noun, plural* **ducks.**

duck² **1.** To push someone under water suddenly. I swam behind my friends and playfully *ducked* them. **2.** To lower the head or bend down quickly. The batter *ducked* to keep from being hit by the ball. **3.** To avoid; evade. I *ducked* the embarrassing question by bringing up another subject.

> **duck** (duk) *verb,* **ducked, ducking.**

duckling A young duck. The *ducklings* followed their parents into the pond.

> **duck·ling** (duk′ling) *noun, plural* **ducklings.**

duct A tube, pipe, or channel that carries a liquid or air. Tears are formed in glands behind the eyes and are carried to the eyes by tiny ducts. Ducts are used in some buildings to carry hot or cold air to control the temperature in rooms.

> **duct** (dukt) *noun, plural* **ducts.**

due **1.** Owed or owing. The rent for the apartment is *due* on the first day of each month. If you don't return your library book when it is *due,* you must pay a fine. **2.** Expected or supposed to arrive or be ready. The train is *due* at noon. **3.** Appropriate; proper. I addressed the principal with *due* respect. Use *due* care when crossing the street. *Adjective.*

—**1.** Something that is owed. You should give the others their *due* and congratulate them for beating you in the contest. **2. dues.** A fee that a person pays to a club for being a member. *Noun.*

—Straight; directly. The explorers walked *due* west toward the setting sun. *Adverb.* ▲ Other words that sound like this are **dew** and **do.**

• **due to.** **1.** Caused by. Our delay was *due to* heavy traffic. **2.** Because of. The project was abandoned *due to* lack of support.

> **due** (dü *or* dū) *adjective; noun, plural* **dues;** *adverb.*

duel A formal fight between two people with swords or pistols. Duels were held to settle an argument or to decide a question of honor. *Noun.*

—To fight a duel. *Verb.* ▲ Another word that sounds like this is **dual.**

> **du·el** (dü′əl *or* dū′əl) *noun, plural* **duels;** *verb,* **dueled, dueling.**

duet A piece of music written for two singers or two musical instruments.

> **du·et** (dü et′ *or* dū et′) *noun, plural* **duets.**

230

dug Past tense and past participle of **dig**. We *dug* a hole and planted a tree in it. Look up **dig** for more information.
dug (dug) *verb*.

dugout **1.** A rough shelter that is made by digging a hole in the ground or in the side of a hill. **2.** A long, low shelter in which baseball players sit during a game when they are not playing. Dugouts are built at the side of the field. **3.** A canoe or boat that is made by hollowing out a large log.
dug·out (dug′out′) *noun, plural* **dugouts**.

duke A nobleman who has the highest rank below a prince.
duke (dük *or* dūk) *noun, plural* **dukes**.

dull **1.** Not sharp or pointed; blunt. The knife was so *dull* that I could not cut the steak. **2.** Not interesting; plain or boring. The movie was so *dull* that we left before it was over. **3.** Slow to learn or understand; not intelligent. A person would have to be very *dull* not to understand that joke. **4.** Not bright, clear, or distinct. The barn was painted a *dull* red. I felt a *dull* ache in my legs the day after the long hike. *Adjective.*
—To make or become dull. Using the kitchen scissors for cutting wire *dulled* them. Cheap knives may *dull* quickly. *Verb.*
dull (dul) *adjective,* **duller, dullest;** *verb,* **dulled, dulling.**

dumb **1.** Not able to speak. Although they were born deaf and *dumb*, those children learned to communicate through sign language. We were struck *dumb* by the surprising news. **2.** Stupid. You have to be really *dumb* to believe such a silly lie.
dumb (dum) *adjective,* **dumber, dumbest.**

dumbbell A short bar with a heavy weight at each end. Dumbbells are lifted to develop the muscles of the arms and back.
dumb·bell (dum′bel′) *noun, plural* **dumbbells.**

dummy **1.** A figure that is made to look like a person. The *dummy* in the department store window was dressed in a wedding gown. **2.** Something that is made to look like something else that is real. The actor's gun was a *dummy*.
dum·my (dum′ē) *noun, plural* **dummies.**

dump To drop, unload, or empty. The truck *dumped* the gravel on the sidewalk. I *dumped* my books on the table. *Verb.*
—A place where garbage and trash are dumped. At the end of the day, the garbage trucks unloaded at the city *dump*. *Noun.*
dump (dump) *verb,* **dumped, dumping;** *noun, plural* **dumps.**

dune A mound or ridge of sand that has been piled up by the wind.
dune (dün *or* dūn) *noun, plural* **dunes.**

dune

dungaree **1.** A heavy cotton cloth that is used to make clothing and sails. **2. dungarees.** Pants or work clothes that are made from this cloth.
dun·ga·ree (dung′gə rē′) *noun, plural* **dungarees.**

<table>
<tr><td>

Word History

The word **dungaree** comes from the country of India, where this kind of cloth was first produced.
</td></tr>
</table>

dungeon A dark prison or cell that is built underground. The royal guards captured the traitors and put them in the *dungeon* of the castle.
dun·geon (dun′jən) *noun, plural* **dungeons.**

duplicate Just like something else. My parents gave me a *duplicate* key to our front door. *Adjective.*
—Something that is just like something else; exact copy. My parents liked the snapshot so much that I had a *duplicate* made for them. *Noun.*
—**1.** To make an exact copy of something. The secretary *duplicated* the letter. **2.** To do again; repeat. Our tennis team tried to *duplicate* last year's victory. *Verb.*
du·pli·cate (dü′pli kit *or* dū′pli kit *for adjective and noun;* dü′pli kāt′ *or* dū′pli kāt′ *for verb*) *adjective; noun, plural* **duplicates;** *verb,* **duplicated, duplicating.**

at; āpe; fär; câre; end; mē; it; īce; pîerce; hot; ōld; sông, fôrk; oil; out; up; ūse; rüle; pull; tûrn; chin; sing; shop; thin; <u>th</u>is; hw in white; zh in treasure. The symbol ə stands for the unstressed vowel sound in about, taken, pencil, lemon, and circus.

durable Able to last a long time in spite of much use or wear. I'm still wearing those *durable* shoes with heavy soles.
du·ra·ble (dûr′ə bəl *or* dyûr′ə bəl) *adjective.*

duration The length of time during which something continues. I stayed in bed for the *duration* of my illness.
du·ra·tion (dù rā′shən *or* dyù rā′shən) *noun, plural* **durations.**

during **1.** Throughout the time of. The trees and grass are green *during* the summer. **2.** At some time in the course of. We were awakened by a telephone call *during* the night.
dur·ing (dùr′ing *or* dyûr′ing) *preposition.*

dusk The time of day just before the sun goes down; twilight. The farmer worked in the fields from dawn to *dusk.*
dusk (dusk) *noun.*

dust Tiny pieces of earth, dirt, or other matter. The horse kicked up a cloud of *dust* as it galloped along the dirt road. *Noun.*
—**1.** To remove the dust from something by brushing or wiping. I *dusted* the table and then polished it with wax. **2.** To cover or sprinkle. The baker *dusted* the doughnuts with powdered sugar. The farmer *dusted* the crops with a chemical that killed insects. *Verb.*
dust (dust) *noun; verb,* **dusted, dusting.**

dusty **1.** Covered with dust. The attic was filled with *dusty* old chairs and pictures. **2.** Like dust. Those flowers give off a *dusty* pollen,
dust·y (dus′tē) *adjective,* **dustier, dustiest.**

Dutch Of or relating to the Netherlands, its people, or their language. *Adjective.*
—**1. the Dutch.** The people of the Netherlands. **2.** The language of the Netherlands. *Noun.*
Dutch (duch) *adjective; noun.*

dutiful Doing what one ought to do; obedient. *Dutiful* children help their parents with chores.
du·ti·ful (dü′ti fəl *or* dū′ti fəl) *adjective.*

duty **1.** Something that a person is supposed to do. Locking up the store at night was one of the manager's *duties.* It is the *duty* of every citizen to vote in elections. **2.** A tax paid on goods that are brought into or taken out of a country.
du·ty (dü′tē *or* dū′tē) *noun, plural* **duties.**

dwarf **1.** A person, animal, or plant that is much smaller than the normal size when fully grown. **2.** A little man in fairy tales who has magical powers. *Noun.*

—To make seem small. The skyscraper *dwarfed* all the buildings around it. *Verb.*
dwarf (dwôrf) *noun, plural* **dwarfs** or **dwarves** (dwôrvz); *verb,* **dwarfed, dwarfing.**

dwell To make one's home; live in a place. After living in the country for many years, they decided to *dwell* in the city.
• **to dwell on** or **to dwell upon.** To think, write, or speak about for a long time. Don't *dwell on* unpleasant memories.
dwell (dwel) *verb,* **dwelt** or **dwelled, dwelling.**

dwelling A place where a person lives. We live in a two-family *dwelling.*
dwell·ing (dwel′ing) *noun, plural* **dwellings.**

dwindle To become less or smaller; shrink slowly. The crowd began to *dwindle* after the parade passed by.
dwin·dle (dwin′dəl) *verb,* **dwindled, dwindling.**

dye A substance that is used to give a particular color to cloth, hair, food, or other materials. *Noun.*
—To color or stain something with a dye. When the blue curtains faded, we *dyed* them red. *Verb.* ⚠ Another word that sounds like this is **die.**
dye (dī) *noun, plural* **dyes;** *verb,* **dyed, dyeing.**

dying Present participle of **die.** Our sailboat slowed because the wind was *dying* down. Look up **die** for more information.
dy·ing (dī′ing) *verb.*

dynamic Having or showing a lot of energy; active; forceful. That *dynamic* young person is sure to become a leader.
dy·nam·ic (dī nam′ik) *adjective.*

dynamite A substance that explodes with great force. Dynamite is used to blow up old buildings and blast openings in rocks. *Noun.*
—To blow something up with dynamite. The builders *dynamited* the rocks so that they could put a road through. *Verb.*
dy·na·mite (dī′nə mīt′) *noun; verb,* **dynamited, dynamiting.**

dynamo An electric motor or generator. Dynamos usually produce a direct current.
dy·na·mo (dī′nə mō′) *noun, plural* **dynamos.**

dynasty A series of rulers who belong to the same family. I read about a *dynasty* of emperors in a book on ancient China.
dy·nas·ty (dī′nə stē) *noun, plural* **dynasties.**

dz. An abbreviation for *dozen.*

E e

1. The oldest form of the letter **E** was used about 4,000 years ago by ancient Middle Eastern tribes. They used it to stand for an *h* sound.

2. The Greeks at first used this letter to stand for both the *h* sound and the *e* sound. Later they used it only for the *e* sound.

3. Then, an ancient tribe that settled near Rome borrowed this letter from the Greeks. Later they turned it around.

4. The Romans borrowed this new form of the Greek letter **E**, gradually changing it to look like the capital **E** we use today.

5. Our modern capital letter **E** looks like it did some 2,400 years ago.

e, E   The fifth letter of the alphabet.
  e, E (ē) *noun, plural* **e's, E's.**

E or E.   An abbreviation for *east* or *eastern.*

each   Every one of two or more things or persons thought of as individuals or one at a time. *Each* player gets a turn. *Adjective.*
  —Every individual person or thing in a group. The farmer gave *each* of us a ride on the horse. *Pronoun.*
  —For each one. These apples are a quarter *each. Adverb.*
  • **each other.**   Each of two or more people or things involved in an action or relationship that is shared by the other or others. The twins love *each other.*
  each (ēch) *adjective; pronoun; adverb.*

eager   Wanting very much to do something. A person who is eager is full of interest and enthusiasm. The children were *eager* to go to the circus.
  ea·ger (ē′gər) *adjective.*

eagle   Any of several large, powerful birds that hunt and feed on small animals and fish. Eagles have sharp eyesight, a hooked bill, and strong claws. One kind of eagle, the bald eagle, is the national symbol of the United States.
  ea·gle (ē′gəl) *noun, plural* **eagles.**

eagle

ear¹   **1.** The organ of the body by which people and animals hear.   **2.** In people and mammals, the outer, visible part of this organ. The rabbit turned its long *ears* toward the sound.   **3.** The sense of hearing. Our singing teacher's voice is pleasing to the *ear.*
  • **to play by ear.**   To play a piece of music without following written music. I *played* a song I had heard on the radio *by ear.*
  ear (îr) *noun, plural* **ears.**

233

ear² The part of certain plants on which the grains or seeds grow. The grains of corn and wheat grow on ears.
  ear (îr) *noun, plural* **ears.**

earache A pain inside the ear.
  ear·ache (îr′āk′) *noun, plural* **earaches.**

eardrum The thin tissue that is stretched like the top of a drum inside the ear. When sound waves strike the eardrum, it vibrates and passes the sound waves on to the hearing nerves.
  ear·drum (îr′drum′) *noun, plural* **eardrums.**

earl A nobleman in Great Britain.
  earl (ûrl) *noun, plural* **earls.**

early **1.** In or near the beginning. We started our hike in the *early* morning. My birthday is *early* in March. **2.** Before the usual time. We had an *early* dinner so we could go to the carnival in the evening. The bus left *early* and I missed it.
  ear·ly (ûr′lē) *adjective,* **earlier, earliest;** *adverb.*

earmuffs A pair of fluffy coverings worn on the ears to protect them from the wind and cold.
  ear·muffs (îr′mufs′) *plural noun.*

earn **1.** To get as pay for work done. I *earned* fifty dollars mowing lawns. **2.** To deserve or win because of hard work or good behavior. The student *earned* high marks by studying hard. ▲ Another word that sounds like this is **urn.**
  earn (ûrn) *verb,* **earned, earning.**

earnest Not joking or fooling about something. Earnest people are sincere about what they say and do. The children were being *earnest* when they said they wanted to help.
  ear·nest (ûr′nist) *adjective.*

earnings Money that has been received as pay, profit, or interest. I put all my *earnings* in the bank to save up for a bicycle.
  earn·ings (ûr′ningz) *plural noun.*

earphone A part of an electrical device that turns electric signals into sound. Earphones are placed over or held next to the ear so that a person can listen to a radio, phonograph, or other device.
  ear·phone (îr′fōn′) *noun, plural* **earphones.**

earring A piece of jewelry worn on or through the ear.
  ear·ring (îr′ring′) *noun, plural* **earrings.**

earth **1.** The planet on which we live. It is the fifth largest planet in our solar system and the third planet in order of distance from the sun. ▲ The word "earth" in this sense is sometimes capitalized. **2.** Dry land; the

ground. After weeks at sea, the sailors were glad to feel the *earth* under their feet. **3.** Soil; dirt. We planted the seeds in the *earth.*
  earth (ûrth) *noun.*

earthen **1.** Made out of earth. The log cabin had an *earthen* floor. **2.** Made of clay that has been baked and made hard. In the museum we saw *earthen* bowls made by American Indians.
  earth·en (ûr′thən) *adjective.*

earthly **1.** Having to do with the earth or this world, rather than with heaven. The couple left all their *earthly* goods to their children. **2.** Possible; that can be imagined. These old shoes are of no *earthly* use.
  earth·ly (ûrth′lē) *adjective.*

earthquake A shaking or trembling of the ground. Earthquakes are caused by rock, lava, or hot gases moving deep inside the earth. Some earthquakes are so powerful that they cause the ground to split and buildings to fall down.
  earth·quake (ûrth′kwāk′) *noun, plural* **earthquakes.**

earthworm A common worm made up of many round segments. Earthworms loosen the soil by making tunnels.
  earth·worm (ûrth′wûrm′) *noun, plural* **earthworms.**

ease Freedom from trouble, pain, or hard work. After working for many years, our neighbors sold their business and lived a life of *ease.* That young child rides a bicycle with *ease. Noun.*
—**1.** To make free from trouble, pain, or worry. The news that the flood would not reach our house *eased* our minds. **2.** To make less; lighten. This medicine will *ease* the ache in your back. **3.** To move slowly or carefully. The driver *eased* the car into the small parking space. *Verb.*
  ease (ēz) *noun; verb,* **eased, easing.**

easels

easel A tall stand or rack. Easels are used to hold blackboards, signs, and paintings.
  ea·sel (ē′zel) *noun, plural* **easels.**

easily 1. Without trouble, pain, or hard work. I can touch my toes *easily*. 2. Without any doubt; certainly. That student is *easily* the best player on the team. 3. Very likely; possibly. If the books are too heavy, you could *easily* drop them.
eas·i·ly (ē′zə lē) *adverb*.

east 1. The direction a person faces to watch the sun rise in the morning. East is one of the four main points of the compass. It is directly opposite west. 2. **East.** Any area or place that is in the east. 3. **the East.** The eastern part of the United States, along the Atlantic coast. 4. **the East.** Asia and the islands close to it. *Noun.*
—1. Toward or in the east. Our school is on the *east* side of town. 2. Coming from the east. An *east* wind was blowing. *Adjective.*
—Toward the east. You bicycle *east* to get to the park. *Adverb.*
east (ēst) *noun; adjective; adverb.*

Easter A Christian holiday that celebrates Jesus's rising from the grave. Easter falls on the Sunday after the first full moon between March 21 and April 25.
East·er (ēs′tər) *noun, plural* **Easters.**

Word History

The word **Easter** comes from the name of a pagan goddess, Eastre. Before Christianity came to England, the pagan people there celebrated Eastre's festival in the spring. Later the new Christian festival of Easter was also held in the spring, so the old name was kept.

---

eastern 1. In or toward the east. There is a large river in the *eastern* part of that state. 2. Coming from the east. An *eastern* breeze was blowing. 3. **Eastern.** Of or in the part of the United States that is in the East. 4. **Eastern.** Of or in Asia and the islands close to it.
east·ern (ēs′tərn) *adjective.*

easterner 1. A person living in the east. 2. **Easterner.** A person living in the eastern part of the United States.
east·ern·er (ēs′tər nər) *noun, plural* **easterners.**

Eastern Hemisphere The half of the earth that includes Europe, Asia, Africa, and Australia.

East Germany A country in north-central Europe.

eastward Toward the east. The river flows *eastward* through the state. *Adverb.*
—Toward or in the east. The *eastward* flight of those ducks will bring them to the lake. *Adjective.*
east·ward (ēst′wərd) *adverb; adjective.*

eastwards Another spelling of the adverb **eastward.** The ship sailed *eastwards.*
east·wards (ēst′wərdz) *adverb.*

easy 1. Needing only a little work; not hard to do. The arithmetic problems were *easy*. 2. Without pain, trouble, or worry. They hope to have an *easy* life if their business is successful. 3. Not strict or difficult to please. We have an *easy* science teacher.
eas·y (ē′zē) *adjective,* **easier, easiest.**

eat 1. To chew on and swallow. I like to *eat* popcorn when I'm at the movies. 2. To have a meal. Our family usually *eats* at six o'clock. 3. To wear away or destroy. Rust has *eaten* away the iron railing on the porch.
eat (ēt) *verb,* **ate, eaten, eating.**

eaves The under part of a roof that hangs over the side of a building.
eaves (ēvz) *plural noun.*

eavesdrop To listen to other people talking without letting them know you are listening. I learned about my own surprise party by *eavesdropping* as my friends planned it.
eaves·drop (ēvz′drop′) *verb,* **eavesdropped, eavesdropping.**

Word History

The word **eavesdrop** once meant the area at the side of a house, where rainwater on the roof would *drop* from the *eaves* to the ground. A person who stood in this place to listen in secret to people talking inside the house was said to be *eavesdropping.*

---

ebb The flowing of the ocean away from the shore. The beach was covered with seaweed and shells at the tide's *ebb. Noun.*
—1. To flow out. We sat on the beach and watched the tide *ebb*. 2. To become less or weaker. Hope of finding the lost plane began to *ebb. Verb.*
ebb (eb) *noun, plural* **ebbs;** *verb,* **ebbed, ebbing.**

---

at; āpe; fär; câre; end; mē; it; īce; pîerce; hot; ōld; sông, fôrk; oil; out; up; ūse; rüle; pùll; tûrn; chin; sing; shop; thin; <u>th</u>is; hw in white; zh in treasure. The symbol ə stands for the unstressed vowel sound in about, taken, pencil, lemon, and circus.

ebony   A hard, black wood. It comes from trees that grow in Africa and Asia. The black piano keys are made of ebony.
eb·on·y (eb′ə nē) *noun, plural* **ebonies.**

eccentric   Not ordinary or normal in behavior or appearance; different and odd. Some people think that my cousin who goes swimming in winter is *eccentric.*
ec·cen·tric (ek sen′trik) *adjective.*

echo   The repeating of a sound. Echoes are caused when sound waves bounce off a surface. We shouted "hello" toward the hill and soon heard the *echo* of our voices. *Noun.*
—**1.** To send back the sound of something. The cave *echoed* the bear's growl. The halls of the school *echoed* with voices and footsteps.   **2.** To be heard again. His warning *echoed* in her ears.   **3.** To repeat or imitate closely. The students *echoed* the words of their teachers. *Verb.*
ech·o (ek′ō) *noun, plural* **echoes;** *verb,* **echoed, echoing.**

eclipse   A darkening or hiding of the sun, a planet, or a moon by another heavenly body. In an eclipse of the sun, the moon passes between the sun and the earth. In an eclipse of the moon, the earth moves between the sun and the moon. *Noun.*
—**1.** To cause an eclipse of. The moon *eclipsed* the sun.   **2.** To be better or more important than. Our team *eclipsed* its rivals to win the championship. *Verb.*
e·clipse (i klips′) *noun, plural* **eclipses;** *verb,* **eclipsed, eclipsing.**

ecology   The science that deals with how plants, animals, and other living things live in relation to each other and to their environment.
e·col·o·gy (ē kol′ə jē) *noun.*

economic   Having to do with economics. The president spoke on television about the need for a new *economic* program.
ec·o·nom·ic (ek′ə nom′ik *or* ē′kə nom′ik) *adjective.*

economical   Using only a small amount of something; not wasting anything. A person who is economical is careful about spending money. A car that is economical doesn't use much gasoline and doesn't cost a lot to run.
ec·o·nom·i·cal (ek′ə nom′i kəl *or* ē′kə nom′i kəl) *adjective.*

economics   The science that studies how money, goods, and services are produced, how they are distributed among people, and how they are used. ▲ The word "economics" is used with a singular verb.
ec·o·nom·ics (ek′ə nom′iks *or* ē′kə nom′iks) *noun.*

economize   **1.** To spend less money; reduce expenses. It is hard to *economize* when prices are so high.   **2.** To be careful to use only a small amount of something; not waste. Everyone had to *economize* on water because there was a shortage.
e·con·o·mize (i kon′ə mīz′) *verb,* **economized, economizing.**

economy   **1.** The way a country produces, distributes, and uses its money, goods, natural resources, and services. The *economy* of the United States is different from that of China.   **2.** The careful use of money and other things to reduce waste. My cousins try to practice *economy* in buying groceries.
e·con·o·my (i kon′ə mē) *noun, plural* **economies.**

ecosystem   All the living and nonliving things in a certain area. Soil, water, algae, insects, fish, and frogs are some of the things that make up the ecosystem of a pond.
ec·o·sys·tem (ek′ō sis′təm *or* ē′kō sis′təm) *noun, plural* **ecosystems.**

ecstasy   A feeling of being very happy, thrilled, or delighted. The children were in *ecstasy* when their parents brought the puppy home.
ec·sta·sy (ek′stə sē) *noun, plural* **ecstasies.**

Ecuador   A country in northwestern South America.
Ec·ua·dor (ek′wə dôr′) *noun.*

-ed   A *suffix* that: **1.** Shows that an action or state is in the past. The word "walked" in the sentence "We walked to work yesterday" is the past tense of "walk." The word "walked" in the sentence "I have walked to work every day this week" is the past participle of "walk."   **2.** Means having or having the quality of. The word "horned" means "having horns."

edge   **1.** A line or place where something ends; side. I wrote my name along the *edge* of my notebook. The pencil rolled off the *edge* of the desk. The house is near the *edge* of the woods.   **2.** The side of a tool that cuts. That knife has a sharp *edge.*   **3.** An advantage. A taller player has an *edge* in basketball. *Noun.*
—**1.** To move slowly or carefully, little by little. The cat *edged* toward the ledge.   **2.** To put an edge on; form an edge on. Please *edge* this handkerchief with lace. *Verb.*
edge (ej) *noun, plural* **edges;** *verb,* **edged, edging.**

edible   Fit or safe to eat. Not all kinds of berries are *edible.*
ed·i·ble (ed′ə bəl) *adjective.*

edit To correct and check something written so that it is ready to be printed. Our neighbor *edits* the town newspaper.
ed·it (ed'it) *verb*, **edited, editing.**

edition 1. The form in which a book is printed. That dictionary is now for sale in a paperback *edition*. 2. The total number of copies of a book, newspaper, or magazine printed at one time. The first *edition* of that novel sold quickly. 3. One of the copies of a book, newspaper, or magazine printed at one time. I buy the morning *edition* of the newspaper.
e·di·tion (i dish'ən) *noun, plural* **editions.**

editor 1. A person who edits. The *editor* made changes in the book after talking with its author. 2. A person who writes editorials. The newspaper *editor* wrote an article in favor of raising city taxes.
ed·i·tor (ed'i tər) *noun, plural* **editors.**

editorial 1. An article in a newspaper or magazine written by the editor. An editorial gives an opinion on some subject. The *editorial* praised Congress for passing the new law. 2. A statement on a television or radio program that gives the opinion of the management of the station. *Noun.*
—Of or having to do with editors or their work. My cousin does *editorial* work at a publishing company. *Adjective.*
ed·i·to·ri·al (ed'i tôr'ē əl) *noun, plural* **editorials;** *adjective.*

educate 1. To teach or train. Teachers *educate* children. 2. To send to school. The cost of *educating* students at college is very high.
ed·u·cate (ej'ə kāt') *verb*, **educated, educating.**

education 1. The act or process of gaining knowledge. A person's *education* at college usually takes four years. 2. The knowledge or skill a person gains by being taught or trained. I wish I had received more *education* in science.
ed·u·ca·tion (ej'ə kā'shən) *noun, plural* **educations.**

educational 1. Of or having to do with education. This state's *educational* system is one of the largest in the country. 2. Giving knowledge or skill. Our class saw an *educational* film about how steel is made.
ed·u·ca·tion·al (ej'ə kā'shə nəl) *adjective.*

eel A long, thin fish that looks like a snake.
eel (ēl) *noun, plural* **eels** or **eel.**

eerie Strange in a scary way; making people frightened or nervous. It was *eerie* that a black cat crossed our yard on Halloween.
ee·rie (îr'ē) *adjective*, **eerier, eeriest.**

effect 1. Something that happens as a result of something else. One *effect* of prices going up was that people began to buy less. 2. The power to change something or to make something happen; influence. Punishment has no *effect* on that naughty child. 3. The condition of being in force or in operation. The new traffic law will be in *effect* next month. 4. *effects.* Belongings; possessions. We lost only a few personal *effects* when the canoe sank. *Noun.*
—To make happen; bring about; cause. The medicine *effected* a cure of my sore throat. *Verb.* ▲ Another word that sounds very similar to this is **affect.**
ef·fect (i fekt') *noun, plural* **effects;** *verb*, **effected, effecting.**

effective 1. Able to change something or to make something happen. The two students used *effective* arguments and got the others to agree with them. The medicine was not *effective* in reducing my fever. 2. In operation. The new rules on riding bicycles in the park become *effective* next week.
ef·fec·tive (i fek'tiv) *adjective.*

efficient Able to get the results wanted with a minimum of time or effort. With our *efficient* new washing machine, the laundry gets done much faster.
ef·fi·cient (i fish'ənt) *adjective.*

effort 1. Hard work. Climbing the steep hill took much *effort*. 2. A hard try. Make an *effort* to get there on time.
ef·fort (ef'ərt) *noun, plural* **efforts.**

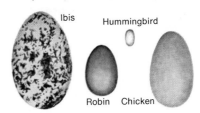

kinds of **eggs**

egg¹ 1. A round or oval body with a shell or other covering produced by certain female animals. Young birds, reptiles, fish, and snakes hatch from eggs. 2. The inside of an egg, especially a chicken egg, that is used for food. 3. A cell produced in the bodies of fe-

at; āpe; fär; câre; end; mē; it; ice; pîerce; hot; ōld; sông, fôrk; oil; out; up; ūse; rūle; pūll; tûrn; chin; sing; shop; thin; **this**; hw in white; zh in treasure. The symbol ə stands for the unstressed vowel sound in about, taken, pencil, lemon, and circus.

male animals that can develop into a new individual after joining with a special cell from a male animal. Human beings, cats, dogs, and many other animals grow from these cells.
> **egg** (eg) *noun, plural* **eggs.**

egg² To urge. The two children began to fight after they were *egged* on by the others in the playground.
> **egg** (eg) *verb,* **egged, egging.**

eggplant An oval-shaped vegetable that usually has a shiny, dark purple skin. Eggplants grow on a plant that is also called an eggplant.
> **egg·plant** (eg′plant′) *noun, plural* **eggplants.**

Egypt A country in the Middle East. Ancient Egypt was the center of one of the world's earliest civilizations.
> **E·gypt** (ē′jipt) *noun.*

eggplant

Egyptian **1.** A person who was born in or is a citizen of Egypt. **2.** A person who lived in ancient Egypt. **3.** The language of the people of Egypt in ancient times. *Noun.*
—Of or having to do with Egypt or its people. *Adjective.*
> **E·gyp·tian** (i jip′shən) *noun, plural* **Egyptians;** *adjective.*

eight One more than seven; 8. ▲ Another word that sounds like this is **ate.**
> **eight** (āt) *noun, plural* **eights;** *adjective.*

eighteen Eight more than ten; 18.
> **eight·een** (ā′tēn′) *noun, plural* **eighteens;** *adjective.*

eighteenth Next after the seventeenth. *Adjective, noun.*
—One of eighteen equal parts; ⅟₁₈. *Noun.*
> **eight·eenth** (ā′tēnth′) *adjective; noun, plural* **eighteenths.**

eighth Next after the seventh. *Adjective, noun.*
—One of eight equal parts; ⅛. *Noun.*
> **eighth** (āth) *adjective; noun, plural* **eighths.**

eightieth Next after the seventy-ninth. *Adjective, noun.*
—One of eighty equal parts; ⅟₈₀. *Noun.*
> **eight·i·eth** (ā′tē ith) *adjective; noun, plural* **eightieths.**

eighty Eight times ten; 80.
> **eight·y** (ā′tē) *noun, plural* **eighties;** *adjective.*

either **1.** One or the other. I would be happy to see *either* movie. **2.** One and the other; each of two. There were tall trees on *either* side of the street. *Adjective.*
—One or the other. Can *either* of you two children help me? *Pronoun.*
—One or the other. The word *either* is used before the first of two or more choices or possibilities that are connected by the word *or. Either* be quiet or leave. They will come *either* tonight, tomorrow, or the day after. *Conjunction.*
—Also; likewise. You can't go to the game, and I can't go *either. Adverb.*
> **ei·ther** (ē′thər *or* ī′thər) *adjective; pronoun; conjunction; adverb.*

eject To throw out; force out. The manager *ejected* the noisy couple from the theater.
> **e·ject** (i jekt′) *verb,* **ejected, ejecting.**

elaborate Worked out or made with great care and in great detail. *Elaborate* plans were made for the wedding. *Adjective.*
—To work out with great care; add details to. The reporters asked the astronauts to *elaborate* on their answer. *Verb.*
> **e·lab·o·rate** (i lab′ər it *for adjective;* i lab′ə rāt′ *for verb) adjective; verb,* **elaborated, elaborating.**

elapse To go by; pass. Three years *elapsed* before we saw each other again.
> **e·lapse** (i laps′) *verb,* **elapsed, elapsing.**

elastic Able to go back to its own shape soon after being stretched, squeezed, or pressed together. Rubber bands, balloons, and metal springs are elastic. *Adjective.*
—A tape or fabric that can stretch. This skirt has *elastic* around the waist. *Noun.*
> **e·las·tic** (i las′tik) *adjective; noun, plural* **elastics.**

elbow **1.** The joint between the upper arm and the lower arm. The elbow allows the arm to bend. **2.** Something having the same shape as a bent elbow. In plumbing, a pipe that curves at a sharp angle is called an elbow. *Noun.*
—To push with the elbows; shove. The bully tried to *elbow* me off the line. *Verb.*
> **el·bow** (el′bō) *noun, plural* **elbows;** *verb,* **elbowed, elbowing.**

elder Born earlier; older. My *elder* cousins are in high school. *Adjective.*
—A person who is older. I have great respect for my *elders. Noun.*
> **eld·er** (el′dər) *adjective; noun, plural* **elders.**

elderly Rather old. Our *elderly* neighbor has no plans to retire.
> **eld·er·ly** (el′dər lē) *adjective.*

E

eldest   Born first; oldest. I am the *eldest* of three children.
eld·est (el′dist) *adjective.*

elect   1. To choose by voting. The people of the town *elected* a new mayor. 2. To make a choice; choose; decide. Will you *elect* to study history in college?
e·lect (i lekt′) *verb,* **elected, electing.**

election   The act of electing. There is an *election* for the president every four years in the United States.
e·lec·tion (i lek′shən) *noun, plural* **elections.**

electric   1. Having to do with electricity; run or produced by electricity. My *electric* clock keeps good time. I got an *electric* shock when I plugged in the lamp. 2. Exciting. The actor's *electric* performance thrilled the audience.
e·lec·tric (i lek′trik) *adjective.*

The train is decorated with **electric** lights.

electrical   Having to do with electricity; electric. Irons and other *electrical* appliances are sold at that store.
e·lec·tri·cal (i lek′tri kəl) *adjective.*

electric eel   A long fish that looks like an eel. It is able to give off electric shocks to protect itself and to catch small fish for food.

electrician   A person who works with electricity or installs or repairs things that are electric, such as wires, motors, and appliances.
e·lec·tri·cian (i lek trish′ən) *noun, plural* **electricians.**

electricity   1. One of the basic forms of energy. Electricity can run motors and produce light and heat. It makes radios, televisions, and telephones work. Electricity can be produced by burning coal, water power, or wind generators. 2. Electric current. *Electricity* is running through those wires.
e·lec·tric·i·ty (i lek tris′i tē) *noun.*

electrocute   To kill by means of a very strong electric shock.
e·lec·tro·cute (i lek′trə kūt′) *verb,* **electrocuted, electrocuting.**

electromagnet   A piece of iron with wire wound around it. It becomes a magnet when an electric current is passed through the wire.
e·lec·tro·mag·net (i lek′trō mag′nit) *noun, plural* **electromagnets.**

electron   A very tiny particle that moves around the nucleus of an atom and has a negative electrical charge.
e·lec·tron (i lek′tron) *noun, plural* **electrons.**

electronic   Of or relating to electrons or electronics.
e·lec·tron·ic (i lek tron′ik) *adjective.*

electronics   The science that deals with electrons and how they act and move. The discoveries of electronics have led to the development of radio, television, and computers. ▲ The word "electronics" is used with a singular verb.
e·lec·tron·ics (i lek tron′iks) *noun.*

elegant   Rich and fine in quality. The museum has a display of *elegant* costumes.
el·e·gant (el′i gənt) *adjective.*

element   1. One of the materials from which all other materials are made. Each element has its own kind of atom. There are more than one hundred known elements. Iron, oxygen, gold, and carbon are elements. 2. One of the parts that something is made of. Words are the *elements* used to build sentences. 3. The natural or most comfortable place to be. The ocean is the whale's *element.* 4. the elements. Rain, wind, snow, and other forces of nature. The mountain climbers struggled against *the elements.*
el·e·ment (el′ə mənt) *noun, plural* **elements.**

elementary   Dealing with the simple parts or beginnings of something. We learned about addition and subtraction when we studied *elementary* arithmetic.
el·e·men·ta·ry (el′ə men′tə rē *or* el′ə men′trē) *adjective.*

elementary school   A school for children from the ages of about six to twelve or fourteen. Elementary schools usually cover the

at; āpe; fär; câre; end; mē; it; īce; pîerce; hot; ōld; sông, fôrk; oil; out; up; ūse; rüle; pùll; tûrn; chin; sing; shop; thin; <u>th</u>is; hw in white; zh in treasure. The symbol ə stands for the unstressed vowel sound in about, taken, pencil, lemon, and circus.

first six or eight grades. An elementary school is also called a **grade school** or a **grammar school**.

elephant

elephant   A huge gray animal with a long trunk, large, floppy ears, and two ivory tusks. Elephants come from parts of Asia and Africa. They are the largest and strongest land animals.
el·e·phant (el′ə fənt) *noun, plural* **elephants** or **elephant**.

elevate   To raise to a higher level; lift up. The workers in the garage *elevated* the car so that they could repair the muffler.
el·e·vate (el′ə vāt′) *verb,* **elevated, elevating.**

elevation   **1.** The act of a raising or lifting up. The cranes beside those docks are used for the *elevation* of boats from the water. **2.** A raised thing or place. The cabin is on a slight *elevation* that looks over the lake. **3.** The height above the earth's surface or above sea level. The plane flew at an *elevation* of 30,000 feet.
el·e·va·tion (el′ə vā′shən) *noun, plural* **elevations.**

elevator   **1.** A small room or cage that can be raised or lowered. It is used for carrying people and things from one floor to another in a building or from one level to another in mines and other places.   **2.** A building for storing grain.
el·e·va·tor (el′ə vā′tər) *noun, plural* **elevators.**

eleven   One more than ten; 11.
e·lev·en (i lev′ən) *noun, plural* **elevens;** *adjective.*

eleventh   Next after the tenth. *Adjective, noun.*
—One of eleven equal parts; ¹⁄₁₁. *Noun.*
e·lev·enth (i lev′ənth) *adjective; noun, plural* **elevenths.**

elf   A kind of fairy who has magical powers. In legends and folk tales, elves are small and are often full of mischief.
elf (elf) *noun, plural* **elves.**

eligible   Having the qualities needed for something; fit to be chosen. A person must be thirty-five years old to be *eligible* to run for president of the United States.
el·i·gi·ble (el′i jə bəl) *adjective.*

eliminate   To get rid of; remove or leave out. The city is trying to *eliminate* pollution. When the family was deciding which house to buy, they *eliminated* all those that didn't have a backyard.
e·lim·i·nate (i lim′ə nāt′) *verb,* **eliminated, eliminating.**

elk   **1.** A large deer of North America. The male elk has very large antlers.   **2.** A moose.
elk (elk) *noun, plural* **elk** or **elks.**

elk

ellipse   A figure that looks like a narrow or flattened circle.
el·lipse (i lips′) *noun, plural* **ellipses.**

elm   A tall tree. Elms were once planted to shade streets and lawns. The hard, heavy wood of this tree is used to make boxes and crates.
elm (elm) *noun, plural* **elms.**

eloquent   Having or showing an ability to use words well. The mayor is an *eloquent* speaker. The lawyer made an *eloquent* plea to the jury to find the accused person innocent of the crime.
el·o·quent (el′ə kwənt) *adjective.*

El Salvador   A country in Central America.
El Sal·va·dor (el sal′və dôr).

else   **1.** Other; different. I mistook that student for someone *else.* Would you like some-

thing *else* instead? **2.** More; further; additional. If anyone *else* comes, we won't have enough chairs. *Adjective.*
—**1.** At a different time or in a different place or manner; instead. What *else* could you have done? **2.** If not; otherwise. We'd better hurry, or *else* we'll miss the train. *Adverb.*
else (els) *adjective; adverb.*

elsewhere In, at, or to another place; somewhere else. We wanted to go to the park, but we'll have to go *elsewhere* because it's raining.
else·where (els′hwâr′ *or* els′wâr′) *adverb.*

elude To avoid or escape by being clever or quick. The bandit *eluded* the police by hiding in an abandoned building.
e·lude (i lüd′) *verb,* **eluded, eluding.**

elves Plural of **elf.** I read a story about some *elves* who turned straw into golden thread. Look up **elf** for more information.
elves (elvz) *plural noun.*

emancipate To set free from slavery or control. President Abraham Lincoln's proclamation *emancipated* the slaves in some states in 1863.
e·man·ci·pate (i man′sə pāt′) *verb,* **emancipated, emancipating.**

embankment A mound of earth, stones, or bricks used to hold up a road or to hold back water.
em·bank·ment (em bangk′mənt) *noun,* *plural* **embankments.**

embankment

embargo **1.** An order by a government that forbids certain ships from entering or leaving its ports. **2.** A restriction that a government puts on the buying and selling of certain goods, especially importing or exporting those goods.
em·bar·go (em bär′gō) *noun, plural* **embargoes.**

embark **1.** To go on board a ship or airplane for a trip. The passengers *embarked* at New York. **2.** To start out or set out. The explorers *embarked* on a dangerous journey.
em·bark (em bärk′) *verb,* **embarked, embarking.**

embarrass To make someone feel shy, uncomfortable, or ashamed. My foolish mistake *embarrassed* me.
em·bar·rass (em bar′əs) *verb,* **embarrassed, embarrassing.**

embarrassment **1.** A feeling of shyness or being ashamed. I turned red with *embarrassment* when the teacher called my name. **2.** Something that embarrasses. My falling asleep during the recital was an *embarrassment.*
em·bar·rass·ment (em bar′əs mənt) *noun, plural* **embarrassments.**

embassy The official home and office in a foreign country of an ambassador and his or her staff.
em·bas·sy (em′bə sē) *noun, plural* **embassies.**

embed To place or set firmly in something. The flagpole was *embedded* in concrete.
em·bed (em bed′) *verb,* **embedded, embedding.**

ember A piece of wood or coal that is still glowing in the ashes of a fire. The campers put water on the *embers* of their fire before they left.
em·ber (em′bər) *noun, plural* **embers.**

embezzle To steal money or goods that one was supposed to take care of. The teller *embezzled* thousands of dollars from the bank.
em·bez·zle (em bez′əl) *verb,* **embezzled, embezzling.**

emblem A sign or figure that stands for something. The shamrock is the *emblem* of Ireland.
em·blem (em′bləm) *noun, plural* **emblems.**

emboss To decorate or cover a surface with a design that is raised. My parents' stationery is *embossed* with their initials.
em·boss (em bôs′) *verb,* **embossed, embossing.**

at; āpe; fär; câre; end; mē; it; īce; pîerce; hot; ōld; sông, fôrk; oil; out; up; ūse; rüle; pùll; tûrn; chin; sing; shop; thin; this; hw in white; zh in treasure. The symbol ə stands for the unstressed vowel sound in about, taken, pencil, lemon, and circus.

embrace   1. To take or hold in the arms as a sign of love or friendship; hug. The children *embraced* their parents as soon as they got off the plane.   2. To take up willingly. We *embraced* the opportunity to visit our cousins in France.   3. To include; contain. Biology *embraces* the study of all things that have life. *Verb.*
—A holding in the arms; hug. The puppy wiggled out of the child's *embrace*. *Noun.*
　em·brace (em brās′) *verb,* **embraced, embracing;** *noun, plural* **embraces.**

embroider   1. To decorate with designs sewn on with thread. I *embroidered* the napkins with flowers.   2. To make a story more interesting by adding parts that have been made up. They *embroidered* their stories about their first day at camp to make us laugh.
　em·broi·der (em broi′dər) *verb,* **embroidered, embroidering.**

embroidering

embroidery   Designs that have been sewn on cloth with thread. The *embroidery* on the wedding dress was beautiful.
　em·broi·der·y (em broi′də rē) *noun, plural* **embroideries.**

embryo   An animal or plant that is just starting to grow, before its birth, hatching, or sprouting. A baby inside its mother, a chick inside an egg, and a plant inside a seed are embryos.
　em·bry·o (em′brē ō′) *noun, plural* **embryos.**

emerald   1. A bright green, clear stone that is very valuable. Emeralds are often used in rings, pins, and other jewelry.   2. A bright green color. *Noun.*
—Having a bright green color. *Adjective.*
　em·er·ald (em′ər əld) *noun, plural* **emeralds;** *adjective.*

emerge   1. To come into view. The sun *emerged* from behind a cloud.   2. To come

out; become known. New facts about the case *emerged* during the trial.
　e·merge (i mûrj′) *verb,* **emerged, emerging.**

emergency   Something serious that comes without any warning and calls for fast action. In case of an *emergency,* the doctor can be reached at home. *Noun.*
—Having to do with an emergency; used during an emergency. There is an *emergency* exit at the back of the theater. *Adjective.*
　e·mer·gen·cy (i mûr′jən sē) *noun, plural* **emergencies;** *adjective.*

emery   A hard black or brown mineral in the form of a powder. Emery is used for grinding and polishing metals or stones.
　em·er·y (em′ə rē) *noun.*

emigrant   A person who leaves his or her own country to live in another. My parents were *emigrants* from China.
　em·i·grant (em′i grənt) *noun, plural* **emigrants.**

emigrate   To leave one's own place or country to live in another. Our neighbors plan to *emigrate* from the United States to Australia.
　em·i·grate (em′i grāt′) *verb,* **emigrated, emigrating.**

Language Note

The verbs **emigrate** and **immigrate** have nearly opposite meanings. **Emigrate** means to leave a country. My grandparents *emigrated* from Italy in 1930. **Immigrate** means to enter a new country to live. Many Irish *immigrated* to the United States in the 1800s.

---

eminent   Above others in rank, power, or achievement; outstanding. George Washington was *eminent* both as a soldier and as president. Our neighbor is an *eminent* lawyer in the town.
　em·i·nent (em′ə nənt) *adjective.*

emit   To send out; give off. The sun *emits* heat and light. You *emitted* a shriek when I surprised you.
　e·mit (i mit′) *verb,* **emitted, emitting.**

emotion   A strong feeling. Love, hate, happiness, sorrow, and fear are emotions.
　e·mo·tion (i mō′shən) *noun, plural* **emotions.**

emotional   1. Having to do with emotion or the feelings a person has. I get *emotional* satisfaction from knowing I've done a job well.   2. Easily moved by emotion. An emo-

E

tional person has strong feelings. **3.** Arousing or attempting to arouse emotion. The general made an *emotional* speech at the ceremony honoring the soldiers who had died in battle.
e·mo·tion·al (i mō′shə nəl) *adjective.*

emperor The ruler of an empire.
em·per·or (em′pər ər) *noun, plural* **emperors.**

emphasis **1.** Special attention or importance given to something. I've been taught to place much *emphasis* on telling the truth. There is an *emphasis* on reading and arithmetic in elementary school. **2.** Special force used when saying a particular word or syllable; stress. The *emphasis* is on the first syllable in the word "empty" and on the second syllable in the word "employ."
em·pha·sis (em′fə sis) *noun, plural* **emphases** (em′fə sēz′).

emphasize To give emphasis to; stress. The mayor's speech *emphasized* the need for a new hospital.
em·pha·size (em′fə sīz′) *verb,* **emphasized, emphasizing.**

empire **1.** A group of countries, lands, or peoples under one government or ruler. The *empire* of ancient Rome was powerful. **2.** A country ruled by an emperor or empress.
em·pire (em′pīr) *noun, plural* **empires.**

employ **1.** To pay someone to do work; hire. The store *employed* extra workers during its big sale. **2.** To use. I *employ* a hoe when weeding the garden. *Verb.*
—Service for pay; employment. That engineer is in the *employ* of a large railroad. *Noun.*
em·ploy (em ploi′) *verb,* **employed, employing;** *noun.*

employee A person who works for some person or business for pay. The store gives its *employees* a raise once a year.
em·ploy·ee (em ploi′ē *or* em′ploi ē′) *noun, plural* **employees.**

employer A person or business that pays a person or group of people to work. My cousin's *employer* has an office in Japan.
em·ploy·er (em ploi′ər) *noun, plural* **employers.**

employment **1.** The work that a person does; job. After the factory closed, it was hard for many of the workers to find new *employment.* **2.** The act of employing or the condition of being employed. *Employment* of more workers made it possible for the automobile company to manufacture cars faster.
em·ploy·ment (em ploi′mənt) *noun, plural* **employments.**

empress **1.** A woman who is the ruler of an empire. **2.** The wife or widow of an emperor.
em·press (em′pris) *noun, plural* **empresses.**

empty **1.** Having nothing in it; without what is usually inside. The bottom drawer of the dresser is *empty,* and you can use it for your shirts. The house was *empty* in August because the family was away on vacation. **2.** Lacking value, force, or meanings. The people didn't want to vote for a candidate who made *empty* promises. *Adjective.*
—**1.** To remove all that is in something. I *emptied* my pockets. Please *empty* the wastebasket. **2.** To become empty. The theater *emptied* when the movie was over. **3.** To pour or flow out. That river *empties* into the sea. *Verb.*
emp·ty (emp′tē) *adjective,* **emptier, emptiest;** *verb,* **emptied, emptying.**

empty set A set that has no members. The set of all even numbers between 8 and 10 is an example of an empty set.

emu A bird of Australia that looks like an ostrich. An emu can be as large as a grown person. Emus cannot fly, but they can run very fast.
e·mu (ē′mū) *noun, plural* **emus.**

emu

enable To make able. The school raised enough money to *enable* the library to buy many new books.
en·a·ble (e nā′bəl) *verb,* **enabled, enabling.**

at; āpe; fär; câre; end; mē; it; īce; pîerce; hot; ōld; sông, fôrk; oil; out; up; ūse; rüle; pull; tûrn; chin; sing; shop; thin; <u>th</u>is; hw in white; zh in treasure. The symbol ə stands for the unstressed vowel sound in about, taken, pencil, lemon, and circus.

enact **1.** To make into law. Congress *enacted* a new bill on education this year. **2.** To act out on stage; play. I am going to *enact* the part of an astronaut in this year's class play.
en·act (e nakt′) *verb*, **enacted, enacting.**

enamel **1.** A smooth, hard coating like glass. Enamel is put on metal, pottery, or other material to protect or decorate it. **2.** A paint that dries to form a hard, glossy surface. They painted the kitchen with white *enamel.* **3.** The hard, white outer layer of the teeth. Decay can eat through a tooth's *enamel. Noun.*
—To cover with enamel. The jeweler *enameled* the bracelet with a pattern of tulips. *Verb.*
e·nam·el (i nam′əl) *noun, plural* **enamels;** *verb,* **enameled, enameling.**

-ence A *suffix* that means: **1.** The state or quality of being. *Independence* means the state or quality of being independent. **2.** The act of. *Occurrence* means the act of occurring.

enchant **1.** To put a magical spell on. The magician had *enchanted* the kingdom and turned its people into statues. **2.** To delight; charm. The children were *enchanted* by the beautiful costumes the dancers wore.
en·chant (en chant′) *verb,* **enchanted, enchanting.**

enchantment The act of enchanting or the condition of being enchanted. The *enchantment* of the kingdom by the magical spell was to last one hundred years.
en·chant·ment (en chant′mənt) *noun, plural* **enchantments.**

encircle **1.** To form a circle around; surround. The soldiers *encircled* the enemy's camp. **2.** To move in a circle around. Many satellites *encircle* the earth.
en·cir·cle (en sûr′kəl) *verb,* **encircled, encircling.**

enclose **1.** To surround on all sides. Our back yard is *enclosed* by a picket fence. **2.** To include with a letter or parcel. They *enclosed* pictures of the children with their letter.
en·close (en klōz′) *verb,* **enclosed, enclosing.**

enclosure **1.** The act of enclosing or the condition of being enclosed. The family finished the *enclosure* of the pool by building a fence. **2.** Something that is enclosed. The check was sent as an *enclosure* with the letter. The dog stays in an *enclosure* in the yard.
en·clo·sure (en klō′zhər) *noun, plural* **enclosures.**

encompass **1.** To form a circle around; surround. A stone wall *encompasses* the castle. **2.** To contain or include. This article *encompasses* the early years of the senator's life.
en·com·pass (en kum′pəs) *verb,* **encompassed, encompassing.**

encore A word meaning "again" that is said by members of an audience to request that a performer continue performing. *"Encore! Encore!"* cried the audience when the musicians had finished their delightful performance. *Interjection.*
—**1.** A demand made by an audience to a performer to go on performing. People usually clap or cheer for a long time to call for an encore. The band received four *encores* at the end of their performance. **2.** Something that is performed in answer to such a demand. As an *encore,* the chorus sang a well-known song. *Noun.*
en·core (äng′kôr) *interjection; noun, plural* **encores.**

encounter **1.** To meet, usually unexpectedly. I *encountered* an old friend on my way to the library. **2.** To face; confront. We *encountered* much opposition to our plan. **3.** To meet in battle. The soldiers *encountered* the enemy and defeated them. *Verb.*
—A usually unexpected meeting. Your *encounter* with the movie star is the talk of the neighborhood. *Noun.*
en·coun·ter (en koun′tər) *verb,* **encountered, encountering;** *noun, plural* **encounters.**

The sheep are going into an **enclosure.**

encourage **1.** To give courage, hope, or confidence to; urge on. The coach *encouraged* the students to try out for the swimming team. **2.** To give help to or help bring about; help or foster. The low price of homes *encouraged* many people to settle in that town.
en·cour·age (en kûr′ij) *verb,* **encouraged, encouraging.**

encouragement **1.** The act of encouraging or the condition of being encouraged. Your *encouragement* of our project helped us to complete it. **2.** Something that encourages. My father's praise of my marks at school has been an *encouragement* to me.
en·cour·age·ment (en kûr′ij mənt) *noun,* *plural* **encouragements.**

encyclopedia A book or set of books giving a great deal of information about many things. Encyclopedias often contain a large number of articles about various subjects.
en·cy·clo·pe·di·a (en sī′klə pē′dē ə) *noun,* *plural* **encyclopedias.**

Word History

The word **encyclopedia** goes back to a Greek phrase meaning "general education." The ancient idea of a total or complete education included training in a variety of fields. The modern encyclopedia also tries to include all areas of knowledge in its coverage.

---

end **1.** The last part. The *end* of the movie was happy. **2.** The part where something starts or stops. They each held an *end* of the rope. We sat at one *end* of the table. Make a left turn at the *end* of the road. My vacation is at an *end*. **3.** Purpose; goal; outcome. The *end* of all their studying was to get into college. *Noun.*
—To bring or come to an end. The heavy rain *ended* their picnic. The ball game *ended* at ten o'clock. *Verb.*
end (end) *noun,* *plural* **ends;** *verb,* **ended, ending.**

endanger **1.** To put in a situation that is dangerous. The flood *endangered* the lives of hundreds of people. **2.** To threaten with becoming extinct. Pollution is *endangering* many different species of animals.
en·dan·ger (en dān′jər) *verb,* **endangered, endangering.**

endangered species A species of wild animals or plants that is close to becoming extinct.
en·dan·gered (en dān′jərd).

endeavor To make an effort; try. The judge always *endeavored* to be fair and just. *Verb.*
—A serious attempt to do or achieve something. My *endeavors* to do well on the test were rewarded with a high mark. *Noun.*
en·deav·or (en dev′ər) *verb,* **endeavored, endeavoring;** *noun,* *plural* **endeavors.**

ending The last or final part. I like stories that have happy *endings*.
end·ing (en′ding) *noun,* *plural* **endings.**

endless **1.** Having no limit or end; going on forever. The drive across the desert seemed *endless*. Our teacher has *endless* patience and never gets angry. **2.** Without ends. A circle is *endless*.
end·less (end′lis) *adjective.*

endorse **1.** To sign one's name on the back of a check or similar paper. You have to *endorse* the check or the bank won't cash it. **2.** To give support or approval to. The senator *endorsed* the president's statement.
en·dorse (en dôrs′) *verb,* **endorsed, endorsing.**

endow **1.** To give money or property to. Many wealthy people have *endowed* that museum with valuable paintings. **2.** To provide with an ability, a talent, or some other good quality at birth. The singer was *endowed* with a beautiful voice.
en·dow (en dou′) *verb,* **endowed, endowing.**

endurance The power to put up with hardships or difficulties. The pioneers who crossed the wilderness in covered wagons had much *endurance*.
en·dur·ance (en dùr′əns *or* en dyùr′əns) *noun.*

endure **1.** To undergo and survive; put up with. The first explorers of the North Pole had to *endure* many hardships. **2.** To continue; last. That great artist's name will *endure* forever.
en·dure (en dùr′ *or* en dyùr′) *verb,* **endured, enduring.**

enemy **1.** A person or group of people who hates or wishes to harm another. Many people were *enemies* of the cruel dictator. **2.** A country that is at war with another country. France and Germany were *enemies* in World

---

at; āpe; fär; câre; end; mē; it; īce; pîerce; hot; ōld; sông, fôrk; oil; out; up; ūse; rüle; pùll; tûrn; chin; sing; shop; thin; this; hw in white; zh in treasure. The symbol ə stands for the unstressed vowel sound in about, taken, pencil, lemon, and circus.

War II.   **3.** Something that is dangerous or harmful. A lack of rain can be a farmer's *enemy*.

> **en·e·my** (en′ə mē) *noun, plural* **enemies.**

energetic   Full of energy. An energetic person is eager and ready to work or do things. After eating lunch the hikers felt *energetic* again.

> **en·er·get·ic** (en′ər jet′ik) *adjective.*

energy   **1.** The strength or eagerness to work or do things. My parents have so much *energy* that they get up early to do exercises. **2.** The capacity for doing work. Some forms of energy are light, heat, and electricity. A windmill uses the *energy* of the wind.

> **en·er·gy** (en′ər jē) *noun, plural* **energies.**

enforce   To make certain that people obey; put or keep in force. The police in that town *enforce* the parking laws strictly.

> **en·force** (en fôrs′) *verb,* **enforced, enforcing.**

Eng.   An abbreviation for *England* or *English.*

engage   **1.** To hire. The automobile factory *engaged* more workers.   **2.** To take the time or attention of. A stranger *engaged* them in a conversation at the bus stop. Practicing the piano *engages* much of my time.   **3.** To involve oneself; take part. The committee *engaged* in a serious discussion of the problem. **4.** To promise; pledge. In 1978 my parents were *engaged* to be married.   **5.** To meet and fight in a battle; fight. After marching all night, the soldiers *engaged* the enemy outside the town.

> **en·gage** (en gāj′) *verb,* **engaged, engaging.**

engagement   **1.** The act or process of engaging or the condition of being engaged. The *engagement* of workers at the printing plant was the job of the recruiter.   **2.** A promise to marry. That young couple's *engagement* was announced last week by their parents. **3.** A meeting with someone at a certain time; appointment. My parents have a dinner *engagement* this evening.

> **en·gage·ment** (en gāj′mənt) *noun, plural* **engagements.**

engine   **1.** A machine that uses energy to run other machines. Engines can get their energy from the burning of oil or gasoline or from steam. The engine of a car provides the power that moves the car.   **2.** A machine that pulls a railroad train; locomotive.

> **en·gine** (en′jin) *noun, plural* **engines.**

engineer   **1.** A person who is trained in engineering. An engineer may plan and design bridges, roads, or airplanes.   **2.** A person

who drives a locomotive. The *engineer* blew the train's whistle as it neared the station.

> **en·gi·neer** (en′jə nîr′) *noun, plural* **engineers.**

engineering   The work that uses scientific knowledge for practical things, such as building bridges and dams, drilling for oil, producing plastics, or designing machines.

> **en·gi·neer·ing** (en′jə nîr′ing) *noun.*

England   A section of the United Kingdom. It is on the southern part of the island of Great Britain.

> **Eng·land** (ing′glənd) *noun.*

Word History

The name **England** comes from Old English and means "Land of the Angles." The Angles were the main tribe of invaders from Germany who conquered Britain around A.D. 450. Their name and their language have been with us for the last 1,500 years.

English   **1.** A language spoken in England, the United States, Canada, India, Australia, and many other places.   **2. the English.** The people of England. *Noun.*
—**1.** Of England or its people. This report tells about various *English* customs.   **2.** Of or in the English language. The book was written in French, but you can buy an *English* translation of it. *Adjective.*

> **Eng·lish** (ing′glish) *noun; adjective.*

English horn   A long, thin musical instrument that resembles the oboe but has a lower tone.

Englishman   A person who was born in or is a citizen of England.

> **Eng·lish·man** (ing′glish mən) *noun, plural* **Englishmen** (ing′glish mən).

Englishwoman   A woman who was born in or is a citizen of England.

> **Eng·lish·wo·man** (ing′glish wùm′ən) *noun, plural* **Englishwomen** (ing′glish wim′ən).

engrave   **1.** To cut or carve letters, figures, or designs into a surface. The jeweler *engraved* my name on the back of my watch. **2.** To print something from a metal plate or other surface that has been cut with letters, figures, or designs. The printer *engraved* the wedding invitations.

> **en·grave** (en grāv′) *verb,* **engraved, engraving.**

engraving   **1.** The art of cutting or carving letters, figures, or designs into a surface. **2.** A picture or design that is printed by us-

ing a surface that has been engraved. This *engraving* shows a famous ancient battle.
en·grav·ing (en grā′ving) *noun, plural* **engravings.**

engulf To swallow up or cover completely, as if by a flood; overwhelm. The waves *engulfed* the small boat.
en·gulf (en gulf′) *verb,* **engulfed, engulfing.**

enhance To make greater; add to. The rose bushes by the front door *enhance* the beauty of the house.
en·hance (en hans′) *verb,* **enhanced, enhancing.**

enjoy **1.** To get joy or pleasure from; be happy with. Our whole family *enjoys* skiing in the winter. **2.** To have as an advantage. That city *enjoys* warm weather throughout the year.
• **to enjoy oneself.** To have a good time. We all *enjoyed ourselves* at the movies.
en·joy (en joi′) *verb,* **enjoyed, enjoying.**

enjoyable Giving joy or happiness; pleasant. The class had an *enjoyable* time at the museum.
en·joy·a·ble (en joi′ə bəl) *adjective.*

enjoyment Pleasure; joy. Many people get *enjoyment* out of collecting stamps.
en·joy·ment (en joi′mənt) *noun, plural* **enjoyments.**

enlarge To make or become larger. We are *enlarging* our house by adding an extra bedroom.
en·large (en lärj′) *verb,* **enlarged, enlarging.**

enlargement **1.** The act of enlarging or the condition of being enlarged. The *enlargement* of the building was achieved by adding another room. **2.** Something, such as a photograph, that has been made larger than the original. Many details could be seen in the *enlargement* of the photograph.
en·large·ment (en lärj′mənt) *noun, plural* **enlargements.**

enlighten To give knowledge or wisdom to. The news reports *enlightened* us about the effect of the drought on this year's harvest.
en·light·en (en lī′tən) *verb,* **enlightened, enlightening.**

enlist **1.** To join or persuade to join the Army, Navy, or some other part of the armed forces. Many *enlisted* in the Navy as soon as the war broke out. The sergeant *enlisted* them in the Army. **2.** To get the help or support of. The mayor *enlisted* the entire town in the drive to clean up the city.
en·list (en list′) *verb,* **enlisted, enlisting.**

enormous Much greater than the usual size or amount; very large. Some dinosaurs were *enormous*. The flood caused an *enormous* amount of damage.
e·nor·mous (i nôr′məs) *adjective.*

The sunglasses are **enormous.**

enough As much or as many as needed. There is not *enough* room for all of us in the car. There were *enough* players for a game of baseball. *Adjective.*
—An amount that is as much or as many as needed. There is *enough* here to feed the whole family. *Noun.*
—To an amount or degree that is wanted or needed. The meat is not cooked *enough*. Are you feeling well *enough* to go out? *Adverb.*
e·nough (i nuf′) *adjective; noun; adverb.*

enrage To make very angry; put into a rage. The dictator's cruel actions *enraged* the people.
en·rage (en rāj′) *verb,* **enraged, enraging.**

enrich **1.** To make rich or richer. The discovery of the shipwreck and its treasure *enriched* the divers. **2.** To improve or make better by adding something. They *enrich* bread at this bakery by adding vitamins to it.
en·rich (en rich′) *verb,* **enriched, enriching.**

enroll To make or become a member. The teacher *enrolled* seven new students in the class. In the summer I am going to *enroll* in camp.
en·roll (en rōl′) *verb,* **enrolled, enrolling.**

enrollment **1.** The act of enrolling or the condition of being enrolled. *Enrollment* at the school takes place during the first week

at; āpe; fär; câre; end; mē; it; īce; pîerce; hot; ōld; sông, fôrk; oil; out; up; ūse; rüle; pull; tûrn; chin; sing; shop; thin; this; hw in white; zh in treasure. The symbol ə stands for the unstressed vowel sound in about, taken, pencil, lemon, and circus.

in September. My *enrollment* in this club entitles me to two free books.   **2.** The number of persons enrolled. The class has an *enrollment* of twenty-five.
  en·roll·ment (en rōl′mənt) *noun, plural* **enrollments.**

en route   On the way. They stopped for lunch *en route* to the movie.
  en route (än rüt′).

ensign   **1.** A flag or banner. The *ensign* of the United States was flying on the ship.
2. A naval officer of the lowest rank. In the United States Navy, an ensign is next below a lieutenant.
  en·sign (en′sən *or* en′sīn *for definition 1;* en′sən *for definition 2*) *noun, plural* **ensigns.**

ensure   **1.** To make sure or certain; guarantee. Careful planning helped to *ensure* the success of the project.   **2.** To make safe; protect. A vaccination will *ensure* you against getting that disease.
  en·sure (en shùr′) *verb,* **ensured, ensuring.**

entangle   To catch in a tangle or net. The kitten *entangled* its claws in the yarn.
  en·tan·gle (en tang′gəl) *verb,* **entangled, entangling.**

enter   **1.** To go or come into or in. The train *entered* the tunnel. Doubts *entered* my mind.
2. To pass through something; pierce. The nail *entered* the sole of my shoe.   **3.** To become a member or part of; join. They will *enter* high school next year.   **4.** To enroll; register. I *entered* my dog in the contest.   **5.** To put down in writing; make a *record of.* The bank *entered* the amount of the deposit in my account.
  en·ter (en′tər) *verb,* **entered, entering.**

enterprise   Something that a person plans or tries to do. An enterprise is often something difficult or important. The search for the treasure was an exciting *enterprise.*
  en·ter·prise (en′tər prīz′) *noun, plural* **enterprises.**

entertain   **1.** To keep interested and amused. The clown *entertained* the children.
2. To have as a guest. They often *entertain* people in their house in the country.   **3.** To keep in mind; consider. Our neighbor is *entertaining* an offer for a new job.
  en·ter·tain (en′tər tān′) *verb,* **entertained, entertaining.**

entertainer   Someone who entertains people for a living. Singers, dancers, and comedians are entertainers.
  en·ter·tain·er (en′tər tā′nər) *noun, plural* **entertainers.**

entertainment   **1.** The act of entertaining. The *entertainment* of guests is the job of a host.   **2.** Something that interests and amuses. The *entertainment* at the party was a puppet show.
  en·ter·tain·ment (en′tər tān′mənt) *noun, plural* **entertainments.**

enthrall   To hold the attention and interest of someone completely. The audience was *enthralled* as they watched the acrobats.
  en·thrall (en thrôl′) *verb,* **enthralled, enthralling.**

The story **enthralls** the children.

enthusiasm   A strong feeling of excitement and interest about something. The children looked forward to the puppet show with *enthusiasm.*
  en·thu·si·asm (en thü′zē az′əm) *noun.*

enthusiastic   Full of enthusiasm. A person who is enthusiastic is very excited, interested, and eager about something. We were all *enthusiastic* about going to the picnic.
  en·thu·si·as·tic (en thü′zē as′tik) *adjective.*

entire   Having all the parts; with nothing left out; whole. Did you eat the *entire* bowl of salad? It took an *entire* morning to clean the attic.
  en·tire (en tīr′) *adjective.*

entirely   In every way or detail; completely. It will be *entirely* your fault if you don't get there on time.
  en·tire·ly (en tīr′lē) *adverb.*

entitle   **1.** To give a right to. Buying a ticket to the amusement park *entitles* you to one free ride.   **2.** To give the title of; call. I *entitled* my story "How Our Cat Got Up the Tree."
  en·ti·tle (en tī′təl) *verb,* **entitled, entitling.**

entrance¹   **1.** A place through which one enters. The *entrance* to the building is in the middle of the block. Only one *entrance* to the

park was open. **2.** The act of entering. Everyone stood up at the judge's *entrance.* **3.** The power, right, or permission to enter. Students were given free *entrance* to the game.
en·trance (en′trəns) *noun, plural* **entrances.**

entrance² **1.** To put into a trance. When a person is hypnotized, he or she is entranced. **2.** To fill with delight or wonder. The children were *entranced* by the tricks that the clown and the dog performed.
en·trance (en trans′) *verb,* **entranced, entrancing.**

entreat To ask earnestly; beg. The prisoners *entreated* the judge to let them go.
en·treat (en trēt′) *verb,* **entreated, entreating.**

entrust **1.** To trust a person with something. We *entrusted* our neighbors with the care of our dog over the weekend. **2.** To put someone or something in the care of a person. I *entrusted* my money to my cousin when I left for vacation.
en·trust (en trust′) *verb,* **entrusted, entrusting.**

entry **1.** The act of entering. At the president's *entry* into the hall, the band began to play. **2.** A place through which one enters; entrance. The ladder blocked the *entry* to the building. **3.** Something written in a book, list, diary, or other record. I made an *entry* in my diary. Each word explained in a dictionary is an *entry.* **4.** A person or thing that is entered in a contest or race. The judges must have all *entries* for the art show by next Friday.
en·try (en′trē) *noun, plural* **entries.**

enunciate To speak or pronounce words. It is difficult to understand someone who does not *enunciate* words clearly.
e·nun·ci·ate (i nun′sē āt′) *verb,* **enunciated, enunciating.**

envelop To wrap or cover completely. Fog *enveloped* the city.
en·vel·op (en vel′əp) *verb,* **enveloped, enveloping.**

envelope A flat covering or container made of paper. Envelopes are used for mailing letters and other papers.
en·ve·lope (en′və lōp′ *or* än′və lōp′) *noun, plural* **envelopes.**

envious Feeling or showing envy; jealous. When people are envious, they often feel dislike for a person who has something they would like to have. I was *envious* of your school's new gymnasium.
en·vi·ous (en′vē əs) *adjective.*

environment **1.** The air, the water, the soil, and all the other things that surround a person, animal, or plant. The environment can affect the growth and health of living things. The zoo tries to make each animal's cage like its natural *environment.* **2.** Surroundings; atmosphere. I loved summer camp because of the friendly *environment.*
en·vi·ron·ment (en vī′rən mənt *or* en vī′ərn mənt) *noun, plural* **environments.**

envy **1.** A feeling of not being happy about another person's good luck or belongings. A person who feels envy wishes that he or she could have what the other person has. I felt *envy* when your grandparents were at our graduation and mine couldn't be. **2.** A person or thing that makes one feel envy. The child's new bicycle was the *envy* of his classmates. *Noun.*
—To feel envy toward or because of. Everyone in our class *envies* you because of your good grades. *Verb.*
en·vy (en′vē) *noun, plural* **envies;** *verb,* **envied, envying.**

eon A very long period of time. That deposit of coal was formed *eons* ago.
e·on (ē′ən *or* ē′on) *noun, plural* **eons.**

epic A long poem that tells of the adventures of heroes in legend or history. *Noun.*
—**1.** Being or having to do with an epic. The class read an *epic* poem about how Rome was founded. **2.** Like something in an epic; great. We admire the *epic* courage of the American pioneers. *Adjective.*
ep·ic (ep′ik) *noun, plural* **epics;** *adjective.*

epidemic An outbreak of a disease that makes many people in an area ill at the same time. In an epidemic the disease may spread very fast.
ep·i·dem·ic (ep′i dem′ik) *noun, plural* **epidemics.**

Word History

The word **epidemic** goes back to a Greek word that means "among the people." An epidemic happens when a disease spreads quickly among many people.

---

at; āpe; fär; câre; end; mē; it; īce; pîerce; hot; ōld; sông; fôrk; oil; out; up; ūse; rüle; pùll; tûrn; chin; sing; shop; thin; this; hw in white; zh in treasure. The symbol ə stands for the unstressed vowel sound in about, taken, pencil, lemon, and circus.

epilepsy A disorder of the brain that can make a person sometimes be unconscious and have convulsions. Sometimes drugs can prevent a person who has epilepsy from becoming unconscious or having convulsions.
ep·i·lep·sy (ep′ə lep′sē) *noun.*

episode One part of a series of events in a story or real life. I watched the third *episode* of that series on television.
ep·i·sode (ep′ə sōd′) *noun, plural* **episodes.**

epoch A period of time during which something important developed or happened. The first airplane flight marked a new *epoch* in travel.
ep·och (ep′ək) *noun, plural* **epochs.**

equal **1.** Being the same, as in amount, size, value, or quality. Four quarts are *equal* to one gallon. Both teams have an *equal* chance to win the game because they both have good players. **2.** Having the same rights and duties. All people are *equal* under the law. *Adjective.*
—A person or thing that is equal. You are my *equal* in softball because you play as well as I do. *Noun.*
—To be equal to. Two plus two *equals* four. *Verb.*
e·qual (ē′kwəl) *adjective; noun, plural* **equals;** *verb,* **equaled, equaling.**

equality The quality or condition of being equal. The Constitution of the United States provides for the *equality* of all Americans under the law.
e·qual·i·ty (i kwol′i tē) *noun.*

equation A statement in mathematics that two quantities are equal. $5 + 4 = 9$ is an equation.
e·qua·tion (i kwā′zhən) *noun, plural* **equations.**

equator An imaginary line around the earth. It is halfway between the North and South Poles. The United States and Canada are north of the equator. Most of South America is south of the equator.
e·qua·tor (i kwā′tər) *noun, plural* **equators.**

The dotted line represents the **equator**.

equatorial **1.** At or near the equator. Some of the countries in South America and Africa are equatorial countries. **2.** Showing the qualities of the area at or near the equator. The *equatorial* heat was unusual for our area.
e·qua·to·ri·al (ē′kwə tôr′ē əl *or* ek′wə tôr′ē əl) *adjective.*

equilateral triangle A triangle in which all three sides are equal in length.
e·qui·lat·er·al triangle (ē′kwə lat′ər əl).

equilibrium Balance. Many tightrope walkers carry poles to help them keep their *equilibrium.*
e·qui·lib·ri·um (ē′kwə lib′rē əm) *noun.*

Word History

The word **equilibrium** goes back to a Latin phrase meaning "equal in weight" or "equal on a scale." Roman scales had two pans. You put an object to be weighed in one pan and little weights in the second pan on the other side. When the two pans were equal in weight, the scale would be balanced, or in *equilibrium.*

---

equinox One of the two days of the year when daytime and nighttime are equal in length all over the earth. During these two days the sun is directly above the equator. The equinoxes take place about March 21 and September 23.
e·qui·nox (ē′kwə noks′) *noun, plural* **equinoxes.**

equip To provide with whatever is needed. The ship was *equipped* with hoses to be used in case of fire.
e·quip (i kwip′) *verb,* **equipped, equipping.**

equipment **1.** Anything that is provided for a particular purpose or use; supplies. The students bought a tent, sleeping bags, and other camping *equipment.* **2.** The act of equipping. The *equipment* of the entire football team with new uniforms cost a lot of money.
e·quip·ment (i kwip′mənt) *noun.*

equivalent Equal. A quarter is *equivalent* to five nickels. Shaking your head from side to side is *equivalent* to saying "no." *Adjective.*
—Something that is equal. Ten dimes are the *equivalent* of one dollar. *Noun.*
e·quiv·a·lent (i kwiv′ə lənt) *adjective; noun, plural* **equivalents.**

-er¹ A *suffix* that means: **1.** A person or thing that does something. *Teacher* means a person who teaches. *Opener* means a tool that opens. The suffix **-or** has the same meaning. **2.** A person who studies or works at something. *Astronomer* means a person who studies astronomy. The suffix **-ist** has the same meaning. **3.** A person living in. *Northerner* means a person living in the north.

-er² A *suffix* that means more. *Colder* means more cold than. The suffix **-er** shows that an adjective or adverb is in its comparative form. *Colder* is the comparative form of *cold. Faster* is the comparative form of *fast.* ▲ The comparative of some words is formed with *more* rather than by adding *-er.* Look up **more** for more information.

era A period of time or of history. An era often begins or ends with an important event. The colonial *era* in American history began when the first permanent settlements of Europeans were established.
e·ra (îr′ə *or* er′ə) *noun, plural* **eras.**

erase **1.** To remove by rubbing, scratching, or wiping off. *Erase* the word that is spelled wrong and write in the correct spelling. Would you please *erase* the blackboard? **2.** To remove recording from. I accidentally *erased* a part of the tape.
e·rase (i rās′) *verb,* **erased, erasing.**

eraser Something used to rub out or remove marks. This pencil has a rubber *eraser* on one end.
e·ras·er (i rā′sər) *noun, plural* **erasers.**

ere Before. ▲ This word is used mainly in poetry and in writing from long ago. ▲ Other words that sound like this are **air** and **heir.**
ere (âr) *preposition; conjunction.*

erect Upright; raised. The dog's ears became *erect* when its owner whistled. *Adjective.*
—**1.** To build. A new apartment house will be *erected* on that lot. **2.** To put or raise into an upright position. They hurried to *erect* the tent so they could get inside before the rain began. *Verb.*
e·rect (i rekt′) *adjective; verb,* **erected, erecting.**

ermine A small animal with short legs that is a member of the weasel family. It has brown fur that changes to white in the winter.
er·mine (ûr′min) *noun, plural* **ermines** or **ermine.**

erode To wear or wash away slowly; eat away. Ocean waves *eroded* the shore. Rust had *eroded* the tin roof of the shed.
e·rode (i rōd′) *verb,* **eroded, eroding.**

erosion A wearing, washing, or eating away. Erosion usually happens gradually over a long time. The trees and grass helped prevent the *erosion* of soil on the hill by protecting it from the wind and rain. This deep canyon was created by *erosion.*
e·ro·sion (i rō′zhən) *noun.*

errand **1.** A short trip to do something. I have to go to the grocery store, stop at the post office, and do several other *errands* this morning. **2.** Something a person is sent to do; the purpose of such a trip. Our *errand* was to buy the newspaper.
er·rand (er′ənd) *noun, plural* **errands.**

erratic **1.** Acting or moving in an irregular or confused way. We knew something was wrong because of the bird's *erratic* flight. **2.** Straying from an accepted or usual standard; eccentric. The captain's *erratic* behavior made the crew of the ship nervous.
er·rat·ic (i rat′ik) *adjective.*

error **1.** Something that is wrong; mistake. There were five spelling *errors* on that test paper. **2.** A poor play made by a fielder in baseball. An error lets a runner get to a base safely or lets a batter remain at bat when either one would have been out if the play had been made correctly.
er·ror (er′ər) *noun, plural* **errors.**

erupt **1.** To break out suddenly and with force. A fight *erupted* between the two hockey teams. **2.** To release lava through a volcano with great force. The volcano *erupted* and covered the surrounding land with lava.
e·rupt (i rupt′) *verb,* **erupted, erupting.**

escalator A moving stairway. It is made of a series of steps pulled by a continuous chain.

an **ermine** in winter

at; āpe; fär; câre; end; mē; it; īce; pîerce; hot; ōld; sông, fôrk; oil; out; up; ūse; rüle; pùll; tûrn; chin; sing; shop; thin; this; hw in white; zh in treasure. The symbol ə stands for the unstressed vowel sound in about, taken, pencil, lemon, and circus.

An escalator is used to carry people from one floor to another.
es·ca·la·tor (es′kə lā′tər) *noun, plural* **escalators.**

escalators

escape **1.** To get free. The bird *escaped* from the cage and flew into the woods. **2.** To remain free from. The workers *escaped* harm when the building collapsed. *Verb.*
—**1.** The act of escaping. The rabbit made its *escape* when its owner forgot to lock the cage door. **2.** A way of escaping. A rope ladder served as an *escape* from the burning house. *Noun.*
  es·cape (e skāp′) *verb,* **escaped, escaping;** *noun, plural* **escapes.**

escort **1.** A person or persons who go along with others. An escort does this to show respect or to honor or protect someone. The president's car had a police *escort.* My *escort* to the party made sure I got home safely. **2.** One or more ships or airplanes that travel with or protect another ship or airplane. The *escort* for the battleship included three destroyers. *Noun.*
—To act as an escort. The police *escorted* the mayor in the parade. *Verb.*
  es·cort (es′kôrt *for noun;* e skôrt′ *for verb*) *noun, plural* **escorts;** *verb,* **escorted, escorting.**

Eskimo A member of a people living in Alaska, northern Canada, and other arctic regions.
  Es·ki·mo (es′kə mō′) *noun, plural* **Eskimo** or **Eskimos.**

esophagus The muscular tube through which food moves from the throat to the stomach.
  e·soph·a·gus (i sof′ə gəs) *noun.*

especially **1.** More than usually; to an unusual degree. Be *especially* careful not to slip on the icy sidewalk. **2.** Mainly; chiefly. We came over *especially* to see your new computer.
  es·pe·cial·ly (e spesh′ə lē) *adverb.*

espionage The use of spies to gather secret information. The government discovered its enemy's plans by using *espionage.*
  es·pi·o·nage (es′pē ə näzh′ *or* es′pē ə nij) *noun.*

essay A short written composition on a subject. I wrote an *essay* about the need for world peace.
  es·say (es′ā) *noun, plural* **essays.**

Word History

The word **essay** comes from a French word meaning "to try." The first essays modestly claimed to be only attempts to set down the writer's thoughts.

essence **1.** Something that makes a thing what it is; necessary and basic part. Respect for each other is the *essence* of a good friendship. **2.** A concentrated substance or solution. We used *essence* of peppermint to add flavoring to the cake we made.
  es·sence (es′əns) *noun, plural* **essences.**

essential Very important or necessary. It is *essential* that we leave now or we'll miss the last train. *Adjective.*
—A necessary or basic part. We brought food, sleeping bags, a tent, and other *essentials* for our camping trip. *Noun.*
  es·sen·tial (i sen′shəl) *adjective; noun, plural* **essentials.**

-est A *suffix* that means most. *Coldest* means the most cold. The suffix *-est* shows that an adjective or adverb is in its superlative form. *Coldest* is the superlative form of *cold. Soonest* is the superlative form of *soon.*
▲ The superlative of some words is formed with *most* rather than by adding *-est.* Look up **most** for more information.

establish **1.** To begin or create; set up. The college *established* a new course for students

interested in computers. The young doctors *established* themselves in their new offices. **2.** To show or prove to be true. The lawyer *established* the fact that the accused people were out of town on the day of the crime.
es·tab·lish (e stab′lish) *verb,* **established, establishing.**

establishment **1.** The act of establishing. The *establishment* of a new hospital for the town took longer than was planned. **2.** Something established. A department store, a school, a business, and a household are establishments.
es·tab·lish·ment (e stab′lish mənt) *noun,* *plural* **establishments.**

estate **1.** A large piece of land, usually with a large house on it. Our neighbors have an *estate* in the country. **2.** Everything that a person owns. The old couple left their entire *estate* to their children.
es·tate (e stāt′) *noun, plural* **estates.**

esteem To think highly of; respect. The captain *esteemed* the soldiers for their bravery. *Verb.*
—High respect and admiration. Many people have great *esteem* for that judge's opinions. *Noun.*
es·teem (e stēm′) *verb,* **esteemed, esteeming;** *noun, plural* **esteems.**

estimate An opinion of the value, quality, size, or cost of something. The worker gave an *estimate* of what it would cost to patch the roof. *Noun.*
—To form an opinion by reasoning. We *estimated* that the trip would take an hour, but it took longer because of heavy traffic. *Verb.*
es·ti·mate (es′tə mit *for noun;* es′tə māt′ *for verb) noun, plural* **estimates;** *verb,* **estimated, estimating.**

estimation An opinion or judgment. In my *estimation,* the project will be finished in two weeks.
es·ti·ma·tion (es′tə mā′shən) *noun, plural* **estimations.**

estuary The mouth of a river where its current meets the sea and is affected by the tides.
es·tu·ar·y (es′chü er′ē) *noun, plural* **estuaries.**

etc. An abbreviation for the Latin words *et cetera,* which mean *and so forth* or *and others.* We went to the store and bought milk, fish, vegetables, *etc.*

etch To engrave a picture or design on metal or glass by letting acid eat away parts of the metal or glass. The artist *etched* a portrait of a couple.
etch (ech) *verb,* **etched, etching.**

etching A picture or design that is printed from a surface that has been etched.
etch·ing (ech′ing) *noun, plural* **etchings.**

eternal **1.** Lasting forever. The laws of nature are *eternal.* **2.** Seeming to last or go on forever. We complained about the *eternal* noise that our neighbors made.
e·ter·nal (i tûr′nəl) *adjective.*

eternity **1.** Time without beginning or end; all time. **2.** A period of time that seems endless. An *eternity* passed before the bus arrived.
e·ter·ni·ty (i tûr′ni tē) *noun, plural* **eternities.**

ether A liquid that burns easily and has a strong smell and no color. It is sometimes used in medicine to make people unconscious during operations.
e·ther (ē′thər) *noun.*

Ethiopia A country in east-central Africa.
E·thi·o·pi·a (ē′thē ō′pē ə) *noun.*

ethnic Having to do with a group of people who have the same language and culture. Many different *ethnic* groups live in our city.
eth·nic (eth′nik) *adjective.*

etiquette Rules of correct behavior. According to *etiquette,* it is not considered proper to eat peas with a knife.
et·i·quette (et′i kit′ *or* et′i ket′) *noun, plural* **etiquettes.**

etymology The history of a word from its beginning to its present form. An etymology tells what other language a word has come from and any changes that have occurred in the word's spelling or meaning. In this dictionary, etymologies are printed in red boxes with the heading "Word History."
et·y·mol·o·gy (et′ə mol′ə jē) *noun, plural* **etymologies.**

Word History

The word **etymology** comes from a Greek term meaning "true word." The ancient Greeks and Romans looked for what they thought was the original meaning of a word. They called this meaning the "true word," or *etymology.*

at; āpe; fär; câre; end; mē; it; īce; pîerce; hot; ōld; sông, fôrk; oil; out; up; ūse; rüle; pu̇ll; tûrn; chin; sing; shop; thin; <u>th</u>is; hw in white; zh in treasure. The symbol ə stands for the unstressed vowel sound in about, taken, pencil, lemon, and circus.

eucalyptus   A tall evergreen tree or shrub that grows in warm climates. Its hard wood is used to make floors, ships, and buildings. Oil made from its leaves is used in medicine.
eu·ca·lyp·tus (ū′kə lip′təs) *noun, plural* **eucalyptuses.**

Europe   The continent that is between Asia and the Atlantic Ocean.
Eu·rope (yùr′əp) *noun.*

European   Of Europe or the people who were born or live there. *Adjective.*
—A person who was born or is living in Europe. *Noun.*
Eu·ro·pe·an (yùr′ə pē′ən) *adjective; noun, plural* **Europeans.**

evacuate   To leave or cause to leave; empty or remove. Firefighters *evacuated* the people from the burning building.
e·vac·u·ate (i vak′ū āt′) *verb,* **evacuated, evacuating.**

evade   To escape from or avoid. The escaped prisoner *evaded* the police by hiding on the roof of an old building. Some people try to *evade* paying their income taxes.
e·vade (i vād′) *verb,* **evaded, evading.**

evaluate   To judge or discover the value of. That test is used to *evaluate* how well students are doing in the reading program.
e·val·u·ate (i val′ū āt′) *verb,* **evaluated, evaluating.**

evaporate   **1.** To change from a liquid or solid into a gas. Water evaporates when it is boiled and becomes steam.   **2.** To fade away or disappear; vanish. Our hopes of winning the game *evaporated* when the other team scored five runs in the ninth inning.
e·vap·o·rate (i vap′ə rāt′) *verb,* **evaporated, evaporating.**

eve   The evening or day before a holiday or other important day. My parents went to a party that our neighbors had on the *eve* of their child's wedding. On the *eve* of the school elections, no one was sure who would be elected class president.
eve (ēv) *noun, plural* **eves.**

even   **1.** Free from changes; regular. We were able to keep up an *even* speed on the highway. My cousin has an *even* temper. **2.** At the same height. The drifts of snow were *even* with the tops of the parked cars. **3.** Completely flat. Our house is built on a piece of *even* ground.   **4.** The same or equal. At the end of the fifth inning the score in the game was *even*.   **5.** Able to be divided by 2 without leaving a remainder. The numbers 4, 28, and 72 are *even* numbers. *Adjective.*
—**1.** As a matter of fact; actually. They were willing, *even* eager, to help us.   **2.** Though it

may seem unlikely. Our dog is always friendly, *even* to strangers.   **3.** Still; yet. Your grade on the test was *even* better than mine.   **4.** At the same moment. Your parents called *even* as you knocked on our door. *Adverb.*
—To make or become even. The workers *evened* the bumpy road by filling in the holes with gravel. That last goal *evened* the score of the hockey game. *Verb.*
e·ven (ē′vən) *adjective; adverb; verb,* **evened, evening.**

evening   The late afternoon and early nighttime. *Noun.*
—Relating to or occurring in the evening. We eat our *evening* meal at seven o'clock. *Adjective.*
eve·ning (ēv′ning) *noun, plural* **evenings;** *adjective.*

event   **1.** Anything that happens, especially anything that is important. We studied the *events* leading up to the American Revolution. The first time I went on an airplane was a big *event* in my life.   **2.** A contest in a program of sports. The mile run was the main *event* at the track meet.
● **in any event.**   No matter what happens; in any case. The train may be late, but *in any event* we'll be there in time for dinner.
e·vent (i vent′) *noun, plural* **events.**

eventual   Happening at the end; final. The *eventual* decision on whether to build a public swimming pool depends on how much money the town can raise.
e·ven·tu·al (i ven′chü əl) *adjective.*

eventually   At the end; finally. We waited and waited for our friends, but *eventually* we went to the movies without them.
e·ven·tu·al·ly (i ven′chü ə lē) *adverb.*

ever   **1.** At any time. Have you *ever* visited the White House?   **2.** At all times; always. Our parents are *ever* willing to listen to what we have to say.   **3.** In any way. How can I *ever* thank you enough for all your help?
ev·er (ev′ər) *adverb.*

everglade   An area of low, swampy ground with dense grasses and many slow-moving streams or small rivers. Everglades are found in warm climates.
ev·er·glade (ev′ər glād′) *noun, plural* **everglades.**

evergreen   Having green leaves or needles all year long. *Adjective.*
—An evergreen shrub, tree, or other plant. Pine trees, spruce trees, and holly trees are evergreens. *Noun.*
ev·er·green (ev′ər grēn′) *adjective; noun, plural* **evergreens.**

everlasting Lasting forever; eternal. The war made the people wish for *everlasting* peace.
ev·er·last·ing (ev′ər las′ting) *adjective.*

every Each person or thing of all the people or things that are part of a group. *Every* student in the class is here today. Answer *every* question on the test.
- **every now and then** or **every now and again.** Once in a while; occasionally. We get to visit my grandparents *every now and then.*
- **every other.** Each second; each alternate. The garbage collector comes to our house *every other* day.
eve·ry (ev′rē) *adjective.*

everybody Every person. *Everybody* in the family went next door to meet the new neighbors.
eve·ry·bod·y (ev′rē bod′ē) *pronoun.*

everyday 1. Having to do with every day; daily. Walking the dog is an *everyday* chore for me. Saving people's lives is an *everyday* event for a firefighter. 2. Fit for normal days; not special. Most people get dressed up to go to a party instead of wearing their *everyday* clothes.
eve·ry·day (ev′rē dā′) *adjective.*

everyone Every person; everybody. There was enough food for *everyone* at the party.
eve·ry·one (ev′rē wun′) *pronoun.*

Everyone in the parade is wearing a uniform.

everything 1. All things or all the things. It is impossible for a person to know *everything.* We showed our parents *everything* we had bought. 2. A very important thing. Getting a good education means *everything* to me.
eve·ry·thing (ev′rē thing′) *pronoun.*

everywhere In every place; in all places.

Have you looked *everywhere* for the book you lost? During autumn there were fallen leaves *everywhere.*
eve·ry·where (ev′rē hwâr′ *or* ev′rē wâr′) *adverb.*

evidence Proof of something. The footprints were *evidence* that the suspect had been near the scene of the crime.
ev·i·dence (ev′i dəns) *noun.*

evident Easily seen or understood; clear. It was *evident* that they didn't like the movie since they left before the end.
ev·i·dent (ev′i dənt) *adjective.*

evil Bad, wicked, or harmful. *Adjective.*
—1. The condition of being wicked. The minister's sermon was about good and *evil.* 2. Something that causes trouble or harm. War is an *evil* that has cursed many people's lives. *Noun.*
e·vil (ē′vəl) *adjective; noun, plural* **evils.**

evolution 1. A development, growth, or change that happens slowly and in steps. The exhibit at the museum showed the *evolution* of the automobile with pictures and models of old and new cars. 2. Changes in the members of a group of plants, animals, or other living things. These changes result from tiny changes in the genes that are passed from one generation to the next over many years. 3. The theory that all living animals and plants slowly developed over millions of years from much earlier and simpler forms of life.
ev·o·lu·tion (ev′ə lü′shən) *noun, plural* **evolutions.**

evolve To develop or grow gradually. The buds of roses *evolve* into beautiful flowers. The plan for the new park *evolved* in discussions between the mayor and the council.
e·volve (i volv′) *verb,* **evolved, evolving.**

ewe A female sheep. ▲ Other words that sound like this are **yew** and **you.**
ewe (ū) *noun, plural* **ewes.**

ex– A *prefix* that means former. *Ex-president* means former president. ▲ This prefix is followed by a hyphen.

exact Without anything wrong; very accurate. This clock always gives the *exact* time. *Adjective.*

at; āpe; fär; câre; end; mē; it; īce; pîerce; hot; ōld; sông, fôrk; oil; out; up; ūse; rüle; pu̇ll; tûrn; chin; sing; shop; thin; <u>th</u>is; hw in white; zh in treasure. The symbol ə stands for the unstressed vowel sound in about, taken, pencil, lemon, and circus.

E

—To demand and get. The criminals *exacted* a ransom from the family of the child that they had kidnapped. *Verb.*
> **ex·act** (eg zakt′) *adjective; verb,* **exacted, exacting.**

exactly   **1.** Without any mistake; in an accurate way. Measure the boards for the bookcase *exactly.*   **2.** In the exact way; quite. The accident happened *exactly* as I told him.
> **ex·act·ly** (eg zakt′lē) *adjective.*

exaggerate   To make something seem larger, greater, or more important than it is. The camper *exaggerated* the size of the fish that had gotten away. You *exaggerated* when you said you ate everything in the refrigerator yesterday.
> **ex·ag·ger·ate** (eg zaj′ə rāt′) *verb,* **exaggerated, exaggerating.**

examination   **1.** The act or process of examining. The dentist's *examination* of my teeth showed that I had no cavities.   **2.** A test. The students prepared for their *examinations* at the end of the year.
> **ex·am·in·a·tion** (eg zam′ə nā′shən) *noun, plural* **examinations.**

examine   **1.** To look at closely and carefully; check. We *examined* the baseball bat to be sure it wasn't cracked. The doctor *examined* me to see if I had the flu.   **2.** To question in a careful way or test, usually to discover what a person knows. The lawyer *examined* the witness during the trial.
> **ex·am·ine** (eg zam′in) *verb,* **examined, examining.**

example   **1.** A thing that is used to show what other similar things are like. Three pictures were hung up as *examples* of the work the class was doing in art.   **2.** A problem given to show how similar problems are solved. The arithmetic *example* on the blackboard was hard to understand.   **3.** A person or thing that ought to be copied. Your good care of your dog is an *example* for all of us.   **4.** Something used to serve as a warning to others. The judge made *examples* of the criminals by giving them harsh sentences.
> • **for example.**   As an example or examples. I would like to visit many foreign countries, *for example,* China and Japan.
> • **to set an example.**   To serve as a model for others. The student's hard work in class *set an example* for the others.
> **ex·am·ple** (eg zam′pəl) *noun, plural* **examples.**

exasperate   To annoy greatly; make angry. The constant barking of our neighbor's dog has *exasperated* our family.
> **ex·as·per·ate** (eg zas′pə rāt′) *verb,* **exasperated, exasperating.**

excavate   **1.** To remove by digging. The workers *excavated* the dirt and rocks with a steam shovel.   **2.** To uncover by digging. The museum sent a group of people to *excavate* the ruins of the ancient city.   **3.** To make by digging. The mining company *excavated* a tunnel in the side of the mountain.
> **ex·ca·vate** (ek′skə vāt′) *verb,* **excavated, excavating.**

exceed   To go beyond or be greater than. The driver *exceeded* the speed limit and was stopped by the police. The money given to the charity *exceeded* $10,000.
> **ex·ceed** (ek sēd′) *verb,* **exceeded, exceeding.**

exceedingly   To an unusual or extreme degree. Last night it was *exceedingly* hot.
> **ex·ceed·ing·ly** (ek sē′ding lē) *adverb.*

excel   To be better or greater than others. I would like to *excel* as a football player.
> **ex·cel** (ek sel′) *verb,* **excelled, excelling.**

excellence   The condition of being very good or outstanding. Your *excellence* as a pitcher is known to everyone in school.
> **ex·cel·lence** (ek′sə ləns) *noun.*

excellent   Very good; outstanding. The teacher told my parents that my work in arithmetic was *excellent.*
> **ex·cel·lent** (ek′sə lənt) *adjective.*

except   With the exception of; not including. The store is open every day *except* Sunday. *Preposition.*
—If it were not for the fact that; only. I would go, *except* that I have work to do. *Conjunction.*
> **ex·cept** (ek sept′) *preposition; conjunction.*

exception   **1.** The act of leaving out or the condition of being left out. Everyone went on the picnic with the *exception* of two students, who were sick.   **2.** A person or thing that is left out or that is different from others. Most birds can fly, but the penguin is an *exception.*
> **ex·cep·tion** (ek sep′shən) *noun, plural* **exceptions.**

exceptional   Not ordinary; unusual; extraordinary. We had an *exceptional* amount of rain this August. This young child is an *exceptional* piano player.
> **ex·cep·tion·al** (ek sep′shə nəl) *adjective.*

excess   An amount greater than what is needed or usual. An *excess* of water in the fish tank caused it to overflow. *Noun.*
—Greater than what is needed or usual; extra. When you travel on an airplane you have to pay for *excess* luggage. *Adjective.*
> **ex·cess** (ek′ses *or* ek ses′) *noun, plural* **excesses;** *adjective.*

excessive   More than is necessary or usual. Don't spend an *excessive* amount of money during your trip.
  ex·ces·sive (ek ses′iv) *adjective.*

exchange   **1.** To give or give up for something else. You can *exchange* the shirt I gave you as a present and get a belt instead. **2.** To give and receive things of the same kind back. My friend and I *exchange* baseball cards. *Verb.*
—**1.** The act of giving one thing for another. The two friends enjoyed their *exchange* of letters. **2.** A place where things are bought, sold, or traded. When we arrived in Mexico, we had to go to the currency *exchange* to trade in our money for Mexican money. **3.** A central office where telephone lines are connected for a town or in part of a large city. *Noun.*
  ex·change (eks chānj′) *verb,* **exchanged, exchanging;** *noun, plural* **exchanges.**

excite   To stir up; arouse. The team's great play *excited* the fans. The old, deserted house *excited* the children's curiosity.
  ex·cite (ek sīt′) *verb,* **excited, exciting.**

excitement   **1.** The condition of being excited. We could hardly sleep because of our *excitement* about starting the trip tomorrow. **2.** Something that stirs up or excites. Winning the contest was an *excitement* I shall never forget.
  ex·cite·ment (ek sīt′mənt) *noun.*

exciting   Causing excitement. For me, the acrobats who walk on the tightrope are the most *exciting* part of the circus.
  ex·cit·ing (ek sī′ting) *adjective.*

exclaim   To speak or shout suddenly, or with force; to express surprise or other strong feeling. "My bicycle's missing!" I *exclaimed.*
  ex·claim (ek sklām′) *verb,* **exclaimed, exclaiming.**

exclamation   **1.** The act of exclaiming. There was no excuse for your constant *exclamations* during the meeting. **2.** Something that is spoken or shouted suddenly or with force. *Hurrah!* and *Ouch!* are exclamations.
  ex·cla·ma·tion (ek′sklə mā′shən) *noun, plural* **exclamations.**

exclamation point or **exclamation mark**   A punctuation mark (!) that is used after a word or group of words that is an exclamation.

exclamatory sentence   A sentence that expresses excitement or strong feelings. An example of an exclamatory sentence is *What a scary movie that was!*
  ex·clam·a·to·ry sentence (ek sklam′ə tôr′ē).

exclude   To keep from entering; shut out. All those who aren't eighteen years old or older are *excluded* from voting.
  ex·clude (ek sklüd′) *verb,* **excluded, excluding.**

exclusive   **1.** Belonging to a single person or group. Because my parents own our family's house together, neither one is the *exclusive* owner. **2.** Open to a certain kind of person or group only. That is an *exclusive* club for lawyers only. **3.** Complete; entire. The students gave the visitor their *exclusive* attention.
  ex·clu·sive (ek sklü′siv) *adjective.*

excrete   To give off waste from the body.
  ex·crete (ek skrēt′) *verb,* **excreted, excreting.**

excursion   **1.** A short trip made for a special reason or for pleasure. Tomorrow the class will take an *excursion* to the zoo. **2.** A trip, as on an airplane or train, at a reduced fare.
  ex·cur·sion (ek skûr′zhən) *noun, plural* **excursions.**

excuse   **1.** To forgive; pardon; overlook. Please *excuse* me for stepping on your toe. We *excused* your rude remark because we knew you were tired. **2.** To let off from duty. I was *excused* from football practice because I had hurt my knee. **3.** To serve as a reason or explanation for. Your illness *excused* your absence from the meeting. *Verb.*
—A reason given to explain something. Waking up late is not a good *excuse* for being late to school. *Noun.*
  • **to excuse oneself.   1.** To apologize for oneself; ask to be pardoned. I *excused myself* for being late. **2.** To ask permission to leave. You should *excuse yourself* if you want to leave the table during dinner.
  ex·cuse (ek skūz′ *for verb;* ek skūs′ *for noun*) *verb,* **excused, excusing;** *noun, plural* **excuses.**

execute   **1.** To carry out or enforce. The captain *executed* the colonel's orders. **2.** To kill according to a legal order. **3.** To make or do by following a plan or design. The two dancers *executed* the unusual steps perfectly.
  ex·e·cute (ek′si kūt′) *verb,* **executed, executing.**

---

at; āpe; fär; câre; end; mē; it; īce; pîerce; hot; ōld; sông, fôrk; oil; out; up; ūse; rüle; pùll; tûrn; chin; sing; shop; thin; this; hw in white; zh in treasure. The symbol ə stands for the unstressed vowel sound in about, taken, pencil, lemon, and circus.

execution   1. The act of executing. The *execution* of the plan to clean up the neighborhood will call for everyone's help.   2. The act of killing according to a legal order.
  ex·e·cu·tion (ek'si kū'shən) *noun, plural* **executions.**

executive   Having to do with directing or managing matters in business or government. My neighbor has an *executive* position as vice president of the company. The president heads the *executive* branch of the United States government. *Adjective.*
  —1. A person who directs or manages. All the *executives* of the company met to discuss ways of selling their new product.   2. The branch of government that manages the affairs of a nation and sees that the laws are carried out. *Noun.*
  ex·ec·u·tive (eg zek'yə tiv) *adjective; noun, plural* **executives.**

exempt   To free from a duty or requirements excuse. One student was *exempted* from taking the final test because of excellent marks during the year. *Verb.*
  —Freed from doing or giving something; excused. Land belonging to a church is usually *exempt* from taxes. *Adjective.*
  ex·empt (eg zempt') *verb,* **exempted, exempting;** *adjective.*

These people are doing **exercises.**

exercise   1. Activity that trains or improves the body or the mind. Walking is good *exercise.* That book has arithmetic *exercises* at the end of each chapter.   2. Use or practice. The *exercise* of power by the dictator led to many cruel acts.   3. A ceremony or program. Graduation *exercises* included speeches by teachers and students. *Noun.*
  —1. To put or go through exercises. I *exercise* my dog in the park. That athlete *exercises* by running five miles every day.   2. To make use of. You should *exercise* your rights as a citizen by voting. *Verb.*
  ex·er·cise (ek'sər sīz') *noun, plural* **exercises;** *verb,* **exercised, exercising.**

exert   To make use of; use. The firefighters had to *exert* all their strength to break down the door.
  ex·ert (eg zûrt') *verb,* **exerted, exerting.**

exhale   To breathe out. The doctor listened to my lungs as I inhaled and *exhaled.*
  ex·hale (eks hāl') *verb,* **exhaled, exhaling.**

exhaust   1. To make very weak or tired. The long, hot hike *exhausted* us.   2. To use up completely. The campers *exhausted* their supply of water, so they drank from a fresh spring. *Verb.*
  —1. The steam or gases that escape from an engine. An automobile has a pipe at the rear to let out the *exhaust.*   2. A pipe or other device that allows used steam or gases to escape. *Noun.*
  ex·haust (eg zôst') *verb,* **exhausted, exhausting;** *noun, plural* **exhausts.**

exhaustion   The act of exhausting or condition of being exhausted. The runner's *exhaustion* was caused by a seven-mile run.
  ex·haus·tion (eg zôs'chən) *noun.*

exhibit   To show. The school *exhibited* the students' best art work. Your cousin *exhibits* great talent in playing the piano. *Verb.*
  —Something shown. We went to see the *exhibit* of African art at the museum. This science *exhibit* won first prize. *Noun.*
  ex·hib·it (eg zib'it) *verb,* **exhibited, exhibiting;** *noun, plural* **exhibits.**

exhibition   1. The act of exhibiting. Being rude is an *exhibition* of bad manners.   2. A public show. The class went to an *exhibition* of rare books shown at the town library.
  ex·hi·bi·tion (ek'sə bish'ən) *noun, plural* **exhibitions.**

exhilarate   To make cheerful, lively, or excited. The brisk air of the mountains *exhilarated* the hikers.
  ex·hil·a·rate (eg zil'ə rāt') *verb,* **exhilarated, exhilarating.**

exile   To send a person away from his or her country or home as a punishment. The country *exiled* the scientist for being a spy for another country. *Verb.*
  —1. The state of being exiled. The government decided that *exile* would be the punishment for the traitors.   2. A person who is sent away from his or her country or home. *Noun.*
  ex·ile (eg'zīl *or* ek'sīl) *verb,* **exiled, exiling;** *noun, plural* **exiles.**

E

exist **1.** To be real. I do not believe that ghosts *exist*. **2.** To have life; live. A person cannot *exist* for long without water. **3.** To be found. Outside of zoos, polar bears *exist* only in arctic regions.
   ex·ist (eg zist') *verb,* **existed, existing.**

existence **1.** The fact of being alive or real. The *existence* of some wild animals is in danger because of pollution. Do you believe in the *existence* of elves? **2.** A way of living; life. The early colonists in America led a dangerous *existence*.
   ex·ist·ence (eg zis'təns) *noun, plural* **existences.**

exit **1.** The way out or off. We left the movies by the *exit* on the left. **2.** The act of leaving. My *exit* from the room was not noticed. *Noun.*
   —To go out; leave; depart. *Exit* by the side door during the fire drill. *Verb.*
   ex·it (eg'zit *or* ek'sit) *noun, plural* **exits;** *verb,* **exited, exiting.**

exotic Foreign; strange; unusual. These *exotic* flowers come from Africa.
   ex·ot·ic (eg zot'ik) *adjective.*

expand To make larger or become larger. Metal *expands* when it is heated.
   ex·pand (ek spand') *verb,* **expanded, expanding.**

expanse A wide, open area. The stagecoach had to cross a large *expanse* of desert to reach the closest town.
   ex·panse (ek spans') *noun, plural* **expanses.**

expansion **1.** The act of expanding or the condition of being expanded. After its *expansion,* the school had thirty new classrooms. **2.** The expanded form of something. This novel is an *expansion* of a story in a magazine.
   ex·pan·sion (ek span'shən) *noun, plural* **expansions.**

expect **1.** To look forward to. I *expect* to see my grandparents at Thanksgiving. **2.** To want something because it is right or necessary. The teacher *expected* an apology from the rude child. **3.** To think; suppose. I *expect* I won't be going to school if I still have the flu tomorrow.
   ex·pect (ek spekt') *verb,* **expected, expecting.**

expectation **1.** The act of expecting. The sailors anchored the boat securely in *expectation* of the coming storm. **2.** A reason for expecting. The student had studied hard and had *expectations* of a good mark on the text.
   ex·pec·ta·tion (ek'spek tā'shən) *noun, plural* **expectations.**

expedition **1.** A journey made for a particular reason. The scientists made an *expedition* to Alaska to study the animals in the area. **2.** The people making such a journey. The *expedition* camped beside the river for the night.
   ex·pe·di·tion (ek'spi dish'ən) *noun, plural* **expeditions.**

expel To drive or force out. They *expelled* the child from school for disobeying everyone.
   ex·pel (ek spel') *verb,* **expelled, expelling.**

expenditure **1.** The spending of time, money, or energy. Building a new house requires the *expenditure* of a great deal of money. **2.** Something that is spent. The *expenditure* for the flowers was $25.00.
   ex·pend·i·ture (ek spen'di chər) *noun, plural* **expenditures.**

expense **1.** Money spent to buy or do something; cost. My family cannot afford the *expense* of a new car. **2.** A cause or reason for spending money. Building the swimming pool was a big *expense*.
   ex·pense (ek spens') *noun, plural* **expenses.**

expensive Having a high price; very costly. The town bought an *expensive* new fire engine.
   ex·pen·sive (ek spen'siv) *adjective.*

experience **1.** Something that a person has done, seen, or taken part in. Our *experience* camping in the national park is something we won't forget. The soldiers told our class about their *experiences* in the army. **2.** The knowledge or skill a person gains from doing something. The youngest firefighter already has three years of *experience*. My friend is the only one on the softball team with *experience* because all the other players are new. *Noun.*
   —To have something happen to one; feel; undergo. I didn't *experience* much pain when the dentist drilled my tooth. *Verb.*
   ex·pe·ri·ence (ek spîr'ē əns) *noun, plural* **experiences;** *verb,* **experienced, experiencing.**

experiment A test that is used to discover or prove something by watching results very

at; āpe; fär; câre; end; mē; it; īce; pîerce; hot; ōld; sông, fôrk; oil; out; up; ūse; rüle; pùll; tûrn; chin; sing; shop; thin; this; hw in white; zh in treasure. The symbol ə stands for the unstressed vowel sound in about, taken, pencil, lemon, and circus.

carefully. The class did an *experiment* to show that a fire needs oxygen to burn. *Noun.* —To make an experiment or experiments. Scientists tested the new drug by *experimenting* with rats. *Verb.*
   ex·per·i·ment (ek sper′ə mənt *for noun;* ek sper′ə ment′ *for verb*) *noun, plural* **experiments;** *verb,* **experimented, experimenting.**

experimental From or relating to experiments. The scientists were working on an *experimental* project in the chemistry laboratory.
   ex·per·i·men·tal (ek sper′ə men′təl) *adjective.*

expert A person who knows a great deal about some special thing. One of our teachers is an *expert* on American history. *Noun.* —Having or showing a great deal of knowledge. The swimming coach gave the team *expert* advice on how to dive. *Adjective.*
   ex·pert (ek′spûrt *for noun;* ek′spûrt *or* ek spûrt′ *for adjective*) *noun, plural* **experts;** *adjective.*

expiration **1.** The act of coming to an end or close. I must get a new library card before the *expiration* of my old one. **2.** The act of breathing out air. The sick child's *expirations* were weak.
   ex·pi·ra·tion (ek′spə rā′shən) *noun, plural* **expirations.**

expire **1.** To come to an end. Your membership at the pool *expires* at the end of the month. **2.** To breathe out; exhale. When we *expire,* our bodies let air out of our lungs.
   ex·pire (ek spīr′) *verb,* **expired, expiring.**

explain **1.** To make something plain or clear; tell the meaning of. *Explain* how to get the answer to this mathematics problem. **2.** To give or have a reason for. Can you *explain* why you were late for school?
   ex·plain (ek splān′) *verb,* **explained, explaining.**

explanation **1.** The act or process of making something plain or clear. My friend's *explanation* of how to make a kite helped me understand how to do it. **2.** A reason or meaning. My parents wanted an *explanation* for why the vase was broken.
   ex·pla·na·tion (ek′splə nā′shən) *noun, plural* **explanations.**

explicit Stated clearly or shown clearly. Our teacher gave *explicit* instructions on how we should do the work.
   ex·plic·it (ek splis′it) *adjective.*

explode **1.** To burst or cause to burst suddenly and with a loud noise; blow up. I pumped too much air into the tire, and it *ex-*

ploded. **2.** To show an emotion noisily or forcefully. The audience *exploded* with laughter at the funny joke.
   ex·plode (ek splōd′) *verb,* **exploded, exploding.**

exploit A brave deed or act. The story is about the daring *exploits* of a knight. *Noun.* —**1.** To use in an unfair or unjust way for selfish reasons. The American colonists felt that the British government *exploited* them by taxing the tea they drank. **2.** To make the fullest possible use of. This new drill will enable us to *exploit* oil buried far under the ground. *Verb.*
   ex·ploit (ek′sploit) *noun, plural* **exploits;** *verb,* **exploited, exploiting.**

exploration The act of exploring. Columbus's *explorations* led to the setting up of trade routes across the Atlantic Ocean.
   ex·plo·ra·tion (ek′splə rā′shən) *noun, plural* **explorations.**

explore **1.** To travel in unknown places for the purpose of discovery. Astronauts *explored* the moon to learn what it is like. **2.** To look through closely; examine. Doctors *explore* the causes of diseases.
   ex·plore (ek splôr′) *verb,* **explored, exploring.**

explorer A person who explores.
   ex·plor·er (ek splôr′ər) *noun, plural* **explorers.**

explosion **1.** The act of bursting or expanding suddenly and noisily. The *explosion* of the bomb broke windows in the buildings nearby. **2.** A sudden outburst. The funny joke caused an *explosion* of laughter.
   ex·plo·sion (ek splō′zhən) *noun, plural* **explosions.**

explosive Likely to explode or cause an explosion. A bomb is an *explosive* device. An *explosive* temper frightens me. *Adjective.* —Something that can explode or cause an explosion. Dynamite is an explosive. *Noun.*
   ex·plo·sive (ek splō′siv) *adjective; noun, plural* **explosives.**

export To send goods to other countries to be sold or traded. Brazil *exports* coffee to the United States. *Verb.* —**1.** Something that is sold or traded to another country. Wheat is an *export* of the United States and Canada. **2.** The act or process of selling or trading to another country. Many farmers depend on the money that comes from the *export* of corn. *Noun.*
   ex·port (ek spôrt′ *or* ek′spôrt′ *for verb;* ek′spôrt′ *for noun*) *verb,* **exported, exporting;** *noun, plural* **exports.**

expose **1.** To leave open or without protection. We were *exposed* to the mumps when a friend had them. The two clowns *exposed* themselves to the laughter of the audience when their magic trick failed to work. **2.** To make something known; reveal. The police *exposed* a gang of thieves who were stealing cars. The magazine article *exposed* the real age of the movie star. **3.** To allow light to reach a photographic film or plate. You will *expose* the film if you load your camera under the lamp.
ex·pose (ek spōz′) *verb,* **exposed, exposing.**

exposition A large public display. There was an *exposition* of camping equipment at the convention center.
ex·po·si·tion (ek′spə zish′ən) *noun, plural* **expositions.**

exposure **1.** The act of exposing. The government's *exposure* of the plot to kill the president shocked the public. **2.** The condition of being exposed. The mountain climbers were suffering from *exposure* after the climb in the terrible cold and wind. **3.** A position in relation to the sun or wind. This room has a southern *exposure,* so it gets a lot of sunlight. **4.** The act of exposing a photographic film to light.
ex·po·sure (ek spō′zhər) *noun, plural* **exposures.**

express To say or show. The dog *expressed* its happiness by wagging its tail. This artist's paintings of plants and animals *express* a love of nature. The Declaration of Independence *expresses* the idea that people are created equal. *Verb.*
—**1.** Special or particular. We came here for the *express* purpose of seeing the monument. **2.** Having to do with fast transportation or delivery. The *express* bus to the city travels on the superhighway. *Adjective.*
—**1.** A system of fast transportation or delivery. I sent my trunk to camp by *express.* **2.** A train, bus, or elevator that is fast and makes few stops. *Noun.*
• **to express oneself.** To put what one thinks or feels into words. I want to learn how to *express myself* clearly when speaking to a large group.
ex·press (ek spres′) *verb,* **expressed, expressing;** *adjective; noun, plural* **expresses.**

expression **1.** The act of putting thoughts or feelings into words or actions. These flowers are an *expression* of our thanks to you. **2.** An outward show; look. The students all had *expressions* of surprise on their faces after the magician performed the trick. **3.** A way of speaking that shows a feeling. The child told the exciting story with *expression.* **4.** A common word or group of words. "Look before you leap" and "A penny saved is a penny earned" are well-known expressions.
ex·pres·sion (ek spresh′ən) *noun, plural* **expressions.**

expressive Full of meaning or feeling. The poet read the poem to the audience in a very *expressive* voice.
ex·pres·sive (ek spres′iv) *adjective.*

expressway A wide highway with several lanes so that cars, trucks, and buses can go long distances without stopping for lights or signs.
ex·press·way (ek spres′wā′) *noun, plural* **expressways.**

expressway

exquisite **1.** Of great beauty or perfection. The view of the sunrise over the lake was *exquisite.* **2.** Of high quality. The detailed sculpture showed *exquisite* workmanship.
ex·qui·site (ek skwiz′it *or* ek′skwi zit) *adjective.*

extend **1.** To make or be longer; stretch out. The bird *extended* its wings and flew away. Our cousins *extended* their visit with us. The driveway *extends* from the house to the street. **2.** To reach; stretch. **3.** To offer or give. We *extended* our welcome to the new neighbors.
ex·tend (ek stend′) *verb,* **extended, extending.**

at; āpe; fär; câre; end; mē; it; īce; pîerce; hot; ōld; sông, fôrk; oil; out; up; ūse; rüle; pùll; tûrn; chin; sing; shop; thin; this; hw in white; zh in treasure. The symbol ə stands for the unstressed vowel sound in about, taken, pencil, lemon, and circus.

extension   **1.** The act of extending or the condition of being extended. The town that was damaged by the tornado accepted the state's *extension* of help.   **2.** Something that extends; addition. They built an *extension* to the house so they would have a room for the new baby.   **3.** An extra telephone added to the same line as the main telephone.
ex·ten·sion (ek sten′shən) *noun, plural* **extensions.**

extensive   Large; great; broad. The flood caused *extensive* damage to the farms in the area.
ex·ten·sive (ek sten′siv) *adjective.*

extent   The space, size, amount, degree, or limit to which something extends. I would go to any *extent* to help a friend. The sheep are allowed to graze over the entire *extent* of the farm.
ex·tent (ek stent′) *noun, plural* **extents.**

exterior   The outer part; outward look or manner. The *exterior* of the building is made of brick. Although you have a calm *exterior,* I think you must feel nervous about running in the race. *Noun.*
—On or having to do with the outside; outer. The *exterior* walls of the house were painted white. *Adjective.*
ex·te·ri·or (ek stîr′ē ər) *noun, plural* **exteriors;** *adjective.*

exterminate   To wipe out; destroy. We used a spray to *exterminate* the bugs.
ex·ter·mi·nate (ek stûr′mə nāt′) *verb,* **exterminated, exterminating.**

external   On or having to do with the outside; outer. The peel of a banana is its *external* covering.
ex·ter·nal (ek stûr′nəl) *adjective.*

extinct   **1.** No longer existing. The dodo became *extinct* because people hunted it for food.   **2.** No longer active or burning. The village is built on an *extinct* volcano.
ex·tinct (ek stingkt′) *adjective.*

extinguish   **1.** To cause to stop burning; put out. The firefighters *extinguished* the fire in about twenty minutes.   **2.** To end; destroy. The heavy rain *extinguished* any hope for a picnic that day.
ex·tin·guish (ek sting′gwish) *verb,* **extinguished, extinguishing.**

extra   More than what is usual, expected, or needed; additional. I spent *extra* time studying so I would get a better grade on that test. *Adjective.*
—**1.** Something added to what is usual, expected, or needed. That car has many *extras,* such as a clock, a radio, and air conditioning.   **2.** A special edition of a newspaper that is printed to report something important. The paper printed an *extra* to announce that the war was over. *Noun.*
—To a degree that is greater than what is usual, expected, or needed. My parents bought an *extra* large cake for my birthday party. *Adverb.*
ex·tra (ek′strə) *adjective; noun, plural* **extras;** *adverb.*

extract   To take, get, or pull out. The dentist *extracted* the tooth. Scientists have found a way to *extract* salt from sea water. *Verb.*
—Something that is extracted. The cake was flavored with vanilla *extract. Noun.*
ex·tract (ek strakt′ *for verb;* ek′strakt *for noun*) *verb,* **extracted, extracting;** *noun, plural* **extracts.**

extraordinary   Very unusual; remarkable. The art teacher said that my friend had *extraordinary* talent.
ex·traor·di·nar·y (ek strôr′də ner′ē *or* ek′strə ôr′də ner′ē) *adjective.*

extraterrestrial   Coming from or existing outside the Earth or its atmosphere. The space explorers hope to find *extraterrestrial* life on other planets. Scientists can determine if a rock is *extraterrestrial* from its chemical composition. *Adjective.*
—A being from another planet. In the movie, *extraterrestrials* came to earth in a spaceship. *Noun.*
ex·tra·ter·res·tri·al (ek′strə tə res′trē əl) *adjective; noun, plural* **extraterrestrials.**

extravagance   The spending of too much money. When our parents go shopping, they avoid *extravagance* and only buy what they need.
ex·trav·a·gance (ek strav′ə gəns) *noun, plural* **extravagances.**

extravagant   Spending too much money; spending in a free or careless way. The *extravagant* movie star bought only very expensive clothes.
ex·trav·a·gant (ek strav′ə gənt) *adjective.*

Word History

The word **extravagant** goes back to a Latin word meaning "wandering outside of the limits." A person who is extravagant in some way has gone beyond the usual limits of behavior.

---

extreme   **1.** Going beyond what is usual; very great or severe. The campers were in *extreme* danger when they were caught in the avalanche. Our neighbor has *extreme* tastes

in clothes. **2.** Very far; farthest. My best friend lives at the *extreme* end of the block. *Adjective.*
—**1.** Farthest points; end. The lighthouse is at one *extreme* of the island. **2. extremes.** Complete opposites. Hot and cold are *extremes* of each other. *Noun.*
> **ex·treme** (ek strēm′) *adjective; noun, plural* **extremes.**

extremely Very. The friends were *extremely* happy when they won the contest. These mountains are *extremely* old.
> **ex·treme·ly** (ek strēm′lē) *adverb.*

eye **1.** One of the organs of the body by which humans and other animals see or sense light. **2.** The colored part of the eye; iris. I have brown *eyes*. **3.** The part of the face around the eye. Many children rub their *eyes* when they are tired. **4. eyes.** The ability to see; vision. My *eyes* are not as good as they used to be. **5.** A look. We cast an *eye* at the bicycle in the store window. **6.** Something like an eye in shape, position, or use. The bud of a potato and the hole in a needle are called *eyes*. A hook attaches to an *eye*. **7.** The center of a hurricane. The eye has no clouds and light winds. *Noun.*
—To watch carefully or closely. The detective *eyed* every move the suspect made. *Verb.* ▲ Other words that sound like this are **aye** and **I.**
- **to catch one's eye.** To attract one's attention. A poster in the shop window *caught my eye* and I stopped to look at it.
- **to keep an eye on.** To watch or tend carefully. I *kept an eye on* the twins when their parents were out for the evening.
- **to see eye to eye.** To agree completely. The team didn't *see eye to eye* on the strategy for the game.
> **eye** (ī) *noun, plural* **eyes;** *verb,* **eyed, eying** or **eyeing.**

eyeball The round part of the eye that is shaped like a ball, without the eyelids or other surrounding parts.
> **eye·ball** (ī′bôl′) *noun, plural* **eyeballs.**

eyebrow **1.** The hair that grows on the bony part of the face above the eye. **2.** The bony ridge above each eye. The eyebrows help to shade and protect the eyes.
> **eye·brow** (ī′brou′) *noun, plural* **eyebrows.**

eyedropper A small glass or plastic tube with a rubber bulb at one end and a hole at the other. It is used to measure and apply drops of medicine to the eye.
> **eye·drop·per** (ī′drop′ər) *noun, plural* **eyedroppers.**

eyeglasses

eyeglasses A pair of lenses in a frame that helps a person to see better.
> **eye·glass·es** (ī′glas′iz) *noun plural.*

eyelash One of the small, stiff hairs growing on the edge of the eyelid. The eyelashes help keep dust out of the eyes.
> **eye·lash** (ī′lash′) *noun, plural* **eyelashes.**

eyelet A small hole in a material for a cord or lace to go through. Shoelaces are put through eyelets. ▲ Another word that sounds like this is **islet.**
> **eye·let** (ī′lit) *noun, plural* **eyelets.**

eyelid The covering of skin that can open and close over the eye. The eyelids protect the eyes and help keep them moist.
> **eye·lid** (ī′lid′) *noun, plural* **eyelids.**

eyesight **1.** The ability to see; vision. They tested our *eyesight* in school by asking us to read a chart. **2.** The range or distance the eye can see; view. The whistling train soon came within *eyesight*.
> **eye·sight** (ī′sīt′) *noun.*

eyetooth Either of the two pointed teeth in the upper jaw between the front teeth and the molars, used for biting or tearing.
> **eye·tooth** (ī′tüth′) *noun, plural* **eyeteeth** (ī′tēth′).

eyewitness A person who has seen something happen, and therefore is able to report or give testimony about it. Reporters interviewed the *eyewitnesses* to the accident.
> **eye·wit·ness** (ī′wit′nis) *noun, plural* **eyewitnesses.**

---

at; āpe; fär; câre; end; mē; it; īce; pîerce; hot; ōld; sông, fôrk; oil; out; up; ūse; rüle; půll; tûrn; chin; sing; shop; thin; this; hw in white; zh in treasure. The symbol ə stands for the unstressed vowel sound in about, taken, pencil, lemon, and circus.

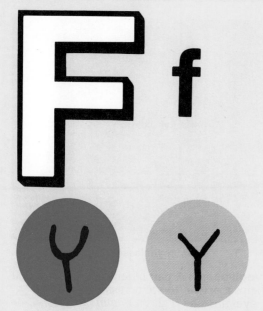

1. The earliest form of the letter **F** was used by ancient tribes in the Middle East. They called it *waw* and used to stand for both a *w* sound and a *u* sound, but not an *f* sound.

2. The ancient Greeks wrote this letter like our modern capital **Y** and used it only for the *u* sound. They used a new letter similar to an **F** for the *w* sound.

3. About 2,800 years ago, an ancient tribe near Rome used both these letters to stand for the *f* sound.

4. The ancient Romans used only the letter that looked like an **F** to stand for the *f* sound.

5. Our capital **F** looks much like the Roman **F**.

f, F   The sixth letter of the alphabet.
  f, F (ef) *noun, plural* **f's, F's.**

F or **F.**   An abbreviation for *Fahrenheit.*

fable   **1.** A story that is meant to teach a lesson. The characters in fables are often animals that talk and act like people.   **2.** A made-up or untrue story. Have you heard the old *fable* about alligators living in the city sewers?
  fa·ble (fā′bəl) *noun, plural* **fables.**

fabric   A material that is woven or knitted; cloth. Fabric is made from natural or synthetic fibers such as cotton, silk, or nylon.
  fab·ric (fab′rik) *noun, plural* **fabrics.**

fabulous   Unbelievable; seeming impossible; amazing. I read a story about dragons and other *fabulous* creatures. They spent *fabulous* amounts of money on books.
  fab·u·lous (fab′yə ləs) *adjective.*

face   **1.** The front of the head. The eyes, nose, and mouth are parts of the face.   **2.** A look on the face; expression. The clown made a sad *face*.   **3.** The front, main, or outward part of something. We could see many people skiing down the *face* of the mountain. There are numbers on the *face* of a clock.   **4.** Importance in the opinion of other people; prestige. If we don't keep our streets clean, our town will lose *face*. *Noun.*
  —**1.** To have or turn the face toward. Please *face* the camera. The school *faces* the park.   **2.** To deal with firmly or courageously. You must *face* the problem immediately. *Verb.*
  face (fās) *noun, plural* **faces;** *verb,* **faced, facing.**

facet   One of the small, polished, flat surfaces of a cut gem.
  fac·et (fas′it) *noun, plural* **facets.**

facets

facial   Of or for the face. A smile is a happy *facial* expression.
  fa·cial (fā′shəl) *adjective.*

facilitate   To make easier; help in the doing of. Zip codes are used to *facilitate* the sorting and delivery of mail.
  fa·cil·i·tate (fə sil′i tāt′) *verb,* **facilitated, facilitating.**

facility   **1.** Ease or skill in doing something. You ride your new bicycle with great *facility*.   **2.** Something that makes a job easier to do or serves a particular purpose. The kitchen *facilities* in our summer cabin consist of a stove, refrigerator, and sink.
  fa·cil·i·ty (fə sil′i tē) *noun, plural* **facilities.**

fact   Something that is known to be true or real; something that has really happened. It is a scientific *fact* that the earth revolves around the sun.

fact (fakt) *noun, plural* **facts.**

factor **1.** Something that helps to bring about a result that affects the course of events. Sunny weather and good food were important *factors* in the success of the picnic. **2.** Any of the numbers that form a product when they are multiplied together. The *factors* of 12 are 12 and 1, 6 and 2, and 3 and 4. *Noun.*
—To find the factors of a product. What answer do you get when you *factor* 6? *Verb.*

fac·tor (fak′tər) *noun, plural* **factors;** *verb,* **factored, factoring.**

factory A building or group of buildings where things are manufactured; plant. Automobiles are made in factories.

fac·to·ry (fak′tə rē) *noun, plural* **factories.**

factual Containing or having to do with facts; true; accurate. This book contains a *factual* account of the battle, without any of the legends about it.

fac·tu·al (fak′chü əl) *adjective.*

faculty **1.** All the teachers of a school, college, or university. The *faculty* had a meeting before the school year began. **2.** A natural power of the mind or body. Hearing and speaking are two human *faculties.* **3.** A special talent or skill for doing something. You have a great *faculty* for making friends.

fac·ul·ty (fak′əl tē) *noun, plural* **faculties.**

fad Something that is very popular for a short period of time. None of us do that dance anymore; it was last year's *fad.*

fad (fad) *noun, plural* **fads.**

fade **1.** To lose or cause to lose color or brightness. Blue jeans may *fade* when they are washed. **2.** To lose freshness; wither. The flowers *faded* after three days. **3.** To become gradually weaker, fainter, or dimmer. The sound of footsteps *faded* away.

fade (fād) *verb,* **faded, fading.**

Fahrenheit The name of a temperature scale on which the freezing point of water is at 32 degrees and the boiling point of water is at 212 degrees. It was 30 degrees *Fahrenheit* and the ice on the pond was frozen.

Fahr·en·heit (far′ən hīt′) *adjective.*

Word History

The word **Fahrenheit** comes from the name of Gabriel Daniel *Fahrenheit.* He was the German scientist who devised this scale for measuring temperature.

fail **1.** To not succeed in doing or getting something. I tried to lift the heaviest weight, but I *failed.* We *failed* to get to the station in time to catch our train. **2.** To get too low a grade in a test or course of study; not pass. I didn't study for the test, so I *failed.* **3.** To be of no use or help to; disappoint. Their friends *failed* them when they refused to keep their promise. The store *failed* the customer by refusing to take back the broken toaster. **4.** To not be enough; run out. The water supply *failed* during the emergency. **5.** To become weaker in strength or health. My cat's eyesight is beginning to *fail.* **6.** To be unable to pay what one owes; go bankrupt. The small store *failed* because it had so few customers. **7.** To not do; neglect. If you *fail* to answer when your name is called, you will be marked absent.

fail (fāl) *verb,* **failed, failing.**

failure **1.** The act of not succeeding in doing or getting something. I was disappointed at the *failure* of the plant to grow. **2.** A person or thing that does not succeed. The school play will not be a *failure* if everyone works hard and cooperates. **3.** The condition of not being large or good enough. The bad weather caused a crop *failure.*

fail·ure (fāl′yər) *noun, plural* **failures.**

faint **1.** Not clear or strong; weak. We heard the *faint* cry of a kitten from the basement. There was a *faint* light at the end of the road. **2.** Weak and dizzy. After bicycling all morning, we were *faint* with hunger by noon. *Adjective.*
—A condition in which a person becomes suddenly unconscious for a short time. *Noun.*
—To become suddenly unconscious for a short time. Two spectators *fainted* from the heat in the stadium. *Verb.* ▲ Another word that sounds like this is **feint.**

faint (fānt) *adjective,* **fainter, faintest;** *noun, plural* **faints;** *verb,* **fainted, fainting.**

fair¹ **1.** Not in favor of any one more than another or others; just. The judges were *fair* in awarding prizes to the contestants. **2.** According to the rules. The referee said it was a *fair* tackle. **3.** Neither too good nor too bad; average. Our team has a *fair* chance

at; āpe; fär; câre; end; mē; it; īce; pîerce; hot; ōld; sông, fôrk; oil; out; up; ūse; rüle; pu̇ll; tûrn; chin; sing; shop; thin; this; hw in white; zh in treasure. The symbol ə stands for the unstressed vowel sound in about, taken, pencil, lemon, and circus.

265

of winning the tennis tournament. **4.** Light in coloring; not dark. Everyone in our family has *fair* hair. **5.** Not cloudy; clear; sunny. The weather for the weekend will be *fair*. **6.** Pleasing to the eye; attractive; beautiful. In the story, the handsome prince married the *fair* young princess. *Adjective.*
—In a fair manner; according to the rules. Our coach encourages us to play *fair,* and not to take advantage of each other. *Adverb.*
▲ Another word that sounds like this is **fare.**
fair (fâr) *adjective,* **fairer, fairest;** *adverb.*

fair² **1.** A public showing of farm products. Fairs are held to show and judge crops and cows, pigs, and other livestock. Fairs often have shows, contests, and entertainment. **2.** Any large showing of products or objects. Many companies had their own exhibits at the photography *fair.* **3.** The showing and selling of things for a particular cause or reason. Our school book *fair* is going to raise money for a new playground. ▲ Another word that sounds like this is **fare.**
fair (fâr) *noun, plural* **fairs.**

fairground An outdoor place where fairs are held.
fair·ground (fâr′ground′) *noun, plural* **fairgrounds.**

fairly **1.** In a fair manner; honestly; justly. Please distribute the toys *fairly,* one to each child. **2.** Somewhat; rather. I saved a *fairly* large amount of money.
fair·ly (fâr′lē) *adverb.*

fairy A tiny being in stories who is supposed to have magic powers.
fair·y (fâr′ē) *noun, plural* **fairies.**

faith **1.** Belief or trust without proof. I have great *faith* in your honesty. **2.** A religion. There are people of many *faiths* in our city.
faith (fāth) *noun, plural* **faiths.**

faithful **1.** Loyal and devoted. My *faithful* friends came to visit me in the hospital. **2.** Accurate; true. This machine will make a *faithful* copy of the drawing.
faith·ful (fāth′fəl) *adjective.*

fake A person or thing that is not what it seems or claims to be. That is not a real fireplace; it's a *fake. Noun.*
—**1.** To take on the appearance of; pretend. Never *fake* illness just to stay home from school. **2.** To make something seem true or real in order to fool. The dishonest clerk stole the money and *faked* the records so that no one would know. *Verb.*
—Not real or genuine; false. I put on a *fake* mustache. *Adjective.*
fake (fāk) *noun, plural* **fakes;** *verb,* **faked, faking;** *adjective.*

falcon A bird that has pointed wings and a long tail. Falcons are powerful flyers and can catch other birds in the air with their feet. Sometimes they are trained to hunt birds and small animals.
fal·con (fôl′kən *or* fal′kən) *noun, plural* **falcons.**

falcon

fall **1.** To come down from a higher place; drop. The mountain climbers held the rope tightly so that they would not *fall.* The leaves of the trees have *fallen.* **2.** To become lower or less. The children's voices *fell* to a whisper. The price of eggs has *fallen* by five cents. **3.** To take place; happen. Christmas *falls* on December 25. Night *fell* quickly. **4.** To pass into a particular condition; become. They *fell* in love. I couldn't come to the party because I *fell* ill. **5.** To be defeated, captured, or overthrown. The city *fell* to the invaders after a long battle. **6.** To hang down. The dress *fell* from the shoulders in soft folds. *Verb.*
—**1.** A coming down from a higher place. A strong wind caused the *fall* from the ladder. The skater took a *fall* on the ice. **2.** The amount of something that comes down. We had a 6-inch *fall* of rain on Saturday. **3.** A loss of power; capture or defeat. The whole country was in confusion after the *fall* of the government. **4.** A lowering or lessening. There was a *fall* in the price of apples last month. **5.** The season of the year coming between summer and winter; autumn. **6. falls.** A fall of water from a higher place; waterfall. *Noun.*
• **to fall back.** To retreat; withdraw. The army *fell back* to a safer position.
• **to fall back on.** To rely on for help; resort to. It's good to have savings to *fall back on* in case of an emergency.
• **to fall behind.** To fail to keep up, as in pace or rate of progress. I *fell behind* in my

266

math studies so I had to study very hard to pass the test at the end of the year.

• **to fall through.** To fail. They were disappointed when their plans *fell through.*
fall (fôl) *verb,* **fell, fallen, falling;** *noun, plural* **falls.**

fallen Past participle of **fall.** All the leaves have *fallen* from the trees. Look up **fall** for more information. *Verb.*
—**1.** Having come down from a higher place; dropped. The *fallen* snow quickly melted in the sun. **2.** Having died in battle. The statue of the soldier in the park is dedicated to all the *fallen* heroes of past wars. *Adjective.*
fall·en (fô′lən) *verb; adjective.*

fallout Radioactive particles that fall to the earth as dust after a nuclear bomb explodes.
fall·out (fôl′out′) *noun.*

false **1.** Not true or correct; wrong. To say that dogs live longer than people is *false.* **2.** Not real; artificial. The actor wore a *false* beard. **3.** Not faithful. Our *false* friends let us down. **4.** Used or intended to deceive. The magician's trunk has a *false* bottom.
false (fôls) *adjective,* **falser, falsest.**

falsehood A statement that is not true. Never hurt a person by telling a *falsehood.*
false·hood (fôls′húd′) *noun, plural* **falsehoods.**

falter **1.** To act or move in an unsteady or hesitating way. The baby *faltered* while trying to take a step. **2.** To pause while speaking because of being unsure or confused; hesitate. The student *faltered* in speaking before so many people.
fal·ter (fôl′tər) *verb,* **faltered, faltering.**

fame The quality of being famous or well-known. The tennis player's *fame* spread across the country.
fame (fām) *noun.*

familiar **1.** Often heard or seen. Cows are a *familiar* sight on a farm. **2.** Known because of having been heard or seen before. The announcer's voice was *familiar.* **3.** Knowing something well. A good mechanic is *familiar* with all sorts of tools. **4.** Friendly or informal; close. Soon I was on *familiar* terms with our new neighbors.
fa·mil·iar (fə mil′yər) *adjective.*

Word History

The word **familiar** goes back to a Latin word meaning "household." People in a household are people with whom you are *familiar.*

family **1.** A group of people who are related and who live together, including parents, children, and sometimes other relatives. The average *family* has three or four members. **2.** The children of a father and mother. My parents raised a large *family.* **3.** A group of people who are related to each other; relatives. The whole *family* will get together for the holidays. **4.** A group of related animals or plants. Zebras and donkeys belong to the horse *family.* **5.** Any group of things that are similar or connected to each other in some way. English and German belong to the same *family* of languages.
fam·i·ly (fam′ə lē *or* fam′lē) *noun, plural* **families.**

famine A great lack of food in an area or country. Many people died of starvation during the *famine* in Ireland in the 1840s.
fam·ine (fam′in) *noun, plural* **famines.**

famous Very well-known; having great fame. Thomas Edison is *famous* for having invented the electric light. A crowd of fans gathered around the *famous* baseball player to ask for his autograph.
fa·mous (fā′məs) *adjective.*

fan¹ **1.** A device that is held in the hand and waved back and forth to make air move. **2.** A mechanical device having several blades that are turned by an electric motor. Fans are used to make air move for cooling or heating. **3.** Anything that looks like a fan. The open tail of the peacock is called a fan. *Noun.*
—To move air toward or on. I am *fanning* the flames of the fire to make it burn more. *Fan* yourself with a newspaper to keep cool. *Verb.*
fan (fan) *noun, plural* **fans;** *verb,* **fanned, fanning.**

fan² A person who is very interested in or enthusiastic about something. Some football *fans* watch games on television all weekend.
fan (fan) *noun, plural* **fans.**

fanatic A person who is much too devoted to a cause or too enthusiastic about something. The teenager was a *fanatic* about sports and even played tennis in the rain. *Noun.*
—Much too devoted or enthusiastic. *Fanatic*

at; āpe; fär; câre; end; mē; it; īce; pîerce; hot; ōld; sông, fôrk; oil; out; up; ūse; rüle; pùll; tûrn; chin; sing; shop; thin; <u>th</u>is; hw in white; zh in treasure. The symbol ə stands for the unstressed vowel sound in about, taken, pencil, lemon, and circus.

chess players sometimes play all night long. *Adjective.*
fa·nat·ic (fə nat′ik) *noun, plural* **fanatics;** *adjective.*

fancy **1.** The picturing of things in the mind; imagination. A unicorn is a creature of *fancy.* **2.** Something that is imagined in a playful or wishful way. Being a movie star was the young teenager's favorite *fancy.* **3.** A liking or fondness. Some writers have a *fancy* for big words. *Noun.*
—Very decorated. The *fancy* dress had ruffles along the hem and a pink sash. *Adjective.*
—**1.** To imagine in a playful or wishful way. I like to *fancy* myself as a famous baseball player. **2.** To be fond of; like. Which of these lovely hats do you *fancy* the most? *Verb.*
fan·cy (fan′sē) *noun, plural* **fancies;** *adjective,* **fancier, fanciest;** *verb,* **fancied, fancying.**

fang A long, pointed tooth used to grip and hold prey. The fangs of certain snakes are hollow and can inject poison.
fang (fang) *noun, plural* **fangs.**

fantastic **1.** Very strange; odd. Driftwood sometimes has *fantastic* shapes. **2.** Very good; excellent. The hikers had a *fantastic* view from the hilltop.
fan·tas·tic (fan tas′tik) *adjective.*

fantasy **1.** Playful or wishful imagination. Your claim that you can fly is pure *fantasy.* **2.** A story with characters, places, or events that are very strange. The author wrote *fantasies* about life on other planets.
fan·ta·sy (fan′tə sē) *noun, plural* **fantasies.**

far **1.** At a great distance; not near. We traveled *far* from home to visit our grandparents. **2.** To or at a certain place, distance, or time. The meeting lasted *far* into the afternoon. **3.** Very much. It would be *far* better if you waited to leave until the rain stops. *Adverb.*
—**1.** At a great distance; distant. New York is *far* from California. Polar bears live in the *far* north. **2.** More distant; farther away. The spacecraft landed on the *far* side of the moon. *Adjective.*
• **as far as.** To the distance, degree, or extent that. *As far as* I know, no one has yet run a mile in less than 3½ minutes.
• **so far.** **1.** Until now. It could rain later, but *so far* it's been a nice day. **2.** To a certain point. The road only goes *so far* into the park; then it becomes a trail.
far (fär) *adverb,* **farther** or **further, farthest** or **furthest;** *adjective,* **farther** or **further, farthest** or **furthest.**

faraway **1.** At a great distance away; remote. The sailor traveled to *faraway* places. **2.** Showing deep thought; dreamy. There is a *faraway* look in the eyes of that quiet child.
far·a·way (fär′ə wā′) *adjective.*

fare **1.** The cost of a ride on a bus, train, airplane, ship, or taxi. The bus driver collected the *fares.* **2.** A passenger who pays a fare. The cab driver had five *fares* during the morning. *Noun.*
—To get along; do. Are you *faring* well at your new school? *Verb.* ▲ Another word that sounds like this is **fair.**
fare (fâr) *noun, plural* **fares;** *verb,* **fared, faring.**

farewell Good-bye and good luck. *"Farewell!"* said the passengers as the ship pulled away. The guests said their *farewells* and left.
fare·well (fâr′wel′) *interjection; noun, plural* **farewells.**

farm **1.** A piece of land that is used to raise crops or animals. **2.** An enclosed area of water in which fish or shellfish are raised. *Noun.*
—**1.** To raise crops or animals on a farm. Most of the people in this valley *farm* for a living. **2.** To cultivate. The settlers had to remove trees and rocks before they could *farm* the land. *Verb.*
farm (färm) *noun, plural* **farms;** *verb,* **farmed, farming.**

farm

farmer A person who owns or works on a farm.
farm·er (fär′mər) *noun, plural* **farmers.**

farming The business of raising crops or animals on a farm; agriculture. Most of the people in that area are involved in *farming.*
farm·ing (fär′ming) *noun.*

farsighted Able to see things that are far away more clearly than things that are close. Many *farsighted* people wear glasses for reading but not for driving.
far·sight·ed (fär′sī′tid) *adjective.*

farther A comparative of **far.** The little boat drifted *farther* from the dock. The *farther* mountain seems smaller than the nearer one. Look up **far** for more information.
far·ther (fär′thər) *adverb; adjective.*

Language Note

Farther and **further** can sometimes be confused. Use **farther** when you are speaking about distances. We live *farther* from town than you do. Use **further** when you mean "additional" or "additionally." There are two *further* points that I want to make.

---

farthest A superlative of **far.** I sat *farthest* from the front of the room. He lives *farthest* from school. The town lies just over the *farthest* hill. Look up **far** for more information.
far·thest (fär′thist) *adverb; adjective.*

fascinate To attract and hold the interest of; charm. The magician's tricks *fascinated* the children in the audience.
fas·ci·nate (fas′ə nāt′) *verb,* **fascinated, fascinating.**

fashion **1.** The current custom or style in dress or behavior. It's the *fashion* now to carry books in backpacks. **2.** Manner or way. During the fire, residents left the building in an orderly *fashion. Noun.*
—To give form to; make; shape. I tried to *fashion* a boat out of a block of wood. *Verb.*
fash·ion (fash′ən) *noun, plural* **fashions;** *verb,* **fashioned, fashioning.**

fast¹ **1.** Acting, moving, or done in a short time; quick; rapid. A *fast* train rushed by. *Fast* thinkers can make decisions quickly. **2.** Ahead of the correct time. My watch is ten minutes *fast.* **3.** Faithful; loyal. Those two have been *fast* friends since they were in college. **4.** Firmly attached; secure. If you can get a *fast* grip on the ladder, I'll climb up. **5.** Not easily faded. Are the colors in this material *fast? Adjective.*
—**1.** In a firm way; tightly; securely. The tent was held *fast* by poles driven into the ground. **2.** Soundly; deeply. You have been *fast* asleep since nine o'clock. **3.** With speed; quickly. The horse ran *fast. Adverb.*
fast (fast) *adjective; adverb,* **faster, fastest.**

fast² To eat little or no food, or only certain kinds of food. In many religions, people *fast* on certain holy days. *Verb.*
—A day or period of fasting. *Noun.*
fast (fast) *verb,* **fasted, fasting;** *noun, plural* **fasts.**

fasten **1.** To attach firmly. Mother *fastened* the gold pin to her dress. **2.** To close so that it will not come loose or open; secure. Please *fasten* the door when you leave. **3.** To direct steadily; fix. He *fastened* his attention on the book he was reading.
fas·ten (fas′ən) *verb,* **fastened, fastening.**

fastener A device that is used to hold things together. A snap, buckle, zipper, and paper clip are all fasteners.
fas·ten·er (fas′ə nər) *noun, plural* **fasteners.**

fast food A food that can be cooked easily and quickly, without much preparation, and then sold to customers.

fat A yellowish or whitish oily substance. Fat is found in certain body tissues of animals and in some plants.
—**1.** Having much fat or flesh on the body. **2.** Having much in it; full. All that money makes your wallet *fat. Adjective.*
fat (fat) *noun, plural* **fats;** *adjective,* **fatter, fattest.**

fatal **1.** Causing death. There are many *fatal* accidents on the highways. **2.** Causing great harm; very bad. Risking all your money in one investment could be a *fatal* mistake.
fa·tal (fā′təl) *adjective.*

fate **1.** The power that is believed to control what is going to happen or how things will turn out. Some gamblers think that *fate* is on their side and will make them win. **2.** What finally happens to someone or something; final outcome. It was my *fate* to be last in line.
fate (fāt) *noun, plural* **fates.**

father **1.** A male parent. **2.** A man who is important in beginning or inventing something. George Washington is called the *father* of his country. **3.** A priest.
fa·ther (fä′thər) *noun, plural* **fathers.**

father-in-law The father of one's husband or wife.
fa·ther-in-law (fä′thər in lô′) *noun, plural* **fathers-in-law.**

fathom A measure of length equal to 6 feet. Fathoms are used mainly in measuring the depth of the ocean.
fath·om (fath′əm) *noun, plural* **fathoms** or **fathom.**

---

at; āpe; fär; câre; end; mē; it; īce; pîerce; hot; ōld; sông, fôrk; oil; out; up; ūse; rüle; pu̇ll; tûrn; chin; sing; shop; thin; this; hw in white; zh in treasure. The symbol ə stands for the unstressed vowel sound in about, taken, pencil, lemon, and circus.

F

fatigue   The condition of being tired. After nine hours on the road, the truck driver was suffering from *fatigue. Noun.*
—To cause to be tired. The long hours of studying *fatigued* me. *Verb.*
fa·tigue (fə tēg′) *noun; verb,* **fatigued, fatiguing.**

fatten   To make or become fat. The farmer *fattened* the turkeys for Thanksgiving. Our pigs *fattened* on grain and scraps.
fat·ten (fat′ən) *verb,* **fattened, fattening.**

faucet   A device for turning on or off the flow of water or another liquid from a pipe, sink, or container.
fau·cet (fô′sit) *noun, plural* **faucets.**

fault   **1.** Something that is wrong with and spoils something else. The roof of the house fell in because of a *fault* in the beams. A bad temper is a serious *fault* in a person. **2.** The responsibility for a mistake. It was my *fault* that I was late to class.   **3.** A mistake; error. The teacher corrected the spelling *faults* on the student's paper.
• **to find fault with.**   To criticize. Why did you *find fault with* my ideas for the party?
fault (fôlt) *noun, plural* **faults.**

favor   **1.** An act of kindness. I did them a *favor* by giving them a ride to school. **2.** Friendliness or approval; liking. The candidate won the *favor* of the voters and was elected.   **3.** A small gift. All the children at the party were given horns, balloons, and other *favors. Noun.*
—**1.** To show kindness or favor to; oblige. Please *favor* us with an answer to our letter. **2.** To approve of; believe in; support. The candidate *favored* a change in the law. **3.** To show special treatment or kindness. The mother cat *favored* the sick kitten over the others.   **4.** To look like; resemble. The baby *favors* his father. *Verb.*
• **in favor of.**   **1.** Approving of; supporting. Everyone in the class was *in favor of* the field trip.   **2.** To the advantage of. The score is three to one *in favor of* the home team.
fa·vor (fā′vər) *noun, plural* **favors;** *verb,* **favored, favoring.**

favorable   **1.** Showing approval or liking; approving. I hoped you would give me a *favorable* answer and say you could come to the party.   **2.** In one's favor; benefiting. If the weather is *favorable,* we'll go on a picnic.
fa·vor·a·ble (fā′vər ə bəl) *adjective.*

favorite   Liked best. What is your *favorite* baseball team? Summer is my *favorite* time of year. *Adjective.*
—A person or thing that is liked best. Mystery and adventure stories are my *favorites. Noun.*
fa·vor·ite (fā′vər it) *adjective; noun, plural* **favorites.**

fawn   A young deer.
fawn (fôn) *noun, plural* **fawns.**

fawn

fear   A strong feeling caused by knowing that danger, pain, or evil is near. The people of the town felt great *fear* when the lion escaped from the zoo. *Noun.*
—**1.** To be afraid of. The baby *fears* the dark.   **2.** To be worried or anxious. I *fear* that we will be late getting to the theater if we don't hurry. *Verb.*
fear (fîr) *noun, plural* **fears;** *verb,* **feared, fearing.**

fearful   **1.** Feeling or showing fear; afraid. The cat was *fearful* of the barking dog. **2.** Causing fear; frightening. The thunder and lightning were *fearful.*
fear·ful (fîr′fəl) *adjective.*

fearless   Feeling or showing no fear; brave. The firefighters seemed calm and *fearless.*
fear·less (fîr′lis) *adjective.*

feast   A large, rich meal on a special occasion. After the wedding, the two families gathered for a *feast. Noun.*
—To have a feast; eat richly. We *feasted* on turkey and stuffing on Thanksgiving. *Verb.*
feast (fēst) *noun, plural* **feasts;** *verb,* **feasted, feasting.**

feat   An act or deed that shows great courage, strength, or skill. Climbing that mountain was quite a *feat.* ▲ Another word that sounds like this is **feet.**
feat (fēt) *noun, plural* **feats.**

feather   One of the light, soft body parts that cover a bird's skin. Feathers protect the bird's skin from injury, help keep the bird warm, and help it to fly. *Noun.*

—To supply, line, or cover with feathers. The birds *feathered* the inside of their nest. *Verb.*

feath·er (fe<u>th</u>′ər) *noun, plural* **feathers;** *verb,* **feathered, feathering.**

fans made of dyed **feathers**

feature 1. A part or quality of something. An important *feature* of the camel is its ability to go for days without water. 2. A part of the face. The eyes, nose, mouth, and chin are features. 3. A motion picture of standard length. We arrived late and missed ten minutes of the *feature.* 4. A story of special interest in a newspaper or magazine. *Noun.*
—To have as a main attraction. The concert *features* a folk singer and a guitar player. *Verb.*

fea·ture (fē′chər) *noun, plural* **features;** *verb,* **featured, featuring.**

Feb. An abbreviation for *February.*

February The second month of the year. February has twenty-eight days except in a leap year, when it has twenty-nine.

Feb·ru·ar·y (feb′rü er′ē *or* feb′ū er′ē) *noun, plural* **Februaries.**

Word History

The word **February** comes from the Latin name of a religious holiday that the ancient Romans used to hold in the middle of this month.

fed Past tense and past participle of **feed.** Have you *fed* the dog today? Look up **feed** for more information.
• **fed up.** Annoyed, bored, or disgusted. After waiting an hour for them, we got *fed up* and left.
fed (fed) *verb.*

federal 1. Formed by an agreement between states or provinces to join together as one nation. The United States has a *federal* government. 2. Having to do with the central government of the United States, thought of as separate from the government of each state. The power to provide for defense is a *federal* power.
fed·er·al (fed′ər əl) *adjective.*

federation A union formed by agreement between states, nations, or other groups. Several countries formed a *federation* to work for world peace.
fed·er·a·tion (fed′ə rā′shən) *noun, plural* **federations.**

fee Money requested or paid for some service or right. We paid a *fee* of ten dollars for a license for our dog.
fee (fē) *noun, plural* **fees.**

feeble Not strong; weak. The *feeble* patient needed a cane to walk.
fee·ble (fē′bəl) *adjective,* **feebler, feeblest.**

feed 1. To give food to. May I *feed* the baby? 2. To give as food. We *fed* oats to the horse. 3. To supply with something. Melting snow from the mountains *feeds* the rivers each spring. I'm learning how to *feed* information into a computer. 4. To take in food; eat. The cows are *feeding* in the pasture. Frogs *feed* on flies. *Verb.*
—Food for farm animals. Grass, hay, and grains are *feed* for cattle. Farmers often buy special *feeds* for their livestock. *Noun.*
feed (fēd) *verb,* **fed, feeding;** *noun, plural* **feeds.**

feel 1. To find out about by touching or handling; touch. The doctor *felt* my pulse. My mother *felt* my forehead to see if I had a temperature. 2. To be aware of by touch. Can you *feel* the rain on your face? 3. To seem to be. The water *feels* warm. 4. To be. I *felt* happy. We're *feeling* tired. 5. To have an impression; think. I *feel* that I haven't done my share. 6. To try to find by touching. We *felt* our way up the stairs in the dark. *Verb.*
—The way that something seems to the touch. I like the warm *feel* of wool against my skin. *Noun.*

at; āpe; fär; câre; end; mē; it; īce; pîerce; hot; ōld; sông, fôrk; oil; out; up; ūse; rüle; pùll; tûrn; chin; sing; shop; thin; <u>th</u>is; hw in white; zh in treasure. The symbol ə stands for the unstressed vowel sound in about, taken, pencil, lemon, and circus.

• **to feel like.** To have an interest in or desire for. Do you *feel like* going to a museum today?
feel (fēl) *verb,* **felt, feeling;** *noun, plural* **feels.**

The mouse **feels** soft.

feeler A part of an animal's body that is used for touching things. Many insects have feelers on their heads.
feel·er (fē′lər) *noun, plural* **feelers.**

feeling **1.** The ability to feel by touching; sense of touch. Rub your cold hands to bring back the *feeling.* **2.** The condition of being aware; awareness; sensation. Having missed breakfast, I had a *feeling* of hunger long before noon. **3.** An emotion. Joy, fear, and anger are feelings. **4. feelings.** The tender or sensitive part of a person's nature. Some people's *feelings* are hurt when you don't say hello to them. **5.** An opinion; belief. It is my *feeling* that you are right about what happened.
feel·ing (fē′ling) *noun, plural* **feelings.**

feet More than one foot. Look up **foot** for more information. ⚠ Another word that sounds like this is **feat.**
feet (fēt) *plural noun.*

feign To put on a false show of; pretend. Opossums *feign* death to escape their enemies.
feign (fān) *verb,* **feigned, feigning.**

feint A blow or movement meant to trick or take away attention from the real or main point of attack. *Noun.*
—To make a feint. The boxer *feinted* with the left hand and then punched with the right. *Verb.* ⚠ Another word that sounds like this is **faint.**
feint (fānt) *noun, plural* **feints;** *verb,* **feinted, feinting.**

fell¹ Past tense of **fall.** The horse slipped on the ice and *fell.* Look up **fall** for more information.
fell (fel) *verb.*

fell² **1.** To hit and knock down; cause to fall. One of the boxers *felled* the other. **2.** To cut down. The lumberjack *felled* the tree.
fell (fel) *verb,* **felled, felling.**

fellow **1.** A man or boy. He is certainly a clever *fellow* to come up with such a good idea. **2.** A person who is like another; companion; associate. Scientists like to talk with their *fellows* at professional meetings. *Noun.*
—Belonging to the same group or kind. On the first day of work I met my *fellow* workers. *Adjective.*
fel·low (fel′ō) *noun, plural* **fellows;** *adjective.*

fellowship **1.** A warm, friendly feeling among people; companionship. We all enjoyed the *fellowship* at the club. **2.** A group of people with common interests or goals.
fel·low·ship (fel′ō ship′) *noun, plural* **fellowships.**

felt¹ Past tense and past participle of **feel.** I *felt* the cold wind against my face. The loss of our best player was *felt* by the whole team. Look up **feel** for more information.
felt (felt) *verb.*

felt² A material made of wool, hair, or fur that is pressed together in layers instead of being woven or knitted. Felt is used to make hats.
felt (felt) *noun, plural* **felts.**

female **1.** Of or having to do with the sex that gives birth to young or produces eggs. A mare is a *female* horse. **2.** Having to do with women or girls; feminine. *Adjective.*
—A female person or animal. Our dog is a *female.* There was an equal number of *females* and males in the medical study. *Noun.*
fe·male (fē′māl) *adjective; noun, plural* **females.**

feminine Of or having to do with women or girls. "Mary" is a *feminine* name.
fem·i·nine (fem′ə nin) *adjective.*

fence **1.** A structure that is used to surround, protect, or mark off an area. There was a white wooden *fence* in front of the house. **2.** A person who buys and sells stolen goods. The thief took the stolen diamonds to a *fence. Noun.*

—1. To put a fence around. We *fenced* our vegetable garden to keep rabbits out. In the spring, part of the park is *fenced* off for a ball field. **2.** To fight with a sword or a foil; take part in the sport of fencing. *Verb.*
fence (fens) *noun, plural* **fences;** *verb,* **fenced, fencing.**

fencing   The art or sport of fighting with a sword or a foil.
fenc·ing (fen′sing) *noun.*

fencing

fender   **1.** A metal piece that sticks out over the wheel of an automobile or bicycle for protection against splashed water or mud. **2.** A metal screen in front of a fireplace to protect against sparks.
fend·er (fen′dər) *noun, plural* **fenders.**

ferment   To undergo or cause a chemical change that results in the formation of bubbles of gas. When the juice of grapes *ferments,* it turns into wine. *Verb.*
—1. Something that causes a substance to ferment. Yeast is used as a *ferment* in making wine. **2.** A state of excitement and activity. The school was in a *ferment* over who would be the new principal. *Noun.*
fer·ment (fər ment′ *for verb;* fûr′ment *for noun*) *verb,* **fermented, fermenting;** *noun, plural* **ferments.**

fern   A plant that has large leaves called fronds and no flowers. Ferns reproduce by means of spores instead of seeds.
fern (fûrn) *noun, plural* **ferns.**

ferocious   Likely to make violent attacks; savage; fierce. A lion can be *ferocious.*
fe·ro·cious (fə rō′shəs) *adjective.*

fern

ferret

ferret   A long, thin animal that is related to the weasel. They are sometimes domesticated and trained to hunt rats, mice, and rabbits. *Noun.*
—1. To hunt with ferrets. **2.** To look for; search. I *ferreted* through my drawers looking for the missing sock. *Verb.*
fer·ret (fer′it) *noun, plural* **ferrets;** *verb,* **ferreted, ferreting.**

Ferris wheel   A large, upright revolving wheel with seats that are hung from the rim. It is used as a ride at fairs and amusement parks.
Fer·ris wheel (fer′is).

ferry   A boat used to carry people, cars, and goods across a river, channel, or other narrow body of water. *Noun.*
—To go or carry in a ferry. We *ferried* to the island in an old steamboat. The rescue workers *ferried* the storm victims to land. *Verb.*
fer·ry (fer′ē) *noun, plural* **ferries;** *verb,* **ferried, ferrying.**

fertile   **1.** Able to produce crops and plants easily and plentifully. There is very *fertile* soil in this valley. **2.** Able to produce eggs, seeds, pollen, or young. An animal is *fertile* when it is able to give birth to young. **3.** Able to develop into or become a new person or animal. An egg must be *fertile* in order for a chick to hatch from it. **4.** Thinking up many good ideas; creative. The poet has a *fertile* imagination.
fer·tile (fûr′təl) *adjective.*

fertilize   **1.** To make fertile. **2.** To put fertilizer on. The farmer *fertilized* the field with manure.
fer·ti·lize (fûr′tə līz′) *verb,* **fertilized, fertilizing.**

fertilizer   A substance that is added to soil to make it better for the growing of crops.

at; āpe; fär; câre; end; mē; it; īce; pîerce; hot; ōld; sông, fôrk; oil; out; up; ūse; rüle; pùll; tûrn; chin; sing; shop; thin; this; hw in white; zh in treasure. The symbol ə stands for the unstressed vowel sound in about, taken, pencil, lemon, and circus.

F

Manure and certain chemicals are used as fertilizers.
fer·ti·liz·er (fûr′tə lī′zər) *noun, plural* **fertilizers.**

festival **1.** A celebration or holiday. Many religious *festivals* take place throughout the year. **2.** A period of special activities or shows. Ten new movies are being shown at this year's film *festival.*
fes·ti·val (fes′tə vəl) *noun, plural* **festivals.**

festivity **1.** The rejoicing and fun that occur during a celebration. The party was full of *festivity.* **2. festivities.** Activities that are part of a celebration. Parades and concerts were among the *festivities* when the town celebrated its hundredth anniversary.
fes·tiv·i·ty (fes tiv′i tē) *noun, plural* **festivities.**

fetch To go after and bring back; get. Please *fetch* two more chairs from the other room.
fetch (fech) *verb,* **fetched, fetching.**

feud A bitter quarrel that lasts for a long time. The *feud* between the two countries resulted in the deaths of many people.
feud (fūd) *noun, plural* **feuds.**

feudalism A political and economic system in the western part of Europe during the Middle Ages. Under feudalism, a lord provided land and protection for people under his rule, who were known as vassals. In return they gave services and a share of their crops to the lord.
feu·dal·ism (fū′də liz′əm) *noun.*

fever A body temperature that is higher than normal. Most people have a fever if their temperature is more than 98.6 degrees Fahrenheit. A fever usually means that a person is fighting an infection.
fe·ver (fē′vər) *noun, plural* **fevers.**

few Not many. *Few* people live to be a hundred years old. *Adjective.*
—A small number of persons or things. Only a *few* of the papers had been sold. *Noun.*
few (fū) *adjective,* **fewer, fewest;** *noun.*

fiancé A man to whom a woman is engaged to be married.
fi·an·cé (fē′än sā′) *noun, plural* **fiancés.**

fiancée A woman to whom a man is engaged to be married.
fi·an·cée (fē′än sā′) *noun, plural* **fiancées.**

fib A lie about something unimportant. I told a *fib* about the size of the fish that I caught. *Noun.*
—To tell a lie about something unimportant. Why did you *fib* about your age? *Verb.*
fib (fib) *noun, plural* **fibs;** *verb,* **fibbed, fibbing.**

fiber **1.** A long, thin piece of material. Cotton *fibers* can be spun into thread. The rope was made of hemp *fibers.* **2.** Material in a plant that cannot be digested by the body; roughage. Fiber helps move food through the intestines. Bran, fruit, vegetables, and whole-wheat bread have much fiber.
fi·ber (fī′bər) *noun, plural* **fibers.**

fiberglass A strong material that is made of fine threads of glass. Fiberglass does not burn easily. It is used for insulation, in textiles, and in the making of boats and automobiles.
fi·ber·glass (fī′bər glas′) *noun.*

fiction **1.** Written works that tell a story or stories about characters and events that are not real. Novels and short stories are fiction. **2.** Something that is imaginary or not true. The monster turned out to be a *fiction.*
fic·tion (fik′shən) *noun, plural* **fictions.**

fiddle A violin. *Noun.*
—**1.** To play a violin. **2.** To make aimless movements with the hands. I *fiddled* nervously with my pencil while I listened. *Verb.*
fid·dle (fid′əl) *noun, plural* **fiddles;** *verb,* **fiddled, fiddling.**

field **1.** A piece of open or cleared land. We could see the farmer in the wheat *field.* **2.** Land that contains or gives a natural resource. There were about ten oil wells in the oil *field.* **3.** An area of land on which a game is played. The players have just come out onto the football *field.* **4.** An area of interest or activity. The two friends both hope to work in the *field* of medicine when they get out of college. *Noun.*
—To catch, stop, or pick up a ball that has been hit in baseball. The shortstop *fielded* the ball and threw it to first base. *Verb.*
field (fēld) *noun, plural* **fields;** *verb,* **fielded, fielding.**

fielder A baseball player who has a position in the field while the other team is at bat.
field·er (fēl′dər) *noun, plural* **fielders.**

field glasses A pair of binoculars.

field trip A trip away from the classroom to see things and learn. Classes take *field trips* to museums, parks, and other places.

fierce **1.** Likely to make violent attacks; dangerous; savage. Bears are shy animals, but they can become *fierce* if they are cornered. **2.** Very strong or violent; raging. The *fierce* storm blew down several trees.
fierce (fîrs) *adjective,* **fiercer, fiercest.**

fiesta A festival or celebration. In many Latin American countries, fiestas are held in honor of certain saints.
fi·es·ta (fē es′tə) *noun, plural* **fiestas.**

F

fife A musical instrument like a flute. The fife makes a high, clear sound and is often used with drums in a marching band.
fife (fīf) *noun, plural* **fifes.**

fifteen Five more than ten; 15.
fif·teen (fif′tēn′) *noun, plural* **fifteens;** *adjective.*

fifteenth Next after the fourteenth. *Adjective, noun.*
—One of fifteen equal parts; ¹⁄₁₅. *Noun.*
fif·teenth (fif′tēnth′) *adjective; noun, plural* **fifteenths.**

fifth Next after the fourth. *Adjective, noun.*
—One of five equal parts; ⅕. *Noun.*
fifth (fifth) *adjective; noun, plural* **fifths.**

fiftieth Next after the forty-ninth. *Adjective, noun.*
—One of fifty equal parts; ¹⁄₅₀. *Noun.*
fif·ti·eth (fif′tē ith) *adjective; noun, plural* **fiftieths.**

fifty Five times ten; 50.
fif·ty (fif′tē) *noun, plural* **fifties;** *adjective.*

fig The sweet fruit of a shrub or small tree that grows in warm regions. Figs have many tiny seeds. Figs are often preserved by drying.
fig (fig) *noun, plural* **figs.**

Halved Fig   Whole Fig   Leaves

fig

fight **1.** A struggle between animals, persons, or groups who use weapons or their bodies against each other. In a fight, each side tries to hurt the other or to protect itself against the other. The two dogs had a *fight* over the bone. **2.** A quarrel. Let's not have a *fight* over which TV program to watch. **3.** A hard effort to gain a goal; struggle. We all admired the child's brave *fight* to recover from the disease. *Noun.*
—**1.** To use weapons or the body to try to hurt or overcome. The parade honored all those who had *fought* in the war. **2.** To struggle against; try to gain power over. The firefighters *fought* the blaze for hours. **3.** To carry on a battle, contest, or struggle. The survivors of the accident *fought* for their lives. I had to *fight* the urge to have another cookie. *Verb.*
fight (fīt) *noun, plural* **fights;** *verb,* **fought, fighting.**

fighter **1.** A person who fights. **2.** A person who boxes; boxer.
fight·er (fī′tər) *noun, plural* **fighters.**

figure **1.** A symbol that stands for a number. 0, 1, 2, 3, 4, and 5 are figures. **2.** An amount given in figures. The population *figures* of the cities and towns are given on the back of the map. **3. figures.** The use of number symbols to solve problems; arithmetic. You're good at *figures.* **4.** A form or outline; shape. I saw the *figure* of a dog in the moonlight. The ballet dancer had a slim *figure.* **5.** A person; character. The mayor is a public *figure.* **6.** A design; pattern. The cloth had bright red *figures* on it. *Noun.*
—**1.** To find out by using numbers; calculate. My parents *figured* the cost of the trip. **2.** To stand out; have importance; appear. Several well-known people *figured* in the news today. *Verb.*
• **to figure out.** To learn, understand, or solve. I couldn't *figure out* how the magician did any of the magic tricks.
fig·ure (fig′yər) *noun, plural* **figures;** *verb,* **figured, figuring.**

figurehead **1.** A carved wooden figure placed on the bow of a ship for decoration. The *figurehead* was carved in the shape of a bird. **2.** A person who has a title that sounds important but who has no real power or responsibility. The king and queen were only *figureheads* because they had no power in the government.
fig·ure·head (fig′yər hed′) *noun, plural* **figureheads.**

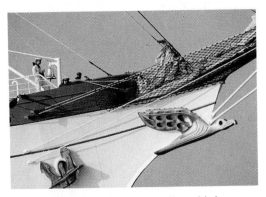

figurehead that looks like a bird

at; āpe; fär; câre; end; mē; it; īce; pîerce; hot; ōld; sông, fôrk; oil; out; up; ūse; rüle; pùll; tûrn; chin; sing; shop; thin; this; hw in white; zh in treasure. The symbol ə stands for the unstressed vowel sound in about, taken, pencil, lemon, and circus.

figure of speech An expression in which words are used in a way that is different from their true or main meanings. Figures of speech are used to make writing or speaking fresher and more expressive. "When I saw I was late, I flew out of the house" is a *figure of speech.*

filament A very fine thread or wire. In an electric light bulb, the filament is a fine wire that gives off light when an electric current passes through it.
fil·a·ment (fil′ə mənt) *noun, plural* **filaments.**

file[1] **1.** A folder, drawer, cabinet, or other container in which papers, cards, or records are arranged in order. **2.** A set of papers, cards, or records arranged in order. I keep a *file* of important addresses on my desk. **3.** A collection of information, program instructions, or words stored on a computer disk. Each file has a name that identifies it. **4.** A line of persons, animals, or things placed one behind the other. We hiked along the trail in a single *file. Noun.*
—**1.** To put away in a set of papers, cards, or records arranged in order. The secretary *filed* the letters in a big cabinet. **2.** To hand in or put on a record. The police officer *filed* a report of the accident. **3.** To march or move in a file. The passengers *filed* off the airplane. *Verb.*
file (fīl) *noun, plural* **files;** *verb,* **filed, filing.**

file[2] A metal tool having many tiny ridges on one or two sides. A file is used to cut, smooth, or grind down hard surfaces. *Noun.*
—To cut, smooth, or grind with a file. I *filed* my fingernails. *Verb.*
file (fīl) *noun, plural* **files;** *verb,* **filed, filing.**

filet A spelling sometimes used for the word **fillet.** Look up **fillet** for more information.
fi·let (fi lā′ *or* fil′ā) *noun, plural* **filets;** *verb,* **fileted, fileting.**

filings Small bits of a material that have been removed by a file. A magnet attracts iron *filings.*
fil·ings (fī′lingz) *plural noun.*

fill **1.** To make or become full. Please *fill* the bucket with water. The room *filled* with fresh air when we opened the window. **2.** To take up the whole space of. The students *filled* the auditorium. **3.** To give or have whatever is asked for or needed. The grocery store *filled* our order. You *fill* the requirements for the job. **4.** To stop up or close up by putting something in. The painter *filled* the hole in the wall with plaster

before painting. The dentist *filled* a cavity in my tooth. **5.** To do the duties or job of. Who will *fill* the office of treasurer when you retire? *Verb.*
—Something used to fill. Gravel was used as *fill* for the hole in the road. *Noun.*
• **to fill in.** **1.** To complete by writing something. *Fill in* all the blanks on the test as quickly as you can. **2.** To write something that is missing or needed. *Fill in* your name and address in the space provided on the form. **3.** To act as a substitute. An assistant *filled in* when our teacher was absent.
• **to fill up.** To make or become completely full. The bathtub *filled up* with water in a few minutes.
fill (fil) *verb,* **filled, filling;** *noun, plural* **fills.**

fillet A slice of meat or fish without bones or fat. *Noun.* This word is sometimes spelled **filet.**
—To cut meat or fish into fillets. *Verb.*
fil·let (fi lā′ *or* fil′ā) *noun, plural* **fillets;** *verb,* **filleted, filleting.**

filling A substance used to fill something. We used cherries as a *filling* for the pie. I broke the *filling* in one of my teeth when I bit into the hard candy.
fill·ing (fil′ing) *noun, plural* **fillings.**

filly A young female horse.
fil·ly (fil′ē) *noun, plural* **fillies.**

film **1.** A very thin layer or covering. The windows were covered with a *film* of dirt. **2.** A thin roll or strip of material coated with a substance that changes when it is exposed to light. It is placed inside a camera and used to take photographs or to make motion pictures. **3.** A motion picture. *Noun.*
—**1.** To cover or become covered with a thin layer of something. The windows of the car were *filmed* with dust. **2.** To take pictures of with a motion-picture camera. We *filmed* the spacecraft as it took off. *Verb.*
film (film) *noun, plural* **films;** *verb,* **filmed, filming.**

filter A device or material with tiny spaces in it. A liquid or gas is passed through a filter in order to clean out any dirt or other matter. The paper *filter* in an air conditioner collects dust. *Noun.*
—**1.** To pass a liquid or air through a filter; strain. The water was *filtered* through sand. **2.** To take out or separate by a filter. The solid pieces of dirt were *filtered* from the water. **3.** To go through very slowly. The sunlight *filtered* through the trees. *Verb.*
fil·ter (fil′tər) *noun, plural* **filters;** *verb,* **filtered, filtering.**

filth Disgusting dirt or other material. The water in the pond was filled with garbage and other *filth*.
    filth (filth) *noun.*

filthy Extremely dirty; foul. No one wanted to swim in the *filthy* river.
    filth·y (fil'thē) *adjective,* **filthier, filthiest.**

fin **1.** One of the thin, flat parts that stick out from the body of a fish. A fish uses its fins to swim and balance itself in the water. Certain other water animals, such as whales and porpoises, also have fins. **2.** Something that has the same shape or use as a fin. Rockets often have fins to keep them steady during flight.
    fin (fin) *noun, plural* **fins.**

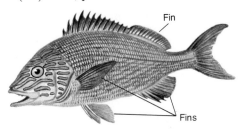

fins on a fish

final **1.** Coming at the end; last. I summed up my thoughts in the *final* paragraph of my essay. What was the *final* score of the game? **2.** Not to be changed. The decision of the judges is *final. Adjective.*
    —**1.** The last examination of a school or college course of study. All the students are studying for their history *finals.* **2.** The last or deciding game or match in a series. Our team played the *final* of the basketball tournament. *Noun.*
    fi·nal (fī'nəl) *adjective; noun, plural* **finals.**

finale The last part of something; conclusion. The band played a lively march as the *finale* of its concert.
    fi·na·le (fi nä'lē) *noun, plural* **finales.**

finalist A person who takes part in the final game or other contest in a series of games or contests. Each of the *finalists* had run 100 meters in less than 15 seconds.
    fi·nal·ist (fī'nə list) *noun, plural* **finalists.**

finally At the end; at last. We *finally* got home at midnight.
    fi·nal·ly (fī'nə lē) *adverb.*

finance **1.** The management of money matters for people, businesses, or governments. The president of that bank is an expert in *finance.* **2. finances.** The amount of money that a person, business, or government has; funds. My parents checked their *finances* to see if the family could afford a vacation. *Noun.*
    —To provide money for. Profits from the bake sale *financed* our field trip. *Verb.*
    fi·nance (fi nans' *or* fī'nans) *noun, plural* **finances;** *verb,* **financed, financing.**

financial Having to do with money matters. Banks, stock exchanges, and insurance companies handle *financial* affairs. Newspapers often have a *financial* section.
    fi·nan·cial (fi nan'shəl *or* fī nan'shəl) *adjective.*

finch A small songbird that has a strong bill that is shaped like a cone. There are many different kinds of finches. They feed mostly on seeds.
    finch (finch) *noun, plural* **finches.**

find **1.** To discover or come upon by accident; happen on. I *found* a wallet on the sidewalk. **2.** To get or learn by thinking or calculating. Please *find* the sum of this column of numbers. **3.** To learn or discover. I *found* that I could not study well with the radio on. Scientists *found* a cure for the disease. **4.** To look for and get something lost or left. I searched through my desk and *found* my old compass. **5.** To come to a decision about and declare. The jury *found* the accused person guilty. *Verb.*
    —Something that is found. I came up with some great *finds* in the attic. *Noun.*
    • **to find out.** To learn. Try to *find out* what time the meeting is.
    find (fīnd) *verb,* **found, finding;** *noun, plural* **finds.**

fine¹ **1.** Of very high quality; very good; excellent. That pianist is a *fine* musician. **2.** Very small or thin. I used a *fine* thread to sew on the button. That book has *fine* print. **3.** Without clouds or rain; clear. We're having *fine* weather. *Adjective.*
    —Very well. Both the children are doing *fine* in school. *Adverb.*
    fine (fīn) *adjective,* **finer, finest;** *adverb.*

fine² An amount of money paid as a punishment for breaking a rule or law. There is a *fine* of fifty dollars for littering. *Noun.*
    —To punish by making pay a fine. The judge *fined* the driver for going through a red light. *Verb.*
    fine (fīn) *noun, plural* **fines;** *verb,* **fined, fining.**

at; āpe; fär; câre; end; mē; it; īce; pîerce; hot; ōld; sông, fôrk; oil; out; up; ūse; rüle; půll; tûrn; chin; sing; shop; thin; this; hw in white; zh in treasure. The symbol ə stands for the unstressed vowel sound in about, taken, pencil, lemon, and circus.

finger **1.** One of the five separate parts at the end of the hand. Usually, a person is said to have four fingers and a thumb. **2.** A part of a glove that covers a finger. *Noun.*
—To touch, handle, or play with the fingers. The pirate *fingered* the gold coins in the treasure chest. *Verb.*
  fin·ger (fing′gər) *noun, plural* **fingers;** *verb,* **fingered, fingering.**

fingernail A thin, hard layer of material that grows at the end of each finger. Fingernails help to protect the tips of the fingers.
  fin·ger·nail (fing′gər nāl′) *noun, plural* **fingernails.**

fingerprint An impression of the markings on the tip of a finger. Fingerprints help to identify people because no two people have the same fingerprints. *Noun.*
—To take the fingerprints of. The police *fingerprinted* the suspect. *Verb.*
  fin·ger·print (fing′gər print′) *noun, plural* **fingerprints;** *verb,* **fingerprinted, fingerprinting.**

finish **1.** To bring to an end; come to the end of; complete. When will you *finish* your homework? When the speaker *finished,* we all applauded. **2.** To use up completely. We *finished* the jar of peanut butter. **3.** To treat the surface of in some way. I used clear varnish to *finish* the cabinet. *Verb.*
—**1.** The last part of something; end. We watched the *finish* of the race. **2.** The surface of something. The table has a shiny *finish.* *Noun.*
  fin·ish (fin′ish) *verb,* **finished, finishing;** *noun, plural* **finishes.**

Finland A country in northern Europe.
  Fin·land (fin′lənd) *noun.*

Finn A person who was born in or is a citizen of Finland. ▲ Another word that sounds like this is **fin.**
  Finn (fin) *noun, plural* **Finns.**

Finnish The language of Finland. *Noun.*
—Of or having to do with Finland, its people, or its language. *Adjective.* ▲ Another word that sounds like this is **finish.**
  Fin·nish (fin′ish) *noun; adjective.*

fiord A spelling sometimes used for **fjord.** Look up **fjord** for more information.
  fiord (fyôrd) *noun, plural* **fiords.**

fir An evergreen tree that is related to the pine. Firs have cones that stand upright on the branch and they are often used as Christmas trees. ▲ Another word that sounds like this is **fur.**
  fir (fûr) *noun, plural* **firs.**

fire **1.** The flame, heat, and light given off when wood, paper, or another material burns. **2.** Something burning. We added another log to the *fire.* **3.** Burning that destroys or causes damage. The bad wiring in the old house started a *fire.* **4.** A very strong emotion or spirit; passion. The angry teenager's eyes were full of *fire.* **5.** The shooting of guns. We heard the sound of rifle *fire* in the distance. *Noun.*
—**1.** To set on fire; cause to burn. We *fired* the heap of leaves. **2.** To dismiss from a job. The company *fired* an employee. **3.** To cause to be excited or stirred up. Stories about pirates *fired* the child's imagination. **4.** To set off or be set off; shoot. The gun *fired* once. The ship *fired* a flare. *Verb.*
• **on fire.** Burning.
• **to catch fire.** To begin to burn. As a result of the explosion in the factory, several nearby houses *caught fire.*
• **under fire.** **1.** Being shot at by an enemy. The soldiers in the trenches were *under fire.* **2.** Being criticized or blamed. The politician was *under fire* from the press.
  fire (fīr) *noun, plural* **fires;** *verb,* **fired, firing.**

firearm A weapon used for shooting. A firearm is usually a weapon that can be carried and fired by one person. Rifles and pistols are firearms.
  fire·arm (fīr′ärm′) *noun, plural* **firearms.**

firecracker A paper tube containing gunpowder and a fuse. Firecrackers make a loud noise when they explode. They are often exploded on holidays and at celebrations.
  fire·crack·er (fīr′krak′ər) *noun, plural* **firecrackers.**

fire department A group set up by a government to prevent and put out fires.

fire engine A truck that carries equipment for fighting and putting out fires.

fire escape A metal stairway attached to the outside of a building. It is used for escape in case of fire.

Needles and Cone

fir

278

fire extinguisher A device containing water, chemicals, or some other substance that can be sprayed on a fire to put it out.
fire·ex·tin·guish·er (ek stĭng′gwĭshər).

firefighter A person whose work is to put out and prevent fires.
fire·fight·er (fīr′fī′tər) *noun, plural* **firefighters.**

firefly A small beetle that flies at night and gives off short flashes of light from its body as a signal to a mate; lightning bug.
fire·fly (fīr′flī′) *noun, plural* **fireflies.**

firehouse A building for firefighters and trucks and equipment for putting out fires.
fire·house (fīr′hous′) *noun, plural* **firehouses** (fīr′hou′zĭz).

fireman 1. A firefighter. 2. A person who takes care of the fire in a furnace or steam engine.
fire·man (fīr′mən) *noun, plural* **firemen** (fīr′mən).

fireplace 1. An opening in a room, with a chimney leading up from it, used for building fires. 2. An outdoor structure of brick or stone in which fires are built.
fire·place (fīr′plās′) *noun, plural* **fireplaces.**

fireplace

fireproof Not able to burn or to burn easily. Steel and concrete are both kinds of fireproof materials.
fire·proof (fīr′prüf′) *adjective.*

fireside 1. The area around a fireplace; hearth. 2. Home; family life. The travelers were happy to be back at their own *fireside.*
fire·side (fīr′sīd′) *noun, plural* **firesides.**

firewood Wood that is used in making a fire.
fire·wood (fīr′wŭd′) *noun.*

fireworks Firecrackers and other devices that are burned or exploded to make loud noises or brilliant shows of light.
fire·works (fīr′wûrks′) *plural noun.*

firm[1] 1. Not giving in much when pressed; solid. This is a very *firm* mattress. 2. Not easily moved; secure. We made sure the fence posts were *firm* in the ground. 3. Not changing; staying the same. It is my *firm* belief that they did the right thing. They had a *firm* friendship for many years. 4. Steady or strong. The minister spoke with a *firm* voice. *Adjective.*
—So as not to move or change. The other team attacked, but we stood *firm. Adverb.*
firm (fûrm) *adjective; adverb,* **firmer, firmest.**

firm[2] A company in which two or more people go into business together. There are five partners in my cousin's law *firm.*
firm (fûrm) *noun, plural* **firms.**

first Before all others. Our team finished in *first* place. George Washington was the *first* president of the United States. *Adjective.*
—1. Before all others. She was ranked *first* in her class in mathematics. 2. For the first time. He *first* heard the news yesterday. *Adverb.*
—1. A person or thing that is first. This invention is the *first* of its kind. 2. The beginning. I liked the new car from the *first. Noun.*
first (fûrst) *adjective; adverb; noun, plural* **firsts.**

first aid Emergency treatment that is given to a sick or injured person before trained medical help is available.

first-class 1. Of the highest rank or best quality. The singer gave a *first-class* performance. 2. Having to do with a class of mail that includes mainly personal letters, packages, and postcards. 3. Having to do with

fireworks

at; āpe; fär; câre; end; mē; it; īce; pîerce; hot; ōld; sông, fôrk; oil; out; up; ūse; rüle; pùll; tûrn; chin; sing; shop; thin; <u>th</u>is; hw in white; zh in treasure. The symbol ə stands for the unstressed vowel sound in about, taken, pencil, lemon, and circus.

279

the best and most expensive seats or rooms on a ship, train, or airplane. We bought *first-class* tickets for our plane trip. *Adjective.*
—By first-class mail or transportation. I sent the package *first-class. Adverb.*
first-class (fûrst′klas′) *adjective; adverb.*

firsthand Direct from the first or original source. That forest ranger has *firsthand* knowledge of these woods. I learned about horses *firsthand* when I worked at a stable.
first·hand (fûrst′hand′) *adjective; adverb.*

first-rate Of the highest quality or importance; excellent. This is an expensive, *first-rate* hotel.
first-rate (fûrst′rāt′) *adjective.*

fish 1. A cold-blooded animal that lives in water. Fish have backbones, gills for breathing, and, usually, fins and scales. Fish are found almost all over the world. 2. The flesh of fish used as food. Are we having meat or *fish* for dinner? *Noun.*
—1. To catch or try to catch fish. We *fished* for trout. 2. To search by groping. I *fished* around in my pocket for the key. *Verb.*
fish (fish) *noun, plural* **fish** or **fishes;** *verb,* **fished, fishing.**

fisherman A person who fishes for a living or for sport.
fish·er·man (fish′ər mən) *noun, plural* **fishermen** (fish′ər mən).

fishery 1. A place for catching fish. 2. A place where fish are bred.
fish·er·y (fish′ə rē) *noun, plural* **fisheries.**

fishhook A hook used for catching fish. A fishhook usually has a barb at its end.
fish·hook (fish′huk′) *noun, plural* **fishhooks.**

fishing rod A long pole made of wood, metal, or fiberglass. It has a hook, line, and usually a reel attached to it and is used for catching fish.

fishy 1. Like a fish in odor or taste. My hands smelled *fishy* after cleaning the fish. 2. Not likely to be true. Our driver gave us a *fishy* excuse for being late.
fish·y (fish′ē) *adjective,* **fishier, fishiest.**

fission The splitting or breaking apart of an atomic nucleus. Large amounts of energy are released during fission.
fis·sion (fish′ən) *noun.*

fist A hand that is tightly closed with the fingers folded into the palm.
fist (fist) *noun, plural* **fists.**

fit¹ 1. Suitable, right, or proper. This dirty water is not *fit* to drink. Only strong people are *fit* for a job loading trucks. 2. In good health; healthy. A person should exercise to keep *fit. Adjective.*

—1. To be suitable, right, or proper for. The part of the witch in the play does not *fit* me. 2. To be the right size or shape for. That coat *fits* you well. 3. To make right, proper, or suitable. *Fit* your speech to the serious nature of the occasion. 4. To supply with what is necessary or suitable; equip. The big store *fitted* the campers with all the supplies needed for the trip. 5. To join, adjust, or put in snugly. We *fitted* the pieces of the jigsaw puzzle together. *Verb.*
—The way in which something fits. The jacket has a tight *fit. Noun.*
fit (fit) *adjective,* **fitter, fittest;** *verb,* **fitted, fitting;** *noun, plural* **fits.**

fit² 1. A sudden, sharp attack of something. I had a *fit* of coughing. 2. A sudden burst. The coach yelled at us in a *fit* of anger.
fit (fit) *noun, plural* **fits.**

five One more than four; 5.
five (fīv) *noun, plural* **fives;** *adjective.*

fix 1. To repair; mend. I *fixed* the broken chair. 2. To get ready or arrange; prepare. I will *fix* dinner tonight. 3. To make firm or secure; fasten tightly. The campers *fixed* the pegs for the tent in the ground. 4. To arrange definitely; settle. Have they *fixed* the date for the wedding? 5. To direct or hold steadily. I *fixed* my eyes straight ahead. 6. To place; put. The police *fixed* the responsibility for the accident on the pedestrian. 7. To try to get something to come out the way one wants. They *fixed* the race by bribing one of the jockeys to lose on purpose. *Verb.*
—Trouble; difficulty. I got myself into quite a *fix* by promising to go to two parties on the same day. *Noun.*
• **to fix up.** 1. To mend; repair. I tried to *fix up* the old car in my free time. 2. To provide with something that is needed or wanted. We *fixed* my cousin *up* with a place to spend the night.
fix (fiks) *verb,* **fixed, fixing;** *noun, plural* **fixes.**

fixture Something that is firmly and permanently fastened into place. A bathtub, a toilet, and a sink are bathroom fixtures.
fix·ture (fiks′chər) *noun, plural* **fixtures.**

fjord A long, narrow inlet of the sea between high cliffs. There are many *fjords* along the coast of Norway. ▲ This word is sometimes spelled **fiord.**
fjord (fyôrd) *noun, plural* **fjords.**

FL Postal abbreviation for *Florida.*

Fla. An abbreviation for *Florida.*

flag A piece of cloth having different colors and designs on it. Flags are used as symbols

of countries or of organizations. Flags are also sometimes used for giving signals. *Noun.*
—To stop or signal. I *flagged* a taxicab by waving my hand. *Verb.*
flag (flag) *noun,* *plural* **flags;** *verb,* **flagged, flagging.**

U.S. flag

flagpole A pole used for raising and flying a flag.
flag·pole (flag′pōl′) *noun, plural* **flagpoles.**

flair A natural talent. You have a *flair* for acting. ▲ Another word that sounds like this is **flare.**
flair (flâr) *noun, plural* **flairs.**

flake A small, thin, flat piece. Large *flakes* of snow covered the window sill. *Noun.*
—To chip or peel off in flakes. The old paint cracked and *flaked* off the wall. *Verb.*
flake (flāk) *noun, plural* **flakes;** *verb,* **flaked, flaking.**

flame 1. One of the streams of light given off by a fire. *Flames* from the burning house could be seen from miles away. 2. Gas or vapor that has been set on fire to give off light or heat. I lowered the *flame* under the frying pan on the stove. 3. The condition of burning. The house burst into *flame. Noun.*
—1. To burn with flames; blaze. The fire *flamed* for hours. 2. To light up or glow. The fighter's eyes *flamed* with anger. *Verb.*
flame (flām) *noun, plural* **flames;** *verb,* **flamed, flaming.**

flamingo A pink or red bird that has a long, thin neck and legs, and webbed feet. Flamingos live near shallow lakes and lagoons in tropical areas throughout the world.
fla·min·go (flə ming′gō) *noun, plural* **flamingos** or **flamingoes.**

flamingo

flammable Able to be set on fire easily. Gasoline is a *flammable* liquid.
flam·ma·ble (flam′ə bəl) *adjective.*

flank 1. The area between the lower ribs and the hip on either side of the body. 2. The left or right side of something, especially a military group. The army was careful to protect its *flanks. Noun.*
—1. To be at the side of. Two statues of lions *flanked* the entrance to the library. 2. To attack or move around the side of. Our ships *flanked* the enemy fleet. *Verb.*
flank (flangk) *noun, plural* **flanks;** *verb,* **flanked, flanking.**

flannel A soft cotton or woolen material. Flannel is used for such things as nightgowns, babies' clothes, and shirts.
flan·nel (flan′əl) *noun, plural* **flannels.**

flap 1. To move up and down. The bird *flapped* its wings. 2. To swing or wave loosely and with noise. The curtain *flapped* in the breeze. *Verb.*
—1. The motion or the noise made by something when it flaps. We could hear the *flap* of the shutters against the house. 2. Something that is attached at only one edge so that its other edge can move freely. The part of an envelope that is folded down to close the envelope is a flap. *Noun.*
flap (flap) *verb,* **flapped, flapping;** *noun, plural* **flaps.**

flapjack A word sometimes used for **pancake.** Look up **pancake** for more information.
flap·jack (flap′jak′) *noun, plural* **flapjacks.**

flare 1. To start to burn with a sudden, very bright light. The match *flared* in the darkness and went out. 2. To break out with sudden or violent feeling. The insulting remark caused my temper to *flare.* 3. To open or spread outward. This new skirt *flares* from the waist. *Verb.*
—1. A sudden bright light. A flare usually lasts only a short time. 2. A fire or burst of light used as a signal or to give light. The captain of the ship in trouble lit up *flares* as a signal for help. *Noun.* ▲ Another word that sounds like this is **flair.**
• **to flare up.** To break out or grow more intense. The infection *flared up* just as the patient seemed to be getting better.
flare (flâr) *verb,* **flared, flaring;** *noun, plural* **flares.**

flash 1. A sudden, short burst of light or flame. A *flash* of lightning lit the sky for an

at; āpe; fär; câre; end; mē; it; īce; pîerce; hot; ōld; sông, fôrk; oil; out; up; ūse; rüle; pùll; tûrn; chin; sing; shop; thin; this; hw in white; zh in treasure. The symbol ə stands for the unstressed vowel sound in about, taken, pencil, lemon, and circus.

instant.   **2.** A very short period of time; instant. The fire engines were at the scene of the fire in a *flash*. *Noun.*
—**1.** To burst out in sudden light or fire. Lightning *flashed* in the sky.   **2.** To be suddenly bright; shine briefly. The speaker's eyes *flashed* with anger.   **3.** To come or move suddenly or quickly. The ambulance *flashed* by. The answer to the riddle *flashed* into my mind. *Verb.*
> **flash** (flash) *noun, plural* **flashes;** *verb,* **flashed, flashing.**

flashlight   An electric light that is powered by batteries and is small enough to be carried around.
> **flash·light** (flash'līt') *noun, plural* **flashlights.**

flask   A small bottle that is used to hold liquids.
> **flask** (flask) *noun, plural* **flasks.**

flat   **1.** Smooth and even; level. It is easy to ride a bicycle on a *flat* road.   **2.** Lying, placed, or stretched at full length; spread out. The dog lay *flat* on its back.   **3.** Not very deep or thick; shallow. The food was served on a large *flat* tray.   **4.** Not changing in amount; fixed. There is a *flat* charge for lunch, no matter which food you order. **5.** Without much interest, energy, or flavor. The singer gave a *flat* performance.   **6.** Containing little or no air. We got a *flat* tire riding over the broken glass.   **7.** Lower than the true or intended musical pitch. I tried to play the right note on my trombone, but it came out *flat*. *Adjective.*
—**1.** A flat part or surface. I hit the table with the *flat* of my hand.   **2.** A tire that has little or no air.   **3.** A musical tone or note that is one half step below its natural pitch. **4.** A symbol (♭) that shows this tone or note. *Noun.*
—**1.** In a flat manner. The fallen tree lay *flat* on the ground.   **2.** Exactly; precisely. The winner ran the race in four minutes *flat*. **3.** Below the true pitch in music. Both cello players were fine, but the violinist played *flat*. *Adverb.*
> **flat** (flat) *adjective,* **flatter, flattest;** *noun, plural* **flats;** *adverb.*

flatcar   A railroad car that has a floor but no roof or sides. It is used for carrying freight.
> **flat·car** (flat'kär') *noun, plural* **flatcars.**

flatfish   A fish that has a flattened body. A flatfish has both eyes on the upper side of the body. Flounder, sole, and halibut are flatfish.
> **flat·fish** (flat'fish') *noun, plural* **flatfish** or **flatfishes.**

flatten   To make or become flat or flatter. The cloth *flattened* out when it was ironed. I *flattened* the dirt with a shovel.
> **flat·ten** (flat'ən) *verb,* **flattened, flattening.**

flatter   **1.** To praise too much or insincerely. If you think you'll change my mind by *flattering* me, you're wrong.   **2.** To show as more attractive than is actually true. I think that picture *flatters* me.
> **flat·ter** (flat'ər) *verb,* **flattered, flattering.**

flattery   Praise that is not sincere or not deserved. It is often easy to tell the difference between genuine praise and mere *flattery*.
> **flat·ter·y** (flat'ə rē) *noun, plural* **flatteries.**

flavor   **1.** A particular taste. Adding pepper to the stew will give it a spicy *flavor*.   **2.** A special or main quality. The speaker's personal experiences as a police officer gave *flavor* to the lecture. *Noun.*
—To give flavor or taste to. The cook *flavored* the fish with lemon juice. *Verb.*
> **fla·vor** (flā'vər) *noun, plural* **flavors;** *verb,* **flavored, flavoring.**

flavoring   Something added to food or drink to give flavor. Did you add your secret *flavoring* to the spaghetti sauce?
> **fla·vor·ing** (flā'vər ing) *noun, plural* **flavorings.**

flaw   A scratch, crack, or other defect. There is a *flaw* in that glass vase. Selfishness is a character *flaw*.
> **flaw** (flô) *noun, plural* **flaws.**

flawless   Having no flaw; perfect. The pianist gave a *flawless* performance.
> **flaw·less** (flô'lis) *adjective.*

flatcars carrying containers

flax   **1.** A fiber that comes from the stem of a certain plant. This fiber is spun into thread,

and the thread is used to make linen. Flax can also be used to make rope and rugs. **2.** The plant that produces this fiber. A kind of oil comes from the seeds of flax plants.
flax (flaks) *noun.*

flax

flea An insect without wings. Fleas feed on the blood of human beings, dogs, cats, and other animals. A flea can sometimes carry a disease and give it to the person or animal it is living on. ▲ Another word that sounds like this is **flee.**
flea (flē) *noun, plural* **fleas.**

fled Past tense and past participle of **flee.** Everyone *fled* from the beach when the storm arose. Look up **flee** for more information.
fled (fled) *verb.*

flee **1.** To run away. The frightened deer *fled* from the field when they saw the hunters. The family *fled* the burning house. **2.** To move or pass away quickly. The days of my vacation *fled* by. ▲ Another word that sounds like this is **flea.**
flee (flē) *verb,* **fled, fleeing.**

fleece The coat of wool covering a sheep. *Noun.*
—To cut the fleece from. The farmer used a pair of electric clippers to *fleece* the sheep. *Verb.*
fleece (flēs) *noun, plural* **fleeces;** *verb,* **fleeced, fleecing.**

fleet¹ **1.** A group of warships under one command. The admiral ordered the *fleet* to sail. **2.** A group of ships, airplanes, or cars. My cousin owns a *fleet* of taxicabs.
fleet (flēt) *noun, plural* **fleets.**

fleet² Capable of moving very quickly; swift. The deer is a *fleet* animal.
fleet (flēt) *adjective,* **fleeter, fleetest.**

fleeting Passing very quickly; very brief. I had only a *fleeting* look at the car because it drove by so fast.
fleet·ing (flē′ting) *adjective.*

flesh **1.** The soft layers of muscle and fat that lie between the bones and the skin. **2.** The soft part of fruit or vegetables that can be eaten. A cantaloupe has greenish skin and orange *flesh.* **3.** The meat of an animal.
flesh (flesh) *noun.*

fleshy Plump; fat. The base of the thumb is the *fleshy* part of the hand.
flesh·y (flesh′ē) *adjective,* **fleshier, fleshiest.**

flew Past tense of **fly.** The bird *flew* away as soon as it saw the cat creeping toward it. Look up **fly** for more information. ▲ Other words that sound like this are **flu** and **flue.**
flew (flü) *verb.*

flex To bend. If your arm is tired, *flex* it to keep it loose.
flex (fleks) *verb,* **flexed, flexing.**

flexible **1.** Able to bend without breaking; not stiff. Rubber is a *flexible* material. **2.** Able to change or adjust when necessary. My schedule is *flexible,* so I can work whenever you want me to.
flex·i·ble (flek′sə bəl) *adjective.*

flick A light, quick snap. I turned the lock with a *flick* of the wrist. *Noun.*
—To hit or move with a quick, light snap. The waiter *flicked* the crumbs off the table before serving the dessert. *Verb.*
flick (flik) *noun, plural* **flicks;** *verb,* **flicked, flicking.**

flicker¹ **1.** To burn with an unsteady or wavering light. The candles *flickered* in the breeze from the open window. **2.** To move back and forth with a quick, unsteady movement. Shadows from the leaves of the trees *flickered* on the barn door. *Verb.*
—**1.** An unsteady or wavering light. The *flicker* of the light from the fireplace made strange shadows on the wall. **2.** A quick, unsteady movement. We watched the *flicker* of the snake's tongue. *Noun.*
flick·er (flik′ər) *verb,* **flickered, flickering;** *noun, plural* **flickers.**

flicker²

flicker² A large woodpecker of North America. It is mostly brown and white, with a curved black mark across its breast.
flick·er (flik′ər) *noun, plural* **flickers.**

at; āpe; fär; câre; end; mē; it; īce; pîerce; hot; ōld; sông; fôrk; oil; out; up; ūse; rüle; půll; tûrn; chin; sing; shop; thin; this; hw in white; zh in treasure. The symbol ə stands for the unstressed vowel sound in about, taken, pencil, lemon, and circus.

flied A past tense of **fly.** The batter *flied* to left field. Look up **fly** for more information.
flied (flīd) *verb.*

flier A person or thing that flies. The eagle is a powerful *flier.* This word is also spelled **flyer.**
fli·er (flī′ər) *noun, plural* **fliers.**

flight[1] **1.** Movement through the air with the use of wings; flying. We watched the graceful *flight* of the gull. **2.** The distance or course traveled by a bird or aircraft. It is a long *flight* from the United States to China. **3.** A group of things flying through the air together. We watched a *flight* of birds heading south for the winter. **4.** A trip in an airplane. Did you have a good *flight* from Canada to New York? **5.** A set of stairs or steps between floors or landings of a building. The movers had to carry the piano up five *flights* of stairs.
flight (flīt) *noun, plural* **flights.**

flight[2] The act of running away; escape. Some people were hurt during their *flight* from the burning building.
flight (flīt) *noun, plural* **flights.**

flight attendant A person who serves passengers on an airplane; a steward or stewardess.

flimsy Without strength; light and thin; frail. I felt cold when the wind blew because I had on a *flimsy* summer shirt. My parents didn't believe my *flimsy* excuse for being late.
flim·sy (flim′zē) *adjective,* **flimsier, flimsiest.**

flinch To draw back from something that is painful, dangerous, or unpleasant. I *flinched* when the doctor gave me the shot.
flinch (flinch) *verb,* **flinched, flinching.**

fling To throw hard or carelessly. Sometimes I just *fling* my books and coat on my bed. *Verb.*
—**1.** A throw. I gave the pebble a *fling* and it landed in the pond. **2.** A time of carefree enjoyment. Our day at the beach was our last *fling* before vacation ended. *Noun.*
fling (fling) *verb,* **flung, flinging;** *noun, plural* **flings.**

flint A very hard, gray stone that makes sparks when steel is struck against it. Before the invention of matches, flint was used to light fires.
flint (flint) *noun, plural* **flints.**

flintlock An old-fashioned gun. In a flintlock, steel is struck against flint to make sparks that set the gunpowder on fire.
flint·lock (flint′lok′) *noun, plural* **flintlocks.**

flip To toss or turn over with a quick, jerking motion. We decided to *flip* a coin to see who would go first. I *flipped* the pages of the book until I came to the part I was looking for. *Verb.*
—**1.** A toss. We'll decide who should start the game by a *flip* of a coin. **2.** A somersault done in the air. The diver did a *flip* before plunging into the pool. *Noun.*
flip (flip) *verb,* **flipped, flipping;** *noun, plural* **flips.**

flipper **1.** A broad, flat limb on a seal, turtle, penguin, or other animal. Flippers are used for swimming and moving along on land. **2.** One of a pair of rubber shoes shaped like a duck's feet. Flippers are worn to make swimming or skin diving easier.
flip·per (flip′ər) *noun, plural* **flippers.**

flirt To act romantic in a playful way. They *flirted* with each other as they danced at the party. *Verb.*
—A person who *flirts. Noun.*
flirt (flûrt) *verb,* **flirted, flirting;** *noun, plural* **flirts.**

flit To move quickly and lightly. We watched the butterflies *flit* among the flowers.
flit (flit) *verb,* **flitted, flitting.**

float **1.** To rest on top of water or other liquid. In swimming class we learned how to *float* on our backs. **2.** To move along slowly in the air or on water. Far above us, a balloon *floated* by. *Verb.*
—**1.** Anything that rests on top of water. A raft anchored in the swimming area of a lake is a float. **2.** A low, flat platform on wheels that carries an exhibit in a parade. Our *float* won first prize in the parade. *Noun.*
float (flōt) *verb,* **floated, floating;** *noun, plural* **floats.**

float

284

F

flock **1.** A group of animals of one kind that is herded or gathered together. The farmer tends a *flock* of sheep. We saw a *flock* of geese flying south. **2.** A large number or group. A *flock* of reporters crowded around the president after the speech. *Noun.*
—To move or gather in crowds. People *flock* to the beaches during the hot summer weather. *Verb.*
  flock (flok) *noun, plural* **flocks;** *verb,* **flocked, flocking.**

floe

floe A mass or sheet of floating ice. ▲ Another word that sounds like this is **flow.**
  floe (flō) *noun, plural* **floes.**

flood **1.** A great flow of water over land that is normally dry. Floods can do much damage. **2.** A great flow of anything. The child's story came out in a *flood* of words mixed with tears. *Noun.*
—**1.** To cover with water. The town was *flooded* when the dam broke. **2.** To fill, cover, or overwhelm. The baseball field was *flooded* with light for the night game. *Verb.*
  flood (flud) *noun, plural* **floods;** *verb,* **flooded, flooding.**

floodlight A lamp that shines brightly over a wide area.
  flood·light (flud′līt′) *noun, plural* **floodlights.**

floor **1.** The surface of a room that people walk or stand on. The kitchen *floor* is covered with tiles. **2.** A surface that is like the floor of a room. The ship sank to the ocean *floor.* **3.** A number of rooms that are the same height from the ground and that make up one level of a building; story. My office is on the second *floor* of the building. *Noun.*
—**1.** To cover with a floor. They decided to *floor* the basement with cement. **2.** To

knock down. **3.** To bewilder or surprise completely. We were *floored* by the news. *Verb.*
  floor (flôr) *noun, plural* **floors;** *verb,* **floored, flooring.**

flop **1.** To drop or fall heavily. I was so tired I couldn't wait to get home and *flop* into bed. **2.** To move around or flap loosely. The dog's ears *flopped* when it ran. **3.** To fail completely. The new restaurant *flopped* after being open for only a month. *Verb.*
—**1.** The act or sound of dropping or falling heavily. The seal landed in the water with a *flop.* **2.** A complete failure. The new television show was a *flop. Noun.*
  flop (flop) *verb,* **flopped, flopping;** *noun, plural* **flops.**

floppy Able to or tending to flop. The hat had a large, *floppy* brim.
  flop·py (flop′ē) *adjective,* **floppier, floppiest.**

floppy disk A flexible piece of plastic that can store information for a computer. Look up **diskette** for more information.

floral Of, relating to, or showing flowers. I received a *floral* arrangement on Valentine's Day. The wallpaper in their room has a *floral* design.
  flo·ral (flôr′əl) *adjective.*

Florida A state in the southeastern United States. Its capital is Tallahassee.
  Flor·i·da (flôr′i də *or* flor′i də) *noun.*

Word History

Florida is a Spanish word that means "flowery." Ponce de Leon landed in Florida during the Spanish festival of flowers. He named the place from the name of the holiday, *Pasqua florida.*

florist A person who sells flowers and indoor plants.
  flo·rist (flôr′ist) *noun, plural* **florists.**

floss **1.** A soft, shiny thread of cotton or silk that is used for embroidering. **2.** A term that is sometimes used for **dental floss.** Look up **dental floss** for more information. *Noun.*

at; āpe; fär; câre; end; mē; it; īce; pîerce; hot; ōld; sông, fôrk; oil; out; up; ūse; rüle; pùll; tûrn; chin; sing; shop; thin; this; hw in white; zh in treasure. The symbol ə stands for the unstressed vowel sound in about, taken, pencil, lemon, and circus.

—To clean between the teeth with dental floss. The dentist said I should *floss* my teeth once a day. *Verb.*

floss (flôs) *noun, plural* **flosses;** *verb,* **flossed, flossing.**

flounder¹ To struggle or stumble about. The colt *floundered* as it tried to walk.

floun·der (floun′dər) *verb,* **floundered, floundering.**

flounder² A flatfish that lives in salt water. Flounder is used as food.

floun·der (floun′dər) *noun, plural* **flounder** or **flounders.**

flour A fine powder that is made by grinding and sifting wheat, rye, or other grains. Flour is used to make bread and cake.

flour (flour) *noun, plural* **flours.**

flourish **1.** To grow or develop strongly and with vigor. Those plants will *flourish* in a sunny garden if they are given plenty of water. A highly developed civilization *flourished* in Mexico long before Europeans discovered the area. **2.** To wave in the air boldly. The guard *flourished* a gun at the escaping prisoners. *Verb.*
—**1.** A showy gesture or sound. The leading actor walked on stage with a *flourish.* The trumpets announced the coming of the king and queen with a *flourish.* **2.** An extra stroke for decoration. I signed my name with a *flourish* below it. *Noun.*

flour·ish (flûr′ish) *verb,* **flourished, flourishing;** *noun, plural* **flourishes.**

flow **1.** To move along steadily in a stream. Water *flows* through these pipes. The crowd *flowed* out of the football stadium when the game was over. **2.** To hang or fall loosely. When I was young, my hair *flowed* to my waist. *Verb.*
—**1.** The act of flowing. The *flow* of the river can be controlled by building a dam. **2.** A long series of things coming steadily one after another; stream. On the crowded highway, the *flow* of cars seemed endless. *Noun.* ▲ Another word that sounds like this is **floe.**

flow (flō) *verb,* **flowed, flowing;** *noun, plural* **flows.**

flower **1.** The part of a plant that makes seeds; blossom. Most flowers have colored petals. **2.** A plant grown for its showy, sometimes brightly colored petals. The garden was full of purple, yellow, and red *flowers. Noun.*
—To produce flowers; blossom. Cherry trees *flower* in the early spring. *Verb.*

flow·er (flou′ər) *noun, plural* **flowers;** *verb,* **flowered, flowering.**

flown Past participle of **fly.** The bird had *flown* out of the cage. Look up **fly** for more information.

flown (flōn) *verb.*

flu A disease that is like a very bad cold. It is caused by a virus and can easily spread from one person to another through coughing and sneezing. This word is a short form of the word **influenza.** ▲ Other words that sound like this are **flew** and **flue.**

flu (flü) *noun, plural* **flus.**

flue The hollow inside part of a chimney that draws the smoke from a fireplace out of the room and into the outside air. ▲ Other words that sound like this are **flew** and **flu.**

flue (flü) *noun, plural* **flues.**

fluff A soft, light material. Some tree seeds are held inside floating bits of *fluff. Noun.*
—To pat or puff into a soft, light mass. I *fluffed* up the cushions on the couch before the guests arrived. *Verb.*

fluff (fluf) *noun; verb,* **fluffed, fluffing.**

fluffy Covered with or like fluff. The *fluffy* baby chicks ran around the barnyard.

fluff·y (fluf′ē) *adjective,* **fluffier, fluffiest.**

fluid A gas or liquid. Fluids can flow easily, and take the shape of any container they are put in. Air and water are fluids. *Noun.*
—Flowing; not solid. Water is *fluid* unless it is frozen. *Adjective.*

flu·id (flü′id) *noun, plural* **fluids;** *adjective.*

Word History

Fluid comes from a Latin word meaning "to flow."

---

flung Past tense and past participle of **fling.** The actor *flung* the glass against the wall in anger. Look up **fling** for more information.

flung (flung) *verb.*

fluorescent **1.** Able to give off light when exposed to electricity or X rays. Fluorescent lamps often are made of glass tubes and are filled with gas. Many schools use *fluorescent* lighting in classrooms and corridors. **2.** Very bright and colorful. Fluorescent colors can attract your attention, so they are sometimes used for warning signs.

fluo·res·cent (flù res′ənt *or* flô res′ənt) *adjective.*

fluoridate To add fluoride to something. The city *fluoridated* its drinking water as a way to reduce tooth decay among the people living there.

fluor·i·date (flùr′i dāt′ *or* flôr′i dāt′) *verb,* **fluoridated, fluoridating.**

F

fluoride A compound that contains fluorine. Fluoride is added to drinking water to help prevent tooth decay.
fluo·ride (flŭr′īd *or* flôr′īd) *noun.*

fluorine A yellow-green gas. Fluorine is a chemical element. It combines very easily with other elements. Compounds of fluorine are added to drinking water to prevent tooth decay.
fluo·rine (flŭr′ēn *or* flôr′ēn) *noun.*

flurry **1.** A brief, light fall of snow. **2.** A sudden outburst. There is always a *flurry* of excitement among the spectators when our star player comes to bat.
flur·ry (flŭr′ē) *noun, plural* **flurries.**

flush¹ **1.** To turn red or cause to turn red; blush. The child's face was *flushed* with excitement. I *flushed* with embarrassment when I saw my mistake. **2.** To flow or rush suddenly. Water *flushed* through the pipes. **3.** To empty or wash with a sudden rush of water. A plumber came to *flush* out the clogged drain. *Verb.*
—**1.** A reddish color or glow. The skiers came home with a healthy *flush* on their cheeks. **2.** A sudden rush or flow. A *flush* of water burst from the broken pipe. **3.** An exciting sensation; thrill. The winner enjoyed the *flush* of success. *Noun.*
flush (flush) *verb,* **flushed, flushing;** *noun, plural* **flushes.**

flush² Even or level. The orange juice was *flush* with the rim of the glass. We tried to fit the shelf *flush* with the wall.
flush (flush) *adjective; adverb.*

fluster To make embarrassed or nervous; confuse. It *flustered* them to be the only couple on the dance floor. *Verb.*
—Nervous confusion. I was in a *fluster* the morning of the wedding. *Noun.*
flus·ter (flus′tər) *verb,* **flustered, flustering;** *noun.*

flute A long, thin musical instrument. A person plays a flute by blowing across a hole at one end. The player makes different notes by covering the holes with the fingers or by pushing down keys that cover the holes.
flute (flüt) *noun, plural* **flutes.**

flutter To move or fly with quick, light, flapping movements. Butterflies *fluttered* among the flowers. *Verb.*
—**1.** A quick, light, flapping movement. We heard a *flutter* of wings, as the pigeons flew by. **2.** A state of excitement or confusion. The appearance of the movie star caused a *flutter* among the crowd of fans. *Noun.*
flut·ter (flut′ər) *verb,* **fluttered, fluttering;** *noun, plural* **flutters.**

fly¹ One of a large group of insects that have two wings. Houseflies, mosquitoes, and gnats are flies.
fly (flī) *noun, plural* **flies.**

fly² **1.** To move through the air with wings. Some birds *fly* south for the winter. **2.** To pilot or travel in an aircraft. My cousin *flies* jets for a large airline. The children *flew* to Puerto Rico to visit their grandparents. **3.** To move, float, or wave in the air. The ocean spray *flew* into our faces. I went to the park to *fly* my kite. A flag *flew* from the ship's mast. **4.** To go swiftly. They *flew* up the stairs when they heard the baby crying. **5.** To hit a baseball high into the air. The batter *flied* to left field. *Verb.*
—**1.** A flap of material that covers buttons or a zipper on a piece of clothing. **2.** A baseball hit high into the air. The batter hit a *fly* to center field. *Noun.*
fly (flī) *verb,* **flew, flown, flying** *(for definitions 1-4)* or **flied, flying** *(for definition 5); noun, plural* **flies.**

flycatcher A songbird that catches flying insects for food. There are many different kinds of flycatchers.
fly·catch·er (flī′kach′ər) *noun, plural* **flycatchers.**

flyer A spelling that is sometimes used for the word **flier.** Look up **flier** for more information.
fly·er (flī′ər).

flutes

flying fish A saltwater fish that has fins that look like wings. The flying fish can leap into the air and use its fins to glide above the surface of the water.

flying saucer A flying object that someone thinks he or she sees but that cannot be identified. Some people think that flying saucers are real and that they are sent by beings from outer space.

foal A young horse, donkey, zebra, or similar animal. *Noun.* The *foal* had long legs and a clumsy gait.
—To give birth to a foal. The mare *foaled* early this morning. *Verb.*
> **foal** (fōl) *noun, plural* **foals**; *verb,* **foaled, foaling.**

foam A mass of tiny bubbles. *Foam* forms on waves as they break against the shore. *Noun.*
—To form or flow in a mass of tiny bubbles. The milk *foamed* when it was poured into the glass. The rushing stream *foamed* over the rocks. *Verb.*
> **foam** (fōm) *noun; verb,* **foamed, foaming.**

foam rubber A firm kind of rubber that is like sponge and is used for seats, mattresses, and pillows.

focus 1. The point at which light rays meet after being bent by a lens. 2. The distance from the lens to the point where the rays meet. The eye of a farsighted person has a longer *focus* than the eye of a person with normal eyesight. 3. An adjustment that gives a clear image. The binoculars were out of *focus*. 4. A center of activity or interest. The speaker was the *focus* of attention for the audience. *Noun.*
—1. To bring to a meeting point or focus. A magnifying glass can be used to *focus* the sun's rays on a piece of paper and start a fire. 2. To bring into focus so as to make a clear image. The photographer *focused* the camera before taking the picture. 3. To fix or direct. The wedding guests *focused* all their attention on the bride and groom as they cut the wedding cake. *Verb.*
> **fo·cus** (fō′kəs) *noun, plural* **focuses**; *verb,* **focused, focusing.**

Word History

The word **focus** comes from Latin; in Latin it meant "fireplace" or "hearth." The fireplace which gave warmth to the room and where cooking was done would be the natural place for a family or others to gather for many activities.

flying fish

fodder Food for horses, cows, and other farm animals. Hay and corn are kinds of fodder.
> **fod·der** (fod′ər) *noun, plural* **fodders.**

foe An enemy. The knight said to the stranger, "Are you friend or *foe?*"
> **foe** (fō) *noun, plural* **foes.**

fog 1. A cloud of small drops of water close to the earth's surface. The thick *fog* made driving dangerous. 2. A state of confusion; daze. After not being able to sleep all night, I was in a *fog* all morning. *Noun.*
—To cover or become covered with fog. We had trouble driving home because the heavy mist had *fogged* the road. *Verb.*
> **fog** (fôg *or* fog) *noun, plural* **fogs**; *verb,* **fogged, fogging.**

foggy 1. Full of or hidden by fog; misty. It was such a *foggy* evening that we could not see the tops of the tallest buildings. 2. Confused or unclear. The lost explorers had only a *foggy* idea of where they were.
> **fog·gy** (fôg′ē *or* fog′ē) *adjective,* **foggier, foggiest.**

foghorn A horn that is sounded to give a warning to boats when fog makes it difficult to see.
> **fog·horn** (fôg′hôrn′ *or* fog′hôrn′) *noun, plural* **foghorns.**

foil¹ To stop from being successful. The clever hero of the story *foiled* the pirates' plan to take over the ship.
> **foil** (foil) *verb,* **foiled, foiling.**

foil² Metal that is formed in very thin, flexible sheets. I wrapped my sandwich in aluminum *foil* to keep it fresh.
> **foil** (foil) *noun, plural* **foils.**

foil³ A long sword used in fencing. The tip of a foil is covered to prevent injury.
> **foil** (foil) *noun, plural* **foils.**

fold¹ 1. To bend or double over on itself. I *folded* the letter and put it in the envelope. 2. To bring together close to the body. I *folded* my hands in my lap and waited. The bird *folded* its wings and went to sleep. *Verb.*
—1. A part that is bent or doubled over on

itself. The dress hung in graceful *folds*. **2.** A mark or crease made by folding. Cut the paper along the *fold. Noun.*
> **fold** (fōld) *verb,* **folded, folding;** *noun, plural* **folds.**

fold² A pen or other closed-in area for sheep. The farmer herded the sheep into the *fold* for the night.
> **fold** (fōld) *noun, plural* **folds.**

folder **1.** A holder for loose papers. A folder is often a folded sheet of thin cardboard. **2.** A booklet made up of folded sheets of paper. Before our trip to Europe, we got travel *folders* about all the places we wanted to see.
> **fold·er** (fōl′dər) *noun, plural* **folders.**

foliage The leaves on a tree or other plant.
> **fo·li·age** (fō′lē ij) *noun.*

folk **1.** People. City *folk* often take their vacations in the country. If you talk to the old *folks* who live here, you can learn a lot about the town's history. **2.** Family or relatives. My *folks* still live in a small town. *Noun.*
—Coming from or belonging to the common people. Modern doctors have learned some interesting things from the *folk* medicine of China. *Adjective.*
> **folk** (fōk) *noun, plural* **folks** or **folk;** *adjective.*

folk dance **1.** A traditional dance that was originally invented by the common people of a region or country. **2.** The music for this kind of dance.

performing a **folk dance**

folklore The tales, beliefs, customs, or other traditions of a group of people that are handed down from one generation to the next.
> **folk·lore** (fōk′lôr′) *noun.*

folk music The traditional music of the common people of a region or country.

folk singer A singer who sings folk songs.

folk song **1.** A traditional song of a region or country that has been handed down among the common people. **2.** A song imitating or in the style of a real folk song.

folktale A traditional story that has been handed down among the common people.
> **folk·tale** (fōk′tāl′) *noun, plural* **folktales.**

follow **1.** To go or come after, behind, or in back of. The lost dog *followed* us down the street. Spring *follows* winter. **2.** To go along. *Follow* this road down the hill and turn left at the stop sign. **3.** To act according to; obey. *Follow* the instructions on the package. **4.** To pay attention to and understand. The listeners *followed* the story with interest. I didn't *follow* the teacher's explanation, so I asked for it to be repeated. **5.** To make a living from. Most people along this coast *follow* the fishing trade.
- **to follow up.** To follow an action with something that strengthens its effect. I wrote a letter of complaint to the company, and I *followed up* with a phone call a few days later.
> **fol·low** (fol′ō) *verb,* **followed, following.**

follower Someone who supports or admires a person or a set of beliefs. The *followers* of the religious leader gathered to listen to the sermon.
> **fol·low·er** (fol′ō ər) *noun, plural* **followers.**

following That comes after in order or time. We'll pack on Thursday evening and start on our trip the *following* morning. *Adjective.*
—A group of supporters. That author has a large *following. Noun.*
> **fol·low·ing** (fol′ō ing) *adjective; noun, plural* **followings.**

folly A lack of good sense; foolishness. It is *folly* to think that you can drive anywhere in this blizzard.
> **fol·ly** (fol′ē) *noun, plural* **follies.**

fond Liking or loving. I'm *fond* of my classmates.
> **fond** (fond) *adjective,* **fonder, fondest.**

font A basin used to hold water for baptism.
> **font** (font) *noun, plural* **fonts.**

---

at; āpe; fär; câre; end; mē; it; īce; pîerce; hot; ōld; sông, fôrk; oil; out; up; ūse; rüle; pùll; tûrn; chin; sing; shop; thin; <u>th</u>is; hw in white; zh in treasure. The symbol ə stands for the unstressed vowel sound in about, taken, pencil, lemon, and circus.

food Something that is eaten or taken in by people, animals, or plants that keeps them alive and helps them grow; nourishment.
food (füd) *noun, plural* **foods.**

food chain A group of living things that form a chain in which the first living thing is eaten by the second, the second is eaten by the third, and so on. An example of a food chain is a peach which is eaten by a fly, which is eaten by a spider, which is eaten by a snake, which is eaten by a hawk.

food processor An appliance for slicing, chopping, grating, and blending foods.
food proc·es·sor (pros′e sər *or* prō′se sər).

fool **1.** A person who does not have good sense. You're a *fool* to think that you can drive all day and all night without any sleep. **2.** A person whose job was to entertain people in the household of a king, queen, or noble. *Noun.*
—**1.** To trick. The prisoner's plan to escape did not *fool* the guards. **2.** To be silly; joke; tease. I said I could swim a mile, but I was only *fooling. Verb.*
fool (fül) *noun, plural* **fools;** *verb,* **fooled, fooling.**

foolish Without good sense; unwise. It is *foolish* to dive into a lake without knowing how deep it is.
fool·ish (fü′lish) *adjective.*

foot **1.** The end part of the leg that humans and other animals walk on or stand on. **2.** The lowest or supporting part. It took all day to hike down to the *foot* of the mountain. Would you hold the *foot* of the ladder steady while I climb up? **3.** The part opposite the head. There is an extra blanket at the *foot* of the bed in case it gets cold during the night. **4.** A measure of length equal to 12 inches. One foot is the same as 0.3048 meters.
- **on foot.** By walking. Some people drove to the park, but we went *on foot.*
- **to put one's foot down.** To act firmly according to one's rights or authority. My friend had kept the borrowed sweater much too long, so I had *to put my foot down* and demand that it be returned the next day.
- **under foot.** Obstructing passage or movement. The kittens were always *under foot.*

foot (füt) *noun, plural* **feet.**

football **1.** A game played by two teams of eleven players each on a large field with goals at each end. Each team tries to make points by carrying, passing, or kicking the ball over the other team's goal. **2.** The oval ball used in this game.
foot·ball (füt′bôl′) *noun, plural* **footballs.**

foothill A low hill near the lower part of a mountain or mountain range. Their home lay in the *foothills* of the great mountains.
foot·hill (füt′hil′) *noun, plural* **foothills.**

footing **1.** The safe or firm placing of the feet. You can easily lose your *footing* on those wet, slippery rocks. **2.** A safe place or support for the feet. The icy ledge provided no *footing* for the mountain climbers. **3.** A position or relationship. We started off on a bad *footing* with our neighbors because we trampled on their garden the day we moved into our new home.
foot·ing (füt′ing) *noun, plural* **footings.**

footlights The row of lights along the front edge of a stage in a theater.
foot·lights (füt′līts′) *plural noun.*

footnote A note or explanation at the bottom of a page.
foot·note (füt′nōt′) *noun, plural* **footnotes.**

footprint A mark made by a foot or shoe. You made *footprints* all over the floor with your dirty feet.
foot·print (füt′print′) *noun, plural* **footprints.**

footstep **1.** The sound made by a step. **2.** A step of the foot.
- **to follow in someone's footsteps.** To imitate or follow the same course as someone. I'm going to *follow in my cousin's footsteps* and become a lawyer.
foot·step (füt′step′) *noun, plural* **footsteps.**

footstool A low stool on which a person can rest the feet while sitting down.
foot·stool (füt′stül′) *noun, plural* **footstools.**

for **1.** Throughout a time or distance of. We worked *for* two hours. The scouts hiked

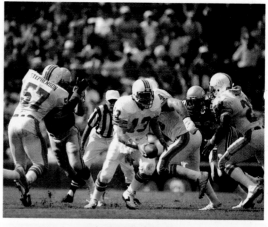

playing **football**

for three miles.   **2.** Intended or reserved to accommodate. This closet is *for* dishes. This room is *for* guests.   **3.** As a result of; because of. We were praised *for* our success in the debate.   **4.** In support or defense of. They were willing to fight *for* their beliefs.   **5.** In the amount of. We received a bill *for* fifty dollars.   **6.** At the cost of. I bought a ticket *for* fifteen dollars.   **7.** Directed to, sent to, given to, or belonging to. This letter is *for* you. **8.** In place of; instead of. They used a cardboard carton *for* a table. *Preposition.*
—Because. We should go, *for* it is late. *Conjunction.* ▲ Other words that sound like this are **fore** and **four**.
> **for** (fôr; *unstressed* fər) *preposition; conjunction.*

forage   Hay, grain, and other food for cows, horses, and similar animals. *Noun.*
—To hunt or search, especially for food or supplies. The birds *foraged* in the snow. *Verb.*
> **for·age** (fôr′ij *or* for′ij) *noun; verb,* **foraged, foraging.**

forbade   Past tense of **forbid**. The teacher *forbade* us to talk during the fire drill. Look up **forbid** for more information.
> **for·bade** (fər bad′ *or* fər bād′) *verb.*

forbid   To order not to do something; prohibit. The school *forbids* eating in the classrooms. I *forbid* you to go swimming.
> **for·bid** (fər bid′) *verb,* **forbade, forbidden, forbidding.**

force   **1.** Power or strength. The batter hit the ball with great *force*. The *force* of the explosion broke the windows.   **2.** Power or strength that is used against a person or thing. The sheriff had to use *force* to pry the top off the box.   **3.** A group of people who work together. The police *force* in this city is one of the best in the country.   **4.** Something that moves a body or stops or changes its motion. The *force* of gravity causes things to fall when they are dropped.   **5.** The power to convince or influence. The *force* of your argument convinced me. *Noun.*
—**1.** To cause someone to do something against his or her wishes; make. The rain *forced* us to cancel the picnic.   **2.** To cause to open by using force. I had to *force* the lock on my suitcase because I lost the key.   **3.** To get or make by using power or strength. They *forced* their way through the crowd. *Verb.*
> • **in force.**   Being observed or enforced; in effect. Despite yesterday's rain, rules for saving water are still *in force*.
> **force** (fôrs) *noun, plural* **forces;** *verb,* **forced, forcing.**

forceful   Having much strength or power;

vigorous. Everyone in the auditorium listened to the candidate's *forceful* speech.
> **force·ful** (fôrs′fəl) *adjective.*

forceps   A small tool for gripping and holding things. Forceps are used by doctors and dentists in operations.
> **for·ceps** (fôr′seps) *noun, plural* **forceps.**

ford   A shallow place where a river or other body of water can be crossed. *Noun.*
—To cross at a shallow place. The riders *forded* the river at its shallowest point. *Verb.*
> **ford** (fôrd) *noun, plural* **fords;** *verb,* **forded, fording.**

fore   At or toward the front. The pilot stood at the *fore* part of the ship. ▲ Other words that sound like this are **for** and **four**.
> **fore** (fôr) *adjective.*

fore-   A *prefix* that means: **1.** At or near the front. *Foreleg* means a front leg.   **2.** Ahead of time; before. *Foresee* means to see ahead of time.

forearm   The part of the arm between the elbow and the wrist.
> **fore·arm** (fôr′ärm′) *noun, plural* **forearms.**

forecast   To tell what will or may happen; predict. Some political experts tried to *forecast* the results of the election. *Verb.*
—A statement that tells what will or may happen; prediction. Let's listen to the weather *forecast* to find out if it's going to rain today. *Noun.*
> **fore·cast** (fôr′kast′) *verb,* **forecast** *or* **forecasted, forecasting;** *noun, plural* **forecasts.**

forefather   An ancestor. My *forefathers* came to America during colonial times.
> **fore·fa·ther** (fôr′fä′thər) *noun, plural* **forefathers.**

forefinger   The finger next to the thumb; index finger.
> **fore·fin·ger** (fôr′fing′gər) *noun, plural* **forefingers.**

forefoot   One of the front feet of an animal that has four feet.
> **fore·foot** (fôr′fut′) *noun, plural* **forefeet.**

foregone   Known or decided ahead of time. My friend's election as captain of the hockey team seemed to be a *foregone* conclusion.
> **fore·gone** (fôr′gôn′ *or* fôr′gon′) *adjective.*

---

at; āpe; fär; câre; end; mē; it; īce; pîerce; hot; ōld; sông, fôrk; oil; out; up; ūse; rüle; pùll; tûrn; chin; sing; shop; thin; <u>th</u>is; hw in white; zh in treasure. The symbol ə stands for the unstressed vowel sound in about, taken, pencil, lemon, and circus.

foreground   The part of a picture or view that is or seems to be nearest to the person looking at it.
fore·ground (fôr′ground′) *noun, plural* **foregrounds.**

Tulips are in the **foreground.**

forehead   The part of the face above the eyebrows.
fore·head (fôr′id *or* fôr′hed′) *noun, plural* **foreheads.**

foreign   **1.** Of or from another country. My neighbor from France speaks English with a *foreign* accent.   **2.** Outside a person's own country. Have you ever visited any *foreign* countries?   **3.** Having to do with other nations or governments. The president makes many decisions on *foreign* policy.
for·eign (fôr′ən) *adjective.*

foreigner   A person who is from another country. The festival I saw in Mexico is not usually seen by *foreigners.*
for·eign·er (fôr′ə nər) *noun, plural* **foreigners.**

foreleg   One of the front legs of an animal that has four or more legs.
fore·leg (fôr′leg′) *noun, plural* **forelegs.**

foreman   **1.** A worker who is in charge of a group of workers. Who is the *foreman* at the factory?   **2.** The chairperson of a jury. The *foreman* announced that the jury had reached a verdict.
fore·man (fôr′mən) *noun, plural* **foremen** (fôr′mən).

foremost   First in position or importance. The judge was considered the *foremost* citizen of the town.
fore·most (fôr′mōst′) *adjective.*

forerunner   **1.** A person or thing that comes before another. The bicycle was the *forerunner* of the motorcycle.   **2.** A sign of something coming. A brisk wind and a dark sky are often *forerunners* of a storm.
fore·run·ner (fôr′run′ər) *noun, plural* **forerunners.**

foresaw   Past tense of **foresee.** The hikers *foresaw* the hot weather and brought plenty of water. Look up **foresee** for more information.
fore·saw (fôr sô′) *verb.*

foresee   To know or see ahead of time. No one can really *foresee* what the world will be like one hundred years from now.
fore·see (fôr sē′) *verb,* **foresaw, foreseen, foreseeing.**

foreseen   Past participle of **foresee.** We should have *foreseen* that we did not have enough gasoline for the long trip. Look up **foresee** for more information.
fore·seen (fôr sēn′) *verb.*

foresight   Care or thought for the future. You showed *foresight* in bringing along an umbrella.
fore·sight (fôr′sīt′) *noun.*

forest   Many trees and plants covering a large area of land; woods.
for·est (fôr′ist) *noun, plural* **forests.**

forest ranger   A person whose job is to protect forests.

foretell   To tell ahead of time; predict. Some people think you can *foretell* a person's future by looking at the stars.
fore·tell (fôr tel′) *verb,* **foretold, foretelling.**

foretold   Past tense and past participle of **foretell.** The prophet *foretold* the king's death. Look up **foretell** for more information.
fore·told (fôr tōld′) *verb.*

forever   **1.** Throughout all time; without ever coming to an end. No one can expect things to remain the same *forever.*   **2.** Without letting up; always; constantly. That grouch is *forever* complaining about things.
for·ev·er (fə rev′ər) *adverb.*

forfeit   To lose or have to give up because of some fault, accident, or mistake. The top player *forfeited* the tennis match because of illness. I had to *forfeit* my place in line because I forgot my wallet. *Verb.*
—Something lost because of some fault, accident, or mistake. The game ended with *forfeit* when one player suffered a severe cramp and could not continue. *Noun.*
for·feit (fôr′fit) *verb,* **forfeited, forfeiting;** *noun, plural* **forfeits.**

forgave Past tense of **forgive**. I *forgave* my friend for forgetting my birthday. Look up **forgive** for more information.
  for·gave (fôr gāv′) *verb.*

forge¹ A furnace or hearth in which metal is heated. The fire softens the metal so that it can be hammered into shape. A blacksmith uses a forge to make horseshoes. *Noun.*
  —**1.** To heat in a forge until very hot and then hammer into shape. Blacksmiths used to *forge* iron into tools as well as horseshoes. **2.** To make or form. Diplomats *forged* a peace agreement between the two warring nations. **3.** To copy in order to trick or cheat. It is a crime to *forge* someone else's signature on the check. *Verb.*
  forge (fôrj) *noun, plural* **forges;** *verb,* **forged, forging.**

forge¹

forge² To move forward slowly but steadily. The tugboat *forged* through the rough waters of the bay.
  forge (fôrj) *verb,* **forged, forging.**

forget **1.** To not be able to remember. I was afraid I would *forget* the address, so I wrote it down. **2.** To fail to think of or do. I *forgot* to tell my parents that I would be late for dinner.
  for·get (fər get′) *verb,* **forgot, forgotten** or **forgot, forgetting.**

forgetful Likely to forget; having a poor memory. My *forgetful* cousin can never remember my telephone number.
  for·get·ful (fər get′fəl) *adjective.*

forget-me-not A low plant that has small blue, pink, or white flowers that are shaped like trumpets and grow in clusters.
  for·get-me-not (fər get′mē not′) *noun, plural* **forget-me-nots.**

forgive To stop blaming or feeling anger toward; pardon or excuse. I said I was sorry for breaking the window, and I asked my parents to *forgive* me.
  for·give (fər giv′) *verb,* **forgave, forgiven, forgiving.**

forgiven Past participle of **forgive.** I have *forgiven* my friend for tearing my sweater. Look up **forgive** for more information.
  for·giv·en (fər giv′ən) *verb.*

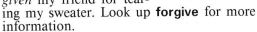

forget-me-not

forgiveness **1.** The act of forgiving; pardon. I beg your *forgiveness* for my being late. **2.** A willingness to forgive. After I heard why my friend had left without me, my heart was full of *forgiveness.*
  for·give·ness (fər giv′nis) *noun.*

forgot Past tense of **forget.** I *forgot* to take my lunch with me to school today. Look up **forget** for more information.
  for·got (fər got′) *verb.*

forgotten Past participle of **forget.** I realized that I had *forgotten* my keys. Look up **forget** for more information.
  for·got·ten (fər got′ən) *verb.*

fork **1.** A tool with a handle at one end and two or more thin pointed parts at the other. One kind of fork is used for eating food. A larger kind of fork is used for pitching hay. **2.** The place where something divides. Turn left at the *fork* in the road. *Noun.*
  —**1.** To lift or pitch with a fork. The farmer *forked* hay into the wagon. **2.** To divide into branches. The river *forks* two miles upstream. *Verb.*
  fork (fôrk) *noun, plural* **forks;** *verb,* **forked, forking.**

form **1.** The outline of something; shape. We could see the dim *form* of the bridge through the fog. **2.** Kind or type. Electricity

at; āpe; fär; câre; end; mē; it; īce; pîerce; hot; ōld; sông, fôrk; oil; out; up; ūse; rüle; pu̇ll; tûrn; chin; sing; shop; thin; this; hw in white; zh in treasure. The symbol ə stands for the unstressed vowel sound in about, taken, pencil, lemon, and circus.

is a *form* of energy.   **3.** A way of behaving or of doing something. I have been working to improve my *form* in diving.   **4.** A sheet of paper with blanks that are to be filled in. Many people who are applying for jobs must fill out forms.   **5.** One of the different ways that a word may appear. "Was" is a *form* of the verb "be." "Data" is a plural *form. Noun.*
—**1.** To make or shape. The artist *formed* a head out of clay. The citizens *formed* a plan to reduce pollution.   **2.** To take shape. The water dripping from the roof *formed* into icicles.   **3.** To make up. Students *formed* the biggest part of the crowd waiting to get into the concert. *Verb.*
> **form** (fôrm) *noun, plural* **forms;** *verb,* **formed, forming.**

formal   **1.** Very stiff and proper. The teacher's manner was so *formal* that the students were a little afraid.   **2.** Following strict custom, ceremony, or rules. At a *formal* dinner, the guest of honor sits to the right of the host.   **3.** Done or made with authority; official. A *formal* agreement has to be written, signed, and witnessed. *Adjective.*
—**1.** A formal dress.   **2.** A formal dance. *Noun.*
> **for·mal** (fôr′məl) *adjective; noun, plural* **formals.**

formation   **1.** The process of forming or making. The *formation* of ice from water requires a temperature below 32 degrees Fahrenheit.   **2.** Something formed or made. Scientists agree that some rock *formations* are several billion years old.   **3.** The way in which the members or units of a group are arranged. The band lined up in parade *formation.* Flocks of geese often fly in a *formation* shaped like a V.
> **for·ma·tion** (fôr mā′shən) *noun, plural* **formations.**

former   **1.** The first of two. Greenland and Madagascar are both islands; the *former* is in the North Atlantic Ocean and the latter is in the Indian Ocean.   **2.** Belonging to or happening in the past; earlier. In *former* times, people used fireplaces to heat their houses.
> **for·mer** (fôr′mər) *adjective.*

formerly   In time past; once. Trains were *formerly* pulled by steam locomotives.
> **for·mer·ly** (fôr′mər lē) *adverb.*

formula   **1.** An explanation of how to prepare a medicine, food, or other mixture. A formula says how much of each ingredient to use. The *formula* for mixing this drink is to add one part powder to three parts of cold water.   **2.** A rule expressed in symbols or numbers. The *formula* for changing miles

into kilometers is: 1 mile equals 1.61 kilometers.   **3.** A way of naming a chemical compound that uses a symbol for each element in a molecule of the compound. The chemical *formula* for water is H_2O.   **4.** A set method for doing or getting something. There is no real *formula* for making friends.
> **for·mu·la** (fôr′myə lə) *noun, plural* **formulas.**

forsake   To give up or leave. I have decided to *forsake* the city and live on a farm.
> **for·sake** (fôr sāk′) *verb,* **forsook, forsaken, forsaking.**

forsaken   Past participle of **forsake.** We took in a stray puppy whose owners had *forsaken* it. Look up **forsake** for more information.
> **for·sak·en** (fôr sā′kən) *verb.*

forsook   Past tense of **forsake.** The shepherd *forsook* the flock when wolves attacked. Look up **forsake** for more information.
> **for·sook** (fôr sùk′) *verb.*

forsythia   A shrub that has yellow flowers shaped like little bells. The flowers grow in clusters along the stem and bloom in the early spring before the leaves appear.
> **for·syth·i·a** (fôr sith′ē ə) *noun, plural* **forsythias.**

forsythia

fort   A strong building or area that can be defended against attacks by an enemy.
> **fort** (fôrt) *noun, plural* **forts.**

forth   **1.** Forward. From that day *forth,* the child was never lonely again.   **2.** Out into view. The buds on the bush burst *forth* on the first warm day of spring. ▲ Another word that sounds like this is **fourth.**
> **forth** (fôrth) *adverb.*

fortieth   Next after the thirty-ninth. *Adjective, noun.*
—One of forty equal parts; 1/40. *Noun.*
> **for·ti·eth** (fôr′tē ith) *adjective; noun, plural* **fortieths.**

fortification   **1.** The act of strengthening something. A high wall was built as part of the *fortification* of the town against attacking armies.   **2.** Something that strengthens, such as a wall or embankment.
> **for·ti·fi·ca·tion** (fôr′tə fi kā′shən) *noun, plural* **fortifications.**

fortify   **1.** To make stronger or more secure. Two thousand years ago the Chinese built a wall on their northern border to *fortify* themselves against invaders. **2.** To add strengthening ingredients to; enrich. This breakfast cereal is *fortified* with vitamins and iron.

for·ti·fy (fôr′tə fī′) *verb,* **fortified, fortifying.**

fortress A strong place that can be defended against attack; fort.

for·tress (fôr′tris) *noun, plural* **fortresses.**

fortunate Having or resulting from good luck; lucky. One *fortunate* person has won the contest twice. Scheduling our picnic for this sunny day was a *fortunate* choice.

for·tu·nate (fôr′chə nit) *adjective.*

fortune **1.** Something either good or bad that will happen to a person. The Gypsy in the circus is going to tell my *fortune.* **2.** Luck. It was my good *fortune* to find a summer job I liked at the first place I looked. **3.** Great wealth; riches. The queen has a *fortune* in jewels.

for·tune (fôr′chən) *noun, plural* **fortunes.**

fortuneteller A person who claims to be able to tell people's fortunes.

for·tune·tell·er (fôr′chən tel′ər) *noun, plural* **fortunetellers.**

forty Four times ten; 40.

for·ty (fôr′tē) *noun, plural* **forties;** *adjective.*

forum **1.** The public square of an ancient Roman city. Business and other important activities took place in the forum. **2.** A meeting to discuss issues or questions of public interest. A *forum* was held at the school to discuss littering in the neighborhood.

fo·rum (fôr′əm) *noun, plural* **forums.**

forward Toward what is in front or ahead. The soldier stepped *forward* to receive the medal. We are looking *forward* to our vacation. *Adverb.*
—**1.** At or toward the front. I took a *forward* seat on the plane. **2.** Bold or rude. Some *forward* children were making fun of the old couple. *Adjective.*
—To send ahead to a new address. My parents *forwarded* the mail I got during the summer to my address at camp. *Verb.*
—A player whose position is near the front of the team in certain games. My cousin plays *forward* on the basketball team. *Noun.*

for·ward (fôr′wərd) *adverb; adjective; verb,* **forwarded, forwarding;** *noun, plural* **forwards.**

forwards Another spelling for the adverb **forward.** The car rolled *forwards.*

for·wards (fôr′wərdz) *adverb.*

fossil The hardened remains or traces of an animal or plant that lived long ago. The *fossils* that we found were imprints of ancient leaves and seashells in rock.

fos·sil (fos′əl) *noun, plural* **fossils.**

fossil fuel A fuel that was formed from the remains of prehistoric plants and animals. Coal and petroleum are fossil fuels.

foster To help the growth or development of. My parents *fostered* my interest in music by giving me piano lessons. *Verb.*
—Giving or receiving care in a family without being related by birth or adoption. The state has a special department that tries to find *foster* parents for children who have no homes of their own. *Adjective.*

fos·ter (fôs′tər) *verb,* **fostered, fostering;** *adjective.*

fought Past tense of **fight.** The armies *fought* a long battle. Look up **fight** for more information.

fought (fôt) *verb.*

foul **1.** Very unpleasant or dirty. There was a *foul* odor in the air when the sewer pipes broke. I would never go swimming in that river because the water is *foul.* **2.** Cloudy, rainy, or stormy. *Foul* weather delayed the ship. **3.** Very bad; evil. The villain in the story had committed all sorts of *foul* deeds. **4.** Breaking the rules; unfair. An umpire or referee applies the rules and prevents any *foul* play. **5.** Outside the foul line in a baseball game. The batter hit a *foul* ball. *Adjective.*
—**1.** A breaking of rules. The basketball player committed a *foul* by knocking down another player. **2.** A baseball that is hit outside the foul line. *Noun.*
—**1.** To make dirty. The factory *fouled* the lake by pumping waste into it. **2.** To tangle or become tangled. The child *fouled* the fishing line in the bushes along the shore. **3.** To hit a foul ball in baseball. The batter *fouled* the ball to the right of first base. *Verb.* ▲ Another word that sounds like this is **fowl.**

foul (foul) *adjective,* **fouler, foulest;** *noun, plural* **fouls;** *verb,* **fouled, fouling.**

foul line Either of the two lines in baseball that go from home plate through first or third base to the limits of the playing field.

---

at; āpe; fär; câre; end; mē; it; īce; pîerce; hot; ōld; sông, fôrk; oil; out; up; ūse; rüle; pùll; tûrn; chin; sing; shop; thin; this; hw in white; zh in treasure. The symbol ə stands for the unstressed vowel sound in about, taken, pencil, lemon, and circus.

found¹   Past tense and past participle of **find.** I *found* the watch I thought I had lost. Look up **find** for more information.
   found (found) *verb.*

found²   To start or bring into being; establish. The students worked together to *found* a science club.
   found (found) *verb,* **founded, founding.**

foundation   **1.** The act of founding. We studied the American Revolution and the *foundation* of the United States.   **2.** The base on which a structure is built. The *foundation* of the house is a big slab of concrete.   **3.** Something that supports or justifies; basis. The story was just a rumor, without *foundation.*
   foun·da·tion (foun dā'shən) *noun, plural* **foundations.**

foundry   A place where metal is melted and formed into different shapes.
   found·ry (foun'drē) *noun, plural* **foundries.**

fountain

fountain   **1.** A stream of water that is made to shoot from the ground or from a structure designed for it. Some fountains are used to drink from, and others are used only as decoration.   **2.** An abundant source of something. That teacher is a *fountain* of knowledge about American history.
   foun·tain (foun'tən) *noun, plural* **fountains.**

fountain pen   A pen that has a little tube inside to hold and feed liquid ink to the writing point.

four   One more than three; 4. ▲ Another word that sounds like this is **for.**
   four (fôr) *noun, plural* **fours;** *adjective.*

Four-H club   One of a group of organizations for young people that teach and pro-

mote skills in farming and maintaining a home. The Four-H clubs are named for their purpose of improving the heads, hearts, hands, and health of their members.
   Four-H club (fôr'āch').

fourteen   Four more than ten; 14.
   four·teen (fôr'tēn') *noun, plural* **fourteens;** *adjective.*

fourteenth   Next after the thirteenth. *Adjective, noun.*
   —One of fourteen equal parts; ¹⁄₁₄. *Noun.*
   four·teenth (fôr'tēnth') *adjective; noun, plural* **fourteenths.**

fourth   Next after the third. *Adjective, noun.*
   —One of four equal parts; ¹⁄₄. *Noun.* ▲ Another word that sounds like this is **forth.**
   fourth (fôrth) *adjective; noun, plural* **fourths.**

Fourth of July   A holiday celebrated in the United States. Look up **Independence Day** for more information.

fowl   One of a number of birds that are used for food. The chicken, turkey, and duck are kinds of fowl. ▲ Another word that sounds like this is **foul.**
   fowl (foul) *noun, plural* **fowl** or **fowls.**

fox   **1.** A wild animal that is closely related to the dog. A fox has a pointed nose and ears, a bushy tail, and thick fur.   **2.** The fur of a fox.   **3.** A sly or cunning person. You were a *fox* to pretend to be sleeping when I came into your room.
   fox (foks) *noun, plural* **foxes.**

fox

foxhound   A hound with a very good sense of smell. It is trained to hunt foxes. A foxhound has a tan, black, and white coat.
   fox·hound (foks'hound') *noun, plural* **foxhounds.**

fraction   **1.** A part of a whole. Only a small *fraction* of the people watching the football game left before it was over.   **2.** A number that stands for one or more of the equal parts of a whole. A fraction shows the division of one number by a second number. ⅔, ¾, and ¹⁄₁₆ are fractions.
   frac·tion (frak'shən) *noun, plural* **fractions.**

fracture To crack or break. The hockey player fell and *fractured* an ankle. *Verb.*
—A crack or break. With care, a *fracture* of a bone will usually heal. *Noun.*
frac·ture (frak′chər) *verb*, **fractured, fracturing**; *noun, plural* **fractures.**

fragile Easily broken; delicate. That china cup is very *fragile.*
frag·ile (fraj′əl) *adjective.*

fragment A part that is broken off; small piece. The students found some *fragments* of Indian pottery in the woods.
frag·ment (frag′mənt) *noun, plural* **fragments.**

fragrance A sweet or pleasing smell. Roses have a beautiful *fragrance.*
fra·grance (frā′grəns) *noun, plural* **fragrances.**

fragrant Having a sweet or pleasing smell. The flowers made the whole room *fragrant.*
fra·grant (frā′grənt) *adjective.*

frail 1. Lacking in strength; weak. The child was too *frail* to play most sports. 2. Easily broken or torn; delicate. That lace is very old and *frail.*
frail (frāl) *adjective*, **frailer, frailest.**

frame 1. A structure that borders or supports something. The window *frame* needs painting. 2. The structure of a person's body; build. That football player has a large *frame. Noun.*
—1. To set in a bordering or supporting structure. The painter *framed* the drawing. 2. To enclose as a picture frame does. The hat *frames* your face nicely. 3. To express or construct carefully. The teacher *framed* each question so that everyone would understand. *Verb.*
frame (frām) *noun, plural* **frames**; *verb,* **framed, framing.**

framework A structure that gives shape or support to something. The *framework* of the building is steel.
frame·work (frām′wûrk′) *noun, plural* **frameworks.**

franc A unit of money and a coin of France, Belgium, Switzerland, and many other countries. ▲ Another word that sounds like this is **frank.**
franc (frangk) *noun, plural* **francs.**

France A country in western Europe.
France (frans) *noun.*

frank Honest and open in expressing one's real thoughts and feelings. Let me be *frank* and tell you that your voice is not good enough for the choir. ▲ Another word that sounds like this is **franc.**
frank (frangk) *adjective*, **franker, frankest.**

frankfurter A sausage made of beef or beef and pork. It is often served on a long roll.
frank·furt·er (frangk′fər tər) *noun, plural* **frankfurters.**

Word History

The word **frankfurter** comes from a German word that means "from Frankfurt." This kind of sausage may have been first made in the city of Frankfurt in Germany.

frantic Wildly excited by worry or fear. The children became *frantic* when they realized they were lost in the crowded department store.
fran·tic (fran′tik) *adjective.*

fraud 1. A tricking of someone in order to cheat. To sell fake diamonds that are supposed to be genuine would be *fraud.* 2. A person or thing that tricks or cheats; fake. Someone who claims to be a doctor but really isn't is nothing but a *fraud.*
fraud (frôd) *noun, plural* **frauds.**

fray To separate into loose threads. Many years of wear had *frayed* the cuffs of the coat.
fray (frā) *verb*, **frayed, fraying.**

freak 1. A person, animal, or plant that has not developed normally. A mouse with two tails would be a freak. 2. Anything odd or unusual.
freak (frēk) *noun, plural* **freaks.**

framework of a house

at; āpe; fär; câre; end; mē; it; īce; pîerce; hot; ōld; sông, fôrk; oil; out; up; ūse; rüle; pùll; tûrn; chin; sing; shop; thin; this; hw in white; zh in treasure. The symbol ə stands for the unstressed vowel sound in about, taken, pencil, lemon, and circus.

freckle A small brownish spot on the skin. The twins have red hair and *freckles*.
freck·le (frek′əl) *noun, plural* **freckles.**

free **1.** Having one's liberty; not under another's control. We kept the injured bird until its wing healed, and then we set it *free*. **2.** Not held back or confined. You are *free* to come and go as you like in the library. **3.** Not troubled or affected by something. They live a life that is *free* from care or worry. The veterinarian said that our dog was *free* from disease. **4.** Not obstructed; clear. The stairway should be kept *free* of toys. **5.** Without cost. We received *free* tickets to the show. *Adjective.*
—Without cost. Children were admitted *free* to the theater. *Adverb.*
—To make or set free. We *freed* the trapped animal. *Verb.*
free (frē) *adjective,* **freer, freest;** *adverb;* *verb,* **freed, freeing.**

freedom **1.** The condition of being free; liberty. The slaves struggled for their *freedom*. **2.** The condition of being able to move or act without being held back. Our dog has complete *freedom* of the house.
free·dom (frē′dəm) *noun, plural* **freedoms.**

freeway A highway with more than two lanes and no intersections or stoplights. A freeway is used for fast and direct driving.
free·way (frē′wā′) *noun, plural* **freeways.**

freeze **1.** To harden because of the cold. When water *freezes*, it becomes ice. **2.** To cover or block with ice. The cold weather *froze* the pipes in our house while we were on vacation. **3.** To make or become very cold. We stood there *freezing* as we waited for the bus. **4.** To become fixed or motionless. The campers *froze* when they saw the snake. **5.** To damage or be damaged by cold or frost. The orange crop in Florida *froze* this winter.
freeze (frēz) *verb,* **froze, frozen, freezing.**

freezer A refrigerator or part of a refrigerator used to freeze food quickly or to store food that is already frozen.
freez·er (frē′zər) *noun, plural* **freezers.**

freight **1.** The carrying of goods by land, air, or water. Most of this airline's business is *freight*. **2.** The goods carried in this way; cargo. It took five hours to unload all the *freight* from the train.
freight (frāt) *noun.*

freighter A ship used for carrying cargo.
freight·er (frā′tər) *noun, plural* **freighters.**

French **1.** The people of France. **2.** The language of France. *Noun.*
—Having to do with France, its people, their language, or their culture. *Adjective.*
French (french) *noun; adjective.*

French fries Thin strips of potatoes that are fried in fat until they are brown and crisp.
French fries (frīz).

French Guiana A territory of France that is on the northeastern coast of South America.
French Gui·a·na (gē ä′nə *or* gē an′ə).

French horn A brass musical instrument. A French horn has a long tube that is coiled in a circle and that then widens into the shape of a bell.

French horn

Frenchman A person who was born in or is a citizen of France.
French·man (french′mən) *noun, plural* **Frenchmen** (french′mən).

Frenchwoman A woman who was born in or is a citizen of France.
French·wom·an (french′wùm′ən) *noun, plural* **Frenchwomen** (french′wim′ən).

frenzy Wild excitement. The people were in a *frenzy* to escape from the bees.
fren·zy (fren′zē) *noun, plural* **frenzies.**

frequency **1.** A happening again and again. The *frequency* of storms this spring caused the pond to overflow. **2.** The number of times something happens or takes place during a period of time. The *frequency* of a person's heartbeat is usually between

sixty and ninety beats a minute. **3.** The number of cycles per second of a radio wave or other kind of wave or radiation.
fre·quen·cy (frē′kwən sē) *noun, plural* **frequencies.**

frequent Happening often; taking place again and again. There are *frequent* thunderstorms in this area in the summer.
fre·quent (frē′kwənt) *adjective.*

fresh **1.** Newly done, made, or gathered. I always buy *fresh* vegetables instead of canned or frozen ones. **2.** New; another. I took out a *fresh* piece of stationery after I made a mistake in my letter. **3.** Clean or refreshing. It was stuffy in the room so we stepped outside for a breath of *fresh* air. **4.** Not salty. Most lakes have *fresh* water. **5.** Rude; impudent. I was kept after school for being *fresh* to the teacher.
fresh (fresh) *adjective,* **fresher, freshest.**

freshen To make or become fresh. The rain *freshened* the air.
fresh·en (fresh′ən) *verb,* **freshened, freshening.**

freshman A student in the first year of high school or college.
fresh·man (fresh′mən) *noun, plural* **freshmen** (fresh′mən).

freshwater Of or living in fresh water rather than in salt water. The perch is a *freshwater* fish.
fresh·wa·ter (fresh′wô′tər) *adjective.*

Fri. An abbreviation for *Friday.*

friar A man who belongs to one of several religious orders of the Roman Catholic Church.
fri·ar (frī′ər) *noun, plural* **friars.**

friction **1.** The rubbing of one thing against another. The *friction* of the rope on the climber's hands was painful. **2.** A force that resists movement between two surfaces that are touching one another. The *friction* between two parts of a machine can be reduced by oiling them. **3.** Conflict or disagreement. There was *friction* between the two neighbors.
fric·tion (frik′shən) *noun.*

Friday The sixth day of the week.
Fri·day (frī′dē *or* frī′dā) *noun, plural* **Fridays.**

fried Past tense and past participle of **fry.** I *fried* an egg for my breakfast this morning. It was *fried* in butter. Look up **fry** for more information.
fried (frīd) *verb.*

friend **1.** A person whom one knows well and likes. I like to play with my *friends* after school. **2.** A person who supports or favors something. The governor is a *friend* of public education.
friend (frend) *noun, plural* **friends.**

friendly **1.** Like or wanting to be a friend; warm and pleasant. My old science teacher greeted me with a *friendly* smile. We said hello to the new student and tried to be *friendly.* **2.** Not angry or fighting; not hostile. Canada and the United States are on *friendly* terms.
friend·ly (frend′lē) *adjective,* **friendlier, friendliest.**

friendship The warm feeling between friends. The two classmates' *friendship* started when they used to walk home together.
friend·ship (frend′ship′) *noun, plural* **friendships.**

fright **1.** A sudden fear or alarm. The people in the burning building were seized with *fright.* **2.** A person or thing that is ugly or shocking. You were a *fright* in the witch costume that you wore on Halloween.
fright (frīt) *noun, plural* **frights.**

frighten **1.** To make or become suddenly afraid or alarmed. The loud explosion *frightened* everyone. Deer *frighten* easily. **2.** To drive away by scaring. The dog *frightened* away the squirrels.
fright·en (frī′tən) *verb,* **frightened, frightening.**

frightful **1.** Causing sudden fear; alarming. I was awakened by a *frightful* noise. **2.** Disgusting or shocking. The amount of litter in the park was *frightful.*
fright·ful (frīt′fəl) *adjective.*

frigid **1.** Very cold. Some animals with heavy fur can survive in a *frigid* climate. **2.** Cold in feeling; unfriendly. The political opponents gave each other a *frigid* greeting when they met on the street.
frig·id (frij′id) *adjective.*

Word History

Friday comes from the Old English word meaning "Frigga's day." Frigga was the queen of the pagan English gods.

at; āpe; fär; câre; end; mē; it; īce; pîerce; hot; ōld; sông, fôrk; oil; out; up; ūse; rüle; pùll; tûrn; chin; sing; shop; thin; this; hw in white; zh in treasure. The symbol ə stands for the unstressed vowel sound in about, taken, pencil, lemon, and circus.

fringe 1. A border of hanging threads or cords. The bedspread has a *fringe* all the way around the edge. 2. Anything like a fringe. A *fringe* of bushes lined the driveway.
  fringe (frinj) *noun, plural* **fringes.**

Frisbee A trademark for a plastic disk that players throw back and forth in a game.
  Fris·bee (friz′bē) *noun, plural* **Frisbees.**

frivolous Lacking seriousness or sense; silly. *Frivolous* people usually aren't able to keep their minds on anything for very long.
  friv·o·lous (friv′ə ləs) *adjective.*

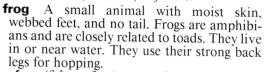

fringe on a jacket

frog A small animal with moist skin, webbed feet, and no tail. Frogs are amphibians and are closely related to toads. They live in or near water. They use their strong back legs for hopping.
  frog (frôg *or* frog) *noun, plural* **frogs.**

frog

frogman A swimmer who is specially trained and equipped to work underwater.
  frog·man (frôg′man′ *or* frog′man′) *noun, plural* **frogmen** (frôg′men′ *or* frog′men′).

frolic To play about happily and gaily. We liked to watch the colts *frolic* in the field.
  frol·ic (frol′ik) *verb,* **frolicked, frolicking.**

from 1. Starting at; beginning with. We flew *from* New York to Chicago. I work *from* nine o'clock to five. 2. With a particular person, place, or thing as the source. I got a letter *from* my friends in Canada. My parents withdrew some money *from* the bank. 3. Off or out of. Take those books *from* the shelves. Two *from* five leaves three. 4. Out of the material of. Their house was made *from* bricks. 5. At a distance relative to. They live ten miles *from* our house. 6. Be-

cause of. We were shivering *from* the cold. 7. As being different from. It's easy to tell lions *from* tigers.
  from (from *or* frum *or unstressed* frəm) *preposition.*

frond The leaf of a fern or palm.
  frond (frond) *noun, plural* **fronds.**

front 1. The part that faces forward or comes first. This jacket has a zipper in the *front.* The introduction comes at the *front* of the book. 2. A place or position ahead of the forward part. He entered the store while I waited in *front.* 3. The land that lies along a street or body of water. We rented a cabin on the lake *front* for the summer. 4. A place where fighting is going on between enemy forces. The general rode all along the *front* to encourage the soldiers. 5. The boundary line between two air masses of different temperatures. The temperature will drop as the cold *front* moves into the area. *Noun.*
  —On or near the front. We knocked on the *front* door. I read the *front* page of the newspaper. *Adjective.*
  —To face. Our house *fronts* on a busy street. *Verb.*
  • **in front of.** In a place or position directly before; ahead of. A tall person sat *in front of* me in the theater, so I couldn't see the stage.
  front (frunt) *noun, plural* **fronts;** *adjective; verb,* **fronted, fronting.**

frontier 1. The far edge of a country, where people are just beginning to settle. The development of the railroad helped to move the American *frontier* farther west. 2. The border between two countries. We crossed the *frontier* between Canada and the United States on our trip. 3. The part of a subject or field of study where new discoveries are being made. Doctors are constantly exploring the *frontiers* of medicine.
  fron·tier (frun tîr′) *noun, plural* **frontiers.**

frost 1. Tiny ice crystals that form on a surface when water vapor in the air freezes. There was *frost* on the windowpanes this morning. 2. Very cold weather during which the temperature is below freezing. *Frost* damaged the orange crop in Florida this winter. *Noun.*
  —1. To cover with frost. The first cold night *frosted* my windows. 2. To cover with frosting or something like frosting. We *frosted* the birthday cake with chocolate icing. *Verb.*
  frost (frôst) *noun, plural* **frosts;** *verb,* **frosted, frosting.**

frostbite Injury to some part of the body caused by exposure to extreme cold. *Noun.*

300

F

—To injure by exposure to extreme cold. The explorer's fingers and toes were *frostbitten* by the cold. *Verb.*
frost·bite (frôst′bīt′) *noun; verb,* **frostbit, frostbitten, frostbiting.**

frosting A mixture of sugar, butter, and flavoring used to cover a cake or cookies; icing.
frost·ing (frôs′ting) *noun, plural* **frostings.**

frosty Cold enough for frost; freezing. Our family loves to take walks on *frosty* winter evenings.
frost·y (frôs′tē) *adjective,* **frostier, frostiest.**

froth A mass of bubbles formed in or on a liquid; foam. A fine *froth* appeared as we slowly boiled the milk. *Noun.*
—To give out or form froth. The tired horse *frothed* at the mouth. The mixture *frothed* as it began to boil. *Verb.*
froth (frôth) *noun, plural* **froths;** *verb,* **frothed, frothing.**

frown A wrinkling of the forehead. A person who is thinking hard or is angry or worried may make a frown. A *frown* came to your face when you were trying to think of an answer to the riddle. *Noun.*
—**1.** To wrinkle the forehead in thought, anger, or worry. The captain *frowned* at the bad news. **2.** To look with anger or disapproval. My parents *frown* on my staying out late at night. *Verb.*
frown (froun) *noun, plural* **frowns;** *verb,* **frowned, frowning.**

froze Past tense of **freeze.** The lake *froze* last night, so we went skating today. Look up **freeze** for more information.
froze (frōz) *verb.*

frozen Past participle of **freeze.** The water dripping from the roof had *frozen* and formed icicles. Look up **freeze** for more information.
fro·zen (frō′zən) *verb.*

frugal **1.** Careful in spending money and using resources; not wasteful. A *frugal* shopper buys only necessary things. **2.** Costing little. The poor family ate a *frugal* meal of beans and bread.
fru·gal (frü′gəl) *adjective.*

fruit **1.** The part of a plant that contains the seeds. Nuts, berries, and pods are fruits. **2.** A plant part that contains seeds and is fleshy or juicy and good to eat. Oranges, apples, melons, bananas, and grapes are fruits.
fruit (früt) *noun, plural* **fruit** or **fruits.**

frustrate **1.** To keep from doing something; prevent. I was *frustrated* in trying to learn the correct address. **2.** To prevent from being fulfilled. The rainy weather *frustrated* our plans for a hike. **3.** To make someone feel helpless or incapable; discourage. My bad luck in not being able to find a job *frustrated* me.
frus·trate (frus′trāt) *verb,* **frustrated, frustrating.**

fry To cook in hot fat. We *fried* bacon and eggs for our breakfast.
fry (frī) *verb,* **fried, frying.**

ft. An abbreviation for *feet, foot,* or *fort.*

fudge A soft candy made out of sugar, milk, butter, and flavoring.
fudge (fuj) *noun, plural* **fudges.**

fuel Something that is burned to provide heat or power. Coal, wood, and oil are fuels.
fu·el (fū′əl) *noun, plural* **fuels.**

fugitive A person who runs away or tries to escape. The police chased and caught the *fugitive.*
fu·gi·tive (fū′ji tiv) *noun, plural* **fugitives.**

-ful A *suffix* that means: **1.** Having the qualities of; full of. *Fearful* means full of fear. **2.** Able to; likely to. *Forgetful* means likely to forget. **3.** The amount that will fill something. *Cupful* means the amount that will fill a cup.

fulcrum The support on which a lever rests or turns when it is moving or lifting something. The farmer used a rock as a *fulcrum* to move the heavy boulder.
ful·crum (fùl′krəm) *noun, plural* **fulcrums.**

fulfill **1.** To carry out or finish. I *fulfilled* my household chores and went out to play. **2.** To meet or satisfy. If you are a citizen and if you are at least eighteen years old, you *fulfill* two requirements for voting.
ful·fill (fùl fil′) *verb,* **fulfilled, fulfilling.**

full **1.** Holding as much or as many as possible. I poured myself a *full* glass of milk. **2.** Having or containing a large number or quantity. We had a house *full* of guests for the party. **3.** Complete; entire. We have a *full* two weeks of vacation. **4.** Having a rounded outline; plump. My cousin has a *full,* round face. *Adjective.*
—Completely; entirely. I filled the pitcher *full* with lemonade. *Adverb.*
full (fùl) *adjective,* **fuller, fullest;** *adverb.*

at; āpe; fär; câre; end; mē; it; īce; pîerce; hot; ōld; sông, fôrk; oil; out; up; ūse; rüle; pùll; tûrn; chin; sing; shop; thin; this; hw in white; zh in treasure. The symbol ə stands for the unstressed vowel sound in about, taken, pencil, lemon, and circus.

full moon　**1.** The moon when all of the side that faces the earth is shining.　**2.** The time when this happens. Tonight is the *full moon.*

fully　**1.** Completely; entirely. I don't *fully* understand that arithmetic problem.　**2.** At least; not less than. The train was *fully* an hour late.
　ful·ly (fŭl′ē) *adverb.*

fumble　**1.** To look for in a clumsy way. I *fumbled* around in my pocket looking for my keys.　**2.** To handle clumsily or drop. The runner *fumbled* the football. *Verb.*
　—The act of fumbling. The quarterback's *fumble* cost us the game. *Noun.*
　fum·ble (fum′bəl) *verb,* **fumbled, fumbling;** *noun, plural* **fumbles.**

fume　A smoke or gas that is harmful or has a bad smell. *Fumes* from automobiles can make a city's air harmful to breathe. *Noun.*
　—To be very angry or irritated. The driver *fumed* while stuck in traffic. *Verb.*
　fume (fūm) *noun, plural* **fumes;** *verb,* **fumed, fuming.**

fun　**1.** Enjoyment or amusement. We had *fun* riding our sleds down the hill.　**2.** Playfulness. My joking friend is always full of *fun.*
　• **to make fun of** or **to poke fun at.** To laugh at; ridicule. They *made fun of* the singer's strange haircut.
　fun (fun) *noun.*

function　**1.** Use or purpose. An usher's *function* is to help people find their seats. The *function* of the heart is to pump blood through the body.　**2.** A formal gathering. All the supporters of the art museum went to a *function* to celebrate the museum's fiftieth anniversary. *Noun.*
　—To work or serve. A motor *functions* best when it is kept well oiled. *Verb.*
　func·tion (fungk′shən) *noun, plural* **functions;** *verb,* **functioned, functioning.**

fund　**1.** A sum of money set aside for a specific purpose. Mr. and Mrs. Black set up a *fund* for their children's college education.　**2.** A supply. This book has a *fund* of information on American Indians.　**3. funds.** Money that is ready for use. The state does not have the *funds* to repair the highway.
　fund (fund) *noun, plural* **funds.**

fundamental　Serving as a basis; essential; basic. Learning the rules is a *fundamental* part of any game. *Adjective.*
　—An essential part. Addition and subtraction are two of the *fundamentals* of arithmetic. *Noun.*
　fun·da·men·tal (fun′də men′təl) *adjective; noun, plural* **fundamentals.**

funeral　The ceremony and services held before the burial of a dead person.
　fu·ner·al (fū′nər əl) *noun, plural* **funerals.**

fungi　More than one fungus.
　fun·gi (fun′jī) *plural noun.*

fungus　One of a large group of living things that have cell walls similar to those of plants but that have no flowers, leaves, or green coloring. Fungi live on plant or animal matter. Mushrooms, mildews, and molds are fungi.
　fun·gus (fung′gəs) *noun, plural* **fungi** or **funguses.**

fungi growing on a tree

funnel　**1.** A utensil that has a wide cone at one end and a thin tube at the other. You can use a funnel to pour something into a container with a small opening without spilling.　**2.** A round chimney or smokestack on a steamship or steam engine.
　fun·nel (fun′əl) *noun, plural* **funnels.**

funny　**1.** Causing laughter or amusement. The comedian told us a very *funny* joke.　**2.** Strange; odd. It seems *funny* that you never told us your real name.
　fun·ny (fun′ē) *adjective,* **funnier, funniest.**

fur　**1.** The soft, thick, hairy coat of certain animals. The raccoon has striped *fur.*　**2.** The skin of an animal that has fur. Fur is used in making clothing, rugs, and many other things.　**3.** A piece of clothing made of fur. ▲ Another word that sounds like this is **fir.**
　fur (fûr) *noun, plural* **furs.**

furious　**1.** Very angry. My folks were *furious* when we missed the train by one minute.　**2.** Violent; fierce. The *furious* thunderstorm knocked down many trees and electrical lines.
　fu·ri·ous (fyûr′ē əs) *adjective.*

furlough An absence from duty for which permission has been given; vacation. The sailors spent their *furlough* seeing the sights in the city.
fur·lough (fûr′lō) *noun, plural* **furloughs.**

furnace A large, enclosed, metal box where heat is produced. A furnace is used to heat a building or to melt metal.
fur·nace (fûr′nis) *noun, plural* **furnaces.**

furnish 1. To supply with furniture. We *furnished* our new den with some old chairs and a Ping-Pong table. 2. To supply or provide. The book *furnished* us with useful facts about the American Revolution.
fur·nish (fûr′nish) *verb,* **furnished, furnishing.**

furniture Tables, chairs, beds, and other movable articles used in a home or office.
fur·ni·ture (fûr′ni chər) *noun.*

furrow A long, narrow groove. Farmers plant seeds in the *furrows* they dig. The wheels of the car made *furrows* in the mud.
fur·row (fûr′ō) *noun, plural* **furrows.**

furry Like fur or covered with fur. The new rug in the living room is soft and *furry*. A hamster is a *furry* little animal.
fur·ry (fûr′ē) *adjective,* **furrier, furriest.**

further A comparative of **far.** We left without *further* delay. I swam to the *further* side of the pond. We'll talk *further* about this later. Let's walk a little *further*. Look up **far** for more information. *Adjective; adverb.*
—To help forward; support. The United Nations was formed to *further* the cause of peace. *Verb.*
fur·ther (fûr′thər) *adjective; adverb; verb,* **furthered, furthering.**

furthermore In addition; moreover; besides. I don't want to go to bed yet, and *furthermore* I still have some homework to do.
fur·ther·more (fûr′thər môr′) *adverb.*

furthest A superlative of **far.** Going swimming is the *furthest* thing from my mind on this cold day. Of all the family, you have gone *furthest* in your education. Look up **far** for more information.
fur·thest (fûr′thist) *adjective; adverb.*

fury 1. Violent anger; rage. I was in a *fury* with myself because I had foolishly locked the keys in the car. 2. Violent or fierce action. The *fury* of the storm raged all night.
fu·ry (fyür′ē) *noun, plural* **furies.**

fuse¹ 1. A strip of metal in an electric circuit. The fuse melts and breaks the circuit if the current becomes too strong. Fuses are used to prevent fires caused by wires that carry too much electricity. 2. A piece of cord that can burn. A fuse is used to explode a bomb or other explosive device.
fuse (fūz) *noun, plural* **fuses.**

fuse² 1. To melt by heating. I *fused* the metal with a torch. 2. To blend or unite. Because gold is such a soft metal, it is *fused* with silver or copper to harden it.
fuse (fūz) *verb,* **fused, fusing.**

fuselage The main body of an airplane, carrying the passengers, cargo, and crew.
fu·se·lage (fū′sə läzh′ *or* fū′sə lij) *noun, plural* **fuselages.**

fusion 1. The act or process of melting or blending. The *fusion* of copper and tin makes bronze. 2. The combining of the nuclei of two atoms to form the nucleus of a heavier atom. Large amounts of energy are released during fusion.
fu·sion (fū′zhən) *noun, plural* **fusions.**

fuss An unnecessary stir or bother over small or unimportant things. There was a big *fuss* over which team should bat first. *Noun.*
—To make an unnecessary stir or bother. You're been *fussing* over your necktie for half an hour. *Verb.*
fuss (fus) *noun, plural* **fusses;** *verb,* **fussed, fussing.**

future Happening in the time after the present; coming. I hope that your *future* work will be better. *Adjective.*
—1. The time that is to come. In the *future*, please call if you are going to be late. 2. Another word for **future tense.** *Noun.*
fu·ture (fū′chər) *adjective; noun.*

future tense A form of a verb that shows that an action will happen or a condition will exist in the future. In the sentence "We will go to the beach tomorrow," "will go" is a verb in the future tense. In the sentence "I will be on time," "will be" is a verb in the future tense. The future tense is also called the **future.**

fuzz Fine, loose fibers or hair. A peach is covered with *fuzz*.
fuzz (fuz) *noun.*

fuzzy 1. Covered with or like fuzz. Some caterpillars are *fuzzy*. The blanket was soft and *fuzzy*. 2. Not clear; blurred. That would be a good photograph except that it's too *fuzzy*.
fuzz·y (fuz′ē) *adjective,* **fuzzier, fuzziest.**

at; āpe; fär; câre; end; mē; it; īce; pîerce; hot; ōld; sông, fôrk; oil; out; up; ūse; rüle; půll; tûrn; chin; sing; shop; thin; this; hw in white; zh in treasure. The symbol ə stands for the unstressed vowel sound in about, taken, pencil, lemon, and circus.

1. In its first form the letter **G** was the third letter (**C**) in the alphabet used by some Middle Eastern tribes.

2. This letter was then borrowed by the Greeks about 3,000 years ago. They pronounced it like the *g* in game.

3. When an ancient tribe near Rome borrowed this letter, they used it to represent both the hard *g* sound, as in *game,* and the *k* sound.

4. The Romans used this letter only for the *k* sound and invented a new letter to stand for the *g* sound.

5. Our modern capital **G** looks very much like the Roman letter.

g, G   The seventh letter of the alphabet.
  g, G (jē) *noun, plural* **g's, G's.**

g   An abbreviation for *gram.*

GA   Postal abbreviation for *Georgia.*

Ga.   An abbreviation for *Georgia.*

gable   The part of an outside wall between the sides of a sloping roof. The gable is shaped like a triangle.
  ga·ble (gā′bəl) *noun, plural* **gables.**

Gabon   A country in west-central Africa.
  Ga·bon (ga bōn′) *noun.*

gadget   A small, useful tool or device. A bottle opener with a corkscrew at one end is a *gadget.*
  gad·get (gaj′it) *noun, plural* **gadgets.**

gag   **1.** Something put in the mouth to keep a person from talking or shouting.   **2.** A joke. The comedian on television told many *gags. Noun.*
  —1. To keep someone from talking or shouting by using a gag. The robbers tied up and *gagged* the clerk.   **2.** To feel as if one were about to vomit; choke. The dog *gagged* when a piece of bone got stuck in its throat. *Verb.*
  gag (gag) *noun, plural* **gags;** *verb,* **gagged, gagging.**

gaiety   Joy and fun; being merry. The *gaiety* of the circus made the child smile.
  gai·e·ty (gā′i tē) *noun, plural* **gaieties.**

gaily   In a gay manner; happily. The campers sang *gaily* around the campfire.
  gai·ly (gā′lē) *adverb.*

gain   **1.** To get or win. Our team *gained* control of the ball. You will *gain* experience by working at the store. The army *gained* an important victory. The car *gained* speed as it moved down the hill.   **2.** To benefit in some way. We all *gained* from the building of the new bridge.   **3.** To get to; reach. The ship *gained* the port before the storm began. *Verb.*
  —Something gained. The football player made a *gain* of ten yards. *Noun.*
  gain (gān) *verb,* **gained, gaining;** *noun, plural* **gains.**

gait   A way of walking or running. They walked with a slow *gait.* The horse's *gait* changed from a trot to a gallop.   ▲ Another word that sounds like this is **gate.**
  gait (gāt) *noun, plural* **gaits.**

gal.   An abbreviation for *gallon.*

gala   Festive; suitable for a celebration. The soldier's return home was marked with a *gala* dinner.
  ga·la (gā′la *or* gal′a) *adjective.*

galaxy   A very large group of stars. There are billions of galaxies in the universe. The

Milky Way is the galaxy that contains our sun and the planets.

gal·ax·y (gal′ək sē) *noun, plural* **galaxies.**

Word History

The first **galaxy** we ever knew about was the Milky Way, which is our own galaxy. The word *galaxy* comes from a Greek word meaning "resembling milk," because the Milky Way looks like a milky white path in the sky.

gale **1.** A very strong wind. The *gale* drove the ship against the rocks. **2.** A loud outburst. The clown's funny tricks sent the children into *gales* of laughter.

gale (gāl) *noun, plural* **gales.**

gallant Good and brave. The *gallant* knight protected the kingdom from its enemies.

gal·lant (gal′ənt) *adjective.*

gallery **1.** A balcony in a theater or large hall. **2.** A room or building where works of art are shown or sold.

gal·ler·y (gal′ə rē) *noun, plural* **galleries.**

galley **1.** A long, low ship used in early times. A galley had sails and oars. **2.** The kitchen of a ship or aircraft.

gal·ley (gal′ē) *noun, plural* **galleys.**

gallon A unit of measure for liquids. A gallon equals four quarts or about 3.8 liters.

gal·lon (gal′ən) *noun, plural* **gallons.**

gallop The fastest gait of a horse or other animal with four feet. *Noun.*
—To move or ride at a gallop. The horses *galloped* to the finish line. *Verb.*

gal·lop (gal′əp) *noun, plural* **gallops;** *verb,* **galloped, galloping.**

a horse **galloping**

gallows A framework from which criminals are hanged.

gal·lows (gal′ōz) *noun, plural* **gallows** or **gallowses.**

galoshes Waterproof overshoes made of rubber or plastic. Galoshes are worn in snowy or rainy weather.

ga·losh·es (gə losh′iz) *plural noun.*

gamble **1.** To play a game for money; bet. The card players *gambled* with dice. I *gambled* a dollar at the bingo game. **2.** To take a chance. The coach decided to *gamble* and use the new player in an important game. *Verb.*
—An act that involves a risk. Buying a used car without driving in it is a *gamble. Noun.*

gam·ble (gam′bəl) *verb,* **gambled, gambling;** *noun, plural* **gambles.**

game **1.** Something done for fun or pleasure. Let's play a *game* of tag. **2.** A sport or contest with certain rules. Are you going to the football *game?* We like the *game* of checkers. In the third inning the *game* was tied. **3.** Materials or equipment needed in playing a game. My grandparents gave me their croquet *game* for a birthday present. **4.** Wild animals, birds, or fish hunted or caught for sport or food. The family went hunting for deer and other *game. Noun.*
—Full of spirit and courage. Are you *game* for a swim in the cold water? *Adjective.*

game (gām) *noun, plural* **games;** *adjective,* **gamer, gamest.**

gander A grown male goose.

gan·der (gan′dər) *noun, plural* **ganders.**

gang **1.** A group of people who do things together. The children went to the fair with a *gang* of their friends. **2.** A group of people who do work together. The workers on the road *gang* are building a new highway. **3.** A group of people who are involved in mischievous or illegal activities. The prisoners were members of the *gang* that took two hostages.

gang (gang) *noun, plural* **gangs.**

gangplank A movable board or bridge used for getting on and off a boat or ship; gangway.

gang·plank (gang′plangk′) *noun, plural* **gangplanks.**

at; āpe; fär; câre; end; mē; it; ice; pîerce; hot; ōld; sông, fôrk; oil; out; up; ūse; rüle; pu̇ll; tûrn; chin; sing; shop; thin; <u>th</u>is; hw in white; zh in treasure. The symbol ə stands for the unstressed vowel sound in about, taken, pencil, lemon, and circus.

G

gangster A member of a gang of criminals.
gang·ster (gang′stər) *noun, plural*
gangsters.

gangway **1.** A passageway on either side
of a ship's deck. **2.** A movable board or
bridge used for getting on or off a boat or
ship; gangplank.
gang·way (gang′wā′) *noun, plural*
gangways.

gap **1.** A break, crack, or opening. Our dog
got out of the yard through a *gap* in the fence.
2. A narrow passage through a mountain
range; mountain pass. **3.** A part or space
where something is missing or blank. There
are several *gaps* in the recording where you
can't hear the music.
gap (gap) *noun, plural* **gaps.**

garage A building where cars and trucks
are parked or repaired.
ga·rage (gə räzh′ *or* gə räj′) *noun, plural*
garages.

garbage Food and other things that are
thrown out.
gar·bage (gär′bij) *noun.*

garden A piece of ground where flowers or
vegetables are grown. Our parents planted a
rose *garden* in the yard. Many people grow
peas, tomatoes, and beets in their *gardens.*
Noun.
—To work in a garden. Our neighbor *gardens* every day after work. *Verb.*
gar·den (gär′dən) *noun, plural* **gardens;**
verb, **gardened, gardening.**

garden

gardener A person who works in a garden.
The city hires *gardeners* to keep its parks
looking beautiful.
gar·den·er (gärd′nər) *noun, plural*
gardeners.

gardenia A yellow or white flower with
petals that have a texture like wax. Gardenias have a sweet smell and grow on a tree or
shrub.
gar·de·nia (gär dēn′yə) *noun, plural*
gardenias.

Word History

The **gardenia** was named after Alexander Garden, a botanist who lived in
the eighteenth century.

gargle To wash or rinse the throat or
mouth with a liquid. The liquid is moved
around by breathing out through the mouth,
which makes a bubbling sound. *Verb.*
—A liquid used for gargling. *Noun.*
gar·gle (gär′gəl) *verb,* **gargled, gargling;**
noun, plural **gargles.**

gargoyle

gargoyle A pipe or spout in the form of an
odd or ugly person or animal. Gargoyles
stick out from the roof of a building and
carry off water.
gar·goyle (gär′goil) *noun, plural*
gargoyles.

garland A wreath of flowers, leaves, or
vines. The winners of the race were honored
with *garlands* of laurel placed on their heads.
gar·land (gär′lənd) *noun, plural* **garlands.**

garlic An herb that has a strong smell and
flavor and is used in cooking. Garlic comes
from the bulb of a plant.
gar·lic (gär′lik) *noun, plural* **garlics.**

garment A piece of clothing. Coats, sweaters, and shirts are garments.
gar·ment (gär′mənt) *noun, plural*
garments.

garnet   A deep red gem that is used in jewelry.
   gar·net (gär′nit) *noun, plural* **garnets.**

garnish   To decorate. The cook *garnished* the fish with slices of lemon. *Verb.*
   —Something placed on or around food to improve the way it looks or tastes. A *garnish* of parsley decorated the bowl of carrots. *Noun.*
   gar·nish (gär′nish) *verb,* **garnished, garnishing;** *noun, plural* **garnishes.**

garrison   A place where soldiers are stationed; military base. A *garrison* protected the town from enemy troops. *Noun.*
   —**1.** To station soldiers in. The general *garrisoned* the town to protect it.   **2.** To station at a military base. That soldier is *garrisoned* at a nearby fort. *Verb.*
   gar·ri·son (gar′ə sen) *noun, plural* **garrisons;** *verb,* **garrisoned, garrisoning.**

garter   A strap or band that holds up a stocking or sock. A garter is usually made of elastic.
   gar·ter (gär′tər) *noun, plural* **garters.**

garter snake   A snake that is green or brown with long yellow stripes on its back. It is harmless to people.

gas   **1.** A form of matter that is not solid or liquid. Gas can move about freely and does not have a definite shape. The air we breathe is made of gases.   **2.** A gaseous substance that is burned as a fuel for heating or cooking. We cook our food with *gas.*   **3.** Gasoline. We filled the car's tank with *gas.* Look up **gasoline** for more information.
   gas (gas) *noun, plural* **gases.**

gaseous   In the form of gas; like gas. The air we breathe is *gaseous.*
   gas·e·ous (gas′ē əs *or* gash′əs) *adjective.*

gas mask   A mask worn over the nose and mouth. It has a filter that keeps a person from breathing poisonous gases and other harmful substances.

gasoline   A clear liquid that burns easily. It is made mostly from petroleum. Gasoline is used as a fuel for cars, trucks, airplanes, and other vehicles.
   gas·o·line (gas′ə lēn′ *or* gas′ə lēn′) *noun, plural* **gasolines.**

gasp   **1.** To draw in air suddenly or with effort. The runner *gasped* for breath after winning the race.   **2.** To utter while breathing in suddenly or with effort. "Lifeguard! Help!" *gasped* the struggling swimmer. *Verb.*
   —The act or sound of gasping. We heard a *gasp* from the frightened child. *Noun.*
   gasp (gasp) *verb,* **gasped, gasping;** *noun, plural* **gasps.**

gate   A movable object like a door that is used to close an opening in a fence or wall.
   ▲ Another word that sounds like this is **gait.**
   gate (gāt) *noun, plural* **gates.**

gateway   **1.** An open place in a fence or wall where a gate is put.   **2.** The way to get somewhere or do something. Some people think that getting a good education is a *gateway* to success.
   gate·way (gāt′wā′) *noun, plural* **gateways.**

gather   **1.** To come or bring together; collect. A crowd *gathered* around the movie star. I *gathered* my books from the table and put them away.   **2.** To increase bit by bit. The sled *gathered* speed as it slid down the hill.   **3.** To reach an opinion; conclude. We *gathered* from the dark clouds that a storm was coming.   **4.** To bring cloth together in folds. I *gathered* the skirt at the waist.
   gath·er (ga<u>th</u>′ər) *verb,* **gathered, gathering.**

gathering   A meeting, assembly, or crowd. There was a large *gathering* of people at the site of the accident.
   gath·er·ing (ga<u>th</u>′ər ing) *noun, plural* **gatherings.**

gaudy   Too bright and showy. That yellow and pink coat with green buttons looks *gaudy.*
   gaud·y (gô′dē) *adjective,* **gaudier, gaudiest.**

gauge   **1.** A standard of measurement. There is a gauge for measuring the barrel of a gun. There is also a gauge for measuring the distance between two rails on a railroad track.   **2.** An instrument for measuring. A barometer is a *gauge* that measures the pressure of the atmosphere. *Noun.*
   —**1.** To measure. Scientists can *gauge* the exact amount of rain that falls during a storm.   **2.** To estimate. How old would you *gauge* this turtle to be? *Verb.*
   gauge (gāj) *noun, plural* **gauges;** *verb,* **gauged, gauging.**

gaunt   So thin that bones show through the skin. The puppies were *gaunt* from not having enough food.
   gaunt (gônt) *adjective,* **gaunter, gauntest.**

G

at; āpe; fär; câre; end; mē; it; ice; pîerce; hot; ōld; sông, fôrk; oil; out; up; ūse; rüle; pùll; tûrn; chin; sing; shop; thin; <u>th</u>is; hw in white; zh in treasure. The symbol ə stands for the unstressed vowel sound in about, taken, pencil, lemon, and circus.

gauze   A very thin cloth that you can see through. It is used in making bandages.
gauze (gôz) *noun.*

gave   Past tense of **give.** I *gave* my parents a gift on their wedding anniversary. Look up **give** for more information.
gave (gāv) *verb.*

gavel   A small wooden hammer. It is used by the person in charge of a meeting or trial to call for order or attention.
gav·el (gav′əl) *noun, plural* **gavels.**

gay   **1.** Full of joy and fun; merry; bright. The birthday party was a *gay* event. **2.** Brightly colored or showy. I bought a *gay* dress with many pink ribbons.
gay (gā) *adjective,* **gayer, gayest.**

gaze   To look at something a long time. We all *gazed* at the beautiful sunset. *Verb.*
—A long, steady look. Our *gaze* rested on the bear and its two playful cubs. *Noun.*
gaze (gāz) *verb,* **gazed, gazing;** *noun, plural* **gazes.**

gazelle   A graceful antelope that can run very fast. It is found in Africa and Asia.
ga·zelle (gə zel′) *noun, plural* **gazelles** or **gazelle.**

gazelle

gear   **1.** A wheel with teeth on the edge. The teeth are made to fit in between the teeth of another gear, so that one gear can cause the other to turn.   **2.** Equipment for a particular purpose. My hiking *gear* includes a knapsack, sleeping bag, and cooking kit. *Noun.*
—To make suitable or right. The school was *geared* to meet the needs of children studying ballet. *Verb.*
gear (gîr) *noun, plural* **gears;** *verb,* **geared, gearing.**

gearshift   A device that connects a set of gears to a motor. An automobile has a gearshift.
gear·shift (gîr′shift′) *noun, plural* **gearshifts.**

geese   Plural of **goose.** Look up **goose** for more information.
geese (gēs) *plural noun.*

Geiger counter   A device used to discover and measure the strength of rays from a radioactive substance.
Gei·ger counter (gī′gər).

Word History

The **Geiger counter** was named after Hans *Geiger.* He was a German scientist who helped invent this device.

gelatin   A substance like jelly. It is made from the skin, bones, and other parts of animals. Gelatin is used in jellies and desserts and in making glue.
gel·a·tin (jel′ə tən) *noun.*

kinds of **gems**

gem   **1.** A precious stone that has been cut and polished; jewel. The necklace was made of rubies, diamonds, and other *gems.* **2.** A person or thing that is thought of as perfect or valuable. Your beautiful garden is a *gem.*
gem (jem) *noun, plural* **gems.**

gene   One of the tiny units of a cell of an animal or plant that determines the characteristics that an offspring inherits from its parent or parents.
gene (jēn) *noun, plural* **genes.**

general   **1.** For all; for the whole. A *general* meeting of the club was held to discuss the new rules. That exhibit is open to the *general* public.   **2.** By all or many; among all or many. There was *general* panic during the landslide.   **3.** Having no limit, restriction, or specialty. After the holiday, that store will have a *general* sale.   **4.** Not concerned with details. The president spoke in a *general* way

about the need to increase taxes. *Adjective.*
—An armed forces officer of the highest rank. The five ranks of general in the United States Army are **brigadier general, major general, lieutenant general, general,** and **general of the army.** The highest rank of general is **general of the army.** *Noun.*

• **in general.** Usually; generally. *In general,* the weather here is very good.
gen·er·al (jen′ər əl) *adjective; noun, plural* **generals.**

generalize **1.** To form a general rule or principle from particular facts or instances. After studying the temperature, rainfall, and other conditions in the city during June, July, and August, we were able to *generalize* about the summer weather there. **2.** To treat a subject in a general way, without discussing details. I had to *generalize* in my report because I did not have enough time to be more specific.
gen·er·al·ize (jen′ər ə līz′) *verb,* **generalized, generalized.**

generally **1.** Almost always; usually. I *generally* walk to school. **2.** To a large extent or great degree. It is *generally* believed that the Vikings visited America before Columbus. **3.** Without discussing the details. *Generally* speaking, the book was good.
gen·er·al·ly (jen′ər ə lē) *adverb.*

generate To bring about or produce. That machine *generates* electricity.
gen·er·ate (jen′ə rāt′) *verb,* **generated, generating.**

generation **1.** A group of persons born around the same time. My parents call me and my friends the younger *generation.* **2.** One step in the line of descent from a common ancestor. A grandparent, parent, and child make up three *generations.* **3.** The period of time, usually about thirty years, between the births of the parents and the births of their children. **4.** The act or process of generating; production. A flashlight needs batteries for the *generation* of light.
gen·er·a·tion (jen′ə rā′shən) *noun, plural* **generations.**

generator A machine that produces electricity, steam, or other energy.
gen·er·a·tor (jen′ə rā′tər) *noun, plural* **generators.**

generic **1.** Of, having to do with, or applied to a whole kind, class, or group; general. "Fruit" is a *generic* term; "apple" is a specific term. **2.** Not having a trademark. *Generic* products often cost less than products with brand names.
ge·ner·ic (jə ner′ik) *adjective.*

generosity The quality of being willing and happy to share with others. Although those people were poor, they were well-known for their *generosity.*
gen·er·os·i·ty (jen′ə ros′i tē) *noun.*

generous **1.** Willing and happy to share; not selfish. Be *generous* with your new bicycle and let your friends ride it. **2.** Large; abundant. The cook gave each person a *generous* helping of stew.
gen·er·ous (jen′ər əs) *adjective.*

genetics The science that deals with how characteristics are passed from a parent or parents to the offspring. The word "genetics" is used with a singular verb.
ge·net·ics (jə net′iks) *noun.*

genie A spirit with magic powers in Middle Eastern fairy tales.
ge·nie (jē′nē) *noun, plural* **genies.**

genius **1.** Great ability to think or to invent or create things. An artist of *genius* painted those great paintings in the art museum. **2.** A person who has this ability. That musician is a *genius.* **3.** A great ability or talent for a particular thing. That student has a *genius* for drawing.
gen·ius (jēn′yəs) *noun, plural* **geniuses.**

gentile or **Gentile** A person who is not a Jew. *Noun.*
—Not Jewish. *Adjective.*
gen·tile or **Gen·tile** (jen′tīl) *noun, plural* **gentiles** or **Gentiles;** *adjective.*

gentle **1.** Mild and kindly. The nurse gave the baby a *gentle* hug. **2.** Soft or low. We heard the *gentle* tapping of the rain on the window. **3.** Easy to handle; tame. The child rode a *gentle* horse. **4.** Not steep. The children slid down the *gentle* slope on their sleds.
gen·tle (jen′tal) *adjective,* **gentler, gentlest.**

G

Word History

The word **gentle** comes from an old French word meaning "noble" or "born of a good family." Because being kind was thought to be a quality of people of noble birth, *gentle* came to be used to mean "mild and kindly."

at; āpe; fär; câre; end; mē; it; īce; pîerce; hot; ōld; sông, fôrk; oil; out; up; ūse; rüle; pull; tûrn; chin; sing; shop; thin; <u>th</u>is; hw in white; zh in treasure. The symbol ə stands for the unstressed vowel sound in about, taken, pencil, lemon, and circus.

gentleman **1.** A man who is polite, kind, and honorable. **2.** A man of high social position. **3.** Any man. "A *gentleman* is here to see you," my cousin said.
gen·tle·man (jen′təl mən) *noun, plural* **gentlemen** (jen′təl mən).

gentlewoman **1.** A woman who is polite, kind, and honorable. **2.** A woman of high social position.
gen·tle·wom·an (jen′təl wùm′ən) *noun, plural* **gentlewomen** (jen′təl wim′ən).

gently In a gentle way. The snow fell *gently.* The child petted the kitten *gently.* The hill *gently* slopes down to the lake.
gent·ly (jent′lē) *adverb.*

genuine **1.** Being what it seems or is claimed to be; real. This belt is made of *genuine* leather. **2.** Sincere; honest. We made a *genuine* effort to get here on time.
gen·u·ine (jen′ū in) *adjective.*

geographical or **geographic** Having to do with geography.
ge·o·graph·i·cal (jē′ə graf′i kəl) or **ge·o·graph·ic** (jē′ə graf′ik) *adjective.*

geography **1.** The science that deals with the surface of the earth and the plant, animal, and human life on it. When you study geography, you learn about the earth's countries and people, and about its climate, oceans and rivers, mountains, and natural resources. **2.** The surface or natural features of a place or region. The Grand Canyon is part of the *geography* of Arizona.
ge·og·ra·phy (jē og′rə fē) *noun, plural* **geographies.**

geological Having to do with geology.
ge·o·log·i·cal (jē′ə loj′i kəl) *adjective.*

geology The science that deals with the structure and physical changes of the earth or other planets that are made mostly of rocks. Geologists study rocks, mountains, and cliffs to find out what the earth or planet is made of and what changes have taken place over the years.
ge·ol·o·gy (jē ol′ə jē) *noun, plural* **geologies.**

geometric **1.** Having to do with geometry. A triangle is a *geometric* form. **2.** Consisting of or decorated with lines, angles, circles, triangles, or similar forms. The rug in my room has a *geometric* design of circles and squares.
ge·o·met·ric (jē′ə met′rik) *adjective.*

geometry The branch of mathematics that deals with the measurement and relation of points, lines, angles, plane figures, and solids.
ge·om·e·try (jē om′i trē) *noun.*

Georgia A state in the southeastern United States. Its capital is Atlanta.
Geor·gia (jôr′jə) *noun.*

Word History

Georgia was named after King *George* II of England. George II gave some people the right to start a colony in part of what is now this state.

geranium A plant with bright red, pink, white, or lavender flowers. The leaves of some geraniums have a scent.
ge·ra·ni·um (jə rā′nē əm) *noun, plural* **geraniums.**

gerbil A small rodent that is native to deserts in Africa and Asia. It lives in a burrow and is sometimes kept as a pet.
ger·bil (jûr′bil) *noun, plural* **gerbils.**

germ A tiny particle that can cause disease. Viruses and bacteria are germs. Germs are so small that they can be seen only through a microscope.
germ (jûrm) *noun, plural* **germs.**

geranium

German **1.** A person who was born in or is a citizen of East or West Germany. **2.** The language of Germany. *Noun.*
—Having to do with Germany, its people, or their language. *Adjective.*
Ger·man (jûr′mən) *noun, plural* **Germans;** *adjective.*

German shepherd A dog that originally came from Germany and was used to herd sheep. It has a thick coat of black, brown, or gray fur.

Germany A former country in north central Europe. It has been divided into the countries of **West Germany** and **East Germany** since 1949.
Ger·ma·ny (jûr′mə nē) *noun.*

germinate To begin growing from a seed; to sprout. The seeds needed water to *germinate.*
ger·mi·nate (jûr′mə nāt′) *verb,* **germinated, germinating.**

gesture **1.** A movement of the hands, head, or other part of the body that shows what a person is thinking or feeling. Holding out your hand with the palm up is a *gesture* that you want something. **2.** Something said or done to express a feeling or for effect. Going to visit your sick classmate was a kind *gesture. Noun.*

—To make or use gestures. The police officer *gestured* for the driver to stop. *Verb.*

ges·ture (jes′chər) *noun, plural* **gestures;** *verb,* **gestured, gesturing.**

get **1.** To come to have or own; receive; gain; earn. I hope to *get* a radio for my birthday. I *got* a good grade on the test. How much do you *get* for mowing the grass? Where did you *get* those shoes? **2.** To come to or reach. When will we *get* home? **3.** To come or go; move. *Get* down from the ladder. **4.** To seek and bring back, capture, or make contact with; catch or fetch. Please *get* me a glass of milk. The police *got* the dog that ran away. In an emergency, the hospital nurse can *get* the doctors very quickly. **5.** To become ill with. Several of my classmates have *got* the flu. **6.** To cause to be, be done, or become. *Get* a haircut. The cook *got* dinner ready. **7.** To be or become. The children *got* lost in the park. Hurry up and *get* ready to go. **8.** To be obliged to. We've *got* to leave by eight o'clock. **9.** To have permission or be able. The campers hoped they would *get* to fish in the lake. **10.** To persuade; convince. Try to *get* them to wear warmer clothes. **11.** To understand. I heard the joke, but I don't *get* it.

• **to get along.** **1.** To be friendly. I try to *get along* with everyone. **2.** To manage to survive. A camel *gets along* on very little water.

• **to get away with.** To do something without being noticed, caught, or punished. No one should *get away with* lying.

• **to get back.** **1.** To come back; return. When did you *get back* from your trip? **2.** To get again something that one used to have; recover; regain. It took me a month to *get back* my strength after I had the flu.

• **to get in.** **1.** To go in; enter. I lost my key to the house so I couldn't *get in.* **2.** To arrive. The train *got in* at noon.

• **to get out.** **1.** To leave; depart. Someone locked the door to my room, and I couldn't *get out.* **2.** To become known; leak out. Do you know how the secret *got out?*

• **to get over.** To recover from. I just *got over* a cold.

• **to get together.** To meet or gather. Let's *get together* for lunch next week.

• **to get up.** **1.** To rise from bed. I usually *get up* at seven o'clock. **2.** To sit up

or stand up. When I fell off my bicycle, I couldn't *get up* for a few minutes.

get (get) *verb,* **got, got** or **gotten, getting.**

geyser A hot, underground spring from which steam and hot water shoot into the air.

gey·ser (gī′zər) *noun, plural* **geysers.**

geyser

Ghana A country in western Africa.

Gha·na (gä′nə) *noun.*

ghastly **1.** Terrible; horrible. The story was a *ghastly* tale of murder. **2.** Very pale; like a ghost. The sick person had a *ghastly* look.

ghast·ly (gast′lē) *adjective,* **ghastlier, ghastliest.**

ghetto A part of a city where members of a certain race or religion live because they are poor or because they are discriminated against.

ghet·to (get′ō) *noun, plural* **ghettos** or **ghettoes.**

ghost The supposed spirit of a dead person.

ghost (gōst) *noun, plural* **ghosts.**

ghostly Of a ghost; like a ghost. We thought we heard *ghostly* sounds coming from the old house. The statue had a *ghostly* appearance in the dim light.

ghost·ly (gōst′lē) *adjective,* **ghostlier, ghostliest.**

ghost town A town that has been deserted. Many ghost towns were left in the western

G

at; āpe; fär; cāre; end; mē; it; īce; pîerce; hot; ōld; sông, fôrk; oil; out; up; ūse; rüle; pùll; tûrn; chin; sing; shop; thin; <u>th</u>is; hw in white; zh in treasure. The symbol ə stands for the unstressed vowel sound in about, taken, pencil, lemon, and circus.

United States after local mines closed or local businesses failed.

giant **1.** An imaginary creature that looks like a huge person. A giant has great strength. **2.** A person or thing that is very large, powerful, or important. That doctor is a *giant* in the field of medicine. That company is a *giant* in automobile manufacturing. *Noun.* —Very large. The scientist looked through a *giant* telescope. *Adjective.*
gi·ant (jī'ənt) *noun, plural* **giants;** *adjective.*

gibbon A small animal that has long arms and no tail. It is a kind of ape. Gibbons live in trees and are found in Asia.
gib·bon (gib'ən) *noun, plural* **gibbons.**

gibbon

giddy **1.** Having a spinning feeling in the head; dizzy. The child felt *giddy* after swinging high on the swing. **2.** Playful; silly. We became so *giddy* that we would laugh at anything.
gid·dy (gid'ē) *adjective,* **giddier, giddiest.**

gift **1.** Something given; present. This basketball was a *gift* from my parents. **2.** Talent; ability. That student has a *gift* for playing the piano.
gift (gift) *noun, plural* **gifts.**

gifted Having natural ability or talent; talented. The *gifted* musician could play ten different instruments.
gift·ed (gif'tid) *adjective.*

gigantic Like a giant; huge and powerful. A *gigantic* whale swam under the ship.
gi·gan·tic (jī gan'tik) *adjective.*

giggle To laugh in a high, silly, or nervous way. The children *giggled* at the funny joke. *Verb.* —A high, silly, or nervous laugh. The youngster gave a *giggle* when the clown slipped and fell. *Noun.*
gig·gle (gig'əl) *verb,* **giggled, giggling;** *noun, plural* **giggles.**

gild To cover with a thin layer of gold or golden color. The artist *gilded* the picture frame. ▲ Another word that sounds like this is **guild.**
gild (gild) *verb,* **gilded** or **gilt, gilding.**

gill The part of a fish and most other water animals that is used for breathing. A gill takes in oxygen from the water.
gill (gil) *noun, plural* **gills.**

gin¹ A colorless alcoholic drink that is flavored with juniper berries.
gin (jin) *noun, plural* **gins.**

gin² A machine for separating cotton from the seeds.
gin (jin) *noun, plural* **gins.**

ginger A hot spice that comes from the root of a tropical plant. Ginger is used in food and medicine.
gin·ger (jin'jər) *noun, plural* **gingers.**

gingerbread A dark, sweet cake or cookie flavored with ginger and molasses.
gin·ger·bread (jin'jər bred') *noun, plural* **gingerbreads.**

gingham A strong cotton fabric. It usually has a pattern of checks, stripes, or plaid.
ging·ham (ging'əm) *noun, plural* **ginghams.**

giraffe A large animal that lives in Africa. The giraffe has a very long neck, long, thin legs, and a coat with brown patches. Giraffes are the tallest living animals.
gi·raffe (jə raf') *noun, plural* **giraffes.**

giraffe

girder A large, heavy beam. Girders are used to support floors and the frameworks of buildings and bridges.
gird·er (gûr'dər) *noun, plural* **girders.**

girl A female child from birth to the time she is a young woman.
girl (gûrl) *noun, plural* **girls.**

Word History

The word **girl** used to mean "a child or young person." The word was used for both boys and girls, and boys were sometimes called "knave girls." Later people began to use *girl* for female children only.

girlhood   **1.** The time of being a girl. **2.** The state of being a girl.
girl·hood (gûrl′hụd′) *noun, plural* **girlhoods.**

girl scout   A member of the Girl Scouts.

Girl Scouts   An organization for girls. It helps girls to develop character and physical fitness.

give   **1.** To hand, pass, present, or grant. My parents *gave* me a dog for my birthday. *Give* the kitten a bowl of milk. The teacher *gave* them permission to leave the room. **2.** To make or do; bring about; cause. The scouts *gave* a shout when they found the cave. The puppy will not *give* you any trouble. The noise *gives* me a headache. **3.** To produce. Both cows and goats *give* milk. The sun *gives* off light. **4.** To break down; yield. If the dam *gives,* the town will be flooded. *Verb.*
—The quality of being able to bend without breaking or yielding to pressure. A hard mattress has very little *give. Noun.*
* **to give away.   1.** To give as a gift. They *gave away* prizes at the party. **2.** To cause to become known; reveal. My friends *gave away* their hiding place when they laughed.
* **to give back.**   To return. I *gave back* the money I had borrowed.
* **to give in.**   To stop being or acting against something; yield. Our parents *gave in* to our request to let us stay up late.
* **to give out.   1.** To distribute. The store is *giving out* free samples of a new perfume. **2.** To become tired, broken down, or used up. The swimmer *gave out* before the end of the race.
* **to give up.   1.** To surrender; yield. We lost the game because our team *gave up* too many points. **2.** To stop or abandon. Our neighbor *gave up* playing golf. No one wants to *give up* the search for the lost dog. **3.** To stop trying. I know the problem is hard to solve, but don't *give up* so soon.

give (giv) *verb,* **gave, given, giving;** *noun.*

given   Past participle of **give.** I have *given* a valentine to each of my classmates. Look up **give** for more information.
giv·en (giv′ən) *verb.*

glacier   A large mass of ice in very cold regions or on the tops of high mountains. A glacier is formed by snow that does not melt.
gla·cier (glā′shər) *noun, plural* **glaciers.**

glad   **1.** Happy; pleased. Our neighbor is *glad* to be home. I am *glad* to meet you. **2.** Causing joy or pleasure. We celebrated when we heard the *glad* news. **3.** Very willing. I was *glad* to help you clean the garage.
glad (glad) *adjective,* **gladder, gladdest.**

gladiator   In ancient Rome, a person who fought another person in an arena to entertain the spectators.
glad·i·a·tor (glad′ē ā′tər) *noun, plural* **gladiators.**

gladiolus   A plant with brightly colored spikes of flowers and leaves shaped like swords.
glad·i·o·lus (glad′ē ō′ləs) *noun, plural* **gladioli** (glad′ē ō′lī) or **gladioluses.**

glamorous   Full of glamour; fascinating, exciting, and charming. The *glamorous* lives of movie stars interest some people.
glam·or·ous (glam′ər əs) *adjective.*

glamour   The quality of being fascinating, exciting, and charming. The *glamour* of the big city made us eager to visit it again. This word is also spelled **glamor.**
glam·our *or* **glam·or** (glam′ər) *noun.*

gladiolus

glance   A quick look. I took one *glance* and knew that you were sad. *Noun.*
—**1.** To take a quick look. I *glanced* in the mirror. **2.** To hit something and move off at a slant. The sword *glanced* off the knight's armor. *Verb.*
glance (glans) *noun, plural* **glances;** *verb,* **glanced, glancing.**

gland   A part inside the body that takes certain substances from the blood and changes them into chemicals that the body uses or gives off. Glands near the eyes make tears.
gland (gland) *noun, plural* **glands.**

glare   **1.** A strong, unpleasant light. The *glare* of the car's headlights hurt my eyes. **2.** An angry look or stare. I gave the cat a *glare* when it refused to come in. *Noun.*
—**1.** To shine with a strong, unpleasant light. The sunlight *glared* at the beach.

G

at; āpe; fär; câre; end; mē; it; īce; pîerce; hot; ōld; sông, fôrk; oil; out; up; ūse; rūle; pụll; tûrn; chin; sing; shop; thin; <u>th</u>is; hw in white; zh in treasure. The symbol ə stands for the unstressed vowel sound in about, taken, pencil, lemon, and circus.

313

2. To give an angry look. The strangers *glared* at the noisy children. *Verb.*

glare (glâr) *noun, plural* **glares;** *verb,* **glared, glaring.**

glaring **1.** Shining with a strong, unpleasant light. We wore sunglasses because of the *glaring* sunlight. **2.** Very easily noticed. It's hard to believe I made this *glaring* error in my addition. **3.** Staring in an angry way. The *glaring* driver told us never to run out into the street without looking.

glar·ing (glâr′ing) *adjective.*

glass **1.** A hard, clear material that breaks easily. Glass is made by heating together sand and certain chemicals. Windows and camera lenses are made of glass. **2.** A container made of glass that is used for drinking. Please fill my *glass* with milk. The runner drank three *glasses* of water. **3. glasses.** A pair of lenses made of glass, used to help a person see better; eyeglasses.

glass (glas) *noun, plural* **glasses.**

gleam **1.** A flash or beam of bright light. I could see the *gleam* of a flashlight. The polished silver has a nice *gleam*. **2.** A faint or short appearance or sign. The doctor was pleased to see a *gleam* of hope in the patient's eyes. *Noun.*
—To shine; glow. The new car *gleamed* in the sunlight. *Verb.*

gleam (glēm) *noun, plural* **gleams;** *verb,* **gleamed, gleaming.**

glee Joy or delight. The little child laughed with *glee* while opening the presents.

glee (glē) *noun.*

glen A small, narrow valley. The campers stayed in a *glen* between the hills.

glen (glen) *noun, plural* **glens.**

glide **1.** To move smoothly along without any effort. The skater *glided* across the ice. The sailboat *glided* along on the lake. **2.** To fly or descend slowly without using a motor for power. The hawk *glided* over the field looking for food. *Verb.*
—The act of gliding. I've always wanted to go for a *glide* in a plane like that. *Noun.*

glide (glīd) *verb,* **glided, gliding;** *noun,* *plural* **glides.**

glider An aircraft that flies without a motor. Rising air currents keep a glider in the air.

glid·er (glī′dər) *noun, plural* **gliders.**

glimmer **1.** A dim, unsteady light. We could see the *glimmer* of a distant star. **2.** A weak sign; hint. There was not even a *glimmer* of hope that we would find the lost dog. *Noun.*
—To shine with a dim, unsteady light;

flicker. The lights on the airplane *glimmered* in the night sky. *Verb.*

glim·mer (glim′ər) *noun, plural* **glimmers;** *verb,* **glimmered, glimmering.**

glimpse A quick look; glance. I caught a *glimpse* of my friend in the crowded store. *Noun.*
—To see for a moment; glance. We *glimpsed* a famous actor when we drove by the theater. *Verb.*

glimpse (glimps) *noun, plural* **glimpses;** *verb,* **glimpsed, glimpsing.**

glisten To shine or sparkle with reflected light. The snow *glistened* in the sun. Tears *glistened* on the child's cheeks.

glis·ten (glis′ən) *verb,* **glistened, glistening.**

glitch A problem or error that prevents a computer or program from operating properly.

glitch (glich) *noun, plural* **glitches.**

glitter To shine with bright flashes; sparkle. The gold ring *glitters* on your finger. Stars *glittered* in the sky. *Verb.*
—**1.** Sparkling brightness or light. We could see the *glitter* of the diamond. **2.** Small bits of sparkling material that are used in decoration. We glued the *glitter* onto our costumes. *Noun.*

glit·ter (glit′ər) *verb,* **glittered, glittering;** *noun.*

a costume covered with **glitter**

gloat   To look at or think about something with great satisfaction. The players *gloated* over their team's big victory.
gloat (glōt) *verb,* **gloated, gloating.**

globe   **1.** The world. The group traveled around the *globe* and saw many interesting countries.   **2.** A round ball with a map of the world on it. We studied the oceans and continents on a *globe* in our classroom.   **3.** Anything shaped like a ball. We bought a new glass *globe* to cover the light bulb in the hall.
globe (glōb) *noun,* *plural* **globes.**

globe

gloom   **1.** Dim light or darkness. You can't see anything in the *gloom* of the forest at night.   **2.** Low spirits; sorrow; sadness. I was filled with *gloom* when my best friend moved away.
gloom (glüm) *noun.*

gloomy   **1.** Sad. The classmates felt *gloomy* because their trip was canceled.   **2.** Dim; dark. Don't be afraid to go into the *gloomy* hallway. It was a *gloomy,* rainy day.
gloom·y (glü′mē) *adjective,* **gloomier, gloomiest.**

glorify   **1.** To praise or worship. The people *glorified* the great hero.   **2.** To cause to appear more glorious or magnificent than it actually is. The television show *glorified* the life of sailors at sea.
glo·ri·fy (glôr′ə fī′) *verb,* **glorified, glorifying.**

glorious   **1.** Full of glory or beauty; grand; magnificent. A *glorious* sunset filled the sky.   **2.** Having or deserving glory; famous. This poem praises a *glorious* military victory.
glo·ri·ous (glôr′ē əs) *adjective.*

glory   **1.** Great praise; honor; fame. They both did the work, but only one got the *glory.*   **2.** A person or thing that brings praise, honor, or fame; source of pride. This great forest is one of the *glories* of our state.   **3.** Great beauty; splendor; magnificence. The sun shone in all its *glory. Noun.*
—To rejoice proudly. The team *gloried* in their unexpected victory. *Verb.*
glo·ry (glôr′ē) *noun,* *plural* **glories;** *verb,* **gloried, glorying.**

gloss   A smooth, bright look; shine; luster. I waxed the floor to give it a nice *gloss.*
gloss (glôs) *noun,* *plural* **glosses.**

glossary   A list of difficult words and their meanings. The words in a glossary are in alphabetical order. Some books have a glossary at the end.
glos·sa·ry (glos′ə rē) *noun,* *plural* **glossaries.**

Word History

Glossary comes from a Greek word meaning "tongue" or "speech." The Romans later borrowed this word and in Latin used it to mean "a difficult word" or "a word needing to be explained." It is from this Latin usage that our word *glossary* comes.

glossy   Having a smooth, bright look; shiny. The photograph has a *glossy* surface. My cat has *glossy* fur.
gloss·y (glô′sē) *adjective,* **glossier, glossiest.**

glove   A covering for the hand. Most gloves have separate parts for each of the four fingers and for the thumb. However, boxing gloves and some baseball gloves hold the four fingers together in one part.
glove (gluv) *noun,* *plural* **gloves.**

glow   **1.** A light or shine. At sunrise, the sky has an orange *glow.* A firefly gives off a *glow.*   **2.** A coloring or appearance that suggests warmth or warm feeling. Your face has the *glow* of good health. *Noun.*
—**1.** To shine or burn without catching on fire. The light bulb *glows* brightly.   **2.** To have a coloring or appearance that suggests warmth or warm feeling. The parents' faces *glowed* as a friend admired their baby. *Verb.*
glow (glō) *noun,* *plural* **glows;** *verb,* **glowed, glowing.**

glue   A substance used for sticking things together. *Noun.*
—**1.** To stick things together with glue. Please *glue* the pieces of the vase together.   **2.** To fasten or hold tightly. The cat kept its eyes *glued* on the bird. *Verb.*
glue (glü) *noun,* *plural* **glues;** *verb,* **glued, gluing.**

gm   An abbreviation for *gram.*

at; āpe; fär; câre; end; mē; it; īce; pîerce; hot; ōld; sông, fôrk; oil; out; up; ūse; rüle; pùll; tûrn; chin; sing; shop; thin; **th**is; hw in white; zh in treasure. The symbol ə stands for the unstressed vowel sound in about, taken, pencil, lemon, and circus.

G

gnarled   Having a rough, twisted, or rugged look. There is a *gnarled* old oak tree beside our house. The old sailor has *gnarled* hands.
   gnarled (närld) *adjective.*

gnat   A small fly. Some gnats bite and suck blood from people and animals. Others feed on plants.
   gnat (nat) *noun, plural* **gnats.**

gnaw   To bite again and again in order to wear away little by little. The dog *gnawed* the bone. A rat had *gnawed* a hole through the fence.
   gnaw (nô) *verb,* **gnawed, gnawing.**

gnome   A kind of dwarf in fairy tales.
   gnome (nōm) *noun, plural* **gnomes.**

gnu   A large animal that lives in Africa. A gnu is a kind of antelope but has a large head and a stocky build like an ox. ▲ Other words that sound like this are **knew** and **new.**
   gnu (nü *or* nū) *noun, plural* **gnus** *or* **gnu.**

gnu

go   **1.** To move from one place to another; move along, ahead, or away. They plan to *go* to the beach today. I have to *go* now, or I'll be late.   **2.** To pass, be spent, or be lost. Time *goes* quickly when you're busy. Where did all the money *go?*   **3.** To reach; lead. The road *goes* east from here. The lamp cord isn't long enough to *go* from the wall to the table. My grandparents' memories *go* back far.   **4.** To be, become, or continue. I always *go* to sleep after the late news.   **5.** To work; run. Our car won't *go.*   **6.** To have as a result; turn out. The game didn't *go* well for the team.   **7.** To be given. First prize *went* to two students.   **8.** To have a place or be suitable; belong or match. These curtains will *go* very well with the new rug.   **9.** To sound or make the sound of. A cow *goes* "moo."   **10.**   To be capable of being divided. How many times does eight *go* into forty?
   • **to go on.   1.** To continue or proceed. The meeting *went on* until midnight.   **2.** To take place; happen; occur. What's *going on* here?

   • **to go out.   1.** To stop burning. The candles *went out* because of the strong wind.   **2.** To go to a social event or have a date. My parents *go out* on Saturday nights.
   • **to let go.   1.** To release or free. The dog had the bone in its mouth and wouldn't *let* it *go.*   **2.** To cause to be without a job; fire; discharge. Because business was bad, the company had to *let* a lot of workers *go.*
   go (gō) *verb,* **went, gone, going.**

goal   **1.** Something that a person wants and tries to get or become; aim; purpose. My *goal* in life is to become a teacher.   **2.** A place in certain games where players must get the ball or puck in order to score. The hockey player shot the puck into the *goal.*   **3.** The point or points made by getting the ball or puck into such a place. The soccer player scored two *goals* in that game.
   goal (gōl) *noun, plural* **goals.**

goalie   The player who defends the goal in soccer, hockey, and some other games.
   goal·ie (gō′lē) *noun, plural* **goalies.**

goat   An animal that is related to the sheep. Goats have short horns and a tuft of hair under their chins that looks like a beard. They are raised in many parts of the world for their milk, hair, meat, and skin.
   goat (gōt) *noun, plural* **goats** *or* **goat.**

goatee   A small pointed beard. It is only large enough to cover the chin and ends in a point just below the chin.
   goat·ee (gō tē′) *noun, plural* **goatees.**

gobble[1]   To eat something quickly and in large chunks. The hungry dog *gobbled* its food and then begged for more.
   gob·ble (gob′əl) *verb,* **gobbled, gobbling.**

gobble[2]   To make the sound that a turkey makes. *Verb.*
   —The sound that a turkey makes. *Noun.*
   gob·ble (gob′əl) *verb,* **gobbled, gobbling;** *noun, plural* **gobbles.**

goblet   A kind of drinking glass. A goblet is tall and is set on a long stem.
   gob·let (gob′lit) *noun, plural* **goblets.**

goblin   An ugly, mischievous spirit or elf.
   gob·lin (gob′lin) *noun, plural* **goblins.**

god   **1.** One of the beings who are supposed to have special powers over the lives and doings of people. The ancient Romans believed in many *gods* and goddesses.   **2.** A person or thing that is considered most important. That greedy person's *god* is money.
   god (god) *noun, plural* **gods.**

God   The being who is worshiped as the only maker and ruler of the universe.
   God (god) *noun.*

goddess A female god. Gods and *goddesses* ruled the world in Greek myths.
 god·dess (god′is) *noun, plural* **goddesses.**

goldfinch

godfather A man who acts as a sponsor, usually at a baptism.
 god·fa·ther (god′fä′<u>th</u>ər) *noun, plural* **godfathers.**

godmother A woman who acts as a sponsor, usually at a baptism.
 god·moth·er (god′mu<u>th</u>′ər) *noun, plural* **godmothers.**

godparent A godfather or godmother.
 god·par·ent (god′pâr′ənt) *noun, plural* **godparents.**

goes A form of the present tense of **go** that is used with *he, she, it,* or the name of a person, place, or thing. That student *goes* to a piano lesson after school. Time *goes* quickly when you're having fun. Look up **go** for more information.
 goes (gōz) *verb.*

goggles Special eyeglasses that fit close to the face. They are worn to protect the eyes from water, glare, wind, dust, or sparks. I brought my *goggles* to the beach so I could swim underwater.
 gog·gles (gog′əlz) *plural noun.*

gold **1.** A soft, heavy yellow metal. Gold is used to make jewelry and coins. Gold is a chemical element. **2.** The yellow color of this metal. *Noun.*
 —**1.** Made of or containing the metal gold. A prospector discovered a *gold* vein in the mountain. **2.** Having the color gold. The leaves are red and *gold* in the fall. *Adjective.*
 gold (gōld) *noun, plural* **golds;** *adjective.*

golden **1.** Made of or containing gold. This pair of *golden* earrings was given to me by my grandparents. **2.** Having the color or shine of gold; bright or shining. The field of *golden* wheat swayed in the wind. The baby's hair is soft and *golden.* **3.** Very good or valuable; excellent. If you join that team, it will be a *golden* opportunity for you to train with an excellent coach. **4.** Very happy, with much success, wealth, or good fortune.

That was the *golden* age of Roman history when the empire was at peace.
 gold·en (gōl′dən) *adjective.*

goldenrod A tall plant that has long stalks of yellow flowers. Goldenrods bloom in late summer and autumn.
 gold·en·rod (gōl′dən rod′) *noun, plural* **goldenrods.**

goldfinch Any of a large group of small birds that have thick bills and brightly colored feathers. The male American goldfinch is yellow with black markings.
 gold·finch (gōld′finch′) *noun, plural* **goldfinches.**

goldfish A fish that is usually orange-gold in color. Goldfish are often raised in home aquariums.
 gold·fish (gōld′fish′) *noun, plural* **goldfish** or **goldfishes.**

golf A game played outdoors on a special course. It is played with a small, hard ball and a set of long, thin clubs with steel or wooden heads. The object of the game is to hit the ball into each of a series of holes with as few strokes at the ball as possible. *Noun.*
 —To play the game of golf. My parents *golf* with our next-door neighbor every Saturday. *Verb.*
 golf (golf) *noun; verb,* **golfed, golfing.**

gondola

gondola **1.** A long, narrow boat with a high peak at each end. It is rowed at one end by

at; āpe; fär; câre; end; mē; it; īce; pîerce; hot; ōld; sông, fôrk; oil; out; up; ūse; rüle; pu̇ll; tûrn; chin; sing; shop; thin; <u>th</u>is; hw in white; zh in treasure. The symbol ə stands for the unstressed vowel sound in about, taken, pencil, lemon, and circus.

G

317

one person with an oar or pole. Gondolas are used to carry passengers on the canals of Venice, Italy. **2.** A compartment under a blimp or large balloon. It is used to carry passengers and equipment.
> **gon·do·la** (gon′də lə) *noun, plural* **gondolas.**

gone Past participle of **go.** My best friend had already *gone* home when I arrived. Look up **go** for more information. *Verb.*
—Used up or spent. The oranges are all *gone. Adjective.*
> **gone** (gôn) *verb; adjective.*

gong A piece of metal shaped like a plate that is used as a musical instrument. It is played with a padded hammer or drumstick. A gong makes a deep sound when it is struck.
> **gong** (gông *or* gong) *noun, plural* **gongs.**

good **1.** Of high quality; not bad or poor. The food at this restaurant is *good.* I thought the movie was very *good.* You are a *good* swimmer. My health has always been *good.* **2.** Nice or pleasant. We had a *good* time. I'm pleased to hear the *good* news. **3.** Giving help or an advantage. The new trade agreement is *good* for the country's economy. **4.** Behaving properly. The children were *good* while you were gone. **5.** Safe or correct; reliable. Our teacher always gives *good* advice. **6.** Real; true; genuine. I have a *good* excuse for being late. *Adjective.*
—**1.** Benefit; advantage. I'm telling you this for your own *good.* **2.** Kindness, honesty, or another quality that is not bad or evil. I feel there is some *good* in everybody. *Noun.*
- **as good as.** Almost; practically. With one team leading by fifteen runs, the baseball game was *as good as* over.
- **for good.** Forever; permanently. The principal said the school might be closing *for good.*
- **no good.** Worthless or useless. That idea is *no good.* It's *no good* trying to please them.
> **good** (gůd) *adjective,* **better, best;** *noun.*

good-bye Farewell. *"Good-bye!"* they called, as we drove down the driveway. After saying our *good-byes,* we left the party. This word is also spelled **good-by.**
> **good-bye** (gůd′bī′) *interjection; noun, plural* **good-byes.**

Word History

Good-bye is a shortened modern form of *God be with ye!* meaning "May God be with you!" This phrase was used as a form of farewell.

Good Friday A Christian holiday on the Friday before Easter marking the anniversary of the day Jesus died.

goodhearted Kind and generous. The *goodhearted* employer treated the workers to lunch on their birthdays.
> **good·heart·ed** (gůd′här′tid) *adjective.*

good-natured Pleasant, kindly, and cheerful toward others. Our neighbor is very *good-natured* and never minds when people drop in without being invited.
> **good-na·tured** (gůd′nā′chərd) *adjective.*

goodness The condition of being good; kindness or generosity. They helped us out of the *goodness* of their hearts. *Noun.*
—A word used to express surprise. My *goodness,* you've grown so much taller since I last saw you! *Interjection.*
> **good·ness** (gůd′nis) *noun; interjection.*

goods **1.** Things that are sold; merchandise. All of the store's *goods* are on sale. **2.** Things that belong to someone; belongings. The family moved all their household *goods* into their new apartment.
> **goods** (gůdz) *plural noun.*

good will **1.** Kindness or friendliness. I always try to show *good will* to my neighbors. **2.** Cheerful agreement to something. Both sides accepted the decision with *good will.* **3.** The advantage a business has because of good relations with its customers. Over the years, the supermarket on our block developed *good will* by charging fairer prices than its competitors. This word is also spelled **goodwill.**

goose

goose **1.** A bird that looks like a duck but is larger and has a longer neck. Geese can swim and they have webbed feet. Many kinds of geese are wild, but others are tame and are raised for food. **2.** A female bird of this kind. A male goose is called a gander.

• **to cook one's goose.** To spoil or destroy one's hopes, plans, or chances. Their *goose was cooked* when they ran out of money for the project.

goose (gŭs) *noun, plural* **geese.**

goose bumps A rough condition of the skin caused by cold or fear. Goose bumps last only a short time.

gopher A small animal that looks like a chipmunk but is larger. Gophers have large pouches in their cheeks. They burrow under the ground to build long tunnels in which they live. Gophers are found throughout North America.

go·pher (gō′fər) *noun, plural* **gophers.**

gopher

gorge A deep, narrow valley or canyon that has steep, rocky walls. *Noun.*
—**1.** To eat food in a greedy way. The children quickly *gorged* their dinner. **2.** To stuff with food. I shouldn't have *gorged* myself with four helpings of spaghetti. *Verb.*

gorge (gôrj) *noun, plural* **gorges;** *verb,* **gorged, gorging.**

gorgeous Very pleasing to look at; very beautiful. We took a drive in the country to see the *gorgeous* colors of the autumn leaves.

gor·geous (gôr′jəs) *adjective.*

gorilla A large, very strong animal that is a kind of ape. Gorillas have big, heavy bodies, short legs, and long arms. They live in Africa. Another word that sounds like this is **guerrilla.**

go·ril·la (gə ril′ə) *noun, plural* **gorillas.**

Word History

The word **gorilla** comes from a Greek word that means "wild, hairy person." Some early explorers in Africa thought that the gorillas were wild people instead of animals.

gospel **1.** The teachings of Jesus and the Apostles. **2.** Gospel. In the Bible, any one of the first four books of the New Testament. They are about the life and teachings of Jesus. **3.** Anything believed as absolutely true. The patients took their doctor's advice as *gospel.*

gos·pel (gos′pəl) *noun, plural* **gospels.**

gossip **1.** Talk or rumors about other people. Gossip is talk that is often untrue and unkind. There's a lot of *gossip* about why the mayor is resigning. **2.** A person who enjoys talking about other people or who repeats rumors to others. Those two are nothing but *gossips,* and I'd never trust them to keep a secret. *Noun.*
—To repeat what one knows or is told about other people; spread gossip. Let's not *gossip* anymore. *Verb.*

gos·sip (gos′ip) *noun, plural* **gossips;** *verb,* **gossiped, gossiping.**

got Past tense and a past participle of **get.** I *got* a new jacket last week. Look up **get** for more information.

got (got) *verb.*

gotten A past participle of **get.** We had *gotten* a letter from them before they called. Look up **get** for more information.

got·ten (got′ən) *verb.*

gouge **1.** A chisel with a curved, hollow blade. A gouge is used for making holes or grooves in wood. **2.** A hole, groove, or cut. We made a *gouge* in the floor when we dragged the table. *Noun.*
—To cut or scoop out. The carpenter *gouged* the wood for the shelves. *Verb.*

gouge (gouj) *noun, plural* **gouges;** *verb,* **gouged, gouging.**

G

gorilla

at; āpe; fär; câre; end; mē; it; īce; pîerce; hot; ōld; sông, fôrk; oil; out; up; ūse; rüle; pùll; tûrn; chin; sing; shop; thin; this; hw in white; zh in treasure. The symbol ə stands for the unstressed vowel sound in about, taken, pencil, lemon, and circus.

gourd A rounded fruit related to the pumpkin or squash. Gourds grow on vines and have a hard outer rind. They are dried and used to make bowls, jugs, and dippers. Gourds are also used for decoration.
gourd (gôrd) *noun, plural* **gourds.**

gourds

gourmet A person who loves fine food and knows a great deal about it.
gour·met (gu̇r mā′ *or* gu̇r′mā) *noun, plural* **gourmets.**

gov. or **Gov.** An abbreviation for *governor* or *government.*

govern To rule, control, or manage. The king and queen *governed* their country wisely. That person's actions were *governed* by a desire to make money.
gov·ern (guv′ərn) *verb,* **governed, governing.**

government **1.** The group of people in charge of ruling or managing a country, state, city, or other place. The *government* in this country is elected by the people. **2.** A way of ruling or governing. The Canadian people have a democratic *government.*
gov·ern·ment (guv′ərn mənt *or* guv′ər mənt) *noun, plural* **governments.**

governor **1.** The person elected to be the head of government of a state of the United States. **2.** A person appointed to govern a province, colony, or territory.
gov·er·nor (guv′ər nər) *noun, plural* **governors.**

govt. An abbreviation for *government.*

gown **1.** A woman's dress. Gowns are usually worn to parties and other special occasions. **2.** A long, loose robe. Students at graduation ceremonies and judges in court wear gowns.
gown (goun) *noun, plural* **gowns.**

grab To take hold of suddenly; seize; snatch. You'd better *grab* your jacket and run to get the bus. The painter *grabbed* the window sill as the ladder began to sway. *Verb.*
—A sudden, snatching movement. The pitcher made a *grab* for the ball, but it flew by too quickly. *Noun.*
grab (grab) *verb,* **grabbed, grabbing;** *noun, plural* **grabs.**

grace **1.** Beautiful or pleasing design, movement, or style. The ballerina danced with *grace.* **2.** A short prayer said before or after a meal. **3.** Kindness and courtesy to others; manners. They had the *grace* to apologize for being so rude. *Noun.*
—To add honor or beauty to. The royal couple *graced* the dinner with their presence. A bouquet of roses *graced* the table. *Verb.*
  • **in someone's good graces.** Liked or approved by someone. I'm not *in their good graces* because I behaved badly at their party.
grace (grās) *noun, plural* **graces;** *verb,* **graced, gracing.**

graceful Beautiful or pleasing in design, movement, or style. The dancer made a *graceful* bow to the audience.
grace·ful (grās′fəl) *adjective.*

gracious Showing kindness and courtesy; full of grace and charm. The host was *gracious* and made each guest feel welcome.
gra·cious (grā′shəs) *adjective.*

grackle A kind of blackbird. It has a long tail and shiny black feathers.
grack·le (grak′əl) *noun, plural* **grackles.**

grackle

grade **1.** A year or level of work in school. Next year I will be in the fourth *grade.* **2.** A number or letter showing how well a student has done in work at school; mark. I got a good *grade* on the geography test. **3.** A degree or step in value, quality, or rank. This beef is of the highest *grade.* **4.** The slope of a road or a railroad track. There was a steep *grade* on the road that went up the side of the mountain. *Noun.*
—**1.** To place or arrange in grades; sort. The farmer *graded* the eggs by size and color.

2. To give a grade to; mark. *The teacher graded the spelling tests.* **3.** To make more level; make less steep. *The bulldozer graded the new road. Verb.*

> **grade** (grād) *noun, plural* **grades;** *verb,* **graded, grading.**

grade school A school for children from the ages of about six to twelve or fourteen. This school is also called an **elementary school** or a **grammar school.**

gradual Happening little by little; moving or changing slowly. *We watched the gradual growth of the seeds into plants in our vegetable garden.*

> **grad·u·al** (graj′ü əl) *adjective.*

graduate **1.** To finish studying at a school or college and be given a diploma. *Our new teacher graduated from college last year.* **2.** To mark with evenly spaced lines for measuring. *This thermometer is graduated in degrees. Verb.*
—A person who has finished studying at a school or college and has been given a diploma. *Noun.*

> **grad·u·ate** (graj′ü āt′ *for verb;* graj′ü it *for noun*) *verb,* **graduated, graduating;** *noun, plural* **graduates.**

graduation **1.** The act or process of graduating. *Certain subjects must be passed for graduation at that college.* **2.** The ceremony of graduating from a school or college. *The whole family went to my graduation from grammar school.*

> **grad·u·a·tion** (graj′ü ā′shən) *noun, plural* **graduations.**

graft **1.** To put a shoot, bud, or branch from one plant into a cut or slit in another plant so that the two pieces will grow together and form one plant. **2.** To transfer a piece of skin or bone onto an injured part of the body. *The material that is grafted may come from another part of the person's body, or from another person or animal, or can be made of synthetic materials. The doctors grafted skin from the patient's leg onto the burned arm. Verb.*
—**1.** A shoot, bud, or branch that has been grafted. **2.** A piece of living or synthetic tissue that is to be grafted. *Noun.*

> **graft** (graft) *verb,* **grafted, grafting;** *noun, plural* **grafts.**

grain **1.** The seed of wheat, corn, rice, oats, and other cereal plants. *That breakfast cereal is made from grains of rice.* **2.** A tiny, hard piece of something. *Grains of sand fell from the castle that we tried to build on the beach.* **3.** The lines and other marks that run through wood, stone, and other things.

> **grain** (grān) *noun, plural* **grains.**

gram A unit of mass or weight in the metric system. One ounce is equal to about 28 grams. One pound is equal to about 450 grams.

> **gram** (gram) *noun, plural* **grams.**

grammar **1.** A system of arranging words in sentences so that the meaning of what is said is clearly communicated. Grammar is based on a series of rules. Most of these rules come naturally to us as we use our language or hear it used by other people. **2.** The use of words in a way that is thought of as standard. *Many people think that the word "ain't" is bad grammar.*

> **gram·mar** (gram′ər) *noun.*

grammar school A school for children from the ages of about six to twelve or fourteen. This school is also called an **elementary school** or a **grade school.**

grammatical **1.** Following the rules of grammar. *The sentence "Bought I shirt a white" is not grammatical, while "I bought a white shirt" is.* **2.** Having to do with grammar. *This book report has several grammatical errors.*

> **gram·mat·i·cal** (grə mat′i kəl) *adjective.*

grand **1.** Large and splendid. *The king and queen lived in a grand palace.* **2.** Including everything; complete. *We raised a grand total of one thousand dollars for our club.* **3.** Most important; main. *The dance was held in the grand ballroom. The grand prize in this contest is a trip.* **4.** Very good or excellent. *We all had a grand time at the birthday party.*

> **grand** (grand) *adjective,* **grander, grandest.**

grandchild A child of one's son or daughter. A grandchild is either a granddaughter or grandson.

> **grand·child** (grand′chīld′) *noun, plural* **grandchildren** (grand′chil′drən).

granddaughter A daughter of one's son or daughter.

> **grand·daugh·ter** (grand′dô′tər) *noun, plural* **granddaughters.**

grandfather The father of one's mother or father.

> **grand·fa·ther** (grand′fä′thər) *noun, plural* **grandfathers.**

G

at; āpe; fär; câre; end; mē; it; īce; pîerce; hot; ōld; sông, fôrk; oil; out; up; ūse; rüle; pùll; tûrn; chin; sing; shop; thin; <u>th</u>is; hw in white; zh in treasure. The symbol ə stands for the unstressed vowel sound in about, taken, pencil, lemon, and circus.

grandfather clock   A clock that is in a tall, narrow cabinet that stands on the floor.

grandmother   The mother of one's mother or father.
   grand·moth·er (grand′mu<u>th</u>′ər) *noun, plural* **grandmothers.**

grandparent   A parent of one's mother or father. A grandparent is either a grandmother or a grandfather.
   grand·par·ent (grand′pâr′ənt) *noun, plural* **grandparents.**

grandson   A son of one's son or daughter.
   grand·son (grand′sun′) *noun, plural* **grandsons.**

grandfather clock

grandstand   The main place where people sit when watching a parade or sports event. It has raised rows of seats that are sometimes covered by a roof.
   grand·stand (grand′stand′) *noun, plural* **grandstands.**

granite   A hard kind of rock. Granite is used to build monuments and buildings.
   gran·ite (gran′it) *noun.*

granola   A food made of oats and other ingredients, such as dried fruit, nuts, and honey. Granola is used as a breakfast cereal and as a snack.
   gra·no·la (grə nō′lə) *noun.*

grant   **1.** To give or allow. The teacher *granted* the student permission to go home early.   **2.** To admit to be true. I'll *grant* that it will be much faster if we ride bikes rather than walk. *Verb.*
—Something that is granted; a gift. The settlers got a *grant* of land from the government. *Noun.*
   • **to take for granted.**   To suppose something to be true or probable. I *took* it *for granted* that you wanted to sleep late, so I turned off the alarm clock.
grant (grant) *verb,* **granted, granting;** *noun, plural* **grants.**

grape   A small, juicy, round fruit that grows in bunches on vines. Grapes have a smooth, thin skin that is usually green, red, or purple in color. They are eaten raw or can be used to

a bunch of **grapes**

make juice, raisins, jelly, jam, and wine.
   grape (grāp) *noun, plural* **grapes.**

grapefruit   A round fruit with a yellow rind and juicy yellow or pink pulp inside. It is like an orange, but larger and more sour.
   grape·fruit (grāp′früt′) *noun, plural* **grapefruits** or **grapefruit.**

grapevine   **1.** A vine that grapes grow on.   **2.** A secret or informal way of spreading news or rumors from person to person. We heard it through the *grapevine* that your birthday is today.
   grape·vine (grāp′vīn′) *noun, plural* **grapevines.**

graph   A drawing that shows the relationship between changing things. The class drew a *graph* to show how the population of the United States has grown over the past one hundred years.
   graph (graf) *noun, plural* **graphs.**

-graph   A *suffix* that means: **1.** An instrument that writes or records. *Seismograph* means an instrument that records earthquakes.   **2.** Something that is written or recorded. *Photograph* means a picture recorded on film.

graphite   A soft, black mineral that is a form of the element carbon. It is used as the writing lead in pencils.
   graph·ite (graf′īt) *noun.*

Word History

The mineral **graphite** takes its name from the Greek word meaning "to write." Graphite can make marks on paper and is used for the lead in pencils.

---

grasp   **1.** To take hold of firmly with or as if with the hand. The batter *grasped* the handle of the bat and swung at the ball.   **2.** To see the meaning of; understand. I had a hard time *grasping* the meaning of that poem. *Verb.*
—**1.** The act of grasping. I lost my *grasp* on the railing and fell down the stairs.   **2.** The power or ability to grasp. The students who had studied felt that passing the test was within their *grasp.*   **3.** Knowledge; understanding. Your classmate has a good *grasp* of the problem. *Noun.*
   grasp (grasp) *verb,* **grasped, grasping;** *noun, plural* **grasps.**

grass   Any of a large number of plants that have narrow leaves called blades. Grasses grow in lawns, fields, and pastures. Horses, cows, and sheep eat grass. Wheat, rye, oats, corn, sugarcane, rice, and bamboo are kinds of grasses.

grass (gras) *noun, plural* **grasses.**

grasshopper An insect that has long, powerful legs which it uses for jumping. It also has wings. Many grasshoppers eat grasses and crops and can become great pests to farmers.

grass·hop·per (gras′hop′ər) *noun, plural* **grasshoppers.**

grasshopper

grassland Land that is covered mainly with grass and has few trees or shrubs on it. It is often used as pasture for animals.

grass·land (gras′land′) *noun, plural* **grasslands.**

grassy Covered with grass. They had a picnic in the *grassy* meadow.

grass·y (gras′ē) *adjective,* **grassier, grassiest.**

grate¹ 1. A frame of iron bars set over a window or other opening. It is used as a cover, guard, or screen. 2. A frame of iron bars for holding burning fuel in a fireplace or furnace. ▲ Another word that sounds like this is **great.**

grate (grāt) *noun, plural* **grates.**

grate² 1. To make into small pieces or shreds by rubbing against a rough surface. The cook *grated* some cheese to sprinkle on top of the spaghetti. 2. To rub or scrape with a harsh, grinding noise. The chalk *grated* on the blackboard. 3. To be annoying, irritating, or unpleasant. A shrill laugh can really *grate* on me. ▲ Another word that sounds like this is **great.**

grate (grāt) *verb,* **grated, grating.**

grateful Full of thanks or warm feelings for a favor that one has received or for something that makes one happy. We were very *grateful* to be inside on such a cold, stormy night.

grate·ful (grāt′fəl) *adjective.*

gratify To give pleasure or satisfaction to; please. I was *gratified* by the good news.

grat·i·fy (grat′ə fī′) *verb,* **gratified, gratifying.**

grating¹ A frame of iron bars set over a window or other opening. It is used as a cover, guard, or screen. Sewers often have gratings over them.

grat·ing (grā′ting) *noun, plural* **gratings.**

grating² 1. Making or having a harsh, grinding sound. There was a loud *grating*

noise as we pulled the rusty lid open. 2. Not pleasant; annoying. I find your habit of chewing your fingernails very *grating.*

grat·ing (grā′ting) *adjective.*

gratitude A feeling of thanks for a favor one has received or for something that makes one happy. Our neighbors were full of *gratitude* for the help that we gave them.

grat·i·tude (grat′i tüd′ *or* grat′i tūd′) *noun.*

grave¹ A hole dug in the ground for burying a person who has died.

grave (grāv) *noun, plural* **graves.**

grave² 1. Thoughtful and solemn; serious. The doctors became *grave* as they described the risks of the operation. 2. Very important. The general had to make *grave* decisions when the war broke out.

grave (grāv) *adjective,* **graver, gravest.**

gravel Pebbles and small pieces of rock. It is used for making driveways and roads.

grav·el (grav′əl) *noun.*

graveyard A place where people who have died are buried; cemetery.

grave·yard (grāv′yärd′) *noun, plural* **graveyards.**

gravitation The force or pull that draws all the bodies in the universe toward one another. Gravitation is the force that keeps the planets in their orbit around the sun. It also keeps people and objects on the surface of the earth.

grav·i·ta·tion (grav′i tā′shən) *noun.*

gravity 1. The force that pulls things toward the center of the earth. Gravity is the force that causes objects to fall when they are dropped. It also pulls them back to earth when they are thrown upward. Gravity causes objects to have weight. 2. Serious nature. Because of the *gravity* of the situation, troops were sent in.

grav·i·ty (grav′i tē) *noun, plural* **gravities.**

gravy A sauce made from the juices that come from meat during cooking.

gra·vy (grā′vē) *noun, plural* **gravies.**

gray A color made by mixing black and white. *Noun.*
—1. Having the color gray. You have *gray* eyes. 2. Dark, gloomy, or dreary. It was *gray* and rainy all week. *Adjective.*

G

at; āpe; fär; câre; end; mē; it; īce; pîerce; hot; ōld; sông, fôrk; oil; out; up; ūse; rüle; pùll; tûrn; chin; sing; shop; thin; this; hw in white; zh in treasure. The symbol ə stands for the unstressed vowel sound in about, taken, pencil, lemon, and circus.

—To make or become gray. The weather has *grayed* the barn's wood over the years. *Verb.* This word is also spelled **grey.**

gray (grā) *noun, plural* **grays;** *adjective,* **grayer, grayest;** *verb,* **grayed, graying.**

graze¹　**1.** To feed on growing grass. The flock of sheep *grazed* on the hillside.　**2.** To put out to feed on growing grass. The farmer *grazes* the cattle in the pasture.

graze (grāz) *verb,* **grazed, grazing.**

cows **grazing** in a field

graze²　To scrape or touch lightly in passing. Did you *graze* your knee when you fell? The tree *grazed* the house when the wind knocked it over.

graze (grāz) *verb,* **grazed, grazing.**

grease　**1.** Melted animal fat. Please clean the *grease* from the pan you used to cook the bacon.　**2.** A very thick, oily material. *Grease* is put on the parts of an automobile engine that move against one another. *Noun.* —To rub or put grease on or in. *Grease* the baking pan so that the cake won't stick. *Verb.*

grease (grēs *for noun;* grēs *or* grēz *for verb*) *noun, plural* **greases;** *verb,* **greased, greasing.**

greasy　**1.** Soiled with grease. The mechanics' uniforms were *greasy* after they repaired the car.　**2.** Containing much grease or fat; oily. This fried chicken is *greasy.*　**3.** Like grease; oily; slick. This lotion feels *greasy.*

greas·y (grē′sē *or* grē′zē) *adjective,* **greasier, greasiest.**

great　**1.** Very large in size, number, or amount. A *great* crowd gathered to welcome the astronauts to the city.　**2.** Very important, excellent, or remarkable. The scientist's cure for this disease was a *great* discovery. **3.** More than is usual; much. We'll never forget your *great* kindness to us when our parents were away. ▲ Another word that sounds like this is **grate.**

great (grāt) *adjective,* **greater, greatest.**

Great Britain　**1.** An island off the western coast of Europe. Great Britain includes England, Scotland, and Wales.　**2.** A term that is sometimes used for **United Kingdom.** Look up **United Kingdom** for more information.

Great Dane　A large, powerful dog. It has a smooth, short coat.

Great Dane (dān).

great-grandchild　The child of one's grandchild.

great-grand·child (grāt′gran′chīld′) *noun, plural* **great-grandchildren** (grāt′grand′chil′drən).

great-grandfather　The father of one's grandparent.

great-grand·fa·ther (grāt′grand′fä′thər) *noun, plural* **great-grandfathers.**

great-grandmother　The mother of one's grandparent.

great-grand·moth·er (grāt′grand′muth′ər) *noun, plural* **great-grandmothers.**

great-grandparent　The mother or father of one's grandparent.

great-grand·par·ent (grāt′grand′pâr′ənt) *noun, plural* **great-grandparents.**

greatly　Very much; highly. We *greatly* appreciated the beautiful gift you gave us.

great·ly (grāt′lē) *adverb.*

Greece　A country in southeastern Europe, on the Mediterranean Sea. In ancient times, Greece was a center of learning and the arts.

Greece (grēs) *noun.*

greed　A very great and selfish desire for more than one's share of something. Because of their *greed* for money, the owners of that store try to cheat their customers.

greed (grēd) *noun, plural* **greeds.**

greedy　Having a great and selfish desire for more than one's share of something. The dictator was *greedy* for power and would go to war to get more land.

greed·y (grē′dē) *adjective,* **greedier, greediest.**

Greek　Having to do with Greece, its people, or their language or culture. *Adjective.* —**1.** A person who was born in or is a citizen of Greece.　**2.** A person who lived in ancient Greece.　**3.** The language of Greece. *Noun.*

Greek (grēk) *adjective; noun, plural* **Greeks.**

green　**1.** The color of growing grass and of leaves in the spring and summer. It is made by mixing blue and yellow.　**2.** Ground covered with grass. The meeting took place near the village *green.*　**3.** On a golf course, the area around the hole that has very thick, closely cut grass.　**4. greens.** Green leaves

and stems of plants that are used for food or decoration. We are having beet *greens* with dinner. *Noun.*
—**1.** Having the color green. Do you like this *green* coat or the red one? **2.** Covered with growing plants, grass, or leaves. The cows grazed over *green* pastures. **3.** Not finished growing or not ripe. I won't eat those *green* tomatoes. **4.** Having little or no training or experience. The pitcher and catcher are *green* compared to the other players on their team. *Adjective.*
> **green** (grēn) *noun, plural* **greens;**
> *adjective,* **greener, greenest.**

greenhouse A room or building with walls and sides made of glass or a strong, clear plastic. Plants can be grown in a greenhouse all year long.
> **green·house** (grēn'hous') *noun, plural* **greenhouses** (grēn'hou'ziz).

greenhouse effect The trapping of heat from the sun within the earth's atmosphere. This can result from an increase in the amount of carbon dioxide and other gases created by the burning of fossil fuels on earth. These gases prevent the heat from escaping into space, just as the glass windows keep heat inside a greenhouse.

green thumb A special talent for growing plants.

greet **1.** To speak to or welcome in a friendly or polite way. The host *greeted* the guests at the door. **2.** To respond to; meet; receive. The principal's announcement that school would end early was *greeted* with cheers. **3.** To present itself to; appear to. A snowy scene *greeted* us when we looked out the window in the morning.
> **greet** (grēt) *verb,* **greeted, greeting.**

greeting **1.** The act or words of a person who greets others. The host of the party gave us a friendly *greeting* at the door. **2.** **greetings.** A friendly message that is sent by someone. My friends send *greetings* to me on my birthday every year.
> **greet·ing** (grē'ting) *noun, plural* **greetings.**

grenade A small bomb that can be thrown by hand or fired by a rifle.
> **gre·nade** (gri nād') *noun, plural* **grenades.**

grew Past tense of **grow.** They *grew* tomatoes on their farm. Look up **grow** for more information.
> **grew** (grü) *verb.*

grey Another spelling for **gray.** Look up **gray** for more information.
> **grey** (grā).

greyhound A slender dog with a smooth coat and a long nose. Greyhounds can run very fast.
> **grey·hound** (grā'hound') *noun, plural* **greyhounds.**

greyhound

grid **1.** An arrangement of parallel or crossing bars or wires, with openings between them; grating. The surface of the bridge is a metal *grid* that lets water drain through. **2.** A pattern of intersecting parallel lines used to divide a map or chart into squares.
> **grid** (grid) *noun, plural* **grids.**

griddle A heavy, flat metal pan with a handle, or a special flat metal surface built into a stove. A griddle is used like a frying pan for cooking pancakes and other food.
> **grid·dle** (grid'əl) *noun, plural* **griddles.**

gridiron **1.** A grill used for broiling food. **2.** A football field.
> **grid·i·ron** (grid'ī'ərn) *noun, plural* **gridirons.**

G

Word History

The Middle English word which gave us **gridiron** meant "a grating or lattice." A football field is called a *gridiron* because it is crisscrossed with yard markings that look like a lattice.

grief A very great feeling of being sad. My *grief* at the death of my dog was something I'll never forget.
> **grief** (grēf) *noun.*

at; āpe; fär; câre; end; mē; it; īce; pîerce; hot; ōld; sông, fôrk; oil; out; up; ūse; rüle; pùll; tûrn; chin; sing; shop; thin; <u>th</u>is; hw in white; zh in treasure. The symbol ə stands for the unstressed vowel sound in about, taken, pencil, lemon, and circus.

grieve **1.** To feel grief; mourn. The entire nation *grieved* at the death of the president. **2.** To make someone feel grief or sorrow. Your unkind words *grieved* your friends.
grieve (grēv) *verb,* **grieved, grieving.**

grill **1.** A framework of metal bars for cooking meat or other food over an open fire. My parents cooked hot dogs on the *grill* in the backyard. **2.** A restaurant that serves mainly food that has been cooked on a grill. *Noun.*
— **1.** To cook on a grill. The campers *grilled* hamburgers for supper. **2.** To question closely, harshly, and for a long time. The sergeant *grilled* the soldiers until they confessed their crime. *Verb.*
grill (gril) *noun, plural* **grills;** *verb,* **grilled, grilling.**

grim **1.** Stern, frightening, and harsh. The football coach had a cold, *grim* expression. **2.** Refusing to give up; very stubborn. The soldiers fought with *grim* determination.
grim (grim) *adjective,* **grimmer, grimmest.**

grimace A twisting of the face. People often make a grimace when they are not comfortable, pleased, or happy about something. *Noun.*
—To make a grimace. The patient *grimaced* at the taste of the bitter medicine. *Verb.*
gri·mace (grim′əs *or* gri mās′) *noun, plural* **grimaces;** *verb,* **grimaced, grimacing.**

grime Dirt that is covering or rubbed into a surface. The windows were covered with *grime.*
grime (grīm) *noun.*

grimy Full of or covered with grime; filthy. The mechanic had *grimy* hands after working on the car.
grim·y (grī′mē) *adjective,* **grimier, grimiest.**

grin To smile very broadly and happily. The grandparents *grinned* and waved at their new grandchild in the hospital. *Verb.*
—A very broad, happy smile. You had a big *grin* on your face when you got first prize in the spelling contest. *Noun.*
grin (grin) *verb,* **grinned, grinning;** *noun, plural* **grins.**

grind **1.** To crush or chop into small pieces or into a fine powder. We watched the butcher *grind* the meat. **2.** To make something smooth or sharp by rubbing it against something rough. The farmer *ground* the ax on the grindstone. **3.** To rub or press down in a harsh or noisy way. I *grind* my teeth whenever I get angry.
grind (grīnd) *verb,* **ground, grinding.**

grindstone A round, flat stone that is set in a frame. By turning it around and around, a person can use it to sharpen knives, axes, and other tools or to polish or smooth things.
grind·stone (grīnd′stōn′) *noun, plural* **grindstones.**

grip **1.** A firm hold; tight grasp. I kept a good *grip* on the dog's collar when it tried to run after the cat. **2.** Firm control or power. The city was in the *grip* of a heavy snowstorm. **3.** A part by which something is held; handle. Get a tight hold on the *grip* of the bat. *Noun.*
—**1.** To take hold of firmly and tightly. I *gripped* the suitcase and carried it off the train. **2.** To attract and keep the interest of. That novel really *gripped* us. *Verb.*
grip (grip) *noun, plural* **grips;** *verb,* **gripped, gripping.**

grit **1.** Very small bits of sand or stone. The strong wind at the beach blew *grit* in my eyes and hair. **2.** Bravery; courage. It takes real *grit* to climb a cliff without using any equipment. *Noun.*
—To press together hard. I *gritted* my teeth before I dove into the cold water of the pool. *Verb.*
grit (grit) *noun; verb,* **gritted, gritting.**

grizzled Gray or mixed with gray. Our old dog has a *grizzled* coat.
griz·zled (griz′əld) *adjective.*

grizzly bear A very large, powerful bear. It has long claws and usually brown or gray fur. Grizzly bears live in western North America.
griz·zly bear (griz′lē).

grizzly bear

groan A deep, sad sound that people sometimes make when they are unhappy, annoyed, or in pain. I let out a *groan* when the dog left dirty footprints all over the floor I had just washed. *Noun.*
—To make a deep, sad sound. I *groaned* when the doctor touched my injured ankle.

Verb. ▲ Another word that sounds like this is **grown.**

groan (grōn) *noun, plural* **groans;** *verb,* **groaned, groaning.**

grocer A person who sells food and household supplies.
gro·cer (grō′sər) *noun, plural* **grocers.**

grocery **1.** A store that sells food and household supplies. **2. groceries.** Food and other things sold by a grocer.
gro·cer·y (grō′sə rē) *noun, plural* **groceries.**

groggy Not fully alert or awake; in a dazed or unsteady condition. When I first wake up in the morning, I am sometimes *groggy.*
grog·gy (grog′ē) *adjective,* **groggier, groggiest.**

groom **1.** A man who has just been married. **2.** A person whose work is taking care of horses. *Noun.*
—**1.** To wash, brush, and take care of horses. My friend worked on a farm *grooming* horses last summer. **2.** To make neat and pleasant in appearance. A barber *grooms* people's hair for a living. *Verb.*
groom (grüm) *noun, plural* **grooms;** *verb,* **groomed, grooming.**

groove A long, narrow cut or dent. The wheels of the car made *grooves* in the dirt road. A phonograph record has *grooves* in it for the needle of the record player. *Noun.*
—To make a groove or grooves in. The carpenter *grooved* the sides of the bookcase so that the shelves would fit into place. *Verb.*
groove (grüv) *noun, plural* **grooves;** *verb,* **grooved, grooving.**

grope **1.** To feel about with the hands. The child *groped* for the light switch in the dark room. **2.** To search for something in a blind or uncertain way. The students *groped* for the right answer while the teacher waited for someone to raise a hand.
grope (grōp) *verb,* **groped, groping.**

gross **1.** With nothing taken out; total; entire. A person's *gross* income is all the money he or she earns before taxes are taken out of it. **2.** Very easily seen or understood. It is a *gross* injustice that this innocent person was sent to prison. **3.** Coarse; vulgar. The guest's *gross* jokes annoyed everyone at dinner. *Adjective.*
—**1.** The total amount received before anything is taken out. The company's *gross* for the year was five million dollars. **2.** Twelve dozen; 144. The tennis coach ordered a *gross* of balls. *Noun.*
gross (grōs) *adjective,* **grosser, grossest;** *noun, plural* **grosses** *(for definition 1)* or **gross** *(for definition 2).*

grotesque Strange, ugly, or not natural in shape or appearance. There were *grotesque* monsters in the movie.
gro·tesque (grō tesk′) *adjective.*

Word History

The word **grotesque** comes from an Italian word meaning "of or from a cave." The Italian word was first used to describe strange paintings found on the walls of caves in Italy. The word *grotesque* is now used for anything that is strange and ugly.

---

grouch A person who is often cross and has a bad temper. A grouch usually complains a great deal.
grouch (grouch) *noun, plural* **grouches.**

grouchy Easily annoyed or angered; in a bad mood. We were unhappy over losing the game and felt a little *grouchy* the next day.
grouch·y (grou′chē) *adjective,* **grouchier, grouchiest.**

ground¹ **1.** The part of the earth that is solid; soil; land. The *ground* was covered with snow. **2. grounds.** The land around a house or other building. The school *grounds* were planted with trees and flowers. **3.** An area or piece of land used for some special purpose. A brook runs through the picnic *grounds.* **4.** The cause for something said, done, or thought; reason. What *grounds* do you have for thinking they are telling the truth? **5. grounds.** The bits that settle at the bottom of a liquid or that are left over in the container that held it. Please wash the coffee *grounds* out of the pot. *Noun.*
—**1.** To force to stay on the ground or to come down to the ground. The airport *grounded* the plane for three hours because of bad weather. **2.** To cause to hit the bottom of a river or other body of water. The captain *grounded* the ship on the sand bar. **3.** To hit a baseball so that it rolls or bounces along the ground. The batter *grounded* to the shortstop. **4.** To fix or base firmly. You must *ground* an argument on facts. **5.** To connect with the ground so that electricity

---

at; āpe; fär; câre; end; mē; it; īce; pîerce; hot; ōld; sông, fôrk; oil; out; up; ūse; rüle; pùll; tûrn; chin; sing; shop; thin; this; hw in white; zh in treasure. The symbol ə stands for the unstressed vowel sound in about, taken, pencil, lemon, and circus.

G

passes into it. Electrical wires or devices are grounded to prevent a person from receiving a shock from any electricity that might collect in them. *Verb.*

ground (ground) *noun, plural* **grounds;** *verb,* **grounded, grounding.**

ground² Past tense and past participle of **grind.** The wheat was *ground* into flour. Look up **grind** for more information.

ground (ground) *verb.*

groundhog A small animal that has a plump body, short legs, and a bushy tail. It is also called a **woodchuck.** Look up **woodchuck** for more information.

ground·hog (ground′hôg′ *or* ground′hog′) *noun, plural* **groundhogs.**

a **group** of children working with balloons

group **1.** A number of persons or things together. A *group* of people gathered on the corner to watch the firefighters put out the fire. **2.** A number of persons or things that belong together or that are put together. The teacher divided the class into *groups* who would read different stories. *Noun.*
—To form or put into a group or groups. The counselor at summer camp *grouped* us by age. The fans *grouped* around the famous actor. *Verb.*

group (grüp) *noun, plural* **groups;** *verb,* **grouped, grouping.**

grouse A plump bird that has brown, black, or gray feathers. Grouse live in forests and on open land. They are often hunted as game.

grouse (grous) *noun, plural* **grouse** or **grouses.**

grove A group of trees standing together. Orange trees are grown in orange *groves.*

grove (grōv) *noun, plural* **groves.**

grow **1.** To become bigger; increase. That plant will *grow* quickly. My friend *grew* two inches last year. **2.** To come into being and live; exist. Cactuses don't *grow* in this part of the country. **3.** To cause to grow. That farmer *grows* corn. **4.** To become. It *grew*

cold as the sun went down. The members of the singing group *grew* rich as their records became popular.

• **to grow up.** To become an adult. I want to be a lawyer when I *grow up.*

grow (grō) *verb,* **grew, grown, growing.**

growl To make a deep, harsh, rumbling sound in the throat. Dogs and other animals often growl when they are angry. The bear *growled* when we got close to its cage. *Verb.*
—A deep, harsh, rumbling sound made in the throat. I greeted our neighbors with a *growl* when I had to get out of the shower to open the door for them. *Noun.*

growl (groul) *verb,* **growled, growling;** *noun, plural* **growls.**

grown Past participle of **grow.** I have *grown* interested in juggling since I visited the circus. These trees have *grown* very tall. Look up **grow** for more information. ▲ Another word that sounds like this is **groan.**

grown (grōn) *verb.*

grown-up **1.** Having come to full growth; adult. Your cousin is a *grown-up* person now. **2.** Of or like an adult. Those children's *grown-up* manners make you think they're older than they are. *Adjective.*
—A person who has come to full growth; an adult. The *grown-ups* watched as the children swam in the pool. *Noun.*

grown-up (grōn′up′ *for adjective;* grōn′up′ *for noun*) *adjective; noun, plural* **grown-ups.**

growth **1.** The process of growing. Our neighbor planted some seeds in the garden and then watched their *growth.* The *growth* of my parents' business has been very rapid. **2.** Something that has grown. A thick *growth* of weeds covered the path leading to the old house.

growth (grōth) *noun, plural* **growths.**

grouse

grub **1.** A beetle or other insect in an early stage of growth, when it looks like a worm. **2.** Food. The pioneers in the wagon train stopped for some *grub* before sunset. *Noun.*
—To dig in the ground; dig up from the

ground. Pigs *grub* for food with their hooves and snouts. *Verb.*

   grub (grub) *noun, plural* **grubs;** *verb,* **grubbed, grubbing.**

grudge Dislike or anger that has been felt for a long time. Those two have held a *grudge* against each other ever since they both ran for class president. *Noun.*
—To be unwilling to give or allow. Although they don't like you, they won't *grudge* you first prize if you deserve it. *Verb.*

   grudge (gruj) *noun, plural* **grudges;** *verb,* **grudged, grudging.**

grueling Very difficult or exhausting. The long bicycle race was *grueling.*

   gru·el·ing (grü′ə ling) *adjective.*

gruesome Causing disgust or fear; horrible. When we walked past the cemetery, we remembered all those *gruesome* stories about ghosts.

   grue·some (grü′səm) *adjective.*

gruff **1.** Deep and rough-sounding. The guard asked me in a *gruff* voice what I was doing in the building so late. **2.** Not friendly, warm, or polite. Some people have a *gruff* manner but are really very kind.

   gruff (gruf) *adjective,* **gruffer, gruffest.**

grumble **1.** To complain in a low voice; mutter in an unhappy way. The child *grumbled* about having to wake up so early. **2.** To make a low, rumbling sound. My stomach *grumbles* when I am hungry. *Verb.*
—**1.** Unhappy complaining or muttering. I answered with a *grumble* that I didn't feel like cleaning my room. **2.** A low, rumbling sound. We heard the *grumble* of thunder in the distance. *Noun.*

   grum·ble (grum′bəl) *verb,* **grumbled, grumbling;** *noun, plural* **grumbles.**

grumpy In a bad mood; cross or grouchy. I sometimes get *grumpy* when people tease me.

   grump·y (grum′pē) *adjective,* **grumpier, grumpiest.**

grunt A short, deep sound. The hog finished eating and lay down with a *grunt.* *Noun.*
—**1.** To make a short, deep sound. The lifeguards *grunted* as they pulled the boat out of the water. **2.** To say with a grunt. The exhausted runner *grunted,* "I did it," at the finish of the race. *Verb.*

   grunt (grunt) *noun, plural* **grunts;** *verb,* **grunted, grunting.**

guarantee **1.** A promise to repair or replace something or to give back the money for it, if anything goes wrong with it before a certain time has passed. This toaster comes with a *guarantee* from the manufacturer.

2. Anything that makes an outcome or condition certain. Wealth is no *guarantee* of happiness. *Noun.*
—**1.** To give a guarantee for. The company *guarantees* this dishwasher for one year. **2.** To make sure or certain. Having that band play will *guarantee* that the dance will be a success. **3.** To promise something. The plumber *guaranteed* the work would be finished on time. *Verb.*

   guar·an·tee (gar′ən tē′) *noun, plural* **guarantees;** *verb,* **guaranteed, guaranteeing.**

The **guard** keeps the children safe on the curb.

guard **1.** To keep safe from harm or danger; protect. The dog *guarded* the house. Using this lotion will *guard* your skin from the sun. **2.** To watch carefully or control the actions of. Two soldiers *guarded* the prisoner. **3.** To try to prevent a player on another team from scoring. I *guarded* the other team's star player during the game. **4.** To do something to prevent a bad thing from happening; take precautions. I always try to *guard* against catching a cold by dressing warmly. *Verb.*
—**1.** A person or group of persons that guards. The museum *guard* collected our tickets at the door. **2.** A careful watch. A sentry kept *guard* at the army camp. **3.** Something that protects. My chin *guard* slipped during the football game, and I got cut in the mouth. **4.** In football, a player at either side of the center. **5.** In basketball, either of two players whose position is near their team's basket and who try to keep the opposing team from scoring points. *Noun.*

at; āpe; fär; câre; end; mē; it; īce; pîerce; hot; ōld; sông, fôrk; oil; out; up; ūse; rüle; pùll; tûrn; chin; sing; shop; thin; this; hw in white; zh in treasure. The symbol ə stands for the unstressed vowel sound in about, taken, pencil, lemon, and circus.

• **on guard** or **on one's guard.** Prepared or watchful, as for danger, difficulties, or attack; alert. The watchdog was *on guard* for burglars.

guard (gärd) *verb*, **guarded, guarding;** *noun, plural* **guards.**

guardian **1.** A person or thing that guards or watches over. It was the judge's duty to be a *guardian* of justice. **2.** A person chosen by law to take care of someone who is young or who is not able to care for himself or herself. After the children's parents died, their grandparents became their *guardians*.

guard·i·an (gär'dē ən) *noun, plural* **guardians.**

Guatemala A country in Central America.

Gua·te·ma·la (gwä'tə mä'lə) *noun.*

guerrilla A member of a small band of soldiers. Guerrillas are not part of the regular army of a country. They often fight the enemy by making quick, surprise attacks. This word is also spelled **guerilla.** ▲ Another word that sounds like this is **gorilla.**

guer·ril·la (gə ril'ə) *noun, plural* **guerrillas.**

guess **1.** To form an opinion without having enough knowledge or facts to be sure. Without a watch, I could only *guess* what time it was. **2.** To get the correct answer by guessing. Did you *guess* the end of the mystery story? **3.** To think; believe; suppose. I *guess* they didn't come because they forgot we were having a party. *Verb.*
—An opinion formed without having enough knowledge or facts to be sure. My *guess* is that it will rain tomorrow. *Noun.*

guess (ges) *verb*, **guessed, guessing;** *noun, plural* **guesses.**

guest **1.** A person who is at another's house for a meal or a visit. We are having *guests* for dinner tonight. **2.** A customer in a restaurant, hotel, or similar place. This motel has enough room for fifty *guests.*

guest (gest) *noun, plural* **guests.**

guidance **1.** The act or process of showing how or directing; direction. I learned how to swim under the *guidance* of an instructor. **2.** Advice concerning one's plans for attending school or getting a job. The school gives *guidance* to students who want to work after graduation.

guid·ance (gī'dəns) *noun.*

guide To show the way; direct. The scout *guided* the campers through the woods. *Verb.*
—A person or thing that shows the way or directs. A *guide* took my aunt and uncle through the museum. *Noun.*

guide (gīd) *verb*, **guided, guiding;** *noun, plural* **guides.**

guided missile A missile that automatically moves along a certain course throughout its flight toward a target. It is guided by an automatic control inside it or by radio signals that it receives from the ground.

guide word A word that appears at the top of a page in dictionaries and some other books. A guide word shows the first or last dictionary entry that appears on a page. The guide words on this page of your dictionary are **guardian** and **guitar.**

guild **1.** In the Middle Ages, a group of people in the same trade or craft who joined together. Guilds were set up to see that the quality of work done was good and to look out for the interests of their members. **2.** An organization of people with the same interests or aims. The amateur actors' *guild* in our city is holding an auction to raise money. ▲ Another word that sounds like this is **gild.**

guild (gild) *noun, plural* **guilds.**

guillotine A machine for executing a person by cutting off the head. A heavy blade is dropped between two posts.

guil·lo·tine (gil'ə tēn') *noun, plural* **guillotines.**

guilt **1.** The condition or fact of having done something wrong or having broken the law. The new evidence proved the couple's *guilt* in the robbery. **2.** A feeling of having done something wrong; shame. I felt *guilt* because I got angry at a good friend.

guilt (gilt) *noun, plural* **guilts.**

guilty **1.** Having done something wrong or having committed a crime; deserving to be blamed or punished. The jury found them *guilty* of armed robbery. We're all *guilty* of losing our temper sometimes. **2.** Feeling or showing guilt or shame. The child had a *guilty* conscience for days after telling the lie.

guilt·y (gil'tē) *adjective*, **guiltier, guiltiest.**

Guinea A country in western Africa.

Guin·ea (gin'ē) *noun.*

guinea pig A small, plump animal with short ears, short legs, and no tail. Guinea pigs are rodents. They are often used in scientific experiments. Guinea pigs are very gentle and are often kept as pets.

guinea pig

guitar A musical instrument with a long neck and six or more strings. It is played by plucking or strumming the strings. Some kinds of guitars use electricity to make their sound louder.

gui·tar (gi tär′) *noun, plural* **guitars.**

guitar

gulch A narrow valley with steep sides; ravine.

gulch (gulch) *noun, plural* **gulches.**

gulf **1.** A part of an ocean or sea that is partly enclosed by land. A gulf is usually larger and deeper than a bay. **2.** A deep opening in the earth; chasm. **3.** A large difference or wide separation. There is a big *gulf* between my age and my teacher's age.

gulf (gulf) *noun, plural* **gulfs.**

gull A bird with gray and white feathers. It lives on or near bodies of water. It has long wings and a thick, slightly hooked beak. It is also called a **sea gull.**

gull (gul) *noun, plural* **gulls.**

gullible Believing or trusting in almost anything; easily fooled, tricked, or cheated. That *gullible* person would believe that bears fly.

gul·li·ble (gul′ə bəl) *adjective.*

gully A narrow ditch made by flowing water. After it rained, there were deep *gullies* along the sides of the road.

gul·ly (gul′ē) *noun, plural* **gullies.**

gulp **1.** To swallow quickly, greedily, or in large amounts. I *gulped* a glass of milk and ran out to catch the bus. **2.** To draw in or swallow air; gasp. I *gulped* when I heard there was going to be a spelling test. *Verb.*
—**1.** The act of gulping. You finished that lemonade in two *gulps*! **2.** The amount that is swallowed at one time. The child took a big *gulp* from the glass. *Noun.*

gulp (gulp) *verb,* **gulped, gulping;** *noun, plural* **gulps.**

gum¹ **1.** A thick, sticky juice that comes from various trees and plants. Gum hardens when it is dry. It is used for sticking paper and other things together and in candy and medicine. **2.** Gum that is made sweet and thick for chewing; chewing gum. *Noun.*
—**1.** To glue or become glued with gum or another sticky substance. I spilled some apple juice and it *gummed* the pages of the book together. **2.** To make or become sticky or clogged. Your fingers are *gummed* with paint. *Verb.*

gum (gum) *noun, plural* **gums;** *verb,* **gummed, gumming.**

gum² The pink flesh around the teeth.

gum (gum) *noun, plural* **gums.**

gumdrop A small piece of candy that is like jelly coated with sugar.

gum·drop (gum′drop′) *noun, plural* **gumdrops.**

gun **1.** A weapon made up of a metal tube through which a bullet or something similar is shot. Pistols, rifles, and cannons are guns. **2.** Something that is like a gun in shape or use. I used a staple *gun* to attach the posters to the wall. **3.** The firing of a gun as a signal or salute. The ship gave the president a twenty-one *gun* salute. *Noun.*
—To shoot or hunt with a gun. The outlaw in the movie tried to *gun* down the sheriff. *Verb.*

gun (gun) *noun, plural* **guns;** *verb,* **gunned, gunning.**

gull

gunner A soldier or other person in the armed forces who handles and fires cannons and other large guns.

gun·ner (gun′ər) *noun, plural* **gunners.**

gunpowder A powder that burns and explodes when touched with fire. It is used in guns, fireworks, and blasting.

gun·pow·der (gun′pou′dər) *noun, plural* **gunpowders.**

G

at; āpe; fär; câre; end; mē; it; īce; pîerce; hot; ōld; sông, fôrk; oil; out; up; ūse; rüle; pùll; tûrn; chin; sing; shop; thin; this; hw in white; zh in treasure. The symbol ə stands for the unstressed vowel sound in about, taken, pencil, lemon, and circus.

gunwale   The upper edge of the side of a ship or boat.
gun·wale (gun′əl) *noun, plural* **gunwales.**

guppy   A very small fish. There are many different kinds of guppies. Some are very colorful. The guppy is often kept as a pet.
gup·py (gup′ē) *noun, plural* **guppies.**

Word History

The **guppy** was named after R. J. L. *Guppy,* a naturalist who knew a great deal about these fish and who gave some of them to a museum.

gurgle   **1.** To flow or run with a bubbling sound. The water *gurgled* as it went down the drain.   **2.** To make a sound like this. The baby *gurgled* and smiled with delight. *Verb.*
—A sound of or like a bubbling liquid. The *gurgle* of the stream could be heard in the woods. *Noun.*
gur·gle (gûr′gəl) *verb,* **gurgled, gurgling;** *noun, plural* **gurgles.**

gush   **1.** To pour out suddenly and in large amounts. Water *gushed* from the broken pipe. The cut finger *gushed* blood until it was bandaged.   **2.** To talk with so much feeling and eagerness that it seems silly. Our neighbors are always *gushing* about their grandchildren. *Verb.*
—A sudden, heavy flow. Oil poured out of the well in a *gush. Noun.*
gush (gush) *verb,* **gushed, gushing;** *noun, plural* **gushes.**

gust   **1.** A sudden, strong rush of wind or air. A *gust* of wind lifted my hat off my head and carried it across the street.   **2.** A short or sudden bursting out of feeling. *Gusts* of laughter greeted the troupe of clowns as they stumbled out into the circus ring.
gust (gust) *noun, plural* **gusts.**

gutter   **1.** A channel or ditch along the side of a street or road to carry off water. The ball rolled off the sidewalk into the *gutter.*   **2.** A pipe or trough along the lower edge of a roof. It carries off rain water.
gut·ter (gut′ər) *noun, plural* **gutters.**

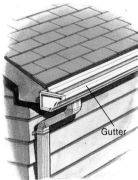

gutter

guy¹   A rope, chain, or wire used to steady or fasten something. Guys are used to steady a tent, a tall antenna, or the masts of a ship.
guy (gī) *noun, plural* **guys.**

guy²   **1.** A boy or man; fellow. Your cousin is a very nice *guy.*   **2. guys.** Persons of either sex; people. Can you please call those *guys* and tell them we're having a party?   ▲ This word is used only in everyday conversation.
guy (gī) *noun, plural* **guys.**

Guyana   A country in northern South America.
Guy·an·a (gī an′ə) *noun.*

gym   **1.** A room or building for physical exercise; gymnasium. The school basketball team practices in the *gym* almost every day after classes.   **2.** A course in physical education that is given in a school or college. We played volleyball in *gym* today.
gym (jim) *noun, plural* **gyms.**

gymnasium   A room or building with equipment for physical exercise or training and for indoor sports.
gym·na·si·um (jim nā′zē əm) *noun, plural* **gymnasiums.**

gymnast   A person skilled in gymnastics or competing in gymnastics. I enjoyed watching the *gymnasts* in the Olympic games.
gym·nast (jim′nast *or* jim′nəst) *noun, plural* **gymnasts.**

gymnastics   **1.** Exercises done to develop strength, balance, and agility.   **2.** The art, practice, or sport of these exercises.   ▲ In this sense, the word "gymnastics" is used with a singular verb.
gym·nas·tics (jim nas′tiks) *plural noun.*

Gypsy   A person belonging to a group of people who came to Europe from India long ago. Gypsies are a wandering people, and they now live scattered throughout the world.
Gyp·sy (jip′sē) *noun, plural* **Gypsies.**

Word History

The word **Gypsy** is short for *Egyptian.* People used to think that Gypsies came from Egypt.

gyroscope   An instrument with a wheel that is mounted so that its axis can point in any direction. A gyroscope is used as a compass and to keep aircraft and ships steady.
gy·ro·scope (jī′rə skōp′) *noun, plural* **gyroscopes.**

H h

1. The letter **H** was first used by several ancient tribes in the Middle East.

2. When the Greeks borrowed this letter, they first wrote it like two boxes, then like a modern **H**.

3. An ancient tribe that settled near Rome used the earlier form of this letter.

4. The ancient Romans also used this letter, but they adopted the later Greek form.

5. Our modern capital **H** comes directly from the Roman letter made some 2,400 years ago.

h, H   The eighth letter of the alphabet.
h, H (āch) *noun, plural* **h's, H's.**

ha   **1.** A word used to show surprise, joy, or victory. "*Ha!* I've found the treasure!" cried the pirate.   **2.** A word used to express laughter. *"Ha, ha, ha,"* laughed the children at the funny joke.
ha (hä) *interjection.*

habit   **1.** An action that you do so often or for so long that you do it without thinking. A habit is hard to stop or control. You have the bad *habit* of biting your fingernails. It is my parents' *habit* to read the newspaper at breakfast.   **2.** A certain kind of clothing. The nun wore a long *habit* of black and white.
hab·it (hab'it) *noun, plural* **habits.**

a rider's **habit**

habitat   The place where an animal or plant naturally lives and grows. The natural *habitat* of fish is water. The zebras' large enclosure at the zoo resembles their *habitat* in Africa.
hab·i·tat (hab'i tat') *noun, plural* **habitats.**

habitual   **1.** Done by habit. Using a seat belt will become *habitual* if you fasten the seat belt whenever you ride in a car.   **2.** Commonly occurring or used; usual. Milk, fish, and fruit are *habitual* foods in a good diet.
ha·bit·u·al (hə bich'ü əl) *adjective.*

hacienda   A large country estate used for farming or for raising cattle. There are ha-

333

ciendas in the southwestern United States and Mexico.

ha·ci·en·da (hä′sē en′də) *noun, plural* **haciendas.**

hack **1.** To cut or chop unevenly with heavy blows. This is often done with a hatchet or cleaver. The explorers *hacked* their way through the thick forest. **2.** To cough with short, harsh sounds.

hack (hak) *verb,* **hacked, hacking.**

had Past tense of **have.** We *had* fun at the party. Look up **have** for more information.

had (had; *unstressed* həd *or* əd) *verb.*

hadn't Shortened form of "had not." I *hadn't* met them until yesterday.

had·n't (had′ənt) *contraction.*

haiku A form of Japanese poetry. A haiku has three lines with five, seven, and five syllables. Many haiku are about nature.

hai·ku (hī′kü) *noun, plural* **haiku.**

hail¹ To greet or attract the attention of by calling or shouting. I *hailed* my friends across the street by calling to them. We *hailed* a taxi by waving our arms. *Verb.*

—A motion or call used as a greeting or to attract attention. *Noun.*

hail (hāl) *verb,* **hailed, hailing;** *noun, plural* **hails.**

hail² **1.** Small round pieces of ice that fall in a shower like rain. The *hail* came down so hard that it crushed many of the flowers in the garden. **2.** A heavy shower of anything. The married couple ran off in a *hail* of rice thrown by the guests. *Noun.*

—**1.** To pour down hail. It *hailed* this afternoon. **2.** To give or send in large amounts; shower. The burning building's collapse *hailed* sparks on the firefighters. *Verb.*

hail (hāl) *noun; verb,* **hailed, hailing.**

hair **1.** A very thin, threadlike growth on the skin of people and animals. **2.** A mass of such growths. My friend's *hair* is brown and wavy. **3.** A very thin, threadlike growth on the outer layer of plants. ⟁ Another word that sounds like this is **hare.**

hair (hâr) *noun, plural* **hairs.**

haircut The act or style of cutting the hair. I went to the barber and got a short *haircut.*

hair·cut (hâr′kut′) *noun, plural* **haircuts.**

hairdo A way of arranging the hair. How do you like my new *hairdo?*

hair·do (hâr′dü′) *noun, plural* **hairdos.**

hairy Covered with hair; having a lot of hair. An ape is a *hairy* animal.

hair·y (hâr′ē) *adjective,* **hairier, hairiest.**

Haiti A country that occupies part of an island in the Caribbean Sea.

Hai·ti (hā′tē) *noun.*

half **1.** One of two equal parts of something. A pint is *half* of a quart. We ate *half* the pie. They will be away at camp for a month and a *half.* **2.** Either of two time periods in certain sports. A football game or a basketball game is divided into two *halves. Noun.*

—Being one of two equal parts. We bought a *half* gallon of ice cream. *Adjective.*

—**1.** To the extent of one half. The glass was *half* full. **2.** Partly; somewhat. I was *half* asleep by the time the movie ended. *Adverb.*

half (haf) *noun, plural* **halves;** *adjective; adverb.*

half brother A brother who shares only one parent with someone else. My *half brother* and I have the same mother, but we have different fathers.

halfhearted Without much hope or spirit. My attempt to catch the ball was *halfhearted,* because it was far over my head.

half·heart·ed (haf′här′tid) *adjective.*

half-mast The position of a flag when it is halfway down from the top of a pole. It is used as a sign of mourning for someone who has died or as a signal of distress.

half-mast (haf′mast′) *noun.*

half sister A sister who shares only one parent with someone else. My *half sister* and I have the same father, but we have different mothers.

halfway To or at half the distance; midway. We climbed *halfway* up the mountain. The movie is *halfway* over. *Adverb.*

—**1.** Half the way between two points. My favorite horse was leading in the race at the *halfway* mark. **2.** Not thorough or adequate; partial. Putting a plank over the hole in the street was just a *halfway* safety measure. *Adjective.*

half·way (haf′wā′) *adverb; adjective.*

halibut A large flatfish with both eyes on the top of the body. It may weigh several hundred pounds. Halibut is found in the northern Atlantic and Pacific oceans and is used as food.

hal·i·but (hal′ə bət) *noun, plural* **halibut** or **halibuts.**

Word History

The word **halibut** comes from two earlier English words that meant "holy" and "flatfish." This fish was called "holy" because it was eaten on holy days when Christians were not allowed to eat meat.

hall **1.** A passageway in a house or other building. A hall has doors or openings that lead into rooms. The students lined up in the *hall* before they went into the auditorium. **2.** A room at the entrance to a building; lobby. We left our wet umbrellas in the *hall*. **3.** A building or large room used for a particular purpose. We went to the concert *hall*. The dining *hall* of our school is in the basement. ▲ Another word that sounds like this is **haul**.
 hall (hôl) *noun, plural* **halls**.

Halloween A holiday on October 31 that is celebrated by dressing up in costumes, collecting treats, and playing tricks.
 Hal·low·een (hal′ə wēn′) *noun, plural* **Halloweens**.

> ### Word History
>
> **Halloween** is short for *All-hallow-even*, meaning "the evening before All Saints (day)." In the ancient pagan religion of Britain, October 31 was considered to be the last day of the old year and a time when witches roamed about. When Christianity came to Britain, the Church made November 1 a holiday honoring all the saints (called "hallows"). But the tradition of imagining witches on the day before All Saints' Day is still part of Halloween.

hallway A hall or passageway. This *hallway* leads to the fire escape.
 hall·way (hôl′wā′) *noun, plural* **hallways**.

halo **1.** A ring of light around the head of a saint or angel in a work of art. **2.** A circle of light that seems to surround the sun, the moon, or another heavenly body.
 ha·lo (hā′lō) *noun, plural* **halos** or **haloes**.

halt A stop for a short time. All work in the factory came to a *halt* at noon. *Noun.*
 —To stop. The troops *halted* when the sergeant gave the order. *Verb.*
 halt (hôlt) *noun, plural* **halts**; *verb,* **halted, halting**.

halter **1.** A rope or strap used for leading or tying an animal. It fits over the animal's nose and over or behind its ears. **2.** A kind of

halter

blouse that fastens behind the neck and leaves the arms and back bare.
 hal·ter (hôl′tər) *noun, plural* **halters**.

halve **1.** To divide into two equal parts. I *halved* an apple so that I could share it with my friend. **2.** To make less by half. We *halved* the pancake recipe so there would be enough for two people instead of four. ▲ Another word that sounds like this is **have**.
 halve (hav) *verb,* **halved, halving**.

halves Plural of **half**. Break these pieces of chalk into *halves* . Look up **half** for more information.
 halves (havz) *plural noun*.

ham **1.** The meat from the back leg or shoulder of a hog. It is usually salted or smoked. **2.** The back part of the thigh of a human being. **3.** An amateur radio operator.
 ham (ham) *noun, plural* **hams**.

hamburger **1.** Ground beef. The recipe calls for a pound of *hamburger*. **2.** A rounded, flat portion of ground beef. It is broiled or fried and usually served on a bun or roll. I like ketchup, mustard, and onions on my *hamburger*.
 ham·burg·er (ham′bûr′gər) *noun, plural* **hamburgers**.

> ### Word History
>
> What we now call **hamburger** used to be called *Hamburger steak* or *Hamburg steak*. This form of meat was named after the city of Hamburg in Germany.

hammer **1.** A tool with a heavy metal head on a handle. A hammer is used for driving nails and for beating or shaping metals. **2.** Anything that is like a hammer in shape or use. The *hammer* of a gun causes it to fire when the trigger is pulled. The padded *hammers* inside a piano strike the strings and produce the sound. *Noun.*
 —**1.** To strike again and again; pound. The carpenter *hammered* nails into the wood. When no one answered, the police officer *hammered* at the door with a fist. **2.** To pound into shape with a hammer. In camp,

at; āpe; fär; câre; end; mē; it; īce; pîerce; hot; ōld; sông, fôrk; oil; out; up; ūse; rüle; pūll; tûrn; chin; sing; shop; thin; <u>th</u>is; hw in white; zh in treasure. The symbol ə stands for the unstressed vowel sound in about, taken, pencil, lemon, and circus.

H

we learned to *hammer* a bowl out of copper. *Verb.*

ham·mer (ham'ər) *noun, plural* **hammers.** *verb,* **hammered, hammering.**

hammock   A swinging bed that is hung between two trees or poles. It is made from a long piece of canvas or netting.

ham·mock (ham'ək) *noun, plural* **hammocks.**

hammock

hamper¹   To get in the way of action or progress. Stalled cars *hampered* efforts to remove the snow from the streets.

ham·per (ham'pər) *verb,* **hampered, hampering.**

hamper²   A large basket or container with a cover. There are food *hampers* for picnics and clothes *hampers* for dirty laundry.

ham·per (ham'pər) *noun, plural* **hampers.**

hamster   A small furry animal that has a plump body, a short tail, and large cheek pouches. Hamsters are rodents. They are often kept as pets.

ham·ster (ham'stər) *noun, plural* **hamsters.**

hamster

hand   **1.** The end part of the arm from the wrist down in humans and some other animals. It is made up of the palm, four fingers, and a thumb. We use our hands to pick up and hold onto things.   **2.** A pointer on a clock, meter, or dial. The *hands* of the clock pointed to three o'clock.   **3. hands.** Control or possession. The town is in enemy *hands.* The decision is in your *hands.*   **4.** A member of a group or crew; laborer. The *hands* on the farm get up early to start their work.   **5.** A way of using the hands. The magician needs a quick *hand* to do magic tricks.   **6.** A

part in something; share; role. Each student had a *hand* in planning the class dance.   **7.** Help; aid. Please give me a *hand* in moving this table.   **8.** A round of applause; clapping. The audience gave the actors a big *hand.*   **9.** One round of a card game.   **10.** The cards a player holds in one round of a card game.   **11.** Handwriting style. The note was written in a large, clear *hand.*   **12.** Either the left or the right side or direction. A nurse was at the doctor's right *hand.*   **13.** A promise of marriage.   **14.** A measurement equal to four inches. It is used to tell the height of a horse. *Noun.*

—To give or pass with the hand. I *handed* the book to the librarian. Please *hand* me the pepper. *Verb.*

- **by hand.**   With the hands. Delicate clothing should be washed *by hand.*
- **on hand.**   Ready or available for use. We always keep canned foods *on hand.*
- **to hand down.**   To transmit, as from a parent to a child or from one generation to another. Certain customs have been *handed down* from the people who founded this country.
- **to hand out.**   To distribute; give out; pass out. I have a job *handing out* advertisements for a department store.

hand (hand) *noun, plural* **hands;** *verb,* **handed, handing.**

handbag   A bag or case used for carrying personal articles, such as a wallet, keys, or cosmetics.

hand·bag (hand'bag') *noun, plural* **handbags.**

handball   **1.** A game in which players take turns hitting a small rubber ball against a wall with the hand.   **2.** The ball used in this game.

hand·ball (hand'bôl') *noun, plural* **handballs.**

handbook   A book that has information or instructions about a subject. I looked up how to make crutches in my scouts' *handbook.*

hand·book (hand'bùk') *noun, plural* **handbooks.**

handcuff   One of two metal rings joined by a chain. Handcuffs are locked around the wrists of a prisoner. *Noun.*

—To put handcuffs on. The police officers *handcuffed* the thieves and led them away. *Verb.*

hand·cuff (hand'kuf') *noun, plural* **handcuffs;** *verb,* **handcuffed, handcuffing.**

handful   **1.** The amount the hand can hold at one time. Each child took a *handful* of peanuts from the jar.   **2.** A small number. Only a *handful* of people showed up for the club meeting.

hand·ful (hand′ful′) *noun, plural* **handfuls.**

handicap **1.** Anything that makes it harder for a person to do well or get ahead. Being short can be a *handicap* in playing basketball. Despite its *handicap*, the injured dog was able to get around the house. **2.** An advantage given to a weaker player or team or a disadvantage given to a stronger player or team at the start of a game. *Noun.*
—To put at a disadvantage; hinder. Poor eyesight *handicaps* me in my work. *Verb.*
hand·i·cap (han′dē kap′) *noun, plural* **handicaps;** *verb,* **handicapped, handicapping.**

handicapped **1.** Having some handicap. We were *handicapped* in the race because we started late. **2.** Having some disability. *Handicapped* people often find it harder to get around the city than others do.
hand·i·capped (han′dē kapt′) *adjective.*

handicraft A trade, work, or art in which skill with the hands is needed. Making pottery and weaving are handicrafts.
hand·i·craft (han′dē kraft′) *noun, plural* **handicrafts.**

handkerchief A square, soft piece of cloth. It is used to wipe the nose or face.
hand·ker·chief (hang′kər chif) *noun, plural* **handkerchiefs.**

handle The part of an object that is made to be grasped by the hand. A frying pan, a suitcase, a tennis racket, a knife, and a broom have handles. *Noun.*
—**1.** To touch or hold with the hand. Please *handle* the glass carefully so that it won't fall and break. **2.** To manage, control, or deal with. I know how to *handle* dogs so they will obey me. The teacher *handled* the problem well. *Verb.*
han·dle (han′dəl) *noun, plural* **handles;** *verb,* **handled, handling.**

handlebars The curved bar on the front of a bicycle or motorcycle. The rider grips the ends of the bars and uses them to steer.
han·dle·bars (han′dəl bärz′) *plural noun.*

handmade Made by hand rather than by machine. That store sells beautiful *handmade* lace.
hand·made (hand′mād′) *adjective.*

handout Money or something else given to a poor person. For a while, the poor family lived on *handouts* from their friends.
hand·out (hand′out′) *noun, plural* **handouts.**

handrail A railing that can be gripped by the hand. Handrails are used on stairways and balconies to support and protect people.
hand·rail (hand′rāl′) *noun, plural* **handrails.**

handshake An act in which two people grip and shake each other's hands. A handshake can be a way of greeting someone, a way of saying good-bye, or a way of marking an agreement. The two business partners ended their talk with a *handshake.*
hand·shake (hand′shāk′) *noun, plural* **handshakes.**

handsome **1.** Having a pleasing appearance. They are a *handsome* couple. That old desk is very *handsome.* **2.** Fairly large or generous. The family gave me a *handsome* reward for finding their pet dog.
hand·some (han′səm) *adjective,* **handsomer, handsomest.**

handspring A kind of somersault in which a person springs forward or backward onto both hands, flips the feet over the head, and then lands back on the feet again.
hand·spring (hand′spring′) *noun, plural* **handsprings.**

handwriting Writing done by hand with a pen or pencil, not with a machine. My *handwriting* is sometimes hard to read.
hand·writ·ing (hand′rī′ting) *noun, plural* **handwritings.**

handy **1.** Within reach; nearby. When I have a cold, I keep a handkerchief *handy.* **2.** Working well with one's hands; skillful. Some people are *handy* with tools. **3.** Easy to use or handle. My parents bought me a *handy* carrying case for all my pencils and drawings.
hand·y (han′dē) *adjective,* **handier, handiest.**

hang **1.** To fasten or be attached from above only, without support from below. We will *hang* our wet bathing suits on the line. Some pictures were *hanging* on the wall. **2.** To fasten or be attached so as to move freely back and forth. We *hung* the gate on hinges. **3.** To put a person to death by hanging by a rope tied around the neck. **4.** To float; hover. A thick fog *hung* over the city. *Verb.*
—**1.** The way something hangs or falls. I did not like the *hang* of my new coat, so I re-

H

at; āpe; fär; câre; end; mē; it; ice; pîerce; hot; ōld; sông, fôrk; oil; out; up; ūse; rüle; půll; tûrn; chin; sing; shop; thin; <u>th</u>is; hw in white; zh in treasure. The symbol ə stands for the unstressed vowel sound in about, taken, pencil, lemon, and circus.

turned it.   **2.** The way of doing something; knack. It takes a while to get the *hang* of riding a bicycle. *Noun.*
• **to hang up.   1.** To put on a hanger or peg. Please *hang up* your clothes in the closet.   **2.** To end a telephone conversation by putting the receiver back on its cradle.
hang (hang) *verb,* **hung** *(for definitions 1, 2, and 4)* or **hanged** *(for definition 3),* **hanging;** *noun.*

hangar   A building or shed to keep aircraft in. ⚠ Another word that sounds like this is **hanger.**
han·gar (hang′ər *or* hang′gər) *noun, plural* **hangars.**

hanger   A frame with three corners that is made of wire, wood, or plastic and has a hook at the top. A hanger is used to hang up a coat or other garment. ⚠ Another word that sounds like this is **hangar.**
hang·er (hang′ər) *noun, plural* **hangers.**

hang glider   A glider that is like a large kite. The person operating it holds on to a frame underneath the wing and launches the hang glider from a cliff or hilltop.

hang glider

hangnail   A piece of skin that hangs loosely at the side or bottom of a fingernail.
hang·nail (hang′nāl′) *noun, plural* **hangnails.**

Hanukkah   A Jewish holiday that lasts for eight days in December. It celebrates the anniversary of the dedication of a certain holy temple in Jerusalem. This word is also spelled **Chanukah.**
Ha·nuk·kah (hä′nə kə) *noun.*

haphazard   Put together or chosen without any order or plan. You'll never find the mate to your sock in that *haphazard* pile of clothing in your closet.
hap·haz·ard (hap haz′ərd) *adjective.*

happen   **1.** To take place; occur. The accident *happened* last week.   **2.** To take place without plan or reason; occur by chance. My

cousin's birthday just *happens* to be the same day as mine.   **3.** To come or go by chance. A police officer *happened* along just after the robbery.   **4.** To be done. Something must have *happened* to the telephone, because it isn't working.
hap·pen (hap′ən) *verb,* **happened, happening.**

happening   Something that happens; event. The community guide tells about movies, fairs, concerts, and other neighborhood *happenings.*
hap·pen·ing (hap′ə ning) *noun, plural* **happenings.**

happily   **1.** With pleasure or gladness. The children played *happily* together. The dog jumped up *happily* when I reached for the leash.   **2.** Luckily. *Happily,* no one was hurt in the fire.
hap·pi·ly (hap′ə lē) *adverb.*

happiness   The condition of being glad or content. Their vacation on the farm was full of *happiness.*
hap·pi·ness (hap′ē nis) *noun.*

happy   **1.** Feeling or showing pleasure or gladness. The children were *happy* when they got a new dog.   **2.** Satisfied and pleased with one's condition; contented. All I need is one good friend to be *happy.*   **3.** Lucky; fortunate. By a *happy* chance, one tennis court was empty.
hap·py (hap′ē) *adjective,* **happier, happiest.**

happy-go-lucky   Without any worries or serious thoughts; carefree. My *happy-go-lucky* friend does not worry about the future.
hap·py-go-luck·y (hap′ē gō luk′ē) *adjective.*

harass   To bother or annoy again and again. The bully *harassed* the younger children by teasing them.
har·ass (har′əs *or* hə ras′) *verb,* **harassed, harassing.**

harbor   A sheltered place along a coast. Ships and boats often anchor in a harbor. *Noun.*
—**1.** To give protection or shelter to. It is against the law to *harbor* a criminal in your home.   **2.** To keep in one's mind. I *harbored* a grudge against the student who had been rude to me. *Verb.*
har·bor (här′bər) *noun, plural* **harbors;** *verb,* **harbored, harboring.**

hard   **1.** Solid and firm to the touch; not soft. Rocks are *hard.*   **2.** Needing or using much effort. Chopping wood is a *hard* job. This is a *hard* arithmetic problem. You are a *hard* worker.   **3.** Full of sorrow, pain, or

worry. Life was *hard* for the family after both parents lost their jobs. **4.** Having great force or strength. The fighter knocked out the opponent with one *hard* blow. **5.** Not gentle or yielding; stern. The judge had a *hard* face. *Adjective.*
—**1.** With effort or energy. They worked *hard* on their farm. **2.** With force or strength. It rained so *hard* yesterday that the roads were flooded. **3.** With difficulty. The runner was breathing *hard* after the race.
4. With great sadness or pain. The family of the accident victim took the bad news *hard*. *Adverb.*
• **hard of hearing.** Partially deaf. My grandfather wears a hearing aid because he is *hard of hearing*.
hard (härd) *adjective,* **harder, hardest;** *adverb.*

hard-boiled Boiled until hard. A *hard-boiled* egg is boiled until its yoke and white are solid.
hard-boiled (härd′boild′) *adjective.*

hard copy Numbers, letters, or pictures from a computer that have been printed on paper.

harden **1.** To make or become hard. The dry weather *hardened* the mud. I put the clay bowl in the sun to *harden*. **2.** To make or become tougher or less sensitive. Seeing crime and pain every day sometimes *hardens* the feelings of police officers.
hard·en (här′dən) *verb,* **hardened, hardening.**

hardly **1.** Just about; barely. We could *hardly* see the path in the dim light. **2.** Not likely; surely not. Since you are sick with a fever, you will *hardly* be able to go to the party tonight.
hard·ly (härd′lē) *adverb.*

hardship Something that causes difficulty, pain, or suffering. The flood was a great *hardship* to the people of the town.
hard·ship (härd′ship′) *noun, plural* **hardships.**

hardware **1.** Metal articles used for making and fixing things. Tools, nails, and screws are hardware. **2.** The electronic and mechanical parts of a computer system, such as the keyboard, the monitor, the printer, and the computer itself.
hard·ware (härd′wâr′) *noun.*

hardwood The usually strong, heavy wood of trees that have leaves rather than needles. Oaks, beeches, and maples are hardwood trees. Hardwood is used for furniture, floors, and sports equipment.
hard·wood (härd′wůd′) *noun, plural* **hardwoods.**

hardy Capable of standing hardship or harsh conditions; robust. The *hardy* pioneers survived the cold winter. Ivy is a *hardy* plant.
har·dy (här′dē) *adjective,* **hardier, hardiest.**

hare An animal of the rabbit family that has very long ears, strong back legs and feet, and a short tail. ⚠ Another word that sounds like this is **hair.**
hare (hâr) *noun, plural* **hares** or **hare.**

hare

harm **1.** Injury or hurt. To make sure no *harm* would come to the children, their parents made them wear life jackets when they went sailing. **2.** An evil; wrong. The bad child saw no *harm* in lying or stealing. *Noun.*
—To do damage to; hurt. The dog looks fierce, but it is quite gentle and will not *harm* you. *Verb.*
harm (härm) *noun, plural* **harms;** *verb,* **harmed, harming.**

harmful Causing harm; damaging. A poor diet can be *harmful* to your health.
harm·ful (härm′fəl) *adjective.*

harmless Not able to cause harm; not damaging. That snake is *harmless*. They played a *harmless* joke on their friend.
harm·less (härm′lis) *adjective.*

harmonica A musical instrument. It is a small case with slots that contain a series of metal reeds. It is played by blowing in and out through the slots.
har·mon·i·ca (här mon′i kə) *noun, plural* **harmonicas.**

harmonize **1.** To arrange, sing, or play in pleasing combinations of sounds. The voices of the church choir *harmonized* in song.

H

at; āpe; fär; câre; end; mē; it; īce; pîerce; hot; ōld; sông, fôrk; oil; out; up; ūse; rüle; půll; tûrn; chin; sing; shop; thin; this; hw in white; zh in treasure. The symbol ə stands for the unstressed vowel sound in about, taken, pencil, lemon, and circus.

2. To go together in a pleasing way. The colors of the curtains and the rug *harmonize* well. **3.** To add notes to a melody to form chords in music.
har·mo·nize (här′mə nīz′) *verb,*
harmonized, harmonizing.

harmony **1.** A combination of musical notes or voices that sound pleasing together. You take the bass part, I'll take the soprano part, and we'll sing in *harmony.* **2.** A pleasing combination of parts. The colors in the plaid dress have a nice *harmony.* **3.** Friendly agreement or cooperation; smooth relation. Often the Indians lived in *harmony* with the first colonists from England.
har·mo·ny (här′mə nē) *noun, plural*
harmonies.

harness The straps, bands, and other gear used to attach a work animal to a cart, plow, or wagon. *Noun.*
—**1.** To put a harness on. The farmer *harnessed* the horses. **2.** To control and make use of. At that dam, engineers *harness* water power to generate electricity. *Verb.*
har·ness (här′nis) *noun, plural*
harnesses; *verb,* **harnessed, harnessing.**

harp A large musical instrument with strings. The strings are set in an upright frame that is shaped like a triangle with a curved top. A harp is played by plucking the strings with the fingers.
harp (härp) *noun, plural* **harps.**

harpoon A weapon similar to a spear with a rope attached. A harpoon is used to kill or capture whales and other sea animals. It is shot from a gun or thrown by hand. *Noun.*
—To strike, catch, or kill with a harpoon. The sailors *harpooned* the whale after a long chase. *Verb.*
har·poon (här pün′) *noun, plural*
harpoons; *verb,* **harpooned, harpooning.**

harpsichord A musical instrument with strings that has a keyboard. It looks like a small piano. The harpsichord was widely used in the sixteenth through eighteenth centuries.
harp·si·chord (härp′si kôrd′) *noun, plural*
harpsichords.

harrow A farm tool that is a heavy frame with upright disks or teeth. It is usually pulled behind a tractor to break up and level plowed land. *Noun.*
—**1.** To drag a harrow over. We plowed and *harrowed* the field. **2.** To make someone suffer or worry very much. The people at the funeral looked *harrowed* by grief. *Verb.*
har·row (har′ō) *noun, plural* **harrows;**
verb, **harrowed, harrowing.**

harsh **1.** Rough or unpleasant to the ear, eye, taste, or touch. The boss shouted orders in a *harsh* voice. The towel felt *harsh* against my sunburned skin. **2.** Very cruel or severe. The prisoners got *harsh* treatment from the guards if they did not obey.
harsh (härsh) *adjective,* **harsher, harshest.**

harvest **1.** The gathering in of a crop when it is ripe. The farmers began the corn *harvest.* **2.** The crop that is gathered. We stored our *harvest* of potatoes in sacks. *Noun.*
—To gather in a crop. We have to *harvest* the fruit now that it is ripe. *Verb.*
har·vest (här′vist) *noun, plural* **harvests;**
verb, **harvested, harvesting.**

The children **harvested** vegetables.

harvester A machine for harvesting crops in fields.
har·vest·er (här′və stər) *noun, plural*
harvesters.

has A form of the present tense of **have** that is used with *he, she, it,* and the name of a person, place, or thing. My friend *has* a new bicycle. Look up **have** for more information.
has (haz) *verb.*

hash **1.** A cooked mixture of chopped meat, potatoes, and other vegetables. **2.** A mess; jumble. I made such a *hash* of the letter that it had to be typed again. *Noun.*
hash (hash) *noun, plural* **hashes.**

hasn't Shortened form of "has not." Our special guest *hasn't* arrived yet.
has·n't (haz′ənt) *contraction.*

haste Quickness in moving or in acting; speed; hurry. We left in great *haste* so we wouldn't miss the bus.
haste (hāst) *noun.*

hasten **1.** To move quickly; hurry. It was getting dark, so I *hastened* home. **2.** To make something happen faster; speed up. The medicine *hastened* the child's recovery.
has·ten (hā′sən) *verb,* **hastened, hastening.**

hasty **1.** Quick; hurried. We barely had time for a *hasty* breakfast. **2.** Too quick; careless or reckless. Don't make a *hasty* decision that you'll be sorry for later.
　hast·y (hās′tē) *adjective*, **hastier, hastiest.**

hat A covering for the head. It often has a brim and crown.
　hat (hat) *noun, plural* **hats.**

hatch¹ **1.** To cause young to come from an egg. The mother robin *hatched* her eggs. The heat from the incubator will *hatch* the chicks. **2.** To come from an egg. The chicks *hatched* by pecking through their shells. **3.** To plan or invent, usually in secret. We *hatched* a plan to catch the thief in the act.
　hatch (hach) *verb*, **hatched, hatching.**

baby birds **hatching**

hatch² **1.** An opening in the deck of a ship. It leads to lower decks or to the cargo hold. **2.** A cover or trap door for such an opening.
　hatch (hach) *noun, plural* **hatches.**

hatchery A place where the eggs of fish or birds are hatched.
　hatch·er·y (hach′ə rē) *noun, plural* **hatcheries.**

hatchet A small ax with a short handle. It is made to be used with one hand.
　hatch·et (hach′it) *noun, plural* **hatchets.**

hate To have very strong feelings against; dislike very much. We *hate* people who treat animals cruelly. I *hate* to clean the house.
　hate (hāt) *verb*, **hated, hating.**

hatred A strong feeling against a person or thing. The people felt *hatred* toward the cruel dictator.
　ha·tred (hā′trid) *noun, plural* **hatreds.**

haughty Thinking of oneself as much better than other people; arrogant. The *haughty* ruler refused to speak to common people.
　haugh·ty (hô′tē) *adjective*, **haughtier, haughtiest.**

haul **1.** To pull or move with force; drag. It took three of us to *haul* the heavy trunk up the stairs. **2.** To carry; transport. Railroads *haul* freight across the country. *Verb.*
　—1. The act of hauling. Give the rope a *haul*. **2.** Something that is gotten by catching or winning. The fishing boat came home with a big *haul* of fish. **3.** The distance something is hauled. It's a long *haul* from here to the garbage dump. *Noun.* ▲ Another word that sounds like this is **hall.**
　haul (hôl) *verb*, **hauled, hauling;** *noun, plural* **hauls.**

haunch A part of the body of a person or animal including the hip and upper thigh. The lion sat on its *haunches*.
　haunch (hônch) *noun, plural* **haunches.**

haunt **1.** To visit or live in. Some people say that ghosts *haunt* the old house. **2.** To come often to the mind of. Memories of the shipwreck he had been in long ago *haunt* the old sailor.
　haunt (hônt) *verb*, **haunted, haunting.**

have **1.** To own; possess. Our neighbors *have* a house in the country. Everyone in my family *has* straight black hair. **2.** To consist of; contain. A year *has* twelve months. **3.** To hold in the mind. I *have* a good idea. **4.** To carry on; engage in. We *had* a discussion in class. **5.** To experience. *Have* a good time! My best friend might *have* chicken pox. **6.** To give birth to. My cat will *have* kittens in about a week. **7.** To be forced or obligated. I *have* to be home by five o'clock. **8.** To receive or obtain; get. You *had* a telephone call while you were out. **9.** To permit; allow. I wanted to keep snakes as pets, but my parents wouldn't *have* it. **10.** To cause something to be done; arrange for. We *had* new wallpaper put up. **11.** Also used as an auxiliary verb to show that the action of the main verb is finished. We *have* done all of our homework. They *have* written a story. ▲ Another word that sounds like this is **halve.**
　● **to have to do with.** To be about, be concerned with, or be related to. That book *has to do with* the history of our

at; āpe; fär; câre; end; mē; it; īce; pîerce; hot; ōld; sông, fôrk; oil; out; up; ūse; rüle; pull; tûrn; chin; sing; shop; thin; this; hw in white; zh in treasure. The symbol ə stands for the unstressed vowel sound in about, taken, pencil, lemon, and circus.

H

state. The judge's anger *had to do with* the lawyer's outrageous behavior in court.
have (hav) *verb,* **had, having.**

haven A place of safety or shelter. The cool woods were a *haven* for the hot and tired hikers. A harbor is a *haven* for boats.
ha·ven (hā′vən) *noun, plural* **havens.**

haven't Shortened form of "have not." I *haven't* been to a dance yet.
have·n't (hav′ənt) *contraction.*

Hawaii An island state of the United States in the Pacific Ocean. Its capital is Honolulu.
Ha·wai·i (hə wī′ē) *noun.*

Word History

Hawaii was originally the name for the biggest island of the state. An ancient island song says that Hawaii was the traditional home of the native people who first lived there. This name was given to the island by later settlers.

hawk¹ A bird with a sharp, hooked beak, strong claws, and sharp eyesight. The hawk hunts and feeds on small animals and is related to the eagle.
hawk (hôk) *noun, plural* **hawks.**

hawk² To offer goods for sale by calling out. The peddler *hawked* fruit in the street.
hawk (hôk) *verb,* **hawked, hawking.**

hawthorn A thorny shrub or tree. The hawthorn has white or pink flowers and small red, orange, purple, or black berries.
haw·thorn (hô′thôrn′) *noun, plural* **hawthorns.**

hawk¹

hay Grass, alfalfa, or clover that is cut and dried for use as feed for livestock. ▲ Another word that sounds like this is **hey.**
hay (hā) *noun, plural* **hays.**

hay fever A condition that causes a stuffy nose, itching eyes, and sneezing. Hay fever is an allergy that is caused by breathing pollen that plants release into the air.

hayloft An upper floor in a barn or stable, used for storing hay.
hay·loft (hā′lôft′) *noun, plural* **haylofts.**

haystack A pile of hay stacked outdoors.
hay·stack (hā′stak′) *noun, plural* **haystacks.**

haystacks

hazard Something that can cause harm or injury; risk; danger. Icy roads are a *hazard* to drivers.
haz·ard (haz′ərd) *noun, plural* **hazards.**

hazardous Likely to cause harm or injury; dangerous. Smoking is *hazardous* to your health because it can cause cancer and heart disease.
haz·ard·ous (haz′ər dəs) *adjective.*

hazardous waste A chemical or nuclear substance that is dangerous to people, animals, or the earth. Hazardous wastes often come from factories and nuclear power plants.

haze Mist, smoke, or dust in the air. The bridge was hidden in the morning *haze.*
haze (hāz) *noun, plural* **hazes.**

hazel **1.** A tree or shrub that has light brown nuts that can be eaten. **2.** A light brown color like the color of this nut. *Noun.* —Having the color hazel; light brown. My cousin has beautiful *hazel* eyes. *Adjective.*
ha·zel (hā′zəl) *noun, plural* **hazels;** *adjective.*

hazy Not clear; blurred or confused. On a *hazy* day, we can see only a dim outline of the mountains. My understanding of how a computer works is *hazy.*
ha·zy (hā′zē) *adjective,* **hazier, haziest.**

H-bomb   A powerful bomb usually called a **hydrogen bomb.** Look up **hydrogen bomb** for more information.
  H-bomb (āch′bom′) *noun, plural* **H-bombs.**

he   **1.** A male person or animal that is being talked about. Bob promised that *he* would be on time.   **2.** A person; anyone. *He* who hesitates is lost. *Pronoun.*
—A male person or animal. Is the kitten a *he* or a *she? Noun.*
  he (hē) *pronoun; noun, plural* **hes.**

head   **1.** The top part of the human body. The head is where the eyes, ears, nose, and mouth are. The brain is inside the head.   **2.** The top or front part of any other animal that is like a human head. Dogs, fish, and birds have heads.   **3.** The top or front part of something. I walked up to the *head* of the stairs. Hit the nail on the *head.*   **4.** A firm, rounded cluster of leaves or flowers. Please buy a *head* of lettuce.   **5.** A person who is above others in rank; chief. The president is the *head* of our country's government.   **6.** A single person or animal. The cowhands rounded up forty *head* of cattle.   **7.** Mental ability. You have a good *head* for figures.   **8. heads.** The side of a coin that shows the main design, usually a picture of a person's head. *Noun.*
—Top, chief, or front. My cousin is the *head* lifeguard at the pool. *Adjective.*
—**1.** To be or go to the top or front of; lead. The scout leader *headed* our troop in the parade.   **2.** To be in charge of. Our best writer *heads* the school newspaper.   **3.** To direct or move in a direction. The captain *headed* the ship to the north. We *head* for the beach on hot days. *Verb.*
  • **over one's head.**   Beyond one's ability to understand or manage. Physics has always been *over my head.*
  • **to head off.**   To get ahead of and cause to stop or turn back. The posse tried to *head off* the bank robbers.
  head (hed) *noun, plural* **heads** *(for definitions 1-5)* or **head** *(for definitions 6 and 7); adjective; verb,* **headed, heading.**

headache   **1.** A pain felt inside the head.   **2.** Something that causes trouble or worry. The flat tire was another *headache* on the long bicycle trip.
  head·ache (hed′āk′) *noun, plural* **headaches.**

headband   A band worn around the head. A headband can hold the hair in place or just be an ornament.
  head·band (hed′band′) *noun, plural* **headbands.**

headdress   A covering or decoration for the head. The Indian wore a *headdress* of feathers.
  head·dress (hed′dres′) *noun, plural* **headdresses.**

headfirst   With the head going in front. The swimmer dived *headfirst* into the water.
  head·first (hed′fûrst′) *adverb.*

heading   A title for a page or chapter.
  head·ing (hed′ing) *noun, plural* **headings.**

headland   A point of high land that sticks out into the water; cape.
  head·land (hed′lənd) *noun, plural* **headlands.**

headlight   A bright light on the front of an automobile or other vehicle. It got dark during the drive home, so the driver turned on the car's *headlights.*
  head·light (hed′līt′) *noun, plural* **headlights.**

headline   A line printed at the top of a newspaper or magazine article. A headline tells what the article is about. It is printed in large or heavy type. "President Addresses Nation," read the *headline. Noun.*
—To be the main attraction of a show. A magic act *headlined* the show. *Verb.*
  head·line (hed′līn′) *noun, plural* **headlines;** *verb,* **headlined, headlining.**

headlong   **1.** With the head first. The runner slid *headlong* into second base.   **2.** In a reckless way; rashly. I rushed *headlong* into buying the used bicycle and didn't notice that it was damaged. *Adverb.*
—Made with the head first. I made a *headlong* dive into the lake. *Adjective.*
  head·long (hed′lông′) *adverb; adjective.*

head-on   With the head or front end first. The car hit the pole *head-on.* The two cars were in a *head-on* crash.
  head-on (hed′ôn′ *or* hed′on′) *adverb; adjective.*

headphone   A radio or telephone receiver that is held against the ear by a band that fits over the head.
  head·phone (hed′fōn′) *noun, plural* **headphones.**

headquarters   A center of operations where leaders work and give orders; main office. The commanders were summoned to

at; āpe; fär; câre; end; mē; it; īce; pîerce; hot; ōld; sông, fôrk; oil; out; up; ūse; rüle; pùll; tûrn; chin; sing; shop; thin; this; hw in white; zh in treasure. The symbol ə stands for the unstressed vowel sound in about, taken, pencil, lemon, and circus.

H

the general's *headquarters.* That company's *headquarters* are in New York. ▲ The word **headquarters** may be used with a singular or plural verb.
    head·quar·ters (hed′kwôr′tərz) *noun.*

headrest A support for the head. Headrests in automobiles are designed to prevent injuries to the neck in a collision. I use a pillow as a *headrest* when I read in bed.
    head·rest (hed′rest′) *noun, plural* **headrests.**

head start An early start or other advantage given to someone starting out in a race or other competition.

headstone A stone set at the head of a grave; tombstone.
    head·stone (hed′stōn′) *noun, plural* **headstones.**

headstrong Insisting on one's own way; stubborn. The *headstrong* child would not listen to advice.
    head·strong (hed′strông′) *adjective.*

headwaters The small streams that come together to form the beginning of a river.
    head·wa·ters (hed′wô′tərz) *plural noun.*

headway Forward movement or progress. It was hard for the small ship to make any *headway* through the high waves. I can't make much *headway* with this arithmetic problem.
    head·way (hed′wā′) *noun.*

heal To make or become healthy or sound again. The doctor *healed* the sick child with medicine. The cut *healed* without leaving a scar. ▲ Other words that sound like this are **heel** and **he'll.**
    heal (hēl) *verb,* **healed, healing.**

health **1.** The condition of being well and without disease or injury. You will lose your *health* if you don't eat the proper foods. **2.** The condition of the body or mind. The doctor examined me and decided that I was in good *health.*
    health (helth) *noun.*

health food Any food that is grown without chemical fertilizers and that is not prepared with additives.

healthful Good for people's health; wholesome. Exercise is *healthful.*
    health·ful (helth′fəl) *adjective.*

healthy Having, showing, or giving good health. A good diet and exercise should make you *healthy.* The athlete's skin had a *healthy* color. I love to breathe this *healthy* country air.
    health·y (hel′thē) *adjective,* **healthier, healthiest.**

heap A collection of things piled together. We left a *heap* of peanut shells on the kitchen table. *Noun.*
—**1.** To make into a pile. We *heaped* the fallen leaves. **2.** To give or fill in large amounts. The cook *heaped* my plate with mashed potatoes. *Verb.*
    heap (hēp) *noun, plural* **heaps;** *verb,* **heaped, heaping.**

hear **1.** To receive sound through the ears. I *hear* someone calling my name. My grandparents can't *hear* very well, so please speak loudly. **2.** To listen to. Please *hear* my side of the quarrel before you decide who is right. **3.** To get information about. The winner of the contest will *hear* the good news soon. I *heard* about the fire on the radio. **4.** To get a letter or other communication. Have you *heard* from your friend in Mexico lately? ▲ Another word that sounds like this is **here.**
    hear (hîr) *verb,* **heard, hearing.**

heard Past tense and past participle of **hear.** I *heard* my brother coming home late last night. Look up **hear** for more information. ▲ Another word that sounds like this is **herd.**
    heard (hûrd) *verb.*

hearing **1.** The ability to hear. You have very good *hearing.* **2.** The act of listening or getting information. *Hearing* that my best friend had won the contest made me very happy. **3.** The chance to be heard. The judge gave both sides a fair *hearing* before making a decision.
    hear·ing (hîr′ing) *noun, plural* **hearings.**

hearing aid A small, electronic device that makes sounds louder. It is worn in or near the ear to make poor hearing better.

hearsay Information that has been heard from someone else. Do you know that for a fact, or is it just *hearsay?*
    hear·say (hîr′sā′) *noun.*

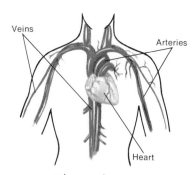

a human **heart**

heart **1.** The hollow organ in the body that pumps blood through the arteries and veins.

The heart is located in the chest. It is divided into four chambers. **2.** The center of a person's feelings. The happy child spoke from the *heart* when thanking us for finding the puppy. **3.** Spirit; courage. The team lost *heart* after their defeat. **4.** The center or middle of anything. We got lost in the *heart* of the forest. Let's get to the *heart* of the problem. **5.** A playing card marked with one or more red figures like this: ♥. **6.** Anything shaped like a heart. We cut out paper *hearts* to make Valentine's Day cards.
- **by heart.** From or by memory. I'm learning my lines for the school play *by heart.*

heart (härt) *noun, plural* **hearts.**

heartbeat One complete pumping motion of the heart.
heart·beat (härt′bēt′) *noun, plural* **heartbeats.**

heartbroken Filled with sorrow or grief. We were *heartbroken* when our dog died.
heart·bro·ken (härt′brō′kən) *adjective.*

hearth **1.** The floor of a fireplace or the space in front of it. **2.** Home.
hearth (härth) *noun, plural* **hearths.**

hearty **1.** Full of warmth, friendliness, or enthusiasm. Our cousins gave us a *hearty* welcome. **2.** Big and satisfying. Thanksgiving dinner is a *hearty* meal at our house.
heart·y (här′tē) *adjective,* **heartier, heartiest.**

heat **1.** High temperature; warmth. Heat is a form of energy. The sun gives off *heat.* The *heat* of the fire warmed the whole room. **2.** Strong feeling, excitement. I slammed the door in the *heat* of anger. *Noun.*
—To make or become hot or warm. We *heated* the milk before giving it to the baby. After the sun came out it *heated* up fast. *Verb.*
heat (hēt) *noun, plural* **heats;** *verb,* **heated, heating.**

heater A device that gives heat. A radiator or a furnace is a kind of heater. We put an electric *heater* in the cold room.
heat·er (hē′tər) *noun, plural* **heaters.**

heath A flat, open piece of land. It is covered with heather or low bushes.
heath (hēth) *noun, plural* **heaths.**

heathen A person who does not believe in the God of the Christians, Jews, or Muslims. *Noun.*
—Having to do with heathens. Ancient *heathen* tribes worshiped many gods. *Adjective.*
hea·then (hē′thən) *noun, plural* **heathens** or **heathen;** *adjective.*

heather A low, evergreen shrub that has pink, purple, or white flowers. Heather grows wild in Scotland and England.
heath·er (heth′ər) *noun, plural* **heathers.**

heave **1.** To lift, raise, pull, or throw using force or effort. The farmers *heaved* bales of hay onto the truck. I *heaved* a rock across the stream. **2.** To give out in a loud or heavy way. I *heaved* a sigh of relief when I found my lost dog. **3.** To rise and fall. The runner's chest *heaved* after the race.
heave (hēv) *verb,* **heaved, heaving.**

heather

heaven **1.** In the Christian religion, the place where God and the angels live. **2. heavens.** The space above and around the earth; sky. You can see many stars in the *heavens* on a clear, dark night.
heav·en (hev′ən) *noun, plural* **heavens.**

heavenly **1.** Having to do with heaven; divine. Angels are *heavenly* beings. **2.** Of or in the sky or outer space. The sun, the moon, and the stars are *heavenly* bodies. **3.** Happy, pleasing, or beautiful. This quiet, shaded place is a *heavenly* spot for a picnic.
heav·en·ly (hev′ən lē) *adjective.*

heavily In a heavy way. The tree fell *heavily* on the ground.
heav·i·ly (hev′ə lē) *adverb.*

at; āpe; fär; câre; end; mē; it; īce; pîerce; hot; ōld; sông, fôrk; oil; out; up; ūse; rüle; pull; tûrn; chin; sing; shop; thin; this; hw in white; zh in treasure. The symbol ə stands for the unstressed vowel sound in about, taken, pencil, lemon, and circus.

H

heavy **1.** Having great weight; hard to lift or move. The desk was too *heavy* for me to move by myself. **2.** Having more than the usual weight. It's so cold that I need a *heavy* blanket to keep me warm. **3.** Large in size or amount. We were late because we got stuck in *heavy* traffic. We had a *heavy* rainfall last night. **4.** Hard to do, carry out, or bear. A parent has *heavy* responsibilities.
heav·y (hev′ē) *adjective,* **heavier, heaviest.**

Hebrew **1.** A member of one of the Jewish tribes of ancient times. **2.** The language spoken by the ancient Jews. The people of Israel speak a form of this language. *Noun.*
—Of the Hebrews or their language. *Adjective.*
He·brew (hē′brü) *noun, plural* **Hebrews;** *adjective.*

hectare A unit of area in the metric system. It is equal to 10,000 square meters, or about 2½ acres.
hec·tare (hek′târ) *noun, plural* **hectares.**

he'd **1.** Shortened form of "he had." *He'd* better hurry. **2.** Shortened form of "he would." *He'd* do it if he could. ▲ Another word that sounds like this is **heed.**
he'd (hēd) *contraction.*

hedge A row of shrubs or small trees planted close together. A hedge is used as a fence. *Noun.*
—**1.** To surround, close in, or separate with a hedge. All the people in our block *hedged* their front yards with bushes. **2.** To avoid answering a question directly. When they asked me if I would help, I *hedged* and said I would think about it. *Verb.*
hedge (hej) *noun, plural* **hedges;** *verb,* **hedged, hedging.**

hedgehog **1.** An animal that has a pointed snout and sharp, hard spines on its back and sides. When it is frightened or attacked, it rolls up into a ball with only its spines showing. Hedgehogs eat insects and are found in western Europe. **2.** A porcupine.
hedge·hog (hej′hôg′ or hej′hog′) *noun, plural* **hedgehogs.**

hedgehog

heed To pay careful attention to; listen or mind. I *heeded* my parents' advice and wore a sweater to the football game. ▲ Another word that sounds like this is **he'd.**
heed (hēd) *verb,* **heeded, heeding.**

heel¹ **1.** The rounded back part of the human foot below the ankle. The heel has many bones in it that carry the weight of the body. **2.** Anything like a heel in shape, use, or position. The heel of the hand is the part of the palm near the wrist. I have to have the *heels* on these shoes fixed. *Noun.*
—To follow closely. The dog was taught to *heel* at its master's side. *Verb.* ▲ Other words that sound like this are **heal** and **he'll.**
heel (hēl) *noun, plural* **heels;** *verb,* **heeled, heeling.**

heel² To lean to one side. The strong winds forced the sailboat to *heel* to the left. ▲ Other words that sound like this are **heal** and **he'll.**
heel (hēl) *verb,* **heeled, heeling.**

heifer A young cow that has not had a calf.
heif·er (hef′ər) *noun, plural* **heifers.**

height **1.** The distance from bottom to top. The *height* of the statue is 11 feet. I measured my *height* by standing next to a pole marked in inches. The mountain stands at a *height* of one mile above sea level. **2.** A high place. The little child was afraid of *heights* and would never climb a tree. **3.** The highest point. The singer retired at the *height* of a brilliant career.
height (hīt) *noun, plural* **heights.**

heighten To make or become high or higher. The carpenters *heightened* the house by adding a third story to it. The excitement *heightened* as the story went on.
height·en (hī′tən) *verb,* **heightened, heightening.**

Heimlich maneuver An emergency treatment used to help a person who is choking on something. You stand behind the person who is choking, put your arms around the person, and press hard into the upper abdomen. This should force the object out.
Heim·lich maneuver (hīm′lik).

Word History

The **Heimlich maneuver** is named after Henry J. Heimlich, the American physician who developed it.

heir A person who is to receive the money or property of a person after that person has died. ▲ Other words that sound like this are **air** and **ere.**
heir (âr) *noun, plural* **heirs.**

heiress A woman who is to receive or has received the money or property of a person after that person has died.
heir·ess (âr′is) *noun, plural* **heiresses.**

heirloom An object that is handed down from generation to generation in a family.
heir·loom (âr′lüm′) *noun, plural* **heirlooms.**

held Past tense and past participle of **hold.** I *held* the ball in my hand. Look up **hold** for more information.
held (held) *verb.*

helicopter An aircraft that is kept in the air by blades that rotate above the craft.
hel·i·cop·ter (hel′i kop′tər) *noun, plural* **helicopters.**

helicopters

helium A very light gas that has no color or odor. Helium is used in balloons and blimps. Helium is a chemical element.
he·li·um (hē′lē əm) *noun.*

Word History

The word **helium** comes from the Greek word for "sun." Helium was first discovered by people who were studying the rays of light that come from the sun.

hell **1.** In the Christian religion, the place where Satan lives and where wicked people will be punished after death. **2.** A place or condition of great suffering. The prison was a *hell* on earth.
hell (hel) *noun, plural* **hells.**

he'll **1.** Shortened form of "he will." *He'll* come to see us when he has time. **2.** Shortened form of "he shall." *He'll* clean his room if I have anything to say about it! ▲ Other words that sound like this are **heal** and **heel.**
he'll (hēl) *contraction.*

hello A word used as a greeting. *"Hello,"* they called, when they met us on the street. The host gave me a warm *hello* when I arrived.
hel·lo (he lō′ *or* hə lō′) *interjection; noun, plural* **hellos.**

helm The part of a ship used for steering. It is usually a wheel or large lever. The captain stood at the *helm* of the ship.
helm (helm) *noun, plural* **helms.**

helmet A covering for the head that is worn for protection. Soldiers, firefighters, football players, and astronauts wear helmets.
hel·met (hel′mit) *noun, plural* **helmets.**

helmets

help **1.** To give or do something that is useful, wanted, or needed; aid; assist. We *helped* the blind person across the street. I *helped* my parents paint the living room. The coach's advice *helped* the team to win. **2.** To make better; ease; relieve. Hot lemon juice and honey will *help* your sore throat. **3.** To stop or avoid. I couldn't *help* laughing when I heard the story. *Verb.*
—**1.** The act of helping. Do you need *help*? **2.** A person or thing that helps. The new vacuum cleaner is a big *help* around the house. *Noun.*
• **to help oneself to.** To take, especially without being urged. The food is on the table, so *help yourself.*
• **to help out.** To provide help, support, or service. I always try to *help out* when we have company for dinner.
help (help) *verb,* **helped, helping;** *noun, plural* **helps.**

helpful Giving help; useful. A bigger child gave me a *helpful* boost, and I got over the fence.
help·ful (help′fəl) *adjective.*

at; āpe; fär; câre; end; mē; it; īce; pîerce; hot; ōld; sông, fôrk; oil; out; up; ūse; rüle; pu̇ll; tûrn; chin; sing; shop; thin; this; hw in white; zh in treasure. The symbol ə stands for the unstressed vowel sound in about, taken, pencil, lemon, and circus.

helping A serving of food for one person. Would you like a second *helping* of string beans?
help·ing (hel′ping) *noun, plural* **helpings.**

helping verb A term that is sometimes used for **auxiliary verb.** Look up **auxiliary verb** for more information.

helpless Not able to take care of oneself. I was made almost *helpless* by my broken ankle. A newborn kitten is *helpless.*
help·less (help′lis) *adjective.*

hem The border of a garment or piece of cloth. It is made by folding under the edge and sewing it down. Dresses, pillowcases, and curtains have hems. *Noun.*
—To fold under the edge of a piece of cloth and sew it down. I *hemmed* the curtains. *Verb.*
  • **to hem in.** To close in; surround. I felt *hemmed in* by the crowd watching the parade.
hem (hem) *noun, plural* **hems;** *verb,* **hemmed, hemming.**

hemisphere One half of the earth or another sphere. The equator divides the earth into the Northern Hemisphere and the Southern Hemisphere. The earth is also divided into the Eastern Hemisphere and the Western Hemisphere. Europe, Africa, Asia, and Australia are in the Eastern Hemisphere. North and South America are in the Western Hemisphere.
hem·i·sphere (hem′ə sfîr′) *noun, plural* **hemispheres.**

hemlock **1.** A tall evergreen tree that has reddish bark, flat needles, and small cones. Its wood is used for pulp and as lumber. **2.** A poisonous plant that has spotted, hollow stems and clusters of white flowers.
hem·lock (hem′lok′) *noun, plural* **hemlocks.**

Needles

Cone

hemlock

hemp A strong, tough fiber made from the stem of a tall plant. It is used to make rope.
hemp (hemp) *noun, plural* **hemps.**

hen **1.** An adult female chicken. **2.** The female of various other birds.
hen (hen) *noun, plural* **hens.**

hence **1.** As a result; therefore. I've seen the movie before, and *hence* I know the story. **2.** From this time or place. The friends agreed to meet two weeks *hence* at the same place.
hence (hens) *adverb.*

her A female person or animal that is being talked about. I invited *her* to the dance. Did you lend *her* the book? *Pronoun.*
—Of, belonging to, or having to do with her. *Her* cousin is my best friend. *Adjective.*
her (hûr) *pronoun; adjective.*

herb **1.** A plant whose leaves, stems, seeds, or roots are used in cooking for flavoring, in medicines, or because they are fragrant. Mint and parsley are herbs. **2.** Any flowering plant that dies at the end of one growing season and does not form a woody stem.
herb (ûrb *or* hûrb) *noun, plural* **herbs.**

herbivore An animal that eats only plants. Cows are herbivores.
her·bi·vore (hûr′bə vôr′) *noun, plural* **herbivores.**

herbivorous Feeding on plants. A cow is a *herbivorous* animal.
her·biv·o·rous (hûr biv′ər əs) *adjective.*

herd A group of animals that live or travel together. A *herd* of cattle grazed in the pasture. *Noun.*
—To group or lead in or like a herd. The cowhands *herded* the cattle and drove them to market. Our tour guide *herded* us into the bus. *Verb.* ▲ Another word that sounds like this is **heard.**
herd (hûrd) *noun, plural* **herds;** *verb,* **herded, herding.**

here **1.** At, in, or to this place. I have been waiting *here* for an hour. Bring the book *here,* and I'll read it to you. **2.** At this time. Let's stop reading *here* and start again later. *Adverb.*
—This place. Can you show me how to get home from *here? Noun.*
—A word used in answering a roll call, calling an animal, or attracting attention. *Interjection.* ▲ Another word that sounds like this is **hear.**
here (hîr) *adverb; noun; interjection.*

hereafter From now on; after this. The guard told me that *hereafter,* I should not run in school halls.
here·af·ter (hîr af′tər) *adverb.*

hereby By means of this. The certificate said, "You are *hereby* entitled to one free admission to the zoo."
here·by (hîr′bī′) *adverb*.

hereditary **1.** Passed on or able to be passed on from an animal or plant to its offspring. Blue eyes are *hereditary*. Some diseases are *hereditary*. **2.** Passed on from an ancestor to an heir. The noble inherited the *hereditary* title from ancestors.
he·red·i·tar·y (hə red′i ter′ē) *adjective*.

heredity **1.** The passing on of characteristics from an animal or plant to its offspring. **2.** The characteristics passed on. Brown hair is part of my *heredity*.
he·red·i·ty (hə red′i tē) *noun, plural* **heredities**.

here's Shortened form of "here is." *Here's* the book I was telling you about.
here's (hîrz) *contraction*.

heritage Something that is handed down from earlier generations or from the past; tradition. The right to free speech is part of the American *heritage*.
her·it·age (her′i tij) *noun, plural* **heritages**.

hermit A person who lives alone and away from other people. A hermit often lives like this for religious reasons.
her·mit (hûr′mit) *noun, plural* **hermits**.

hero **1.** A person who is looked up to by others because of his or her great achievements or fine qualities. The swimmer who saved the child from drowning was a *hero*. **2.** The main male character in a play, story, or poem. The actor played the *hero* with great skill. **3.** A big sandwich on a long roll with a thick crust. I had a meatball *hero* for lunch.
he·ro (hîr′ō) *noun, plural* **heroes**.

heroic **1.** Very brave; courageous. The firefighter made a *heroic* attempt to save the family from the burning apartment. **2.** Describing the deeds of heroes. We read a *heroic* poem about a great warrior.
he·ro·ic (hi rō′ik) *adjective*.

heroin An illegal drug that is addictive. ▲ Another word that sounds like this is **heroine**.
her·o·in (her′ō in) *noun*.

heroine **1.** A woman or girl who is looked up to by others for great achievements or fine qualities. Our school doctor is my *heroine*, because I want to be a doctor too some day. **2.** The main female character in a play, story, or poem. The audience awaited the entrance of the *heroine*. ▲ Another word that sounds like this is **heroin**.
her·o·ine (her′ō in) *noun, plural* **heroines**.

heron A bird with a long slender neck, a long pointed bill, and long thin legs.
her·on (her′ən) *noun, plural* **herons**.

herring A small saltwater fish that is a member of a family that includes shad and sardines. Herring are found in the northern Atlantic Ocean. They can be eaten smoked, fresh, or canned.
her·ring (her′ing) *noun, plural* **herring** or **herrings**.

heron

hers The one or ones that belong or have to do with her. Whose book is it, his or *hers?*
hers (hûrz) *pronoun*.

herself **1.** Her own self. The scientist should not have blamed *herself* for the failure of the experiment. The principal *herself* is opposed to the plan. **2.** Her usual, normal, or true self. Mother has not been *herself* since she caught a cold.
her·self (hûr self′) *pronoun*.

he's **1.** Shortened form of "he is." *He's* going to come with us. **2.** Shortened form of "he has." *He's* seen that movie three times.
he's (hēz) *contraction*.

hesitant Waiting or pausing because of feeling unsure; not quite willing. I was *hesitant* about jumping into the cold lake.
hes·i·tant (hez′i tənt) *adjective*.

hesitate **1.** To wait or stop a moment, especially because of feeling unsure. The speaker *hesitated* and looked down at some notes. **2.** To be unwilling. I *hesitated* to telephone you because it was late. **3.** To wait to act because of doubt or fear. If you *hesitate* too long, you will lose your chance to get the job.
hes·i·tate (hez′i tāt′) *verb,* **hesitated, hesitating**.

at; āpe; fär; câre; end; mē; it; īce; pîerce; hot; ōld; sông, fôrk; oil; out; up; ūse; rüle; pull; tûrn; chin; sing; shop; thin; this; hw in white; zh in treasure. The symbol ə stands for the unstressed vowel sound in about, taken, pencil, lemon, and circus.

hesitation A delay or pause because of fear, uncertainty, or forgetting. The brave child picked up the garden snake without *hesitation.*
  hes·i·ta·tion (hez′i tā′shən) *noun, plural* **hesitations.**

hey A word used to attract attention or to show surprise or pleasure. "*Hey!* Watch where you're going when you're crossing the street!" ▲ Another word that sounds like this is **hay.**
  hey (hā) *interjection.*

hi A word used to say "hello." ▲ Another word that sounds like this is **high.**
  hi (hī) *interjection.*

HI Postal abbreviation for *Hawaii.*

H.I. An abbreviation for *Hawaiian Islands.*

hibernate To spend the winter sleeping. Some bears, woodchucks, frogs, and snakes hibernate.
  hi·ber·nate (hī′bər nāt′) *verb,* **hibernated, hibernating.**

Word History

  Hibernate comes from a Latin word meaning "winter quarters." The Roman legions usually did not fight during the winter season; instead they would stay near camp until spring. *Hibernate* now refers to how animals become inactive during the winter.

---

hiccup **1.** A quick catching of the breath that one cannot control. A hiccup is caused by a short spasm of the breathing muscles. **2. hiccups.** The condition of having one hiccup after another. *Noun.*
—To have hiccups. I waited until I stopped *hiccupping* before I tried to sing along. *Verb.*
  hic·cup (hik′up) *noun, plural* **hiccups.**
  verb, **hiccupped, hiccupping.**

hickory A tall tree of North America. The hickory has nuts that are used as food and strong, hard wood.
  hick·o·ry (hik′ə rē) *noun, plural* **hickories.**

hid Past tense and a past participle of **hide.** The pirates *hid* the treasure in a cave. Look up **hide** for more information.
  hid (hid) *verb.*

hidden A past participle of **hide.** The dog has *hidden* its bone. Look up **hide** for more information.
  hid·den (hid′ən) *verb.*

hide¹ **1.** To put or keep out of sight. I *hid* my letters in a tree hole so that no one else would see them. We tried to *hide* in a closet, but the others found us. The heavy snow *hid* the deer's tracks. **2.** To keep secret. The lost children tried to *hide* their fears from each other.
  hide (hīd) *verb,* **hid, hidden** or **hid, hiding.**

hide² The skin of an animal. Leather shoes are made from hides.
  hide (hīd) *noun, plural* **hides.**

hide-and-seek A children's game in which one player has to find all of the other players who are hiding.
  hide-and-seek (hīd′ən sēk′) *noun.*

hideous Very ugly; horrible. My cousin dressed up as a *hideous* monster for Halloween.
  hid·e·ous (hid′ē əs) *adjective.*

hideout A place where someone can hide. The thieves used a cave as their *hideout* from the police.
  hide·out (hīd′out′) *noun, plural* **hideouts.**

hieroglyphics

hieroglyphic A picture or symbol that stands for a word, sound, or idea. The ancient Egyptians used hieroglyphics in their writing.
  hi·er·o·glyph·ic (hī′ər ə glif′ik) *noun, plural* **hieroglyphics.**

Leaves

hickory

high **1.** Tall. That mountain is very *high*. The building is forty stories *high*. **2.** At a great distance from the ground. The bird was *high* in the sky. **3.** Above or more important than others. A general has a *high* rank in the army. **4.** Greater than others. *High* winds swept the snow into drifts. The racing car was going at a *high* speed. I am trying to sell my bicycle for a *high* price. **5.** Above other sounds in pitch. The soprano sang a *high* note. **6.** Noble or lofty. Their *high* ideals made them refuse a reward for the diamond necklace that they found and returned. *Adjective.*
—At or to a high place. The hikers climbed *high* up the hill. *Adverb.*
—**1.** A high place or point. The temperature today reached a new *high* for the year. **2.** The arrangement of gears in an automobile, bicycle, or other vehicle that gives the greatest speed. *Noun.* ▴ Another word that sounds like this is **hi.**
  • **high and dry.** **1.** Completely up out of water. The ship was stranded *high and dry* on the rocks. **2.** Without aid or assistance; alone; abandoned. The outlaws drove off in the stagecoach, leaving the passengers *high and dry.*
  high (hī) *adjective,* **higher, highest;** *adverb; noun, plural* **highs.**

high jump A contest in which a person jumps as high as possible over a bar set between two upright poles.

highland A high or hilly part of a country.
  high·land (hī′lənd) *noun, plural* **highlands.**

highly **1.** Very much; very. I thought the movie was *highly* entertaining. Mercury is *highly* poisonous. **2.** With much praise or admiration. The students think *highly* of their teacher. **3.** At a high price. I was not *highly* paid for mowing the neighbor's lawn.
  high·ly (hī′lē) *adverb.*

Highness A title of respect used when speaking to or about a member of a royal family. A king is spoken of as "His *Highness,*" and a queen is spoken of as "Her *Highness.*"
  High·ness (hī′nis) *noun, plural* **Highnesses.**

high-rise A very tall building.
  high-rise (hī′rīz′) *noun, plural* **high-rises.**

high school A school attended after elementary school or junior high school. High school goes up to the twelfth grade.

high seas The open waters of an ocean. The high seas are not under the control of any country.

high-strung Very tense or nervous by nature. That *high-strung* dog is frightened easily.
  high-strung (hī′strung′) *adjective.*

high tide The tide when the level of the ocean is at its highest.

highway A main road. Main Street becomes a *highway* just outside of town.
  high·way (hī′wā′) *noun, plural* **highways.**

highwayman A robber who holds up travelers on a road.
  high·way·man (hī′wā′mən) *noun, plural* **highwaymen** (hī′wā′mən).

hijack To take over a truck, airplane, or other vehicle by force. Two passengers with machine guns *hijacked* the airplane.
  hi·jack (hī′jak′) *verb,* **hijacked, hijacking.**

hike To take a long walk. The scout troop *hiked* to their camp by the lake. *Verb.*
—A long walk. We took a long *hike* in the woods. *Noun.*
  hike (hīk) *verb,* **hiked, hiking;** *noun, plural* **hikes.**

hilarious Very funny. The guest told a *hilarious* story that made us all laugh.
  hi·lar·i·ous (hi lâr′ē əs) *adjective.*

hill **1.** A raised, rounded part of the earth's surface. A hill is not as high as a mountain. **2.** A small heap or mound. Ants have made *hills* in our backyard.
  hill (hil) *noun, plural* **hills.**

hillside The side or slope of a hill. We sledded down the snowy *hillside.*
  hill·side (hil′sīd′) *noun, plural* **hillsides.**

hilltop The top of a hill. We climbed to the *hilltop* for our picnic.
  hill·top (hil′top′) *noun, plural* **hilltops.**

hilly Having many hills. It's hard to bicycle over *hilly* country.
  hill·y (hil′ē) *adjective,* **hillier, hilliest.**

hilt The handle of a sword or dagger.
  hilt (hilt) *noun, plural* **hilts.**

him A male person or animal that is being talked about. We saw *him* last night at the game. I lent a book to *him.* ▴ Another word that sounds like this is **hymn.**
  him (him *or* im) *pronoun.*

himself **1.** His own self. Jim hit *himself* by accident with the hammer. Ted is annoyed at

H

at; āpe; fär; câre; end; mē; it; īce; pîerce; hot; ōld; sông, fôrk; oil; out; up; ūse; rüle; pull; tûrn; chin; sing; shop; thin; this; hw in white; zh in treasure. The symbol ə stands for the unstressed vowel sound in about, taken, pencil, lemon, and circus.

himself for missing the movie. Bob promised that he would cook *himself* dinner. **2.** His usual, normal, or true self. Mike just wasn't *himself* during the game today.
him·self (him self') *pronoun.*

hind At the back; rear. Our dog sometimes stands on its *hind* legs.
hind (hīnd) *adjective.*

hinder To hold back the progress of. The snowstorm *hindered* the search for the missing plane.
hin·der (hin'dər) *verb,* **hindered, hindering.**

hindrance Something that gets in the way of progress; obstacle. The noisy traffic outside was a *hindrance* to our conversation.
hin·drance (hin'drəns) *noun, plural* **hindrances.**

Hinduism A religion, philosophy, and social system that originated in India. The supreme being of Hinduism takes many different forms.
Hin·du·ism (hin'dü iz'əm) *noun.*

hinge A joint on which a door, gate, or lid moves back and forth or up and down. The *hinges* on the old gate squeak when you open or close it. *Noun.*
—**1.** To put hinges on; attach by hinges. The carpenter *hinged* the cupboard doors. **2.** To depend. The team's chances of winning the championship *hinge* on next week's game. *Verb.*
hinge (hinj) *noun, plural* **hinges;** *verb,* **hinged, hinging.**

hint A slight sign or suggestion. If you can't guess the answer to the riddle, I'll give you a *hint.* There is a *hint* of spring in the air this morning. *Noun.*
—To give a slight sign or suggestion. My parents *hinted* that I might be getting a bicycle for my birthday. *Verb.*
hint (hint) *noun, plural* **hints;** *verb,* **hinted, hinting.**

hip The part on either side of the body just below the waist; the joint where either leg meets the body.
hip (hip) *noun, plural* **hips.**

hippopotamus A very large, heavy animal that eats plants. It lives in and near rivers and lakes in Africa. Hippopotamuses have short legs and thick skin with no hair.
hip·po·pot·a·mus (hip'ə pot'ə məs) *noun, plural* **hippopotamuses.**

hire **1.** To give a job to; employ. The school *hired* three new teachers this year. **2.** To get the temporary use of something in return for payments; rent. We *hired* a car to drive to Florida. *Verb.*

—The act of hiring. I couldn't afford the *hire* of a rowboat. *Noun.*
hire (hīr) *verb,* **hired, hiring;** *noun, plural* **hires.**

his The one or ones that belong or have to do with him. This book is mine and that book is *his. Pronoun.*
—Of, belonging to, or having to do with him. *His* best friend lives four doors away from him. *Adjective.*
his (hiz) *pronoun; adjective.*

Hispanic Of or having to do with Spain or Latin America, or with the people of Spain or Latin America. *Adjective.*
—A person who lives in the United States and has Spanish or Latin American parents or ancestors. *Noun.*
His·pan·ic (hi span'ik) *adjective; noun, plural* **Hispanics.**

historian A person who knows a great deal about history. Historians write history books.
his·to·ri·an (hi stôr'ē ən) *noun, plural* **historians.**

historic Important in history. The committee tried to preserve all the *historic* old houses in town.
his·tor·ic (hi stôr'ik) *adjective.*

historical Having to do with history. This book has *historical* information, such as how our town began, how it changed, and who its leaders have been.
his·tor·i·cal (hi stôr'i kəl) *adjective.*

history The story or record of what has happened in the past. The *history* of the United States as a nation goes back over 200 years. That old house has an interesting *history.*
his·to·ry (his'tə rē) *noun, plural* **histories.**

hit **1.** To give a blow to; strike. The bully *hit* my friend with a stick. **2.** To send by striking with a bat or racket. The batter *hit* the ball over the fence. **3.** To come against with force. The arrow *hit* the target. **4.** To

hippopotamus

come to; reach. The speeding car *hit* ninety miles per hour. We finally *hit* upon the answer. **5.** To have a strong effect on; impress. The unhappy news *hit* us hard. *Verb.*
—**1.** A blow or strike. The *hit* on the head stunned me. **2.** A person or thing that is successful or popular. The band's music made them the *hit* of the party. The new movie is a big *hit.* **3.** The hitting of a baseball so that the batter gets on base. *Noun.*
• **to hit it off.** To like or get along with one another. When I first met the twins, we didn't *hit it off.*
hit (hit) *verb,* **hit, hitting;** *noun, plural* **hits.**

hitch **1.** To fasten with a rope, strap, or hook. The farmer *hitched* the horse to the wagon. **2.** To move or lift with a jerk. I *hitched* up my suspenders. *Verb.*
—**1.** A fastening. The *hitch* between the car and the trailer broke. **2.** An unexpected delay or problem. A sudden storm put a *hitch* in their plans to leave that day. **3.** A quick, upward, pull or tug. I straightened my tie and gave my trousers a *hitch.* **4.** A kind of knot used to attach things together temporarily. *Noun.*
hitch (hich) *verb,* **hitched, hitching;** *noun, plural* **hitches.**

hitchhike To travel by getting free rides from cars or trucks that are passing by. The two friends *hitchhiked* into town.
hitch·hike (hich′hīk′) *verb,* **hitchhiked, hitchhiking.**

hive **1.** A box or house for bees to live in. **2.** All the bees that live together in the same hive.
hive (hīv) *noun, plural* **hives.**

hives A rash of raised red or white bumps that itch. Hives are often caused by an allergy.
hives (hīvz) *plural noun.*

hoard To save and store or hide away. I *hoarded* my allowance until I had enough money to buy a camera. *Verb.*
—Something that is stored or hidden away. We keep a *hoard* of canned goods in the basement. *Noun.* ▲ Another word that sounds like this is **horde.**
hoard (hôrd) *verb,* **hoarded, hoarding;** *noun, plural* **hoards.**

hoarse **1.** Having a rough or harsh, deep sound. The teacher's voice was *hoarse* from a bad cold. **2.** Having a harsh voice. I was *hoarse* after all the shouting I did at the game. ▲ Another word that sounds like this is **horse.**
hoarse (hôrs) *adjective,* **hoarser, hoarsest.**

hoax A trick or made-up story meant to fool people. The report that a sea monster was seen in the bay turned out to be nothing but a *hoax.*
hoax (hōks) *noun, plural* **hoaxes.**

hobble **1.** To move or walk awkwardly with a limp. I *hobbled* around with a sprained ankle for two weeks. **2.** To keep from moving easily or freely. You *hobble* a horse by tying its front legs or its back legs together. *Verb.*
—A rope, strap, or other thing used to hobble a horse or other animal. *Noun.*
hob·ble (hob′əl) *verb,* **hobbled, hobbling;** *noun, plural* **hobbles.**

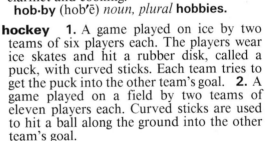
hobble

hobby Something done regularly in one's spare time for pleasure. My *hobbies* are playing the clarinet and cooking.
hob·by (hob′ē) *noun, plural* **hobbies.**

hockey **1.** A game played on ice by two teams of six players each. The players wear ice skates and hit a rubber disk, called a puck, with curved sticks. Each team tries to get the puck into the other team's goal. **2.** A game played on a field by two teams of eleven players each. Curved sticks are used to hit a ball along the ground into the other team's goal.
hock·ey (hok′ē) *noun.*

hoe A tool with a wide, thin blade set across the end of a long handle. Hoes are used to loosen the soil around plants and dig up weeds. *Noun.*
—To dig with a hoe. We *hoe* the vegetable garden once a week to keep the soil loose. *Verb.*
hoe (hō) *noun, plural* **hoes;** *verb,* **hoed, hoeing.**

hog **1.** A fully grown pig. Hogs are raised for their meat. **2.** Any of several wild animals in the pig family. **3.** A greedy or dirty person. *Noun.*

H

at; āpe; fär; câre; end; mē; it; īce; pîerce; hot; ōld; sông, fôrk; oil; out; up; ūse; rüle; pull; tûrn; chin; sing; shop; thin; this; hw in white; zh in treasure. The symbol ə stands for the unstressed vowel sound in about, taken, pencil, lemon, and circus.

353

—To take more than one's share. The truck *hogged* the narrow road so that no cars could pass. *Verb.*

hog (hôg *or* hog) *noun, plural* **hogs;** *verb,* **hogged, hogging.**

hogan   A house made of stones or logs with a roof of branches covered with earth. Some Navajo Indians live in hogans.

ho·gan (hō′gän) *noun, plural* **hogans.**

hogan

hoist   To lift or pull up. The sailors *hoisted* the cargo onto the ship's deck with a crane. We *hoisted* the flag up the pole. *Verb.*
—**1.** A device used to lift or pull up something heavy. The mechanic at the garage put the car on a *hoist* to raise it.   **2.** A lift. Someone gave me a *hoist* up the tree. *Noun.*

hoist (hoist) *verb,* **hoisted, hoisting;** *noun, plural* **hoists.**

hold¹   **1.** To take and keep in the hands or arms; grasp; grip. If you will *hold* the packages, I will unlock the door.   **2.** To keep from falling; support. Will this chair *hold* my weight?   **3.** To keep in a certain place or position. The baby would not *hold* still. The dam *held* back the flooding river. A good book *holds* your attention.   **4.** To remain attached or fastened. The ship's anchor *held* even in rough seas.   **5.** To contain. This bottle *holds* two quarts. The bus will *hold* fifty people.   **6.** To take part in; carry on. We were *holding* an interesting conversation when the phone rang. The club will *hold* a meeting on Saturday.   **7.** To have in the mind. I *hold* strong opinions about religion. **8.** To believe to be; think. The judge *held* them responsible for the accident. *Verb.*
—**1.** A grasp; grip. I didn't have a good *hold* on the heavy lamp, and I dropped it. **2.** Something that can be gripped. The hikers couldn't find enough *holds* to climb the side of the cliff.   **3.** A mark or symbol in music that shows a pause. *Noun.*
• **to hold back.**   To restrain; control. I tried *to hold back* the tears, but I couldn't. The police *held back* the excited crowd.

• **to hold out.**   **1.** To last; continue. Our food supply will *hold out* for another week.   **2.** To keep fighting or resisting. The troops in the fort *held out* for weeks.
• **to hold up.**   **1.** To support; keep from falling. These columns *hold up* the roof. **2.** To raise in order to show or display. *Hold up* your hand if you want to ask a question.   **3.** To last or continue. These shoes have *held up* for years. If this good weather *holds up,* we'll go on a picnic. **4.** To stop or delay. Heavy traffic *held* us *up.*   **5.** To rob while threatening with a weapon. A gang *held up* three stores.

hold (hōld) *verb,* **held, holding;** *noun, plural* **holds.**

hold²   A space in a ship or airplane where cargo is stored.

hold (hōld) *noun, plural* **holds.**

holder   **1.** A person who holds something; owner. To get this job you must be the *holder* of a driver's license.   **2.** A thing that is used to hold something else with. That jar will make a good *holder* for pencils.

hold·er (hōl′dər) *noun, plural* **holders.**

holdup   **1.** A robbery by someone who is armed. There was a *holdup* in the jewelry store last week.   **2.** A stopping or delay. There was a *holdup* of traffic because of the snowstorm.

hold·up (hōld′up′) *noun, plural* **holdups.**

hole   **1.** A hollow place in something solid. There was a big *hole* in the street after the heavy rain. The dog dug a *hole* in the ground to hide its bone.   **2.** An opening through something. I wore a *hole* in the elbow of my old sweater.   **3.** A small hollow place on the green of a golf course. The ball is hit into the hole.   **4.** The burrow of an animal. The rabbit disappeared down its *hole.* ◢ Another word that sounds like this is **whole.**

hole (hōl) *noun, plural* **holes.**

holiday   **1.** A day on which most people do not work. Many holidays celebrate the anniversaries of great events. The Fourth of July and Thanksgiving Day are American holidays.   **2.** A vacation. My neighbor is home from college for the spring *holidays.*

hol·i·day (hol′i dā′) *noun, plural* **holidays.**

Word History

The word **holiday** comes from an Old English word that meant "holy day." In England long ago, the only days when people did not work were days set aside as special religious feast days.

Holland   A country in northwestern Europe. This country is also called **the Netherlands.**
Hol·land (hol′ənd) *noun.*

hollow   **1.** Having a hole or an empty space inside; not solid. A water pipe is *hollow.* **2.** Curved in like a cup or bowl; sunken. The thin child had *hollow* cheeks.   **3.** Deep and echoing. Our footsteps made a *hollow* sound as we walked through the empty tunnel. *Adjective.*
—**1.** A hole or empty space. The car bounced over a *hollow* in the dirt road.   **2.** A valley. The farm nestled in the *hollow* between the hills. *Noun.*
—**1.** To make hollow. Woodpeckers had *hollowed* out the dead tree trunk.   **2.** To make by digging out. The rabbits *hollowed* out a burrow in the ground. *Verb.*
hol·low (hol′ō) *adjective,* **hollower, hollowest;** *noun, plural* **hollows;** *verb,* **hollowed, hollowing.**

holly   An evergreen tree or shrub. Holly usually has very shiny leaves with sharp, pointed edges and bright red berries. Its leaves and berries are often used as Christmas decorations.
hol·ly (hol′ē) *noun, plural* **hollies.**

hollyhock   A tall plant that has round wrinkled leaves and spikes of large, brightly colored flowers.
hol·ly·hock (hol′ē hok′) *noun, plural* **hollyhocks.**

a **holly** branch

holocaust   A great or complete destruction, as by fire. The *holocaust* leveled the city.
hol·o·caust (hol′ə kôst′ *or* hō′lə kôst′) *noun, plural* **holocausts.**

Word History

The word **holocaust** comes from a Greek word meaning "burnt up whole." This was the term applied to an ancient form of sacrifice to a particular god. In this ritual an animal was killed, and then all or part of it was burned on an altar.

holster   A leather case for carrying a gun. Holsters for pistols are often worn on a belt around a person's waist.
hol·ster (hōl′stər) *noun, plural* **holsters.**

holy   **1.** Belonging to or set apart for the worship of God; sacred. The priest stood at the *holy* altar.   **2.** Close to God; very religious and pure. The nun led a *holy* life.
▲ Another word that sounds like this is **wholly.**
ho·ly (hō′lē) *adjective,* **holier, holiest.**

home   **1.** The place where a person lives. Our *home* is in an apartment house. My best friend's *home* is that house up the road.   **2.** A person's family; household. I grew up in a happy *home.*   **3.** The place that a person comes from. Colorado has always been my *home.*   **4.** The goal or place of safety in some sports and games. The person who gets *home* first wins.   **5.** A place for the shelter and care of certain people. That big house is a *home* for elderly people. *Noun.*
—**1.** At or to the place where a person lives. The whole family will come *home* for Christmas.   **2.** To the place or mark aimed at. The camper shot at the tree and the arrow hit *home. Adverb.*
• **at home.**   As if one were in one's own home; comfortable; relaxed. Whenever I visit your family, they always make me feel *at home.*
home (hōm) *noun, plural* **homes;** *adverb.*

homeland   A country where a person was born or has a home. Their *homeland* is Sweden, although they have been living in New York for three years.
home·land (hōm′land′) *noun, plural* **homelands.**

homeless   Having no home. *Homeless* people have been sleeping in the streets and parks of this city.
home·less (hōm′lis) *adjective.*

homely   **1.** Having a plain appearance; not handsome or pretty. Our old dog is *homely,* but we love it.   **2.** Simple and modest; not fancy or special. The hotel manager's *homely* manners put us at ease.
home·ly (hōm′lē) *adjective,* **homelier, homeliest.**

homemade   Made at home or by hand. My parents bake *homemade* bread on Saturdays. We have a *homemade* swing on a tree in the yard.
home·made (hōm′mād′) *adjective.*

at; āpe; fär; câre; end; mē; it; īce; pîerce; hot; ōld; sông, fôrk; oil; out; up; ūse; rüle; pull; tûrn; chin; sing; shop; thin; **this**; hw in white; zh in treasure. The symbol ə stands for the unstressed vowel sound in about, taken, pencil, lemon, and circus.

H

home plate

home plate The place where a baseball player stands to hit a pitched ball. A runner must touch home plate after rounding the bases in order to score a run.

homer A short form of the word **home run.** Look up **home run** for more information.
hom·er (hō′mər) *noun, plural* **homers.**

homeroom A classroom to which all the pupils in a class go in the mornings. Attendance is checked and special announcements are made there.
home·room (hōm′rüm′ *or* hōm′rùm′) *noun, plural* **homerooms.**

home run A hit in baseball that lets the batter go around all the bases to home plate and score a run.

homesick Sad because of being away from one's home or family. The soldier was *homesick* during the first month in the army.
home·sick (hōm′sik′) *adjective.*

homespun A cloth that is woven by hand at home, instead of in a factory by big machines.
home·spun (hōm′spun′) *noun.*

homestead **1.** A farm with its house and other buildings. **2.** A piece of land that was given by the United States government to a settler for farming.
home·stead (hōm′sted′) *noun, plural* **homesteads.**

homeward Toward home. The hikers turned *homeward* for the walk back. This train ticket is good for our *homeward* trip.
home·ward (hōm′wərd) *adverb; adjective.*

homework A school assignment that is meant to be done at home, not in the classroom.
home·work (hōm′wûrk′) *noun.*

hominy Kernels of white corn that are hulled and ground up. Hominy is mixed with water and boiled before it is eaten.
hom·i·ny (hom′ə nē) *noun.*

homogenize To mix milk so that the cream is spread evenly throughout and will not separate and rise to the top.
ho·mog·e·nize (hə moj′ə nīz′) *verb,* **homogenized, homogenizing.**

homograph A word with the same spelling as another, but with a different origin and meaning and, sometimes, a different pronunciation. *Bow* meaning "to bend forward" and *bow* meaning "a weapon for shooting arrows" are homographs.
hom·o·graph (hom′ə graf′) *noun, plural* **homographs.**

homonym A word with the same pronunciation as another, but with a different meaning and, often, a different spelling. *Lean* meaning "to bend" and *lean* meaning "thin" are homonyms.
hom·o·nym (hom′ə nim′) *noun, plural* **homonyms.**

homophone A word with the same pronunciation as another, but with a different meaning and spelling. *Know* and *no* are homophones.
hom·o·phone (hom′ə fōn′) *noun, plural* **homophones.**

Honduras A country in Central America.
Hon·du·ras (hon dùr′əs *or* hon dyùr′əs) *noun.*

honest **1.** Truthful, fair, or trustworthy. An honest person does not cheat, lie, or steal. **2.** Earned or gotten fairly. That farmer earns an *honest* living.
hon·est (on′ist) *adjective.*

honesty The quality of being honest; truthfulness. Answer the questions with *honesty.*
hon·es·ty (on′ə stē) *noun.*

honey **1.** A thick, sweet liquid made by bees. Bees collect nectar from flowers and make honey, which they store in honeycombs. **2.** A very dear person or thing.
hon·ey (hun′ē) *noun, plural* **honeys.**

honeybee A bee that makes and stores honey.
hon·ey·bee (hun′ē bē′) *noun, plural* **honeybees.**

honeycomb **1.** A wax structure made by bees to store their eggs and honey in. A honeycomb is made up of layers of cells that have six sides. **2.** Something that looks like a bee's honeycomb. There was a *honeycomb* of subway tunnels under the city. *Noun.*
—To make full of tunnels or cells like a bee's honeycomb. Secret passages *honeycombed* the castle. *Verb.*
hon·ey·comb (hun′ē kōm′) *noun, plural* **honeycombs;** *verb,* **honeycombed, honeycombing.**

honeydew melon   A kind of melon that has light green pulp and a smooth green or yellow rind.
   hon·ey·dew melon (hun′ē dü′).

honeymoon   A vacation taken by a couple who have just been married. *Noun.*
   —To be or go on a honeymoon. *Verb.*
   hon·ey·moon (hun′ē mün′) *noun, plural* **honeymoons;** *verb,* **honeymooned, honeymooning.**

honeysuckle   A shrub or vine that has many small, sweet-smelling flowers.
   hon·ey·suck·le (hun′ē suk′əl) *noun, plural* **honeysuckles.**

Hong Kong   A colony of Great Britain on the southern coast of China. It will become part of China in 1997.
   Hong Kong (hong′kong′).

honeysuckle

honk   **1.** The cry of a goose or a sound like it. **2.** A sound made by an automobile horn. The *honk* of our car's horn scared the deer. *Noun.*
   —To make the cry of a goose or the sound of an automobile horn. We heard the geese *honk* as they flew overhead. The angry drivers *honked* their horns. *Verb.*
   honk (hongk) *noun, plural* **honks;** *verb,* **honked, honking.**

honor   **1.** A sense of what is right or honest; high moral standards. If you are a person of *honor,* you will not let another person be blamed for your mistake.   **2.** A good name or reputation. When the bully called me a coward, I felt my *honor* was at stake. **3.** Something given or done to show great respect or appreciation. The hero received a medal, a certificate, and other *honors.* **4. Honor.** A title of respect used in speaking to or of a judge, mayor, or other official. Everyone at the trial called the judge "Your *Honor." Noun.*
   —To show or feel great respect for a person or thing. The city *honored* the astronauts with a parade. *Verb.*
   hon·or (on′ər) *noun, plural* **honors;** *verb,* **honored, honoring.**

hood   **1.** A covering for the head and neck. A hood is often attached to the collar of a coat.   **2.** The metal cover that is over the engine of an automobile.   **3.** Something that looks like a hood or is used as a cover. There is a metal *hood* above our stove. A cobra has a fold of loose skin called a *hood* that it can stretch open around its head.
   hood (hùd) *noun, plural* **hoods.**

hoodlum   A rough and nasty person who causes trouble for other people. Several young *hoodlums* broke some store windows on Main Street last night.
   hood·lum (hüd′ləm *or* hùd′ləm) *noun, plural* **hoodlums.**

hoof   **1.** The hard covering on the feet of horses, cattle, deer, and some other animals. **2.** A foot with this covering. The horse's *hoof* pawed the ground.
   hoof (hùf *or* hüf) *noun, plural* **hooves** or **hoofs.**

hook   **1.** A bent piece of metal, wood, or other strong material that is used to hold or fasten something. There is a row of coat *hooks* along the wall in our classroom. **2.** Anything bent or shaped like a hook. A curved piece of wire with a barb at one end used for catching fish is a hook. *Noun.*
   —**1.** To hang, fasten, or attach with a hook. We *hooked* the wire picture hanger over the nail.   **2.** To catch with or on a hook. By the end of the day, we had *hooked* three fish. **3.** To have or make into the shape of a hook. The tired youngster *hooked* a leg over the arm of the chair. *Verb.*
   hook (hùk) *noun, plural* **hooks;** *verb,* **hooked, hooking.**

hoop   A ring made of wood, metal, or other material. Metal *hoops* hold together the staves of a barrel. Lions leap through flaming *hoops* in the circus. ▲ Another word that sounds like this is **whoop.**
   hoop (hüp *or* hùp) *noun, plural* **hoops.**

hooray   Another form of the word **hurrah.** Look up **hurrah** for more information.
   hoo·ray (hù rā′) *noun, plural* **hoorays;** *interjection.*

hoot   **1.** The sound that an owl makes. **2.** A shout that expresses dislike, scorn, or disbelief. Our friends gave a *hoot* when we said we saw a ghost in the old house. *Noun.*
   —To make the sound of an owl or a shout of scorn or disbelief. The fans *hooted* when the other team made an error. *Verb.*
   hoot (hüt) *noun, plural* **hoots;** *verb,* **hooted, hooting.**

at; āpe; fär; câre; end; mē; it; īce; pîerce; hot; ōld; sông, fôrk; oil; out; up; ūse; rüle; pùll; tûrn; chin; sing; shop; thin; this; hw in white; zh in treasure. The symbol ə stands for the unstressed vowel sound in about, taken, pencil, lemon, and circus.

H

hooves Plural of **hoof.** Look up **hoof** for more information.
  hooves (hŭvz *or* hüvz) *plural noun.*

hop **1.** To make a short jump on one foot. When you play hopscotch, you have to *hop* from one square to another. **2.** To move by jumping on both feet or all feet at once. Rabbits and frogs *hop.* **3.** To jump over. We *hopped* the fence instead of walking around to the gate. *Verb.*
  —**1.** A short jump or leap. The bunny took three *hops* and was gone. **2.** A bounce. The ball took a high *hop* over the shortstop's head. *Noun.*
  hop (hop) *verb,* **hopped, hopping;** *noun, plural* **hops.**

hope To wish for something very much, usually with some belief that it could happen. I *hope* that you will feel better soon. The family *hoped* for a sunny day so that they could go to the beach. *Verb.*
  —**1.** A strong wish and belief that a thing will happen. We *hope* you enjoy your vacation. **2.** Something that is wished for. My *hope* is that we will catch enough fish for dinner. *Noun.*
  hope (hōp) *verb,* **hoped, hoping;** *noun, plural* **hopes.**

hopeful **1.** Having or showing hope. The many branches on the tree made me *hopeful* that I could climb it. **2.** Giving promise that what is wished for will happen. A clear moon is a *hopeful* sign of good weather to come.
  hope·ful (hōp′fəl) *adjective.*

hopeless Having or giving no hope. The student had studied hard and felt *hopeless* after failing the test.
  hope·less (hōp′lis) *adjective.*

hopper **1.** A person or an animal that hops. Grasshoppers, rabbits, and kangaroos are hoppers. **2.** A container that is wide open at the top with a small opening at the bottom. A hopper is used to store grain, coal, or other material and then to empty it into another container.
  hop·per (hop′ər) *noun, plural* **hoppers.**

hopscotch A children's game on numbered squares that are drawn on the ground. The players hop into the squares in a certain order and try to pick up a stone or other object that has been tossed into one of the squares.
  hop·scotch (hop′skoch′) *noun.*

horde A very large group that is close together; a crowd or swarm. A *horde* of ants came out of the anthill. A *horde* of people pushed their way into the baseball stadium.

▲ Another word that sounds like this is **hoard.**
  horde (hôrd) *noun, plural* **hordes.**

horizon **1.** The line where the sky and the ground or the sea seem to meet. We could see a rocky island on the *horizon.* **2.** The limit of a person's knowledge, interests, or experience. You can widen your *horizons* by reading different kinds of books.
  ho·ri·zon (hə rī′zən) *noun, plural* **horizons.**

The road is **horizontal.** The trees are vertical.

horizontal Flat and straight across; parallel to the horizon. We made a cross by nailing a *horizontal* stick to an upright post.
  hor·i·zon·tal (hôr′ə zon′təl) *adjective.*

hopscotch

hormone A chemical made by certain glands in the body. Hormones travel through

the bloodstream and help control growth, digestion, and other body processes.
hor·mone (hôr′mōn) *noun, plural* **hormones.**

horn **1.** A hard, pointed growth on the head of some animals that have hooves. Deer, sheep, and rhinoceroses have horns. **2.** Something that looks like the horn of an animal. Some owls have tufts of feathers on their heads called horns. **3.** A brass musical instrument. Horns have a narrow end that you blow into to play them. **4.** A device used to make a loud warning sound. The bus driver honked the *horn* at the children in the street.
horn (hôrn) *noun, plural* **horns.**

horns

horned toad A lizard that has spikes that look like horns on its head and scales on its body. Horned toads live in the southwestern United States.

horned toad

hornet A large wasp that can give a very painful sting.
hor·net (hôr′nit) *noun, plural* **hornets.**

horny **1.** Made of horn. **2.** Being hard like a horn. A deer's antlers are *horny* growths.
horn·y (hôr′nē) *adjective,* **hornier, horniest.**

horrible **1.** Causing great fear or shock. It was *horrible* to see the house burn to the ground. Murder is a *horrible* crime. **2.** Very bad, ugly, or unpleasant. There was a *horrible* smell by the garbage heap.
hor·ri·ble (hôr′ə bəl) *adjective.*

horrid **1.** Causing great fear or shock; horrible. We thought the monster movie was so *horrid* that we left before it was over. **2.** Very bad, ugly, or unpleasant. My best friend thinks spinach tastes *horrid,* but I like the way it tastes.
hor·rid (hôr′id) *adjective.*

horrify To cause great fear or shock. Seeing the two cars crash *horrified* them.
hor·ri·fy (hôr′ə fī′) *verb,* **horrified, horrifying.**

horror **1.** A feeling of great fear and dread. They watched with *horror* as the passenger ship sank. I have a *horror* of being alone in the dark. **2.** A strong feeling of dislike or shock. We looked around the dirty old house with *horror.* **3.** A person or thing that causes great fear, shock, or dislike. They all felt that war was a *horror.*
hor·ror (hôr′ər) *noun, plural* **horrors.**

horse **1.** A large animal with four legs, hooves, and a long, flowing mane and tail. Horses are used for riding and pulling heavy loads. **2.** Any mammal belonging to the horse family that includes horses, zebras, and asses. **3.** A frame with legs, used to hold things like wood being sawed. **4.** A heavy leather pad on supporting legs, used in gymnastics for doing certain exercises. ▲ Another word that sounds like this is **hoarse.**
horse (hôrs) *noun, plural* **horses.**

horse

horseback The back of a horse. The mail was delivered by riders on *horseback. Noun.* —On the back of a horse. Some of us are going to ride *horseback* to the camp. *Adverb.*
horse·back (hôrs′bak′) *noun; adverb.*

horsefly A large fly with two black wings. The female gives a painful bite to horses and other animals and to humans.
horse·fly (hôrs′flī′) *noun, plural* **horseflies.**

horseman **1.** A person who rides on a horse. **2.** A person who is skilled in riding or handling horses.
horse·man (hôrs′mən) *noun, plural* **horsemen** (hôrs′mən).

at; āpe; fär; câre; end; mē; it; īce; pîerce; hot; ōld; sông, fôrk; oil; out; up; ūse; rüle; půll; tûrn; chin; sing; shop; thin; this; hw in white; zh in treasure. The symbol ə stands for the unstressed vowel sound in about, taken, pencil, lemon, and circus.

horseplay Rough, lively play. We started wrestling for fun, but the *horseplay* ended with both of us getting hurt.
horse·play (hôrs′plā′) *noun.*

horsepower A unit for measuring the power of an engine. One horsepower is equal to the energy needed to raise 550 pounds one foot in one second.
horse·pow·er (hôrs′pou′ər) *noun.*

horseshoe **1.** A metal U-shaped plate that is curved to fit the shape of a horse's hoof. A horseshoe is nailed onto the hoof to protect it. **2. horseshoes.** A game played by throwing U-shaped plates toward a post so that they will land around the post.
horse·shoe (hôrs′shü′) *noun, plural* **horseshoes.**

horsewoman **1.** A woman who rides on a horse. **2.** A woman who is skilled in riding or handling horses.
horse·wom·an (hôrs′wùm′ən) *noun, plural* **horsewomen** (hôrs′wim′ən).

hose **1.** A tube of rubber or other material that will bend easily. Hoses are used to carry water or other fluids from one place to another. I watered the garden with a *hose*. Gasoline is pumped through a *hose* into a car. **2.** Stockings or socks. *Noun.*
—To wash or water with a hose. We *hosed* down the car before we waxed it. Will you *hose* off the front porch? *Verb.*
hose (hōz) *noun, plural* **hoses** *(for definition 1)* or **hose** *(for definition 2); verb,* **hosed, hosing.**

firefighters using a **hose**

hosiery Stockings and socks.
ho·sier·y (hō′zhə rē) *noun.*

hospitable Making a guest or visitor feel welcome and comfortable; friendly. The *hospitable* couple who owned the hotel greeted us warmly, showed us our room, and offered us food.
hos·pi·ta·ble (hôs′pi tə bəl *or* ho spit′ə bəl) *adjective.*

hospital A place where people who are sick or hurt are taken care of.
hos·pi·tal (hos′pi təl) *noun, plural* **hospitals.**

Word History

The word **hospital** comes from a Latin word meaning "a place where travelers can find rest and food." These places often also took care of the needs of poor people who could not pay to stay at other places. *Hospital* then was used to mean "a place for the care of poor sick people." Today, a *hospital* is "a place for the care of sick people."

---

hospitality A friendly welcome and treatment of guests or visitors. We thanked our friends for their *hospitality* to us last week.
hos·pi·tal·i·ty (hos′pi tal′i tē) *noun, plural* **hospitalities.**

hospitalize To put a person in a hospital for medical care. The skier was *hospitalized* for a week with a broken leg.
hos·pi·tal·ize (hos′pi tə līz′) *verb,* **hospitalized, hospitalizing.**

host¹ A person who invites people to visit as guests. We thanked our *host* for a wonderful party.
host (hōst) *noun, plural* **hosts.**

host² A large number. On a clear night, you can see a *host* of stars in the sky.
host (hōst) *noun, plural* **hosts.**

hostage A person who is held as a prisoner by someone until money is paid or promises are kept. The passengers and crew of the hijacked plane were held as *hostages* until a ransom was paid.
hos·tage (hos′tij) *noun, plural* **hostages.**

hostel A place that gives simple, cheap lodging to travelers, especially young people on bicycle tours or hikes. ▲ Another word that sounds like this is **hostile.**
hos·tel (hos′təl) *noun, plural* **hostels.**

hostess **1.** A woman who invites people to come to her home as her guests. My aunt was the *hostess* at a large dinner party. **2.** A woman who serves food and greets people in a restaurant or on an airplane.
host·ess (hōs′tis) *noun, plural* **hostesses.**

hostile Feeling or showing hatred or dislike. After their fight, the students wouldn't talk to each other for a week, and just gave each other *hostile* looks. ▲ Another word that sounds like this is **hostel.**
hos·tile (hos′təl) *adjective.*

hostility **1.** A readiness to fight; unfriendliness; antagonism. There was still *hostility* between the two old enemies. **2. hostilities.** Acts of war; warfare. *Hostilities* between the two countries ended when a peace agreement was signed.

> **hos·til·i·ty** (ho stil′i tē) *noun, plural* **hostilities.**

hot **1.** Having a high temperature. I burned my hand when I touched the *hot* iron. We were *hot* after sitting in the sun. **2.** Having a burning, sharp taste. We put *hot* mustard on our frankfurters. **3.** Showing anger or passion; violent. My friend has a *hot* temper. **4.** Following very closely. The police were in *hot* pursuit of the robbers. **5.** Just made or heard; fresh. This is *hot* news.

> **hot** (hot) *adjective,* **hotter, hottest.**

hot dog A long, thin sausage; frankfurter. It is often served hot on a long roll.

hotel A building with many rooms that people pay to sleep in. Most hotels serve meals.

> **ho·tel** (hō tel′) *noun, plural* **hotels.**

hothouse A heated building made mainly of glass where plants are grown; greenhouse.

> **hot·house** (hot′hous′) *noun, plural* **hothouses** (hot′hou′ziz).

hot spring A spring whose water is heated naturally in the earth.

hound A dog that has been raised and trained to hunt by scent or sight. Beagles and bloodhounds are two kinds of hounds. *Noun.*
—To keep urging; pester. My parents *hounded* me about cleaning up my room. *Verb.*

> **hound** (hound) *noun, plural* **hounds;** *verb,* **hounded, hounding.**

hour **1.** A unit of time equal to sixty minutes. There are twenty-four hours in a day. We waited for one *hour,* from four o'clock to five o'clock, for the bus to come. **2.** A time of the day that is shown on a clock or watch. At what *hour* should we leave for the station? **3.** The time for anything. The doctor's office *hours* are from nine o'clock to four o'clock. A good friend is someone who will help you in an *hour* of need. ▲ Another word that sounds like this is **our.**

> **hour** (our) *noun, plural* **hours.**

hourglass A device for measuring time used in former times. It is a glass tube with a narrow middle. A quantity of sand runs from the top part of

hourglass

the tube to the bottom part in one hour.

> **hour·glass** (our′glas′) *noun, plural* **hourglasses.**

hourly Done or happening every hour. There are *hourly* airplane flights from New York to California. *Adjective.*
—Every hour. The weather is reported *hourly* on the radio. *Adverb.*

> **hour·ly** (our′lē) *adjective; adverb.*

house **1.** A building in which people live; home. Our friends asked us to come to their *house* for dinner. **2.** The people who live in a house. Our whole *house* was awakened by the noise. **3.** Any building used for a special purpose. The town has a new movie *house.* **4.** A group of people who make laws. The United States Congress is made up of two *houses,* the House of Representatives and the Senate. **5.** An audience. There was a full *house* for the opening of the new show. **6.** A royal or noble family. *Noun.*
—To give a place to live or stay. We *housed* our friends until their new home was ready. The horses are *housed* in a barn. *Verb.*

> **house** (hous *for noun;* houz *for verb) noun, plural* **houses** (hou′ziz); *verb,* **housed, housing.**

houseboat A boat that people can live on.

> **house·boat** (hous′bōt′) *noun, plural* **houseboats.**

housefly A grayish black fly with transparent wings that lives in and near people's houses. It eats food and garbage.

> **house·fly** (hous′flī′) *noun, plural* **houseflies.**

household **1.** A place where people live; home. Our *household* was very busy the week before Christmas. **2.** All the people who live in a home. The *household* took a vote on what to have for dinner. *Noun.*
—Having to do with a household. On Saturday, we all helped with cleaning, ironing, and other *household* chores. *Adjective.*

> **house·hold** (hous′hōld′) *noun, plural* **households;** *adjective.*

housekeeper A person whose job is to take care of a home. A housekeeper is responsible for housework and sometimes child care.

> **house·keep·er** (hous′kē′pər) *noun, plural* **housekeepers.**

---

at; āpe; fär; câre; end; mē; it; īce; pîerce; hot; ōld; sông, fôrk; oil; out; up; ūse; rüle; pùll; tûrn; chin; sing; shop; thin; <u>th</u>is; hw in white; zh in treasure. The symbol ə stands for the unstressed vowel sound in about, taken, pencil, lemon, and circus.

H

House of Commons One of the houses of the British or Canadian Parliament. The members of the House of Commons are elected.

House of Lords One of the houses of the British Parliament. The members of the House of Lords are nobles or members of the clergy.

House of Representatives One of the two houses of the United States Congress.

houseplant A plant grown indoors.
house·plant (hous'plant') *noun, plural* **houseplants.**

housewife A woman who takes care of a home and the needs of a family.
house·wife (hous'wīf') *noun, plural* **housewives** (hous'wīvz').

housework Washing, ironing, cleaning, cooking, and other work that has to be done in taking care of a home.
house·work (hous'wûrk') *noun.*

housing **1.** A number of houses. There is a lot of new *housing* being built in our town. **2.** A covering for the moving parts of a machine. The *housing* on the drill gets very hot when the drill is used for a long time.
hous·ing (hou'zing) *noun, plural* **housings.**

hover **1.** To stay in the air, flying right above one place. The bees *hovered* over the flowers. Helicopters can *hover,* but airplanes cannot. **2.** To stay close by. The reporters *hovered* around the candidate while waiting to ask their questions.
hov·er (huv'ər *or* hov'ər) *verb,* **hovered, hovering.**

how **1.** In what way; by what means. *How* will you go home, by bus or by train? **2.** To what degree, amount, or extent. *How* cold is it outside? *How* did you like the circus? **3.** In what condition. *How* are you today? **4.** For what reason; why. *How* did you happen to be so late?
• **how about.** What do you think of. *How about* playing a game of cards?
• **how come.** Why does it happen that. *How come* I didn't think of that?
how (hou) *adverb.*

however In spite of that; yet. It is the middle of winter; *however,* it is very warm outside. *Conjunction.*
—**1.** In whatever way. You may each draw the house *however* you like. **2.** To whatever degree. *However* far our dogs wander, they always come home. *Adverb.*
how·ev·er (hou ev'ər) *conjunction; adverb.*

howl To make a loud, wailing cry. Dogs and wolves both howl. The wind howls when it blows hard. I *howled* when I hurt my toe. We *howled* with laughter. *Verb.*
—A loud, wailing cry. We heard the *howl* of the wind in the rafters of the old barn. *Noun.*
howl (houl) *verb,* **howled, howling;** *noun, plural* **howls.**

hr. An abbreviation for *hour.*

ht. An abbreviation for *height.*

hub **1.** The middle part of a wheel. A round cap covers the *hub* of a car wheel. **2.** A center of interest or movement. The refreshment table was the *hub* of activity during the party.
hub (hub) *noun, plural* **hubs.**

huckleberry A small, shiny, dark blue berry. They are like blueberries but are smaller, darker, and have harder seeds. These berries grow on a small, low shrub that is also called a huckleberry.
huck·le·ber·ry (huk'əl ber'ē) *noun, plural* **huckleberries.**

huckleberries

huddle To gather close together in a bunch. The scouts *huddled* around the campfire to keep warm. The hen *huddled* the baby chicks under its wings at night. *Verb.*
—A group of people or animals that are gathered close together. The football players formed a *huddle* to plan their next play. *Noun.*
hud·dle (hud'əl) *verb,* **huddled, huddling;** *noun, plural* **huddles.**

hue A color or a shade of a color. The sunset had an orange *hue.*
hue (hū) *noun, plural* **hues.**

huff A sudden feeling of anger, resentment, or hurt pride. You shouldn't have left the party in a *huff* just because you didn't win the prize for best costume. *Noun.*
—To take in or give out a quick, noisy breath; puff. We were *huffing* and puffing from the long climb. *Verb.*
huff (huf) *noun, plural* **huffs;** *verb,* **huffed, huffing.**

hug **1.** To put the arms around a person or thing and hold close and tightly. I *hugged* my grandparents because I was so glad to see them. **2.** To keep close to. Try to *hug* the curb when you're bicycling on a busy street. *Verb.*
—A close, tight clasp with the arms. I gave my dog a big *hug* when I got home. *Noun.*
hug (hug) *verb,* **hugged, hugging;** *noun, plural* **hugs.**

huge Great in size or amount; very big; enormous. An elephant is a *huge* animal. I took such a *huge* helping of turkey that I couldn't eat it all.
huge (hūj) *adjective*, **huger, hugest.**

hull **1.** The outer covering of a nut, grain, or other seed. **2.** The small leaves around the stem of a strawberry and certain other fruits. **3.** The sides and bottom of a boat or ship. *Noun.*
—To remove the hull from a seed or fruit. I *hulled* the strawberries and then sliced them. *Verb.*
hull (hul) *noun, plural* **hulls;** *verb,* **hulled, hulling.**

Hull

hull

hum **1.** To make a soft, murmuring sound for a long time, like a bee. If you keep saying "m" with your mouth closed, you are humming. The bumblebees were *humming* in the garden. **2.** To sing with the lips closed and without saying words. I didn't know the words to the song so I just *hummed* the tune. *Verb.*
—A soft, murmuring sound that keeps going. The *hum* of the air conditioner seemed loud in the small room. *Noun.*
hum (hum) *verb,* **hummed, humming;** *noun, plural* **hums.**

human Being or having to do with a person or persons. Men, women, and children are *human* beings. Is that an animal track or a *human* footprint? *Adjective.*
—A person. Every man, woman, and child is a *human. Noun.*
hu·man (hū′mən) *adjective; noun, plural* **humans.**

human being A man, woman, or child; person; human.

humane Having sympathy for others; wanting to prevent pain. The *humane* doctor helped many sick people, even if they could not pay.
hu·mane (hū mān′) *adjective.*

humanity **1.** People; all human beings. Keeping our air and water clean will help all *humanity.* **2.** Deep concern for the suffering of others; human sympathy. The volunteers showed great *humanity* in caring for the flood victims.
hu·man·i·ty (hū man′i tē) *noun.*

humble **1.** Not proud; modest. A humble person does not think he or she is better than other people. The musicians remained *humble* even after their records became famous.

2. Not big or important; lowly. They lived in a *humble* cottage on a farm. *Adjective.*
—To make humble. We were *humbled* when we saw what good work the others had done without our help. *Verb.*
hum·ble (hum′bəl) *adjective,* **humbler, humblest;** *verb,* **humbled, humbling.**

humid Having a lot of water vapor in the air; damp; moist. It was a hot, *humid* summer day.
hu·mid (hū′mid) *adjective.*

humidity Water vapor in the air; dampness. The high *humidity* that day made us feel warm and uncomfortable. An air conditioner is designed to take *humidity* out of the air.
hu·mid·i·ty (hū mid′i tē) *noun.*

humiliate To make a person feel very ashamed or foolish. I was *humiliated* when I failed the test after telling everyone that I thought I would do well.
hu·mil·i·ate (hū mil′ē āt′) *verb,* **humiliated, humiliating.**

hummingbird A tiny bird with brightly colored feathers and a long, narrow bill. The hummingbird beats its wings so fast that they make a humming sound. It can fly backward or sideways, and can hover above flowers while it drinks their nectar.
hum·ming·bird (hum′ing bûrd′) *noun, plural* **hummingbirds.**

hummingbird

humor **1.** The funny part of something. Humor is what makes a person laugh. The *humor* in the story came from the silly rabbit that could talk. **2.** The ability to make people laugh or to enjoy funny things. Our guests must have lacked *humor,* because they never even smiled at any of our jokes. **3.** The state of mind that a person is in; mood. We were in a good *humor* after having such a nice day fishing. *Noun.*
—To give in to what a person wants. When

at; āpe; fär; câre; end; mē; it; īce; pîerce; hot; ōld; sông, fôrk; oil; out; up; ūse; rüle; pùll; tûrn; chin; sing; shop; thin; this; hw in white; zh in treasure. The symbol ə stands for the unstressed vowel sound in about, taken, pencil, lemon, and circus.

H

I was sick, my mother *humored* me by reading my favorite story several times. *Verb.*
hu·mor (hū′mər) *noun, plural* **humors;** *verb,* **humored, humoring.**

humorous Making people laugh; funny; comical. They saw a *humorous* movie about a fish that thought it could fly.
hu·mor·ous (hū′mər əs) *adjective.*

hump A rounded lump or bump. Some camels have two *humps* on their backs.
hump (hump) *noun, plural* **humps.**

humus A dark part of the soil. Humus comes from dead plants.
hu·mus (hū′məs) *noun.*

hunch To draw up or bend. The cold wind made me *hunch* my shoulders. *Verb.*
—A guess or feeling about what will happen. We had a *hunch* our friends might visit, so we made extra sandwiches. *Noun.*
hunch (hunch) *verb,* **hunched, hunching;** *noun, plural* **hunches.**

hundred Ten times ten; 100.
hun·dred (hun′drid) *noun, plural* **hundreds;** *adjective.*

hundredth Next after the ninety-ninth. *Adjective, noun.*
—One of a hundred equal parts; $\frac{1}{100}$. *Noun.*
hun·dredth (hun′dridth) *adjective; noun, plural* **hundredths.**

hung A past tense and a past participle of **hang.** We *hung* new curtains last night. Look up **hang** for more information.
hung (hung) *verb.*

Hungary A country in east-central Europe.
Hun·ga·ry (hung′gə rē) *noun.*

hunger 1. Pain or weakness caused by not eating enough food. During the long, cold winter many wild animals died of *hunger.* 2. The feeling of wanting or needing food. My *hunger* made me gobble my lunch. 3. A strong wish or need for something. The dictator had a *hunger* for power. *Noun.*
—To have a strong wish or need for something. I *hungered* for pizza after camping for two weeks. The students *hungered* for praise from their teacher. *Verb.*
hun·ger (hung′gər) *noun, plural* **hungers;** *verb,* **hungered, hungering.**

hungry 1. Wanting or needing food. We were *hungry* all morning because we didn't have time to eat breakfast. 2. Having a strong wish or need for anything. The orphans were *hungry* for love.
hun·gry (hung′grē) *adjective,* **hungrier, hungriest.**

hunk A large lump or piece; chunk. Take a *hunk* of bread to eat with your cheese.
hunk (hungk) *noun, plural* **hunks.**

hunt 1. To chase wild animals in order to catch or kill. The hunters *hunted* deer. Most owls *hunt* at night and rest during the day. 2. To look hard to try to find something or someone. The police *hunted* the robbers. We *hunted* all over for the keys. *Verb.*
—1. A chase made to catch or kill wild animals. The Indians went on a buffalo *hunt.* 2. A search to try to find something or someone. The best part of the party was the *hunt* for the hidden presents. *Noun.*
hunt (hunt) *verb,* **hunted, hunting;** *noun, plural* **hunts.**

hunter 1. A person who chases wild animals in order to kill or catch them. 2. An animal that chases other animals for its own food or to help human beings. Our cat is a good *hunter.* 3. A person who searches for something. A fossil *hunter* looks for the remains of animals and plants that lived long ago.
hunt·er (hun′tər) *noun, plural* **hunters.**

hurdles

hurdle 1. A barrier that has to be jumped over in a race. The horse cleared the *hurdle.* 2. **hurdles.** A race in which the runners must jump over barriers while they run. 3. A difficulty or problem. Passing final exams was the last *hurdle* before graduating from high school. *Noun.*
—To jump over while running. The farmer had to *hurdle* a fence to get away from the angry bull. *Verb.*
hur·dle (hûr′dəl) *noun, plural* **hurdles;** *verb,* **hurdled, hurdling.**

hurl To throw hard and fast; fling. The pitcher turned and *hurled* the ball to first base. We *hurled* the pebbles far out into the water.
    hurl (hûrl) *verb,* **hurled, hurling.**

hurrah A shout of joy or encouragement. "Let's hear a big *hurrah* for our team!" yelled the fan. *Noun.*
    —A word used to express joy. "Hurrah!" I yelled when my sister crossed the finish line. *Interjection.*
    hur·rah (hə rä′) *noun, plural* **hurrahs;** *interjection.*

hurricane A storm with very strong winds and heavy rain.
    hur·ri·cane (hûr′i kān′) *noun, plural* **hurricanes.**

hurried Done or made quickly or too quickly. I wrote a *hurried* note to tell my family where I was going and then ran for the bus.
    hur·ried (hûr′ēd) *adjective.*

hurry To move faster than is usual; rush; speed. If we don't *hurry* we'll miss the train. We *hurried* our parents along so we could be first in line. *Verb.*
    —**1.** The act of moving very quickly. In your *hurry* to pack, you forgot your toothbrush. **2.** The wish or need to act or move very quickly. The children were in a *hurry* to go outside and play. *Noun.*
    hur·ry (hûr′ē) *verb,* **hurried, hurrying;** *noun, plural* **hurries.**

hurt **1.** To cause pain or injury. I fell on the rocks and *hurt* my arm. The doctor said the needle would not *hurt.* It *hurt* my feelings when my classmates laughed at me. **2.** To be painful. My knee *hurts* because I twisted it. **3.** To be bad for; harm. Being sick so often *hurt* the child's chances of making the team. *Verb.*
    —A pain or injury. *Noun.*
    hurt (hûrt) *verb,* **hurt, hurting;** *noun, plural* **hurts.**

husband A man who is married.
    hus·band (huz′bənd) *noun, plural* **husbands.**

Word History

    The word **husband** comes from an old Scandinavian word meaning "master of a household." In Old English times, any man who was head of his own household could be a "husband." Only later did *husband* mean that the man was married, even if he did not own his own land.

---

hush A silence or stillness that comes when noise suddenly stops. When the speaker raised a hand, there was a *hush* in the auditorium. *Noun.*
    —**1.** To make quiet or silent. The dimming of the lights *hushed* the audience. **2.** To keep secret. They all agreed to *hush* up about the party so they could surprise the couple. *Verb.*
    —Be quiet. "*Hush,*" the babysitter said, "or you will wake the baby." *Interjection.*
    hush (hush) *noun, plural* **hushes;** *verb,* **hushed, hushing;** *interjection.*

husk The dry, outside covering of some vegetables and fruits. We took the green *husks* off the corn before we cooked it. *Noun.*
    —To take off the husk from. We cracked and *husked* the coconut. *Verb.*
    husk (husk) *noun, plural* **husks;** *verb,* **husked, husking.**

husky¹ **1.** Big and strong. There are several *husky* players on the football team. **2.** Rough and deep in sound. My voice gets *husky* when I have a cold.
    husk·y (hus′kē) *adjective,* **huskier, huskiest.**

husky² A strong dog with a thick coat of hair and a bushy tail. Huskies are used to pull sleds in the Arctic.
    husk·y (hus′kē) *noun, plural* **huskies.**

hustle To move or do something very quickly and with energy. We had to *hustle* to finish all our work in an hour.
    hus·tle (hus′əl) *verb,* **hustled, hustling.**

hut A small, roughly built house or shelter. There is a *hut* on the beach that we use to keep our fishing equipment in.
    hut (hut) *noun, plural* **huts.**

hutch A house for rabbits or other small animals.
    hutch (huch) *noun, plural* **hutches.**

hyacinth A plant that has a thick stem with small flowers growing on it. Hyacinths grow from bulbs and have long leaves that grow up from the ground.
    hy·a·cinth (hī′ə sinth′) *noun, plural* **hyacinths.**

hyacinth

H

at; āpe; fär; câre; end; mē; it; īce; pîerce; hot; ōld; sông, fôrk; oil; out; up; ūse; rüle; pull; tûrn; chin; sing; shop; thin; this; hw in white; zh in treasure. The symbol ə stands for the unstressed vowel sound in about, taken, pencil, lemon, and circus.

365

hybrid   The offspring of two different kinds of plants or animals. A mule is a hybrid because its father is a donkey and its mother is a horse. *Noun.*
—Having to do with or being a hybrid. Our neighbor raises *hybrid* roses. *Adjective.*
hy·brid (hī′brid) *noun, plural* **hybrids;** *adjective.*

hydrant   A wide, covered pipe that sticks out of the ground and is attached underground to a water supply. Firefighters attach hoses to hydrants to get water to put out fires.
hy·drant (hī′drənt) *noun, plural* **hydrants.**

hydroelectric   Relating to electricity created by generators run by rapidly flowing water. There is a *hydroelectric* power station at the waterfall.
hy·dro·e·lec·tric (hī′drō i lek′trik) *adjective.*

hydrogen   A gas that has no color, taste, or odor and that burns very easily. Hydrogen is a chemical element. It is the lightest and most abundant element in the universe.
hy·dro·gen (hī′drə jən) *noun.*

Word History

The word **hydrogen** is formed from two Greek words, one meaning "water" and the other meaning "forming." Hydrogen combines with oxygen to form water.

hydrogen bomb   A very powerful bomb that explodes with great force. The fusion of atoms of hydrogen to form atoms of helium causes the explosion. The hydrogen bomb is more powerful than the atomic bomb. It is also called an **H-bomb.**

hyena

hyena   An animal that has a large head and front legs that are longer than the back legs. Hyenas are meat eaters and live in Africa and Asia.
hy·e·na (hī ē′nə) *noun, plural* **hyenas.**

hygiene   Things that must be done to keep people and places healthy and clean. Washing yourself and brushing your teeth are part of your personal *hygiene.*
hy·giene (hī′jēn) *noun.*

hygienist   A person who is trained to know what must be done to keep people and places healthy and clean. A dental *hygienist* cleans teeth and instructs people in how to care for them.
hy·gien·ist (hī jē′nist *or* hī′jē en′ist) *noun, plural* **hygienists.**

hymn   A song of praise to God. ▲ Another word that sounds like this is **him.**
hymn (him) *noun, plural* **hymns.**

hymnal   A book of hymns.
hym·nal (him′nəl) *noun, plural* **hymnals.**

hyphen   A punctuation mark (-) that is used to connect two or more words or parts of words to form a compound word, as in the word *merry-go-round.* A hyphen is also used to connect the syllables of a word that has been divided at the end of a line.
hy·phen (hī′fən) *noun, plural* **hyphens.**

hyphenate   To put a hyphen or hyphens in a word. We must *hyphenate* a word when it has to be divided between two lines.
hy·phen·ate (hī′fə nāt′) *verb,* **hyphenated, hyphenating.**

hypnotize   To put someone into a special kind of sleep in which one can still hear and see. People who are hypnotized sometimes remember things that they had forgotten, and they respond to what the hypnotizer says to them.
hyp·no·tize (hip′nə tīz′) *verb,* **hypnotized, hypnotizing.**

hypocrite   Someone who pretends to be one sort of person but acts or behaves differently. A hypocrite is often a person who pretends to be honest, thoughtful, loyal, or religious, and is not.
hyp·o·crite (hip′ə krit) *noun, plural* **hypocrites.**

hypotenuse   The side of a right triangle that is opposite the 90 degree angle. The hypotenuse is always the longest side of a right triangle.
hy·pot·e·nuse (hī pot′ə nüs′ *or* hī pot′ə nūs′) *noun.*

hysterical   **1.** Emotionally violent and uncontrollable. The frightened child burst into *hysterical* crying. **2.** Crying or laughing uncontrollably, usually because of an emotional upset. If you ever get lost in the woods, keep calm and don't become *hysterical.*
hys·ter·i·cal (hi ster′i kəl) *adjective.*

1. The letter **I** was first used in the alphabets of several ancient Middle Eastern tribes. They called this letter *yod*.

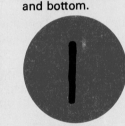

2. When the early Greeks adopted this letter, they wrote it as a long line with a short stroke at the top and bottom.

3. Later, the Greeks wrote this letter as a single, straight line. This form of the letter was adopted by an ancient tribe near Rome.

4. The ancient Romans borrowed this form of the letter **I**, which they used for either the *i* sound or the *j* sound.

5. Our modern capital **I** is almost always written with a short stroke at the top and bottom of the letter.

i, I The ninth letter of the alphabet.
   i, I (ī) *noun, plural* **i's, I's.**

I The person who is speaking or writing. *I* have a dog and a cat. ▲ Other words that sound like this are **aye** and **eye.**
   I (ī) *pronoun.*

Ia. An abbreviation for *Iowa.*

IA Postal abbreviation for *Iowa.*

–ic or **–ical** *Suffixes* that mean: **1.** Of or having to do with. *Symbolic* means having to do with symbols. *Mythical* means having to do with myths. **2.** Like. *Poetic* means like a poem. **3.** Made of; containing. *Alcoholic* means containing alcohol.

ice **1.** Water that is solid because it is below 32 degrees Fahrenheit; frozen water. We cut a hole through the *ice* on the lake. **2.** A frozen dessert made with sweetened water and fruit flavors. *Noun.*
   —1. To become covered with ice. The lake *ices* over in the winter. **2.** To decorate with icing. The baker *iced* the cake after it had cooled. *Verb.*
   ice (īs) *noun, plural* **ices;** *verb,* **iced, icing.**

ice age A period on earth or another planet when temperatures are very cold over a long period of time, usually for millions of years. These cold temperatures cause glaciers to form over vast areas. The most recent ice age on earth ended about 10,000 years ago.

iceberg A very large piece of floating ice that has broken off from a glacier. Most of an iceberg is underwater. The ship was damaged when it hit an *iceberg.*
   ice·berg (īs'bûrg') *noun, plural* **icebergs.**

I

iceberg

icebox **1.** A box or chest cooled with blocks of ice. It is used for storing food and drinks. **2.** A refrigerator.
ice·box (īs′boks′) *noun, plural* **iceboxes.**

icebreaker A specially designed ship that is used to break a passage through ice.
ice·break·er (īs′brā′kər) *noun, plural* **icebreakers.**

icecap A sheet of ice with a high center. It covers an area of land and moves out from the center in all directions as it becomes larger.
ice·cap (īs′kap′) *noun, plural* **icecaps.**

ice cream A frozen dessert. It is made from milk products, sweeteners, and flavoring.

Iceland An island country northwest of Europe in the Atlantic Ocean.
Ice·land (īs′lənd) *noun.*

ice-skate To skate on ice.
ice-skate (īs′skāt′) *verb,* **ice-skated, ice-skating.**

ice skate A shoe with a metal blade on the bottom. It is used for ice-skating.

icicle A pointed, hanging piece of ice. It is formed by water that freezes as it drips.
i·ci·cle (ī′si kəl) *noun, plural* **icicles.**

icicles

icing A mixture of sugar, butter, flavoring and sometimes eggs. Icing is used to cover or decorate cakes or other baked goods.
ic·ing (ī′sing) *noun, plural* **icings.**

icy **1.** Made of or covered with ice. I slipped on the *icy* sidewalk. **2.** Very cold. When the *icy* winds blew, it grew cold in the house. **3.** Cold and unfriendly. My friend gave me an *icy* stare the next time we met after our big argument.
i·cy (ī′sē) *adjective,* **icier, iciest.**

ID Postal abbreviation for *Idaho.*

I'd **1.** Shortened form of "I had." They asked me if I'd seen their dog. **2.** Shortened form of "I would." *I'd* go if you would.
I'd (īd) *contraction.*

Ida. An abbreviation for *Idaho.*

Idaho A state in the western United States. Its capital is Boise.
I·da·ho (ī′də hō′) *noun.*

Word History

The Apache and the Comanche are two tribes of American Indians who live in the West. The word **Idaho** probably comes from the Apache used to mean "Comanche." The name was first used in the area that is now Colorado, but the United States Senate officially gave the name *Idaho* to a nearby territory. This other territory kept the name when it became the state of Idaho.

---

idea **1.** A picture or thought formed in the mind. The author had an *idea* for a new novel. **2.** A belief; opinion. My parents have some firm *ideas* about religion. **3.** The purpose. The *idea* of the game of baseball is to score runs for your team. **4.** The main meaning; point. Do you understand the *idea* of the poem?
i·de·a (ī dē′ə) *noun, plural* **ideas.**

ideal **1.** A person or thing thought of as perfect. That star quarterback was my *ideal* when I played football. **2.** The best or most perfect goal or result. Justice is the *ideal* that a judge tries to achieve. *Noun.*
—Being exactly what one would hope for; perfect. The breeze makes it an *ideal* day for going sailing. *Adjective.*
i·de·al (ī dē′əl) *noun, plural* **ideals;** *adjective.*

identical **1.** The very same. This is the *identical* hotel we stayed at two years ago. **2.** Exactly alike. The twins always wore *identical* clothes.
i·den·ti·cal (ī den′ti kəl) *adjective.*

identification **1.** The act of saying who a person is or what a thing is. I had to make an *identification* of my lost wallet before the principal could return it to me.   **2.** Something used to show who a person is. Many people use their driver's license as *identification*.

i·den·ti·fi·ca·tion (ī den′tə fi kā′shən) *noun, plural* **identifications.**

identify   To find out or tell exactly who a person is or what a thing is; recognize. Can you *identify* the keys that you lost? Can you *identify* this strange object?

i·den·ti·fy (ī den′tə fī′) *verb,* **identified, identifying.**

identity   **1.** Who a person is or what a thing is. Famous people sometimes hide their *identity* so that they can have some privacy. **2.** The condition of being exactly the same. The *identity* of the twins made it hard for their friends to tell them apart.

i·den·ti·ty (ī den′ti tē) *noun, plural* **identities.**

idiom   A phrase or expression whose meaning cannot be understood from the ordinary meanings of the separate words in it. "To put off " is an idiom that means "to delay or postpone." "To pull a person's leg" is an idiom that means "to trick or tease."

id·i·om (id′ē əm) *noun, plural* **idioms.**

Language Note

Idioms are a part of everyday language. People who have grown up speaking English use them without thinking about the fact that they have a special meaning. For someone learning English as a foreign language, though, idioms do not make sense and can be very confusing. Imagine, for example, what a student of English thinks when he or she first hears someone say, "I don't believe you; you're pulling my leg."

---

idiot   A very silly or foolish person. Only an *idiot* would believe that such a fantastic story was true.

id·i·ot (id′ē ət) *noun, plural* **idiots.**

idle   **1.** Not wanting to be active; lazy. The *idle* children seldom helped with the chores. **2.** Having little worth or usefulness. I exchanged some *idle* chatter with the person waiting in front of me in line. **3.** Not working or being used; not busy. The piano in our house is *idle* because two keys are broken. *Adjective.*
—1. To spend time doing nothing. Instead of doing my homework, I *idled* around the house all evening. We *idled* away the afternoon.   **2.** To run slowly and out of gear. We left the car *idling* in the driveway while we

delivered the package. *Verb.* ▲ Another word that sounds like this is **idol.**

i·dle (ī′dəl) *adjective,* **idler, idlest;** *verb,* **idled, idling.**

idol   **1.** A statue or other object that is worshiped as a god.   **2.** A person who is greatly loved or admired. That movie star is an *idol* to people around the world. ▲ Another word that sounds like this is **idle.**

i·dol (ī′dəl) *noun, plural* **idols.**

if   **1.** In case; in the event that; supposing that. *If* I hurt your feelings, I'm sorry. *If* I were older, I'm sure I would better understand such things.   **2.** With the requirement or agreement that; on condition that; provided. I can go to the movies *if* I finish my chores first.   **3.** Whether. I don't know *if* they'll be there.

if (if) *conjunction.*

igloo   A hut shaped like a dome that is used by the Eskimo to live in. It is usually built of blocks of hardened snow.

ig·loo (ig′lü) *noun, plural* **igloos.**

igloo

igneous   Produced with great heat or by a volcano. An *igneous* rock is formed when lava from a volcano hardens.

ig·ne·ous (ig′nē əs) *adjective.*

ignite   **1.** To set on fire. We *ignited* the sticks for the campfire with a match.   **2.** To begin to burn; catch on fire. You must be careful with how you store oily rags because they *ignite* easily.

ig·nite (ig nīt′) *verb,* **ignited, igniting.**

ignition   **1.** The act of igniting. The *ignition* of the rockets sent the spacecraft on its way to the moon.   **2.** A system for starting a car, a boat, or some other vehicle. The ignition

---

at; āpe; fär; câre; end; mē; it; īce; pîerce; hot; ōld; sông, fôrk; oil; out; up; ūse; rüle; pùll; tûrn; chin; sing; shop; thin; this; hw in white; zh in treasure. The symbol ə stands for the unstressed vowel sound in about, taken, pencil, lemon, and circus.

starts the fuel and air burning in the engine.
ig·ni·tion (ig nish′ən) *noun, plural* **ignitions.**

ignorance   A lack of knowledge; being ignorant. My *ignorance* of current affairs meant that I couldn't join the debate team this year.
ig·no·rance (ig′nər əns) *noun.*

ignorant   **1.** Having or showing a lack of knowledge. The young cowhands were *ignorant* at first of how to brand cattle, but they learned quickly.   **2.** Not informed or aware. I wasn't wearing my watch, so I was *ignorant* of the time.
ig·no·rant (ig′nər ənt) *adjective.*

ignore   To pay no attention to. I tried to *ignore* the noise of the subway as I read my book. The police officer gave a ticket to the driver who *ignored* the stop sign.
ig·nore (ig nôr′) *verb,* **ignored, ignoring.**

iguana   A large greenish brown lizard that has a ridge of scales down its back. It is found in the very warm parts of Central and South America.
i·gua·na (i gwä′nə) *noun, plural* **iguanas.**

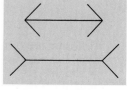
iguana

IL   Postal abbreviation for *Illinois.*

ill   **1.** Not healthy or well; sick. Many children in our class were *ill* with colds last week.   **2.** Bad or evil. The destruction of homes and crops were two *ill* results of the flood. *Adjective.*
—Unkindly; badly. Don't speak *ill* of anyone. *Adverb.*
—Trouble, evil, or misfortune. War is one of the *ills* of humanity. *Noun.*
ill (il) *adjective,* **worse, worst;** *adverb; noun, plural* **ills.**

Ill.   An abbreviation for *Illinois.*

I'll   Shortened form of "I will" or "I shall." *I'll* win the contest no matter what it takes. *I'll* go if you will. ▲ Other words that sound like this are **aisle** and **isle.**
I'll (īl) *contraction.*

illegal   Not legal; against laws or rules. It is *illegal* to shoot off fireworks in that town.
il·le·gal (i lē′gəl) *adjective.*

illegible   Very hard or impossible to read. The handwriting on the envelope was *illegible.*
il·leg·i·ble (i lej′ə bəl) *adjective.*

Illinois   A state in the north-central United States. Its capital is Springfield.
Il·li·nois (il′ə noi′ *or* il′ə noiz′) *noun.*

illiterate   Not able to read or write. The *illiterate* person needed help in filling out the form.
il·lit·er·ate (i lit′ər it) *adjective.*

illness   A sickness or disease. Many illnesses can be cured by taking the right medicine.
ill·ness (il′nis) *noun, plural* **illnesses.**

illuminate   To light up; give light to. A lamp *illuminated* one corner of the dark room.
il·lu·mi·nate (i lü′mə nāt′) *verb,* **illuminated, illuminating.**

illusion   A false impression or belief; misleading idea. We were under the *illusion* that the party was on Friday and not Saturday.
il·lu·sion (i lü′zhən) *noun, plural* **illusions.**

This picture gives the **illusion** that the bottom line is longer.

illustrate   **1.** To make clear or explain. The teacher *illustrated* how the human eye works by comparing it to a camera.   **2.** To draw a picture or diagram to explain or decorate something written. The famous artist *illustrated* a book about birds.
il·lus·trate (il′ə strāt′ *or* i lus′trāt′) *verb,* **illustrated, illustrating.**

illustration   **1.** An example or comparison that is given to explain, teach, or show something. The teacher showed us how to solve

the arithmetic problem as an *illustration* of how to do other problems of the same kind. **2.** A picture or diagram used to explain or decorate something written. The *illustrations* in this dictionary help to explain words that have been defined.
    il·lus·tra·tion (il′ə strā′shən) *noun, plural* **illustrations.**

illustrator An artist who makes illustrations for books, magazines, or other works.
    il·lus·tra·tor (il′ə strā′tər) *noun, plural* **illustrators.**

ill will Unfriendly feeling. After their argument, the two classmates felt *ill will* toward each other.

im- A prefix that means: **1.** Not or a lack of. *Imperfect* means not perfect. *Impatience* means a lack of patience. **2.** In or into. *Imperil* means to put in peril or danger. ▲ *Im-* has the same meaning as *in-*. It is used instead of *in-* before words or roots that begin with the letters *b, m,* or *p.*

I'm Shortened form of "I am." *I'm* going to the zoo today.
    I'm (īm) *contraction.*

image **1.** A picture or other likeness of a person or thing. A penny has an *image* of Abraham Lincoln on one side of it. **2.** A picture of an object formed by a mirror or lens. **3.** A person who looks very similar to someone else. That girl is the *image* of her mother.
    im·age (im′ij) *noun, plural* **images.**

imaginary Existing only in the mind; unreal. Most people believe that ghosts are *imaginary.*
    i·mag·i·nar·y (i maj′ə ner′ē) *adjective.*

imagination **1.** The forming in a person's mind of pictures or ideas of things that are elsewhere or not real. I pictured my summer vacation over and over in my *imagination* because it had been such fun. Your *imagination* led you to believe that you and I might be cousins, but we aren't. **2.** The ability or power to create or form new images or ideas. It took great *imagination* to write such a clever story.
    i·mag·i·na·tion (i maj′ə nā′shən) *noun, plural* **imaginations.**

imaginative **1.** Having a good imagination. The *imaginative* child made up stories to tell the younger children. **2.** Showing imagination. The author wrote an *imaginative* story about a genie who had magical powers.
    i·mag·i·na·tive (i maj′ə nə tiv) *adjective.*

imagine **1.** To picture a person or thing in the mind. Try to *imagine* a dragon breathing

fire. **2.** To suppose; guess. I don't *imagine* we will go on a picnic if it rains.
    i·mag·ine (i maj′in) *verb,* **imagined, imagining.**

imitate **1.** To try to act or behave just as another person does; copy. People often *imitate* other people whom they admire. **2.** To look like; resemble. The wooden floors were painted to *imitate* marble.
    im·i·tate (im′i tāt′) *verb,* **imitated, imitating.**

imitation **1.** The act of copying. That student does a great *imitation* of the president's voice. **2.** Something that is a copy of something else. We bought an *imitation* of a famous painting. *Noun.*
—Made to look like something real; not real. An *imitation* diamond ring should cost less than a genuine one. *Adjective.*
    im·i·ta·tion (im′i tā′shən) *noun, plural* **imitations;** *adjective.*

immaculate Extremely clean or neat. The shirt was *immaculate* after we washed it. The living room is always *immaculate.*
    im·mac·u·late (i mak′yə lit) *adjective.*

Word History

Immaculate comes from a Latin word meaning "without spots" or "without stains."

---

immature **1.** Not having reached full growth; not mature. *Immature* corn is not ready to pick and eat. **2.** Foolish or childish. The *immature* visitor fussed about not liking the food at the party.
    im·ma·ture (im′ə chùr′ *or* im′ə tùr′ *or* im′ə tyùr′) *adjective.*

immeasurable Unable to be measured; very great. The help you gave us was *immeasurable.*
    im·meas·ur·able (i mezh′ər ə bəl) *adjective.*

immediate **1.** Done or happening right away; without delay. When you do an arithmetic problem on a calculator, you get an *immediate* answer. **2.** Close in time or space; near. I can remember the *immediate*

at; āpe; fär; câre; end; mē; it; īce; pîerce; hot; ōld; sông, fôrk; oil; out; up; ūse; rüle; pùll; tûrn; chin; sing; shop; thin; this; hw in white; zh in treasure. The symbol ə stands for the unstressed vowel sound in about, taken, pencil, lemon, and circus.

past better than what happened five years ago.

im·me·di·ate (i mē′dē it) *adjective.*

immediately   Right away; now. If we leave *immediately,* we can get to the movie in time.

im·me·di·ate·ly (i mē′dē it lē) *adverb.*

immense   Of great size; very large; huge. The whale is an *immense* animal that can grow as long as 100 feet.

im·mense (i mens′) *adjective.*

immerse   **1.** To cover completely by dipping into water or another liquid. We *immersed* our feet in the pool.   **2.** To involve or occupy completely. I did not hear the doorbell because I was *immersed* in a good book.

im·merse (i mûrs′) *verb,* **immersed, immersing.**

immigrant   A person who comes to live in a country in which he or she was not born. My grandparents were *immigrants* to the United States from Italy.

im·mi·grant (im′i grənt) *noun, plural* **immigrants.**

immigrate   To come to live in a country where one was not born. My grandparents *immigrated* to Canada from Poland.

im·mi·grate (im′i grāt′) *verb,* **immigrated, immigrating.**

immigration   The act of coming to a new country to make one's home.

im·mi·gra·tion (im′i grā′shən) *noun.*

imminent   Expected to happen; likely to occur or take place very soon. The dark clouds made me think that a storm was *imminent.*

im·mi·nent (im′ə nənt) *adjective.*

immoral   Wicked; evil; not moral. Lying about a friend is an *immoral* thing to do.

im·mor·al (i môr′əl) *adjective.*

immortal   Living, lasting, or remembered forever.

im·mor·tal (i môr′təl) *adjective.*

immune   **1.** Protected from a disease. The doctor gave me a vaccination that made me *immune* to measles.   **2.** Safe from undergoing something; not subject. No one is *immune* from criticism.

im·mune (i mūn′) *adjective.*

immune system   The system that protects the body from disease. In humans, the immune system includes white blood cells and antibodies.

immunity   The ability of the body to resist a disease. A person can gain immunity to a disease by being inoculated or vaccinated.

im·mu·ni·ty (i mū′ni tē) *noun, plural* **immunities.**

impact   **1.** The action of one object striking against another. The *impact* of the car crashing into the pole smashed the front fender.   **2.** A strong, immediate effect. That book has an emotional *impact* on its readers.

im·pact (im′pakt) *noun, plural* **impacts.**

impair   To lessen the quality or strength of; weaken. The heavy fog *impaired* the driver's vision.

im·pair (im pâr′) *verb,* **impaired, impairing.**

impala   A small, slender antelope that lives in Africa. It has a reddish or golden brown coat and a black line down the hind part of each thigh. The impala can leap great distances.

im·pal·a (im pal′ə) *noun, plural* **impalas.**

impartial   Not favoring one more than others; fair. The judges of a contest should be *impartial.*

im·par·tial (im pär′shəl) *adjective.*

impala

impatience   An inability to put up with delay or opposition calmly and without anger. When I wouldn't clean my room, my parents' *impatience* grew until they finally scolded me. The teacher could sense the children's *impatience* for summer vacation to begin.

im·pa·tience (im pā′shəns) *noun.*

impatient   Not able to put up with delay or opposition calmly and without anger. Toward the end of the movie, the children became *impatient* to leave.

im·pa·tient (im pā′shənt) *adjective.*

impeach   To bring formal charges of wrong conduct against a public official. An official can be removed from office if he or she is found guilty of the charges.

im·peach (im pēch′) *verb,* **impeached, impeaching.**

imperative   Absolutely necessary; urgent. If we are to arrive on time, it is *imperative* that we leave right away.

im·per·a·tive (im per′ə tiv) *adjective.*

imperative sentence   A sentence that tells or asks someone to do something. An example of an imperative sentence is "Go to the store and buy some bread."

imperfect Having a mistake, defect, or fault. The fit was *imperfect* but I liked the shoes so much that I bought them anyway.
im·per·fect (im pûr′fikt) *adjective.*

imperial **1.** Having to do with an empire or an emperor or empress. The emperor and empress live in the *imperial* palace. **2.** Having to do with one country's control over another or others. The United States was formed from a group of colonies under the *imperial* rule of England.
im·pe·ri·al (im pîr′ē əl) *adjective.*

impersonate To copy the appearance and actions of in order to amuse or deceive. My friend can *impersonate* famous actors. It is illegal to *impersonate* a police officer.
im·per·son·ate (im pûr′sə nāt′) *verb,* **impersonated, impersonating.**

impertinent Very rude or bold; impudent. It would be *impertinent* to interrupt someone who is speaking.
im·per·ti·nent (im pûr′tə nənt) *adjective.*

impetuous Acting or done too quickly, without enough planning or thought. I later regretted my *impetuous* decision.
im·pet·u·ous (im pech′ü əs) *adjective.*

implant To put an organ or a device into the body. *Verb.*
—An organ or a device placed in the body by surgery. *Noun.*
im·plant (im plant′ *for verb;* im′plant′ *for noun*) *verb* **implanted, implanting;** *noun,* *plural* **implants.**

implement An object used to do a particular job; tool. Hoes, rakes, and spades are gardening *implements.*
im·ple·ment (im′plə mənt) *noun, plural* **implements.**

imply To suggest without saying directly. Did you *imply* that I'm old-fashioned when you said my clothes were out of style?
im·ply (im plī′) *verb,* **implied, implying.**

Language Note

People often confuse the verbs **imply** and **infer** because the words describe two sides of the same idea. Someone who hints at something is implying. The frown on your face *implied* that something was wrong. Someone who reaches a conclusion by examining things is inferring. I *inferred* from your smile that you won the game.

impolite Having or showing bad manners; not polite; rude. It is *impolite* to arrive late for dinner.
im·po·lite (im′pə līt′) *adjective.*

import To bring in goods from another country for sale or use. The United States *imports* tea from India. *Verb.*
—Something that is imported. *Noun.*
im·port (im pôrt′ *for verb;* im′pôrt′ *for noun*) *verb,* **imported, importing;** *noun,* *plural* **imports.**

importance The state of being important. Rain is of great *importance* to farmers since crops can't grow without water.
im·por·tance (im pôr′təns) *noun.*

important **1.** Having great value or meaning. A proper diet is *important* to good health. **2.** Having a high position or much power. Members of the city council are *important* civic figures.
im·por·tant (im pôr′tənt) *adjective.*

impose **1.** To put or set on a person. The judge *imposed* a sentence of three years. **2.** To make unfair or impolite demands. I won't *impose* on you by taking your time.
im·pose (im pōz′) *verb,* **imposed, imposing.**

impossible Not able to happen or be done. It is *impossible* for a person to fly by flapping the arms.
im·pos·si·ble (im pos′ə bəl) *adjective.*

impostor A person who tries to trick others by pretending to be someone else.
im·pos·tor (im pos′tər) *noun, plural* **impostors.**

impracticable Not capable of being done or carried out. We rejected the plan because it was clearly *impracticable.*
im·prac·ti·ca·ble (im prak′ti kə bəl) *adjective.*

impress **1.** To have a strong effect on the mind or feelings. The height of the skyscraper *impressed* me. **2.** To fix in the mind. Our parents tried to *impress* a sense of right and wrong on each of us.
im·press (im pres′) *verb,* **impressed, impressing.**

impression **1.** An effect on the mind or feelings. What was your *impression* of the new student in our class? **2.** An uncertain belief, notion, or memory; feeling. I had the

at; āpe; fär; câre; end; mē; it; īce; pîerce; hot; ōld; sông, fôrk; oil; out; up; ūse; rüle; pùll; tûrn; chin; sing; shop; thin; this; hw in white; zh in treasure. The symbol ə stands for the unstressed vowel sound in about, taken, pencil, lemon, and circus.

impression that they were related, but I was wrong.   **3.** A mark or design produced by pressing or stamping. We made *impressions* of our hands in the wet concrete.   **4.** Imitation. The clown did a very funny *impression* of a monkey.
im·pres·sion (im presh′ən) *noun, plural* **impressions.**

The boy is putting his hands into **impressions** of an adult's hands.

impressive   Making a strong impression. Their science project was so *impressive* that the judges awarded them first prize.
im·pres·sive (im pres′iv) *adjective.*

imprint   **1.** A mark made by pressing or stamping. Your boots have made *imprints* in the snow.   **2.** A mark or effect. Age has left its *imprint* on the crumbling building. *Noun.*
—1. To mark by pressing or stamping. The store *imprinted* envelopes with my name and address.   **2.** To fix firmly in the mind. That beautiful scene became *imprinted* in my memory. *Verb.*
im·print (im′print′ *for noun;* im print′ *for verb) noun, plural* **imprints;** *verb,* **imprinted, imprinting.**

imprison   To put or keep in prison; lock up.
im·pris·on (im priz′ən) *verb,* **imprisoned, imprisoning.**

improper   **1.** Not correct. A screwdriver is an *improper* tool for driving nails.   **2.** Showing bad manners or bad taste. It is *improper* to talk with food in your mouth.
im·prop·er (im prop′ər) *adjective.*

improper fraction   A fraction that is equal to or greater than 1. ⅘ and 6/6 are both improper fractions because ⅘ is equal to 1⅗ and 6/6 is equal to 1.

improve   To make or become better. I am taking lessons to *improve* my singing. My tennis has *improved* greatly since I began practicing.
im·prove (im prüv′) *verb,* **improved, improving.**

improvement   **1.** The act of improving or the state of being improved. A balanced diet

and exercise will lead to *improvement* of your health.   **2.** A change or a thing added that improves something. The new yellow curtains are an *improvement* to the room.   **3.** A person or thing that is better than another. This new wagon is an *improvement* over our old rusty one.
im·prove·ment (im prüv′mənt) *noun, plural* **improvements.**

improvise   **1.** To make up and perform without planning beforehand. The class *improvised* a program of skits and songs for the unexpected visitors.   **2.** To make out of whatever materials are around. The children *improvised* bookcases out of some old wooden crates.
im·pro·vise (im′prə vīz′) *verb,* **improvised, improvising.**

impudent   Bold and rude. The *impudent* student talked back to the teacher.
im·pu·dent (im′pyə dənt) *adjective.*

impulse   **1.** A sudden feeling that makes a person act without thinking. An *impulse* made me give the new baseball mitt to my best friend.   **2.** A sudden force that causes motion; push. The *impulse* of the falling water turned the water wheel.
im·pulse (im′puls′) *noun, plural* **impulses.**

impulsive   **1.** Acting without thinking or planning. It's hard to guess what an *impulsive* person will do next.   **2.** Done because of a sudden feeling or urge; not planned or thought out. When I had to pay the bill, I regretted my *impulsive* shopping trip.
im·pul·sive (im pul′siv) *adjective.*

impure   **1.** Not clean; dirty. *Impure* water may be harmful to drink.   **2.** Containing another substance that is not as good. This *impure* gold has traces of other metals in it.
im·pure (im pyur′) *adjective.*

in   **1.** Surrounded by; inside or within. The suitcase is *in* the closet. I held the cat *in* my arms.   **2.** To or toward the inside of; into. We all got *in* the car. Go *in* the entrance on the left.   **3.** While, during, or after. The weather here is cold *in* the winter.   **4.** Affected by or having. The astronauts are *in* good health. The new worker is *in* trouble because of lateness. *Preposition.*
—1. To or toward a place inside. Come *in* out of the cold.   **2.** At a certain place; at one's home or an office. I stayed *in* because I had a cold. Is the doctor *in*? *Adverb.* ▲ Another word that sounds like this is **inn.**
• **ins and outs.**   All of the details of some activity or process. I'm learning the *ins and outs* of my family's business.
in (in) *preposition; adverb.*

in- A *prefix* that means: **1.** Not. *Inappropriate* means not appropriate. **2.** In or into. *Inborn* means born in a person. *Intake* means the amount of something taken in.
▲ *In-* has the same meaning as *im-*. *Im-* is used instead of *in-* before words or roots that begin with *b, m,* or *p.*

in. An abbreviation for *inch.*

IN Postal abbreviation for *Indiana.*

inability Lack of power or ability to do something. My *inability* to sing well kept me from joining the school chorus.
in·a·bil·i·ty (in′ə bil′i tē) *noun.*

inaccurate Not correct or accurate; wrong. I got lost because the directions were *inaccurate.*
in·ac·cu·rate (in ak′yər it) *adjective.*

inappropriate Not suitable or correct; not appropriate. A formal suit is *inappropriate* for a beach party.
in·ap·pro·pri·ate (in′ə prō′prē it) *adjective.*

inaugurate **1.** To put a person in office with a formal ceremony. The president of the United States is *inaugurated* in January after the election. **2.** To open or begin to use formally. The governor *inaugurated* the new bridge by riding in the first car to drive across it.
in·au·gu·rate (in ô′gyə rāt′) *verb,* **inaugurated, inaugurating.**

Word History

The word **inaugurate** comes from a Latin word meaning "to look for omens." The Romans believed that such things as the flight of birds were signs, or omens, that could be used to help predict the future. They watched for these signs when they *inaugurated* someone into public office.

inauguration **1.** The ceremony of putting a person in office. At the *inauguration,* the new president took the oath of office. **2.** A formal beginning or opening. We went to the *inauguration* of the city's new swimming pool.
in·au·gu·ra·tion (in ô′gyə rā′shən) *noun, plural* **inaugurations.**

inborn Born in a person; natural. That youngster seems to have an *inborn* talent for playing musical instruments.
in·born (in′bôrn′) *adjective.*

Inca A member of an American Indian people of the Andes Mountains of South America. The Inca developed an advanced civilization and controlled an empire in the fifteenth and sixteenth centuries.
In·ca (ing′kə) *noun, plural* **Inca** or **Incas.**

incapable Lacking the necessary power or skill to do something; not capable. An infant is *incapable* of walking.
in·ca·pa·ble (in kā′pə bəl) *adjective.*

incense¹ A substance that has a fragrant smell when it is burned. After the *incense* was lighted, it created a spicy smell in the room.
in·cense (in′sens′) *noun, plural* **incenses.**

incense² To make very angry. I was *incensed* when I discovered my bike was missing.
in·cense (in sens′) *verb,* **incensed, incensing.**

incentive Something that urges a person on. The possibility of a higher allowance was a powerful *incentive* for me to do extra chores.
in·cen·tive (in sen′tiv) *noun, plural* **incentives.**

incessant Going on without stopping; continuous. The campers were bothered by the *incessant* buzz of mosquitoes.
in·ces·sant (in ses′ənt) *adjective.*

inch A measure of length that equals ¹⁄₁₂ of a foot. Twelve inches equal 1 foot. One inch is the same as 2.54 centimeters. *Noun.*
—To move very slowly. We *inched* our way along the narrow ledge. *Verb.*
inch (inch) *noun, plural* **inches;** *verb,* **inched, inching.**

inchworm A kind of moth caterpillar that has legs in the front and the back but not in the middle. It moves by pulling the rear of its body up toward the front and then stretching the front end forward.
inch·worm (inch′wûrm′) *noun, plural* **inchworms.**

inchworm

at; āpe; fär; câre; end; mē; it; īce; pîerce; hot; ōld; sông, fôrk; oil; out; up; ūse; rüle; pùll; tûrn; chin; sing; shop; thin; this; hw in white; zh in treasure. The symbol ə stands for the unstressed vowel sound in about, taken, pencil, lemon, and circus.

I

incident Something that happens; event. My neighbors told us some of the funny *incidents* of their trip to Florida.
in·ci·dent (in'si dənt) *noun, plural* **incidents.**

incidentally By the way. Let's play catch; *incidentally*, do you still have my baseball?
in·ci·den·tal·ly (in'si den'tə lē *or* in'si dent'lē) *adverb.*

incinerator A furnace that burns garbage or trash.
in·cin·er·a·tor (in sin'ə rā'tər) *noun, plural* **incinerators.**

inclination **1.** A natural tendency. My *inclination* to check small details often helps me in planning projects. **2.** A liking. I have an *inclination* to go to the movies rather than stay home. **3.** A slope; slant. The steep *inclination* of the hill makes it great for sledding.
in·cli·na·tion (in'klə nā'shən) *noun, plural* **inclinations.**

incline To slope or slant. The road is hard to climb because it *inclines* upward. *Verb.*
—A surface that slopes. The ball rolled down the *incline* to the bottom of the hill. *Noun.*
in·cline (in klīn' *for verb;* in'klīn' *or* in klīn' *for noun) verb,* **inclined, inclining;** *noun, plural* **inclines.**

The children are taking a wagon up an **incline.**

include **1.** To have as part of the whole; contain. You don't have to buy batteries with that toy because they are already *included* in the box. **2.** To put in a group or total. Besides our relatives, we *included* some of our close friends in the list of people invited to the party.
in·clude (in klüd') *verb,* **included, including.**

inclusion **1.** The act of including. The *inclusion* of pictures in a book sometimes makes the book more interesting. **2.** Something that is included.
in·clu·sion (in klü'zhən) *noun, plural* **inclusions.**

income Money received for work or from property or other things that are owned.
in·come (in'kum') *noun, plural* **incomes.**

income tax A tax on a person's income.

incompetent Not having or showing enough ability, knowledge, or skill; not competent. Only an *incompetent* typist could make so many mistakes on just one page.
in·com·pe·tent (in kom'pi tənt) *adjective.*

incomplete Not complete; not finished. The report was *incomplete* because certain information was still missing.
in·com·plete (in'kəm plēt') *adjective.*

inconspicuous Not easily seen or noticed; not attracting attention; not conspicuous. The plaid of my shirt helped to make the mend *inconspicuous.*
in·con·spic·u·ous (in'kən spik'ū əs) *adjective.*

inconvenience **1.** Lack of comfort or ease; trouble or bother. I don't like the *inconvenience* of living far away from school. **2.** Something that causes trouble or bother. Not having a telephone is an *inconvenience. Noun.*
—To cause bother to; trouble. We hope the bus delay won't *inconvenience* you. *Verb.*
in·con·ven·ience (in'kən vēn'yəns) *noun, plural* **inconveniences;** *verb,* **inconvenienced, inconveniencing.**

incorporate To include something as part of a larger thing. I *incorporated* the photographs into our big picture album.
in·cor·po·rate (in kôr'pə rāt') *verb,* **incorporated, incorporating.**

incorrect Not right or correct; not proper. You must do this problem over because your answer is *incorrect.*
in·cor·rect (in'kə rekt') *adjective.*

increase To make or become larger in number or size. The library has *increased* its collection of mystery books. The number of students trying out for the band has *increased* this year. *Verb.*
—An amount by which something is made larger. I got an *increase* of fifty cents in my allowance. *Noun.*
in·crease (in krēs' *for verb;* in'krēs' *for noun) verb,* **increased, increasing;** *noun, plural* **increases.**

incredible **1.** Hard or impossible to believe. Your excuse that the dog ate your homework is *incredible.* **2.** Amazing; astonishing. The amount of money they spend on fancy clothes is *incredible.*
in·cred·i·ble (in kred'ə bəl) *adjective.*

incredulous Not able to believe something. Many people were *incredulous* when the workers from the mine said they had found gold.

in·cred·u·lous (in krej′ə ləs) *adjective*.

incubate To sit on eggs and keep them warm for hatching. A hen *incubates* her eggs.
in·cu·bate (ing′kyə bāt′) *verb*, **incubated, incubating.**

incubator **1.** A heated container that is used to hatch eggs. **2.** A similar container that supplies heat, moisture, and oxygen to babies who are born too early.
in·cu·ba·tor (ing′kyə bā′tər) *noun, plural* **incubators.**

incurable Not capable of being cured. Some diseases are *incurable*.
in·cur·a·ble (in kyùr′ə bəl) *adjective*.

indebted **1.** Owing money; in debt. Until I pay back this loan, I am *indebted* to the bank. **2.** Owing gratitude to another for a favor. I am *indebted* to you for all your help.
in·debt·ed (in det′id) *adjective*.

Ind. An abbreviation for *Indiana*.

indeed Really; truly. They do *indeed* have a talking parrot, just as they said they did.
in·deed (in dēd′) *adverb*.

indefinite **1.** Not clear, set, or exact; vague. Our plans for the summer are still *indefinite*. **2.** Having no limits; not fixed. I will be in the hospital for an *indefinite* number of days.
in·def·i·nite (in def′ə nit) *adjective*.

indefinite article Either of the articles *a* or *an*. An indefinite article is used to refer to an indefinite person or thing. In the sentence "I'd like a piece of fruit," the indefinite article "a" refers to an indefinite "piece."

indent To start a written line farther in than the other lines. We *indent* the first sentence of a paragraph.
in·dent (in dent′) *verb*, **indented, indenting.**

independence Freedom from the control of another or others. The American colonies fought to win *independence* from England.
in·de·pend·ence (in′di pen′dəns) *noun*.

Independence Day A holiday in the United States that falls on the fourth of July. It celebrates the anniversary of the signing of the Declaration of Independence in 1776. This holiday is also called the **Fourth of July.**

independent Free from the control or rule of another or others; separate. Mexicans fought against the Spanish to make Mexico an *independent* country. They did exactly what they wanted, *independent* of anyone's wishes.
in·de·pend·ent (in′di pen′dənt) *adjective*.

index An alphabetical list at the end of a book. An index tells on what page or pages a particular subject or name can be found. To find information about robins, look up the word "robin" in the *indexes* of some books on birds. *Noun*.
—To make an index for. The editor *indexed* the book about Indians so the reader could look up information easily. *Verb*.
in·dex (in′deks) *noun, plural* **indexes;** *verb*, **indexed, indexing.**

Word History

The word **index** comes from a Latin word that means "to show or point out." In Latin, the word *index* was first used to mean "forefinger," which is the finger we use for pointing.

---

index finger The finger next to the thumb; forefinger.

India A country in southern Asia.
In·di·a (in′dē ə) *noun*.

Indian **1.** A member of one of the peoples who have been living in North and South America since before the Europeans discovered the continents; Native American. **2.** A person who was born in or is a citizen of India. *Noun*.
—**1.** Having to do with American Indians; Native American. **2.** Having to do with India or its people. *Adjective*.
In·di·an (in′dē ən) *noun, plural* **Indians;** *adjective*.

Indiana A state in the north-central United States. Its capital is Indianapolis.
In·di·an·a (in′dē an′ə) *noun*.

Word History

The name **Indiana** comes from a modern Latin word meaning "Indian." There were many American Indians living in this region when other Americans began to settle there. This name was used for the territory and then the state.

---

at; āpe; fär; câre; end; mē; it; īce; pîerce; hot; ōld; sông, fôrk; oil; out; up; ūse; rüle; pùll; tûrn; chin; sing; shop; thin; this; hw in white; zh in treasure. The symbol ə stands for the unstressed vowel sound in about, taken, pencil, lemon, and circus.

I

Indian corn A plant whose grain grows on large ears. Look up **corn** for more information.

Indian Ocean An ocean south of Asia, between Africa and Australia.

indicate **1.** To be a sign of; show. A high fever *indicates* that a person is sick. **2.** To point out. The guide *indicated* the best path for us to take. **3.** To say or express briefly. By nodding, I *indicated* that I agreed.
in·di·cate (in′di kāt′) *verb,* **indicated, indicating.**

indication Something that indicates; a sign. Good grades are often an *indication* of hard work.
in·di·ca·tion (in′di kā′shən) *noun, plural* **indications.**

indict To accuse and charge a person with committing a crime. A person is indicted by a special jury and then is given a trial.
in·dict (in dīt′) *verb,* **indicted, indicting.**

indifferent Having or showing a lack of interest, concern, or care. The football game was so exciting that the fans were *indifferent* to the rain that was pouring down.
in·dif·fer·ent (in dif′ər ənt *or* in dif′rənt) *adjective.*

indigestion Difficulty or discomfort in digesting foods. Food that is very spicy may cause *indigestion.*
in·di·ges·tion (in′di jes′chən *or* in′dī jes′chən) *noun.*

indignant Filled with anger about something unfair, wrong, or bad. People in the town became *indignant* when they learned of plans to turn the park into a garbage dump.
in·dig·nant (in dig′nənt) *adjective.*

indigo **1.** A very dark blue dye. It can be obtained from various plants but is now usually made artificially. **2.** A plant that usually has purple or red flowers from which this dye is obtained. **3.** A deep violet-blue color. *Noun.*
—Having the color indigo; deep violet-blue. *Adjective.*

indigo

in·di·go (in′di gō′) *noun, plural* **indigos** or **indigoes;** *adjective.*

indirect **1.** Not in a straight line; roundabout. We took the *indirect* route through small towns because it is prettier than the main highway. **2.** Not straight to the point. Yawning is an *indirect* way of saying that you are bored. **3.** Not directly connected.
in·di·rect (in′də rekt′ *or* in′dī rekt′) *adjective.*

indirect object A word or group of words in a sentence to whom, to what, for whom, or for what the action of a verb is done. In the sentence "I showed them how to solve the problem," the pronoun "them" is the indirect object of the verb "showed."

individual **1.** Of or for one person or thing. You can announce your party to the whole class, or you can send out *individual* invitations. **2.** Single; separate. The coffee was served with *individual* packets of sugar. **3.** Characteristic of a particular person or thing. My cousin has an *individual* way of laughing. *Adjective.*
—A single person or thing. In this group picture, the tallest *individual* stands out. *Noun.*
in·di·vid·u·al (in′də vij′ü əl) *adjective; noun, plural* **individuals.**

individuality A quality that makes one person or thing different from others. Some people try to express their *individuality* in the way they dress.
in·di·vid·u·al·i·ty (in′də vij′ü al′i tē) *noun, plural* **individualities.**

individually One at a time. The teacher explained the assignment to the class as a whole and then answered our questions *individually.*
in·di·vid·u·al·ly (in′də vij′ü ə lē) *adverb.*

indivisible Not able to be divided or separated. The United States is an *indivisible* nation.
in·di·vis·i·ble (in′də viz′ə bəl) *adjective.*

Indonesia A country made up of a group of islands in southeastern Asia.
In·do·ne·sia (in′də nē′zhə) *noun.*

indoor Used, done, or built within a house or building. The school had an *indoor* swimming pool.
in·door (in′dôr′) *adjective.*

indoors In or into a house or building. We went *indoors* when it began to rain.
in·doors (in′dôrz′) *adverb.*

indulge **1.** To allow oneself to have, do, or enjoy something. I *indulged* in an hour of relaxation after I finished all my chores. **2.** To give in to the wishes of. Grandparents sometimes *indulge* children by giving them everything they ask for.
in·dulge (in dulj′) *verb,* **indulged, indulging.**

industrial **1.** Having to do with or produced by industry. Iron smelting, coal min-

ing, and the production of plastics are *industrial* processes. **2.** Having highly developed industries. Canada is an *industrial* country.
in·dus·tri·al (in dus′trē əl) *adjective.*

industrialize To set up or develop industry in an area or country. The governor wanted to *industrialize* the state in order to provide more jobs.
in·dus·tri·al·ize (in dus′trē ə līz′) *verb,* **industrialized, industrializing.**

industrious Working hard. The *industrious* student finished the report a week before it was due.
in·dus·tri·ous (in dus′trē əs) *adjective.*

The **industrious** children are working on their art projects.

industry **1.** Making of things on a large scale, especially by people and machines working together. *Industry* came to the town when a tire factory and an electric power plant were opened. **2.** A branch of business, trade, or manufacturing. The tourist *industry* employs many people in Hawaii. The making of lumber and other forest products is an important *industry* in Oregon. **3.** Hard work; steady effort. The students showed much *industry* in preparing their homework.
in·dus·try (in′də strē) *noun, plural* **industries.**

inedible Not fit as food; not suitable for eating. The burned meat was *inedible.*
in·ed·i·ble (in ed′ə bəl) *adjective.*

inequality The condition of not being equal. Often there is an *inequality* between what we hope for and what we get.
in·e·qual·i·ty (in′i kwol′i tē) *noun, plural* **inequalities.**

inert Not able to move or act; not moving. A mountain is *inert.*
in·ert (i nûrt′) *adjective.*

inevitable Not able to be avoided; bound to happen. An *inevitable* result of closing your eyes is not being able to see.
in·ev·i·ta·ble (i nev′i tə bəl) *adjective.*

inexpensive Not expensive; reasonable in price. I bought *inexpensive* shorts for the summer.
in·ex·pen·sive (in′ek spen′siv) *adjective.*

inexperienced Lacking the knowledge or skill gained from doing something. The new members of the team are still *inexperienced* players. The driver was *inexperienced* in driving through snow.
in·ex·pe·ri·enced (in′ek spîr′ē ənst) *adjective.*

infant A child during the earliest period of life; baby. *Noun.*
—1. Having to do with a baby. **2.** In an early stage of growth; young. The United States was an *infant* republic when its constitution was written. *Adjective.*
in·fant (in′fənt) *noun, plural* **infants;** *adjective.*

infantry Soldiers trained and equipped to fight on foot. The *infantry* was very important in winning the war.
in·fan·try (in′fən trē) *noun, plural* **infantries.**

Word History

The word **infantry** comes from an Italian word that means both "boy" and "foot soldier." This word has these two meanings because the soldiers who served a knight were usually young and fought on foot.

---

infect **1.** To spread a disease that is caused by a germ. Mosquitoes *infected* many of the workers in the jungle with malaria. **2.** To enter a living thing and cause disease. The doctor said that bacteria had *infected* the cut on my hand.
in·fect (in fekt′) *verb,* **infected, infecting.**

infection **1.** The process of infecting. The *infection* of the wound was caused by bacteria. **2.** A disease that is caused by germs entering the body. I got a very bad *infection* in my foot after stepping on some pieces of broken glass.
in·fec·tion (in fek′shən) *noun, plural* **infections.**

---

at; āpe; fär; câre; end; mē; it; īce; pîerce; hot; ōld; sông, fôrk; oil; out; up; ūse; rüle; pùll; tûrn; chin; sing; shop; thin; this; hw in white; zh in treasure. The symbol ə stands for the unstressed vowel sound in about, taken, pencil, lemon, and circus.

infectious   Spread by infection. Many infectious diseases spread from one person to another. Mumps is an *infectious* disease.
　　in·fec·tious (in fek′shəs) *adjective.*

infer   To find out by reasoning; conclude. From your high grades, I *inferred* that you were a good student. ▲ Look up **imply** for a Language Note about this word.
　　in·fer (in fûr′) *verb,* **inferred, inferring.**

inferior   1. Of poor quality; below average. The food at that restaurant is *inferior*. 2. Low or lower in quality, importance, or value. The rank of private is *inferior* to the rank of sergeant.
　　in·fe·ri·or (in fîr′ē ər) *adjective.*

infield   1. The area of a baseball field that is inside and around the bases.   2. In baseball, the people who play the positions at first base, second base, third base, and shortstop.
　　in·field (in′fēld′) *noun, plural* **infields.**

infinite   1. Without limits or an end. Outer space seems to be *infinite*. 2. Very great. The artist painted the tiny figures with *infinite* care.
　　in·fi·nite (in′fə nit) *adjective.*

infinitive   A simple verb form. An infinitive is often preceded by the word "to." In the sentence "I like to swim," "to swim" is an infinitive.
　　in·fin·i·tive (in fin′i tiv) *noun, plural* **infinitives.**

inflame   1. To excite greatly; stir up. The plan to turn the park into a parking lot *inflamed* the whole town.   2. To make hot, red, or swollen. The infection in the cut *inflamed* my finger.
　　in·flame (in flām′) *verb,* **inflamed, inflaming.**

inflammable   Easily set on fire; flammable. Gasoline is an *inflammable* liquid.
　　in·flam·ma·ble (in flam′ə bəl) *adjective.*

inflammation   A condition of a part of the body in which there is heat, redness, swelling, and pain. It is usually caused by an infection or injury.
　　in·flam·ma·tion (in′flə mā′shən) *noun, plural* **inflammations.**

inflate   To cause to swell by filling with air or gas. Use a pump to *inflate* the bicycle tire.
　　in·flate (in flāt′) *verb,* **inflated, inflating.**

inflation   1. The act or process of inflating. The *inflation* of the balloons for the party took all morning.   2. A rise in the usual prices of goods and services.
　　in·fla·tion (in flā′shən) *noun, plural* **inflations.**

influence   1. The power of a person or thing to produce an effect on others without using force or a command. Use your *influence* to persuade your friend to study harder. 2. A person or thing that has the power to produce an effect on others. Working with that classmate has had a good *influence* on my study habits. *Noun.*
—To have an effect on; especially by giving suggestions or by serving as an example. The older members of my family *influence* me in many ways. *Verb.*
　　in·flu·ence (in′flü əns) *noun, plural* **influences;** *verb,* **influenced, influencing.**

influential   Having or using influence. Some *influential* teachers persuaded the principal to change the rule.
　　in·flu·en·tial (in′flü en′shəl) *adjective.*

influenza   A disease that causes fever, coughing, and muscle pains. Influenza is caused by a virus. It is also called **flu.**
　　in·flu·en·za (in′flü en′zə) *noun.*

inform   1. To give information to; tell. Please *inform* us of the date you will arrive. 2. To tell secret or damaging information.
　　in·form (in fôrm′) *verb,* **informed, informing.**

informal   Without ceremony; not formal; casual. We gave a very *informal* party where everyone wore old clothes.
　　in·for·mal (in fôr′məl) *adjective.*

information   1. Knowledge or facts about something. Where can I ask for *information* about the bus schedule? You can get the *information* you need for your report on Italy from the encyclopedia. 2. A person or service that answers questions and gives facts. You can call *information* for the telephone number of the school.
　　in·for·ma·tion (in′fər mā′shən) *noun.*

infrequent   Not happening or seen often; not frequent; occasional. Serious accidents are *infrequent* on our quiet street. They are *infrequent* visitors to our town.
　　in·fre·quent (in frē′kwənt) *adjective.*

infuriate   To make very angry; make furious. Their constant teasing *infuriates* me.
　　in·fu·ri·ate (in fyùr′ē āt′) *verb,* **infuriated, infuriating.**

–ing   A *suffix* that: 1. Forms the present participle of verbs. The word *talking* is the present participle of *talk.* We are *talking* about something important.   2. Forms nouns from verbs. The noun that is formed names the action that the verb describes. *Talking* is not allowed in the halls.

ingenious   Clever, imaginative, and original. My friend is *ingenious* at thinking of new ideas for class projects.
　　in·gen·ious (in jēn′yəs) *adjective.*

ingenuity The quality of being clever and imaginative. You showed *ingenuity* in making bookcases out of orange crates.
in·ge·nu·i·ty (in′jə nü′i tē) *noun.*

ingot A mass of metal that is often shaped like a bar or block.
in·got (ing′gət) *noun, plural* **ingots.**

gold **ingots**

ingredient Any one of the parts that go into a mixture. Flour, eggs, sugar, and butter are the main *ingredients* of this cake.
in·gre·di·ent (in grē′dē ənt) *noun, plural* **ingredients.**

inhabit To live in or on. Many birds *inhabit* the woods.
in·hab·it (in hab′it) *verb,* **inhabited, inhabiting.**

inhabitant A person or animal that lives in a place.
in·hab·it·ant (in hab′i tənt) *noun, plural* **inhabitants.**

inhale To take into the lungs; breathe in. I *inhaled* the fresh, clean mountain air.
in·hale (in hāl′) *verb,* **inhaled, inhaling.**

inherit 1. To receive the property or money of a person who has died. We *inherited* this house from our grandparents. 2. To get from one's parent or parents. The little boy *inherited* his mother's black hair.
in·her·it (in her′it) *verb,* **inherited, inheriting.**

inheritance Something that is inherited. We set aside my *inheritance* from my grandparents for my college education.
in·her·it·ance (in her′i təns) *noun, plural* **inheritances.**

inhuman Without kindness, pity, or mercy; cruel; brutal. Making the tired old horse work in the heat was *inhuman.*
in·hu·man (in hū′mən) *adjective.*

initial Coming at the beginning; first. The *initial* letter of the word "ring" is "r." My *initial* response to their request was "no." *Adjective.*
—The first letter of a word or a name. "B.R." are the *initials* of Betsy Ross. *Noun.*
—To mark or sign with one's initial or initials. The teacher *initialed* the report after reading it. *Verb.*
i·ni·tial (i nish′əl) *adjective; noun, plural* **initials;** *verb,* **initialed, initialing.**

initiate 1. To be the first to do; begin; start. The new librarian *initiated* the practice of lending books for a month. 2. To make a person a member of an organization or club. The new members were *initiated* into the club at a special ceremony.
i·ni·ti·ate (i nish′ē āt′) *verb,* **initiated, initiating.**

initiative 1. The first step in doing or beginning something. I took the *initiative* at the party by introducing myself to the people I didn't know. 2. The ability or willingness to take a first step in doing or learning something. The new campers showed *initiative* by setting up the tent without being asked.
i·ni·tia·tive (i nish′ə tiv) *noun.*

inject 1. To force a liquid through the skin into a muscle, vein, or other part of the body. The doctor *injected* the vaccine into my arm. 2. To put in. The principal tried to *inject* some humor into the speech by telling several jokes.
in·ject (in jekt′) *verb* **injected, injecting.**

injection The forcing of a liquid through the skin into the body for a medical purpose. The veterinarian gave the dog an *injection* with a needle.
in·jec·tion (in jek′shən) *noun, plural* **injections.**

injure To cause harm to; damage or hurt. I *injured* myself when I fell off my bicycle. Failing the test *injured* my friend's pride.
in·jure (in′jər) *verb,* **injured, injuring.**

injury Harm or damage done to a person or thing. The accident caused an *injury* to my leg.
in·ju·ry (in′jə rē) *noun, plural* **injuries.**

injustice 1. The lack of justice; unfairness. The class protested against the *injustice* of

I

at; āpe; fär; câre; end; mē; it; īce; pîerce; hot; ōld; sông, fôrk; oil; out; up; ūse; rüle; pùll; tûrn; chin; sing; shop; thin; <u>th</u>is; hw in white; zh in treasure. The symbol ə stands for the unstressed vowel sound in about, taken, pencil, lemon, and circus.

punishing everyone because one student was noisy. **2.** Something unjust. You do your friends an *injustice* when you lie to them.
in·jus·tice (in jus′tis) *noun, plural* **injustices.**

ink A colored liquid used for writing, drawing, or printing.
ink (ingk) *noun, plural* **inks.**

inkwell A container for ink.
ink·well (ingk′wel′) *noun, plural* **inkwells.**

inland Away from the coast or border. Kansas is an *inland* state. *Adjective.*
—In or toward the inner part of a country or region. We drove *inland* from the coast for many miles. *Adverb.*
in·land (in′lənd) *adjective; adverb.*

inkwells

inlet A narrow body of water leading inland from a larger body of water.
in·let (in′let′) *noun, plural* **inlets.**

inn A small hotel. An inn is usually in the country. ▲ Another word that sounds like this is **in.**
inn (in) *noun, plural* **inns.**

inner **1.** Farther in. The principal's office is in the *inner* room. **2.** More private; personal. I hid my *inner* feelings of disappointment at having lost the contest.
in·ner (in′ər) *adjective.*

inning One of the parts into which a baseball or softball game is divided. Both teams bat during an inning until three players on each team are put out.
in·ning (in′ing) *noun, plural* **innings.**

innkeeper A person who owns or manages an inn.
inn·keep·er (in′kē′pər) *noun, plural* **innkeepers.**

innocence The state or quality of being innocent. The *innocence* of the prisoner was proven during the trial.
in·no·cence (in′ə səns) *noun.*

innocent **1.** Free from guilt or wrong. An *innocent* person was accused of the crime, but a jury found the person not guilty. **2.** Not doing harm; harmless. The children hid from their parents as an *innocent* joke.
in·no·cent (in′ə sənt) *adjective.*

innovation Something new that is introduced. The development of the first antibiotic was a great *innovation* in medicine.
in·no·va·tion (in′ə vā′shən) *noun, plural* **innovations.**

inoculate To give a healthy person or animal a small amount of a substance that contains weakened disease germs. This helps the body protect itself against the disease. A person can be inoculated against diseases such as smallpox and typhoid fever.
in·oc·u·late (in ok′yə lāt′) *verb,* **inoculated, inoculating.**

input Information that is put into a computer.
in·put (in′pùt′) *noun.*

inquire To try to get information or knowledge about by asking questions. We stopped at a gas station to *inquire* the way to the park.
in·quire (in kwīr′) *verb,* **inquired, inquiring.**

inquiry **1.** A looking for information or knowledge; investigation. The fire department is making an *inquiry* into the cause of the fire. **2.** A request for information. There were many *inquiries* about the summer job that was advertised in the paper.
in·quir·y (in kwīr′ē *or* in′kwə rē) *noun, plural* **inquiries.**

inquisitive Eager to know; curious. An *inquisitive* student asks a lot of questions.
in·quis·i·tive (in kwiz′i tiv) *adjective.*

insane **1.** Not having a healthy mind; not sane; crazy. **2.** Of or for insane people. The state runs that *insane* asylum. **3.** Very foolish. It is *insane* to think that you can fly.
in·sane (in sān′) *adjective.*

insanity A state in which the mind is seriously sick.
in·san·i·ty (in san′i tē) *noun, plural* **insanities.**

inscribe To write, carve, engrave, or mark words or letters on something. The locket was *inscribed* with initials.
in·scribe (in skrīb′) *verb,* **inscribed, inscribing.**

The artist **inscribes** a picture in ivory.

insect **1.** Any of a large group of small animals without a backbone. The body of an insect is divided into three parts. Insects have three pairs of legs and usually two pairs of wings. Flies, ants, grasshoppers, and beetles are insects. **2.** An animal that is similar to an insect. Ticks and spiders are sometimes called insects but they are another kind of animal.
in·sect (in′sekt) *noun, plural* **insects.**

Word History

The word **insect** comes from a Latin word that means "cut into." An insect was called "an animal that has been cut into" because its body is divided into three sections.

---

insecticide A chemical for killing insects.
in·sec·ti·cide (in sek′tə sīd′) *noun, plural* **insecticides.**

insecure **1.** Likely to fail; not firm or stable. The latch was so *insecure* that the wind could blow the door open. **2.** Not safe from danger, harm, or loss. The fort was *insecure* because there were not enough troops to defend it. **3.** Not confident; fearful. The student felt nervous and *insecure* before the start of the spelling contest.
in·se·cure (in′si kyür′) *adjective.*

insert To put, set, or place in. I *inserted* a coin in the vending machine. Please *insert* the cork in the bottle. *Verb.*
—Something inserted. The Sunday edition of the newspaper has an eight-page color *insert* on vacations. *Noun.*
in·sert (in sûrt′ *for verb;* in′sûrt′ *for noun*) *verb,* **inserted, inserting;** *noun, plural* **inserts.**

inside **1.** The inner side or part; interior. The *inside* of the house was dark. **2. insides.** The internal organs of the body. *Noun.*
—**1.** On or in the inside. I took an *inside* seat on the train. **2.** Known or done by only a few. The reporter got the *inside* story on the mayor's meeting with the governor. *Adjective.*
—**1.** On, in, or into the inner side or part of within. I opened the door of the house and stepped *inside.* **2.** Indoors. The children played *inside* because of the rain. *Adverb.*
—In, into, or on the inner side or part of. I looked *inside* the closet for my coat. *Preposition.*
• **inside out.** **1.** So that the inside is facing out. Your sweater is turned *inside out.*

2. Completely; thoroughly. They had worked at the office so many years that they knew their job *inside out.*
in·side (in′sīd′ *or* in sīd′ *or* in′sīd′) *noun, plural* **insides;** *adjective; adverb; preposition.*

insignia A badge, medal, or other mark showing a person's rank, position, or membership. The police officer wore the *insignia* of a captain.
in·sig·ni·a (in sig′nē ə) *noun, plural* **insignias.**

insignificant Having little or no importance or meaning. My problems seem *insignificant* compared to the difficulties of others.
in·sig·nif·i·cant (in′sig nif′i kənt) *adjective.*

insincere Not sincere; dishonest. It is *insincere* to say that you like a person when you really don't.
in·sin·cere (in′sin sîr′) *adjective.*

insist To demand or say in a strong, firm manner. The doctor *insisted* that the sick patient stay in bed. I *insisted* that my answer was right.
in·sist (in sist′) *verb,* **insisted, insisting.**

inspect **1.** To look at closely and carefully. The official *inspected* our car and declared that it was safe to drive. **2.** To look at formally or officially. The general *inspected* the troops.
in·spect (in spekt′) *verb,* **inspected, inspecting.**

inspection The act of inspecting. The mechanic's *inspection* of the elevator took an hour.
in·spec·tion (in spek′shən) *noun, plural* **inspections.**

inspector A person who makes inspections.
in·spec·tor (in spek′tər) *noun, plural* **inspectors.**

inspiration **1.** The stirring of the mind, feelings, or imagination, especially so that some good idea comes. Hoping for *inspiration,* I looked at a list of possible topics for my essay. **2.** A person or thing that stirs the mind, feelings, or imagination. The author's family was the *inspiration* for many of the characters in the novel. **3.** A sudden, bright

---

at; āpe; fär; câre; end; mē; it; īce; pîerce; hot; ōld; sông, fôrk; oil; out; up; ūse; rüle; pùll; tûrn; chin; sing; shop; thin; _this_; hw in white; zh in treasure. The symbol ə stands for the unstressed vowel sound in about, taken, pencil, lemon, and circus.

idea. Your plan to put your bed on a platform was an *inspiration*.
in·spi·ra·tion (in′spə rā′shən) *noun, plural* **inspirations.**

inspire **1.** To stir the mind, feelings, or imagination of. The senator's speech *inspired* the audience. **2.** To fill with a strong, encouraging feeling. Success in school *inspired* me with hope for the future. **3.** To move to action. What *inspired* you to take up knitting?
in·spire (in spīr′) *verb,* **inspired, inspiring.**

install **1.** To put in place for use or service. We had a new air conditioner *installed* today. **2.** To place a person in an office with a ceremony. The new club president will be *installed* at the next meeting.
in·stall (in stôl′) *verb,* **installed, installing.**

installment **1.** One of the parts of a sum of money that is owed and is to be paid at particular times. My parents paid for our new car in thirty-six monthly *installments*. **2.** A part of a story that is issued or shown separately. The book was first published in a magazine in weekly *installments*.
in·stall·ment (in stôl′mənt) *noun, plural* **installments.**

instance An example; case. There are many *instances* of immigrants becoming famous Americans.
• **for instance.** As an example or illustration. I enjoy many team sports, *for instance,* baseball, football, basketball, and hockey.
in·stance (in′stəns) *noun, plural* **instances.**

instant **1.** A very short period of time; moment. For an *instant,* lightning lit up the sky. **2.** A particular moment. I want you to leave this *instant! Noun.*
—1. Without delay; immediate. The computer gave us an *instant* reply to our question. **2.** Very important or necessary; urgent. The town had an *instant* need for help during the flood. **3.** Needing only additional liquid to prepare. I added hot water to the *instant* mashed potatoes for dinner. *Adjective.*
in·stant (in′stənt) *noun, plural* **instants;** *adjective.*

instantly At once; without delay. I picked up a very hot frying pan and *instantly* dropped it.
in·stant·ly (in′stənt lē) *adverb.*

instead In place of another person or thing. When my friend got sick and couldn't baby-sit, I baby-sat *instead*. The recipe called for butter, but we used margarine *instead*.

• **instead of.** As a substitute for; in place of. We watched television *instead of* going to the movies.
in·stead (in sted′) *adverb.*

instep The arched upper part of the human foot between the toes and the ankle.
in·step (in′step′) *noun, plural* **insteps.**

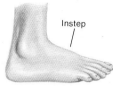
instep

instill To put in or introduce little by little. The English teachers *instilled* a love of books into their pupils.
in·still (in stil′) *verb,* **instilled, instilling.**

instinct A way of acting or behaving that a person or animal is born with and does not have to learn. Birds build nests by *instinct*.
in·stinct (in′stingkt′) *noun, plural* **instincts.**

instinctive Having to do with a way of acting or behaving that a person or animal is born with and does not have to learn. Building a nest is *instinctive* behavior in a bird.
in·stinc·tive (in stingk′tiv) *adjective.*

institute A school or other organization that is set up for a special purpose. Both of my parents are doctors at the medical *institute* for cancer research. *Noun.*
—To set up; establish. The people living on the block got together and *instituted* a weekly clean-up campaign. *Verb.*
in·sti·tute (in′sti tüt′ *or* in′sti tūt′) *noun, plural* **institutes;** *verb,* **instituted, instituting.**

institution **1.** An organization that is set up for a special purpose. A school is an *institution* of learning. **2.** A custom or practice that has been followed for a long time. Having Thanksgiving dinner at my grandparents' house is an *institution* in our family.
in·sti·tu·tion (in′sti tü′shən *or* in′sti tū′shən) *noun, plural* **institutions.**

instruct **1.** To show how to do or use something; teach. Has someone *instructed* you in the correct use of the saw? **2.** To give directions or orders to. Our folks *instructed* us to lock the door when we left.
in·struct (in strukt′) *verb,* **instructed, instructing.**

instruction **1.** The act of teaching. We learned how to swim from the coach's *instruction*. **2.** An explanation or direction. If you follow the *instructions,* you can put the model airplane together easily.
in·struc·tion (in struk′shən) *noun, plural* **instructions.**

instructor A person who instructs; teacher. My friend is a swimming *instructor* at the town pool.
   in·struc·tor (in struk′tər) *noun, plural* **instructors.**

The **instructor** uses his own body to teach anatomy.

instrument **1.** A device used for doing a certain kind of work; tool. The dental hygienist used a sharp *instrument* to scrape my teeth. **2.** A device for producing musical sounds. Our music teacher plays the guitar, flute, and several other *instruments.*
   in·stru·ment (in′strə mənt) *noun, plural* **instruments.**

insulate To cover or surround with a material that slows or stops the flow of electricity, heat, or sound. The electrician *insulated* the electric wire with rubber. Our house is *insulated* so that it stays warm inside in winter.
   in·su·late (in′sə lāt′) *verb,* **insulated, insulating.**

insulation **1.** The act of insulating or the condition of being insulated. *Insulation* of the water pipes keeps them from freezing in winter. **2.** Material that is used to slow or stop the flow of electricity, heat, or sound. The builders put fiberglass *insulation* under the roof of our new house.
   in·su·la·tion (in′sə lā′shən) *noun.*

insult To hurt the feelings or pride of. You *insulted* your friends when you refused to attend their party. *Verb.*
—A remark or action that hurts someone's feelings or pride. My old friend wouldn't say hello to me, and this was a painful *insult.* *Noun.*
   in·sult (in sult′ *for verb;* in′sult′ *for noun*) *verb,* **insulted, insulting;** *noun, plural* **insults.**

insurance Protection against loss or damage. A person who wants insurance agrees to pay a small amount of money at regular times to a company. In exchange, the company promises to pay a certain amount in case of death, accident, fire, or theft. My parents' medical *insurance* paid for the doctors' bills when I broke my arm.
   in·sur·ance (in shùr′əns) *noun.*

insure To protect by insurance. The car is *insured* against accident or theft.
   in·sure (in shùr′) *verb,* **insured, insuring.**

intake **1.** The amount of something taken in. I was advised to increase my *intake* of liquids while I had a cold. **2.** A place in a channel or pipe where a liquid or gas is taken in.
   in·take (in′tāk′) *noun, plural* **intakes.**

integrate **1.** To make open to people of all races. The town *integrated* all its schools long ago. **2.** To bring parts together into a whole. The reporter tried to *integrate* all the different accounts of the accident into one clear story.
   in·te·grate (in′ti grāt′) *verb,* **integrated, integrating.**

integration The act of making something open to people of all races. In 1954 the Supreme Court ruled that there should be *integration* of the public schools of the United States.
   in·te·gra·tion (in′ti grā′shən) *noun.*

integrity Complete honesty. A person who lies has no *integrity.*
   in·teg·ri·ty (in teg′ri tē) *noun.*

intellect The power of the mind to think, learn, and understand, especially when this power is developed and trained; intelligence. That chemistry professor is a scientist of great *intellect.*
   in·tel·lect (in′tə lekt′) *noun.*

intellectual **1.** Having to do with the power to think, learn, and understand. It

I

at; āpe; fär; câre; end; mē; it; īce; pîerce; hot; ōld; sông, fôrk; oil; out; up; ūse; rüle; pùll; tûrn; chin; sing; shop; thin; this; hw in white; zh in treasure. The symbol ə stands for the unstressed vowel sound in about, taken, pencil, lemon, and circus.

385

takes *intellectual* ability to solve difficult problems.   **2.** Having or showing highly developed intelligence. *Intellectual* people often like to think and to express ideas. *Adjective.*
—A person who has a highly developed and trained intelligence. The person who wrote that book was one of the great *intellectuals* of the time. *Noun.*
in·tel·lec·tu·al (in′tə lek′chü əl) *adjective; noun, plural* **intellectuals.**

intelligence   1. The ability to think, learn, and understand.   **2.** Information, especially about foreign countries or enemy forces. The army's *intelligence* showed that the enemy was going to attack at dawn.
in·tel·li·gence (in tel′i jəns) *noun.*

intelligent   Having or showing the ability to think, learn, and understand. *Intelligent* people learn from their mistakes.
in·tel·li·gent (in tel′i jənt) *adjective.*

intend   1. To have in mind as a purpose; plan. I can't play tennis, but I *intend* to learn. What do you *intend* to do with this money?   **2.** To mean for a particular person or purpose. That present is *intended* for you.
in·tend (in tend′) *verb,* **intended, intending.**

intense   1. Very great or strong; extreme. The heat from the iron was so *intense* that it burned a hole in the cloth.   **2.** Having or showing strong feeling, purpose, or effort; concentrated. The worried parent had an *intense* look.
in·tense (in tens′) *adjective.*

intensity   1. The state or quality of being intense. The light from the searchlight shone with great *intensity.*   **2.** Amount or degree of something that varies. The *intensity* of my toothache lessened after I took aspirin.
in·ten·si·ty (in ten′si tē) *noun, plural* **intensities.**

intent   1. Something that is intended; purpose; aim. My *intent* has always been to go to college.   **2.** Meaning; significance. What was the precise *intent* of what you said? *Noun.*
—Having the mind firmly fixed on something. I asked them to stay, but they were *intent* on leaving. We sat quietly, *intent* on our reading. *Adjective.*
in·tent (in tent′) *noun, plural* **intents;** *adjective.*

intention   Something that is intended; purpose; plan. Our *intention* is to wash all the windows before dinner.
in·ten·tion (in ten′shən) *noun, plural* **intentions.**

intentional   Done on purpose; planned; meant. I know that your bumping into me was not *intentional.*
in·ten·tion·al (in ten′shə nəl) *adjective.*

intercept   To stop or take something on its way from one person or place to another. I tried to pass the ball to a teammate, but an opposing player *intercepted* it.
in·ter·cept (in′tər sept′) *verb,* **intercepted, intercepting.**

The player in the blue shirt
intercepts the ball.

interchangeable   Capable of being put or used in place of each other. These typewriter ribbons are *interchangeable,* although they were made by different companies.
in·ter·change·a·ble (in′tər chān′jə bəl) *adjective.*

intercom   A radio or telephone system between different parts of a building, airplane, or ship. The pilot welcomed the passengers over the *intercom.*
in·ter·com (in′tər kom′) *noun, plural* **intercoms.**

interest   1. A desire or eagerness to know about or take part in something. Do you have any *interest* in football?   **2.** Something that causes such a desire. Collecting records is my main *interest* now.   **3.** The power to cause such a desire. That book about horses had little *interest* for us.   **4.** Advantage; benefit. A selfish person cares only about his or her own *interests.*   **5.** Money that is paid for the use of borrowed or deposited money. When a person keeps money in a bank, the bank pays the person a certain amount of interest.   **6.** A right or share. The four partners each have a one-quarter *interest* in the business they own. *Noun.*
—**1.** To cause to want to know about or take part in something. The teacher *interested* me in gardening by giving me several books on the subject.   **2.** To persuade to do or take something. Could I *interest* you in a walk? *Verb.*

in·ter·est (in′trist *or* in′tər ist) *noun, plural* **interests;** *verb,* **interested, interesting.**

interesting Causing or holding interest or attention. The pictures in this book on underwater photography are *interesting.*
in·ter·est·ing (in′tris ting *or* in′tə res′ting) *adjective.*

interfere 1. To take part in the affairs of others without having been asked; meddle. Our neighbor is always *interfering* by giving us advice that we don't want. 2. To disturb or interrupt; prevent or hinder. That loud music *interferes* with my studying.
in·ter·fere (in′tər fîr′) *verb,* **interfered, interfering.**

interference The act of interfering.
in·ter·fer·ence (in′tər fîr′əns) *noun.*

interior 1. The inner side, surface, or part. The *interior* of the cave was dark. 2. The part of a country or region that is away from the coast or border. The *interior* of Australia is mostly desert. *Noun.*
—Having to do with or on the inner side; inside. The *interior* walls of the building are painted gray. *Adjective.*
in·te·ri·or (in tîr′ē ər) *noun, plural* **interiors;** *adjective.*

interjection A word or phrase that shows strong feeling. An interjection can be used alone. "Oh!" and "Hey!" are interjections.
in·ter·jec·tion (in′tər jek′shən) *noun, plural* **interjections.**

intermediate In the middle; being between. The school offers beginning, *intermediate,* and advanced classes in gymnastics.
in·ter·me·di·ate (in′tər mē′dē it) *adjective.*

intermission A time of rest or stopping between periods of activity. There was an *intermission* of ten minutes between the first and second acts of the play.
in·ter·mis·sion (in′tər mish′ən) *noun, plural* **intermissions.**

intern A doctor who has just graduated from medical school and is working in a hospital under more experienced doctors.
in·tern (in′tûrn′) *noun, plural* **interns.**

internal 1. Having to do with or on the inside; interior. The stomach and kidneys are *internal* organs of the body. 2. Having to do with matters within a country; domestic. A national government deals with *internal* affairs as well as foreign policy.
in·ter·nal (in tûr′nəl) *adjective.*

international Having to do with or made up of two or more countries. The United Nations is an *international* organization.
in·ter·na·tion·al (in′tər nash′ə nəl) *adjective.*

interplanetary Having to do with or operating in the space between the planets in the solar system. The movie was about an *interplanetary* flight from Earth to Mars and beyond.
in·ter·plan·e·tar·y (in′tər plan′i ter′ē) *adjective.*

interpret 1. To explain the meaning of. The teacher *interpreted* what the author meant in the poem. 2. To change from one language to another; translate. Since my friends couldn't speak Spanish, I *interpreted* what my cousin from Mexico was saying. 3. To take as meaning; understand. You can usually *interpret* a nod as meaning "yes." 4. To perform so as to bring out the meaning. The pianist *interpreted* the musical piece with great feeling.
in·ter·pret (in tûr′prit) *verb,* **interpreted, interpreting.**

interpretation 1. An explanation of the meaning of something. The two students disagreed in their *interpretation* of the poem. 2. A performance of a work of art that shows the performer's idea of its meaning.
in·ter·pre·ta·tion (in tûr′pri tā′shən) *noun, plural* **interpretations.**

interrogative Having the form of a question. *Adjective.*
—A word or form used in asking a question. In the sentence "Who is it?" the word "who" is an interrogative. *Noun.*
in·ter·rog·a·tive (in′tə rog′ə tiv) *adjective; noun, plural* **interrogatives.**

interrogative sentence A sentence that asks a question. An example of an interrogative sentence is "Where are you going tonight?"

interrupt 1. To break in upon or stop a person who is acting or speaking. Please do not *interrupt* me when I'm talking. 2. To stop for a time; break off. I *interrupted* my work to answer the telephone. A special announcement about the election *interrupted* the television show.
in·ter·rupt (in′tə rupt′) *verb,* **interrupted, interrupting.**

interruption 1. The state of being interrupted. There was an *interruption* in the radio program for a special report. 2. Some-

I

at; āpe; fär; câre; end; mē; it; īce; pîerce; hot; ōld; sông, fôrk; oil; out; up; ūse; rüle; pùll; tûrn; chin; sing; shop; thin; <u>th</u>is; hw in white; zh in treasure. The symbol ə stands for the unstressed vowel sound in about, taken, pencil, lemon, and circus.

thing that interrupts. Please make no *interruption* while the principal is addressing the class.

in·ter·rup·tion (in'tə rup'shən) *noun,*
plural **interruptions.**

intersect **1.** To divide by passing through or cutting across. The river *intersects* the valley. **2.** To meet and cross each other. The two roads *intersect* near our house.

in·ter·sect (in'tər sekt') *verb,* **intersected,**
intersecting.

intersection The place where two or more things meet and cross each other. There was a traffic signal at the *intersection* of the two roads.

in·ter·sec·tion (in'tər sek'shən *or*
in'tər sek'shən) *noun, plural*
intersections.

interstate Between or among two or more states of the United States. We traveled on an *interstate* highway.

in·ter·state (in'tər stāt') *adjective.*

interval A time or space between two things. There was a long *interval* of rain before the sun came out again. There is an *interval* of 20 yards between each streetlight on our block.

• **at intervals.** **1.** With spaces between. Signs were placed *at intervals* along the road. **2.** Now and then; occasionally. We visited them *at intervals* during the summer.

in·ter·val (in'tər vəl) *noun, plural*
intervals.

interview **1.** A meeting in which people talk face to face. I had an *interview* with the store manager for a summer job. **2.** A meeting in which someone, such as a reporter or television commentator, obtains information. The magazine writer arranged for an *interview* with the scientist. **3.** A written or broadcast reproduction of the information obtained at such a meeting. *Noun.*
—To have an interview with. The mayor was *interviewed* about the growing traffic problem. *Verb.*

in·ter·view (in'tər vū') *noun, plural*
interviews; *verb,* **interviewed,**
interviewing.

intestine A long tube that extends down from the stomach. The intestine is part of the digestive system. It carries and digests food and stores waste products. The intestine is divided into the small intestine and the large intestine.

in·tes·tine (in tes'tin) *noun, plural*
intestines.

intimate **1.** Close and familiar; well-acquainted. The two neighbors have been *intimate* friends for years. **2.** Very personal; private. Do you keep a diary of your *intimate* thoughts?

in·ti·mate (in'tə mit) *adjective.*

into **1.** To or toward the inside of. We walked *into* the house. I bit *into* the apple. **2.** So as to make contact with; against. The child bumped *into* the door. **3.** To the form or condition of. The water turned *into* ice. The dish broke *into* pieces. You'll get *into* trouble if you do that. **4.** Dividing. 8 *into* 16 is 2.

in·to (in'tü *or* in'tə) *preposition.*

intolerant Not willing to accept or respect different opinions, practices, or people. I used to be *intolerant* of people who disagreed with my religious beliefs.

in·tol·er·ant (in tol'ər ənt) *adjective.*

intoxicate **1.** To make drunk. Drinking too much liquor will *intoxicate* a person. **2.** To excite greatly. The sights and sounds of the circus *intoxicated* the children.

in·tox·i·cate (in tok'si kāt') *verb,*
intoxicated, intoxicating.

intransitive verb A verb that cannot have a direct object. In the sentence "The clock stopped," "stopped" is an intransitive verb.

in·tran·si·tive verb (in tran'si tiv).

The woman on the left is being **interviewed.**

intricate Very involved or complicated; complex. I took the back off the watch and

looked at its *intricate* parts. This *intricate* dance takes weeks of practice to learn.
in·tri·cate (in'tri kit) *adjective.*

an **intricate** design

intrigue To make curious or interested; fascinate. The story of the sailor's adventures *intrigued* us all.
in·trigue (in trēg') *verb,* **intrigued, intriguing.**

introduce 1. To make known or acquainted. My parents *introduced* me to the dinner guests. 2. To bring into use, knowledge, or notice. The potato was *introduced* to Europe from the New World. 3. To begin; start. The lecturer *introduced* the poem with a short explanation.
in·tro·duce (in'trə düs' *or* in'trə dūs') *verb,* **introduced, introducing.**

introduction 1. The act of introducing or the state of being introduced. We shook hands after our *introduction.* 2. A beginning part that explains what is going to follow. Many books have *introductions.*
in·tro·duc·tion (in'trə duk'shən) *noun, plural* **introductions.**

introductory Giving an introduction; preliminary. The speaker's *introductory* remarks told us what the lecture would be about.
in·tro·duc·to·ry (in'trə duk'tə rē) *adjective.*

Inuit An Eskimo of North America.
I·nu·it (in'ü it, in'ū it) *noun, plural* **Inuit** or **Inuits.**

invade 1. To go or and attack in order to conquer. Enemy troops *invaded* the country. 2. To go or break into something without being asked or wanted. You *invade* my privacy when you read my mail without asking.
in·vade (in vād') *verb,* **invaded, invading.**

invalid¹ A person who is not able to take care of himself or herself because of a sickness or injury. A broken hip made our neighbor an *invalid* for several months.
in·va·lid (in'və lid) *noun, plural* **invalids.**

invalid² Not valid; no longer in force. My bus pass is *invalid* on weekends.
in·val·id (in val'id) *adjective.*

invaluable Having a value or worth that is too great to be measured; extremely valuable; precious. My grandparents own some *invaluable* antiques. My neighbor's *invaluable* advice helped me solve my problem.
in·val·u·a·ble (in val'ū ə bəl) *adjective.*

invasion 1. The entrance of an army into a region in order to conquer it. Throughout its history that country had survived the *invasion* of several enemies. 2. A breaking into something without being asked or wanted.
in·va·sion (in vā'zhən) *noun, plural* **invasions.**

invent 1. To make or think of for the first time; create. Do you know who *invented* the phonograph? 2. To make up. I'm ashamed to say I *invented* an excuse for being late.
in·vent (in vent') *verb,* **invented, inventing.**

Word History

The word **invent** comes from a Latin word meaning "to come upon" or "find." At first the word *invent* was used to describe the finding of an answer, the solution to a problem, or the means to do something. This use led to our modern meaning "to make or think of for the first time."

invention 1. The act of inventing. The *invention* of the airplane had a great effect on travel. 2. Something that is invented. Such *inventions* as the telephone and the computer have changed our way of life. 3. A false or untrue story. Their story about seeing a monster is nothing but an *invention.*
in·ven·tion (in ven'chən) *noun, plural* **inventions.**

inventive Good at thinking up new things; creative. The *inventive* campers kept their

at; āpe; fär; câre; end; mē; it; īce; pîerce; hot; ōld; sông; fôrk; oil; out; up; ūse; rüle; pùll; tûrn; chin; sing; shop; thin; this; hw in white; zh in treasure. The symbol ə stands for the unstressed vowel sound in about, taken, pencil, lemon, and circus.

food cool by putting it in a closed jar in the river.

in·ven·tive (in ven'tiv) *adjective.*

inventor   A person who invents. Alexander Graham Bell was the *inventor* of the telephone.

in·ven·tor (in ven'tər) *noun, plural* **inventors.**

inventory   **1.** A detailed list of articles on hand. The *inventory* showed all the goods the clothing store had on its shelves.   **2.** The articles that are on such a list. The store has a large *inventory* of sports equipment.

in·ven·to·ry (in'vən tôr'ē) *noun, plural* **inventories.**

invert   **1.** To turn upside down. *Invert* the bank and try to shake some coins out. **2.** To reverse the order or position of. If you *invert* the letters of the word "star," you have the word "rats."

in·vert (in vûrt') *verb,* **inverted, inverting.**

invertebrate   Having to do with an animal that does not have a backbone. *Adjective.* —An animal that does not have a backbone. Sponges, worms, lobsters, and insects are invertebrates. *Noun.*

in·ver·te·brate (in vûr'tə brit *or* in vûr'tə brāt') *adjective; noun, plural* **invertebrates.**

invest   **1.** To use money to buy something that will make more money. Some people *invest* their savings in stocks and bonds. **2.** To give or spend time or effort. We *invested* many hours in planning the annual class trip.

in·vest (in vest') *verb,* **invested, investing.**

investigate   To look into carefully in order to find facts and get information. The police are responsible for *investigating* crimes.

in·ves·ti·gate (in ves'ti gāt') *verb,* **investigated, investigating.**

investigation   The act of investigating. The *investigation* of the moon has been accomplished by astronauts.

in·ves·ti·ga·tion (in ves'ti gā'shən) *noun, plural* **investigations.**

investment   **1.** The act of investing money, time, or effort. They made a lot of money on that *investment* in real estate. **2.** The amount of money that is invested. How large is your *investment* in your friend's business?   **3.** Something in which money is invested. That savings certificate was a good *investment.*

in·vest·ment (in vest'mənt) *noun, plural* **investments.**

investor   A person or company that invests money.

in·ves·tor (in ves'tər) *noun, plural* **investors.**

invisible   Not able to be seen; not visible. Oxygen is an *invisible* gas.

in·vis·i·ble (in viz'ə bəl) *adjective.*

invitation   A written or spoken request to do something. Have you received an *invitation* to the party?

in·vi·ta·tion (in'vi tā'shən) *noun, plural* **invitations.**

invite   **1.** To ask someone to go somewhere or to do something. Please *invite* your friends to come with us to the concert.   **2.** To ask for; request. The teacher *invited* questions from the students on the arithmetic lesson. **3.** To risk causing. To fail to do your homework is to *invite* trouble.

in·vite (in vīt') *verb,* **invited, inviting.**

involuntary   **1.** Not done willingly or by choice; not voluntary. I let out an *involuntary* cry when I accidentally stuck myself with the pin.   **2.** Happening without a person's control. Breathing is an *involuntary* action.

in·vol·un·tar·y (in vol'ən ter'ē) *adjective.*

involve   **1.** To have as a necessary part; include. This job as a salesperson *involves* a great deal of traveling.   **2.** To bring into difficulty. I tried not to become *involved* in the argument.   **3.** To take up completely; absorb. We were *involved* all day in household chores.

in·volve (in volv') *verb,* **involved, involving.**

inward   Toward the inside or center. The front gate opens *inward. Adverb.* —Of or toward the inside. I opened the heavy door with an *inward* push. *Adjective.*

in·ward (in'wərd) *adverb; adjective.*

inwardly   **1.** Toward the inside; inward. **2.** In the mind; privately. Although the tightrope walkers seemed calm, they were *inwardly* terrified.

in·ward·ly (in'wərd lē) *adverb.*

inwards   Another spelling of the adverb **inward.** Both the front door and the back door open *inwards.* Look up **inward** for more information.

in·wards (in'wərdz) *adverb.*

iodine   **1.** A chemical element that occurs as shiny gray crystals. It is found in seaweed and saltwater. Iodine is used in medicine and in photography.   **2.** A brown medicine that contains iodine. It is put on cuts to kill germs.

i·o·dine (ī'ə dīn' *or* ī'ə dēn') *noun.*

ion An atom or group of atoms that has an electrical charge.

　i·on (ī′ən *or* ī′on) *noun, plural* **ions.**

-ion A *suffix* that means: **1.** The act of. *Discussion* means the act of discussing. **2.** The condition of being. *Confusion* means the state of being confused. The suffix *-tion* has the same meanings.

Iowa A state in the north-central United States. Its capital is Des Moines.

　I·o·wa (ī′ə wə) *noun.*

Word History

　The name **Iowa** comes from a name of a tribe of American Indians who lived in what is now Iowa. Pioneers gave this name to the area's largest river. Later it was chosen as the name of the state.

Iran A country in southwestern Asia. This country was formerly known as **Persia.**

　I·ran (i ran′) *noun.*

Iraq A country in southwestern Asia.

　I·raq (i rak′) *noun.*

Ireland **1.** An island west of Great Britain that is divided into two countries, **Ireland** and **Northern Ireland.** **2.** The country called the **Republic of Ireland** that is in the southern part of this island.

　Ire·land (īr′lənd) *noun.*

iris **1.** The round, colored part of the eye. The iris is between the cornea and the lens. It controls the amount of light that enters the eye. **2.** A plant that has long leaves shaped like swords and large, showy flowers.

　i·ris (ī′ris) *noun, plural irises.*

Irish **1.** The people of Ireland or their descendants in other countries. **2.** A language spoken in Ireland.

　I·rish (ī′rish) *noun.*

iris

Irish setter A hunting dog that originally came from Ireland. It has a coat of silky, reddish hair.

iron **1.** A gray-white metal. Iron is the most important metal and is used in making steel. It is magnetic and is a good conductor of heat and electricity. All plants and animals need iron. Iron is a chemical element. **2.** Any of various tools made of iron or a similar metal.

The cowhand branded the cattle with a hot *iron.* **3.** An appliance with a flat surface that is heated and used to press or smooth cloth. The laundry used a large *iron* to press shirts. **4. irons.** Heavy chains that are used to keep a prisoner from moving. *Noun.*
—**1.** Made of iron. The lion's cage has *iron* bars. **2.** Strong and hard. I have an *iron* will once I make up my mind to do something. *Adjective.*
—To press or smooth with a heated iron. Can you *iron* your own shirt? *Verb.*

　• **to iron out.** To settle, adjust, or eliminate. We talked for an hour and *ironed out* our differences. *Verb.*

　i·ron (ī′ərn) *noun, plural* **irons;** *adjective; verb,* **ironed, ironing.**

irony A way of speaking or writing in which what a person says is the opposite of what he or she really means or feels. To say "Oh, wonderful!" when you hear bad news is irony.

　i·ro·ny (ī′rə nē) *noun.*

Iroquois A member of a confederation of American Indian tribes of New York.

　Ir·o·quois (ir′ə kwoi′) *noun, plural* **Iroquois.**

irregular **1.** Not following a pattern; unequal or uneven in length, shape, or spacing. The *irregular* row of trees had gaps and clusters in it. My work hours are *irregular;* some days I work for eight hours and some for only two. **2.** Not smooth; bumpy or rugged. The surface of the moon is *irregular.* **3.** Not going by a rule, custom, or habit; unusual. It's *irregular* to call a teacher by his or her first name.

　ir·reg·u·lar (i reg′yə lər) *adjective.*

irregularity **1.** The quality of being irregular. The *irregularity* of rainfall in this area makes it hard for farmers to know when to plant. **2.** Something that goes against a pattern, rule, or custom. That lone hill is the only *irregularity* in the flat landscape.

　ir·reg·u·lar·i·ty (i reg′yə lar′i tē) *noun, plural* **irregularities.**

irresistible Not capable of being resisted or opposed. The delicious watermelon was *irresistible* to the children.

　ir·re·sist·i·ble (ir′i zis′tə bəl) *adjective.*

---

at; āpe; fär; câre; end; mē; it; īce; pîerce; hot; ōld; sông, fôrk; oil; out; up; ūse; rüle; pull; tûrn; chin; sing; shop; thin; this; hw in white; zh in treasure. The symbol ə stands for the unstressed vowel sound in about, taken, pencil, lemon, and circus.

I

irresponsible   Not trustworthy or reliable; not responsible. It would be *irresponsible* to borrow a book and not return it.
ir·re·spon·si·ble (ir′i spon′sə bəl) *adjective.*

irrigate   To supply land with water through streams, channels, or pipes. The farmer *irrigated* the dry land so that crops could be grown.
ir·ri·gate (ir′i gāt′) *verb,* **irrigated, irrigating.**

irrigation   The act of supplying land with water. *Irrigation* made it possible for crops to grow in the desert.
ir·ri·ga·tion (ir′i gā′shən) *noun.*

irrigation

irritate   **1.** To make angry or impatient, especially over a small thing. Your constant teasing *irritates* me. **2.** To make sore or sensitive. The smoke *irritated* my eyes.
ir·ri·tate (ir′i tāt′) *verb,* **irritated, irritating.**

is   A form of the present tense of **be** that is used with *he, she, it,* or the name of a person, place, or thing. She *is* not home. He *is* four years old. Who *is* at the door?
is (iz) *verb.*

-ish   A *suffix* that means: **1.** Of or having to do with. *Polish* means of or having to do with Poland.   **2.** Like. *Childish* means like a child.   **3.** Somewhat. *Yellowish* means somewhat yellow.

island   **1.** A body of land that is completely surrounded by water. An island is smaller than a continent. Ireland is an island. **2.** Something that looks like an island. There was an *island* of floating ice in the middle of the lake.
is·land (ī′lənd) *noun, plural* **islands.**

islander   A person who was born or is living on an island.
is·land·er (ī′lən dər) *noun, plural* **islanders.**

isle   An island. Isles are usually small islands. ▲ Other words that sound like this are **aisle** and **I'll.**
isle (īl) *noun, plural* **isles.**

islet   A little island. ▲ Another word that sounds like this is **eyelet.**
is·let (ī′lit) *noun, plural* **islets.**

isn't   Shortened form of "is not." Our dog *isn't* a puppy anymore.
is·n't (iz′ənt) *contraction.*

isolate   To place or set apart; separate from others. I was *isolated* from my sister and brother when I had the mumps so that they wouldn't get it.
i·so·late (ī′sə lāt′) *verb,* **isolated, isolating.**

isosceles triangle   A triangle with two sides of equal length.
i·sos·ce·les triangle (ī sos′ə lēz).

Israel   A country in the Middle East.
Is·ra·el (iz′rē əl *or* iz′rā əl) *noun.*

Israeli   A person who was born in or is a citizen of Israel. *Noun.*
—Having to do with Israel or the people of Israel. *Adjective.*
Is·rae·li (iz rā′lē) *noun, plural* **Israelis;** *adjective.*

issue   **1.** The act of sending or giving out. I was in charge of the *issue* of tents to all the campers.   **2.** Something that is sent or given out. Do you have the latest *issue* of this magazine?   **3.** A subject that is being discussed or considered. The student council debated the *issue* of safety in the hallways. *Noun.*
—To send or give out. The Department of the Treasury *issues* paper money and coins. The teacher *issued* books to all the students. *Verb.*
is·sue (ish′ü) *noun, plural* **issues;** *verb,* **issued, issuing.**

-ist   A *suffix* that means: **1.** A person who does or makes something. *Tourist* means a person who tours. *Novelist* means a person who writes novels.   **2.** A person who is skilled in or works at something. *Biologist* means a person who is skilled in biology. *Machinist* means a person who is skilled in using machinery.   **3.** A person who supports or is in favor of. *Socialist* means a person who is in favor of socialism.

isthmus   A narrow strip of land that connects two larger land areas. An isthmus has water on two sides. North America and South America are connected by an isthmus.
isth·mus (is′məs) *noun, plural* **isthmuses.**

it   **1.** A thing, person, or situation that is being talked about. My cousin threw the ball to me and I caught *it*. I met someone interesting today; do you know who *it* was?   **2.** *It* is used with some verbs that show an action or condition. *It* is raining hard. *It* isn't very cold this morning. *Pronoun.*

—In certain children's games, the person who has to do something special. In playing tag, the person who is *it* has to chase the other players. *Noun.*

   it (it) *pronoun; noun.*

Italian   **1.** A person who was born in or is a citizen of Italy.   **2.** The language spoken in Italy. *Noun.*

—Of or having to do with Italy, its people, or their language. *Adjective.*

   I·tal·ian (i tal′yən) *noun, plural* **Italians;** *adjective.*

italic   Of or having to do with a style of type whose letters slant to the right. *This sentence is printed in italic type. Adjective.*

—**italics.** Italic type. Print the sentence in *italics. Noun.*

   i·tal·ic (i tal′ik) *adjective; noun, plural* **italics.**

italicize   To print in italics.

   i·tal·i·cize (i tal′ə sīz′) *verb,* **italicized, italicizing.**

Italy   A country in southern Europe.

   It·a·ly (it′ə lē) *noun.*

itch   **1.** A tickling or stinging feeling in the skin. An itch is relieved by scratching or rubbing.   **2.** A restless, uneasy feeling or longing. Some people have an *itch* to travel around the world. *Noun.*

—**1.** To have or cause a tickling or stinging feeling in the skin. The rash on my hand *itches.*   **2.** To have a restless, uneasy feeling or desire. The bully was *itching* for a fight. *Verb.*

   itch (ich) *noun, plural* **itches;** *verb,* **itched, itching.**

item   **1.** A single thing in a group or list. There are many rare *items* in that stamp collection. The shopping list has ten *items* on it.   **2.** A bit of news. There was an *item* in the newspaper about the football team's victory.

   i·tem (ī′təm) *noun, plural* **items.**

itemize   To make a list of each item in a group. If you *itemize* all your expenses, you can make up a budget.

   i·tem·ize (ī′tə mīz′) *verb,* **itemized, itemizing.**

it'll   Shortened form of "it will." *It'll* soon be spring. *It'll* take me an hour to get home.

   it'll (it′əl) *contraction.*

its   Of, belonging to, or having to do with it. The cat licked *its* paw. The last volume of the encyclopedia is not in *its* proper place. ▲ Another word that sounds like this is **it's.**

   its (its) *adjective.*

it's   **1.** Shortened form of "it is." *It's* cold out today.   **2.** Shortened form of "it has." *It's* been nice to see you. ▲ Another word that sounds like this is **its.**

   it's (its) *contraction.*

itself   Its own self. The cat washed *itself.* The yard is full of weeds, but the house *itself* is in good condition.

   it·self (it self′) *pronoun.*

-ity   A *suffix* that means the state or quality of being. The word *finality* means the state or quality of being final.

-ive   A *suffix* that means doing or tending to do something. The word *destructive* means tending to destroy.

I've   Shortened form of "I have." *I've* no money. *I've* been home all day.

   I've (īv) *contraction.*

ivory   **1.** A smooth, hard, white substance. It forms the tusks of elephants, walruses, and certain other animals. Piano keys are often made of ivory.   **2.** A creamy white color. *Noun.*

—**1.** Made of or like ivory. The piano has *ivory* keys.   **2.** Having the color ivory. The room was *ivory* with red trim. *Adjective.*

   i·vo·ry (ī′və rē) *noun, plural* **ivories;** *adjective.*

The elephants' tusks are **ivory.**

Ivory Coast   A country in western Africa.

ivy   **1.** A vine with shiny, evergreen leaves. Some kinds of ivy climb up walls or grow along the ground.   **2.** Any plant that climbs up walls or grows along the ground.

   i·vy (ī′vē) *noun, plural* **ivies.**

I

at; āpe; fär; câre; end; mē; it; īce; pîerce; hot; ōld; sông, fôrk; oil; out; up; ūse; rüle; půll; tûrn; chin; sing; shop; thin; **th**is; hw in white; zh in treasure. The symbol ə stands for the unstressed vowel sound in about, taken, pencil, lemon, and circus.

J j

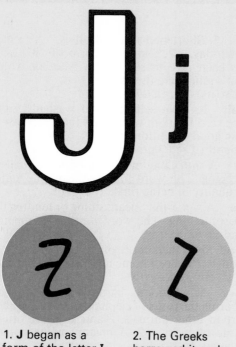

1. **J** began as a form of the letter **I** in the Middle East nearly 4,000 years ago.

2. The Greeks borrowed it and wrote it as a straight line with a short stroke at either end.

3. An ancient tribe near Rome borrowed the letter about 2,800 years ago, writing it without the top or bottom strokes.

4. The Romans borrowed this form of the letter and used it to represent the vowel sound *i* and the consonant sound *j*.

5. Later, the older letter, **I**, was used only for the vowel sound, while **J** was used for the consonant sound.

---

j, J The tenth letter of the alphabet.
  j, J (jā) *noun, plural* **j's, J's.**

jab To poke with something pointed. I accidentally *jabbed* my finger with a pin while I was sewing. *Verb.*
  —A poke with something pointed. Please give me a *jab* if I start to fall asleep during the movie. *Noun.*
  jab (jab) *verb,* **jabbed, jabbing;** *noun, plural* **jabs.**

jack **1.** A tool that is used for lifting heavy objects a short distance above the ground. The mechanic raised the front end of the car with a *jack* in order to change the flat tire. **2.** A playing card with a picture of a young man on it. **3. jacks.** A game that is played with a small rubber ball and little pieces of metal that are also called jacks. A player has to pick up a number of the metal jacks while bouncing and catching the ball with the same hand. *Noun.*
  —To lift with a jack. The mechanic at the gas station *jacked* the car up so we could see what needed to be repaired. *Verb.*
  jack (jak) *noun, plural* **jacks;** *verb,* **jacked, jacking.**

Word History

The word **jack** comes from the man's name *Jack.* Tools and other objects are often named after personal names. This same word *jack* is also found in the words *jack-in-the-box, jackknife, jack-o'-lantern, jackpot,* and *jackrabbit.*

jackal An animal that looks like a small dog. A jackal has a pointed face, a bushy tail, and ears that point straight up. Jackals live on plains in Africa and Asia. They eat plants, small animals, and the remains of other animals' prey.
  jack·al (jak'əl) *noun, plural* **jackals.**

jacket **1.** A short coat. Our team wears *jackets* with the name of the team across the back. **2.** An outer covering for a record or book. On the back of this book *jacket* there is a picture of the author.
  jack·et (jak'it) *noun, plural* **jackets.**

jack-in-the-box A toy that is made up of a box that a doll pops out of when the lid is opened.
  jack-in-the-box (jak' in thə boks') *noun, plural* **jack-in-the-boxes.**

jackknife A large pocketknife.
  jack·knife (jak'nīf') *noun, plural* **jackknives** (jak'nīvz').

jack-o'-lantern A pumpkin that has been hollowed out and carved to look like a face. Jack-o'-lanterns are used at Halloween as lanterns or decorations.
jack-o'-lan·tern (jak′ə lan′tərn) *noun, plural* **jack-o'-lanterns.**

jack-o'-lantern

jackpot The largest prize in a game or contest. That game show has a *jackpot* of $100,000.
• **to hit the jackpot. 1.** To win a jackpot. Someone from our town *hit the jackpot* on a television game show. **2.** To have a great success or unexpected good fortune. My parents' friends *hit the jackpot* with their new business.
jack·pot (jak′pot′) *noun, plural* **jackpots.**

jackrabbit A large hare of western North America that has very long ears and strong back legs for leaping.
jack·rab·bit (jak′rab′it) *noun, plural* **jackrabbits.**

jade A hard, green stone that is used for jewelry and carved ornaments.
jade (jād) *noun, plural* **jades.**

jagged Having sharp points that stick out. Some eagles build nests on *jagged* cliffs.
jag·ged (jag′id) *adjective.*

jaguar A large animal that belongs to the cat family. The short fur of a jaguar is golden and is marked with black rings with spots in their centers. Jaguars are found in Mexico, Central America, and South America.
jag·uar (jag′wär) *noun, plural* **jaguars.**

jaguar

jail A building where people who are waiting for a trial or who have been found guilty of breaking the law are kept; prison. *Noun.*
—To put or keep in a jail. The police *jailed* the people they caught robbing the bank. *Verb.*
jail (jāl) *noun, plural* **jails;** *verb,* **jailed, jailing.**

jam¹ 1. To press or squeeze into a tight space. The traveler tried to *jam* too many clothes into one small suitcase. People *jammed* onto the bus to get to work. **2.** To fill or block completely. Cars *jammed* the road to the beach. The store was *jammed* with customers. **3.** To become or cause to become stuck so as not to work. The rifle *jammed* when the soldier tried to fire it. Rust and dirt *jammed* the lock on the gate. **4.** To push hard. The driver *jammed* on the brakes to stop the car. **5.** To bruise or crush. I *jammed* my hand when I closed the drawer on it. *Verb.*
—**1.** A mass of people or things so crowded together that it is difficult to move. We were three hours late because we got stuck in a traffic *jam* in the city. **2.** A difficult situation. The tourists were in a real *jam* when the police found the stolen money in their car. *Noun.*
jam (jam) *verb,* **jammed, jamming;** *noun, plural* **jams.**

jam² A sweet food made by boiling fruit and sugar together until it is thick. Jam is used as a spread on bread or other foods.
jam (jam) *noun, plural* **jams.**

Jamaica An island country in the Caribbean Sea.
Ja·mai·ca (jə mā′kə) *noun.*

Jan. An abbreviation for *January.*

jangle 1. To make or cause to make a harsh or unpleasant sound. The metal blinds *jangled* in the wind. The janitor *jangled* a bunch of keys. **2.** To irritate or upset. The noise from the party at my neighbor's apartment *jangled* me and made it hard to concentrate. *Verb.*
—A harsh or unpleasant sound. Everything fell from the shelf with a loud *jangle. Noun.*
jan·gle (jang′gəl) *verb,* **jangled, jangling;** *noun, plural* **jangles.**

janitor A person whose job is to take care of and clean a building.
jan·i·tor (jan′i tər) *noun, plural* **janitors.**

J

at; āpe; fär; câre; end; mē; it; īce; pîerce; hot; ōld; sông, fôrk; oil; out; up; ūse; rüle; pu̇ll; tûrn; chin; sing; shop; thin; this; hw in white; zh in treasure. The symbol ə stands for the unstressed vowel sound in about, taken, pencil, lemon, and circus.

January The first month of the year. January has thirty-one days.
Jan·u·ar·y (jan′ū er′ē) *noun.*

Word History

The Romans named **January** after *Janus*, their god of doors and gates. A holiday in his honor was held during this month. Janus was shown with two faces that looked in opposite directions. His holiday was probably held in January because this month looks in two directions, back on the year that has passed and ahead to the year to come.

Japan An island country in the Pacific Ocean. It is off the eastern coast of Asia.
Ja·pan (jə pan′) *noun.*

Japanese **1.** A person who was born in or is a citizen of Japan. **2.** The language of Japan. *Noun.*
—Having to do with Japan, its people, or their language. *Adjective.*
Jap·a·nese (jap′ə nēz′ *or* jap′ə nēs′) *noun, plural* **Japanese;** *adjective.*

Japanese beetle A beetle that came to the United States from Asia. Its head parts are blue-green and its wings are copper colored. The larvae feed on roots, and the adults eat leaves and flowers and can be serious pests.

Japanese beetle

jar¹ **1.** A container that has a wide mouth. A jar is usually made out of glass, plastic, or pottery. Peanut butter, pickles, and jelly often come in jars. **2.** The amount that is contained in a jar. This recipe calls for a small *jar* of olives.
jar (jär) *noun, plural* **jars.**

jar² **1.** To shake or vibrate. The explosion *jarred* the building. **2.** To have a harsh, unpleasant effect on. The sudden clatter of dishes *jarred* my nerves. *Verb.*
—A shake or sudden movement; shock. We wrapped the glass bowl well so all the *jars* and bumps it would get in the mail would not break it. *Noun.*
jar (jär) *verb,* **jarred, jarring;** *noun, plural* **jars.**

javelin **1.** A light spear that was once used as a weapon. **2.** A long, thin spear of metal that is thrown in athletic contests. The athlete who throws it the farthest wins.
jave·lin (jav′lin) *noun, plural* **javelins.**

jaw **1.** The lower or upper bony part of the mouth. The jaws give shape to the mouth and hold the teeth in place. **2.** A similar mouth part or parts in insects and other animals without backbones. **3.** One of two parts of a tool that can be closed to grasp or hold something. The *jaws* of this vise hold the piece of wood tight while I sand it.
jaw (jô) *noun, plural* **jaws.**

jay Any of various noisy, brightly colored birds that belong to the crow family. Some jays, like the common blue jay, have crests on their heads.
jay (jā) *noun, plural* **jays.**

jay

jaywalk To cross the street without paying attention to the traffic lights or laws.
jay·walk (jā′wôk′) *verb,* **jaywalked, jaywalking.**

jazz Music that has strong rhythm and accented notes that fall in unexpected places. Jazz was originated by American blacks in the late nineteenth century. Musicians frequently add notes of their own as they play a jazz piece.
jazz (jaz) *noun.*

jealous **1.** Fearful of losing someone's love to another person. A young child will often be *jealous* of a new baby in the family. **2.** Having envy of a person, or what a person has or can do. I used to be *jealous* of my friend's ability to play football well.
jeal·ous (jel′əs) *adjective.*

jealousy A jealous feeling. My *jealousy* over my friend's new bicycle was silly.
jeal·ous·y (jel′ə sē) *noun, plural* **jealousies.**

jeans Pants made from denim or similar strong cloth and worn for work or informal dress. I wore old *jeans* while cleaning the house.
jeans (jēnz) *plural noun.*

jeep A small, powerful automobile that

moves easily over poor, rough roads. The jeep was originally used by soldiers.

jeep (jēp) *noun, plural* **jeeps.**

jelly A soft, firm food. The most common kind of jelly is made from fruit juice boiled with sugar and is eaten with bread, toast, muffins, and other foods. Peanut butter and *jelly* sandwiches are my favorite. *Noun.*
—To make into or become jelly. My neighbor *jellies* plums every fall. *Verb.*

jel·ly (jel′ē) *noun, plural* **jellies;** *verb,* **jellied, jellying.**

jellyfish A sea animal with a body that is soft and firm like jelly and has the shape of an umbrella. There are many long, slender tentacles hanging down from this body. The jellyfish uses its tentacles to sting its prey and move the prey to its mouth.

jel·ly·fish (jel′ē fish′) *noun, plural* **jellyfish** or **jellyfishes.**

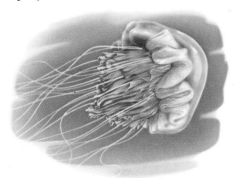

jellyfish

jeopardy The danger of loss, injury, or death. Firefighters are in *jeopardy* when they enter burning buildings.

jeop·ard·y (jep′ər dē) *noun.*

jerk A sudden, sharp pull or twist; start. The worker gave the rope a *jerk.* The car moved forward with a *jerk. Noun.*
—To move with a sudden, sharp motion. I *jerked* my head around when I heard the loud noise. The fishing rod *jerked* when the fish bit the bait. *Verb.*

jerk (jûrk) *noun, plural* **jerks;** *verb,* **jerked, jerking.**

jerkin A short, tight jacket that does not have sleeves. Jerkins were worn by men and boys in the 1500s and 1600s.

jer·kin (jûr′kin) *noun, plural* **jerkins.**

jersey 1. A cloth that is knitted by machine out of wool, cotton, or other materials. Jersey is very soft and is used to make clothing. 2. A sweater or shirt made out of this cloth. It is pulled on over the head.

jer·sey (jûr′zē) *noun, plural* **jerseys.**

jest A playful joke; prank. I meant my remark as a *jest,* and I'm sorry it hurt your feelings. *Noun.*
—To speak or act in a playful way. You must be *jesting;* I can't believe what you're saying is true. *Verb.*

jest (jest) *noun, plural* **jests;** *verb,* **jested, jesting.**

Jesus The founder of the Christian religion. He was born in about 4 B.C. and died in about 29 A.D. He is also called Christ or Jesus Christ.

Je·sus (jē′zəs).

jet 1. A stream of liquid, gas, or vapor that comes with force from a small opening. This fountain is a *jet* of water that rises fifty feet into the air. 2. An aircraft that is driven by a stream of hot gas. When we went to Puerto Rico, we flew on a *jet. Noun.*
—To shoot forth in a stream; spurt. Water *jetted* onto the street from the break in the water pipe. *Verb.*

jet (jet) *noun, plural* **jets;** *verb,* **jetted, jetting.**

jet-propelled Driven by a stream or jet of hot gas. The *jet-propelled* rocket was launched into an orbit around the earth.

jet-pro·pelled (jet′prə peld′) *adjective.*

jet propulsion A method of moving an airplane, rocket, or other vehicle in one direction by using a stream or jet of hot gas forced out in the opposite direction.

jetty

jetty 1. A wall that is built out into a body of water. Jetties can be built of rocks, wood,

at; āpe; fär; câre; end; mē; it; īce; pîerce; hot; ōld; sông, fôrk; oil; out; up; ūse; rüle; pull; tûrn; chin; sing; shop; thin; this; hw in white; zh in treasure. The symbol ə stands for the unstressed vowel sound in about, taken, pencil, lemon, and circus.

concrete, or steel. Jetties are used to control the flow of a river or to protect the coast from breaking waves. **2.** A platform where boats and ships can dock; wharf.

jet·ty (jet′ē) *noun, plural* **jetties.**

Jew **1.** A person who is descended from the ancient Hebrews. **2.** A person whose religion is Judaism.

Jew (jü) *noun, plural* **Jews.**

jewel **1.** A precious stone; gem. Jewels are used in rings and bracelets because of their beauty. They are also used in watches or machines because they are very hard and last a long time. **2.** A valuable necklace, pin, bracelet, or other ornament that is decorated with precious stones. **3.** A person or thing that has great value or excellence. That battleship is the *jewel* of the navy.

jew·el (jü′əl) *noun, plural* **jewels.**

jeweler A person who makes, repairs, or sells jewelry or watches.

jew·el·er (jü′ə lər) *noun, plural* **jewelers.**

jewelry

jewelry Necklaces, pins, bracelets, or other ornaments. Jewelry is often decorated with precious stones.

jew·el·ry (jü′əl rē) *noun.*

Jewish Having to do with Jews, their religion, or their culture.

Jew·ish (jü′ish) *adjective.*

jib A sail in the shape of a triangle that is set in front of the mast and is attached to the bow.

jib (jib) *noun, plural* **jibs.**

jiffy A very short time; moment. Wait for me; I'll be there in a *jiffy.*

jif·fy (jif′ē) *noun.*

jig **1.** A fast, lively dance. **2.** The music for this dance. The bagpipes played a *jig,* and everyone danced. *Noun.*
—**1.** To dance a jig. **2.** To move with a rapid jerking or bobbing motion. As I watched, the float on my fishing line *jigged* up and down. *Verb.*

jig (jig) *noun, plural* **jigs;** *verb,* **jigged, jigging.**

jigsaw A saw that has a narrow blade set vertically in a frame. A jigsaw is used to cut along wavy or curved lines.

jig·saw (jig′sô′) *noun, plural* **jigsaws.**

jigsaw puzzle A puzzle made up of small pieces that have irregular shapes and can be fitted together to make a picture.

jingle To make or cause to make a tinkling or ringing sound. Whenever the kitten moved, the bell on its collar *jingled.* The child shook the bank to *jingle* the coins inside. *Verb.*
—**1.** A tinkling or ringing sound. Whenever the cowhands walked you could hear the *jingle* of their spurs. **2.** A light, short tune that is easy to remember. I can't stop humming a new *jingle* I've heard on the radio. *Noun.*

jin·gle (jing′gəl) *verb,* **jingled, jingling;** *noun, plural* **jingles.**

jinx **1.** A person or thing that is believed to bring bad luck. **2.** A spell of bad luck. There seems to be a *jinx* on this garden, because nothing will grow. *Noun.*
—To bring or try to bring bad luck to. Some people think a black cat will jinx you if it walks in front of you. *Verb.*

jinx (jingks) *noun, plural* **jinxes;** *verb,* **jinxed, jinxing.**

job **1.** A position of work; employment. Did you get a *job* in the grocery store for the summer? **2.** Something that has to be done; piece of work. It's my *job* to feed and walk the dog. The repair *job* on the television set will cost fifty dollars.

job (job) *noun, plural* **jobs.**

jockey A person who rides horses in races.

jock·ey (jok′ē) *noun, plural* **jockeys.**

jog To run or move at a slow, steady pace. My parents *jog* in the park every morning for exercise. *Verb.*
—A slow, steady pace. The runner moved at a *jog. Noun.*

jog (jog) *verb,* **jogged, jogging;** *noun, plural* **jogs.**

join **1.** To put or fasten together so as to become one. Tie a knot to *join* the two ends of the rope. We all *joined* hands and formed a circle. **2.** To come together or come together with. Where do the two rivers *join?*

This road *joins* the main highway just ahead.
3. To become a member of. Two students who are graduating from high school plan to *join* the army.   **4.** To come into the company of; get together with. Our friends at the other table *joined* us after they had finished eating.   **5.** To take part with others. Many people *joined* in singing the old songs.

join (join) *verb,* **joined, joining.**

joint   **1.** The place or part where two or more bones meet or come together. The knee and the elbow are joints. Most joints act like hinges, allowing the bones to move in one or more directions.   **2.** The part or space between two joints. The ring was stuck on the middle *joint* of my finger.   **3.** The place or part where any two or more things meet or come together. The old chair was very unsteady because the *joint* in one of its legs was coming loose. *Noun.*
—Belonging to or done by two or more people. You and I have a *joint* responsibility to feed and walk the dog after school. My parents are *joint* owners of a gas station. *Adjective.*

joint (joint) *noun, plural* **joints;** *adjective.*

joke   Something that is said or done to make people laugh. The child started to tell a *joke* but forgot the funny line at the end. My parents pretended to forget my birthday as a *joke. Noun.*
—To tell or make jokes. At the party everyone laughed and *joked. Verb.*

joke (jōk) *noun, plural* **jokes;** *verb,* **joked, joking.**

jolly   Full of fun; merry and cheerful. The person who was dressed as a clown was very *jolly.* We sat around the campfire singing songs and having a *jolly* time.

jol·ly (jol′ē) *adjective,* **jollier, jolliest.**

jolt   To move or cause to move with a sudden, rough jerk or jerks. The jeep *jolted* along the dirt road. When the car behind us hit our car, we were *jolted* out of our seats. *Verb.*
—**1.** A jerk or jar. The bus stopped with a *jolt.* **2.** A surprise or shock. The bad news gave us quite a *jolt. Noun.*

jolt (jōlt) *verb,* **jolted, jolting;** *noun, plural* **jolts.**

jonquil   A fragrant

jonquils

yellow flower that is a kind of daffodil. A jonquil has a short center petal shaped like a cup. Jonquils grow from bulbs. The flower garden in the park is full of *jonquils* and tulips in the spring.

jon·quil (jong′kwəl) *noun, plural* **jonquils.**

Jordan   A country in the Middle East.

Jor·dan (jôr′dən) *noun.*

jostle   To bump or push roughly. A group of people at the stage door *jostled* one another to get a chance to meet the actors after the show. *Verb.*
—A bump or push. I accidentally gave the person next to me a *jostle* as I tried to get to the back of the bus. *Noun.*

jos·tle (jos′əl) *verb,* **jostled, jostling;** *noun, plural* **jostles.**

jot   To write quickly or briefly. I always keep a pad by the telephone so I can *jot* down messages before I forget them.

jot (jot) *verb,* **jotted, jotting.**

journal   **1.** A regular record or account. A diary is one kind of journal. Each student was told to keep a *journal* during the summer. The scientist entered the results of the experiments in a *journal.*   **2.** A magazine or newspaper. The medical *journal* published a report on the doctor's most recent discoveries.

jour·nal (jûr′nəl) *noun, plural* **journals.**

journalism   The writing and publishing of articles on news and opinions in newspapers, magazines, and similar publications.

jour·nal·ism (jûr′nə liz′əm) *noun.*

journalist   A writer who works for a newspaper or magazine.

jour·nal·ist (jûr′nə list) *noun, plural* **journalists.**

journey   A long trip. The Pilgrims crossed the Atlantic on their *journey* to the New World. *Noun.*
—To make a trip; travel. My cousin wants to *journey* through Africa after graduating from college. *Verb.*

jour·ney (jûr′nē) *noun, plural* **journeys;** *verb,* **journeyed, journeying.**

joust   A formal contest or combat between two knights on horseback. Each knight was armed with a lance and wore armor. *Noun.*
—To fight or take part in a joust. The two

at; āpe; fär; câre; end; mē; it; īce; pîerce; hot; ōld; sông, fôrk; oil; out; up; ūse; rūle; pùll; tûrn; chin; sing; shop; thin; this; hw in white; zh in treasure. The symbol ə stands for the unstressed vowel sound in about, taken, pencil, lemon, and circus.

J

knights *jousted* to win the favor of the royal couple. *Verb.*

joust (joust) *noun, plural* **jousts;** *verb,* **jousted, jousting.**

joust

jovial   Full of fun; merry; jolly. I'm always in a *jovial* mood on my birthday.
jo·vi·al (jō′vē əl) *adjective.*

jowl   Heavy, loose flesh hanging from or under the lower jaw.
jowl (joul) *noun, plural* **jowls.**

joy   **1.** A strong feeling of happiness or delight. The young children jumped with *joy* when their grandparents arrived for a visit. **2.** A person or thing that causes a strong feeling of happiness. The friendly, helpful children were a *joy* to their neighbors.
joy (joi) *noun, plural* **joys.**

joyful   Feeling, showing, or causing great happiness; glad. The parents had *joyful* looks on their faces when they saw that their child was not hurt in the accident. The couple's wedding anniversary was a *joyful* occasion.
joy·ful (joi′fəl) *adjective.*

joyous   Joyful or happy. The wedding was a *joyous* occasion for the families of the bride and groom.
joy·ous (joi′əs) *adjective.*

joystick   A control shaped like a rod that is attached to some computers. The joystick controls figures on the monitor. This word is also spelled **joy stick.**
joy·stick (joi′stik′) *noun, plural* **joysticks.**

jr. or **Jr.**   An abbreviation for *junior.*

jubilant   Feeling or showing great joy. The players were *jubilant* over their victory.
ju·bi·lant (jü′bə lənt) *adjective.*

Judaism   The religion of the Jews. It is based chiefly on a belief in one God and the teachings of the Old Testament.
Ju·da·ism (jü′dē iz′əm) *noun.*

judge   **1.** To agree on a verdict or make a decision about a case in a court of law. The court could not *judge* the case properly because of a lack of evidence.   **2.** To settle or decide. Three men and three women have been chosen to *judge* the dog show.   **3.** To form an opinion of. *Judge* the movie by seeing it yourself; don't listen to what other people say about it.   **4.** To find something wrong with. Don't be quick to *judge* other people. *Verb.*
—**1.** A person who decides on questions and disagreements in a court of law. A judge can be chosen by a government official or elected by the voters.   **2.** A person who decides the winner in a contest or dispute.   **3.** A person who knows enough about a subject to give an opinion about it. My cousin is a good *judge* of horses. *Noun.*
judge (juj) *verb,* **judged, judging;** *noun, plural* **judges.**

judgment   **1.** The ability to decide or judge. They showed good *judgment* in deciding to buy this car.   **2.** An opinion. In my *judgment,* that student is very good at drawing.   **3.** A verdict agreed on or a decision made by a court of law. It was the *judgment* of the court that the accused person was guilty.
judg·ment (juj′mənt) *noun, plural* **judgments.**

judicial   Having to do with courts of law or judges. It is the responsibility of the *judicial* branch of government to make the meaning of the law clear.
ju·di·cial (jü dish′əl) *adjective.*

judo   A way of fighting and defending oneself without weapons.
ju·do (jü′dō) *noun.*

Word History

The word **judo** comes from a Japanese word that means "gentle way." This method of fighting is not so rough as other ways of fighting.

jug   A rounded container that has a handle and a narrow neck. A jug is used for holding liquids and is usually made out of pottery, glass, or plastic.
jug (jug) *noun, plural* **jugs.**

juggle   **1.** To keep balls or other objects in continuous motion from the hands into the air by skillful tossing and catching. That clown can *juggle*

jug

three oranges at once without letting one drop to the floor. **2.** To change in order to cheat or deceive. The criminals *juggled* the records to hide the theft from the company.

jug·gle (jug′əl) *verb,* **juggled, juggling.**

juice **1.** The liquid from vegetables, fruits, or meats. I love fresh orange *juice.* **2.** A fluid produced inside the body. The stomach releases digestive *juices* when we eat.

juice (jüs) *noun, plural* **juices.**

juicy Having much juice. The *juicy* peach squirted my shirt when I bit into it.

juic·y (jü′sē) *adjective,* **juicier, juiciest.**

July The seventh month of the year. July has thirty-one days.

Ju·ly (jů lī′) *noun.*

Word History

The Romans named the month of **July** in honor of *Julius* Caesar because he was born in this month.

---

jumble To mix or throw into confusion. All the toys were *jumbled* together in the box. *Verb.*

—A confused mixture or condition; mess. The child threw everything in the closet into a *jumble* in trying to find a missing shoe. *Noun.*

jum·ble (jum′bəl) *verb,* **jumbled, jumbling;** *noun, plural* **jumbles.**

jumbo Extremely large.

jum·bo (jum′bō) *adjective.*

Word History

The word **jumbo** comes from *Jumbo,* the name of a large elephant that appeared about one hundred years ago in a famous circus.

---

jump **1.** To use a push from one's feet to move through or into the air. The shortstop had to *jump* to catch the ball. I can *jump* off the high diving board. **2.** To move or get up suddenly. The students *jumped* to their feet when they heard the fire alarm ring. **3.** To pass over through the air. The horse *jumped* the fence. **4.** To increase or rise in a quick or unexpected way. The price of gasoline *jumped. Verb.*

—**1.** The act of jumping. The fox made a *jump* across the stream. **2.** The distance covered by jumping. The athlete made a *jump* of 20 feet. **3.** A sudden move or start.

4. A sudden increase or rise. My parents complained about the *jump* in the price of milk. *Noun.*

• **to jump at.** To accept quickly and eagerly. I *jumped at* the chance to work at the library during the summer.

jump (jump) *verb,* **jumped, jumping;** *noun, plural* **jumps.**

jumper A dress that is in one piece and does not have sleeves. A jumper is usually worn over a blouse or sweater.

jump·er (jum′pər) *noun, plural* **jumpers.**

jump rope **1.** A game played by swinging a rope over the head and under the feet of one-self or another person or persons who jump up to let the rope pass underneath. Jump rope may be played alone, or two people may swing the rope while one or more other players jump. **2.** The rope used to play this game.

jump ropes

junction **1.** A place where things meet or cross. A place where railroad tracks meet is called a junction. **2.** The act of joining or the condition of being joined.

junc·tion (jungk′shən) *noun, plural* **junctions.**

June The sixth month of the year. June has thirty days.

June (jün) *noun.*

Word History

The Romans named the month of **June** in honor of *Juno,* queen of the gods in Roman mythology.

---

at; āpe; fär; câre; end; mē; it; īce; pîerce; hot; ōld; sông, fôrk; oil; out; up; ūse; rüle; půll; tûrn; chin; sing; shop; thin; <u>th</u>is; hw in white; zh in treasure. The symbol ə stands for the unstressed vowel sound in about, taken, pencil, lemon, and circus.

J

401

jungle Land in tropical areas that is covered with a thick mass of trees, vines, and bushes.
  jun·gle (jung′gəl) *noun, plural* **jungles.**

junior **1.** The younger of two. The word "junior" is used after the name of a son who has the same name as his father. Robert Edwards, *Junior,* is the son of Robert Edwards, Senior. **2.** Of or for younger people. The twins are playing in the *junior* tennis tournament. **3.** Having to do with the year before the last year in high school or college. **4.** Having a lower position or rank. A *junior* executive does not have as important a job as a senior executive. *Adjective.*
—**1.** A person who is younger than another. My cousin is my *junior* by three years. **2.** A student who is in the year before the last year of high school or college. *Noun.*
  jun·ior (jün′yər) *adjective; noun, plural* **juniors.**

junior high school A school between elementary school and high school. It usually includes grades seven and eight and sometimes grades six or nine.

juniper An evergreen shrub or tree. Junipers have purple cones that look like berries.
  ju·ni·per (jü′nə pər) *noun, plural* **junipers.**

junk¹ Old pieces of metal, wood, rags, or other things that are thrown away; trash.
  junk (jungk) *noun.*

junk² A sailing ship usually found in China and southeastern Asia.
  junk (jungk) *noun, plural* **junks.**

junk food Food that has a large amount of sugar or fat and small amounts of other nutrients.

junkyard A place where junk is collected and stored, especially a place for cars that are old or wrecked.
  junk·yard (jungk′yärd′) *noun, plural* **junkyards.**

Jupiter The largest planet in our solar system. It is the fifth closest planet to the sun.
  Ju·pi·ter (jü′pi tər) *noun.*

juror A member of a jury. The *jurors* left the court to decide on their verdict.
  ju·ror (jür′ər) *noun, plural* **jurors.**

jury **1.** A group of people chosen to hear the facts in a matter that has been brought before a court of law. The jury makes a decision on the matter based on the facts they hear and on the law. **2.** A group of people who choose the winners and award the prizes in a contest.
  ju·ry (jür′ē) *noun, plural* **juries.**

just Fair and right; honest. The principal is a stern but *just* person. *Adjective.*
—**1.** Not more or less than; exactly. You said *just* what I was going to say. **2.** A little while ago. If you're looking for your parents, I *just* saw them in the garage. **3.** By very little; barely. Because of all the traffic, they *just* made their plane on time. **4.** No more than; only. I'm not really hurt; it's *just* a scratch. *Adverb.*
  just (just) *adjective; adverb.*

justice **1.** Fair or right treatment or action. The lawyer demanded *justice* for the innocent person. **2.** The quality or condition of being fair and right. *Justice* demands that all people be treated as equals in a court of law. **3.** A judge of the Supreme Court of the United States.
  jus·tice (jus′tis) *noun, plural* **justices.**

justify **1.** To show to be fair or reasonable. You *justified* our teacher's faith in you when you won the scholarship. **2.** To prove to be without blame or guilt. The lawyer tried to *justify* the suspect's action.
  jus·ti·fy (jus′tə fī′) *verb,* **justified, justifying.**

jut To stick out. The lighthouse is on a piece of land that *juts* into the sea.
  jut (jut) *verb,* **jutted, jutting.**

jute A strong fiber that is used to make heavy cord or a coarse material called burlap. Jute comes from a plant that is grown mostly in tropical areas of Asia.
  jute (jüt) *noun, plural* **jutes.**

juvenile **1.** Of or for children or young people. Our town library keeps its collection of *juvenile* books on the second floor. **2.** Childish. The teenagers were criticized for their *juvenile* behavior. *Adjective.*
—A young person. Our youth center offers many activities for *juveniles. Noun.*
  ju·ve·nile (jü′və nəl *or* jü′və nīl′) *adjective; noun, plural* **juveniles.**

Jupiter

K k

1. The earliest form of the letter **K** was a symbol used by ancient tribes in the Middle East. It looked something like a hand.

2. In the early Hebrew alphabet, this letter was written a little differently.

3. When the ancient Greeks borrowed this letter, they first made it like a backwards capital **K**.

4. Several hundred years later, the Greeks turned this letter around.

5. The ancient Romans borrowed this new form of the letter and did not change it very much.

6. Our modern capital **K** in English looks similar to the capital **K** as it was written 2,000 years ago.

k, K   The eleventh letter of the alphabet.
   k, K (kā) *noun, plural* **k's, K's.**

kaleidoscope   A tube that contains mirrors and often small pieces of colored glass or other colored objects at one end. When the other end of the tube is held up to the eye and turned, the mirrors reflect a series of changing patterns.
   ka·lei·do·scope (kə lī′də skōp′) *noun, plural* **kaleidoscopes.**

Kampuchea   A country in southeastern Asia. It is also called **Cambodia.**
   Kam·pu·che·a (kam′pü chē′ə) *noun.*

kangaroo   An animal that has small front legs, very strong back legs for leaping, and a long, powerful tail for balance. The female carries her young in a pouch for about six months after birth. Kangaroos are marsupials and live in Australia and New Guinea.
   kan·ga·roo (kang′gə rü′) *noun, plural* **kangaroos** or **kangaroo.**

kangaroos

Kans.   An abbreviation for *Kansas.*

Kansas   A state in the west-central United States. Its capital is Topeka.
   Kan·sas (kan′zəs) *noun.*

Word History

Kansas was named for a river in the northeastern part of the state. The word was an Indian name for a tribe that used to live near this river.

katydid   A large, green insect that resembles a grasshopper. A katydid has two long antennae and wings that look like leaves. By rubbing its two wings together, the male katydid can make a shrill noise that sounds like its name.
   ka·ty·did (kā′tē did′) *noun, plural* **katydids.**

K

kayaks

kayak **1.** A canoe first used by the Eskimo, who made it by stretching animal skins over a frame. There is an opening in the center where a person can sit. **2.** A light canoe that looks like this, usually made of fiberglass.
kay·ak (kī′ak) *noun, plural* **kayaks.**

keel A wooden or metal piece that runs along the center of the bottom of many ships and boats. The keel supports the whole structure of a boat and helps keep it balanced.
• **to keel over.** **1.** To turn upside down; capsize. The little sailboat *keeled over* in the strong wind. **2.** To fall over suddenly; collapse. The heat in the crowded subway caused two people to *keel over.*
keel (kēl) *noun, plural* **keels.**

keen **1.** Sharp or quick in seeing, hearing, or thinking. That hound has a *keen* sense of smell. **2.** Full of enthusiasm; eager. I am *keen* about sports of all kinds. **3.** Having a sharp cutting edge or point. A *keen* knife is an important tool in any kitchen.
keen (kēn) *adjective,* **keener, keenest.**

keep **1.** To continue to have, hold, or do. My parents let me *keep* the kitten that followed me home. *Keep* mixing the batter until it is smooth. **2.** To continue or cause to continue in a certain place or condition; stay or cause to stay. The teacher asked the class to *keep* quiet. The doctor *kept* the sick patient in the hospital for a week. **3.** To store or put. Do you *keep* your shoes in the closet? **4.** To hold back or stop. The cold weather may *keep* the plants from budding. **5.** To be faithful to; fulfill. I *kept* my promise and mowed the lawn. **6.** To take care of. That farmer *keeps* a big herd of cows. **7.** To write or make entries in. Do you *keep* a diary? *Verb.*
—**1.** Food and a place to live. When the children grew up, they all left home and started earning their own *keep.* **2.** The strongest part in a castle or fort. *Noun.*

• **to keep up.** To continue. The noise of the machines *kept up* all through the night.
keep (kēp) *verb,* **kept, keeping;** *noun, plural* **keeps.**

keep

keeping **1.** The condition of being in charge of or having control over something. We left the key to our house in our neighbor's *keeping* while we were on vacation. **2.** Agreement or harmony. Your jokes were not in *keeping* with the serious nature of the occasion.
keep·ing (kē′ping) *noun.*

keg A small metal or wooden barrel. Beer is often put in kegs.
keg (keg) *noun, plural* **kegs.**

kelp A large, brown seaweed that grows in cold waters along ocean coasts. Kelp provides food for people and animals and is used to make many products.
kelp (kelp) *noun.*

kennel **1.** A building where dogs are kept. **2.** A place where dogs are raised and trained or cared for while an owner is away.
ken·nel (ken′əl) *noun, plural* **kennels.**

Kentucky A state in the east-central United States. Its capital is Frankfort.
Ken·tuck·y (kən tuk′ē) *noun.*

Word History

Kentucky comes from an Indian name for this area that probably meant "meadowland" or "flat land." Later the name was used for the river running through this flat land south of the Ohio River. When Virginia established a county in this area in 1776, it used the name *Kentucky.* When the county was made a state, it kept the same name.

Kenya A country in east-central Africa.
Ken·ya (ken′yə *or* kēn′yə) *noun*.

kept Past tense and past participle of **keep**.
I *kept* the ball I found in the playground
when no one claimed it. Look up **keep** for
more information.
kept (kept) *verb*.

kerchief A piece of cloth that is worn over
the head or around the neck.
ker·chief (kûr′chif) *noun, plural*
kerchiefs.

kernel **1.** The whole grain or seed of wheat,
corn, and some other plants. When we eat
corn on the cob, we are eating the kernels.
2. The soft part inside the shell of a seed,
fruit, or nut. **3.** The central or most necessary part. There is a *kernel* of truth in what
our opponent says. ▲ Another word that
sounds like this is **colonel**.
ker·nel (kûr′nəl) *noun, plural* **kernels**.

kerosene A thin, colorless oil that is made
from petroleum. Kerosene was once used as
a fuel for lamps before the electric light bulb
was invented. Today it is used in fuel for jet
engines, portable heaters, and farm equipment.
ker·o·sene (ker′ə sēn′) *noun*.

ketchup A thick red sauce that is made of
tomatoes, onions, vinegar, salt, sugar, and
spices. Ketchup is used to give flavor to
hamburgers, french fries, and many other
foods. This word is also spelled **catsup**.
ketch·up (kech′əp) *noun*.

kettle A metal pot used for boiling liquids
or for cooking foods.
ket·tle (ket′əl) *noun, plural* **kettles**.

kettledrum A drum, shaped like a bowl,
that is made of copper or brass with a thin
material called parchment stretched over the
top.
ket·tle·drum (ket′əl drum′) *noun, plural*
kettledrums.

key[1] **1.** A shaped piece of metal that can
open a lock on a door, drawer, or other thing.
We lost the *key,* so we can't unlock the front
door. **2.** Anything that is used or shaped
like such a piece of metal. I used a roller
skate *key* to tighten the skates on my shoes.
3. Something that solves or explains. The
detective found the *key* to the mystery. There
is a *key* to the pronunciations in this dictionary at the bottom of this page. **4.** Something that leads to or is a way of getting
something. Hard work can sometimes be the
key to success. **5.** The part on a machine or
musical instrument that is pressed down to
make it work. The keys of a typewriter or
computer are marked with different num-

bers, symbols, and letters of the alphabet. A
piano has black and white keys. **6.** A group
of notes in which all the notes are related to
each other and are based on the lowest note
in the group. *Noun*.
—Very important; chief. The quarterback
holds a *key* position on a football team. *Ad-*
jective.
—To regulate or adjust the musical pitch of.
The musicians in the orchestra have to *key*
their instruments before a performance.
Verb. ▲ Another word that sounds like this
is **quay**.
key (kē) *noun, plural* **keys;** *adjective; verb,*
keyed, keying.

key[2] A low island or reef. There are keys
along the southern tip of Florida. ▲ Another
word that sounds like this is **quay**.
key (kē) *noun, plural* **keys**.

keyboard A set or row of keys. A piano, a
typewriter, or a computer has a keyboard.
key·board (kē′bôrd′) *noun, plural*
keyboards.

keyhole The hole in a lock where a key is
put.
key·hole (kē′hōl′) *noun, plural* **keyholes**.

keystone The top stone in the middle of
an arch. The keystone
holds the other stones
of the arch together.
key·stone (kē′stōn′)
noun, plural
keystones.

kg An abbreviation
for *kilogram*.

khaki **1.** A dull, yellowish brown color.
2. A heavy cotton
cloth of this color.
Khaki is most often
used to make military
uniforms.
3. khakis. A military
uniform or other
clothing made from khaki. *Noun*.
khak·i (kak′ē *or* kä′kē) *noun, plural*
khakis.

Keystone

keystone

kick **1.** To hit or strike out with the foot.
The mule *kicked* the fence. Knowing how to

at; āpe; fär; câre; end; mē; it; īce; pîerce; hot; ōld;
sông, fôrk; oil; out; up; ūse; rüle; pull; tûrn; chin;
sing; shop; thin; <u>this</u>; hw in white; zh in treasure.
The symbol ə stands for the unstressed vowel
sound in about, taken, pencil, lemon, and circus.

kick correctly is important when you are learning to swim.   **2.** To move by hitting with the foot. The child *kicked* a stone along on the way home from school.   **3.** To spring back when fired. The rifle *kicked* so hard that it hurt the hunter's shoulder. *Verb.*

—**1.** A hit or blow with the foot. The police opened the door with a *kick.*   **2.** The sudden springing back of a gun when it is fired. The *kick* of the gun bruised my shoulder.   **3.** A feeling of excitement; thrill. Did you get a *kick* out of going for your first ride on an airplane? *Noun.*

> **kick** (kik) *verb,* **kicked, kicking;** *noun, plural* **kicks.**

kickoff   A kick of the ball in football or soccer that begins the action. The crowd in the stands stood up to watch the opening *kickoff* of the football game.

> **kick·off** (kik′ôf′) *noun, plural* **kickoffs.**

kid   **1.** A young goat.   **2.** A child. ▲ This meaning is used mostly in everyday conversation.   **3.** A kind of leather that is made from the skin of a young goat. These gloves are made of tan *kid. Noun.*

—To make fun of or tease. My friends *kidded* me about my new short haircut. I was only *kidding* when I told my parents there wouldn't be any school today. *Verb.*

> **kid** (kid) *noun, plural* **kids;** *verb,* **kidded, kidding.**

kidnap   To seize or hold a person by force. Three people *kidnaped* the rich couple and demanded one million dollars for their release.

> **kid·nap** (kid′nap′) *verb,* **kidnaped** or **kidnapped, kidnaping** or **kidnapping.**

kidney   **1.** Either of two organs in the body that are shaped like a very large bean. The kidneys are located underneath the lowest ribs in the back. They filter out waste from the bloodstream and pass it to the bladder in the form of urine.   **2.** The kidneys of certain animals when used as food.

> **kid·ney** (kid′nē) *noun, plural* **kidneys.**

kill   **1.** To end the life of. Automobile accidents *kill* thousands of Americans every year. Many deer are *killed* during the hunting season.   **2.** To end; destroy. Failing the test *killed* the student's chances of getting an A in the course.   **3.** To use up. While we were waiting for the bus, we *killed* fifteen minutes by looking in store windows.   **4.** To cause much pain to; hurt very much. I hurt my back and it's *killing* me. *Verb.*

—**1.** The act of killing. Once the dogs had chased the animal up a tree, the hunters moved in for the *kill.*   **2.** An animal that is killed. The wolf dragged its *kill* back to the den to feed its family. *Noun.*

> **kill** (kil) *verb,* **killed, killing;** *noun, plural* **kills.**

killdeer

killdeer   A noisy bird whose song sounds like its name. The killdeer is a plover of North America, Central America, and western South America. It has brownish feathers with two black stripes along the breast.

> **kill·deer** (kil′dîr′) *noun, plural* **killdeers** or **killdeer.**

kiln   A furnace or oven for burning, baking, or drying. A kiln is used in making bricks, pottery, and charcoal.

> **kiln** (kiln *or* kil) *noun, plural* **kilns.**

kilo–   A *prefix* that means 1,000. A *kilowatt* means 1,000 watts.

kilogram   A unit of weight and mass in the metric system. A kilogram is equal to 1,000 grams, or about two pounds and three ounces.

> **kil·o·gram** (kil′ə gram′) *noun, plural* **kilograms.**

kilometer   A unit of length in the metric system. A kilometer is equal to 1,000 meters, or about 0.62 of a mile.

> **ki·lom·e·ter** (ki lom′i tər *or* kil′ə mē′tər) *noun, plural* **kilometers.**

kilowatt   A unit of electrical power. A kilowatt is equal to 1,000 watts.

> **kil·o·watt** (kil′ə wot′) *noun, plural* **kilowatts.**

kilt   A pleated, plaid skirt that reaches to the knees. Scottish men sometimes wear kilts.

> **kilt** (kilt) *noun, plural* **kilts.**

kilt

kimono   A loose robe that is tied with a sash. Kimonos are worn traditionally by both men and women in Japan.

ki·mo·no (ki mō′nə) *noun, plural* **kimonos.**

kimonos

kin A person's whole family; relatives. All of my neighbor's *kin* live in Alabama.
kin (kin) *noun.*

kind¹ Gentle, generous, and friendly. A kind person is thoughtful of others. It was *kind* of you to help me.
kind (kīnd) *adjective,* **kinder, kindest.**

kind² **1.** A group of things that are the same in some way. The whales are one *kind* of mammal. That store sells many different *kinds* of sports equipment. **2.** One of a group of people or things that are different or special in some way. That's not the *kind* of saw that can cut a metal pipe.
kind (kīnd) *noun, plural* **kinds.**

kindergarten A class in school for children between the ages of four and six. It comes before first grade.
kin·der·gar·ten (kin′dər gär′tən) *noun, plural* **kindergartens.**

Word History

The word **kindergarten** comes from a German word that means "children's garden."

kindle **1.** To begin burning or cause to burn. The campers *kindled* the logs of the campfire. The trash *kindled* when a spark landed on it. **2.** To stir or excite. The factory's pollution of the river *kindled* the anger of the people who lived nearby.
kin·dle (kin′dəl) *verb,* **kindled, kindling.**

kindling Small pieces of dry material, such as twigs and leaves, used to start a fire. The campers searched the woods for *kindling* to light the campfire.
kind·ling (kind′ling) *noun.*

kindly Having or showing kindness. I looked for the *kindly* faces of my friends in the audience before I gave my speech. *Adjective.*
—1. In a kind or gentle manner. The police officer spoke *kindly* to the lost child. **2.** As a favor; please. *Kindly* mail this letter for me on your way to school. **3.** Very much; sincerely. Thank you *kindly* for your help. *Adverb.*
kind·ly (kīnd′lē) *adjective,* **kindlier, kindliest;** *adverb.*

kindness **1.** The quality or condition of being kind. The *kindness* of my friends when I was sick made me very grateful. **2.** A thoughtful, friendly act; favor. The guests thanked their hosts for their many *kindnesses.*
kind·ness (kīnd′nis) *noun, plural* **kindnesses.**

king **1.** A man who rules a country. A man usually becomes king because he is related to the ruler before him and usually rules until he dies. **2.** A person or thing that is the best of its group. The lion is often called the *king* of the jungle. **3.** A playing card with a picture of a king on it. **4.** An important piece in a game of chess or checkers.
king (king) *noun, plural* **kings.**

kingdom **1.** A country that is ruled by a king or a queen. **2.** One of the main divisions of living things, such as the animal kingdom, the plant kingdom, and the fungus kingdom.
king·dom (king′dəm) *noun, plural* **kingdoms.**

kingfisher Any of various birds that have a short tail and a long beak. A kingfisher can

K

at; āpe; fär; câre; end; mē; it; īce; pîerce; hot; ōld; sông, fôrk; oil; out; up; ūse; rüle; pùll; tûrn; chin; sing; shop; thin; <u>th</u>is; hw in white; zh in treasure. The symbol ə stands for the unstressed vowel sound in about, taken, pencil, lemon, and circus.

dive from a tree branch into the water to catch small fish.

king·fish·er (king′fish′ər) *noun, plural* **kingfishers.**

kingfisher

king-size   Larger or longer than is ordinary. After I bought a *king-size* bed, I had to move my other furniture to make room for it.

king-size (king′sīz′) *adjective.*

kink   **1.** A tight curl of hair, wire, rope, or something similar. Damp weather always makes my hair full of *kinks.* The water wouldn't flow because the hose had a *kink.* **2.** A pain in a muscle; cramp. You got a *kink* in your back because you tried to move the heavy piano alone. *Noun.*
—To form a kink or kinks. The thread *kinked* as I was sewing the button onto the coat. *Verb.*

kink (kingk) *noun, plural* **kinks;** *verb,* **kinked, kinking.**

kiss   To touch with the lips as a sign of greeting or affection. I *kissed* my aunt and uncle before they left. *Verb.*
—**1.** A touch with the lips as a sign of greeting or affection. The children gave each parent a *kiss* before going to bed.   **2.** A small piece of candy that is sometimes wrapped in foil. The store had chocolate *kisses* on sale. *Noun.*

kiss (kis) *verb,* **kissed, kissing;** *noun, plural* **kisses.**

kit   **1.** A set of parts or materials to be put together. Have you ever built a model of a rocket from a *kit?*   **2.** A collection of tools or equipment for a particular purpose. My sewing *kit* has a thimble, needles, pins, and thread.

kit (kit) *noun, plural* **kits.**

kitchen   A room or place where food is cooked.

kitch·en (kich′ən) *noun, plural* **kitchens.**

kitchenette   A very small kitchen.

kitch·en·ette (kich′ə net′) *noun, plural* **kitchenettes.**

kite   **1.** A light, wooden frame that is covered with paper, plastic, or cloth. A kite can be flown in the air at the end of a long string. **2.** A hawk that has a hooked bill and long, narrow wings. Some kites have a forked tail.

kite (kīt) *noun, plural* **kites.**

flying a **kite**

kitten   A young cat. The cat gave birth to four *kittens.*

kit·ten (kit′ən) *noun, plural* **kittens.**

kitty   A young cat; a kitten. I called my pet by saying, "Here, *kitty!"*

kit·ty (kit′ē) *noun, plural* **kitties.**

kiwi[1]   A bird that lives in New Zealand. The kiwi has a round body covered with brown feathers that look like fur. It cannot fly.

ki·wi (kē′wē) *noun, plural* **kiwis.**

kiwi[2]   A small, round fruit grown in New Zealand. It has brown, fuzzy skin and green flesh. The kiwi was first grown in China, where it is called the Chinese gooseberry.

ki·wi (kē′wē) *noun, plural* **kiwis.**

km.   An abbreviation for *kilometer.*

knack   A special ability or skill for doing something easily. My classmate has a *knack* for repairing things.

knack (nak) *noun.*

knapsack   A bag made of canvas, leather, or other material that is used for carrying clothes, equipment, or other supplies. A knapsack is strapped over the shoulders and carried on the back.

knap·sack (nap′sak′) *noun, plural* **knapsacks.**

knead To mix and press together with the hands. The baker had to *knead* the dough before baking it. ▴ Another word that sounds like this is **need**.
knead (nēd) *verb*, **kneaded, kneading.**

knee 1. The joint between the thigh and the lower leg. 2. Something that works or looks like a knee.
knee (nē) *noun, plural* **knees.**

kneecap A flat, movable bone in front of the knee. The kneecap protects the knee joint from getting injured.
knee·cap (nē′kap′) *noun, plural* **kneecaps.**

kneel To go down on a bent knee or knees. The knights and ladies *kneeled* before the royal couple.
kneel (nēl) *verb*, **knelt** or **kneeled, kneeling.**

knelt A past tense and a past participle of **kneel**. The scouts *knelt* beside the campfire. Look up **kneel** for more information.
knelt (nelt) *verb*.

knew Past tense of **know**. Who *knew* the answer to the question? Look up **know** for more information. ▴ Other words that sound like this are **gnu** and **new**.
knew (nü *or* nū) *verb*.

knickknack A small object used as an ornament. The mantel was crowded with small figures of animals and other *knicknacks*.
knick·knack (nik′nak′) *noun, plural* **knicknacks.**

knife 1. A tool that is used for cutting. A knife has a sharp blade attached to a handle. 2. The part of a tool or machine that cuts; blade. *Noun*.
—To cut or stab with a knife. *Verb*.
knife (nīf) *noun, plural* **knives;** *verb*, **knifed, knifing.**

knight 1. A soldier in the Middle Ages. A knight gave his loyalty to a king or lord and in return was given the right to hold land. A man had to serve as a page and squire before he could become a knight. 2. A man who holds this title today as an honor for service to his country. In Great Britain, a knight uses the word "Sir" before his name. 3. One of the pieces in a game of chess. A knight is usually in the shape of a horse's head. *Noun*.
—To raise to the rank of knight. The king and queen *knighted* two soldiers for their courage and loyalty. *Verb*. ▴ Another word that sounds like this is **night**.
knight (nīt) *noun, plural* **knights;** *verb*, **knighted, knighting.**

knighthood The rank of a knight. After many years of service to the country, the page was awarded *knighthood* at a grand ceremony.
knight·hood (nīt′hůd′) *noun*.

knit 1. To make cloth or clothing by looping yarn together, either by hand with long needles, or by a machine. I *knitted* a sweater for my grandchild. 2. To join or come together closely and securely. The doctor said that broken bone would take six months to *knit*.
knit (nit) *verb*, **knitted** or **knit, knitting.**

knives Plural of **knife**. These *knives* are not very sharp. Look up **knife** for more information.
knives (nīvz) *plural noun*.

knob 1. A rounded handle for opening a door or drawer, or for working a radio, television, or other machine. The *knob* on the drawer came off in my hand. 2. A rounded lump. There were *knobs* all over the trunk of the huge old tree.
knob (nob) *noun, plural* **knobs.**

knock 1. To strike with a sharp, hard blow or blows; hit. The branch *knocked* the hunter on the head. I *knocked* on the door but no one answered. 2. To push and cause to fall. The cat jumped on the table and *knocked* the lamp over. 3. To make a pounding or rattling noise. The engine of the old car *knocked*. 4. To find something wrong with. It's a good idea; don't *knock* it. *Verb*.
—1. A sharp, hard blow; hit. The player got a *knock* on the head in the soccer game. I heard a *knock* on the door. 2. A pounding or rattling noise. Our old car had a *knock* in the engine. *Noun*.
● **to knock out.** To hit so hard as to make unconscious. The blow on the head *knocked out* the football player.
knock (nok) *verb*, **knocked, knocking;** *noun, plural* **knocks.**

knocker A metal knob or ring that is attached to a door with a hinge. A knocker is used to knock on a door.
knock·er (nok′ər) *noun, plural* **knockers.**

knoll A small, rounded hill.
knoll (nōl) *noun, plural* **knolls.**

knot 1. The place where pieces of thread, string, or cord are tied around each other. Tie

K

at; āpe; fär; câre; end; mē; it; īce; pîerce; hot; ōld; sông, fôrk; oil; out; up; ūse; rüle; půll; tûrn; chin; sing; shop; thin; this; hw in white; zh in treasure. The symbol ə stands for the unstressed vowel sound in about, taken, pencil, lemon, and circus.

the rope around the tree with a tight *knot*. **2.** A tangle or lump. There were *knots* in the dog's coat because it hadn't been brushed for a long time. **3.** A small group of people or things. A *knot* of people waited on the platform for the train. **4.** A dark, hard, round spot in a board. A knot is the spot where a branch grew out of the trunk of a tree. **5.** A measurement of speed used on ships, boats, and aircraft. A knot is the same as one nautical mile per hour, which equals 6,076 feet per hour. *Noun.*
—To tie or tangle in or with a knot or knots. I *knotted* the string around the package. Your hair is all *knotted* from the wind. *Verb.* ▲ Another word that sounds like this is **not**.
> **knot** (not) *noun, plural* **knots;** *verb,* **knotted, knotting.**

knotty **1.** Having, covered with, or full of knots. We used *knotty* wood to make this table. **2.** Difficult to understand or solve. No one got the correct answer to the *knottiest* problem on the test.
> **knot·ty** (not′ē) *adjective,* **knottier, knottiest.**

know **1.** To understand clearly; be certain of the facts or truth of. The police *know* how the accident happened. Do you *know* what causes lightning? **2.** To be acquainted or familiar with. I am a friend of theirs, but I don't *know* their parents. **3.** To have skill or experience with. That student *knows* how to type very well. ▲ Another word that sounds like this is **no**.
> **know** (nō) *verb,* **knew, known, knowing.**

know–how The knowledge of how to do something; practical skill. To fix this lawn mower, you'll need some *know-how* with small engines.
> **know-how** (nō′hou′) *noun.*

knowledge **1.** An understanding that is gained through experience or study. I have enough *knowledge* of football to be able to follow a game. I have no *knowledge* of Dutch. **2.** The fact of knowing. The *knowledge* that the car could slide on the icy road made the driver more careful.
> **knowl·edge** (nol′ij) *noun.*

known Past participle of **know**. A great deal is *known* about the harmful effects of pollution. Look up **know** for more information.
> **known** (nōn) *verb.*

knuckle A joint of a finger.
- **to knuckle under.** To give in; yield. The general refused to *knuckle under* to the enemy's demands.
> **knuck·le** (nuk′əl) *noun, plural* **knuckles.**

koala A furry, chubby animal that lives in Australia. It has large bushy ears, a black nose, and hands that help it grasp the limbs of trees. Koalas are marsupials. The female carries her young in a pouch.
> **ko·a·la** (kō ä′lə) *noun, plural* **koalas.**

koala

Koran The sacred book of Muslims, containing the religious and moral code of Islam.
> **Ko·ran** (kô ran′ *or* kô rän′) *noun.*

Korea A former country in east-central Asia. It is now divided into **North Korea** and **South Korea**.
> **Ko·re·a** (kə rē′ə) *noun.*

Korean **1.** A person who was born in or is a citizen of North Korea or South Korea. **2.** The language spoken in North Korea and South Korea. *Noun.*
—Of or having to do with North Korea or South Korea, its people, or its language. *Adjective.*
> **Ko·re·an** (kə rē′ən) *noun, plural* **Koreans;** *adjective.*

kosher **1.** Prepared according to Jewish ceremonial law. Milk and meat are not served together at a *kosher* meal. **2.** Selling or preparing kosher food. There is a *kosher* butcher's shop on the main street in our neighborhood.
> **ko·sher** (kō′shər) *adjective.*

KS Postal abbreviation for *Kansas.*

Kuwait A country in southwestern Asia.
> **Ku·wait** (kü wāt′) *noun.*

Ky. An abbreviation for *Kentucky.*

KY Postal abbreviation for *Kentucky.*

L

1. Ancient tribes in the Middle East were the first people to use a form of the letter **L** in their alphabets.

2. When the ancient Greeks borrowed this letter, they wrote it by turning it upside down and backwards.

3. Later, the Greeks wrote this letter like an upside-down V.

4. An ancient tribe that settled near Rome went back to the earlier form of **L**.

5. When the Romans borrowed this letter from them, they too used the early form.

6. By about 2,400 years ago, the Romans were writing their **L** much as we write our modern capital **L** today.

I, L The twelfth letter of the alphabet.
I, L (el) *noun, plural* **I's, L's.**

l An abbreviation for *liter.*

La. An abbreviation for *Louisiana.*

LA Postal abbreviation for *Louisiana.*

lab A short form of the word "laboratory." Look up **laboratory** for more information.
lab (lab) *noun, plural* **labs.**

label A piece of cloth, paper, or other material that is fastened to something and gives information about it. The *label* inside the shirt tells the brand name. *Noun.*
—**1.** To put a label on. I can *label* the package you want to mail. **2.** To describe as, using a word or short phrase. The teacher *labeled* the picnic a success. *Verb.*
la·bel (lā′bəl) *noun, plural* **labels;** *verb,* **labeled, labeling.**

labor **1.** Hard work; toil. The farmers were tired after their *labor.* **2.** People who work at jobs that require physical strength or skills, or are members of a union of workers. *Labor* supported the senator for another new term. *Noun.*
—**1.** To do hard work. **2.** To move slowly and with difficulty. The tired runners *labored* up the steep hill. *Verb.*
la·bor (lā′bər) *noun, plural* **labors;** *verb,* **labored, laboring.**

laboratory A room used for doing scientific experiments or for teaching science.
lab·o·ra·to·ry (lab′ər ə tôr′ē *or* lab′rə tôr′ē) *noun, plural* **laboratories.**

Labor Day A holiday in the United States that honors working people. It is celebrated on the first Monday in September.

labor union An association of workers formed to protect and advance their interests. Labor unions help workers obtain better wages and working conditions.

lace **1.** A string or cord used to pull or hold parts together. The *lace* on this shoe broke. **2.** An open fabric of fine threads that form elaborate designs. The dress was trimmed with *lace. Noun.*
—To pull or tighten together with a string or cord. *Lace* up your skates. *Verb.*
lace (lās) *noun, plural* **laces;** *verb,* **laced, lacing.**

Word History

The word **lace** comes from a Latin word meaning "snare" or "noose." *Lace* later came to be used for any cord or string used for tying things together.

L

411

lack To be without or have too little of; need. The town *lacks* a good park. That movie *lacked* excitement. *Verb.*
—**1.** The condition of needing something. The *lack* of rain caused the crops to fail. **2.** Something that is needed or is missing. The most serious *lack* in that person's character is honesty. *Noun.*
> **lack** (lak) *verb,* **lacked, lacking;** *noun, plural* **lacks.**

lacquer A liquid that is put on wood or metal. Lacquer dries quickly to form a shiny coat. *Noun.*
—To coat with lacquer. The worker *lacquered* the wooden chairs. *Verb.*
> **lac·quer** (lak′ər) *noun, plural* **lacquers.** *verb,* **lacquered, lacquering.**

lacrosse A game played by two teams of ten players each. The players use sticks with a net on one end to throw, catch, and carry a ball. Points are scored by getting the ball into a goal.
> **la·crosse** (lə krôs′) *noun.*

> ## Word History
>
> The name **lacrosse** comes from the French word for the staff that a bishop carries. French explorers first saw lacrosse played by Indians in Canada. Supposedly, they thought that a lacrosse stick looked like a bishop's staff.

lad A boy or young man. Our proud neighbors always said that their grandson was a fine *lad.*
> **lad** (lad) *noun, plural* **lads.**

ladder A device used for climbing. A ladder is made of two long side pieces joined together by short pieces, called rungs, which are used as steps. I stood on a *ladder* to paint the ceiling.
> **lad·der** (lad′ər) *noun, plural* **ladders.**

laden Filled; loaded. The pirate's chest was *laden* with jewels.
> **lad·en** (lā′dən) *adjective.*

ladle A spoon with a long handle and a bowl shaped like a cup. It is used to scoop up liquids.
> **la·dle** (lā′dəl) *noun, plural* **ladles.**

lady **1.** Any woman. There is a *lady* at the door to see you. **2.** A girl or woman who is polite or has good manners. **3.** A woman who has a high social position. **4. Lady.** In Great Britain, a title for a woman of noble rank.
> **la·dy** (lā′dē) *noun, plural* **ladies.**

ladybug A small, round, bright red or orange beetle with black spots. Ladybugs eat insects that are harmful to plants.

> **la·dy·bug** (lā′dē bug′) *noun, plural* **ladybugs.**

ladybug

lag To move less quickly and follow. That little child always *lags* behind the older children. *Verb.*
—An act, amount, or example of moving less quickly and following. After we saw the lightning, there was a *lag* of a few seconds before we heard the thunder. *Noun.*
> **lag** (lag) *verb,* **lagged, lagging;** *noun, plural* **lags.**

lagoon A shallow body of water usually connected to a larger body of water.
> **la·goon** (lə gün′) *noun, plural* **lagoons.**

laid Past tense and past participle of **lay.** I *laid* the book on the table. Look up **lay¹** for more information.
> **laid** (lād) *verb.*

lain Past participle of **lie.** The toys have *lain* on the floor all day. Look up **lie²** for more information. ▲ Another word that sounds like this is **lane.**
> **lain** (lān) *verb.*

lair A place where a wild animal lives or rests; den. The fox's *lair* was in a hole in the ground.
> **lair** (lâr) *noun, plural* **lairs.**

ladders

lake A body of water completely or almost completely surrounded by land. A lake is larger than a pond.
lake (lāk) *noun, plural* **lakes.**

lamb **1.** A young sheep. **2.** The meat from a lamb.
lamb (lam) *noun, plural* **lambs.**

lame **1.** Not able to walk well. The *lame* horse won't be able to run in this race. **2.** Stiff and painful. My back is *lame* from moving the heavy chest. **3.** Poor or weak. The student had a *lame* excuse for not doing the homework. *Adjective.*
—To make lame. The accident had *lamed* the runner. *Verb.*
lame (lām) *adjective,* **lamer, lamest;** *verb,* **lamed, laming.**

lamp A device that produces light. Some lamps hold light bulbs and work by electricity. Other lamps burn oil, kerosene, or gas to provide light.
lamp (lamp) *noun, plural* **lamps.**

lance A long spear. A lance is made of a wooden pole with a sharp metal point at one end. *Noun.*
—To cut open with a sharp instrument. The doctor *lanced* the boil so that the pus could drain. *Verb.*
lance (lans) *noun, plural* **lances;** *verb,* **lanced, lancing.**

land **1.** All or any part of the earth's surface that is not water; ground. **2.** A country or region. The tourists went to Europe to visit foreign *lands. Noun.*
—**1.** To come or bring to the ground. The airplane *landed* safely at the airport. The pilot *landed* the helicopter in the field. **2.** To come or bring ashore. The marines have *landed.* The ship *landed* its cargo at the dock. **3.** To bring to land or into a boat; catch. After fishing for an hour, we *landed* only one fish. **4.** To end up or cause to end up. Stealing could *land* you in jail. *Verb.*
land (land) *noun, plural* **lands;** *verb,* **landed, landing.**

lance

landing **1.** The act or process of coming to the ground or to land, or coming ashore. The airplane had a smooth *landing.* The capture of the island began with the *landing* of the Marines. **2.** The place on a dock or pier where people and goods are brought ashore or put on a boat. **3.** A level area at the end of a flight of stairs.
land·ing (lan′ding) *noun, plural* **landings.**

landlady A woman who owns houses, apartments, or rooms that she rents to other people.
land·la·dy (land′lā′dē) *noun, plural* **landladies.**

landlord A person or organization that owns houses, apartments, or rooms to be rented to other people.
land·lord (land′lôrd′) *noun, plural* **landlords.**

landmark **1.** An object that is familiar and serves as a guide. The church steeple is a well-known *landmark* in our town. **2.** An important building, structure, or place. This Civil War battlefield is a national *landmark.* **3.** An important event. The first landing of astronauts on the moon was a *landmark* in history.
land·mark (land′märk′) *noun, plural* **landmarks.**

landscape **1.** The stretch of land that can be seen from a place; view. The train passengers watched the passing *landscape.* **2.** A picture of such a view. The artist painted a *landscape. Noun.*
—To make an area of land more beautiful by planting trees, shrubs, and other plants and by designing gardens. A gardener *landscaped* the grounds around these offices. *Verb.*
land·scape (land′skāp′) *noun, plural* **landscapes;** *verb,* **landscaped, landscaping.**

landslide **1.** The sliding down a slope of rocks and soil. The rumble of the *landslide* echoed in the valley. **2.** Rocks and soil that slide down a slope. The road was buried under a *landslide.* **3.** A great victory in an election. The mayor won the election by a *landslide.*
land·slide (land′slīd′) *noun, plural* **landslides.**

at; āpe; fär; câre; end; mē; it; īce; pîerce; hot; ōld; sông, fôrk; oil; out; up; ūse; rüle; pull; tûrn; chin; sing; shop; thin; this; hw in white; zh in treasure. The symbol ə stands for the unstressed vowel sound in about, taken, pencil, lemon, and circus.

lane   **1.** A narrow way or road. The child walked down the country *lane.*   **2.** A route for traffic going in one direction. The cars kept in the right-hand *lane* on the highway.   **3.** A long, narrow path down which bowling balls are rolled; alley.   ▲ Another word that sounds like this is **lain.**
   lane (lān) *noun, plural* **lanes.**

language   **1.** Spoken or written words; human speech. We are able to express our thoughts and feelings by means of language.   **2.** The speech of a country or group. In Mexico, people speak the Spanish *language.*   **3.** A way of expressing thoughts and feelings without words. Many deaf people use sign *language.*   **4.** A set of words and symbols that are used to give instructions to a computer and to write programs; computer language.
   lan·guage (lang′gwij) *noun, plural* **languages.**

Word History

   The word **language** comes from a Latin word that means "tongue." In Latin and the languages closely related to it, such as English, the word for "tongue" can also be used to mean "speech" and "language."

---

lantern   A covering or container for a light. Some lanterns are made of metal with sides of glass. Most lanterns can be carried. The camper used a *lantern* to light the path.
   lan·tern (lan′tərn) *noun, plural* **lanterns.**

Laos   A country in southeastern Asia.
   La·os (lä′ōs *or* lā′os) *noun.*

lap¹   The front part of the body between the waist and the knees of a person who is seated.
   lap (lap) *noun, plural* **laps.**

lap²   To lie partly over another; extend over; overlap. The shingles on a roof *lap* over each other. *Verb.*
   —One time around or over the entire length of something. The athlete ran three *laps* around the track. *Noun.*
   lap (lap) *verb,* **lapped, lapping;** *noun, plural* **laps.**

lap³   **1.** To drink a liquid by lifting it up with the tongue. The kitten *lapped* its milk.   **2.** To wash or move gently against. The waves *lapped* against the shore. *Verb.*
   —The act of lapping. The dog drank all its water in a few *laps. Noun.*
   lap (lap) *verb,* **lapped, lapping;** *noun, plural* **laps.**

lapel   The front part of a coat or jacket that is folded back. Will you pin this carnation to the *lapel* of my jacket?
   la·pel (lə pel′) *noun, plural* **lapels.**

lapse   **1.** A slight mistake or failure. The report was perfect except for a few *lapses* in grammar.   **2.** An amount of time between events; interval. We met again after a *lapse* of a year. *Noun.*
   —**1.** To slip or fall gradually. The old building *lapsed* into ruin.   **2.** To end or be discontinued. My insurance policy *lapsed* when I failed to make the monthly payment. *Verb.*
   lapse (laps) *noun, plural* **lapses;** *verb,* **lapsed, lapsing.**

larch   A tall tree with small cones and needles that turn yellow and drop off in the fall. The hard wood of the *larch* is often used for telephone poles.
   larch (lärch) *noun, plural* **larches.**

lard   A soft, white grease. Lard is obtained by melting the fat of pigs and hogs. It is used in cooking. *Noun.*
   —To add lard to or cover with lard. This recipe says to *lard* the pan before using it. *Verb.*
   lard (lärd) *noun, plural* **lards;** *verb,* **larded, larding.**

large   Big in size or amount. That *large* house has twenty rooms. The museum has a *large* stamp collection.
   • **at large.**   **1.** Free. The police are searching for the thieves who are still *at large.*   **2.** Of or representing an entire area. The United States senators from each state are elected by the people *at large.*
   large (lärj) *adjective,* **larger, largest.**

large intestine   The lower section of the intestines including the appendix, colon, and rectum. The large intestine is the part of the digestive system that removes water from digested food.

largely   To a great extent; mostly. The houses on that street are *largely* made of wood.
   large·ly (lärj′lē) *adverb.*

lariat   A long rope with a loop at one end; lasso. It is used to catch animals. The rancher used a *lariat* to rope the calf.
   lar·i·at (lar′ē ət) *noun, plural* **lariats.**

lark¹   A small songbird with gray-brown feathers. Larks live in most parts of the world. The lark is known for its beautiful song.
   lark (lärk) *noun, plural* **larks.**

lark²   Something done for fun. The children went running and sliding through the snow for a *lark.*
   lark (lärk) *noun, plural* **larks.**

larkspur A plant that has tall stalks of blue, purple, or white flowers.
lark·spur (lärk′spûr′) *noun, plural* **larkspurs.**

larva The newly hatched form of some insects and other animals without backbones. A larva has a soft body that looks like a worm and has no wings. A caterpillar is the larva of a moth or butterfly, and a grub is the larva of a beetle.
lar·va (lär′və) *noun, plural* **larvae** (lär′vē).

larkspur

Word History

The word **larva** comes from a Latin word that means "mask." People used to think that this stage in an insect's growth hid or "masked" the way the insect would finally look.

laryngitis Inflammation of the larynx. A person with laryngitis sounds hoarse.
lar·yn·gi·tis (lar′in jī′tis) *noun.*

larynx The top part of the windpipe. The larynx holds the vocal cords.
lar·ynx (lar′ingks) *noun, plural* **larynxes.**

laser A device that makes a very narrow but strong beam of light. A laser may be used to perform surgery, cut metal, or send electronic messages.
la·ser (lā′zər) *noun, plural* **lasers.**

lash¹ 1. A blow with a whip. 2. A movement like a whip makes. The *lash* of the dog's tail knocked the lamp over. 3. A small, stiff hair that grows on the edge of the eyelid; eyelash. *Noun.*
— 1. To beat with a whip. The farmer *lashed* the stubborn mule. 2. To strike against with force. Violent winds *lashed* the trees. 3. To move back and forth quickly. The tiger *lashed* its tail in anger. *Verb.*
lash (lash) *noun, plural* **lashes;** *verb,* **lashed, lashing.**

lash² To tie with a rope. The shipwrecked sailors *lashed* some boards together to make a raft.
lash (lash) *verb,* **lashed, lashing.**

lass A girl or young woman.
lass (las) *noun, plural* **lasses.**

lasso A long rope with a loop. It is used to catch animals. *Noun.*

—To catch with a lasso. The cowhands will *lasso* the steer. *Verb.*
las·so (las′ō *or* la sü′) *noun, plural* **lassos** or **lassoes;** *verb,* **lassoed, lassoing.**

a cowhand throwing a **lasso**

last¹ 1. Coming at the end; final. December is the *last* month of the year. 2. Being the only one that is left. I spent my *last* dollar on a gift for my friend. 3. Coming just before this; most recent; latest. How old were you on your *last* birthday? We watched television *last* night. 4. Most unlikely. A giraffe is the *last* thing you would expect to see in the middle of Main Street. *Adjective.*
—1. At the end. Wash the dishes first and the pots and pans *last*. 2. Most recently. When did your cousin *last* write to you? I *last* saw the mayor two weeks ago. *Adverb.*
—A person or thing that is last. I was the *last* in line in the cafeteria. *Noun.*
• **at last.** After a long time or much effort; finally. *At last* it's stopped raining.
last (last) *adjective; adverb; noun.*

last² 1. To go on; continue. The television show will *last* an hour. 2. To stay in good condition. That coat will *last* if you take care of it.
last (last) *verb,* **lasted, lasting.**

latch A small piece of metal or wood for holding a door, window, or gate closed. Please lift the *latch* and open the gate. *Noun.*

at; āpe; fär; câre; end; mē; it; īce; pîerce; hot; ōld; sông, fôrk; oil; out; up; ūse; rüle; pùll; tûrn; chin; sing; shop; thin; this; hw in white; zh in treasure. The symbol ə stands for the unstressed vowel sound in about, taken, pencil, lemon, and circus.

L

—To fasten or close the latch of something. We were in a hurry and forgot to *latch* the back door. *Verb.*

latch (lach) *noun, plural* **latches;** *verb,* **latched, latching.**

late **1.** Coming after the usual time. I was *late* to school today. The campers had a *late* lunch. **2.** Coming near the end. It was *late* afternoon when we started our trip. **3.** Done, made, or happening not long ago. My parents bought a *late* model car. **4.** Recently dead. The *late* senator had served for thirty years. *Adjective.*
—**1.** After the usual time. We arrived *late* at the party. They came home *late* last night. **2.** Near or toward the end. The football team scored its first touchdown *late* in the second quarter. *Adverb.*

late (lāt) *adjective; adverb,* **later, latest.**

lately Not long ago; recently. Have you seen the principal *lately*?

late·ly (lāt′lē) *adverb.*

lateral On, from, or to the side. A lateral pass in football is a pass made to a side of the field rather than forward or backward.

lat·er·al (lat′ər əl) *adjective.*

lathe A machine that spins around a piece of wood or metal while a cutting tool is pressed against the spinning piece to shape it. The table leg was shaped on a *lathe*.

lathe (lāth) *noun, plural* **lathes.**

lather **1.** Foam made by mixing soap and water. This shampoo makes a thick *lather*. **2.** Foam caused by sweating. The horse was covered with *lather* from pulling the plow. *Noun.*
— **1.** To cover with lather. The barber *lathered* the customer's face before shaving it. **2.** To form a lather. This soap does not *lather* well in cold water. *Verb.*

lath·er (lath′ər) *noun, plural* **lathers;** *verb,* **lathered, lathering.**

Latin **1.** The language of the ancient Romans. **2.** A person who speaks a language that developed from Latin. The Italians, Spanish, French, and Portuguese are Latins. *Noun.*
— **1.** Having to do with Latin. The class is studying *Latin* grammar. **2.** Having to do with the people or countries that use languages coming from Latin. Spain and Mexico are *Latin* countries. *Adjective.*

Lat·in (lat′in) *noun, plural* **Latins;** *adjective.*

Latin America The countries of North America and South America that are south of the United States, where languages based on Latin are spoken.

Latin American A person who was born in or is a citizen of a country in Latin America. *Noun.*
—Of or having to do with Latin America or its people. *Adjective.*

latitude Distance measured on the earth's surface north and south of the equator. On a map or globe, lines of latitude are drawn running east and west. Latitude is expressed in degrees. Each degree is equal to around sixty-nine miles.

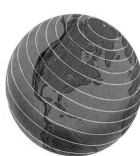

lat·i·tude (lat′i tüd′ or lat′i tūd′) *noun, plural* **latitudes.**

lines of **latitude**

latter **1.** The second of two things mentioned. Of baseball and football, our friends like the *latter* sport better. **2.** Near the end; later. I spend the *latter* part of each day doing my homework.

lat·ter (lat′ər) *adjective.*

lattice A framework of thin strips of wood or metal placed across each other with open spaces between them. The roses grew over a white wooden *lattice*.

lat·tice (lat′is) *noun, plural* **lattices.**

laugh To make sounds that show amusement, happiness, or ridicule. The children *laughed* at the silly monkeys in the zoo. We *laughed* at the idea of losing. *Verb.*
—The act or sound of laughing. The *laughs* of the audience filled the theater. *Noun.*

laugh (laf) *verb,* **laughed, laughing;** *noun, plural* **laughs.**

laughable Causing or likely to cause a person to laugh. It was *laughable* to think that all those clowns could fit in one tiny car.

laugh·a·ble (laf′ə bəl) *adjective.*

laughter The act or sound of laughing. We could hear *laughter* coming from the playground.

laugh·ter (laf′tər) *noun.*

launch¹ **1.** To start in motion; send off. The scientists at the space center will *launch* a rocket. **2.** To put into the water. The sailors *launched* the sailboat. **3.** To start something. The company *launched* its store by having a big sale. *Verb.*
—The act or process of launching. The *launch* of the rocket began with the countdown. *Noun.*

launch (lônch) *verb,* **launched, launching;** *noun, plural* **launches.**

launch² An open motorboat.
    launch (lônch) *noun, plural* **launches.**

launch pad A platform from which a rocket or missile is launched.

launder To wash or wash and iron clothing and linens. I sometimes help *launder* my family's clothes.
    laun·der (lôn′dər) *verb,* **laundered, laundering.**

Laundromat A trademark for a laundry where people can wash their own clothes. It has washing machines and clothes dryers that work when coins are put in them.
    Laun·dro·mat (lôn′drə mat′) *noun, plural* **Laundromats.**

launch pad

laundry 1. Clothes and linens that are to be or have been washed. I folded the *laundry*. 2. A place where clothes, sheets, and other things are washed. We sent the shirts to the *laundry*.
    laun·dry (lôn′drē) *noun, plural* **laundries.**

laurel An evergreen tree that has stiff, pointed leaves. In ancient times, people placed wreaths made of laurel leaves on the heads of heroes.
    lau·rel (lôr′əl) *noun, plural* **laurels.**

lava 1. Very hot, melted rock that comes out of a volcano when it erupts. 2. Rock formed by lava that has cooled and hardened.
    la·va (lä′və *or* lav′ə) *noun.*

lavatory 1. A room with toilets and sinks; bathroom. 2. A sink for washing.
    lav·a·to·ry (lav′ə tôr′ē) *noun, plural* **lavatories.**

lavender 1. A plant that has fragrant purple flowers. The dried leaves and flowers of lavender are used in chests or closets to give a pleasant odor to clothes and sheets. Oil from the flowers is used in perfumes. 2. A light purple color. *Noun.*

lavender

—Having the color lavender; light purple. At sunset the sky was *lavender* and orange. *Adjective.*
    lav·en·der (lav′ən dər) *noun, plural* **lavenders;** *adjective.*

lavish 1. Giving or spending in great amounts; extravagant. I was so *lavish* with the shampoo that I used the whole bottle in a week. 2. Being or costing a great amount or an amount that is greater than usual. The wedding was followed by a *lavish* dinner. *Adjective.*
—To give or spend in great amounts. Our grandparents always *lavished* presents on us. *Verb.*
    lav·ish (lav′ish) *adjective; verb,* **lavished, lavishing.**

law 1. A rule made by a government for all the people in a town, state, or country. The state and city police enforce the *laws* against driving too fast. 2. A set or system of such rules. The *law* of the United States is based on the system used in England. 3. The profession of a lawyer. My cousin is interested in *law* as a career. 4. Any rule or custom. This book covers the *laws* of English grammar. 5. A statement that says a group of scientific events will always happen the same way when all the conditions are the same. This science book tells us about the *law* of gravity.
    law (lô) *noun, plural* **laws.**

lawful Allowed by the law. It is not *lawful* to park near a fire hydrant.
    law·ful (lô′fəl) *adjective.*

lawn An area with grass that is kept mowed. The *lawn* around the old house was full of weeds.
    lawn (lôn) *noun, plural* **lawns.**

lawn mower A machine with blades for cutting grass. Some lawn mowers are run by motors powered by gasoline.

lawsuit A legal case begun in a court by one person who claims something from another; suit.
    law·suit (lô′süt′) *noun, plural* **lawsuits.**

lawyer A person who has studied the law and can give legal advice and represent people in court.
    law·yer (lô′yər) *noun, plural* **lawyers.**

L

at; āpe; fär; câre; end; mē; it; īce; pîerce; hot; ōld; sông; fôrk; oil; out; up; ūse; rüle; pull; tûrn; chin; sing; shop; thin; this; hw in white; zh in treasure. The symbol ə stands for the unstressed vowel sound in about, taken, pencil, lemon, and circus.

lay¹ **1.** To put or place. May I *lay* my coat over this chair? *Lay* the plates on the table. **2.** To place or spread upon a surface. They *laid* new sod on our front yard. The workers will *lay* the new carpet. **3.** To produce an egg or eggs. These chickens *lay* almost every day. ▲ Another word that sounds like this is **lei.**

• **to lay aside** or **to lay away** or **to lay by.** To save or reserve. I try to *lay aside* a little of my allowance every week.

lay (lā) *verb,* **laid, laying.**

lay² Past tense of **lie.** The tired dog *lay* down to rest. Look up **lie²** for more information. ▲ Another word that sounds like this is **lei.**

lay (lā) *verb.*

layer **1.** One thickness of something. A *layer* of dust covered the table. The wall has several *layers* of paint. **2.** A chicken that lays eggs.

lay·er (lā'ər) *noun, plural* **layers.**

lazy Not willing to work. The *lazy* child would not help us clean the garage.

la·zy (lā'zē) *adjective,* **lazier, laziest.**

lb. An abbreviation for *pound¹.*

lead¹ **1.** To show the way. The guide *led* the scouts through the cave. **2.** To go or be first; be ahead of others. The general will *lead* the parade. Our team *leads* by a score of three to nothing. You now *lead* the class in arithmetic. **3.** To be a way; go. This hall *leads* to the cafeteria. **4.** To be the head of; direct. That teacher *leads* the school orchestra. **5.** To live. Our doctor *leads* a busy life. *Verb.*

—**1.** The first position; being ahead. The fastest runner took the *lead* in the race. **2.** The amount or extent by which one is ahead. Our team has a *lead* of seven points. **3.** Clue. The detectives don't know who stole the money yet, but they have a few *leads.* **4.** The main actor or role in a play, motion picture, or the like. They want a well-known actor for the *lead* in that movie. *Noun.*

lead (lēd) *verb,* **led, leading;** *noun, plural* **leads.**

lead² **1.** A heavy, soft, gray metal. Lead is easy to bend and melt. It is used to make pipes and solder. Lead is a chemical element. **2.** The soft black substance in a pencil. ▲ Another word that sounds like this is **led.**

lead (led) *noun, plural* **leads.**

leader A person who leads. My friend is the *leader* of the school band. The youngest swimmer was the *leader* in the race.

lead·er (lē'dər) *noun, plural* **leaders.**

leaf **1.** One of the flat, green parts growing from a stem of a plant. Some leaves are made up of smaller parts called leaflets. **2.** A sheet of paper. The student tore a *leaf* out of the notebook. **3.** A movable flat part of the top of a table. We added a *leaf* to make the table bigger. *Noun.*

—**1.** To grow leaves. Many trees *leaf* in the spring. **2.** To turn pages and glance at them quickly. I *leafed* through a magazine while waiting in the dentist's office. *Verb.*

leaf (lēf) *noun, plural* **leaves;** *verb,* **leafed, leafing.**

kinds of **leaves**

leaflet **1.** A single printed sheet of paper or pamphlet. The candidate for mayor handed out *leaflets* to people on the street. This game comes with a *leaflet* that gives the rules. **2.** A small or young leaf. In the spring this tree has fuzzy *leaflets.* **3.** One part of a larger leaf. This leaf is made up of six *leaflets.*

leaf·let (lēf'lit) *noun, plural* **leaflets.**

league¹ A number of people, groups, or countries joined together for a common purpose. Those two baseball teams belong to the same *league.*

league (lēg) *noun, plural* **leagues.**

league² A measure of distance that was used in the past. A league is equal to about three miles.

league (lēg) *noun, plural* **leagues.**

leak A hole or tear that lets something pass through by accident. The *leak* in the milk carton let the milk drip on the table. The tire went flat because of a *leak. Noun.*

—**1.** To have a leak. The roof of that old house *leaks.* **2.** To pass or cause to pass through a hole or tear. All the air *leaked* out of the tire. **3.** To allow or be allowed to become no longer secret. The official *leaked* the government secret to the newspapers. *Verb.* ▲ Another word that sounds like this is **leek.**

leak (lēk) *noun, plural* **leaks;** *verb,* **leaked, leaking.**

lean¹   **1.** To be at a slant; bend. The walls of the old shed *lean* out.   **2.** To rest or rely on a person or thing for support or help. The monkey *leaned* against the branch. Whom do you *lean* on when you have a problem? **3.** To put something at a slant. *Lean* the fishing pole against the wall.
 lean (lēn) *verb,* **leaned, leaning.**

lean²   **1.** Having little or no fat; not fat. That student is tall and *lean.* Did you buy this *lean* meat from the butcher? **2.** Not producing much; poor. That was a *lean* year for farmers.
 lean (lēn) *adjective,* **leaner, leanest.**

leap   To jump. The soldiers *leaped* to their feet. The horse *leaped* the fence. *Verb.*
 —A jump. The cat made a *leap* from the chair. *Noun.*
 leap (lēp) *verb,* **leaped** or **leapt, leaping;** *noun, plural* **leaps.**

leapfrog   A game in which players take turns leaping over the backs of other players.
 leap·frog (lēp′frôg′ *or* lēp′frog′) *noun.*

leapt   A past tense and a past participle of *leap.* The squirrel *leapt* from the branch to the garage. Look up **leap** for more information.
 leapt (lept) *verb.*

leap year   A year that has an extra day, February 29. The years 1992, 1996, and 2000 will be leap years.

learn   **1.** To get to know through study or practice; gain knowledge or skill. I want to *learn* to speak French. The children *learned* how to swim this summer. **2.** To memorize. The students had to *learn* their lines for the school play quickly. **3.** To get information about. The police never *learned* who had taken the bicycle.
 learn (lûrn) *verb,* **learned** or **learnt, learning.**

learned   Having or showing knowledge. Our teacher is a *learned* person.
 learn·ed (lûr′nid) *adjective.*

learning   Knowledge gained by careful study. This book about the ancient Greeks was written by a person of *learning.*
 learn·ing (lûr′ning) *noun, plural* **learnings.**

learnt   A past tense and a past participle of **learn.** The child had *learnt* how to spell all the words on the list. Look up **learn** for more information.
 learnt (lûrnt) *verb.*

lease   A written agreement for renting a house, apartment, or land. My parents have signed a *lease* for this apartment for three years. *Noun.*
 —To rent. The family *leased* a cabin for the summer. *Verb.*
 lease (lēs) *noun, plural* **leases;** *verb,* **leased, leasing.**

leash   A strap, cord, or chain for holding or tying an animal. Fasten the *leash* to the dog's collar. *Noun.*
 —To fasten to a leash. The child *leashed* the puppy before taking it for a walk. *Verb.*
 leash (lēsh) *noun, plural* **leashes;** *verb,* **leashed, leashing.**

dogs on **leashes**

least   Smallest; littlest. A second is the *least* amount of time that is shown on most watches. Of all my houseplants, the cactus requires the *least* care. *Adjective.*
 —The smallest thing or amount. Saying you are sorry for breaking the vase is the *least* you can do. *Noun.*
 —In the smallest degree. This year's crop is the *least* abundant in years. *Adverb.*
 • **at least.**   **1.** Not less or fewer than. *At least* twenty people will come to the party. **2.** No matter what happens; at any rate. We may not succeed with our project, but *at least* we'll try.
 least (lēst) *adjective; noun; adverb.*

leather   A material made from an animal skin that has been cleaned and tanned. Leather is used for making shoes, gloves, jackets, and many other things.
 leath·er (leth′ər) *noun, plural* **leathers.**

leave¹   **1.** To go from a place; go away. We have to *leave* and go home. The plane *leaves*

at; āpe; fär; câre; end; mē; it; īce; pîerce; hot; ōld; sông, fôrk; oil; out; up; ūse; rüle; pull; tûrn; chin; sing; shop; thin; this; hw in white; zh in treasure. The symbol ə stands for the unstressed vowel sound in about, taken, pencil, lemon, and circus.

419

at six o'clock. You may *leave* the table if you have finished eating.   **2.** To withdraw from; quit. I must *leave* the softball team. At the end of the summer, I will *leave* my job.   **3.** To let something stay behind. *Leave* the note on the desk. The spilled grape juice *left* a stain on my shirt. Did you *leave* your notebook at school?   **4.** To let stay in a certain way. Why did you *leave* your work unfinished? *Leave* the dog alone. The good news *left* us feeling happy.   **5.** To let another do something. Why don't you *leave* the cooking to me tonight?   **6.** To give in a will. The collection of paintings was *left* to the museum.   **7.** To have remaining. 10 minus 3 *leaves* 7.

* **to leave off.**   To stop. Where did we *leave off* in our discussion?
* **to leave out.**   To omit. We didn't have enough onions for the stew, so I *left* them *out*.

leave (lēv) *verb,* **left, leaving.**

leave²   **1.** Permission; consent. Our parents gave us *leave* to go camping overnight. **2.** Permission to be absent. The soldier asked for a *leave* to visit a sick friend.

* **on leave.**   Away from one's duty with permission. The sailors decided to see a play while they were *on leave*.

leave (lēv) *noun, plural* **leaves.**

leaves   Plural of **leaf.** We raked the *leaves* into a pile. Look up **leaf** for more information.

leaves (lēvz) *plural noun.*

Lebanon   A country in the Middle East.
Leb·a·non (leb′ə non′) *noun.*

lecture   **1.** A talk given to an audience. The writer gave a *lecture* on the poets of Japan. **2.** A scolding. I got a *lecture* from my parents for breaking the window. *Noun.*
—**1.** To give a lecture. The scientist *lectures* on the history of aviation at the college. **2.** To scold. The teacher *lectured* us for not doing our homework. *Verb.*
lec·ture (lek′chər) *noun, plural* **lectures;** *verb,* **lectured, lecturing.**

led   Past tense and past participle of **lead¹.** The guide *led* the hunters through the forest. Look up **lead¹** for more information. ▲ Another word that sounds like this is **lead².**
led (led) *verb.*

ledge   A narrow shelf or surface like a shelf. A window *ledge* juts out from the wall of a building. The climbers rested on a *ledge* of the mountain.
ledge (lej) *noun, plural* **ledges.**

lee   The side of a ship sheltered from the wind. *Noun.*

—Sheltered from the wind. The sailors stayed on the *lee* side of the ship. *Adjective.*
lee (lē) *noun, plural* **lees;** *adjective.*

leech   A kind of worm that sucks the blood of animals. Leeches are found in ponds, rivers, and damp soil.
leech (lēch) *noun, plural* **leeches.**

leek   A plant with long, thick leaves. It tastes like a mild onion. The leaves and bulb of the leek are eaten as vegetables. ▲ Another word that sounds like this is **leak.**
leek (lēk) *noun, plural* **leeks.**

left¹   On the west side of your body when you face north. I write with my *left* hand. Walk on the *left* side of the road. *Adjective.*
—The left side. Who's that standing on your *left* in the photograph? *Noun.*
—Toward the left. Turn *left* at the next corner. *Adverb.*
left (left) *adjective; noun; adverb.*

left²   Past tense and past participle of **leave.** I *left* my books at home. Look up **leave** for more information.
left (left) *verb.*

left-hand   **1.** On or toward the left. Look in the *left-hand* drawer.   **2.** For the left hand. I lost my *left-hand* glove.
left-hand (left′hand′) *adjective.*

left-handed   **1.** Using the left hand more easily than the right hand. My parents are both *left-handed*.   **2.** Done with the left hand. The quarterback made a *left-handed* pass.   **3.** Made to be held in or used by the left hand. These are *left-handed* scissors.
left-hand·ed (left′han′did) *adjective.*

leftover   Something that remains unused or not eaten. We had the *leftovers* from last night's dinner for our lunch. *Noun.*
—Unused or uneaten; remaining. We ate the *leftover* pizza for lunch. *Adjective.*
left·o·ver (left′ō′vər) *noun, plural* **leftovers;** *adjective.*

leg   **1.** One of the parts of the body that a person or animal stands and walks on. **2.** Something like a leg. The *leg* of the chair is broken.   **3.** One part of a trip or journey. On the first *leg* of our trip, we'll travel 300 miles.

* **to pull one's leg.**   To trick or tease. I was only *pulling your leg* when I told you we would get six feet of snow.

leg (leg) *noun, plural* **legs.**

legal   **1.** Having to do with law. Go to a lawyer for *legal* advice.   **2.** Allowed by or according to the law or the rules; lawful. They're the *legal* owners of the farm. That's not a *legal* move in checkers.
le·gal (lē′gəl) *adjective.*

legend **1.** A story passed down through the years that many people believe, but that is not entirely true. There are many *legends* about the knights of the Middle Ages.
leg·end (lej′ənd) *noun, plural* **legends.**

legendary Of or having to do with a legend or legends. The story told of a *legendary* king and queen.
leg·end·ar·y (lej′ən der′ē) *adjective.*

leggings Outer coverings for the legs, made of cloth or leather. When I was younger, I wore *leggings* when I played in the snow.
leg·gings (leg′ingz) *plural noun.*

legible Easily read. This sloppy writing is not *legible.*
leg·i·ble (lej′ə bəl) *adjective.*

legion **1.** A unit of the army of ancient Rome. A legion had several thousand soldiers and several hundred more on horseback. **2.** An army. The enemy sent its *legions* to conquer the small country. **3.** A great number of persons or things. *Legions* attended the county fair.
le·gion (lē′jən) *noun, plural* **legions.**

legislation **1.** The making or passing of laws. The work of the Senate and House of Representatives is *legislation.* **2.** The laws that are made or passed. Congress passed new *legislation* dealing with housing.
leg·is·la·tion (lej′is lā′shən) *noun, plural* **legislations.**

legislative **1.** Of or having to do with making or passing laws. Senators and Representatives have *legislative* duties. **2.** Having the power to make or pass laws. Congress is the *legislative* branch of the United States government.
leg·is·la·tive (lej′is lā′tiv) *adjective.*

legislature A body of persons that has the power to make or pass laws. The state *legislature* voted on a new tax bill.
leg·is·la·ture (lej′is lā′chər) *noun, plural* **legislatures.**

legitimate According to what is right or lawful. The judge ruled that the state was the *legitimate* owner of the land. The student could not give a *legitimate* excuse for being late.
le·git·i·mate (li jit′ə mit) *adjective.*

legume A plant whose seeds grow in pods. Peas, beans, lentils, and peanuts grow on plants that are legumes.
leg·ume (leg′ūm *or* li gūm′) *noun, plural* **legumes.**

lei A wreath of flowers, leaves, or other material. Leis are often worn around the neck in Hawaii. ▲ Another word that sounds like this is **lay.**
lei (lā) *noun, plural* **leis.**

leis

leisure The time to do what one likes; free time. The busy farmer did not have much *leisure. Noun.*
—Not taken up by work, school, or duty. I spend my *leisure* time reading. *Adjective.*
lei·sure (lē′zhər *or* lezh′ər) *noun; adjective.*

lemon A yellow fruit with a sour taste. Lemons have an oval or round shape, a rind, and juicy pulp. Lemons grow on small, thorny trees in warm regions. *Noun.*
—Made from or flavored with lemon. The bakery sells *lemon* pies. *Adjective.*

lemons

lem·on (lem′ən) *noun, plural* **lemons;** *adjective.*

lemonade A drink made from lemon juice, water, and sugar.
lem·on·ade (lem′ə nād′) *noun, plural* **lemonades.**

lend **1.** To let a person have or use something for a while. Please *lend* me your base-

at; āpe; fär; câre; end; mē; it; īce; pîerce; hot; ōld; sông, fôrk; oil; out; up; ūse; rüle; pull; tûrn; chin; sing; shop; thin; this; hw in white; zh in treasure. The symbol ə stands for the unstressed vowel sound in about, taken, pencil, lemon, and circus.

L

ball glove for the game. **2.** To give a person money to use for a certain period of time. When the money is repaid, the person also pays interest. The bank will *lend* my parents money to buy a car. **3.** To provide; give. Bright lights *lend* excitement to the city.
lend (lend) *verb,* **lent, lending.**

length **1.** The distance from one end to the other end. The *length* of a football field is 100 yards. **2.** The amount or extent from beginning to end. My vacation was three months in *length*. **3.** A piece of something. Did you buy a *length* of rope?
length (lengkth *or* length) *noun, plural* **lengths.**

lengthen To make or become longer. Can you *lengthen* this dress? The days *lengthened* as summer grew near.
length·en (lengk'thən *or* leng'thən) *verb,* **lengthened, lengthening.**

lengthwise In the same direction as the length. Split these logs *lengthwise*. These towels should have *lengthwise* folds.
length·wise (lengkth'wīz' *or* length'wīz') *adverb; adjective.*

lenient Tolerant or merciful; not strict. My parents are *lenient* about my staying up late.
len·i·ent (lē'nē ənt *or* lēn'yənt) *adjective.*

lens **1.** A piece of glass or other clear material that is curved to make light rays move apart or come together. A lens can make an object look larger or closer. Lenses are used in eyeglasses, telescopes, and cameras. **2.** The curved, clear part of the eye that focuses light on the retina. The lens is located behind the pupil.
lens (lenz) *noun, plural* **lenses.**

lent Past tense and past participle of **lend.** I *lent* my classmate a pencil for the test. Look up **lend** for more information.
lent (lent) *verb.*

Lent The forty days before Easter, not including Sundays. In many Christian churches, Lent is observed as a time to pray, fast, and repent for sins.
Lent (lent) *noun.*

lentil A flat, round seed that grows on a certain kind of legume. Lentils are cooked as a vegetable, especially in soups.
len·til (len'təl) *noun, plural* **lentils.**

leopard A large animal that belongs to the cat family. Leopards have short fur that is usually yellow or gray with black spots grouped in circles. They live in Africa and southern Asia.
leop·ard (lep'ərd) *noun, plural* **leopards.**

leotard A single garment that fits tightly from the neck to the top of the legs or to the feet. Acrobats and dancers wear leotards.
le·o·tard (lē'ə tärd') *noun, plural* **leotards.**

leprosy A disease that attacks the nerves, skin, and muscles. People with leprosy lose sensation in parts of their bodies and can easily injure themselves without knowing it. Leprosy is caused by an infection.
lep·ro·sy (lep'rə sē) *noun.*

less Not as much. I have *less* work to do today than I had yesterday. *Adjective.*
—To a smaller extent or degree. This watch is *less* expensive than that one. *Adverb.*
—A smaller number or quantity. I finished *less* of the work than I had planned. *Noun.*
—With the subtraction of; minus. 10 *less* 7 is 3. *Preposition.*
less (les) *adjective; adverb; noun; preposition.*

Language Note

It isn't difficult to remember when to use **less** and when to use **fewer.** Use "less" when you are speaking about something that cannot be counted. There is *less* sugar in the bowl. Use "fewer" when you are speaking about something that can be counted. *Fewer* students attended the game.

-less A *suffix* that means: **1.** Having no; without. *Hopeless* means having no hope. **2.** That cannot be. *Countless* means that cannot be counted.

lessen To make or become less. The teacher *lessened* the amount of homework we had to do. The pain of the sprained ankle *lessened* after the ankle was soaked in cold water. ⚠ Another word that sounds like this is **lesson.**
less·en (les'ən) *verb,* **lessened, lessening.**

lesser Smaller or less in number, size, degree, or importance. From the high peak, we

leopard

could see the *lesser* mountains around us.
less·er (les′ər) *adjective.*

lesson   **1.** Something to be learned, taught, or studied. Today's arithmetic *lesson* was on the addition of fractions. We have five more *lessons* to study in our social studies book. **2.** A period of time given to instruction; class or course of study. Do you have a piano *lesson* today? My cousin is taking skating *lessons.* ▲ Another word that sounds like this is **lessen.**
les·son (les′ən) *noun, plural* **lessons.**

let   **1.** To allow; permit. Mom and Dad *let* me go to the party. Do you *let* your friends ride your bicycle? **2.** To allow to pass or go. The hole in the roof *lets* in the rain. Open the cage and *let* the bird out. **3.** To cause or make. I will *let* my parents know what I would like for my birthday. **4.** To rent. Does your family *let* a cabin for the summer every year?
- **to let down.**   To disappoint. I *let down* my friends when I didn't help them.
- **to let out.**   **1.** To utter. At one point in the scary movie, the person sitting next to me *let out* a scream. **2.** To make larger. These jeans will have to be *let out.*
- **to let up.**   To lessen or stop. It seemed the rain would never *let up.*
let (let) *verb,* **let, letting.**

let's   Shortened form of "let us." *Let's* go for a walk.
let's (lets) *contraction.*

letter   **1.** A mark that stands for a spoken sound. The word "run" has three *letters.* **2.** A written message. I wrote a *letter* to my friend.   **3.** The initial of a school or college that is given to a student as an award. The pitcher for that high school team has received a *letter* every year for playing so well.
let·ter (let′ər) *noun, plural* **letters.**

letter carrier   A person who carries and delivers mail.

lettering   Letters that have been drawn, painted, or formed by some other means. The *lettering* on this statue is carefully carved.
let·ter·ing (let′ər ing) *noun, plural* **letterings.**

lettuce   A plant with large green or reddish leaves. Lettuce is eaten in salads. There are many different kinds of lettuce.
let·tuce (let′is) *noun, plural* **lettuces.**

lettuce

level   **1.** Having a flat, horizontal surface; even. The airport was built on *level* ground. **2.** At the same height or position. The top of the tree is *level* with the roof of the house. *Adjective.*
—**1.** Height. The flood in the basement rose to a *level* of two feet.   **2.** A position or rank in a process, series, or order. Our neighbor has risen to the *level* of manager of the store. The students in this class read at a high *level.* **3.** A floor or story of a structure. The car is parked on the lower *level.*   **4.** A tool used to show whether a surface is flat. A level is a long, narrow box with a liquid inside that indicates when the surface that it is on is flat. The carpenter put a *level* on the shelf to make sure it was straight. *Noun.*
—**1.** To make flat. The workers *leveled* the hilly land with a bulldozer.   **2.** To bring to the level of the ground; destroy. The fire *leveled* the house. *Verb.*
lev·el (lev′əl) *adjective; noun, plural* **levels;** *verb,* **leveled, leveling.**

lever   **1.** A rod or bar used to lift things or pry things open. A crowbar is a kind of lever. **2.** A rod or bar attached to a machine that is used to work or control it. The operator moved a *lever* to lower the arm of the crane.
lev·er (lev′ər *or* lē′vər) *noun, plural* **levers.**

levy   To impose or collect by lawful actions or force. The county plans to *levy* new taxes. *Verb.*
—**1.** A tax. The legislature has passed a new *levy* on gasoline.   **2.** The act of levying. The *levy* of new taxes angered many citizens. *Noun.*
lev·y (lev′ē) *verb,* **levied, levying;** *noun, plural* **levies.**

liable   **1.** Likely; apt. You are *liable* to be cold if you don't wear a jacket.   **2.** Responsible by law. The driver of the car is *liable* for the damage done to the other car.
li·a·ble (lī′ə bəl) *adjective.*

liar   A person who tells lies.
li·ar (lī′ər) *noun, plural* **liars.**

liberal   **1.** Generous. The family gave a *liberal* donation to the library.   **2.** More than enough; plentiful. The school has a *liberal* supply of chalk.   **3.** Favoring change as a way of improving things in political and so-

at; āpe; fär; câre; end; mē; it; īce; pîerce; hot; ōld; sông, fôrk; oil; out; up; ūse; rüle; pùll; tûrn; chin; sing; shop; thin; **this**; hw in white; zh in treasure. The symbol ə stands for the unstressed vowel sound in about, taken, pencil, lemon, and circus.

423

cial matters; favoring progress and reform. The two candidates in the election were a *liberal* politician and a conservative one. **4.** Not limited or narrow; broad. Science and literature are two parts of a *liberal* education. **5.** Not narrow in one's thinking; tolerant. *Adjective.*
—A person who is liberal. *Noun.*
> **lib·er·al** (lib′ər əl) *adjective; noun, plural* **liberals.**

liberate To set free. The soldiers *liberated* the prisoners.
> **lib·er·ate** (lib′ə rāt′) *verb,* **liberated, liberating.**

Liberia A country in western Africa.
> **Li·be·ri·a** (lī bîr′ē ə) *noun.*

liberty **1.** The ability to act, speak, or think the way one pleases. The people lost their *liberty* under the dictator's rule. **2.** Freedom from another's control. England was forced to give the American colonies their *liberty.* **3.** Time granted to a sailor in the navy to go ashore. During their *liberty,* the sailors watched a bullfight.
> • **at liberty.** **1.** Not confined; free. The escaped prisoners are still *at liberty.* **2.** Permitted; allowed. I am not *at liberty* to tell you.
> **lib·er·ty** (lib′ər tē) *noun, plural* **liberties.**

librarian A person who is in charge of or works in a library.
> **li·brar·i·an** (lī brâr′ē ən) *noun, plural* **librarians.**

library **1.** A collection of books, magazines, and newspapers. Many libraries also have records, films, and videotapes. My parents gave me some books for my *library.* **2.** A room or building for such a collection. You can study in the school *library.*
> **li·brar·y** (lī′brer′ē) *noun, plural* **libraries.**

Libya A country in northern Africa.
> **Lib·y·a** (lib′ē ə) *noun.*

lice Plural of **louse.** The dog was scratching because it had *lice.* Look up **louse** for more information.
> **lice** (līs) *plural noun.*

license A card, paper, or other object showing that a person has legal permission to do or have something. The police officer asked the drivers in the accident for their *licenses. Noun.*
— To give a license to or for. Doctors are *licensed* to practice medicine. *Verb.*
> **li·cense** (lī′səns) *noun, plural* **licenses;** *verb,* **licensed, licensing.**

lichen A special organism that is made up of a kind of algae and a fungus. Lichens grow on tree trunks, rocks, or the ground.
> **li·chen** (lī′kən) *noun, plural* **lichens.**

lick **1.** To move the tongue over something. I *licked* the envelope to seal it. **2.** To eat or drink something by taking it up with the tongue. The dog *licked* the water. **3.** To defeat. Our football team can *lick* their team. **4.** To move over or touch lightly or quickly. The flames began to *lick* the tree above the burning shed. *Verb.*
—**1.** A movement of the tongue over something. The cat gave the milk a *lick.* **2.** Salt that animals can lick. The farmer put a block of salt in the pasture as a *lick* for the cows. **3.** A small amount; bit. The lazy child wouldn't do a *lick* of work. *Noun.*
> **lick** (lik) *verb,* **licked, licking;** *noun, plural* **licks.**

licorice **1.** A plant whose sweet-tasting root is used in medicine and candy. **2.** A candy flavored with licorice.
> **lic·o·rice** (lik′ər is *or* lik′ər ish) *noun.*

lid **1.** A movable cover. I lifted the *lid* off the garbage can. **2.** Either of the upper or lower protective coverings of the eye; eyelid.
> **lid** (lid) *noun, plural* **lids.**

lie¹ Something a person says that he or she knows is not true. You told a *lie* when you said you were at school today. *Noun.*
—To say something that is not true; tell a lie. Those two students *lie* so often that you never know when to believe them. *Verb.*
▲ Another word that sounds like this is **lye.**
> **lie** (lī) *noun, plural* **lies;** *verb,* **lied, lying.**

lie² **1.** To put oneself in a flat position on a surface. I like to *lie* on the grass and watch the clouds. **2.** To be or rest on something. The book *lies* on the table. **3.** To stay in a certain place or condition. The treasure *lies* hidden at the bottom of the ocean. **4.** To be located or placed. Mexico *lies* south of the United States. **5.** To be found; exist. The problem with the car *lies* in the ignition.
▲ Another word that sounds like this is **lye.**
> **lie** (lī) *verb,* **lay, lain, lying.**

Language Note

The verbs **lie** and **lay,** and their inflected forms, are easy to confuse. Remember that **lay** is followed by a noun or pronoun that is used as a direct object. **Lie** does not take a direct object. Here are the various inflected forms of **lie** and **lay:**

Present	lie	lay
Past	lay	laid
Past Participle	lain	laid

lieutenant An officer in the armed forces. In the United States Army, Marine Corps, and Air Force, a lieutenant is next below a captain in rank. The two ranks of lieutenant in the Army, Air Force, and Marines are **second lieutenant** and **first lieutenant**. In the United States Navy and Coast Guard, a lieutenant is next below a commander. The two ranks of lieutenant in the Navy and Coast Guard are **lieutenant junior grade** and **lieutenant**.
  lieu·ten·ant (lü ten′ənt) *noun, plural* **lieutenants.**

life 1. The quality that makes it possible for things to grow and reproduce. Plants and animals have life. Rocks do not have life. 2. The fact of having this quality. Don't risk your *life* in a dangerous stunt. 3. A living being; person. Firefighters save many *lives* every year. 4. Living beings. There was no plant *life* in the cave. 5. The period from birth to death. My grandparents had long and happy *lives.* 6. The period during which something lasts or works. Poor driving can shorten the *life* of a car. 7. A way of living. *Life* in the city can be exciting. 8. A story of a person's life. I am reading the *life* of a great scientist. 9. Energy; spirit. You are always full of *life.*
  life (līf) *noun, plural* **lives.**

lifeboat A boat used for saving lives at sea or along the shore. A lifeboat is often carried on a larger ship.
  life·boat (līf′bōt′) *noun, plural* **lifeboats.**

life cycle The sequence of changes each living thing passes through during its life. The life cycle of animals includes birth, development, reproduction, growing old, and death.

lifeguard A person who is hired to protect and help swimmers at a beach or pool. The *lifeguard* blew a whistle to warn the swimmers that they were too far from shore.
  life·guard (līf′gärd′) *noun, plural* **lifeguards.**

lifeless Not having life.
  life·less (līf′lis) *adjective.*

lifelike Like something that is alive or real. The doll was so *lifelike* that for a moment we thought it was a real baby.
  life·like (līf′līk′) *adjective.*

lifelong Lasting or continuing through a person's life. The children became *lifelong* friends.
  life·long (līf′lông′) *adjective.*

life preserver A device used to keep a person floating in water. A life preserver can be a belt, a vest, or a ring. It is filled with air or made with a material that floats. I wear a *life preserver* whenever I go sailing.
  life pre·ser·ver (pri zûr′vər).

children wearing **life preservers**

lifesaving The skill or method of saving a person's life. Lifeguards and firefighters are trained in lifesaving. *Noun.*
—Used or made for saving a person's life. The fire engine carried *lifesaving* equipment. *Adjective.*
  life·sa·ving (līf′sā′ving) *noun; adjective.*

life span The period of time that a person, animal, or plant is expected to live.

lifetime The period of time that the life of a person or thing lasts. My grandparents have seen many changes in their *lifetime.*
  life·time (līf′tīm′) *noun, plural* **lifetimes.**

lift 1. To raise or be raised; pick up. I can't *lift* this heavy suitcase. The team's spirits *lifted* after their victory over the league champions. 2. To rise into the air. The jet *lifted* from the runway. 3. To rise or seem to rise and go; disappear. When the fog *lifted,* we had a beautiful, clear day. *Verb.*
—1. The act of lifting. Give me a *lift* into the tree. 2. A free ride given to a person. Our neighbor gave us a *lift* into town. 3. A happy feeling. Your compliment about my new outfit gave me a *lift. Noun.*
  lift (lift) *verb,* **lifted, lifting;** *noun, plural* **lifts.**

lift-off The movement of a rocket or spacecraft as it rises from its launch pad. After the *lift-off,* the rocket went into orbit.
  lift-off (lift′ôf′) *noun, plural* **lift-offs.**

at; āpe; fär; câre; end; mē; it; īce; pîerce; hot; ōld; sông, fôrk; oil; out; up; ūse; rüle; pùll; tûrn; chin; sing; shop; thin; this; hw in white; zh in treasure. The symbol ə stands for the unstressed vowel sound in about, taken, pencil, lemon, and circus.

ligament A band of strong tissue. A ligament connects bones or holds an organ of the body in place.
lig·a·ment (lig′ə mənt) *noun, plural* **ligaments.**

light¹ **1.** The form of energy that makes it possible for us to see. The sun gives off light. **2.** Something that gives off light or brightness. Candles and lamps are lights. We could see the dim *lights* of the distant town. **3.** Something used to set fire to something else. A flame and a spark are lights. Give me a *light* so I can start the logs burning. **4.** The time of day when the sun first shines; daybreak. Because I deliver newspapers, I have to wake up before *light*. **5.** Knowledge or information; understanding. The scientist's study shed new *light* on ways to prevent pollution. **6.** Public knowledge. Some new clues to the mystery have come to *light*. **7.** The way that someone thinks about something. The information caused us to see the problem in a new *light*. *Noun.*
—**1.** To burn or cause to burn. Wet wood will not *light* easily. We will *light* candles if the electricity goes off. **2.** To cause to give off light. When you *light* that lamp, it makes the whole room bright. **3.** To give brightness to. One large bulb *lights* the long hallway. **4.** To make or become bright or lively. Your face *lighted* up when you heard you had passed the test. **5.** To show the way by means of a light or lights. Please *light* our way up these dark steps with your flashlight. *Verb.*
—**1.** Bright; not dark. The room was *light* and airy. **2.** Pale in color. I have a *light* complexion and sunburn easily. *Adjective.*
light (līt) *noun, plural* **lights;** *verb,* **lighted** or **lit, lighting;** *adjective,* **lighter, lightest.**

light² **1.** Having little weight; not heavy. The empty box was *light*. **2.** Not great in amount or force. A *light* rain fell. The leaves hardly moved in the *light* breeze. **3.** Easy to do or bear; not hard. We did some *light* cleaning in the living room. **4.** Moving easily; graceful; nimble. Good dancers are *light* on their feet. **5.** Happy; cheerful. We whistled a *light* tune. **6.** Entertaining; amusing; not serious. I read a good, *light* novel last week. **7.** Few or slight; not serious. The army suffered *light* losses in the battle.
light (līt) *adjective,* **lighter, lightest.**

lighten¹ To make or become brighter or lighter. The sky *lightened* after the thunderstorm ended.
light·en (līt′ən) *verb,* **lightened, lightening.**

lighten² **1.** To make or become less heavy or harsh. You'll have to *lighten* that suitcase because no one can lift it. The teacher *lightened* the homework assignment. **2.** To make or become more cheerful; ease. My spirits *lightened* when the test was over.
light·en (līt′ən) *verb,* **lightened, lightening.**

lighthearted Not bothered by worries; cheerful; gay. The *lighthearted* child was always laughing.
light·heart·ed (līt′här′tid) *adjective.*

lighthouse A tower with a strong light on top. It is built near a dangerous place in the water to warn or guide ships.
light·house (līt′hous′) *noun, plural* **lighthouses** (līt′hou′ziz).

lighthouse

lighting The system or arrangement of lights in a room, building, or area. This room is too dark; we need better *lighting*.
light·ing (līt′ting) *noun.*

lightning A flash of light in the sky. It is caused by electricity moving between clouds or between a cloud and the ground. *Lightning* struck our house during the storm.
light·ning (līt′ning) *noun.*

lightning bug A small beetle that gives off flashes of light as a signal to a mate; firefly.

light pen An instrument that is shaped like a pen and is used to draw or change images on a computer screen or to give commands to the computer.

light–year The distance that light travels through space in one year. Since light moves at a speed of about 186,000 miles per second, it travels about 5,880,000 miles in one year. If a star is 30 *light-years* away, it takes 30 years for its light to reach the earth.
light-year (līt′yîr′) *noun, plural* **light-years.**

likable Easy to like; agreeable; pleasant. It's hard to argue with someone who is so *likable*. This word is also spelled **likeable**.
lik·a·ble *or* like·a·ble (lī′kə bəl) *adjective*.

-like A *suffix* that means similar to; like. *Lifelike* means like life.

like¹ **1.** Almost the same as; similar to. Your bicycle is *like* mine. **2.** In the same or a similar way as. I tried to crow *like* a rooster. **3.** Such as. I do well in subjects *like* math and science. **4.** Having the desire to; inclined to. Do you feel *like* watching television or playing a game? **5.** Giving a promise or indication of; likely to. It looks *like* rain. *Preposition.*
—Similar or equal. The twins wore *like* outfits. The boss gave me a fifty-dollar bonus and a *like* amount to all the other workers. *Adjective.*
—**1.** In the way that; as. This soup doesn't taste *like* it has enough salt. **2.** As if; as though. It looks *like* it will snow today. *Conjunction.*
like (līk) *preposition; adjective; conjunction.*

like² To be fond of; enjoy. Do you *like* sports? Out of the litter, I *like* the brown puppy the most. I *like* swimming in the ocean. *Verb.*
—**likes.** The things a person enjoys or prefers. My cousin has strong *likes* and dislikes in clothes. *Noun.*
like (līk) *verb,* **liked, liking;** *plural noun.*

likelihood The condition or quality of being expected. Is there any *likelihood* that it will rain tonight? In all *likelihood*, I will leave tomorrow.
like·li·hood (līk′lē hu̇d′) *noun.*

likely **1.** Seeming to be true; probable. The damp weather is the *likely* cause of this year's poor strawberry crop. **2.** To be expected. The weather announcer says it is *likely* to rain tomorrow. We are *likely* to finish painting the fence by sundown. **3.** Right for the time or purpose; suitable. That student has many good ideas and is a *likely* candidate for school president. *Adjective.*
—Almost certainly, probably. Judging from the nice porch they built, they're most *likely* good carpenters. *Adverb.*
like·ly (līk′lē) *adjective,* **likelier, likeliest;** *adverb.*

likeness **1.** The condition of looking alike; resemblance. The girl's *likeness* to her mother was very strong. **2.** A portrait. A one-dollar bill has a *likeness* of George Washington on it.
like·ness (līk′nis) *noun, plural* **likenesses.**

likewise **1.** In a like way; similarly. Watch what the swimming teacher does and then do *likewise*. **2.** Also. The class president is a fine athlete and a good student *likewise*.
like·wise (līk′wīz′) *adverb.*

liking A feeling of being fond or preferring. I have a *liking* for folk music.
lik·ing (lī′king) *noun, plural* **likings.**

lilac **1.** A shrub that has clusters of purple, pink, or white flowers. Some lilacs have flowers that smell very sweet. **2.** A pale, pinkish purple color. *Noun.*
—Having a pale, pinkish purple color. *Adjective.*
li·lac (lī′lək) *noun, plural* **lilacs;** *adjective.*

lily **1.** A large, showy flower that is shaped like a trumpet. The lily grows from a bulb. **2.** Any plant like a lily. A water lily grows in the water.
lil·y (lil′ē) *noun, plural* **lilies.**

lily of the valley A plant that grows from a bulb and has tiny flowers growing down one side of its stem. The flowers smell very sweet and are shaped like bells.

lily of the valley

lima bean A flat, pale green bean that is cooked and eaten as a vegetable.
li·ma bean (lī′mə).

limb **1.** A part of a body used in moving or grasping. Arms, legs, wings, and flippers are limbs. **2.** One of the large branches of a tree. We hung a swing from a *limb* of the old tree.
limb (lim) *noun, plural* **limbs.**

lime¹ A white substance like powder that is made up of calcium and oxygen. Lime is found in seashells or is made by burning limestone. Lime is used in making plaster and cement and as a fertilizer.
lime (līm) *noun.*

lime² A small, yellowish green citrus fruit. The lime has an oval or round shape, a thin

at; āpe; fär; câre; end; mē; it; īce; pîerce; hot; ōld; sông, fôrk; oil; out; up; ūse; rüle; pu̇ll; tûrn; chin; sing; shop; thin; this; hw in white; zh in treasure. The symbol ə stands for the unstressed vowel sound in about, taken, pencil, lemon, and circus.

L

rind, and a juicy pulp. It grows on a thorny evergreen tree.

lime (līm) *noun, plural* **limes.**

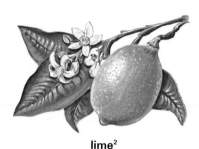

lime²

limerick A funny poem five lines long. An example of a limerick is: There once was a man named Paul/ Who went to a masquerade ball./ He decided to risk it/ And go as a biscuit/ But a dog ate him up in the hall.
lim·er·ick (lim′ər ik) *noun, plural* **limericks.**

Word History

The word **limerick** comes from the name of a place in Ireland. It was the custom at parties to take turns making up funny poems. At the end of a poem, everyone would sing, "Will you come up to Limerick?" This may be how these funny poems got their name.

limestone A hard rock used for building and for making lime. Most limestone is light gray.
lime·stone (līm′stōn′) *noun.*

limit The point at which something ends or must end. Stay inside the *limits* of the park. That car was going faster than the speed *limit. Noun.*
—To keep within a bound or bounds; restrict. I have to *limit* my spending because I'm trying to save money. *Verb.*
lim·it (lim′it) *noun, plural* **limits;** *verb,* **limited, limiting.**

limp¹ To walk unevenly or with difficulty. The dog is *limping* because it hurt its leg. *Verb.*
—A lame or uneven walk. An accident on the court caused the basketball player's *limp. Noun.*
limp (limp) *verb,* **limped, limping;** *noun, plural* **limps.**

limp² Not stiff or firm. After three days of heat, the flowers became *limp* and died.
limp (limp) *adjective,* **limper, limpest.**

Lincoln's Birthday A holiday on February 12 observed in some states to celebrate Abraham Lincoln's birthday. This holiday is observed by many states on **Presidents' Day.** Look up **Presidents' Day** for more information.
Lin·coln's Birthday (ling′kənz).

line¹ **1.** A long, thin mark or stroke. White *lines* divide the lanes of the highway. **2.** Anything like a line. Your forehead is full of *lines* from frowning. **3.** A limit or boundary; edge. That row of trees marks the *line* of our property. **4.** A number of persons or things arranged one after the other; row. We waited in a long *line* outside the movie theater. **5.** A row of words or letters on a page. The journalist wrote a column of thirty *lines* for the newspaper. **6.** A short letter, note, or verse. While you're at camp, don't forget to drop us a *line* once in a while. **7. lines.** The words spoken by a person in a play. I was so nervous in front of the large audience that I forgot my *lines.* **8.** A kind of goods. That store is selling a new *line* of bicycles. **9.** A system of transportation in which vehicles travel over a route on a regular schedule. The bus *line* runs buses on most of the main streets of the city. **10.** A cord, rope, wire, or cable that is used for a special purpose. We hung the wash on the *line* to dry. I telephoned you, but your *line* was busy. **11.** A pipe that carries a fluid from one place to another. The water *line* broke, and our neighborhood was without water for three days. *Noun.*
—**1.** To mark or cover with lines. I always *line* blank paper before I write on it. **2.** To form a line along. Trees *lined* the edge of the road. *Verb.*
• **in line.** **1.** In a line or row. We waited *in line* for tickets. **2.** In agreement. Most of your ideas are *in line* with mine.
• **to line up.** **1.** To form or cause to form a line. The workers *lined up* to get their pay. The teacher *lined* the students *up* according to their height. **2.** To obtain or gather. The mayor is trying *to line up* supporters for the new tax law.
line (līn) *noun, plural* **lines;** *verb,* **lined, lining.**

line² **1.** To cover the inside of. The tailor *lined* the wool suit with silk. **2.** To be used as a lining or covering for. Paintings *lined* the walls of the museum.
line (līn) *verb,* **lined, lining.**

linear Having to do with length. Feet, miles, centimeters, and inches are *linear* measurements.
lin·e·ar (lin′ē ər) *adjective.*

linen **1.** A cloth woven from fibers of flax. **2. linens.** Household things made of linen or a similar cloth. Sheets, tablecloths, towels, and napkins are linens. *Noun.*
—Made of linen. *Adjective.*
lin·en (lin′ən) *noun, plural* **linens;** *adjective.*

liner A ship or airplane that belongs to a transportation line.
lin·er (lī′nər) *noun, plural* **liners.**

linger To stay on as if not wanting to leave; move slowly. The fans *lingered* outside the stadium to see the players on the team.
lin·ger (ling′gər) *verb,* **lingered, lingering.**

lining The layer or coating that covers the inside of something. The fur *lining* of the jacket made it very warm.
lin·ing (lī′ning) *noun, plural* **linings.**

link **1.** One of the rings or loops of a chain. **2.** Anything that joins or connects. That museum provides a *link* to our country's history. **3.** Something that looks like a link in a chain, such as links of sausage. *Noun.*
—To join or be joined; connect. We *linked* arms to form a circle. *Verb.*
link (lingk) *noun, plural* **links;** *verb,* **linked, linking.**

linking verb A verb that links a subject with a predicate noun or a predicate adjective. A linking verb does not express action. In the sentence "The movie was a thrilling mystery," "was" is a linking verb.

linoleum A floor covering that is made with a hardened mixture of linseed oil and finely ground cork or wood put on a canvas back. It is nailed or glued in place.
li·no·le·um (li nō′lē əm) *noun, plural* **linoleums.**

linseed oil An oil from the seed of certain flax plants, used to make paints, varnish, ink, patent leather, and linoleum.
lin·seed oil (lin′sēd′).

lion A large, strong animal of the cat family. The lion lives mainly in Africa and southern Asia. It has a yellowish brown coat of short, coarse hair. The male has long, shaggy hair around its neck, head, and shoulders.
li·on (lī′ən) *noun, plural* **lions.**

lioness A female lion.
li·on·ess (lī′ə nis) *noun, plural* **lionesses.**

lip **1.** Either of the two soft flaps of flesh that form the opening to the mouth. **2.** The edge or rim of an opening. I chipped the *lip* of the pitcher.
lip (lip) *noun, plural* **lips.**

lipstick A stick of oily material used as a cosmetic for coloring the lips.
lip·stick (lip′stik′) *noun, plural* **lipsticks.**

liquid A form of matter that is not a solid or a gas. A liquid can flow easily. It can take on the shape of any container into which it is poured. Water, milk, and ink are liquids. *Noun.*
—In the form of a liquid; not solid or gaseous. The nurse gave me the *liquid* medicine with a spoon. *Adjective.*
liq·uid (lik′wid) *noun, plural* **liquids;** *adjective.*

liquor A kind of alcoholic drink. Whiskey and gin are liquors.
liq·uor (lik′ər) *noun, plural* **liquors.**

lira A unit of money in Italy.
li·ra (lîr′ə) *noun, plural* **lire** (lîr′ā).

lisp A way of speaking in which a person says the sound of *s* as the sound of *th* in *thing* and the sound of *z* as the sound of *th* in *them. Noun.*
—To speak with a lisp. *Verb.*
lisp (lisp) *noun, plural* **lisps;** *verb,* **lisped, lisping.**

list¹ A series of names, numbers, or other things. Make a *list* of the groceries we need to buy. *Noun.*
—To make a list of or enter in a list. The teacher *listed* the students in the class. Is your name *listed* in the telephone book? *Verb.*
list (list) *noun, plural* **lists;** *verb,* **listed, listing.**

list² A leaning to one side. The *list* of the sailboat was caused by the strong wind. *Noun.*
—To lean to one side; tilt. The ship *listed* sharply in the bad storm. *Verb.*
list (list) *noun, plural* **lists;** *verb,* **listed, listing.**

L

lion

at; āpe; fär; câre; end; mē; it; ice; pîerce; hot; ōld; sông, fôrk; oil; out; up; ūse; rüle; pùll; tûrn; chin; sing; shop; thin; <u>th</u>is; hw in white; zh in treasure. The symbol ə stands for the unstressed vowel sound in about, taken, pencil, lemon, and circus.

listen To try to hear; pay attention in order to hear. *Listen* for the sound of the school bus.
lis·ten (lis′ən) *verb,* **listened, listening.**

lit A past tense and a past participle of **light**[1]. Have you *lit* the fire yet? Look up **light**[1] for more information.
lit (lit) *verb.*

liter A unit of measurement in the metric system. A liter is a little larger than a quart of liquid.
li·ter (lē′tər) *noun, plural* **liters.**

literacy The ability to read and write. *Literacy* is essential in the modern world.
lit·er·a·cy (lit′ər ə sē) *noun.*

literally 1. Considering each word; word for word. The class translated the story from Spanish into English *literally.* 2. Really; actually. The village was *literally* destroyed by the earthquake.
lit·er·al·ly (lit′ər ə lē) *adverb.*

literate Able to read and write.
lit·er·ate (lit′ər it) *adjective.*

literature 1. Writing that has lasting value. Literature includes plays, poems, and novels. My cousin studies American *literature* in college. 2. Printed matter of any kind. Some *literature* came with the new dryer.
lit·er·a·ture (lit′ər ə chər *or* lit′ər ə chùr′) *noun.*

litmus paper A paper soaked in a dye and used in chemistry experiments. Red litmus paper turns blue in a base solution, and blue litmus paper turns red in an acid solution.
lit·mus paper (lit′məs).

litter 1. Bits or scraps of paper or other rubbish; mess. Broken bottles and other *litter* filled the empty lot. 2. A group of young animals born at one time to the same mother. Our cat gave birth to a *litter* of five

a **litter** of puppies on a bed

kittens. 3. A stretcher for carrying a sick or injured person. *Noun.*
—To scatter or leave bits of rubbish around; make dirty with litter. *Verb.*
lit·ter (lit′ər) *noun, plural* **litters;** *verb,* **littered, littering.**

little 1. Small in size or amount. A pebble is a *little* stone. Give the plant a *little* water. 2. Short in time or distance. We will be home in a *little* while. *Adjective.*
—Not much; slightly. Snow is *little* seen in warm, dry places. *Adverb.*
—1. A small amount. I ate only a *little* because I wasn't hungry. 2. A short time or distance. Step back a *little* so that I can get by you. *Noun.*
lit·tle (lit′əl) *adjective,* **less** or **lesser** or **littler, least** or **littlest;** *adverb,* **less, least;** *noun.*

Little Dipper A group of seven stars in the northern sky. They form the outline of a dipper. The star at the end of the Little Dipper's handle is called the North Star.

live[1] 1. To be alive; have life. That ruler *lived* during the Middle Ages. 2. To stay alive. Most fish cannot *live* out of water. 3. To support oneself. That family *lives* on a small income. 4. To feed. Some birds *live* on bugs and worms. 5. To make one's home. We *live* on the east side of town. This kind of spider *lives* in the desert.
live (liv) *verb,* **lived, living.**

live[2] 1. Having life; living. The hunter brought back a *live* elephant to the zoo. 2. Burning. Be careful because there are still *live* coals in the fireplace. 3. Carrying an electric current. After the thunderstorm, we had to be careful of *live* wires that were blown down across the road. 4. Seen while actually happening; not taped. We saw a *live* television show. 5. Containing an explosive; capable of exploding. The police discovered a *live* bomb in the suitcase.
live (līv) *adjective.*

livelihood The means of staying alive or supporting life. A journalist earns a *livelihood* by writing articles for newspapers or magazines.
live·li·hood (līv′lē hùd′) *noun, plural* **livelihoods.**

lively 1. Full of life or energy; gay or cheerful. The *lively* kitten played with the ball of string. The band played a *lively* tune. 2. Bright and strong. The colors of the clown's costume were very *lively. Adjective.*
—In a lively manner; with vigor. The horses stepped *lively. Adverb.*
live·ly (līv′lē) *adjective,* **livelier, liveliest;** *adverb.*

liver **1.** A large, reddish brown organ in the body. The liver cleans the blood, stores fats and sugars, and makes bile. **2.** The liver of certain animals when used as food.
liv·er (liv′ər) *noun, plural* **livers.**

livery **1.** A uniform worn by servants or the members of a profession. The *livery* of the cook included a white hat and apron. **2.** A stable where horses are cared for and rented out.
liv·er·y (liv′ə rē) *noun, plural* **liveries.**

lives Plural of **life.** The firefighters saved many *lives* during the fire. Look up **life** for more information.
lives (līvz) *plural noun.*

livestock Animals raised on a farm or ranch for profit. Cows, horses, sheep, and pigs are livestock. We enjoy seeing the *livestock* when we go to the county fair.
live·stock (līv′stok′) *noun.*

livid **1.** Having a pale, usually bluish, color. Your face was *livid* with anger. **2.** Changed in color because of a bruise. I had a *livid* mark on my arm where the ball had hit me.
liv·id (liv′id) *adjective.*

living **1.** Having life; alive. All animals are *living* creatures. We read a book on famous *living* artists. **2.** Of or for life. *Living* conditions in the town were bad after the flood. **3.** Still active or in use. Russian is a *living* language. *Adjective.*
—**1.** The condition or fact of being alive. I enjoy *living* by the sea. **2.** A means of maintaining the condition of being alive; livelihood. My cousin earns a *living* as a firefighter. **3.** A way of life. The athlete believed in healthy *living. Noun.*
liv·ing (liv′ing) *adjective; noun, plural* **livings.**

living room A room in a home for the general use of the family or for entertaining guests.

lizard An animal with a scaly body, four legs, and a long tail. Lizards are reptiles and are related to snakes and alligators.
liz·ard (liz′ərd) *noun, plural* **lizards.**

lizard

llama A shaggy animal that belongs to the camel family. Llamas live in the mountains of South America. They are used for carrying heavy loads.
lla·ma (lä′mə) *noun, plural* **llamas.**

llama

load **1.** Something carried. The wagon has a *load* of hay. **2.** The amount or number that can be carried. Just one *load* of bricks will be enough to build the patio. **3.** Something that burdens the mind or heart. Finishing my book report a day before it was due took a *load* off my mind. *Noun.*
—**1.** To put a load in or on something. I *loaded* the box with old clothes. The workers *loaded* the rocks onto the truck. **2.** To put something needed into a device. The photographer *loaded* the camera with film. Our teacher will show us how to *load* the program into the computer. **3.** To put a charge of gunpowder or ammunition into a gun. The hunter *loaded* the rifle. *Verb.* ⬥ Another word that sounds like this is **lode.**
load (lōd) *noun, plural* **loads;** *verb,* **loaded, loading.**

loaf¹ **1.** Bread baked in one piece. **2.** Any mass of food in the shape of a loaf of bread. We had a meat *loaf* for dinner.
loaf (lōf) *noun, plural* **loaves.**

loaf² To spend time doing little or nothing. I sometimes *loaf* when I'm on vacation.
loaf (lōf) *verb,* **loafed, loafing.**

loan **1.** The act of lending something. Thank you for the *loan* of your pencil during the test. **2.** Something that is lent. Our neighbor received a *loan* of five thousand dollars from the bank. *Noun.*
—To lend. Please *loan* me your bicycle for tomorrow. I *loaned* my friend a dollar. *Verb.*
⬥ Another word that sounds like this is **lone.**
loan (lōn) *noun, plural* **loans;** *verb,* **loaned, loaning.**

L

loathe To dislike strongly; to feel disgust toward. I *loathe* small animals that crawl, but my cousin finds them interesting.
loathe (lōth) *verb,* **loathed, loathing.**

loathsome Extremely disgusting or hateful. The *loathsome* monster in the movie had five red eyes and slimy skin.
loath·some (lōth'səm) *adjective.*

loaves Plural of **loaf**¹. The *loaves* of bread were delivered by the bakery. Look up **loaf**¹ for more information.
loaves (lōvz) *plural noun.*

lobby 1. A hall or room at the entrance to a building. The movie theater had a large *lobby*. 2. A person or group that tries to convince legislators to vote in a certain way. *Noun.*
—To try to convince legislators to vote in a certain way. A group of citizens *lobbied* against the bill to build a new highway. *Verb.*
lob·by (lob'ē) *noun, plural* **lobbies;** *verb,* **lobbied, lobbying.**

lobster A saltwater animal that has a hard shell and five pairs of legs. The front pair of legs ends in large claws. Lobsters are crustaceans and are eaten as food.
lob·ster (lob'stər) *noun, plural* **lobsters.**

lobster

local 1. Having to do with a particular place. We went to the *local* library. My neighbor writes for the *local* newspaper. 2. Stopping at all or most of the stops along a route; not an express. We rode the *local* train. 3. Having to do with or affecting only a part of the body. The dentist gave the patient a *local* anesthetic. *Adjective.*
—A train, bus, or subway that stops at all or most of the stops along its route. *Noun.*
lo·cal (lō'kəl) *adjective; noun, plural* **locals.**

locality A place and the area around it. You'll like the camp's *locality* because it is on a lake.
lo·cal·i·ty (lō kal'i tē) *noun, plural* **localities.**

locate 1. To find the place or position of. He could not *locate* his lost book. She *located* Kansas on the map. 2. To put or settle in a particular place. The baker *located* the bak-

ery in the new shopping center. The family left the large city to *locate* in a small town.
lo·cate (lō'kāt) *verb,* **located, locating.**

location 1. The place where something is located; site. Where is the *location* of your school? Their new house is in a beautiful *location* on top of a hill. 2. The act of locating. Your *location* of the North Pole on the map was correct.
lo·ca·tion (lō kā'shən) *noun, plural* **locations.**

locks in a canal

lock¹ 1. A fastener for a door, window, chest, or other thing. Many locks can be opened with a key or combination. 2. A part of a canal or other waterway through which water can be pumped in or out to raise or lower ships. Ships use a lock to pass from one body of water to another that is at a different level. *Noun.*
—1. To fasten with a lock. Be sure to *lock* the front door. 2. To shut in or out of a place. The owner of the store *locked* the money in a metal box. We were *locked* out of the house. 3. To join or hold firmly. The two cars *locked* bumpers in the accident. *Verb.*
lock (lok) *noun, plural* **locks;** *verb,* **locked, locking.**

lock² 1. A piece of hair, cotton, or wool. 2. **locks.** The hair on a person's head. The child's *locks* were soft and curly.
lock (lok) *noun, plural* **locks.**

locker A small closet, cabinet, or chest that can be locked. At school, we have metal *lockers* to keep our coats, books, and other belongings in.
lock·er (lok'ər) *noun, plural* **lockers.**

locket A small case for holding a picture of someone. It is often worn on a chain around the neck.
lock·et (lok'it) *noun, plural* **lockets.**

lockjaw A disease caused by germs that enter the body through a wound. One of the first signs of this disease is tight muscles in

the jaw. This disease is also called **tetanus**. Look up **tetanus** for more information.
lock·jaw (lok′jô′) *noun.*

locksmith A person who makes or fixes locks and keys. We had to call a *locksmith* when we locked ourselves out of the house.
lock·smith (lok′smith′) *noun, plural* **locksmiths.**

locomotion The act or capability of moving from place to place. A powerful steam engine provided the *locomotion* of the freight train.
lo·co·mo·tion (lō′kə mō′shən) *noun.*

locomotive An engine that moves on its own power. It is used to pull railroad cars.
lo·co·mo·tive (lō′kə mō′tiv) *noun, plural* **locomotives.**

Word History

The word **locomotive** comes from two Latin words that mean "place" and "moving." *Locomotive* first meant "moving from place to place."

locust 1. A type of large grasshopper that travels in huge swarms and destroys crops. 2. A tree that has small leaves and fragrant white, pink, or purple flowers.
lo·cust (lō′kəst) *noun, plural* **locusts.**

Leaf

locust

lode A deposit of a metal in the earth. The prospectors discovered and mined a *lode* of silver. ▲ Another word that sounds like this is **load**.
lode (lōd) *noun, plural* **lodes.**

lodestone A stone containing iron that acts as a magnet.
lode·stone (lōd′stōn′) *noun, plural* **lodestones.**

lodge 1. A small house, cottage, or cabin. The hunters stayed at a *lodge* in the mountains. 2. A branch of a club or other organization. *Noun.*
—1. To live in a place for a while. People *lodged* in the school during the flood. 2. To provide with a place to live for a while; rent rooms to. That couple *lodges* tourists in their home. 3. To become stuck or fixed in a place. A pebble *lodged* in my shoe and made walking very uncomfortable. 4. To bring to someone in authority. We *lodged* a complaint with the owner of the building about our noisy neighbors. *Verb.*
lodge (loj) *noun, plural* **lodges;** *verb,* **lodged, lodging.**

lodger A person who rents a room or rooms in someone else's home.
lodg·er (loj′ər) *noun, plural* **lodgers.**

lodging 1. A place to live in for a while. The family wanted *lodging* for the weekend. 2. **lodgings.** A rented room or rooms in someone else's home.
lodg·ing (loj′ing) *noun, plural* **lodgings.**

loft 1. The upper floor, room, or space in a building. Lofts in office buildings are used as work or storage areas. Lofts in stables and barns are used for storing hay. 2. An upper floor or balcony in a large hall or church. The choir sang in the choir *loft.* 3. A large, open room in a building. The owner of the building divided the *loft* into three apartments.
loft (lôft) *noun, plural* **lofts.**

lofty 1. Very high; towering. We saw many *lofty* skyscrapers in the city. The hikers climbed to the *lofty* mountain peak. 2. High and noble. Many knights of olden times believed in *lofty* ideals. 3. Too proud; haughty. A *lofty* manner can offend people.
loft·y (lôf′tē) *adjective,* **loftier, loftiest.**

log 1. A piece of a tree cut with the bark still on. The pioneer family used *logs* to build a cabin. 2. The record of the voyage of a ship or the flight of an airplane. The captain of the ship kept a *log. Noun.*
—1. To cut down trees in a forest and shape them into logs. 2. To make a record of a ship's voyage in a log. *Verb.*
—Made of logs. The hunters slept in a *log* cabin. *Adjective.*
log (lôg *or* log) *noun, plural* **logs;** *verb,* **logged, logging;** *adjective.*

at; āpe; fär; câre; end; mē; it; īce; pîerce; hot; ōld; sông, fôrk; oil; out; up; ūse; rüle; pùll; tûrn; chin; sing; shop; thin; this; hw in white; zh in treasure. The symbol ə stands for the unstressed vowel sound in about, taken, pencil, lemon, and circus.

loganberry The reddish purple fruit of a thorny shrub. It has a sharp taste.
lo·gan·ber·ry (lō′gən ber′ē) *noun, plural* **loganberries.**

logger A person who logs trees; lumberjack.
log·ger (lô′gər *or* log′ər) *noun, plural* **loggers.**

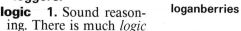

loganberries

logic 1. Sound reasoning. There is much *logic* in your argument. 2. Any method of reasoning. I don't understand the *logic* behind planting flowers in winter. 3. The study of the rules for reasoning and for proving things by reasoning.
log·ic (loj′ik) *noun.*

logical 1. Having to do with or done by sound reasoning. The dealer gave a *logical* explanation for how the gears on my bicycle work. 2. Capable of reasoning correctly. You have a *logical* mind. 3. Naturally to be expected. It is *logical* that if you make fun of them, you will hurt their feelings.
log·i·cal (loj′i kəl) *adjective.*

LOGO A computer language that is very easy to learn. LOGO can be used to draw pictures.
LOGO (lō′gō) *noun.*

loin 1. The part of a person or animal between the ribs and hip on each side of the body. 2. A cut of meat from this part of an animal.
loin (loin) *noun, plural* **loins.**

loiter 1. To stand around; be idle. A group of students *loitered* in the hall. 2. To move slowly. I *loitered* on my way to the dentist.
loi·ter (loi′tər) *verb,* **loitered, loitering.**

lollipop A piece of hard candy on the end of a stick.
lol·li·pop (lol′ē pop′) *noun, plural* **lollipops.**

lone 1. Away from others; alone; solitary. A *lone* star twinkled in the early evening sky. 2. Only; sole. The pilot was the *lone* survivor of the airplane crash. ▲ Another word that sounds like this is **loan.**
lone (lōn) *adjective.*

lonely 1. Unhappy from being alone. The student felt *lonely* at the new school. 2. Away from others; alone. A *lonely* house stood by itself on the hill. 3. Not often visited or used by people; deserted. We were the only people on the *lonely* beach.
lone·ly (lōn′lē) *adjective,* **lonelier, loneliest.**

lonesome 1. Unhappy from being alone. Were you *lonesome* when your best friend was away at camp? 2. Not often visited or used by people; deserted. We drove along the dark, *lonesome* road.
lone·some (lōn′səm) *adjective.*

long[1] 1. Of or having great length; not short. It's a *long* way from our school to the lake. There was a *long* wait before the movie started. 2. Having or lasting for a certain length. The room is ten feet *long*. The program was an hour *long*. 3. Taking more time to pronounce. The "e" in the word "be" is a *long* vowel. *Adjective.*
—1. For a long time. Our guests did not stay *long*. 2. Throughout the length of. It snowed all morning *long*. 3. At a time in the far past. That castle was built *long* ago. *Adverb.*
—A long time. They should return before *long*. *Noun.*
long (lông) *adjective,* **longer, longest;** *adverb; noun.*

long[2] To want very much; yearn. I *longed* to see my old friends again.
long (lông) *verb,* **longed, longing.**

long-distance 1. Covering or capable of covering a long distance. These trucks are *long-distance* carriers. 2. Connecting distant locations. We made a *long-distance* call to our grandparents on their anniversary. *Adjective.*
—By means of a long-distance connection. I called my friend *long-distance*. *Adverb.*
long-dis·tance (lông′dis′təns) *adjective; adverb.*

longhand Writing that is done by hand. When you write in longhand, you write the words out in full.
long·hand (lông′hand′) *noun.*

longhorn A breed of cattle with very long horns. Longhorns were once common in the southwestern United States.
long·horn (lông′hôrn′) *noun, plural* **longhorns.**

longhorn

longing A feeling of strong desire; yearning. The children have a *longing* to visit the zoo. *Noun.*
—Feeling or showing a strong desire. The hungry child cast *longing* glances at the food. *Adjective.*
long·ing (lông′ing) *noun, plural* **longings;** *adjective.*

longitude Distance that is measured on the earth's surface east and west of an imaginary line passing through the town of Greenwich, England. On a map or globe, lines of longitude are drawn from the North Pole to the South Pole. Longitude is expressed in degrees.

lines of **longitude**

lon·gi·tude (lôn′ji tüd′ *or* lôn′ji tūd′) *noun, plural* **longitudes.**

look 1. To use one's eyes; see. I *looked* at my friend's stamp collection. *Look* carefully before you cross the street. 2. To turn one's eyes or attention. *Look* at the camera and smile! 3. To make a search or examination. I *looked* through the magazine to find the article on fishing. 4. To appear; seem. You *look* tired. 5. To face in a certain direction or have a certain view. These windows *look* north. *Verb.*
—1. The act of looking; a glance or inspection. Take a *look* at this new bicycle. Don't buy the car if you haven't had a good *look* at it. 2. Appearance. The guest had a cheerful *look*. The new car has a shiny *look*. 3. **looks.** The outward appearance. I don't like the *looks* of those clouds. *Noun.*
- **to look after.** To take care of. I *looked after* the neighbor's dog for a week.
- **to look down on.** To have a feeling of dislike for and of being better than. Don't *look down on* people who are different from you.
- **to look forward to.** To wait for eagerly. We *look forward to* our vacation.
- **to look into.** To ask questions about, examine, or search for. The police *looked into* the reason for the accident.
- **to look up.** 1. To search for and find. The librarian *looked up* the date of the battle in an encyclopedia. 2. To locate and visit. When I got to the city, I *looked up* an old friend. 3. To get better; improve. Business is *looking up*.

- **to look up to.** To respect. People in the United States *look up to* the Supreme Court.
look (lük) *verb,* **looked, looking;** *noun, plural* **looks.**

looking glass A surface made with glass that reflects light; mirror.

lookout 1. A careful watch for someone or something. When crossing the street, be on the *lookout* for cars. 2. A person who keeps a careful watch. The *lookout* in the tower warned the town when enemy soldiers appeared. 3. A place from which to keep a careful watch. The high tower of the castle served as a *lookout*.
look·out (lük′out′) *noun, plural* **lookouts.**

loom¹ A machine or frame for weaving thread into cloth.
loom (lüm) *noun, plural* **looms.**

loom¹

loom² To appear as large and dangerous or full of trouble. A ship *loomed* in the fog. The most important test for the new airplane still *loomed* ahead.
loom (lüm) *verb,* **loomed, looming.**

at; āpe; fär; câre; end; mē; it; īce; pîerce; hot; ōld; sông, fôrk; oil; out; up; ūse; rüle; pùll; tûrn; chin; sing; shop; thin; this; hw in white; zh in treasure. The symbol ə stands for the unstressed vowel sound in about, taken, pencil, lemon, and circus.

loon A water bird with short legs and webbed feet that dives and swims in the water for fish. The loon has a loud, laughing call.
loon (lün) *noun, plural* **loons.**

loon

loop 1. The rounded shape formed by the part of a string, wire, or rope that crosses itself. 2. Anything like a loop. The curly ribbon on the package had many *loops*. The belt goes through the *loops* of the pants. 3. A series of commands for a computer that is repeated until the computer is instructed to stop. *Noun.*
—To make a loop or loops in something; form a loop or loops. You *loop* the laces when you tie your shoes. As the dog ran, the chain *looped* around the tree. *Verb.*
loop (lüp) *noun, plural* **loops;** *verb,* **looped, looping.**

loose 1. Not fastened or attached firmly. A page was *loose* in the book. A *loose* wire caused the radio to stop playing. 2. Free. The canary is *loose* in the house. 3. Not tight. My friend wears a *loose* jacket. 4. Not tied or joined together. I carry *loose* keys in my pocket. 5. Not in a package or container. We bought some *loose* carrots at the store. 6. Not packed or pressed tightly together. The workers put *loose* gravel on the driveway. The tablecloth has a *loose* weave. *Adjective.*
—1. To set free; let go. We *loosed* the dog in the field. 2. To make or become less tight; loosen or unfasten. You *loosed* the knot. *Verb.*
loose (lüs) *adjective,* **looser, loosest;** *verb,* **loosed, loosing.**

loose-leaf 1. Holding or made to hold pages that have holes and are easily removed. I keep my book reports in a *loose-leaf* notebook. 2. Made to be put in and removed from a special notebook that has rings that open. *Loose-leaf* paper is available with two or three holes.
loose-leaf (lüs′lēf′) *adjective.*

loosen 1. To make or become loose or looser. *Loosen* your necktie. I *loosened* my

hold on the rope. 2. To set free or release. The dog had been *loosened* from its leash.
loos·en (lü′sən) *verb,* **loosened, loosening.**

loot Things that have been stolen. The thieves hid their *loot* in a barn. *Noun.*
—To steal valuable things from; plunder. The enemy soldiers *looted* the town. *Verb.*
▲ Another word that sounds like this is **lute.**
loot (lüt) *noun; verb,* **looted, looting.**

lopsided Larger or heavier on one side than on the other; leaning more to one side than to the other. The dog's uneven ears gave it a *lopsided* appearance.
lop·sid·ed (lop′sī′did) *adjective.*

lord 1. A person who has power over others or is of noble rank. In the Middle Ages, a lord was a powerful man who lived in a castle and had many people under his rule. 2. **Lord.** In Great Britain, a title for a man of noble rank. 3. **Lord. a.** God. **b.** Jesus.
lord (lôrd) *noun, plural* **lords.**

Word History

The word **lord** comes from an Old English word that meant "keeper of the loaf." The lady of the house made the bread, and the lord kept the bread and distributed it to the other members of the household.

---

lose 1. To have no longer; be without. I *lost* my pencil. We don't want to *lose* your friendship. The roof *lost* some of its shingles in the storm. 2. To fail to keep. Do you *lose* your temper easily? Those acrobats never *lose* their balance. 3. To fail to win. The team *lost* the game. 4. To fail to use; waste. The travelers will *lose* time if the bus breaks down.
lose (lüz) *verb,* **lost, losing.**

loss 1. The act of losing something or the condition of being lost. The *loss* of the game was a disappointment to the team. I'm worried about the *loss* of my wallet. 2. Something that has been lost. The owner suffered great *losses* in the fire in the store. 3. The suffering or damage that is caused by losing something. We had a strong feeling of *loss* when our neighbors moved.
• **at a loss.** Puzzled; confused. Their sudden departure left me *at a loss.*
loss (lôs) *noun, plural* **losses.**

lost Past tense and past participle of **lose.** I *lost* my gloves. The team has *lost* the game. Look up **lose** for more information. *Verb.*

—**1.** That cannot be found; missing. The child looked for the *lost* toy.   **2.** No longer possessed. They thought sadly about their *lost* fortune.   **3.** Not knowing where one is or the way to go. The *lost* driver asked the police officer for directions. That dog looks *lost* to me.   **4.** Not won or able to be won. The team played well, but the game was *lost*.   **5.** Not used; wasted. They drove all night to try to make up for *lost* time.   **6.** Ruined; destroyed. Many lives were *lost* in the fire. *Adjective.*

• **lost in.**   So busy with or interested in something that one is not aware of other things. I was *lost in* thought and didn't hear your question.

lost (lôst) *verb; adjective.*

lot   **1.** A great amount. There are a *lot* of cars on this road. This horse eats *lots* of hay.   **2.** A number or group of persons or things. This is a poor *lot* of vegetables.   **3.** A piece of land. We play baseball on an empty *lot*.   **4.** A bit of paper, wood, straw, or other material used to decide something by chance. The children drew *lots* to decide who would be first at bat in the game.   **5.** Fate or fortune in life. It was the hermit's *lot* to live alone.

• **a lot.**   By a great amount or to a great degree; much. I don't want to be *a lot* taller than I am now.

lot (lot) *noun, plural* **lots.**

There are a **lot** of pumpkins in the field.

lotion   A special liquid that is used on the skin. A lotion heals, soothes, softens, or cleans the skin.

lo·tion (lō′shən) *noun, plural* **lotions.**

lotus   A plant with large pink, white, or yellow flowers. The roots of the lotus grow under water, and the leaves and flowers grow above water.

lo·tus (lō′təs) *noun, plural* **lotuses.**

loud   **1.** Having a strong sound; not quiet. The jet plane made a *loud* noise.   **2.** Too bright; gaudy. Do you really want to wear that *loud* tie? *Adjective.*
—In a loud way. We hear you *loud* and clear. *Adverb.*

loud (loud) *adjective,* **louder, loudest;** *adverb.*

loudspeaker   A device that can change electrical signals into sounds and make the sounds louder. Loudspeakers are used in radios and phonographs.

loud·speak·er (loud′spē′kər) *noun, plural* **loudspeakers.**

Louisiana   A state in the southern United States. Its capital is Baton Rouge.

Lou·i·si·an·a (lü ē′zē an′ə *or* lü′ə zē an′ə) *noun.*

Word History

A French explorer named the Mississippi Valley **Louisiana** after King *Louis* XIV of France. When the land was divided into states, *Louisiana* became the name of one of the states.

---

lounge   To stand, sit, or lie down in a comfortable or lazy way. Don't *lounge* on the sofa for the entire afternoon. *Verb.*
—**1.** A place where a person may lounge. The hotel has a *lounge* where guests may relax.   **2.** A long seat for more than one person that has a back and arms; sofa; couch. *Noun.*

lounge (lounj) *verb,* **lounged, lounging;** *noun, plural* **lounges.**

louse   A tiny insect without wings. It lives on people and animals by biting them and sucking their blood. Lice can spread some diseases.

louse (lous) *noun, plural* **lice.**

lovable   Having qualities that make one easy to love or worthy of being loved. This word is also spelled **loveable.**

lov·a·ble (luv′ə bəl) *adjective.*

love   **1.** A strong, warm feeling for another; deep affection.   **2.** A strong liking for some-

---

at; āpe; fär; câre; end; mē; it; īce; pîerce; hot; ōld; sông, fôrk; oil; out; up; ūse; rüle; pùll; tûrn; chin; sing; shop; thin; this; hw in white; zh in treasure. The symbol ə stands for the unstressed vowel sound in about, taken, pencil, lemon, and circus.

thing. They go to concerts because of their *love* of music. **3.** Someone that is loved or something that is liked very much. Playing chess is a *love* of mine. *Noun.*
—**1.** To have a strong, warm feeling for another. The mother and father *love* their children. **2.** To have a strong liking for something. That student *loves* to read. My cousin *loves* fresh, raw carrots. *Verb.*
love (luv) *noun, plural* **loves;** *verb,* **loved, loving.**

lovely **1.** Having a beautiful appearance or a warm character. The *lovely* flowers were a gift. Our neighbor is a kind, *lovely* person. **2.** Enjoyable. We had a *lovely* time at your party.
love·ly (luv′lē) *adjective,* **lovelier, loveliest.**

loving Feeling or showing love. The parents were very *loving* toward their children.
lov·ing (luv′ing) *adjective.*

low **1.** Not high or tall. A *low* wall surrounds the yard. The branches of the tree are *low* enough for me to reach. **2.** Below the usual level. The river was *low.* The car was going at a *low* speed. **3.** Below what is regarded as average; below others. I got a *low* grade on that test. That meat is *low* in quality. **4.** Not favorable; bad. I have a *low* opinion of people who are cruel to animals. **5.** Not having enough. Our car is *low* on gasoline. **6.** Not loud; soft. Speak in a *low* voice. **7.** Deep in pitch. You can sing very *low* notes. **8.** Not lively or happy; sad; gloomy. Everyone on the team felt *low* after losing that important game. *Adjective.*
—At or to a low place or level. The airplane flew *low* over the town. The campers' supplies ran *low* after they had been in the woods for two weeks. *Adverb.*
—**1.** A low place or point. The temperature reached a new *low* during the night. **2.** The position of gears in an automobile that gives the lowest speed and greatest power. The driver of the car shifted into *low* to go up the steep hill. *Noun.*
low (lō) *adjective,* **lower, lowest;** *adverb; noun, plural* **lows.**

lower Comparative of **low.** They live on a *lower* floor of the apartment house. Our supply of heating oil is *lower* than it should be. Look up **low** for more information. *Adjective.*
—**1.** To move or cause to move from one position to another that is not as high. The soldiers will *lower* the flag at dusk. I *lowered* my arm when the teacher called my name. **2.** To make or become less; lessen. The store *lowered* its prices during the sale. **3.** To

make soft or less loud. *Lower* your voice. *Verb.*
low·er (lō′ər) *adjective; verb,* **lowered, lowering.**

lower case Letters that are not capitals. The letters a, b, c, and d are printed in lower case.

low tide The tide when the level of the ocean or a lake is at its lowest.

loyal Having or showing strong and lasting affection and support for someone or something. The old friends were *loyal* to each other. The *loyal* soldiers refused to betray their country.
loy·al (loi′əl) *adjective.*

loyalty Strong and lasting affection and support; allegiance. You showed your *loyalty* to your friends by helping them when they were in need.
loy·al·ty (loi′əl tē) *noun, plural* **loyalties.**

lubricate **1.** To put oil or grease on the parts of a machine that move against each other so that the parts will move easily. The mechanic *lubricated* the car's wheels and axles. **2.** To help the parts of a machine move easily. That oil *lubricated* the fan well.
lu·bri·cate (lü′bri kāt′) *verb,* **lubricated, lubricating.**

luck **1.** What seems to happen to a person by chance. It was good playing and not *luck* that caused the team to win. Some of their problems were the result of bad *luck.* **2.** Good fortune. Wish me *luck!* They had no *luck* in looking for the lost ring.
luck (luk) *noun.*

luckily By or with good fortune. *Luckily,* they found my missing wallet.
luck·i·ly (luk′ə lē) *adverb.*

lucky **1.** Having or bringing good luck. You were very *lucky* to win the prize. The child believed the rabbit's foot was *lucky.* **2.** Happening as a result of good fortune; caused by good luck. That home run was just a *lucky* hit.
luck·y (luk′ē) *adjective,* **luckier, luckiest.**

lug To carry or drag with much trouble or effort. I didn't want to *lug* that heavy suitcase upstairs.
lug (lug) *verb,* **lugged, lugging.**

luggage The suitcases, trunks, and bags that a traveler takes along on a trip; baggage.
lug·gage (lug′ij) *noun.*

lukewarm **1.** Slightly warm; neither hot nor cold. **2.** Having or showing little enthusiasm; indifferent. The audience's response to the new play was only *lukewarm.*
luke·warm (lük′wôrm′) *adjective.*

lull To make or become calm. The sound of rain on the roof *lulled* the baby to sleep. The storm finally *lulled. Verb.*
—A short period of calm or quiet. There was a *lull* in the wind. *Noun.*
lull (lul) *verb,* **lulled, lulling;** *noun, plural* **lulls.**

lullaby A song that is sung to lull a baby to sleep.
lul·la·by (lul′ə bī′) *noun, plural* **lullabies.**

lumber¹ Boards cut from logs. The carpenter bought *lumber* to build a shed.
lum·ber (lum′bər) *noun.*

lumber¹

lumber² To move about in a clumsy, noisy way. The wagon *lumbered* down the dirt road. The elephant *lumbered* along the trail.
lum·ber (lum′bər) *verb,* **lumbered, lumbering.**

lumberjack A person who cuts down trees and gets logs ready for the sawmill.
lum·ber·jack (lum′bər jak′) *noun, plural* **lumberjacks.**

luminous Bright; shining. We could see the *luminous* glow of a campfire through the trees.
lu·mi·nous (lü′mə nəs) *adjective.*

lump **1.** A shapeless piece of something; chunk. The sculptor took the *lump* of clay and made a figure of a dog with it. **2.** A swollen place; bump. You have a *lump* on your head where the ball hit you. *Noun.*
—**1.** To put or bring together. The teenagers *lumped* their allowances to buy a camera. **2.** To form lumps. Oatmeal sometimes *lumps* when it cools. *Verb.*
lump (lump) *noun, plural* **lumps;** *verb,* **lumped, lumping.**

lunar Of or having to do with the moon. The astronauts brought back *lunar* rocks for study. A *lunar* eclipse is the darkening of the moon when the earth moves between the sun and the moon.
lu·nar (lü′nər) *adjective.*

lunch A meal eaten between breakfast and dinner. *Noun.*
—To eat lunch. We *lunched* at noon. *Verb.*
lunch (lunch) *noun, plural* **lunches;** *verb,* **lunched, lunching.**

luncheon A lunch. We went to a formal *luncheon* given by the school.
lunch·eon (lun′chən) *noun, plural* **luncheons.**

lung One of two organs for breathing in the chest of human beings and other animals with backbones. The lungs supply the blood with oxygen and rid the blood of carbon dioxide.
lung (lung) *noun, plural* **lungs.**

lunge A sudden movement forward. The catcher made a *lunge* for the ball. *Noun.*
—To move forward suddenly. The shortstop *lunged* to catch the ball. *Verb.*
lunge (lunj) *noun, plural* **lunges;** *verb,* **lunged, lunging.**

lure **1.** A strong attraction. The explorer felt the *lure* of adventure in the unknown land. **2.** Artificial bait used in fishing. I used a plastic worm as a *lure* to catch the fish. *Noun.*
—To attract strongly. We were *lured* to the park by the sound of music. *Verb.*
lure (lùr) *noun, plural* **lures;** *verb,* **lured, luring.**

lush Thick, rich, and abundant. That land is covered with *lush* forests.
lush (lush) *adjective,* **lusher, lushest.**

luster A bright shine; glow. You can give the table a nice *luster* by waxing it.
lus·ter (lus′tər) *noun, plural* **lusters.**

lute A musical instrument with strings that has a

lute

at; āpe; fär; câre; end; mē; it; īce; pîerce; hot; ōld; sông; fôrk; oil; out; up; ūse; rüle; pull; tûrn; chin; sing; shop; thin; this; hw in white; zh in treasure. The symbol ə stands for the unstressed vowel sound in about, taken, pencil, lemon, and circus.

body shaped like a pear. It is played by plucking the strings. ▲ Another word that sounds like this is **loot**.
lute (lüt) *noun, plural* **lutes.**

Luxembourg A country in northwestern Europe.
Lux·em·bourg (luk′səm bûrg′) *noun.*

luxuriant **1.** Having thick or abundant growth of plants. The jungle was *luxuriant* and green after the rainy season. **2.** Rich in decoration; very fancy. The drapes behind the king and queen's throne were *luxuriant*.
lux·u·ri·ant (luk shùr′ē ənt *or* lug zhùr′ē ənt) *adjective.*

luxurious **1.** Giving much comfort and pleasure. The family stayed at a *luxurious* hotel on the beach. **2.** Fond of luxuries or luxury. Don't get a *luxurious* taste for jewels and furs.
lux·u·ri·ous (luk shùr′ē əs *or* lug zhùr′ē əs) *adjective.*

luxury **1.** Something that gives much comfort and pleasure but is not really necessary. Eating dinner at the fancy restaurant was a *luxury* for our family. **2.** A way of life that gives comfort and pleasure. The opera star is used to *luxury*.
lux·u·ry (luk′shə rē *or* lug′zhə rē) *noun, plural* **luxuries.**

-ly¹ A *suffix* that means: **1.** In a certain way or manner. *Perfectly* means in a perfect way. **2.** To a certain degree or extent. *Highly* means to a high degree.

-ly² A *suffix* that means: **1.** Like. *Friendly* means like a friend. **2.** Happening at a certain period of time. *Weekly* means happening every week.

lye A strong substance used in making soap and detergents. Lye is obtained by soaking wood ashes in water. ▲ Another word that sounds like this is **lie**.
lye (lī) *noun.*

lying¹ Present participle of **lie**¹. They are *lying* if they say they don't know what happened. Look up **lie**¹ for more information. *Verb.*
—The act of telling lies. You will be punished if you are caught *lying*. *Noun.*
ly·ing (lī′ing) *verb; noun.*

lying² Present participle of **lie**². The dog is *lying* on the rug. Look up **lie**² for more information.
ly·ing (lī′ing) *verb.*

lymph A clear, yellowish liquid in the tissues of the body. Lymph contains water, proteins, and white blood cells.
lymph (limf) *noun.*

lynx A wild animal in the cat family that is about the size of a large domestic cat. It has yellowish brown fur with black spots and has black tufts on the ears. Lynx are found in eastern Europe and Asia.
lynx (lingks) *noun, plural* **lynx** or **lynxes.**

lynx

lyre A musical instrument with strings that is like a harp. The lyre was played by ancient Egyptians, Hebrews, and Greeks.
lyre (līr) *noun, plural* **lyres.**

lyric Expressing a strong, personal emotion. The poet wrote *lyric* poems about nature. *Adjective.*
—1. A poem that expresses a strong personal emotion. **2. lyrics.** The words of a song. I wrote both the *lyrics* and the melody of this song. *Noun.*
lyr·ic (lir′ik) *adjective; noun, plural* **lyrics.**

Word History

The word **lyric** comes from a Greek word meaning "of a lyre." Lyric poetry was originally sung accompanied by a lyre.

lyrical Expressing a strong, personal emotion; lyric. The *lyrical* poem was about love.
lyr·i·cal (lir′i kəl) *adjective.*

M m

3. Around 3,000 years ago, the Greeks borrowed this letter and changed it.

1. The oldest form of **M** was used about 4,000 years ago by tribes in the Middle East.

5. Around 2,400 years ago the Romans went back to the Greeks (3.) for their form of the letter **M**.

4. An ancient tribe north of Rome borrowed the Middle Eastern **M** 2,800 years ago.

2. In the early Hebrew alphabet, this letter was turned on its side.

6. The form of the capital letter **M** we use today is similar to the one used by the Greeks and Romans.

m, M   The thirteenth letter of the alphabet.
   m, M (em) *noun, plural* **m's, M's.**

m.   An abbreviation for *meter.*

MA   Postal abbreviation for *Massachusetts.*

ma'am   Madam. Excuse me, *ma'am;* do you know what time it is? ▲ This word is used mostly in everyday conversation.
   ma'am (mam) *noun, plural* **ma'ams.**

macaroni   A food that is made from dough and then dried. It is usually shaped like short, hollow tubes. The way to cook macaroni is by boiling it in water.
   mac·a·ro·ni (mak′ə rō′nē) *noun.*

machine   **1.** A device that does some particular job. It is made up of a number of moving or fixed parts that work together. A lawn mower, a hair dryer, and a printing press are machines.   **2.** A simple device that lessens the force needed to move an object. A lever and a pulley are simple machines.
   ma·chine (mə shēn′) *noun, plural* **machines.**

machine gun   A rifle that keeps firing bullets as long as the trigger is pressed.

machinery   **1.** Machines or parts of machines. The mechanics fixed the *machinery* of the elevator.   **2.** A group of things or people that make something work. The president and Congress are part of the *machinery* of the federal government.
   ma·chin·er·y (mə shē′nə rē) *noun.*

machinist   A skilled worker who operates machinery that makes tools and parts.
   ma·chin·ist (mə shē′nist) *noun, plural* **machinists.**

mackerel   A fish that lives in salt water and is used for food. It has a silver-colored body with wavy dark markings on its back.
   mack·er·el (mak′ər əl) *noun, plural* **mackerels** or **mackerel.**

macron   A short line (¯) that is placed over a vowel to show that it has a long sound.
   ma·cron (mā′kron) *noun, plural* **macrons.**

mad   **1.** Feeling or showing anger; angry. I was *mad* when I found that my new bicycle was scratched.   **2.** Crazy; insane.   **3.** Very foolish or reckless; not wise or sensible. The character in the movie had the *mad* idea of walking across the canyon on a tightrope.   **4.** Very enthusiastic. My family is *mad* about camping.   **5.** Wild and excited. We made a *mad* dash to the airport to make the plane.   **6.** Sick with rabies.
   mad (mad) *adjective,* **madder, maddest.**

Madagascar   An island country in the Indian Ocean. It is off the coast of southeastern Africa.
   Mad·a·gas·car (mad′ə gas′kər) *noun.*

M

madam A title for a woman. May I help you, *madam?*
mad·am (mad′əm) *noun, plural*
mesdames (mā däm′) or **madams.**

madame The French title for a married woman or a widow.
mad·ame (mə dam′) *noun, plural*
mesdames.

made Past tense and past participle of **make.** We *made* a map of our neighborhood. Look up **make** for more information. ▲ Another word that sounds like this is **maid.**
made (mād) *verb.*

mademoiselle The French title for a girl or an unmarried woman.
mad·e·moi·selle (mad′ə mə zel′) *noun, plural* **mademoiselles** or
mesdemoiselles (mād mwä zel′).

made-up 1. Not real or true. The author used *made-up* names for the characters in the book. 2. Wearing make-up.
made-up (mād′up′) *adjective.*

magazine 1. A printed collection of stories, articles, and pictures. A magazine is usually bound in a paper cover. Most magazines are issued every week or every month. 2. A room or building for storing ammunition. 3. The part of a gun or rifle that holds the bullets.
mag·a·zine (mag′ə zēn′ *or* mag′ə zēn′) *noun, plural* **magazines.**

maggot A fly that has just come out of its egg; fly larva. It has a thick body with no legs.
mag·got (mag′ət) *noun, plural* **maggots.**

magic 1. The power to control forces of nature and events by using special charms or spells. The fairy tale told of witches and wizards who used *magic.* 2. The art or skill of doing tricks to entertain people. *Noun.*
—Using magic; done by or seeming to be done by magic. The *magic* trick was done with mirrors. *Adjective.*
mag·ic (maj′ik) *noun; adjective.*

magical Using or done by magic. The wizard used *magical* powers to disappear.
mag·i·cal (maj′i kəl) *adjective.*

magician 1. A person who entertains people by doing magic tricks. 2. A person who is thought to have magical powers; wizard.
ma·gi·cian (mə jish′ən) *noun, plural* **magicians.**

magma Melted rock material that exists below the surface of the earth. Magma rises to the surface of the earth and hardens into rock or flows as lava out of volcanoes.
mag·ma (mag′mə) *noun.*

magnesium A silver-white metal. Magnesium is very light in weight and is used in alloys. It burns with a brilliant, white light, and is often used in making fireworks. Magnesium is a chemical element.
mag·ne·si·um (mag nē′zē əm *or* mag nē′zhəm) *noun.*

magnet A piece of stone, metal, or other material that can attract iron or steel. Magnets are often made in the shape of a bar or horseshoe.
mag·net (mag′nit) *noun, plural* **magnets.**

Word History

The word **magnet** comes from the the Greek name of the city of *Magnesia,* in western Asia. The first magnets were discovered there.

---

magnetic 1. Acting like a magnet; having to do with magnets or magnetism. The *magnetic* needle of a compass points to the earth's *magnetic* poles. 2. Able to attract or fascinate people. That movie star has a *magnetic* personality.
mag·net·ic (mag net′ik) *adjective.*

magnetic field The space around a magnet in which the magnet has the power to attract other metals.

magnetic pole 1. Either of the two points of a magnet where its magnetic force seems to be strongest. 2. Either of the two points on the earth's surface toward which the needle of a compass points. One of these points is near the North Pole and the other is near the South Pole. They are the points where the earth's magnetic pull is strongest.

magnetic tape Tape that has a special coating that is magnetic. Magnetic tape is

magician

used for recording and playing sound, and for recording and displaying images. A videocassette contains magnetic tape.

magnetism **1.** The power to attract iron, steel, and certain other materials. Certain stones and metals and all electric currents have magnetism. **2.** The ability to attract or fascinate people. Many political leaders have strong personal *magnetism.*
  mag·net·ism (mag′ni tiz′əm) *noun.*

magnetize To cause an object to act like a magnet; give the power of magnetism to a metal. We *magnetized* the iron bar by setting it against a strong magnet for a few days.
  mag·net·ize (mag′ni tīz′) *verb,*
  magnetized, magnetizing.

magnificence The quality of being magnificent; great beauty; splendor. We were amazed at the *magnificence* of the royal palace.
  mag·nif·i·cence (mag nif′ə səns) *noun.*

magnificent Very beautiful and grand; splendid. The house on the top of the hill has a *magnificent* view of the valley.
  mag·nif·i·cent (mag nif′ə sənt) *adjective.*

magnify **1.** To make something look bigger than it really is. The microscope *magnified* the cells one hundred times. **2.** To make something seem more important than it really is; exaggerate. Some people always *magnify* their health problems.
  mag·ni·fy (mag′nə fī′) *verb,* **magnified, magnifying.**

magnifying glass

magnifying glass A lens or combination of lenses that make things look bigger than they really are.

magnitude **1.** Greatness of size. We could only guess at the *magnitude* of the mountain. **2.** Importance. The discovery of America was an event of great *magnitude.*
  mag·ni·tude (mag′ni tüd′ *or* mag′ni tūd′) *noun.*

magnolia A tree or shrub that has large white, pink, purple, or yellow flowers.
  mag·no·lia (mag nōl′yə) *noun, plural* **magnolias.**

magpie A bird that has a long tail and a thick bill. Magpies have a noisy, chattering call. They are related to crows.
  mag·pie (mag′pī′) *noun, plural* **magpies.**

magpie

mahogany **1.** An evergreen tree that grows in warm parts of North America and South America. The reddish brown wood of this tree is strong and hard. It is often used in making furniture. **2.** A dark reddish brown color. *Noun.*
  —Having the color mahogany; dark reddish brown. *Adjective.*
  ma·hog·a·ny (mə hog′ə nē) *noun, plural* **mahoganies;** *adjective.*

maid **1.** A woman who is paid to do housework. A *maid* comes once a week to clean their house. **2.** A girl or young woman who is not married. ⚠ Another word that sounds like this is **made.**
  maid (mād) *noun, plural* **maids.**

maiden A girl or young woman who is not married. *Noun.*
  —First or earliest. That ship's *maiden* voyage was from England to New York. *Adjective.*
  maid·en (mā′dən) *noun, plural* **maidens;** *adjective.*

maiden name The original last name of a woman who has married and changed her last name.

maid of honor An unmarried woman who is the main female attendant of the bride at a wedding.

mail **1.** Letters, cards, and packages that are sent or received through a post office. I received three birthday cards in yesterday's *mail.* **2.** The system by which mail is sent, moved, or delivered. It is usually run by the

M

at; āpe; fär; câre; end; mē; it; īce; pîerce; hot; ōld; sông, fôrk; oil; out; up; ūse; rüle; pu̇ll; tûrn; chin; sing; shop; thin; this; hw in white; zh in treasure. The symbol ə stands for the unstressed vowel sound in about, taken, pencil, lemon, and circus.

government of a country. We received a party invitation by *mail. Noun.*
—To send by mail. I *mailed* the letter I wrote to my grandparents. *Verb.* ⓘ Another word that sounds like this is **male.**
mail (māl) *noun, plural* **mails;** *verb,* **mailed, mailing.**

mailbox **1.** A box in which letters are put so that they can be picked up by a mail carrier. **2.** A box into which a person's mail is put when it is delivered.
mail·box (māl′boks′) *noun, plural* **mailboxes.**

mail carrier A person who carries and delivers mail.

mailman A person whose job is carrying and delivering mail; mail carrier; postman.
mail·man (māl′man′) *noun, plural* **mailmen** (māl′men′).

main Greatest in size or importance. The *main* branch of the library is in the center of the city. The *main* idea of the game is to score points. *Adjective.*
—A large pipe or cable that is usually underground. Mains are used to carry water, gas, and electricity to homes or other buildings. *Noun.* ⓘ Other words that sound like this are **Maine** and **mane.**
main (mān) *adjective; noun, plural* **mains.**

Maine A state in the northeastern United States, on the Atlantic Ocean. Its capital is Augusta. ⓘ Other words that sound like this are **main** and **mane.**
Maine (mān) *noun.*

Word History

The name **Maine** comes from the earlier English words "the *maine,*" which meant "mainland." People who explored this region used these words to show the difference between the North American continent and the islands along the coast in this area.

---

mainframe A powerful computer that is much larger than a microcomputer. Mainframes are usually used by big companies and organizations to process large amounts of information.
main·frame (mān′frām′) *noun, plural* **mainframes.**

mainland The chief land mass of a country or continent, as distinguished from an island. Hong Kong is an island located off the *mainland* of China.
main·land (mān′land′ *or* mān′lənd′) *noun.*

mainly For the most part; chiefly. Although they are interested *mainly* in popular music, they sometimes listen to classical music too.
main·ly (mān′lē) *adverb.*

mainstay **1.** A heavy rope or cable that supports or steadies the mast of a sailing ship. **2.** A person or thing that is the main support of something. My cousin is the *mainstay* of the debating team. Agriculture is the *mainstay* of our state.
main·stay (mān′stā′) *noun, plural* **mainstays.**

maintain **1.** To continue to have or do; go on with; keep. The truck *maintained* a speed of fifty miles an hour on the highway. It was hard for the skiers to *maintain* their balance on the icy hill. **2.** To take care of. The town hired gardeners to *maintain* the park. Both of my parents work hard to *maintain* our large family. **3.** To say in a firm and sure way. No matter what you say, I still *maintain* that I am right.
main·tain (mān tān′) *verb,* **maintained, maintaining.**

maintenance **1.** A maintaining or being maintained. The city government is responsible for the *maintenance* of streets and sidewalks. **2.** Money, food, and shelter needed for living; means of support. My job provides a comfortable *maintenance.*
main·te·nance (mān′tə nəns) *noun.*

maize A grain that grows in rows on the ears of a tall plant. This grain is usually called **corn.** Look up **corn** for more information. ⓘ Another word that sounds like this is **maze.**
maize (māz) *noun.*

majestic Grand and noble; dignified. The *majestic* mountains rose thousands of feet above the valley.
ma·jes·tic (mə jes′tik) *adjective.*

majesty **1.** Great dignity; grandness. The crowds along the streets were thrilled by the *majesty* of the royal procession. **2. Majesty.** A title used in speaking to or about a king, queen, or other royal ruler.
maj·es·ty (maj′ə stē) *noun, plural* **majesties.**

major Bigger or more important. The *major* expense of my vacation was the cost of the airplane ticket. *Adjective.*
—An officer in the armed forces. In the United States Army, Marine Corps, or Air Force, a major ranks below a colonel but above a captain. *Noun.*
ma·jor (mā′jər) *adjective; noun, plural* **majors.**

majority 1. The larger number or part of something; more than half. The *majority* of the students voted for you for class president. 2. The amount by which a larger number is greater than a smaller number. I won the election by twenty-five votes to ten votes, so I had a *majority* of fifteen votes. 3. The age at which a person is legally permitted to manage his or her own affairs. In the United States this age is different in different states.

    ma·jor·i·ty (mə jôr′i tē) *noun, plural* **majorities.**

make 1. To cause to be, become, or happen. A robin has begun to *make* a nest in the tree outside my window. Slamming a door *makes* a loud noise. The principal *made* a speech to the class. The smell of food *made* me hungry. 2. To cause or force to do. A funny movie always *makes* me laugh. The babysitter *made* the child eat the vegetables. 3. To add up to; amount to. Ten and three *make* thirteen. Thirty-six inches *make* a yard. 4. To earn. I *made* ten dollars a day by delivering newspapers. The author *makes* a living by writing novels. 5. To go or get to. I woke up late and had to rush to *make* the bus on time. 6. To win a place or position on. My friend hopes to *make* the school basketball team this year. *Verb.*
—The style or type of something that is made and sold; brand. Our new car is the same *make* as our old car. *Noun.*

    • **to make believe.** To pretend. The two playmates like to *make believe* that they are firefighters.
    • **to make it.** To succeed. That movie actor has also *made it* in television.
    • **to make up.** 1. To become friends again. The two friends argue a lot, but they always *make up* afterwards. 2. To put cosmetics on. The actor *made up* before going on stage. 3. To invent in the mind. The babysitter *made up* a funny story to amuse us. 4. To be the parts of; form. Nine players *make up* a baseball team.

    make (māk) *verb,* **made, making;** *noun, plural* **makes.**

make-believe Imagination. The book contained stories of ghosts and witches and other tales of *make-believe. Noun.*
—Not real; imaginary. The attic became the children's *make-believe* castle. *Adjective.*

    make-be·lieve (māk′bi lēv′) *noun; adjective.*

makeshift Something used for a time in place of the correct or usual thing. When the Venetian blind broke, we used a sheet as a *makeshift. Noun.*

—Used for a time in place of the correct or usual thing. We sometimes use our sofa as a *makeshift* bed. *Adjective.*

    make·shift (māk′shift′) *noun, plural* **makeshifts;** *adjective.*

makeup 1. Lipstick, powder, and other cosmetics that are put on the face. 2. The way in which something is put together. The *makeup* of the kennel is half dogs and half cats. 3. A person's nature; personality. You are such a polite person that it is not in your *makeup* to be rude to anyone.

    makeup (māk′up′) *noun, plural* **makeups.**

makeup

malaria A disease that causes chills, a high fever, and sweating. Malaria is spread by the bite of a certain type of mosquito that carries the disease from infected persons.
    ma·lar·i·a (mə lâr′ē ə) *noun.*

Malawi A country in southeastern Africa.
    Ma·la·wi (mə lä′wē) *noun.*

Malaysia A country in southeastern Asia.
    Ma·lay·sia (mə lā′zhə) *noun.*

male 1. Of or having to do with men or boys. The school play will have four *male* parts and four female parts. 2. Having to do with or belonging to the sex that can fertilize female eggs. A *male* deer is called a buck. *Adjective.*
—A male person or animal. *Noun.* ▴ Another word that sounds like this is **mail.**
    male (māl) *adjective; noun, plural* **males.**

Mali A country in northwestern Africa.
    Ma·li (mä′lē) *noun.*

M

at; āpe; fär; câre; end; mē; it; īce; pîerce; hot; ōld; sông, fôrk; oil; out; up; ūse; rüle; pull; tûrn; chin; sing; shop; thin; <u>th</u>is; hw in white; zh in treasure. The symbol ə stands for the unstressed vowel sound in about, taken, pencil, lemon, and circus.

445

malice The desire to cause harm or pain to someone; ill will; spite. It was *malice* that made the child spread the nasty rumor.
mal·ice (mal′is) *noun*.

malicious Feeling, showing, or caused by malice. *Malicious* lies can hurt others.
ma·li·cious (mə lish′əs) *adjective*.

malign To tell damaging lies about; speak ill of; slander. During the election campaign, many people *maligned* the mayor. *Verb.*
ma·lign (mə līn′) *verb*, **maligned, maligning.**

malignant **1.** Tending to spread disease through the body. The surgeon operated to remove the *malignant* growth. **2.** Showing ill will; harmful. The soldiers spread *malignant* lies about their new commander.
ma·lig·nant (mə lig′nənt) *adjective*.

mallard A common wild duck of North America, Europe and Asia. The male mallard has a green head, a white band around the neck, a reddish brown chest, and a grayish back.
mal·lard (mal′ərd) *noun, plural* **mallards** or **mallard.**

mallard

mallet A type of hammer with a head made of wood or another soft material. Mallets with short handles are used as tools. In some sports, such as croquet or polo, mallets with long handles are used to hit the ball.
mal·let (mal′it) *noun, plural* **mallets.**

malnutrition An unhealthy condition of the body, caused by not eating enough food or not eating the right kinds of food.
mal·nu·tri·tion (mal′nü trish′ən *or* mal′nū trish′ən) *noun*.

malt Barley or another grain that is soaked in warm water until it sprouts and then is dried. Malt is used in making beer and ale.
malt (môlt) *noun*.

malted milk A drink made by mixing milk and sometimes ice cream with a powder made of malt.

mama Mother. Some children call their mothers "Mama."
ma·ma (mä′mə) *noun, plural* **mamas.**

mammal A kind of animal that is warm-blooded and has a backbone. Female mammals have glands that produce milk to feed their young. Most mammals are covered with fur or have some hair. Human beings, cattle, dogs, cats, and whales are mammals.
mam·mal (mam′əl) *noun, plural* **mammals.**

mammoth

mammoth A kind of elephant that lived long ago. Mammoths had long, curving tusks and shaggy, brown hair. They were larger than the elephants that live today. The last mammoths on earth died about 10,000 years ago. *Noun.*
—Very large; gigantic; huge. Building that cabin was a *mammoth* job. *Adjective.*
mam·moth (mam′əth) *noun, plural* **mammoths;** *adjective.*

man **1.** An adult male person. The boy grew up to be a handsome *man*. Until 1920, only *men* were allowed to vote in the U.S. **2.** A human being or the human race; a person or all people. All *men* are created equal. *Man* is the only animal that can speak. **3.** One of the pieces used in playing chess, checkers, and other games. *Noun.*
—To supply with people who do a certain job. Ten soldiers *manned* the fort. *Verb.*
man (man) *noun, plural* **men;** *verb,* **manned, manning.**

manage **1.** To direct or control. The president of the company *managed* its business affairs. Only a very good rider could *manage* such a wild horse. **2.** To succeed at doing something; be able to. Our team *managed* to win, even though our best player was sick.
man·age (man′ij) *verb*, **managed, managing.**

management **1.** The act or process of directing or controlling. The business failed be-

cause of bad *management*.   **2.** The person or persons who manage something, such as a business.   The company's *management* planned to hire more workers.
man·age·ment (man'ij mənt) *noun.*

manager   A person who manages something. The *manager* of the baseball team decided which player would pitch.
man·ag·er (man'i jər) *noun, plural* **managers.**

mandarin   **1.** A high public official in imperial China.   **2. Mandarin.** A dialect of the Chinese language. It is the official language of the Chinese government.   **3.** A small citrus fruit with a loose rind that is easy to peel. It is also called a **mandarin orange.**
man·da·rin (man'dər in) *noun, plural* **mandarins.**

mandate   **1.** Instruction or support given by voters to their representatives in government through the votes cast in an election. The president got a *mandate* to work for tax reform.   **2.** An official command or order. *Noun.*
—To demand or require. Trouble with the lights *mandated* moving the slide show to another room. *Verb.*
man·date (man'dāt) *noun, plural* **mandates;** *verb,* **mandated, mandating.**

mandolin   A musical instrument that is like a guitar. It has a pear-shaped body and metal strings.
man·do·lin (man'də lin' *or* man'də lin') *noun, plural* **mandolins.**

mane   The long, thick hair on the neck of certain animals. Horses and male lions have manes. ⚠ Other words that sound like this are **main** and **Maine.**
mane (mān) *noun, plural* **manes.**

maneuver   **1.** A planned movement of soldiers or ships. The generals discussed a *maneuver* to capture the enemy's supplies. **2.** A skillful or clever move or plan. The candidate used many *maneuvers* to win. *Noun.*
—**1.** To cause soldiers or ships to move in a certain way. The captain *maneuvered* the soldiers into a position for attacking the enemy. **2.** To move or manage skillfully or cleverly. We *maneuvered* our way to the front of the crowd so we could see the parade. *Verb.*
ma·neu·ver (mə nü'vər) *noun, plural* **maneuvers;** *verb,* **maneuvered, maneuvering.**

manganese   A brittle, silver gray metal. Manganese is used in making steel. Manganese is a chemical element.
man·ga·nese (mang'gə nēz' *or* mang'gə nēs') *noun.*

manger   A large box that holds food for horses or cattle.
man·ger (mān'jər) *noun, plural* **mangers.**

mango   A yellowish red fruit that has a sweet, spicy taste and a hard seed in the center. It grows on a tropical evergreen tree.
man·go (mang'gō) *noun, plural* **mangoes** or **mangos.**

manhole   An opening or hole, usually in a street, through which a worker can go to build or repair a sewer, wires, pipes, or the like. Manholes have lids that can be removed.
man·hole (man'hōl') *noun, plural* **manholes.**

manhood   **1.** The condition or the time of being an adult male person. The adolescent boy will soon enter *manhood*.   **2.** Men as a group. The *manhood* and womanhood of our country always respond well in a national crisis.
man·hood (man'hùd') *noun.*

manicure   A cleaning, shaping, and, sometimes, polishing of the fingernails. *Noun.*
—To give a manicure to. *Verb.*
man·i·cure (man'i kyùr') *noun, plural* **manicures;** *verb,* **manicured, manicuring.**

Manitoba   A province in central Canada. Its capital is Winnipeg.
Man·i·to·ba (man'i tō'bə) *noun.*

mankind   The human race; human beings as a group. The exploration of outer space is one of the greatest achievements of *mankind*.
man·kind (man'kīnd') *noun.*

man–made   Made by people rather than by nature. Glass, steel, and plastic are *man-made;* water, coal, and wood are not.
man-made (man'mād') *adjective.*

manner   **1.** The way in which something is done. The guests came in and dropped their jackets on the floor in a careless *manner*. **2.** A way of acting or behaving. Our librarian has a warm and friendly *manner*.   **3. manners.** Polite ways of behaving or acting. Those children are too young to have good table *manners*. ⚠ Another word that sounds like this is **manor.**
man·ner (man'ər) *noun, plural* **manners.**

M

at; āpe; fär; câre; end; mē; it; īce; pîerce; hot; ōld; sông, fôrk; oil; out; up; ūse; rüle; pùll; tûrn; chin; sing; shop; thin; <u>th</u>is; hw in white; zh in treasure. The symbol ə stands for the unstressed vowel sound in about, taken, pencil, lemon, and circus.

man-of-war A warship. A man-of-war is usually a sailing ship.
  man-of-war (man′əv wôr′) *noun, plural* **men-of-war** (men′əv wôr′).

manor **1.** A large estate belonging to a lord in the Middle Ages. The lord lived on part of the land and the rest was divided among peasants, who paid rent to the lord in the form of goods or work. **2.** A mansion.
▲ Another word that sounds like this is **manner.**
  man·or (man′ər) *noun, plural* **manors.**

mansion A very large and grand home. The rich family lived in a beautiful old *mansion* by the ocean.
  man·sion (man′shən) *noun, plural* **mansions.**

manslaughter The crime of killing someone without having planned to do so. A driver who accidentally kills someone may be guilty of *manslaughter.*
  man·slaugh·ter (man′slô′tər) *noun.*

mantel **1.** The structure that surrounds a fireplace opening. **2.** The shelf above a fireplace. This is also called a **mantelpiece.**
  man·tel (man′təl) *noun, plural* **mantels.**

manual Done with or using the hands. Carpenters use many *manual* skills in their work. We grew up on a farm and are used to doing *manual* labor. *Adjective.*
—A book that gives instructions or information about something; handbook. You have to study a driver's *manual* carefully before you take the test to get a driver's license. *Noun.*
  man·u·al (man′ū əl) *adjective; noun, plural* **manuals.**

manufacture **1.** To make or process something, especially in quantity and with the use of machinery. That company *manufactures* bicycles. The mill *manufactured* wool into cloth. **2.** To make up; invent. I *manufactured* an excuse for forgetting my friend's birthday. *Verb.*
—The act or process of manufacturing. That city is famous for the *manufacture* of automobiles. *Noun.*
  man·u·fac·ture (man′yə fak′chər) *verb,* **manufactured, manufacturing;** *noun.*

manure Waste matter from animals that is used to fertilize soil.
  ma·nure (mə nùr′ *or* mə nyùr′) *noun.*

manuscript A book or article that is written or typed by hand. Manuscripts are sent to a publisher or printer to be made into printed books or magazines.
  man·u·script (man′yə skript′) *noun, plural* **manuscripts.**

many Made up of a large number. There are *many* books on American history in our library. *Adjective.*
—A large number. The meeting of the club was canceled because *many* of the members could not be there. *Noun.*
—A large number of people or things. *Many* were late for school because of the bad weather. *Pronoun.*
  man·y (men′ē) *adjective,* **more, most;** *noun; pronoun.*

map

map A drawing that shows the surface features of an area, as of a state or country. Maps of large areas usually show cities, rivers, oceans, and other features. *Noun.*
—**1.** To make a map of; show on a map. The explorers *mapped* the wilderness as they traveled through it. **2.** To plan in detail; arrange. The committee *mapped* out a campaign to raise money for a new hospital. *Verb.*
  map (map) *noun, plural* **maps;** *verb,* **mapped, mapping.**

maple A tree that has leaves with deep notches. Its seeds are contained in a small fruit that looks like two wings. Its wood is hard and is used in making furniture.
  ma·ple (mā′pəl) *noun, plural* **maples.**

maple syrup A sweet syrup made by boiling the sap of a certain kind of maple tree.

Mar. An abbreviation for *March.*

marathon **1.** A race for runners over a course of 26 miles and 385 yards. **2.** A long race or competition testing endurance. The baseball game turned into a *marathon* of six hours, because neither team could score any runs.
  mar·a·thon (mar′ə thon′) *noun, plural* **marathons.**

marble **1.** A type of hard, smooth stone. Marble is white, or streaked with different colors. It is often used in building and sculpture. **2.** A small, hard ball of glass used in games.
mar·ble (mär′bəl) *noun, plural* **marbles.**

march **1.** To walk with regular, measured steps as soldiers do. People who march walk in step with others in an orderly group. The firefighters and police from our town *marched* in the parade. **2.** To move forward steadily. Time *marches* on. *Verb.*
—**1.** The act of marching. The parade started its *march* at noon. **2.** A musical piece that has a strong rhythm and is suitable for marching. The band played a military *march. Noun.*
march (märch) *verb,* **marched, marching;** *noun, plural* **marches.**

March The third month of the year. March has thirty-one days.
March (märch) *noun.*

Word History

The Romans named the month of **March** in honor of *Mars,* the god of war in Roman mythology.

---

mare The female of the horse, donkey, zebra, or certain other animals.
mare (mâr) *noun, plural* **mares.**

margarine A food that is used as a spread or in cooking and baking. It may contain animal or vegetable oil, milk, water, and salt. Margarine was originally made as a substitute for butter. Another word for this is **oleomargarine.**
mar·ga·rine (mär′jər in) *noun, plural* **margarines.**

margin **1.** The blank space around the written or printed part of a page. I wrote down the address in the *margin* of my notebook. **2.** An edge or border. There was a high fence around the *margin* of the property. **3.** An extra amount; amount in addition to what is necessary. You'd better allow a *margin* of fifteen minutes for your trip in case the traffic is heavy. Our team won the game by a very small *margin.*
mar·gin (mär′jin) *noun, plural* **margins.**

marigold A garden plant that bears yellow, orange, or red flowers in summer.
mar·i·gold (mar′i gōld′) *noun, plural* **marigolds.**

marine **1.** Having to do with or living in the sea. Whales are *marine* animals.

2. Having to do with ships or navigation. Several stores in the harbor sold *marine* supplies. **3.** Having to do with the Marine Corps. *Adjective.*
—**Marine.** A member of the Marine Corps. *Noun.*
ma·rine (mə rēn′) *adjective; noun, plural* **Marines.**

Marine Corps A branch of the United States armed forces that is trained to fight both on land and at sea. The Marine Corps band is famous all over the world.

marionette A doll or puppet moved by strings or wires that are held from above. It is usually made of wood.
mar·i·o·nette (mar′ē ə net′) *noun, plural* **marionettes.**

marionettes

maritime **1.** Of or having to do with the sea, ships, or sea travel. The Coast Guard enforces *maritime* laws. **2.** Close to or living near the sea. That *maritime* nation has a large fishing fleet.
mar·i·time (mar′i tīm′) *adjective.*

mark¹ **1.** A spot or trace made on one thing by another. A line, scratch, stain, or scar is a mark. The wet glass made a *mark* on our wooden table. **2.** A sign or symbol. I put

at; āpe; fär; câre; end; mē; it; īce; pîerce; hot; ōld; sông, fôrk; oil; out; up; ūse; rüle; pùll; tûrn; chin; sing; shop; thin; **th**is; hw in white; zh in treasure. The symbol ə stands for the unstressed vowel sound in about, taken, pencil, lemon, and circus.

M

my initials on my notebook cover as an identification *mark*. Does this sentence end with a question *mark?* **3.** A letter or number that shows how good a person's work is. I get better *marks* in history than in arithmetic. **4.** A line or object that shows position. The white pole was the halfway *mark* on the race track. **5.** Something that is aimed at; target or goal. The arrow missed the *mark. Noun.*
—**1.** To make or put a mark or marks on. My dirty boots *marked* the kitchen floor. **2.** To show clearly. A stone wall *marks* the end of the farmer's land. **3.** To be a sign or feature of. Happiness *marked* the occasion of their wedding. **4.** To give a mark to; grade. The teacher *marked* the spelling tests. *Verb.*
- **to make one's mark.** To become famous or successful. Our state senators have *made their mark* in this session of Congress.
- **to mark down.** To reduce the price of. Our local grocery store *marked down* the apples and pears this week.
- **to mark up.** To increase the price of. The manager of the store has *marked up* these jackets since the last time I was here.

mark (märk) *noun, plural* **marks;** *verb,* **marked, marking.**

mark² A unit of money in Germany.
mark (märk) *noun, plural* **marks.**

market **1.** A place or store where food or goods are for sale. I bought shrimp at the fish *market.* **2.** A demand for something that is for sale. There is a very large *market* for television sets in this country. *Noun.*
—To buy or sell goods at a market. I go *marketing* for groceries every weekend. The rancher *marketed* the cattle in town. *Verb.*
mar·ket (mär′kit) *noun, plural* **markets;** *verb,* **marketed, marketing.**

marketplace A place where food and other products are bought and sold. In old towns the *marketplace* was often in a square.
mar·ket·place (mär′kit plās′) *noun, plural* **marketplaces.**

marking A mark or marks; patch or patches of color. The bird had brown and white *markings* on its wings.
mark·ing (mär′king) *noun, plural* **markings.**

marmalade A type of jam made with fruit and sugar. It is usually made with citrus fruits and their peel.
mar·ma·lade (mär′mə lād′) *noun, plural* **marmalades.**

maroon¹ A dark brownish red color. *Noun.*
—Having the color maroon. *Adjective.*
ma·roon (mə rün′) *noun, plural* **maroons;** *adjective.*

maroon² To leave a person alone on a deserted island or coast. The pirates *marooned* their prisoner on a tiny, lonely island.
ma·roon (mə rün′) *verb,* **marooned, marooning.**

marquis A nobleman ranking next below a duke and above an earl or count.
mar·quis (mär′kwis *or* mär kē′) *noun, plural* **marquises** or **marquis.**

marquise **1.** The wife or widow of a marquis. **2.** A noblewoman whose rank equals that of a marquis.
mar·quise (mär kēz′) *noun, plural* **marquises.**

marriage **1.** The state of being married. My grandparents' *marriage* was a happy one. **2.** The act of marrying. The couple's *marriage* took place in June.
mar·riage (mar′ij) *noun, plural* **marriages.**

marrow The soft substance that fills the hollow parts of bones. The marrow makes cells for the bloodstream.
mar·row (mar′ō) *noun.*

marry **1.** To take as a husband or wife; wed. They plan to *marry* when they finish college. **2.** To join as husband and wife. The minister *married* them in a church.
mar·ry (mar′ē) *verb,* **married, marrying.**

Mars The seventh largest planet in our solar system. It is the fourth planet in order of distance from the sun.
Mars (märz) *noun.*

Mars

marsh Low, wet land. Grasses and reeds grow in marshes.
marsh (märsh) *noun, plural* **marshes.**

marshal **1.** An officer of a federal court who has the duties of a sheriff. **2.** A person who arranges certain ceremonies. *Noun.*
—To arrange in proper order. The general *marshaled* all the troops for battle. *Verb.*

⌃ Another word that sounds like this is **martial**.

mar·shal (mär′shəl) *noun, plural* **marshals;** *verb,* **marshaled, marshaling.**

marshmallow A soft, white candy with a texture like a sponge. Marshmallows are sometimes roasted before being eaten.

marsh·mal·low (märsh′mel′ō *or* märsh′mal′ō) *noun, plural* **marshmallows.**

marsupial A kind of animal. The female has a pouch in which young are carried. Kangaroos and opossums are marsupials.

mar·su·pi·al (mär sü′pē əl) *noun, plural* **marsupials.**

martial Of, having to do with, or suitable for war or military life. In some societies *martial* training was required of everyone.
⌃ Another word that sounds like this is **marshal**.

mar·tial (mär′shəl) *adjective.*

martin One of several kinds of swallows. Martins eat insects that they catch while in flight. Martins live throughout the world.

mar·tin (mär′tən) *noun, plural* **martins.**

Martin Luther King Day A holiday observed on the third Monday in January to celebrate the birthday of Martin Luther King, Jr., the black civil-rights leader.

martyr A person who chooses to suffer or die rather than give up his or her beliefs.

mar·tyr (mär′tər) *noun, plural* **martyrs.**

marvel A wonderful or astonishing thing. Travel in space is one of the *marvels* of modern science. *Noun.*
—To feel wonder and astonishment. We *marveled* at the acrobat's skill. *Verb.*

mar·vel (mär′vəl) *noun, plural* **marvels;** *verb,* **marveled, marveling.**

marvelous **1.** Causing wonder or amazement. The story tells of *marvelous* events. **2.** Outstanding; excellent. I went to a *marvelous* birthday party yesterday.

mar·vel·ous (mär′və ləs) *adjective.*

Maryland A state in the eastern United States. Its capital is Annapolis.

Mar·y·land (mer′ə lənd) *noun.*

Word History

Maryland was named for Queen Henrietta *Maria* of England. The person who started the colony of Maryland got the land from Queen Henrietta Maria's husband, King Charles I.

mascot An animal, person, or thing that is supposed to bring good luck. Sports teams often keep a pet animal as a *mascot.*

mas·cot (mas′kot) *noun, plural* **mascots.**

masculine Having to do with a man; like that of a man. My cousin has a deep, *masculine* voice.

mas·cu·line (mas′kyə lin) *adjective.*

mash **1.** A soft mass or mixture. **2.** A mixture of grains that is fed to livestock or poultry. *Noun.*
—To make into a soft mass. After I boiled the potatoes, I *mashed* them. *Verb.*

mash (mash) *noun, plural* **mashes;** *verb,* **mashed, mashing.**

mask **1.** A covering worn to hide or protect the face. The children wore *masks* to the Halloween party. The baseball bounced off of the catcher's *mask.* **2.** Anything that hides or covers up something. Their boasting is just a *mask* to hide their lack of self-confidence. *Noun.*
—**1.** To cover with a mask. The surgeons *masked* their faces before the operation. **2.** To hide or cover up. A high stone wall *masked* the house from the road. I tried to *mask* my disappointment with a smile. *Verb.*

mask (mask) *noun, plural* **masks;** *verb,* **masked, masking.**

mason A person whose work is building with stone, bricks, or cement.

ma·son (mā′sən) *noun, plural* **masons.**

masquerade **1.** A party at which masks and costumes are worn. The children dressed as famous people from history for the *masquerade.* **2.** A false appearance; disguise. The spy's *masquerade* of friendship fooled the soldier into revealing secret information. *Noun.*
—To disguise oneself; put on a false appearance. We *masqueraded* as pirates for the dance. *Verb.*

mas·quer·ade (mas′kə rād′) *noun, plural* **masquerades;** *verb,* **masqueraded, masquerading.**

mass **1.** A body of matter that has no particular shape. A *mass* of snow piled up along the fence. **2.** A large quantity or number. A *mass* of people showed up for the football

M

at; āpe; fär; câre; end; mē; it; īce; pîerce; hot; ōld; sông, fôrk; oil; out; up; ūse; rüle; pùll; tûrn; chin; sing; shop; thin; this; hw in white; zh in treasure. The symbol ə stands for the unstressed vowel sound in about, taken, pencil, lemon, and circus.

451

game.   **3.** Size or bulk. An elephant has great *mass.*   **4.** The main or larger part; majority. The *mass* of voters turned out for the election.   **5.** The quantity of matter that a body contains. *Noun.*
—Involving many people or things. There was a *mass* meeting in front of the library. *Adjective.*
—To gather or form into a mass. The people *massed* together in front of the theater before the performance. The police *massed* the crowds along the sidewalk so that the parade could pass through. *Verb.*
  mass (mas) *noun, plural* **masses;** *adjective; verb,* **massed, massing.**

Mass   The main religious ceremony in the Roman Catholic Church and certain other churches.
  Mass (mas) *noun, plural* **Masses.**

Mass.   An abbreviation for *Massachusetts.*

Massachusetts   A state in the northeastern United States. Its capital is Boston.
  Mas·sa·chu·setts (mas′ə chü′sits) *noun.*

Word History

Massachusetts was the name of an American Indian village by some hills near Boston. The word means "at the big hill." English settlers used the name for the tribe that lived in the village, and then later for the colony and the state.

---

massacre   A brutal, bloody killing of many people or animals. Many Indians died in the *massacre. Noun.*
—To kill many people or animals in a brutal, bloody way. The cruel ruler ordered the army to *massacre* the enemy. *Verb.*
  mas·sa·cre (mas′ə kər) *noun, plural* **massacres;** *verb,* **massacred, massacring.**

massage   The rubbing or kneading of the muscles and joints of the body. A massage relaxes the muscles and helps the circulation of the blood. *Noun.*
—To give a massage to. The trainer *massaged* the athlete's sore back after a long practice session. *Verb.*
  mas·sage (mə säzh′ *or* mə säj′) *noun, plural* **massages;** *verb,* **massaged, massaging.**

massive   Of great size or extent; very big; large and solid. The safe in the bank has *massive* steel doors.
  mas·sive (mas′iv) *adjective.*

mass production of light bulbs

mass production   The process or technique of making things in large quantities, especially by using machinery.

mass transit   A system of buses and trains used to carry many people from place to place within a city. The city plans to extend its *mass transit* to the new neighborhood.

mast   **1.** A tall pole on a sailing ship or boat that supports the sails and rigging.   **2.** Any long pole or post.
  mast (mast) *noun, plural* **masts.**

master   **1.** A person who has power or control over something. The dogs came when their *master* called them.   **2.** A person who has great skill or knowledge about something. That author is a *master* of the mystery novel.   **3.** A male teacher.   **4. Master.** A title for a young boy. "Will Master Charles be dining with his parents tonight?" the cook asked. *Noun.*
—**1.** Very skillful in an art or trade. The work on the new house was done by a *master* carpenter.   **2.** Most important; main. The *master* bedroom was larger than the other bedrooms. All the lights in the building were controlled by a *master* switch. *Adjective.*
—**1.** To gain control over. I finally *mastered* my fears and dived from the high diving board.   **2.** To become expert in. That student *mastered* French easily. *Verb.*
  mas·ter (mas′tər) *noun, plural* **masters;** *adjective; verb,* **mastered, mastering.**

masterful   **1.** Tending to control or dominate; showing power. I use a *masterful* voice when I give my dog a command.   **2.** Having great skill or knowledge. The singer gave a *masterful* performance.
  mas·ter·ful (mas′tər fəl) *adjective.*

masterpiece   **1.** Something that is done with great skill. Several *masterpieces* were sold at the art auction.   **2.** A person's greatest achievement or finest work. This novel is considered the author's *masterpiece.*

mas·ter·piece (mas′tər pēs′) *noun, plural* **masterpieces.**

mat **1.** A small, flat piece of material used as a floor covering or placed in front of a door. Mats are often made of rubber or woven material. **2.** A small, flat piece of material that is put under a dish, vase, or other object. It is used for decoration or to protect a surface. **3.** A large, thick pad or covering that is put on the floor to protect wrestlers, gymnasts, or other athletes. **4.** A thick, tangled mass. There was a *mat* of hair in the bathtub drain. *Noun.*
—To become tangled in a thick mass. The dog's coat was *matted* with rain and mud. *Verb.*

mat (mat) *noun, plural* **mats;** *verb,* **matted, matting.**

match¹ **1.** A person or thing that is suitable with or very much like another. I bought a pocketbook that was a perfect *match* for my shoes. You are a good tennis player, but you're no *match* for the team captain. **2.** A game or contest. They challenged us to a bowling *match. Noun.*
—**1.** To be suitable with, equal to, or like something. The new curtains *match* the rug very well. These gloves don't *match.* **2.** To find or bring together things that are exactly equal to or like one another. After I washed the socks, I *matched* them in pairs. **3.** To compete with as an equal. No one on their team could *match* our pitcher. *Verb.*

match (mach) *noun, plural* **matches;** *verb,* **matched, matching.**

match² A short, thin piece of wood or cardboard used to start a fire. Matches are coated on one end with a chemical substance that makes a flame when it is struck against something.

match (mach) *noun, plural* **matches.**

mate **1.** One of a pair. I've lost the *mate* to this sock. **2.** A husband or wife. **3.** The male or female of a pair of animals. The lion guarded its *mate* and their cubs. **4.** An officer on a ship who is lower in rank than the captain. The *mate* gave orders to mop the deck. **5.** A friend or companion. *Noun.*
—To join in a pair for breeding. Birds *mate* in the spring. *Verb.*

mate (māt) *noun, plural* **mates;** *verb,* **mated, mating.**

material What something is made of or used for. My winter coat is made of heavy *material.* Stone, wood, bricks, and cement are building *materials.* I used my experiences in camp as *material* for my story. *Noun.*

—**1.** Made from or having to do with matter; physical. Scientists study things that exist in the *material* world. **2.** Having to do with the body or physical well-being. Food, clothing, and shelter are *material* needs. *Adjective.*

ma·te·ri·al (mə tîr′ē əl) *noun, plural* **materials;** *adjective.*

maternal **1.** Of or like a mother; motherly. My *maternal* instincts come out when I am around small children. **2.** Related through one's mother. Your *maternal* grandparents are your mother's parents.

ma·ter·nal (mə tûr′nəl) *adjective.*

mathematical Having to do with or using mathematics. My classmate helped me solve the *mathematical* problem.

math·e·mat·i·cal (math′ə mat′i kəl) *adjective.*

mathematician A person who works or specializes in mathematics.

math·e·ma·ti·cian (math′ə mə tish′ən) *noun, plural* **mathematicians.**

mathematics The study of numbers, quantities, measurements, and shapes, and how they relate to each other. Arithmetic, algebra, and geometry are parts of mathematics. *Mathematics* is my favorite subject. ▲ The word "mathematics" is used with a singular verb.

math·e·mat·ics (math′ə mat′iks) *noun.*

matinee A play or other performance given in the afternoon. The *matinee* starts at two o'clock.

mat·i·nee (mat′ə nā′) *noun, plural* **matinees.**

matter **1.** Anything that has weight and takes up space. All things are made of matter. Matter can be a solid, liquid, or gas. **2.** A subject of discussion, interest, or action. The secretary talked on the telephone about a business *matter.* I talked with the principal about a personal *matter.* **3.** Problem; trouble. I went to the dentist to find out what was the *matter* with my tooth. **4.** Written or printed material. The store sells books, newspapers, and other reading *matter.* **5.** An amount or quantity. It's only a *matter* of minutes before the train arrives. *Noun.*
—To be of importance. It doesn't *matter* to me which movie we go to see. *Verb.*

at; āpe; fär; câre; end; mē; it; īce; pîerce; hot; ōld; sông, fôrk; oil; out; up; ūse; rüle; pùll; tûrn; chin; sing; shop; thin; this; hw in white; zh in treasure. The symbol ə stands for the unstressed vowel sound in about, taken, pencil, lemon, and circus.

M

453

- **as a matter of fact.** Truly; actually. I know them very well; *as a matter of fact,* they're my good friends.
- **no matter.** Regardless of; it makes no difference. *No matter* how hard we try, we cannot always succeed.

mat·ter (mat′ər) *noun, plural* **matters;** *verb,* **mattered, mattering.**

mattress A thick pad that is used as a bed or part of a bed. It is usually covered with cloth and stuffed with cotton, foam rubber, or hair.

mat·tress (mat′ris) *noun, plural* **mattresses.**

mature **1.** Having reached full growth or development; ripe. When a puppy becomes *mature* it is called a dog. The farmer harvested the corn when it was *mature.* **2.** Like or having the qualities of a mature person; adult. My classmate did the *mature* thing by not hitting back. *Adjective.*
—To become fully grown or developed. The tomatoes are *maturing* fast. *Verb.*

ma·ture (mə chùr′ *or* mə tùr′ *or* mə tyùr′) *adjective; verb,* **matured, maturing.**

Mauritania A country in western Africa.
Mau·ri·ta·ni·a (môr′i tā′nē ə) *noun.*

maximum **1.** The greatest possible number or amount. Six dollars was the *maximum* that we could spend on supplies. **2.** The highest point or degree reached or recorded. The temperature rose to a *maximum* of 98 degrees today. *Noun.*
—The greatest possible. The *maximum* number of people allowed on the merry-go-round at any one time is forty. *Adjective.*

max·i·mum (mak′sə məm) *noun, plural* **maximums** or **maxima** (mak′sə mə); *adjective.*

may An auxiliary verb that is used in the following ways: **1.** To ask or give permission. *May* I leave the table? Yes, you *may.* **2.** To say that something is possible or likely. It *may* snow today. **3.** To express hope or a wish. *May* you have a happy life. ⏺ Look up **can** for a Language Note about this word.
may (mā) *verb.*

May The fifth month of the year. May has thirty-one days.
May (mā) *noun.*

Word History

The Romans named the month of **May** in honor of *Maia,* the earth goddess in Roman mythology.

Maya A member of an American Indian people of southern Mexico and Central America. The Maya had an advanced civilization that flourished until about A.D. 1000.
Ma·ya (mä′yə) *noun, plural* **Maya** or **Mayas.**

maybe Possibly; perhaps. I don't agree with you, but *maybe* you are right.
may·be (mā′bē) *adverb.*

mayonnaise A thick, creamy sauce or dressing. It is made of egg yolks, oil, and vinegar or lemon juice. Mayonnaise is often used on sandwiches and in salads.
may·on·naise (mā′ə nāz′ *or* mā′ə nāz′) *noun.*

mayor The person who is the official head of a city or town government.
may·or (mā′ər) *noun, plural* **mayors.**

maze A confusing series of paths or passageways through which people may have a hard time finding their way. I got lost in the *maze* of hallways in my new school. ⏺ Another word that sounds like this is **maize.**
maze (māz) *noun, plural* **mazes.**

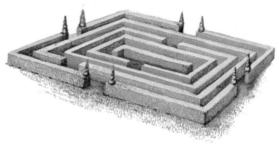

maze

MB Postal abbreviation for *Manitoba.*

Md. An abbreviation for *Maryland.*

MD Postal abbreviation for *Maryland.*

M.D. An abbreviation meaning *doctor of medicine.*

me The person who is speaking or writing. The bus takes *me* to school. My cousin sent *me* a birthday card. Send your answer to *me* as soon as you get this letter.
me (mē) *pronoun.*

Me. An abbreviation for *Maine.*

ME Postal abbreviation for *Maine.*

meadow A field of grassy land. It is often used for growing hay or as a pasture for animals.
mead·ow (med′ō) *noun, plural* **meadows.**

meadowlark A songbird that has a yellow breast with a black bar across it. It has a pointed bill and a short tail. Meadowlarks live in North America, Central America, and South America.

mead·ow·lark (med′ō lärk′) *noun, plural* **meadowlarks.**

meadowlark

meager Very little; hardly enough. The sick child ate a *meager* meal of tea and toast.
mea·ger (mē′gər) *adjective.*

meal¹ The food served or eaten at one time. Breakfast is the first *meal* of the day.
meal (mēl) *noun, plural* **meals.**

meal² Grain or other food that has been ground. I mixed corn *meal* into the batter.
meal (mēl) *noun, plural* **meals.**

mean¹ **1.** To have in mind; want to do or say. I do not know what you *mean* by that remark. **2.** To have as a purpose; intend. I didn't *mean* to hurt your feelings. **3.** To be defined as; have a particular sense. "To start" *means* "to begin."
mean (mēn) *verb,* **meant, meaning.**

mean² **1.** Cruel; not kind; not nice. It was *mean* to tease the new student. **2.** Low in quality or rank. The politician grew up in *mean* conditions, but still achieved fame and success. **3.** Hard to deal with; difficult. You'd better drive slowly because there's a *mean* curve in the road just ahead.
mean (mēn) *adjective,* **meaner, meanest.**

mean³ **1.** Something that is halfway between two extremes. Warmth is a happy *mean* between freezing cold and great heat. **2. means.** The way that something is or may be done. The president of the company is accused of getting money through dishonest *means.* We used the back door as a *means* of escape. **3. means.** Money or property; wealth. The money for the new hospital was donated by a family of *means. Noun.*
—Halfway between two extremes; average. The *mean* temperature for last Saturday was 60 degrees. *Adjective.*
• **by means of.** By the use of; with the help of. They climbed out of the window *by means of* a ladder.
mean (mēn) *noun, plural* **means;** *adjective.*

meaning An idea or sense that is meant or intended. Do you understand the *meaning* of that poem? The word "run" has many *meanings.*

mean·ing (mē′ning) *noun, plural* **meanings.**

meant Past tense and past participle of **mean¹.** I *meant* to bring my umbrella with me, but I forgot. Look up **mean¹** for more information.
meant (ment) *verb.*

meantime The time between. I'll be gone for an hour; in the *meantime,* please answer the telephone if it rings.
mean·time (mēn′tīm′) *noun.*

meanwhile **1.** In or during the time between. The train doesn't leave for an hour; *meanwhile,* I'm going to read a book. **2.** At the same time. My cousin washed the car; *meanwhile,* I mowed the lawn.
mean·while (mēn′hwīl′ *or* mēn′wīl′) *adverb.*

measles A disease that causes a rash of small red spots, a fever, and the symptoms of a bad cold. It is caused by a virus. ▲ The word "measles" is used with a singular or plural verb.
mea·sles (mē′zəlz) *noun.*

measure **1.** To find or show the size, weight, or amount of something. The doctor *measured* me and found that I had grown two inches in a year. We *measured* the room before buying a new rug for it. The thermometer *measured* the temperature in the house. **2.** To have as a measurement. The painting *measured* three feet long and two feet high. **3.** To mark off or set apart by measuring. I *measured* out two cups of flour for the cake. *Verb.*
—**1.** The size, weight, or amount of something. Without a ruler, I could only guess at the *measure* of the piece of wood. **2.** A unit, standard, or system of measurement. Inches and meters are *measures* of length. Grades are not always a true *measure* of a student's intelligence. **3.** An instrument, container, or other device used for measuring. The cook used a cup *measure* to add milk to the pancake batter. **4.** An amount, degree, or portion that can be measured. Our success was due in large *measure* to your help. **5.** Something that is done to make something else happen. The police took harsh *measures* to stop crime in the town. **6.** A bill or law. The Senate and the House of Representatives

M

at; āpe; fär; câre; end; mē; it; īce; pîerce; hot; ōld; sông, fôrk; oil; out; up; ūse; rüle; pull; tûrn; chin; sing; shop; thin; <u>th</u>is; hw in white; zh in treasure. The symbol ə stands for the unstressed vowel sound in about, taken, pencil, lemon, and circus.

have passed the *measure.* **7.** A bar of music. *Noun.*
>**meas·ure** (mezh′ər) *verb,* **measured, measuring;** *noun, plural* **measures.**

measurement **1.** The act of measuring. Rulers and scales are used for *measurement.* **2.** Something found or shown by measuring; the size, height, or amount of something. The carpenter used a ruler to get the *measurements* of the shelf. **3.** A system of measuring. Metric *measurement* is used in most countries of the world.
>**meas·ure·ment** (mezh′ər mənt) *noun, plural* **measurements.**

meat **1.** The parts of an animal used as food. The flesh of a cow, pig, or lamb is meat. **2.** The part of a fruit or nut that can be eaten. The solid, white part of a coconut is called the *meat.* **3.** The most important part of something. The story of the author's childhood was the *meat* of the book. ▲ Another word that sounds like this is **meet.**
>**meat** (mēt) *noun, plural* **meats.**

meatball A small ball made from ground meat and other ingredients and then cooked.
>**meat·ball** (mēt′bôl′) *noun, plural* **meatballs.**

mechanic A person who is skilled in repairing and operating machines. A *mechanic* fixed our car when it wouldn't start.
>**me·chan·ic** (mi kan′ik) *noun, plural* **mechanics.**

mechanical **1.** Using or having to do with machines or machinery. The *mechanical* toy was run by a small motor. **2.** Like or suitable for a machine; lacking feeling. A *mechanical* task like folding clothes can be more pleasant if you do it with someone else.
>**me·chan·i·cal** (mi kan′i kəl) *adjective.*

mechanism The working parts of a machine; a mechanical device. The jeweler said that the only thing wrong with the *mechanism* of my watch was a broken spring.
>**mech·a·nism** (mek′ə niz′əm) *noun, plural* **mechanisms.**

medal A flat piece of metal that is often similar in shape to a coin and attached to a ribbon. Medals are sometimes given as a reward for bravery or achievement. ▲ Another word that sounds like this is **meddle.**
>**med·al** (med′əl) *noun, plural* **medals.**

meddle To take part in another person's business without being asked or wanted; interfere. It is often wise not to *meddle* in other people's affairs. ▲ Another word that sounds like this is **medal.**
>**med·dle** (med′əl) *verb,* **meddled, meddling.**

media **1.** Plural of **medium.** Look up **medium** for more information. **2. the media.** Sources of news and information, such as newspapers, television, and magazines. The president's trip abroad was reported on television and in other news *media.*
>**me·di·a** (mē′dē ə) *plural noun.*

median The middle number in a series of numbers arranged in order from smallest to largest. If the series has an even number of elements, the median equals the average of the two middle numbers.
>**me·di·an** (mē′dē ən) *noun, plural* **medians.**

medic **1.** An informal word for a medical doctor. Our family *medic* fixed my broken arm. **2.** An intern. The young *medic* listened carefully as the chief surgeon explained the operation. **3.** Someone who is trained to give first aid or medical assistance in an emergency or on a battlefield. As soon as the ambulance arrived, the *medics* began to help the accident victim.
>**med·ic** (med′ik) *noun, plural* **medics.**

medical Having to do with doctors and medicine. Doctors are trained in *medical* schools. My neighbor went to the hospital for *medical* treatment.
>**med·i·cal** (med′i kəl) *adjective.*

medicine **1.** A drug or other substance used to prevent or cure disease or to relieve pain. I took the cough *medicine* every three hours. **2.** The science or practice of detecting, treating, or preventing disease or injury.

medals

456

Some of the students in the Biology Club plan to have a career in *medicine*.
med·i·cine (med′ə sin) *noun, plural* **medicines.**

medicine man A person in certain North American Indian tribes who was called upon to cure sickness and was believed to have magic powers.

medieval Having to do with or belonging in the Middle Ages.
me·di·e·val (mē′dē ē′vəl *or* mid ē′vəl) *adjective.*

meditate To think seriously, carefully, and quietly; reflect. I looked for a peaceful spot to *meditate* for a while.
med·i·tate (med′i tāt′) *verb,* **meditated, meditating.**

Mediterranean A large sea between southern Europe, western Asia, and northern Africa.
Med·i·ter·ra·ne·an (med′i tə rā′nē ən) *noun.*

medium 1. Something that is in the middle. I try to find a happy *medium* between working too hard and not doing anything. 2. A substance or means through which something acts or is done. The newspaper is a *medium* of communication. The air is a *medium* for sound waves. 3. The substance or conditions in which something lives. The ideal *medium* for growing potatoes is moist, sandy, soil. *Noun.*
—Having a middle position in size, amount, quality, or degree. Although my parents are both short, I am of *medium* height. *Adjective.*
me·di·um (mē′dē əm) *noun, plural* **media** or **mediums;** *adjective.*

medley 1. A mixture of things that usually don't belong together; jumble. The dinner was a *medley* of Chinese, Italian, and Mexican dishes that tasted awful when they were combined on one plate. 2. A series of musical compositions or parts of musical compositions combined into a single piece of music. The orchestra played a *medley* of songs from popular movies.
med·ley (med′lē) *noun, plural* **medleys.**

meet 1. To come to a place where one is facing someone or something coming from another direction. While walking downtown, they *met* a friend they hadn't seen in months. 2. To be introduced to. I hope to *meet* your parents some day soon. 3. To keep an appointment with. We'll *meet* you outside of school at three o'clock. 4. To be equal to; satisfy. These supplies should *meet* your needs. 5. To come into contact with; join. The Mississippi River *meets* the Gulf of Mexico in southern Louisiana. 6. To come together; assemble. The school board will *meet* again next Thursday. *Verb.*
—A meeting or contest. Our school won first prize in the swimming *meet. Noun.* ▴ Another word that sounds like this is **meat.**
• **to meet with.** 1. To receive. My suggestion *met with* everyone's approval. 2. To experience; undergo. The explorers *met with* danger in the jungle.
meet (mēt) *verb,* **met, meeting;** *noun, plural* **meets.**

meeting 1. A gathering of people. All the members of the club came to the *meeting.* 2. The act of coming together. We had a chance *meeting* with some old friends. 3. The place where things meet. The town was located at the *meeting* of two rivers. *Noun.*
meet·ing (mē′ting) *noun, plural* **meetings.**

megaphone A device used to make the voice sound louder so that it can be heard far away. It is usually shaped like a cone.
meg·a·phone (meg′ə fōn′) *noun, plural* **megaphones.**

melancholy 1. Low in spirits; sad; gloomy. I was in a *melancholy* mood because I didn't want the party to end. 2. Causing low spirits or sadness. I don't want to listen to such *melancholy* music. *Adjective.*
—Low spirits; a mood of sadness. *Melancholy* filled the town when the mayor died. *Noun.*
mel·an·chol·y (mel′ən kol′ē) *adjective; noun.*

mellow 1. Soft, sweet, and juicy from being ripe. Those peaches are *mellow* and ready to eat. 2. Full, soft, and rich; not harsh. As this cheese ages, it becomes more *mellow.* The room echoed with the *mellow* sound of the violin. 3. Made wise and understanding by age. You used to get angry easily, but now you are more *mellow.*
mel·low (mel′ō) *adjective,* **mellower, mellowest.**

melodious Making agreeable sounds; pleasant to hear. The *melodious* voice of the teacher captured the attention of the children.
me·lo·di·ous (mə lō′dē əs) *adjective.*

M

at; āpe; fär; câre; end; mē; it; ice; pîerce; hot; ōld; sông, fôrk; oil; out; up; ūse; rüle; pùll; tûrn; chin; sing; shop; thin; this; hw in white; zh in treasure. The symbol ə stands for the unstressed vowel sound in about, taken, pencil, lemon, and circus.

melody A series of musical notes that make up a tune. That song has a pleasing *melody*.
mel·o·dy (mel′ə dē) *noun, plural* **melodies.**

melon A large, juicy fruit that grows on a vine. Melons have a sweet, soft pulp that can be eaten. Cantaloupes and watermelons are types of melons.
mel·on (mel′ən) *noun, plural* **melons.**

melt **1.** To change from a solid to a liquid by heating. The warm sun *melted* the ice on the pond. **2.** To slowly become a liquid; dissolve. The lump of sugar *melted* in the tea. **3.** To disappear or fade away gradually. The clouds *melted* away. **4.** To become gentle or understanding; soften. My heart *melted* when the child began to cry.
melt (melt) *verb,* **melted, melting.**

member **1.** A person, animal, or thing that belongs to a group. The *members* of the club elected a new president. The lion is a *member* of the cat family. **2.** A limb of a person or an animal. A leg or arm is a member.
mem·ber (mem′bər) *noun, plural* **members.**

membership **1.** The condition of being a member. You must pay your dues every year to keep your *membership* in the club. **2.** All of the members of a group. The union *membership* voted to strike. **3.** The number of members in a group. *Membership* in the society has been growing each year.
mem·ber·ship (mem′bər ship′) *noun, plural* **memberships.**

membrane A thin, flexible layer of skin or tissue. Membranes line parts of the body.
mem·brane (mem′brān) *noun, plural* **membranes.**

memento Something that is kept or given as a reminder of someone or some place or event. This rock collection is a *memento* of my trip to the West.
me·men·to (mə men′tō) *noun, plural* **mementos** or **mementoes.**

memo A short note. The principal sent a *memo* about holidays to all the teachers at the school.
mem·o (mem′ō) *noun, plural* **memos.**

memorable Not to be forgotten; worth remembering; notable. Our trip to Europe was *memorable*.
mem·o·ra·ble (mem′ər ə bəl) *adjective.*

memorial Something that is a reminder of a person or event. Monuments and statues often serve as memorials. The town built a *memorial* to honor soldiers who had died in the war. *Noun.*
—Serving as a reminder. The *memorial* pa-

rade was held every year on the anniversary of the founding of the city. *Adjective.*
me·mo·ri·al (mə môr′ē əl) *noun, plural* **memorials;** *adjective.*

The Vietnam **Memorial** in Washington, D.C.

Memorial Day A holiday in the United States honoring Americans who have died while fighting in wars. Memorial Day is observed on the last Monday in May.

memorize To learn by heart; fix in the memory. I *memorized* the words of the poem by repeating them over and over.
mem·o·rize (mem′ə rīz′) *verb,* **memorized, memorizing.**

memory **1.** The ability to remember things. In studying history it is helpful to have a good *memory* for facts and dates. **2.** A person or thing that is remembered. The trip to Canada was one of their happiest *memories*. The statue was built to honor the *memory* of George Washington. **3.** All that a person can remember. The student recited the poem from *memory*. **4.** The length of time in the past that is remembered. It was the worst snowstorm in our *memory*. **5.** The part of a computer that very quickly stores information that can be retrieved very quickly. RAM and ROM are different kinds of memory.
mem·o·ry (mem′ə rē) *noun, plural* **memories.**

men Plural of **man**. Look up **man** for more information.
men (men) *plural noun.*

menace A person or thing that is a danger or a threat. Careless drivers are a *menace* to everyone else on the road. *Noun.*
—To threaten something; put in danger. The sudden storm *menaced* the small ship. *Verb.*
men·ace (men′is) *noun, plural* **menaces;** *verb,* **menaced, menacing.**

mend **1.** To put in good condition again; fix or repair. I used glue to *mend* the broken cup. **2.** To heal; improve. The doctor said that my sprained ankle is *mending* nicely. *Verb.*
—A mended place. You could see the *mend* where the hole in the sock had been sewed up. *Noun.*
• **on the mend.** Getting better; improving. I was sick for a week, but now I'm *on the mend.*
mend (mend) *verb,* **mended, mending;** *noun, plural* **mends.**

-ment A *suffix* that means: **1.** The act of. *Development* means the act of developing. **2.** The state of being. *Amazement* means the state of being amazed. **3.** The result or product of. *Improvement* means the result of improving.

mental **1.** Done by or having to do with the mind. Learning to speak is one stage of a child's *mental* development. **2.** Having to do with or affected by a disease of the mind. The hospital treated many *mental* patients.
men·tal (men′təl) *adjective.*

mention To speak about or refer to. I *mentioned* your party in the letter I wrote to my friend. *Verb.*
—A short remark or statement. There was no *mention* of the parade in this morning's newspaper. *Noun.*
men·tion (men′shən) *verb,* **mentioned, mentioning;** *noun.*

menu **1.** A list of the food that is available in a restaurant or other eating place. We wanted to order fried chicken but it wasn't on the *menu.* **2.** A list of operations to choose from on a computer screen.
men·u (men′ū) *noun, plural* **menus.**

meow The sound that a cat or kitten makes. *Noun.*
—To make this sound. The cat *meowed* because it was hungry. *Verb.*
me·ow (mē ou′) *noun, plural* **meows;** *verb,* **meowed, meowing.**

merchandise Things that are for sale; goods. The hardware store sells tools, paint, and other *merchandise.*
mer·chan·dise (mûr′chən dīz′ or mûr′chən dīs′) *noun.*

merchant **1.** A person whose business is buying goods and selling them for profit. My grandparents were clothing *merchants.* **2.** A person who owns or runs a store. All the *merchants* in town decorated their store windows during the holiday season.
mer·chant (mûr′chənt) *noun, plural* **merchants.**

merchant marine **1.** The ships of a nation that are used to carry cargo and passengers. **2.** The officers and crews of these ships.

mercury A heavy, silver-colored metal. Mercury is a liquid at normal temperatures. It is used in thermometers and barometers. Mercury is a chemical element.
mer·cu·ry (mûr′kyə rē) *noun.*

Mercury The second smallest planet in our solar system. It is the closest planet to the sun.
Mer·cu·ry (mûr′kyə rē) *noun.*

mercy **1.** Kindness or forgiveness that is more than what is expected or deserved. The ruler showed no *mercy* to the rebels. **2.** Something to be thankful for; blessing. Your help on the project was a real *mercy.*
• **at the mercy of.** Under the control of; subject to. The troops were *at the mercy of* the enemy.
mer·cy (mûr′sē) *noun, plural* **mercies.**

mere Nothing more than; only. The *mere* thought of having to do all that work made me feel tired.
mere (mîr) *adjective.*

merge To join and become one; come together. The two paths *merged* at the foot of the hill.
merge (mûrj) *verb,* **merged, merging.**

meridian **1.** An imaginary line on the earth's surface. It passes through the North and South poles. Meridians are shown on maps and globes and are used in navigation. **2.** The highest point that the sun or a star reaches in the sky. The sun's *meridian* is reached at about noon.
me·rid·i·an (mə rid′ē ən) *noun, plural* **meridians.**

M

Word History

The word **meridian** comes from two Latin words meaning "middle" and "day." At the middle of the day, the sun is highest in the sky and directly south. From this come both the meanings "highest point in the sky" and "the imaginary line from north to south."

at; āpe; fär; câre; end; mē; it; ice; pîerce; hot; ōld; sông, fôrk; oil; out; up; ūse; rüle; pu̇ll; tûrn; chin; sing; shop; thin; this; hw in white; zh in treasure. The symbol ə stands for the unstressed vowel sound in about, taken, pencil, lemon, and circus.

merit **1.** Goodness, worth, or value. Your idea has great *merit.* **2. merits.** The actual facts of a matter. A fair judge will always decide a case on its *merits. Noun.*
—To deserve; be worthy of. The book report you wrote *merits* a very good grade. *Verb.*
mer·it (mer′it) *noun, plural* **merits;** *verb,* **merited, meriting.**

mermaid An imaginary creature believed to live in the sea. A mermaid is supposed to have the head and body of a woman and the tail of a fish.
mer·maid (mûr′mād′) *noun, plural* **mermaids.**

merry Cheerful and jolly; full of fun. During the holidays we sang *merry* songs.
mer·ry (mer′ē) *adjective,* **merrier, merriest.**

merry-go-round A round platform that has wooden animals and seats on which people ride while the platform turns.
mer·ry-go-round (mer′ē gō round′) *noun, plural* **merry-go-rounds.**

merry-go-round

merrymaking The act of being merry and having fun; gaiety.
mer·ry·mak·ing (mer′ē mā′king) *noun.*

mesa A hill or mountain with a flat top and steep sides; a high plateau.
me·sa (mā′sə) *noun, plural* **mesas.**

Word History

Mesa comes from a Spanish word which means "table." The Spanish called a raised area of land a *mesa* because it resembled a large rock table.

mesh A net made of threads or wires woven together with openings between them. The screen on a window is a mesh. *Noun.*
—To fit together. The teeth on a zipper *mesh* very closely. *Verb.*
mesh (mesh) *noun, plural* **meshes;** *verb,* **meshed, meshing.**

mess **1.** A dirty or disorderly condition; untidy group of things. Please clean up the *mess* in your room. **2.** An unpleasant, difficult, or confusing state. Problems with our car made a *mess* of our vacation. **3.** A group of people, such as soldiers or campers, who eat their meals together. **4.** A meal eaten by a group, such as soldiers or campers. *Noun.*
—**1.** To make dirty or disorderly. Our dirty boots *messed* the clean kitchen floor. **2.** To spoil or confuse. The rain *messed* up our plans for a picnic. *Verb.*
mess (mes) *noun, plural* **messes;** *verb,* **messed, messing.**

message **1.** Words or information sent from one person or group to another. I left a *message* for them to call me when they got home. **2.** An official speech or other communication. The president's *message* to the nation was broadcast on television.
mes·sage (mes′ij) *noun, plural* **messages.**

messenger A person who delivers messages or runs errands. A *messenger* brought the telegram to our house.
mes·sen·ger (mes′ən jər) *noun, plural* **messengers.**

messy **1.** In a sloppy or dirty condition; not tidy. Our attic is *messy.* **2.** Unpleasant or difficult. Cleaning the oven is a *messy* job.
mes·sy (mes′ē) *adjective,* **messier, messiest.**

met Past tense and past participle of **meet.** They *met* in front of the school. Look up **meet** for more information.
met (met) *verb.*

metabolism All of the chemical and biological changes that take place in a living thing. Metabolism is the means by which our bodies make use of the food we eat.
me·tab·o·lism (mə tab′ə liz′əm) *noun, plural* **metabolisms.**

metal A substance that usually has a shiny surface, can be melted, and can conduct heat and electricity. Iron, silver, copper, lead, brass, and bronze are metals.
met·al (met′əl) *noun, plural* **metals.**

metallic Of or containing a metal. The box was made of a *metallic* substance. There are gold *metallic* threads in the material.
me·tal·lic (mə tal′ik) *adjective.*

metamorphic **1.** Of or having to do with metamorphosis. A caterpillar goes through

metamorphic changes to become a butterfly.
2. Produced beneath the surface of the earth by processes that change the texture, structure, and mineral makeup of rocks. Marble is a *metamorphic* rock that began as limestone.
met·a·mor·phic (met′ə môr′fik) *adjective.*

metamorphosis **1.** The series of changes in shape and function that certain animals go through as they develop from an egg to an adult. Caterpillars become butterflies and tadpoles become frogs through the process of metamorphosis. **2.** A complete change in form or appearance.
met·a·mor·pho·sis (met ə môr′fə sis) *noun, plural* **metamorphoses** (met′ə môr′fə sēz′).

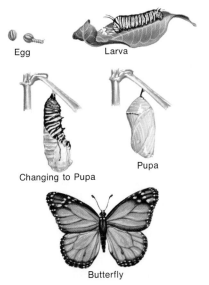

Egg

Larva

Changing to Pupa

Pupa

Butterfly

metamorphosis

metaphor A statement in which one thing is compared to another to suggest a similarity. Metaphors are often used in writing, especially poetry. "You are the sunshine of my life" is an example of a metaphor.
met·a·phor (met′ə fôr′) *noun, plural* **metaphors.**

Word History

The word **metaphor** comes from the Greek word meaning "to carry over" or "transfer." In a *metaphor,* the meaning of one word is carried over to another to make a comparison.

meteor A mass of metal or stone that comes into the earth's atmosphere from space. As it passes through the atmosphere at high speed, it becomes very hot and burns with a bright light as it falls to the earth. This is also called a **shooting star.**
me·te·or (mē′tē ər) *noun, plural* **meteors.**

meteorite A meteor that has fallen to earth.
me·te·or·ite (mē′tē ə rīt′) *noun, plural* **meteorites.**

meteorologist A person who studies meteorology or who knows a great deal about meteorology. The *meteorologist* on television predicted that it would snow.
me·te·or·ol·o·gist (mē′tē ə rol′ə jist) *noun, plural* **meteorologists.**

meteorology The science that studies the earth's atmosphere and the changes that take place within it. One important branch of meteorology is the study of the weather.
me·te·or·ol·o·gy (mē′tē ə rol′ə jē) *noun.*

meter[1] The basic unit of length in the metric system. A meter is equal to 39.37 inches, or slightly more than 3¼ feet.
me·ter (mē′tər) *noun, plural* **meters.**

meter[2] **1.** The regular pattern of rhythm that accented and unaccented syllables give to a line of poetry. **2.** The basic pattern of rhythm that accented notes or beats give to a piece of music.
me·ter (mē′tər) *noun, plural* **meters.**

meter[3] A device that measures or records. Meters are used to show how much electricity, water, or gas is used in a house or building or how fast a car is moving.
me·ter (mē′tər) *noun, plural* **meters.**

methane A gas with no color or odor. Methane burns easily. The gas that we use for heating or cooking is mostly methane.
meth·ane (meth′ān) *noun.*

method **1.** A way of doing something. Speaking on the telephone is a *method* of communicating with another person. **2.** Order or system. I could not find the book I wanted because the books had been put on the shelves without *method.*
meth·od (meth′əd) *noun, plural* **methods.**

metric Of or having to do with the metric system. The gram is a *metric* measurement.
met·ric (met′rik) *adjective.*

at; āpe; fär; câre; end; mē; it; īce; pîerce; hot; ōld; sông, fôrk; oil; out; up; ūse; rüle; pùll; tûrn; chin; sing; shop; thin; this; hw in white; zh in treasure. The symbol ə stands for the unstressed vowel sound in about, taken, pencil, lemon, and circus.

metric system A system of measurement based on counting by tens. In the metric system, the meter is the basic unit of length, the gram is the basic unit of weight, and the liter is the basic unit of capacity.

metronome A device with a pendulum that can be adjusted to swing back and forth at different speeds. Musicians use a metronome to help them keep time when they practice playing music.
met·ro·nome (met′rə nōm′) *noun, plural* **metronomes.**

metropolis A large and important city.
me·trop·o·lis (mə trop′ə lis) *noun, plural* **metropolises.**

metropolitan Belonging to or having to do with a metropolis. There were more than 5,000 officers on the *metropolitan* police force.
met·ro·pol·i·tan (met′rə pol′i tən) *adjective.*

Mexican A person who was born in Mexico or is a citizen of Mexico. *Noun.*
—Of or having to do with Mexico or its people. *Adjective.*
Mex·i·can (mek′si kən) *noun, plural* **Mexicans;** *adjective.*

Mexico A country in North America, south of the United States.
Mex·i·co (mek′si kō′) *noun.*

mg An abbreviation for *milligram.*

mi. An abbreviation for *mile.*

MI Postal abbreviation for *Michigan.*

mice Plural of **mouse.** Look up **mouse** for more information.
mice (mīs) *plural noun.*

Mich. An abbreviation for *Michigan.*

Michigan A state in the north-central United States. Its capital is Lansing.
Mich·i·gan (mish′i gən) *noun.*

Word History

Michigan is the way French explorers wrote an Indian name for Lake Michigan that meant "big water." The state was named for Lake Michigan.

microbe A very tiny living thing; a microorganism. Some microbes cause disease.
mi·crobe (mī′krōb) *noun, plural* **microbes.**

microchip A small, thin slice of special material that usually contains a large number of tiny electronic parts.
mi·cro·chip (mī′krə chip′) *noun, plural* **microchips.**

microcomputer A small computer that is usually designed to be used by one person at a time. Although they are small, microcomputers are powerful enough to perform many tasks. A microcomputer is also called a **personal computer.**
mi·cro·com·put·er (mī′krō kəm pū′tər) *noun, plural* **microcomputers.**

microorganism A living thing that is too small to be seen with the naked eye. Bacteria are microorganisms.
mi·cro·or·gan·ism (mī′krō ôr′gə niz′əm) *noun, plural* **microorganisms.**

microphone A device that is used to transmit sound or to make it louder. A microphone changes sound waves into electrical signals. Speak into the *microphone* and your voice will be recorded on the tape.
mi·cro·phone (mī′krə fōn′) *noun, plural* **microphones.**

microscope A device that is used to look at things that are too small to be seen with the naked eye. It has one or more lenses that produce an enlarged image of anything seen through it. The biologist studied the leaf under a *microscope.*
mi·cro·scope (mī′krə skōp′) *noun, plural* **microscopes.**

microwave **1.** A type of radio wave that can pass through solid objects and other materials, such as fog, that would block light waves. Microwaves are used to transmit messages over long distances and to cook food in microwave ovens. **2.** A short form of the term "microwave oven." Look up **microwave oven** for more information.
mi·cro·wave (mī′krə wāv′) *noun, plural* **microwaves.**

microwave oven An oven that cooks or heats food very quickly by means of microwaves instead of the heat from electricity or burning gas.

an enlarged view of a **microchip**

mid   Being at or near the middle. My older cousin was born in the *mid* 1960s.
   mid (mid) *adjective.*

midday   The middle of the day; noon. We ate our lunch at *midday.*
   mid·day (mid′dā′) *noun.*

middle   Halfway between two things, sides, times, or the like. We sat in the *middle* row of the class. *Adjective.*
   —Something that is halfway between two things, sides, times, or the like. There is a white line down the *middle* of the road. *Noun.*
   mid·dle (mid′əl) *adjective; noun, plural* **middles.**

middle-aged   In the time of life between youth and old age, between about forty and sixty-five years old. My grandparents are *middle-aged.*
   mid·dle-aged (mid′əl ājd′) *adjective.*

Middle Ages   The period of European history from about A.D. 400 to 1450.

middle class   The class of people between the rich and the poor.

Middle East   A region made up of Israel, Egypt, Syria, Turkey, Iran, and other countries. The Middle East consists of parts of northeastern Africa and southwestern Asia.

Middle English   The English language as it was spoken and written in the period between about 1100 and 1500.

Middle West   A region of the north-central United States. This area is also called the **Midwest.**

midget   A very small person or thing. A person who is a midget is much smaller than, but has the same proportions as, a normal adult.
   midg·et (mij′it) *noun, plural* **midgets.**

midland   The middle or interior part of a country or region. Kansas is in the *midland* of the United States. *Noun.*
   —Of or located in the midland. Iowa is a *midland* state. *Adjective.*
   mid·land (mid′lənd) *noun, plural* **midlands;** *adjective.*

midnight   Twelve o'clock at night; the middle of the night.
   mid·night (mid′nīt′) *noun.*

midst   **1.** The middle; center. The child got lost in the *midst* of the crowd. The telephone call came in the *midst* of a very important meeting.   **2.** A position in the middle of a group of people or things. The soldiers were afraid that there was a spy in their *midst.*
   midst (midst) *noun.*

midway   In the middle; halfway. The sailors reached the *midway* point in their voyage. Their house is *midway* between my house and yours. *Adjective, Adverb.*
   —A place for games, rides, and other amusements at a circus, carnival, or fair. *Noun.*
   mid·way (mid′wā′) *adjective; adverb; noun, plural* **midways.**

Midwest   A region of the north-central United States. This area is also called the **Middle West.**
   Mid·west (mid′west′) *noun.*

might¹   An auxiliary verb that is used in the following ways: **1.** To express the past tense of **may.** I asked the teacher if I *might* leave.   **2.** To say that something is possible. The story we heard *might* be true, but I'm not sure.   **3.** To ask permission. *Might* I borrow your dictionary?   **4.** To offer a suggestion. You *might* try using a pencil so that you can erase your mistakes. ⟁ Another word that sounds like this is **mite.**
   might (mīt) *verb.*

might²   Power or strength. The door made a loud bang because I slammed it with all my **might.** ⟁ Another word that sounds like this is **mite.**
   might (mīt) *noun.*

mighty   Great in power, size, or amount. The Pacific is a *mighty* ocean.
   might·y (mī′tē) *adjective,* **mightier, mightiest.**

migrant   A person or animal that migrates. These birds are *migrants* from South America. *Noun.*
   —Migrating. *Migrant* workers go from farm to farm looking for work. *Adjective.*
   mi·grant (mī′grənt) *noun, plural* **migrants;** *adjective.*

migrate   To move from one place to another. Many birds *migrate* to the south in the fall.
   mi·grate (mī′grāt) *verb,* **migrated, migrating.**

migration   The act of moving from one place to another. During their *migration,* geese stop at a pond near our house.
   mi·gra·tion (mī grā′shən) *noun, plural* **migrations.**

mild   Gentle or calm; not harsh or sharp. A *mild* winter is not very cold and snowy.
   mild (mīld) *adjective,* **milder, mildest.**

M

at; āpe; fär; câre; end; mē; it; īce; pîerce; hot; ōld; sông, fôrk; oil; out; up; ūse; rüle; pùll; tûrn; chin; sing; shop; thin; this; hw in white; zh in treasure. The symbol ə stands for the unstressed vowel sound in about, taken, pencil, lemon, and circus.

mildew A kind of fungus that looks like white powder or fuzz. It grows on plants and materials such as cloth, leather, and paper when they are left damp.
mil·dew (mil′dü) *noun, plural* **mildews.**

mile A measure of distance equal to 5,280 feet.
mile (mīl) *noun, plural* **miles.**

mileage 1. Distance traveled in miles. The *mileage* on our old car is about 150,000 miles. 2. The distance in miles that a vehicle can travel on a given amount of fuel. Small cars usually get better *mileage* than large ones.
mile·age (mī′lij) *noun.*

milestone 1. A marker made of stone placed at the side of a road. It gives the distance in miles to some place or places. 2. An important event or development. The invention of the telephone was a *milestone* in the history of communications.
mile·stone (mīl′stōn′) *noun, plural* **milestones.**

military 1. Having to do with the armed forces, soldiers, or war. My cousin wants to follow a *military* career in the Marine Corps. **2. the military.** The armed forces as a whole. The army, navy, and air force are branches of *the military.*
mil·i·tar·y (mil′i ter′ē) *adjective.*

militia A group of citizens who are trained to fight and help in emergencies. Each state in the United States has a militia called the National Guard.
mi·li·tia (mi lish′ə) *noun, plural* **militias.**

milk 1. A white liquid food produced by glands in female mammals. The milk of all mammals is used to feed their babies. The milk of cows is used as food by people. 2. A white liquid like this that is made in plants. Coconuts are filled with milk that people use as food. *Noun.*
—To take milk from a cow or other animal. The farmer *milked* the cows early each evening and early each morning. *Verb.*
milk (milk) *noun; verb,* **milked, milking.**

Milky Way A galaxy that includes billions of stars. Our sun, the earth, and the rest of the solar system are part of the Milky Way. On clear nights, the Milky Way appears as a cloudy white path stretching across the sky.
Mil·ky Way (mil′kē).

mill 1. A building where there are machines to grind grain into flour or meal. 2. A machine that grinds grain or other seeds. 3. A building where there are machines to make raw materials into finished products. Steel *mills* make steel. *Noun.*

—1. To grind. The machines *milled* the wheat into flour. 2. To move around in a confused way. The frightened sheep *milled* around in the pen. *Verb.*
mill (mil) *noun, plural* **mills;** *verb,* **milled, milling.**

milli– A *prefix* that means one thousandth ($^1/_{1000}$) of. A *milliliter* is $^1/_{1000}$ of a liter.

millimeter A unit of length in the metric system. A millimeter is equal to one thousandth of a meter, or about .039 of an inch.
mil·li·me·ter (mil′ə mē′tər) *noun, plural* **millimeters.**

million 1. One thousand times one thousand; 1,000,000. 2. A very large number. It looks like there are a *million* stars in the sky tonight.
mil·lion (mil′yən) *noun, plural* **millions;** *adjective.*

millionaire A person who has money or property worth a million or more dollars.
mil·lion·aire (mil′yə nâr′) *noun, plural* **millionaires.**

mimeograph A machine that makes copies of written pages using an ink process. Our teacher made copies of our test questions on the *mimeograph.*
mim·e·o·graph (mim′ē ə graf′) *noun, plural* **mimeographs.**

mimic To imitate, especially in order to make fun of. The comedian could *mimic* the voices and gestures of famous people. *Verb.*
—A person or thing that imitates. *Noun.*
mim·ic (mim′ik) *verb,* **mimicked, mimicking;** *noun, plural* **mimics.**

min. An abbreviation for *minute.*

minaret A tall, slender tower on top of a mosque. A person calls people to prayer from a balcony near the top of a minaret.
min·a·ret (min′ə ret′) *noun, plural* **minarets.**

mince To chop into very small pieces. I *minced* onions and garlic to put in the spaghetti sauce.
mince (mins) *verb,* **minced, mincing.**

mincemeat A filling for pies. Mincemeat is a mixture of finely

minaret

chopped apples, raisins, currants, sugar, spices, and sometimes meat.
mince·meat (mins′mēt′) *noun.*

mind **1.** The part of a person that thinks, knows, learns, remembers, understands, and feels. That student has a good *mind* and learns things quickly. Keep your *mind* on what you're doing. **2.** A wish or opinion. I changed my *mind* about visiting when I heard you were sick. *Noun.*
—**1.** To pay attention to or worry about. *Mind* your manners at the dinner table. **2.** To take care of. A babysitter *minded* the children when their parents went out. **3.** To not like something; object to. Do you *mind* going to the movies alone? *Verb.*
• **never mind.** To not worry or pay attention. *Never mind* about the dirty dishes; we can wash them later.
• **to make up one's mind.** To decide. After thinking for a while, I *made up my mind* to go to the movie.
mind (mīnd) *noun, plural* **minds;** *verb,* **minded, minding.**

mine¹ The one or ones that belong to me. The bicycle that used to belong to my older cousin is now *mine.*
mine (mīn) *pronoun.*

mine² **1.** A large area dug out in or under the ground. Coal, gold, diamonds, and other minerals are dug out of mines. **2.** Any rich source or supply. The book was a *mine* of information about life under the sea. **3.** A bomb that is put underground or underwater. *Noun.*
—**1.** To take a mineral from the ground by digging. Workers *mine* coal in Pennsylvania. **2.** To put bombs in. The navy divers *mined* the harbor during the war. *Verb.*
mine (mīn) *noun, plural* **mines;** *verb,* **mined, mining.**

mineral A substance found in nature that is not an animal or a plant. Salt, coal, and gold are minerals. *Noun.*
—Containing minerals. *Mineral* water is water that has natural salts in it. *Adjective.*
min·er·al (min′ər əl) *noun, plural* **minerals;** *adjective.*

mingle **1.** To put or come together; mix; join. This stream *mingles* with many others to form a river. **2.** To move about freely; join; associate. We *mingled* with the other guests at the party.
min·gle (ming′gəl) *verb,* **mingled, mingling.**

miniature Much smaller than the usual size. My parents made *miniature* furniture for my doll house. *Adjective.*
—A model or copy of something in a much smaller size. We bought a *miniature* of the Statue of Liberty as a souvenir of our trip to New York. *Noun.*
min·i·a·ture (min′ē ə chər *or* min′ə chər) *adjective; noun, plural* **miniatures.**

a **miniature** village

minimum **1.** The smallest or least possible amount. I will need a *minimum* of two weeks to finish my report. **2.** The lowest point or number reached. The temperature reached a *minimum* of 20 degrees today. *Noun.*
—Lowest; smallest. The *minimum* pay for the job was five dollars an hour. *Adjective.*
min·i·mum (min′ə məm) *noun, plural* **minimums** or **minima** (min′ə mə); *adjective.*

mining The act, process, or industry of digging for minerals in the ground. Gold, coal, and diamonds are produced by *mining.*
min·ing (mī′ning) *noun.*

minister **1.** A person who is authorized to conduct religious services; member of the clergy; pastor. **2.** A person who is in charge of a department of the government. **3.** A person who represents his or her government in a foreign country. *Noun.*

at; āpe; fär; câre; end; mē; it; īce; pîerce; hot; ōld; sông, fôrk; oil; out; up; ūse; rüle; pùll; tûrn; chin; sing; shop; thin; this; hw in white; zh in treasure. The symbol ə stands for the unstressed vowel sound in about, taken, pencil, lemon, and circus.

M

—To take care of. Nurses *minister* to sick people. *Verb.*
min·is·ter (min′ə stər) *noun, plural* **ministers;** *verb,* **ministered, ministering.**

mink **1.** A slender animal of the weasel family with short legs and soft, thick fur. Minks live in woods near water. **2.** The fur of this animal.
mink (mingk) *noun, plural* **mink** or **minks.**

mink

Minn. An abbreviation for *Minnesota.*

Minnesota A state in the north-central United States. Its capital is St. Paul.
Min·ne·so·ta (min′ə sō′tə) *noun.*

Word History

Minnesota was an Indian name for the Minnesota River. It means "water the color of the sky" or "cloudy water." Congress gave this name to the area that became the state of Minnesota.

minnow A very small, freshwater fish.
min·now (min′ō) *noun, plural* **minnows.**

minor Small in importance or size. The teacher read my report and found a few *minor* errors in spelling. *Adjective.*
—A person who is not old enough to vote or be legally responsible for his or her own affairs. *Noun.*
mi·nor (mī′nər) *adjective; noun, plural* **minors.**

minority **1.** The smaller part of a group or whole; less than half. Out of twenty students, a *minority* of only six voted for the new plan. **2.** A group of people that is thought of as different from the larger group of which it is a part because of race, religion, politics, or nationality.
mi·nor·i·ty (mə nôr′i tē *or* mī nôr′i tē) *noun, plural* **minorities.**

mint¹ **1.** A plant that has fragrant leaves that are used as flavoring and in medicine. Peppermint and spearmint are kinds of mint. **2.** A candy flavored with mint.
mint (mint) *noun, plural* **mints.**

mint² **1.** A place where metal is made into coins, usually under government authority. **2.** A large amount of money. A fancy car like this must cost a *mint. Noun.*
—To make coins. The government *minted* new half dollars this year. *Verb.*
mint (mint) *noun, plural* **mints;** *verb,* **minted, minting.**

minuend The number from which another number is subtracted. In the equation $6 - 2 = 4$, the minuend is 6.
min·u·end (min′ū end′) *noun, plural* **minuends.**

minus **1.** Decreased by; less. Ten *minus* seven is three. **2.** Lacking; without. The chair was *minus* a leg. *Preposition.*
—**1.** Less than zero. It was *minus* four degrees this morning. **2.** Lower than or less than. I got a grade of A *minus* on my paper. **3.** Showing that something is to be or has been taken away. A minus sign means that the number following it is to be subtracted. *Adjective.*
—A sign ($-$) that shows something is to be or has been subtracted. In the equation $9 - 6 = 3$, the sign between 9 and 6 is a minus. *Noun.*
mi·nus (mī′nəs) *preposition; adjective; noun, plural* **minuses.**

minute¹ **1.** A unit of time equal to sixty seconds. There are sixty minutes in an hour. **2.** A moment in time; instant. I knew who you were the *minute* you walked into the room. **3.** **minutes.** A written report of what was said and done at a meeting.
min·ute (min′it) *noun, plural* **minutes.**

minute² **1.** Very small; tiny. A *minute* piece of dust blew into my eye. **2.** Paying close attention to details; very careful and thorough. The detective made a *minute* examination of the desk for fingerprints.
mi·nute (mī nüt′ *or* mī nūt′) *adjective.*

minuteman A volunteer soldier who was not part of the regular army during the American Revolution, but was ready to fight at a minute's notice.
min·ute·man (min′it man′) *noun, plural* **minutemen** (min′it men′).

miracle **1.** Something amazing or wonderful that cannot be explained by the laws of nature. **2.** An amazing or wonderful thing. It was a *miracle* that our team won the championship.
mir·a·cle (mir′ə kəl) *noun, plural* **miracles.**

miraculous **1.** Impossible to explain by the laws of nature. The child's recovery from the loss of hearing seemed *miraculous*. **2.** Amazing; marvelous. The magician made a *miraculous* escape from a locked trunk.
mi·rac·u·lous (mi rak′yə ləs) *adjective*.

mirage An illusion in which an object that is seen at a distance is not really there. A common mirage is the appearance of a sheet of water that you see ahead of you on a highway on a hot day. A mirage is caused by light rays that are bent by layers of air at different temperatures.
mi·rage (mi räzh′) *noun, plural* **mirages**.

mirror **1.** A smooth, polished surface that shows the image of the person or thing in front of it by reflecting light. Most mirrors are made of glass with an aluminum or silver coating on the back. **2.** Something that gives a true picture. This story is a *mirror* of life in colonial America. *Noun*.
—To reflect a picture or image. I can see myself *mirrored* in your sunglasses. *Verb*.
mir·ror (mir′ər) *noun, plural* **mirrors;** *verb*, **mirrored, mirroring**.

mis– A *prefix* that means: **1.** Bad; wrong. *Misfortune* means bad fortune. **2.** In a bad or wrong way. *Mispronounce* means to pronounce in the wrong way.

misbehave To do something that is wrong; behave badly. The child *misbehaved* by writing on the wall.
mis·be·have (mis′bi hāv′) *verb*, **misbehaved, misbehaving**.

miscellaneous Made up of different kinds of things. There was a *miscellaneous* collection of papers, toys, and clothes in the dresser drawer.
mis·cel·la·ne·ous (mis′ə lā′nē əs) *adjective*.

mischief An action or conduct that may seem playful but that causes harm or trouble. Our parents asked us not to get into any *mischief* while they were away.
mis·chief (mis′chif) *noun*.

mischievous **1.** Full of mischief; playful but naughty. That *mischievous* child hid my slippers again. **2.** Causing trouble; harmful. The candidate was hurt by the *mischievous* rumors being spread by opponents.
mis·chie·vous (mis′chə vəs) *adjective*.

miscount To count incorrectly. The votes in our school election were *miscounted*. *Verb*.
—An incorrect count. Because of a *miscount* of the tickets sold, extra seats had to be brought into the auditorium. *Noun*.
mis·count (mis kount′ *for verb;* mis′kount′ *for noun*) *verb*, **miscounted, miscounting;** *noun, plural* **miscounts**.

miser A person who prefers to live poorly and save money rather than spend it; a stingy person.
mi·ser (mī′zər) *noun, plural* **misers**.

miserable **1.** Very unhappy; wretched. We all felt *miserable* about losing our dog. **2.** Causing discomfort or unhappiness. I had a *miserable* cold. **3.** Of little or no value; poor. They did such a *miserable* job of fixing the chair that it broke again.
mis·er·a·ble (miz′ər ə bəl) *adjective*.

misery Great unhappiness or suffering. The flood caused *misery* for many people.
mis·er·y (miz′ə rē) *noun, plural* **miseries**.

misfortune **1.** Bad luck. It was my *misfortune* to lose my new watch. **2.** An unlucky event or happening. The pitcher's injury was a great *misfortune* for our baseball team.
mis·for·tune (mis fôr′chən) *noun, plural* **misfortunes**.

misgiving A feeling of doubt, suspicion, or worry. We had *misgivings* about making the long trip with so little money.
mis·giv·ing (mis giv′ing) *noun, plural* **misgivings**.

mislay To put in a place that is later forgotten. I *mislaid* my skates and couldn't find them for a week.
mis·lay (mis lā′) *verb*, **mislaid, mislaying**.

mislead **1.** To lead or guide in the wrong direction. Our map *misled* us so we never found the way to the beach. **2.** To lead into a mistaken or wrong thought or action. The advertisement for this product *misled* us.
mis·lead (mis lēd′) *verb*, **misled** (mis led′), **misleading**.

misleading Causing a mistake or wrong idea. The witnesses told the detective a *misleading* story because they did not want the police to know what really happened.
mis·lead·ing (mis lē′ding) *adjective*.

misplace **1.** To put something in a place and forget where it is; lose. I *misplaced* my key and had to get a new one. **2.** To put in the wrong place. In the sentence "If you go please, tell me first," the comma after "please" is *misplaced*. It should be after "go."
mis·place (mis plās′) *verb*, **misplaced, misplacing**.

M

at; āpe; fär; câre; end; mē; it; īce; pîerce; hot; ōld; sông, fôrk; oil; out; up; ūse; rüle; pùll; tûrn; chin; sing; shop; thin; this; hw in white; zh in treasure. The symbol ə stands for the unstressed vowel sound in about, taken, pencil, lemon, and circus.

mispronounce   To pronounce a word or sound in the wrong way. If you pronounce the "k" in the word "knife," you are *mispronouncing* it.
> **mis·pro·nounce** (mis′prə nouns′) *verb,* **mispronounced, mispronouncing.**

misread   To read or understand incorrectly. We *misread* the sign on the highway and drove past the turn.
> **mis·read** (mis rēd′) *verb,* **misread** (mis red′), **misreading.**

miss¹   **1.** To fail to do something attempted or planned; fail to get, reach, hit, meet, find, or catch. The player swung the bat and *missed* the ball. We *missed* the bus. You *missed* your appointment with the dentist. The driver *missed* the exit on the highway and had to turn around.   **2.** To notice or feel the absence or loss of a person or thing. I *missed* my parents when they went away for vacation. I didn't *miss* my watch until I looked to see what time it was.   **3.** To get away from; escape. We just *missed* being hit by the falling rock.   **4.** To be without; lack. This coat is *missing* a button. *Verb.*
—A failure to hit or reach something. I shot five arrows at the target without a *miss.* *Noun.*
> **miss** (mis) *verb,* **missed, missing;** *noun,* *plural* **misses.**

miss²   A title for a girl or for a woman who is not married. When "miss" is used with a person's name, it is written with a capital "M." Our friend, *Miss* Lane, will be visiting this weekend. "Yes, *miss,* may I help you?" asked the clerk.
> **miss** (mis) *noun,* *plural* **misses.**

Miss.   An abbreviation for *Mississippi.*

missile   **1.** Anything that is thrown or shot through the air. An arrow, a bullet, and a rock can be missiles.   **2.** A rocket that is used to launch a space capsule, satellite, or weapon. We all watched as the *missile* rose from the launching pad.
> **mis·sile** (mis′əl) *noun,* *plural* **missiles.**

missing   **1.** Lost; not to be found. I finally found the *missing* sock under the bed.   **2.** Not there; absent or lacking. This jigsaw puzzle has a *missing* piece.
> **miss·ing** (mis′ing) *adjective.*

mission   **1.** A group of people who are sent somewhere to do a special job. Four rangers formed a rescue *mission* to search for the lost child.   **2.** A special job or task. The astronauts went on a *mission* to the moon.   **3.** A church or other place where a group of missionaries work.
> **mis·sion** (mish′ən) *noun,* *plural* **missions.**

missionary   A person who is sent by a religious group to spread the religion and promote good will in another country. My grandparents were *missionaries* in India.
> **mis·sion·ar·y** (mish′ə ner′ē) *noun,* *plural* **missionaries.**

Mississippi   **1.** A state in the southern United States. Its capital is Jackson.   **2.** The longest river in the United States. It flows from Minnesota to the Gulf of Mexico.
> **Mis·sis·sip·pi** (mis′ə sip′ē) *noun.*

Word History

Mississippi comes from two American Indian words that mean "big river," "great water," or "father of the waters." The name was first used in the northern part of the country for what is now called the Mississippi River, but French explorers carried it down the Mississippi River. Congress gave the name to the area at the southern end of the river that became the state of Mississippi.

Missouri   **1.** A state in the central United States. Its capital is Jefferson City.   **2.** A large river in the United States. It flows from Montana to the Mississippi River.
> **Mis·sou·ri** (mi zùr′ē *or* mi zùr′ə) *noun.*

Word History

Missouri is an American Indian word that means "people with the big canoes." It was the name of a tribe that lived near the mouth of the Missouri River when French explorers first went there. Later the name was used for the river near this tribe's home, and finally it was given to the state.

misspell   To spell a word incorrectly. I *misspelled* "until" on the test because I spelled it with two l's at the end.
> **mis·spell** (mis spel′) *verb,* **misspelled** or **misspelt, misspelling.**

mist   A cloud of tiny drops of water or other liquid in the air; fog. Early this morning, there was a heavy *mist* over the lake. *Noun.*
—**1.** To be or become covered with a mist. My glasses *misted* in the fog.   **2.** To rain in fine drops; drizzle. It *misted* in the morning, but by noon the sky was clear. *Verb.*
> **mist** (mist) *noun; verb,* **misted, misting.**

mistake Something that is not correctly done, said, or thought; error. I made two spelling *mistakes* on the test. It was a *mistake* to mention the party, since it was supposed to be a surprise. *Noun.*
—To make an error about something. It is easy to *mistake* one twin for the other because they look exactly alike. *Verb.*
mis·take (mis tāk′) *noun, plural* **mistakes;** *verb,* **mistook, mistaken, mistaking.**

mistaken In error; wrong. We had a *mistaken* idea about what time the party was to begin. *Adjective.*
—Past participle of **mistake.** I've *mistaken* your coat for mine because they're the same color. Look up **mistake** for more information. *Verb.*
mis·tak·en (mis tā′kən) *adjective; verb.*

mister A title for a man. When "mister" is used with a man's name, it is written with a capital "M" or more often abbreviated as "Mr." *Mr.* Jackson lives next door to us. "Excuse me, *mister,* can you direct me to the library?" I asked.
mis·ter (mis′tər) *noun, plural* **misters.**

mistletoe A plant that has small, yellowish green leaves and bunches of little white berries. Mistletoe is a parasite that grows on the branches of trees. Mistletoe is used as a Christmas decoration.
mis·tle·toe (mis′əl tō′) *noun, plural* **mistletoes.**

mistletoe

mistook Past tense of **mistake.** I *mistook* your gloves for mine. Look up **mistake** for more information.
mis·took (mis tùk′) *verb.*

mistreat To be cruel, rough, or unkind to; treat badly. The child *mistreated* the cat by pulling its tail.
mis·treat (mis trēt′) *verb,* **mistreated, mistreating.**

mistress A woman who is in charge or control of something. A woman who has a home is mistress of the household.
mis·tress (mis′tris) *noun, plural* **mistresses.**

mistrust A lack of trust or confidence; suspicion; doubt. I discussed my *mistrust* of the plan with the committee. *Noun.*
—To have no trust or confidence in; be suspicious of; doubt. I *mistrust* a lot of television commercials. *Verb.*
mis·trust (mis trust′) *noun; verb,* **mistrusted, mistrusting.**

misty **1.** Covered or clouded with mist. The harbor was *misty* with the morning fog. The sad child's eyes were *misty* with tears. **2.** Not clear; vague. I have only a *misty* memory of what my grandparents looked like.
mist·y (mis′tē) *adjective,* **mistier, mistiest.**

misunderstand To understand someone or something incorrectly. I *misunderstood* the instructions and wrote my answers in pencil instead of ink.
mis·un·der·stand (mis′un dər stand′) *verb,* **misunderstood, misunderstanding.**

misunderstanding **1.** The failure to understand correctly. *Misunderstanding* sometimes leads to mistakes. **2.** A disagreement between people. The two friends settled their *misunderstanding* by discussing it.
mis·un·der·stand·ing (mis′un dər stan′ding) *noun, plural* **misunderstandings.**

misunderstood Past tense of **misunderstand.** We *misunderstood* your directions and got lost. Look up **misunderstand** for more information.
mis·un·der·stood (mis′un dər stùd′) *verb.*

misuse Wrong or incorrect use. The teacher warned us that *misuse* of laboratory equipment can be dangerous. *Noun.*
—**1.** To use wrongly or incorrectly. My essay was criticized because I *misused* pronouns in several sentences. **2.** To treat badly. We *misused* our new car by driving on rocky roads. *Verb.*
mis·use (mis ūs′ *for noun;* mis ūz′ *for verb*) *noun, plural* **misuses;** *verb,* **misused, misusing.**

mite **1.** A tiny animal that is similar to a spider. Most mites are parasites and live on animals. **2.** A very small object or creature. The baby was a *mite* compared to the adults. **3.** A small amount. ▲ Another word that sounds like this is **might.**
mite (mīt) *noun, plural* **mites.**

M

at; āpe; fär; câre; end; mē; it; īce; pîerce; hot; ōld; sông, fôrk; oil; out; up; ūse; rüle; pùll; tûrn; chin; sing; shop; thin; this; hw in white; zh in treasure. The symbol ə stands for the unstressed vowel sound in about, taken, pencil, lemon, and circus.

mitt 1. A type of glove used in baseball. Mitts have padding to protect a person's hand when a ball is caught. 2. A glove that covers the palm of the hand but not the fingers.
mitt (mit) *noun, plural* **mitts.**

mitten A warm covering for the hand. A mitten covers four fingers together and the thumb separately.
mit·ten (mit'ən) *noun, plural* **mittens.**

mix 1. To put two or more different things together. We *mixed* yellow roses and white roses in the bouquet. 2. To blend, combine, or join. Oil and water will not *mix*. 3. To get along with other people. It was a great party because all the guests *mixed* well. *Verb.*
—Something that is made by mixing; mixture. We bought a pancake *mix* at the store. *Noun.*
• **to mix up.** 1. To confuse. I was so *mixed up* by your directions that I got lost. 2. To involve. The police suspect that the gang was *mixed up* in the robberies.
mix (miks) *verb,* **mixed, mixing;** *noun, plural* **mixes.**

mixed number A number made up of a whole number and a fraction. The number $4\frac{7}{8}$ is a mixed number.

mixer A machine for mixing different things together. A cement *mixer* mixes cement, water, and sand to make concrete. I used an electric *mixer* to mix the cake batter.
mix·er (mik'sər) *noun, plural* **mixers.**

mixture 1. Something made up of different things that are put together. The color pink is a *mixture* of red and white. 2. The act or process of mixing. The *mixture* of oil, vinegar, and spices makes a salad dressing.
mix·ture (miks'chər) *noun, plural* **mixtures.**

mix-up An instance or condition of confusion. We missed the bus because of a *mix-up* in the schedule.
mix-up (miks'up') *noun, plural* **mix-ups.**

ml An abbreviation for *milliliter.*

mm An abbreviation for *millimeter.*

MN Postal abbreviation for *Minnesota.*

mo. An abbreviation for *month.*

Mo. An abbreviation for *Missouri.*

MO Postal abbreviation for *Missouri.*

moan A long, low sound. A moan usually shows that a person or animal feels pain or grief. The patient's *moans* were heard by everyone in the dentist's office. *Noun.*
—To make or say with a long, low sound. I *moaned* when I accidentally bumped my sore arm. *Verb.* ⚠ Another word that sounds like this is **mown.**
moan (mōn) *noun, plural* **moans;** *verb,* **moaned, moaning.**

moat A deep, wide ditch that surrounds a castle or town for protection against an enemy. Moats are usually filled with water. A drawbridge is lowered over the moat so that people can cross it.
moat (mōt) *noun, plural* **moats.**

mob A large number of people; crowd. A mob is sometimes made up of people who are so angry or upset about something that they break the law and cause damage. An angry *mob* gathered in front of the jail to demand that the prisoner be set free. *Noun.*
—To crowd around in excitement or anger. Shoppers *mobbed* the store during the big sale. *Verb.*
mob (mob) *noun, plural* **mobs;** *verb,* **mobbed, mobbing.**

mobile Capable of moving or being moved. The crew set up *mobile* television cameras to tape the opening of the new theater. *Adjective.*
—A kind of sculpture with movable parts that are usually hung from rods or thin wires. These parts can be easily moved by currents of air. *Noun.*
mo·bile (mō'bəl *or* mō'bēl *for adjective;* mō'bēl *for noun*) *adjective; noun, plural* **mobiles.**

mobile home A large trailer that people can live in.

moccasin A soft leather shoe or slipper with no heel. Moccasins were first worn by American Indians.
moc·ca·sin (mok'ə sin) *noun, plural* **moccasins.**

Word History

The word **moccasin** comes from the American Indian word for this sort of leather shoe.

---

mock 1. To make fun of in a mean way. Instead of helping, they laughed and *mocked* me when I fell off my bike. 2. To imitate or copy in a joking or rude way. That comedian *mocks* several famous politicians and actors. *Verb.*
—Not real; imitation. In history class we had a *mock* battle with cardboard shields and wooden swords. *Adjective.*
mock (mok) *verb,* **mocked, mocking;** *adjective.*

mockingbird A bird that can imitate the calls of other birds. Mockingbirds live in North and Central America. Most of them have dark gray feathers with white markings. **mock·ing·bird** (mok′ing bûrd′) *noun, plural* **mockingbirds.**

mockingbird

mode¹ A way of doing something. Automobiles are a popular *mode* of transportation. **mode** (mōd) *noun, plural* **modes.**

mode² A style of dress, fashion, or behavior that is popular at a particular time. Hats with wide brims will be the *mode* next spring. **mode** (mōd) *noun, plural* **modes.**

model **1.** A small-sized copy of something. I like to make car *models* from kits. **2.** A person or thing that is a good example of something and is copied. The U.S. Constitution is used as a *model* by many new governments. **3.** A person who poses for an artist or photographer. **4.** A person whose job is to wear new clothes so that customers can see what they look like. Models may work in stores or in fashion shows, or be photographed for magazines. **5.** A style or type of thing. That car is a very old *model. Noun.* —**1.** Worthy of being imitated. The children showed *model* behavior during their visit to the museum. **2.** Serving as or being a small copy. We built the *model* airplane from a kit. *Adjective.* —**1.** To make or design something. The sculptor *modeled* a pony in clay. **2.** To follow or copy someone or something. I hope to *model* my career after my favorite teacher's. **3.** To work as a model. My cousin *models* for a local clothing store. *Verb.* **mod·el** (mod′əl) *noun, plural* **models;** *adjective; verb,* **modeled, modeling.**

moderate Not too much or too little; not extreme. The price of this coat was *moderate.* We have had *moderate* temperatures this winter. *Adjective.* —To become or make less extreme or violent. The heavy winds *moderated* during the night. *Verb.* **mod·er·ate** (mod′ər it *for adjective;* mod′ə rāt′ *for verb) adjective; verb,* **moderated, moderating.**

modern **1.** Having to do with the present time or recent time. Airplanes are a fairly *modern* means of transportation. Nuclear energy as a source of power is a *modern* development. **2.** Having to do with the period from about the year 1400 to the present. Last year, we studied ancient history; now we are learning about *modern* history. **3.** Up-to-date; not old-fashioned. The laboratory was filled with the most *modern* equipment available. **mod·ern** (mod′ərn) *adjective.*

modernize To make or become modern or up-to-date. We *modernized* our kitchen by installing a new dishwasher and a microwave oven. **mod·ern·ize** (mod′ər nīz′) *verb,* **modernized, modernizing.**

modest **1.** Not thinking too highly of oneself. A modest person does not brag or show off. **2.** Within reason; limited or restrained; not extreme. We spent only a *modest* amount of money on the trip. **mod·est** (mod′ist) *adjective.*

modify **1.** To change in some way. We *modified* our plan for the new kitchen and added a small dining area at one end. **2.** To make less; reduce. The union leaders decided to *modify* their demands for better working conditions. **3.** To limit the meaning of a word. In the sentence "They live in a white house," the adjective "white" *modifies* the noun "house." **mod·i·fy** (mod′ə fī′) *verb,* **modified, modifying.**

module A part of a spacecraft that has a special use and can be separated from the rest of the craft. A lunar module is the small craft in which astronauts landed on the moon. **mod·ule** (moj′ül *or* mod′ūl) *noun, plural* **modules.**

Mohawk A member of a tribe of American Indians of New York. The Mohawk are part of the Iroquois confederation. **Mo·hawk** (mō′hôk) *noun, plural* **Mohawk** or **Mohawks.**

moist Slightly wet; damp. I wiped the shelves with a *moist* cloth. The air was *moist* and chilly this morning. **moist** (moist) *adjective,* **moister, moistest.**

M

moisten   To make or become slightly wet. I *moistened* the soil around the plant.
moist·en (moi′sən) *verb*, **moistened, moistening.**

moisture   Water or other liquid in the air or on a surface; slight wetness. There was *moisture* on the window from the steam in the kitchen.
mois·ture (mois′chər) *noun*.

molar   Any one of the large teeth at the back of the mouth. Molars have broad surfaces for grinding food.
mo·lar (mō′lər) *noun, plural* **molars.**

molasses   A sweet, thick, yellowish brown syrup that is made from sugarcane.
mo·las·ses (mə las′iz) *noun.*

mold¹   A hollow form that is made in a special shape. A liquid or soft material is poured into a mold. When it hardens, it takes the shape of the mold. *Noun.*
—**1.** To make into a special shape; form. We *molded* the clay with our hands.   **2.** To influence and give form to. Our parents help *mold* our habits. *Verb.*
mold (mōld) *noun, plural* **molds;** *verb,* **molded, molding.**

mold²   A furry-looking covering of fungus that grows on food and damp surfaces. *Noun.*
—To become covered with mold. The bread *molded* because it wasn't refrigerated. *Verb.*
mold (mōld) *noun, plural* **molds;** *verb,* **molded, molding.**

molding   A strip of wood, plaster, or other material that is used along the edges of walls, windows, or doorways for decoration.
mold·ing (mōl′ding) *noun, plural* **moldings.**

mole¹   A small, often raised, brown spot on the skin.
mole (mōl) *noun, plural* **moles.**

mole²   A small animal with very soft, grayish fur that burrows holes underground. Moles have long claws and very small eyes.
mole (mōl) *noun, plural* **moles.**

mole²

molecule   The smallest particle into which a substance can be divided without being changed chemically. For example, a molecule of water has two atoms of hydrogen and one atom of oxygen.
mol·e·cule (mol′ə kūl′) *noun, plural* **molecules.**

mollusk   Any of a group of animals without backbones that usually have a soft body protected by a hard shell. Mollusks often live in or near water. Clams, snails, and oysters are mollusks.
mol·lusk (mol′əsk) *noun, plural* **mollusks.**

molt   To shed the hair, feathers, skin, or shell and grow a new covering. Birds and snakes molt.
molt (mōlt) *verb,* **molted, molting.**

molten   Melted by heat. Lava from a volcano is *molten* rock.
mol·ten (mōl′tən) *adjective.*

mom   Mother. I call my mother *Mom.*
mom (mom) *noun, plural* **moms.**

moment   **1.** A short period of time. I'll answer your question in just a *moment.*   **2.** A particular point in time. Please come home the *moment* I call you or your dinner will get cold.
mo·ment (mō′mənt) *noun, plural* **moments.**

momentary   Lasting only a short time. There was a *momentary* lull in the storm and then it rained heavily again.
mo·men·tar·y (mō′mən ter′ē) *adjective.*

momentous   Having great importance. The end of the war was a *momentous* event for all.
mo·men·tous (mō men′təs) *adjective.*

momentum   The force or speed that an object has when it is moving. A rock gains *momentum* as it rolls down a hill.
mo·men·tum (mō men′təm) *noun, plural* **momentums.**

Mon.   An abbreviation for *Monday.*

monarch   **1.** A king, queen, or other ruler of a state or country.   **2.** A large orange and black butterfly found in North America.
mon·arch (mon′ərk) *noun, plural* **monarchs.**

monarchy   **1.** Government by a king, queen, or other monarch.   **2.** A nation or state that is ruled by a monarch.
mon·ar·chy (mon′ər kē) *noun, plural* **monarchies.**

monastery   A place where monks live and work together.
mon·as·ter·y (mon′ə ster′ē) *noun, plural* **monasteries.**

Monday The second day of the week.
Mon·day (mun′dē *or* mun′dā) *noun, plural*
Mondays.

Word History

The Romans dedicated the second day of the week to the moon. This name was translated as an Old English word meaning "moon's day," or **Monday** as it became in modern English.

monetary Of, in, or having to do with money or currency. This vase has great *monetary* value. The dollar is the *monetary* unit of the United States.
mon·e·tar·y (mon′i ter′ē) *adjective*.

money The coins and paper currency of a country. Money is used to buy goods and pay people for services. Nickels, dimes, and dollar bills are money.
mon·ey (mun′ē) *noun, plural* **moneys.**

Mongolia A country in central Asia.
Mon·go·li·a (mong gō′lē ə) *noun*.

mongoose A slender animal that has a pointed face, a long tail, and rough, shaggy fur. Mongooses live in Africa and Asia. They eat rats and mice and are very quick.
mon·goose (mong′güs′) *noun, plural* **mongooses.**

mongoose

mongrel An animal, especially a dog, or a plant that is a mixture of breeds.
mon·grel (mung′grəl *or* mong′grəl) *noun, plural* **mongrels.**

monitor **1.** A student who is given a special duty to do. Some monitors help take attendance and others help keep order. **2.** Any person who warns or keeps watch. The sailor's job was to be *monitor* of the radar screen. **3.** The screen that a computer uses to display numbers, letters, and pictures. It is similar to a television screen. *Noun.*
—To watch over or observe something. Our teacher *monitored* the fire drill. *Verb.*
mon·i·tor (mon′i tər) *noun, plural* **monitors;** *verb,* **monitored, monitoring.**

monk A man who has joined a religious order, lives in a monastery, and is bound by religious vows.
monk (mungk) *noun, plural* **monks.**

monkey **1.** Any of a group of intelligent, furry animals with long tails and hands and feet that can grasp things. Most monkeys live in trees in tropical areas of the world. Monkeys are primates. **2.** A playful or naughty child. *Noun.*
—To fool or play around in a mischievous way. The lifeguard asked us to quit *monkeying* around in the water. Don't *monkey* with the stove or you might get burned. *Verb.*

monkey

mon·key (mung′kē) *noun, plural* **monkeys;** *verb,* **monkeyed, monkeying.**

monkey wrench A wrench with a jaw that can be adjusted to fit different sizes of nuts and bolts.

monogram A design made by combining two or more initials of a person's name. You see monograms on such things as clothing, towels, and stationery.
mon·o·gram (mon′ə gram′) *noun, plural* **monograms.**

monologue **1.** A long dramatic or comic speech or performance given by one person. The audience wept during the actor's *monologue* in the second act of the play. **2.** A long speech made by one person who is part of a group.
mon·o·logue (mon′ə lôg′ *or* mon′ə log′) *noun, plural* **monologues.**

monopolize **1.** To get or have a monopoly of. **2.** To get, have, or use all of. Don't *monopolize* the teacher's attention.
mo·nop·o·lize (mə nop′ə līz′) *verb,* **monopolized, monopolizing.**

monopoly **1.** The sole control of a product or service by a person or company. That bus

at; āpe; fär; câre; end; mē; it; īce; pîerce; hot; ōld; sông, fôrk; oil; out; up; ūse; rüle; půll; tûrn; chin; sing; shop; thin; this; hw in white; zh in treasure. The symbol ə stands for the unstressed vowel sound in about, taken, pencil, lemon, and circus.

M

company has a *monopoly* on public transportation in our town. **2.** A person or company that has such control.
mo·nop·o·ly (mə nop′ə lē) *noun, plural* **monopolies.**

monorail **1.** A train or other vehicle that runs on or is suspended from a single rail. We took a ride on the new *monorail*. **2.** A railroad track that has only one rail instead of two. Some modern trains run on *monorails*.
mon·o·rail (mon′ə rāl′) *noun, plural* **monorails.**

monorail

monotone Speech or vocal sound uttered with no change in tone. The announcer's dull *monotone* made the program very boring.
mon·o·tone (mon′ə tōn′) *noun.*

monotonous Tiring or not interesting because it does not change in any way. The announcer's *monotonous* voice never changes in tone. That job is *monotonous* because you have to do the same thing over and over.
mo·not·o·nous (mə not′ə nəs) *adjective.*

monsieur The French title for a man.
mon·sieur (mə syûr′) *noun, plural* **messieurs** (mes′ ərz).

monsoon A very strong wind that blows in the Indian Ocean and southern Asia. In the summer, it blows from the ocean toward the land and brings very heavy rains. In the winter, it blows from the land toward the ocean.
mon·soon (mon sün′) *noun, plural* **monsoons.**

monster **1.** An imaginary creature that is huge and frightening. In fairy tales, there is sometimes a dragon or other terrible *monster*. **2.** A huge animal, plant, or thing. **3.** A wicked, cruel person. **4.** An animal or plant that is not normal in form or appearance.
mon·ster (mon′stər) *noun, plural* **monsters.**

monstrous **1.** Horrible or frightening. The dragon in the story was a *monstrous* creature. **2.** Very, very large; enormous. The child thought the elephant at the zoo was a *monstrous* animal. **3.** Very evil. Murder is a *monstrous* crime.
mon·strous (mon′strəs) *adjective.*

Mont. An abbreviation for *Montana*.

Montana A state in the northwestern United States. Its capital is Helena.
Mon·tan·a (mon tan′ə) *noun.*

Word History

Montana probably comes from a Spanish word meaning "mountainous." The name was first given to a mining town in the mountains of Colorado and later to the territory east of Idaho.

month One of the twelve parts of a year.
month (munth) *noun, plural* **months.**

monthly **1.** Done or happening once a month. Our camera club has *monthly* meetings. **2.** Of or for a month. The *monthly* rainfall for April was 12 inches. *Adjective.*
—Once a month; every month. The bill from the grocery store arrives *monthly. Adverb.*
—A magazine that is published once a month. *Noun.*
month·ly (munth′lē) *adjective; adverb; noun, plural* **monthlies.**

monument **1.** A building, statue, or other object that is made to honor a person or event. The Lincoln Memorial in Washington, D.C., is a *monument* to Abraham Lincoln. **2.** An achievement of lasting importance. The discovery of a polio vaccine was a *monument* in medical research.
mon·u·ment (mon′yə mənt) *noun, plural* **monuments.**

moo The sound that a cow makes. *Noun.*
—To make this sound. *Verb.*
moo (mü) *noun, plural* **moos;** *verb,* **mooed, mooing.**

mood The way that a person feels at a certain time. Our moods change; sometimes we are happy and other times we are sad. Learn-

ing to swim put me in a good *mood*.
mood (müd) *noun, plural* **moods.**

moody **1.** Tending to change moods often. You can never predict the reactions of such a *moody* person. **2.** Being in or showing a gloomy or sullen mood. Some people are *moody* because of rainy weather.
mood·y (mü′dē) *adjective,* **moodier, moodiest.**

moon **1.** A heavenly body that revolves around the earth from west to east once every 29½ days. The moon seems to shine because it reflects light from the sun. The moon is the earth's satellite. **2.** A satellite of any planet. Mars has two *moons.*
moon (mün) *noun, plural* **moons.**

moonbeam A ray of light from the moon.
moon·beam (mün′bēm′) *noun, plural* **moonbeams.**

moonlight The light that shines from the moon.
moon·light (mün′līt′) *noun.*

moor¹ To fasten or tie a boat in place. We *moored* the sailboat at the dock with a rope.
moor (mùr) *verb,* **moored, mooring.**

moor² An open area of wild land with few trees. There are moors in England and Scotland that are often covered with heather and have wet, marsh-like ground.
moor (mùr) *noun, plural* **moors.**

moose A large, heavy animal related to the deer that lives in forests in cold northern regions of North America, Europe, and Asia. The male has enormous, broad antlers.
moose (müs) *noun, plural* **moose.**

moose

mop **1.** A cleaning device made of a bundle of yarn or cloth or a sponge attached to a long handle. **2.** A thick, tangled mass, as of hair. Please comb that *mop* of hair. *Noun.*
—To clean or dry with a mop. I *mopped* the kitchen floor. *Verb.*
mop (mop) *noun, plural* **mops;** *verb,* **mopped, mopping.**

moped A heavy bicycle with a small engine.
mo·ped (mō′ped) *noun, plural* **mopeds.**

moral **1.** Good and honest in behavior and character. A *moral* person would admit to breaking the window. **2.** Having to do with what is right and wrong. Whether or not to report that your friend cheated is a *moral* question. *Adjective.*
—**1.** A lesson about right and wrong that is taught in a story, event, or fable. The *moral* of the story was "Don't put off until tomorrow what you can do today." **2. morals.** The beliefs that a person has about what is right and what is wrong. *Noun.*
mor·al (môr′əl) *adjective; noun, plural* **morals.**

morale The way a person or a group of people feel in general; attitude or spirit. The team's *morale* was low after they lost the game.
mo·rale (mə ral′) *noun.*

more **1.** Greater in number, amount, or degree. A gallon is *more* than a quart. **2.** Additional; further. I need *more* charcoal for the fire. *Adjective.*
—**1.** To a greater amount or degree. Be *more* careful. **2.** In addition; again. I will only tell you once *more. Adverb.*
—An extra amount. Our dogs always want *more* to eat. *Noun.*
more (môr) *adjective; adverb; noun.*

Language Note

More is used to make the comparative form of some adjectives and adverbs. Most English comparatives are formed by adding *-er* to the end of a word. For example, *tall* + *-er* forms the comparative *taller.* But many words would sound awkward if we added *-er* to the end of the word. So instead we put the word "more" in front of it. We would say "more familiar," not "familiarer."

moreover In addition to what has been said; not only that. It's dark and cold, and *moreover* it's raining.
more·o·ver (môr ō′vər) *adverb.*

at; āpe; fär; câre; end; mē; it; īce; pîerce; hot; ōld; sông, fôrk; oil; out; up; ūse; rüle; pùll; tûrn; chin; sing; shop; thin; this; hw in white; zh in treasure. The symbol ə stands for the unstressed vowel sound in about, taken, pencil, lemon, and circus.

morning The early part of the day. Morning ends at noon. ▴ Another word that sounds like this is **mourning**.
morn·ing (môr′ning) *noun, plural* **mornings.**

morning glory A white, pink, purple, or blue flower that is shaped like a trumpet and grows on a vine. The flower opens in early morning and then closes later in the day.

morning glories

Morocco A country in northwestern Africa.
Mo·roc·co (mə rok′ō) *noun.*

morsel A small bite of food or piece of something. The birds ate every *morsel* of bread we put out for them.
mor·sel (môr′səl) *noun, plural* **morsels.**

mortal 1. Certain to die. All things that live are *mortal.* 2. Causing death. The soldier was given a *mortal* wound by the enemy. 3. Very great; intense. I have a *mortal* fear of wasps. 4. Very hostile. *Adjective.*
—A person; human being. *Noun.*
mor·tal (môr′təl) *adjective; noun, plural* **mortals.**

mortar¹ A building material made of sand, water, and lime. Mortar is used like cement to hold bricks or stones together.
mor·tar (môr′tər) *noun.*

mortar² A thick, heavy bowl in which things are crushed or ground by using a pestle. Look up **pestle** for a picture of a mortar.
mor·tar (môr′tər) *noun, plural* **mortars.**

mosaic A picture or design made by fitting together bits of stone, glass, or tile of different colors, and cementing them in place.
mo·sa·ic (mō zā′ik) *noun, plural* **mosaics.**

mosaic

Moslem Another spelling for **Muslim.** Look up **Muslim** for more information.
Mos·lem (moz′ləm) *adjective; noun, plural* **Moslems.**

mosque A Muslim temple or place of worship.
mosque (mosk) *noun, plural* **mosques.**

mosquito A small insect with two wings. The female gives a sting or bite that itches. Some mosquitoes carry malaria and other diseases.
mos·qui·to (mə skē′tō) *noun, plural* **mosquitoes** or **mosquitos.**

moss A small green plant that grows in groups to form a soft, thick mat on the ground, on rocks, or on trees. Mosses grow in shady places where it is damp.
moss (môs) *noun, plural* **mosses.**

most 1. Greatest in number, amount, or degree. Who received the *most* votes in the election? 2. The majority of. *Most* children like to play games. *Adjective.*
—The greatest number, amount, or degree. One dollar is the *most* I can give you now. *Noun.*
—1. Very. That musician is a *most* unusual person. 2. To the greatest degree. That was the *most* interesting book I have ever read. *Adverb.*
most (mōst) *adjective; noun; adverb.*

Language Note

Most is used to make the superlative form of some adjectives and adverbs. Most English superlatives are formed by adding -*est* to the end of a word. For example, *fast* + -*est* forms the superlative *fastest.* But many words would sound awkward if we added -*est* to the end of the word. So instead we put the word "most" in front of it. We would say "most famous," not "famousest."

---

mostly For the most part; mainly; chiefly. It has been *mostly* cloudy today. The dress is *mostly* blue with a little white trim.
most·ly (mōst′lē) *adverb.*

motel A kind of hotel that is built near a main road. Travelers can drive up to it easily and park their cars near their rooms.
mo·tel (mō tel′) *noun, plural* **motels.**

moth An insect that looks like a butterfly. Unlike butterflies, moths have thick bodies and fly mostly at night. The larvae of some moths eat holes in wool and other fabrics.
moth (môth) *noun, plural* **moths.**

mother **1.** A female parent. **2.** The source or origin of something. Necessity is the *mother* of invention. *Noun.*
—To produce or care for something as a mother does. Our cat *mothered* four kittens. We *mothered* the injured bird until it was well enough to fly. *Verb.*
—**1.** That is a mother. We saw a *mother* hen and many chicks at the farm. **2.** Relating to or characteristic of a mother. **3.** Being related or attached to something as a mother is to her children. After three years in a foreign land they longed to return to their *mother* country. *Adjective.*
moth·er (mu<u>th</u>′ər) *noun, plural* **mothers;** *verb,* **mothered, mothering;** *adjective.*

mother-in-law The mother of one's husband or wife.
moth·er-in-law (mu<u>th</u>′ər in lô′) *noun, plural* **mothers-in-law.**

motherly Of, having to do with, or like a mother. The doctor treated the patients with *motherly* care.
moth·er·ly (mu<u>th</u>′ər lē) *adjective.*

motion **1.** The act of changing place or position; movement. The steady *motion* of the boat made me feel sick. The police officer waved us on with a quick *motion* of the arm. **2.** A formal suggestion made at a meeting. I made a *motion* to take a vote on the proposal. *Noun.*
—To move the hand or another part of the body as a sign of something. The teacher *motioned* for everyone to sit down. *Verb.*
mo·tion (mō′shən) *noun, plural* **motions;** *verb,* **motioned, motioning.**

motionless Not moving; without motion. The deer stood *motionless* at the edge of the meadow.
mo·tion·less (mō′shən lis) *adjective.*

motion picture A series of pictures on a film. They are projected onto a screen at such a high speed that it appears to the viewer that the people and things in the pictures are moving. This is also called a **moving picture** or **movie.**

motive The reason that a person does something. A desire to go to college can be a strong *motive* for trying to get good marks. Fear of being caught and scolded was their *motive* for telling the lie.
mo·tive (mō′tiv) *noun, plural* **motives.**

motor A machine that provides motion or power to make things run or work. Some motors use electricity and others burn fuel. The *motor* of a fan makes the fan blades turn. The *motor* of a car makes the car go. *Noun.*
—**1.** Having to do with a motor or some-

thing run by a motor. A car is a *motor* vehicle. We are going on a *motor* trip in Canada. **2.** Having to do with the nerves of a person's body that control motion. Pulling your hand back from a hot object is a *motor* reflex. *Adjective.*
—To travel by car. We *motored* through New England. *Verb.*
mo·tor (mō′tər) *noun, plural* **motors;** *adjective; verb,* **motored, motoring.**

motorboat A boat that is run by a motor. The police *motorboat* made a loud noise as it sped by.
mo·tor·boat (mō′tər bōt′) *noun, plural* **motorboats.**

motorcycle A vehicle with two wheels that is bigger and heavier than a bicycle and is powered by an engine.
mo·tor·cy·cle (mō′tər sī′kəl) *noun, plural* **motorcycles.**

motto A short sentence or phrase that says what someone believes or what something stands for. The Latin phrase, "E pluribus unum," which means "out of many, one," is the *motto* on the seal of the United States.
mot·to (mot′ō) *noun, plural* **mottoes** or **mottos.**

mound **1.** A hill or heap of earth, stones, or other material. There are *mounds* of garbage at the dump. **2.** A slightly higher area in the center of a baseball diamond. The pitcher stands on the mound to pitch the ball. *Noun.*
—To pile in a hill or heap. I like to *mound* ice cream on top of my pie. *Verb.*
mound (mound) *noun, plural* **mounds;** *verb,* **mounded, mounding.**

mount[1] **1.** To go up; climb. The firefighters *mounted* the stairs two at a time. **2.** To get up on. The sheriff *mounted* the horse and rode off. **3.** To set in place. I *mounted* the stamps in my new album. **4.** To rise or increase. The cost of meat has been *mounting* steadily this year. *Verb.*
—**1.** A horse or other animal for riding. The rider stopped for a fresh *mount* at the midway point of the journey. **2.** A stand, frame, or other object used to hold something. We bought a wooden frame as a *mount* for the picture. *Noun.*
mount (mount) *verb,* **mounted, mounting;** *noun, plural* **mounts.**

M

at; āpe; fär; câre; end; mē; it; īce; pîerce; hot; ōld; sông, fôrk; oil; out; up; ūse; rüle; půll; tûrn; chin; sing; shop; thin; <u>th</u>is; hw in white; zh in treasure. The symbol ə stands for the unstressed vowel sound in about, taken, pencil, lemon, and circus.

mount²   A hill or mountain.
   mount (mount) *noun, plural* **mounts.**

mountain   **1.** A mass of land that rises very high above the surrounding area. The *mountain* was tall and very difficult to climb. **2.** A very large pile or amount of something. There was a *mountain* of trash at the dump.
   moun·tain (moun′tən) *noun, plural* **mountains.**

mountain

mountaineer   **1.** A person who lives in the mountains. The *mountaineer's* shack was stocked with food for the winter. **2.** A person who climbs mountains as a sport. The *mountaineers* prepared their equipment for the climb.
   moun·tain·eer (moun′tə nîr′) *noun, plural* **mountaineers.**

mountain lion   A large wild cat that lives in the mountains of North and South America. This animal is usually called a **cougar.** Look up **cougar** for more information.

mountainous   **1.** Having many mountains. There is good skiing in that *mountainous* area. **2.** Very big; huge. The storm piled up *mountainous* drifts of snow.
   moun·tain·ous (moun′tə nəs) *adjective.*

mountain range   A series of mountains that form a group.

mourn   To feel or show sorrow or grief. We *mourned* for all the people who died in the war.
   mourn (môrn) *verb,* **mourned, mourning.**

mourning   **1.** The act of showing sorrow or grief. They were in *mourning* for the victims of the terrible fire. **2.** Black clothing or some other symbol worn to show grief over a person's death. ▲ Another word that sounds like this is **morning.**
   mourn·ing (môr′ning) *noun.*

mouse   **1.** A small, furry animal with a pointed nose, small ears, and a long, thin tail. Mice that live in houses are often gray. Mice are rodents, as are rats and squirrels.

2. A small instrument that can be connected to a computer to move the cursor on a monitor. A mouse is moved by hand across the top of a desk or table to control the movement of the cursor.
   mouse (mous) *noun, plural* **mice.**

moustache   Another spelling for **mustache.** Look up **mustache** for more information.

mouth   **1.** The opening through which people and animals take in food. The human mouth contains the tongue and the teeth. Many animals make sounds through their mouths. **2.** Any opening that is like a mouth. We entered the *mouth* of the cave. The *mouth* of a river is where it empties into another body of water. *Noun.*
   —To say or repeat in a false or insincere way. Try to recite the poem with feeling and not just *mouth* the words. *Verb.*
   mouth (mouth *for noun;* mou<u>th</u> *for verb*) *noun, plural* **mouths** (mou<u>th</u>z); *verb,* **mouthed, mouthing.**

mouthful   The amount of food or drink that is taken into the mouth at one time. I had a *mouthful* of the pudding.
   mouth·ful (mouth′fùl′) *noun, plural* **mouthfuls.**

mouth organ   Another word for **harmonica.** Look up **harmonica** for more information.

mouthpiece   The part of a musical instrument, telephone, or other object that is put between or near the lips.
   mouth·piece (mouth′pēs′) *noun, plural* **mouthpieces.**

movable   **1.** Able to be moved. The shelves in that cabinet are *movable.* **2.** That changes from one date to another in different years. Thanksgiving is a *movable* holiday. This word is also spelled **moveable.**
   mov·a·ble (mü′və bəl) *adjective.*

move   **1.** To change the place or direction of something. We had to *move* to different seats to get a good view of the movie screen. *Move* the chair closer to the window. **2.** To change the location of a home or business. Our family is going to *move* to a new city. **3.** To go forward; advance. Time *moves* quickly when you are having fun. **4.** To put in motion. Wind *moves* a windmill. **5.** To cause someone to do something. The teacher waited at first, but finally was *moved* by curiosity to open the package. **6.** To stir a person's feelings. I was *moved* to tears when I found the starving puppies. **7.** To make a suggestion at a meeting. The secretary *moved* that the meeting be ended. *Verb.*

—**1.** The act of moving. The basketball player made a quick *move* toward the basket. **2.** An action planned to bring about a result. It was a smart *move* to shop early before the store got crowded. **3.** A person's turn to move a playing piece in certain games. The player with the white chess pieces makes the first *move*. *Noun.*
> **move** (müv) *verb,* **moved, moving;** *noun,* plural **moves.**

movement **1.** The act of moving. A fan causes *movement* of air in a room. **2.** A group of moving parts that make something work. The *movement* of a watch turns the hands. **3.** The actions of a group of people to reach some goal. The civil rights *movement* is working for equal opportunities for people of all races. **4.** A tendency or trend. After the president's speech there was a *movement* toward reform in the school system. **5.** A part of a long musical piece, such as a symphony. The orchestra practiced the first *movement* several times.
> **move·ment** (müv′mənt) *noun, plural* **movements.**

mover A person or company whose job is to move people's furniture and other things from one house or office to another.
> **mov·er** (mü′vər) *noun, plural* **movers.**

movie **1.** A series of pictures on a film that is projected onto a screen; motion picture. **2. movies.** The showing of a motion picture. I went to the *movies* last weekend.
> **mov·ie** (mü′vē) *noun, plural* **movies.**

moving **1.** That moves or is able to move. It's hard to hit a *moving* target. **2.** Causing or producing action or motion. The mayor was a *moving* force behind the passage of the new law. **3.** Affecting the emotions; touching. The actor's *moving* performance left the audience in tears.
> **mov·ing** (mü′ving) *adjective.*

mow To cut grass, grain, or hay with a sharp blade or machine. My parents asked me to *mow* the lawn.
> **mow** (mō) *verb,* **mowed, mowed** or **mown, mowing.**

mower A device or person that mows.
> **mow·er** (mō′ər) *noun, plural* **mowers.**

mown Past participle of **mow.** After the grass was *mown,* I raked it into piles. Look up **mow** for more information. ▲ Another word that sounds like this is **moan.**
> **mown** (mōn) *verb.*

Mozambique A country in southeastern Africa.
> **Mo·zam·bique** (mō′zəm bēk′) *noun.*

mpg or **m.p.g.** An abbreviation for *miles per gallon.*

mph or **m.p.h.** An abbreviation for *miles per hour.*

Mr. The abbreviation for *Mister,* used before a man's name. "Dear *Mr.* Andrews," I wrote.
> **Mr.** (mis′tər) *plural* **Messrs.**

Mrs. A title used before the name of a married woman or a widow. *Mrs.* Whitney was my kindergarten teacher.
> **Mrs.** (mis′iz) *plural* **Mmes.**

Ms. A title used before a woman's name. *Ms.* Simpson is the school principal.
> **Ms.** (miz *or* em′es′) *plural* **Mses.**

MS Postal abbreviation for *Mississippi.*

Mt. An abbreviation for *Mount* or *Mountain.*

MT Postal abbreviation for *Montana.*

much Great in amount or degree. I don't have *much* money left after buying that gift. We had too *much* rain this week. *Adjective.*
—**1.** To a great degree; very. I was very *much* upset when I lost my keys. **2.** Just about; nearly. They feel *much* the same as you do. *Adverb.*
—A great amount. *Much* has been written about the Civil War. *Noun.*
> **much** (much) *adjective,* **more, most;** *adverb,* **more, most;** *noun.*

mucilage A sticky substance made from plants; glue.
> **mu·ci·lage** (mū′sə lij) *noun, plural* **mucilages.**

mucus A slimy fluid that coats and protects the inside of the mouth, nose, throat, and other parts of the body.
> **mu·cus** (mū′kəs) *noun.*

mud Soft, wet, sticky earth or dirt. We tracked *mud* into the house after it rained.
> **mud** (mud) *noun.*

muddle A confused condition; mess. My cousin's business accounts are in a *muddle.* *Noun.*
—**1.** To cause to be in a confused condition; mix up. The two speakers *muddled* the issues in their debate. **2.** To make a mess of; do in a bad or clumsy way. We tried hard, but we *muddled* the job. *Verb.*
> **mud·dle** (mud′əl) *noun, plural* **muddles;** *verb,* **muddled, muddling.**

---

at; āpe; fär; câre; end; mē; it; ice; pîerce; hot; ōld; sông, fôrk; oil; out; up; ūse; rüle; pùll; tûrn; chin; sing; shop; thin; this; hw in white; zh in treasure. The symbol ə stands for the unstressed vowel sound in about, taken, pencil, lemon, and circus.

muff   A roll of fur that is made so a person can put one hand in each end. Muffs keep the hands warm.
   muff (muf) *noun, plural* **muffs.**

muffin   A small, cup-shaped cake or bread.
   muf·fin (muf'in) *noun, plural* **muffins.**

muffle   **1.** To soften the sound that something makes. The carpet in the hallway *muffled* our footsteps. I *muffled* my laughter by burying my face in a pillow.   **2.** To wrap or cover so as to soften the sound or protect. The carpenter *muffled* the hammer with a cloth. I *muffled* my face against the cold wind.
   muf·fle (muf'əl) *verb,* **muffled, muffling.**

muffler   **1.** A warm scarf that is wrapped around the neck in cold weather.   **2.** A device that reduces the noise made by an engine. Cars have mufflers.
   muf·fler (muf'lər) *noun, plural* **mufflers.**

The snowman has a **muffler** around its neck.

mug   A large drinking cup with a handle. Mugs are often made of pottery or metal. *Noun.*
   mug (mug) *noun, plural* **mugs.**

muggy   Warm and damp. It was a *muggy* day with no breeze.
   mug·gy (mug'ē) *adjective,* **muggier, muggiest.**

Muhammad   An Arab religious leader who founded Islam. He was born around A.D. 570 and died in 632.
   Mu·ham·mad (mủ ham'əd).

mulberry   A tree with sweet, dark reddish purple berries that look like blackberries and can be eaten. The leaves of some mulberry trees are fed to silkworms.
   mul·ber·ry (mul'ber'ē) *noun, plural* **mulberries.**

mule   **1.** An animal that is the offspring of a female horse and a male donkey. A mule is as large as a horse, but it has longer ears and a tail like a donkey. Mules are used to carry and pull things.   **2.** A person who is stubborn.
   mule (mūl) *noun, plural* **mules.**

multiple   Having or involving many parts; made up of more than one. I got *multiple* cuts and bruises when I fell off my bicycle. *Adjective.*
   —A number that is the product of multiplying one number by another. The numbers 8 and 12 are *multiples* of 4. *Noun.*
   mul·ti·ple (mul'tə pəl) *adjective; noun, plural* **multiples.**

multiplicand   A number that is to be multiplied by another number. If you multiply 2 times 4, the *multiplicand* is 4.
   mul·ti·pli·cand (mul'tə pli kand') *noun, plural* **multiplicands.**

multiplication   The mathematical operation of taking a number and adding it to itself a certain number of times. In the multiplication of 2 times 4, you are adding 2 sets of 4, which equals 8.
   mul·ti·pli·ca·tion (mul'tə pli kā'shən) *noun.*

multiplier   A number that tells how many times to multiply another number. If you multiply 2 times 4, the *multiplier* is 2.
   mul·ti·pli·er (mul'tə plī'ər) *noun, plural* **multipliers.**

multiply   **1.** To add a number to itself a certain number of times. If we *multiply* 2 times 4, we get 8.   **2.** To grow in number. The longer you wait to ask for help, the more your problems *multiply.*
   mul·ti·ply (mul'tə plī') *verb,* **multiplied, multiplying.**

multitude   A great number of people or things. A *multitude* of people came to the outdoor music festival.
   mul·ti·tude (mul'ti tüd' *or* mul'ti tūd') *noun, plural* **multitudes.**

mumble   To speak low and unclearly, as with the mouth partly closed. The shy student *mumbled* the answer.
   mum·ble (mum'bəl) *verb,* **mumbled, mumbling.**

mummy   A dead body that has been wrapped in cloth and specially treated to preserve it. Some ancient Egyptian mummies are 3,000 years old.
   mum·my (mum'ē) *noun, plural* **mummies.**

mumps   A disease that causes the glands at the sides of the face to become swollen and sore. The mumps spreads from person to person. It is caused by a virus. ⏴ The word "mumps" can be used with a singular or plural verb.

mumps (mumps) *noun.*

munch   To chew something in a noisy way. My pet rabbit *munches* carrots.

munch (munch) *verb,* **munched, munching.**

municipal   Having to do with the government and affairs of a city or town. We are having a *municipal* election this week to elect a new town sheriff.

mu·nic·i·pal (mū nis′ə pəl) *adjective.*

mural   A picture painted on a wall or ceiling. A mural usually covers most of the wall.

mu·ral (myùr′əl) *noun, plural* **murals.**

mural

murder   The deliberate and unlawful killing of a person. *Noun.*
—To kill a person deliberately and unlawfully. The robber *murdered* the storekeeper during the robbery. *Verb.*

mur·der (mûr′dər) *noun, plural* **murders;** *verb,* **murdered, murdering.**

murky   Dark and gloomy. We couldn't see beneath the surface of the *murky* water in the pond.

murk·y (mûr′kē) *adjective,* **murkier, murkiest.**

murmur   A low, soft sound. We heard the *murmur* of the brook in the distance. When in the library I always speak in a *murmur. Noun.*
—To make or say with a low, soft sound. I heard you *murmur* in your sleep. *Verb.*

mur·mur (mûr′mər) *noun, plural* **murmurs;** *verb,* **murmured, murmuring.**

muscle   **1.** A tissue in the body that is made of strong fibers. Muscles can be tightened or relaxed to make the body move. Most muscles, like those that move our arms and legs, are controlled by us. Other muscles, like

those that make the heart beat, work by themselves.   **2.** A bundle of this tissue that moves a particular part of the body. The biceps *muscle* is tightened to move the arm. **3.** Strength. We'll need some *muscle* if we're going to move that piano. ⏴ Another word that sounds like this is **mussel.**

mus·cle (mus′əl) *noun, plural* **muscles.**

Word History

The word **muscle** comes from the Latin word meaning "little mouse." Muscles under the skin reminded the Romans of little mice.

muscular   **1.** Having strong or well-developed muscles. My arms were *muscular* after a summer of working on the farm.   **2.** Having to do with muscle. The pain in my leg is from a *muscular* strain.

mus·cu·lar (mus′kyə lər) *adjective.*

museum   A building where objects of art, science, or history are kept and displayed for people to see.

mu·se·um (mū zē′əm) *noun, plural* **museums.**

mush   **1.** A kind of porridge made by boiling cornmeal in water or milk.   **2.** Any soft, thick mass. An increase in temperature turned the snow into *mush.*

mush (mush) *noun.*

mushroom   A fast-growing fungus that is shaped like a small umbrella. Some mushrooms can be eaten, but others are poisonous. *Noun.*
—To grow or appear suddenly and quickly. New office buildings have *mushroomed* all over the city. *Verb.*

mush·room (mush′rüm′ or mush′rùm′) *noun, plural* **mushrooms;** *verb,* **mushroomed, mushrooming.**

mushrooms

at; āpe; fär; câre; end; mē; it; īce; pîerce; hot; ōld; sông, fôrk; oil; out; up; ūse; rüle; pùll; tûrn; chin; sing; shop; thin; this; hw in white; zh in treasure. The symbol ə stands for the unstressed vowel sound in about, taken, pencil, lemon, and circus.

M

481

music 1. A pleasing or beautiful combination of sounds. 2. The art of creating a pleasing combination of sounds. 3. A musical composition. Does the pianist know the *music* to that song? 4. The written or printed signs that tell a person what sounds are used for a musical composition. Can you read *music?*
mu·sic (mū′zik) *noun.*

musical Having to do with or producing music. The trombone is a *musical* instrument. *Adjective.*
—A play that has songs and dancing in it. *Noun.*
mu·si·cal (mū′zi kəl) *adjective; noun, plural* **musicals.**

music box A box containing a device that plays music mechanically. Many music boxes have to be wound in order to play.

musician A person who is skilled in playing a musical instrument, composing music, or singing.
mu·si·cian (mū zish′ən) *noun, plural* **musicians.**

musket A gun with a long barrel like a rifle. It was used in warfare before modern rifles were invented.
mus·ket (mus′kit) *noun, plural* **muskets.**

musketeer A soldier armed with a musket.
mu·ske·teer (mus′ki tîr′) *noun, plural* **musketeers.**

muskmelon A large, juicy fruit; a type of melon. Cantaloupes are muskmelons.
musk·mel·on (musk′mel′ən) *noun, plural* **muskmelons.**

musk ox A shaggy, dark brown animal that chews its cud. Musk oxen have horns that lie flat over the forehead and sides of the head and curve upward at the tips. They live in northern Canada and Greenland.
musk ox (musk).

muskrat A small North American animal that looks like a large rat. Muskrats live in and near the water. A muskrat has webbed back feet and a flat tail that help it to swim.
musk·rat (musk′rat′) *noun, plural* **muskrat** or **muskrats.**

muskrat

Muslim Having to do with Islam, the religion founded by Muhammad. *Adjective.*
—A person who follows the religion founded by Muhammad. *Noun.*
Mus·lim (muz′lim) *adjective; noun, plural* **Muslims.**

muslin A cotton cloth that is used to make sheets and some clothing.
mus·lin (muz′lin) *noun.*

muss To make untidy; mess. The wind and rain *mussed* their hair.
muss (mus) *verb,* **mussed, mussing.**

mussel An animal that looks like a clam. Saltwater mussels have bluish black shells and are used as food. The shells of freshwater mussels are used to make buttons and jewelry. A mussel is a kind of mollusk. ▲ Another word that sounds like this is **muscle.**
mus·sel (mus′əl) *noun, plural* **mussels.**

must An auxiliary verb that is used to express the following meanings: 1. To be obliged to; have to. I *must* return this book to the library by Saturday. 2. To be forced or required to. People *must* eat in order to survive. 3. To be likely to. They *must* have forgotten about the meeting.
must (must) *verb.*

mustache Hair that grows above the upper lip. My grandfather has a big *mustache* that curls up at each end. This word is also spelled **moustache.**
mus·tache (mus′tash *or* mə stash′) *noun, plural* **mustaches.**

mustang A wild horse that lives on the American plains; bronco.
mus·tang (mus′tang) *noun, plural* **mustangs.**

mustard A sharp-tasting yellow paste or powder that is made from the seeds of a plant. Mustard is used to flavor food. The mustard plant has bunches of small, yellow flowers.
mus·tard (mus′tərd) *noun, plural* **mustards.**

muster 1. To bring or call together; assemble. The captain *mustered* all of the troops for the day's march. 2. To gather from within oneself. The shy child *mustered* up the courage to read aloud in class. *Verb.*
—An assembled group, as of military units. *Noun.*
mus·ter (mus′tər) *verb,* **mustered, mustering;** *noun, plural* **musters.**

mustn't Shortened form of "must not." We *mustn't* run through the hall. Look up **must** for more information.
must·n't (mus′ənt) *contraction.*

musty Having a stale or moldy smell or taste, often because of dampness or decay.

After the flood, the house smelled *musty.*
mus·ty (mus′tē) *adjective,* **mustier, mustiest.**

mute **1.** Not able to speak because of an illness, birth defect, or injury. **2.** Not willing to speak; silent. The student stood *mute* and would not answer the principal's questions. **3.** Not pronounced. The "b" in "lamb" is *mute. Adjective.*
—**1.** A person who cannot speak. **2.** A device put on a musical instrument to soften the tone. Mutes are usually used with trumpets and other brass instruments. *Noun.*
mute (mūt) *adjective; noun, plural* **mutes.**

mutineer A person who takes part in a mutiny. The *mutineers* tied up their captain and seized control of the ship.
mu·tin·eer (mū′tə nîr′) *noun, plural* **mutineers.**

mutiny An open rebellion against authority. The sailors who took part in the *mutiny* were punished. *Noun.*
—To take part in an open rebellion; revolt. They *mutinied* against their captain. *Verb.*
mu·ti·ny (mū′tə nē) *noun, plural* **mutinies;** *verb,* **mutinied, mutinying.**

mutt A dog, especially one that is a mixture of breeds; a mongrel. The *mutt* was part collie and part beagle.
mutt (mut) *noun, plural* **mutts.**

mutter To speak in a low, unclear way with the mouth almost closed. I *muttered* to myself that I would be late if I didn't hurry. *Verb.*
—Words spoken in a low, unclear way. There was a *mutter* of disapproval when the children kept giggling during the movie. *Noun.*
mut·ter (mut′ər) *verb,* **muttered, muttering;** *noun.*

mutton Meat from an adult sheep.
mut·ton (mut′ən) *noun.*

mutual Given and received equally; shared. My friend and I have a *mutual* interest in sports.
mu·tu·al (mū′chü əl) *adjective.*

muzzle **1.** The part of the head of an animal made up of the nose, mouth, and jaws. A collie has a long *muzzle.* **2.** A set of straps that are made to fit over the muzzle of an animal to keep it from biting. **3.** The opening at the front end of a gun. The bullet comes out through the muzzle. *Noun.*
—To put a muzzle on an animal. *Verb.*
muz·zle (muz′əl) *noun, plural* **muzzles;** *verb,* **muzzled, muzzling.**

my Of, belonging to, or done by me. That is *my* pencil.
my (mī) *adjective.*

myrtle **1.** An evergreen tree that has white or pink flowers and shiny leaves. **2.** A vine that grows along the ground and has shiny leaves and blue, pink, or white flowers.
myr·tle (mûr′təl) *noun, plural* **myrtles.**

myself **1.** My own self. I cut *myself.* I can cook for *myself.* I *myself* will do the job. **2.** My usual, normal, or true self. I haven't been *myself* since the accident.
my·self (mī self′) *pronoun.*

mysterious Very hard or impossible to explain or understand; full of mystery. We heard *mysterious* sounds from the deserted house.
mys·te·ri·ous (mi stîr′ē əs) *adjective.*

mystery **1.** Something that is not or cannot be known, explained, or understood. The identity of the poem's author is a *mystery.* It is a *mystery* to us how you can be so alert when you've had so little sleep. **2.** A book, play, or other story about a crime that is puzzling.
mys·ter·y (mis′tə rē) *noun, plural* **mysteries.**

mystify To confuse or puzzle; bewilder. The audience was *mystified* by the magician's tricks.
mys·ti·fy (mis′tə fī′) *verb,* **mystified, mystifying.**

myth **1.** A story that tells about a belief of a group of people. Myths often tell about gods and heroes. They were made up as an explanation or reason for something that happens in nature or for a custom. Long ago people explained thunder by the *myth* that it was the noise made by the chariot of the god Thor as he rode across the skies. **2.** A person or thing that is not real or true. The idea that a person gets warts from touching a frog is a *myth.*
myth (mith) *noun, plural* **myths.**

mythical Having to do with myths. A unicorn is a *mythical* creature. Apollo was a *mythical* god.
myth·i·cal (mith′i kəl) *adjective.*

mythology A group or collection of myths and legends. All the myths that were told and written in ancient Greece are known as Greek *mythology.*
my·thol·o·gy (mi thol′ə jē) *noun, plural* **mythologies.**

M

at; āpe; fär; câre; end; mē; it; īce; pîerce; hot; ōld; sông, fôrk; oil; out; up; ūse; rüle; půll; tûrn; chin; sing; shop; thin; this; hw in white; zh in treasure. The symbol ə stands for the unstressed vowel sound in about, taken, pencil, lemon, and circus.

N n

1. The earliest form of the letter **N** was used by ancient tribes in the Middle East. They used this symbol to mean "fish."

2. When the early Greeks borrowed this letter about 3,000 years ago, they changed its shape somewhat.

3. Later, the Greeks turned their **N** around, giving the letter its modern shape.

4. The Romans borrowed this form of the letter **N** directly from the Greeks.

5. By about 2,400 years ago, the Romans were writing the letter **N** almost exactly as we write it today.

n, N The fourteenth letter of the alphabet.
n, N (en) *noun, plural* **n's, N's.**

N or **N.** An abbreviation for *north* or *northern.*

nag¹ To annoy with scolding and complaining. My parents sometimes *nag* me about the way I dress.
nag (nag) *verb,* **nagged, nagging.**

nag² A horse, especially a worn-out old horse. We had to buy a new horse when our *nag* could no longer pull the wagon.
nag (nag) *noun, plural* **nags.**

nail **1.** A thin piece of metal that is pointed at one end and flat at the other. A nail is hammered into pieces of wood to hold them together. **2.** The thin, hard layer of tough material at the end of a finger or toe. *Noun.*
—To fasten with a nail or nails. The carpenter *nailed* pieces of wood together to make a bookcase. Will you *nail* that picture to the wall? *Verb.*
nail (nāl) *noun, plural* **nails;** *verb,* **nailed, nailing.**

naked **1.** Without clothing or covering of any kind. A person is *naked* when taking a bath or shower. The tree was *naked* after the caterpillars ate every leaf on it. **2.** Without anything added. I'm telling you the *naked* truth. **3.** Without the aid of any device. You don't need a telescope; you can see that star with the *naked* eye.
na·ked (nā′kid) *adjective.*

name **1.** The word or words by which a person, animal, place, or thing is known. The mayor's *name* is Taylor. Salmon is the *name* of a kind of fish. Denver is the *name* of a city. **2.** A bad or insulting word or words used to refer to someone or something. The bully called everyone *names.* **3.** Reputation or character. That company has a *name* for making products of high quality. *Noun.*
—**1.** To give a name or names to. The couple *named* their first child Leslie. **2.** To speak of; mention. The newspaper article *named* the topics of the coming debate. *Name* some of your favorite songs. **3.** To appoint or choose. The president *named* three senators to the commission. *Verb.*
name (nām) *noun, plural* **names;** *verb,* **named, naming.**

namely In other words. We visited two southern states, *namely* Mississippi and Louisiana.
name·ly (nām′lē) *adverb.*

nap¹ A short sleep. The baby is taking an afternoon *nap. Noun.*
—**1.** To sleep for a short while. The host *napped* for an hour before the guests came.

2. To be not prepared or ready. The storm caught us *napping. Verb.*
nap (nap) *noun, plural* **naps;** *verb,* **napped, napping.**

nap² The soft, fuzzy surface of cloth. This coat is so old that all the *nap* has worn off.
nap (nap) *noun.*

napkin A piece of cloth or paper used at meals for protecting clothing and for wiping the lips and hands.
nap·kin (nap′kin) *noun, plural* **napkins.**

narcissus A plant that has yellow or white flowers and long, thin leaves. The daffodil is a kind of narcissus.
nar·cis·sus (när sis′əs) *noun, plural* **narcissuses.**

narcotic A drug that dulls the senses, produces sleep, and eases pain when used in small doses. People can become addicted to narcotics.
nar·cot·ic (när kot′ik) *noun, plural* **narcotics.**

narrate To tell or relate. The reporter *narrated* an interesting story of travels in Africa.
nar·rate (nar′āt *or* na rāt′) *verb,* **narrated, narrating.**

narrator A person who tells a story. The *narrator* of the film started by explaining the historical background of the story.
nar·ra·tor (nar′ā tər *or* na rā′tər) *noun, plural* **narrators.**

narrow **1.** Not wide or broad. The deer jumped across the *narrow* stream. **2.** Limited or small. The small library had only a *narrow* choice of books. People with *narrow* minds don't like new ideas. **3.** Barely successful; close. The firefighter saved the child, but they had a *narrow* escape. *Adjective.*
—To make or become narrow. The workers *narrowed* the sidewalk when the street was made wider. The river *narrows* at the bridge. *Verb.*
—**narrows.** The narrow part of a body of water. The bridge was built across the *narrows. Noun.*
nar·row (nar′ō) *adjective,* **narrower, narrowest;** *verb,* **narrowed, narrowing;** *plural noun.*

nasal **1.** Having to do with the nose. A cold usually stuffs up the *nasal* passages and makes it hard to breathe through the nose. **2.** Spoken by releasing the breath through the nose rather than the mouth. The "m" sound is nasal.
na·sal (nā′zəl) *adjective.*

nasturtium A plant that has yellow, orange, or red flowers. Nasturtiums have sharp-tasting flower buds and leaves that are sometimes used in salads. The seeds are used in pickles.
na·stur·tium (nə stûr′shəm) *noun, plural* **nasturtiums.**

nasty **1.** Resulting from hate or spite; mean. That *nasty* rumor is not true. **2.** Disagreeable or unpleasant. The weather today is cold and *nasty.* The filthy canal had a *nasty* smell. **3.** Harmful or severe. I took a *nasty* fall while skiing last weekend.
nas·ty (nas′tē) *adjective,* **nastier, nastiest.**

nasturtium

nation **1.** A group of people living in a particular area under one government, usually sharing the same history, culture, and language. Presidents often address the *nation* on television to gain support for their proposals. **2.** A particular land where such a people live; country. Canada is a *nation.*
na·tion (nā′shən) *noun, plural* **nations.**

national **1.** Having to do with a land united under one government. The *national* government of the United States is headed by the president. **2.** Characteristic of or having to do with the people who make up a nation. Their *national* costume is very colorful. **3.** Covering or having to do with an entire land. The *national* road system is very impressive. *Adjective.*
—A citizen of a country. Only *nationals* may vote in some elections. *Noun.*
na·tion·al (nash′ə nəl) *adjective; noun, plural* **nationals.**

national anthem A special song that expresses love for one's country. People sing the national anthem of their country at public occasions and special events as a way of honoring the country and showing patriotism.

nationalism A feeling of deep loyalty to one's nation.
na·tion·al·ism (nash′ə nə liz′əm) *noun.*

at; āpe; fär; câre; end; mē; it; īce; pîerce; hot; ōld; sông, fôrk; oil; out; up; ūse; rüle; půll; tûrn; chin; sing; shop; thin; this; hw in white; zh in treasure. The symbol ə stands for the unstressed vowel sound in about, taken, pencil, lemon, and circus.

485

nationality 1. The fact or condition of belonging to a particular nation. That painter's *nationality* is French. 2. A group of people who share the same language, culture, and history. People of many *nationalities* work at the United Nations.
na·tion·al·i·ty (nash′ə nal′i tē) *noun, plural* **nationalities.**

native 1. A person who was born in a particular country or place. One of my classmates is a *native* of Germany. The mayor is a *native* of this town. 2. One of the original people, animals, or plants of a region or country. The *natives* of America are called American Indians. The kangaroo is a *native* of Australia. *Noun.*
—1. Born in a particular country or place. 2. Belonging to a person by birth. My grandparents' *native* language is Italian. 3. Originally living or growing in a region or country. Raccoons are *native* to America. *Adjective.*
na·tive (nā′tiv) *noun, plural* **natives;** *adjective.*

Native American A member of any of the peoples, except the Eskimo, who have lived in North and South America since long before European settlers arrived; American Indian.

natural 1. Found in nature; not made by people; not artificial. *Natural* rock formations overlook the river. 2. Possessed or being from birth; not resulting from teaching or training. Is your musical talent *natural*, or did you take lessons? The new sergeant was a *natural* leader. 3. Happening in the normal course of things. My grandparents both died of *natural* causes when they were very old. 4. Closely following nature; lifelike. This painting of the garden is very *natural*. 5. Not pretending to feel what one does not; sincere. Their *natural* hospitality made us feel at home. *Adjective.*
—A person who is good at something because of a special talent or ability. My cousin is a *natural* at basketball. *Noun.*
nat·u·ral (nach′ər əl) *adjective; noun, plural* **naturals.**

natural gas A gas that is found beneath the surface of the earth. Natural gas burns very easily and is used for cooking and heating.

naturalist A person who specializes in the study of things in nature, especially animals and plants.
nat·u·ral·ist (nach′ər ə list) *noun, plural* **naturalists.**

naturalize To make a citizen of someone who was born in another country. After living in the United States for several years, the immigrants passed a test and were *naturalized.*
nat·u·ral·ize (nach′ər ə līz′) *verb,* **naturalized, naturalizing.**

naturally 1. As would be expected; of course. *Naturally* I'll help you. 2. By nature. I sleep late *naturally*. 3. In a normal manner. I was too nervous to act *naturally.*
nat·u·ral·ly (nach′ər ə lē) *adverb.*

natural resources Materials found in nature that are useful or necessary for life. Water, forests, and minerals are natural resources.

nature 1. The basic character and quality of a person or thing. The doctor has a kindly *nature*. It is the *nature* of fire to be hot. 2. The physical universe; all the things that are not made by people. The mountains, the woods, and the oceans are parts of *nature*. 3. Sort or kind; variety. I enjoy books about camping, hiking, and things of that *nature.*
na·ture (nā′chər) *noun, plural* **natures.**

naught 1. Nothing. All our plans came to *naught*. 2. Zero. Five plus *naught* equals five.
naught (nôt) *noun.*

naughty Behaving badly; mischievous or disobedient. The teacher is making us stay after school because we were *naughty* today.
naugh·ty (nô′tē) *adjective,* **naughtier, naughtiest.**

nausea A sick feeling in the stomach. I take special pills to prevent *nausea* whenever I go on a boat.
nau·sea (nô′zē ə *or* nô′shə) *noun.*

nautical Having to do with ships, sailors, or navigation. A shop at the harbor sells *nautical* equipment.
nau·ti·cal (nô′ti kəl) *adjective.*

nautical mile A measurement of distance used by sailors. It is equal to about 6,076 feet.

Navajo A member of a tribe of American Indians of the southwestern United States. This word is also spelled **Navaho.**
Na·va·jo (nav′ə hō′) *noun, plural* **Navajo, Navajos,** or **Navajoes.**

naval 1. Having to do with a navy. *Naval* supplies are kept in storehouses near the docks. 2. Having a navy. England was once the greatest *naval* power in the world. ▲ Another word that sounds like this is **navel.**
na·val (nā′vəl) *adjective.*

navel A round scar in the middle of the abdomen. The navel results when the cord that connected a newborn baby to its mother is cut or falls off. ▲ Another word that sounds like this is **naval.**
na·vel (nā′vəl) *noun, plural* **navels.**

navigate   **1.** To sail, steer, or direct the course of. They *navigated* the ship through the storm.   **2.** To sail on or across. Ships can *navigate* the Atlantic in under a week.
  nav·i·gate (nav′i gāt′) *verb*, **navigated, navigating.**

navigation   **1.** The act of navigating a ship or aircraft. The captain found *navigation* almost impossible in the high winds.   **2.** The art or science of figuring out the position and course of boats, ships, and aircraft. Knowing the position of the stars and the sun is useful in *navigation*.
  nav·i·ga·tion (nav′i gā′shən) *noun*.

navigator   **1.** A person on a boat, ship, or aircraft who is in charge of determining or steering a course.   **2.** A person who explores by ship. The *navigator* Ferdinand Magellan organized the first voyage around the world.
  nav·i·ga·tor (nav′i gā′tər) *noun, plural* **navigators.**

The **navigator** sits at the right in the cockpit.

navy   **1.** All the warships of a country. The United States has one of the most powerful *navies* in the world.   **2.** The large, organized group of sailors who are trained to fight at sea. ▲ The word *navy* is often capitalized. Our neighbor is a lieutenant in the *Navy*.   **3.** A very dark blue color; navy blue. *Noun.*
—Having the color navy. *Adjective.*
  na·vy (nā′vē) *noun, plural* **navies;** *adjective.*

navy blue   A very dark blue color.

nay   No. "*Nay,*" said the knight, "I do not know the way to Westwood Castle." *Adverb.* ▲ This word was once common, but is not used often today.
—A vote or voter against. A narrow majority of *nays* defeated the proposal. *Noun.* ▲ Another word that sound like this is **neigh.**
  nay (nā) *adverb; noun, plural* **nays.**

NB   Postal abbreviation for *New Brunswick.*

N.B.   An abbreviation for *New Brunswick.*

NC   Postal abbreviation for *North Carolina.*

N.C.   An abbreviation for *North Carolina.*

ND   Postal abbreviation for *North Dakota.*

N.D. or **N. Dak.**   An abbreviation for *North Dakota.*

NE   Postal abbreviation for *Nebraska.*

NE or **N.E.**   An abbreviation for *northeast.*

near   **1.** Not far or distant. Night is drawing *near.*   **2.** Almost; nearly. We were *near* exhausted when we got home. *Adverb.*
—**1.** Not far or distant. Will I see you in the *near* future?   **2.** Done or missed by only a small amount; narrow. The people in that building had a *near* escape from the fire.   **3.** Close in feeling or association. You can rely on help from those who are *near* to you.   **4.** Being the closer of two. The telephone is on the *near* side of the street. *Adjective.*
—Close to or by. My grandparents live *near* the beach. *Preposition.*
—To come or draw near. The airplane *neared* the landing field. The animals fled as the hunters *neared. Verb.*
  near (nîr) *adverb; adjective,* **nearer, nearest;** *preposition; verb,* **neared, nearing.**

nearby   A short distance away; not far off. My parents work in a *nearby* town. My neighbor and I go to school *nearby.*
  near·by (nîr′bī′) *adjective; adverb.*

nearly   All but; almost. I *nearly* forgot your birthday. It is *nearly* midnight.
  near·ly (nîr′lē) *adverb.*

nearsighted   Able to see objects that are close by more clearly than those that are far away. A *nearsighted* person should not drive a car without wearing eyeglasses.
  near·sight·ed (nîr′sī′tid) *adjective.*

neat   **1.** Clean and orderly; tidy. You have *neat* handwriting.   **2.** Having or showing care for keeping things in order. My cousin is *neater* than I am and has a tidy room.   **3.** Done in a clever way. We learned a *neat* trick in school today.   **4.** Wonderful or fine. I had a *neat* time at the party.
  neat (nēt) *adjective,* **neater, neatest.**

N

at; āpe; fär; câre; end; mē; it; īce; pîerce; hot; ōld; sông, fôrk; oil; out; up; ūse; rüle; pull; tûrn; chin; sing; shop; thin; this; hw in white; zh in treasure. The symbol ə stands for the unstressed vowel sound in about, taken, pencil, lemon, and circus.

Neb. or **Nebr.** An abbreviation for *Nebraska*.

Nebraska A state in the central United States. Its capital is Lincoln.
Ne·bras·ka (nə bras′kə) *noun.*

Word History

Nebraska was an American Indian name for the Platte River. It means "flat water." The river's name was changed, but the Indian name was kept for the state.

---

necessarily As a certain result. Tall people are not *necessarily* good basketball players.
nec·es·sar·i·ly (nes′ə ser′ə lē) *adverb.*

necessary **1.** That must be had or done; needed; required. Proper food is *necessary* for good health. **2.** That cannot be avoided; certain. Low grades were a *necessary* result of the student's poor work. *Adjective.*
—Something that cannot be done without; necessity; essential. We can't go on without *necessaries* like fresh water. *Noun.*
nec·es·sar·y (nes′ə ser′ē) *adjective; noun, plural* **necessaries.**

necessity **1.** Something that cannot be done without; requirement. Food, clothing, and shelter are the *necessities* of life. **2.** The fact of being necessary. I realize the *necessity* of finishing school if I want to be a doctor.
ne·ces·si·ty (ni ses′i tē) *noun, plural* **necessities.**

neck **1.** The part of the body of a person or animal that connects the head and the shoulders. **2.** The part of a piece of clothing that fits around the neck. I like to leave the *neck* of my shirt open in hot weather. **3.** A narrow part that is like a neck in shape or position. This bottle has a stopper that fits into its *neck*. We have a summer cottage on a little *neck* of land that juts out into the lake.
neck (nek) *noun, plural* **necks.**

neckerchief A scarf or kerchief that is worn around the neck.
neck·er·chief (nek′ər chif) *noun, plural* **neckerchiefs.**

necklace A string of beads or other piece of jewelry that is worn around the neck for decoration.
neck·lace (nek′lis) *noun, plural* **necklaces.**

necktie A piece of cloth that is worn around the neck by putting it under a shirt collar and knotting it in front. A person usually wears a necktie with a suit.
neck·tie (nek′tī′) *noun, plural* **neckties.**

nectar The sweet liquid formed in flowers. Bees use nectar to make honey.
nec·tar (nek′tər) *noun, plural* **nectars.**

nectarine A kind of peach that has a smooth skin.
nec·tar·ine (nek′tə rēn′) *noun, plural* **nectarines.**

need **1.** A lack of something necessary, useful, or desired. The team's defeat showed their *need* for practice. **2.** Something that is necessary, useful, or desired. What are the *needs* for our camping trip? **3.** A necessity or obligation. There is no *need* to stay any longer. **4.** A condition or time of trouble or want. When I sprained my ankle, you were truly a friend in *need* to help me get home. **5.** Poverty or hardship. They lived in *need*, barely having enough food. *Noun.*
—**1.** To lack or require. I *need* a new coat. The town *needs* a library. **2.** To have to. Do you *need* to wait for them? *Verb.* ▲ Another word that sounds like this is **knead.**
need (nēd) *noun, plural* **needs;** *verb,* **needed, needing.**

needle **1.** A thin, pointed instrument with a hole in one end. It is used in sewing. The thread is passed through the hole and the needle carries the thread through the cloth. **2.** A pointer on a compass or dial. The *needle* on the compass shows that north is to our right. **3.** A sharp, thin, hollow tube that is used to put fluid into or take fluid out of the body. The doctor stuck a *needle* in my arm to give me a flu shot. **4.** A thin rod that is used in knitting. The baby's sweater was knitted on very small *needles*. **5.** The thin, pointed leaves on a fir tree or pine tree. The *needles* of the pine tree do not fall off when winter comes. **6.** Anything that is thin and pointed like a needle. The *needle* on our record player is wearing. *Noun.*
—To annoy or tease. My friends *needled* me about my new haircut. *Verb.*
nee·dle (nē′dəl) *noun, plural* **needles;** *verb,* **needled, needling.**

needless Not needed; unnecessary. Buying a new stove would be a *needless* expense.
need·less (nēd′lis) *adjective.*

needlework Work, such as sewing or embroidery, that is done with a needle.
nee·dle·work (nē′dəl wûrk′) *noun.*

needn't Shortened form of "need not." You *needn't* hurry because we have plenty of time.
need·n't (nē′dənt) *contraction.*

needy Not having enough to live on; very poor. The church helps *needy* families.
need·y (nē′dē) *adjective,* **needier, neediest.**

negative **1.** Saying or indicating "no." I accompanied my *negative* answer to the question with a *negative* shake of my head. **2.** Not helpful. If you have a *negative* attitude toward learning French, you will never be good at it. **3.** Less than zero. The result of 6 minus 8 is a *negative* number. **4.** Having one of two opposite kinds of electric charge. Magnets have a *negative* pole at one end and a positive pole at the other. **5.** Not showing a certain disease or condition. The doctor knew that it was not a broken leg because the X rays were *negative. Adjective.*
—**1.** A photographic image that is created when film is developed. In a negative, the areas that were light in the original subject are dark and those that were dark are light. Prints can be made from a negative. **2.** A word or phrase that expresses a denial or says "no." "Not" is a negative. *Noun.*
> **neg·a·tive** (neg′ə tiv) *adjective; noun, plural* **negatives.**

neglect **1.** To fail to give proper attention or care to. I *neglected* my plants and they died. **2.** To fail to do. You *neglected* to make your bed this morning. *Verb.*
—**1.** A failure to give proper attention; lack of care. *Neglect* of a pet may cause it to get sick. **2.** The condition of not being cared for. The house fell into *neglect. Noun.*
> **neg·lect** (ni glekt′) *verb,* **neglected, neglecting;** *noun.*

negligent Not showing proper care or concern; careless or neglectful. The *negligent* waiter forgot to bring us our drinks.
> **neg·li·gent** (neg′li jənt) *adjective.*

negotiate **1.** To talk over and arrange the terms of. The factory owners met with the workers to *negotiate* an end to the strike. **2.** To have a discussion in order to bring about an agreement. The two warring countries refused to *negotiate.*
> **ne·go·ti·ate** (ni gō′shē āt′) *verb,* **negotiated, negotiating.**

negotiation A discussion for the purpose of bringing about an agreement. The *negotiations* to end the war between the two countries are going well.
> **ne·go·ti·a·tion** (ni gō′shē ā′shən) *noun, plural* **negotiations.**

Negro A member of one of the major divisions of the human race; black. Negroes have dark skin. The native peoples of southern and central Africa are Negroes. *Noun.*
—Of or having to do with Negroes; black. *Adjective.* ▲ In recent times, the word **black** has replaced the word **Negro.**
> **Ne·gro** (nē′grō) *noun, plural* **Negroes;** *adjective.*

neigh The sound that a horse makes. *Noun.*
—To make the sound of a horse. *Verb.* ▲ Another word that sounds like this is **nay.**
> **neigh** (nā) *noun, plural* **neighs;** *verb,* **neighed, neighing.**

neighbor **1.** A person who lives in a house or apartment next to or near one's own. Our *neighbor* down the street took care of our dog while we were away on vacation. **2.** A person, place, or thing that is next to or near another. Mexico is a *neighbor* of the United States. **3.** A fellow human being. Concern for our *neighbors* is important to society.
> **neigh·bor** (nā′bər) *noun, plural* **neighbors.**

Word History

The word **neighbor** goes back to two Old English words that meant "near" and "a person who dwells." A person's neighbor is someone who dwells nearby.

neighborhood **1.** A small area or district in a town or city where people live. The *neighborhood* near the river is one of the oldest in town. **2.** The people living in the same area or district. The whole *neighborhood* is talking about the fire last night. **3.** An area near something. In the *neighborhood* of the factory it is very noisy and crowded.
> **neigh·bor·hood** (nā′bər hůd′) *noun, plural* **neighborhoods.**

neither **1.** Not either. The word *neither* is used before the first of two or more negative choices or possibilities connected by *nor.* When I was sick I could *neither* eat nor drink. **2.** Nor. My parents don't want to see the movie; *neither* do I. *Conjunction.*
—Not one or the other; not either. *Neither* team played well in the game. *Adjective.*
—Not the one nor the other. I tried on two coats, but *neither* fit me. *Pronoun.*
> **nei·ther** (nē′thər *or* nī′thər) *conjunction; adjective; pronoun.*

neon A gas that has no color or odor. It makes up a very small part of the air. Neon glows when electricity passes through it.

N

at; āpe; fär; câre; end; mē; it; īce; pîerce; hot; ōld; sông, fôrk; oil; out; up; ūse; rüle; půll; tûrn; chin; sing; shop; thin; <u>th</u>is; hw in white; zh in treasure. The symbol ə stands for the unstressed vowel sound in about, taken, pencil, lemon, and circus.

Tubes filled with neon are used in electric signs. Neon is a chemical element.
ne·on (nē′on) *noun.*

neon

Word History

The word **neon** comes from the Greek word meaning "new." The gas *neon* was given this name late in the nineteenth century because it was at that time the newest gas discovered.

Nepal A country in central Asia.
Ne·pal (nə pôl′ *or* nə päl′) *noun.*

nephew **1.** The son of one's brother or sister. **2.** The son of one's brother-in-law or sister-in-law.
neph·ew (nef′ū) *noun, plural* **nephews.**

Neptune The fourth largest planet in our solar system. It is the eighth planet in order of distance from the sun. Neptune can be seen from earth only with the aid of a telescope.
Nep·tune (nep′tün *or* nep′tūn) *noun.*

nerve **1.** A bundle of fibers that carries messages between the brain and spinal cord and other parts of the body. If a person touches a hot stove, the brain receives a message of pain from the nerves in the hand. The brain then sends a message through the nerves to the hand that makes the hand pull away from the stove. **2.** Courage or bravery. The diver did not have the *nerve* to jump off the high diving board. **3. nerves.** The way one feels; state of mind. It's important to have calm *nerves* when handling dangerous materials.
• **to get on one's nerves.** To annoy or irritate one. Their constant bragging *gets on my nerves.*
nerve (nûrv) *noun, plural* **nerves.**

nervous **1.** Not able to relax; tense. Loud noises make me *nervous.* **2.** Fearful or timid. I am very *nervous* about taking the exam. **3.** Having to do with nerves or the nervous system. A rash may be caused by a *nervous* reaction to something upsetting.
nerv·ous (nûr′vəs) *adjective.*

nervous system The system in the body that includes the brain, spinal cord, and nerves. The nervous system controls all the actions and reactions of the body.

–ness A *suffix* that means the state or quality of being. *Likeness* means the state of being similar or alike. *Kindness* means the quality of being kind.

nest **1.** A place built by a bird for laying its eggs and raising its young. A nest can be made out of grass, twigs, mud, or many other materials. **2.** A place made by insects, fish, turtles, or other animals for laying their eggs or raising their young. Some fish make nests by making a hole in the mud or sand with their tails. **3.** A group of birds, insects, or other animals living in a nest. There was a *nest* of robins in the maple tree by the barn. **4.** A cozy place or shelter. The kitten made a *nest* among the rags in the closet and fell asleep. *Noun.*
—To build or live in a nest. Every spring the sparrows *nest* under the attic roof. *Verb.*
nest (nest) *noun, plural* **nests;** *verb,* **nested, nesting.**

nest

nestle To get very close to; snuggle; cuddle. The kittens *nestled* against their mother.
nes·tle (nes′əl) *verb,* **nestled, nestling.**

net¹ **1.** A fabric made of threads, cords, ropes or wires that are woven together so as to leave evenly spaced holes. Net is used to make stockings, veils, and other articles of clothing. **2.** A device made of such fabric. We used a *net* to catch the fish and pull them out of the water. If you don't hit the tennis ball high enough, it will hit the *net. Noun.*

nets

—To catch with or as if with a net. I *netted* three large fish on my first day of fishing. *Verb.*

net (net) *noun, plural* **nets;** *verb,* **netted, netting.**

net² Remaining after all costs and deductions or after allowances are made for other factors. A storekeeper's *net* profit is the money left over from selling goods after the rent and the other costs of running the business are paid. *Adjective.*

—To earn or get as a profit. The sale of a new car may *net* the dealer a good sum of money. *Verb.*

net (net) *adjective; verb,* **netted, netting.**

Netherlands A country in northwestern Europe. This country is also called **Holland.**

Neth·er·lands (ne<u>th</u>'ər ləndz) *noun.*

network **1.** A system of lines or structures that cross. An electric system is often a *network* of wires. A railroad yard is a *network* of tracks. **2.** A group of radio or television stations that usually broadcast many of the same programs, often at the same time.

net·work (net'wûrk') *noun, plural* **networks.**

neutral **1.** Not taking or belonging to either side in a conflict. During the war many people fled to a *neutral* country. **2.** Having no particular shade or tint. Gray is a *neutral* color. **3.** Neither an acid nor a base in chemistry. The right mixture of an acid and a base will produce a *neutral* salt. *Adjective.*

—**1.** A person or country that is neutral. Switzerland and Sweden were *neutrals* in World War II. **2.** A position of gears in an automobile. When a car is in neutral, the engine cannot transmit power to the wheels to make the car move. *Noun.*

neu·tral (nü'trəl *or* nū'trəl) *adjective; noun, plural* **neutrals.**

neutron A small particle that is part of the nucleus, or center, of every atom except that of hydrogen. A neutron has no electric charge. It is a little heavier than a proton.

neu·tron (nü'tron *or* nū'tron) *noun, plural* **neutrons.**

Nev. An abbreviation for *Nevada.*

Nevada A state in the western United States. Its capital is Carson City.

Ne·vad·a (nə vad'ə *or* nə vä'də) *noun.*

Word History

The name **Nevada** comes from the Spanish word meaning "snowy" or "covered with snow." Spanish explorers gave this name to the Sierra Nevada mountains. The state of *Nevada* takes its name from these mountains.

never **1.** At no time; not ever. I have *never* been to China. **2.** In no way; not at all. We *never* thought this work would be so hard.

nev·er (nev'ər) *adverb.*

nevertheless In spite of that; in any case; however. It was a cloudy day; *nevertheless,* we went to the beach.

nev·er·the·less (nev'ər <u>th</u>ə les') *adverb.*

new **1.** Having existed only a short time; recently grown or made. In spring there are *new* leaves on the trees. The *new* boat was launched yesterday. **2.** Seen, known, made, or thought of for the first time; strange; unfamiliar. When I came back to school there were *new* faces in my class. They are slow to act on *new* ideas. On the expedition we found several *new* rocks for the collection. The sailors discovered a *new* land. **3.** Not yet familiar or experienced. I was still *new* to the job. **4.** Having recently come into a certain state, relationship, position, or role. I made lots of *new* friends when we moved. The *new* mayor acted quickly to improve the traffic situation. **5.** Not yet used or worn. Do you like my *new* shoes? Our house has a *new* coat of paint. **6.** Coming or beginning again. Tomorrow is a *new* day. The *new* year began with a heavy snowstorm.

at; āpe; fär; câre; end; mē; it; īce; pîerce; hot; ōld; sông, fôrk; oil; out; up; ūse; rüle; pùll; tûrn; chin; sing; shop; thin; <u>th</u>is; hw in white; zh in treasure. The symbol ə stands for the unstressed vowel sound in about, taken, pencil, lemon, and circus.

7. Changed, as for the better. Today I feel like a *new* person. ⬥ Other words that sound like this are **gnu** and **knew**.
   new (nü *or* nū) *adjective*, **newer, newest.**

newborn **1.** Born very recently. A *newborn* baby sleeps most of the time. **2.** As if born again; fresh. After resting we started to climb again with *newborn* determination.
   new·born (nü'bôrn' *or* nū'bôrn') *adjective.*

New Brunswick A province in southeastern Canada. Its capital is Fredericton.
   New Bruns·wick (brunz'wik) *noun.*

newcomer A person who has recently arrived. I'm a *newcomer* in town.
   new·com·er (nü'kum'ər *or* nū'kum'ər) *noun, plural* **newcomers.**

New England A region of the northeastern United States. Maine, Vermont, New Hampshire, Massachusetts, Rhode Island, and Connecticut are the New England states.

Newf. An abbreviation for *Newfoundland.*

newfangled New and different. My grandparents don't like *newfangled* appliances.
   new·fan·gled (nü'fang'gəld *or* nū'fang'gəld) *adjective.*

Newfoundland An island province in northeastern Canada. Its capital is St. John's.
   New·found·land (nü'fənd lənd *or* nū'fənd lənd) *noun.*

New Hampshire A state in the northeastern United States. Its capital is Concord.
   New Hamp·shire (hamp'shər).

New Jersey A state in the eastern United States. Its capital is Trenton.
   New Jer·sey (jûr'zē).

newly Lately; recently. This bread is so *newly* made that it is still warm.
   new·ly (nü'lē *or* nū'lē) *adverb.*

New Mexico A state in the southwestern United States. Its capital is Santa Fe.
   New Mex·i·co (mek'si kō').

new moon The moon when it cannot be seen or when it appears as a thin crescent with the hollow part on the right side. A new moon happens every month.

news A report or information of something that happened recently. People at home heard no *news* from the traveler. Everyone was excited by the *news* that the spacecraft had landed safely on the moon.
   news (nüz *or* nūz) *noun.*

newscast A radio or television program that presents the news. Our family watches a *newscast* every evening.
   news·cast (nüz'kast' *or* nūz'kast') *noun, plural* **newscasts.**

newspaper A publication printed on sheets of paper that contain news, opinions on local and national happenings, and advertisements. Most newspapers are published every day or every week.
   news·pa·per (nüz'pā'pər *or* nūz'pā'pər) *noun, plural* **newspapers.**

newsstand A place where newspapers and magazines are sold.
   news·stand (nüz'stand' *or* nūz'stand') *noun, plural* **newsstands.**

newt A small, brightly colored salamander that lives in or around water.
   newt (nüt *or* nūt) *noun, plural* **newts.**

New Testament The second part of the Christian Bible. It contains the life and teachings of Jesus and his disciples.

New World North and South America; the Western Hemisphere.

newt

New Year's Day A holiday that celebrates the first day of the year, January 1.

New York A state in the eastern United States. Its capital is Albany.
　New York (yôrk).

Word History

When the English took over the Dutch colony of New Netherland, the English king gave the colony to his brother, the Duke of York. It was renamed **New York** in honor of its official protector, who was later crowned King James II.

New Zealand A country made up of two islands in the Pacific Ocean. It is off the east coast of Australia.
　New Zea·land (zē'lənd).

next **1.** Following immediately in time or order. It rained on Thursday, but the *next* morning it was sunny. **2.** Nearest. The *next* house is my cousin's. *Adjective.*
—**1.** Immediately afterward. January is the first month, and February comes *next*. **2.** At the first time after this. When you are *next* in town, we'll visit the zoo. *Adverb.*
　• **next door.** In or at the building, house, or apartment that is nearest. My best friend lives *next door* to me.
　• **next to.** **1.** Almost; nearly. Fixing the old toaster was *next to* impossible. **2.** Beside. I was standing *next to* you.
　next (nekst) *adjective; adverb.*

next–door In the nearest building, house, or apartment. Our *next-door* neighbors share a driveway with us.
　next-door (nekst'dôr') *adjective.*

Nez Percé A member of a tribe of American Indians of the northwestern United States.
　Nez Percé (nez'pûrs') *noun, plural* **Nez Percé** or **Nez Percés.**

Nfld. An abbreviation for *Newfoundland.*

NH Postal abbreviation for *New Hampshire.*

N.H. An abbreviation for *New Hampshire.*

nibble **1.** To eat quickly and with small bites. The mouse *nibbled* the cheese. **2.** To bite gently. *Verb.*
—A small bite. A fish took a *nibble* at the bait but swam away. *Noun.*
　nib·ble (nib'əl) *verb,* **nibbled, nibbling;** *noun, plural* **nibbles.**

Nicaragua A country in Central America.
　Nic·a·ra·gua (nik'ə rä'gwə) *noun.*

nice **1.** Pleasant or agreeable. The weather was *nice* yesterday. We had a *nice* time at the dance. **2.** Kind and thoughtful. It was *nice* of you to ask us to the party. **3.** Showing or needing care and skill; fine. Those wooden cabinets are a *nice* piece of work. **4.** Having or showing good manners; polite. It isn't *nice* to grab things at dinner.
　nice (nīs) *adjective,* **nicer, nicest.**

niche **1.** A hollow in a wall used as a setting for statues or vases; recess. **2.** A place, position, or situation especially suitable for someone or something. I've found my *niche* in the science club.
　niche (nich) *noun, plural* **niches.**

nick A place on a surface or edge that has been cut or chipped. The mirror made a *nick* in the table when it fell. *Noun.*
—To make a cut or chip on the surface or edge of. I *nicked* another car when I was backing mine into a parking space. *Verb.*
　• **in the nick of time.** Just before it is too late; just in time. The lifeguard reached the drowning swimmer *in the nick of time.*
　nick (nik) *noun, plural* **nicks;** *verb,* **nicked, nicking.**

nickel **1.** A hard, silver-colored metal. Nickel is added to alloys to make them strong. Nickel is a chemical element. **2.** A coin of the United States equal to five cents.
　nick·el (nik'əl) *noun, plural* **nickels.**

nickname A name that is used instead of or in addition to a person's real name. Walter's nickname is "Ace." "Sandy" is a *nickname* for Sandra or Alexandra. *Noun.*
—To give a nickname to. I was *nicknamed* "Red" because of my red hair. *Verb.*
　nick·name (nik'nām') *noun, plural* **nicknames;** *verb,* **nicknamed, nicknaming.**

nicotine A poisonous, oily substance that is found in the leaves, roots, and seeds of the tobacco plant. It is what makes people addicted to cigarettes.
　nic·o·tine (nik'ə tēn') *noun.*

niece **1.** The daughter of one's brother or sister. **2.** The daughter of one's brother-in-law or sister-in-law.
　niece (nēs) *noun, plural* **nieces.**

Niger A country in north-central Africa.
　Ni·ger (nī'jər) *noun.*

Nigeria A country in west-central Africa.
　Ni·ge·ri·a (nī jîr'ē ə) *noun.*

at; āpe; fär; câre; end; mē; it; īce; pîerce; hot; ōld; sông, fôrk; oil; out; up; ūse; rüle; pùll; tûrn; chin; sing; shop; thin; <u>th</u>is; hw in white; zh in treasure. The symbol ə stands for the unstressed vowel sound in about, taken, pencil, lemon, and circus.

N

493

night **1.** The time when it is dark; time between the setting and rising of the sun. The baby slept quietly all *night* long. **2.** The darkness of night. The soldier slipped behind the enemy's lines under the cover of *night*. **3.** The beginning of night; nightfall. *Night* comes earlier in the autumn. ▲ Another word that sounds like this is **knight**.
  night (nīt) *noun, plural* **nights.**

nightfall The beginning of night; the end of the day. My parents told me to be sure to be home before *nightfall*.
  night·fall (nīt′fôl′) *noun.*

nightgown A loose gown that is worn to bed.
  night·gown (nīt′goun′) *noun, plural* **nightgowns.**

nightingale A small bird that lives in Europe and western Asia. The nightingale has brown wings and a white chest. Male nightingales are known for their beautiful song.
  night·in·gale (nī′tən gāl′ *or* nī′ting gāl′) *noun, plural* **nightingales.**

nightingale

nightly Done or happening every night. My parents watch the *nightly* news show after dinner. *Adjective.*
—Every night. Brush your teeth *nightly*. *Adverb.*
  night·ly (nīt′lē) *adjective; adverb.*

nightmare **1.** A bad or frightening dream. My cousin had a *nightmare* about being chased by a lion. **2.** Any bad or frightening experience. Being lost in the big city was a *nightmare* for the children.
  night·mare (nīt′mâr′) *noun, plural* **nightmares.**

Word History

The word **nightmare** is made up of the word *night* and an Old English word for an imaginary monster. The word was first used for an imaginary creature that was supposed to sit on people when they were asleep so that they could not breathe.

nighttime The time when it is dark; night. Our parents didn't like us going out alone at *nighttime*.
  night·time (nīt′tīm′) *noun.*

nimble **1.** Light and quick in movement. The circus has *nimble* acrobats. **2.** Quick to understand or respond. In a debate, a *nimble* mind helps.
  nim·ble (nim′bəl) *adjective,* **nimbler, nimblest.**

nine One more than eight; 9.
  nine (nīn) *noun, plural* **nines;** *adjective.*

nineteen Nine more than ten; 19.
  nine·teen (nīn′tēn′) *noun, plural* **nineteens;** *adjective.*

nineteenth Next after the eighteenth. *Adjective, noun.*
—One of nineteen equal parts; $\frac{1}{19}$. *Noun.*
  nine·teenth (nīn′tēnth′) *adjective; noun, plural* **nineteenths.**

ninetieth Next after the eighty-ninth. *Adjective, noun.*
—One of ninety equal parts; $\frac{1}{90}$. *Noun.*
  nine·ti·eth (nīn′tē ith) *adjective; noun, plural* **ninetieths.**

ninety Nine times ten; 90.
  nine·ty (nīn′tē) *noun, plural* **nineties;** *adjective.*

ninth Next after the eighth. *Adjective, noun.*
—One of nine equal parts; $\frac{1}{9}$. *Noun.*
  ninth (nīnth) *adjective; noun, plural* **ninths.**

nip **1.** To bite or pinch quickly and not hard. The parrot *nipped* my finger. **2.** To cut by pinching. The gardener *nipped* the dead leaves off the branch. **3.** To cause to smart or sting. The cold night air *nipped* our faces. **4.** To stop or destroy the growth of. Bad weather *nipped* our plans for the weekend. *Verb.*
—**1.** A bite or pinch. I pulled my foot away when I felt the *nip* of a crab on my toe. **2.** A sharp, biting cold. There is a *nip* in the air today. *Noun.*
  nip (nip) *verb,* **nipped, nipping;** *noun, plural* **nips.**

nipple **1.** The small rounded tip in the center of a breast or udder. A baby or other newly born mammal sucks milk from its mother's nipple. **2.** The rubber tip or mouthpiece of a baby's bottle. A baby sucks on the nipple to get milk or other liquids.
  nip·ple (nip′əl) *noun, plural* **nipples.**

nitrogen A gas that has no color or smell. Nitrogen makes up almost $\frac{4}{5}$ of the air on earth. All living things need nitrogen. Nitrogen is a chemical element.
  ni·tro·gen (nī′trə jən) *noun.*

NJ Postal abbreviation for *New Jersey.*

N.J. An abbreviation for *New Jersey.*

NM Postal abbreviation for *New Mexico.*

N.M. or **N. Mex.** An abbreviation for *New Mexico.*

no¹ **1.** Not so. *No,* this is not the road to the shore. **2.** Not at all; not any. The bird was *no* larger than your hand. ▲ In this sense, the word "no" is used with the comparative form of an adjective. *Adverb.*
—A word used to show surprise, wonder, or disbelief. *No!* I can't believe it! *Interjection.*
—**1.** The saying of the word "no"; denial; refusal. I thought they would accept the invitation, but they gave me a *no* instead. **2.** A vote or voter against. The *noes* were in the majority, so the proposal lost. *Noun.* ▲ Another word that sounds like this is **know.**
 no (nō) *adverb; interjection; noun, plural* **noes** or **nos.**

no² **1.** Not any. It was a clear day, with *no* clouds in the sky. **2.** Not a. The old car had not been running well, and it was *no* surprise when it stopped altogether. *Adjective.*
 no (nō) *adjective.*

no. An abbreviation for *number.*

nobility **1.** A class of people who have a high rank or title. Dukes, duchesses, earls, and countesses belong to the nobility. **2.** Greatness of character. Courage and honesty are two elements of *nobility.*
 no·bil·i·ty (nō bil′i tē) *noun, plural* **nobilities.**

noble **1.** Having high rank or title. The duke and duchess come from *noble* families. **2.** Having or showing greatness of character. The fight for freedom is a *noble* cause. **3.** Impressive in appearance; magnificent. It is a *noble* view from the top of the mountain. *Adjective.*
—A person of high rank or title. The royal family is often accompanied by *nobles. Noun.*
 no·ble (nō′bəl) *adjective,* **nobler, noblest;** *noun, plural* **nobles.**

nobleman A man of high rank or title.
 no·ble·man (nō′bəl mən) *noun, plural* **noblemen** (nō′bəl mən).

noblewoman A woman of high rank or title.
 no·ble·wom·an (nō′bəl wùm′ən) *noun, plural* **noblewomen** (nō′bəl wim′ən).

nobody No person; no one. I rang the doorbell, but *nobody* answered. *Pronoun.*
—A person of no importance or rank. *Noun.*
 no·bod·y (nō′bod′ē) *pronoun; noun, plural* **nobodies.**

nocturnal **1.** Happening or appearing at night. We sat quietly on our porch and listened to the *nocturnal* sounds. **2.** Active at night. The raccoon is *nocturnal* and spends a large part of the day sleeping.
 noc·tur·nal (nok tûr′nəl) *adjective.*

nod **1.** To move the head up and down. *Nod* if you understand, and shake your head if you don't. **2.** To let the head fall forward with a quick motion. The student sat *nodding* over the dull book and finally fell asleep. **3.** To show by quickly moving the head up and down. The judge *nodded* approval of our request. **4.** To bend forward with a swaying motion. The wheat *nodded* in the breeze. *Verb.*
—A movement up and down of the head. My friend greeted me with a *nod. Noun.*
 nod (nod) *verb,* **nodded, nodding;** *noun, plural* **nods.**

noise **1.** A sound that is loud and harsh. The *noise* of the traffic outside the window made it hard to sleep. **2.** Any sound. I heard a *noise* in the bushes.
 noise (noiz) *noun, plural* **noises.**

noisy Making much noise. The usher told the *noisy* children to leave the theater.
 nois·y (noi′zē) *adjective,* **noisier, noisiest.**

nomad **1.** A member of a group or tribe that does not have a permanent home. Nomads wander from place to place looking for food for themselves or for their animals. **2.** A person who wanders from place to place. I was a *nomad* for years before I settled down.
 no·mad (nō′mad) *noun, plural* **nomads.**

nomadic Having to do with nomads or with wandering from place to place. Many Eskimo are *nomadic.*
 no·mad·ic (nō mad′ik) *adjective.*

nominate **1.** To choose as a candidate. The political parties *nominate* candidates for president. **2.** To appoint to an office or name for an honor. The mayor *nominated* a new police chief.
 nom·i·nate (nom′ə nāt′) *verb,* **nominated, nominating.**

nomination **1.** The choice of a person to run for an office. The *nominations* for pres-

N

at; āpe; fär; câre; end; mē; it; īce; pîerce; hot; ōld; sông, fôrk; oil; out; up; ūse; rüle; pùll; tûrn; chin; sing; shop; thin; <u>this</u>; hw in white; zh in treasure. The symbol ə stands for the unstressed vowel sound in about, taken, pencil, lemon, and circus.

ident took place this summer. **2.** The appointment of a person to an office, or the naming of a person for an honor. We'll celebrate your *nomination* as town manager.

nom·i·na·tion (nom′ə nā′shən) *noun, plural* **nominations.**

nominee A person who is nominated.

nom·i·nee (nom′ə nē′) *noun, plural* **nominees.**

non- A *prefix* that means not or the opposite of. *Nonfiction* means not fiction. *Nonsense* means the opposite of sense. ▲ If the root word begins with a capital letter, we use a hyphen when we add *non-*. For example, *non-Chinese* is written with a hyphen. *Non-Chinese* means not Chinese.

none **1.** No one; not one. All the children tried to catch the rabbit, but *none* could run fast enough. **2.** No part; not any. *None* of the stolen money was ever found. *Pronoun.*
—Not at all. Help came *none* too soon. *Adverb.* ▲ Another word that sounds like this is **nun.**

none (nun) *pronoun; adverb.*

nonfiction Writing that is not fiction. Nonfiction deals with real people and events. Biographies and history books are examples of *nonfiction.*

non·fic·tion (non fik′shən) *noun.*

nonsense **1.** A way of talking or acting that is silly and makes no sense. A little baby talks *nonsense.* **2.** Language or behavior that is annoying or lacking in good sense. I don't want to hear any more *nonsense* about not being able to sleep!

non·sense (non′sens) *noun.*

nonstop Not making any stops. Your reservation is on a *nonstop* flight. *Adjective.*
—Without stops. We flew *nonstop* from Boston to Denver. *Adverb.*

non·stop (non′stop′) *adjective; adverb.*

noodle A flat strip of dried dough. Noodles are made out of flour, water, and eggs.

noo·dle (nü′dəl) *noun, plural* **noodles.**

noon Twelve o'clock in the daytime; the middle of the day.

noon (nün) *noun.*

no one No person; nobody. I thought I heard the doorbell ring, but *no one* was there.

noontime Twelve o'clock in the daytime; noon. "It's *noontime;* let's eat!"

noon·time (nün′tīm′) *noun.*

noose A loop of rope with a special knot that lets the loop tighten when the end of the rope is pulled.

noose (nüs) *noun, plural* **nooses.**

nor **1.** A word that is used as a connector between a word or group of words that begins with *neither* or some other negative and one or more other words or groups of words. Neither Mom *nor* Dad *nor* I saw the eclipse. We could neither watch television *nor* listen to the radio. **2.** A word that is used in place of *and* and *not* to continue a negative idea. They didn't like the concert, *nor* did I.

nor (nôr) *conjunction.*

normal **1.** Conforming to a standard, pattern, or model; regular; usual. Heavy rain is *normal* at this time of year. **2.** Having or showing average mental or physical development; healthy. We were happy to hear that the baby is *normal* in every way. *Adjective.*
—The usual or regular condition or level. This year's rainfall is above *normal. Noun.*

nor·mal (nôr′məl) *adjective; noun.*

Norse Of or having to do with ancient Scandinavia.

Norse (nôrs) *adjective.*

north **1.** The direction to your right as you watch the sun set in the evening. North is one of the four main points of the compass. It is located directly opposite south. **2. North.** Any region or place that is in this direction. **3. the North.** The region of the United States that is north of Maryland, the Ohio River, and Missouri. *Noun.*
—**1.** Toward or in the north. The oak tree is on the *north* side of the backyard. **2.** Coming from the north. A *north* wind was blowing. *Adjective.*
—Toward the north. We hiked *north* for a mile and then rested. *Adverb.*

north (nôrth) *noun; adjective; adverb.*

North America A continent in the Western Hemisphere. North America lies between the Atlantic and Pacific oceans. North America contains the countries of Mexico, the United

making **noodles**

States, and Canada. It is the third largest continent.

North American 1. A person who was born or is living in North America. 2. Having to do with North America or its people.

North Carolina A state in the United States on the Atlantic Ocean. Its capital is Raleigh.
North Car·o·li·na (kar′ə lī′nə).

Word History

North Carolina was created from the northern part of the English colony of Carolina. The founder of the colony had asked that it be given the Latin name *Carolana,* which means "from Charles" or "belonging to Charles," in honor of Charles I, who was then king of England. King Charles II later changed the name to *Carolina.*

North Dakota A state in the north-central United States. Its capital is Bismarck.
North Da·ko·ta (də kō′tə).

Word History

North Dakota was made from the northern part of the Dakota Territory. The territory was named after the Dakota Indians, who lived there. Their name is an American Indian word that means "allied tribes."

northeast 1. The direction halfway between north and east. 2. A region or place in this direction. The *northeast* of the island has few trees. 3. the Northeast. The region in the north and east of the United States, including New England and New York. *Noun.*
—1. Toward or in the northeast. Do you live in the *northeast* section of town? 2. Coming from the northeast. A *northeast* wind was blowing. *Adjective.*
—Toward the northeast. *Adverb.*
north·east (nôrth′ēst′) *noun; adjective; adverb.*

northeastern 1. Toward or in the northeast. The *northeastern* sky grew darker in the afternoon. 2. Characteristic of or having to do with the northeast or Northeast. *Northeastern* summers are cool and pleasant. 3. Coming from the northeast. The *northeastern* storm blew all the leaves off the trees.
north·east·ern (nôrth′ēs′tərn) *adjective.*

northerly 1. Toward the north. We traveled in a *northerly* direction. 2. From the north. The wind blew *northerly* for days.
north·er·ly (nôr′thər lē) *adjective; adverb.*

northern 1. In or toward the north. There is a large lake in the *northern* part of that state. I spent my vacation in *northern* Michigan. 2. Coming from the north. A cold *northern* breeze was blowing. 3. Northern. Of or in the part of the United States that is in the north.
north·ern (nôr′thərn) *adjective.*

northerner 1. A person born or living in the north. 2. Northerner. A person born or living in the northern part of the United States.
north·ern·er (nôr′thər nər) *noun, plural* northerners.

Northern Hemisphere The half of the earth that is north of the equator. Europe and North America and most of Asia and Africa are located in the Northern Hemisphere.

Northern Ireland A country in the northeastern part of Ireland. It is a part of the United Kingdom. Look up **Ireland** for more information.

northern lights

northern lights Shining bands or streams of light sometimes seen in the northern sky

at; āpe; fär; câre; end; mē; it; īce; pîerce; hot; ōld; sông, fôrk; oil; out; up; ūse; rüle; pùll; tûrn; chin; sing; shop; thin; this; hw in white; zh in treasure. The symbol ə stands for the unstressed vowel sound in about, taken, pencil, lemon, and circus.

N

at night; aurora borealis. Look up **aurora borealis** for more information.

North Korea A country in east-central Asia.

    North Ko·re·a (kô rē′ə) *noun.*

North Pole The point on earth that is farthest north. It is the northern end of the earth's axis.

North Star A bright star that is in the northern sky above the North Pole.

northward Toward the north. The train sped *northward. Adverb.*

—Toward or in the north. The *northward* slope is often covered with ice. *Adjective.*

    north·ward (nôrth′wərd) *adverb; adjective.*

northwards Another spelling of the adverb **northward.** The storm traveled *northwards.* Look up **northward** for more information.

    north·wards (nôrth′wərdz) *adverb.*

northwest 1. The direction halfway between north and west. 2. A region or place in this direction. The *northwest* is a region of forests. 3. **the Northwest.** The region in the north and west of the United States. Oregon is in the *Northwest. Noun.*

—1. Toward or in the northwest. We drove to the *northwest* part of town. 2. Coming from the northwest. A *northwest* wind was blowing. *Adjective.*

—Toward the northwest. Turn *northwest* at the next corner. *Adverb.*

    north·west (nôrth′west′) *noun; adjective; adverb.*

northwestern 1. Toward or in the northwest. The army's *northwestern* advance was slowed by the coming of winter. 2. Characteristic of or having to do with the northwest or Northwest. Washington is a *northwestern* state. 3. Coming from the northwest. A *northwestern* wind brought the temperature down.

    north·west·ern (nôrth′wes′tərn) *adjective.*

Northwest Territories A division of Canada located in the north-central part of the country. Its capital is Yellowknife.

Norway A country in northern Europe.

    Nor·way (nôr′wā) *noun.*

Norwegian 1. A person who was born in or is a citizen of Norway. 2. The language spoken in Norway. *Noun.*

—Of or having to do with Norway, its people, or its language. *Adjective.*

    Nor·we·gian (nôr wē′jən) *noun, plural* **Norwegians;** *adjective.*

nose 1. The part of the face or head that is used for breathing and smelling. Air comes into and goes out of the nose through the nostrils. 2. The sense of smell. Dogs have

good *noses.* 3. The point or front of something that sticks out. The *nose* of the plane points slightly upward when it takes off. *Noun.*

—1. To find or notice by smell. The dog *nosed* the rabbit in the bushes. 2. To push or move forward slowly and gently. Our dog *nosed* the back door open. The big car *nosed* around the corner. *Verb.*

    • **under one's nose.** In a place that is clearly visible. I felt silly when I found the pen I'd lost right *under my nose.*

    nose (nōz) *noun, plural* **noses;** *verb,* **nosed, nosing.**

nosebleed A bleeding from the nose.

    nose·bleed (nōz′blēd′) *noun, plural* **nosebleeds.**

nose cone The front part of a rocket sent into space. It is in the shape of a cone. The nose cone separates from the rest of the rocket during flight. It often has a special shield that protects it from the enormous heat that builds up when it comes back into the earth's atmosphere.

nostril One of two outer openings of the nose. Air is taken in and let out through the nostrils.

    nos·tril (nos′trəl) *noun, plural* **nostrils.**

Word History

The word **nostril** goes back to two Old English words meaning "nose" and "hole."

---

not An adverb that is used in the following ways: 1. To mean at no time, or in no way. It did *not* rain this week. 2. To make a statement mean the opposite of what it says, or make it negative. You may *not* sit there. 3. After a statement to represent the negative or opposite. Sometimes I'm hungry, sometimes *not.* ▲ Another word that sounds like this is **knot.**

    not (not) *adverb.*

notable Worthy of notice; important or remarkable. The author's first book was a *notable* success. A *notable* scientist spoke to us last night. *Adjective.*

—A person who is important. The mayor and other *notables* led the parade. *Noun.*

    no·ta·ble (nō′tə bəl) *adjective; noun, plural* **notables.**

notation 1. A system of signs or symbols that are used to represent numbers, words, or other information. The sign ÷ is a *notation* in arithmetic that means "divided by."

2. A quick note, as to assist memory or help organize information. Many students make *notations* in the margins of the books they are reading.
no·ta·tion (nō tā'shən) *noun, plural* **notations.**

notch **1.** A nick or cut on the edge or surface of something. The scouts made *notches* in the trees as they went along so they could find their way back to camp. **2.** A narrow pass between mountains. There is a stream at the bottom of the *notch. Noun.*
—To make a notch or notches in. Some Indians counted things like the passing days by *notching* sticks. *Verb.*
notch (noch) *noun, plural* **notches;** *verb,* **notched, notching.**

note **1.** A word, phrase, or short sentence that is written down to help a person remember what was in a talk or book. I took *notes* during the history class. **2.** A comment that explains a word or part of a book. Our poetry book has *notes* at the bottom of the pages. **3.** A short message or letter. Send your grandparents a *note* thanking them for the birthday present. **4.** Careful notice; regard. Take *note* of how long it takes you to get to my house. **5.** Importance. A judge is a person of *note.* **6.** A hint or suggestion; indication. We thought we heard a *note* of jealousy in their voices. **7.** A single sound in music, or a sign that represents such a sound. **8.** A piece of paper with a written promise to pay someone a sum of money. *Noun.*
—**1.** To put down in writing. I will *note* your telephone number in my address book. **2.** To take careful notice of; regard. Please *note* the enclosed newspaper article. *Verb.*
note (nōt) *noun, plural* **notes;** *verb,* **noted, noting.**

notebook A book with blank pages for notes. I have a *notebook* for each of the five subjects I take at school.
note·book (nōt'bŏok') *noun, plural* **notebooks.**

noted Noticed for a particular reason; well-known; famous. A *noted* speaker has been invited to talk at our graduation.
not·ed (nō'tid) *adjective.*

nothing **1.** No thing; not anything. We bought *nothing* at the store. They were so shy that they sat in a corner and said *nothing.* **2.** A person or thing that is of no importance. One dollar is *nothing* to a rich person. **3.** Zero. The final score in the soccer game was two to *nothing. Noun.*
—In no way; not at all. You look *nothing* like your parents. *Adverb.*
noth·ing (nuth'ing) *noun; adverb.*

notice **1.** The condition of being seen or observed. The children quietly tiptoed out of the room to escape *notice.* **2.** The act of seeing or observing. This problem deserves your *notice.* **3.** A warning or announcement. The ship's horn gave *notice* that it was about to sail. The enemy attacked without *notice.* **4.** A printed or written announcement. There were *notices* about the circus posted up all over town. *Noun.*
—To become aware of; observe. I *noticed* that the room was getting cooler. We *noticed* that the roses were in bloom. *Verb.*
no·tice (nō'tis) *noun, plural* **notices;** *verb,* **noticed, noticing.**

notify To tell about something; inform. The store *notified* us of the sale.
no·ti·fy (nō'tə fī') *verb,* **notified, notifying.**

notion **1.** An idea or belief. I haven't the slightest *notion* of what you're talking about. Where did you get the silly *notion* that I'm angry at you? **2.** A desire or whim. We all had a sudden *notion* to go swimming this afternoon. **3. notions.** Ribbons, pins, needles, and other small, useful items.
no·tion (nō'shən) *noun, plural* **notions.**

notorious Well-known for something bad. Who do you think was the most *notorious* outlaw in the old West?
no·to·ri·ous (nō tôr'ē əs) *adjective.*

noun A word that names a person, place, or thing. In the sentence "My parents took the dog to the country," "parents", "dog", and "country" are nouns.
noun (noun) *noun, plural* **nouns.**

nourish **1.** To provide food needed for life and growth. Milk *nourishes* a baby or newborn animal. Sun, rain, and good soil *nourish* plants and trees. **2.** To provide with other things that promote life, growth, development, or success. Studying at the university *nourished* the scientist's career.
nour·ish (nûr'ish) *verb,* **nourished, nourishing.**

nourishment Something needed for life and growth. It is important that children who are still growing get good *nourishment.*
nour·ish·ment (nûr'ish mənt) *noun, plural* **nourishments.**

N

at; āpe; fär; câre; end; mē; it; īce; pîerce; hot; ōld; sông, fôrk; oil; out; up; ūse; rüle; pŭll; tûrn; chin; sing; shop; thin; <u>th</u>is; hw in white; zh in treasure. The symbol ə stands for the unstressed vowel sound in about, taken, pencil, lemon, and circus.

Nov. An abbreviation for *November*.

Nova Scotia A province in southeastern Canada. Its capital is Halifax.

No·va Sco·tia (nō′və skō′shə) *noun*.

novel¹ A long story about imaginary people and events. A novel usually tells about events that might really take place and people like those in real life.

nov·el (nov′əl) *noun, plural* **novels**.

novel² New and unusual. We need a *novel* design for the cover of the book so that people will notice it.

nov·el (nov′əl) *adjective*.

novelist A person who writes novels. Jane Austen and Charles Dickens were famous English *novelists*.

nov·el·ist (nov′ə list) *noun, plural* **novelists**.

novelty **1.** The quality of being new. Once the *novelty* of mowing the lawn wore off, I got bored. **2.** Something that is new or unusual. Riding the city's subway trains was a *novelty* for the children who lived on a farm. **3. novelties.** Small, cheap toys and decorations.

nov·el·ty (nov′əl tē) *noun, plural* **novelties**.

November The eleventh month of the year. November has thirty days.

No·vem·ber (nō vem′bər) *noun*.

Word History

> **November** comes from the Latin word for "nine." The early Roman calendar began with March, making November the ninth month.

---

novice **1.** A person who is new to something; beginner. Some of the drivers are *novices* taking part in their first race. **2.** A person who is taken into a religious order for a trial period of time before taking vows for that order. Monks and nuns must go through a time as novices.

nov·ice (nov′is) *noun, plural* **novices**.

now **1.** At this time; at this moment. My friends are at the beach *now*, while I'm here working. **2.** Without delay; immediately. Eat your food *now*, before it gets cold. **3.** Under the present conditions or circumstances. The tire is flat, and *now* we must walk. **4.** A short while ago. Just *now* I finished the book I've been reading. **5.** At that time; then. The war was finally over, and *now* the job of rebuilding the city lay ahead. *Adverb*.
—Since. *Now* that the rain has stopped, the game can go on. *Conjunction*.
—The present time. The time to act is *now*. *Noun*.
—A word used to express warning, sympathy, or disapproval. *Now*, stop that! *Interjection*.
• **now and again** or **now and then.** At times; once in a while; occasionally.

now (nou) *adverb; conjunction; noun; interjection*.

nowadays In the present day. Most people travel by airplane *nowadays* if they are going a long distance.

now·a·days (nou′ə dāz′) *adverb*.

nowhere To, at, or in no place; not anywhere. I've looked all over the house, but the cat is *nowhere* to be found. *Adverb*.
—**1.** No place. There is *nowhere* you can hide that I can't find you. **2.** A condition of being unknown. The new baseball star rose quickly from *nowhere*. *Noun*.

no·where (nō′hwâr′ *or* nō′wâr′) *adverb; noun*.

nozzle A spout at the end of a hose or pipe. Turn the *nozzle* on the hose to make the water come out in a spray.

noz·zle (noz′əl) *noun, plural* **nozzles**.

nozzle

NS Postal abbreviation for *Nova Scotia*.

N.S. An abbreviation for *Nova Scotia*.

NT Postal abbreviation for *Northwest Territories*.

nuclear **1.** Of or forming a nucleus. Protons and neutrons are *nuclear* particles. The *nuclear* membrane is a thin layer that surrounds the nucleus. **2.** Coming from or having to do with energy that is created when the nucleus of an atom is split or combined. Some electricity is made from *nuclear* energy.

nu·cle·ar (nü′klē ər *or* nū′klē ər) *adjective*.

nuclear energy Energy that can be released from the nucleus of an atom. The release of this energy may be uncontrolled, as in the explosion of an atomic bomb. It may also be controlled and used to produce electric power, to run ships, and to treat certain diseases. This is also called **atomic energy.**

nuclei Plural of **nucleus.** Look up **nucleus** for more information.
> **nu·cle·i** (nü′klē ī′ *or* nū′klē ī′) *plural noun.*

nucleus **1.** The center point or core around which other things gather. The *nucleus* of the party was the table where the food and drinks were. **2.** The small oval center of a plant or animal cell. The nucleus controls important activities in the cell, such as cell growth and cell division. It also contains the genes that control heredity. **3.** The center of an atom. The nucleus of an atom is made up of protons and neutrons. The nucleus carries a positive charge of electricity.
> **nu·cle·us** (nü′klē əs *or* nū′klē əs) *noun,* *plural* **nuclei** or **nucleuses.**

Word History

The word **nucleus** comes from a Latin word meaning "kernel" or "inner part of a nut."

nudge To push or touch gently in order to attract attention. My friend *nudged* me when the teacher called my name. *Verb.*
—A gentle push or touch. My dog gave me a *nudge* to get my attention. *Noun.*
> **nudge** (nuj) *verb,* **nudged, nudging;** *noun, plural* **nudges.**

nugget A solid lump. Gold as it is found in nature is often in *nuggets.*
> **nug·get** (nug′it) *noun, plural* **nuggets.**

nuisance A person, thing, or action that annoys or offends. The radios some people play very loud are a *nuisance.* I think it's a *nuisance* having to get up early.
> **nui·sance** (nü′səns *or* nū′səns) *noun,* *plural* **nuisances.**

numb **1.** Lacking or having lost feeling or movement. The skier's face was *numb* with cold. Ten minutes after the dentist gave me the shot, my mouth was completely *numb.* **2.** Lacking or seeming to lack feelings. When I spoke to them about the loss of their dog, they were still *numb. Adjective.*
—To make or become numb. The cold *numbed* their fingers. *Verb.*
> **numb** (num) *adjective,* **number, numbest;** *verb,* **numbed, numbing.**

number **1.** The total amount of things in a group; how many there are of something. The *number* of children in our family is three. **2.** A symbol or word that tells how many or which one. 2, 5, 77, and 396 are numbers. Their apartment *number* is 2D. Do you have my telephone *number?* **3.** A total or sum. The person who guesses the right *number* of peanuts in the jar will win a prize. **4.** A large quantity or group. A *number* of people gathered outside the store before the sale started. *Noun.*
—**1.** To find out the number of; count. The police officers *numbered* the crowd at about 1,000. **2.** To give a number or numbers to. The teacher told us to *number* the pages of our book reports before turning them in. **3.** To amount to or include; contain. The sixth grade *numbered* fifty-two students. **4.** To limit. The days are *numbered* before summer vacation ends. *Verb.*
> **num·ber** (num′bər) *noun, plural* **numbers;** *verb,* **numbered, numbering.**

number line A line on which points are marked with numbers.

numeral A figure or group of figures that stand for a number. The *numerals* 7 and VII both stand for seven.
> **nu·mer·al** (nü′mər əl *or* nū′mər əl) *noun, plural* **numerals.**

numerator The number above or to the left of the line in a fraction. In the fraction ½, 1 is the numerator and 2 is the denominator.
> **nu·mer·a·tor** (nü′mə rā′tər *or* nū′mə rā′tər) *noun, plural* **numerators.**

numerical Having to do with or expressed by a number or numbers. 2 + 3 = 5 is a *numerical* equation; a + b = c is not.
> **nu·mer·i·cal** (nü mer′i kəl *or* nū mer′i kəl) *adjective.*

numerous **1.** Forming a large number; many. Our parents have *numerous* friends in this neighborhood. **2.** Containing a large number; large. Counting all my cousins, this is a *numerous* family.
> **nu·mer·ous** (nü′mər əs *or* nū′mər əs) *adjective.*

nun A woman who has taken special vows and belongs to a religious order. Many nuns live in convents, while others live and work

at; āpe; fär; câre; end; mē; it; ice; pîerce; hot; ōld; sông, fôrk; oil; out; up; ūse; rüle; pùll; tûrn; chin; sing; shop; thin; this; hw in white; zh in treasure. The symbol ə stands for the unstressed vowel sound in about, taken, pencil, lemon, and circus.

N

in different communities. ▲ Another word that sounds like this is **none.**

nun (nun) *noun, plural* **nuns.**

nurse **1.** A person who is trained to take care of sick people and to teach people how to stay healthy. The school *nurse* taught us to wash our hands before meals. **2.** A person who is hired to take care of children. *Noun.*
—**1.** To take care of. We *nursed* the injured rabbit until it recovered. **2.** To feed a baby or young animal from a nipple. A mother cat *nurses* her kittens until they are able to eat food by themselves. **3.** To be fed from a nipple. At first, the puppies did nothing but *nurse* and sleep. **4.** To treat with care. I *nursed* my sore elbow until it felt better. *Verb.*

nurse (nûrs) *noun, plural* **nurses;** *verb,* **nursed, nursing.**

Word History

The word **nurse** goes back to a Latin word meaning "nourishing" or "the nourishing one." Originally, a *nurse* was the woman who tended and fed babies.

nursery **1.** A baby's bedroom. **2.** A place where young children are taken care of during the day. **3.** A place where plants and trees are raised and sold.

nurs·er·y (nûr′sə rē) *noun, plural* **nurseries.**

nursery school A school for children who are too young to go to kindergarten.

nut **1.** The dry fruit of a plant. Nuts have a hard outer shell and a softer kernel inside that usually can be eaten. **2.** The edible inside kernel of a nut. **3.** A piece of metal with a hole in the center. The nut screws onto a bolt and helps keep the bolt in place. **4.** A crazy or silly person.

nut (nut) *noun, plural* **nuts.**

nutcracker **1.** A tool that is used for breaking open the hard outer shell of a nut. **2.** A bird with a tough pointed beak for feeding on nuts. Nutcrackers are related to crows.

nut·crack·er (nut′krak′ər) *noun, plural* **nutcrackers.**

nutmeg The hard seed of a tropical evergreen tree. Nutmeg is dried and is then either ground or grated and used in flavoring foods.

nut·meg (nut′meg′) *noun, plural* **nutmegs.**

nutrient Something that is needed by people, animals, or plants for life and growth. The protein in meat is a nutrient for people and many animals. Plants use the nutrients in water and in the air to grow.

nu·tri·ent (nü′trē ənt *or* nū′trē ənt) *noun, plural* **nutrients.**

nutrition **1.** Food; nourishment. The lack of proper *nutrition* made the child sick. **2.** The process by which food is taken in and used by a living thing. We are studying plant *nutrition* in science this month.

nu·tri·tion (nü trish′ən *or* nū trish′ən) *noun.*

nutritious Giving nourishment; useful as a food. It is important for children to have *nutritious* food.

nu·tri·tious (nü trish′əs *or* nū trish′əs) *adjective.*

nuzzle To touch or rub with the nose. The dog *nuzzled* its owner when it wanted to be fed.

nuz·zle (nuz′əl) *verb,* **nuzzled, nuzzling.**

NV Postal abbreviation for *Nevada.*

NW or **N.W.** An abbreviation for *northwest.*

N.W.T. An abbreviation for *Northwest Territories.*

NY Postal abbreviation for *New York.*

N.Y. An abbreviation for *New York.*

nylon A strong fabric manufactured from chemicals. Nylon is used to make thread, clothes, stockings, tires for automobiles, tents for camping, and many other things.

ny·lon (nī′lon) *noun.*

nymph **1.** In old legends, a goddess that lived in forests, hills, or rivers. Nymphs usually took the form of beautiful young women. **2.** A newly hatched insect that looks like a tiny adult. A newly hatched grasshopper is a nymph.

nymph (nimf) *noun, plural* **nymphs.**

1. The letter **O** first appeared in the alphabets of several Middle Eastern tribes.

2. In the early Hebrew alphabet, this letter was sometimes written as an oval.

3. This letter was then borrowed by the Greeks.

4. The Romans, too, borrowed the letter **O**, writing it much the same way.

5. Today we still write the letter **O** almost exactly like the Romans did 2,400 years ago.

o, O   The fifteenth letter of the alphabet.
   o, O (ō) *noun, plural* **o's, O's.**

O.   An abbreviation for *Ohio.*

oak   Any of a large group of trees or shrubs that bear acorns. Oaks have a strong, heavy wood that is used in making furniture and boats and for covering floors.
   oak (ōk) *noun, plural* **oaks.**

oar   A long pole with a flat or curved blade at one end. Oars are usually made of wood. They are used to row or steer a boat. ▲ Other words that sound like this are **or** and **ore.**
   oar (ôr) *noun, plural* **oars.**

oasis   A place in a desert where trees, shrubs, and other plants can grow because there is a supply of water.
   o·a·sis (ō ā′sis) *noun, plural* **oases.**

oasis

oat   The grain of a plant that is related to grass. Oats are used as food by humans and as feed for horses, cattle, and other animals.
   oat (ōt) *noun, plural* **oats.**

oath   **1.** A statement or promise in which a person swears that what he or she says is true. The witness took an *oath* to tell the truth about the accident. **2.** A strong or foul word used by someone who is angry; curse.
   oath (ōth) *noun, plural* **oaths.**

oatmeal   **1.** Meal that is made by grinding or rolling oats. **2.** A cooked cereal that is made from this meal.
   oat·meal (ōt′mēl′) *noun, plural* **oatmeals.**

obedient   Tending or willing to obey. The *obedient* children went right to bed.
   o·be·di·ent (ō bē′dē ənt) *adjective.*

obese   Very fat. This special diet helps *obese* people to lose weight.
   o·bese (ō bēs′) *adjective.*

obey   **1.** To carry out the orders, wishes, or instructions of. I *obeyed* my parents and came home before dark. **2.** To carry out or

O

follow. The driver *obeyed* the law and didn't go faster than the speed limit.

o·bey (ō bā′) *verb,* **obeyed, obeying.**

obi A wide sash worn with a kimono.

o·bi (ō′bē) *noun, plural* **obis.**

object 1. Anything that can be seen and touched; thing. What is that large, round *object* you hold in your hand? 2. A person or thing toward which feeling, thought, or action is directed. The children were the *object* of their parents' love. 3. A thing that one wants to achieve; purpose; goal. The *object* of my telephone call was to invite you to the party. 4. A word or group of words in a sentence that tells who or what receives or is affected by the action of a verb. In the sentence "I already gave them permission," the pronoun "them" and the noun "permission" are objects of the verb "gave." 5. A noun or pronoun that ends a phrase begun with a preposition. In the sentence "I threw the ball over the fence," the noun "fence" is the object of the preposition "over." *Noun.*

—To be against; have or raise an objection. I *object* to your using my baseball glove without asking me first. *Verb.*

ob·ject (ob′jikt *for noun;* əb jekt′ *for verb*) *noun, plural* **objects;** *verb,* **objected, objecting.**

objection 1. A cause or reason for not liking or approving of something. My teacher's *objection* to my answer was that it was too vague. 2. A feeling of not liking or approving. They showed their *objection* to the meeting by not attending.

ob·jec·tion (əb jek′shən) *noun, plural* **objections.**

objective Not influenced by one's personal feelings or opinions. The witnesses to the accident tried to be *objective* when they talked to the police. *Adjective.*

—Something that one wants to achieve; purpose; goal. What was your *objective* in going to see the mayor? *Noun.*

ob·jec·tive (əb jek′tiv) *adjective; noun, plural* **objectives.**

obligate To make a person do something because of a law, promise, or sense of duty. A driver is *obligated* to obey the traffic laws.

ob·li·gate (ob′li gāt′) *verb,* **obligated, obligating.**

obligation Something a person is supposed to do; duty; responsibility. It is the *obligation* of all citizens to vote.

ob·li·ga·tion (ob′li gā′shən) *noun, plural* **obligations.**

oblige 1. To make a person do something by a law, promise, or sense of duty. My par-

ents were *obliged* to pay for the window I broke. 2. To make thankful for a service or favor. We are *obliged* to you for the help you have given us.

o·blige (ə blīj′) *verb,* **obliged, obliging.**

oblique angle Any angle that is not a right angle.

o·blique angle (ə blēk′).

oblong Longer than wide. The necktie was in an *oblong* box. *Adjective.*

—An object or shape that is oblong. A rectangle that is not square is an *oblong. Noun.*

ob·long (ob′lông′) *adjective; noun, plural* **oblongs.**

oboe A musical instrument that makes a high tone. The oboe is played by blowing into a mouthpiece made from two reeds.

o·boe (ō′bō) *noun, plural* **oboes.**

obscure 1. Hard to understand; not clearly expressed. The poem was full of symbols and very *obscure.* 2. Not clearly seen, felt, or heard. I could not recognize the *obscure* figure in the faded picture. 3. Not well-known. Few people have read a book by that *obscure* writer. *Adjective.*

—To hide; conceal. Fog *obscured* the moon. *Verb.*

ob·scure (əb skyůr′) *adjective; verb,* **obscured, obscuring.**

observation 1. The act or power of noticing. The detective's careful *observation* helped the police to solve the crime. 2. The condition of being seen; notice. The thief escaped *observation* in the darkness. 3. Something said; comment; remark. I made an *observation* about the weather.

ob·ser·va·tion (ob′zər vā′shən) *noun, plural* **observations.**

observatory A place or building that has telescopes for observing and studying the sun, moon, planets, and stars.

ob·serv·a·to·ry (əb zûr′və tôr′ē) *noun, plural* **observatories.**

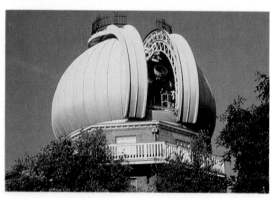

observatory

observe **1.** To see or notice. I *observed* a large truck parked in front of our neighbor's house. **2.** To make a careful study of. The scientist *observed* how the mice acted after they were given the medicine. **3.** To follow, obey, or celebrate. The driver of the car *observed* the speed limit. We *observe* Thanksgiving with my grandparents. **4.** To comment; remark. "We have a strong team," the coach *observed*.
ob·serve (əb zûrv′) *verb,* **observed, observing.**

obsolete No longer in use or practice; out-of-date. Stagecoaches are *obsolete*.
ob·so·lete (ob′sə lēt′ *or* ob′sə lēt′) *adjective.*

obstacle A person or thing that stands in the way or blocks progress. The heavy snowstorm was an *obstacle* to traffic.
ob·sta·cle (ob′stə kəl) *noun, plural* **obstacles.**

obstruct **1.** To fill and block. Fallen trees *obstructed* the road after the storm. **2.** To stand or be in the way of. The large hat on the person sitting in front of me *obstructed* my view of the stage.
ob·struct (əb strukt′) *verb,* **obstructed, obstructing.**

Word History

The word **obstruct** comes from two Latin words meaning "in the way" and "to build." To *obstruct* means "to build something in the way" and thus block a path or action.

---

obstruction **1.** Something that obstructs; obstacle; block. The tree that fell in the road was an *obstruction* to traffic. **2.** The act of obstructing or the condition of being obstructed. Your *obstruction* of this road is illegal.
ob·struc·tion (əb struk′shən) *noun, plural* **obstructions.**

obtain To get through effort; gain. In order to *obtain* the information I need for my report, I have to go to the library.
ob·tain (əb tān′) *verb,* **obtained, obtaining.**

obtuse angle Any angle that is greater than a right angle.
ob·tuse angle (əb tüs′ *or* əb tūs′).

obvious Easily seen or understood. The dog made it *obvious* that it didn't want to

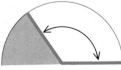

obtuse angle

take a bath. It is *obvious* that the answer is wrong.
ob·vi·ous (ob′vē əs) *adjective.*

occasion **1.** The time when something happens. I cannot remember the *occasion,* but I have met that person before. **2.** An important or special event. The baby's first birthday was an *occasion.* **3.** A suitable time; good opportunity. I haven't had many *occasions* to talk to them since they moved.
oc·ca·sion (ə kā′zhən) *noun, plural* **occasions.**

occasional Happening or appearing now and then; not frequent. The weather report said there will be *occasional* showers today.
oc·ca·sion·al (ə kā′zhə nəl) *adjective.*

occupant A person or thing that occupies a place or position. The *occupant* of the house is away for the day.
oc·cu·pant (ok′yə pənt) *noun, plural* **occupants.**

occupation **1.** The work that a person does in order to earn a living; profession. Our neighbor's *occupation* is teaching school. **2.** The act of occupying or the condition of being occupied. The enemy soldiers' *occupation* of the town lasted for months.
oc·cu·pa·tion (ok′yə pā′shən) *noun, plural* **occupations.**

occupy **1.** To take up time or space; fill. Running errands for my parents *occupied* most of the morning. **2.** To take and keep control of. Enemy soldiers *occupied* the fort. **3.** To live in. They *occupy* the house just down the street. **4.** To keep busy. The children *occupied* themselves by working on model airplanes. **5.** To have as one's own; possess. Two of our neighbors *occupy* a position in the town's government.
oc·cu·py (ok′yə pī′) *verb,* **occupied, occupying.**

occur **1.** To take place; happen. The fire *occurred* in the middle of the night. **2.** To be found; appear. How many times does the word "to" *occur* on this page? **3.** To come into one's thoughts; suggest itself. It did not *occur* to me to take my umbrella.
oc·cur (ə kûr′) *verb,* **occurred, occurring.**

occurrence **1.** The act of occurring. The *occurrence* of snow at this time of year is

---

at; āpe; fär; câre; end; mē; it; īce; pîerce; hot; ōld; sông, fôrk; oil; out; up; ūse; rüle; pull; tûrn; chin; sing; shop; thin; this; hw in white; zh in treasure. The symbol ə stands for the unstressed vowel sound in about, taken, pencil, lemon, and circus.

rare. **2.** Something that takes place or happens. Rain is an unusual *occurrence* in the desert.
oc·cur·rence (ə kûr′əns) *noun, plural* **occurrences.**

ocean **1.** The whole body of salt water that covers nearly three fourths of the earth's surface. **2.** Any one of the four main parts of this body of water: the Atlantic, Pacific, Indian, or Arctic Ocean.
o·cean (ō′shən) *noun, plural* **oceans.**

ocean floor The land lying at the bottom of the ocean. The diver found many exotic fish while exploring the *ocean floor.*

oceanography The science that deals with the ocean and the animals and plants that live in it.
o·cean·og·ra·phy (ō′shə nog′rə fē) *noun.*

ocelot A wildcat of medium size that has yellow fur with black stripes on its face and spots on its body. Ocelots live in the southwestern United States and in Central and South America.
o·ce·lot (os′ə lot′ *or* ō′sə lot′) *noun, plural* **ocelots.**

ocelot

o'clock Of or according to the clock. They will meet us at two *o'clock.*
o'clock (ə klok′) *adverb.*

Oct. An abbreviation for *October.*

octagon A figure having eight sides and eight angles.
oc·ta·gon (ok′tə gon′) *noun, plural* **octagons.**

octave **1.** The musical interval between the first and last notes of a scale. **2.** All the notes or keys of an instrument that make up this interval. Most pianos have a range of seven and one half octaves.
oc·tave (ok′tiv) *noun, plural* **octaves.**

October The tenth month of the year. October has thirty-one days.
Oc·to·ber (ok tō′bər) *noun.*

Word History

October comes from the Latin word for "eight." The early Roman calendar began with March, making October the eighth month.

octopus An animal that lives in salt water and has a soft, rounded body and eight arms. The octopus has suckers on its arms that help it move along the ocean bottom and catch food.
oc·to·pus (ok′tə pəs) *noun, plural* **octopuses.**

octopus

odd **1.** Different from the usual or normal; strange; peculiar. The radio was making an *odd* sound, so we took it to be fixed. It is *odd* that they never answered my letter. **2.** Remaining from a pair or set. I have an *odd* glove and can't find its mate. This is an *odd* plate left from the set of old dishes. **3.** Happening or appearing now and then; occasional. I do *odd* jobs after school. **4.** Leaving a remainder of one when divided by two. 5, 7, and 19 are *odd* numbers.
odd (od) *adjective,* **odder, oddest.**

oddity **1.** A person or thing that is odd or strange. An animal with two heads would be quite an *oddity.* **2.** The condition or quality of being odd or strange. The *oddity* of their green hair made the clowns look funnier than ever.
odd·i·ty (od′i tē) *noun, plural* **oddities.**

odds The difference in favor of or against something being true or happening. The *odds* are ten to one against that horse's winning the race. The *odds* are in favor of your being elected class president.
• **at odds.** Disagreeing or quarreling. The twins are often *at odds* with each other.
odds (odz) *plural noun.*

odor Smell; scent. The *odor* of flowers filled the room. The *odor* of garbage bothered the people who lived near the town dump.
o·dor (ō′dər) *noun, plural* **odors.**

odorless Having no smell; without an odor. Some gases are *odorless.*
 o·dor·less (ō′dər lis) *adjective.*

of **1.** Belonging to. The cover *of* the book is red. Are you a member *of* the club? **2.** Away from. We live five miles north *of* the city. **3.** That is or that is called. The city *of* Boston is very historic. **4.** Characterized by; having; with. The senator is a politician *of* distinction. **5.** Having to do with; concerning; about. I thought *of* you last night. **6.** Resulting from; caused by. The plant died *of* the cold. **7.** Having or containing. I drank a glass *of* milk. **8.** Made from or with. A wall *of* bricks surrounded the yard.
 of (uv *or* ov *or unstressed* əv) *preposition.*

off No longer on, attached to, or connected with; away from. Take the books *off* the shelf, please. A button is *off* my jacket. *Preposition.*
 —**1.** So as to be no longer on, attached, or connected. The coin rolled to the edge of the table and fell *off.* I broke a piece of bread *off* from the loaf. **2.** So as to be no longer working or functioning. Please switch *off* the lights in the living room. **3.** So as to be away from work or duty. Did you take yesterday *off? Adverb.*
 —**1.** No longer working, continuing, or taking place. Is the electricity *off?* **2.** Away from work or duty. The students are *off* for the day. **3.** Not accurate or correct. Your addition of the bill was *off* by three cents. *Adjective.*
 • **off and on.** Stopping and starting with periods of time between; not continuously. Yesterday it rained *off and on* all day.
 off (ôf) *preposition; adverb; adjective.*

offend To cause to be angry or unhappy. Your rude remark *offended* me.
 of·fend (ə fend′) *verb,* **offended, offending.**

offense **1.** The act of breaking the law or a rule. The thieves will be punished for their *offense.* **2.** The act of causing anger or unhappiness. I meant no *offense* when I said that you aren't a good dancer. **3.** The attacking team or players in a game. Our football team has a good *offense.*
 of·fense (ə fens′ *for definitions 1 and 2;* ô′fəns *for definition 3) noun, plural* **offenses.**

offensive **1.** Causing anger or unhappiness. They got into an argument over an *offensive* remark. **2.** Not pleasing; unpleasant; disagreeable. There was an *offensive* smell in the garbage can. **3.** Used for attack. A knife is an *offensive* weapon. *Adjective.*
 —A position or course, or attitude of attack. The enemy took the *offensive* and surrounded the fort. *Noun.*
 of·fen·sive (ə fen′siv) *adjective; noun, plural* **offensives.**

offer **1.** To present to be accepted or turned down. I *offered* an apology for being late. They *offered* some suggestions for the party. We *offered* ten dollars for the book. **2.** To show a desire to do or give something; volunteer. My friend *offered* to help me wash the car. **3.** To make a show of. The enemy *offered* little resistance when the soldiers attacked. *Verb.*
 —**1.** The act of offering. We accept your *offer* of help. **2.** Something offered. The salesperson turned down our *offer* of $500 for the old car. *Noun.*
 of·fer (ô′fər) *verb,* **offered, offering;** *noun, plural* **offers.**

office **1.** A place where the work of a business or profession is done. The door to the doctor's *office* was open. That company's *office* is upstairs. **2.** All the people who work in such a place. The *office* gave the secretary a birthday party. **3.** A position of authority, trust, or responsibility. Who is running for the *office* of mayor?
 of·fice (ô′fis) *noun, plural* **offices.**

office

officer **1.** A person who has the power to command and lead others in the army or navy. Captains, generals, and admirals are officers. **2.** A person who has a position of

at; āpe; fär; câre; end; mē; it; īce; pîerce; hot; ōld; sông, fôrk; oil; out; up; ūse; rüle; pùll; tûrn; chin; sing; shop; thin; this; hw in white; zh in treasure. The symbol ə stands for the unstressed vowel sound in about, taken, pencil, lemon, and circus.

authority, trust, or responsibility. The president and vice president of a company are two of its *officers*.   **3.** A member of the police; policeman or policewoman. We asked the *officer* for directions.
of·fi·cer (ô′fə sər) *noun, plural* **officers.**

official   A person who holds a certain office or position. The president and vice president are the two highest *officials* in the executive branch of the United States government. *Noun.*
—**1.** Of or having to do with an office or position of authority. Taking notes at each meeting is one of the *official* duties of the club secretary.   **2.** Coming from or approved by an authority. The governor made an *official* statement to the press.   **3.** Having the authority to do a specific job. Our neighbor was the *official* referee at the basketball game.   **4.** Formal and proper. There was an *official* reception for the visiting ruler. *Adjective.*
of·fi·cial (ə fish′əl) *noun, plural* **officials;** *adjective.*

offset   To act against or lessen the effect of; make up for. The teacher's kindness *offset* the strict rules of the school.
off·set (ôf′set′) *verb,* **offset, offsetting.**

offshoot   Something that develops or grows from something else. A shoot or stem that grows from the main stem of a plant is an offshoot.
off·shoot (ôf′shüt′) *noun, plural* **offshoots.**

offshore   Moving or in a direction away from the shore. We saw some people doing *offshore* fishing from their boats. *Adjective.*
—Away from the shore. The storm has moved *offshore. Adverb.*
off·shore (ôf′shôr′) *adjective; adverb.*

offspring   The young of a person, animal, or plant. We went to the zoo and saw a mother lion and three *offspring.*
off·spring (ôf′spring′) *noun, plural* **offspring.**

often   Many times; frequently. We went swimming *often* this summer.
of·ten (ô′fən) *adverb.*

ogre   **1.** A monster or giant that eats people. Ogres appear in fairy tales and legends.   **2.** A person who is cruel and frightening. Our neighbor is an *ogre* who yells often.
o·gre (ō′gər) *noun, plural* **ogres.**

oh   A word used to express surprise, happiness, sadness, pain, or other feeling. *Oh!* I didn't hear you come into the room! ▲ Another word that sounds like this is **owe.**
oh (ō) *interjection.*

OH   Postal abbreviation for *Ohio.*

Ohio   **1.** A state in the north-central United States. Its capital is Columbus.   **2.** A river in the east-central United States.
O·hi·o (ō hī′ō) *noun.*

Word History

Ohio was an American Indian name for the Ohio River that means "fine, great, beautiful river." Settlers used the name for the land around the river. When this land was made a county of Virginia, it was called *Ohio,* too. When the county became a separate state, it kept the same name.

oil   **1.** Any one of a large group of substances that are greasy and will dissolve in alcohol but not in water. Oils are usually liquid or will easily become liquid when warmed. Oil comes from animals, vegetables, and minerals.   **2.** A liquid that is found beneath the earth's surface; petroleum. Look up **petroleum** for more information. *Noun.*
—To cover, polish, or supply with oil. I helped *oil* the furniture. The worker *oiled* the rusty hinges of the door. *Verb.*
oil (oil) *noun, plural* **oils;** *verb,* **oiled, oiling.**

oil paint   A paint that is made by mixing colored powders with oil.

oil well   A well that is dug or drilled in the earth to get petroleum.

oil well

oily   **1.** Of or like oil. The suntan lotion was *oily.*   **2.** Containing, covered, or soaked with oil. We threw away the *oily* rags.
oil·y (oi′lē) *adjective,* **oilier, oiliest.**

ointment   A soft, oily substance that is put on the skin to heal, protect, or soften it.

Ointments frequently contain medicine.
oint·ment (oint′mənt) *noun, plural*
ointments.

OK¹ All right. Everything is *OK.* Is it *OK* if
I borrow your book? *OK!* I'll do it! *Adjective;
adverb; interjection.*
—Agreement or approval. We need the
teacher's *OK* to have a party. *Noun.*
—To approve or agree to. The teacher *OK'd*
our project. *Verb.* This word is also spelled
O.K. and **okay.**
  OK (ō′kā′) *adjective; adverb; interjection;
  noun, plural* **OK's;** *verb,* **OK'd, OK'ing.**

OK² Postal abbreviation for *Oklahoma.*

Okla. An abbreviation for *Oklahoma.*

Oklahoma A state in the south-central
United States. Its capital is Oklahoma City.
  O·kla·ho·ma (ō′klə hō′mə) *noun.*

Word History

In an Indian treaty of 1866, one tribe
used the name **Oklahoma** for its lands.
This American Indian word means "red
people." The name was given to a railroad station that used to be where Oklahoma City is today. Later it was chosen
as the name for the state.

okra The green pods of a plant. Okra is soft
and sticky inside. It is used in soups and eat-
en as a vegetable.
  o·kra (ō′krə) *noun.*

old **1.** Having lived or existed for a long period of time. That church is a very *old* building. **2.** Of a certain age. Our car is three
years *old.* **3.** From the past; not new or recent. The comedian told an *old* joke.
4. Known for a long time; familiar. We are
old friends. **5.** Former. This is my *old*
neighborhood. **6.** Worn-out; used. We gave
away all our *old* clothes. *Adjective.*
—A time in the past; former times. We read
a story of the knights of *old. Noun.*
  old (ōld) *adjective,* **older** or **elder, oldest**
  or **eldest;** *noun.*

olden Very old or ancient. Chariots were
used in *olden* days.
  old·en (ōl′dən) *adjective.*

Old English The oldest form of the English
language, used until about the year 1100.

old-fashioned **1.** Attached to or favoring
old ways, ideas, or customs. My grandparents are a little *old-fashioned* in the way they
think. **2.** Out-of-date; no longer in fashion.
I found an *old-fashioned* hat in the attic.
  old-fash·ioned (ōld′fash′ənd) *adjective.*

Old Testament A collection of writings
that make up the Jewish Bible and form the
first part of the Christian Bible.

Old World The part of the world that includes Europe, Asia, and Africa. Columbus
sailed from the *Old World* to the New World.

oleomargarine A substitute for butter.
This is also called **margarine.** Look up **margarine** for more information.
  o·le·o·mar·ga·rine (ō′lē ō mär′jər in)
  noun, plural **oleomargarines.**

olive **1.** The small, oily fruit of an evergreen tree. Olives
have a single hard
seed and firm
flesh. They are of-
ten eaten pickled
and are used to
make olive oil.
2. A dull yellowish
green color. *Noun.*
—Having the color
olive; dull yellow-
ish green. *Adjective.*

olives

  ol·ive (ol′iv) *noun, plural* **olives;** *adjective.*

olive oil A yellow or green oil obtained
from olives. It is used in salads and in cooking.

Olympic games **1.** An ancient Greek festival during which a series of competitions in
athletics, poetry, and dancing were held.
2. A modern series of athletic contests in
which athletes from many countries take
part. The Olympic games are held in winter
and summer every four years. These games
are also called the **Olympics.**
  O·lym·pic games (ō lim′pik).

Word History

The **Olympic games** were named after *Olympia,* the city in Greece where the
first games were held in 776 B.C.

omelet A food that is made of eggs that
have been beaten, cooked in a pan, and then
folded over. Omelets often have fillings.
  om·e·let (om′lit *or* om′ə lit) *noun, plural*
  omelets.

at; āpe; fär; câre; end; mē; it; īce; pîerce; hot; ōld;
sông, fôrk; oil; out; up; ūse; rüle; pùll; tûrn; chin;
sing; shop; thin; this; hw in white; zh in treasure.
The symbol ə stands for the unstressed vowel
sound in about, taken, pencil, lemon, and circus.

O

omen Something that is supposed to be a sign of good or bad luck to come. Breaking a mirror is thought to be a bad *omen*.
o·men (ō′mən) *noun, plural* **omens.**

ominous Telling of trouble or bad luck to come; threatening. There were *ominous* black storm clouds coming in from the sea.
om·i·nous (om′ə nəs) *adjective.*

omit To leave out; not include. Did you *omit* butter from the recipe?
o·mit (ō mit′) *verb,* **omitted, omitting.**

omnivore An animal that eats both animal flesh and plants. Bears and opossums are omnivores.
om·ni·vore (om′nə vôr′) *noun, plural* **omnivores.**

on **1.** In a position above and supported by; atop. The coats are *on* the bed. **2.** So as to be in contact with. Please spread butter *on* the bread. **3.** In a position at, near, or next to. Their house is *on* the lake. **4.** In the direction of; toward; to. Our house in *on* the left. **5.** In the condition or process of. The nurse was *on* duty. **6.** About; concerning. The lecture was *on* the art of the Eskimo. **7.** During the time, course or occasion of. We left for camp *on* Wednesday. **8.** Connected or associated with as a member. I am *on* the committee that is planning the spring dance. **9.** For the purpose of. They went to the city *on* business. *Preposition.*
—**1.** In or into contact with something. I'm putting some water *on* to boil. **2.** Forward in time or space; onward. Please move *on* so that others can pass by. **3.** In, to, or into action, operation, or movement. Switch the light *on* in the den. The riders urged their horses *on. Adverb.*
—**1.** In operation or use. Why is the light *on* in the cellar? **2.** Taking place; happening: The war is still *on. Adjective.*
• **on and on.** Without stopping. The speaker talked *on and on* for two hours.
on (ôn *or* on) *preposition; adverb; adjective.*

ON Postal abbreviation for *Ontario.*

once **1.** One time. I have a piano lesson *once* a week. **2.** In a time now past; before. Parents were *once* children. *Adverb.*
—One single time. May I borrow your bicycle just this *once? Noun.*
—As soon as; when. The game is easy, *once* you learn the rules. *Conjunction.*
• **at once.** **1.** Without any delay; now. Come here *at once.* **2.** At the same time. Everyone in class tried to talk *at once.*
• **once in a while.** Not often; occasionally. We visit our cousins only *once in a while.*

• **once upon a time.** At some time in the past; long ago. *Once upon a time* there were knights who wore armor.
once (wuns) *adverb; noun; conjunction.*

oncoming Approaching; coming nearer. The *oncoming* car had its lights off.
on·com·ing (ôn′kum′ing *or* on′kum′ing) *adjective.*

one **1.** The first and lowest number; 1. **2.** A single person, thing, or unit. Someone's been eating the cherries; there's only *one* left. *Noun.*
—**1.** Being a single person or thing. I have only *one* pencil. **2.** Being a particular person, thing, or group. The squirrel ran from *one* side of the yard to the other. **3.** Some. Practical jokes will get you in trouble *one* day. *Adjective.*
—**1.** A particular person or thing. *One* of the paintings won an award. **2.** Any person. *One* can see the tall buildings of the city in the distance. *Pronoun.* ▲ Another word that sounds like this is **won.**
• **one by one.** One after another; each following the preceding one. We entered the bus *one by one.*
one (wun) *noun, plural* **ones;** *adjective; pronoun.*

oneself One's own self. Seeing *oneself* on television would be exciting.
one·self (wun self′) *pronoun.*

one-sided **1.** For or showing only one side; unfair; partial. Your story of the argument is *one-sided.* **2.** Not even or equal. The basketball game was very *one-sided,* with our team losing by forty points.
one-sid·ed (wun′sī′did) *adjective.*

one-way Moving or allowing movement in one direction only. That is a *one-way* street.
one-way (wun′wā′) *adjective.*

onion The round or oval bulb of a plant that is also known as an onion. Onions have a strong, sharp taste and smell. They are eaten as a vegetable either raw or cooked.
on·ion (un′yən) *noun, plural* **onions.**

kinds of onions

only **1.** Alone of its kind; solitary. My friend is an *only* child. This is the *only* hat I own. **2.** Best of all. You are the *only* singer for the role. *Adjective.*
—**1.** No more than. I have *only* two dollars. **2.** No one or nothing other than. *Only* you remembered that today is my birthday. **3.** No time or no place except. My dog comes indoors *only* at night. *Adverb.*
—Except that; but. I would have gone to the park, *only* it was raining. *Conjunction.*
on·ly (ōn′lē) *adjective; adverb; conjunction.*

onset **1.** The beginning of something. At the *onset* of summer, we move to the seashore. **2.** An attack; assault. The town withstood the enemy's *onset.*
on·set (ôn′set′ *or* on′set′) *noun, plural* **onsets.**

Ont. An abbreviation for *Ontario.*

Ontario A province in central Canada. Its capital is Toronto.
On·tar·i·o (on târ′ē ō) *noun.*

onto To a position on. The door opens *onto* the porch. The actor walked *onto* the stage.
on·to (ôn′tü *or* on′tü) *preposition.*

Language Note

Do not confuse **onto** and **on to.** Onto is a preposition, and it is written as one word. *On to* is a combination of the adverb *on* and the preposition *to* and so is written as two words. After looking at the lions, we walked *on to* the next exhibit at the zoo. The cat jumped *onto* the back of the chair.

---

onward Toward the front. They climbed *onward* to the top of the hill. *Adverb.*
—Moving or directed toward a point in front; forward. It was impossible to stop the *onward* flow of the flood. *Adjective.*
on·ward (ôn′wərd *or* on′wərd) *adverb; adjective.*

ooze To leak or pass out slowly through small holes or openings; seep. The mud *oozed* between my toes.
ooze (üz) *verb,* **oozed, oozing.**

opal A mineral used as a gem. Opals are white, blue, yellow, or black. They change color slightly when moved in the light.
o·pal (ō′pəl) *noun, plural* **opals.**

opaque **1.** Not letting light through; not transparent. *Opaque* curtains keep sunlight out of the room. **2.** Not shining; dull. The table was painted an *opaque* black.
o·paque (ō pāk′) *adjective.*

open **1.** Allowing movement in, out, or through. The bird flew in through the *open* window. **2.** Not having its lid, door, or other covering closed. There is an *open* box of tissues on the self. **3.** Not closed in or covered; having no barriers. The horses ran across the *open* meadow. **4.** Spread out or unfolded. The *open* umbrella blew away in the wind. **5.** Free to be used, taken, entered, or attended; available. The job of school secretary is still *open.* The meeting of the city council is *open* to the public. **6.** Able or ready to take in new ideas, facts, or beliefs. Our teacher is always *open* to suggestions. **7.** Honest; frank. I am very *open* with my best friend about my problems. **8.** Ready to do business. That store is *open* every day but Sunday. **9.** Having spaces, holes, or gaps between the parts. A net used for fishing has an *open* weave. *Adjective.*
—**1.** To make or become open. *Open* the envelope and read the letter. The door creaked as it *opened.* **2.** To have an opening. The room *opens* onto a porch. **3.** To spread out; unfold. The petals of the flower *opened.* **4.** To set up or become available. The pool *opens* in June. **5.** To begin; start. The governor *opened* the speech with a joke. *Verb.*
—Any space or area that is not closed in or hidden. The party was held in the *open.* *Noun.*
o·pen (ō′pən) *adjective; verb,* **opened, opening;** *noun.*

opener **1.** A tool that is used to open closed or sealed containers, such as cans or bottles. **2.** The first thing or part in a series. We won the *opener* of the baseball season.
o·pen·er (ō′pə nər) *noun, plural* **openers.**

opening **1.** An empty or clear space. We squeezed through an *opening* in the fence. **2.** The first part; beginning. The *opening* of the book was not interesting. **3.** A job that is not filled. There is an *opening* for a clerk at the grocery store. **4.** The first time something is performed or open for business. The *opening* of the school play is tomorrow. **5.** The act of becoming open or being made open. The real *opening* of the West took place when the railroads were built.
o·pen·ing (ō′pə ning) *noun, plural* **openings.**

---

at; āpe; fär; câre; end; mē; it; īce; pîerce; hot; ōld; sông, fôrk; oil; out; up; ūse; rüle; půll; tûrn; chin; sing; shop; thin; <u>th</u>is; hw in white; zh in treasure. The symbol ə stands for the unstressed vowel sound in about, taken, pencil, lemon, and circus.

O

opera   A play in which all or most of the words are sung. Operas include costumes, scenery, acting, and music.
op·er·a (op′ər ə) *noun, plural* **operas.**

operate   **1.** To go or run; work; function. The car's motor *operates* well.   **2.** To cause to work or control the working of. How do you *operate* the elevator? I know how to *operate* a computer.   **3.** To perform surgery on the body of a person or animal. The doctors *operated* on the patient to fix a broken bone.
op·er·ate (op′ə rāt′) *verb,* **operated, operating.**

operation   **1.** The act or way of working or directing. The *operation* of the business took up a lot of the owner's time. I would like to learn about the *operation* of car engines.   **2.** The condition of being at work. The machine is in *operation*.   **3.** Treatment that is performed on the body of a sick or hurt person or animal by surgery. Two classmates had *operations* to remove their tonsils.
op·er·a·tion (op′ə rā′shən) *noun, plural* **operations.**

operator   A person who operates a machine or other device. My cousin is a telephone *operator*. The elevator *operator* has worked here for many years.
op·er·a·tor (op′ə rā′tər) *noun, plural* **operators.**

operetta   A short opera that is funny. An operetta includes music and songs combined with spoken parts and dancing.
op·er·et·ta (op′ə ret′ə) *noun, plural* **operettas.**

opinion   **1.** A belief that is based on what a person thinks rather than what is proved or known to be true. It is my *opinion* that our team will win the race. What is your *opinion* of that movie?   **2.** A formal statement or decision made by an expert. My parents wanted to get a lawyer's *opinion* before they signed the contract.
o·pin·ion (ə pin′yən) *noun, plural* **opinions.**

opossum   A furry American animal that

opossums

lives in trees. Female opossums carry their young in a pouch as kangaroos do. When frightened, the opossum lies still as if it were dead. This animal is also called a **possum.**
o·pos·sum (ə pos′əm) *noun, plural* **opossums.**

opponent   A person who is against another in a fight, contest, or discussion. The soccer team beat its *opponent* and won the championship.
op·po·nent (ə pō′nənt) *noun, plural* **opponents.**

opportunity   A good chance; favorable time. When the pond froze, we had an *opportunity* to go ice skating.
op·por·tu·ni·ty (op′ər tü′ni tē *or* op′ər tū′ni tē) *noun, plural* **opportunities.**

oppose   **1.** To be against; resist. The people in the town *opposed* the plan to raise taxes.   **2.** To be the opposite of; contrast. Good is *opposed* to evil.
op·pose (ə poz′) *verb,* **opposed, opposing.**

opposite   **1.** On the other side of or across from another person or thing; facing. They live on the *opposite* side of the street from me. That student sits *opposite* me.   **2.** Turned or moving the other way. We passed a red car going in the *opposite* direction from us.   **3.** Completely different. Hot is *opposite* to cold. *Adjective.*
—A person or thing that is completely different from another. Summer and winter are *opposites*. Night is the *opposite* of day. *Noun.*
—Across from. Stand *opposite* me. *Preposition.*
op·po·site (op′ə zit) *adjective; noun, plural* **opposites;** *preposition.*

opposition   **1.** Action against. My *opposition* to the plan surprised my friends.   **2.** A political party that is opposed to the party in power.
op·po·si·tion (op′ə zish′ən) *noun, plural* **oppositions.**

oppress   **1.** To control or rule by cruel and unjust means. The dictator's army *oppressed* the people of the country.   **2.** To be a burden to; trouble or depress. The long drought *oppressed* the farmers.
op·press (ə pres′) *verb,* **oppressed, oppressing.**

optical   **1.** Having to do with the sense of sight. A mirage is an *optical* illusion.   **2.** Designed to help one see. Microscopes and eyeglasses are *optical* devices.
op·ti·cal (op′ti kəl) *adjective.*

optimistic   Tending to look on the favorable side of things and believe that everything will turn out for the best. The students were very *optimistic* about their chances of getting summer jobs.

op·ti·mis·tic (op′tə mis′tik) *adjective.*

optional Left to one's choice; not required. Going to the class party is *optional.*

op·tion·al (op′shə nəl) *adjective.*

or **1.** A word that is used to connect words, phrases, and clauses that represent choices. Is the water warm *or* cold? Eat lunch, *or* you will be hungry later. **2.** A word that is used to introduce the second of two choices when the first is introduced by *either* or *whether.* Either write *or* phone me. We didn't know whether to stay *or* leave. **3.** A word that is used to introduce a word or phrase that means the same as something already mentioned. We saw a cougar, *or* mountain lion, at the zoo. ▲ Other words that sound like this are **oar** and **ore.**

or (ôr) *conjunction.*

-or A *suffix* that means a person or thing that does something. *Inventor* means a person who invents. *Generator* means a machine that produces or generates something. The suffix *-er* sometimes has the same meaning. Look up **-er¹** for more information.

OR Postal abbreviation for *Oregon.*

oral **1.** Not written; using speech; spoken. Each student must give an *oral* report on a favorite book. **2.** Having to do with the mouth. Brushing your teeth after every meal is good *oral* hygiene.

o·ral (ôr′əl) *adjective.*

orange **1.** A round citrus fruit that has a thick orange or yellow skin and a sweet juice. Oranges grow on evergreen trees in warm climates. **2.** A reddish yellow color. *Noun.*
—Having the color orange; reddish yellow. *Adjective.*

or·ange (ôr′inj or or′inj) *noun, plural* **oranges;** *adjective.*

oranges

orangeade A drink made of orange juice and water and sweetened with sugar.

or·ange·ade (ôr′in jād′ or or′in jād′) *noun, plural* **orangeades.**

orangutan A large ape that lives in trees in certain parts of Asia. Orangutans have very long, strong arms, a shaggy coat of reddish brown hair, and no tail.

o·rang·u·tan (ô rang′ü tan′) *noun, plural* **orangutans.**

orbit **1.** The path that a planet or other heavenly body follows as it moves in a circle around another heavenly body. The *orbit* of the earth around the sun takes about 365 days. **2.** One complete trip of a spacecraft along such a path. The scientists sent a satellite into *orbit* around the earth. *Noun.*
—To move in an orbit around a heavenly body. The earth *orbits* the sun. *Verb.*

or·bit (ôr′bit) *noun, plural* **orbits;** *verb,* **orbited, orbiting.**

orchard An area of land where fruit trees are grown.

or·chard (ôr′chərd) *noun, plural* **orchards.**

orchestra **1.** A group of musicians playing together on various instruments. **2.** The violins, horns, drums, and other instruments played by such a group. **3.** The main floor of a theater. **4.** The area just in front of a stage in which the orchestra plays.

or·ches·tra (ôr′kə strə) *noun, plural* **orchestras.**

Word History

The word **orchestra** comes from a Greek word meaning "dance area." In the theater of ancient Greece, one section of the stage was called the *orchestra.* It was there that a chorus of performers danced and sang during a performance.

---

orchid A plant with flowers that grow in various shapes and colors.

or·chid (ôr′kid) *noun, plural* **orchids.**

ordain **1.** To decide or order by law or authority. The law *ordains* the punishment that a convicted criminal will receive. **2.** To admit formally to the clergy or other religious office. My cousin was *ordained* as a minister.

or·dain (ôr dān′) *verb,* **ordained, ordaining.**

orchids

O

---

at; āpe; fär; câre; end; mē; it; īce; pîerce; hot; ōld; sông, fôrk; oil; out; up; ūse; rüle; půll; tûrn; chin; sing; shop; thin; this; hw in white; zh in treasure. The symbol ə stands for the unstressed vowel sound in about, taken, pencil, lemon, and circus.

ordeal   A very hard or painful experience or test. Living through the earthquake was quite an *ordeal*.
   or·deal (ôr dēl′) *noun, plural* **ordeals.**

order   **1.** A command to do something. The soldier obeyed *orders*.   **2.** The way in which things are arranged; position in a series. The teacher called the students' names in alphabetical *order*.   **3.** A condition in which laws or rules are obeyed. The police restored *order* after the riot.   **4.** Clean, neat, or proper condition. Please keep your room in *order*.   **5.** A request for goods. I called the grocery store and gave them our *order*.   **6.** Goods that have been requested or supplied. The waiter delivered their *order*.   **7.** A group of people who live under the same rules or belong to the same organization. Nuns and monks belong to religious *orders*.   **8.** A related group of animals, plants, or other living things. Each order is made up of several families. Mice and squirrels are both in the rodent *order*. *Noun.*
   —**1.** To tell to do something; give an order to; command. The police officer *ordered* the thieves to put up their hands.   **2.** To place an order for; ask for. We *ordered* eggs and bread from the grocery store.   **3.** To put into proper order; arrange neatly or properly. I *ordered* the books on my shelves. *Verb.*
   • **in order to.**   So as to be able to. The child stood on a chair *in order to* see better.
   • **out of order.**   Not working in the proper way. The broken telephone had been *out of order* for a week.
   or·der (ôr′dər) *noun, plural* **orders;** *verb,* **ordered, ordering.**

orderly   **1.** Arranged in a certain way or order; having order. The children marched in an *orderly* line. I keep my room *orderly*.   **2.** Not causing or making trouble or noise. An *orderly* crowd of people waited outside of the White House for the president to come out. *Adjective.*
   —**1.** A worker in a hospital who cleans and does other jobs.   **2.** A soldier assigned to an officer or group of officers. An orderly carries messages and does other tasks. *Noun.*
   or·der·ly (ôr′dər lē) *adjective; noun, plural* **orderlies.**

ordinal number   A number that shows position in a series. First, second, and third are ordinal numbers.
   or·di·nal number (ôr′də nəl)

ordinarily   In normal conditions or circumstances; usually. *Ordinarily,* the museum is open on Sundays.
   or·di·nar·i·ly (ôr′də ner′ə lē) *adverb.*

ordinary   **1.** Commonly used; regular; usual. My *ordinary* tone of voice is soft.   **2.** Not different in any way from others; average. I thought the movie was very *ordinary.*
   or·di·nar·y (ôr′də ner′ē) *adjective.*

ore   A mineral or rock that is mined for the metal or other substance it contains. ⊿ Other words that sound like this are **oar** and **or.**
   ore (ôr) *noun, plural* **ores.**

Ore. or **Oreg.**   An abbreviation for *Oregon.*

Oregon   A state in the northwestern United States on the Pacific. Its capital is Salem.
   Or·e·gon (ôr′i gon′ *or* ôr′i gən) *noun.*

Word History

   The origin of the name **Oregon** is not definitely known. Somehow, the American Indian name for the Wisconsin River was written incorrectly on a map. When explorers in the Northwest found the Columbia River, they thought it was the river on the map. The river's name was later changed to the Columbia River, but the name Oregon was kept as the name of the state that lies south of this river.

---

organ   **1.** A musical instrument made up of pipes of different lengths which are sounded by air blown from a bellows. The organ is played by means of one or more keyboards.   **2.** A similar musical instrument that has no pipes and uses electricity and loudspeakers to produce sound.   **3.** A part of an animal or plant that is made up of several kinds of tissues and that does a particular job. The heart, liver, and eyes are *organs* of the body. Leaves and flowers are plant *organs.*
   or·gan (ôr′gən) *noun, plural* **organs.**

organic   **1.** Having to do with or coming from living things. Decaying leaves, grass, vegetables, and other *organic* matter can be used to make soil fertile.   **2.** Using or grown by farming or gardening methods in which manufactured chemicals are not used.
   or·gan·ic (ôr gan′ik) *adjective.*

organism   A living thing. Animals, plants, amebas, and bacteria are all organisms.
   or·gan·ism (ôr′gə niz′əm) *noun, plural* **organisms.**

organization   **1.** The act of organizing. The class president was in charge of the *organization* of the school dance.   **2.** The condition or way of being organized. In our li-

brary, the *organization* of books is by subject. **3.** A group of people joined together for a particular purpose. I belong to an *organization* that does work for various charities.
  or·gan·i·za·tion (ôr′gə nə zā′shən) *noun, plural* **organizations.**

organize **1.** To arrange or put together in an orderly way. I *organize* the stamps in my collection according to what country they are from. Who is in charge of *organizing* the trip to the zoo? **2.** To cause to join together in a labor union or other organization.
  or·gan·ize (ôr′gə nīz′) *verb,* **organized, organizing.**

Orient The countries of Asia. China and Japan are countries of the Orient.
  O·ri·ent (ôr′ē ənt) *noun.*

Oriental Having to do with or belonging to the Orient. *Adjective.*
  —A member of one of the peoples living in the Orient. *Noun.*
  O·ri·en·tal (ôr′ē en′təl) *adjective; noun, plural* **Orientals.**

origin **1.** The cause or source of something; what something begins or comes from. The *origin* of the fire was in the basement. **2.** Parents; ancestors. Are your grandparents of foreign *origin?*
  or·i·gin (ôr′i jin *or* or′i jin) *noun, plural* **origins.**

original **1.** Made, done, thought of, or used for the first time; new. The idea for my story is *original.* **2.** Able to do, make, or think of something new or different. An inventor must be an *original* thinker. **3.** Having to do with or belonging to the origin or beginning of something; first. The *original* owner of the house still lives there. *Adjective.*
  —Something that is original; not a copy, imitation, or translation. That painting is an *original* by a famous artist. *Noun.*
  o·rig·i·nal (ə rij′ə nəl) *adjective; noun, plural* **originals.**

originality **1.** The quality of being new or unusual. The *originality* of this painting fascinates me. **2.** The ability to do, make, or think of something new or unusual. That sculptor shows great *originality.*
  o·rig·i·nal·i·ty (ə rij′ə nal′i tē) *noun.*

originally At or from the start. Basketball was *originally* played in the United States.
  o·rig·i·nal·ly (ə rij′ə nə lē) *adverb.*

originate **1.** To bring into being; start. Who *originated* the design for this new airplane? **2.** To come into being; begin. The fire *originated* in an old, deserted building.
  o·rig·i·nate (ə rij′ə nāt′) *verb,* **originated, originating.**

oriole Any of various brightly colored songbirds that are found in most parts of the world. The males are usually bright orange or yellow with black markings.
  o·ri·ole (ôr′ē ōl′) *noun, plural* **orioles.**

oriole

ornament Something that is used as a decoration. The Christmas tree *ornaments* were painted bright colors. *Noun.*
  —To decorate with ornaments. *Verb.*
  or·na·ment (ôr′nə mənt *for noun;* ôr′nə ment′ *for verb*) *noun, plural* **ornaments;** *verb,* **ornamented, ornamenting.**

ornate Having much decoration. The palace was filled with *ornate* furniture.
  or·nate (ôr nāt′) *adjective.*

an **ornate** throne

at; āpe; fär; câre; end; mē; it; īce; pîerce; hot; ōld; sông, fôrk; oil; out; up; ūse; rüle; pull; tûrn; chin; sing; shop; thin; <u>th</u>is; hw in white; zh in treasure. The symbol ə stands for the unstressed vowel sound in about, taken, pencil, lemon, and circus.

orphan A child whose parents are dead. *Noun.*
—To make an orphan of. The war *orphaned* hundreds of children. *Verb.*
  or·phan (ôr′fən) *noun, plural* **orphans;** *verb,* **orphaned, orphaning.**

orphanage A place that takes in and cares for orphans.
  or·phan·age (ôr′fə nij) *noun, plural* **orphanages.**

orthodontist A dentist whose work is straightening the teeth.
  or·tho·don·tist (ôr′thə don′tist) *noun, plural* **orthodontists.**

orthodox **1.** The same or almost the same as what most people believe or accept. My parents' opinions on politics are very *orthodox.* **2.** Holding or following widely accepted or traditional beliefs or practices. That family is very *orthodox* in their religious beliefs.
  or·tho·dox (ôr′thə doks′) *adjective.*

ostrich A large bird that has a long neck, long, strong legs, and a small, flat head. The ostrich is the largest of all living birds. It cannot fly, but it can run very fast. Ostriches are found in Africa.
  os·trich (ôs′trich *or* os′trich) *noun, plural* **ostriches.**

other **1.** Different from the one or ones already mentioned. If you can't help me, maybe some *other* person can. **2.** Remaining. The *other* guests haven't arrived yet. **3.** More, extra, or further. I have no *other* gloves. **4.** Not very long ago. Our cousins just called us the *other* day. *Adjective.*
—**1.** A different or additional person or thing. If you don't like that hat we have *others.* **2.** The remaining one. I didn't know the *others* at the party. *Pronoun.*
—In a different way; otherwise. I could not feel *other* than surprised. *Adverb.*
  oth·er (uth′ər) *adjective; pronoun, plural* **others;** *adverb.*

otherwise **1.** In other respects besides that. It rained a little during the picnic, but *otherwise* the picnic was a success. **2.** If the circumstances were different. We were lucky we brought an umbrella; we would have gotten wet *otherwise.* **3.** In a different way or in any other way. I cannot believe *otherwise* but that our team will win. *Adverb.*
—Different; other. The spy's story sounds true, but the facts are *otherwise. Adjective.*
—Because if not; or else. The roof must be fixed, *otherwise* it'll leak if it rains. *Conjunction.*
  oth·er·wise (uth′ər wīz′) *adverb; adjective; conjunction.*

otter A water animal that looks like a weasel. Otters have webbed feet, long, slightly flattened tails, and brown, shiny fur.
  ot·ter (ot′ər) *noun, plural* **otters** *or* **otter.**

otter

ouch A word used to express sudden pain. *Ouch!* I burned my finger on the stove!
  ouch (ouch) *interjection.*

ought An auxiliary verb that is used in the following ways: **1.** To express an obligation or responsibility. You *ought* to obey the law. **2.** To express what is expected or likely. I put in new batteries, so the radio *ought* to work. **3.** To offer advice. You *ought* to take care of yourself so you won't get sick.
  ought (ôt) *verb.*

ounce **1.** A unit of weight equal to 1/16 of a pound. Sixteen ounces equal one pound. **2.** A unit of measure for liquids. Thirty-two ounces equal one quart. **3.** A small bit. The runners didn't have an *ounce* of energy left when they reached the end of the long race.
  ounce (ouns) *noun, plural* **ounces.**

our Of, belonging to, or having to do with us. *Our* house is on Oak Street. ▲ Another word that sounds like this is **hour.**
  our (our) *adjective.*

ours The one or ones that belong or have to do with us. Their dog is larger than *ours.* The error was *ours.*
  ours (ourz) *pronoun.*

ourselves **1.** Our own selves. We hurt *ourselves* in the game. We cooked for *ourselves* when our parents were away. We *ourselves* made the decision. **2.** Our usual, normal, or true self. We're not feeling *ourselves* in this hot, humid weather.
  our·selves (our selvz′) *pronoun.*

-ous A *suffix* that means having or full of. *Malicious* means having malice. *Dangerous* means full of danger.

oust To force out; drive out; expel. The player was *ousted* from the game for arguing with the umpire.
  oust (oust) *verb,* **ousted, ousting.**

out   **1.** Away from the center or from inside. I turned on the faucet, and water gushed *out*. The children went *out* to play.   **2.** Away from one's home or business. The doctor went *out* to visit a patient.   **3.** So as to be no longer active or available. Our supplies will soon run *out*.   **4.** Into view or to the attention of the public. The sun just came *out*. The book came *out* last month. *Adverb.*
—**1.** Not active, being used, or in proper condition. The road is *out* because of the flood.   **2.** Not successful in reaching a base in a baseball game.   **3.** Away or outside. I was *out* when you phoned. *Adjective.*
—Through. I looked *out* the window. *Preposition.*
   out (out) *adverb; adjective; preposition.*

out–   A *prefix* that means: **1.** Forth; away. *Outburst* means a bursting forth.   **2.** More than; longer than; better than. *Outnumber* means to number more than. *Outdo* means to do better than.   **3.** Away from; outside. *Outlying* means lying outside. *Outpost* means a post away from the main post.

outboard motor   A motor attached to the outside of the stern of a small boat.
   out·board motor (out′bôrd′).

outbreak   A breaking out of something. There was an *outbreak* of flu last winter.
   out·break (out′brāk′) *noun, plural* **outbreaks.**

outburst   A bursting forth of something. We were surprised by your *outburst* of anger.
   out·burst (out′bûrst′) *noun, plural* **outbursts.**

outcome   A result; end. We are waiting to hear the *outcome* of the election.
   out·come (out′kum′) *noun, plural* **outcomes.**

outcry   **1.** A strong objection or protest. There was an immediate *outcry* when it was announced that train service had been canceled.   **2.** A cry; shout. An *outcry* from the backyard brought us to the windows.
   out·cry (out′krī′) *noun, plural* **outcries.**

outdated   No longer used or fashionable; out-of-date. That kind of hat is *outdated*.
   out·dat·ed (out′dā′tid) *adjective.*

outdid   Past tense of **outdo.** Look up **outdo** for more information.
   out·did (out′did′) *verb.*

outdo   To do better than. I tried to *outdo* the rest of the class in geography.
   out·do (out′dü′) *verb,* **outdid, outdone, outdoing.**

outdone   Past participle of **outdo.** Look up **outdo** for more information.
   out·done (out′dun′) *verb.*

outdoor   Used or done out in the open instead of inside a house or other building. Baseball is an *outdoor* game.
   out·door (out′dôr′) *adjective.*

outdoors   Not in a house or other building; out under the sky. We ate *outdoors. Adverb.*
—The world that is outside houses or other buildings. We took a walk in the *outdoors. Noun.*
   out·doors (out′dôrz′) *adverb; noun.*

outer   On the outside. We wear warm *outer* clothes in the winter.
   out·er (ou′tər) *adjective.*

outer space   The space beyond the earth's atmosphere. The planets and stars are in outer space.

outfield   The part of a baseball field beyond the infield and between the foul lines.
   out·field (out′fēld′) *noun.*

outfit   **1.** All the articles or pieces of equipment needed for doing something. These shoes and helmets are part of the football team's new *outfits*.   **2.** A set of clothes. I wore my new *outfit* on the first day of school.   **3.** A group of people who work or belong together. What army *outfit* did that general lead during the war? *Noun.*
—To give or sell articles or equipment needed for doing something. The store *outfitted* the campers. *Verb.*
   out·fit (out′fit′) *noun, plural* **outfits;** *verb,* **outfitted, outfitting.**

outgoing   **1.** Friendly and liking to talk. An *outgoing* person makes friends easily.   **2.** Going out or departing. The *outgoing* governor lost the last election. When is the first *outgoing* bus tomorrow?
   out·go·ing (out′gō′ing) *adjective.*

outgrew   Past tense of **outgrow.** Look up **outgrow** for more information.
   out·grew (out′grü′) *verb.*

outgrow   **1.** To grow too big for. The baby will soon *outgrow* these clothes.   **2.** To leave behind or lose as one grows older. I *outgrew* my fear of the dark.   **3.** To grow bigger than. I have *outgrown* everyone in the class.
   out·grow (out′grō′) *verb,* **outgrew, outgrown, outgrowing.**

outgrown   Past participle of **outgrow.** Look up **outgrow** for more information.
   out·grown (out′grōn′) *verb.*

O

at; āpe; fär; câre; end; mē; it; īce; pîerce; hot; ōld; sông, fôrk; oil; out; up; ūse; rüle; pùll; tûrn; chin; sing; shop; thin; this; hw in white; zh in treasure. The symbol ə stands for the unstressed vowel sound in about, taken, pencil, lemon, and circus.

outing A short trip for pleasure. All the students enjoyed the school *outing* to the park.
out·ing (ou′ting) *noun, plural* **outings.**

outlaw A person who constantly breaks the law; criminal. The sheriff searched for the *outlaws. Noun.*
—To make illegal; prohibit. The state *outlawed* the sale of fireworks. *Verb.*
out·law (out′lô′) *noun, plural* **outlaws;** *verb,* **outlawed, outlawing.**

outlet **1.** A place at which something comes out. Dead leaves clogged the *outlets* of the gutters. **2.** A means of expressing or getting rid of something. Playing tennis is a good *outlet* for a person's energy. **3.** A place in an electric wiring system where appliances are plugged in. **4.** A store that usually sells the goods of only one manufacturing company. Our family shopped for bargains at a clothing *outlet.*
out·let (out′let′) *noun, plural* **outlets.**

outline **1.** The shape of an object formed by following along its outer edges. We saw the *outline* of a passing ship through the fog. **2.** A summary of a story, speech, or other writing. Make a brief *outline* of your report before you write it. *Noun.*
—**1.** To give a summary of. The general *outlined* the plan for the attack. **2.** To draw the outline of. Each student *outlined* oak and maple leaves. *Verb.*
out·line (out′līn′) *noun, plural* **outlines;** *verb,* **outlined, outlining.**

a flower and its **outline**

outlook **1.** A view into the future; situation that is expected. The weather *outlook* for tomorrow is not good. **2.** A way of looking at or thinking about something. Most people have a happy *outlook* during a holiday.
out·look (out′lùk′) *noun, plural* **outlooks.**

outlying Located far from the center of something. The zoo is located in an *outlying* district of the city.
out·ly·ing (out′lī′ing) *adjective.*

outnumber To be greater in number than. The home team's fans *outnumbered* the visiting team's at the football game.
out·num·ber (out′num′bər) *verb,* **outnumbered, outnumbering.**

out-of-date No longer in style or use; old-fashioned. We found those *out-of-date* clothes in the attic at our grandparents' house.
out-of-date (out′əv dāt′) *adjective.*

outpost A small military station that controls an area and guards against attack.
out·post (out′pōst′) *noun, plural* **outposts.**

output **1.** The amount of something produced. The employees increased their *output* by working extra hours. **2.** Information that a computer displays on its screen or prints on paper.
out·put (out′pùt′) *noun.*

outrage **1.** An act of great violence or cruelty. The dictator committed many *outrages* against the people of the country. **2.** Great anger. The people of the city felt *outrage* at the mayor's accepting a bribe. *Noun.*
—To cause to feel great anger. The attack against the small country *outraged* many people. *Verb.*
out·rage (out′rāj′) *noun, plural* **outrages;** *verb,* **outraged, outraging.**

outrageous Shocking. Insulting people in front of friends is an *outrageous* thing to do.
out·ra·geous (out rā′jəs) *adjective.*

outran Past tense of **outrun.** The winner of the race *outran* fifteen other athletes. Look up **outrun** for more information.
out·ran (out′ran′) *verb.*

outrigger A frame that is attached to the outside of a canoe. It keeps the canoe from turning over.
out·rig·ger (out′rig′ər) *noun, plural* **outriggers.**

outrigger on a canoe

outright Complete; total. Saying you will be home when you know you won't is an *outright* lie. *Adjective.*
—1. In a direct or honest way; openly. Please say *outright* what you think about my idea. 2. Completely and all at once. We paid for the bicycle *outright*. *Adverb.*
out·right (out′rīt′) *adjective; adverb.*

outrun To run faster or farther than. That horse *outran* all the others in the race.
out·run (out′run′) *verb,* **outran, outrun, outrunning.**

outside The outer side, surface, or part. The *outside* of the house was painted white. *Noun.*
—1. On the outside; outer. The *outside* layer of paint was peeling. 2. Extremely slight; not likely. There is only an *outside* chance that we will be able to go to the movies. *Adjective.*
—On or to the outside; outdoors. Do you want to go *outside* for some fresh air? We played *outside* all day. *Adverb.*
—Beyond the limits or range of. They live just *outside* Philadelphia. *Preposition.*
out·side (out′sīd′ *or* out′sīd′ *or* out′sīd′) *noun, plural* **outsides;** *adjective; adverb; preposition.*

outskirts The region or area that is outside or at the edge of a town or city. They live in a house on the *outskirts* of town.
out·skirts (out′skûrts′) *plural noun.*

outsmart To get the better of; be cleverer than. I sometimes *outsmart* my parents at chess.
out·smart (out′smärt′) *verb,* **outsmarted, outsmarting.**

outspoken Honest or open. Many people were very *outspoken* in their criticism of the county's plan for a new garbage dump.
out·spo·ken (out′spō′kən *or* out′spō′kən) *adjective.*

outstanding 1. So good as to stand out from others of its kind. That famous pitcher was an *outstanding* athlete. The student wrote an *outstanding* book report. 2. Not paid or settled. The business has an *outstanding* debt of $1,000.
out·stand·ing (out′stan′ding) *adjective.*

outward To or toward the outside. The gate opens *outward*. This word is also spelled **outwards.** *Adverb.*
—1. Toward or on the outside. The knight's *outward* armor was made of sheets of metal. 2. Capable of being seen from the outside. There was no *outward* sign of anyone's being at home. *Adjective.*
out·ward (out′wərd) *adverb; adjective.*

outwards Another spelling for the adverb **outward.** The eyes on many kinds of fish look *outwards.*
out·wards (out′wərdz) *adverb.*

outwit To get the better of; be more clever than. The rabbit *outwitted* the fox that was chasing it.
out·wit (out′wit′) *verb,* **outwitted, outwitting.**

oval Shaped like an egg or an ellipse. The turkey was on an *oval* platter. *Adjective.*
—Something shaped like an egg or an ellipse. *Noun.*
o·val (ō′vəl) *adjective; noun, plural* **ovals.**

The glass in the center is an **oval.**

ovary 1. The part of a female animal that produces eggs. 2. The part of a flowering plant in which seeds are formed.
o·va·ry (ō′və rē) *noun, plural* **ovaries.**

oven An enclosed space that is used to heat, bake, or roast food that is placed inside. A kitchen stove usually has an oven.
ov·en (uv′ən) *noun, plural* **ovens.**

over 1. In a place or position higher than; above. A flock of birds flew *over* our heads. 2. Upon so as to cover. The nurse put a blanket *over* the patient. I spread wax *over* the

at; āpe; fär; câre; end; mē; it; īce; pîerce; hot; ōld; sông, fôrk; oil; out; up; ūse; rüle; pull; tûrn; chin; sing; shop; thin; <u>th</u>is; hw in white; zh in treasure. The symbol ə stands for the unstressed vowel sound in about, taken, pencil, lemon, and circus.

O

floor. **3.** From one side or end to the other; across or along. The horse jumped *over* the fence. **4.** During the time of; throughout. School is closed *over* the holidays. **5.** More than. We spent *over* twenty dollars to buy groceries. **6.** Concerning; about. Are you upset *over* the arithmetic test? *Preposition.*
—**1.** In a higher place or position; above. We could see a plane flying *over.* **2.** Above and beyond the top or edge. The water in the pot boiled *over.* **3.** Across a distance or space; from another place. Come *over* to my house for dinner. **4.** From an upright or erect position. The cat knocked the vase *over.* **5.** Once more; again. If you make a mistake, start *over. Adverb.*
—At an end; finished. The game is *over. Adjective.*
   o·ver (ō′vər) *preposition; adverb; adjective.*

over- A *prefix* that means: **1.** Too much. *Overwork* means to work too much. **2.** Above; across; beyond. *Overhead* means above the head. *Overseas* means across the sea. *Overflow* means to flow beyond normal bounds. **3.** From above to below; down. *Overthrow* means to throw down.

overalls Loose-fitting trousers. Overalls usually have a piece that covers the chest with suspenders attached.
   o·ver·alls (ō′vər ôlz′) *plural noun.*

overboard Over the side of a ship into the water. The sailor slipped and fell *overboard.*
   o·ver·board (ō′vər bôrd′) *adverb.*

overcame Past tense of **overcome.** I *overcame* my fear of the water and learned to swim. Look up **overcome** for more information.
   o·ver·came (ō′vər kām′) *verb.*

overcast Covered with clouds; cloudy. The rain stopped at noon, but the sky was *overcast* for the rest of the day.
   o·ver·cast (ō′vər kast′) *adjective.*

overcoat A heavy outer coat worn over other clothing for warmth.
   o·ver·coat (ō′vər kōt′) *noun, plural* **overcoats.**

overcome **1.** To get the better of; beat or conquer. The tired runner couldn't *overcome* the others in the race. Our soldiers *overcame* the enemy. **2.** To get over or deal with. You must *overcome* your fear of water before you can learn how to swim. **3.** To make tired or helpless. Many people in the crowd were *overcome* by the heat and smoke from the fire. I was *overcome* with emotion while watching the play.
   o·ver·come (ō′vər kum′) *verb,* **overcame, overcome, overcoming.**

overdid Past tense of **overdo.** I'm still stiff from when I *overdid* my exercises. Look up **overdo** for more information.
   o·ver·did (ō′vər did′) *verb.*

overdo **1.** To do or use too much; carry too far. The other politicians gave the mayor so much praise that they *overdid* it. **2.** To cook food too much. Be careful not to *overdo* the steak. ▲ Another word that sounds like this is **overdue.**
   o·ver·do (ō′vər dü′) *verb,* **overdid, overdone, overdoing.**

overdone Past participle of **overdo.** The steak was *overdone.* It's hard to laugh when a person has *overdone* a joke. Look up **overdo** for more information.
   o·ver·done (ō′vər dun′) *verb.*

overdose Too large an amount of a medicine or drug. Follow directions on bottles of medicine to avoid taking an *overdose.*
   o·ver·dose (ō′vər dōs′) *noun, plural* **overdoses.**

overdress To dress in clothes that are too formal or too warm for the occasion. Don't *overdress;* this will be a very casual party.
   o·ver·dress (ō′vər dres′) *verb,* **overdressed, overdressing.**

overdue **1.** Not paid even though the date when payment is due has passed. The rent is *overdue.* **2.** Not on time; late. The plane from New York is twenty minutes *overdue.* ▲ Another word that sounds like this is **overdo.**
   o·ver·due (ō′vər dü′ *or* ō′vər dū′) *adjective.*

overeat To eat too much. I *overate* at dinner.
   o·ver·eat (ō′vər ēt′) *verb,* **overate** (ō′vər āt′), **overeaten** (ō′vər ē′tən), **overeating.**

overflow **1.** To flow beyond the usual limits. Water from the kitchen sink *overflowed* onto the floor. **2.** To be so full that the contents flow over. The bathtub *overflowed.* **3.** To flow over the top edge of. The water *overflowed* the glass. **4.** To flow or spread over; flood. When the dam burst, water *overflowed* the town. *Verb.*
—Something that flows over. We mopped up the *overflow* of water from the bathtub. *Noun.*
   o·ver·flow (ō′vər flō′ *for verb;* ō′vər flō′ *for noun*) *verb,* **overflowed, overflowed** or **overflown, overflowing;** *noun.*

overflown A past participle of **overflow.** Because of the heavy rain, the river has *overflown.* Look up **overflow** for more information.
   o·ver·flown (ō′vər flōn′) *verb.*

overgrew Past tense of **overgrow.** The weeds *overgrew* the flowers in the garden. Look up **overgrow** for more information.
o·ver·grew (ō′vər grü′) *verb.*

overgrow To grow over. The gardeners pulled up the weeds that were *overgrowing* the park.
o·ver·grow (ō′vər grō′) *verb,* **overgrew, overgrown, overgrowing.**

overgrown Past participle of **overgrow.** The hedge around the old house was *overgrown* with poison ivy. Look up **overgrow** for more information.
o·ver·grown (ō′vər grōn′) *verb.*

The wall is **overgrown** with ivy.

overhand Done with the hand raised above the elbow or the arm raised above the shoulders. Throw the ball with an *overhand* pitch. *Adjective.*
—With an overhand style or motion. That pitcher throws *overhand. Adverb.*
o·ver·hand (ō′vər hand′) *adjective; adverb.*

overhaul **1.** To examine completely and make needed repairs or changes. The mechanic *overhauled* the car's engine. **2.** To catch up with. The large motorboat quickly *overhauled* the small sailboat. *Verb.*
—The act of overhauling. The car's engine needs an *overhaul. Noun.*
o·ver·haul (ō′vər hôl′ *or* ō′vər hôl′ *for verb;* ō′vər hôl′ *for noun) verb,* **overhauled, overhauling;** *noun, plural* **overhauls.**

overhead Above one's head. Birds flew *overhead.* The light was on *overhead. Adverb.*
—The general expenses of running a business. Money spent for rent, taxes, heating, and lighting is part of the overhead. *Noun.*
—Above one's head. Please turn on the *overhead* lights. *Adjective.*
o·ver·head (ō′vər hed′ *for adverb;* ō′vər hed′ *for noun and adjective) adverb; noun, plural* **overheads;** *adjective.*

overhear To hear something one is not supposed to hear. Did you *overhear* the con-

versation of the people sitting behind us on the train?
o·ver·hear (ō′vər hîr′) *verb,* **overheard, overhearing.**

overheard Past tense and past participle of **overhear.** I *overheard* my parents talking about a surprise party. Look up **overhear** for more information.
o·ver·heard (ō′vər hûrd′) *verb.*

overjoy To make very happy. We were *overjoyed* when we heard that our school's team had won the championship.
o·ver·joy (ō′vər joi′) *verb,* **overjoyed, overjoying.**

overlap To rest on top of something and partly cover it. The magazines on the table were arranged so that one *overlapped* the other.
o·ver·lap (ō′vər lap′) *verb,* **overlapped, overlapping.**

overload To put too much of something in or on. Our car was *overloaded* with suitcases. We can't make a phone call because all of the circuits are *overloaded* with calls.
o·ver·load (ō′vər lōd′) *verb,* **overloaded, overloading.**

overlook **1.** To not see, notice, or think of. The thief *overlooked* the possibility that the house had a burglar alarm. **2.** To think of as never having happened; ignore. I *overlooked* your rudeness because I knew you were angry. **3.** To have a view of from a place above. The house on the hill *overlooks* a river.
o·ver·look (ō′vər lùk′) *verb,* **overlooked, overlooking.**

overnight **1.** During or through the night. A storm struck the farm *overnight.* **2.** Very quickly; suddenly. The town seemed to grow into a city *overnight. Adverb.*
—**1.** For one night. We had an *overnight* guest. **2.** Lasting through or happening during the night. We took an *overnight* flight from California to New York. **3.** Used or made for short trips. I packed everything I needed for my weekend visit in an *overnight* bag. *Adjective.*
o·ver·night (ō′vər nīt′ *or* ō′vər nīt′ *for adverb;* ō′vər nīt′ *for adjective) adverb; adjective.*

at; āpe; fär; câre; end; mē; it; īce; pîerce; hot; ōld; sông, fôrk; oil; out; up; ūse; rüle; pùll; tûrn; chin; sing; shop; thin; this; hw in white; zh in treasure. The symbol ə stands for the unstressed vowel sound in about, taken, pencil, lemon, and circus.

O

521

overpass A bridge or road that crosses above another road or a railroad.
o·ver·pass (ō′vər pas′) *noun, plural* **overpasses.**

overpower 1. To beat or conquer by greater strength or power. The prisoner *overpowered* the guard and escaped. 2. To make helpless. Our family was *overpowered* by sadness when our dog died.
o·ver·pow·er (ō′vər pou′ər) *verb,* **overpowered, overpowering.**

overran Past tense of **overrun.** Poison ivy *overran* the shrubs around the empty house. Look up **overrun** for more information.
o·ver·ran (ō′vər ran′) *verb.*

overrule 1. To rule against by higher authority. The Supreme Court *overruled* the decision of another court. 2. To decide against. I thought we should leave on Friday, but the rest of the group *overruled* me, and we left on Saturday.
o·ver·rule (ō′vər rül′) *verb,* **overruled, overruling.**

overrun 1. To spread or swarm over or throughout. Weeds have *overrun* the flower garden. The enemy had *overrun* the fort. 2. To flow over. The river *overran* its banks. 3. To run beyond. That baseball player always *overruns* second base.
o·ver·run (ō′vər run′) *verb,* **overran, overrun, overrunning.**

overseas Over, across, or beyond the sea; abroad. We plan to travel *overseas* this summer, visiting France and Italy. *Adverb.*
—1. Working, located, or serving overseas. That company has an *overseas* office. 2. Having to do with countries across the sea; foreign. Many farmers depend on our nation's *overseas* trade. *Adjective.*
o·ver·seas (ō′vər sēz′) *adverb; adjective.*

overshoe A shoe or boot that is worn over an ordinary shoe to protect against cold, snow, water, or mud. Overshoes are usually made of rubber.
o·ver·shoe (ō′vər shü′) *noun, plural* **overshoes.**

oversight 1. A careless mistake that was not made on purpose. Leaving your name off the list of people I invited to the party was an *oversight.* 2. The act or process of watching over with care and guiding. That committee is in charge of the *oversight* of the state's hospitals.
o·ver·sight (ō′vər sīt′) *noun, plural* **oversights.**

overtake 1. To move from being behind to being inside or ahead of; catch up with or pass. The police car tried to *overtake* the car speeding down the highway. 2. To come upon in a sudden or unexpected way. The rain *overtook* the campers as they hiked in the woods.
o·ver·take (ō′vər tāk′) *verb,* **overtook, overtaken, overtaking.**

overtaken Past participle of **overtake.** That runner has *overtaken* the others in the race and might win. Look up **overtake** for more information.
o·ver·taken (ō′vər tā′kən) *verb.*

overthrew Past tense of **overthrow.** Look up **overthrow** for more information.
o·ver·threw (ō′vər thrü′) *verb.*

overthrow 1. To cause to lose power; defeat, as by force or a struggle. After years of suffering, the people *overthrew* the dictator. 2. To cause to turn or fall over; upset. I accidentally *overthrew* a vase. *Verb.*
—The loss of power; defeat. The *overthrow* of the tyrant was celebrated by huge crowds. *Noun.*
o·ver·throw (ō′vər thrō′ *for verb;* ō′vər thrō′ *for noun) verb,* **overthrew, overthrown, overthrowing;** *noun.*

overthrown Past participle of **overthrow.** Look up **overthrow** for more information.
o·ver·thrown (ō′vər thrōn′) *verb.*

overtime Time worked beyond the regular working hours. You will be paid for the *overtime* you will have to work today. *Noun.*
—Beyond the hours one is usually expected to work. I worked three hours *overtime* this week. My family worked *overtime* to get ready for the wedding. *Adverb.*
—Of or for overtime. Do you get *overtime* pay at your job? *Adjective.*
o·ver·time (ō′vər tīm′) *noun; adverb; adjective.*

overtook Past tense of **overtake.** The brown horse *overtook* the black one and won the race. Look up **overtake** for more information.
o·ver·took (ō′vər tůk′) *verb.*

overture 1. A musical composition played by an orchestra to introduce an opera, ballet, or other large musical work. 2. An offer to begin something; suggestion or proposal. We made *overtures* of friendship to our new classmate.
o·ver·ture (ō′vər chər) *noun, plural* **overtures.**

overweight Having more than the normal or needed weight. I dieted because the doctor said I was *overweight.*
o·ver·weight (ō′vər wāt′) *adjective.*

overwhelm 1. To overcome completely; overpower or make helpless. The enemy

overwhelmed our soldiers.   **2.** To cover or bury completely. The waves *overwhelmed* the small island during the storm.
   o·ver·whelm (ō′vər hwelm′ *or* ō′vər welm′) *verb,* **overwhelmed, overwhelming.**

overwork   To cause to work too much. The farmer *overworked* the mule. *Verb.*
—Too much work. *Overwork* was the cause of your illness. *Noun.*
   o·ver·work (ō′vər wûrk′ *for verb;* ō′vər wûrk′ *for noun) verb,* **overworked, overworking;** *noun.*

owe   **1.** To have to pay. I still *owe* my parents some money for the bicycle they helped me buy.   **2.** To have to give. I *owe* you an apology for being so late.   **3.** To be obliged for. I *owe* a great deal to my brother and sister for all the help they gave me with my report. ▲ Another word that sounds like this is **oh.**
   owe (ō) *verb,* **owed, owing.**

owl   A bird that has a round head with large, staring eyes and a hooked bill, a short square tail, and soft feathers. Owls eat mice, frogs, snakes, and insects and usually hunt for them at night.
   owl (oul) *noun, plural* **owls.**

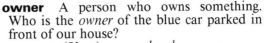
owl

own   Of, having to do with, or belonging to oneself or itself. I use my *own* baseball bat even though our school has them. The accident was your *own* fault. *Adjective.*
—Something that belongs to one. That bicycle is my *own. Noun.*
—**1.** To have as belonging to one; possess. That farmer *owns* all the land between here and the river.   **2.** To admit doing something; confess; acknowledge. The children *owned* that they had broken the window by accident. *Verb.*
   • **on one's own.** Relying or dependent only on oneself or one's own efforts, as for support or success. I know exactly what to do when I'm *on my own* in the woods.
   • **to hold one's own.** To do well, as against opposition or competition. I was pleased that I was able *to hold my own* in the debate.
   own (ōn) *adjective; noun; verb,* **owned, owning.**

owner   A person who owns something. Who is the *owner* of the blue car parked in front of our house?
   own·er (ō′nər) *noun, plural* **owners.**

ox   **1.** The adult male of domestic cattle. It is used as a work animal or for beef. An ox cannot father young.   **2.** Any of various animals related to the ox. Buffaloes, bison, and yaks are also called oxen.
   ox (oks) *noun, plural* **oxen.**

oxcart   A cart pulled by an ox or oxen.
   ox·cart (oks′kärt′) *noun, plural* **oxcarts.**

oxen   Plural of **ox.** Two *oxen* were pulling the cart. Look up **ox** for more information.
   ox·en (ok′sən) *plural noun.*

oxford   A shoe that is laced over the top of the foot.
   ox·ford (oks′fərd) *noun, plural* **oxfords.**

oxide   A compound of oxygen and one or more chemical elements.
   ox·ide (ok′sīd) *noun, plural* **oxides.**

oxidize   To combine a chemical substance with oxygen.
   ox·i·dize (ok′si dīz′) *verb,* **oxidized, oxidizing.**

oxygen   A gas that has no color or smell. Oxygen makes up about one fifth of the air. Living things need oxygen to live, and fires need it to burn. Oxygen is a chemical element.
   ox·y·gen (ok′si jən) *noun.*

oyster   An animal that has a soft body and a rough, hinged shell. Oysters are found in shallow waters along coasts. Some kinds of oysters are used for food, while other kinds are raised for the pearls they produce.
   oys·ter (oi′stər) *noun, plural* **oysters.**

oz.   An abbreviation for *ounce* or *ounces.*

ozone   A form of oxygen. It is formed by lightning or other electricity in the air. Ozone is used to kill germs and freshen the air.
   o·zone (ō′zōn) *noun.*

Word History

Ozone goes back to a Greek word meaning "smelling." The gas ozone was named for its sharp odor.

---

at; āpe; fär; câre; end; mē; it; īce; pîerce; hot; ōld; sông, fôrk; oil; out; up; ūse; rüle; pùll; tûrn; chin; sing; shop; thin; this; hw in white; zh in treasure. The symbol ə stands for the unstressed vowel sound in about, taken, pencil, lemon, and circus.

O

P p

1. The letter **P** first appeared in the alphabets of several Middle Eastern tribes. It had a shape like a hook.

2. When the ancient Greeks borrowed the letter, they wrote it in much the same way, sometimes reversing it.

3. The ancient Romans then borrowed the letter **P**, at first giving it the same form as the Greeks did.

4. The Romans later changed the way they wrote this letter, adding a closed loop at the top.

5. Our modern capital **P** has been written almost the same way for the last 2,400 years.

---

p, P   The sixteenth letter of the alphabet.
p, P (pē) *noun, plural* **p's, P's.**

p.   An abbreviation for *page.*

Pa.   An abbreviation for *Pennsylvania.*

PA   Postal abbreviation for *Pennsylvania.*

pace   **1.** A single step. The soldiers took two *paces* forward.   **2.** The length of a single step. I was about six *paces* from the edge of the cliff.   **3.** The rate of speed in walking, running, or moving. We walked home at a fast *pace.*   **4.** A way of stepping or moving; gait. The trot is one of the *paces* of a horse. *Noun.*
—**1.** To walk back and forth across. The tiger *paced* its cage.   **2.** To measure by taking paces. The treasure hunter *paced* off five feet from the tree and began to dig. *Verb.*
pace (pās) *noun, plural* **paces;** *verb,* **paced, pacing.**

Pacific   The ocean that separates North America and South America from Asia and Australia. This is also called the **Pacific Ocean.** *Noun.*
—Of the Pacific. *Adjective.*
Pa·cif·ic (pə sif'ik) *noun; adjective.*

Word History

The name **Pacific** comes from a Latin word meaning "peaceful." The explorer Magellan named this ocean "pacific" because it seemed calm compared to the Atlantic.

---

pacify   To make calm or quiet. I *pacified* the baby by singing.
pac·i·fy (pas'ə fī') *verb,* **pacified, pacifying.**

pack   **1.** A group of things wrapped or tied together for carrying; bundle. I strapped the books together to form a secure *pack.*   **2.** A sturdy bag for carrying things on the back of a person or animal. The camper's *pack* was filled with supplies.   **3.** A set or group of things that are alike. A large *pack* of wolves lives in those mountains.   **4.** A large quantity; a lot. *Noun.*
—**1.** To place in something for storing or carrying. We had to *pack* all our dishes in boxes.   **2.** To fill up with things. *Pack* your suitcase for the trip.   **3.** To press together tightly. The child *packed* the snow into a ball.   **4.** To fill by crowding together. The audience *packed* the theater. *Verb.*
pack (pak) *noun, plural* **packs;** *verb,* **packed, packing.**

package   **1.** A thing or group of things packed, wrapped up, or tied together; bundle.

I received a large *package* on my birthday. **2.** A box, case, or other container in which something is packed. Follow the directions on the *package* to make the soup. *Noun.*
—To make or put into a package. My favorite cereal is *packaged* in a red box. *Verb.*
 pack·age (pak′ij) *noun, plural* **packages;** *verb,* **packaged, packaging.**

pack animal An animal used for carrying loads. Horses and mules are used as pack animals.

packet A small package or parcel.
 pack·et (pak′it) *noun, plural* **packets.**

pact An agreement between persons or countries; treaty. The two nations signed a peace *pact.* The friends made a secret *pact.*
 pact (pakt) *noun, plural* **pacts.**

pad **1.** A soft piece of thick material used as stuffing or for protection or comfort. The football player put on shoulder *pads.* **2.** A number of sheets of paper that are glued together along one edge. We leave a *pad* and pencil by the telephone. **3.** A part like a small, soft cushion on the bottom of the feet of dogs, foxes, and some other animals. **4.** A block of cloth soaked with ink and used with a rubber stamp. *Noun.*
—**1.** To cover, stuff, or line with a pad. The chair was *padded* so that it would be more comfortable. **2.** To make longer by adding unnecessary material. The report was too short, so the writer *padded* it. *Verb.*
 pad (pad) *noun, plural* **pads;** *verb,* **padded, padding.**

paddle **1.** A short oar with a flat, wide blade. A paddle is used to move and steer a canoe or other small boat. **2.** A small, broad board with a short handle. It is used to hit the ball in table tennis and other games. **3.** A flat, wooden tool. Paddles are used for beating, stirring, or mixing things. *Noun.*
—**1.** To move a canoe or other boat with a paddle or paddles. You can *paddle* across the lake in fifteen minutes. **2.** To hit with a paddle or with the hand; spank. *Verb.*
 pad·dle (pad′əl) *noun, plural* **paddles;** *verb,* **paddled, paddling.**

paddle wheel A large wheel with broad boards, or paddles, fixed around it. Paddle wheels are used to move steamboats.

paddock **1.** A small field or area that is fenced in. Animals can graze or exercise in a paddock. **2.** A small, fenced area near a racetrack. Horses are saddled and walked in a paddock before a race.
 pad·dock (pad′ək) *noun, plural* **paddocks.**

paddy A field where rice is grown.
 pad·dy (pad′ē) *noun, plural* **paddies.**

padlock A lock with a U-shaped bar that is hinged on one end. The other end of the bar can be put through an opening or link and then snapped shut. Padlocks can be opened with a key or a dial. *Noun.*
—To fasten or lock with a padlock. *Verb.*
 pad·lock (pad′lok′) *noun, plural* **padlocks;** *verb,* **padlocked, padlocking.**

pagan A person who is not a Christian, Jew, or Muslim. Some pagans believe in many gods or no god at all.
 pa·gan (pā′gən) *noun, plural* **pagans.**

page¹ One side of a sheet of paper in a book, newspaper, or magazine. Find the exact *page* where the lesson begins. How many pages are in that book?
 page (pāj) *noun, plural* **pages.**

page² **1.** A young person who runs errands and carries messages. Pages help members of Congress and other legislatures. **2.** Long ago, a boy working as a servant or helper for an important person. *Noun.*
—To try to find someone by calling out his or her name. They *paged* the doctor over the loudspeaker in the hospital. *Verb.*
 page (pāj) *noun, plural* **pages;** *verb,* **paged, paging.**

pageant **1.** A kind of play that is about events in history or legend. Our school gave a *pageant* about the first Thanksgiving. **2.** A colorful parade or ceremony for an im-

paddle wheel

portant event. The wedding of the king and queen was a magnificent *pageant.*

pag·eant (paj′ənt) *noun, plural* **pageants.**

pagoda A temple or tower that is many stories high. The roof of each story usually curves upward. There are pagodas in Asia.

pa·go·da (pə gō′də) *noun, plural* **pagodas.**

pagoda

paid Past tense and past participle of **pay.** They *paid* for their meal and left. Look up **pay** for more information.

paid (pād) *verb.*

pail A round, open container with a flat bottom and a curved handle; bucket. It is used for carrying sand, water, or other things. ▲ Another word that sounds like this is **pale.**

pail (pāl) *noun, plural* **pails.**

pain 1. A feeling of being hurt; suffering. The blister gave me *pain.* I eased the *pain* of being left alone by watching television. 2. **pains.** Care or effort. I took *pains* to put the model airplane together neatly. *Noun.*
—To cause pain to. My sprained ankle still *pained* me. It *pains* me to hear people quarreling. *Verb.* ▲ Another word that sounds like this is **pane.**

pain (pān) *noun, plural* **pains;** *verb,* **pained, paining.**

painful Causing pain. A bee can give a *painful* sting.

pain·ful (pān′fəl) *adjective.*

painless Causing no pain. The nurse gave me a *painless* shot.

pain·less (pān′lis) *adjective.*

paint A mixture of pigments and water, oil, or some other liquid. Paint is spread on a surface to color it or protect it. *Noun.*
—1. To cover with paint. We helped *paint* the kitchen walls. 2. To make a picture or design of something by using paint. This artist likes to *paint* mountain scenes. *Verb.*

paint (pānt) *noun, plural* **paints;** *verb,* **painted, painting.**

painter 1. A person who paints pictures. That artist is a talented *painter* and sculptor. 2. A person whose work is painting things like walls and houses. The landlord sent the *painters* over to paint our apartment.

paint·er (pān′tər) *noun, plural* **painters.**

painting 1. Something painted; picture. A *painting* of the family hangs over the sofa. 2. The act or art of using paints. I hope to study drawing and *painting.*

paint·ing (pān′ting) *noun, plural* **paintings.**

pair 1. A set of two things meant to be used together. Try on this *pair* of shoes. 2. A single thing made up of two parts. You will find a *pair* of scissors in the top drawer. 3. Two persons or animals that are alike or that go together; couple. A *pair* of black horses were pulling the wagon. *Noun.*
—1. To join or match in a pair. They *paired* the two tallest band members to lead the march. 2. To form into pairs. The whole class *paired* off for the square dance. *Verb.* ▲ Other words that sound like this are **pare** and **pear.**

pair (pâr) *noun, plural* **pairs** or **pair;** *verb,* **paired, pairing.**

pajamas A set of clothes to sleep in. They are usually made up of a shirt and trousers.

pa·ja·mas (pə jä′məz *or* pə jam′əz) *plural noun.*

Pakistan A country in south-central Asia.

Pakistan (pak′ə stan′ *or* pä′kə stän′) *noun.*

pal A close friend. I play softball with my *pals* every day after school.

pal (pal) *noun, plural* **pals.**

palace A very large, grand building where a king, queen, or other ruler lives.

pal·ace (pal′is) *noun, plural* **palaces.**

Word History

The word **palace** goes back to the Latin word for the *Palatine.* The Palatine is a hill in Rome where the first Roman emperor, Augustus, built his palace.

palate 1. The roof of the mouth. The bony part in the front is called the **hard palate,** and the fleshy part in the back is called the **soft palate.** 2. The sense of taste. Ripe peaches please my *palate.* ▲ Other words that sound like this are **palette** and **pallet.**

pal·ate (pal′it) *noun, plural* **palates.**

pale 1. Having skin color that is light. My friend is blond and has a *pale* complexion. The sick child looked weak and *pale.*

2. Not bright in color. The lake glimmered in the *pale* moonlight. *Adjective.*
—To turn pale. Their faces *paled* when they heard about the accident. *Verb.* ⚠ Another word that sounds like this is **pail**.
pale (pāl) *adjective,* **paler, palest;** *verb,* **paled, paling.**

Paleozoic Belonging to or having to do with the era in the earth's early history from about 570 million years ago to about 230 million years ago. During this time, fish, insects, and reptiles began to appear.
Pa·le·o·zo·ic (pā′lē ə zō′ik) *adjective.*

Palestine A region in southwestern Asia. In biblical times, Palestine was the land of the Jews. The area is now occupied by Israel and Jordan.
Pal·es·tine (pal′ə stīn) *noun.*

palette A thin, oval board with a hole for the thumb at one end. Artists place and mix their paints on palettes. ⚠ Other words that sound like this are **palate** and **pallet**.
pal·ette (pal′it) *noun, plural* **palettes.**

palisades A line of steep cliffs that rise along a river.
pal·i·sades (pal′ə sādz′) *plural noun.*

pallet **1.** A bed or mattress made of straw. **2.** A small, hard, or temporary bed. During the flood, we slept on *pallets* at the emergency shelter. ⚠ Other words that sound like this are **palate** and **palette**.
pal·let (pal′it) *noun, plural* **pallets.**

palm¹ The inside surface of the hand between the wrist and the fingers. *Noun.*
—**1.** To hold or hide in the hand. The magician *palmed* the cards so we would think they had disappeared. **2.** To get rid of by fooling someone. The crook *palmed* off the cheap stone as a diamond. *Verb.*
palm (päm) *noun, plural* **palms;** *verb,* **palmed, palming.**

palm² Any of a number of trees, shrubs, or vines that grow in warm climates. They have large leaves like feathers or fans that grow at the very top of a tall trunk.
palm (päm) *noun, plural* **palms.**

palmetto A kind of palm that grows in the southern United States and some other warm areas. It has leaves shaped like fans.
pal·met·to (pal met′ō) *noun, plural* **palmettos** or **palmettoes.**

palomino A light tan or golden horse having a white or yellowish white mane and tail.
pal·o·mi·no (pal′ə mē′nō) *noun, plural* **palominos.**

pamper To treat too well; spoil. The parents *pampered* their only child.
pam·per (pam′pər) *verb,* **pampered, pampering.**

pamphlet A small book that has a paper cover. The board game came with a *pamphlet* of playing instructions.
pam·phlet (pam′flit) *noun, plural* **pamphlets.**

pan **1.** A metal dish used for cooking or baking. Pans are usually broad and shallow and do not have a cover. **2.** A shallow container that is like a cooking pan. Pans are used to wash gold ore from gravel. *Noun.*
—To wash soil or gravel in a pan to separate the gold in it. The prospector *panned* for gold. *Verb.*
pan (pan) *noun, plural* **pans;** *verb,* **panned, panning.**

Panama A country in Central America.
Pan·a·ma (pan′ə mä′) *noun.*

pancake A flat, thin cake made of batter. It is cooked in a pan or on a griddle.
pan·cake (pan′kāk′) *noun, plural* **pancakes.**

pancreas A gland near the stomach. The pancreas makes digestive juices and hormones such as insulin.
pan·cre·as (pan′krē əs) *noun, plural* **pancreases.**

panda **1.** A large animal that looks like a bear. It has thick, black and white fur and lives in western China. It is also called the **giant panda.** **2.** A reddish brown animal that looks like a raccoon. It has short legs, a long bushy tail marked with darker rings, and a white face. It is also called the **lesser panda.**

panda

pan·da (pan′də) *noun, plural* **pandas.**

pane A sheet of glass in a window or door. ⚠ Another word that sounds like this is **pain**.
pane (pān) *noun, plural* **panes.**

panel **1.** A part or section of something that is different in some way from what is around it because it is raised, sunken, or bor-

at; āpe; fär; câre; end; mē; it; īce; pîerce; hot; ōld; sông, fôrk; oil; out; up; ūse; rüle; pùll; tûrn; chin; sing; shop; thin; this; hw in white; zh in treasure. The symbol ə stands for the unstressed vowel sound in about, taken, pencil, lemon, and circus.

dered. A panel may be in a door or a wall, part of a piece of furniture, or a section of a garment. **2.** A group of persons gathered together to talk about or judge something. The *panel* of judges for the baking contest awarded the prizes. **3.** A board containing the dials, instruments, and controls for running something. My electric train has a control *panel*. *Noun.*
—To arrange in panels; decorate with panels. The walls of the living room are *paneled* in pine. *Verb.*
pan·el (pan′əl) *noun, plural* **panels;** *verb,* **paneled, paneling.**

pang A sudden, sharp feeling. I get *pangs* of hunger just before lunch. The thief began to feel *pangs* of guilt.
pang (pang) *noun, plural* **pangs.**

panic A strong feeling of fear that makes a person lose self-control and want to run away. When the theater caught fire, *panic* spread through the crowd. *Noun.*
—To fill with or have a feeling of great fear. The lightning *panicked* the horses. *Verb.*
pan·ic (pan′ik) *noun, plural* **panics;** *verb,* **panicked, panicking.**

panorama A wide or complete view of an area. You can see a *panorama* of the whole valley from the top of the mountain.
pan·o·ram·a (pan′ə ram′ə *or* pan′ə rä′mə) *noun, plural* **panoramas.**

pansy A plant with flowers that have five flat petals overlapping each other. Pansies have flowers of many colors.
pan·sy (pan′zē) *noun, plural* **pansies.**

pansies

pant 1. To breathe quickly and hard; gasp for breath. After the race, the runners stood *panting* at the finish line. **2.** To say while gasping for breath. "Help me," the stranger *panted*.
pant (pant) *verb,* **panted, panting.**

panther A leopard that is so dark that it looks almost black.
pan·ther (pan′thər) *noun, plural* **panthers** or **panther.**

pantomime 1. The telling of a story without talking, through the use of gestures, body movements, and facial expressions. **2.** A play acted in this way. The class put on a *pantomime* of the first Thanksgiving. *Noun.*

—To act or show in pantomime. The clown *pantomimed* riding on a subway. *Verb.*
pan·to·mime (pan′tə mīm′) *noun, plural* **pantomimes;** *verb,* **pantomimed, pantomiming.**

pantry A small room for storing food, dishes, or silverware.
pan·try (pan′trē) *noun, plural* **pantries.**

pants A garment for the part of the body below the waist. Pants are divided so that they cover each leg separately.
pants (pants) *plural noun.*

papaya A yellowish orange fruit that grows on a tropical American tree. It looks like a melon and has a sweet taste.
pa·pa·ya (pə pä′yə) *noun, plural* **papayas.**

paper 1. A material that is used for writing and printing, wrapping things, covering walls, and many other purposes. Paper is made from ground wood, rags, or certain grasses. It is usually made in thin pieces called sheets. **2.** A piece or sheet of paper. Write your name at the top of the *paper*. **3.** A piece of paper with writing or printing on it; document. These *papers* prove that we own the house. **4.** A written report or essay for school. My history *paper* is finished. **5.** A newspaper. We buy the evening *paper*. *Noun.*
—To cover with wallpaper. The workers *papered* the hall. *Verb.*
pa·per (pā′pər) *noun, plural* **papers;** *verb,* **papered, papering.**

Word History

The earliest writing material that was like the paper we use today was made from the papyrus plant. The word **paper** goes back to the Greek word meaning "papyrus."

paperback A book that has a soft paper cover.
pa·per·back (pā′pər bak′) *noun, plural* **paperbacks.**

panther

paper clip A small piece of bent wire that is used to hold sheets of paper together.

papoose A North American Indian baby or small child.
pa·poose (pa püs′) *noun, plural* **papooses.**

paprika A reddish orange powder used as a spice and to add color to food. It is made from sweet red peppers.
pap·ri·ka (pa prē′kə *or* pap′ri kə) *noun, plural* **paprikas.**

Papua New Guinea An island country in southeastern Asia.
Pap·u·a New Guinea (pap′ū ə *or* pä′pü ä′).

papyrus 1. A tall plant that grows in swamps and along rivers in parts of Africa and Europe. 2. A material like paper that is made from this plant. The ancient Egyptians used this material to write on.
pa·py·rus (pə pī′rəs) *noun, plural* **papyri** (pə pī′rī).

par 1. An average or normal amount, condition, or degree. Their work is above *par.* 2. An equal level. The skills of the two athletes are not on a *par.*
par (pär) *noun, plural* **pars.**

parachute A device that allows a person or object attached to it to be dropped slowly and safely from an airplane or other high place. Parachutes are made of fabric and open out like an umbrella when unfolded. *Noun.*
—To come or send down by parachute. The pilot *parachuted* from the burning plane. The air force *parachuted* supplies to the soldiers who were surrounded by the enemy. *Verb.*
par·a·chute (par′ə shüt′) *noun, plural* **parachutes;** *verb,* **parachuted, parachuting.**

Word History

The word **parachute** comes from a French word that originally meant "guarding against a fall."

parade A march or procession in honor of a person or event. Every year we go downtown to watch the Fourth of July *parade. Noun.*
—1. To march in a parade. The soldiers *paraded* through town. 2. To make a great show of; show off. Some people like to *parade* their knowledge before everyone they meet. *Verb.*
pa·rade (pə rād′) *noun, plural* **parades;** *verb,* **paraded, parading.**

paradise 1. Heaven. 2. A place or state of great happiness. The island where they spent their vacation was a *paradise* of peace and beauty.
par·a·dise (par′ə dīs′) *noun.*

paraffin A white substance like wax. It is used for making candles and waxed paper, and for sealing jars.
par·af·fin (par′ə fin) *noun.*

paragraph A part of something written, made up of one or more sentences about a particular subject or idea. It begins on a new line that is indented from the rest of the lines.
par·a·graph (par′ə graf′) *noun, plural* **paragraphs.**

Word History

The word **paragraph** goes back to a Greek word that means "to write beside." The Greeks used this word for a symbol drawn beside a piece of writing to mark the beginning of a new idea or topic. This was also the first meaning of *paragraph* in English. Later the word came to mean a section of writing containing a single topic or idea.

Paraguay A country in central South America.
Par·a·guay (par′ə gwī′ *or* par′ə gwā′) *noun.*

P

parade

at; āpe; fär; câre; end; mē; it; ice; pîerce; hot; ōld; sông, fôrk; oil; out; up; ūse; rüle; pull; tûrn; chin; sing; shop; thin; this; hw in white; zh in treasure. The symbol ə stands for the unstressed vowel sound in about, taken, pencil, lemon, and circus.

529

parakeet A small parrot. It has a slender body, a long, pointed tail, and brightly colored feathers. Parakeets are often kept as pets.
par·a·keet (par′ə kēt′) *noun, plural* **parakeets.**

parakeet

parallel 1. Being the same distance apart at all points. If lines are parallel, they never meet or cross each other. The rails of a railroad track are *parallel.* 2. Alike in some way; similar. These children live in different cities but have *parallel* experiences. *Adjective.*
—1. A parallel line or surface. The teacher drew a line and then drew a *parallel.* 2. A being alike; similarity. There are many *parallels* in the lives of pioneers. 3. Any of the imaginary lines that circle the earth in the same direction as the equator. They are used to mark latitude. *Noun.*
—1. To be or lie in the same direction and always the same distance apart. The railroad tracks *parallel* the road. 2. To be similar to. The growth of the small town *paralleled* that of the city nearby. *Verb.*
—Always the same distance apart. The road runs *parallel* to the river. *Adverb.*
par·al·lel (par′ə lel′) *adjective; noun, plural* **parallels;** *verb,* **paralleled, paralleling;** *adverb.*

parallelogram A flat figure with four sides. The opposite sides of a parallelogram are both equal in length and parallel.
par·al·lel·o·gram (par′ə lel′ə gram′) *noun, plural* **parallelograms.**

paralysis A loss of the power to move or feel in a part of the body.
pa·ral·y·sis (pə ral′ə sis) *noun, plural* **paralyses** (pa ral′ə sēz).

paralyze 1. To take away the power to move or feel in a part of the body. After the accident, my right arm was *paralyzed.* 2. To make unable to move or act; make helpless. The bus strike *paralyzed* the city.
par·a·lyze (par′ə līz′) *verb,* **paralyzed, paralyzing.**

paramecium A tiny living thing that has only one cell and lives in fresh water. It can be seen only through a microscope.
par·a·me·ci·um (par′ə mē′shē əm *or* par′ə mē′sē əm) *noun, plural* **paramecia** (par′ə mē′shē ə *or* par′ə mē′sē ə).

paramount Above all others, as in influence or importance; greatest; highest. Taking care of this is of *paramount* importance.
par·a·mount (par′ə mount′) *adjective.*

parasite An animal or plant that lives on or in another animal or plant, which is called a host. A parasite gets food or shelter from its host. Fleas and tapeworms are parasites on animals. Mistletoe is a parasite on trees.
par·a·site (par′ə sīt′) *noun, plural* **parasites.**

parasol A small, light umbrella. Parasols are used as a protection against the sun.
par·a·sol (par′ə sôl′) *noun, plural* **parasols.**

paratrooper A soldier trained to parachute from an airplane into an area of battle.
par·a·troop·er (par′ə trü′pər) *noun, plural* **paratroopers.**

parcel 1. Something wrapped up; bundle or package. I received three *parcels* on my birthday. 2. A piece or section. *Noun.*
—To divide into sections; give out in parts. The coach *parceled* equipment. *Verb.*
par·cel (pär′səl) *noun, plural* **parcels;** *verb,* **parceled, parceling.**

parch 1. To make very dry. The summer drought *parched* the fields. 2. To make very hot and thirsty. Hiking *parched* us.
parch (pärch) *verb,* **parched, parching.**

parchment The skin of sheep, goats, or other animals prepared so that it can be written on, or paper made to look like this skin. Diplomas are often written on parchment.
parch·ment (pärch′mənt) *noun, plural* **parchments.**

pardon 1. To free a person from punishment. The governor *pardoned* the prisoner. 2. To not have hard feelings about; not want to blame or punish. *Verb.*
—1. A freeing from punishment. The prisoner received a *pardon* from the governor. 2. The act of refusing to blame or punish; forgiveness. I beg your *pardon* if I hurt you. *Noun.*
par·don (pär′dən) *verb,* **pardoned, pardoning;** *noun, plural* **pardons.**

paramecium

530

pare **1.** To cut or peel off the outer part of something. *Pare* the apple with a knife. **2.** To make less little by little; cut down. The family tried to *pare* expenses. ▲ Other words that sound like this are **pair** and **pear**.
pare (pâr) *verb,* **pared, paring.**

parent **1.** A father or mother. **2.** A living thing, as an animal or plant, that has produced offspring.
par·ent (pâr′ənt) *noun, plural* **parents.**

parenthesis Either one of two curved lines, ( ), that are used to enclose and set apart a word or group of words in a sentence. Parentheses are also used to enclose numbers and mathematical symbols.
pa·ren·the·sis (pə ren′thə sis) *noun, plural* **parentheses** (pə ren′ thə sēz′).

parish **1.** An area that has its own church and minister or priest. **2.** The people who live in this area and belong to this church.
par·ish (par′ish) *noun, plural* **parishes.**

park **1.** A piece of land, often having benches, trees, paths, and playgrounds, used by people for enjoyment and recreation. **2.** A large area of land that is left in its natural state by the government. *Noun.*
—To leave an automobile or other vehicle in a place for a time. We *parked* the car next to the supermarket and went in. *Verb.*
park (pärk) *noun, plural* **parks;** *verb,* **parked, parking.**

parka A warm fur or cloth jacket with a hood. Eskimo often wear fur parkas.
par·ka (pär′kə) *noun, plural* **parkas.**

parkway A highway or wide road with trees, bushes, or grass planted along it.
park·way (pärk′wā′) *noun, plural* **parkways.**

parliament **1.** A group of people who make the laws of a country. A parliament also chooses the leaders of a government. **2.** Parliament. A group like this in Great Britain or Canada.
par·lia·ment (pär′lə mənt) *noun, plural* **parliaments.**

parlor **1.** A room in a house used for entertaining. **2.** A room or rooms used as a shop. An ice cream *parlor* opened in town.
par·lor (pär′lər) *noun, plural* **parlors.**

Word History

The word **parlor** comes from an old French word for a place in a monastery where a monk could talk to a visitor. The old French word came from a Latin word meaning "to talk."

---

parochial Of or run by a church or parish. Our neighborhood has a public school and *parochial* school.
pa·ro·chi·al (pə rō′kē əl) *adjective.*

parole The release of a person from prison before his or her full sentence has been served. People are usually put on parole for good behavior, and they must then obey certain rules for a time. *Noun.*
—To release a person from prison before his or her full sentence is served. The burglar was *paroled* after four years in prison. *Verb.*
pa·role (pə rōl′) *noun, plural* **paroles;** *verb,* **paroled, paroling.**

parrot A bird with a wide, curved bill, a long, pointed tail, and glossy, brightly colored feathers. Some parrots can imitate speech and other sounds. Parrots are sometimes kept as pets. *Noun.*
—To repeat or imitate what someone else has said without thinking about it or understanding it. The little child *parroted* everything the older children said. *Verb.*
par·rot (par′ət) *noun, plural* **parrots;** *verb,* **parroted, parroting.**

parrot

parsley A small herb with leaves that are used to flavor and decorate food.
pars·ley (pär′slē) *noun, plural* **parsleys.**

parsnip The thick, white root of a plant that is related to the carrot. This root is cooked and eaten as a vegetable.
pars·nip (pär′snip) *noun, plural* **parsnips.**

parson A member of the Protestant clergy who is in charge of a church; minister.
par·son (pär′sən) *noun, plural* **parsons.**

part **1.** Something less than the whole. We liked the last *part* of the movie the best. I ate only *part* of my dinner. **2.** A piece that helps make up a machine or device. The technician replaced the broken *part* in the

at; āpe; fär; câre; end; mē; it; īce; pîerce; hot; ōld; sông, fôrk; oil; out; up; ūse; rüle; pùll; tûrn; chin; sing; shop; thin; <u>th</u>is; hw in white; zh in treasure. The symbol ə stands for the unstressed vowel sound in about, taken, pencil, lemon, and circus.

P

computer.   **3.** A share. They all did their *part* to make the picnic a success.   **4.** One of the sides in an argument or contest. When the disagreement started, I took my friend's *part*.   **5.** A line made to divide one's hair when combing it. I used a comb to make my *part* straight.   **6.** A character or role in a movie or play. You can play the *part* of the lawyer in the school play. *Noun.*
—**1.** To separate by coming between; force or hold apart. The referee *parted* the two boxers.   **2.** To go in different directions; separate. They shook hands and *parted* at the corner.   **3.** To comb the hair so as to make it fall on either side of a line. I *part* my hair in the middle. *Verb.*
—In some degree; partly. The sled is *part* mine and *part* yours. *Adverb.*
—Not full or complete; partial. Each of the partners is *part* owner of the store. *Adjective.*
- **to part with.**   To give away; give up. I refused *to part with* the stray kitten.
- **to take part.**   To join with others, as in an activity. I will *take part* in the race.
part (pärt) *noun, plural* **parts;** *verb,* **parted, parting;** *adverb; adjective.*

partial   **1.** Not complete; not total. We have a *partial* list of club members.   **2.** Showing more favor than is fair to one side, person, or group. The umpire should not be *partial* to the home team.   **3.** Having a strong liking; fond. I'm *partial* to plums.
par·tial (pär′shəl) *adjective.*

participate   To join with others; take part. Everyone *participated* in the rally.
par·tic·i·pate (pär tis′ə pāt′) *verb,* **participated, participating.**

participle   A form of a verb that is used with a helping verb to form certain tenses. A participle also can act as a noun or adjective. In the sentence "I am going to the movies now that my homework is finished," the words "going" and "finished" are participles.
par·ti·ci·ple (pär′tə sip′əl) *noun, plural* **participles.**

particle   A very small bit or piece of something. A *particle* of dirt flew into my eye.
par·ti·cle (pär′ti kəl) *noun, plural* **particles.**

particular   **1.** Taken by itself; apart from others. This *particular* suitcase is too small for me.   **2.** Having to do with some one person or thing. This artist's *particular* talent is drawing plants.   **3.** Unusual in some way; special. That book should be of *particular* interest to you.   **4.** Very careful about details; hard to please. I'm *particular* about keeping my room neat. *Adjective.*

—A single and separate fact or part; detail. All the *particulars* of the robbery were in the morning paper. *Noun.*
par·tic·u·lar (pər tik′yə lər) *adjective; noun, plural* **particulars.**

partition   A wall or panel that divides space. We use a movable *partition* to make two separate areas in our classroom. *Noun.*
—**1.** To divide into parts. The large farm was *partitioned* into small lots for houses.   **2.** To separate by a wall or panel. The workers *partitioned* off a small room in the basement for the washing machine and dryer. *Verb.*
par·ti·tion (pär tish′ən) *noun, plural* **partitions;** *verb,* **partitioned, partitioning.**

Partitions create private offices.

partly   In some degree; to some extent; in part. You were *partly* to blame for my being late.
part·ly (pärt′lē) *adverb.*

partner   **1.** A person who runs a business with one or more other persons and who shares the profits and losses of the business. My mother and my uncle are *partners* in a law firm.   **2.** A person who plays with another person on the same side in a game. My classmate and I were tennis *partners* today.   **3.** A person who dances with another. Choose a *partner* for the first dance.
part·ner (pärt′nər) *noun, plural* **partners.**

partnership A business that is run by two or more persons who share the profits and losses. The bakery on the corner is a *partnership* run by three friends.
part·ner·ship (pärt′nər ship′) *noun, plural* **partnerships.**

part of speech A class of words that have the same purpose when used in sentences. The eight parts of speech into which the English language is divided are noun, pronoun, adjective, verb, adverb, preposition, conjunction, and interjection. Many words can be used as more than one part of speech.

partridge 1. A plump bird that is hunted as game. Partridges have gray, brown, and white feathers.
2. Another word for **quail.** Look up **quail** for more information.
par·tridge (pär′trij) *noun, plural* **partridge** or **partridges.**

partridge

part-time For only part of the usual working time. I tried to get a *part-time* job working Saturdays at the grocery store. *Adjective.*
—On a part-time schedule. Some students work *part-time* after school. *Adverb.*
part-time (pärt′tīm′) *adjective; adverb.*

party 1. A gathering of people to have a good time. Are you haveing a birthday *party?* 2. A group of people who are doing something together. A search *party* went through the woods looking for the lost child. 3. An organization working to gain political power or control. Each political *party* chose a candidate for office. 4. A person who takes part in an action or plan. I refused to be a *party* to their practical joke. 5. A person. The *party* I telephoned was not there.
par·ty (pär′tē) *noun, plural* **parties.**

pass 1. To go past; move or go by. I *pass* the park on my way to school. The hours *passed* slowly. 2. To go from one place or state to another; move. Many thoughts *passed* through my mind as I waited. 3. To hand or move from one person to another. Please *pass* the salt. The center *passed* the basketball to the forward. 4. To complete a test or course of study with success. To become a lifeguard, you have to *pass* a swimming test. 5. To come to an end. The storm raged for an hour and then *passed.* 6. To use or spend time. As I waited, I *passed* the time by reading a magazine. 7. To approve or make into law. The Senate *passed* the bill quickly. 8. To happen. Tell me everything that *passed* at the meeting. *Verb.*
—1. A written permission. No one was allowed to enter the building without showing a *pass.* 2. A free ticket. The prize in the contest was two *passes* to a baseball game. 3. A gap or passage in a mountain range. 4. A moving or throwing of a ball from one player to another. The quarterback made a long *pass* to another player on the team. *Noun.*
• **to pass away** or **to pass on.** To die. My grandparents have *passed away.*
• **to pass out.** 1. To distribute; give out. The teacher *passed out* books to everyone in the class. 2. To lose consciousness; faint. Several marchers in the parade *passed out* from the heat.
pass (pas) *verb,* **passed, passing;** *noun, plural* **passes.**

passage 1. A short part of a piece of music or writing. The teacher read a *passage* from a long poem. 2. A route, path, or other way by which a person or thing can pass. The prisoners escaped by using an underground *passage.* 3. A trip or voyage. The ship's *passage* across the Atlantic was rough. 4. A passing or moving. The *passage* of time in the play was shown by dimming the lights. 5. A making into law; approval. *Passage* of the bill in Congress seemed certain.
pas·sage (pas′ij) *noun, plural* **passages.**

passageway A way along which a person or thing can pass. You can cross the highway safely by using an underground *passageway.*
pas·sage·way (pas′ij wā′) *noun, plural* **passageways.**

passenger A person who travels in an automobile, bus, airplane, or other vehicle.
pas·sen·ger (pas′ən jər) *noun, plural* **passengers.**

passing 1. Going or moving by. Many people watched the *passing* parade. The family grew richer with the *passing* years. 2. Not lasting; brief. My classmate had a *passing* interest in video games. 3. Given or done quickly, without pausing. After a *passing* glance at my identification card, the

at; āpe; fär; câre; end; mē; it; ice; pîerce; hot; ōld; sông, fôrk; oil; out; up; ūse; rüle; pùll; tûrn; chin; sing; shop; thin; this; hw in white; zh in treasure. The symbol ə stands for the unstressed vowel sound in about, taken, pencil, lemon, and circus.

P

guard let me in.   **4.** Allowing one to pass a test or course of study. Try to get at least a *passing* grade on the test. *Adjective.*
—A going by or past. With the *passing* of summer, the weather turns cool. *Noun.*
 pass·ing (pas′ing) *adjective; noun, plural* **passings.**

passion   **1.** A very strong feeling. Love, hate, and anger are passions.   **2.** A very strong liking. Everyone in the fan club has a *passion* for baseball.
 pas·sion (pash′ən) *noun, plural* **passions.**

passionate   Having, showing, or resulting from very strong feelings. The mayor delivered a *passionate* speech today about the need for a new high school.
 pas·sion·ate (pash′ə nit) *adjective.*

Passover   A Jewish holiday celebrated for seven or eight days in March or April. Passover celebrates the anniversary of the Jews' escape from slavery in Egypt.
 Pass·o·ver (pas′ō′vər) *noun.*

passport   A document given to a person to show what country the person is a citizen of. It helps to identify a person traveling in foreign countries.
 pass·port (pas′pôrt′) *noun, plural* **passports.**

password   A secret word or phrase that a person must say to be allowed to pass a guard.
 pass·word (pas′wûrd′) *noun, plural* **passwords.**

past   **1.** Gone by; ended; over. Vacation is *past. Past* events are described in history books.   **2.** Gone by just before the present time; just ended. I've seen three movies in the *past* week.   **3.** Of time gone by; former. Our neighbor is a *past* mayor of the town. *Adjective.*
—**1.** A time that has gone by. Dinosaurs lived in the distant *past.*   **2.** Things that have happened; history. We studied our state's *past.*   **3.** The past tense. Look up **past tense** for more information. *Noun.*
—Beyond in place, time, or amount. The pitcher threw the ball *past* the catcher. My grandparents are *past* seventy. *Preposition.*
—So as to pass or go by. We watched the train roll *past. Adverb.*
 past (past) *adjective; noun, plural* **pasts;** *preposition; adverb.*

pasta   A food made from flour paste or dough. Macaroni and spaghetti are pasta.
 pas·ta (pä′stə) *noun.*

paste   **1.** A mixture used to stick things together. Paste is usually made of flour and water.   **2.** Any soft, smooth, very thick mix-

ture. The cook put tomato *paste* into the spaghetti sauce. *Noun.*
—**1.** To stick with paste. We decided to *paste* the photographs into an album.   **2.** To cover with something stuck on with paste. The students *pasted* the walls of the classroom with travel posters. *Verb.*
 paste (pāst) *noun, plural* **pastes;** *verb,* **pasted, pasting.**

pastel   **1.** A crayon that is like chalk. Pastels are used in drawing.   **2.** A picture drawn with such crayons.   **3.** A pale, soft shade of a color. *Noun.*
—**1.** Drawn with pastels.   **2.** Having a pale, soft shade. The towel was a *pastel* blue. *Adjective.*
 pas·tel (pas tel′) *noun, plural* **pastels;** *adjective.*

drawing with **pastels**

pasteurize   To heat milk or other liquids to a specific temperature for a given period of time. The heat kills germs that may be living in the milk.
 pas·teur·ize (pas′chə rīz′) *verb,* **pasteurized, pasteurizing.**

Word History

The word **pasteurize** comes from the name of Louis *Pasteur.* Louis Pasteur was a French scientist who lived from 1822 to 1895. He discovered this way of killing certain germs in milk without changing its taste or food value.

pastime   Something that makes time pass in a pleasant and happy way. We played word games in the car as a *pastime* during the long drive.

pas·time (pas′tīm′) *noun, plural* **pastimes.**

pastor A minister or priest in charge of a parish or church.

pas·tor (pas′tər) *noun, plural* **pastors.**

past participle A form of a verb that can be used with an auxiliary verb to show that an action or condition is completed. In the sentences "They had already gone," and "I have been sick," "gone" and "been" are past participles.

pastry 1. Pies, tarts, and other sweet baked goods. 2. Crust made of dough. The meat pie was topped with a layer of *pastry.*

pas·try (pās′trē) *noun, plural* **pastries.**

past tense A form of a verb that shows that an action happened or that a condition existed in the past. In the sentence "We drove to the city yesterday," the verb "drove" is in the past tense. In the sentence "I felt sick last night," the verb "felt" is in the past tense. The past tense is also called the **past.**

pasture 1. A field or other piece of land on which cows, horses, sheep, or other animals graze. 2. Grass and other growing plants that animals feed on. This valley provides excellent *pasture* for livestock. *Noun.*
—To put animals in a pasture to graze. The farmer *pastured* the ponies. *Verb.*

pas·ture (pas′chər) *noun, plural* **pastures;** *verb,* **pastured, pasturing.**

pat To tap or stroke gently with the hand. I *patted* my dog when it obeyed. *Verb.*
—1. A gentle tap or stroke. The child finished the mud pie with three *pats.* 2. A small, flat slice. The cook topped the stack of pancakes with a *pat* of butter. *Noun.*

pat (pat) *verb,* **patted, patting;** *noun, plural* **pats.**

patch 1. A small piece of material. Patches are often used to cover holes or worn spots in clothing. They are also used as decorations, badges, or bandages. I sewed a *patch* over the hole in my blue jeans. The pirate captain wore a *patch* over one eye. 2. A small area that is different from what is around it. The car skidded on a *patch* of ice. 3. A small piece of ground where something grows. The children went out to pick berries in the strawberry *patch. Noun.*
—1. To cover or repair with a patch; put a patch on. You can *patch* the hole in the elbow of your sweater. 2. To fix or put together in a hasty or careless way. We tried to *patch* the engine in the car. *Verb.*

• **to patch up.** To smooth over; settle. We *patched up* our quarrel and became friends again.

patch (pach) *noun, plural* **patches;** *verb,* **patched, patching.**

patchwork Pieces of cloth of different colors and shapes that are sewed together. The quilt was a *patchwork.*

patch·work (pach′wûrk′) *noun.*

patent A piece of paper issued to a person or company by the government. It gives someone the right to be the only one to make, use, or sell a new invention for a certain number of years. The engineer took out a *patent* on the new motor. *Noun.*
—To get a patent for. The company *patented* the new machine so that no one else would be able to make it. *Verb.*

pat·ent (pat′ənt) *noun, plural* **patents;** *verb,* **patented, patenting.**

patent leather A leather with a very smooth and shiny surface. The child's shoes were made of black *patent leather.*

paternal 1. Of or like a father. The old storekeeper had *paternal* feelings for the little child. 2. Related through one's father. My *paternal* grandparents come from China.

pa·ter·nal (pə tûr′nəl) *adjective.*

path 1. A trail or way for walking. We had to shovel a *path* through the snow to our garage. 2. The line along which a person or thing moves. The scientist traced the *path* of the comet around the sun.

path (path) *noun, plural* **paths.**

pathetic Causing pity or sorrow. The wet, frightened puppy was a *pathetic* sight.

pa·thet·ic (pə thet′ik) *adjective.*

patience The quality or fact of being able to put up with hardship, pain, trouble, or delay without getting angry or upset. The crowd showed great *patience* as they waited in the rain to buy tickets to the movie.

pa·tience (pā′shəns) *noun.*

patient Having or showing an ability to put up with hardship, pain, trouble, or delay without getting angry or upset. I tried to be *patient* while I waited in the line at the post office. The teacher repeated the instructions several times in a *patient* voice. *Adjective.*

at; āpe; fär; câre; end; mē; it; ice; pîerce; hot; ōld; sông, fôrk; oil; out; up; ūse; rüle; pull; tûrn; chin; sing; shop; thin; this; hw in white; zh in treasure. The symbol ə stands for the unstressed vowel sound in about, taken, pencil, lemon, and circus.

—A person who is under the care or treatment of a doctor. *Noun.*
pa·tient (pā′shənt) *adjective; noun, plural* **patients.**

patio 1. A paved outdoor space for cooking, eating, and relaxing. Our neighbors have a barbecue on their *patio* every weekend. 2. An inner court or yard that has no roof and is open to the sky. Many houses in Spain and Latin America are built around patios.
pat·i·o (pat′ē ō′) *noun, plural* **patios.**

patriarch 1. The father and head of a family or tribe. 2. An old man who is respected and honored. Many people go to the *patriarch* of the village for advice.
pa·tri·arch (pā′trē ärk′) *noun, plural* **patriarchs.**

patriot A person who loves his or her country and defends or supports it. We studied the lives of many American *patriots.*
pa·tri·ot (pā′trē ət) *noun, plural* **patriots.**

patriotic Characterized by or showing love and loyal support of one's country. The parade for the Fourth of July was planned by a group of *patriotic* citizens.
pa·tri·ot·ic (pā′trē ot′ik) *adjective.*

patriotism Love and loyal support of one's country. A time of war is a great test of a people's *patriotism.*
pa·tri·ot·ism (pā′trē ə tiz′əm) *noun.*

Word History

Patriotism goes back to the Latin word for "native land." Someone who has patriotism has a sense of pride in the land or country of his or her birth.

---

patrol To go through or around an area to guard it or make sure that everything is all right. The mayor promised that extra police cars would *patrol* the neighborhood. *Verb.*
—1. A going through or around an area to guard it or make sure that everything is all right. The scouts went on *patrol* to find enemy troops. 2. A group of people or vehicles that do this. The night *patrol* of the building is made up of two guards. *Noun.*
pa·trol (pə trōl′) *verb,* **patrolled, patrolling;** *noun, plural* **patrols.**

patron 1. A person who regularly shops at a particular store or regularly uses the services of a particular business establishment. Some of this restaurant's *patrons* have been coming to it for more than twenty years. 2. A person, especially one who is rich or powerful, who supports or helps another person, a group, or a cause. That banker who gave money to build the new concert hall has always been a *patron* of the arts.
pa·tron (pā′trən) *noun, plural* **patrons.**

patronize To shop at or use the services of regularly. We *patronize* the grocery on the corner.
pa·tron·ize (pā′trə nīz′) *verb,* **patronized, patronizing.**

pattern 1. The way in which colors, shapes, or lines are arranged or repeated in some order; design. The wallpaper was printed with a pretty flower *pattern.* 2. A guide or model to be followed when making something. The kit for sewing a dress included a *pattern.* 3. A set of actions or qualities that is repeated or that does not change. The scientist noticed *patterns* in the way the animals in the experiment behaved. *Noun.*
—To make according to a pattern. I decided to *pattern* my singing style after my favorite singer. *Verb.*
pat·tern (pat′ərn) *noun, plural* **patterns;** *verb,* **patterned, patterning.**

patty 1. A small, round, flat piece of chopped or ground food. We had hamburger *patties* for lunch. 2. A small, flat piece of candy.
pat·ty (pat′ē) *noun, plural* **patties.**

pauper A very poor person, especially one supported by charity or welfare. The state's laws provide for the care of *paupers.*
pau·per (pô′pər) *noun, plural* **paupers.**

pause To stop for a short time. The grown-ups *paused* to let the children catch up. *Verb.*
—A short stop or rest. After a *pause* because of rain, the game continued. *Noun.*
pause (pôz) *verb,* **paused, pausing;** *noun, plural* **pauses.**

pave To cover a road or street with a hard surface. The workers were paving the road.
pave (pāv) *verb,* **paved, paving.**

pavement A hard covering or surface for a street, road, or sidewalk. A pavement is usually made from concrete or asphalt.
pave·ment (pāv′mənt) *noun, plural* **pavements.**

pavilion 1. A building or other structure that is used for a show or exhibit, or for recreation. A pavilion often has open sides. The dance was held at a *pavilion* in the park. 2. One of a group of buildings, such as those that make up a hospital.
pa·vil·ion (pə vil′yən) *noun, plural* **pavilions.**

paw The foot of an animal that has four feet and nails or claws. Dogs and cats have paws. *Noun.*

—**1.** To strike or scrape something with a paw or a hoof. The angry bull *pawed* the ground and then charged toward the gate. **2.** To touch or handle roughly, clumsily, or without care. The shoppers *pawed* the fruit that was on sale. *Verb.*
paw (pô) *noun, plural* **paws;** *verb,* **pawed, pawing.**

pawn¹ To leave something valuable with a lender of money in order to get a loan. The lender gets to keep the valuable object if the person who borrowed the money does not pay it back. I *pawned* a watch for ten dollars.
pawn (pôn) *verb,* **pawned, pawning.**

pawn² **1.** One of the pieces used in the game of chess. The pawn is the piece of lowest value used in the game. **2.** A person or thing used by someone to gain some advantage. The robbers used their hostage as a *pawn* to bargain for a safe escape.
pawn (pôn) *noun, plural* **pawns.**

pay **1.** To give money to someone in return for things or work. We had to *pay* fifteen dollars to have the radio fixed. *Pay* the salesperson for the coat. **2.** To give money in order to settle. The driver who was caught speeding had to *pay* a fine. **3.** To be worthwhile or good for someone. It *pays* to get plenty of sleep. **4.** To give or suffer something in return. They *paid* for their bad eating habits by having poor health. **5.** To make or give. I *paid* my cousin a visit in the hospital. Please *pay* attention. *Verb.*
—Money given in return for things or work. The factory workers went on strike because they wanted higher *pay. Noun.*
• **to pay back.** To return what one has borrowed; repay. I want to *pay back* the money you lent me.
pay (pā) *verb,* **paid, paying;** *noun.*

payment **1.** The act of paying. *Payment* has to be made for the television set when it is delivered. **2.** Something that is paid. I ordered some seeds from the catalog and mailed the *payment* in.
pay·ment (pā′mənt) *noun, plural* **payments.**

payroll **1.** A list of people to be paid and the amount that each one is to receive. The company added the new employees' names to the *payroll* as soon as they began working. **2.** The total amount of money to be paid.
pay·roll (pā′rōl′) *noun, plural* **payrolls.**

PE Postal abbreviation for *Prince Edward Island.*

pea A small, round green vegetable. It grows in a pod and is a seed.
pea (pē) *noun, plural* **peas.**

peace **1.** Freedom from fighting or conflict. After the war, a period of *peace* began. **2.** A lack of noise or disorder; quiet or calm. My grandparents love the *peace* and quiet of the country. **3.** Public order and safety. The police department's job is to keep *peace.* ▲ Another word that sounds like this is **piece.**
peace (pēs) *noun.*

peaceful **1.** Free from war or disorder; quiet and calm. Everyone who visited the *peaceful* valley never forgot its beauty. **2.** Liking peace; avoiding fights and disorder. They are *peaceful* people and do not keep an army.
peace·ful (pēs′fəl) *adjective.*

peace pipe A long pipe smoked by North American Indians as a symbol of peace or friendship.

peach **1.** A round, sweet, juicy fruit. It has a fuzzy, yellow or reddish skin. It grows on a tree that is also called a peach. **2.** A yellowish pink color. *Noun.*
—Having a yellowish pink color. *Adjective.*
peach (pēch) *noun, plural* **peaches;** *adjective.*

peacock A large bird that is related to a pheasant. The male peacock has shiny blue feathers on its head, neck, and body. The peacock's tail has bright green and gold feathers with spots like eyes on them. When the peacock raises its tail, its feathers spread out like a fan.
pea·cock (pē′kok′) *noun, plural* **peacocks** or **peacock.**

P

peacock

peak **1.** A high mountain, or the pointed top of a high mountain. We could see the snowy *peaks* in the distance. **2.** A sharp or pointed end or top. If you stand on the *peak* of our roof, you can see the ocean. **3.** The highest point or greatest level. Traffic reached its *peak* during the late afternoon. **4.** The brim or front part of a cap that sticks out. A baseball player's cap has a peak. ▲ Another word that sounds like this is **peek**.
peak (pēk) *noun, plural* **peaks.**

peal A loud, long sound or series of sounds. A *peal* of bells came from the church tower. *Peals* of laughter greeted the clown. *Noun.*
—To sound or ring out in a peal. The church bells *pealed* loudly on Sunday morning. *Verb.* ▲ Another word that sounds like this is **peel**.
peal (pēl) *noun, plural* **peals;** *verb,*
pealed, pealing.

peanut A seed like a nut that grows in a pod under the ground. Peanuts are eaten for food and are also used to make peanut butter. The oil from peanuts is used for cooking.
pea·nut (pē′nut′) *noun, plural* **peanuts.**

peanut butter A soft, creamy food made from ground, roasted peanuts. It is used as a spread on crackers and in sandwiches.

pear A sweet, juicy fruit that grows on trees. Pears are shaped like bells and usually have smooth, yellow, or brown skins. ▲ Other words that sound like this are **pair** and **pare**.
pear (pâr) *noun, plural* **pears.**

pears

pearl **1.** A small, round gem that is white or cream in color and has a soft, glowing shine. Pearls are formed inside the shells of certain kinds of oysters. **2.** Something that looks like a pearl. *Pearls* of dew covered the flowers.
pearl (pûrl) *noun, plural* **pearls.**

peasant A person who works on a farm or owns a small farm.
peas·ant (pez′ənt) *noun, plural* **peasants.**

peat A kind of soil made up of decayed plants. It is found in wet areas and is used as a fertilizer and as fuel.
peat (pēt) *noun.*

pebble A small stone that is usually round and smooth.
peb·ble (peb′əl) *noun, plural* **pebbles.**

pecan A nut that has a sweet taste. It grows on a large tree and has a thin shell.
pe·can (pi kän′ *or* pi kan′) *noun, plural* **pecans.**

peck¹ **1.** A unit of measure used for fruits, vegetables, grains, and other dry things. A peck is equal to eight quarts, or one fourth of a bushel. **2.** A large amount. You'll get into a *peck* of trouble if you break a window.
peck (pek) *noun, plural* **pecks.**

peck² To strike or pick up something with the beak in a short, quick movement. The parakeet *pecked* the bars of its cage. The hen *pecked* at the crumbs. *Verb.*
—**1.** A short, quick stroke made with the beak. The canary gave me a *peck* on the finger. **2.** A quick kiss. The parents gave each child a *peck* on the cheek as the children went to bed. *Noun.*
peck (pek) *verb,* **pecked, pecking;** *noun,*
plural **pecks.**

peculiar **1.** Not usual; strange; queer. It's *peculiar* that the sky is so dark at noon. **2.** Belonging to a certain person, group, place, or thing. The kangaroo is *peculiar* to Australia and New Guinea.
pe·cul·iar (pi kūl′yər) *adjective.*

peculiarity **1.** Something that is peculiar. The *peculiarities* of the old house included a sloping floor and a main entrance in the back. **2.** The quality of being peculiar.
pe·cu·li·ar·i·ty (pi kū′lē ar′i tē) *noun,*
plural **peculiarities.**

pedal A lever or other device that is moved by the foot to run or control something. The pedals on a bicycle make it go. The pedals on a piano change the length and loudness of the notes played. *Noun.*
—To work or use the pedals of something. I *pedaled* my bicycle hard to catch up with the others. *Verb.* ▲ Another word that sounds like this is **peddle**.
ped·al (ped′əl) *noun, plural* **pedals;** *verb,*
pedaled, pedaling.

peddle To carry goods from place to place and offer them for sale. I *peddle* newspapers downtown after school. ▲ Another word that sounds like this is **pedal**.
ped·dle (ped′əl) *verb,* **peddled, peddling.**

peddler A person who travels from place to place with goods for sale. I bought an apple for my lunch from a *peddler* on a street corner.
ped·dler (ped′lər) *noun, plural* **peddlers.**

pedestal **1.** A base on which a column or statue stands. A statue of our first mayor stands upon a marble *pedestal* in front of city hall. **2.** The base or other part of something that supports it. The *pedestal* of the lamp was cracked.

ped·es·tal (ped′ə stəl) *noun, plural* **pedestals.**

The statue stands on a **pedestal.**

pedestrian A person who travels on foot; walker. Sidewalks are for *pedestrians.*
ped·es·tri·an (pə des′trē ən) *noun, plural* **pedestrians.**

pediatrician A doctor who takes care of and treats babies and children.
pe·di·a·tri·cian (pē′dē ə trish′ən) *noun, plural* **pediatricians.**

pedigree A line of ancestors; descent. This dog's *pedigree* includes many prize-winning champions.
ped·i·gree (ped′i grē′) *noun, plural* **pedigrees.**

peek To look quickly or secretly. The children were told not to *peek* into the box holding the present. *Verb.*
—A quick or secret look. I took a *peek* in the oven to see what was cooking. *Noun.* ⚊ Another word that sounds like this is **peak.**
peek (pēk) *verb,* **peeked, peeking;** *noun, plural* **peeks.**

peel The skin or outer covering of certain fruits and vegetables. Don't slip on that banana *peel. Noun.*
—1. To take off the skin or outer covering of something. Please *peel* these potatoes.
2. To remove or strip. Can you *peel* the label

off the jar? 3. To come off in pieces or strips. The paint is *peeling* from the walls.
4. To lose or shed an outer covering or layer. My sunburned back is *peeling. Verb.* ⚊ Another word that sounds like this is **peal.**
peel (pēl) *noun, plural* **peels;** *verb,* **peeled, peeling.**

peep¹ 1. To look secretly or quickly through a narrow opening or from a hiding place. The actors *peeped* through an opening in the curtain to see how many people were in the audience. 2. To come slowly or partly into view; show slightly. The moon *peeped* through the clouds. *Verb.*
—A secret or quick look. The children took a *peep* at the rabbit through the bushes so they would not frighten it. *Noun.*
peep (pēp) *verb,* **peeped, peeping;** *noun, plural* **peeps.**

peep² A short, sharp sound like that made by a young bird or chicken. We could hear the *peep* of the chicks in the barn. *Noun.*
—To make a peep. The chicks *peeped* as we let them out of the box. *Verb.*
peep (pēp) *noun, plural* **peeps;** *verb,* **peeped, peeping.**

peer¹ 1. A person who is the same as another in age, status, or ability; equal. As a baseball player, our star pitcher has few *peers.* 2. A member of British nobility. ⚊ Another word that sounds like this is **pier.**
peer (pîr) *noun, plural* **peers.**

peer² 1. To look hard or closely, as if trying to see something clearly. The scientist *peered* at the slide through a microscope. 2. To come slightly into view. The sun *peered* over the mountain. ⚊ Another word that sounds like this is **pier.**
peer (pîr) *verb,* **peered, peering.**

peg A piece of wood, metal, or other material that can be fitted or driven into a surface. Pegs are used to fasten parts together, to hang things on, or to mark the score in a game. *Noun.*
—To fasten with pegs. We watched the workers *peg* down the circus tents. *Verb.*
peg (peg) *noun, plural* **pegs;** *verb,* **pegged, pegging.**

P.E.I. An abbreviation for *Prince Edward Island.*

at; āpe; fär; câre; end; mē; it; īce; pîerce; hot; ōld; sông, fôrk; oil; out; up; ūse; rüle; pull; tûrn; chin; sing; shop; thin; this; hw in white; zh in treasure. The symbol ə stands for the unstressed vowel sound in about, taken, pencil, lemon, and circus.

539

Pekingese A small dog with a long, silky coat. It has a flat, wrinkled face. The Pekingese originated in China.
Pe·king·ese (pē′kə nēz′ *or* pē′king ēz′) *noun, plural* **Pekingese.**

pelican A large bird that lives near the water and has a pouch under its long bill. A pelican uses this pouch to catch and store fish.
pel·i·can (pel′i kən) *noun, plural* **pelicans.**

pelican

pellet A small, hard ball of something. I put food *pellets* in the cage for my pet mice. *Pellets* of ice hit the windshield as we drove through the storm.
pel·let (pel′it) *noun, plural* **pellets.**

pell-mell In a jumbled or confused way. Clothing had been thrown *pell-mell* into the closet. The frightened pickpocket ran *pell-mell* through the crowd.
pell-mell (pel′mel′) *adverb.*

pelt¹ To strike over and over with small hard things. The children *pelted* each other with snowballs. Hail *pelted* the roof.
pelt (pelt) *verb,* **pelted, pelting.**

pelt² The skin of an animal with its fur or hair still on it. Pelts are used to make clothing and rugs.
pelt (pelt) *noun, plural* **pelts.**

pen¹ A long, thin tool for writing or drawing with ink.
pen (pen) *noun, plural* **pens.**

pen² **1.** A small, fenced yard for cows, pigs, sheep, or other animals. **2.** Any small area that is enclosed. *Noun.*
—To hold or shut up in a pen. The farmer *penned* the horses. *Verb.*
pen (pen) *noun, plural* **pens;** *verb,* **penned, penning.**

penalize To give a penalty or punishment to. The referee *penalized* the football team for taking too much time between plays.
pe·nal·ize (pē′nə līz′) *verb,* **penalized, penalizing.**

penalty **1.** A punishment. The *penalty* for illegal parking in this city is a fine of thirty dollars. **2.** A disadvantage or punishment placed on a player or team for breaking the rules. The referee called a *penalty* of five yards against the team.
pen·al·ty (pen′əl tē) *noun, plural* **penalties.**

pencil A long, thin tool for writing or drawing. It is usually made of a stick of graphite enclosed in a case of wood. *Noun.*
—To write, draw, or mark with a pencil. I *penciled* in the form. *Verb.*
pen·cil (pen′səl) *noun, plural* **pencils;** *verb,* **penciled, penciling.**

pendant An ornament that hangs from something. Jewels or lockets are often worn as pendants.
pend·ant (pen′dənt) *noun, plural* **pendants.**

pendulum A weight that is hung from a fixed point in such a way that it can swing back and forth. Pendulums are used in some clocks.
pen·du·lum (pen′jə ləm) *noun, plural* **pendulums.**

a clock with a **pendulum**

penetrate **1.** To go into or pass through. The sword *penetrated* the knight's shield. The headlights of the car could not *penetrate* the thick evening fog. **2.** To find the meaning of; understand. Science tries to *penetrate* the mysteries of nature.
pen·e·trate (pen′i trāt′) *verb,* **penetrated, penetrating.**

penguin A bird whose feathers are black or gray on the back and white on the front. Penguins cannot fly. Their wings look like flippers and are used for swimming. Most of them live in or near Antarctica.

pen·guin (pen′gwin *or* peng′gwin) *noun, plural* **penguins.**

penicillin   A powerful drug that destroys bacteria and is used to treat many diseases. It is made from a fungus mold.

pen·i·cil·lin (pen′ə sil′ən) *noun.*

peninsula   A piece of land that sticks out into water from a larger body of land. The southern part of Florida is a peninsula.

pen·in·su·la (pə nin′sə lə *or* pə nin′syə lə) *noun, plural* **peninsulas.**

Word History

The word **peninsula** goes back to two Latin words that mean "almost" and "island."

---

penitentiary   A prison for people who have been found guilty of serious crimes.

pen·i·ten·tia·ry (pen′i ten′shə rē) *noun, plural* **penitentiaries.**

penknife   A small pocketknife, once used to make and sharpen quill pens.

pen·knife (pen′nīf′) *noun, plural* **penknives** (pen′nīvz′).

penmanship   The art or a style of handwriting.

pen·man·ship (pen′mən ship′) *noun.*

Penn. or **Penna.**   An abbreviation for *Pennsylvania.*

pen name   A made-up name that an author uses instead of his or her real name. The *pen name* of Samuel Clemens was Mark Twain.

pennant   A long, narrow flag that is shaped like a triangle. Pennants are used for signaling and as emblems, decorations, and prizes.

pen·nant (pen′ənt) *noun, plural* **pennants.**

penniless   Having no money at all. After paying all my bills, I was *penniless.*

pen·ni·less (pen′i lis) *adjective.*

Pennsylvania   A state in the eastern United States. Its capital is Harrisburg.

Penn·syl·va·nia (pen′səl vān′yə) *noun.*

Word History

The word **Pennsylvania** comes from the last name of William *Penn* and a Latin word meaning "woods." King Charles II of England named this colony when he gave it to William Penn.

---

penny   **1.** A coin that is worth one cent. It is used in the United States and Canada. One hundred pennies equal one dollar.   **2.** A British coin. One hundred pennies equal one pound.

pen·ny (pen′ē) *noun, plural* **pennies** .

pension   A sum of money that is paid regularly to a retired or disabled person. Many companies pay pensions to people who retire after working for them for a long time.

pen·sion (pen′shən) *noun, plural* **pensions.**

pentagon   A figure that has five sides.

pen·ta·gon (pen′tə gon′) *noun, plural* **pentagons.**

penthouse   An apartment or house built on the roof of a building.

pent·house (pent′hous′) *noun, plural* **penthouses** (pent′hou′ziz).

peony   A garden plant with large pink, red, or white flowers.

pe·o·ny (pē′ə nē) *noun, plural* **peonies.**

peonies

people   **1.** Men, women, and children; persons. This theater can seat 500 *people.*   **2.** All of the persons making up a nation, race, tribe, or group. The museum exhibit shows the crafts of African *peoples.* Many of the *people* of Israel originally came from other lands.   **3.** The public; persons in general. This country was founded on a belief in government by the *people.*   **4.** Family; relatives. My teacher's *people* came from Cuba. *Noun.*
—To fill with people; inhabit. A great number of human beings *people* the earth. *Verb.*

peo·ple (pē′pəl) *noun, plural* **people** or **peoples** *(for definition 2); verb,* **peopled, peopling.**

pep   A lively, vital quality; activity; spirit. After the brisk walk outside, I was full of *pep. Noun.*

---

at; āpe; fär; câre; end; mē; it; īce; pîerce; hot; ōld; sông, fôrk; oil; out; up; ūse; rūle; pùll; tûrn; chin; sing; shop; thin; <u>th</u>is; hw in white; zh in treasure. The symbol ə stands for the unstressed vowel sound in about, taken, pencil, lemon, and circus.

P

—To make lively or energetic. Whenever I need to be *pepped* up I do some exercises. *Verb.*

pep (pep) *noun; verb,* **pepped, pepping.**

pepper   **1.** A spice that is used to flavor foods. Black pepper is ground from the whole, dried berries of a tropical plant. White pepper comes from the seeds inside these berries.   **2.** The hollow green, red, or yellow fruit of any of a group of plants. The fruit of many plants can be eaten and may be sweet or hot. *Noun.*

—**1.** To flavor with pepper. The cook salted and *peppered* the fried eggs.   **2.** To cover or sprinkle. The gardener *peppered* the ground with grass seed. *Verb.*

pep·per (pep′ər) *noun, plural* **peppers;** *verb,* **peppered, peppering.**

peppermint   **1.** A kind of mint plant. The oil from peppermint leaves is used in medicine and to flavor candy, chewing gum, and toothpaste.   **2.** A candy that is flavored with peppermint oil.

pep·per·mint (pep′ər mint′) *noun, plural* **peppermints.**

per   For each. My summer job paid sixty dollars *per* week.

per (pûr *or unstressed* pər) *preposition.*

perceive   **1.** To become aware of through seeing, hearing, tasting, smelling, or feeling. I *perceived* a faint knocking at the door. **2.** To understand; comprehend. The teacher soon *perceived* that the students did not understand the explanation.

per·ceive (pər sēv′) *verb,* **perceived, perceiving.**

percent   The number of parts in every hundred. Two *percent* of fifty is one. Twenty *percent* of the class was out sick with chicken pox. The symbol for "percent" when it is written with a number is %. For example, "five percent" is also written "5%."

per·cent (pər sent′) *noun.*

percentage   **1.** The proportion of something, expressed as the number of hundredths. What *percentage* of the class passed the test?   **2.** A part of a whole; portion. A large *percentage* of students walk to school.

per·cent·age (pər sen′tij) *noun, plural* **percentages.**

perception   **1.** The act or power of perceiving. A cat's *perception* of colors is poor. **2.** The understanding, comprehension, or knowledge that is the result of perceiving. The astronauts' *perception* of the problems that arose during their flight saved their lives.

per·cep·tion (pər sep′shən) *noun, plural* **perceptions.**

perch¹   **1.** A bar, branch, or anything else a bird can rest on. Our pet canary uses a swinging bar in its cage as a *perch.*   **2.** Any raised place for sitting or standing. The lifeguard watched the swimmers from a *perch* above the pool. *Noun.*

—To sit or rest on a perch. The bird *perched* on the fence. The cat loved to *perch* itself on a window ledge in the sun. *Verb.*

perch (pûrch) *noun, plural* **perches;** *verb,* **perched, perching.**

perch²   **1.** A small fish that is found in fresh water in North America and most parts of Europe. It is used for food.   **2.** A similar fish that lives in salt water.

perch (pûrch) *noun, plural* **perch** or **perches.**

perch²

percussion   **1.** The striking of one thing against another with force; collision. Over a long time, the *percussion* of shoes on stone wore out the pavement.   **2.** The sound or vibration that results when one thing strikes another with force. We could hear the *percussion* of the waves on the rocks.

per·cus·sion (pər kush′ən) *noun.*

percussion instrument   A musical instrument that is played by striking one thing against another. The drum, cymbal, and xylophone, are percussion instruments.

perennial   **1.** Lasting or existing through the year or through many years. The ice in this cave is *perennial.*   **2.** Lasting for a long time; enduring. Peace is a *perennial* dream. **3.** Of plants, living more than two years. Roses are *perennial* plants. *Adjective.*

—A plant that lives and produces flowers for more than two years. This part of the garden is full of *perennials. Noun.*

per·en·ni·al (pə ren′ē əl) *adjective; noun, plural* **perennials.**

perfect   **1.** Without a mistake or fault. This *perfect* apple doesn't have one bruise or bad spot.   **2.** Not missing anything; complete; exact. You can draw a *perfect* circle with the use of a compass. The picture the artist drew was a *perfect* likeness of my mother. **3.** Very great. My father told me that I was making a *perfect* nuisance of myself. *Adjective.*

—To make or complete without any mistakes or faults. I went to Mexico to *perfect* my Spanish. *Verb.*
per·fect (pûr′fikt *for adjective;* pər fekt′ *for verb*) *adjective; verb,* **perfected, perfecting.**

perfection **1.** The condition of being perfect or without fault; excellence. The athlete practiced the dive over and over, striving for *perfection.* **2.** The act or process of making perfect. The *perfection* of a ballet dancer's ·technique takes many years of practice.
per·fec·tion (pər fek′shən) *noun.*

perfectly **1.** In an excellent way; without fault. That suit fits you *perfectly.* **2.** Completely; entirely. I had a *perfectly* wonderful time at the party.
per·fect·ly (pûr′fikt lē) *adverb.*

perforate To make a hole or holes through. We *perforated* the box with a pencil so the kitten could breathe more easily. Sheets of stamps are *perforated* to make it easy to tear off one or two at a time.
per·fo·rate (pûr′fə rāt′) *verb,* **perforated, perforating.**

perform **1.** To carry out; do. A soldier is trained to *perform* certain duties. The doctor *performed* a difficult operation. **2.** To sing, act, or do something in public that requires skill. Our band *performed* at the game.
per·form (pər fôrm′) *verb,* **performed, performing.**

performance **1.** A public presentation of something meant to entertain. The audience enjoyed last night's *performance* of the school play. **2.** The act of carrying out an action. You may watch the factory workers, but don't interfere with the *performance* of their jobs. **3.** The way in which something works; operation. The advertisement said that the *performance* of the car had been tested on rough country roads.
per·form·ance (pər fôr′məns) *noun, plural* **performances.**

performer A person who sings, acts, or does some form of entertainment in public. Dancers and clowns are performers.
per·form·er (pər fôr′mər) *noun, plural* **performers.**

perfume **1.** A liquid that is used to give people or things a pleasant smell. **2.** A pleasant smell. The *perfume* from the flowers filled the room. *Noun.*
—To fill with a pleasant smell. The roses *perfumed* the air. *Verb.*
per·fume (pûr′fūm *or* pər fūm′ *for noun;* pər fūm′ *for verb*) *noun, plural* **perfumes;** *verb,* **perfumed, perfuming.**

perhaps Maybe; possibly. *Perhaps* it will rain tomorrow. I disagree, but *perhaps* you're right.
per·haps (pər haps′) *adverb.*

peril **1.** A chance or risk of harm or loss; danger. A firefighter's life is often in *peril.* **2.** Something dangerous. Crocodiles, quicksand, and hostile natives were some of the *perils* faced by the jungle explorers.
per·il (per′əl) *noun, plural* **perils.**

perimeter The boundary of a figure or an area. The *perimeter* of a square is equal to four times the length of one side.
pe·rim·e·ter (pə rim′i tər) *noun, plural* **perimeters.**

period **1.** A portion of time. A day is a *period* of twenty-four hours. Our team made a goal in the second *period* of the hockey game. **2.** A punctuation mark (.) used at the end of a declarative sentence or an imperative sentence or at the end of an abbreviation.
pe·ri·od (pîr′ē əd) *noun, plural* **periods.**

periodic Happening again and again at regular times. Everyone in our family makes *periodic* visits to the dentist.
pe·ri·od·ic (pîr′ē od′ik) *adjective.*

periodical A magazine that is printed at regular times. Most periodicals come out every week, every month, or every three months.
pe·ri·od·i·cal (pîr′ē od′i kəl) *noun, plural* **periodicals.**

periscope A device that looks like a telescope and sticks out from the top of a submarine. It is used to see ships, land, or other things above the surface of the water.
per·i·scope (per′ə skōp′) *noun, plural* **periscopes.**

perish To be destroyed; die. Many people *perished* when the ship sank.
per·ish (per′ish) *verb,* **perished, perishing.**

perishable Likely to spoil or decay quickly. Milk, meat and other *perishable* foods should be kept in a refrigerator.
per·ish·a·ble (per′i shə bəl) *adjective.*

perjury The act or crime of lying after swearing under oath to tell the truth.
per·ju·ry (pûr′jə rē) *noun, plural* **perjuries.**

P

at; āpe; fär; câre; end; mē; it; īce; pîerce; hot; ōld; sông, fôrk; oil; out; up; ūse; rüle; pu̇ll; tûrn; chin; sing; shop; thin; <u>th</u>is; hw in white; zh in treasure. The symbol ə stands for the unstressed vowel sound in about, taken, pencil, lemon, and circus.

permanent Lasting or meant to last; enduring. After graduating from college, I started looking for a *permanent* job.
per·ma·nent (pûr′mə nənt) *adjective.*

permission A consent from someone in authority. You should ask your parents for *permission* to stay overnight at my house.
per·mis·sion (pər mish′ən) *noun.*

permit To allow or let. My parents will not *permit* me to play outside after it is dark. *Verb.*
—A written order giving permission to do something. You must have a *permit* to fish in this stream. *Noun.*
per·mit (pər mit′ *for verb;* pûr′mit *or* pər mit′ *for noun*) *verb,* **permitted, permitting;** *noun, plural* **permits.**

The beams are **perpendicular** to the upright supports.

perpendicular 1. Straight up and down; upright. The expert mountain climber climbed the *perpendicular* face of the cliffs. 2. At right angles to a given line or surface. The telephone pole is *perpendicular* to the road.
per·pen·dic·u·lar (pûr′pən dik′yə lər) *adjective.*

perpetual 1. Lasting for a very long time or forever. Some of the highest mountains in the world are covered by *perpetual* snow. 2. Continuing without stopping. The *perpetual* rise and fall of the tides is influenced by the moon and sun.
per·pet·u·al (pər pech′ü əl) *adjective.*

perpetuate To keep alive or active; preserve. Holidays *perpetuate* important traditions.
per·pet·u·ate (pər pech′ü āt′) *verb,* **perpetuated, perpetuating.**

perplex To confuse; puzzle. Some words in the poem *perplexed* me, so I asked the teacher what they meant.
per·plex (pər pleks′) *verb,* **perplexed, perplexing.**

persecute To treat continually in a cruel and unjust way. The rebels *persecuted* the people who were loyal to the king.
per·se·cute (pûr′si kūt′) *verb,* **persecuted, persecuting.**

persecution Continual cruel treatment. The refugees fled their country after years of *persecution.*
per·se·cu·tion (pûr′si kū′shən) *noun, plural* **persecutions.**

Persia 1. An ancient empire of southwestern Asia. 2. The former name of **Iran.**
Per·sia (pûr′zhə) *noun.*

Persian 1. A person who lived in ancient Persia. 2. The language of ancient Persia or modern Iran. *Noun.*
—Of or having to do with Persia, its people, or their language. *Adjective.*
Per·sian (pûr′zhən) *noun, plural* **Persians;** *adjective.*

persimmon A round fruit that has thin orange or yellow skin and grows on a tree or shrub. Persimmons are sweet when they are fully ripe.
per·sim·mon (pər sim′ən) *noun, plural* **persimmons.**

persimmons

persist To continue firmly and steadily. The rainy weather *persisted* all week. If you *persist* in misbehaving, you will be punished.
per·sist (pər sist′) *verb,* **persisted, persisting.**

persistent **1.** Continuing firmly and steadily. A *persistent* person does not give up when faced with trouble. **2.** Lasting a long time. I had a *persistent* cough for a month.
per·sist·ent (pər sis′tənt) *adjective.*

person **1.** A man, woman, or child; human being. Every ten years, the government takes an official count of every *person* living in this country. **2.** The body of and clothing worn by a human being. I usually keep a handkerchief somewhere on my *person.* **3.** Any of three groups of personal pronouns and verb forms. The words of the *first person* are used for the speaker or speakers. The words of the *second person* are used for the one or ones spoken to. And the words of the *third person* are used for the one or ones spoken of.
• **in person.** Physically present. The movie star looked better *in person.*
per·son (pûr′sən) *noun, plural* **persons.**

personal **1.** Private; not public. My diary is *personal,* so please don't read it. **2.** Done or made in person. The movie stars made *personal* appearances at the opening of their movie. **3.** Having to do with a person's body. In health class, we learned the importance of *personal* cleanliness.
per·son·al (pûr′sə nəl) *adjective.*

personal computer A small computer for use by one person. Look up **microcomputer** for more information.

personality **1.** All of a person's characteristics, habits, behavior, and other qualities. A person's personality makes him or her different from everybody else. The class chose a student with a friendly *personality* to greet and guide the foreign visitors. **2.** A well-known person. This magazine tells the life stories of television *personalities.*
per·son·al·i·ty (pûr′sə nal′i tē) *noun, plural* **personalities.**

personally **1.** Without the help of others; by oneself. The senator answered my letter *personally.* **2.** As far as oneself is concerned; for oneself. *Personally,* I am in favor of going camping. **3.** As a person or individual. I don't like our neighbor *personally.*
per·son·al·ly (pûr′sə nə lē) *adverb.*

personnel The group of people working for a company or other organization. The *personnel* in this company are given two weeks of vacation a year.
per·son·nel (pûr′sə nel′) *noun.*

perspective **1.** The way in which a picture that is on a flat surface can show objects that seem to be at a distance. **2.** A point of view. From the *perspective* of a child, the house seemed very large. **3.** The relation of things to one another; relative size or importance. If you see things in their proper *perspective,* you won't worry about small matters.
per·spec·tive (pər spek′tiv) *noun, plural* **perspectives.**

Perspective makes the parallel rows of plants appear to meet in the distance.

perspiration **1.** Moisture that is given off through the pores of the skin; sweat. **2.** The process of sweating. When a person's body gets too hot, it cools off through perspiration.
per·spi·ra·tion (pûr′spə rā′shən) *noun.*

perspire To give off perspiration; sweat. I *perspire* when I play tennis on a hot day.
per·spire (pər spīr′) *verb,* **perspired, perspiring.**

persuade To cause to do or believe something by pleading or giving reasons; convince. The principal *persuaded* the students to stop littering the school playground.
per·suade (pər swād′) *verb,* **persuaded, persuading.**

persuasion **1.** The act or power of persuading. I used *persuasion* to get people to contribute to our fund for homeless people. **2.** A firm belief; conviction. People of different religious *persuasions* can still be friends.
per·sua·sion (pər swā′zhən) *noun, plural* **persuasions.**

at; āpe; fär; câre; end; mē; it; īce; pîerce; hot; ōld; sông, fôrk; oil; out; up; ūse; rüle; pùll; tûrn; chin; sing; shop; thin; this; hw in white; zh in treasure. The symbol ə stands for the unstressed vowel sound in about, taken, pencil, lemon, and circus.

P

pertain   **1.** To be connected or related. I have a collection of programs, autographs, and other objects *pertaining* to professional baseball. **2.** To belong. Some important duties *pertain* to that office.
per·tain (pər tān′) *verb,* **pertained, pertaining.**

pertinent   Having to do with what is being discussed or considered; relevant. The weather forecast is *pertinent* because we're planning to have our party in the garden.
per·ti·nent (pûr′tə nənt) *adjective.*

Peru   A country in western South America.
Pe·ru (pə rü′) *noun.*

peso   A unit of money in Mexico and in several South American countries.
pe·so (pā′sō) *noun, plural* **pesos.**

pessimistic   Having a negative attitude about things; expecting the worst. Since our best player was sick, we were all *pessimistic* about winning the game.
pes·si·mis·tic (pes′ə mis′tik) *adjective.*

pest   A person or thing that is troublesome or annoying; nuisance.
pest (pest) *noun, plural* **pests.**

pester   To trouble or bother; annoy again and again. Please don't *pester* me.
pes·ter (pes′tər) *verb,* **pestered, pestering.**

pesticide   A chemical substance used to kill insects, mice, rats, or other animal pests.
pest·i·cide (pes′tə sīd′) *noun, plural* **pesticides.**

pestle   A tool that is shaped like a club. It is used for pounding, grinding, or mixing something in a bowl called a mortar.
pes·tle (pes′əl *or* pes′təl) *noun, plural* **pestles.**

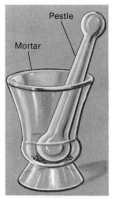

pestle

pet   **1.** An animal that is kept in a person's home for fun and companionship. Dogs, cats, and birds are common pets. **2.** A person who is treated with special kindness or favor; favorite. My friend felt that I was the teacher's *pet.* *Noun.*
—Kept or treated as a pet. My friend has a *pet* rabbit. *Adjective.*
—To stroke or pat in a gentle or loving way. The cat purrs whenever we *pet* it. *Verb.*
pet (pet) *noun, plural* **pets;** *adjective; verb,* **petted, petting.**

petal   One of the parts of a flower. Petals come in many colors and shapes. The *petals* of a daisy are usually white and are arranged in a circle.
pet·al (pet′əl) *noun, plural* **petals.**

petition   A formal request that is made to a person in authority. All the people on our street signed a *petition* asking the city to put a stop sign on the corner. *Noun.*
—To make a formal request to. The students in our school *petitioned* the principal to keep the library open on weekends. *Verb.*
pe·ti·tion (pi tish′ən) *noun, plural* **petitions;** *verb,* **petitioned, petitioning.**

petrify   **1.** To turn into stone. Petrified wood forms when water seeps through the dead wood of fallen trees and leaves minerals inside the wood cells. The minerals eventually take the place of the wood cells when they decay. **2.** To make helpless with fear. The sudden bolt of lightning *petrified* us.
pet·ri·fy (pet′rə fī′) *verb,* **petrified, petrifying.**

petroleum   An oily liquid that is found beneath the surface of the earth. Petroleum is made into gasoline, kerosene, oil for heating buildings, and many other products.
pe·tro·le·um (pi trō′lē əm) *noun.*

Word History

The word **petroleum** comes from two Greek words meaning "rock" and "oil." *Petroleum* is oil that comes from the ground instead of from olives or some other fruit.

petticoat   A skirt that is made to be worn under a dress or outer skirt.
pet·ti·coat (pet′ē kōt′) *noun, plural* **petticoats.**

petty   **1.** Of little value or importance; insignificant. Try not to be upset by *petty* problems. **2.** Mean or intolerant. It's *petty* to gossip about people.
pet·ty (pet′ē) *adjective,* **pettier, pettiest.**

petunia   A garden plant that has flowers that are shaped like trumpets. The flowers come in many colors.
pe·tu·nia (pi tün′yə *or* pi tūn′yə) *noun, plural* **petunias.**

pew   A long bench in church for people to sit on. Pews have backs and are arranged in rows.
pew (pū) *noun, plural* **pews.**

pewter   A metal that is made by combining tin, copper, and other metals. Pewter is used to make plates, pitchers, mugs, and candle-sticks.

pew·ter (pū′tər) *noun.*

pg. An abbreviation for *page.*

phantom Something that appears to be real but is not.

phan·tom (fan′təm) *noun, plural* **phantoms.**

Pharaoh The title of the kings of ancient Egypt.

Phar·aoh (fâr′ō) *noun, plural* **Pharaohs.**

pharmacist A person who is trained to pre-pare and dispense drugs and medicines. I asked my *pharmacist* if the medicine would make me sleepy.

phar·ma·cist (fär′mə sist) *noun, plural* **pharmacists.**

pharmacy A store where drugs and medi-cines are sold; drugstore.

phar·ma·cy (fär′mə sē) *noun, plural* **pharmacies.**

phase **1.** A stage of development. Most ba-bies go through a *phase* when they try to put everything in their mouths. **2.** A part or side; aspect. Advertising, accounting, and selling are some of the *phases* of many busi-nesses. **3.** The appearance and shape of the moon or a planet as it is seen at a particular time, which depends on how much of its lighted side can be seen from the earth.

phase (fāz) *noun, plural* **phases.**

pheasant A large bird that has a long tail and brightly colored feathers. Pheasants live on the ground. Peacocks, partridges and quails are special kinds of pheasants.

pheas·ant (fez′ənt) *noun, plural* **pheasants.**

pheasant

phenomenon **1.** A fact or event that can be seen or sensed. The strange *phenomenon* in the sky was a meteor that exploded. **2.** A person or thing that is extraordinary or re-markable.

phe·nom·e·non (fə nom′ə non′) *noun, plural* **phenomena** or **phenomenons.**

philanthropist A person who helps other people by giving his or her money or time to good causes. The new wing of the museum was paid for by a local *philanthropist.*

phil·an·thro·pist (fə lan′thrə pist) *noun, plural* **philanthropists.**

Philippines A country that is a group of is-lands in southeastern Asia.

Phil·ip·pines (fil′ə pēnz′ *or* fil′ə pēnz′) *noun.*

philodendron A vine that grows in the tropical Americas. There are many different kinds of philodendrons, and they are often grown indoors.

phil·o·den·dron (fil′ə den′drən) *noun, plural* **philodendrons.**

philosopher A person who studies or spe-cializes in philosophy. Philosophers often try to answer basic questions about reality, mat-ter, knowledge, or life.

phi·los·o·pher (fə los′ə fər) *noun, plural* **philosophers.**

philosophy **1.** The study of the basic na-ture of reality, matter, knowledge, and life. **2.** A person's principles and beliefs. My par-ents' *philosophy* is to be kind to others.

phi·los·o·phy (fə los′ə fē) *noun, plural* **philosophies.**

phlox A plant that has groups of small white, pink, red, purple, or blue flowers.

phlox (floks) *noun, plural* **phloxes.**

phlox

phone A tele-phone. *Noun.* —To call on the telephone. Will you please *phone* me tomor-row? *Verb.*

phone (fōn) *noun, plural* **phones;** *verb,* **phoned, phoning.**

phonetic Having to do with or represent-ing speech sounds. We use the *phonetic* symbol ô to show how to pronounce the sound of the letter "o" in "fork."

pho·net·ic (fə net′ik) *adjective.*

phonograph An instrument that repro-duces sound from records. The needle of a

at; āpe; fär; câre; end; mē; it; ice; pîerce; hot; ōld; sông, fôrk; oil; out; up; ūse; rūle; půll; tûrn; chin; sing; shop; thin; <u>th</u>is; hw in white; zh in treasure. The symbol ə stands for the unstressed vowel sound in about, taken, pencil, lemon, and circus.

P

phonograph picks up the sounds that have been recorded in the grooves of a record as the record turns. It plays them through loudspeakers so they can be heard.
pho·no·graph (fō′nə graf′) *noun, plural* **phonographs.**

phosphorus A substance that looks like white or yellow wax. Phosphorus glows in the dark. Plants and animals need phosphorus. Phosphorus is a chemical element.
phos·pho·rus (fos′fər əs) *noun.*

photo A short form of the word "photograph." Look up **photograph** for more information.
pho·to (fō′tō) *noun, plural* **photos.**

photograph A picture that is made by using a camera. *Noun.*
—To take a picture of with a camera. We *photographed* the beautiful sunset from the balcony. *Verb.*
pho·to·graph (fō′tə graf′) *noun, plural* **photographs;** *verb,* **photographed, photographing.**

photographer A person who takes photographs for fun or as a job.
pho·tog·ra·pher (fə tog′rə fər) *noun, plural* **photographers.**

photography The art of using a camera to take pictures, of developing film, and of printing photographs.
pho·tog·ra·phy (fə tog′rə fē) *noun.*

photosynthesis The process by which green plants use carbon dioxide, water, and sunlight to make their own food.
pho·to·syn·the·sis (fō′tə sin′thə sis) *noun.*

phrase **1.** A group of words that expresses a thought but does not contain both a subject and a predicate. In the sentence "We walked to town," "to town" is a phrase. **2.** A short expression. "Lower taxes!" was the *phrase* that the marchers chanted. *Noun.*
—To express in chosen words. The teacher *phrased* the questions very carefully. *Verb.*
phrase (frāz) *noun, plural* **phrases;** *verb,* **phrased, phrasing.**

physical **1.** Having to do with the body. An elephant has great *physical* strength. **2.** Having to do with matter and energy. Chemistry and physics are *physical* sciences. **3.** Having to do with nature or natural objects. The map shows mountains, lakes, and other *physical* features of the country.
phys·i·cal (fiz′i kəl) *adjective.*

physical fitness A state of good health that comes from exercising often and eating nutritious food.
physical fit·ness (fit′nis).

physician A person who is trained and licensed to treat sickness or injury; doctor.
phy·si·cian (fə zish′ən) *noun, plural* **physicians.**

physicist A person who works or specializes in physics.
phys·i·cist (fiz′ə sist) *noun, plural* **physicists.**

physics The science that deals with matter and energy and the laws governing them. Physics includes the study of motion, light, heat, sound, and electricity and force. ▲ The word "physics" is used with a singular verb.
phys·ics (fiz′iks) *noun.*

pi The symbol π. It represents the ratio of the circumference of a circle to its diameter. Pi is equal to about 3.1416. ▲ Another word that sounds like this is **pie.**
pi (pī) *noun, plural* **pis.**

pianist A person who plays the piano.
pi·an·ist (pē an′ist *or* pyan′ist *or* pē′ə nist) *noun, plural* **pianists.**

piano A musical instrument. A piano usually is a wooden box shaped like a rectangle or harp and has a keyboard. The keys control little hammers inside the box that strike metal strings to produce tones.
pi·an·o (pē an′ō *or* pyan′ō) *noun, plural* **pianos.**

piano

piccolo A small flute. The piccolo has a higher pitch than an ordinary flute.
pic·co·lo (pik′ə lō′) *noun, plural* **piccolos.**

pick¹ **1.** To take from a number offered; select or choose. *Pick* a card from the deck. **2.** To gather with the fingers. We *picked* blueberries for a pie. **3.** To remove with the fingers or something pointed. Our dog loves to *pick* the meat off a bone. **4.** To pull at and let go; pluck. The folk singer *picked* the strings of a guitar. **5.** To cause on purpose. The bully *picked* a fight with me after school. **6.** To steal the contents of. The thief *picked* the subway rider's pocket. **7.** To open with a wire or something pointed instead of a key. The burglar *picked* the lock on the door. **8.** To eat in small amounts. The children *picked* at their food. *Verb.*

—**1.** The best one or ones. That puppy is the *pick* of the litter. **2.** An act of choosing; selection. Take your *pick* of the books on the table. **3.** A small, thin piece of plastic or other material. It is used to pluck the strings of a guitar or similar instrument. *Noun.*

• **to pick on.** To treat or tease someone smaller or weaker in a mean way. Older children sometimes *pick on* younger children.

• **to pick out.** To choose. The parents *picked out* a name for their new baby.

• **to pick up. 1.** To take and lift up. We *picked up* pebbles and shells on the beach. **2.** To get without much planning or by chance. I *pick up* extra money by doing odd jobs. **3.** To stop for and take on. The bus *picked up* two passengers. **4.** To manage to receive or record. Sometimes my radio *picks up* police conversations. **5.** To get better; improve. Business is *picking up.* **6.** To learn. My cousin *picked up* Italian after a few months in Italy.

pick (pik) *verb,* **picked, picking;** *noun, plural* **picks.**

pick² **1.** A tool with a wooden handle and a metal head that is pointed at one end or both. A pick is used for breaking rocks and loosening dirt. It is also called a **pickax. 2.** A pointed tool. An ice pick can be used to break up ice.

pick (pik) *noun, plural* **picks.**

pickax A pick, especially one with a head that has a point at one end and a blade like that of a chisel at the other end. Look up **pick²** for more information. ▲ This word is also spelled **pickaxe.**

pick·ax or **pick·axe** (pik′aks′) *noun, plural* **pickaxes.**

pickerel A freshwater fish that has a thin body and a pointed head. Pickerels are members of the pike family. They live in North America and are used for food.

pick·er·el (pik′ər əl) *noun, plural* **pickerel** or **pickerels.**

picket **1.** A pointed stake that is driven into the ground to hold something in place or to be part of a fence. **2.** A person who stands or walks outside a place to protest or demand something. The *pickets* outside the

store carried signs asking customers to support an employees' strike by not shopping there. *Noun.*

—To stand in front of or walk about as a picket. The workers *picketed* the steel factory to demand better pay. *Verb.*

pick·et (pik′it) *noun, plural* **pickets;** *verb,* **picketed, picketing.**

pickle Any food that has been preserved and flavored in salt water or vinegar. Cucumbers are often prepared in this way. *Noun.*

—To preserve in salt water or vinegar. My grandparents *pickle* beets every year. *Verb.*

pick·le (pik′əl) *noun, plural* **pickles;** *verb,* **pickled, pickling.**

pickpocket A person who steals from other people's pockets or purses.

pick·pock·et (pik′pok′it) *noun, plural* **pickpockets.**

pickup **1.** The act of getting hold of and lifting or taking something. The shortstop made a good *pickup* of the batted ball. There is a *pickup* of mail this afternoon. **2.** A small truck with an open back that is used for carrying light loads.

pick·up (pik′up′) *noun, plural* **pickups.**

picnic A party or trip for which food is taken along and eaten outside. We made sandwiches and lemonade for a *picnic* on the beach. *Noun.*

—To go on or have a picnic. We *picnicked* in the park. *Verb.*

pic·nic (pik′nik) *noun, plural* **picnics;** *verb,* **picnicked, picnicking.**

picture **1.** A painting, drawing, or photograph that represents a person or thing. I knew how my cousins would look because I

pickerel

at; āpe; fär; câre; end; mē; it; īce; pîerce; hot; ōld; sông, fôrk; oil; out; up; ūse; rüle; pùll; tûrn; chin; sing; shop; thin; this; hw in white; zh in treasure. The symbol ə stands for the unstressed vowel sound in about, taken, pencil, lemon, and circus.

549

had seen a *picture* of them.   **2.** An image that is seen on a television, motion-picture, or computer screen. This television set's *picture* is not very clear.   **3.** A description in words. A student from Germany visited our class and gave us a very good *picture* of life in that country.   **4.** A likeness or perfect example. That child is the *picture* of health. **5.** A motion picture; movie. *Noun.*
—**1.** To draw or paint a picture of. The artist *pictured* an old couple sitting on a bench. **2.** To give a description of. The writer *pictured* the horrors of war.   **3.** To imagine. It is hard for me to *picture* what our town will be like in ten years. *Verb.*

> **pic·ture** (pik′chər) *noun, plural* **pictures;** *verb,* **pictured, picturing.**

picturesque   Being a good subject for a picture; pleasant or interesting to look at or imagine. A cottage by the sea is *picturesque.*

> **pic·tur·esque** (pik′chə resk′) *adjective.*

pie   A pastry shell that is filled with fruit, meat, or other foods. Pies are baked in an oven and can be eaten for dessert or for a main course. ▲ Another word that sounds like this is **pi.**

> **pie** (pī) *noun, plural* **pies.**

piece   **1.** A part that has been broken, cut, or torn from something; fragment. There are *pieces* of broken glass all over the floor. **2.** One of a group or set of similar things. We're missing two chess *pieces.*   **3.** A work of art, music, or literature. I'm learning a new *piece* of music for the piano.   **4.** An example or instance. What a *piece* of luck! **5.** A coin. A dime is a ten-cent *piece. Noun.*
—To join the parts or pieces of. It was hard to *piece* the jigsaw puzzle together. The police were able to *piece* together the evidence and solve the crime. *Verb.* ▲ Another word that sounds like this is **peace.**

> **piece** (pēs) *noun, plural* **pieces;** *verb,* **pieced, piecing.**

pier   **1.** A structure built out over the water. It is used as a landing place for boats or ships.   **2.** A pillar or other kind of support that is used to hold up a bridge. Modern bridges have steel piers to support them. ▲ Another word that sounds like this is **peer.**

> **pier** (pîr) *noun, plural* **piers.**

pierce   **1.** To make a hole through. A nail *pierced* the tire of my bicycle.   **2.** To pass through; penetrate. A shrill cry *pierced* the stillness of the night.

> **pierce** (pîrs) *verb,* **pierced, piercing.**

pig   **1.** An animal that has a stout body, short legs with hooves, a short snout, and a short, curly tail; a young hog. Some pigs are raised for their meat, which is called pork.

2. A person who is messy or greedy.

> **pig** (pig) *noun, plural* **pigs.**

pigeon   A bird that has a plump body, a small head, and thick, soft feathers; dove. Pigeons live in the wild, but are also found in nearly every city of the world.

> **pi·geon** (pij′ən) *noun, plural* **pigeons.**

piggyback   On the back or shoulders. Those children love it when grown-ups give them *piggyback* rides. *Adjective.*
—On the back or shoulders. The guide had to carry the injured climber *piggyback. Adverb.*

> **pig·gy·back** (pig′ē bak′) *adjective; adverb.*

The child is riding **piggyback.**

pigment   **1.** A substance that is used for coloring. A pigment is often a powder that is mixed with a liquid to make a paint or dye. **2.** A substance in a plant or in animal tissue that gives it color. Chlorophyll is the green *pigment* in leaves.

> **pig·ment** (pig′mənt) *noun, plural* **pigments.**

pigpen   **1.** An enclosed place where pigs are kept; sty. This place is also called a **pigsty.**

> **pig·pen** (pig′pen′) *noun, plural* **pigpens.**

pigsty   An enclosed place where pigs are kept; pigpen.

> **pig·sty** (pig′stī′) *noun, plural* **pigsties.**

pigtail   A braid or fastened bunch of hair hanging from the head. I used to wear my hair in two *pigtails.*

> **pig·tail** (pig′tāl′) *noun, plural* **pigtails.**

pike   A large freshwater fish that has a long, thin body, a large mouth, and sharp teeth.

> **pike** (pīk) *noun, plural* **pikes** or **pike.**

pile¹ **1.** A number of things lying one on top of the other; heap. There is a *pile* of newspapers on the floor. **2.** A large amount. I have to finish a *pile* of homework. *Noun.*
—**1.** To form or put into a heap or mass. *Pile* the dirty dishes in the sink. **2.** To cover with a large amount. The carpenters *piled* their table with lumber and tools. *Verb.*
   pile (pīl) *noun, plural* **piles;** *verb,* **piled, piling.**

pile² A heavy, upright post that is driven into the ground to support a bridge or pier.
   pile (pīl) *noun, plural* **piles.**

pile³ The soft, thick fibers on the surface of a rug or a piece of cloth. Pile is often made of loops of yarn.
   pile (pīl) *noun.*

pilgrim **1.** A person who travels to a sacred place for a religious purpose. For centuries, Christian *pilgrims* have been going to Palestine to pray and worship in the places where Jesus lived. **2.** Pilgrim. One of a group of English settlers who founded the colony of Plymouth in New England in 1620.
   pil·grim (pil′grəm) *noun, plural* **pilgrims.**

Word History

The word **pilgrim** comes from a Latin word that means "foreigner." Pilgrims often travel far from home, to places where they are foreigners.

pill A small tablet of medicine. A pill is made either to be swallowed or chewed.
   pill (pil) *noun, plural* **pills.**

pillar A column that is used as support for a building or that stands alone as a monument. The roof of the porch is supported by *pillars.*
   pil·lar (pil′ər) *noun, plural* **pillars.**

pillory A frame of wood with holes for a person's head and hands. A pillory used to be set up in a public place, and people were put in it as a punishment.
   pil·lo·ry (pil′ə rē) *noun, plural* **pillories.**

pillow A bag or case that is filled with feathers or other soft material. Pillows are used to support the head when resting or sleeping.
   pil·low (pil′ō) *noun, plural* **pillows.**

pillowcase A cloth case open at one end, used to cover a pillow.
   pil·low·case (pil′ō kās′) *noun, plural* **pillowcases.**

pilot **1.** A person who operates an aircraft or spacecraft. **2.** A person who steers large ships into and out of a harbor or through dangerous waters. *Noun.*
—To act as a pilot. The captain *piloted* the airplane safely through the dangerous thunderstorm. *Verb.*
   pi·lot (pī′lət) *noun, plural* **pilots;** *verb,* **piloted, piloting.**

pimple A small, red bump on the skin. Pimples are often painful and filled with pus.
   pim·ple (pim′pəl) *noun, plural* **pimples.**

pin **1.** A short piece of wire with a pointed end, used for holding things together. Some pins are stiff and straight. Others are U-shaped, like pins for the hair. Others can be closed, with the pointed end covered, like safety pins. **2.** An ornament or badge that has a clasp for attaching it to clothing. I wore a *pin* in the shape of a butterfly on my collar. **3.** A short, slender, round piece of wood or other hard material. A pin fits into a hole in each of two parts of something, so that the parts are held together. The doctors put a metal *pin* into the badly broken bone. **4.** One of ten pieces of wood shaped like bottles that are used in bowling. *Noun.*
—**1.** To hold together or attach with a pin or pins. My dress was too long, so I *pinned* the hem up. **2.** To hold fast in one position. In wrestling, you try to *pin* your opponent to the mat. *Verb.*
   • **on pins and needles.** Very nervous or anxious. I was *on pins and needles* until I found out I had gotten the job I wanted.
   pin (pin) *noun, plural* **pins;** *verb,* **pinned, pinning.**

pinch **1.** To squeeze between the finger and thumb or between other surfaces. Somebody sneaked up behind me and *pinched* my arm. I *pinched* my finger in the drawer when I closed it. **2.** To make thin or wrinkled. The child's face was *pinched* from the cold weather. *Verb.*
—**1.** A sharp squeeze. My friend gave me a *pinch* to keep me awake during the movie. **2.** An amount that can be held between the thumb and a finger. The recipe said to add a *pinch* of salt. **3.** A time of need or emergency. I can lend you money if you are in a *pinch. Noun.*
   pinch (pinch) *verb,* **pinched, pinching;** *noun, plural* **pinches.**

at; āpe; fär; câre; end; mē; it; īce; pîerce; hot; ōld; sông, fôrk; oil; out; up; ūse; rüle; pùll; tûrn; chin; sing; shop; thin; <u>th</u>is; hw in white; zh in treasure. The symbol ə stands for the unstressed vowel sound in about, taken, pencil, lemon, and circus.

P

pincushion A small, firm cushion into which needles and pins are stuck when they are not being used.

pin·cush·ion (pin′kush′ən) *noun, plural* **pincushions.**

pine An evergreen tree that has cones and leaves that look like needles. The wood from the pine is used in building and in making turpentine.

pine (pīn) *noun, plural* **pines.**

pineapple A large, oval fruit. The outside of a pineapple is hard and prickly, but the yellow meat inside is sweet and juicy. Pineapples grow on a tropical plant that has long, stiff leaves.

pine·ap·ple (pīn′ap′əl) *noun, plural* **pineapples.**

pineapples

Ping-Pong The trademark for the game of table tennis. Look up **table tennis** for more information.

Ping-Pong (ping′pong′) *noun.*

pink **1.** A light red color. It is made by mixing red and white. **2.** A garden plant that has pink, red, white, or sometimes yellow flowers with a sweet fragrance. *Noun.*
—Having the color pink. *Adjective.*

pink (pingk) *noun, plural* **pinks;** *adjective,* **pinker, pinkest.**

pinkeye A disease of the eye that causes the covering on the eyeball and on the inside of the eyelid to become red and sore.

pink·eye (pingk′ī′) *noun.*

pinpoint To locate or fix exactly. The rescue team used a helicopter to *pinpoint* the place where the airplane had crashed.

pin·point (pin′point′) *verb,* **pinpointed, pinpointing.**

pint A unit of measurement. It is equal to half a quart.

pint (pīnt) *noun, plural* **pints.**

pinto A horse or pony that has spots or patches of two or more colors.

pin·to (pin′tō) *noun, plural* **pintos.**

pinwheel A toy made of colored paper or plastic that is pinned to a stick. It spins when the wind blows it.

pin·wheel (pin′hwēl′ *or* pin′wēl′) *noun, plural* **pinwheels.**

pioneer **1.** A person who is among the first to explore and settle a region. *Pioneers* set-

tled the American West. **2.** A person who is among the first to develop an area of thought or research. The Wright brothers were *pioneers* in aviation. *Noun.*
—To be among the first to explore for others. American scientists *pioneered* in sending human beings to the moon. *Verb.*

pi·o·neer (pī′ə nîr′) *noun, plural* **pioneers;** *verb,* **pioneered, pioneering.**

pious **1.** Very religious; devout. The *pious* couple went to church every day. **2.** Of or relating to religious devotion. They studied the *pious* writings of religious leaders.

pi·ous (pī′əs) *adjective.*

pipe **1.** A tube of metal, glass, or other material used for carrying a gas or liquid. The water in our house flows through copper *pipes.* **2.** A tube with a bowl of wood or clay at one end that is used for smoking tobacco. **3.** A musical instrument that is in the shape of a tube. A person plays a pipe by blowing into it at one end. *Noun.*
—**1.** To carry by means of a pipe or pipes. The farmer *piped* water to the fields. **2.** To play on a pipe. The band *piped* a tune during the parade. *Verb.*

pipe (pīp) *noun, plural* **pipes;** *verb,* **piped, piping.**

pipeline A line of pipes for carrying a liquid or gas over a long distance. There is a *pipeline* that carries oil across Alaska.

pipe·line (pīp′līn′) *noun, plural* **pipelines.**

piracy The robbing of ships at sea.

pi·ra·cy (pī′rə sē) *noun, plural* **piracies.**

pirate A person who robs ships at sea.

pi·rate (pī′rit) *noun, plural* **pirates.**

pistachio A small, green nut. It has a tan shell that sometimes is dyed red.

pis·ta·chi·o (pi stash′ē ō) *noun, plural* **pistachios.**

pinto

pistil The tiny stalk in the center of a flower. The pistil is the female part of a flower. Seeds develop in the pistil. ▲ Another word that sounds like this is **pistol**.
pis·til (pis′təl) *noun, plural* **pistils.**

pistol A small gun that is held and fired with one hand. ▲ Another word that sounds like this is **pistil**.
pis·tol (pis′təl) *noun, plural* **pistols.**

piston A cylinder that fits closely inside a tube or hollow cylinder where it moves back and forth. The movement of the pistons in an automobile engine turns the car wheels.
pis·ton (pis′tən) *noun, plural* **pistons.**

pit¹ 1. A hole in the ground that is natural or dug. The workers dug a deep *pit* in the backyard for the pool. 2. A sunken or indented area on a surface. Acne sometimes leaves scars that are *pits* on the skin. *Noun.*
—1. To make pits in; mark with sunken areas. Pebbles thrown against the window *pitted* the glass. Craters *pit* the surface of the moon. 2. To set against each other in a contest. The World Series *pits* the two champion baseball teams against each other. *Verb.*
pit (pit) *noun, plural* **pits;** *verb,* **pitted, pitting.**

pit² The single hard seed that is in some fruits. Peaches and plums have pits. *Noun.*
—To remove a pit from. We *pitted* the cherries before serving them for dessert. *Verb.*
pit (pit) *noun, plural* **pits;** *verb,* **pitted, pitting.**

pitch¹ 1. To throw or toss. We spent the afternoon trying to *pitch* horseshoes around a stake. 2. To set up. The campers *pitched* their tents. 3. To fall or plunge forward. The ship *pitched* and rolled in the rough seas. *Verb.*
—1. A throw of the ball from the pitcher to a batter in baseball. The batter struck out on three *pitches.* 2. A high point or degree. We worked ourselves up to a *pitch* of excitement just before the big festival. 3. The highness or lowness of a sound in music. The music director hummed the *pitch* for the chorus before each song. 4. A slope. The roof of the ski lodge had a steep *pitch. Noun.*
pitch (pich) *verb,* **pitched, pitching;** *noun, plural* **pitches.**

pitch² A dark, sticky substance that is made from tar. Pitch is used to make the roof of houses waterproof and to pave streets.
pitch (pich) *noun.*

pitcher¹ A container with a handle and a lip or spout. A pitcher is used for holding and pouring milk, water, and other liquids.
pitch·er (pich′ər) *noun, plural* **pitchers.**

pitcher² A baseball player who throws the ball to the batter. The pitcher stands near the middle of the diamond facing home plate.
pitch·er (pich′ər) *noun, plural* **pitchers.**

pitchfork A tool that looks like a large fork. It is used to lift and throw hay.
pitch·fork (pich′fôrk′) *noun, plural* **pitchforks.**

pith 1. The soft tissue that is in the center of the stems of certain plants. The pith is important in storing food. 2. Any soft tissue that is like this. The pith of an orange is the soft white part that is inside the rind.
pith (pith) *noun.*

pitiful 1. Arousing sorrow and sympathy. The lost puppy looked so *pitiful* that we took it home and kept it as a pet. 2. Arousing scorn or contempt. That's a *pitiful* excuse.
pit·i·ful (pit′i fəl) *adjective.*

pity 1. A feeling of sorrow and sympathy for the troubles of another. We felt *pity* for the family who lost everything when their house burned down. 2. A cause for regret. What a *pity* you have a cold and can't come to the party. *Noun.*
—To feel sorrow and sympathy for. We *pity* the people who lost their homes in the flood. *Verb.*
pit·y (pit′ē) *noun, plural* **pities;** *verb,* **pitied, pitying.**

pivot A fixed point, shaft, or pin that something else turns on. The hands of a clock turn on a *pivot. Noun.*
—To turn on a pivot or as if on a pivot. The gun on that tank can *pivot* and fire in any direction. The basketball player *pivoted* and passed the ball to another player. *Verb.*
piv·ot (piv′ət) *noun, plural* **pivots;** *verb,* **pivoted, pivoting.**

pixel The very small shape that is used in combinations to form numbers, letters, and pictures on a computer's monitor.
pix·el (pik′səl) *noun, plural* **pixels.**

pizza An Italian pie that is made of a flat crust covered with tomato sauce and cheese. Sometimes extra ingredients such as sausage, peppers, and mushrooms are added before the pizza is baked.
piz·za (pēt′sə) *noun, plural* **pizzas.**

P

at; āpe; fär; câre; end; mē; it; īce; pîerce; hot; ōld; sông, fôrk; oil; out; up; ūse; rüle; pùll; tûrn; chin; sing; shop; thin; this; hw in white; zh in treasure. The symbol ə stands for the unstressed vowel sound in about, taken, pencil, lemon, and circus.

pl. An abbreviation for *plural*.

place 1. A part of space; location; area. We visited many interesting *places* on our trip. The *place* where I hit my elbow is still sore. 2. A home. My parents have rented a *place* in the country. 3. A passage in a book or other writing. I marked my *place* in the book. 4. A space or seat for a person. Would you save my *place*? 5. A position in an order or series; rank. My poem won third *place* in the contest. 6. A proper or usual position. When we finished cleaning, everything was in its *place*. 7. Duty or business. It is not your *place* to criticize their work. *Noun.*
—1. To put or be in a particular spot or location. *Place* the napkin beside the plate. My friend *placed* third in the swimming race. 2. To identify by connecting with the correct time and location. I know I've seen you, but I can't *place* you. *Verb.*
• **to take place.** To happen. The band concert *took place* in the park.
place (plās) *noun, plural* **places**; *verb,* **placed, placing.**

placid Calm and peaceful. There was no wind, so the lake was *placid*. The *placid* child was seldom excited or disturbed.
plac·id (plas′id) *adjective.*

plague 1. A very serious disease that spreads quickly among the people in an area. A plague often causes death. 2. Anything that causes great misfortune. The trees were destroyed by a *plague* of caterpillars. *Noun.*
—To trouble or annoy. Mosquitoes started to *plague* the hikers. *Verb.*
plague (plāg) *noun, plural* **plagues**; *verb,* **plagued, plaguing.**

The kilts are **plaid**.

plaid A pattern of stripes of different colors and widths crossing each other. Cloth with a pattern of plaid is used to make clothing, blankets, and other things.
plaid (plad) *noun, plural* **plaids.**

plain 1. Clearly seen, heard, or understood. As the airplane descended for a landing, the people and houses on the ground came into *plain* view. My friends made it *plain* that they did not agree with me. 2. Straightforward; direct; frank. I will be *plain* with you and tell you the truth. 3. Without decoration. You can wear your *plain* black dress with a silver necklace. 4. Not rich or highly seasoned. When I was sick I could eat only *plain* foods. 5. Common or ordinary. *Plain* people as well as famous people have a right to vote. 6. Not beautiful. That child has a *plain* but sweet face. *Adjective.*
—An area of flat or almost flat land. Buffaloes used to roam the Western *plains*. *Noun.*
▲ Another word that sounds like this is **plane.**
plain (plān) *adjective,* **plainer, plainest;** *noun, plural* **plains.**

planning a trip

plan 1. A way of doing something that has been thought out ahead of time. Our *plan* for climbing the mountain is to zigzag up the south slope. 2. Something that a person intends to do. I have no *plans* for this weekend. 3. A drawing that shows how the parts of something are arranged. We looked at a *plan* of the museum to find out where the dinosaur bones were. *Noun.*
—1. To think out a way of doing something ahead of time. We *planned* the dinner so that there would be plenty of food for everyone.

2. To have an intention; intend. I *plan* to go to college someday. **3.** To make a drawing of. The town hired a famous architect to *plan* the new school. *Verb.*

plan (plan) *noun, plural* **plans;** *verb,* **planned, planning.**

plane¹ **1.** A level or grade. The book was on such a high *plane* that I couldn't understand it. **2.** An aircraft that has an engine and wings that are not movable; airplane. Look up **airplane** for more information. *Noun.*
—Level or flat. This highway has a *plane* surface. *Adjective.* ▲ Another word that sounds like this is **plain.**

plane (plān) *noun, plural* **planes;** *adjective.*

plane² A hand tool with a sharp blade that sticks out from the bottom. A plane is used for smoothing wood. *Noun.*
—To smooth with a plane. The carpenter *planed* the door down a little so it would fit the door opening exactly. *Verb.* ▲ Another word that sounds like this is **plain.**

plane (plān) *noun, plural* **planes;** *verb,* **planed, planing.**

planet One of nine large heavenly bodies that orbit the sun. The planets in our solar system are Mercury, Venus, Earth, Mars, Jupiter, Saturn, Uranus, Neptune, and Pluto.

plan·et (plan′it) *noun, plural* **planets.**

Word History

The word **planet** goes back to a Greek word meaning "wandering star." People noticed that most stars held the same positions night after night, but that the planets shifted their positions and "wandered" among the other stars.

planetarium A building in which there is a device that shows the movements of the sun, moon, planets, and stars by projecting their images on a curved ceiling.

plan·e·tar·i·um (plan′i tãr′ē əm) *noun, plural* **planetariums** or **planetaria** (plan′i tãr′ē ə).

plank A long, flat piece of sawed wood that is thicker than a board.

plank (plangk) *noun, plural* **planks.**

plankton Very small plants and animals that float in seas and lakes. Many fish and whales feed on plankton.

plank·ton (plangk′tən) *noun.*

plant **1.** A living thing that, unlike animals, stays in one place, makes its own food, and has rigid cell walls. Shrubs, trees, mosses, and most algae are plants. **2.** A building or group of buildings containing equipment used in making something. A power *plant* produces electricity. *Noun.*
—**1.** To set or place in the ground so that it will take root and grow. We *planted* our tomato seeds in May. **2.** To place or set firmly in position. The donkey *planted* its feet on the ground and refused to move. *Verb.*

plant (plant) *noun, plural* **plants;** *verb,* **planted, planting.**

plantain A kind of banana. Plantains contain a lot of starch. They are cooked before being eaten.

plan·tain (plan′tən) *noun, plural* **plantains.**

plantation A large estate or farm worked by laborers who live there. Before the Civil War, cotton, tobacco, and rice were grown on *plantations* in the South.

plan·ta·tion (plan tā′shən) *noun, plural* **plantations.**

planter **1.** A person or machine that plants seeds. **2.** A person who owns or manages a plantation. **3.** A container for plants.

plant·er (plan′tər) *noun, plural* **planters.**

plaque **1.** A flat piece of wood or metal that is decorated and hung on a wall. **2.** A sticky film of bacteria, food, and saliva that forms on the teeth.

plaque (plak) *noun, plural* **plaques.**

plasma The clear, yellow liquid that forms the watery part of blood. Blood cells, salts, antibodies, and other things carried by the blood are suspended in the plasma.

plas·ma (plaz′mə) *noun, plural* **plasmas.**

plaster A mixture of lime, sand, and water that becomes hard when dry. Plaster is used for covering walls and ceilings. Artists sometimes use plaster to make statues and molds. *Noun.*
—**1.** To cover with plaster. We *plastered* the ceiling to repair the damage done by the leak. **2.** To cover thoroughly. The workers *plastered* the sides of buildings with posters advertising the circus. *Verb.*

plas·ter (plas′tər) *noun; verb,* **plastered, plastering.**

at; āpe; fär; câre; end; mē; it; īce; pîerce; hot; ōld; sông, fôrk; oil; out; up; ūse; rüle; pull; tûrn; chin; sing; shop; thin; this; hw in white; zh in treasure. The symbol ə stands for the unstressed vowel sound in about, taken, pencil, lemon, and circus.

plastic Any of a number of artificially made substances that can be molded and shaped into materials or objects. Dishes, furniture, food wrappers, raincoats, film, false teeth, and eyeglasses can all be made of plastic. *Noun.*
—**1.** Capable of being molded and shaped. Wax is a *plastic* material when it is heated. **2.** Made of plastic. The radio has a *plastic* case. The *plastic* seats in this car are made to look like leather. *Adjective.*
  plas·tic (plas′tik) *noun, plural* **plastics;** *adjective.*

plastic dishes

plate **1.** A flat or shallow dish. Food is served or eaten from *plates.* **2.** A flat, thin piece of metal. Modern warships are covered with plates of steel. A knight's armor was made of metal *plates.* **3.** A piece of metal on which something is or can be engraved. In printing, the words or pictures to be printed are copied onto metal plates that fit into a printing press. **4.** Home plate in a baseball game. **5.** One of the very large parts of the earth's crust on which the continents and oceans rest. These plates move very slowly over millions of years and sometimes cause earthquakes. *Noun.*
—To cover with a coat of silver, gold, or other metal. The jeweler *plated* the steel box with gold. *Verb.*
  plate (plāt) *noun, plural* **plates;** *verb,* **plated, plating.**

plateau An area of flat land that is raised above the surrounding country.
  pla·teau (pla tō′) *noun, plural* **plateaus.**

platform **1.** A raised, flat surface. The speaker stood on a *platform.* We waited on the *platform* for the train. **2.** A statement of the principles or beliefs of a group. The political party adopted a *platform* that called for lowering the voting age.
  plat·form (plat′fôrm′) *noun, plural* **platforms.**

platinum A soft, heavy metal that looks like silver. Platinum does not tarnish. It is used in jewelry and alloys. Platinum is a chemical element.
  plat·i·num (plat′ə nəm) *noun.*

platoon A military unit that includes two or more squads. A *platoon* is usually commanded by a lieutenant.
  pla·toon (plə tün′) *noun, plural* **platoons.**

platter A large, shallow dish. It is used for serving food.
  plat·ter (plat′ər) *noun, plural* **platters.**

platypus An animal that has a wide flat bill, webbed feet, and soft brown fur. The platypus is one of the only mammals that lay eggs. It lives near streams in Australia.
  plat·y·pus (plat′ə pəs) *noun, plural* **platypuses.**

play **1.** Activity that is done for fun or pleasure; sport. Many children were at *play* in the playground. **2.** A move or turn in a game. The quarterback made a great *play.* It is your *play* next. **3.** A story that is written to be acted out on stage. We saw a *play* about the American Revolution. **4.** Action or operation. The engine was in full *play.* **5.** A quick flickering movement. The painter tried to capture the *play* of light on the water. *Noun.*
—**1.** To do something for fun or pleasure. The children *played* all morning in the backyard. **2.** To be in or have a game. Let's *play* tag. Some members of the basketball team never got a chance to *play.* **3.** To compete against in a game. Our team *played* the champions in a chess tournament. **4.** To act carelessly with something. Don't *play* with matches. **5.** To act the part of. The star of the movie *played* an old sailor. **6.** To make or cause to make music or other sounds. I'm learning how to *play* the piano. Let's *play* a record on the phonograph. **7.** To act or behave. An honest person *plays* fair with everyone. *Verb.*
  play (plā) *noun, plural* **plays;** *verb,* **played, playing.**

player **1.** A person who plays in a sport or game. My cousins are all good tennis *players.* **2.** A person who performs. That restaurant has a piano *player* every night. **3.** A machine that produces music or other sounds. The neighbors complained that our record *player* was too loud.
  play·er (plā′ər) *noun, plural* **players.**

playful **1.** Wanting or liking to play; lively. The *playful* kitten chased the leaf. **2.** Meant to amuse or tease; humorous. The speaker made some *playful* remarks before discussing serious matters.
  play·ful (plā′fəl) *adjective.*

556

playground An outdoor area for children to play in. Playgrounds often have slides, swings, and sandboxes.
play·ground (plā′ground′) *noun, plural* **playgrounds.**

playground

playing card A card used in playing games. The most common group of playing cards has fifty-two cards and is divided into four suits called clubs, diamonds, hearts, and spades.

playmate A child who plays with another child.
play·mate (plā′māt′) *noun, plural* **playmates.**

playpen A small pen that folds up easily. It is used for a baby or small child to play in.
play·pen (plā′pen′) *noun, plural* **playpens.**

plaything A thing to play with; toy.
play·thing (plā′thing′) *noun, plural* **playthings.**

playwright A person who writes plays. William Shakespeare was a very famous English *playwright.*
play·wright (plā′rīt′) *noun, plural* **playwrights.**

plaza A public square or open space in a city or town. There is a *plaza* with benches and a large fountain at the center of town.
pla·za (plä′zə *or* plaz′ə) *noun, plural* **plazas.**

plea 1. A sincere request. The Red Cross made a *plea* for money to aid the victims of the flood. 2. An answer given to a charge in a court of law. The prisoner made a *plea* of not guilty at the start of the trial.
plea (plē) *noun, plural* **pleas.**

plead 1. To make a sincere request; beg. I *pleaded* with my friend not to swim near the rocks. 2. To give as an excuse. I *pleaded* ill-

ness when they asked me why I was not coming to the party. 3. To speak in defense of someone in a court of law. The lawyer agreed to *plead* the accused person's case. 4. To give as an answer to a charge in a court of law. The prisoner will *plead* guilty.
plead (plēd) *verb,* **pleaded** or **pled, pleading.**

pleasant 1. Giving pleasure. It's a *pleasant* feeling to lie on a soft bed. 2. Behaving in a pleasing way; friendly. The bus driver was *pleasant* to all the people who got on.
pleas·ant (plez′ənt) *adjective,* **pleasanter, pleasantest.**

please 1. To give pleasure to. My shiny new bicycle *pleases* me. 2. To want or prefer. The children may buy whatever they *please.* 3. To be so kind as to. *Please* give me some more beans. Close the door, *please.*
please (plēz) *verb,* **pleased, pleasing.**

pleasing Giving pleasure; pleasant; agreeable. Our baby-sitter has a *pleasing* personality.
pleas·ing (plē′zing) *adjective.*

pleasure 1. A feeling of enjoyment or happiness. The circus clowns gave *pleasure* to the children in the audience. A good nurse takes *pleasure* in helping others. 2. Something that gives a feeling of enjoyment or happiness. It was a *pleasure* to see my old classmate again.
pleas·ure (plezh′ər) *noun, plural* **pleasures.**

pleat A flat fold made by doubling cloth upon itself and fastening or pressing it into place. Skirts often have pleats. *Noun.*
—To make pleats in. I decided to *pleat* the skirt I was making. *Verb.*
pleat (plēt) *noun, plural* **pleats;** *verb,* **pleated, pleating.**

pled A past tense and a past participle of **plead.** The prisoner *pled* not guilty. Look up **plead** for more information.
pled (pled) *verb.*

pledge 1. A serious promise. The children made a *pledge* to keep the secret. My parents made a *pledge* to give money to the hospital. 2. Something given to another person for a time, as part of an agreement. I gave the storekeeper my watch as a *pledge* that I

at; āpe; fär; câre; end; mē; it; īce; pîerce; hot; ōld; sông, fôrk; oil; out; up; ūse; rüle; pull; tûrn; chin; sing; shop; thin; this; hw in white; zh in treasure. The symbol ə stands for the unstressed vowel sound in about, taken, pencil, lemon, and circus.

P

would come back and pay what I owed. *Noun.*
—**1.** To promise. The children *pledge* allegiance to the flag each morning. **2.** To give something as a pledge. The borrower *pledged* a valuable violin for the loan. *Verb.*
> **pledge** (plej) *noun, plural* **pledges;** *verb,* **pledged, pledging.**

plentiful In a large amount; more than enough; abundant. We have a *plentiful* supply of wood for our fireplace.
> **plen·ti·ful** (plen′ti fəl) *adjective.*

plenty A large amount; more than enough of something. There is *plenty* of milk left.
> **plen·ty** (plen′tē) *noun.*

plesiosaur A huge dinosaur with a long neck and legs shaped like paddles. It lived in the sea millions of years ago. This dinosaur is also called **plesiosaurus.**
> **ple·si·o·saur** (plē′sē ə sôr′) *noun, plural* **plesiosaurs.**

pliers A tool that has a pair of jaws for gripping or bending things. Some pliers can also cut wire.
> **pli·ers** (plī′ərz) *plural noun.*

plod **1.** To move in a slow, heavy way. The children *plodded* through the deep snow. **2.** To work in a slow, steady way. I *plodded* through all my homework.
> **plod** (plod) *verb,* **plodded, plodding.**

plot **1.** A secret plan. The outlaws formed a *plot* to rob the stagecoach. **2.** The main story in a novel, play, or movie. That movie has an exciting *plot.* **3.** A small piece of ground. We had our picnic on a grassy *plot* in the shade. The gardener prepared the *plot* for vegetables. *Noun.*
—**1.** To make a secret plan. The army officers *plotted* to take over the government. **2.** To make a chart or map of. The captain will *plot* the ship's course. *Verb.*
> **plot** (plot) *noun, plural* **plots;** *verb,* **plotted, plotting.**

plover A bird with a short bill and long, pointed wings. Plovers run along shores and beaches in search of food.
> **plo·ver** (pluv′ər *or* plō′vər) *noun, plural* **plovers.**

plow **1.** A heavy farm tool for cutting through and turning over soil. A farmer uses a plow to prepare soil for planting

plover

seeds. A plow is usually drawn by a tractor or by animals. **2.** A device for clearing away or pushing aside matter in its path. A snowplow is a plow for removing snow from roads and sidewalks. *Noun.*
—**1.** To cut through and turn over with a plow. The farmer *plowed* the field for planting corn. **2.** To move ahead in a steady, strong way, as a plow does. The ship *plowed* through the waves. *Verb.*
> **plow** (plou) *noun, plural* **plows;** *verb,* **plowed, plowing.**

pluck **1.** To pull off; pick. The butcher *plucked* the feathers from the chicken. I *plucked* a rose from the rose bush. **2.** To pull off hair or feathers from. We *plucked* the chicken. **3.** To pull at and quickly let go. The banjo player *plucked* the strings quickly. **4.** To give a quick, short pull; tug. The child *plucked* at the grown-up's coat for attention. *Verb.*
—**1.** A quick, short pull; tug. The musician gave a *pluck* to the strings of the guitar. **2.** Courage. It takes a lot of *pluck* to stand up to the school bully. *Noun.*
> **pluck** (pluk) *verb,* **plucked, plucking;** *noun, plural* **plucks.**

plug **1.** A piece of rubber, wood or some other thing used to stop up a hole. Don't forget to pull out the *plug* to let the water out of the bathtub. **2.** A device with prongs, placed on the end of a cord or wire. It is put into an electrical outlet to make a connection with a source of electricity. *Noun.*
—**1.** To stop up. I *plugged* the big jug of cider with a stopper. Grease *plugged* the kitchen drain. **2.** To put the electrical plug of a machine, appliance, or cord into an outlet. *Plug* in the radio. **3.** To work in a slow, steady way. We *plugged* away at the giant jigsaw puzzle until we finally finished it. *Verb.*
> **plug** (plug) *noun, plural* **plugs;** *verb,* **plugged, plugging.**

plum A soft, juicy fruit with smooth red or purple skin and a pit. It grows on a tree that has oval leaves and small white or pink flowers. Dried plums are called prunes. ▲ Another word that sounds like this is **plumb.**
> **plum** (plum) *noun, plural* **plums.**

plumage The feathers of a bird. The male cardinal has bright red *plumage.*
> **plum·age** (plü′mij) *noun.*

plumb To test or measure by means of a marked line with a weight at one end. *Plumb* the well to see how deep the water is. *Verb.*
—A weight at the end of a line marked with units of length. It is used to test whether something is straight up and down, or to

measure how deep something is. *Noun.*
▲ Another word that sounds like this is
plum.
> **plumb** (plum) *verb,* **plumbed, plumbing;**
> *noun, plural* **plumbs.**

plumber A person who puts in and repairs water and sewage pipes in buildings. A *plumber* came to the house to connect the washing machine.
> **plumb·er** (plum′ər) *noun, plural* **plumbers.**

Word History

The word **plumber** comes from a Latin word meaning "someone who works with lead." Water pipes were originally made out of lead.

---

plumbing The pipes for bringing water in and taking water and sewage out of a building. The *plumbing* in that old house leaks.
> **plumb·ing** (plum′ing) *noun.*

plume A large, fluffy feather. Ostriches have long *plumes* on their tails and wings.
> **plume** (plüm) *noun, plural* **plumes.**

plump Full and round; nicely fat. That healthy baby has *plump,* rosy cheeks.
> **plump** (plump) *adjective,* **plumper, plumpest.**

plunder To steal from; rob. The soldiers *plundered* the town. *Verb.*
—Something stolen. The outlaws hid their *plunder* in an old shed. *Noun.*
> **plun·der** (plun′dər) *verb,* **plundered, plundering;** *noun.*

plunge **1.** To put in suddenly. I *plunged* my hand into the water to try to catch the fish. **2.** To dive or fall suddenly. The swimmer *plunged* into the pool. The kite *plunged* to the ground. *Verb.*
—The act of plunging. The campers enjoy an early morning *plunge* in the lake. *Noun.*
> **plunge** (plunj) *verb,* **plunged, plunging;** *noun, plural* **plunges.**

plural Of or having to do with a form of a word that names or refers to more than one person or more than one thing. "Chairs" and "oxen" are plural nouns. "Chair" and "ox" are singular nouns. *Adjective.*
—The form of a word that names or refers to more than one person or more than one thing. The nouns "chickens" and "baskets" are in the plural. The nouns "chicken" and "basket" are in the singular. *Noun.*
> **plu·ral** (plůr′əl) *adjective; noun, plural* **plurals.**

Language Note

Most nouns add *-s* or *-es* to form what we call regular plurals. Other nouns form irregular plurals:

child, children	mouse, mice
foot, feet	ox, oxen
goose, geese	woman, women

---

plus With the addition of. Two *plus* two is four. Dinner *plus* dessert costs eight dollars at that restaurant. *Preposition.*
—Somewhat higher than. The student got a grade of B *plus* on the test. *Adjective.*
—A sign (+) showing that something is to be added. *Noun.*
> **plus** (plus) *preposition; adjective; noun, plural* **pluses.**

Pluto The smallest planet in our solar system. It is the planet farthest from the sun. Pluto can be seen from earth only with the aid of a telescope.
> **Plu·to** (plü′tō) *noun.*

plutonium A silver-colored radioactive metal. Plutonium is a rare chemical element. It is not found in nature but is made in nuclear reactors.
> **plu·to·ni·um** (plü tō′nē əm) *noun.*

plywood A strong board made of thin layers of wood glued together.
> **ply·wood** (plī′wůd′) *noun.*

p.m. or **P.M.** An abbreviation meaning the time of day between noon and midnight.

Word History

P.M. comes from the first letters of the Latin words *post meridiem. Post meridiem* means "after noon."

---

pneumonia A disease in which the lungs become inflamed and fill with thick fluid. Pneumonia is caused by a virus. A person who has pneumonia might cough or have a hard time breathing.
> **pneu·mo·nia** (nü mōn′yə *or* nü mōn′yə) *noun.*

---

at; āpe; fär; câre; end; mē; it; īce; pîerce; hot; ōld; sông, fôrk; oil; out; up; ūse; rüle; půll; tûrn; chin; sing; shop; thin; this; hw in white; zh in treasure. The symbol ə stands for the unstressed vowel sound in about, taken, pencil, lemon, and circus.

P

P.O. An abbreviation for *post office.*

pocket **1.** A small bag or pouch that is sewn on or into a garment, suitcase, or purse. Pockets are for holding coins, papers, keys, and other small things. **2.** A place in the earth that contains ore. The miners drilled into a *pocket* of iron ore. *Noun.*
—Small enough to be carried in the pocket. My grandparents gave me an old *pocket* watch. *Adjective.*
—To put in a pocket. The customer *pocketed* the coins. *Verb.*
pock·et (pok′it) *noun, plural* **pockets;** *adjective; verb,* **pocketed, pocketing.**

pocketbook A bag for carrying money, keys, and other small things; handbag; purse.
pock·et·book (pok′it bùk′) *noun, plural* **pocketbooks.**

pocketknife A small knife with one or more blades that fold into the handle.
pock·et·knife (pok′it nīf′) *noun, plural* **pocketknives.** (pok′it nīvz′).

pod A part of a plant that holds a number of seeds as they grow. A pod splits open along the side when it is ripe. Beans and peas grow in pods.
pod (pod) *noun, plural* **pods.**

poem A form of writing that expresses imaginative thought or strong feeling. A poem is usually written with a rhythmic arrangement of words and often with rhyme.
po·em (pō′əm) *noun, plural* **poems.**

pods

poet A person who writes poetry.
po·et (pō′it) *noun, plural* **poets.**

poetic Of or like poetry. *Poetic* language is chosen for its sound as well as its meaning.
po·et·ic (pō et′ik) *adjective.*

poetry **1.** Poems. I like to read *poetry.* **2.** The art of writing poems. Some writers are skilled in *poetry* as well as prose.
po·et·ry (pō′i trē) *noun.*

poinsettia A plant with small flowers and large, bright red, pink, or white leaves that look like flower petals. Poinsettias are used for decoration during Christmas.
poin·set·ti·a (poin set′ē ə *or* poin set′ə) *noun, plural* **poinsettias.**

point **1.** A fine, sharp end. The knife has a *point.* You write with the *point* of your pen-

cil. **2.** A piece of land with a sharp end sticking out into the water. A lighthouse was built on the *point.* **3.** A dot; mark. We use a *point* to separate dollars and cents when we write $3.50. **4.** A place, position, step, or degree. Tourists visit the *points* of interest in our town. The chapter ended at an exciting *point* in the story. **5.** A particular time; moment. At that *point,* everyone left the room. **6.** The main part, idea, or purpose. What is the *point* of that joke? **7.** A special quality; trait. Honesty is one of my friend's good *points.* **8.** A score in a game. Our football team is ahead by six *points.* **9.** One of the thirty-two marks that show direction on a compass. *Noun.*
—**1.** To show where something is by aiming a finger or other thing at it. I *pointed* at the bicycle I liked best. The road sign *points* in the direction of town. **2.** To aim; direct. I *pointed* the telescope at the moon. *Verb.*
- **beside the point.** Not related to a subject; not changing a fact or judgment. It is illegal to go through a red light; whether you are driving a car or riding a bicycle is *beside the point.*
- **to point out.** To show; indicate. The teacher read our tests and *pointed out* our mistakes to us.
- **to the point.** Related to the subject; relevant. The mayor's speech was brief and *to the point.*
point (point) *noun, plural* **points;** *verb,* **pointed, pointing.**

pointer **1.** A long stick or other object for pointing out things. **2.** A hunting dog that has a short coat and long ears. A pointer will stand very still and point its body toward any game it senses. **3.** A piece of advice; hint. Can you give me some *pointers* on fishing?
point·er (poin′tər) *noun, plural* **pointers.**

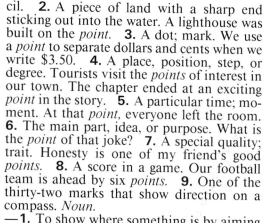

pointer

point of view A way of looking at or thinking about something. From my *point of view,* reading a good book is much more interesting than watching television.

poise 1. Calmness and confidence. The child spoke in front of the class with *poise*. 2. Balance. The acrobat walked across the tightrope with perfect *poise*. *Noun.*
—To be or keep in balance. The dancer *poised* on one foot. *Verb.*
poise (poiz) *noun; verb*, **poised, poising.**

poison A drug or other substance that harms or kills by chemical action. *Noun.*
—1. To give poison to. The farmer *poisoned* the insect pests that damaged the crops. 2. To put poison in. The villain had *poisoned* the victim's food. 3. To have a bad effect on. The gossip *poisoned* the minds of others with lies. *Verb.*
poi·son (poi′zən) *noun, plural* **poisons;** *verb*, **poisoned, poisoning.**

poison ivy A plant that has shiny leaves with three leaflets. It may grow along the ground, as a shrub, or as a vine. It causes a rash that itches if you touch the leaves.

poisonous Containing poison; having the effects of a poison. Many household cleaning products are *poisonous*.
poi·son·ous (poi′zə nəs) *adjective.*

poke 1. To push with something pointed; jab. I *poked* the frog with a stick to make it jump. 2. To stick out quickly; thrust. The woodchuck *poked* its head out of the burrow. 3. To move slowly. The little children *poked* along behind us. *Verb.*
—A push with something pointed; jab. A friend gave me a *poke* to wake me up. *Noun.*
poke (pōk) *verb*, **poked, poking;** *noun, plural* **pokes.**

poker¹ A metal rod for stirring a fire.
pok·er (pō′kər) *noun, plural* **pokers.**

poker² A card game in which the players bet on cards that they hold.
pok·er (pō′kər) *noun.*

Poland A country in east-central Europe.
Po·land (pō′lənd) *noun.*

polar Of or having to do with the North Pole or the South Pole. That explorer has led many *polar* expeditions.
po·lar (pō′lər) *adjective.*

polar bear A large bear that lives in the Arctic. Polar bears have thick, white fur and are strong swimmers.

pole¹ A long, thin piece of wood, metal, or other hard material. ⚠ Another word that sounds like this is **poll.**
pole (pōl) *noun, plural* **poles.**

pole² 1. Either end of the earth's axis. The North Pole is opposite the South Pole.

2. Either end of a magnet or battery where the force is strongest. ⚠ Another word that sounds like this is **poll.**
pole (pōl) *noun, plural* **poles.**

Pole A person who was born in or is a citizen of Poland.
Pole (pōl) *noun, plural* **Poles.**

polecat 1. A European animal that belongs to the weasel family. The polecat gives off a strong-smelling spray similar to that of a skunk. 2. The skunk of North America.
pole·cat (pōl′kat′) *noun, plural* **polecats.**

pole vault A contest in which a person uses a long pole to leap over a very high bar.

police A group of persons given power by a government to keep order and to enforce the law. ⚠ The word "police" may be used with a singular or plural verb. The state *police* patrols the highways. *Noun.*
—To keep order in. Guards *policed* the city streets. *Verb.*
po·lice (pə lēs′) *noun; verb*, **policed, policing.**

policeman A man who is a member of the police.
po·lice·man (pə lēs′mən) *noun, plural* **policemen** (pə lēs′mən).

police officer A member of the police; policeman or policewoman.

policewoman A woman who is a member of the police.
po·lice·wom·an (pə lēs′wùm′ən) *noun, plural* **policewomen** (pə lēs′wim′ən).

policy¹ A guiding belief or plan that people use to help them make decisions. What is the school's *policy* about pets in class?
pol·i·cy (pol′ə sē) *noun, plural* **policies.**

P

polar bear

at; āpe; fär; câre; end; mē; it; īce; pîerce; hot; ōld; sông, fôrk; oil; out; up; ūse; rüle; pùll; tûrn; chin; sing; shop; thin; <u>th</u>is; hw in white; zh in treasure. The symbol ə stands for the unstressed vowel sound in about, taken, pencil, lemon, and circus.

policy²   A written contract that is an agreement between an insurance company and the person being insured.
pol·i·cy (pol′ə sē) *noun, plural* **policies.**

polio   A short form of the word "poliomyelitis." Look up **poliomyelitis** for more information.
po·li·o (pō′lē ō′) *noun.*

poliomyelitis   A disease that can cause paralysis by attacking the spinal cord. It is caused by a virus and affects mainly children. There are two vaccines that help to prevent the disease. This disease is also called **polio.**
po·li·o·my·e·li·tis (pō′lē ō mī′ə lī′tis) *noun.*

polish   **1.** The smoothness or shine of a surface. The waxed floor had a bright *polish.*
2. A substance used to give a shine to something. Use plenty of shoe *polish* on those boots. *Noun.*
—To shine. We waxed and *polished* the oak table. *Verb.*
pol·ish (pol′ish) *noun, plural* **polishes;**
verb, **polished, polishing.**

Polish   The language of Poland. *Noun.*
—Of or having to do with Poland, the Poles, or their language. *Adjective.*
Po·lish (pō′lish) *noun; adjective.*

polite   Having good manners; showing consideration for others; courteous. It is *polite* to say "thank you" and "please."
po·lite (pə līt′) *adjective,* **politer, politest.**

political   Of or having to do with politics, politicians, or government. Democracy is one kind of *political* system. A *political* party helps people to get elected or appointed to government offices.
po·lit·i·cal (pə lit′i kəl) *adjective.*

politician   A person who holds or seeks a government office.
pol·i·ti·cian (pol′i tish′ən) *noun, plural* **politicians.**

politics   **1.** The work or study of government; the management of public affairs. The young person went into *politics* and ran for Congress.   **2.** The activities of political leaders, candidates, and parties. Around election time, *politics* is always in the news.
3. Opinions or beliefs about government. My parents' *politics* are conservative.   ▲ The word "politics" is used with a singular verb in definitions 1 and 2, and with a plural verb in definition 3.
pol·i·tics (pol′i tiks) *noun.*

polka   A lively dance that originated in central Europe.
pol·ka (pōl′kə *or* pō′kə) *noun, plural* **polkas.**

polka dot   One of many round dots that are spaced evenly to form a pattern on cloth or other material. This pattern is used on scarves, ties, blouses, and other things.

poll   **1.** A collecting of votes or opinions. A public opinion poll is the collecting of answers to questions about important issues or happenings.   **2. polls.** A place where votes are cast and recorded. *Noun.*
—**1.** To receive votes. The winner of the election *polled* twice as many votes as the loser.   **2.** To question a group of people to get their opinions. The newspaper reporter *polled* the town to find out what people thought about the president's decision. *Verb.*
▲ Another word that sounds like this is **pole.**
poll (pōl) *noun, plural* **polls;** *verb,* **polled, polling.**

Word History

The word **poll** comes from a Middle English word meaning "head" or "top of the head." In a crowd of people, someone could determine the number of people present by counting heads or "taking a poll." Since this count could also indicate the number of people in favor of something or against it, the word later came to mean "counting votes."

pollen   A yellowish powder made in the anthers of flowers. Pollen is made up of the male cells of flowering plants. It fertilizes the female cells so that they can form seeds.
pol·len (pol′ən) *noun.*

The bee is covered with **pollen.**

pollination   The transfer of pollen from the stamen to the pistil of the same flower or another flower. After pollen reaches the pistil, the plant can form seeds. The wind and some insects, birds, and animals help with pollination.
pol·li·na·tion (pol′ə nā′shən) *noun.*

pollute To make dirty or impure. Exhaust from automobiles *pollutes* the air.
pol·lute (pə lüt′) *verb,* **polluted, polluting.**

pollution 1. Harmful materials such as certain gases, chemicals, and wastes that pollute the air, water, or soil. *Pollution* in the pond killed the reeds that once grew there. 2. The act or process of polluting.
pol·lu·tion (pə lü′shən) *noun.*

polo A game played on horseback with mallets that have long handles. The object of the game is to hit a wooden ball through the other team's goal posts.
po·lo (pō′lō) *noun.*

polygon A figure that has three or more straight sides. A square is a polygon.
pol·y·gon (pol′ē gon′) *noun, plural* **polygons.**

polyp A small sea animal that has a tube-shaped body. The polyp's mouth has tentacles around it that catch food. Corals are polyps that live close together in large colonies.
pol·yp (pol′ip) *noun, plural* **polyps.**

pomegranate A round reddish yellow fruit that has a tough skin, a juicy red pulp, and many seeds. The pomegranate grows on a tree in warm areas.
pome·gran·ate (pom′gran′it) *noun, plural* **pomegranates.**

Whole Fruit

Split Fruit

pomegranates

pomp Stately and splendid display; magnificence; splendor. The foreign rulers were greeted with great *pomp*.
pomp (pomp) *noun.*

poncho A cloak made of one piece of cloth or other material. It has a hole in the middle for the head.
pon·cho (pon′chō) *noun, plural* **ponchos.**

pond A body of water surrounded by land. A pond is smaller than a lake.
pond (pond) *noun, plural* **ponds.**

ponder To think about something carefully. They *pondered* what to do next.
pon·der (pon′dər) *verb,* **pondered, pondering.**

pony A small kind of horse.
po·ny (pō′nē) *noun, plural* **ponies.**

pony express A postal service in which relays of riders on horseback carried mail across the western United States. The pony express ran from 1860 to 1861.

ponytail A way of wearing one's hair. The hair is pulled back and fastened behind the head, where it hangs down like a pony's tail.
po·ny·tail (pō′nē tāl′) *noun, plural* **ponytails.**

poodle A dog with thick curly hair. Poodles vary in size from large to very small. A poodle's hair is sometimes cut in a fancy way.
poo·dle (pü′dəl) *noun, plural* **poodles.**

pool¹ 1. A tank of water to swim in, either indoors or outdoors. 2. A small body of still water. 3. A small amount of any liquid. A *pool* of spilled gravy was on the table.
pool (pül) *noun, plural* **pools.**

pool² 1. A game played with hard balls and a long stick called a cue. Pool is played on a large table that has six pockets. The object of the game is to hit the balls into the pockets by striking one ball against another with the cue. 2. An arrangement in which a number of people share something. There is a typing *pool* at that office. *Noun.*
—To put into a common fund or group effort. The children *pooled* their money to buy a present for their teacher. *Verb.*
pool (pül) *noun, plural* **pools;** *verb,* **pooled, pooling.**

poor 1. Having little money. We are too *poor* to buy a car. 2. Below standard; bad. The farmer had a *poor* wheat crop. 3. Unfortunate. The *poor* child was crying over the lost dog.
poor (pùr) *adjective,* **poorer, poorest.**

pop 1. To make or cause to make a short, sharp sound. The balloon will *pop* if you squeeze it. 2. To move or appear quickly or without being expected. Our neighbor *popped* in to see us. The dog *popped* its head out the car window. *Verb.*
—1. A short, sharp sound. The firecracker exploded with a loud *pop*. 2. A soft drink. We each drank a bottle of *pop*. *Noun.*
pop (pop) *verb,* **popped, popping;** *noun, plural* **pops.**

P

at; āpe; fär; câre; end; mē; it; īce; pîerce; hot; ōld; sông; fôrk; oil; out; up; ūse; rüle; pùll; tûrn; chin; sing; shop; thin; this; hw in white; zh in treasure. The symbol ə stands for the unstressed vowel sound in about, taken, pencil, lemon, and circus.

popcorn   A kind of corn having kernels that burst open with a pop when heated. The kernels become white and fluffy, and can be eaten.
   pop·corn (pop′kôrn′) *noun.*

pope   The head of the Roman Catholic Church.
   pope (pōp) *noun, plural* **popes.**

poplar   A tall tree that grows rapidly and has wide leaves. The wood of the poplar is used to make pulp for paper and cardboard.
   pop·lar (pop′lər) *noun, plural* **poplars.**

poppy   A garden plant with round red, yellow, or white flowers.
   pop·py (pop′ē) *noun, plural* **poppies.**

popular   **1.** Liked or accepted by many people. The beach is a *popular* place on summer afternoons. It is a *popular* belief that a four-leaf clover brings good luck.   **2.** Having many friends; liked by many. That *popular* student is always getting invited to parties. That *popular* actor plays in many movies.   **3.** Of or for the people. Since 1913, United States senators have been elected by *popular* vote.
   pop·u·lar (pop′yə lər) *adjective.*

poppy

popularity   The condition of being popular. You could tell the *popularity* of the library book by how worn its cover was.
   pop·u·lar·i·ty (pop′yə lar′i tē) *noun.*

population   **1.** The number of people who live in a place. What is the *population* of your city?   **2.** The people or animals living in a place; inhabitants. The entire *population* was forced to leave the town because of the flood.
   pop·u·la·tion (pop′yə lā′shən) *noun, plural* **populations.**

populous   Having many people. New York is a *populous* city. China and India are *populous* countries.
   pop·u·lous (pop′yə ləs) *adjective.*

porcelain   A kind of hard, fine pottery. It is thin enough to see through when held to the light. Cups, plates, and other dishes are sometimes made of porcelain.
   por·ce·lain (pôr′sə lin) *noun.*

porch   An area with a roof that is built onto the outside of a house by a door. We play on our front *porch* in the summer. I left my galoshes on the *porch* before going in.
   porch (pôrch) *noun, plural* **porches.**

porcupine

porcupine   A forest animal whose body is covered with sharp quills.
   por·cu·pine (pôr′kyə pīn′) *noun, plural* **porcupines.**

pore¹   A very small opening in the skin or other surface. Perspiration passes through the *pores* in our skin.   ▲ Another word that sounds like this is **pour.**
   pore (pôr) *noun, plural* **pores.**

pore²   To read or study carefully. I *pored* over my notes the night before the test.   ▲ Another word that sounds like this is **pour.**
   pore (pôr) *verb,* **pored, poring.**

pork   The meat of a pig used as food.
   pork (pôrk) *noun.*

porous   Having or full of pores. Water seeped through the *porous* bricks.
   po·rous (pôr′əs) *adjective.*

porpoise   An animal that lives in the sea. The porpoise is a mammal and is related to the dolphin and whale. It looks like a dolphin but has a rounded head and a short snout.
   por·poise (pôr′pəs) *noun, plural* **porpoises** or **porpoise.**

porridge   A soft food made by boiling ground grains in water or milk. It is usually eaten for breakfast.
   por·ridge (pôr′ij)

port   **1.** A place where boats and ships can dock or anchor safely; harbor.   **2.** A city with a harbor.
   port (pôrt) *noun, plural* **ports.**

portable   Easy to carry from place to place. We took a *portable* radio on our trip.
   port·a·ble (pôr′tə bəl) *adjective.*

porter   **1.** A person who carries baggage. The *porter* at the hotel carried our suitcases to our room.   **2.** A person who waits on the passengers on a train.
   por·ter (pôr′tər) *noun, plural* **porters.**

porthole   A small round window in the side of a boat or ship. It lets in air and light.
   port·hole (pôrt′hōl′) *noun, plural* **portholes.**

portico A porch or covered walk. A portico usually has columns supporting its roof. Some churches, courthouses, and large homes have porticoes at the entrance.
por·ti·co (pôr′ti kō′) *noun, plural* **porticoes** or **porticos.**

portion 1. A part or share of something. I spent a *portion* of the day running errands. 2. An amount of food served to one person. Each of us had a *portion* of potatoes. *Noun.*
—To divide and give out in parts; distribute. We *portioned* out the cheese so that each camper had some. *Verb.*
por·tion (pôr′shən) *noun, plural* **portions;** *verb,* **portioned, portioning.**

portrait A picture of someone. The artist painted a *portrait* of the famous explorer.
por·trait (pôr′trit *or* pôr′trāt) *noun, plural* **portraits.**

portray 1. To make a picture of someone or something. The artist *portrayed* the family in a painting. 2. To picture in words; describe. In the book, the author *portrays* life in a small town. 3. To play the part of. The star *portrays* a sheriff in the movie.
por·tray (pôr trā′) *verb,* **portrayed, portraying.**

Portugal A country in southwestern Europe.
Por·tu·gal (pôr′chə gəl) *noun.*

Portuguese 1. A person who was born in or is a citizen of Portugal. 2. The language of Portugal and Brazil. *Noun.*
—Of or having to do with Portugal, its people, their language, or their culture. *Adjective.*
Por·tu·guese (pôr′chə gēz′ *or* pôr′chə gēs′) *noun, plural* **Portuguese;** *adjective.*

pose 1. A position of the body. I took a sitting *pose* for the next photograph. 2. A way of behaving or looking that hides the truth. The new student adopted a *pose* of self-confidence. *Noun.*
—1. To hold a position, such as for a painting, photograph, or sculpture. We all *posed* for the class photograph. 2. To take on a false manner or appearance. The thief *posed* as a plumber to get into the house. *Verb.*
pose (pōz) *noun, plural* **poses;** *verb,* **posed, posing.**

position 1. The place where a person or thing is. From my *position* at the window, I could see the whole parade. 2. A way of being placed. The teacher was seated in a comfortable *position.* 3. A way of thinking about something; point of view. What is the senator's *position* on the proposal to increase taxes? 4. Rank; standing. That judge is a person of high *position.* 5. A job. My cousin has held the same *position* with a company for many years.
po·si·tion (pə zish′ən) *noun, plural* **positions.**

positive 1. Certain; sure. I am *positive* that I locked the door. 2. Helpful or favorable. The teacher made some *positive* comments about my work. 3. Saying or meaning yes; consenting. Their answer to our invitation was *positive.* 4. More than zero. Five is a *positive* number. 5. Having one of two opposite kinds of electric charge. Magnets have a *positive* pole at one end and a negative pole at the other.
pos·i·tive (poz′i tiv) *adjective.*

posse A group of people gathered by a sheriff to help him or her capture a criminal.
pos·se (pos′ē) *noun, plural* **posses.**

possess 1. To have or own. That singer *possesses* a fine voice. The family *possesses* great wealth. 2. To have an influence over. A desire for ice cream *possessed* me, and I ordered a sundae.
pos·sess (pə zes′) *verb,* **possessed, possessing.**

possession 1. The act or condition of having or owning something. The two prospectors fought for *possession* of the gold. 2. Something owned. The family lost all their *possessions* in the fire. 3. A place under the control of a foreign country. The

The children **pose** for the camera.

at; āpe; fär; câre; end; mē; it; īce; pîerce; hot; ōld; sông, fôrk; oil; out; up; ūse; rüle; pùll; tûrn; chin; sing; shop; thin; this; hw in white; zh in treasure. The symbol ə stands for the unstressed vowel sound in about, taken, pencil, lemon, and circus.

Philippine Islands were once a *possession* of the United States.

pos·ses·sion (pə zesh′ən) *noun, plural* **possessions.**

possessive **1.** The form of a word that shows possession. In the sentence "The child's hat blew off," the noun "child's" is in the possessive. **2.** A word in the form that shows possession. In the sentence "The books are theirs," the pronoun "theirs" is a possessive. *Noun.*

—Having to do with or showing possession. *My* is the possessive form of the pronoun *I. Cousin's* is the possessive form of the noun *cousin. Adjective.*

pos·ses·sive (pə zes′iv) *noun, plural* **possessives;** *adjective.*

possibility **1.** The fact of being possible. The *possibility* that you might come to visit made me clean up my room. **2.** Something that may happen. The weather report says that snow is a *possibility* on Monday.

pos·si·bil·i·ty (pos′ə bil′i tē) *noun, plural* **possibilities.**

possible **1.** Capable of being, being done, or happening. It is not *possible* to be in two places at the same time. **2.** Capable of being used or considered. The park is a *possible* place for our picnic.

pos·si·ble (pos′ə bəl) *adjective.*

possibly **1.** In any way that is possible. I can't *possibly* get to your house before noon. **2.** Perhaps; maybe. I'll see you tonight, or *possibly* tomorrow.

pos·si·bly (pos′ə blē) *adverb.*

possum A small, furry animal; opossum. Look up **opossum** for more information.

pos·sum (pos′əm) *noun, plural* **possums.**

post– A *prefix* that means after. *Postwar* means after a war.

post¹ A piece of wood or other hard material that is set firmly upright to support or mark something. We started building the fence by digging holes for the *posts. Posts* supported the roof of the cabin. *Noun.*

—To put up a notice of something. The teacher *posted* the names of the winners of the drawing contest.

post (pōst) *noun, plural* **posts;** *verb,* **posted, posting.**

post² **1.** A place where a soldier, police officer, or guard must be to do his or her duty. A guard was assigned to the *post* in front of police headquarters. **2.** A place where soldiers work or are trained. There is an army *post* near our town. **3.** A job; position. The diplomat was named to the *post* of ambassador. *Noun.*

—To assign to a post. The police *posted* a guard near the valuable painting. *Verb.*

post (pōst) *noun, plural* **posts;** *verb,* **posted, posting.**

post³ **1.** A system for picking up and delivering mail. I will send the letter by *post.* **2.** A delivery of mail. The package came in today's *post.* *Noun.*

—**1.** To put in a mailbox. I will *post* the package right away. **2.** To let know; inform of news. Please keep me *posted. Verb.*

post (pōst) *noun, plural* **posts;** *verb,* **posted, posting.**

postage The amount of money charged for sending something by mail.

post·age (pōs′tij) *noun.*

postage stamp A small printed piece of paper issued by a government. It is placed on mail to show that postage has been paid.

postal Of or having to do with mail. A mail carrier is a *postal* worker.

post·al (pōs′təl) *adjective.*

Postal Service The independent government agency in the United States that is in charge of delivering the mail.

postcard A card that can be sent through the mail without an envelope. Some postcards have a picture on one side.

post·card (pōst′kärd′) *noun, plural* **postcards.**

poster A large printed sign that often has a picture. A poster usually has a notice or advertisement for the public to see.

post·er (pōs′tər) *noun, plural* **posters.**

A **poster** for the circus.

postman A person who delivers mail; mail carrier.

post·man (pōst′mən) *noun, plural* **postmen** (pōst′mən).

postmark An official mark stamped on mail. A postmark cancels the postage stamp and shows the place and date of mailing.

post·mark (pōst′märk′) *noun, plural* **postmarks.**

postmaster The person in charge of a post office.
> **post·mas·ter** (pōst′mas′tər) *noun, plural* **postmasters.**

postmistress The woman in charge of a post office.
> **post·mis·tress** (pōst′mis′tris) *noun, plural* **postmistresses.**

post office **1.** A department of a government in charge of handling mail. **2.** A place where mail is brought and made ready for delivery and stamps are sold.

postpone To put off until later. We *postponed* the baseball game until next Sunday because of rain.
> **post·pone** (pōst pōn′) *verb,* **postponed, postponing.**

postscript A message or note added to a letter after the writer's signature. In a *postscript,* I put the time of my train's arrival.
> **post·script** (pōst′skript′) *noun, plural* **postscripts.**

posture The way a person holds the body when sitting, standing, or walking. Your *posture* is good, because your back is straight and your shoulders are relaxed.
> **pos·ture** (pos′chər) *noun, plural* **postures.**

postwar Having to do with the period after a war. Foods that were scarce during the war were easier to obtain in the *postwar* period.
> **post·war** (pōst′wôr′) *adjective.*

pot A deep, round container for cooking or for holding things. Pots are made of baked clay, metal, glass, or another hard material. The stew simmered in a big copper *pot.*
> **pot** (pot) *noun, plural* **pots.**

potassium A soft, silver-colored metal. Potassium is a chemical element. Compounds that contain potassium are used to make soap, fertilizers, and explosives.
> **po·tas·si·um** (pə tas′ē əm) *noun.*

potato The thick, rounded underground stem of a leafy plant. Potatoes are eaten as a vegetable and can be prepared in many ways.
> **po·ta·to** (pə tā′tō) *noun, plural* **potatoes.**

potatoes

potential Capable of becoming something; possible but not yet actual. A board with rusty nails sticking out is a *potential* danger.
> **po·ten·tial** (pə ten′shəl) *adjective.*

potter A person who makes pottery.
> **pot·ter** (pot′ər) *noun, plural* **potters.**

pottery Pots, bowls, dishes, and other things made from clay.
> **pot·ter·y** (pot′ə rē) *noun.*

pottery

pouch **1.** A bag; sack. The mail carrier took the letters out of a *pouch.* **2.** A pocket of skin in some animals. Kangaroos and opossums carry their young in pouches. Squirrels carry nuts in the pouches of their cheeks.
> **pouch** (pouch) *noun, plural* **pouches.**

poultry Chickens, turkeys, geese, and other birds raised for their eggs or meat.
> **poul·try** (pōl′trē) *noun.*

pounce To come down suddenly and take hold of; leap or swoop suddenly. The kitten *pounced* on the rubber ball. *Verb.*
—The act of leaping or swooping on something. *Noun.*
> **pounce** (pouns) *verb,* **pounced, pouncing;** *noun, plural* **pounces.**

pound¹ **1.** A unit of weight. A pound is equal to 16 ounces. One pound is equal to 2.2 kilograms. **2.** A unit of money in Great Britain and certain other countries.
> **pound** (pound) *noun, plural* **pounds** or **pound.**

pound² **1.** To hit with heavy blows. I *pounded* the nails in with a hammer. The waves *pounded* against the rocks during the storm. **2.** To beat heavily. My heart was *pounding* with fright.
> **pound** (pound) *verb,* **pounded, pounding.**

pound³ A place where stray dogs and other animals are kept.
> **pound** (pound) *noun, plural* **pounds.**

pour **1.** To flow or cause to flow. The cook *poured* a cup of rice into the boiling water. The crowd *poured* out of the theater. **2.** To rain hard. It *poured* all day. ▲ Another word that sounds like this is **pore.**
> **pour** (pôr) *verb,* **poured, pouring.**

---

at; āpe; fär; câre; end; mē; it; īce; pîerce; hot; ōld; sông, fôrk; oil; out; up; ūse; rüle; pùll; tûrn; chin; sing; shop; thin; <u>th</u>is; hw in white; zh in treasure. The symbol ə stands for the unstressed vowel sound in about, taken, pencil, lemon, and circus.

P

567

pout   To thrust out the lips to show displeasure. The children *pouted* when they were scolded.
pout (pout) *verb*, **pouted, pouting.**

poverty   **1.** A lack of money; the condition of being poor. That family lives in *poverty*. **2.** The lack of what is needed. The *poverty* of the soil caused the farmer to give up the farm.
pov·er·ty (pov′ər tē) *noun*.

powder   **1.** Fine bits made by grinding, crushing, or crumbling something. When I rubbed the plaster, a white *powder* came off on my hand. **2.** Anything in the form of small dry particles. I put some *powder* on my hot, tired feet. We washed our clothes with soap *powder*. *Noun*.
—**1.** To make or turn into fine bits. We *powdered* the dried herbs by grinding them. **2.** To cover with fine bits. I *powdered* my face after I finished putting on my makeup for the play. The baker *powdered* the rolling pin with flour. *Verb*.
pow·der (pou′dər) *noun, plural* **powders;** *verb*, **powdered, powdering.**

power   **1.** The ability to do or bring about something; strength. I used all my *power* to lift the heavy box. Human beings have the *power* of speech. The witch in the story had magical *powers*. **2.** The right to do something; authority. Congress has the *power* to declare war. **3.** A person, thing, or nation that has strength or influence. The two world *powers* signed a trade agreement. **4.** Energy that can do work. Toasters, irons, and other household appliances are run by electric *power*. **5.** The product of a number that is multiplied by itself a given number of times. 5 to the second *power* is 25. *Noun*.
—To provide with power. That lawn mower is *powered* by a gasoline motor. *Verb*.
pow·er (pou′ər) *noun, plural* **powers;** *verb*, **powered, powering.**

powerful   Having great power. The Speaker of the House of Representatives is one of the most *powerful* members of Congress. This big truck has a *powerful* engine.
pow·er·ful (pou′ər fəl) *adjective*.

pp.   An abbreviation for *pages*.

PQ   Postal abbreviation for *Quebec*.

PR   Postal abbreviation for *Puerto Rico*.

P.R.   An abbreviation for *Puerto Rico*.

practical   **1.** Having to do with real life; coming from experience. I gained much *practical* knowledge of farming by working on a farm last summer. **2.** Easy to use, do, or put into effect. Those heavy clothes are not *practical* for a hike on a hot day.

3. Having or showing good sense; sensible. A *practical* person sets goals that can be achieved.
prac·ti·cal (prak′ti kəl) *adjective*.

practical joke   A prank or trick. Putting salt in the sugar bowl is a practical joke.

practically   **1.** Nearly; almost. My homework is *practically* finished. It is *practically* time for us to leave. **2.** In a practical way; sensibly. When you travel, dress *practically*.
prac·ti·cal·ly (prak′ti kə lē *or* prak′ti klē) *adverb*.

practice   **1.** The doing of some action over and over again to gain skill. You need more *practice* before you can be a good tennis player. *Practice* will help you to learn to speak Spanish. **2.** The usual way of doing something; habit. You may skip a meal once in a while, but don't make a *practice* of it. **3.** Actual use or performance. The idea seemed good, but it did not work in *practice*. **4.** The business of a doctor or other professional. The young lawyer has a small *practice*. *Noun*.
—**1.** To do some action over and over again to gain skill. I *practice* the violin every day. **2.** To do as a habit. Try to *practice* doing good deeds instead of just talking about it. **3.** To work at a profession. I hope someday to *practice* medicine. *Verb*.
prac·tice (prak′tis) *noun, plural* **practices;** *verb*, **practiced, practicing.**

prairie   Flat or rolling land covered with grass. A prairie has few or no trees.
prai·rie (prâr′ē) *noun, plural* **prairies.**

prairie dog   An animal that is related to the squirrel and that lives in underground dens in the prairies of the western United States. The prairie dog is a small, plump animal with a short tail and a grayish brown coat. Prairie dogs can be pests to farmers.

prairie dog

prairie schooner   A covered wagon used by American pioneers to cross the prairies.

praise   Words that show high regard and approval. Your good work at school deserves much *praise*. *Noun*.
—**1.** To express high regard and approval of. The teacher *praised* the student's fine draw-

ing. **2.** To worship. The minister *praised* God in the sermon. *Verb.*
> **praise** (prāz) *noun, plural* **praises;** *verb,* **praised, praising.**

prance **1.** To move in a proud, happy way. The children *pranced* around the house in their fancy costumes. **2.** To spring forward on the hind legs. The colt *pranced* and leaped about the field.
> **prance** (prans) *verb,* **pranced, prancing.**

prank A playful or mischievous act meant to trick or tease someone. As a *prank,* I hid my friend's notebook.
> **prank** (prangk) *noun, plural* **pranks.**

pray **1.** To speak to God to give thanks. Many people *pray* before dinner. **2.** To ask earnestly from God. We *prayed* for the safe return of the lost child. **3.** To be so kind as to; please. *Pray* be quiet. ▲ Another word that sounds like this is **prey.**
> **pray** (prā) *verb,* **prayed, praying.**

prayer **1.** The act of praying to God. The people in the mosque were on their knees in *prayer.* **2.** The words said when praying. I say a *prayer* every night before I go to sleep. **3.** Something prayed for. The farmer's *prayers* were granted and it finally began to rain.
> **prayer** (prâr) *noun, plural* **prayers.**

praying mantis An insect that is related to the grasshopper. The praying mantis has front legs for seizing the smaller insects it feeds upon.
> **praying man·tis** (man′tis) *noun, plural* **mantises** or **mantes.**

Word History

This insect is called a **praying mantis** because it holds its front legs in a way that looks like hands folded in prayer. *Mantis* comes from a Greek word that means "religious teacher" or "prophet."

---

pre- A *prefix* that means before or ahead of time. *Prehistoric* means before history was written down. *Prepaid* means paid for ahead of time.

preach **1.** To give a talk on a religious subject; give a sermon. The minister *preaches* each Sunday. **2.** To give advice; urge. My parents always *preach* about saving money.
> **preach** (prēch) *verb,* **preached, preaching.**

preacher A person who preaches, especially a Protestant minister.
> **preach·er** (prē′chər) *noun, plural* **preachers.**

precaution Something done beforehand to prevent harm or danger. Looking both ways is a good *precaution* to take before crossing the street.
> **pre·cau·tion** (pri kô′shən) *noun, plural* **precautions.**

precede To come or go before. The number 3 *precedes* the number 7. Lightning *precedes* thunder.
> **pre·cede** (pri sēd′) *verb,* **preceded, preceding.**

precedent An action or decision that may serve as an example to be followed in the future. The decision of the court set a *precedent* for how similar cases would be settled.
> **prec·e·dent** (pres′i dənt) *noun, plural* **precedents.**

preceding Coming or going before; earlier. I didn't understand something, so I went back to the *preceding* chapter of the textbook.
> **pre·ced·ing** (pri sē′ding) *adjective.*

precinct A part of a town or city. Each police *precinct* in our city has a police station.
> **pre·cinct** (prē′singkt′) *noun, plural* **precincts.**

precious **1.** Having great value. Gold is a *precious* metal. **2.** Dear; beloved. The stray dog became a *precious* pet in our family.
> **pre·cious** (presh′əs) *adjective.*

precipitate **1.** To make something happen suddenly; bring on. The unkind remark *precipitated* an argument. **2.** To change from vapor in the air into rain, sleet, hail, or snow.
> **pre·cip·i·tate** (pri sip′i tāt′) *verb,* **precipitated, precipitating.**

precipitation The falling of water in the form of rain, sleet, hail, or snow. The weather forecast warned of some *precipitation* during the day.
> **pre·cip·i·ta·tion** (pri sip′i tā′shən) *noun.*

precise **1.** Definite; exact. "8:03 A.M." is a *precise* time; "about eight o'clock" is not. **2.** Strict or careful. The teacher speaks in a clear and *precise* way.
> **pre·cise** (pri sīs′) *adjective.*

precision Accuracy; exactness. This watch keeps time with great *precision.*
> **pre·ci·sion** (pri sizh′ən) *noun.*

P

---

at; āpe; fär; câre; end; mē; it; īce; pîerce; hot; ōld; sông, fôrk; oil; out; up; ūse; rüle; pùll; tûrn; chin; sing; shop; thin; <u>th</u>is; hw in white; zh in treasure. The symbol ə stands for the unstressed vowel sound in about, taken, pencil, lemon, and circus.

precocious   Having more skill, talent, or knowledge than is usual at an early age. The *precocious* child read books at age three.
  pre·co·cious (pri kō′shəs) *adjective.*

predator   An animal that lives by hunting other animals for food. Lions, wolves, sharks, and owls are predators.
  pred·a·tor (pred′ə tər) *noun, plural* **predators.**

predecessor   A person who held an office or position before another person. President Ronald Reagan was President George Bush's *predecessor* in the White House.
  pred·e·ces·sor (pred′ə ses′ər) *noun, plural* **predecessors.**

predicament   An unpleasant or difficult situation; fix. Look at the *predicament* you're in because you accepted two invitations for the same evening!
  pre·dic·a·ment (pri dik′ə mənt) *noun, plural* **predicaments.**

predicate   A word or group of words in a sentence that tells what the subject does or what is done to the subject. The predicate may also give some descriptive information about the subject. In the sentence "Because of the rain our car skidded," the verb "skidded" is the predicate.
  pred·i·cate (pred′i kit) *noun, plural* **predicates.**

predicate adjective   An adjective that follows a linking verb in a sentence and that describes the subject. In the sentence "The flowers were lovely," "lovely" is a predicate adjective.

predicate noun   A noun that follows a linking verb in a sentence and that tells who or what the subject is. In the sentence "They are doctors," "doctors" is a predicate noun.

predict   To tell beforehand. Tomorrow's weather report *predicts* rain.
  pre·dict (pri dikt′) *verb,* **predicted, predicting.**

prediction   **1.** The act of predicting something. The weather forecaster's job is the *prediction* of the weather.   **2.** Something predicted. My *prediction* that our team would win has come true.
  pre·dic·tion (pri dik′shən) *noun, plural* **predictions.**

preface   An introduction to a book or speech. Our spelling book has a short *preface* written by the author.
  pref·ace (pref′is) *noun, plural* **prefaces.**

prefer   To like better. Which sport do you *prefer*, tennis or basketball?
  pre·fer (pri fûr′) *verb,* **preferred, preferring.**

preference   Something liked better; first choice. My *preference* is to go to the seashore rather than to the mountains this summer.
  pref·er·ence (pref′ər əns) *noun, plural* **preferences.**

prefix   A syllable or group of syllables that is added to the beginning of a word or root to change the meaning and form a new word. The word *dislike* is made up of the prefix *dis-* and the word *like.*
  pre·fix (prē′fiks′) *noun, plural* **prefixes.**

Language Note

Many words that begin with **prefixes** are not listed in this dictionary. To find out the meaning of most of these words, first look up the meaning of the word or root that the prefix is attached to. Then look up the meaning of the prefix. Put the prefix meaning and the meaning of the word or root together. The word *reestablish* is formed from the prefix *re-* and the word *establish. Establish* means to set something up or prove something true. The prefix *re-* means again. Therefore *reestablish* means to set something up again or prove something true again.

pregnant   Having one or more unborn young developing within the body. A woman is pregnant for about nine months before she gives birth to a baby.
  preg·nant (preg′nənt) *adjective.*

prehistoric   Belonging to a time before people started writing history. Dinosaurs were *prehistoric* animals.
  pre·his·tor·ic (prē′his tôr′ik) *adjective.*

prehistoric drawings on a rock

prejudice   **1.** An opinion that has been formed beforehand or before all the facts are known; bias. A judge must patiently hear a whole case without *prejudice.*   **2.** Hatred or

unfair treatment of a particular group, such as members of a race or religion. Because of *prejudice,* the owners of the company only hired workers of their own religion. *Noun.*
—To cause to have prejudice. Being hurt once by a dentist *prejudiced* me against all dentists. *Verb.*
prej·u·dice (prej′ə dis) *noun, plural* **prejudices;** *verb,* **prejudiced, prejudicing.**

preliminary Coming before the main part. We bought food and made other *preliminary* arrangements for the party.
pre·lim·i·nar·y (pri lim′ə ner′ē) *adjective.*

premature Arriving, happening, existing, or done before the usual or proper time; too early or too soon. Don't you think shopping for Christmas presents in July is *premature?*
pre·ma·ture (prē′mə chùr′ *or* prē′mə tùr′) *adjective.*

premier A person who is the chief minister in a government; prime minister.
pre·mier (pri mîr′) *noun, plural* **premiers.**

premise 1. A statement that is accepted as true without needing proof. A premise is used as a starting point for a line of reasoning or argument. 2. **premises.** Land and the buildings on it. The owner of the warehouse hired someone to guard the *premises.*
prem·ise (prem′is) *noun, plural* **premises.**

preparation 1. The act of making something ready, or the condition of being made ready. The cook was busy with the *preparation* of dinner. 2. An action needed to make something ready. Putting on costumes and make-up are some of the *preparations* for going on stage. 3. Something put together for a purpose. That medicine is a *preparation* to help stop coughing.
prep·a·ra·tion (prep′ə rā′shən) *noun, plural* **preparations.**

prepare To make or get ready. We *prepared* for the race by doing some exercises.
pre·pare (pri pâr′) *verb,* **prepared, preparing.**

preposition A word that shows the relation between another word and a noun or pronoun. In the sentence "The neighbors across the street never argue with us," the words "across" and "with" are prepositions.
prep·o·si·tion (prep′ə zish′ən) *noun, plural* **prepositions.**

prepositional Having a preposition or serving as a preposition. In the sentence "I drew with a crayon," "with a crayon" is a prepositional phrase.
prep·o·si·tion·al (prep′ə zish′ə nəl) *adjective.*

prescribe To order for use as a medical treatment. The doctor *prescribed* an ointment for my rash.
pre·scribe (pri skrīb′) *verb,* **prescribed, prescribing.**

prescription 1. An order written by a doctor to a pharmacist for medicine. The doctor gave me a *prescription* for cough medicine. 2. Medicine ordered by a prescription.
pre·scrip·tion (pri skrip′shən) *noun, plural* **prescriptions.**

presence 1. The fact of being in a place at a certain time. The *presence* of the growling dog in the room made me nervous. 2. The area around or near a person. The document had to be signed in the *presence* of a witness.
pres·ence (prez′əns) *noun.*

present¹ 1. In a place at a certain time. Were you *present* at the graduation ceremony? 2. Going on at this time; being or happening now. Do you know who the *present* mayor of your town is? *Adjective.*
—1. The time that is going on now. At *present,* there are two supermarkets in town. 2. The present tense. Look up **present tense** for more information. *Noun.*
pres·ent (prez′ənt) *adjective; noun.*

present² 1. To introduce a person to another person. I *presented* my new friend to my parents. 2. To bring or place before another person or group. The two candidates for mayor *presented* themselves at the town meeting. 3. To give in a formal way. The principal *presented* the awards to the students with the highest marks. 4. To put before an audience; display; show. The class *presented* a puppet show. *Verb.*
—Something given; gift. I made a necklace and gave it to my friend as a *present. Noun.*
pre·sent (pri zent′ *for verb;* prez′ənt *for noun*) *verb,* **presented, presenting;** *noun, plural* **presents.**

presentation The act of presenting something. The whole school attended the ceremony for the *presentation* of athletic awards.
pres·en·ta·tion (prez′ən tā′shən *or* prē′zən tā′shən) *noun, plural* **presentations.**

presently 1. In a little while; soon. The bus arrived *presently.* 2. At the present

at; āpe; fär; câre; end; mē; it; īce; pîerce; hot; ōld; sông, fôrk; oil; out; up; ūse; rüle; pùll; tûrn; chin; sing; shop; thin; this; hw in white; zh in treasure. The symbol ə stands for the unstressed vowel sound in about, taken, pencil, lemon, and circus.

time; now. Our geography class is *presently* studying Mexico.

pre·sent·ly (prez′ənt lē) *adverb.*

present participle   A form of a verb that can be used with an auxiliary verb to show that an action or condition continues. In the sentences "What are you reading?" and "I am being very quiet," "reading" and "being" are present participles.

present tense   A form of a verb that shows that an action is happening or that a condition exists at the present time. In the sentence "I like this book," the verb "like" is in the present tense. The present tense is also called the **present.**

preservation   Protection from loss, damage, or decay. Freezing is a method of food *preservation.* We encourage the *preservation* of our country's forests.

pre·ser·va·tion (prez′ər vā′shən) *noun.*

preservative   A substance that keeps something from spoiling or being damaged. Salt is used as a *preservative* for meat.

pre·serv·a·tive (pri zûr′və tiv) *noun, plural* **preservatives.**

preserve   **1.** To keep from being lost, damaged, or decayed; protect. You can *preserve* the wood of the old table by waxing it. It is important that we *preserve* our freedoms in this country.   **2.** To fix food so that it won't spoil. *Verb.*
—**1.** An area set aside for the protection of plants and animals. Rare birds and mammals breed in that nature *preserve.*   **2. preserves.** Fruit that has been boiled with sugar and then put in glass jars for later use. We made some strawberry *preserves. Noun.*

pre·serve (pri zûrv′) *verb,* **preserved, preserving;** *noun, plural* **preserves.**

preside   **1.** To be in the position of authority, as at a meeting. The mayor *presides* at town meetings.   **2.** To exert authority. The mayor *presides* over the town's affairs.

pre·side (pri zīd′) *verb,* **presided, presiding.**

presidency   **1.** The office of president. The young manager hoped someday to gain the *presidency* of the company.   **2.** The time during which a president is in office. The Civil War took place during the *presidency* of Abraham Lincoln.

pres·i·den·cy (prez′i dən sē) *noun, plural* **presidencies.**

president   **1.** A person who is head of the government of a republic, such as the United States. ▲ The word "president" is often capitalized when it means the president of the United States. The *President* answered ques-

tions at a news conference yesterday.   **2.** The person in charge of a company, a college or university, or other organization.

pres·i·dent (prez′i dənt) *noun, plural* **presidents.**

president-elect   A person who has been elected president, but has not yet been inaugurated.

pres·i·dent-e·lect (prez′i dənt i lekt′) *noun, plural* **presidents-elect.**

Presidents' Day   A holiday observed in most of the United States on the third Monday in February to celebrate the birthdays of George Washington and Abraham Lincoln.

newspapers printed by a **press**

press   **1.** To use force on something; push. You have to *press* the button to start the machine.   **2.** To push forward; go on. We *pressed* through the crowd of people.   **3.** To squeeze. I *pressed* juice from the grapefruit.   **4.** To iron. The tailor *pressed* the pants.   **5.** To hold close; hug. I *pressed* the kitten to my chest.   **6.** To try to persuade; urge. We *pressed* our guests to stay. *Verb.*
—**1.** A pushing on something. A *press* of the button started the elevator.   **2.** A tool or machine for pressing. We put the apples into a *press* to squeeze out the juice.   **3.** A machine for printing things; printing press.   **4.** Newspapers and magazines and the peo-

ple who write them. The president's speech was described in the *press*. *Noun*.
  press (pres) *verb*, **pressed, pressing;** *noun, plural* **presses.**

pressure **1.** Force caused by one thing pushing against another thing. The *pressure* of the driver's foot on the gas pedal made the car go faster. **2.** Strong influence or persuasion. The parents put *pressure* on their children to do well in school. **3.** A burden; strain. They went camping to get away from the *pressure* of city life. *Noun*.
  —To urge strongly. The salesperson tried to *pressure* people into buying things they didn't need. *Verb*.
  pres·sure (presh′ər) *noun, plural* **pressures;** *verb*, **pressured, pressuring.**

prestige Respect from others; high regard. The scientists' discovery brought them *prestige* and also brought *prestige* to their laboratory.
  pres·tige (pre stēzh′ *or* pre stēj′) *noun*.

presume **1.** To believe to be true without question; take for granted; assume. I *presumed* you would want to go to the game, so I bought you a ticket. **2.** To attempt without permission or authority; dare. Don't *presume* to tell me how to run my own business.
  pre·sume (pri züm′) *verb*, **presumed, presuming.**

pretend **1.** To claim. I like to play chess, but I don't *pretend* to be an expert at the game. **2.** To give a false show. The children *pretended* to be asleep. **3.** To make believe. We *pretended* that we were pirates.
  pre·tend (pri tend′) *verb*, **pretended, pretending.**

pretty Sweetly pleasing; attractive; charming. Your cousin is very *pretty*. The teacher read a *pretty* poem about spring. *Adjective*.
  —Fairly; quite. It is raining *pretty* hard. *Adverb*.
  pret·ty (prit′ē) *adjective*, **prettier, prettiest;** *adverb*.

pretzel A crisp food baked in the shape of a knot or stick and salted on the outside.
  pret·zel (pret′səl) *noun, plural* **pretzels.**

prevent **1.** To keep something from happening. Putting out campfires helps *prevent* forest fires. **2.** To keep someone from doing something; hinder. The noise outside our window *prevented* us from sleeping.
  pre·vent (pri vent′) *verb*, **prevented, preventing.**

prevention The act of preventing. Traffic lights are helpful in the *prevention* of accidents at street corners.
  pre·ven·tion (pri ven′shən) *noun*.

preventive Helping to prevent something. Locking your windows is a *preventive* against theft. *Adjective*.
  —Something that prevents, as a drug. A vaccine is a *preventive* against a disease. *Noun*.
  pre·ven·tive (pri ven′tiv) *adjective; noun*.

preview A showing of something ahead of time. My parents went to a *preview* of the film before it opened in the theaters.
  pre·view (prē′vū) *noun, plural* **previews.**

previous Coming before; earlier. We were introduced at the *previous* meeting.
  pre·vi·ous (prē′vē əs) *adjective*.

prey **1.** An animal that is hunted by another animal for food. Rabbits, birds, and snakes are the *prey* of foxes. **2.** The habit of hunting animals for food. A tiger is a beast of *prey*. **3.** A person who is the object of an attack; victim. The customer was the *prey* of a dishonest salesperson. *Noun*.
  —**1.** To hunt for food. Owls *prey* on small animals. **2.** To take advantage of. The bully *preyed* upon the smaller children. **3.** To trouble; distress. Worry about failing the test *preyed* on the student's mind. *Verb*. ▲ Another word that sounds like this is **pray.**
  prey (prā) *noun, plural* **preys;** *verb*, **preyed, preying.**

price **1.** The amount of money for which something is sold or offered for sale. What is the *price* of that radio? **2.** The cost at which something is gained. The country won the war, but paid a great *price* in lives lost. *Noun*.
  —**1.** To set a price on. The store manager *priced* the bicycle at $99. **2.** To find out the price of. We went into the shop to *price* the coats on display in the window. *Verb*.
  price (prīs) *noun, plural* **prices;** *verb*, **priced, pricing.**

priceless So valuable that it cannot be measured by a price. The *priceless* ancient statue is always guarded.
  price·less (prīs′lis) *adjective*.

prick To make a small hole with a sharp point. I *pricked* my finger on a pin. *Verb*.
  —A small hole in something. Make several *pricks* on the top of the pie crust. *Noun*.
  prick (prik) *verb*, **pricked, pricking;** *noun, plural* **pricks.**

P

at; āpe; fär; câre; end; mē; it; īce; pîerce; hot; ōld; sông, fôrk; oil; out; up; ūse; rüle; pùll; tûrn; chin; sing; shop; thin; <u>th</u>is; hw in white; zh in treasure. The symbol ə stands for the unstressed vowel sound in about, taken, pencil, lemon, and circus.

prickly   **1.** Having small, sharp thorns or points. We planted *prickly* rose bushes along the fence.   **2.** Stinging or tingling. Do you ever get a *prickly* sensation in your foot?
prick·ly (prik′lē) *adjective,* **pricklier, prickliest.**

prickly pear   A cactus that has yellow flowers and pear-shaped fruit.

pride   **1.** A feeling that one has worth and importance; self-respect. It is important to keep your *pride* even during difficult times. **2.** Too high an opinion of oneself. They knew they were wrong, but their foolish *pride* kept them from apologizing. **3.** Pleasure or satisfaction in something that one does or is connected with. The mechanics in this shop take *pride* in their work. *Noun.*

prickly pear

—**to pride oneself.** To feel pride; be proud. I *pride* myself on always being on time. *Verb.* ⌧ Other words that sound like this are **pried[1]** and **pried[2].**
pride (prīd) *noun; verb,* **prided, priding.**

pried[1]   Past tense and past participle of **pry[1].** Sometimes the newspaper reporter *pried* into other people's business. Look up **pry[1]** for more information. ⌧ Another word that sounds like this is **pride.**
pried (prīd) *verb.*

pried[2]   Past tense and past participle of **pry[2].** We *pried* the cover off the jar. Look up **pry[2]** for more information. ⌧ Another word that sounds like this is **pride.**
pried (prīd) *verb.*

priest   In certain Christian churches, a member of the clergy.
priest (prēst) *noun, plural* **priests.**

primary   **1.** First or greatest in importance; main. The travelers' *primary* concern was finding a place to stay for the night.   **2.** First in order or in time. Digging a foundation is one of the *primary* stages of building a house. *Adjective.*
—An election in which members of the same political party run against one another. The winner becomes the party's candidate for an office in a later, general election. *Noun.*
pri·ma·ry (prī′mer ē) *adjective; noun, plural* **primaries.**

primary color   One of the basic colors from which all other colors can be made. In mixing paint, red, yellow, and blue are the primary colors.

primary school   A school that includes the first three or four grades of elementary school. It sometimes includes kindergarten.

primate   A group of mammals that includes humans, apes, and monkeys. All primates have large brains, eyes that look forward, and fingers and thumbs that can grasp things.
pri·mate (prī′māt) *noun, plural* **primates.**

prime   **1.** First or greatest in importance or value; main. My *prime* concern was getting home safely.   **2.** Of the best quality; excellent. We get *prime* beef from the butcher. *Adjective.*
—The best stage or condition. This bouquet is past its *prime. Noun.*
—To get ready by putting something in or on. You should *prime* the woodwork before painting it. *Verb.*
prime (prīm) *adjective; noun, plural* **primes;** *verb,* **primed, priming.**

prime minister   The leader of a governing group of ministers. Both Great Britain and Canada have prime ministers.

prime number   A number that can be divided evenly only by itself and the number 1. The number 13 is a prime number.

primitive   **1.** Having to do with an early or first stage of development. A worm is a *primitive* form of life.   **2.** Very simple or crude. A stone ax is a *primitive* tool.
prim·i·tive (prim′i tiv) *adjective.*

primrose   A small garden plant with brightly colored flowers. It grows in moist, shady areas.
prim·rose (prim′rōz′) *noun, plural* **primroses.**

prince   **1.** A male member of a royal family other than a king. **2.** A nobleman of very high rank.
prince (prins) *noun, plural* **princes.**

primrose

Prince Edward Island   An island province in eastern Canada. Its capital is Charlottetown.
Prince Ed·ward Island (ed′wərd).

princess   **1.** A female member of a royal family other than a queen.   **2.** The wife of a prince.   **3.** A noblewoman of very high rank.

prin·cess (prin′sis *or* prin′ses) *noun, plural* **princesses.**

principal   Greatest or first in importance; chief. Our *principal* task this weekend is to weed the garden. *Adjective.*
—**1.** The person who is the head of a school. **2.** A person who leads or plays an important role in some activity. After the performance, the *principals* in the play came out for a special bow. *Noun.* ◣ Another word that sounds like this is **principle.**

prin·ci·pal (prin′sə pəl) *adjective; noun, plural* **principals.**

principle   **1.** A basic truth, law, or belief. Our legal system is based on the *principle* that a person is innocent until proven guilty. **2.** A rule of behavior that a person chooses to live by. I make it a *principle* to answer all my mail promptly. ◣ Another word that sounds like this is **principal.**

prin·ci·ple (prin′sə pəl) *noun, plural* **principles.**

print   **1.** To put letters, words, or pictures on a surface by pressing, stamping, or photographing. Machines *print* words and pictures on paper for books and magazines. **2.** To make something appear in a book, magazine, or newspaper; publish. Our town newspaper *printed* the poem that I wrote. **3.**   To write in separated letters like the letters in books. We *print* our names before we learn to write them in script. *Verb.*
—**1.** Letters that are made by printing. That book has large *print.* **2.** A mark that is made by pressing into something. There were *prints* in the snow where the dog had walked.   **3.** A picture made by pressing paper against an engraved or raised surface covered with ink. **4.** A photograph made from a negative. We had *prints* made of the class picture. **5.** Cloth with a design on it. I made a dress from a cotton *print. Noun.*

print (print) *verb,* **printed, printing;** *noun, plural* **prints.**

printer   **1.** A person or company whose business is to print books, magazines, or other material. **2.** An instrument that can be connected to a computer to produce a printed copy of a file that is stored on a disk.

print·er (prin′tər) *noun, plural* **printers.**

printing   **1.** The business or process of making books, magazines, and other printed material. **2.** Writing in which the letters are separated like the letters in books.

print·ing (prin′ting) *noun.*

printing press   A machine that prints letters or words on paper.

printout   A printed paper copy of the output from a computer.

print·out (print′out′) *noun, plural* **printouts.**

prism   A solid object that is transparent. A prism can be made of glass or crystal and can break up a ray of light into the colors of the rainbow. A prism has three sides shaped like rectangles that are equal in area and two triangular ends that are parallel to one another.

prism (priz′əm) *noun, plural* **prisms.**

prison   A building or other place where people who are accused or convicted of crimes are forced to stay.

pris·on (priz′ən) *noun, plural* **prisons.**

prisoner   **1.** A person who is forced to stay in a prison. **2.** Any person who is captured by someone else; captive. The kidnapers kept the hostage a *prisoner* in the basement of the old house.

pris·on·er (priz′ə nər) *noun, plural* **prisoners.**

privacy   The condition of being alone or private. The writer went to a cabin in the mountains in order to have *privacy* to finish a novel.

pri·va·cy (prī′və sē) *noun.*

private   **1.** Belonging to a particular person or group. That is a *private* driveway, not a town road. **2.** Not meant to be shared with others; not public. Our telephone conversation was *private.* **3.** Not holding a public office. The senator retired and became a *private* citizen. *Adjective.*
—A soldier of the lowest rank. A private is next below a corporal. *Noun.*
• **in private.**   Without other people being present. May I speak to you *in private?*

pri·vate (prī′vit) *adjective; noun, plural* **privates.**

privilege   A special right given to a person or group. The older children were given the *privilege* of staying up late on Friday night.

priv·i·lege (priv′ə lij) *noun, plural* **privileges.**

privileged   Having special rights or advantages. The seniors are a *privileged* group, because they are allowed to eat lunch outside.

priv·i·leged (priv′ə lijd) *adjective.*

P

at; āpe; fär; câre; end; mē; it; īce; pîerce; hot; ōld; sông, fôrk; oil; out; up; ūse; rüle; pùll; tûrn; chin; sing; shop; thin; this; hw in white; zh in treasure. The symbol ə stands for the unstressed vowel sound in about, taken, pencil, lemon, and circus.

prize¹   Something that is won in a contest or game. The blue ribbon was the top *prize* in the dog show. *Noun.*
—That has won or is good enough to win a prize. The farmer's children raised a *prize* calf for the state fair. *Adjective.*
   prize (prīz) *noun, plural* **prizes;** *adjective.*

The squash won first **prize.**

prize²   To think very highly of. I *prize* this fossil because I found it on my birthday.
   prize (prīz) *verb,* **prized, prizing.**

pro   A person who is a professional, not an amateur. A tennis *pro* gives lessons at the town tennis courts.
   pro (prō) *noun, plural* **pros.**

probability   **1.** The chances of something happening; likelihood. Bad weather increases the *probability* of accidents on the roads. **2.** A thing that is likely to happen. Rain today is a strong *probability.*
   prob·a·bil·i·ty (prob'ə bil'i tē) *noun, plural* **probabilities.**

probable   Likely to happen or be true. Our team is far ahead, so it is *probable* that we will win the game.
   prob·a·ble (prob'ə bəl) *adjective.*

probably   Almost surely; most likely. We are about the same size, so my coat will *probably* fit you. We will *probably* need to buy some groceries before the weekend.
   prob·a·bly (prob'ə blē) *adverb.*

probation   A period of time for testing a person's ability, behavior, or qualifications. After a month of *probation,* the new worker was accepted as a permanent employee.
   pro·ba·tion (prō bā'shən) *noun, plural* **probations.**

probe   **1.** A thorough investigation of something. The newspaper report led to a *probe* of prison conditions. **2.** A tool or device used to test or explore. A doctor might use a *probe* to look into an injured ear. A space *probe* is a spacecraft used to gather information about outer space. *Noun.*
—To investigate or explore thoroughly. The police *probed* the details of the bank's dishonest practices. *Verb.*
   probe (prōb) *noun, plural* **probes;** *verb,* **probed, probing.**

problem   **1.** A question to be thought about and answered. There were ten *problems* on the arithmetic test. **2.** A condition or fact that causes trouble and must be dealt with. Being nearsighted can be a *problem.*
   prob·lem (prob'ləm) *noun, plural* **problems.**

procedure   A proper way of doing something, usually by a series of steps. When the alarm rang, we followed the *procedure* for leaving the building in an emergency.
   pro·ce·dure (prə sē'jər) *noun, plural* **procedures.**

proceed   To move on or continue, especially after a stop. The speaker waited for the applause to stop and then *proceeded.*
   pro·ceed (prə sēd') *verb,* **proceeded, proceeding.**

proceeds   Money that is raised for a special purpose by selling something. The *proceeds* from the cake sale will pay for the class trip.
   pro·ceeds (prō'sēdz) *plural noun.*

process   A series of actions that are done in making or doing something. The *process* of making bread is simple but takes time. *Noun.*
—To treat or change something by a special series of steps. That factory *processes* cheese and other foods. *Verb.*
   proc·ess (pros'es) *noun, plural* **processes;** *verb,* **processed, processing.**

procession   **1.** A continuous forward movement of something or someone. We followed the *procession* of the parade along the avenue. **2.** A group of persons moving forward in a line or in a certain order. The wedding *procession* started down the aisle.
   pro·ces·sion (prə sesh'ən) *noun, plural* **processions.**

proclaim   To announce publicly. The mayor *proclaimed* a town holiday.
   pro·claim (prə klām') *verb,* **proclaimed, proclaiming.**

proclamation An official announcement of something. Abraham Lincoln made a *proclamation* in 1863 that freed slaves in many states.

proc·la·ma·tion (prok′lə mā′shən) *noun, plural* **proclamations.**

prod **1.** To push with something sharp or pointed; jab or poke. My friend *prodded* me with a pencil to wake me. **2.** To make do something; urge. I *prodded* my grandparents into singing a song. *Verb.*
—**1.** A push or jab. **2.** Something pointed. The shepherds used *prods* to keep the sheep moving through the gates. *Noun.*

prod (prod) *verb,* **prodded, prodding;** *noun, plural* **prods.**

produce **1.** To make or create something. That factory *produces* automobiles. A cow *produces* milk. **2.** To bring forth; show. The lawyer *produced* new evidence at the trial. **3.** To prepare a play or movie and present it to the public. The two partners *produced* a movie based on a popular book. *Verb.*
—Something that is made or yielded. The market sells lettuce, tomatoes, carrots, and other garden *produce. Noun.*

pro·duce (prə düs′ *or* prə dūs′ *for verb;* prod′üs *or* prod′ūs *or* prō′düs *or* prō′dūs *for noun*) *verb,* **produced, producing;** *noun.*

producer A person, company, or thing that makes or creates something. That company is a leading *producer* of automobiles. The *producer* hired actors for a new film.

pro·duc·er (prə dü′sər *or* prə dū′sər) *noun, plural* **producers.**

product **1.** Anything that is made or created. Milk, butter, and yogurt are dairy *products.* A made-up story is a *product* of the imagination. **2.** A number that is gotten by multiplying two other numbers. When you multiply 3 times 4, the *product* is 12.

prod·uct (prod′əkt) *noun, plural* **products.**

production **1.** The act of making or creating something. The *production* of steel is an important industry in that town. **2.** Something that is made or created. The opera was an elaborate *production.*

pro·duc·tion (prə duk′shən) *noun, plural* **productions.**

productive **1.** Making or yielding large amounts of something. This is fertile and *productive* land. **2.** Having good results. The talks were *productive* and an agreement was reached.

pro·duc·tive (prə duk′tiv) *adjective.*

profess **1.** To make known; declare. They *professed* their love for each other. **2.** To say that something is true when it isn't; pretend. They *professed* to be interested in the show, but they were really bored.

pro·fess (prə fes′) *verb,* **professed, professing.**

profession **1.** An occupation that requires special education and training. Medicine is a *profession* that requires years of study. **2.** The act of declaring something. The knight made a *profession* of loyalty to the king.

pro·fes·sion (prə fesh′ən) *noun, plural* **professions.**

professional **1.** Having to do with an occupation that requires special education. An architect is a *professional* person. **2.** Making money by doing something that other people do for fun. *Professional* athletes cannot compete in the Olympic games. *Adjective.*
—**1.** A person who has an occupation that requires special education. Doctors, lawyers, engineers, and architects are professionals. **2.** A person who works for money doing something that other people do for fun. After years of being an amateur golfer, my cousin decided to become a *professional. Noun.*

pro·fes·sion·al (prə fesh′ə nəl) *adjective; noun, plural* **professionals.**

professor A teacher having a high rank in a college or university.

pro·fes·sor (prə fes′ər) *noun, plural* **professors.**

profiles of three relatives

profile **1.** A side view or outline of a person's head or of something else. There is a

P

profile of George Washington on a quarter. **2.** A short description of someone or something. The newspaper printed a *profile* of the new mayor.

pro·file (prō′fīl) *noun, plural* **profiles.**

profit **1.** The amount of money left after all the costs of running a business have been paid. We bought the old boat for $100, spent $50 fixing it, and sold it for $200, which gave us a *profit* of $50. **2.** Anything that is gained by doing something; advantage; benefit. It will be to our *profit* to study hard for the test. *Noun.*
—To gain or benefit in some way. It will *profit* you to go to summer school because you will be better prepared for next year. A wise person *profits* from past mistakes. *Verb.*
▲ Another word that sounds like this is **prophet.**

prof·it (prof′it) *noun, plural* **profits;** *verb,* **profited, profiting.**

profitable Giving a profit. The person who runs that coffee shop has a very *profitable* business.

prof·it·a·ble (prof′i tə bəl) *adjective.*

profound **1.** Showing great understanding or knowledge. That book contains a *profound* analysis of ancient ideas about life. **2.** Very great or deep. We felt *profound* sorrow when we heard of our friend's death.

pro·found (prə found′) *adjective.*

profuse **1.** Very abundant; plentiful. In spring, the flowers in the meadow are *profuse.* **2.** Given or giving in a generous way; lavish. Our dinner guests were *profuse* in their compliments.

pro·fuse (prə fūs′) *adjective.*

program **1.** A list telling what will be done and who will do it in a play, concert, or other presentation. Photographs of the players on the baseball team appeared in the *program* sold at the stadium. **2.** A play or other presentation or performance. The class planned an interesting *program* for their parents. What is your favorite television *program?* **3.** A plan of what will be done. We have a new *program* to fight crime in our city. **4.** A series of instructions that a computer follows in order to perform some task.

pro·gram (prō′gram) *noun, plural* **programs.**

programmer A person who writes programs for computers.

pro·gram·mer (prō′gram ər) *noun, plural* **programmers.**

progress A forward movement. A storm slowed the ship's *progress* across the ocean. Are you making any *progress* with your book report? *Noun.*
—To move forward. The building of the new house *progressed* rapidly. *Verb.*

prog·ress (prog′res *for noun;* prə gres′ *for verb*) *noun; verb,* **progressed, progressing.**

progressive **1.** Moving forward; developing. Some diseases cause *progressive* deterioration of health. **2.** In favor of reform or improvement. The new senator had many *progressive* ideas for protecting the environment against pollution. *Adjective.*
—A person who favors improvement or reform in politics or some other area. *Noun.*

pro·gres·sive (prə gres′iv) *adjective; noun, plural* **progressives.**

prohibit To not allow; forbid or prevent. Smoking is *prohibited* in the bus.

pro·hib·it (prō hib′it) *verb,* **prohibited, prohibiting.**

The signs **prohibit** pedestrians and bicycles on this road.

project **1.** A plan or activity to be done. Our *project* for science class was to raise a baby chicken. **2.** A group of apartment buildings that are designed as a unit. That is the new housing *project. Noun.*
—**1.** To throw or propel. A slingshot *projects* stones into the air. **2.** To cause light, a shadow, or an image to fall on a surface. The movie was *projected* on a screen. **3.** To imagine or predict what will happen. The newspapers took polls to *project* the winner of the election. **4.** To stick out; protrude. Fine hairs *project* from the sides of some kinds of caterpillars. *Verb.*

proj·ect (proj′ekt *for noun;* prə jekt′ *for verb*) *noun, plural* **projects;** *verb,* **projected, projecting.**

projectile Any object that can be thrown or shot through the air. A bullet is a projectile.
pro·jec·tile (prə jek′tīl) *noun, plural* **projectiles.**

projection **1.** The act of throwing something forward. The *projection* of objects onto the rink is forbidden. **2.** The picture or other image that is projected onto a screen or other surface. The *projection* of the slide was so clear that we could see every detail. **3.** A prediction that is based on certain information. The network announced its *projection* of who would win the election. **4.** Something that sticks out or projects. The surface of the moon has many rocky *projections.*
pro·jec·tion (prə jek′shən) *noun, plural* **projections.**

projector A machine that is used to show a movie, photographic slides, or other material on a screen or other surface.
pro·jec·tor (prə jek′tər) *noun, plural* **projectors.**

prolong To make longer, expecially in time; extend. New medical treatments can *prolong* people's lives.
pro·long (prə lông′) *verb,* **prolonged, prolonging.**

prominent **1.** Well-known or important. The town council was made up of five *prominent* citizens. **2.** Very easy to see because it stands out in some way; noticeable. The lone tree was *prominent* in the open field.
prom·i·nent (prom′ə nənt) *adjective.*

promise **1.** A statement made by a person, saying that something will or will not be done or happen. I gave a *promise* that I would clean my room. **2.** Something that gives a reason for expecting success or progress in the future. You show *promise* as a writer. *Noun.*
—**1.** To give one's word that something will or will not be done or happen. I *promise* to be home by 5:30. **2.** To give reason to expect something. The beautiful red sunset *promises* a sunny day for tomorrow. *Verb.*
prom·ise (prom′is) *noun, plural* **promises;** *verb,* **promised, promising.**

promontory A high piece of land that sticks out into a body of water. There was an old lighthouse on the *promontory.*
prom·on·to·ry (prom′ən tôr′ē) *noun, plural* **promontories.**

promote **1.** To give a higher rank or importance to. Everyone in the class was *promoted* from third to fourth grade. **2.** To help in doing or contribute to something. Eating too much sugar *promotes* tooth decay.
pro·mote (prə mōt′) *verb,* **promoted, promoting.**

promotion **1.** A change to a higher rank, position, or grade. "Congratulations on your *promotion* to manager!" **2.** The act of promoting. The candidate needed a great deal of money for the *promotion* of the campaign.
pro·mo·tion (prə mō′shən) *noun, plural* **promotions.**

prompt Quick or on time. The restaurant gave very *prompt* service. *Adjective.*
—**1.** To cause someone to do something. The sound of thunder *prompted* me to close the windows. **2.** To remind an actor or speaker of what to say if he or she forgets. Your job is to *prompt* the actors. *Verb.*
prompt (prompt) *adjective,* **prompter, promptest;** *verb,* **prompted, prompting.**

prone **1.** Lying flat with the face downward. I stretched out *prone* on the floor. **2.** Having the wish or tendency to do something. Some people are *prone* to eat too much.
prone (prōn) *adjective.*

prong One of the pointed ends of an antler or of a fork or other tool.
prong (prông *or* prong) *noun, plural* **prongs.**

pronoun A word that takes the place of one or more nouns or noun phrases. In the sentence "We gave it to them yesterday," "We," "it," and "them" are pronouns.
pro·noun (prō′noun′) *noun, plural* **pronouns.**

pronounce **1.** To make the sound of a letter or word. People from different parts of the country *pronounce* certain words differ-

promontory

at; āpe; fär; câre; end; mē; it; īce; pîerce; hot; ōld; sông, fôrk; oil; out; up; ūse; rüle; pùll; tûrn; chin; sing; shop; thin; this; hw in white; zh in treasure. The symbol ə stands for the unstressed vowel sound in about, taken, pencil, lemon, and circus.

ently. If you look up the word "adult," you will see that there are two ways to *pronounce* this word, and both ways are correct. **2.** To say or declare. The judge *pronounced* the prisoner not guilty.
pro·nounce (prə nouns') *verb*, **pronounced, pronouncing.**

pronunciation A way of making the sound of a letter, a word, or words. In many dictionaries, the *pronunciation* of each word is shown.
pro·nun·ci·a·tion (prə nun'sē ā'shən) *noun*, *plural* **pronunciations.**

proof Facts or evidence showing that something is true. The lawyer had *proof* of the accused person's innocence.
proof (prüf) *noun*, *plural* **proofs.**

proofread To read written or printed material to find and correct mistakes. You should *proofread* your report before you give it to the teacher.
proof·read (prüf'rēd') *verb*, **proofread** (prüf'red'), **proofreading.**

prop To hold up or hold in place by putting something under or against; support. We *propped* up the sagging roof with some pieces of lumber. *Verb.*
—A thing used to hold something in a position. They used a large stone as a *prop* to keep the door open. *Noun.*
prop (prop) *verb*, **propped, propping;** *noun*, *plural* **props.**

propaganda Information or ideas that are deliberately spread to try to influence the thinking of other people. Often propaganda is not completely true or fair. That government publishes *propaganda* criticizing the way of life in other countries.
prop·a·gan·da (prop'ə gan'də) *noun.*

propel To cause to move forward or onward. This plane is *propelled* by jet engines.
pro·pel (prə pel') *verb*, **propelled, propelling.**

propeller A device that is made up of blades mounted on a hub. When a propeller turns, it moves air or water and provides the force to drive a boat or aircraft forward.
pro·pel·ler (prə pel'ər) *noun*, *plural* **propellers.**

proper **1.** Correct or suitable for a certain purpose or occasion. A carpenter must have the *proper* tools to do good work. *Proper* attire should be worn at the wedding. **2.** Thought of in a strict sense. The village we live in is not part of the city *proper.*
prop·er (prop'ər) *adjective.*

proper adjective An adjective that is formed from a proper noun. In the sentence "We will visit several European countries," "European" is a proper adjective.

properly **1.** In a correct or suitable way. The dentist showed us how to brush *properly.* **2.** In a strict sense. *Properly* speaking, that book is not a novel; it is a biography.
prop·er·ly (prop'ər lē) *adverb.*

proper noun A noun that names a particular person, place, or thing. A proper noun is always capitalized. In the sentence "George Washington was born in Virginia," "George Washington" and "Virginia" are proper nouns.

property **1.** Anything that is owned by a person or organization. The school building was town *property.* That coat is my *property.* **2.** A piece of land. We bought some *property* near the ocean. **3.** A characteristic of something. Heat is a *property* of fire.
prop·er·ty (prop'ər tē) *noun*, *plural* **properties.**

prophecy **1.** Something that a person says will happen in the future; prediction. They believe a *prophecy* that there will be a great flood in ten years. **2.** The act of predicting.
proph·e·cy (prof'ə sē) *noun*, *plural* **prophecies.**

prophet **1.** A person who tells others a message that is believed to be from God. **2.** A person who tells what will happen in the future. ▲ Another word that sounds like this is **profit.**
proph·et (prof'it) *noun*, *plural* **prophets.**

proportion **1.** The relation of one thing to another with regard to size, number, or amount. The *proportion* of boys to girls in the class is two to one. **2. proportions.** The size or dimensions of something. We measured the *proportions* of the room.
pro·por·tion (prə pôr'shən) *noun*, *plural* **proportions.**

proposal **1.** A plan or suggestion that is presented to others for consideration. The committee wrote a *proposal* to change some of the rules of the school. **2.** An offer of marriage.
pro·pos·al (prə pō'zəl) *noun*, *plural* **proposals.**

propose **1.** To suggest something or someone to other people for their consideration. The governor *proposed* increased taxes for next year. Several of the students have *proposed* you for class president. **2.** To intend or plan to do something. My friend *proposes* to study to be a doctor. **3.** To make an offer of marriage.
pro·pose (prə pōz') *verb*, **proposed, proposing.**

580

proposition   1. Something that is suggested for consideration. They accepted our *proposition* to mow their lawn in exchange for the use of their pool.   2. A statement or subject to be discussed. The *proposition* for debate was whether taxes should be increased.
   pro·po·si·tion (prop′ə zish′ən) *noun, plural* **propositions.**

propulsion   The force that moves something forward or onward. The spacecraft was launched by means of rocket *propulsion.*
   pro·pul·sion (prə pul′shən) *noun.*

prose   Written or spoken language that is like normal speech, rather than like poetry.
   prose (prōz) *noun.*

prosecute   To investigate or examine a person accused of a crime in a court of law. They *prosecuted* two people for the theft.
   pros·e·cute (pros′i kūt′) *verb,* **prosecuted, prosecuting.**

prosecution   1. The act or process of prosecuting. The evidence resulted in the *prosecution* of the gang for arson.   2. The person or group that prosecutes. My cousin testified as a witness for the *prosecution* in the trial.
   pros·e·cu·tion (pros′i kū′shən) *noun,* *plural* **prosecutions.**

prospect   1. Something that is looked forward to or expected. I was excited at the *prospect* of owning a bike.   2. A person who will probably do something that is expected. The salesperson thought I was a good *prospect* for buying the vacuum cleaner. *Noun.*
   —To search or explore. Many have gone *prospecting* for gold in Alaska. *Verb.*
   pros·pect (pros′pekt) *noun, plural* **prospects;** *verb,* **prospected, prospecting.**

prospector   A person who explores for gold or other minerals.
   pros·pec·tor (pros′pek tər) *noun, plural* **prospectors.**

The **prospector** pans for gold.

prosper   To be successful; do very well. The town *prospered* when several companies moved their offices there.
   pros·per (pros′pər) *verb,* **prospered, prospering.**

prosperity   Success, wealth, or good fortune in life. Since it had been a good season for crops, the farmers enjoyed *prosperity.*
   pros·per·i·ty (pros per′i tē) *noun.*

prosperous   Having success, wealth, or good fortune. The *prosperous* family tried to help others less fortunate than they.
   pros·per·ous (pros′pər əs) *adjective.*

protect   To keep from harm; defend. Football players wear helmets to *protect* their heads. That law *protects* our right to vote.
   pro·tect (prə tekt′) *verb,* **protected, protecting.**

Goggles **protect** the eyes.

protection   1. The keeping of someone or something from harm. Our state has game preserves for the *protection* of wild animals. 2. A person or thing that protects. I put lotion on my skin as a *protection* against sunburn.
   pro·tec·tion (prə tek′shən) *noun.*

protective   Keeping from harm; protecting. A turtle has a *protective* shell. We put a *protective* coating of wax on the floors.
   pro·tec·tive (prə tek′tiv) *adjective.*

protein   A substance that is found in all living cells of animals and plants. It is necessary for growth and life. Meat, eggs, and milk contain protein.
   pro·tein (prō′tēn) *noun, plural* **proteins.**

---

at; āpe; fär; câre; end; mē; it; īce; pîerce; hot; ōld; sông, fôrk; oil; out; up; ūse; rüle; pùll; tûrn; chin; sing; shop; thin; <u>this</u>; hw in white; zh in treasure. The symbol ə stands for the unstressed vowel sound in about, taken, pencil, lemon, and circus.

P

protest An objection or complaint against something. The people of the town made a *protest* against the building of the new highway. The parents ignored the child's *protests* about going to bed early. *Noun.*
—To make a protest; object to. The students *protested* against closing the library. *Verb.*
pro·test (prō′test *for noun;* prə test′ *for verb*) *noun, plural* **protests;** *verb,* **protested, protesting.**

Protestant A member of any Christian church other than the Roman Catholic Church or the Orthodox Church.
Prot·es·tant (prot′ə stənt) *noun, plural* **Protestants.**

proton A tiny particle found in the nucleus of an atom. A proton has a positive electrical charge.
pro·ton (prō′ton) *noun, plural* **protons.**

protoplasm A substance that is like a jelly and is the living matter of all cells.
pro·to·plasm (prō′tə plaz′əm) *noun.*

protozoan A cell that captures its food. Protozoans are so small that they can be seen only through a microscope. An ameba is one kind of protozoan.
pro·to·zo·an (prō′tə zō′ən) *noun, plural* **protozoans** or **protozoa.** (prō′tə zō′ə).

protrude To stick out. Rocks *protruded* from the snow.
pro·trude (prō trüd′) *verb,* **protruded, protruding.**

proud 1. Having a strong sense of satisfaction in a person or thing. I am *proud* of the bookcase I made. 2. Having self-respect. They were too *proud* to ask their friends for money.
proud (proud) *adjective,* **prouder, proudest.**

prove 1. To show that something is what it is supposed to be, or does what it is supposed to do. They asked the salesperson to *prove* that the soap would really get clothes cleaner. The lawyer *proved* the innocence of the prisoner. 2. To have a certain result. The new play *proved* to be a great success.
prove (prüv) *verb,* **proved, proved** or **proven, proving.**

proven Past participle of **prove.** You have *proven* that you are a loyal friend. Look up **prove** for more information.
prov·en (prü′vən) *verb.*

proverb A short saying that expresses something that many people believe to be true. "Haste makes waste" is a proverb.
prov·erb (prov′ərb) *noun, plural* **proverbs.**

provide 1. To give what is needed or wanted; supply. The art teacher *provided* paper, brushes, and paint. Trees *provide* shade from the sun. 2. To set as a rule or condition. The law *provides* that a person is innocent until proven guilty. 3. To take care of a present or future need. They *provide* for their family by working.
pro·vide (prə vīd′) *verb,* **provided, providing.**

provided On the condition that; if. I'll lend you my bicycle, *provided* you return it tomorrow.
pro·vid·ed (prə vī′did) *conjunction.*

province 1. One of the divisions of some countries. Canada is made up of ten provinces. 2. An area of activity or authority. Representing a person in a court of law is within the *province* of a lawyer. 3. the **provinces.** The regions of a country away from the main cities.
prov·ince (prov′ins) *noun, plural* **provinces.**

provincial 1. Of or having to do with a province. They are running for office in the *provincial* government. 2. Belonging to or characteristic of a certain province. On holidays the people of the village wear *provincial* costumes.
pro·vin·cial (prə vin′shəl) *adjective.*

provision 1. The act of giving something that is needed. The coach was responsible for the *provision* of equipment to the team. 2. The act of planning ahead for a future need. Has any *provision* been made for the party if it rains? 3. A condition or requirement. A *provision* for voting is being a citizen. 4. **provisions.** A supply of food. The ship has *provisions* for one month.
pro·vi·sion (prə vizh′ən) *noun, plural* **provisions.**

provoke 1. To make angry. Their rudeness *provoked* me. 2. To stir; excite. Unfair laws *provoked* the people to riot. 3. To bring out; arouse. The newspaper article *provoked* much discussion.
pro·voke (prə vōk′) *verb,* **provoked, provoking.**

prow The front part of a boat or ship; bow.
prow (prou) *noun, plural* **prows.**

prow

prowl To move or roam quietly or secretly. The tiger *prowled* through the forest. The thief *prowled* the streets at night.
prowl (proul) *verb,* **prowled, prowling.**

prudence Good judgment and caution. You show *prudence* in spending your money.
pru·dence (prü′dəns) *noun.*

prudent Having or showing good judgment or planning; cautious; sensible. It is *prudent* to have the car checked before starting on a long trip.
pru·dent (prü′dənt) *adjective.*

prune¹ A plum that has been dried.
prune (prün) *noun, plural* **prunes.**

prune² To cut off or cut out parts from something. We *pruned* dead branches from the tree.
prune (prün) *verb,* **pruned, pruning.**

pry¹ To look or inquire too closely or curiously. They obviously don't want to discuss the matter, so please don't *pry.*
pry (prī) *verb,* **pried, prying.**

pry² 1. To move or raise by force. The worker *pried* the top off the crate with a crowbar. 2. To get with much effort. The reporter tried to *pry* information about the accident from the victims.
pry (prī) *verb,* **pried, prying.**

P.S. An abbreviation for *postscript* or *public school.*

psalm A sacred song or poem. There is a collection of *psalms* in the Bible.
psalm (säm) *noun, plural* **psalms.**

psychiatrist A doctor who treats emotional and mental illness.
psy·chi·a·trist (si kī′ə trist *or* sī kī′ə trist) *noun, plural* **psychiatrists.**

psychiatry A branch of medicine that deals with emotional and mental illness.
psy·chi·a·try (si kī′ə trē *or* sī kī′ə trē) *noun.*

psychological 1. Having to do with the study of the mind and the way people behave. 2. Having to do with the mind or the way people behave. Scientists study the *psychological* effects of noise on people.
psy·cho·log·i·cal (sī′kə loj′i kəl) *adjective.*

psychologist A person who works or specializes in psychology.
psy·chol·o·gist (sī kol′ə jist) *noun, plural* **psychologists.**

psychology The study of the mind and of the way people or animals behave.
psy·chol·o·gy (sī kol′ə jē) *noun.*

pt. An abbreviation for *pint* or *pints.*

pterodactyl A flying reptile that lived in prehistoric times. The pterodactyl's wings were membranes that stretched from the sides of its body and arms to its fourth fingers.
pter·o·dac·tyl (ter′ə dak′təl) *noun, plural* **pterodactyls.**

public 1. Having to do with or for all the people. The mayor made a *public* announcement over the radio. A *public* beach is for anybody to use. 2. Working for the government of a town, city, or country. A judge is a *public* official. *Adjective.*
—All the people of a town, city, or country. The museum is open to the *public* every day. *Noun.*
• **in public.** In a place where other people are present, sometimes a large number of people. The singer has talent but has never appeared *in public.*
pub·lic (pub′lik) *adjective; noun.*

publication A magazine, newspaper, book, or any other printed material that is published. We subscribe to several *publications* about nature.
pub·li·ca·tion (pub′li kā′shən) *noun, plural* **publications.**

publicity 1. Information given out to bring a person or thing to the attention of the public. The *publicity* about the singers brought a large crowd to hear them. 2. The attention of the public. Most politicians like *publicity.*
pub·lic·i·ty (pu blis′i tē) *noun.*

public school A free school that is supported by people's taxes.

publish To print a newspaper, magazine, book, or other material and offer it for sale. The high school *publishes* a weekly newspaper.
pub·lish (pub′lish) *verb,* **published, publishing.**

publisher A person or company that publishes books, magazines, newspapers, or other material.
pub·lish·er (pub′li shər) *noun, plural* **publishers.**

puck A thick, black disk made of hard rubber. A puck is used in playing ice hockey.
puck (puk) *noun, plural* **pucks.**

pudding A sweet, soft dessert that is cooked.
pud·ding (pùd′ing) *noun, plural* **puddings.**

P

at; āpe; fär; câre; end; mē; it; īce; pîerce; hot; ōld; sông, fôrk; oil; out; up; ūse; rüle; pùll; tûrn; chin; sing; shop; thin; <u>th</u>is; hw in white; zh in treasure. The symbol ə stands for the unstressed vowel sound in about, taken, pencil, lemon, and circus.

puddle A small pool of water or other liquid that is not very deep. There were *puddles* in the road after the rain. There was a *puddle* of spilled milk on the floor.
pud·dle (pud′əl) *noun, plural* **puddles.**

pueblo **1.** An American Indian village consisting of adobe and stone houses that are joined together. Pueblo are built by certain Indian tribes in the southwestern United States. **2. Pueblo.** A member of an American Indian tribe of New Mexico and Arizona.
pueb·lo (pweb′lō) *noun, plural* **pueblo** *for definition 1;* **Pueblo** *or* **Pueblos** *for definition 2.*

pueblo

Puerto Rican **1.** A person who was born or is living in Puerto Rico. **2.** Having to do with Puerto Rico or its people.
Puer·to Ri·can (pwer′tō rē′kən *or* pôr′tə rē′kən).

Puerto Rico An island in the Caribbean Sea. It is a territory of the United States.
Puer·to Ri·co (pwer′tō rē′kō *or* pôr′tə rē′kō).

puff **1.** A short, gentle burst of air, breath, smoke, or something similar. A *puff* of smoke came out of the chimney. **2.** Anything soft, round, and fluffy. The chicks were *puffs* of yellow down. *Noun.*
—**1.** To blow or breathe in a puff or puffs. The engine *puffed* smoke. We *puffed* from climbing the stairs. **2.** To swell up or out.

My finger *puffed* up from the bee sting. The little bird *puffed* out its feathers. *Verb.*
puff (puf) *noun, plural* **puffs;** *verb,* **puffed, puffing.**

puffin A bird that lives in Arctic waters and coastal regions. Puffins have black and white feathers, a plump body, and a large, brightly colored bill.
puf·fin (puf′in) *noun, plural* **puffins.**

puffin

pull **1.** To grab or hold something and move it forward or toward oneself. Two horses *pulled* the wagon. I *pulled* the closet door open. **2.** To remove or tear out something. The dentist had to *pull* my tooth. **3.** To go or move. The ferry *pulled* away from the dock. *Verb.*
—**1.** The work done or the force used in moving something by pulling it. It was a long, hard *pull* to the top of the hill with the supplies on the sled. The strong *pull* of the magnet attracted the nails. **2.** The act of pulling something. Give a *pull* on the rope and the bell will ring. *Noun.*
• **to pull through.** To manage to exist through a difficult or dangerous situation. The puppies were very sick with distemper, but they all *pulled through.*
pull (pu̇l) *verb,* **pulled, pulling;** *noun, plural* **pulls.**

pulley A wheel with a groove around it that a rope or chain can be pulled over. Pulleys are used to lift heavy weights.
pul·ley (pu̇l′ē) *noun, plural* **pulleys.**

pulp **1.** The soft, juicy part of fruits and vegetables. **2.** Any soft, wet mass of material. Wood pulp is used to make paper. **3.** The soft inner part of a tooth.
pulp (pulp) *noun, plural* **pulps.**

pulpit A platform in a church from which sermons are given.
pul·pit (pu̇l′pit *or* pul′pit) *noun, plural* **pulpits.**

pulse **1.** The rhythmic beat of the arteries caused by the beating of the heart. I felt my *pulse* by resting my fingers on blood vessels in my wrist. **2.** Any regular, rhythmic beat. We heard the steady *pulse* of the train engine.
pulse (puls) *noun, plural* **pulses.**

puma A wild cat that lives in North America and South America. This animal is usually called a **cougar**. Look up **cougar** for more information.

pu·ma (pū'mə *or* pü'mə) *noun, plural* **pumas.**

pump A machine that is used to move water or other liquids or a gas from one place to another. The car drove up to the gasoline *pump. Noun.*
—**1.** To move a liquid or gas from one place to another with a pump. We *pumped* water into the swimming pool. My cousin *pumps* gas at the gas station on weekends. **2.** To fill with air or other gas. I *pumped* up the flat tire. **3.** To get or try to get information from by questioning closely. The police *pumped* the suspects about their friends. *Verb.*

pump (pump) *noun, plural* **pumps;** *verb,* **pumped, pumping.**

pumpkin A large, yellowish orange fruit with a hard outer rind and a soft pulp inside. Pumpkins grow on vines.

pump·kin (pump'kin *or* pung'kin) *noun, plural* **pumpkins.**

pun A joke in which something can have two meanings. A pun can contain two different meanings of one word or two words that sound

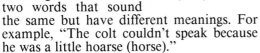

pumpkin

the same but have different meanings. For example, "The colt couldn't speak because he was a little hoarse (horse)."

pun (pun) *noun, plural* **puns.**

punch¹ **1.** To hit a person or thing with the fist or part of the hand. The boxers *punched* each other. I *punched* the elevator button for the eighth floor. **2.** To herd or drive. The cowhands *punched* cattle in the fall. *Verb.*
—A blow with the fist or part of the hand. The detective knocked out the thief with one powerful *punch. Noun.*

punch (punch) *verb,* **punched, punching;** *noun, plural* **punches.**

punch² A tool for making holes in or putting a design on a surface. One kind of *punch* can fix plain paper so that it will fit into a looseleaf notebook. *Noun.*
—To make holes in or press a design on with a punch. I *punched* another hole in the belt so I could tighten it. *Verb.*

punch (punch) *noun, plural* **punches;** *verb,* **punched, punching.**

punch³ A drink made by mixing different fruit juices, sodas, or other ingredients.

punch (punch) *noun, plural* **punches.**

punctual On time; prompt. I always try to be *punctual* for appointments.

punc·tu·al (pungk'chü əl) *adjective.*

punctuate To mark written material with punctuation marks.

punc·tu·ate (pungk'chü āt') *verb,* **punctuated, punctuating.**

Word History

The word **punctuate** comes from a Latin word meaning "point." Latin writing was marked by dots and other "points" to show where sentences began or ended and to give other information.

---

punctuation **1.** The use of periods, commas, and other punctuation marks to make the meaning of written material clear. Your spelling is excellent, but you are poor at *punctuation.* **2.** One or more punctuation marks. The *punctuation* of the poem will help you read it correctly.

punc·tu·a·tion (pungk'chü ā'shən) *noun.*

punctuation mark Any of a group of marks used to make the meaning of written material clear. Periods, commas, semicolons, hyphens, quotation marks, and question marks are punctuation marks.

puncture To make a hole in something with a sharp object. I *punctured* the balloon with a pin. *Verb.*
—A hole made by a sharp object. The mechanic patched the *puncture* in the tire. *Noun.*

punc·ture (pungk'chər) *verb,* **punctured, puncturing;** *noun, plural* **punctures.**

pungent Sharp or strong to the taste or smell. I like a *pungent* mustard on frankfurters. Ammonia has an unpleasant, *pungent* odor.

pun·gent (pun'jənt) *adjective.*

punish **1.** To make a person suffer for a wrong he or she has done. The law *punishes* criminals. **2.** To treat or handle roughly. The bumpy dirt road *punished* our old car.

pun·ish (pun'ish) *verb,* **punished, punishing.**

---

at; āpe; fär; câre; end; mē; it; īce; pîerce; hot; ōld; sông, fôrk; oil; out; up; ūse; rüle; pùll; tûrn; chin; sing; shop; thin; <u>th</u>is; hw in white; zh in treasure. The symbol ə stands for the unstressed vowel sound in about, taken, pencil, lemon, and circus.

P

punishment **1.** The act of punishing. The *punishment* of criminals is left to the courts. **2.** The penalty for a crime or wrong. Their *punishment* was five years in prison.
pun·ish·ment (pun′ish mənt) *noun, plural* **punishments.**

pup **1.** A young dog; puppy. **2.** One of the young of certain other animals. The young of foxes, wolves, and seals are called pups.
pup (pup) *noun, plural* **pups.**

pupa An insect at the stage after it is a larva and before it is an adult. A caterpillar in its cocoon is a pupa.
pu·pa (pū′pə) *noun, plural* **pupas.**

pupil¹ A person who is studying in school or with a teacher; student.
pu·pil (pū′pəl) *noun, plural* **pupils.**

pupil² The opening in the center of the iris of the eye. Light enters the eye through the pupil. The pupil gets smaller in bright light and larger in darkness.
pu·pil (pū′pəl) *noun, plural* **pupils.**

puppet A doll that looks like a person or animal and has parts that can be moved. Some puppets fit over a person's hand and are made to move by the fingers. Other puppets have strings attached to parts of their bodies and are moved by pulling the strings.
pup·pet (pup′it) *noun, plural* **puppets.**

puppets

puppy A young dog.
pup·py (pup′ē) *noun, plural* **puppies.**

purchase To get something by paying money; buy. We *purchased* our train tickets at the station. *Verb.*
—**1.** The act of purchasing. I saved for the *purchase* of a new bike. **2.** Something that is gotten by being paid for. They piled their *purchases* on the table. *Noun.*
pur·chase (pûr′chəs) *verb,* **purchased, purchasing;** *noun, plural* **purchases.**

pure **1.** Not mixed with anything else. I bought a scarf of *pure* silk. **2.** Not dirty or polluted; clean. We drank *pure* water from a stream. **3.** Nothing but. It was *pure* luck that we won. **4.** Free from evil or guilt; innocent. The young child had a *pure* mind.
pure (pyùr) *adjective,* **purer, purest.**

purebred Having ancestors that are all the same breed or kind of animal. My dog is a *purebred* Irish setter.
pure·bred (pyùr′bred′) *adjective.*

purify To make pure or clean. The filter will *purify* the water.
pu·ri·fy (pyùr′ə fī′) *verb,* **purified, purifying.**

Puritan A member of a group of Protestants in England during the 1500s and 1600s. The Puritans wanted simpler forms of worship and stricter morals than those of the national church of England. Some Puritans fled England and settled in America.
Pu·ri·tan (pyùr′i tən) *noun, plural* **Puritans.**

purity The condition of being pure or clean. We tested the *purity* of the water in the pool.
pu·ri·ty (pyùr′i tē) *noun.*

purple The color that is made by mixing red and blue. *Noun.*
—Having the color purple. *Adjective.*
pur·ple (pûr′pəl) *noun, plural* **purples;** *adjective.*

purpose The reason for which something is made or done. What is the *purpose* of that hook on the wall?
• **on purpose.** Not by accident; deliberately. Did you slip *on purpose*?
pur·pose (pûr′pəs) *noun, plural* **purposes.**

purposeful **1.** Having a purpose or meaning. **2.** Having determination. They made a *purposeful* effort to learn French.
pur·pose·ful (pûr′pəs fəl) *adjective.*

purposely On purpose; deliberately. We *purposely* left the radio on when we left.
pur·pose·ly (pûr′pəs lē) *adverb.*

purr A soft, murmuring sound like the one made by a cat when it's happy. The *purr* of the car's motor satisfied the mechanic. *Noun.*
—To make a soft, murmuring sound. The kitten *purred* when I petted it. *Verb.*
purr (pûr) *noun, plural* **purrs;** *verb,* **purred, purring.**

purse **1.** A pocketbook or handbag. **2.** A small bag or case used to carry money. *Noun.*
—To draw together. The babysitter's lips were *pursed* in anger. *Verb.*
purse (pûrs) *noun, plural* **purses;** *verb,* **pursed, pursing.**

pursue **1.** To follow in order to catch up to or capture. The police *pursued* the thief down the street. **2.** To follow or carry out. I see that you *pursue* your hobby very seriously.
pur·sue (pər sü′) *verb,* **pursued, pursuing.**

pursuit **1.** The act of pursuing. The police were in *pursuit* of the speeding car. **2.** A hobby or other interest a person has. Making model cars is one of my *pursuits*.
pur·suit (pər süt′) *noun, plural* **pursuits.**

pus A yellowish fluid that collects in an infection. Pus is made up of dead germs and white blood cells.
pus (pus) *noun.*

push **1.** To press on something in order to move it. I *pushed* the shopping cart through the market. You have to *push* hard against that door to open it. **2.** To move forward with effort. We had to *push* through the crowd. **3.** To work hard to do or sell something. The senator *pushed* for the passage of tax reform. The store is *pushing* canned soup this week. *Verb.*
—A shove or strong effort to move forward or accomplish something. They made a big *push* to finish the work by five o'clock. *Noun.*
push (push) *verb,* **pushed, pushing;** *noun, plural* **pushes.**

push–up An exercise in which a person lies face down and raises and lowers the body by straightening and bending the arms while keeping the rest of the body straight.
push-up (push′up′) *noun, plural* **push-ups.**

pussy willow A shrub that has silver-colored, furry flowers that grow on long straight branches.
pus·sy willow (pus′ē).

pussy willow

put **1.** To cause a thing or a person to be in a certain place, condition, or position; place; set. *Put* the box on the table. Your warm smile *put* them at ease. **2.** To cause to undergo or experience. You *put* them to a lot of trouble by being late. **3.** To apply. We *put* our knowledge of machinery to use in repairing the engine. **4.** To state or express. *Put* your question clearly. **5.** To impose; levy. The government *puts* a tax on cigarettes.

- **to put off.** To delay or postpone. It's not wise to *put off* going to the dentist.
- **to put on.** To present or perform. The class *put on* a Christmas play.
- **to put up with.** To bear patiently; endure. My parents do not *put up with* yelling in the house.
put (pùt) *verb,* **put, putting.**

putty A soft material that is like clay and that is used to fill cracks in wood or plaster, or to fasten panes of glass to window frames.
put·ty (put′ē) *noun.*

puzzle **1.** Something that confuses. It is a *puzzle* to me how you got here so fast. **2.** A toy, game, or other object that presents a problem to solve. We tried to fit together the pieces of the *puzzle*. *Noun.*
—**1.** To confuse or be hard to understand. The arithmetic problem *puzzled* me. The twins' pranks *puzzled* their friends. **2.** To think hard in order to answer or solve something. I *puzzled* over the last question. *Verb.*
puz·zle (puz′əl) *noun, plural* **puzzles;** *verb,* **puzzled, puzzling.**

pyramid **1.** An object that has triangular sides that meet at a point at the top. Its base is usually square. **2. the Pyramids.** Huge stone structures that are in the shape of a pyramid. The Pyramids were built in ancient Egypt as royal tombs.
pyr·a·mid (pir′ə mid′) *noun, plural* **pyramids.**

pyramid

python A large snake that coils around its prey and suffocates it.
py·thon (pī′thon) *noun, plural* **pythons.**

at; āpe; fär; câre; end; mē; it; īce; pîerce; hot; ōld; sông, fôrk; oil; out; up; ūse; rüle; pùll; tûrn; chin; sing; shop; thin; this; hw in white; zh in treasure. The symbol ə stands for the unstressed vowel sound in about, taken, pencil, lemon, and circus.

P

Q q

1. The letter **Q** was first used by ancient tribes in the Middle East. They used it to stand for a *k* sound.

2. When the ancient Greeks borrowed this letter, they changed it very little.

3. An ancient tribe near Rome borrowed the letter **Q** and used it only before the letter *u*, just as we do.

4. The ancient Romans borrowed the letter **Q** and used it in much the same way.

5. By about 2,000 years ago, the Romans were writing this letter almost the same way we do today.

q, Q   The seventeenth letter of the alphabet.
   q, Q (kū) *noun, plural* **q's, Q's.**

qt.   An abbreviation for *quart* or *quarts.*

quack¹   The harsh, flat sound that a duck makes. *Noun.*
   —To make the sound that a duck makes. *Verb.*
   quack (kwak) *noun, plural* **quacks;** *verb,* **quacked, quacking.**

quack²   A dishonest person who pretends to be a doctor or an expert. The *quack* claimed that the tonic of sugar and water would cure the flu. *Noun.*
   —Of, having to do with, or like a quack. Don't follow *quack* advice on how to invest your money. *Adjective.*
   quack (kwak) *noun; adjective.*

quadrilateral   A design or figure having four sides and four angles. A square and a rectangle are quadrilaterals.
   quad·ri·lat·er·al (kwod'rə lat'ər əl) *noun, plural* **quadrilaterals.**

quadruped   An animal that has four feet.
   quad·ru·ped (kwod'rə ped') *noun, plural* **quadrupeds.**

quadruplet   **1.** One of four children or animals born at the same time to the same mother.   **2.** A group of four.
   quad·rup·let (kwo drü'plit) *noun, plural* **quadruplets.**

quahog   A round clam that has a thick shell. It lives in shallow waters along the Atlantic coast of North America. It is used for food.
   qua·hog (kwô'hôg' *or* kwô'hog') *noun, plural* **quahogs.**

quail   A bird that has a plump body and brown or gray feathers often dotted with white. This bird is also called a **partridge.**
   quail (kwāl) *noun, plural* **quail** or **quails.**

quail

quaint   Pleasant or attractive in an old-fashioned or amusing way. We walked down the narrow streets of the *quaint* old village.
   quaint (kwānt) *adjective,* **quainter, quaintest.**

quake To shake or tremble. The kitten *quaked* with terror when it first went outside. The thunder made the house *quake*. *Verb.*
—**1.** A trembling or shaking. We felt a *quake* as the train went by. **2.** A shaking or trembling of the ground; earthquake. There was a small *quake* last night. Look up **earthquake** for more information. *Noun.*
   quake (kwāk) *verb,* **quaked, quaking;** *noun, plural* **quakes.**

Quaker A person who is a member of a Christian religion founded by George Fox in England around 1650.
   Quak·er (kwā′kər) *noun, plural* **Quakers.**

qualification **1.** Something that makes a person or thing fit for a job or task. The ability to swim well is one of the *qualifications* for the job of lifeguard. **2.** Something that limits or restricts. You are, without *qualification,* the best tennis player I know.
   qual·i·fi·ca·tion (kwol′ə fi kā′shən) *noun, plural* **qualifications.**

qualify **1.** To make or be fit for something. Their years of experience *qualify* them to go on the difficult hike. **2.** To limit or restrict. I *qualified* my statement that children like the circus with the word "usually." **3.** To limit the meaning of; modify. Adjectives *qualify* nouns, and adverbs *qualify* verbs, adjectives, and adverbs.
   qual·i·fy (kwol′ə fī′) *verb,* **qualified, qualifying.**

quality **1.** Something that makes a person or thing what it is. You have all the *qualities* needed for success. The most obvious *quality* of water is wetness. **2.** Degree of excellence. That market sells meat of the highest *quality.*
   qual·i·ty (kwol′i tē) *noun, plural* **qualities.**

qualm **1.** A feeling that something is bad or wrong. The suspect had no *qualms* about lying to the police. I have *qualms* about cheating on tests. **2.** A sudden feeling of doubt or uneasiness. I had *qualms* about being away from home for the first time.
   qualm (kwäm) *noun, plural* **qualms.**

quantity **1.** A number or amount. The recipe calls for a small *quantity* of milk. **2.** A large number or amount. That restaurant buys food in *quantity.*
   quan·ti·ty (kwon′ti tē) *noun, plural* **quantities.**

quarantine The keeping of a person, animal, or thing away from others to stop the spreading of a disease. The camper who had chicken pox was put in *quarantine* to keep the disease from spreading to anyone else. *Noun.*
—To put a person or thing in quarantine.

During the cruise, the passengers with measles were *quarantined.* *Verb.*
   quar·an·tine (kwôr′ən tēn′) *noun, plural* **quarantines;** *verb,* **quarantined, quarantining.**

Word History

In the past, ships that came from foreign lands and might be bringing diseases were often made to wait forty days before landing in a port and unloading. If no disease had broken out on the ships, the ships were allowed to dock. The word **quarantine** comes from the Italian word for "forty," because of this forty-day waiting period.

quarrel An angry argument or disagreement. The children had a *quarrel* about whose turn it was to wash the dishes. *Noun.*
—**1.** To have an angry argument or disagreement. We *quarreled* about who would ride the bicycle first. **2.** To find fault. I won't *quarrel* with your decision. *Verb.*
   quar·rel (kwôr′əl) *noun, plural* **quarrels;** *verb,* **quarreled, quarreling.**

quarry A place where stone is cut or blasted out. Quarries supply stone for use in building.
   quar·ry (kwôr′ē) *noun, plural* **quarries.**

quart A unit of measure that equals 2 pints, or ¼ of a gallon. A quart is slightly less than a liter.
   quart (kwôrt) *noun, plural* **quarts.**

quarter **1.** One of four equal parts. We divided the pie into *quarters.* Fifteen minutes is a *quarter* of an hour. Three months is a *quarter* of a year. **2.** A coin of the United States and Canada equal to twenty-five cents or ¼ of a dollar. **3.** The moment at the end of each fourth of an hour. I left the house at *quarter* after seven.

quarter of a pie

at; āpe; fär; câre; end; mē; it; īce; pîerce; hot; ōld; sông, fôrk; oil; out; up; ūse; rüle; pùll; tûrn; chin; sing; shop; thin; this; hw in white; zh in treasure. The symbol ə stands for the unstressed vowel sound in about, taken, pencil, lemon, and circus.

Q

4. One of four periods of about seven days each that together make up the time it takes for the moon to revolve around the earth; phase. **5.** One of the four equal time periods into which certain games are divided. **6.** A section or district. Their house was in the old *quarter* of the city. **7. quarters.** A place to live or stay. The soldiers' *quarters* were at the edge of the base. *Noun.*
—**1.** To divide into four equal units. I *quartered* the pie. **2.** To give a place to live. The soldiers are *quartered* in tents. *Verb.*
  quar·ter (kwôr′tər) *noun, plural* **quarters;** *verb,* **quartered, quartering.**

quarterback The football player who leads the team when they are trying to score. A quarterback usually throws the passes.
  quar·ter·back (kwôr′tər bak′) *noun, plural* **quarterbacks.**

quarterly Happening or done once every three months. The bank pays *quarterly* interest on my savings account. *Adjective.*
—Once every three months. That magazine is published *quarterly. Adverb.*
  quar·ter·ly (kwôr′tər lē) *adjective; adverb.*

quartet **1.** A musical piece written for four singers or musicians. **2.** A group of four singers or musicians performing together. **3.** Any group of four people or things.
  quar·tet (kwôr tet′) *noun, plural* **quartets.**

quartz A kind of clear, hard rock. It is the most common mineral and is the main ingredient of sand.
  quartz (kwôrts) *noun.*

quasar A heavenly body similar to a star. Quasars send out huge quantities of light or of very powerful radio waves.
  qua·sar (kwā′zär *or* kwā′sär) *noun, plural* **quasars.**

quay A landing place for boats or ships. Quays are usually made of stone. ▲ Another word that sounds like this is **key.**
  quay (kē) *noun, plural* **quays.**

Que. An abbreviation for *Quebec.*

Quebec A province in eastern Canada. Its capital is also called Quebec.
  Que·bec (kwi bek′) *noun.*

queen **1.** The wife or widow of a king. **2.** A woman who rules a kingdom. A woman usually becomes queen because she is related to the ruler before her and usually rules until she dies. **3.** A woman or thing that is beautiful or important. Some people call that singer the *queen* of jazz. **4.** A female bee or other insect that lays eggs. **5.** A playing card that has a picture of a queen. **6.** The most powerful piece in the game of chess.
  queen (kwēn) *noun, plural* **queens.**

queer Different from what is normal or usual; strange; peculiar. My classmate has some *queer* ideas about studying.
  queer (kwîr) *adjective,* **queerer, queerest.**

quench **1.** To put an end to by satisfying. I *quenched* my thirst with a long drink of water. **2.** To make something stop burning; put out; extinguish. I *quenched* the fire.
  quench (kwench) *verb,* **quenched, quenching.**

query A question. Any *queries* from the audience may be put to the speaker after the speech is over. *Noun.*
—**1.** To ask about. They *queried* my reasons for quitting. **2.** To express doubt about. The teacher *queried* the facts in my report. *Verb.*
  que·ry (kwîr′ē) *noun, plural* **queries;** *verb,* **queried, querying.**

quest A search or pursuit. The explorers went in *quest* of gold.
  quest (kwest) *noun, plural* **quests.**

question **1.** Something asked in order to get an answer or find out something. The tourist asked us a few *questions* about the history of our town. **2.** A matter to be talked over. The meeting dealt with the *question* of who would be the next president of the club. **3.** Doubt; uncertainty. My friend is, without *question,* the best student in the class. *Noun.*
—**1.** To ask questions of or about. The police *questioned* the witness to the robbery. **2.** To express doubt about. I *question* the truth of your story. *Verb.*
  ques·tion (kwes′chən) *noun, plural* **questions;** *verb,* **questioned, questioning.**

question mark A punctuation mark (?) that is used at the end of a question or at the end of an interrogative sentence.

quetzal A bird of Central America that has a bright red breast and a shiny green head, back, and long, drooping tail.
  quet·zel (ket säl′) *noun, plural* **quetzals.**

quetzal

590

quick **1.** Done or happening in a short time; fast. We made a *quick* trip to the store. **2.** Thinking, learning, or reacting easily and rapidly. That child has a very *quick* mind.
quick (kwik) *adjective*, **quicker, quickest.**

quicksand Very deep, wet sand. A person or thing that moves or stands on quicksand will sink into it.
quick·sand (kwik′sand′) *noun.*

quiet **1.** Making little or no noise; without noise. It is always very *quiet* in the library. **2.** With little or no disturbance or motion; not busy; peaceful. Our family spent a *quiet* weekend at home. *Adjective.*
—The condition of being quiet. I enjoy the peace and *quiet* of my own room. *Noun.*
—To make or become quiet. The babysitter *quieted* the crying baby. *Verb.*
qui·et (kwī′it) *adjective*, **quieter, quietest;** *noun;* *verb*, **quieted, quieting.**

quill **1.** A large, stiff feather. **2.** A pen made from the hollow stem of a feather. **3.** One of the sharp spines of a porcupine or other animal.
quill (kwil) *noun, plural* **quills.**

quilt A bed covering made of two pieces of cloth that are stuffed with soft material. The two pieces of cloth are held together by lines of stitching that are sewn all over the surface of the cloth. *Noun.*
—**1.** To make a quilt or quilts. *Verb.* **2.** To stitch together with a soft lining.
quilt (kwilt) *noun, plural* **quilts;** *verb,* **quilted, quilting.**

sewing a **quilt**

quintuplet **1.** One of five children or animals born at the same time to the same mother. **2.** A group of five.
quin·tu·plet (kwin tup′lit) *noun, plural* **quintuplets.**

quit **1.** To stop doing something. I *quit* reading to go outside for a walk. **2.** To go away from; leave. I may *quit* my job and look for a new one. **3.** To give up or stop trying. You refused to *quit,* even though you knew you couldn't win the race.
quit (kwit) *verb*, **quit or quitted, quitting.**

quite **1.** Very much or completely. The sign made it *quite* clear which road we should take. **2.** Really; actually. Climbing the mountain was *quite* an achievement.
quite (kwīt) *adverb.*

quiver[1] To shake slightly; shiver. The leaves *quivered* in the breeze. *Verb.*
—The act or motion of quivering. There was a *quiver* in my voice before I started to cry. *Noun.*
quiv·er (kwiv′ər) *verb*, **quivered, quivering;** *noun, plural* **quivers.**

quiver[2] A case for holding arrows.
quiv·er (kwiv′ər) *noun, plural* **quivers.**

quiz A short or informal test. The teacher gave us a spelling *quiz* today. *Noun.*
—To question. The class was *quizzed* on last week's work. *Verb.*
quiz (kwiz) *noun, plural* **quizzes;** *verb,* **quizzed, quizzing.**

quota A certain share or amount due to or from a person, group, or organization. Each soldier received a daily *quota* of rations.
quo·ta (kwō′tə) *noun, plural* **quotas.**

quotation **1.** A person's words repeated exactly by another person. The book began with a *quotation* from the Bible. **2.** The act of quoting.
quo·ta·tion (kwō tā′shən) *noun, plural* **quotations.**

quotation mark One of a pair of punctuation marks (" ") used mainly to indicate the beginning and end of a quotation.

quote To repeat the exact words of. The newspaper *quoted* the mayor's speech. *Verb.*
—A quotation. *Noun.*
quote (kwōt) *verb*, **quoted, quoting;** *noun, plural* **quotes.**

quotient A number obtained by dividing one number by another. If you divide 12 by 4, the *quotient* is 3.
quo·tient (kwō′shənt) *noun, plural* **quotients.**

Q

1. The earliest form of the letter **R** appears in the alphabets of the ancient Middle East.

2. The ancient Greeks borrowed this letter about 3,000 years ago, writing it in much the same way.

3. Several hundred years later, the Greeks changed their **R** by reversing it and rounding it.

4. The ancient Romans borrowed the Greek letter and later added a short line to it.

5. By about 2,400 years ago, the Romans were making their **R** almost like our modern capital **R**.

r, R   The eighteenth letter of the alphabet.
- **the three R's.**   Reading, writing, and arithmetic. The idiom *the three R's* originated in the humorous spelling *reading, 'riting, and 'rithmetic.*

r, R (är) *noun, plural* **r's, R's.**

rabbi   A teacher of the Jewish religion. A rabbi is usually the leader of a Jewish congregation.

rab·bi (rab′ ī) *noun, plural* **rabbis.**

Word History

The word **rabbi** comes from a Hebrew word meaning "my master." The word was used as a term of respect for the leader of a synagogue.

---

rabbit   **1.** A small animal that has long ears, a short tail, and soft fur. Rabbits live in burrows that they dig in the ground.   **2.** A hare.   **3.** The fur of the rabbit.

rab·bit (rab′it) *noun, plural* **rabbits.**

rabies   A disease that can affect people, dogs, bats, and all other warm-blooded animals. A person almost always dies of it if not treated. Rabies is caused by a virus. People get rabies if they are bitten by an animal that already has the disease.

ra·bies (rā′bēz) *noun.*

raccoon   A small animal with brownish gray fur. It has a pointed face with black markings that look like a mask and a long, bushy tail marked with black rings. Raccoons live in wooded areas near water and feed at night on plants, fish, and other foods.

rac·coon (ra kün′) *noun, plural* **raccoons.**

raccoon

race¹   **1.** A contest to find out who is fastest. Our horse won the *race.*   **2.** Any contest. There are three candidates in the *race* for governor. *Noun.*
—**1.** To take part in a contest of speed; be in a race against. The two children *raced* each other to school.   **2.** To move or go very fast. I *raced* down the stairs to answer the door.

3. To cause to move or go too fast. The driver *raced* the engine of the car to keep it from stalling. *Verb.*
> **race** (rās) *noun, plural* **races;** *verb,* **raced, racing.**

race² A very large group of people having certain physical characteristics in common. These characteristics are passed on from one generation to another.
> **race** (rās) *noun, plural* **races.**

racer **1.** A person, animal, or vehicle that competes in races. That horse is a fine *racer.* **2.** Any of a group of American snakes that moves very quickly.
> **rac·er** (rā′sər) *noun, plural* **racers.**

racetrack An area used for racing.
> **race·track** (rās′trak′) *noun, plural* **racetracks.**

racial Of or having to do with a race of human beings. *Racial* prejudice is prejudice against people because of their race.
> **ra·cial** (rā′shəl) *adjective.*

rack A frame or stand for hanging, storing, or showing things. The store had many *racks* of suits. *Noun.*
—To cause great pain or suffering to. The injured victim was *racked* with pain. *Verb.*
> **rack** (rak) *noun, plural* **racks;** *verb,* **racked, racking.**

racket¹ **1.** A loud or confusing noise. I could hardly hear what you were saying because of the *racket* in the bus. **2.** A dishonest plan or way to get money from someone.
> **rack·et** (rak′it) *noun, plural* **rackets.**

racket² A round or oval frame with a network of strings and a thin handle. Rackets are usually made of wood, metal, or some other material and are used to hit the ball in tennis and other games.
> **rack·et** (rak′it) *noun, plural* **rackets.**

racquetball A game in which two or four players use short rackets to hit a small ball off the floor, walls, and ceiling of an enclosed court.
> **rac·quet·ball** (rak′it bôl′) *noun.*

radar A device used to find and track objects such as aircraft and automobiles. It uses reflected radio waves.
> **ra·dar** (rā′där) *noun.*

Word History

The word **radar** is short for *radio detecting and ranging.* It is made up of the first two letters of *radio* and the beginning letter of each of the other three words.

radiant **1.** Shining brightly; beaming. We shielded our eyes from the *radiant* summer sun. The child's face was *radiant* from the excitement of winning. **2.** Given off in waves or made up of waves. The warmth we get from the sun is *radiant* heat.
> **ra·di·ant** (rā′dē ənt) *adjective.*

radiant energy Energy that is sent off in waves. Heat, radio waves, light, and X rays are kinds of radiant energy.

radiate **1.** To give off rays. The lamp *radiated* light through the room. **2.** To be given off in rays. Heat and light *radiate* from the sun. **3.** To move or branch outward from a center. Many spokes *radiated* from the hub of the bicycle wheel. **4.** To show. Your face *radiates* happiness.
> **ra·di·ate** (rā′dē āt′) *verb,* **radiated, radiating.**

radiation Energy that is given off in the form of waves or very tiny particles. Light, X rays, heat, and radio waves are forms of radiation.
> **ra·di·a·tion** (rā′dē ā′shən) *noun.*

radiator **1.** A device for heating a room. It is made up of a series of pipes or coils through which steam or hot water passes. **2.** A device for cooling something. The radiator in a car's engine holds and cools a liquid that is passed through the engine.
> **ra·di·a·tor** (rā′dē ā′tər) *noun, plural* **radiators.**

radical **1.** Going to or affecting the most important part; basic. Moving from the country to the city caused a *radical* change in my life. **2.** Favoring extreme changes or reforms. My parents do not agree with my *radical* political beliefs. *Adjective.*
—A person who favors extreme changes or reforms. *Noun.*
> **rad·i·cal** (rad′i kəl) *adjective; noun, plural* **radicals.**

Word History

The word **radical** comes from a Latin word meaning "root" or "origin." Something that is *radical* affects even the roots of a problem or situation.

at; āpe; fär; câre; end; mē; it; īce; pîerce; hot; ōld; sông, fôrk; oil; out; up; ūse; rüle; pùll; tûrn; chin; sing; shop; thin; this; hw in white; zh in treasure. The symbol ə stands for the unstressed vowel sound in about, taken, pencil, lemon, and circus.

radii A plural of **radius**. Measure the *radii* of these two circles. Look up **radius** for more information.
ra·di·i (rā'dē ī') *plural noun.*

radio 1. A way of sending messages, programs, music, or other sounds through the air without the use of wires. 2. A device for receiving or sending such sounds. *Noun.*
—To send a message to or report by radio. The pilot *radioed* the airport for permission to land. *Verb.*
ra·di·o (rā'dē ō') *noun, plural* **radios;** *verb,* **radioed, radioing.**

radioactive Of, caused by, or having radioactivity. Uranium is *radioactive.*
ra·di·o·ac·tive (rā'dē ō ak'tiv) *adjective.*

radioactivity The giving off of energy in the form of rays. The rays are given off during a process in which atoms of one element split apart.
ra·di·o·ac·tiv·i·ty (rā'dē ō ak tiv'i tē) *noun.*

radish The small, thick, red or white root of a plant. Radishes have a strong, sharp taste and are usually eaten raw in salads.
rad·ish (rad'ish) *noun, plural* **radishes.**

radish

radium A white metal that is highly radioactive. Radium is a chemical element.
ra·di·um (rā'dē əm) *noun.*

radius 1. A line going from the center to the outside of a circle or sphere. Look up **circle** for a picture of this. 2. A circular area that is measured by the length of its radius. There are no houses within a three mile *radius* of the farm.
ra·di·us (rā'dē əs) *noun, plural* **radii** or **radiuses.**

radon A heavy, radioactive gas found in soil and rocks. Radon is produced by the element radium. Doctors use small amounts of radon to treat cancer. Radon is a chemical element.
ra·don (rā'don) *noun.*

raft A kind of flat boat made of logs or boards that have been fastened together.
raft (raft) *noun, plural* **rafts.**

rag 1. A small piece of cloth. It is usually made of worn or torn material. 2. **rags.** Old clothing that is torn or worn out.
rag (rag) *noun, plural* **rags.**

rage 1. Violent or great anger. Those spoiled children go into a *rage* if they can't have what they want. 2. A fad; fashion. Floppy hats were the *rage* last year. *Noun.*
—To talk or act in a violent way. I *raged* at the bullies who had hurt my dog. The storm *raged* along the coast. *Verb.*
rage (rāj) *noun, plural* **rages;** *verb,* **raged, raging.**

ragged 1. Worn or torn into rags. After a few years, my jacket became stained and *ragged.* 2. Wearing torn or worn out clothing. The *ragged* beggar asked us for money to get some food. 3. Rough and uneven. *Ragged* cliffs rose over the beach.
rag·ged (rag'id) *adjective.*

ragweed A common weed whose pollen is a cause of hay fever in the autumn.
rag·weed (rag'wēd') *noun, plural* **ragweeds.**

raid A sudden, surprise attack. The soldiers were prepared for a *raid* at dawn. *Noun.*
—To make a raid on. Enemy troops *raided* the village during the night. *Verb.*
raid (rād) *noun, plural* **raids;** *verb,* **raided, raiding.**

rail 1. A long, narrow bar of wood, metal, or other material. It is used as a guard or support. The long metal bars on which a train rides are rails. 2. A railroad. My folks prefer traveling by *rail* to driving a car.
rail (rāl) *noun, plural* **rails.**

railing A fence or barrier made of a rail or rails. Hold onto the *railing* when you go down the steep stairs.
rail·ing (rā'ling) *noun, plural* **railings.**

railroad 1. The metal tracks on which a train runs. The *railroad* runs near our house. 2. All the tracks, stations, and cars that are part of a system of transportation by rail. That *railroad* has been in operation since 1872. Another word for this is **railway.**
rail·road (rāl'rōd') *noun, plural* **railroads.**

railway 1. A railroad. 2. The tracks on which a train runs.
rail·way (rāl'wā') *noun, plural* **railways.**

rain 1. Water that falls in drops from clouds to the earth. *Rain* came in the open window and soaked the rug. 2. A falling of rain; storm or shower. Don't go out in the *rain* without an umbrella. 3. A heavy or rapid fall of anything. A *rain* of rice hit the bride and groom as they left the church. *Noun.*
—1. To fall in drops of water. We put off our picnic because it *rained.* 2. To fall or pour like rain. Bullets *rained* on the soldiers. *Verb.*
▲ Other words that sound like this are **reign** and **rein.**

• **to rain out.** To cancel or postpone because of rain. The game was *rained out*.
rain (rān) *noun, plural* **rains;** *verb,* **rained, raining.**

rainbow A curve of colored light seen in the sky. It is caused by the sun's shining through tiny drops of water in the air. A rainbow is made up of seven colors: red, orange, yellow, green, blue, indigo, and violet.
rain·bow (rān′bō′) *noun, plural* **rainbows.**

rainbow

raincoat A waterproof coat that keeps a person dry when it is raining.
rain·coat (rān′kōt′) *noun, plural* **raincoats.**

raindrop A drop of rain.
rain·drop (rān′drop′) *noun, plural* **raindrops.**

rainfall The amount of rain, snow, sleet, or hail that falls on an area in a certain period of time. The yearly *rainfall* in that city is over 30 inches.
rain·fall (rān′fôl′) *noun, plural* **rainfalls.**

rain forest A dense forest that receives a large amount of rain during the year.

rainy Having much rain. It is important to drive carefully in *rainy* weather.
rain·y (rā′nē) *adjective,* **rainier, rainiest.**

raise **1.** To move or cause to move to a higher position, place, degree, or amount. I *raised* my arm above my head. My parents *raised* my allowance. Many people *raise* their voice when they are angry. **2.** To cause to rise or appear. The bee sting *raised* a bump on the child's arm. **3.** To gather together; collect. The town *raised* the money to build a new school. **4.** To take care of and help to grow. My grandparents *raised* four children. They *raise* horses and cattle on that ranch. **5.** To ask or bring up. My classmate *raised* an interesting question about the story we were reading. **6.** To build. A new house was *raised* on that empty lot. **7.** To stir up;

bring about. Someone was *raising* a commotion in the hall. *Verb.*
—An increase in amount. The worker received a *raise* in pay of five dollars a week. *Noun.*
raise (rāz) *verb,* **raised, raising;** *noun, plural* **raises.**

raisin A sweet, dried grape.
rai·sin (rā′zin) *noun, plural* **raisins.**

rake A tool that has a long handle with teeth or prongs attached at one end. It is used to gather leaves or hay together or to smooth down earth. *Noun.*
—**1.** To gather or smooth with a rake. We *raked* the fallen leaves. **2.** To search carefully. I *raked* through my desk for a pen. *Verb.*
rake (rāk) *noun, plural* **rakes;** *verb,* **raked, raking.**

rally **1.** To bring or come together for some purpose. The general tried to *rally* the scattered troops. The farmers *rallied* to rebuild the burned barn. **2.** To come to the aid or support of a person or thing. My friends *rallied* behind me when I was teased. **3.** To recover strength, energy, or health. Our team *rallied* to win the game. With the doctor's help, the patient began to *rally*. *Verb.*
—A meeting for a particular purpose. Hundreds of people were at the political *rally* for the presidential candidate. *Noun.*
ral·ly (ral′ē) *verb,* **rallied, rallying;** *noun, plural* **rallies.**

ram

ram **1.** A male sheep. **2.** A device or part of a machine used to batter, crush, or force something. The firefighters used a *ram* to break down the door. *Noun.*

---

at; āpe; fär; câre; end; mē; it; īce; pîerce; hot; ōld; sông, fôrk; oil; out; up; ūse; rüle; pûll; tûrn; chin; sing; shop; thin; this; hw in white; zh in treasure. The symbol ə stands for the unstressed vowel sound in about, taken, pencil, lemon, and circus.

R

—**1.** To strike or strike against with great force. In the train wreck one train *rammed* into the other's back. **2.** To force or drive down or into something. The worker *rammed* the post into the ground. *Verb.*
> **ram** (ram) *noun, plural* **rams;** *verb,* **rammed, ramming.**

RAM Memory in a computer that can be added to or altered by the person using the computer. The computer uses this memory to store and retrieve information quickly.
> **RAM** (ram) *noun.*

ramble **1.** To wander about; roam. We *rambled* through the fields before having our picnic. **2.** To talk or write in a confused way. The speaker *rambled* on and never came to the point of the story. *Verb.*
—A pleasant stroll or walk. *Noun.*
> **ram·ble** (ram′bəl) *verb,* **rambled, rambling;** *noun, plural* **rambles.**

ramp A sloping platform or passageway connecting two different levels.
> **ramp** (ramp) *noun, plural* **ramps.**

ramrod **1.** A rod used to ram the gunpowder down the barrel of a gun that is loaded through the muzzle. **2.** A rod used to clean the barrel of a gun.
> **ram·rod** (ram′rod′) *noun, plural* **ramrods.**

ran Past tense of **run.** We were so late that we *ran* all the way to school. Look up **run** for more information.
> **ran** (ran) *verb.*

ranch A large farm on which large herds of cattle, sheep, and horses are raised. *Noun.*
—To manage or work on a ranch. *Verb.*
> **ranch** (ranch) *noun, plural* **ranches;** *verb,* **ranched, ranching.**

Word History

The word **ranch** comes from a Spanish word that means "a camp" or "a small farm." Today a *ranch* is often a very large estate.

random Made or done with no clear pattern; made or done by chance. The teacher made a *random* choice of three students to help pass out the new books.
• **at random.** With no pattern or method. I picked up a magazine *at random* from the pile.
> **ran·dom** (ran′dəm) *adjective.*

rang Past tense of **ring.** The mail carrier *rang* the doorbell twice, but no one was home. Look up **ring** for more information.
> **rang** (rang) *verb.*

range **1.** The distance or extent between certain limits. There is a *range* in ticket prices from $7 to $20. **2.** The distance or area over which something can travel or extend. A rifle has a greater *range* than a bow and arrow. Our *range* of vision was limited by the fog. **3.** A place set aside for shooting practice or for testing rockets. The police officers did some target shooting on the pistol *range.* **4.** A large area of land on which livestock roam and graze. The cowhands rounded up the cattle on the open *range.* **5.** A row or series of mountains. A *range* of mountains rises from the coastline. **6.** A large stove having burners and an oven. **7.** The extent of the tones that can be produced by a particular singing voice or musical instrument. *Noun.*
—**1.** To go between certain limits. The prices for those bicycles *range* from one hundred to two hundred dollars. **2.** To wander or roam. Cattle *ranged* over the prairie. **3.** To stretch out or extend in some direction. The hills *range* west from the shore. *Verb.*
> **range** (rānj) *noun, plural* **ranges;** *verb,* **ranged, ranging.**

ranger **1.** A person whose work is looking after and guarding a forest or other natural area. **2.** A member of a group of armed people who go through an area to keep law and order.
> **ran·ger** (rān′jər) *noun, plural* **rangers.**

The **ranger** is wearing a uniform.

rank¹ **1.** A position or grade. The soldier was promoted to the *rank* of sergeant. I have a high *rank* in my class at school. **2.** High position or grade. The governor of the state is a person of *rank.* **3. ranks.** The common soldiers of an army. *Noun.*

—1. To put in or have a certain position or grade. The students were *ranked* according to their grades.   **2.** To arrange in a row or rows. The students were *ranked* for the fire drill. *Verb.*
  rank (rangk) *noun, plural* **ranks;** *verb,* **ranked, ranking.**

rank² **1.** Having a strong, bad smell or taste. The cheese became *rank* after a week. **2.** Complete; extreme. The soldier was accused of being a *rank* coward.
  rank (rangk) *adjective,* **ranker, rankest.**

ransom **1.** The release of a captive in return for payment of money. The ambassador was kidnapped and was being held for *ransom.*   **2.** The amount of money paid or demanded before a captive is set free. *Noun.*
  —To pay money for a captive to be set free. *Verb.*
  ran·som (ran′səm) *noun, plural* **ransoms;** *verb,* **ransomed, ransoming.**

rap A quick, sharp knock or tap. We heard a *rap* on the window. *Noun.*
  —To knock or tap sharply. I *rapped* on the door but there was no answer. *Verb.* ▲ Another word that sounds like this is **wrap.**
  rap (rap) *noun, plural* **raps;** *verb,* **rapped, rapping.**

rapid Very quick; fast. The train went at a *rapid* pace. *Adjective.*
  —rapids. A part of a river where the water flows very fast. It was dangerous to go over the *rapids* in a canoe. *Noun.*
  rap·id (rap′id) *adjective; plural noun.*

rapture Great happiness, delight, or joy; ecstasy. We stared in *rapture* at the beautiful scenery.
  rap·ture (rap′chər) *noun.*

rare¹ **1.** Not often happening, seen, or found. Thunderstorms are *rare* at this time of year.   **2.** Unusually fine; excellent. The cliffs have a *rare* beauty.   **3.** Not dense; thin. The air is *rare* at high altitudes.
  rare (râr) *adjective,* **rarer, rarest.**

rare² Cooked for only a short time. Do you like your hamburgers *rare?*
  rare (râr) *adjective,* **rarer, rarest.**

rarely Not often; seldom. We *rarely* go to the movies.
  rare·ly (râr′lē) *adverb.*

rascal **1.** A mischievous person. That pup is a *rascal.*   **2.** A dishonest person; rogue.
  ras·cal (ras′kəl) *noun, plural* **rascals.**

rash¹ Too hasty; not careful. We made a *rash* decision that we regretted later.
  rash (rash) *adjective,* **rasher, rashest.**

rash² A condition in which red spots appear on the skin. Poison ivy causes a *rash.*
  rash (rash) *noun, plural* **rashes.**

rasp To make a harsh, grating sound. The iron gate *rasped* because the hinges were rusty. *Verb.*
  —A harsh, grating sound. I spoke with a *rasp* because I had a sore throat. *Noun.*
  rasp (rasp) *verb,* **rasped, rasping;** *noun, plural* **rasps.**

raspberry A small, sweet fruit of a prickly plant. Raspberries are usually red or black.
  rasp·ber·ry (raz′ber′ē) *noun, plural* **raspberries.**

rat **1.** An animal that looks like a large mouse. A rat has a long nose, round ears, and a long, thin tail.   **2.** A mean or dishonest person.
  rat (rat) *noun, plural* **rats.**

raspberries

rate **1.** An amount or number measured against the amount or number of something else. The car was going at a *rate* of 60 miles per hour.   **2.** The price or charge for something. Telephone *rates* went up last year.   **3.** A rank or class. Your school work has always been of the first *rate. Noun.*
  —1. To consider; regard. My friend *rated* the movie as very good.   **2.** To place in or have a certain class or rank. Our team is *rated* first in its league. *Verb.*
  rate (rāt) *noun, plural* **rates;** *verb,* **rated, rating.**

rather **1.** More willingly. I would *rather* stay home than go out tonight.   **2.** More properly; instead. Our team *rather* than theirs deserved to win.   **3.** More correctly. The airplane is landing at about noon or, *rather,* at 12:10 P.M.   **4.** Somewhat. It is *rather* cold today.
  rath·er (rath′ər) *adverb.*

ratify To agree to officially; approve. Congress *ratified* the trade agreement.
  rat·i·fy (rat′ə fī′) *verb,* **ratified, ratifying.**

ratio A comparison in number or quantity between two things. The ratio is the number or times the second thing can be divided into

at; āpe; fär; câre; end; mē; it; īce; pîerce; hot; ōld; sông, fôrk; oil; out; up; ūse; rüle; pùll; tûrn; chin; sing; shop; thin; <u>th</u>is; hw in white; zh in treasure. The symbol ə stands for the unstressed vowel sound in about, taken, pencil, lemon, and circus.

R

the first thing. If there are 12 girls and 6 boys in a class, the *ratio* of girls to boys is 2 to 1.
ra·ti·o (rā′shē ō′) *noun, plural* **ratios.**

ration A fixed portion or share, especially of food. The mountain climber carried *rations* in a pack. *Noun.*
—**1.** To give out in portions. Supplies were *rationed* to victims of the flood. **2.** To limit to fixed portions. The government *rationed* meat during the war. *Verb.*
ra·tion (rash′ən *or* rā′shən) *noun, plural* **rations;** *verb,* **rationed, rationing.**

rational **1.** Based on reason or logic; sensible. The writer used *rational* arguments to support each idea. **2.** Able to think or think clearly. Humans are *rational* animals.
ra·tion·al (rash′ə nəl) *adjective.*

rattle **1.** To make or cause to make a series of short, sharp sounds. The doors and windows *rattled* when the wind blew. **2.** To talk or say quickly. My classmate *rattled* off the names of all the states. **3.** To confuse or embarrass. I was *rattled* by the mistake I made in answering the question. *Verb.*
—**1.** A series of short, sharp sounds. We could tell by the *rattle* of the doorknob that someone was trying to get into the room. **2.** A baby's toy or other thing that makes a rattling noise when it is shaken. *Noun.*
rat·tle (rat′əl) *verb,* **rattled, rattling;** *noun, plural* **rattles.**

rattlesnake A poisonous American snake. A rattlesnake has a number of horny rings at the end of its tail that rattle when it shakes its tail.
rat·tle·snake (rat′əl snāk′) *noun, plural* **rattlesnakes.**

rattlesnake

rave **1.** To talk in a wild or crazy way. A high fever caused the patient to *rave* . **2.** To talk with much or too much enthusiasm. They *raved* about their new car.
rave (rāv) *verb,* **raved, raving.**

ravel To separate into loose threads; fray. Pulling the piece of yarn made the cuff of the sweater *ravel.*
rav·el (rav′əl) *verb,* **raveled, raveling.**

raven A bird that looks very much like a crow but is larger. It has shiny black feathers and a harsh cry. *Noun.*
—Shiny and black. The horse's *raven* coat shone in the sun. *Adjective.*
ra·ven (rā′vən) *noun, plural* **ravens;** *adjective.*

raven

ravine A deep, narrow valley.
ra·vine (rə vēn′) *noun, plural* **ravines.**

raw **1.** Not cooked. Carrots may be eaten *raw.* **2.** Not treated or processed; natural. Milk before it is pasteurized is *raw.* **3.** Not trained or experienced. The army trains *raw* recruits. **4.** Having the skin rubbed off. My heel was *raw* from my new shoe. **5.** Damp and cold. We've had *raw* weather.
raw (rô) *adjective,* **rawer, rawest.**

rawhide The hide of cattle or other animals that has not been tanned. The cowhand wore boots made of *rawhide.*
raw·hide (rô′hīd′) *noun.*

raw material A substance that has not been treated, processed, or prepared. Wood is the *raw material* used in making paper.

ray¹ **1.** A narrow beam of light or other radiant energy. The sun's *rays* shone brightly. **2.** One of a group of lines or parts coming from a center. The arms of a starfish are *rays.* **3.** A very small amount. There was only a *ray* of hope for the lost sailors.
ray (rā) *noun, plural* **rays.**

ray² A fish that has a broad, flat body, broad fins, and a skeleton made of cartilage.
ray (rā) *noun, plural* **rays.**

rayon A fiber or cloth made from cellulose.
ray·on (rā′on) *noun.*

razor A device with a sharp blade used for shaving or for cutting hair.
ra·zor (rā′zər) *noun, plural* **razors.**

Rd. An abbreviation for *Road* used in a written address.

R.D. An abbreviation for *rural delivery.*

re– A *prefix* that means: **1.** Again. *Reelect* means to elect again. **2.** Back. *Recall* means to call back.

Language Note

A word formed with **re-** is written with a hyphen if it is spelled the same way as another word with a different meaning. For example, the word *re-cover* means to cover again, but *recover* means to get something back again. The hyphen helps us to tell the words apart.

reach **1.** To arrive at; come to. We *reached* the cabin after walking for two miles through the woods. **2.** To touch or grasp. I can't *reach* the top shelf of the bookcase. **3.** To stretch or extend. The draperies *reached* from the ceiling to the floor. **4.** To stretch the arm or hand out. Our dinner guest *reached* across the table for the salt. **5.** To try to grasp something. I *reached* into my pocket for my keys. **6.** To get in touch with; contact. I tried to *reach* you by phone. *Verb.* —**1.** The distance covered in reaching. A person would have to have a long *reach* to get that box off the closet shelf. **2.** As much as a person is able to do or understand. Our coach knew that a victory was within our *reach*. **3.** The act of reaching. With a *reach* of my arm I pulled the apple from the tree. **4.** A stretch of something; extent. The camels crossed the vast reaches of desert. *Noun.*
> **reach** (rēch) *verb*, **reached, reaching;** *noun*, *plural* **reaches.**

react To act because something has happened or has been done; respond. My friend *reacted* to the good news by smiling.
> **re·act** (rē akt′) *verb*, **reacted, reacting.**

reaction An action in response to something that has happened or has been done. What was your parents' *reaction* when they saw your report card?
> **re·ac·tion** (rē ak′shən) *noun*, *plural* **reactions.**

reactor A device that produces atomic energy for making electricity. It splits atoms without causing an atomic explosion.
> **re·ac·tor** (rē ak′tər) *noun*, *plural* **reactors.**

read **1.** To look at and understand the meaning of something that is written. I learned to *read* when I was in first grade. I *read* an article about football in the newspaper. **2.** To say aloud something that is written. The teacher *read* a story to the class. **3.** To learn by reading. Do you like to *read* about horses? **4.** To get the meaning of; understand. Sometimes my parents seem to be able to *read* my thoughts. **5.** To give or show; register. The thermometer *read* 70 degrees this morning. ▲ Another word that sounds like this is **reed.**
> **read** (rēd) *verb*, **read** (red), **reading.**

Word History

The word **read** goes back to Old English and originally meant "to think or consider." Later it came to mean "to figure out the meaning of." This use of *read* led to the meaning "to discover the meaning of something written" and finally to our modern use of *read.*

readable Easy or interesting to read. Your handwriting is not *readable.*
> **read·a·ble** (rē′də bəl) *adjective.*

reader **1.** A person who reads. **2.** A textbook that is used to teach reading.
> **read·er** (rē′dər) *noun*, *plural* **readers.**

readily **1.** In a prompt and willing way. I *readily* followed my parents' advice. **2.** Without difficulty; easily. The story was *readily* understood by everyone in the class.
> **read·i·ly** (red′ə lē) *adverb.*

reading **1.** The act of looking at and understanding something that is written. I prefer *reading* to playing baseball. **2.** The act of saying aloud something that is written. The writer gave a *reading* of a new poem. **3.** Something read or to be read. This book is interesting *reading.* **4.** The information shown on a meter or other instrument. The gas company took a *reading* from our meter.
> **read·ing** (rē′ding) *noun*, *plural* **readings.**

ready **1.** Prepared for use or action. When I finish packing I'll be *ready* for the trip. **2.** Willing. I am *ready* to work hard. **3.** Likely to do something. The dynamite was *ready* to explode any minute. **4.** Quick; prompt. The politician had a *ready* answer for the reporter's questions. **5.** Easy to get at. My parents keep some *ready* cash at home in case of emergency. *Adjective.* —To make ready; prepare. The mechanics *ready* the plane before it can take off. *Verb.*
> **read·y** (red′ē) *adjective*, **readier, readiest;** *verb*, **readied, readying.**

at; āpe; fär; câre; end; mē; it; īce; pîerce; hot; ōld; sông, fôrk; oil; out; up; ūse; rüle; pùll; tûrn; chin; sing; shop; thin; this; hw in white; zh in treasure. The symbol ə stands for the unstressed vowel sound in about, taken, pencil, lemon, and circus.

R

real **1.** Actual or true; not imagined. Our adventures were *real;* we did not make them up. **2.** Genuine; not imitation. These flowers are *real,* not plastic.
re·al (rē′əl *or* rēl) *adjective.*

Language Note

Real is an adjective, so it modifies a noun or pronoun. Is that a *real* arrowhead? Ghosts are not *real.* **Really** is an adverb, so it modifies a verb, an adjective, or another adverb. Did you *really* go to the beach? I was *really* tired. The plane traveled *really* fast.

---

real estate Land together with the buildings, trees, water, and other things on it.

realistic **1.** Showing people, things, or events as they appear in everyday life. I admire the skill needed to create a *realistic* painting. **2.** Tending to see and accept things as they are; practical. You need to be *realistic* about your chances of winning.
re·al·is·tic (rē′ə lis′tik) *adjective.*

reality **1.** The state or quality of being real. Some people doubted the *reality* of the story. **2.** Something that is real. Their dream of owning a horse had become a *reality.*
re·al·i·ty (rē al′i tē) *noun, plural* **realities.**

realization **1.** The act of understanding completely. The *realization* that we were lost in the fog made us anxious. **2.** Something that is made real. Buying their own house was the *realization* of one of their dreams.
re·al·i·za·tion (rē′ə lə zā′shən) *noun, plural* **realizations.**

realize **1.** To understand completely. I didn't *realize* how late it was. **2.** To make real. Years of saving money helped us to *realize* our dream of owning a house.
re·al·ize (rē′ə līz′) *verb,* **realized, realizing.**

really **1.** In fact; actually. My neighbor told the police what had *really* caused the accident. Although we argue sometimes, we are *really* good friends. **2.** Truly; very. We spent a *really* pleasant afternoon in the park.
re·al·ly (rē′ə lē *or* rē′lē) *adverb.*

realm **1.** A kingdom. The king and queen ruled their *realm* wisely. **2.** An area or field of interest, knowledge, or power. I enjoy almost everything in the *realm* of science.
realm (relm) *noun, plural* **realms.**

reap **1.** To cut down and gather; harvest. The workers used sickles to *reap* the grain. **2.** To cut down or harvest a crop from. The farmer *reaped* the fields in the autumn. **3.** To get as a reward. The child's good behavior *reaped* high praise.
reap (rēp) *verb,* **reaped, reaping.**

reappear To come into sight again; be seen again. It stopped raining and the sun *reappeared.*
re·ap·pear (rē′ə pîr′) *verb,* **reappeared, reappearing.**

rear¹ **1.** The part that is behind or in the back. I sat in the *rear* of the car. **2.** The part of a military force that is farthest from the fighting area. *Noun.*
—At or in the back. We left the house by the *rear* door. *Adjective.*
rear (rîr) *noun, plural* **rears;** *adjective.*

rear² **1.** To take care of and help to grow up. My grandparents *reared* three children. **2.** To go up on the back legs. The frightened horse *reared* and threw its rider. **3.** To lift up. The lion *reared* its head.
rear (rîr) *verb,* **reared, rearing.**

The horse on the left is **rearing.**

rearrange To arrange again, especially in a different way. I *rearranged* my furniture.
re·ar·range (rē′ə rānj′) *verb,* **rearranged, rearranging.**

reason **1.** A cause or motive. I have no *reason* to doubt you. **2.** A statement that explains something; excuse. The student could give no *reason* for being late. **3.** The ability to think clearly. The sudden shock made me lose all *reason. Noun.*
—**1.** To think or think about clearly. I was able to *reason* out the answer to the arithmetic problem. **2.** To try to change a person's mind. They are so stubborn that it is useless to *reason* with them. *Verb.*
rea·son (rē′zən) *noun, plural* **reasons;** *verb,* **reasoned, reasoning.**

reasonable **1.** Showing or using good sense and thinking; not foolish. A *reasonable* person will always listen to both sides of an argument. **2.** Not asking too much; fair. Their asking to borrow our lawn mower was a *reasonable* request. **3.** Not too expensive. The grocery store's prices are *reasonable*.
rea·son·a·ble (rē′zə nə bəl *or* rēz′nə bəl) *adjective.*

reasoning **1.** The process of drawing conclusions from facts; clear and sensible thinking. To do well in mathematics, you must be good at *reasoning*. **2.** Reasons or arguments. I don't agree with your *reasoning*.
rea·son·ing (rē′zə ning *or* rēz′ning) *noun.*

reassure To restore confidence or courage in. Before the curtain rose, the director *reassured* the actors.
re·as·sure (rē′ə shůr′) *verb*, **reassured, reassuring.**

rebel **1.** A person who fights against or will not obey authority. The *rebels* attacked the palace. **2. Rebel.** A soldier who fought against the North in the Civil War. *Noun.*
—**1.** To fight against authority. I *rebelled* at being ordered to do something I thought was wrong. **2.** To feel or show great dislike. The sick child *rebelled* against taking the medicine because it tasted bad. *Verb.*
reb·el (reb′əl *for noun;* ri bel′ *for verb*) *noun, plural* **rebels;** *verb,* **rebelled, rebelling.**

Word History

The word **rebel** goes back to a Latin word that means "to make war again." The word was used to talk about people who had been conquered in war and started another war against the people who had beaten them.

---

rebellion **1.** An armed fight against one's government. The American Revolution was a *rebellion* by the colonists against the British. **2.** A struggle against any authority.
re·bel·lion (ri bel′yən) *noun, plural* **rebellions.**

recall **1.** To bring back to mind; remember. Your face is familiar, but I don't *recall* your name. **2.** To take or order back. The auto manufacturer *recalled* the defective cars. The troops were *recalled* from the front. *Verb.*
—The act of recalling. I have little *recall* of the book because I read it so long ago. *Noun.*
re·call (ri kôl′ *for verb;* ri kôl′ *or* rē′kôl′ *for noun*) *verb,* **recalled, recalling;** *noun, plural* **recalls.**

recapture **1.** To catch or capture again. The police *recaptured* the prisoner who had escaped from jail. **2.** To bring back to mind; recall. They tried to *recapture* their childhood by visiting their birthplace.
re·cap·ture (rē kap′shər) *verb,* **recaptured, recapturing.**

recede To move back or away. The waves *receded* from the shore.
re·cede (ri sēd′) *verb,* **receded, receding.**

receipt **1.** A written statement showing that a package, mail, or money has been received. The clerk in the store gave me a *receipt* for my purchase. **2. receipts.** The amount of money that has been received. The store's *receipts* for the week were over $1,000. **3.** A receiving or being received. We thanked them on *receipt* of their gift.
re·ceipt (ri sēt′) *noun, plural* **receipts.**

The woman on the right is **receiving** an award.

receive **1.** To take or get. I *received* a watch for my birthday. **2.** To greet or welcome. The host and hostess *received* the guests at the door.
re·ceive (ri sēv′) *verb,* **received, receiving.**

receiver **1.** A person or thing that receives. **2.** A device that changes electrical impulses or radio waves into pictures or sounds. The part of a telephone that you hold to your ear is a receiver.
re·ceiv·er (ri sē′vər) *noun, plural* **receivers.**

recent Done, made, or happening not long ago. The radio program reported the most *re-*

---

at; āpe; fär; câre; end; mē; it; īce; pîerce; hot; ōld; sông, fôrk; oil; out; up; ūse; rüle; půll; tûrn; chin; sing; shop; thin; **this**; hw in white; zh in treasure. The symbol ə stands for the unstressed vowel sound in about, taken, pencil, lemon, and circus.

R

cent election news. The computer is one of the most useful inventions of *recent* times.
re·cent (rē′sənt) *adjective.*

receptacle An object used to hold something; container. We use a large metal can as a *receptacle* for garbage.
re·cep·ta·cle (ri sep′tə kəl) *noun, plural* **receptacles.**

reception **1.** The act or way of receiving. The play got a warm *reception* from everyone in the audience. **2.** A party or gathering where guests are received. **3.** The quality of the sound of a radio or the sound and picture of a television. The new antenna improved our television's *reception.*
re·cep·tion (ri sep′shən) *noun, plural* **receptions.**

recess **1.** A time during which work or other activity stops. We played baseball during *recess* at school. **2.** A part of a wall that is set back from the rest; niche. **3.** A hidden place or part. Many thoughts are buried in the *recesses* of our minds. *Noun.*
—To stop work or other activity for a time. The trial started again after the court had *recessed* for lunch. *Verb.*
re·cess (rē′ses *or* ri ses′) *noun, plural* **recesses;** *verb,* **recessed, recessing.**

recession A period when business is slower and more people than usual are out of work. A recession is less severe and shorter than a depression.
re·ces·sion (ri sesh′ən) *noun, plural* **recessions.**

recipe A list of ingredients and instructions for making something to eat or drink.
rec·i·pe (res′ə pē′) *noun, plural* **recipes.**

Word History

The word **recipe** comes from a Latin word that means "Take!" Doctors wrote this word in prescriptions to tell a druggist to "take" certain drugs and combine them to make the medicine.

---

recital **1.** A performance or concert of music or dance. We went to a piano *recital* in the auditorium. **2.** A story or account. Your *recital* of your experiences in Africa was interesting.
re·cit·al (ri sī′təl) *noun, plural* **recitals.**

recite **1.** To repeat something from memory. Can you *recite* the names of all the fifty states and their capitals? I had to *recite* at the school assembly. **2.** To tell the story of. I *recited* my adventures at camp to the class.

3. To repeat a lesson or answer questions in class. The teacher asked me to *recite.*
re·cite (ri sīt′) *verb,* **recited, reciting.**

reckless Not careful. It was *reckless* of them to have skated out onto the thin ice.
reck·less (rek′lis) *adjective.*

reckon **1.** To count or calculate. Income tax is *reckoned* according to the amount of money a person makes. **2.** To think or consider. I *reckon* my best friend to be the smartest student in the class.
reck·on (rek′ən) *verb,* **reckoned, reckoning.**

recline To lean back; lie down. I *reclined* on the sofa.
re·cline (ri klīn′) *verb,* **reclined, reclining.**

recognition **1.** A recognizing or being recognized. **2.** An accepting of something as being true, right, or valid. They demanded *recognition* of their rights as citizens. **3.** Favorable attention or notice. That band has gained *recognition* for its songs and records.
rec·og·ni·tion (rek′əg nish′ən) *noun.*

recognize **1.** To know and remember from before; identify. I didn't *recognize* you at first. **2.** To understand and accept as being true, right, or valid. We *recognized* that it was our duty to report the crime to the police.
rec·og·nize (rek′əg nīz′) *verb,* **recognized, recognizing.**

recollect To remember; recall. I cannot *recollect* their address at the moment.
re·col·lect (rek′ə lekt′) *verb,* **recollected, recollecting.**

recollection **1.** The act or power of remembering. My *recollection* of the accident is no longer very clear. **2.** A thing remembered. I have happy *recollections* of camp.
re·col·lec·tion (rek′ə lek′shən) *noun, plural* **recollections.**

recommend **1.** To speak in favor of. The librarian *recommended* this book. **2.** To advise; suggest. The nurse *recommended* that I stay home until my cold was better. **3.** To make acceptable or pleasing. Your excellent skills *recommend* you for this job.
rec·om·mend (rek′ə mend′) *verb,* **recommended, recommending.**

recommendation **1.** The act of recommending. Your *recommendation* of the movie makes me want to see it. **2.** Something recommended; advice; suggestion. You should follow the doctor's *recommendations.*
re·com·men·da·tion (rek′ə men dā′shən) *noun, plural* **recommendations.**

record **1.** A written account of something. The school keeps a *record* of each student's

attendance. The story the witness told was in the *record* of the trial.   **2.** All the facts about what a person, group, or thing has done. Your school *record* is excellent. The football team had an even *record* of wins and losses. **3.** A performance or act that is better than all others. The runner set a new *record* for the event.   **4.** A disk on which music or other sounds have been recorded to be played back on a phonograph. *Noun.*
—**1.** To set down in writing. I *recorded* my feelings about my new school in my diary. **2.** To indicate or show. This thermometer *records* temperatures up to 120 degrees. **3.** To put music or other sounds on a phonograph record or a magnetic tape. *Verb.*
rec·ord (rek′ərd *for noun;* ri kôrd′ *for verb*) *noun, plural* **records;** *verb,* **recorded, recording.**

recorder   **1.** A person whose job is taking notes and keeping records.   **2.** A machine that records sound on magnetic tape.   **3.** A musical instrument similar to a flute. It is usually made of wood or hard plastic.
re·cord·er (ri kôr′dər) *noun, plural* **recorders.**

recording   **1.** A phonograph record or magnetic tape. I have a new *recording* of that song.   **2.** The sound recorded on a phonograph record or a magnetic tape. The quality of the *recording* is poor.
re·cord·ing (ri kôr′ding) *noun, plural* **recordings.**

recover   **1.** To get back. The police *recovered* the two missing bicycles.   **2.** To make up for. We took the short route to *recover* the time we had lost.   **3.** To return to a normal condition or position. My friend is *recovering* from the measles.
re·cov·er (ri kuv′ər) *verb,* **recovered, recovering.**

re-cover   To cover again. After the chair's cover was worn out, we *re-covered* it.
re-cov·er (rē kuv′ər) *verb,* **re-covered, re-covering.**

recovery   The act of recovering. I was given a reward for my *recovery* of the lost wallet. The patient's speedy *recovery* was due to good medical care.
re·cov·er·y (ri kuv′ə rē) *noun, plural* **recoveries.**

recreation   Something that is done for amusement or relaxation. Sports, games, and hobbies are kinds of recreation.
rec·re·a·tion (rek′rē ā′shən) *noun, plural* **recreations.**

recruit   **1.** A newly enlisted soldier or sailor.   **2.** A new member of any group or organization. *Noun.*

—To get to join. The coach *recruited* nine players for the baseball team. *Verb.*
re·cruit (ri krüt′) *noun, plural* **recruits;** *verb,* **recruited, recruiting.**

rectangle   A figure with four sides that has four right angles. A square is a rectangle whose four sides are equal.
rec·tan·gle (rek′tang′gəl) *noun, plural* **rectangles.**

rectangle

recuperate   To get better and stronger after being sick. It took me several weeks to *recuperate* after having pneumonia.
re·cu·per·ate (ri kü′pə rāt′ *or* ri kū′pə rāt′) *verb,* **recuperated, recuperating.**

recur   To happen or appear again. The pain *recurs* every time I lift something heavy.
re·cur (ri kûr′) *verb,* **recurred, recurring.**

recycle   To make fit to be used again. Our city *recycles* cans and bottles.
re·cy·cle (rē sī′kəl) *verb,* **recycled, recyling.**

red   **1.** The color of blood.   **2.** Something having this color. The artist used a bright *red* to paint a picture of the fire engine. *Noun.*
—**1.** Having the color red.   **2.** Blushing. I was *red* with embarrassment. *Adjective.*
• **in the red.**   Losing or owing money. The school fair was not a success, and we found ourselves *in the red.*

at; āpe; fär; câre; end; mē; it; īce; pîerce; hot; ōld; sông, fôrk; oil; out; up; ūse; rüle; pull; tûrn; chin; sing; shop; thin; this; hw in white; zh in treasure. The symbol ə stands for the unstressed vowel sound in about, taken, pencil, lemon, and circus.

• **to see red.** To be or become very angry. Those people were so nasty to me that I *saw red.*
red (red) *noun, plural* **reds;** *adjective,* **redder, reddest.**

red blood cell A cell in the blood that picks up oxygen in the lungs and carries it to the cells and tissues of the body.

redcoat A British soldier during the American Revolution and other wars of that period. At those times, a red coat was part of the British military uniform.
red·coat (red′kōt′) *noun, plural* **redcoats.**

Red Cross An international organization whose main purpose is to take care of victims of war and of floods, fires, earthquakes, and other disasters.

red-handed In the act of doing something wrong. The police caught them *red-handed.*
red-hand·ed (red′han′did) *adjective.*

reduce **1.** To make or become less or smaller in size, number, or degree. Drivers should *reduce* their speed if the road is slippery. I *reduced* by going on a diet. The store *reduced* its prices. **2.** To bring to a lesser form, condition, or position. The forest was *reduced* to ashes by the fire.
re·duce (ri düs′ *or* ri dūs′) *verb,* **reduced, reducing.**

reduction **1.** The act of reducing or the state of being reduced. The *reduction* of the speed limit resulted in fewer traffic accidents. **2.** The amount by which something is reduced. The store is offering a 10-percent *reduction* on the price of summer clothes.
re·duc·tion (ri duk′shən) *noun, plural* **reductions.**

redwood One of the largest trees in the world. It is evergreen and has thick reddish brown bark. Its wood is used as timber. Redwoods grow along the western coast of North America.
red·wood (red′wůd′) *noun, plural* **redwoods.**

reed **1.** A tall grass having long, narrow leaves and jointed stems. Reeds usually grow in marshes and other wet places. **2.** A thin piece of wood, reed, metal, or plastic that is used in some musical instruments. A reed makes a sound when air passes over it and makes it vibrate. Reeds are found in wind instruments, accordions, and certain organs.
▲ Another word that sounds like this is **read.**
reed (rēd) *noun, plural* **reeds.**

reef A ridge of sand, rock, or coral that lies at or near the surface of the ocean or another body of water.
reef (rēf) *noun, plural* **reefs.**

reel[1] **1.** A spool or similar device on which something is wound. Fishing line, motion picture film, and magnetic tape are wound on reels. **2.** The amount of film or other material wound on a reel. There are two *reels* of film left. *Noun.*
—**1.** To wind on a reel. The sailor *reeled* the rope. **2.** To pull by winding a line on a reel. My friend *reeled* in a huge swordfish. *Verb.*
• **to reel off.** To say or write quickly and easily. I *reeled off* all the answers.
reel (rēl) *noun, plural* **reels;** *verb,* **reeled, reeling.**

reel[2] **1.** To be thrown off balance; stagger. I *reeled* when someone ran into me. **2.** To turn or seem to turn around and around. The merry-go-round ride made my head *reel.*
reel (rēl) *verb,* **reeled, reeling.**

reel[3] A lively folk dance. It is performed by two or more couples who form two lines facing each other.
reel (rēl) *noun, plural* **reels.**

reelect To elect again. The president was *reelected* and served another four years.
re·e·lect (rē′i lekt′) *verb,* **reelected, reelecting.**

redwoods

reentry **1.** An entering again. **2.** The return of a spacecraft or missile from space into the earth's atmosphere.
re·en·try (rē en′trē) *noun, plural* **reentries.**

refer **1.** To send or direct to someone or something. The doctor *referred* me to a specialist. **2.** To turn to for help or information. The speaker *referred* to written notes. **3.** To call or direct attention. The speaker *referred* to a movie I have not seen. **4.** To turn over to someone else. The teacher will *refer* the problem to the principal.

re·fer (ri fûr′) *verb,* **referred, referring.**

referee An official in certain sports and games who enforces the rules. *Noun.*
—To act as a referee in. Our teacher *refereed* the hockey game. *Verb.*

ref·er·ee (ref′ə rē′) *noun, plural* **referees;** *verb,* **refereed, refereeing.**

reference **1.** A statement that calls or directs attention to something. The authors made a *reference* to their other book. **2.** A person or thing that is referred to; source of information or help. The encyclopedia was the *reference* for my report. **3.** A statement about a person's ability or character. I have good *references* from the people I worked for. **4.** Connection; relation. I am writing to you in *reference* to your letter of last week.

ref·er·ence (ref′ər əns *or* ref′rəns) *noun, plural* **references.**

reference book A book that has information arranged in an orderly, convenient way. Dictionaries, encyclopedias, atlases, and almanacs are reference books.

refill To fill again. The hiker *refilled* the canteen with water. *Verb.*
—Something that replaces the material that first filled a container. I had to buy a *refill* for my pen when it ran out of ink. *Noun.*

re·fill (rē fil′ *for verb;* rē′fil′ *for noun*) *verb,* **refilled, refilling;** *noun, plural* **refills.**

refine To make fine and pure. Crude oil is *refined* before it can be used for gasoline.

re·fine (ri fīn′) *verb,* **refined, refining.**

refinery A place where crude oil, sugar, or some other substance is refined.

re·fin·er·y (ri fī′nə rē) *noun, plural* **refineries.**

reflect **1.** To turn or throw back. Sand *reflects* light and heat from the sun. **2.** To give back an image of something. I saw myself *reflected* in the pond. **3.** To think seriously or carefully. I often *reflect* on what I have done. **4.** To bring blame or discredit. Your actions *reflect* on your character. **5.** To bring or give back as a result. Their brave acts *reflected* honor upon their families. **6.** To show or express. Your clothes *reflect* your good taste.

re·flect (ri flekt′) *verb,* **reflected, reflecting.**

reflection **1.** An image given back by a reflecting surface. I looked at my *reflection* in the water. **2.** Something that is reflected.

The *reflection* of the sun on the car windshield made the driver squint. **3.** Serious or careful thinking. Upon *reflection,* I decided to take the job. **4.** A statement or idea that results from careful thinking. What are your *reflections* on the problem? **5.** Something that shows or expresses something else. My smile was a *reflection* of my happiness. **6.** Something that causes blame or discredit. My parents think my behavior is a *reflection* on them.

re·flec·tion (ri flek′shən) *noun, plural* **reflections.**

reflection of a mountain in a lake

reflector A device or surface that throws back light, heat, or sound. My bicycle is easy to see at night because it has *reflectors.*

re·flec·tor (ri flek′tər) *noun, plural* **reflectors.**

reforest To plant trees on land that was once a forest to replace those that have been cut down or destroyed by fire.

re·for·est (rē fôr′ist *or* rē for′ist) *verb,* **reforested, reforesting.**

reform **1.** To make a change for the better in; correct; improve. The government tried to *reform* the prison system. **2.** To become better. The criminal promised to *reform* and live an honest life. *Verb.*
—A change for the better. The town planned several *reforms* in the schools. *Noun.*

re·form (ri fôrm′) *verb,* **reformed, reforming;** *noun, plural* **reforms.**

reformatory A special school for young people who have broken the law.

re·form·a·to·ry (ri fôr′mə tôr′ē) *noun, plural* **reformatories.**

at; āpe; fär; câre; end; mē; it; īce; pîerce; hot; ōld; sông, fôrk; oil; out; up; ūse; rüle; pùll; tûrn; chin; sing; shop; thin; this; hw in white; zh in treasure. The symbol ə stands for the unstressed vowel sound in about, taken, pencil, lemon, and circus.

R

refrain A part of a song or poem that is repeated several times.
re·frain (ri frān′) *noun, plural* **refrains.**

refresh To make fresh again; revive. The cold drink *refreshed* us after the hike. I have to read my notes to *refresh* my memory.
re·fresh (ri fresh′) *verb,* **refreshed, refreshing.**

refreshment 1. Food or drink. What *refreshments* will you serve at the party? 2. A refreshing or being refreshed. I needed *refreshment* after working hard all day.
re·fresh·ment (ri fresh′mənt) *noun, plural* **refreshments.**

refrigerate To make or keep cool or cold. *Refrigerate* the meat to keep it from spoiling.
re·frig·er·ate (ri frij′ə rāt′) *verb,* **refrigerated, refrigerating.**

refrigerator An appliance, box, or room with a cooling system. Refrigerators are used to keep food and other things from spoiling.
re·frig·er·a·tor (ri frij′ə rā′tər) *noun, plural* **refrigerators.**

refuge 1. Shelter or protection from danger or trouble. The frightened puppy took *refuge* under the bed. 2. A place that gives shelter or protection. There were many kinds of animals in the wildlife *refuge.*
ref·uge (ref′ūj) *noun, plural* **refuges.**

refugee A person who flees from a place to find safety or protection. The *refugees* left their homeland for another country.
ref·u·gee (ref′yù jē′) *noun, plural* **refugees.**

refund To give or pay back. The store *refunded* my money. *Verb.*
—1. The return of money that has been paid. I returned my pants for a *refund.* 2. The amount of money returned. I got a *refund* of five dollars. *Noun.*
re·fund (ri fund′ *for verb;* rē′fund′ *for noun) verb,* **refunded, refunding;** *noun, plural* **refunds.**

refuse[1] 1. To say no to; reject. I *refused* their offer of help. 2. To be unwilling to do, give, or allow something. My parents *refused* to let me stay up late.
re·fuse (ri fūz′) *verb,* **refused, refusing.**

refuse[2] Anything thrown away as useless or worthless; trash or rubbish. The street was littered with *refuse* after the parade.
ref·use (ref′ūs) *noun.*

regain 1. To get back again; recover. The dog *regained* its health. 2. To get back to. We *regained* the highway after a detour.
re·gain (rē gān′) *verb,* **regained, regaining.**

regard 1. To think of; consider. I *regard* you as my best friend. 2. To look at closely. The stranger *regarded* us with suspicion. 3. To respect or consider. Always *regard* other people's feelings. 4. To have to do with; concern. The speech *regarded* plans for the new year. 5. To pay attention to. We *regarded* our parents' warnings. *Verb.*
—1. Careful thought, attention, or consideration. Have some *regard* for other people. 2. Respect or affection. I hold you in high *regard.* 3. **regards.** Best wishes. Give my *regards* to your family. 4. Connection; relation. My question *regards* your future. *Noun.*
• **in regard to** or **with regard to.** About; concerning. My parents spoke to me *in regard to* plans for our vacation.
re·gard (ri gärd′) *verb,* **regarded, regarding;** *noun, plural* **regards.**

regarding Having to do with; concerning; about. I wrote a letter to the company *regarding* their new product.
re·gard·ing (ri gär′ding) *preposition.*

regardless In spite of everything; nevertheless. I know that book's expensive, but I'm going to buy it, *regardless.*
• **regardless of.** In spite of. Let's do this play, *regardless of* the work it will take.
re·gard·less (ri gärd′lis) *adverb.*

regime A system of government. The people suffered under the *regime* of the dictator.
re·gime (rə zhēm′ *or* rā zhēm′) *noun, plural* **regimes.**

regiment A military unit made up of several battalions.
reg·i·ment (rej′ə mənt) *noun, plural* **regiments.**

region Any large area or territory. This plant grows in desert *regions.*
re·gion (rē′jən) *noun, plural* **regions.**

register 1. An official list or record or a book used for this. Guests signed the hotel *register.* 2. A machine that automatically records and counts. A cash *register* records money it takes in. 3. An opening or a similar device that controls the passage of air in a heating or ventilating system. 4. The range of a voice or musical instrument. *Noun.*
—1. To write in a list or record. The teacher *registered* the names of students who were absent. 2. To have one's name placed on a list or record. Voters must *register* before they can vote. 3. To show or express. Your face *registered* your joy. 4. To show or record, as on a scale or meter. The temperature *registered* 50 degrees. 5. To have officially recorded at the post office by paying a fee. This mail is *registered. Verb.*
reg·is·ter (rej′ə stər) *noun, plural* **registers;** *verb,* **registered, registering.**

registered nurse A nurse who has a license from a state government to practice nursing.

regret To feel sorry about. I *regret* having said unkind things to my friends. *Verb.*
—**1.** A feeling of sadness or sorrow. They felt no *regret* about their decision to move to another city. **2. regrets.** A polite apology for turning down an invitation. I couldn't go to the party, so I sent my *regrets* to the host and hostess. *Noun.*
> **re·gret** (ri gret′) *verb*, **regretted, regretting;** *noun, plural* **regrets.**

regretful Feeling regret; sorry; sad. I am *regretful* that I missed seeing the race you won.
> **re·gret·ful** (ri gret′fəl) *adjective.*

regular **1.** Normal; usual. Our *regular* teacher is absent. **2.** Happening again and again at the same time. The *regular* ticking of the clock made me drowsy. **3.** According to habit or usual behavior. I am a *regular* customer there. **4.** Evenly shaped, spaced, or arranged. The dentist said I have *regular* teeth. **5.** Following a rule. The *regular* ending for a plural noun is "-s" or "-es."
> **reg·u·lar** (reg′yə lər) *adjective.*

regulate **1.** To control, manage, or set. Valves *regulate* the flow of blood through your heart. **2.** To put or keep in good working order or at some standard. The jeweler *regulated* my watch to make it keep better time. Turn the dial to *regulate* the flow of air.
> **reg·u·late** (reg′yə lāt′) *verb*, **regulated, regulating.**

Word History

The word **regulate** comes from a Latin word meaning "a rule" or "a standard." When you *regulate* something, you put it in order according to rules or standards.

---

regulation **1.** A law, rule, or order. Smoking is against school *regulations*. **2.** The act of regulating or the state of being regulated. A thermostat controls the *regulation* of heat in the building.
> **reg·u·la·tion** (reg′yə lā′shən) *noun, plural* **regulations.**

rehearsal A practicing in order to prepare for a performance. The actors had many *rehearsals* before the play opened.
> **re·hears·al** (ri hûr′səl) *noun, plural* **rehearsals.**

rehearse To practice or train in order to prepare for a performance. The dancers *rehearsed* the ballet. The director *rehearsed* the actors until they knew all their lines.
> **re·hearse** (ri hûrs′) *verb*, **rehearsed, rehearsing.**

reign **1.** The period of time that a monarch rules. That building was designed during the *reign* of Queen Victoria. **2.** The power or rule of a monarch. The people lived in peace under the *reign* of the new king. *Noun.*
—**1.** To hold or have the power of a monarch. The king and queen *reigned* together for nearly sixty years. **2.** To be widespread; exist everywhere. Peace and prosperity *reigned* for many years. *Verb.* ▲ Other words that sound like this are **rain** and **rein.**
> **reign** (rān) *noun, plural* **reigns;** *verb,* **reigned, reigning.**

rein **1.** One of two or more narrow straps that are attached to a bridle or bit. Reins are used to guide and control a horse or other animal. **2.** Any means of control. I kept a tight *rein* on my temper. *Noun.*
—To guide, control, or hold back. The rider *reined* the galloping horse. *Verb.* ▲ Other words that sound like this are **rain** and **reign.**
> **rein** (rān) *noun, plural* **reins;** *verb,* **reined, reining.**

reindeer A large deer that has a white, gray, or brown coat and branching antlers. It is found in northern regions. In some parts of the world reindeer have been tamed and used to pull sleds or are raised for their milk and meat.
> **rein·deer** (rān′dîr′) *noun, plural* **reindeer.**

reindeer

---

at; āpe; fär; câre; end; mē; it; ice; pîerce; hot; ōld; sông, fôrk; oil; out; up; ūse; rüle; pu̇ll; tûrn; chin; sing; shop; thin; **this**; **hw** in white; **zh** in treasure. The symbol ə stands for the unstressed vowel sound in about, taken, pencil, lemon, and circus.

R

reinforce   To give more strength to by adding new or extra parts, materials, or people. They *reinforced* the dam with bags of sand.
re·in·force (rē′in fôrs′) *verb,* **reinforced, reinforcing.**

reject   To refuse to accept, allow, or approve. The voters *rejected* the tax plan.
re·ject (ri jekt′) *verb,* **rejected, rejecting.**

rejoice   To show or feel great joy. My parents *rejoiced* at the good news.
re·joice (ri jois′) *verb,* **rejoiced, rejoicing.**

relapse   A falling or slipping back into a former condition. Just when I thought I was over the flu, I had a *relapse.*
re·lapse (rē′laps′) *noun, plural* **relapses.**

relate   **1.** To tell the story of. The witness *related* how the accident occurred.   **2.** To connect or be connected in thought or meaning. The teacher *related* my improved grades to better study habits. My answer *relates* to a question you asked me this morning.
re·late (ri lāt′) *verb,* **related, relating.**

related   Belonging to the same family. You and your sisters, brothers, cousins, aunts, uncles, and grandparents are all *related.*
re·lat·ed (ri lā′tid) *adjective.*

relation   **1.** A connection in thought, meaning, action, or condition between two or more things. The doctor explained the *relation* between a good diet and good health. **2.** A connection or dealings between one person or thing and another. The two countries improved their *relations.*   **3.** A person who belongs to the same family as someone else; relative. The young couple sent wedding invitations to all their close *relations.*
re·la·tion (ri lā′shən) *noun, plural* **relations.**

relationship   The condition of being related; connection. There was a *relationship* between the amount of time we rehearsed and how well we performed.
re·la·tion·ship (ri lā′shən ship′) *noun, plural* **relationships.**

relative   Having meaning only in relation or comparison to something else. The words "right" and "left" are *relative* because their meaning depends on which way a person looks at something. *Adjective.*
—A person who belongs to the same family as someone else. *Noun.*
rel·a·tive (rel′ə tiv) *adjective; noun, plural* **relatives.**

relax   **1.** To make or become less tense. A hot bath helps to *relax* me. I like to *relax* by reading.   **2.** To make less strict. The principal *relaxed* the rule about proper dress.
re·lax (ri laks′) *verb,* **relaxed, relaxing.**

relaxation   **1.** The act of relaxing. *Relaxation* is easy when my chores are done. **2.** The condition of being relaxed. I enjoy the *relaxation* I feel after swimming. **3.** Something that relaxes, as an activity, hobby, or pastime. Reading is my favorite form of *relaxation.*
re·lax·a·tion (rē′lak sā′shən) *noun.*

relay   A fresh set, team, or supply that replaces or relieves another. The stagecoaches that carried mail across the plains used several *relays* of horses. *Noun.*
—To pass along. If I'm not home, my parents will *relay* your message. *Verb.*
re·lay (rē′lā *for noun;* rē′lā *or* ri lā′ *for verb*) *noun, plural* **relays;** *verb,* **relayed, relaying.**

relay race   A race between two or more teams. Each team member goes a certain distance and then is replaced by another team member.

relay race

release   **1.** To set free; let go. The hostage was *released* after being held prisoner for ten days.   **2.** To allow to be seen, published, or broadcast. The film was *released* today. *Verb.*
—The act of releasing or the state of being released. The criminal's *release* from prison came after two years. *Noun.*
re·lease (ri lēs′) *verb,* **released, releasing;** *noun, plural* **releases.**

relent   To become less severe, strict, or harsh; to be more lenient. My teacher *relented* and gave me a later deadline.
re·lent (ri lent′) *verb,* **relented, relenting.**

relevant   Having to do with what is being discussed or considered; pertinent. Your question was *relevant* to our discussion.
rel·e·vant (rel′ə vənt) *adjective.*

reliable Able to be depended on and trusted. That worker is a *reliable* person who finishes every job on time.
re·li·a·ble (ri līʹə bəl) *adjective.*

relic **1.** A thing from the past. We found arrowheads and other Indian *relics.* **2.** An object belonging to a holy person.
rel·ic (relʹik) *noun, plural* **relics.**

relief[1] **1.** The freeing from discomfort or pain; comfort, help, or aid. The medicine gave me *relief* from my headache. It was a *relief* when our lost dog came home. The government sent *relief* for the flood victims. **2.** Freedom from a job or duty. The guard got *relief* at seven o'clock.
re·lief (ri lēfʹ) *noun, plural* **reliefs.**

relief[2] A figure or design that stands out from a flat background.
re·lief (ri lēfʹ) *noun, plural* **reliefs.**

relief map A map that shows how high or low all the places in a certain area are.

relieve **1.** To free from discomfort or pain; comfort, help, or aid. The doctor gave me medicine to *relieve* my cough. The good news *relieved* us of our worries. **2.** To free from a job or duty. The lifeguards stayed on duty until they were *relieved.*
re·lieve (ri lēvʹ) *verb,* **relieved, relieving.**

religion **1.** Belief in or worship of God, or a god or gods. **2.** A particular system of belief and worship. Judaism, Christianity, Islam, Hinduism, and Buddhism are some of the world's major *religions.*
re·li·gion (ri lijʹən) *noun, plural* **religions.**

religious **1.** Showing devotion to a religion. Are you from a *religious* family? **2.** Of or having to do with religion. My friend's *religious* beliefs are not the same as mine. **3.** Very careful and exact; strict. The artist paid *religious* attention to details.
re·li·gious (ri lijʹəs) *adjective.*

relish **1.** A mixture of spices, pickles, olives, chopped vegetables, and the like. It is used as a side dish and to flavor food. **2.** Interest or pleasure; enjoyment. The child opened the presents with *relish. Noun.*
—To take pleasure in; enjoy. We all *relished* the delicious holiday meal. *Verb.*
rel·ish (relʹish) *noun, plural* **relishes;** *verb,* **relished, relishing.**

reluctant Unwilling. I am *reluctant* to lend you the book because you seldom return what you borrow.
re·luc·tant (ri lukʹtənt) *adjective.*

rely To trust; depend. You can *rely* on friends to be of help when you need them.
re·ly (ri līʹ) *verb,* **relied, relying.**

remain **1.** To stay behind or in the same place. I *remained* at home while my family went out. **2.** To go on being. We *remained* friends for years. **3.** To be left. All that *remains* of the ancient city is ruins.
re·main (ri mānʹ) *verb,* **remained, remaining.**

remainder **1.** A remaining part. I gave my friend the *remainder* of my sandwich. **2.** The number found when one number is subtracted from another. If you subtract 3 from 10, the *remainder* is 7. **3.** The number left over when a number cannot be divided evenly. If you divide 3 into 10, the answer is 3 with a *remainder* of 1.
re·main·der (ri mānʹdər) *noun, plural* **remainders.**

remains **1.** Things that are left. The explorers found the *remains* of an ancient city. **2.** A dead body. The victim's *remains* were buried in a local cemetery.
re·mains (ri mānzʹ) *plural noun.*

remark A short statement or comment. The farmer made a few *remarks* about the weather. *Noun.*
—**1.** To say; comment; mention. Our teacher *remarked* that we had all done well on the test. **2.** To notice; observe. I *remarked* that two classmates were absent yesterday. *Verb.*
re·mark (ri märkʹ) *noun, plural* **remarks;** *verb,* **remarked, remarking.**

remarkable Worthy of being noticed; not ordinary; unusual. Your science project is *remarkable.*
re·mark·a·ble (ri märʹkə bəl) *adjective.*

remedy Something that heals, improves, or gets rid of a bad condition. The scientists hoped to discover a *remedy* for the common cold. *Noun.*
—To heal, improve, or get rid of. The city government hoped to *remedy* the air pollution in the town. *Verb.*
rem·e·dy (remʹi dē) *noun, plural* **remedies;** *verb,* **remedied, remedying.**

remember **1.** To bring back to mind; recall. Do you *remember* where you left your jacket? **2.** To keep in mind carefully. Please *remember* that you have to see the dentist today. **3.** To reward or present with a gift. My

---

at; āpe; fär; câre; end; mē; it; ice; pîerce; hot; ōld; sông, fôrk; oil; out; up; ūse; rūle; pull; tûrn; chin; sing; shop; thin; this; hw in white; zh in treasure. The symbol ə stands for the unstressed vowel sound in about, taken, pencil, lemon, and circus.

R

parents *remember* all their favorite charities once a year. **4.** To send greetings from. *Remember* me to your family.
re·mem·ber (ri mem′bər) *verb,*
remembered, remembering.

remind To make think of someone or something; cause to remember. The person I met yesterday *reminds* me of you. The note *reminded* me of my cousin's birthday.
re·mind (ri mīnd′) *verb,* **reminded, reminding.**

remission A temporary end to the pain or other symptoms of a disease.
re·mis·sion (ri mish′ən) *noun, plural* **remissions.**

remodel To change the design, structure, or purpose of. The architect *remodeled* the store.
re·mod·el (rē mod′əl) *verb,* **remodeled, remodeling.**

remote **1.** Not near; far away. The explorer traveled to *remote* regions. **2.** Far from cities or towns. The *remote* mountain village was visited by very few tourists. **3.** Small; slight. There was only a *remote* possibility that our team would win.
re·mote (ri mōt′) *adjective,* **remoter, remotest.**

remote control The controlling of a machine or device from a distance. Some televisions are run by remote control.

removal The act of removing or the condition of being removed. *Removal* of the books from the shelf took a few minutes.
re·mov·al (ri mü′vəl) *noun, plural* **removals.**

remove **1.** To take or move away or off. The waiter *removed* the dishes from the table. I *removed* my sweater because the room was warm. **2.** To do away with; get rid of. The pilot's calm words *removed* our fear. **3.** To dismiss from an office or position. The mayor was *removed* from office.
re·move (ri müv′) *verb,* **removed, removing.**

render **1.** To cause to be or become; make. The surprise gift *rendered* me speechless. **2.** To give or present; deliver. The jury *rendered* a verdict of not guilty.
ren·der (ren′dər) *verb,* **rendered, rendering.**

rendezvous **1.** An appointment to meet at a certain place at a certain time. The scouts made a *rendezvous* to meet at the camp at noon. **2.** A place for meeting or gathering. Our favorite *rendezvous* is the playground.
ren·dez·vous (rän′də vü′) *noun, plural* **rendezvous.**

renew **1.** To make new or as if new again. The carpenter *renewed* the finish on the table. **2.** To begin again. After a long separation, they *renewed* their friendship. **3.** To cause to continue for a period of time. I *renewed* my subscription to the magazine. **4.** To replace with more; fill again. The ship *renewed* its supply of food.
re·new (ri nü′ *or* ri nū′) *verb,* **renewed, renewing.**

renovate To make like new; restore. The landlord *renovated* the entire building.
ren·o·vate (ren′ə vāt′) *verb,* **renovated, renovating.**

renowned Known and honored by many people; famous. The doctors were *renowned* for their successes in heart surgery.
re·nowned (ri nound′) *adjective.*

rent A payment for the use of something. My parents pay the *rent* every month for our apartment. *Noun.*
—**1.** To get the right to use in return for paying rent. We *rented* a car for the weekend. **2.** To give the right to use in return for the paying of rent. The store *rents* out bicycles. **3.** To be available for renting. The apartment *rents* for $500 a month. *Verb.*
• **for rent.** Available for use in return for the payment of rent. Is that apartment *for rent?*
rent (rent) *noun, plural* **rents;** *verb,* **rented, renting.**

repaid Past tense and past participle of **repay.** The couple *repaid* the borrowed money. Look up **repay** for more information.
re·paid (ri pād′) *verb.*

repairing a car

repair **1.** To put into good condition again; fix; mend. We *repaired* the broken leg of the table. **2.** To make good or right; correct.

610

I *repaired* all of my spelling mistakes. *Verb.*
—**1.** The act of repairing. The old chair was beyond *repair.* The *repairs* cost a lot of money. **2.** The condition that something is in. I keep my bicycle in good *repair. Noun.*
re·pair (ri pâr´) *verb,* **repaired, repairing;** *noun, plural* **repairs.**

repay **1.** To pay or give back. The family promised to *repay* the loan quickly. **2.** To pay or give something back to. You forgot to *repay* me for the money you borrowed. **3.** To give, make, or do in return. I will *repay* your kindness to me someday.
re·pay (ri pā´) *verb,* **repaid, repaying.**

repeal To do away with officially. Congress voted to *repeal* the old law. *Verb.*
—The act of repealing. The president supported the *repeal* of the law. *Noun.*
re·peal (ri pēl´) *verb,* **repealed, repealing;** *noun, plural* **repeals.**

repeat To say, do, or make again. The teacher *repeated* the question to the class. Please don't *repeat* my secret to anyone. I am careful not to *repeat* my mistakes. *Verb.*
—Something that is repeated. That television show is a *repeat* from last season. *Noun.*
re·peat (ri pēt´) *verb,* **repeated, repeating;** *noun, plural* **repeats.**

repel **1.** To drive back or away. The soldiers *repelled* the enemy's attack. **2.** To cause to feel dislike or disgust. I was *repelled* by the violence in that movie. **3.** To keep off or out. This raincoat *repels* water.
re·pel (ri pel´) *verb,* **repelled, repelling.**

repetition The act of repeating. *Repetition* of numbers helps me to remember them.
rep·e·ti·tion (rep´i tish´ən) *noun, plural* **repetitions.**

replace **1.** To take or fill the place of. Who will *replace* you as team captain? **2.** To get or give something similar in place of. We *replaced* the broken toy. **3.** To put back. I *replaced* the book on the shelf.
re·place (ri plās´) *verb,* **replaced, replacing.**

reply To answer in speech, writing, or action. The mayor *replied* to my letter. I *replied* that I enjoyed the movie. When we waved, the child *replied* with a smile. *Verb.*
—Something said, written, or done in answer. You gave the correct *reply* to the teacher's question. *Noun.*
re·ply (ri plī´) *verb,* **replied, replying;** *noun, plural* **replies.**

report An account, statement, or announcement, often formal or prepared for the public. I wrote a book *report* . A *report* of the game is in today's paper. *Noun.*
—**1.** To make or give a report of. My neighbor *reported* the crime to the police. **2.** To present oneself. Two students were asked to *report* to the principal's office. *Verb.*
re·port (ri pôrt´) *noun, plural* **reports;** *verb,* **reported, reporting.**

report card A written report of a student's grades and behavior.

reporter A person whose job is to gather and report news for a newspaper, magazine, or television or radio show.
re·port·er (ri pôr´tər) *noun, plural* **reporters.**

represent **1.** To be a sign or symbol of; stand for. The dots on the map *represent* towns and cities. The letters of the alphabet *represent* sounds. **2.** To speak or act for. Two senators *represent* the citizens of each state. **3.** To give a picture of. This painting *represents* the artist's grandparents.
rep·re·sent (rep´ri zent´) *verb,* **represented, representing.**

representative **1.** A person who is chosen to speak or act for others. The members of Congress are our elected *representatives.* **2.** A person or thing that is characteristic of a group or kind. The lion is a *representative* of the cat family. *Noun.*
—**1.** Characteristic of a group or kind. The museum has a *representative* collection of modern art. **2.** Made up of or based on representatives. Congress is a *representative* body. *Adjective.*
rep·re·sent·a·tive (rep´ri zen´tə tiv) *noun, plural* **representatives;** *adjective.*

reproduce **1.** To produce, form, or bring about again. The tape recorder *reproduced* my voice. **2.** To produce offspring. Most plants *reproduce* by means of seeds.
re·pro·duce (rē´prə düs´ *or* rē´prə dūs´) *verb,* **reproduced, reproducing.**

reproduction **1.** The process by which living things produce offspring or others like themselves. **2.** Something that is reproduced. That picture is a *reproduction* of a famous painting.
re·pro·duc·tion (rē´prə duk´shən) *noun, plural* **reproductions.**

reptile One of a class of cold-blooded animals with a backbone. Reptiles have dry,

at; āpe; fär; câre; end; mē; it; īce; pîerce; hot; ōld; sông; fôrk; oil; out; up; ūse; rüle; půll; tûrn; chin; sing; shop; thin; this; hw in white; zh in treasure. The symbol ə stands for the unstressed vowel sound in about, taken, pencil, lemon, and circus.

R

scaly skin. They move by crawling on their stomachs or creeping on short legs. Most reptiles reproduce by laying eggs. Lizards, snakes, alligators, and turtles are reptiles.
rep·tile (rep′təl *or* rep′tīl) *noun, plural* **reptiles.**

republic 1. A form of government in which the authority belongs to the people. The people elect representatives to manage the government. A *republic* is usually headed by a president, rather than a royal ruler. 2. A country that has such a form of government. The United States is a *republic.*
re·pub·lic (ri pub′lik) *noun, plural* **republics.**

Word History

The word **republic** goes back to two Latin words that mean "public thing." Since citizens in a republic vote for their rulers, the government is a thing that belongs to the public.

republican Of or like a republic. The rebels overthrew the dictator and set up a *republican* government. *Adjective.*
—1. A person who believes in or supports a republic as a form of government. 2. **Republican.** A person who is a member of the Republican Party. *Noun.*
re·pub·li·can (ri pub′li kən) *adjective; noun, plural* **republicans.**

Republican Party One of the two main political parties of the United States.

reputation What most people think of a person or thing. That judge has a *reputation* for being fair and honest. That restaurant has a bad *reputation.*
rep·u·ta·tion (rep′yə tā′shən) *noun, plural* **reputations.**

request To ask or ask for. I *requested* permission to leave early. The host *requested* that we be on time for the party. *Verb.*
—1. The act of asking for something. The teacher's *request* for attention made the class quiet down. 2. Something that is asked for. My parents felt that three dollars more allowance a week was too large a *request. Noun.*
re·quest (ri kwest′) *verb,* **requested, requesting;** *noun, plural* **requests.**

require 1. To have a need of. All human beings *require* food and sleep. 2. To force, order, or demand. The law *requires* people to stop their cars at a red light.
re·quire (ri kwīr′) *verb,* **required, requiring.**

requirement Something that is necessary; demand or need. Good grades are a *requirement* for getting into that college. Eating properly is a *requirement* for good health.
re·quire·ment (ri kwīr′mənt) *noun, plural* **requirements.**

reread To read again. I enjoyed the book so much that I'm going to *reread* it.
re·read (rē rēd′) *verb,* **reread** (rē red′), **rereading.**

rescue To save or free. The lifeguard *rescued* the drowning child. *Verb.*
—The act of rescuing. The firefighters all got medals for their daring *rescue. Noun.*
res·cue (res′kū) *verb,* **rescued, rescuing;** *noun, plural* **rescues.**

research A careful study or investigation in order to find and learn facts. I did *research* in the library for my report. *Noun.*
—To do research on or for. I *researched* my speech by reading many books on the subject. *Verb.*
re·search (ri sûrch′ *or* rē′sûrch′) *noun, plural* **researches;** *verb,* **researched, researching.**

resemblance A likeness in appearance. There is a close *resemblance* between us.
re·sem·blance (ri zem′bləns) *noun, plural* **resemblances.**

resemble To be like or similar to. That blue hat *resembles* mine.
re·sem·ble (ri zem′bəl) *verb,* **resembled, resembling.**

These girls **resemble** each other.

resent To feel anger or bitterness at or toward. I *resent* your unkind remark.
re·sent (ri zent′) *verb,* **resented, resenting.**

resentment A feeling of anger or bitterness. That child is filled with *resentment.*
re·sent·ment (ri zent′mənt) *noun, plural* **resentments.**

reservation **1.** An arrangement to have something kept for a particular person or persons. We called the restaurant to make dinner *reservations*. **2.** Land set aside by the government for a special purpose. Reservations have been set aside for Indian tribes to live on. Places where wild animals can live without danger of being killed are also called reservations. **3.** Something that limits or causes doubt. I had some *reservations* about walking home alone at night.
res·er·va·tion (rez′ər vā′shən) *noun, plural* **reservations.**

reserve **1.** To arrange to have something kept for a particular person or purpose. My parents *reserved* rooms in a hotel. **2.** To save or keep for a future or special purpose. *Reserve* your strength for the race. My neighbors *reserve* their weekends for gardening. **3.** To keep for oneself. I *reserve* the right to make up my own mind. *Verb.*
—**1.** Something that is saved or available for future use; store; supply. The squirrel had a large *reserve* of nuts for the winter. **2.** Land used for a special purpose. There is a wildlife *reserve* near our house. **3.** The habit of keeping one's feelings or thoughts to oneself. My *reserve* makes it hard for me to make friends quickly. **4. reserves.** The part of the armed forces that is kept ready for service in an emergency. *Noun.*
re·serve (ri zûrv′) *verb,* **reserved, reserving;** *noun, plural* **reserves.**

reservoir A place where water is stored. The water system in many towns and cities uses water from reservoirs.
res·er·voir (rez′ər vwär′) *noun, plural* **reservoirs.**

reside To make one's home for a long period of time. My family *resides* in Florida.
re·side (ri zīd′) *verb,* **resided, residing.**

residence **1.** A place where a person lives. Is this the Smith *residence*? **2.** A period of time spent living in a place. After ten years' *residence* in the city, my family moved.
res·i·dence (rez′i dəns) *noun, plural* **residences.**

resident A person who lives in a particular place. They are *residents* of this town.
res·i·dent (rez′i dənt) *noun, plural* **residents.**

residential Having to do with or suitable for residences. A *residential* neighborhood does not have factories or office buildings.
res·i·den·tial (rez′i den′shəl) *adjective.*

resign To give up a job, position, or office. I *resigned* as captain of the team.
re·sign (ri zīn′) *verb,* **resigned, resigning.**

resignation **1.** The act of resigning. We were surprised by the club treasurer's *resignation*. **2.** A formal notice that a person is resigning. I handed my *resignation* to my boss. **3.** A giving in to something without complaint. We accepted the defeat with *resignation*.
res·ig·na·tion (rez′ig nā′shən) *noun, plural* **resignations.**

resin A yellow or brown sticky substance that comes from pine, balsam, and certain other trees. Resin is used especially in paints and plastics and in making glue and rubber.
res·in (rez′in) *noun, plural* **resins.**

resist **1.** To keep from giving in to. My friend can't *resist* telling me secrets. **2.** To fight against or overcome. The country *resisted* attack. **3.** To overcome the effect or action of. This metal *resists* corrosion.
re·sist (ri zist′) *verb,* **resisted, resisting.**

resistance **1.** The act of resisting. The soldiers could not put up much *resistance* to the enemy. **2.** The ability to overcome something. I caught a cold because my *resistance* was low. **3.** A force that opposes or works against the motion of another. Race cars are designed to overcome air *resistance*.
re·sist·ance (ri zis′təns) *noun.*

resolution **1.** Something that is decided upon. My cousin made a *resolution* to go on a diet. The town council passed a *resolution* to clean up the park. **2.** The state or quality of being very determined. They approached the difficult task with *resolution*.
res·o·lu·tion (rez′ə lü′shən) *noun, plural* **resolutions.**

resolve **1.** To decide; determine. My friends have *resolved* to go to college. **2.** To settle, explain, or solve. I *resolved* the argument about the baseball player by looking up the statistics. *Verb.*
—Firmness of purpose; determination. It takes great *resolve* to do well in school. *Noun.*
re·solve (ri zolv′) *verb,* **resolved, resolving;** *noun.*

resonant **1.** Able to amplify sounds or make them last longer. The wood of a guitar is *resonant*. **2.** Having a full, rich sound. The famous actor had a *resonant* voice.
res·o·nant (rez′ə nənt) *adjective.*

---

at; āpe; fär; câre; end; mē; it; ice; pîerce; hot; ōld; sông, fôrk; oil; out; up; ūse; rüle; pùll; tûrn; chin; sing; shop; thin; this; hw in white; zh in treasure. The symbol ə stands for the unstressed vowel sound in about, taken, pencil, lemon, and circus.

R

resort To use or go to for help or protection. I *resort* to my family whenever I'm in trouble. *Verb.*
—**1.** A place where people go for fun or relaxation. We are going to a *resort* in the mountains to ski. **2.** A person or thing that is used or gone to for help or protection. The dictionary is your best *resort* when you need information about a word. *Noun.*
re·sort (ri zôrt′) *verb,* **resorted, resorting;** *noun, plural* **resorts.**

resound **1.** To be filled with sound. The stadium *resounded* with cheers when the home team scored a touchdown. **2.** To make a loud, long, or echoing sound. Thunder *resounded* in the air.
re·sound (ri zound′) *verb,* **resounded, resounding.**

resource **1.** Something that is used or gone to for help or support. The library is a great *resource* for students. **2. resources.** The wealth of a country or its way of producing wealth. Oil is one of that country's largest natural *resources.* **3.** Skill and cleverness in dealing with situations. You showed great *resource* in finding enough wood for a campfire. **4.** The action or means used in an emergency or a difficult time. Your only *resource* may be to ask others for help.
re·source (rē′sôrs′ *or* ri sôrs′ *or* rē′zôrs′ *or* ri zôrs′) *noun, plural* **resources.**

respect **1.** High regard or consideration. You must *respect* the rights and opinions of others. **2.** A favorable opinion; admiration. The mayor had little *respect* in the town. **3.** Affectionate regard, honor, or esteem. The twins had *respect* for their elders. **4.** A special way; particular point. In some *respects,* you are a better student than I am. **5.** Relation; reference. You show improvement with *respect* to grades. **6. respects.** Regards or greetings. Please give my *respects* to your family. *Noun.*
—To have or show honor or consideration for. We are taught to *respect* our elders. They *respected* my privacy. *Verb.*
re·spect (ri spekt′) *noun, plural* **respects;** *verb,* **respected, respecting.**

respectable **1.** Honest and decent; having a good reputation. Our neighbors are *respectable* people. **2.** Better than average; fairly good or large. Your grades are *respectable.* **3.** Fit to be seen or used. Wear a *respectable* suit to your job interview.
re·spect·a·ble (ri spek′tə bəl) *adjective.*

respectful Having or showing respect. I am always *respectful* when I talk to my teacher.
re·spect·ful (ri spekt′fəl) *adjective.*

respective Belonging to each. The children went to their *respective* homes after school.
re·spec·tive (ri spek′tiv) *adjective.*

respectively Regarding each in the order given. The train and the bus leave at 2:00 P.M. and 3:00 P.M., *respectively.*
re·spec·tive·ly (ri spek′tiv lē) *adverb.*

respiration The act or process of breathing. *Respiration* is more difficult at high altitudes because the air has less oxygen.
res·pi·ra·tion (res′pə rā′shən) *noun.*

respiratory Having to do with respiration or the organs used in respiration. A disease that affects the lungs is a *respiratory* disease.
res·pi·ra·to·ry (res′pər ə tôr′ē) *adjective.*

respond **1.** To give an answer. The witness did not *respond* to the lawyer's question. **2.** To act in return; react. The patient *responded* well to the medicine.
re·spond (ri spond′) *verb,* **responded, responding.**

response Something said or done in answer. What was the salesperson's *response* to your question?
re·sponse (ri spons′) *noun, plural* **responses.**

responsibility **1.** The quality or condition of being responsible. I feel a great deal of *responsibility* for my pet. **2.** Something for which a person is responsible; job or duty. Setting the table is your *responsibility.*
re·spon·si·bil·i·ty (ri spon′sə bil′i tē) *noun, plural* **responsibilities.**

responsible **1.** Having as a job, duty, or concern. I am *responsible* for collecting the class dues. **2.** Able to be trusted; trustworthy; reliable. We have a very *responsible* baby-sitter. **3.** Being the main cause. Careless driving is *responsible* for many accidents. **4.** Involving important duties. Being president of a large bank is a *responsible* job.
re·spon·si·ble (ri spon′sə bəl) *adjective.*

rest¹ **1.** A time of ease or relaxation; stopping of work or activity. The plumber took a *rest* before finishing the job. **2.** Freedom from work or anything that troubles or disturbs; quiet. The patient needs two more weeks' *rest* to recover fully. **3.** Sleep. I did not get enough *rest* last night. **4.** The state of not being in motion. The butterfly came to *rest* on the flower. **5.** Something that acts as a stand or support for something else. This chair has a foot *rest.* **6.** A silence in music. *Noun.*
—**1.** To stop work or activity; take a rest. The children *rested* on the porch after their game. **2.** To be quiet or at ease. The parents couldn't *rest* until they knew where their

children were.   **3.** To support or be supported. My hands *rested* in my lap. I *rested* my arm on the table.   **4.** To give rest to. The rider *rested* the horse after the race.   **5.** To be directed or fixed. The hungry child's eyes *rested* on the cake.   **6.** To lie in death. May the earthquake victims *rest* in peace. *Verb.*
  rest (rest) *noun, plural* **rests;** *verb,* **rested, resting.**

rest²   **1.** Something that is left; remainder. I ate the *rest* of the cake after everyone left.   **2.** Those people or things remaining; others. The *rest* will meet us in the park. *Noun.*
—To continue to be; remain. The responsibility for the money *rests* with you. *Verb.*
  rest (rest) *noun; verb,* **rested, resting.**

restaurant   A place where food is prepared and served to customers. In many restaurants customers serve themselves.
  res·tau·rant (res′tər ənt *or* res′tə ränt′) *noun, plural* **restaurants.**

Word History

The word **restaurant** comes from a French word meaning "to restore." At a *restaurant* people can sit down, eat, and feel refreshed, or "restored."

---

restless   **1.** Not able to rest. We got *restless* because the speech was so long.   **2.** Not giving rest. The patient spent a *restless* night.
  rest·less (rest′lis) *adjective.*

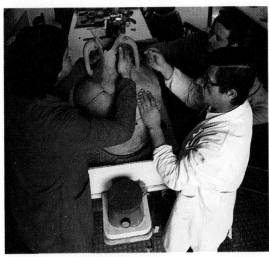
restoring a pot

restore   **1.** To bring back; establish again. The police tried to *restore* order in the crowd after the fight broke out.   **2.** To bring back to a former or original state or condition. The old house has been *restored* by its new owners.   **3.** To give or put back. The police *restored* the bicycle to its owner.
  re·store (ri stôr′) *verb,* **restored, restoring.**

restrain   **1.** To hide or keep secret; keep in. We tried to *restrain* our laughter.   **2.** To keep from doing something; hold back. We *restrained* the child from running.
  re·strain (ri strān′) *verb,* **restrained, restraining.**

restrict   To keep within certain limits. Use of the gym is *restricted* to students. Please *restrict* your speech to three minutes.
  re·strict (ri strikt′) *verb,* **restricted, restricting.**

restriction   **1.** Something that restricts. There are *restrictions* on who can use the pool.   **2.** The act of restricting or the condition of being restricted. Club membership is open to students of all ages without *restriction.*
  re·stric·tion (ri strik′shən) *noun, plural* **restrictions.**

restroom   A room with toilets and sinks in a public building.
  rest·room (rest′rüm′ *or* rest′rüm′) *noun, plural* **restrooms.**

result   Something that happens or is brought about because of something else. The accident was a *result* of carelessness. I won the race as a *result* of my greater speed. *Noun.*
—**1.** To be a result. High grades *result* from good study habits.   **2.** To have as a result. The lack of rain *resulted* in a poor crop. *Verb.*
  re·sult (ri zult′) *noun, plural* **results;** *verb,* **resulted, resulting.**

resume   **1.** To go on again after stopping. I *resumed* talking after taking a drink.   **2.** To take again. We *resumed* our places after recess.
  re·sume (ri züm′) *verb,* **resumed, resuming.**

resuscitate   To bring back to life; make conscious again; revive. The lifeguard *resuscitated* the child who almost drowned.
  re·sus·ci·tate (ri sus′i tāt′) *verb,* **resuscitated, resuscitating.**

---

at; āpe; fär; câre; end; mē; it; īce; pîerce; hot; ōld; sông, fôrk; oil; out; up; ūse; rüle; pu̇ll; tûrn; chin; sing; shop; thin; **th**is; hw in white; zh in treasure. The symbol ə stands for the unstressed vowel sound in about, taken, pencil, lemon, and circus.

R

615

retail The sale of goods in small amounts directly to customers. That store deals in the *retail* of sporting equipment. *Noun.*
—Having to do with the selling of goods directly to customers. That is a *retail* clothing store. *Adjective.*
re·tail (rē′tāl) *noun; adjective.*

retain **1.** To continue to have or hold; keep. Our family *retained* ownership of our old house. The cracked jar would not *retain* water. **2.** To keep in mind; remember. I *retained* all the important dates and battles of the American Revolution. **3.** To hire the services of by paying a fee. The family *retained* a lawyer to give them legal advice.
re·tain (ri tān′) *verb,* **retained, retaining.**

retarded Slow, especially in mental development. A retarded person cannot learn as fast or as much as most other people.
re·tard·ed (ri tär′did) *adjective.*

retina The lining of the back of the eyeball. It is made up of several layers of cells that are sensitive to the light that enters the eye. These cells send messages to the brain, which translates the messages into pictures.
ret·i·na (ret′ə nə) *noun, plural* **retinas.**

retire **1.** To take oneself away from a business, job, or office. My parents plan to *retire* when they are sixty-five. **2.** To go to bed. We *retired* early last night. **3.** To go away to rest or be alone. They often *retire* to the country on weekends.
re·tire (ri tīr′) *verb,* **retired, retiring.**

retirement The act of retiring or the state of being retired. They took up gardening after their *retirement* from business.
re·tire·ment (ri tīr′mənt) *noun, plural* **retirements.**

retiring Avoiding people or publicity; shy. The child has a *retiring* nature.
re·tir·ing (ri tīr′ing) *adjective.*

retreat To draw or move back. The soldiers *retreated* to their original position. *Verb.*
—**1.** The act of retreating. The soldiers surrendered soon after their *retreat.* **2.** A place in which to rest or relax. We have a summer *retreat.* **3.** A signal for soldiers to retreat. *Retreat* was sounded by the bugler. *Noun.*
re·treat (ri trēt′) *verb,* **retreated, retreating;** *noun, plural* **retreats.**

retrieve **1.** To get back; recover. The golfer *retrieved* the ball from the pond. **2.** To find and bring back dead or wounded game. Our dog is trained to *retrieve.*
re·trieve (ri trēv′) *verb,* **retrieved, retrieving.**

retriever A dog that is trained to retrieve game for a hunter.
re·triev·er (ri trē′vər) *noun, plural* **retrievers.**

retriever

retrorocket A small rocket that is attached to a larger rocket, a spacecraft, or an aircraft. It is fired in a direction opposite to the direction in which the vehicle is traveling. A retrorocket decreases the vehicle's speed.
ret·ro·rock·et (ret′rō rok′it) *noun.*

return **1.** To come or go back. I *returned* home to get the book I had forgotten. **2.** To happen or take place again. Winter *returns* every year. **3.** To take, bring, send, give, or put back. The student *returned* the book to the library. **4.** To give or put back in the same way. My friend *returned* my compliment by saying that my coat was nice. **5.** To report in an official way. The jury *returned* a verdict of not guilty. *Verb.*
—**1.** The act of returning. I'll call you after my *return.* **2.** An official report. I mailed my tax *return* on time. **3.** An amount of money made as a profit. The *returns* from the cake sale were fifty dollars. *Noun.*
re·turn (ri tûrn′) *verb,* **returned, returning;** *noun, plural* **returns.**

reunion A coming or bringing together again of family, friends, or other groups of people. My cousin's college class is holding its tenth *reunion* this year.
re·un·ion (rē ūn′yən) *noun, plural* **reunions.**

reveal **1.** To make known. Don't *reveal* my secret. **2.** To show; display. The magician opened the lid to *reveal* a bunny.
re·veal (ri vēl′) *verb,* **revealed, revealing.**

revenge Injury, harm, or punishment done to pay back a wrong. The couple swore to get *revenge* on their attacker. *Noun.*
—To return or pay back by causing injury, harm, or punishment. It is often wise not to try to *revenge* an insult. *Verb.*
re·venge (ri venj′) *noun; verb,* **revenged, revenging.**

616

revenue **1.** The money that is made from property or other investments. **2.** The money that is made by a government from taxes and other sources.
rev·e·nue (rev′ə nü′ or rev′ə nū′) *noun,* *plural* **revenues.**

reverence A feeling of deep love and respect. All the people of the town had *reverence* for the old doctor.
rev′er·ence (rev′ər əns or rev′rəns) *noun.*

reverent Feeling or showing deep love and respect. Each guest gave the royal couple a *reverent* bow.
rev·er·ent (rev′ər ənt or rev′rənt) *adjective.*

reverse **1.** Something that is the direct opposite of something else; contrary. You did the *reverse* of what I told you to do. **2.** The position of gears in a machine that makes them move in a direction that is opposite to the usual direction. You have to put the car in *reverse* to back up. **3.** The back side of something. The song I like is on the *reverse* of that record. **4.** A change of luck from good to bad. The store owners had a *reverse* in the first year of their business. *Noun.*
—Opposite in position or direction. An eagle is on the *reverse* side of the coin. The driver put the car in *reverse* gear. *Adjective.*
—**1.** To turn around, upside down, or inside out. I *reversed* the sock to mend the hole. **2.** To change to the opposite. I *reversed* my opinion once I heard all the facts. *Verb.*
re·verse (ri vûrs′) *noun,* *plural* **reverses;** *adjective; verb,* **reversed, reversing.**

review **1.** To study, go over, or examine again. I *reviewed* my notes. **2.** To go over in one's mind; look back on. I *reviewed* the day's events with a smile. **3.** To give a critical account of. My neighbor *reviews* new movies for a newspaper. **4.** To make a formal or official inspection of. The general *reviewed* the troops. *Verb.*
—**1.** A studying, going over, or examining again. Let's *review* what we talked about. **2.** A looking back. The magazine's *review* of the past year is in this issue. **3.** An account of a movie, play, book, or other work given to praise or criticize it. The author's latest book got very good *reviews.* **4.** A formal or official inspection. There was a *review* of the troops before the parade. *Noun.*
re·view (ri vū′) *verb,* **reviewed, reviewing;** *noun,* *plural* **reviews.**

revise **1.** To change in order to correct or make better. The author *revised* a confusing paragraph. **2.** To make different. I *revised* my opinion after I learned more.
re·vise (ri vīz′) *verb,* **revised, revising.**

revival **1.** The act of reviving or the condition of being revived. There has been a *revival* of interest in jazz. **2.** A showing of an old movie or a new production of an old play. Our drama club plans two *revivals* this season. **3.** A special service or series of services held to renew interest in religion. The preacher held a *revival* in our town.
re·viv·al (ri vī′vəl) *noun,* *plural* **revivals.**

revive **1.** To bring back to consciousness. The firefighter *revived* the unconscious child. **2.** To bring back into use, interest, or notice. The old movie was *revived* with great success. **3.** To give new strength or freshness to. A good meal *revived* the hungry children.
re·vive (ri vīv′) *verb,* **revived, reviving.**

revoke To cancel or make no longer good or useful. A driver's license can be *revoked* if the driver does not obey traffic laws.
re·voke (ri vōk′) *verb,* **revoked, revoking.**

revolt An uprising or rebellion against a government or other authority. The citizens staged a *revolt* against the cruel ruler. *Noun.*
—**1.** To rebel against a government or other authority. The prisoners *revolted.* **2.** To cause to feel sick or disgusted. The smell of the garbage *revolted* us. *Verb.*
re·volt (ri vōlt′) *noun,* *plural* **revolts;** *verb,* **revolted, revolting.**

revolution **1.** The overthrow of a system of government and the setting up of a new or different system of government. Revolutions are often carried out through the use of force. **2.** A sudden or complete change. The development of modern machines brought about a *revolution* in industry. **3.** Movement in a circle around a central point or object. The spacecraft made three *revolutions* around the moon before landing.
rev·o·lu·tion (rev′ə lü′shən) *noun,* *plural* **revolutions.**

revolutionary Having to do with or tending to bring about a revolution. The *revolutionary* leaders invaded the palace. The steam engine was a *revolutionary* invention.
rev·o·lu·tion·ar·y (rev′ə lü′shə ner′ē) *adjective.*

Revolutionary War The war the American colonies fought to become independent.

at; āpe; fär; câre; end; mē; it; īce; pîerce; hot; ōld; sông, fôrk; oil; out; up; ūse; rüle; pùll; tûrn; chin; sing; shop; thin; <u>th</u>is; hw in white; zh in treasure. The symbol ə stands for the unstressed vowel sound in about, taken, pencil, lemon, and circus.

R

Look up **American Revolution** for more information.

revolve　**1.** To move in a circle around a central point or object. The planets *revolve* around the sun.　**2.** To spin or turn around a central point. Wheels *revolve* when in motion.　**3.** To depend on. My whole life *revolves* around my family and my work.
　re·volve (ri volv′) *verb,* **revolved, revolving.**

This ride **revolves.**

revolver　A pistol that can be fired several times without putting more bullets into it. The bullets are held in a cylinder that revolves.
　re·volv·er (ri vol′vər) *noun, plural* **revolvers.**

reward　**1.** Something given or received in return for something done. The student received a medal as a *reward* for getting the best marks in English.　**2.** Money offered or given for the return of lost property or the capture of criminals. We offered a *reward* for the return of our lost dog. *Noun.*
　—1. To give a reward to. I *rewarded* the children with ten dollars for finding my watch.　**2.** To give a reward for. Our country *rewards* bravery in battle. *Verb.*
　re·ward (ri wôrd′) *noun, plural* **rewards;** *verb,* **rewarded, rewarding.**

reword　To put into different words. I *reworded* the question because the teacher did not understand it.
　re·word (rē wûrd′) *verb,* **reworded, rewording.**

RFD or **R.F.D.**　An abbreviation for *rural free delivery.*

rheumatic fever　A disease that usually affects children and causes fever, pain, and swelling in the joints. It can damage the heart.
　rheu·mat·ic fever (rü mat′ik).

rheumatism. Pain or stiffness in the muscles and joints of the body.
　rheu·ma·tism (rü′mə tiz′əm) *noun.*

rhinoceros　A very large animal having thick skin and one or two horns rising from the snout. Rhinoceroses live in open, grassy areas of Africa and Asia.
　rhi·noc·er·os (rī nos′ər əs) *noun, plural* **rhinoceroses** or **rhinoceros.**

Rhode Island　A state in the northeastern United States. It is the smallest state in the country. Its capital is Providence.
　Rhode Island (rōd).

Word History

　Rhode Island was named after the island of *Rhodes* in the Aegean Sea. An Italian explorer gave this name to an island near what is now known as Rhode Island because he thought that the island was about the size of Rhodes. This name was later used for the whole colony and then for the state.

rhododendron　An evergreen shrub that has clusters of flowers shaped like bells and shiny leaves.
　rho·do·den·dron (rō′də den′drən) *noun, plural* **rhododendrons.**

rhododendron

rhombus　A flat figure with four sides of equal length. The opposite sides of a rhombus are parallel.
　rhom·bus (rom′bəs) *noun, plural* **rhombuses** or **rhombi** (rom′bī).

rhubarb　A plant with green or reddish stalks that have a slightly sour taste. The stalks are cooked in pies and sauces.
　rhu·barb (rü′bärb) *noun, plural* **rhubarbs.**

rhyme　**1.** The repetition of similar sounds at the ends of lines of verse. For example, in the verse "Humpty Dumpty sat on a wall, Humpty Dumpty had a great fall," there is a rhyme with the words "wall" and "fall."　**2.** A word that sounds like or the same as another. "Mail" is a *rhyme* for "pail."　**3.** Verse or poetry having sounds at the ends of lines that are alike or the same. *Noun.*
　—To make a rhyme. "Wide" rhymes with "side." *Verb.*
　rhyme (rīm) *noun, plural* **rhymes;** *verb,* **rhymed, rhyming.**

rhythm A regular or orderly repeating of sounds or movements. We marched to the *rhythm* of drums beating steadily.
rhythm (ri<u>th</u>′əm) *noun, plural* **rhythms.**

rhythmic or **rhythmical** Relating to or having rhythm. That poem is *rhythmic.*
rhyth·mic or rhyth·mi·cal (ri<u>th</u>′mik *or* ri<u>th</u>′mi kəl) *adjective.*

RI Postal abbreviation for *Rhode Island.*

R.I. An abbreviation for *Rhode Island.*

rib **1.** One of the curved bones that are attached to the backbone and curve around to enclose the chest cavity. The ribs protect the heart and lungs. **2.** Something that looks like or acts as a rib. An umbrella has ribs.
rib (rib) *noun, plural* **ribs.**

ribbon **1.** A band of cloth or other material that is used for decoration. The gift was tied with *ribbons.* **2.** A band of material that is like a ribbon but that is not used for decoration. I need a new typewriter *ribbon.*
rib·bon (rib′ən) *noun, plural* **ribbons.**

rice The grains of a grass plant that is grown in many warm areas of the world. Rice is an important food crop.
rice (rīs) *noun.*

rich **1.** Having much money, land, or other valuable things. **2.** Having a lot of something. Our country is *rich* in natural resources. **3.** Able to produce much; fertile. The soil on this farm is very *rich.* **4.** Deep and full. That singer has a *rich* voice. **5.** Having a heavy, strong taste or having large amounts of butter or other fat, eggs, sugar, or flavoring. This is a very *rich* sauce.
rich (rich) *adjective,* **richer, richest.**

riches Much money, land, and other valuable things; wealth. The royal family has great *riches.*
rich·es (rich′iz) *plural noun.*

rickety Likely to fall or break; shaky. We were afraid to cross the *rickety* bridge.
rick·et·y (rik′i tē) *adjective.*

rid To clear or free of something that is not wanted. How do we *rid* the house of ants?
• **to get rid of.** **1.** To get free from. It's hard to *get rid of* a cold. **2.** To destroy. Poison *got rid of* the bugs in the house.
rid (rid) *verb,* **rid** or **ridded, ridding.**

ridden Past participle of **ride.** Have you ever *ridden* a horse? Look up **ride** for more information.
rid·den (rid′ən) *verb.*

riddle[1] A question or problem that is hard to figure out or understand. For example: What has two hands but no fingers? Answer: A clock.
rid·dle (rid′əl) *noun, plural* **riddles.**

riddle[2] To make many holes in. The soldier *riddled* the target with bullets.
rid·dle (rid′əl) *verb,* **riddled, riddling.**

ride **1.** To sit on a vehicle or animal and make it move in order to be carried by it. He *rides* his bicycle to school. She likes to *ride* horses. **2.** To travel on or in a car, train, or other vehicle. We *rode* through the town on the bus. **3.** To be carried along. The sailboat *rode* smoothly over the waves. *Verb.*
—**1.** A short trip on an animal or in a car, train, or other vehicle. We took a *ride* around the block on our bicycles. **2.** A device on which people ride for amusement. We tried all the *rides* at the fair. *Noun.*
ride (rīd) *verb,* **rode, ridden, riding;** *noun, plural* **rides.**

rider A person who rides. There were a number of horseback *riders* in the park.
rid·er (rī′dər) *noun, plural* **riders.**

ridge **1.** The long and narrow upper part of something. The animal had a black and white spot on the *ridge* of its back. **2.** A raised, narrow strip. Corduroy has *ridges.* **3.** A long and narrow chain of hills or mountains. **4.** The line where the two slanting sides of a roof come together.
ridge (rij) *noun, plural* **ridges.**

ridicule To make fun of. That mean bully often *ridicules* other children. *Verb.*
—Words or actions that make fun of a person or thing. Your strange way of dressing leaves you open to *ridicule. Noun.*
rid·i·cule (rid′i kūl′) *verb,* **ridiculed, ridiculing;** *noun.*

ridiculous Very silly or foolish. One of the guests wore a *ridiculous* hat with fruit and flowers on it to the costume party.
ri·dic·u·lous (ri dik′yə ləs) *adjective.*

rifle A firearm that is meant to be fired from the shoulder.
ri·fle (rī′fəl) *noun, plural* **rifles.**

rig **1.** To fit a boat or ship with masts, sails, lines, and the like. The workers *rigged* the entire boat in two weeks. **2.** To fit out; equip. We *rigged* our car with a special rack for carrying skis. **3.** To make or build in a hurry or by using odd bits and pieces of material. We *rigged* up a radio from used parts. *Verb.*
—**1.** An arrangement of masts, sails, lines,

at; āpe; fär; câre; end; mē; it; īce; pîerce; hot; ōld; sông, fôrk; oil; out; up; ūse; rüle; pùll; tûrn; chin; sing; shop; thin; <u>th</u>is; hw in white; zh in treasure. The symbol ə stands for the unstressed vowel sound in about, taken, pencil, lemon, and circus.

R

and the like on a boat or ship.   **2.** Equipment used for a special purpose. We bought a new fishing *rig* for our trip. The field is filled with oil drilling *rigs. Noun.*
rig (rig) *verb,* **rigged, rigging;** *noun, plural* **rigs.**

rigging   **1.** All the lines of a boat or ship. The rigging includes such things as ropes, chains, and wires.   **2.** Equipment used for a special purpose. The workers set up the *rigging* for drilling the oil well.
rig·ging (rig′ing) *noun, plural* **riggings.**

rigging on a ship

right   **1.** Correct or true; free from mistakes. The student gave the *right* answer to the arithmetic problem.   **2.** Just, moral, or good. Telling the truth was the *right* thing to do.   **3.** On or toward the side of the body that is to the east when one is facing north. He writes with his *right* hand. She sat on the *right* side of the room.   **4.** Proper; suitable. You are the *right* person to head the committee.   **5.** Healthy; well. I don't feel *right.* **6.** Meant to be seen. Which is the *right* side of this cloth? *Adjective.*
—**1.** Something that is just, moral, or good. The parents tried to teach their children to do *right.*   **2.** A just, moral, or lawful claim. Every citizen is guaranteed the *right* to free speech.   **3.** The right side or direction. Our house is on your *right. Noun.*
—**1.** Correctly. You didn't spell my name *right.*   **2.** According to what is just, moral, or good. You must do *right* and return the wallet you found.   **3.** In a proper way; suitably. This tape doesn't work *right.*   **4.** Exactly. Put the book *right* here.   **5.** Without

delay; immediately. Let's leave *right* after lunch.   **6.** To or toward the right. Turn *right* at the corner.   **7.** Completely. The rain soaked *right* through.   **8.** In a straight line. I went *right* up to the window. *Adverb.*
—**1.** To make good, just, or correct. I *righted* the wrong I had done.   **2.** To put or get back into a proper or normal position. We *righted* the raft after it turned over. *Verb.* ⊿ Another word that sounds like this is **write.**
 • **right away** or **right off.**   At once; immediately. I'll be there *right away.*
right (rīt) *adjective; noun, plural* **rights;** *adverb; verb,* **righted, righting.**

right angle   An angle of 90 degrees. It is formed by two lines that are perpendicular to each other.

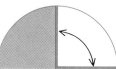

right angle

right-hand   **1.** On or toward the right. We drive on the *right-hand* side of the street.   **2.** For the right hand. I have lost my *right-hand* glove.
right-hand (rīt′hand′) *adjective.*

right-handed   **1.** Using the right hand more often and more easily than the left hand.   **2.** Done with the right hand. The pitcher made a *right-handed* throw.
right-hand·ed (rīt′han′did) *adjective.*

right triangle   A triangle with a right angle.

rigid   **1.** Not bending or giving; stiff. *Rigid* steel beams are used in building.   **2.** Not changing; fixed. We have a *rigid* schedule.
rig·id (rij′id) *adjective.*

rim   The outer edge or border of something. The *rim* of the glass is chipped. *Noun.*
—To form a rim around. The mountains *rimmed* the valley. *Verb.*
rim (rim) *noun, plural* **rims;** *verb,* **rimmed, rimming.**

rind   A firm outer covering or skin. Oranges, lemons, and watermelons have rinds. Some cheeses also have rinds.
rind (rīnd) *noun, plural* **rinds.**

ring¹   **1.** A closed, curved line; circle. The children sat in a *ring* around the teacher.   **2.** A band of metal or other material in the shape of a circle. I wear a *ring* on my finger.   **3.** An enclosed area. Rings are used for circus performances or for sports events. *Noun.*
—To put or form a ring around. Trees *ringed* the pond. *Verb.* ⊿ Another word that sounds like this is **wring.**
ring (ring) *noun, plural* **rings;** *verb,* **ringed, ringing.**

ring²   **1.** To make a clear sound like that of a bell. Did you hear the telephone *ring?*

620

2. To cause to make a clear sound. The visitor *rang* the doorbell.   **3.** To be full of loud and clear sounds; echo. Shots *rang* out. **4.** To hear a ringing or buzzing sound in the ear or ears. My ears *rang* from the music. **5.** To call or announce by ringing a bell. I *rang* for the hotel clerk.   **6.** To seem to be; sound. That story does not *ring* true. *Verb.*
—**1.** A clear sound like that made by a bell. The loud *ring* of the alarm clock woke me up.   **2.** A telephone call. I'll give you a *ring*. **3.** A certain impression or quality. Their words had the *ring* of sincerity. *Noun.* ▲ Another word that sounds like this is **wring**.
ring (ring) *verb,* **rang, rung, ringing;** *noun, plural* **rings.**

rink   A place that has a surface for ice-skating or roller-skating.
rink (ringk) *noun, plural* **rinks.**

ice-skating **rink**

rinse   **1.** To wash with clear water; take out soap or other matter with water. I *rinsed* the shirt before hanging it up to dry.   **2.** To wash lightly. Please *rinse* the glass before you put it in the dishwasher. *Verb.*
—The act of rinsing. I gave my hair a *rinse* after I got out of the pool. *Noun.*
rinse (rins) *verb,* **rinsed, rinsing;** *noun, plural* **rinses.**

riot   **1.** A noisy and violent disorder caused by a group or crowd of people.   **2.** A person or thing that is very funny. *Noun.*
—To take part in a noisy and violent disorder. The prisoners threatened to *riot. Verb.*
ri·ot (rī′ət) *noun, plural* **riots;** *verb,* **rioted, rioting.**

rip   To tear or pull apart. I *ripped* my pants on the fence. *Verb.*
—A torn place; tear. You have a *rip* in your shirt. *Noun.*
rip (rip) *verb,* **ripped, ripping;** *noun, plural* **rips.**

ripe   **1.** Fully grown and ready to be eaten. The tomatoes in the garden are *ripe* now. **2.** Ready; well prepared. Political unrest made the country *ripe* for revolution.
ripe (rīp) *adjective,* **riper, ripest.**

ripen   To make or become ripe. The heat and sun have *ripened* the pears.
rip·en (rī′pən) *verb,* **ripened, ripening.**

ripple   **1.** A very small wave. The breeze made *ripples* on the surface of the pond. **2.** Anything that is like a ripple. The wind makes *ripples* in the curtains.   **3.** A sound that is like the sound made by the flowing of very small waves. There was only a *ripple* of applause when the speaker finished. *Noun.*
—To have or cause to have ripples. The stone I threw *rippled* the water. *Verb.*
rip·ple (rip′əl) *noun, plural* **ripples;** *verb,* **rippled, rippling.**

rise   **1.** To get up from a sitting, kneeling, or lying position; stand up. Everyone had to *rise* when the judge entered.   **2.** To get out of bed. We *rise* at 7:00 every morning.   **3.** To move from a lower to a higher place; go upward. Smoke *rose* from the chimney. **4.** To reach upward. The building *rises* above the others.   **5.** To become greater, larger, or higher. Yeast makes bread dough *rise*. **6.** To go upward in position, rank, or importance. The artist *rose* to a prominent position.   **7.** To start; begin. That river *rises* in the mountains. **8.** To rebel; revolt. The people *rose* against the cruel dictator. *Verb.*
—**1.** A moving upward. There was a *rise* in temperature today.   **2.** An upward slope. The campers were so tired that they could not climb the *rise* of the hill. *Noun.*
rise (rīz) *verb,* **rose, risen, rising;** *noun, plural* **rises.**

risen   Past participle of **rise.** The sun has *risen.* Look up **rise** for more information.
ris·en (riz′ən) *verb.*

risk   A chance of loss or harm; danger. There is great *risk* in skydiving. *Noun.*
—**1.** To put in danger of loss or harm. The firefighters *risked* their lives every day. **2.** To take the risk of. My parents *risked* losing money when they bought a store. *Verb.*
risk (risk) *noun, plural* **risks;** *verb,* **risked, risking.**

at; āpe; fär; câre; end; mē; it; īce; pîerce; hot; ōld; sông, fôrk; oil; out; up; ūse; rüle; pùll; tûrn; chin; sing; shop; thin; this; hw in white; zh in treasure. The symbol ə stands for the unstressed vowel sound in about, taken, pencil, lemon, and circus.

R

ritual A system or fixed form of special ceremonies. Baptism is part of the *ritual* of many churches.
rit·u·al (rich′ü əl) *noun, plural* **rituals.**

rival A person who is, or tries to be, as good as or better than another. The two students were *rivals* for class president. My cousin has no *rival* as a chess player. *Noun.*
—**1.** To be the equal of. Nothing *rivals* the enjoyment I get from fishing. **2.** To try to be as good as or better than. *Verb.*
—Trying to get the same thing as another; competing. The two *rival* teams both practiced hard before the game. *Adjective.*
ri·val (rī′vəl) *noun, plural* **rivals;** *verb,* **rivaled, rivaling;** *adjective.*

river **1.** A large natural stream of water that empties into a lake, ocean, or other river. **2.** Anything that is like a river. A *river* of oil spilled from the truck when it turned over.
riv·er (riv′ər) *noun, plural* **rivers.**

rivet A metal bolt that is used to fasten pieces of metal together. *Noun.*
—**1.** To fasten with a rivet. The workers *riveted* the steel beams together. **2.** To hold or fasten firmly. The children's attention was *riveted* on the puppet show. *Verb.*
riv·et (riv′it) *noun, plural* **rivets;** *verb,* **riveted, riveting.**

roach A brown or black insect often found as a pest in homes. This insect is also called a **cockroach.** Look up **cockroach** for more information.
roach (rōch) *noun, plural* **roaches.**

road **1.** A strip of pavement or cleared ground that people or vehicles use to go from one place to another. **2.** A way for going or moving toward something wanted. Many people helped the actor on the *road* to fame.
▲ Another word that sounds like this is **rode.**
road (rōd) *noun, plural* **roads.**

road map A map that shows the streets and highways of an area.

roadrunner A bird that has brownish black streaked feathers, a long tail tipped with white, and a shaggy crest on top of its head. Roadrunners usually run very fast instead of flying. They are found in the southwestern United States.
road·run·ner (rōd′run′ər) *noun, plural* **roadrunners.**

roadside An area along the side of a road. We pulled up on the *roadside* to rest. *Noun.*
—Located along the side of the road. We stopped at a *roadside* stand. *Adjective.*
road·side (rōd′sīd′) *noun, plural* **roadsides;** *adjective.*

roam To go or move around without any particular place to go; wander. We *roamed* through the woods.
roam (rōm) *verb,* **roamed, roaming.**

roar **1.** To make a loud, deep sound or cry. The lion *roared.* The jet engine *roared.* **2.** To laugh loudly. They all *roared* at my jokes. *Verb.*
—A loud, deep sound or cry. I heard the *roar* of the ocean. The engine's *roar* faded. *Noun.*
roar (rôr) *verb,* **roared, roaring;** *noun, plural* **roars.**

roast **1.** To cook in an oven or over an open fire or hot coals. We *roasted* a chicken for dinner. The children *roasted* marshmallows over the barbecue. **2.** To dry and brown by heat. Coffee beans are *roasted* and ground. **3.** To be or make too hot. I'm *roasting* in this coat. *Verb.*
—A piece of meat that has been roasted or is ready to be roasted. We had a *roast* of pork for dinner. *Noun.*
—Roasted. My whole family likes *roast* beef. *Adjective.*
roast (rōst) *verb,* **roasted, roasting;** *noun, plural* **roasts;** *adjective.*

rob To take away from by using force or violence; steal from. Have the police found who *robbed* the jewelry store in town?
rob (rob) *verb,* **robbed, robbing.**

robber A person who robs.
rob·ber (rob′ər) *noun, plural* **robbers.**

robbery The act of taking something by the use of force or violence; theft. Did you read about the bank *robbery* on Tuesday?
rob·ber·y (rob′ə rē) *noun, plural* **robberies.**

robe **1.** A loose piece of clothing that is worn as a covering. I bought a yellow *robe* to wear over my pajamas. **2.** A piece of clothing that is worn to show one's office, profession, or rank. Members of the clergy and judges sometimes wear robes. *Noun.*
—To put a robe on. Servants *robed* the emperor before the ceremony. *Verb.*
robe (rōb) *noun, plural* **robes;** *verb,* **robed, robing.**

roadrunner

robin A bird that lives in North America and Europe. The robin that lives in North America has a reddish orange breast and a black head and tail.
rob·in (rob′in) *noun, plural* **robins.**

robot A machine that can do some of the same things that a human being can do.
ro·bot (rō′bət *or* rō′bot) *noun, plural* **robots.**

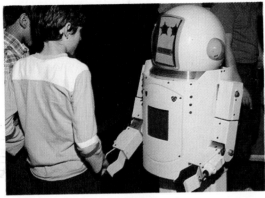
robot

robust Having strength and energy; in good health. The football player was very *robust.*
ro·bust (rō bust′ *or* rō′bust) *adjective.*

Word History

The word **robust** comes from a Latin word meaning "made of oak." Oak is a strong, hard wood, so the Latin word came to mean "strong."

rock¹ **1.** A piece of stone. The children threw *rocks* into the lake. **2.** A large mass of stone forming a cliff or peak. The boat was thrown against the *rocks* by the large waves. **3.** A mass of mineral matter that is formed naturally and is part of the earth's crust. Granite, limestone, and slate are rocks. **4.** Something that is like a rock in hardness or strength; strong support. My cousin was our *rock* during the family crisis.
rock (rok) *noun, plural* **rocks.**

rock² **1.** To move back and forth or from side to side in a gentle way. I *rocked* the baby in my arms. **2.** To move or shake violently. The explosion *rocked* the building. *Verb.*
—**1.** A rocking motion. Give the baby a *rock* in the cradle. **2.** Rock 'n' roll. *Noun.*
rock (rok) *verb,* **rocked, rocking;** *noun, plural* **rocks.**

rocker **1.** A rocking chair. **2.** One of the two curved pieces on which a cradle, rocking chair, or other object rocks.
rock·er (rok′ər) *noun, plural* **rockers.**

rocket A device that is driven through the air by a stream of hot gases that are released from the rear. Rockets are used as fireworks and weapons and to propel spacecraft. *Noun.*
—To move or rise very quickly. The price of food is *rocketing. Verb.*
rock·et (rok′it) *noun, plural* **rockets;** *verb,* **rocketed, rocketing.**

rocking chair A chair that is mounted on rockers or springs so that it can rock.

rocking horse A toy horse mounted on rockers. It is large enough for a child to ride.

rock 'n' roll A kind of popular music that has a strong, steady beat.
rock 'n' roll (rok′ən rōl′).

rocky¹ Full of rocks. The *rocky* beach was hard to walk on.
rock·y (rok′ē) *adjective,* **rockier, rockiest.**

rocky² Likely to fall or sway. Don't sit in that *rocky* old chair.
rock·y (rok′ē) *adjective,* **rockier, rockiest.**

rod **1.** A thin, straight piece of metal, wood, or other material. **2.** A long pole used for fishing. This is also called a **fishing rod.** Look up **fishing rod** for more information. **3.** A stick or bundle of sticks used to beat or punish. **4.** A unit for measuring. It is equal to 5½ yards or 16½ feet.
rod (rod) *noun, plural* **rods.**

rode Past tense of **ride.** My friend *rode* a bicycle. Look up **ride** for more information. ▲ Another word that sounds like this is **road.**
rode (rōd) *verb.*

rodent Any of a large group of animals that have a pair of big front teeth used for gnawing. Rats, mice, squirrels, guinea pigs, and beavers are rodents.
ro·dent (rō′dənt) *noun, plural* **rodents.**

Word History

The word **rodent** comes from a Latin word meaning "to gnaw." *Rodents* are "gnawing animals."

at; āpe; fär; câre; end; mē; it; īce; pîerce; hot; ōld; sông, fôrk; oil; out; up; ūse; rüle; pùll; tûrn; chin; sing; shop; thin; <u>th</u>is; hw in white; zh in treasure. The symbol ə stands for the unstressed vowel sound in about, taken, pencil, lemon, and circus.

R

rodeo   A show with contests in horseback riding, roping, and other similar skills.
   ro·de·o (rō′dē ō′ *or* rō dā′ō) *noun, plural* **rodeos.**

roe¹   The eggs of fish. ▲ Another word that sounds like this is **row.**
   roe (rō) *noun.*

roe²   A small deer that has a reddish brown coat. It is found in the forests of Europe and northern Asia. ▲ Another word that sounds like this is **row.**
   roe (rō) *noun, plural* **roes** *or* **roe.**

rogue   **1.** A person who is dishonest; cheat. **2.** A person who is playful or mischievous.
   rogue (rōg) *noun, plural* **rogues.**

role   **1.** A character or part played by an actor. I have a *role* in the play.   **2.** A part played by a person or thing; position. Our teacher took the *role* of guide on our trip. ▲ Another word that sounds like this is **roll.**
   role (rōl) *noun, plural* **roles.**

Word History

   The word **role** comes from a French word that was first used to mean "a roll of paper on which an actor's part or lines are written."

roll   **1.** To move by turning over and over. The ball *rolled* away.   **2.** To move or be moved on wheels or rollers. The wagon *rolled* down the hill. I *rolled* the cart down the street.   **3.** To turn over many times. The dog *rolled* in the grass.   **4.** To move in an up-and-down motion or from side to side. The tide *rolled* in. The ship *rolled* in the storm.   **5.** To make a deep, continuous sound; rumble. The drums *rolled.*   **6.** To wrap around on itself or on something else. *Roll* up the sleeping bag. *Roll* the clay into a ball.   **7.** To wrap in a covering. I *rolled* the fish in paper.   **8.** To spread out or make flat with a roller. I *rolled* dough for the cookies.   **9.** To pronounce with a trill.   **10.** To pass or go. The days *rolled* by. *Verb.*
— **1.** Something that is rolled up. Please buy a *roll* of stamps.   **2.** A list of names of people belonging to a group. The teacher called the *roll.*   **3.** A piece of baked bread. I put the hamburger on a *roll.*   **4.** A rolling or swaying motion. The *roll* of the boat made me dizzy.   **5.** A quick, continuous series of short sounds, as those made by beating on a drum. *Noun.* ▲ Another word that sounds like this is **role.**
   roll (rōl) *verb,* **rolled, rolling;** *noun, plural* **rolls.**

roller   **1.** A cylinder on which something is rolled or wound up. A window shade is on a *roller.*   **2.** A cylinder that smooths, spreads out, flattens, or crushes. We painted the walls with a *roller.*   **3.** A small wheel on which something is rolled or moved. They had to move the piano on *rollers.*   **4.** A long, swelling wave that breaks on the shore.
   roll·er (rō′lər) *noun, plural* **rollers.**

roller coaster   A ride in an amusement park or fair. On a roller coaster, people sit in a car that moves very fast over a track having sharp turns and sudden, steep inclines.

roller-skate   To skate on roller skates. The children *roller-skated* down the street.
   roll·er-skate (rō′lər skāt′) *verb,* **roller-skated, roller-skating.**

roller skate   A skate that has small wheels on the bottom. Roller skates are used for skating on flat surfaces, such as sidewalks.

rolling pin   A smooth cylinder used to roll out dough. Rolling pins are often made of wood and have a handle at each end.

The boy is using a **rolling pin.**

ROM   A type of memory that is installed in a computer and that cannot be changed. The information stored in ROM is permanent.
   ROM (rom) *noun.*

Roman   **1.** Of or having to do with ancient or modern Rome, its people, or their culture. **2. roman.** Of or having to do with the style of type most widely used in printing. The letters of roman type are upright. This sentence is printed in roman type. *Adjective.*
—**1.** A person who was born or is living in Rome.   **2.** A person who lived in ancient Rome.   **3. roman.** Roman type or lettering. *Noun.*
   Ro·man (rō′mən) *adjective; noun, plural* **Romans.**

Roman Catholic   **1.** Having to do with the Roman Catholic Church.   **2.** A member of the Roman Catholic Church.

Roman Catholic Church   The Christian church that recognizes the pope as its head.

romance   **1.** A love affair. The story of Sleeping Beauty is about a *romance* that she has with a prince.   **2.** A quality of love, excitement, mystery, or adventure. The dim lights gave a sense of *romance* to the room.   **3.** A story or poem that tells of heroes and their deeds, of adventure, and of love.
   ro·mance (rō mans' *or* rō'mans) *noun, plural* **romances.**

Word History

The word **romance** comes from an old French word that meant "something written in a *Romance* language." In the Middle Ages, stories of love and adventure were usually written in one of these Romance languages instead of in Latin, which was used in more serious writings.

Romance language   One of the languages that developed from Latin. French, Spanish, Italian, and Portuguese are Romance languages.

Romania   A country in southeastern Europe. This word is also spelled **Rumania.**
   Ro·ma·ni·a (rō mā'nē ə) *noun.*

Roman numeral   Any one of the letters used in a numbering system based on that used by the ancient Romans. In this system I = 1, V = 5, X = 10, L = 50, C = 100, D = 500, and M = 1,000.

romantic   **1.** Having to do with or marked by romance. My friend's head is full of *romantic* dreams.   **2.** Having thoughts and feelings of love and adventure.   **3.** Suitable for love or romance. The candles gave the room a *romantic* atmosphere.
   ro·man·tic (rō man'tik) *adjective.*

Rome   The capital of Italy, in the central part of the country. In ancient times, Rome was the center of the Roman Empire.
   Rome (rōm) *noun.*

romp   To play in a lively and noisy way. The children *romped* in the waves. *Verb.*
   —Lively and noisy play. I took my dog along for a *romp* in the woods. *Noun.*
   romp (romp) *verb,* **romped, romping;** *noun, plural* **romps.**

roof   **1.** The outer covering of the top of a building. I hit a ball over the *roof.* The workers replaced the shingles on the *roof.*
2. Something that is like a roof in position or use. I burned the *roof* of my mouth *Noun.*
—To cover with a roof. Our new house will be *roofed* this week. *Verb.*
   roof (rüf *or* rüf) *noun, plural* **roofs;** *verb,* **roofed, roofing.**

rook¹   A bird that is related to the crow. It looks like a crow with a gray beak. Rooks nest in colonies and live in Europe and Asia.
   rook (rùk) *noun, plural* **rooks.**

rook²   A piece that is used in the game of chess. The rook moves any number of spaces across or up and down the board parallel to the sides.
   rook (rùk) *noun, plural* **rooks.**

rookie   **1.** A person who has just joined a group and has had no experience. Those police officers are *rookies.*   **2.** An athlete who has just started playing a professional sport.
   rook·ie (rùk'ē) *noun, plural* **rookies.**

room   **1.** An area that is or may be taken up by something; space. There was no *room* to park the car in the lot. Is there *room* for this book in the suitcase?   **2.** An area in a house or other building that is separated or set off by walls. Our house has seven *rooms.*   **3.** The people in a room. The whole *room* was laughing.   **4.** A chance or opportunity; possibility. There is *room* for improvement in your schoolwork. *Noun.*
—To live in a room or rooms. They *roomed* together at college. *Verb.*
   room (rüm *or* rùm) *noun, plural* **rooms;** *verb,* **roomed, rooming.**

roommate   A person with whom one shares a room or rooms.
   room·mate (rüm'māt' *or* rùm'māt') *noun, plural* **roommates.**

roomy   Having plenty of room; large. They live in a *roomy* old house.
   room·y (rü'mē *or* rùm'ē) *adjective,* **roomier, roomiest.**

roost   **1.** A perch on which birds rest or sleep.   **2.** A building or other place for birds to rest or sleep for the night. *Noun.*
—To rest or sleep on a roost as a bird does. *Verb.*
   roost (rüst) *noun, plural* **roosts;** *verb,* **roosted, roosting.**

---

at; āpe; fär; câre; end; mē; it; īce; pîerce; hot; ōld; sông, fôrk; oil; out; up; ūse; rüle; pùll; tûrn; chin; sing; shop; thin; this; hw in white; zh in treasure. The symbol ə stands for the unstressed vowel sound in about, taken, pencil, lemon, and circus.

R

rooster An adult male chicken.
roost·er (rüs′tər) *noun, plural* **roosters.**

root[1] **1.** The part of a plant that grows down into the ground. Roots hold the plant in the soil and take in water and minerals to feed the plant. **2.** A part that acts as or looks like a root. Teeth and hair have roots. **3.** A part where something begins; origin. Get to the *root* of the problem. **4.** A word to which a prefix or suffix is added to make other words. "Faith" is the *root* of "faithful," and "bear" is the root of "bearable" and "unbearable." *Noun.*
—**1.** To develop roots and begin to grow. The cuttings will *root* soon . **2.** To fix or establish firmly. Fear *rooted* me to the spot. **3.** To pull, tear, or get rid of completely. We *rooted* weeds from the lawn. *Verb.* ▲ Another word that sounds like this is **route.**
root (rüt *or* rùt) *noun, plural* **roots;** *verb,* **rooted, rooting.**

rooster

kinds of **roots**

root[2] **1.** To dig in the earth with the snout. The pig *rooted* about for food. **2.** To search for something; rummage. I *rooted* through the closet for my other shoe. ▲ Another word that sounds like this is **route.**
root (rüt *or* rùt) *verb,* **rooted, rooting.**

root[3] To support a team or a person in a contest. Who are we *rooting* for? ▲ Another word that sounds like this is **route.**
root (rüt *or* rùt) *verb,* **rooted, rooting.**

rope **1.** A strong cord made of twisted or woven strands of wire, fiber, or other material. Ropes are used for pulling, lifting, or hanging objects. **2.** A number of things joined together by twisting or stringing. I wore a *rope* of pearls around my neck. *Noun.*
—**1.** To tie, bind, or fasten with a rope. The clerk *roped* the boxes together to make them easier to carry. **2.** To separate or enclose with a rope or ropes. The police *roped* off the area. **3.** To catch with a lasso or rope. The cowhand *roped* the calf. *Verb.*
rope (rōp) *noun, plural* **ropes;** *verb,* **roped, roping.**

rose[1] **1.** A flower that grows on a thorny bush or vine. Roses are usually red, pink, yellow, or white and often have a sweet smell. **2.** A pinkish red color. *Noun.*
—Having the color rose. *Adjective.*
rose (rōz) *noun, plural* **roses;** *adjective.*

rose[2] Past tense of **rise.** Everyone *rose* when the principal entered the room. Look up **rise** for more information.
rose (rōz) *verb.*

rosebud The bud of a rose.
rose·bud (rōz′bud′) *noun, plural* **rosebuds.**

Rosh Hashanah A holiday celebrating the first day of the Jewish year, which occurs in September or October.
Rosh Ha·sha·nah (rōsh′ hə shä′nə).

rosy **1.** Having the color rose; pinkish red. The baby's cheeks were *rosy* from the cold. **2.** Full of hope; bright; cheerful. The college graduate had a *rosy* outlook on the future.
ros·y (rō′zē) *adjective,* **rosier, rosiest.**

rot To make or become rotten; decay. The apples will *rot* on the tree if we don't pick them. The damp air in the basement will *rot* the old wooden chest. *Verb.*
—**1.** The process of rotting. *Rot* ruined the books in the damp basement. **2.** One of several diseases of plants or animals caused by any of various fungi or bacteria. *Noun.*
rot (rot) *verb,* **rotted, rotting;** *noun; plural* **rots.**

rotary Having a part or parts that turn or rotate. Some telephones have a rotary dial.
ro·ta·ry (rō′tə rē) *adjective.*

rotate **1.** To turn or cause to turn around on an axis. The earth *rotates* from west to east. Electricity *rotates* the wheel of the machine. **2.** To change in a fixed order; take turns regularly. The guards will *rotate* every four hours. Farmers *rotate* their crops to keep the soil fertile.
ro·tate (rō′tāt) *verb,* **rotated, rotating.**

rotation The act or process of turning on an

axis. The *rotation* of the earth takes 24 hours.

ro·ta·tion (rō tā′shən) *noun, plural*
rotations.

rotor **1.** The part of a motor or other machine that turns or rotates. **2.** A set of large, turning blades that lifts and moves a helicopter or other aircraft.

ro·tor (rō′tər) *noun, plural* **rotors.**

rotten **1.** Decayed; spoiled. That is a *rotten* apple. This meat is *rotten*. **2.** Likely to break, crack, or give way; weak. The wood in this old floor is *rotten*. **3.** Very bad or unpleasant. That was a *rotten* movie.

rot·ten (rot′ən) *adjective,* **rottener, rottenest.**

rouge A red or pink cosmetic used to color the cheeks.

rouge (rüzh) *noun, plural* **rouges.**

rough **1.** Having an uneven surface; not smooth or level. The bark of the tree is *rough*. Our car bounced over the *rough* road. **2.** Marked by or showing force or violence. Football can be a *rough* game. The little boat tossed on the *rough* waters. **3.** Not having or showing gentleness or politeness; rude. I would never speak in such a *rough* way. **4.** Not completely or perfectly finished or made. The artist made a *rough* sketch before painting. The mechanic gave us a *rough* estimate of the repair costs. **5.** In a natural or unfinished state. Jewelers cut *rough* diamonds into smaller stones. **6.** Hard or unpleasant. I had a *rough* day. *Adjective.*
—To plan, sketch, or shape in an incomplete way. The builder *roughed* out a plan for the house. I *roughed* in the details of the drawing. *Verb.* ▲ Another word that sounds like this is **ruff.**

rough (ruf) *adjective,* **rougher, roughest;**
verb, **roughed, roughing.**

round **1.** Shaped like a ball or globe. A grapefruit is *round*. **2.** Shaped like a circle; circular. Tires and hoops are *round*. **3.** Having a curved outline or surface. The chair has a *round* back. *Adjective.*
—**1.** Something that has a round shape. The cook cut the cookie dough into *rounds*. **2.** Movement in a circle or about an axis; revolution. The spacecraft made two *rounds* of the moon before it landed. **3. rounds.** A fixed or regular course or route. The guards made their *rounds* every hour. **4.** A series of happenings or actions. There is a *round* of parties over the holidays. **5.** A single outburst. Let's have a *round* of applause. **6.** A complete game or a section of a game or contest. There are ten *rounds* in the boxing match. We played a *round* of golf this afternoon. **7.** A short song that is sung by three

or more voices. Each voice begins the song at a different time. "Row, Row, Row Your Boat" is a round. **8.** A single discharge of a gun or other firearm or the ammunition needed for this. The police officer fired three *rounds* at the target. *Noun.*
—**1.** To make or become round. I *rounded* the corners of the table I was making. **2.** To pass or travel to the other side of; go around. The car *rounded* the corner. *Verb.*
—Around. The top spun *round* and *round*. The children gathered *round* the teacher. *Adverb, preposition.*

• **to round off.** To make into a round number. I *rounded off* 49.8 to 50.

• **to round out.** To make complete. That coin *rounds out* my collection.

• **to round up.** To drive or gather together. The farmer *rounded up* the stray cows. I *rounded up* a bunch of my friends.

round (round) *adjective,* **rounder, roundest;** *noun, plural* **rounds;** *verb,* **rounded, rounding;** *adverb; preposition.*

roundabout Not straight or direct. We took a *roundabout* route home.

round·a·bout (round′ə bout′ *or*
round′ə bout′) *adjective.*

roundhouse A round building with a turntable inside. A roundhouse is used to store or repair locomotives.

round·house (round′hous′) *noun, plural*
roundhouses (round′hou′ziz).

roundhouse

R

round number A number given in terms of the nearest whole number or in tens, hundreds, thousands, and the like. The number 500 is the *round number* for 498, and 6 is the *round number* for 5⅞.

round trip A trip to a place and back to the starting point. We took a *round trip* from Florida to New York and back to Florida

roundup **1.** The act of driving or gathering scattered cattle together for counting, branding, or selling. **2.** A gathering together of people or things. The announcer presented a *roundup* of the latest news items.
   round·up (round′up′) *noun, plural* **roundups.**

rouse **1.** To awaken from sleep, rest, or the like. The loud noise *roused* us. **2.** To stir up; excite. The touchdown *roused* the crowd.
   rouse (rouz) *verb,* **roused, rousing.**

rout¹ A complete defeat, or a disorderly retreat following such a defeat. The surprise attack resulted in a *rout* of the enemy. *Noun.*
—**1.** To beat completely. Our team *routed* theirs by twenty points. **2.** To force to retreat. Our soldiers *routed* the enemy. *Verb.*
   rout (rout) *noun, plural* **routs;** *verb,* **routed, routing.**

rout² **1.** To find or uncover by searching; discover. I *routed* my old shoes from the closet. **2.** To drive out; make leave. They *routed* us from our tents at seven o'clock.
   rout (rout) *verb,* **routed, routing.**

route **1.** A road or other course used for traveling. We drove along the ocean *route* to the beach. **2.** A regular course or territory covered by a person who delivers or sells something. I have a newspaper *route*. *Noun.*
—**1.** To arrange the route for. The travel agency *routed* our trip for us. **2.** To send by a certain route. The company *routes* its mail through New York. *Verb.* ▲ Another word that sounds like this is **root.**
   route (rüt *or* rout) *noun, plural* **routes;** *verb,* **routed, routing.**

routine **1.** A regular way of doing something. Shopping for groceries is part of my weekly *routine*. **2.** Sameness of actions or ways of doing things. The children became bored with the *routine* of camp life. *Noun.*
—According to or using routine; regular. Making my bed is one of my *routine* chores. *Adjective.*
   rou·tine (rü tēn′) *noun, plural* **routines;** *adjective.*

row¹ **1.** A series of people or things arranged in a line. A *row* of trees was planted in front of the house. **2.** A line of chairs or seats. We sat in the last *row* of the theater. ▲ Another word that sounds like this is **roe.**
   row (rō) *noun, plural* **rows.**

row² **1.** To use oars to make a boat move. We *rowed* to shore. **2.** To carry in a rowboat. Will you *row* me across the lake? *Verb.*
—A trip in a rowboat. It is a long *row* across the river. *Noun.* ▲ Another word that sounds like this is **roe.**
   row (rō) *verb,* **rowed, rowing;** *noun, plural* **rows.**

row³ A noisy quarrel or fight. They had a *row* over who would use the bathroom first.
   row (rou) *noun, plural* **rows.**

rowboat A boat that is moved by oars.
   row·boat (rō′bōt′) *noun, plural* **rowboats.**

rowboat

royal **1.** Of or having to do with a king or queen or their family. The *royal* family lives in the palace. **2.** Belonging to or serving a king or queen or their family. The queen lives in the *royal* palace. **3.** Coming from or by a king or queen or their family. The king issued a *royal* command. **4.** Suitable for or like a king or queen or their family. We were given a *royal* welcome when we arrived.
   roy·al (roi′əl) *adjective.*

royalty **1.** A royal person or persons. Kings, queens, princes, and princesses are royalty. **2.** The position or power of a king or queen or other member of a royal family. The crown is a symbol of *royalty*.
   roy·al·ty (roi′əl tē) *noun, plural* **royalties.**

R.R. An abbreviation for *railroad.*

Rte. An abbreviation for *route.*

rub **1.** To press something back and forth over; move back and forth with pressure. The nurse *rubbed* my leg to ease the cramp. **2.** To spread by using pressure. I *rubbed* lotion on my sunburned arms. **3.** To move against something else or against each other. I *rubbed* my cold hands together to make them warm. **4.** To apply pressure to in order to clean, polish, or make smooth. I *rubbed* the table with wax. **5.** To take away

by applying pressure. I used my foot to *rub* out what I had written in the sand. *Verb.*
—The act of rubbing. The coach gave my sore shoulder a good *rub. Noun.*
rub (rub) *verb,* **rubbed, rubbing;** *noun, plural* **rubs.**

rubber 1. A strong, elastic, waterproof substance that comes from the milky liquid in certain tropical trees. Rubber is used to make tires. 2. A short boot or overshoe that protects shoes from water.
rub·ber (rub′ər) *noun, plural* **rubbers.**

Word History

The word **rubber** comes from the word *rub.* This material was first used to rub out, or erase, pencil marks.

rubber band An elastic loop of rubber. It is used to hold things together.

rubber stamp A stamp made of rubber, with raised printing or a design. When it is pressed on a pad containing ink, it can be used to print dates, names, and the like.

rubbish 1. Useless waste material; trash. Put all the *rubbish* in a pile by the back door. 2. Worthless talk or thoughts; nonsense. Those rumors were just a lot of *rubbish.*
rub·bish (rub′ish) *noun.*

rubble Rough, broken pieces of stone, rock, or other solid material. The rescue workers searched through the *rubble* of the bombed building.
rub·ble (rub′əl) *noun.*

ruble A unit of money in the Soviet Union.
ru·ble (rü′bəl) *noun, plural* **rubles.**

ruby 1. A clear, red precious stone. 2. A deep red color. *Noun.*
—Having the color ruby; deep red. *Adjective.*
ru·by (rü′bē) *noun, plural* **rubies;** *adjective.*

rudder 1. A broad, flat, movable piece of wood, metal, or other material that is attached to the rear of a boat or ship. It is used in steering. 2. A piece that is like the rudder of a boat or ship, attached at the tail of an aircraft.
rud·der (rud′ər) *noun, plural* **rudders.**

ruddy Having a healthy redness. That child has a *ruddy* complexion.
rud·dy (rud′ē) *adjective,* **ruddier, ruddiest.**

rude 1. Having or showing bad manners; not polite. The bus driver gave a very *rude* answer to my question. I've never met such a *rude* person. 2. Roughly made or done; primitive. Cave dwellers used *rude* tools.
rude (rüd) *adjective,* **ruder, rudest.**

ruff 1. A ring of feathers or hairs growing around the neck of a bird or other animal. 2. A stiff, round frill, worn as a collar by men and women in former times. ⚠ Another word that sounds like this is **rough.**
ruff (ruf) *noun, plural* **ruffs.**

ruffle 1. To disturb the smoothness or calmness of. The wind *ruffled* the water. The bird *ruffled* its feathers. 2. To disturb or upset. The noisy crowd didn't *ruffle* the speaker. *Verb.*
—A strip of ribbon, lace, or other material gathered along one edge. It is used for trimming or decoration on clothes, curtains, bedspreads, and other things. *Noun.*
ruf·fle (ruf′əl) *verb,* **ruffled, ruffling;** *noun, plural* **ruffles.**

rug A piece of heavy fabric used to cover part of a floor. There was a small *rug* in front of the fireplace.
rug (rug) *noun, plural* **rugs.**

rugged 1. Having a sharp, rough outline or surface; rough and uneven. The mountain has many *rugged* peaks. 2. Very strong and sturdy. Our school has a *rugged* football team. 3. Hard to do or put up with; harsh. Life on the frontier was very *rugged.*
rug·ged (rug′id) *adjective.*

ruins

ruin 1. Destruction, damage, or collapse. The storekeeper faced financial *ruin.*

at; āpe; fär; câre; end; mē; it; īce; pîerce; hot; ōld; sông, fôrk; oil; out; up; ūse; rüle; pùll; tûrn; chin; sing; shop; thin; this; hw in white; zh in treasure. The symbol ə stands for the unstressed vowel sound in about, taken, pencil, lemon, and circus.

2. ruins. The remains of something destroyed or decayed. They found the *ruins* of an ancient city. **3.** Something that causes destruction, damage, or collapse. Money and fame will be the *ruin* of them. *Noun.*
—To bring to ruin; harm or damage greatly. The earthquake *ruined* the town. My broken ankle *ruined* my chances of being chosen for the team. *Verb.*
ru·in (rü′in) *noun, plural* **ruins;** *verb,* **ruined, ruining.**

rule **1.** A direction or principle that serves as a guide for behavior or action. Baseball, football, and other games have rules. Clubs and other organizations have rules for members to follow. One *rule* of good manners is not to speak when your mouth is full. **2.** Control or government; reign. The people were happy under the *rule* of the king and queen. **3.** Something that usually or normally happens or is done. Getting up early is the *rule* in our house. **4.** An instrument for measuring; ruler. *Noun.*
—**1.** To have power or control over; govern. The king and queen did not *rule* their subjects fairly. **2.** To make a decision with authority. The court *ruled* in their favor. **3.** To mark with straight lines. I write on paper that is *ruled. Verb.*
• **to rule out.** To decide against; exclude from consideration. The mayor *ruled out* higher taxes as a way of raising money.
rule (rül) *noun, plural* **rules;** *verb,* **ruled, ruling.**

ruler **1.** A person who rules. **2.** A strip of wood, plastic, metal, or other material that is marked off in measuring units, such as inches. It is used for drawing straight lines and for measuring.
rul·er (rü′lər) *noun, plural* **rulers.**

rum An alcoholic liquor made from molasses or the juice of sugar cane.
rum (rum) *noun, plural* **rums.**

Rumania Another spelling for the word **Romania.** Look up **Romania** for more information.
Ru·ma·ni·a (rù mā′nē ə) *noun.*

rumble **1.** To make a heavy, deep, rolling sound. Thunder *rumbled* in the distance. **2.** To move with such a sound. The tanks *rumbled* down the road. *Verb.*
—A heavy, deep, rolling sound. We heard the *rumble* of thunder. *Noun.*
rum·ble (rum′bəl) *verb,* **rumbled, rumbling;** *noun, plural* **rumbles.**

rummage To search completely by moving things around. I *rummaged* in the closet for my missing shoe. *Verb.*
—A complete search made by moving things

around. My *rummage* through the drawer did not turn up the missing glove. *Noun.*
rum·mage (rum′ij) *verb,* **rummaged, rummaging;** *noun, plural* **rummages.**

rumor **1.** A story or statement that is passed from one person to another as truth without anything to prove it. I heard a *rumor* that the game was canceled. **2.** What people are saying; general talk. *Rumor* has it that school will close early. *Noun.*
—To spread or tell by rumor. It is *rumored* that our teacher is getting married. *Verb.*
ru·mor (rü′mər) *noun, plural* **rumors;** *verb,* **rumored, rumoring.**

rump **1.** The part of an animal's body where the back and legs are joined. **2.** A cut of meat from this part.
rump (rump) *noun, plural* **rumps.**

run **1.** To go or cause to go quickly; move at a faster pace than a walk. The child had to *run* to catch the bus. I *ran* for help when I saw the fire break out. **2.** To do by or as if by running. The athlete *ran* the race in 3 minutes and 40 seconds. I *ran* an errand for my parents. **3.** To leave quickly; escape. The teenager *ran* away from home. **4.** To operate; work. I oiled the lawn mower so it would *run* better. **5.** To go or travel regularly. A bus *runs* every hour from Boston to New York. **6.** To move or cause to move freely and easily. We let our cats *run* in the house. I *ran* my eyes over the page. I *ran* the water for my bath. **7.** To take part in or enter a race or contest. Seven horses *ran* in the fifth race. Who do you think should *run* for mayor? **8.** To pass into or bring to a particular place or condition. If you *run* into any trouble, just call me. **9.** To keep on going or happening; continue. The road *runs* north about ten miles before it ends. The sale will *run* for one week. Blond hair *runs* in my family. **10.** To be in charge of. I *ran* today's meeting. Our friend *runs* the grocery store. **11.** To spread and mix together when exposed to water. The colors in this shirt *ran* after the first washing. **12.** To suffer from; have. The patient was *running* a high fever.

13. To have the stitches break at some point and come undone. My stocking *ran*. **14.** To get past or through. The ship tried to *run* the blockade. **15.** To give out liquid. My nose is *running*. **16.** To give to a computer as an instruction. *Run* that program again. **17.** To read and follow the instructions in a program. The computer is now *running* that new program. *Verb.*
—**1.** The act of running. I took the dog for a *run*. **2.** A pace that is faster than a walk. The children broke into a *run* as they neared the park. **3.** A trip. We took a *run* into town. This train makes four *runs* a day. **4.** The freedom to move about or use. Our friends gave us the *run* of the house. **5.** A period of time during which something continues to happen. We had a *run* of hot weather. The play had a six-month *run*. **6.** A place where stitches have broken and come undone. You have a *run* in your stocking. **7.** In baseball, a score that is made by touching home plate after touching the three bases. The shortstop scored the winning *run*. **8.** A sudden demand. There was a *run* on eggs at our local store. **9.** A steep pathway or track. There is a ski *run* near here. *Noun.*

- **in the long run.** In the last part of a course of events; at the end; finally. The project started well, but *in the long run,* we abandoned it.
- **to run across.** To meet or find by chance. If you *run across* any bargains at the book sale, buy something for me.
- **to run into.** **1.** To meet or find by chance. I *ran into* my dentist when I was leaving the library. **2.** To collide with. The car *ran into* a truck.
- **to run out of.** To use up the supply of. We have *run out of* eggs.

run (run) *verb,* **ran, run, running;** *noun, plural* **runs.**

runaway A person or animal that runs away. A horse that has broken away from the rider's control is a runaway. *Noun.*
—Running away; fleeing; escaping. We finally caught the *runaway* horse. *Adjective.*
run·a·way (run′ə wā′) *noun, plural* **runaways;** *adjective.*

run-down **1.** Having bad health; tired or sick. I felt *run-down* after working so hard. **2.** In need of repair; falling apart. They bought a large, *run-down* house.
run-down (run′doun′) *adjective.*

rung¹ Past participle of **ring.** The telephone has *rung* three times. Look up **ring** for more information. ▲ Another word that sounds like this is **wrung.**
rung (rung) *verb.*

rungs of a ladder

rung² **1.** A piece that forms a step of a ladder. **2.** A piece that is placed between the legs of a chair or forms part of the back of a chair. ▲ Another word that sounds like this is **wrung.**
rung (rung) *noun, plural* **rungs.**

runner **1.** A person or animal that runs. The greyhound is a fast *runner.* **2.** One of the long narrow parts or blades on which a sled or an ice skate moves. **3.** A narrow strip of rug, carpet, or other material. We have a *runner* on the floor in the hall. **4.** The thin stem of certain plants that trails along the ground and puts down roots to produce new plants. Strawberry plants have runners.

runner

run·ner (run′ər) *noun, plural* **runners.**

runner-up A person, group, or team that finishes in second place in a contest.
run·ner-up (run′ər up′) *noun, plural* **runners-up.**

at; āpe; fär; câre; end; mē; it; īce; pîerce; hot; ōld; sông; fôrk; oil; out; up; ūse; rüle; pùll; tûrn; chin; sing; shop; thin; this; hw in white; zh in treasure. The symbol ə stands for the unstressed vowel sound in about, taken, pencil, lemon, and circus.

running The act of a person, animal, or thing that runs. *Running* on the beach is fun. *Running* a business is hard work. *Noun.*
—**1.** Going quickly, moving at a run. The book had a picture of *running* gazelles. **2.** Flowing. We could hear *running* water. **3.** Operating; working. We left the engine *running.* **4.** Going on without a break; continuous. During the show, our teacher made *running* comments. **5.** Discharging mucus or pus. I have a *running* nose. **6.** Done with or during a run. The player made a *running* catch. *Adjective.*
> **run·ning** (run′ing) *noun, plural* **runnings;** *adjective.*

running mate A candidate for office from the same political party as another. A running mate is a candidate for the less important office. A presidential candidate's running mate is the candidate for vice president.

runway A long, narrow area where an airplane can take off and land.
> **run·way** (run′wā′) *noun, plural* **runways.**

rupture **1.** The act of breaking open or bursting. The *rupture* of the main water pipe caused a flood. **2.** A break in a friendship between people or nations. *Noun.*
—To break open or off. I *ruptured* a tiny blood vessel in my leg. *Verb.*
> **rup·ture** (rup′chər) *noun, plural* **ruptures;** *verb,* **ruptured, rupturing.**

rural In, having to do with, or like the country. The farm family lives in a *rural* area.
> **ru·ral** (rur′əl) *adjective.*

rush¹ **1.** To move, go, or come quickly. We'll have to *rush* or we'll be late. Water *rushed* out of the faucet. The police *rushed* the child to the hospital. **2.** To act or do in a quick or hasty way. Don't *rush* your work or you will make a mistake. *Verb.*
—**1.** The act of rushing; sudden, quick movement. There was a *rush* of water from the broken dam. **2.** Busy or hurried activity or movement. There was such a *rush* in the store that I couldn't find a clerk to help me. **3.** A busy or hurried state. They were in a *rush* to leave. *Noun.*
—Needing to be done quickly; urgent. Typing this letter is a *rush* job. *Adjective.*
> **rush** (rush) *verb,* **rushed, rushing;** *noun, plural* **rushes;** *adjective.*

rush² A plant that looks like grass. It usually has slender, hollow stems and bunches of small green or brown flowers.
> **rush** (rush) *noun, plural* **rushes,**

Russia **1.** A country in eastern Europe and in Asia. This country is now called the **Soviet Union.** Look up **Soviet Union** for more information. **2.** A former empire in eastern Europe and northern Asia.
> **Rus·sia** (rush′ə) *noun.*

Russian **1.** A person who was born in or is a citizen of Russia. **2.** The language of Russia. *Noun.*
—Of or having to do with Russia, its people, or their language. *Adjective.*
> **Rus·sian** (rush′ən) *noun, plural* **Russians;** *adjective.*

rust **1.** A reddish brown or orange coating that forms on iron when it is exposed to moisture or air. **2.** A plant disease that causes reddish brown spots to appear on leaves and stems. Rust is caused by a fungus. **3.** A reddish brown or orange color. *Noun.*
—To become covered with rust. The hinges on the old gate *rusted. Verb.*
—Having the color rust. *Adjective.*
> **rust** (rust) *noun, plural* **rusts;** *verb,* **rusted, rusting;** *adjective.*

rustic Of, relating to, or like the country. The artist is famous for painting *rustic* scenes.
> **rus·tic** (rus′tik) *adjective.*

rustle **1.** To make or cause to make soft, fluttering sounds. The leaves *rustled* in the wind. **2.** To steal cattle. *Verb.*
—A soft, fluttering sound of things being rubbed together or stirred about. We heard the *rustle* of papers in the next room. *Noun.*
> **rus·tle** (rus′əl) *verb,* **rustled, rustling;** *noun, plural* **rustles.**

rusty **1.** Covered with rust. Let's replace the *rusty* nails in the fence. **2.** Made by rust. There are *rusty* spots on these metal chairs. **3.** Not as good as it used to be because of not being used. My piano playing is a bit *rusty* because I haven't practiced for a while.
> **rust·y** (rus′tē) *adjective,* **rustier, rustiest.**

rut **1.** A track or groove made in the ground by a wheel or by constant use. The tractor left *ruts* in the dirt road. **2.** A fixed way of living, thinking, or acting; boring routine or sameness. Don't get yourself into a *rut* by doing the same things every day. *Noun.*
—To make ruts in. The heavy trucks *rutted* the road. *Verb.*
> **rut** (rut) *noun, plural* **ruts;** *verb,* **rutted, rutting.**

ruthless Not having pity or mercy. The dictator was a *ruthless* ruler.
> **ruth·less** (rüth′lis) *adjective.*

rye A grass plant that has slender stems. The grain of this plant is used as food for animals and in making flour and whiskey and other alcoholic liquors. ▲ Another word that sounds like this is **wry.**
> **rye** (rī) *noun, plural* **ryes.**

S s

1. The earliest form of the letter **S** was used in the ancient Middle East to represent the word "tooth."

2. The ancient Greeks then borrowed this letter, writing it something like a backwards Z.

3. The letter was then adopted by an ancient tribe that settled north of Rome.

4. The Romans borrowed this form of the letter **S** and gave it a more rounded shape.

5. By about 2,200 years ago, the Romans were writing their **S** much like our modern capital **S**.

s, S   The nineteenth letter of the alphabet.
s, S (es) *noun, plural* **s's, S's.**

S or **S.**   An abbreviation for *south* or *southern.*

Sabbath   The day of the week that is used for worship. Sunday is the Sabbath for most Christians. Saturday is the Sabbath for Jews.
Sab·bath (sab′əth) *noun, plural* **Sabbaths.**

saber   A heavy sword that has a long, usually curved blade and one cutting edge.
sa·ber (sā′bər) *noun, plural* **sabers.**

saber-toothed tiger   A large animal that lived millions of years ago. They had long, curved teeth in the upper jaw. They are closely related to lions, tigers, and other cats.
sa·ber-toothed tiger (sā′bər tütht′).

saber-toothed tiger

sable   A small animal that looks like a weasel. Its soft, brown fur is very valuable.
sa·ble (sā′bəl) *noun, plural* **sables.**

sabotage   The deliberate damage or destruction of buildings, machinery, or other property, or the interference with some activity. Sabotage is used during a time of war against an enemy. *Noun.*
—To damage, destroy, or interfere with by using sabotage. Enemy agents *sabotaged* the radar of two air force bases. *Verb.*
sab·o·tage (sab′ə täzh′) *noun; verb,*
sabotaged, sabotaging.

sac   A part in a plant or animal that is shaped like a bag and usually holds liquid. ⬩ Another word that sounds like this is **sack.**
sac (sak) *noun, plural* **sacs.**

sack¹   A large bag that is made of coarse, strong material. We bought a *sack* of potatoes at the market. ⬩ Another word that sounds like this is **sac.**
sack (sak) *noun, plural* **sacks.**

sack²   To steal all the valuable things from a town or city that has been captured in a war. The army *sacked* the town. *Verb.*
—The act of sacking. *Noun.* ⬩ Another word that sounds like this is **sac.**
sack (sak) *verb,* **sacked, sacking;** *noun, plural* **sacks.**

sacred   **1.** Belonging to God or a god; having to do with religion. Our choir sings *sa-*

cred music. **2.** Deserving to be treated with great respect. The memory of the dead hero was *sacred* to the town.

sa·cred (sā′krid) *adjective.*

sacrifice **1.** The ceremony of offering something to God or a god as an act of worship. The *sacrifice* of animals once was common in many religions. **2.** Something that is offered in an act of worship. The ancient Greeks often killed a sheep on the altar as a *sacrifice* to a god. **3.** The giving up of something that is wanted. A sacrifice is made for the sake of someone else or something else. The parents made many *sacrifices* in order to send their children to college. *Noun.*
—**1.** To offer as a sacrifice to God or a god. Ancient peoples *sacrificed* animals to their gods. **2.** To give up for the sake of someone else or something else. I *sacrificed* a chance to go skiing because I had promised to help my parents. *Verb.*

sac·ri·fice (sak′rə fīs′) *noun, plural* **sacrifices;** *verb,* **sacrificed, sacrificing.**

sad **1.** Unhappy or sorrowful. I was *sad* when my friend moved to another city. **2.** Causing unhappiness or sorrow. The wet and hungry dog was a *sad* sight.

sad (sad) *adjective,* **sadder, saddest.**

sadden To make or become sad. The death of our dog *saddened* us. I *saddened* at the thought of not being able to see my friend.

sad·den (sad′ən) *verb,* **saddened, saddening.**

saddle **1.** A seat for a rider on the back of a horse or similar animal. Saddles are usually made of leather. **2.** Something that is used like or looks like a saddle. The seat of a bicycle is often called a saddle. *Noun.*
—**1.** To put a saddle on. The cowhand *saddled* the horse. **2.** To load or burden. The club *saddled* me with all the work. *Verb.*

sad·dle (sad′əl) *noun, plural* **saddles;** *verb,* **saddled, saddling.**

safari A hunting trip. Many hunters once went on *safaris* in Africa.

sa·fa·ri (sə fär′ē) *noun, plural* **safaris.**

safe **1.** Free from or giving protection from harm or danger. It is not *safe* to skate on thin ice. The spy found a *safe* place to hide the secret paper. **2.** Without a chance of failure or error. It is a *safe* guess that it will rain today. **3.** Careful. My parents are very *safe* drivers. **4.** Having reached a base in baseball without being put out. *Adjective.*
—A strong metal box or other container. It is used to store money, jewelry, or other valuable things. *Noun.*

safe (sāf) *adjective,* **safer, safest;** *noun, plural* **safes.**

safeguard Something that protects. We put a screen in front of the fireplace as a *safeguard* against escaping sparks. *Noun.*
—To protect or guard. The dam *safeguarded* the town against a flood. *Verb.*

safe·guard (sāf′gärd′) *noun, plural* **safeguards;** *verb,* **safeguarded, safeguarding.**

safety Freedom from harm or danger. The police work for the *safety* of us all.

safe·ty (sāf′tē) *noun.*

safety belt A strong band of cloth, leather, or other material that is used to hold a person in place or to prevent a person from falling. Window washers use *safety belts* when working outside on tall buildings.

safety pin A pin that is bent so as to form a spring. It has a guard at one end to cover the point.

sag **1.** To sink or hang down. The old bed *sagged* in the middle. **2.** To become less firm or lose strength. Our spirits *sagged* after we lost four games in a row.

sag (sag) *verb,* **sagged, sagging.**

sage A very wise person, usually also old and very respected. People of the village consulted the *sage* for advice. *Noun.*
—Having or showing great wisdom and sound judgment. My grandparents often give me *sage* advice. *Adjective.*

sage (sāj) *noun, plural* **sages;** *adjective,* **sager, sagest.**

sagebrush A plant that has silver-white leaves and small yellow or white flowers. Sagebrush grows on the dry plains of western North America.

sage·brush (sāj′brush′) *noun.*

said Past tense and past participle of **say.** I *said* that I would like some more fruit. Look up **say** for more information.

said (sed) *verb.*

sail **1.** A large piece of canvas or other material that is attached to a boat or ship. It is used to catch the wind and move the boat forward in the water. **2.** Something that is like a sail in shape or use. The flat part of the arm of a windmill is called a sail. **3.** A trip or ride in a boat. We went for a *sail. Noun.*
—**1.** To move through or travel over the water. The boat *sailed* to sea. **2.** To begin a trip by water. The ship *sails* for Hawaii in two weeks. **3.** To steer or run a boat. I am going to learn how to *sail.* **4.** To move smoothly and without difficulty. The hawk *sailed* across the sky. *Verb.* ▲ Another word that sounds like this is **sale.**

sail (sāl) *noun, plural* **sails;** *verb,* **sailed, sailing.**

sailboat A boat that is moved by the wind blowing against its sail or sails.
sail·boat (sāl′bōt′) *noun, plural* **sailboats.**

sailor A person whose work is sailing or working on a boat. A sailor may work for a steamship company or be in the navy.
sail·or (sā′lər) *noun, plural* **sailors.**

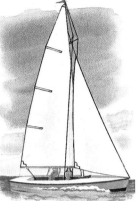

sailboat

saint 1. A very holy person. Some churches publicly honor such holy people after they have died. 2. A person who is very kind to or patient with other people. The sick patient thought the helpful nurse was a *saint.*
saint (sānt) *noun, plural* **saints.**

Saint Bernard A large, strong, reddish brown and white dog that has a big head.
Saint Ber·nard (bər närd′).

Saint Bernard

sake 1. Benefit or advantage; good. My grandparents moved to a warmer climate for the *sake* of their health. 2. Purpose or reason. Did you take the new job for the *sake* of making more money?
sake (sāk) *noun, plural* **sakes.**

salad A cold dish that is made with lettuce, tomatoes, or other vegetables and often served with a dressing. Meat, fish, eggs, or fruit are also used in salads.
sal·ad (sal′əd) *noun, plural* **salads.**

salamander An animal that looks like a small lizard. Salamanders are amphibians and are related to frogs and toads. They live in or near fresh water.
sal·a·man·der (sal′ə man′dər) *noun, plural* **salamanders.**

salary A fixed amount of money that is paid to someone for work done. It is paid at regular times. That job pays a good *salary.*
sal·a·ry (sal′ə rē) *noun, plural* **salaries.**

sale 1. An exchange of goods or property for money. A real estate agent arranged for the *sale* of our house. 2. The selling of something for less than it usually costs. The store is having a *sale* on bathing suits. ▲ Another word that sounds like this is **sail.**
• **for sale.** Available for purchase. Is that house *for sale?*
• **on sale.** Available for purchase at a price that is lower than usual. Furniture is *on sale* at our local department store.
sale (sāl) *noun, plural* **sales.**

salesman A man whose job is selling things.
sales·man (sālz′mən) *noun, plural* **salesmen** (sālz′mən).

salesperson A salesman or saleswoman.
sales·per·son (sālz′pûr′sən) *noun, plural* **salespersons.**

The **salesperson** is putting the shoe on the child.

saleswoman A woman whose job is selling things.
sales·wom·an (sālz′wùm′ən) *noun, plural* **saleswomen** (sālz′wim′ən).

saliva A clear liquid that is given off into the mouth by glands. It keeps the mouth moist, helps in chewing, and starts digestion.
sa·li·va (sə lī′və) *noun.*

at; āpe; fär; câre; end; mē; it; īce; pîerce; hot; ōld; sông, fôrk; oil; out; up; ūse; rüle; pùll; tûrn; chin; sing; shop; thin; this; hw in white; zh in treasure. The symbol ə stands for the unstressed vowel sound in about, taken, pencil, lemon, and circus.

635

S

salmon   **1.** A large fish with a silver-colored body. Most salmon live in salt water but swim to fresh water to lay their eggs.   **2.** A yellowish pink color. *Noun.*
—Having the color salmon. *Adjective.*
sal·mon (sam′ən) *noun, plural* **salmon** or **salmons;** *adjective.*

salmon

salt   **1.** A white substance that is found in sea water and in the earth. Salt is used to season and preserve foods.   **2.** A chemical substance that is formed by the reaction of an acid with a base. *Noun.*
—Containing or preserved with salt. The ocean is made up of *salt* water. *Adjective.*
—To season or preserve with salt. Please don't *salt* my vegetables. *Verb.*
  • **with a grain of salt.**   With some doubt; not too seriously. Since they were not reliable, I took their advice *with a grain of salt.*
salt (sôlt) *noun, plural* **salts;** *adjective;* *verb,* **salted, salting.**

saltwater   Of, having to do with, or living in salt water. A shark is a *saltwater* fish.
salt·wa·ter (sôlt′wô′tər) *adjective.*

salty   Containing or tasting of salt. The food was too *salty* to eat.
salt·y (sôl′tē) *adjective,* **saltier, saltiest.**

salute   **1.** To show formal respect by raising the right hand to the forehead. The sailor *saluted* when the flag was raised.   **2.** To greet with friendly or respectful words or actions. The visiting speaker *saluted* the audience with words of praise for their city. *Verb.*
—The act or gesture of saluting. The president was greeted by a twenty-one gun *salute.* *Noun.*
sa·lute (sə lüt′) *verb,* **saluted, saluting;** *noun, plural* **salutes.**

Word History

The word **salute** comes from a Latin word that means "to wish good health to."

salvage   To save from being lost or destroyed. Our friends were able to *salvage* some furniture from their burning house. *Verb.*
—The rescue of something from being lost or destroyed. The tugboats helped in the *salvage* of the sinking ship. *Noun.*
sal·vage (sal′vij) *verb,* **salvaged, salvaging;** *noun.*

salvation   **1.** The saving or freeing from difficulty, danger, evil, or sin.   **2.** A person or thing that saves or frees.
sal·va·tion (sal vā′shən) *noun.*

salve   A soft, often greasy substance that heals or soothes wounds or sores; ointment. The nurse put *salve* on my scraped knee.
salve (sav) *noun, plural* **salves.**

same   **1.** Like another in every way. Two people wore the *same* costume to the party.   **2.** Being the very one; not another; identical. That is the *same* person I sat next to on the bus yesterday.   **3.** Not changed. You are the *same* kind, friendly person you were a year ago. *Adjective.*
—A person or thing that is alike or identical. My friend ordered a slice of melon for dessert, and I asked for the *same. Noun.*
same (sām) *adjective; noun.*

sample   A small part or piece of anything that shows what the whole is like. Show me a *sample* of the carpet you like. *Noun.*
—To test or judge a part of. The cook *sampled* the soup to see how it tasted. *Verb.*
sam·ple (sam′pəl) *noun, plural* **samples;** *verb,* **sampled, sampling.**

sanctuary   **1.** Safety or protection. The escaped prisoners found *sanctuary* in the woods.   **2.** A natural area where birds and animals are protected.   **3.** A holy or sacred place.
sanc·tu·ar·y (sangk′chü er′ē) *noun, plural* **sanctuaries.**

sand   Tiny, loose grains of crushed rocks. Sand is found on beaches and in deserts. *Noun.*
—**1.** To scrape and smooth with sandpaper or sand. *Sand* the edges before you paint.   **2.** To sprinkle or cover with sand. The city *sanded* the roads after the snowstorm. *Verb.*
sand (sand) *noun; verb,* **sanded, sanding.**

sandal   A shoe with a sole that is held to the foot by one or more straps.
san·dal (san′dəl) *noun, plural* **sandals.**

sandbar   A ridge or bank of sand built up by the action of waves or currents. Sandbars can form in rivers or bays or along the shore.
sand·bar (sand′bär′) *noun, plural* **sandbars.**

sandbox A large, low box or enclosed area that is filled with sand for children to play in.
sand·box (sand′boks′) *noun, plural* **sandboxes.**

sandpaper A strong, heavy paper with a rough coating of sand or other material on one side. It is used for smoothing and cleaning wood and other surfaces. *Noun.*
—To smooth and clean by rubbing with sandpaper. The worker *sandpapered* the old door until it was smooth. *Verb.*
sand·pa·per (sand′pā′pər) *noun; verb,* **sandpapered, sandpapering.**

sandpiper A bird that has a long, thin bill, long legs, and brown or grayish feathers. Sandpipers live along the seashore.
sand·pip·er (sand′pī′pər) *noun, plural* **sandpipers.**

sandpiper

sandstone A kind of rock that is made up mainly of grains of sand held together by a kind of natural cement.
sand·stone (sand′stōn′) *noun.*

sandwich Two or more slices of bread with meat, cheese, or some other filling between them. *Noun.*
—To fit or squeeze in tightly. The book was *sandwiched* between two others on the top shelf. *Verb.*
sand·wich (sand′wich) *noun, plural* **sandwiches;** *verb,* **sandwiched, sandwiching.**

Word History

The word **sandwich** comes from the name of the Earl of *Sandwich.* It is said that he invented the sandwich so that he would not have to leave the table in the middle of a card game to eat a regular meal.

sandy **1.** Containing or like sand. The road to the beach is *sandy* and full of bumps. The cactus is a plant that grows in *sandy* soil. **2.** Yellowish brown in color. You have *sandy* hair.
sand·y (san′dē) *adjective,* **sandier, sandiest.**

sane **1.** Having a healthy mind; not crazy. **2.** Having or showing good sense. My friend gave me some *sane* advice. ▲ Another word that sounds like this is **seine.**
sane (sān) *adjective,* **saner, sanest.**

sang A past tense of **sing.** We *sang* a cheerful song in the school play. Look up **sing** for more information.
sang (sang) *verb.*

sanitation The protection of people's health by keeping living conditions clean. Sanitation includes getting rid of garbage and keeping drinking water clean.
san·i·ta·tion (san′i tā′shən) *noun.*

sanity A healthy state of mind.
san·i·ty (san′i tē) *noun.*

sank A past tense of **sink.** The ship *sank* during a hurricane. Look up **sink** for more information.
sank (sangk) *verb.*

sap A liquid that flows through a plant. Sap carries water and food from one part of a plant to another. The *sap* of the maple tree is used to make syrup.
sap (sap) *noun, plural* **saps.**

sapling A young tree. The thin trunk of the *sapling* bent easily.
sap·ling (sap′ling) *noun, plural* **saplings.**

sapphire A precious stone that is clear and deep blue in color.
sap·phire (saf′īr) *noun, plural* **sapphires.**

sarcastic Using sharp or bitter words that are meant to hurt or make fun of someone or something. Your *sarcastic* answer hurt my feelings.
sar·cas·tic (sär kas′tik) *adjective.*

sardine A small fish that lives in salt water and is used for food. Sardines are packed tightly in oil in flat cans. We had *sardines* and crackers for lunch.
sar·dine (sär dēn′) *noun, plural* **sardines** or **sardine.**

sari A piece of clothing worn by women of India and Pakistan. A sari is one long piece

at; āpe; fär; câre; end; mē; it; īce; pîerce; hot; ōld; sông, fôrk; oil; out; up; ūse; rüle; pùll; tûrn; chin; sing; shop; thin; <u>th</u>is; hw in white; zh in treasure. The symbol ə stands for the unstressed vowel sound in about, taken, pencil, lemon, and circus.

S

of cloth that is wrapped around the body to form a skirt and cover one shoulder.

sa·ri (sär′ē) *noun, plural* **saris.**

saris

sash¹ A broad piece of cloth that is worn around the waist or over one shoulder. This dress has a bright pink *sash* instead of a belt.

sash (sash) *noun, plural* **sashes.**

sash² The frame that holds the glass in a window or door.

sash (sash) *noun, plural* **sashes.**

Sask. An abbreviation for *Saskatchewan.*

Saskatchewan A province in central Canada. Its capital is Regina.

Sas·katch·e·wan (sas kach′ə won′) *noun.*

sat Past tense and past participle of **sit.** We *sat* on a bench while we waited. Look up **sit** for more information.

sat (sat) *verb.*

Sat. An abbreviation for *Saturday.*

Satan The evil spirit that is thought to rule hell; the Devil.

Sa·tan (sā′tən) *noun.*

satellite 1. A heavenly body that moves in an orbit around another body larger than itself. The moon is the earth's only natural satellite. 2. A spacecraft that moves in an orbit around the earth, the moon, or other bodies in space. Satellites are used to forecast

the weather, to connect radio, telephone, and television communications, and to provide information about conditions in space. 3. A country that is dependent on or controlled by another, more powerful country.

sat·el·lite (sat′ə līt′) *noun, plural* **satellites.**

Word History

The word **satellite** comes from a Latin word meaning "bodyguard" or "attendant." A satellite such as the moon moves around the earth the way an attendant or bodyguard accompanies an important person.

satin A fabric that has a smooth, shiny surface. It is made of silk or similar materials.

sat·in (sat′in) *noun, plural* **satins.**

satisfaction The condition of being satisfied or the act of satisfying. Don't you get a lot of *satisfaction* from doing your homework well?

sat·is·fac·tion (sat′is fak′shən) *noun.*

satisfactory Good enough to meet a need, desire, or standard; giving satisfaction. Your high grade on the arithmetic test is more than *satisfactory.*

sat·is·fac·to·ry (sat′is fak′tə rē) *adjective.*

satisfy 1. To be or give enough to meet the need, desire, or demand of. The sandwich will *satisfy* me until dinner. The team's performance in the championship game did not *satisfy* the coach. 2. To make free from doubt; convince. The children's explanation of where they had been all afternoon *satisfied* their parents.

sat·is·fy (sat′is fī′) *verb,* **satisfied, satisfying.**

saturate To soak or fill completely. The spilled milk *saturated* the rug.

sat·u·rate (sach′ə rāt′) *verb,* **saturated, saturating.**

Saturday The seventh day of the week.

Sat·ur·day (sat′ər dē *or* sat′ər dā′) *noun, plural* **Saturdays.**

Word History

Saturday is named after Saturn, the Roman god of farming. The planet *Saturn* is also named for this god.

Saturn The second largest planet in our solar system. It is the sixth planet in order of

distance from the sun. Saturn is surrounded by large rings and many moons.
Sat·urn (sat'ərn) *noun.*

Saturn

sauce **1.** A liquid or creamy mixture that is served with food to make it taste better. The chef made a lemon *sauce* for the fish. **2.** A food consisting of fruit that has been stewed. I like cranberry *sauce* with turkey.
sauce (sôs) *noun, plural* **sauces.**

saucepan A small pot with a handle, used for cooking.
sauce·pan (sôs'pan') *noun, plural* **saucepans.**

saucer A small, shallow dish that is used for holding a cup.
sau·cer (sô'sər) *noun, plural* **saucers.**

Saudi Arabia A country in southwestern Asia.
Sa·u·di A·ra·bi·a (sä ü'dē ə rā'bē ə *or* sô'dē ə rā'bē ə) *noun.*

sausage Finely chopped meat that is mixed with spices. It is often stuffed into a thin case like a tube. Frankfurters are sausages.
sau·sage (sô'sij) *noun, plural* **sausages.**

savage **1.** Cruel or fierce. There was *savage* fighting all day on the battlefield. **2.** Not tamed; wild. The leopard is a *savage* animal. **3.** Not civilized. The *savage* people used wooden spears for hunting. *Adjective.*
—**1.** A person who is cruel, fierce, or brutal. **2.** A person who belongs to a tribe or group that is not civilized. *Noun.*
sav·age (sav'ij) *adjective; noun, plural* **savages.**

save **1.** To free from harm; make safe. The firefighters *saved* the child from the burning house. **2.** To set aside money or anything else for use in the future. I am *saving* my al-lowance to buy a baseball mitt. They *saved* the leftover food from the party. **3.** To keep from being lost, spent, or damaged. You can *save* time by shopping close to home. **4.** To keep from being needed. We borrowed a cup of flour and *saved* a trip to the store. **5.** To avoid expense or waste. We *save* on food by buying what is on sale.
save (sāv) *verb,* **saved, saving.**

savings Money that is saved. It will take all of your *savings* to buy that camera.
sav·ings (sā'vingz) *plural noun.*

saw¹ A tool or machine that has a sharp metal blade with teeth. It is used for cutting wood, metal, or other hard materials. *Noun.*
—To cut or be cut with a saw. The lumberjack *sawed* the log in half. This wood *saws* more easily than I thought it would. *Verb.*
saw (sô) *noun, plural* **saws;** *verb,* **sawed, sawed** or **sawn, sawing.**

saw² Past tense of **see.** Who *saw* the helicopter? Look up **see** for more information.
saw (sô) *verb.*

sawdust The fine particles that fall from wood as it is being sawed.
saw·dust (sô'dust') *noun.*

sawmill A place where machines saw logs into lumber.
saw·mill (sô'mil') *noun, plural* **sawmills.**

sawn A past participle of **saw¹.** They have already *sawn* all the wood. Look up **saw¹** for more information.
sawn (sôn) *verb.*

saxophone A musical instrument that has a curved metal body with keys fitted along it. It is played by blowing into the mouthpiece and pushing down the keys with the fingers.
sax·o·phone (sak'sə fōn') *noun, plural* **saxophones.**

say **1.** To speak or pronounce words. What did you *say?* I *said,* "Hello, how are you?" **2.** To make known or express in words; declare. They *said* that they enjoyed meeting you. **3.** To estimate or suppose. How much money would you *say* that cashier earns? **4.** To repeat; recite. The class *said* the pledge of allegiance to the flag. *Verb.*
—**1.** The right or chance to speak. You'll have your *say.* **2.** The right or power to in-

at; āpe; fär; câre; end; mē; it; īce; pîerce; hot; ōld; sông, fôrk; oil; out; up; ūse; rüle; pull; tûrn; chin; sing; shop; thin; this; hw in white; zh in treasure. The symbol ə stands for the unstressed vowel sound in about, taken, pencil, lemon, and circus.

S

fluence or decide. The mayor had a strong *say* in hiring more police officers. *Noun.*

say (sā) *verb,* **said, saying;** *noun.*

saying A familiar statement that contains some truth or common sense; proverb. "A stitch in time saves nine" is a saying.

say·ing (sā'ing) *noun, plural* **sayings.**

SC Postal abbreviation for *South Carolina.*

S.C. An abbreviation for *South Carolina.*

scab A crust that forms over a sore or wound to protect it as it heals.

scab (skab) *noun, plural* **scabs.**

scabbard A case for the blade of a sword, dagger, or similar weapon; sheath.

scab·bard (skab'ərd) *noun, plural* **scabbards.**

scaffold A platform that workers stand on as they work on a building.

scaf·fold (skaf'əld) *noun, plural* **scaffolds.**

scale[1]

scale[1] A device used to find out how heavy something is. It works by balancing the thing to be weighed against another weight or against the force of a spring.

scale (skāl) *noun, plural* **scales.**

scale[2] **1.** One of the thin, flat plates that cover the body of fish, snakes, and lizards. **2.** A thin, flat piece of something. The old paint is coming off the house in *scales. Noun.*
—To take off the scales from. The clerk in the fish store *scaled* the fish for us. *Verb.*

scale (skāl) *noun, plural* **scales;** *verb,* **scaled, scaling.**

scale[3] **1.** A series of marks made along a line at regularly spaced points. A scale is used for measuring. The *scale* of that ruler is in inches. **2.** The size of a plan, map, or model compared with what it represents. The *scale* of the map is one inch for every 200 miles. **3.** A series of steps or degrees. The pay *scale* for that job is from $100 per week to $175 per week. **4.** Relative size or extent. The artist worked on a large *scale.* **5.** A series of musical tones that go up or down in pitch. A scale is usually made up of eight notes. *Noun.*
—**1.** To climb to or over the top of. The climbers *scaled* the steep cliff. **2.** To change by a fixed amount. The two countries *scaled* down the building of weapons. *Verb.*

scale (skāl) *noun, plural* **scales;** *verb,* **scaled, scaling.**

scalene triangle A triangle with each of its three sides a different length.

sca·lene triangle (skā lēn')

scallion A kind of onion that has a small bulb and long green leaves.

scal·lion (skal'yən) *noun, plural* **scallions.**

scallop **1.** A sea animal enclosed by two shells that have ridges. These shells close to protect the soft body inside, and open to let in food and water. The scallop is a mollusk. **2.** One of a series of curves that looks like the edge of a scallop shell. The dress had *scallops* along the bottom. *Noun.*
—To shape or make with a series of curves. The edges of the quilt were *scalloped. Verb.*

scal·lop (skol'əp *or* skal'əp) *noun, plural* **scallops;** *verb,* **scalloped, scalloping.**

scalp The skin that covers the head. The scalp is usually covered with hair. *Noun.*
—To cut or tear the scalp from. *Verb.*

scalp (skalp) *noun, plural* **scalps;** *verb,* **scalped, scalping.**

scaly Covered or partly covered with scales. Fish and snakes are *scaly.*

scal·y (skā'lē) *adjective,* **scalier, scaliest.**

scamper To run or to move quickly. The rabbit *scampered* into the woods.

scam·per (skam'pər) *verb,* **scampered, scampering.**

scan **1.** To look at closely and carefully. The sailor *scanned* the horizon for land. **2.** To read quickly or glance over. We *scanned* the newspaper headlines.

scan (skan) *verb,* **scanned, scanning.**

scandal **1.** Something that shocks people's sense of what is right and wrong and disgraces those who are involved in it. There was a *scandal* when the mayor stole city funds. **2.** Talk that harms a person's good name; harmful gossip. The old couple did not believe the *scandal* about their neighbor.

scan·dal (skan'dəl) *noun, plural* **scandals.**

Scandinavia **1.** A part of north-central Europe consisting of Denmark, Norway, and Sweden. Sometimes Finland and Iceland are considered part of Scandinavia. **2.** A large peninsula in north-central Europe. Norway and Sweden are on this peninsula.
Scan·di·na·vi·a (skan′də nā′vē ə) *noun.*

Scandinavian A person who was born in or is a citizen of a country in Scandinavia. *Noun.*
—Of or relating to Scandinavia, its peoples, or its languages. *Adjective.*
Scan·di·na·vi·an (skan′də nā′vē ən) *noun, plural* **Scandinavians;** *adjective.*

scant **1.** Not enough or barely enough. We brought only *scant* supplies for the trip. **2.** A little less than full; not quite full. The recipe calls for a *scant* teaspoon of salt.
scant (skant) *adjective,* **scanter, scantest.**

scar **1.** A mark on the skin left by a cut or burn that has healed. I have a *scar* on my knee. **2.** Any mark that is like this. The burning cigar left an ugly *scar* on the table. *Noun.*
—To mark with a scar or scars. Our dog *scarred* the door by scratching it. *Verb.*
scar (skär) *noun, plural* **scars;** *verb,* **scarred, scarring.**

scarce Difficult to get or find. Water is *scarce* in the desert.
scarce (skârs) *adjective,* **scarcer, scarcest.**

scarcely **1.** Only just or almost not; barely or hardly. I had *scarcely* come in when the phone rang. There was *scarcely* a person on the street. **2.** Certainly not. I would *scarcely* go back to visit them.
scarce·ly (skârs′lē) *adverb.*

scare To frighten or become afraid. The loud thunder *scared* the children. My older cousin doesn't *scare* easily. *Verb.*
—**1.** A sudden fear or fright. The explosion gave us quite a *scare.* **2.** A condition of widespread fear or fright; panic. There was a bomb *scare* on the plane. *Noun.*
scare (skâr) *verb,* **scared, scaring;** *noun, plural* **scares.**

scarecrow A figure of a person used to scare crows and other

scarecrow

birds away from crops. A scarecrow is often dressed in old clothes.
scare·crow (skâr′krō′) *noun, plural* **scarecrows.**

scarf A piece of cloth worn about the neck or head. A scarf is worn for warmth or decoration.
scarf (skärf) *noun, plural* **scarves** or **scarfs.**

scarlet A bright red color. *Noun.*
—Having the color scarlet. I like *scarlet* roses. *Adjective.*
scar·let (skär′lit) *noun; adjective.*

scary Causing alarm or fear; frightening. It was *scary* to be all alone in the big old house.
scar·y (skâr′ē) *adjective,* **scarier, scariest.**

scatter **1.** To spread or throw about in various places. The wind *scattered* the leaves all over the yard. **2.** To separate or cause to separate and go in different directions. The mob *scattered* when the police arrived. The loud thunder *scattered* the cattle.
scat·ter (skat′ər) *verb,* **scattered, scattering.**

scattering leaves

scavenger **1.** An animal that feeds on carcasses or decaying plant matter. **2.** A person who searches through trash for

at; āpe; fär; câre; end; mē; it; īce; pîerce; hot; ōld; sông, fôrk; oil; out; up; ūse; rüle; pùll; tûrn; chin; sing; shop; thin; this; hw in white; zh in treasure. The symbol ə stands for the unstressed vowel sound in about, taken, pencil, lemon, and circus.

S

641

things that can be used or sold to others.
scav·en·ger (skav′ən jər) *noun, plural*
scavengers.

scene **1.** The place where something happens. The police arrived on the *scene* just as the thieves were escaping. **2.** A part of an act in a play or movie. **3.** View; sight. The *scene* of the valley from the porch was beautiful. **4.** A show of strong feeling in front of others. The child made a *scene* when it was time to go to bed. ⚠ Another word that sounds like this is **seen.**
scene (sēn) *noun, plural* **scenes.**

scenery **1.** The general appearance of a place; the group of views or sights in an area. They drove to the mountains to look at the *scenery.* **2.** The painted pictures or objects that are used to make the setting of a play or movie. The *scenery* looked realistic.
scen·er·y (sē′nə rē) *noun, plural* **sceneries.**

scenic Of, having to do with, or full of attractive natural scenery. I was impressed by the *scenic* wonders of the West.
sce·nic (sē′nik) *adjective.*

scent **1.** A smell. The *scent* of lilacs was in the air. **2.** The trail by which someone or something can be traced or found. Hunting dogs are able to track foxes by their *scent.* The false clue threw the detective off the *scent* of the robbers. **3.** The sense of smell. Bloodhounds are known for their keen *scent.* **4.** A liquid with a pleasant smell; perfume. What *scent* is that you're wearing? *Noun.*
—To sense by or as if by the sense of smell. The dogs *scented* the rabbit. I *scent* trouble. *Verb.* ⚠ Other words that sound like this are **cent** and **sent.**
scent (sent) *noun, plural* **scents;** *verb,* **scented, scenting.**

scepter A rod or staff that is carried by a king or queen. A scepter is used as a symbol of royal office or power.
scep·ter (sep′tər) *noun, plural* **scepters.**

schedule **1.** A list of times, events, or things to do. Check the bus *schedule* before you go. The orchestra's *schedule* shows that it will play in our town tonight. **2.** The time at which something is supposed to happen. The train was running behind *schedule* because of the weather. *Noun.*
—To put in or on a schedule; plan or arrange for a particular time. I *scheduled* an appointment with my dentist for Friday. *Verb.*
sched·ule (skej′ül) *noun, plural* **schedules;** *verb,* **scheduled, scheduling.**

scheme **1.** A plan or plot for doing something. The crooks had a *scheme* for robbing

the bank. **2.** An orderly arrangement of related things; design. You can choose the color *scheme* for your room. *Noun.*
—To plan or plot. The rebels *schemed* to capture the king and queen. *Verb.*
scheme (skēm) *noun, plural* **schemes;** *verb,* **schemed, scheming.**

scholar **1.** A person who has much knowledge. **2.** A person who attends school.
schol·ar (skol′ər) *noun, plural* **scholars.**

scholarship **1.** Money that is given to a student to help pay for his or her studies. **2.** Knowledge or learning.
schol·ar·ship (skol′ər ship′) *noun, plural* **scholarships.**

school¹ **1.** A place for teaching and learning. They are classmates of mine at *school.* **2.** The students, teachers, and other people who work at such a place. The entire *school* went on the trip. **3.** A period or time of teaching at a school. There is no *school* today. **4.** The process of being educated at a school. I found *school* very difficult when I was your age. **5.** A department of a college or university for teaching in a particular field. My cousin attends the university's *school* of medicine. *Noun.*
—To train or teach. Doctors must *school* themselves to handle emergencies. *Verb.*
school (skül) *noun, plural* **schools;** *verb,* **schooled, schooling.**

school² A large group of fish or water animals swimming together.
school (skül) *noun, plural* **schools.**

schoolhouse A building used as a school.
school·house (skül′hous′) *noun, plural* **schoolhouses** (skül′hou′ziz).

schooner A ship that has two or more masts and sails that are set lengthwise.
schoon·er (skü′nər) *noun, plural* **schooners.**

schooner

schwa The symbol (ə) used in English for a vowel sound that is spoken without any force. The *a* in *ago* and the *o* in *lemon* are represented by a schwa.
schwa (shwä) *noun, plural* **schwas.**

science **1.** Knowledge about things in nature and the universe. Science is based on facts that are learned from experiments and careful study. **2.** Any particular branch of such knowledge. Biology, chemistry, and physics are sciences.
sci·ence (sī′əns) *noun, plural* **sciences.**

scientific Having to do with or used in science. All of the students in our class had to plan and carry out a *scientific* experiment.
sci·en·tif·ic (sī′ən tif′ik) *adjective.*

scientist A person who works or specializes in a branch of science. Biologists, chemists, and physicists are scientists.
sci·en·tist (sī′ən tist) *noun, plural* **scientists.**

scissors A tool used for cutting paper, thread, cardboard, cloth, and many other kinds of material. Scissors have two blades held together in the middle. When the blades are brought together, they form a double cutting edge.
scis·sors (siz′ərz) *plural noun.*

scold To find fault with; speak sharply to. The teacher *scolded* the student. *Verb.*
—A person who scolds. *Noun.*
scold (skōld) *verb,* **scolded, scolding;** *noun, plural* **scolds.**

scoop **1.** A tool that is shaped like a small shovel. It is used for taking up flour, sugar, or other soft substances. **2.** The large bucket of a steam shovel. It is used for picking up dirt, sand, or other material from the ground. **3.** A tool shaped like a cup attached to a handle. It is used to take up portions of food. **4.** The amount any scoop holds. I only want one *scoop* of mashed potatoes. *Noun.*
—To take up with a scoop, or as if with a scoop. Please *scoop* a cup of flour and add it to this dough. The children *scooped* up their books and ran off to school. *Verb.*
scoop (sküp) *noun, plural* **scoops;** *verb,* **scooped, scooping.**

scope The range or extent of an idea, action, or a person's understanding. Landing a spacecraft on Mars is within the *scope* of modern science. The lecture on nuclear energy was beyond my *scope.*
scope (skōp) *noun.*

scorch **1.** To burn slightly on the surface. I *scorched* my shirt with the iron. **2.** To dry up with heat. The hot sun *scorched* the grass. *Verb.*
—A slight burn. A necktie will cover the *scorch* on the front of that shirt. *Noun.*
scorch (skôrch) *verb,* **scorched, scorching;** *noun, plural* **scorches.**

score **1.** The points or a record of the points made in a game or on a test. The final *score* was 5 to 4. What was your *score* on the test? **2.** A set or group of twenty. A *score* of people came to the meeting. **3.** Written or printed music. A score shows all the parts for instruments and voices. *Noun.*
—**1.** To make a point or points in a game or test. I *scored* twenty points in the game. **2.** To keep a record of points made or assign points in a game or test. A judge *scored* the divers. The teacher *scored* our tests right after we finished. **3.** To achieve or win. You *scored* a great success by winning all three races. *Verb.*
score (skôr) *noun, plural* **scores;** *verb,* **scored, scoring.**

scorn A feeling of hatred for someone or something thought of as low or bad. The defeated villain slipped away as the play's hero and heroine looked on with *scorn. Noun.*
—To treat or reject as low or bad. The whole town *scorned* the idea of turning the playground into a parking lot. *Verb.*
scorn (skôrn) *noun; verb,* **scorned, scorning.**

scornful Feeling or showing scorn. The villain in the story had a *scornful* attitude toward the law.
scorn·ful (skôrn′fəl) *adjective.*

scorpion A small animal that is related to the spider. It has four pairs of legs and a long tail with a poisonous stinger on the end.
scor·pi·on (skôr′pē ən) *noun, plural* **scorpions.**

scorpion

Scot A person who was born in or is a citizen of Scotland.
Scot (skot) *noun, plural* **Scots.**

S

Scotch Of or having to do with Scotland. I have a skirt made of *Scotch* plaid. ⚠ This term is usually used only in compound words referring to Scottish things, not people or places.

Scotch (skoch) *adjective*.

Scotland A section of the United Kingdom. It occupies the northern part of the island of Great Britain.

Scot·land (skot'lənd) *noun*.

Scottish 1. **the Scottish.** The people of Scotland. 2. The dialect of English spoken in Scotland. *Noun.*
—Of or having to do with Scotland, its people, or its language. *Adjective.*

Scot·tish (skot'ish) *noun; adjective*.

scoundrel A wicked or dishonest person; villain; rogue. The gang was a bunch of *scoundrels* who had stolen a lot of money.

scoun·drel (skoun'drəl) *noun, plural* **scoundrels**.

scour[1] 1. To clean or polish by rubbing hard, as with steel wool or a cleanser. I *scoured* the pots to make them shiny. 2. To remove by rubbing hard. I *scoured* the grime off the bathtub. 3. To clean or remove something that clogs, as by flushing. We have to *scour* our kitchen drain.

scour (skour) *verb*, **scoured, scouring**.

scour[2] To go through or examine in search of something. We *scoured* the house for signs of termites.

scour (skour) *verb*, **scoured, scouring**.

scout 1. A soldier, ship, or plane sent to find out and bring back information. The *scout* brought back word that the enemy was camped nearby. 2. A person who belongs to the Boy Scouts or Girl Scouts. *Noun.*
—To look at or explore in order to find out and bring back information. Two campers went ahead to *scout* the trail. Planes were sent out to *scout* for the enemy. *Verb.*

scout (skout) *noun, plural* **scouts;** *verb,* **scouted, scouting**.

scoutmaster An adult who leads a troop of Boy Scouts.

scout·mas·ter (skout'mas'tər) *noun, plural* **scoutmasters**.

scowl An angry frown. Dad had a *scowl* on his face. *Noun.*
—To frown in an angry way. The mother *scowled* at her child's rude behavior. *Verb.*

scowl (skoul) *noun, plural* **scowls;** *verb,* **scowled, scowling**.

scramble 1. To mix together; mix up. We *scrambled* the pieces of the puzzle. 2. To cook eggs with the whites and yolks mixed together. 3. To move or climb quickly. The children *scrambled* down the rocks. 4. To struggle or compete with others. The players *scrambled* for the ball. *Verb.*
—1. The act of moving or climbing quickly. The *scramble* up the hill left everyone tired. 2. A struggle or competition. There was a *scramble* for the best seats. *Noun.*

scram·ble (skram'bəl) *verb,* **scrambled, scrambling;** *noun, plural* **scrambles**.

scrap 1. A small piece or little bit of something. I wrote a note on a *scrap* of paper. We fed *scraps* to the dog. 2. Worn or used material that can be used again in some way. They sold the car for *scrap*. *Noun.*
—1. To throw away or give up as useless. We decided to *scrap* the idea of going on a picnic. 2. To break up into scrap. The navy decided to *scrap* the old battleship. *Verb.*

scrap (skrap) *noun, plural* **scraps;** *verb,* **scrapped, scrapping**.

scrapbook A book with blank pages on which pictures, newspaper clippings, and other items may be mounted and kept.

scrap·book (skrap'bùk') *noun, plural* **scrapbooks**.

scrape 1. To injure or scratch by rubbing against something sharp or rough. The runner *scraped* a knee sliding into first base. 2. To rub or move with a harsh, grating sound. I *scraped* the chalk on the blackboard. 3. To clean or smooth by rubbing. We *scraped* the food off our plates. 4. To get or collect with difficulty. The cycling club *scraped* up enough money for a trip. *Verb.*
—1. A mark made on a surface by rubbing or scratching against something sharp or rough. There is a big *scrape* on the car. 2. A harsh, grating sound. We heard the *scrape* of sleds on the road. 3. A difficult, unpleasant situation. We got into a *scrape*. *Noun.*

scrape (skrāp) *verb,* **scraped, scraping;** *noun, plural* **scrapes**.

scratch 1. To scrape or cut with nails, claws, or anything else that is sharp and pointed. The cat *scratched* my arm. The broken glass *scratched* the table. 2. To rub or scrape in order to stop itching. 3. To rub with a harsh, grating sound. Is that the puppy *scratching* at the door? 4. To cancel or strike out. *Scratch* my name off the list. *Verb.*
—1. A mark made by scraping or cutting. I had *scratches* on my legs. 2. A harsh, grating sound. The *scratch* of the branch against the window startled us. *Noun.*
• **from scratch.** From the beginning; with no resources. When their business failed, they had to start again *from scratch*.

scratch (skrach) *verb,* **scratched, scratching;** *noun, plural* **scratches**.

scream To make a loud, shrill, piercing cry or sound. I *screamed* when the monster appeared in the movie. *Verb.*
—A loud, shrill, piercing cry or sound. The *scream* of a train whistle broke the silence of the night. *Noun.*
  scream (skrēm) *verb*, **screamed, screaming**; *noun, plural* **screams.**

screech To make a shrill, harsh cry or sound. The monkeys *screeched* at feeding time. The car's brakes *screeched*. *Verb.*
—A shrill, harsh cry or sound. We heard a *screech* as the car came to a stop. *Noun.*
  screech (skrēch) *verb*, **screeched, screeching**; *noun, plural* **screeches.**

screen 1. Wire mesh or netting in a frame. We use *screens* on the windows in the summer to keep out the flies. 2. A covered frame that is used to hide or divide. In our house, there is a *screen* that separates the dining area from the kitchen. 3. Anything like a screen. A *screen* of bushes hides the house. 4. A surface that reflects light, on which motion pictures or slides are projected. 5. The front surface of a television set or computer monitor. *Noun.*
—To hide or protect with a screen. We *screened* in the porch to keep out bugs. A hat will *screen* your eyes from the sun. *Verb.*
  screen (skrēn) *noun, plural* **screens**; *verb,* **screened, screening.**

screw A kind of nail with ridges cut around its length and a slot on its head. It is twisted or turned into place with a screwdriver to hold things together. *Noun.*
—1. To attach or fasten with a screw or screws. I *screwed* a lock onto the door. 2. To fix in place by twisting or turning. *Screw* a new light bulb into the socket. *Verb.*
  screw (skrü) *noun, plural* **screws**; *verb,* **screwed, screwing.**

screwdriver A tool for turning screws. One end is a handle and the other end fits into the slot on the head of a screw.
  screw·driv·er (skrü′drī′vər) *noun, plural* **screwdrivers.**

scribble To write or draw quickly or carelessly. I *scribbled* a note to my friend. *Verb.*
—Writing or drawing that is made by scribbling. The

screwdriver

piece of paper was covered with messy *scribbles. Noun.*
  scrib·ble (skrib′əl) *verb*, **scribbled, scribbling**; *noun, plural* **scribbles.**

scribe A person who writes down or copies letters, books, or other written materials.
  scribe (skrīb) *noun, plural* **scribes.**

script 1. Handwriting in which the letters are joined together. Our teacher taught us how to write *script*. 2. The written text of a play, movie, or television or radio show. We hope to say our lines without looking at the *script.*
  script (skript) *noun, plural* **scripts.**

scroll A roll of paper, parchment, or other material with writing on it. Each end of a scroll is often rolled around a rod.
  scroll (skrōl) *noun, plural* **scrolls.**

scrub To rub in order to wash or clean. You'll have to *scrub* your hands to get them clean. *Verb.*
—The act of scrubbing. I gave the kitchen floor a good *scrub. Noun.*
  scrub (skrub) *verb*, **scrubbed, scrubbing**; *noun.*

scruple A feeling about what is right and wrong that keeps one from doing something. I couldn't lie because of my *scruples.*
  scru·ple (skrü′pəl) *noun, plural* **scruples.**

scrupulous 1. Very careful to do what is right or proper; moral. My neighbor is *scrupulous* in dealing with others. 2. Very careful about details. The *scrupulous* clerk made sure everything was ready for the sale.
  scru·pu·lous (skrü′pyə ləs) *adjective.*

scuba diving Swimming underwater with the help of special breathing equipment. The equipment includes a cylinder of compressed air, which is strapped to the diver's back, and a hose through which the diver can breathe the compressed air.
  scu·ba diving (skü′bə)

scuff To scratch the surface of by scraping or wear. The child *scuffed* the new shoes on the gravel. *Verb.*
—The act or result of scuffing. There is a *scuff* on the new floor. *Noun.*
  scuff (skuf) *verb*, **scuffed, scuffing**; *noun, plural* **scuffs.**

at; āpe; fär; câre; end; mē; it; īce; pîerce; hot; ōld; sông, fôrk; oil; out; up; ūse; rüle; pùll; tûrn; chin; sing; shop; thin; this; hw in white; zh in treasure. The symbol ə stands for the unstressed vowel sound in about, taken, pencil, lemon, and circus.

S

645

scuffle   A confused struggle or fight. Two hockey players had a *scuffle. Noun.*
—To struggle or fight in a confused way. The two dogs *scuffled* on the street. *Verb.*
   scuf·fle (skuf′əl) *noun, plural* **scuffles;** *verb,* **scuffled, scuffling.**

sculptor   A person who makes or carves figures in stone, clay, metal, or any other material.
   sculp·tor (skulp′tər) *noun, plural* **sculptors.**

sculpture

sculpture   **1.** The art of carving or making figures or designs that occupy space. Sculpture usually is done by carving stone, wood, or marble, modeling in clay, or casting in bronze or another metal.   **2.** The figure or design that is made in this way. That statue is a beautiful piece of *sculpture. Noun.*
—To carve, model, or cast figures or designs. The artist *sculptured* a lion. *Verb.*
   sculp·ture (skulp′chər) *noun, plural* **sculptures;** *verb,* **sculptured, sculpturing.**

scurry   To go or move in a hurry. The children *scurried* after their parents.
   scur·ry (skûr′ē) *verb,* **scurried, scurrying.**

scurvy   A disease that is caused by a lack of vitamin C. A person with scurvy feels very weak and has bleeding gums. Scurvy can be prevented by eating vegetables and fruits that contain a large amount of vitamin C.
   scur·vy (skûr′vē) *noun.*

scythe   A tool with a long curved blade and a long bent handle. It is swung from side to side to mow or cut grasses and crops by hand.
   scythe (sīth) *noun, plural* **scythes.**

SD   Postal abbreviation for *South Dakota.*

S.D. or **S. Dak.**   An abbreviation for *South Dakota.*

SE or **S.E.**   An abbreviation for *southeast.*

sea   **1.** The large body of salt water that covers almost three fourths of the earth's surface; ocean.   **2.** A large part of this body of salt water, usually partly enclosed by land.   **3.** The movement of the water of the ocean; wave or waves. The crew struggled to keep the ship afloat in the rough *seas.*   **4.** An overwhelming amount or number. A *sea* of soldiers stormed the fort.   ⊿ Another word that sounds like this is **see.**
   • **at sea.**   **1.** Out on the ocean. We were *at sea* for a week.   **2.** Confused; bewildered. I was *at sea* about what to do.
   • **to go to sea.**   **1.** To become a sailor. They joined the navy and *went to sea.*   **2.** To begin a voyage at sea. They *went to sea* a week ago.
   sea (sē) *noun, plural* **seas.**

sea anemone   A sea animal that is shaped like a tube and that attaches itself to rocks and other objects.

seaboard   The land on or near the sea. California is on the Pacific *seaboard.*
   sea·board (sē′bôrd′) *noun, plural* **seaboards.**

seacoast   Land that is near the sea or bordering the sea.
   sea·coast (sē′kōst′) *noun, plural* **seacoasts.**

seafaring   **1.** Making a living by working at sea. The *seafaring* merchant visited many lands.   **2.** Of or having to do with the sea or sailors. The sailor told *seafaring* tales.
   sea·far·ing (sē′fâr′ing) *adjective.*

seafood   Saltwater fish or shellfish used for food.
   sea·food (sē′füd′) *noun, plural* **seafoods.**

sea gull   A white and gray bird with long wings that lives near the sea. Look up **gull** for more information.

sea horse   A kind of fish with a head that looks like that of a horse. It has a curling tail that it uses to hold onto underwater plants.

seal¹   A sea animal that lives in coastal waters and has flippers instead of feet. Seals spend some of their time on land. Seals are mammals.
   seal (sēl) *noun, plural* **seals** or **seal.**

sea horse

seal²   **1.** A design that is stamped on wax, paper, or other soft material or a picture of such a design. A seal is used to show who owns something or that something is genuine.   **2.** Something that closes tightly and completely. The *seal* of this envelope is a flap with glue on it.   **3.** The condition of being closed tightly. The *seal* on the jar was so tight that we had to put the top under hot water to loosen it.   **4.** A stamp or sticker. Some kinds of seals are sold to raise money for a cause, and people who buy seals usually put them on letters and packages. *Noun.*
—**1.** To close tightly and completely. Please *seal* the envelope. The worker *sealed* the cracks in the wall with plaster before painting.   **2.** To settle or decide. The two neighbors *sealed* their agreement by shaking hands.   **3.** To place a seal on. The diploma was stamped and *sealed* by the college. *Verb.*
  seal (sēl) *noun, plural* **seals;** *verb,* **sealed, sealing.**

sea lion   One of several large seals that are found in the Pacific Ocean.

sea lion

seam   **1.** A line formed by sewing together the edges of two or more pieces of cloth, leather, or other material. One of the *seams* in this coat is coming apart.   **2.** Any mark or line like a seam. Water leaked into the rowboat because the *seams* were no longer sealed.   **3.** A layer of a mineral or metal in the earth. The mining company found a *seam* of coal in the mountain. ▲ Another word that sounds like this is **seem.**
  seam (sēm) *noun, plural* **seams.**

seaman   **1.** A sailor.   **2.** A sailor of the lowest rank in the navy and coast guard.
  sea·man (sē′mən) *noun, plural* **seamen** (sē′mən).

seamstress   A woman whose job is sewing.
  seam·stress (sēm′stris) *noun, plural* **seamstresses.**

seaplane   An airplane with floats attached to its underside. The floats allow a seaplane to take off from and land on water.
  sea·plane (sē′plān′) *noun, plural* **seaplanes.**

seaport   A port or harbor, or a town or city with a harbor that is used by ships that travel on the sea.
  sea·port (sē′pôrt′) *noun, plural* **seaports.**

search   To look, look through, or examine carefully in order to find something. We've *searched* through the house for your keys. I've *searched* all my drawers, but my notebook is still missing. *Verb.*
—The act of searching. The police led a *search* through the building. *Noun.*
  search (sûrch) *verb,* **searched, searching;** *noun, plural* **searches.**

searchlight   A special lamp that produces a very strong beam of light. The battleship used a *searchlight* to spot enemy airplanes at night.
  search·light (sûrch′līt′) *noun, plural* **searchlights.**

seashell   The shell of an oyster, clam, or other sea animal.
  sea·shell (sē′shel′) *noun, plural* **seashells.**

kinds of **seashells**

seashore   The land near or on the sea.
  sea·shore (sē′shôr′) *noun, plural* **seashores.**

seasick   Sick and dizzy because of the rolling motion of a boat or ship.
  sea·sick (sē′sik′) *adjective.*

season   **1.** One of the four parts of the year; spring, summer, fall, or winter.   **2.** Any special part of the year. There is almost no rain during the dry *season* in parts of Africa. *Noun.*

at; āpe; fär; câre; end; mē; it; īce; pîerce; hot; ōld; sông, fôrk; oil; out; up; ūse; rüle; pùll; tûrn; chin; sing; shop; thin; <u>this</u>; hw in white; zh in treasure. The symbol ə stands for the unstressed vowel sound in about, taken, pencil, lemon, and circus.

S

—**1.** To add seasoning to food in order to bring out the flavor. I *seasoned* the stew with pepper and other spices. **2.** To make or become right for use. They let the newly cut logs dry to *season* them for firewood. *Verb.*
- **in season.** **1.** Available or in the best condition for eating. Peaches are *in season*. **2.** Legally permitted to be hunted or caught. Salmon are now *in season*.
- **out of season.** Not in season. Are pumpkins *out of season* in the summer?

sea·son (sē′zən) *noun, plural* **seasons;** *verb,* **seasoned, seasoning.**

Word History

The word **season** comes from a French word that originally meant "the season of spring," or "planting time." The French word came from a Latin word meaning "seed time" or "sowing."

seasonal Of, happening at, or influenced by a certain season or seasons. The blooming of flowers is a *seasonal* event.
sea·son·al (sē′zə nəl) *adjective.*

seasoning Something that is used to bring out the flavor of food. Salt, pepper, and herbs are seasonings.
sea·son·ing (sē′zə ning) *noun, plural* **seasonings.**

seat **1.** Something to sit on. A chair, stool, or bench is a seat. We have enough *seats* for everyone. **2.** A place to sit. I couldn't get a *seat* on the bus. **3.** The part of a thing that one sits on. The *seat* of this bicycle is uncomfortable. **4.** The part of the body that one sits on, or the clothes covering it. Those pants have a rip in the *seat*. **5.** A membership or position. Our neighbor has a *seat* on the town council. **6.** A center. A college is a *seat* of learning. *Noun.*
—**1.** To place on or lead to a seat. The barber *seated* the little child in the chair. The usher *seated* us. **2.** To have seats for. That theater *seats* 500 people. *Verb.*
- **to be seated.** To sit down. Will you please *be seated?*

seat (sēt) *noun, plural* **seats;** *verb,* **seated, seating.**

seat belt A strap that is fastened to hold a person in the seat of a car, truck, airplane, or other vehicle in case of a crash, bump, or jolt.

sea urchin A sea animal that has a round shell covered with hard spines. The spines help the sea urchin move and protect itself.
sea ur·chin (ûr′chin)

seaweed A plant that grows in the sea, especially certain kinds of algae. Seaweeds are green, brown, or red in color. All seaweeds need sunlight to make their own food.
sea·weed (sē′wēd′) *noun, plural* **seaweeds.**

sec. An abbreviation for *second.*

secede To withdraw from a group or organization. South Carolina was the first Southern state to *secede* from the Union before the Civil War.
se·cede (si sēd′) *verb,* **seceded, seceding.**

second¹ **1.** Next after the first. I liked the movie better the *second* time I saw it. **2.** Below the first or best. He is the *second* pitcher on the team. **3.** Another. May I have a *second* helping of potatoes, please? **4.** Skipping one after each. We receive that magazine every *second* month. *Adjective.*
—In second place; after the first. My friend finished first, and I finished *second*. *Adverb.*
—**1.** A person or thing that is next after the first. She was the *second* in line. **2.** Something lower in quality. The shirts were sold as *seconds* because some buttons were missing. *Noun.*
—To help or support. Who will *second* the motion to end the meeting? *Verb.*
sec·ond (sek′ənd) *adjective; adverb; noun, plural* **seconds;** *verb,* **seconded, seconding.**

second² **1.** One of the sixty equal parts of a minute. **2.** Any very short period of time. I'll come outside in a *second*.
sec·ond (sek′ənd) *noun, plural* **seconds.**

fastening a **seat belt**

secondary After the first or main thing; not as important. The bus took a *secondary* road during the blizzard because the main road was closed.
sec·ond·ar·y (sek′ən der′ē) *adjective.*

secondary school A school that is attended after elementary or grade school.

secondhand **1.** Already used or owned by someone else; gotten from another. My cousin bought a *secondhand* car. We have only *secondhand* knowledge of how the accident happened. **2.** Selling goods that someone else has owned or used. I bought my bicycle at a *secondhand* store.
sec·ond·hand (sek′ənd hand′) *adjective.*

secrecy **1.** The condition of being secret or being kept secret. The rebels made their plans in *secrecy*. **2.** The ability or practice of keeping things secret. Our *secrecy* about the party helped make it a real surprise.
se·cre·cy (sē′krə sē) *noun.*

secret **1.** Known only to oneself or a few; hidden. The pirates buried the treasure in a *secret* place. **2.** Acting in a hidden way. The *secret* agent spied on the enemy. *Adjective.*
—**1.** Something that is secret. I'll tell you a *secret*. **2.** A hidden reason or cause. Hard work is the *secret* of my success. The scientist sought to learn the *secrets* of nature. *Noun.*
• **in secret.** In a private place or in a manner that prevents other people from knowing. The two old friends discussed their plans *in secret*.
se·cret (sē′krit) *adjective; noun, plural* **secrets.**

secretary **1.** A person whose work is writing letters and keeping records for another person, a business, or an organization. I was elected *secretary* of the stamp club. **2.** A person who is the head of a department of a government. The *Secretary* of Defense heads the Defense Department. **3.** A piece of furniture. It has a writing surface, drawers, and sometimes shelves.
sec·re·tar·y (sek′rə ter′ē) *noun, plural* **secretaries.**

secretary

secrete To produce and release a chemical substance into the body. The thyroid gland *secretes* a hormone that controls growth.
se·crete (si krēt′) *verb,* **secreted, secreting.**

sect A group of people sharing the same beliefs and practices, especially a religious group that has separated from the religion of which it was a part.
sect (sekt) *noun, plural* **sects.**

section **1.** A part taken from a whole; portion. Please cut the apple into four *sections*. They planted vegetables in one *section* of the garden. **2.** A part of something written. I always read the sports *section* of the newspaper. **3.** A part of an area or group. We visited the old *section* of the city. The trumpet player plays in the brass *section* of the orchestra. **4.** A picture or model of something that shows what it would look like if it were cut open. This lengthwise *section* of a flower shows all the inner parts. *Noun.*
—To cut into parts or divide. Please *section* the watermelon. *Verb.*
sec·tion (sek′shən) *noun, plural* **sections;** *verb,* **sectioned, sectioning.**

secure **1.** Safe from harm or loss. The basement was a *secure* place to be during the tornado. The jewels were *secure* in a safe. **2.** Firm; steady; sound. The old ladder is not *secure* enough to climb. **3.** Certain or guaranteed. Our victory seemed *secure*. *Adjective.*
—**1.** To get. They *secured* tickets to the game. **2.** To fasten firmly. I *secured* the lock on the suitcase. **3.** To make safe. The guards in the armored truck *secured* the gold against robbers. *Verb.*
se·cure (si kyùr′) *adjective,* **securer, securest;** *verb,* **secured, securing.**

security **1.** Protection from harm or loss; safety. I ran to the *security* of the school during the storm. Having money in the bank gives me a feeling of *security*. **2.** Something that gives protection. A burglar alarm is *security* against thieves. **3.** Something that is given to make sure that an agreement will be fulfilled. The pawnbroker accepted a gold ring as *security* for the loan.
se·cu·ri·ty (si kyùr′i tē) *noun, plural* **securities.**

at; āpe; fär; câre; end; mē; it; īce; pîerce; hot; ōld; sông; fôrk; oil; out; up; ūse; rüle; pùll; tûrn; chin; sing; shop; thin; this; hw in white; zh in treasure. The symbol ə stands for the unstressed vowel sound in about, taken, pencil, lemon, and circus.

S

sedan An automobile with a roof. It has two or four doors, and seats in both the front and the back.
se·dan (si dan′) *noun, plural* **sedans.**

sediment **1.** Small pieces of matter that settle at the bottom of a liquid. There was *sediment* at the bottom of the bottle. **2.** Rocks, dirt, or other solid matter carried and left by water, glaciers, or wind. The flood left a layer of *sediment* on the streets and sidewalks.
sed·i·ment (sed′ə mənt) *noun.*

sedimentary Formed from particles of stone or animal remains that have been deposited by water, wind, or ice over millions of years. Sedimentary rocks usually show layers of the materials that formed them.
sed·i·men·ta·ry (sed′ə men′tə rē) *adjective.*

see **1.** To look or look at with the eyes; view. I *see* better with glasses. Do you want to go *see* a movie? **2.** To understand. I *see* what you mean. **3.** To find out. Please *see* who is at the door. **4.** To make sure. *See* that you finish your homework. **5.** To go with; accompany. I'll *see* you to the door. **6.** To visit or meet with. The dentist will *see* you now. **7.** To experience. Those old shoes have *seen* much wear. ▴ Another word that sounds like this is **sea.**
• **to see off.** To go with to a place of departure. I'll see you *off* at the airport.
• **to see through.** **1.** To continue with to the end. This project is difficult, but I'm going to *see* it *through.* **2.** To help or take care of during a period of difficulty. We *saw* the dogs *through* a serious case of distemper. **3.** To understand the real meaning or nature of. We *saw through* their story.
• **to see to.** To attend to; take care of. Please *see to* this task immediately.
see (sē) *verb,* **saw, seen, seeing.**

seed **1.** The part of a flowering plant from which a new plant will grow. Many seeds are in the form of a small nut or kernel surrounded by a hard shell. My neighbors have planted the *seeds* for their vegetable garden. **2.** The source or cause of something. A lack of sleep was the *seed* of my bad mood. *Noun.*
—**1.** To plant land with seeds. We *seeded* the lawn. **2.** To take seeds out of. The cook *seeded* the watermelon. *Verb.*
seed (sēd) *noun, plural* **seeds** or **seed;** *verb,* **seeded, seeding.**

seedling A young plant grown from a seed.
seed·ling (sēd′ling) *noun, plural* **seedlings.**

seek **1.** To try to find; go in search of. The police were *seeking* a stolen car. **2.** To try.

Every candidate in the election will *seek* to win. **3.** To try to get; ask for. The victims of the flood *sought* help.
seek (sēk) *verb,* **sought, seeking.**

seem **1.** To appear to be. The dark clouds make it *seem* later than it really is. That book *seems* easy to read. **2.** To appear to oneself. I *seem* to have forgotten your name. ▴ Another word that sounds like this is **seam.**
seem (sēm) *verb,* **seemed, seeming.**

seen Past participle of **see.** I have not *seen* that movie yet. Look up **see** for more information. ▴ Another word that sounds like this is **scene.**
seen (sēn) *verb.*

seep To flow or spread slowly. Water *seeped* into the ground after the rain.
seep (sēp) *verb,* **seeped, seeping.**

seesaw A device used for play. It is made of a long board with a support in the middle. When a person sits on each end of the board, one end goes up as the other end goes down. *Noun*
—**1.** To move up and down on a seesaw. **2.** To move or act up and down or back and forth. The small boat *seesawed* in the waves. *Verb.*
see·saw (sē′sô′) *noun, plural* **seesaws;** *verb,* **seesawed, seesawing.**

segment One of the parts into which a whole is or can be divided; section. You can separate the *segments* of a grapefruit with your fingers. I cut the string into *segments.*
seg·ment (seg′mənt) *noun, plural* **segments.**

segregation The practice of setting one racial group apart from another. There are laws against the *segregation* of black children and white children in the public schools.
seg·re·ga·tion (seg′ri gā′shən) *noun.*

seine A fishing net. It has floats on the top edge and weights on the bottom edge. ▴ An-

Apple

Avocado

Elm

Maple

Milkweed

Sunflower

Dandelion

kinds of **seeds**

other word that sounds like this is **sane.**
seine (sān) *noun, plural* **seines.**

seismograph An instrument used to measure the power of earthquakes.
seis·mo·graph (sīz′mə graf′) *noun, plural* **seismographs.**

seismograph

seize **1.** To take hold of; grab. The dog *seized* the bone. **2.** To get control of; capture. The soldiers *seized* the fort.
seize (sēz) *verb,* **seized, seizing.**

seldom Not often; rarely. I *seldom* see my friend who moved to another city.
sel·dom (sel′dəm) *adverb.*

select To pick out; choose. Would you *select* this red coat or that green one? *Verb.*
—Picked or chosen because of a special ability or quality. A *select* group of athletes will compete in the games. *Adjective.*
se·lect (si lekt′) *verb,* **selected, selecting;** *adjective.*

selection **1.** The selecting of something. The magician had me make a *selection* of a card from the deck. **2.** A person or thing that is or can be selected. What are the *selections* on the menu?
se·lec·tion (si lek′shən) *noun, plural* **selections.**

self **1.** One's own person apart from all other persons. I know my own *self* best. **2.** The way that one feels, looks, or acts. You were very angry and so unlike your usual *self.*
self (self) *noun, plural* **selves.**

self- A *prefix* that means oneself. *Self-respect* means respect for oneself. ▲ The prefix *self-* is always followed by a hyphen.

self-addressed Addressed to oneself. They will reply only if you send a *self-addressed* envelope along with your letter.
self-ad·dressed (self′ə drest′) *adjective.*

self-confidence Faith in one's own ability or worth. The pitcher's *self-confidence* inspired the rest of the softball team.
self-con·fi·dence (self′kon′fi dəns) *noun.*

self-conscious Too concerned about what other people think of one's appearance, thoughts, or actions. The *self-conscious* student had difficulty speaking to the class.
self-con·scious (self′kon′shəs) *adjective.*

self-control Control over one's own emotions and actions. When I hurt myself, it took a lot of *self-control* to keep from crying.
self-con·trol (self′kən trōl′) *noun.*

selfish Thinking only of oneself; not thinking of others. A selfish person is not interested in the wishes and feelings of other people.
self·ish (sel′fish) *adjective.*

self-respect Proper regard for one's own worth or importance; respect for oneself. Anyone with *self-respect* would defy a bully.
self-re·spect (self′ri spekt′) *noun.*

sell **1.** To give something in return for money. We *sold* the old bicycle for twenty-five dollars. **2.** To deal in. That store *sells* shoes. **3.** To be offered for sale. This candy *sells* for twenty-five cents. ▲ Another word that sounds like this is **cell.**
sell (sel) *verb,* **sold, selling.**

selves Plural of **self.** The dog and cat don't seem to be their usual *selves* today. Look up **self** for more information.
selves (selvz) *plural noun.*

semaphore A post with lights or flags on movable arms, used to give signals to railroad trains.
sem·a·phore (sem′ə fôr′) *noun, plural* **semaphores.**

These **semaphore** signals mean ''stop,'' ''slow,'' and ''go ahead.''

at; āpe; fär; câre; end; mē; it; īce; pîerce; hot; ōld; sông, fôrk; oil; out; up; ūse; rüle; pùll; tûrn; chin; sing; shop; thin; <u>th</u>is; hw in white; zh in treasure. The symbol ə stands for the unstressed vowel sound in about, taken, pencil, lemon, and circus.

S

semester   One of two terms into which a school or college year may be divided.
se·mes·ter (si mes′tər) *noun, plural* **semesters.**

semicircle   Half a circle. The children sat in a *semicircle* around the campfire.
sem·i·cir·cle (sem′ē sûr′kəl) *noun, plural* **semicircles.**

semicolon   A punctuation mark (;) that is used to separate parts of a sentence. A semicolon marks a greater separation than a comma does.
sem·i·co·lon (sem′ē kō′lən) *noun, plural* **semicolons.**

semifinal   A game or match that comes right before the final one in a series. Our team made it to the *semifinal. Noun.*
—Coming right before the final game or match in a series. We played in the *semifinal* game. *Adjective.*
sem·i·fi·nal (sem′ē fī′nəl) *noun, plural* **semifinals;** *adjective.*

seminary   A school that trains students to be priests, ministers, or rabbis.
sem·i·nar·y (sem′ə ner′ē) *noun, plural* **seminaries.**

Seminole   A member of a tribe of American Indians that settled in Florida. Many of the Seminole now live in Oklahoma.
Sem·i·nole (sem′ə nōl′) *noun, plural* **Seminole** or **Seminoles.**

senate   **1.** One of the branches of an assembly that makes laws. The legislatures of most states of the United States have senates. **2. Senate.** One of the branches of the United States Congress.
sen·ate (sen′it) *noun, plural* **senates.**

Word History

The word **senate** comes from a Latin word that means "old man." In Rome, the government council known as the senate was made up of the heads of noble families, who were old men.

---

senator   A member of a senate.
sen·a·tor (sen′i tər) *noun, plural* **senators.**

send   **1.** To cause to go from one place to another. Do you *send* birthday cards to your friends? The batter *sent* the ball into left field.   **2.** To cause to go, come, or be. The soft music *sent* me to sleep. *Send* a reply to the letter right away.
• **to send for.   1.** To ask someone to come; summon. Did you *send for* the po-

lice?   **2.** To ask that something be brought or sent. We *sent for* a free booklet.
send (send) *verb,* **sent, sending.**

Senegal   A country in western Africa.
Sen·e·gal (sen′i gôl′ *or* sen′i gäl′) *noun.*

senior   **1.** The older of two. "Senior" is used after the name of a father whose son has the same name. William Lawrence, *Senior,* is the father of William Lawrence, Junior.   **2.** Higher in rank, longer in service, or older in age. A general is a *senior* officer. Our senator is a *senior* member of Congress.   **3.** Of or having to do with the last year of high school or college. Next year I will be a *senior* in high school. *Adjective.*
—**1.** A person who is older than another or higher in rank than another. My sister is my *senior* by five years.   **2.** A student who is in the last year of high school or college. *Noun.*
sen·ior (sēn′yər) *adjective; noun, plural* **seniors.**

senior citizen   An elderly person, especially one who is over 65 years of age and has retired. My grandparents are *senior citizens.*

señor   The Spanish title for a man.
se·ñor (sen yôr′) *noun, plural* **señores.**

señora   The Spanish title for a married woman or for a widow.
se·ño·ra (sen yôr′ə) *noun, plural* **señoras.**

señorita   The Spanish title for a girl or unmarried woman.
se·ño·ri·ta (sen′yə rē′tə) *noun, plural* **señoritas.**

sensation   **1.** The power or ability to see, hear, smell, taste, or touch.   **2.** A condition of being aware; feeling. The little children felt a *sensation* of fear when they saw the big dog.   **3.** Great excitement; strong feeling. The news caused a *sensation.*   **4.** A person or thing that causes great excitement or interest. The new invention was a *sensation.*
sen·sa·tion (sen sā′shən) *noun, plural* **sensations.**

sensational   Causing or meant to cause great excitement or strong feeling. The football player made a *sensational* catch. That magazine publishes *sensational* stories.
sen·sa·tion·al (sen sā′shə nəl) *adjective.*

sense   **1.** A power of a living being to know about its surroundings and about changes in its own body. Sight, hearing, smell, taste, and touch are the five senses.   **2.** Feeling. I had a *sense* of failure after losing the race.   **3.** Understanding or appreciation. You have a good *sense* of humor.   **4.** Intelligence; good judgment. The puppy hasn't *sense* enough to come in out of the rain.   **5.** Use; reason. What is the *sense* of keeping that old radio if it doesn't work? **6.** Meaning. The word "run" has many different *senses*. *Noun.*

—To feel; understand. We could *sense* that you were glad to be home. *Verb.*

• **to make sense.** To have a clear meaning; be reasonable, logical, or understandable. This paragraph doesn't *make sense* to me.

sense (sens) *noun, plural* **senses;** *verb,* **sensed, sensing.**

sense organ An organ in the body that takes in information from its surroundings. In humans, the eyes, ears, nose, taste buds, and skin are sense organs.

sensible Having or showing good sense; wise. It is *sensible* to look both ways before crossing the street.

sen·si·ble (sen′sə bəl) *adjective.*

sensitive **1.** Easily affected or hurt. A baby's skin is very *sensitive*. A *sensitive* person can become very upset if criticized. **2.** Having deep feelings; very aware. A poet must be a *sensitive* person. **3.** Able to react to a certain thing or condition. The film in a camera is very *sensitive* to light.

sen·si·tive (sen′si tiv) *adjective.*

sent Past tense and past participle of **send.** I *sent* a package to my grandparents and they received it a week later. Look up **send** for more information. ▲ Other words that sound like this are **cent** and **scent.**

sent (sent) *verb.*

sentence **1.** A group of words that gives a complete thought. A sentence states something or asks a question. "The dog and cat" is not a sentence. "The dog and cat are fighting" is a sentence. **2.** A punishment for crime set by a court. The judge gave the thief a *sentence* of three years in the state prison. *Noun.*

—To set the punishment of. The judge *sentenced* them to thirty days in jail for refusing to pay their parking fines. *Verb.*

sen·tence (sen′təns) *noun, plural* **sentences;** *verb,* **sentenced, sentencing.**

sentiment Feeling or emotion. There is much *sentiment* in our town against closing the park on Sundays.

sen·ti·ment (sen′tə mənt) *noun, plural* **sentiments.**

sentimental Having or showing tender feeling. The couple in the movie sang a *sentimental* song.

sen·ti·men·tal (sen′tə men′təl) *adjective.*

sentry A person stationed to keep watch and warn others of danger; guard. A *sentry*

sentry

guarded the palace twenty-four hours a day.

sen·try (sen′trē) *noun, plural* **sentries.**

sepal One of a ring of parts shaped like leaves that lies at the base of a flower. Sepals are usually green. They cover and protect the flower when it is a bud and fold back from the flower when it blooms.

se·pal (sē′pəl) *noun, plural* **sepals.**

separate **1.** To keep apart; divide. A fence *separates* our yard from theirs. **2.** To set apart; place apart. We *separated* the old books from the new ones. **3.** To go in different directions; part. The two friends *separated* and went home for dinner. *Verb.*

—Set apart; not joined. The twins have *separate* rooms. *Adjective.*

sep·a·rate (sep′ə rāt′ *for verb;* sep′ər it *or* sep′rit *for adjective*) *verb,* **separated, separating;** *adjective.*

separation **1.** The act of separating things. The recipe called for the *separation* of the egg's white and yolk. **2.** The condition of being separated. The friends were happy to see each other again after a year's *separation*.

sep·a·ra·tion (sep′ə rā′shən) *noun, plural* **separations.**

Sept. An abbreviation for *September.*

at; āpe; fär; câre; end; mē; it; īce; pîerce; hot; ōld; sông, fôrk; oil; out; up; ūse; rüle; pull; tûrn; chin; sing; shop; thin; this; hw in white; zh in treasure. The symbol ə stands for the unstressed vowel sound in about, taken, pencil, lemon, and circus.

S

653

September   The ninth month of the year. September has thirty days.
Sep·tem·ber (sep tem′bər) *noun.*

Word History

September comes from the Latin word for "seven." The early Roman calendar began with March, making September the seventh month.

sequence   **1.** The coming of one thing after another in a fixed order. Winter, spring, summer, and fall follow each other in *sequence*.   **2.** A series of things that are related in some way. This *sequence* of photos shows how the explosion happened.
se·quence (sē′kwəns) *noun, plural* **sequences.**

sequoia   A huge evergreen tree. It has thick, reddish brown bark, sharply pointed leaves, and hard cones that stay on the tree for years. Sequoias grow in California.
se·quoi·a (si kwoi′ə) *noun, plural* **sequoias.**

Leaves and Cone

sequoia

serene   Calm and peaceful; quiet. The lake was *serene* after the storm had passed.
se·rene (sə rēn′) *adjective,* **serener, serenest.**

serf   In olden times, a person who was like a slave. Serfs were forced to stay on the land where they lived and were sold along with the land. ▲ Another word that sounds like this is **surf.**
serf (sûrf) *noun, plural* **serfs.**

sergeant   **1.** An army or marine officer who ranks below a lieutenant but above a corporal.   **2.** An air force enlisted person who ranks above an airman.
ser·geant (sär′jənt) *noun, plural* **sergeants.**

serial   A long story divided into parts. The parts are presented on television or radio or published in a magazine or newspaper at scheduled times. ▲ Another word that sounds like this is **cereal.**
se·ri·al (sîr′ē əl) *noun, plural* **serials.**

series   A number of similar things coming one after another. The famous explorer gave a *series* of talks at the school. I like to watch that nature *series* on television.
se·ries (sîr′ēz) *noun, plural* **series.**

serious   **1.** Having a thoughtful, solemn manner; grave. The judge is a *serious* person.   **2.** Not joking; sincere. Were you *serious* about taking piano lessons?   **3.** Important. Failing in school is a *serious* matter.   **4.** Dangerous. Cancer is a *serious* illness.
se·ri·ous (sîr′ē əs) *adjective.*

sermon   **1.** A public talk about religion or morals. A sermon is given by a member of the clergy.   **2.** Any serious talk. The parents gave their child a *sermon* about sharing.
ser·mon (sur′mən) *noun, plural* **sermons.**

serpent   A snake.
ser·pent (sûr′pənt) *noun, plural* **serpents.**

serum   **1.** A thin, clear liquid that separates from blood when a clot forms.   **2.** The serum of an animal that has already had a disease and is now immune to it. This serum can be taken from the animal and used to protect humans and other animals from getting the disease.
se·rum (sîr′əm) *noun, plural* **serums.**

servant   A person hired to work for the comfort or protection of others. Employees in a household are servants. Mail carriers and mayors are public servants.
serv·ant (sûr′vənt) *noun, plural* **servants.**

serve   **1.** To set food before; place food on a table. The waiter *served* us quickly. I helped *serve* dinner.   **2.** To supply enough for. That stew will *serve* ten people.   **3.** To be a servant to; do certain duties for; work. The butler *served* the family for many years.   **4.** To spend or work for a period of time. The thief had to *serve* five years in jail. The sailor *served* in the navy.   **5.** To be used. This sofa can *serve* as a bed.   **6.** To be of use or help to. This airport *serves* many people. The senator thanked them for *serving* their country.   **7.** In some games, to hit a ball in order to begin playing.   **8.** To give; present. The driver was *served* with a summons. *Verb.*
—In some games, the act of hitting a ball in

order to begin playing. The tennis player's *serve* was good. *Noun.*

• **to serve one right.** To be just what one deserves. It *served them right* to fail the test since they tried to cheat.

serve (sûrv) *verb,* **served, serving;** *noun,* *plural* **serves.**

service **1.** A helpful act; useful work. Our neighbor spends much time in *service* to the poor. The sick patient needs the *services* of a doctor. **2.** Employment as a servant. The maid and butler have been in the *service* of the family for many years. **3.** Use or help. "How may I be of *service* to you?" said the salesperson. **4.** A system or way of giving something needed or requested by a person or people. Mail *service* is good in our town. The *service* in this restaurant is slow today. **5.** A branch of the armed forces. My cousin spent three years in the *service.* **6.** A branch or department of a government. The diplomat works in the foreign *service.* **7.** A religious ceremony. The wedding *service* lasted an hour. **8.** The act of repairing or keeping ready for use. The old car needed *service.* **9.** A set of things needed for use while eating. This china *service* is for eight people. *Noun.*
—To make or keep ready for use. The mechanic *serviced* the car. *Verb.*

serv·ice (sûr′vis) *noun, plural* **services;** *verb,* **serviced, servicing.**

service station A place to buy gasoline, oil, and other things necessary for the operation of cars, trucks, and other motor vehicles. Service stations also provide repairs.

session **1.** A meeting of a group, such as a court or legislature. We attended a *session* of the Supreme Court. **2.** A series of such meetings. This *session* of Congress ends today. **3.** A time or period when students attend classes at a school or college.

• **in session.** Meeting. Court is now *in session.* Classes won't be *in session* until after the holidays.

ses·sion (sesh′ən) *noun, plural* **sessions.**

set **1.** To place; put. *Set* your books on the table. The child *set* the toy horse on its feet. **2.** To put in a useful or the correct order; arrange; fix. Please *set* the table. *Set* your watch by the clock. The doctor *set* my broken arm. **3.** To cause to be or become; put in some condition. We *set* our pet mouse free. *Set* the logs on fire. **4.** To begin; start. I *set* to work on my report. **5.** To fix or establish. Have they *set* a date for the party? **6.** To achieve or provide. The runner *set* a new record. **7.** To go down below the horizon. The sun will *set* in an hour. **8.** To become firm or

hard. This glue *sets* in five minutes. *Verb.*
—**1.** Fixed or decided. Most games have *set* rules. **2.** Stubborn about changing. My mind is *set.* **3.** Ready; prepared. We are all *set* to leave. *Adjective.*
—**1.** A group of things or persons. We have a new *set* of dishes. **2.** A device for sending out or receiving by radio, television, telephone, or telegraph. The television *set* broke. **3.** The scenery for a play or motion picture. **4.** One group of games in tennis. *Noun.*

• **to set aside.** To keep available or save for a special use or reason. I *set aside* an hour each day to practice playing the drums. *Set aside* a little money each week.

• **to set forth.** **1.** To make known; state; declare. The speakers *set forth* their ideas. **2.** To start to go, as on a journey. The pioneers *set forth* on their journey.

• **to set in.** To begin. Fall *set in* early.

• **to set off.** **1.** To make more prominent by contrast. Dark hair *sets off* a fair complexion. **2.** To start to go or to begin. We'll *set off* for the beach in an hour. **3.** To explode. We *set off* fireworks.

• **to set out.** To begin a trip. The ship *set out* for Australia yesterday.

• **to set up.** **1.** To assemble, erect, or prepare for use. The scout *set up* a tent. **2.** To establish; found. We *set up* a car wash.

set (set) *verb,* **set, setting;** *adjective;* *noun, plural* **sets.**

setter

setter One of several breeds of hunting dogs that crouch in a set position when they

S

find game. A setter has large, drooping ears and a long, silky coat.

set·ter (set′ər) *noun, plural* **setters.**

settle **1.** To agree about something; decide. The two children could not *settle* their argument. **2.** To come to rest. The bird *settled* on the branch. **3.** To make a home in a place. We decided to *settle* in a small town. **4.** To sink. The pebble *settled* to the bottom of the pond. **5.** To make calm. The medicine *settled* my stomach.
• **to settle down. 1.** To become calm or quiet. The class *settled down* quickly after recess. **2.** To devote effort and attention. After dinner I *settled down* to two hours of studying.
set·tle (set′əl) *verb,* **settled, settling.**

settlement **1.** The act of settling or the condition of being settled. The *settlement* of Jamestown, Virginia, took place in 1607. **2.** A small village or group of houses. During the 1800s, pioneers built many *settlements* in the American West. **3.** A colony. Part of Canada was once a French *settlement.*
set·tle·ment (set′əl mənt) *noun, plural* **settlements.**

settler A person who settles in a new land or country. The first European *settlers* of Florida were from Spain.
set·tler (set′lər) *noun, plural* **settlers.**

seven One more than six; 7.
sev·en (sev′ən) *noun, plural* **sevens;** *adjective.*

seventeen Seven more than ten; 17.
sev·en·teen (sev′ən tēn′) *noun, plural* **seventeens;** *adjective.*

seventeenth Next after the sixteenth. *Adjective, noun.*
—One of seventeen equal parts; ¹/₁₇. *Noun.*
sev·en·teenth (sev′ən tēnth′) *adjective; noun, plural* **seventeenths.**

seventh Next after the sixth. *Adjective, noun.*
—One of seven equal parts; ¹/₇. *Noun.*
sev·enth (sev′ənth) *adjective; noun, plural* **sevenths.**

seventieth Next after the sixty-ninth. *Adjective, noun.*
—One of seventy equal parts; ¹/₇₀. *Noun.*
sev·en·ti·eth (sev′ən tē ith) *adjective; noun, plural* **seventieths.**

seventy Seven times ten; 70.
sev·en·ty (sev′ən tē) *noun, plural* **seventies;** *adjective.*

several More than two, but not many. We saw *several* of our friends at the parade.
sev·er·al (sev′ər əl *or* sev′rəl) *adjective; noun.*

severe **1.** Very strict; harsh. The dictator established many *severe* laws. **2.** Dangerous; serious. The soldier had a *severe* wound. **3.** Causing great difficulty or suffering; violent or sharp. A *severe* storm is expected.
se·vere (sə vîr′) *adjective,* **severer, severest.**

sew To make, fasten, or close things with a needle and thread. A person can sew by hand or with a sewing machine. I *sew* clothes as a hobby. *Sew* the button on your shirt. The doctor *sewed* up the wound on my leg. ▲ Other words that sound like this are **so** and **sow.**
sew (sō) *verb,* **sewed, sewed** or **sewn, sewing.**

sewage Waste that is carried off from sinks, toilets, and other devices in houses and factories by sewers and drains.
sew·age (sü′ij) *noun.*

sewer A pipe or channel under the ground for carrying off waste from sinks, toilets, and other devices in houses and factories.
sew·er (sü′ər) *noun, plural* **sewers.**

sewing machine A machine for sewing things. Most sewing machines are run by electric motors.

sewing machine

sewn A past participle of **sew.** The tailor has *sewn* the rip in my coat. Look up **sew** for more information. ▲ Another word that sounds like this is **sown.**
sewn (sōn) *verb.*

sex **1.** One of the two divisions, male and female, that people and most other living things are divided into. **2.** The fact or character of being male or female. The club is open to all children, regardless of *sex.*
sex (seks) *noun, plural* **sexes.**

shabby **1.** Worn-out and faded. The beggar wore a *shabby* coat. **2.** Mean or unfair.

It's cruel and *shabby* to make fun of other people.
shab·by (shab′ē) *adjective,* **shabbier, shabbiest.**

shack A small, roughly built hut or cabin.
shack (shak) *noun, plural* **shacks.**

shad A fish related to the herring. Shad are caught to be used as food. They live along the coasts of Europe and North America and swim up freshwater rivers to lay their eggs.
shad (shad) *noun, plural* **shad** or **shads.**

shade **1.** A place sheltered from the sun; place darker than the area around it. They rested in the *shade* of a tree. **2.** Something that shuts out or reduces light. Please lower the *shades* on the living room windows. We bought a new *shade* for the lamp. **3.** A particular variety of a color. The pants are a light *shade* of green. **4.** A small amount or difference. You are a *shade* taller than your friend. The word "run" has many *shades* of meaning. *Noun.*
—**1.** To shelter from heat or light. The umbrella *shaded* us from the sun. **2.** To mark with different amounts of darkness. The artist *shaded* the faces in the painting. *Verb.*
shade (shād) *noun, plural* **shades;** *verb,* **shaded, shading.**

shadow **1.** A dark area or figure made when rays of light are blocked by a person or thing. The child cast a *shadow*. **2.** A slight amount; suggestion. There is not a *shadow* of a doubt that they are lying. *Noun.*
—To follow and watch another person closely and secretly. The detective *shadowed* the suspected criminal. *Verb.*
shad·ow (shad′ō) *noun, plural* **shadows;** *verb,* **shadowed, shadowing.**

shady **1.** Full of or giving shade. We sat in a *shady* part of the yard. A big *shady* tree is next to the house. **2.** Not completely honest. The dishonest manager tried to carry out a *shady* business deal.
shad·y (shā′dē) *adjective,* **shadier, shadiest.**

shaft **1.** A long, thin part connected to the head of an arrow or spear, or the entire arrow or spear. **2.** The long handle of a hammer, golf club, hockey stick, or the like. **3.** A bar in a machine that supports parts or carries motion to other parts. **4.** A ray or beam. *Shafts* of light came through the window. **5.** A deep passage that goes straight down. An elevator goes up and down an elevator *shaft*.
shaft (shaft) *noun, plural* **shafts.**

shaggy **1.** Covered with long, rough hair or something like hair. The dog is large and *shaggy.* **2.** Long, bushy, and rough. That person's hair is very *shaggy.*
shag·gy (shag′ē) *adjective,* **shaggier, shaggiest.**

a **shaggy** dog

shake **1.** To move quickly up and down, back and forth, or from side to side. *Shake* the bottle to mix the salad dressing. The house *shakes* when the trains go by. **2.** To remove or throw by moving up and down or from side to side. The dog *shook* the water from its coat. **3.** To tremble or cause to tremble. The cold wind made me *shake*. **4.** To weaken. Nothing will *shake* our friendship. **5.** To upset. The news has *shaken* us. *Verb.*
—The act of shaking. The child scared the dog away with a *shake* of a big stick. *Noun.*
• **to shake hands.** To clasp another's hand, as in greeting or agreement.
• **to shake up.** To disturb mentally or physically; shock. The argument I had with my best friend *shook* me *up*.
shake (shāk) *verb,* **shook, shaken, shaking;** *noun, plural* **shakes.**

at; āpe; fär; câre; end; mē; it; īce; pîerce; hot; ōld; sông, fôrk; oil; out; up; ūse; rüle; püll; tûrn; chin; sing; shop; thin; **this;** hw in white; zh in treasure. The symbol ə stands for the unstressed vowel sound in about, taken, pencil, lemon, and circus.

S

shaky   **1.** Trembling; shaking. The frightened person answered in a *shaky* voice. **2.** Not firm; unsound. The old bridge is *shaky.*
    shak·y (shā′kē) *adjective,* **shakier, shakiest.**

shale   A rock formed from mud that has hardened. Shale is found in thin layers.
    shale (shāl) *noun.*

shall   An auxiliary verb that is used in the following ways: **1.** To express future actions and conditions. I *shall* be happy to see you.   **2.** To express a requirement. You *shall* do as I say.   **3.** To ask a question that extends an invitation or offers a suggestion. *Shall* we dance? *Shall* we go for a walk?
    shall (shal) *verb.*

shallow   Not deep. The water in the pond is *shallow. Adjective.*
  —**shallows.** A shallow part of a body of water. They waded in the *shallows* of the stream. *Noun.* ▲ This word can be used with a singular or plural verb.
    shal·low (shal′ō) *adjective,* **shallower, shallowest;** *plural noun.*

shame   **1.** A painful feeling caused by having done something wrong or foolish. He felt *shame* for having cheated.   **2.** Dishonor; disgrace. Her arrest for robbery brought *shame* to her family.   **3.** A thing to be sorry for. It is a *shame* that our team lost. *Noun.*
  —**1.** To cause to feel shame. I was *shamed* by my foolish mistake.   **2.** To force by causing shame or the fear of shame. Did your friends *shame* you into helping them? *Verb.*
    shame (shām) *noun; verb,* **shamed, shaming.**

shampoo   To wash hair, rugs, or furniture coverings with a special soap. I *shampoo* my hair twice a week. *Verb.*
  —**1.** A special soap used to wash hair, rugs, or furniture coverings.   **2.** An act of washing with shampoo. Give the dog a *shampoo. Noun.*
    sham·poo (sham pü′) *verb,* **shampooed, shampooing;** *noun, plural* **shampoos.**

shamrock   A leaf with three parts or leaflets that is an emblem of Ireland. A clover leaf with three leaflets is a shamrock.
    sham·rock (sham′rok′) *noun, plural* **shamrocks.**

shape   **1.** Form; figure. All circles have the same *shape.* A lion has a different *shape* from a bear. This jar has the *shape* of a pumpkin. **2.** Condition. The runner was in bad *shape* after the fall.   **3.** Regular, proper, or good form or condition. Get your room in *shape.* My parents exercise to keep in *shape. Noun.*

  —**1.** To give form to; mold. I *shaped* the wire into the figure of a dog. A baker *shapes* dough into loaves.   **2.** To change the form of. The tailor can *shape* this jacket to fit you better. *Verb.*
    shape (shāp) *noun, plural* **shapes;** *verb,* **shaped, shaping.**

share   **1.** The part that is given or belongs to one person. Each of us will do a *share* of the work on this project. Did you eat my *share* of the orange?   **2.** One of the equal parts into which the ownership of a company or business is divided. Each partner owns ten *shares* of stock in the company. *Noun.*
  —**1.** To use with another or others. Two of us *shared* a tent.   **2.** To divide into portions and give to others as well as to oneself. I *shared* my sandwich.   **3.** To have a share; take part. We all *shared* in the fun. *Verb.*
    share (shâr) *noun, plural* **shares;** *verb,* **shared, sharing.**

shark   A fish that lives in the sea. A shark has gray scales, a skeleton made of cartilage, and a large mouth with sharp teeth. Sharks eat other fish, and some kinds of sharks will attack people.
    shark (shärk) *noun, plural* **sharks.**

shark

sharp   **1.** Having an edge or point that cuts or pierces easily. That knife has a *sharp* blade. A needle has a *sharp* point.   **2.** Having a pointed end; not rounded. That mountain has a *sharp* peak. This table has *sharp* edges.   **3.** Harsh or biting. The strong cheese had a *sharp* taste. The winter wind is very *sharp.*   **4.** Having a sudden change in direction. The road ahead has a *sharp* curve. **5.** Clear. Your camera takes *sharp* pictures. **6.** Watchful; alert. Keep a *sharp* lookout. The dog has *sharp* ears.   **7.** Quick and strong. The falling book gave me a *sharp* blow on the head. *Adjective.*
  —**1.** At the moment that is mentioned and not any other. We must leave at ten o'clock *sharp.*   **2.** In a sharp manner. Look *sharp* or you will miss the turn. *Adverb.*
  —**1.** A tone or note in music that is one half

note above its natural pitch. **2.** A symbol (♯) that shows this tone or note. *Noun.*
  sharp (shärp) *adjective,* **sharper, sharpest;** *adverb; noun, plural* **sharps.**

sharpen To make or become sharp. *Sharpen* the knife. My vision *sharpened* when I got my new glasses.
  sharp·en (shär′pən) *verb,* **sharpened, sharpening.**

shatter **1.** To break into pieces. The glass *shattered* when I dropped it. The ball *shattered* the window. **2.** To destroy completely or damage very much; ruin. The storm *shattered* our hopes of going sailing.
  shat·ter (shat′ər) *verb,* **shattered, shattering.**

shave **1.** To remove hair or remove hair from with a razor. My cousin *shaves* with an electric razor. Do you plan to *shave* your beard off? The barber *shaved* the customer. **2.** To cut off in thin strips. The carpenter *shaved* the board with a plane. *Verb.*
—The removing of hair with a razor. You can go to the barber for a *shave. Noun.*
  shave (shāv) *verb,* **shaved, shaved** or **shaven, shaving;** *noun, plural* **shaves.**

shaving A thin piece or slice. The floor of the workshop was covered with wood *shavings.*
  shav·ing (shā′ving) *noun, plural* **shavings.**

shawl A piece of cloth that is worn over the shoulders or head.
  shawl (shôl) *noun, plural* **shawls.**

she A female person or animal that is being talked about. Betty told us that *she* would come to our party. *Pronoun.*
—A female person or animal. Is the puppy a *she* or a he? *Noun.*
  she (shē) *pronoun; noun, plural* **shes.**

shear **1.** To cut or clip with shears or scissors. Please *shear* the hedge. **2.** To cut or cut off; remove. The farmer *sheared* wool from the sheep. The side of the building was *sheared* off by the explosion. ▲ Another word that sounds like this is **sheer.**
  shear (shîr) *verb,* **sheared, sheared** or **shorn, shearing.**

shears A cutting instrument like scissors. There are shears for cutting grass and cutting metal.
  shears (shîrz) *plural noun.*

sheath A case for the blade of a sword, dagger, or similar weapon; scabbard.
  sheath (shēth) *noun, plural* **sheaths** (shē*th*z).

she'd **1.** Shortened form of "she had." *She'd* better do her homework. **2.** Short-

ened form of "she would." *She'd* come if she could.
  she'd (shēd) *contraction.*

shed¹ A small building used for storing or sheltering things.
  shed (shed) *noun, plural* **sheds.**

shed² **1.** To let fall or cause to flow. I *shed* a few tears when we moved away. **2.** To lose or drop. A dog *sheds* hair. Many trees *shed* their leaves in the fall. **3.** To send out. The moon *shed* little light last night because it was just a crescent.
  shed (shed) *verb,* **shed, shedding.**

sheep **1.** An animal with a thick, heavy coat that is raised on farms for its wool and meat. **2.** Any of several less common kinds of sheep that live wild in mountain regions. **3.** A person who follows the ideas or actions of another person without thinking.
  sheep (shēp) *noun, plural* **sheep.**

sheep

sheer **1.** So thin that one can see through it; very fine and thin. The window has *sheer* curtains. **2.** Total; utter. This is *sheer* nonsense! **3.** Steep. There is a *sheer* drop of 400 feet from the edge of the cliff. ▲ Another word that sounds like this is **shear.**
  sheer (shîr) *adjective,* **sheerer, sheerest.**

sheet **1.** A large piece of cotton, linen, or other cloth. It is used to cover a bed. **2.** A thin, broad piece or surface of something. We bought four *sheets* of plywood. A *sheet* of ice covered the sidewalk.
  sheet (shēt) *noun, plural* **sheets.**

at; āpe; fär; câre; end; mē; it; īce; pîerce; hot; ōld; sông, fôrk; oil; out; up; ūse; rüle; pull; tûrn; chin; sing; shop; thin; *th*is; hw in white; zh in treasure. The symbol ə stands for the unstressed vowel sound in about, taken, pencil, lemon, and circus.

S

659

sheik A leader or chief of an Arab clan, tribe, or village.
  sheik (shēk *or* shāk) *noun, plural* **sheiks.**

shelf **1.** A thin piece of wood, metal, or other material fastened to a wall or frame. It is used to hold books, dishes, and other things. **2.** Anything like a shelf. The ship was stuck on an underwater *shelf* of sand.
  shelf (shelf) *noun, plural* **shelves.**

shell **1.** A hard outer covering. A shell helps protect what it holds inside. Turtles, snails, eggs and nuts have shells. **2.** Something like a shell. I filled the pasta *shells* with cheese. The framework of a building is called a *shell.* **3.** A case of metal or cardboard filled with explosives or bits of metal. It is fired from a cannon or gun. *Noun.*
  —**1.** To take something out of its shell. Will you help by *shelling* the peanuts for the party? **2.** To bombard with shells. The army *shelled* the city. *Verb.*
  shell (shel) *noun, plural* **shells;** *verb,* **shelled, shelling.**

she'll **1.** Shortened form of "she will." *She'll* come tomorrow. **2.** Shortened form of "she shall." *She'll* take care of the dog.
  she'll (shēl) *contraction.*

shellac A liquid used as a varnish on floors and furniture to protect them and make them shine. *Noun.*
  —To coat with shellac. I'm going to *shellac* the table. *Verb.*
  shel·lac (shə lak') *noun, plural* **shellacs;** *verb,* **shellacked, shellacking.**

shellfish An animal with a shell that lives in water. Shrimps, crabs, and clams are shellfish. Shellfish are not actually fish.
  shell·fish (shel'fish') *noun, plural* **shellfish** or **shellfishes.**

shelter **1.** Something that covers or protects. The hikers used an old barn as a *shelter* during the thunderstorm. **2.** The condition of being covered or protected. An umbrella will give you *shelter* from rain. **3.** A place where a person or an animal who is lost or doesn't have a home can stay. The victims of the flood slept in the emergency *shelter.* We got our dog from the animal *shelter. Noun.*
  —To give shelter to. The tent *sheltered* us from the rain. We *sheltered* the puppy. *Verb.*
  shel·ter (shel'tər) *noun, plural* **shelters;** *verb,* **sheltered, sheltering.**

shelves Plural of **shelf.** There are 5,000 books on the *shelves* of this library. Look up **shelf** for more information.
  shelves (shelvz) *plural noun.*

shepherd A person who takes care of sheep. *Noun.*
—**1.** To take care of as a shepherd. Who *shepherds* this flock of sheep? **2.** To guide or watch over. The teacher *shepherded* the class through the museum. *Verb.*
  shep·herd (shep'ərd) *noun, plural* **shepherds;** *verb,* **shepherded, shepherding.**

sherbet A frozen dessert. It is made of fruit juices, water, sugar, and a small amount of egg whites or milk.
  sher·bet (shûr'bit) *noun, plural* **sherbets.**

sheriff The main officer responsible for enforcing the law in a county. The sheriff is also in charge of taking care of the jails.
  sher·iff (sher'if) *noun, plural* **sheriffs.**

she's **1.** Shortened form of "she is." *She's* late this morning. **2.** Shortened form of "she has." *She's* been doing her homework.
  she's (shēz) *contraction.*

Shetland pony A small pony that originally came from the Shetland Islands of Scotland. It has a rough coat and a long mane and tail.
  Shet·land (shet'lənd)

shied Past tense and past participle of **shy.** The horse *shied* when it saw the snake on the trail. Look up **shy** for more information.
  shied (shīd) *verb.*

shield **1.** A piece of armor used in olden times. It was carried on the arm to protect the body or head during a battle. **2.** A person or thing that defends or protects. She stood as a *shield* between her little brother and the growling dog. The umbrella was a *shield* against the rain. **3.** Something shaped like a shield. A police officer's badge is called a shield. *Noun.*
  —To defend or protect. I *shielded* my eyes from the bright sun with my hand. *Verb.*
  shield (shēld) *noun, plural* **shields;** *verb,* **shielded, shielding.**

shift To move or change. We helped to *shift* the heavy table to the other side of the room. I *shifted* my position in the chair. The driver of the car *shifted* from first gear into second gear. *Verb.*
  —**1.** A movement or change. The camper's sudden *shift* in the canoe tipped it over. **2.** A group of workers, or the time that they work. My cousin works during the day *shift* at the factory. **3.** A device that connects a set of gears to a motor; gearshift. *Noun.*
  shift (shift) *verb,* **shifted, shifting;** *noun, plural* **shifts.**

shilling A coin that was once used in Great Britain. Twenty shillings were equal to one pound.
  shil·ling (shil'ing) *noun, plural* **shillings.**

shimmer To shine with a faint, flickering light; glimmer. The lake *shimmered* in the moonlight.
shim·mer (shim′ər) *verb,* **shimmered, shimmering.**

shin The front part of the leg from the knee to the ankle. *Noun.*
—To climb by using the arms and legs. I like to *shin* up trees. *Verb.*
shin (shin) *noun, plural* **shins;** *verb,* **shinned, shinning.**

shine **1.** To give or reflect light. The stars *shine* at night. The surface of the lake *shone* in the bright sunshine. **2.** To be or make bright. Their faces *shone* with happiness. I'm going to *shine* my shoes. **3.** To do very well. You *shine* in arithmetic at school. *Verb.*
—**1.** Light or brightness. The *shine* from the lamp hurts my eyes. The polished floor has a nice *shine.* **2.** The act of polishing. Those shoes need a *shine. Noun.*
shine (shīn) *verb,* **shone** or **shined, shining;** *noun, plural* **shines.**

shingle A thin piece of wood or other material. Shingles are placed in overlapping rows to cover the roofs and sometimes the walls of buildings. *Noun.*
—To cover with shingles. The workers will *shingle* the roof. *Verb.*
shin·gle (shing′gəl) *noun, plural* **shingles;** *verb,* **shingled, shingling.**

shingles

shiny Shining; bright. We have a *shiny* car.
shin·y (shī′nē) *adjective,* **shinier, shiniest.**

ship **1.** A large boat that travels across deep water. **2.** An airplane, airship, or spacecraft. *Noun.*
—**1.** To send by ship, train, truck, or airplane. They will *ship* the bed by truck. **2.** To go on a ship as a member of the crew. My cousin *shipped* as a cook. *Verb.*
ship (ship) *noun, plural* **ships;** *verb,* **shipped, shipping.**

-ship A *suffix* that means: **1.** The state or quality of being. *Friendship* means the state of being a friend. **2.** The art or skill of. *Workmanship* means the art or skill of a workman.

shipment **1.** The shipping of goods. The farmer's crops were loaded for *shipment* to market. **2.** Something that is shipped or an amount of something that is shipped. The *shipment* hasn't arrived yet. Several *shipments* of books arrived at the library.
ship·ment (ship′mənt) *noun, plural* **shipments.**

shipping **1.** The act or business of sending goods by ship, train, truck, or airplane. **2.** Ships. That harbor is open to the world's *shipping.*
ship·ping (ship′ing) *noun, plural* **shippings.**

shipshape In good or proper condition. The inspector found the new house to be *shipshape. Adjective.*
—In a neat manner. *Adverb.*
ship·shape (ship′shāp′) *adjective; adverb.*

shipwreck **1.** The destruction or loss of a ship at sea. All those aboard survived the *shipwreck.* **2.** The remains of a wrecked ship. Divers explored the *shipwreck. Noun.*
—**1.** To cause to be destroyed or lost. The storm *shipwrecked* the boat. **2.** To cause to experience the destruction or loss of a ship at sea. The sailor was *shipwrecked* and stranded on an island. *Verb.*
ship·wreck (ship′rek′) *noun, plural* **shipwrecks;** *verb,* **shipwrecked, shipwrecking.**

shipyard A place where ships are built or repaired.
ship·yard (ship′yärd′) *noun, plural* **shipyards.**

shirk To avoid or neglect doing something that should be done. They *shirked* their chores and went swimming.
shirk (shûrk) *verb,* **shirked, shirking.**

shirt A piece of clothing worn on the upper part of the body. One kind of shirt has a collar, sleeves, and buttons down the front.
shirt (shûrt) *noun, plural* **shirts.**

shiver To shake; tremble. They *shivered* in the cold room. *Verb.*
—The act or instance of shivering. The story about ghosts sent *shivers* up my back. *Noun.*
shiv·er (shiv′ər) *verb,* **shivered, shivering;** *noun, plural* **shivers.**

shoal A place in a river, lake, or ocean where the water is shallow.
shoal (shōl) *noun, plural* **shoals.**

at; āpe; fär; câre; end; mē; it; īce; pîerce; hot; ōld; sông; fôrk; oil; out; up; ūse; rüle; pull; tûrn; chin; sing; shop; thin; this; hw in white; zh in treasure. The symbol ə stands for the unstressed vowel sound in about, taken, pencil, lemon, and circus.

S

shock¹ **1.** A sudden, violent upsetting of the mind or emotions. The parents never got over the *shock* of their child's death. **2.** A sudden, violent blow or jolt. The *shock* caused by the explosion broke windows in nearby buildings. **3.** A feeling caused by electricity passing through the body. I felt a *shock* when we shook hands. **4.** A serious weakening of the body caused by injury, disease, or emotional upset. A person is said to be in shock when too little blood reaches the body's tissues. *Noun.*
—**1.** To disturb the mind or emotions of. My friend's rudeness *shocked* me. **2.** To give an electric shock. *Verb.*
  shock (shok) *noun, plural* **shocks;** *verb,* **shocked, shocking.**

shock² A bundle of wheat, corn, or other grain stalks propped up on end in a field to dry.
  shock (shok) *noun, plural* **shocks.**

shock³ A thick, bushy mass. We recognized you in the crowd by your *shock* of blond hair.
  shock (shok) *noun, plural* **shocks.**

shocking Causing horror, surprise, or disgust. We heard some *shocking* news.
  shock·ing (shok′ing) *adjective.*

shod Past tense and past participle of **shoe.** The blacksmith *shod* the horse. Look up **shoe** for more information.
  shod (shod) *verb.*

shoe **1.** An outer covering for the foot. Shoes are usually made of leather. **2.** A piece of metal curved to fit the shape of a horse's hoof; horseshoe. *Noun.*
—To provide with a shoe or shoes. The blacksmith will *shoe* the horse. *Verb.*
  shoe (shü) *noun, plural* **shoes;** *verb,* **shod, shoeing.**

shoelace A string or cord used to pull and hold together the sides of a shoe.
  shoe·lace (shü′lās′) *noun, plural* **shoelaces.**

shone A past tense and past participle of **shine.** The light *shone* in the window. Look up **shine** for more information.
  shone (shōn) *verb.*

shook Past tense of **shake.** I *shook* my head. Look up **shake** for more information.
  shook (shuk) *verb.*

shoot **1.** To hit with a bullet, arrow, or the like. Hunters *shoot* deer with rifles. **2.** To send forth from a weapon. I *shot* an arrow at the target. **3.** To cause a weapon to send forth bullets, arrows, or the like; fire. Soldiers *shoot* cannons. The sheriff *shot* at the escaping outlaw. **4.** To move or cause to move fast. The train *shot* by. The snake *shot* out its

tongue. **5.** To come forth; sprout; grow. The bean plants are *shooting* up from the ground. **6.** To photograph or film. That movie was *shot* in Rome. *Verb.*
—A new or young plant or stem; sprout. *Noun.* ▲ Another word that sounds like this is **chute.**
  shoot (shüt) *verb,* **shot, shooting;** *noun, plural* **shoots.**

shooting star A mass of metal or stone that falls to earth from space; meteor. Look up **meteor** for more information.

shop **1.** A place where goods are sold. Can we go to the pet *shop*? **2.** A place where a particular kind of work is done. The broken radio is at the repair *shop*. *Noun.*
—To visit stores in order to look at and buy goods. I *shopped* for a new coat. *Verb.*
  shop (shop) *noun, plural* **shops;** *verb,* **shopped, shopping.**

shoplift To steal merchandise from a store while pretending to be a shopper there.
  shop·lift (shop′lift′) *verb,* **shoplifted, shoplifting.**

shopping center A group of stores and other business establishments. Shopping centers are usually built in suburbs and usually have a lot of space for parking cars.

shopping center

shore **1.** The land along the edge of an ocean, lake, or large river. We walked along the *shore*. **2.** Land. The sailors were glad to be back on *shore* after the long voyage.
  shore (shôr) *noun, plural* **shores.**

short **1.** Not long or tall. The grass is cut very *short*. It's a *short* trip to the store. That was a *short* speech. **2.** Not having or being enough. The hikers were *short* of food. **3.** Taking less time to pronounce. The "i" in "bit" is a *short* vowel. *Adjective.*

—**1.** In a sudden or unexpected way; suddenly. The horse stopped *short,* and the rider fell off. **2.** Not quite up to. The golf ball stopped *short* of the hole. *Adverb.*
—**1.** A short circuit. **2. shorts.** Pants that are worn above the knee. **3. shorts.** Short pants worn by men as underwear. *Noun.*
• **for short.** As a shortened or shorter form. A taxicab is called a cab *for short.*
• **short for.** A shorter form of. "Phone" is *short for* "telephone."
short (shôrt) *adjective,* **shorter, shortest;** *adverb; noun, plural* **shorts.**

shortage Too small an amount or supply; lack. There is a *shortage* of water.
short·age (shôr′tij) *noun, plural* **shortages.**

short circuit A connection that allows a flow of electric current that is not wanted or is greater than is wanted. It is usually formed by accident, as when two bare wires touch each other.

shortcoming A fault, defect, or weakness, as in character or behavior. The habit of breaking promises is a serious *shortcoming.*
short·com·ing (shôrt′kum′ing) *noun, plural* **shortcomings.**

shorten To make or become short or shorter. The tailor has to *shorten* these pants. The days *shorten* during fall.
short·en (shôr′tən) *verb,* **shortened, shortening.**

shortening Any of various fats that are used in cooking. Butter, lard, and vegetable oil are kinds of shortening.
short·en·ing (shôr′tə ning) *noun.*

shorthorn A kind of cattle with short horns. Some are raised for beef, and others are raised for milk.
short·horn (shôrt′hôrn′) *noun, plural* **shorthorns.**

shorthorn

shortly In a short time; soon. The doctor will see you *shortly.*
short·ly (shôrt′lē) *adverb.*

shortsighted **1.** Not thinking about, caring about, or planning for the future. We were *shortsighted* in bringing so little food for the long hike. **2** Not able to see distant objects clearly; nearsighted. Look up **nearsighted** for more information.
short·sight·ed (shôrt′sī′tid) *adjective.*

shortstop A baseball or softball player whose position is between second and third base.
short·stop (shôrt′stop′) *noun, plural* **shortstops.**

shot¹ **1.** The firing of a gun or other weapon. Did you hear a *shot?* **2.** A person who fires a gun or other weapon. That hunter is a good *shot.* **3.** A ball or balls of metal that are fired from a gun or cannon. **4.** The launching of a rocket or missile into space. We watched the moon *shot* on television. **5.** The distance over which something can travel; range. The soldier waited to shoot until the enemy was within rifle *shot.* **6.** An injection of medicine. I had to get a measles *shot.* **7.** A throw or stroke in certain games. I need a few practice *shots* before we start the game. **8.** An attempt; try. Let's give it a *shot.*
shot (shot) *noun, plural* **shots** or **shot** *(for definition 3).*

shot² Past tense and past participle of **shoot.** The police officer *shot* the gun. Look up **shoot** for more information.
shot (shot) *verb.*

should An auxiliary verb that is used in the following ways: **1.** To express obligation or duty. A judge *should* know the law. **2.** To offer advice. You *should* see a doctor. **3.** To say that something is probable or expected. They *should* be here soon. **4.** To express a possible condition or action. If anyone *should* call, take a message.
should (shủd) *verb.*

shoulder **1.** The area on either side of the body at which an arm, foreleg, or wing joins the trunk. **2. shoulders.** Both shoulders plus the part of the back that lies between them. **3.** The part of a shirt, dress, or other piece of clothing that covers the shoulder. I ripped my sweater at the *shoulder.* **4.** The edge or border on either side of a road or

at; āpe; fär; câre; end; mē; it; ice; pîerce; hot; ōld; sông, fôrk; oil; out; up; ūse; rüle; pùll; tûrn; chin; sing; shop; thin; <u>th</u>is; hw in white; zh in treasure. The symbol ə stands for the unstressed vowel sound in about, taken, pencil, lemon, and circus.

S

highway. The driver pulled onto the *shoulder* of the road to change the flat tire. *Noun.*
—To push with the shoulder or shoulders. I *shouldered* my way onto the train. *Verb.*
> **shoul·der** (shōl′dər) *noun, plural* **shoulders;** *verb,* **shouldered, shouldering.**

shoulder blade One of two flat, triangular bones in the upper corners of the back.

shouldn't Shortened form of "should not." You *shouldn't* play in the street.
> **should·n't** (shud′ənt) *contraction.*

shout To call loudly; yell. I *shouted* "Hello!" to the people in the boat. *Verb.*
—A loud call; yell. I gave a *shout* when I found the lost puppy. *Noun.*
> **shout** (shout) *verb,* **shouted, shouting;** *noun, plural* **shouts.**

shove 1. To push along or forward from behind. The mechanic *shoved* open the door to the garage. We *shoved* the bed closer to the wall. 2. To push in a rude or rough way. The bully *shoved* the young child. *Verb.*
—A strong push. You need to give this door a *shove* to close it. *Noun.*
> **shove** (shuv) *verb,* **shoved, shoving;** *noun, plural* **shoves.**

shovel 1. A tool or machine with a broad scoop. A shovel is used for digging and moving dirt, snow, and other loose material. 2. The amount a shovel holds. Throw a few *shovels* of dirt on the campfire. *Noun.*
—1. To move or dig with a shovel. The worker *shoveled* dirt into the back of the truck. I *shoveled* a path through the snow. 2. To move or throw in large amounts. Stop *shoveling* food into your mouth. *Verb.*
> **shov·el** (shuv′əl) *noun, plural* **shovels;** *verb,* **shoveled, shoveling.**

show 1. To bring to sight or view; make able to be seen. Please *show* your ticket at the gate. The theater *showed* that movie last week. 2. To be able to be seen; be in sight. The light *showed* through the curtains. 3. To make or be made known or clear. I *showed* my anger by stamping my foot. The trial will *show* who is lying. Your worry *shows* in your face. 4. To point out or lead. *Show* us the way to the zoo. I *showed* them out. 5. To explain to. The mechanic *showed* me how to change a tire. 6. To grant or give. The judge *showed* mercy in the decision. *Verb.*
—1. Something that is seen in public; display. We went to a horse *show.* 2. Any program or entertainment in the theater or on radio or television. Did you see that nature *show* last night? 3. A display meant to at-

tract attention or give a false impression. The older students made a *show* of their knowledge. The traitor fooled everyone with a *show* of loyalty. *Noun.*
- **to show off.** 1. To display in a proud or showy way. I *showed off* my new coat to my friends. 2. To behave in a way that calls attention to oneself. The twins love to *show off* at parties.
- **to show up.** 1. To reveal; expose. You *showed up* those frauds for what they really are. 2. To arrive; come. When do you think they'll *show up?*
> **show** (shō) *verb,* **showed, shown** or **showed, showing;** *noun, plural* **shows.**

shower 1. A brief fall of rain. The forecast is for *showers* today. 2. A fall of anything in large numbers. I saw a *shower* of sparks when the fireworks went off. 3. A bath in which water is sprayed on a person from overhead. 4. A room or device that is used for such a bath. I was in the *shower* when you called. 5. A party where gifts are given to a future bride or a pregnant woman. *Noun.*
—1. To fall or make fall in a shower. It *showered* all day, so I stayed home. The wedding guests *showered* rice on the bride and groom. 2. To bathe by taking a shower. They *showered* and got dressed. 3. To wet with water or another liquid. We were *showered* by water from the sprinkler. 4. To give freely and in large amounts. The astronauts were *showered* with praise. *Verb.*
> **show·er** (shou′ər) *noun, plural* **showers;** *verb,* **showered, showering.**

shown A past participle of **show.** We were *shown* many sights in Arizona. Look up **show** for more information. ▲ Another word that sounds like this is **shone.**
> **shown** (shōn) *verb.*

show-off A person who behaves in a way that gets attention.
> **show-off** (shō′ôf′) *noun, plural* **show-offs.**

showy 1. Attracting attention by being bright or colorful. I bought a bunch of *showy* flowers. 2. Too bright or colorful; gaudy. I don't like *showy* clothing.
> **show·y** (shō′ē) *adjective,* **showier, showiest.**

shrank A past tense of **shrink.** My new shirt *shrank* when I washed it. Look up **shrink** for more information.
> **shrank** (shrangk) *verb.*

shred 1. A small piece or narrow strip torn or cut off. Put *shreds* of paper in the puppies' box. 2. A small amount; bit. There is not a *shred* of truth to the story. *Noun.*

—To tear or cut into small pieces or narrow strips. I *shredded* cabbage for the salad. *Verb.*
shred (shred) *noun, plural* **shreds;** *verb,* **shredded** or **shred, shredding.**

shrew A small animal that looks like a mouse but has a long, pointed nose. Shrews eat insects and are related to moles and hedgehogs.
shrew (shrü) *noun, plural* **shrews.**

shrew

shrewd Clever and sharp. The *shrewd* customer found a bargain.
shrewd (shrüd) *adjective,* **shrewder, shrewdest.**

shriek A loud, sharp cry or sound. The child let out a *shriek* of laughter. *Noun.*
—To utter a loud, sharp cry or sound. We all *shrieked* with laughter when the twins fell into the pool with all their clothes on. *Verb.*
shriek (shrēk) *noun, plural* **shrieks;** *verb,* **shrieked, shrieking.**

shrill Having a sharp, high sound. The officer used a *shrill* whistle to direct traffic.
shrill (shril) *adjective,* **shriller, shrillest.**

shrimp A sea animal that is covered with a thin shell and has a long tail. Shrimp are related to lobsters and crabs and are often used for food.
shrimp (shrimp) *noun, plural* **shrimp** or **shrimps.**

shrimp

shrine 1. A holy place for worship. A shrine often marks the tomb of a saint, contains a holy object, or is in memory of a religious person or event. 2. A place or thing that is honored and visited because it is connected with something important. The site of the great victory became a national *shrine.*
shrine (shrīn) *noun, plural* **shrines.**

shrink 1. To make or become smaller because of heat, cold, or wetness. That wool sweater will *shrink* if it's washed in hot wa-

ter. 2. To draw back in fear or horror. The child *shrank* from the barking dog.
shrink (shringk) *verb,* **shrank** or **shrunk, shrunk** or **shrunken, shrinking.**

shrivel To shrink, wrinkle, or wither. The plant *shriveled* because it was too hot in the room. Drought *shriveled* the flowers.
shriv·el (shriv'əl) *verb,* **shriveled, shriveling.**

shrub A woody plant that is smaller than a tree. A shrub has many stems that branch out at or near the ground.
shrub (shrub) *noun, plural* **shrubs.**

shrug To raise or draw up the shoulders to show doubt or lack of interest. *Verb.*
—The act of shrugging. Please don't answer my question with a *shrug. Noun.*
shrug (shrug) *verb,* **shrugged, shrugging;** *noun, plural* **shrugs.**

shrunk A past tense and a past participle of **shrink.** My sweater *shrunk* in the wash. Look up **shrink** for more information.
shrunk (shrungk) *verb.*

shrunken A past participle of **shrink.** The hot water had *shrunken* the shirt. Look up **shrink** for more information.
shrun·ken (shrung'kən) *verb.*

shudder To tremble suddenly from fear or cold. Strange sounds make me *shudder. Verb.*
—The act of trembling suddenly from fear or cold. The child awoke from the nightmare with a *shudder. Noun.*
shud·der (shud'ər) *verb,* **shuddered, shuddering;** *noun, plural* **shudders.**

shuffle 1. To drag the feet while walking. The tired runner *shuffled* around the track. Don't *shuffle* your feet when you walk. 2. To mix playing cards to change the order. When you play cards, you should *shuffle* them after each game. 3. To move from one place to another. The customer *shuffled* the books on the display. *Verb.*
—An act of shuffling. They walked with a *shuffle.* Give the cards a *shuffle. Noun.*
shuf·fle (shuf'əl) *verb,* **shuffled, shuffling;** *noun, plural* **shuffles.**

shun To keep away from deliberately; avoid on purpose. That family *shuns* the city.
shun (shun) *verb,* **shunned, shunning.**

at; āpe; fär; câre; end; mē; it; īce; pîerce; hot; ōld; sông, fôrk; oil; out; up; ūse; rüle; pùll; tûrn; chin; sing; shop; thin; <u>th</u>is; hw in white; zh in treasure. The symbol ə stands for the unstressed vowel sound in about, taken, pencil, lemon, and circus.

S

665

shut **1.** To move something so as to block or cover up an entrance or opening; close. We *shut* the window because it was cold. *Shut* your eyes and count to ten. **2.** To become closed. The door *shut* behind me. **3.** To make or force to stay; confine. The dog was *shut* inside.
- **to shut down.** To stop operating or cause to stop operating, usually for a short time. The factory had to *shut down* because of the strike.
- **to shut off.** To stop the flow, passage or operation of. *Shut* the water *off.*
- **to shut out.** **1.** To keep from entering; exclude. That building next door *shuts out* sunlight. **2.** To prevent the opposing team from scoring in a contest.
- **to shut up.** To stop talking or cause to stop talking. Please *shut up!*

shut (shut) *verb,* **shut, shutting.**

shutter **1.** A movable cover for a window, usually attached to the frame by hinges. Shutters are used to shut out light and to keep people from looking in. **2.** The part of a camera that snaps open and shuts quickly to let light onto the film when a picture is taken.

shut·ter (shut'ər) *noun, plural* **shutters.**

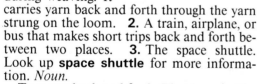
shutters

shuttle **1.** A device on a loom during weaving. It carries yarn back and forth through the yarn strung on the loom. **2.** A train, airplane, or bus that makes short trips back and forth between two places. **3.** The space shuttle. Look up **space shuttle** for more information. *Noun.*
—To move back and forth. That bus *shuttles* guests from the hotel to the airport. The doctor *shuttled* between the two hospitals. *Verb.*

shut·tle (shut'əl) *noun, plural* **shuttles;** *verb,* **shuttled, shuttling.**

shy **1.** Not comfortable around other people; bashful. The *shy* little child wouldn't come into the room. **2.** Easily frightened; timid. Animals that live in the woods are usually too *shy* to get close to people. **3.** Being or having less than a certain amount or not having enough; short. We are three cents *shy* of five dollars. *Adjective.*

—To move back or aside suddenly in fear. The horse *shied* at the loud noise. *Verb.*

shy (shī) *adjective,* **shyer** or **shier, shyest** or **shiest;** *verb,* **shied, shying.**

Siamese cat A breed of cat that has a long, narrow body and short hair. A Siamese cat's ears, paws, and tail are often a darker color than the rest of its body.

Si·a·mese (sī'ə mēz' *or* sī'ə mēs')

sick **1.** Suffering from a disease or having poor health; ill. My friend was *sick* with the flu for a week. **2.** Having to do with sickness or illness. When several children were ill at camp, two rooms were set up as *sick* rooms. **3.** Feeling nausea. The carnival ride made me *sick.* **4.** Upset; disturbed. We were *sick* at having to miss the party. **5.** Tired or disgusted. I bought new curtains because I was *sick* of the old ones.

sick (sik) *adjective,* **sicker, sickest.**

sickle A tool having a sharp, curved blade that is attached to a short handle. A sickle is used for cutting grass or grain by hand.

sick·le (sik'əl) *noun, plural* **sickles.**

sickly **1.** Usually or always sick. The *sickly* child often stayed home from school. **2.** Caused by or showing sickness. The patient had a pale and *sickly* complexion.

sick·ly (sik'lē) *adjective,* **sicklier, sickliest.**

sickness **1.** Illness or poor health. There has been quite a lot of *sickness* in our family this year. **2.** A disease or illness. Chicken pox is usually a childhood *sickness.*

sick·ness (sik'nis) *noun, plural* **sicknesses.**

side **1.** A line or surface that encloses or forms something. A triangle has three *sides.* The workers painted one *side* of the house. **2.** One of the two surfaces of a piece of paper or cloth or any other flat object. One *side* of the coin is worn. **3.** The place or space away from a central line, point, or thing. Put the chairs on the left *side* of the room. We live on the south *side* of the river. **4.** The right or left part of the body of a person or animal. I got a pain in my *side.* **5.** The area next to a person. Come stand at my *side.* **6.** One of two opposing groups or persons. Which *side* won the game? He was on his friend's *side* during the argument. **7.** A point of view or position. I want to hear your *side* of the story. **8.** A series or group of people that have a common ancestor. I am a cousin of that senator on my mother's *side. Noun.*
—**1.** At or near one side. Use the *side* entrance. **2.** Coming from or directed toward

one side. The army surprised the enemy with a *side* attack. **3.** Less important or not the main. We will discuss the *side* issues later. I'd like a *side* order of salad. *Adjective.*
- **side by side.** Next to each other. The twins walked down the street *side by side.*
- **to side with.** To agree with or support a person or group that disagrees with or opposes another person or group. Only one newspaper *sided with* the mayor in the disagreement with the town council.

side (sīd) *noun, plural* **sides;** *adjective.*

sideline 1. A line along each side of the playing area in certain sports. The spectators sat behind the *sidelines* at the tennis match. **2.** Work done in addition to one's usual job. The lawyer's *sideline* is coaching basketball.

side·line (sīd′līn′) *noun, plural* **sidelines.**

sideshow A small show that is part of a larger show or entertainment. I like to see the *sideshows* at the circus.

side·show (sīd′shō′) *noun, plural* **sideshows.**

sidestep 1. To step to one side. I had to *sidestep* to get out of the way of the bicycle. **2.** To avoid or delay; dodge. The candidate cleverly *sidestepped* the newspaper reporter's questions.

side·step (sīd′step′) *verb,* **sidestepped, sidestepping.**

sidetrack A short railroad track that is connected to the main track. *Noun.*
—**1.** To move a train from the main track to a sidetrack. The local train was *sidetracked* to let an express train pass by. **2.** To turn away from what is most important; distract. I was *sidetracked* by the television show and didn't finish my homework. *Verb.*

side·track (sīd′trak′) *noun, plural* **sidetracks;** *verb,* **sidetracked, sidetracking.**

sidewalk A path by a side of a street or road where people can walk. A sidewalk is usually paved.

side·walk (sīd′wôk′) *noun, plural* **sidewalks.**

sideways 1. Toward or from one side. I have to move *sideways* to let you go by. **2.** With one side forward. Turn that box *sideways* or we won't be able to fit it through the door. *Adverb.*
—Moving or directed toward one side. I gave the child a *sideways* glance. *Adjective.*

side·ways (sīd′wāz′) *adverb; adjective.*

siege The surrounding of an enemy fort or position for a long time in order to cut off food and other supplies and force surrender.

siege (sēj) *noun, plural* **sieges.**

sierra A chain of hills or mountains with sharp peaks. There are many sierras in the western part of the United States.

si·er·ra (sē er′ə) *noun, plural* **sierras.**

Word History

Sierra comes from the Spanish word for "saw." *Sierra* refers to the jagged appearance of the mountain ridges, which look like the teeth of a saw.

Sierra Leone A country in western Africa.

Si·er·ra Le·o·ne (sē er′ə lē ō′nē) *noun.*

siesta An afternoon nap or rest.

si·es·ta (sē es′tə) *noun, plural* **siestas.**

sieve A utensil that has a bottom with many holes in it. A sieve is used for sifting or draining.

sieve (siv) *noun, plural* **sieves.**

sift 1. To separate large pieces from small pieces by using a sieve. I helped *sift* stones out of the garden soil. **2.** To put through a sieve to take out lumps or make finer. *Sift* the flour before measuring it. **3.** To fall loosely as if through a sieve. Snow *sifted* through the cracks in the roof. **4.** To look at closely. The police *sifted* the evidence carefully.

sift (sift) *verb,* **sifted, sifting.**

sigh 1. To make a long, deep breathing sound because of sadness, tiredness, or relief. I *sighed* with relief when I found my lost watch. **2.** To make a sound like this. The wind *sighed* through the trees. *Verb.*
—The act or sound of sighing. I uttered a *sigh* of relief. *Noun.*

sigh (sī) *verb,* **sighed, sighing;** *noun, plural* **sighs.**

sight 1. The power or ability to see. My glasses helped improve my *sight.* **2.** The act of seeing. I recognized you at first *sight.* **3.** The range or distance a person can see. The soldiers kept out of the enemy's *sight.* **4.** The presence of something in the range that a person can see. The *sight* of the strangers frightened the baby. **5.** Something that is seen or is worth seeing. The sunset was a

at; āpe; fär; cāre; end; mē; it; īce; pîerce; hot; ōld; sông, fôrk; oil; out; up; ūse; rüle; pùll; tûrn; chin; sing; shop; thin; this; hw in white; zh in treasure. The symbol ə stands for the unstressed vowel sound in about, taken, pencil, lemon, and circus.

S

beautiful *sight*. **6.** Something that is unpleasant, funny, or odd to look at. You're a *sight* in that hat. **7.** Something on a gun or other object that helps in aiming or seeing. Line up the target in the *sight. Noun.*
—To see with the eyes. The group finally *sighted* the cabin. *Verb.* ▲ Other words that sound like this are **cite** and **site.**
  sight (sīt) *noun, plural* **sights;** *verb,* **sighted, sighting.**

sightless Not able to see; blind. Kangaroos are *sightless* at birth.
  sight·less (sīt′lis) *adjective.*

sightseeing The act of visiting places of interest. We went *sightseeing* in Washington, D.C. *Noun.*
—Visiting or used for visiting places of interest. We took a *sightseeing* tour. The *sightseeing* bus was late. *Adjective.*
  sight·see·ing (sīt′sē′ing) *noun; adjective.*

sign **1.** Something that stands for, shows, or suggests something else. ÷ is a *sign* for division. I nodded as a *sign* that I agreed with what they said. A fever is a *sign* of illness. The dark clouds were a *sign* of an approaching storm. **2.** A notice or board with writing on it that gives information. The *sign* said "Closed on Sundays." **3.** Something that warns or points out what is to come. Some people believe that breaking a mirror is a *sign* of bad luck.

This **sign** means that railroad tracks cross the road.

4. A trace. There was no *sign* of our pet cat. **5.** One of the twelve parts of the zodiac. **6.** Sign language. Look up **sign language** for more information. *Noun.*
—**1.** To write one's name on. I *signed* my name at the bottom of the letter. **2.** To communicate using sign language. *Verb.*
• **to sign off.** To announce the end of broadcasting and to stop broadcasting. This radio station *signs off* at midnight.
• **to sign up.** To sign a written agreement in order to join an organization or group or in order to obtain something. I *signed up* for a pottery class. My parents *signed up* for some additional life insurance.
  sign (sīn) *noun, plural* **signs;** *verb,* **signed, signing.**

signal Something that warns, directs, or informs. The red light on the dashboard is a *signal* that the car needs oil. A gun was fired as the *signal* for the race to begin. *Noun.*

—**1.** To make a signal to. The people on the sinking ship *signaled* for help. **2.** To make known by a signal or signals. A bell *signals* the end of the school day. *Verb.*
—Used as a signal. The *signal* light showed that a train was coming. *Adjective.*
  sig·nal (sig′nəl) *noun, plural* **signals;** *verb,* **signaled, signaling;** *adjective.*

signature **1.** The name of a person written in his or her own handwriting. We need your *signature* on this petition. **2.** A sign or signs at the beginning of each section of music. The signature shows the pitch, key, and time of a piece of music.
  sig·na·ture (sig′nə chər) *noun, plural* **signatures.**

significance Special value or meaning; importance. The election of a new president is an event of great *significance*. What was the *significance* of that remark?
  sig·nif·i·cance (sig nif′i kəns) *noun.*

significant Having special value or meaning; important. July 20, 1969, was a *significant* date in history because it was the day of the first moon landing.
  sig·nif·i·cant (sig nif′i kənt) *adjective.*

sign language A way of communicating in which gestures, especially hand motions, are used instead of speech. Sign language is used especially by the deaf.

using **sign language**

silence **1.** A lack of sound; complete quiet. There was *silence* in the deep cave. **2.** The condition of being or keeping quiet or silent. The audience listened in *silence*. Does your *silence* mean you agree with me? *Noun.*
—To make or keep silent. The judge banged a gavel to *silence* the noisy spectators. *Verb.*
  si·lence (sī′ləns) *noun, plural* **silences;** *verb,* **silenced, silencing.**

silent **1.** Completely quiet; still. She crept through the *silent* house. **2.** Not speaking,

668

or saying little. The children remained *silent* during the play. He is a shy, *silent* boy. **3.** Not spoken or expressed; not said out loud. The "k" in "know" is *silent*. A *silent* fear filled my heart when the alarm sounded.
si·lent (sī′lənt) *adjective.*

silhouette **1.** A picture or drawing showing the outline of a figure or object and filled in with black or another solid color. **2.** A dark outline seen against a lighter background. From our window at dusk, you can see the *silhouette* of the mountains against the sky. *Noun.*
—To show as a dark outline against a lighter background. The horse standing on the hill was *silhouetted* against the sky. *Verb.*
sil·hou·ette (sil′ü et′) *noun, plural* **silhouettes;** *verb,* **silhouetted, silhouetting.**

silicon A chemical element found in rocks and sand. Silicon is used in making glass, transistors, and computer chips.
si·li·con (sil′i kən *or* sil′i kon′) *noun.*

silk **1.** A soft, shiny cloth that is made from threads that are spun by silkworms. Silk is used to make scarves, ties, blouses, and many other pieces of clothing. **2.** Anything that is like silk. The tassels on an ear of corn are called silk. *Noun.*
—Made of or like silk. The *silk* blouse was very expensive. *Adjective.*
silk (silk) *noun, plural* **silks;** *adjective.*

silkworm A caterpillar that makes silk thread to spin its cocoon. Silkworms were originally found in China. They are raised on farms, and their silk is gathered and used to make silk cloth.
silk·worm (silk′wûrm′) *noun, plural* **silkworms.**

silky Like silk in the way it looks and feels; shiny and soft. The horse's mane was long and *silky.*
silk·y (sil′kē) *adjective,* **silkier, silkiest.**

Silkworm

Cocoon

silkworm

sill The piece of wood, stone, or other material at the bottom of a door or window.
sill (sil) *noun, plural* **sills.**

silly Without judgment or common sense; foolish. Don't be *silly;* you can't drive home in this snowstorm. Before the airplane was invented, some people thought that flying was a *silly* idea.
sil·ly (sil′ē) *adjective,* **sillier, silliest.**

silo **1.** A tall, round tower that is used to store food for farm animals. Silos are made out of metal, concrete, or other material. **2.** An underground structure in which missiles are stored.
si·lo (sī′lō) *noun, plural* **silos.**

silo

silt Fine particles of sand, clay, dirt, and other material. Silt is carried by flowing water, as in a river, and eventually it settles to the bottom.
silt (silt) *noun.*

silver **1.** A shiny white metal that is soft and easily shaped. It is used to make coins, jewelry, spoons, forks, and knives. Silver is a chemical element. **2.** Coins that are made from silver; change. **3.** Spoons, forks, or other things made of or coated with silver. **4.** The color of silver. *Noun.*
—**1.** Made of, coated with, or containing silver. You haven't polished the *silver* tray. **2.** Having the color of silver. *Adjective.*
—To coat with silver or a metal like silver. Take the old bowl to a jeweler to have it *silvered. Verb.*
sil·ver (sil′vər) *noun, plural* **silvers;** *adjective; verb,* **silvered, silvering.**

silversmith A person who makes or repairs objects of silver.
sil·ver·smith (sil′vər smith′) *noun, plural* **silversmiths.**

at; āpe; fär; câre; end; mē; it; īce; pîerce; hot; ōld; sông, fôrk; oil; out; up; ūse; rüle; pùll; tûrn; chin; sing; shop; thin; this; hw in white; zh in treasure. The symbol ə stands for the unstressed vowel sound in about, taken, pencil, lemon, and circus.

S

silverware 1. Spoons, forks, dishes, or anything else for the table that is made of or coated with silver. 2. Spoons, forks, or knives. I'll bring the plates and napkins for the picnic if you'll bring the *silverware*.
sil·ver·ware (sil′vər wâr′) *noun.*

similar Having many but not all qualities the same; alike. Our dresses are *similar*.
sim·i·lar (sim′ə lər) *adjective.*

similarity 1. The quality or condition of being similar; likeness. There is a *similarity* between you and your brother. 2. A way in which things are similar or alike. There are several *similarities* between those two houses.
sim·i·lar·i·ty (sim′ə lar′i tē) *noun, plural* **similarities.**

simmer To cook at or just below the boiling point. *Simmer* the soup for two hours.
sim·mer (sim′ər) *verb,* **simmered, simmering.**

simple 1. Easy to understand or do. That test was *simple*. Learning to ride a bicycle is not so *simple*. 2. Without anything added or any ornament; plain. A *simple* "yes" or "no" will do. The architect made a *simple* design. 3. Natural and honest. Our neighbor is a *simple* soul. 4. Foolish.
sim·ple (sim′pəl) *adjective,* **simpler, simplest.**

simple sentence A sentence that expresses only one complete thought. A simple sentence cannot be divided into shorter sentences. "Our dog is still a puppy" is a simple sentence.

simplicity 1. The condition or quality of being simple or plain. The instructions that came with the toy were written with *simplicity*. 2. The quality of being natural and sincere; honesty. The young children charmed us with their *simplicity*.
sim·plic·i·ty (sim plis′i tē) *noun, plural* **simplicities.**

simplify To make easier. The teacher *simplified* the arithmetic problem.
sim·pli·fy (sim′plə fī′) *verb,* **simplified, simplifying.**

simply 1. In a clear or natural way. The lecturer spoke *simply*. 2. Without decoration; plainly. I dressed *simply*. 3. Merely; only. If you need help, it is *simply* a matter of asking. 4. To the greatest degree; absolutely. That picture is *simply* beautiful.
sim·ply (sim′plē) *adverb.*

simultaneous Done, existing, or happening at the same time. Three acrobats performed *simultaneous* somersaults.
si·mul·ta·ne·ous (sī′məl tā′nē əs) *adjective.*

sin 1. An act that goes against a religious law. In many religions, murder is a *sin*. 2. Any wrong or bad act. It's a *sin* to be cruel to animals. *Noun.*
—To go against a religious law. They asked to be forgiven for having *sinned*. *Verb.*
sin (sin) *noun, plural* **sins;** *verb,* **sinned, sinning.**

since 1. From a particular time in the past until now. My cousin left last week and has been away ever *since*. 2. At some time between a particular time in the past and now. I was sick last month but have *since* recovered. 3. Before now; ago. Our neighbors have long *since* moved away. *Adverb.*
—During the time after. My parents had been gone *since* noon. There have been many changes in American life *since* 1945. *Preposition.*
—1. During the period after. I haven't seen the twins *since* they graduated. 2. For the reason that; because. *Since* the car isn't working, we'll have to take the bus. *Conjunction.*
since (sins) *adverb; preposition; conjunction.*

sincere Not false or pretended; honest and true. We gave them our *sincere* thanks.
sin·cere (sin sîr′) *adjective,* **sincerer, sincerest.**

sinew A strong cord or band of tissue that joins a muscle to a bone; a tendon. The sinews make it possible for the muscles to move an arm, leg, or other part of the body.
sin·ew (sin′ū) *noun, plural* **sinews.**

sing 1. To utter words or make sounds with musical tones. The school choir *sings* beautifully. The whole class *sang* the national anthem. The birds *sang* in the trees. 2. To make a whistling or humming sound. The tea kettle *sang* when the water boiled.
sing (sing) *verb,* **sang** or **sung, sung, singing.**

Singapore 1. An island country in southeastern Asia. 2. The capital city of this country.
Sin·ga·pore (sing′ə pôr′) *noun.*

singer A person or bird that sings. I am one of the *singers* in the school chorus. My friend's canary is a good *singer*.
sing·er (sing′ər) *noun, plural* **singers.**

single 1. Only one. There was a *single* flower in the vase. 2. To be used by one person only. The traveler asked for a *single* room at the hotel. 3. Not married. My older cousin is *single*. *Adjective.*
—A hit in baseball or softball that allows the batter to reach first base safely. *Noun.*
—1. To pick or choose from others. They

singled out the black cat as their favorite. **2.** To hit a single in a baseball or softball game. I *singled* my first time at bat. *Verb.*
sin·gle (sing′gəl) *adjective; noun, plural* **singles;** *verb,* **singled, singling.**

single-handed Without the help or support of anyone. The firefighter's *single-handed* rescue of the baby won great praise.
sin·gle-hand·ed (sing′gəl han′did) *adjective.*

singular Of or having to do with a form of a word that names or refers to one person or thing. *Child* and *tree* are singular nouns. *Children* and *trees* are plural nouns. *Adjective.*
—The form of a word that names or refers to one person or thing. The nouns *neighbor* and *box* are in the singular. The nouns *neighbors* and *boxes* are in the plural. *Noun.*
sin·gu·lar (sing′gyə lər) *adjective; noun, plural* **singulars.**

sinister Evil or suggesting evil. The dark old house looked *sinister* at night. In the story, the genie gave a *sinister* laugh.
sin·is·ter (sin′ə stər) *adjective.*

sink **1.** To go down or cause to go down partly or completely below a surface. The car *sank* into the mud. The canoe could *sink* if it has a hole. The bomb hit and *sank* the ship. **2.** To become less. Our voices *sank* to a whisper. **3.** To fall into a certain state. I *sank* into a deep sleep as soon as I got into bed. **4.** To dig. We *sunk* a well in the yard. **5.** To go or cause to go through or into deeply. The rain *sank* into the soil. *Sink* your teeth into this. *Verb.*
—A basin of metal, porcelain, or other material that is used to hold water for washing. A sink has faucets to turn water on and off and a drain to take water away. *Noun.*
sink (singk) *verb,* **sank** or **sunk, sunk** or **sunken, sinking;** *noun, plural* **sinks.**

sinus A hollow space in the bones of the face. There are sinuses above the eyes and on each side of the nose.
si·nus (sī′nəs) *noun, plural* **sinuses.**

Sioux A member of a group of American Indian tribes of the North American plains; Dakota.
Sioux (sü) *noun, plural* **Sioux.**

sip To drink little by little. I *sipped* the cold water. *Verb.*
—**1.** A small amount to drink. Can I have a *sip* of your juice? **2.** The act of sipping. Have a short *sip* of water. *Noun.*
sip (sip) *verb,* **sipped, sipping;** *noun, plural* **sips.**

siphon A bent tube with one side longer than the other. A siphon is used to move a liquid from one container to another. The liquid is moved by air pressure.
si·phon (sī′fən) *noun, plural* **siphons.**

sir **1.** A title used in place of a man's name. I said to the man, "May I help you, *sir?*" **2.** Sir. A title used before a knight's name. *Sir* Lancelot was a brave knight.
sir (sûr) *noun, plural* **sirs.**

siren A device that makes a loud, shrill sound. It is used as a signal or warning. Ambulances and police cars have sirens.
si·ren (sī′rən) *noun, plural* **sirens.**

sister **1.** A girl or woman with the same mother and father as another person. **2.** A woman who belongs to a religious order; nun. **3.** A woman who has the same interest or is a member of the same organization as another person.
sis·ter (sis′tər) *noun, plural* **sisters.**

sisterhood **1.** The close feeling between sisters or women. **2.** A group of women who are united by a common interest or aim.
sis·ter·hood (sis′tər hùd′) *noun, plural* **sisterhoods.**

sister-in-law **1.** The sister of one's husband or wife. **2.** The wife of one's brother.
sis·ter-in-law (sis′tər in lô′) *noun, plural* **sisters-in-law.**

sit **1.** To be in a position in which the weight of the body rests on the lower back part and not the feet. *Sit* in a chair. **2.** To cause to sit; seat. We *sat* the children around the table. **3.** To rest on a perch; roost. The bird *sat* on a branch. **4.** To take care of a child or children while the parents are away for a time; babysit. Can you *sit* for us tonight? **5.** To cover eggs in order to hatch them. Hens *sit* on their eggs. **6.** To be placed or be kept. The cabin *sits* in the woods. **7.** To hold a position for an artist or photographer. The governor *sat* for a portrait. **8.** To be a member of a group of officials. My cousin *sits* in the state assembly. **9.** To hold a session or meeting. This court will *sit* next week.
• **to sit down.** To lower oneself so that one is in a sitting position. When everyone *sat down,* the meeting began.
• **to sit up.** **1.** To raise oneself so that one is in a sitting position. The patient had to

at; āpe; fär; câre; end; mē; it; īce; pîerce; hot; ōld; sông, fôrk; oil; out; up; ūse; rüle; pùll; tûrn; chin; sing; shop; thin; **this;** hw in white; zh in treasure. The symbol ə stands for the unstressed vowel sound in about, taken, pencil, lemon, and circus.

S

sit up when lunch was served.   **2.** To sit with the upper part of the body in an upright position. *Sit up* straight!   **3.** To stay up; not go to bed. My parents and their guest *sat up* for half the night.
sit (sit) *verb,* **sat, sitting.**

Language Note

The verbs **sit** and **set** each have many different meanings. Their most common meanings, however, are sometimes confused. Remember that *set* means to put or place something in a certain position. Please *set* the books over there. *Sit* means to be in or take a certain position. We were *sitting* on the couch in the living room. Please *sit* down.

---

site   The position or location of something. Our house is in a mountain *site* with a beautiful view. That town is the *site* of a major battle in the Civil War. ▲ Other words that sound like this are **cite** and **sight.**
site (sīt) *noun, plural* **sites.**

situate   To give a position to; place. A large garden was *situated* alongside the house.
sit·u·ate (sich′ü āt′) *verb,* **situated, situating.**

situation   **1.** A condition or state of affairs; circumstance. We found ourselves in a difficult *situation* when our car broke down. **2.** The work one is hired and paid to do; job. What is your *situation* with that company?
sit·u·a·tion (sich′ü ā′shən) *noun, plural* **situations.**

sit-up   A kind of exercise in which a person lying with the back flat on the floor rises to a sitting position without lifting the feet and then returns to the original position.
sit-up (sit′up′) *noun, plural* **sit-ups.**

six   One more than five; 6.
six (siks) *noun, plural* **sixes;** *adjective.*

sixteen   Six more than ten; 16.
six·teen (siks′tēn′) *noun, plural* **sixteens;** *adjective.*

sixteenth   Next after the fifteenth. *Adjective, noun.*
—One of sixteen equal parts; ¹⁄₁₆. *Noun.*
six·teenth (siks′tēnth′) *adjective; noun, plural* **sixteenths.**

sixth   Next after the fifth. *Adjective, noun.*
—One of six equal parts; ¹⁄₆. *Noun.*
sixth (siksth) *adjective; noun, plural* **sixths.**

sixtieth   Next after the fifty-ninth. *Adjective, noun.*

—One of sixty equal parts; ¹⁄₆₀. *Noun.*
six·ti·eth (siks′tē ith) *adjective; noun, plural* **sixtieths.**

sixty   Six times ten; 60.
six·ty (siks′tē) *noun, plural* **sixties;** *adjective.*

sizable   Quite large. A *sizable* amount of my salary is spent on rent. This word is also spelled **sizeable.**
siz·a·ble (sī′zə bəl) *adjective.*

size   **1.** The amount of space something takes up; the length, width, and height of something. Your room is the same *size* as mine.   **2.** Amount or number. Did you ask your parents to increase the *size* of your allowance? Our dancing class has increased in *size* since last year.   **3.** One of a series of measurements used for shoes, clothing, and other things sold in stores. What *size* shirt do you wear?
size (sīz) *noun, plural* **sizes.**

sizzle   To make a hissing or sputtering sound. The bacon *sizzled* as it cooked in the frying pan.
siz·zle (siz′əl) *verb,* **sizzled, sizzling.**

SK   Postal abbreviation for *Saskatchewan.*

skate¹   **1.** A special shoe with a metal runner attached to the sole; ice skate. It is used for moving over ice.   **2.** A special shoe with small wheels attached to the sole; roller skate. It is used for moving over a flat surface, like a sidewalk. *Noun.*
—To glide or move along on skates. The children can *skate* when the ice on the pond is thicker. *Verb.*
skate (skāt) *noun, plural* **skates;** *verb,* **skated, skating.**

doing a **sit-up**

skate²   A broad, flat fish that lives in salt water off the Pacific coast of the United States. Skates are related to sharks and rays.
skate (skāt) *noun, plural* **skates** or **skate.**

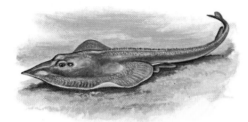

skate²

skateboard   A low, flat board that has wheels on the bottom, used for riding.
skate·board (skāt′bôrd′) *noun, plural* **skateboards.**

skeleton   1. A framework that supports and protects the body of an animal. Birds, fish, and humans have skeletons made up of bones or cartilage.   2. Any framework or structure used as a support. The workers built the steel *skeleton* of the building first.
skel·e·ton (skel′i tən) *noun, plural* **skeletons.**

skeptical   Having or showing doubt or disbelief. My classmates were *skeptical* of my plan to get the governor to visit our class.
skep·ti·cal (skep′ti kəl) *adjective.*

sketch   1. A rough, quick drawing. The artist made several *sketches* of the model before starting the painting.   2. A short piece of writing; essay or story. This *sketch* describes a room in a run-down hotel. *Noun.*
—1. To make a sketch of. I *sketched* an old barn for my art class.   2. To make a sketch or sketches. I want to learn to *sketch. Verb.*
sketch (skech) *noun, plural* **sketches;** *verb,* **sketched, sketching.**

sketchy   1. Done without detail; rough. The *sketchy* drawing showed only a few outlines of the buildings.   2. Incomplete; lacking much detail. The police got only a *sketchy* description of the suspect.
sketch·y (skech′ē) *adjective,* **sketchier, sketchiest.**

ski   1. One of a pair of long, narrow strips of wood, metal, or plastic that curve upward at the front. Skis are made to be attached to boots and are used for gliding over snow.   2. One of a pair of similar strips that are used for gliding over water; water ski. *Noun.*
—To glide on skis. We *skied* down the mountain. *Verb.*
ski (skē) *noun, plural* **skis;** *verb,* **skied, skiing.**

skid   To slide or slip out of control or sideways. The car *skidded* out of control. *Verb.*
—The act of skidding. The car went into a *skid* on the wet road. *Noun.*
skid (skid) *verb,* **skidded, skidding;** *noun, plural* **skids.**

skill   The power or ability to do something. Skill comes from practice, study, or experience. You show great *skill* in playing the piano. My neighbor works with children who have poor reading *skills.*
skill (skil) *noun, plural* **skills.**

skilled   1. Having or showing skill and ability. That *skilled* mechanic repairs old cars.   2. Requiring special ability or training. The factory is hiring workers for *skilled* jobs.
skilled (skild) *adjective.*

skillet   A shallow pan with a handle. A skillet is used for frying.
skil·let (skil′it) *noun, plural* **skillets.**

skillful   Having or showing skill; expert. The gymnasts were *skillful.* That is a *skillful* portrait.
skill·ful (skil′fəl) *adjective.*

skim   1. To remove something that is floating from the surface of a liquid. The cook *skimmed* the fat from the soup.   2. To read quickly. *Skim* the newspaper for the baseball scores.   3. To move or move over lightly and swiftly. The sailboat *skimmed* easily across the lake. The kite *skimmed* the top of the tree.   4. To throw so as to bounce lightly across a surface. Let's see who can *skim* a stone the farthest across the pond.
skim (skim) *verb,* **skimmed, skimming.**

skim milk   Milk from which the cream has been removed. Another name for this is **skimmed milk.**

skin   1. The outer covering of the body of a person or other animal with a backbone. The skin protects the organs inside the body and is the sense organ for touch, temperature, and pain.   2. The outer covering or hide that is removed from a dead animal. The skins of such animals as calves and snakes are used to make shoes, handbags, and clothing.   3. Anything that is like skin. This apple has a bright red *skin. Noun.*
—To take off the skin from. I *skinned* my

at; āpe; fär; câre; end; mē; it; ice; pîerce; hot; ōld; sông, fôrk; oil; out; up; ūse; rüle; pu̇ll; tûrn; chin; sing; shop; thin; this; hw in white; zh in treasure. The symbol ə stands for the unstressed vowel sound in about, taken, pencil, lemon, and circus.

S

673

knees when I fell off my bicycle. The early trappers in America made a living by *skinning* animals and selling the hides. *Verb.*
• **by the skin of one's teeth.** By a very narrow margin; only just; barely. I passed the test *by the skin of my teeth.*
skin (skin) *noun, plural* **skins;** *verb,* **skinned, skinning.**

skin diving Swimming underwater for long periods of time. A face mask and flippers, and sometimes an oxygen tank or a snorkel, are used in skin diving.

skinny Very thin. You were very *skinny* when you were sick.
skin·ny (skin′ē) *adjective,* **skinnier, skinniest.**

skip **1.** To spring or bound along, hopping lightly on one foot and then on the other. The children *skipped* down the path. **2.** To jump or leap over. We *skipped* rope in the playground. **3.** To pass by or leave out. *Skip* the arithmetic problems you can't do. **4.** To bounce or cause to bounce across a surface. The boat *skipped* across the water. Let's *skip* stones across the pond. **5.** To not go to or attend. They *skipped* the meeting last night. **6.** To be promoted to the next higher grade without attending. The bright student *skipped* fifth grade. *Verb.*
—A light springing or jumping step. I took a *skip* to avoid the puddle. *Noun.*
skip (skip) *verb,* **skipped, skipping;** *noun, plural* **skips.**

skirt **1.** A piece of clothing that is worn by women or girls. It hangs down from the waist. Skirts are worn with a blouse, sweater, or other garment on top. **2.** The part of a dress or similar piece of clothing that hangs down from the waist. *Noun.*
—To move or lie along the border or edge of. The airplane *skirted* the canyon. The highway *skirts* the town. *Verb.*
skirt (skûrt) *noun, plural* **skirts;** *verb,* **skirted, skirting.**

skit A short, usually funny play. Our class wrote a *skit* to perform for Thanksgiving.
skit (skit) *noun, plural* **skits.**

skull The bony framework of the head in animals that have a backbone. The skull serves to protect the brain.
skull (skul) *noun, plural* **skulls.**

skunk **1.** An animal of the

skunk

weasel family that has a bushy tail and black fur with white stripes along its back. Skunks can spray a strong, bad-smelling liquid when frightened or attacked. They are found only in North and South America. **2.** A mean person who is worthy of contempt.
skunk (skungk) *noun, plural* **skunks.**

sky The space or air above the earth. On clear days, the sky has a light blue color.
sky (skī) *noun, plural* **skies.**

skydiving The act or sport of jumping from an airplane and falling as far as is safe before opening a parachute.
sky·div·ing (skī′dī′ving) *noun.*

skylark A small European bird that sings while it is flying. The skylark has brown feathers with marks of black and white.
sky·lark (skī′lärk′) *noun, plural* **skylarks.**

skylight A window in a ceiling or roof. Some skylights can be opened and closed.
sky·light (skī′līt′) *noun, plural* **skylights.**

skyline **1.** The outline of buildings, mountains, or other objects as seen against the sky. We saw the city's *skyline* as we drove over the bridge. **2.** The line at which the earth and sky seem to come together; horizon. The sunset turned the *skyline* red and orange.
sky·line (skī′līn′) *noun, plural* **skylines.**

skyrocket A kind of firecracker that explodes high in the air and produces a shower of colored sparks. *Noun.*
—To rise suddenly and quickly. The cost of food *skyrocketed* last year. *Verb.*
sky·rock·et (skī′rok′it) *noun, plural* **skyrockets;** *verb,* **skyrocketed, skyrocketing.**

skyscrapers

skyscraper A very tall building. Big cities often have have many *skyscrapers.*
sky·scrap·er (skī′skrā′pər) *noun, plural* **skyscrapers.**

slab A broad, flat, thick piece or slice of stone, bread, or other material. The workers had to remove the concrete *slabs*.
slab (slab) *noun, plural* **slabs**.

slack **1.** Not tight or firm; loose. Tighten the *slack* rope. **2.** Slow and not rushed. We walked at a *slack* pace. *Adjective.*
—A part that hangs loose. Pull the rope tight to remove the *slack*. *Noun.*
slack (slak) *adjective,* **slacker, slackest;** *noun, plural* **slacks**.

slacks Long pants for casual wear.
slacks (slaks) *plural noun.*

slain Past participle of **slay**. The dragon was *slain*. Look up **slay** for more information.
slain (slān) *verb.*

slam **1.** To close with force and a loud noise. Please don't *slam* the door. **2.** To throw, move, or put with force and a loud noise. I'm sorry I *slammed* the phone down. **3.** To strike or hit with force and a loud noise. The batter *slammed* the ball. *Verb.*
—A forceful and noisy closing or striking. The door closed with a *slam*. *Noun.*
slam (slam) *verb,* **slammed, slamming;** *noun, plural* **slams**.

slander A false statement made to damage a person's reputation. The *slander* kept the senator from being reelected. *Noun.*
—To utter false and damaging statements about a person. The mayor said the governor had *slandered* the city officials. *Verb.*
slan·der (slan′dər) *noun; verb.*

slang An informal kind of language used in everyday conversation. Slang uses new words and new and different meanings for old words. The use of slang helps to keep language lively and interesting.
slang (slang) *noun.*

Language Note

Most **slang** is used for only a short time, and then it disappears from the language. Some slang words and phrases that people once said but we no longer use today are *skiddoo*, meaning "go away," and *the cat's pajamas*, meaning "wonderful." There are other words, however, that were slang at first and are now part of our standard language. *Kidnap, skyscraper,* and *jazz* were all considered slang at one time. Slang words do make our language interesting, but in most cases you should use slang only in everyday conversation, not in writing and formal speaking.

slant To run or slope away from a straight line. The roof *slants* toward the ground. I *slanted* the ladder against the wall. *Verb.*
—A sloping direction, line, or surface. Hang the picture straight, not on a *slant*. *Noun.*
slant (slant) *verb,* **slanted, slanting;** *noun, plural* **slants**.

slap A sharp, quick blow with the open hand or something flat. He greeted his friend with a *slap* on the back. *Noun.*
—**1.** To hit with a sharp, quick blow. She *slapped* the fly with an old magazine. **2.** To put or throw with noise and force. Don't *slap* your books down on the desk. *Verb.*
slap (slap) *noun, plural* **slaps;** *verb,* **slapped, slapping**.

slash **1.** To cut or try to cut with a sweeping stroke of a knife or another sharp object. The vandals *slashed* the tires of our car. The sailor *slashed* at the rope with a knife. **2.** To lower or decrease greatly. The store *slashed* its prices. After the war, the country *slashed* the size of its army. *Verb.*
—**1.** A sweeping stroke with great force. The *slash* of the whip made a sound like a crack. **2.** A long cut or wound. The patient had a *slash* on the leg. **3.** A great lowering or decrease. The store advertised a *slash* in the prices of all its clothing. *Noun.*
slash (slash) *verb,* **slashed, slashing;** *noun, plural* **slashes**.

slat A thin, flat strip of wood, metal, or other material. The *slats* on the back of the chair are coming loose.
slat (slat) *noun, plural* **slats**.

slate **1.** A bluish gray rock that splits easily into thin layers. Slate is used to make blackboards and garden walks, and to cover roofs. **2.** A piece of this rock that has been cut for some use. The roof had many broken *slates*. **3.** A dark, bluish gray color.
slate (slāt) *noun, plural* **slates**.

slaughter **1.** The act of killing an animal or animals for use as food. **2.** A brutal killing; massacre. *Noun.*
—**1.** To kill for use as food. **2.** To kill in a brutal way; massacre. *Verb.*
slaugh·ter (slô′tər) *noun, plural* **slaughters;** *verb,* **slaughtered, slaughtering**.

at; āpe; fär; câre; end; mē; it; īce; pîerce; hot; ōld; sông, fôrk; oil; out; up; ūse; rüle; pùll; tûrn; chin; sing; shop; thin; this; hw in white; zh in treasure. The symbol ə stands for the unstressed vowel sound in about, taken, pencil, lemon, and circus.

S

675

slave   **1.** A person who is owned by another person.   **2.** A person who is controlled by another person, a habit, or other influence. When I do my math homework, I try not to be a *slave* to my calculator.   **3.** A person who works or is made to work hard and long. *Noun.*
—To work hard and long. The writer *slaved* at the assignment for hours. *Verb.*
  slave (slāv) *noun, plural* **slaves;** *verb,* **slaved, slaving.**

Word History

The word **slave** comes from a Latin word meaning "Slav." The Slavs are a group of people who live in eastern and central Europe. In the Middle Ages, many Slavs had been conquered and made to work as slaves.

---

slavery   **1.** The practice of owning slaves. **2.** The condition of being a slave.
  slav·er·y (slā′və rē) *noun.*

slay   To kill in a violent way. In this story, a brave knight *slays* a large, frightening dragon.   ▲ Another word that sounds like this is **sleigh.**
  slay (slā) *verb,* **slew, slain, slaying.**

sled   A wooden framework mounted on runners. A sled is used to carry people or loads over the snow. *Noun.*
—To ride on a sled. The children *sledded* down the hill. *Verb.*
  sled (sled) *noun, plural* **sleds;** *verb,* **sledded, sledding.**

sledgehammer   A heavy hammer that has a long handle that is held with both hands.
  sledge·ham·mer (slej′ham′ər) *noun, plural* **sledgehammers.**

sleek   **1.** Smooth and shiny. That cat with the new kittens has *sleek* black fur. **2.** Looking healthy and well cared for. A *sleek* horse won the race.
  sleek (slēk) *adjective,* **sleeker, sleekest.**

sleep   **1.** A time or condition of rest that occurs naturally and regularly in humans and other animals. During sleep, a person becomes unaware of most things, and the body regains its strength and energy.   **2.** A condition that resembles sleep. A hibernating bear is sometimes said to be sleeping. *Noun.*
—**1.** To be in a state of sleep; be asleep. A baby *sleeps* a large part of the day.   **2.** To be in a state that resembles sleep. *Verb.*
  sleep (slēp) *noun; verb,* **slept, sleeping.**

sleeping bag   A long bag that is lined or padded to keep a person warm. It is often used for sleeping outdoors.

sleepy   **1.** Ready for or needing sleep. I feel *sleepy.*   **2.** Dull or quiet. We live in a *sleepy* little town.
  sleep·y (slē′pē) *adjective,* **sleepier, sleepiest.**

sleet   Frozen or partly frozen rain. *Noun.*
—To shower sleet. The roads were very slippery because it had *sleeted* all day. *Verb.*
  sleet (slēt) *noun; verb,* **sleeted, sleeting.**

sleeve   The part of a piece of clothing that covers all or part of the arm.
  sleeve (slēv) *noun, plural* **sleeves.**

sleigh   A carriage on runners that is drawn by a horse. A sleigh is used for traveling over snow or ice.   ▲ Another word that sounds like this is **slay.**
  sleigh (slā) *noun, plural* **sleighs.**

slender   **1.** Not big around; thin. Everyone in my family is *slender.* The new dining room chairs have *slender* legs.   **2.** Small in size or amount. The candidate won the election by only a *slender* margin.
  slen·der (slen′dər) *adjective,* **slenderer, slenderest.**

slept   Past tense and past participle of **sleep.** I was very tired and *slept* until noon. Look up **sleep** for more information.
  slept (slept) *verb.*

slew   Past tense of **slay.** The hunter *slew* the deer. Look up **slay** for more information.
  slew (slü) *verb.*

slice   A thin, flat piece cut from something larger. May I have a *slice* of bread? *Noun.*
—**1.** To cut into a thin, flat piece or pieces. I *sliced* the bread.   **2.** To move or cut through like a knife. The shark's fin *sliced* the water. The saw *sliced* through the board. *Verb.*
  slice (slīs) *noun, plural* **slices;** *verb,* **sliced, slicing.**

slick   **1.** Smooth and shiny. The horse had a *slick* brown coat.   **2.** Smooth and slippery. A newly waxed floor is *slick. Adjective.*
—A smooth or slippery place on a surface. The boat left a *slick* of oil on the water. *Noun.*
  slick (slik) *adjective,* **slicker, slickest;** *noun, plural* **slicks.**

slid   The past tense and a past participle of **slide.** Look up **slide** for more information.
  slid (slid) *verb.*

slidden   A past participle of **slide.** Look up **slide** for more information.
  slid·den (slid′ən) *verb.*

slide **1.** To move or cause to move smoothly, easily, or quietly. The wet bar of soap *slid* across the floor. My friend *slid* into the seat next to me. **2.** To fall or move suddenly from a position. The truck *slid* off the icy road into a ditch. *Verb.*
—**1.** The act of sliding. Let's *slide* down the hill on our sleds. **2.** A smooth surface for sliding. I like the *slide* in the playground. **3.** A small sheet of glass or plastic. Objects are put on a glass slide and looked at under a microscope. Slides with pictures on them are put in a projector and shown on a screen. **4.** The fall of a mass of rock, snow, or other material down a slope. The road was closed because of rock *slides. Noun.*
slide (slīd) *verb,* **slid, slid** or **slidden, sliding;** *noun, plural* **slides.**

slide

slight **1.** Not much or not important; small. There is a *slight* chance of rain. **2.** Not big around; thin. My older cousin is very *slight* and weighs only 100 pounds. *Adjective.*
—To treat as unimportant; not pay enough attention to. I felt I had been *slighted* when I was not invited to your picnic. *Verb.*
—The act of treating someone or something as unimportant. They weren't invited to the party, and they resented the *slight. Noun.*
slight (slīt) *adjective,* **slighter, slightest;** *verb,* **slighted, slighting;** *noun, plural* **slights.**

slim **1.** Small in thickness; thin. The fashion model had a very *slim* figure. **2.** Small in amount; slight. The team felt it had only a *slim* chance of winning the championship game. *Adjective.*
—To become slim. You can *slim* down by dieting. *Verb.*
slim (slim) *adjective,* **slimmer, slimmest;** *verb,* **slimmed, slimming.**

slime **1.** Wet, soft, sticky mud. **2.** A thin, sticky substance given off by some animals, such as snails.
slime (slīm) *noun.*

slimy Of, covered with, or like slime; disgusting. Don't go in the *slimy* pond.
slim·y (slī′mē) *adjective,* **slimier, slimiest.**

sling **1.** A device for throwing stones. A sling is usually made of a piece of leather with a string fastened to each end. **2.** A loop of cloth hanging down from the neck to support an injured arm or hand. When I broke my arm, I had to wear a *sling. Noun.*
—**1.** To hang with a sling or strap. The workers *slung* bags of potatoes over their shoulders. **2.** To hang or throw loosely. The campers *slung* the hammock between two trees. *Verb.*
sling (sling) *noun, plural* **slings;** *verb,* **slung, slinging.**

slingshot A Y-shaped piece of wood, metal, or other material with an elastic band fastened to the tips of the two upper ends. A slingshot is used to shoot stones or other small objects.
sling·shot (sling′shot′) *noun, plural* **slingshots.**

slip¹ **1.** To move suddenly from a position or out of control; slide. The man *slipped* on the icy sidewalk. The soapy glass *slipped* out of her hands. **2.** To move or go quietly. The thief *slipped* out of the house. **3.** To move or cause to move smoothly and easily. A little oil will help the ring to *slip* off your finger. **4.** To put or give quietly and quickly. Don't *slip* each other notes during class. **5.** To fail to be noticed or remembered. Summer vacation always seems to *slip* by. I know you, but your name *slips* my mind. **6.** To put on or take off clothing quickly and easily. He *slipped* into his pajamas. **7.** To make a mis-

at; āpe; fär; câre; end; mē; it; īce; pîerce; hot; ōld; sông, fôrk; oil; out; up; ūse; rüle; pull; tûrn; chin; sing; shop; thin; this; hw in white; zh in treasure. The symbol ə stands for the unstressed vowel sound in about, taken, pencil, lemon, and circus.

S

take. She only *slipped* once during the test.
8. To become worse or lower. Your score
slipped on this test. *Verb.*
—**1.** The act of slipping. I fell as a result of a
slip on the icy sidewalk. **2.** A piece of clothing worn under a woman's or girl's dress or
skirt. A slip is made out of a light material
like cotton or nylon. **3.** A mistake or error.
The thieves would have been successful, but
one little *slip* gave them away. *Noun.*
• **to slip up.** To make a mistake. I *slipped
up* on the first question of the test.
slip (slip) *verb,* **slipped, slipping;** *noun,*
plural **slips.**

slip² **1.** A small piece of paper, cloth, or any
other material. I wrote my friend's telephone
number on a *slip* of paper. **2.** A small shoot
or twig cut from a plant.
slip (slip) *noun, plural* **slips.**

slipper A light, low shoe that is easily
slipped on or off the foot. Slippers are worn
indoors.
slip·per (slip′ər) *noun, plural* **slippers.**

slippery **1.** Causing or likely to cause slipping or sliding. Rain made the roads *slippery.*
2. Slipping or sliding away easily. The wet
fish was *slippery.* **3.** Not trustworthy. The
villain was a *slippery* character.
slip·per·y (slip′ə rē) *adjective,* **slipperier,
slipperiest.**

slit A long, narrow cut or opening. I opened
the door a little and looked through the *slit.*
Cut two *slits* in the paper. *Noun.*
—To cut or make a slit or slits in. *Slit* open
the envelope with a dull knife. *Verb.*
slit (slit) *noun, plural* **slits;** *verb,* **slitted,
slitting.**

slither To slide or glide like a snake. The
snake *slithered* across the hot sand.
slith·er (slith′ər) *verb,* **slithered,
slithering.**

sliver A thin, often pointed piece that has
been broken, cut, or torn off; splinter. I got a
sliver of wood in my toe. I'd like a *sliver* of
pie.
sliv·er (sliv′ər) *noun, plural* **slivers.**

slogan A phrase or motto. Slogans are used
by a person, a group, or a business. "No taxation without representation" was a *slogan*
used by American colonists.
slo·gan (slō′gən) *noun, plural* **slogans.**

Word History

The word **slogan** comes from a word
meaning "battle cry" in the language
spoken in the highlands of Scotland.

sloop A sailboat with one mast and sails
that run from front to rear.
sloop (slüp) *noun, plural* **sloops.**

slope To lie or cause to lie at an angle between flat and upright. The road *slopes* toward the river. *Verb.*
—**1.** A line, piece of ground, or any surface
that is not flat or level. The house was built
on a *slope.* **2.** The amount that something
slopes or slants. The river bank has a steep
slope at this point. *Noun.*
slope (slōp) *verb,* **sloped, sloping;** *noun,*
plural **slopes.**

sloppy **1.** Not neat; messy. Your clothes
looked very *sloppy* after you had slept overnight in them. **2.** Careless. *Sloppy* addition
gave you the wrong answer. **3.** Very wet or
covered with mud or slush. The roads are
sloppy from the snow and rain today.
slop·py (slop′ē) *adjective,* **sloppier,
sloppiest.**

slot A narrow, straight opening or groove.
Put the coin in the *slot.*
slot (slot) *noun, plural* **slots.**

sloth **1.** A slow-moving animal that lives
in the forests of
South America.
Sloths use their
long arms and
legs and their
curved claws to
hang upside
down from trees.
2. Laziness.
sloth (slôth *or*
slōth) *noun,*
plural **sloths.**

sloth

slouch **1.** To
sit, stand, or walk in a loose, drooping way.
Sit up and don't *slouch.* **2.** To hang or bend
down. Don't *slouch* your shoulders. *Verb.*
—**1.** A drooping of the head and shoulders
while sitting, standing, or walking. The tired
hikers walked with a *slouch.* **2.** An awkward, lazy, or sloppy person. Do your share
of the work; don't be a *slouch. Noun.*
slouch (slouch) *verb,* **slouched,
slouching;** *noun, plural* **slouches.**

slovenly Untidy or careless, especially in
dress or appearance. It's important not to
look *slovenly* at work.
slov·en·ly (sluv′ən lē) *adjective,*
slovenlier, slovenliest.

slow **1.** Acting, moving, or happening with
little speed; not fast or quick. The student
was *slow* to answer the question. It was a
slow climb up the mountain. **2.** Behind the
correct time. Your watch is *slow.* **3.** Not

quick to learn or understand. I am *slow* in arithmetic. **4.** Not easily excited or moved. I'm *slow* to anger. **5.** Not busy or interesting; dull. It was *slow* at work. *Adjective.*
—In a slow manner. Drive *slow. Adverb.*
—To make or become slow or slower. The car *slowed* to a halt. *Verb.*
slow (slō) *adjective,* **slower, slowest;** *adverb; verb,* **slowed, slowing.**

slug¹ **1.** An animal that looks like a snail, but either has a very small shell or none at all. Some slugs eat plants and can become harmful pests in gardens. **2.** A piece of lead or other metal that is fired from a gun. **3.** A round, flat piece of metal. A slug is used in place of a coin in a vending machine or other device that requires coins. It is against the law to use slugs.
slug (slug) *noun, plural* **slugs.**

slug² To strike or hit hard. The batter *slugged* the ball over the fence. *Verb.*
—A hard or heavy strike or hit. Give that nail a good *slug* with the hammer. *Noun.*
slug (slug) *verb,* **slugged, slugging;** *noun, plural* **slugs.**

sluggish **1.** Not energetic or alert. I feel *sluggish* today because I did not get enough sleep. **2.** Slow in movement or action. Ice cream sales are *sluggish* in the winter and very active in the summer.
slug·gish (slug′ish) *adjective.*

sluice **1.** An artificially made channel for water that has a gate or valve for controlling the amount of flow. **2.** The gate or valve of such a channel. **3.** A long, sloping trough through which water is run. A sluice is often used for separating gold ore from dirt.
sluice (slüs) *noun, plural* **sluices.**

slum A poor, crowded section of a city. Bad housing and dirty living conditions are some of the problems in slums.
slum (slum) *noun, plural* **slums.**

slumber **1.** To sleep or spend in sleeping. The baby *slumbered* peacefully. You *slumbered* all day. **2.** To be quiet or calm. The town *slumbered. Verb.*
—A sleep. In the fairy tale, the prince woke the princess from her long *slumber. Noun.*
slum·ber (slum′bər) *verb,* **slumbered, slumbering;** *noun.*

slump To fall or sink suddenly or heavily. I *slumped* in my favorite chair. *Verb.*
—A sharp, sudden fall or decline. This store has had a *slump* in sales every summer. The baseball team was in a *slump* and had lost six of its last seven games. *Noun.*
slump (slump) *verb,* **slumped, slumping;** *noun, plural* **slumps.**

slung Past tense and past participle of **sling.** I *slung* the backpack over my shoulder. Look up **sling** for more information.
slung (slung) *verb.*

slush Partly melted snow or ice.
slush (slush) *noun.*

sly **1.** Clever and shrewd; crafty. The *sly* thief was never caught. **2.** Mischievous in a playful way. One child gave me a *sly* glance.
● **on the sly.** In a secret or crafty way. The treasurer was stealing part of the club's funds *on the sly.*
sly (slī) *adjective,* **slier** or **slyer, sliest** or **slyest.**

smack **1.** To press together and open quickly so as to make a sharp sound. The boy *smacked* his lips when he saw the food. **2.** To strike or hit sharply. The car *smacked* into the fence. **3.** To kiss loudly. I *smacked* my mother on the cheek. *Verb.*
—**1.** A loud slap. The dog got a *smack* for chewing on the furniture. **2.** A loud kiss. The boy got a *smack* on his cheek from his sister for the gift he had given her. *Noun.*
—Directly or squarely. The child rode the bicycle *smack* into a tree. *Adverb.*
smack (smak) *verb,* **smacked, smacking;** *noun, plural* **smacks;** *adverb.*

sluice

small **1.** Not large; little. A mouse is a *small* animal. The *small* town has only three stores. The *small* audience sat in just three rows of seats. **2.** Not important. We had a *small* problem trying to decide who should

at; āpe; fär; câre; end; mē; it; īce; pîerce; hot; ōld; sông, fôrk; oil; out; up; ūse; rüle; pˇull; tûrn; chin; sing; shop; thin; <u>th</u>is; hw in white; zh in treasure. The symbol ə stands for the unstressed vowel sound in about, taken, pencil, lemon, and circus.

S

679

give the speech. **3.** Soft or weak. The shy student replied in a *small* voice. **4.** Buying and selling goods or doing some other activity in a limited way. Each one of these shops is a *small* business. *Adjective.*
—A small or narrow part. Be careful you don't strain the *small* of your back when you lift that heavy carton. *Noun.*
> **small** (smôl) *adjective*, **smaller, smallest;** *noun.*

small intestine   A part of the digestive system that forms a long, coiled tube which connects the stomach and the large intestine. As food passes through the small intestine it is broken down into materials the body can use, and these materials are absorbed into the bloodstream.

small letter   A letter that is not a capital letter. The letter "a" is a *small letter,* and "A" is a capital letter.

smallpox   A certain very contagious disease caused by a virus. People with smallpox have a high fever and bumps on the skin that can leave permanent scars.
> **small·pox** (smôl′poks′) *noun.*

smart   **1.** Clever or intelligent; bright. She is a *smart* girl who does well in school. It was very *smart* of him to figure out the answer. **2.** Amusing and clever in a way that fails to show respect. My parents told me not to act so *smart.* **3.** Neat and trim. You look very *smart.* **4.** Stylish or fashionable. That store is selling *smart* new dresses. **5.** Quick or brisk; lively. The soldiers marched at a *smart* pace. *Adjective.*
—**1.** To cause or feel a sharp, stinging pain. The soap *smarted* when it got in my eyes. Our faces *smarted* from the icy cold wind. **2.** To feel hurt. The twins *smarted* from the scolding their parents gave them. *Verb.*
> **smart** (smärt) *adjective*, **smarter, smartest;** *verb*, **smarted, smarting.**

smash   **1.** To break violently into pieces. The child accidentally *smashed* the window. The plate fell and *smashed* on the floor. **2.** To hit with a hard blow. The car *smashed* into a tree. **3.** To destroy, crush, or defeat completely. The soldiers *smashed* the enemy. *Verb.*
—The act or sound of breaking violently. We heard the *smash* of glass from the next room. *Noun.*
> **smash** (smash) *verb*, **smashed, smashing;** *noun, plural* **smashes.**

smear   **1.** To cover or make dirty with something wet, sticky, or greasy. The girl had *smeared* her dress with mud. **2.** To spread something wet, sticky, or greasy on something else. He *smeared* paint all over his

hands. **3.** To become or cause to become blurred or messy. The wet paint *smeared* when I touched it. **4.** To harm a person's reputation. One candidate for governor *smeared* the others by saying that they were crooks. *Verb.*
—A mark or stain made by smearing. There was a *smear* of dirt on the cat's fur. *Noun.*
> **smear** (smîr) *verb*, **smeared, smearing;** *noun, plural* **smears.**

smell   **1.** To sense an odor by using the nose. Do you *smell* gas? **2.** To test or sample by smelling; sniff. The dog *smells* everyone that comes into the house. **3.** To have or give off an odor. The kitchen *smelled* of fish. **4.** To have or give off an unpleasant odor. The spoiled milk *smelled. Verb.*
—**1.** The sense by which odors are recognized. Taste and *smell* are often affected by colds. **2.** An odor or scent. I love the *smell* of the sea. **3.** The act of smelling. Won't you have a *smell* of this rose? *Noun.*
> **smell** (smel) *verb*, **smelled** or **smelt, smelling;** *noun, plural* **smells.**

smelt¹   A small, thin, silver-colored fish found in cold waters of the Northern Hemisphere. It is caught for food.
> **smelt** (smelt) *noun, plural* **smelts** or **smelt.**

smelt¹

smelt²   To melt ore in order to separate the metal from it. The first step in making steel is to *smelt* iron ore.
> **smelt** (smelt) *verb*, **smelted, smelting.**

smile   An expression of the face that is made by turning up the corners of the mouth. A smile can show that a person is happy, amused, or being friendly. *Noun.*
—To have or give a smile. The children *smiled* when they saw the clown. *Verb.*
> **smile** (smīl) *noun, plural* **smiles;** *verb*, **smiled, smiling.**

smock   A loose garment that looks like a long shirt. A smock is worn over other clothing to protect it.
> **smock** (smok) *noun, plural* **smocks.**

smog A combination of smoke and fog in the air. Smog is found especially over cities where there are factories and many cars.
smog (smog) *noun.*

Word History

The word **smog** was made using the first two letters of *smoke* and the last two letters of *fog.*

smoke **1.** A gas given off by something that is burning. The carbon particles in smoke give it a gray color. **2.** The act of drawing in and breathing out smoke from burning tobacco. *Noun.*
—**1.** To send out or produce smoke. We could see a chimney *smoking* in the distance. **2.** To draw in and breathe out smoke from burning tobacco. **3.** To preserve food by exposing it to smoke. This company *smokes* ham and sausage. *Verb.*
smoke (smōk) *noun, plural* **smokes;** *verb,* **smoked, smoking.**

smoke alarm A device that warns people of a fire by giving off a loud noise when smoke is present. Smoke alarms are often installed in homes, schools, and offices.

smokestack A tall chimney or pipe from which smoke is released. Smokestacks are used by factories and big ships.
smoke·stack (smōk'stak') *noun, plural* **smokestacks.**

smokestacks

smoky **1.** Giving off or filled with smoke. We moved away from the *smoky* campfire. It was hard to see across the *smoky* room. **2.** Like the color or taste of smoke. They own a beautiful *smoky* gray cat.
smok·y (smō'kē) *adjective,* **smokier, smokiest.**

smolder **1.** To burn and smoke with few or no flames. When I awoke, the campfire was still *smoldering.* **2.** To exist or continue in a hidden condition. Anger against the dictator *smoldered* in the minds of the people.
smol·der (smōl'dər) *verb,* **smoldered, smoldering.**

smooth **1.** Having a surface that is not uneven or rough. The baby has such *smooth* skin. **2.** Even or gentle in movement. The pilot made a *smooth* landing. **3.** Free from difficulties or trouble. We are making *smooth* progress in our plans to start a gardening club. **4.** Able and skillful. That *smooth* skater made difficult turns appear easy. *Adjective.*
—**1.** To make even or level or remove what is keeping something from being smooth. We *smoothed* the dirt around the shrubs we had planted. **2.** To free from difficulty; make easy. The club president *smoothed* the way for the vice-president to become president next year. *Verb.*
smooth (smū̱th) *adjective,* **smoother, smoothest;** *verb,* **smoothed, smoothing.**

smother **1.** To keep from or kill by keeping from breathing air. The avalanche *smothered* several climbers. **2.** To be kept from breathing air. The cat will *smother* in that small box. **3.** To put out or cause to burn less by covering. We used dirt to *smother* our campfire. **4.** To cover thickly. The cook *smothered* the steak with onions. **5.** To hide or hold back. I *smothered* a yawn.
smoth·er (smuth'ər) *verb,* **smothered, smothering.**

smudge To make or become dirty or smeared. My dirty hands *smudged* the white towel. Wet ink *smudges* easily. *Verb.*
—A dirty mark or stain. Someone's dirty hand left a *smudge* on the wall. *Noun.*
smudge (smuj) *verb,* **smudged, smudging;** *noun, plural* **smudges.**

at; āpe; fär; câre; end; mē; it; īce; pîerce; hot; ōld; sông, fôrk; oil; out; up; ūse; rüle; pu̇ll; tûrn; chin; sing; shop; thin; <u>th</u>is; hw in white; zh in treasure. The symbol ə stands for the unstressed vowel sound in about, taken, pencil, lemon, and circus.

S

681

smug So certain or pleased about one's own worth that one annoys other people. The contest winners were so *smug* that no one else would talk to them.
smug (smug) *adjective.*

smuggle 1. To take in or out of a country secretly and against the law. The thief tried to *smuggle* the jewels out of the country. 2. To take or carry secretly. Who *smuggled* a gun to one of the prisoners?
smug·gle (smug'əl) *verb,* smuggled, smuggling.

snack A small amount of food or drink eaten between regular meals.
snack (snak) *noun, plural* snacks.

snail 1. An animal that has a soft body protected by a shell shaped like a spiral. Snails are mollusks and are found in water and on land. 2. A person who moves very slowly.
snail (snāl) *noun, plural* snails.

snail

snake 1. A kind of animal that has a long body covered with scales and no legs, arms, or wings. Snakes are reptiles that move by curving and then straightening out their bodies. Some snakes have a poisonous bite. 2. A person who is sly or evil or cannot be trusted.
snake (snāk) *noun, plural* snakes.

snap 1. To make or cause to make a sudden, sharp sound. The dry wood *snapped* as it burned. If you *snap* your fingers, the dog will come. 2. To break suddenly and sharply. The twig *snapped* when I stepped on it. 3. To move, act, or speak quickly and sharply. The soldiers *snapped* to attention as the general walked by. 4. To open, close, or move into a position with a sudden, sharp sound. We closed the door and the lock *snapped* shut. 5. To seize or snatch suddenly or eagerly. The fish *snapped* at the bait. 6. To take a photograph. I *snapped* a picture of my cousin. *Verb.*
—1. A sudden, sharp or breaking sound or action. The stem of the glass broke with a *snap.* 2. A fastener or clasp that makes a snapping sound. My jacket has *snaps.* 3. A sudden bite or snatch. The dog took a *snap* at the mail carrier. 4. A short period of cold weather. 5. A thin, crisp cookie. The bakery sells lemon and ginger *snaps.* 6. Something that is easy to do. That spelling test was a *snap. Noun.*

—Made or done quickly and with little thought. You think about things for a while and never make a *snap* decision. *Adjective.*
snap (snap) *verb,* snapped, snapping; *noun, plural* snaps; *adjective.*

snapdragon A garden plant that has spikes of flowers in yellow, pink, white, or many other colors.
snap·dra·gon (snap'drag'ən) *noun, plural* snapdragons.

snapshot An informal photograph that is taken with a small, often inexpensive camera.
snap·shot (snap'shot') *noun, plural* snapshots.

snare A trap for catching small animals. A snare has a noose that jerks tight around the animal when the trap is set off. *Noun.*
—To catch with or as if with a snare. The hunter *snared* a rabbit. The police *snared* the thief. *Verb.*
snare (snâr) *noun, plural* snares; *verb,* snared, snaring.

snapdragon

snare drum A small drum with wires or strings stretched across the bottom part. When the top of the drum is struck, the wires vibrate and give the drum a rattling sound.

snarl[1] 1. To growl while showing the teeth. The dog *snarled* at the stranger. 2. To speak in an angry, growling way. The plumber *snarled* at the leaking pipe. *Verb.*
—An angry growl. *Noun.*
snarl (snärl) *verb,* snarled, snarling; *noun, plural* snarls.

snarl[2] 1. A tangled or knotted mass. Please help me brush the *snarls* out of my hair. 2. A confused condition. The accident caused a traffic *snarl* on the highway. *Noun.*
—1. To make or become tangled or knotted. The wind and rain *snarled* your hair. The kite's string could *snarl* in that tree. 2. To make or become confused. The snowstorm *snarled* the highways. *Verb.*
snarl (snärl) *noun, plural* snarls; *verb,* snarled, snarling.

snatch To seize or grab suddenly or quickly. My parents scolded me for *snatching* the grapes from the counter. *Verb.*
—1. The act of seizing or grabbing suddenly and quickly. 2. A small amount. We could

hear *snatches* of the conversation at the next table. *Noun.*
> **snatch** (snach) *verb,* **snatched, snatching;** *noun, plural* **snatches.**

sneak   To move, act, or take in a secret or sly way. The children *sneaked* into the theater by a side door. Did you *sneak* an extra orange from the kitchen? *Verb.*
—A person who is sly and dishonest. Those two students are such *sneaks* that I wouldn't trust them to tell the truth. *Noun.*
—Done, planned, or acting in a secret or sly manner. The army was surprised by the *sneak* attack. *Adjective.*
> **sneak** (snēk) *verb,* **sneaked** or **snuck, sneaking;** *noun, plural* **sneaks;** *adjective.*

sneaker   A shoe made of canvas or other material with a rubber sole.
> **sneak·er** (snē'kər) *noun, plural* **sneakers.**

sneaky   Like a sneak; secret and sly. It was *sneaky* of them to go out by the back door so that their parents wouldn't know.
> **sneak·y** (snē'kē) *adjective,* **sneakier, sneakiest.**

sneer   An expression of the face or remark that shows hatred or scorn. The rude child answered our question with a *sneer. Noun.*
—To show or say with a sneer. The thief *sneered* at the police. She *sneered* an answer to the insult. *Verb.*
> **sneer** (snîr) *noun, plural* **sneers;** *verb,* **sneered, sneering.**

sneeze   To put forth air from the nose and mouth in a sudden, violent way. Ever since I caught this cold I have been *sneezing. Verb.*
—The act of sneezing. I found my handkerchief just in time to cover my *sneeze. Noun.*
> **sneeze** (snēz) *verb,* **sneezed, sneezing;** *noun, plural* **sneezes.**

snicker   A sly, disrespectful laugh. I heard *snickers* from the audience when my false beard fell off during the play. *Noun.*
—To laugh in a sly, disrespectful way. Some of the students *snickered* during the boring speech. *Verb.*
> **snick·er** (snik'ər) *noun, plural* **snickers;** *verb,* **snickered, snickering.**

sniff   **1.** To take in air through the nose in a short, quick breath. The kitten *sniffed* at its food.   **2.** To take in through the nose. We *sniffed* the clean mountain air.   **3.** To smell by sniffing. *Sniff* this flower. *Verb.*
—The act or sound of sniffing. *Noun.*
> **sniff** (snif) *verb,* **sniffed, sniffing;** *noun, plural* **sniffs.**

sniffle   To sniff again and again because of a cold or to keep from crying. The unhappy child sat in the corner and *sniffled. Verb.*

—**the sniffles.** A condition that causes sniffing, such as a cold. My case of *the sniffles* didn't prevent me from going to the baseball game. *Noun.*
> **snif·fle** (snif'əl) *verb,* **sniffled, sniffling;** *plural noun.*

snip   To cut with scissors in short, quick strokes. *Snip* those loose threads off the dress. *Verb.*
—**1.** The act of snipping. The barber made a few last *snips* and finished the haircut.   **2.** A small piece that is snipped off. We took a *snip* of fabric to see if we could match it. *Noun.*
> **snip** (snip) *verb,* **snipped, snipping;** *noun, plural* **snips.**

snipe   A bird with a long bill and brown feathers that are spotted with black and white. Snipes live in marshes and swamps.
> **snipe** (snīp) *noun, plural* **snipes** or **snipe.**

snipe

snob   **1.** A person who places great value on wealth and social position.   **2.** A person who feels he or she is better than others.
> **snob** (snob) *noun, plural* **snobs.**

snooze   To sleep for a short time; nap; doze. I *snoozed* during the movie. *Verb.*
—A short sleep; nap. *Noun.*
> **snooze** (snüz) *verb,* **snoozed, snoozing;** *noun, plural* **snoozes.**

snore   To make harsh, rattling breathing sounds while sleeping. My roommate *snored* so loudly that I couldn't sleep. *Verb.*
—A harsh, rattling breathing sound made while sleeping. The sleeper let out a long, loud *snore. Noun.*
> **snore** (snôr) *verb,* **snored, snoring;** *noun, plural* **snores.**

snorkel   A tube through which a person can breathe while swimming with the face held underwater. We used masks with *snorkels* to look at the fish around the reef.
> **snor·kel** (snôr'kəl) *noun, plural* **snorkels.**

---

at; āpe; fär; câre; end; mē; it; ice; pîerce; hot; ōld; sông, fôrk; oil; out; up; ūse; rüle; pull; tûrn; chin; sing; shop; thin; this; hw in white; zh in treasure. The symbol ə stands for the unstressed vowel sound in about, taken, pencil, lemon, and circus.

S

683

snort   To force air through the nose noisily and with great force. The horse *snorted* and threw back its head. *Verb.*
—The sound or act of forcing air through the nose noisily and with great force. I showed my disbelief with a *snort. Noun.*
> **snort** (snôrt) *verb,* **snorted, snorting;** *noun, plural* **snorts.**

snout   The front part of an animal's head, including the nose, mouth, and jaws.
> **snout** (snout) *noun, plural* **snouts.**

snow   **1.** Soft, white crystals of ice that fall to earth as precipitation. Snow is formed when water vapor freezes in the air.   **2.** A fall of snow. *Noun.*
—To fall as snow. It *snowed* all day. *Verb.*
- **to snow in.**   To cover or surround with so much snow that a person cannot leave a place. After the blizzard, we were *snowed in* for two days.
> **snow** (snō) *noun, plural* **snows;** *verb,* **snowed, snowing.**

snowball   A ball made of snow packed together.
> **snow·ball** (snō′bôl′) *noun, plural* **snowballs.**

snowflake   One of the small ice crystals that fall as snow.
> **snow·flake** (snō′flāk′) *noun, plural* **snowflakes.**

snowman   A figure of a person made by shaping a mass of snow.
> **snow·man** (snō′man′) *noun, plural* **snowmen** (snō′men′).

snowmobile   A vehicle for travel on the snow. It has a motor and runners or skis.
> **snow·mo·bile** (snō′mō bēl′) *noun, plural* **snowmobiles**

snowplow   A wide, curved metal blade used to push snow off a road or other surface, or a vehicle having such a blade.
> **snow·plow** (snō′plou′) *noun, plural* **snowplows.**

snowshoe   A flat, webbed frame that is attached to boots and used for walking over deep snow without sinking into it.
> **snow·shoe** (snō′shü′) *noun, plural* **snowshoes.**

snowstorm   A storm with strong winds and much snow.
> **snow·storm** (snō′stôrm′) *noun, plural* **snowstorms.**

snowy   **1.** Covered with or having a lot of snow. The *snowy* streets looked clean and beautiful.   **2.** White like snow. The tree was covered with *snowy* blossoms.
> **snow·y** (snō′ē) *adjective,* **snowier, snowiest.**

snub   To treat someone coldly or with contempt, especially by ignoring the person. Do you know why my friend *snubbed* me and didn't come to my party? *Verb.*
—Treatment that is cold, full of contempt, or lacking in respect. *Noun.*
> **snub** (snub) *verb,* **snubbed, snubbing;** *noun, plural* **snubs.**

snug   **1.** Comfortable, warm, and cozy. It is nice to get into a *snug* bed on a cold night.   **2.** Fitting very closely or tightly. The sweater is a bit *snug,* but I can still wear it.
> **snug** (snug) *adjective,* **snugger, snuggest.**

snuggle   To lie close to or hold closely for warmth or protection, or to show love. The wolf cubs *snuggled* against their parents.
> **snug·gle** (snug′əl) *verb,* **snuggled, snuggling.**

so   **1.** To this or that extent or degree. It was *so* cold that we stayed indoors.   **2.** Very. I am *so* glad.   **3.** Very much. They love their parents *so.*   **4.** For this or that reason; therefore. We were tired, and *so* we went home early.   **5.** Too; also. I sing, and *so* does my friend.   **6.** In this or that way. Hold the tennis racket *so. Adverb.*
—True. I found out that what the author says is *so. Adjective.*
—For the purpose that. Please turn off the light *so* I can go to sleep. *Conjunction.*
—**1.** More or less. We will be away for a month or *so.*   **2.** The same. That is a lazy dog and will always be *so. Pronoun.*
—The word *so* is also used to express or to introduce another thought. So! You decided to come to the concert after all. *Interjection.*
▲ Other words that sound like this are **sew** and **sow.**
- **so as** or **so that.**   With the purpose or result. We divided the food carefully *so as*

snowy city streets

to have enough for everyone. I run every day *so that* I'll be in good condition.
so (sō) *adverb; adjective; conjunction; pronoun; interjection.*

soak **1.** To make very wet. We were *soaked* by the sudden thunderstorm. **2.** To take in; absorb. The sponge *soaked* up the spilled juice. **3.** To let something stay in water or other liquid. We left the dirty clothes to *soak* overnight. *Verb.*
—The act or process of soaking. Give those dirty clothes a *soak*. *Noun.*
soak (sōk) *verb,* **soaked, soaking;** *noun,* *plural* **soaks.**

soap A substance used for washing and cleaning. Soap is usually made with fats and lye. Soaps are made in the form of bars, powders, and liquids. *Noun.*
—To rub or cover with soap. Did you *soap* your hands well? *Verb.*
soap (sōp) *noun,* *plural* **soaps;** *verb,* **soaped, soaping.**

soapy **1.** Containing soap. Wash the dishes in hot, *soapy* water. **2.** Covered with soap. The *soapy* toy slipped out of the child's hands and hit the side of the tub. **3.** Like soap. The drink tasted *soapy.*
soap·y (sō′pē) *adjective.*

soar **1.** To fly high in the air. The birds *soared* in the sky. **2.** To go very high. The price of food *soared* this year. ▲ Another word that sounds like this is **sore.**
soar (sôr) *verb,* **soared, soaring.**

sob To cry with short gasps of breath. The little boy *sobbed* when he was told he couldn't go with his friends. *Verb.*
—The act or sound of crying with short gasps of breath. *Noun.*
sob (sob) *verb,* **sobbed, sobbing;** *noun,* *plural* **sobs.**

sober **1.** Not drunk. A person who drives a car should be *sober.* **2.** Serious and solemn. The room was decorated in a *sober* way, with no bright colors. *Adjective.*
—To make or become sober. The sad news *sobered* the people at the party. *Verb.*
so·ber (sō′bər) *adjective,* **soberer, soberest;** *verb,* **sobered, sobering.**

soccer A game in which the players try to move a round ball into a goal by kicking it or striking it with any part of their bodies except the hands and arms. Soccer is played by two teams of eleven players each.
soc·cer (sok′ər) *noun.*

sociable Liking to be with other people; friendly. I am a *sociable* person and like to go to parties.
so·cia·ble (sō′shə bəl) *adjective.*

social **1.** Having to do with people as a group. A family is a *social* unit. Geography and history are *social* studies. **2.** Having to do with people being together in a friendly way. We paid a *social* visit to our neighbor. **3.** Liking to be with other people; friendly; sociable. They're very *social* people and like to have visitors. **4.** Having to do with the part of society that is wealthy or that sets or follows current fashions. **5.** Living together in organized communities. A bee is a *social* insect. *Adjective.*
—A party or other friendly gathering. We are going to a *social* tonight. *Noun.*
so·cial (sō′shəl) *adjective;* *noun,* *plural* **socials.**

socialism An economic system in which the major businesses, factories, farms, and other means of producing and distributing goods are owned and run by the government or by the people as a whole, rather than by individuals.
so·cial·ism (sō′shə liz′əm) *noun.*

socialist A person who favors or supports socialism.
so·cial·ist (sō′shə list) *noun,* *plural* **socialists.**

social studies In an elementary school or a secondary school, a course of study that includes geography, history, and civics.

society **1.** Human beings as a group; all people. Having enough food may become one of *society's* biggest problems. **2.** A club or other group of people who join together

soccer

at; āpe; fär; câre; end; mē; it; īce; pîerce; hot; ōld; sông, fôrk; oil; out; up; ūse; rüle; pùll; tûrn; chin; sing; shop; thin; <u>th</u>is; hw in white; zh in treasure. The symbol ə stands for the unstressed vowel sound in about, taken, pencil, lemon, and circus.

S

685

because of an interest they all share. My parents belong to a *society* that performs operas. **3.** The people who are wealthy or who set or follow current fashions in a group or community. **4.** Companionship; company. We enjoy our neighbors' *society* and invite them to dinner often.
 so·ci·e·ty (sə sī′i tē) *noun, plural* **societies.**

sock A knitted or woven cloth covering for the foot and the lower leg.
 sock (sok) *noun, plural* **socks.**

socket An opening into which something fits. We screwed the light bulb into the *socket.* Our eyes are set in *sockets.*
 sock·et (sok′it) *noun, plural* **sockets.**

sod The top layer of soil that has grass growing on it. People who do not want to plant grass seed to start a lawn buy pieces of sod. *Noun.*
 —To plant with sod. We *sodded* our front yard. *Verb.*
 sod (sod) *noun; verb,* **sodded, sodding.**

soda **1.** A sweet drink made with soda water, flavoring, and sometimes ice cream. **2.** A white powder made with sodium that is used in cooking, medicine, and in making soaps and other cleaners; baking soda. **3.** A soft drink. **4.** Soda water.
 so·da (sō′də) *noun, plural* **sodas.**

soda fountain A counter where ice cream, ice cream sodas, sundaes, and soft drinks are served.

soda water A drink that has bubbles. It is made of water that has been mixed with carbon dioxide gas.

sodium A soft, silver-colored metal. Salt is a compound that contains sodium. Sodium is a chemical element.
 so·di·um (sō′dē əm) *noun.*

sofa A long seat that has a back and arms and is upholstered; couch. A sofa has room for two or more people.
 so·fa (sō′fə) *noun, plural* **sofas.**

soft **1.** Easy to shape; not hard. The *soft* clay was easy to mold. I like to rest my head on a *soft* pillow. **2.** Smooth to the touch; not rough. A baby has very *soft* skin. **3.** Gentle or light; not harsh or sharp. The police officer's *soft* voice calmed the lost child. The *soft* spring breeze felt warm. **4.** Kind or easily influenced by emotions. He has a *soft* heart for his friends. **5.** Weak. Her muscles were *soft* after her broken leg mended.
 soft (sôft) *adjective,* **softer, softest.**

softball **1.** A game that is like baseball, but is played on a smaller field and with a larger,

softer ball. **2.** The ball used in this game.
 soft·ball (sôft′bôl′) *noun, plural* **softballs.**

soft drink A sweet drink that is made with soda water. It has no alcohol in it.

soften To make or become soft or softer. You can *soften* your skin with a lotion. Butter will *soften* in a warm room.
 soft·en (sô′fən) *verb,* **softened, softening.**

software Programs that a computer uses to perform tasks. Software is put on a storage device, such as a diskette.
 soft·ware (sôft′wâr′) *noun.*

soggy Very wet or damp; soaked. The ground was *soggy* after the heavy rain.
 sog·gy (sog′ē) *adjective,* **soggier, soggiest.**

soil¹ **1.** The top part of the ground in which plants grow; dirt; earth. There is sandy *soil* near the coast. **2.** A country or land. The United States has fought in many wars on foreign *soil.*
 soil (soil) *noun, plural* **soils.**

soil² To make or become dirty. I *soiled* my jacket when I dropped it on the ground. White clothes *soil* easily.
 soil (soil) *verb,* **soiled, soiling.**

solar **1.** Having to do with or coming from the sun. This *solar* telescope will be used for studying the sun. *Solar* energy is sometimes used to heat homes. **2.** Using or powered by the energy of the sun. This *solar* car uses sunshine for energy.
 so·lar (sō′lər) *adjective.*

solar energy Energy from the sun that is used for heating or for generating electricity.

solar system The sun and all the planets, satellites, asteroids, and comets that revolve around it.

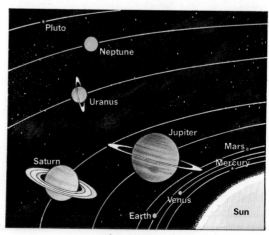

solar system

sold Past tense and past participle of **sell**. We *sold* our house last week. Look up **sell** for more information.
  sold (sōld) *verb.*

solder Any metal that can be melted and used to join two other metal surfaces together. A mixture of tin and lead is often used as solder. *Noun.*
  —To join, fasten, or fix with solder. The electrician *soldered* the wires together. *Verb.*
  sol·der (sod′ər) *noun, plural* **solders;** *verb,* **soldered, soldering.**

soldier A person who is a member of an army.
  sol·dier (sōl′jər) *noun, plural* **soldiers.**

sole¹ The bottom part of the foot or of a boot, shoe, or sock. The skin on the *soles* of your feet gets tougher when you walk barefoot. The *soles* of shoes are made of leather or rubber. *Noun.*
  —To put a sole on a shoe or other foot covering. *Verb.* ▲ Another word that sounds like this is **soul.**
  sole (sōl) *noun, plural* **soles;** *verb,* **soled, soling.**

sole² **1.** Being the only one or ones; only. Those two people were the *sole* survivors of the fire. **2.** Belonging to a single person or group. The company has *sole* rights to make that machine. ▲ Another word that sounds like this is **soul.**
  sole (sōl) *adjective.*

sole³ A kind of flatfish used as food. ▲ Another word that sounds like this is **soul.**
  sole (sōl) *noun, plural* **soles** or **sole.**

solemn Serious; grave. They made a *solemn* promise never to reveal the secret.
  sol·emn (sol′əm) *adjective.*

solid **1.** Having shape and hardness; not liquid or gaseous. Melted wax becomes *solid* when it cools. Water in its *solid* form is ice. **2.** Of one material, color, or kind; not mixed or hollow. Those rabbits are *solid* chocolate. The carpet is *solid* green. **3.** Not interrupted or broken. I slept for twelve *solid* hours. **4.** Very strong or hard; not weak or loose. The foundation of a house must be *solid.* **5.** Having a good character; reliable. Our neighbors are all *solid* citizens. **6.** Having length, width, and thickness. A cube is a *solid* figure. *Adjective.*
  —**1.** A form of matter that has shape and hardness. A solid is not a liquid or a gas. **2.** An object in geometry that has length, width, and thickness. A cube, sphere, and pyramid are solids. *Noun.*
  sol·id (sol′id) *adjective; noun, plural* **solids.**

solitary **1.** Alone. We saw a *solitary* person ahead on the trail. **2.** Single. Not a *solitary* customer came into the store. **3.** Made, done, or spent alone. That family leads a *solitary* life in a cabin in the mountains.
  sol·i·tar·y (sol′i ter′ē) *adjective.*

solo Music that one person sings or plays on an instrument by himself or herself. The drummer had a *solo* in the concert. *Noun.*
  —**1.** Played by one instrument or sung by one person alone. There are three *solo* parts in the concert. **2.** Made or done by one person alone. She was excited about her first *solo* airplane flight. *Adjective.*
  —By oneself; alone. He sang *solo. Adverb.*
  so·lo (sō′lō) *noun, plural* **solos;** *adjective; adverb.*

Word History

The word **solo** comes from an Italian word that means "alone." This Italian word came from a Latin word meaning "only" or "the only one."

soloist A person who performs a solo.
  so·lo·ist (sō′lō ist) *noun, plural* **soloists.**

soloist

at; āpe; fär; câre; end; mē; it; īce; pîerce; hot; ōld; sông, fôrk; oil; out; up; ūse; rüle; pùll; tûrn; chin; sing; shop; thin; this; hw in white; zh in treasure. The symbol ə stands for the unstressed vowel sound in about, taken, pencil, lemon, and circus.

S

soluble Capable of being dissolved in a liquid. Soap is *soluble* in water.
sol·u·ble (sol′yə bəl) *adjective.*

solution **1.** The answer to a problem. We tried to find the *solution* to the puzzle. **2.** The act, process, or method of finding an answer to a problem. The detectives worked on the *solution* of the crime for a year. **3.** A mixture formed by a substance dissolved in a liquid. Salt in water forms a *solution.*
so·lu·tion (sə lü′shən) *noun, plural* **solutions.**

solve To find the answer to. I *solved* all the arithmetic problems correctly.
solve (solv) *verb,* **solved, solving.**

Somalia A country in east-central Africa.
So·ma·lia (sō mäl′yə) *noun.*

somber Dark or gloomy. The sky became gray and *somber* before the thunderstorm. Why are you in such a *somber* mood?
som·ber (som′bər) *adjective.*

sombrero A hat with a broad brim that is worn in Mexico and the southwestern United States.
som·brer·o (som brâr′ō) *noun, plural* **sombreros.**

Word History

The word **sombrero** comes from the Spanish word for this hat. The Spaniards named the hat from their word for "shade" because the hat shades a person's face from the sun.

some **1.** Being one or ones not named or known. *Some* birds cannot fly. *Some* friend of yours called. **2.** Being of a number or amount that is not stated. We met *some* weeks ago. Have *some* dessert. *Adjective.*
—A number or amount that is not stated. *Some* of my friends want to start a football team. Please eat *some* of the salad. *Pronoun.*
—Approximately; about. The club has *some* forty members. *Adverb.* ⬥ Another word that sounds like this is **sum.**
some (sum) *adjective; pronoun; adverb.*

somebody A person not named or known; someone. *Somebody* took my hat. *Pronoun.*
—A person who is important or famous. Some of the guests at the party were real *somebodies. Noun.*
some·bod·y (sum′bod′ē) *pronoun; noun, plural* **somebodies.**

someday At some future time. *Someday* I'm going to Europe.
some·day (sum′dā′) *adverb.*

somehow In a way not known or stated. Don't worry, we'll do it *somehow.*
some·how (sum′hou′) *adverb.*

someone A person who is not named or known; somebody. *Someone* is at the front door.
some·one (sum′wun′) *pronoun.*

somersault To roll the body by turning the heels over the head. The acrobat *somersaulted* ten times without stopping. *Verb.*
—A roll of the body done by turning the heels over the head. *Noun.*
som·er·sault (sum′ər sôlt′) *verb,* **somersaulted, somersaulting;** *noun, plural* **somersaults.**

Word History

The word **somersault** comes from an old French word meaning "leap." This French word comes from two Latin words meaning "over" and "to jump."

something A thing that is not known or stated. *Something* is wrong with our car. I brought *something* for you. *Pronoun.*
—To some extent; somewhat. Your house looks *something* like ours. *Adverb.*
some·thing (sum′thing′) *pronoun; adverb.*

sometime At a time not known or stated. I saw that movie *sometime* last year.
some·time (sum′tīm′) *adverb.*

sometimes At some times; on certain occasions. *Sometimes* we spend a weekend in the country.
some·times (sum′tīmz′) *adverb.*

somewhat To some extent; rather. You look *somewhat* upset. *Adverb.*
—Some part, amount, or degree. That movie lost *somewhat* of its excitement when I saw it a second time. *Noun.*
some·what (sum′hwut′ *or* sum′hwot′ *or* sum′wut′ *or* sum′wot′) *adverb; noun.*

somewhere **1.** In, at, or to some place not known or stated. We'll stop for lunch *somewhere* along the highway. **2.** At some point, as in time, space, or amount. Be there *somewhere* between noon and one o'clock. *Adverb.*
—A place that is not known or stated. We will find *somewhere* to stay when we get to the lake. *Noun.*
some·where (sum′hwâr′ *or* sum′wâr′) *adverb; noun.*

son A male child. A man or a boy is the son of his mother and father. ⬥ Another word that sounds like this is **sun.**
son (sun) *noun, plural* **sons.**

sonar An instrument that sends out radio waves to discover and locate objects under the water.
so·nar (sō'när) *noun, plural* **sonars.**

song **1.** A piece of music that has words or other vocal sounds set to it. **2.** The musical call of a bird, whale, or other animal.
song (sông) *noun, plural* **songs.**

songbird A bird that has a musical call. The canary and the lark are songbirds.
song·bird (sông'bûrd') *noun, plural* **songbirds.**

son-in-law The husband of one's daughter.
son-in-law (sun'in lô') *noun, plural* **sons-in-law.**

soon **1.** In a short time. Come to visit us again *soon.* **2.** Before the expected time; early. The guests arrived too *soon,* and we weren't ready. **3.** Without a delay; quickly. I'll be there as *soon* as I can. **4.** Readily. I would just as *soon* do it now as later.
soon (sün) *adverb.*

soot A black, greasy powder that forms when such fuels as wood, coal, and oil are burned.
soot (sut *or* süt) *noun.*

soothe To quiet, calm, or ease. The nurse *soothed* the crying child by singing a lullaby. The lotion *soothed* my sunburn.
soothe (sü<u>th</u>) *verb,* **soothed, soothing.**

sophisticated Having or showing much knowledge and experience of the world. They had developed *sophisticated* tastes from living in many different countries.
so·phis·ti·cat·ed (sə fis'ti kā'tid) *adjective.*

sophomore A student in the second year of a four-year high school or college.
soph·o·more (sof'ə môr') *noun, plural* **sophomores.**

soprano **1.** The highest singing voice of women and boys. **2.** A singer who has such a voice. *Noun.*
—Able to sing or play the range of the highest singing voice. I am learning to play a *soprano* saxophone. *Adjective.*
so·pran·o (sə pran'ō) *noun, plural* **sopranos;** *adjective.*

Word History

The word **soprano** comes from an Italian word meaning "above." The *soprano* part is written "above" the other voices, because a *soprano* has a higher voice than other singers.

---

sore **1.** Painful; hurting. The mover's back was *sore* from lifting so many heavy boxes. **2.** Feeling anger; annoyed. Don't be *sore* just because we forgot your birthday. **3.** Causing misery or distress. My friend's better report card was a *sore* subject. *Adjective.*
—A place on the body that has been hurt. There was a *sore* on my arm where the blister had been. *Noun.* ▲ Another word that sounds like this is **soar.**
sore (sôr) *adjective,* **sorer, sorest;** *noun, plural* **sores.**

sorrel A plant that has long clusters of small green or red flowers. The leaves of some kinds of sorrel are eaten either raw or cooked.
sor·rel (sôr'əl) *noun, plural* **sorrels.**

sorrow **1.** A strong feeling of loss and being unhappy; sadness or grief. People feel sorrow when someone they love dies. **2.** A cause of sadness or grief. The fire that destroyed many homes was a *sorrow* to the town.
sor·row (sor'ō) *noun, plural* **sorrows.**

sorrel

sorrowful Feeling or showing sorrow; very sad.
sor·row·ful (sor'ō fəl) *adjective.*

sorry **1.** Feeling sadness, sympathy, or regret. I am *sorry* to hear that you have been so sick. **2.** Not very good; poor. The rusty old car was a *sorry* sight.
sor·ry (sor'ē) *adjective,* **sorrier, sorriest.**

sort A group of people or things that are alike in some way; kind; type. This *sort* of plant grows best in the shade. *Noun.*
—To place or separate according to kind or type. We *sorted* the socks by color and size. *Verb.*
sort (sôrt) *noun, plural* **sorts;** *verb,* **sorted, sorting.**

SOS A call or signal for help. The ship sent an *SOS* when the engines broke down.
SOS (es'ō'es').

---

at; āpe; fär; câre; end; mē; it; īce; pîerce; hot; ōld; sông, fôrk; oil; out; up; ūse; rüle; pull; tûrn; chin; sing; shop; thin; <u>th</u>is; hw in white; zh in treasure. The symbol ə stands for the unstressed vowel sound in about, taken, pencil, lemon, and circus.

S

sought Past tense and past participle of **seek.** I *sought* help from the librarian. Look up **seek** for more information.
    sought (sôt) *verb.*

soul **1.** The part of a person that is thought to control what he or she thinks, feels, and does; spirit. **2.** A person. Don't tell another *soul* what I just told you. **3.** A person's ability and desire to do things; energy and emotion. I put all my *soul* into winning that game. **4.** A person who leads or inspires. That captain is the *soul* of this ship and its crew. ▲ Another word that sounds like this is **sole.**
    soul (sōl) *noun, plural* **souls.**

sound¹ **1.** What can be heard. Sounds are vibrations that move through the air and produce sensation in the ear. **2.** One of the noises that make up human speech. The word "cat" begins with a "k" *sound.* **3.** The distance a sound can be heard. The house was within the *sound* of the stream. *Noun.*
  —1. To make or cause to make a noise that can be heard. The bell *sounded* at nine o'clock. **2.** To pronounce or be pronounced. "Doe" and "dough" *sound* alike. **3.** To seem to be. Your excuse for being late *sounds* reasonable. **4.** To announce by means of a sound. The trumpets *sounded* the arrival of the royal couple. *Verb.*
    sound (sound) *noun, plural* **sounds;** *verb,* **sounded, sounding.**

sound² **1.** Strong and healthy. The doctor said my arm had healed and was perfectly *sound.* **2.** Free from any damage, flaw, decay, or weakness. The old house was built on a *sound* foundation. **3.** Based on facts, truth, or good sense; sensible. The teacher gave us *sound* advice. **4.** Deep and not interrupted. I had a *sound* sleep. *Adjective.*
  —Deeply and completely. The baby is *sound* asleep. *Adverb.*
    sound (sound) *adjective,* **sounder, soundest;** *adverb.*

sound³ **1.** To measure the depth of water. One way to *sound* water is to drop a line or rope with a weight on the end until it touches bottom. **2.** To dive deeply and quickly. Whales *sound* when they sense danger.
    sound (sound) *verb,* **sounded, sounding.**

sound⁴ **1.** A long, narrow passage of water between two larger bodies of water or between the mainland and an island. **2.** A long inlet or arm of the sea.
    sound (sound) *noun, plural* **sounds.**

soundproof Not letting sound pass in or out. The singer recorded the songs in a *soundproof* studio. *Adjective.*
  —To make soundproof. *Verb.*

sound·proof (sound′prüf′) *adjective; verb,* **soundproofed, soundproofing.**

soup A liquid food made by boiling meat, fish, or vegetables in water.
    soup (süp) *noun, plural* **soups.**

sour **1.** Having a sharp taste. Lemons and green apples are *sour.* **2.** Bad or unpleasant. I had a *sour* look on my face. *Adjective.*
  —To get or cause to get a sharp taste. The milk *soured* because it wasn't kept cold. *Verb.*
    sour (sour *or* sou′ər) *adjective,* **sourer, sourest;** *verb,* **soured, souring.**

source The person, place, or thing from which something comes or begins. Who was the *source* of that news? A mountain lake is the *source* of this river.
    source (sôrs) *noun, plural* **sources.**

south **1.** The direction to your left as you watch the sun set in the evening. South is one of the four main points of the compass. It is located directly opposite north. **2. South.** Any region or place that is in this direction. **3. the South.** The region of the United States that is south of Pennsylvania, the Ohio River, and Missouri, especially those states that fought as the Confederacy in the Civil War. *Noun.*
  —1. Toward or in the south. The *south* side of our house usually gets a lot of sunlight. **2.** Coming from the south. A *south* wind was blowing. *Adjective.*
  —Toward the south. Many birds travel *south* in the winter. *Adverb.*
    south (south) *noun; adjective; adverb.*

South Africa A country in southern Africa.

South America A continent in the Western Hemisphere. It is southeast of North America. It is the fourth largest continent.

South American **1.** A person who was born in or is a citizen of a country in South America. **2.** Of or having to do with South America or its people.

South Carolina A state in the southeastern United States. Its capital is Columbia.
    South Car·o·li·na (kar′ə lī′nə).

Word History

South Carolina was created from the southern part of the English colony of Carolina. The founder of the colony had asked that it be given the Latin name *Carolana,* which means "from Charles" or "belonging to Charles," in honor of Charles I, who was then king of England.

South Dakota A state in the north-central United States. Its capital is Pierre.
South Da·ko·ta (də kō′tə).

Word History

South Dakota used to be the southern part of the Dakota Territory. The territory was named after the *Dakota* Indians, who lived there. Their name is an Indian word that means "allied tribes."

---

southeast **1.** The direction halfway between south and east. **2.** The point of the compass showing this direction. **3.** A region or place that is in this direction. **4. the Southeast.** The region in the south and east of the United States. *Noun.*
—**1.** Toward or in the southeast. The bus stops at the *southeast* corner of the street. **2.** Coming from the southeast. A *southeast* wind was blowing. *Adjective.*
—Toward the southeast. The plane was traveling *southeast. Adverb.*
south·east (south′ēst′) *noun; adjective; adverb.*

southeastern **1.** Toward or in the southeast. **2.** Characteristic of or having to do with the southeast or Southeast. **3.** Coming from the southeast.
south·east·ern (south′ēs′tərn) *adjective.*

southern **1.** In or toward the south. Australia is a *southern* continent. **2.** Coming from the south. A *southern* breeze was blowing. **3.** Of or in the part of the United States that is in the South.
south·ern (su<u>th</u>′ərn) *adjective.*

southerner **1.** A person who was born or is living in the southern part of a country or region. **2. Southerner.** A person who was born or is living in the southern part of the United States.
south·ern·er (su<u>th</u>′ər nər) *noun, plural* **southerners.**

Southern Hemisphere The half of the earth that is located south of the equator. Australia, most of South America, and parts of Africa and Asia are located in the Southern Hemisphere.

Southern Yemen A country in southwestern Asia.
Southern Yem·en (yem′ən).

South Korea A country in east-central Asia.
South Ko·re·a (kə rē′ə).

South Pole The point on the earth that is farthest south. The South Pole is the southern end of the earth's axis.

southward Toward the south. We traveled *southward* along the rim of the hill. *Adverb.*
—Toward or in the south. We skied on the *southward* slope of the mountain. *Adjective.*
south·ward (south′wərd) *adverb; adjective.*

southwards Another spelling of the adverb **southward.** They drove *southwards.*
south·wards (south′wərdz) *adverb.*

southwest **1.** The direction halfway between south and west. **2.** The point of the compass showing this direction. **3.** A region or place that is in this direction. **4. the Southwest.** The region in the south and west of the United States. *Noun.*
—**1.** Toward or in the southwest. That house is on the *southwest* corner of the street. **2.** Coming from the southwest. A *southwest* wind was blowing. *Adjective.*
—Toward the southwest. The ship sailed *southwest. Adverb.*
south·west (south′west′) *noun; adjective; adverb.*

southwester A waterproof hat with a wide brim. It covers the back of the neck as well as the head.
south·west·er (south′wes′tər *or* sou′wes′tər) *noun, plural* **southwesters.**

southwestern **1.** Toward or in the southwest. **2.** Characteristic of or having to do with the southwest or Southwest. **3.** Coming from the southwest.
south·west·ern (south′wes′tərn) *adjective.*

souvenir Something that is kept because it reminds one of a person, place, or event. I bought a pennant as a *souvenir* of the baseball game.
sou·ve·nir (sü′və nîr′ *or* sü′və nîr′) *noun, plural* **souvenirs.**

sovereign A king or queen. *Noun.*
—**1.** Having the greatest power or highest rank or authority. The king and queen were the *sovereign* rulers of the country. **2.** Not controlled by others; independent. Mexico is a *sovereign* nation. *Adjective.*
sov·er·eign (sov′ər ən *or* sov′rən) *noun, plural* **sovereigns;** *adjective.*

---

at; āpe; fär; câre; end; mē; it; īce; pîerce; hot; ōld; sông, fôrk; oil; out; up; ūse; rüle; pull; tûrn; chin; sing; shop; thin; <u>th</u>is; hw in white; zh in treasure. The symbol ə stands for the unstressed vowel sound in about, taken, pencil, lemon, and circus.

S

Soviet A person who was born in or is a citizen of the Soviet Union. *Noun.*
—Of or having to do with the Soviet Union or its people. *Adjective.*
So·vi·et (sō′vē et′) *noun, plural* **Soviets;** *adjective.*

Soviet Union A large country in eastern Europe and northern Asia. It is also called the **U.S.S.R.** This country was formerly called **Russia.**

sow¹ **1.** To scatter seeds over the ground; plant. The farmer will *sow* corn in this field. **2.** To spread or scatter. The clown *sowed* happiness among the children. ▲ Other words that sound like this are **sew** and **so.**
sow (sō) *verb,* **sowed, sown** or **sowed, sowing.**

sow² An adult female pig.
sow (sou) *noun, plural* **sows.**

soybean A seed that is rich in oil and protein and is used as food. Soybeans grow in pods on bushy plants.
soy·bean (soi′bēn′) *noun, plural* **soybeans.**

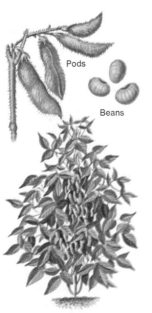

Pods

Beans

soybeans

space **1.** The area in which the whole universe exists. It has no limits. The planet earth and everything and everyone on it exist in space. **2.** The region beyond the earth's atmosphere; outer space. The rocket was launched into *space.* **3.** A distance or area between things. There is not much *space* between our house and the house next door. **4.** An area reserved or available for some purpose. We had a hard time finding a parking *space* downtown. **5.** A period of time. Both jets landed in the *space* of ten minutes. *Noun.*
—To put space in between. The architect *spaced* the houses far apart. *Verb.*
space (spās) *noun, plural* **spaces;** *verb,* **spaced, spacing.**

spacecraft A vehicle used for flight in outer space. This is also called a **spaceship.**
space·craft (spās′kraft′) *noun, plural* **spacecraft.**

spaceship A vehicle that is launched into outer space. Spaceships have carried astronauts to the moon and cameras and equipment to other planets.
space·ship (spās′ship′) *noun, plural* **spaceships.**

space shuttle A spacecraft that carries a crew into space and returns to land on earth. The same space shuttle can be used again. A space shuttle is also called a **shuttle.**

space station A spaceship that orbits around the earth like a satellite and on which a crew can live for long periods of time.

spacesuit Special clothing worn by an astronaut in space. A spacesuit covers an astronaut's entire body and has equipment to help the astronaut breathe.
space·suit (spās′süt′) *noun, plural* **spacesuits.**

spacewalk

spacewalk A period of activity during which an astronaut in space is outside a spacecraft.
space·walk (spās′wôk′) *noun, plural* **spacewalks.**

spade¹ A tool used for digging. It has a long handle and a flat blade that can be pressed into the ground with the foot. *Noun.*
—To dig with a spade. We *spaded* the garden and then raked it. *Verb.*
spade (spād) *noun, plural* **spades;** *verb,* **spaded, spading.**

spade² **1.** A playing card marked with one or more figures shaped like this: ♠. **2. spades.** The suit of cards marked with this figure.
spade (spād) *noun, plural* **spades.**

spaghetti   A food that looks like long, thin strings. It is made of a mixture of flour and water. Spaghetti is a kind of pasta.
spa·ghet·ti (spə get′ē) *noun.*

Word History

The word **spaghetti** comes from an Italian word meaning "strings" or "little cords." Spaghetti looks like little strings.

Spain   A country in southwestern Europe.
Spain (spān) *noun.*

span   **1.** The distance or part between two supports. The *span* of that bridge is very long.   **2.** The full reach or length of anything. Some people accomplish a great deal in the *span* of their lives. *Noun.*
—To extend over or across. A bridge *spans* this river three miles from here. *Verb.*
span (span) *noun, plural* **spans;** *verb,* **spanned, spanning.**

Spaniard   A person who was born in or is a citizen of Spain.
Span·iard (span′yərd) *noun, plural* **Spaniards.**

spaniel   Any of various dogs of small to medium size with long, drooping ears, a silky, wavy coat, and short legs. The larger types are used in hunting.
span·iel (span′yəl) *noun, plural* **spaniels.**

spaniel

Spanish   **1.** The people of Spain. ⚠ The word "Spanish" in this sense is used with a plural verb.   **2.** The language spoken in Spain. It is also spoken in many countries south of the United States. *Noun.*
—Of or having to do with Spain, its people, or the Spanish language. *Adjective.*
Span·ish (span′ish) *noun; adjective.*

spank   To hit with the open hand or something flat as punishment.
spank (spangk) *verb,* **spanked, spanking.**

spare   **1.** To not hurt or injure; show mercy to. They tried to *spare* my feelings by not telling me what a poor job I had done.   **2.** To give or get along without. Can you *spare* a dollar?   **3.** To free from the need to make, do, or take; save. Your hard work *spared* us much trouble.   **4.** To have remaining as extra or not used. There's no room to *spare* in the crowded closet.   **5.** To fail to use or spend; use or spend only in small amounts. Don't *spare* any effort to do your best. *Verb.*
—**1.** More than is needed; extra. We have a *spare* tire in the trunk.   **2.** Small in amount or quantity. I had to eat *spare* meals when I dieted.   **3.** Not fat; thin. That skinny child is too *spare. Adjective.*
—**1.** One or an amount of something that is extra. In case you get a flat tire, it is wise to always carry a *spare.*   **2.** The knocking down of all the pins in bowling with two rolls of the ball. I bowled eight *spares* in that game. *Noun.*
spare (spâr) *verb,* **spared, sparing;** *adjective,* **sparer, sparest;** *noun, plural* **spares.**

spark   **1.** A small bit of burning or glowing material. Sparks fly off burning wood.   **2.** A flash of light. One kind of spark is the small flash caused by electricity passing through the air.   **3.** A small amount; trace. The bored student didn't show a *spark* of interest. *Noun.*
—**1.** To send out sparks. The burning logs in the fireplace hissed and *sparked.*   **2.** To be the force or influence that causes or arouses. The question *sparked* a lively discussion. The pitcher *sparked* the whole baseball team to victory. *Verb.*
spark (spärk) *noun, plural* **sparks;** *verb,* **sparked, sparking.**

sparkle   **1.** To shine in quick, bright flashes; glitter. The diamonds *sparkled.* Their eyes *sparkled* with laughter.   **2.** To bubble like soda water. Soft drinks *sparkle.*   **3.** To be brilliant and lively. Your conversation *sparkled* and delighted our guests. *Verb.*
—A bright, glittering look. The *sparkle* of the sun on the water was beautiful. *Noun.*
spar·kle (spär′kəl) *verb,* **sparkled, sparkling;** *noun, plural* **sparkles.**

at; āpe; fär; câre; end; mē; it; īce; pîerce; hot; ōld; sông, fôrk; oil; out; up; ūse; rüle; pùll; tûrn; chin; sing; shop; thin; this; hw in white; zh in treasure. The symbol ə stands for the unstressed vowel sound in about, taken, pencil, lemon, and circus.

S

sparrow A common, small bird with brown, white, and gray feathers. The sparrow has a short bill shaped for eating seeds.
spar·row (spar′ō) *noun, plural* **sparrows.**

sparrow

sparse Not living or growing close together. The population and vegetation in the desert area were *sparse*.
sparse (spärs) *adjective,* **sparser, sparsest.**

spasm A movement of a muscle that is sudden and cannot be controlled.
spasm (spaz′əm) *noun, plural* **spasms.**

spat[1] A short, unimportant argument or disagreement. They had a *spat* about which television program they would watch.
spat (spat) *noun, plural* **spats.**

spat[2] A past tense and past participle of **spit**. The cat *spat* when the dog got close. Look up **spit** for more information.
spat (spat) *verb.*

spatter To scatter in or splash with drops or small bits. Mud *spattered* on my boots.
spat·ter (spat′ər) *verb,* **spattered, spattering.**

spatula A small tool with a flat blade. Spatulas are used to lift and turn over foods, and also to spread thick, soft foods.
spat·u·la (spach′ə lə) *noun, plural* **spatulas.**

spawn The eggs of fish, frogs, and some other animals that live in water. *Noun.*
—To produce eggs. *Verb.*
spawn (spôn) *noun; verb,* **spawned, spawning.**

speak 1. To use or utter words; talk. The baby cannot *speak* yet. 2. To make known or express an idea, fact, or feeling. Did you *speak* to him about going fishing? She always *speaks* the truth. 3. To make a speech. The senator *spoke* at our graduation. 4. To use or be able to use in speaking. You *speak* French very well. 5. To have a conversation. We *spoke* with our cousins yesterday.
• **to speak out** or **to speak up.** 1. To speak loudly and clearly enough to be understood. *Speak up* so that we can hear you. 2. To say what one really believes; be frank. The mayor *spoke out* against crime.
speak (spēk) *verb,* **spoke, spoken, speaking.**

speaker 1. A person who speaks. People who give speeches are called speakers. 2. **Speaker.** The person who heads a meeting of a legislature. 3. A device that changes electrical signals into sounds, as in a stereo system; loudspeaker.
speak·er (spē′kər) *noun, plural* **speakers.**

spear 1. A weapon with a sharp, pointed head attached to a long shaft. 2. A long, thin stalk, blade, or sprout of a plant. Asparagus grows in spears. *Noun.*
—To stab with something sharp. *Verb.*
spear (spîr) *noun, plural* **spears;** *verb,* **speared, spearing.**

spears of asparagus

spearmint A kind of mint. The leaves of this plant are used to flavor candy and foods.
spear·mint (spîr′mint′) *noun, plural* **spearmints.**

special Different from others in a certain way; not ordinary; unusual. The sports fan had a *special* interest in hockey. My birthday is a *special* day for me. An electrician must have *special* training.
spe·cial (spesh′əl) *adjective.*

specialist A person who knows a great deal about something. A veterinarian is a *specialist* in the treatment and care of animals.
spe·cial·ist (spesh′ə list) *noun, plural* **specialists.**

specialize To learn a great deal about a special thing or area. That doctor *specializes* in surgery on the heart.
spe·cial·ize (spesh′ə līz′) *verb,* **specialized, specializing.**

specialty 1. A special thing that a person knows a great deal about. This mechanic's *specialty* is repairing old motorcycles. 2. A special product or service. Italian food is the *specialty* of this restaurant.
spe·cial·ty (spesh′əl tē) *noun, plural* **specialties.**

species A group of animals or plants that have many characteristics in common. Members of the same species can mate and have offspring. Poodles and beagles belong to the same species. Beagles and wolves belong to different species.
spe·cies (spē′shēz) *noun, plural* **species.**

specific **1.** Exact; particular. Nine hundred dollars is the *specific* amount of money you need to buy this used car. **2.** Stated in a way that is easily understood; clear. Please make your questions as *specific* as you can.
spe·cif·ic (spi sif′ik) *adjective*.

specimen A single person or thing that shows what the whole group is like; sample. I collect *specimens* of different kinds of butterflies.
spec·i·men (spes′ə mən) *noun, plural* specimens.

speck A very small bit, spot, or mark. There are greasy *specks* on this shirt.
speck (spek) *noun, plural* specks.

spectacle **1.** A very unusual sight or show. The sunrise was a magnificent *spectacle*. **2.** spectacles. A pair of lenses in a frame that help a person see better; eyeglasses.
spec·ta·cle (spek′tə kəl) *noun, plural* spectacles.

spectacular Very unusual or impressive. There is a *spectacular* view from the top of that mountain.
spec·tac·u·lar (spek tak′yə lər) *adjective*.

spectator A person who watches something but does not take part; observer. There were many *spectators* at the game.
spec·ta·tor (spek′tā tər) *noun, plural* spectators.

spectrum **1.** A band of colors into which white light is separated by being passed through a prism or by other means. A rainbow is a spectrum caused by sunlight passing through raindrops. The colors of the spectrum are red, orange, yellow, green, blue, indigo, and violet. **2.** The whole range of colors that exist in nature, including those that cannot be seen by a human being's eyes.
spec·trum (spek′trəm) *noun, plural* spectrums.

speculate **1.** To think of reasons or answers for something. The children *speculated* about what was in the boxes. **2.** To risk losses in an attempt to make a profit. They lost money when they *speculated* in real estate.
spec·u·late (spek′yə lāt′) *verb*, speculated, speculating.

sped A past tense and past participle of **speed.** I *sped* down the hill on my bicycle. Look up **speed** for more information.
sped (sped) *verb*.

speech **1.** The ability to use spoken words to express ideas, thoughts, and feelings. Animals do not have the power of speech. **2.** Something that is spoken; talk. The president's *speech* was broadcast on television.

3. A way in which someone speaks. Your *speech* shows no trace of an accent.
speech (spēch) *noun, plural* speeches.

speechless Not able to say anything. You were *speechless* when we yelled "Surprise!"
speech·less (spēch′lis) *adjective*.

speed **1.** Quick or fast motion. She ran with great *speed* and won the race. **2.** The rate of motion. He drove the car at a *speed* of forty miles per hour. *Noun.*
—**1.** To go or cause to go quickly or rapidly. We *sped* down the hill on our sleds. **2.** To drive faster than is safe or lawful. They were arrested because they were *speeding*. *Verb.*
speed (spēd) *noun, plural* speeds; *verb*, sped or speeded, speeding.

speedometer A device that shows how fast a car or other vehicle is moving.
speed·om·e·ter (spē dom′i ter) *noun, plural* speedometers.

spell¹ **1.** To write or say the letters of a word in the right order. You *spell* "speak" s-p-e-a-k. We are learning how to *spell*. **2.** To be the letters that form. D-o-g *spells* "dog." **3.** To mean. The player's injury *spelled* defeat for the team.
• **to spell out.** To explain clearly and completely. The official *spelled out* the rules for sailing in the harbor to us.
spell (spel) *verb*, spelled or spelt, spelling.

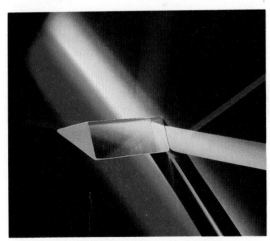

a **spectrum** created by a prism

S

695

spell² **1.** A word or words supposed to have magic power. The wicked magician cast a *spell* that put everyone in the kingdom to sleep. **2.** The power to attract or delight greatly. It was hard to resist the *spell* of the beautiful music.

spell (spel) *noun, plural* **spells.**

spell³ **1.** A period of time. Sit and rest for a short *spell.* **2.** A period of a certain kind of weather. We have had a long cold *spell.* **3.** An attack of something. I had a dizzy *spell* a few minutes ago. *Noun.*
—To take a person's place at doing something for a time. If you're tired, I'll *spell* you at mowing the lawn for a while. *Verb.*

spell (spel) *noun, plural* **spells;** *verb,* **spelled** or **spelt, spelling.**

speller **1.** A person who spells words. Who is the best *speller* in your class? **2.** A book used to teach spelling.

spell·er (spel'ər) *noun, plural* **spellers.**

spelling **1.** The way words are spelled. We all have to study to learn *spelling.* **2.** The writing or saying of the letters of a word in the right order. K-e-t-c-h-u-p and c-a-t-s-u-p are two *spellings* of the same word.

spell·ing (spel'ing) *noun, plural* **spellings.**

spelt A past tense and past participle of **spell¹.** You and I *spelt* every word on the test correctly. Look up **spell¹** for more information.

spelt (spelt) *verb.*

spend **1.** To pay money. You *spent* too much for your bike. **2.** To pass. We *spent* the weekend in the country. **3.** To use up. The mechanic *spent* a lot of time working on the car.

spend (spend) *verb,* **spent, spending.**

sperm A special male cell which, if it is joined with a female egg, can develop into offspring.

sperm (spûrm) *noun, plural* **sperm** or **sperms.**

sperm whale A large whale with a square head. Sperm whales produce a valuable oil called sperm oil.

sperm whale

sphere **1.** A round body like a ball. All the points on the surface of a sphere are the same distance from its center. **2.** An area of interest, knowledge, or activity. Chemistry is outside my *sphere* of knowledge.

sphere (sfîr) *noun, plural* **spheres.**

sphinx **1.** A mythical creature having the head of a human and the body of a lion. **2. the Sphinx.** a large statue of this creature in Egypt.

sphinx (sfingks) *noun, plural* **sphinxes.**

the Sphinx

spice **1.** The seeds or other parts of certain plants that are used to flavor food. Pepper, cloves, and cinnamon are spices. **2.** Something that adds interest or excitement. The speaker called variety "the *spice* of life." *Noun.*
—**1.** To flavor with a spice or spices. I *spiced* the hamburgers with pepper. **2.** To add interest or excitement to. A good speaker often *spices* a speech with funny stories. *Verb.*

spice (spīs) *noun, plural* **spices;** *verb,* **spiced, spicing.**

spicy Seasoned with or full of spice. This sausage is very *spicy.*

spic·y (spī'sē) *adjective,* **spicier, spiciest.**

spider A small animal with four pairs of legs, a body that is divided into two parts, and no wings. Most spiders spin webs to catch insects for food.

spi·der (spī'dər) *noun, plural* **spiders.**

spied Past tense and past participle of **spy.** The secret agent *spied* on the enemy. Look up **spy** for more information.

spied (spīd) *verb.*

spike¹ **1.** A large, heavy nail. Spikes are used to hold rails to railroad ties. **2.** Any sharp, pointed object or part that sticks out. Baseball and soccer shoes have *spikes* on the soles.

spike (spīk) *noun, plural* **spikes.**

spike² **1.** An ear of grain. Wheat has spikes. Corn ears are spikes. **2.** A long cluster of flowers that grow on one stem.
spike (spīk) *noun, plural* **spikes.**

spill **1.** To make or let something fall, run out, or flow. The child *spilled* milk on the tablecloth. **2.** To fall or flow out. Water *spilled* from the glass onto the floor. **3.** To cause to tumble or fall out or off. The canoe tipped and *spilled* us into the stream. **4.** To make known; reveal. I didn't mean to *spill* the secret. *Verb.*
—**1.** An act or instance of spilling or the amount spilled. The *spill* of oil polluted the river. I cleaned up the *spill* with a mop. **2.** A tumble or fall. The jockey was hurt in a *spill* from a horse. *Noun.*
spill (spil) *verb,* **spilled** or **spilt, spilling;** *noun, plural* **spills.**

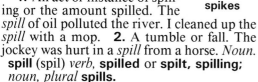
spikes

spin **1.** To turn around quickly. The car's wheels *spun* in the mud. The child *spun* the top. **2.** To make thin fibers into thread. **3.** To make a web or cocoon by giving off a sticky substance that hardens into thread. Spiders *spin* webs. Silkworms *spin* cocoons. **4.** To tell. Our counselor at camp was good at *spinning* ghost stories. **5.** To feel dizzy. The hot sun made my head *spin. Verb.*
—**1.** A quick turning motion. Give the wheel a *spin.* **2.** A quick ride. I took a *spin* on my bicycle. *Noun.*
spin (spin) *verb,* **spun, spinning;** *noun, plural* **spins.**

spinach The dark green leaves of a garden plant. They are eaten as a vegetable.
spin·ach (spin′ich) *noun.*

spinal column The column of bones in the back; backbone. Look up **backbone** for more information.
spi·nal column (spī′nəl)

spinal cord A thick cord of nerve tissue running through the center of the backbone. The spinal cord links the brain to the rest of the nerves in the body.

spindle A stick or rod on or around which something is turned. Fibers of cotton are spun into thread from a spindle.
spin·dle (spin′dəl) *noun, plural* **spindles.**

spine **1.** The column of bones in the back; backbone. Look up **backbone** for more information. **2.** A sharp, pointed growth on a plant or animal. The quills of a porcupine are spines.
spine (spīn) *noun, plural* **spines.**

spinning wheel A large wheel and a spindle on a stand. It is used to spin thread. A spinning wheel is turned with the hand or by a pedal pressed with the foot.

spiral A curve that keeps winding. A spiral may wind inward and outward or downward and upward. Some springs are *spirals. Noun.*
—To move in or take the shape of a spiral. The staircase *spirals* to the attic. *Verb.*
—Having the shape or form of a spiral. The *spiral* staircase goes to the tower. *Adjective.*
spi·ral (spī′rəl) *noun, plural* **spirals;** *verb,* **spiraled, spiraling;** *adjective.*

a shell that forms a **spiral**

spire A tall, narrow structure that tapers to a point at the top. Spires are built on top of towers.
spire (spīr) *noun, plural* **spires.**

spirit **1.** The part of a person that is thought to control what he or she thinks, feels, and does; soul. **2.** A supernatural being; ghost. **3.** Enthusiasm and pep. They danced with *spirit.* **4. spirits.** The way a person thinks or feels. I was in good *spirits* after passing the test. **5.** The real meaning or intent. The *spirit* of a law is more than just what is written down.
spir·it (spir′it) *noun, plural* **spirits.**

spirited Full of spirit; lively; vigorous. The team played a *spirited* game.
spir·it·ed (spir′i tid) *adjective.*

spiritual **1.** Of or having to do with the spirit. **2.** Of or having to do with religion.

at; āpe; fär; câre; end; mē; it; īce; pîerce; hot; ōld; sông, fôrk; oil; out; up; ūse; rüle; pull; tûrn; chin; sing; shop; thin; <u>th</u>is; hw in white; zh in treasure. The symbol ə stands for the unstressed vowel sound in about, taken, pencil, lemon, and circus.

S

697

Priests, ministers, and rabbis are *spiritual* leaders. *Adjective.*
—A religious folk song. Spirituals were originally sung by the blacks of the southern United States. *Noun.*
> **spir·i·tu·al** (spir′i chü əl) *adjective; noun, plural* **spirituals.**

spit¹ To force out saliva or another substance from the mouth. The cat *spit* at the dog. *Verb.*
—A clear liquid given off into the mouth; saliva. *Noun.*
> **spit** (spit) *verb,* **spit** or **spat, spitting;** *noun.*

spit² **1.** A slender, pointed rod on which meat is roasted over a fire. **2.** A narrow piece of land extending into a body of water.
> **spit** (spit) *noun, plural* **spits.**

spite A feeling of ill will toward another. *Noun.*
—To show ill will toward someone. *Verb.*
> • **in spite of.** Without being hindered or prevented by; despite; regardless of. We are going on the hike *in spite of* the rain.
> **spite** (spīt) *noun; verb,* **spited, spiting.**

splash **1.** To throw water or other liquid about. The children had fun *splashing* in the pool. The passing car *splashed* mud on my coat. **2.** To fall, strike, or move with the throwing about of water. The diver *splashed* into the pool. *Verb.*
—**1.** The act or sound of throwing water about. When you dove, you hit the water with a loud *splash.* **2.** A spot of water or other liquid, or a spot of color. The black horse had a *splash* of white on its nose. *Noun.*
> **splash** (splash) *verb,* **splashed, splashing;** *noun, plural* **splashes.**

splashdown The landing of a spacecraft in water, especially the ocean.
> **splash·down** (splash′doun′) *noun, plural* **splashdowns.**

splendid **1.** Very beautiful or magnificent. A peacock's tail has a *splendid* display of colors. **2.** Very good; excellent. Having a party was a *splendid* idea.
> **splen·did** (splen′did) *adjective.*

splendor Great beauty or magnificence. The child had never seen anything like the *splendor* of the royal palace.
> **splen·dor** (splen′dər) *noun, plural* **splendors.**

splint A piece of wood or other material used to hold a broken bone in place. A splint is often used until a cast can be put on.
> **splint** (splint) *noun, plural* **splints.**

splinter A thin, sharp piece broken off from something hard or brittle. I got a *splin-*

ter in my hand from the wooden board. *Noun.*
—To break into thin, sharp pieces. The glass window *splintered* when the ball hit it. *Verb.*
> **splin·ter** (splin′tər) *noun, plural* **splinters;** *verb,* **splintered, splintering.**

split To break apart or divide into parts or layers. The jacket *split* at the seam. The search party *split* into two groups. *Split* these logs for firewood. *Verb.*
—**1.** A break or division in something. The heavy wind made a *split* in the sail. There was a *split* in the political party over the tax issue. **2.** A movement in which a person's body slides to the floor with the legs spread out in opposite directions. *Noun.*
> **split** (split) *verb,* **split, splitting;** *noun, plural* **splits.**

spoil **1.** To damage or hurt in some way. Too much salt *spoiled* the taste of the soup. **2.** To raise poorly so that a child is not guided to form a good character. I think you *spoil* children if you always give them whatever they want. **3.** To become so bad it cannot be eaten. The meat *spoiled* because we forgot to put it back in the refrigerator. *Verb.*
—**spoils.** Property that has been seized by force. The soldiers carried away jewels and other *spoils* from the conquered city. *Noun.*
> **spoil** (spoil) *verb,* **spoiled** or **spoilt, spoiling;** *plural noun.*

spoilt A past tense and a past participle of **spoil.** Look up **spoil** for more information.
> **spoilt** (spoilt) *verb.*

spoke¹ Past tense of **speak.** I *spoke* to them yesterday. Look up **speak** for more information.
> **spoke** (spōk) *verb.*

spoke² One of the rods or bars that connect the rim of a wheel to the hub.
> **spoke** (spōk) *noun, plural* **spokes.**

spoken Past participle of **speak.** Have you *spoken* to your neighbor lately? Look up **speak** for more information. *Verb.*
—Said in speech; oral. People communicate by the *spoken* word. *Adjective.*
> **spo·ken** (spō′kən) *verb; adjective.*

sponge **1.** A simple water animal that has a body that is full of holes and absorbs water easily. Many sponges live in large colonies attached to rocks. The dried skeletons of some sponge colonies are used for cleaning and washing. **2.** A cleaning pad that looks like the skeleton of a sponge colony. *Noun.*
—To clean with a sponge. We *sponged* and dried the dirty walls. *Verb.*
> **sponge** (spunj) *noun, plural* **sponges;** *verb,* **sponged, sponging.**

sponsor 1. A person who is responsible in some way for another person or a thing. That senator is the *sponsor* of the bill. The *sponsors* of that television program paid the costs of making the program. 2. A person who attends the baptism of a child and agrees to help with the child's religious training; godparent. *Noun.*
—To act as a sponsor for. The school *sponsored* the fair to raise money. *Verb.*
spon·sor (spon′sər) *noun, plural* **sponsors;** *verb,* **sponsored, sponsoring.**

spontaneous 1. Not planned or forced. There was a *spontaneous* burst of applause when the batter hit a home run. 2. Happening without any apparent outside cause. There was a *spontaneous* explosion at the factory.
spon·ta·ne·ous (spon tā′nē əs) *adjective.*

spool A piece of wood or other material shaped like a cylinder. Wire, thread, and tape are wound around spools.
spool (spül) *noun, plural* **spools.**

spools of yarn

spoon A utensil with a small, shallow bowl at one end of a handle. A spoon is used for eating, measuring, or stirring. *Noun.*
—To lift up or move with a spoon. I *spooned* the food into the baby's mouth. *Verb.*
spoon (spün) *noun, plural* **spoons;** *verb,* **spooned, spooning.**

spore A cell that can develop into a new organism. Ferns, mushrooms, bacteria, and certain other living things produce spores.
spore (spôr) *noun, plural* **spores.**

sport 1. A game in which a person is physically active and often is competing with someone else. Baseball, bowling, swimming, and sailing are kinds of sports. 2. Amusement; fun. They collect butterflies for *sport.* 3. A person who has a definite attitude and behavior in games, contests, and sports.

They were good *sports* to congratulate us when we beat them. *Noun.*
—To amuse oneself; play. We watched the colts *sporting* in the field. *Verb.*
sport (spôrt) *noun, plural* **sports;** *verb,* **sported, sporting.**

sportsmanship 1. Conduct or behavior in playing a sport. You got a low grade in gym because of poor *sportsmanship.* 2. Good conduct in playing a sport; fair play. Both athletes are admired for their *sportsmanship.*
sports·man·ship (spôrts′mən ship′) *noun.*

spot 1. A mark or stain left by dirt, food, or other matter. There is a *spot* of gravy on your necktie. 2. A mark or area on something that is different from the rest. My dog is white with black *spots.* 3. A place. That park is a pleasant *spot* for a picnic. *Noun.*
—1. To mark or be marked with a stain or blot. The paint *spotted* the floor. 2. To see; recognize. I *spotted* you in the crowd. *Verb.*
• **on the spot.** 1. At the place referred to. We had the good luck to be *on the spot* when the movie star arrived at the hotel. 2. Without delay; immediately; at once. The manager refunded my money *on the spot.* 3. In a difficult or embarrassing condition or situation. I was *on the spot* when I didn't have bus fare.
spot (spot) *noun, plural* **spots;** *verb,* **spotted, spotting.**

spotless Without a spot or flaw. My white shirt must be *spotless* for the ceremony. The company's reputation for quality is *spotless.*
spot·less (spot′lis) *adjective.*

spotlight 1. A strong beam of light pointed at a particular person, place, or object. 2. A lamp projecting a beam of light onto a person, place, or object. The theater *spotlights* are on a platform high over the stage. 3. Public attention. Politicians live their lives in the *spotlight.*
spot·light (spot′līt′) *noun, plural* **spotlights.**

spouse A husband or wife.
spouse (spous) *noun, plural* **spouses.**

spout 1. To force out water or other liquid through a narrow opening. The elephant *spouted* water from its trunk. 2. To flow with force from an opening. Water *spouted* from the fire hydrant. *Verb.*

at; āpe; fär; câre; end; mē; it; īce; pîerce; hot; ōld; sông, fôrk; oil; out; up; ūse; rüle; pull; tûrn; chin; sing; shop; thin; <u>th</u>is; hw in white; zh in treasure. The symbol ə stands for the unstressed vowel sound in about, taken, pencil, lemon, and circus.

S

—A narrow opening through which a liquid flows or is poured. The teakettle has a curved *spout*. At a water fountain, the water comes up out of a *spout*. *Noun.*
 spout (spout) *verb,* **spouted, spouting;** *noun, plural* **spouts.**

spout

sprain To injure a joint or muscle of the body by twisting or straining it. The runner *sprained* an ankle in the race. *Verb.*
—An injury to a joint or muscle caused by twisting or straining. A bad *sprain* kept our best pitcher from playing. *Noun.*
 sprain (sprān) *verb,* **sprained, spraining;** *noun, plural* **sprains.**

sprang A past tense of **spring.** I *sprang* out of the chair suddenly when the phone rang. Look up **spring** for more information.
 sprang (sprang) *verb.*

sprawl **1.** To lie or sit with the body stretched out in an awkward or careless manner. I *sprawled* in the chair with one leg hooked over the arm. **2.** To spread out in a way that is not regular or organized. New houses *sprawl* across the countryside.
 sprawl (sprôl) *verb,* **sprawled, sprawling.**

spray **1.** Water or other liquid in tiny drops. The *spray* from the ocean waves felt cool. **2.** A device used to produce a spray or the substance put out by such a device. We used a *spray* to kill the mosquitoes in the tent. *Noun.*
—To put on or send out in a spray. The workers *sprayed* paint on the wall. *Verb.*
 spray (sprā) *noun, plural* **sprays;** *verb,* **sprayed, spraying.**

spread **1.** To open wide or stretch out. We *spread* the blanket on the sand. The bird *spread* its wings and flew away. **2.** To put or make a thin layer or covering on. I *spread* peanut butter on my toast. **3.** To scatter or reach out over an area; extend. The farmer *spread* fertilizer over the fields. The fire *spread* through the house. **4.** To make or become known by more people. Who *spread* the rumor that school would be closed tomorrow? News of the accident *spread* quickly. *Verb.*
—**1.** The act of spreading. Medicines can stop the *spread* of some diseases. **2.** The amount or extent to which something opens wide. The *spread* of the robin's wings was 15 inches from the tip of one wing to the other.

3. A cloth covering for a bed. **4.** Food that is soft enough to be spread. We had sandwiches made with chicken *spread*. *Noun.*
 spread (spred) *verb,* **spread, spreading;** *noun, plural* **spreads.**

spring **1.** To move forward or jump up quickly; leap. The dog had to *spring* out of the way to avoid the bicycle. **2.** To move or snap quickly. The door *sprang* shut behind me. **3.** To come or appear suddenly. The words *sprang* from my lips. After the rain, weeds *sprang* up on our lawn. **4.** To make known or cause to happen suddenly. They heard the good news yesterday, but they didn't *spring* it on us until tonight. *Verb.*
—**1.** A jump or leap. The acrobat made a beautiful *spring* from one trapeze to the next. **2.** An elastic device that can be stretched or bent and will move back to its original shape when it is released. This bed has metal *springs* shaped like spirals inside it. **3.** A place where underground water comes out of the earth. **4.** The season of the year that comes between winter and summer. *Noun.*
 spring (spring) *verb,* **sprang** or **sprung, sprung, springing;** *noun, plural* **springs.**

springboard A board that helps a person who is diving or tumbling to spring higher.
 spring·board (spring′bôrd′) *noun, plural* **springboards.**

sprinkle **1.** To scatter something in small drops or bits. We *sprinkled* sugar on the cookies. **2.** To rain gently. It *sprinkled* for a few minutes, and then the sun came out.
 sprin·kle (spring′kəl) *verb,* **sprinkled, sprinkling.**

sprinkler A device that is used to water gardens or lawns.
 sprin·kler (spring′klər) *noun, plural* **sprinklers.**

sprint To run fast for a short distance. We *sprinted* across the football field. *Verb.*
—A short, fast run or race. The 50-yard dash is a *sprint*. *Noun.*
 sprint (sprint) *verb,* **sprinted, sprinting;** *noun, plural* **sprints.**

sprout To begin to grow. The seeds that I planted a week ago have just *sprouted*. *Verb.*
—A young shoot from a seed or plant. The *sprouts* grew into new leaves. *Noun.*
 sprout (sprout) *verb,* **sprouted, sprouting;** *noun, plural* **sprouts.**

spruce An evergreen tree with drooping cones and short leaves shaped like needles. Its wood is used in making pulp for paper.
 spruce (sprüs) *noun, plural* **spruces.**

sprung A past tense and the past participle of **spring.** Flowers have *sprung* up in our

yard. Look up **spring** for more information.
sprung (sprung) *verb.*

spun Past tense and past participle of **spin.** The football player *spun* around and caught the ball. Look up **spin** for more information.
spun (spun) *verb.*

spur A sharp metal piece worn on the heel of a horse rider's boot. A horse is pricked with a spur to make it go faster. *Noun.*
—**1.** To prick a horse with a spur or spurs. The rider *spurred* the horse so it would run faster. **2.** To urge on. The crowd's cheers *spurred* the home team to victory. *Verb.*
spur (spûr) *noun, plural* **spurs;** *verb,* **spurred, spurring.**

spurs

spurt To pour out suddenly in a stream. Water *spurted* from the broken pipe. *Verb.*
—A sudden pouring out or bursting forth. A *spurt* of water came out of the hose. *Noun.*
spurt (spûrt) *verb,* **spurted, spurting;** *noun, plural* **spurts.**

sputter **1.** To make popping or spitting noises. The hot oil *sputtered* when I put the onions in it. **2.** To speak quickly in a confused way. The child *sputtered* with anger. **3.** To throw out saliva or small bits of food when speaking in a quick or excited way. The baby *sputtered* when trying to speak. *Verb.*
—The act or sound of sputtering. *Noun.*
sput·ter (sput′ər) *verb,* **sputtered, sputtering;** *noun, plural* **sputters.**

spy A person who watches others secretly. A person is sometimes hired as a spy by a government to discover secret information about another government. *Noun.*
—**1.** To watch others secretly; act as a spy. The submarine was sent to *spy* on enemy ships. **2.** To catch sight of; spot. The sailor *spied* a ship on the horizon. *Verb.*
spy (spī) *noun, plural* **spies;** *verb,* **spied, spying.**

spyglass A small telescope.
spy·glass (spī′glas′) *noun, plural* **spyglasses.**

sq. An abbreviation for *square.*

squabble To argue noisily over something of little importance. They *squabbled* over who would sit in the big chair. *Verb.*
—A noisy argument over something of little importance. *Noun.*

squab·ble (skwob′əl) *verb,* **squabbled, squabbling;** *noun, plural* **squabbles.**

squad **1.** A small group of soldiers who train, work, or fight together. **2.** A small group of people working together. The counselor picked a *squad* to clean our cabin.
squad (skwod) *noun, plural* **squads.**

squadron A group of airplanes, ships, or other military units.
squad·ron (skwod′rən) *noun, plural* **squadrons.**

squall A strong gust of wind that arises very suddenly. Squalls often bring rain, snow, or sleet.
squall (skwôl) *noun, plural* **squalls.**

The windowpanes have a **square** shape.

square **1.** A figure having four sides that are all the same length and four right angles. **2.** Something having the shape of a square. A checkerboard is covered with light and dark *squares.* **3.** An open space in a city or town that has streets on all sides. Squares are often planted with grass, trees, or flowers and used as parks. **4.** An instrument shaped like an **L** or a **T** that is used to draw or measure right angles. The architect used a *square* to draw the design. **5.** The number obtained when a number is multiplied by itself. The *square* of 4 is 16 because $4 \times 4 = 16$. **6.** A person who is not interested in

at; āpe; fär; câre; end; mē; it; īce; pîerce; hot; ōld; sông, fôrk; oil; out; up; ūse; rüle; pull; tûrn; chin; sing; shop; thin; <u>th</u>is; hw in white; zh in treasure. The symbol ə stands for the unstressed vowel sound in about, taken, pencil, lemon, and circus.

S

701

new fashions or trends. Don't be such a *square*—you might enjoy this new kind of music. *Noun.*
—**1.** Having four sides that are all the same length and four right angles. Is this sheet of paper *square* or triangular? **2.** Shaped somewhat like a cube. The hat came in a *square* box. **3.** Forming a right angle. This desk has *square* corners. **4.** Being a square or squares with each side equal to one unit of the named length, used for measuring area. Our back yard is 50 feet wide and 100 feet long, so its total area is 5,000 *square* feet. **5.** Fair or just; honest. That car dealer promises to give all customers a *square* deal. **6.** Conservative or not interested in new fashions or trends; old-fashioned. *Adjective.*
—**1.** To make into the form of a right angle; make look like part of a square. The carpenter *squared* the door frame so the door would close easily. **2.** To mark in a square or squares. The children *squared* off part of the playing field for their game. **3.** To fit or match with something else; agree. The witness's story doesn't *square* with the facts. **4.** To multiply a number by itself. Two *squared* equals four because $2 \times 2 = 4$. *Verb.*
—Directly and firmly. The truck hit the car *square* on its fender. *Adverb.*

square (skwâr) *noun, plural* **squares;** *adjective,* **squarer, squarest;** *verb,* **squared, squaring;** *adverb.*

square dance A dance performed by groups of couples who are arranged in a square at the start of the dance.

square root A number that, when multiplied by itself, will produce a certain number. The *square root* of 36 is 6 because $6 \times 6 = 36$.

kinds of **squash**

squash¹ **1.** To squeeze or press into a soft or flat mass; crush. I *squashed* the flower when I accidentally stepped on it. **2.** To force or squeeze into a small area. We *squashed* our clothes into a small suitcase. *Verb.*
—A game somewhat like tennis and hand-ball. It is played by two or four people with rackets and a rubber ball in a court with walls. *Noun.*

squash (skwosh) *verb,* **squashed, squashing;** *noun.*

squash² Any of several vegetables of various shapes that grow on vines. Squashes are usually yellow or green in color.

squash (skwosh) *noun, plural* **squashes.**

squat To crouch or sit with the knees bent and drawn close to the body. I *squatted* to pet the cat. *Verb.*
—Short and thick; low and broad. That *squat* vase was a present. *Adjective.*

squat (skwot) *verb,* **squatted** or **squat, squatting;** *adjective.*

squawk **1.** To make a shrill, harsh cry like that of a frightened chicken. The parrot *squawked* when I waved a cracker in front of it. **2.** To complain loudly or harshly. Don't *squawk* about your chores. *Verb.*
—**1.** A shrill, harsh cry, such as one made by a frightened chicken. We could hear the *squawks* of the chickens in the barnyard. **2.** A complaint. I don't want to hear another *squawk* from you! *Noun.*

squawk (skwôk) *verb,* **squawked, squawking;** *noun, plural* **squawks.**

squeak A short, thin, high sound or cry. We heard the *squeak* of the rusty hinges as someone opened the gate. *Noun.*
—To make a short, thin, high sound or cry. The mouse *squeaked* and ran when it saw the cat. *Verb.*

squeak (skwēk) *noun, plural* **squeaks;** *verb,* **squeaked, squeaking.**

squeal To make a loud, shrill cry or sound. The child *squealed* with delight upon seeing all the presents. *Verb.*
—A loud, shrill cry or sound. There was a *squeal* of brakes as the speeding car came to a halt. *Noun.*

squeal (skwēl) *verb,* **squealed, squealing;** *noun, plural* **squeals.**

squeeze **1.** To press hard. *Squeeze* the tube of toothpaste from the bottom. **2.** To get by squeezing or by putting on pressure. I *squeezed* the juice from an orange. **3.** To hug or clasp in affection. The mother *squeezed* the child in her arms. **4.** To force by pushing or shoving. Don't *squeeze* your shirts into the drawer. The rabbit could barely *squeeze* through the opening in the fence. *Verb.*
—The act of squeezing. Dad gave my hand a gentle *squeeze* to let me know everything would be all right. *Noun.*

squeeze (skwēz) *verb,* **squeezed, squeezing;** *noun, plural* **squeezes.**

squid   A sea animal that looks something like an octopus. A squid has ten arms and a body shaped like a tube.
  squid (skwid) *noun, plural* **squids** or **squid.**

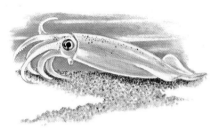

squid

squint   To partly close the eyes. The bright sunlight made me *squint*.
  squint (skwint) *verb,* **squinted, squinting.**

squirm   **1.** To turn or twist the body; wriggle. The children were bored and began to *squirm* in their seats.   **2.** To feel uncomfortable or nervous. The lawyer's clever questions made the witness *squirm. Verb.*
  —A turn or twist of the body. With a *squirm*, the puppy jumped out of my arms. *Noun.*
  squirm (skwûrm) *verb,* **squirmed, squirming;** *noun, plural* **squirms.**

squirrel   A small animal with a long, bushy tail. Squirrels live in trees and feed mainly on nuts.
  squir·rel (skwûr′əl) *noun, plural* **squirrels.**

squirrel

squirt   **1.** To force out liquid in a thin stream through a narrow opening. The worker *squirted* oil on the rusty hinge.   **2.** To come out in a thin stream. Ink *squirted* from the fountain pen. *Verb.*
  —The act of squirting or the amount squirted. I added a few *squirts* of yellow to the orange paint. *Noun.*
  squirt (skwûrt) *verb,* **squirted, squirting;** *noun, plural* **squirts.**

Sr.   An abbreviation for *Senior.*

Sri Lanka   An island country in the Indian Ocean. It is off the southeastern coast of India.
  Sri Lan·ka (srē läng′kə) *noun.*

St.   An abbreviation for *Street* used in a written address and for *Saint.*

stab   **1.** To wound or make a hole with a pointed weapon. In the movie, the hero *stabbed* the villian with a sword.   **2.** To stick or drive something pointed into something. I *stabbed* a fork into the steak. *Verb.*
  —**1.** A blow or thrust made with a pointed weapon or as if with a pointed weapon. My *stab* at the peas made them roll off the plate.   **2.** A sharp but brief feeling; pang. You'll feel a *stab* of pain if you try to move your sprained ankle.   **3.** An attempt; try. I'm going to take a *stab* at skiing. *Noun.*
  stab (stab) *verb,* **stabbed, stabbing;** *noun, plural* **stabs.**

stability   The condition of not being easily moved, shaken, or overthrown. This kind of rowboat has great *stability*. The government's *stability* was threatened by the rebels.
  sta·bil·i·ty (stə bil′i tē) *noun.*

stable¹   A building where horses or cattle are kept and fed. *Noun.*
  —To put or keep in a stable. *Verb.*
  sta·ble (stā′bəl) *noun, plural* **stables;** *verb,* **stabled, stabling.**

stable²   Not easily moved, shaken, or changed. The wooden bridge over the river is *stable* and can support a lot of weight. That new country does not have a *stable* government.
  sta·ble (stā′bəl) *adjective.*

stack   **1.** A large, neat pile of hay, straw, or grain. The farmer arranged the hay in *stacks* all over the field.   **2.** A number of things piled up one on top of the other; pile. I had a *stack* of pancakes for breakfast. *Noun.*
  —To pile or arrange in a stack. Please *stack* the records in the corner. *Verb.*
  stack (stak) *noun, plural* **stacks;** *verb,* **stacked, stacking.**

stadium   A structure made up of rows of seats built around an open field. People sit in stadiums to watch sports contests and concerts.
  sta·di·um (stā′dē əm) *noun, plural* **stadiums.**

staff   **1.** A stick, rod, or pole. In the painting, the shepherd stood holding a *staff*.   **2.** A pole for flying a flag; flagpole.   **3.** A group of people who work for an institution, company, or person. A hospital *staff* includes doctors and nurses.   **4.** The lines and spaces on which music is written. *Noun.*

at; āpe; fär; câre; end; mē; it; īce; pîerce; hot; ōld; sông, fôrk; oil; out; up; ūse; rüle; pull; tûrn; chin; sing; shop; thin; this; hw in white; zh in treasure. The symbol ə stands for the unstressed vowel sound in about, taken, pencil, lemon, and circus.

S

703

—To provide with workers. The new library won't open until it is *staffed. Verb.*
staff (staf) *noun, plural* **staves** (stāvz) *(for definitions 1 and 4)* or **staffs** *(for definitions 2 and 3); verb,* **staffed, staffing.**

stag   A fully grown male deer.
stag (stag) *noun, plural* **stags.**

stage   **1.** A raised platform on which actors, dancers, singers, or other entertainers perform.   **2.** A place where something important takes place. Europe was the principal *stage* of World War I.   **3.** A single step, period, or degree in a process or development. During the last *stage* of their journey, the explorers had very little food left.   **4.** A short form of the word "stagecoach." Look up **stagecoach** for more information.   **5.** A section of a rocket that has its own engine and fuel. It is usually separated from the rest of the rocket when its fuel is used up. *Noun.*
—To plan, put on, or present. The children *staged* a play for Thanksgiving. The workers *staged* a protest in front of the factory. *Verb.*
stage (stāj) *noun, plural* **stages;** *verb,* **staged, staging.**

stagecoach   A large, closed coach pulled by horses. Stagecoaches were once used for carrying passengers, mail, and baggage.
stage·coach (stāj′kōch′) *noun, plural* **stagecoaches.**

stagger   **1.** To move or cause to move with a swaying motion. You *staggered* because you were dizzy from spinning around.   **2.** To stun; shock. The nation was *staggered* by the news of war.   **3.** To arrange by scheduling at different times. The school *staggered* the lunch hours so that the cafeteria would be less crowded. *Verb.*
—An unsteady or swaying motion. I walked with a *stagger* after the boat ride. *Noun.*
stag·ger (stag′ər) *verb,* **staggered, staggering;** *noun, plural* **staggers.**

stagnant   **1.** Without motion; still. The air in the closed room was *stagnant.*   **2.** Foul from being still. The water in the swamp is *stagnant.*   **3.** Not active, changing, or developing. Business in the department store becomes *stagnant* after a big sale.
stag·nant (stag′nənt) *adjective.*

stain   **1.** A mark or spot. The spilled ink left a *stain* on the rug.   **2.** A cause of shame or dishonor. They vowed to wipe out the *stain* on their family's reputation.   **3.** A dye or other substance used to color something. I put a brown *stain* on the bookcase. *Noun.*
—**1.** To spot or soil. They *stained* the towels with their greasy hands.   **2.** To color with a dye or something like a dye. They *stained* the bookcase brown.   **3.** To bring shame or dishonor to. The dishonesty of one person *stained* the reputation of the group. *Verb.*
stain (stān) *noun, plural* **stains;** *verb,* **stained, staining.**

stair   **1. stairs.** A set of steps for going from one level or floor to another.   **2.** A step in such a set.   ▲ Another word that sounds like this is **stare.**
stair (stâr) *noun, plural* **stairs.**

staircase   A set of stairs with the railing and framework that support it. This is also called a **stairway.**
stair·case (stâr′kās′) *noun, plural* **staircases.**

staircase

stairway   A staircase.
stair·way (stâr′wā′) *noun, plural* **stairways.**

stake   **1.** A stick or post pointed at one end so that it can be driven into the ground. The campers drove *stakes* into the ground and tied the corners of the tent to them.   **2.** An amount of money or anything else that is risked in a bet or gamble.   **3.** An interest or share in something. My folks have a large *stake* in the business. *Noun.*
—**1.** To fasten or hold up with a stake. The gardener *staked* the tomatoes and the beans.   **2.** To mark the boundaries of a piece of land; claim. Each of the prospectors *staked* a claim.   **3.** To risk something in a bet or gamble. They *staked* all their savings on their invention. *Verb.*   ▲ Another word that sounds like this is **steak.**
stake (stāk) *noun, plural* **stakes;** *verb,* **staked, staking.**

stalactite A piece of stone that looks like an icicle and hangs from the roof of a cave. A stalactite is formed by drips of water that contain lime.
sta·lac·tite (stə lak′tīt) *noun, plural* **stalactites.**

stalagmite A piece of stone that is shaped like a cone and is built up from the floor of a cave. A stalagmite is formed by drips of water that contain lime.
sta·lag·mite (stə lag′mīt) *noun, plural* **stalagmites.**

stale **1.** Not fresh. The old bread was very *stale.* **2.** Not new or interesting. The audience was bored with the *stale* jokes.
stale (stāl) *adjective,* **staler, stalest.**

stalk¹ **1.** The main stem of a plant or part of a plant. The flower and leaves of a rose grow on the stalk. **2.** Something that is shaped like a plant's stalk. In some crabs, each eye is located at the end of a short stalk.
stalk (stôk) *noun, plural* **stalks.**

stalk² **1.** To follow someone or something quietly and carefully in order to catch it. The lion *stalked* the antelope. **2.** To walk in a stiff, proud manner. I was so angry that I *stalked* out of the room.
stalk (stôk) *verb,* **stalked, stalking.**

stall¹ **1.** A place in a barn or stable for an animal. **2.** A counter or booth where things are shown for sale. *Noun.*
—To stop running. The engine of our old car sometimes *stalls* on cold days. *Verb.*
stall (stôl) *noun, plural* **stalls;** *verb,* **stalled, stalling.**

stall² To delay or prevent. The neighborhood wants a traffic light installed at this corner, but the city has been *stalling.Verb.*
—Something used to delay or prevent. Complaints about the new chairperson were a *stall* to keep us from voting. *Noun.*
stall (stôl) *verb,* **stalled, stalling;** *noun, plural* **stalls.**

stallion An adult male horse.
stal·lion (stal′yən) *noun, plural* **stallions.**

stamen The part of a flower that produces pollen. A stamen consists of a long stalk with a pollen sac at the end. The stamens of a flower are usually surrounded by the petals.
sta·men (stā′mən) *noun, plural* **stamens.**

Pistil

Stamens

stamens

stamina Strength; endurance. That athlete had the *stamina* to practice long and hard.
stam·i·na (stam′ə nə) *noun.*

stammer To speak or say with difficulty. A person who stammers might repeat the same sound several times when trying to say a word. *Verb.*
—The act of stammering. I sometimes speak with a *stammer* when I'm nervous. *Noun.*
stam·mer (stam′ər) *verb,* **stammered, stammering;** *noun, plural* **stammers.**

stamp **1.** A small piece of paper that is stuck on letters or packages to show that a mailing fee has been paid; postage stamp. Look up **postage stamp** for more information. **2.** A tool for cutting, shaping, or pressing a design, numbers, or letters on paper, wax, metal, or other material. The librarian used a rubber *stamp* to put the date on the library card. **3.** A bringing down of one's foot with force. With a *stamp* of the foot, the child refused to go to bed. *Noun.*
—**1.** To bring down one's foot or feet with force. The spoiled children *stamped* their feet in anger. **2.** To mark with a tool that makes or prints a design, numbers, or letters. The salesperson *stamped* the bill to show it had been paid. **3.** To put a postage stamp on. I sealed the envelope and *stamped* it. *Verb.*
• **to stamp out.** To put out, stop, or do away with. Citizens of our town are doing their best to *stamp out* pollution.
stamp (stamp) *noun, plural* **stamps;** *verb,* **stamped, stamping.**

stamps

at; āpe; fär; câre; end; mē; it; ice; pîerce; hot; ōld; sông, fôrk; oil; out; up; ūse; rüle; pùll; tûrn; chin; sing; shop; thin; this; hw in white; zh in treasure. The symbol ə stands for the unstressed vowel sound in about, taken, pencil, lemon, and circus.

S

stampede **1.** A sudden, wild running of a frightened herd of animals. The thunderstorm frightened the cattle and caused a *stampede.* **2.** A sudden, wild rush of many people. There was a *stampede* toward the exit when the fire broke out in the theater. *Noun.*
—To make a sudden, wild rush. The wild horses *stampeded* when they heard the helicopter coming. *Verb.*
stam·pede (stam pēd′) *noun, plural* stampedes; *verb,* stampeded, stampeding.

stand **1.** To be upright on one's feet. We had to *stand* because there were no more seats. **2.** To get up on one's feet. The crowd *stood* to sing the national anthem. **3.** To be or put upright. A ladder *stood* against the side of the barn. We *stood* the barrel on its end. **4.** To be in a particular place, condition, or situation. The village *stands* at the foot of the hill. The door at the end of the hall *stood* open. **5.** To stay the same; be unchanged. The rule against chewing gum in class still *stands.* **6.** To be patient about; bear. I can't *stand* all this noise. **7.** To have an opinion or point of view. How does the mayor *stand* on that issue? *Verb.*
—**1.** A position or opinion. What is the candidate's *stand* on lowering taxes? **2.** A stop or halt for battle. The troops made a *stand* by the river. **3.** A place where someone or something should be or usually is. I took my *stand* at the door. **4.** A rack or something like it to put things on or in. There's an umbrella *stand* in the hall. **5.** A booth, counter, or other small place where things are sold. You can get a newspaper at the *stand* on the corner. **6.** A raised place where people can sit or stand. The mayor watched the parade from the reviewing *stand.* We sat in the *stands* at the baseball game. *Noun.*
- **to stand by.** **1.** To support or defend. My friends *stood by* me when I was having trouble with the bully. **2.** To be or become ready; wait in preparation. The radio announcer said to *stand by* for an important message.
- **to stand for.** **1.** To mean, represent, or symbolize. What does the contraction "can't" *stand for?* **2.** To allow or endure; put up with. This is a terrible situation, and I won't *stand for it.*
- **to stand out.** To be easy to see; stick out. Your red hair certainly makes you *stand out* in this picture.

stand (stand) *verb,* stood, standing; *noun, plural* stands.

standard **1.** Anything used to set an example or serve as something to be copied. New cars must meet safety *standards* before they can be sold. **2.** A flag or emblem. I carried my school's *standard* in the parade. *Noun.*
—**1.** Used as a standard. A pound is a *standard* measure of weight. **2.** Widely used or usual. It's our *standard* practice to send bills on the first day of the month. **3.** Thought of as excellent or as an authority. This is the *standard* book on gardening. *Adjective.*
stand·ard (stan′dərd) *noun, plural* standards; *adjective.*

stanza A group of lines in poetry that are arranged in a particular pattern. A stanza forms one of the parts of a poem or song.
stan·za (stan′zə) *noun, plural* stanzas.

staple[1] A piece of wire or metal that is bent into the shape of a **U**. Staples are used to hold papers, fabrics, and various other materials together. *Noun.*
—To hold together or attach with a staple. I *stapled* the pages of my book report. *Verb.*
sta·ple (stā′pəl) *noun, plural* staples; *verb,* stapled, stapling.

staple[2] **1.** A very important product that everyone needs or uses. Flour, salt, and sugar are staples. **2.** A very important crop or product of a country or region.
sta·ple (stā′pəl) *noun, plural* staples.

stapler A device used to staple things together.
sta·pler (stā′plər) *noun, plural* staplers.

star **1.** A heavenly body that shines by its own light, which comes from burning gases. Our sun is the nearest star to earth. Other stars are so far away that they look like tiny points of light in the night sky. **2.** A figure that has five or more points. A starfish has the shape of a *star.* **3.** A person who is very good or outstanding in some field. They are the *stars* of our school's basketball team. **4.** An actor who plays a leading role in a play, movie, or television show. *Noun.*
—**1.** To mark with a star. I *starred* the words that I still need to study. **2.** To play a leading role in a play, movie, or television show. My favorite actor *stars* in this movie. *Verb.*
—Leading; best. You are the *star* speller in our class. *Adjective.*
star (stär) *noun, plural* stars; *verb,* starred, starring; *adjective.*

starboard The right side of a boat, ship, or aircraft when a person standing on deck faces forward. *Noun.*
—On the right side of a boat, ship, or aircraft. The tugboat moved toward the *starboard* side of the ship. *Adjective.*
star·board (stär′bərd) *noun; adjective.*

starch **1.** A white food substance that is made and stored in most plants. It has no

taste or smell. Potatoes, wheat, corn, and rice contain starch. **2.** A substance used to make clothes or cloth stiffer or stiff. *Noun.*
—To make stiffer or stiff by using starch. The laundry *starched* your shirts. *Verb.*
 starch (stärch) *noun, plural* **starches;** *verb,* **starched, starching.**

stare To look very hard or very long with the eyes wide open. We *stared* at the fancy watches in the store window. *Verb.*
—A long, fixed look with the eyes wide open. *Noun.* ▲ Another word that sounds like this is **stair.**
 stare (stâr) *verb,* **stared, staring;** *noun, plural* **stares.**

starfish A sea animal that has a flat body shaped like a star. A starfish is not a fish.
 star·fish (stär′fish′) *noun, plural* **starfish** or **starfishes.**

starling A bird with a plump body and brown or greenish black feathers. Starlings originally lived only in Europe and Australia but are now found in most parts of the world.
 star·ling (stär′ling) *noun, plural* **starlings.**

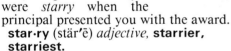
starling

starry **1.** With many stars in the sky; lighted by stars. It was a cold, *starry* night. **2.** Shining like a star; bright. Your eyes were *starry* when the principal presented you with the award.
 star·ry (stär′ē) *adjective,* **starrier, starriest.**

Stars and Stripes The flag of the United States. It has red and white stripes, and a blue rectangle with white stars on it in the upper left corner. The stripes represent the thirteen original colonies, and the fifty stars represent the fifty states.

Star-Spangled Banner The national anthem of the United States.
 Star-Span·gled Banner (stär′spang′gəld).

start **1.** To begin to act, move, or happen. If everyone is ready, we can *start.* The car *started* easily when it got warmer. What time does the game *start?* **2.** To make something act, move, or happen. You turn the key to *start* the car's engine. My cousin has *started* a new business in town. **3.** To move suddenly from surprise or fear. The kitten *started* when I tapped it on the back. *Verb.*
—**1.** The act of starting; beginning. We got an early *start* and reached the lake before noon. At the *start* of the movie, the two main characters met. **2.** A sudden movement. I woke with a *start* when the phone rang. *Noun.*
 start (stärt) *verb,* **started, starting;** *noun, plural* **starts.**

the **start** of a race

startle **1.** To excite or cause to move suddenly, as with surprise or fright. A spider dropped from the ceiling and *startled* me. **2.** To become excited or move suddenly, as with surprise or fright. Deer *startle* easily.
 star·tle (stär′təl) *verb,* **startled, startling.**

starve **1.** To suffer from or die of hunger. **2.** To be very hungry. It's almost time for lunch, and I'm *starving.* **3.** To need or want very much. The lost puppy was *starving* for attention.
 starve (stärv) *verb,* **starved, starving.**

state **1.** The condition of a person or thing. They were very upset after the accident and were in no *state* to see anyone. Water in its solid *state* is ice. **2.** A group of people living together under one government; nation. Africa has many newly independent *states.* **3.** A group of people living in a political unit that is part of a larger government. Hawaii is a *state* of the United States. **4.** The area where the people of a state live. **5. the States.** The United States. *Noun.*
—To show or explain in words; express. The test question asked us to *state* the causes of the Civil War. *Verb.*
—**1.** Having to do with a state. Their *state* highway system is one of the best in the na-

at; āpe; fär; câre; end; mē; it; īce; pîerce; hot; ōld; sông, fôrk; oil; out; up; ūse; rüle; pull; tûrn; chin; sing; shop; thin; **this;** hw in white; zh in treasure. The symbol ə stands for the unstressed vowel sound in about, taken, pencil, lemon, and circus.

S

707

tion. **2.** Having to do with an official ceremony; formal. A *state* dinner was planned for the visiting diplomat. *Adjective.*

    state (stāt) *noun, plural* **states;** *verb,* **stated, stating;** *adjective.*

stately Grand and graceful in appearance or manner; dignified; majestic. The orchestra played a *stately* march.

    state·ly (stāt′lē) *adjective,* **statelier, stateliest.**

statement **1.** Something stated. The police took a *statement* from the witness about the robbery. **2.** A report of financial matters. Every month my parents receive a *statement* from the bank telling how much is in their account.

    state·ment (stāt′mənt) *noun, plural* **statements.**

statesman A person who has shown skill or wisdom in politics or government. Benjamin Franklin was an American *statesman.*

    states·man (stāts′mən) *noun, plural* **statesmen** (stāts′mən).

static Showing little or no growth, change, or movement; staying the same. The town's population has remained *static. Adjective.*
—Electrical charges in the air. Static causes the crackling or hissing sounds that may interfere with radio broadcasts. *Noun.*

    stat·ic (stat′ik) *adjective; noun.*

static electricity A quantity of electricity that builds up on an object and does not flow away. Static electricity can be created by combing dry hair with a dry comb.

station **1.** A regular stopping place along a route. There are stations along railroad and bus routes where passengers can get on or off. **2.** A building or place used by a business or other organization. My cousin works at a gas *station.* There is a police *station* on the next block. **3.** The place or position in which a person or thing stands or is supposed to stand. The guards could not leave their *stations.* **4.** A place where radio or television programs are recorded or transmitted. *Noun.*
—To place in a post or position. We *stationed* ourselves by the door. *Verb.*

    sta·tion (stā′shən) *noun, plural* **stations;** *verb,* **stationed, stationing.**

stationary **1.** Standing still; not moving. Traffic leaving the resort was nearly *stationary.* **2.** Not able to be moved. The old desks in the classroom were *stationary* because they were bolted to the floor. **3.** Staying the same; not changing. The price of eggs has been *stationary* for months. ▲ Another word that sounds like this is **stationery.**

    sta·tion·ar·y (stā′shə ner′ē) *adjective.*

stationery Paper, envelopes, and other materials used for writing. ▲ Another word that sounds like this is **stationary.**

    sta·tion·er·y (stā′shə ner′ē) *noun.*

station wagon An automobile that has one or more rows of seats in the rear that can be folded down or taken out. A station wagon also has a door across the back.

statistics Numbers, facts, and other data that are collected about a particular subject.

    sta·tis·tics (stə tis′tiks) *plural noun.*

statue A likeness of a person or animal that is made out of stone, bronze, clay, or some other solid material.

    stat·ue (stach′ü) *noun, plural* **statues.**

status **1.** The position or rank of someone when compared with other people. Did your *status* change when you got your new job? **2.** The condition or situation of a person or thing; state. Where the form asked for job *status,* the woman wrote "employed."

    sta·tus (stā′təs *or* stat′əs) *noun.*

statute A law or rule, especially a law passed by a legislature.

    stat·ute (stach′üt) *noun, plural* **statutes.**

stave One of the long, narrow strips of wood that make up the sides of a barrel or keg.

    stave (stāv) *noun, plural* **staves.**

staves **1.** A plural of **staff.** The shepherds' *staves* were made from tree branches. Look up **staff** for more information. **2.** The plural of **stave.** The barrel was too full and so the *staves* broke. Look up **stave** for more information.

    staves (stāvz) *plural noun.*

staves of a basket

stay¹ **1.** To wait in one place; not leave; remain. *Stay* where you are so that you don't get lost in the crowd. **2.** To continue being. We *stayed* friends for many years after I moved away. **3.** To live for a short time. Did you *stay* at a hotel during your vacation? *Verb.*
—A visit or stop. After a brief *stay* at the seashore, they returned home. *Noun.*

    stay (stā) *verb,* **stayed, staying;** *noun, plural* **stays.**

stay² **1.** A strong rope or wire used to support the mast of a ship. **2.** Something used as a support.
stay (stā) *noun, plural* **stays.**

steadfast Not changing or moving; constant. She was *steadfast* in her determination to become a doctor. He looked at me with a *steadfast* gaze.
stead·fast (sted′fast′) *adjective.*

steady **1.** Firm in movement or position; not shaky. Make sure the ladder is *steady.* **2.** Going at an even rate. We walked at a *steady* pace. **3.** Not changing; regular. This drugstore has many *steady* customers. **4.** Not easily upset; calm. When the fire started, the students showed courage and *steady* nerves. *Adjective.*
—To make or become steady. I *steadied* myself on the end of the diving board. *Verb.*
stead·y (sted′ē) *adjective,* **steadier, steadiest;** *verb,* **steadied, steadying.**

steak A thick piece of meat or fish for broiling or frying. ▲ Another word that sounds like this is **stake.**
steak (stāk) *noun, plural* **steaks.**

steal **1.** To take something that does not belong to one. I hope no one *steals* my bicycle. **2.** To take in a secret or tricky way. We *stole* a glance behind the curtain. **3.** To get, take, or win by surprise or charm. The cute kitten *stole* my heart. **4.** To move or pass secretly, quietly, or without being noticed. They *stole* past the guard and into the stadium. **5.** To get to the next base in baseball without the help of a hit or error. The catcher *stole* second base in that inning. *Verb.*
—**1.** The act of stealing a base in baseball. **2.** Something bought at a low price; bargain. *Noun.* ▲ Another word that sounds like this is **steel.**
steal (stēl) *verb,* **stole, stolen, stealing;** *noun, plural* **steals.**

steam **1.** Water in the form of a gas. Water turns into steam when it is heated to the boiling point. Steam is often used to heat buildings and to run engines. **2.** Power; energy. By the end of the game, we had run out of *steam. Noun.*
—**1.** To cook with steam or apply steam to. The cook *steamed* the clams. I *steamed* the wrinkles out of my shirt. **2.** To give off steam. The boiling water *steamed.* **3.** To be covered with steam or mist. My eyeglasses *steamed* up when I came into the warm building. **4.** To move by means of steam power. The boat *steamed* into port. *Verb.*
steam (stēm) *noun; verb,* **steamed, steaming.**

steamboat

steamboat A boat powered by steam.
steam·boat (stēm′bōt′) *noun, plural* **steamboats.**

steam engine An engine run by steam.

steamer **1.** A boat powered by steam; steamboat or steamship. **2.** A pot or device for cooking things with steam. **3.** A clam with a soft shell that is used for food.
steam·er (stē′mər) *noun, plural* **steamers.**

steamroller A large engine on wide, heavy rollers that is powered by steam. It is used to press and to smooth the material used in making roads.
steam·roll·er (stēm′rō′lər) *noun, plural* **steamrollers.**

steamship A large ship powered by steam.
steam·ship (stēm′ship′) *noun, plural* **steamships.**

steed A horse.
steed (stēd) *noun, plural* **steeds.**

steel A hard, strong metal made of iron, carbon, and other materials. Steel is used to make machines, tools, automobiles, and many other things. *Noun.*
—Made of steel. This knife has a *steel* blade. *Adjective.*
—To make hard or strong like steel. We *steeled* ourselves for the bad news. *Verb.*
▲ Another word that sounds like this is **steal.**
steel (stēl) *noun; adjective; verb,* **steeled, steeling.**

at; āpe; fär; câre; end; mē; it; īce; pîerce; hot; ōld; sông, fôrk; oil; out; up; ūse; rüle; pull; tûrn; chin; sing; shop; thin; this; hw in white; zh in treasure. The symbol ə stands for the unstressed vowel sound in about, taken, pencil, lemon, and circus.

S

709

steel wool   A pad made from fine threads of steel. It is used for cleaning and polishing things.

steep[1]   Having a very sharp slope. It was difficult to ride our bicycles up the *steep* hill.
steep (stēp) *adjective*, **steeper, steepest.**

steep[2]   **1.** To soak in water or another liquid. I *steeped* tea leaves in hot water.   **2.** To be full of something. The disappearance of the painting was *steeped* in mystery.
steep (stēp) *verb*, **steeped, steeping.**

steeple   A high tower that narrows to a point and is built on a roof. Many churches have steeples.
stee·ple (stē′pəl) *noun, plural* **steeples.**

steer[1]   **1.** To guide the course of. We *steered* our bicycles around the hole.   **2.** To be guided. A large truck does not *steer* as easily as a car.   **3.** To follow or direct one's course. The people in the sailboat *steered* a course for the dock.
steer (stîr) *verb*, **steered, steering.**

steer[2]   A young bull that is raised to produce meat rather than to produce young.
steer (stîr) *noun, plural* **steers.**

stegosaurus   A dinosaur that had bony plates sticking up along its backbone. It ate only plants and walked on all four feet.
steg·o·sau·rus (steg′ə sôr′əs) *noun, plural* **stegosauri** (steg′ə sôr′ī).

stem[1]   **1.** The main part of a plant that supports the leaves and flowers. Water and food travel through the stem to all parts of the plant.   **2.** Anything that is like the stem of a plant in shape or purpose. The *stem* of the wine glass broke. *Noun.*
—**1.** To remove the stem of. We *stemmed* the cherries before serving them.   **2.** To originate; begin. The air pollution in our town *stems* from the refinery. *Verb.*
stem (stem) *noun, plural* **stems;** *verb,* **stemmed, stemming.**

stem[2]   To stop. The plumber *stemmed* the flow of water from the leak in the pipe.
stem (stem) *verb,* **stemmed, stemming.**

stencil   **1.** A thin sheet of paper, metal, plastic, or other material with a pattern or letters cut out. When a stencil is placed on a surface and ink or paint is spread on it, the pattern or letters appear on the surface.   **2.** The pattern or letters produced by using a stencil. *Noun.*
—To mark or paint with a stencil. We *stenciled* our names on the boxes. *Verb.*
sten·cil (sten′səl) *noun, plural* **stencils;** *verb,* **stenciled, stenciling.**

step   **1.** The movement of lifting the foot and putting it down again in a new position. I took two *steps* across the porch.   **2.** The distance that can be walked with a step. The store is only a few *steps* from our house.   **3.** Any place to put the foot in going up or coming down. A stair or the rung of a ladder is a step.   **4.** **steps.** A set or flight of steps; stairs. We climbed the *steps* to the second floor.   **5.** An action or stage in a series. Learning to float is the first *step* in learning to swim.   **6.** The sound made by putting the foot down. Our dog starts barking whenever it hears *steps* in the hall.   **7.** A pattern or rhythm of walking or dancing. Can you teach me the new dance *step? Noun.*
—**1.** To move by taking a step or steps. The driver asked everyone to *step* to the rear of the bus.   **2.** To put or press the foot. Don't *step* on the broken glass. *Verb.* ▲ Another word that sounds like this is **steppe.**
• **in step.**   With the feet or body moving in a certain pattern or rhythm. The soldiers marched *in step* with each other.
• **out of step.**   With the feet or body not moving in a certain pattern or rhythm. The dancers were *out of step* with the beat.
• **step by step.**   Gradually and steadily, advancing from one stage to the next. We learned to make pottery *step by step.*
• **to step up.**   To increase or accelerate. The company had to *step up* production to fill all its orders.
step (step) *noun, plural* **steps;** *verb,* **stepped, stepping.**

stepfather   A man who has married a person's mother after the death or divorce of the natural father.
step·fa·ther (step′fä′thər) *noun, plural* **stepfathers.**

stepmother   A woman who has married a person's father after the death or divorce of the natural mother.
step·moth·er (step′muth′ər) *noun, plural* **stepmothers.**

steppe   A large grassy plain. Steppes are found in southeastern Europe and parts of Asia. ▲ Another word that sounds like this is **step.**
steppe (step) *noun, plural* **steppes.**

stereo   A phonograph that produces sound through two or more sets of speakers.
ster·e·o (ster′ē ō′ *or* stîr′ē ō′) *noun, plural* **stereos.**

sterilize   To free from dirt or germs. We *sterilized* the test tubes in boiling water.
ster·i·lize (ster′ə līz′) *verb,* **sterilized, sterilizing.**

sterling   **1.** A metal that is made of 92.5 percent silver. It is also called **sterling sil-**

ver.   **2.** The British system of money. *Noun.*
—**1.** Made of sterling silver. We use the *sterling* tea set on special occassions.   **2.** Of very fine quality; excellent. That senator has a *sterling* character. *Adjective.*
   ster·ling (stûr′ling) *noun; adjective.*

stern¹   **1.** Harsh or strict. Our parents became *stern* when they realized that we had lied to them.   **2.** Not wavering or giving in; firm; hard. The *stern* determination of the settlers helped them bear the icy winter.
   stern (stûrn) *adjective,* **sterner, sternest.**

stern²   The rear part of a boat or ship.
   stern (stûrn) *noun, plural* **sterns.**

stethoscope   An instrument used by doctors and nurses to listen to heartbeats and other sounds in the body.
   steth·o·scope (steth′ə skōp′) *noun, plural* **stethoscopes.**

Word History

The word **stethoscope** comes from two Greek words that mean "chest" and "to examine."

stew   A dish made of pieces of meat or fish and vegetables cooked together in a liquid. We had beef *stew* for dinner. *Noun.*
—To cook food slowly in a liquid. The chef let the prunes *stew* on the stove. *Verb.*
   stew (stü *or* stū) *noun, plural* **stews;** *verb,* **stewed, stewing.**

steward   **1.** A man in charge of food and other services for passengers on ships, airplanes, and trains.   **2.** Someone who takes care of the property of another. A *steward* is in charge of the estate when the owners are away.
   stew·ard (stü′ərd *or* stū′ərd) *noun, plural* **stewards.**

stewardess   A woman who serves passengers on an airplane; female flight attendant.
   stew·ard·ess (stü′ər dis *or* stū′ər dis) *noun, plural* **stewardesses.**

stick¹   **1.** A long, thin piece of wood. I put a *stick* on the fire.   **2.** Something shaped like a stick. The candy store sells peppermint *sticks.*
   stick (stik) *noun, plural* **sticks.**

stick²   **1.** To push something pointed or sharp into something else; pierce; stab. I *stuck* my finger with the needle.   **2.** To make something stay on something else; fasten; attach. *Stick* a stamp on the envelope be-

fore you mail it.   **3.** To hold fast or close. The wet shirt *stuck* to my back.   **4.** To be or become set or fixed in place. The thorn *stuck* in the dog's paw.   **5.** To put in a place or position. I *stuck* my hand in the water to check the temperature.   **6.** To keep from moving. They were *stuck* in traffic.   **7.** To continue something; keep on. I better *stick* to practicing, if I want to play in the recital.
• **to stick out.**   **1.** To project or extend out from something else. A nail *stuck out* from the board.   **2.** To be easy to see; stand out. The family in the red hats *sticks out* from the rest of the spectators.
• **to stick up for.**   To support or defend; stand up for. I *stick up for* my friends.
   stick (stik) *verb,* **stuck, sticking.**

sticker   A piece of paper, plastic, or other material that has glue on one side. I covered my notebook with *stickers.*
   stick·er (stik′ər) *noun, plural* **stickers.**

sticky   **1.** Tending to stick to anything it touches. This glue is *sticky.*   **2.** Covered with something sticky. My hands were *sticky* after I ate the jelly sandwich.
   stick·y (stik′ē) *adjective,* **stickier, stickiest.**

stiff   **1.** Not easily bent. The new leather belt was *stiff.*   **2.** Not able to move or flow easily. The glue in the open jar became *stiff.*   **3.** Not natural or easy in manner; formal. The guard made a *stiff* bow to the king and queen.   **4.** Hard to deal with; severe. There was *stiff* competition in the swim meet.   **5.** Greater than usual. They're asking a *stiff* price for their house. *Adjective.*
—Completely; extremely. I was bored *stiff* by the movie. *Adverb.*
   stiff (stif) *adjective,* **stiffer, stiffest;** *adverb.*

stifle   **1.** To hold back; stop. I *stifled* a yawn.   **2.** To make breathing difficult for; smother. The smoke *stifled* the people in the burning building.   **3.** To be unable to breathe normally; feel smothered. I opened the window because I was *stifling.*
   sti·fle (stī′fəl) *verb,* **stifled, stifling.**

still   **1.** Without motion. The pond was *still.*   **2.** Without sound; silent. The house was *still* after everyone went to bed. *Adjective.*

at; āpe; fär; câre; end; mē; it; īce; pîerce; hot; ōld; sông; fôrk; oil; out; up; ūse; rüle; pùll; tûrn; chin; sing; shop; thin; this; hw in white; zh in treasure. The symbol ə stands for the unstressed vowel sound in about, taken, pencil, lemon, and circus.

S

—To make or become quiet or calm. I held the kitten to *still* its shivering. *Verb.*

—Quiet and calm; silence. In the *still* of the night I heard an owl hoot far away. *Noun.*

—**1.** Without motion; not moving. I tried to sit *still*. **2.** Up to this or that time; as before. They *still* live on the same street. **3.** Beyond this; even; yet. After I fell off the bicycle, I tried *still* harder to learn how to ride it. **4.** Nevertheless. You're the shortest one on the basketball team, but you're *still* the best player. *Adverb.*

—In spite of that. The children were tired; *still* they wanted to wait up for their parents to come home. *Conjunction.*

still (stil) *adjective*, **stiller, stillest;** *verb*, **stilled, stilling;** *noun; adverb.*

stilts

stilt **1.** One of a pair of long sticks with a small block on which the foot can rest. By using stilts, a person can stand or walk several feet above the ground. **2.** One of the posts that holds a building or other structure above ground or water.

stilt (stilt) *noun, plural* **stilts.**

stimulate To make more active or excited. The fantastic video *stimulated* my imagination.

stim·u·late (stim′yə lāt′) *verb*, **stimulated, stimulating.**

stimuli Plural of **stimulus.** Look up **stimulus** for more information.

stim·u·li (stim′yə lī′) *plural noun.*

stimulus **1.** Something that causes a living thing to react. The plant grew toward the *stimulus* of light. **2.** Anything that causes action or excites. The coach's speech was a *stimulus* to the team.

stim·u·lus (stim′yə ləs) *noun, plural* **stimuli.**

sting **1.** To prick or wound with a small, sharp point. A bee is one kind of insect that *stings*. **2.** To have or cause to have sharp, burning pain or hurt. My finger *stings* where I scraped it. *Verb.*

—**1.** A sharp, pointed part of an insect or animal; stinger. **2.** A wound made by a stinger. The bee *sting* on my arm is red and swollen. **3.** A sharp, burning pain. This lotion will ease the *sting* of your sunburn. *Noun.*

sting (sting) *verb*, **stung, stinging;** *noun, plural* **stings.**

stinger A sharp, pointed part of an insect or animal. It is used to prick or wound.

sting·er (sting′ər) *noun, plural* **stingers.**

stingray A broad, flat fish that lives in the ocean. It has a long tail with stingers that can cause painful wounds.

sting·ray (sting′rā′) *noun, plural* **stingrays.**

stingy **1.** Not willing to give or share; not generous. You were *stingy* when you wouldn't share your peanuts. **2.** Too small in amount. We were hungry after a *stingy* lunch.

stin·gy (stin′jē) *adjective*, **stingier, stingiest.**

stink A strong, bad smell. As we drove past the city dump, we smelled the *stink* of burning garbage. *Noun.*

—To give off or have a strong, bad smell. Those rotten eggs *stink*. *Verb.*

stink (stingk) *noun, plural* **stinks;** *verb*, **stank** or **stunk, stunk, stinking.**

stir **1.** To mix something by moving it around with a spoon, stick, or similar object. I *stirred* the milk into my tea. **2.** To move or cause to move about. The wind *stirred* the leaves. **3.** To affect; move the feelings of. The speaker *stirred* the audience. **4.** To excite; awake. The stories *stirred* my desire to travel. *Verb.*

—**1.** A burst of activity or excitement. The arrival of the star caused a *stir*. **2.** The act of stirring. Please give the soup a *stir*. *Noun.*

stir (stûr) *verb*, **stirred, stirring;** *noun, plural* **stirs.**

stirrup One of a pair of metal or leather loops that hang from either side of a saddle and hold a rider's foot.

stir·rup (stûr′əp) *noun, plural* **stirrups.**

stitch **1.** One complete movement made with a needle and thread. Stitches are made in sewing and in closing up wounds or cuts. **2.** Any similar movement made with a needle and thread or yarn in knitting, crocheting, and embroidering. *Noun.*
—To make, fasten, or mend with stitches; sew. I *stitched* up the tear in my shirt. *Verb.*
stitch (stich) *noun, plural* **stitches;** *verb,* **stitched, stitching.**

stock **1.** A supply of things kept to be sold or used. This store has a large *stock* of fishing rods. **2.** Cattle, sheep, and other animals raised on a farm or ranch; livestock. **3.** Family or race; descent. My grandparents come from German *stock.* **4.** Shares in the owning of a company or business. My cousin owns *stock* in an automobile company. **5. stocks.** A wooden frame with holes for a person's ankles and, sometimes, hands. People used to be put in stocks as a punishment for certain crimes. **6.** A liquid in which meat, poultry, or fish has been cooked. It is often used in making soup or gravy. **7.** The part of something that is used as a handle or support. Place the *stock* of the rifle against your shoulder and then aim. *Noun.*
—**1.** To fill or supply something with a stock. They *stocked* the cabin with enough food for a week. **2.** To put in, have, or keep a stock or supply of something. The hardware store *stocks* all kinds of tools. *Verb.*
—Kept in stock or on hand. Greeting cards are a *stock* item in that store. *Adjective.*
stock (stok) *noun, plural* **stocks;** *verb,* **stocked, stocking;** *adjective.*

stockade **1.** An area closed off by a fence made of strong posts that are set upright. A stockade serves as a barrier against an attack. **2.** A jail for military personnel.
stock·ade (sto kād′) *noun, plural* **stockades.**

stockade

stocking A snug, knitted covering for the foot and leg. Stockings are made of cotton, nylon, wool, and other materials.
stock·ing (stok′ing) *noun, plural* **stockings.**

stocky Having a solid, sturdy form or build. You are tall and thin, but your friend is short and *stocky.*
stock·y (stok′ē) *adjective,* **stockier, stockiest.**

stockyard A place with pens and sheds where livestock are kept before being shipped or slaughtered.
stock·yard (stok′yärd′) *noun, plural* **stockyards.**

stoke To tend or feed fuel to a fire or furnace. The workers *stoked* the furnace all through the night.
stoke (stōk) *verb,* **stoked, stoking.**

stole Past tense of **steal.** Who *stole* my pencil? Look up **steal** for more information.
stole (stōl) *verb.*

stolen Past participle of **steal.** A number of books have been *stolen* from the library. Look up **steal** for more information.
sto·len (stō′lən) *verb.*

stomach **1.** In humans and other animals with backbones, a large muscular pouch that receives food and helps to break it down. The stomach lies between the esophagus and the small intestine. It is part of the digestive system. **2.** The part of the body containing the stomach; belly. *Noun.*
—To be patient about; bear. I just can't *stomach* the way you make fun of people. *Verb.*
stom·ach (stum′ək) *noun, plural* **stomachs;** *verb,* **stomached, stomaching.**

stomp **1.** To walk heavily or violently on the floor. The angry child *stomped* out of the room. **2.** To bring down the foot or feet heavily and with force; stamp. I was so angry that I *stomped* my feet.
stomp (stomp) *verb,* **stomped, stomping.**

stone **1.** The hard material that rocks are made of. Stone is used for building. **2.** A piece of this material. They threw small *stones* into the pond. **3.** A valuable jewel;

at; āpe; fär; câre; end; mē; it; īce; pîerce; hot; ōld; sông, fôrk; oil; out; up; ūse; rūle; pull; tûrn; chin; sing; shop; thin; this; hw in white; zh in treasure. The symbol ə stands for the unstressed vowel sound in about, taken, pencil, lemon, and circus.

S

gem. The *stones* in the necklace are diamonds. **4.** The hard pit of cherries, peaches and some other fruits. *Noun.*
—Made of stone. We climbed over the *stone* wall. *Adjective.*
—To throw stones at. *Verb.*
stone (stōn) *noun, plural* **stones;** *adjective; verb,* **stoned, stoning.**

Stone Age The earliest period of human culture. During the Stone Age, people developed stone tools and weapons.

stood Past tense and past participle of **stand.** We *stood* at the window. I've *stood* here for twenty minutes. Look up **stand** for more information.
stood (stŭd) *verb.*

stool **1.** A seat without a back or arms. We sat on *stools* at the counter. **2.** A low bench used to rest the feet on.
stool (stül) *noun, plural* **stools.**

stoop¹ **1.** To bend forward and downward. The teacher *stooped* to pick up the pencil. **2.** To stand or walk with the head and shoulders bent forward. I *stoop* when I walk because my back hurts. **3.** To lower or degrade oneself to do something. I would never *stoop* to cheating. *Verb.*
—A bending forward of the head and shoulders. *Noun.*
stoop (stüp) *verb,* **stooped, stooping;** *noun, plural* **stoops.**

stoop² A small porch with stairs at the entrance of a house or other building.
stoop (stüp) *noun, plural* **stoops.**

stop **1.** To keep from moving or doing something. The driver *stopped* the car. Our baby-sitter told us to *stop* making so much noise. **2.** To keep from continuing; end. The firefighters *stopped* the spread of the fire. **3.** To come to an end or halt. The snow may *stop* soon. **4.** To close up. I used a cork to *stop* the bottle. *Verb.*
—**1.** The act of stopping or the state of being stopped. Make a *stop* at the traffic light. **2.** A place where a stop is made. The bus *stop* is at the corner. **3.** Something that stops. Please put the rubber *stop* back in the bottle. *Noun.*
stop (stop) *verb,* **stopped, stopping;** *noun, plural* **stops.**

stoplight A device used to direct the flow of traffic; traffic light. Look up **traffic light** for more information.
stop·light (stop′līt′) *noun, plural* **stoplights.**

stopper Something used to stop the opening of a bottle or other container.
stop·per (stop′ər) *noun, plural* **stoppers.**

stopwatch A watch used to time races or contests. It has a button that can be pressed to stop or start a hand instantly so that the exact time can be measured.
stop·watch (stop′woch′) *noun, plural* **stopwatches.**

storage **1.** The act of storing things or the condition of being stored. The furniture was picked up for *storage* today. **2.** A place for storing things. The chest is used as a *storage* for our toys. **3.** A place in a computer system for keeping information until it is needed. Memory and disks are two different kinds of storage.
stor·age (stôr′ij) *noun.*

store **1.** A place where goods are sold. They went to the grocery *store.* **2.** A supply of things put away for future use. A *store* of firewood is in the garage. *Noun.*
—To put away for future use. The farmer *stored* food and supplies for the winter. *Verb.*
• **in store.** Set aside; waiting. There is a surprise *in store* for you when you get home.
store (stôr) *noun, plural* **stores;** *verb,* **stored, storing.**

storehouse **1.** A place or building where things are stored. **2.** A large supply; good source. Our history teacher is a *storehouse* of information.
store·house (stôr′hous′) *noun, plural* **storehouses** (stôr′hou′ziz).

storekeeper A person who owns or runs a store.
store·keep·er (stôr′kē′pər) *noun, plural* **storekeepers.**

stoplight

714

stork A wading bird with long legs, a long neck, and a long, pointed bill. Storks live in marshes and grasslands.
  stork (stôrk) *noun, plural* **storks** or **stork.**

stork

storm **1.** A strong wind with heavy rain, hail, sleet, or snow. Storms may also have thunder and lightning. **2.** A sudden, strong outburst. The baby's *storm* of tears made us worry. **3.** A sudden, violent attack. The soldiers took the town by *storm. Noun.*
  —**1.** To blow hard with rain, hail, sleet, or snow. It *stormed* all day. **2.** To rush with violence and anger. After our argument, I *stormed* out of the house. **3.** To attack violently. Troops *stormed* the fort. *Verb.*
  storm (stôrm) *noun, plural* **storms;** *verb,* **stormed, storming.**

stormy **1.** Of or having to do with storms. We had *stormy* weather all day. **2.** Violent and angry. My friend and I had a *stormy* argument.
  storm·y (stôr′mē) *adjective,* **stormier, stormiest.**

story¹ **1.** An account of something that happened. The newspaper has a *story* about the circus. **2.** An account that has been made up to entertain people. We sat around the fire and told scary *stories.* **3.** A lie. They told a *story* about why they were late.
  sto·ry (stôr′ē) *noun, plural* **stories.**

story² A level or floor of a building. That office building has twenty-five *stories.*
  sto·ry (stôr′ē) *noun, plural* **stories.**

stout **1.** Thick and heavy; fat. The *stout* dog found it hard to climb our stairs. **2.** Having courage; brave. The *stout* soldier wasn't afraid. **3.** Having strength; strong. *Stout* beams held up the roof.
  stout (stout) *adjective,* **stouter, stoutest.**

stove An object made of metal, used for cooking or heating. Some stoves burn wood, coal, or gas, and others work by electricity.
  stove (stōv) *noun, plural* **stoves.**

stow To put away or load; store or pack. The campers *stowed* their gear in the empty tent. We *stowed* the suitcase in the car's trunk.
  stow (stō) *verb,* **stowed, stowing.**

stowaway A person who hides on a ship or airplane in order to get a free ride.
  stow·a·way (stō′ə wā′) *noun, plural* **stowaways.**

straggle To wander or stray. The tired hikers *straggled* back to camp.
  strag·gle (strag′əl) *verb,* **straggled, straggling.**

straight **1.** Not bent, curved, or crooked. I used a ruler to draw a *straight* line. **2.** In proper order. Please keep your closet *straight.* **3.** Direct and truthful; honest; upright. The witness gave a *straight* answer to the lawyer's question. *Adjective.*
  —**1.** In a straight way. Stand up *straight.* **2.** Without delay; immediately. We went *straight* home from school. *Adverb.* ▴ Another word that sounds like this is **strait.**
  straight (strāt) *adjective,* **straighter, straightest;** *adverb.*

straighten **1.** To make or become straight. The picture on the wall slanted to the left, so I *straightened* it. **2.** To put into proper order. I asked you to *straighten* your room.
  straight·en (strā′tən) *verb,* **straightened, straightening.**

straightforward Honest; truthful. My cousin is a *straightforward* person who never tries to deceive people. Please give a *straightforward* answer.
  straight·for·ward (strāt′fôr′wərd) *adjective.*

strain¹ **1.** To draw or pull tight; pull with force. The large dog *strained* at the leash. **2.** To hurt or weaken by using too much or stretching too far. I *strained* my eyes reading in dim light. **3.** To use or drive to the utmost. The porter *strained* every muscle to lift the heavy trunk. **4.** To press or pour through a strainer. We always *strain* the fresh orange juice we make. *Verb.*
  —**1.** Great force or weight. The *strain* on the wire made it snap. **2.** A hurt; injury. The runner suffered a muscle *strain.* **3.** Harmful pressure caused by worry or too much

at; āpe; fär; câre; end; mē; it; īce; pîerce; hot; ōld; sông, fôrk; oil; out; up; ūse; rüle; pûll; tûrn; chin; sing; shop; thin; <u>th</u>is; hw in white; zh in treasure. The symbol ə stands for the unstressed vowel sound in about, taken, pencil, lemon, and circus.

S

715

work; stress; tension. The coach's headache was caused by nervous *strain. Noun.*
strain (strān) *verb,* **strained, straining;** *noun, plural* **strains.**

strain² **1.** Line of descent or ancestors. That dog has a collie *strain.* **2.** A characteristic or tendency that is inherited. Our family has a musical *strain.* **3.** A melody; tune. We listened to the *strains* of the folk song.
strain (strān) *noun, plural* **strains.**

strainer A utensil, such as a sieve, used to separate liquids from solids.
strain·er (strā′nər) *noun, plural* **strainers.**

strait **1.** A narrow channel between two larger bodies of water. **2.** **straits.** Distress or difficulty. The family was in terrible *straits* after their house burned down. ▲ Another word that sounds like this is **straight.**
strait (strāt) *noun, plural* **straits.**

strand¹ To leave in a helpless position. We were *stranded* when our car broke down.
strand (strand) *verb,* **stranded, stranding.**

strand² **1.** One of the threads or wires twisted together to form a rope, cord, or cable. **2.** Something similar to a thread. *Strands* of hair fell across the baby's face.
strand (strand) *noun, plural* **strands.**

strange **1.** Odd or unusual. She painted a picture of a strange animal with green hair. **2.** Not familiar. We heard a *strange* voice on the telephone. **3.** Ill at ease; uncomfortable. I felt *strange* when I was first at camp.
strange (strānj) *adjective,* **stranger, strangest.**

stranger **1.** A person whom one does not know. A *stranger* rang our doorbell. **2.** A person from another place or country.
stran·ger (strān′jər) *noun, plural* **strangers.**

strangle **1.** To kill by squeezing the throat to stop the breath. **2.** To choke.
stran·gle (strang′gəl) *verb,* **strangled, strangling.**

strap A long strip of leather, cloth, or other material. It is used to hold things together or in place. This bag hangs by a *strap* from the shoulder. *Noun.*
—To fasten or hold with a strap. *Strap* your knapsack to your back for the hike. *Verb.*
strap (strap) *noun, plural* **straps;** *verb,* **strapped, strapping.**

strategy **1.** The planning and directing of the movements of troops and ships during a war. **2.** A plan for achieving a goal. What is the team's *strategy* for winning the game?
strat·e·gy (strat′i jē) *noun, plural* **strategies.**

stratosphere The layer of the earth's atmosphere that begins about 8 miles (13 kilometers) above the earth and ends about 30 miles (50 kilometers) above the earth. The air in the stratosphere is very thin and cold.
strat·o·sphere (strat′ə sfîr′) *noun.*

Word History

The word **stratosphere** comes from a Latin word meaning "bed" or "layer," and a Greek word meaning "ball." The stratosphere is one layer of our atmosphere.

---

straw **1.** A tube used to suck up a liquid. **2.** The dry stalks of rye, oats, wheat, or other grains after they have been cut and threshed.
straw (strô) *noun, plural* **straws.**

strawberry The sweet red fruit of a plant that grows close to the ground.
straw·ber·ry (strô′ber′ē) *noun, plural* **strawberries.**

stray To wander away. The kitten *strayed* from the yard. Please don't *stray* from the point of your story. *Verb.*
—**1.** Wandering or lost. A *stray* dog followed me home. **2.** Found here and there; scattered. A few *stray* flowers grew in the yard. *Adjective.*
—A lost or homeless animal. *Noun.*
stray (strā) *verb,* **strayed, straying;** *adjective; noun, plural* **strays.**

strawberries

streak **1.** A long, thin mark. *Streaks* of lightning flashed across the sky. **2.** A trace of anything. That bully has a mean *streak.* **3.** A short period of time or brief series. Our team's winning *streak* ended last night. *Noun.*
—**1.** To mark with streaks. After the game, the soccer player's face was *streaked* with dirt. **2.** To move at great speed. *Verb.*
streak (strēk) *noun, plural* **streaks;** *verb,* **streaked, streaking.**

stream **1.** A body of flowing water. **2.** A steady flow or movement. A *stream* of people came out of the theater. *Noun.*
—**1.** To move steadily; flow. Light *streamed* into the room. **2.** To wave or float. The school banners *streamed* in the wind. *Verb.*
stream (strēm) *noun, plural* **streams;** *verb,* **streamed, streaming.**

streamer A long, narrow flag or strip. We hung paper *streamers* from the ceiling.
stream·er (strē'mər) *noun, plural* **streamers.**

streamline 1. To design and build something so that it has the least possible resistance to air or water. 2. To make something work better. The new mayor *streamlined* the city government.
stream·line (strēm'līn') *verb,* **streamlined, streamlining.**

street A public way in a town or city, often with sidewalks and buildings on both sides.
street (strēt) *noun, plural* **streets.**

streetcar A vehicle for carrying passengers. Streetcars run on rails through city streets.
street·car (strēt'kär') *noun, plural* **streetcars.**

streetlight A light on a street or road. A streetlight is usually attached to a tall pole.
street·light (strēt'līt') *noun, plural* **streetlights.**

The friends are testing each other's **strength.**

strength 1. The quality of being strong; energy, power, or force. I lift weights to develop my *strength.* 2. The ability to take much strain; firmness. We tested the *strength* of the rope. 3. The degree of power or force; intensity. What is the *strength* of this medicine?
strength (strengkth *or* strength) *noun, plural* **strengths.**

strengthen To make or become strong. I *strengthened* my muscles by lifting weights.
strength·en (strengk'thən *or* streng'thən) *verb,* **strengthened, strengthening.**

strenuous 1. Needing much effort. Cutting down the tree was *strenuous* work. 2. Very active; energetic. There was *strenuous* opposition to the plan to build a mall.
stren·u·ous (stren'ū əs) *adjective.*

stress 1. The force, pressure, or strain put on one thing by another. A rocket withstands great *stress.* 2. A special importance. Our baby-sitter puts much *stress* on courtesy. 3. A stronger tone of voice given to a word or syllable of a word; accent. In the word "table," the *stress* is on the first syllable. 4. Harmful pressure caused by worry or too much work; strain; tension. *Noun.*
—1. To give special importance to. The teacher *stressed* the need for good study habits. 2. To pronounce a word or syllable of a word with stress. When you say the word "begin," you *stress* the second syllable. *Verb.*
stress (stres) *noun, plural* **stresses;** *verb,* **stressed, stressing.**

stretch 1. To spread out one's arms, legs, or body to full length. I got up and *stretched.* 2. To reach; extend. The elephant *stretched* its trunk for the nut. 3. To spread out when pulled. Rubber is a material that *stretches* easily. *Verb.*
—1. An unbroken space or area. The campers canoed along a *stretch* of the river. 2. The act of stretching. I can touch the ceiling with a *stretch* of my arms. *Noun.*
stretch (strech) *verb,* **stretched, stretching;** *noun, plural* **stretches.**

stretcher A piece of canvas or other material stretched across a frame. A stretcher is used to carry a sick or injured person.
stretch·er (strech'ər) *noun, plural* **stretchers.**

stricken A past participle of **strike.** The tree had been *stricken* by a disease. Look up **strike** for more information. *Verb.*
—Affected or hurt by something. Aid was sent to the *stricken* towns after the flood. *Adjective.*
strick·en (strik'ən) *verb; adjective.*

strict 1. Following or enforcing a rule in a careful, exact way. The teacher is *strict* about spelling. 2. To be followed in a careful, exact way; carefully enforced. That school has *strict* rules. 3. Complete; absolute. We kept the secret in *strict* confidence.
strict (strikt) *adjective,* **stricter, strictest.**

stridden Past participle of **stride.** Look up **stride** for more information.
strid·den (strid'ən) *verb.*

at; āpe; fär; câre; end; mē; it; īce; pîerce; hot; ōld; sông, fôrk; oil; out; up; ūse; rüle; pull; tûrn; chin; sing; shop; thin; <u>th</u>is; hw in white; zh in treasure. The symbol ə stands for the unstressed vowel sound in about, taken, pencil, lemon, and circus.

S

717

stride **1.** To walk with long steps. We watched the models *stride* in their fancy clothes. **2.** To pass over with a long step. I *strode* across the mud puddle. *Verb.*
—**1.** A long step. My friend has a quick *stride.* **2.** Progress or improvement. Science has made *strides* in fighting disease. *Noun.*
stride (strīd) *verb,* **strode, stridden, striding;** *noun, plural* **strides.**

strike **1.** To give a blow to; hit. I *struck* the dog for chewing on my shoes. The car *struck* the tree. **2.** To make an impression on. What they said *struck* me as funny. **3.** To find or discover suddenly. The prospectors hope to *strike* oil. **4.** To set on fire by rubbing or hitting. We *struck* a match. **5.** To give the time by sounding. The clock *struck* twelve. **6.** To stop work in order to get higher pay, better working conditions, or some other improvement or benefit. *Verb.*
—**1.** The stopping of work. The workers went on *strike* for higher pay. **2.** A sudden discovery. The gold *strike* made them rich. **3.** In baseball, a pitched ball that the batter swings at and misses or hits foul, or a pitched ball that passes through the strike zone. *Noun.*
strike (strīk) *verb,* **struck, struck** or **stricken, striking;** *noun, plural* **strikes.**

string **1.** A thin line of twisted threads or wire. I held the kite by a *string.* **2.** Something like a string. The violinist needs new *strings* for the violin. **3.** A series or row of persons, things, or events. **4. strings.** Musical instruments with strings. They are played with a bow or plucked. *Noun.*
—**1.** To put on a string. My cousin likes to *string* beads. **2.** To provide with strings. I *strung* my guitar. **3.** To stretch from one place to another. Our neighbors *strung* a wire from their television to the antenna. **4.** To arrange in a row or series. *Verb.*
string (string) *noun, plural* **strings;** *verb,* **strung, stringing.**

string bean A long, green bean pod that is eaten as a vegetable.

strip¹ **1.** To take off the clothing or covering; undress. **2.** To pull off. I *stripped* the bark from the log.
strip (strip) *verb,* **stripped, stripping.**

Pod

Seed

string beans

strip² A long, narrow piece of something. They tore the paper into *strips.*
strip (strip) *noun, plural* **strips.**

stripe A long, narrow band. Your shirt has red and white *stripes.* Zebras and tigers have *stripes. Noun.*
—To mark with a stripe or stripes. The work table was *striped* with spilled paint. *Verb.*
stripe (strīp) *noun, plural* **stripes;** *verb,* **striped, striping.**

strive To make a great effort; try hard. I always *strive* to win in sports.
strive (strīv) *verb,* **strove** or **strived, striven** or **strived, striving.**

striven A past participle of **strive.** Look up **strive** for more information.
striv·en (striv′ən) *verb.*

The cat's fur has **stripes.**

strode Past tense of **stride.** The two friends *strode* through the park together in the afternoon. Look up **stride** for more information.
strode (strōd) *verb.*

stroke¹ **1.** The act of striking. That lumberjack can split a log with one *stroke* of an ax. **2.** An unexpected event. Winning that money was a *stroke* of good luck! **3.** A mark made by a pen, pencil, or brush. The student finished the drawing with a few *strokes* of the crayon. **4.** A sudden weakness or sickness caused by the breaking or blocking of a blood vessel in the brain. **5.** A combination of arm and leg movements used in swimming. I learned a new *stroke* at the swimming pool today.
stroke (strōk) *noun, plural* **strokes.**

stroke² To rub gently. I *stroked* the puppy.
stroke (strōk) *verb,* **stroked, stroking.**

stroll To walk in a slow, relaxed way. We *strolled* through the park. *Verb.*
—A slow, relaxed walk. Let's take a *stroll* after dinner. *Noun.*
stroll (strōl) *verb,* **strolled, strolling;** *noun, plural* **strolls.**

strong **1.** Having much power, force, or energy; full of strength. Are you *strong* enough to move the table? The *strong* winds damaged trees and buildings. **2.** Able to resist; firm. The house has *strong* walls. You are *strong* in your beliefs.
strong (strông) *adjective,* **stronger, strongest.**

stronghold A place protected against attack or danger. The *stronghold* of the castle was a stone tower in the center.
strong·hold (strông′hōld′) *noun, plural* **strongholds.**

strove A past tense of **strive.** We *strove* to do better in school. Look up **strive** for more information.
strove (strōv) *verb.*

struck The past tense and a past participle of **strike.** You *struck* your head on the table when you fell. Look up **strike** for more information.
struck (struk) *verb.*

structure 1. Anything that is built. A house, office building, or bridge is a structure. 2. An arrangement of parts, or the way parts are arranged. We saw the *structure* of a plant cell through a microscope.
struc·ture (struk′chər) *noun, plural* **structures.**

struggle 1. To make a great effort. The children *struggled* through the heavy snow. 2. To fight; battle. The soldiers *struggled* bravely with the enemy. *Verb.*
—1. A great effort. It was a *struggle* to learn French. 2. A fight, battle, or war. The *struggle* resulted in a tremendous amount of bloodshed. *Noun.*
strug·gle (strug′əl) *verb,* **struggled, struggling;** *noun, plural* **struggles.**

strum To play in an easy, relaxed, or unskilled way. I like to *strum* on my guitar.
strum (strum) *verb,* **strummed, strumming.**

strung Past tense and past participle of **string.** I *strung* the beads that you gave me. Look up **string** for more information.
strung (strung) *verb.*

stub A short part that remains after the rest has been used, broken, or torn off. I tried to write with the *stub* of a pencil, but it was difficult. *Noun.*
—To strike one's toe or foot against something. What did you *stub* your toe on? *Verb.*
stub (stub) *noun, plural* **stubs;** *verb,* **stubbed, stubbing.**

stubble 1. Short stalks of grain left standing after the crop has been cut. *Stubble* covered the corn field through the winter. 2. A short, rough growth. The sailor's face was covered with the *stubble* of his beard.
stub·ble (stub′əl) *noun.*

stubborn 1. Not yielding. The *stubborn* children would not admit that they were wrong. 2. Hard to overcome or deal with. My *stubborn* cold lasted a month.
stub·born (stub′ərn) *adjective.*

stuck Past tense and past participle of **stick.** I *stuck* myself with a pin. Look up **stick** for more information.
stuck (stuk) *verb.*

student 1. A person who is going to a school. The fourth grade has thirty *students.* 2. A person who studies something. That scientist is a *student* of how animals behave.
stu·dent (stü′dənt *or* stū′dənt) *noun, plural* **students.**

studio 1. A place where an artist or craftsperson works. We went to the photographer's *studio* to have our pictures taken. 2. A place where motion pictures are filmed. 3. A place where radio or television programs are broadcast or recorded.
stu·di·o (stü′dē ō′ *or* stū′dē ō′) *noun, plural* **studios.**

an artist's **studio**

study 1. To try to learn by reading about, thinking about, or looking carefully at something. Our class *studied* the planets of the solar system. 2. To look at closely; examine. I *studied* the face in the picture to see if I knew the person. *Verb.*
—1. The act of studying. Many hours of *study* are needed to learn French well. 2. A close look at something; examination. Make a careful *study* of the photograph to see if you know anyone in it. 3. A thing studied; sub-

at; āpe; fär; câre; end; mē; it; īce; pîerce; hot; ōld; sông, fôrk; oil; out; up; ūse; rüle; pull; tûrn; chin; sing; shop; thin; <u>th</u>is; hw in white; zh in treasure. The symbol ə stands for the unstressed vowel sound in about, taken, pencil, lemon, and circus.

S

ject. How are you doing in your *studies?*
4. A room used for studying. We use the extra bedroom as a *study. Noun.*
stud·y (stud'ē) *verb,* **studied, studying;** *noun, plural* **studies.**

stuff **1.** Material used to make something. What kind of *stuff* did you use to make that sheep costume? **2.** Useless matter or things. The box was full of *stuff* to be thrown away. **3.** Things of any sort. What sort of *stuff* do you keep in your scrapbook? *Noun.*
—**1.** To pack full. We *stuffed* the suitcase with clothes. **2.** To force in. I *stuffed* the papers into the drawer. **3.** To fill. I *stuffed* myself at dinner. **4.** To fill the skin of a dead animal in order to make it look natural or alive. **5.** To put stuffing into a food to be cooked. *Verb.*
stuff (stuf) *noun; verb,* **stuffed, stuffing.**

stuffing Something used to fill or pack another thing. A mixture of bread crumbs and other food is used as *stuffing* for turkey. Feathers are used as *stuffing* for pillows.
stuff·ing (stuf'ing) *noun, plural* **stuffings.**

stuffy **1.** Without fresh air; close. The room is *stuffy;* please open a window. **2.** Dull and uninteresting; boring. The professor gave a *stuffy* talk.
stuff·y (stuf'ē) *adjective,* **stuffier, stuffiest.**

stumble **1.** To lose one's balance; trip. I *stumbled* over the rake. **2.** To move or speak in a clumsy way. We *stumbled* around in the dark room. **3.** To discover by chance. The detective *stumbled* on a clue.
stum·ble (stum'bəl) *verb,* **stumbled, stumbling.**

stump **1.** The lower part of a tree trunk that is left when the tree has been cut down. **2.** The part of anything left after the main part is gone. The artist drew with a *stump* of chalk. *Noun.*
—To puzzle; confuse. This arithmetic problem has *stumped* me. *Verb.*
stump (stump) *noun, plural* **stumps;** *verb,* **stumped, stumping.**

stun **1.** To make unconscious. The robin was *stunned* when it flew into the window. **2.** To shock. We were *stunned* by the news.
stun (stun) *verb,* **stunned, stunning.**

stung Past tense and past participle of **sting.** The bee *stung* the pony. Look up **sting** for more information.
stung (stung) *verb.*

stunk A past tense and the past participle of **stink.** The garbage *stunk.* Look up **stink** for more information.
stunk (stungk) *verb.*

stunt¹ To slow or hinder growth. Lack of light and water *stunted* the plant.
stunt (stunt) *verb,* **stunted, stunting.**

stunt² An act that shows skill or strength. The acrobat performed many *stunts* on the high trapeze.
stunt (stunt) *noun, plural* **stunts.**

stupid Lacking common sense or intelligence. It would be *stupid* to drive in this blizzard.
stu·pid (stü'pid *or* stū'pid) *adjective.*

sturdy **1.** Strong; hardy. Heavy trucks were able to drive on the *sturdy* bridge. **2.** Hard to overcome. Their football team put up a *sturdy* defense, but our team won.
stur·dy (stûr'dē) *adjective,* **sturdier, sturdiest.**

sturgeon A large fish that has bony, pointed scales. Sturgeons are caught for food.
stur·geon (stûr'jən) *noun, plural* **sturgeons** or **sturgeon.**

sturgeon

stutter To repeat sounds when speaking. Many people who stutter often repeat sounds at the beginning of a word. *Verb.*
—The act or condition of stuttering. *Noun.*
stut·ter (stut'ər) *verb,* **stuttered, stuttering;** *noun.*

sty¹ A pen or enclosed yard where pigs are kept; pigpen.
sty (stī) *noun, plural* **sties.**

sty² A small, sore, white or red bump on the eyelid. A sty is caused by an infection.
sty (stī) *noun, plural* **sties.**

style **1.** A particular way of saying or doing something. That writer has a clear and simple *style.* **2.** Fashion. Models wear clothes in the latest *style.* **3.** A beautiful or excellent quality or manner. That skater really has *style.*
style (stīl) *noun, plural* **styles.**

subdivide **1.** To divide into smaller parts something that has already been divided. **2.** To divide a tract of land into lots for sale. The property was *subdivided* and many small houses were built on it.
sub·di·vide (sub'di vīd' *or* sub'di vīd') *verb,* **subdivided, subdividing.**

subdue **1.** To defeat; conquer. The soldiers *subdued* the enemy in battle. **2.** To control or overcome. I managed to *subdue* my anger. **3.** To reduce the intensity or strength of. The drapes *subdued* the light.
sub·due (səb dü′ *or* səb dū′) *verb,*
subdued, subduing.

subject **1.** Something thought or talked about. The *subject* of the student's report was birds' nests. **2.** A course or field that is studied. Math is my favorite *subject* in school. **3.** A person or thing that experiences something. The scientist used mice as *subjects* in an experiment. **4.** A person that is under the control of another. The people were loyal *subjects* of the king and queen. **5.** A word or group of words in a sentence that tells whom or what the sentence is about. In the sentence "Astronauts get a lot of training," "Astronauts" is the subject. *Noun.*
—**1.** Under the control of a person or organization. The members are *subject* to the club's rules. **2.** Likely to be affected; liable to have. Some people are *subject* to colds. **3.** Depending on. You may go on the trip, *subject* to your parents' approval. *Adjective.*
—**1.** To bring under control. The dictator *subjected* the people to tyranny. **2.** To cause to experience. If you wear those clothes, you will *subject* yourself to teasing. *Verb.*
sub·ject (sub′jikt *for noun and adjective;* səb jekt′ *for verb*) *noun, plural* **subjects;** *adjective; verb,* **subjected, subjecting.**

submarine **1.** A ship that can travel under water. **2.** A sandwich made with one long loaf of bread. *Noun.*
—Growing or lying underwater. Seaweed is a *submarine* plant. *Adjective.*
sub·mar·ine (sub′mə rēn′ *for noun;* sub′mə rēn′ *for adjective*) *noun, plural* **submarines;** *adjective.*

submerge **1.** To cover with a liquid. The dock was *submerged* during the flood. **2.** To go beneath the surface of water or another liquid. The diver *submerged* to look for the sunken ship.
sub·merge (səb mûrj′) *verb,* **submerged, submerging.**

submit **1.** To yield to some power or authority. The children *submitted* to their parents' wishes. **2.** To present. You will *submit* your book reports on Monday.
sub·mit (səb mit′) *verb,* **submitted, submitting.**

subordinate Lower in rank or importance. Colonels are *subordinate* to generals. *Adjective.*
—A person or thing that is lower in rank or importance. The president of that company listens to the advice of *subordinates. Noun.*
—To make lower in rank or importance. *Verb.*
sub·or·di·nate (sə bôr′də nit) *adjective; noun, plural* **subordinates;** *verb,* **subordinated, subordinating.**

subscribe **1.** To agree to receive and pay for. We *subscribe* to the local newspaper. **2.** To give or show one's agreement or approval. They *subscribe* to the belief that world peace is possible.
sub·scribe (səb skrīb′) *verb,* **subscribed, subscribing.**

subscription An arrangement by which one agrees to receive and pay for something. I have a *subscription* to a newspaper.
sub·scrip·tion (səb skrip′shən) *noun, plural* **subscriptions.**

subsequent Happening after; coming as a result. *Subsequent* experiments showed the same results as the first experiment.
sub·se·quent (sub′si kwənt) *adjective.*

The diver is **submerged.**

at; āpe; fär; câre; end; mē; it; īce; pîerce; hot; ōld; sông, fôrk; oil; out; up; ūse; rüle; pull; tûrn; chin; sing; shop; thin; <u>th</u>is; hw in white; zh in treasure. The symbol ə stands for the unstressed vowel sound in about, taken, pencil, lemon, and circus.

S

721

subset A set whose members are all members of another set. The set of even whole numbers, for example, is a subset of the set of whole numbers.
sub·set (sub′set′) *noun*, *plural* **subsets.**

subside **1.** To sink to a lower level. It took a week for the flood waters to *subside*. **2.** To become less. My anger *subsided* after my friend apologized.
sub·side (səb sīd′) *verb*, **subsided, subsiding.**

substance **1.** The material that something is made of. Wood is the main *substance* in paper. **2.** Material of a certain kind. The floor was covered with a greasy *substance*. **3.** The important part of something; meaning. The *substance* of the letter was that they were homesick.
sub·stance (sub′stəns) *noun*, *plural* **substances.**

substantial **1.** Large in amount; ample. We ate a *substantial* dinner. **2.** Strong; firm. That *substantial* bridge can support heavy trucks and buses.
sub·stan·tial (səb stan′shəl) *adjective*.

substitute A person who does something in place of another; a thing used instead of another. The baker used margarine as a *substitute* for butter. *Noun.*
—**1.** To put in place of another. The coach *substituted* a new player for the pitcher. **2.** To take the place of another. The principal *substituted* for our regular teacher. *Verb.*
sub·sti·tute (sub′sti tüt′ *or* sub′sti tūt′) *noun*, *plural* **substitutes;** *verb*, **substituted, substituting.**

subtle Not obvious; faint and delicate. That flower has a *subtle* smell.
sub·tle (sut′əl) *adjective*, **subtler, subtlest.**

subtract To take away from. If you *subtract* 3 from 7, you get 4.
sub·tract (səb trakt′) *verb*, **subtracted, subtracting.**

subtraction The subtracting of one number from another number to find the difference. $5 - 2 = 3$ is an example of subtraction.
sub·trac·tion (səb trak′shən) *noun*, *plural* **subtractions.**

subtrahend The number to be subtracted from another number. When you subtract 4 from 11, the number 4 is the subtrahend.
sub·tra·hend (sub′trə hend′) *noun*, *plural* **subtrahends.**

suburb An area with homes and stores next to or near a city. We live in the *suburbs*, so my parents have to drive to work in the city.
sub·urb (sub′ûrb) *noun*, *plural* **suburbs.**

suburban Of or having to do with a suburb. My parents commute between the city and our *suburban* community.
sub·ur·ban (sə bûr′bən) *adjective*.

subway A railroad in a city that runs under the ground. Subways are run by electricity.
sub·way (sub′wā′) *noun*, *plural* **subways.**

subway

succeed **1.** To have a good result; manage; do well. The team *succeeded* in winning the award. **2.** To come after and take the place of. If the president dies, the vice-president *succeeds* to the office of president.
suc·ceed (sək sēd′) *verb*, **succeeded, succeeding.**

success **1.** A result that has been hoped for; favorable end. The coach was pleased with the *success* of the team. **2.** A person or thing that does or goes well. The party was a big *success*.
suc·cess (sək ses′) *noun*, *plural* **successes.**

successful Having success. The writer's book was *successful* and sold many copies.
suc·cess·ful (sək ses′fəl) *adjective*.

succession **1.** A group of persons or things following one after another. The football team has had a *succession* of victories. **2.** The coming of one person or thing after another. The claps of thunder came in quick *succession*.
suc·ces·sion (sək sesh′ən) *noun*, *plural* **successions.**

successive Following one after another. Our team has had three *successive* defeats.
suc·ces·sive (sək ses′iv) *adjective*.

successor A person or thing that comes next after or takes the place of another. The retiring senators wished their *successors* luck.
suc·ces·sor (sək ses′ər) *noun*, *plural* **successors.**

such **1.** Of the same kind; of that kind. I have never seen *such* weather. How could they have done *such* a thing? **2.** Similar; like. We bought tomatoes, lettuce, and other

such vegetables for a salad.   **3.** So much of. It is *such* a surprise to see you. *Adjective.*
—A person or thing of that kind. We need paper plates and *such* for the picnic. *Pronoun.*

such (such) *adjective; pronoun.*

suck   **1.** To draw something into the mouth. I *sucked* the apple juice through a straw.   **2.** To draw liquid from something with the mouth. The baby *sucked* a bottle.   **3.** To hold in the mouth and lick. I *sucked* on a piece of ice.   **4.** To draw in. A vacuum cleaner *sucks* in dust.

suck (suk) *verb,* **sucked, sucking.**

sucker   **1.** A part of the body of certain animals that is used to stick onto things. An octopus has suckers on its tentacles.   **2.** A piece of candy that is held in the mouth and licked. Some lollipops are suckers.

suck·er (suk′ər) *noun, plural* **suckers.**

suction   The pulling of a gas or liquid into a space from which part or all of the air has been removed. A vacuum cleaner works by suction.

suc·tion (suk′shən) *noun.*

Sudan   A country in northeastern Africa.

Su·dan (sü dan′) *noun.*

sudden   **1.** Happening without warning; not expected. A *sudden* storm caught me without an umbrella.   **2.** Hasty; quick. A *sudden* decision may not be the best one.

sud·den (sud′ən) *adjective.*

suds   Soapy water with foam or bubbles.

suds (sudz) *plural noun.*

sue   To start a case against in a court of law.

sue (sü) *verb,* **sued, suing.**

suede   Leather with a soft, fuzzy surface. It is used to make clothes, shoes, belts, and other articles.

suede (swād) *noun.*

suffer   **1.** To have pain or sorrow. I have *suffered* from a sore throat all week.   **2.** To have or feel. Are you *suffering* pain from your broken leg?   **3.** To be harmed or damaged. My grades *suffer* if I don't study.

suf·fer (suf′ər) *verb,* **suffered, suffering.**

suffering   The feeling of pain or sorrow. The doctor will give you some medicine to ease your *suffering.*

suf·fer·ing (suf′ər ing) *noun, plural* **sufferings.**

sufficient   As much as is needed; enough. Do we have *sufficient* supplies for our trip?

suf·fi·cient (sə fish′ənt) *adjective.*

suffix   A syllable or group of syllables that is added to the end of a word or root to change its meaning. The word *painter* is

made up of the word *paint* and the suffix *-er.*

suf·fix (suf′iks) *noun, plural* **suffixes.**

Language Note

Many words that end with a **suffix** are not listed in this dictionary. To find out the meaning of most of these words, first look up the meaning of the root. Then look up the meaning of the suffix. Put the meaning of the root and the suffix together. For example, the word *properly* is formed from the root *proper* and the suffix *-ly. Proper* means correct or suitable. The suffix *-ly* means in a certain way or manner. Therefore, *properly* means in a correct or suitable way.

The spelling of a root may change when a suffix is added. This often happens when the root ends in the letter *y.* For example, *philosopher* is formed from *philosophy* and *-er.* When *-er* is added, the *y* at the end of *philosophy* is dropped. *Merciless* is formed from *mercy* and *-less.* When *-less* is added, the *y* at the end of *mercy* becomes *i.*

suffocate   **1.** To kill by keeping from breathing.   **2.** To die from a lack of air. A pet can *suffocate* in a box that has no holes for air.   **3.** To keep or be kept from breathing easily. I was *suffocating* in the hot room.

suf·fo·cate (suf′ə kāt′) *verb,* **suffocated, suffocating.**

suffrage   The right to vote. The nineteenth amendment to the United States Constitution established *suffrage* for women.

suf·frage (suf′rij) *noun.*

sugar   A white or brown sweet substance. Sugar comes mainly from sugar beets and sugarcane.

sug·ar (shüg′ər) *noun, plural* **sugars.**

sugar beet   A plant whose long, thick roots are a source of sugar.

sugarcane   A tall grass with a woody stem. The juice in its stem is a source of sugar.

sug·ar·cane (shüg′ər kān′) *noun.*

suggest   **1.** To offer as something to think

at; āpe; fär; câre; end; mē; it; īce; pîerce; hot; ōld; sông, fôrk; oil; out; up; ūse; rüle; pull; tûrn; chin; sing; shop; thin; **this**; hw in white; zh in treasure. The symbol ə stands for the unstressed vowel sound in about, taken, pencil, lemon, and circus.

S

about. Who *suggested* that we play baseball? **2.** To come or bring into the mind. The color red *suggests* warmth. **3.** To hint. Your smile *suggests* that you are happy.

sug·gest (səg jest′ *or* sə jest′) *verb,* **suggested, suggesting.**

suggestion **1.** The act of suggesting something. We went to that movie because of your *suggestion.* **2.** Something suggested. Buying a lock for my bicycle was my friend's *suggestion.* **3.** A hint; trace. There is a *suggestion* of roses in that perfume.

sug·ges·tion (səg jes′chən *or* sə jes′chən) *noun, plural* **suggestions.**

suicide **1.** The killing of oneself on purpose. **2.** A person who has committed suicide.

su·i·cide (sü′ə sīd′) *noun, plural* **suicides.**

suit **1.** A set of clothes made to be worn together. A suit has trousers or a skirt, a jacket, and sometimes a vest. **2.** A case brought to a court of law. I brought a *suit* against the driver whose car hit me. **3.** Any of the four sets of playing cards in a deck. The suits are spades, hearts, diamonds, and clubs. *Noun.*
—**1.** To meet the needs of; be right for. The lively music *suits* my happy mood. **2.** To be convenient to; please; satisfy. Stay as long as it *suits* you. **3.** To be becoming to. The yellow jacket *suits* you perfectly. *Verb.*

suit (süt) *noun, plural* **suits;** *verb,* **suited, suiting.**

suitable Right; proper. The soil in our backyard is *suitable* for growing tomatoes.

suit·a·ble (sü′tə bəl) *adjective.*

suitcase A flat bag for carrying clothes when traveling.

suit·case (süt′kās′) *noun, plural* **suitcases.**

suite **1.** A group of rooms that are connected. The family took a *suite* at the hotel. **2.** A set of matching or similar things. Mom and Dad bought a *suite* of furniture for the dining room. ⚠ Another word that sounds like this is **sweet.**

suite (swēt) *noun, plural* **suites.**

suitor A man who courts a woman.

suit·or (sü′tər) *noun, plural* **suitors.**

sulfur A yellow substance that is used to make matches, fertilizers, and explosives. Sulfur is a chemical element. This word is sometimes spelled **sulphur.**

sul·fur (sul′fər) *noun.*

sullen **1.** Gloomy and silent from anger. The child was *sullen* after being scolded. **2.** Gloomy; dismal.

sul·len (sul′ən) *adjective.*

sulphur Another spelling for **sulfur.** Look up **sulfur** for more information.

sul·phur (sul′fər) *noun.*

sultan The king of certain Muslim countries. Turkey was once ruled by a sultan.

sul·tan (sul′tən) *noun, plural* **sultans.**

sum **1.** The number that results from adding two or more numbers together. The *sum* of 6 plus 8 is 14. **2.** An amount of money. I was paid the *sum* of ten dollars for mowing their lawn. ⚠ Another word that sounds like this is **some.**

sum (sum) *noun, plural* **sums.**

sumac A tree or shrub that has pointed leaves and clusters of flowers and berries. One kind of sumac can cause a rash that itches.

su·mac (shü′mak *or* sü′mak) *noun, plural* **sumacs.**

summarize To make a summary of. My friend *summarized* the movie for me.

sum·ma·rize (sum′ə rīz′) *verb,* **summarized, summarizing.**

sumac

summary A brief account that contains the main points of something. The radio announcer gave a *summary* of the day's news.

sum·ma·ry (sum′ə rē) *noun, plural* **summaries.**

summer The season of the year that comes between spring and autumn. *Noun.*
—To spend the summer. The family will *summer* in the mountains. *Verb.*

sum·mer (sum′ər) *noun, plural* **summers;** *verb,* **summered, summering.**

summit The highest point. They climbed to the *summit* of the mountain.

sum·mit (sum′it) *noun, plural* **summits.**

summon **1.** To ask to come. We *summoned* the police to the car accident. **2.** To stir up; arouse. I *summoned* my courage and dove off the high diving board.

sum·mon (sum′ən) *verb,* **summoned, summoning.**

summons An official notice or command to appear somewhere or do something. I received a *summons* to appear in court.

sum·mons (sum′ənz) *noun, plural* **summonses.**

sun **1.** The star around which the earth and other planets revolve. The sun gives light and heat. **2.** Light and heat from the sun. The plants need plenty of *sun. Noun.*

—To be in the light and heat of the sun. We *sunned* ourselves on the beach. *Verb.* ▲ Another word that sounds like this is **son**.
sun (sun) *noun; verb,* **sunned, sunning.**

Sun. An abbreviation for *Sunday.*

sunbathe To lie in the sun. Our neighbors sometimes *sunbathe* in their backyard.
sun·bathe (sun′bā<u>th</u>′) *verb,* **sunbathed, sunbathing.**

sunburn A redness or burn on the skin caused by the sun. *Noun.*
—To burn the skin by exposure to the sun. *Verb.*
sun·burn (sun′bûrn′) *noun, plural* **sunburns;** *verb,* **sunburned** or **sunburnt, sunburning.**

sunburnt A past tense and past participle of **sunburn**. Look up **sunburn** for more information.
sun·burnt (sun′bûrnt′) *verb.*

sundae Ice cream served with syrup, fruit, or nuts on top.
sun·dae (sun′dē *or* sun′dā) *noun, plural* **sundaes.**

Sunday The first day of the week.
Sun·day (sun′dē *or* sun′dā) *noun, plural* **Sundays.**

Word History

The Romans dedicated the second day of their week to the sun. The Latin name was translated into an Old English word meaning "sun's day," which became **Sunday.**

sundial A device that consists of a plate with numbers and a pointer that casts a shadow. It shows the time of day by the movement of the shadow across the numbers.
sun·dial (sun′dī′əl) *noun, plural* **sundials.**

sundown The setting of the sun.
sun·down (sun′doun′) *noun, plural* **sundowns.**

sunflower A large flower that grows on a tall plant. A sunflower has a brown center and yellow petals.
sun·flow·er (sun′flou′ər) *noun, plural* **sunflowers.**

sunflower

sung Past participle of **sing**. The choir has *sung* many songs. Look up **sing** for more information.
sung (sung) *verb.*

sunglasses A pair of dark pieces of glass or plastic in a frame that help to protect the eyes from the glare of the sun.
sun·glass·es (sun′glas′iz) *plural noun.*

sunk A past tense and a past participle of **sink**. The rock I threw has *sunk* to the bottom of the pond. Look up **sink** for more information.
sunk (sungk) *verb.*

sunken 1. Having sunk below the surface. The divers looked for *sunken* treasure. 2. Placed below the area around it. There is a *sunken* garden in our backyard. 3. Hollow. The thin child had *sunken* cheeks. *Adjective.*
—A past participle of **sink**. Look up **sink** for more information. *Verb.*
sunk·en (sung′kən) *adjective; verb.*

sunlight The light of the sun.
sun·light (sun′līt′) *noun.*

sunny 1. Full of sunlight; warmed by sunlight. We sat on the *sunny* porch. 2. Cheerful; happy. The child had a *sunny* smile.
sun·ny (sun′ē) *adjective,* **sunnier, sunniest.**

sunrise The rising of the sun.
sun·rise (sun′rīz′) *noun, plural* **sunrises.**

sunset The setting of the sun.
sun·set (sun′set′) *noun, plural* **sunsets.**

sunset

at; āpe; fär; câre; end; mē; it; īce; pîerce; hot; ōld; sông, fôrk; oil; out; up; ūse; rüle; pùll; tûrn; chin; sing; shop; thin; <u>th</u>is; hw in white; zh in treasure. The symbol ə stands for the unstressed vowel sound in about, taken, pencil, lemon, and circus.

S

sunshine   The light that comes from the sun.
   sun·shine (sun′shīn′) *noun.*

suntan   A dark coloring of the skin that comes from exposure to the sun.
   sun·tan (sun′tan′) *noun, plural* **suntans.**

superb   Very fine; excellent. The actor gave a *superb* performance.
   su·perb (sü pûrb′) *adjective.*

superintendent   A person who directs or manages something. The superintendent of police is the head of the police department.
   su·per·in·tend·ent (sü′pər in ten′dənt) *noun, plural* **superintendents.**

superior   1. Higher, greater, or better. The champion baseball team has *superior* players.   2. Proud; haughty. Those children have a *superior* attitude because their parents are famous. *Adjective.*
   —A person who is in a higher position. The principal of a school is the teachers' *superior. Noun.*
   su·pe·ri·or (sə pîr′ē ər) *adjective; noun, plural* **superiors.**

superiority   The state or quality of being superior. The football team showed its *superiority* by winning the state championship.
   su·pe·ri·or·i·ty (sə pîr′ē ôr′i tē) *noun.*

superlative   Of the highest sort; above all others. Landing astronauts on the moon was a *superlative* achievement. *Adjective.*
   —The form of an adjective or adverb that shows the greatest degree of whatever is expressed by the basic form. For example, *darkest* is the superlative of *dark. Noun.*
   su·per·la·tive (sə pûr′lə tiv) *adjective; noun, plural* **superlatives.**

supermarket   A large store that sells food and household goods.
   su·per·mar·ket (sü′pər mär′kit) *noun, plural* **supermarkets.**

supernatural   Having an existence not limited by the laws of nature. Ghosts and demons are *supernatural* creatures.
   su·per·nat·u·ral (sü′pər nach′ər əl) *adjective.*

superstition   A belief based on ignorance and fear. The belief that a black cat will bring bad luck is a *superstition.*
   su·per·sti·tion (sü′pər stish′ən) *noun, plural* **superstitions.**

superstitious   Having or showing superstition.
   su·per·sti·tious (sü′pər stish′əs) *adjective.*

supervise   To watch over and direct. The manager *supervised* workers at the plant.
   su·per·vise (sü′pər vīz′) *verb,* **supervised, supervising.**

supervisor   A person who watches over and directs the work of other people.
   su·per·vi·sor (sü′pər vī′zər) *noun, plural* **supervisors.**

supper   The last meal of the day.
   sup·per (sup′ər) *noun, plural* **suppers.**

supple   1. Easy to bend; not stiff. I used *supple* branches to weave the basket.   2. Able to adapt to changes or new things. A person with a *supple* mind learns easily.
   sup·ple (sup′əl) *adjective,* **suppler, supplest.**

supplement   Something added to complete or improve another thing. My history book has a *supplement* in the back that lists all the presidents of the United States. *Noun.*
   —To add as a supplement. I *supplement* my allowance by earning money mowing lawns. *Verb.*
   sup·ple·ment (sup′lə mənt *for noun;* sup′lə ment′ *for verb*) *noun, plural* **supplements;** *verb,* **supplemented, supplementing.**

supply   To provide with something needed or wanted. Rain *supplies* water. *Verb.*
   —A quantity of something that is needed or ready for use. We have bought the *supplies* for our camping trip. *Noun.*
   sup·ply (sə plī′) *verb,* **supplied, supplying;** *noun, plural* **supplies.**

support   1. To hold up. The columns *support* the roof.   2. To provide for. Our parents *support* our family by working.   3. To help or back. Many people *support* that candidate for mayor.   4. To give strength or comfort to. The family *supported* each other during a difficult time.   5. To show to be true. The facts *support* your story. *Verb.*
   —1. The supporting of something or someone. My friends gave me *support* when I ran for club president.   2. A person or thing that supports. The center pole is the main *support* of the tent. *Noun.*
   sup·port (sə pôrt′) *verb,* **supported, supporting;** *noun, plural* **supports.**

suppose   1. To imagine to be possible. *Suppose* that we were able to fly by flapping our arms.   2. To believe; guess. I *suppose* that I'll be finished with my homework soon.   3. To expect or require. My friend is *supposed* to be here by now.
   sup·pose (sə pōz′) *verb,* **supposed, supposing.**

supreme   1. Greatest in power or authority; most important. The dictator was *supreme* in that country.   2. Highest; utmost. We made a *supreme* effort to lift the box.
   su·preme (sə prēm′) *adjective.*

Supreme Court   The highest court in the United States.

sure   **1.** Having no doubt; confident. I am *sure* that you are right.   **2.** Certain to be; dependable. Our team is a *sure* winner.   **3.** Steady; firm. You should have a *sure* grip on the bat when you swing it. *Adjective.*
—Surely; certainly. *Sure*, I'm going. *Adverb.*
sure (shùr) *adjective*, **surer, surest;** *adverb.*

surely   Without any doubt; truly. I will *surely* be there.
sure·ly (shùr′lē) *adverb.*

surf   The rise and splash of the waves of the sea on the shore. *Noun.*
—To ride on a wave with a surfboard. My cousin *surfs* where the waves are big. *Verb.*
▲ Another word that sounds like this is **serf.**
surf (sûrf) *noun; verb,* **surfed, surfing.**

surf

surface   **1.** The outside of a thing. The *surface* of the stone is rough. The astronauts explored the *surface* of the moon.   **2.** Outer look or appearance. The problem seemed simple on the *surface. Noun.*
—Of or having to do with a surface; on a surface. We scraped off the *surface* rust from the metal. *Adjective.*
—**1.** To come or rise to the surface. The submarine *surfaced.*   **2.** To cover the surface of. Our driveway is *surfaced* with tar. *Verb.*
sur·face (sûr′fis) *noun, plural* **surfaces;** *adjective; verb,* **surfaced, surfacing.**

surfboard   A long, flat board used to ride on the crest of a wave.
surf·board (sûrf′bôrd′) *noun, plural* **surfboards.**

surge   To swell and move with force like a wave. The flood waters *surged* over the river banks. The crowd *surged* forward. *Verb.*
—**1.** A swelling movement. The *surge* of the waves tossed the ship.   **2.** A sudden rise. There was a *surge* in the price of food. *Noun.*

surge (sûrj) *verb,* **surged, surging;** *noun, plural* **surges.**

surgeon   A doctor who performs surgery.
sur·geon (sûr′jən) *noun, plural* **surgeons.**

surgery   **1.** The branch of medicine that deals with the removal and repair of diseased or damaged parts of the body.   **2.** An operation performed by a surgeon.
sur·ger·y (sûr′jə rē) *noun.*

Suriname   A country in northeastern South America.
Su·ri·name (sùr′ə näm′) *noun.*

surname   A last name; family name. My *surname* is Banks.
sur·name (sûr′nām′) *noun, plural* **surnames.**

surpass   **1.** To be better, greater, or stronger than. I am a good runner, but two of my friends *surpass* me.   **2.** To be beyond the power or reach of; exceed. A few problems on the math test *surpassed* my ability.
sur·pass (sər pas′) *verb,* **surpassed, surpassing.**

surplus   An amount greater than what is used or needed; quantity remaining. We have a *surplus* of furniture in the attic. *Noun.*
—Greater than what is needed. The farmer gave the *surplus* fruit to a charity. *Adjective.*
sur·plus (sûr′plus′) *noun; adjective.*

surprise   **1.** To cause to feel sudden wonder or amazement. You *surprised* us with all the gifts you brought.   **2.** To find suddenly and unexpectedly. One morning we *surprised* two deer in our backyard. *Verb.*
—**1.** A feeling of wonder or amazement caused by something unexpected. Winning the contest filled me with *surprise.*   **2.** Something that causes surprise. Was the party a *surprise* to you?   **3.** The act of coming upon someone suddenly and unexpectedly. We caught them by *surprise. Noun.*
sur·prise (sər prīz′) *verb,* **surprised, surprising;** *noun, plural* **surprises.**

surrender   To yield. The outlaw *surrendered* to the sheriff. *Verb.*
—The act of surrendering. *Noun.*
sur·ren·der (sə ren′dər) *verb,* **surrendered, surrendering;** *noun, plural* **surrenders.**

at; āpe; fär; câre; end; mē; it; īce; pîerce; hot; ōld; sông, fôrk; oil; out; up; ūse; rüle; pùll; tûrn; chin; sing; shop; thin; <u>th</u>is; hw in white; zh in treasure. The symbol ə stands for the unstressed vowel sound in about, taken, pencil, lemon, and circus.

S

surround To be on all sides of; fórm a circle around. A fence *surrounds* our yard.
sur·round (sə round′) *verb,* **surrounded, surrounding.**

surroundings The things or conditions that surround a person. We moved to the country for the quiet *surroundings.*
sur·round·ings (sə roun′dingz) *plural noun.*

survey **1.** To look at or study in detail. The mayor *surveyed* the damage to the city after the storm. **2.** To measure land to fix or find out its boundaries. They *surveyed* the property before it was divided into lots. *Verb.*
—**1.** A detailed study. The company made a *survey* to find out who might buy its products. **2.** A measuring of land. That family had a *survey* made of their property. *Noun.*
sur·vey (sər vā′ *for verb;* sûr′vā *or* sər vā′ *for noun*) *verb,* **surveyed, surveying;** *noun, plural* **surveys.**

surveyor A person whose work is surveying land.
sur·vey·or (sər vā′ər) *noun, plural* **surveyors.**

survival **1.** The act of surviving. The *survival* of all the bus passengers in the accident seemed a miracle. **2.** A thing that survives. The custom of throwing rice at a bride and groom is a *survival* from the past.
sur·viv·al (sər vī′vəl) *noun.*

survive **1.** To live through. The passengers *survived* the plane crash. **2.** To continue to exist. These plants need water to *survive.*
sur·vive (sər vīv′) *verb,* **survived, surviving.**

survivor A person or thing that survives. There were two *survivors* of the crash.
sur·vi·vor (sər vī′vər) *noun, plural* **survivors.**

suspect **1.** To think that something is possible or true. I *suspect* that they have already gone. **2.** To think someone is guilty without proof. The sheriff *suspected* the stranger of the crime. **3.** To not believe or trust; doubt. We *suspected* their honesty. *Verb.*
—A person who is suspected of committing a crime. The *suspect* is in jail. *Noun.*
sus·pect (sə spekt′ *for verb;* sus′pekt′ *for noun*) *verb,* **suspected, suspecting;** *noun, plural* **suspects.**

suspend **1.** To attach so as to hang down. We *suspended* the swing from a tree branch. **2.** To support while allowing movement. Bits of lemon were *suspended* in the lemonade. **3.** To stop or cause to stop for a time. Why did you *suspend* payments on your car? **4.** To take away the privilege of using or at-

tending. The principal *suspended* the student from school for breaking the rules.
sus·pend (sə spend′) *verb,* **suspended, suspending.**

suspenders Two straps worn over the shoulders to hold up trousers or a skirt.
sus·pend·ers (sə spen′dərz) *plural noun.*

suspense The condition of being in doubt and worried about what will happen. The exciting movie kept me in *suspense.*
sus·pense (sə spens′) *noun.*

suspension The act of suspending. My *suspension* from school lasted a week.
sus·pen·sion (sə spen′shən) *noun, plural* **suspensions.**

suspension bridge A bridge suspended from cables or chains that are strung from towers.

suspension bridge

suspicion **1.** The act or instance of suspecting. My *suspicion* that the apple was rotten turned out to be correct. **2.** The condition of being suspected. Members of the gang were under *suspicion* for several crimes.
sus·pi·cion (sə spish′ən) *noun, plural* **suspicions.**

suspicious **1.** Causing suspicion. The person outside the bank acted in a *suspicious* manner. **2.** Feeling or showing suspicion. That farmer is *suspicious* of strangers.
sus·pi·cious (sə spish′əs) *adjective.*

SW or **S.W.** An abbreviation for *southwest.*

swallow¹ **1.** To cause food to pass from the mouth to the stomach. **2.** To take in and cover. The sea *swallowed* the ship. **3.** To take or keep back. I *swallowed* my pride and apologized for being rude. **4.** To believe something without questioning

whether it makes sense or is true. That story is just too fantastic to *swallow. Verb.*
—**1.** The act of swallowing. With a quick *swallow* I finished my milk.   **2.** The amount that can be swallowed at a time. I took a *swallow* of water before I dashed out. *Noun.*
> **swal·low** (swol′ō) *verb,* **swallowed, swallowing;** *noun, plural* **swallows.**

swallow²   A small bird with long wings. Swallows are very good fliers.
> **swal·low** (swol′ō) *noun, plural* **swallows.**

swam   Past tense of **swim.** We *swam* in the pool. Look up **swim** for more information.
> **swam** (swam) *verb.*

swamp   An area of wet land. Swamps may have trees and shrubs growing in them. *Noun.*
—To fill with water. The high waves *swamped* the boat and made it sink. *Verb.*
> **swamp** (swomp) *noun, plural* **swamps;** *verb,* **swamped, swamping.**

swan   A large water bird that has a long, graceful neck and webbed feet.
> **swan** (swon) *noun, plural* **swans.**

swan

swarm   **1.** A group of bees that leave their hive to start a new colony.   **2.** A large group of people or animals. *Swarms* of tourists visited the beach. *Noun.*
—**1.** To leave a hive together to start a new colony. The bees *swarmed.*   **2.** To move in a large group. People *swarmed* out of the theater.   **3.** To be filled. The river *swarmed* with alligators. *Verb.*
> **swarm** (swôrm) *noun, plural* **swarms;** *verb,* **swarmed, swarming.**

sway   **1.** To move or cause to move back and forth. The dancers *swayed* to the music.   **2.** To change the thinking of; influence. Can I *sway* you from quitting your job? *Verb.*
—**1.** The act of swaying. We felt the *sway* of the bus.   **2.** Influence or control. The nation was under the dictator's *sway. Noun.*
> **sway** (swā) *verb,* **swayed, swaying;** *noun, plural* **sways.**

swear   **1.** To make a solemn statement, often by calling on God or another sacred being or thing. The witness *swore* on a Bible to tell the truth during the trial.   **2.** To promise in a solemn way. I *swear* that I'm telling the truth.   **3.** To say words that show hatred and anger; curse.
> **swear** (swâr) *verb,* **swore, sworn, swearing.**

sweat   **1.** A salty fluid given off through the skin. Sweat helps to keep the body cool.   **2.** Moisture formed in drops on a surface. *Sweat* formed on the glass of cold water.   **3.** The condition of sweating. I was so nervous that I broke into a *sweat. Noun.*
—**1.** To give off sweat. The horse *sweated* in the hot sun.   **2.** To gather moisture in drops from the surrounding air. The glass of cold lemonade *sweated* in the warm room. *Verb.*
> **sweat** (swet) *noun; verb,* **sweated, sweating.**

sweater   A warm, knitted piece of clothing worn over the upper part of the body.
> **sweat·er** (swet′ər) *noun, plural* **sweaters.**

sweatshirt   A heavy, knitted shirt that usually has long sleeves and no collar.
> **sweat·shirt** (swet′shûrt′) *noun, plural* **sweatshirts.**

Sweden   A country in northern Europe.
> **Swe·den** (swē′dən) *noun.*

Swedish   The language spoken in Sweden. *Noun.*
—Of or having to do with Sweden, its people, or its language. *Adjective.*
> **Swed·ish** (swē′dish) *noun; adjective.*

sweep   **1.** To clean with a broom or brush. Please *sweep* the floor.   **2.** To clear away or take up. We *swept* the crumbs from the floor.   **3.** To move or carry quickly and with force. The fire *swept* through the barn.   **4.** To pass over with a quick, steady motion. The sailor's eyes *swept* the horizon. *Verb.*
—Any quick, sweeping motion. The cat batted the ball with a *sweep* of its paw. *Noun.*
> **sweep** (swēp) *verb,* **swept, sweeping;** *noun, plural* **sweeps.**

sweet   **1.** Having a taste like that of sugar or honey. This apple is *sweet* and juicy.   **2.** Pleasing to the smell. A rose has a *sweet*

at; āpe; fär; câre; end; mē; it; īce; pîerce; hot; ōld; sông, fôrk; oil; out; up; ūse; rüle; pùll; tûrn; chin; sing; shop; thin; this; hw in white; zh in treasure. The symbol ə stands for the unstressed vowel sound in about, taken, pencil, lemon, and circus.

odor. **3.** Not sour; fresh. Store the cream in the refrigerator to keep it *sweet*. **4.** Not salted. The baker would only use *sweet* butter. **5.** Pleasing and kindly; good-natured. Our camp counselor is a *sweet* person. *Adjective.*
—Something that tastes sweet. That store sells cookies, candy, and other *sweets. Noun.* ▲ Another word that sounds like this is **suite.**
> **sweet** (swēt) *adjective,* **sweeter, sweetest;** *noun, plural* **sweets.**

sweeten To make or become sweet or sweeter. The cook *sweetened* the lemonade with sugar.
> **sweet·en** (swē′tən) *verb,* **sweetened, sweetening.**

sweetener A substance that sweetens. Sugar and honey are natural sweeteners, and there are also synthetic sweeteners that have been developed as substitutes for them.
> **sweet·en·er** (swē′tə nər) *noun, plural* **sweeteners.**

sweetheart A person who is loved by and loves another.
> **sweet·heart** (swēt′härt′) *noun, plural* **sweethearts.**

sweet pea A flower with a sweet smell. Sweet peas may be purple, pink, red, or white. They grow on climbing plants.

sweet potato The sweet, orange root of a vine. The sweet potato is cooked and eaten as a vegetable.

swell **1.** To grow or cause to grow in size. The sprain *swelled* my wrist. **2.** To rise above the normal level. The river *swells* in the spring. This symphony *swells* to a loud ending. *Verb.*
—A wave or series of waves. The boat rose and fell on the ocean *swells. Noun.*
—Fine; excellent. You look *swell* in your new clothes. *Adjective.* ▲ This meaning is used mostly in everyday conversation.
> **swell** (swel) *verb,* **swelled, swollen** or **swelled, swelling;** *noun, plural* **swells;** *adjective,* **sweller, swellest.**

sweet peas

swelling A swollen part. I had a *swelling* on my leg where the baseball hit me.
> **swell·ing** (swel′ing) *noun, plural* **swellings.**

swept Past tense and past participle of **sweep.** We *swept* the floor of the cabin. Look up **sweep** for more information.
> **swept** (swept) *verb.*

swerve To turn aside suddenly. The driver *swerved* to avoid hitting a dog. *Verb.*
—The act of swerving. The *swerve* of the bus caused a passenger to fall to the floor. *Noun.*
> **swerve** (swûrv) *verb,* **swerved, swerving;** *noun, plural* **swerves.**

swift **1.** Moving or able to move very quickly. The rider had a *swift* horse. **2.** Happening quickly; quick. The frog made a *swift* leap into the pond. *Adjective.*
—A bird with narrow wings and dark gray, brown, or bluish feathers. *Noun.*
> **swift** (swift) *adjective,* **swifter, swiftest;** *noun, plural* **swifts.**

swim **1.** To move in the water by using the arms and legs or the fins and tail. We watched the fish *swimming* in the pond. **2.** To move across something in this way. How fast can you *swim* the length of the pool? **3.** To be in a liquid or be covered with a liquid. The turkey was *swimming* in gravy. The child's eyes *swam* with tears. **4.** To have a dizzy feeling. The rocking of the boat made my head *swim. Verb.*
—The act, time, or distance of swimming. Let's take a quick *swim* before lunch. *Noun.*
> **swim** (swim) *verb,* **swam, swum, swimming;** *noun, plural* **swims.**

swimmer A person or animal that swims.
> **swim·mer** (swim′ər) *noun, plural* **swimmers.**

swindle To take someone's money or property in a dishonest way; cheat. The dealer *swindled* me and never delivered the goods as promised. *Verb.*
—The act of swindling. *Noun.*
> **swin·dle** (swin′dəl) *verb,* **swindled, swindling;** *noun, plural* **swindles.**

swine A member of the pig family; pig or hog.
> **swine** (swīn) *noun, plural* **swine.**

swing **1.** To move back and forth. We like to *swing* on the tire that hangs from the tree. **2.** To move or turn in a curved motion. The player *swung* the bat. *Verb.*
—**1.** The swinging of something. A *swing* of the golf club sent the ball flying. **2.** A seat hung by chains or ropes in which a person can sit and swing. We play on the *swings* at the playground. *Noun.*
> **swing** (swing) *verb,* **swung, swinging;** *noun, plural* **swings.**

swirl To move around and around. The wind *swirled* the dry leaves. *Verb.*

—**1.** A spinning or twisting motion. The breeze made the smoke of the campfire rise with a *swirl*. **2.** Something shaped like a curl. My signature ends in a *swirl*. *Noun.*
swirl (swûrl) *verb,* **swirled, swirling;** *noun, plural* **swirls.**

swish To move with a soft, brushing sound. My long coat *swished* as I walked. *Verb.*
—A swishing movement or sound. I listened to the *swish* of the tide. *Noun.*
swish (swish) *verb,* **swished, swishing;** *noun, plural* **swishes.**

Swiss the Swiss. The people of Switzerland. *Noun.*
—Of or having to do with Switzerland or its people. *Adjective.*
Swiss (swis) *noun; adjective.*

switch **1.** A long, thin stick or rod used for whipping. **2.** A stroke or lash. The cow brushed flies off with a *switch* of its tail. **3.** A change. The coach made a *switch* to a new pitcher in the ninth inning. **4.** A device used to open or close an electric circuit. Where is the *switch* for the light? **5.** A device by which a train can change from one track to another. *Noun.*
—**1.** To strike with a switch. **2.** To move or swing with a quick motion. The cat *switched* its tail. **3.** To change. Let's *switch* seats. **4.** To turn on or off by means of an electrical switch. I *switched* the light on. **5.** To move a train from one track to another. *Verb.*
switch (swich) *noun, plural* **switches;** *verb,* **switched, switching.**

switchboard A device used to connect telephone lines or other electrical circuits.
switch·board (swich′bôrd′) *noun, plural* **switchboards.**

Switzerland A country in central Europe.
Switz·er·land (swit′sər lənd) *noun.*

swivel A device that allows parts attached to it to move freely. My lamp has a *swivel* that lets me raise or lower it. *Noun.*
—To turn on a swivel. I *swiveled* on the piano stool. *Verb.*
swiv·el (swiv′əl) *noun, plural* **swivels;** *verb,* **swiveled, swiveling.**

swollen A past participle of **swell.** Your sore toe has *swollen* since yesterday. Look up **swell** for more information. *Verb.*
—Made larger by swelling. I can't get my ring on my *swollen* finger. *Adjective.*
swol·len (swō′lən) *verb; adjective.*

swoop To rush down suddenly. The hawk *swooped* on the rabbit. The outlaws *swooped* out of the hills to attack the stagecoach. *Verb.*

—The act of swooping. With a *swoop*, the eagle caught the squirrel. *Noun.*
swoop (swüp) *verb,* **swooped, swooping;** *noun, plural* **swoops.**

sword A weapon that has a long, sharp blade set in a handle.
sword (sôrd) *noun, plural* **swords.**

swordfish A large saltwater fish with a long, flat, bony part like a sword that sticks out from the upper jaw. People catch swordfish for food and for sport.
sword·fish (sôrd′fish′) *noun, plural* **swordfish** or **swordfishes.**

swordfish

swore Past tense of **swear.** The witness *swore* to tell the truth. Look up **swear** for more information.
swore (swôr) *verb.*

sworn Past participle of **swear.** They have *sworn* to be friends forever. Look up **swear** for more information.
sworn (swôrn) *verb.*

swum Past participle of **swim.** That child has *swum* in the lake all day. Look up **swim** for more information.
swum (swum) *verb.*

swung Past tense and past participle of **swing.** I *swung* the bat at the ball. Look up **swing** for more information.
swung (swung) *verb.*

sycamore A tree with smooth, colorful bark that peels off in thin layers.
syc·a·more (sik′ə môr′) *noun, plural* **sycamores.**

at; āpe; fär; câre; end; mē; it; īce; pîerce; hot; ōld; sông, fôrk; oil; out; up; ūse; rüle; pull; tûrn; chin; sing; shop; thin; this; hw in white; zh in treasure. The symbol ə stands for the unstressed vowel sound in about, taken, pencil, lemon, and circus.

S

731

syllable **1.** A spoken sound without interruption that forms a word or part of a word. The word "break" has one syllable. The word "important" has three syllables. **2.** A letter or group of letters that form a syllable.
syl·la·ble (sil′ə bəl) *noun, plural* **syllables.**

symbol Something that represents something else. The dove is a *symbol* of peace. ▲ Another word that sounds like this is **cymbal.**
sym·bol (sim′bəl) *noun, plural* **symbols.**

symbolize To be a symbol of; stand for. The owl *symbolizes* wisdom.
sym·bol·ize (sim′bə līz′) *verb,* **symbolized, symbolizing.**

symmetric or **symmetrical** Having or showing symmetry.
sym·met·ric or **sym·met·ri·cal** (si met′rik *or* si met′rī kəl) *adjective.*

symmetry A balanced grouping of parts on either side of a line or around a center.
sym·me·try (sim′i trē) *noun, plural* **symmetries.**

The shape of a starfish shows **symmetry.**

sympathetic **1.** Feeling or showing kindness and pity toward others. A *sympathetic* neighbor brought flowers to me when I was sick. **2.** In agreement. The counselor is *sympathetic* to our plans for a picnic.
sym·pa·thet·ic (sim′pə thet′ik) *adjective.*

sympathize **1.** To feel and understand the sorrow or troubles of others; have or show compassion. I *sympathized* with my neighbors when their cat ran away. **2.** To be in agreement. My parents *sympathize* with my plan to be an actor.
sym·pa·thize (sim′pə thīz′) *verb,* **sympathized, sympathizing.**

sympathy **1.** The ability to feel and understand the sorrow or troubles of others. I had *sympathy* for the hurt dog. **2.** Agreement. The teacher is in *sympathy* with us.
sym·pa·thy (sim′pə thē) *noun, plural* **sympathies.**

symphony **1.** A long musical work written for an orchestra. **2.** A large orchestra.
sym·pho·ny (sim′fə nē) *noun, plural* **symphonies.**

symptom A sign of something. A sore throat often is a *symptom* of a cold.
symp·tom (simp′təm) *noun, plural* **symptoms.**

synagogue A building that is used by Jews for worship and religious instruction.
syn·a·gogue (sin′ə gog′ *or* sin′ə gôg′) *noun, plural* **synagogues.**

synonym A word that has the same or almost the same meaning as another word. "Large" is a *synonym* for "big."
syn·o·nym (sin′ə nim) *noun, plural* **synonyms.**

Language Note

A **synonym** is a word that can be used instead of another word. Synonyms help us make our writing clearer and more interesting. Some words are so close in meaning that they can replace each other in a sentence. For example, the synonyms *gift* and *present* can be used in the same sentence: I received four gifts (presents) for my birthday.

Some synonyms, such as *make, form,* and *manufacture,* are not close enough in meaning to be substituted for one another. The meaning of these synonyms must be understood before they can be used properly in a sentence.

synonymous Having the same or almost the same meaning. The words "leap" and "jump" are *synonymous.*
syn·on·y·mous (si non′ə məs) *adjective.*

synthetic Made by people; not found in nature; artificial. Plastic is synthetic.
syn·thet·ic (sin thet′ik) *adjective.*

Syria A country in the Middle East.
Syr·i·a (sîr′ē ə) *noun.*

syrup A thick, sweet liquid. Some syrups are made by boiling sugar and water or juice.
syr·up (sir′əp *or* sûr′əp) *noun, plural* **syrups.**

system **1.** A group of things that form a whole. Our state has a good *system* of roads. **2.** A group of laws, beliefs, or facts. In school, we study different *systems* of government. **3.** An orderly method. You have a good *system* for studying.
sys·tem (sis′təm) *noun, plural* **systems.**

1. The letter **T** was the last letter of the alphabet for many ancient tribes in the Middle East.

2. In the early Hebrew alphabet, this letter was sometimes written like an *x*.

3. The ancient Greeks borrowed this letter and put the short line at the top, rather than in the middle of the letter.

4. An ancient tribe that settled near Rome about 2,800 years ago used the **T** also, changing it only slightly.

5. The ancient Romans then borrowed the letter **T** and used it in their alphabet.

6. By about 2,400 years ago, the Romans were writing their letter **T** just like our capital **T**.

t, T   The twentieth letter of the alphabet.
t, T (tē) *noun, plural* **t's, T's.**

tab   A small flap that sticks out from something. The *tab* on the file folder was marked with the name of a customer.
tab (tab) *noun, plural* **tabs.**

table   **1.** A piece of furniture with a flat top supported by one or more legs. The *table* in the dining room can seat eight people. **2.** The people seated at a table. The *table* next to us was very noisy.   **3.** A list of facts or information. A *table* in my history book lists all the states and their capitals.
• **ta·ble** (tā′bəl) *noun, plural* **tables.**

tablecloth   A cloth used to cover a table.
ta·ble·cloth (tā′bəl klôth′) *noun, plural* **tablecloths.**

tablespoon   A large spoon that is used to serve and measure food. A tablespoon holds the same amount as three teaspoons.
ta·ble·spoon (tā′bəl spün′) *noun, plural* **tablespoons.**

tablet   **1.** A number of sheets of paper glued together at one edge; pad. I bought a *tablet* of writing paper at the stationery store.   **2.** A small, flat piece of medicine or candy. Those red *tablets* will help your hay fever.   **3.** A thin, flat slab of wood or stone that has writing on it.
tab·let (tab′lit) *noun, plural* **tablets.**

table tennis   A game played on a table with a low net stretched across it. Players use paddles to hit a small ball back and forth.

table tennis

tack **1.** A short nail that has a sharp point and a broad, flat head. **2.** A course of action. We weren't succeeding, so we tried a new *tack. Noun.*
—**1.** To fasten with a tack or tacks. Let's *tack* posters to the walls of the room. **2.** To attach or add. I think you should *tack* a small pocket onto the dress right here. *Verb.*
> **tack** (tak) *noun, plural* **tacks;** *verb,* **tacked, tacking.**

tackle **1.** The equipment used for some activity or sport. The store sold rods, line, hooks, nets, and other fishing *tackle.* **2.** A system of ropes and pulleys used for raising and lowering heavy loads. Tackle is used for raising and lowering the sails on a ship. **3.** The act of stopping and bringing to the ground. The football player made a good *tackle* of the ball carrier. *Noun.*
—**1.** To deal with; work on. First we mowed the front lawn, then we *tackled* the backyard. **2.** To stop and bring to the ground. The farmer *tackled* the fleeing pig. *Verb.*
> **tack·le** (tak'əl) *noun, plural* **tackles;** *verb,* **tackled, tackling.**

taco A tortilla wrapped around a filling, such as cheese, ground beef, or chicken.
> **ta·co** (tä'kō) *noun, plural* **tacos.**

tact The ability to say or do the right thing when dealing with people or difficult situations. I tried to use *tact* when thanking my aunt for a gift I didn't like.
> **tact** (takt) *noun.*

tadpole A very young frog or toad when it still lives under water and has gills, a tail, and no legs.
> **tad·pole** (tad'pōl') *noun, plural* **tadpoles.**

tadpole

taffy A chewy candy made of brown sugar or molasses mixed with butter.
> **taf·fy** (taf'ē) *noun, plural* **taffies.**

tag¹ A piece of paper or other material that is attached to something. The price *tag* says this shirt costs ten dollars. *Noun.*
— **1.** To attach a tag to. My suitcases are *tagged* with my name and address. **2.** To follow closely. The dog *tagged* along wherever the children went. *Verb.*
> **tag** (tag) *noun, plural* **tags;** *verb,* **tagged, tagging.**

tag² A game in which one player chases the other players until he or she touches one. The player who is touched must then chase the others. *Noun.*
—**1.** To touch or tap in the game of tag. I *tagged* you, so now you chase us. **2.** To put a runner out in baseball by touching the runner with the ball. *Verb.*
> **tag** (tag) *noun; verb,* **tagged, tagging.**

tail **1.** A slender, flexible part of an animal's body that sticks out from the back end. Our dog wags its *tail* when it sees us coming home from school. **2.** Anything that is shaped like a tail. The *tail* of a comet always points away from the sun. **3.** The end or rear part of anything. The airplane had an emergency exit in the *tail.* **4. tails.** The reverse side of a coin. *Noun.*
—To follow closely and secretly. The secret agent *tailed* the spy. *Verb.* ▲ Another word that sounds like this is **tale.**
> **tail** (tāl) *noun, plural* **tails;** *verb,* **tailed, tailing.**

tailor A person who makes, alters, or repairs clothing. *Noun.*
—To make as a tailor does. Suits *tailored* at that store always fit well. *Verb.*
> **tai·lor** (tā'lər) *noun, plural* **tailors;** *verb,* **tailored, tailoring.**

Taiwan An island country in the Pacific Ocean. It is off the eastern coast of China.
> **Tai·wan** (tī'wän') *noun.*

take **1.** To get a hold of; grasp. I reached down to *take* the child's hand as we crossed the street. The student *took* a book from the shelf. **2.** To capture or win by using force or skill. The invading army *took* many prisoners. My friend's painting *took* first prize. **3.** To obtain; get. The nurse *took* my temperature. **4.** To carry with one; bring. My parents only *took* two suitcases on their trip. **5.** To make use of. Please *take* a seat. Let's *take* the bus home. **6.** To move or remove. *Take* the trash to the town dump. If you *take* 3 from 5, you get 2. **7.** To lead or conduct. This staircase will *take* you to the street. I *took* the dog for a walk. **8.** To receive or accept. I *take* a vitamin pill every morning. *Take* my advice and get a good night's sleep. **9.** To make or do. I have to *take* a history test this morning. I *took* a photograph of the deer in the meadow. **10.** To need or require. It *takes* practice to learn how to play the guitar. **11.** To have a sense of; feel. Some collectors *take* great pride in their

734

rare coins. **12.** To put up with; tolerate; endure. Our teacher won't *take* rude behavior.
- **to take after.** To look like or be like. I don't *take after* either of my parents.
- **to take in.** **1.** To reduce the size of; make smaller. I have to *take in* this jacket. **2.** To understand. The lecture was so full of information that I couldn't *take* it all *in*.
- **to take off.** **1.** To remove. *Take off* your hat. **2.** To rise up in flight. The airplane *took off* on time.
- **to take up.** **1.** To make shorter or smaller. You'll have to *take up* those jeans. **2.** To begin, as a hobby or a course of instruction. I'm going to *take up* tennis. **3.** To consume or fill; occupy. Collecting stamps *takes up* some of my spare time. That truck *takes up* a lot of space. **4.** To gather or collect. We *took up* a collection to buy a present for our friend.

take (tāk) *verb,* **took, taken, taking.**

taken Past participle of **take.** Is this seat *taken?* Look up **take** for more information.
tak·en (tā′kən) *verb.*

takeoff The act of leaving the ground. The *takeoff* of the space shuttle is scheduled for noon.
takeoff (tāk′ôf′) *noun, plural* **takeoffs.**

takeoff

tale **1.** A story. What a good *tale* about life at sea! **2.** A story that is not true; falsehood. Stop telling *tales* and give us the truth. ▲ Another word that sounds like this is **tail.**
tale (tāl) *noun, plural* **tales.**

talent **1.** A natural ability or skill. You have a *talent* for playing the piano. **2.** A person or persons who have talent. We need more *talent* for our play.
tal·ent (tal′ənt) *noun, plural* **talents.**

talented Having or showing talent. That ballet student is a very *talented* dancer.
tal·ent·ed (tal′ən tid) *adjective.*

talk **1.** To say words; speak. The baby cannot *talk* yet. **2.** To discuss. You should *talk* with the doctor about the pain in your back. **3.** To bring or persuade by speech. The salesperson *talked* me into buying two pairs of shoes. *Verb.*
—**1.** An exchange of spoken words; conversation. The two friends had a long *talk.* **2.** An informal speech or lecture. The speaker gave a *talk* about Africa. *Noun.*
talk (tôk) *verb,* **talked, talking;** *noun, plural* **talks.**

talkative Talking or tending to talk a lot. I am not *talkative* early in the morning.
talk·a·tive (tô′kə tiv) *adjective.*

tall **1.** Higher than average; not short or low. Two *tall* people in front of me blocked my view. **2.** Measured from the bottom to the top; having a certain height. I am four feet *tall.* **3.** Made-up or exaggerated. I think stories about ghosts are *tall* tales.
tall (tôl) *adjective,* **taller, tallest.**

tallow The fat from cattle and sheep. Tallow is used in making candles and soap.
tal·low (tal′ō) *noun.*

talon The strong, sharp claw of an eagle, hawk, or other bird of prey.
tal·on (tal′ən) *noun, plural* **talons.**

tambourine A small drum that has metal disks attached loosely around the rim.
tam·bou·rine (tam′bə rēn′) *noun, plural* **tambourines.**

tame **1.** Taken from a wild or natural state by human beings and made gentle or obedient. *Tame* elephants are a favorite sight at the circus. **2.** Not fearful or shy. The goat was *tame* enough to let us feed it. *Adjective.*
—To take from a wild or natural state and make gentle or obedient. They *tame* wild horses at that ranch. *Verb.*
tame (tām) *adjective,* **tamer, tamest;** *verb,* **tamed, taming.**

tamper To interfere in an improper manner. If you *tamper* with this recipe, the bread won't rise.
tam·per (tam′pər) *verb,* **tampered, tampering.**

tan **1.** To make into leather by soaking in a special solution. That company *tans* animal

at; āpe; fär; câre; end; mē; it; īce; pîerce; hot; ōld; sông, fôrk; oil; out; up; ūse; rüle; pull; tûrn; chin; sing; shop; thin; this; hw in white; zh in treasure. The symbol ə stands for the unstressed vowel sound in about, taken, pencil, lemon, and circus.

T

hides to make purses and belts. **2.** To make or become brown by exposure to the sun. Sunlight *tanned* the climber's face. *Verb.*
—**1.** A yellowish brown color. **2.** The brown color given to a person's skin by exposure to the sun. The lifeguard had a deep *tan* from being at the beach every day. *Noun.*
—Having the color tan. *Adjective.*
tan (tan) *verb,* **tanned, tanning;** *noun,* plural **tans;** *adjective,* **tanner, tannest.**

tang A sharp or strong taste, flavor, or odor. I love the *tang* of fresh grapefruit.
tang (tang) *noun, plural* **tangs.**

tangerine A small, sweet, juicy fruit that is like an orange. A tangerine has a reddish orange skin that peels easily.
tan·ge·rine (tan′jə rēn′) *noun, plural* **tangerines.**

tangle To twist together in a confused mass; snarl. The strong wind *tangled* my hair. *Verb.*
—A twisted, confused mass. The yarn was in a *tangle* after the kitten played with it. *Noun.*
tan·gle (tang′gəl) *verb,* **tangled, tangling;** *noun, plural* **tangles.**

tank **1.** A large container for holding liquid or gas. The driver filled the gas *tank* of the car. **2.** An enclosed, armored vehicle used in combat. It has machine guns and a cannon and moves on two continuous belts.
tank (tangk) *noun, plural* **tanks.**

tanker A ship, truck, or airplane that has tanks for carrying oil or other liquid.
tank·er (tang′kər) *noun, plural* **tankers.**

tantrum An outburst of temper or anger.
tan·trum (tan′trəm) *noun, plural* **tantrums.**

Tanzania A country in southeastern Africa.
Tan·za·ni·a (tan′zə nē′ə) *noun.*

tap¹ **1.** To hit or strike lightly. The teacher *tapped* on the desk with a ruler for attention. **2.** To make or do by striking or hitting lightly again and again. I *tapped* out the beat of the music with my foot. *Verb.*
—A light or gentle blow. I turned around when I felt a *tap* on my shoulder. *Noun.*
tap (tap) *verb,* **tapped, tapping;** *noun, plural* **taps.**

tap² A device for starting or stopping the flow of water or another liquid from a pipe, sink, or container; faucet. Our kitchen sink has two *taps. Noun.*
—**1.** To put a hole in to draw liquid from. Our grandparents *tap* the trunks of sugar maple trees to collect sap for making syrup. **2.** To make a hidden connection in order to listen to someone's conversations. The spy *tapped* the enemy's telephone lines. *Verb.*
tap (tap) *noun, plural* **taps;** *verb,* **tapped, tapping.**

tape **1.** A long narrow strip of cloth, paper, plastic, or some other material. The runner broke the *tape* that was stretched across the finish line. **2.** A specially treated plastic band that is used to record and play sounds or images. My music collection includes many *tapes. Noun.*
—**1.** To fasten with a tape. *Tape* the two pieces of paper together. **2.** To record on a specially treated plastic tape. The television station *taped* the president's speech. *Verb.*
tape (tāp) *noun, plural* **tapes;** *verb,* **taped, taping.**

tape measure A long strip of cloth, plastic, or steel marked off in units for measuring.

taper **1.** To make or become gradually smaller at one end. The tailor *tapered* the legs of the slacks. **2.** To become less and less. The rain finally *tapered* off. ▲ Another word that sounds like this is **tapir.**
ta·per (tā′pər) *verb,* **tapered, tapering.**

tape recorder A machine that records and plays sound on a kind of plastic tape.

tapestry A cloth that has designs and pictures woven into it.
tap·es·try (tap′ə strē) *noun, plural* **tapestries.**

tapir An animal that looks like a large pig but is related to horses and rhinoceroses. Tapirs live in Central and South America and

tap²

Asia. ▲ Another word that sounds like this is **taper**.

ta·pir (tā′pər) *noun, plural* **tapirs**.

tapir

taps A bugle call that is played at the end of the day in military camps as a signal that all lights must be put out. It is also played at military funerals.

taps (taps) *noun*.

tar A dark, sticky substance that is made from coal or wood. Tar is used to pave roads and to waterproof roofs and sheds. *Noun.*
—To cover or coat with tar. The workers *tarred* the new highway. *Verb.*

tar (tär) *noun; verb,* **tarred, tarring**.

tarantula A hairy spider that is found in warm areas. It has a painful bite.

ta·ran·tu·la (tə ran′chə lə) *noun, plural* **tarantulas**.

tardy Arriving or happening after the appointed time; late. Those students were *tardy* for class because their bus got a flat tire.

tar·dy (tär′dē) *adjective,* **tardier, tardiest**.

target 1. A mark or object that is aimed at. When we practice archery, we use a piece of cardboard as a *target*. 2. A person or thing that is made fun of or criticized. I was the *target* for teasing after I struck out.

tar·get (tär′git) *noun, plural* **targets**.

tariff A charge or tax that a government puts on goods coming into a country. The government placed a *tariff* on imported cars.

tar·iff (tar′if) *noun, plural* **tariffs**.

tarnish 1. To dull the shine or color of. Sulfur in the air can *tarnish* silver. 2. To lose shine or color. The old candlesticks have *tarnished. Verb.*
—A surface coating that results from tarnishing. Polish will take that *tarnish* off. *Noun.*

tar·nish (tär′nish) *verb,* **tarnished, tarnishing;** *noun*.

tart¹ Sharp in taste; not sweet. This apple is crisp and *tart*.

tart (tärt) *adjective,* **tarter, tartest**.

tart² A pastry shell containing a custard, fruit, or other filling.

tart (tärt) *noun, plural* **tarts**.

tartan A woolen cloth with a plaid pattern. Each Scottish clan has its own special tartan.

tar·tan (tär′tən) *noun, plural* **tartans**.

tartar A yellowish substance that forms on teeth and becomes hard if not removed.

tar·tar (tär′tər) *noun*.

task A piece of work to be done. My classroom *task* is to wash the blackboard.

task (task) *noun, plural* **tasks**.

tassel 1. A hanging group of threads or cords that are tied together at one end. The cord on our window shade ends in a *tassel*. 2. Anything that is like this in shape. An ear of corn has a silky *tassel* at one end.

tas·sel (tas′əl) *noun, plural* **tassels**.

taste 1. The sense by which the flavor of something in the mouth is noticed. 2. A particular flavor of food or anything else that is taken into the mouth. The four basic tastes are sweet, bitter, sour, and salty. 3. A small amount; sample. May I have a *taste* of your fish? 4. A liking or preference. I found a shirt to my *taste*. 5. A feeling of appreciation for what is good or beautiful. My friend has good *taste* in music. *Noun.*
—1. To recognize the flavor of something by means of the sense of taste. I can *taste* the garlic in this stew. 2. To have a particular flavor. The sauce *tastes* too sweet. 3. To find out the flavor of something by taking a little of it into the mouth. *Taste* the soup to see if it needs pepper. *Verb.*

taste (tāst) *noun, plural* **tastes;** *verb,* **tasted, tasting**.

tasteless 1. Having little or no flavor. The soup was *tasteless,* so I added some pepper. 2. Having or showing little sense of what is good, beautiful, or appropriate. It was *tasteless* to joke at such a serious event.

taste·less (tāst′lis) *adjective*.

tasty Pleasing to the sense of taste. This is a very *tasty* dessert.

tast·y (tās′tē) *adjective,* **tastier, tastiest**.

tattered Torn or hanging in shreds. I like to wear that old *tattered* shirt.

tat·tered (tat′ərd) *adjective*.

tattle To tell secrets. Speak softly, or someone might hear and *tattle* on us.

tat·tle (tat′əl) *verb,* **tattled, tattling**.

at; āpe; fär; câre; end; mē; it; īce; pîerce; hot; ōld; sông, fôrk; oil; out; up; ūse; rüle; pull; tûrn; chin; sing; shop; thin; <u>th</u>is; hw in white; zh in treasure. The symbol ə stands for the unstressed vowel sound in about, taken, pencil, lemon, and circus.

T

tattletale   A person who tells the secrets of others. Never tell a *tattletale* anything you don't want others to know.
   tat·tle·tale (tat′əl tāl′) *noun, plural* **tattletales.**

tattoo   A colored figure or design made on the skin with needles that have been dipped in colors. The sailor had *tattoos* of ships on each arm.
   tat·too (ta tü′) *noun, plural* **tattoos.**

taught   Past tense and past participle of **teach.** I *taught* my cousin how to play volleyball. That experienced teacher has *taught* hundreds of children. Look up **teach** for more information. ▲ Another word that sounds like this is **taut.**
   taught (tôt) *verb.*

taut   Tightly drawn or stretched; not loose. The campers made sure the ropes on the tent were *taut*. ▲ Another word that sounds like this is **taught.**
   taut (tôt) *adjective,* **tauter, tautest.**

tavern   A place where travelers stay overnight; inn.
   tav·ern (tav′ərn) *noun, plural* **taverns.**

tax   **1.** Money that people or businesses must pay the government for its support. **2.** A heavy burden or demand; strain. The delay was a *tax* on our patience. *Noun.*
   —**1.** To put a tax on. Our state *taxes* gasoline and uses the money to build highways. **2.** To make a heavy demand on; strain. The difficult arithmetic problems *taxed* my brain. *Verb.*
   tax (taks) *noun, plural* **taxes;** *verb,* **taxed, taxing.**

taxation   The practice or system of taxing. Taxation gives the government money to provide schools, hospitals, clean water, and many other services.
   tax·a·tion (tak sā′shən) *noun.*

taxi   An automobile that can be hired to take a person somewhere; taxicab. *Noun.*
   — To move slowly along the ground or over the surface of the water. The airplane *taxied* out to the runway to take off. *Verb.*
   tax·i (tak′sē) *noun, plural* **taxis;** *verb,* **taxied, taxiing** or **taxying.**

taxicab   An automobile that can be hired to carry passengers where they want to go. A taxicab usually has a meter that records the fare to be paid.
   tax·i·cab (tak′sē kab′) *noun, plural* **taxicabs.**

tbs. or **tbsp.**   An abbreviation for *tablespoon.*

tea   **1.** A drink that is made by pouring boiling water over the dried leaves of a shrub that is grown in China, Japan, and India. **2.** This shrub or its dried and crumbled leaves.   **3.** A drink prepared in the same way from other dried leaves.   **4.** A light meal or gathering held in the late afternoon, during which tea and other refreshments are served.
   tea (tē) *noun, plural* **teas.**

teach   To help a person to learn; show how. My neighbor *teaches* swimming in a camp and *taught* me to swim last summer.
   teach (tēch) *verb,* **taught, teaching.**

teacher   A person who gives lessons or classes. The science *teacher* began the class by doing an experiment.
   teach·er (tē′chər) *noun, plural* **teachers.**

teakettle   A small covered kettle with a spout and handle. It is used to boil water.
   tea·ket·tle (tē′ket′əl) *noun, plural* **teakettles.**

teal   A small duck with a short neck.
   teal (tēl) *noun, plural* **teal** or **teals.**

teal

team   **1.** A group that plays, acts, or works together. A *team* of scientists discovered a cure for the disease.   **2.** Two or more horses or other animals that are harnessed together to do work. In many parts of the world, a *team* of oxen is used to pull a plow. *Noun.*
   —To work together; form a team. The children *teamed* up to carry away the old bricks from the vacant lot. *Verb.* ▲ Another word that sounds like this is **teem.**
   team (tēm) *noun, plural* **teams;** *verb,* **teamed, teaming.**

teammate   A person who is a member of the same team. Many of my basketball *teammates* have become my friends.
   team·mate (tēm′māt′) *noun, plural* **teammates.**

tear¹   **1.** To pull or become pulled apart by force. I *tore* the envelope open. *Tear* off a sheet from the pad of paper. **2.** To make a hole or cut into by force; rip. I *tore* my shirt when I caught it on a nail. To move very quickly; rush. When the door was opened, the dog *tore* out of the house. *Verb.*

—A torn part or place. The tailor sewed the *tear* in my coat. *Noun.*

tear (târ) *verb,* **tore, torn, tearing;** *noun,* plural **tears.**

tear² **1.** A drop of clear, salty liquid that comes from the eye. Tears help keep the eye clean. **2. tears.** The act of crying. The baby fell and burst into *tears.* ⚠ Another word that sounds like this is **tier.**

tear (tîr) *noun,* plural **tears.**

tease To annoy or make fun of in a playful way. Don't *tease* the cat or it will scratch you. *Verb.*

—A person who annoys or makes fun of people. A *tease* in my class keeps kidding me about my hair. *Noun.*

tease (tēz) *verb,* **teased, teasing;** *noun,* plural **teases.**

teaspoon A spoon that is used to eat with and to measure food. Three teaspoons hold the same amount as one tablespoon.

tea·spoon (tē′spün′) *noun,* plural **teaspoons.**

technical **1.** Having to do with the special skills, facts, or terms that belong to a science, art, or profession. The judge explained the case in the *technical* language of the law. **2.** Having to do with engineering or any of the mechanical or industrial arts. You can learn to be an electrician at a *technical* school.

tech·ni·cal (tek′ni kəl) *adjective.*

technician A person who is trained in the techniques of a certain job or science. The dental *technician* cleaned the patient's teeth.

tech·ni·cian (tek nish′ən) *noun,* plural **technicians.**

technique A method or way of bringing about a desired result in a science, art, sport, or profession. *Techniques* for growing crops are taught at agricultural schools.

tech·nique (tek nēk′) *noun,* plural **techniques.**

technology **1.** The use of science for practical purposes, especially in engineering and industry. **2.** Methods, machines, and devices that are used in doing things in a science or profession. X rays were an important advance in medical *technology.*

tech·nol·o·gy (tek nol′ə jē) *noun.*

tedious Long and tiring; boring. Washing all the windows in our house is a *tedious* job.

te·di·ous (tē′dē əs *or* tē′jəs) *adjective.*

teem To be full; swarm. The creek near our house *teems* with fish. By noon the beach was *teeming* with people. ⚠ Another word that sounds like this is **team.**

teem (tēm) *verb,* **teemed, teeming.**

teenager A person who is between the ages of thirteen and nineteen.

teen·ag·er (tēn′ā′jər) *noun,* plural **teenagers.**

teens The years of a person's life between thirteen and nineteen. When I was still in my *teens,* we moved from New York to Ohio.

teens (tēnz) *plural noun.*

tee shirt Another spelling for **T-shirt.** Look up **T-shirt** for more information.

tee (tē) *noun,* plural **tee shirts.**

teeth Plural of **tooth.** Most grown-ups have thirty-two permanent teeth. Look up **tooth** for more information.

teeth (tēth) *plural noun.*

teethe To grow teeth. Many babies chew on rubber rings when they are *teething.*

teethe (tē<u>th</u>) *verb,* **teethed, teething.**

telecast To broadcast for television. That network will *telecast* the president's speech. *Verb.*

—A program that is broadcast by television. I saw that *telecast* last fall. *Noun.*

tel·e·cast (tel′i kast′) *verb,* **telecasted, telecasting;** *noun,* plural **telecasts.**

telegram A message sent by telegraph.

tel·e·gram (tel′i gram′) *noun,* plural **telegrams.**

telegraph A system or equipment used for sending messages by wire over a long distance. The message is sent in code over wires by means of electricity. *Noun.*

—To send by telegraph. Let's *telegraph* the news to your parents. *Verb.*

tel·e·graph (tel′i graf′) *noun,* plural **telegraphs;** *verb,* **telegraphed, telegraphing.**

telephone **1.** A system for sending sound or other information by wire or radio waves over a long distance. **2.** An instrument used to send sound or other information over a long distance. A telephone includes a part for speaking into and a part for listening. It can also be used to send messages between computers. *Noun.*

at; āpe; fär; câre; end; mē; it; īce; pîerce; hot; ōld; sông, fôrk; oil; out; up; ūse; rüle; pu̇ll; tûrn; chin; sing; shop; thin; <u>th</u>is; hw in white; zh in treasure. The symbol ə stands for the unstressed vowel sound in about, taken, pencil, lemon, and circus.

T

—**1.** To talk with someone by telephone. I will *telephone* you tomorrow. **2.** To send by telephone. My cousin *telephoned* love and good wishes on my birthday. *Verb.*
tel·e·phone (tel′ə fōn′) *noun, plural* **telephones;** *verb,* **telephoned, telephoning.**

Word History

The word **telephone** comes from two Greek words that mean "far away" and "sound or voice." A telephone lets someone hear sounds from far away.

---

telescope   An instrument that makes distant objects seem larger and nearer. Telescopes are very useful for studying the stars and other heavenly bodies.
tel·e·scope (tel′ə skōp′) *noun, plural* **telescopes.**

telescope

televise   To send by television. All the major stations *televised* the president's speech.
tel·e·vise (tel′ə vīz′) *verb,* **televised, televising.**

television   **1.** A system for sending and receiving pictures and sound over long distances by means of electricity. **2.** A set or device on which these pictures are seen and the sound is heard.
tel·e·vi·sion (tel′ə vizh′ən) *noun, plural* **televisions.**

tell   **1.** To put in words; say. When we were little, Mom and Dad used to *tell* us a story before we went to sleep. *Tell* us about your vacation. **2.** To give an order to; command. The librarian *told* us where to find the atlas. **3.** To reveal something secret. I know who did it, but I won't *tell.* **4.** To recognize; identify. Can you *tell* the twins apart?
tell (tel) *verb,* **told, telling.**

teller   **1.** A person who tells or relates. The old sea captain is a wonderful *teller* of tales of adventure. **2.** A person who works in a bank giving out and receiving money.
tell·er (tel′ər) *noun, plural* **tellers.**

temper   **1.** A tendency to become angry or irritated. I have quite a *temper* when someone insults me. **2.** A usual state of mind; disposition. The members of my family have an even *temper,* and few things really upset them. **3.** Control over the emotions. I lost my *temper* and ran from the house. *Noun.*
—To lessen the harshness of; soften. The teacher *tempered* the criticism of my work by saying that it was improving. *Verb.*
tem·per (tem′pər) *noun, plural* **tempers;** *verb,* **tempered, tempering.**

temperate   Not too hot and not too cold. Most areas of the United States have a *temperate* climate.
tem·per·ate (tem′pər it) *adjective.*

temperature   The degree of heat or cold. Temperature is often measured with a thermometer. The nurse sent me home from school today with a high *temperature.* The *temperature* outside is going down.
tem·per·a·ture (tem′pər ə chər) *noun, plural* **temperatures.**

temple¹   A building that is used for the worship of a god or gods. In Greece, we saw the ruins of the ancient *temples.* People of the Jewish religion worship in *temples.*
tem·ple (tem′pəl) *noun, plural* **temples.**

temple¹

temple² The flattened part on either side of the forehead. The temple is above the cheek and in front of the ear.
tem·ple (tem′pəl) *noun, plural* **temples.**

temporary Lasting or used for a short time only. Some students try to find *temporary* jobs for the summer.
tem·po·rar·y (tem′pə rer′ē) *adjective.*

tempt **1.** To give someone thoughts of doing something wrong or foolish. Don't *tempt* me with chocolate; I'm allergic to it. **2.** To appeal strongly to; attract. The clothing in that store *tempts* me.
tempt (tempt) *verb,* **tempted, tempting.**

temptation **1.** The act of tempting or the condition of being tempted. I resisted the *temptation* to sleep late. **2.** Something that tempts. Although I try to eat only healthful food, candy is a *temptation* for me.
temp·ta·tion (temp tā′shən) *noun, plural* **temptations.**

ten One more than nine; 10.
ten (ten) *noun, plural* **tens;** *adjective.*

tenant A person who pays money to use a house, apartment, office, or land that belongs to someone else.
ten·ant (ten′ənt) *noun, plural* **tenants.**

tend¹ **1.** To be likely or apt. Some people *tend* to gain weight easily. **2.** To have a general direction. The road *tends* to the left just ahead.
tend (tend) *verb,* **tended, tending.**

tend² To take care of; look after. Our neighbor *tended* our plants while we were away on vacation.
tend (tend) *verb,* **tended, tending.**

tendency A likelihood of behaving or thinking in a certain way; inclination. The chain on this old bike has a *tendency* to slip.
tend·en·cy (ten′dən sē) *noun, plural* **tendencies.**

tender **1.** Not tough or hard; soft. This steak is very *tender.* **2.** Not strong; delicate. The *tender* leaves of the young plant became limp in the hot sun. **3.** Kind or loving. Both parents were especially *tender* toward their new baby. **4.** Very sensitive; painful. My thumb was still *tender* after the cut had healed. Yesterday's baseball game is a *tender* subject with us because we played so badly.
ten·der (ten′dər) *adjective.*

tendon A strong cord or band of tissue that attaches a muscle to a bone or other part of the body.
ten·don (ten′dən) *noun, plural* **tendons.**

tenement An old apartment building usually in poor condition.
ten·e·ment (ten′ə mənt) *noun, plural* **tenements.**

Tenn. An abbreviation for *Tennessee.*

Tennessee A state in the southeastern United States. Its capital is Nashville.
Ten·nes·see (ten′ə sē′) *noun.*

Word History

Tennessee comes from the name that the Cherokee had for their ancient capital. The name was given to a stream near the city, and later the river into which the stream flows was also called Tennessee. The name of the state came from the Tennessee River.

tennis A game in which two or four players hit a small ball over a net with a racket. Tennis is played on grass, clay, concrete, or other courts.
ten·nis (ten′is) *noun.*

tenor **1.** A man's singing voice that is lower than an alto and higher than a bass. **2.** A singer who has such a voice. **3.** A musical instrument that has the range of a tenor voice.
ten·or (ten′ər) *noun, plural* **tenors.**

tense¹ **1.** Stretched or drawn tight; strained. When you lift something heavy, your arm muscles become *tense.* **2.** Showing or causing strain or suspense. Our argument made me feel *tense. Adjective.*
—To make or become tense. *Tense* your leg muscle. *Verb.*
tense (tens) *adjective,* **tenser, tensest;** *verb,* **tensed, tensing.**

tense² A form of a verb that shows the time of the action or condition that the verb expresses. In the sentence "I am taller than you," the verb "am" is in the present tense. In the sentence "I ran home," the verb "ran" is in the past tense.
tense (tens) *noun, plural* **tenses.**

tension **1.** The force that affects objects that are pulled or stretched. That rope will break if you apply more *tension.* **2.** A harmful feeling of pressure caused by worry or too much work.
ten·sion (ten′shən) *noun, plural* **tensions.**

at; āpe; fär; câre; end; mē; it; īce; pîerce; hot; ōld; sông, fôrk; oil; out; up; ūse; rüle; pùll; tûrn; chin; sing; shop; thin; <u>th</u>is; hw in white; zh in treasure. The symbol ə stands for the unstressed vowel sound in about, taken, pencil, lemon, and circus.

T

tent A portable shelter that is usually made out of canvas or nylon. A tent is held up by one or more poles or flexible rods.
tent (tent) *noun, plural* **tents.**

tents

tentacle A long, thin body part of certain animals. Tentacles are used to feel, grasp, and move. An octopus has eight tentacles.
ten·ta·cle (ten′tə kəl) *noun, plural* **tentacles.**

tenth Next after the ninth. *Adjective; noun.* —One of ten equal parts; ¹/₁₀. *Noun.*
tenth (tenth) *adjective; noun, plural* **tenths.**

tepee A tent shaped like a cone. A tepee is made from animal skins stretched over poles. North American Indians who lived on the plains used tepees..
te·pee (tē′pē′) *noun, plural* **tepees.**

Word History

Tepee comes from an American Indian word for this kind of tent. This word came from two other words that meant "to be used for living."

term **1.** A word or group of words that has a specific meaning. "Serve," "set," and "racket" are *terms* used in tennis. **2.** A definite or limited period of time. The *term* of office for the president of the United States is four years. **3. terms.** A relationship between people. We are on good *terms* with our neighbors. **4.** A condition that is part of an agreement or a legal document. The *terms* of the peace treaty called for an immediate end to the fighting. *Noun.* —To call or name. Hurricanes in the western Pacific Ocean are *termed* "typhoons." *Verb.*
term (tûrm) *noun, plural* **terms;** *verb,* **termed, terming.**

terminal **1.** A station at either end of a railroad, bus, air, or other transportation line. **2.** A keyboard and a monitor that can be connected to a computer.
ter·mi·nal (tûr′mə nəl) *noun, plural* **terminals.**

termite An insect that has a white body. Termites live in large groups and eat wood, paper, and other similar material.
ter·mite (tûr′mīt) *noun, plural* **termites.**

terrace **1.** A paved outdoor space next to a house. A terrace is used for relaxing. **2.** A balcony of an apartment house. **3.** A raised bank of earth with a flat top and sloping sides. Farmers often build terraces on hillsides to make a level area for growing crops.
ter·race (ter′is) *noun, plural* **terraces.**

terrarium A container that is used for growing small plants or raising small animals. It is usually made of glass.
ter·rar·i·um (tə râr′ē əm) *noun, plural* **terrariums** or **terraria** (tə râr′ē ə).

terrestrial **1.** Of or having to do with the earth or its inhabitants. **2.** Of or having to do with land instead of water or air. Elephants are *terrestrial* creatures; fish are not.
ter·res·tri·al (tə res′trē əl) *adjective.*

terrible **1.** Causing fear or terror; awful. The volcano erupted with a *terrible* roar. **2.** Very bad. We had *terrible* weather on our vacation.
ter·ri·ble (ter′ə bəl) *adjective.*

terrier One of various lively, small dogs that can have either a smooth or curly coat.
ter·ri·er (ter′ē ər) *noun, plural* **terriers.**

terrier

terrific **1.** Unusually great or severe. Today's *terrific* heat melted the tar on our roof. **2.** Causing terror; frightening. That was a *terrific* storm. **3.** Extremely good; wonderful. That's a *terrific* idea!
ter·rif·ic (tə rif′ik) *adjective.*

terrify To fill with terror; frighten greatly. The child was *terrified* by the bad dream.
ter·ri·fy (ter′ə fī′) *verb,* **terrified, terrifying.**

territory **1.** Any large area of land; region. The plane was shot down over enemy *terri-*

tory. **2.** Land that is under the control of a distant government. A territory does not have the full rights of a state or province. Hawaii was a *territory* of the United States until it became a state in 1959.
ter·ri·to·ry (ter′i tôr′ē) *noun, plural* **territories.**

terror **1.** Great fear. That movie about monsters filled me with *terror.* **2.** A person or thing that causes great fear. That vicious dog is a *terror* to the whole neighborhood.
ter·ror (ter′ər) *noun, plural* **terrors.**

terrorize To fill with great fear. The pirates *terrorized* the ship's passengers.
ter·ror·ize (ter′ə rīz′) *verb,* **terrorized, terrorizing.**

test **1.** A set of problems or tasks; examination. A test is used to determine a person's knowledge or skill. The teacher announced that there would be a spelling *test* on Friday. **2.** Any method of finding out the nature or quality of something. I gave the new bicycle a *test* on the road before buying it. The doctor gave me several *tests* to find out why I felt sick. *Noun.*
—To give a test to or check. The teacher *tested* the class in arithmetic. The baker opened the oven and *tested* the bread. *Verb.*
test (test) *noun, plural* **tests;** *verb,* **tested, testing.**

Testament Either of two main divisions of the Bible, the Old Testament or the New Testament.
Tes·ta·ment (tes′tə mənt) *noun, plural* **Testaments.**

testify To make a statement after promising to tell the truth. During a legal trial, witnesses *testify* to what they saw and heard.
tes·ti·fy (tes′tə fī′) *verb,* **testified, testifying.**

testimony **1.** A statement made under oath by a witness in a court of law. The jury listened carefully to the *testimony* of each witness. **2.** Proof or evidence. Your good report card is *testimony* of your hard work.
tes·ti·mo·ny (tes′tə mō′nē) *noun, plural* **testimonies.**

test tube A narrow glass tube that is closed at one end. A test tube is used in laboratory tests and experiments.

tetanus A serious disease that is caused by a germ that enters the body through a deep, narrow wound. Tetanus causes extreme stiffness of some muscles, especially those that control the jaw. This disease is also called **lockjaw.**
tet·a·nus (tet′ə nəs) *noun.*

Tex. An abbreviation for *Texas.*

Texas A state in the south-central United States. Its capital is Austin.
Tex·as (tek′səs) *noun.*

Word History

Texas comes from an American Indian word that means "friends." Spanish explorers used the name for the Indians who lived in what is now part of Texas. These Spaniards also heard Indian tales of an area called "the great kingdom of Texas." This led Spanish settlers to name this region *Texas,* and the name was then kept for the state.

text **1.** The main body of reading matter in a book. The *text* in each chapter of our history book is followed by questions. **2.** The original or actual words of a writer or speaker. The newspaper printed the full *text* of the president's speech. **3.** A textbook. Please remember to bring your *texts* to class tomorrow.
text (tekst) *noun, plural* **texts.**

test tubes

at; āpe; fär; câre; end; mē; it; īce; pîerce; hot; ōld; sông, fôrk; oil; out; up; ūse; rüle; pùll; tûrn; chin; sing; shop; thin; this; hw in white; zh in treasure. The symbol ə stands for the unstressed vowel sound in about, taken, pencil, lemon, and circus.

T

textbook   A book that is used in school for the study of a particular subject. Read the first chapter of your history *textbook*.
text·book (tekst′bùk′) *noun, plural* **textbooks.**

textile   A fabric that is made by weaving or knitting. *Noun.*
—Having to do with textiles or their manufacture. Our class visited a *textile* factory to see how cloth is made. *Adjective.*
tex·tile (teks′tīl *or* teks′təl) *noun, plural* **textiles;** *adjective.*

texture   The look and feel of something. Sandpaper has a rough *texture*.
tex·ture (teks′chər) *noun, plural* **textures.**

Thailand   A country in southeastern Asia.
Thai·land (tī′land′) *noun.*

than   **1.** In comparison with. My cousin is older *than* I am.   **2.** Except; but; besides. Haven't you any fruit other *than* apples?
than (<u>th</u>an *or unstressed* <u>th</u>ən) *conjunction.*

thank   **1.** To say that one is grateful to. I *thanked* the teacher for helping me.   **2.** To hold responsible; blame. I have you to *thank* for getting us into this mess.
thank (thangk) *verb,* **thanked, thanking.**

thankful   Feeling or expressing thanks; grateful. The thirsty traveler was *thankful* for the water that I offered. Let's be *thankful* for all the blessings of life.
thank·ful (thangk′fəl) *adjective.*

thankless   **1.** Not likely to be rewarded or appreciated. I'm afraid that sweeping this sidewalk is a *thankless* task.   **2.** Not feeling or showing gratitude; not grateful. Our *thankless* guests left their room in a mess.
thank·less (thangk′lis) *adjective.*

thanks   I thank you. *Thanks* for the help. *Interjection.*
—An expression or feeling of gratitude. The family gave *thanks* that no one had been hurt in the fire. *Noun.*
• **thanks to.**   Because of; as a result of. *Thanks to* your efforts, the party was a success.
thanks (thangks) *interjection; plural noun.*

Thanksgiving   **1.** A holiday in the United States observed on the fourth Thursday in November to celebrate the anniversary of the first Pilgrims' harvest feast that was held in 1621.   **2. thanksgiving.** An act of giving thanks. After winning the battle, the commander declared a day of *thanksgiving*.
Thanks·giv·ing (thangks′giv′ing) *noun, plural* **Thanksgivings.**

that   **1.** Used to indicate a person or thing being looked at or already mentioned. *That* teacher is very popular. Who wrote that book?   **2.** Used to indicate something more distant than or contrasted with another thing. *That* mountain is higher than this one. *Adjective.*
—**1.** The person or thing being looked at or already mentioned. *That* is my best friend. *That* was a close race.   **2.** Something more distant than or contrasted with another thing. This is an easy recipe for muffins, but *that* is my favorite.   **3.** Who, whom, or which. The children *that* live next door are my classmates. *Pronoun.*
—**1.** Used to introduce a clause in a sentence. I think *that* I will accept the job.   **2.** Used to show reason or cause. I'm sorry *that* you can't come to the party.   **3.** Used to show result. We ate so much for lunch *that* we couldn't eat dinner. *Conjunction.*
—To that extent; so. Was it really *that* cold yesterday? *Adverb.*
that (<u>th</u>at) *adjective; pronoun, plural,* **those;** *conjunction; adverb.*

thatch   Straw, reeds, or similar material that is used to cover a roof. *Noun.*
—To cover with thatch. The farmer *thatched* the roof of the house with straw. *Verb.*
thatch (thach) *noun; verb,* **thatched, thatching.**

The roof of this house is made of **thatch.**

that's   Shortened form of "that is." *That's* the book I left here yesterday.
that's (<u>th</u>ats) *contraction.*

thaw   **1.** To free or become free of frost or ice; melt. The sun *thawed* the snow on the roof.   **2.** To become warm. The ice skaters *thawed* out in front of a large fire.   **3.** To become friendlier. The unfriendly relations between the two countries began to *thaw. Verb.*
—Weather that is warm enough to melt ice and snow. When the spring *thaw* came, water from melting snow flooded the river. *Noun.*
thaw (thô) *verb,* **thawed, thawing;** *noun, plural* **thaws.**

the¹ Used before a noun that stands for a particular person, thing, or group. *The* president made a speech today. Close *the* door. *The* birds ate *the* seeds quickly.
 the (th͟ə *before a consonant or* th͟ē *before a vowel*) *definite article.*

the² To that degree; by that much. *The* sooner you finish your homework, *the* more time you will have to play outside.
 the (th͟ə *before a consonant or* th͟ē *before a vowel*) *adverb.*

theater **1.** A building or other place where plays or motion pictures are presented. **2.** The writing and performing of plays. I'm reading a book on the history of the *theater.* This word is sometimes spelled **theatre.**
 the·a·ter (thē′ə tər) *noun, plural* **theaters.**

thee An old form of the word "you."
 thee (th͟ē) *pronoun.*

theft The act of stealing. The person who stole the car was arrested for *theft.*
 theft (theft) *noun, plural* **thefts.**

their Of, belonging to, or having to do with them. The neighbors and *their* friends played tennis all afternoon. Our house is smaller than *their* house. ▲ Other words that sound like this are **there** and **they're.**
 their (th͟âr) *adjective.*

theirs The one or ones that belong to or have to do with them. Our car is new; *theirs* is old. Was the party your idea or *theirs?*
 theirs (th͟ârz) *pronoun.*

them The persons or things being talked about. I ran to my grandparents and hugged *them.* Carrots are good for you; eat *them* often.
 them (th͟em *or unstressed* th͟əm) *pronoun.*

theme **1.** The main subject or idea of something. The *theme* of the book was the loyalty of a dog to its master. **2.** The main melody in a piece of music. **3.** A short piece of writing on one subject; essay.
 theme (thēm) *noun, plural* **themes.**

themselves **1.** Their own selves. The dinner guests seated *themselves* around the table. **2.** Their usual, normal, or true selves. The players on the losing team were not *themselves* today.
 them·selves (th͟em selvz′ *or* th͟əm selvz′) *pronoun.*

then **1.** At that time. That was five years ago; I was the only child *then.* **2.** After that; next. I ate a sandwich and *then* an apple. **3.** In that case; if that is so. If you want to come with us, *then* get ready now. *Adverb.*
 —Acting or serving at that time. The *then* governor of our state decided to run for president. *Adjective.*
 —That time. The deadline is Friday; we must finish our project before *then. Noun.*
 then (th͟en) *adverb; adjective; noun.*

theory **1.** A group of ideas or principles that explain why or how something happens. The *theory* of gravity explains why a leaf falls to the ground when it comes off a tree. **2.** An opinion based on some evidence but not proved. The fire department has a *theory* about how the fire started.
 the·o·ry (thē′ə rē) *noun, plural* **theories.**

therapy Treatment for a disability, injury, psychological problem, or illness. The doctor suggested swimming as a *therapy* for my injured leg.
 ther·a·py (ther′ə pē) *noun, plural* **therapies.**

there **1.** At, in, or to that place. Put the box down *there.* The lake is nearby; you can walk *there* in ten minutes. **2.** Used to introduce a sentence in which a linking verb such as "be" comes before the subject. *There* is some milk in the refrigerator. *There* are two squirrels in the tree now. *Adverb.*
 —That place. Do you know the way home from *there? Noun.*
 —A word used to express satisfaction or sympathy. *There!* I did it! *There, there,* don't cry. *Interjection.* ▲ Other words that sound like this are **their** and **they're.**
 there (th͟âr) *adverb; noun; interjection.*

thereafter From that time on; after that. The sun shone the first day of our vacation, but it rained every day *thereafter.*
 there·af·ter (th͟âr af′tər) *adverb.*

thereby By that means; in that way. I cut the straw in half, *thereby* forming two short straws.
 there·by (th͟âr bī′) *adverb.*

therefore For that reason; as a result. Our star runner injured a leg and *therefore* could not run.
 there·fore (th͟âr′fôr′) *adverb.*

there's Shortened form of "there is." *There's* some cheese in the refrigerator.
 there's (th͟ârz) *contraction.*

thermometer A device for measuring temperature. Some thermometers are glass tubes containing mercury or alcohol that moves as

at; āpe; fär; câre; end; mē; it; īce; pîerce; hot; ōld; sông, fôrk; oil; out; up; ūse; rüle; pùll; tûrn; chin; sing; shop; thin; th͟is; hw in white; zh in treasure. The symbol ə stands for the unstressed vowel sound in about, taken, pencil, lemon, and circus.

T

the temperature changes. Other thermometers show the temperature in other ways.

ther·mom·e·ter (thər mom′i tər) *noun, plural* **thermometers.**

thermometer

thermos bottle   A container made to keep liquids hot or cold for many hours.
ther·mos bottle (thûr′məs)

thermostat   A device that automatically controls temperature, as in furnaces, ovens, cars, and refrigerators.
ther·mo·stat (thûr′mə stat′) *noun, plural* **thermostats.**

thesaurus   A book or list of synonyms and antonyms.
the·sau·rus (thə sôr′əs) *noun, plural* **thesauri** (thə sôr′ī) or **thesauruses.**

Word History

Thesaurus comes from a Greek word meaning "storehouse for treasure" or just "treasure." A thesaurus is a kind of treasure chest of words.

these   Plural of **this.** Do you prefer *these* flowers or the ones over there? I prefer *these.* Look up **this** for more information.
these (t͟hēz) *adjective; plural pronoun.*

they   **1.** The persons or things being talked about. The travelers were late because *they* missed the bus.   **2.** Some people. *They* say that cats have nine lives.
they (t͟hā) *plural pronoun.*

they'd   **1.** Shortened form of "they had." *They'd* better leave now or they will be late for the show.   **2.** Shortened form of "they would." *They'd* be too polite to leave without saying good-bye.
they'd (t͟hād) *contraction.*

they'll   Shortened form of "they will." *They'll* be back before you know it.
they'll (t͟hāl) *contraction.*

they're   Shortened form of "they are." *They're* supposed to be in school by nine o'clock. ▲ Other words that sound like this are **their** and **there.**
they're (t͟hâr) *contraction.*

they've   Shortened form of "they have." *They've* played this game before.
they've (t͟hāv) *contraction.*

thick   **1.** Having much space between one side or surface and the other; not thin. The outside walls of this brick building are very *thick.*   **2.** Measured from one side or surface to the other. That stone wall is 3 feet *thick.*   **3.** Not flowing or pouring easily. We made a delicious *thick* pea soup.   **4.** Growing or being close together; dense. The hikers had trouble walking through the *thick* forest. *Adjective.*
—So as to be thick. The butcher always cuts the steaks *thick. Adverb.*
—The part or place of greatest activity or danger. The brave soldier was in the *thick* of the fight. *Noun.*
thick (thik) *adjective,* **thicker, thickest;** *adverb; noun.*

thicken   To make or become thick or thicker. The cook *thickened* the gravy.
thick·en (thik′ən) *verb,* **thickened, thickening.**

thicket   A thick growth of shrubs or bushes.
thick·et (thik′it) *noun, plural* **thickets.**

thickness   **1.** The quality of being thick. The *thickness* of the walls makes the house quiet.   **2.** The distance between two sides or surfaces of something; the measurement other than the length or width. The *thickness* of this board is 1 inch.
thick·ness (thik′nis) *noun, plural* **thicknesses.**

thief   A person who steals. The *thief* broke into the house and stole the television.
thief (thēf) *noun, plural* **thieves.**

thigh   The part of the leg between the hip and the knee.
thigh (thī) *noun, plural* **thighs.**

thimble   A small plastic or metal cap that is worn on the finger to protect it when pushing the needle through material in sewing.
thim·ble (thim′bəl) *noun, plural* **thimbles.**

thin   **1.** Having little space between one side or surface and the other; not thick. The *thin* wrapping paper did not hide the title of the book.   **2.** Not fat; slender or lean. Horses have *thin,* long faces.   **3.** Flowing or pouring easily; watery. The first course of the dinner

was a clear, *thin* broth. **4.** Easily seen through; flimsy. Light came through the *thin* curtains. That's a *thin* excuse for being late to class. **5.** Not dense. The air is *thin* on the mountain. **6.** Having a faint, shrill sound; weak. The sick patient spoke in a *thin* voice. *Adjective.*
—So as to be thin. I like my roast beef sliced *thin. Adverb.*
—To make or become thin. Please *thin* this gravy with a little water. *Verb.*
> **thin** (thin) *adjective,* **thinner, thinnest;** *adverb; verb,* **thinned, thinning.**

thing **1.** Whatever is spoken of, thought of, or done. That was an unkind *thing* to say. **2.** Something that can be touched, seen, heard, smelled, or tasted but is not a human being. A book, a tree, and the moon are all things. **3.** A person or animal. A young kitten is a soft little *thing.* **4.** Affair; matter. I have to settle this *thing* before I can leave. **5. things.** The general state of affairs. How are *things* at school? **6. things.** Belongings. I packed my *things* for the trip.
> **thing** (thing) *noun, plural* **things.**

think **1.** To use the mind to form ideas or to make decisions. *Think* carefully before you answer. **2.** To have or form in the mind as an opinion, belief, or idea. The teacher *thought* we were related because we have the same last name. It's getting dark; I *think* we should go home. **3.** To call to mind or remember. I often *think* of last summer. **4.** To have care or consideration. A person who is selfish seldom *thinks* of others first.
> **think** (thingk) *verb,* **thought, thinking.**

third Next after the second. *Adjective; noun.*
—One of three equal parts; ⅓. *Noun.*
> **third** (thûrd) *adjective; noun, plural* **thirds.**

thirst **1.** An uncomfortable feeling of dryness in the mouth and throat. Thirst is caused by the need to drink water. **2.** The desire or need for something to drink. This juice should satisfy your *thirst.* **3.** A strong desire for something. Some people have a *thirst* for adventure and excitement.
> **thirst** (thûrst) *noun, plural* **thirsts.**

thirsty **1.** Feeling the need to drink something. The *thirsty* softball players drank lots of water. **2.** Lacking water or moisture. The plants became *thirsty* in the hot sun.
> **thirst·y** (thûrs'tē) *adjective,* **thirstier, thirstiest.**

thirteen Three more than ten; 13.
> **thir·teen** (thûr'tēn') *noun, plural* **thirteens;** *adjective.*

thirteenth Next after the twelfth. *Adjective; noun.*
—One of thirteen equal parts; ¹/₁₃. *Noun.*
> **thir·teenth** (thûr'tēnth') *adjective; noun, plural* **thirteenths.**

thirtieth Next after the twenty-ninth. *Adjective; noun.*
—One of thirty equal parts; ¹/₃₀. *Noun.*
> **thir·ti·eth** (thûr'tē ith) *adjective; noun, plural* **thirtieths.**

thirty Three times ten; 30.
> **thir·ty** (thûr'tē) *noun, plural* **thirties;** *adjective.*

this **1.** Used to indicate a person or thing that is present, nearby, or just mentioned. *This* house is ten years old. **2.** Used to indicate something that is nearer than or contrasted with another thing. *This* house is larger than the one across the street. That novel is very interesting, but *this* one is more exciting. *Adjective.*
—**1.** The person or thing that is present, nearby, or just mentioned. Is *this* your coat? **2.** Something that is nearer than or contrasted with another thing. *This* is mine; that is yours. That is a fascinating computer game, but *this* is more fun to play. **3.** Something about to be said or explained. *This* is what I mean. *Pronoun.*
—To this extent or degree. Is it *this* hot here every day? *Adverb.*
> **this** (<u>th</u>is) *adjective; pronoun, plural* **these;** *adverb.*

thistle A prickly plant with white, yellow, red, or purple flowers.
> **this·tle** (this'əl) *noun, plural* **thistles.**

thong **1.** A narrow strip of leather or other material that is used for fastening. The prisoner's hands were tied with a *thong.* **2.** A sandal that is held on the foot by a small strap that fits between the first two toes.
> **thong** (thông *or* thong) *noun, plural* **thongs.**

thorax **1.** The part of the body between the

thistle

neck and the abdomen, including the heart, lungs, and ribs. **2.** The part of an insect's body that is between the head and the abdomen. The thorax includes the wings and legs.

tho·rax (thôr′aks) *noun, plural* **thoraxes.**

thorn **1.** A sharp point on a branch or stem. Roses and various other plants have thorns. **2.** A tree or shrub that has thorns.

thorn (thôrn) *noun, plural* **thorns.**

thorny **1.** Full of thorns; prickly. Rose bushes are very *thorny.* **2.** Causing trouble; difficult. This is going to be a *thorny* problem to solve.

thorn·y (thôr′nē) *adjective,* **thornier, thorniest.**

thorough Leaving nothing out; careful and complete. I emptied all my shelves and drawers in a *thorough* search for the missing key.

thor·ough (thûr′ō) *adjective.*

thorns

those Plural of **that.** Do you prefer *those* shirts or the ones here on the shelf? I prefer *those.* Look up **that** for more information.

those (thōz) *adjective; plural pronoun.*

thou An old form of the word "you."

thou (thou) *pronoun.*

though **1.** In spite of the fact that. I was late for school, *though* I got up early. **2.** But; yet; however. The movie was good, *though* it could have been better. *Conjunction.*

—Nevertheless; however. The salad was not very fresh; the dressing was good, *though. Adverb.*

• **as though.** In the way it would be if. You look *as though* you need to take a nap.

though (thō) *conjunction; adverb.*

thought Past tense and past participle of **think.** I *thought* about the movie as I walked home. Look up **think** for more information. *Verb.*

—**1.** The act of thinking. My friend sat alone, deep in *thought.* **2.** A product of thinking; an idea or opinion. What are your *thoughts* on how to solve this problem? **3.** Careful attention or consideration. The teacher advised us to give some *thought* to the questions on the test before writing the answers. *Noun.*

thought (thôt) *verb; noun, plural* **thoughts.**

thoughtful **1.** Thinking or looking as if one is thinking. The reader looked up with a *thoughtful* expression. **2.** Showing careful thought. The student paused and then gave a *thoughtful* answer. **3.** Showing concern and care for others; considerate. It was *thoughtful* of you to send me a birthday card.

thought·ful (thôt′fəl) *adjective.*

thousand Ten times a hundred; 1,000.

thou·sand (thou′zənd) *noun, plural* **thousands;** *adjective.*

thousandth Next after the 999th. *Adjective; noun.*

—One of a thousand equal parts; $\frac{1}{1,000}$. *Noun.*

thou·sandth (thou′zəndth) *adjective; noun, plural* **thousandths.**

thrash **1.** To give a beating to. The farmer warned us that any child caught stealing cherries would be *thrashed.* **2.** To make wild movements; toss violently. The animal *thrashed* about trying to escape from its cage.

thrash (thrash) *verb,* **thrashed, thrashing.**

thread **1.** A very thin cord that is used in sewing and in weaving cloth. **2.** Anything that is thin and long like a thread. *Threads* of paint dripped from the brush. **3.** The main idea or thought that connects the parts of a story or speech. The *thread* of the story was the lost dog's struggle to find its way home again. **4.** A curved ridge that twists around a screw or nut. The threads of a screw make it hold tightly to whatever it is inserted or driven into. *Noun.*

—**1.** To pass a thread through. Please *thread* this needle for me. **2.** To put on a thread; string. I *threaded* the beads and made a necklace. **3.** To make one's way through a narrow or obstructed place. I *threaded* my way through the crowd to see what all the excitement was about. *Verb.*

thread (thred) *noun, plural* **threads;** *verb,* **threaded, threading.**

The girl is sewing with **thread.**

threadbare Worn out so much that the threads show through; shabby. You ought to get a new coat because your old one is *threadbare*.
thread·bare (thred′bâr′) *adjective.*

threat **1.** A statement of something that will be done to hurt or punish. The hunters heeded our *threat* to call the sheriff if they trespassed on our land. **2.** A person or thing that might cause harm; danger. The outbreak of flu was a *threat* to everyone in the community. **3.** A sign or possibility of some danger or harm that might happen. The *threat* of rain made us cancel our trip to the beach.
threat (thret) *noun, plural* **threats.**

threaten **1.** To say what will be done to hurt or punish; make a threat of or against. The teacher *threatened* punishment if we kept making noise. **2.** To be the cause of danger or harm. The lack of rain *threatened* the farmer's crops. **3.** To be a sign or possibility of. The dark clouds *threatened* rain.
threat·en (thret′ən) *verb,* **threatened, threatening.**

three One more than two; 3.
three (thrē) *noun, plural* **threes;** *adjective.*

thresh To separate the grain or the seeds from a cereal plant or grass. Farmers today use machines to thresh their crops.
thresh (thresh) *verb,* **threshed, threshing.**

thresher **1.** Someone or something that threshes. **2.** A machine that separates the grain from cereal plants.
thresh·er (thresh′ər) *noun, plural* **threshers.**

threshold **1.** A piece of wood, stone, or metal that forms the bottom of a door frame. **2.** A point of entering or beginning. The scientist was on the *threshold* of an important discovery.
thresh·old (thresh′ōld) *noun, plural* **thresholds.**

threw Past tense of **throw.** I caught the ball and *threw* it back. Look up **throw** for more information. ▲ Another word that sounds like this is **through.**
threw (thrü) *verb.*

thrift Careful management of money or of anything valuable; lack of waste. If you practice *thrift,* you can have that bicycle.
thrift (thrift) *noun.*

thrifty Very careful in using money and resources. A *thrifty* person does not waste food, clothing, or other things.
thrift·y (thrif′tē) *adjective,* **thriftier, thriftiest.**

thrill **1.** A sudden feeling of pleasure or excitement. Seeing the ocean for the first time gave me a great *thrill.* **2.** Something that gives such a sudden feeling of pleasure or excitement. It was a *thrill* to see the famous athlete in person. *Noun.*
—To fill with pleasure or excitement. The home team's victory *thrilled* the crowd. *Verb.*
thrill (thril) *noun, plural* **thrills;** *verb,* **thrilled, thrilling.**

Word History

The word **thrill** comes from an Old English word meaning "to pierce or pass through quickly." At first, *thrill* was only used to refer to objects. For example, "A spear *thrilled* through the shield." Later this word was used to describe how an emotion sharply affects a person.

thrive To be successful; do well. This plant *thrives* in the sun.
thrive (thrīv) *verb,* **thrived** or **throve, thrived** or **thriven, thriving.**

throat **1.** The passage in the body between the mouth and the esophagus. Food and air pass through the throat. **2.** The front of the neck. My new summer dress is open at the *throat.* **3.** A narrow opening that is like the throat. Hold the bottle by the *throat* and twist off the cap.
throat (thrōt) *noun, plural* **throats.**

throb To beat or pound heavily and fast. I could feel my heart *throbbing* with excitement. *Verb.*
—A heavy, fast beat or sensation. A *throb* of pain shot through my ankle as I fell. *Noun.*
throb (throb) *verb,* **throbbed, throbbing;** *noun, plural* **throbs.**

throne **1.** The chair that a king or queen sits on during ceremonies and other special occasions. **2.** The power or authority of a king or queen. The young prince came to the *throne* after the death of his mother, the queen. ▲ Another word that sounds like this is **thrown.**
throne (thrōn) *noun, plural* **thrones.**

at; āpe; fär; câre; end; mē; it; īce; pîerce; hot; ōld; sông, fôrk; oil; out; up; ūse; rüle; pull; tûrn; chin; sing; shop; thin; this; hw in white; zh in treasure. The symbol ə stands for the unstressed vowel sound in about, taken, pencil, lemon, and circus.

T

throng A large number of people; crowd. A *throng* of people watched the parade. *Noun.*
—To move in a large group; crowd. People from all over *thronged* to the state fair. *Verb.*
throng (thrông *or* throng) *noun, plural* **throngs;** *verb,* **thronged, thronging.**

throttle A valve that controls the amount of steam or gasoline that flows to an engine. The railroad engineer opened the *throttle* to make the train go faster.
throt·tle (throt'əl) *noun, plural* **throttles.**

through 1. From the beginning to the end of. I read *through* the book in one day. 2. In one side and out the other side of. Hammer two nails *through* this board. 3. In or to various places in. We plan to travel *through* New England this summer. 4. In the midst of; among. We strolled *through* the cherry trees. 5. Because of. My cousin got a promotion *through* hard work. 6. By means of. We heard the news *through* a friend. 7. Finished with; at the end of. When will you be *through* high school? *Preposition.*
—1. From one side or end to the other side or end. The farmer opened a gate and the cattle went *through.* 2. Completely; totally. After just a short time in the storm, my clothes were soaked *through. Adverb.*
—1. Allowing passage from one place to another with no obstruction. Is this a *through* street or a dead end? 2. Having reached a point of completion; finished. Are you *through* with your work yet? *Adjective.* ▲ Another word that sounds like this is **threw.**
through (thrü) *preposition; adverb; adjective.*

throughout 1. In every part of; everywhere in. The senator is famous *throughout* the state. 2. During the whole time or course of. They visited us frequently *throughout* the summer. *Preposition.*
—In, to, or through every part; everywhere. The color of the walls of the apartment is the same *throughout. Adverb.*
through·out (thrü out') *preposition; adverb.*

throughway Another spelling for **thruway.** Look up **thruway** for more information.
through·way (thrü'wā') *noun, plural* **throughways.**

throve A past tense of **thrive.** Look up **thrive** for more information.
throve (thrōv) *verb.*

throw 1. To send up into or through the air. The two players *threw* a ball back and forth. *Throw* me the magazine that's on the table. 2. To make fall to the ground. The

horse reared and *threw* its rider. 3. To put quickly and carelessly. The happy child *threw* a coat on and ran out to play. 4. To put or place suddenly in a certain position or condition. The fire alarm *threw* the crowd into a panic. *Verb.*
—The act of throwing; toss. The shortstop made the *throw* to third base. *Noun.*
• **to throw away.** 1. To get rid of; dispose of; discard. I'm going to *throw away* some old clothes. 2. To waste or not take advantage of. I *threw away* an opportunity by not taking that trip.
• **to throw up.** To vomit.
throw (thrō) *verb,* **threw, thrown, throwing;** *noun, plural* **throws.**

thrown Past participle of **throw.** Look up **throw** for more information. ▲ Another word that sounds like this is **throne.**
thrown (thrōn) *verb.*

thrush One of a number of birds that are known for their song. The robin, the bluebird, and the nightingale are thrushes.
thrush (thrush) *noun, plural* **thrushes.**

thrust To push or shove suddenly or with force. She *thrust* the knife into the pumpkin. He *thrust* the note into his pocket. *Verb.*
—A sudden, strong drive or push. The army made a *thrust* into enemy territory. *Noun.*
thrust (thrust) *verb,* **thrust, thrusting;** *noun, plural* **thrusts.**

thruway A wide highway with several lanes used for rapid, long-distance travel. This word is also spelled **throughway.**
thru·way (thrü'wā') *noun, plural* **thruways.**

thud A dull, heavy sound. We heard the *thud* of footsteps in the room above.
thud (thud) *noun, plural* **thuds.**

thumb 1. The short, thick finger on the hand. The thumb makes it easier to pick things up and grip things. 2. The part of a glove or mitten that covers the thumb. *Noun.*
—To turn and look through pages quickly. The patient *thumbed* through a magazine while waiting to see the dentist. *Verb.*
thumb (thum) *noun, plural* **thumbs;** *verb,* **thumbed, thumbing.**

thumbtack A tack with a flat, round head that can be pressed into a wall or board with the thumb. Notices are posted on bulletin boards with thumbtacks.
thumb·tack (thum'tak') *noun, plural* **thumbtacks.**

thump A dull, heavy sound. The heavy suitcase dropped with a *thump. Noun.*
—1. To beat or hit so as to make a dull,

heavy sound. The speaker *thumped* the table with a fist to get our attention. **2.** To beat rapidly. My heart *thumped* as I stepped up to the microphone. *Verb.*
thump (thump) *noun, plural* **thumps;** *verb,* **thumped, thumping.**

thunder **1.** A loud rumbling or cracking sound that follows lightning. **2.** A noise that is like thunder. The soldiers could hear the *thunder* of cannons in the distance. *Noun.*
—To make thunder or a noise that is like thunder. It stopped *thundering* as the storm moved away from our area. The express train *thundered* through the station. *Verb.*
thun·der (thun′dər) *noun; verb,* **thundered, thundering.**

thundercloud A dark cloud of great height that produces thunder and lightning.
thun·der·cloud (thun′dər kloud′) *noun, plural* **thunderclouds.**

thunderstorm A storm that has thunder and lightning.
thun·der·storm (thun′dər stôrm′) *noun, plural* **thunderstorms.**

Thurs. An abbreviation for *Thursday.*

Thursday The fifth day of the week.
Thurs·day (thûrz′dē *or* thûrz′dā) *noun, plural* **Thursdays.**

Word History

Thursday comes from the Old English word meaning "Thor's day." Thor was the pagan English god of thunder.

thus **1.** In this way. The dance teacher said, "The waltz is done *thus,*" and then demonstrated the steps. **2.** As a result; therefore. You did not study and, *thus,* you failed the test. **3.** To this extent; so. We have not heard from them *thus* far.
thus (thus) *adverb.*

thwart To prevent someone or something from succeeding. We thought we would win, but we were *thwarted* by our rivals.
thwart (thwôrt) *verb,* **thwarted, thwarting.**

thy An old form of the word "your."
thy (thī) *pronoun.*

thyme A low plant with fragrant leaves that are used to flavor foods. ⌃ Another word that sounds like this is **time.**
thyme (tīm) *noun, plural* **thymes.**

tiara A band for the head that looks like a crown. Tiaras are worn by women and are often decorated with precious stones.
ti·ar·a (tē ar′ə *or* tē är′ə) *noun, plural* **tiaras.**

The queen is wearing a **tiara.**

tick¹ A light, clicking sound. Many clocks mark time with a tick. *Noun.*
—**1.** To make a light, clicking sound. The clock stopped *ticking.* **2.** To pass. The minutes *ticked* away. **3.** To mark with a dot, slash, or other mark; check. They *ticked* off each item on the grocery list. *Verb.*
tick (tik) *noun, plural* **ticks;** *verb,* **ticked, ticking.**

tick² A tiny animal that looks like a spider. Ticks attach themselves to the skin of humans and other animals to suck their blood.
tick (tik) *noun, plural* **ticks.**

ticket **1.** A card or piece of paper that gives the person who holds it the right to be admitted or to get a service. You need a *ticket* to ride the train. **2.** A tag or label that is attached to something to show its price or give other information. The *ticket* on the sweater said that it cost twenty dollars. **3.** A notice that orders a person to pay a fine or come to court. I was given a parking *ticket* *Noun.*
—**1.** To attach a tag or label to. The clerk at the airport *ticketed* our suitcases for the flight to Washington. **2.** To give a traffic ticket to. The police officer *ticketed* the driver for driving through a red light. *Verb.*
tick·et (tik′it) *noun, plural* **tickets;** *verb,* **ticketed, ticketing.**

at; āpe; fär; câre; end; mē; it; īce; pîerce; hot; ōld; sông, fôrk; oil; out; up; ūse; rüle; p ll; tûrn; chin; sing; shop; thin; this; hw in white; zh in treasure. The symbol ə stands for the unstressed vowel sound in about, taken, pencil, lemon, and circus.

T

tickle **1.** To touch the body in a way that causes a tingling feeling. *It makes me laugh whenever someone* tickles *my feet.* **2.** To have a tingling feeling. *The dust in the air made my nose* tickle. **3.** To please or delight. *The children were* tickled *by the sight of so many clowns in a little car.* Verb.
—A tingling feeling. *The* tickle *in my throat made me cough.* Noun.
tick·le (tik′əl) *verb,* **tickled, tickling;** *noun, plural* **tickles.**

tic-tac-toe A game played on a block of nine squares arranged in three rows of three squares. Two players take turns putting an X or O into an empty square. The first player to get three X's or O's in a row wins.
tic-tac-toe (tik′tak tō′) *noun.*

tidal Of, having to do with, caused by, or having tides. *This shore has suffered a great amount of* tidal *erosion.*
ti·dal (tī′dəl) *adjective.*

tidal wave A huge, powerful ocean wave that is caused by an underwater earthquake or volcanic eruption.

tide **1.** The regular rise and fall of the water level of the oceans and other large bodies of water that is caused by the pull of the moon and sun on the earth. *High tide and low tide each occur about twice a day.* **2.** A movement or tendency that is hard to resist. *The* tide *of the battle turned against the invading army.*
tide (tīd) *noun, plural* **tides.**

tidy **1.** Clean and neat. *My closet is not very* tidy. **2.** Quite large. *That new bicycle must have cost a* tidy *sum.* Adjective.
—To make clean and neat. *Please* tidy *up your room.* Verb.
ti·dy (tī′dē) *adjective,* **tidier, tidiest;** *verb,* **tidied, tidying.**

tie **1.** To fasten or attach with a bow or knot. *How old were you when you learned to* tie *your own shoes?* **2.** To draw together or join closely. *A common interest in football* tied *the two friends together.* **3.** To equal the score or total of. *The two baseball teams were* tied *at five to five.* Verb.
—**1.** A cord, string, or line that is used to fasten things together. *This apron has a* tie *in back.* **2.** A strip of cloth that is worn around the neck; necktie. **3.** A feeling or relationship that holds people together; bond. *There are very strong* ties *of friendship between us.* **4.** An equal score. *The game ended in a* tie. **5.** A timber or rod that holds together and strengthens other parts. *The rails of a railroad track are attached to wooden* ties. Noun.
tie (tī) *verb,* **tied, tying;** *noun, plural* **ties.**

tier One of a series of layers or rows that are arranged one above another. *The football stadium has* tiers *of seats for the spectators.* ▲ Another word that sounds like this is **tear²**.
tier (tîr) *noun, plural* **tiers.**

tiger A large animal that is a member of the cat family. Most tigers have an orange or yellow coat with black or brown stripes. Tigers live in Asia.
ti·ger (tī′gər) *noun, plural* **tigers.**

tiger

tiger lily A lily that has dark orange flowers with black spots.

tight **1.** Held firmly; secure. *Make a* tight *knot so the string won't come loose.* **2.** Made so that the parts are close together. *This sweater is very warm because it has such a* tight *knit.* **3.** Fitting the body closely. *My belt was* tight *after I ate that big dinner.* **4.** Having little time or space to spare. *I'll try to fit that chore into my* tight *schedule.* **5.** Hard to deal with; difficult. *The question put me in a* tight *spot.* **6.** Not generous; stingy. *The customer was too* tight *to leave a generous tip.* **7.** Evenly matched; close. *The race is very* tight; *it's hard to tell who will win.* Adjective.
—Firmly; securely. *Be sure to twist the lid* tight *on the jar.* Adverb.
tight (tīt) *adjective; adverb,* **tighter, tightest.**

tighten To make or become tight or tighter. *Tighten that knot so that the rope won't come loose. The leash* tightened *when the dog tried to walk faster.*
tight·en (tī′tən) *verb,* **tightened, tightening.**

tightrope A wire or rope that is stretched taut and placed high above the ground. *Acrobats perform on a tightrope.*
tight·rope (tīt′rōp′) *noun, plural* **tightropes.**

tights A closely fitting covering for the lower part of the body and the legs. *Tights are worn by dancers.*
tights (tīts) *plural noun.*

tile A thin, flat piece of hard material used for covering roofs, floors, or walls. Most tiles are made of baked clay. *Noun.*
  tile (tīl) *noun, plural* **tiles.**

till¹ **1.** Up to the time of; until. Wait *till* tomorrow before deciding. **2.** Before; until. They won't arrive *till* Sunday. *Preposition.*
  —**1.** Up to the time when or that; until. Wait *till* you hear from me before writing. **2.** Before; until. Don't leave *till* you finish doing the dishes. *Conjunction.*
  till (til) *preposition; conjunction.*

till² To prepare and use land for growing crops. Farmers use a plow to *till* the soil.
  till (til) *verb,* **tilled, tilling.**

till³ A drawer where money is kept. The cashier put the money in the *till.*
  till (til) *noun, plural* **tills.**

tiller A bar or handle used to turn the rudder of a boat.
  till·er (til'ər) *noun, plural* **tillers.**

tilt To raise one end or side of; tip. Don't *tilt* your chair back or you may fall over. *Verb.*
  —A sloping or slanting position. The *tilt* of the dog's head suggested that it was listening very carefully. *Noun.*
  tilt (tilt) *verb,* **tilted, tilting;** *noun, plural* **tilts.**

timber **1.** Wood that is used in building things; lumber. **2.** A large, heavy piece of wood; beam. **3.** Trees; forest. New England was mostly covered with *timber* when European settlers first came to America.
  tim·ber (tim'bər) *noun, plural* **timbers.**

No trees grow above the **timberline.**

timberline **1.** The highest place where trees can grow on a mountain. **2.** The farthest northern place where trees can grow in the arctic regions.
  tim·ber·line (tim'bər līn') *noun, plural* **timberlines.**

time **1.** The period during which all events, conditions, and actions happen or continue. The changing of summer into fall shows the passing of *time.* Dinosaurs lived a long *time* ago. **2.** An exact point in time. The clock showed that the *time* was three o'clock. It's *time* for lunch. **3.** A portion of time available or taken for some purpose. The runner's *time* for the mile was four minutes. **4.** A portion of time in history. That was the style of dress during colonial *times.* **5.** A person's experience. We had a great *time* flying the model plane. **6.** One of a number of repeated actions or happenings. We saw that movie four *times.* **7.** The beat or rhythm of a piece of music. That music was written in waltz *time. Noun.*
  —**1.** To arrange or set according to time. The alarm clock was *timed* to go off at seven o'clock. **2.** To measure the time or rate of. The coach *timed* the runners. *Verb.* ▲ Another word that sounds like this is **thyme.**
  • **ahead of time.** Before the time when one is due or expected; early. Because there was very little traffic on the road, we arrived *ahead of time.*
  • **in time.** **1.** Before it is too late. Please come *in time* for lunch. **2.** In the correct beat or rhythm. We all clapped our hands *in time* with the music.
  • **on time.** At the correct time; according to schedule. Did you get to the concert *on time?*
  • **times.** Multiplied by. Two *times* two equals four.
  time (tīm) *noun, plural* **times;** *verb,* **timed, timing.**

timetable A schedule that shows at what time certain events are to take place. Timetables are used to show arrivals and departures of buses and trains.
  time·ta·ble (tīm'tā'bəl) *noun, plural* **timetables.**

time zone A region in which all the clocks are set to the same time. There are seven time zones in the United States and Canada, including those for Alaska and Hawaii.

timid Easily frightened; lacking courage or boldness; shy. The *timid* child was afraid to speak up in class.
  tim·id (tim'id) *adjective.*

at; āpe; fär; câre; end; mē; it; īce; pîerce; hot; ōld; sông, fôrk; oil; out; up; ūse; rüle; pùll; tûrn; chin; sing; shop; thin; *th*is; hw in white; zh in treasure. The symbol ə stands for the unstressed vowel sound in about, taken, pencil, lemon, and circus.

T

tin 1. A soft, silver-white metal that does not rust easily. Tin is used to coat steel cans. Tin is a chemical element. 2. A can or other container that is made of a metal coated with tin. *Noun.*
—Made out of tin or a metal coated with tin. Food is preserved in *tin* cans. *Adjective.*
tin (tin) *noun, plural* **tins;** *adjective.*

tinfoil A very thin, flexible sheet of tin or aluminum that is used as a wrapping.
tin·foil (tin′foil′) *noun.*

tingle To have a slight stinging feeling. The skater's face *tingled* from the cold. *Verb.*
—A slight stinging feeling. I felt a *tingle* of excitement as I got ready for my first airplane ride. *Noun.*
tin·gle (ting′gəl) *verb,* **tingled, tingling;** *noun, plural* **tingles.**

tinkle To make a light, ringing sound. The chimes *tinkled* in the wind. *Verb.*
—A light, ringing sound. We heard the *tinkle* of sleigh bells in the distance. *Noun.*
tin·kle (ting′kəl) *verb,* **tinkled, tinkling;** *noun, plural* **tinkles.**

tint A shade of a color. We added a little red to white paint to get a pink *tint.* *Noun.*
—To give a slight color to. The windows on our new car are *tinted.* *Verb.*
tint (tint) *noun, plural* **tints;** *verb,* **tinted, tinting.**

tiny Very small. Babies' hands are *tiny.*
ti·ny (tī′nē) *adjective,* **tinier, tiniest.**

tip¹ 1. The end part or point. The *tips* of the fingers are very sensitive. 2. A small piece that forms the end of something. The cane had a shiny, rounded *tip.*
tip (tip) *noun, plural* **tips.**

tip² 1. To raise one end or side of; tilt. The hungry diner *tipped* the bowl slightly to get out the last few drops of soup. 2. To knock or turn over. My aunt accidentally *tipped* over her glass. 3. To raise or touch one's hat as a greeting. Grandfather *tips* his hat to friends he meets on the street.
tip (tip) *verb,* **tipped, tipping.**

tip³ 1. An extra sum of money that is given as a way of thanking someone for good service. We gave the airport porter a *tip* for helping us with our baggage. 2. A piece of useful information. The mechanic gave us a *tip* about the care of our new car. *Noun.*
—1. To give an extra sum of money as a way of thanking someone for good service. We paid our bill, *tipped* the waiter, and left the restaurant. 2. To give a piece of useful information to. My friend *tipped* me off about the sale on phonograph records. *Verb.*
tip (tip) *noun, plural* **tips;** *verb,* **tipped, tipping.**

tiptoe To walk quietly on or as if on the tips of one's toes. I *tiptoed* out of the room so I wouldn't wake the baby.
tip·toe (tip′tō′) *verb,* **tiptoed, tiptoeing.**

tire¹ 1. To make or become weak from too much work or use. The long walk *tired* us. Sick people *tire* easily. 2. To lose or cause to lose interest; bore or become bored. The long lecture *tired* the audience. I *tired* of the dull game.
tire (tīr) *verb,* **tired, tiring.**

tire² A band of rubber that fits around a wheel of a vehicle, such as a car or bicycle. Most tires are filled with air.
tire (tīr) *noun, plural* **tires.**

tired 1. Worn-out; weary. The *tired* tennis player sat down to rest. 2. Bored. I'm *tired* of cereal for breakfast; let's have eggs today.
tired (tīrd) *adjective.*

tissue 1. A group of cells in a plant or animal that are similar in form and in function. The bark that protects a tree is a kind of plant tissue. In animals, the nervous tissue sends messages from the brain to other parts of the body. 2. A soft, thin paper.
tis·sue (tish′ü) *noun, plural* **tissues.**

tissue paper A very thin paper that is used for wrapping or packing.

title 1. The name of a book, painting, song, or other work of art. 2. A word or group of words used to show a person's status, rank, or occupation. "Miss," "vice president," and "doctor" are titles. 3. A championship. Our school's team won the state soccer *title* last year.
ti·tle (tī′təl) *noun, plural* **titles.**

TN Postal abbreviation for *Tennessee.*

to 1. In the direction of; toward. Turn *to* the left. 2. On, upon, or against. Tack the carpet *to* the floor. 3. Into a condition of; into. The glass was smashed *to* bits when it fell. 4. For the purpose of; for. The police came *to* our aid. 5. Until. The store is open from nine *to* six. 6. Earlier than; before. It's five minutes *to* three. 7. As compared with. Our team won by a score of three *to* one. 8. About; concerning; regarding. What did you say *to* that? 9. A word that is used to show who receives the action of a verb. I gave the letter *to* them. 10. A word that is used before a verb to form an infinitive. We started *to* leave at dawn. ▲ Other words that sound like this are **too** and **two.**
to (tü *or unstressed* tu̇ *or* tə) *preposition.*

toad An animal that looks something like a frog. A toad has rough, dry skin and spends most of its time on land rather than in water. Toads are amphibians.
toad (tōd) *noun, plural* **toads.**

toadstool 1. A mushroom. Many people use the word "toadstool" to mean a poisonous mushroom.
toad·stool (tōd′stül′) *noun, plural* **toadstools.**

toadstool

toast¹ Sliced bread that has been browned by heat. *Noun.*
—1. To brown by heating. We *toasted* marshmallows over the campfire. 2. To warm thoroughly. Our guests *toasted* their cold feet next to the radiator. *Verb.*
toast (tōst) *noun; verb,* **toasted, toasting.**

toast² The act of drinking in honor of or to the health of a person or thing. There were several *toasts* to the bride and groom at the wedding party. *Noun.*
—To drink in honor of or to the health of. Mother *toasted* Grandfather on his ninetieth birthday. *Verb.*
toast (tōst) *noun, plural* **toasts;** *verb,* **toasted, toasting.**

toaster An appliance that toasts bread.
toast·er (tōs′tər) *noun, plural* **toasters.**

tobacco A tall plant whose broad leaves are dried, chopped up, and used for chewing and for making cigarettes and cigars.
to·bac·co (tə bak′ō) *noun, plural* **tobaccos.**

toboggan A long, flat sled without runners. A toboggan has a front end that is curled upward. It is used to travel over snow. *Noun.*
—To ride on a toboggan. The children *tobogganed* down the hill. *Verb.*
to·bog·gan (tə bog′ən) *noun, plural* **toboggans;** *verb,* **tobogganed, tobogganing.**

Word History

The word **toboggan** comes from the American Indian name for this kind of sled.

---

today The present day or time. *Noun.*
—1. On or during the present day. Do you want to go ice skating *today?* 2. At the present time. *Today* most people in this country light their houses with electricity. *Adverb.*
to·day (tə dā′) *noun; adverb.*

toe 1. One of the slender parts that stick out from a foot. People have five toes on each foot. 2. The part of a sock, shoe, or stocking that covers the toes. The *toe* of my sock has a big hole in it. ▲ Another word that sounds like this is **tow.**
toe (tō) *noun, plural* **toes.**

toga A loose outer piece of clothing worn by the citizens of ancient Rome.
to·ga (tō′gə) *noun, plural* **togas.**

together 1. With one another. The friends walked to school *together.* 2. Into one gathering or mass. Mix the butter and sugar *together.* 3. In agreement or cooperation. Let's work *together* to solve this problem. 4. Considered as a whole. Alaska is larger than Texas, California, and Montana *together.*
to·geth·er (tə geth′ər) *adverb.*

toil Hard and exhausting work or effort. Planting the vegetables was easy, but soon the *toil* of weeding began. *Noun.*
—1. To do hard and exhausting work. We *toiled* for hours to clear the snow. 2. To move with difficulty, weariness, or pain. The old horse *toiled* up the hill. *Verb.*
toil (toil) *noun; verb,* **toiled, toiling.**

toilet 1. A bowl or box with a seat on it, used for getting rid of body wastes. Most toilets are filled with water that can be flushed away down a sewer. 2. A bathroom.
toi·let (toi′lit) *noun, plural* **toilets.**

token 1. Something that is a sign of something else; symbol. We gave a gift to our teacher as a *token* of our appreciation. 2. A piece of metal that looks like a coin and is used in place of money. You need a *token* to ride on this subway.
to·ken (tō′kən) *noun, plural* **tokens.**

told Past tense and past participle of **tell.** The clerk *told* us to wait. Have I *told* you that story before? Look up **tell** for more information.
told (tōld) *verb.*

---

at; āpe; fär; câre; end; mē; it; īce; pîerce; hot; ōld; sông, fôrk; oil; out; up; ūse; rüle; pùll; tûrn; chin; sing; shop; thin; this; hw in white; zh in treasure. The symbol ə stands for the unstressed vowel sound in about, taken, pencil, lemon, and circus.

T

tolerance   **1.** Willingness to respect the customs, ideas, or beliefs of others; lack of prejudice. They showed *tolerance* even though they did not agree with me.   **2.** The ability to put up with something; endurance. I have a great *tolerance* for cold.
   tol·er·ance (tol′ər əns) *noun.*

tolerant   Willing to respect or try to understand customs, ideas, or beliefs that are different from one's own.
   tol·er·ant (tol′ər ənt) *adjective.*

tolerate   To put up with; endure; stand. I can't *tolerate* people who talk during a movie.
   tol·er·ate (tol′ə rāt′) *verb,* **tolerated, tolerating.**

toll¹   To sound with slow, regular strokes. Bells in the town hall *toll* at noon. *Verb.*
   —The stroke or sound of a bell tolling. We could hear the faint *toll* of bells from the other side of the valley. *Noun.*
   toll (tōl) *verb,* **tolled, tolling;** *noun, plural* **tolls.**

toll²   A tax or fee paid for the right to do or use something. Some highways, bridges, and tunnels charge a *toll* to drivers.
   toll (tōl) *noun, plural* **tolls.**

tomahawk   A small ax. It was once used as a tool or weapon by certain Indians in North America. It is now used in ceremonies.
   tom·a·hawk (tom′ə hôk′) *noun, plural* **tomahawks.**

tomato   **1.** The round, juicy fruit of a plant. The fruit is usually red when it is ripe and is eaten either raw or cooked. **2.** The plant that produces this fruit.
   to·ma·to (tə mā′tō *or* tə mä′tō) *noun, plural* **tomatoes.**

tomb   A grave or building in which a dead body is placed.
   tomb (tüm) *noun, plural* **tombs.**

tomboy   A girl who likes to do things that were once thought to be preferred by boys.
   tom·boy (tom′boi′) *noun, plural* **tomboys.**

tomatoes

tombstone   A stone that marks a grave. Tombstones often show the dead person's name and dates of birth and death.
   tomb·stone (tüm′stōn′) *noun, plural* **tombstones.**

tomcat   A male cat.
   tom·cat (tom′kat′) *noun, plural* **tomcats.**

tomorrow   **1.** The day after today. If today is Saturday, then *tomorrow* is Sunday. **2.** The future. I wonder if people will live in outer space in the world of *tomorrow. Noun.*
   —On the day after today. We are going on a trip *tomorrow. Adverb.*
   to·mor·row (tə môr′ō *or* tə mor′ō) *noun; adverb.*

tom-tom   A small drum. Tom-toms are usually played by being beaten with the hands.
   tom-tom (tom′tom′) *noun, plural* **tom-toms.**

ton   A measure of weight equal to 2,000 pounds in the United States and Canada, and 2,240 pounds in Great Britain.
   ton (tun) *noun, plural* **tons.**

tone   **1.** A single sound, thought of in terms of its quality, length, pitch, or loudness. The musician produced soft *tones* on the violin. **2.** The difference in pitch between two musical notes. The notes C and D are one *tone* apart.   **3.** A way of speaking or writing that shows a person's feelings or attitude. I knew you were angry by your *tone* of voice. **4.** The main style or character of something. The *tone* of the essay was serious.   **5.** A shade of a color. The artist used several *tones* of red to paint the flowers.
   tone (tōn) *noun, plural* **tones.**

tongs   A tool used to pick up things. It usually has two movable arms.
   tongs (tongz *or* tôngz) *plural noun.*

tongue   **1.** A movable piece of flesh in the mouth. It is used for tasting and swallowing. People also use their tongues to speak. **2.** An animal's tongue cooked and used as food.   **3.** A language. My mother is from Puerto Rico, and Spanish is her native *tongue.*   **4.** The ability to speak. Dad was so shocked that he lost his *tongue* for a moment.   **5.** Something that is shaped like a tongue, such as the piece of material under the laces of a shoe.
   tongue (tung) *noun, plural* **tongues.**

tonight   The night of this day. The rain should stop by *tonight. Noun.*
   —On or during this night. I am going to go to sleep early *tonight. Adverb.*
   to·night (tə nīt′) *noun; adverb.*

tonsil   Either of two small, oval pieces of flesh in the throat at the back of the mouth.
   ton·sil (ton′səl) *noun, plural* **tonsils.**

tonsillitis   An illness in which the tonsils become red, sore, and swollen.
   ton·sil·li·tis (ton′sə lī′tis) *noun.*

too **1.** In addition; also. I love to read, but I like movies, *too*. **2.** More than is needed or wanted. I am *too* short to touch the ceiling. That toy costs *too* much. **3.** Very. I'm not *too* pleased with the way this drawing turned out. ▲ Other words that sound like this are **to** and **two**.
  too (tü) *adverb*.

took Past tense of **take**. I *took* a book off the shelf. Look up **take** for more information.
  took (tùk) *verb*.

tool **1.** An object that is specially made to help people do work. Tools are held in the hand. A hammer, a saw, and a screwdriver are tools. **2.** A person or thing that is used to help someone accomplish things. A good memory is a useful *tool* for learning. *Noun*.
  —To work, shape, or mark with a tool or tools. The craftsperson *tooled* a design on the leather belt. *Verb*.
  tool (tül) *noun, plural* **tools;** *verb,* **tooled, tooling.**

toolbox A box for storing or carrying tools.
  tool·box (tül'boks') *noun, plural* **toolboxes.**

toot The short, quick noise that a horn or whistle makes. *Noun*.
  —To make or cause to make a short, quick blast of sound. The bus driver *tooted* the horn to get our attention. *Verb*.
  toot (tüt) *noun, plural* **toots;** *verb,* **tooted, tooting.**

tooth **1.** One of the hard, white, bony parts in the mouth. Teeth are used for biting and chewing food and also in speaking. **2.** One of a row of pointed parts that stick out from something, as on a comb or saw.
  tooth (tüth) *noun, plural* **teeth.**

toothache A pain in a tooth or teeth.
  tooth·ache (tüth'āk') *noun, plural* **toothaches.**

toothbrush A small, narrow brush with a handle. It is used to clean the teeth.
  tooth·brush (tüth'brush') *noun, plural* **toothbrushes.**

toothpaste A paste for cleaning the teeth.
  tooth·paste (tüth'pāst') *noun, plural* **toothpastes.**

toothpick A small, narrow piece of wood or other material that is used to remove food from between the teeth.
  tooth·pick (tüth'pik') *noun, plural* **toothpicks.**

top¹ **1.** The highest or upper part of something. Write your name at the *top* of the page. A bird built a nest near the *top* of the tree. **2.** The highest position or rank. That stu-dent is at the *top* of the class. **3.** A cover or lid. Put the *top* on the bottle. **4.** A piece of clothing for the upper half of the body. I am going to wear a blue skirt and a white *top*. **5.** The highest pitch or degree. I shouted for help at the *top* of my voice. *Noun*.
  —**1.** Of or at the top. The socks are in the *top* drawer. **2.** Highest or greatest. Run the electric mixer at *top* speed. *Adjective*.
  —**1.** To put a top on. I *topped* the dessert with nuts. **2.** To be on the top of something. An antenna *topped* the office building. **3.** To be or do better than. The runner's time in the 1,500 meter race *topped* the previous record. *Verb*.
  top (top) *noun, plural* **tops;** *adjective; verb,* **topped, topping.**

top² A child's toy shaped like a cone that can be made to spin on its pointed end.
  top (top) *noun, plural* **tops.**

topaz A precious stone. Most topazes are light brown or yellow.
  to·paz (tō'paz) *noun, plural* **topazes.**

topic What a speech, discussion, or piece of writing is about; subject. The senator spoke on the *topic* of forest conservation.
  top·ic (top'ik) *noun, plural* **topics.**

topography The shapes and forms of the land in a particular region. The topography of a region includes mountains, valleys, plains, lakes, rivers, and other features.
  to·pog·ra·phy (tə pog'rə fē) *noun, plural* **topographies.**

topple To fall or make fall forward. The bookcase *toppled* over with a loud crash.
  top·ple (top'əl) *verb,* **toppled, toppling.**

topsoil The top part of the soil that has most of the foods that plants need to grow.
  top·soil (top'soil') *noun*.

topsy-turvy **1.** Upside down. I hung *topsy-turvy* from the bar. **2.** In or into complete confusion or disorder. My life turned *topsy-turvy* when I moved to a new city. *Adverb*.
  —**1.** Turned upside down. Did you notice the *topsy-turvy* picture in the newspaper? **2.** Completely confused or disordered. The store was *topsy-turvy* after the sale. *Adjective*.
  top·sy-tur·vy (top'sē tûr'vē) *adverb; adjective*.

---

at; āpe; fär; câre; end; mē; it; īce; pîerce; hot; ōld; sông, fôrk; oil; out; up; ūse; rüle; pùll; tûrn; chin; sing; shop; thin; <u>th</u>is; hw in white; zh in treasure. The symbol ə stands for the unstressed vowel sound in about, taken, pencil, lemon, and circus.

T

757

A **torch** burns during the Olympic Games.

torch 1. A flaming light that can be carried in the hand. 2. A tool that has a hot flame, used to burn through or soften metal.
torch (tôrch) *noun, plural* **torches.**

tore Past tense of **tear**. I *tore* my pants. Look up **tear** for more information.
tore (tôr) *verb.*

torment To cause someone great pain or suffering. Mosquitoes *tormented* us all night. *Verb.*
—Great pain or suffering. Bad burns can cause *torment*. *Noun.*
tor·ment (tôr ment′ *for verb;* tôr′ment *for noun*) *verb,* **tormented, tormenting;** *noun, plural* **torments.**

torn Past participle of **tear**. The sheet was *torn*. Look up **tear** for more information.
torn (tôrn) *verb.*

tornado A powerful storm with winds that whirl in a dark cloud shaped like a funnel. It can cause great destruction.
tor·na·do (tôr nā′dō) *noun, plural* **tornadoes** or **tornados.**

torpedo A large metal shell shaped like a cigar. It moves underwater and explodes when it hits something. *Noun.*
—To hit with a torpedo. The submarine *torpedoed* the enemy battleship. *Verb.*
tor·pe·do (tôr pē′dō) *noun, plural* **torpedoes;** *verb,* **torpedoed, torpedoing.**

torrent A fast, heavy stream of water or other liquid. When the dam broke, *torrents* of water flowed over the land.
tor·rent (tôr′ənt) *noun, plural* **torrents.**

torrid Very hot. Central Africa has a *torrid* climate.
tor·rid (tôr′id *or* tor′id) *adjective.*

tortilla A thin, round, flat bread made from water and cornmeal.
tor·til·la (tôr tē′yə) *noun, plural* **tortillas.**

tortoise A turtle that lives on land.
tor·toise (tôr′təs) *noun, plural* **tortoises.**

torture To cause severe pain or suffering to. Nightmares of the accident *tortured* the survivors. *Verb.*
—1. The act of causing severe pain, especially as a punishment or as a way of forcing someone to do something. The cruel ruler ordered the *torture* of the prisoners. 2. A cause of great pain or suffering. Wearing the tight shoes was *torture*. *Noun.*
tor·ture (tôr′chər) *verb,* **tortured, torturing;** *noun.*

toss 1. To throw lightly into or through the air. Please *toss* me a towel. 2. To move back and forth. The waves *tossed* the little boat. 3. To throw a coin into the air in order to decide something depending on which side lands face up. Let's *toss* a coin to see who has to wash the dishes. *Verb.*
—A throw. We decided which team was going to bat first by a *toss* of a coin. *Noun.*
toss (tôs) *verb,* **tossed, tossing;** *noun, plural* **tosses.**

The boy **tosses** the salad.

tot A young child.
tot (tot) *noun, plural* **tots.**

total 1. Being all there is; making up the whole; entire. I paid the *total* amount of the bill. 2. Complete; utter. The experiment was a *total* failure. *Adjective.*
—The whole amount. The cost of repairing the TV came to a *total* of seventy dollars. *Noun.*

—**1.** To find the sum of; add up. I *totaled* the long column of numbers. **2.** To amount to. The bill *totaled* ten dollars. *Verb.*

to·tal (tō′təl) *adjective; noun, plural* **totals;** *verb,* **totaled, totaling.**

totally Completely; entirely. No one can see anything in a *totally* dark room.

to·tal·ly (tō′tə lē) *adverb.*

tote To carry or haul. The shopper *toted* the heavy packages home from the store.

tote (tōt) *verb,* **toted, toting.**

totem An animal, plant, or object that is the symbol of a family or a clan. Certain North American Indians carved these symbols on poles that stood outside their homes.

to·tem (tō′təm) *noun, plural* **totems.**

totem pole A pole carved or painted with symbols that are called totems.

toucan A bird that has a heavy body, a very large beak, and colorful feathers. Toucans are found in tropical America.

tou·can (tü′kan) *noun, plural* **toucans.**

touch **1.** To put a hand or other part of the body on or against something. I *touched* the hot stove and burned my finger. **2.** To bring something against something else. The camper *touched* the match to the paper to start the fire. **3.** To come or be in contact. Our hands *touched.* **4.** To affect a person's feelings or emotions; move. I was *touched* that my friend remembered my birthday. *Verb.*

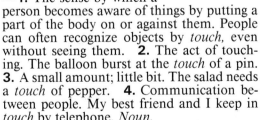

totem pole

—**1.** The sense by which a person becomes aware of things by putting a part of the body on or against them. People can often recognize objects by *touch,* even without seeing them. **2.** The act of touching. The balloon burst at the *touch* of a pin. **3.** A small amount; little bit. The salad needs a *touch* of pepper. **4.** Communication between people. My best friend and I keep in *touch* by telephone. *Noun.*

touch (tuch) *verb,* **touched, touching;** *noun, plural* **touches.**

touchdown **1.** A score made in football by carrying the ball across the other team's goal line. It counts six points. **2.** The act or moment of landing an aircraft or spacecraft.

touch·down (tuch′doun′) *noun, plural* **touchdowns.**

touching Stirring or affecting a person's feelings. My family's reunion was a *touching* experience.

touch·ing (tuch′ing) *adjective.*

tough **1.** Not easy to break, cut, or damage; strong. Canvas is a *tough* cloth. **2.** Able to put up with difficulty, strain, or hardship. The pioneers had to be *tough.* **3.** Rough; violent. Let's stay away from those *tough* kids. **4.** Hard to deal with or do; demanding. Clearing the field for planting was a *tough* job. **5.** Not giving in easily; stubborn. This cleaning fluid removes the *toughest* stains.

tough (tuf) *adjective,* **tougher, toughest.**

tour A trip or journey in which many places are visited or many things are seen. *Noun.*
—To travel in or through a place. *Verb.*

tour (tùr) *noun, plural* **tours;** *verb,* **toured, touring.**

tourist A person who is traveling for pleasure or to learn about other places.

tour·ist (tùr′ist) *noun, plural* **tourists.**

tournament A series of contests between two or more people or teams. People from all over the world met for the chess *tournament.*

tour·na·ment (tùr′nə mənt *or* tûr′nə mənt) *noun, plural* **tournaments.**

tourniquet Something, such as a bandage twisted snug with a stick, used to stop bleeding by putting pressure on a blood vessel.

tour·ni·quet (tûr′ni kit) *noun, plural* **tourniquets.**

tow To pull or drag behind. The tugboat *towed* the barge up the river. ⚠ Another word that sounds like this is **toe.**

tow (tō) *verb,* **towed, towing.**

toward *or* **towards** **1.** In the direction of. The puppy ran *toward* the house. **2.** In regard to; concerning; about. The nurse showed great kindness *toward* the patients. **3.** Near in time; shortly before. The snow stopped *toward* morning.

to·ward *or* **to·wards** (tə wôrd′ *or* tôrd; tə wôrdz′ *or* tôrdz) *preposition.*

towel A piece of paper or cloth that is used for wiping or drying something. *Noun.*
—To wipe or dry with a towel. The swimmers *toweled* off quickly. *Verb.*

tow·el (tou′əl) *noun, plural* **towels;** *verb,* **toweled, toweling.**

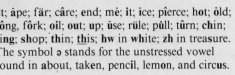
at; āpe; fär; câre; end; mē; it; īce; pîerce; hot; ōld; sông, fôrk; oil; out; up; ūse; rüle; pùll; tûrn; chin; sing; shop; thin; this; hw in white; zh in treasure. The symbol ə stands for the unstressed vowel sound in about, taken, pencil, lemon, and circus.

T

tower A tall, narrow building or structure. The castle had a *tower* at each corner. *Noun.*
—To rise high up in the air. The skyscraper *towered* above the city. *Verb.*
tow·er (tou′ər) *noun, plural* **towers;** *verb,* **towered, towering.**

town An area with buildings where people live and work. It is usually larger than a village but smaller than a city.
town (toun) *noun, plural* **towns.**

toxic Having to do with or caused by a poison; poisonous. Those factories no longer dump *toxic* wastes in the river.
tox·ic (tok′sik) *adjective.*

tower

toy Something for a person to play with. A doll, a kite, and a ball are toys. *Noun.*
— To handle in a careless way; play with. I was nervous and *toyed* with the button on my jacket. *Verb.*
toy (toi) *noun, plural* **toys;** *verb* **toyed, toying.**

trace A small bit or sign left behind showing that something was there. They found pieces of pottery and other *traces* of an old village when digging in the field. *Noun.*
—1. To follow the trail, course, or path of. The explorers *traced* the river to its source. The police *trace* missing persons. 2. To copy by following lines seen through a piece of thin paper. I *traced* the map so that my copy would be exact. 3. To study or describe thoroughly, step by step. The book *traces* the history of science. *Verb.*
trace (trās) *noun, plural* **traces;** *verb,* **traced, tracing.**

track 1. A mark or marks left by a person, animal, or object as it moves over a surface. We saw deer *tracks* in the snow. The tire *tracks* on the road showed where the car had skidded. 2. A path, race course, or other trail. The horses raced around the *track.* 3. A group of sports events held at a running track; track and field. 4. A set of rails on which trains move. *Noun.*
—1. To follow the marks, path, or course of. The dogs *tracked* the fox. The scientists *tracked* the flight of the missile on their radar screens. 2. To make marks on something. I *tracked* mud on the carpet. *Verb.*
track (trak) *noun, plural* **tracks;** *verb,* **tracked, tracking.**

track and field A group of sports events that includes running, jumping, and throwing contests.

tract 1. A piece of land; area. There is a *tract* of wooded land for sale near our house. 2. A group of parts or organs in the body that work together. The stomach and the intestines are part of the digestive *tract.*
tract (trakt) *noun, plural* **tracts.**

traction The grip that a moving object has on a surface. Traction keeps a car wheel or a rock climber's shoe from slipping.
trac·tion (trak′shən) *noun.*

tractor A vehicle with heavy tires or tracks. Tractors are used to pull heavy loads over rough ground.
trac·tor (trak′tər) *noun, plural* **tractors.**

tractor

trade 1. The business of buying and selling goods; commerce. The United States engages in much foreign *trade.* 2. The giving of one thing in return for something else. The farmers made a *trade* of milk for eggs. 3. A kind of job or work. I hope to work in the building *trade* some day. *Noun.*
—1. To buy or sell as a business. At the stock exchange, people *trade* in stocks and bonds. 2. To give one thing in return for something else. I'll *trade* you three of my pictures for two of yours. Let's *trade* seats. *Verb.*
trade (trād) *noun, plural* **trades;** *verb,* **traded, trading.**

trademark A picture, word, or mark that a manufacturing company uses on its product. Only a trademark's owner may use it legally.
trade·mark (trād′märk′) *noun, plural* **trademarks.**

trader A person who buys and sells things as a business.
trad·er (trā′dər) *noun, plural* **traders.**

trading post A store set up in a frontier region where people get food and supplies in exchange for things like hides or furs.

tradition   1. The practice of passing down customs, beliefs, or other knowledge from parents to their children.   2. A custom or belief that is passed on in this way.
tra·di·tion (trə dish′ən) *noun, plural* **traditions.**

traditional   According to tradition. Turkey is the *traditional* Thanksgiving dinner.
tra·di·tion·al (trə dish′ə nəl) *adjective.*

traffic   1. Automobiles, airplanes, ships, or people moving along a route. There is heavy *traffic* during holiday weekends.   2. A buying and selling of goods; trade. The police work to stop *traffic* in illegal guns. *Noun.*
—To buy or sell; deal. The store manager was *trafficking* in stolen goods. *Verb.*
traf·fic (traf′ik) *noun; verb,* **trafficked, trafficking.**

traffic light   A device for directing the flow of vehicles or pedestrians through streets or highways. It has a red, amber, or green light or a combination of these.

tragedy   1. A serious story or play about great misfortunes, usually with a sad ending.   2. A sad or dreadful event; disaster. The explosion in the coal mine was a great *tragedy.*
trag·e·dy (traj′i dē) *noun, plural* **tragedies.**

tragic   1. Having to do with serious stories about great misfortunes. A *tragic* hero is a great person who fails or dies in a noble way.   2. Very sad or dreadful. The plane crash was a *tragic* accident.
trag·ic (traj′ik) *adjective.*

trail   1. A path through an area that is wild or not lived in. The hikers followed the *trail* through the woods.   2. A mark, scent, or path made by a person or animal. The hunters followed the bear's *trail.*   3. Something that follows along behind. The jet left a *trail* of smoke in the sky. *Noun.*
— 1. To follow behind. The children *trailed* the parade.   2. To follow the scent or path of. The photographer *trailed* the family of deer.   3. To drag or be dragged behind. My long robe *trailed* along the floor.   4. To be behind or losing in a game or contest. Our team *trailed* by ten points. *Verb.*
trail (trāl) *noun, plural* **trails;** *verb,* **trailed, trailing.**

trailer   A vehicle that is pulled by a car or a truck. Some trailers are used to carry goods, and some are made for people to live in.
trail·er (trā′lər) *noun, plural* **trailers.**

train   1. A line of railroad cars connected together. Some trains carry passengers; other trains carry only freight.   2. A group of people, animals, or vehicles traveling together in a long line. A *train* of mules carried supplies over the mountains.   3. A connected series of events, ideas, or parts. It was hard for me to follow the writer's *train* of thought.   4. A part of a dress or robe that trails on the ground behind the person who wears it. The bride's gown had a long *train. Noun.*
—1. To teach to behave, think, or grow up in a certain way; bring up. The parents *trained* their children to respect the rights of others.   2. To teach how to do something; instruct. We *trained* the dog to stay in the yard.   3. To get ready for something by practicing, exercising, or learning how. Boxers have to *train* for a fight.   4. To make something grow or go a certain way. We *trained* the vine to cover the fence. *Verb.*
train (trān) *noun, plural* **trains;** *verb,* **trained, training.**

training   1. Teaching; education. The sergeant took charge of the *training* of the new soldiers.   2. The state of being in good physical condition. The football players stayed in *training* by practicing every day.
train·ing (trā′ning) *noun, plural* **trainings.**

trait   A quality of a person or animal; characteristic. Bravery is a necessary *trait* for a firefighter.
trait (trāt) *noun, plural* **traits.**

traitor   A person who does something to harm his or her own country or friends; one who betrays a group or cause. The *traitors* gave secrets to the enemy.
trai·tor (trā′tər) *noun, plural* **traitors.**

tramp   1. To walk or step heavily. Don't *tramp* on the flowers!   2. To travel on foot; walk or hike. They spent the day *tramping* through the woods. *Verb.*
—1. A person who wanders from place to place and has no home or job. The *tramp* went to the farmer's door and asked for food.   2. The sound of a heavy step. We heard the *tramp* of the soldiers marching down the street. *Noun.*
tramp (tramp) *verb,* **tramped, tramping;** *noun, plural* **tramps.**

trample   To step on heavily and crush. Do not *trample* the new grass.
tram·ple (tram′pəl) *verb,* **trampled, trampling.**

at; āpe; fär; câre; end; mē; it; ice; pîerce; hot; ōld; sông, fôrk; oil; out; up; ūse; rüle; pùll; tûrn; chin; sing; shop; thin; this; hw in white; zh in treasure. The symbol ə stands for the unstressed vowel sound in about, taken, pencil, lemon, and circus.

T

761

trampoline   A piece of canvas attached by springs to a metal frame. People do tumbling exercises on trampolines.
tram·po·line (tram′pə lēn′ *or* tram′pə lēn′) *noun, plural* **trampolines.**

trampoline

tranquil   Free from noise or disturbance; calm; peaceful.
tran·quil (trang′kwəl) *adjective.*

transfer   To move from one person or place to another. Next year we have to *transfer* to a new school. *Verb.*
—**1.** A move from one person or place to another. The secretary hoped for a *transfer* to the company's main office in New York. **2.** A ticket that lets a person change from one bus, train, or plane to another without paying more money. *Noun.*
trans·fer (trans fûr′ *or* trans′fər *for verb;* trans′fər *for noun*) *verb,* **transferred, transferring;** *noun, plural* **transfers.**

transform   To change in shape, appearance, or nature. The yellow paint *transformed* the dark room into a bright one.
trans·form (trans fôrm′) *verb,* **transformed, transforming.**

transfusion   The transfer of one person's blood to another person.
trans·fu·sion (trans fū′zhən) *noun, plural* **transfusions.**

transistor   A very small electronic device that controls the electric current in television sets, radios, computers, and other equipment.
tran·sis·tor (tran zis′tər) *noun, plural* **transistors.**

transit   **1.** The act of passing across or through; movement from one place to another. The sun makes a *transit* across the sky each day. **2.** The act of carrying things from one place to another. The fresh tomatoes were damaged in *transit.* **3.** A system for carrying passengers on subway, buses, and other public vehicles.
trans·it (tran′sit *or* tran′zit) *noun, plural* **transits.**

transition   A change or movement from one place or condition to another. I made a smooth *transition* to the new school.
tran·si·tion (tran zish′ən) *noun, plural* **transitions.**

transitive verb   A verb that has a direct object. In the sentence "I put jam on the bread," "put" is a transitive verb and "jam" is its direct object.
tran·si·tive verb (tran′si tiv *or* tran′zi tiv)

translate   To say in or change into another language. The class had to *translate* the story from English to French.
trans·late (trans lāt′) *verb,* **translated, translating.**

translation   A changing of a speech or piece of writing into another language. We read an English *translation* of the Spanish story.
trans·la·tion (trans lā′shən) *noun, plural* **translations.**

translucent   Allowing some light to pass through. The frosted glass is *translucent.*
trans·lu·cent (trans lü′sənt) *adjective.*

transmission   **1.** The act of sending or passing from one person or place to another. Insects cause the *transmission* of some diseases. **2.** The broadcasting of radio or television waves. **3.** A series of gears in an automobile that causes power to be transferred from the engine to the wheels.
trans·mis·sion (trans mish′ən) *noun, plural* **transmissions.**

transmit   **1.** To send, pass, or cause to go from one person or place to another. A telegraph system *transmits* messages across long distances. **2.** To send out signals by radio or television. That station *transmits* the news twenty-four hours a day.
trans·mit (trans mit′) *verb,* **transmitted, transmitting.**

transmitter   A device that sends out radio or television signals.
trans·mit·ter (trans mit′ər) *noun, plural* **transmitters.**

transom   A small window above a door or another window.
tran·som (tran′səm) *noun, plural* **transoms.**

transparent **1.** Allowing light to pass through so that things on the other side can be clearly seen. The lenses in eyeglasses are *transparent.* **2.** Easy to understand; obvious. That excuse is a *transparent* lie.
trans·par·ent (trans pâr′ənt *or* trans par′ənt) *adjective.*

transplant **1.** To take from one place and put in another. We *transplanted* the bush from the front yard to the backyard. **2.** To transfer skin or an organ from one person or animal to another.
trans·plant (trans plant′) *verb,* **transplanted, transplanting.**

transport **1.** To bring or carry from one place to another. The new automobiles were *transported* across the ocean by ship. **2.** To fill with joy or some other strong emotion. The powerful music *transported* us. *Verb.*
—**1.** The act of transporting. Trucks are used for the *transport* of vegetables from farms to markets. **2.** A ship or airplane used to carry people or freight. *Noun.*
trans·port (trans pôrt′ *for verb;* trans′pôrt *for noun*) *verb,* **transported, transporting;** *noun, plural* **transports.**

transportation The act or means of carrying or moving something from one place to another. A bicycle provides my *transportation* to school.
trans·por·ta·tion (trans′pər tā′shən) *noun.*

trap **1.** A device that catches animals that step into or on it. **2.** A trick used to catch a person or get a person to do something not intended. The lawyer's question was a *trap* to get the witness to tell the truth. *Noun.*
—To catch in a trap. The hunter *trapped* the tiger in a pit covered with branches. *Verb.*
trap (trap) *noun, plural* **traps;** *verb,* **trapped, trapping.**

trapdoor A door in a ceiling or floor.
trap·door (trap′dôr′) *noun, plural* **trapdoors.**

trapeze A short bar hung between two ropes, used by acrobats.
tra·peze (tra pēz′) *noun, plural* **trapezes.**

trapper A person who traps wild animals for their fur.
trap·per (trap′ər) *noun, plural* **trappers.**

trash Unwanted things that are to be thrown away. We cleared the garage of old newspapers and other *trash.*
trash (trash) *noun.*

travel **1.** To go from one place to another; make a trip. We *traveled* through England. **2.** To pass or move from one point to another. Sound *travels* in waves. *Verb.*
—**1.** The act of traveling. Camels are used for desert *travel.* **2. travels.** A long trip or series of trips; journeys. *Noun.*
trav·el (trav′əl) *verb,* **traveled, traveling;** *noun, plural* **travels.**

Word History

The word **travel** comes from a similar English word that means "to work hard or labor." This word came from an old French word meaning both "to labor" and "to journey." The meaning of *travel* became limited to the work of getting from one place to another.

traveler A person who travels.
trav·el·er (trav′ə lər) *noun, plural* **travelers.**

trawl A strong net that is shaped like a bag. Trawls are dragged slowly over the ocean bottom to catch fish. *Noun.*
—To fish with a trawl. *Verb.*
trawl (trôl) *noun, plural* **trawls;** *verb,* **trawled, trawling.**

tray A flat, open container with a low rim, used to carry or display things. Waiters often carry food on large *trays.*
tray (trā) *noun, plural* **trays.**

treacherous **1.** Betraying one's country or friends; disloyal. The *treacherous* soldier gave the army's secret plans to the enemy. **2.** Full of danger; hazardous. Many ships have sunk in those *treacherous* waters.
treach·er·ous (trech′ər əs) *adjective.*

treachery A breaking or betraying of trust; disloyal behavior.
treach·er·y (trech′ə rē) *noun, plural* **treacheries.**

tread **1.** To go on foot; walk. It felt good to *tread* the sand barefoot. **2.** To step heavily; trample. The dog *trod* on the flowers and broke their stems. *Verb.*
—**1.** The way or sound of walking; footstep. I listened for the letter carrier's *tread.* **2.** The outer, grooved surface of a tire. The *tread* on those old tires is worn. **3.** The horizontal part of a step in a staircase. *Noun.*
tread (tred) *verb,* **trod, trodden** or **trod, treading;** *noun, plural* **treads.**

at; āpe; fär; câre; end; mē; it; īce; pîerce; hot; ōld; sông, fôrk; oil; out; up; ūse; rüle; pùll; tûrn; chin; sing; shop; thin; this; hw in white; zh in treasure. The symbol ə stands for the unstressed vowel sound in about, taken, pencil, lemon, and circus.

T

763

treadmill A device turned by animals or persons walking on moving steps or on a belt formed into a loop. Treadmills produce motion to run machines, raise water from wells, and perform other tasks.
tread·mill (tred′mil′) *noun, plural* **treadmills.**

treason The betraying of one's country by helping an enemy. Giving the army's battle plans to the enemy was an act of *treason*.
trea·son (trē′zən) *noun.*

treasure Money, jewels, or other things that are valuable. A chest of gold coins was part of the pirates' *treasure. Noun.*
—To think of as being of great value or importance; cherish. We *treasure* the memory of our grandparents. *Verb.*
treas·ure (trezh′ər) *noun, plural* **treasures;** *verb,* **treasured, treasuring.**

treasurer A person responsible for taking care of the money of a club or business.
treas·ur·er (trezh′ər ər) *noun, plural* **treasurers.**

treasury 1. The money or other funds of a business, government, or other group. The club paid for a party out of its *treasury.* 2. **Treasury.** A department of the government in charge of the country's finances.
treas·ur·y (trezh′ə rē) *noun, plural* **treasuries.**

treat 1. To behave toward or deal with in a certain way. The principal *treated* the student fairly. 2. To talk or write about; consider or discuss. The Sunday paper *treats* the week's sports events in detail. 3. To give medical care to. The doctor *treated* my burned hand with an ointment. 4. To subject to a process. You can *treat* cloth with a chemical to make it waterproof. 5. To pay for the entertainment of another person. I will *treat* you to the movie. *Verb.*
—Something that is a special pleasure. Going to the circus was a *treat. Noun.*
treat (trēt) *verb,* **treated, treating;** *noun, plural* **treats.**

treatment 1. The way something or someone is treated. That scratched record has had rough *treatment.* 2. The care or medicine used to help cure a sick or injured person. Rest was the recommended *treatment.*
treat·ment (trēt′mənt) *noun, plural* **treatments.**

treaty A formal agreement between countries. A *treaty* was signed to end the war.
trea·ty (trē′tē) *noun, plural* **treaties.**

tree A plant with a single main stem or trunk that is made up of solid, woody tissue. Trees have branches and leaves at a distance above the ground. *Noun.*

—To chase up a tree. The dog *treed* the squirrel. *Verb.*
tree (trē) *noun, plural* **trees;** *verb,* **treed, treeing.**

trellis A frame of crossed strips of wood or metal for a plant to grow on.
trel·lis (trel′is) *noun, plural* **trellises.**

trellis

tremble 1. To shake with cold, fear, weakness, or anger. The wet kitten *trembled.* We *trembled* at the sound of thunder. 2. To move or vibrate. The building *trembled* from the explosion.
trem·ble (trem′bəl) *verb,* **trembled, trembling.**

tremendous Very large or great; enormous. A *tremendous* clap of thunder shook the house.
tre·men·dous (tri men′dəs) *adjective.*

tremor A shaking or trembling. Earthquakes cause *tremors* in the earth.
trem·or (trem′ər) *noun, plural* **tremors.**

trench A long, narrow ditch. The soldiers fought from *trenches* in the battlefield.
trench (trench) *noun, plural* **trenches.**

trend A direction or course that seems to be followed; tendency. There is a *trend* toward higher prices in this country.
trend (trend) *noun, plural* **trends.**

trespass To go on another person's property without permission. The swimmers *trespassed* on the private beach. *Verb.*
—A sin. *Noun.*
tres·pass (tres′pəs *or* tres′pas′) *verb,* **trespassed, trespassing;** *noun, plural* **trespasses.**

trestle A framework used to hold up a railroad bridge or other raised structure.
tres·tle (tres′əl) *noun, plural* **trestles.**

tri– A *prefix* that means having or involving three. A *triangle* is a figure with three sides.

trial 1. The examination of a person accused of a crime in a court of law. 2. A trying or testing of something. 3. A test of someone's strength, patience, or faith; hardship. The cold winter was a *trial* for the Pilgrims.
tri·al (trī′əl) *noun, plural* **trials.**

triangle

triangle **1.** A figure or object with three sides and three angles. **2.** A musical instrument made of a metal bar bent in the shape of a triangle. A triangle sounds like a bell when it is hit.
tri·an·gle (trī′ang′gəl) *noun, plural* **triangles.**

triangular Having to do with or like a triangle. The tent had a *triangular* shape.
tri·an·gu·lar (trī ang′yə lər) *adjective.*

tribal Having to do with a tribe. We studied African *tribal* customs.
trib·al (trī′bəl) *adjective.*

a **tribal** gathering

tribe A group of people who have the same ancestors, social customs, and other characteristics. There are many Native American *tribes.*
tribe (trīb) *noun, plural* **tribes.**

tribesman A member of a tribe.
tribes·man (trībz′mən) *noun, plural*
tribesmen (trībz′mən).

tributary A river or stream that flows into a larger river. The Tennessee River is a main *tributary* of the Ohio River.
trib·u·tar·y (trib′yə ter′ē) *noun, plural*
tributaries.

tribute Something done or given to show thanks or respect. The statue was a *tribute* to the soldiers who had died in the war.
trib·ute (trib′ūt) *noun, plural* **tributes.**

triceratops A dinosaur that had a long horn over each eye, a short horn on its snout, and a bony collar over the back of its head.
tri·cer·a·tops (trī ser′ə tops′) *noun, plural*
triceratopses.

trick **1.** An action done to fool or cheat someone. **2.** A clever or skillful act. The magician pulled a rabbit out of a hat and did many other *tricks.* **3.** A joke or prank. On Halloween, children play *tricks* and ask for treats. *Noun.*
—To fool or cheat with a trick. We tried to *trick* the teacher into letting us leave early. *Verb.*
trick (trik) *noun, plural* **tricks;** *verb,*
tricked, tricking.

trickle To flow or fall drop by drop or in a thin stream. The rain *trickled* down the window. *Verb.*
—A small flow or thin stream. There was a *trickle* of milk down the side of the carton. *Noun.*
trick·le (trik′əl) *verb,* **trickled, trickling;**
noun, plural **trickles.**

tricky **1.** Using or marked by tricks. The magician could do some *tricky* things with cards. **2.** Hard in an unexpected way; needing careful handling. The last question on the test was *tricky* and needed much thought.
trick·y (trik′ē) *adjective,* **trickier,**
trickiest.

tricycle A vehicle with two wheels in the back and one in front. It is moved by pedaling and steered with handlebars.
tri·cy·cle (trī′si kəl) *noun, plural* **tricycles.**

tried Past tense and past participle of **try.** I *tried* to reach the top shelf. Have you *tried* this new breakfast cereal? Look up **try** for more information.
tried (trīd) *verb.*

trifle Something that is small in amount or importance. One twin is just a *trifle* taller than the other. *Noun.*

at; āpe; fär; câre; end; mē; it; īce; pîerce; hot; ōld;
sông, fôrk; oil; out; up; ūse; rüle; pull; tûrn; chin;
sing; shop; thin; this; hw in white; zh in treasure.
The symbol ə stands for the unstressed vowel
sound in about, taken, pencil, lemon, and circus.

T

765

—To treat something in a careless way. Don't *trifle* with the camera. *Verb.*
tri·fle (trī′fəl) *noun, plural* **trifles;** *verb,* **trifled, trifling.**

trigger A small lever that is pulled or pressed to shoot a gun. *Noun.*
—To start or cause something. A spark from a campfire *triggered* the forest fire. *Verb.*
trig·ger (trig′ər) *noun, plural* **triggers;** *verb,* **triggered, triggering.**

trim 1. To cut away or remove parts to make something neat and orderly. Please *trim* the hedge evenly. 2. To add ornaments or decorations to. They *trimmed* the gym with red and white balloons. *Verb.*
—1. Something that decorates or ornaments. I put white lace *trim* on the curtains. 2. A good, fit condition. *Noun.*
trim (trim) *verb,* **trimmed, trimming;** *noun, plural* **trims.**

trimming 1. Something used as a decoration or ornament. The dress had velvet *trimming* on the sleeves. 2. **trimmings.** Things that usually go with something. We had roast turkey, stuffing, and all the *trimmings.*
trim·ming (trim′ing) *noun, plural* **trimmings.**

trio 1. A group of three persons or things. 2. A musical piece written for three singers or musicians.
tri·o (trē′ō) *noun, plural* **trios.**

trip The act of traveling or going from one place to another. The bus ride was a long, slow *trip. Noun.*
—1. To catch one's foot on something and stumble or fall. I *tripped* on the edge of the rug. 2. To cause someone to stumble or fall. The wire on the floor might *trip* someone. 3. To make or cause to make a mistake. I *tripped* up on the third question of the test. *Verb.*
trip (trip) *noun, plural* **trips;** *verb,* **tripped, tripping.**

tripe The stomach walls of the ox and certain other grazing animals used for food.
tripe (trīp) *noun.*

triple 1. Made up of three parts. Three movies were shown in a special *triple* feature. 2. Three times as much or as many. The capital is *triple* the size of our town. *Adjective.*
—To make or become three times as much or as many. The population of our state *tripled* in ten years. *Verb.*
tri·ple (trip′əl) *adjective; verb,* **tripled, tripling.**

triplet One of three children or animals born at the same time to the same mother.
tri·plet (trip′lit) *noun, plural* **triplets.**

tripod A stand with three legs used to hold up a telescope or some other instrument. The camera was mounted on a *tripod.*
tri·pod (trī′pod′) *noun, plural* **tripods.**

triumph 1. A great success or victory. The discovery of a polio vaccine was a medical *triumph.* 2. Great happiness caused by success or victory. The winning runner shouted in *triumph* at the finish line. *Noun.*
—To succeed or win. Our soldiers *triumphed* over the enemy. *Verb.*
tri·umph (trī′umf) *noun, plural* **triumphs;** *verb,* **triumphed, triumphing.**

triumphant Successful or victorious. Our team was *triumphant* in the game.
tri·um·phant (trī um′fənt) *adjective.*

The team is **triumphant.**

trivial Of little or no importance. When you tell a story, leave out the *trivial* details.
triv·i·al (triv′ē əl) *adjective.*

trod Past tense and a past participle of **tread.** We *trod* home after a day of shopping. Someone had *trod* on the radish seedlings. Look up **tread** for more information.
trod (trod) *verb.*

trodden A past participle of **tread.** The path through the woods was well *trodden.* Look up **tread** for more information.
trod·den (trod′ən) *verb.*

troll¹ To fish with a line that is moving, usually by dragging it behind a moving boat.
troll (trōl) *verb,* **trolled, trolling.**

troll² A dwarf or giant in stories who lives underground or in a cave.
troll (trōl) *noun, plural* **trolls.**

trolley

trolley **1.** A small wheel that moves along an overhead wire and picks up electricity to run a streetcar, train, or bus. **2.** A kind of streetcar that runs on tracks and gets its power from a trolley.
trol·ley (trol′ē) *noun, plural* **trolleys.**

trombone A brass musical instrument. A trombone is made up of two long, U-shaped tubes. The pitch is changed by sliding one of the tubes back and forth.
trom·bone (trom bōn′ *or* trom′bōn) *noun, plural* **trombones.**

troop **1.** A group of persons doing something together. A *troop* of ten volunteers cleaned the park. **2. troops.** Soldiers. The enemy *troops* surrendered. **3.** A group of soldiers on horseback or in vehicles. *Noun.*
—To walk or march in a group. When recess was over, the students *trooped* back into the classroom. *Verb.*
troop (trüp) *noun, plural* **troops;** *verb,* **trooped, trooping.**

trooper A police officer. The state *trooper* patrolled the highway.
troop·er (trü′pər) *noun, plural* **troopers.**

trophy A cup, small statue, or other prize given to someone for winning a contest or race or doing something outstanding. The captain of the basketball team accepted the championship *trophy.*
tro·phy (trō′fē) *noun, plural* **trophies.**

tropical Having to do with or found in the tropics. Most monkeys live in *tropical* forests. The heat last summer felt *tropical.*
trop·i·cal (trop′i kəl) *adjective.*

tropics A region of the earth that is near the equator. It is always warm in the tropics.
trop·ics (trop′iks) *plural noun.*

trot **1.** The gait of an animal that is faster than a walk. In a graceful *trot,* the horse circled the ring. **2.** A slow run; jog. I headed for school at a *trot. Noun.*
—**1.** To move or ride at a trot. The horse *trotted* toward the stable. **2.** To run slowly; jog. The little children *trotted* after the grown-ups. *Verb.*
trot (trot) *noun, plural* **trots;** *verb,* **trotted, trotting.**

trouble **1.** A difficult or dangerous situation. The people in the valley will be in serious *trouble* if the dam breaks. **2.** Extra work or effort. We all went to a lot of *trouble* to make this dinner a success. **3.** A cause of difficulty. The *trouble* with your plan is that it will take too much time. *Noun.*
—**1.** To disturb or make uncomfortable. Does your headache still *trouble* you? **2.** To cause someone to make an extra effort. May I please *trouble* you for a glass of water? *Verb.*
trou·ble (trub′əl) *noun, plural* **troubles;** *verb,* **troubled, troubling.**

trough A long, deep, narrow box or other container to hold food for animals.
trough (trôf) *noun, plural* **troughs.**

trousers A piece of clothing that reaches from the waist to the ankles and covers each leg separately; pants.
trou·sers (trou′zərz) *plural noun.*

trout A fish that lives in fresh water. Some trout have speckles on their bodies.
trout (trout) *noun, plural* **trout** or **trouts.**

trout

trowel **1.** A tool with a flat blade that is used for spreading and smoothing wet plaster, cement, or a similar substance. **2.** A tool that is shaped like a small scoop. It is used for digging.
trow·el (trou′əl) *noun, plural* **trowels.**

at; āpe; fär; câre; end; mē; it; īce; pîerce; hot; ōld; sông, fôrk; oil; out; up; ūse; rüle; pull; tûrn; chin; sing; shop; thin; this; hw in white; zh in treasure. The symbol ə stands for the unstressed vowel sound in about, taken, pencil, lemon, and circus.

767

truce A short stop in fighting. A truce is agreed to by both sides, who then sometimes try to reach a peace agreement.
truce (trüs) *noun, plural* **truces.**

Word History

The word **truce** comes from a Middle English word meaning "agreement." The Middle English word comes from an Old English word meaning "true" or "faithful." In a *truce,* both sides must be faithful to their agreement.

---

truck A large motor vehicle that is made to carry heavy loads. Some trucks are open in the back and some are closed. *Noun.*
—To move something by truck. When we moved, we *trucked* all our furniture to the new house. *Verb.*
truck (truk) *noun, plural* **trucks;** *verb,* **trucked, trucking.**

trudge To walk slowly and with effort. The tired hikers *trudged* up the hill. *Verb.*
—A slow, tiring walk. The campers had a long *trudge* back to their camp. *Noun.*
trudge (truj) *verb,* **trudged, trudging;** *noun, plural* **trudges.**

true 1. Agreeing with the facts; not false, wrong, or made-up. The movie was based on a *true* story. Everything they said was *true.* 2. Faithful to someone or something; loyal. A *true* friend will always try to help you. 3. Genuine; real. The koala is not a *true* bear.
true (trü) *adjective,* **truer, truest.**

truly In a real, genuine, or honest way; sincerely. I am *truly* sorry I forgot to call you.
tru·ly (trü′lē) *adverb.*

trumpet

trumpet 1. A brass musical instrument. A trumpet is made up of a long tube coiled into a loop with a flared end. 2. A sound like the sound made with a trumpet. The cry of an elephant is called a *trumpet. Noun.*
—To make a sound like a trumpet. The elephant *trumpeted* loudly. *Verb.*
trum·pet (trum′pit) *noun, plural* **trumpets;** *verb,* **trumpeted, trumpeting.**

trunk 1. The main stem of a tree. The branches grow out from the trunk. 2. A large, sturdy box used for carrying and storing things. 3. The covered space in an automobile where things are stored and carried. 4. The long snout of an elephant. 5. **trunks.** Short pants. Trunks are worn by men and boys for swimming and other sports. 6. The main part of the human body, apart from the legs, arms, and head.
trunk (trungk) *noun, plural* **trunks.**

trust 1. To believe to be true, honest, or reliable. We should not have *trusted* the weather report. I *trust* you to keep this secret. 2. To feel sure; hope or expect confidently. I *trust* that you will enjoy this movie. *Verb.*
—1. A belief that someone or something is true, honest, or reliable; confidence. I have complete *trust* in your ability to direct the school play. 2. The care or keeping of someone or something. The neighbor's dog was left in my *trust* for the week. *Noun.*
trust (trust) *verb,* **trusted, trusting;** *noun.*

trustworthy Able to be trusted; reliable. I told my secret to a *trustworthy* friend.
trust·wor·thy (trust′wûr′ṯẖē) *adjective.*

trusty Capable of being trusted or relied on. My *trusty* watch never failed me.
trust·y (trus′tē) *adjective,* **trustier, trustiest.**

truth 1. Something that is true. They taught their children to tell the *truth.* 2. The quality of being true, honest, or sincere. My friend's criticisms were painful, but there was some *truth* in them.
truth (trüth) *noun, plural* **truths.**

truthful Telling the truth. I gave a *truthful* answer to my parent's question.
truth·ful (trüth′fəl) *adjective.*

try 1. To make an effort to do something; attempt. I *tried* moving the box alone, but it was too heavy. Please *try* not to be late in arriving at the theater. 2. To make a test of. *Try* the bicycle's brakes before you start down the hill. 3. To examine a person accused of a crime in a court of law. The accused person was *tried* for robbery and found guilty. 4. To put a strain on; tax. The long wait at the airport *tried* my patience. *Verb.*
—An effort or attempt. I hit the target with an arrow on my third *try. Noun.*

- **to try on.** To put on to test the fit or appearance. When I *tried on* the shoes, I found that they were tight.
- **to try out. 1.** To demonstrate one's skill or ability in order to show that one is suitable or fit. Are you going to *try out* for the basketball team? **2.** To test. My parents *tried out* the new car before they bought it.

try (trī) *verb*, **tried, trying;** *noun, plural* **tries.**

tryout A test to see if a person can do something well. *Tryouts* for parts in the new play will be held this afternoon.
try·out (trī′out′) *noun, plural* **tryouts.**

T-shirt A light, knit undershirt or outer shirt with short sleeves and no collar. This word is sometimes spelled **tee shirt.**
T-shirt (tē′shûrt′) *noun, plural* **T-shirts.**

tsp. An abbreviation for *teaspoon.*

tsunami A huge, powerful ocean wave that is caused by an earthquake or a volcanic eruption on the floor of the ocean. A tsunami can destroy buildings and kill people. It is sometimes called a **tidal wave.**
tsu·na·mi (tsü nä′mē) *noun, plural* **tsunamis.**

tub 1. A large open container used for taking a bath; bathtub. **2.** A round container used to hold butter, honey, or other foods.
tub (tub) *noun, plural* **tubs.**

tuba A very large brass musical instrument that has a deep, mellow tone.
tu·ba (tü′bə *or* tū′bə) *noun, plural* **tubas.**

tube 1. A hollow piece of glass, rubber, plastic, or metal in the shape of a long pipe, used to carry liquids or gases. A garden hose is a long tube. **2.** Something that is like a tube in shape or use. A tunnel is a tube. **3.** A container of soft metal or plastic from which the contents are removed by squeezing. Tubes are used for holding toothpaste, shampoo, and other products.
tube (tüb *or* tūb) *noun, plural* **tubes.**

tuberculosis A disease that is caused by bacteria and usually affects the lungs.
tu·ber·cu·lo·sis (tù bûr′kyə lō′sis *or* tyù bûr′kyə lō′sis) *noun.*

tuck 1. To push or fold the edge or ends of something in place. I *tucked* my shirt in. **2.** To put into a hidden, safe, or covered space. There is a wasp's nest *tucked* under the eaves. *Verb.*
—A fold sewed in a piece of clothing to make it fit better or to decorate it. Let's make a *tuck* in the waist of the coat. *Noun.*
tuck (tuk) *verb,* **tucked, tucking;** *noun, plural* **tucks.**

Tues. An abbreviation for *Tuesday.*
Tuesday The third day of the week.
Tues·day (tüz′dē *or* tüz′dā *or* tūz′dē *or* tūz′dā) *noun, plural* **Tuesdays.**

tuft A bunch of hair, grass, threads, or other things that grows or is fastened together at one end and is loose at the other. The bird had a *tuft* of feathers on its head.
tuft (tuft) *noun, plural* **tufts.**

tug To give a pull on something. The little child *tugged* at my sleeve to get my attention. The horses *tugged* the heavy wagon. *Verb.*
—A hard pull. Suddenly I felt a *tug* on the fishing line. *Noun.*
tug (tug) *verb,* **tugged, tugging;** *noun, plural* **tugs.**

tugboat A small, powerful boat that is used to push or pull barges and other boats. The *tugboat* guided the ocean liner into its berth.
tug·boat (tug′bōt′) *noun, plural* **tugboats.**

tugboats

tuition Money paid for instruction or teaching. Some students take part-time jobs to help pay for their *tuition* at college.
tu·i·tion (tü ish′ən *or* tū ish′ən) *noun, plural* **tuitions.**

at; āpe; fär; câre; end; mē; it; ice; pîerce; hot; ōld; sông, fôrk; oil; out; up; ūse; rüle; pùll; tûrn; chin; sing; shop; thin; <u>th</u>is; hw in white; zh in treasure. The symbol ə stands for the unstressed vowel sound in about, taken, pencil, lemon, and circus.

tulip   A flower that is shaped like a cup. The plant that it grows on is also called a tulip. Tulips grow from bulbs.
tu·lip (tü′lip *or* tū′lip) *noun, plural* **tulips.**

tumble   **1.** To fall in a helpless or clumsy way. When our sled tipped over, we *tumbled* down the icy hill. **2.** To roll or toss about. We could hear the pail *tumbling* around in the trunk of the car.   **3.** To do somersaults, handsprings, or similar feats. *Verb.*
—A fall. The skater slipped on the ice and took a *tumble. Noun.*
tum·ble (tum′bəl)
verb, **tumbled,**
tumbling; *noun, plural* **tumbles.**

tulips

tumbler   **1.** An acrobat who does somersaults or other stunts.   **2.** A tall glass for drinking. Use the blue *tumbler* for juice.
tum·bler (tum′blər) *noun, plural* **tumblers.**

tumbleweed   A bushy plant that grows in the deserts and plains of western North America. In the autumn, the tumbleweed breaks off from its roots and is blown about by the wind.
tum·ble·weed (tum′bəl wēd′) *noun, plural* **tumbleweeds.**

tumor   A group of cells in the body that grow much faster than normal cells.
tu·mor (tü′mər *or* tū′mər) *noun, plural* **tumors.**

tuna   A large fish found in warm seas all over the world. It is used for food.
tu·na (tü′nə) *noun, plural* **tuna** *or* **tunas.**

tundra   A huge plain with no trees that lies in arctic regions.
tun·dra (tun′drə) *noun, plural* **tundras.**

tune   **1.** A series of musical tones that form a pleasing, easily remembered unit; melody. We hummed the *tune* when we couldn't remember the words. **2.** A song. The band played a few popular *tunes*. **3.** The right pitch or key. The old piano was out of *tune*. **4.** Agreement or harmony. The opinions expressed by the speaker were not in *tune* with modern ideas. *Noun.*
—To adjust a musical instrument so that it plays notes of the right pitch. I learned how to *tune* my guitar. *Verb.*
tune (tün *or* tūn) *noun, plural* **tunes;** *verb,* **tuned, tuning.**

tunic   **1.** A piece of clothing that looks like a shirt and reaches to the knees. **2.** A short jacket that fits closely. Tunics are often worn as part of a military or police uniform.
tu·nic (tü′nik *or* tū′nik) *noun, plural* **tunics.**

Tunisia   A country in northern Africa.
Tu·ni·sia (tü nē′zhə *or* tū nē′zhə) *noun.*

tunnel   A long passage built underneath the ground or water or through a mountain. There is a *tunnel* under the river. *Noun.*
—To make a tunnel under or through something. The dog *tunneled* under the fence and got loose. *Verb.*
tun·nel (tun′əl) *noun, plural* **tunnels;** *verb,* **tunneled, tunneling.**

turban   A long scarf that is wound around the head and worn like a hat.
tur·ban (tûr′bən) *noun, plural* **turbans.**

turbine   An engine that is run by a stream of gas or liquid moving against the blades or vanes of a rotating wheel.
tur·bine (tûr′bin *or* tûr′bīn) *noun, plural* **turbines.**

turf   The surface layer of the soil, including the tangled plant roots that make it like a mat.
turf (tûrf) *noun.*

turkey   A large North American bird with black and brown feathers and a tail shaped like a fan.
tur·key (tûr′kē) *noun, plural* **turkeys.**

turkey

Turkey   A country in western Asia and southeastern Europe.
Tur·key (tûr′kē) *noun.*

Turkish   The language of Turkey. *Noun.*
—Of or having to do with Turkey, its people, or their language. *Adjective.*
Turk·ish (tûr′kish) *noun; adjective.*

turmoil   Great confusion or disorder. The airport was in *turmoil* during the snowstorm.
tur·moil (tûr′moil) *noun.*

turn **1.** To move or cause to move around in a circle or part of a circle; rotate or revolve. The earth *turns*. The key *turned* in the lock. Power from the car engine *turns* the wheels. **2.** To go or make go a certain or different way. The driver *turned* the car left at the corner. *Turn* the pancakes over. Let's *turn* to the next question. **3.** To change or cause to change in nature or condition. Leaves *turn* brown in the fall. In the fairy tale, the frog *turned* into a prince. **4.** To have or cause to have different feelings. Our neighbors *turned* against us when our dog kept chasing their cat. **5.** To make or become sick. My stomach *turned* when the roller coaster went down the big hill. *Verb.*
—**1.** A movement around in a circle or part of a circle. I had to make a quick *turn* to catch the ball. **2.** A change in position or direction. Make a left *turn* at the corner. There is a sharp *turn* in the road ahead. **3.** A time, occasion, or chance at something. It's the pitcher's *turn* at bat. *Noun.*

• **to turn down.** **1.** To reject or refuse. I decided to *turn down* the invitation. **2.** To reduce the volume, intensity, or flow of. *Turn down* your radio.

• **to turn in.** **1.** To turn and go in; enter. *Turn in* when you get to the next driveway. **2.** To give or return. The teacher asked us to *turn in* our tests. **3.** To go to bed. I think I'll *turn in* early tonight.

• **to turn off.** To cause to stop flowing or operating. Please *turn off* the water.

• **to turn on.** To cause to flow or to operate. *Turn* the gas *on* in the oven. *Turn on* the lamp in the den.

• **to turn out.** **1.** To produce. The machine *turns out* fifty copies per minute. **2.** To come; assemble; show up. A large crowd *turned out* for the game. **3.** To end or result. How did the movie *turn out*? **4.** To cause to stop operating. *Turn out* the lights before you leave.

• **to turn up.** **1.** To appear unexpectedly. The sweater I had misplaced *turned up* at school. **2.** To discover or be discovered. The police *turned up* new evidence in the case. **3.** To increase the volume, intensity, or flow of. I'll *turn up* the music.

turn (tûrn) *verb,* **turned, turning;** *noun,* *plural* **turns.**

turnip A round, white or yellow vegetable that is the root of a certain plant.
tur·nip (tûr′nip) *noun, plural* **turnips.**

turnout A gathering of people for a certain purpose. There was a poor *turnout* at the football game because of the rain.
turn·out (tûrn′out′) *noun, plural* **turnouts.**

turnpike A highway with more than two lanes and no intersections or stoplights. Turnpikes are used for fast travel between cities.
turn·pike (tûrn′pīk′) *noun, plural* **turnpikes.**

turnstile A revolving gate or movable bar at an exit or entrance. People pass through a turnstile one at a time.
turn·stile (tûrn′stīl′) *noun, plural* **turnstiles.**

turntable A round platform that turns things around. Phonographs have turntables that turn the records.
turn·ta·ble (tûrn′tā′bəl) *noun, plural* **turntables.**

turpentine A liquid that is mixed with paints and other substances to make them thinner.
tur·pen·tine (tûr′pən tīn′) *noun.*

turquoise **1.** A greenish blue mineral used as a gem. **2.** A greenish blue color. *Noun.*
—Having the color turquoise. *Adjective.*
tur·quoise (tûr′kwoiz *or* tûr′koiz) *noun, plural* **turquoises;** *adjective.*

working with **turquoise**

at; āpe; fär; câre; end; mē; it; īce; pîerce; hot; ōld; sông, fôrk; oil; out; up; ūse; rüle; pull; tûrn; chin; sing; shop; thin; <u>th</u>is; hw in white; zh in treasure. The symbol ə stands for the unstressed vowel sound in about, taken, pencil, lemon, and circus.

turret   **1.** A small tower on a building. Some castles have *turrets* at each corner. **2.** A structure on top of a military tank or ship that holds guns or cannons.
  tur·ret (tûr′it) *noun, plural* **turrets.**

turtle   **1.** An animal with a low, wide body covered by a hard, rounded shell. A turtle can pull its head, legs, and tail into its shell for protection. Turtles are reptiles. They live on land and in water. **2.** A small triangle that appears on a computer monitor when the computer language LOGO is used.

  turtle
  tur·tle (tûr′təl) *noun, plural* **turtles.**

turtleneck   A sweater or other garment with a high collar that fits snugly around the neck and is usually worn turned down.
  tur·tle·neck (tûr′təl nek′) *noun, plural* **turtlenecks.**

tusk   A long, pointed tooth that sticks out of each side of the mouth in certain animals. Elephants and walruses have tusks.
  tusk (tusk) *noun, plural* **tusks.**

tutor   A teacher who gives private lessons to a pupil. When I was sick for three months, I had a *tutor* at home. *Noun.*
  —To teach privately; act as a tutor. The college student made extra money by *tutoring* French. I'll *tutor* you in arithmetic. *Verb.*
  tu·tor (tü′tər *or* tū′tər) *noun, plural* **tutors;** *verb,* **tutored, tutoring.**

Word History

The word **tutor** comes from a Latin word meaning "defender" or "guardian." Later, in some English universities, the word *tutor* was used for a graduate responsible for a younger student. From this meaning came the sense of "a private teacher."

TV   Television. We watched *TV* for an hour.

tweed   A rough, wool cloth woven with two or more colors of yarn.
  tweed (twēd) *noun, plural* **tweeds.**

tweezers   A small instrument with two prongs. It is used for plucking out hairs or for picking up tiny objects.
  tweez·ers (twē′zərz) *plural noun.*

twelfth   Next after the eleventh. *Adjective; noun.*
—One of twelve equal parts; ¹/₁₂. *Noun.*
  twelfth (twelfth) *adjective; noun, plural* **twelfths.**

twelve   Two more than ten; 12.
  twelve (twelv) *noun, plural* **twelves;** *adjective.*

twentieth   Next after the nineteenth. *Adjective; noun.*
—One of twenty equal parts; ¹/₂₀. *Noun.*
  twen·ti·eth (twen′tē ith) *adjective; noun, plural* **twentieths.**

twenty   Two times ten; 20.
  twen·ty (twen′tē) *noun, plural* **twenties;** *adjective.*

twice   Two times. I rang the doorbell *twice.* Twenty is *twice* as much as ten.
  twice (twīs) *adverb.*

twig   A small branch of a tree or other woody plant. We gathered dry *twigs* to start a campfire.
  twig (twig) *noun, plural* **twigs.**

twilight   The time just after sunset or just before sunrise when there is a soft, hazy light.
  twi·light (twī′līt′) *noun.*

twin   One of two children or animals born at the same time to the same mother. Some twins look exactly alike. *Noun.*
—**1.** Being a twin. Those two are *twin* sisters. *Twin* lambs were born to our sheep. **2.** Being identical or very much alike. Look at the *twin* mountain peaks. *Adjective.*
  twin (twin) *noun, plural* **twins;** *adjective.*

twine   A strong string made of two or more strands twisted together. *Noun.*
—To wind or coil one thing around another. Ivy *twined* around the gate post. A ribbon was *twined* through the lace. *Verb.*
  twine (twīn) *noun, plural* **twines;** *verb,* **twined, twining.**

twinge   A sudden, sharp pain. I felt a *twinge* in my sore ankle when I stood up.
  twinge (twinj) *noun, plural* **twinges.**

twinkle   To shine with flashes of light. Stars seem to *twinkle* in the sky at night. The child's eyes *twinkled* with laughter. *Verb.*
—A flash of light or brightness. We saw the *twinkle* of the city lights in the distance. *Noun.*
  twin·kle (twing′kəl) *verb,* **twinkled, twinkling;** *noun, plural* **twinkles.**

twirl   To spin around quickly. A drum majorette *twirled* a baton at the head of the parade. The dancers *twirled* around the floor.
  twirl (twûrl) *verb,* **twirled, twirling.**

twist   **1.** To wind or turn around something. The dog's chain was *twisted* around the tree. The road *twisted* around the mountain.   **2.** To change the natural or usual

shape of. Anger *twisted* the child's face. **3.** To change the meaning of; distort. If you argue, don't *twist* the words of your opponent. **4.** To hurt a part of the body by turning it suddenly or too far. I *twisted* my ankle when I slipped off the ladder. *Verb.*
—A turn or bend in something. I can't straighten this *twist* in the wire. *Noun.*
　twist (twist) *verb,* **twisted, twisting;** *noun, plural* **twists.**

twister A dark, whirling column of wind; tornado.
　twist·er (twis′tər) *noun, plural* **twisters.**

twitch To move or pull with a sudden jerk or tug. The rabbit's nose *twitched.*
　twitch (twich) *verb,* **twitched, twitching.**

twitter **1.** A series of short, light, chirping sounds made by a bird or birds. We heard the *twitter* of birds **2.** A nervous or excited state. Everyone was in a *twitter* on the last day of school. *Noun.*
—To make short, light, chirping sounds. The sparrows *twittered* in the trees. *Verb.*
　twit·ter (twit′ər) *noun, plural* **twitters;** *verb,* **twittered, twittering.**

two One more than one; 2. ▲ Other words that sound like this are **to** and **too.**
　two (tü) *noun, plural* **twos;** *adjective.*

TX Postal abbreviation for *Texas.*

tycoon A wealthy, powerful businessman or businesswoman.
　ty·coon (tī kün′) *noun, plural* **tycoons.**

tying Present participle of **tie.** This string is good for *tying* packages. Look up **tie** for more information.
　ty·ing (tī′ing) *verb.*

type **1.** A group of things that are alike or have the same qualities; kind. A collie is a *type* of dog. **2.** Small pieces of metal with raised letters or numbers on their surfaces. Type is coated with ink and pressed onto paper in printing. **3.** Printed or typewritten letters or numbers. *Noun.*
— To write with a typewriter. I *typed* a letter to my friend at college. *Verb.*
　type (tīp) *noun, plural* **types;** *verb,* **typed, typing.**

typewriter A machine with keys for each letter of the alphabet, for numbers, and for punctuation marks. When you press a key, the letter is printed on a piece of paper.
　type·writ·er (tīp′rī′tər) *noun, plural* **typewriters.**

typhoon A tropical storm with violent winds. Typhoons occur in the western Pacific Ocean.
　ty·phoon (tī fün′) *noun, plural* **typhoons.**

Word History

　The word **typhoon** is derived from two words in the Chinese language that mean "great wind."

---

typical Showing the qualities or characteristics of a certain type. A *typical* movie lasts about ninety minutes. It's *typical* for me to sleep late on Saturday morning.
　typ·i·cal (tip′i kəl) *adjective.*

tyrannical Of or like a tyrant; cruel or unjust. The *tyrannical* dictator was hated by the citizens of the country.
　ty·ran·ni·cal (ti ran′i kəl) *adjective.*

tyrannosaurus A huge dinosaur that lived in North America in prehistoric times. It walked upright on its hind feet.
　ty·ran·no·sau·rus (ti ran′ə sôr′əs) *noun, plural* **tyrannosauruses.**

tyranny The unjust use of power; harsh or cruel government. The people rose up against the dictator's *tyranny.*
　tyr·an·ny (tir′ə nē) *noun, plural* **tyrannies.**

tyrant A person who uses power in a cruel or unjust way. The king was a *tyrant* who put anyone who disagreed with him in prison.
　ty·rant (tī′rənt) *noun, plural* **tyrants.**

---

at; āpe; fär; câre; end; mē; it; īce; pîerce; hot; ōld; sông; fôrk; oil; out; up; ūse; rüle; pùll; tûrn; chin; sing; shop; thin; this; hw in white; zh in treasure. The symbol ə stands for the unstressed vowel sound in about, taken, pencil, lemon, and circus.

T

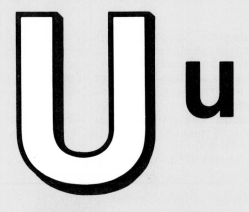

U u

1. **U** developed from the letter **V**, which was first used by ancient tribes in the Middle East.

2. The Greeks borrowed this letter, writing it like a modern capital **Y**.

3. An ancient tribe near Rome also borrowed this letter, changing it to look like a **V**.

4. The ancient Romans began using this letter about 2,400 years ago, writing it in the same way.

5. Our modern **U** was first used about 1,000 years ago instead of a **V** when it fell in the middle of a word. Later it became a separate letter.

u, U   The twenty-first letter of the alphabet.
u, U (ū) *noun, plural* **u's, U's.**

udder   A sac that hangs from the underside of certain female animals, especially cows, goats, ewes, and mares. It contains the glands that make milk. Each gland is connected to a nipple where a baby animal can nurse.
ud·der (ud'ər) *noun, plural* **udders.**

Uganda   A country in central Africa.
U·gan·da (ū gan'də *or* ü gän'də) *noun.*

ugly   **1.** Not nice or pleasing to look at. That is an *ugly* painting. **2.** Unpleasant; offensive. My classmate started an *ugly* rumor about me. **3.** Likely to cause trouble or harm. Dark clouds told us that an *ugly* storm was coming. **4.** Bad-tempered; cross. I am in an *ugly* mood today.
ug·ly (ug'lē) *adjective,* **uglier, ugliest.**

ukulele   A small guitar that has four strings. It is played by plucking the strings.
u·ku·le·le (ū'kə lā'lē) *noun, plural* **ukuleles.**

ultimate   **1.** Coming at the end; final. The *ultimate* cost of building that highway was 40 million dollars. **2.** Most basic; original. Hard work was the *ultimate* cause of the student's success in school.
ul·ti·mate (ul'tə mit) *adjective.*

umbrella   A circular piece of cloth or plastic stretched on a framework that can be folded up when the umbrella is not needed. An umbrella is used to give protection from the rain or sun.
um·brel·la (um brel'ə) *noun, plural* **umbrellas.**

umbrellas

Word History

The word **umbrella** comes from the Italian word for this device. The Italian word came from a Latin word meaning "shade" or "shadow."

umpire A person who rules on plays in baseball or certain other sports. *Noun.*
—To act as an umpire of. My neighbor will *umpire* our softball game on Saturday. *Verb.*
um·pire (um′pīr) *noun, plural* **umpires;** *verb,* **umpired, umpiring.**

un– A *prefix* that means: **1.** The opposite of; not. *Unexpected* means not expected. *Unemployment* means the opposite of employment. **2.** To do the opposite of. *Unlock* means to do the opposite of lock.

UN An abbreviation for *United Nations.*

unable Not having the power or skill to do something; not able. I was *unable* to reach the top shelf.
un·a·ble (un ā′bəl) *adjective.*

unaccented Not accented. In the word "ago," the "a" is *unaccented.*
un·ac·cent·ed (un ak′sen tid) *adjective.*

unanimous In or showing total agreement. The family was *unanimous* in wanting to go on a picnic. My friend was elected club president by a *unanimous* vote.
u·nan·i·mous (ū nan′ə məs) *adjective.*

Word History

The word **unanimous** comes from a Latin word that means "of one mind." When people are *unanimous* about something, they have all made up their minds in the same way about it.

---

unaware Not knowing or realizing; not aware. We were *unaware* that the road ahead was closed.
un·a·ware (un′ə wâr′) *adjective.*

unbearable Not able to be tolerated or endured. The icy water of the lake was *unbearable.*
un·bear·a·ble (un bâr′ə bəl) *adjective.*

unbecoming **1.** Not flattering or attractive; not becoming. Hats are *unbecoming* on some people. **2.** Not suitable or proper. Such childish behavior is *unbecoming* for someone of your age!
un·be·com·ing (un′bi kum′ing) *adjective.*

unbelievable **1.** Hard to believe. The child told an *unbelievable* story about seeing a ghost. **2.** Remarkable; amazing. The circus acrobats did *unbelievable* tricks.
un·be·liev·a·ble (un′bi lē′və bəl) *adjective.*

unbreakable Not able to be broken or not easily broken. These plastic plates are *unbreakable.*
un·break·a·ble (un brā′kə bəl) *adjective.*

unbroken **1.** Not broken. I dropped my glasses, but luckily they were *unbroken.* **2.** Not interrupted. We drove through miles of *unbroken* desert. The football team has had an *unbroken* series of victories. **3.** Not beaten; not surpassed. The athlete's swimming record is still *unbroken.* **4.** Not weakened or tamed. The rider could not handle the *unbroken* horse.
un·bro·ken (un brō′kən) *adjective.*

uncanny **1.** Strange and mysterious. We heard *uncanny* sounds coming from the deserted house. **2.** Remarkable; extraordinary. You have an *uncanny* ability to know what other people are thinking.
un·can·ny (un kan′ē) *adjective.*

uncertain **1.** Not known for sure; not certain. It is still *uncertain* whether our team will win the game. **2.** Not dependable; changing. The weather was *uncertain,* so we canceled the picnic.
un·cer·tain (un sûr′tən) *adjective.*

unchanged Not changed. The patient's condition was *unchanged.*
un·changed (un chānjd′) *adjective.*

uncle **1.** The brother of one's mother or father. **2.** The husband of one's aunt.
un·cle (ung′kəl) *noun, plural* **uncles.**

uncomfortable **1.** Causing discomfort or uneasiness. That chair is hard and *uncomfortable.* An *uncomfortable* situation arose when unexpected guests arrived at dinner time. **2.** Feeling discomfort. I am *uncomfortable* in these tight shoes.
un·com·fort·a·ble (un kum′fər tə bəl *or* un kumf′tə bəl) *adjective.*

uncommon Unusual; rare. That bird is *uncommon* in this part of the country.
un·com·mon (un kom′ən) *adjective.*

unconcerned Not interested, troubled, or worried; not concerned. The neighbors were *unconcerned* that their dog had trampled our flower bed.
un·con·cerned (un′kən sûrnd′) *adjective.*

unconscious **1.** Not conscious. I was knocked *unconscious* when I fell out of the tree and hit my head. **2.** Not knowing; not aware. They were *unconscious* of how sloppy they looked. **3.** Not done on purpose. I

at; āpe; fär; câre; end; mē; it; īce; pîerce; hot; ōld; sông, fôrk; oil; out; up; ūse; rüle; pùll; tûrn; chin; sing; shop; thin; this; hw in white; zh in treasure. The symbol ə stands for the unstressed vowel sound in about, taken, pencil, lemon, and circus.

U

made an *unconscious* mistake when I called you by the wrong name.

un·con·scious (un kon′shəs) *adjective*.

unconstitutional Not in keeping with the constitution of a state or country. The Supreme Court declared the new state law *unconstitutional*.

un·con·sti·tu·tion·al (un′kon sti tü′shə nəl *or* un′kon sti tū′shə nəl) *adjective*.

uncover 1. To take away the cover from. The cook *uncovered* the pan. 2. To discover; make known. The detective *uncovered* some new clues.

un·cov·er (un kuv′ər) *verb*, **uncovered, uncovering.**

undecided 1. Not having one's mind made up. I am still *undecided* about what I would like for my birthday. 2. Not yet settled. The result of the school election is still *undecided*.

un·de·cid·ed (un′di sī′did) *adjective*.

under 1. In or to a place lower than; beneath; below. I found the paper *under* a pile of books. 2. Less than. The book cost *under* five dollars. 3. Subject to or affected by the authority or guidance of. My cousin studied painting in Paris *under* a famous artist. 4. According to. *Under* the new rules, the swimming pool is open five nights a week. 5. During the reign or rule of. *Under* the last king and queen, the country grew rich and powerful. *Preposition.*
—In or into a position lower than something. The canoe went *under* when it reached the rapids. *Adverb.*

un·der (un′dər) *preposition; adverb*.

underbrush Bushes and other plants growing under big trees in a forest or woods.

un·der·brush (un′dər brush′) *noun*.

underclothes Clothing worn under a person's outer clothing; underwear.

un·der·clothes (un′dər klōz′ *or* un′dər klōᵗhz′) *plural noun*.

underdeveloped 1. Not fully or properly developed. Lack of proper exercise can lead to *underdeveloped* muscles. 2. Behind other countries in economic growth or development. The rich country sent aid to the *underdeveloped* country.

un·der·de·vel·oped (un′dər di vel′əpt) *adjective*.

underdog A person or group that is thought most likely to lose, as in a contest or game. Our school team started the tournament as the *underdog* but won the championship.

un·der·dog (un′dər dôg′) *noun, plural* **underdogs.**

underfoot 1. In the way. The baby's toys are always *underfoot*. 2. Beneath the feet; on the ground. Because of the rain it was wet *underfoot*.

un·der·foot (un′dər fůt′) *adverb*.

undergo To go through; experience. The street will *undergo* repairs during the summer months. The early settlers of America had to *undergo* many hardships.

un·der·go (un′dər gō′) *verb*, **underwent, undergone, undergoing.**

undergone Past participle of **undergo**. The patient has *undergone* surgery and is now recovering. Look up **undergo** for more information.

un·der·gone (un′dər gôn′) *verb*.

underground 1. Below the earth's surface. The workers built an *underground* passage for the subway. 2. Secret; hidden. The spies belonged to an *underground* organization. *Adjective.*
—1. A place below the earth's surface. 2. A group working in secret. The *underground* in the country continued to fight against the government. *Noun.*
—1. Below the earth's surface. Moles live *underground*. 2. In or into hiding. The outlaws went *underground* because the police were looking for them. *Adverb.*

un·der·ground (un′dər ground′ *for adjective and adverb;* un′dər ground′ *for noun*) *adjective; noun, plural* **undergrounds;** *adverb*.

undergrowth Small plants growing under large trees in a forest; underbrush.

un·der·growth (un′dər grōth′) *noun*.

underhanded Not open and honest; secret and unfair. The newspaper accused the candidate of using *underhanded* methods to be elected.

un·der·handed (un′dər han′did) *adjective*.

underline To draw a line under. The teacher *underlined* the words that I had spelled wrong on the test.

un·der·line (un′dər līn′) *verb*, **underlined, underlining.**

underneath In or to a place or position lower than; under; beneath. The ball rolled *underneath* the chair. *Preposition.*
—In a place or position below. Pack the records on top and the books *underneath*. *Adverb.*

un·der·neath (un′dər nēth′) *preposition; adverb*.

underpass A section of road that goes under a bridge or another road.

un·der·pass (un′dər pas′) *noun, plural* **underpasses.**

underprivileged Lacking the advantages or rights that other people have, usually because one is poor.
un·der·priv·i·leged (un′dər priv′ə lijd) *adjective.*

undersea Lying, done, or used below the surface of the sea. The wreck of the sunken ship was found during an *undersea* exploration.
un·der·sea (un′dər sē′ *or* un′dər sē′) *adjective.*

undershirt A shirt with short sleeves or no sleeves that is worn under a person's outer clothing.
un·der·shirt (un′dər shûrt′) *noun, plural* **undershirts.**

underside The bottom side or surface of something. The bird had brown wings and a red *underside.*
un·der·side (un′dər sīd′) *noun, plural* **undersides.**

understand **1.** To get the meaning of; comprehend. I didn't *understand* the teacher's question. **2.** To know very well. My parents *understand* French because they lived for a time in France. **3.** To be in sympathy or agreement with. The two friends are very close and *understand* each other completely. **4.** To be told; hear; learn. I *understand* that you hope to go to college. **5.** To take as a fact; assume. I *understand* that I can return the tickets before the game and get my money back.
un·der·stand (un′dər stand′) *verb,* **understood, understanding.**

understanding **1.** A grasping of the meaning of something; knowledge. You have a good *understanding* of arithmetic. **2.** Opinion; belief; conclusion. It was my *understanding* that we would meet at three o'clock. **3.** Sympathy or agreement. My parents always show *understanding* when I bring them my problems. The two friends reached an *understanding* that ended their quarrel. *Noun.*
—Feeling or showing sympathy. The teacher gave the nervous student an *understanding* look. *Adjective.*
un·der·stand·ing (un′dər stan′ding) *noun, plural* **understandings;** *adjective.*

understood Past tense and past participle of **understand.** I *understood* the meaning of the poem. Look up **understand** for more information.
un·der·stood (un′dər stŭd′) *verb.*

undertake **1.** To try to do; start. The explorers planned to *undertake* a journey over the mountain ridge. **2.** To agree to do; ac-

cept as a duty. I will *undertake* the care of my sick grandparents.
un·der·take (un′dər tāk′) *verb,* **undertook, undertaken, undertaking.**

undertaker A person whose job is arranging funerals and preparing dead people for burial.
un·der·tak·er (un′dər tā′kər) *noun, plural* **undertakers.**

undertook Past tense of **undertake.** The company *undertook* to deliver the merchandise in two weeks. Look up **undertake** for more information.
un·der·took (un′dər tük′) *verb.*

undertow A strong current just below the surface of a body of water, such as a river or the ocean. It usually moves in a different direction than the surface current moves, and it can pull swimmers away from shore or safe swimming areas.
un·der·tow (un′dər tō′) *noun, plural* **undertows.**

underwater Lying, used, or done below the surface of the water. An *underwater* tunnel connected the island and the mainland. The book had photographs of *underwater* plants. *Adjective.*
—Below the surface of the water. I like to swim *underwater. Adverb.*
un·der·wa·ter (un′dər wô′tər) *adjective; adverb.*

underwear Clothing worn under a person's outer clothing; underclothes.
un·der·wear (un′dər wâr′) *noun.*

underweight Having less than the normal or needed weight. The child was a little *underweight* after being sick.
un·der·weight (un′dər wāt′) *adjective.*

underwent Past tense of **undergo.** I *underwent* an operation to remove my tonsils. Look up **undergo** for more information.
un·der·went (un′dər went′) *verb.*

undid Past tense of **undo.** I *undid* the laces of my shoes. Look up **undo** for more information.
un·did (un did′) *verb.*

undisturbed Not disturbed or bothered. The baby was *undisturbed* by the noise.
un·dis·turbed (un′dis tûrbd′) *adjective.*

---

at; āpe; fär; câre; end; mē; it; īce; pîerce; hot; ōld; sông, fôrk; oil; out; up; ūse; rüle; pùll; tûrn; chin; sing; shop; thin; this; hw in white; zh in treasure. The symbol ə stands for the unstressed vowel sound in about, taken, pencil, lemon, and circus.

U

undo **1.** To loosen something that is fastened or tied. This is a hard knot to *undo*. Let me help you *undo* the package. **2.** To do away with; wipe out. The storm *undid* the farmer's hard work. **3.** To bring to ruin; destroy. Nasty rumors finally *undid* the politician.
▸ **un·do** (un dü′) *verb,* **undid, undone, undoing.**

undoing Ruin or the cause of ruin. Carelessness on the test was the student's *undoing*.
▸ **un·do·ing** (un dü′ing) *noun.*

undone¹ Not finished or done. I left the last question on the test *undone*.
▸ **un·done** (un dun′) *adjective.*

undone² Past participle of **undo**. The mistakes we make can often be *undone*. Look up **undo** for more information.
▸ **un·done** (un dun′) *verb.*

undress To take clothes off. The tired child *undressed* and went to bed.
▸ **un·dress** (un dres′) *verb,* **undressed, undressing.**

undying Without an end; lasting forever; eternal. The monarchs had the *undying* loyalty of their subjects.
▸ **un·dy·ing** (un dī′ing) *adjective.*

unearth **1.** To dig up out of the earth. The dog *unearthed* a bone it had buried. **2.** To search for and find; discover. My grandparents *unearthed* some old family photographs in the attic.
▸ **un·earth** (un ûrth′) *verb,* **unearthed, unearthing.**

The man **unearthed** a skeleton.

uneasy **1.** Worried; nervous; restless. My parents were *uneasy* about my staying out so late. I finally dropped off into an *uneasy* sleep. **2.** Embarrassed or awkward. The

speaker's rude remark was followed by an *uneasy* silence in the group.
▸ **un·eas·y** (un ē′zē) *adjective,* **uneasier, uneasiest.**

unemployed Not having a job; out of work. The closing of the factory left many people *unemployed*.
▸ **un·em·ployed** (un′em ploid′) *adjective.*

unemployment **1.** The condition of being without a job. The workers' *unemployment* ended when the closed factory opened again. **2.** The number of people who are without a job. *Unemployment* has risen this year.
▸ **un·em·ploy·ment** (un′em ploi′mənt) *noun.*

unequal **1.** Not the same; uneven. We complained that the cake was divided into *unequal* pieces. The sleeves of the sweater are of *unequal* length. **2.** Not well matched; unfair. When the older children played the younger children in football, it was an *unequal* contest.
▸ **un·e·qual** (un ē′kwəl) *adjective.*

uneven **1.** Not straight, smooth, or regular. The hem of the dress was *uneven*. The car bounced along the *uneven* road. **2.** Being an odd number. 1, 3, and 5 are *uneven*. **3.** Not well matched; unfair. There was no way our team could win the *uneven* contest. **4.** Not always the same; changing. Our school plays were *uneven* in quality.
▸ **un·e·ven** (un ē′vən) *adjective.*

unexpected Coming or happening without warning; not expected. The train was late because of an *unexpected* delay.
▸ **un·ex·pect·ed** (un′ek spek′tid) *adjective.*

unfair Not fair or just. The older child had an *unfair* advantage over the younger child in the fight.
▸ **un·fair** (un fâr′) *adjective.*

unfamiliar **1.** Not well known or easily recognized; strange. The handwriting on the envelope is *unfamiliar* to me. **2.** Not acquainted. The librarian was *unfamiliar* with the book I wanted.
▸ **un·fa·mil·iar** (un′fə mil′yər) *adjective.*

unfeeling Not feeling or showing sympathy; without pity. Only someone who is *unfeeling* would make such nasty remarks about poor people.
▸ **un·feel·ing** (un fē′ling) *adjective.*

unfold **1.** To open or spread out something folded. Please *unfold* the tablecloth. **2.** To make or become known gradually. The general *unfolded* a daring plan. We listened as the strange story *unfolded*. **3.** To become open. The petals of the flowers *unfolded*.
▸ **un·fold** (un fōld′) *verb,* **unfolded, unfolding.**

unfortunate **1.** Not fortunate; unlucky. It was very *unfortunate* that their luggage was stolen during their vacation. **2.** Not proper or suitable. The speaker offended the audience with an *unfortunate* joke about their town. *Adjective.*
un·for·tu·nate (un fôr′chə nit) *adjective.*

unfriendly **1.** Feeling or showing dislike; not friendly. We tried to get to know our new neighbors, but they were *unfriendly* to us. **2.** Not pleasant or favorable. The Arctic is known for its cold, *unfriendly* climate.
un·friend·ly (un frend′lē) *adjective,* **unfriendlier, unfriendliest.**

unhappy **1.** Without happiness or joy; sad. My cousin is *unhappy* about having to move to a different town. **2.** Not suitable. Red and green was an *unhappy* choice of colors for the living room.
un·hap·py (un hap′ē) *adjective,* **unhappier, unhappiest.**

unhealthy Not having, showing, or giving good health; not healthy. Our best cow has been *unhealthy* this winter so her milk production has been lower than usual. Lack of exercise is *unhealthy.*
un·heal·thy (un hel′thē) *adjective,* **unhealthier, unhealthiest.**

unheard-of Not known or happening before; unknown. Before the use of jet planes, travel across the Atlantic in six hours was *unheard-of.*
un·heard-of (un hûrd′uv′ *or* un hûrd′ov′) *adjective.*

uni– A *prefix* that means one or single. *Unicycle* means a vehicle that has one wheel.

unicorn An imaginary animal that looks like a white horse with a long pointed horn in the middle of its forehead.
u·ni·corn (ū′ni kôrn′) *noun, plural* **unicorns.**

unicycle A vehicle that has pedals and a seat like a bicycle but has only one wheel and no handlebars. It is used mostly by acrobats and other entertainers.
u·ni·cy·cle (ū′nə sī′kəl) *noun, plural* **unicycles.**

uniform **1.** Always the same; not changing. The plants in our greenhouse need to be kept at a *uniform* temperature. **2.** Showing little or no difference; all alike. The houses on that street are of *uniform* design. *Adjective.*
—The special or official clothes that the members of a particular group wear. Soldiers, police officers, mail carriers, and students at some schools wear uniforms. *Noun.*
un·i·form (ū′nə fôrm′) *adjective; noun, plural* **uniforms.**

unify To cause to be or feel like one thing; bring or join together; unite. Fear of being invaded *unified* the people of the small country.
u·ni·fy (ū′nə fī′) *verb,* **unified, unifying.**

unimportant Of no special value, meaning, or interest; not important. The newspaper didn't bother to print a story on the *unimportant* incident. It is *unimportant* what color the car is as long as it runs well.
un·im·por·tant (un′im pôr′tənt) *adjective.*

union **1.** A joining together of two or more people or things. The new town was formed by the *union* of three small villages. **2.** Something formed by a joining together; confederation. The three countries formed a *union* to increase trade among them. **3. the Union. a.** The United States of America. **b.** The states that stayed loyal to the federal government during the Civil War. **4.** A group of workers joined together to protect their interests and improve their working conditions.
un·ion (ūn′yən) *noun, plural* **unions.**

unicycle

at; āpe; fär; câre; end; mē; it; ice; pîerce; hot; ōld; sông, fôrk; oil; out; up; ūse; rüle; pull; tûrn; chin; sing; shop; thin; <u>th</u>is; hw in white; zh in treasure. The symbol ə stands for the unstressed vowel sound in about, taken, pencil, lemon, and circus.

U

Union of Soviet Socialist Republics
The official name for **Soviet Union.** Look up **Soviet Union** for more information.

unique   Not having an equal; being the only one of its kind. Being the first person to set foot on the moon was a *unique* achievement.
u·nique (ū nēk′) *adjective.*

unison   **In unison.** Making the same sounds or movements at the same time. The students recited the poem *in unison.* The acrobats did two cartwheels *in unison.*
u·ni·son (ū′nə sən *or* ū′nə zən) *noun.*

Word History

The word **unison** goes back to two Latin words meaning "one" and "sound."

unit   **1.** A single person, thing, or group that is part of a larger group. That apartment building contains fifty *units.*   **2.** A fixed quantity or amount that is used as a standard of measurement. An hour is a *unit* of time.   **3.** A piece of equipment having a special purpose. The builder installed an air conditioning *unit* in the house.   **4.** The smallest whole number; one.
u·nit (ū′nit) *noun, plural* **units.**

unite   To bring or join together; make or become one. The two families were *united* by marriage. All the people in the country *united* in the battle against the enemy.
u·nite (ū nīt′) *verb,* **united, uniting.**

United Kingdom   The country that includes England, Scotland, Wales, and Northern Ireland. It is also called **Great Britain.**

United Nations   An international organization that includes most of the countries of the world as its members. It was founded in 1945 to keep world peace. Its headquarters are in New York City.

United States   A country that has forty-nine states in North America and the state of Hawaii in the Pacific Ocean. Its capital is Washington, D. C. This country is also called the **United States of America.**

unity   **1.** The condition of being one. The candidates expressed *unity* on foreign trade.   **2.** The condition of harmony. The goal of the United Nations is *unity* in the world.
u·ni·ty (ū′ni tē) *noun, plural* **unities.**

universal   **1.** Of, for, or shared by all. There was *universal* joy when the war ended.   **2.** Being everywhere; affecting everything. Disease is *universal* throughout the world.
u·ni·ver·sal (ū′nə vûr′səl) *adjective.*

universe   Everything that exists, including the earth, the planets, the stars, and all of space.
u·ni·verse (ū′nə vûrs′) *noun, plural* **universes.**

Word History

The word **universe** comes from a Latin word that means "the whole world."

university   A school that is made up of one or more colleges. It also may have special schools that give training in many professions.
u·ni·ver·si·ty (û′nə vûr′si tē) *noun, plural* **universities.**

unjust   Not fair or just. The lawyer complained that the judge's decision had been *unjust.*
un·just (un just′) *adjective.*

unkempt   **1.** Not combed or groomed. The campers were *unkempt* after several days in the woods.   **2.** Not neat, tidy, or clean. Your room is *unkempt.*
un·kempt (un kempt′) *adjective.*

unkind   Not kind; cruel. Your *unkind* remark hurt my feelings.
un·kind (un kīnd′) *adjective,* **unkinder, unkindest.**

unknown   Not known; not familiar. That person's name is *unknown* to me. The sailors were shipwrecked on an *unknown* island. *Adjective.*
—A person or thing that is unknown. *Noun.*
un·known (un nōn′) *adjective; noun, plural* **unknowns.**

unless   Except on the condition that. *Unless* you return the library books you have borrowed, you cannot borrow any more.
un·less (un les′) *conjunction.*

unlike   **1.** Different from. *Unlike* most of my friends, I enjoy dancing.   **2.** Not usual for. It is *unlike* you to be rude. *Preposition.*
—Not the same; different. A deer and a mouse are *unlike* animals. *Adjective.*
un·like (un līk′) *preposition; adjective.*

unlikely   **1.** Not likely or not probable. It is *unlikely* that it will rain today.   **2.** Not likely to succeed. The two friends had an *unlikely* plan for making money.
un·like·ly (un līk′lē) *adjective,* **unlikelier, unlikeliest.**

unlimited   Without any limits. This card will give you *unlimited* use of the town library.
un·lim·it·ed (un lim′i tid) *adjective.*

unload   **1.** To take off or remove from a vehicle. The workers *unloaded* the cargo from the ship.   **2.** To remove a load from. We *unloaded* the car when we got home.   **3.** To remove ammunition from. The soldier *unloaded* the gun.
   un·load (un lōd′) *verb*, **unloaded, unloading.**

unlock   **1.** To open the lock of. This key will *unlock* the front door.   **2.** To make known. The detective *unlocked* the mystery of the missing car.
   un·lock (un lok′) *verb*, **unlocked, unlocking.**

unlucky   **1.** Not having good luck. The *unlucky* travelers were stranded when their car broke down for the third time.   **2.** Causing bad luck. Some people believe that thirteen is an *unlucky* number.
   un·luck·y (un luk′ē) *adjective*, **unluckier, unluckiest.**

unmanned   Without a human crew. The *unmanned* spacecraft landed on Mars.
   un·manned (un mand′) *adjective*.

unmistakable   Not capable of being mistaken; plain; clear. There was an *unmistakable* note of anger in the teacher's voice.
   un·mis·tak·a·ble (un′mis tā′kə bəl) *adjective*.

unnatural   Going against or different from what is usual or normal in nature; not natural. The cat grew to an *unnatural* size. We all have *unnatural* smiles in the class photograph.
   un·nat·u·ral (un nach′ər əl) *adjective*.

unnecessary   Not necessary; needless. It was *unnecessary* for you to repeat your question, because I heard it the first time.
   un·nec·es·sar·y (un nes′ə ser′ē) *adjective*.

unofficial   Not official. One of the spectators volunteered to act as the *unofficial* umpire for the game.
   un·of·fi·cial (un′ə fish′əl) *adjective*.

unpack   **1.** To open and take things out of. I *unpacked* my suitcase when I got home.   **2.** To take out from a container or package. We *unpacked* glasses from the box.
   un·pack (un pak′) *verb*, **unpacked, unpacking.**

unpleasant   Not pleasing; disagreeable. There was an *unpleasant* odor coming from the sewer.
   un·pleas·ant (un plez′ənt) *adjective*.

unpopular   Not generally liked or accepted. I am afraid I might be *unpopular* at my new school. The politician had a number of ideas that were *unpopular* with the voters.
   un·pop·u·lar (un pop′yə lər) *adjective*.

unprepared   **1.** Not ready; not prepared. I was *unprepared* for the test because I didn't have time to study.   **2.** Not prepared at an earlier time. Your class president gave an *unprepared* speech to our class.
   un·pre·pared (un′pri pârd′) *adjective*.

unreasonable   **1.** Not showing or using good sense; not reasonable. You are being *unreasonable* in wanting your own way all the time.   **2.** Too great. The prices at that restaurant were *unreasonable*.
   un·rea·son·a·ble (un rē′zə nə bəl *or* un rēz′nə bəl) *adjective*.

unreliable   Not to be trusted. That car is *unreliable;* you never know if it will start in the morning.
   un·re·li·a·ble (un′ri lī′ə bəl) *adjective*.

unrest   A disturbed or discontented condition. There was political *unrest* in the country under the dictator's rule.
   un·rest (un rest′) *noun*.

unruly   Hard to control or manage. The police tried to control the *unruly* mob. After I wash my hair, it is *unruly* and hard to comb.
   un·ru·ly (un rü′lē) *adjective*, **unrulier, unruliest.**

unsatisfactory   Not good enough to meet a need, desire, or hope; not satisfactory. I won't hire those painters again because their work was *unsatisfactory*.
   un·sa·tis·fac·to·ry (un′sat is fak′tə rē) *adjective*.

unsettled   **1.** Not peaceful, calm, or orderly. There were *unsettled* conditions in the country after the war.   **2.** Not decided or determined. The question of how much the club should charge new members for dues is still *unsettled*.   **3.** Not paid. The old farmer died and left behind a lot of *unsettled* medical bills.   **4.** Not being lived in; not inhabited. Many areas of Alaska are still *unsettled*.   **5.** Changing; uncertain. We called off our trip to the beach because of the *unsettled* weather.
   un·set·tled (un set′əld) *adjective*.

unsightly   Not pleasant to look at; ugly. The park was covered with *unsightly* litter after the big picnic.
   un·sight·ly (un sīt′lē) *adjective*, **unsightlier, unsightliest.**

---

at; āpe; fär; câre; end; mē; it; īce; pîerce; hot; ōld; sông, fôrk; oil; out; up; ūse; rüle; pull; tûrn; chin; sing; shop; thin; <u>th</u>is; hw in white; zh in treasure. The symbol ə stands for the unstressed vowel sound in about, taken, pencil, lemon, and circus.

U

unskilled 1. Not having special skills, training, or experience. An *unskilled* worker generally gets paid less than a skilled worker does. 2. Not needing special skills, training, or experience. The new factory will provide many *unskilled* jobs for the town.
un·skilled (un skild′) *adjective.*

unsound 1. Not strong or solid; not in good condition. That old wooden bridge is *unsound.* 2. Not based on truth or good judgment. My friends gave me *unsound* advice about buying this old bicycle.
un·sound (un sound′) *adjective.*

unstable 1. Not firmly fixed; easily moved. The chair is *unstable* because one leg is broken. 2. Likely to change. A group of army officers tried to overthrow the *unstable* government of that country.
un·sta·ble (un stā′bəl) *adjective.*

unsteady Not firm; shaky. This ladder is *unsteady* because it is not standing on level ground. I fought back my tears and answered in an *unsteady* voice.
un·stead·y (un sted′ē) *adjective,*
unsteadier, unsteadiest.

unthinkable Not able to be thought about as possible. It is *unthinkable* that my friend could have lied to me.
un·think·a·ble (un thing′kə bəl) *adjective.*

untie To loosen or undo; set free. I *untied* the ribbon on my birthday gift. They *untied* the dog as soon as they got home.
un·tie (un tī′) *verb,* **untied, untying.**

until 1. Up to the time of. Wait *until* eight o'clock before you call me. 2. Before. Tickets for the play are not available *until* Wednesday. *Preposition.*
—1. Up to the time when. Wait here *until* I get back. 2. Before. We can't leave *until* we finish our chores. *Conjunction.*
un·til (ən til′ *or* un til′) *preposition; conjunction.*

untold 1. Too great or too many to be counted or measured. An *untold* number of stars appeared in the clear night sky. 2. Not told. That secret will remain *untold.*
un·told (un tōld′) *adjective.*

unused 1. Not in use; not put to use. Put those books on the *unused* shelf in the bookcase. 2. Never having been used; new. I have an *unused* toothbrush I could give you.
un·used (un ūzd′) *adjective.*

unusual Not usual, common, or ordinary; rare. It is very *unusual* for them not to want to go to a hockey game.
un·u·su·al (un ū′zhü əl) *adjective.*

up 1. From a lower to a higher place or position. I climbed *up* to the top of the ladder.
2. In, on, or at a higher place. They're spending the summer *up* in the mountains. 3. To a higher point or degree. My weight went *up* during the winter. 4. In or to an upright position. A kind person helped me *up* when I fell off my skateboard. 5. Out of bed. When did you get *up* this morning? 6. Entirely; completely. We used *up* our potatoes in the soup. *Adverb.*
—1. At a higher point or degree. The price of food was *up* again this month. 2. Above the horizon. The sun is *up.* 3. Out of bed. They get *up* at six o'clock. *Adjective.*
—1. To or at a point further along or higher on. The spider climbed *up* the wall. Their house is *up* the block. 2. To or toward the source, interior, or upper part of. We paddled for hours *up* the river. *Preposition.*
• **up to.** 1. Doing or about to do. What are you *up to?* 2. Having the skill, training, power, or other qualities necessary for. I hope I'm *up to* the difficult task that's been assigned to me. 3. Depending on; being the responsibility of. It's *up to* the governor to try to lower taxes in our state.
up (up) *adverb; adjective; preposition.*

upheld Past tense and past participle of **uphold.** Look up **uphold** for more information.
up·held (up held′) *verb.*

uphold 1. To support or defend. All public officials must promise to *uphold* the laws. Duels have been fought to *uphold* a family's honor. 2. To keep from falling; hold up. Columns *uphold* the roof of the porch.
up·hold (up hōld′) *verb,* **upheld, upholding.**

upholster To fit with pads, cushions, or coverings. The cat tore up our couch so badly that it had to be *upholstered* again.
up·hol·ster (up hōl′stər *or* ə pōl′stər) *verb,* **upholstered, upholstering.**

upkeep 1. The keeping of something in good condition; maintenance. Much money is needed for the *upkeep* of the city's parks. 2. The cost of this maintenance. The *upkeep* of that mansion must be very high.
up·keep (up′kēp′) *noun.*

upland Land that is higher than the land surrounding it. A plateau is one kind of *upland. Noun.*
—Of or on such land. Sheep grazed on the *upland* meadow. *Adjective.*
up·land (up′lənd) *noun, plural* **uplands;** *adjective.*

upon In a position above and supported by; atop; on. The king and queen sat *upon* their thrones.
up·on (ə pôn′ *or* ə pon′) *preposition.*

upper Higher in position or rank. The people who live in the *upper* stories of that building have a beautiful view of the city.
up·per (up′ər) *adjective.*

upper case Letters that are capitals; capital letters. The letters A, B, C, and D are upper case; a,b,c, and d are lower case.

upper hand A position of control; advantage. Our team gained the *upper hand* in the last half of the basketball game.

uppermost **1.** Farthest up; highest. I can't reach the *uppermost* shelf of the kitchen cabinet. **2.** Having the most importance; foremost. The campers were so hungry that food was *uppermost* in their thoughts all day. *Adjective.*
—In the highest or most important place, position, or rank. The committee placed your problem *uppermost* on the list of things it has to consider. *Adverb.*
up·per·most (up′ər mōst′) *adjective; adverb.*

upright **1.** Straight up and down; vertical. Only a few trees remained *upright* after the storm. **2.** Good; honest. An *upright* person would never lie or cheat. *Adjective.*
—In a straight up and down position. I placed the chair *upright* after the dog knocked it over. *Adverb.*
—Something that stands straight up. *Noun.*
up·right (up′rīt′) *adjective; adverb; noun, plural* **uprights.**

uprising A revolt against a government or other authority; rebellion. The dictator used troops to put down the people's *uprising.*
up·ris·ing (up′rī′zing) *noun, plural* **uprisings.**

uproar **1.** A noisy and excited disturbance. The crowd was in an *uproar* when the player hit a home run to win the game. **2.** A loud, confused noise. I can't sleep because of the *uproar* in the street.
up·roar (up′rôr′) *noun, plural* **uproars.**

uproot **1.** To tear or pull up by the roots. The bulldozers *uprooted* bushes and trees to make way for the new highway. **2.** To cause to leave; displace. The flood *uprooted* many families from their homes.
up·root (up rüt′ *or* up rut′) *verb,* **uprooted, uprooting.**

upset **1.** To turn or knock over. I accidentally *upset* the glass of milk. **2.** To interfere with; throw into confusion. The rain *upset* our plans for a picnic. **3.** To make nervous and worried; disturb. The news of my cousin's accident *upset* me greatly. **4.** To make sick. Eating your food too quickly will *upset* your stomach. **5.** To defeat unexpectedly.

The young tennis player *upset* the city champion. *Verb.*
—**1.** Turned or knocked over. The *upset* glass of milk spilled all over me. **2.** Nervous and worried. They were *upset* about missing their plane. **3.** Sick. I got an *upset* stomach from eating too much at the picnic. *Adjective.*
—An unexpected defeat of a team or player. *Noun.*
up·set (up set′ *for verb and adjective;* up′set′ *for noun*) *verb,* **upset, upsetting;** *adjective; noun, plural* **upsets.**

upside down **1.** So that the top side or part becomes the bottom side or part. You're holding the book *upside down.* **2.** In or into complete disorder or confusion. I turned my room *upside down* looking for the missing keys.
up·side down (up′sīd′).

upstairs **1.** Up the stairs. I ran *upstairs* to get my baseball glove. **2.** On or to an upper floor. My parents are watching television *upstairs. Adverb.*
—On an upper floor. We live in an *upstairs* apartment. *Adjective.*
—An upper floor or floors. The *upstairs* of the house is not yet finished. *Noun.* ▲ The noun "upstairs" is used with a singular verb.
up·stairs (up′stârz′) *adverb; adjective; noun.*

upstream Toward or at the source of a stream; against the current. We rowed *upstream. Adverb.*

The tree was **uprooted.**

at; āpe; fär; câre; end; mē; it; īce; pîerce; hot; ōld; sông, fôrk; oil; out; up; ūse; rüle; pùll; tûrn; chin; sing; shop; thin; <u>th</u>is; hw in white; zh in treasure. The symbol ə stands for the unstressed vowel sound in about, taken, pencil, lemon, and circus.

U

— The *upstream* fishing is good today. *Adjective.*

up·stream (up′strēm′) *adverb; adjective.*

salmon swimming **upstream**

up-to-date Using or showing the latest developments or style; modern. You can tell this is an *up-to-date* map because it shows the new highway. The fashion model always wore the most *up-to-date* clothes.

up-to-date (up′tə dāt′) *adjective.*

upward From a lower to a higher place or level. The people on the street looked *upward* to see the plane fly overhead. The cost of food has climbed steadily *upward. Adverb.*
—Moving from a lower to a higher place or level. The road we were on had a long *upward* slope. *Adjective.*

up·ward (up′wərd) *adverb; adjective.*

upwards Another spelling of the adverb **upward**. The balloon sailed *upwards* into the cloudless sky. Look up **upward** for more information.

up·wards (up′wərdz) *adverb.*

uranium A silver-colored metal that is radioactive. It is used as a source of nuclear energy. Uranium is a chemical element.

u·ra·ni·um (yu rā′nē əm) *noun.*

Word History

Scientists named **uranium** after the planet *Uranus,* which had just recently been discovered. Both the planet Uranus and the metal uranium were named after *Uranus,* a god of the sky in Roman and Greek mythology.

Uranus The third largest planet in our solar system. It is the seventh planet in distance from the sun. Uranus is surrounded by rings.

U·ra·nus (yur′ə nəs *or* yu rā′nəs) *noun.*

urban In, having to do with, or like a city or city life. In this country the *urban* population is much larger than the rural population.

ur·ban (ûr′bən) *adjective.*

urge **1.** To try to convince or persuade. They *urged* their friend to try out for the football team. **2.** To drive or force on. The rider *urged* the horse on to win the race. **3.** To speak or argue strongly for. The group of citizens *urged* improvements in conditions in the city's prisons. *Verb.*
—A strong desire or impulse. I had a sudden *urge* for a hamburger. *Noun.*

urge (ûrj) *verb,* **urged, urging;** *noun, plural* **urges.**

urgent Needing or demanding immediate action or attention. My boss left the country on *urgent* business. The hospital made an *urgent* request for people to give blood.

ur·gent (ûr′jənt) *adjective.*

urinary system The parts of the body that make, store, and release urine. In humans and other mammals, the urinary system includes the kidneys, the bladder, and the tubes that carry urine.

urine A clear, yellow liquid made up of water and wastes taken out of the blood by the kidneys. Urine is stored in the bladder. From time to time the bladder empties and urine flows out of the body.

u·rine (yur′in) *noun.*

urn **1.** A vase set on a base. Urns are used for decoration or to hold plants. **2.** A container with a faucet that is used to serve coffee or tea. ▲ Another word that sounds like this is **earn.**

urn (ûrn) *noun, plural* **urns.**

Uruguay A country in southeastern South America.

U·ru·guay (yur′ə gwā′ *or* ur′ə gwī′) *noun.*

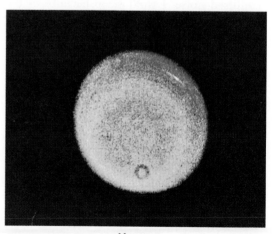

Uranus

us The persons who are speaking or writing. The neighbors invited *us* to a barbecue. Please write to *us* as soon as you can.
us (us *or unstressed* əs) *pronoun.*

U.S. An abbreviation for *United States.*

U.S.A. An abbreviation for *United States of America.*

usable Fit, suitable, or ready for use. This old cup is chipped but still *usable.* This word is also spelled **useable.**
us·a·ble (ū′zə bəl) *adjective.*

usage 1. A way of using or handling something. 2. The usual way in which people use words in speaking or writing. This dictionary gives many examples of English *usage.*
us·age (ū′sij *or* ū′zij) *noun, plural* **usages.**

use To put into service for a particular purpose. May I *use* your scissors? We *use* a dictionary to find out the meanings of words. *Verb.*
—1. The act of using or the state of being used. We made the bookcase with the *use* of a saw and a hammer and nails. The auditorium is in *use* until later this afternoon. 2. The quality of being useful or helpful. There's no *use* worrying about things you can't change. 3. A need or purpose for which something is used. Do you have any *use* for these empty bottles? This tool has many *uses.* 4. The right or ability to use something. May I have the *use* of your bicycle while you are away? 5. The way of using something. My neighbor taught me the proper *use* of a hammer. *Noun.*
• **to make use of.** To use; employ. The carpenter *made use of* the wood scraps.
• **used to.** 1. Did at a time in the past. I *used to* ride a tricycle, but now I ride a bicycle. 2. Familiar with. They live on a farm and are not *used to* the city.
• **to use up.** To use all of. We've *used up* the ketchup, so we'll have to buy more before the barbecue.
use (ūz *for verb;* ūs *for noun*) *verb,* **used, using;** *noun, plural* **uses.**

useable Another spelling of **usable.** Look up **usable** for more information.
use·a·ble (ū′zə bəl) *adjective.*

used That has been used by someone else; not new. I intend to buy a *used* car.
used (ūzd) *adjective.*

useful Serving a good use or purpose; helpful. A pocketknife can be very *useful* on a camping trip.
use·ful (ūs′fəl) *adjective.*

usher A person who leads people to their seats in a church, theater, stadium, or other place. *Noun.*
—To act as an usher; lead. The waiter

ushered us to a table by the window. *Verb.*
ush·er (ush′ər) *noun, plural* **ushers;** *verb,* **ushered, ushering.**

U.S.S.R. An abbreviation for *Union of Soviet Socialist Republics,* the official name for the **Soviet Union.**

usual Common or expected; customary. Hot weather is *usual* for July and August.
u·su·al (ū′zhü əl) *adjective.*

UT Postal abbreviation for *Utah.*

Utah A state in the western United States. Its capital is Salt Lake City.
U·tah (ū′tô *or* ū′tä) *noun.*

Word History

Utah comes from the name of a tribe of American Indians who lived where Colorado and Utah are now. The Indian word may have meant "the people." Congress used this name for the territory of Utah, and the name was later given to the state.

---

utensil An object or tool that is useful or necessary in doing or making something. I keep all my cooking *utensils* in a drawer.
u·ten·sil (ū ten′səl) *noun, plural* **utensils.**

utility 1. The quality of being useful. Scientists are looking into the *utility* of the sun's rays as a source of energy on earth. 2. A company that provides service to the public. Telephone companies are *utilities.*
u·til·i·ty (ū til′i tē) *noun, plural* **utilities.**

utmost Greatest or highest. Everyone in school has the *utmost* respect for our principal. *Adjective.*
—The most or greatest possible. I did my *utmost* to help our team win the game. *Noun.*
ut·most (ut′mōst′) *adjective; noun.*

utter¹ To give voice to; express out loud. We all *uttered* a sigh of relief when the test was over.
ut·ter (ut′ər) *verb,* **uttered, uttering.**

utter² Complete or perfect; total. When the light bulb blew out, we found ourselves in *utter* darkness.
ut·ter (ut′ər) *adjective.*

---

at; āpe; fär; câre; end; mē; it; īce; pîerce; hot; ōld; sông, fôrk; oil; out; up; ūse; rüle; pull; tûrn; chin; sing; shop; thin; this; hw in white; zh in treasure. The symbol ə stands for the unstressed vowel sound in about, taken, pencil, lemon, and circus.

U

1. The first people to write the letter **V** were ancient tribes in the Middle East. They made it like a hook.

2. Ancient Greeks borrowed this letter and wrote it like a capital **Y**, but pronounced it like a *u* sound.

3. An ancient tribe north of Rome wrote this letter as a **V** and used it for both a vowel and a consonant sound.

4. The ancient Romans continued to write and pronounce this letter in the same way.

5. We adopted the **V** from the Romans and eventually used it only for the *v* sound.

v, V   The twenty-second letter of the alphabet.
 v, V (vē) *noun, plural* **v's, V's.**
Va.   An abbreviation for *Virginia.*
VA   Postal abbreviation for *Virginia.*
vacant   **1.** Not having anyone or anything in it; empty. You can sit in the *vacant* chair. The office of president was *vacant* for two months.   **2.** Lacking or seeming to lack intelligence or awareness. The dazed child had a *vacant* stare.
 va·cant (vā′kənt) *adjective.*
vacation   A period of rest or freedom from school, business, or other activity. Summer *vacation* begins next week. Our family took a *vacation* at the shore. *Noun.*
—To take or spend a vacation. We *vacationed* in Canada. *Verb.*
 va·ca·tion (vā kā′shən) *noun, plural* **vacations;** *verb,* **vacationed, vacationing.**
vaccinate   To give a vaccine to.
 vac·ci·nate (vak′sə nāt′) *verb,* **vaccinated, vaccinating.**
vaccination   The act or practice of vaccinating. Our state requires the *vaccination* of dogs for rabies.
 vac·ci·na·tion (vak′sə nā′shən) *noun, plural* **vaccinations.**
vaccine   A liquid that contains the dead or weakened germs of a certain disease. This liquid is swallowed or injected into the body, where it helps the body protect itself against this disease
 vac·cine (vak sēn′ *or* vak′sēn) *noun, plural* **vaccines.**

Word History

The word **vaccine** comes from the Latin word meaning "of a cow." The first vaccine was made from cowpox, a mild disease that people catch from cattle, and was used to vaccinate people against the disease smallpox.

vacuum   **1.** A space that is completely empty of matter. Scientists have not been able to make a perfect vacuum. Therefore, the word *vacuum* usually refers to a space with most but not all of the matter removed. **2.** A vacuum cleaner. *Noun.*
—To clean with a vacuum cleaner. I *vacuumed* the rug before the party. *Verb.*
 vac·u·um (vak′ū əm *or* vak′ūm) *noun, plural* **vacuums;** *verb,* **vacuumed, vacuuming.**

vacuum cleaner A machine that is used for cleaning carpets, floors, and other objects and spaces. A vacuum cleaner works by sucking dirt into its tank or bag.

vague Not clear or definite. I have only a *vague* idea of how to get to the theater. We could see only the *vague* outline of the building in the fog. The candidate's *vague* response contained few facts.
vague (vāg) *adjective,* **vaguer, vaguest.**

vain **1.** Too proud of one's looks, abilities, or accomplishments; conceited. It is *vain* to spend a lot of time looking at yourself in the mirror. **2.** Not successful. The mechanic made a *vain* effort to fix our car. ▲ Other words that sound like this are **vane** and **vein.**
• **in vain.** Without success. The crew's attempts to keep the ship from sinking were *in vain.*
vain (vān) *adjective,* **vainer, vainest.**

valentine **1.** A greeting card sent on Valentine's Day to one's sweetheart or another person. **2.** A sweetheart chosen on Valentine's Day.
val·en·tine (val′ən tīn′) *noun, plural* **valentines.**

Valentine's Day The day, February 14, named in honor of Saint Valentine, an early Christian saint. It is celebrated by the sending of valentines.

valiant Full of or showing courage; brave. The small group of soldiers carried on a *valiant* fight against the enemy. A *valiant* sailor saved the passenger from drowning.
val·iant (val′yənt) *adjective.*

valid **1.** Soundly based on facts or evidence; true. The experiment proved that the scientist's theory was *valid.* **2.** Acceptable under the law or rules. Your library card is not *valid* unless you sign it.
val·id (val′id) *adjective.*

valley **1.** An area of low land between hills or mountains. Valleys often have rivers flowing through them. **2.** An area drained by a river system. The state of Louisiana is in the Mississippi *Valley.*
val·ley (val′ē) *noun, plural* **valleys.**

valuable **1.** Worth much money. The museum has a very *valuable* coin collection. **2.** Having great use or importance. My summer job was a *valuable* experience for me. *Adjective.*
—**valuables.** Things that have great value. The robbers broke in and stole the couple's jewelry and other *valuables. Noun.*
val·u·a·ble (val′ū ə bəl *or* val′yə bəl) *adjective; plural noun.*

value **1.** The worth, usefulness, or importance of something. He places great *value* on her friendship. **2.** The worth of something in money or exchange. The *value* of land in this area has gone up in recent years. **3.** A number, amount, or quantity. What is the *value* of x if $x + 5 = 8$? *Noun.*
—**1.** To think of as being worth an amount in money or exchange; set a price for. The jeweler *valued* the necklace at three thousand dollars. **2.** Think highly of. They have always *valued* their parents' advice. *Verb.*
val·ue (val′ū) *noun, plural* **values;** *verb,* **valued, valuing.**

valve A device that controls the flow of liquid or gases through a pipe or other container. The faucet on the sink works a *valve* that turns the water on and off. The *valves* of the heart control the flow of blood into and out of the heart.
valve (valv) *noun, plural* **valves.**

van **1.** A large, covered truck that is used to move furniture, animals, or other large items. **2.** A small, covered truck with two or more seats inside. It is used for carrying people or things or for recreation.
van (van) *noun, plural* **vans.**

vane A flat or curved blade that is made of wood, metal, or another material. The vanes of a windmill catch the wind and provide the force for the windmill to do work. ▲ Other words that sound like this are **vain** and **vein.**
vane (vān) *noun, plural* **vanes.**

vane

vanilla A flavoring that is used in candies, ice cream, cookies, and other foods. Vanilla comes from the seed pods of a tropical plant that is a type of orchid.
va·nil·la (və nil′ə) *noun.*

---

at; āpe; fär; câre; end; mē; it; īce; pîerce; hot; ōld; sông, fôrk; oil; out; up; ūse; rüle; pùll; tûrn; chin; sing; shop; thin; **th**is; **hw** in white; **zh** in treasure. The symbol ə stands for the unstressed vowel sound in about, taken, pencil, lemon, and circus.

V

vanish To go out of sight or existence; disappear. The airplane *vanished* above the clouds. All hope of winning the game *vanished* when our star player was injured.
van·ish (van'ish) *verb,* **vanished, vanishing.**

vanity Too much pride in one's looks, abilities, or accomplishments; conceit.
van·i·ty (van'i tē) *noun.*

vanquish To defeat or overcome. Our soldiers *vanquished* the enemy in battle.
van·quish (vang'kwish) *verb,* **vanquished, vanquishing.**

vapor Small particles of mist, steam, or smoke that can be seen in the air. When water boils in a pot, you can see the *vapor* rising into the air. My breath formed clouds of *vapor* in the cold air.
va·por (vā'pər) *noun.*

variable 1. Likely to change. The weather is so *variable* at this time of year that I don't know what clothes to pack for my trip. 2. Able to be changed. This wrench has *variable* jaws for different jobs. *Adjective.*
—Something that changes or is likely to change. The temperature is a *variable* at this time of the year. *Noun.*
var·i·a·ble (vâr'ē ə bəl) *adjective; noun,* *plural* **variables.**

variation 1. A change. In the tropics, there is little *variation* in temperature between seasons. 2. The amount by which something changes. There was a *variation* of 15 degrees in temperature between the city and the suburbs. 3. A different form of something. This story is a *variation* of one I heard before.
var·i·a·tion (vâr'ē ā'shən) *noun,* *plural* **variations.**

variety 1. Change or difference; lack of sameness. A job that has no *variety* can become boring. 2. A number of different things. We bought a *variety* of foods at the grocery store. That amusement park has a wide *variety* of rides. 3. A different kind or form of something. This is a new *variety* of umbrella, not quite like any I have seen.
va·ri·e·ty (və rī'i tē) *noun,* *plural* **varieties.**

various 1. Different from one another; of different kinds. Students of *various* backgrounds and nationalities go to our school. 2. More than one; many. We stayed in *various* towns on our vacation.
var·i·ous (vâr'ē əs) *adjective.*

varnish A liquid that gives a hard, clear coating to wood, metal, or other materials it is spread on. *Noun.*
—To put varnish on; cover with varnish. The workers *varnished* the floor. *Verb.*
var·nish (vär'nish) *noun, plural* **varnishes;** *verb,* **varnished, varnishing.**

vary 1. To make or become different; change. The store tries to *vary* its merchandise from season to season. The color of the stone seems to *vary* as you move it around in the light. 2. To be different; differ. The flowers in our garden *vary* widely in color.
var·y (vâr'ē) *verb,* **varied, varying.**

vase A container that is usually higher than it is wide. Vases are mostly used for holding flowers or for decoration.
vase (vās *or* vāz *or* väz) *noun, plural* **vases.**

vases

vassal A person in the Middle Ages who received land and protection from a lord in return for loyalty and service.
vas·sal (vas'əl) *noun, plural* **vassals.**

vast Very great in extent, size, or amount. That ranch covers a *vast* area. A *vast* number of people came to watch the football game.
vast (vast) *adjective,* **vaster, vastest.**

vat A large tank or container used for holding liquids.
vat (vat) *noun, plural* **vats.**

vault 1. An arched structure serving as a roof or ceiling. The *vault* of the tunnel curved up into darkness. 2. A safe room or compartment that is used to store money or other things of value. Banks keep their money in steel *vaults.* 3. A burial chamber. The body of the ruler lay in a marble *vault.*
vault (vôlt) *noun, plural* **vaults.**

VCR The abbreviation for *videocassette recorder.*

VDT The abbreviation for *video display terminal.*

veal The meat of a calf.
veal (vēl) *noun.*

vegetable A plant whose roots, leaves, or other parts are used as food. Carrots, celery, potatoes, lettuce, and beans are vegetables. *Noun.*
—Having to do with or made from vegetables or other plants. On our way back from the country, we stopped at a *vegetable* stand and bought fresh corn. I had *vegetable* soup for lunch. *Adjective.*
veg·e·ta·ble (vej′i tə bəl *or* vej′tə bəl) *noun, plural* **vegetables;** *adjective.*

vegetarian A person who eats only plants and their products and no meat, fish, or poultry. No one at the barbecue was a *vegetarian. Noun.*
—Having to do with eating only plants. Some people prefer a *vegetarian* diet. *Adjective.*
veg·e·tar·i·an (vej′i târ′ē ən) *noun, plural* **vegetarians;** *adjective.*

vegetation Plant life. Jungles have very thick *vegetation.*
veg·e·ta·tion (vej′i tā′shən) *noun.*

vehicle **1.** A means of carrying or transporting people or goods. Automobiles, ships, and airplanes are vehicles. **2.** A means of expressing, communicating, or achieving something. Some writers use poetry as a *vehicle* for their ideas.
ve·hi·cle (vē′i kəl) *noun, plural* **vehicles.**

veil **1.** A piece of very thin material that is worn over the head and shoulders or to conceal the face. **2.** Something that hides. A *veil* of secrecy surrounded the army's plans for the attack. *Noun.*
—To cover or hide with a veil or something like a veil. Some women in the countries of the Middle East *veil* their faces. He tried to *veil* his anger with a smile. *Verb.*
veil (vāl) *noun, plural* **veils;** *verb,* **veiled, veiling.**

vein **1.** One of the blood vessels that carry blood from all parts of the body to the heart. **2.** One of the stiff tubes that form the framework of a leaf or an insect's wing. The veins in a leaf carry food and water to the cells in the leaf. The veins in an insect's wing make the wing strong and firm. **3.** A band of a mineral deposited in a rock. The miners found a *vein* of silver in the mine. **4.** A streak of a different color in marble or other stone or in

veins in an insect's wings

wood. This slab of marble is completely white except for a few black *veins.* **5.** A quality or mood. There was a humorous *vein* in everything that the speaker said. ▲ Other words that sound like this are **vain** and **vane.**
vein (vān) *noun, plural* **veins.**

velocity The rate of motion; speed. Light has a *velocity* of about 186,000 miles per second. The baseball was pitched at a *velocity* close to 95 miles per hour.
ve·loc·i·ty (və los′i tē) *noun, plural* **velocities.**

velvet A fabric with a soft, thick pile. Velvet can be made out of silk, nylon, or other materials. *Noun.*
—**1.** Made of or covered with velvet. The room was furnished with red *velvet* curtains. **2.** That is like velvet in smoothness or softness. My little black kitten has *velvet* fur. *Adjective.*
vel·vet (vel′vit) *noun; adjective.*

vending machine A machine that is worked by putting coins into a slot. Vending machines are used to sell candy, soft drinks, and many other small items.
vend·ing machine (ven′ding).

vendor A person who sells something. I bought an apple from the fruit *vendor* on the corner.
ven·dor (ven′dər) *noun, plural* **vendors.**

Venetian blind A blind used at a window to keep out light. It has a series of horizontal wooden, metal, or plastic slats that can be opened or closed. The blind can be raised or lowered by using cords that are attached to the side.
Ve·ne·tian blind (və nē′shən).

Word History

This kind of shade may be called a **Venetian blind** because it was first made and used in the Italian city of *Venice.*

Venezuela A country in northern South America.
Ven·e·zue·la (ven′ə zwā′lə *or* ven′ə zwē′lə) *noun.*

---

at; āpe; fär; câre; end; mē; it; īce; pîerce; hot; ōld; sông, fôrk; oil; out; up; ūse; rüle; pùll; tûrn; chin; sing; shop; thin; <u>th</u>is; hw in white; zh in treasure. The symbol ə stands for the unstressed vowel sound in about, taken, pencil, lemon, and circus.

V

venison   The meat of a deer.
ven·i·son (ven′ə sən *or* ven′ə zən) *noun.*

venom   The poison of some snakes, spiders, and other animals. The venom can be passed to prey or an enemy by a bite or sting.
ven·om (ven′əm) *noun, plural* **venoms.**

vent   **1.** A hole or other opening through which a gas or liquid passes. A *vent* above the stove lets air out of the kitchen.   **2.** A means of letting something out. They used exercise as a *vent* for their tension. *Noun.*
—To let out. The children *vented* their anger by kicking the door. *Verb.*
vent (vent) *noun, plural* **vents;** *verb,* **vented, venting.**

ventilation   The circulation or change of air. This room gets very good *ventilation* when all the windows are open.
ven·ti·la·tion (ven′tə lā′shən) *noun.*

ventilator   A device or an opening that brings fresh air into a room or other space. A small fan served as a *ventilator* in the attic.
ven·ti·la·tor (ven′tə lā′tər) *noun, plural* **ventilators.**

ventricle   Either of the two lower chambers of the heart. The ventricles receive blood from the auricles and pump it through the arteries to the lungs and the rest of the body.
ven·tri·cle (ven′tri kəl) *noun, plural* **ventricles.**

venture   A task or undertaking that involves risk or danger. The plan to invade the enemy's territory was a *venture* that called for great courage. *Noun.*
—**1.** To put in danger; risk. The firefighters *ventured* their lives by entering the burning building.   **2.** To go despite risk or danger. The sailors *ventured* into the storm searching for the missing boat.   **3.** To express at the risk of criticism. If I had to *venture* a guess, I would say it won't rain today. *Verb.*
ven·ture (ven′chər) *noun, plural* **ventures;** *verb,* **ventured, venturing.**

Venus   The sixth largest planet in our solar system. It is the second planet in order of distance from the sun and the one nearest earth.
Ve·nus (vē′nəs) *noun.*

veranda   An open porch that runs along one or more sides of a building. A veranda usually has a roof. This word is also spelled **verandah.**
ve·ran·da (və ran′də) *noun, plural* **verandas.**

verb   A word that is used to express an action or condition. *Run, buy, be, build, feel, read,* and *seem* are verbs.
verb (vûrb) *noun, plural* **verbs.**

verbal   **1.** Expressed in words; spoken. The police officer asked me to give a *verbal* description of the missing bracelet.   **2.** Having to do with words. My teacher has good *verbal* ability and can explain things well.
ver·bal (vûr′bəl) *adjective.*

verdict   **1.** The decision of a jury in a trial. The jurors agreed on a *verdict* of "guilty."   **2.** A decision or conclusion. The audience's *verdict* was that the play was worth seeing.
ver·dict (vûr′dikt) *noun, plural* **verdicts.**

Vermont   A state in the northeastern United States. Its capital is Montpelier.
Ver·mont (vər mont′) *noun.*

Word History

The area now known as **Vermont** was once known by English settlers as "Green Mountains." The name *Vermont* probably comes from the French words for "green mountain." This name became popular and was chosen as the official name after the area declared itself independent in 1777.

---

versatile   **1.** Able to do many different things well. The *versatile* athlete could play most games with skill.   **2.** Having many uses. A hammer is a *versatile* tool.
ver·sa·tile (vûr′sə təl) *adjective.*

verse   **1.** Words that are written in a particular rhythmic pattern and often in rhyme; poetry.   **2.** A section of a poem or song; stanza. I only know the first *verse* of that song.   **3.** One of the short parts into which the chapters of the Bible are divided.
verse (vûrs) *noun, plural* **verses.**

version   **1.** An account or description given from a particular point of view. There were several different *versions* of who had started the fight.   **2.** A translation from one lan-

veranda

guage into another. I read the English *version* of the story written by the French author.

ver·sion (vûr′zhən) *noun, plural* **versions.**

vertebra One of the small bones that make up the backbone.

ver·te·bra (vûr′tə brə) *noun, plural* **vertebrae** (vûr′tə brē′) or **vertebras.**

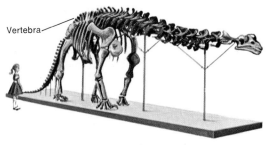

vertebra

vertebrate One of a large group of animals that has a backbone. Fish, amphibians, reptiles, birds, and mammals are vertebrates. *Noun.*

—Having a backbone. Humans are *vertebrate* animals. *Adjective.*

ver·te·brate (vûr′tə brāt′ *or* vûr′tə brit) *noun, plural* **vertebrates;** *adjective.*

vertical Straight up and down; upright. The walls of a building are in a *vertical* position. Look up **horizontal** for a picture of this.

ver·ti·cal (vûr′ti kəl) *adjective.*

very 1. To a high degree; to a great extent. I am *very* sorry that you are not feeling well. 2. Truly; absolutely; exactly. That is the *very* best movie I have ever seen. *Adverb.*

—1. Mere; by itself. The *very* idea of having to get up so early makes me groan. 2. Exact; precise. Your gift was the *very* thing I have been wanting. 3. Absolute; utter. That horse is at the *very* top of its career. *Adjective.*

ver·y (ver′ē) *adverb; adjective.*

Word History

The word **very** comes from an old French word meaning "true."

---

vessel 1. A ship or large boat. Both passenger ships and *vessels* carrying freight were docked at the pier. 2. A hollow container or holder. Vases, cups, and bowls are vessels. 3. A duct in the body for carrying blood or other fluids. Arteries and veins are vessels.

ves·sel (ves′əl) *noun, plural* **vessels.**

vest A short, sleeveless piece of clothing that is worn over a shirt or blouse. *Noun.*

—To give authority or power to. The new president was *vested* with all the rights and powers of the office. *Verb.*

vest (vest) *noun, plural* **vests;** *verb,* **vested, vesting.**

vestige A trace, sign, or evidence of something that no longer exists. The archaeologists discovered *vestiges* of an ancient village.

ves·tige (ves′tij) *noun, plural* **vestiges.**

veteran 1. A person who has had a lot of experience. The actor was a *veteran* of the stage. 2. A person who has been in the armed forces. The police chief is an army *veteran. Noun.*

—Having had a lot of experience. The newspaper sent a *veteran* reporter to cover the important story. *Adjective.*

vet·er·an (vet′ər ən) *noun, plural* **veterans;** *adjective.*

Veterans Day A holiday in the United States that is celebrated on November 11. It honors the people who have served in the armed forces and have fought in wars for the United States.

veterinarian A doctor who treats animals.

vet·er·i·nar·i·an (vet′ər ə nâr′ē ən) *noun, plural* **veterinarians.**

The **veterinarian** is examining the iguana.

veto The power of a president, governor, or official group to keep an act or measure from taking effect. The president can exercise a *veto* over any bill passed by Congress. *Noun.*

—To refuse to approve; stop or prevent by a veto. The governor *vetoed* the bill passed by

---

at; āpe; fär; câre; end; mē; it; īce; pîerce; hot; ōld; sông, fôrk; oil; out; up; ūse; rüle; pull; tûrn; chin; sing; shop; thin; this; hw in white; zh in treasure. The symbol ə stands for the unstressed vowel sound in about, taken, pencil, lemon, and circus.

V

791

the legislature. Our grandparents *vetoed* our idea of going swimming after lunch. *Verb.*
ve·to (vē′tō) *noun, plural* **vetoes;** *verb,* **vetoed, vetoing.**

Word History

The word **veto** comes from a Latin word that means "I forbid." In ancient Rome, there was a government official who was supposed to speak for the common people and protect them from unfair laws. If he did not like a law that the Senate was trying to pass, he would say *veto*—"I forbid."

via By way of. I drove home *via* the highway.
vi·a (vī′ə *or* vē′ə) *preposition.*

vibrate To move or cause to move rapidly back and forth or up and down. The strings of a guitar *vibrate* when they are plucked. I *vibrated* the line to scare the birds away from the wet clothes.
vi·brate (vī′brāt) *verb,* **vibrated, vibrating.**

vibration Rapid movement back and forth or up and down. People many miles away could feel the *vibration* from the earthquake.
vi·bra·tion (vī brā′shən) *noun, plural* **vibrations.**

vice president An officer who ranks second to a president. A vice president takes the place of a president when necessary.
vice pres·i·dent (vīs′ prez′i dənt) *noun, plural* **vice presidents.**

vice versa The opposite in order; the other way around. My brother helps me with my homework, and *vice versa.*
vi·ce ver·sa (vī′sə vûr′sə) *adverb.*

vicinity The area near or surrounding a particular place; neighborhood. There are several parks and playgrounds in the *vicinity* of our house.
vi·cin·i·ty (və sin′i tē) *noun, plural* **vicinities.**

vicious 1. Wicked; evil. The kidnapers planned a *vicious* crime. 2. Full of spite; malicious. They told *vicious* lies to try to put the blame on someone else. 3. Fierce or dangerous. The *vicious* dog bit two children.
vi·cious (vish′əs) *adjective.*

victim 1. A person who is injured, killed, or ruined. A friend of ours was the *victim* of an automobile accident. 2. A person who is cheated or tricked. My friend was the *victim*

of a dishonest lawyer and lost $200.
vic·tim (vik′təm) *noun, plural* **victims.**

victorious 1. Having won a victory. The *victorious* army was welcomed home. 2. Having to do with victory. The nation hoped for a *victorious* end of the war.
vic·to·ri·ous (vik tôr′ē əs) *adjective.*

victory The defeat of an enemy or opponent. Our team gained its first *victory* of the season in yesterday's game. *Victory* over hunger in the world is not impossible.
vic·to·ry (vik′tə rē) *noun, plural* **victories.**

video Having to do with the picture part of television or with the display on a computer screen. *Adjective.*
—The picture part of television. *Noun.*
vid·e·o (vid′ē ō′) *adjective; noun, plural* **videos.**

videocassette A videotape in a cassette. It can be recorded on and played by a videocassette recorder.
vid·e·o·cas·sette (vid′ē ō kə set′) *noun, plural* **videocassettes.**

videocassette recorder An electronic device that records on and plays videotapes.

video display terminal A keyboard and monitor for a computer. A video display terminal can be used to type information to be put into the computer and to retrieve information from the computer for display on the monitor.

video game A game that is played on a television or computer screen. A player can move images on the screen with the help of special controls.

videotape 1. A strip of magnetic tape on which pictures as well as sound can be recorded. 2. A recording made on this kind of tape. Our friends made a *videotape* of their wedding. *Noun.*
—To make a recording of something on videotape. We *videotaped* the fire next door, and the tape was shown on the local news. *Verb.*
vid·e·o·tape (vid′ē ō tāp′) *noun, plural* **videotapes;** *verb,* **videotaped, videotaping.**

Vietnam A country in southeastern Asia.
Vi·et·nam (vē′et näm′) *noun.*

Vietnamese 1. the Vietnamese. The people of Vietnam. 2. The language spoken in Vietnam. *Noun.*
—Of or having to do with Vietnam, its people, or its language. *Adjective.*
Vi·et·nam·ese (vē′et nə mēz′ *or* vē et′nə mēs′) *noun; adjective.*

view 1. The act of looking or seeing; sight. The sailors got their first *view* of land after many weeks at sea. 2. The range or extent

of seeing. The airplane suddenly came into *view*. **3.** Something that is seen or can be seen. We have a lovely *view* of the lake from our window. **4.** A particular way of thinking about something; opinion. The two friends had different *views* on who would make the best class president. *Noun.*
—**1.** To look at or see. Many people *viewed* the exhibit at the museum. **2.** To think about; consider. The people *viewed* the president's new education bill with approval. *Verb.*
   view (vū) *noun, plural* **views;** *verb,* **viewed, viewing.**

vigor **1.** Active power or force; strength. The mayor opposed with *vigor* the proposal to widen the highway. **2.** Healthy strength. Even though my grandparents are both over eighty, they are still full of *vigor*.
   vig·or (vig′ər) *noun.*

vigorous Full of or done with vigor. Our dog is still just as *vigorous* as it was when it was a puppy.
   vig·or·ous (vig′ər əs) *adjective.*

Viking A member of a people who lived in Norway, Sweden, Denmark, and Iceland. The Vikings built ships, raided the coasts of Europe, and voyaged to North America during the eighth to eleventh centuries.
   Vi·king (vī′king) *noun, plural* **Vikings.**

village **1.** A small group of houses. A village is usually smaller than a town. The countryside was dotted with *villages*. **2.** The people who live in a village. The whole *village* came to the wedding.
   vil·lage (vil′ij) *noun, plural* **villages.**

villain A wicked or evil person. In the story, the *villains* tried to trick the child into going away with them.
   vil·lain (vil′ən) *noun, plural* **villains.**

vine A plant with a long, thin stem that grows along the ground or climbs on trees, fences, or other supports. Grapes, melons, and squash grow on vines.
   vine (vīn) *noun, plural* **vines.**

vinegar A sour liquid that is made by fermenting cider, wine, or juice. Vinegar is used in salad dressing and to flavor and preserve food.
   vin·e·gar (vin′i gər) *noun, plural* **vinegars.**

Word History

The word **vinegar** comes from two old French words meaning "wine" and "sour."

vineyard An area where grapes are grown.
   vine·yard (vin′yərd) *noun, plural* **vineyards.**

vinyl A flexible, shiny plastic used to make floor tiles, raincoats, phonograph records, and other products.
   vi·nyl (vī′nəl) *noun, plural* **vinyls.**

viola A musical instrument that looks like a violin but is a little larger.
   vi·o·la (vē ō′lə) *noun, plural* **violas.**

violate **1.** To fail to obey or keep; break. The driver *violated* the law by going through a red light. **2.** To break in on; disrupt. The quiet of the afternoon was *violated* by the loud radio.
   vi·o·late (vī′ə lāt′) *verb,* **violated, violating.**

violence **1.** Strong physical force used to harm. The robbers threatened to use *violence* if the banker did not open the vault. **2.** Great or destructive force or action. The *violence* of the hurricane left few houses standing.
   vi·o·lence (vī′ə ləns) *noun.*

violent **1.** Acting with, characterized by, or resulting from strong physical force. The falling branch gave the gardener a *violent* blow on the head. **2.** Caused by or showing strong feeling or emotion. My friend has a *violent* temper.
   vi·o·lent (vī′ə lənt) *adjective.*

violet A small purple, white, or pink flower that grows on a low plant. Many violets grow wild, while others are grown in gardens and indoors.
   vi·o·let (vī′ə lit) *noun, plural* **violets.**

violin A musical instrument that has four strings and is played with a bow.
   vi·o·lin (vī′ə lin′) *noun, plural* **violins.**

violets

at; āpe; fär; câre; end; mē; it; īce; pîerce; hot; ōld; sông, fôrk; oil; out; up; ūse; rüle; půll; tûrn; chin; sing; shop; thin; <u>th</u>is; hw in white; zh in treasure. The symbol ə stands for the unstressed vowel sound in about, taken, pencil, lemon, and circus.

V

violinists

violinist A person who plays the violin. A solo *violinist* performed with the symphony last night.
vi·o·lin·ist (vī'ə lin'ist) *noun, plural* **violinists.**

virgin Not yet used or touched. We made footprints in the *virgin* snow. The early settlers in America cut down *virgin* forests to make way for farms.
vir·gin (vûr'jin) *adjective.*

Virginia A state in the eastern United States. Its capital is Richmond.
Vir·gin·ia (vûr jin'yə) *noun.*

Word History

Virginia takes its name from a poetic title, "the Virgin Queen," that was given to the English queen Elizabeth I. The colony of Virginia was founded during the reign of Queen Elizabeth and named in her honor.

Virgin Islands A group of islands in the Caribbean Sea. Some of them belong to the United States, and the others belong to the United Kingdom.

virtually In almost every way; practically. The twins are *virtually* identical.
vir·tu·al·ly (vûr'chü ə lē) *adverb.*

virtue 1. Moral goodness in one's thinking and behavior. Their *virtue* is shown in the thoughtful things they do for other people. 2. A particular type of moral goodness. Honesty is a *virtue*. 3. Any good quality or characteristic. This small car has the *virtue* of fitting into tiny parking spaces.
vir·tue (vûr'chü) *noun, plural* **virtues.**

virus 1. A very tiny particle that can reproduce only when it is inside a living cell. Vi-ruses cause many diseases, such as polio, measles, and the common cold. 2. A disease caused by a virus.
vi·rus (vī'rəs) *noun, plural* **viruses.**

vise A device with two jaws that are opened and closed with a screw or lever. A vise is used to hold an object firmly in place while it is being worked on.
vise (vīs) *noun, plural* **vises.**

visibility 1. The condition or quality of being visible. I painted my bicycle silver to improve its *visibility* at night. 2. The distance that the eye can see under particular physical conditions, such as the amount of light or the weather. Because of the fog, *visibility* is only a quarter of a mile today.
vis·i·bil·i·ty (viz'ə bil'i tē) *noun.*

visible 1. Able to be seen. Their house is *visible* from the road. 2. Easily seen or understood. The new mayor has made many promises, but there has been no *visible* improvement in the city government.
vis·i·ble (viz'ə bəl) *adjective.*

vision 1. The act or power of seeing; sense of sight. Your *vision* can weaken as you grow older. 2. Something that is or has been seen. A vision is usually something beautiful. The flower garden was a *vision* in red and yellow. 3. The ability to plan ahead; foresight. Designing a new highway is a job that calls for *vision*. 4. Something that is imagined or dreamed. The young writer had *visions* of success and fame.
vi·sion (vizh'ən) *noun, plural* **visions.**

visit 1. To go or come to see. We *visited* my grandparents last Sunday. 2. To stay with as a guest. Friends from Massachusetts *visited* us for the weekend. 3. To go to for pleasure. We *visited* the shore last week. *Verb.*
—A short stay or call. We paid a *visit* to my old friend last night. *Noun.*
vis·it (viz'it) *verb,* **visited, visiting;** *noun, plural* **visits.**

visitor A person who visits; guest. We have to clean up our rooms because we are having *visitors* this afternoon.
vis·i·tor (viz'i tər) *noun, plural* **visitors.**

visor A brim that sticks out on the front of a cap. A visor is made to shade the eyes from the sun.
vi·sor (vī'zər) *noun, plural* **visors.**

visual 1. Having to do with or used in seeing. Eyeglasses are used to correct *visual* defects. 2. Able to be seen; visible. The teacher used charts, slides, and other *visual* aids to help explain how the heart works.
vis·u·al (vizh'ü əl) *adjective.*

vital **1.** Having to do with life. The victim's heartbeat and other *vital* signs began to weaken. **2.** Necessary to or supporting life. The lungs are *vital* organs. **3.** Full of life and energy. My best friend has a *vital* personality and is interested in many things. **4.** Very important or necessary. Proper clothing is *vital* for our camping trip.
vi·tal (vī′təl) *adjective.*

vitamin One of a group of substances that are needed in small amounts for the health and the normal working of the body. We get most of the vitamins we need from eating the right kinds of food.
vi·ta·min (vī′tə min) *noun, plural* **vitamins.**

Word History

The word **vitamin** comes from a Latin word meaning "life." Vitamins are essential to life.

vivid **1.** Bright and strong; brilliant. The room was painted a *vivid* yellow. **2.** Clear and sharp. Some old people have *vivid* memories of their childhood. The witness gave a *vivid* description of the robber. **3.** Active; lively. You must have a *vivid* imagination to be able to write such good stories.
viv·id (viv′id) *adjective.*

vocabulary **1.** All the words used or understood by a person or group. English has one of the largest vocabularies of any language. Doctors use a special *vocabulary* when they talk to each other about medical matters. **2.** A list of words and their meanings in alphabetical order.
vo·cab·u·lar·y (vō kab′yə ler′ē) *noun, plural* **vocabularies.**

vocal **1.** Having to do with or expressed by the voice. Babies produce *vocal* sounds before they learn how to talk. **2.** Performed by or composed for the voice. Our glee club performs all kinds of *vocal* music. **3.** Readily expressing one's views in speech. My cousins are so *vocal* that they offend some people.
vo·cal (vō′kəl) *adjective.*

vocal cords Two folds of skin found in the part of the throat called the larynx. There are two pairs of vocal cords in the larynx. Air from the lungs passes through the lower pair and causes them to vibrate. This makes the sound of the voice.

voice **1.** The sound that is produced through the mouth by speaking, singing, or shouting. I knew you were home from work because I could hear your *voice* downstairs. **2.** The ability to produce sound through the mouth; speech. I lost my *voice* yesterday because of a sore throat. **3.** The right to express a view, opinion, or choice. We believe that the people must have a *voice* in the running of their government. *Noun.*
—To express or utter. The teacher encouraged the students to *voice* their opinions in class. *Verb.*
voice (vois) *noun, plural* **voices;** *verb,* **voiced, voicing.**

volcano An opening in the surface of the earth through which lava, gases, and ashes are forced out. Volcanoes often look like mountains that have the shape of a cone.
vol·ca·no (vol kā′nō) *noun, plural* **volcanoes** or **volcanos.**

volcano

Word History

The English word **volcano** comes from the Italian word for the same thing. The Italian word comes from the name *Vulcan,* the Roman god of fire.

volleyball **1.** A game in which two teams stand on either side of a high net and hit a ball back and forth with their hands. Each side tries not to let the ball touch the ground. **2.** The ball that is used in this game.
vol·ley·ball (vol′ē bôl′) *noun, plural* **volleyballs.**

at; āpe; fär; câre; end; mē; it; īce; pîerce; hot; ōld; sông, fôrk; oil; out; up; ūse; rüle; pùll; tûrn; chin; sing; shop; thin; <u>th</u>is; hw in white; zh in treasure. The symbol ə stands for the unstressed vowel sound in about, taken, pencil, lemon, and circus.

V

795

volt A unit for measuring the force of an electric current.
  volt (vōlt) *noun, plural* **volts.**

Word History

The word **volt** comes from the name of Alessandro *Volta,* an Italian scientist who invented the first electric battery.

voltage The force of an electric current measured in volts.
  vol·tage (vōl′tij) *noun, plural* **voltages.**

volume **1.** A book. Our school has a library of 10,000 *volumes.* **2.** One of a set or series of related books, newspapers, or magazines. The first *volume* of that encyclopedia has an article on Africa. **3.** The amount of space occupied. The *volume* of a room can be found by multiplying its height by its length by its width. **4.** The amount of sound. Please turn down the *volume* on the radio.
  vol·ume (vol′ūm) *noun, plural* **volumes.**

voluntary **1.** Done, made, or acting of one's own free will; not forced. The robber made a *voluntary* confession to the police. **2.** Doing something freely; volunteering. There are many *voluntary* workers in that hospital. **3.** Controlled by the will. Raising an arm is done by *voluntary* muscles, but digesting food in the stomach is not.
  vol·un·tar·y (vol′ən ter′ē) *adjective.*

volunteer **1.** A person who offers to help or does something by choice and often without pay. The teacher asked for *volunteers* for the decorating committee. Many *volunteers* are helping in my cousin's campaign for mayor. **2.** A person who makes a voluntary decision to join the armed forces. *Noun.*
  —**1.** To offer to help or do something of one's own free will. My friend *volunteered* to coach the baseball team. **2.** To give or offer readily. I *volunteered* an answer to the question. *Verb.*
  —Having to do with or serving as a volunteer. My cousin is a *volunteer* firefighter in our town. *Adjective.*
  vol·un·teer (vol′ən tîr′) *noun, plural* **volunteers;** *verb,* **volunteered, volunteering;** *adjective.*

vomit To bring up food and other substances from the stomach and expel them through the mouth. *Verb.*
  —The matter that comes out of the stomach when a person vomits. *Noun.*
  vom·it (vom′it) *verb,* **vomited, vomiting;** *noun.*

vote **1.** The formal expression of a wish or choice. A vote can be taken by ballot, by voice, or by a show of hands. **2.** A decision made by such means. The group's *vote* was to end the meeting. **3.** The right of expressing such a wish or choice. In some countries large groups of people have not been given the *vote.* **4.** The number of votes cast. The *vote* for the proposal was 250 to 150. *Noun.*
  —**1.** To express one's wish or choice by a vote. At our club meetings, we *vote* by a show of hands. **2.** To give or establish by a vote. The school board *voted* money for a new library. *Verb.*
  vote (vōt) *noun, plural* **votes;** *verb,* **voted, voting.**

Word History

The word **vote** comes from a Latin word meaning "a vow," "a promise," or "a wish."

vow A solemn promise or pledge. The soldiers took a *vow* of loyalty to the government. *Noun.*
  —To promise or pledge solemnly. The bride and groom *vowed* to love and support each other. *Verb.*
  vow (vou) *noun, plural* **vows;** *verb,* **vowed, vowing.**

vowel **1.** A speech sound made by not blocking the flow of air through the mouth. **2.** A letter that represents such a sound. *A, e, i, o, u,* and sometimes *y* are vowels.
  vow·el (vou′əl) *noun, plural* **vowels.**

voyage **1.** A journey by water or through space. The ship's *voyage* across the Atlantic took one week. **2.** A long journey. *Noun.*
  —To journey by water or through space. Astronauts *voyaged* to the moon in 1969. *Verb.*
  voy·age (voi′ij) *noun, plural* **voyages;** *verb,* **voyaged, voyaging.**

Vt. An abbreviation for *Vermont.*

VT Postal abbreviation for *Vermont.*

vulgar **1.** Showing or marked by a lack of good manners or taste. The motel had the most *vulgar* decorations I had ever seen. **2.** Offensive in words. The driver told a *vulgar* joke.
  vul·gar (vul′gər) *adjective.*

vulture **1.** A large bird that has dark, dull feathers and a bald head and neck. Vultures are related to hawks and eagles. They feed on the meat of dead animals. **2.** A person who cheats or preys upon a weaker person.
  vul·ture (vul′chər) *noun, plural* **vultures.**

1. Our letter **W** began as an early form of **V**, which was first used by ancient tribes in the Middle East.

2. The ancient Greeks borrowed this letter, making it like a capital **Y**. They used it for the *u* sound.

3. An ancient tribe that settled near Rome then borrowed the letter, changing it to the shape of a **V**.

4. About 2,400 years ago the ancient Romans gave this letter both a vowel and a consonant sound.

5. When **U** became a separate letter, people put two **U**'s together to make a "double U." From this, our **W** developed.

w, W   The twenty-third letter of the alphabet.
  w, W (dub′əl ū′) *noun, plural* **w's, W's.**
W or **W.**   An abbreviation for *west* or *western.*
WA   Postal abbreviation for *Washington.*
wad   **1.** A small, tightly packed lump of soft material. The nurse cleaned my cut with a *wad* of cotton. I stepped on a *wad* of chewing gum.   **2.** A tight roll of paper. The train conductor took out a large *wad* of dollar bills and gave me my change. *Noun.*
  —To roll, press, or pack into a wad. I *wadded* up the letter and threw it away. *Verb.*
  wad (wod) *noun, plural* **wads;** *verb,* **wadded, wadding.**
waddle   To walk or move with short steps, swaying the body from side to side. The duck *waddled* across the yard. *Verb.*
  —A swaying or rocking walk. The audience laughed at the clown's *waddle. Noun.*
  wad·dle (wod′əl) *verb,* **waddled, waddling;** *noun, plural* **waddles.**
wade   **1.** To walk in or through water or mud. We *waded* in the shallow pool.   **2.** To move or make one's way slowly and with difficulty. The secretary had to *wade* through a pile of papers to find the missing letter.
  wade (wād) *verb,* **waded, wading.**
wafer   A thin, crisp cookie or cracker.
  wa·fer (wā′fər) *noun, plural* **wafers.**
waffle   A crisp cake made of batter. Waffles have crisscross markings on them that are made by the utensil they are cooked in.
  waf·fle (wof′əl) *noun, plural* **waffles.**
wag   To move quickly from side to side or up and down. The friendly dog *wagged* its tail when the visitors arrived. *Verb.*
  —The act of wagging; wagging motion. The puppy greeted us with a *wag* of its tail. *Noun.*
  wag (wag) *verb,* **wagged, wagging;** *noun, plural* **wags.**
wage   Payment for work done. The factory pays a *wage* of $6.50 per hour to the workers. *Noun.*
  —To carry on or take part in. The rebels are *waging* a war against the government. *Verb.*
  wage (wāj) *noun, plural* **wages;** *verb,* **waged, waging.**
wager   An agreement or promise to give or pay something to another person if he or she is right about something and you are wrong; bet. They made a *wager* on which team would win the football game. *Noun.*
  —To make a wager; bet. I'll *wager* a dollar that you can't beat me at this game. *Verb.*
  wa·ger (wā′jər) *noun, plural* **wagers;** *verb,* **wagered, wagering.**

W

wagon **1.** A vehicle that has four wheels. It is used for carrying heavy loads. Wagons are usually drawn by a horse or horses. **2.** A low vehicle with four wheels that is pulled by a long handle.
wag·on (wag′ən) *noun, plural* **wagons.**

The boy pulls the **wagon.**

waif A homeless, lost, or abandoned person or animal, especially a young child. I read a sad story about a city filled with poor *waifs* who were cold and hungry.
waif (wāf) *noun, plural* **waifs.**

wail To make a long, sad cry or sound. The unhappy child sat down and *wailed.* The wind *wailed* all through the night. *Verb.*
—A long, sad cry or sound. The children were frightened by the *wail* of the wind. *Noun.*
wail (wāl) *verb,* **wailed, wailing;** *noun, plural* **wails.**

waist **1.** The part of the human body between the ribs and the hips. **2.** A piece of clothing or part of a piece of clothing that covers this part of the body. The dress had a high *waist.* ⚠ Another word that sounds like this is **waste.**
waist (wāst) *noun, plural* **waists.**

wait **1.** To stay in a place until someone comes or something happens. "*Wait* for me!" called my friend. *Wait* until it stops raining before you leave. **2.** To be put off or delayed. The job of cleaning out the garage can *wait* until next week. *Verb.*
—The act of waiting or the amount of time spent waiting. There will be a two-hour *wait* before the next plane. *Noun.* ⚠ Another word that sounds like this is **weight.**
• **to wait on.** To serve or help. A nice salesperson *waited on* us at the book store.
wait (wāt) *verb,* **waited, waiting;** *noun, plural* **waits.**

waiter A man whose job is serving food or drink in a restaurant or other place.
wait·er (wā′tər) *noun, plural* **waiters.**

waiting room A room or area in which people wait, as in a doctor's office or at an airport. I sat in the *waiting room* for hours because my flight was delayed.

waitress A woman whose job is serving food or drink in a restaurant or other place.
wait·ress (wā′tris) *noun, plural* **waitresses.**

wake¹ To stop or cause to stop sleeping. I *waked* at nine o'clock this morning. Be quiet or you will *wake* the baby. *Verb.*
—A watch over the body of a dead person before burial. *Noun.*
• **to wake up.** To stop or cause to stop sleeping. I usually *wake up* at 7 A.M. A fire engine's siren *woke* us *up* last night.
wake (wāk) *verb,* **waked** or **woke, waked** or **woken, waking;** *noun, plural* **wakes.**

wake² The track of waves or foam left by a boat, ship, or other thing moving through water.
wake (wāk) *noun, plural* **wakes.**

waken **1.** To stop or cause to stop sleeping; wake. Do you need an alarm clock, or will you *waken* by yourself? If you're not quiet, you will *waken* the dogs. **2.** To make active; stir up. Visiting the art museum *wakened* my interest in learning how to paint.
wak·en (wā′kən) *verb,* **wakened, wakening.**

Wales A section of the United Kingdom. It is in the southwestern part of the island of Great Britain.
Wales (wālz) *noun.*

walk **1.** To move or travel on foot at a normal, slow pace. A person walks by placing one foot on the ground before lifting the other. **2.** To move through, over, or across on foot. Let's *walk* the beach after we swim. **3.** To go with on foot. I'll *walk* you to the corner. **4.** To make or help to walk. We *walk* the dog twice a day. **5.** To go or allow a batter to go to first base in baseball because four balls have been pitched. *Verb.*
—**1.** The act of walking. We took a *walk* around the park. **2.** A distance covered or a time spent walking. It's a long *walk* to your house. The beach is only a ten-minute *walk* from here. **3.** A path or area set apart for walking. There is a shady *walk* along the lake. **4.** A particular social position or occupation. People from all *walks* of life live in this neighborhood. *Noun.*
walk (wôk) *verb,* **walked, walking;** *noun, plural* **walks.**

walkie-talkie   A portable electronic device that is used to send and receive voice messages by radio over short distances.
walk·ie-talk·ie (wô′kē tô′kē) *noun, plural* **walkie-talkies.**

wall   **1.** A solid structure that forms a side of a building, room, or space. That school building has brick *walls.* The *walls* of my room are decorated with pictures. A stone *wall* separates our yard from the neighbor's. **2.** Something hard to get over that blocks the way; barrier. A *wall* of fire kept the firefighters from getting near the burning house. *Noun.*
—To divide, surround, or block with a wall or walls. The workers *walled* up the old entrance to the building. *Verb.*
wall (wôl) *noun, plural* **walls;** *verb,* **walled, walling.**

wallet   A flat, folding case for holding money, cards, or photographs.
wal·let (wol′it *or* wô′lit) *noun, plural* **wallets.**

wallop   **1.** To give a beating to; thrash. **2.** To hit hard; smack. The batter *walloped* the ball out of the stadium. *Verb.*
—A hard, powerful blow. *Noun.*
wal·lop (wol′əp) *verb,* **walloped, walloping;** *noun, plural* **wallops.**

wallow   To toss or roll about in something. Pigs *wallow* in mud to stay cool.
wal·low (wol′ō) *verb,* **wallowed, wallowing;** *noun, plural* **wallows.**

wallpaper   Paper that is pasted on the walls of a room to decorate them. Wallpaper is usually colored or has designs or patterns printed on it. *Noun.*
—To put wallpaper on the walls of. The roommates *wallpapered* their room. *Verb.*
wall·pa·per (wôl′pā′pər) *noun, plural* **wallpapers;** *verb,* **wallpapered, wallpapering.**

walnut   A sweet, oily nut that has a hard shell. Walnuts grow on tall trees. The wood of the walnut tree is used to make furniture.
wal·nut (wôl′nut′) *noun, plural* **walnuts.**

Kernel

Nut

walnut

walrus   A large animal that lives in water in Arctic regions. Walruses have flippers like seals but are larger and have a pair of long ivory tusks and a tough hide.
wal·rus (wôl′rəs *or* wol′rəs) *noun, plural* **walruses** or **walrus.**

walrus

Word History

The word **walrus** comes from the Dutch name for this animal. The Dutch word means "whale horse."

waltz   **1.** A whirling, gliding dance that is performed by a couple.   **2.** The music for this dance. *Noun.*
—To dance a waltz. *Verb.*
waltz (wôlts) *noun, plural* **waltzes;** *verb,* **waltzed, waltzing.**

wampum   Small, polished beads made from shells and strung together or woven into belts, collars, and necklaces. Wampum was used by some American Indians as money.
wam·pum (wom′pəm *or* wôm′pəm) *noun.*

wand   A thin rod or stick. The magician waved a *wand* over the hat and flowers appeared.
wand (wond) *noun, plural* **wands.**

wander   **1.** To go or move about with no particular place to go. We *wandered* through the woods looking for flowers.   **2.** To lose one's way; stray. They *wandered* off the trail and got lost.   **3.** To stray from a subject. My mind *wandered* during the play.
wan·der (won′dər) *verb,* **wandered, wandering.**

at; āpe; fär; câre; end; mē; it; īce; pîerce; hot; ōld; sông, fôrk; oil; out; up; ūse; rüle; pu̇ll; tûrn; chin; sing; shop; thin; <u>th</u>is; hw in white; zh in treasure. The symbol ə stands for the unstressed vowel sound in about, taken, pencil, lemon, and circus.

W

want **1.** To feel an impulse to have or do something; wish for; desire. My neighbor *wanted* a new bicycle. I *want* to go home. **2.** To have need of; lack. Those curtains *want* washing. *Verb.*
—**1.** An impulse to have or do something; desire. They live simply, and their *wants* are few. **2.** A need; lack. For *want* of wood, the first settlers on the prairie built their house of sod. **3.** Lack of money and necessary things; poverty. The homeless people lived in great *want. Noun.*
> **want** (wont *or* wônt) *verb,* **wanted, wanting;** *noun, plural* **wants.**

wanting Missing; lacking. The only thing *wanting* is mustard for the hot dogs.
> **want·ing** (won′ting *or* wôn′ting) *adjective.*

war **1.** A state or time of armed fighting between countries or different groups within a country. The two nations could not settle their disagreements peacefully, and *war* broke out. **2.** A long struggle or fight. Many millions of dollars are spent each year in the *war* against cancer. *Noun.*
—To carry on a war; fight. The two countries *warred* for many years before a peace treaty was finally signed. *Verb.* ▲ Another word that sounds like this is **wore.**
> **war** (wôr) *noun, plural* **wars;** *verb,* **warred, warring.**

warbler Any of a number of small, lively American song-birds. Most warblers have bright feathers.
> **war·bler** (wôr′ blər) *noun, plural* **warblers.**

warbler

ward **1.** A large room or section of a hospital. A number of patients are taken care of in a ward. The children's *ward* has one hundred beds. **2.** A person who is under the care or control of a court or another person acting as guardian. **3.** A division of a city or town. Cities and towns are divided into wards for purposes of local government. *Noun.*
> • **to ward off.** To keep or force away. Our soldiers *warded off* the enemy attack.
> **ward** (wôrd) *noun, plural* **wards;** *verb,* **warded, warding.**

warden **1.** A person who is in charge of prison. **2.** An official who patrols an area

and sees that certain laws are obeyed there. The game *warden* reminded us that we could only catch three trout in the lake.
> **ward·en** (wôr′dən) *noun, plural* **wardens.**

wardrobe **1.** A collection of clothing. That opera company has a large *wardrobe* of costumes. **2.** A piece of furniture or a closet for keeping clothes. Instead of a closet, the hotel room had a large wooden *wardrobe.*
> **ward·robe** (wôr′drōb′) *noun.*

Word History

The word **wardrobe** comes from an old French word used for a place to keep clothes. The French word was made up of two words that mean "to guard" and "a piece of clothing."

---

ware **1. wares.** Things for sale. The street vendors put their *wares* on display in the public square. **2.** Dishes, pots, and other things used for cooking or eating. We bought a new piece of ceramic *ware* at the fair. ▲ Another word that sounds like this is **wear.**
> **ware** (wâr) *noun, plural* **wares.**

warehouse A building where merchandise is stored. The new sofa we ordered will be sent from the *warehouse.*
> **ware·house** (wâr′hous′) *noun, plural* **warehouses** (wâr′hou′zīz).

warfare Armed fighting between countries or groups; war.
> **war·fare** (wôr′fâr′) *noun.*

warlike **1.** Favoring war; quick to go to war. Some of the native people in that country were *warlike,* and some were peaceful. **2.** Threatening war; hostile. Sinking the foreign ship was a *warlike* act.
> **war·like** (wôr′līk′) *adjective.*

warm **1.** Somewhat hot; not cold. The fire made the room *warm.* I'm going to take a *warm* bath. **2.** Having a feeling of heat in or on the body. My hands were *warm* inside my mittens. **3.** Giving off heat. The *warm* fire made the autumn night less chilly. **4.** Holding in heat. We all wore *warm* clothing on the camping trip. **5.** Full of or showing strong, usually friendly feelings. A hug is a *warm* greeting. I was grateful for my teacher's *warm,* encouraging words. *Adjective.*
—**1.** To make or become warm or heated. Please *warm* the milk for the baby. The soup will *warm* quickly on the stove. **2.** To fill or be filled with strong, usually friendly feelings. The sight of home *warmed* their hearts. The family *warmed* to the little puppy. *Verb.*

• **to warm up.   1.** To make warm. Please *warm up* the rolls in the oven.   **2.** To get ready by practicing or exercising. The team *warmed up* before the game.   **3.** To make or become more friendly or enthusiastic. The two strangers started to talk and soon *warmed up* to each other.
warm (wôrm) *adjective,* **warmer, warmest;** *verb,* **warmed, warming.**

warm-blooded   Having a body temperature that stays the same even when the temperature of the air or of other surroundings changes. Mammals and birds are warm-blooded. Snakes and turtles are cold-blooded.
warm·blood·ed (wôrm′blud′id) *adjective.*

warmth   The state or quality of being warm. We felt the *warmth* of the sun on our faces. The actor was pleased by the *warmth* of the audience's applause.
warmth (wôrmth) *noun.*

warn   1. To tell beforehand about something that may happen; put on guard; alert. The news on the radio *warned* us of the coming storm. The flashing yellow light *warned* of danger ahead.   **2.** To give advice to. Dentists *warn* us not to eat too much candy.
warn (wôrn) *verb,* **warned, warning.**

warning   Notice or advice given beforehand of a danger or a possible bad result. The *warning* on the label said the bottle contained poison.
warn·ing (wôr′ning) *noun, plural* **warnings.**

warrant   An official paper that gives the police authority for an arrest, a search, or some other action. A judge gave the police a *warrant* to search the house. *Noun.*
—To give good reason for; justify; deserve. Your courage *warrants* high praise. *Verb.*
war·rant (wôr′ənt *or* wor′ənt) *noun, plural* **warrants;** *verb,* **warranted, warranting.**

warrior   A person who fights or is experienced in fighting battles.
war·ri·or (wôr′ē ər *or* wor′ē ər) *noun, plural* **warriors.**

warship   A ship built and armed for use in war.
war·ship (wôr′ship′) *noun, plural* **warships.**

wart   1. A small, hard lump that grows on the skin. A wart is caused by a virus.   **2.** A small lump that grows on part of a plant.
wart (wôrt) *noun, plural* **warts.**

wary   Watching carefully; alert; cautious. Always be *wary* when crossing a busy street.
war·y (wâr′ē) *adjective,* **warier, wariest.**

was   A form of the past tense of **be** that is used with *I, he, she, it,* or the name of a person, place, or thing. I *was* at home yesterday. The robin *was* building a nest. Look up **be** for more information.
was (wuz *or* woz *or unstressed* wəz) *verb.*

wash   1. To make free of dirt, germs, or the like by using water or soap and water. I *washed* my face.   **2.** To take out or away by using water or soap and water. I *washed* the gravy stain out of the tablecloth.   **3.** To clean oneself.   **4.** To carry away, wear away, or destroy by flowing water. The rain *washed* away the fertilizer on the lawn. *Verb.*
—**1.** The act of washing. I gave my hands a quick *wash.*   **2.** The amount of clothes or other things washed at one time. I hung the *wash* on the line to dry.   **3.** A flow or rush of water, or the sound made by this. We could hear the *wash* of the waves on the beach.   **4.** A special liquid that is used for bathing, rinsing, or cleansing. The doctor gave me a *wash* for my infected eye. *Noun.*
wash (wôsh *or* wosh) *verb,* **washed, washing;** *noun, plural* **washes.**

Wash.   An abbreviation for *Washington.*

washer   1. A person who washes.   **2.** A machine for washing.   **3.** A flat ring of metal, rubber, or other material. It is placed between a nut and a bolt to give a tighter fit. The leaking faucet needs a new *washer.*
wash·er (wô′shər *or* wosh′ər) *noun, plural* **washers.**

washing machine   A machine for washing clothes and other things.

Washington   1. A state in the northwestern United States. Its capital is Olympia.   **2.** The capital of the United States. It lies between Maryland and northern Virginia, and includes all of the District of Columbia. It is also called **Washington, D.C.**
Wash·ing·ton (wô′shing tən *or* wosh′ing tən) *noun.*

Word History

Washington was named after George Washington. It is the only state that is named for a president.

---

at; āpe; fär; câre; end; mē; it; īce; pîerce; hot; ōld; sông, fôrk; oil; out; up; ūse; rüle; pùll; tûrn; chin; sing; shop; thin; this; hw in white; zh in treasure. The symbol ə stands for the unstressed vowel sound in about, taken, pencil, lemon, and circus.

W

Washington's Birthday A holiday that used to be observed on February 22 to celebrate George Washington's birthday. It is now observed on the third Monday in February. This holiday is also called **Presidents' Day.**

wasn't Shortened form of "was not." My friend *wasn't* home when I called. I *wasn't* planning to get up early, but the sunlight woke me.
  was·n't (wuz′ənt *or* woz′ənt) *contraction.*

wasp An insect that has wings and a thin body with a narrow waist. Female wasps can give a painful sting.
  wasp (wosp) *noun, plural* **wasps.**

wasp

waste 1. To use or spend in a careless or useless way. You *wasted* your money when you bought that old broken bicycle. I *wasted* the whole afternoon daydreaming. 2. To use up, wear away, or exhaust. The long sickness *wasted* the old dog's strength. 3. To destroy; ruin. The forest fire *wasted* everything in its path. 4. To lose energy, strength, or health slowly but steadily. The homeless kitten was *wasting* away from lack of food when we found it. *Verb.*
—1. The act of wasting or the condition of being wasted. It's a *waste* of time trying to mend that sock. Avoid the *waste* of water. 2. Material that has been thrown away or is left over; refuse. There was a lot of *waste* floating in the dirty river. 3. Material that has not been digested and is eliminated from the body. *Noun.*
—Left over or worthless. Some of the products sold in the lumber store are made from *waste* materials that have been recycled. *Adjective.*

• **to go to waste.** To be unused or used in the wrong way. After the party, we froze all of the leftovers so they wouldn't *go to waste.* ▲ Another word that sounds like this is **waist.**
  waste (wāst) *verb,* **wasted, wasting;** *noun, plural* **wastes;** *adjective.*

wastebasket A basket or other open container used for scraps of paper or other things to be thrown away.
  waste·bas·ket (wāst′bas′kit) *noun, plural* **wastebaskets.**

wasteful Using or spending in a careless or useless way. It's *wasteful* to throw out leftovers.
  waste·ful (wāst′fəl) *adjective.*

wasteland A piece of land or an area where there are few or no living things. A desert is a wasteland.
  waste·land (wāst′land′) *noun, plural* **wastelands.**

watch 1. To look at a person or thing carefully. If you *watch* the magician's tricks a few times, you may learn how they're done. 2. To guard; take care of. Please *watch* my dog while I'm in the store. 3. To wait and look in a careful, alert way. The prisoner *watched* for a chance to escape. *Verb.*
—1. The act of looking carefully or guarding. Please keep *watch* for the bus while I get a newspaper. 2. One or more persons whose work is guarding something. My cousin is part of the night *watch* at the museum. 3. The period of time when a person or persons guard something. The sailor's *watch* lasted for eight hours. 4. A small device that measures and shows the time. Watches are usually worn on the wrist or carried in the pocket. *Noun.*

• **to watch over.** To take care of, be in charge of, or guard. A nurse will *watch over* the patient during the night. The manager *watches over* the work of twenty salespersons. Two soldiers *watched over* the prisoner.
  watch (woch) *verb,* **watched, watching;** *noun, plural* **watches.**

Word History

The word **watch** goes back to an Old English word meaning "to be awake." Sometimes people would stay awake deliberately, or *watch,* as a religious duty or to tend a sick person. This led to the meaning of staying awake on purpose to look out for something. From this meaning, *watch* came to mean "to look at with attention."

---

watchdog A dog that is kept to guard a house or property.
  watch·dog (woch′dôg′) *noun, plural* **watchdogs.**

watchful Watching carefully; alert. The babies played while their *watchful* parents sat nearby.
  watch·ful (woch′fəl) *adjective.*

watchman A person whose work is guarding a building or property. A watchman usually works during the night when a place is empty.
  watch·man (woch′mən) *noun, plural* **watchmen** (woch′mən).

water   **1.** The liquid that falls as rain and forms the earth's oceans, rivers, lakes, and ponds. Water has no color, smell, or taste in its pure form. We use water for washing and drinking.   **2.** A body of water. We swam in the warm Florida *waters*. ▲ The word "water" in this sense is usually used in the plural form. *Noun.*
—**1.** To put water into or on. I *water* the plants every day.   **2.** To give water to for drinking. We stopped to *water* the horses. **3.** To give forth water from the body. The smoke made my eyes *water*. *Verb.*
   wa·ter (wô′tər) *noun, plural* **waters;** *verb,* **watered, watering.**

water buffalo   A black buffalo of Asia that has long horns that curve backward. The water buffalo is used for carrying or pulling heavy loads.

water buffalo

watercolor   **1.** A paint that is made by mixing pigment with water.   **2.** The art of painting with watercolors.   **3.** A picture or design made with watercolors.
   wa·ter·col·or (wô′tər kul′ər) *noun, plural* **watercolors.**

watercress   A plant that grows in running water or wet soil. It's leaves have a sharp taste and are used in salads.
   wa·ter·cress (wô′tər kres′) *noun, plural* **watercresses.**

waterfall   A natural stream of water falling from a high place.
   wa·ter·fall (wô′tər fôl′) *noun, plural* **waterfalls.**

waterfront   Land or a part of a city or town that is beside a body of water. Our cottage at the lake is on the *waterfront*.
   wa·ter·front (wô′tər frunt′) *noun, plural* **waterfronts.**

water lily   A plant that grows in freshwater ponds and lakes. Water lilies have large, showy flowers and leaves that float on the water.

watermelon   A large, juicy fruit that usually has a thick green rind, a watery pulp that

is pink, red, or yellow, and many seeds. Watermelons grow on vines.
   wa·ter·mel·on (wô′tər mel′ən) *noun, plural* **watermelons.**

watermelons

water moccasin   A kind of poisonous snake; cottonmouth. Look up **cottonmouth** for more information.

waterproof   Not letting water pass through. Our roof is covered with *waterproof* shingles. *Adjective.*
—To make waterproof. My boots have been *waterproofed* with a rubber coating. *Verb.*
   wa·ter·proof (wô′tər prüf′) *adjective; verb,* **waterproofed, waterproofing.**

watershed   **1.** A ridge or other high land area that separates two different river basins. **2.** The total land area from which water drains into a river or lake. Nebraska is part of the *watershed* of the Mississippi River.
   wa·ter·shed (wô′tər shed′) *noun, plural* **watersheds.**

water-ski   To glide over the surface of the water on water skis while being pulled by a rope attached to a boat.
   water-ski (wô′tər skē′) *verb,* **water-skied, water-skiing.**

water ski   One of a pair of short, wide skis used when water-skiing.

watertight   Constructed so that water cannot leak into, leak out of, or move through something. Submarines must be completely *watertight*.
   wa·ter·tight (wô′tər tīt′) *adjective.*

waterway   A river, canal, or other body of water that is used as a route for ships.
   wa·ter·way (wô′tər wā′) *noun, plural* **waterways.**

at; āpe; fär; câre; end; mē; it; īce; pîerce; hot; ōld; sông, fôrk; oil; out; up; ūse; rüle; pùll; tûrn; chin; sing; shop; thin; <u>th</u>is; hw in white; zh in treasure. The symbol ə stands for the unstressed vowel sound in about, taken, pencil, lemon, and circus.

W

waterwheel A wheel that is turned by the weight or pressure of water falling on it or flowing under it. Waterwheels are used to provide power.
wa·ter·wheel (wô′tər hwēl′ *or* wô′tər wēl′) *noun, plural* **waterwheels.**

waterwheel

waterworks **1.** The entire system for supplying water to a city or town. Reservoirs, machinery, pipes, and buildings are part of a waterworks. **2.** A building in which the machinery for pumping water to a city or town is located.
wa·ter·works (wô′tər wûrks′) *plural noun.*

watery **1.** Covered with or containing water. My eyes get *watery* when I go out in the cold. The ground is still *watery* from yesterday's heavy rains. **2.** Too much like water; too liquid. This gravy is *watery.*
wa·ter·y (wô′tə rē) *adjective,* **waterier, wateriest.**

watt A unit for measuring electric power.
watt (wot) *noun, plural* **watts.**

Word History

The word **watt** comes from the name of James *Watt.* He was a Scottish engineer and inventor.

wave **1.** To move freely back and forth or up and down; move with a swaying motion. The stalks of wheat *waved* in the wind. The children *waved* their flags as the parade passed by. **2.** To show or signal by raising and moving the hand or something held in the hand. Our friends *waved* good-bye to us as the train pulled out. The guard *waved* for us to stop. **3.** To have or give a curving form or appearance to. I'm tired of having straight hair, so I'm going to *wave* it. *Verb.*
—**1.** A long, moving ridge of water on the surface of a body of water. The ship rode gently over the *waves.* **2.** A motion that transmits energy through matter or space, moving somewhat like a water wave. Sound, heat, and light move in waves. **3.** The act of waving with the hand or with something held in the hand. The garage attendant signaled for us to come in with a *wave* of the hand. **4.** A sudden rush or increase. We had a heat *wave* last week and temperatures rose into the high nineties. **5.** A curve or series of curves. *Noun.*
wave (wāv) *verb,* **waved, waving;** *noun, plural* **waves.**

waver **1.** To move in an unsteady way up and down or from side to side; sway. The ladder *wavered* and then fell over. **2.** To show doubt; be uncertain. The class *wavered* between having a picnic and an indoor party.
wa·ver (wā′vər) *verb,* **wavered, wavering.**

wavy Having a curving movement or shape; full of waves. My friend has *wavy* hair.
wav·y (wā′vē) *adjective,* **wavier, waviest.**

wax¹ **1.** Any of various substances that are like fat and come from plants or animals. Bees make a wax called beeswax that is used in making their honeycombs. Wax also forms inside the human ear. **2.** A substance that is like or contains wax. Wax is used to polish furniture and cars, and to make candles. *Noun.*
—To cover or polish with wax. We *waxed* the floors this afternoon. *Verb.*
wax (waks) *noun, plural* **waxes;** *verb,* **waxed, waxing.**

candles made of **wax**

wax² **1.** To become larger in size, brightness, or strength. The moon *waxes* as it gets nearer to the full moon. **2.** To become. They *waxed* enthusiastic when they spoke about plans for the camping trip.
wax (waks) *verb*, **waxed, waxing.**

way **1.** A course of action for doing or getting something; method. One *way* to paint the ceiling is to stand on a stool. Being kind to others is a good *way* to make friends. **2.** How something is done; manner. The visitor said "hello" in a friendly *way*. **3.** A road or path that leads from one place to another. That road is the quickest *way* to town. **4.** A direction. The storm is heading this *way*. **5.** A moving along a particular route or in a particular direction. I bought bread on my *way* home from school. **6.** Distance. They walked a long *way* before finding the right house. **7.** Something that a person wants to have or do; wish. Some people become angry if they cannot have their *way*. **8.** A particular detail or feature. In many *ways*, the plan is a good one. **9.** Space for passing; room. The cars pulled over to make *way* for the fire engine. *Noun.*
—At or to a distance; far. The water from the breaking waves came *way* up on the beach. *Adverb.* ▲ Another word that sounds like this is **weigh.**
• **by the way.** An expression used to introduce a topic that is new but usually related to the one that is being discussed. *By the way*, we're leaving at four o'clock.
• **to give way.** **1.** To withdraw or retreat. The rebels *gave way* after a long battle with government troops. **2.** To collapse. The bridge *gave way* under the heavy load.
• **under way.** Moving, happening, or being carried out. The plane was *under way* after a delay of an hour. Plans for the party are *under way*.
way (wā) *noun, plural* **ways;** *adverb.*

we The persons who are speaking. *We* won the baseball game. ▲ Another word that sounds like this is **wee.**
we (wē) *plural pronoun.*

weak **1.** Likely to fall or give way. The legs of the old chair are *weak*. **2.** Not having strength, force, or power. Lack of food made the lost hikers *weak*. The light is too *weak* to read by. ▲ Another word that sounds like this is **week.**
weak (wēk) *adjective*, **weaker, weakest.**

weaken To make or become weak or weaker. I *weakened* the tea by adding water. The runner *weakened* near the finish line.
weak·en (wē′kən) *verb*, **weakened, weakening.**

weakly In a weak way. The sick patient called out *weakly* for the nurse. ▲ Another word that sounds like this is **weekly.**
weak·ly (wēk′lē) *adverb.*

weakness **1.** The state or quality of being weak. *Weakness* from the illness kept the child in bed. **2.** A weak point; flaw. My biggest character *weakness* is being lazy. **3.** A special liking; fondness. My cousin has a *weakness* for fancy clothing.
weak·ness (wēk′nis) *noun, plural* **weaknesses.**

wealth **1.** A great amount of money or valuable things; riches. That big house belongs to a family of great *wealth*. **2.** A great amount of anything. The class came up with a *wealth* of ideas for the science project.
wealth (welth) *noun.*

wealthy Having wealth; rich. Some *wealthy* people founded this museum.
wealth·y (wel′thē) *adjective*, **wealthier, wealthiest.**

weapon **1.** Something that is used in fighting to attack or defend. Guns and knives are weapons. **2.** Any means used to attack or defend. The dictator used the threat of prison as a *weapon* against opponents.
weap·on (wep′ən) *noun, plural* **weapons.**

wear **1.** To carry or have on the body. We *wear* warm clothes in the winter. **2.** To have or show. She *wears* her hair long. He *wore* a big smile. **3.** To damage or reduce by long use or exposure. The ocean *wore* the rocks until they were smooth. **4.** To cause or make by rubbing or scraping. You'll *wear* holes in your socks if you don't wear slippers. **5.** To last or hold out. These trousers did not *wear* well. *Verb.*
—**1.** The act of wearing or the state of being worn. This suit has had five years of *wear*. **2.** Clothing. This store sells both women's *wear* and men's *wear*. **3.** Damage caused by use or age. Noun. ▲ Another word that sounds like this is **ware.**
• **to wear out.** **1.** To use until no longer fit or able to be used. The runner *wore out* the soles of the shoes after only two months. **2.** To make tired; exhaust. We were *worn out* from the long hike.
wear (wâr) *verb*, **wore, worn, wearing;** *noun.*

at; āpe; fär; câre; end; mē; it; īce; pîerce; hot; ōld; sông, fôrk; oil; out; up; ūse; rüle; pull; tûrn; chin; sing; shop; thin; this; hw in white; zh in treasure. The symbol ə stands for the unstressed vowel sound in about, taken, pencil, lemon, and circus.

805

weary Very tired. The carpenter was *weary* after the day's hard work. *Adjective.*
—To make or become weary; tire. The long walk *wearied* the children. I *weary* of watching the same television shows. *Verb.*
  wea·ry (wîr′ē) *adjective,* **wearier, weariest;** *verb,* **wearied, wearying.**

weasel A small animal that has a slender body, short legs, a long neck, and soft, thick, brownish fur. Weasels eat rabbits and other small animals, snakes, and small birds.
  wea·sel (wē′zəl) *noun, plural* **weasels** or **weasel.**

weather The condition of the air or atmosphere at a particular time and place. The *weather* has been cold and rainy for the past week. *Noun.*
—**1.** To cause to be dried, bleached, or aged by the weather. The salt air and sun *weathered* the houses at the beach. **2.** To come safely through. The little boat *weathered* the storm. *Verb.*
  weath·er (weth′ər) *noun; verb,* **weathered, weathering.**

weathercock A weather vane that is in the shape of a rooster.
  weath·er·cock (weth′ər kok′) *noun, plural* **weathercocks.**

weatherman A person who studies and forecasts the weather.
  weath·er·man (weth′ər man′) *noun, plural* **weathermen** (weth′ər men′).

weather vane A device that is moved by the wind and is usually placed on the top of a roof. It shows the direction in which the wind is blowing.

weathercock

weave 1. To make something by passing strands or lengths of material over and under one another. This machine *weaves* yarn into cloth. I *wove* a basket out of straw. **2.** To spin a web or cocoon. Spiders *weave* webs. **3.** To move or make by turning and twisting. The police had to *weave* their way through the crowd to reach the accident. *Verb.*
—A way or kind of weaving. The rug has a tight *weave. Noun.* ◢ Another word that sounds like this is **we've.**
  weave (wēv) *verb,* **wove** or *(for definition 3)* **weaved, woven** or *(for definition 3)* **weaved, weaving;** *noun, plural* **weaves.**

web 1. A network of fine threads that are spun by a spider; cobweb. **2.** A crisscross pattern; network. We got lost in the *web* of streets in the old part of town. **3.** The skin between the toes of ducks, frogs, and other animals that swim.
  web (web) *noun, plural* **webs.**

webbed Having or joined by a web. A duck has *webbed* feet.
  webbed (webd) *adjective.*

web-footed Having the toes joined by a web. Ducks and geese are *web-footed.*
  web-foot·ed (web′fŭt′id) *adjective.*

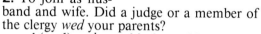

a duck with **webbed** feet

wed 1. To become husband and wife. The engaged couple will *wed* next Saturday. **2.** To join as husband and wife. Did a judge or a member of the clergy *wed* your parents?
  wed (wed) *verb,* **wedded, wedded** or **wed, wedding.**

we'd 1. Shortened form of "we would." *We'd* be happy to drive you home. **2.** Shortened form of "we had." *We'd* just left when the rain began. **3.** Shortened form of "we should." The postal clerk said *we'd* get the package tomorrow. ◢ Another word that sounds like this is **weed.**
  we'd (wēd) *contraction.*

Wed. An abbreviation for *Wednesday.*

wedding 1. A marriage ceremony. We are going to my cousin's *wedding* today. **2.** The anniversary of a marriage. A golden wedding is a celebration of fifty years of marriage.
  wed·ding (wed′ing) *noun, plural* **weddings.**

wedge 1. A piece of wood, metal, or plastic that is thick at one end and narrow at the other. A wedge is pounded into logs to split them. It is also used to fill a space tightly or to hold a door open. **2.** Something that has the shape of a wedge. We served a *wedge* of cheese with some crackers. *Noun.*
—**1.** To separate or split by driving a wedge into. The workers *wedged* the floor boards apart. **2.** To fasten or fix in place with a wedge. The door was *wedged* open with a piece of wood. **3.** To drive, push, or crowd.

I *wedged* the book into place on the crowded shelf. *Verb.*

wedge (wej) *noun, plural* **wedges;** *verb,* **wedged, wedging.**

Wednesday The fourth day of the week.
Wednes·day (wenz′dē *or* wenz′dā) *noun, plural* **Wednesdays.**

Word History

The word **Wednesday** comes from the Old English word meaning "Woden's day." Woden was the king of the English gods.

wee 1. Very small; tiny. The *wee* baby was asleep in the cradle. 2. Early. We stayed awake until the *wee* hours of the morning. ▲ Another word that sounds like this is **we.**
wee (wē) *adjective,* **weer, weest.**

weed A plant that is useless or harmful or grows where it is not wanted. We pulled the *weeds* out of our vegetable garden. *Noun.*
—1. To take out the weeds from. The gardener used a hoe to *weed* the garden. 2. To take out what is harmful or not wanted. The coach *weeded* out the worst players from the baseball team. *Verb.* ▲ Another word that sounds like this is **we'd.**
weed (wēd) *noun, plural* **weeds;** *verb,* **weeded, weeding.**

week 1. A period of seven days. A week is usually thought of as starting with Sunday. 2. The part of a seven-day period during which a person works or goes to school. Many companies require their employees to work a forty-hour *week*. Our school *week* begins Monday morning. ▲ Another word that sounds like this is **weak.**
week (wēk) *noun, plural* **weeks.**

weekday Any day of the week except Saturday and Sunday.
week·day (wēk′dā′) *noun, plural* **weekdays.**

weekend The period of time from Friday night or Saturday morning until Sunday night or Monday morning. We went to the country for the *weekend*.
week·end (wēk′end′) *noun, plural* **weekends.**

weekly 1. For or having to do with a week or weekdays. Our family has a *weekly* grocery budget. 2. Done, happening, or published once a week. The *weekly* newspaper comes out every Thursday. *Adjective.*
—A newspaper or magazine published once a week. *Noun.*
—Once each week; every week. I go to dance class *weekly*. *Adverb.* ▲ Another word that sounds like this is **weakly.**
week·ly (wēk′lē) *adjective; noun, plural* **weeklies;** *adverb.*

weep To show sorrow, joy, or other strong emotion by crying. The sad story made us *weep*.
weep (wēp) *verb,* **wept, weeping.**

weevil A beetle with a long snout that curves downward. Weevils eat cotton, grain, and other crops and are serious pests to farmers.
wee·vil (wē′vəl) *noun, plural* **weevils.**

weigh 1. To find out the weight or heaviness of a person or thing. The grocer *weighed* the tomatoes on a scale. 2. To have, amount to, or be equal to a named weight. The car *weighs* 3,744 pounds. How much do you *weigh*? 3. To think about or examine carefully. They *weighed* their chances of winning the game. You should *weigh* your words before answering. 4. To lie heavily on; burden. The heavy snow *weighed* down the branches of the trees. Guilt about having lied *weighed* on my conscience. ▲ Another word that sounds like this is **way.**
weigh (wā) *verb,* **weighed, weighing.**

The girl **weighs** the substance on a scale.

weight 1. The amount of heaviness of a person or thing. My *weight* is 70 pounds. 2. The quality of a thing that comes from the

at; āpe; fär; câre; end; mē; it; īce; pîerce; hot; ōld; sông, fôrk; oil; out; up; ūse; rüle; pull; tûrn; chin; sing; shop; thin; this; hw in white; zh in treasure. The symbol ə stands for the unstressed vowel sound in about, taken, pencil, lemon, and circus.

W

pull of gravity upon it. Weight tends to pull things toward the center of the earth. The *weight* of helium is less than the *weight* of air, so a balloon filled with helium will rise in the air.   **3.** A unit or system of units for expressing weight. The pound and the kilogram are different *weights*.   **4.** A heavy object that is used to hold down things or to keep something steady. We put rocks as *weights* at the corners of the beach towel.   **5.** An object whose weight is known. Lifting *weights* will help you build your muscles.   **6.** A burden or load. The *weight* of all this homework is discouraging.   **7.** Strong influence; importance. The old chief's advice carried much *weight* with the tribe. ▴ Another word that sounds like this is **wait.**
   weight (wāt) *noun, plural* **weights.**

weightless   **1.** Having little or no weight. A feather is practically *weightless*.   **2.** Not influenced by the pull of gravity. The spacecraft was *weightless* when it was in space.
   weight·less (wāt′lis) *adjective.*

weird   Strange or mysterious; odd. *Weird* sounds came from the deserted old house.
   weird (wîrd) *adjective,* **weirder, weirdest.**

welcome   **1.** To greet someone in a pleasant and friendly way. My father *welcomed* the guests when they arrived at the party.   **2.** To receive or accept with pleasure or gladness. My mother works so hard that she *welcomes* a summer vacation. *Verb.*
   —A glad and friendly greeting. We received a warm *welcome* at our grandparents' house. *Noun.*
   —**1.** Received kindly and with pleasure. You are always a *welcome* visitor to our house.   **2.** Free to use, have, or enjoy. Anyone is *welcome* to the newspaper after I've finished reading it.   **3.** *Welcome* is used in the phrase "You are welcome," a polite answer to someone who has thanked you. *Adjective.*
   wel·come (wel′kəm) *verb,* **welcomed, welcoming;** *noun, plural* **welcomes;** *adjective.*

weld   To join pieces of metal or plastic by heating until soft enough to be hammered or pressed together. The plumber *welded* the broken pieces of pipe together.
   weld (weld) *verb,* **welded, welding.**

welfare   **1.** The condition of being happy and healthy; well-being. The parents were concerned about their children's *welfare,* so they fed and raised them well.   **2.** Money or other aid given by the government to people who are in need.
   wel·fare (wel′fâr′) *noun.*

we'll   Shortened form of "we will" or "we shall." *We'll* see you at the party. *We'll* go to the picnic if it doesn't rain.
   we'll (wēl) *contraction.*

well¹   **1.** In a good or satisfactory way. Everything went *well* at the rehearsal of the play.   **2.** In a complete way; thoroughly. Be sure to mix the flour and salt *well*.   **3.** To a considerable degree; much. The piano weighs *well* over 300 pounds.   **4.** In a close or personal way. Do you know your neighbors *well? Adverb.*
   —**1.** In good health; healthy. The doctor examined me and said I was *well*. After resting, I felt *well* again.   **2.** Good; fortunate. It is *well* that you called now because we were just leaving. *Adjective.*
   —A word used to show surprise or to bring in another idea or thought. *Well!* How nice to see you. *Well,* I think that it's time to leave now. *Interjection.*
   • **as well.**   In addition; also. I play the flute and the guitar *as well*.
   • **as well as.**   In addition to; besides. The twins, *as well as* their parents, came to visit us.
   well (wel) *adverb,* **better, best;** *adjective; interjection.*

well²   **1.** A deep hole that is made in the ground to get water, oil, or natural gas.   **2.** A natural spring or fountain.   **3.** Something that is like a well in shape or use. The old desk has a *well* for ink. An encyclopedia is a *well* of information. *Noun.*
   —To rise or fill. Tears *welled* in the lost child's eyes. *Verb.*
   well (wel) *noun, plural* **wells;** *verb,* **welled, welling.**

well-balanced   Evenly balanced. A *well-balanced* meal includes a variety of healthful foods.
   well-bal·anced (wel′bal′ənst) *adjective.*

well-behaved   Having or showing good conduct or manners. The *well-behaved* children played quietly.
   well-be·haved (wel′bi hāvd′) *adjective.*

well-being   Health and happiness; welfare. Lots of exercise is good for the *well-being* of a dog.
   well-be·ing (wel′bē′ing) *noun.*

well-known   Known to many people; generally or widely known. The *well-known* movie actor attracted a crowd.
   well-known (wel′nōn′) *adjective.*

well-mannered   Having or showing good manners; polite. The *well-mannered* child thanked the hosts of the birthday party.
   well-man·nered (wel′man′ərd) *adjective.*

Welsh **1. the Welsh.** The people of Wales. **2.** The original language of the Welsh. The English language is now more common in Wales. *Noun.*
—Of or having to do with Wales, its people, or their original language. *Adjective.*
  Welsh (welsh) *noun; adjective.*

went Past tense of **go.** I *went* to bed early last night. Look up **go** for more information.
  went (went) *verb.*

wept Past tense and past participle of **weep.** Some of our players *wept* when we lost the championship game. Look up **weep** for more information.
  wept (wept) *verb.*

were A form of the past tense of **be** that is used with *you, we, they,* or the plural form of a noun. We *were* at home all day. They *were* glad to see the puppy. *Were* you there? Look up **be** for more information.
  were (wûr) *verb.*

we're Shortened form of "we are." *We're* going home now.
  we're (wîr) *contraction.*

weren't Shortened form of "were not." They *weren't* home this afternoon.
  weren't (wûrnt *or* wûr′ənt) *contraction.*

west **1.** The direction you face when you watch the sun set in the evening. West is one of the four main points of the compass. It is located directly opposite east. **2. West.** Any region or place that is in this direction. **3. the West.** The region of the United States that is west of the Mississippi River. *Noun.*
—**1.** Toward or in the west. The grocery store is on the *west* side of the street. **2.** Coming from the west. A *west* wind was blowing. *Adjective.*
—Toward the west. Christopher Columbus sailed *west* from Europe to cross the Atlantic Ocean. *Adverb.*
  west (west) *noun; adjective; adverb.*

western **1.** In or toward the west. California is a *western* state. **2.** Coming from the west. **3. Western.** Of or in the part of the United States that is west of the Mississippi river. *Adjective.*
—A story, book, or movie about frontier life in the western United States. *Noun.*
  west·ern (wes′tərn) *adjective; noun, plural* **westerns.**

westerner **1.** A person who was born or is living in the western part of a country or region. **2. Westerner.** A person living in the western part of the United States.
  west·ern·er (wes′tər nər) *noun, plural* **westerners.**

Western Hemisphere The half of the earth that includes North America and South America.

West Germany A country in northwestern Europe.

West Indies A group of islands in the Caribbean Sea.
  West In·dies (in′dēz).

West Virginia A state in the eastern United States. Its capital is Charleston.

Word History

Like Virginia, **West Virginia** takes its name from a title given to the English queen Elizabeth I. Since she never married, she was called "the Virgin Queen." The colony of Virginia, founded under Queen Elizabeth, included what is now West Virginia. But when Virginia seceded from the Union at the start of the Civil War, the people of the western part of that state decided to remain with the Union. This area became the state of West Virginia.

---

westward Toward the west. The airplane flew *westward* into the sunset. *Adverb.*
—Toward or in the west. The pioneers began their *westward* journey. *Adjective.*
  west·ward (west′wərd) *adverb; adjective.*

westwards Another spelling of the adverb **westward.** The storm moved *westwards.* Look up **westward** for more information.
  west·wards (west′wərdz) *adverb.*

wet **1.** Covered, soaked, or moist with water or other liquid. My bathing suit is still *wet* from my swim. **2.** Not yet hardened. A footprint was made in the *wet* cement. **3.** Having rainfall; rainy. *Adjective.*
—To make wet. The directions said to *wet* the ground before planting the seeds. *Verb.*
  wet (wet) *adjective,* **wetter, wettest;** *verb,* **wet** *or* **wetted, wetting.**

we've Shortened form of "we have." *We've* enjoyed seeing you. ⑃ Another word that sounds like this is **weave.**
  we've (wēv) *contraction.*

---

at; āpe; fär; câre; end; mē; it; īce; pîerce; hot; ōld; sông; fôrk; oil; out; up; ūse; rüle; pu̇ll; tûrn; chin; sing; shop; thin; this; hw in white; zh in treasure. The symbol ə stands for the unstressed vowel sound in about, taken, pencil, lemon, and circus.

whale A large animal that has a body like a fish. Whales are found in all oceans and in certain fresh waters. A whale is a mammal.
whale (hwāl *or* wāl) *noun, plural* **whales** or **whale.**

whale

whaler **1.** A person whose job is hunting and killing whales. **2.** A ship or boat used in whaling.
whal·er (hwā′lər *or* wā′lər) *noun, plural* **whalers.**

whaling The act or work of hunting and killing whales for their oil, meat, and bone.
whal·ing (hwā′ling *or* wā′ling) *noun.*

wharf A structure built along a shore as a landing place for boats and ships; dock.
wharf (hworf *or* wôrf) *noun, plural* **wharves** or **wharfs.**

what **1.** Used to ask questions about persons or things. *What* is today's date? **2.** The thing that. They knew *what* I was thinking. **3.** Anything that; whatever. Choose *what* you want for dinner. *Pronoun.*
—**1.** Which one or ones. *What* books are missing from the shelf? **2.** Any that; whatever. Take *what* you need for the trip. *Adjective.*
—In which way; how much; how. *What* does it matter? *Adverb.*
—Used to show surprise, disbelief, anger, or other feeling. *What!* That's not possible! *Interjection.*
• **what for.** For which reason; why. *What* did you do that *for*?
what (hwut *or* hwot *or* wut *or* wot) *pronoun; adjective; adverb; interjection.*

whatever **1.** Anything that. Take *whatever* you want to eat from the refrigerator. **2.** No matter what. *Whatever* you say, I still think I'm right. *Pronoun.*
—**1.** Any that. Buy *whatever* supplies you need for the hike. **2.** Of any kind. No person *whatever* could be kinder than you. *Adjective.*
what·ev·er (hwət ev′ər *or* wət ev′ər) *pronoun; adjective.*

what's **1.** Shortened form of "what is." *What's* the difference? **2.** Shortened form of "what has." *What's* happened?
what's (hwuts *or* hwots *or* wuts *or* wots) *contraction.*

wheat A kind of grass whose seeds are used to make flour and other foods. Wheat is a very important food for human beings and animals.
wheat (hwēt *or* wēt) *noun.*

wheel **1.** A round frame or solid object. Some wheels have a middle part that is connected to its outside rim by spokes. A wheel turns on its center and is used on cars, wagons, and other vehicles and as a machine part. **2.** Any machine or other thing that has or uses a wheel. A spinning *wheel* is used for making thread. *Noun.*
—**1.** To turn. My friend *wheeled* around when I called out. **2.** To move or roll on wheels. I *wheeled* the cart around the grocery store. *Verb.*
• **at the wheel.** Doing the steering or driving. Who was *at the wheel* when the car crashed?
wheel (hwēl *or* wēl) *noun, plural* **wheels;** *verb,* **wheeled, wheeling.**

wheelbarrow A small cart with one or two wheels at the front end and two handles at the back for pushing. Wheelbarrows are used to move small loads for short distances.
wheel·bar·row (hwēl′bar′ō *or* wēl′bar′ō) *noun, plural* **wheelbarrows.**

wheelchair A chair on wheels that is used by someone who cannot walk to get from one place to another.
wheel·chair (hwēl′chär′ *or* wēl′chär′) *noun, plural* **wheelchairs.**

wheelchair

wheeze To breathe with a hoarse, whistling sound. People with a bad cold or asthma sometimes *wheeze*.
   wheeze (hwēz *or* wēz) *verb*, **wheezed, wheezing.**

whelk A large snail that lives in salt water. Whelks have spiral shells.
   whelk (hwelk *or* welk) *noun, plural* **whelks.**

whelk

when At what or which time. *When* did they arrive? *Adverb.*
   —**1.** At the time that. I'll come *when* you call me. **2.** At any time that; whenever. *When* I am embarrassed, my face turns red. **3.** And then; at which time. The children played until noon, *when* they had lunch. **4.** Although; but. I wore a light sweater *when* I should have worn a heavy coat. **5.** Considering that. How can we go to the party *when* we haven't been invited? *Conjunction.*
   when (hwen) *adverb; conjunction.*

whenever At whatever time. We can eat dinner *whenever* you're hungry.
   when·ev·er (hwen ev′ər *or* wen ev′ər) *conjunction.*

where In, at, to, or from what place. *Where* did they go? *Where* did you buy that book? *Adverb.*
   —**1.** In, at, or to the place in which, at which, or to which. The keys are *where* you left them last night. Why can't I go *where* you're going? **2.** In or at which place. Let's go inside *where* we can sit. *Conjunction.*
   —What place. *Where* did those people come from? *Pronoun.*
   where (hwâr *or* wâr) *adverb; conjunction; pronoun.*

whereabouts In or near what place; where. *Whereabouts* did you last see the lost dog? *Adverb.*
   —The place where something or someone is; location. The *whereabouts* of the hidden treasure is a secret. The suspect's *whereabouts* are unknown. *Noun.* ▲ The noun form of the word "whereabouts" may be used with a singular or a plural verb.
   where·a·bouts (hwâr′ə bouts′ *or* wâr′ə bouts′) *adverb; noun.*

whereupon At which time; after which; and then. Finally my friends finished their work, *whereupon* we all went to the concert.
   where·up·on (hwâr′ə pôn′ *or* hwâr′ə pon′ *or* wâr′ə pôn′ *or* wâr′ə pon′) *conjunction.*

wherever In, at, or to whatever place. *Wherever* were you all afternoon? I'll go *wherever* you go.
   where·ev·er (hwâr ev′ər *or* wâr ev′ər) *adverb; conjunction.*

whether **1.** A word that is used to introduce a choice between things. You must decide *whether* to take the train or to go by plane. **2.** If. Let me know *whether* you can come to my party.
   wheth·er (hwe<u>th</u>′ər *or* we<u>th</u>′ər) *conjunction.*

whew A word used to show relief, surprise, or dismay. *Whew!* We just made the train.
   whew (hwū) *interjection.*

whey The watery part of milk that separates from the curd when milk turns sour or thickens.
   whey (hwā *or* wā) *noun.*

which **1.** What one or ones. *Which* of the players did you think was best? **2.** Any one or ones that; whichever. Choose *which* of the records you want to hear. **3.** Used to introduce a clause that refers to a thing or things mentioned before. That jacket, *which* I bought last year, is my favorite. *Pronoun.*
   —What one or ones. *Which* skates are yours? *Which* highway is the most direct route to the mountains? *Adjective.*
   which (hwich) *pronoun; adjective.*

whichever **1.** Any one that. Buy *whichever* you like best. **2.** No matter which. *Whichever* you choose is fine. *Pronoun.*
   —**1.** Any one that. You can have *whichever* picture you like best. **2.** No matter which. *Whichever* road you follow, you'll arrive at the train station in ten minutes. *Adjective.*
   which·ev·er (hwich ev′ər *or* wich ev′ər) *pronoun; adjective.*

whiff A sudden light puff, breath, or smell A *whiff* of smoke rose from the fire. The *whiff* of bacon made me hungry.
   whiff (hwif *or* wif) *noun, plural* **whiffs.**

while A period of time. We stopped walking and rested for a *while. Noun.*
   —**1.** During or in the time that. Did anyone call *while* I was away? **2.** In spite of the fact that; although. *While* they are our neighbors, we don't know them well. *Conjunction.*

---

at; āpe; fär; câre; end; mē; it; īce; pîerce; hot; ōld; sông, fôrk; oil; out; up; ūse; rüle; pùll; tûrn; chin; sing; shop; thin; <u>th</u>is; hw in white; zh in treasure. The symbol ə stands for the unstressed vowel sound in about, taken, pencil, lemon, and circus.

W

811

—To pass or spend time in a relaxed, pleasant way. We *whiled* away the afternoon listening to records. *Verb.*

while (hwīl *or* wīl) *noun; conjunction; verb,* **whiled, whiling.**

whim A sudden idea or wish to do something. I went to the movie on a *whim.*

whim (hwim *or* wim) *noun, plural* **whims.**

whimper To cry with weak, broken sounds. The puppy *whimpered* for its mother.

whim·per (hwim′pər *or* wim′pər) *verb,* **whimpered, whimpering.**

whine To cry in a soft, high, complaining voice. The tired child *whined* in the back seat of the car.

whine (hwīn *or* wīn) *verb,* **whined, whining.**

whinny To neigh in a low, gentle way. My horse *whinnied* when it saw me. *Verb.*

—A soft neigh. We heard the *whinnies* of the horses. *Noun.*

whin·ny (hwin′ē *or* win′ē) *verb,* **whinnied, whinnying;** *noun, plural* **whinnies.**

whip **1.** To hit with a strap, rod, or something similar. The driver of the carriage *whipped* the horses to make them go faster. **2.** To beat eggs, cream, or the like until it forms a foam. The baker *whipped* cream for the cake. **3.** To move, take, or throw suddenly. We *whipped* the clean clothes from the line just as the storm began. *Verb.*

—A rod or strap that bends easily and has a handle. Whips are used for driving horses and other animals. *Noun.*

whip (hwip *or* wip) *verb,* **whipped, whipping;** *noun, plural* **whips.**

whippoorwill A plump bird having feathers spotted with brown, gray, and black. The whippoorwill lives in eastern North America. Its call sounds like its name.

whip·poor·will (hwip′ər wil′ *or* wip′ər wil′) *noun, plural* **whippoorwills.**

whir To move or turn with a whizzing or buzzing sound. The helicopter *whirred* overhead. *Verb.*

—A whizzing or buzzing sound. *Noun.*

whir (hwûr *or* wûr) *verb,* **whirred, whirring;** *noun, plural* **whirs.**

whippoorwill

whirl **1.** To turn or cause to turn quickly in a circle. The blades of a fan whirl. The breeze *whirled* the bits of paper around in the air. **2.** To move or turn around suddenly or quickly. The guards *whirled* when they heard the noise. *Verb.*

—**1.** A quick turn in a circle; whirling movement. We watched the skaters make graceful leaps and *whirls* on the ice. **2.** A confused or dizzy condition. My head was in a *whirl* after I was hit by the ball. *Noun.*

whirl (hwûrl *or* wûrl) *verb,* **whirled, whirling;** *noun, plural* **whirls.**

whirlpool A current of water that moves quickly in a circle.

whirl·pool (hwûrl′pül′ *or* wûrl′pül′) *noun, plural* **whirlpools.**

whisk **1.** To brush lightly. The waiter *whisked* the crumbs off the table with a napkin. **2.** To move or carry quickly. The taxi *whisked* us to the airport.

whisk (hwisk *or* wisk) *verb,* **whisked, whisking.**

whisker **1. whiskers.** The hair growing on a man's face; a beard or part of a beard. **2.** A stiff hair that grows on the face. Cats and dogs have whiskers.

whisk·er (hwis′kər *or* wis′kər) *noun, plural* **whiskers.**

whiskey A strong alcoholic drink made from rye, corn, or other grains.

whis·key (hwis′kē *or* wis′kē) *noun, plural* **whiskeys.**

Word History

The word **whiskey** comes from a word in a language that was once spoken by people in Scotland and Ireland. In this language, the word meant "water of life."

whisper To speak or say very softly. My friend *whispered* a secret to me. *Verb.*

—A very soft way of speaking, or something said in this way. The teacher heard *whispers* from the back of the room. *Noun.*

whis·per (hwis′pər *or* wis′pər) *verb,* **whispered, whispering;** *noun, plural* **whispers.**

whistle **1.** To make a clear, sharp sound by forcing air out through rounded lips or through the teeth. **2.** To make or move with a sound like this. The kettle *whistled* when the water boiled. **3.** To call or signal by whistling. The police officer *whistled* for us to stop. *Verb.*

—1. A device that makes a clear, sharp sound when air is blown through it. The lifeguard blew a *whistle* to warn the swimmers. **2.** A whistling sound. The dog came when it heard my *whistle. Noun.*
> whis·tle (hwis′əl *or* wis′əl) *verb,* **whistled, whistling;** *noun, plural* **whistles.**

white **1.** Having the lightest of all colors; having the color of fresh snow. A *white* cloud floated by. **2.** Light in color. I like the *white* meat of turkey better than the dark. The child's face was *white* with fear. **3.** Pale gray. My grandparents have *white* hair. **4.** Belonging to a race of people having light skin. Both *white* and black people live on our block. **5.** Not harmful. I told a *white* lie about my age. **6.** Snowy. Let's hope for a *white* Christmas. *Adjective.*
—1. The lightest of all colors; the opposite of black. White is the color of fresh snow. **2.** Something that is white or light-colored. The recipe called for the *whites* of four eggs. **3.** A member of a race of people that has light skin. *Noun.*
> white (hwīt *or* wīt) *adjective,* **whiter, whitest;** *noun, plural* **whites.**

white blood cell A colorless cell found in the blood. White blood cells protect the body against infection by destroying germs that carry disease. They are a part of the immune system.

White House **1.** The official home of the president of the United States. The White House is in Washington, D.C. **2.** The office of the president of the United States. The *White House* announced the president's decision.

whiten To make or become white. Bleach *whitens* clothes. Our faces must have *whitened* in fear when the door began to open.
> whit·en (hwī′tən *or* wī′tən) *verb,* **whitened, whitening.**

whitewash A watery, white paint used on walls, wood fences, and other surfaces.
> white·wash (hwīt′wôsh′ *or* hwīt′wosh′ *or* wīt′wôsh′ *or* wīt′wosh′) *noun.*

whittle **1.** To cut small bits or pieces from wood or soap with a knife. We *whittled* the wood into interesting shapes. **2.** To make or shape by cutting away small bits with a knife. I *whittled* a dog from a bar of soap.
> whit·tle (hwit′əl *or* wit′əl) *verb,* **whittled, whittling.**

whiz To make a buzzing sound while moving quickly. The plane *whizzed* over the tops of the trees.
> whiz (hwiz *or* wiz) *verb,* **whizzed, whizzing.**

who **1.** What or which person or persons. *Who* gave you that pen? **2.** That. The student *who* wrote that story has a good sense of humor.
> who (hü) *pronoun.*

whoa A word used as a command to stop. *"Whoa,"* the rider said to the horse.
> whoa (hwō *or* wō) *interjection.*

who'd **1.** Shortened form of "who would." *Who'd* say such a thing about you? **2.** Shortened form of "who had." Our guide knew someone *who'd* climbed that mountain.
> who'd (hüd) *contraction.*

whoever **1.** Any person who; whatever person. *Whoever* wants to come along is welcome. **2.** No matter who. *Whoever* those strangers are, I like them. **3.** What or which person. *Whoever* told you such a story?
> who·ev·er (hü ev′ər) *pronoun.*

whole Having all its parts; entire; complete. Have you read the *whole* book already? Fifty-two cards make a *whole* deck. Is this *whole* milk or skim milk? *Adjective.*
—All the parts that make up a thing. I spent the *whole* of my allowance on the present. Two halves make a *whole. Noun.* ▲ Another word that sounds like this is **hole.**
> • **on the whole.** Considering everything. *On the whole* I thought the party was a success.
> whole (hōl) *adjective; noun.*

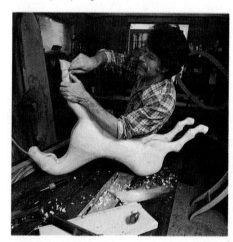
The man **whittles** a horse from wood.

at; āpe; fär; câre; end; mē; it; ice; pîerce; hot; ōld; sông, fôrk; oil; out; up; ūse; rüle; pull; tûrn; chin; sing; shop; thin; this; hw in white; zh in treasure. The symbol ə stands for the unstressed vowel sound in about, taken, pencil, lemon, and circus.

W

813

whole number   A number that tells how many complete things there are. 0, 1, 2, and 21 are whole numbers; ¾, ⅞, and other fractions are not whole numbers.

wholesome   **1.** Good for the health. Exercise and a proper diet are *wholesome*. This polluted air is not *wholesome*.   **2.** Having habits and attitudes that give good health. *Wholesome* people don't smoke cigarettes.
   whole·some (hōl′səm) *adjective.*

whole-wheat   Made from the whole grain of wheat. This bread is made with *whole-wheat* flour only.
   whole-wheat (hōl′hwēt′ *or* hōl′wēt′) *adjective.*

who'll   Shortened form of "who will" or "who shall." *Who'll* bake the cake?
   who'll (hül) *contraction.*

wholly   To the whole amount or extent; entirely; completely. I am *wholly* to blame for what happened. ⌁ Another word that sounds like this is **holy.**
   whol·ly (hō′lē) *adverb.*

whom   What or which person or persons. *Whom* do you suspect? I don't know *whom* I liked best in the play.
   whom (hüm) *pronoun.*

whomever   Any person whom; whatever person. I asked *whomever* I liked to come to the party.
   whom·ev·er (hüm ev′ər) *pronoun.*

whoop   A loud cry or shout. You gave a *whoop* when you caught the fish. *Noun.*
   —To give a loud cry or shout. We *whooped* with laughter when we heard what had happened. *Verb.* ⌁ Another word that sounds like this is **hoop.**
   whoop (hüp *or* hwüp *or* wüp) *noun, plural* **whoops;** *verb,* **whooped, whooping.**

whooping crane   A crane that has a white body, wings with black tips, and a red face. It is four feet high and the tallest of all North American birds. The whooping crane is nearly extinct.

whooping crane

who's   **1.** Shortened form of "who is." *Who's* going to be at the meeting this morning?   **2.** Shortened form of "who has." *Who's* been eating my porridge? ⌁ An-

other word that sounds like this is **whose.**
   who's (hüz) *contraction.*

whose   **1.** Of or belonging to whom or which. *Whose* house is that? We tried to help the neighbor *whose* dog had run away.   **2.** The one or ones belonging to what person or persons. *Whose* are those books? ⌁ Another word that sounds like this is **who's.**
   whose (hüz) *pronoun.*

why   For what reason or purpose. *Why* are you laughing? *Why* do you want to go swimming today? *Adverb.*
   —The reason or purpose for which. Do you know *why* they didn't come to the party? *Conjunction.*
   —A word used to show mild surprise or other feelings. *Why,* look who's here! *Interjection.*
   why (hwī *or* wī) *adverb; conjunction; interjection.*

WI   Postal abbreviation for *Wisconsin.*

wick   A cord in an oil lamp, candle, or cigarette lighter that soaks up the fuel and burns when it is lit.
   wick (wik) *noun, plural* **wicks.**

wicked   Evil, mean, and very bad. The villain in the story was a *wicked* person who liked to harm other people.
   wick·ed (wik′id) *adjective.*

wicker   Thin twigs that are easily bent and are woven together to make baskets and furniture. *Noun.*
   —Made of wicker. We have *wicker* furniture on our porch. *Adjective.*
   wick·er (wik′ər) *noun; adjective.*

wide   **1.** Made up of or covering a large area from side to side. There is a *wide* porch across the back of the house.   **2.** Having a certain distance from side to side. The room is 12 feet *wide*.   **3.** Fully opened. The child's eyes were *wide* with excitement.   **4.** Including many different things; various. This store carries a *wide* selection of furniture.   **5.** Far away from a specific place. My arrow was *wide* of the target. *Adjective.*
   —**1.** Over a large area. The writer traveled far and *wide* to learn about different countries.   **2.** To a large or full extent. The hippopotamus opened its mouth *wide* and yawned. Please open the window *wide*. *Adverb.*
   wide (wīd) *adjective,* **wider, widest;** *adverb.*

widen   To make or become wide or wider. If we get a bigger car, we'll have to *widen* the driveway. The road *widens* just ahead.
   wid·en (wī′dən) *verb,* **widened, widening.**

widespread **1.** Happening over a large area or to many people. The flu epidemic was *widespread* in the country. **2.** Fully open. They greeted us with *widespread* arms.
wide·spread (wīd′spred′) *adjective.*

widow A woman whose husband is dead and who has not married again.
wid·ow (wid′ō) *noun, plural* **widows.**

widower A man whose wife is dead and who has not married again.
wid·ow·er (wid′ō ər) *noun, plural* **widowers.**

width The distance from one side of something to the other side. The *width* of a football field is 52⅓ yards.
width (width) *noun, plural* **widths.**

wife A married woman.
wife (wīf) *noun, plural* **wives.**

Word History

The word **wife** comes from Old English. It used to mean "a woman," whether she was married or not.

wig A covering for the head made of real or artificial hair.
wig (wig) *noun, plural* **wigs.**

wiggle To move from side to side in short, sudden movements. I *wiggled* my loose tooth with my finger.
wig·gle (wig′əl) *verb,* **wiggled, wiggling.**

wigwam A hut made of poles covered with bark, leaves, or hides. Some North American Indian tribes built wigwams to live in.
wig·wam (wig′wom *or* wig′wôm) *noun, plural* **wigwams.**

wig

Word History

The word **wigwam** comes from the American Indian name for this kind of house.

wild **1.** Not controlled by people; living or growing naturally. There are *wild* ponies on that island. The forest is full of *wild* plants.

2. Not disciplined or orderly. Those *wild* children often play rough games and hurt themselves. **3.** Crazy or fantastic. I have a *wild* idea for a Halloween costume. *Adjective.*
—Not under the control of people; naturally. Blueberries grow *wild* in that field. *Adverb.*
wild (wīld) *adjective,* **wilder, wildest;** *adverb.*

wildcat A bobcat, lynx, or other small cat that is not tamed. A wildcat is larger than a domestic cat but smaller than a lion.
wild·cat (wīld′kat′) *noun, plural* **wildcats.**

wilderness A natural place where no people live. In a wilderness there may be a dense forest and many wild animals.
wil·der·ness (wil′dər nis) *noun, plural* **wildernesses.**

wildflower Any flower of a wild plant.
wild·flow·er (wīld′flou′ər) *noun, plural* **wildflowers.**

wildlife Wild animals that live naturally in an area.
wild·life (wīld′līf′) *noun.*

will¹ **1.** An auxiliary verb that is used to express future actions and states. I *will* be ten next month. The team *will* play here tomorrow. **2.** To have the intention to. I *will* help with the dishes. **3.** To be required to; have to; must. You *will* be on time from now on. **4.** To be able to; can. That chair *will* not support your weight. This camera *will* not work.
will (wil) *verb.*

will² **1.** The power to decide what to do and to keep wanting and trying to do it. A person with a strong *will* endeavors to achieve goals in spite of all obstacles. **2.** Firm purpose; determination. The young business executive had a *will* to succeed. **3.** A wish; desire. "What is your *will?*" the servant asked. **4.** A legal document that states what a person wants done with everything he or she owns after the person dies. *Noun.*
—**1.** To use the power of the mind to decide what to do. The runner *willed* herself to keep going even though her leg hurt badly. **2.** To give away what one owns by a will. The rich man *willed* all his money to charity. *Verb.*
will (wil) *noun, plural* **wills;** *verb,* **willed, willing.**

at; āpe; fär; câre; end; mē; it; īce; pîerce; hot; ōld; sông, fôrk; oil; out; up; ūse; rüle; pùll; tûrn; chin; sing; shop; thin; this; hw in white; zh in treasure. The symbol ə stands for the unstressed vowel sound in about, taken, pencil, lemon, and circus.

willing Wanting or ready to do something. Are you *willing* to help us? To be hypnotized, you have to be a *willing* subject.
  will·ing (wil'ing) *adjective.*

willow A tree or bush that has long, thin branches that bend easily and narrow leaves. Willows usually grow in wet areas.
  wil·low (wil'ō) *noun, plural* **willows.**

wilt To become limp; droop. The flowers *wilted* soon after they were cut.
  wilt (wilt) *verb,* **wilted, wilting.**

win **1.** To do better than any other in a race or contest; gain a victory. The home team *won* the hockey game. We flipped a coin, and I *won.* **2.** To get as a prize. The winner of the baking contest will *win* a set of bread pans. **3.** To get by effort; gain. The explorer is *winning* new fame as an author. *Verb.*
  —A victory or success. The team had six *wins* and five losses this season. *Noun.*
  win (win) *verb,* **won, winning;** *noun, plural* **wins.**

wince To draw back slightly from something painful, dangerous, or unpleasant. The child *winced* when the doctor gave the injection.
  wince (wins) *verb,* **winced, wincing.**

winch A machine for lifting or pulling things. A winch is made up of a large spool or pulley with a rope or chain around it. Ships' anchors are hoisted on a winch.
  winch (winch) *noun, plural* **winches.**

wind¹ **1.** Air that is moving over the earth. The *wind* blew my hat off. The strong *winds* made the trees bend and sway. **2.** The power to breathe; breath. The hard blow knocked the *wind* out of me. *Noun.*
  —To cause someone to be out of breath. Climbing the long flight of stairs *winded* us. *Verb.*
  • **to get wind of.** To receive information or hints about. If my cousin *gets wind of* the party, the surprise will be ruined.
  wind (wind) *noun, plural* **winds;** *verb,* **winded, winding.**

wind² **1.** To wrap something around on itself or on something else. Please *wind* this loose yarn into a ball. The vine *wound* around the pole. **2.** To move or cause to move in one direction and then another. The road *winds* through the mountains. I *wound* through the traffic on my bicycle. **3.** To give a machine power by tightening its spring. Don't forget to *wind* your alarm clock. *Verb.*
  • **to wind up.** **1.** To end; finish; conclude. Let's *wind up* the work today. The meeting *wound up* at six o'clock. **2.** To make movements with the arms and body

before pitching a ball. The batter watched carefully while the pitcher *wound up.*
  wind (wīnd) *verb,* **wound, winding.**

wind instrument A musical instrument that is played by blowing into it. Trumpets and flutes are wind instruments.
  wind instrument (wind).

windmill A machine that uses the power of the wind to turn vanes or sails at the top of a tower. Windmills are used to pump water, grind grain, or generate electricity.
  wind·mill (wind'mil') *noun, plural* **windmills.**

windmill

window An opening in a wall or roof that lets in air and light. Panes of glass fill the openings of most windows.
  win·dow (win'dō) *noun, plural* **windows.**

Word History

The word **window** comes from two Scandinavian words meaning "wind" and "eye." A window was thought of as an opening, or "eye," in a wall to let the wind through.

---

windowpane A single pane of glass in a window.
  win·dow·pane (win'dō pān') *noun, plural* **windowpanes.**

windpipe The tube in the body that carries air from the throat to the lungs.
  wind·pipe (wind'pīp') *noun, plural* **windpipes.**

windshield A glass or plastic screen attached near the front of an automobile, motorcycle, or other vehicle. A windshield protects the driver and riders from the wind.
  wind·shield (wind'shēld') *noun, plural* **windshields.**

windy Having or swept by strong winds. We need a *windy* day for flying our kites.
wind·y (win′dē) *adjective*, **windier, windiest.**

wine An alcoholic drink made from the fermented juice of grapes or other fruits.
wine (wīn) *noun, plural* **wines.**

wing **1.** A movable part of the body that is used in flying. Birds, insects, and bats have wings. **2.** A structure that sticks out from the side of an airplane. Wings are shaped to help a moving airplane rise and fly. **3.** A part that is attached to and sticks out from the main part of a structure. We added a new *wing* with two bedrooms to our house. **4.** The part on either side of a stage that is not seen by the audience. The actors waited in the *wings. Noun.*
—To fly. Many birds *wing* their way south in the fall. *Verb.*
wing (wing) *noun, plural* **wings;** *verb*, **winged, winging.**

winged Having wings. Bats are *winged* animals.
winged (wingd *or* wing′id) *adjective.*

wingspan or **wingspread** The distance between the tip of one wing and the tip of another on an airplane or a bird, bat, or insect when it opens its wings wide. The *wingspan* of that airplane is 40 feet. Some eagles have a *wingspread* of 7½ feet.
wing·span or **wing·spread** (wing′span′ *or* wing′spred′) *noun, plural* **wingspans** or **wingspreads.**

wink To close and open one or both eyes quickly. People usually wink with one eye as a signal. Mother *winked* at me to let me know she knew the secret. *Verb.*
—**1.** A quick closing and opening of one or both eyes. Dad gave me a *wink* to show that he was just joking. **2.** A very short time. I didn't get a *wink* of sleep last night. *Noun.*
wink (wingk) *verb*, **winked, winking;** *noun, plural* **winks.**

winner A person or thing that wins. My friend was the *winner* of the spelling bee.
win·ner (win′ər) *noun, plural* **winners.**

winning **1.** Victorious or successful. The *winning* team received a trophy. Who scored the *winning* goal? **2.** Charming or attractive. The salesperson had a very *winning* smile. *Adjective.*
—**winnings.** Something that is won. My family plays cards for pennies and we get to keep our *winnings. Noun.*
win·ning (win′ing) *adjective; plural noun.*

winter The season of the year between fall and spring. *Noun.*
—To spend the winter. My grandparents *winter* in Florida. *Verb.*
win·ter (win′tər) *noun, plural* **winters;** *verb*, **wintered, wintering.**

wintergreen A low evergreen plant with white flowers and red berries. Oil from the wintergreen is used in medicine or for flavoring.
win·ter·green (win′tər grēn′) *noun, plural* **wintergreens.**

wintergreen

wintry Having to do with or like winter. It was a cold, *wintry* day with gray skies overhead.
win·try (win′trē) *adjective*, **wintrier, wintriest.**

wipe **1.** To clean or dry by rubbing with or on something. If you wash the dishes, I will *wipe* them dry. Please *wipe* your shoes on the mat before coming into the house. **2.** To take away by cleaning or drying. Please *wipe* the mud off your shoes.
• **to wipe out.** To destroy totally. The epidemic *wiped out* the population of the village.
wipe (wīp) *verb*, **wiped, wiping.**

wire **1.** A thin metal thread or a bunch of metal threads. Wire is used for fastening, for making such things as fences and screens, and for carrying electricity. **2.** A telegram. *Noun.*
—Made of wire. We put the eggs into a *wire* basket. *Adjective.*
—**1.** To put in wires for electricity. The new house was *wired* but the plumbing was not in yet. **2.** To fasten with a wire. I *wired* the broken gate together. **3.** To send a telegram. *Verb.*
wire (wīr) *noun, plural* **wires;** *adjective; verb*, **wired, wiring.**

wireless Sending messages or signals without using wires. Radio is a form of *wireless* communication. *Adjective.*

at; āpe; fär; câre; end; mē; it; īce; pîerce; hot; ōld; sông, fôrk; oil; out; up; ūse; rüle; pùll; tûrn; chin; sing; shop; thin; this; hw in white; zh in treasure. The symbol ə stands for the unstressed vowel sound in about, taken, pencil, lemon, and circus.

w

817

—A radio. *Noun.*
wire·less (wīr′lis) *adjective; noun, plural* **wirelesses.**

wiring A system of wires that carry electric current. The *wiring* in our house is connected to a fuse box.
wir·ing (wīr′ing) *noun.*

Wis. or **Wisc.** An abbreviation for *Wisconsin.*

Wisconsin A state in the north-central United States. Its capital is Madison.
Wis·con·sin (wis kon′sən) *noun.*

Word History

Wisconsin was named after the *Wisconsin* River, which is the main river in the state. This name is the English form of an earlier French name. The French name probably came from an American Indian word that means "at the big river" or "the place where the waters come together."

---

wisdom Good judgment and intelligence in knowing what is right, good, and true. We grow in *wisdom* as we gain more experience and knowledge.
wis·dom (wiz′dəm) *noun.*

wise Having or showing good judgment and intelligence. The *wise* counselor gave sound advice. It's *wise* to stay away from fighting dogs.
wise (wīz) *adjective,* **wiser, wisest.**

wish **1.** A feeling of wanting something; a strong desire. My *wish* to be a firefighter gets stronger every day. **2.** An expression of what a person wants. Make a *wish* and blow out the candles. Don't go against your parents' *wishes.* **3.** A thing that a person wants. I hoped for a compass for my birthday, and I got my *wish. Noun.*
—**1.** To want something very much; have a wish. I *wish* that summer would last longer. **2.** To think of or express a wish. I *wish* you good luck and a safe journey. *Verb.*
wish (wish) *noun, plural* **wishes;** *verb,* **wished, wishing.**

wishbone A forked bone in front of the breastbone of chickens and other birds. Some people make wishes on wishbones. One person holds one end, another person holds the other end, and they pull to break the bone. The person who gets the longer piece is supposed to have a wish come true.
wish·bone (wish′bōn′) *noun, plural* **wishbones.**

wisp A small bit or piece of something. The farmer's shirt was covered with *wisps* of hay. *Wisps* of smoke drifted up from the chimney.
wisp (wisp) *noun, plural* **wisps.**

wisteria A vine with a woody stem that has long, drooping clusters of white, pink, blue, or purple flowers.
wis·te·ri·a (wi stîr′ē ə) *noun.*

wisteria

wistful Sadly wishful. The little children were *wistful* as they looked at all the toys in the shop window.
wist·ful (wist′fəl) *adjective.*

wit **1.** The ability to make clever, amusing, and unusual comments. The speaker's *wit* delighted and stimulated the audience. **2.** A person who has this ability. We asked the class *wit* to think of something to write on the birthday card. **3.** The ability to think and reason; understanding. If a fire ever starts, try to keep your *wits* about you. ▲ The word "wit" in this sense is usually used in the plural.
wit (wit) *noun, plural* **wits.**

witch A person who is thought to have magic powers. In old fairy tales and legends, a witch is usually a woman who does evil things.
witch (wich) *noun, plural* **witches.**

with **1.** In the company or keeping of. We went to the movie *with* friends. We left our keys *with* a neighbor when we went on va-

cation.   **2.** Having or possessing. We need someone *with* good skills for this job.   **3.** By means of; by using. We work *with* a very powerful microscope in biology class.   **4.** In a way that shows. The skaters glided across the ice *with* the grace of dancers.   **5.** As an accompaniment to; in addition to. We had fruit *with* our cereal.   **6.** In regard to. Are you pleased *with* your gift?   **7.** In an association that involves. I talked on the phone *with* my friend in California. How often do you correspond *with* your grandparents? **8.** In opposition to; against. I seldom argue *with* my friends.   **9.** In support of; on the side of. Are you *with* us or against us? *Preposition.*
   with (wi<u>th</u> *or* with) *preposition.*

withdraw   **1.** To take away; remove. The captain *withdrew* the troops from the battle. He will have to *withdraw* money from the bank to pay for the gifts.   **2.** To take back. She *withdrew* her offer to buy the house. **3.** To leave a place; go away. A servant brought food on a tray and then *withdrew.*
   with·draw (wi<u>th</u> drô′ *or* with drô′) *verb,* **withdrew, withdrawn, withdrawing.**

withdrawn   Past participle of **withdraw.** The soldiers were *withdrawn* from the patrol. Look up **withdraw** for more information. *Verb.*
—Very shy or quiet. We decided to invite a *withdrawn* classmate whom no one knew very well. *Adjective.*
   with·drawn (wi<u>th</u> drôn′ *or* with drôn′) *verb; adjective.*

withdrew   Past tense of **withdraw.** Yesterday I *withdrew* five dollars from my savings account. Look up **withdraw** for more information.
   with·drew (wi<u>th</u> drü′ *or* with drü′) *verb.*

wither   To dry up or shrivel. The flowers *withered* soon after they were cut. The hot sun *withered* the crops.
   with·er (wi<u>th</u>′ər) *verb,* **withered, withering.**

within   **1.** In or into the inner part or parts of. The troops camped *within* the walls of the fort.   **2.** Not beyond the limits or extent of. I promise to return *within* an hour. It is *within* their power to help us. *Preposition.*
—In or into the inner part or parts of. I heard a noise *within* that sounded like an explosion. *Adverb.*
   with·in (wi<u>th</u> in′ *or* with in′) *preposition; adverb.*

without   **1.** Not having; lacking. We were exhausted after a night *without* sleep. **2.** Not accompanied by. They went to the movie *without* you.   **3.** In a way that ne-

glects or avoids. They slipped out *without* saying good-bye.
   with·out (wi<u>th</u> out′ *or* with out′) *preposition.*

withstand   To resist the effects of; hold out against. The little boat *withstood* the storm and reached the shore safely.
   with·stand (with stand′ *or* wi<u>th</u> stand′) *verb,* **withstood, withstanding.**

withstood   Past tense and past participle of **withstand.** The strong table *withstood* the weight of the heavy sculpture. Look up **withstand** for more information.
   with·stood (with stùd′ *or* wi<u>th</u> stùd′) *verb.*

witness   A person who has seen or heard something, and so can answer questions about what happened. She was a *witness* to the accident and had to testify in court. *Noun.*
—To be present to see or hear something. Who *witnessed* the fight? Two friends of the old man *witnessed* the signing of his will. *Verb.*
   wit·ness (wit′nis) *noun, plural* **witnesses;** *verb,* **witnessed, witnessing.**

witty   Clever and amusing; having wit. We all laughed at the *witty* remark.
   wit·ty (wit′ē) *adjective,* **wittier, wittiest.**

wives   Plural of **wife.** The husbands and *wives* of the teachers are invited to the school celebration. Look up **wife** for more information.
   wives (wīvz) *plural noun.*

wizard   **1.** A person who is thought to have magic powers. In old fairy tales and legends, a wizard is usually a man.   **2.** A person who is very clever and skillful. My cousin is a *wizard* at arithmetic.
   wiz·ard (wiz′ərd) *noun, plural* **wizards.**

wk.   An abbreviation for *week.*

wobble   To move from side to side in an unsteady or shaky way. The old chair *wobbled* because the legs were loose.
   wob·ble (wob′əl) *verb,* **wobbled, wobbling.**

woe   Great sadness or suffering. The story told of the hunger, sickness, and other *woes* of the early settlers in America.
   woe (wō) *noun, plural* **woes.**

---

at; āpe; fär; câre; end; mē; it; īce; pîerce; hot; ōld; sông, fôrk; oil; out; up; ūse; rüle; pùll; tûrn; chin; sing; shop; thin; <u>th</u>is; hw in white; zh in treasure. The symbol ə stands for the unstressed vowel sound in about, taken, pencil, lemon, and circus.

W

woke A past tense of **wake.** I *woke* early this morning. Look up **wake** for more information.
woke (wōk) *verb.*

woken A past participle of **wake.** I was *woken* by the barking dog. Look up **wake** for more information.
wo·ken (wō′kən) *verb.*

wolf A wild animal that looks like a dog. Wolves have thick fur, a pointed muzzle, and a bushy tail. They live and hunt in packs. *Noun.*
—To eat very quickly and hungrily. The children *wolfed* down their lunch so they could get back outside to play. *Verb.*
wolf (wu̇lf) *noun, plural* **wolves;** *verb,* **wolfed, wolfing.**

wolf

wolverine A stout, meat-eating animal that is related to the weasel. It has dark brown fur and a long, bushy tail. Wolverines now live in northern Canada and Alaska.
wol·ver·ine (wu̇l′və rēn′) *noun, plural* **wolverines.**

wolves Plural of **wolf.** *Wolves* sometimes howl at night. Look up **wolf** for more information.
wolves (wu̇lvz) *plural noun.*

woman **1.** An adult female person. **2.** Adult female people as a group.
wom·an (wu̇m′ən) *noun, plural* **women.**

womanhood The condition or the time of being an adult female person. The girl had not yet reached *womanhood.*
wom·an·hood (wu̇m′ən hu̇d′) *noun.*

womb The organ in a female body that holds and nourishes a baby until it is born.
womb (wüm) *noun, plural* **wombs.**

wombat A stout animal that has coarse fur, short legs, and a large head with small eyes and pointed ears. The female wombat has a pouch in which she carries her young. Wombats are found in Australia.
wom·bat (wom′bat) *noun, plural* **wombats.**

women Plural of **woman.** Two *women* run the store. Look up **woman** for more information.
wom·en (wim′ən) *plural noun.*

won Past tense and past participle of **win.** Who *won* the first prize? We've *won* more games than we've lost. Look up **win** for more information. ▲ Another word that sounds like this is **one.**
won (wun) *verb.*

wonder **1.** An unusual, surprising, or very impressive thing. This huge waterfall is a natural *wonder.* That tightrope walker is a *wonder* to behold. **2.** The feeling caused by something unusual, surprising, or very impressive. I watched with *wonder* as the artist sketched the scene with just a few strokes of a pencil. *Noun.*
—**1.** To want to know or learn; be curious about. I *wonder* why the sky is blue. **2.** To feel or be surprised or impressed. The child *wondered* at the giraffe's long neck. *Verb.*
won·der (wun′dər) *noun, plural* **wonders;** *verb,* **wondered, wondering.**

wonderful **1.** Causing wonder; remarkable. The kangaroo is a strange and *wonderful* animal. **2.** Very good; fine. Our friends cooked a *wonderful* dinner for us.
won·der·ful (wun′dər fəl) *adjective.*

won't Shortened form of "will not." The painters *won't* be able to finish the work today.
won't (wōnt) *contraction.*

wood **1.** The hard material that makes up the trunk and branches of a tree or bush. Wood is cut and prepared for use as building material and fuel. **2.** An area of trees growing naturally; forest. *Noun.* ▲ The word "wood" in this sense is often used in the plural form.
—Made of or consisting of wood; wooden. We have *wood* furniture on our porch. *Adjective.* ▲ Another word that sounds like this is **would.**
wood (wu̇d) *noun, plural* **woods;** *adjective.*

woodchuck A stout animal with short legs that has coarse, brown fur. Woodchucks live underground in holes that they dig. They eat leaves and grass. This animal is also called a **groundhog.**

woodchuck

wood·chuck (wu̇d′chuk′) *noun, plural* **woodchucks.**

woodcutter   A person whose work is cutting down trees or chopping wood.
wood·cut·ter (wŭd′kut′ər) *noun, plural* **woodcutters.**

wooded   Having trees or woods. We had a picnic in a *wooded* area near our house.
wood·ed (wŭd′id) *adjective.*

wooden   Made of wood. I keep my clothes in a *wooden* chest of drawers.
wood·en (wŭd′ən) *adjective.*

woodpecker   Any of a number of birds that have strong, pointed bills. Woodpeckers use their bills to make holes in trees in order to get insects to eat. They are found in forests throughout the world.
wood·peck·er (wŭd′pek′ər) *noun, plural* **woodpeckers.**

woodpecker

woodsman   A woodcutter, hunter, or other person who lives or works in the woods.
woods·man (wŭdz′mən) *noun, plural* **woodsmen** (wŭdz′mən).

woodwind   A wind instrument that was originally made of wood, but that is now often made of metal or plastic. Flutes, oboes, clarinets, and saxophones are woodwinds.
wood·wind (wŭd′wind′) *noun, plural* **woodwinds.**

woodwork   Parts or things that are made out of wood. Window and door frames are parts of the woodwork of a house.
wood·work (wŭd′wûrk′) *noun.*

woodworking   The art of making things out of wood.
wood·work·ing (wŭd′wûr′king) *noun.*

woody   **1.** Containing wood. *Woody* plants have wood trunks and branches rather than soft green stems. **2.** Having many trees. We sailed to one of the small, *woody* islands in the bay.
wood·y (wŭd′ē) *adjective,* **woodier, woodiest.**

wool   **1.** The soft, thick, curly hair of sheep and some other animals such as the llama and alpaca. Wool is spun into yarn which is made into cloth. **2.** Cloth or yarn made of wool. **3.** Any substance made of a thick mass of fibers. We used steel *wool* to smooth my bike's fender before we painted it. *Noun.*
—Made of wool. I wear a *wool* coat in the winter. *Adjective.*
wool (wŭl) *noun, plural* **wools;** *adjective.*

woolen   Made of wool. I have a red *woolen* jacket.
wool·en (wŭl′ən) *adjective.*

word   **1.** A sound or group of sounds having meaning and forming a unit of a language.   **2.** A written or printed letter or group of letters standing for such a sound. The *word* "house" has five letters.   **3.** A short conversation or statement. I'd like a *word* with you.   **4.** A promise or vow. Give me your *word* that you won't tell a soul. **5.** A message or news. We received *word* of our team's victory. *Noun.*
—To put into words. *Word* your question so that we can understand. *Verb.*
• **word for word.**   In exactly the same words. Copy this message *word for word.*
word (wûrd) *noun, plural* **words;** *verb,* **worded, wording.**

wording   The way of saying or writing something in words. Which *wording* do you think is better: "Wanted, Buyer for Bike" or "Bicycle for Sale"?
word·ing (wûr′ding) *noun, plural* **wordings.**

word processing   The creating, changing, storing, and printing of words by means of a computer.

wordy   Using too many words. The *wordy* speaker went on and on.
word·y (wûr′dē) *adjective,* **wordier, wordiest.**

wore   Past tense of **wear.** I *wore* my new coat. Look up **wear** for more information.
▲ Another word that sounds like this is **war.**
wore (wôr) *verb.*

work   **1.** The use of a person's energy or ability to do something; effort. Work can be done by the mind, as in writing a paper, or by the body, as in chopping wood.   **2.** What a person does to earn money; a job or occupation. What kind of *work* does your cousin do?   **3.** Something that is done or is to be done; task. We finished our *work* early. **4.** Something that has been made or done. The painting was a beautiful *work* of art. **5. works.** The moving parts of a machine, watch, or other device. *Noun.*
—**1.** To use one's energy or ability in order to do or get something. If we *work* hard, we'll

at; āpe; fär; câre; end; mē; it; īce; pîerce; hot; ōld; sông, fôrk; oil; out; up; ūse; rüle; pŭll; tûrn; chin; sing; shop; thin; <u>th</u>is; hw in white; zh in treasure. The symbol ə stands for the unstressed vowel sound in about, taken, pencil, lemon, and circus.

W

finish the job today. **2.** To have a job. My cousin *works* in a business office. **3.** To act or make act properly; operate. Can you *work* the tape recorder? Did the medicine *work?* **4.** To make happen; bring about. We'll have to *work* a miracle to finish on time. **5.** To shape, as by pressing and rolling; mold. *Work* the clay in your hands until it becomes soft. *Verb.*

- **out of work.** Without a job; unemployed. I lost my job last month and have been *out of work* ever since.
- **to work out. 1.** To develop or improve. *Work out* your ideas before you begin to write the essay. **2.** To solve. Can you *work out* the problem yourself? **3.** To end or result; turn out. Did your suggestions *work out* in the way that you hoped? **4.** To train or do exercises. I *work out* at the gym every day.

work (wûrk) *noun, plural* **works;** *verb,* **worked, working.**

workable 1. Capable of being accomplished or used. We decided the plan was *workable*, so we went ahead with it. **2.** Capable of being molded, forged, or otherwise shaped into something. To make the clay *workable*, add a little more water to it.
work·a·ble (wûr′kə bəl) *adjective.*

workbench A strong table used for working. Carpenters use workbenches.
work·bench (wûrk′bench′) *noun, plural* **workbenches.**

workbook A book that has questions and exercises to be answered or done by a student.
work·book (wûrk′bük′) *noun, plural* **workbooks.**

worker 1. A person who works. There were over one hundred *workers* in the factory. **2.** A female bee, ant, termite, or other insect that does most of the work in a colony.
work·er (wûr′kər) *noun, plural* **workers.**

working 1. In operation; functioning properly. Is that telephone *working?* **2.** Having to do with or doing a job. Our *working* hours are 9:00 A.M. to 5:00 P.M. *Working* people are often tired in the evening.
work·ing (wûr′king) *adjective.*

workman A person who works with his or her hands or with machines. Many *workmen* have been hired to build the new school.
work·man (wûrk′mən) *noun, plural* **workmen** (wûrk′mən).

workmanship The skill with which a thing is made. The beautifully carved cabinet showed excellent *workmanship.*
work·man·ship (wûrk′mən ship′) *noun.*

workshop 1. A room or building in which work is done by hand or with machines. We keep our tools in a *workshop* in the basement. The garage has a *workshop* where cars are repaired. **2.** A group of people who are studying or working together on a special subject. The school has a *workshop* in child care this summer.
work·shop (wûrk′shop′) *noun, plural* **workshops.**

workshop

world 1. The earth. Old whaling ships sometimes sailed around the *world.* **2.** A part of the earth. The United States is in the western *world.* **3.** All the people who live on the earth. The *world* waited for news of the first astronauts to land on the moon. **4.** A field of activity, interest, or life. We studied the *world* of fish and the sea. Many people who work are part of the business *world.* **5.** A large amount; great deal. The rain did the corn crop a *world* of good.
world (wûrld) *noun, plural* **worlds.**

World War I A war fought between 1914 and 1918 mainly in Europe. Great Britain, France, Russia, Italy, the United States, and their allies fought against Germany and its allies.

World War II A war fought between 1939 and 1945 mainly in Europe, northern Africa, and Asia and the Atlantic and Pacific oceans. Great Britain, France, the Soviet Union, the United States, China, and their allies fought against Germany, Italy, Japan, and their allies.

worldwide All over the world. That movie star has won *worldwide* fame.
world·wide (wûrld′wīd′) *adjective.*

worm 1. A long, thin animal with a soft body, no legs, and no backbone. Worms crawl or creep. **2. worms.** A disease caused

by certain worms that live as parasites inside another animal. *Noun.*
—**1.** To move by wiggling or creeping like a worm. It took me ten minutes to *worm* my way through the crowd to the door. **2.** To get by a sly method. They tried to *worm* the secret out of us. **3.** To get rid of worms that live inside an animal. We *wormed* our dog by giving it medicine every morning. *Verb.*
worm (wûrm) *noun, plural* **worms;** *verb,* **wormed, worming.**

worn Past participle of **wear.** I have *worn* this coat for three years. Look up **wear** for more information. *Verb.*
—Damaged by use or wear. Those pants are *worn* at the knees. *Adjective.*
worn (wôrn) *verb; adjective.*

worn-out **1.** Used or worn so much that it should not or cannot be used any more. It's time to replace those *worn-out* shoes. **2.** Very tired. The *worn-out* hikers finally reached the camp.
worn-out (wôrn'out') *adjective.*

worry **1.** To feel or cause to feel uneasy or troubled. The parents *worried* when the sick child's fever would not go down. That leak in the ceiling *worries* me. **2.** To pull or bite at something with the teeth. The puppy *worried* at the rug. *Verb.*
—Something that causes an uneasy or troubled feeling. Their biggest *worry* was that it might rain on the day of the picnic. *Noun.*
wor·ry (wûr'ē) *verb,* **worried, worrying;** *noun, plural* **worries.**

worse **1.** More inferior; less good. I am a bad speller, but my friend is *worse.* **2.** More unfavorable. The weather was *worse* yesterday than it is today. **3.** In poorer health; less well. The doctor said that the patient was *worse. Adjective.*
—In a worse way. Our team seems to play *worse* during practice. *Adverb.*
—Something that is worse. The soup was pretty bad, but I have tasted *worse. Noun.*
worse (wûrs) *adjective; adverb; noun.*

worship Prayer, religious services, and other acts done in honor of God or a god. Churches, temples, and mosques are places of *worship. Noun.*
—**1.** To pay honor to God or a god. The ancient Romans *worshiped* in this temple. **2.** To give great love or devotion to. My little sister *worships* her older brother. *Verb.*
wor·ship (wûr'ship) *noun; verb,* **worshiped** or **worshipped, worshiping** or **worshipping.**

worst **1.** Most inferior; least good. Throwing water on a grease fire is the *worst* thing you can do. **2.** Most unfavorable. That's

the *worst* news I've heard all week. **3.** Most harmful or severe. The *worst* storm we had last year knocked over our big walnut tree. *Adjective.*
—In the worst way. My sore throat hurts *worst* in the morning. *Adverb.*
—Something that is worst. None of these photographs is good, but this one is the *worst. Noun.*
worst (wûrst) *adjective; adverb; noun.*

worth **1.** Good enough for; deserving of. That movie was *worth* seeing. **2.** Having the same value as. This old coin is *worth* thirty dollars today. **3.** Having wealth that amounts to. That banker is *worth* millions of dollars. *Preposition.*
—**1.** The quality that makes a person or thing good or useful; excellence. My raincoat proved its *worth* by keeping me dry during the storm. **2.** The amount of money that something can be exchanged for; value in money. That diamond's *worth* is said to be $50,000. **3.** The amount that a certain sum of money will buy. The customer asked for a dollar's *worth* of cherries. *Noun.*
worth (wûrth) *preposition; noun.*

worthless Not good or useful; without value. This pot is *worthless* because it has a hole in the bottom.
worth·less (wûrth'lis) *adjective.*

worthwhile Good enough or important enough to spend time, effort, or money on. Doing volunteer work at the hospital is a *worthwhile* activity.
worth·while (wûrth'hwīl' *or* wûrth'wīl') *adjective.*

worthy **1.** Having value; good or worthwhile. The prize should go to a *worthy* person. **2.** Having enough value; deserving. The idea is at least *worthy* of consideration.
wor·thy (wûr'thē) *adjective,* **worthier, worthiest.**

would An auxiliary verb that is used in the following ways: **1.** To express something that might have happened if something else had happened first. We *would* be cooler if we had opened the windows. **2.** To express something that might happen later. We sat on the platform, wondering if the train *would* be on time. **3.** To express something that

at; āpe; fär; câre; end; mē; it; īce; pîerce; hot; ōld; sông, fôrk; oil; out; up; ūse; rüle; pùll; tûrn; chin; sing; shop; thin; **this;** hw in white; zh in treasure. The symbol ə stands for the unstressed vowel sound in about, taken, pencil, lemon, and circus.

W

was planned or intended. The scouts promised that they *would* return soon. **4.** To express something that happened often or commonly. During the summer we *would* sit by the lake and talk for hours. **5.** To express a request. *Would* you please turn off the radio? ▲ Another word that sounds like this is **wood.**

would (wŭd) *verb.*

wouldn't Shortened form of "would not." I *wouldn't* do that if I were you.

would·nt (wŭd'ənt) *contraction.*

wound¹ **1.** A cut or other injury to a part of the body. **2.** A hurt to a person's feelings. It took a long time to recover from the *wound* of that insult. *Noun.*
—**1.** To hurt or injure by cutting, piercing, or tearing the skin. The soldier was *wounded* during the war. **2.** To hurt a person's feelings. The singer's pride was *wounded* when the leading role went to someone else. *Verb.*

wound (wünd) *noun, plural* **wounds;** *verb,* **wounded, wounding.**

wound² Past tense of **wind².** I *wound* the clock before I went to bed. Look up **wind²** for more information.

wound (wound) *verb.*

wove A past tense of **weave.** Yesterday we *wove* baskets out of reeds. Look up **weave** for more information.

wove (wōv) *verb.*

woven A past participle of **weave.** The robin had *woven* twigs together to make a nest. Look up **weave** for more information.

wo·ven (wō'vən) *verb.*

wrap **1.** To cover by putting something around. We *wrapped* the presents in colored tissue paper. **2.** To fold or wind as a covering. The nurse *wrapped* a blanket around the baby. **3.** To hide by covering. The top of the mountain was *wrapped* in fog. **4.** To clasp or fold. The monkey *wrapped* its arms around the animal trainer. ▲ Another word that sounds like this is **rap.**

wrap (rap) *verb,* **wrapped, wrapping.**

wrapper A piece of paper or other covering for something. Be sure to put food *wrappers* in the wastebasket.

wrap·per (rap'ər) *noun, plural* **wrappers.**

wrapping Paper or other covering for something. We burned the *wrappings* from the birthday presents in the fireplace.

wrap·ping (rap'ing) *noun, plural* **wrappings.**

wrath Very great anger. In the story, the wizard's tricks aroused the *wrath* of the monster.

wrath (rath) *noun.*

wreath A circle of leaves or flowers woven together. We hung a holiday *wreath* on the front door.

wreath (rēth) *noun, plural* **wreaths** (rēthz *or* rēths).

wreck To destroy or ruin. The builders *wrecked* the old house to clear the land. The dishonest behavior of the store owners *wrecked* their business. *Verb.*
—What is left of something that has been ruined or damaged. There are many automobile *wrecks* in the junkyard. The room was a *wreck* after the party. *Noun.*

wreck (rek) *verb,* **wrecked, wrecking;** *noun, plural* **wrecks.**

wreckage What is left of something that has been ruined or destroyed. We went to look at the *wreckage* after the building burned down.

wreck·age (rek'ij) *noun.*

wren A small songbird with brown feathers, a narrow bill, and a short tail that often sticks upward.

wren (ren) *noun, plural* **wrens.**

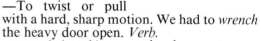

wren

wrench **1.** A very hard, sharp twist or pull. I gave the doorknob a *wrench* but the door was stuck. **2.** A tool with jaws that is used to grip and turn a nut or bolt. *Noun.*
—To twist or pull with a hard, sharp motion. We had to *wrench* the heavy door open. *Verb.*

wrench (rench) *noun, plural* **wrenches;** *verb,* **wrenched, wrenching.**

wrestle **1.** To struggle by grasping and trying to force and hold one's opponent to the ground, without punching. The children *wrestled* on the lawn. **2.** To force by grasping. The champion *wrestled* his opponent to the mat. **3.** To struggle very hard. She *wrestled* with the last problem on the arithmetic test.

wres·tle (res'əl) *verb,* **wrestled, wrestling.**

wrestling A sport in which two people struggle by grasping each other. Each person tries to force and hold the other to the ground. Punching is not allowed in wrestling.

wres·tling (res'ling) *noun.*

wretched **1.** Very unhappy, poor, or uncomfortable. My fever made me feel *wretched.* **2.** Very bad or evil. The cruel soldiers were *wretched* people.

wretch·ed (rech'id) *adjective.*

wriggle **1.** To twist or turn from side to side with short, quick moves; squirm. The bored children *wriggled* in their seats. The snake *wriggled* through the grass. **2.** To get into or out of a position by tricky means. You always try to *wriggle* out of having to wash the dishes.
   wrig·gle (rig′əl) *verb*, **wriggled, wriggling.**

wring **1.** To squeeze or twist so that liquid is forced out. You must *wring* the wet clothes before hanging them up to dry. **2.** To force out liquid by squeezing or twisting. I *wrung* the water from my bathing suit. **3.** To get by force. The soldiers said they would *wring* the truth out of the spy. **4.** To hold tightly and press or twist. Some of the people waiting in the dentist's office were *wringing* their hands nervously. ⚠ Another word that sounds like this is **ring.**
   wring (ring) *verb*, **wrung, wringing.**

wrinkle A small fold, ridge, or line in a smooth surface. He ironed the *wrinkles* out of his shirt. She had small *wrinkles* at the corners of her eyes. *Noun.*
—To make or have a fold, ridge, or line in a smooth surface. Some people *wrinkle* their foreheads when they frown. Silk clothing *wrinkles* easily. *Verb.*
   wrin·kle (ring′kəl) *noun, plural* **wrinkles;** *verb,* **wrinkled, wrinkling.**

wrist The joint between the hand and the arm.
   wrist (rist) *noun, plural* **wrists.**

wristwatch A watch that is worn on a strap around the wrist.
   wrist·watch (rist′woch′) *noun, plural* **wristwatches.**

write **1.** To form letters, words, or symbols on paper or some other surface. The teacher *wrote* his name on the blackboard. **2.** To be the author of. My aunt *writes* children's stories. **3.** To send a letter. Please *write* to us when you are on vacation. ⚠ Another word that sounds like this is **right.**
   write (rīt) *verb,* **wrote, written, writing.**

writer A person who writes stories, poems, or articles; author.
   writ·er (rī′tər) *noun, plural* **writers.**

writing **1.** Letters, words, or symbols that are written by hand. Do you know whose *writing* this is? **2.** A book, play, or other thing that has been written. We study the *writings* of many authors in English class.
   writ·ing (rī′ting) *noun, plural* **writings.**

written Past participle of **write.** Has your friend *written* you a letter yet? Look up **write** for more information.
   writ·ten (rit′ən) *verb.*

wrong **1.** Not correct or true. Some of your answers were right, and some were *wrong.* **2.** Not moral or good; bad. It is *wrong* to steal. **3.** Not proper; not suitable. A heavy sweater is the *wrong* thing to wear on a hot day. **4.** Out of order; not working. Something is *wrong* with my watch. *Adjective.*
—Something that is not moral or good. Injustice is a great *wrong. Noun.*
—In a way that is not right; incorrectly. I spelled several words *wrong* in my report. *Adverb.*
—To treat in an unjust or bad way. The salesperson *wronged* us by accusing us of stealing. *Verb.*
   wrong (rông) *adjective; noun, plural* **wrongs;** *adverb; verb,* **wronged, wronging.**

wrote Past tense of **write.** We all *wrote* down what the teacher said. Look up **write** for more information.
   wrote (rōt) *verb.*

wrung Past tense and past participle of **wring.** I *wrung* out the wet shirt and hung it up to dry. Look up **wring** for more information. ⚠ Another word that sounds like this is **rung.**
   wrung (rung) *verb.*

wt. An abbreviation for *weight.*

WV Postal abbreviation for *West Virginia.*

W. Va. An abbreviation for *West Virginia.*

WY Postal abbreviation for *Wyoming.*

Wyo. An abbreviation for *Wyoming.*

Wyoming A state in the western United States. Its capital is Cheyenne.
   Wy·o·ming (wī ō′ming) *noun.*

Word History

The name **Wyoming** comes from a word used by eastern American Indians to mean "flat area between mountains." The Indians used this name for a valley in Pennsylvania. Congress later gave this name to a new territory in the western plains. The name *Wyoming* was kept when the territory became a state.

---

at; āpe; fär; câre; end; mē; it; īce; pîerce; hot; ōld; sông, fôrk; oil; out; up; ūse; rüle; pu̇ll; tûrn; chin; sing; shop; thin; this; hw in white; zh in treasure. The symbol ə stands for the unstressed vowel sound in about, taken, pencil, lemon, and circus.

W

825

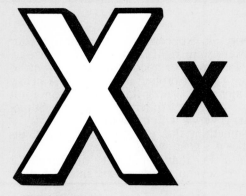

1. One of the oldest forms of the letter **X** was used by the ancient Greeks. They wrote it either like a plus sign or an X.

2. Several hundred years later, the Greeks were making their "cross sign," very much like a modern **X**.

3. An ancient tribe that settled near Rome about 2,800 years ago also used the "cross sign."

4. The ancient Romans then borrowed the letter **X**, giving it the same form.

5. We write our capital letter **X** much the same way as the Romans did 2,400 years ago.

x, X   The twenty-fourth letter of the alphabet.
  x, X (eks) *noun, plural* **x's, X's.**

Xerox   A trademark for a process or machine for making photographic copies of written or printed materials. *Noun.*
  —To make a copy of something written or printed by using a Xerox machine. I *Xeroxed* the schedule of events and distributed it to the class. *Verb.*
  Xe·rox (zîr′oks) *noun; verb,* **Xeroxed, Xeroxing.**

Xmas   Christmas. Look up **Christmas** for more information.
  X·mas (kris′məs *or* eks′məs) *noun, plural* **Xmases.**

X-ray   To examine, photograph, or treat with X rays. The doctor *X-rayed* my arm to see if any bones had been broken.
  X-ray (eks′rā′) *verb,* **X-rayed, X-raying.**

X ray   **1.** A kind of radiation that can pass through substances that ordinary rays of light cannot pass through. Doctors use X rays to take pictures of parts inside the body that cannot be seen from outside. X rays can be used to see if a bone has been broken or to see if there is a cavity in a hidden part of a tooth.   **2.** A photograph made with X rays. The doctor looked at the *X ray* of the dog's injured leg.

xylophone   A musical instrument that is made up of one or two rows of wooden bars. The bars are of different lengths, and they are sounded by hitting them with small wooden hammers.
  xy·lo·phone (zī′lə fōn′) *noun, plural* **xylophones.**

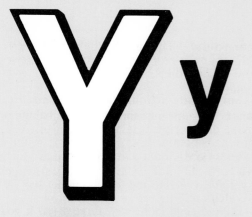

1. The letter **Y** has the same history as the letter **V**. It was first used by ancient tribes in the Middle East.

2. When the ancient Greeks borrowed this letter, they made it very much like a modern capital **Y**.

3. The ancient Romans adopted this letter twice from the Greeks. The first time they used it to form the letter **V**.

4. Later, the Romans again adopted this letter, this time to write words they had borrowed from the Greeks.

5. The form of our modern capital **Y** can be traced back to both the Greeks and the Romans.

y, Y The twenty-fifth letter of the alphabet. **y, Y** (wī) *noun, plural* **y's, Y's.**

-y A *suffix* that is often added to a noun to form an adjective and that means: **1.** Full of; having. *Dirty* means full of dirt. **2.** Like. *Wintry* means like winter. **3.** Tending to. *Sticky* means tending to stick.

yacht A small ship used for pleasure trips. **yacht** (yot) *noun, plural* **yachts.**

yak

yak An ox that has long hair and is found in Asia. Yaks are raised for their meat and milk. They are also used to carry heavy loads. There are very few wild yaks left. **yak** (yak) *noun, plural* **yaks.**

yam **1.** The root of a trailing tropical vine. It is ground into flour or eaten baked or broiled. **2.** A kind of sweet potato. Look up **sweet potato** for more information. **yam** (yam) *noun, plural* **yams.**

yank To pull something in a sharp, sudden way; jerk; tug. The selfish child *yanked* the toy truck away from the baby. *Verb.* —A sharp, sudden pull. With one *yank* on the ribbon, I untied the bow on my birthday present. *Noun.* **yank** (yangk) *verb,* **yanked, yanking;** *noun, plural* **yanks.**

yams

Yankee **1.** A person who was born or is living in a state in New England or another Northern state. **2.** A person who fought for the Union during the Civil War. **3.** A person who was born in or is a citizen of the United States; American. **Yan·kee** (yang′kē) *noun, plural* **Yankees.**

yard¹ **1.** An area of ground next to or surrounding a house, school, or other building.

We have a vegetable garden in our *yard*. We play games in the *yard* behind the school. **2.** An enclosed area used for carrying on some work or business. Wood for building can be bought at a lumber *yard*. A train *yard* is where trains are stored and switched.
yard (yärd) *noun, plural* **yards.**

yard² **1.** A measure of length equal to 36 inches, or 3 feet. A yard is slightly shorter than a meter. **2.** A long rod fastened across the mast of a ship to support a sail.
yard (yärd) *noun, plural* **yards.**

yardstick **1.** A flat strip of wood, plastic, or metal one yard long and marked with units of length. It is used in measuring. **2.** Any standard used in making a judgment or comparison. One *yardstick* of the quality of a car is the number of miles it can travel using a gallon of gas.
yard·stick (yärd′stik′) *noun, plural* **yardsticks.**

yarn **1.** Fibers that have been twisted into long strands. Yarn is used in knitting or weaving. It is made from cotton, wool, silk, nylon, or other fiber. **2.** A long story; tale. The old sailors liked to tell *yarns* about their sea voyages.
yarn (yärn) *noun, plural* **yarns.**

yawn **1.** To open the mouth wide and take a deep breath. People yawn because they are tired or bored. **2.** To be wide open. The entrance to the huge cave *yawned* in front of them. *Verb.*
—The act of opening the mouth wide and taking a deep breath. The bored listener tried to hide a *yawn* as the speaker went on and on. *Noun.*
yawn (yôn) *verb,* **yawned, yawning;** *noun, plural* **yawns.**

yd. An abbreviation for *yard.*

ye You. ▲ This word was common in the past, but it is not often used today.
ye (yē) *pronoun.*

year **1.** A period of time made up of the twelve months from January 1 to December 31. A year contains 365 days. There are 366 days in a leap year. **2.** Any period of twelve months. We moved to this house two *years* ago. **3.** A part of a year spent in a particular activity. During the school *year* I get up at 7:30 in the morning.
year (yîr) *noun, plural* **years.**

yearly **1.** Happening or returning once a year. We make a *yearly* trip to my grandparents' house at Thanksgiving. **2.** Measured by the year. The *yearly* average rainfall in our city is about 42 inches.
year·ly (yîr′lē) *adjective.*

year-round Throughout the year. The athletes follow a *year-round* routine of exercises and special diets. This hotel is open *year-round.*
year-round (yîr′round′) *adjective; adverb.*

yeast A substance that is used in baking to make dough rise. It is made up of tiny cells of fungus plants.
yeast (yēst) *noun, plural* **yeasts.**

yell To call loudly; shout; cry. My sister got mad and *yelled* at me for taking her bicycle. "Watch out!" he *yelled. Verb.*
—A loud call; shout; cry. Give a *yell* if you need any help. *Noun.*
yell (yel) *verb,* **yelled, yelling;** *noun, plural* **yells.**

yellow **1.** The color of gold, butter, or ripe lemons. **2.** The yolk of an egg. The recipe calls for two egg *yellows. Noun.*
—Having the color yellow. A daisy has a *yellow* center. *Adjective.*
—**1.** To make or become yellow. The old newspaper had *yellowed* with age. *Verb.*
yel·low (yel′ō) *noun, plural* **yellows;** *adjective,* **yellower, yellowest;** *verb,* **yellowed, yellowing.**

yellow jacket A kind of wasp that has black and bright yellow markings.

Yemen **1.** A country in southwestern Asia. **2.** Another name for a nearby country called **Southern Yemen.** Look up **Southern Yemen** for more information.
Yem·en (yem′ən) *noun.*

yellow jacket

yen¹ A unit of money in Japan.
yen (yen) *noun, plural* **yen.**

yen² A strong desire, longing. I have a *yen* to travel to sunny places.
yen (yen) *noun, plural* **yens.**

yes A word used to show agreement or acceptance. *Yes,* you are right. *Yes,* you may borrow my calculator. *Adverb.*
—**1.** An answer that shows agreement or acceptance. Six people said *yes* to our party invitation. **2.** A vote in favor of something. The hikers voted on whether to stop for lunch, and there were three *yeses* and one no. *Noun.*
yes (yes) *adverb; noun, plural* **yeses.**

yesterday The day before today. *Yesterday* was sunny, but by this morning it had begun to rain. *Noun.*
—On the day before today. I started to read

the book *yesterday* and finished it by this afternoon. *Adverb.*

yes·ter·day (yes′tər dē *or* yes′tər dā′) *noun, plural* **yesterdays;** *adverb.*

yet   **1.** At the present time; now. I'm not *yet* old enough to drive a car.   **2.** Up to the present time; so far. They have never *yet* been late for a meeting.   **3.** Continuously up to this or that time; still. The farmers went to the fields early and are working *yet*.   **4.** At some future time; eventually. The mystery will be solved *yet*.   **5.** In addition. There are three days *yet* to go until our vacation. *Adverb.*
—Nevertheless; however; but. I thought I knew the way, *yet* I soon got lost. *Conjunction.*
• **as yet.**   Up to the present time; so far. We have not *as yet* received the package you sent us.
yet (yet) *adverb; conjunction.*

yew   An evergreen tree that has reddish brown bark, flat, needle-shaped leaves, and a seed with a red, fleshy covering. It is native to Europe and Asia. The wood of this tree is used to make bows for archery.   ▲ Other words that sound like this are **ewe** and **you.**
yew (ū) *noun, plural* **yews.**

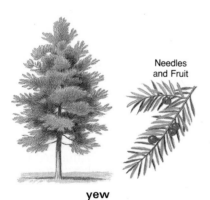

Needles and Fruit

yew

yield   **1.** To produce. The field *yielded* a large crop of wheat.   **2.** To give control or possession of to another. The defeated army *yielded* the town to the enemy.   **3.** To stop fighting or disagreeing. We *yielded* in the argument when we realized that we were wrong.   **4.** To give way to force or pressure. The lock on the door of the old house was broken, and it *yielded* when we pushed against it. *Verb.*
—An amount produced. The farm's *yield* of corn was greater this year than last year. *Noun.*
yield (yēld) *verb,* **yielded, yielding;** *noun, plural* **yields.**

yogurt   A thick, soft food that is made by adding certain bacteria to milk. Yogurt is often sweetened and flavored with fruit.
yo·gurt (yō′gərt) *noun, plural* **yogurts.**

Word History

The word **yogurt** comes from the Turkish name for this food.

yoke   **1.** A wooden frame used to join together two work animals.   **2.** A pair of animals joined by a yoke. The wagon was pulled by a *yoke* of oxen.   **3.** The part of a shirt, dress, or other piece of clothing that fits around the shoulders and neck. The *yoke* on that dress is trimmed with lace. *Noun.*
—To join with a yoke or harness. The farmer *yoked* the oxen to the plow. *Verb.*   ▲ Another word that sounds like this is **yolk.**
yoke (yōk) *noun, plural* **yokes** *(for definitions 1 and 3)* or **yoke** *(for definition 2); verb,* **yoked, yoking.**

The cattle are in a **yoke.**

yolk   The yellow part of an egg. The yolk provides food for the young chick or other animal until it hatches. The recipe calls for three egg *yolks*.   ▲ Another word that sounds like this is **yoke.**
yolk (yōk) *noun, plural* **yolks.**

at; āpe; fär; câre; end; mē; it; īce; pîerce; hot; ōld; sông, fôrk; oil; out; up; ūse; rüle; pu̇ll; tûrn; chin; sing; shop; thin; this; hw in white; zh in treasure. The symbol ə stands for the unstressed vowel sound in about, taken, pencil, lemon, and circus.

Y

Yom Kippur   A Jewish holiday that occurs ten days after Rosh Hashana, which is the first day of the Jewish year. Yom Kippur is a day of fasting and prayer. It is the holiest Jewish holiday.
Yom Kip·pur (yom kip′ər *or* yōm′ kē pùr′)

yonder   In that place; over there. *Yonder* stands the castle of the king and queen of this land.
yon·der (yon′dər) *adverb.*

you   **1.** The person or persons that are spoken or written to. I'll meet *you* on the corner at six o'clock. We'll go with *you* to the concert.   **2.** A person; anyone. *You* have to be at least eighteen years old to be able to vote.   ⚠ Other words that sound like this are **ewe** and **yew**.
you (ū *or unstressed* yə) *pronoun.*

you'd   **1.** Shortened form of "you had." *You'd* better not forget to lock the door at night.   **2.** Shortened form of "you would." *You'd* have liked the movie our family saw yesterday evening.
you'd (ūd) *contraction.*

you'll   Shortened form of "you will" or "you shall." *You'll* probably grow up to be taller than your parents.
you'll (ūl *or unstressed* yùl) *contraction.*

young   **1.** In the early part of life or growth. These picture books are for *young* readers. A lamb is a *young* sheep. The age of space travel is still *young.*   **2.** Having the look or qualities of a young person. My grandmother is a very active woman and is quite *young* for her age.   **3.** Of or belonging to the early part of life. Our neighbor spent his *younger* years in England. *Adjective.*
—Young offspring. The lion caught an antelope to feed its *young. Noun.*
young (yung) *adjective,* **younger, youngest;** *noun, plural* **young.**

youngster   A young person. Many of the *youngsters* in the neighborhood helped to clean up the vacant lot.
young·ster (yung′stər) *noun, plural* **youngsters.**

your   Of or belonging to you. Let's meet tomorrow at *your* house. Is this *your* coat?   ⚠ Another word that sounds like this is **you're.**

your (yùr *or* yôr *or unstressed* yər) *adjective.*

you're   Shortened form of "you are" *You're* almost as tall as I am.   ⚠ Another word that sounds like this is **your.**
you·re (yùr *or* yôr *or unstressed* yər) *contraction.*

yours   The one or ones that belong to or have to do with you. If this hat is mine, the other must be *yours.* Their plan is good, but *yours* is even better.
yours (yùrz *or* yôrz) *pronoun.*

yourself   **1.** Your own self. You *yourself* know that what you did was wrong. Be careful of the fire or you will burn *yourself.*   **2.** Your usual, normal, or true self. After a good night's sleep you will feel like *yourself* again.
your·self (yùr self′ *or* yôr self′ *or* yər self′) *pronoun, plural* **yourselves.**

youth   **1.** The condition or quality of being young. The new player has *youth* but lacks experience. Many old people keep the fresh outlook and attitudes of *youth.*   **2.** The time of life after childhood and before becoming an adult. In his *youth,* my father wanted to be a soldier.   **3.** The beginning or early stage of something. Aviation was still in its *youth* when my grandmother first flew.   **4.** A young person. The car was driven by a *youth* of about eighteen years of age.
youth (ūth) *noun, plural* **youths** *or* **youth.**

you've   Shortened form of "you have." *You've* been talking on the telephone for nearly half an hour.
you've (ūv *or* yùv) *contraction.*

yo-yo   A toy that has two disks attached at their centers with a peg. A yo-yo goes up and down on a string that is attached to the peg.
yo-yo (yō′yō) *noun, plural* **yo-yos.**

yr.   An abbreviation for *year.*

YT   Postal abbreviation for *Yukon Territory.*

Yugoslavia   A country in southeastern Europe.
Yu·go·sla·vi·a (ū′gō slä′vē ə) *noun.*

Yukon Territory   A territory in northwestern Canada. Its capital is Whitehorse.
Yu·kon Territory (ū′kon) *noun.*

z, Z The twenty-sixth and last letter of the alphabet.
z, Z (zē) *noun, plural* **z's, Z's.**

Zaire A country in central Africa.
Za·ire (zä îr′) *noun.*

Zambia A country in south-central Africa.
Zam·bi·a (zam′bē ə) *noun.*

zebra A wild animal that looks like a horse with a black-and-white striped coat. Zebras come from southern and eastern Africa.
ze·bra (zē′brə) *noun, plural* **zebras** or **zebra.**

zebra

zenith **1.** The point in the sky directly above the place where a person stands. **2.** The highest or greatest point. The musician's recent concert was the *zenith* of a great career.
ze·nith (zē′nith) *noun, plural* **zeniths.**

Word History

The word **zenith** goes back to an Arabic word meaning "way or path." It was used in an Arabic phrase that meant "the way over one's head." The zenith is the spot in the sky directly overhead.

zero **1.** The number 0, which means no quantity or amount at all. When you add zero to any number or subtract zero from any number, the number remains the same. **2.** A point on a thermometer or other scale at which numbering or measurement begins. The temperature outside is ten degrees above *zero* Fahrenheit. **3.** Nothing. The business did not lose money, but its profit was *zero*. *Noun.*
—**1.** Of, being, or at zero. The temperature dropped to *zero* degrees Fahrenheit last night. **2.** None at all; not any. The team had *zero* victories last season. *Adjective.*
ze·ro (zîr′ō) *noun, plural* **zeros** or **zeroes;** *adjective.*

1. The letter **Z** first appeared in the alphabets of several ancient tribes in the Middle East. They wrote it much like our capital letter **I**.

2. When the ancient Greeks borrowed this letter, they changed its shape to look more like our modern capital **Z**.

3. The ancient Romans then adopted this letter, using it in words they had borrowed from the Greek language.

4. Today, we write the letter Z in the same way that the Romans wrote it almost 2,400 years ago.

The word **zero** comes from an Arabic word meaning "empty." The Muslims were the best mathematicians and scientists of the Middle Ages, and many mathematical and scientific terms come from their language, Arabic.

zigzag   A line, pattern, or course that moves in or has a series of short, sharp turns from one side to the other. The clown wore a big bright tie with *zigzags* of different colors. *Noun.*
—To move in or form a zigzag. The dog *zigzagged* down the street. *Verb.*
zig·zag (zig′zag′) *noun, plural* **zigzags;** *verb,* **zigzagged, zigzagging.**

Zimbabwe   A country in south-central Africa.
Zim·bab·we (zim bäb′wē) *noun.*

zinc   A grayish white metal. It is used to make alloys and in electric batteries. Zinc is a chemical element.
zinc (zingk) *noun.*

zinnia   A garden plant that has rounded, brightly colored flowers.
zin·ni·a (zin′ē ə) *noun, plural* **zinnias.**

zinnias

zip   To fasten or close with a zipper. It was cold, so I *zipped* up my coat.
zip (zip) *verb,* **zipped, zipping.**

zip code or **ZIP Code**   A number that identifies a postal delivery area in the United States. The zip code is written after the state in an address on a letter, package, or other piece of mail.

zipper   A fastener made up of two rows of teeth that fit into each other. The teeth can be joined or separated by pulling a sliding device up or down. Zippers are used on clothing, suitcases, and other articles.
zip·per (zip′ər) *noun, plural* **zippers.**

zither   A musical instrument made up of a shallow, wooden box with thirty to forty-five strings stretched across it. It is played by plucking the strings.
zith·er (zith′ər *or* zith′ər) *noun, plural* **zithers.**

zodiac   An imaginary belt in the heavens. The sun, moon, and most of the planets seem to travel on paths through the zodiac during the year. The zodiac is divided into twelve parts, and each part is named for a constellation.
zo·di·ac (zō′dē ak′) *noun.*

zone   **1.** A region or area that has some special quality, condition, or use. Cars are not allowed to go more than 15 miles per hour in the school *zone.* The area at the end of a football field is called the end *zone.* **2.** Any of the five regions of the earth's surface divided according to the climate found there. There is a torrid zone, two temperate zones, and two frigid zones. *Noun.*
—To divide into zones. The city government *zones* the city, so that certain areas are only for private homes, and other areas are only for stores and businesses. *Verb.*
zone (zōn) *noun, plural* **zones;** *verb,* **zoned, zoning.**

zoo   A park or other public place where wild animals are kept for people to see.
zoo (zü) *noun, plural* **zoos.**

The word **zoo** comes from a Greek word meaning "animal." The full name of this kind of park is *zoological garden.*

zoology   The science that deals with the study of animals.
zo·ol·o·gy (zō ol′ə jē) *noun.*

zoom   To move or climb suddenly and quickly. The airplane *zoomed* into the clouds. A police officer *zoomed* past on a motorcycle.
zoom (züm) *verb,* **zoomed, zooming.**

*C*ontents

*W*riter's Resources

THE WRITING PROCESS

Writing is an important skill. You may write a story or a report, or a note to a friend. When you write, you want readers to understand what you are trying to say. You can help make sure they will understand by thinking like your readers. What do they need to know? Are you telling them enough? Can they understand how your ideas are related or connected?

PREWRITING STRATEGIES

You can use some strategies, or plans, to get ready to write. Some prewriting strategies you can use are listed below.

- **BRAINSTORMING** is thinking about a topic or problem and writing down all the ideas that come to your mind. You can brainstorm by yourself, with a partner, or with a small group.

- **CLUSTERING** is another way to organize your ideas for writing. When you cluster your ideas, you put them into groups. A clustering model like the one below can help.

- **TIME LINES** can help you organize events that happen in a certain order, or sequence. You can also use a time line to show the steps in a process.

Harriet Tubman	
1821	born
1844	married John Tubman
1849	escaped to the North
1869	biography by Sarah Bradford published
1896	helped to found National Association of Colored Women

- **CHARTING** is a way to organize your ideas about a topic. The headings for a chart will be different for different kinds of writing. You might use the following chart, for example, when getting ready to write a persuasive paragraph.

Opinions	Reasons

- **OUTLINING** is a useful strategy for getting ready to write longer pieces such as research reports. When you outline, you give a summary by listing main ideas and important details. In the final report, each main idea becomes a paragraph.

Report Topic
I.   Introduction
II. Main Idea
   A. Detail
   B. Detail
III. Main Idea
   A. Detail
   B. Detail
   C. Detail
IV. Conclusion

- **FREEWRITING** is a strategy you can use to get your thoughts down on paper as quickly as possible. The purpose of freewriting is to get some words, phrases, and sentences on paper. Reading your freewriting will help you find the ideas you can write more about.

- **LISTING** is a strategy you can use to organize ideas or events in their order of importance.

Why I Exercise
1. It helps make my heart and lungs strong.
2. I'm on the basketball team.
3. It relaxes me.
4. I enjoy it.

WRITING PROCESS CHECKLISTS

Writing is a process. Like other processes, writing involves certain steps. Prewriting is just the first step in the writing process. The steps that make up the complete writing process are:

1. Prewriting
2. Writing a First Draft
3. Revising
4. Proofreading
5. Publishing

Asking yourself some key questions as you go through the steps of the writing process can help you write clearly. Use the checklists that follow as you complete the steps in *your* writing process.

Prewrite
Checklist for Prewriting

1. What is my topic? What thoughts do I have about my topic?
2. What kind of writing am I planning to do? How should I get ready to do that kind of writing?
3. Who will read my writing? What does that person already know about my topic?
4. What is my purpose for writing? Am I describing, explaining, telling a story, or persuading?
5. How do I begin? What is the main idea of what I want to say? How can I tell the main idea in a general way?

Write a First Draft
Checklist for Writing a First Draft

1. Am I thinking of my reader as I write? Will my reader enjoy and understand my writing?
2. Did I tell the main idea of my writing in my first or last sentence? If not, how can I fix that now?
3. Did I use the rest of my paragraph to tell more about the main idea? How can I improve my details?

Revise
Checklist for Revising

1. Have I shared my writing with someone? Was I careful to listen to what that person had to say?
2. Should I go back to my notes and find more ideas to add to my paragraph? How can I help my reader picture what I am writing about?
3. Do I need to combine short sentences and break up long sentences?
4. Should I change the order of my sentences to make my meaning clearer?
5. Have I connected my ideas? Do I need to start my sentences with words such as *first, next,* and *last*?

Proofread
Checklist for Proofreading
1. Should I check the spelling of any words by looking in the dictionary?
2. Have I used the correct punctuation in my sentences?
3. Have I indented my paragraph by beginning the first line further in than the rest?
4. Did I use my best handwriting?

Publish
Suggestions for Sharing
How would I like to share my writing with others?
- Make a class book
- Create a bulletin board display
- Read aloud to others
- Perform a skit
- Publish a newspaper
- Make a tape recording

PROOFREADING MARKS		
Mark	**Meaning**	**Example**
⌐¶	indent	¶The beach is lovely in summer. The sand is warm and the water cool.
∧	add this	*love* I to dig in the sand.
Sp	spelling	My mother enjoys the ocean *breeze* breze. Sp
⌐	move this	The lifeguard for sharks watches.
ℐ	take this out	Where is my suntan oil lotion?
≡	capital letter	after swimming I feel hungry.
/	lower-case letter	I wish the Summer would never end.

THESAURUS

A **thesaurus** is a reference tool that can help you when you write. It provides synonyms for many common words. Synonyms are words that mean almost the same thing.

The thesaurus can help you choose more interesting words and more exact words. For example, you may write this sentence:

Joey **walked** across the street.

Walked is not a very interesting word, and it says very little about Joey. If you looked up the word *walk* in the thesaurus, you will find these words: *march, stride, stroll, strut.* Using one of these words would make your sentence more interesting and more exact.

USING THE THESAURUS

The words in a thesaurus are listed in alphabetical order. You look up words in a thesaurus as you do in a dictionary. If the word is listed in the thesaurus, you will find an entry.

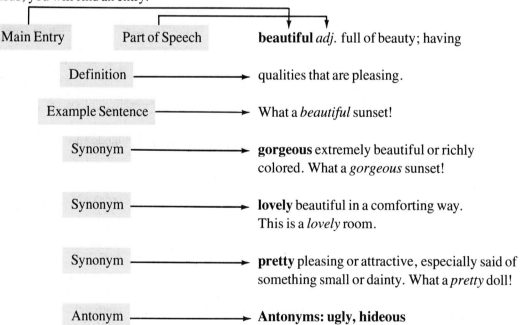

Main Entry   Part of Speech   **beautiful** *adj.* full of beauty; having

Definition ⟶ qualities that are pleasing.

Example Sentence ⟶ What a *beautiful* sunset!

Synonym ⟶ **gorgeous** extremely beautiful or richly colored. What a *gorgeous* sunset!

Synonym ⟶ **lovely** beautiful in a comforting way. This is a *lovely* room.

Synonym ⟶ **pretty** pleasing or attractive, especially said of something small or dainty. What a *pretty* doll!

Antonym ⟶ **Antonyms: ugly, hideous**

The word *beautiful* is called an **entry word**. The information that follows is called the **entry**.

Cross-references. Sometimes you will find cross-references in the thesaurus. The cross-reference for **large** tells you to look under **big.**

large See **big.**

The thesaurus can make you a better writer by helping you find just the right word for what you want to say.

On the pages that follow, you will find a thesaurus. Use it as a resource to locate just the right word for your writing. The following abbreviations are used in the thesaurus:

adj. adjective   *n.* noun   *v.* verb

A

angry *adj.* feeling or showing anger. Don's remark made me *angry.*
　enraged filled with rage; angry beyond control. The *enraged* lion growled loudly.
　furious extremely angry. Marty was *furious* at me.

awful *adj.* causing fear, dread, or awe. The storm was *awful.*
　terrible causing terror or great trouble. We saw a *terrible* accident today.
　dreadful causing great fear or unhappiness. We heard a *dreadful* scream.

B

beautiful *adj.* full of beauty; having qualities that are pleasing. What a *beautiful* sunset!
　gorgeous extremely beautiful or richly colored. What a *gorgeous* sunset!
　lovely beautiful in a soothing or peaceful way. This is a *lovely* room.
　pretty pleasing or attractive, often said of something small or dainty. What a *pretty* doll!
　Antonyms: ugly, hideous

big *adj.* of great size. He works on a *big* farm.
　huge extremely big. That is a *huge* tree!
　enormous much greater than the usual size. We saw an *enormous* mushroom on the front lawn.
　large of great size. What *large* feet you have!
　Antonyms: *See* **little**.

brave *adj.* willing to face danger. The *brave* firefighter raced into the burning house.
　bold showing courage. The *bold* explorer marched through the dark jungle.
　courageous having courage. A *courageous* woman jumped into the icy water to save the young girl.

daring willing to take risks. The *daring* boy stood ready to jump from the tree limb.
　Antonyms: afraid, fearful

bright *adj.* filled with light; shining. The sun was so *bright* I had to wear sunglasses.
　brilliant shining or sparkling with light. The sky was filled with *brilliant* stars.
　shiny reflecting brightly. I could see the *shiny* coin in the water.
　Antonyms: dark, dull

C

cold *adj.* having a low temperature; lacking warmth or heat. The desert has hot days and *cold* nights.
　chilly uncomfortably cool. The first day was wet and *chilly.*
　frigid extremely cold. The North Pole is *frigid* all the time.

cry/hard

icy very cold. An *icy* wind stung our cheeks.
Antonyms: *See* **hot**.

cry *v.* to shed tears. Julie did not know what to do when the baby started to *cry*.
sob to cry with short gasps. Tina *sobbed* as she told us what had happened.
weep to show grief, joy, or other strong emotions by crying. James began to *weep* every time he thought of his grandmother.
Antonyms: *See* **laugh**.

D

do *v.* to carry out. Mrs. Riley will *do* the job right.
execute to do what has been ordered. The soldier *executed* the command.
perform to carry out to completion. The doctor *performed* the operation.

dry *adj.* not wet; free of moisture. Please bring me a *dry* towel.
arid dry as a result of having little rainfall. The Gobi Desert is an *arid* place.
parched dried out by heat. It was so hot that my throat was *parched*.
Antonyms: *See* **wet**.

F

fast *adj.* moving or done with speed. We rode on a *fast* train.

quick done in a very short time. That was a *quick* game.
rapid with great speed. She kept up a *rapid* pace for the whole race.
swift moving with great speed, often said of animals or people. The *swift* horse flew across the field.
Antonym: slow

funny *adj.* causing laughter. Dick told us a *funny* joke.
amusing causing smiles or enjoyment. That was an *amusing* story.
comical causing laughter through actions. The clowns were *comical*.
humorous funny or joking. Jessica told a *humorous* story.
hilarious very funny, causing noisy laughter. That movie was *hilarious*.

G

get *v.* to go for and return with. Please *get* me a sandwich.
acquire to come into possession of through effort or merit. He *acquired* a new house.
earn to gain through effort. She *earned* the A's on her report card.
obtain to get as one's own, often with some difficulty. Lily worked hard to *obtain* her job.

good *adj.* above average in quality. This is a *good* book.
excellent extremely good. Marie always does *excellent* work.
fair somewhat good; of average quality. Jeremy did a *fair* painting of the castle.
fine of high quality; very good. She made a *fine* dinner for us.
Antonyms: bad, poor

H

happy *adj.* having or showing pleasure. Today, Mr. Carson is a *happy* man.
glad feeling or expressing joy or pleasure. Lisa was *glad* to meet Mrs. James.
joyful very happy; filled with joy. Danny was *joyful* when he heard his father was coming home.
merry happy and cheerful. Christmas was a *merry* occasion.
pleased satisfied or content. Harry was *pleased* with his new coat.
Antonyms: *See* **sad**.

hard *adj.* not easy to do or deal with. Mowing the lawn is *hard* work.
difficult hard to do; requiring effort. Steering the ship through the storm was a *difficult* task.
tough difficult to do, often in a physical sense. Catching

wild horses is a *tough* job.
Antonym: easy

hot *adj.* having a high temperature; having much heat. The oven is *hot*.
fiery as hot as fire; burning. The spaceship flew toward a *fiery* sun.
scalding hot enough to burn, often said of liquids. A pot of *scalding* water fell on the floor.
torrid extremely hot, often said of weather. The weather was *torrid* yesterday.
Antonyms: *See* cold.

hurt *v.* to cause pain or damage. Did you *hurt* your knee?
harm to do damage to. A good rider would never *harm* a horse.
injure to cause physical damage. Jon fell and *injured* his leg.

I

interesting *adj.* arousing or holding interest or attention. It was an *interesting* book.
captivating capturing and holding the attention of by beauty or excellence. Grandpa told us a *captivating* ghost story.
fascinating causing and holding interest through a special quality or charm. The snake charmer's act was *fascinating*.
inspiring having a rousing effect; arousing interest. His

speech was so *inspiring* that I stood up and cheered.
Antonyms: dull, boring

L

large *See* **big**.

laugh *v.* to make the sounds and facial movements that show amusement. He *laughs* at my jokes.
chuckle to laugh softly, especially to oneself. Carla *chuckled* when she read my note.
giggle to laugh in a silly, high-pitched, or nervous way. Jill *giggled* and turned red.
guffaw to laugh loudly. Henry *guffawed* so hard he had to hold his sides.
Antonyms: *See* cry.

let *v.* to give permission to. Mom won't *let* me go to the game.
allow to grant permission to or for, often in relation to rules. The police do not *allow* fishing at the beach.
permit to allow (a person) to do something. He will *permit* you to use the pool if you ask him first.
Antonyms: refuse, deny, forbid

little *adj.* small in size; not big. Vanna found a *little* puppy.
small not large. Wally needs a *small* box for his gift.
tiny extremely small. We

saw three *tiny* birds in the nest.
wee very small. The kitten was just a *wee* thing when it was born.
Antonyms: *See* big.

look *v.* to see with one's eyes. She *looked* at the moon.
glance to look quickly. Kenny *glanced* at the book and put it aside.
peer to look closely. Moe *peered* at the map but could not find the town.
stare to look at for a long time. Sue was so surprised she just *stared* at me.

loud *adj.* having a strong sound. We heard a *loud* crash from the kitchen.
deafening extremely loud. The dam broke with a *deafening* roar.
noisy full of sounds, often unpleasant. The *noisy* crowd kept yelling for their team.
Antonyms: *See* quiet.

M

mad *See* **angry**.

many *adj.* consisting of a large number. Dave has *many* pairs of socks.
numerous a great many. I have asked you *numerous* times.
several more than a few but less than many. Cheryl has played in *several* games this season.

mean/rich

plenty (of) enough, or more than enough, suggesting a large number. We have *plenty* of plates.
Antonym: few

mean *adj.* lacking in kindness or understanding. Joe was very *mean* to us.
cruel willing to cause pain or suffering to others. He is a very *cruel* man.
nasty resulting from hate. That was a *nasty* trick he played on us.
selfish concerned only about oneself. Kelly is too *selfish* to care about how I feel.
spiteful filled with ill feelings toward others. Pat is a *spiteful* person.
Antonyms: *See* **nice**.

N

neat *adj.* orderly. His work is always *neat*.
tidy neat and clean, well-organized. She likes to keep this room *tidy*.
well-groomed carefully dressed and groomed. Marvin always looks *well-groomed*.
Antonyms: messy, untidy, sloppy

nice *adj.* agreeable or pleasing. Lynn is a *nice* person.
gentle mild and kindly in manner. He is so *gentle* with the children.
kind gentle and friendly; good-hearted. Uncle Bob was very *kind* to send you a gift.

pleasant agreeable and friendly. She has a *pleasant* way of making me feel welcome.
sweet having or marked by agreeable or pleasing qualities. Jenny has a *sweet* personality.
Antonyms: *See* **mean**.

O

old *adj.* having lived or existed for a long time. My grandfather is an *old* man.
aged having grown old. Minnie helps take care of her *aged* aunt.
ancient of great age; very old; of times long past. Dr. Tyrell found an *ancient* coin in Egypt.
Antonym: young

P

proud *adj.* having a sense of one's own worth, usually in a positive way. She was *proud* of her accomplishments in science.
conceited having too high an opinion of oneself, in a negative way. Shelly is too *conceited* to talk to me.
haughty having or showing too much pride in oneself. He is *haughty* because he has an expensive bike.
vain overly concerned with or proud of oneself. He is so *vain* that he spends hours in front of the mirror.
Antonym: humble

Q

quiet *adj.* with little or no noise. The house was *quiet* after everyone had gone.
calm free of excitement. Everyone remained *calm* during the fire drill.
peaceful calm; undisturbed. The camp is so *peaceful* in early morning.
silent completely quiet; without noise. We stood in the *silent* field after the snow had ended.
still without sound or movement; silent. The forest was *still*.
Antonyms: loud, noisy

R

ready *adj.* fit for use or action. Everything is *ready* for the party.
prepared ready or fit for a particular purpose. Jim was *prepared* for the test.
set ready or prepared to do something. Willie was all *set* to go to school.

rich *adj.* having great wealth. The Duchess is a *rich* woman.
affluent wealthy, prosperous. *Affluent* customers shop at that expensive store.
opulent showing wealth or affluence. Their *opulent* mansion even had silver doorknobs.

wealthy having many material goods or riches. Mr. Harris' invention made him a *wealthy* man.
Antonym: poor

rude *adj.* not polite; ill-mannered. Jack made a *rude* remark to me.
discourteous without good manners. You have no reason to be *discourteous* to Mrs. Braun.
impolite not showing good manners. They were *impolite* to everyone at the party.
Antonyms: polite, courteous

S

sad *adj.* feeling or showing unhappiness or sorrow. Jake was *sad* when he lost his dog.
depressed feeling sad. Tim was *depressed* when he could not go to the game.
downcast low in spirits. She was *downcast* when she did not make the team.
miserable extremely unhappy. Mary was *miserable* after her brother left home.
Antonyms: *See* happy.

say *v.* to make known or express in words. Mel *said* that he wanted to go home.
declare to make known publicly or formally. The mayor *declared* that the town needed more money.
speak to express an idea, fact, or feeling. Wendy *spoke* to us about the new shopping mall.
state to express or explain

fully in words. Mr. Coombs *stated* his opinion during the meeting.
talk to express ideas or information by means of speech; to speak. Ken *talked* about his new model airplane. *See also* **tell**.

scared *adj.* afraid; alarmed. She got *scared* when she heard a noise.
afraid feeling fear, often in a continuing way or for a long time. Jerry is *afraid* of the dark.
fearful filled with fear. Donna was *fearful* of the thunder.
frightened scared, often suddenly or for a short time. When all the lights in the house went out, Lauren was *frightened*.
terrified extremely scared; filled with terror. Pete was *terrified* when he heard the scream.

shy *adj.* uncomfortable in the presence of others. Paula is too *shy* to stand in front of the class.
bashful easily embarrassed. Carl was too *bashful* to step out from behind the chair.
timid showing a lack of courage; easily frightened. The *timid* little boy would not go near the cows.
Antonym: bold

small *See* **little**.

smart *adj.* intelligent; bright; having learned a lot. Leah is a *smart* girl for her age.
clever mentally sharp; quick-

witted. He is a *clever* fellow.
intelligent able to learn, understand, and reason. Shana is an *intelligent* girl, but she does not try hard enough.
wise able to know or judge what is right, good, or true. The chief was a *wise* old man.
Antonym: stupid

smile *v.* to have, show, or give a smile. May Li *smiled* when she saw the puppy.
grin to smile with amusement. Keith *grinned* when he saw my costume.
smirk to smile in a silly or self-satisfied way. Pat *smirked* at him because she knew the answer.
Antonyms: frown, scowl

strange *adj.* differing from the usual or the ordinary. That is a *strange* little dog.
odd not expected or appropriate. She wore some very *odd* clothes to the party.
peculiar strange or odd, but in an interesting or curious way. Bill has a *peculiar* habit of looking up when he speaks.
weird strange or odd in a frightening or mysterious way. A *weird* man came out of the house.
See also **unusual**.

strong *adj.* having great strength or physical power. Football players have to be *strong*.
muscular having well-developed muscles; strong.

talk/wet

Neil has become *muscular* from lifting weights.
powerful having great strength, influence, or authority. The governor is a *powerful* woman.
Antonym: weak

T

talk *See* **say**.

tell *v.* to put or express in written or spoken words. Mandy *told* us about summer camp.
announce to state or make known publicly or formally. Mrs. Grimes *announced* that she would be leaving.
narrate to tell about events, especially a story. The camp leader *narrated* a ghost story.
relate to tell or report events or details. Paul *related* the story of how we got lost in the woods.
See also **say**.

thin *adj.* not fat. He was small and *thin* until he was ten years old.
lean with little or no fat, but often strong. A runner must have a *lean* body.
skinny very thin, in a way that suggests poor health. She got so *skinny* that she felt weak.
slim thin, in a good or healthy way. Dennis has gotten *slim* since he started exercising.
Antonyms: fat, plump, chubby

U

unusual *adj.* not usual, common, or ordinary. Her eyes are an *unusual* color.
extraordinary very unusual; beyond the ordinary. That painting is an *extraordinary* work of art.
rare seldom happening, seen, or found. Bald eagles are *rare* birds.
uncommon not happening often. Snowstorms are *uncommon* in this area. *See also* **strange**.
Antonyms: usual, common

upset *adj.* feeling uneasy; distressed. Tina was *upset* when no one came to the party.
anxious uneasy or fearful of what may happen. Melinda is *anxious* about her first day at the new school.
concerned troubled or worried. Mom was *concerned* when my brother did not come home for supper.
worried uneasy or troubled about something. Jack was *worried* that the river would flood.
Antonym: calm

W

walk *v.* to move or travel on foot at a normal or comfortable speed. Ruth *walked* across the street.
march to walk with regular steps. The band *marched* down the street.
stride to walk with long steps, usually with a purpose. We watched him *stride* down the hall.
stroll to walk in a relaxed or leisurely manner. Amy and Sally *strolled* through the park.
strut to walk in a vain or very proud way. Joe likes to *strut* up and down in his new clothes.

want *v.* to have a desire or wish for. Lenny *wanted* to have lunch.
crave to want badly. Sue *craved* ice cream so much that she ran all the way to the store.
desire to have a strong wish for. Molly *desired* a lot of money.
wish to have a longing or strong need for. Gary *wished* he had blond hair.
yearn to feel a strong and deep desire. Grandpa *yearned* for the warm days of summer.

wet *adj.* covered or soaked with water or other liquid. Her hair was *wet* after she went swimming.
damp slightly wet. After sitting in the sun for half an hour, our bathing suits are still *damp*.
moist slightly wet; damp. Use a *moist* cloth to wipe up the dust.
sopping extremely wet; dripping. Lisa's clothes were *sopping* by the time she got home.
Antonyms: *See* dry.

SPELLING HELPS

In your writing, it is very important to spell every word correctly. Otherwise, the meaning of what you write may not be clear. Follow the steps below to help improve your spelling.

1. Learn some basic spelling rules.
2. Learn to spell some commonly misspelled words.
3. Check your work carefully when you have finished writing.
4. Whenever you have a question about how a word should be spelled, check the spelling in the dictionary.

VOWEL SOUNDS

Sometimes the way you pronounce a word can help you spell the word correctly.

Words with *ie* and *ei*. Spell the word with *ie* when the word has the long *e* vowel sound, except after *c*. For example:

> **long *e* vowel sound: believe, chief, field, piece**
> **except after *c*: ceiling, deceive, receive**

Spell the word with *ei* when the word does not have the long *e* vowel sound, especially if the word has the long *a* vowel sound. For example:

> **long *a* vowel sound: eight, neighbor, sleigh, weigh**

There are some exceptions to this rule: **either, friend, seize, weird**

PLURAL NOUNS

Sometimes when you make a noun plural, the spelling of the word changes. Here are some rules to help you spell these words correctly.
Adding *s* and *es*. In most cases, *s* can be added to a noun without changing the spelling.

> **club + s = club   room + s = rooms   pail + s = pails**

If the word ends in *ch, s, sh, x* or *z,* add *es*.

> **buzz/buzzes   match/matches   fox/foxes**

PLURAL NOUNS

Changing *f* to *v*. If the word ends in *f* or *fe*, change the *f* to *v* when adding *s* or *es*.

> **leaf/leaves**   **shelf/shelves**   **life/lives**

Irregular nouns. Some words become plural in irregular ways.

> **woman/women**   **child/children**   **mouse/mice**   **tooth/teeth**

INFLECTIONAL ENDINGS

With many kinds of words, if you add an ending such as *es, ed, ing, er,* or *est*, the spelling of the word may change. Here are some rules.

Changing *y* to *i*. If the word ends in a consonant and *y*, change the *y* to *i* before any ending that does not begin with *i*.

> **story + es = stories**   **jolly + er = jollier**
> **worry + ed = worried**   **tiny + est = tiniest**

However, for most words that end in a vowel and *y*, keep the *y* when adding an ending.

> **donkey + s = donkeys**   **delay + ed = delayed**
> **enjoy + ing = enjoying**   **toy + s = toys**

Doubling the final consonant. In most cases, if a one-syllable word ends in one vowel and one consonant, double the consonant when adding an ending that begins with a vowel.

> **trip + ed = tripped**   **sad + er = sadder**
> **rub + ing = rubbing**   **fat + est = fattest**

Silent *e*. If the word ends in a silent *e*, drop the *e* when adding an ending that begins with a vowel.

> **dive + ing = diving**   **pale + er = paler**
> **hike + ed = hiked**   **large + est = largest**

PREFIXES AND SUFFIXES

When a prefix is added to a word, the spelling of the word stays the same.

> **re + write = rewrite**   **mis + place = misplace**
> **pre + view = preview**   **dis + appear = disappear**

When a suffix is added to a word, the spelling of the word may change. If the word ends in silent *e*, drop the *e* when adding a suffix that begins with a vowel.

> **bake + er = baker**   **love + able = lovable**
> **shake + y = shaky**

However, for most words ending in silent *e*, keep the *e* when adding a suffix that begins with a consonant.

> **peace + ful = peaceful**   **pave + ment = pavement**
> **lone + ly = lonely**

HOMOPHONES

Homophones are words that sound alike but are spelled differently, and they have different meanings. These kinds of words are commonly misspelled. Knowing what these words mean will help you choose—and spell—the correct word when you use it in your writing. Here are some examples. If you are not sure what these words mean, look them up in the dictionary.

ate	brake	heal	hole	made	more	right	stair
eight	break	heel	whole	maid	moor	write	stare

CONTRACTIONS AND POSSESSIVES

Use an apostrophe in a contraction to show where one or more letters have been left out.

> **he + is = he's**   **was + not = wasn't**
> **they + will = they'll**

Do not use an apostrophe with a possessive pronoun: **hers, ours, yours.**

Some contractions and possessives are actually homophones and should not be confused. Here are some examples:

Contraction:	you're	it's	there's	they're
Possessive pronoun:	your	its	theirs	their

GRAMMAR, MECHANICS, USAGE HANDBOOK

This handbook is a reference you can use when you revise your writing or when you want to check a rule of grammar, capitalization, punctuation, or usage. The **Grammar** section describes sentences and parts of speech. The **Mechanics** section gives rules for capitalization and punctuation. The **Usage** section gives rules that will help you use language effectively and write correctly.

GRAMMAR

SENTENCES

A **sentence** is a group of words that states a complete thought. A **sentence fragment** is a group of words that does not state a complete thought.

Sentence:	We took a trip last summer.
Sentence Fragment:	Watched the space flight.

There are four kinds of sentences. A **declarative** sentence makes a statement or tells something. It ends with a period (.). An **interrogative** sentence asks something. It has the form of a question and ends with a question mark (?). An **exclamatory** sentence shows strong feeling. It ends with an exclamation point or exclamation mark (!). An **imperative** sentence tells or asks someone to do something. It ends with a period (.).

Declarative:	The players were ready.
Interrogative:	When does the game start?
Exclamatory:	What a game the team played!
Imperative:	Watch this game.

SUBJECTS AND PREDICATES

Every sentence has a subject and a predicate. The **subject part** tells whom or what the sentence is about. The **predicate part** tells what action the subject does.

A group of students started a club.

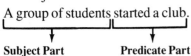

Subject Part   **Predicate Part**

The **simple subject** is the main word of the subject part. The **simple predicate** is the main word of the predicate part.

A loud noise echoed through the forest.

Simple Subject   Simple Predicate

A compound subject has two or more simple subjects joined by **and.**

Alligators and crocodiles live in the water.

A **compound predicate** has two or more simple predicates joined by **and.**

The girls **washed and waxed** the bike.

A **simple sentence** has one subject part and one predicate part. A **compound sentence** contains two or more simple sentences joined by **and.**

Simple Sentences:	Zoos have animals. Aquariums have fish.
Compound Sentence:	Zoos have animals, **and** aquariums have fish.

COMBINING SENTENCES

Avoid repeating words in your writing by combining sentences. Sentences can be combined by joining the subject parts, the predicate parts, or other parts to make one sentence. Use the word **and** to join the parts.

Combining Subjects:	Randy milked the cows. Scott milked the cows. *Randy and Scott milked the cows.*
Combining Predicates:	Cynthia loves animals. She has two dogs. *Cynthia loves animals and has two dogs.*
Combining Other Words:	The woods were cold. The woods were covered with snow. *The woods were cold and covered with snow.*

PARTS OF SPEECH

Definitions	Examples	
A **noun** is a word that names a person, place, thing, or idea.	girl town game love	Sally Miami Monopoly happiness
A **verb** is a word that is used to express action, feeling, or a state of being.	She **dried** the dishes. I **feel** awful. Dave **is** late.	
A **pronoun** is a word that takes the place of one or more nouns.	Jan called Ben and Joe. **She** called **them.**	
An **adjective** is a word that describes or modifies a noun or pronoun. It tells how many, what kind, or which one.	**several** boys a **large** house **these** books	
An **adverb** is a word that describes or modifies a verb, an adjective, or another adverb. It tells how, when, or where.	He sings **sweetly.** They sing **often.**	
A **preposition** is a word that relates a noun or a pronoun to another word in the sentence.	Rain fell **from** the sky. The teacher sat **behind** the desk. She stood **in front of** him.	
A **conjunction** is a word that joins words or groups of words in a sentence.	Some alligators live in Florida, **but** others live in China.	
An **interjection** is a word or group of words that shows strong feeling.	**Oh,** no, I'm late! **Wow!** That was great!	

MECHANICS
RULES FOR CAPITALIZATION

1. Capitalize the first word of a sentence or a direct quotation.

   My sister goes ice skating in the winter.

   Katy said, ''**W**e read a poem about winter sports.''

2. Capitalize the first word in the opening and in the closing of a letter.

   Dear Bobby,   **Y**our friend,

3. Capitalize a person's name, a person's initials, and titles that appear before a person's name.

Henry Lodge   **D.B.** Carson   **Dr.** Spock

Queen Anne   Mary **A.** Blake   **Ms.** Kelly

4. Capitalize words that show family relationships when used as titles or subtitles for a person's name, but not when they follow a possessive noun or pronoun.

Aunt Beth   Father got a new job.

his aunt, Tony's aunt   My father got a new job.

5. Capitalize the pronoun *I*.

Jody and **I** went to see Mr. Wilkins.

6. Capitalize all important words in the names of cities, states, countries, continents, bodies of water, and geographical features.

Cheyenne, Wyoming   Mexico   Europe

Atlantic Ocean   Gulf of St. Lawrence   Hudson Bay

7. Capitalize the names of parts of the country.

New England   the Midwest   the East Coast

8. Capitalize the names of streets and highways, bridges, buildings, and monuments.

Hyde Street   Hollywood Freeway   Route 17

Empire State Building   Washington Monument   Bay Bridge

9. Capitalize the names of stars and planets, but not *sun* or *moon*.

Mercury   North Star   Pluto

10. Capitalize the names of schools, clubs, and businesses.

Girl Scouts   Franklin Middle School

Nabisco   the American Red Cross

11. Capitalize names from history.

American Revolution   Declaration of Independence

12. Capitalize the names of days of the week, months of the year, and holidays. Do not capitalize the names of the seasons.

Monday   August   Thanksgiving Day   winter

13. Capitalize all important words in the title of a book, play, short story, poem, essay, article, movie, TV series, song, magazine, newspaper, and chapter of a book.

A Wrinkle in Time   Star Trek

Miami Herald   "Billie Jean"

RULES FOR PUNCTUATION

End Punctuation

1. Use a period at the end of a declarative or imperative sentence, after an abbreviation, and after a person's initials.
   Dr. Milton works at the I.J. Stone Hospital.
2. Use a question mark at the end of an interrogative sentence.
   Where does Dr. Milton work?
3. Use an exclamation point (or exclamation mark) at the end of an exclamatory sentence and after an interjection.
   Wow! What a wonderful invention!

Commas

1. Use commas to separate three or more items in a series.
   Beets, radishes, and carrots are root crops.
2. Use commas to separate two or more adjectives.
   Marty found a smooth, glassy rock.
3. Use a comma to separate the name of the day from the date, and the month and day from the year.
   Kathy was born on Monday, June 6, 1988.
4. Use a comma to separate the name of a city and state.
   She lives in Tacoma, Washington.
5. Use a comma to set off **too** when used to mean *also*.
   I want to visit Aunt Betsy, too.
6. Use a comma after the opening of a friendly letter and after the closing of a friendly letter or business letter.
   Dear Tina,   Yours truly,   Best wishes,
7. Use a comma before **and** when this word joins simple sentences in a compound sentence.
   We went to the lake, and Timmy went swimming.
8. Use a comma to show a pause after the word **yes** or **no** when it begins a sentence.
   Yes, we won the game.
9. Use a comma to set off the name of a person who is spoken to directly.
   Jill, please bring me the paint.

Quotation Marks

1. Use quotation marks around the exact words a speaker says. Use a comma or commas to separate the quotation from the rest of the sentence.

> "Music is my favorite subject," said Alice.
> "The flute," said May, "is a woodwind instrument."

2. Place a period inside the quotation marks. Place a quotation mark or exclamation point (or exclamation mark) inside the quotation marks.

> Mr. Yen said, "Flutes are now made of metal."
> Donna asked, "Is a piccolo smaller than a flute?"

3. Use quotation marks around the title of a short story, essay, poem, song, magazine or newspaper article, and chapter from a book.

> Short story: "The Open Boat"   Song: "Yesterday"

Apostrophes

1. Use an apostrophe + s to form the possessive of a singular noun or the possessive of a plural noun that does not end in s.

> the girl's hat   the men's club
> James's coat   the children's hour

2. Use an apostrophe to form the possessive of a plural noun that ends in s.

> the girls' hats   the cities' mayors

3. Use an apostrophe to show missing letters in a contraction.

> it + is = it's   we + are = we're   did + not = didn't

USAGE

SUBJECT-VERB AGREEMENT

A subject and its verb must agree in number. If a subject is singular, the verb must be singular. If the subject is plural, the verb must be plural. When the subject of a sentence is a singular noun or *he, she,* or *it,* add s or es to the verb. When the subject of a sentence is a plural noun or *I, we, you,* or *they,* do not add s or es to the verb.

> The girl walks home.   The girls walk home.
> She watches a TV program.   They watch a TV program.

A compound subject has two or more simple subjects joined by the word **and.** When a compound subject is joined by **and,** it takes a plural verb.

> Lauren and Brian **listen** to music.
> New York and Los Angeles **are** big cities.

IRREGULAR VERBS

The past tense of most verbs is formed by adding **ed** to the verb. Irregular verbs, however, do not follow this rule. The following chart shows forms of some commonly used irregular verbs. If you have a question about a verb in your writing, check the dictionary.

Verb	Past	Past Participle
be	was, were	been
begin	began	begun
do	did	done
get	got	got, gotten
know	knew	known
make	made	made
run	ran	run
take	took	taken
write	wrote	written

SUBJECT AND OBJECT PRONOUNS

A **subject pronoun** can be used as the subject of a sentence. Subject pronouns include: *I, you, she, it, we, they.*

Meg and **I** cut the grass.

Object pronouns are used in the predicate parts of sentences. Object pronouns include: *me, you, him, her, it, us, you, them.*

She gave the basket to **me.**

Avoid mistakes in the use of pronouns in compound subjects and compound objects.

Correct: You and **I** will feed the birds.
Incorrect: You and **me** will feed the birds.
Correct: She gave the presents to you and **me.**
Incorrect: She gave the presents to you and **I.**

RUN-ON SENTENCES

A run-on sentence should be written as two or more separate sentences.

Run-on: The artist drew a picture the picture had bright colors.
Correct: The artist drew a picture. The picture had bright colors.

ADJECTIVES AND ADVERBS

Some adjectives and adverbs change completely when they are used to compare. Some examples of these adjectives are listed below.

Adjective	More	Most
good	better	best
bad	worse	worst
well	better	best
many	more	most
little	less	least

Good and **bad** are adjectives. These words describe nouns.

Jane is a **good** baseball player.	The weather is **bad.**
Jane is a **better** baseball player than I.	The weather is **worse** than it was yesterday.
Jane is the **best** baseball player of all.	This is the **worst** weather I have ever seen.

Well and **badly** are adverbs. These words describe actions.

Jane plays **well.**	The team played **badly.**
Peter plays **better** than Jane.	The other team played **worse** than ours.
Sue plays **best** of all.	Kenny played **worst** of all.

Always be careful when you use these words. If you have questions about the correct form of a word, check the dictionary.

DOUBLE NEGATIVES

Negative words say *no* in a sentence. These words include: **no, not,** contractions with **not, none, no one, never, nobody, nothing,** and **nowhere.**

In a sentence, use only one negative word. Never use a double negative in the same sentence. You can avoid using a double negative by changing one of the words to an **affirmative word.** Some affirmative words are **a, any, ever, anywhere, anybody, anything, anyone.**

Correct:	I did not see anybody.
Correct:	I saw nobody.
Incorrect:	I did not see nobody.

Reader's Resources

If you wanted to find the meaning of a word, you would look in the dictionary. The dictionary can be very helpful for readers. If you wanted to find other kinds of information, you would use different kinds of reference books. You can find these references in a library.

ALMANAC

An **almanac** is a reference book that contains facts ands figures on many different subjects. A new almanac is published every year. The almanac gives information on current events. It also gives facts about many different subjects. It is a good place to look for short, quick answers to certain kinds of questions. The almanac can also tell you about certain things that have happened in the last year.

For example, if you wanted to know the answers to these kinds of questions, you can find them in an almanac.

What is the tallest building in the United States?

How many people live in Chicago?

Who was the governor of Texas in 1986?

Who won the Super Bowl in 1987?

Two of the best known almanacs are the *World Almanac and Book of Facts* and the *Information Please Almanac*.

To find information in an almanac, you must use the index. The index can help you find the pages where certain answers can be found. To find the right pages, you must know what word or topic to look under. Think of the key word or words in the question you want to answer. For example, supopose you want to know who the president of Mexico is. You would look under *Mexico*. There you would find *subtopics* and page numbers.

Mexico . . .
Cities 595
Government 595
Mountain Peaks 536

If you look under the subtopic *Government* on page 595, you will find the answer to your question.

In some cases, you may look up a topic and find a *cross-reference*. For example, suppose you want to know who won the Olympic gold medals in figure skating in 1984. You might look under *Figure Skating*. There you would find a cross-reference: (see *Skating*). Under *Skating* you would find the subtopic *Figure—Olympic Records* (1908–1988).

ATLAS

An **atlas** is a book of maps. The title of the atlas tells you what parts of the world are shown on the maps. A **world atlas**, for example, has maps of all parts of the world. A **United States atlas** has maps of the United States. Most atlases give information about places by using maps that show land forms, bodies of water, roads, yearly rainfall, and so on.

To find information in an atlas, you use the index. It lists every place name that appears on a map. It tells you the page on which the map can be found. It also tells you where to find each place on a certain map by giving numbers or letters, called **coordinates**. These coordinates are listed on the sides of each map to help you find places.

Atlases are most useful for answering questions about places that can be found on maps. Here are some examples.

Where is the Indian Ocean?

How far is it from Los Angeles to San Francisco?

What are the names of the Great Lakes?

ENCYCLOPEDIA

An **encyclopedia** is a book or set of books with articles on many different subjects. These subjects include people, places, events, ideas, and general topics. Many encyclopedias have a number of books, or volumes, and an index. The articles are arranged in alphabetical order. Letters on each book help you find information on a topic beginning with a certain letter of the alphabet.

When you want to find the answer to a question, you must look for the key word or words in the question. For example, if you want to find information about Martin Luther King, Jr., you would look for *King*, under **K**. Or, suppose you want to find out what kinds of dinosaurs lived in North America. You should look for *dinosaurs*, under **D**.

In most encyclopedias, the last volume is an index of all the places where information on a topic can be found. For example, you may find information on Abraham Lincoln in the volume that covers the letter **L.** By using the index, you would discover that information on Abraham Lincoln also appears in other articles

in other volumes. For each topic, the index lists the volumes which have information. And it lists the page numbers where the information in each volume can be found.

Most encyclopedias also publish a **yearbook**. The yearbook gives information about things that have happened since the encyclopedia was printed. For example, suppose you want information about an event that happened in 1990, but your encyclopedia was published in 1988. You could probably find the information in the encyclopedia yearbook.

CARD CATALOG

Sometimes you need information that cannot be found in a reference book, such as a dictionary or encyclopedia. You can go to the library and find the information in other ways. One place to look is the card catalog. The **card catalog** is a list of books in the library. The listings are usually kept on small cards arranged alphabetically in a cabinet. (Some libraries keep the list in a book or on a computer, but the information and how it is arranged are much the same.)

For every nonfiction book in the library, there are three cards: an **author card**, a **title card**, and a **subject card**. All three cards contain the same information arranged in different ways. The cards are filed in alphabetical order in the drawers of the cabinet. Here are examples of the three cards for a single book.

Author Card

```
539    Jackson, Annabel C.
Ja

       A Lot of Hot Air. Baltimore: Sky
       High Publishers, Inc., 1988.
       276 p.: il.

       Describes types of hot air balloons
       and how they work.
```

Title Card

```
       A Lot of Hot Air.

539    Jackson, Annabel C.
Ja

       A Lot of Hot Air. Baltimore: Sky
       High Publishers, Inc., 1988.
       276 p.: il.

       Describes types of hot air balloons
       and how they work.
```

Subject Card

```
       SPORTS—HOT AIR BALLOONING

539    Jackson, Annabel C.
Ja

       A Lot of Hot Air. Baltimore: Sky
       High Publishers, Inc., 1988.
       276 p.: il.

       Describes types of hot air balloons
       and how they work.
```

Each card gives the author of the book, the title, the place and date of publication, and the name of the publisher. The card also has a **call number** in the upper left-hand corner. This number tells where to find the book in the library. The call number on all three cards is the same.

If you know the author of a book, you can look for the author card. An author card lists the author's last name first. If you know the title of a book, you can look for the title card. This card lists the title first. If you are looking for books on a certain subject, you can look up the subject card. For example, suppose you want to find a book about Christopher Columbus. You can look under *Columbus*. There you will find a card for every book in the library about Columbus.

Many catalog cards also give you other information. A card may tell the number of pages in the book. It may tell if the book is illustrated (il.). It may also describe the information you can find in the book.

READERS' GUIDE TO PERIODICAL LITERATURE

The card catalog will help you find books in the library. But suppose you want to find magazine articles about a certain subject. You would use a different kind of reference.

One reference you could use is the *Readers' Guide to Periodical Literature*. This is a set of books that lists magazine articles. All the articles are listed in alphabetical order by subject and by author. The listing gives the name of the magazine, the date, and the page numbers. Some libraries have this information on microfilm instead of in books. Some libraries use a computerized system called

Magazine Index. Both of these work in much the same way as the *Readers' Guide*.

For example, suppose you want to find magazine articles about the Everglades in Florida. You would look under *Everglades*. There you would find a listing of all the articles written about the Everglades in different magazines. The articles would be listed in alphabetical order by title. The listing might look like this example.

Everglades
See also
Florida
Alligators in the Everglades.
    J. Crock. il. *Deep South* 10: 31–33
    Ag 7 '88
Visiting the Everglades. M. Parson. il.
    Florida 52:12–15 Jl 10 '88

This example lists two articles about the Everglades. Each entry gives the name of the article and the first initial and last name of the author. If the article is illustrated, the entry says *il*. The entry also gives the name of the magazine in which the article appeared. And it gives the volume, page numbers, and the date. The note *See also* means that other articles on this subject are listed under other topics, such as *Florida*.

You might also want to find articles written by a certain author, such as Jay Blake or Margaret Collins. You could look under *Blake, Jay* or *Collins, Margaret*. There you would find a list of all the articles written by the author during a given year.

The *Readers' Guide to Periodical Literature* has a book of listings for every year. It also has a small paperback volume of the *Readers' Guide* that is published every two weeks, every month, and every three months (quarterly). At the end of each year, all these paperback volumes are put together in one book for the whole year.

When you use the *Readers' Guide*, you may use it in one of two ways. You can look in each yearly volume under a certain topic, such as *Space Exploration*. You would find listings of all the articles written about this topic. Or, you might want to find articles about a certain event. Then you would look in the volume covering the date of that event. For example, suppose you want to read about the first landing on the moon. You would look for the volume of the *Readers' Guide* that covers July, 1969.

Suppose you want to know about something that happened in the past year. You could look in the quarterly or monthly paperback. For example, articles about an event that happened in February of this year would be listed in the volume for January–March.

MULTIMEDIA RESOURCES

Most libraries also have other materials which are not books or magazines. Check with your own library to see what kinds of nonprint materials may be there.

The **vertical file** is a collection of folders, newspaper clippings, pictures, and other things. Most of these materials are fairly new and will not be kept for a long time. All materials in the vertical file are kept in alphabetical order by subject. The materials

for each subject are kept in labeled folders in a special cabinet or in marked boxes. The index for the vertical file tells what subjects you will find there.

Audiovisual materials have sound and/or pictures. These might include records, listening tapes, videotapes, filmstrips, and so on. The library usually has an index or listing of these materials.

Computers are available at some libraries. And the library often has software programs for using the computer. The software might include video games, educational programs, and "how-to" materials for learning how to do something.

Many libraries also have **microfilm** and **microfiche** equipment. Both are used to store copies of books, magazines, newspapers, indexes, and such. Microfilm is a piece of film that works like a filmstrip. Microfiche looks like a set of index cards. Both types use a special machine for viewing.

Time Line of United States History

1492

1513

1585

1620

1636

1718

1733

1750

Many groups of American Indians had been living in North America for thousands of years before European explorers arrived.

1492 Christopher Columbus leaves Spain, seeking to find a sea route to the Far East, but he lands in San Salvador. Europeans honor him as the discoverer of America.

1513 Ponce de Léon explores and names Florida and claims it for Spain.

1565 Spaniards found St. Augustine on the Atlantic Coast in Florida. It is the oldest city in the U.S.

1585 The settlement by the English on Roanoke Island begins. This is their first attempt to begin colonizing North America, and it later proves unsuccessful.

1607 A group of about one hundred English colonists found Jamestown, the first permanent British settlement in North America.

1610 Santa Fe, in the area that would later become New Mexico, is founded by the Spanish.

1620 The Pilgrims found Plymouth Colony in Massachusetts. It is the second permanent British settlement in North America.

1625 New Amsterdam, later named New York, is founded by the Dutch.

1636 Harvard, the first North American college, is founded.

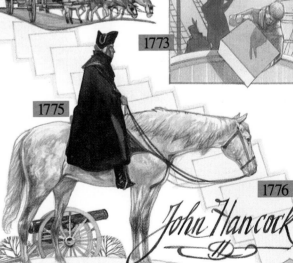

1773

1775

1776

John Hancock

1647 Massachusetts establishes first public school system.

1673 Father Jacques Marquette and fur trader Louis Jolliet explore the upper Mississippi.

1718 San Antonio, in what would later become Texas, is founded by the Spanish.

1733 Georgia becomes the thirteenth colony. Each colony has its own governing body, but all are under the rule of Britain.

1750 The first Conestoga wagons carry pioneers and freight to new settlements in the West.

1754 French and Indian War begins.

1763 Britain defeats France in the French and Indian War and gains control of a large section of the country. Because the war has cost the British a great deal, they increase taxes on the colonists.

1773 Colonists dump cargo of tea on British ships into Boston Harbor (the Boston Tea Party) in protest to buying tea from British East India Company.

1775 The Revolutionary War between the colonists and Great Britain begins at Lexington and Concord.

1776 On July 4, the colonists adopt the Declaration of Independence and form the United States of America.

1781 The Americans defeat the British at Yorktown, Virginia, in the last major battle of the Revolutionary War.

1787 The Northwest Ordinance is passed, outlining provisions that allow a territory to become a state.

The Founding Fathers write the Constitution.

1789 George Washington is elected the nation's first President.

1791 The Bill of Rights goes into effect. It guarantees civil liberties to every citizen.

1793 Eli Whitney invents the cotton gin. His invention helps to make the U.S. the world's largest cotton producer.

1803 The Louisiana Purchase doubles the size of the U.S. The government buys the land from France for $15 million.

1811 Work begins on the Cumberland Road, which starts the national system of transportation in the U.S.

1812-1815 British interference in American shipping and the practice of forcing American seamen into service on British ships results in the War of 1812.

1820 The Missouri Compromise temporarily settles disagreements about slavery by defining areas in which slavery is forbidden.

1823 The Monroe Doctrine declares North and South America off limits to European interference.

1825 The Erie Canal opens, providing a water route from the Atlantic Ocean to the Great Lakes.

1837 Samuel F. B. Morse demonstrates the first successful telegraph in the U.S.

1846 The Mexican War begins.

1848 Victory in the Mexican War gives the U.S. new territory in the West, including what would later become California, Utah, Texas, New Mexico, Nevada, and parts of other states.

Lucretia Coffin Mott and Elizabeth Cady Stanton meet with a group of women at Seneca Falls, NY, to inaugurate the women's rights movement.

The discovery of gold in California starts a Gold Rush.

1857 The Dred Scott decision denies citizen rights to slaves and rules the Missouri Compromise unconstitutional.

1860-1861 Eleven Southern states leave the Union in disagreement with the North about slavery and states' rights to form the Confederate States of America.

1861 The Civil War begins when Confederate troops fire on Fort Sumter in Charleston, South Carolina.

1863 The Emancipation Proclamation is signed by President Lincoln. The proclamation declares freedom for all slaves in Confederate-held territory.

President Lincoln describes the meaning of the Civil War in his Gettysburg Address.

1865 The Civil War ends when General Lee surrenders to General Grant at Appomattox Court House, Virginia.

1811

1837

1867

1803

Louisiana Purchase

1865

1865-1870

1848

1820

LUCRETIA MOTT

1793

1789

ELIZABETH STANTON

EQUALITY

1879

1914

1939

1960s

1876

1908

1927

1929

1945

1958

1865-1870 The Thirteenth Amendment to the Constitution outlaws slavery; the Fourteenth gives citizenship to former slaves; the Fifteenth opens voting to all men, regardless of race.

1867 The United States buys Alaska from Russia for a little more than $7 million.

1869 The first transcontinental railroad is completed when a golden spike joins the Central Pacific and Union Pacific railroads near Ogden, Utah.

1876 Alexander Graham Bell invents the telephone.

1879 Thomas Alva Edison invents the electric light bulb.

1886 The American Federation of Labor is formed. It calls for better wages and working conditions and for employers to talk and bargain with their workers.

1898 The U.S. defeats Spain in the Spanish-American War. Under the terms of the peace treaty, the U.S.

receives Guam, Puerto Rico, and the Philippines.

1903 The Wright Brothers make the first successful airplane flight.

1908 Henry Ford brings out the Model T automobile and demonstrates the value of the assembly line.

1914 The first ship travels through the Panama Canal.

World War I begins.

1920 The Nineteenth Amendment to the Constitution gives women the right to vote.

1927 The first solo transatlantic flight flown by Charles Lindbergh helps to start the Air Age.

1929 A stock market crash brings financial ruin to thousands and starts the Great Depression.

1933 The New Deal program to end the Depression begins under President Franklin D. Roosevelt. Many government public work projects provide work and wages for the unemployed.

1939 World War II begins.

1941-1945 After the bombing of Pearl Harbor, the U.S. joins the Allies in World War II. War against Japan, Germany, and Italy is declared.

1945 The United Nations is founded.

1950-1953 The U.S. joins with other members of the United Nations in trying to help restore peace in Korea.

1958 The U.S. creates the National Aeronautics and Space Administration (NASA) in response to challenge posed by Soviets, who launch *Sputnik I* into outer space.

U.S. launches *Explorer I.*

1960s Civil rights organizations become active in demanding civil rights for African Americans, Hispanic Americans, American Indians, and other minorities.

1962 John Glenn is the first American to orbit the Earth.

1963

1965

1968

1969

1979

1981

1976

1986

1987

1988

1990

1963 Martin Luther King, Jr., leads civil rights march in Washington, D.C.
President Kennedy is assassinated.

1965 U.S. sends troops to Vietnam to support South Vietnam in its effort to remain independent.

1968 Martin Luther King, Jr., is assassinated.

1969 Astronauts Neil A. Armstrong and Edwin Aldrin are the first people to walk on the moon.

1970 Clean Air Act is passed, and the Environmental Protection Agency is created.

1972 SALT I treaty, limiting nuclear arms, is signed.
President Nixon visits China, becoming the first American President to do so.
Break-in at Democratic National Committee headquarters is the first of a series of events leading to a loss of confidence in President Nixon.

1973 U.S. involvement in the Vietnam War ends.

1974 President Nixon resigns.

1976 The Bicentennial of the signing of the Declaration of Independence is celebrated.

1979 Full diplomatic relations are established between the U.S. and China. U.S. ends diplomatic relations with The Republic of China in Taiwan.
President Carter, Israeli Prime Minister Begin, and Egyptian

President Sadat sign Camp David peace agreements.
President Carter and Soviet President Brezhnev sign SALT II treaty.
Iranians seize U.S. embassy in Tehran and take more than 60 Americans hostage.

1980 U.S. military mission to rescue hostages in Iran fails.

1981 American hostages in Iran are freed after 444 days of captivity.
Columbia, the first reusable space shuttle, is launched by the U.S.
Sandra O'Connor is the first woman associate justice of the U.S. Supreme Court.

1985 U.S.–Soviet Summit takes place in Geneva, Switzerland.

1986 U.S. space shuttle, *Challenger,* explodes, killing all onboard including Christa McAuliffe—the first teacher to

participate in the space shuttle program.

1987 President Reagan and General Secretary Gorbachev meet for summit meeting in Washington, D.C., and sign treaty to reduce the size of U.S. and Soviet nuclear arsenals.

1988 U.S. space shuttle *Discovery* is launched thirty-two months after the *Challenger* tragedy.

1990 International Literacy Year.

R32

*S*tates of the United States

ALABAMA

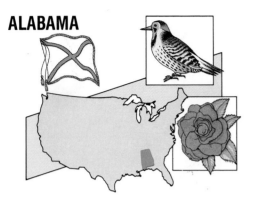

U.S. Postal Abbreviation	AL
Capital	Montgomery
Population	4,083,000
Area	51,609 (sq. mi.)
	133,667 (sq. km)
State Nicknames	Yellowhammer State; Heart of Dixie; Cotton State
State Flower	Camellia
State Bird	Yellowhammer
Year Admitted to Union	1819
Order of Admission	22

ALASKA

U.S. Postal Abbreviation	AK
Capital	Juneau
Population	525,000
Area	586,412 (sq. mi.)
	1,518,800 (sq. km)
State Nickname	The Last Frontier
State Flower	Forget-Me-Not
State Bird	Willow Ptarmigan
Year Admitted to Union	1959
Order of Admission	49

ARIZONA

U.S. Postal Abbreviation	AZ
Capital	Phoenix
Population	3,386,000
Area	113,909 (sq. mi.)
	295,023 (sq. km)
State Nickname	Grand Canyon State
State Flower	Blossom of the Saguaro Cactus
State Bird	Cactus Wren
Year Admitted to Union	1912
Order of Admission	48

ARKANSAS

U.S. Postal Abbreviation	AR
Capital	Little Rock
Population	2,388,000
Area	53,104 (sq. mi.)
	137,539 (sq. km)
State Nickname	Land of Opportunity
State Flower	Apple Blossom
State Bird	Mockingbird
Year Admitted to Union	1836
Order of Admission	25

CALIFORNIA

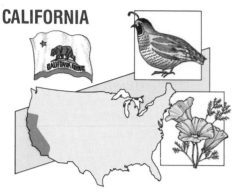

U.S. Postal Abbreviation	CA
Capital	Sacramento
Population	27,663,000
Area	158,706 (sq. mi.)
	411,013 (sq. km)
State Nickname	Golden State
State Flower	Golden Poppy
State Bird	California Valley Quail
Year Admitted to Union	1850
Order of Admission	31

COLORADO

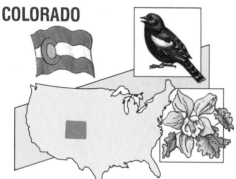

U.S. Postal Abbreviation	CO
Capital	Denver
Population	3,296,000
Area	104,247 (sq. mi.)
	269,998 (sq. km)
State Nickname	Centennial State
State Flower	Rocky Mountain Columbine
State Bird	Lark Bunting
Year Admitted to Union	1876
Order of Admission	38

CONNECTICUT

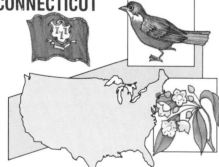

U.S. Postal Abbreviation	CT
Capital	Hartford
Population	3,211,000
Area	5,009 (sq. mi.)
	12,973 (sq. km)
State Nicknames	Constitution State; Nutmeg State
State Flower	Mountain Laurel
State Bird	Robin
Year Admitted to Union	1788
Order of Admission	5

DELAWARE

U.S. Postal Abbreviation	DE
Capital	Dover
Population	644,000
Area	2,057 (sq. mi.)
	5,328 (sq. km)
State Nicknames	First State; Diamond State
State Flower	Peach Blossom
State Bird	Blue Hen Chicken
Year Admitted to Union	1787
Order of Admission	1

FLORIDA

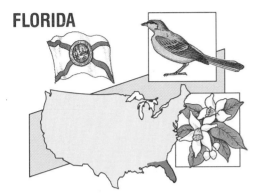

U.S. Postal Abbreviation	FL
Capital	Tallahassee
Population	12,023,000
Area	58,560 (sq. mi.)
	151,670 (sq. km)
State Nickname	Sunshine State
State Flower	Orange Blossom
State Bird	Mockingbird
Year Admitted to Union	1845
Order of Admission	27

GEORGIA

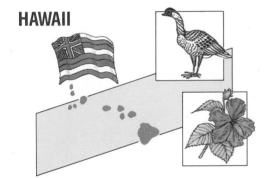

U.S. Postal Abbreviation	GA
Capital	Atlanta
Population	6,222,000
Area	58,876 (sq. mi.)
	152,488 (sq. km)
State Nicknames	Empire State of the South; Peach State; Goober State
State Flower	Cherokee Rose
State Bird	Brown Thrasher
Year Admitted to Union	1788
Order of Admission	4

HAWAII

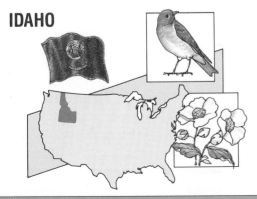

U.S. Postal Abbreviation	HI
Capital	Honolulu
Population	1,083,000
Area	6,450 (sq. mi.)
	16,705 (sq. km)
State Nickname	Aloha State
State Flower	Hibiscus
State Bird	Nene (Hawaiian Goose)
Year Admitted to Union	1959
Order of Admission	50

IDAHO

U.S. Postal Abbreviation	ID
Capital	Boise
Population	998,000
Area	83,557 (sq. mi.)
	216,412 (sq. km)
State Nickname	Gem State
State Flower	Mock Orange
State Bird	Mountain Bluebird
Year Admitted to Union	1890
Order of Admission	43

ILLINOIS

U.S. Postal Abbreviation	IL
Capital	Springfield
Population	11,582,000
Area	56,400 (sq. mi.)
	146,075 (sq. km)
State Nicknames	Prairie State; Land of Lincoln
State Flower	Violet
State Bird	Cardinal
Year Admitted to Union	1818
Order of Admission	21

INDIANA

U.S. Postal Abbreviation	IN
Capital	Indianapolis
Population	5,531,000
Area	36,291 (sq. mi.)
	93,993 (sq. km)
State Nickname	Hoosier State
State Flower	Peony
State Bird	Cardinal
Year Admitted to Union	1816
Order of Admission	19

IOWA

U.S. Postal Abbreviation	IA
Capital	Des Moines
Population	2,834,000
Area	56,290 (sq. mi.)
	145,790 (sq. km)
State Nickname	Hawkeye State
State Flower	Wild Rose
State Bird	Eastern Goldfinch
Year Admitted to Union	1846
Order of Admission	29

KANSAS

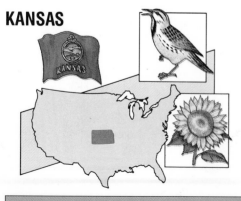

U.S. Postal Abbreviation	KS
Capital	Topeka
Population	2,476,000
Area	82,264 (sq. mi.)
	213,063 (sq. km)
State Nickname	Sunflower State
State Flower	Sunflower
State Bird	Western Meadowlark
Year Admitted to Union	1861
Order of Admission	34

KENTUCKY

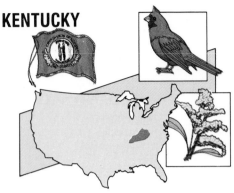

U.S. Postal Abbreviation	KY
Capital	Frankfort
Population	3,727,000
Area	40,409 (sq. mi.)
	104,623 (sq. km)
State Nickname	Bluegrass State
State Flower	Goldenrod
State Bird	Cardinal
Year Admitted to Union	1792
Order of Admission	15

LOUISIANA

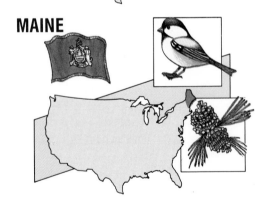

U.S. Postal Abbreviation	LA
Capital	Baton Rouge
Population	4,461,000
Area	48,523 (sq. mi.)
	125,674 (sq. km)
State Nickname	Pelican State
State Flower	Magnolia
State Bird	Brown Pelican
Year Admitted to Union	1812
Order of Admission	18

MAINE

U.S. Postal Abbreviation	ME
Capital	Augusta
Population	1,187,000
Area	33,215 (sq. mi.)
	86,026 (sq. km)
State Nickname	Pine Tree State
State Flower	White Pine Cone and Tassel
State Bird	Chickadee
Year Admitted to Union	1820
Order of Admission	23

MARYLAND

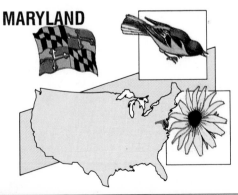

U.S. Postal Abbreviation	MD
Capital	Annapolis
Population	4,535,000
Area	10,577 (sq. mi.)
	27,394 (sq. km)
State Nicknames	Old Line State; Free State
State Flower	Black-Eyed Susan
State Bird	Baltimore Oriole
Year Admitted to Union	1788
Order of Admission	7

MASSACHUSETTS

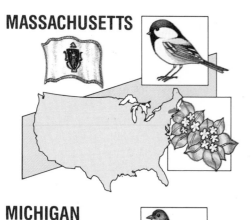

U.S. Postal Abbreviation	MA
Capital	Boston
Population	5,855,000
Area	8,257 (sq. mi.)
	21,386 (sq. km)
State Nicknames	Bay State; Old Colony State
State Flower	Mayflower
State Bird	Chickadee
Year Admitted to Union	1788
Order of Admission	6

MICHIGAN

U.S. Postal Abbreviation	MI
Capital	Lansing
Population	9,200,000
Area	58,216 (sq. mi.)
	150,779 (sq. km)
State Nickname	Wolverine State
State Flower	Apple Blossom
State Bird	Robin
Year Admitted to Union	1837
Order of Admission	26

MINNESOTA

U.S. Postal Abbreviation	MN
Capital	St. Paul
Population	4,246,000
Area	84,068 (sq. mi.)
	217,735 (sq. km)
State Nicknames	North Star State; Gopher State
State Flower	Pink and White Lady's Slipper
State Bird	Common Loon
Year Admitted to Union	1858
Order of Admission	32

MISSISSIPPI

U.S. Postal Abbreviation	MS
Capital	Jackson
Population	2,625,000
Area	47,716 (sq. mi.)
	123,584 (sq. km)
State Nickname	Magnolia State
State Flower	Magnolia
State Bird	Mockingbird
Year Admitted to Union	1817
Order of Admission	20

MISSOURI

U.S. Postal Abbreviation	MO
Capital	Jefferson City
Population	5,103,000
Area	69,686 (sq. mi.)
	180,486 (sq. km)
State Nickname	Show Me State
State Flower	Hawthorn
State Bird	Bluebird
Year Admitted to Union	1821
Order of Admission	24

MONTANA

U.S. Postal Abbreviation	MT
Capital	Helena
Population	809,000
Area	147,138 (sq. mi.)
	381,086 (sq. km)
State Nickname	Treasure State
State Flower	Bitterroot
State Bird	Western Meadowlark
Year Admitted to Union	1889
Order of Admission	41

NEBRASKA

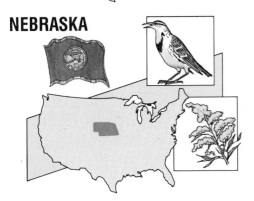

U.S. Postal Abbreviation	NE
Capital	Lincoln
Population	1,594,000
Area	77,227 (sq. mi.)
	200,017 (sq. km)
State Nickname	Cornhusker State
State Flower	Goldenrod
State Bird	Western Meadowlark
Year Admitted to Union	1867
Order of Admission	37

NEVADA

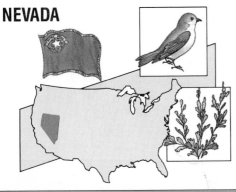

U.S. Postal Abbreviation	NV
Capital	Carson City
Population	1,007,000
Area	110,540 (sq. mi.)
	286,297 (sq. km)
State Nicknames	Silver State; Sagebrush State
State Flower	Sagebrush
State Bird	Mountain Bluebird
Year Admitted to Union	1864
Order of Admission	36

NEW HAMPSHIRE

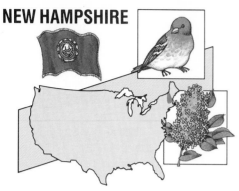

U.S. Postal Abbreviation	NH
Capital	Concord
Population	1,057,000
Area	9,304 (sq. mi.)
	24,097 (sq. km)
State Nickname	Granite State
State Flower	Purple Lilac
State Bird	Purple Finch
Year Admitted to Union	1788
Order of Admission	9

NEW JERSEY

U.S. Postal Abbreviation	NJ
Capital	Trenton
Population	7,672,000
Area	7,836 (sq. mi.)
	20,295 (sq. km)
State Nickname	Garden State
State Flower	Purple Violet
State Bird	Eastern Goldfinch
Year Admitted to Union	1787
Order of Admission	3

NEW MEXICO

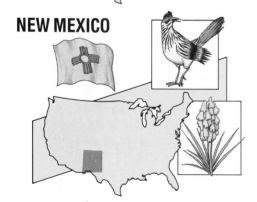

U.S. Postal Abbreviation	NM
Capital	Sante Fe
Population	1,500,000
Area	121,666 (sq. mi.)
	315,113 (sq. km)
State Nickname	Land of Enchantment
State Flower	Yucca
State Bird	Roadrunner
Year Admitted to Union	1912
Order of Admission	47

NEW YORK

U.S. Postal Abbreviation	NY
Capital	Albany
Population	17,825,000
Area	49,576 (sq. mi.)
	128,401 (sq. km)
State Nickname	Empire State
State Flower	Rose
State Bird	Bluebird
Year Admitted to Union	1788
Order of Admission	11

NORTH CAROLINA

U.S. Postal Abbreviation	NC
Capital	Raleigh
Population	6,413,000
Area	52,586 (sq. mi.)
	136,197 (sq. km)
State Nickname	Tar Heel State
State Flower	Dogwood
State Bird	Cardinal
Year Admitted to Union	1789
Order of Admission	12

NORTH DAKOTA

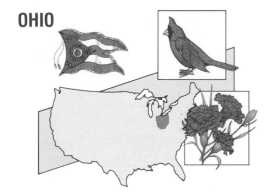

U.S. Postal Abbreviation	ND
Capital	Bismarck
Population	672,000
Area	70,665 (sq. mi.)
	183,022 (sq. km)
State Nicknames	Flickertail State; Sioux State
State Flower	Wild Prairie Rose
State Bird	Western Meadowlark
Year Admitted to Union	1889
Order of Admission	39

OHIO

U.S. Postal Abbreviation	OH
Capital	Columbus
Population	10,784,000
Area	41,222 (sq. mi.)
	106,764 (sq. km)
State Nickname	Buckeye State
State Flower	Scarlet Carnation
State Bird	Cardinal
Year Admitted to Union	1803
Order of Admission	17

OKLAHOMA

U.S. Postal Abbreviation	OK
Capital	Oklahoma City
Population	3,272,000
Area	69,919 (sq. mi.)
	181,089 (sq. km)
State Nickname	Sooner State
State Flower	Mistletoe
State Bird	Scissor-Tailed Flycatcher
Year Admitted to Union	1907
Order of Admission	46

OREGON

U.S. Postal Abbreviation	OR
Capital	Salem
Population	2,724,000
Area	96,981 (sq. mi.)
	251,180 (sq. km)
State Nickname	Beaver State
State Flower	Oregon Grape
State Bird	Western Meadowlark
Year Admitted to Union	1859
Order of Admission	33

PENNSYLVANIA

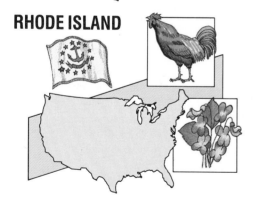

U.S. Postal Abbreviation	PA
Capital	Harrisburg
Population	11,936,000
Area	45,333 (sq. mi.)
	117,412 (sq. km)
State Nickname	Keystone State
State Flower	Mountain Laurel
State Bird	Ruffed Grouse
Year Admitted to Union	1787
Order of Admission	2

RHODE ISLAND

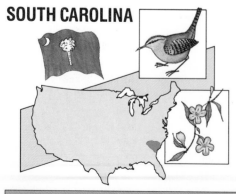

U.S. Postal Abbreviation	RI
Capital	Providence
Population	986,000
Area	1,214 (sq. mi.)
	3,144 (sq. km)
State Nickname	Ocean State
State Flower	Violet
State Bird	Rhode Island Red
Year Admitted to Union	1790
Order of Admission	13

SOUTH CAROLINA

U.S. Postal Abbreviation	SC
Capital	Columbia
Population	3,425,000
Area	31,055 (sq. mi.)
	80,432 (sq. km)
State Nickname	Palmetto State
State Flower	Yellow Jessamine
State Bird	Carolina Wren
Year Admitted to Union	1788
Order of Admission	8

SOUTH DAKOTA

U.S. Postal Abbreviation	SD
Capital	Pierre
Population	709,000
Area	77,047 (sq. mi.)
	199,551 (sq. km)
State Nicknames	Sunshine State; Coyote State
State Flower	Pasqueflower
State Bird	Ring-Necked Pheasant
Year Admitted to Union	1889
Order of Admission	40

TENNESSEE

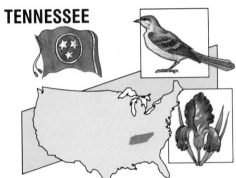

U.S. Postal Abbreviation	TN
Capital	Nashville
Population	4,855,000
Area	42,244 (sq. mi.)
	109,411 (sq. km)
State Nickname	Volunteer State
State Flower	Iris
State Bird	Mockingbird
Year Admitted to Union	1796
Order of Admission	16

TEXAS

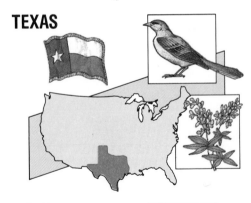

U.S. Postal Abbreviation	TX
Capital	Austin
Population	16,789,000
Area	267,338 (sq. mi.)
	692,402 (sq. km)
State Nickname	Lone Star State
State Flower	Bluebonnet
State Bird	Mockingbird
Year Admitted to Union	1845
Order of Admission	28

UTAH

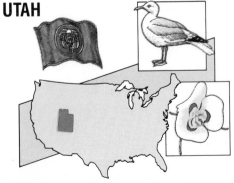

U.S. Postal Abbreviation	UT
Capital	Salt Lake City
Population	1,680,000
Area	84,916 (sq. mi.)
	219,931 (sq. km)
State Nickname	Beehive State
State Flower	Sego Lily
State Bird	Sea Gull
Year Admitted to Union	1896
Order of Admission	45

VERMONT

U.S. Postal Abbreviation	VT
Capital	Montpelier
Population	548,000
Area	9,609 (sq. mi.)
	24,887 (sq. km)
State Nickname	Green Mountain State
State Flower	Red Clover
State Bird	Hermit Thrush
Year Admitted to Union	1791
Order of Admission	14

VIRGINIA

U.S. Postal Abbreviation	VA
Capital	Richmond
Population	5,904,000
Area	40,817 (sq. mi.)
	105,716 (sq. km)
State Nickname	Old Dominion
State Flower	Dogwood
State Bird	Cardinal
Year Admitted to Union	1788
Order of Admission	10

WASHINGTON

U.S. Postal Abbreviation	WA
Capital	Olympia
Population	4,538,000
Area	68,192 (sq. mi.)
	176,616 (sq. km)
State Nickname	Evergreen State
State Flower	Rhododendron
State Bird	Willow Goldfinch
Year Admitted to Union	1889
Order of Admission	42

WEST VIRGINIA

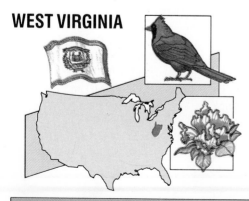

U.S. Postal Abbreviation	WV
Capital	Charleston
Population	1,897,000
Area	24,181 (sq. mi.)
	62,628 (sq. km)
State Nickname	Mountain State
State Flower	Rhododendron
State Bird	Cardinal
Year Admitted to Union	1863
Order of Admission	35

WISCONSIN

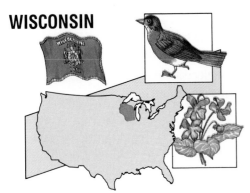

U.S. Postal Abbreviation	WI
Capital	Madison
Population	4,807,000
Area	56,154 (sq. mi.)
	145,438 (sq. km)
State Nickname	Badger State
State Flower	Wood Violet
State Bird	Robin
Year Admitted to Union	1848
Order of Admission	30

WYOMING

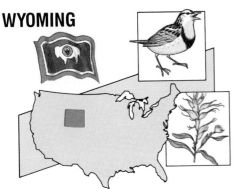

U.S. Postal Abbreviation	WY
Capital	Cheyenne
Population	490,000
Area	97,914 (sq. mi.)
	253,596 (sq. km)
State Nickname	Equality State
State Flower	Indian Paintbrush
State Bird	Meadowlark
Year Admitted to Union	1890
Order of Admission	44

*P*residents of the United States

According to the Constitution, the President of the United States must be a natural-born citizen of at least 35 years of age who has lived in the United States for 14 years. The President may serve two 4-year terms, but not more than two. On January 20 following the election, the President is inaugurated. On that day, the President takes this oath of office:

> "I do solemnly swear (or affirm) that I will faithfully execute the office of President of the United States, and will to the best of my ability, preserve, protect, and defend the Constitution of the United States."

The Presidents of the United States are listed below and on the pages that follow.

In Office: 1789–1797
Age When Inaugurated: 57
Political Party: Federalist
Native State: Virginia
Vice President: John Adams
First Lady: Martha Dandridge
　　　　　Washington

GEORGE WASHINGTON (1732–1799)

In Office: 1797–1801
Age When Inaugurated: 61
Political Party: Federalist
Native State: Massachusetts
Vice President: Thomas Jefferson
First Lady: Abigail Smith Adams

JOHN ADAMS (1735–1826)

In Office: 1801–1809
Age When Inaugurated: 57
Political Party: Democratic-Republican
Native State: Virginia
Vice Presidents: Aaron Burr (1801–1805)
　　George Clinton (1805–1809)
No First Lady in his Administration

THOMAS JEFFERSON (1743–1826)

In Office: 1809–1817
Age When Inaugurated: 57
Political Party: Democratic-Republican
Native State: Virginia
Vice Presidents:
　　George Clinton (1809–1812)
　　Elbridge Gerry (1813–1814)
First Lady: Dolley Payne Madison

JAMES MADISON (1751–1836)

In Office: 1817–1825
Age When Inaugurated: 58
Political Party: Democratic-Republican
Native State: Virginia
Vice President: Daniel D. Tompkins
First Lady: Elizabeth Kortright Monroe

JAMES MONROE (1758–1831)

In Office: 1825–1829
Age When Inaugurated: 57
Political Party: Democratic-Republican
Native State: Massachusetts
Vice President: John C. Calhoun
First Lady: Louisa Johnson Adams

JOHN QUINCY ADAMS (1767–1848)

In Office: 1829–1837
Age When Inaugurated: 61
Political Party: Democratic
Native State: South Carolina
Vice Presidents:
    John C. Calhoun (1829–1832)
    Martin Van Buren (1833–1837)
No First Lady in his Administration

ANDREW JACKSON (1767–1845)

In Office: 1837–1841
Age When Inaugurated: 54
Political Party: Democratic
Native State: New York
Vice President: Richard M. Johnson
No First Lady in his Administration

MARTIN VAN BUREN (1782–1862)

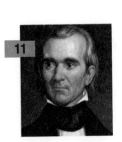

In Office: 1841 (one month)
Age When Inaugurated: 68
Political Party: Whig
Native State: Virginia
Vice President: John Tyler*
First Lady: Anna Symmes Harrison

WILLIAM HENRY HARRISON (1773–1841)

In Office: 1841–1845
Age When Inaugurated: 51
Political Party: Whig
Native State: Virginia
No Vice President in his Administration
First Ladies:
    Letitia Christian Tyler (1841–1842)
    Julia Gardiner Tyler (1844–1845)

JOHN TYLER (1790–1862)

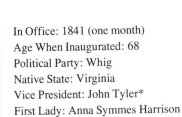

In Office: 1845–1849
Age When Inaugurated: 49
Political Party: Democratic
Native State: North Carolina
Vice President: George M. Dallas
First Lady: Sarah Childress Polk

JAMES K. POLK (1795–1849)

In Office: 1849–1850
Age When Inaugurated: 64
Political Party: Whig
Native State: Virginia
Vice President: Millard Fillmore*
First Lady: Margaret Smith Taylor

ZACHARY TAYLOR (1784–1850)

*Succeeded from the vice presidency on the death of the President.

13

In Office: 1850–1853
Age When Inaugurated: 50
Political Party: Whig
Native State: New York
No Vice President in his Administration
First Lady: Abigail Powers Fillmore

MILLARD FILLMORE (1800–1874)

14

In Office: 1853–1857
Age When Inaugurated: 48
Political Party: Democratic
Native State: New Hampshire
Vice President: William R. King (1853)
First Lady: Jane Appleton Pierce

FRANKLIN PIERCE (1804–1869)

15

In Office: 1857–1861
Age When Inaugurated: 65
Political Party: Democratic
Native State: Pennsylvania
Vice President: John C. Breckinridge
No First Lady in his Administration

JAMES BUCHANAN (1791–1868)

16

In Office: 1861–1865
Age When Inaugurated: 52
Political Party: Republican
Native State: Kentucky
Vice Presidents:
    Hannibal Hamlin (1861–1865)
    Andrew Johnson* (1865)
First Lady: Mary Todd Lincoln

ABRAHAM LINCOLN (1809–1865)

17

In Office: 1865–1869
Age When Inaugurated: 56
Political Party: Democratic
Native State: North Carolina
No Vice President in his Administration
First Lady: Eliza McCardle Johnson

ANDREW JOHNSON (1808–1875)

18

In Office: 1869–1877
Age When Inaugurated: 46
Political Party: Republican
Native State: Ohio
Vice Presidents:
    Schuyler Colfax (1869–1873)
    Henry Wilson (1873–1875)
First Lady: Julia Dent Grant

ULYSSES S. GRANT (1822–1885)

19

In Office: 1877–1881
Age When Inaugurated: 54
Political Party: Republican
Native State: Ohio
Vice President: William A. Wheeler
First Lady: Lucy Webb Hayes

RUTHERFORD B. HAYES (1822–1893)

20

In Office: 1881 (6 months)
Age When Inaugurated: 49
Political Party: Republican
Native State: Ohio
Vice President: Chester A. Arthur*
First Lady: Lucretia Rudolph Garfield

JAMES A. GARFIELD (1831–1881)

*Succeeded from the vice presidency on the death of the President.

In Office: 1881–1885
Age When Inaugurated: 50
Political Party: Republican
Native State: Vermont
No Vice President in his
    Administration
No First Lady in his Administration

CHESTER A. ARTHUR (1829–1886)

In Office: 1885–1889
Age When Inaugurated: 47
Political Party: Democratic
Native State: New Jersey
Vice President:
    Thomas A. Hendricks (1885)
First Lady: Frances Folsom Cleveland

• **GROVER CLEVELAND** (1837–1908)

In Office: 1889–1893
Age When Inaugurated: 55
Political Party: Republican
Native State: Ohio
Vice President: Levi P. Morton
First Lady: Caroline Scott Harrison

BENJAMIN HARRISON (1833–1901)

In Office: 1893–1897
Age When Inaugurated: 56
Political Party: Democratic
Native State: New Jersey
Vice President:
    Adlai E. Stevenson (1893–1897)
First Lady: Frances Folsom Cleveland

GROVER CLEVELAND (1837–1908)

In Office: 1897–1901
Age When Inaugurated: 54
Political Party: Republican
Native State: Ohio
Vice Presidents:
    Garret A. Hobart (1897–1899)
    Theodore Roosevelt* (1901)
First Lady: Ida Saxton McKinley

WILLIAM McKINLEY (1843–1901)

In Office: 1901–1909
Age When Inaugurated: 42
Political Party: Republican
Native State: New York
Vice President: Charles W. Fairbanks
    (1905–1909)
First Lady: Edith Carow Roosevelt

THEODORE ROOSEVELT (1858–1919)

In Office: 1909–1913
Age When Inaugurated: 51
Political Party: Republican
Native State: Ohio
Vice President: James S. Sherman
    (1909–1912)
First Lady: Helen Herron Taft

WILLIAM HOWARD TAFT (1857–1930)

In Office: 1913–1921
Age When Inaugurated: 56
Political Party: Democratic
Native State: Virginia
Vice President: Thomas R. Marshall
First Ladies:
    Ellen Louise Wilson (1913–1914)
    Edith Bolling Wilson (1915–1921)

WOODROW WILSON (1856–1924)

•Cleveland was elected for a second term after Benjamin Harrison.

*Succeeded from the vice presidency on the death of the President.

In Office: 1921–1923
Age When Inaugurated: 56
Political Party: Republican
Native State: Ohio
Vice President: Calvin Coolidge*
First Lady: Florence Kling Harding

WARREN G. HARDING (1865–1923)

In Office: 1923–1929
Age When Inaugurated: 51
Political Party: Republican
Native State: Vermont
Vice President: Charles G. Dawes
  (1925–1929)
First Lady: Grace Goodhue Coolidge

CALVIN COOLIDGE (1872–1933)

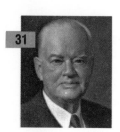

In Office: 1929–1933
Age When Inaugurated: 54
Political Party: Republican
Native State: Iowa
Vice President: Charles Curtis
First Lady: Lou Henry Hoover

HERBERT HOOVER (1874–1964)

In Office: 1933–1945
Age When Inaugurated: 51
Political Party: Democratic
Native State: New York
Vice Presidents: John N. Garner (1933–194
  Henry A. Wallace (1941–1945)
  Harry S. Truman* (1945)
First Lady: Anna Eleanor Roosevelt

FRANKLIN DELANO ROOSEVELT (1882–1945)

In Office: 1945–1953
Age When Inaugurated: 60
Political Party: Democratic
Native State: Missouri
Vice President: Alben W. Barkley
  (1949–1953)
First Lady: Elizabeth (Bess) W. Truman

HARRY S. TRUMAN (1884–1972)

In Office: 1953–1961
Age When Inaugurated: 62
Political Party: Republican
Native State: Texas
Vice President: Richard M. Nixon
First Lady: Marie (Mamie) Doud
  Eisenhower

DWIGHT D. EISENHOWER (1890–1969)

In Office: 1961–1963
Age When Inaugurated: 43
Political Party: Democratic
Native State: Massachusetts
Vice President: Lyndon B. Johnson*
First Lady: Jacqueline Bouvier Kennedy

JOHN F. KENNEDY (1917–1963)

In Office: 1963–1969
Age When Inaugurated: 55
Political Party: Democratic
Native State: Texas
Vice President: Hubert H. Humphrey
First Lady: Claudia (Lady Bird) Taylor
  Johnson

LYNDON BAINES JOHNSON (1908–1973)

*Succeeded from the vice presidency on the death of the President.

In Office: 1969–1974
Age When Inaugurated: 56
Political Party: Republican
Native State: California
Vice Presidents:
    Spiro T. Agnew (1969–1973)
    Gerald R. Ford** (1973–1974)
First Lady: Patricia (Pat) Ryan Nixon

RICHARD M. NIXON (1913–)

In Office: 1974–1977
Age When Inaugurated: 61
Political Party: Republican
Native State: Nebraska
Vice President: Nelson A. Rockefeller
First Lady: Elizabeth (Betty) B. Ford

GERALD R. FORD (1913–)

In Office: 1977–1981
Age When Inaugurated: 52
Political Party: Democratic
Native State: Georgia
Vice President: Walter F. Mondale
First Lady: Rosalynn Smith Carter

JAMES EARL CARTER (1924–)

In Office: 1981–1989
Age When Inaugurated: 69
Political Party: Republican
Native State: Illinois
Vice President: George Bush
First Lady: Nancy Davis Reagan

RONALD W. REAGAN (1911–)

In Office: 1989–
Age When Inaugurated: 64
Political Party: Republican
Native State: Massachusetts
Vice President: James
    Danforth Quayle
First Lady: Barbara Pierce Bush

GEORGE BUSH (1924–)

**Succeeded from the vice presidency on the resignation of the President.

THE UNITED STATES: Political

⊗ National capital ★ State capital • Other city

0   100   200   300 Miles

0   100   200   300   400 Kilometers

THE WORLD
Political

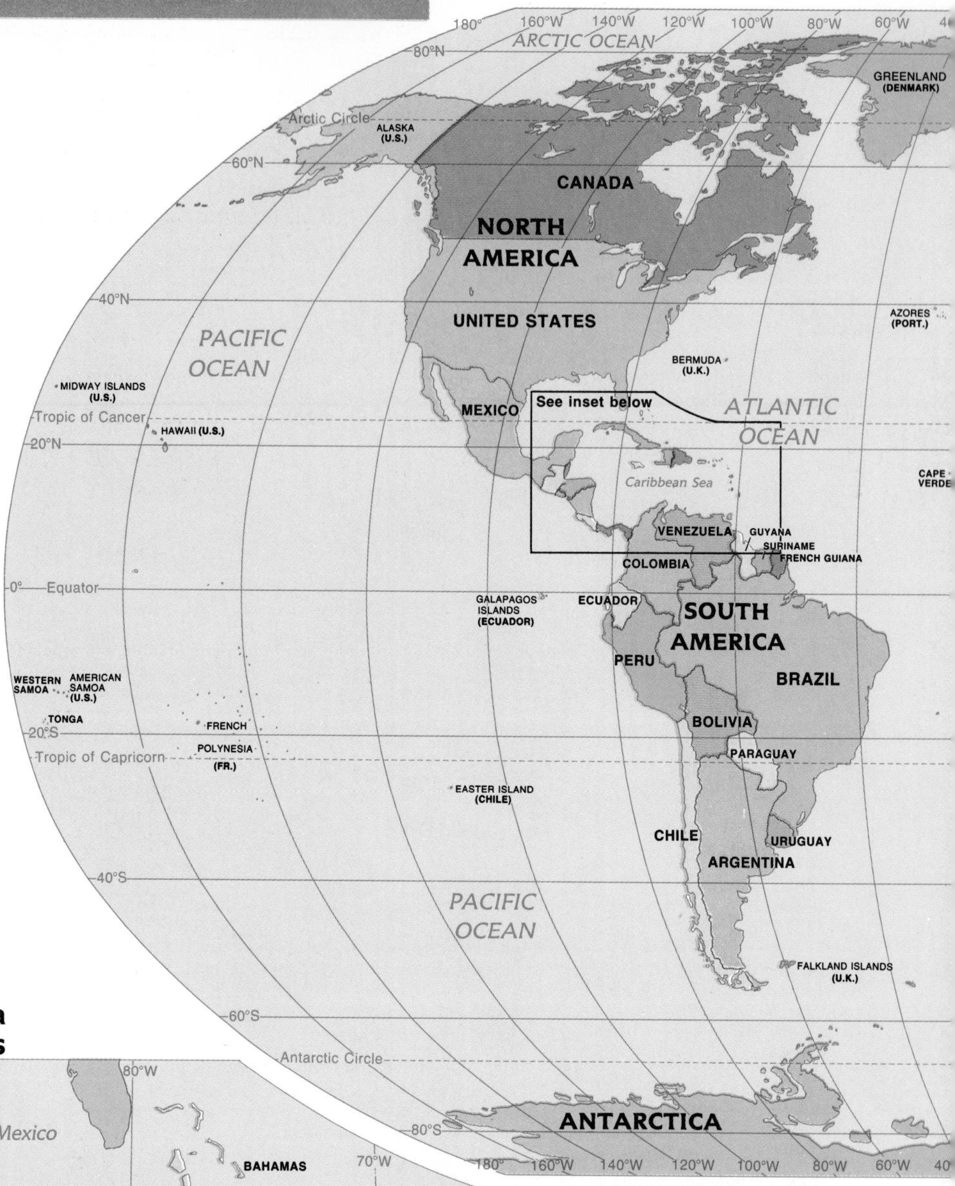

ARCTIC OCEAN

80°N

GREENLAND (DENMARK)

Arctic Circle

ALASKA (U.S.)

60°N

CANADA

NORTH AMERICA

40°N

UNITED STATES

AZORES (PORT.)

PACIFIC OCEAN

MIDWAY ISLANDS (U.S.)

BERMUDA (U.K.)

Tropic of Cancer

See inset below

ATLANTIC OCEAN

20°N

HAWAII (U.S.)

MEXICO

Caribbean Sea

CAPE VERDE

VENEZUELA   GUYANA
SURINAME
FRENCH GUIANA

COLOMBIA

0° Equator

GALAPAGOS ISLANDS (ECUADOR)

ECUADOR

SOUTH AMERICA

WESTERN SAMOA   AMERICAN SAMOA (U.S.)

PERU

BRAZIL

TONGA

20°S

FRENCH

BOLIVIA

Tropic of Capricorn

POLYNESIA (FR.)

PARAGUAY

EASTER ISLAND (CHILE)

CHILE   URUGUAY

ARGENTINA

40°S

PACIFIC OCEAN

FALKLAND ISLANDS (U.K.)

60°S

Antarctic Circle

ANTARCTICA

80°S

180° 160°W 140°W 120°W 100°W 80°W 60°W 40°

Central America and West Indies

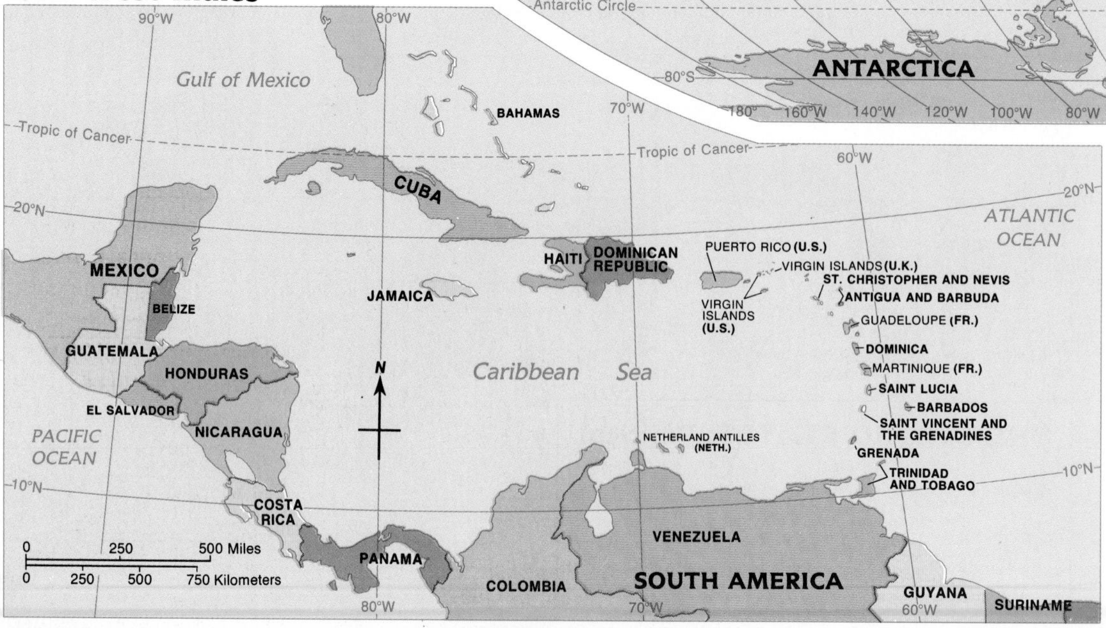

90°W   80°W

Gulf of Mexico

70°W

BAHAMAS

Tropic of Cancer

Tropic of Cancer

60°W

ATLANTIC OCEAN

20°N

CUBA

20°N

MEXICO

HAITI DOMINICAN REPUBLIC

PUERTO RICO (U.S.)

VIRGIN ISLANDS (U.K.)
ST. CHRISTOPHER AND NEVIS

BELIZE

JAMAICA

VIRGIN ISLANDS (U.S.)

ANTIGUA AND BARBUDA

GUADELOUPE (FR.)

GUATEMALA

N

Caribbean   Sea

DOMINICA

MARTINIQUE (FR.)

HONDURAS

SAINT LUCIA

EL SALVADOR

BARBADOS
SAINT VINCENT AND THE GRENADINES

PACIFIC OCEAN

NICARAGUA

NETHERLAND ANTILLES (NETH.)

GRENADA

10°N

TRINIDAD AND TOBAGO

10°N

COSTA RICA

| 0 | 250 | 500 Miles |
| 0 | 250 | 500 | 750 Kilometers |

PANAMA

VENEZUELA

COLOMBIA

SOUTH AMERICA

GUYANA

SURINAME

80°W   70°W   60°W

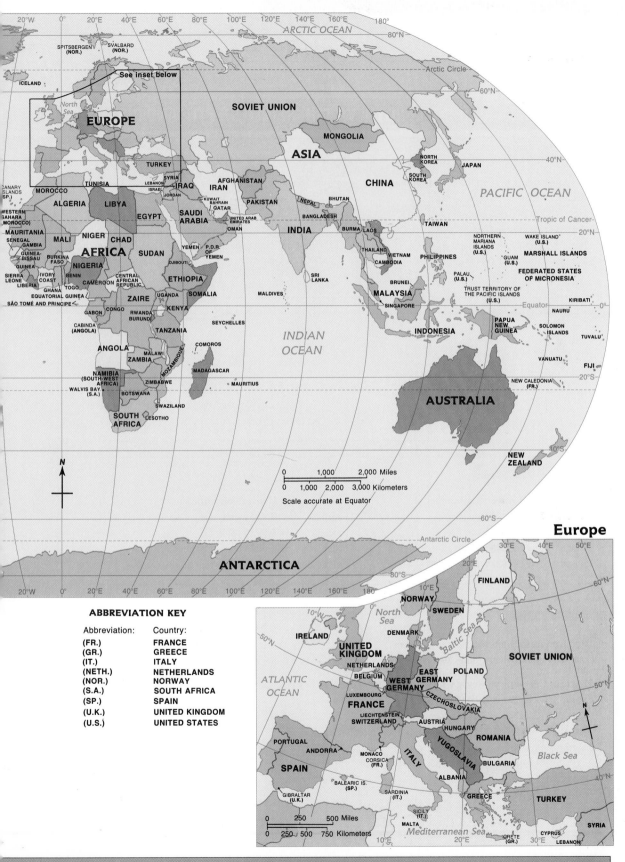

ARCTIC OCEAN

SPITSBERGEN (NOR.)   SVALBARD (NOR.)

ICELAND

Arctic Circle

North Sea

EUROPE

See inset below

SOVIET UNION

MONGOLIA

ASIA

NORTH KOREA   JAPAN

SOUTH KOREA

PACIFIC OCEAN

TURKEY

TUNISIA   SYRIA   LEBANON   ISRAEL   JORDAN   IRAQ   IRAN   AFGHANISTAN   CHINA

CANARY ISLANDS (SP.)   MOROCCO   ALGERIA   LIBYA   EGYPT   SAUDI ARABIA   KUWAIT   BAHRAIN   QATAR   PAKISTAN   NEPAL   BHUTAN   TAIWAN   Tropic of Cancer

WESTERN SAHARA (MOROCCO)   UNITED ARAB EMIRATES   OMAN   INDIA   BANGLADESH   BURMA   LAOS   20°N

MAURITANIA   MALI   NIGER   CHAD   SUDAN   YEMEN   P.D.R. OF YEMEN   THAILAND   VIETNAM   CAMBODIA   PHILIPPINES   NORTHERN MARIANA ISLANDS (U.S.)   WAKE ISLAND (U.S.)   MARSHALL ISLANDS

SENEGAL   GAMBIA   GUINEA-BISSAU   BURKINA FASO   GUINEA   AFRICA   NIGERIA   SRI LANKA   GUAM (U.S.)   FEDERATED STATES OF MICRONESIA

SIERRA LEONE   LIBERIA   IVORY COAST   BENIN   TOGO   GHANA   CAMEROON   CENTRAL AFRICAN REPUBLIC   ETHIOPIA   MALDIVES   BRUNEI   PALAU (U.S.)   TRUST TERRITORY OF THE PACIFIC ISLANDS (U.S.)   KIRIBATI

EQUATORIAL GUINEA   SÃO TOMÉ AND PRINCIPE   GABON   CONGO   ZAIRE   UGANDA   SOMALIA   MALAYSIA   SINGAPORE   Equator   NAURU   0°

CABINDA (ANGOLA)   RWANDA   BURUNDI   KENYA   SEYCHELLES   INDONESIA   PAPUA NEW GUINEA   SOLOMON ISLANDS   TUVALU

ANGOLA   TANZANIA   COMOROS   INDIAN OCEAN   VANUATU   FIJI   20°S

MALAWI   ZAMBIA   MOZAMBIQUE   MADAGASCAR   MAURITIUS   NEW CALEDONIA (FR.)

NAMIBIA (SOUTH-WEST AFRICA)   ZIMBABWE   AUSTRALIA

WALVIS BAY (S.A.)   BOTSWANA   SWAZILAND

SOUTH AFRICA   LESOTHO   NEW ZEALAND   40°S

N

0   1,000   2,000 Miles
0   1,000   2,000   3,000 Kilometers
Scale accurate at Equator

60°S

Antarctic Circle   80°S

ANTARCTICA

20°W   0°   20°E   40°E   60°E   80°E   100°E   120°E   140°E   160°E   180°

Europe

ABBREVIATION KEY

Abbreviation:	Country:
(FR.)	FRANCE
(GR.)	GREECE
(IT.)	ITALY
(NETH.)	NETHERLANDS
(NOR.)	NORWAY
(S.A.)	SOUTH AFRICA
(SP.)	SPAIN
(U.K.)	UNITED KINGDOM
(U.S.)	UNITED STATES

FINLAND

NORWAY   SWEDEN

North Sea

IRELAND   DENMARK   Baltic Sea   SOVIET UNION

UNITED KINGDOM

NETHERLANDS   EAST GERMANY   POLAND

ATLANTIC OCEAN   BELGIUM   WEST GERMANY   CZECHOSLOVAKIA

LUXEMBOURG   FRANCE   LIECHTENSTEIN   SWITZERLAND   AUSTRIA   HUNGARY   ROMANIA

PORTUGAL   ANDORRA   MONACO (FR.)   CORSICA (FR.)   ITALY   YUGOSLAVIA   Black Sea   N

SPAIN   BALEARIC IS. (SP.)   SARDINIA (IT.)   BULGARIA   ALBANIA

GIBRALTAR (U.K.)   SICILY (IT.)   GREECE   TURKEY

MALTA   CRETE (GR.)   CYPRUS   LEBANON   SYRIA

Mediterranean Sea

0   250   500 Miles
0   250   500   750 Kilometers

*T*ables of Weights and Measures and

UNITS FOR MEASURING LENGTH, WIDTH, HEIGHT, DEPTH, AND DISTANCE

METRIC UNITS

1 centimeter (cm) = 10 millimeters (mm)
1 decimeter (dm) = 10 centimeters
1 meter (m) = 100 centimeters
1 dekameter (dam) = 10 meters
1 hectometer (hm) = 100 meters
1 kilometer (km) = 1,000 meters

*A penny is about 1 millimeter in thickness.
A stack of ten pennies is about 1 centimeter in
height.*

CUSTOMARY UNITS

1 foot (ft.) = 12 inches (in.)
1 yard (yd.) = 3 feet
1 mile (mi.) = 1,760 yards = 5,280 feet

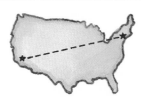

*The distance from New York City to Los Angeles is
about 3,000 miles.*

CONVERSION TABLE

Unit	Conversion Number		Unit	Conversion Number
1 inch	= 2.54 centimeters		1 yard	= 0.914 meter
1 centimeter	= 0.3937 inch		1 meter	= 1.0936 yards
1 foot	= 0.3048 meter		1 mile	= 1.609 kilometers
1 meter	= 3.2808 feet		1 kilometer	= 0.621 mile

CONVERSION FORMULA

To convert metric units to customary units or
customary units to metric units, use the following formula:

Metric to Customary: Metric Unit × *Conversion Number = Customary Unit
Example: 12 inches × 2.54 (conversion number) = 30.48
       12 inches = 30.48 centimeters
Customary to Metric: Customary Unit × *Conversion Number = Metric Unit
Example: 6 centimeters × 0.3937 (conversion number) = 2.36
       6 centimeters = 2.36 inches

*See Conversion Tables

Conversion Tables

UNITS FOR MEASURING MASS OR WEIGHT

METRIC UNITS

1 gram (g)   = 1,000 milligrams (mg)
1 kilogram (kg) = 1,000 grams
1 metric ton (t) = 1,000 kilograms

A key weighs about 4 grams.

CUSTOMARY UNITS

1 pound (lb.) = 16 ounces (oz.)
1 ton (tn.) = 2,000 pounds

A car weighs about 1 ton.

CONVERSION TABLE

Unit	Conversion Number
1 ounce	= 28.35 grams
1 gram	= 0.0353 ounce
1 pound	= 0.4536 kilogram
1 kilogram	= 2.2 pounds
1 ton	= 907.2 kilograms
1 kilogram	= 0.001 ton

A bag of potatoes weighs about 5 pounds;
2,268 grams; or 2.268 kilograms.

UNITS FOR MEASURING TEMPERATURE

METRIC UNITS

Celsius (C)
Freezing Point of Water = 0°C
Boiling Point of Water = 100°C
Normal Body Temperature = 37°C

CUSTOMARY UNITS

Fahrenheit (F.)
Freezing Point of Water = 32°F.
Boiling Point of Water = 212°F.
Normal Body Temperature = 98.6°F.

CONVERSION FORMULA

To convert Celsius to Fahrenheit or Fahrenheit to Celsius, use the following formula:

Celsius to Fahrenheit:
Celsius unit × 1.8; then add 32.
Example: 20° × 1.8 = 36 + 32 = 68°
       20°C = 68°F.

Fahrenheit to Celsius:
Fahrenheit unit − 32; then divide by 1.8.
Example: 80° − 32 = 48 ÷ 1.8 = 26.6°
       80°F. = 26.6°C

UNITS FOR MEASURING CAPACITY

METRIC UNITS

1 liter (L)   = 1,000 milliliters (mL)
1 kiloliter (kL) = 1,000 liters

A large soda bottle holds 2 liters.

CUSTOMARY UNITS

Liquid Measure
1 cup (c.) = 8 fluid ounces (oz.)
1 pint (pt.) = 2 cups
1 quart (qt.) = 2 pints
1 gallon (gal.) = 4 quarts

Dry Measure
2 pints = 1 quart
8 quarts = 1 peck (pk.)
4 pecks = 1 bushel (bu.)

LIQUID VOLUME CONVERSION TABLE

Unit	Conversion Number
1 fluid ounce	= 29.57 milliliters
1 milliliter	= 0.0338 fluid ounce
1 quart	= 0.946 liter
1 liter	= 1.057 quarts
1 gallon	= 3.785 liters
1 liter	= 0.264 gallon

An average drinking glass holds about 10 ounces of lemonade.

DRY MEASURE CONVERSION TABLE

Unit	Conversion Number
1 dry quart	= 1.101 liters
1 liter	= 0.908 dry quart
1 peck	= 8.810 liters
1 liter	= 0.114 peck
1 bushel	= 35.24 liters
1 liter	= 0.028 bushel

A peck of peaches   *A bushel of apples*

UNITS FOR MEASURING AREA

METRIC UNITS

1 square meter (m²) = 10,000 square centimeters (cm²)

1 square centimeter (1 cm²)

CUSTOMARY UNITS

1 square foot (ft.²) = 144 square inches (in.²)
1 square yard (yd.²) = 9 square feet
1 acre (a.) = 43,560 square feet = 4,840 square yards

CONVERSION TABLE

Unit	Conversion Number
1 square inch	= 6.45 square centimeters
1 square centimeter	= 0.155 square inch
1 square foot	= 0.093 square meter
1 square meter	= 10.76 square feet
1 square yard	= 0.836 square meter

A small rug has an area of about 300 square centimeters.

Unit	Conversion Number
1 square meter	= 1.196 square yards
1 square mile	= 2.59 square kilometers
1 square kilometer	= 0.386 square mile

UNITS FOR MEASURING VOLUME

METRIC UNITS

1 cubic meter (m³) = 1,000,000 cubic centimeters (cm³)

1 cubic centimeter (1 cm³)

CUSTOMARY UNITS

1 cubic foot (ft.³) = 1,728 cubic inches
1 cubic yard (yd.³) = 27 cubic feet

CONVERSION TABLE

Unit	Conversion Number
1 cubic inch	= 16.387 cubic centimeters
1 cubic centimeter	= 0.061 cubic inch
1 cubic yard	= 0.765 cubic meter
1 cubic meter	= 1.31 cubic yards
1 cubic foot	= 0.028 cubic meter
1 cubic meter	= 35.315 cubic feet

A small box has a volume of about 600 cubic centimeters.

Geometric Figures

The word *geometry* comes from two Greek words meaning "to measure the earth." Probably the first use of geometry was measuring land to set up boundaries. From the Greek and Latin languages come many of the words still used today to describe geometric figures. For example, the word *angle* comes from a Greek word for *knee*. Can you guess why?

The word *triangle* is made from the word *angle* and the prefix *tri-,* which means "three." A triangle has three angles. There are several different kinds of **triangles.**

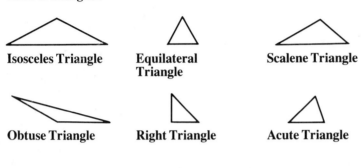

Isosceles Triangle **Equilateral Triangle** **Scalene Triangle**

Obtuse Triangle **Right Triangle** **Acute Triangle**

Quadrilaterals are four-sided figures. *Quad* comes from a Latin word meaning "four." *Lateral* comes from a Latin word meaning "side." There are several different kinds of quadrilaterals.

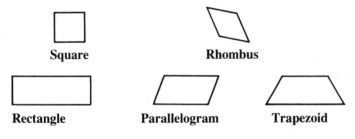

Square **Rhombus**

Rectangle **Parallelogram** **Trapezoid**

A five-sided figure is called a **pentagon.** *Penta* means "five" and *gon* means "angle." A pentagon has five angles. You can figure out what many other geometric figures look like by referring to the chart below.

Numerical Prefix	Meaning	Numerical Prefix	Meaning
uni-	one	hexa-	six
bi-	two	sept-	seven
tri-	three	octa-, octo-	eight
quad-, quadri-,]	four	nona-	nine
tetra-		deca-, deka-	ten
penta-	five	poly-, multi-	many

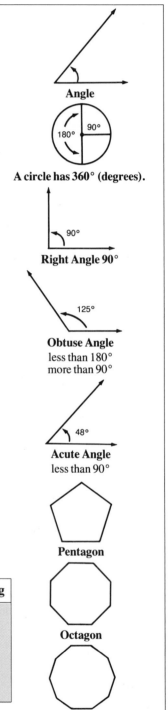

Angle

A circle has 360° (degrees).

Right Angle 90°

125°

Obtuse Angle
less than 180°
more than 90°

48°

Acute Angle
less than 90°

Pentagon

Octagon

Decagon

The Solar System

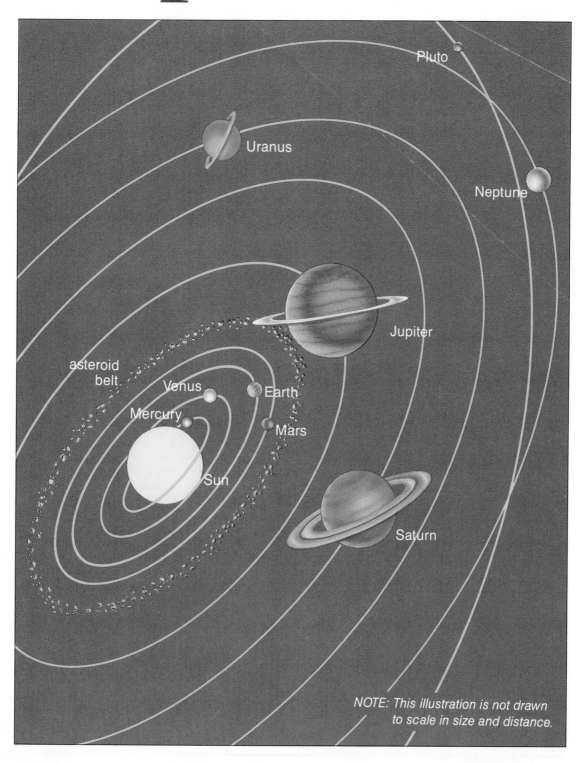

Pluto

Uranus

Neptune

Jupiter

asteroid belt

Venus

Earth

Mercury

Mars

Sun

Saturn

NOTE: This illustration is not drawn to scale in size and distance.

PLANET	AVERAGE DISTANCE FROM SUN	PERIOD OF ROTATION	PERIOD OF REVOLUTION
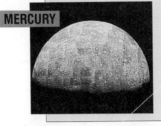 MERCURY	36,000,000 mi. (57,900,000 km)	59 days	88 days

FACTS *Mercury has no atmosphere to protect it from the rays of the sun. The side facing the sun becomes very hot. The side facing away from the sun becomes very cold. Mercury has no moons.*

	AVERAGE DISTANCE FROM SUN	PERIOD OF ROTATION	PERIOD OF REVOLUTION
 VENUS	67,250,000 mi. (108,230,000 km)	243 days	225 days

FACTS *Venus has a thick, cloudy atmosphere, made largely of carbon dioxide. The atmosphere produces a "greenhouse" effect, trapping heat near its surface. Temperatures may reach 878°F. (470°C). Venus has no moons.*

	AVERAGE DISTANCE FROM SUN	PERIOD OF ROTATION	PERIOD OF REVOLUTION
 EARTH	93,000,000 mi. (150,000,000 km)	23 hrs./56 mins.	365 days

FACTS *Earth is rich in oxygen, water, and nitrogen. It is the only planet that is known to support life. The Earth has one moon.*

	AVERAGE DISTANCE FROM SUN	PERIOD OF ROTATION	PERIOD OF REVOLUTION
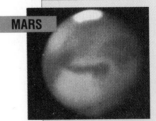 MARS	141,700,000 mi. (228,000,000 km)	24 hrs./37 mins.	687 days

FACTS *Mars has a thin atmosphere and reddish-brown, desertlike regions on its surface. Like the Earth, it has a tilted axis. As a result, it has changes in seasons as it revolves around the sun. Mars has two moons.*

	AVERAGE DISTANCE FROM SUN	PERIOD OF ROTATION	PERIOD OF REVOLUTION
 JUPITER	483,700,000 mi. (778,400,000 km)	9 hrs./55 mins.	12 years

FACTS *Jupiter's atmosphere has colored bands of clouds. The Great Red Spot resembles a large hurricane and seems to consist of spinning masses of gases. Jupiter has a single, faint ring and 17 known moons. One moon has active volcanoes.*

PLANET	AVERAGE DISTANCE FROM SUN	PERIOD OF ROTATION	PERIOD OF REVOLUTION
SATURN 	885,200,000 mi. (1,424,600,000 km)	10 hrs./39 mins.	29.5 years

FACTS *Saturn has a complex ring system. Each ring is made up of smaller rings of ice and rock particles. Saturn has at least 22 known moons.*

URANUS 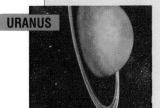	1,781,000,000 mi. (2,866,900,000 km)	17 hours	84.1 years

FACTS *Uranus's greenish color is a result of its thick atmosphere. Uranus has several dark rings and at least 15 known moons.*

NEPTUNE 	2,788,000,000 mi. (4,486,100,000 km)	18–20 hours	165 years

FACTS *Neptune is similar in size and color to Uranus. It has three known moons. One moon, Triton, is one of the largest moons in the solar system.*

PLUTO 	3,660,000,000 mi. (5,890,000,000 km)	6 days	248 years

FACTS *Pluto, the smallest planet, is about the size of Earth's moon. It may well be the coldest planet, with temperatures ranging from −342° to −369°F. (−208° to −223°C). Pluto has one known moon.*

NOTE: The planets are not shown to scale in size.

*I*nside the Earth

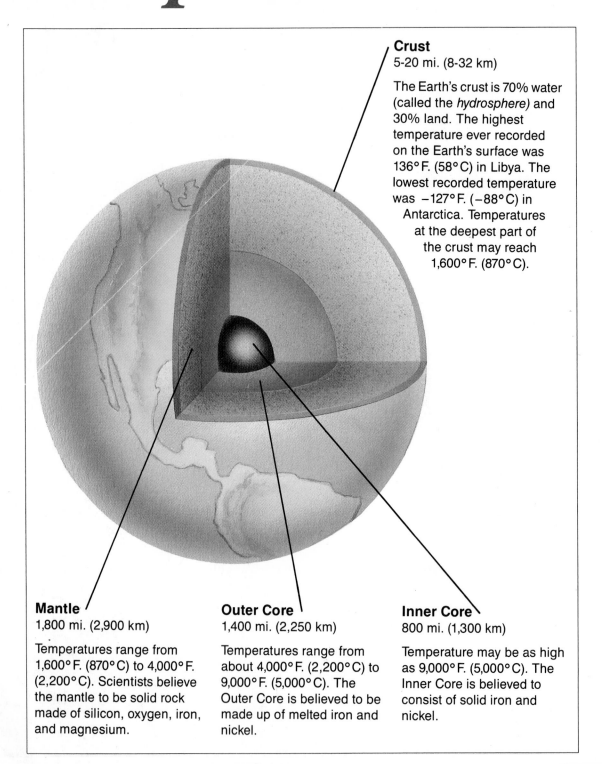

Crust
5-20 mi. (8-32 km)

The Earth's crust is 70% water (called the *hydrosphere)* and 30% land. The highest temperature ever recorded on the Earth's surface was 136° F. (58° C) in Libya. The lowest recorded temperature was −127° F. (−88° C) in Antarctica. Temperatures at the deepest part of the crust may reach 1,600° F. (870° C).

Mantle
1,800 mi. (2,900 km)

Temperatures range from 1,600° F. (870° C) to 4,000° F. (2,200° C). Scientists believe the mantle to be solid rock made of silicon, oxygen, iron, and magnesium.

Outer Core
1,400 mi. (2,250 km)

Temperatures range from about 4,000° F. (2,200° C) to 9,000° F. (5,000° C). The Outer Core is believed to be made up of melted iron and nickel.

Inner Core
800 mi. (1,300 km)

Temperature may be as high as 9,000° F. (5,000° C). The Inner Core is believed to consist of solid iron and nickel.